Gale Biographical Index Series
Number 2

CHILDREN'S AUTHORS AND ILLUSTRATORS: AN INDEX TO BIOGRAPHICAL DICTIONARIES

FIFTH EDITION

Joyce Nakamura, Editor

Gale Research Inc.
An International Thomson Publishing Company

ITP

NEW YORK • LONDON • BONN • BOSTON • DETROIT • MADRID
MELBOURNE • MEXICO CITY • PARIS • SINGAPORE • TOKYO
TORONTO • WASHINGTON • ALBANY NY • BELMONT CA • CINCINNATI OH

Editor: Joyce Nakamura

Consulting Editor: Barbara McNeil

Associate Editors: Linda R. Andres, Shelly Andrews, Julie K. Karmazin, Michael J. Tyrkus

Assistant Editors: Marilyn O'Connell Allen, Aileen Collins, Sheryl Eichstaedt

Manager, Technical Support Services: Theresa Rocklin
Programmer: Ida M. Wright

Production Director: Mary Beth Trimper
Production Assistant: Shanna Philpott Heilveil

Library of Congress Catalog Number 86-27035
ISBN 0-8103-2899-2

Printed in the United States of America

Gale Research Inc., an International Thomson Publishing Company.

I(T)P™ **Gale Research Inc., an International Thomson Publishing Company.**
ITP logo is a trademark under license.

10 9 8 7 6 5 4 3 2 1

CHILDREN'S AUTHORS AND ILLUSTRATORS:

AN INDEX TO BIOGRAPHICAL DICTIONARIES

The Gale Biographical Index Series

Biography and Genealogy Master Index
Second Edition, Supplements and Annual Volumes
(GBIS Number 1)

Children's Authors and Illustrators
Fifth Edition
(GBIS Number 2)

Author Biographies Master Index
(GBIS Number 3)

Journalist Biographies Master Index
(GBIS Number 4)

Performing Arts Biography Master Index
Second Edition
(GBIS Number 5)

Writers for Young Adults: Biographies Master Index
(GBIS Number 6)

Historical Biographical Dictionaries Master Index
(GBIS Number 7)

Twentieth-Century Author Biographies Master Index
(GBIS Number 8)

Artist Biographies Master Index
(GBIS Number 9)

Business Biography Master Index
(GBIS Number 10)

Abridged Biography and Genealogy Master Index
(GBIS Number 11)

Contents

Introduction

The fifth edition of *Children's Authors & Illustrators (CA&I)* updates and augments the fourth edition published in 1987, citing over 200,000 biographies of approximately 30,000 individuals found in 550 reference books. Including new editions of sources previously indexed as well as new titles, nearly 2,000 biographical sources are represented. For anyone interested in the study of children's literature—students from upper elementary school through college, teachers, librarians, and general researchers—*CA&I* is a research tool that provides quick and easy access to biographical information about the people who create books for young readers. As the amount of that biographical information steadily increases, *CA&I* grows in usefulness, eliminating the need to search source-by-source through hundreds of biographical dictionaries.

Concept and Scope

■ Comprehensiveness

CA&I's intent is to include all known writers and illustrators of children's books whose work is accessible in the English language. In the case of those prominent authors and illustrators for whom biographical information is readily available, *CA&I* conveniently consolidates references to a wide variety of sources. For the less prominent person, *CA&I* often provides the clue to a rare, hard-to-find biography.

■ Extensive coverage

The writers listed in this index represent the spectrum of literature read by young people. Included here are the authors who have written directly for children (like Dr. Seuss), as well as those whose writings for adults have been adopted by children (like Mark Twain), and even those authors whose writings are often required reading for class assignments (like John Steinbeck).

■ Variety of sources

Because *CA&I* aims to be comprehensive, a broad variety of biographical sources is included. *CA&I* provides all citations for a given author or illustrator that occur in biographical sources researched for this index. Users' needs for information may vary widely and some sources may be unavailable in some libraries. For these reasons, *CA&I* attempts to provide the maximum information from which the user can make his or her own best selection.

CA&I is limited to citing biographical reference books and necessarily excludes most material published in journals, magazines, and newspapers, with the exception of periodicals included in *Biography Index.*

Editorial Practices

The fifth edition of *Children's Authors & Illustrators* retains material included in the previous editions. All new books (or new editions of previously indexed books) devoted exclusively to children's authors and illustrators were indexed in their entirety *(Something about the Author* or *Sixth Book of Junior Authors & Illustrators,* for example).

Names were then computer-matched against update sources in Gale Research's data bank of more than nine million biographical citations. The computer-generated information was reviewed to:

- Verify in the original reference sources that similar names did, in fact, represent the same individual.

  For example, the match on James Robert Davis (better known as cartoonist Jim Davis, creator of "Garfield") also produced citations for a mayor, a curator, an executive, and a professor of plant pathology.

- Establish links between "real names" and pseudonyms (or name variants)

Unlike previous editions, the fifth edition of *CA&I* does not establish a standardized form of the person's real name. References to names that are identical in spelling and dates are consolidated under a single name and date entry; otherwise, names from update biographical sources appear as they are listed in the original source:

Alexander, Lloyd *BioIn 14, –15, –16, –17, InvtTCA2*

Alexander, Lloyd 1924- *Au&Arts 1, ConAu 24NR, DcLB 52, MajTwCW, ScF&Fl 92, SmATA 49, . . .*

Alexander, Lloyd Chudley 1924- *AnCL, AuByP 2, –3, Au&Wr 71, BioIn 5, –9, –10, ChlLr 1, –5, ConAu1R, –1NR, –38NR, . . .*

Despite the variations in the form of the name, it is apparent that the same person is referred to in the above citations. In some instances, the existence of such variations can be of importance to anyone attempting to determine biographical details about an individual.

How To Use This Book

Entries in *CA&I* provide:

- **The author or illustrator's real name**

- **Links to and from pseudonyms**

Within an entry or cluster of entries, "Pseud./variant" listings of names may lead the user to additional biographical sources:

Allan, Mabel Esther 1915- *AuBYP 2, –3, Au&Wr 71, BioIn 7, –10, 1–14, –16, . . .*
Pseud./variant:
Estoril, Jean
Hagon, Priscilla
Pilgrim, Anne

Likewise, a "Main entry" listing will lead the user to additional sources listed under an entrant's real name or most commonly cited of variants. Multiple names may be cited if the same pseudonym has been used by more than one person.

Allen, Betsy *AuBYP 2, –3, ConAu X, CurBio 50, InWom SUP, MajAI, SmATA X, TwCCChW 83, –89, . . .*
Main entry: Cavanna, Betty

Carroll, Elizabeth *ConAu 135, SmATA X, WrDr 90, –92, –94*
Main entry: Barkin, Carol
James, Elizabeth

The user is cautioned that some book sources cited within the pseudonym entry may, in fact, be cross-references directing the reader to a main entry in that book. Other sources may give the primary information at the pseudonym, particularly in the case of authors better known by a pseudonym (for example, the main entry for Charles Dodgson vs. the pseudonym entry for his better-known pen name, Lewis Carroll).

CA&I does not eliminate those citations that represent cross-references in the original sources. Therefore, users are advised to investigate first the sources cited within a main entry and then the unduplicated sources cited within a pseudonym entry.

- **Birth and death dates, if known**

If a source has indicated dates may not be accurate, or if discrepancies in dates were found among various sources, the questionable dates are preceded by a *c.* (circa) or followed by a question mark. In some instances, flourished dates are indicated by the abbreviation *fl.* and centuries by *cent.* If there is no year of birth, the death date is preceded by a lowercase *d.*

- **One or more biographical sources, represented by an alphabetic code**

When a name appears in more than one edition or volume of an indexed work, the title code for the book is given only once and followed by the various codes for the editions. In the example below, the name appears once in *ChlLR 17, FifBJA, MajAI,* and *MichAU 80,* and otherwise in multiple volumes/editions of sources cited:

Aardema, Verna 1911- *AuBYP 2S, –3, BioIn 9, –12, –17, ChlLR 17, ConAu 5R, –X, –39NR, FifBJA, MajAI, MichAu 80, SmATA 4, –68, 8AS, WrDr 76, –80, –82, –84, –88, –92, –94*

The key to book codes is printed on the endpapers and within the complete bibliography which follows this introduction.

Workbook Format

This edition retains the "workbook" format of the previous edition. Space has been allotted for librarians' use according to their particular needs; for example, entering additional information like Dewey or LC numbers or perhaps local information sources to which the *CA&I* editors do not have access. Cataloguers, in particular, may find this index helpful in the difficult task of identifying pseudonyms.

Suggestions are Welcome

Any comments or suggestions regarding future publications of *Children's Authors & Illustrators* will be most welcome.

Bibliographic Key to Source Codes

Code	*Book Indexed*
AfSS	*Africa South of the Sahara.* London: Europa Publications, 1980-1982.
	AfSS 80 10th edition, 1980-1981; 1980.
	AfSS 81 11th edition, 1981-1982; 1981.
	AfSS 82 12th edition, 1982-1983; 1982.
	Biographies are located in the "Who's Who in Africa South of the Sahara" section.
AfrAmBi	*African American Biographies.* Profiles of 558 current men and women. By Walter L. Hawkins. Jefferson, NC: McFarland & Co., 1992.
AfrAmW	*African American Writers.* Edited by Valerie Smith, Lea Baechler, and A. Walton Litz. New York: Charles Scribner's Sons, 1991.
AfrA	*African Authors.* A Companion to Black African Writing. Volume I: 1300-1973. By Donald E. Herdeck. Washington, DC: Black Orpheus Press, 1973.
AfrAmAl 6	*The African-American Almanac.* Sixth edition. Detroit: Gale Research, 1994. Formerly published as *The Negro Almanac.*
	Use the Index to locate biographies.
AfroAA	*Afro-American Artists.* A bio-bibliographical directory. Compiled and edited by Theresa Dickason Cederholm. Boston: Trustees of the Boston Public Library, 1973.
AgeMat	*The Age of Maturity, 1929-1941.* Concise Dictionary of American Literary Biography Series. Detroit: Gale Research, 1989.
ALA	*The ALA Yearbook.* A review of library events 1979. Volume 5, 1980. Chicago: American Library Association, 1980.
	ALA 80 Biographies begin on page 73.
	ALA 80N Obituary section begins on page 227.
Alli	*Allibone's Critical Dictionary of English Literature.* British and American authors living and deceased from the earliest accounts to the latter half of the Nineteenth Century. Three volumes. By S. Austin Allibone. Philadelphia: J.B. Lippincott & Co., 1858-1871. Reprint. Detroit: Gale Research, 1965.

Alli SUP *Allibone's Critical Dictionary of English Literature: A Supplement.* British and American authors. Two volumes. By John Foster Kirk. Philadelphia: J.B. Lippincott & Co., 1891. Reprint. Detroit: Gale Research, 1965.

AlmAP 78 *The Almanac of American Politics.* The senators, the representatives, the governors--their records, states, and districts. 1978 edition. By Michael Barone, Grant Ujifusa, and Douglas Matthews. New York: E.P. Dutton, 1977.

Use the "Names Index" to locate biographies.

AlmAP 82 *The Almanac of American Politics.* The president, the senators, the representatives, the governors: their records and election results, their states and districts. 1982 edition. By Michael Barone and Grant Ujifusa. Washington, DC: Barone & Co., 1981.

Use the "Index of Persons" to locate biographies.

AlmAP *The Almanac of American Politics.* The senators, the representatives, the governors: their records and election results, their states and districts. By Michael Barone and Grant Ujifusa. Washington, DC: National Journal, 1983-1991.

AlmAP 84	1984 edition; 1983. Use the "Index of People" to locate biographies.
AlmAP 88	1988 edition; 1987. Use the "Index of People" to locate biographies.
AlmAP 92	1992 edition; 1991. Use the index to locate biographies.

AmArch 70 *American Architects Directory.* Third edition. Edited by John F. Gane. New York: R.R. Bowker Co., 1970.

AmArt *American Artists.* An illustrated survey of leading contemporary Americans. Edited by Les Krantz. New York: Facts on File Publications, 1985.

AmAu *American Authors, 1600-1900.* A biographical dictionary of American literature. Edited by Stanley J. Kunitz and Howard Haycraft. Wilson Authors Series. New York: H.W. Wilson Co., 1938.

AmAu&B *American Authors and Books.* 1640 to the present day. Third revised edition. By W.J. Burke and Will D. Howe. Revised by Irving Weiss and Anne Weiss. New York: Crown Publishers, 1972.

AmCath 80 *The American Catholic Who's Who.* Volume 23, 1980-1981. Edited by Joy Anderson. Washington, DC: National Catholic News Service, 1979.

AmComp *American Composers.* A biographical dictionary. By David Ewen. New York: G.P. Putnam's Sons, 1982.

AmEA 74 *American Economic Association, Directory of Members, 1974.* Edited by Rendigs Fels. Published as Volume 64, Number 5 (October, 1974) of *The American Economic Review.*

AmGrD *American Graphic Designers.* Thirty years of design imagery. By RitaSue Siegel. New York: McGraw-Hill Book Co., 1984.

Use the Table of Contents to locate listings.

AmLY *The American Literary Yearbook.* A biographical and bibliographical dictionary of living North American authors. Volume 1, 1919. Edited by Hamilton Traub. Henning, MN: Paul Traub, 1919. Reprint. Detroit: Gale Research, 1968.

- ***AmLY*** "Biographical and Bibliographical Dictionary of Living North American Authors" section begins on page 57.
- ***AmLY X*** "Pen-names and Pseudonyms" section begins on page 49.

AmMWSc *American Men & Women of Science.* A biographical directory of today's leaders in physical, biological and related sciences. New Providence, NJ: R.R. Bowker Co., 1971-1992.

- ***AmMWSc 73P*** 12th edition, Physical & Biological Sciences Seven volumes; 1971.
- ***AmMWSc 73S*** 12th edition, Social & Behavioral Sciences. Two volumes; 1973.
- ***AmMWSc 76P*** 13th edition, Physical & Biological Sciences Seven volumes; 1976.
- ***AmMWSc 78S*** 13th edition, Social & Behavioral Sciences. One volume; 1978.
- ***AmMWSc 82*** 15th edition. Seven volumes; 1982.
- ***AmMWSc 86*** 16th edition. Eight volumes; 1986.
- ***AmMWSc 89*** 17th edition. Eight volumes; 1989.
- ***AmMWSc 92*** 18th edition, 1992-1993. Eight volumes; 1992.

AmNov *American Novelists of Today.* By Harry R. Warfel. New York: American Book Co., 1951. Reprint. Westport, Conn.: Greenwood Press, 1976.

- ***AmNov X*** "Index of Married Names and Pseudonyms" begins on page 477.

AmPeW *American Peace Writers, Editors, and Periodicals.* A dictionary. By Nancy L. Roberts. New York: Greenwood Press, 1991.

AmPB *American Picturebooks from "Noah's Ark" to "The Beast Within."* By Barbara Bader. New York: Macmillan Publishing Co.; London: Collier Macmillan Publishers, 1976.

AmPolW 80 *American Political Women.* Contemporary and historical profiles. By Esther Stineman. Littleton, CO: Libraries Unlimited, 1980.

- ***AmPolW 80A*** Appendix I: "Women of the Congress 1917-1980" begins on page 191.
- ***AmPolW 80C*** Appendix III: "Women Chiefs of Mission 1933-1980" begins on page 199.
- ***AmPolW 80E*** Appendix V: "Women Currently Serving in Government in Key Departmental, Agency, and White House Positions" begins on page 204.

AmSong *American Songwriters.* By David Ewen. New York: H.W. Wilson Co., 1987.

AmWomD *American Women Dramatists of the Twentieth Century.* A bibliography. By Brenda Coven. Metuchen, NJ: Scarecrow Press, 1982.

AmWomM *American Women Managers and Administrators.* A selective biographical dictionary of twentieth-century leaders in business, education, and government. By Judith A. Leavitt. Westport, CT: Greenwood Press, 1985.

AmWomPl *American Women Playwrights, 1900-1930.* A checklist. Compiled by Frances Diodato Bzowski. Bibliographies and Indexes in Women's Studies, no. 15. Westport, CT: Greenwood Press, 1992.

AmWomWr *American Women Writers.* A critical reference guide from colonial times to the present. Four volumes. Edited by Lina Mainiero. New York: Frederick Ungar Publishing Co., 1979-1982.

AmWomWr 92 *American Women Writers.* Diverse voices in prose since 1945. Edited by Eileen Barrett and Mary Cullinan. New York: St. Martin's Press, 1992.

Use the Table of Contents to locate biographies.

AmWr *American Writers.* A collection of literary biographies. New York: Charles Scribner's Sons, 1974-1991.

AmWr	Four volumes. Edited by Leonard Unger; 1974.
AmWr S1	Supplement I. Two parts. Edited by Leonard Unger; 1979.
AmWr S2	Supplement II. Two parts. Edited by A. Walton Litz; 1981.
AmWr S3	Supplement III. Two parts. Edited by Lea Baechler and A. Walton Litz; 1991.

AmWrBE *American Writers before 1800.* A biographical and critical dictionary. Three volumes. Edited by James A. Levernier and Douglas R. Wilmes. Westport, CT: Greenwood Press, 1983.

AnObit *The Annual Obituary.* New York: St. Martin's Press, 1981-1983.

AnObit 1980	*1980* ; 1981.
AnObit 1981	*1981* ; 1982.
AnObit 1982	*1982* ; 1983.

Use the "Alphabetical Index of Entrants" to locate biographies.

AnObit *The Annual Obituary.* Detroit: St. James Press, 1984-1993.

AnObit 1983	*1983* ; 1984.
AnObit 1984	*1984* ; 1985.
AnObit 1985	*1985* ; 1988.
AnObit 1986	*1986* ; 1989.
AnObit 1987	*1987* ; 1990.
AnObit 1988	*1988* ; 1990.
AnObit 1989	*1989* ; 1990.
AnObit 1990	*1990* ; 1991.
AnObit 1991	*1991* ; 1992.
AnObit 1992	*1992* ; 1993.

Use the "Alphabetical Index of Entrants" to locate biographies.

AnCL *Anthology of Children's Literature.* Fourth edition. Edited by Edna Johnson, Evelyn R. Sickels, and Frances Clarke Sayers. Boston: Houghton Mifflin Co., 1970.

Biographies begin on page 1217.

AnMV 1926 *Anthology of Magazine Verse for 1926 and Yearbook of American Poetry.* Edited by William Stanley Braithwaite. New York: G. Sully, 1926. Reprint. Granger Index Reprint Series. Freeport, N.Y.: Books for Libraries Press, 1972.

The "Biographical Dictionary of Poets in the United States" section begins on page 3 of part 4.

ArizL *Arizona in Literature.* A collection of the best writings of Arizona authors from early Spanish days to the present time. By Mary G. Boyer. Glendale, CA: Arthur H. Clark Co., 1935. Reprint. Ann Arbor, Mich.: Gryphon Books, 1971.

Use the Index to locate biographies.

ArtCS *The Art of the Comic Strip.* By Judith O'Sullivan. College Park, MD: University of Maryland, Department of Art, 1971.

Biographies begin on page 60.

ArtclWW 2 *Articles on Women Writers.* Volume 2, 1976-1984: A bibliography. By Narda Lacey Schwartz. Santa Barbara, CA: ABC-Clio, 1986.

ArtsAmW 2 *Artists of the American West.* A biographical dictionary. Volume II. By Doris Ostrander Dawdy. Chicago: Sage Books/Swallow Press, 1981.

ArtsAmW 3 *Artists of the American West.* A biographical dictionary. Volume III, *Artists Born before 1900.* By Doris Ostrander Dawdy. Athens, OH: Swallow Press/Ohio University Press, 1985.

ArtsCL *Artists of a Certain Line.* A selection of illustrations for children's books. By John Ryder. London: The Bodley Head, 1960.

ArtsEM *Artists of Early Michigan.* A biographical dictionary of artists native to or active in Michigan, 1701-1900. Compiled by Arthur Hopkin Gibson. Detroit: Wayne State University Press, 1975.

ArtsNiC *Artists of the Nineteenth Century and Their Works.* A handbook containing two thousand and fifty biographical sketches. Revised edition. Two volumes. By Clara Erskine Clement and Laurence Hutton. Boston: J.R. Osgood & Co., 1885. Reprint. Two volumes in one. St. Louis: North Point, 1969.

ASCAP 66 *The ASCAP Biographical Dictionary.* Third edition. New York: American Society of Composers, Authors and Publishers, 1966.

AsBiEn *Asimov's Biographical Encyclopedia of Science and Technology.* The lives and achievements of 1,195 great scientists from ancient times to the present, chronologically arranged. New revised edition. By Isaac Asimov. New York: Avon, 1976.

Use the "Alphabetic List of Biographical Entries" to locate biographies.

AtlBL *Atlantic Brief Lives.* A biographical companion to the arts. Edited by Louis Kronenberger. Boston: Little, Brown & Co., 1971.

AuLitCr *Australian Literary Criticism: 1945-1988.* An annotated bibliography. By Robert L. Ross. Garland Reference Library of the Humanities, vol. 1075. New York: Garland Publishing, 1989.

Biographies are located in the "Major Writers" section, which begins on page 155.

AuWomWr *Australian Women Writers.* A bibliographic guide. By Debra Adelaide. London: Pandora, 1988.

AuSpks — *The Author Speaks.* Selected "PW" interviews, 1967-1976. By *Publishers Weekly* editors and contributors. New York: R.R. Bowker Co., 1977.

Au&Arts — *Authors & Artists for Young Adults.* Detroit: Gale Research, 1989-1994.

Au&Arts 1	Volume 1; 1989.
Au&Arts 2	Volume 2; 1989.
Au&Arts 3	Volume 3; 1990.
Au&Arts 4	Volume 4; 1990.
Au&Arts 5	Volume 5; 1990.
Au&Arts 6	Volume 6; 1991.
Au&Arts 7	Volume 7; 1991.
Au&Arts 8	Volume 8; 1992.
Au&Arts 9	Volume 9; 1992.
Au&Arts 10	Volume 10; 1993.
Au&Arts 11	Volume 11; 1993.
Au&Arts 12	Volume 12; 1994.

AuBYP — *Authors of Books for Young People.* By Martha E. Ward et al. Metuchen, NJ: Scarecrow Press, 1971-1990.

AuBYP 2	Second edition; 1971.
AuBYP 2S	Supplement to the second edition; 1979.
AuBYP 2SA	Supplement to the second edition; 1979. Addendum to the Supplement begins on page 301.
AuBYP 3	Third edition; 1990.

Au&ICB — *Authors and Illustrators of Children's Books.* Writings on their lives and works. By Miriam Hoffman and Eva Samuels. New York: R.R. Bowker Co., 1972.

AuNews — *Authors in the News.* A compilation of news stories and feature articles from American newspapers and magazines covering writers and other members of the communications media. Edited by Barbara Nykoruk. Detroit: Gale Research, 1976.

AuNews 1	Volume 1.
AuNews 2	Volume 2.

Au&Wr 71 — *The Author's and Writer's Who's Who.* Sixth edition. Darien, CT: Hafner Publishing Co., 1971.

Baker 84 — *Baker's Biographical Dictionary of Musicians.* Seventh edition. Revised by Nicolas Slonimsky. New York: Macmillan, Schirmer Books, 1984.

Baker 92 — *Baker's Biographical Dictionary of Musicians.* Eighth edition. Revised by Nicolas Slonimsky. New York: Macmillan, 1992.

Ballpl 90 — *The Ballplayers.* Baseball's ultimate biographical reference. Edited by Mike Shatzkin. New York: William Morrow and Co., 1990.

Benet 87 — *Benet's Reader's Encyclopedia.* Third edition. New York: Harper & Row, 1987.

BenetAL 91 — *Benet's Reader's Encyclopedia of American Literature.* First edition. Edited by George Perkins, Barbara Perkins, and Phillip Leininger. New York: HarperCollins Publishers, 1991.

BestSel *Bestsellers.* Books and authors in the news. Detroit: Gale Research, 1989-1991.

BestSel 89-1	89, Issue 1; 1989.
BestSel 89-2	89, Issue 2; 1989.
BestSel 89-3	89, Issue 3; 1989.
BestSel 89-4	89, Issue 4; 1990.
BestSel 90-1	90, Issue 1; 1990.
BestSel 90-2	90, Issue 2; 1990.
BestSel 90-3	90, Issue 3; 1991.
BestSel 90-4	90, Issue 4; 1991.

BibAL 8 *Bibliography of American Literature.* Volume 8. Compiled by Jacob Blanck; edited and completed by Michael Winship. New Haven, CT: Yale University Press, 1990.

BbD *The Bibliophile Dictionary.* A biographical record of the great authors, with bibliographical notices of their principal works from the beginning of history. Originally published as Volumes 29 and 30 of *The Bibliophile Library of Literature, Art, and Rare Manuscripts.* Compiled and arranged by Nathan Haskell Dole, Forrest Morgan, and Caroline Ticknor. New York: International Bibliophile Society, 1904. Reprint. Detroit: Gale Research, 1966.

BbtC *Bibliotheca Canadensis.* Or, A manual of Canadian literature. By Henry J. Morgan. Ottawa: G.E. Desbarats, 1867. Reprint. Detroit: Gale Research, 1968.

BiGAW *A Bio-Bibliography of German-American Writers, 1670-1970.* By Robert E. Ward. White Plains, NY: Kraus International Publications, 1985.

BiNAW *A Biobibliography of Native American Writers, 1772-1924: A Supplement.* By Daniel F. Littlefield, Jr. and James W. Parins. Native American Bibliography Series, no. 5. Metuchen, NJ: Scarecrow Press, 1985.

BiNAW Sup	Part I: "A Bibliography of Native American Writers."
BiNAW SupB	Part III: "Biographical Notes" begins on page 165.

BiDAfM *Biographical Dictionary of Afro-American and African Musicians.* By Eileen Southern. Westport, CT: Greenwood Press, 1982.

BiDAmAr *Biographical Dictionary of American Architects, Deceased.* By Henry F. Withey and Elsie Rathburn Withey. Los Angeles: New Age Publishing Co., 1956.

BiDAmBL 83 *Biographical Dictionary of American Business Leaders.* By John N. Ingham. Westport, CT: Greenwood Press, 1983.

Use the Index to locate biographies.

BiDAmJo *Biographical Dictionary of American Journalism.* Edited by Joseph P. McKerns. New York: Greenwood Press, 1989.

BiDAmL *Biographical Dictionary of American Labor.* Edited by Gary M. Fink. Westport, CT: Greenwood Press, 1984.

Biographies begin on page 83.

BiDAmSp *Biographical Dictionary of American Sports.* Edited by David L. Porter. Westport, CT: Greenwood Press, 1987-1992.

BiDAmSp BB	*Baseball*; 1987.

BiDAmSp BK	*Basketball and Other Indoor Sports* ; 1989. Use the index to locate biographies.
BiDAmSp FB	*Football.*; 1987.
BiDAmSp OS	*Outdoor Sports* ; 1988. Use the Index to locate biographies.
BiDAmSp Sup	1989-1992 supplement for baseball, football, basketball, and other sports; 1992. Use the Index to locate biographies.

BiDBrF 2 *The Biographical Dictionary of British Feminists.* Volume Two: A supplement, 1900-1945. By Olive Banks. New York: New York University Press, 1990.

BiDConC *Biographical Dictionary of Contemporary Catholic American Writing.* Edited by Daniel J. Tynan. New York: Greenwood Press, 1989.

BiDD *Biographical Dictionary of Dance.* By Barbara Naomi Cohen-Stratyner. New York: Macmillan Publishing Co., Schirmer Books; London: Collier Macmillan Publishers, 1982.

BiDEWW *A Biographical Dictionary of English Women Writers, 1580-1720.* By Maureen Bell, George Parfitt, and Simon Shepherd. Boston: G.K. Hall & Co., 1990.

BiDExR *Biographical Dictionary of the Extreme Right since 1890.* By Philip Rees. New York: Simon & Schuster, 1990.

BiDFedJ *Biographical Dictionary of the Federal Judiciary.* Compiled by Harold Chase, Samuel Krislov, Keith O. Boyum, and Jerry N. Clark. Detroit: Gale Research, 1976.

BiDFilm *A Biographical Dictionary of Film.* First edition. By David Thomson. New York: William Morrow & Co., 1976.

BiDFrPL *Biographical Dictionary of French Political Leaders since 1870.* Edited by David S. Bell, Douglas Johnson, and Peter Morris. New York: Simon & Schuster, 1990.

BiDHisL *Biographical Dictionary of Hispanic Literature in the United States.* The literature of Puerto Ricans, Cuban Americans, and other Hispanic writers. Edited by Nicolas Kanellos. New York: Greenwood Press, 1989.

BiDInt *Biographical Dictionary of Internationalists.* Edited by Warren F. Kuehl. Westport, CT: Greenwood Press, 1983.

BiDIrW *A Biographical Dictionary of Irish Writers.* By Anne M. Brady and Brian Cleeve. New York: St. Martin's Press, 1985.

BiDIrW	"Writers in English" section begins on page 1.
BiDIrW B	"Writers in Irish and Latin" section begins on page 255.

BiDJaL *Biographical Dictionary of Japanese Literature.* By Sen'ichi Hisamatsu. Tokyo: Kodansha International, 1976. Distributed by Harper & Row, New York.

Use the Index to locate biographies.

BiDJaz — *Biographical Dictionary of Jazz.* By Charles Eugene Claghorn. Englewood Cliffs, NJ: Prentice-Hall, 1982.

BiDLA — *A Biographical Dictionary of the Living Authors of Great Britain and Ireland.* Comprising literary memoirs and anecdotes of their lives; and a chronological register of their publications. London: Printed for Henry Colburn, Public Library, Hanover Square, 1816. Reprint. Detroit: Gale Research, 1966.

BiDLA SUP — "Supplement of Additions and Corrections" begins on page 407.

BiDPara — *Biographical Dictionary of Parapsychology, 1964-1966.* Edited by Helene Pleasants. New York: Garrett Publications, Helix Press, 1964.

BiDPsy — *Biographical Dictionary of Psychology.* By Leonard Zusne. Westport, CT: Greenwood Press, 1984. A continuation of *Names in the History of Psychology: A Biographical Sourcebook.*

BiDRP&D — *A Biographical Dictionary of Renaissance Poets and Dramatists, 1520-1650.* By J.W. Saunders. Sussex, England: Harvester Press; Totowa, NJ: Barnes & Noble Books, 1983.

BiDScF — *A Biographical Dictionary of Science Fiction and Fantasy Artists.* By Robert Weinberg. New York: Greenwood Press, 1988.

BiDSA — *Biographical Dictionary of Southern Authors.* Compiled by Lucian Lamar Knight. Atlanta: Martin & Hoyt Co., 1929. Reprint. Detroit: Gale Research, 1978. Originally published as *Library of Southern Literature, Volume 15, Biographical Dictionary of Authors.*

BiD&SB — *Biographical Dictionary and Synopsis of Books Ancient and Modern.* Edited by Charles Dudley Warner. Akron, OH: Werner Co., 1902. Reprint. Detroit: Gale Research, 1965.

BiDrACP 79 — *Biographical Directory of the American College of Physicians.* 1979 edition. New York: R.R. Bowker Co., 1979.

Use the Index, which begins on page 1789, to locate biographies.

BiDrAPH 79 — *Biographical Directory of the American Public Health Association.* 1979 edition. New York: R.R. Bowker Co., 1979.

BiDrAPA 77 — *Biographical Directory: Fellows and Members of the American Psychiatric Association.* 1977 edition. New York: R.R. Bowker Co., 1977.

BiDrAPA 89 — *Biographical Directory: Fellows and Members of the American Psychiatric Association.* 1989 edition. Washington, DC: American Psychiatric Association, 1989. Distributed by American Psychiatric Press, Washington, DC.

BiDrLUS 70 — *A Biographical Directory of Librarians in the United States and Canada.* Fifth edition. Edited by Lee Ash. Chicago: American Library Association, 1970.

BiDrUSC 89 *Biographical Directory of the United States Congress, 1774-1989.* The Continental Congress, September 5, 1774 to October 21, 1788 and the Congress of the United States from the first through the one hundredth Congresses, March 4, 1789, to January 3, 1989, inclusive. Bicentennial Edition. Washington, DC: U.S. Government Printing Office, 1989.

Biographies begin on page 507.

BiDrUSE 89 *Biographical Directory of the United States Executive Branch. 1774-1989.* Edited by Robert Sobel. New York: Greenwood Press, 1990.

BiESc *A Biographical Encyclopedia of Scientists.* Two volumes. Edited by John Daintith, Sarah Mitchell, and Elizabeth Tootill. New York: Facts on File, 1981.

BiE&WWA *The Biographical Encyclopaedia and Who's Who of the American Theatre.* Edited by Walter Rigdon. New York: James H. Heineman, 1966. Revised edition published as *Notable Names in the American Theatre.*

The "Biographical Who's Who" section begins on page 227.

BiInAmS *Biographical Index to American Science.* The seventeenth century to 1920. Compiled by Clark A. Elliott. Bibliographies and Indexes in American History, no. 16. New York: Greenwood Press, 1990.

BioAmW *Biographies of American Women.* An annotated bibliography. By Patricia E. Sweeney. Santa Barbara, CA: ABC-Clio, 1990.

BioIn *Biography Index.* A cumulative index to biographical material in books and magazines. New York: H.W. Wilson Co., 1949-1992.

BioIn 1	Volume 1: January, 1946-July, 1949; 1949.
BioIn 2	Volume 2: August, 1949-August, 1952; 1953.
BioIn 3	Volume 3: September, 1952-August, 1955; 1956.
BioIn 4	Volume 4: September, 1955-August, 1958; 1960.
BioIn 5	Volume 5: September, 1958-August, 1961; 1962.
BioIn 6	Volume 6: September, 1961-August, 1964; 1965.
BioIn 7	Volume 7: September, 1964-August, 1967; 1968.
BioIn 8	Volume 8: September, 1967-August, 1970; 1971.
BioIn 9	Volume 9: September, 1970-August, 1973; 1974.
BioIn 10	Volume 10: September, 1973-August, 1976; 1977.
BioIn 11	Volume 11: September, 1976-August, 1979; 1980.
BioIn 12	Volume 12: September, 1979-August, 1982; 1983.
BioIn 13	Volume 13: September, 1982-August, 1984; 1984.
BioIn 14	Volume 14: September, 1984-August, 1986; 1986.
BioIn 15	Volume 15: September, 1986-August, 1988; 1988.
BioIn 16	Volume 16: September, 1988-August, 1990; 1990.
BioIn 17	Volume 17: September, 1990-August, 1992; 1992.

BioNews *Biography News.* A compilation of news stories and feature articles from American news media covering personalities of national interest in all fields. Edited by Frank E. Bair. Detroit: Gale Research, 1974-1975.

BioNews 74	Volume 1, Numbers 1-12; 1974.
BioNews 75	Volume 2, Number 1, January-February; 1975.

BlkAWP *Black American Writers Past and Present.* A biographical and bibliographical dictionary. Two volumes. By Theressa Gunnels Rush, Carol Fairbanks Myers, and Esther Spring Arata. Metuchen, NJ: Scarecrow Press, 1975.

BlkAuIl *Black Authors and Illustrators of Children's Books.* By Barbara Rollock. New York: Garland Publishing, 1988-1992.

BlkAuIl First edition. Garland Reference Library of the Humanities, vol. 660; 1988.

BlkAuIl 92 Second edition. Garland Reference Library of the Humanities, vol. 1316; 1992.

BlkLC *Black Literature Criticism.* Excerpts from criticism of the most significant works of Black authors over the past 200 years. Three volumes. Detroit: Gale Research, 1992.

BlkWWr *Black Women Writers (1950-1980).* A critical evaluation. Edited by Mari Evans. Garden City, NY: Anchor Press/Doubleday, 1984.

BlkWr *Black Writers.* A selection of sketches from *Contemporary Authors.* Detroit: Gale Research, 1989-1994.

BlkWr 1 First edition. 1989.
BlkWr 2 Second edition. 1994.

BlkWrNE *Black Writers in New England.* A bibliography, with biographical notes, of books by and about Afro-American writers associated with New England in the *Collection of Afro-American Literature.* By Edward Clark. Boston: National Park Service, 1985.

BlkWrNE A Section II, "Afro-American writers associated with New England not represented with books by or about them in the *Collection of Afro-American Literature,*" begins on page 70.

BlksAmF *Blacks in American Films and Television.* An encyclopedia. By Donald Bogle. Garland Reference Library of the Humanities, vol. 604. New York: Garland Publishing, 1988.

Biographies are located in the "Profiles" section which begins on page 353.

BlksScM *Blacks in Science and Medicine.* By Vivian Ovelton Sammons. New York: Hemisphere Publishing, 1990.

BlmGEL *The Bloomsbury Guide to English Literature.* The new authority on English literature. Edited by Marion Wynne-Davies. New York: Prentice Hall General Reference, 1990. Originally published in hardcover as the *Prentice Hall Guide to English Literature.*

Biographies begin on page 295.

BlmGWL *The Bloomsbury Guide to Women's Literature.* Edited by Claire Buck. New York: Prentice Hall General Reference, 1992.

Biographies begin on page 247.

BlueB 76 *The Blue Book.* Leaders of the English-speaking world. 1976 edition. London: St. James Press; New York: St. Martin's Press, 1976. Reprint. In two volumes by Gale Research, Detroit, 1979.

BlueB 76N Obituary section begins on page 1837.

BkC *The Book of Catholic Authors.* Informal self-portraits of famous modern Catholic writers. Edited by Walter Romig. Detroit: Walter Romig & Co., (n.d.).

BkC 1 First series; 1942.
BkC 2 Second series; 1943.
BkC 3 Third series; 1945.

BkC 4	Fourth series.
BkC 5	Fifth series.
BkC 6	Sixth series.

BkCL — *A Book of Children's Literature.* Third edition. Edited by Lillian Hollowell. New York: Holt, Rinehart & Winston, 1966.

Biographies begin on page 553.

BkIE — *Book Illustrators in Eighteenth-Century England.* By Hanns Hammelmann. Edited and completed by T.S.R. Boase. New Haven, CT: Yale University Press, 1975.

BkP — *Books Are by People.* Interviews with 104 authors and illustrators of books for young children. By Lee Bennett Hopkins. New York: Citation Press, 1969.

BriB — *Brilliant Bylines.* A biographical anthology of notable newspaperwomen in America. By Barbara Belford. New York: Columbia University Press, 1986.

BriEAA — *The Britannica Encyclopedia of American Art.* Chicago: Encyclopaedia Britannica Educational Corp., 1973. Distributed by Simon & Schuster, New York.

BritAS — *British and American Sporting Authors: Their Writings and Biographies.* By A. Henry Higginson. London: Hutchinson & Co., 1951.

Use the Index to locate biographies.

BritAu — *British Authors before 1800.* A biographical dictionary. Edited by Stanley J. Kunitz and Howard Haycraft. Wilson Authors Series. New York: H.W. Wilson Co., 1952.

BritAu 19 — *British Authors of the Nineteenth Century.* Edited by Stanley J. Kunitz. Wilson Authors Series. New York: H.W. Wilson Co., 1936.

BritCA — *British Children's Authors.* Interviews at Home. By Cornelia Jones and Olivia R. Way. Chicago: American Library Association, 1976.

BritWr — *British Writers.* New York: Charles Scribner's Sons, 1979-1992.

BritWr 1	Volume I: William Langland to The English Bible; 1979.
BritWr 2	Volume II: Thomas Middleton to George Farquhar; 1979.
BritWr 3	Volume III: Daniel Defoe to The Gothic Novel; 1980.
BritWr 4	Volume IV: William Wordsworth to Robert Browning; 1981.
BritWr 5	Volume V: Elizabeth Gaskell to Francis Thompson; 1982.
BritWr 6	Volume VI: Thomas Hardy to Wilfred Owen; 1983.
BritWr 7	Volume VII: Sean O'Casey to Poets of World War II; 1984.
BritWr S1	Supplement 1; 1987.
BritWr S2	Supplement 2; 1992.

Use the "List of Subjects" to locate biographies.

BroV — *Broadening Views, 1968-1988.* Concise Dictionary of American Literary Biography Series. Detroit: Gale Research, 1989.

BroadAu *Broadside Authors and Artists.* An illustrated biographical directory. Compiled and edited by Leaonead Pack Bailey. Detroit: Broadside Press, 1974.

BusPN *Business People in the News.* A compilation of news stories and feature articles from American newspapers and magazines covering people in industry, finance, and labor. Volume 1. Edited by Barbara Nykoruk. Detroit: Gale Research, 1976.

Cald 1938 *Caldecott Medal Books: 1938-1957.* With the artist's acceptance papers & related material chiefly from the *Horn Book Magazine.* Edited by Bertha Mahony Miller and Elinor Whitney Field. Horn Book Papers, volume II. Boston: Horn Book, 1957.

CamGEL *The Cambridge Guide to English Literature.* Edited by Michael Stapleton. Cambridge: Cambridge University Press; Middlesex, England: Newnes Books, 1983.

CamGLE *The Cambridge Guide to Literature in English.* Edited by Ian Ousby. Cambridge: Cambridge University Press; London: Hamlyn Publishing Group, 1988.

CamGWoT *The Cambridge Guide to World Theatre.* Edited by Martin Banham. Cambridge: Cambridge University Press, 1988.

CamHAL *The Cambridge Handbook of American Literature.* Edited by Jack Salzman. Cambridge: Cambridge University Press, 1986.

CaW *Canada Writes!* The members' book of the Writers' Union of Canada. Edited by K.A. Hamilton. Toronto: Writers' Union of Canada, 1977.

CanNov *Canadian Novelists, 1920-1945.* By Clara Thomas. Toronto: Longmans, Green & Co., 1946. Reprint. Folcroft, Penn.: Folcroft Library Editions, 1970.

CanWW 70 *Canadian Who's Who.* A biographical dictionary of notable living men and women. Volume 12, 1970-1972. Toronto: Who's Who Canadian Publications, 1972.

CanWW *Canadian Who's Who.* A biographical dictionary of notable living men and women. Edited by Kieran Simpson. Toronto: University of Toronto Press, 1979-1989.

CanWW 79	Volume 14; 1979.
CanWW 80	Volume 15; 1980.
CanWW 81	Volume 16; 1981.
CanWW 83	Volume 18; 1983.
CanWW 89	Volume 24; 1989.

CanWr *Canadian Writers.* A biographical dictionary. New edition, revised and enlarged. Edited by Guy Sylvestre, Brandon Conron, and Carl F. Klinck. Toronto: Ryerson Press, 1966.

CarSB *The Carolyn Sherwin Bailey Historical Collection of Children's Books.* A catalogue. Edited and compiled by Dorothy R. Davis. New Haven, CT: Southern Connecticut State College, 1966.

Not in strict alphabetic sequence.

CasWL *Cassell's Encyclopaedia of World Literature.* Two volumes. Edited by S.H. Steinberg. Revised and enlarged in three volumes by J. Buchanan-Brown. New York: William

Morrow & Co., 1973.

Biographies are found in Volumes 2 and 3 of the revised edition.

CathA *Catholic Authors.* Contemporary biographical sketches. Edited by Matthew Hoehn. Newark, NJ: St. Mary's Abbey, 1948-1952.

CathA 1930	First volume: 1930-1947; 1948.
CathA 1952	Second volume; 1952.

CelCen *Celebrities of the Century.* Being a dictionary of men and women of the nineteenth century. Two volumes. Edited by Lloyd C. Sanders. London: Cassell & Co., 1887. Reprint. Ann Arbor: Gryphon Books, 1971.

CelR *Celebrity Register.* Third edition. Edited by Earl Blackwell. New York: Simon & Schuster, 1973.

CelR 90 *Celebrity Register, 1990.* Detroit: Gale Research, 1990.

CenC *A Century of Ceramics in the United States, 1878-1978.* A study of its development. By Garth Clark. New York: E.P. Dutton, 1979.

Biographies begin on page 269.

Chambr *Chambers's Cyclopaedia of English Literature.* A history critical and biographical of authors in the English tongue from the earliest times till the present day with specimens of their writings. Edited by David Patrick, revised by J. Liddell Geddie. Philadelphia: J.B. Lippincott, 1938. Reprint. Detroit: Gale Research, 1978.

Chambr 1	Volume I: 7th-17th Century.
Chambr 2	Volume II: 18th Century.
Chambr 3	Volume III: 19th-20th Century.

Use the Index to locate biographies.

ChiLit *Chicano Literature: A Reference Guide.* Edited by Julio A. Martinez and Francisco A. Lomeli. Westport, CT: Greenwood Press, 1985.

ChiSch *Chicano Scholars and Writers.* A bio-bibliographical directory. Edited and compiled by Julio A. Martinez. Metuchen, NJ: Scarecrow Press, 1979.

ChhPo *Childhood in Poetry.* A catalogue, with biographical and critical annotations, of the books of English and American poets comprising the Shaw Childhood in Poetry Collection in the Library of the Florida State University. By John Mackay Shaw. Detroit: Gale Research, 1967-1976.

ChhPo	First edition; 1967.
ChhPo S1	First Supplement; 1972.
ChhPo S2	Second Supplement; 1976.

ChlBIlD *Children's Book Illustration and Design.* Edited by Julie Cummins. Library of Applied Design. New York: PBC International, 1992. Distributed by Rizzoli International Publications, New York.

ChlFicS *Children's Fiction Sourcebook.* A survey of children's books for 6-13 year olds. By Margaret Hobson, Jennifer Madden, and Ray Prytherch. Brookfield, VT: Ashgate Publishing Co., 1992.

ChlLR *Children's Literature Review.* Excerpts from reviews, criticism, and commentary on books for children and young people. Detroit: Gale Research, 1976-1994.

ChlLR 1	Volume 1; 1976.
ChlLR 2	Volume 2; 1976.
ChlLR 3	Volume 3; 1978.
ChlLR 4	Volume 4; 1982.
ChlLR 5	Volume 5; 1983.
ChlLR 6	Volume 6; 1984.
ChlLR 7	Volume 7; 1984.
ChlLR 8	Volume 8; 1985.
ChlLR 9	Volume 9; 1985.
ChlLR 10	Volume 10; 1986.
ChlLR 11	Volume 11; 1986.
ChlLR 12	Volume 12; 1987.
ChlLR 13	Volume 13; 1987.
ChlLR 14	Volume 14; 1988.
ChlLR 15	Volume 15; 1988.
ChlLR 16	Volume 16; 1989.
ChlLR 17	Volume 17; 1989.
ChlLR 18	Volume 18; 1989.
ChlLR 19	Volume 19; 1990.
ChlLR 20	Volume 20; 1990.
ChlLR 21	Volume 21; 1990.
ChlLR 22	Volume 22; 1991.
ChlLR 23	Volume 23; 1991.
ChlLR 24	Volume 24; 1991.
ChlLR 25	Volume 25; 1991.
ChlLR 26	Volume 26; 1992.
ChlLR 27	Volume 27; 1992.
ChlLR 28	Volume 28; 1992.
ChlLR 29	Volume 29; 1993.
ChlLR 30	Volume 30; 1993.
ChlLR 31	Volume 31; 1994.
ChlLR 32	Volume 32; 1994.

ChrP *The Children's Poets.* Analyses and appraisals of the greatest English and American poets for children. By Walter Barnes. Yonkers-on-Hudson, NY: World Book Co., 1924.

ChsFB *The Child's First Books.* A critical study of pictures and texts. By Donnarae MacCann and Olga Richard. New York: H.W. Wilson Co., 1973.

ChsFB A	"Author Biographies" begin on page 96.
ChsFB I	"Illustrator Biographies" begin on page 47.

CivR 74 *Civil Rights: A Current Guide to the People, Organizations, and Events.* Second edition. By Joan Martin Burke. New York: R.R. Bowker Co., 1974.

Biographies begin on page 21.

CivWDc *The Civil War Dictionary.* By Mark Mayo Boatner, III. New York: David McKay Co., 1959.

ClaDrA *The Classified Directory of Artists' Signatures, Symbols, & Monograms.* Second edition, enlarged and revised. By H.H. Caplan. London: George Prior Publishers, 1982. Distributed by Gale Research, Detroit.

ClDMEL 47 *Columbia Dictionary of Modern European Literature.* First edition. Edited by Horatio Smith. New York: Columbia University Press, 1947.

CmCal — *A Companion to California.* By James D. Hart. New York: Oxford University Press, 1978.

CmMov — *A Companion to the Movies: From 1903 to the Present Day.* A guide to the leading players, directors, screenwriters, composers, cameramen and other artistes who have worked in the English-speaking cinema over the last 70 years. By Roy Pickard. New York: Hippocrene Books, 1972.

Use the "Who's Who Index" to locate biographies.

CmScLit — *Companion to Scottish Literature.* By Trevor Royle. Detroit: Gale Research, 1983.

CmpEPM — *The Complete Encyclopedia of Popular Music and Jazz, 1900-1950.* Three volumes. By Roger D. Kinkle. New Rochelle, NY: Arlington House Publishers, 1974.

Biographies are located in Volumes 2 and 3.

CompSN SUP — *Composers since 1900.* A biographical and critical guide. *First Supplement.* Compiled and edited by David Ewen. New York: H.W. Wilson Co., 1981.

CpmDNM — *Composium Directory of New Music.* Annual index of contemporary compositions. Sedro Woolley, WA: Crystal Musicworks, 1981-1983.

CpmDNM 81	1981 edition; 1981.
CpmDNM 82	1982/83 edition; 1983.

CnDAL — *Concise Dictionary of American Literature.* Edited by Robert Fulton Richards. New York: Philosophical Library, 1955. Reprint. New York: Greenwood Press, 1969.

CnDBLB — *Concise Dictionary of British Literary Biography.* Detroit: Gale Research, 1992.

CnDBLB 1	Volume 1: *Writers of the Middle Ages and Renaissance before 1660* ; 1992.
CnDBLB 2	Volume 2: *Writers of the Restoration and Eighteenth Century, 1660-1789* ; 1992.
CnDBLB 3	Volume 3: *Writers of the Romantic Period, 1789-1832* ; 1992.
CnDBLB 4	Volume 4: *Victorian Writers, 1832-1890* ; 1991.
CnDBLB 5	Volume 5: *Late Victorian and Edwardian Writers, 1890-1914* ; 1991.
CnDBLB 6	Volume 6: *Modern Writers, 1914-1945* ; 1991.
CnDBLB 7	Volume 7: *Writers After World War II, 1945-1960* ; 1991.
CnDBLB 8	Volume 8: *Contemporary Writers, 1960 to the Present* ; 1992.

CnE&AP — *The Concise Encyclopedia of English and American Poets and Poetry.* Edited by Stephen Spender and Donald Hall. New York: Hawthorn Books, 1963.

CnMD — *The Concise Encyclopedia of Modern Drama.* By Siegfried Melchinger. Translated by George Wellwarth. Edited by Henry Popkin. New York: Horizon Press, 1964.

CnMD	Biographies begin on page 159.
CnMD SUP	"Additional Entries" section begins on page 287.

CnMWL — *The Concise Encyclopedia of Modern World Literature.* Second edition. Edited by Geoffrey Grigson. London: Hutchinson & Co., 1970.

CnThe *A Concise Encyclopedia of the Theatre.* By Robin May. Reading, England: Osprey Publishing, 1974.

Use the Index to locate biographies.

CngDr *Congressional Directory.* Washington, DC: United States Government Printing Office, 1989-1991.

CngDr 89	101st Congress, 1989-1990; 1989.
CngDr 91	102d Congress, 1991-1992; 1991.

Use the "Name Index" to locate biographies.

ConAmA *Contemporary American Authors.* A critical survey and 219 bio-bibliographies. By Fred B. Millett. New York: Harcourt, Brace & World, 1940. Reprint. New York: AMS Press, 1970.

Biographies begin on page 207.

ConAmC *Contemporary American Composers.* A biographical dictionary. Compiled by E. Ruth Anderson. Boston: G.K. Hall & Co., 1976-1982.

ConAmC 76	First edition; 1976.
ConAmC 76A	First edition; 1976. Addendum begins on page 495.
ConAmC 82	Second edition; 1982.

ConAmL *Contemporary American Literature.* Bibliographies and study outlines. By John Matthews Manly and Edith Rickert. Revised by Fred B. Millett. New York: Harcourt, 1929. Reprint. New York: Haskell House Publishers, 1974.

Biographies begin on page 101.

ConAmTC *Contemporary American Theater Critics.* A directory and anthology of their works. Compiled by M.E. Comtois and Lynn F. Miller. Metuchen, NJ: Scarecrow Press, 1977.

ConAmWS *Contemporary American Women Sculptors.* By Virginia Watson-Jones. Phoenix, AZ: Oryx Press, 1986.

ConArt *Contemporary Artists.* Contemporary Arts Series. New York: St. Martin's Press, 1977-1983.

ConArt 77	First edition. Edited by Colin Naylor and Genesis P-Orridge; 1977.
ConArt 83	Second edition. Edited by Muriel Emanuel et al; 1983.

ConArt 89 *Contemporary Artists.* Third edition. Edited by Colin Naylor. Contemporary Arts Series. Chicago: St. James Press, 1989. Distributed by Gale Research, Detroit.

ConAu *Contemporary Authors.* A bio-bibliographical guide to current writers in fiction, general nonfiction, poetry, journalism, drama, motion pictures, television, and other fields. Detroit: Gale Research, 1967-1994.

ConAu 1R	Volumes 1-4, 1st revision; 1967.
ConAu 5R	Volumes 5-8, 1st revision; 1969.
ConAu 9R	Volumes 9-12, 1st revision; 1974.
ConAu 13R	Volumes 13-16, 1st revision; 1975.
ConAu 17R	Volumes 17-20, 1st revision; 1976.
ConAu 21R	Volumes 21-24, 1st revision; 1977.
ConAu 25R	Volumes 25-28, 1st revision; 1977.

ConAu 29R	Volumes 29-32, 1st revision; 1978.
ConAu 33R	Volumes 33-36, 1st revision; 1978.
ConAu 37R	Volumes 37-40, 1st revision; 1979.
ConAu 41R	Volumes 41-44, 1st revision; 1979.
ConAu 45	Volumes 45-48; 1974.
ConAu 49	Volumes 49-52; 1975.
ConAu 53	Volumes 53-56; 1975.
ConAu 57	Volumes 57-60; 1976.
ConAu 61	Volumes 61-64; 1976.
ConAu 65	Volumes 65-68; 1977.
ConAu 69	Volumes 69-72; 1978.
ConAu 73	Volumes 73-76; 1978.
ConAu 77	Volumes 77-80; 1979.
ConAu 81	Volumes 81-84; 1979.
ConAu 85	Volumes 85-88; 1980.
ConAu 93	Volumes 93-96; 1980.
ConAu 97	Volumes 97-100; 1981.
ConAu 101	Volume 101; 1981.
ConAu 102	Volume 102; 1981.
ConAu 103	Volume 103; 1982.
ConAu 104	Volume 104; 1982.
ConAu 105	Volume 105; 1982.
ConAu 106	Volume 106; 1982.
ConAu 107	Volume 107; 1983.
ConAu 108	Volume 108; 1983.
ConAu 109	Volume 109; 1983.
ConAu 110	Volume 110; 1984.
ConAu 111	Volume 111; 1984.
ConAu 112	Volume 112; 1985.
ConAu 113	Volume 113; 1985.
ConAu 114	Volume 114; 1985.
ConAu 115	Volume 115; 1985.
ConAu 116	Volume 116; 1986.
ConAu 117	Volume 117; 1986.
ConAu 118	Volume 118; 1986.
ConAu 119	Volume 119; 1987.
ConAu 120	Volume 120; 1987.
ConAu 121	Volume 121; 1987.
ConAu 122	Volume 122; 1988.
ConAu 123	Volume 123; 1988.
ConAu 124	Volume 124; 1988.
ConAu 125	Volume 125; 1989.
ConAu 126	Volume 126; 1989.
ConAu 127	Volume 127; 1989.
ConAu 128	Volume 128; 1990.
ConAu 129	Volume 129; 1990.
ConAu 130	Volume 130; 1990.
ConAu 131	Volume 131; 1991.
ConAu 132	Volume 132; 1991.
ConAu 133	Volume 133; 1991.
ConAu 134	Volume 134; 1992.
ConAu 135	Volume 135; 1992.
ConAu 136	Volume 136; 1992.
ConAu 137	Volume 137; 1992.
ConAu 138	Volume 138; 1993.
ConAu 139	Volume 139; 1993.
ConAu 140	Volume 140; 1993.
ConAu 141	Volume 141; 1994.
ConAu 142	Volume 142; 1994.

ConAu *Contemporary Authors, Autobiography Series.* Detroit: Gale Research, 1984-1994.

ConAu 1AS	Volume 1; 1984.
ConAu 2AS	Volume 2; 1985.
ConAu 3AS	Volume 3; 1986.
ConAu 4AS	Volume 4; 1986.
ConAu 5AS	Volume 5; 1987.
ConAu 6AS	Volume 6; 1988.
ConAu 7AS	Volume 7; 1988.
ConAu 8AS	Volume 8; 1989.
ConAu 9AS	Volume 9; 1989.
ConAu 10AS	Volume 10; 1989.
ConAu 11AS	Volume 11; 1990.
ConAu 12AS	Volume 12; 1990.
ConAu 13AS	Volume 13; 1991.
ConAu 14AS	Volume 14; 1991.
ConAu 15AS	Volume 15; 1992.
ConAu 16AS	Volume 16; 1992.
ConAu 17AS	Volume 17; 1993.
ConAu 18AS	Volume 18; 1994.

ConAu *Contemporary Authors, Bibliographical Series.* Detroit: Gale Research, 1986-1989.

ConAu 1BS	Volume 1: *American Novelists.* Edited by James J. Martine; 1986.
ConAu 2BS	Volume 2: *American Poets.* Edited by Ronald Baughman; 1986.
ConAu 3BS	Volume 3: *American Dramatists.* Edited by Matthew C. Roudane; 1989.

ConAu X *Contemporary Authors, Index.* A bio-bibliographical guide to current writers in fiction, general nonfiction, poetry, journalism, drama, motion pictures, television, and other fields. Detroit: Gale Research, (n.d.).

This code refers to Pseudonym Entries which appear only as Cross-References in the Cumulative Index.

ConAu *Contemporary Authors, New Revision Series.* A bio-bibliographical guide to current writers in fiction, general nonfiction, poetry, journalism, drama, motion pictures, television, and other fields. Detroit: Gale Research, 1981-1994.

ConAu 1NR	Volume 1; 1981.
ConAu 2NR	Volume 2; 1981.
ConAu 3NR	Volume 3; 1981.
ConAu 4NR	Volume 4; 1981.
ConAu 5NR	Volume 5; 1982.
ConAu 6NR	Volume 6; 1982.
ConAu 7NR	Volume 7; 1982.
ConAu 8NR	Volume 8; 1983.
ConAu 9NR	Volume 9; 1983.
ConAu 10NR	Volume 10; 1983.
ConAu 11NR	Volume 11; 1984.
ConAu 12NR	Volume 12; 1984.
ConAu 13NR	Volume 13; 1984.
ConAu 14NR	Volume 14; 1985.
ConAu 15NR	Volume 15; 1985.
ConAu 16NR	Volume 16; 1986.
ConAu 17NR	Volume 17; 1986.
ConAu 18NR	Volume 18; 1986.
ConAu 19NR	Volume 19; 1987.
ConAu 20NR	Volume 20; 1987.
ConAu 21NR	Volume 21; 1987.

ConAu 22NR	Volume 22; 1988.
ConAu 23NR	Volume 23; 1988.
ConAu 24NR	Volume 24; 1988.
ConAu 25NR	Volume 25; 1989.
ConAu 26NR	Volume 26; 1989.
ConAu 27NR	Volume 27; 1989.
ConAu 28NR	Volume 28; 1990.
ConAu 29NR	Volume 29; 1990.
ConAu 30NR	Volume 30; 1990.
ConAu 31NR	Volume 31; 1990.
ConAu 32NR	Volume 32; 1991.
ConAu 33NR	Volume 33; 1991.
ConAu 34NR	Volume 34; 1991.
ConAu 35NR	Volume 35; 1992.
ConAu 36NR	Volume 36; 1992.
ConAu 37NR	Volume 37; 1992.
ConAu 38NR	Volume 38; 1993.
ConAu 39NR	Volume 39; 1992.
ConAu 40NR	Volume 40; 1993.
ConAu 41NR	Volume 41; 1994.
ConAu 42NR	Volume 42; 1994.
ConAu 43NR	Volume 43; 1994.

ConAu *Contemporary Authors, Permanent Series.* A bio-bibliographical guide to current authors and their works. Detroit: Gale Research, 1975-1978.

ConAu P-1	Volume 1; 1975.
ConAu P-2	Volume 2; 1978.

ConBlAP 88 *Contemporary Black American Playwrights and Their Plays.* A biographical directory and dramatic index. By Bernard L. Peterson, Jr. New York: Greenwood Press, 1988.

ConBlB *Contemporary Black Biography.* Profiles from the international black community. Detroit: Gale Research, 1992-1994.

ConBlB 1	Volume 1; 1992.
ConBlB 2	Volume 2; 1992.
ConBlB 3	Volume 3; 1993.
ConBlB 4	Volume 4; 1993.
ConBlB 5	Volume 5; 1994.
ConBlB 6	Volume 6; 1994.

ConBrA 79 *Contemporary British Artists.* Edited by Charlotte Parry-Crooke. New York: St. Martin's Press, 1979.

Biographies are found in the "Directory" section.

ConCom 92 *Contemporary Composers.* Edited by Brian Morton and Pamela Collins. Chicago: St. James Press, 1992.

ConDes 84 *Contemporary Designers.* First edition. Edited by Ann Lee Morgan. Contemporary Arts Series. Detroit: Gale Research, 1984.

ConDes 90 *Contemporary Designers.* Second edition. Edited by Colin Naylor. Contemporary Arts Series. Chicago: St. James Press, 1990.

Author Index" to locate entries.

ConLC 45	Volume 45; 1987.
ConLC 46	Volume 46; 1988.
ConLC 47	Volume 47; 1988.
ConLC 48	Volume 48; 1988.
ConLC 49	Volume 49; 1988.
ConLC 50	Volume 50: Yearbook 1987; 1988. Use the "Cumulative Author Index" to locate entries.
ConLC 51	Volume 51; 1989.
ConLC 52	Volume 52; 1989.
ConLC 53	Volume 53; 1989.
ConLC 54	Volume 54; 1989.
ConLC 55	Volume 55: Yearbook 1988; 1989. Use the "Cumulative Author Index" to locate entries.
ConLC 56	Volume 56; 1989.
ConLC 57	Volume 57; 1990.
ConLC 58	Volume 58; 1990.
ConLC 59	Volume 59: Yearbook 1989; 1990. Use the "Cumulative Author Index" to locate entries.
ConLC 60	Volume 60; 1990.
ConLC 61	Volume 61; 1990.
ConLC 62	Volume 62; 1991.
ConLC 63	Volume 63; 1991.
ConLC 64	Volume 64; 1991.
ConLC 65	Volume 65: Yearbook 1990; 1991. Use the "Cumulative Author Index" to locate entries.
ConLC 66	Volume 66; 1991.
ConLC 67	Volume 67; 1992.
ConLC 68	Volume 68; 1992.
ConLC 69	Volume 69; 1992.
ConLC 70	Volume 70: Yearbook 1991; 1992. Use the "Cumulative Author Index" to locate entries.
ConLC 71	Volume 71; 1992.
ConLC 72	Volume 72; 1992.
ConLC 73	Volume 73; 1993.
ConLC 74	Volume 74; 1993.
ConLC 75	Volume 75; 1993.
ConLC 76	Volume 76: Yearbook 1992; 1993. Use the "Cumulative Author Index" to locate entries.
ConLC 77	Volume 77; 1993.
ConLC 78	Volume 78; 1994.
ConLC 79	Volume 79; 1994.
ConLC 80	Volume 80; 1994.
ConLC 81	Volume 81: Yearbook 1993; 1994. Use the "Cumulative Author Index" to locate entries.

ConLCrt 77 *Contemporary Literary Critics*. First edition. By Elmer Borklund. London: St. James Press; New York: St. Martin's Press, 1977.

ConLCrt 82 *Contemporary Literary Critics*. Second edition. By Elmer Borklund. Detroit: Gale Research, 1982.

ConMus *Contemporary Musicians*. Profiles of the people in music. Detroit: Gale Research, 1989-1994.

ConMus 1	Volume 1; 1989.
ConMus 2	Volume 2; 1990.
ConMus 3	Volume 3; 1990.
ConMus 4	Volume 4; 1991.
ConMus 5	Volume 5; 1991.

ConMus 6	Volume 6; 1992.
ConMus 7	Volume 7; 1992.
ConMus 8	Volume 8; 1993.
ConMus 9	Volume 9; 1993.
ConMus 10	Volume 10; 1994.

ConNews *Contemporary Newsmakers.* A biographical guide to people in the news in business, education, technology, social issues, politics, law, economics, international affairs, religion, entertainment, labor, sports, design, psychology, medicine, astronautics, ecology, and other fields. Detroit: Gale Research, 1985-1988.Later editions published as *Newsmakers.*

ConNews 85-2	1985, Issue 2; 1985.
ConNews 86-2	1986, Issue 2; 1986.
ConNews 87-2	1987, Issue 2; 1987.
ConNews 87-3	1987, Issue 3; 1988.
ConNews 88-1	1988, Issue 1; 1988.

Use the "Cumulative Newsmaker Index" to locate entries in each quarterly edition.

ConNov *Contemporary Novelists.* Chicago: St. James Press, 1972-1991.

ConNov 72	First edition. Edited by James Vinson; 1972.
ConNov 76	Second edition. Edited by James Vinson; 1976.
ConNov 82	Third edition. Edited by James Vinson; 1982.
ConNov 82A	Third edition. Edited by James Vinson; 1982. The Appendix is located at the back of this edition.
ConNov 86	Fourth edition. Edited by D.L. Kirkpatrick; 1986.
ConNov 86A	Fourth edition. Edited by D.L. Kirkpatrick; 1986. The Appendix is located at the back of this edition.
ConNov 91	Fifth edition. Edited by Lesley Henderson; 1991.

ConPhot 82 *Contemporary Photographers.* Edited by George Walsh, Colin Naylor, and Michael Held. Contemporary Arts Series. New York: St. Martin's Press, 1982.

ConPhot 88 *Contemporary Photographers.* Second edition. Edited by Colin Naylor. Chicago: St. James Press, 1988. Distributed by Gale Research, Detroit.

ConPo *Contemporary Poets.* Chicago: St. James Press, 1970-1991.

ConPo 70	First edition. Edited by Rosalie Murphy; 1970.
ConPo 75	Second edition. Edited by James Vinson; 1975.
ConPo 80	Third edition. Edited by James Vinson; 1980.
ConPo 80A	Third edition. Edited by James Vinson; 1980. The Appendix is located at the back of this edition.
ConPo 85	Fourth edition. Edited by James Vinson and D.L. Kirkpatrick; 1985.
ConPo 85A	Fourth edition. Edited by James Vinson and D.L. Kirkpatrick; 1985. The Appendix is located at the back of this edition.
ConPo 91	Fifth edition. Edited by Tracy Chevalier; 1991.

ConSFA *Contemporary Science Fiction Authors.* First edition. Compiled and edited by R. Reginald. New York: Arno Press, 1975. Previously published as *Stella Nova: The Contemporary Science Fiction Authors.* Los Angeles: Unicorn & Son, Publishers, 1970.

ConSFF	*Contemporary Science Fiction, Fantasy, and Horror Poetry.* A resource guide and biographical directory. By Scott E. Green. New York: Greenwood Press, 1989. Biographies are found in the "Biographical Directory of Poets" section which begins on page 85.
ConTFT	*Contemporary Theatre, Film, and Television.* A biographical guide featuring performers, directors, writers, producers, designers, managers, choreographers, technicians, composers, executives, dancers, and critics in the United States and Great Britain. Detroit: Gale Research, 1984-1994. Earlier editions published as *Who's Who in the Theatre.*

ConTFT 1	Volume 1; 1984.
ConTFT 2	Volume 2; 1986.
ConTFT 3	Volume 3; 1986.
ConTFT 4	Volume 4; 1987.
ConTFT 5	Volume 5; 1988.
ConTFT 6	Volume 6; 1989.
ConTFT 7	Volume 7; 1989.
ConTFT 8	Volume 8; 1990.
ConTFT 9	Volume 9; 1992.
ConTFT 10	Volume 10; 1993.
ConTFT 11	Volume 11; 1994.

ConWorW 93 — *Contemporary World Writers.* Second edition. Edited by Tracy Chevalier. Contemporary Writers of the English Language Series. Detroit: St. James Press, 1993. First edition published as *Contemporary Foreign-Language Writers.*

ContDcW 89 — *The Continuum Dictionary of Women's Biography.* Second edition. Edited by Jennifer S. Uglow. New York: Continuum Publishing, 1989. First edition published as *The International Dictionary of Women's Biography.*

Conv — *Conversations.* Conversations series. Detroit: Gale Research, 1977-1978.

Conv 1	Volume 1: *Conversations with Writers*; 1977.
Conv 3	Volume 3: *Conversations with Writers II*; 1978.

CorpD — *Corpus Delicti of Mystery Fiction.* A guide to the body of the case. By Linda Herman and Beth Stiel. Metuchen, NJ: Scarecrow Press, 1974.

Biographies begin on page 31.

CreCan — *Creative Canada.* A biographical dictionary of twentieth-century creative and performing artists. Compiled by the Reference Division, McPherson Library, University of Victoria, British Columbia. Toronto: University of Toronto Press, 1971-1972.

CreCan 1	Volume 1; 1971.
CreCan 2	Volume 2; 1972.

CrtSuMy — *Critical Survey of Mystery and Detective Fiction.* Four volumes. Edited by Frank N. Magill. Pasadena, CA: Salem Press, 1988.

CrtT — *The Critical Temper.* A survey of modern criticism on English and American literature from the beginnings to the twentieth century. Edited by Martin Tucker. A Library of Literary Criticism. New York: Frederick Ungar Publishing Co., 1969.

CrtT 1	Volume I: From Old English to Shakespeare.
CrtT 2	Volume II: From Milton to Romantic Literature.
CrtT 3	Volume III: Victorian Literature and American Literature.

CroCAP *Crowell's Handbook of Contemporary American Poetry.* By Karl Malkoff. New York: Thomas Y. Crowell Co., 1973.

Biographies begin on page 43.

CroCD *Crowell's Handbook of Contemporary Drama.* By Michael Anderson et al. New York: Thomas Y. Crowell Co., 1971.

CroE&S *Crowell's Handbook of Elizabethan & Stuart Literature.* By James E. Ruoff. New York: Thomas Y. Crowell Co., 1975.

CurBio *Current Biography Yearbook.* New York: H.W. Wilson Co., 1940-1993.

CurBio 40 *1940* ; 1940.
CurBio 41 *1941* ; 1941.
CurBio 42 *1942* ; 1942.
CurBio 43 *1943* ; 1943.
CurBio 44 *1944* ; 1944.
CurBio 45 *1945* ; 1945.
CurBio 46 *1946* ; 1946.
CurBio 47 *1947* ; 1947.
CurBio 48 *1948* ; 1948.
CurBio 49 *1949* ; 1949.
CurBio 50 *1950* ; 1950.
CurBio 51 *1951* ; 1951.
CurBio 52 *1952* ; 1952.
CurBio 53 *1953* ; 1953.
CurBio 54 *1954* ; 1954.
CurBio 55 *1955* ; 1955.
CurBio 56 *1956* ; 1956.
CurBio 57 *1957* ; 1957.
CurBio 58 *1958* ; 1958.
CurBio 59 *1959* ; 1959.
CurBio 60 *1960* ; 1960.
CurBio 61 *1961* ; 1961.
CurBio 62 *1962* ; 1962.
CurBio 63 *1963* ; 1963.
CurBio 64 *1964* ; 1964.
CurBio 65 *1965* ; 1965.
CurBio 66 *1966* ; 1966.
CurBio 67 *1967* ; 1967.
CurBio 68 *1968* ; 1968.
CurBio 69 *1969* ; 1969.
CurBio 70 *1970* ; 1970.
CurBio 71 *1971* ; 1971.
CurBio 72 *1972* ; 1972.
CurBio 73 *1973* ; 1973.
CurBio 74 *1974* ; 1974.
CurBio 75 *1975* ; 1975.
CurBio 75N *1975.*; 1975. Obituary Section located in the back of the volume.
CurBio 76 *1976* ; 1976.
CurBio 76N *1976.*; 1976. Obituary Section located in the back of the volume.
CurBio 77 *1977* ; 1977.
CurBio 77N *1977.*; 1977. Obituary Section located in the back of the volume.
CurBio 78 *1978* ; 1978.
CurBio 78N *1978.*; 1978. Obituary Section located in the back of the volume.

CurBio 79 — *1979*; 1979.
CurBio 79N — *1979.*; 1979. Obituary Section located in the back of the volume.
CurBio 80 — *1980*; 1980.
CurBio 80N — *1980.*; 1980. Obituary Section located in the back of the volume.
CurBio 81 — *1981*; 1981.
CurBio 81N — *1981.*; 1981. Obituary Section located in the back of the volume.
CurBio 82 — *1982*; 1982.
CurBio 82N — *1982.*; 1982. Obituary Section located in the back of the volume.
CurBio 83 — *1983*; 1983.
CurBio 83N — *1983.*; 1983. Obituary Section located in the back of the volume.
CurBio 84 — *1984*; 1985.
CurBio 84N — *1984.*; 1985. Obituary Section located in the back of the volume.
CurBio 85 — *1985*; 1985.
CurBio 85N — *1985.*; 1985. Obituary Section located in the back of the volume.
CurBio 86 — *1986*; 1987.
CurBio 86N — *1986.*; 1987. Obituary Section located in the back of the volume.
CurBio 87 — *1987*; 1988.
CurBio 87N — *1987.*; 1988. Obituary Section located in the back of the volume.
CurBio 88 — *1988*; 1989.
CurBio 88N — *1988.*; 1989. Obituary Section located in the back of the volume.
CurBio 89 — *1989*; 1990.
CurBio 89N — *1989.*; 1990. Obituary section located in the back of the volume.
CurBio 90 — *1990*; 1990.
CurBio 90N — *1990.*; 1990. Obituary section located in the back of the volume.
CurBio 91 — *1991*; 1991.
CurBio 91N — *1991.*; 1991. Obituary section located in the back of the volume.
CurBio 92 — *1992*; 1992.
CurBio 92N — *1992.*; 1992. Obituary section located in the back of the volume.
CurBio 93 — *1993*; 1993.
CurBio 93N — *1993.*; 1993. Obituary section located in the back of the volume.

CyAG — *Cyclopedia of American Government.* Three volumes. Edited by Andrew C. McLaughlin and Albert Bushnell Hart. New York: D. Appleton & Co., 1914. Reprint. Gloucester, Mass.: Peter Smith, 1963.

CyAL — *Cyclopaedia of American Literature.* Embracing personal and critical notices of authors, and selections from their writings, from the earliest period to the present day; with portraits, autographs, and other illustrations. Two volumes. By Evert A. Duyckinck and George L. Duyckinck. Philadelphia: William Rutter & Co., 1875. Reprint. Detroit: Gale Research Co., 1965.

Use the Index in volume 2 to locate biographies.

CyEd — *A Cyclopedia of Education.* Five volumes. Edited by Paul Monroe. New York: Macmillan Co., 1911. Reprint. Detroit: Gale Research, 1968.

CyWA 58 *Cyclopedia of World Authors.* Edited by Frank N. Magill. New York: Harper & Row, Publishers, 1958. Also published as *Masterplots Cyclopedia of World Authors.*

CyWA 89 *Cyclopedia of World Authors II.* Four volumes. Edited by Frank N. Magill. Pasadena, CA: Salem Press, 1989.

DcAfHiB 86 *Dictionary of African Historical Biography.* Second edition. By Mark R. Lipschutz and R. Kent Rasmussen. Berkeley, CA and Los Angeles: University of California Press, 1986.

DcAfAmP *Dictionary of Afro-American Performers.* 78 RPM and cylinder recordings of opera, choral music, and songs, c. 1900-1949. By Patricia Turner. Garland Reference Library of the Humanities, vol. 590. New York: Garland Publishing, 1990.

DcAfL *Dictionary of Afro-Latin American Civilization.* By Benjamin Nunez. Westport, CT: Greenwood Press, 1980.

DcAmAu *A Dictionary of American Authors.* Fifth edition, revised and enlarged. By Oscar Fay Adams. New York: Houghton Mifflin Co., 1904. Reprint. Detroit: Gale Research, 1969.

Biographies are found in the "Dictionary of American Authors" section which begins on page 1 and in the "Supplement" which begins on page 441.

DcAmB *Dictionary of American Biography.* New York: Charles Scribner's Sons; London: Collier Macmillan Publishers, 1928-1988.

DcAmB	Volumes 1-20; 1928.
DcAmB S1	Supplement 1; 1944.
DcAmB S2	Supplement 2; 1958.
DcAmB S3	Supplement 3; 1973.
DcAmB S4	Supplement 4; 1974.
DcAmB S5	Supplement 5; 1977.
DcAmB S6	Supplement 6; 1980.
DcAmB S7	Supplement 7; 1981.
DcAmB S8	Supplement 8, 1966-1970; 1988.

DcAmBC *Dictionary of American Book Collectors.* By Donald C. Dickinson. New York: Greenwood Press, 1986.

DcAmChF *Dictionary of American Children's Fiction.* Books of recognized merit. By Alethea K. Helbig and Agnes Regan Perkins. Westport, CT: Greenwood Press, 1986-1993.

DcAmChF 1960	*1960-1984.*; 1986.
DcAmChF 1985	*1985-1989.*; 1993.

DcAmDH *Dictionary of American Diplomatic History.* By John E. Findling. New York: Greenwood Press, 1980-1989.

DcAmDH 80	First edition; 1980.
DcAmDH 89	Second edition; 1989.

DcAmImH *Dictionary of American Immigration History.* Edited by Francesco Cordasco. Metuchen, NJ: Scarecrow Press, 1990.

DcAmMeB *Dictionary of American Medical Biography.* Lives of eminent physicians of the United States and Canada, from the earliest times. By Howard A. Kelly and Walter L. Burrage. New York: D. Appleton & Co., 1928. Reprint. Road Town, Tortola, British Virgin Islands: Longwood Press, 1979.

DcAmMeB 84 *Dictionary of American Medical Biography.* Two volumes. Edited by Martin Kaufman, Stuart Galishoff, and Todd L. Savitt. Westport, CT: Greenwood Press, 1984.

DcAmNB *Dictionary of American Negro Biography.* Edited by Rayford W. Logan and Michael R. Winston. New York: W.W. Norton & Co., 1982.

DcAmReB 2 *Dictionary of American Religious Biography.* Second edition. By Henry Warner Bowden. Westport, CT: Greenwood Press, 1993.

DcAmSR *A Dictionary of American Social Reform.* By Louis Filler. New York: Philosophical Library, 1963.

DcBiA *A Dictionary of Biographies of Authors Represented in the Authors Digest Series.* With a supplemental list of later titles and a supplementary biographical section. Edited by Rossiter Johnson. New York: Authors Press, 1927. Reprint. Detroit: Gale Research, 1974.

"Biographies of Authors" begin on page 3 and "Biographies of Authors Whose Works Are in Volume XVIII" begin on page 437.

DcBiPP *A Dictionary of Biography, Past and Present.* Containing the chief events in the lives of eminent persons of all ages and nations. Edited by Benjamin Vincent. Haydn Series. London: Ward, Lock, & Co., 1877. Reprint. Detroit: Gale Research, 1974.

DcBiPP A Addenda begin on page 638.

DcBrAmW *A Dictionary of British and American Women Writers, 1660-1800.* Edited by Janet Todd. Totowa, NJ: Rowman & Allanheld, 1985.

Biographies begin on page 27.

DcBrAr *Dictionary of British Artists Working 1900-1950.* By Grant M. Waters. Eastbourne, England: Eastbourne Fine Art Publications, 1975-1976.

DcBrAr 1 Volume I, 1975.
DcBrAr 2 Volume II, 1976.

DcBrBI *The Dictionary of British Book Illustrators and Caricaturists, 1800-1914.* By Simon Houfe. Woodbridge, England: Antique Collectors' Club, 1978.

Biographies begin on page 215.

DcBrECP *The Dictionary of British Eighteenth Century Painters in Oils and Crayons* By Ellis Waterhouse. Woodbridge, England: Antique Collectors' Club, 1981.

DcCanB *Dictionary of Canadian Biography.* Toronto: University of Toronto Press, 1966-1990.

DcCanB 1 *Volume I: 1000 to 1700.* Edited by George W. Brown; 1966.
DcCanB 2 *Volume II: 1701 to 1740.* Edited by David M. Hayne; 1969.
DcCanB 3 *Volume III: 1741 to 1770.* Edited by Francess G.

Halpenny; 1974.

DcCanB 4	*Volume IV: 1771 to 1800.* Edited by Francess G. Halpenny; 1979.
DcCanB 5	*Volume V: 1801 to 1820.* Edited by Francess G. Halpenny; 1983.
DcCanB 6	*Volume VI: 1821-1835.* Edited by Francess G. Halpenny; 1987.
DcCanB 7	*Volume VII: 1836 to 1850.* Edited by Francess G. Halpenny; 1988.
DcCanB 8	*Volume VIII: 1851-1860.* Edited by Francess G. Halpenny; 1985.
DcCanB 9	*Volume IX: 1861 to 1870.* Edited by Francess G. Halpenny; 1976.
DcCanB 10	*Volume X: 1871 to 1880.* Edited by Marc La Terreur; 1972.
DcCanB 11	*Volume XI: 1881 to 1890.* Edited by Henri Pilon; 1982.
DcCanB 12	*Volume XII: 1891 to 1900.* Edited by Francess G. Halpenny; 1990.

DcCathB *Dictionary of Catholic Biography.* By John J. Delaney and James Edward Tobin. Garden City, NY: Doubleday & Co., 1961.

DcChlFi *Dictionary of Children's Fiction from Australia, Canada, India, New Zealand, and Selected African Countries.* Books of recognized merit. By Alethea K. Helbig and Agnes Regan Perkins. Westport, CT: Greenwood Press, 1992.

DcCAA *Dictionary of Contemporary American Artists.* By Paul Cummings. New York: St. Martin's Press; London: St. James Press, 1971-1988.

DcCAA 71	Second edition; 1971.
DcCAA 77	Third edition; 1977.
DcCAA 88	Fifth edition; 1988.

DcCAr 81 *Dictionary of Contemporary Artists.* Edited by V. Babington Smith. Oxford: Clio Press, 1981.

DcCLAA *A Dictionary of Contemporary Latin American Authors.* Compiled by David William Foster. Tempe, AZ: Center for Latin American Studies, Arizona State University, 1975.

DcCM *Dictionary of Contemporary Music.* Edited by John Vinton. New York: E.P. Dutton & Co., 1974.

This book ignores prefixes in filing surnames.

DcD&D *Dictionary of Design & Decoration.* A Studio Book. New York: Viking Press, 1973.

DcEnA *A Dictionary of English Authors, Biographical and Bibliographical.* Being a compendious account of the lives and writings of upwards of 800 British and American writers from the year 1400 to the present time. New edition, revised with an appendix. By R. Farquharson Sharp. London: Kegan Paul, Trench, Trubner & Co., 1904. Reprint. Detroit: Gale Research, 1978.

DcEnA A	Appendix begins on page 311.

DcEnL *Dictionary of English Literature.* Being a comprehensive guide to English authors and their works. Second edition. By W. Davenport Adams. London: Cassell Petter & Galpin, (n.d.). Reprint. Detroit: Gale Research, 1966.

DcEuL *A Dictionary of European Literature.* Designed as a companion to English studies. Second, revised edition. By Laurie Magnus. London: George Routledge & Sons; New York: E.P. Dutton & Co., 1927. Reprint. Detroit: Gale Research, 1974.

The Appendix begins on page 595.

DcFM *Dictionary of Film Makers.* By Georges Sadoul. Translated, edited, and updated by Peter Morris. Berkeley, CA and Los Angeles: University of California Press 1972. Originally published as *Dictionnaire des Cineastes,* 1965.

DcInB *Dictionary of Indian Biography.* By C.E. Buckland. London: Swan Sonnenschein & Co., 1906. Reprint. Detroit: Gale Research, 1968.

DcInv *Dictionary of Inventions & Discoveries.* Edited by E.F. Carter. Stevenage, England: Robin Clark, 1978.

DcIrB 88 *A Dictionary of Irish Biography.* Second edition. By Henry Boylan. New York: St. Martin's Press, 1988.

DcIrL *Dictionary of Irish Literature.* Edited by Robert Hogan. Westport, CT: Greenwood Press, 1979. Also published as *The Macmillan Dictionary of Irish Literature.* London: Macmillan Press, 1980.

DcIrW 1 *Dictionary of Irish Writers.* Volume 1: Fiction. By Brian Cleeve. Cork, Ireland: Mercier Press, 1967.

DcItL *Dictionary of Italian Literature.* Edited by Peter Bondanella and Julia Conaway Bondanella. Westport, CT: Greenwood Press, 1979.

DcLB *Dictionary of Literary Biography.* Detroit: Gale Research, 1978-1994.

- ***DcLB 1*** Volume 1: *The American Renaissance in New England.* Edited by Joel Myerson; 1978.
- ***DcLB 2*** Volume 2: *American Novelists since World War II.* Edited by Jeffrey Helterman and Richard Layman; 1978.
- ***DcLB 3*** Volume 3: *Antebellum Writers in New York and the South.* Edited by Joel Myerson; 1979.
- ***DcLB 4*** Volume 4: *American Writers in Paris, 1920-1939.* Edited by Karen Lane Rood; 1980.
- ***DcLB 5*** Volume 5: *American Poets since World War II.* Two parts. Edited by Donald J. Greiner; 1980.
- ***DcLB 6*** Volume 6: *American Novelists since World War II.* Second Series. Edited by James E. Kibler, Jr; 1980.
- ***DcLB 7*** Volume 7: *Twentieth-Century American Dramatists.* Two parts. Edited by John MacNicholas; 1981.
- ***DcLB 8*** Volume 8: *Twentieth-Century American Science-Fiction Writers.* Two parts. Edited by David Cowart and Thomas L. Wymer; 1981.
- ***DcLB 9*** Volume 9: *American Novelists, 1910-1945.* Three parts. Edited by James J. Martine; 1981.
- ***DcLB 10*** Volume 10: *Modern British Dramatists, 1900-1945.* Two parts. Edited by Stanley Weintraub; 1982.

DcLB 11	Volume 11: *American Humorists, 1800-1950.* Two parts. Edited by Stanley Trachtenberg; 1982.
DcLB 12	Volume 12: *American Realists and Naturalists.* Edited by Donald Pizer and Earl N. Harbert; 1982.
DcLB 13	Volume 13: *British Dramatists since World War II.* Two parts. Edited by Stanley Weintraub; 1982.
DcLB 14	Volume 14: *British Novelists since 1960.* Two parts. Edited by Jay L. Halio; 1983.
DcLB 15	Volume 15: *British Novelists, 1930-1959.* Two parts. Edited by Bernard Oldsey; 1983.
DcLB 16	Volume 16: *The Beats: Literary Bohemians in Postwar America.* Two parts. Edited by Ann Charters; 1983.
DcLB 17	Volume 17: *Twentieth-Century American Historians.* Edited by Clyde N. Wilson; 1983.
DcLB 18	Volume 18: *Victorian Novelists after 1885.* Edited by Ira B. Nadel and William E. Fredeman; 1983.
DcLB 19	Volume 19: *British Poets, 1880-1914.* Edited by Donald E. Stanford; 1983.
DcLB 20	Volume 20: *British Poets, 1914-1945.* Edited by Donald E. Stanford; 1983.
DcLB 21	Volume 21: *Victorian Novelists before 1885.* Edited by Ira B. Nadel and William E. Fredeman; 1983.
DcLB 22	Volume 22: *American Writers for Children, 1900-1960.* Edited by John Cech; 1983.
DcLB 23	Volume 23: *American Newspaper Journalists, 1873-1900.* Edited by Perry J. Ashley; 1983.
DcLB 24	Volume 24: *American Colonial Writers, 1606-1734.* Edited by Emory Elliott; 1984.
DcLB 25	Volume 25: *American Newspaper Journalists, 1901-1925.* Edited by Perry J. Ashley; 1984.
DcLB 26	Volume 26: *American Screenwriters.* Edited by Robert E. Morsberger, Stephen O. Lesser, and Randall Clark; 1984.
DcLB 27	Volume 27: *Poets of Great Britain and Ireland, 1945-1960.* Edited by Vincent B. Sherry, Jr; 1984.
DcLB 28	Volume 28: *Twentieth-Century American-Jewish Fiction Writers.* Edited by Daniel Walden; 1984.
DcLB 29	Volume 29: *American Newspaper Journalists, 1926-1950.* Edited by Perry J. Ashley; 1984.
DcLB 30	Volume 30: *American Historians, 1607-1865.* Edited by Clyde N. Wilson; 1984.
DcLB 31	Volume 31: *American Colonial Writers, 1735-1781.* Edited by Emory Elliott; 1984.
DcLB 31A	Volume 31: *American Colonial Writers, 1735-1781.* Edited by Emory Elliott; 1984. Appendix I: "Eighteenth-Century Philosophical Background." Use the Table of Contents to locate entries.
DcLB 32	Volume 32: *Victorian Poets before 1850.* Edited by William E. Fredeman and Ira B. Nadel; 1984.
DcLB 33	Volume 33: *Afro-American Fiction Writers after 1955.* Edited by Thadious M. Davis and Trudier Harris; 1984.
DcLB 34	Volume 34: *British Novelists, 1890-1929: Traditionalists.* Edited by Thomas F. Staley; 1985.
DcLB 35	Volume 35: *Victorian Poets after 1850.* Edited by William E. Fredeman and Ira B. Nadel; 1985.
DcLB 36	Volume 36: *British Novelists, 1890-1929: Modernists.* Edited by Thomas F. Staley; 1985.
DcLB 37	Volume 37: *American Writers of the Early Republic.* Edited by Emory Elliott; 1985.
DcLB 38	Volume 38: *Afro-American Writers after 1955: Dramatists and Prose Writers.* Edited by Thadious M. Davis and Trudier Harris; 1985.

DcLB 39	Volume 39: *British Novelists, 1660-1800.* Two parts. Edited by Martin C. Battestin; 1985.
DcLB 40	Volume 40: *Poets of Great Britain and Ireland since 1960.* Two parts. Edited by Vincent B. Sherry, Jr; 1985.
DcLB 41	Volume 41: *Afro-American Poets since 1955.* Edited by Trudier Harris and Thadious M. Davis; 1985.
DcLB 42	Volume 42: *American Writers for Children before 1900.* Edited by Glenn E. Estes; 1985.
DcLB 43	Volume 43: *American Newspaper Journalists, 1690-1872.* Edited by Perry J. Ashley; 1985.
DcLB 44	Volume 44: *American Screenwriters.* Second Series. Edited by Randall Clark; 1986.
DcLB 45	Volume 45: *American Poets, 1880-1945.* First Series. Edited by Peter Quartermain; 1986.
DcLB 47	Volume 47: *American Historians, 1866-1912.* Edited by Clyde N. Wilson; 1986.
DcLB 48	Volume 48: *American Poets, 1880-1945.* Second Series. Edited by Peter Quartermain; 1986.
DcLB 50	Volume 50: *Afro-American Writers before the Harlem Renaissance.* Edited by Trudier Harris; 1986.
DcLB 51	Volume 51: *Afro-American Writers from the Harlem Renaissance to 1940.* Edited by Trudier Harris; 1987.
DcLB 52	Volume 52: *American Writers for Children since 1960: Fiction.* Edited by Glenn E. Estes; 1986.
DcLB 53	Volume 53: *Canadian Writers since 1960.* First Series. Edited by W.H. New; 1986.
DcLB 54	Volume 54: *American Poets, 1880-1945.* Third Series. Two parts. Edited by Peter Quartermain; 1987.
DcLB 55	Volume 55: *Victorian Prose Writers before 1867.* Edited by William B. Thesing; 1987.
DcLB 56	Volume 56: *German Fiction Writers, 1914-1945.* Edited by James Hardin; 1987.
DcLB 57	Volume 57: *Victorian Prose Writers after 1867.* Edited by William B. Thesing; 1987.
DcLB 58	Volume 58: *Jacobean and Caroline Dramatists.* Edited by Fredson Bowers; 1987.
DcLB 59	Volume 59: *American Literary Critics and Scholars, 1800-1850.* Edited by John W. Rathbun; 1987.
DcLB 60	Volume 60: *Canadian Writers since 1960.* Second Series. Edited by W.H. New; 1987.
DcLB 61	Volume 61: *American Writers for Children since 1960: Poets, Illustrators, and Nonfiction Authors.* Edited by Glenn E. Estes; 1987.
DcLB 62	Volume 62: *Elizabethan Dramatists.* Edited by Fredson Bowers; 1987.
DcLB 63	Volume 63: *Modern American Critics, 1920-1955.* Edited by Gregory S. Jay; 1988.
DcLB 64	Volume 64: *American Literary Critics and Scholars, 1850-1880.* Edited by John W. Rathbun and Monica M. Grecu; 1988.
DcLB 65	Volume 65: *French Novelists, 1900-1930.* Edited by Catharine Savage Brosman; 1988.
DcLB 66	Volume 66: *German Fiction Writers, 1885-1913.* Two parts. Edited by James Hardin; 1988.
DcLB 67	Volume 67: *Modern American Critics since 1955.* Edited by Gregory S. Jay; 1988.
DcLB 68	Volume 68: *Canadian Writers, 1920-1959.* First Series. Edited by W.H. New; 1988.
DcLB 69	Volume 69: *Contemporary German Fiction Writers.* First Series. Edited by Wolfgang D. Elfe; 1988.
DcLB 70	Volume 70: *British Mystery Writers, 1860-1919.* Edited

by Bernard Benstock; 1988.

DcLB 71 Volume 71: *American Literary Critics and Scholars, 1880-1900.* Edited by John W. Rathbun and Monica M. Grecu; 1988.

DcLB 72 Volume 72: *French Novelists, 1930-1960.* Edited by Catharine Savage Brosman; 1988.

DcLB 73 Volume 73: *American Magazine Journalists, 1741-1850.* Edited by Sam G. Riley; 1988.

DcLB 74 Volume 74: *American Short-Story Writers before 1880.* Edited by Bobby Ellen Kimbel; 1988.

DcLB 75 Volume 75: *Contemporary German Fiction Writers.* Second Series. Edited by Wolfgang D. Elfe and James Hardin; 1988.

DcLB 76 Volume 76: *Afro-American Writers, 1940-1955.* Edited by Trudier Harris; 1988.

DcLB 77 Volume 77: *British Mystery Writers, 1920-1939.* Edited by Bernard Benstock and Thomas F. Staley; 1989.

DcLB 78 Volume 78: *American Short-Story Writers, 1880-1910.* Edited by Bobby Ellen Kimbel; 1989.

DcLB 79 Volume 79: *American Magazine Journalists, 1850-1900.* Edited by Sam G. Riley; 1989.

DcLB 80 Volume 80: *Restoration and Eighteenth-Century Dramatists.* First Series. Edited by Paula R. Backscheider; 1989.

DcLB 81 Volume 81: *Austrian Fiction Writers, 1875-1913.* Edited by James Hardin and Donald G. Daviau; 1989.

DcLB 82 Volume 82: *Chicano Writers.* First Series. Edited by Francisco A. Lomeli and Carl R. Shirley; 1989.

DcLB 83 Volume 83: *French Novelists since 1960.* Edited by Catharine Savage Brosman; 1989.

DcLB 84 Volume 84: *Restoration and Eighteenth-Century Dramatists.* Second Series. Edited by Paula R. Backscheider; 1989.

DcLB 85 Volume 85: *Austrian Fiction Writers after 1914.* Edited by James Hardin and Donald G. Daviau; 1989.

DcLB 86 Volume 86: *American Short-Story Writers, 1910-1945.* First Series. Edited by Bobby Ellen Kimbel; 1989.

DcLB 87 Volume 87: *British Mystery and Thriller Writers since 1940.* First Series. Edited by Bernard Benstock and Thomas F. Staley; 1989.

DcLB 88 Volume 88: *Canadian Writers, 1920-1959.* Second Series. Edited by W.H. New; 1989.

DcLB 89 Volume 89: *Restoration and Eighteenth-Century Dramatists.* Third Series. Edited by Paula R. Backscheider; 1989.

DcLB 90 Volume 90: *German Writers in the Age of Goethe, 1789-1832.* Edited by James Hardin and Christoph E. Schweitzer; 1989.

DcLB 91 Volume 91: *American Magazine Journalists 1900-1960.* First Series. Edited by Sam G. Riley; 1990.

DcLB 92 Volume 92: *Canadian Writers, 1890-1920.* Edited by W.H. New; 1990.

DcLB 93 Volume 93: *British Romantic Poets, 1789-1832.* First Series. Edited by John R. Greenfield; 1990.

DcLB 94 Volume 94: *German Writers in the Age of Goethe: Sturm und Drang to Classicism.* Edited by James Hardin and Christoph Schweitzer; 1990.

DcLB 95 Volume 95: *Eighteenth-Century British Poets.* First Series. Edited by John Sitter; 1990.

DcLB 96 Volume 96: *British Romantic Poets, 1789-1832.* Second Series. Edited by John R. Greenfield; 1990.

DcLB 97	Volume 97: *German Writers from the Enlightenment to Sturm und Drang, 1720-1764.* Edited by James Hardin and Christoph E. Schweitzer; 1990.
DcLB 98	Volume 98: *Modern British Essayists.* First Series. Edited by Robert Beum; 1990.
DcLB 99	Volume 99: *Canadian Writers before 1890.* Edited by W.H. New; 1990.
DcLB 100	Volume 100: *Modern British Essayists.* Second Series. Edited by Robert Beum; 1990.
DcLB 101	Volume 101: *British Prose Writers, 1660-1800.* First Series. Edited by Donald T. Siebert; 1991.
DcLB 102	Volume 102: *American Short-Story Writers, 1910-1945.* Second Series. Edited by Bobby Ellen Kimbel; 1991.
DcLB 103	Volume 103: *American Literary Biographers.* First Series. Edited by Steven Serafin; 1991.
DcLB 104	Volume 104: *British Prose Writers, 1660-1800.* Second Series. Edited by Donald T. Siebert; 1991.
DcLB 105	Volume 105: *American Poets since World War II.* Second Series. Edited by R.S. Gwynn; 1991.
DcLB 106	Volume 106: *British Literary Publishing Houses, 1820-1880.* Edited by Patricia J. Anderson and Jonathan Rose; 1991.
DcLB 107	Volume 107: *British Romantic Prose Writers, 1789-1832.* First Series. Edited by John R. Greenfield; 1991.
DcLB 108	Volume 108: *Twentieth-Century Spanish Poets.* First Series. Edited by Michael L. Perna; 1991.
DcLB 109	Volume 109: *Eighteenth-Century British Poets.* Second Series. Edited by John Sitter; 1991.
DcLB 110	Volume 110: *British Romantic Prose Writers, 1789-1832.* Second Series. Edited by John R. Greenfield; 1991.
DcLB 111	Volume 111: *American Literary Biographers.* Second Series. Edited by Steven Serafin; 1991.
DcLB 112	Volume 112: *British Literary Publishing Houses, 1881-1965.* Edited by Jonathan Rose and Patricia J. Anderson; 1991.
DcLB 113	Volume 113: *Modern Latin-American Fiction Writers.* First Series. Edited by William Luis; 1992.
DcLB 114	Volume 114: *Twentieth-Century Italian Poets.* First Series. Edited by Giovanna Wedel De Stasio, Glauco Cambon, and Antonio Illiano; 1992.
DcLB 115	Volume 115: *Medieval Philosophers.* Edited by Jeremiah Hackett; 1992.
DcLB 116	Volume 116: *British Romantic Novelists, 1789-1832.* Edited by Bradford K. Mudge; 1992.
DcLB 117	Volume 117: *Twentieth-Century Caribbean and Black African Writers.* First Series. Edited by Bernth Lindfors and Reinhard Sander; 1992.
DcLB 118	Volume 118: *Twentieth-Century German Dramatists, 1889-1918.* Edited by Wolfgang D. Elfe and James Hardin; 1992.
DcLB 119	Volume 119: *Nineteenth-Century French Fiction Writers: Romanticism and Realism, 1800-1860.* Edited by Catharine Savage Brosman; 1992.
DcLB 120	Volume 120: *American Poets since World War II.* Third Series. Edited by R.S. Gwynn; 1992.
DcLB 121	Volume 121: *Seventeenth-Century British Nondramatic Poets.* First Series. Edited by M. Thomas Hester; 1992.
DcLB 122	Volume 122: *Chicano Writers.* Second Series. Edited by Francisco A. Lomeli and Carl R. Shirley; 1992.
DcLB 123	Volume 123: *Nineteenth-Century French Fiction Writers: Naturalism and Beyond, 1860-1900.* Edited by Catharine

Savage Brosman; 1992.

DcLB 124 Volume 124: *Twentieth-Century German Dramatists, 1919-1992.* Edited by Wolfgang D. Elfe and James Hardin; 1992.

DcLB 125 Volume 125: *Twentieth-Century Caribbean and Black African Writers.* Second Series. Edited by Bernth Lindfors and Reinhard Sander; 1993.

DcLB 126 Volume 126: *Seventeenth-Century British Nondramatic Poets.* Second Series. Edited by M. Thomas Hester; 1993.

DcLB 127 Volume 127: *American Newspaper Publishers, 1950-1990.* Edited by Perry J. Ashley; 1993.

DcLB 128 Volume 128: *Twentieth-Century Italian Poets.* Second Series. Edited by Giovanna Wedel De Stasio, Glauco Cambon, and Antonio Illiano; 1993.

DcLB 129 Volume 129: *Nineteenth-Century German Writers, 1841-1900.* Edited by James Hardin and Siegfried Mews; 1993.

DcLB 130 Volume 130: *American Short-Story Writers since World War II.* Edited by Patrick Meanor; 1993.

DcLB 131 Volume 131: *Seventeenth-Century British Nondramatic Poets.* Third Series. Edited by M. Thomas Hester; 1993.

DcLB 132 Volume 132: *Sixteenth-Century British Nondramatic Writers.* First Series. Edited by David A. Richardson; 1993.

DcLB 133 Volume 133: *Nineteenth-Century German Writers to 1840.* Edited by James Hardin and Siegfried Mews; 1993.

DcLB 134 Volume 134: *Twentieth-Century Spanish Poets.* Second Series. Edited by Jerry Phillips Winfield; 1994.

DcLB 135 Volume 135: *British Short-Fiction Writers, 1880-1914: The Realist Tradition.* Edited by William B. Thesing; 1994.

DcLB 136 Volume 136: *Sixteenth-Century British Nondramatic Writers.* Second Series. Edited by David A. Richardson; 1994.

DcLB 137 Volume 137: *American Magazine Journalists, 1900-1960.* Second Series. Edited by Sam G. Riley; 1994.

DcLB 138 Volume 138: *German Writers and Works of the High Middle Ages: 1170-1280.* Edited by James Hardin and Will Hasty; 1994.

DcLB 139 Volume 139: *British Short-Fiction Writers, 1945-1980.* Edited by Dean Baldwin; 1994.

DcLB 140 Volume 140: *American Book-Collectors and Bibliographers.* First Series. Edited by Joseph Rosenblum; 1994.

DcLB *Dictionary of Literary Biography, Documentary Series.* An illustrated chronicle. Detroit: Gale Research, 1982-1992.

DcLB DS1 Volume 1. Edited by Margaret A. Van Antwerp; 1982.

DcLB DS2 Volume 2. Edited by Margaret A. Van Antwerp; 1982.

DcLB DS3 Volume 3. Edited by Mary Bruccoli; 1983.

DcLB DS4 Volume 4. Edited by Margaret A. Van Antwerp and Sally Johns; 1984.

DcLB DS5 Volume 5; 1987.

DcLB DS6 Volume 6. Edited by Matthew J. Bruccoli and Richard Layman; 1989.

DcLB DS7 Volume 7. Edited by Karen L. Rood; 1989.

DcLB DS8 Volume 8. Edited by Jeffrey Louis Decker; 1991.

DcLB DS9 Volume 9. Edited by Ronald Baughman; 1991.

DcLB DS10 Volume 10. Edited by Edward L. Bishop; 1992.

Use the Table of Contents to locate entries; multiple essays for the same name are often provided. Volumes 5 and 11 contain no biographies.

DcLB *Dictionary of Literary Biography, Yearbook.* Detroit: Gale Research, 1981-1994.

DcLB Y80A *1980 Yearbook.* Edited by Karen L. Rood, Jean W. Ross, and Richard Ziegfeld; 1981. "Updated Entries" section begins on page 3.

DcLB Y80B *1980 Yearbook.* Edited by Karen L. Rood, Jean W. Ross, and Richard Ziegfeld; 1981. "New Entries" section begins on page 127.

DcLB Y81A *1981 Yearbook.* Edited by Karen L. Rood, Jean W. Ross, and Richard Ziegfeld; 1982. "Updated Entries" section begins on page 21.

DcLB Y81B *1981 Yearbook.* Edited by Karen L. Rood, Jean W. Ross, and Richard Ziegfeld; 1982. "New Entries" section begins on page 139.

DcLB Y82A *1982 Yearbook.* Edited by Richard Ziegfeld; 1983. "Updated Entries" section begins on page 121.

DcLB Y82B *1982 Yearbook.* Edited by Richard Ziegfeld; 1983. "New Entries" section begins on page 203.

DcLB Y83A *1983 Yearbook.* Edited by Mary Bruccoli and Jean W. Ross; 1984. "Updated Entries" section begins on page 155.

DcLB Y83B *1983 Yearbook.* Edited by Mary Bruccoli and Jean W. Ross; 1984. "New Entries" section begins on page 175.

DcLB Y83N *1983 Yearbook.* Edited by Mary Bruccoli and Jean W. Ross; 1984. Obituaries section begins on page 103.

DcLB Y84A *1984 Yearbook.* Edited by Jean W. Ross; 1985. "Updated Entry" section begins on page 219.

DcLB Y84B *1984 Yearbook.* Edited by Jean W. Ross; 1985. "New Entries" section begins on page 225.

DcLB Y84N *1984 Yearbook.* Edited by Jean W. Ross; 1985. Obituaries section begins on page 163.

DcLB Y85A *1985 Yearbook.* Edited by Jean W. Ross; 1986. "Updated Entries" section begins on page 279.

DcLB Y85B *1985 Yearbook.* Edited by Jean W. Ross; 1986. "New Entries" section begins on page 319.

DcLB Y85N *1985 Yearbook.* Edited by Jean W. Ross; 1986. Obituaries section begins on page 253.

DcLB Y86A *1986 Yearbook.* Edited by J.M. Brook; 1987. "Updated Entries" section begins on page 247.

DcLB Y86B *1986 Yearbook.* Edited by J.M. Brook; 1987. "New Entries" section begins on page 271.

DcLB Y86N *1986 Yearbook.* Edited by J.M. Brook; 1987. Obituaries section begins on page 199.

DcLB Y87A *1987 Yearbook.* Edited by J.M. Brook; 1988. "Updated Entries" section begins on page 241.

DcLB Y87B *1987 Yearbook.* Edited by J.M. Brook; 1988. "New Entries" section begins on page 293.

DcLB Y87N *1987 Yearbook.* Edited by J.M. Brook; 1988. Obituaries section begins on page 219.

DcLB Y88 *1988 Yearbook.* Edited by J.M. Brook; 1989. The Nobel Prize entry begins on page 3.

DcLB Y88N *1988 Yearbook.* Edited by J.M. Brook; 1989. Obituaries section begins on page 199.

DcLB Y89 *1989 Yearbook.* Edited by J.M. Brook; 1990. The Nobel Prize entry begins on page 3.

DcLB Y89N *1989 Yearbook.* Edited by J.M. Brook; 1990. Obituaries section begins on page 170.

DcLB Y91 *1991 Yearbook.* Edited by James W. Hipp; 1992. Use the

	Table of Contents to locate entries.
DcLB Y91N	*1991 Yearbook.* Edited by James W. Hipp; 1992. Obituaries section begins on page 224.
DcLB Y92	*1992 Yearbook.* Edited by James W. Hipp; 1993. Use the Table of Contents to locate entries.
DcLB Y92N	*1992 Yearbook.* Edited by James W. Hipp; 1993. Obituaries section begins on page 286.
DcLB Y93	*1993 Yearbook.* Edited by James W. Hipp; 1994. Use the Table of Contents to locate entries.

DcLEL *A Dictionary of Literature in the English Language.* Compiled and edited by Robin Myers. Oxford: Pergamon Press, 1970-1978.

DcLEL	*From Chaucer to 1940* ; 1970.
DcLEL 1940	*From 1940 to 1970* ; 1978.

DcMexL *Dictionary of Mexican Literature.* Edited by Eladio Cortes. Westport, CT: Greenwood Press, 1992.

DcNaB *The Dictionary of National Biography.* London: Oxford University Press, 1953-1993.

DcNaB	The Concise Dictionary. Part 1, From the beginnings to 1900; 1953. Contains abstracts of the biographies found in *The Dictionary of National Biography* (21 volumes, New York: Macmillan Co.; London: Smith, Elder & Co., 1908).
DcNaB C	The Concise Dictionary. Part 1, From the beginnings to 1900; 1953. Corrigenda begins on page 1457.
DcNaB S1	The Concise Dictionary. Part 1, From the beginnings to 1900. First Supplement; 1953. Contains abstracts of the biographies found in *The Dictionary of National Biography, First Supplement* (Volume 22, New York: Macmillan Co.; London: Smith, Elder & Co., 1909).
DcNaB 1912	*1912-1921.* Edited by H.W.C. Davis and J.R.H. Weaver; 1927.
DcNaB 1922	*1922-1930.* Edited by J.R.H. Weaver; 1937.
DcNaB 1931	*1931-1940.* Edited by L.G. Wickham Legg; 1949.
DcNaB 1941	*1941-1950.* Edited by L.G. Wickham Legg and E.T. Williams; 1959.
DcNaB 1951	*1951-1960.* Edited by E.T. Williams and Helen M. Palmer; 1971.
DcNaB 1961	*1961-1970.* Edited by E.T. Williams and C.S. Nicholls; 1981.
DcNaB 1971	*1971-1980.* Edited by Lord Blake and C.S. Nicholls; 1986.
DcNaB 1981	*1981-1985.* Edited by Lord Blake and C.S. Nicholls; 1990.
DcNaB MP	*Missing Persons.* Edited by C. S. Nicholls; 1993.

DcNaB S2 *The Dictionary of National Biography.* Second Supplement. Three volumes. Edited by Sir Sidney Lee. New York: Macmillan Co.; London: Smith, Elder & Co., 1912.

DcNAA *A Dictionary of North American Authors Deceased before 1950.* Compiled by W. Stewart Wallace. Toronto: Ryerson Press, 1951. Reprint. Detroit: Gale Research, 1968.

DcNCBi *Dictionary of North Carolina Biography.* Edited by William S. Powell. Chapel Hill, NC: University of North Carolina Press, 1979-1991.

DcNCBi 1	Volume 1, A-C; 1979.

DcNCBi 2 Volume 2, D-G; 1986.
DcNCBi 3 Volume 3, H-K; 1988.
DcNCBi 4 Volume 4, L-O; 1991.

DcOrL *Dictionary of Oriental Literatures.* New York: Basic Books, 1974.

DcOrL 1 Volume I: East Asia. Edited by Zbigniew Slupski.
DcOrL 2 Volume II: South and South-East Asia. Edited by Dusan Zbavitel.

DcPol *A Dictionary of Politics.* Revised edition. Edited by Walter Laqueur. New York: Macmillan Publishing Co., Free Press, 1974.

DcRusL *Dictionary of Russian Literature.* By William E. Harkins. New York: Philosophical Library, 1956. Reprint. Westport, Conn.: Greenwood Press, 1971.

DcRusLS *Dictionary of Russian Literature since 1917.* By Wolfgang Kasack. New York: Columbia University Press, 1988.

DcScanL *Dictionary of Scandinavian Literature.* Edited by Virpi Zuck. New York: Greenwood Press, 1990.

DcScB *Dictionary of Scientific Biography.* New York: Charles Scribner's Sons, 1970-1990.

DcScB Volumes I-XIV. Edited by Charles Coulston Gillispie; 1970.
DcScB S2 Volumes 17-18, Supplement II. Edited by Frederic L. Holmes; 1990.

DcSeaP *Dictionary of Sea Painters.* By E.H.H. Archibald. Woodbridge, England: Antique Collectors' Club, 1980.

Biographies begin on page 59.

DcSoc *A Dictionary of Sociology.* Edited by G. Duncan Mitchell. Chicago: Aldine Publishing Co., 1968.

DcSpL *Dictionary of Spanish Literature.* By Maxim Newmark. New York: Philosophical Library, 1956. Reprint. Totowa, N.J.: Littlefield, Adams & Co., 1970.

DcTwHis *Dictionary of Twentieth-Century History, 1914-1990.* By Peter Teed. Oxford: Oxford University Press, 1992.

DcVicP 2 *The Dictionary of Victorian Painters.* Second edition. By Christopher Wood. Woodbridge, England: Antique Collectors' Club, 1978.

DcWomA *Dictionary of Women Artists.* An international dictionary of women artists born before 1900. By Chris Petteys. Boston: G.K. Hall & Co., 1985.

DrAF 76 *A Directory of American Fiction Writers.* Names and addresses of more than 800 contemporary fiction writers whose work has been published in the United States. 1976 edition. New York: Poets & Writers, 1976.

Use the Index to locate listings.

DrAP 75 *A Directory of American Poets.* Names and addresses of more than 1,500 contemporary poets whose work has been published in the United States. 1975 edition. New York: Poets & Writers, 1974.

Use the Index to locate listings.

DrAPF *A Directory of American Poets and Fiction Writers.* Names and addresses of contemporary poets and fiction writers whose work has been published in the United States. New York: Poets & Writers, 1983-1992.

DrAPF 83	1983-1984 edition; 1983.
DrAPF 85	1985-1986 edition; 1985.
DrAPF 87	1987-1988 edition; 1987.
DrAPF 89	1989-1990 edition; 1989.
DrAPF 91	1991-1992 edition; 1990.
DrAPF 93	1993-1994 edition; 1992.

Use the Index to locate listings.

DrAS *Directory of American Scholars.* New York: R.R. Bowker Co., 1974-1982.

DrAS 74E	Sixth edition, Volume 2: English, Speech, & Drama; 1974.
DrAS 74F	Sixth edition, Volume 3: Foreign Languages, Linguistics, & Philology; 1974.
DrAS 74H	Sixth edition, Volume 1: History; 1974.
DrAS 74P	Sixth edition, Volume 4: Philosophy, Religion, & Law; 1974.
DrAS 78E	Seventh edition, Volume 2: English, Speech, & Drama; 1978.
DrAS 78F	Seventh edition, Volume 3: Foreign Languages, Linguistics, & Philology; 1978.
DrAS 78H	Seventh edition, Volume 1: History; 1978.
DrAS 78P	Seventh edition, Volume 4: Philosophy, Religion, & Law; 1978.
DrAS 82E	Eighth edition, Volume 2: English, Speech, & Drama; 1982.
DrAS 82F	Eighth edition, Volume 3: Foreign Languages, Linguistics, & Philology; 1982.
DrAS 82H	Eighth edition, Volume 1: History; 1982.
DrAS 82P	Eighth edition, Volume 4: Philosophy, Religion, & Law; 1982.

DrBlPA 90 *Directory of Blacks in the Performing Arts.* Second edition. By Edward Mapp. Metuchen, NJ: Scarecrow Press, 1990.

DrLC 69 *Directory of Library Consultants.* Edited by John N. Berry, III. New York: R.R. Bowker Co., 1969.

Dis&D *Disease and Destiny.* A bibliography of medical references to the famous. By Judson Bennett Gilbert. Additions and introduction by Gordon E. Mestler. London: Dawsons of Pall Mall, 1962.

DramC *Drama Criticism.* Criticism of the most significant and widely studied dramatic works from all the world's literature. Detroit: Gale Research, 1991-1994.

DramC 1	Volume 1; 1991.
DramC 2	Volume 2; 1992.
DramC 3	Volume 3; 1993.
DramC 4	Volume 4; 1994.

DrmM 2 — *Dream Makers.* The uncommon men & women who write science fiction. Volume II. Interviews by Charles Platt. New York: Berkley Books, 1983.

Use the Table of Contents to locate interviews.

EarABI — *Early American Book Illustrators and Wood Engravers, 1670-1870.* A catalogue of a collection of American books illustrated for the most part with woodcuts and wood engravings in the Princeton University Library. By Sinclair Hamilton. Princeton, NJ: Princeton University Press, 1958-1968.

EarABI	Volume I: Main Catalogue; 1958.
EarABI SUP	Volume II: Supplement; 1968.

EarBlAP — *Early Black American Playwrights and Dramatic Writers.* A biographical directory and catalog of plays, films, and broadcasting scripts. By Bernard L. Peterson, Jr. New York: Greenwood Press, 1990.

EncAACR — *Encyclopedia of African-American Civil Rights.* From emancipation to the present. Edited by Charles D. Lowery and John F. Marszalek. Westport, CT: Greenwood Press, 1992.

EncAB-H — *Encyclopedia of American Biography.* Edited by John A. Garraty. New York: Harper & Row Publishers, 1974.

EncAB-A — *Encyclopedia of American Biography.* New York and West Palm Beach, FL: The American Historical Society, 1934-1970.

Number after the source code indicates volume number. Use the Index to locate biographies.

EncABHB 6 — *Encyclopedia of American Business History and Biography. Banking and Finance to 1913.* Edited by Larry Schweikart. New York: Facts on File, 1990.

EncACom — *The Encyclopedia of American Comics.* Edited by Ron Goulart. New York: Facts on File, 1990.

EncAFC — *Encyclopedia of American Film Comedy.* By Larry Langman. Garland Reference Library of the Humanities, vol. 744. New York: Garland Publishing, 1987.

EncAHmr — *Encyclopedia of American Humorists.* Edited by Steven H. Gale. New York: Garland Publishing, 1988.

EncAI&E — *The Encyclopedia of American Intelligence and Espionage.* From the Revolutionary War to the present. By G.J.A. O'Toole. New York: Facts on File, 1988.

EncAJ — *The Encyclopedia of American Journalism.* By Donald Paneth. New York: Facts on File Publications, 1983.

EncAR — *Encyclopedia of the American Revolution.* By Mark Mayo Boatner, III. New York: David McKay Co., 1966.

EncBrWW — *An Encyclopedia of British Women Writers.* Edited by Paul Schlueter and June Schlueter. Garland Reference Library of the Humanities, vol. 818. New York: Garland Publishing, 1988.

EncCoWW *An Encyclopedia of Continental Women Writers.* Two volumes. Edited by Katharina M. Wilson. Garland Reference Library of the Humanities, vol. 698. New York: Garland Publishing, 1991.

EncFCWM *The Encyclopedia of Folk, Country & Western Music.* By Irwin Stambler and Grelun Landon. New York: St. Martin's Press, 1969-1983.

EncFCWM 69	First edition; 1969.
EncFCWM 83	Second edition; 1983.

EncFWF *Encyclopedia of Frontier and Western Fiction.* Edited by Jon Tuska and Vicki Piekarski. New York: McGraw-Hill Book Co., 1983.

EncJap *Encyclopedia of Japan.* Japanese history and culture, from abacus to zori. By Dorothy Perkins. New York: Facts on File, 1991.

EncJzS *Encyclopedia of Jazz in the Seventies.* By Leonard Feather and Ira Gitler. New York: Horizon Press, 1976.

EncLatA *Encyclopedia of Latin America.* Edited by Helen Delpar. New York: McGraw-Hill Book Co., 1974.

EncMT *Encyclopaedia of the Musical Theatre.* By Stanley Green. New York: Dodd, Mead & Co., 1976.

EncMys *Encyclopedia of Mystery and Detection.* By Chris Steinbrunner and Otto Penzler. New York: McGraw-Hill Book Co., 1976.

EncO&P *Encyclopedia of Occultism & Parapsychology.* A compendium of information on the occult sciences, magic, demonology, superstitions, spiritism, mysticism, metaphysics, psychical science, and parapsychology, with biographical and bibliographical notes and comprehensive indexes. Edited by Leslie A. Shepard. Detroit: Gale Research, 1978-1991.

EncO&P 1	First edition; 1978.
EncO&P 1S1	First edition, *Occultism Update,* Issue Number 1; 1978.
EncO&P 1S2	First edition, *Occultism Update,* Issue Number 2; 1980.
EncO&P 2	Second edition; 1984.
EncO&P 2S1	Second edition, *Occultism Update.*; 1987.
EncO&P 3	Third edition. Two volumes; 1991.

EncPaPR 91 *The Encyclopedia of Parapsychology and Psychical Research.* By Arthur S. Berger and Joyce Berger. New York: Paragon House, 1991.

EncRk 88 *Encyclopedia of Rock.* By Phil Hardy and Dave Laing. New York: Schirmer Books, 1988.

EncSF 93 *The Encyclopedia of Science Fiction.* Edited by John Clute and Peter Nicholls. New York: St. Martin's Press, 1993.

EncSoA *Encyclopaedia of Southern Africa.* Sixth edition. Compiled and edited by Eric Rosenthal. London: Frederick Warne & Co., 1973.

EncSoB *Encyclopedia of Southern Baptists.* Nashville, TN: Broadman Press, 1958-1971.

- ***EncSoB*** Two volumes; 1958.
- ***EncSoB SUP*** Volume III, Supplement; 1971.

EncSoH *The Encyclopedia of Southern History.* Edited by David C. Roller and Robert W. Twyman. Baton Rouge, LA: Louisiana State University Press, 1979.

EncTwCJ *Encyclopedia of Twentieth-Century Journalists.* By William H. Taft. Garland Reference Library of the Humanities, vol. 493. New York: Garland Publishing, 1986.

EncUrb *Encyclopedia of Urban Planning.* Edited by Arnold Whittick. New York: McGraw-Hill Book Co., 1974.

EncWB *Encyclopedia of World Biography: 20th Century Supplement.* Three volumes. Palatine, IL: Jack Heraty & Associates, 1987-1988. Earlier volumes published as *The McGraw-Hill Encyclopedia of World Biography.*

EncWL *Encyclopedia of World Literature in the 20th Century.* New York: Frederick Ungar Publishing Co., 1967-1984.

- ***EncWL*** First edition. Three volumes and supplement. Edited by Wolfgang Bernard Fleischmann; 1967-1975.
- ***EncWL 2*** Revised edition. Four volumes. Edited by Leonard S. Klein; 1981-1984.

EncWM *The Encyclopedia of World Methodism.* Two volumes. Edited by Nolan B. Harmon. Nashville, TN: United Methodist Publishing House, 1974.

EncWT *The Encyclopedia of World Theater.* Translated by Estella Schmid, edited by Martin Esslin. New York: Charles Scribner's Sons, 1977. Based on *Friedrichs Theaterlexikon,* by Karl Groning and Werner Kliess.

EngPo *English Poetry of the Second World War.* A Biobibliography. By Catherine W. Reilly. Boston: G.K. Hall & Co., 1986.

Biographies begin on page 21.

Entr *Entrepreneurs.* The men and women behind famous brand names and how they made it. By Joseph J. Fucini and Suzy Fucini. Boston: G.K. Hall & Co., 1985.

Use the Index to locate biographies.

EuAu *European Authors, 1000-1900.* A biographical dictionary of European literature Edited by Stanley J. Kunitz and Vineta Colby. Wilson Authors Series. New York: H.W. Wilson Co., 1967.

EuWr *European Writers.* New York: Charles Scribner's Sons, 1983-1990.

- ***EuWr 1*** Volume 1: *The Middle Ages and the Renaissance.* Edited by William T.H. Jackson and George Stade; 1983.
- ***EuWr 2*** Volume 2: *The Middle Ages and the Renaissance.* Edited by William T.H. Jackson and George Stade; 1983.
- ***EuWr 3*** Volume 3: *The Age of Reason and the Enlightenment.* Edited by George Stade; 1984.
- ***EuWr 4*** Volume 4: *The Age of Reason and the Enlightenment.* Edited by George Stade; 1984.

EuWr 5 Volume 5: *The Romantic Century*. Edited by Jacques Barzun and George Stade; 1985.
EuWr 6 Volume 6: *The Romantic Century*. Edited by Jacques Barzun and George Stade; 1985.
EuWr 7 Volume 7: *The Romantic Century*. Edited by Jacques Barzun and George Stade; 1985.
EuWr 8 Volume 8: *The Twentieth Century*. Edited by George Stade; 1989.
EuWr 9 Volume 9: *The Twentieth Century*. Edited by George Stade; 1989.
EuWr 10 Volume 10: *The Twentieth Century*. Edited by George Stade; 1990.
EuWr 11 Volume 11: *The Twentieth Century*. Edited by George Stade; 1990.
EuWr 12 Volume 12: *The Twentieth Century*. Edited by George Stade; 1990.
EuWr 13 Volume 13: *The Twentieth Century*. Edited by George Stade; 1990.

Use the "List of Subjects" to locate biographies.

EvEuW *Everyman's Dictionary of European Writers*. By W.N. Hargreaves-Mawdsley. London: J.M. Dent & Sons; New York: E.P. Dutton & Co., 1968.

EvLB *Everyman's Dictionary of Literary Biography, English and American*. Compiled after John W. Cousin by D.C. Browning. Revised edition. London: J.M. Dent & Sons; New York: E.P. Dutton & Co., 1960.

Expl 93 *Explorers and Discoverers of the World*. First edition. Edited by Daniel B. Baker. Detroit: Gale Research, 1993.

Use the Table of Contents to locate biographies.

FamA&A *Famous Actors and Actresses on the American Stage*. Documents of American theater history. Two volumes. By William C. Young. New York: R.R. Bowker Co., 1975.

FamAIYP *Famous Author-Illustrators for Young People*. By Norah Smaridge. New York: Dodd, Mead & Co., 1973.

FamAYP *Famous Authors for Young People*. By Ramon P. Coffman and Nathan G. Goodman. New York: Dodd, Mead & Co., 1943.

FamMS *Famous Modern Storytellers for Young People*. By Norah Smaridge. New York: Dodd, Mead & Co., 1969.

FamPYP *Famous Poets for Young People*. By Laura Benet. New York: Dodd, Mead & Co., 1964.

FamSYP *Famous Storytellers for Young People*. By Laura Benet. New York: Dodd, Mead & Co., 1968.

FarE&A *The Far East and Australasia*. A survey and directory of Asia and the Pacific. London: Europa Publications, 1980-1981.

FarE&A 80 1980-1981 edition; 1980.
FarE&A 81 1981-1982 edition; 1981.

Biographies are found in the "Who's Who in the Far East and Australasia" section.

FemPA — *The Female Poets of America.* With portraits, biographical notices, and specimens of their writings. Seventh edition, revised. By Thomas Buchanan Read. Philadelphia: E.H. Butler & Co., 1857. Reprint. Detroit: Gale Research, 1978.

FemiCLE — *The Feminist Companion to Literature in English.* Women writers from the Middle Ages to the present. By Virginia Blain, Patricia Clements, and Isobel Grundy. New Haven, CT: Yale University Press, 1990.

FifBJA — *Fifth Book of Junior Authors & Illustrators.* Edited by Sally Holmes Holtze. New York: H.W. Wilson Co., 1983.

FifIDA — *Fifth International Directory of Anthropologists.* Current Anthropology Resource Series, edited by Sol Tax. Chicago: University of Chicago Press, 1975.

FifCWr — *Fifty Caribbean Writers.* A bio-bibliographical critical sourcebook. Edited by Daryl Cumber Dance. New York: Greenwood Press, 1986.

FifSWrB — *Fifty Southern Writers before 1900.* A bio-bibliographical sourcebook. Edited by Robert Bain and Joseph M. Flora. New York: Greenwood Press, 1987.

FifSWrA — *Fifty Southern Writers after 1900.* A bio-bibliographical sourcebook. Edited by Joseph M. Flora and Robert Bain. New York: Greenwood Press, 1987.

FilmgC — *The Filmgoer's Companion.* Fourth edition. By Leslie Halliwell. New York: Hill & Wang, 1974. Later editions published as *Halliwell's Filmgoer's Companion.*

ForWC 70 — *Foremost Women in Communications.* A biographical reference work on accomplished women in broadcasting, publishing, advertising, public relations, and allied professions. New York: Foremost Americans Publishing Corp., 1970.

ForIl — *Forty Illustrators and How They Work.* By Ernest W. Watson. Cincinnati: Watson-Guptil Publications, 1946. Reprint. Freeport, New York: Books for Libraries Press, 1970.

FourBJA — *Fourth Book of Junior Authors & Illustrators.* Edited by Doris De Montreville and Elizabeth D. Crawford. New York: H.W. Wilson Co., 1978.

FrenWW — *French Women Writers.* A bio-bibliographical source book. Edited by Eva Martin Sartori and Dorothy Wynne Zimmerman. New York: Greenwood Press, 1991.

Future — *The Future.* A guide to information sources. Second edition. Edited by Edward S. Cornish. Washington: World Future Society, 1979.

Biographies begin on page 125.

GayLL — *Gay & Lesbian Literature.* Detroit: St. James Press, 1994.

GolEC — *Golombek's Encyclopedia of Chess.* Edited by Harry Golombek. New York: Crown Publishers, 1977.

GrAmP *Great American Prints, 1900-1950.* 138 lithographs, etchings and woodcuts. By June Kraeft and Norman Kraeft. New York: Dover Publications, 1984.

Biographies begin on page 139.

GrBIl *The Great Bird Illustrators and Their Art, 1730-1930.* By Peyton Skipwith. New York: Hamlyn Publishing Group, 1979.

GrBr *Great Britons.* Twentieth-century lives. By Harold Oxbury. Oxford: Oxford University Press, 1985.

GrFLW *Great Foreign Language Writers.* Edited by James Vinson and Daniel Kirkpatrick. Great Writers Series. New York: St. Martin's Press, 1984.

GuFrLit *Guide to French Literature.* By Anthony Levi. Detroit: St. James Press, 1992-1994.

GuFrLit 1 1789 to the present; 1992.
GuFrLit 2 Beginnings to 1789; 1994.

GuPsyc *A Guide to Psychologists and Their Concepts.* By Vernon J. Nordby and Calvin S. Hall. San Francisco: W.H. Freeman & Co., 1974.

HalFC *Halliwell's Filmgoer's Companion.* By Leslie Halliwell. New York: Charles Scribner's Sons, 1984-1988. Earlier editions published as *The Filmgoer's Companion.*

HalFC 84 Eighth edition; 1984.
HalFC 88 Ninth edition; 1988.

HanAmWH *Handbook of American Women's History.* Edited by Angela Howard Zophy. Garland Reference Library of the Humanities, vol. 696. New York: Garland Publishing, 1990.

HanRL *Handbook of Russian Literature.* Edited by Victor Terras. New Haven, CT: Yale University Press, 1985.

HarlReB *Harlem Renaissance and Beyond.* Literary biographies of 100 black women writers, 1900-1945. By Lorraine Elena Roses and Ruth Elizabeth Randolph. Boston: G. K. Hall & Co., 1990.

HarEnUS *Harper's Encyclopaedia of United States History: From 458 A.D. to 1915.* New edition entirely revised and enlarged. 10 volumes. By Benson John Lossing. New York: Harper & Brothers Publishers, 1915. Reprint. Detroit: Gale Research, 1974.

HerW *Her Way.* A guide to biographies of women for young people. Chicago: American Library Association, 1976-1984.

HerW First edition. By Mary-Ellen Kulkin; 1976.
HerW 84 Second edition. By Mary-Ellen Siegel; 1984.

HispLC *Hispanic Literature Criticism.* Two volumes. Detroit: Gale Research, 1994.

HispWr *Hispanic Writers.* A selection of sketches from *Contemporary Authors.* Detroit: Gale Research, 1991.

HispAmA *The Hispanic-American Almanac.* A reference work on Hispanics in the United States. By Nicolas Kanellos. Detroit: Gale Research, 1993.

Use the Index to locate biographies.

HisEWW *The Historical Encyclopedia of World War II.* Edited by Marcel Baudot et al. New York: Facts on File, 1980. Originally published as *Encyclopedie de la Guerre 1939-1945.* Paris: Editions Casterman, 1977.

HsB&A *The House of Beadle and Adams and Its Dime and Nickel Novels.* The Story of a Vanished Literature. By Albert Johannsen. Norman, OK: University of Oklahoma Press, 1950-1962.

HsB&A	Volumes I-II; 1950. Biographies are found in volume II.
HsB&A SUP	Volume III, Supplement, Addenda, Corrigenda; 1962.

ICPEnP *ICP (International Center of Photography) Encyclopedia of Photography.* New York: Crown Publishers, 1984.

ICPEnP A	"Appendix 1" begins on page 576.

IlBBlP *An Illustrated Bio-Bibliography of Black Photographers, 1940-1988.* By Deborah Willis-Thomas. Garland Reference Library of the Humanities, vol. 760. New York: Garland Publishing, 1989.

IlDcG *An Illustrated Dictionary of Glass.* 2,442 entries, including definitions of wares, materials, processes, forms, and decorative styles, and entries on principal glass-makers, decorators, and designers, from antiquity to the present. By Harold Newman. London: Thames & Hudson, 1977.

IlEncMy *An Illustrated Encyclopaedia of Mysticism and the Mystery Religions.* By John Ferguson. London: Thames & Hudson, 1976.

IlrAm 1880 *The Illustrator in America, 1880-1980.* A century of illustration. By Walt Reed and Roger Reed. New York: Madison Square Press, 1984. Distributed by Robert Silver Associates, New York.

Use the Index to locate biographies.

IlrAm *The Illustrator in America, 1900-1960's.* Compiled and edited by Walt Reed. New York: Reinhold Publishing Corp., 1966.

IlrAm A	"The Decade: 1900-1910" begins on page 13.
IlrAm B	"The Decade: 1910-1920" begins on page 43.
IlrAm C	"The Decade: 1920-1930" begins on page 77.
IlrAm D	"The Decade: 1930-1940" begins on page 113.
IlrAm E	"The Decade: 1940-1950" begins on page 167.
IlrAm F	"The Decade: 1950-1960" begins on page 211.
IlrAm G	"The Decade: 1960's" begins on page 239.

IlsBYP *Illustrators of Books for Young People.* Second edition. By Martha E. Ward and Dorothy A. Marquardt. Metuchen, NJ: Scarecrow Press, 1975.

IlsCB *Illustrators of Children's Books.* Boston: Horn Book, 1947-1978.

IlsCB 1744	*1744-1945.* Compiled by Bertha E. Mahony, Louise Payson Latimer, and Beulah Folmsbee; 1947. Biographies begin on page 267.

IlsCB 1946 *1946-1956.* Compiled by Ruth Hill Viguers, Marcia Dalphin, and Bertha Mahony Miller; 1958. Biographies begin on page 62.

IlsCB 1957 *1957-1966.* Compiled by Lee Kingman, Joanna Foster, and Ruth Giles Lontoft; 1968. Biographies begin on page 70.

IlsCB 1967 *1967-1976.* Compiled by Lee Kingman, Grace Allen Hogarth, and Harriet Quimby; 1978. Biographies begin on page 93.

InB&W *In Black and White.* A guide to magazine articles, newspaper articles, and books concerning Black individuals and groups. Edited by Mary Mace Spradling. Detroit: Gale Research, 1980-1985.

InB&W 80 Third edition. Two volumes; 1980.

InB&W 85 Third edition, Supplement; 1985.

InSci *Index to Scientists of the World from Ancient to Modern Times.* Biographies and portraits. By Norma Olin Ireland. Boston: F.W. Faxon Co., 1962.

InWom SUP *Index to Women of the World from Ancient to Modern Times: A Supplement.* By Norma Olin Ireland. Metuchen, NJ: Scarecrow Press, 1988.

IndAu 1816 *Indiana Authors and Their Books, 1816-1916.* Biographical sketches of authors who published during the first century of Indiana statehood with lists of their books. Compiled by R.E. Banta. Crawfordsville, IN: Wabash College, 1949.

IndAu 1917 *Indiana Authors and Their Books, 1917-1966.* A continuation of *Indiana Authors and Their Books, 1816-1916,* and containing additional names from the earlier period. Compiled by Donald E. Thompson. Crawfordsville, IN: Wabash College, 1974.

IntAu&W *The International Authors and Writers Who's Who.* Cambridge: International Biographical Centre, 1977-1991.

IntAu&W 77 Eighth edition. Edited by Adrian Gaster; 1977.

IntAu&W 77X Eighth edition. Edited by Adrian Gaster; 1977. "Pseudonyms of Included Authors" section begins on page 1131.

IntAu&W 82 Ninth edition. Edited by Adrian Gaster; 1982.

IntAu&W 82X Ninth edition. Edited by Adrian Gaster; 1982. "Pseudonyms of Included Authors" section begins on page 719.

IntAu&W 86 10th edition. Edited by Ernest Kay; 1986.

IntAu&W 86X 10th edition. Edited by Ernest Kay; 1986. "Pseudonyms of Authors and Writers" section begins on page 796.

IntAu&W 89 11th edition. Edited by Ernest Kay; 1989.

IntAu&W 91 12th edition. Edited by Ernest Kay; 1991.

IntAu&W 91X 12th edition. Edited by Ernest Kay; 1991. "Pseudonyms of Authors" section begins on page 940.

IntDcAA 90 *International Dictionary of Art and Artists: Artists.* Edited by James Vinson. Chicago: St. James Press, 1990.

IntDcT 2 *International Dictionary of Theatre.* Volume 2: *Playwrights.* Edited by Mark Hawkins-Dady. Detroit: St. James Press, 1994.

IntDcWB *The International Dictionary of Women's Biography.* Compiled and edited by Jennifer S. Uglow. New York: Continuum Publishing Co., 1982. Later edition published as *The Continuum Dictionary of Women's Biography.*

IntEnSS 79 *International Encyclopedia of the Social Sciences.* Volume 18: Biographical Supplement. Edited by David L. Sills. New York: Macmillan Publishing Co., 1979.

IntLitE *International Literature in English.* Essays on the major writers. Edited by Robert L. Ross. New York: Garland Publishing, 1991.

Use the Index to locate biographies.

IntMed 80 *International Medical Who's Who.* A biographical guide in medical research. First edition. Two volumes. Harlow, United Kingdom: Longman Group, 1980.

IntMPA *International Motion Picture Almanac.* New York: Quigley Publishing Co., 1975-1992.

IntMPA 75	1975 edition; 1975.
IntMPA 76	1976 edition; 1976.
IntMPA 77	1977 edition; 1977.
IntMPA 78	1978 edition; 1978.
IntMPA 81	1981 edition; 1981.
IntMPA 82	1982 edition; 1982.
IntMPA 84	1984 edition; 1984.
IntMPA 86	1986 edition; 1986.
IntMPA 88	1988 edition; 1988.
IntMPA 92	1992 edition; 1992.

Biographies are found in the "Who's Who in Motion Pictures and Television" section.

IntWW *The International Who's Who.* London: Europa Publications, 1974-1991. Distributed by Gale Research, Detroit.

IntWW 74	38th edition, 1974-1975; 1974.
IntWW 75	39th edition, 1975-1976; 1975.
IntWW 75N	39th edition, 1975-1976; 1975. The Obituary section is located at the front of the volume.
IntWW 76	40th edition, 1976-1977; 1976.
IntWW 76N	40th edition, 1976-1977; 1976. The Obituary section is located at the front of the volume.
IntWW 77	41st edition, 1977-1978; 1977.
IntWW 77N	41st edition, 1977-1978; 1977. The Obituary section is located at the front of the volume.
IntWW 78	42nd edition, 1978-1979; 1978.
IntWW 78N	42nd edition, 1978-1979; 1978. The Obituary section is located at the front of the volume.
IntWW 79	43rd edition, 1979-1980; 1979.
IntWW 79N	43rd edition, 1979-1980; 1979. The Obituary section is located at the front of the volume.
IntWW 80	44th edition, 1980-1981; 1980.
IntWW 81	45th edition, 1981-1982; 1981.
IntWW 81N	45th edition, 1981-1982; 1981. The Obituary section is located at the front of the volume.
IntWW 82	46th edition, 1982-1983; 1982.
IntWW 82N	46th edition, 1982-1983; 1982. The Obituary section is located at the front of the volume.
IntWW 83	47th edition, 1983-1984; 1983.
IntWW 83N	47th edition, 1983-1984; 1983. The Obituary section is located at the front of the volume.

IntWW 89	53rd edition, 1989-1990; 1989.
IntWW 89N	53rd edition, 1989-1990; 1989. The Obituary section is located at the front of the volume.
IntWW 91	55th edition, 1991-1992; 1991.
IntWW 91N	55th edition, 1991-1992; 1991. The Obituary section is located at the front of the volume.

IntWWE *International Who's Who in Energy and Nuclear Sciences.* Harlow, United Kingdom: Longman Group, 1983.

IntWWM *International Who's Who in Music and Musicians' Directory.* Cambridge: International Who's Who in Music, 1984-1990. Distributed by Taylor and Francis International Publication Services, Bristol, Pa.

IntWWM 85	10th edition; 1984.
IntWWM 90	12th edition, 1990-1991; 1990.

IntWWP *International Who's Who in Poetry.* Sixth edition. Edited by Ernest Kay. Cambridge: International Biographical Centre, 1982. 1982 edition is combined with *The International Authors and Writers Who's Who.*

IntWWP 82	Biographies begin on page 759.
IntWWP 82X	"Pseudonyms of Included Poets" section begins on page 1035.

IntYB *The International Year Book and Statesmen's Who's Who.* West Sussex, England: Kelly's Directories, 1980-1981.

IntYB 80	1980 edition; 1980.
IntYB 81	1981 edition; 1981.

Biographies are found in Part 3.

IntYB 82 *The International Yearbook and Statesmen's Who's Who.* 1982 edition. West Sussex, England: Thomas Skinner Directories, 1982.

Biographies are found in Part 3.

IntvTCA 2 *Interviews and Conversations with 20th-Century Authors Writing in English.* An index. Series II. By Stan A. Vrana. Metuchen, NJ: Scarecrow Press, 1986.

IntvWPC *Interviews with Writers of the Post-Colonial World.* Edited by Feroza Jussawalla and Reed Way Dasenbrock. Jackson, MS: University Press of Mississippi, 1992.

Use the Table of Contents to locate biographies.

JeAmFiW *Jewish American Fiction Writers.* An annotated bibliography. By Gloria L. Cronin, Blaine H. Hall, and Connie Lamb. Garland Reference Library of the Humanities, vol. 972. New York: Garland Publishing, 1991.

JeAmHC *Jewish-American History and Culture.* An encyclopedia. Edited by Jack Fischel and Sanford Pinkser. Garland Reference Library of the Social Sciences, vol. 429. New York: Garland Publishing, 1992.

JrnUS *Journalists of the United States.* Biographical sketches of print and broadcast news shapers from the late 17th century to the present. By Robert B. Downs and Jane B. Downs. Jefferson, NC: McFarland & Co., 1991.

JBA *The Junior Book of Authors.* Edited by Stanley J. Kunitz and Howard Haycraft. Wilson Authors Series. New York: H.W. Wilson Co., 1934-1951.

JBA 34 First edition; 1934.
JBA 51 Second edition, revised; 1951.

LadLa 86 *The Lady Laureates.* Women who have won the Nobel Prize. Second edition. By Olga S. Opfell. Metuchen, NJ: Scarecrow Press, 1986.

Use the Index to locate biographies.

LatAmWr *Latin American Writers.* Three volumes. Edited by Carlos A. Sole and Maria Isabel Abreu. New York: Charles Scribner's Sons, 1989.

Use the Index, which begins on page 1459 of Volume 3, to locate biographies.

Law&B 92 *Law & Business Directory of Corporate Counsel.* 1992-1993 edition. Englewood Cliffs, NJ: Prentice Hall, 1992.

Use the "Corporate Individual Name Index," which begins on page I-95, to locate biographies.

LEduc 74 *Leaders in Education.* Fifth edition. New York: R.R. Bowker Co., 1974.

LElec *Leaders in Electronics.* New York: McGraw-Hill Book Co., 1979. Title page reads *McGraw-Hill's Leaders in Electronics.*

LesBEnT *Les Brown's Encyclopedia of Television.* By Les Brown. New York: New York Zoetrope, 1982. Earlier edition published as *The New York Times Encyclopedia of Television.*

LesBEnT 92 *Les Brown's Encyclopedia of Television.* Third edition. By Les Brown. Detroit: Gale Research, 1992.

LiExTwC *Literary Exile in the Twentieth Century.* An analysis and biographical dictionary. Edited by Martin Tucker. New York: Greenwood Press, 1991.

Biographies begin on page 47.

LiHiK *A Literary History of Kentucky.* By William S. Ward. Knoxville, TN: University of Tennessee Press, 1988.

Use the Index to locate biographies.

LitC *Literature Criticism from 1400 to 1800.* Excerpts from criticism of the works of fifteenth-, sixteenth-, seventeenth-, and eighteenth-century novelists, poets, playwrights, philosophers, and other creative writers, from the first published critical appraisals to current evaluations. Detroit: Gale Research, 1984-1992.

LitC 1 Volume 1; 1984.
LitC 2 Volume 2; 1985.
LitC 3 Volume 3; 1986.
LitC 4 Volume 4; 1986.
LitC 5 Volume 5; 1987.
LitC 6 Volume 6; 1987.
LitC 7 Volume 7; 1988.
LitC 8 Volume 8; 1988.
LitC 9 Volume 9; 1989.
LitC 10 Volume 10; 1989.
LitC 11 Volume 11; 1990.

LitC 12	Volume 12; 1990.
LitC 13	Volume 13; 1990.
LitC 14	Volume 14; 1991.
LitC 15	Volume 15; 1991.
LitC 16	Volume 16; 1991.
LitC 17	Volume 17; 1992.

LivgBAA *Living Black American Authors.* A biographical directory. By Ann Allen Shockley and Sue P. Chandler. New York: R.R. Bowker Co., 1973.

LivgFWS *The Living Female Writers of the South.* Edited by Mary T. Tardy. Philadelphia: Claxton, Remsen & Haffelfinger, 1872. Reprint. Detroit: Gale Research, 1978.

LngCEL *Longman Companion to English Literature.* Second edition. By Christopher Gillie. London: Longman Group, 1977. Also published as *A Companion to British Literature.* Detroit: Grand River Books, 1980.

LngCTC *Longman Companion to Twentieth Century Literature.* By A.C. Ward. London: Longman Group, 1970.

LuthC 75 *Lutheran Cyclopedia.* Revised edition. Edited by Erwin L. Lueker. St. Louis: Concordia Publishing House, 1975.

MacBEP *Macmillan Biographical Encyclopedia of Photographic Artists & Innovators.* By Turner Browne and Elaine Partnow. New York: Macmillan Publishing Co.; London: Collier Macmillan Publishers, 1983.

MacEA *Macmillan Encyclopedia of Architects.* Four volumes. Edited by Adolf K. Placzek. New York: Macmillan Publishing Co., Free Press; London: Collier Macmillan Publishers, 1982.

Use the "Index of Names," which begins on page 533 of Volume 4, to locate biographies.

MagSAmL *Magill's Survey of American Literature.* Six volumes. Edited by Frank N. Magill. North Bellmore, NY: Marshall Cavendish, 1991.

MagSWL *Magill's Survey of World Literature.* Six volumes. Edited by Frank N. Magill. North Bellmore, NY: Marshall Cavendish, 1993.

MajAI *Major Authors and Illustrators for Children and Young Adults.* A selection of sketches from *Something about the Author.* Six volumes. Detroit: Gale Research, 1993.

MajMD *Major Modern Dramatists.* A Library of Literary Criticism. New York: Ungar Publishing Co., 1984-1986.

MajMD 1	Volume I. Compiled and edited by Rita Stein and Friedhelm Rickert; 1984.
MajMD 2	Volume II. Compiled and edited by Blandine M. Rickert, et al; 1986.

Use the "Dramatists Included" list on page ix to locate biographies.

MajTwCW *Major Twentieth-Century Writers.* A selection of sketches from *Contemporary Authors.* Four volumes. Detroit: Gale Research, 1991.

MakMC *Makers of Modern Culture.* Edited by Justin Wintle. New York: Facts on File, 1981.

MarqDCG 84 *Marquis Who's Who Directory of Computer Graphics.* First edition. Chicago: Marquis Who's Who, 1984.

McGEWB *The McGraw-Hill Encyclopedia of World Biography.* New York: McGraw-Hill Book Co., 1973. Supplemental volumes published as *Encyclopedia of World Biography: 20th Century Supplement.*

McGEWD *McGraw-Hill Encyclopedia of World Drama.* New York: McGraw-Hill Book Co., 1972-1984.

McGEWD 72	First edition. Four volumes; 1972.
McGEWD 84	Second edition. Five volumes; 1984.

McGMS 80 *McGraw-Hill Modern Scientists and Engineers.* Three volumes. New York: McGraw-Hill Book Co., 1980.

MedHR *Medal of Honor Recipients, 1863-1978.* 96th Congress, 1st Session, Senate Committee Print No. 3. Prepared by the Committee on Veterans' Affairs, United States Senate. Washington, DC: U.S. Government Printing Office, 1979.

Use the "Medal of Honor Alphabetical Index," which begins on page 1023, to locate biographies.

MedPD *Media Personnel Directory.* An alphabetical guide to names, addresses, and telephone numbers of key editorial and business personnel at over 700 United States and international periodicals. Edited by Alan E. Abrams. Detroit: Gale Research Co., 1979.

MemAm *Memorable Americans, 1750-1950.* By Robert B. Downs, John T. Flanagan, and Harold W. Scott. Littleton, CO: Libraries Unlimited, 1983.

MexAmB *Mexican American Biographies.* A historical dictionary, 1836-1987. By Matt S. Meier. New York: Greenwood Press, 1988.

MichAu 80 *Michigan Authors.* Second edition. By the Michigan Association for Media in Education. Ann Arbor, MI: Michigan Association for Media in Education, 1980.

MidE *The Middle East and North Africa.* London: Europa Publications, 1980-1982.

MidE 80	27th edition, 1980-1981; 1980.
MidE 81	28th edition, 1981-1982; 1981.
MidE 82	29th edition, 1982-1983; 1982.

Biographies are found in the "Who's Who in the Middle East and North Africa" section.

MinnWr *Minnesota Writers.* A collection of autobiographical stories by Minnesota prose writers. Edited and annotated by Carmen Nelson Richards. Minneapolis: T.S. Denison & Co., 1961.

Use the Table of Contents to locate biographies.

ModAL *Modern American Literature.* A Library of Literary Criticism. New York: Frederick Ungar Publishing Co., 1969-1985.

ModAL Fourth edition. Volumes 1-3. Compiled and edited by Dorothy Nyren Curley, Maurice Kramer, and Elaine Fialka Kramer; 1969.

ModAL S1 Volume 4, Supplement. Compiled and edited by Dorothy Nyren, Maurice Kramer, and Elaine Fialka Kramer; 1976.

ModAL S2 Volume 5, Second Supplement. Compiled and edited by Paul Schlueter and June Schlueter; 1985.

ModAWP *Modern American Women Poets.* By Jean Gould. New York: Dodd, Mead & Co., 1984.
Use the Table of Contents to locate biographies.

ModAWWr *Modern American Women Writers.* Edited by Elaine Showalter, Lea Baechler, and A. Walton Litz. New York: Charles Scribner's Sons, 1991.

ModArCr 1 *Modern Arts Criticism.* A biographical and critical guide to painters, sculptors, photographers, and architects from the beginning of the modern era to the present. Volume 1. Detroit: Gale Research, 1991.

ModBlW *Modern Black Writers.* Compiled and edited by Michael Popkin. A Library of Literary Criticism. New York: Frederick Ungar Publishing Co., 1978.

ModBrL *Modern British Literature.* A Library of Literary Criticism. New York: Frederick Ungar Publishing Co., 1966-1985.

ModBrL Volumes 1-3. Compiled and edited by Ruth Z. Temple and Martin Tucker; 1966.

ModBrL S1 Volume 4, Supplement. Compiled and edited by Martin Tucker and Rita Stein; 1975.

ModBrL S2 Volume 5, Second Supplement. Compiled and edited by Denis Lane and Rita Stein; 1985.

ModCmwL *Modern Commonwealth Literature.* Compiled and edited by John H. Ferres and Martin Tucker. A Library of Literary Criticism. New York: Frederick Ungar Publishing Co., 1977.

ModFrL *Modern French Literature.* Two volumes. Compiled and edited by Debra Popkin and Michael Popkin. A Library of Literary Criticism. New York: Frederick Ungar Publishing Co., 1977.

ModGL *Modern German Literature.* Two volumes. Compiled and edited by Agnes Korner Domandi. A Library of Literary Criticism. New York: Frederick Ungar Publishing Co., 1972.

ModIrL *Modern Irish Literature.* Compiled and edited by Denis Lane and Carol McCrory Lane. A Library of Literary Criticism. New York: Ungar Publishing Co., 1988.

ModRL *Modern Romance Literatures.* Compiled and edited by Dorothy Nyren Curley and Arthur Curley. A Library of Literary Criticism. New York: Frederick Ungar Publishing Co., 1967.

ModSL *Modern Slavic Literatures.* A Library of Literary Criticism. New York: Frederick Ungar Publishing Co., 1972-1976.

ModSL 1 Volume 1: Russian Literature. Compiled and edited by

Vasa D. Mihailovich; 1972.

ModSL 2 Volume 2: Bulgarian, Czechoslovak, Polish, Ukrainian and Yugoslav Literatures. Compiled and edited by Vasa D. Mihailovich et al; 1976.

Use the alphabetic listing of authors to locate biographies.

ModSpP *Modern Spanish and Portuguese Literatures.* Compiled and edited by Marshall J. Schneider and Irwin Stern. A Library of Literary Criticism. New York: Continuum, 1988.

ModSpP P Biographies of Portuguese writers are located in the "Portugal" section, which begins on page 455.

ModSpP S Biographies of Spanish writers are located in the "Spain" section.

ModWD *Modern World Drama.* An encyclopedia. By Myron Matlaw. New York: E.P. Dutton & Co., 1972.

MorBMP *More Books by More People.* Interviews with sixty-five authors of books for children. By Lee Bennett Hopkins. New York: Citation Press, 1974.

MorJA *More Junior Authors.* Edited by Muriel Fuller. Wilson Authors Series. New York: H.W. Wilson Co., 1963.

MorMA *More Memorable Americans, 1750-1950.* By Robert B. Downs, John T. Flanagan, and Harold W. Scott. Littleton, CO: Libraries Unlimited, 1985.

MotPP *Motion Picture Performers.* A bibliography of magazine and periodical articles, 1900-1969. Compiled by Mel Schuster. Metuchen, NJ: Scarecrow Press, 1971.

MouLC *Moulton's Library of Literary Criticism.* English and American authors through the beginning of the twentieth century. Abridged, revised, and with additions by Martin Tucker. New York: Frederick Ungar Publishing Co., 1966.

MouLC 1 Volume 1: The beginnings to the seventeenth century.
MouLC 2 Volume 2: Neo-Classicism to the Romantic period.
MouLC 3 Volume 3: The Romantic period to the Victorian age.
MouLC 4 Volume 4: The mid-nineteenth century to Edwardianism.

Use the alphabetic listing at the front of the volume to locate biographies.

MovMk *The Movie Makers.* By Sol Chaneles and Albert Wolsky. Secaucus, NJ: Derbibooks, 1974.

The "Directors" section begins on page 506.

NamesHP *Names in the History of Psychology.* A biographical sourcebook. By Leonard Zusne. Washington, DC: Hemisphere Publishing Corp., 1975. Distributed by John Wiley & Sons, Halstead Press, New York. Continued by *Biographical Dictionary of Psychology.*

Use the "Alphabetic List of Names," which begins on page ix, to locate biographies.

NatCAB *The National Cyclopaedia of American Biography.* New York: James T. White & Co., 1979-1984.

NatCAB 58 Volume 58; 1979. Use the Index to locate biographies.
NatCAB 59 Volume 59; 1980. Use the Index to locate biographies.

NatCAB 60 Volume 60; 1981. Use the Index to locate biographies.
NatCAB 61 Volume 61; 1982. Use the Index to locate biographies.
NatCAB 62 Volume 62; 1984. Use the Index to locate biographies.
NatCAB 63 Volume 63; 1984. Use the Index which begins on page 353 to locate biographies.
NatCAB 63N Volume 63; 1984. Use the Index which begins on page 349 to locate biographies.

NatPD *National Playwrights Directory.* Edited by Phyllis Johnson Kaye. Waterford, CT: The O'Neill Theater Center, 1977-1981.

NatPD 77 First edition; 1977.
NatPD 81 Second edition; 1981.

NegAl 76 *The Negro Almanac.* A reference work on the Afro American. Third edition. Edited by Harry A. Ploski and Warren Marr, II. New York: Bellwether Co., 1976. Later edition published as *The African-American Almanac.*

Use the Index to locate biographies.

NegAl 83 *The Negro Almanac.* A reference work on the Afro-American. Fourth edition. Compiled and edited by Harry A. Ploski and James Williams. New York: John Wiley & Sons, 1983.

Use the Index to locate biographies.

NegAl *The Negro Almanac.* A reference work on the African American. Fifth edition. Detroit: Gale Research, 1989. Later edition published as *The African-American Almanac.*

NegAl 89 Use the Index to locate biographies.
NegAl 89A Unindexed biographies in "The Black Voter and Elected Office Holder" chapter are located on pages 386-468.

NewAmDM *The New American Dictionary of Music.* By Philip D. Morehead with Anne MacNeil. New York: Dutton, 1991.

NewC *The New Century Handbook of English Literature.* Revised edition. Edited by Clarence L. Barnhart with the assistance of William D. Halsey. New York: Appleton-Century-Crofts, 1967.

NewCBMT *New Complete Book of the American Musical Theater.* By David Ewen. New York: Holt, Rinehart & Winston, 1970.

Biographies are found in the "Librettists, Lyricists and Composers" section which begins on page 607.

NewCon *The New Consciousness, 1941-1968.* Concise Dictionary of American Literary Biography Series. Detroit: Gale Research, 1987.

NewEScF *The New Encyclopedia of Science Fiction.* Edited by James Gunn. New York: Viking, 1988.

NewGrDA 86 *The New Grove Dictionary of American Music.* Four volumes. Edited by H. Wiley Hitchcock and Stanley Sadie. London: Macmillan Press, 1986.

NewOxM *The New Oxford Companion to Music.* Two volumes. Edited by Denis Arnold. Oxford: Oxford University Press, 1983.

NewYTBE *The New York Times Biographical Edition.* A compilation of current biographical information of general interest. New York: Arno Press, 1970-1973.Continued by *The New York Times Biographical Service.*

NewYTBE 70	Volume 1, Numbers 1-12; 1970.
NewYTBE 71	Volume 2, Numbers 1-12; 1971.
NewYTBE 72	Volume 3, Numbers 1-12; 1972.
NewYTBE 73	Volume 4, Numbers 1-12; 1973.

Use the annual Index to locate biographies.

NewYTBS *The New York Times Biographical Service.* A compilation of current biographical information of general interest. New York: Arno Press, 1974-1981.A continuation of *The New York Times Biographical Edition.*

NewYTBS 74	Volume 5, Numbers 1-12; 1974.
NewYTBS 75	Volume 6, Numbers 1-12; 1975.
NewYTBS 76	Volume 7, Numbers 1-12; 1976.
NewYTBS 77	Volume 8, Numbers 1-12; 1977.
NewYTBS 78	Volume 9, Numbers 1-12; 1978.
NewYTBS 79	Volume 10, Numbers 1-12; 1979.
NewYTBS 80	Volume 11, Numbers 1-12; 1980.
NewYTBS 81	Volume 12, Numbers 1-12; 1981.

Use the annual Index to locate biographies.

NewYTBS *The New York Times Biographical Service.* A compilation of current biographical information of general interest. Sanford, NC: Microfilming Corp. of America, 1982-1983.

NewYTBS 82	Volume 13, Numbers 1-12; 1982.
NewYTBS 83	Volume 14, Numbers 1-12; 1983.

Use the annual Index to locate biographies.

NewYTBS *The New York Times Biographical Service.* A compilation of current biographical information of general interest. Ann Arbor, MI: University Microfilms International, 1984-1993.

NewYTBS 84	Volume 15, Numbers 1-12; 1984.
NewYTBS 85	Volume 16, Numbers 1-12; 1985.
NewYTBS 86	Volume 17, Numbers 1-12; 1986.
NewYTBS 87	Volume 18, Numbers 1-12; 1987.
NewYTBS 88	Volume 19, Numbers 1-12; 1988.
NewYTBS 89	Volume 20, Numbers 1-12; 1989.
NewYTBS 90	Volume 21, Numbers 1-12; 1990.
NewYTBS 91	Volume 22, Numbers 1-12; 1991.
NewYTBS 92	Volume 23, Numbers 1-12; 1992.
NewYTBS 93	Volume 24, Numbers 1-12; 1993.

Use the annual Index to locate biographies.

NewYTET *The New York Times Encyclopedia of Television.* By Les Brown. New York: New York Times Book Co., 1977. Later editions published as *Les Brown's Encyclopedia of Television.*

NewbC *Newbery and Caldecott Medal Books.* With acceptance papers, biographies and related material chiefly from the *Horn Book Magazine.* Edited by Lee Kingman. Boston: Horn Book, 1965-1975.

NewbC 1956	*1956-1965* ; 1965.
NewbC 1966	*1966-1975* ; 1975.

NewbMB 1922 *Newbery Medal Books, 1922-1955.* With their authors' acceptance papers and related material chiefly from the *Horn Book Magazine.* Edited by Bertha Mahony Miller and Elinor Whitney Field. Horn Book Papers, vol. 1. Boston: Horn Book, 1955.

News *Newsmakers.* The people behind today's headlines. Detroit: Gale Research, 1990-1994.Issues prior to 1988, Issue 2, were published as *Contemporary Newsmakers.*

News 89	1989 Cumulation; 1990.
News 90	1990 Cumulation; 1990.
News 91	1991 Cumulation; 1991.
News 92	1992 Cumulation; 1992.
News 93	1993 Cumulation; 1993.
News 88-2	1988, Issue 2; 1988.
News 88-3	1988, Issue 3; 1988.
News 89-1	1989, Issue 1; 1989.
News 89-2	1989, Issue 2; 1989.
News 89-3	1989, Issue 3; 1989.
News 90-1	1990, Issue 1; 1990.
News 90-2	1990, Issue 2; 1990.
News 90-3	1990, Issue 3; 1990.
News 91-1	1991, Issue 1; 1990.
News 91-2	1991, Issue 2; 1991.
News 91-3	1991, Issue 3; 1991.
News 92-1	1992, Issue 1; 1992.
News 92-2	1992, Issue 2; 1992.
News 92-3	1992, Issue 3; 1992.
News 93-1	1993, Issue 1; 1993.
News 93-2	1993, Issue 2; 1993.
News 93-3	1993, Issue 3; 1993.
News 94-1	1994, Issue 1; 1994.

Use the "Cumulative Newsmaker Index" to locate entries. Biographies in each quarterly issue can also be located in the annual cumulation.

NinCLC *Nineteenth-Century Literature Criticism.* Excerpts from criticism of the works of novelists, poets, playwrights, short story writers, philosophers, and other creative writers who died between 1800 and 1899, from the first published critical appraisals to current evaluations. Detroit: Gale Research, 1981-1994.

NinCLC 1	Volume 1; 1981.
NinCLC 2	Volume 2; 1982.
NinCLC 3	Volume 3; 1983.
NinCLC 4	Volume 4; 1983.
NinCLC 5	Volume 5; 1984.
NinCLC 6	Volume 6; 1984.
NinCLC 7	Volume 7; 1984.
NinCLC 8	Volume 8; 1985.
NinCLC 9	Volume 9; 1985.
NinCLC 10	Volume 10; 1985.
NinCLC 11	Volume 11; 1986.
NinCLC 12	Volume 12; 1986.
NinCLC 13	Volume 13; 1986.
NinCLC 14	Volume 14; 1987.
NinCLC 15	Volume 15; 1987.
NinCLC 16	Volume 16; 1987.
NinCLC 17	Volume 17; 1988.
NinCLC 18	Volume 18; 1988.
NinCLC 19	Volume 19; 1988.
NinCLC 20	Volume 20; 1989. Contains no biographies.
NinCLC 21	Volume 21; 1989.
NinCLC 22	Volume 22; 1989.
NinCLC 23	Volume 23; 1989.

NinCLC 24	Volume 24; 1989. Contains no biographies.
NinCLC 25	Volume 25; 1990.
NinCLC 26	Volume 26; 1990.
NinCLC 27	Volume 27; 1990.
NinCLC 28	Volume 28; 1990. Contains no biographies.
NinCLC 29	Volume 29; 1991.
NinCLC 30	Volume 30; 1991.
NinCLC 31	Volume 31; 1991.
NinCLC 32	Volume 32; 1991. Contains no biographies.
NinCLC 33	Volume 33; 1992.
NinCLC 34	Volume 34; 1992.
NinCLC 35	Volume 35; 1992.
NinCLC 36	Volume 36; 1992. Contains no biographies.
NinCLC 37	Volume 37; 1993.
NinCLC 38	Volume 38; 1993.
NinCLC 39	Volume 39; 1993.
NinCLC 40	Volume 40; 1993. Contains no biographies.
NinCLC 41	Volume 41; 1994.
NinCLC 42	Volume 42; 1994.

NobelP *Nobel Prize Winners.* New York: H.W. Wilson Co., 1987-1992.

NobelP	Edited by Tyler Wasson; 1987.
NobelP 91	Supplement 1987-1991. Edited by Paula McGuire; 1992.
NobelP 91N	Supplement 1987-1991. Edited by Paula McGuire; 1992. "Nobel Prize Winners Who Have Died since 1986" section appears on page 25.

NotAW MOD *Notable American Women, The Modern Period.* A biographical dictionary. Edited by Barbara Sicherman and Carol Hurd Green. Cambridge: Harvard University Press, Belknap Press, 1980.

NotBlAW 92 *Notable Black American Women.* Edited by Jessie Carney Smith. Detroit: Gale Research, 1992.

NotHsAW 93 *Notable Hispanic American Women.* First edition. Detroit: Gale Research, 1993.

NotNAT *Notable Names in the American Theatre.* Clifton, NJ: James T. White & Co., 1976. Earlier edition published as *The Biographical Encyclopaedia and Who's Who of the American Theatre.*

NotNAT	"Notable Names in the American Theatre" section begins on page 489.
NotNAT A	"Biographical Bibliography" section begins on page 309.
NotNAT B	"Necrology" section begins on page 343.

This book often alphabetizes by titles of address, e.g.: Dr., Mrs., and Sir.

NotWoAT *Notable Women in the American Theatre.* A biographical dictionary. Edited by Alice M. Robinson, Vera Mowry Roberts, and Milly S. Barranger. New York: Greenwood Press, 1989.

Novels *Novels and Novelists.* A guide to the world of fiction. Edited by Martin Seymour-Smith. New York: St. Martin's Press, 1980.

Biographies are located in the "Novelists: An Alphabetical Guide" section, which begins on page 87.

ObitOF 79 — *Obituaries on File.* Two volumes. Compiled by Felice Levy. New York: Facts on File, 1979.

ObitT — *Obituaries from the Times.* Compiled by Frank C. Roberts. Reading, England: Newspaper Archive Developments, 1979-1978.

ObitT 1951	*1951-1960* ; 1979.
ObitT 1961	*1961-1970* ; 1975.
ObitT 1971	*1971-1975* ; 1978.

OhA&B — *Ohio Authors and Their Books.* Biographical data and selective bibliographies for Ohio authors, native and resident, 1796-1950. Edited by William Coyle. Cleveland: World Publishing Co., 1962.

OxCAmH — *The Oxford Companion to American History.* By Thomas H. Johnson. New York: Oxford University Press, 1966.

OxCAmL — *The Oxford Companion to American Literature.* By James D. Hart. New York: Oxford University Press, 1965-1983.

OxCAmL 65	Fourth edition; 1965.
OxCAmL 83	Fifth edition; 1983.

OxCAmT 84 — *The Oxford Companion to American Theatre.* By Gerald Bordman. New York: Oxford University Press, 1984.

OxCArt — *The Oxford Companion to Art.* Edited by Harold Osborne. Oxford: Oxford University Press, Clarendon Press, 1970.

OxCAusL — *The Oxford Companion to Australian Literature.* By William H. Wilde, Joy Hooton, and Barry Andrews. Melbourne, Australia: Oxford University Press, 1985.

OxCCan — *The Oxford Companion to Canadian History and Literature.* Toronto: Oxford University Press, 1967-1973.

OxCCan	By Norah Story; 1967.
OxCCan SUP	Supplement. Edited by William Toye; 1973.

OxCCanL — *The Oxford Companion to Canadian Literature.* Edited by William Toye. Toronto: Oxford University Press, 1983.

OxCCanT — *The Oxford Companion to Canadian Theatre.* Edited by Eugene Benson and L.W. Conolly. Toronto: Oxford University Press, 1989.

OxCChiL — *The Oxford Companion to Children's Literature.* By Humphrey Carpenter and Mari Prichard. Oxford: Oxford University Press, 1984.

OxCClL 89 — *The Oxford Companion to Classical Literature.* Second edition. Edited by M.C. Howatson. Oxford: Oxford University Press, 1989.

OxCEng — *The Oxford Companion to English Literature.* Oxford: Oxford University Press, 1967-1985.

OxCEng 67	Fourth edition. Compiled and edited by Sir Paul Harvey,

revised by Dorothy Eagle; 1967.
OxCEng 85 Fifth edition. Edited by Margaret Drabble; 1985.

OxCFilm *The Oxford Companion to Film.* Edited by Liz-Anne Bawden. New York: Oxford University Press, 1976.

OxCFr *The Oxford Companion to French Literature.* Compiled and edited by Sir Paul Harvey and J.E. Heseltine. Oxford: Oxford University Press, 1959. Reprinted with corrections, 1966.

OxCGer *The Oxford Companion to German Literature.* Oxford: Oxford University Press, 1976-1986.
OxCGer 76 By Henry Garland and Mary Garland; 1976.
OxCGer 86 Second edition. By Mary Garland; 1986.

OxCLaw *The Oxford Companion to Law.* By David M. Walker. Oxford: Oxford University Press, Clarendon Press, 1980.

OxCLiW 86 *The Oxford Companion to the Literature of Wales.* Compiled and edited by Meic Stephens. Oxford: Oxford University Press, 1986.

OxCMus *The Oxford Companion to Music.* 10th edition (corrected). By Percy A. Scholes. Edited by John Owen Ward. London: Oxford University Press, 1974.

OxCPMus *The Oxford Companion to Popular Music.* By Peter Gammond. Oxford: Oxford University Press, 1991.

OxCShps *The Oxford Companion to Ships and the Sea.* Edited by Peter Kemp. London: Oxford University Press, 1976.

OxCThe *The Oxford Companion to the Theatre.* Edited by Phyllis Hartnoll. Oxford Oxford University Press, 1967-1983.
OxCThe 67 Third edition; 1967.
OxCThe 83 Fourth edition; 1983.

OxCTwCA *The Oxford Companion to Twentieth-Century Art.* Edited by Harold Osborne. Oxford: Oxford University Press, 1981.

OxDcArt *The Oxford Dictionary of Art.* Edited by Ian Chilvers and Harold Osborne. Oxford: Oxford University Press, 1988.

PenC *The Penguin Companion to World Literature.* New York: McGraw-Hill Book Co., 1971-1969.
PenC AM *American Literature.* Edited by Malcolm Bradbury, Eric Mottram, and Jean Franco; 1971. Biographies are found in the "U.S.A." and "Latin America" sections.
PenC CL *Classical, Oriental and African Literature.* Edited by D.M. Lang and D.R. Dudley; 1969. Biographies are found in the "Classical," "Byzantine," "Oriental," and "African" sections.
PenC ENG *English Literature.* Edited by David Daiches; 1971.
PenC EUR *European Literature.* Edited by Anthony Thorlby; 1969.

PenDiMP — *The Penguin Dictionary of Musical Performers.* A biographical guide to significant interpreters of classical music - singers, solo instrumentalists, conductors, orchestras and string quartets - ranging from the seventeenth century to the present day. By Arthur Jacobs. London: Viking, 1990.

- ***PenDiMP A*** — Biographies located in the "Index of Composers" begin on page 239.

PenEncH — *The Penguin Encyclopedia of Horror and the Supernatural.* Edited by Jack Sullivan. New York: Viking Penguin, 1986.

PenEncP — *The Penguin Encyclopedia of Popular Music.* Edited by Donald Clarke. New York: Viking, 1989.

PhDcTCA 77 — *Phaidon Dictionary of Twentieth-Century Art.* Second edition. Oxford: Phaidon Press; New York: E.P. Dutton, 1977.

PiP — *The Pied Pipers.* Interviews with the influential creators of children's literature. By Justin Wintle and Emma Fisher. New York: Paddington Press, 1974.

Use the Table of Contents to locate biographies.

PlP&P — *Plays, Players, and Playwrights.* An illustrated history of the theatre. By Marion Geisinger. Updated by Peggy Marks. New York: Hart Publishing Co., 1975.

- ***PlP&P*** — Use the Index, which begins on page 575, to locate biographies.
- ***PlP&P A*** — Use the Supplemental Index to the last chapter, which begins on page 797, to locate biographies.

PoeCrit — *Poetry Criticism.* Excerpts from criticism of the works of the most significant and widely studied poets of world literature. Detroit: Gale Research, 1991-1994.

- ***PoeCrit 1*** — Volume 1; 1991.
- ***PoeCrit 2*** — Volume 2; 1991.
- ***PoeCrit 3*** — Volume 3; 1991.
- ***PoeCrit 4*** — Volume 4; 1992.
- ***PoeCrit 5*** — Volume 5; 1992.
- ***PoeCrit 6*** — Volume 6; 1993.
- ***PoeCrit 7*** — Volume 7; 1994.
- ***PoeCrit 8*** — Volume 8; 1994.

PoChrch — *The Poets of the Church.* A series of biographical sketches of hymn-writers with notes on their hymns. By Edwin F. Hatfield. New York: Anson D.F. Randolph & Co., 1884. Reprint. Detroit: Gale Research, 1978.

PoIre — *The Poets of Ireland.* A biographical and bibliographical dictionary of Irish writers of English verse. By D.J. O'Donoghue. Dublin, Ireland: Hodges Figgis & Co.; London: Henry Frowde, Oxford University Press, 1912. Reprint. Detroit: Gale Research, 1968.

"The Poets of Ireland" begins on page 5. The Appendices begin on page 495.

PoLE — *The Poets Laureate of England.* Being a history of the office of poet laureate, biographical notices of its holders, and a collection of the satires, epigrams, and lampoons directed against them. By Walter Hamilton. London: Elliot Stock, 1879. Reprint. Detroit: Gale Research, 1968.

Use the Index to locate biographies.

PolBiDi — *Polish Biographical Dictionary.* Profiles of nearly 900 Poles who have made lasting contributions to world civilization. By Stanley S. Sokol and Sharon F. Mrotek Kissane. Wauconda, IL: Bolchazy-Carducci Publishers, 1992.

PolsAm 84 — *Politics in America.* Members of Congress in Washington and at home. Edited by Alan Ehrenhalt. Washington: Congressional Quarterly, 1983.

Use the Index to locate biographies.

PorAmW — *Portraits of American Women.* From settlement to the present. By G.J. Barker-Benfield and Catherine Clinton. New York: St. Martin's Press, 1991.

Use the Table of Contents to locate biographies.

PostFic — *Postmodern Fiction.* A bio-bibliographical guide. Edited by Larry McCaffery. Movements in the Arts, no. 2. New York: Greenwood Press, 1986.

Biographies begin on page 247.

PrintW — *The Printworld Directory of Contemporary Prints & Prices.* Edited by Selma Smith. Bala Cynwyd, PA: Printworld, 1983-1985.

PrintW 83	*1983/84,* second edition; 1983.
PrintW 85	*1985/86,* third edition; 1985.

Not in strict alphabetical order.

Profile — *Profiles.* Authors and illustrators, children's literature in Canada. Edited by Irma McDonough. Ottawa: Canadian Library Association, 1975-1982.

Profile 1	Revised edition; 1975.
Profile 2	*Profiles 2*; 1982.

PueRA — *Puerto Rican Authors.* A biobibliographic handbook. By Marnesba D. Hill and Harold B. Schleifer. Translation of entries into Spanish by Daniel Maratos. Metuchen, NJ: Scarecrow Press, 1974.

RAdv — *The Reader's Adviser.* A layman's guide to literature. New York: R.R. Bowker Co., 1974-1988.

RAdv 1	12th edition. Volume 1: *The Best in American and British Fiction, Poetry, Essays, Literary Biography, Bibliography, and Reference.* Edited by Sarah L. Prakken; 1974.
RAdv 13-1	13th edition. Volume 1: *The Best in American and British Fiction, Poetry, Essays, Literary Biography, Bibliography, and Reference.* Edited by Fred Kaplan; 1986.
RAdv 13-2	13th edition. Volume 2: *The Best in American and British Drama and World Literature in English Translation.* Edited by Maurice Charney; 1986.
RAdv 13-3	13th edition. Volume 3: *The Best in General Reference Literature, the Social Sciences, History, and the Arts.* Edited by Paula T. Kaufman; 1986.
RAdv 13-4	13th edition. Volume 4: *The Best in the Literature of Philosophy and World Religions.* Edited by William L. Reese; 1988.
RAdv 13-5	13th edition. Volume 5: *The Best in the Literature of Science, Technology, and Medicine.* Edited by Paul T. Durbin; 1988.

Use the "Name Index" to locate biographies.

RComAH — *The Reader's Companion to American History.* Edited by Eric Foner and John A. Garraty. Boston: Houghton Mifflin Co., 1991.

RComWL — *The Reader's Companion to World Literature.* Second edition. Revised and updated by Lillian Herlands Hornstein, Leon Edel, and Horst Frenz. New York: New American Library, 1973.

REn — *The Reader's Encyclopedia.* Second edition. By William Rose Benet. New York: Thomas Y. Crowell Co., 1965.

REnAL — *The Reader's Encyclopedia of American Literature.* By Max J. Herzberg. New York: Thomas Y. Crowell Co., 1962.

REnWD — *The Reader's Encyclopedia of World Drama.* Edited by John Gassner and Edward Quinn. New York: Thomas Y. Crowell Co., 1969.

RGAfL — *A Reader's Guide to African Literature.* Compiled and edited by Hans M. Zell and Helene Silver. New York: Africana Publishing Corp., 1971.

Biographies begin on page 113.

RGTwCSF — *Reader's Guide to Twentieth-Century Science Fiction.* Edited by Marilyn P. Fletcher. Chicago: American Library Association, 1989.

RealN — *Realism, Naturalism, and Local Color, 1865-1917.* Concise Dictionary of American Literary Biography Series. Detroit: Gale Research, 1988.

RfGAmL 87 — *Reference Guide to American Literature.* Second edition. Edited by D.L. Kirkpatrick. Chicago: St. James Press, 1987. Distributed by Gale Research, Detroit.

RfGEnL 91 — *Reference Guide to English Literature.* Second edition. Three volumes. Edited by D.L. Kirkpatrick. Chicago: St. James Press, 1991.

RfGShF — *Reference Guide to Short Fiction.* Edited by Noelle Watson. Detroit: St. James Press, 1994.

RkOn 74 — *Rock On.* The illustrated encyclopedia of rock n' roll. Volume 1: *The Solid Gold Years.* By Norm N. Nite. New York: Thomas Y. Crowell Co., 1974.

RkOn 85 — *Rock On.* The illustrated encyclopedia of rock n' roll. Volume 3: *The Video Revolution, 1978-Present.* By Norm N. Nite. New York: Harper & Row, 1985.

RolSEnR 83 — *The Rolling Stone Encyclopedia of Rock & Roll.* Edited by Jon Pareles and Patricia Romanowski. New York: Rolling Stone Press/Summit Books, 1983.

ScF&FL 92 — *Science Fiction & Fantasy Literature, 1975-1991.* A bibliography of science fiction, fantasy, and horror fiction books and nonfiction monographs. By Robert Reginald. Detroit: Gale Research, 1992.

ScFSB — *The Science Fiction Source Book.* Edited by David Wingrove. New York: Van Nostrand Reinhold Co., 1984.

Listings are located in the "Science Fiction Writers: A Consumers' Guide" section, which begins on page 87.

ScFEYrs *Science Fiction: The Early Years.* A full description of more than 3,000 science-fiction stories from earliest times to the appearance of the genre magazines in 1930. By Everett F. Bleiler. Kent, OH: Kent State University Press, 1990.

ScFEYrs A First Addenda begins on page 843.

SelBAAf *Selected Black American, African, and Caribbean Authors.* A bio-bibliography. Compiled by James A. Page and Jae Min Roh. Littleton, CO: Libraries Unlimited, 1985.

SelBAAu *Selected Black American Authors.* An illustrated bio-bibliography. Compiled by James A. Page. Boston: G.K. Hall & Co., 1977.

SenS *A Sense of Story.* Essays on contemporary writers for children. By John Rowe Townsend. London: Longman Group, 1971.

ShSCr *Short Story Criticism.* Excerpts from criticism of the works of short fiction writers. Detroit: Gale Research, 1988-1994.

ShSCr 1	Volume 1; 1988.
ShSCr 2	Volume 2; 1989.
ShSCr 3	Volume 3; 1989.
ShSCr 4	Volume 4; 1990.
ShSCr 5	Volume 5; 1990.
ShSCr 6	Volume 6; 1990.
ShSCr 7	Volume 7; 1991.
ShSCr 8	Volume 8; 1991.
ShSCr 9	Volume 9; 1992.
ShSCr 10	Volume 10; 1992.
ShSCr 11	Volume 11; 1992.
ShSCr 12	Volume 12; 1993.
ShSCr 13	Volume 13; 1993.
ShSCr 14	Volume 14; 1994.

ShSWr *Short Story Writers & Their Work.* A guide to the best. By Brad Hooper. Chicago: American Library Association, 1988.

Use the "Author Index" to locate biographies.

SingR *Singing Roads.* A guide to Australian children's authors and illustrators. Edited by Hugh Anderson. Surry Hills, Australia: Wentworth Books, 1970-1972.

SingR 1	Part 1, Fourth edition; 1972.
SingR 2	Part 2; 1970.

SixBJA *Sixth Book of Junior Authors & Illustrators.* Edited by Sally Holmes Holtze. New York: H.W. Wilson Co., 1989.

SixAP *Sixty American Poets, 1896-1944.* Revised edition. Selected, with preface and critical notes by Allen Tate. Washington, DC: Library of Congress, 1954. Reprint Detroit: Gale Research, 1969.

SmATA *Something about the Author.* Facts and pictures about authors and illustrators of books for young people. Detroit: Gale Research, 1971-1994.

SmATA 1	Volume 1; 1971.
SmATA 2	Volume 2; 1971.
SmATA 3	Volume 3; 1972.
SmATA 4	Volume 4; 1973.
SmATA 5	Volume 5; 1973.
SmATA 6	Volume 6; 1974.
SmATA 7	Volume 7; 1975.
SmATA 8	Volume 8; 1976.
SmATA 9	Volume 9; 1976.
SmATA 10	Volume 10; 1976.
SmATA 11	Volume 11; 1977.
SmATA 12	Volume 12; 1977.
SmATA 13	Volume 13; 1978.
SmATA 14	Volume 14; 1978.
SmATA 15	Volume 15; 1979.
SmATA 16	Volume 16; 1979.
SmATA 17	Volume 17; 1979.
SmATA 18	Volume 18; 1980.
SmATA 19	Volume 19; 1980.
SmATA 20	Volume 20; 1980.
SmATA 20N	Volume 20, Obituary Notice; 1980.
SmATA 21	Volume 21; 1980.
SmATA 21N	Volume 21, Obituary Notice; 1980.
SmATA 22	Volume 22; 1981.
SmATA 22N	Volume 22, Obituary Notice; 1981.
SmATA 23	Volume 23; 1981.
SmATA 23N	Volume 23, Obituary Notice; 1981.
SmATA 24	Volume 24; 1981.
SmATA 24N	Volume 24, Obituary Notice; 1981.
SmATA 25	Volume 25; 1981.
SmATA 25N	Volume 25, Obituary Notice; 1981.
SmATA 26	Volume 26; 1982.
SmATA 26N	Volume 26, Obituary Notice; 1982.
SmATA 27	Volume 27; 1982.
SmATA 27N	Volume 27, Obituary Notice; 1982.
SmATA 28	Volume 28; 1982.
SmATA 28N	Volume 28, Obituary Notice; 1982.
SmATA 29	Volume 29; 1982.
SmATA 29N	Volume 29, Obituary Notice; 1982.
SmATA 30	Volume 30; 1983.
SmATA 30N	Volume 30, Obituary Notice; 1983.
SmATA 31	Volume 31; 1983.
SmATA 31N	Volume 31, Obituary Notice; 1983.
SmATA 32	Volume 32; 1983.
SmATA 32N	Volume 32, Obituary Notice; 1983.
SmATA 33	Volume 33; 1983.
SmATA 33N	Volume 33, Obituary Notice; 1983.
SmATA 34	Volume 34; 1984.
SmATA 34N	Volume 34, Obituary Notice; 1984.
SmATA 35	Volume 35; 1984.
SmATA 35N	Volume 35, Obituary Notice; 1984.
SmATA 36	Volume 36; 1984.
SmATA 36N	Volume 36, Obituary Notice; 1984.
SmATA 37	Volume 37; 1985.
SmATA 37N	Volume 37, Obituary Notice; 1985.
SmATA 38	Volume 38; 1985.
SmATA 38N	Volume 38, Obituary Notice; 1985.
SmATA 39	Volume 39; 1985.
SmATA 39N	Volume 39, Obituary Notice; 1985.
SmATA 40	Volume 40; 1985.
SmATA 40N	Volume 40, Obituary Notice; 1985.

SmATA 41	Volume 41; 1985.
SmATA 41N	Volume 41, Obituary Notice; 1985.
SmATA 42	Volume 42; 1986.
SmATA 42N	Volume 42, Obituary Notice; 1986.
SmATA 43	Volume 43; 1986.
SmATA 43N	Volume 43, Obituary Notice; 1986.
SmATA 44	Volume 44; 1986.
SmATA 44N	Volume 44, Obituary Notice; 1986.
SmATA 45	Volume 45; 1986.
SmATA 45N	Volume 45, Obituary Notice; 1986.
SmATA 46	Volume 46; 1987.
SmATA 46N	Volume 46, Obituary Notice; 1987.
SmATA 47	Volume 47; 1987.
SmATA 47N	Volume 47, Obituary Notice; 1987.
SmATA 48	Volume 48; 1987.
SmATA 48N	Volume 48, Obituary Notice; 1987.
SmATA 49	Volume 49; 1987.
SmATA 49N	Volume 49, Obituary Notice; 1987.
SmATA 50	Volume 50; 1988.
SmATA 50N	Volume 50, Obituary Notice; 1988.
SmATA 51	Volume 51; 1988.
SmATA 51N	Volume 51, Obituary Notice; 1988.
SmATA 52	Volume 52; 1988.
SmATA 52N	Volume 52, Obituary Notice; 1988.
SmATA 53	Volume 53; 1988.
SmATA 53N	Volume 53, Obituary Notice; 1988.
SmATA 54	Volume 54; 1989.
SmATA 54N	Volume 54, Obituary Notice; 1989.
SmATA 55	Volume 55; 1989.
SmATA 55N	Volume 55, Obituary Notice; 1989.
SmATA 56	Volume 56; 1989.
SmATA 56N	Volume 56, Obituary Notice; 1989.
SmATA 57	Volume 57; 1989.
SmATA 58	Volume 58; 1990.
SmATA 59	Volume 59; 1990.
SmATA 60	Volume 60; 1990.
SmATA 61	Volume 61; 1990.
SmATA 62	Volume 62; 1990.
SmATA 63	Volume 63; 1991.
SmATA 64	Volume 64; 1991.
SmATA 65	Volume 65; 1991.
SmATA 66	Volume 66; 1991.
SmATA 67	Volume 67; 1992.
SmATA 68	Volume 68; 1992.
SmATA 69	Volume 69; 1992.
SmATA 70	Volume 70; 1993.
SmATA 71	Volume 71; 1993.
SmATA 72	Volume 72; 1993.
SmATA 73	Volume 73; 1993.
SmATA 74	Volume 74; 1993.
SmATA 75	Volume 75; 1994.
SmATA 76	Volume 76; 1994.
SmATA 77	Volume 77; 1994.

SmATA *Something about the Author, Autobiography Series.* Detroit: Gale Research, 1986-1994.

SmATA 1AS	Volume 1; 1986.
SmATA 2AS	Volume 2; 1986.
SmATA 3AS	Volume 3; 1987.
SmATA 4AS	Volume 4; 1987.
SmATA 5AS	Volume 5; 1988.

SmATA 6AS	Volume 6; 1988.
SmATA 7AS	Volume 7; 1989.
SmATA 8AS	Volume 8; 1989.
SmATA 9AS	Volume 9; 1990.
SmATA 10AS	Volume 10; 1990.
SmATA 11AS	Volume 11; 1991.
SmATA 12AS	Volume 12; 1991.
SmATA 13AS	Volume 13; 1992.
SmATA 14AS	Volume 14; 1992.
SmATA 15AS	Volume 15; 1993.
SmATA 16AS	Volume 16; 1993.
SmATA 17AS	Volume 17; 1994.
SmATA 18AS	Volume 18; 1994.

SmATA X *Something about the Author, Index.* Facts and pictures about authors and illustrators of books for young people. Detroit: Gale Research, (n.d.).

This code refers to pseudonym entries which appear only as cross-references in the cumulative index to *Something about the Author.*

SouSt *A Sounding of Storytellers.* New and revised essays on contemporary writers for children. By John Rowe Townsend. New York: J.B. Lippincott, 1979.

SourALJ *A Sourcebook of American Literary Journalism.* Representative writers in an emerging genre. Edited by Thomas B. Connery. New York: Greenwood Press, 1992.

Use the Index to locate biographies.

SouBlCW *Southern Black Creative Writers, 1829-1953.* Biobibliographies. Compiled by M. Marie Booth Foster. Bibliographies and Indexes in Afro-American and African Studies, no. 22. New York: Greenwood Press, 1988.

SpAmA *Spanish American Authors.* The twentieth century. By Angel Flores. New York: H.W. Wilson Co., 1992.

SpAmWW *Spanish American Women Writers.* A bio-bibliographical source book. Edited by Diane E. Marting. New York: Greenwood Press, 1990.

SpyFic *Spy Fiction.* A connoisseur's guide. By Donald McCormick and Katy Fletcher. New York: Facts on File, 1990.

StaCVF *The Stanford Companion to Victorian Fiction.* By John Sutherland. Stanford, CA: Stanford University Press, 1989.

Str&VC *Story and Verse for Children.* Third edition. By Miriam Blanton Huber. New York: Macmillan Co., 1965.

Biographies begin on page 793.

SupFW *Supernatural Fiction Writers.* Fantasy and horror. Two volumes. Edited by E.F. Bleiler. New York: Charles Scribner's Sons, 1985.

Use the Index to locate biographies.

TelT *Tellers of Tales.* British authors of children's books from 1800 to 1964. Revised edition. By Roger Lancelyn Green. New York: Franklin Watts, 1964.

TexWr *Texas Writers of Today.* By Florence Elberta Barns. Dallas: Tardy Publishing Co., 1935. Reprint. Ann Arbor, Mich.: Gryphon Books, 1971.

ThTwC 87 *Thinkers of the Twentieth Century.* Second edition. Edited by Roland Turner. Chicago: St. James Press, 1987.

ThrBJA *Third Book of Junior Authors.* Edited by Doris De Montreville and Donna Hill. Wilson Authors Series. New York: H.W. Wilson Co., 1972.

ThrtnMM *Thirteen Mistresses of Murder.* By Elaine Budd. New York: Ungar Publishing Co., 1986.
Use the Table of Contents to locate biographies.

Tw *The Twenties, 1917-1929.* Concise Dictionary of American Literary Biography. Detroit: Gale Research, 1989.

TwCA *Twentieth Century Authors.* A biographical dictionary of modern literature. Wilson Authors Series. New York: H.W. Wilson Co., 1942-1955.

- ***TwCA*** Edited by Stanley J. Kunitz and Howard Haycraft; 1942.
- ***TwCA SUP*** First Supplement. Edited by Stanley J. Kunitz; 1955.

TwCPaSc *Twentieth Century Painters and Sculptors.* By Frances Spalding. Dictionary of British Art, vol. 6. Suffolk, England: Antique Collectors' Club, 1990.

TwCWr *Twentieth Century Writing.* A reader's guide to contemporary literature. Edited by Kenneth Richardson. Levittown, NY: Transatlantic Arts, 1971.

TwCChW *Twentieth-Century Children's Writers.* Edited by D.L. Kirkpatrick. Twentieth-Century Writers Series. New York: St. Martin's Press, 1978-1983.

- ***TwCChW 78*** First edition; 1978.
- ***TwCChW 78A*** First edition; 1978. Appendix begins on page 1391.
- ***TwCChW 78B*** First edition; 1978. "Children's Books in Translation" section begins on page 1481.
- ***TwCChW 83*** Second edition; 1983.
- ***TwCChW 83A*** Second edition; 1983. Appendix begins on page 859.
- ***TwCChW 83B*** Second edition; 1983. "Foreign-Language Writers" section begins on page 893.

TwCChW 89 *Twentieth-Century Children's Writers.* Third edition. Edited by Tracy Chevalier. Chicago: St. James Press, 1989.

- ***TwCChW 89A*** Appendix begins on page 1083.
- ***TwCChW 89B*** "Foreign-Language Writers" section begins on page 1119.

TwCCr&M *Twentieth-Century Crime and Mystery Writers.* Edited by John M. Reilly. Twentieth-Century Writers Series. New York: St. Martin's Press, 1980-1985.

- ***TwCCr&M 80*** First edition; 1980.
- ***TwCCr&M 80A*** First edition; 1980. "Nineteenth-Century Writers" section begins on page 1525.
- ***TwCCr&M 80B*** First edition; 1980. "Foreign-Language Writers" section begins on page 1537.
- ***TwCCr&M 85*** Second edition; 1985.
- ***TwCCr&M 85A*** Second edition; 1985. "Nineteenth-Century Writers" section begins on page 931.

TwCCr&M 85B	Second edition; 1985. "Foreign-Language Writers" section begins on page 939.

TwCCr&M 91 *Twentieth-Century Crime and Mystery Writers.* Third edition. Edited by Lesley Henderson. Twentieth-Century Writers Series. Chicago: St. James Press, 1991.

TwCCr&M 91A	"Nineteenth-Century Writers" section begins on page 1121.
TwCCr&M 91B	"Foreign-Language Writers" section begins on page 1129.

TwCLC *Twentieth-Century Literary Criticism.* Excerpts from criticism of the works of novelists, poets, playwrights, short story writers, and other creative writers who lived between 1900 and 1960, from the first published critical appraisals to current evaluations. Detroit: Gale Research, 1978-1994.

TwCLC 1	Volume 1; 1978.
TwCLC 2	Volume 2; 1979.
TwCLC 3	Volume 3; 1980.
TwCLC 4	Volume 4; 1981.
TwCLC 5	Volume 5; 1981.
TwCLC 6	Volume 6; 1982.
TwCLC 7	Volume 7; 1982.
TwCLC 8	Volume 8; 1982.
TwCLC 9	Volume 9; 1983.
TwCLC 10	Volume 10; 1983.
TwCLC 11	Volume 11; 1983.
TwCLC 12	Volume 12; 1984.
TwCLC 13	Volume 13; 1984.
TwCLC 14	Volume 14; 1984.
TwCLC 15	Volume 15; 1985.
TwCLC 16	Volume 16; 1985.
TwCLC 17	Volume 17; 1985.
TwCLC 18	Volume 18; 1985.
TwCLC 19	Volume 19; 1986.
TwCLC 20	Volume 20; 1986.
TwCLC 21	Volume 21; 1986.
TwCLC 22	Volume 22; 1987.
TwCLC 23	Volume 23; 1987.
TwCLC 24	Volume 24; 1987.
TwCLC 25	Volume 25; 1988.
TwCLC 26	Volume 26; 1988. Contains no biographies.
TwCLC 27	Volume 27; 1988.
TwCLC 28	Volume 28; 1988.
TwCLC 29	Volume 29; 1988.
TwCLC 30	Volume 30; 1989. Contains no biographies.
TwCLC 31	Volume 31; 1989.
TwCLC 32	Volume 32; 1989.
TwCLC 33	Volume 33; 1989.
TwCLC 34	Volume 34; 1990. Contains no biographies.
TwCLC 35	Volume 35; 1990.
TwCLC 36	Volume 36; 1990.
TwCLC 37	Volume 37; 1991.
TwCLC 38	Volume 38; 1991. Contains no biographies.
TwCLC 39	Volume 39; 1991.
TwCLC 40	Volume 40; 1991.
TwCLC 41	Volume 41; 1991.
TwCLC 42	Volume 42; 1992. Contains no biographies.
TwCLC 43	Volume 43; 1992.
TwCLC 44	Volume 44; 1992.
TwCLC 45	Volume 45; 1992.
TwCLC 46	Volume 46; 1992. Contains no biographies.

TwCLC 47	Volume 47; 1993.
TwCLC 48	Volume 48; 1993.
TwCLC 49	Volume 49; 1993.
TwCLC 50	Volume 50; 1993. Contains no biographies.
TwCLC 51	Volume 51; 1994.
TwCLC 52	Volume 52; 1994.

TwCRHW 90 *Twentieth-Century Romance and Historical Writers.* Second edition. Edited by Lesley Henderson. Chicago: St. James Press, 1990.

TwCSFW *Twentieth-Century Science-Fiction Writers.* Twentieth-Century Writers Series. Chicago: St. James Press, 1986-1991.

TwCSFW 86	Second edition. Edited by Curtis C. Smith; 1986.
TwCSFW 86A	Second edition. Edited by Curtis C. Smith; 1986. "Foreign-Language Writers" section begins on page 837.
TwCSFW 86B	Second edition. Edited by Curtis C. Smith; 1986. "Major Fantasy Writers" section begins on page 863.
TwCSFW 91	Third edition. Edited by Noelle Watson and Paul E. Schellinger; 1991.
TwCSFW 91A	Third edition. Edited by Noelle Watson and Paul E. Schellinger; 1991. "Foreign-Language Writers" section begins on page 913.

TwCWW 91 *Twentieth-Century Western Writers.* Second edition. Edited by Geoff Sadler. Twentieth-Century Writers Series. Chicago: St. James Press, 1991.

TwCYAW *Twentieth-Century Young Adult Writers.* First edition. Twentieth-Century Writers Series. Detroit: St. James Press, 1994.

UFOEn *The UFO Encyclopedia.* By Margaret Sachs. New York: G.P. Putnam's Sons, 1980.

WebAB *Webster's American Biographies.* Edited by Charles Van Doren. Springfield, MA: G. & C. Merriam Co., 1974-1979.

WebAB 74	1974 edition; 1974.
WebAB 79	1979 edition; 1979.

WebAMB *Webster's American Military Biographies.* Springfield, MA: G. & C. Merriam Co., 1978.

WebE&AL *Webster's New World Companion to English and American Literature.* Edited by Arthur Pollard. New York: World Publishing Co., 1973.

WhDW *Who Did What.* The lives and achievements of the 5,000 men and women -- leaders of nations, saints and sinners, artists and scientists -- who shaped our world. Edited by Gerald Howat. New York: Crown Publishers, 1974.

WhAm *Who Was Who in America.* A companion biographical reference work to *Who s Who in America.* Chicago: A.N. Marquis Co., 1943-1963.

WhAm 1	Volume 1, 1897-1942; 1943.
WhAm 2	Volume 2, 1943-1950; 1963.

WhAm *Who Was Who in America.* Chicago: Marquis Who's Who, 1966-1993.

WhAm 3	Volume 3, 1951-1960; 1966.

WhAm 3A	Volume 3, 1951-1960; 1966. Addendum begins on page 952.
WhAm 4	Volume 4, 1961-1968; 1968.
WhAm 4A	Volume 4, 1961-1968; 1968. Addendum begins on page 1049.
WhAm 5	Volume 5, 1969-1973; 1973.
WhAm 6	Volume 6, 1974-1976; 1976.
WhAm 7	Volume 7, 1977-1981; 1981.
WhAm 8	Volume 8, 1982-1985; 1985.
WhAm 9	Volume 9, 1985-1989; 1989.
WhAm 10	Volume 10, 1989-1993; 1993.
WhAm HS	Historical Volume, 1607-1896. Revised Edition; 1967.
WhAm HSA	Historical Volume, 1607-1896. Revised Edition; 1967. Addendum begins on page 677.

WhAmArt 85 *Who Was Who in American Art.* Compiled from the original thirty-four volumes of *American Art Annual: Who's Who in Art, Biographies of American Artists Active from 1898-1947.* Edited by Peter Hastings Falk. Madison, CT: Sound View Press, 1985.

WhAmP *Who Was Who in American Politics.* A biographical dictionary of over 4,000 men and women who contributed to the United States political scene from colonial days up to and including the immediate past. By Dan and Inez Morris. New York: Hawthorn Books, 1974.

WhCiWar *Who Was Who in the Civil War.* By Stewart Sifakis. New York: Facts on File Publications, 1988.

WhFla *Who Was Who in Florida.* Written and compiled by Henry S. Marks. Huntsville, AL: Strode Publishers, 1973.

WhJnl *Who Was Who in Journalism, 1925-1928.* A consolidation of all material appearing in the 1928 edition of *Who's Who in Journalism,* with unduplicated biographical entries from the 1925 edition of *Who's Who in Journalism,* originally compiled by M.N. Ask (1925 and 1928 editions) and S. Gershanek (1925 edition). Gale Composite Biographical Dictionary Series, Number 4. Detroit: Gale Research, 1978.

WhJnl SUP	The "1925 Supplement" begins on page 639.

WhNaAH *Who Was Who in Native American History.* Indians and non-Indians from early contacts through 1900. By Carl Waldman. New York: Facts on File, 1990.

WhNAA *Who Was Who among North American Authors, 1921-1939.* Compiled from *Who's Who among North American Authors,* Volumes 1-7, 1921-1939. Two volumes. Gale Composite Biographical Dictionary Series, Number 1. Detroit: Gale Research, 1976.

WhScrn 74 *Who Was Who on Screen.* First edition. By Evelyn Mack Truitt. New York: R.R. Bowker Co., 1974.

WhScrn 77 *Who Was Who on Screen.* Second edition. By Evelyn Mack Truitt. New York: R.R. Bowker, 1977.

WhScrn 83 *Who Was Who on Screen.* Third edition. By Evelyn Mack Truitt. New York: R.R. Bowker Co., 1983.

Who *Who's Who.* An annual biographical dictionary. New York and London: St. Martin's Press, 1974-1992.

Who 74	126th Year of Issue, 1974-1975; 1974.
Who 82	134th Year of Issue, 1982-1983; 1982.
Who 82N	134th Year of Issue, 1982-1983; 1982. Obituary section.
Who 83	135th Year of Issue, 1983-1984; 1983.
Who 83N	135th Year of Issue, 1983-1984; 1983. Obituary section.
Who 85	137th Year of Issue, 1985-1986; 1985.
Who 85N	137th Year of Issue, 1985-1986; 1985. Obituary section.
Who 85S	137th Year of Issue, 1985-1986; 1985. Supplement.
Who 88	140th Year of Issue, 1988; 1988.
Who 88N	140th Year of Issue, 1988; 1988. Obituary section.
Who 90	142nd Year of Issue, 1990; 1990.
Who 90N	142nd Year of Issue, 1990; 1990. Obituary section.
Who 92	144th Year of Issue, 1992; 1992.
Who 92N	144th Year of Issue, 1992; 1992. Obituary section.

WhoAdv *Who's Who in Advertising.* Monroe, NY: Redfield Publishing Co., 1972-1980.

WhoAdv 72	Second edition. Edited by Robert S. Morgan; 1972. Biographies are found in "U.S. Advertising Executives," beginning on page 1; "Canadian Advertising Executives," beginning on page 585; and the Addendum beginning on page 637.
WhoAdv 80	Third edition. Edited by Catherine Quinn Serie; 1980.

WhoAm *Who's Who in America.* New Providence, NJ: Marquis Who's Who, 1974-1993.

WhoAm 74	38th edition, 1974-1975; 1974.
WhoAm 76	39th edition, 1976-1977; 1976.
WhoAm 78	40th edition, 1978-1979; 1978.
WhoAm 80	41st edition, 1980-1981; 1980.
WhoAm 82	42nd edition, 1982-1983; 1982.
WhoAm 84	43rd edition, 1984-1985; 1984.
WhoAm 86	44th edition, 1986-1987; 1986.
WhoAm 88	45th edition, 1988-1989; 1988.
WhoAm 90	46th edition, 1990-1991; 1990.
WhoAm 92	47th edition, 1992-1993; 1992.
WhoAm 94	48th edition, 1994; 1993.

WhoAmA *Who's Who in American Art.* New Providence, NJ: R.R. Bowker Co., 1973-1990.

WhoAmA 73	11th edition; 1973.
WhoAmA 78	13th edition; 1978.
WhoAmA 78N	13th edition; 1978. The Necrology is located at the back of the volume.
WhoAmA 80	14th edition; 1980.
WhoAmA 80N	14th edition; 1980. The Necrology is located at the back of the volume.
WhoAmA 82	15th edition; 1982.
WhoAmA 82N	15th edition; 1982. The Necrology is located at the back of the volume.
WhoAmA 84	16th edition; 1984.
WhoAmA 86	17th edition; 1986.
WhoAmA 86N	17th edition; 1986. The Necrology is located at the back of the volume.
WhoAmA 89	18th edition, 1989-1990; 1989.
WhoAmA 89N	18th edition, 1989-1990; 1989. The Necrology is located at the back of the volume.
WhoAmA 91	19th edition, 1991-1992; 1990.

WhoAmA 91N — 19th edition, 1991-1992; 1990. The Necrology begins on page 1387.

WhoAmJ 80 — *Who's Who in American Jewry.* Incorporating *The Directory of American Jewish Institutions.* 1980 edition. Los Angeles: Standard Who's Who, 1980.

WhoAmL — *Who's Who in American Law.* New Providence, NJ: Marquis Who's Who, 1978-1994.

WhoAmL 78	First edition; 1978.
WhoAmL 83	Third edition; 1983.
WhoAmL 85	Fourth edition, 1985-1986; 1985.
WhoAmL 87	Fifth edition, 1987-1988; 1987.
WhoAmL 90	Sixth edition, 1990-1991; 1989.
WhoAmL 92	Seventh edition, 1992-1993; 1991.
WhoAmL 94	Eighth edition, 1994-1995; 1994.

WhoAmM 83 — *Who's Who in American Music: Classical.* First edition. New York: R.R. Bowker Co., 1983.

WhoAmP — *Who's Who in American Politics.* New Providence, NJ: R.R. Bowker, 1973-1993.

WhoAmP 73	Fourth edition, 1973-1974; 1973.
WhoAmP 75	Fifth edition, 1975-1976; 1975.
WhoAmP 77	Sixth edition, 1977-1978; 1977.
WhoAmP 81	Eighth edition, 1981-1982; 1981.
WhoAmP 83	Ninth edition, 1983-1984; 1983.
WhoAmP 85	10th edition, 1985-1986; 1985.
WhoAmP 87	11th edition, 1987-1988; 1987.
WhoAmP 89	12th edition, 1989-1990; 1989.
WhoAmP 91	13th edition, 1991-1992; 1991.
WhoAmP 93	14th edition, 1993-1994; 1993.

Use the Index to locate biographies.

WhoAmW 72 — *Who's Who of American Women.* Seventh edition, 1972-1973. Wilmette, IL: Marquis Who's Who, 1971.

WhoAmW 74 — *Who's Who of American Women* Eighth edition, 1974-1975. Wilmette, IL: Marquis Who's Who, 1973.

WhoAmW — *Who's Who of American Women.* New Providence, NJ: Marquis Who's Who, 1975-1993.

WhoAmW 75	Ninth edition, 1975-1976; 1975.
WhoAmW 77	10th edition, 1977-1978; 1978.
WhoAmW 81	12th edition, 1981-1982; 1981.
WhoAmW 83	13th edition, 1983-1984; 1983.
WhoAmW 85	14th edition, 1985-1986; 1984.
WhoAmW 87	15th edition, 1987-1988; 1986.
WhoAmW 89	16th edition, 1989-1990; 1988.
WhoAmW 91	17th edition, 1991-1992; 1991.
WhoAmW 93	18th edition, 1993-1994; 1993.

WhoArab 81 — *Who's Who in the Arab World.* Sixth edition, 1981-1982. Edited by Gabriel M. Bustros. Beirut, Lebanon: Publitec Publications, 1981.

Biographies are located in Part III.

WhoArt *Who's Who in Art.* Biographies of leading men and women in the world of art today -- artists, designers, craftsmen, critics, writers, teachers and curators, with an appendix of signatures. Havant, England: Art Trade Press, 1980-1984.

WhoArt 80	19th edition; 1980.
WhoArt 80N	19th edition; 1980. The Obituary section is located at the back of the volume.
WhoArt 82	20th edition; 1982.
WhoArt 82N	20th edition; 1982. The Obituary section is located at the back of the volume.
WhoArt 84	21st edition; 1984.
WhoArt 84N	21st edition; 1984. The Obituary section is located at the back of the volume.

WhoAsA 94 *Who's Who among Asian Americans.* 1994-1995 edition. Detroit: Gale Research, 1994.

WhoAtom 77 *Who's Who in Atoms.* Sixth edition. Edited by Ann Pernet. Guernsey, England: Francis Hodgson, 1977.

WhoBlA *Who's Who among Black Americans.* Northbrook, IL: Who's Who among Black Americans, 1976-1981.

WhoBlA 75	First edition, 1975-1976; 1976.
WhoBlA 77	Second edition, 1977-1978; 1978.
WhoBlA 80	Third edition, 1980-1981; 1981.

WhoBlA *Who's Who among Black Americans.* Lake Forest, IL: Educational Communications, 1985-1988.

WhoBlA 85	Fourth edition, 1985; 1985.
WhoBlA 88	Fifth edition, 1988; 1988.

WhoBlA *Who's Who among Black Americans.* Detroit: Gale Research, 1990-1994.

WhoBlA 90	Sixth edition, 1990/1991; 1990.
WhoBlA 90N	Sixth edition, 1990/1991; 1990. The Obituary section is located in the back of the volume.
WhoBlA 92	Seventh edition, 1992/1993; 1992.
WhoBlA 92N	Seventh edition, 1992/1993; 1992. The Obituary section is located in the back of the volume.
WhoBlA 94	Eighth edition, 1994/1995; 1994.
WhoBlA 94N	Eighth edition, 1994/1995; 1994. The Obituaries section is located in the back of the volume.

WhoCan *Who's Who in Canada.* An illustrated biographical record of men and women of the time in Canada. Toronto: International Press, 1973-1982.

WhoCan 73	1973-1974 edition; 1973.
WhoCan 75	1975-1976 edition; 1975.
WhoCan 77	1977-1978 edition; 1977.
WhoCan 80	1980-1981 edition; 1980.
WhoCan 82	1982-1983 edition; 1982.

Use the Index at the front of the volume to locate biographies.

WhoCan 84 *Who's Who in Canada.* An illustrated biographical record of Canada's leading men and women in business, government and academia. 1984-1985 edition. Agincourt, ON, Canada: Gage Publishing, Global Press, 1984.

WhoCanL *Who's Who in Canadian Literature.* By Gordon Ripley and Anne Mercer. Teeswater, ON, Canada: Reference Press, 1985-1992.

WhoCanL 85	1985-1986 edition; 1985.
WhoCanL 87	1987-1988 edition; 1987.
WhoCanL 92	1992-1993 edition; 1992.

WhoChL *The Who's Who of Children's Literature.* Compiled and edited by Brian Doyle. New York: Schocken Books, 1968.

Biographies are found in "The Authors," beginning on page 1, and "The Illustrators," beginning on page 303.

WhoCom *Who's Who in Comedy.* Comedians, comics, and clowns from vaudeville to today's stand-ups. By Ronald L. Smith. New York: Facts on File, 1992.

WhoE *Who's Who in the East.* New Providence, NJ: Marquis Who's Who, 1974-1992.

WhoE 74	14th edition, 1974-1975; 1974.
WhoE 75	15th edition, 1975-1976; 1975.
WhoE 77	16th edition, 1977-1978; 1977.
WhoE 81	18th edition, 1981-1982; 1981.
WhoE 83	19th edition, 1983-1984; 1983.
WhoE 85	20th edition, 1985-1986; 1984.
WhoE 85A	20th edition, 1985-1986; 1984. The Addendum is located at the back of the volume.
WhoE 86	21st edition, 1986-1987; 1986.
WhoE 89	22nd edition, 1989-1990; 1988.
WhoE 91	23rd edition, 1991-1992; 1990.
WhoE 93	24th edition, 1993-1994; 1992.

WhoEc *Who's Who in Economics.* A biographical dictionary of major economists, 1700-1986. Cambridge: MIT Press, 1983-1986.

WhoEc 81	First edition. Edited by Mark Blaug and Paul Sturges; 1983.
WhoEc 86	Second edition. Edited by Mark Blaug; 1986.

WhoEnt 92 *Who's Who in Entertainment.* Second edition, 1992-1993. Wilmette, IL: Marquis Who's Who, 1992.

WhoEIO 82 *Who's Who in European Institutions and Organizations.* A biographical encyclopedia of the international red series containing some 4,000 biographies of the top administrators, chairmen, politicians and other leading personalities working with European institutions and organizations, and international institutions in Europe. First edition. Edited by Karl Strute and Theodor Doelken. Zurich, Switzerland: Who's Who, 1982.

WhoFI *Who's Who in Finance and Industry.* New Providence, NJ: Marquis Who's Who, 1974-1993.

WhoFI 74	18th edition, 1974-1975; 1974.
WhoFI 75	19th edition, 1975-1976; 1975.
WhoFI 77	20th edition, 1977-1978; 1977.
WhoFI 81	22nd edition, 1981-1982; 1981.
WhoFI 83	23rd edition, 1983-1984; 1983.
WhoFI 85	24th edition, 1985-1986; 1985.
WhoFI 87	25th edition, 1987-1988; 1987.
WhoFI 89	26th edition, 1989-1990; 1989.

WhoFI 92	27th edition, 1992-1993; 1991.
WhoFI 94	28th edition, 1994-1995; 1993.

WhoFla *Who's Who in Florida, 1973/74.* A composite of biographical sketches of outstanding men and women of the State of Florida. First edition. Lexington, KY: Names of Distinction, 1974.

WhoFtbl 74 *Who's Who in Football.* By Ronald L. Mendell and Timothy B. Phares. New Rochelle, NY: Arlington House, 1974.

WhoFrS 84 *Who's Who in Frontier Science and Technology.* First edition, 1984-1985. Chicago: Marquis Who's Who, 1984.

WhoGen 81 *Who's Who in Genealogy & Heraldry.* Volume 1. Edited by Mary Keysor Meyer and P. William Filby. Detroit: Gale Research, 1981.

WhoGov *Who's Who in Government.* Chicago: Marquis Who's Who, 1972-1977.

WhoGov 72	First edition, 1972-1973; 1972.
WhoGov 75	Second edition, 1975-1976; 1975.
WhoGov 77	Third edition, 1977; 1977.

WhoGrA 62 *Who's Who in Graphic Art.* An illustrated book of reference to the world's leading graphic designers, illustrators, typographers and cartoonists. First edition. Edited by Walter Amstutz. Zurich: Amstutz & Herdeg Graphis Press, 1962.

Use the "Index of Artists' Names," which begins on page 576, to locate biographies.

WhoGrA 82 *Who's Who in Graphic Art.* An illustrated world review of the leading contemporary graphic and typographic designers, illustrators and cartoonists. Volume Two. Edited and designed by Walter Amstutz. Dubendorf, Switzerland: De Clivo Press, 1982.

Use the "Index of Artists' Names," which begins on page 886, to locate biographies.

WhoHisp *Who's Who among Hispanic Americans.* Detroit: Gale Research, 1991-1994.

WhoHisp 91	First edition, 1991-1992; 1991.
WhoHisp 92	Second edition, 1992-1993; 1992.
WhoHisp 94	Third edition, 1994-1995; 1994.

WhoHcky 73 *Who's Who in Hockey.* By Harry C. Kariher. New Rochelle, NY: Arlington House, 1973.

WhoHol *Who's Who in Hollywood, 1900-1976.* By David Ragan. New Rochelle, NY: Arlington House, 1976.

WhoHol A	The "Living Players" section begins on page 11.
WhoHol B	The "Late Players (1900-1974)" section begins on page 539.
WhoHol C	The "Players Who Died in 1975 and 1976" section begins on page 845.

WhoHr&F *Who's Who in Horror and Fantasy Fiction.* By Mike Ashley. London: Elm Tree Books, 1977.

WhoIns 93 *Who's Who in Insurance.* 1993 edition. Englewood, NJ: Underwriter Printing & Publishing Co., 1993.

WhoJazz 72 *Who's Who of Jazz: Storyville to Swing Street.* By John Chilton. Philadelphia: Chilton Book Co., 1972.

WhoLib 54 *Who's Who in Librarianship.* Edited by Thomas Landau. Cambridge: Bowes & Bowes, 1954.

WhoLib 72 *Who's Who in Librarianship and Information Science.* Second edition. Edited by T. Landau. London: Abelard-Schuman, 1972.

WhoLibI 82 *Who's Who in Library and Information Services.* Edited by Joel M. Lee. Chicago: American Library Association, 1982.

WhoLibS 55 *Who's Who in Library Service.* A biographical directory of professional librarians of the United States and Canada. Third edition. Edited by Dorothy Ethlyn Cole. New York: Grolier Society, 1955.

WhoLibS 66 *Who's Who in Library Service.* A biographical directory of professional librarians in the United States and Canada. Fourth edition. Edited by Lee Ash. Hamden, CT: Shoe String Press, 1966.

WhoLA *Who's Who among Living Authors of Older Nations.* Covering the literary activities of living authors and writers of all countries of the world except the United States of America, Canada, Mexico, Alaska, Hawaii, Newfoundland, the Philippine Islands, the West Indies, and Central America. Volume 1, 1931-1932. Edited by A. Lawrence. Los Angeles: Golden Syndicate Publishing Co., 1931. Reprint. Detroit: Gale Research, 1966.

WhoMW *Who's Who in the Midwest.* New Providence, NJ: Marquis Who's Who, 1974-1994.

WhoMW 74	14th edition, 1974-1975; 1974.
WhoMW 76	15th edition, 1976-1977; 1976.
WhoMW 78	16th edition, 1978-1979; 1978.
WhoMW 80	17th edition, 1980-1981; 1980.
WhoMW 82	18th edition, 1982-1983; 1982.
WhoMW 84	19th edition, 1984-1985; 1984.
WhoMW 86	20th edition, 1986-1987; 1985.
WhoMW 88	21st edition, 1988-1989; 1987.
WhoMW 90	22nd edition, 1990-1991; 1989.
WhoMW 92	23rd edition, 1992-1993; 1992.
WhoMW 93	24th edition, 1994-1995; 1994.

WhoMus 72 *Who's Who in Music and Musicians' International Directory.* Sixth edition. New York: Hafner Publishing Co., 1972. Later editions published as *International Who's Who in Music and Musicians' Directory.*

WhoNob *Who's Who of Nobel Prize Winners.* Edited by Bernard S. Schlessinger and June H. Schlessinger. Phoenix, AZ: Oryx Press, 1986-1991.

WhoNob	First edtion; 1986. Use the "Name Index," which begins on page 195, to locate biographies.
WhoNob 90	Second edition; 1991.

WhoOcn 78 *Who's Who in Ocean and Freshwater Science.* First edition. Edited by Allen Varley. Essex, England: Longman Group, Francis Hodgson, 1978.

WhoOp 76 *Who's Who in Opera.* An international biographical directory of singers, conductors, directors, designers, and administrators. Also including profiles of 101 opera companies. Edited by Maria F. Rich. New York: Arno Press, 1976.

WhoPNW *Who's Who among Pacific Northwest Authors.* Second edition. Edited by Frances Valentine Wright. Missoula, MT: Pacific Northwest Library Association, 1969.

Biographies are arranged alphabetically by state. Use the "Index of Authors" to locate listings.

WhoPolA *Who's Who in Polish America.* A biographical directory of Polish-American leaders and distinguished Poles resident in the Americas. Third edition. Edited by Francis Bolek. New York: Harbinger House, 1943. Reprint. The American Immigration Collection - Series II. New York: Arno Press and The New York Times, 1970.

WhoRel *Who's Who in Religion.* Wilmette, IL: Marquis Who's Who, 1975-1992.

WhoRel 75	First edition, 1975-1976; 1975.
WhoRel 77	Second edition, 1977; 1977.
WhoRel 92	Fourth edition, 1992-1993; 1992.

WhoSciF *Who's Who in Science Fiction.* By Brian Ash. London: Elm Tree Books, 1976.

WhoSSW *Who's Who in the South and Southwest.* New Providence, NJ: Marquis Who's Who, 1973-1993.

WhoSSW 73	13th edition, 1973-1974; 1973.
WhoSSW 75	14th edition, 1975-1976; 1975.
WhoSSW 76	15th edition, 1976-1977; 1976.
WhoSSW 78	16th edition, 1978-1979; 1978.
WhoSSW 80	17th edition, 1980-1981; 1980.
WhoSSW 82	18th edition, 1982-1983; 1982.
WhoSSW 84	19th edition, 1984-1985; 1984.
WhoSSW 86	20th edition, 1986-1987; 1986.
WhoSSW 88	21st edition, 1988-1989; 1988.
WhoSSW 91	22nd edition, 1991-1992; 1990.
WhoSSW 93	23rd edition, 1993-1994; 1993.

WhoSpc *Who's Who in Space.* The First 25 Years. By Michael Cassutt. Boston: G.K. Hall & Co., 1987.

Use the Index to locate biographies.

WhoSpyF *Who's Who in Spy Fiction.* By Donald McCormick. London: Elm Tree Books, 1977.

WhoTech 82 *Who's Who in Technology Today.* Third edition. Four volumes. Edited by Jan W. Churchwell. Highland Park, IL: J. Dick & Co., 1982.

Use the "Index of Names," which begins on page 667 of Volume 4, to locate biographies.

WhoTech 84 *Who's Who in Technology Today.* Fourth edition. Five volumes. Edited by Barbara A. Tinucci. Lake Bluff, IL: Research Publications, J. Dick Publishing, 1984.

Use the "Index of Names," which begins on page 1125 of Volume 5, to locate biographies.

WhoThe *Who's Who in the Theatre.* A biographical record of the contemporary stage. London: Pitman Publishing; Detroit: Gale Research, 1972-1981. Continued as *Contemporary Theatre, Film, and Television.*

WhoThe 72	15th edition. Compiled by John Parker; 1972.
WhoThe 77	16th edition. Edited by Ian Herbert; 1977.
WhoThe 81	17th edition. Edited by Ian Herbert; 1981.
WhoThe 81N	17th edition. Edited by Ian Herbert; 1981. Obituary section begins on page 743.

WhoTr&F 73 *Who's Who in Track and Field.* By Reid M. Hanley. New Rochelle, NY: Arlington House, 1973.

WhoTwCL *Who's Who in Twentieth Century Literature.* By Martin Seymour-Smith. New York: Holt, Rinehart & Winston, 1976.

WhoUSWr 88 *Who's Who in U.S. Writers, Editors & Poets.* A biographical directory. Second edition. Edited by Curt Johnson. Highland Park, IL: December Press, 1988.

WhoWest *Who's Who in the West.* New Providence, NJ: Marquis Who's Who, 1974-1993.

WhoWest 74	14th edition, 1974-1975; 1974.
WhoWest 76	15th edition, 1976-1977; 1976.
WhoWest 78	16th edition, 1978-1979; 1978.
WhoWest 80	17th edition, 1980-1981; 1980.
WhoWest 82	18th edition, 1982-1983; 1982.
WhoWest 84	19th edition, 1984-1985; 1983.
WhoWest 87	21st edition, 1987-1988; 1987.
WhoWest 89	22nd edition, 1989-1990; 1989.
WhoWest 92	23rd edition, 1992-1993; 1992.
WhoWest 94	24th edition, 1994-1995; 1993.

WhoWor *Who's Who in the World.* New Providence, NJ: Marquis Who's Who, 1973-1992.

WhoWor 74	Second edition, 1974-1975; 1973.
WhoWor 78	Fourth edition, 1978-1979; 1978.
WhoWor 80	Fifth edition, 1980-1981; 1980.
WhoWor 82	Sixth edition, 1982-1983; 1982.
WhoWor 84	Seventh edition, 1984-1985; 1984.
WhoWor 87	Eighth edition, 1987-1988; 1986.
WhoWor 89	Ninth edition, 1989-1990; 1988.
WhoWor 91	10th edition, 1991-1992; 1990.
WhoWor 93	11th edition, 1993-1994; 1992.

WhoWorJ 72 *Who's Who in World Jewry.* A biographical dictionary of outstanding Jews. Edited by I.J. Carmin Karpman. New York: Pitman Publishing Corp., 1972.

WhoWorJ 78 *Who's Who in World Jewry.* A biographical dictionary of outstanding Jews. Edited by I.J. Carmin Karpman. Tel-Aviv, Israel: Olive Books of Israel, 1978.

WhoWrEP *Who's Who in Writers, Editors & Poets.* United States & Canada. Edited by Curt Johnson. Highland Park, IL: December Press, 1989-1992.

WhoWrEP 89	Third edition, 1989-1990; 1989.
WhoWrEP 92	Fourth edition, 1992-1993; 1992.

WisWr *Wisconsin Writers.* Sketches and studies. By William A. Titus. Chicago, 1930. Reprint. Detroit: Gale Research, 1974.

Use the Table of Contents to locate biographies.

WomWWA 14 *Woman's Who's Who of America.* A biographical dictionary of contemporary women of the United States and Canada, 1914-1915. Edited by John William Leonard. New York: American Commonwealth Co., 1914. Reprint. Detroit: Gale Research, 1976.

WomNov *Women Novelists, 1891-1920.* An index to biographical and autobiographical sources. By Doris Robinson. Garland Reference Library of the Humanities, vol. 491. New York: Garland Publishing, 1984.

WomSc *Women in Science.* Antiquity through the Nineteenth Century. By Marilyn Bailey Ogilvie. Cambridge: MIT Press, 1986.

WomWMM *Women Who Make Movies.* By Sharon Smith. Cinema Study Series. New York: Hopkinson & Blake, 1975.

WomWMM	"Overview" section. Biographies can be located through the index beginning on page 299.
WomWMM A	"The New Filmmakers" begin on page 145.
WomWMM B	"Directory" begins on page 221.

WomWrGe *Women Writers of Germany, Austria, and Switzerland.* An annotated bio-bibliographical guide. Edited by Elke Frederiksen. Bibliographies and Indexes in Women's Studies, no. 8. New York: Greenwood Press, 1989.

WomWrSA *Women Writers of Spanish America.* An annotated bio-bibliographical guide. Edited by Diane E. Marting. Bibliographies and Indexes in Women's Studies, no. 5. New York: Greenwood Press, 1987.

WorAlBi *The World Almanac Biographical Dictionary.* By the editors of *The World Almanac.* New York: World Almanac, 1990.

WorAl *The World Almanac Book of Who.* Edited by Hana Umlauf Lane. New York: World Almanac Publications, 1980.

Use the "Name Index," which begins on page 326, to locate biographies.

WorArt 1950 *World Artists, 1950-1980.* Edited by Claude Marks. New York: H.W. Wilson Co., 1984.

WorArt 1980 *World Artists, 1980-1990.* Edited by Claude Marks. New York: H.W. Wilson Co., 1991.

WorAu *World Authors.* Wilson Authors Series. New York: H.W. Wilson Co., 1975-1991.

WorAu 1950	*1950-1970.* Edited by John Wakeman; 1975.
WorAu 1975	*1975-1980.* Edited by Vineta Colby; 1985.
WorAu 1980	*1980-1985.* Edited by Vineta Colby; 1991.

WorECar *The World Encyclopedia of Cartoons.* Two volumes. Edited by Maurice Horn. Detroit: Gale Research, 1980. Published in association with Chelsea House Publishers, New

York.

WorECar A "Notes on the Contributors" section begins on page 631.

WorEFlm *The World Encyclopedia of the Film.* Edited by John M. Smith and Tim Cawkwell. New York: A. & W. Visual Library, 1972.

WorFDir *World Film Directors.* Edited by John Wakeman. New York: H.W. Wilson Co., 1987-1988.

WorFDir 1 Volume 1: 1890-1945; 1987.
WorFDir 2 Volume 2: 1945-1985; 1988.

WorLitC *World Literature Criticism.* 1500 to the present. A selection of major authors from Gale's Literary Criticism Series. Six volumes. Detroit: Gale Research, 1992.

WrChl *Writers for Children.* Critical studies of major authors since the seventeenth century. Edited by Jane M. Bingham. New York: Charles Scribner's Sons, 1988.

WrDr *The Writers Directory.* London: St. James Press; New York: St. Martin's Press, 1976-1979.

WrDr 76 Third edition, 1976-1978; 1976.
WrDr 80 Fourth edition, 1980-1982; 1979.

WrDr 82 *The Writers Directory.* Fifth edition, 1982-1984. Detroit: Gale Research, 1981.

WrDr *The Writers Directory.* Detroit: St. James Press, 1983-1994.

WrDr 84 Sixth edition, 1984-1986; 1983.
WrDr 86 Seventh edition, 1986-1988; 1986.
WrDr 88 Eighth edition, 1988-1990; 1988.
WrDr 90 Ninth edition, 1990-1992; 1990.
WrDr 92 10th edition, 1992-1994; 1991.
WrDr 94 11th edition, 1994-1996; 1994.
WrDr 94N 11th edition, 1994-1996; 1994. The Obituaries section is located in the back of the volume.

WrPh *Writers and Philosophers.* A sourcebook of philosophical influences on literature. By Edmund J. Thomas and Eugene G. Miller. New York: Greenwood Press, 1990.

WrPh P "Profiles of Philosophers" section begins on page 215.

YABC *Yesterday's Authors of Books for Children.* Facts and pictures about authors and illustrators of books for young people, from early times to 1960. Edited by Anne Commire. Detroit: Gale Research, 1977-1978.

YABC 1 Volume 1; 1977.
YABC 2 Volume 2; 1978.

YABC X *Yesterday's Authors of Books for Children, Index.* Facts and pictures about authors and illustrators of books for young people, from early times to 1960. Detroit: Gale Research, 1977-1978.

This code refers to pseudonym entries which appear only as cross-references in the cumulative index to *Yesterday's Authors of Books for Children.*

CHILDREN'S AUTHORS AND ILLUSTRATORS:

AN INDEX TO BIOGRAPHICAL DICTIONARIES

A

Aardema, Verna 1911- *AuBYP 2S, -3, BioIn 9, -12, -17, ChILR 17, ConAu 5R, -X, -39NR, FifBJA, MajAI, MichAu 80, SmATA 4, -68, -8AS, WrDr 76, -80, -82, -84, -88, -92, -94*

Aaron, Anna 1931- *BioIn 17, SmATA X*
Main entry: Selden, Neil Roy

Aaron, Chester 1923- *AuBYP 2S, -3, BioIn 11, -16, ConAu 21R, -8NR, -38NR, MajAI, ScF&FL 92, SixBJA, SmATA 9, -74, -12AS, TwCChW 83, -89, WhoWest 74, WrDr 86, -92, -94*

Aaseng, Nate *ConAu X, -36NR, MajAI, SmATA X*

Aaseng, Nathan *BioIn 15*

Aaseng, Nathan 1953- *ConAu 106, -36NR, MajAI, SixBJA, SmATA 38, -51, -12AS*

Aaseng, Nathan 1956- *BioIn 16*

Aaseng, Rolf E 1923- *ConAu 49*

Abbott, Alice *BioIn 14, ConAu X, MichAu 80, SmATA X, WrDr 86, -88, -92, -94*
Main entry: Borland, Kathryn Kilby
Speicher, Helen Ross

Abbott, Berenice 1898- *AmAu&B, BioAmW, BioIn 1, -7, -9, -10, -11, -12, -13, -14, -15, -16, ConAu 106, ConPhot 82, -88, ContDcW 89, CurBio 42, ICPEnP, InWom SUP, IntDcWB, MacBEP, NewYTBS 80, -83, WhAmArt 85, WhoAm 82, -84, -88, -90, WorAlBi, WorAl*

Abbott, Berenice 1898-1991 *AnObit 1991, BioIn 17, ConAu 136, CurBio 92N, NewYTBS 91, WhAm 10*

Abbott, Cynthia 1908- *ArtsCL, BioIn 6*

Abbott, Frank Frost 1860-1924 *AmLY, DcAmAu, DcNAA, WhAm 1*

Abbott, Jacob 1803-1879 *Alli, -SUP, AmAu, AmAu&B, BenetAL 91, BbD, BiD&SB, BioIn 1, -3, -13, -15, CarSB, CnDAL, CyAL, CyEd, DcAmAu, DcBiPP, DcEnL, DcLB 42, DcNAA, HarEnUS, JBA 34, OxCAmH, OxCAmL 65, -83, OxCChiL, REnAL, SmATA 22, TwCChW 89A, WhAm HS*

Abbott, Jacob Bates 1896-1950 *BioIn 2*

Abbott, John Sheldon 1926- *DrAS 82P, WhoAm 80, -82, -84, -86, -88, -90, -92, -94, WhoAmL 85, -92*

Abbott, John Stevens Cabot 1805-1877 *Alli, -SUP, AmAu, AmAu&B, BbD, BiD&SB, CarSB, ChhPo, -S1, CyAL, DcAmAu, DcEnL, DcNAA, EvLB, HarEnUS, REnAL, WhAm HS*

Abbott, Manager Henry *ConAu X, MajAI*
Main entry: Stratemeyer, Edward L

Abbott, R Tucker 1919- *BioIn 17, IntAu&W 89, SmATA 61, WrDr 86, -88, -90, -92*

Abbott, Robert Tucker 1919- *AmMWSc 73P, AuBYP 2S, -3, BioIn 17, ConAu 9R, -37NR, WhoAm 80, -82, -84, -86, -88, -90, -92, -94, WhoE 74, WhoOcn 78, WhoTech 84, WhoUSWr 88, WhoWrEP 89, -92, WrDr 76, -80, -94*

Abbott, Sarah *AuBYP 2S, -3, ConAu X, -38NR, InWom SUP, MajAI, SmATA X*

Abdul, Raoul 1929- *BioIn 11, -16, BlkAuII, -92, ChhPo S2, ConAu 29R, DrBlPA 90, InB&W 80, SelBAAf, SmATA 12, WhoBlA 75, -80, -85, -88, -90, -92, -94, WhoE 81*

Abeita, Louise 1926- *AmPB, AnCL*
Pseud./variant:
E-Yeh-Shure

Abel, Raymond 1911- *BioIn 11, -12, IlsCB 1967, SmATA 12*

Abeles, Elvin 1907- *ConAu 104*

Abell, Kathleen 1938- *BioIn 11, ConAu 49, SmATA 9*

Abels, Harriette Sheffer 1926- *BioIn 16, ConAu 121, SmATA 50*

Pseud./variant:
Sheffer, H R

Abelson, Ann 1918- *SmATA X*
Main entry: Cavallaro, Ann

Abercrombie, Barbara 1939- *BioIn 12, SmATA 16*

Abernethy, Robert Gordon 1927- *BioIn 10, ConAu 21R, SmATA 5, WhoAm 74, –80, –82*

Abisch, Roslyn Kroop *AuBYP 3*

Abisch, Roslyn Kroop 1927- *AuBYP 2S, BioIn 11, ChhPo S1, ConAu 21R, –10NR, SmATA 9, WhoAmW 74*
Pseud./variant:
Abisch, Roz
McGillicuddy, Mr.
Roche, A K
Sniff, Mr.

Abisch, Roz
Main entry: Abisch, Roslyn Kroop

Abodaher, David J 1919- *AuBYP 2S, –3, BioIn 12, ConAu 17R, –10NR, MichAu 80, SmATA 17*

Abolafia, Yossi 1944- *BioIn 15, –16, –17, ConAu 142, SixBJA, SmATA 46, –60*

Abrahall, Clare Hoskyns *ChhPo S1, ConAu X, SmATA X*
Main entry: Hoskyns-Abrahall, Clare

Abrahams, Hilary Ruth 1938- *BioIn 8, –12, –13, IlsBYP, IlsCB 1957, –1967, SmATA 29*

Abrahams, Robert David 1905- *AmAu&B, AuBYP 2, –3, BioIn 8, –9, ConAu P-2, SmATA 4, WhoAm 74, –80, –82, –84, –86, –88, –90, –92, –94, WhoAmL 83, WhoE 74, WhoWor 82, WhoWorJ 72, –78*

Abrahamson, Una *OxCCan SUP*

Abramovitz *AuBYP 3*

Abrams, Joy 1941- *BioIn 12, SmATA 16*

Abrams, Lawrence F *BioIn 16, ConAu 124, SmATA 47*

Abrams, Lawrence F 1944- *SmATA 58*

Abrams, Lester *IlsBYP*

Abrashkin, Raymond 1911-1960 *AuBYP 2S, –3, BioIn 5, –16, ConAu 115, ObitOF 79, ScF&FL 92, SmATA 50*
Pseud./variant:
Ashley, Ray

Abrecht, Mary Ellen *BioIn 11*

Achebe, Chinua 1930- *AfSS 80, –81, –82, AfrA, Au&Wr 71, Benet 87, BioIn 7, –8, –9, –10, –12, –13, –14, –15, –16, –17, BlkAuII, –92, BlkLC, BlkWr 1, BlmGEL, CamGEL, CamGLE, CasWL, ChlLR 20, ConAu 1R, –6NR, –26NR, ConBlB 6, ConLC 1, –3, –5, –11, –26, –51, –75, ConNov 72, –76, –82, –86, –91, ConPo 75, –80, –85, –91, CurBio 92, CyWA 89, DcAfHiB 86, DcTwHis, EncWL, –2, InB&W 80, –85, IntAu&W 82, –89, –91, IntLitE, IntWW 74, –78, –79, –80, –81, –82, –83, –89, –91, IntvTCA 2, IntvWPC, LongCTC, MagSWL, MajAI MajTwCW, McGEWB, ModBlW, ModCmwL, Novels, OxCChiL, OxCEng 85, PenC CL, –ENG, RAdv 13-2, RGAfL, RfGEnL 91, SelBAAf, SmATA 38, –40, TwCChW 83, –89, TwCWr, WebE&AL, Who 74, –82, –83, –85, –88, –90, –92, WhoTwCL, WhoWor 74, –80, –82, –84, –87, –89, –91, –93, WorAlBi, WorAu 1950, WorLitC, WrDr 76, –80, –82, –84, –86, –88, –90, –92, –94*

Acheson, Patricia Castles 1924- *AuBYP 2, –3, BioIn 8, ConAu 1R, WhoAmW 93*

Acker, Helen *AuBYP 2, –3, BioIn 8, ConAu 73*

Ackerman, Eugene 1888-1974 *SmATA 10*

Ackerman, Karen *AuBYP 3*

Ackley, Peggy Jo 1955- *BioIn 16, SmATA 58, WhoWest 89*

Acs, Laszlo Bela 1931- *BioIn 12, IlsCB 1967, SmATA 32, –42*

Acuff, Selma Boyd 1924- *ConAu 111, SmATA 45*
Pseud./variant:
Boyd, Selma

Ada, Alma Flor 1938- *BioIn 15, ConAu 123, SmATA 43*

Adair, Cecil *BioIn 8, ConAu X, WhoChL, WomNov*
Main entry: Everett-Green, Evelyn

Adair, Ian 1942- *BioIn 16, IntAu&W 91, SmATA 53, WrDr 86, –88, –90*

Adair, Ian Hugh 1940- *WhoWor 87, –89*

Adair, Ian Hugh 1942- *Au&Wr 71, ConAu 69, IntAu&W 77, WhoWor 80, –82, –84, WrDr 76, –80*

Adair, Margaret Weeks d1971 *BioIn 11, ConAu P-1, SmATA 10*

Adam, Cornel *BioIn 13, ConAu X, IntWWP 82X, SmATA X*
Main entry: Lengyel, Cornel Adam

Adam, Ruth Augusta 1907- *Au&Wr 71, ConAu 21R, WrDr 76*

Adams, Adrienne *BioIn 14*

Adams, Adrienne 1906- *AmPB, BioIn 5, –7, –8, –9, –10, –11, –12, BkP, ChhPo, –S1, –S2, ConAu 49, –1NR, –35NR, IlsBYP, IlsCB 1946, –1957, –1967, SmATA 8, ThrBJA*
Pseud./variant:
Anderson, Adrienne Adams

Adams, Andy 1859-1935 *AmAu&B, AmLY, BenetAL 91, BiDSA, BioIn 2, –7, –8, –11, –15, CamGEL, CamGLE, CamHAL, CnDAL, DcAmAu, DcLEL, DcNAA, EncFWF, IndAu 1816, JBA 34, –51, OxCAmH, OxCAmL 65, –83, REnAL, TexWr, TwCWW 91, WebAB 74, –79, WhAm 2, WhNAA, YABC 1*

Adams, Barbara Johnston 1943-
Pseud./variant:
Shiels, Barbara

Adams, Barbara Johnston 1943-1990 *BioIn 17, SmATA 60*

Adams, Charlotte *Alli SUP, ChhPo*

Adams, Charlotte 1899- *AuBYP 2S, –3, ConAu 107*

Adams, Christopher *SmATA X*
Main entry: Hopkins, Kenneth

Adams, Clifton 1919- *ConAu 13R, –21NR, EncFWF, IntAu&W 91, WrDr 84, –86, –88, –90*
Pseud./variant:
Gant, Jonathan

Adams, Clifton 1919-1971 *TwCWW 91*

Adams, Dale *SmATA X*
Main entry: Quinn, Elisabeth

Adams, Edith *SmATA 71*
Main entry: Shine, Deborah

Adams, Florence 1932- *ConAu 49, SmATA 61*

Adams, Gerald Drayson *IntMPA 86, –88, –92*

Adams, Gerald Drayson 1904- *HalFC 84, –88, IntMPA 76, –78, –81, –82, –84, –86*

Adams, Harriet S 1892?-1982 *ConAu 27NR*

Adams, Harriet S 1893?-1982 *AmAu&B, AnObit 1982, AuNews 2, BioIn 9, –10, –11, ConAu 17R, –106, EncMys, NewYTBS 82, SmATA 1, –29N, WhAm 8, WhoAm 78, –80, –82*
Pseud./variant:
Appleton, Victor, II
Barton, May Hollis
Dixon, Franklin W
Hope, Laura Lee
Keene, Carolyn

Adams, Harriet Stratemeyer 1893?-1982 *BioIn 17, EncSF 93, MajAI, ScF&FL 92*

Adams, Harrison *ConAu X*
Main entry: Stratemeyer, Edward L

Adams, Hazard Simeon 1926- *BioIn 10, ConAu 9R, DrAS 74E, –78E, IntAu&W 77, LEduc 74, SmATA 6, WhoAm 74, –76, –80, –82, –84, –86, –88, –90, –92, –94, WhoWest 74, –76, WrDr 76, –80*

Adams, Helen Simmons 1897- *AmAu&B*

Adams, Henry Brooks 1838-1918 *Alli SUP, AmAu, AmAu&B, AmWr, AtlBL, BbD, BiD&SB, BioIn 1, –2, –3, –4, –5, –6, –7, –8, –9, –10, –11, CamGEL, CasWL, CnDAL, CyWA 58, DcAmAu, DcBiA, DcLEL, DcNAA, EncAB-H, EvLB, LongCTC, McGEWB, ModAL, –S1, OxCAmL 65, OxCEng 67, –85, PenC AM, RAdv 1, RComWL, REn, REnAL, TwCWr, WebAB 74, –79, WebE&AL, WhAm 1, WhAmP, WhCiWar, WhoTwCL, WorAlBi, WorAl*

Adams, John *BioIn 14, ChhPo S2*

Adams, John 1750?-1814 *CarSB, DcNaB*

Adams, John Anthony 1944- *BioIn 17, ConAu 134, SmATA 67, WrDr 94*

Adams, John D 1943- *WhoBlA 77, –80*

Adams, Julia Davis *AmAu&B, BioIn 2, –6, –10, IntAu&W 77*
Main entry: Davis, Julia

Adams, Julia Davis d1993 *NewYTBS 93*

Adams, Julia Davis 1900- *BioIn 14, IntAu&W 86, –89, –91*

Adams, Katharine *AmAu&B, BioIn 2, JBA 34, –51*

Adams, Laurie 1941- *ConAu 53, SmATA 33, WrDr 76, –80, –82, –84, –86, –88, –90, –92, –94*
Pseud./variant:
Schneider, Laurie

Adams, Lowell *ConAu X, IntAu&W 86X*
Main entry: Joseph, James Herz

Adams, Pauline Batchelder 1897- *BioIn 2, IlsBYP*

Adams, Richard 1920- *AuBYP 3, BioIn 14, –15, –17, CamGLE, ChlFicS, ChlLR 20, ConAu 35NR, ConNov 86, –91, CyWA 89, HalFC 88, MajTwCW, ScF&FL 92, ScFSB, SmATA 69, TwCChW 89, WrDr 86, –88, –90, –92*

Adams, Richard George 1920- *AuBYP 2S, AuNews 1, –2, BioIn 10, –11, –12, ChhPo S2, ConAu 49, –3NR, ConLC 4, –5, –18, CurBio 78, HalFC 84, IntAu&W 77, –89, –91, IntWW 78, –79, –80, –81, –82, –83, –89, –91, MajAI, Novels, OxCChiL, PenEncH, PiP, SmATA 7, TwCChW 78, –83, TwCYAW, Who 82, –83, –85, –88, –90, –92, WhoAm 80, –82, –84, –86, –88, –90, –92, –94, WhoEnt 92, WhoWor 82, –84, –87, –89, –91, –93, WrDr 76, –80, –82, –84, –94*

Adams, Ruth Joyce *AuBYP 2, –3, BioIn 8, –12, SmATA 14*

Adams, Samuel Hopkins 1871-1958 *AmAu&B, AmLY, AmNov, AuBYP 2, –3, BenetAL 91, BiDAmJo, BioIn 1, –2, –3, –4, –5, –6, –8, –16, CnDAL, DcAmSR, Dis&D, EncAB-A 28, EncAJ, EncMys, EncSF 93, JrnUS, NotNAT B, ObitOF 79, OxCAmL 65, –83, REn, REnAL, ScFEYrs, TwCA, –SUP, WebAB 74, –79, WhAm 3, WhNAA*

Adams, William 1814-1848 *DcNaB, OxCChiL*

Adams, William Taylor 1822-1897 *Alli SUP, AmAu, AmAu&B, BenetAL 91, BbD, BiD&SB, BioIn 13, –15, CarSB, ChhPo, –S2, CnDAL, CyAL, CyEd, DcAmAu, DcEnL, DcLB 42, DcNAA, HarEnUS, HsB&A, –SUP, OxCAmL 65, –83, OxCChiL, REn, REnAL, SmATA 28, WebAB 74, –79, WhAm HS*
Pseud./variant:
Ashton, Warren T
Brown, Irving
Hunter, Clingham
McCormick, Brooks
Optic, Oliver
Winterton, Gayle

Adam Smith, Janet 1905- *ConAu 35NR, SmATA 63, Who 88, –90, –92*

Adam Smith, Janet Buchanan 1905- *Au&Wr 71, LongCTC, Who 74*
Pseud./variant:
Smith, Janet Buchanan Adam

Adamson, Anthony 1906- *CanWW 70, –80, –81, –83, –89*

Adamson, Gareth 1925-1982? *BioIn 14, –15, ConAu 13R, –106, –11NR, OxCChiL, SmATA 30N, –46, WrDr 76, –80, –82, –84*

Adamson, George 1906-1989 *AnObit 1989, ConAu 129, NewYTBS 89, News 90, –90-2, SmATA 63*

Adamson, George Worsley 1913- *BioIn 5, –8, –12, –14, ChhPo S1, –S2, ClaDrA, ConAu 107, IlsBYP, IlsCB 1946, –1957, –1967, SmATA 30, WhoArt 80, –82, –84*

Adamson, Graham *BioIn 11, ConAu X, SmATA X*
Main entry: Groom, Arthur William

Adamson, Jean *OxCChiL*

Adamson, Joy 1910-1980 *AnObit 1980, –1981, Au&Wr 71, BioIn 7, –8, –9, –11, –12, –13, –16, –17, ConAu 69, –93, –22NR, ConHero 1, ConLC 17, ContDcW 89, CurBio 72, –80N, FourBJA, HalFC 84, –88, InWom SUP, IntAu&W 77, IntDcWB, MajTwCW, NewYTBS 80, SmATA 11, –22N, WhAm 7, WhoAm 74, –76, –78, WhoAmW 74, –75*

Adamson, Wendy Wriston 1942- *ConAu 53, SmATA 22*

Addams, Charles 1912- *WrDr 86, –88*

Addams, Charles 1912-1988 *AnObit 1988, BenetAL 91, BioIn 16, ConAu 126, CurBio 88N, NewYTBS 88, News 89-1, SmATA 55, WhoAmA 89N, –91N, WorAlBi*

Addams, Charles Samuel d1988 *IntWW 89N*

Addams, Charles Samuel 1912- *AmAu&B, BiDScF, BioIn 2, –3, –6, –7, –8, –10, CelR, ConAu 61, CurBio 54, EncTwCJ, IntWW 74, –75, –76, –77, –78, –79, –80, –81, –82, –83, WebAB 74, –79, WhoAm 74, –76, –78, –80, –82, –84, –86, –88, WhoAmA 73, –78, –80, –82, –84, –86, WhoUSWr 88, WhoWor 74, –78, –80, –82, –84, –87, WorAl, WrDr 76, –80*

Addams, Charles Samuel 1912-1988 *WhAm 9*

Addie, Pauline Betz 1919?- *AuBYP 2S, –3, BiDAmSp OS, BioIn 14, ConAu 105*

Addison, Ottelyn *OxCCan SUP*

Addona, Angelo F 1925- *BioIn 12, ConAu 25R, SmATA 14, WrDr 76, –80, –82, –84, –86*

Addy, Ted *BioIn 11, ConAu X, SmATA X*
Main entry: Winterbotham, R R

Adelberg, Doris *AuBYP 3, ChhPo S1, ConAu X, IntAu&W 91X, SmATA 7, WrDr 84, –86, –88, –90, –92, –94*
Main entry: Orgel, Doris

Adelberg, Roy P 1928- *ConAu 17R*

Adelman, Robert 1930- *BioIn 7, –10, ConAu 69, ICPEnP A, WhoE 74*

Adelson, Leone 1908- *AuBYP 2, –3, BioIn 8, –11, ConAu 61, SmATA 11*

Ades, Dawn 1943- *ConAu 103, IntAu&W 91, WrDr 80, –82, –84, –86, –88, –90, –92, –94*

Adkins, Jan 1944- *AuBYP 2S, –3, BioIn 11, –12, ChlLR 7, ConAu 33R, FifBJA, IlsCB 1967, MajAI, SmATA 8, –69, WhoE 77*

Adler, Bill
Main entry: Adler, William

Adler, Bill 1929- *BioIn 7, –13, ConAu X, WhoE 74*

Adler, C S *DrAPF 91*

Adler, C S 1932- *Au&Arts 4, BioIn 16, –17, ConAu 19NR, ConLC 35, DrAPF 83, –85, –87, –89, –93, ScF&FL 92, SixBJA, SmATA 26, –63, –15AS, WhoUSWr 88, WhoWrEP 89, WrDr 88, –90, –92*

Adler, Carole S 1932- *AuBYP 3*

Adler, Carole Schwerdtfeger 1932- *ConAu 40NR, DcAmChF 1985, MajAI, TwCYAW, WhoWrEP 92, WrDr 94*

Adler, David A 1947- *BioIn 12, –16, ConAu 57, –7NR, –23NR, MajAI, SixBJA, SmATA 14, –70, WhoWrEP 89, –92*

Adler, David Avram 1947- *BiDrAPA 89, WhoAm 92, –94, WhoE 91*

Adler, Helmut E 1920- *WrDr 86, –88, –90, –92, –94*

Adler, Helmut Ernest 1920- *AmMWSc 73S, –78S, ConAu 33R, WhoE 83, –86, –93, WhoWorJ 72, WrDr 76, –80, –82, –84*

Adler, Irene *AuBYP 2S, ConAu X, –35NR, SmATA X*
Main entry: Penzler, Otto
Storr, Catherine

Adler, Irving 1913- *AmAu&B, AuBYP 2, –3, Au&Wr 71, BioIn 7, –9, –13, ChlLR 27, ConAu 5R, –2NR, IntAu&W 91, MajAI, SmATA 1, –29, –15AS, ThrBJA, WhoE 91, –93, WhoFrS 84, WhoWor 93*
Pseud./variant:
Irving, Robert

Adler, Larry *NewYTBS 85*

Adler, Larry 1914- *Baker 92, BioIn 14, ConTFT 4, HalFC 88, IntWW 89, –91, IntWWM 90, NewAmDM, NewGrDA 86, OxCPMus, PenDiMP, PenEncP, Who 88, –90, –92, WhoEnt 92*

Adler, Larry 1938- *WhoAm 86, –88, –90, –92, –94*

Adler, Larry 1939- *BioIn 14, ConAu 105, SmATA 36*

Adler, Peggy *AuBYP 2, –3, BioIn 8, –13, SmATA 22*

Adler, Peggy 1942- *WhoAmW 93, WhoE 93, WhoEnt 92, WhoFI 92, –94, WhoWor 93*

Adler, Ruth 1915-1968 *AuBYP 2, –3, BioIn 7, –8, –9, ConAu 5R, –25R, –4NR, SmATA 1, ThrBJA, WhAmArt 85*

Adler, Samuel Hans 1928- *AmComp, ASCAP 66, BioIn 7, –8, ConAmC 76, DcCM, IntWWM 85, WhoAm 80, –82, –84, –85, –88, –90, –92, –94, WhoAmJ 80, WhoAmM 83, WhoE 75, –77, –81, –83, –85, –86, –89, WhoEnt 92, WhoWorJ 72, –78*

Adler, Sophie *ForWC 70*

Adler, Warren *BioIn 17, NewYTBS 91*

Adler, Warren 1927- *ConAu 69, –11NR, IntAu&W 91, SpyFic, WhoAm 92, –94 WhoEnt 92, WrDr 80, –82, –84, –86, –88, –90, –92, –94*

Adler, William 1929- *ConAu 9R, –7NR*
Pseud./variant:
Adler, Bill

Adoff, Arnold 1935- *Au&Arts 3, AuBYP 2, –3, AuNews 1, BioIn 10, –16, ChhPo S1, –S2, ChlLR 7, ConAu 41R, –20NR, –37NR, FourBJA, IntAu&W 91, MajAI, MorBMP, SmATA 5, –57, –15AS, TwCChW 83, –89, TwCYAW, WrDr 86, –88, –90, –92, –94*

Adorjan, Carol M *DrAPF 91, –93*

Adorjan, Carol Madden 1934- *BioIn 11, ConAu 41R, DrAPF 83, IntAu&W 77, SmATA 10, –71, WhoAmW 87, WhoUSWr 88, WhoWrEP 89, –92*

Adrian, Frances *ConAu 37NR, IntAu&W 86X, MajAI, SmATA 68, WrDr 86, –88, –90, –92, –94*
Main entry: Polland, Madeleine Angela Cahill

Adrian, Mary *AuBYP 2, –3, BioIn 8, ConAu X, ForWC 70, SmATA X, WhoAmW 74, –75*
Main entry: Jorgensen, Mary Venn

Adshead, Gladys Lucy 1896- *AmAu&B, BioIn 2, –6, –9, ConAu 29R, MorJA, SmATA 3, WhAm 7*

Adshead, Mary *Who 88, –90, –92*

Adshead, Mary 1904- *BioIn 5, –14, DcBrAr 1, DcCAr 81, IlsCB 1946, TwCPaSc, Who 74, –82, –83, –85*

Aeby, Jacquelyn *ConAu 29R, –24NR*

Aelfric 955?-1012? *RfGEnL 91*

Aelfric 955?-1020? *Benet 87, BlmGEL, CamGEL, CamGLE, OxCChiL*

Aesop 620?BC-564?BC *AnCL, AtlBL, BiD&SB, BioIn 1, –5, –8, –9, –10, –17, BlmGEL, CarSB, CasWL, ChhPo, –S1, –S2, ChlLR 14, CyEd, CyWA 58, DcEnL, Dis&D, LongCEL, NewC, OxCChiL, OxCClL 89, OxCEng 67, –85, PenC CL, RAdv 13-2, RComWL, REn, WhDW, WhoChL, WorAl*

Aesop 620?BC-560?BC *Benet 87, MajAI, SmATA 64, WorAlBi*

Aesop, Abraham *MajAI, SmATA X*
Main entry: Newbery, John

Afanasyev, Alexander Nikolayevich 1826-1871 *CasWL, EvEuW*

Affabee, Eric *ScF&FL 92, SmATA 76, TwCYAW*
Main entry: Stine, Robert Lawrence

Afonsky, N *ArtCS*

Afonsky, Nicholas 1892-1943 *EncACom*

Agapida, Fray Antonio *YABC X*
Main entry: Irving, Washington

Agard, John *TwCChW 89, WrDr 90, –92, –94*

Agard, John 1930- *BlkAuII 92*

Agard, Nadema 1948- *BioIn 12, SmATA 18*

Agassi, Joseph 1927- *CanWW 89, ConAu 41R, –15NR, –41NR, DrAS 74P, –78P, –82P, WhoAm 74, –76, –78, –80, –82, WhoAmJ 80, WhoE 83, WhoWor 91, WhoWorJ 78*

Agee, Tommie Lee 1942- *BioIn 9, WhoAm 74, WhoBlA 75, –77*

Aghill, Gordon *MajAI*

Agle, Nan Hayden 1905- *AuBYP 2, –3, ConAu 1R, –3NR, FourBJA, IntAu&W 77, –91, SmATA 3, –10AS, WrDr 76, –80, –82, –84, –86, –88, –90*

Agnew, Edith J 1897- *BioIn 11, ChhPo, ConAu P-1, SmATA 11*
Pseud./variant:
Marcelino

Agnew, Seth Marshall 1921?-1967 *AuBYP 2S, –3, BioIn 8*

Agostinelli, Maria Enrica 1929- *ConAu 33R*

Agree, Rose H 1913- *BiDrLUS 70, BioIn 8, ChhPo S1, ConAu 21R, WhoAmW 74, WhoLibS 66*

Ahern, Margaret McCrohan 1921- *BioIn 11, ConAu 13R, SmATA 10*
Pseud./variant:
O'Connell, Peg

Ahern, Mary Eileen 1860-1938 *BioIn 15, InWom SUP*

Ahern, Mary Eileen 1865?-1938 *BioIn 2, –6, –10, WhAm 1, WomWWA 14*

Ahern, Mary Eileen 1868-1938 *HanAmWH*

Ahl, Anna Maria 1926- *BioIn 14, SmATA 32*

Ahlberg, Allan 1938- *AuBYP 3, BioIn 14, –17, ChlFicS, ChlLR 18, ConAu 111, –114, –38NR, FifBJA, IntAu&W 91, MajAI, OxCChiL, SmATA 35, –68, TwCChW 83, –89, WrDr 86, –88, –92, –94*

Ahlberg, Janet 1944- *AuBYP 3, BioIn 14, –17, ChlLR 18, ConAu 111, –114, FifBJA, MajAI, OxCChiL, SmATA 32, –68*

Ahnstrom, Doris N 1915- *AuBYP 3*

Ahnstrom, Doris Newell *WhoE 86, –89*

Ahnstrom, Doris Newell 1915- *AuBYP 2, BioIn 8, ConAu 5R, IntAu&W 86, WhoAmW 77, –81, WhoE 81, –83, –85, WhoSSW 76, –78*

Ahrenhold, Novie Moffat *IlsBYP*

Aichinger, Helga 1937- *BioIn 9, –12, ConAu 25R, –19NR, FourBJA, IlsBYP, IlsCB 1967, SmATA 4, WhoWor 78*

Aiken, Clarissa Lorenz 1899- *BioIn 11, ConAu P-2, SmATA 12*

Aiken, Conrad 1889-1973 *AgeMat, AuBYP 3, Benet 87, BenetAL 91, BioIn 14, –15, –16, –17, CamGEL, CamGLE, CamHAL, ConLC 52, CyWA 89, DcLB 102, EncWB, IntvTCA 2, MajTwCW, NewGrDA 86, PenEncH, RAdv 13-1, RfGAmL 87, ShSCr 9, WorAlBi, WrPh*

Aiken, Conrad Potter 1889-1973 *AmAu&B, AmLY, –X, AmWr, AnCL, AuBYP 2, BioIn 1, –2, –3, –4, –5, –6, –7, –8, –9, –10, –11, –12, –13, CasWL, Chambr 3, ChhPo, –S1, –S2, CnDAL, CnE&AP, CnMD, CnMWL, ConAmA, ConAmL, ConAu 5R, –45, –4NR, ConLC 1,*

-3, -5, -10, ConNov 72, ConPo 70, CurBio 70, -73, DcLB 9, -45, DcLEL, EncWL, -2, EvLB, IntAu&W 77, -82, LongCTC, MakMC, ModAL, -S1, ModWD, NewYTBE 73, Novels, ObitOF 79, ObitT 1971, OxCAmL 65, -83, OxCEng 67, -85, PenC AM, RAdv 1, REn, REnAL, RfGShF, SixAP, SmATA 3, -30, TwCA, -SUP, TwCWr, WebAB 74, -79, WebE&AL, WhDW, WhAm 6, WhNAA, WhoAm 74, WhoE 74, WhoTwCL, WhoWor 74, WorAl
Pseud./variant:
Jeake, Samuel, Jr.

Aiken, Joan 1924- *Au&Arts 1, AuBYP 3, BioIn 14, -15, -16, -17, BlmGWL, CamGLE, ChlLR 19, ConAu 23NR, -34NR, FemiCLE, MajTwCW, ScF&FL 92, TwCChW 89, TwCCr&M 91, TwCRHW 90, WrDr 86, -88, -90, -92*

Aiken, Joan Delano 1924- *AuBYP 2, Au&Wr 71, BioIn 8, -9, -10, -11, BritCA, ChlFicS, ChlLR 1, ConAu 9R, -4NR, ConLC 35, EncSF 93, IntAu&W 82, -89, -91, MajAI, OxCChiL, SenS, SmATA 2, -30, -73, -1AS, ThrBJA, TwCChW 78, -83, TwCCr&M 80, -85, TwCYAW, Who 82, -83, -85, -88, -90, -92, WhoHr&F, WrDr 76, -80, -82, -84, -94*

Aiken, John 1747-1822 *OxCChiL*

Aikin, Lucy 1781-1864 *ArtclWW 2, BioIn 2, -16, BlmGWL, DcBiPP, DcNaB, FemiCLE, OxCChiL*

Aimard, Gustave 1818-1883 *BiD&SB, CelCen, CmCal, DcBiPP, Dis&D, EvEuW, HsB&A, OxCAmL 65, -83*

Ainsworth, Catherine Harris 1910- *BioIn 16, SmATA 56, WhoUSWr 88, WhoWrEP 89, -92*
Pseud./variant:
Harris, Catherine

Ainsworth, Harriet *ConAu 57, -X, IntAu&W 91X, TwCRHW 90, WrDr 84, -86, -88, -90*
Main entry: Cadell, Elizabeth

Ainsworth, Harriet 1903- *BioIn 14*

Ainsworth, Harrison 1805-1882 *OxCChiL*

Ainsworth, Leonard Herbert 1919- *WhoE 75, -77*

Ainsworth, Norma Paul Ruedi *BioIn 11, ConAu 13R, ForWC 70, SmATA 9, WhoAmW 75, WhoE 74, -75, -77*
Pseud./variant:
Ruedi, Norma Paul

Ainsworth, Ruth 1908- *IntAu&W 91, ScF&FL 92, TwCChW 89, WrDr 86, -88, -90*

Ainsworth, Ruth Gallard 1908- *Au&Wr 71, BioIn 8, -10, ChhPo, -S1, ConAu X, -37NR, MajAI, OxCChiL, SmATA 7, -73, TwCChW 78, -83, WhoChL, WrDr 76, -80, -82, -84*
Pseud./variant:
Gilbert, Ruth Gallard Ainsworth

Ainsworth, William Harrison 1805-1882 *Alli, -SUP, BbD, BiD&SB, BioIn 3, -4, -5, -8, -9, -12, -13, -14, -15, -16, BlmGEL, BritAu 19, CamGEL, CamGLE, CasWL, CelCen, Chambr 3, ChhPo, -S1, CyWA 58, DcBiA, DcBiPP, DcEnA, -A, DcEnL, DcEuL, DcLB 21, DcLEL, DcNaB, EvLB, LongCEL, NewC, NinCLC 13, Novels, OxCEng 67, -85, PenC ENG, PenEncH, REn, RfGEnL 91, SmATA 24, StaCVF, SupFW, TelT, WebE&AL, WhoChL*
Pseud./variant:
Brown, Will
Ticheburn, Cheviot

Aistrop, Jack Bentley 1916- *AuBYP 2, -3, Au&Wr 71, BioIn 8, -12, ConAu 1R, SmATA 14*

Aitchison, Janet 1962- *ConAu 57*

Aitken, Amy 1952- *ConAu 108, SmATA 40, -54*

Aitken, Dorothy 1916- *BioIn 11, ConAu 49, -2NR, SmATA 10*

Aitmatov, Chingiz 1928- *Au&Wr 71, Benet 87, BioIn 10, -14, -16, -17, ConAu 103, ConLC 71, HanRL, IntAu&W 77, IntWW 74, -75, -76, -77, -78, MajTwCW, ScF&FL 92, SmATA 56, TwCChW 78B, -83B, -89B, WhoWor 74, WorAu 1975*

Aitmatov, Chingiz Torekulovich 1928- *ConAu 38NR, EncSF 93, RfGShF*

Akaba, Suekichi 1910- *BioIn 15, SmATA 46*

Akens, David Strode 1921- *ConAu 25R -12NR, WhoAm 78, -80*

Akens, Floyd *AmAu&B, ThrBJA*
Main entry: Baum, Lyman Frank

Akers, Elizabeth Chase 1832-1911 *Alli SUP, AmAu, AmAu&B, ChhPo, DcAmAu, DcNAA, EvLB, OxCAmL 65, PoIre, REnAL*
Pseud./variant:
Allen, Elizabeth Ann Akers

Akers, Floyd *AuBYP 2, -3, ConAu 133 -X, DcNAA, EncSF 93, MajAI, MajTwCW, SmATA X, TwCChW 83, -89*
Main entry: Baum, Lyman Frank

Akino, Fuku 1908- *BioIn 8, ChhPo S2, IlsBYP, IlsCB 1957, -1967*

Akiyama, Kazuo *AuBYP 2, –3, BioIn 8*

Akrigg, George Philip Vernon *WrDr 86, –88, –90, –92, –94*

Akrigg, George Philip Vernon 1913- *CanWW 80, –81, –83, –89, ConAu 25R, DrAS 74E, –82E, IntAu&W 82, WhoAm 74, –80, WrDr 76, –80, –82, –84*

Aks, Patricia 1926- *BioIn 17, ConAu 136, SmATA 68, WrDr 94*
Pseud./variant:
Chase, Emily

Aksenov, Vassily 1932- *ConAu 53, –X, IntWW 74, WhoWor 74, WorAu 1950*

Akutagawa, Ryunosuke 1892-1927 *BiDJaL, BioIn 10, –15, CasWL, ConAu 117, CyWA 89, DcOrL 1, EncWL 2, PenC CL, RAdv 13-2, REn, RfGShF, TwCLC 16, WorAu 1950*

Alain *AmAu&B, IlsBYP, IlsCB 1957, SmATA X*
Main entry: Brustlein, Daniel

Alain 1868-1951 *TwCLC 41*

Alajalov, Constantin 1900- *BioIn 1, –2, –5, CurBio 42, ForIl, IlrAm 1880, –D, IlsBYP, IlsCB 1744, –1946, WhAmArt 85, WhoAm 74, –76, –78, –80, –82, –84, –86, WhoAmA 73, –78, –80, –82, –84, –86, WhoE 86, WorECar*

Alajalov, Constantin 1900-1987 *BioIn 15, –16, –17, ConAu 123, CurBio 88N, NewYTBS 87, SmATA 53N, WhAm 9*

Albala, Leila *AuBYP 3*

Albert, Burton, Jr. 1936- *BioIn 13, ConAu 61, –8NR, –23NR, IntAu&W 82, –86, –89, SmATA 22, WhoWrEP 89, –92*
Pseud./variant:
Healey, Brooks

Albert, Louise 1928- *ConAu 69*

Albert, Marvin H *AuBYP 3, BioIn 14, HalFC 88, IntAu&W 91, TwCWW 91, WrDr 86, –88, –90, –92, –94*

Albert, Marvin H 1924- *AuBYP 2, BioIn 8, ConAu 73, –30NR, HalFC 84, TwCCr&M 85, WrDr 84*

Alberts, Frances Jacobs 1907- *BioIn 12, ConAu 5R, ForWC 70, SmATA 14*

Albinson, James P 1932- *ConAu 57*

Albion, Lee Smith *BioIn 13, IlsBYP, IlsCB 1957, SmATA 29*
Pseud./variant:
Smith, Lee

Albrecht, Lillie 1894- *BioIn 11, ConAu 5R, SmATA 12*

Alcock, Gudrun *DcAmChF 1960, SmATA 33*

Alcock, Gudrun d1985 *BioIn 14*

Alcock, Gudrun 1908- *BioIn 16, SmATA 56*

Alcock, Vivian Dolores 1924- *ChlFicS*

Alcock, Vivien 1924- *Au&Arts 8, AuBYP 3, BioIn 15, –16, ChlLR 26, ConAu 110, –41NR, IntAu&W 86, –89, –91, MajAI, ScF&FL 92, SixBJA, SmATA 38, –45, –76, TwCChW 83, –89*

Alcock, Vivien 1926- *WrDr 86, –88, –90, –92*

Alcock, Vivien Dolores 1924- *TwCYAW*

Alcock, Vivien Dolores 1926- *WrDr 94*

Alcorn, John 1935- *AmArt, BioIn 8, –9, –14, ChhPo, –S1, IlsBYP, IlsCB 1957, SmATA 30, –31, ThrBJA*

Alcorn, John 1935-1992 *BioIn 17*

Alcorn, Robert Hayden 1909- *WhoE 75*

Alcott, Louisa May 1832-1888 *Alli SUP, AmAu, AmAu&B, AmWomWr 92, AmWr S1, ArtclWW 2, AtlBL, AuBYP 2, –3, Benet 87, BenetAL 91, BbD, BiD&SB, BioAmW, BioIn 1, –2, –3, –4, –5, –6, –7, –8, –9, –10, –11, –12, –14, –15, –16, –17, BlmGWL, CamGEL, CamGLE, CamHAL, CarSB, CasWL, CelCen, Chambr 3, ChhPo, ChlLR 1, CivWDc, CnDAL, ContDcW 89, CrtT 3, CyAL, CyWA 58, DcAmAu, DcBiA, DcBiPP, DcEnL, DcLB 1, –42, –79, DcLEL, DcNAA, EncAB-H, EvLB, FamAYP, FemiCLE, FilmgC, HalFC 84, –88, HanAmWH, HarEnUS, HerW, –84, InWom SUP, IntDcWB, JBA 34, MagSAmL, MajAI, McGEWB, MorMA, MouLC 4, NinCLC 6, Novels, OxCAmH, OxCAmL 65, –83, OxCChiL, OxCEng 67, –85, PenC AM, PenEncH, RComAH, REn, REnAL, RealN, RfGAmL 87, Str&VC, TwCChW 78A, –83A, –89A, TwCYAW, WebAB 74, –79, WhAm HS, WhCiWar, WhoChL, WorAlBi, WorAl, WorLitC, WrChl, YABC 1*

Alda, Arlene 1933- *BioIn 12, –14, –15, ConAu 114, NewYTBS 81, SmATA 36, –44*

Aldan, Daisy *DrAPF 87, –89, –91, –93, InWom SUP, IntvTCA 2*

Aldan, Daisy 1923- *AmAu&B, ArtclWW 2, ConAu 13R, –8NR, –25NR, DrAP 75, DrAPF 83, –85, ForWC 70, IntAu&W 86, WhoUSWr 88, WhoWrEP 89, –92, WomWMM B*

Alden, Betty 1898-1948 *WhScrn 83*

Alden, Carella *ConAu X*
Main entry: Remington, Ella-Carrie

Alden, Isabella Macdonald 1841-1930 *Alli SUP, AmAu&B, AmLY, BbD, BiD&SB, BioIn 4, –12, CarSB, DcAmAu, DcLB 42, DcNAA, InWom SUP, LongCTC, OhA&B, OxCAmL 65, –83, OxCChiL, WhAm 1, YABC 2*
Pseud./variant:
Pansy

Alden, Jack *AuBYP 3*

Alden, Raymond Macdonald 1873-1924 *Alli SUP, AmAu&B, AmLY, BioIn 1, ChhPo, DcAmAu, DcNAA, WhAm 1*

Alden, Sue *WrDr 80, –82, –84, –86, –88, –90, –92, –94*

Alden, William Livingston 1837-1908 *Alli SUP, AmAu, AmAu&B, BbD, BiD&SB, CarSB, ChhPo, –S2, DcAmAu, DcNAA, JrnUS, ScFEYrs, WhAm 1*

Alder, Francis A 1937- *ConAu 61*

Alderman, Clifford Lindsey 1902- *AuBYP 2, –3, BioIn 8, –9, ConAu 1R, –3NR, SmATA 3*

Alderson, Brian Wouldhave 1930- *IntAu&W 89, –91, OxCChiL, Who 82, –83, –85, –88, –90, –92*

Alderson, Sue Ann 1940- *BioIn 13, –16, CanWW 89, Profile 2, SmATA 48, –59, TwCChW 89, WhoCanL 87, –92, WrDr 90, –92, –94*

Alderson, William Thomas 1926- *WhoAm 86, –88, –90, –92, –94, WhoE 86, WhoSSW 88, –91, –93*

Alderson, William Thomas, Jr. 1926- *BiDrLUS 70, ConAu 9R, DrAS 74H, –78H, –82H, EncAB-A 32, WhoAm 74, –76, –78, –80, –82, –84, WhoE 83, WhoLibI 82, WhoLibS 66, WhoSSW 73*

Aldhelm 640?-709 *CyEd, DcNaB, LuthC 75, OxCChiL*

Aldhelm, Saint d709 *CamGEL*

Aldhelm, Saint d710 *CamGLE*

Aldin, Cecil Charles Windsor 1870-1935 *BioIn 2, –5, –12, BritAS, ChhPo S1, –S2, ClaDrA, ConICB, DcBrAr 1, DcBrBI, StaCVF*

Aldis, Dorothy 1896-1966 *AuBYP 3, BioIn 14, ConAu 34NR*

Aldis, Dorothy 1897?-1966 *AmAu&B, AnCL, AuBYP 2, BioIn 2, –7, –8, –9, BkCL, ChhPo, –S1, ConAu 1R, DcLB 22, JBA 34, –51, SmATA 2, Str&VC, WhAm 4, WhNAA*

Aldiss, Brian W 1925- *Benet 87, CamGLE, ConAu 28NR, ConLC 40, CyWA 89, IntvTCA 2, MajTwCW, RGTwCSF, ScF&FL 92, ScFSB, TwCSFW 91*

Aldiss, Brian W 1926- *NewEScF*

Aldiss, Brian Wilson 1925- *Au&Wr 71, BioIn 11, –14, –15, –17, BlueB 76, ConAu 5R, –2AS, –5NR, ConLC 5, ConNov 72, –76, ConSFA, DcLB 14, DcLEL 1940, EncSF 93, IntAu&W 77, –82, –89, –91, IntWW 74, –75, –76, –77, –78, –79, –80, –81, –82, –83, –89, –91, Novels, OxCEng 85, SmATA 34, TwCWr, Who 74, –82, –83, –85, –88, –90, –92, WhoAm 90, –92, –94, WhoSciF, WhoWor 74, –78, –82, –84, –87, –89, –91, –93, WorAl, WrDr 76, –80*
Pseud./variant:
Shackleton, C C

Aldon, Adair *AuBYP 2, –3, ConAu X, MajAI, SmATA 6, TwCChW 83, TwCYAW*
Main entry: Meigs, Cornelia Lynde

Aldous, Allan 1911- *DcChlFi*

Aldous, Allan Charles 1911- *Au&Wr 71, BioIn 13, OxCAusL, SingR 1, SmATA 27*

Aldrich, Ann *BioIn 12, ConAu X, –37NR, MajAI, MajTwCW, SmATA X, TwCYAW, WhoMW 93*
Main entry: Meaker, Marijane

Aldrich, Bess Streeter 1881-1954 *AmAu&B, AmNov, ArtclWW 2, BenetAL 91, BioIn 6, –17, BlmGWL, EncAB-A 6, ObitOF 79, OxCAmL 65, –83, REn, REnAL, TwCA, –SUP, TwCWW 91, WhAm 3, WhNAA*

Aldrich, Thomas Bailey 1836-1907 *Alli, –SUP, AmAu, AmAu&B, AuBYP 2S, Benet 87, BenetAL 91, BbD, BiD&SB, BioIn 1, –2, –3, –5, –7, –12, –15, CamGEL, CamGLE, CamHAL, CarSB, CasWL, CelCen, Chambr 3, ChhPo, –S1, –S2, CnDAL, ConAu 111, CrtSuMy, CyAL, CyWA 58, DcAmAu, DcBiA, DcEnA A, DcEnL, DcLB 42, –71, –74 –79, DcLEL, DcNAA, EncAJ, EncMys, EncSF 93, EvLB, JBA 34, NewGrDA 86, NotNAT B, OxCAmL 65, –83, OxCChiL, OxCEng 67, –85, PenC AM, REn, REnAL, SmATA 17, TwCChW 78A, –83A, –89A, WebAB 74, –79, WhAm 1*

Aldridge, Adele *DrAPF 87, –89, –91, –93*

Aldridge, Adele 1934- *ConAu 49, –28NR, DrAP 75, DrAPF 83, –85*

Aldridge, Alan *BioIn 14*

Aldridge, Alan 1943- *BioIn 8, –10, ConAu 125, ConDes 84, –90, DcCAr 81, SmATA 33*

Aldridge, Harold Edward James 1918- *DcChlFi, TwCYAW, WrDr 94*

Aldridge, James 1918- *Au&Wr 71, BioIn 2, –4, –6, –10, ConAu 61, –13NR, ConNov 72, –76, –82, –91, CurBio 43, IntAu&W 77, –89, –91, IntWW 83, –89, –91, Novels, OxCAusL, TwCA SUP, TwCChW 89, Who 74, –82, –83, –85, –88, –90, –92, WrDr 76, –80, –82, –84, –86, –88, –90, –92*

Aldridge, Josephine Haskell *AuBYP 2, –3, BioIn 8, –12, ConAu 73, SmATA 14*

Alegria, Ricardo E 1921- *AmMWSc 73S, BioIn 10, ConAu 25R, –15NR, –32NR, HispWr, PueRA, SmATA 6, WhoHisp 92, –94, WhoWor 74*

Aleichem, Sholem
Main entry: Rabinowitz, Solomon J

Aleichem, Sholem 1859-1916 *AmAu&B, AtlBL, BioIn 1, –2, –3, –4, –5, –6, –7, –8, –9, –10, –11, –14, –15, –16, –17, CasWL, EncWL, HalFC 84, –88, LongCTC, NotNAT B, PlP&P, REn, TwCA, –SUP, TwCLC 1*

Aleksin, Anatolii Georgievich 1924- *BioIn 11, ConAu 29NR, SmATA 36*

Alenov, Lydia 1948- *BioIn 17, SmATA 61*

Alex, Ben 1946- *BioIn 15, ConAu 114, SmATA 45*

Alex, Marlee 1948- *BioIn 15, ConAu 114, SmATA 45*

Alexander, Anna 1913- *AuBYP 3*

Alexander, Anna Barbara Cooke 1913- *AuBYP 2, ConAu 57, SmATA 1*
Pseud./variant:
Alexander, Anne
Cooke, Barbara

Alexander, Anne *AuBYP 3*
Main entry: Alexander, Anna Barbara Cooke

Alexander, Arthur 1927- *ChhPo S1, ConAu 5R*

Alexander, Cecil Frances 1818-1895 *Alli SUP, BiD&SB, BioIn 17, BkCL, BritAu 19, Chambr 3, ChhPo, –S1, –S2, ContDcW 89, DcEnL, DcIrB 88, DcNaB S1, EvLB, FemiCLE, OxCChiL, PoChrch, PoIre*

Alexander, David 1907-1973 *AuBYP 2S, –3, Au&Wr 71, BioIn 9, ConAu 1R, –41R, EncMys, LiHiK, TwCCr&M 85, –91*

Alexander, David 1907-1983 *BioIn 14*

Alexander, Frances Laura 1888- *AnCL, BioIn 9, ConAu 25R, IntAu&W 77, SmATA 4, TexWr, WhoAmW 75, WrDr 76, –80*

Alexander, Janet
Main entry: McNeill, Janet

Alexander, Janet 1907- *AuBYP 3, Au&Wr 71, ConAu 4NR, IntAu&W 77, –82, –86, WrDr 76, –80*

Alexander, Jocelyn Anne Arundel 1930- *AuBYP 2, –3, ConAu 1R, –4NR, SmATA 22*
Pseud./variant:
Arundel, Anne
Arundel, Jocelyn

Alexander, Linda Lewann 1935- *BioIn 9, ConAu 21R, ForWC 70, SmATA 2, WrDr 76, –80*

Alexander, Lloyd *BioIn 14, –15, –16, –17, IntvTCA 2*

Alexander, Lloyd 1924- *Au&Arts 1, ConAu 24NR, DcLB 52, MajTwCW, ScF&FL 92, SmATA 49, SupFW, TwCChW 89, WrDr 86, –88, –90, –92*

Alexander, Lloyd Chudley 1924- *AnCL, AuBYP 2, –3, Au&Wr 71, BioIn 5, –9, –10, ChlLR 1, –5, ConAu 1R, –1NR, –38NR, ConLC 35, DcAmChF 1960, –1985, MajAI, MorBMP, NewbC 1966, OxCChiL, PiP, SmATA 3, SupFW, ThrBJA, TwCChW 78, –83, TwCYAW, WhoAm 74, –76, –78, –80, –82, –84, –86, –88, –90, –92, –94, WhoE 74, WhoHr&F, WhoUSWr 88, WhoWor 78, WhoWrEP 89, –92, WrDr 80, –82, –84, –94*

Alexander, Louis George 1932- *Au&Wr 71, IntAu&W 77, –89, –91, WrDr 76, –80, –82, –84, –86, –88, –90, –92, –94*

Alexander, Marge *ConAu X*
Main entry: Edwards, Roselyn

Alexander, Martha 1920- *AuBYP 3, BioIn 11, FourBJA, IlsBYP, IlsCB 1967, SmATA 11*

Alexander, Martha G 1920- *MajAI, SmATA 70*

Alexander, Martha Kathleen 1910- *Au&Wr 71*
Pseud./variant:
Robinson, Martha

Alexander, Marthann 1907- *ConAu 53*

Alexander, Rae Pace *ConAu X, SmATA X*
Main entry: Alexander, Raymond Pace

Alexander, Raymond Pace 1898-1974 *BioIn 8, –10, –13, BioNews 75, ConAu 97, InB&W 80, ObitOF 79, SmATA 22, WhAm 6, WhoAm 74,*

WhoAmP 73, WhoBlA 75
Pseud./variant:
Alexander, Rae Pace

Alexander, Sue 1933- *BioIn 11, –16, ConAu 53, –4NR, –19NR, IntAu&W 91, SixBJA, SmATA 12, –15AS, WrDr 88, –90, –92, –94*

Alexander, Taylor Richard 1915- *AmMWSc 73P, –76P, –82, –86, –89, –92, ConAu 107*

Alexander, Thomas Williamson, Jr. 1930- *ConAu 9R*

Alexander, Vincent Arthur 1925-1980 *BioIn 12, –13, ConAu 101, SmATA 23N*

Alexander Schmorell *DcAmChF 1960*

Alexeieff, Alexandre A 1901- *BioIn 12, DcFM, FilmgC, OxCFilm, SmATA 14, WhoGrA 62, WorEFlm*

Alexenberg, Melvin Leonard 1937- *WhoAmA 78, WhoWor 78*

Alger, Horatio 1832-1899 *BioIn 14, –15, –17, CamGLE, CamHAL, RfGAmL 87, TwCChW 89A*

Alger, Horatio 1834?-1899 *Alli SUP, AmAu, AmAu&B, BbD, BiD&SB, BioIn 1, –2, –3, –4, –5, –6, –7, –8, –9, –10, –11, –12, –13, CamGEL, CarSB, CasWL, ChhPo, –S1, –S2, CnDAL, CyAL, DcAmAu, DcLB 42, DcNAA, EncAB-H, EvLB, McGEWB, NinCLC 8, OxCAmH, OxCAmL 65, –83, OxCChiL, PenC AM, REn, REnAL, SmATA 16, TwCChW 83A, WebAB 74, –79, WebE&AL, WhAm 1, WhoChL, WorAl*
Pseud./variant:
Putnam, Arthur Lee

Alger, Horatio, Jr. *MajAI, SmATA 67*
Main entry: Stratemeyer, Edward L

Alger, Horatio, Jr. 1832-1899 *Benet 87, BenetAL 91, WorAlBi*

Alger, Horatio, Jr. 1834-1899 *MemAm*

Alger, Leclaire Gowans 1898-1969 *AuBYP 2, –3, BioIn 8, –9, –12, ConAu 73, MajAI, SmATA 15, ThrBJA*
Pseud./variant:
Leodhas, Sorche Nic
Nic Leodhas, Sorche

Aliki *AmPB, AuBYP 2, –3, BioIn 14, ChlLR 9, ConAu X, –30NR, IlsCB 1957, –1967, IntAu&W 82X, –86X, MajAI, SmATA 2, –75, –X, ThrBJA, WhoAm 94, WhoAmA 78, –80, –82, –84, –86, –89, –91, WrDr 76, –80, –82, –84, –86, –88, –90, –92, –94*
Main entry: Brandenberg, Aliki Liacouras

Alimayo, Chikuyo *ConAu X*
Main entry: Franklin, Harold L

Alkema, Chester Jay 1932- *BioIn 11, ConAu 53, MichAu 80, SmATA 12*

Allamand, Pascale 1942- *BioIn 11, ConAu 69, –12NR, SmATA 12*

Allan, Elizabeth Preston 1848-1933 *Alli SUP, AmAu&B, BiDSA, CarSB, DcNAA*

Allan, Iris *OxCCan SUP*

Allan, Mabel Esther 1915- *AuBYP 2, –3, Au&Wr 71, BioIn 7, –10, –14, –16, ConAu 5R, –2NR, –18NR, EngPo, IntAu&W 77, –82, –89, –91, MajAI, OxCChiL, ScF&FL 92, SixBJA, SmATA 5, –32, –75, –11AS, TwCChW 78, –83, –89, WrDr 76, –80, –82, –84, –86, –88, –90, –92, –94*
Pseud./variant:
Estoril, Jean
Hagon, Priscilla
Pilgrim, Anne

Allan, Ted *IntMPA 86, –88, –92, ScF&FL 92*

Allan, Ted 1916- *CanWW 89, ConDr 88, –93, DcLB 68, IntAu&W 86, –91, OxCCanT, WhoCanL 87, –92, WrDr 86, –88, –90, –92, –94*

Allan, Ted 1918- *BioIn 10, CanWW 70, –79, –80, –81, –83, ConAu 77, ConDr 73, –77, –82, IntMPA 75, –77, OxCCan, OxCCanL, WhoAm 78, WhoCanL 85, WrDr 76, –80, –82, –84*

Allard, Harry, Jr. 1928- *AuBYP 2S, –3, BioIn 15, –16, ConAu 113, FifBJA, SmATA 42*

Allard, Harry Grover, Jr. 1928- *ConAu 38NR, MajAI*

Allardyce, Paula *ConAu X, –28NR, TwCCr&M 80, –85, –91, TwCRHW 90, WrDr 76, –80, –82, –84, –86, –88, –90, –92*
Main entry: Torday, Ursula

Allee, Marjorie Hill 1890-1945 *AmAu&B, BioIn 1, –2, –14, CurBio 45, DcNAA, IndAu 1917, JBA 34, –51, SmATA 17, WhAm 2, WhNAA*

Alleman, Herbert Christian 1868-1953 *BioIn 3, WhAm 3*

Allen, A B 1903-1975 *ConAu P-2*

Allen, Adam *AuBYP 2, –3, ConAu X, –39NR, MorJA, OhA&B, SmATA X*

Main entry: Epstein, Beryl Williams
Epstein, Samuel

Allen, Agnes 1898-1959 *BioIn 2, –5, –8, FourBJA, WhoChL*

Allen, Alex B *ConAu X, MajAI, SmATA 69, –X, TwCChW 83, –89, WhoWrEP 89, –92, WrDr 86, –88, –90, –92, –94*
Main entry: Heide, Florence Parry

Allen, Allyn *AuBYP 2, –3, ConAu X, SmATA X*
Main entry: Eberle, Irmengarde

Allen, Betsy *AuBYP 2, –3, ConAu X, CurBio 50, InWom SUP, MajAI, SmATA X, TwCChW 83, –89, TwCYAW, WrDr 80*
Main entry: Cavanna, Betty

Allen, Bob 1961- *SmATA 76*

Allen, Carl *ConAu 69*

Allen, Cecil J 1889-1973 *ConAu P-2*

Allen, Chris 1929- *ConAu 29R*

Allen, Don B *AmAu&B, BioIn 7, WhoAtom 77*
Main entry: Dimmittz, Arthur Luther

Allen, Durward L 1910- *WrDr 86, –88, –90, –92*

Allen, Durward Leon 1910- *AmMWSc 73P, –76P, –82, –86, –89, –92, BioIn 14, ConAu 41R, MichAu 80, WhoAm 74, –76, –78, –80, –82, –84, –86, –88, –90, –92, –94, WhoGov 77, –72, –75, WhoMW 93, WrDr 82, –84, –94*

Allen, Elizabeth 1794?-1849 *ChhPo, –S1, DcNAA*

Allen, Elizabeth Ann Akers
Main entry: Akers, Elizabeth Chase

Allen, Elizabeth Ann Akers 1832-1911 *Alli SUP, AmAu, AmAu&B, BiD&SB, ChhPo, –S1, –S2, CyAL, DcAmAu, DcNAA*

Allen, Elizabeth Anne Chase Akers 1832-1911 *InWom SUP*

Allen, Eric 1908-1968 *TwCChW 83, –89*

Allen, Ethan d1993 *NewYTBS 93*

Allen, Ethan 1904- *BioIn 3, CurBio 54, OhA&B*

Allen, Ethan Nathan 1904-1993 *CurBio 93N*

Allen, Forrest Claire 1885-1974 *BiDAmSp BK, BioIn 4, –9, –10, NewYTBS 74*

Allen, Frederick Lewis *IntvTCA 2*

Allen, Frederick Lewis 1890-1954 *AmAu&B, BenetAL 91, BioIn 1, –3, –4, –5, –6, –10, –12, CnDAL, DcLB 137, EncAJ, EncTwCJ, JrnUS, ObitOF 79, OxCAmL 65, –83, REn, REnAL, TwCA, –SUP, WebAB 74, –79, WhAm 3*

Allen, Gertrude Elizabeth 1888- *BioIn 11, ConAu 61, SmATA 9*

Allen, Gina *WhoAm 86, –88, –90, –92, –94, WhoAmW 87, –89, –91, –93*

Allen, Gina 1918- *AmAu&B, ConAu 1R, –43NR, WhoAm 74, –76, –78, –80, –82, –84, WhoAmW 74*

Allen, Henry 1912- *AmAu&B*
Pseud./variant:
Fisher, Clay
Henry, Will

Allen, Henry W 1912- *BenetAL 91, BioIn 15, –16*

Allen, Henry W 1912-1991 *BioIn 17*

Allen, Henry Wilson *AuBYP 3*

Allen, Henry Wilson 1912- *IntAu&W 91, TwCWW 91, WrDr 86, –88, –90, –92, –94*

Allen, Henry Wilson 1912-1991 *ConAu 135, EncSF 93, ScF&FL 92*

Allen, Jack 1899- *BioIn 13, FourBJA, SmATA 29*

Allen, James L d1992 *NewYTBS 92*

Allen, James Lamar 1936- *AmMWSc 92*

Allen, James Lane 1849?-1925 *AmAu, AmAu&B, AmLY, BenetAL 91, BbD, BiDSA, BiD&SB, BioIn 1, –7, –8, –12, CamGEL, CamGLE, CamHAL, CarSB, CasWL, ChhPo S1, –S2, CnDAL, ConAmL, DcAmAu, DcBiA, DcLB 71, DcLEL, DcNAA, HarEnUS, LiHiK, LongCTC, OxCAmL 65, –83, REn, REnAL, RfGAmL 87, WhAm 1*

Allen, Jeffrey 1948- *BioIn 15, ConAu 112, IntAu&W 86, SmATA 42*

Allen, Jeffrey Blynne 1948- *WhoWest 89*

Allen, Judy *ChlFicS*

Allen, Jules Verne 1883- *TexWr*

Allen, Kenneth Sydney 1913- *Au&Wr 71, BioIn 16, ConAu 77, IntAu&W 77, SmATA 56, WhoWor 78, WrDr 76, –80, –82*
Pseud./variant:
Carter, Avis Morton
Scott, Alastair

Allen, Kenneth Sydney 1913-1981 *ConAu 32NR*

Allen, Laura Jean *BioIn 16, ConAu 110, –133, SmATA 53, WrDr 94*

Allen, Lee 1915-1969 *AuBYP 2, –3, Ballpl 90, BioIn 8, ConAu 1R, –1NR, OhA&B*

Allen, Leroy 1912- *BioIn 11, ConAu 65, SmATA 11*

Allen, Linda *ChlFicS*

Allen, Linda 1925- *ConAu 102, SmATA 33*

Allen, Marie Louise *AuBYP 2, –3, BioIn 8, ChhPo*

Allen, Marjorie 1931- *BioIn 13, ConAu 69, SmATA 22*

Allen, Maury 1932- *Ballpl 90, BioIn 13, –16, ConAu 17R, –11NR, SmATA 26*

Allen, Mel *BioIn 14, –16, LesBEnT 92*

Allen, Mel 1913- *AuBYP 2, –3, Ballpl 90, BioIn 2, –4, –5, –6, –7, –8, –9, –10, –11, CurBio 50, IntMPA 75, –76, –78, –81, –82, –84, –86, –88, –92, –77, LesBEnT, NewYTET, WhoAm 74, –76, –78, WhoWorJ 72, –78, WorAlBi, WorAl*

Allen, Merritt Parmelee 1892-1954 *AuBYP 2, –3, BioIn 2, –3, –7, –13, JBA 51, SmATA 22, WhNAA*

Allen, Nina 1935- *BioIn 13, SmATA 22*

Allen, Oswald 1816-1878 *LuthC 75*

Allen, Pamela *AuBYP 3*

Allen, Pamela 1934- *ConAu 126, IntAu&W 91, SmATA 50*

Allen, Patricia H *BioIn 7*

Allen, Richard J *AuBYP 2, –3, BioIn 8*

Allen, Robert *ConAu X*
Main entry: Garfinkel, Bernard

Allen, Robert Day 1927- *AmMWSc 73P, –76P, –82, –86, BioIn 13, ConAu 107, IntAu&W 86, WhoAm 74, –76, –78, –80, –82, –84, WhoTech 82, –84, WhoWor 74*

Allen, Robert Day 1927-1986 *ConAu 125, WhAm 9*

Allen, Rodney F 1938- *BioIn 13, ConAu 61, SmATA 27, WhoSSW 91, –93*

Allen, Ruth *ConAu X, SmATA X*
Main entry: Peterson, Esther Allen

Allen, Samuel W *BlkWr 1, ConAu 26NR, DrAPF 87, –89, –91, –93*

Allen, Samuel Washington 1917- *BioIn 11, BlkAWP, BroadAu, ChhPo S2, ConAu 49, DcLB 41, DrAP 75, DrAPF 83, –85, DrAS 74E, –78E, –82E, InB&W 80, –85, IntAu&W 82, –86, IntWWP 82, LivgBAA, SelBAAf, SelBAAu, SmATA 9, WhoAm 76, –78, –80, –82, –84, –86, –88, –90, WhoBlA 77, –80, –85, –88, –90, –92, –94*
Pseud./variant:
Vesey, Paul

Allen, Steve 1921- *AmAu&B, ASCAP 66, AuBYP 2S, –3, BenetAL 91, BiDJaz, BiE&WWA, BioIn 2, –3, –4, –5, –6, –8, –10, –12, –13, –16, –17, BioNews 75, CelR, –90, CmpEPM, ConAu 25R, ConTFT 4, CurBio 51, –82, EncAFC, EncJzS, EncTwCJ, FilmgC, HalFC 84, –88, IntMPA 75, –76, –78, –81, –82, –84, –86, –88, –92, –77, IntvTCA 2, LesBEnT, –92, NewAmDM, NewGrDA 86, NewYTBS 81, NewYTET, PenEncP, REnAL, WebAB 74, –79, WhoCom, WhoHol A, WorAlBi, WorAl, WrDr 76, –80, –82, –84, –86, –88, –90, –92, –94*

Allen, Steve 1946- *WhoWest 89*

Allen, Terril Diener 1908- *AmAu&B, ConAu 5R, –2NR, DrAPF 83, –85, SmATA 35, WhoWest 74, –76, –78, –80, –82, –84, WhoWor 84, –87, –89*

Allen, Terry D 1908- *BioIn 14, ConAu X, SmATA X, TwCWW 91*

Allen, Thomas B *ChlBIlD*

Allen, Thomas B 1929- *BioIn 10, ConAu 5NR, –20NR, SmATA 45*

Allen, Tom *ConAu X, SmATA X*

Allen, Willis Boyd 1855-1938 *Alli SUP, AmAu&B, BiD&SB, CarSB, ChhPo, –S1, –S2, DcAmAu, DcNAA, WhAm 1, WhNAA*

Allerton, Mary *AuBYP 3, BioIn 11, ConAu X, SmATA X, WrDr 76, –80, –82, –84, –85, –88*
Main entry: Govan, Christine Noble

Alleyn, Ellen *MajAI, SmATA X*
Main entry: Rossetti, Christiana Georgina

Allfrey, Katherine *AuBYP 2, –3, BioIn 8*

Allingham, Margery Louise 1904-1966 *BioIn 2, –4, –7, –9, BlmGWL, ConAu 5R, –25R, CorpD, DcLEL, DcNaB 1961, EncMys, EvLB, LongCTC, NewC, TwCA, –SUP, TwCWr, WhoSpyF*

Allingham, William 1824?-1889 *Alli SUP, AnCL, BbD, BiDIrW, BiD&SB, BioIn 6, –8, –9, –10, –14, –16, –17, BritAu 19, CamGEL, CamGLE, CasWL, CelCen, Chambr 3, ChhPo, –S1, –S2, DcBiPP, DcEnL, DcIrB 88, DcIrL, DcIrW 1, DcLB 35, DcLEL, DcNaB S1, EvLB, FamPYP, NewC, NinCLC 25, OxCChiL, OxCEng 85, PenC ENG, PoIre, REn, RfGEnL 91, Str&VC, WebE&AL*

Allington, Richard L 1947- *ConAu 112, –30NR, SmATA 35, –39*

Allinson, Beverly 1936- *BioIn 10, CaW, ConAu 49, Profile 1*

Allison, Bob *AuBYP 2, –3, BioIn 8, –12, SmATA 14*

Allison, Linda 1948- *BioIn 15, ConAu 113, SmATA 43*

Allison, Rand *AuBYP 3*

Allison, Rosemary 1953- *BioIn 13, CaW, ConAu 93, Profile 2, WhoCanL 85, –87*

Allmendinger, David Frederick, Jr. 1938- *ConAu 61, DrAS 74H, –78H, –82H, SmATA 35*

Allred, Gordon Thatcher 1930- *BioIn 11, ConAu 17R, –10NR, DrAS 74E, –78E, –82E, SmATA 10*

Allsop, Kenneth 1920-1973 *Au&Wr 71, BioIn 9, –10, –12, ConAu 1R, –6NR, DcLEL 1940, SmATA 17, WhoWor 74, WorAu 1950*

Allward, Maurice Frank 1923- *Au&Wr 71, ConAu 5R, IntAu&W 77, –82, WhoWor 78, WrDr 76, –80*

Allyn, Paul *ConAu X*
Main entry: Schosberg, Paul Alan

Almedingen, E M 1898-1971 *AuBYP 2S, –3, Au&Wr 71, ConAu 1R, –X, ConLC 12, EncSF 93, LongCTC, OxCChiL, ScF&FL 92, SmATA 3, ThrBJA, TwCChW 78, –83, –89, WorAu 1950*
Pseud./variant:
Almedingen, Martha Edith Von
VonAlmedingen, Martha Edith

Almedingen, Martha Edith Von 1898-1971 *BioIn 2, –3, –6, –8, –9, –10, ConAu 1NR, SmATA 3*

Almedingen, Martha Edith Von
Main entry: Almedingen, E M

Almond, Linda Stevens d1987 *BioIn 16*

Almond, Linda Stevens 1881?-1987 *ConAu 121, SmATA 50N*

Almquist, Don 1929- *BioIn 5, –11, ChhPo, IlsBYP, SmATA 11, WhoAm 86, –88, –90, –92, –94, WhoGrA 82*

A L O E *CelCen, Chambr 3, ChhPo, DcEnL, InWom SUP, NewC, OxCChiL, WhoChL, WomNov*
Main entry: Tucker, Charlotte Maria

Aloise, Frank *IlsBYP*

Alpert, Helen *WhoAmW 77*

Alsop, Mary O'Hara 1885-1980 *BioIn 9, –12, –13, –14, ConAu 9R, –102, –4NR, MajAI, NewYTBS 80, SmATA 2, –24N, –34, WrDr 80, –82*
Pseud./variant:
O'Hara, Mary
Sture-Vasa, Mary

Alsop, Reese Fell *AuBYP 3*

Alsop, Reese Fell 1913- *AuBYP 2, BioIn 8*

Alter, Judith MacBain 1938- *BioIn 16, ConAu 81, WhoAmW 77, –81*

Alter, Judith McBain 1938- *ConAu 31NR, SmATA 52*

Alter, Robert Edmond 1925-1965 *AuBYP 2, –3, BioIn 7, –8, –11, ConAu 1R, –1NR, SmATA 9*
Pseud./variant:
Retla, Robert

Alth, Max Octavious 1927- *ConAu 41R, –17NR, IntAu&W 77, WhoE 77*
Pseud./variant:
Collins, Harry C

Althea *ConAu X, IntAu&W 82X, OxCChiL, SmATA X*
Main entry: Braithwaite, Althea

Altman, Frances Evelyn 1937- *ConAu 65, WrDr 76, –80*

Altschuler, Franz 1923- *BioIn 4, –15, SmATA 45, WhoAmA 78, –80*

Altsheler, Joseph A 1862-1919 *AuBYP 3, TwCChW 89*

Altsheler, Joseph Alexander 1862-1919 *AmAu&B, AuBYP 2, BiDSA, BioIn 7, –11, DcAmAu, DcNAA, JBA 34, LiHiK, OxCChiL, REnAL, TwCA, –SUP, TwCChW 83, WhAm 1, YABC 1*

Alvarez, John *ConAu 141, EncSF 93, MajTwCW, SmATA 76*
Main entry: del Rey, Lester

Alvarez, Joseph A 1930- *BioIn 12, ConAu 33R, -17NR, SmATA 18*

Alyer, Philip A *MajAI*

Alzada, Juan Sanchez
Main entry: Joseph, James Herz

Amacher, Richard Earl 1917- *ConAu 1R, -3NR, DrAS 74E, -78E, -82E, WhoAm 82, -84, -86, -88, -90, -92, -94*

Amadio, Nadine *SingR 2*

Amadon, Dean 1912- *AmMWSc 73P, -76P, BioIn 4, ConAu 61, WhoAm 74, -76*

Amaral, Anthony 1930-1982 *ConAu 21R, -11NR*

Ambler, Christopher Gifford 1886- *BioIn 5, -13, IlsBYP, IlsCB 1946, SmATA 29*

Ambler, Eric 1909- *AmAu&B, Au&Wr 71, Benet 87, BioIn 4, -5, -10, -12, -14, -15, -16, -17, BlueB 76, CamGLE, CnMWL, ConAu 9R, -7NR, -38NR, ConLC 4, -6, -9, ConNov 72, -76, -82, -86, -91, CorpD, CrtSuMy, CurBio 75, CyWA 89, DcLB 77, DcLEL, EncMys, EncWB, FilmgC, HalFC 84, -88, IntAu&W 82, -89, -91, IntWW 83, -89, -91, LongCTC, MajTwCW, NewC, NewYTBS 81, Novels, OxCEng 85, OxCFilm, REn, SpyFic, TwCA SUP, TwCCr&M 80, -85, -91, TwCWr, Who 74, -82, -83, -85, -88, -90, -92, WhoAm 86, -88, -90, -92, -94, WhoSpyF, WhoWor 74, -82, -84, -91, WorAlBi, WorAl, WrDr 76, -80, -82, -84, -86, -88, -90, -92, -94*

Ambrose, Stephen Edward 1936- *ConAu 1R, -3NR, -43NR, DrAS 74H, -78H, -82H, SmATA 40, WhoAm 92, -94*

Ambrus, Gyozo Victor Laszlo 1935- *MajAI*

Ambrus, Victor G *ConAu 28NR, MajAI*

Ambrus, Victor G 1935- *BioIn 14, -15, SmATA 4AS*

Ambrus, Victor Gyozo Laszlo 1935- *BioIn 7, -8, -9, -11, -12, BritCA, ChhPo S1, -S2, ConAu 25R, -11NR, IlsBYP, IlsCB 1957, -1967, IntAu&W 77, OxCChiL, SmATA 1, -41, ThrBJA, WhoArt 80, -82, -84, WhoChL*

Amdur, Nikki 1950- *AuBYP 3*

Amerman, Lockhart 1911-1969 *AuBYP 2, -3, BioIn 8, -9, ConAu P-2, SmATA 3*

Ames, Delano 1906- *Au&Wr 71, BioIn 14, OhA&B, TwCCr&M 91*

Ames, Delano L 1906- *WrDr 94*

Ames, Evelyn d1990 *NewYTBS 90*

Ames, Evelyn 1908- *ConAu 57, SmATA 13*

Ames, Evelyn 1908-1990 *ConAu 130, SmATA 64*

Ames, Gerald 1906- *AuBYP 2S, -3, BioIn 9, -11, BkP, ConAu 73, SmATA 11, ThrBJA*

Ames, Gerald 1906-1993 *ConAu 140, SmATA 74*

Ames, Lee J 1921- *BioIn 16, ScF&FL 92*

Ames, Lee Judah 1921- *AuBYP 2, -3, BioIn 5, -8, -9, ConAu 1R, -3NR, -18NR, IlsCB 1946, -1957, -1967, SixBJA, SmATA 3, WhoAmA 73, -78, -80, -82, -84, -86, -89, -91*
Pseud./variant:
David, Jonathan

Ames, Mildred 1919- *BioIn 13, -16, ConAu 69, -11NR, EncSF 93, FifBJA, ScF&FL 92, SmATA 22*

Ames, Noel *AuBYP 3*

Ames, Rose Wyler 1909- *ThrBJA*
Pseud./variant:
Thayer, Peter
Wyler, Rose

Amicis, Edmondo De 1846-1908 *BioIn 1, -5, -7, OxCChiL*

Ammerman, Gale Richard 1923- *AmMWSc 73P, -89, -92, ConAu 107, IntAu&W 77*

Amoaku, J K 1936- *ConAu 45*

Amon, Aline 1928- *AuBYP 2S, -3, BioIn 11, ConAu 61, -8NR, SmATA 9*

Amory, Cleveland *BioIn 15, -17, IntAu&W 91*

Amory, Cleveland 1917- *AmAu&B, AuNews 1, BenetAL 91, BioIn 2, -4, -5, -7, -10, -11, -12, -13, BioNews 75, CelR, -90, ConAu 69, -29NR, REnAL, TwCA SUP, WhoAm 74, -76, -78, -80, -82, -84, -86, -88, -90, -92, -94, WhoUSWr 88, WhoWor 74, WhoWrEP 89, -92, WrDr 76, -80, -82, -84, -86, -88, -90, -92, -94*

Amoss, Berthe 1925- *BioIn 10, ConAu 21R, -14NR, SmATA 5, WhoAmA 78, -80, -82, -84, -86, -89, -91*

Amoss, Berthe Marks 1925- *DcAmChF 1960*

Amundsen, Richard E *IlsBYP*

Anand, Mulk Raj 1905- *Au&Wr 71, BioIn 9, -10, -14, -17, CamGLE, CasWL, ConAu 65, -32NR, ConLC 23, ConNov 72, -76, -82, -86, -91, DcOrL 2, EncWL 2, FarE&A 80, -81, IntAu&W 77, -86, -89, -91, IntLitE, IntWW 74, -75, -76, -77, -78, -79, -80, -81, -82, -83, -89, -91, MajTwCW, ModCmwL, Novels, OxCEng 85, PenC ENG, REn, RfGEnL 91, WebE&AL, WhoWor 74, WorAu 1950, WrDr 76, -80, -82, -84, -86, -88, -90, -92, -94*

Anastasio, Dina 1941- *BioIn 14, -15, ConAu 107, SmATA 30, -37*

Anckarsvard, Karin Inez Maria 1915-1969 *AuBYP 2, -3, BioIn 7, -9, -10, ConAu 9R, -103, SmATA 6, ThrBJA*

Ancona, George 1929- *AuBYP 2S, -3, BioIn 11, -16, ConAu 53, -4NR, -19NR, SixBJA, SmATA 12, -18AS, WrDr 88, -90, -92, -94*

Ancona, George Ephraim 1929- *WhoAm 92*

Andersdatter, Karla M *DrAPF 87, -89, -91, -93*
Pseud./variant:
Margaret, Karla

Andersdatter, Karla M 1938- *BioIn 14, ConAu 104, -21NR, DrAPF 83, -85, SmATA 34, WhoUSWr 88, WhoWrEP 89, -92*

Andersen, Doris 1909- *BioIn 13, CaW, ConAu 21R, -11NR, DcChlFi, IntAu&W 91, Profile 2, TwCChW 78, -83, WhoCanL 85, -87, -92, WrDr 80, -82, -84, -86, -88, -90*

Andersen, Hans Christian 1805-1875 *AnCL, AtlBL, AuBYP 2, -3, Benet 87, BbD, BiD&SB, BioIn 1, -2, -3, -4, -5, -6, -7, -8, -9, -10, -11, -12, -13, -15, -16, -17, BlmGEL, CarSB, CasWL, CelCen, ChhPo, -S1, -S2, ChlLR 6, CyWA 58, DcBiA, DcBiPP, DcEnL, DcEuL, DcScanL, Dis&D, EncSF 93, EuAu, EuWr 6, EvEuW, FamAYP, FamSYP, FilmgC, GrFLW, HalFC 84, -88, JBA 34, -51, LongCEL, MajAI, McGEWB, NewC, NinCLC 7, NotNAT B, Novels, OxCChiL, OxCEng 67, -85, PenC EUR, RAdv 13-2, RComWL, REn, RfGShF, ShSCr 6, Str&VC, WhDW, WhoChL, WorAlBi, WorAl, WorLitC, WrChl, YABC 1*
Pseud./variant:
Walter, Villiam Christian

Andersen, Ted *AuBYP 2S, -3, ConAu X, SmATA X*
Main entry: Boyd, Waldo T

Andersen, Yvonne 1932- *AuBYP 2S, -3, BioIn 10, -13, ConAu 29R, SmATA 27, WomWMM A, -B*

Anderson, Adrienne Adams *ThrBJA*
Main entry: Adams, Adrienne

Anderson, Alan H, Jr. 1943- *ConAu 69*

Anderson, Alexander 1775-1870 *ArtsNiC, BioIn 2, -8, -15, DcAmMeB, HarEnUS, OxCChiL*

Anderson, Bernice G 1894- *BioIn 14, ConAu 101, SmATA 33*

Anderson, Brad J 1924- *AmAu&B, BioIn 10, ConAu 106, SmATA 31, -33, WhoAmA 73, -80, -82, -84, -86, -89, -91*

Anderson, C C *SmATA 72*
Main entry: Anderson, Catherine Corley

Anderson, C W *TwCChW 89*

Anderson, Carl Thomas d1948 *WhoAmA 86N*

Anderson, Carl Thomas 1865-1948 *AmAu&B, ArtCS, BioIn 1, WhAm 2, WhoAmA 78N, -80N, -82N, -89N, -91N*

Anderson, Catherine C *SmATA 72*
Main entry: Anderson, Catherine Corley

Anderson, Catherine Corley 1909- *ConAu 1R, SmATA 72*
Pseud./variant:
Anderson, C C
Anderson, Catherine C
Anderson, Melvin, Mrs.
Cora Lee
Coralie

Anderson, Chester Grant 1923- *ConAu 25R, DrAS 74E, -78E, -82E, WhoAm 80, -82, -84, -86, -88, -90, -92, -94*

Anderson, Chuck 1933- *ConAu 49*

Anderson, Clarence William 1891-1971 *AuBYP 2, -3, BioIn 1, -2, -5, -7, -8, -9, -11, BkP, ConAu 29R, -73, IlsCB 1744, -1946, -1957, JBA 51, OxCChiL, SmATA 11, Str&VC, ThrBJA, TwCChW 83, WhAmArt 85*

Anderson, Clary *NewYTBE 72*

Anderson, Clifford *ConAu X, SmATA X*
Main entry: Gardner, Richard M

Anderson, Dave *AuNews 2, SmATA X*
Main entry: Anderson, David Poole

Anderson, David Poole 1929- *BiDAmSp Sup, SmATA 60, WhoAm 86, -88, -90, -92, -94, WhoE 86, -89, WhoUSWr 88, WhoWrEP 89, -92*
Pseud./variant:
Anderson, Dave

Anderson, Doug 1919- *BioIn 2, WhoAmA 73, –78, –80, –82*

Anderson, Edna A *BioIn 6, MinnWr*

Anderson, Edna Matsner 1907- *BioIn 10*

Anderson, Ella *BioIn 12, IntAu&W 82X, –86X, –91X, SmATA X, WrDr 76, –80, –82, –84, –86, –88, –90, –92, –94*
Main entry: MacLeod, Ellen Jane

Anderson, Eloise Adell 1927- *BioIn 11, ConAu 53, SmATA 9*

Anderson, Erica 1914-1976 *BioIn 4, –11, ConAu 57, CurBio 57, –76N, ForWC 70, WhAm 7, WhoAm 74, –76, WhoAmW 74, WomWMM B*

Anderson, Erica Kellner Collier 1914-1976 *InWom SUP*

Anderson, Ethel Todd *AuBYP 2, –3, BioIn 8, OhA&B*

Anderson, Freddie 1932- *AfroAA*

Anderson, George *BioIn 11, ConAu X, SmATA X*
Main entry: Groom, Arthur William

Anderson, Grace Fox 1932- *BioIn 15, ConAu 121, SmATA 43*
Pseud./variant:
Fox, Grace

Anderson, Gunnar *IlsBYP*

Anderson, Gunnar Donald 1927- *WhoAmA 86, –91*

Anderson, Jean 1931- *AuBYP 2S, –3, ConAu 41R, –14NR, –31NR, ForWC 70, WhoAm 86, –88, WhoAmW 75, –77, –81, –83, –85, –87, WhoE 77, –81, –83, –85, WhoWor 84, –87*

Anderson, John 1909- *WrDr 76, –80, –82, –84, –86, –88, –90, –92, –94*

Anderson, John Lonzo 1905- *AuBYP 2S, –3, ConAu 25R, IntAu&W 77X, –82*
Pseud./variant:
Anderson, Lonzo

Anderson, John Merrick 1917- *WhoE 75*

Anderson, John Richard Lane 1911-1981 *Au&Wr 71, BioIn 12, –13, ConAu 25R, –104, –18NR, IntAu&W 77, –82, SmATA 15, –27N, WrDr 76, –80, –82*

Anderson, Joy 1928- *BioIn 9, ConAu 25R, SmATA 1*

Anderson, Kevin J 1962- *ScF&FL 92*

Anderson, Kevin James 1962- *EncSF 93, SmATA 74*

Anderson, LaVere Francis Shoenfelt 1907- *BioIn 13, ConAu 101, SmATA 27, WhoAmW 75, –77, –81, WhoSSW 76, –78, –80*

Anderson, Leone Castell 1923- *BioIn 16, ConAu 126, IntAu&W 91, SmATA 49, –53*

Anderson, Lonzo *ConAu 35NR*
Main entry: Anderson, John Lonzo

Anderson, Lonzo 1905- *BioIn 9, BkP, ConAu X, IntAu&W 77X, –82X, SmATA 2, ThrBJA*

Anderson, Lucia 1922- *AmMWSc 73P, BioIn 11, ConAu 41R, SmATA 10, WhoAmW 77, WhoE 74*
Pseud./variant:
Lewis, Lucia Z

Anderson, Madeleine Paltenghi 1899- *ConAu P-1*
Pseud./variant:
Paltenghi, Madeleine

Anderson, Madelyn Klein *ConAu 69, –11NR, –28NR, SmATA 28*

Anderson, Margaret J 1931- *ConAu 26NR, ScF&FL 92, SmATA 8AS*

Anderson, Margaret Jean 1931- *BioIn 13, ConAu 69, –11NR, FifBJA, SmATA 27*

Anderson, Mary 1939- *AuBYP 2S, –3, BioIn 10, ConAu 49, –1NR, –16NR, IntAu&W 77, –82, SixBJA, SmATA 7*

Anderson, Melvin, Mrs *SmATA 72*
Main entry: Anderson, Catherine Corley

Anderson, Mildred Napier *ChhPo*

Anderson, Mildred Travers *ChhPo*

Anderson, Mona 1910- *ConAu 6NR, SmATA 40, WrDr 82, –84*

Anderson, Neil *AuBYP 2, –3*
Main entry: Beim, Jerrold

Anderson, Norman Dean 1928- *BioIn 13, ConAu 33R, –15NR, –42NR, LEduc 74, SmATA 22, WhoSSW 91, –93*

Anderson, Paul Leroy 1935- *AmMWSc 82, –86, –89, –92*

Anderson, Paul Lewis 1880-1956 *BioIn 4, MacBEP, WhAm 3, WhNAA*

Anderson, Peggy Perry *AuBYP 3*

Anderson, Poul *ConSFF, DrAPF 87, –89, –91, –93, IntvTCA 2*

Anderson, Poul 1926- *AmAu&B, Au&Arts 5, AuBYP 2S, –3, BioIn 3, –10, –12, –13, –15, –17, ConAu 1R, –2AS, –2NR, –15NR, –34NR, ConLC 15, ConSFA, DcLB 8, DrAPF 83, –85, DrmM 2, MajTwCW, NewEScF, Novels, RGTwCSF, ScF&FL 92, ScFSB, SmATA 39, SupFW, TwCSFW 86, –91, WhoAm 74, –76, WhoHr&F, WhoSciF, WorAu 1950, WrDr 76, –80, –82, –84, –86, –88, –90, –92, –94*
Pseud./variant:
Craig, A A
Karageorge, Michael
Sanders, Winston P

Anderson, Poul William 1926- *EncSF 93*

Anderson, Rachel 1943- *BioIn 14, –17, ConAu 9NR, –24NR, IntAu&W 91, SmATA 34, –18AS, WrDr 82, –84, –86, –88, –90, –92, –94*

Anderson, Ruth Irene 1919- *AuBYP 2, –3, BioIn 8, ConAu 1R, –18NR, ForWC 70, IntAu&W 77, LEduc 74, WhoAmW 75, –77, –83, WrDr 76, –80, –82, –84*

Anderson, Sydney 1927- *AmMWSc 73P, –76P, –82, –86, –89, –92, ConAu 106, WhoAm 76, –78, –80, –82, –90, –92, –94, WhoE 75, –77*

Anderson, Wayne 1946- *BioIn 12, ConAu 107, IlsCB 1967, SmATA 56*

Andre, Evelyn Marie 1924- *BioIn 13, ConAu 69, –11NR, SmATA 27*

Andreassen, Karl *AuBYP 3*

Andree, Louise *ConAu X, SmATA X*
Main entry: Coury, Louise Andree

Andrew, Prudence 1924- *IntAu&W 91, TwCChW 89, WrDr 86, –88, –90, –92, –94*

Andrew, Prudence Hastings 1924- *Au&Wr 71, ConAu 1R, –1NR, TwCChW 78, –83, WrDr 76, –80, –82, –84*

Andrews, Benny 1930- *AfroAA, BioIn 9, –14, –16, –17, ChhPo S1, ConAu 106, DcCAr 81, IlsBYP, InB&W 80, –85, NegAl 89, OxCTwCA, SelBAAf, SmATA 31, WhoAm 74, –76, –78, –80, –82, –84, –86, –94, WhoAmA 73, –78, –80, –82, –84, –86, –89, –91, WhoBlA 75, –77, –80, –85, –88, –90, –92, –94, WhoE 74, WorArt 1950*

Andrews, Douglas Guy 1917- *AmMWSc 73P, –82, –86, –89, –92, CanWW 89, IntWWE, WhoAtom 77*

Andrews, Eleanor Lattimore *AuBYP 3*

Andrews, F Emerson 1902-1978 *AmAu&B, BioIn 11, –13, ConAu 1R, –81, –1NR, ScF&FL 92, SmATA 22, WhAm 7, WhoAm 74, –76, –78*

Andrews, J S 1934- *ConAu 29R, SmATA 4, TwCChW 89, WrDr 90, –92*

Andrews, James Sydney 1934- *AuBYP 2S, –3, Au&Wr 71, BioIn 9, WrDr 94*

Andrews, Jan 1942- *BioIn 16, ConAu 122, SixBJA, SmATA 49, –58*

Andrews, Jane 1833-1887 *Alli SUP, AmAu&B, BenetAL 91, BiD&SB, CarSB, DcAmAu, DcNAA, InWom SUP, OxCAmL 65, –83, OxCChiL, REnAL*

Andrews, Julie 1935- *AuBYP 2S, –3, Baker 92, BiDFilm, BiE&WWA, BioIn 3, –4, –5, –6, –7, –8, –9, –10, –11, –12, –13, –14, –15, –16, –17, BlueB 76, CelR, –90, CmMov, ConAu 37R, ConMus 4, ConTFT 1, –7, ContDcW 89, CurBio 56, EncAFC, EncMT, FamA&A, FilmgC, HalFC 84, –88, InWom SUP, IntMPA 75, –76, –78, –81, –82, –84, –86, –88, –92, –77, IntWW 74, –75, –76, –77, –78, –79, –80, –81, –82, –83, –89, –91, MotPP, MovMk, NewAmDM, NewGrDA 86, NewYTBS 82, –87, NotNAT, –A, OxCAmT 84, OxCFilm, OxCPMus, OxCThe 83, PenEncP, PlP&P, SmATA 7, Who 74, –82, –83, –85, –88, –90, –92, WhoAm 74, –76, –78, –80, –82, –84, –86, –88, –90, –92, –94, WhoAmW 74, –83, –85, –87, –89, –91, –93, WhoEnt 92, WhoHol A, WhoThe 72, –81, WhoWor 74, –78, –84, –87, –89, –91, –93, WorAlBi, WorAl, WorEFlm, WrDr 76, –80, –82, –84, –86, –88, –90, –92, –94*
Pseud./variant:
Edwards, Julie

Andrews, Laura *ConAu X, SmATA X*
Main entry: Coury, Louise Andree

Andrews, Mary Raymond Shipman 1865?-1936 *AmAu&B, AmWomPl, BenetAL 91, ChhPo, ConAmL, DcNAA, InWom SUP, JBA 34, LiHiK, REnAL, TwCA, WhAm 1, WhNAA, WomNov*

Andrews, Peter Ferguson 1931- *ConAu 17R, –11NR, WhoAm 74, –80*

Andrews, Roy Chapman 1884-1960 *AmAu&B, AsBiEn, AuBYP 2, –3, BenetAL 91, BiESc, BioIn 1, –2, –3, –4, –5, –6, –7, –9, –11, –12, –14, –16, –17, CurBio 41, –53, –60, EvLB, InSci, McGEWB, MorMA, ObitOF 79, ObitT 1951, REnAL, SmATA 19, TwCA, –SUP, WebAB 74, –79, WhAm 3A, WhNAA, WorAlBi, WorAl*

Andrews, V C *BioIn 15, -16, -17, PenEncH*

Andrews, V C d1986 *Au&Arts 4, ConAu 121, -21NR, MajTwCW, NewYTBS 86, SmATA 50N, TwCYAW*

Andrews, V C 1936?-1986 *AnObit 1986*

Andrews, Wendy *ConAu 40NR, MajAI, SmATA 74*
Main entry: Sharmat, Marjorie Weinman

Andrews, William G 1930- *SmATA 74*

Andrews, William George 1930- *WhoAm 86, -88, -90*

Andrezel, Pierre *BioIn 14, -15, -16, -17, BlmGWL, InWom SUP, IntDcWB, MajTwCW, Novels, SmATA X*
Main entry: Blixen, Karen

Andriola, Alfred J 1912-1983 *ArtCS, BioIn 13, ConAu 109, EncTwCJ, SmATA 34N, WhoAm 78, -80, -82*

Andrist, Ralph K 1914- *AuBYP 2S, -3, BioIn 15, ConAu 9R, -5NR, -20NR, SmATA 45*

Anelay, Henry 1817-1883 *DcBrBI, DcVicP 2*

Anfousse, Ginette 1944- *BioIn 13, -16, Profile 2, SmATA 48, WhoCanL 85, -87, -92*

Angel, Heather 1941- *BioIn 15, -16, ConAu 69, -25NR, ConPhot 88, ICPEnP A, IntAu&W 89, -91, Who 92, WrDr 80, -82, -84, -86, -88, -90, -92, -94*

Angel, Marie 1923- *SmATA 47*

Angel, Marie Felicity 1923- *BioIn 12, ChhPo S1, -S2, ConAu 29R, IlsBYP, IlsCB 1967, WhoWor 80*

Angeles, Peter Adam 1931- *DrAS 82P, SmATA 40, WhoWest 92, -94*

Angeli, Marguerite De *DcWomA, JBA 51*
Main entry: DeAngeli, Marguerite Lofft

Angeli, Marguerite de 1889-1987 *AnObit 1987*

Angell, Judie 1937- *Au&Arts 11, BioIn 13, -16, ConAu 77, ScF&FL 92, SixBJA, SmATA 22*

Angell, Madeline 1919- *BioIn 12, ConAu 65, -10NR, SmATA 18, WhoMW 80, -82, -84, -86, -88*

Angell, Tony 1940- *ConAu 53, -4NR, WhoAmA 80, -82, -84, -86, -89, -91*

Angelo, Valenti 1897- *AmAu&B, ArtsAmW 2, AuBYP 2, -3, BioIn 1, -2, -3, -5, -7, -8, -12, -14, BkC 6, CathA 1952, ChhPo, ConAu 73, IlsCB 1744, -1946, -1957, JBA 51, SmATA 14, TwCChW 78, -83, WhAmArt 85*

Angelou, Maya 1928- *AmWomD, AmWomWr 92, ArtclWW 2, Au&Arts 7, Benet 87, BenetAL 91, BioIn 14, -15, -16, -17, BlkLC, BlkWWr, BlkWr 1, -2, BlmGWL, CamGLE, CamHAL, ConAu 19NR, ConBlAP 88, ConBlB 1, ConHero 1, ConLC 64, ConPo 91, ConTFT 10, ContDcW 89, CyWA 89, DrAPF 87, -89, -91, -93, DrBlPA 90, EncWB, FemiCLE, HanAmWH, InB&W 85, InWom SUP, IntAu&W 91, IntWW 89, -91, MajTwCW, ModAL S2, ModAWWr, NegAl 89, NotBlAW 92, NotWoAT, SmATA 49, TwCYAW, WhoAm 86, -88, -90, -92, -94, WhoBlA 85, -88, -90, -92, WhoUSWr 88, WhoWrEP 89, -92, WrDr 86, -88, -90, -92*

Angier, Bradford *AuBYP 2S, -3, BioIn 11, ConAu 5R, -7NR, SmATA 12*

Angle, Paul McClelland 1900-1975 *AmAu&B, BioIn 3, -4, -10, -12, ConAu 57, -P-2, CurBio 55, -75N, DrAS 74H, NewC, ObitOF 79, REnAL, SmATA 20N, TwCA SUP, WhAm 6, WhoAm 74*

Anglund, Joan Walsh 1926- *AmAu&B, AuBYP 2, -3, Au&Wr 71, BioIn 6, -7, -8, -9, -10, ChhPo S1, -S2, ChlLR 1, ConAu 5R, -15NR, FamAIYP, IlsCB 1957, InWom SUP, IntAu&W 91, OxCChiL, SmATA 2, ThrBJA, TwCChW 78, WhoAm 74, -76, -78, -80, WhoAmW 74, -83, -85, WrDr 80, -82, -84, -86, -88, -90, -92, -94*

Angrist, Stanley W 1933- *AmMWSc 86, -89, -92*

Angrist, Stanley Wolff 1933- *AmMWSc 73P, -82, BioIn 9, ConAu 25R, SmATA 4*

Anholt, Catherine 1958- *SmATA 74*

Anholt, Laurence 1959- *SmATA 74*

Anita *SmATA X*
Main entry: Daniel, Anita

Anker, Charlotte 1934- *ConAu 93*

Anker, Charlotte Miriam 1934- *WhoAmW 87, WhoEnt 92*

Annett, Cora *AuBYP 2, -3, BioIn 8, ConAu X, SmATA X*
Main entry: Scott, Cora Annett

Annett, Cora Scott 1931- *DcAmChF 1960*

Annie Johnston *DcAmChF 1960*

Annixter, Jane *AuBYP 2, -3, BioIn 8, -9, ConAu X, ForWC 70, MichAu 80, SmATA 1, WhoAmW 75*
Main entry: Sturtzel, Jane Levington

Annixter, Paul *AuBYP 3, BioIn 6, -9, ConAu X, SmATA 1*
Main entry: Sturtzel, Howard A

Anno, Mitsumasa *ChlBlID, TwCChW 89B*

Anno, Mitsumasa 1926- *BioIn 10, -12, -15, -17, ChlLR 2, -14, ConAu 49, -4NR, FourBJA, IlsBYP, IlsCB 1967, IntAu&W 77, MajAI, OxCChiL, SmATA 5, -38, -77, TwCChW 83B*

Anobile, Richard J 1947- *ScF&FL 92*

Anobile, Richard Joseph 1947- *ConAu 53, -5NR*

Anrooy, Frans Van *BioIn 9, SmATA 2*
Main entry: VanAnrooy, Francine

Anstey, F 1856-1934 *Alli SUP, BiD&SB, CamGEL, CamGLE, Chambr 3, ChhPo, -S2, ConAu X, DcBiA, DcEnA A, DcLEL, DcNaB 1931, EncSF 93, EvLB, FilmgC, HalFC 84, -88, LongCTC, ModBrL, NewC, NewEScF, NotNAT B, OxCChiL, OxCEng 67, -85, REn, ScFSB, StaCVF, SupFW, TelT, TwCA, -SUP, TwCChW 83A, -89A, WhoChL, WhoHr&F*

Antell, Will D 1935- *BioIn 9, ConAu 104, LEduc 74, SmATA 31*

Anthony, Barbara 1932- *Au&Wr 71, BioIn 13, ConAu 103, -21NR, IntAu&W 77, SmATA 29*
Pseud./variant:
Barber, Antonia

Anthony, C L *Chambr 3, ConAu X, -37NR, DcLEL, IntAu&W 77X, -82X, LongCTC, MajAI, NewC, SmATA 4, -65, Who 74, -82, -83, -85, -88, -90, WrDr 76, -80, -82, -84, -86, -88*
Main entry: Smith, Dodie

Anthony, C L *BlmGWL, ConAu 133, WrDr 90*

Anthony, Edward 1895-1971 *AmAu&B, AuBYP 2, -3, BioIn 5, -8, -9, -12, BkCL, ChhPo, ConAu 33R, -73, NewYTBE 71, REnAL, SmATA 21, WhAm 5*

Anthony, Evelyn
Main entry: Ward-Thomas, Evelyn Bridget Stephens

Anthony, Evelyn 1928- *Au&Wr 71, BioIn 14, ConAu X, InWom SUP, IntAu&W 77, -82, -91, Novels, SpyFic, TwCCr&M 80, -85, -91, TwCRHW 90, Who 82, -83, -85, -88, -90, -92, WhoSpyF, WorAl, WrDr 76, -80, -82, -84, -86, -88, -90, -92, -94*

Anthony, John *ConAu 33NR, MajAI, MajTwCW, SmATA 65*
Main entry: Ciardi, John

Anthony, John Peter 1941- *WhoWest 94*

Anthony, Piers *BioIn 15, -17, IntvTCA 2*

Anthony, Piers 1934- *Au&Arts 11, ConAu 28NR, DrmM 2, EncSF 93, IntAu&W 91, MajTwCW, NewEScF, RGTwCSF, ScF&FL 92, ScFSB, SupFW, TwCSFW 86, -91, TwCYAW, WhoAm 94, WrDr 86, -88, -90, -92, -94*

Anticaglia, Elizabeth Ahlfors 1939- *BioIn 11, ConAu 45, -1NR, SmATA 12, WhoAmW 81, -83*

Antolini, Margaret Fishback d1985 *BioIn 14, -15*

Antolini, Margaret Fishback 1904-1985 *ConAu 117, SmATA 45N*
Pseud./variant:
Fishback, Margaret

Anton, Michael J 1940- *BioIn 11, ConAu 57, MichAu 80, SmATA 12*

Antonacci, Robert J 1916- *ConAu 5R, -9NR, MichAu 80, SmATA 37, -45*

Antonacci, Robert Joseph 1916- *BioIn 15*

Antoncich, Betty 1913- *AuBYP 2, -3, BioIn 8, ConAu 13R*

Antrobus, John 1933- *ChlFicS*

Aoki, Hisako 1942- *BioIn 15, ConAu 115, SmATA 45*

Apenfels, Ethel J *WhoAmW 74*

Apfel, Necia H *BioIn 15*

Apfel, Necia H 1930- *BioIn 16, ConAu 107, -23NR, IntAu&W 86, -89, -91, SmATA 41, -51*

Apfel, Necia Halpern 1930- *WhoMW 90*

Aphrodite, J *ConAu X, SmATA X*
Main entry: Livingston, Carole

Apilado, Tony *IlsBYP*

Apion d48 *AnCL, DcBiPP*

Appel, Benjamin *IntvTCA 2*

Appel, Benjamin 1907- *ScFSB*

Appel, Benjamin 1907-1977 *AmAu&B, AmNov, BioIn 1, -2, -4, -11, -12, -15, ConAu 13R, -69, -6NR, DcLEL, EncSF 93, IntAu&W 77, OxCAmL 65, -83, ScF&FL 92, SmATA 21N, -39, TwCA, -SUP, WhAm 7, WhoAm 74, -76*

Appel, David *AuBYP 2, -3, BioIn 8*

Appel, Martin E 1948- *ConAu 85, -15NR, SmATA 45*

Appel, Martin Eliot 1948- *WhoE 91, WhoEnt 92*

Appiah, Peggy 1921- *Au&Wr 71, BioIn 12, ChlFicS, ConAu 41R, IntAu&W 91, OxCChiL, SmATA 15, TwCChW 78, -83, -89, WrDr 76, -80, -82, -84, -86, -88, -90, -92, -94*

Apple, Margot *SmATA 42, -64*

Applebaum, Stan 1929?- *ASCAP 66, ConAmC 76, ConAu 85, IntWWM 85, SmATA 45, WhoAmM 83*
Pseud./variant:
Keith, Robert

Appleton, Victor *AmAu&B, ConAu P-2, EncSF 93, ScF&FL 92, ScFEYrs, SmATA 1, -67, WebAB 74, -79*
Main entry: Stratemeyer, Edward L

Appleton, Victor, II *AmAu&B, ConAu 17R, ScF&FL 92, SmATA 1, -67, -X*
Main entry: Adams, Harriet S
Stratemeyer, Edward L

Appleyard, Dev *IlsBYP*

Apsler, Alfred 1907- *AuBYP 2S, -3, BioIn 11, ConAu 5R, -3NR, IntAu&W 77, SmATA 10, WhoPNW, WrDr 76, -80, -82, -84*

Aquillo, Don *SmATA X*
Main entry: Prince, Jack Harvey

Aragones, Sergio 1937- *BioIn 15, -16, ConAu 122, SmATA 39, -48, WhoAm 82, -84, -86*

Arango, Jorge Sanin 1916- *AmArch 70, ConAu 61, WhoAm 74, -76, -78, -80, -82, -84, -86, -88, -90, -92, -94, WhoSSW 73, -75, -76, -78, WhoWor 78, -80, -82, -84, -87, -89*

Arason, Steingrimur *AuBYP 2, -3, BioIn 8*

Arbeiter, Jean S 1937- *AuBYP 2S, -3, ConAu 106*

Arbuckle, Dorothy Fry 1910-1982 *BioIn 14, ConAu 108, SmATA 33N, WhoAmW 81, -83, -85, WhoMW 80, -82, WhoWor 80, -82*

Arbuckle, Wanda Rector Samson 1910- *ConAu 41R, WhoAmW 74, WhoWest 74, -76*

Arbuthnot, May Hill 1884-1969 *AuBYP 2, -3, BioIn 4, -5, -6, -7, -9, -15, ChhPo, -S2, ConAu 9R, InWom SUP, NotAW MOD OhA&B, SmATA 2, WhAm 5*

Arch, E L *ConAu 49, -X, ConSFA, IntAu&W 77X, -82X*
Main entry: Payes, Rachel Cosgrove

Arch, E L 1922- *EncSF 93*

Archambault, John *ConAu 135, MajAI, SixBJA, SmATA 67, WrDr 94*

Archer, Frank *ConAu X, SmATA X, TwCCr&M 80*
Main entry: O'Connor, Richard

Archer, Janet 1942- *BioIn 12, IlsCB 1967*

Archer, Jules 1915- *AuBYP 2, -3, BioIn 8, -9, -14, -16, ConAu 9R, -6NR, ConLC 12, FifBJA, IntAu&W 77, SmATA 4, -5AS, WhoUSWr 88, WhoWrEP 89, -92, WrDr 80, -82, -84, -86, -88, -90, -92, -94*

Archer, Marion Fuller 1917- *BioIn 11, ConAu 5R, ForWC 70, SmATA 11, WhoAmW 75*

Archer, Sellers G 1908-1980 *ConAu 17R, -134*

Archibald, John J 1925- *ConAu 5R*

Archibald, Joseph 1898-1986 *AuBYP 3*

Archibald, Joseph S 1898- *AuBYP 2, BioIn 7, -9, ConAu 9R, -5NR, SmATA 3*

Archibald, Joseph S 1898-1986 *BioIn 16, ConAu 118, SmATA 47N*

Arden, Barbi *ConAu X, SmATA 3, ThrBJA*
Main entry: Stoutenburg, Adrien

Arden, William *ConAu X, EncMys, IntAu&W 91X, SmATA X, TwCCr&M 80, -85, -91, WhoUSWr 88, WhoWrEP 89, -92, WrDr 82, -84, -86, -88, -90, -92, -94*
Main entry: Lynds, Dennis

Ardizzone, Edward 1900-1979 *AuBYP 3, BioIn 14, CamGLE, OxDcArt, TwCChW 89, TwCPaSc, WhoAmA 86N, -89N, -91N, WrChl*

Ardizzone, Edward Jeffery Irving 1900-1979 *DcNaB 1971*

Ardizzone, Edward Jeffrey 1900-1979 *ArtsCL, AuBYP 2, Au&ICB, Au&Wr 71, BioIn 1, -4, -5, -6, -7, -8, -9, -10, -11, -12, -13, BlueB 76, BritCA, ChhPo, -S1, -S2, ChlLR 3, ConArt 77, ConAu 5R, -8NR, CurBio 64,*

–80N, DcBrAr 1, IlsCB 1744, –1946, –1957, –1967, IntWW 74, –75, –76, –77, –78, –79, LongCTC, MorJA, OxCChiL, OxCEng 85, PhDcTCA 77, PiP, SmATA 1, –21N, –28, TwCChW 78, –83, Who 74, WhoAmA 80N, –82N, WhoArt 80, WhoChL, WhoWor 74, –78, WrDr 76, –80

Ardizzone, Edward Jeffrey Irving 1900-1979 *MajAI*

Ardley, Neil 1937- *BioIn 15, ConAu 115, SmATA 43*

Ardley, Neil Richard 1937- *ConAu 39NR, IntAu&W 91*

Arehart-Treichel, Joan 1942- *BioIn 13, ConAu 57, –6NR, SmATA 22*

Arem, Joel Edward 1943- *WhoE 77, –86*

Arenella, Roy 1939- *BioIn 12, SmATA 14*

Arenella, Roy Edward 1939- *WhoE 93*

Aresty, Esther Bradford *ConAu 9R, ForWC 70, WhoAm 92, WhoAmW 74, –75, –81, –83, –87, –89, –91, WrDr 76, –80, –82, –84, –86, –88, –90*

Argenzio, Victor 1902- *ConAu 53*

Argus, Arabella *Alli, CarSB, OxCChiL*

Ariane *AmPB*
Main entry: Duplaix, Georges

Arkhurst, Joyce 1921- *AuBYP 3, BioIn 16, BlkAuII, –92*

Arkhurst, Joyce Cooper 1921- *AuBYP 2S, BlkAWP, ConAu 17R, ForWC 70, LivgBAA, WhoBlA 90, –92, –94, WrDr 76, –80, –82, –84, –86, –88, –90*

Arkin, Alan 1934- *ASCAP 66, BiE&WWA, BioIn 7, –8, –9, –10, –11, –14, –15, –16, CelR, ConAu 110, –112, ConTFT 2, –11, CurBio 67, EncAFC, EncFCWM 69, FilmgC, HalFC 84, –88, IntMPA 75, –76, –78, –81, –82, –84, –86, –88, –92, –77, MotPP, MovMk, NewYTBE 70, NewYTBS 86, NotNAT, ScF&FL 92, SmATA 32, –59, WhoAm 74, WhoCom, WhoHol A, WhoThe 72, –77, –81, WhoWor 74, WorAlBi*
Pseud./variant:
Short, Roger

Arkin, David 1906- *ASCAP 66, AuBYP 2S, –3, ConAu 21R, WrDr 76, –80, –82*

Arkle, Phyllis 1910- *ChlFicS*

Arkley, Arthur James 1919- *ConAu 112, IntAu&W 77, –89, WrDr 76, –80, –82, –84, –86, –88, –90, –92, –94*

Arlandson, Leone 1917- *ConAu 29R*
Pseud./variant:
Ryland, Lee

Arlen, Michael J 1930- *AmAu&B, AuSpks, BioIn 8, –10, –11, –13, ConAu 61, –13NR, DcLEL 1940, EncTwCJ, LiExTwC, WhoAm 74, –76, –78, –80, –82, –84, –86, –88, –90, –92, –94, WhoE 74, WhoUSWr 88, WhoWor 89, –91, –93, WhoWrEP 89, –92, WorAu 1975, WrDr 80, –82, –84, –86, –88, –90, –92, –94*

Arlen, Michael John 1930- *IntAu&W 89, –91*

Armer, Alberta Roller 1904- *BioIn 11, ConAu 5R, ForWC 70, IndAu 1917, SmATA 9*

Armer, Laura Adams 1874-1963 *AmAu&B, ArtsAmW 2, AuBYP 2, –3, BioIn 1, –2, –4, –6, –7, –14, ConAmA, ConAu 65, IlsCB 1744, InWom SUP, JBA 34, –51, MajAI, NewbMB 1922, SmATA 13, TwCChW 83, –89*

Armer, Sidney 1871- *ArtsAmW 2, BioIn 1, IlsCB 1744*

Armfield, Maxwell 1881?-1972 *Au&Wr 71, BioIn 1, ChhPo S1, ClaDrA, DcBrBI, IlsCB 1744, PhDcTCA 77, TwCPaSc, WhAmArt 85*

Armitage, Alfred *DcVicP 2*

Armitage, Angus 1902-1976 *Au&Wr 71, BioIn 11, ConAu P-1, WrDr 76, –80*

Armitage, David 1943- *SmATA 38*

Armitage, Ronda 1943- *BioIn 15, –16, ConAu 121, IntAu&W 91, OxCChiL, SmATA 38, –47, TwCChW 83, –89, WrDr 88, –90, –92*

Armitage, Ronda Jacqueline 1943- *WrDr 94*

Armour, Margaret d1943 *CarSB, ChhPo S2, EngPo*

Armour, Richard 1906- *EncAHmr, IntAu&W 91, WhoAm 86, –88, WhoWor 87, –89, WrDr 86, –88, –90*

Armour, Richard 1906-1989 *AuBYP 3*

Armour, Richard Willard 1906- *AmAu&B, AnCL, AuBYP 2, Au&Wr 71, BioIn 2, –5, –7, –8, –12, –15, ChhPo, –S1, –S2, ConAu 1R, –4NR, CurBio 58, DrAS 74E, –78E, –82E, FifBJA, IntAu&W 77, –82, REnAL, SmATA 14, TwCChW 78, WhoAm 74, –76,*

–78, –80, –82, –84, WhoWor 74, –78, –80, –82, –84, WorAl, WrDr 76, –80, –82, –84

Armour, Richard Willard 1906-1989 *BenetAL 91, BioIn 16, –17, ConAu 128, –32NR, CurBio 89N, NewYTBS 89, SmATA 61, WhAm 10, WorAlBi*

Armstrong, Anthony *TwCSFW 86, –91*

Armstrong, Anthony 1897?-1976 *Au&Wr 71, BioIn 3, ConAu X, DcLEL, EncMys, EncSF 93, EvLB, IntAu&W 77X, IntWW 74, –75, –76N, LongCTC, ScF&FL 92, Who 74, WhoThe 81N, WhoWor 74*

Armstrong, Edward Allworthy 1900-1978 *Au&Wr 71, ConAu 5R, –4NR, DcNaB MP, IntAu&W 77, WrDr 76, –80*

Armstrong, George D 1927- *BioIn 11, SmATA 10*

Armstrong, Gerry 1929- *BioIn 11, ConAu 13R, SmATA 10*

Armstrong, Jennifer 1961- *SmATA 77*
Pseud./variant:
Winfield, Julia

Armstrong, Louise *AuBYP 2S, –3, ConAu 111, –117, SmATA 33, –43, WhAmArt 85*

Armstrong, Richard 1903- *AuBYP 2, –3, Au&Wr 71, BioIn 2, –8, –9, –11, ConAu 77, OxCChiL, SmATA 11, ThrBJA, TwCChW 78, –83, WhoChL, WrDr 80, –82, –84, –86*
Pseud./variant:
Renton, Cam

Armstrong, Richard 1903-1986 *TwCChW 89*

Armstrong, Tom *IlsBYP*

Armstrong, William H 1914- *SmATA 7AS, TwCChW 89, WrDr 86, –88, –90, –92*

Armstrong, William Howard 1914- *AuBYP 2, –3, AuNews 1, BioIn 8, –9, –10, BioNews 74, ChlLR 1, ConAu 17R, –9NR, DcAmChF 1960, MajAI, MorBMP, NewbC 1966, OxCChiL, SmATA 4, ThrBJA, TwCChW 78, –83, TwCYAW, WhoAm 74, –76, –78, –80, –82, –84, –86, –88, –90, WhoE 74, WrDr 76, –80, –82, –84, –94*

Arndt, Ursula *BioIn 15, –16, ChhPo S1, ForWC 70, IlsBYP, SmATA 39, –56*

Arneson, D J 1935- *BioIn 15, ConAu 106, SmATA 37*

Arneson, DJ 1935- *ScF&FL 92*

Arnett, Caroline *ConAu X, SmATA X*
Main entry: Cole, Lois Dwight

Arnette, Robert *MajAI*

Arnim, Countess Von 1866-1941 *OxCChiL*

Arnim, Achim Von *OxCChiL*

Arno, Enrico 1913-1981 *BioIn 13, –15, ChhPo S1, –S2, FourBJA, IlsBYP, IlsCB 1946, –1957, –1967, SmATA 28N, –43*

Arnold, Arnold 1921- *ChhPo S2, ConAu 17R, –10NR, –27NR*

Arnold, Caroline *BioIn 14*

Arnold, Caroline 1944- *AuBYP 3, BioIn 16, ConAu 107, –24NR, SmATA 34, –36*

Arnold, Edmund Clarence 1913- *BlueB 76, ConAu 1R, –3NR, MichAu 80, WhoWor 74, WrDr 76, –80, –82, –84, –86, –88, –90, –92, –94*

Arnold, Edwin, Sir 1823-1904 *CamGLE*

Arnold, Edwin, Sir 1832-1904 *Alli, –SUP, BbD, BiD&SB, BioIn 3, –6, –14, BritAu 19, CamGEL, CelCen, Chambr 3, ChhPo, –S1, –S2, DcBiPP, DcEnA, –A, DcEnL, DcEuL, DcInB, DcLB 35, DcLEL, DcNaB S2, EvLB, LongCTC, NewC, OxCEng 67, –85, REn*

Arnold, Edwin L 1857-1935 *ScFSB, TwCSFW 86, –91*

Arnold, Edwin Lester 1856?-1935 *Alli SUP, BiD&SB, BioIn 3, ConAu 109, TelT, WhoHr&F, WhoLA, WhoSciF*

Arnold, Edwin Lester 1857-1935 *EncSF 93, ScF&FL 92, ScFEYrs, StaCVF*

Arnold, Elliott 1912-1980 *AmAu&B, AmNov, AnObit 1980, AuBYP 2, –3, Au&Wr 71, BioIn 2, –4, –8, –10, –12, –13, BlueB 76, ConAu 17R, –97, –24NR, EncFWF, NewYTBS 80, SmATA 5, –22N, TwCA SUP, TwCWW 91, WhAm 7, WhoAm 74, –76, –78, –80, WhoWest 74, –76, –78, –80, WhoWor 74, –78, –80, WrDr 76, –80*

Arnold, Emily *AuBYP 3, WhoUSWr 88, WhoWrEP 89, –92*

Arnold, Emily 1939- *BioIn 16, MajAI, SmATA 50, –76*
Pseud./variant:
McCully, Emily Arnold 1939-

Arnold, Eric H *AuBYP 3*

Arnold, Francena H 1888- *ConAu P-1*

Arnold, Janet 1932- *ConAu 93, IntAu&W 77, –82, –86, –89, –91, WrDr 76, –80, –82, –84, –86, –88, –90, –92, –94*

Arnold, Mary Ann 1918- *ConAu 65*

Arnold, Oren 1900- *BioIn 3, -9, -10, ConAu 5R, -2NR, SmATA 4*

Arnold, Pauline 1894-1974 *ConAu 1R, -2NR*

Arnold, Peter 1943- *ConAu 49, -1NR, IntAu&W 77, WrDr 76, -80, -82, -84, -86, -88, -90, -92, -94*

Arnold, Ralph *AuBYP 3*

Arnold, Ralph 1906-1970 *AuBYP 2, BioIn 8, ObitT 1961*

Arnold, Richard 1912- *Au&Wr 71, ConAu 3NR*

Arnold, Rollo Davis 1926- *ConAu 21R, WrDr 76, -80, -82, -84, -86, -88, -90, -92, -94*

Arnold, Susan 1951- *BioIn 16, SmATA 58*

Arnold, Tedd *AuBYP 3*

Arnold, Tedd 1949- *ConAu 137, SmATA 69*

Arnold, Thomas 1795-1842 *BioIn 2, -3, -5, -8, -9, -10, -14, -15, -16, BlmGEL, CamGEL, CamGLE, CelCen, CyEd, DcBiPP, DcLB 55, DcNaB, LuthC 75, NinCLC 18, OxCChiL, OxCEng 85, WhDW, WorAlBi, WorAl*

Arnoldy, Julie *AuBYP 3, ConAu X, SmATA X*
Main entry: Bischoff, Julia Bristol

Arnosky, Jim *ChlBIID, ConAu 32NR*

Arnosky, Jim 1946- *AuBYP 3, BioIn 13, ChlLR 15, ConAu 69, -12NR, FifBJA, MajAI, SmATA 22, -70*

Arnothy, Christine 1930- *Au&Wr 71, BlmGWL, ConAu 65, -10NR, IntAu&W 77, REn*

Arnott, Anne *IntAu&W 86X*

Arnott, Anne 1916- *ConAu 73, -13NR, IntAu&W 77X, -82X, WrDr 76, -80, -82, -84, -86, -88, -90*

Arnott, Kathleen 1914- *BioIn 12, ConAu 57, SmATA 20*

Arnov, Boris, Jr. 1926- *AuBYP 2, -3, BioIn 7, -11, ConAu 1R, -3NR, SmATA 12*

Arnow, Harriette Louisa Simpson 1908- *AmAu&B, AmNov, BioIn 2, -3, -4, -10, -11, -13, ConAu 14NR, ConLC 2, -7, -18, ConNov 76, -82, CurBio 54, DcLB 6, InWom SUP, MichAu 80, OxCAmL 83, SmATA 42, WorAu 1950, WrDr 76, -80, -82, -84*

Arnow, Harriette Louisa Simpson 1908-1986 *BenetAL 91, BioIn 14, -15, -16, -17, BlmGWL, ConAu 118, CurBio 86N, LiHiK, MajTwCW, SmATA 47N*
Pseud./variant:
Simpson, Harriette

Arnsteen, Katy Keck 1934- *BioIn 17, ConAu 136, SmATA 68, WrDr 94*

Arnstein, Helene Solomon 1915- *BioIn 11, ConAu 57, SmATA 12, WhoAmW 77*

Arntson, Herbert Edward 1911- *BioIn 11, ConAu 17R, DrAS 74E, -78E, -82E, SmATA 12, WhoPNW*

Aronin, Ben 1904-1980 *BioIn 2, -12, -13, ConAu 102, ScF&FL 92, SmATA 25N*

Aronoff, Frances Webber 1915- *IntWWM 85, LEduc 74, WhoAmM 83*

Aronsten, Joan *SingR 1*

Arora, Shirley Lease 1930- *BioIn 9, ConAu 1R, DcAmChF 1960, DrAS 74F, -78F, -82F, SmATA 2, WhoAm 90, -92, -94*

Arquette, Lois *AuBYP 3*

Arquette, Lois Duncan *ScF&FL 92*

Arquette, Lois S 1934- *BioIn 9, -12, SmATA 1*
Pseud./variant:
Cardozo, Lois S
Duncan, Lois
Kerry, Lois

Arre, Helen *ConAu 130, -X, WrDr 84, -86, -88, -90*
Main entry: Ross, Zola Helen

Arre, John *ConAu X*
Main entry: Holt, John Robert

Arriola, Gustavo Montano 1917- *ArtCS, BioIn 1, MexAmB, WhoAm 78, WhoHisp 91, -92, -94*

Arrowood, Clinton L 1939- *SmATA 19*

Arrowsmith, Pat 1930- *FemiCLE, SmATA X, Who 88, -90, -92*
Main entry: Barton, Pat

Artes, Dorothy Beecher 1919- *ConAu 57*

Arthur, Eric Ross 1898-1982 *BioIn 5, -13, BlueB 76, CanWW 70, -80, -81, OxCCan, -SUP*

Arthur, Robert *IntMPA 86*
Main entry: Feder, Robert Arthur

Arthur, Robert d1969 *BioIn 14*

Arthur, Robert 1909- *IntMPA 86*

Arthur, Robert 1909-1969 *AuBYP 2S, -3, BioIn 8, ConAu X, HalFC 84, IntMPA 81, -82, -84, -86, SmATA X, WhoHr&F*

Arthur, Robert 1909-1986 *BioIn 15, ConTFT 4, HalFC 88*

Arthur, Ruth 1905-1979 *TwCChW 89*

Arthur, Ruth M 1905-1979 *ScF&FL 92*

Arthur, Ruth Mabel 1905-1979 *AuBYP 2S, -3, Au&Wr 71, BioIn 10, -11, -13, ChhPo, ConAu 9R, -85, -4NR, ConLC 12, FifBJA, IntAu&W 77, OxCChiL, SmATA 7, -26N, TwCChW 78, -83, WrDr 80*

Arthur, Timothy Shay *Benet 87*

Arthur, Timothy Shay 1809-1885 *Alli, -SUP, AmAu, AmAu&B, BenetAL 91, BbD, BiD&SB, BioIn 4, -12, -15, CarSB, CasWL, ChhPo, -S1, -S2, CyAL, DcAmAu, DcBiA, DcEnL, DcLB 42, -79, DcNAA, OxCAmH, OxCAmL 65, -83, PenC AM, REn, REnAL, RfGAmL 87, WebAB 74, -79, WhAm HS*

Artis, Vicki Kimmel 1945- *BioIn 11, ConAu 53, IntAu&W 77, SmATA 12, WhoAmW 77, -81*

Artzybasheff, Boris 1899-1965 *AuBYP 3, BiDScF, BioIn 14, -15*

Artzybasheff, Boris Mikhailovic 1899-1965 *AmAu&B, AmPB, AnCL, AuBYP 2, BioIn 1, -2, -3, -5, -7, -8, ChhPo S2, ConICB, CurBio 45, -65, ForIl, IlsCB 1744, JBA 34, -51, SmATA 14, Str&VC, WhAm 4, WhoAmA 78N, WhoGrA 62*

Aruego, Ariane *BioIn 10, ConAu X, SmATA 7*
Main entry: Dewey, Ariane

Aruego, Jose *BioIn 15, -17*

Aruego, Jose 1932- *BioIn 10, -11, ChhPo S2, ChlLR 5, ConAu 37R, FourBJA, IlsBYP, IlsCB 1967, MajAI, SmATA 6, -68*

Aruego, Jose Espiritu 1932- *ConAu 42NR*

Arundel, Anne *AuBYP 2*
Main entry: Alexander, Jocelyn Anne Arundel

Arundel, Honor 1919-1973 *AuBYP 3, EngPo, TwCChW 89*

Arundel, Honor Morfydd 1919-1973 *AuBYP 2S, Au&Wr 71, BioIn 9, -10, -13, ConAu 41R, -P-2, ConLC 17, FourBJA, OxCChiL, SmATA 4, -24N, TwCChW 78, -83*

Arundel, Jocelyn *AuBYP 3*
Main entry: Alexander, Jocelyn Anne Arundel

Arundel, Jocelyn 1930- *AuBYP 2, BioIn 8, -13, ConAu X, SmATA X*

Arundel, Louis *CarSB*

Asare, Meshack 1945- *ConAu 61, -11NR, TwCChW 89, WrDr 90, -92*

Asare, Meshack Yaw 1945- *WrDr 94*

Asbjornsen, Peter Christen 1812-1885 *AnCL, BbD, BiD&SB, BioIn 1, -2, -7, -8, -12, CarSB, CasWL, CelCen, DcEuL, EuAu, EvEuW, MajAI, OxCChiL, SmATA 15, Str&VC, WhoChL, WrChl*

Asbjornsen, Peter Christian 1812-1885 *Benet 87*

Asbjornsen And Moe *WrChl*

Asch, Frank *BioIn 16, -17*

Asch, Frank 1946- *AuBYP 3, ScF&FL 92, SmATA 66, TwCChW 89, WrDr 86, -88, -90, -92, -94*

Asch, Frank Edward 1946- *AmPB, AuBYP 2S, BioIn 10, ConAu 41R, FourBJA, IlsCB 1967, SmATA 5, WrDr 76, -80*

Ascham, Roger 1515-1568 *Benet 87, BioIn 12, -15, BlmGEL, CamGEL, CamGLE, CyEd, DcBiPP, DcNaB, OxCChiL, OxCEng 85, RfGEnL 91*

Aschmann, Helen Tann *ConAu 13R*

Ash, Brian 1936- *ConAu 114, EncSF 93, IntAu&W 91, ScF&FL 92, WrDr 80, -82, -84, -86, -88, -90*

Ash, Jutta 1942- *BioIn 12, IlsCB 1967, SmATA 38*

Ashabranner, Brent 1921- *Au&Arts 6, BioIn 9, BlueB 76, ConAu 5R, -10NR, -27NR, SixBJA, SmATA 1, -67, -14AS, WhoAm 74*

Ashabranner, Brent K 1921- *BioIn 17*

Ashabranner, Brent Kenneth 1921- *ChlLR 28, MajAI, TwCYAW*

Ashby, Gwynneth Margaret 1922- *Au&Wr 71, ConAu 25R, IntAu&W 77, -82, -91, SmATA 44, WhoWor 78, WrDr 76, -80, -82, -84, -86, -88, -90, -92, -94*

Ashe, Arthur *BioIn 14, -15, -16, -17, NewYTBS 85, -92*

Ashe, Arthur 1943- *ConAu 35NR, ConBlB 1, ConHero 2, NegAl 89, SmATA 65, WhoAm 86, WorAlBi, WrDr 90, -92*

Ashe, Arthur, Jr. 1943- *AfrAmBi, CelR 90*

Ashe, Arthur R, Jr. 1943- *WhoBlA 85, -88, -90, -92*

Ashe, Arthur Robert 1943- *IntWW 89, -91*

Ashe, Arthur Robert, Jr. 1943- *BiDAmSp OS, BioIn 6, -7, -8, -9, -10, -11, -12, -13, BioNews 74, BlueB 76, CelR, ConAu 65, -18NR, CurBio 66, InB&W 80, -85, IntWW 79, -80, -81, -82, -83, NegAl 76, -83, NewYTBS 85, WebAB 74, -79, WhoAm 74, -76, -78, -80, -82, -84, -88, -90, -92, WhoBlA 75, -80, -85, WhoE 89, -91, -93, WhoSSW 73, -75, -76, WorAl*

Ashe, Arthur Robert, Jr. 1943-1993
ConAu 42NR, CurBio 93N, News 93-3, WhoBlA 94N, WrDr 94N

Ashe, Geoffrey Thomas 1923- *Au&Wr 71, BioIn 12, ConAu 5R, IntAu&W 82, -86, -89, -91, SmATA 17, WhoWor 74, WrDr 76, -80, -82, -84, -86, -88, -90, -92, -94*

Ashe, Gordon *ConAu X, EncMys, EncSF 93, LongCTC, MajTwCW, ScF&FL 92, TwCCr&M 80, -85, -91, WhoSpyF, WorAu 1950*

Ashe, Mary Ann *ConAu X, -43NR, SmATA X, TwCCr&M 85, -91, WrDr 82, -84, -86, -88*
Main entry: Lewis, Mary Christianna Milne

Asher, Sandra Fenichel 1942- *MajAI*

Asher, Sandy 1942- *BioIn 14, -16, ConAu 105, DcLB Y83B, IntAu&W 86, SmATA 34, -36, -13AS, TwCYAW*

Asher, Sandy Fenichel 1942- *SmATA 71*

Asheron, Sara *MajAI*

Ashey, Bella *BioIn 11, ConAu X, SmATA X*
Main entry: Breinburg, Petronella Alexandrina

Ashford, Daisy *WomNov*
Main entry: Ashford, Margaret Mary

Ashford, Daisy 1881?-1972 *BioIn 9, -10, -11, -16, BlmGWL, CamGLE, CarSB, ConAu X, ContDcW 89, DcLEL, EvLB, FemiCLE, InWom SUP, LongCTC, NewYTBE 72, ObitT 1971, OxCChiL, OxCEng 85, PenC ENG, REn, SmATA X, StaCVF, WhoChL*

Ashford, Daisy 1882-1972 *Benet 87*

Ashford, Jeffrey *AuBYP 2, -3, Au&Wr 71, ConAu X, EncMys, IntAu&W 91X, TwCCr&M 80, -85, -91, WrDr 76, -80, -82, -84, -86, -88, -90, -92, -94*
Main entry: Jeffries, Roderic

Ashford, Jeffrey 1926- *BioIn 14*

Ashford, Margaret Mary 1881?-1972
ConAu 33R, NewC, SmATA 10, WomNov
Pseud./variant:
Ashford, Daisy

Ashford, Margaret Mary Julia 1881-1972
DcNaB 1971

Ashlee, Ted *OxCCan SUP*

Ashley, Bernard *BioIn 15*

Ashley, Bernard 1926- *BioIn 16*

Ashley, Bernard 1935- *BioIn 16, ChlFicS, ChlLR 4, ConAu 93, -25NR, IntAu&W 82, -86, -89, -91, MajAI, OxCChiL, SmATA 39, -47, TwCChW 78, -83, -89, TwCYAW, WrDr 80, -82, -84, -86, -88, -90, -92, -94*

Ashley, Elizabeth *ConAu X, SmATA X, WrDr 76, -80, -82, -84*
Main entry: Salmon, Annie Elizabeth

Ashley, Ray
Main entry: Abrashkin, Raymond

Ashley, Robert Paul, Jr. 1915- *AuBYP 2, -3, BioIn 8, ConAu 17R, DrAS 74E, -78E, -82E, LEduc 74, WhoAm 74, -76, -78, -80, -82, -84, -86, -88, -90, -92, -94*

Ashmead, Gordon *AuBYP 2, -3, BioIn 8*

Ashmun, Margaret Eliza d1940 *AmAu&B, BioIn 2, CurBio 40, DcNAA, JBA 34, -51, WhAm 1, WhNAA, WisWr*

Ashner, Sonie Shapiro 1938- *ConAu 57*

Ashton, Warren T *SmATA X*
Main entry: Adams, William Taylor

Ashton-Warner, Sylvia 1905-1984
ContDcW 89

Ashton-Warner, Sylvia 1908- *ArtclWW 2, Benet 87*

Ashton-Warner, Sylvia 1908-1978
InWom SUP

Ashton-Warner, Sylvia 1908-1984
AnObit 1984, BioIn 8, -9, -10, -12, -13, -14, -15, -16, -17, BlueB 76, CamGLE, ConAu 69, -112, -29NR, ConLC 19, ConNov 72, -76, -82, FemiCLE, IntAu&W 77, IntDcWB, LongCTC, MajTwCW,

ModCmwL, NewYTBS 84, Novels, PenC ENG, RAdv 1, TwCWr, WorAu 1950, WrDr 76, –80, –82, –84

Ashton-Warner, Sylvia Constance 1908-1984 *BlmGWL*

Ashworth, Mae Hurley *IndAu 1917*

Asimov, Isaac 1920- *AmAu&B, AmMWSc 73P, –76P, –82, –86, –89, –92, AsBiEn, AuBYP 2, –3, Au&Wr 71, Benet 87, BenetAL 91, BestSel 90-2, BioIn 3, –7, –8, –9, –10, –11, –12, –13, –14, –15, –16, BlueB 76, CamGLE, CasWL, CelR, –90, ChlLR 12, ConAu 1R, –2NR, –19NR, –36NR, ConLC 1, –3, –9, –19, –26, ConNov 72, –76, –82, –86, –91, ConSFA, ConSFF, CurBio 53, –68, CyWA 89, DcLB 8, DcLEL 1940, DrAF 76, DrAPF 83, –85, –87, –89, –91, EncMys, Future, IntAu&W 77, –82, –86, –89, –91, IntWW 74, –75, –76, –77, –78, –79, –80, –81, –82, –83, –89, –91, IntvTCA 2, JeAmHC, LongCTC, MajTwCW, MakMC, NewEScF, Novels, OxCAmL 83, PenC AM, RAdv 13-5, REn, REnAL, RGTwCSF, ScFSB, ScFEYrs, SmATA 1, –26, ThrBJA, TwCCr&M 80, –85, –91, TwCSFW 86, –91, TwCWr, WebAB 74, –79, WebE&AL, Who 82, –83, –85, –88, –90, –92, WhoAm 74, –76, –78, –80, –82, –84, –86, –88, –90, WhoAmJ 80, WhoE 74, –81, –83, WhoEnt 92, WhoSciF, WhoUSWr 88, WhoWor 74, –78, –80, –82, –84, –87, –89, –91, WhoWorJ 78, WhoWrEP 89, –92, WorAlBi, WorAl, WorAu 1950, WrDr 76, –80, –82, –84, –86, –88, –90, –92*
Pseud./variant:
French, Paul

Asimov, Isaac 1920-1990 *WhAm 10*

Asimov, Isaac 1920-1992 *AnObit 1992, BioIn 17, ConAu 137, ConLC 76, CurBio 92N, DcLB Y92N, EncSF 93, MajAI, NewYTBS 92, News 92, –92-3, ScF&FL 92, SmATA 74, TwCYAW*
Pseud./variant:
Dale, George E
Dr. A

Asimov, Janet 1926- *ConAu 36NR, SmATA 54*

Asimov, Janet Jeppson 1926- *ScF&FL 92*
Pseud./variant:
Jeppson, J O

Asimov, Janet Opal Jeppson 1926- *EncSF 93, IntAu&W 89*

Asinof, Eliot 1919- *BioIn 3, –10, ConAu 9R, –7NR, SmATA 6, WrDr 76, –80, –82, –84, –86, –88, –90, –92, –94*

Aska, Warabe 1944- *BioIn 16, CanWW 89, SmATA 56*
Pseud./variant:
Masuda, Takeshi

Asmussen, Des *IlsBYP*

Aspin, Jehosaphat *BioIn 2, BritAS, CarS3*

Aspinwall, Alicia *CarSB, ChhPo, DcAmAu, WomWWA 14*

Asquith, Herbert 1881-1947 *BioIn 1, BkCL, ChhPo, –S1, –S2, EngPo, LongCTC, NewC, ObitOF 79, Str&VC, WhoLA*

Astley, Juliet *ConAu X, SmATA X, TwCRHW 90, WrDr 82, –84*
Main entry: Lofts, Norah

Aston, James *BioIn 11, –12, –13, ConAu X, –37NR, LongCTC, MajAI, SmATA X*
Main entry: White, Terence Hanbury

Astor, Gerald *IntAu&W 91, WrDr 86, –88, –90, –92, –94*

Astor, Gerald 1926- *ConAu 24NR, WrDr 76, –80, –82, –84*

Atene, Anna 1922- *BioIn 11, SmATA 12*

Atheling, William, Jr. *SmATA 66*
Main entry: Blish, James

Atkey, Philip *TwCCr&M 91*

Atkey, Philip 1908- *BioIn 14, ConAu 112, EncMys, TwCCr&M 80, –85, WrDr 82, –84, –86*

Atkey, Philip 1908-1985 *ConAu 118*

Atkin, Flora B 1919- *WrDr 86, –88, –90, –92, –94*

Atkin, Flora Blumenthal 1919- *ConAu 93, –16NR, –37NR, IntAu&W 89, TwCChW 78, WhoAm 82, WhoAmW 75, WrDr 80, –82, –84*

Atkin, Flora Blumethal 1919- *IntAu&W 91*

Atkin, Mary Gage 1929- *ConAu 81*

Atkinson, Allen *SmATA 46*

Atkinson, Allen d1987 *BioIn 15, –16, –17, NewYTBS 87*

Atkinson, Allen 1953?-1987 *SmATA 60*

Atkinson, Allen G 1953?-1987 *SmATA 55N*

Atkinson, Eleanor 1863-1942 *AmAu&B, BioIn 2, –4, CurBio 43, DcNAA, InWom SUP, IndAu 1816, JBA 34, TwCA, –SUP, WhAm 2, WhNAA, WomWWA 14, WomNov*

Atkinson, M E 1899-1974 *TwCChW 89*

Atkinson, Margaret Fleming *AuBYP 2, -3, BioIn 12, ConAu 73, SmATA 14*

Atkinson, Mary Evelyn
Main entry: Frankau, Mary Evelyn Atkinson

Atkinson, Mary Evelyn 1899- *Au&Wr 71, BioIn 8, ConAu X, OxCChiL, SmATA 4, TwCChW 78, -83, WhoChL*

Atkinson, Mary Jourdan 1898- *TexWr*

Atkinson, W A *ClaDrA, DcVicP 2*

Atticus *ConAu 135, -X, MajTwCW, SmATA X*
Main entry: Davies, Hunter
Fleming, Ian

Atticus 109BC-32BC *BlmGEL*

Attwell, Mabel Lucie 1879-1964 *BioIn 7, -8, -14, -17, ChhPo, -S1, DcBrAr 1, DcBrBI, DcNaB 1961, DcWomA, OxCChiL, WhoChL, WorECar*

Atwater, C Elizabeth 1923- *ConAu 13R*

Atwater, Florence *ChlLR 19*

Atwater, Florence 1896-1979 *ConAu 135, SmATA 66*

Atwater, Florence Carroll *BioIn 14*

Atwater, Florence Carroll 1896-1979 *BioIn 17*

Atwater, Florence Hasseltine *BioIn 1, -6, -12, MorJA, OxCChiL, SmATA 16*

Atwater, Florence Hasseltine Carroll 1896-1979 *MajAI*

Atwater, James David 1928- *ConAu 101, WhoAm 76, -78, -80, -82, -84, -86, -88, -90, -92, -94, WhoMW 86, -90*

Atwater, Montgomery Meigs 1904- *AuBYP 2, -3, BioIn 6, -7, -12, ConAu 73, MorJA, SmATA 15, WhoPNW*

Atwater, Richard 1892-1938? *SmATA 66*

Atwater, Richard Tupper 1892-1938? *AmAu&B, BioIn 1, -6, -13, BkCL, ChhPo S1, ChlLR 19, ConAu 111, -135, MorJA, OxCChiL, SmATA 27, -54, TwCChW 78, -83, -89*

Atwater, Richard Tupper 1892-1948 *BioIn 14, -16, -17, MajAI*
Pseud./variant:
Riq

Atwood, Ann 1913- *AuBYP 3, IntAu&W 91, WrDr 86, -88, -90*

Atwood, Ann Margaret 1913- *AuBYP 2S, BioIn 10, ConAu 41R, FourBJA, IntAu&W 82, -86, SmATA 7, WhoAm 74, -76, -78, -80, -82, -84, -86, -88, -90, -92, WhoAmW 74*

Atwood, Margaret 1939- *ArtclWW 2, Au&Arts 12, Benet 87, BenetAL 91, BestSel 89-2, BioIn 15, -16, -17, BlmGEL, CamGLE, CanWW 89, ConAu 24NR, -33NR, ConLC 44, ConNov 86, -91, ConPo 91, ContDcW 89, CyWA 89, DcLB 53, DrAPF 87, -89, -91, -93, FemiCLE, IntAu&W 86, -89, -91, IntLitE, IntWW 89, -91, IntvTCA 2, MagSWL, MajTwCW, NewYTBS 86, RAdv 13-1, RfGEnL 91, ScF&FL 92, ShSCr 2, SmATA 50, Who 88, -90, -92, WhoCanL 87, -92, WorLitC, WrDr 86, -88, -90, -92*

Atwood, Margaret Eleanor 1939- *EncSF 93, RfGShF, TwCYAW*

Aubry, Claude B 1914-1984 *BioIn 3, -6, -7, -10, -13, CanWW 70, -80, -81, -83, ConAu 106, OxCCan SUP, Profile 1, SmATA 29, -40N, WhoAm 80, WhoCanL 85, -87, -92, WhoLibS 55, -66*

Auclair, Joan 1960- *SmATA 68*

Audubon, John James 1785?-1851 *AfroAA, Alli, AmAu, AmAu&B, ArtsNiC, AsBiEn, AtlBL, Benet 87, BenetAL 91, BbD, BiDSA, BiD&SB, BiESc, BilnAmS, BioIn 1, -2, -3, -4, -5, -6, -7, -8, -9, -10, -11, -12, -13, -14, -15, -16, -17, BriEAA, CamGEL, CamGLE, CamHAL, CelCen, CnDAL, CyAL, DcAmAu, DcBiPP, DcLEL, DcNAA, DcScB, Dis&D, EncAB-H, EncSoH, GrBIl, HarEnUS, InSci, McGEWB, MemAm, MouLC 3, NegAl 89, OhA&B, OxCAmH, OxCAmL 65, -83, OxCArt, OxCCan, OxCEng 67, -85, OxDcArt, PenC AM, RAdv 13-5, RComAH, REn, REnAL, WebAB 74, -79, WhAm HS, WhFla, WorAlBi, WorAl*

Auer, Martin 1951- *SmATA 77*

Auerbach, Marjorie 1932- *AuBYP 2S, -3, BioIn 8, ConAu 9R, IlsCB 1957*

Augarde, Stephen Andre 1950- *BioIn 12, -13, ConAu 104, IlsCB 1967, SmATA 25*

Augelli, John P 1921- *SmATA 46*

Augelli, John Pat 1921- *WhoAm 88, -90, -92, -94, WhoMW 92*

Augustine, Mildred *ConAu 134, MajAI, SmATA 65, WrDr 94*
Main entry: Benson, Mildred Augustine Wirt

Aulaire, Edgar Parin D'
Main entry: D'Aulaire, Edgar Parin

Aulaire, Edgar Parin D' 1898- *AmPB, AnCL, BioIn 1, –2, –4, –5, –7, –8, –10, CurBio 40, JBA 34, –51*

Aulaire, Ingri D'
Main entry: D'Aulaire, Ingri Mortenson Parin

Aulaire, Ingri D' 1904-1980 *AmPB, AnCL, BioIn 1, –2, –4, –5, –7, –8, –10, JBA 34, –51*

Aulaire, Ingri D'Mortenson 1904- *InWom SUP*

Aulnoy, Marie C, Comtesse
Main entry: D'Aulnoy, Marie Catherine, Comtesse

Aulnoy, Marie-Catherine 1649-1705 *FemiCLE*

Aulnoy, Marie Catherine, Comtesse D' 1650?-1705 *BiD&SB, BioIn 8, –10, BlmGWL, CarSB, CasWL, DcEuL, OxCChiL, OxCFr*
Pseud./variant:
D'Aulnoy, Marie C, Comtesse D'

Ault, Norman 1880-1950 *BioIn 1, –2, –14, ChhPo, –S1, ConICB, DcBrBI, IlsCB 1744*

Ault, Phillip H 1914- *AuBYP 2S, BioIn 1, –13, ConAu 101, –18NR, IntYB 80, –81, –82, SmATA 23, WhoAm 74, –76, –78, –80, WhoMW 74, –76, –78*

Ault, Phillip Halliday 1914- *AuBYP 3*

Ault, Rosalie Sain 1942- *ConAu 107, SmATA 38*
Pseud./variant:
Ault, Roz

Ault, Roz *ConAu X, SmATA X*
Main entry: Ault, Rosalie Sain

Aung, Maung Htin 1909- *SmATA 21*
Pseud./variant:
Aung, U Htin
Fourth Brother, The

Aung, U Htin
Main entry: Aung, Maung Htin

Aunt Charlotte *OxCChiL*

Aunt Effie 1811-1898 *OxCChiL*

Aunt Friendly 1824-1906 *OxCChiL*

Auntie Deb *ConAu X, SmATA X*
Main entry: Coury, Louise Andree

Auntie Louise *ConAu X, SmATA X*
Main entry: Coury, Louise Andree

Aunt Irene *NewbC 1966*

Aunt Louisa 1814-1899 *OxCChiL*

Aunt Mary *OxCChiL*

Austen, Jane 1775-1817 *Alli, ArtclWW 2, AtlBL, Benet 87, BbD, BiD&SB, BioIn 1, –2, –3, –4, –5, –6, –7, –8, –9, –10, –11, –12, –13, –14, –15, –16, –17, BlmGEL, BlmGWL, BritAu 19, BritWr 4, CamGEL, CamGLE, CasWL, CelCen, Chambr 2, CnDBLB 3, ContDcW 89, CrtT 2, CyWA 58, DcBiA, DcBiPP, DcEnA, DcEnL, DcEuL, DcLB 116, DcLEL, DcNaB, Dis&D, EncBrWW, EvLB, FemiCLE, HalFC 84, –88, HerW, –84 InWom SUP, IntDcWB, LongCEL, MagSWL, McGEWB, MouLC 2, NewC, NewOxM, NinCLC 1, –13, –19, –33, Novels, OxCEng 67, –85, PenC ENG, RAdv 1, –13-1, RComWL, REn, RfGEnL 91, WebE&AL, WhDW, WorAlBi, WorAl, WorLitC*

Austen, John 1886- *BioIn 1, ChhPo, –S1, –S2, IlsCB 1744*

Austen, John 1886-1948 *BioIn 14*

Austin, Elizabeth 1907- *AuBYP 3*

Austin, Elizabeth S 1907- *AuBYP 2S, BioIn 10, ConAu P-2, IntAu&W 77, SmATA 5*

Austin, Frank *ConAu X, EncFWF, TwCWW 91, WebAB 79*

Austin, Frederick Britten 1885-1941 *NewC, ScFEYrs, WhoLA*

Austin, Jane Goodwin 1831-1894 *Alli SUP, AmAu, AmAu&B, BenetAL 91, BbD, BiD&SB, BioIn 3, CarSB, DcAmAu, DcBiA, DcNAA, JBA 34, OxCAmL 65, –83, REnAL, WhAm HS*

Austin, Margot *AuBYP 2, –3, BioIn 7, –11, ConAu P-1, MorJA, SmATA 11*

Austin, Margot d1990 *BioIn 17, NewYTBS 90*

Austin, Margot 1909?-1990 *ConAu 132, SmATA 66*

Austin, Mary Hunter 1868-1934 *AmAu&B, AmLY, AmWomPl, AmWomWr 92, AnCL, BioAmW, BioIn 1, –2, –7, –8, –14, –15, –16, –17, BkCL, ChhPo, –S1, –S2, CnDAL ConAmA, ConAmL, DcAmAu, DcLEL, DcNAA, EncFWF, InWom SUP, OxCAmL 65, REnAL, Str&VC, TwCA, –SUP, WebAB 74, WhAm 1, WhNAA, WomWWA 14*

Austin, Oliver L, Jr. 1903-1988 *BioIn 16, ConAu 127, NewYTBS 89, SmATA 59*

Austin, Oliver Luther, Jr. 1903- *AmMWSc 73P, -76P, -82, -86, -89, -92, AuBYP 2S, -3, BioIn 10, ConAu 49, SmATA 7, WhoSSW 73*

Austin, Phil 1910- *BioIn 9, IlsBYP, WhoAmA 73, -78, -80, -82, -84, -86, -89, -91*

Austin, R G
Main entry: Gelman, Rita Golden

Austin, Stella d1893 *Alli SUP, OxCChiL, TelT*

Austin, Tom *SmATA X*
Main entry: Jacobs, Linda C

Austing, Ronald 1932?- *BioIn 6, -10*

Auth, William Anthony, Jr. 1942- *ConGrA 3, SmATA 51*

Averill, Esther 1902- *TwCChW 89, WrDr 86, -88, -90, -92*

Averill, Esther Holden 1902- *AmAu&B, AmPB, AuBYP 2, -3, BioIn 2, -3, -5, -7, -8, -9, -12, -13, BkCL, ConAu 29R, -12NR, ForWC 70, IlsCB 1946, -1957, -1967, JBA 51, SmATA 1, -28, TwCChW 78, -83, WhoAmW 74, -75, -77, WrDr 76, -80, -82, -84, -94*
Pseud./variant:
Domino, John

Averill, Esther Holden 1902-1992 *ConAu 139, SmATA 72*

Averill, Naomi *AmPB*

Avery, Al *AmAu&B, AuBYP 2, -3, ConAu X, SmATA 3, WrDr 76, -80, -82, -84, -86, -88*
Main entry: Montgomery, Rutherford George

Avery, Gillian 1926- *IntAu&W 91, SmATA 6AS, TwCChW 89, WrDr 86, -88, -90, -92*

Avery, Gillian Elise 1926- *AuBYP 2, -3, BioIn 8, -10, ConAu 9R, -4NR, FourBJA, IntAu&W 77, -82, -86, -89, MajAI, OxCChiL, SmATA 7, -75, TwCChW 78, -83, Who 82, -83, -85, -88, -90, -92, WhoChL, WhoWor 80, WrDr 80, -82, -84, -94*

Avery, Harold 1867-1943 *BioIn 8, OxCChiL, StaCVF, TwCChW 83, -89, WhoChL*

Avery, Kay 1908- *BioIn 10, ConAu 1R, SmATA 5*

Avery, Lynn *AuBYP 2, -3, ConAu X, SmATA X*
Main entry: Cole, Lois Dwight

Avi 1937- *Au&Arts 10, BioIn 15, -16, ChlLR 24, ConAu X, -42NR, DcAmChF 1960, -1985, FifBJA, ScF&FL 92, SmATA 71, -X, TwCChW 89, TwCYAW, WhoAm 92, -94, WrDr 90, -92, -94*
Main entry: Wortis, Avi

Avinoff, Andrey d1948 *WhoAmA 86N*

Avinoff, Andrey 1884-1948 *WhoAmA 89N, -91N*

Avinoff, Andrey 1884-1949 *BioIn 1, -2, -3, -12, IlsCB 1744, InSci, ObitOF 79, WhAmArt 85, WhoAmA 78N, -80N, -82N*

Avis, Walter Spencer 1919- *DrAS 74F, -82F*

Avison, George 1885- *BioIn 1, -5, ConICB, IlsBYP, IlsCB 1744, -1946, WhAmArt 85*

Avi-Yonah, Michael 1904- *ConAu 5R, WhoWorJ 72, -78*

Avrett, Robert William 1901- *ChhPo S1, ConAu 1R, DcSpL, TexWr, WhoSSW 73*

Awdry, Christopher Vere 1940- *ConAu 136, SmATA 67, WrDr 94*

Awdry, W V 1911- *ChlLR 23, IntAu&W 91, TwCChW 89, WrDr 86, -88, -90, -92*

Awdry, Wilbert Vere 1911- *Au&Wr 71, BioIn 8, ConAu 103, IntAu&W 77, -82, -86, -89, OxCChiL, SmATA 67, TwCChW 83, Who 92, WhoChL, WrDr 76, -80, -82, -84, -94*

Awdry, Wilbert Vere, Rev 1911- *Who 90*

Axeman, Lois *IlsBYP*

Axtell, James Lewis 1941- *ConAu 108, -25NR, DrAS 78H, -82H, WhoAm 90, -92, -94*

Axton, David *ConAu 36NR, EncSF 93, MajTwCW, TwCCr&M 91, TwCYAW, WrDr 86, -88, -90, -92*

Axton, David 1945- *BioIn 14, -15, -17, WrDr 94*

Ayars, Albert Lee 1917- *AmMWSc 73S, BlueB 76, ConAu 29R, IntAu&W 77, -91, LEduc 74, WhoAm 74, -76, -78, -80, -82, -84, -86, -88, -90, -92, -94, WhoSSW 80, -82, WhoWest 89, WhoWor 74, WrDr 76, -80, -82, -84, -86, -88, -90, -92, -94*

Ayars, James Sterling 1898- *AuBYP 2, -3, BioIn 8, -9, ConAu 5R, -2NR, IntAu&W 77, -82, MichAu 80, SmATA 4, WhoMW 74, -82, -84, WrDr 76, -80, -82, -84, -86*

Ayars, Rebecca Caudill *AuBYP 3*

Ayer, Jacqueline Brandford 1930- *BioIn 8, -9, ConAu 69, IlsBYP, IlsCB 1957, -1967,*

InB&W 85, SmATA 13, ThrBJA, TwCChW 78, WrDr 80

Ayer, Margaret d1981 *BioIn 5, -6, -12, ConAu 65, -13NR, ForWC 70, IlsBYP, IlsCB 1946, MorJA, SmATA 15, WhAmArt 85*

Aylesworth, Jim 1943- *ConAu 106, -22NR, SmATA 38, WhoWrEP 89, -92*

Aylesworth, Thomas G 1927- *ConAu 26NR, ScF&FL 92, SmATA 17AS*

Aylesworth, Thomas Gibbons 1927- *AmMWSc 73P, -76P, -82, -86, -89, -92, AuBYP 2S, -3, BioIn 9, ChlLR 6, ConAu 25R, -10NR, IndAu 1917, LEduc 74, SmATA 4, WhoAm 84, -86, -88, -90, -92, -94, WhoE 74, -75, -77, -81, -83, -85, -86, -89, WhoUSWr 88, WhoWrEP 89, -92*

Ayling, Keith 1898-1976 *BioIn 11, ConAu 69, -73*

Aylward, William J *WhoAmA 86N*

Aylward, William J 1875-1958 *WhoAmA 89N, -91N*

Aylward, William James 1875-1956 *BioIn 1, -4, IlrAm 1880, -B, IlsCB 1744, ObitOF 79, WhAmArt 85, WhoAmA 80N, -82N*

Aymar, Brandt 1911- *BioIn 13, ConAu 1R, -16NR, -37NR, SmATA 22, WhNAA*

Aymar, Gordon Christian 1893- *Au&Wr 71, ConAu 5R, IntAu&W 77, WhAm 10, WhoAm 74, -76, -78, -80, -82, -84, -86, -88, WhoAmA 73, -78, -80, -82, -84, -86, WhoE 86, WrDr 76, -80, -82*

Ayme, Marcel *TwCChW 89B*

Ayme, Marcel 1902-1967 *Benet 87, BiE&WWA, BioIn 1, -2, -4, -8, -14, CasWL, ChlLR 25, ClDMEL 47, CnMD, CnThe, ConLC 11, DcLB 72, EncWL, -2, EncWT, EuWr 12, EvEuW, GuFrLit 1, LongCTC, McGEWD 72, -84, ModFrL, ModRL, ModWD, NotNAT B, Novels, ObitOF 79, ObitT 1961, OxCChiL, OxCFr, PenC EUR, RAdv 13-2, REn, RfGShF, TwCA SUP, TwCChW 78B, -83B, TwCWr, WhAm 4A*

Ayme, Marcel Andre 1902-1967 *EncSF 93*

Ayre, Robert Hugh 1900- *AuBYP 2, -3, BioIn 7, CanWW 70, -79, ConAu 1R, OxCCan, -SUP, WhoAmA 73*

Ayres, Carole Briggs
Main entry: Briggs, Carole S

Ayres, Patricia Miller d1985 *BioIn 14, -15*

Ayres, Patricia Miller 1923-1985 *SmATA 46N*

Azaid *BioIn 16, -17, ConAu 131, -X, SmATA 66, -X*
Main entry: Zaidenberg, Arthur
Zaidenberg, Arthur

B

"B" *ScF&FL 92, SmATA X*
Main entry: Gilbert, William Schwenck, Sir

B, Tania *SmATA X*
Main entry: Blixen, Karen

Baastad, Babbis Friis *ConAu 134, –X, SmATA 7*
Main entry: Friis-Baastad, Babbis Ellinor

Bab *ConAu X, SmATA X*
Main entry: Gilbert, William Schwenck, Sir

Baba, Meher
Main entry: Meher Baba

Baba, Meher 1894-1969 *BioIn 8, –10, –11, –13, ConAu 106, –109, ObitOF 79*

Babbis, Eleanor *AuBYP 2S, –3, ConAu 134, –X, SmATA 7, ThrBJA*
Main entry: Friis-Baastad, Babbis Ellinor

Babbitt, Natalie *BioIn 14, –15, –16, –17, WrDr 86, –88, –90, –92*

Babbitt, Natalie 1932- *AuBYP 2S, –3, BioIn 10, –12, ChhPo S2, ChlLR 2, ConAu 49, –2NR, –19NR, DcLB 52, FourBJA, IlsCB 1967, IntAu&W 77, MorBMP, OxCChiL, ScF&FL 92, SmATA 6, –68, –5AS, TwCChW 78, –83, –89, WrDr 76, –80, –82, –84, –94*

Babbitt, Natalie Moore 1932- *DcAmChF 1960*

Babbitt, Natalie Zane Moore 1932- *ConAu 38NR, MajAI*

Babbitt, Robert *WrDr 76, –80, –82, –84, –86, –88, –90*
Main entry: Bangs, Robert Babbitt

Babbitt, Samuel Fisher 1929- *Au&Wr 71, DrAS 74E, –78E, LEduc 74, WhoAm 84, –86, –88, –90, –92, –94, WhoE 75, –77, –86*

Babcock, Dennis Arthur 1948- *BioIn 13, ConAu 61, SmATA 22, WhoMW 78*

Bach, Alice *BioIn 14*

Bach, Alice 1942- *AuBYP 3*

Bach, Alice Hendricks 1942- *AuBYP 2S, BioIn 13, ConAu 101, FifBJA, ForWC 70, SmATA 27, –30, TwCYAW*

Bach, Mickey 1909- *WhoAmA 78*

Bach, Richard David 1936- *AuNews 1, BioIn 9, –10, –11, BioNews 74, ConAu 9R, CurBio 73, EncO&P 1S1, IntAu&W 77, SmATA 13, WhoAm 76, –78, –80, –94, WhoAmL 83, WorAl, WrDr 76, –80*

Bacharach, Herman Ilfeld 1899- *ArtsAmW 2, ConICB, WhAmArt 85*

Bacheller, Irving *IntvTCA 2*

Bacheller, Irving 1859-1950 *AmAu&B, BenetAL 91, BiD&SB, BioIn 1, –2, –4, Chambr 3, ChhPo, –S1, –S2, ConAmL, DcAmAu, DcBiA, DcLEL, JBA 34, ObitOF 79, OxCAmL 65, –83, REn, TwCA SUP, TwCRHW 90, WhAm 2, WhNAA*

Bachman, Fred 1949- *BioIn 11, ConAu 53, SmATA 12*

Bachman, Richard *ConAu 30NR, ConTFT 8, EncSF 93, MajTwCW, ScF&FL 92, TwCYAW, WorAu 1980, WrDr 86, –88, –90, –92, –94*
Main entry: King, Stephen

Back, George 1796-1878 *Expl 93*

Back, George, Sir 1796-1873? *DcBiPP*

Back, George, Sir 1796-1878? *Alli, BiD&SB, CelCen, DcCanB 10, DcNaB, OxCCan, OxCShps*

Backus, James Gilmore 1913-1989 *ConAu 129, SmATA 63*
Pseud./variant:
Backus, Jim

Backus, Jim 1913-1989 *AnObit 1989, ConAu 129, ConTFT 6, EncAFC, HalFC 88, IntMPA 86, –88, NewYTBS 89, News 90, –90-1, SmATA X, WhAm 10, WhoCom,*

WorAlBi
Main entry: Backus, James Gilmore

Bacmeister, Rhoda W 1893-1991 *ConAu 133*

Bacmeister, Rhoda Warner 1893- *ChhPo, ConAu P-1, ForWC 70, SmATA 11*

Bacon, Elizabeth 1914- *BioIn 9, ConAu 29R, SmATA 3, WhoWest 74*
Pseud./variant:
Morrow, Betty

Bacon, Frances Atchinson 1903- *ConAu 1R, MichAu 80*

Bacon, Joan Chase *BioIn 15, –16, SmATA X*
Main entry: Bowden, Joan Chase

Bacon, Josephine Dodge 1876-1961 *BenetAL 91, SmATA 48, WomNov*

Bacon, Josephine Dodge Daskam 1876-1961 *AmAu&B, AmWomPl, BioIn 4, –6, –16, ChhPo, –S2, ConAu 97, DcAmAu, REnAL, Str&VC, TwCA, –SUP, WhAm 5, WhNAA, WomWWA 14*
Pseud./variant:
Lovell, Ingraham

Bacon, Margaret Frances 1895-1987 *SmATA 50N*
Pseud./variant:
Bacon, Peggy 1895-1987

Bacon, Margaret Hope 1921- *BioIn 10, ConAu 25R, SmATA 6, WrDr 76*

Bacon, Martha 1917-1981 *ScF&FL 92, TwCChW 89*

Bacon, Martha Sherman 1917-1981 *AuBYP 2S, –3, BioIn 12, –13, ChlLR 3, ConAu 85, –104, DcAmChF 1960, SmATA 18, –27N, TwCChW 78, –83*

Bacon, Paul 1913- *AuBYP 2, –3, BioIn 2, –7*

Bacon, Peggy 1895- *AmAu&B, AmPB, BioIn 1, –5, –8, –9, –10, BriEAA, ChhPo, –S2, ConAu P-2, ConICB, CurBio 40, DcWomA, GrAmP, IlsBYP, IlsCB 1744, –1946, –1957, –1967, InWom SUP, OxCAmL 65, –83, REnAL, SmATA 2, Str&VC, WhAmArt 85, WhoAm 74, –76, –78, –82, –84, WhoAmA 73, –78, –80, –82, –84, –86, WhoAmW 74, –85*

Bacon, Peggy 1895-1987 *BenetAL 91, BioIn 15, –16, ConAu 121, ConGrA 3, CurBio 87N, NewYTBS 87, ScF&FL 92, WhAm 9, WhoAmA 89N, –91N*
Main entry: Bacon, Margaret Frances

Bacon, Phillip 1922- *AmMWSc 73S, –76P, BioIn 10, ConAu 41R, WhoAm 74, –76, –78, –80, –82, –84, –86, –88, –90, –92, –94, WhoSSW 73, –75, –76, –78, –80, WhoUSWr 88, WhoWor 74, –91, –93, WhoWrEP 89, –92*

Bacon, R L 1924- *TwCChW 89, WrDr 86, –88, –90, –92*

Bacon, Ronald Leonard 1924- *BioIn 13, ConAu 104, OxCChiL, SmATA 26, TwCChW 78, –83, WrDr 80, –82, –84, –94*

Baden, Robert 1936- *SmATA 70*

Baden-Powell, Robert S Smyth, Baron 1857-1941 *BioIn 1, –3, –4, –5, –6, –7, –8, –9, –10, –12, –13, ConAu 114, DcBrBI, DcNaB 1941, EncSoA, HarEnUS, LongCTC, ObitOF 79, OxCChiL, SmATA 16, WhLW, WhoChL, WhoLA, WorAl*

Baden-Powell, Robert Stephenson Smyth 1857-1941 *DcAfHiB 86, DcTwHis, GrBr, WorAlBi*

Bader, Barbara *AuBYP 2S, –3, BioIn 10, ChhPo S2, MedPD, WhoLibS 66*

Badmin, Stanley Roy d1989 *Who 90N*

Badmin, Stanley Roy 1906- *BioIn 5, –14, DcBrAr 1, IlsCB 1946, Who 74, –82, –83, –85, –88*

Baehr, Patricia 1952- *ConAu 35NR, SmATA 65*

Baehr, Patricia Goehner *BioIn 17*

Baer, Edith R 1920- *ConAu 21NR*

Baer, Edith Ruth 1920- *Au&Wr 71, ConAu 104*

Baer, Judy 1951- *SmATA 71*
Pseud./variant:
Kaye, Judy

Baerg, Harry John 1909- *BioIn 11, –12, ConAu 9R, –4NR, IntAu&W 77, –91, SmATA 12, WrDr 76, –80, –82, –84, –86, –88, –90, –92, –94*

Bagley, John Joseph 1908- *Au&Wr 71, ConAu 5R, IntAu&W 77, –82, –86, –89, –91, WrDr 76, –82, –84, –86, –88, –90, –92*

Bagley, John Joseph 1908-1989 *WrDr 94N*

Bagnold, Enid *BioIn 14, –15, –16, WomNov*

Bagnold, Enid 1889-1981 *AnObit 1981, AuBYP 2, –3, Benet 87, BiE&WWA, BioIn 2, –4, –6, –7, –8, –9, –10, –12, –13, BlmGWL, BlueB 76, CamGLE, CamGWoT, ChhPo S2, CnMD, ConAu 5R, –103, –5NR, –40NR, ConDr 73, –77, ConLC 25, ConNov 76, CurBio 64, –81N, DcLB 13, DcLEL, EncBrWW, EncWT, EvLB, FemiCLE,*

FourBJA, IntAu&W 77, IntWW 78, –79, –80, –81, –81N, LongCTC, MajAI, ModWD, NewC, NewYTBS 81, NotNAT, –A, Novels, OxCChiL, OxCEng 67, OxCThe 83, PlP&P, REn, RfGEnL 91, SmATA 1, –25, TwCA, –SUP, TwCChW 83, –89, TwCWr, WhAm 7, Who 74, –82N, WhoAmW 74, WhoChL, WhoThe 72, –77, –81, WhoWor 74, –78, WorAlBi, WorAl, WrDr 76, –80, –82
Pseud./variant:
Lady Of Quality, A

Bagnold, Enid 1962-1981 *ConDr 93*

Bahadur, K P 1924- *ConAu 57, –28NR*

Bahlke, Valerie Worth 1933- *ConAu 41R, –15NR*
Pseud./variant:
Worth, Valerie

Bahr, Robert 1940- *ConAu 9NR, SmATA 38, WrDr 82, –84, –86, –88, –90, –92, –94*

Bahti, Tom *IlsBYP, SmATA 31*

Bahti, Tom 1926-1972 *SmATA 57*

Bailey, Alice Cooper 1890- *BioIn 11, ConAu P-1, ForWC 70, SmATA 12, WhoAmW 74, –75, –77*

Bailey, Anne 1958- *SmATA 71*

Bailey, Bernadine Freeman 1901- *AuBYP 2, –3, BioIn 2, –7, ConAu 5R, ForWC 70, IntAu&W 77, SmATA 14, WhoAmW 74, –75*

Bailey, Carolyn Sherwin 1875-1961 *AmAu&B, AmWomPl, AnCL, AuBYP 2, –3, BioIn 1, –2, –6, –7, –8, –14, BkCL, CarSB, ChhPo, –S1, –S2, ConAu 73, CurBio 48, JBA 51, MajAI, NewbMB 1922, OxCChiL, SmATA 14, Str&VC, TwCChW 78, –83, –89, WomWWA 14*

Bailey, Charles Waldo 1929- *EncSF 93, WhoWrEP 92, WrDr 86, –88, –90, –92*

Bailey, Charles Waldo, II 1929- *BioIn 7, –13, ConAu 1R, –1NR, EncTwCJ, IntAu&W 91, WhoAm 74, –76, –78, –80, –82, –84, –86, –88, –90, –92, –94, WhoUSWr 88, WhoWrEP 89, WrDr 76, –80, –82, –84, –94*

Bailey, Donna 1938- *SmATA 68*

Bailey, Donna Veronica Anne 1938- *ConAu 136*
Pseud./variant:
Bonar, Veronica

Bailey, Flora *AuBYP 2, –3, BioIn 7*

Bailey, Jane H 1916- *BioIn 11, ConAu 53, –4NR, SmATA 12, WhoAmW 77*

Bailey, Jean *BioIn 4, InB&W 80*

Bailey, John *AuBYP 2, –3, BioIn 8*

Bailey, John 1940- *SmATA 52*

Bailey, Maralyn Collins 1941- *BioIn 11, ConAu 53, IntAu&W 77, SmATA 12*

Bailey, Matilda *BioIn 10, ConAu X, SmATA 6*
Main entry: Radford, Ruby Lorraine

Bailey, Maurice Charles 1932- *BioIn 11, ConAu 53, SmATA 12*

Bailey, Ralph Edgar 1893- *BioIn 11, ConAu P-1, SmATA 11*

Bailey-Jones, Beryl 1912- *BioIn 5, IlsBYP, IlsCB 1946*
Pseud./variant:
Jones, Beryl Bailey

Baillie, Allan 1943- *ChlFicS, ConAu 118, DcChlFi, TwCYAW*

Baillie, Allan Stuart 1943- *ConAu 42NR, IntAu&W 91*

Bain, Edward Ustick *AuBYP 2, –3, BioIn 7*

Bain, R Nisbet 1854-1909 *Str&VC*

Baines, John David 1943- *SmATA 71*

Baird, Bil d1987 *NewYTBS 87*

Baird, Bil 1904- *BiE&WWA, BioIn 1, –3, –5, –10, –14, BioNews 74, CelR, ChhPo S2, ConAu 106, CurBio 54, SmATA 30, WhoThe 81, WorAl*

Baird, Bil 1904-1987 *AnObit 1987, BioIn 15, –16, ConTFT 5, CurBio 87N, SmATA 52N*

Baird, David McCurdy 1920- *AmMWSc 73P, –82, –86, –89, BioIn 15, BlueB 76, CanWW 80, –81, –83, –89, WhoAm 80, –82, WrDr 80, –82, –84, –86, –88, –90*

Baird, Eva-Lee *AuBYP 2S, –3*

Baird, Thomas 1923- *ConAu 21NR, WhoUSWr 88, WhoWrEP 89, WrDr 86, –88, –90*

Baird, Thomas 1923-1990 *ConAu 131, SmATA 64*

Baird, Thomas P 1923- *AmAu&B, AuBYP 2S, –3, BioIn 15, ConAu 53, –4NR, SmATA 39, –45, WrDr 76, –80, –82, –84*

Baird, Thomas P 1923-1990 *BioIn 16, –17, ScF&FL 92*

Baity, Elizabeth Chesley 1907- *AmAu&B, AnCL, BioIn 3, –6, –9, –14, ConAu 29R, MorJA, SmATA 1*

Bakacs, George *IlsBYP*

Bakeless, John Edwin 1894-1973 *AmAu&B, AuBYP 2, Au&Wr 71, BioIn 4, –7, –11, ConAu 5R, DrAS 74E, REnAL, SmATA 9, TwCA, –SUP, WhNAA, WhoAm 74, –76, –78, WhoWor 74, WrDr 76*

Bakeless, John Edwin 1894-1978 *AuBYP 3, BioIn 13, EncAI&E*

Bakeless, Katherine Little *AuBYP 3*

Bakeless, Katherine Little 1895- *Au&Wr 71, BioIn 11, ConAu 5R, SmATA 9, WhoE 74, WrDr 76, –80, –82, –84*

Baker, Alan 1951- *BioIn 13, ConAu 97, –16NR, –38NR, SmATA 22*

Baker, Augusta *NegAl 89*

Baker, Augusta 1911- *BiDrLUS 70, BioIn 8, –9, –10, –11, BlkAWP, BlkAull, –92, BlkWr 1, ConAu 1R, –17NR, LivgBAA, NegAl 76, –83, NotBlAW 92, SelBAAf, SelBAAu, SmATA 3, WhoAmW 74, –75, WhoLibI 82, WhoLibS 55, –66*

Baker, Barbara *AuBYP 3*

Baker, Betty 1928- *AmAu&B, AuBYP 2, BioIn 8, –9, –10, ConAu X, DcAmChF 1960, IntAu&W 91, SmATA 5, ThrBJA, TwCChW 78, –83, WhoAmW 74, –75, WhoWest 74, –76, WrDr 84, –86, –88*
Pseud./variant:
Venturo, Betty Lou Baker

Baker, Betty 1928-1987 *ScF&FL 92, SmATA 54N, TwCChW 89*

Baker, Betty Lou 1928-1987 *AuBYP 3, ConAu 38NR, MajAI, SmATA 73*

Baker, Charlotte
Main entry: Montgomery, Charlotte Baker

Baker, Charlotte 1910- *AuBYP 2, –3, BioIn 5, –7, –9, ConAu 17R, DcAmChF 1960, IlsCB 1946, IntAu&W 77X, SmATA 2*

Baker, Denys Val 1917- *BioIn 14, –15*

Baker, Denys Val 1917-1984 *ConAu 9R, –113, –6NR, PenEncH, ScF&FL 92, WhoHr&F*

Baker, Elizabeth
Main entry: Baker, Mary Elizabeth Gillette

Baker, Elizabeth 1923- *AuBYP 2S, ConAu 1R, –3NR, WrDr 76, –80, –82, –84, –86, –88, –90*

Baker, Emilie Kip *AmAu&B, Str&VC, WhAm 5*

Baker, Eugene H *SmATA 50*

Baker, Gayle Cunningham 1950- *ConAu 105, SmATA 39*

Baker, Harriette Newell 1815?-1893 *Alli SUP, AmAu&B, BbD, BiD&SB, CarSB, DcAmAu, DcNAA, WhAm HS*

Baker, James Lawrence 1941- *ConAu 53, WhoE 77*

Baker, James W 1924- *BioIn 13, SmATA 22*

Baker, James W 1926- *SmATA 65, WrDr 94*

Baker, Janice E 1941- *BioIn 13, ConAu 57, SmATA 22*

Baker, Jeannie 1950- *BioIn 13, ChlLR 28, ConAu 97, SmATA 23, WrDr 82, –84, –86, –88, –90, –92, –94*

Baker, Jeffrey John Wheeler 1931- *AmMWSc 73P, –76P, –82, –86, –89, –92, BioIn 10, ConAu 49, –1NR, SmATA 5, WhoE 83*

Baker, Jerry *AuNews 2, BioIn 11, ConAu 105*

Baker, Laura Nelson 1911- *AuBYP 2, –3, Au&Wr 71, BioIn 6, –8, –9, ConAu 5R, –5NR, ForWC 70, MinnWr, SmATA 3, WrDr 76, –80, –84*

Baker, Liva 1930- *AuBYP 2S, –3, ConAu 29R*

Baker, Lucinda 1916- *ConAu 65, WhoAmW 75, –77, –81, WrDr 80, –82, –84, –86, –88, –90, –92, –94*

Baker, Margaret 1890- *Au&Wr 71, BioIn 2, –9, ChhPo S2, ConAu 13R, –6NR, JBA 34, –51, SmATA 4, WrDr 76, –80*

Baker, Margaret J 1918- *ConAu 22NR, IntAu&W 91, SmATA 8AS, TwCChW 89, WrDr 86, –88, –90, –92*

Baker, Margaret Joyce 1918- *AuBYP 2 –3, Au&Wr 71, BioIn 6, –7, –11, ConAu 13R, –7NR, IntAu&W 77, –82, MorJA, SmATA 12, TwCChW 78, –83, WrDr 76, –80, –82, –84, –94*

Baker, Mary 1897- *BioIn 1, –2, –5, –14, ConICB, DcWomA, IlsCB 1744, –1946, JBA 34, –51*

Baker, Mary Elizabeth 1923- *AuBYP 3*

Baker, Mary Elizabeth Gillette 1923- *BioIn 10, SmATA 7*

Pseud./variant:
Baker, Elizabeth

Baker, Mary Gladys Steel 1892-1974 *BioIn 11, ConAu P-1, SmATA 12*
Pseud./variant:
Stuart, Sheila

Baker, Michael 1938- *BioIn 9, ConAu 25R, SmATA 4, WrDr 76, –80, –82, –84, –86, –88, –90*

Baker, Nina Brown 1888-1957 *AmAu&B, AuBYP 2, –3, BioIn 1, –2, –4, –7, CurBio 47, –57, JBA 51, ScF&FL 92, SmATA 15*

Baker, Olaf *BioIn 2, JBA 34, –51*

Baker, Olaf 187-?- *ConAu 129*

Baker, Pamela J 1947- *BioIn 17, ConAu 127, SmATA 66*

Baker, Rachel 1904-1978 *AuBYP 2, BioIn 6, –7, –9, –13, BkCL, ConAu 5R, –103, MorJA, SmATA 2, –26N*

Baker, Rachel Mininberg 1904-1978 *AuBYP 3*

Baker, Ray Stannard 1870-1946 *AmAu&B, AmLY, AmPeW, BenetAL 91, BiDAmJo, BiDInt, BioIn 1, –2, –3, –4, –5, –6, –7, –8, –12, –15, –16, –17, CarSB, ChhPo S2, ConAmL, ConAu 118, CurBio 40, –46, DcAmAu, DcAmSR, DcLEL, DcNAA, EncAB-H, EvLB, JrnUS, LongCTC, McGEWB, MichAu 80, ObitOF 79, OxCAmH, OxCAmL 65, –83, REn, REnAL, TwCA, –SUP, TwCLC 47, TwCWr, WebAB 74, –79, WhAm 2, WhNAA, WisWr*
Pseud./variant:
Grayson, David

Baker, Richard St Barbe 1889-1982 *AnObit 1982, Au&Wr 71, BioIn 9, –13, –14, –15, BlueB 76, ConAu 110, –P-1, IntAu&W 77, –82, IntWW 74, Who 74, –82, –83N, WhoWor 74*

Baker, Robert H 1883- *WhNAA*

Baker, Samm Sinclair *BioIn 15*

Baker, Samm Sinclair 1909- *BioIn 11, ConAu 5R, –3NR, –21NR, IntAu&W 77, –86, –89, SmATA 12, WhoUSWr 88, WhoWrEP 89, –92*

Baker, Samuel White 1821-1893 *BioIn 17, DcAfHiB 86, Expl 93, WorAlBi*

Baker, Samuel White, Sir 1821-1893 *Alli SUP, BbD, BiD&SB, BioIn 2, –3, –4, –5, –6, –9, –12, BritAu 19, CelCen, Chambr 3, DcBiPP, DcBrBI, DcEnL, DcNaB S1, EvLB, McGEWB, NewC, OxCEng 67, –85, WhDW, WorAl*

Baker, Sarah Schoonmaker 1824-1906 *Alli SUP, CarSB, ChhPo, DcAmAu, DcNAA, WhAm 1*

Baker, Susan 1942- *BioIn 13, ConAu 105, SmATA 29*
Pseud./variant:
Richards, Kay

Baker, William C 1891- *AuBYP 2, –3, BioIn 8, WhAm 9*

Baker, William Howard *ConAu X, –28NR*

Baker, William Hudson 1911- *AmMWSc 76P, WhoAm 74, –76, –78, –80*

Balaam *BioIn 17, ConAu X, IntAu&W 91X, LongCEL, SmATA X, WrDr 76, –80, –82, –84, –86, –88, –90, –92, –94*
Main entry: Lamb, Geoffrey Frederick

Balch, Glenn 1902- *AmAu&B, AuBYP 2, –3, BioIn 6, –7, –9, ConAu 1R, –3NR, MorJA, SmATA 3, WhoAm 74, –76, –78, –80, –82, –84, –86, –88, WhoPNW, WhoUSWr 88, WhoWest 74, –76, –78, WhoWrEP 89, –92*

Balch, Glenn 1902-1989 *SmATA 11AS*

Balderson, Margaret *IntAu&W 91, WrDr 86, –88*

Balderson, Margaret 1915- *DcChlFi*

Balderson, Margaret 1935- *AuWomWr, ConAu 25R, FourBJA, OxCAusL, TwCChW 78, –83, –89, WrDr 80, –82, –84, –90, –92, –94*

Baldridge, Cyrus LeRoy 1889-1975 *AfroAA, ArtsAmW 2, BioIn 1, –3, –5, –13, IlsBYP, IlsCB 1744, –1946, SmATA 29, WhAmArt 85, WhNAA*

Baldry, Cherith 1947- *SmATA 72*

Balducci, Carolyn *DrAPF 87, –89, –91, –93*

Balducci, Carolyn 1946- *AuBYP 3*

Balducci, Carolyn Feleppa 1946- *AuBYP 2S, BioIn 10, ConAu 33R, SmATA 5, WhoAmW 81, –83*

Baldwin, Anne 1938- *AuBYP 3*

Baldwin, Anne Norris 1938- *AuBYP 2S, BioIn 10, ConAu 29R, IntAu&W 89, –91, SmATA 5, WhoAmW 74, –75, WrDr 76, –80, –82, –84, –86, –88, –90, –92, –94*

Baldwin, Arthur H *AuBYP 2, –3*

Baldwin, Bates *AuBYP 3*

Baldwin, Clara *BioIn 11, ConAu 61, ForWC 70, SmATA 11*

Baldwin, Gordo *AuBYP 3, IntAu&W 91X, TwCWW 91*
Main entry: Baldwin, Gordon C

Baldwin, Gordon 1908- *WrDr 94*

Baldwin, Gordon C 1908- *AuBYP 2S, –3, BioIn 11, ConAu 1R, –3NR, IntAu&W 91, SmATA 12, TwCWW 91, WrDr 84, –86, –88, –90, –92*
Pseud./variant:
Baldwin, Gordo
Gordon, Lew

Baldwin, James *DrAPF 87, IntvTCA 2*

Baldwin, James 1841-1925 *Alli SUP, AmAu&B, AmLY, AnCL, AuBYP 2, –3, BioIn 2, –7, –13, CarSB, ChhPo, ConAu 111, DcNAA, HarEnUS, IndAu 1816, JBA 34, –51, OxCChiL, REnAL, SmATA 24, WhAm 1*

Baldwin, James 1924- *AmAu&B, AmWr S1, BioIn 3, –5, –6, –7, –8, –9, –10, –11, –14, BlkAWP, BlueB 76, CamGEL, CamHAL, CasWL, CelR, CivR 74, ConAu 1R, –1BS, –3NR, ConDr 73, –77, –82, ConLC 1, –2, –3, –4, –5, –8, –13, –15, –17, –42, ConNov 72, –76, –82, –86, ConTFT 3, CroCD, CurBio 59, –64, DcLB 2, –7, –33, DrAF 76, EncAB-H, EncAJ, EncWL, –2, EncWT, IntAu&W 77, IntWW 74, LivgBAA, LongCTC, McGEWD 72, –84, ModAL, –S1, –S2, ModBlW, ModWD, NatPD 81, NegAl 76, –83, NewCon, NewYTBE 72, NotNAT, –A, Novels, OxCAmL 65, –83, OxCEng 85, PenC AM, RAdv 1, –13-1, REn, REnAL, RfGAmL 87, SelBAAf, SelBAAu, SmATA 9, TwCWr, WebAB 74, –79, WebE&AL, WhDW, Who 74, –82, –83, –85, –88, WhoAm 74, –76, –78, –80, –82, –84, –86, WhoBlA 75, –77, –80, –85, –88, WhoE 74, –75, WhoTwCL, WhoUSWr 88, WhoWor 74, –78, WorAl, WorAu 1950, WrDr 76, –80, –82, –84, –86, –88*
Pseud./variant:
Dudley, Robert

Baldwin, James 1924-1987 *AfrAmAl 6, AfrAmW, AnObit 1987, Au&Arts 4, Benet 87, BenetAL 91, BioIn 15, –16, –17, BlkLC, BlkWr 1, CamGLE, ConAu 124, –24NR, ConBlB 1, ConDr 88, ConGAN, ConLC 50, –67, CurBio 88N, CyWA 89, DcLB Y87N, DrBlPA 90, DramC 1, EncAACR, LiExTwC, MagSAmL, MajTwCW, NegAl 89, NewYTBS 87, News 88-2, RComAH, ShSCr 10, SmATA 54N, WhAm 9, WhoBlA 90N, WorAlBi, WorLitC*

Baldwin, James 1925-1987 *ConBlAP 88*

Baldwin, James Arthur 1924-1987 *ConDr 93, GayLL, TwCYAW*

Baldwin, Margaret *ConAu X, –34NR, SmATA X*
Main entry: Weis, Margaret

Baldwin, Stan 1929- *BioIn 13, ConAu 2NR, –17NR, SmATA 28, –62*

Baldwin, Stanley C 1929- *ConAu 38NR*

Baldwin-Ford, Pamela *IlsBYP*

Bales, Carol Ann 1940- *BioIn 13, ConAu 45, SmATA 29, –57*

Balet, Jan Bernard 1913- *AuBYP 2, –3, BioIn 1, –2, –3, –5, –7, –9, –11, ConAu 85, IlsCB 1946, –1967, SmATA 11, ThrBJA*

Balian, Lorna 1929- *AuBYP 2S, –3, BioIn 11, ChhPo, ConAu 53, –4NR, –19NR, –40NR, FifBJA, IntAu&W 91, SmATA 9, WrDr 76, –80, –82, –84, –86, –88, –90, –92, –94*

Ball, Brian N 1932- *ConAu 33R, ConSFA, EncSF 93, IntAu&W 91, ScFSB, TwCSFW 86, WrDr 88, –90*
Pseud./variant:
Kinsey-Jones, Brian

Ball, Duncan 1941- *SmATA 73*

Ball, John 1911- *AuBYP 3, CrtSuMy, IntAu&W 89, –91, WrDr 86, –88*

Ball, John 1911-1988 *AnObit 1988, ConAu 126, NewYTBS 88, ScF&FL 92, TwCCr&M 91*

Ball, John Dudley 1911- *BioIn 14, WorAlBi*

Ball, John Dudley 1911-1988 *BioIn 16*

Ball, John Dudley, Jr. 1911- *AmAu&B, AuBYP 2, Au&Wr 71, BlueB 76, ConAu 5R, ConSFA, EncMys, IntAu&W 77, –82 –86, WhoAm 74, –76, –78, –80, –82, –84, –86, –88, WhoWest 74, –76, –78, WhoWor 80, –82, –89, WorAl, WrDr 76, –80*

Ball, John Dudley, Jr. 1911-1988 *EncSF 93, WhAm 9*

Ball, Robert 1918- *BioIn 5, DcBrAr 1, IlsBYP, IlsCB 1946, TwCPaSc, WhoArt 80, –82, –84*

Ball, Walter William Rouse 1850?-1925 *Alli SUP*

Ball, Zachary *AuBYP 2, –3, BioIn 3, –7, –9, ConAu X, CurBio 53, FourBJA, SmATA 3*
Main entry: Masters, Kelly Ray

Ball, Zachary 1897- *DcAmChF 1960*

Ballantine, Bill Oliver 1921- *AmPB, WhoE 74*

Ballantine, Lesley Frost
Main entry: Frost, Lesley

Ballantine, Lesley Frost d1983 *BioIn 14*

Ballantine, Lesley Frost 1899?-1983 *ConAu X, NewYTBS 83, SmATA X*

Ballantine, William Gay 1848-1937 *AmAu&B, ChhPo, –S1, DcAmAu, DcNAA, OhA&B, WhAm 1, WhNAA*

Ballantyne, Lereine 1891- *WhNAA*

Ballantyne, R M 1825-1894 *CamGEL, CamGLE, CmScLit, RfGEnL 91, StaCVF, TwCChW 89A*

Ballantyne, Robert Michael 1825-1894 *Alli SUP, BbD, BbtC, BiD&SB, BioIn 3, –7, –8, –12, –13, BritAu 19, CarSB, CasWL, Chambr 3, ChhPo, –S1, DcCanB 12, DcEnL, DcLEL, DcNaB S1, EncSoA, EvLB, NewC, Novels, OxCCan, OxCCanL, OxCChiL, OxCEng 67, –85, PenC ENG, SmATA 24, TelT, TwCChW 78A, –83A, WhoChL*
Pseud./variant:
Comus

Ballard, Lowell C 1904-1986 *ConAu 120*

Ballard, Lowell Clyne 1904- *BioIn 11, ConAu P-1, SmATA 12*

Ballard, Lowell Clyne 1904-1986 *SmATA 49N*

Ballard, Lowell Clyne 1904-1988 *BioIn 16*

Ballard, Martin 1929- *Au&Wr 71, BioIn 9, ConAu 25R, SmATA 1, TwCChW 78, –83, WrDr 80, –82, –84, –86, –88, –90*

Ballard, Mignon Franklin 1934- *BioIn 16, –17, ConAu 121, SmATA 49, –64*

Ballinger, William A *ConAu X*

Ballou, Arthur W 1915- *ConAu 25R*

Ballou, Arthur W 1915-1981 *ConAu 134, ScF&FL 92*

Balmer, Edwin 1883-1959 *AmAu&B, BioIn 14, ConAu 114, EncMys, EncSF 93, NewEScF, ObitOF 79, REnAL, ScFEYrs, TwCCr&M 80, –85, –91, WhAm 3, WhNAA*

Balogh, Penelope 1916- *WrDr 86, –88*

Balogh, Penelope 1916-1975 *Au&Wr 71, BioIn 9, –14, ConAu P-2, SmATA 1, –34N, WrDr 76, –80, –82, –84*
Pseud./variant:
Fox, Petronella

Balow, Tom 1931- *BioIn 11, ConAu 45, SmATA 12*

Balterman, Marcia Ridlon 1942- *ConAu 25R*
Pseud./variant:
Ridlon, Marci 1942-

Baltimore, J *ConAu 38NR, MajAI, SmATA 74*
Main entry: Catherall, Arthur

Baltzer, Hans 1900- *BioIn 8, –15, IlsBYP, IlsCB 1957, SmATA 40*

Bambara, Toni Cade *ArtclWW 2, BioIn 14, –17, BlkWWr, DrAPF 87, –89, –91, –93, InWom SUP*

Bambara, Toni Cade 1931- *FemiCLE*

Bambara, Toni Cade 1939- *AmWomWr 92, Au&Arts 5, BenetAL 91, BioIn 13, BlkAWP, BlkLC, BlkWWr, BlkWr 1, BlmGWL, ConAu 29R, –24NR, ConLC 19, DcLB 38, DrAPF 83, –85, InB&W 80, –85, LivgBAA, MajTwCW, RfGShF, SelBAAf, SelBAAu, WhoBlA 75, –77, –80, –85, –88, –90, –92, WorAu 1975*
Pseud./variant:
Cade, Toni

Bamfylde, Walter *BioIn 12, YABC X*
Main entry: Bevan, Tom

Bamman, Henry A 1918- *BioIn 11, ConAu 5R, –7NR, LEduc 74, SmATA 12*

Banat, D R *SmATA X*
Main entry: Bradbury, Ray

Bancroft, Griffing 1907- *AuBYP 2, –3, AuNews 1, BioIn 10, ConAu 29R, SmATA 6*

Bancroft, Jessie Hubbell 1867-1952 *BioIn 3, –5, –12, ChhPo S2, InWom SUP, NotAW MOD, ObitOF 79, WhAm 4, WhNAA, WomWWA 14*

Bancroft, Laura *ConAu 133, –X, EncSF 93, MajAI, MajTwCW, SmATA X, ThrBJA*
Main entry: Baum, Lyman Frank

Bandel, Betty 1912- *BioIn 16, ConAu 106, DrAS 74E, –78E, –82E, SmATA 47*

Banel, Joseph 1943- *ConAu 45*

Baner, Skulda Vanadis 1897-1964 *BioIn 11, ConAu P-1, SmATA 10*

Banet, Doris Beatrice Robinson 1925- *BioIn 11, MinnWr*

Banfield, Alexander William Francis 1918- *AmMWSc 73P, –82, –86, –89, –92, BlueB 76, CanWW 70, –80, –81, –83, –89, ConAu 61, WhoCan 82, WrDr 80*

Bang, Betsy 1912- *SmATA 48*

Bang, Betsy Garrett 1912- *ConAu 102, FifBJA, SmATA 37*

Bang, Garrett *ConAu X, SmATA X*
Main entry: Bang, Molly Garrett

Bang, Molly 1943- *SmATA 69*

Bang, Molly Garrett 1943- *AuBYP 3, BioIn 13, ChlLR 8, ConAu 102, FifBJA, MajAI, SmATA 24*
Pseud./variant:
Bang, Garrett

Bangert, Ethel Elizabeth 1912- *ConAu 45, –1NR, IntAu&W 82*

Bangham, Mary Dickerson 1896- *ChhPo, ConAu P-2*

Bangs, Edward 1756-1818 *ChhPo*

Bangs, John Kendrick 1862-1922 *AmAu&B, BenetAL 91, BbD, BiD&SB, BioIn 4, –6, –15, CarSB, ChhPo, –S1, –S2, ConAu 110, DcAmAu, DcLB 11, –79, DcLEL, DcNAA, EncAHmr, EncAJ, EncMys, EncSF 93, NotNAT B, OxCAmL 65, –83, REnAL, Str&VC, TwCA, –SUP, WhAm 1, WhoHr&F*

Bangs, Robert B 1914- *WrDr 86, –88, –90*

Bangs, Robert Babbitt 1914- *AmMWSc 73S, ConAu 37R, WhoGov 72, –75, WrDr 76, –80, –82, –84*
Pseud./variant:
Babbitt, Robert

Banister, Manly 1914- *ConAu 41R*

Banister, Manly 1914-1986 *ScF&FL 92*

Banister, Manly Miles 1914- *EncSF 93*

Bank-Jensen, Thea *ConAu X, IntAu&W 77*
Main entry: Ottesen, Thea Tauber

Banks, Laura Stockton Voorhees 1908?-1980 *BioIn 13, ConAu 101, SmATA 23N*

Banks, Lynne Reid *BlmGWL, ScF&FL 92, SixBJA*

Banks, Lynne Reid 1929- *AuBYP 3, BioIn 13, –16, –17, ChlFicS, ConLC 23, ConNov 72, –76, –86, –91, DcLEL 1940, InWom SUP, IntAu&W 82, –86, –89, –91, Novels, OxCChiL, TwCChW 83, –89, TwCWr, Who 88, –90, –92*
Main entry: Reid Banks, Lynne

Banks, Sara 1937- *BioIn 13, SmATA 26*
Pseud./variant:
Harrell, Sara Gordon

Banner, Angela
Main entry: Maddison, Angela Mary

Banner, Angela 1923- *BioIn 11, ChlLR 24, ConAu X, IntAu&W 77X, –91, OxCChiL, SmATA X, TwCChW 78, –83, –89, WrDr 76, –80, –82, –84, –86, –88, –90, –92, –94*

Banner, Rachel *SmATA X*
Main entry: Roddy, Lee

Bannerman, Helen 1862?-1946 *ArtclWW 2, BioIn 14, –16, ChlLR 21, CmScLit, FemiCLE, TwCChW 89*

Bannerman, Helen 1863-1946 *InWom SUP*

Bannerman, Helen Brodie Cowan 1862?-1946 *BioIn 1, –2, –8, –12, CarSB, ConAu 111, IlsCB 1744, JBA 51, ObitOF 79, OxCChiL, OxCEng 85, SmATA 19, TelT, TwCChW 78, –83, WhoChL*

Bannerman, Helen Brodie Cowan Watson 1862?-1946 *ConAu 136, MajAI*

Banning, Evelyn Irene 1903- *ConAu 73, SmATA 36, WrDr 76, –80, –82, –84, –86*

Bannister, Pat *AuBYP 3*

Bannon, Laura May d1963 *AuBYP 2, –3, BioIn 1, –2, –5, –6, –7, –8, –10, ConAu 1R, IlsCB 1744, –1946, –1957, MorJA, SmATA 6*

Bapu *ConAu X*
Main entry: Khare, Narayan Bhaskar

Baraka, Imamu Amiri *ConTFT 7, IntvTCA 2, WrDr 86, –88, –90, –92*
Main entry: Jones, LeRoi

Baraka, Imamu Amiri 1934- *Benet 87, BiDAfM, BioIn 14, –15, –16, –17, BlkAWP, BroadAu, CelR, CivR 74, ConAu X, ConDr 73, –77, ConLC 1, –2, –3, –5, –10, ConNov 72, –76, ConPo 75, CroCAP, CurBio 70, DcLEL 1940, DrAP 75, EncWL, –SUP, EncWT, InB&W 80, –85, IntAu&W 77X, LivgBAA, McGEWB, McGEWD 72, –84, NatPD 81, NegAl 76, –83, –89, NewYTBE 72, NotNAT, Novels, OxCAmL 83, RAdv 13-1, –13-2, SelBAAf, SelBAAu, WebAB 74, –79, WhoAm 76, –78, –84, WhoBlA 75, –77, –80, –85, –88, –90, –92, WhoE 74, WhoThe 77, –81, WorAlBi, WorAu 1950, WrDr 76, –80, –82, –84, –94*

Barasch, Lynne 1939- *SmATA 74*

Barbalet, Margaret 1949- *AuWomWr, SmATA 77*

Barbalet, Margaret Evelyn Hardy 1949- *IntAu&W 89*

Barbary, James *ConAu X, EncSF 93, SmATA X*
Main entry: Baumann, Amy Brown Beeching
Beeching, Jack

Barbauld, Anna Laetitia 1743-1824 *BlmGEL*

Barbauld, Anna Laetitia 1743-1825 *CamGEL, CamGLE, DcBrAmW, DcLB 107, –109, EncBrWW, FemiCLE, InWom SUP*

Barbauld, Anna Laetitia Aikin 1743-1824 *BioIn 2, –3, –5, –10, –11, CelCen, DcBiPP, DcNaB, DcWomA, IntDcWB, OxCChiL, OxCEng 85*

Barbauld, Anna Laetitia Aikin 1743-1825 *BlmGWL*

Barbauld, Anna Letitia Aikin 1743-1825 *BioIn 16, –17, ContDcW 89*

Barbe, Walter Burke 1926- *BioIn 15, ConAu 13R, LEduc 74, SmATA 45, WhoAm 74, –76, –78, –80, –82, –84, –86, –88, –90, –92, –94, WhoWor 78, –80, –82, –84, –87, –89, –91*

Barbeau, Marius 1883-1969 *Baker 84, –92, BioIn 2, –5, –8, –17, CanWr, ConAu 25R, CreCan 2, DcLB 92, ObitOF 79, OxCCan, OxCCanL, WhNAA*

Barber, Antonia *ConAu X, IntAu&W 77X, SmATA X*
Main entry: Anthony, Barbara

Barber, D F 1940- *ConAu 61, –21NR*
Pseud./variant:
Fletcher, David

Barber, Elsie Oakes 1914- *AmAu&B, AmNov, BioIn 2*

Barber, Linda *SmATA X*

Barber, Richard 1941- *ConAu 33R, –13NR, –32NR, ScF&FL 92, SmATA 35, WhoOcn 78, WrDr 80, –82, –84, –86, –88, –90, –92*

Barber, Richard William 1941- *WrDr 94*

Barbera, Joe
Main entry: Barbera, Joseph R

Barbera, Joseph R *IntMPA 86, –88*

Barbera, Joseph R 1911- *IntMPA 92, SmATA 51*
Pseud./variant:
Barbera, Joe

Barberis, Franco 1905- *ConAu 25R*

Barberis, Juan Carlos 1920- *SmATA 61*
Pseud./variant:
Kumpa
My

Barbour, John Anderson 1915- *WhoRel 75, –77*

Barbour, Karen 1956- *ConAu 127, SmATA 63*

Barbour, Ralph Henry 1870-1944 *AmAu&B, AuBYP 2, –3, BenetAL 91, BioIn 1, –2, –7, –12, –14, CarSB, ChhPo, CurBio 44, DcAmAu, DcLB 22, DcNAA, JBA 34, –51, ObitOF 79, OxCChiL, REnAL, SmATA 16, WhAm 2*
Pseud./variant:
Powell, Richard Stillman

Barclay, Barbara 1938- *ConAu 29R, WhoAmW 77*

Barclay, Isabel *Au&Wr 71, ConAu X, SmATA X*
Main entry: Dobell, Isabel Marian Barclay

Barclay, William 1907-1978 *Au&Wr 71, BioIn 11, –14, BlueB 76, ConAu 73, –77, –29NR, Who 74*

Barclay, William Ewert *ConAu 38NR*

Bard, Bernard 1927- *ConAu 25R, WhoE 83, –85, –86, –91*

Bardi, Pietro Maria 1900- *ConAu 85, –19NR, –42NR, WhoWor 74, –78, –80, –82, –84*

Bardill, Donald Ray 1934- *WhoAm 90, –92, WhoE 75, –77, WhoSSW 80, –84*

Bard Of Avondale *ConAu X*
Main entry: Jacobs, Howard

Bare, Arnold Edwin 1920- *BioIn 1, –5, –12, –14, IlsBYP, IlsCB 1744, –1946, SmATA 16, WhAmArt 85*

Bare, Colleen Stanley *ConAu 102, SmATA 32*

Barenholtz, Bernard 1914-1989 *SmATA 64*

Barenholtz, Bernard M *WhoE 86*

Barenholtz, Bernard M d1989 *BioIn 16*

Barenholtz, Bernard M 1914-1989 *BioIn 17*

Barfoot, Audrey Ilma 1918-1964 *ConAu 5R*

Bargar, Gary W 1947-1985 *SmATA 63*

Barham, Richard Harris 1788-1845 *Alli, BbD, BiD&SB, BioIn 4, –8, –12, BritAu 19, CamGEL, CarSB, CasWL, CelCen, Chambr 3, ChhPo, –S1, –S2, DcBiPP, DcEnA, DcEnL,*

DcEuL, DcLEL, DcNaB, EvLB, NewC, OxCEng 67, RfGEnL 91, WhoHr&F

Baring-Gould, Sabine 1834-1924? *BbD, BiD&SB, BioIn 4, –8, –9, –11, –12, BritAu 19, CamGLE, CarSB, CathA 1952, CelCen, Chambr 3, ChhPo, –S1, DcBiA, DcBiPP, DcEnA, –A, DcEnL, DcLEL, DcNaB 1922, EvLB, LongCTC, LuthC 75, NewC, Novels, OxCChiL, OxCEng 67, –85, OxCMus, PenC ENG, RfGEnL 91, WebE&AL*

Barish, Matthew 1907- *AuBYP 2S, –3, BioIn 11, ConAu 57, SmATA 12*

Barkan, Joanne *SmATA 77*
Pseud./variant:
Wright, J B

Barker, Albert W 1900- *BioIn 11, ConAu 73, –14NR, SmATA 8*
Pseud./variant:
King, Reefe
Macrae, Hawk

Barker, Arthur James 1918- *ConAu 13R, Who 74, WhoWor 80*

Barker, Carol Minturn 1938- *ArtsCL, BioIn 6, –8, ChhPo S1, ConAu 107, IlsBYP, IlsCB 1957, –1967, SmATA 31*

Barker, Cicely Mary 1895-1973 *BioIn 14, –15, –16, ChhPo, –S1, –S2, ClaDrA, ConAu 117, –121, DcBrAr 1, DcWomA, OxCChiL, SmATA 39, –49, TwCChW 83, –89*

Barker, Elsa M 1906- *Au&Wr 71, ConAu P-2, WrDr 76, –80*

Barker, Melvern J 1907- *BioIn 5, –11, ConAu P-1, IlsCB 1946, SmATA 11*

Barker, S Omar 1894- *BioIn 11, ConAu P-2, EncFWF, IntAu&W 77, IntWWP 82, SmATA 10, WhNAA, WrDr 76, –80, –82, –84, –86, –88, –90*
Pseud./variant:
Canusi, Jose
Scott, Dan
Squires, Phil

Barker, S Omar 1894-1985 *TwCWW 91*

Barker, Shirley Frances 1911-1965 *AmAu&B, BioIn 2, –4, –7, ChhPo, –S1, TwCA SUP*

Barker, Will 1913-1983 *AuBYP 2, –3, Au&Wr 71, BioIn 8, –11, ConAu 9R, –110, SmATA 8*
Pseud./variant:
Demarest, Doug

Barkhouse, Joyce 1913- *BioIn 13, CaW, ConAu 93, Profile 2, SmATA 48, WhoCanL 85, –87, –92*

Barkhouse, Joyce C 1913- *BioIn 16*

Barkin, Carol *AuBYP 3, ConAu 118, SmATA 42*

Barkin, Carol 1944- *BioIn 16, ConAu 135, SmATA 52, WrDr 90, –92, –94*
Pseud./variant:
Carroll, Elizabeth
Hastings, Beverly

Barklem, Jill 1951- *ChlLR 31*

Barkley, James Edward 1941- *BioIn 10, –12, IlsBYP, IlsCB 1967, SmATA 6*

Barks, Carl 1901- *ConAu 115, EncACom, SmATA 37*

Barksdale, Lena *AmAu&B, AuBYP 2, –3, BioIn 8*

Barlow, Genevieve 1910- *AuBYP 2S, –3, ConAu 21R*

Barlow, Roger *AuBYP 3, ConAu X*
Main entry: Leckie, Robert

Barnaby, Ralph S d1986 *NewYTBS 86*

Barnaby, Ralph S 1893-1986 *BioIn 14, –15*

Barnaby, Ralph Stanton 1893- *AuBYP 2S, –3, BioIn 11, ConAu 61, InSci, SmATA 9*

Barnard, A M *MajAI*

Barnard, C D 1895-1971 *ObitT 1971*

Barnard, Frederick 1846-1896 *DcVicP 2*

Barnard, Frederick 1847?-1896 *BioIn 4, ChhPo S1, ClaDrA, DcBiPP, DcBrBI, DcNaB S1, DcVicP 2*

Barnard, Peggy *SingR 1*

Barnardo, Thomas John 1845-1905 *BioIn 3, –4, –6, –7, –8, –9, –10, –12, –16, –17, DcIrB 88, DcNaB S2, LuthC 75, OxCChiL*

Barne, Kitty 1883- *AmWomPl*

Barne, Kitty 1883-1957 *AuBYP 2S, –3, BioIn 2, –8, ConAu X, JBA 51, OxCChiL, TwCChW 78, –83, –89, WhoChL*

Barne, Marion Catherine *AuBYP 3*

Barner, Bob 1947- *BioIn 13, ConAu 93, SmATA 29*

Barnes, Catherine J 1918- *BioIn 3, –5, ChhPo, IlsBYP, IlsCB 1946, WhAmArt 85*

Barnes, Eric Wollencott 1907- *AuBYP 3*

Barnes, Eric Wollencott 1907-1962 *AmAu&B, AuBYP 2, BioIn 6, -8, -13, SmATA 22, WhAm 4*

Barnes, Gregory Allen 1934- *ConAu 25R, -10NR, -25NR*

Barnes, Leola Christie 1889- *TexWr*

Barnes, Malcolm 1909?-1984 *BioIn 15, ConAu 114, SmATA 41N*

Barnes, Michael 1934- *SmATA 55*
Pseud./variant:
Wesley, Alison

Barnes, Mildred Jane *WhoAmW 75*

Barness, Richard 1917- *ConAu 65*

Barnes-Svarney, Patricia L 1953- *ConAu 135, SmATA 67*

Barnes-Svarney, Patricia Lou 1953- *WrDr 94*

Barnett, Dick 1936- *BioIn 7*

Barnett, Isa 1924- *BioIn 2, IlrAm 1880, -F, WhAmArt 85*

Barnett, Ivan 1947- *SmATA 70*

Barnett, L David *AuBYP 3*

Barnett, Leo 1925- *AuBYP 2S, -3, ConAu 29R*

Barnett, Lincoln Kinnear 1909-1979 *AmAu&B, BioIn 10, -12, -14, ConAu 102, SmATA 36, WhAm 7, WorAu 1950*

Barnett, Moneta 1922?-1976 *BioIn 11, -12, -14, -16, BlkAuII, -92, IlsBYP, IlsCB 1967, SmATA 33*

Barnett, Naomi 1927- *ConAu 7NR, SmATA 40*
Pseud./variant:
Buchheimer, Naomi Barnett

Barney, Maginel Wright 1881-1966 *BioIn 1, -7, -14, -15, ConAu 111, IlrAm 1880, -C, IlsCB 1744, SmATA 32, -39, WhAmArt 85*
Pseud./variant:
Enright, Maginel Wright

Barnhart, Clarence L 1900- *SmATA 48, WorAlBi*

Barnhart, Clarence Lewis d1993 *NewYTBS 93*

Barnhart, Clarence Lewis 1900- *AmAu&B, BioIn 2, -3, -11, -14, -16, BlueB 76, ConAu 13R, CurBio 54, DrAS 74F, WhoAm 74, -76, -78, -80, -82, -84, -86, -88, -90, -92, -94, WhoUSWr 88, WhoWor 74, WhoWrEP 89, -92, WorAl*

Barnhart, Nancy 1889- *BioIn 1, -2, -5, ChhPo, IlsBYP, IlsCB 1744, -1946*

Barnouw, Adriaan Jacob 1877-1968 *ArtsAmW 2, AuBYP 2, -3, BioIn 1, -7, -13, ChhPo S1, ConAu 104, SmATA 27N, WhAm 5, WhAmArt 85, WhNAA*

Barnouw, Victor 1915- *AmMWSc 73S, -76P, BioIn 13, -15, ConAu 85, FifIDA, SmATA 28, -43, WhoAm 74*

Barnouw, Victor 1915-1989 *BioIn 17*

Barnstone, Aliki *DrAPF 87, -89, -91, -93*

Barnstone, Aliki 1956- *ChhPo S1, ConAu 105, DrAPF 83, -85*

Barnstone, Willis *DrAPF 87, -89, -91, -93*

Barnstone, Willis 1927- *BioIn 12, ConAu 17R, -15AS, DrAP 75, DrAPF 83, -85, DrAS 74F, -78F, -82F, IntAu&W 86, IntWWP 82, SmATA 20, WhoAm 78, -80, -82, -84, -86, -88, -90, -92, -94, WhoUSWr 88, WhoWrEP 89, -92*

Barnum, Jay Hyde d1962 *BioIn 14*

Barnum, Jay Hyde 1888?-1962 *AuBYP 2, -3, BioIn 5, -6, -7, -12, IlsCB 1946, SmATA 20*

Barnum, P T, Jr. *MajAI*

Barnum, Richard *ConAu 26NR, -P-2, SmATA 1, -67*
Main entry: Stratemeyer, Edward L

Barnum, Theodore *MajAI*

Barnwell, D Robinson 1915- *AuBYP 2S, -3, ConAu 17R, DcAmChF 1960*

Baron, Nancy *AuBYP 3*

Baron, Virginia Olsen 1931- *AuBYP 2S, -3, BioIn 13, -15, ConAu 25R, SmATA 28, -46*

Baron-Hall, Daria *AuBYP 3*

Barr, Donald 1921- *AuBYP 2S, -3, BioIn 9, -12, ConAu 9R, EncSF 93, ScF&FL 92, ScFSB, SmATA 20, WhoAm 74*

Barr, George 1907- *AmAu&B, AuBYP 2, -3, BioIn 8, -9, ConAu 1R, -1NR, SmATA 2*

Barr, Jene *ConAu 42NR*

Barr, Jene 1900-1985 *AmAu&B, AuBYP 2, -3, BioIn 2, -7, -12, -15, ConAu 5R, -X, -3NR, SmATA 42N, WhoAmW 74, -75*
Pseud./variant:
Cohen, Jene Barr

WhoAm 74, –76, –78, –80, –82, WhoAmW 74, –75

Barry, Dan 1923- *ArtCS, EncACom*

Barry, James E *IlsBYP*

Barry, James P 1918- *ConAu 24NR, IntAu&W 86, –89, –91, WhoMW 86, –88, –90, WrDr 86, –88, –90, –92, –94*

Barry, James Potvin 1918- *BioIn 12, ConAu 37R, IntAu&W 77, –82, SmATA 14, WhoAm 94, WhoMW 76, –78, –80, –82, –84, –86, –92, –93, WhoWor 91, –93, WrDr 76, –80, –82, –84*

Barry, Joseph Amber 1917- *ConAu 57, IntAu&W 86, WhoWor 91, –93*

Barry, Katharina Watjen 1936- *AuBYP 2, BioIn 7, –8, –9, ChhPo, ConAu 9R, IlsCB 1957, SmATA 4*

Barry, Katharina Watzen 1936- *AuBYP 3*

Barry, Lucy 1934- *ConAu 17R, ForWC 70*

Barry, Margaret Stuart 1927- *ChlFicS, ConAu 106, –25NR, IntAu&W 91, OxCChiL, TwCChW 83, –89, WrDr 86, –88, –90, –92, –94*

Barry, Robert E 1931- *WhoAmA 86, –89, –91*

Barry, Robert Everett 1931- *AuBYP 2, –3, BioIn 7, –8, –10, ConAu 5R, IlsCB 1957, IntAu&W 77, –82, SmATA 6, WhoAmA 78, –80, –82, –84, WhoE 91, WrDr 76, –80, –82, –84, –86, –88, –90, –92, –94*

Barry, Scott 1952- *BioIn 14, SmATA 32*

Barry, Seymour *EncACom*

Barry, Seymour 1928- *ArtCS, WhoAm 80, –82, –84, –86, –88, –90*

Barsis, Max 1894?-1973 *BioIn 10, ConAu 41R*

Barss, William 1916- *BioIn 8, ChhPo S1, IlsBYP, IlsCB 1957*

Bartel, Pauline C 1952- *WhoUSWr 88, WhoWrEP 89, –92*

Bartel, Pauline Christine 1952- *ConAu 81, IntAu&W 89*

Bartenbach, Jean 1918- *ConAu 115, SmATA 40*

Barth, Edna 1914-1980 *AuBYP 2S, –3, BioIn 10, –12, –13, ConAu 41R, –102, –27NR, ForWC 70, SmATA 7, –24N, WhoAm 74, WhoAmW 77*
Pseud./variant:
Weiss, Edna

Barthelme, Donald *DrAPF 87, –89, IntvTCA 2, ScFSB*

Barthelme, Donald 1931- *AmAu&B, AuBYP 2S, Benet 87, BioIn 9, –10, –11, –12, –13, BlueB 76, CamGLE, CamHAL, CelR, –90, ConAu 21R, –20NR, ConLC 1, –2, –3, –5, –6, –8, –13, –23, –46, ConNov 72, –76, –82, –86, CurBio 76, DcLB 2, –Y80A, DcLEL 1940, DrAF 76, DrAPF 83, –85, EncAHmr, EncWL 2, IntAu&W 77, ModAL S1, –S2, Novels, OxCAmL 83, PenC AM, PostFic, RAdv 1, –13-1, RfGAmL 87, ShSCr 2, ShSWr, SmATA 7, WhoAm 74, –76, –78, –80, –84, –86, –88, WhoE 75, –77, WhoUSWr 88, WhoWrEP 89, WorAl, WorAu 1950, WrDr 76, –80, –82, –84, –86, –88*

Barthelme, Donald 1931-1989 *AnObit 1989, AuBYP 3, BenetAL 91, ConAu 129, ConLC 59, CurBio 89N, CyWA 89, DcLB Y89N, MagSAmL, MajTwCW, NewYTBS 89, ScF&FL 92, SmATA 62, WhAm 10, WorAlBi, WrDr 90*

Barthelme, Donald 1933-1989 *EncSF 93*

Bartholomew, Barbara 1941- *ConAu 118, –135, EncSF 93, ScF&FL 92, SmATA 42*

Bartholomew, Jean *ConAu 134, IntAu&W 91X, SmATA 68, –73, WrDr 86, –88, –90, –92*
Main entry: Beatty, Patricia Robbins

Bartholomew, Jean 1922-1991 *WrDr 94N*

Bartlett, Evelyn *SingR 1, WhAmArt 85*

Bartlett, Margaret Abbott 1892-1949 *ChhPo S1, WhAm 3*

Bartlett, Margaret Farrington 1896- *ConAu 5R, –5NR*

Bartlett, Philip A *ConAu 26NR, –P-2, SmATA 1*
Main entry: Stratemeyer, Edward L

Bartlett, Robert Merrill 1899- *AmAu&B, BioIn 11, ConAu 5R, –2NR, IndAu 1917, SmATA 12, WhoAm 74, –76, –78, –80*

Bartlett, Ruth *ConAu 17R*

Bartlett, Susan *BioIn 5*

Bartlett, Vernon 1894-1983 *Au&Wr 71, BioIn 4, –5, –10, BlueB 76, ConAu 61, –108, DcNaB 1981, IntAu&W 77, IntWW 74, –75, –76, –77, –78, –79, –80, –81, –82, –83N, LongCTC, NewC, ScF&FL 92, TwCA, –SUP, Who 74, –82, –83, WhoLA, WrDr 76, –80, –82, –84*

Bartlett, Vernon Oldfield 1894-1983 *EncSF 93*

Barton, Byron 1930- *AuBYP 2S, -3, BioIn 11, -12, ConAu 57, -13NR, FifBJA, IlsCB 1967, SmATA 9*

Barton, Carl *OxCCan SUP*

Barton, Clara H 1821-1912 *BioAmW*

Barton, Clara Harlowe 1821-1912 *AmAu&B, BioIn 1, -2, -3, -4, -5, -6, -7, -8, -9, -10, -11, -12, -13, DcNAA, EncAB-H, HerW, InWom SUP, McGEWB, REn, REnAL, WebAB 74, WebAMB, WhAm 1*

Barton, Harriett *SmATA 43*

Barton, Jillian 1940- *SmATA 75*

Barton, May Hollis *ConAu 26NR, -P-2, SmATA 1, -67, -X*
Main entry: Adams, Harriet S
Stratemeyer, Edward L

Barton, Pat *WhoUSWr 88, WhoWrEP 89, -92*

Barton, Pat 1928- *SmATA 59*
Pseud./variant:
Arrowsmith, Pat

Barton, Thomas Frank 1905-1985 *BioIn 15*

Barton, Thomas Frank, Sr. 1905- *BioIn 7, ConAu 45, -1NR, WhoAm 74, -76, -80, -82, -84, WhoUSWr 88, WhoWor 74, WhoWrEP 89, -92*

Barton, Thomas Frank, Sr. 1905-1985 *WhAm 9*

Bartos-Hoeppner, Barbara 1923- *Au&Wr 71, BioIn 10, ConAu 25R, -10NR, FourBJA, IntAu&W 77, SmATA 5, TwCChW 78B, -83B*

Bartos-Hoppner, Barbara *TwCChW 89B*

Bartram, George *ChhPo S1*

Bartsch, Jochen 1906- *BioIn 8, -15, IlsBYP, IlsCB 1957, SmATA 39*

Baruch, Dorothy Walter 1899-1962 *AmAu&B, AmPB, ChhPo, SmATA 21, Str&VC, WhAm 4*

Bar-Zohar, Michael J 1938- *ConAu 21R, WhoWorJ 72, -78*

Bas, Rutger *ConAu X, EncCoWW, IntAu&W 82X, SmATA X*

Base, Graeme *AuBYP 3, ChlBIlD*

Base, Graeme 1958- *BioIn 16, -17, ChlLR 22, ConAu 134, SmATA 67*

Base, Graeme Rowland 1958- *MajAI, WrDr 94*

Bashevis, Isaac *ConAu 134, -X, -39NR, IntAu&W 91X, MajAI, MajTwCW, SmATA 3, -68, -X*
Main entry: Singer, Isaac Bashevis

Basho *Benet 87*

Basho 1644-1694 *BioIn 3, -5, -9, -16, CasWL, DcOrL 1, EncJap, GrFLW, PenC CL, RAdv 13-2, REn*

Basile, Giambattista 1575?-1632 *BioIn 7, CarSB, CasWL, DcItL, EuAu, EvEuW, PenC EUR, REn*

Basilevsky, Helen 1939- *IlsBYP*

Baskin, Leonard 1922- *AmArt, BioIn 4, -5, -6, -7, -8, -9, -11, -12, -13, BriEAA, ConArt 83, -89, ConAu 106, CurBio 64, DcCAA 71, -77, -88, DcCAr 81, FifBJA, IlsCB 1967, OxCTwCA, OxDcArt, PhDcTCA 77, PrintW 83, -85, SmATA 27, -30, WebAB 74, -79, WhoAm 74, -76, -78, -80, -86, -88, -90, -92, -94, WhoAmA 73, -78, -80, -82, -84, -86, -89, -91, WhoGrA 62, -82, WhoWor 74, WorArt 1950*

Baskin, Wade 1924- *ConAu P-2, WhoSSW 73*

Bason, Lillian 1913- *AuBYP 2S, -3, BioIn 12, ConAu 69, SmATA 20*

Bass, Milton Ralph 1923- *Au&Wr 71, ConAmTC, ConAu 25R, WhoUSWr 88, WhoWrEP 89, -92*

Bass, Virginia W 1905- *ConAu 61*

Basser, Veronica *DcChlFi, SingR 1*

Bassermann, Lujo *ConAu X, -36NR, IntAu&W 77X, -86X, WrDr 76, -80, -82, -84, -86, -88*
Main entry: Schreiber, Hermann Otto Ludwig

Bassett, Jeni 1959- *SmATA 64*

Bassett, Jeni 1960?- *SmATA 43*

Bassett, John Keith *AuBYP 2, -3, ConAu X, SmATA X*
Main entry: Keating, Lawrence Alfred

Bassett, Lisa *AuBYP 3*

Bassett, Lisa 1958- *ConAu 126, SmATA 61*

Batchelor, Joy 1914- *BioIn 13, ContDcW 89, DcFM, FilmgC, HalFC 84, -88, IntDcWB, IntMPA 75, -76, -78, -81, -82, -84, -86, -88, -77, OxCFilm, SmATA 29, WomWMM, -B, WorECar, WorEFlm*

Batchelor, Joy 1914-1991 *AnObit 1991*

Bate, Lucy 1939- *BioIn 12, ConAu 69, ForWC 70, SmATA 18*

Bate, Norman Arthur 1916- *AuBYP 3*

Bate, Norman Arthur 1916-1980 *AuBYP 2, BioIn 5, –8, –10, ConAu 1R, IlsCB 1946, SmATA 5, WhoAmA 73, –78, –80, –82N, –86N, –89N, –91N, WrDr 76, –80, –82, –84*

Bateman, Henry Mayo 1887-1970 *BioIn 1, –8, –12, –13, –14, DcBrAr 1, DcBrBI, DcNaB 1961, GrBr, IlsCB 1744*

Bateman, Robert 1922- *ScFSB*

Bateman, Robert 1922-1973 *Au&Wr 71, ConAu 5R, –7NR, ConSFA*

Bateman, Robert Moyes Carruthers 1922-1973 *EncSF 93*

Bateman, Walter L 1916- *ConAu 29R*

Bates, Arlo 1850-1918 *Alli SUP, AmAu, AmAu&B, BenetAL 91, BbD, BiD&SB, CarSB, ChhPo, DcAmAu, DcBiA, DcNAA, OxCAmL 65, –83, REnAL, WhAm 1*

Bates, Barbara Snedeker 1919- *BioIn 11, ConAu 17R, ForWC 70, SmATA 12, WhoAmW 74, –85, –87, WhoLibI 82*
Pseud./variant:
Cuyler, Stephen
Roberts, Jim

Bates, Betty
Main entry: Bates, Elizabeth

Bates, Betty 1921- *BioIn 12, ConAu X, –32NR, SmATA 19*

Bates, Daisy *NegAl 89, WhoBlA 88, –90, –92, –94*

Bates, Daisy 1861-1951 *BioIn 2, –3, –7, –8, –9, –10, ContDcW 89, IntDcWB, ObitOF 79, ObitT 1951, OxCAusL*

Bates, Daisy 1863-1951 *AuWomWr, BlmGWL*

Bates, Elizabeth 1921- *ConAu 77, –14NR, –32NR*
Pseud./variant:
Bates, Betty

Bates, Gordon *CarSB, Who 85*

Bates, Harriet Leonora 1856-1886 *Alli SUP, AmAu&B, BiD&SB, CarSB, DcAmAu, DcNAA, WhAm HS*

Bates, Katharine Lee 1850-1929 *BenetAL 91*

Bates, Katharine Lee 1859-1929 *Alli SUP, AmAu&B, AmLY, AmWomPl, AnMV 1926, BiD&SB, BioAmW, BioIn 2, –3, –4, –5, –6, –11, CarSB, ChhPo, –S1, –S2, CnDAL, DcAmAu, DcLB 71, DcNAA, EvLB, FemiCLE, JBA 34, OxCAmL 65, OxCMus, REnAL, TwCA, –SUP, TwCWr, WebAB 74, –79, WhAm 1, WhNAA*

Bates, Marston 1906-1974 *AmAu&B, AmMWSc 73P, –76P, BioIn 4, –10, ConAu 5R, –49, –7NR, CurBio 56, –74, DcScB S2, InSci, NewYTBS 74, ObitOF 79, WhAm 6, WhoAm 74, WhoWor 74*

Batey, Tom *WrDr 90, –92*

Batey, Tom 1946- *ConAu 107, SmATA 41, –52*
Pseud./variant:
Tomkins, Jasper

Bath, Philip Ernest 1898- *Au&Wr 71, ConAu P-1*

Batherman, Muriel
Main entry: Sheldon, Muriel

Batherman, Muriel 1926?- *AuBYP 2S, –3, BioIn 2, ConAu X, SmATA X*

Batiuk, Thomas Martin 1947- *ConAu 69, EncTwCJ, SmATA 40, WhoAm 80, –82, –84, –86, –88, –90, –92, –94, WhoWest 94*

Batson, Larry 1930- *BioIn 14, ConAu 57, SmATA 35*

Batson, Larry Floyd 1930- *WhoAm 90, –92*

Battaglia, Aurelius *IlsBYP, SmATA 33*

Battaglia, Aurelius 1910- *BioIn 14, –16, SmATA 50*

Batten, Harry Mortimer 1888-1958 *ConAu 112, SmATA 25, WhoChL, WhoLA*

Batten, Jack Hubert 1932- *CaW, CanWW 83, –89, ConAu 49, OxCCan SUP*

Batten, John Dickson 1860-1932 *ClaDrA, DcBrAr 1, DcVicP 2*

Batten, Mary 1937- *AuBYP 2S, –3, BioIn 10, ConAu 41R, SmATA 5*

Batterberry, Ariane Ruskin *AuBYP 3*

Batterberry, Ariane Ruskin 1935- *ConAu 69, –13NR, SmATA 13, WhoAmW 77*
Pseud./variant:
Ruskin, Ariane

Batterberry, Michael Carver 1932- *AuBYP 2S, –3, ConAu 77, SmATA 32*

Battle, Gerald N 1914- *ConAu 57*

Battles, Edith 1921- *AuBYP 3, ScF&FL 92, WhoUSWr 88, WhoWrEP 89*

Battles, Edith Baker 1921- *AuBYP 2S, BioIn 10, ConAu 41R, IntAu&W 82, SmATA 7*

Baudouy, Michel-Aime 1909- *BioIn 10, ConAu P-2, IntAu&W 82, SmATA 7, ThrBJA*

Bauer, Caroline Feller *WhoAm 92, –94, WhoAmW 87, –89, –91, WhoWest 89, –92*

Bauer, Caroline Feller 1935- *AuBYP 3, BioIn 15, –16, –17, ConAu 77, IntAu&W 89, –91, SmATA 46, –52, WhoAmW 85, WhoLibI 82, WhoWest 76, –84, WhoWor 84, WrDr 90, –92, –94*

Bauer, E Charles 1916- *ConAu 9R*

Bauer, Ernst Waldemar 1926- *WhoWor 78*

Bauer, Fred 1934- *ConAu 29R, –13NR, SmATA 36*

Bauer, Helen 1900- *BioIn 9, ConAu 5R, ForWC 70, SmATA 2*

Bauer, Marion Dane 1938- *ConAu 69, –11NR, –26NR, DcAmChF 1960, –1985, FifBJA, MajAI, SmATA 20, –69, –9AS, TwCYAW, WhoAm 92, –94*

Bauernschmidt, Marjorie 1926- *BioIn 5, –12, IlsBYP, IlsCB 1946, SmATA 15*

Baughman, Dorothy 1940- *ConAu 65, SmATA 61, WhoUSWr 88*

Baum, Allyn Zelton 1924- *BioIn 12, ConAu 17R, SmATA 20, WhoE 74, –75, –77, WhoFI 89, –92*

Baum, Betty *AuBYP 2, –3, BioIn 8*

Baum, L Frank
Main entry: Thompson, Ruth Plumly

Baum, L Frank 1856-1919 *Benet 87, BenetAL 91, BioIn 14, –15, –17, CamGLE, ChlLR 15, ConAu 133, HalFC 88, MajTwCW, RfGAmL 87, ScF&FL 92, ScFSB, ScFEYrs, TwCChW 89, WorAlBi, WrChl*

Baum, L Frank 189-?-1976 *ConAu 134, SmATA 66*

Baum, Louis 1948- *ConAu 124, SmATA 52, –64, WrDr 90, –92, –94*

Baum, Louis F *MajAI*

Baum, Lyman Frank 1856-1919 *AmAu&B, AuBYP 2, –3, BioIn 4, –5, –7, –8, –9, –11, –12, –13, –14, –15, –17, CarSB, ChhPo, –S2, CnDAL, ConAu 108, DcAmAu, DcLB 22, DcNAA, EncAB-A 6, EncSF 93, FamSYP, HalFC 84, LongCTC, MajAI, NotNAT B, Novels, OxCAmL 65, –83, OxCChiL, PenC AM, REn, REnAL, SmATA 18, ThrBJA, TwCA, TwCChW 78, –83, TwCLC 7, WebAB 74, –79, WhoChL, WorAl*
Pseud./variant:
Akens, Floyd
Akers, Floyd
Bancroft, Laura
Fitzgerald, Captain Hugh
Metcalf, Suzanne
Stanton, Schuyler
Staunton, Schuyler
VanDyne, Edith

Baum, Patricia *AuBYP 2S, –3*

Baum, Thomas 1940- *ConAu 65, ScF&FL 92*

Baum, Willi 1931- *BioIn 9, ConAu 29R, SmATA 4*

Bauman, Elizabeth Hershberger 1924- *IndAu 1917*

Baumann, Amy Brown Beeching 1922- *BioIn 11, ConAu 21R, SmATA 10*
Pseud./variant:
Barbary, James
Brown, Alexis

Baumann, Elwood D *AuBYP 2S, –3, ConAu 111, SmATA 33*

Baumann, Hans *TwCChW 89B*

Baumann, Hans 1914- *Au&Wr 71, BioIn 9, ConAu 5R, –3NR, IntAu&W 77, –82, OxCChiL, SmATA 2, ThrBJA, TwCChW 78B, –83B, WhoWor 74*

Baumann, Kurt 1935- *BioIn 12, ConAu 77, –13NR, SmATA 21*

Baumer, Lewis 1870- *BioIn 1, ChhPo, IlsCB 1744*

Baumhauer, Hans 1913- *BioIn 5, IlsBYP, IlsCB 1946*

Baur, John Edward 1922- *ConAu 9R, DrAS 74H, –78H, –82H, WrDr 76, –80, –82, –84, –86, –88, –90, –92, –94*

Bausch, William John 1929- *ConAu 29R, –11NR, WhoRel 77*

Bawden, Edward 1903- *BioIn 1, –2, –5, –12, –14, –15, BlueB 76, ClaDrA, ConDes 84, DcBrAr 1, DcD&D, IlsCB 1946, IntWW 74, –75, –76, –77, –78, –79, –80, –81, –82, –83, –89, OxCArt, OxCTwCA, OxDcArt, PhDcTCA 77, Who 74, –82, –83, –85, –88, –90, WhoArt 84, WhoGrA 62, WhoWor 74*

Bawden, Edward 1903-1989 *AnObit 1989, ConDes 90, TwCPaSc*

Bawden, Nina 1925- *AuBYP 2S, -3, Au&Wr 71, BioIn 9, -10, -11, -13, -16, BritCA, CamGLE, ChlFicS, ChlLR 2, ConAu X, -29NR, ConNov 72, -76, -82, -86, -91, DcLB 14, EncBrWW, FemiCLE, FourBJA, InWom SUP, IntAu&W 77, -82, -86, Novels, OxCChiL, ScF&FL 92, SmATA 4, -16AS, SouSt, TwCChW 78, -83, -89, TwCCr&M 80, TwCYAW, Who 74, WrDr 76, -80, -82, -84, -86, -88, -90, -92*
Pseud./variant:
Kark, Nina Mary

Bawden, Nina Mary 1925- *WrDr 94*

Bawden, Nina Mary Mabey 1925- *MajAI, SmATA 72*

Baxendale, Leo 1930- *BioIn 12, OxCChiL*

Baxter, Caroline 1956- *WrDr 80, -82, -84*

Baxter, George Owen *ConAu X, EncFWF, TwCWW 91, WebAB 74, -79*

Baxter, Valerie *ConAu 128, -X, TwCChW 83, -89, WrDr 82, -84, -86, -88*
Main entry: Meynell, Laurence Walter

Baxter, Valerie 1899-1989 *SmATA X*

Bayefsky, Aba 1923- *BioIn 5, -6, CanWW 70, -80, -81, -83, -89, CreCan 1, WhoAmA 73, -80, -82, -84, -86, -89, -91*

Bayer, Jane E d1985 *ConAu 116, SmATA 44N*

Bayley, Dorothy *ChhPo*

Bayley, Nicola 1949- *BioIn 12, -14, -15, -16, -17, ChlBIlD, ConAu 118, IlsCB 1967, MajAI, OxCChiL, SixBJA, SmATA 41, -69*

Baylor, Byrd *BioIn 15*
Main entry: Schweitzer, Byrd Baylor

Baylor, Byrd 1924- *AuBYP 2S, -3, BioIn 12, ChlLR 3, ConAu 81, FourBJA, MajAI, SmATA 16, -69*

Bayly, George *Alli SUP*

Bayne-Jardine, Colin Charles 1932- *ConAu 25R*

Baynes, Ernest Harold 1868-1925 *AmLY, BioIn 2, DcNAA, JBA 34, -51, Str&VC, WhAm 1*

Baynes, Pauline 1922- *BioIn 14, -16, ConAu 120, SmATA 59*

Baynes, Pauline Diana 1922- *BioIn 5, -8, -9, -12, ChhPo, -S2, ConAu 37NR, IlsBYP, IlsCB 1946, -1957, -1967, MajAI, OxCChiL, SmATA 19, ThrBJA, Who 82, -83, -85, -88, -90, -92, WhoArt 80, -82, -84, WhoChL*

B B *BioIn 12, -14, -15, -17, BritAS, ConAu 132, -X, -38NR, IntAu&W 77X, -91X, LongCTC, OxCChiL, SmATA 6, -66, ThrBJA, TwCChW 78, -83, -89, Who 83, -85, -88, -90, WhoChL*
Main entry: Watkins-Pitchford, Denys James

Beach, Charles *SmATA X*
Main entry: Reid, Mayne

Beach, Charles Amory *CarSB, ConAu 26NR, -P-2, SmATA 1*
Main entry: Stratemeyer, Edward L

Beach, Edward L *DrAPF 87, -89, -91, -93*

Beach, Edward L 1918- *WrDr 86, -88, -90, -92, -94*

Beach, Edward Latimer 1918- *Au&Wr 71, BioIn 3, -5, -6, -11, -13, ConAu 5R, -6NR, CurBio 60, DrAPF 83, -85, Novels, SmATA 12, WebAMB, WhoAm 92, -94, WhoAmP 73, -75, -77, WhoE 91, WhoGov 77, -72, -75, WrDr 76, -80, -82, -84*

Beach, Lynn *EncSF 93, ScF&FL 92, SmATA 76*
Main entry: Lance, Kathryn

Beach, Stewart Taft 1899-1979 *AmAu&B, AuBYP 2, -3, BioIn 1, -7, -11, -13, ConAu 85, -93, SmATA 23, WhAm 7*

Beachcroft, Nina 1931- *BioIn 12, ConAu 97, -19NR, ScF&FL 92, SmATA 18, TwCChW 78, -83, -89, WrDr 80, -82, -84, -86, -88, -90, -92, -94*

Beagle, Peter S *DrAPF 87, -89, -91, -93*

Beagle, Peter S 1939- *ScF&FL 92, ScFSB, SmATA 60, SupFW, WrDr 86, -88, -90, -92*

Beagle, Peter Soyer 1939- *BioIn 12, ConAu 9R, -4NR, ConLC 7, ConSFA, DcLB Y80B, DrAF 76, DrAPF 83, -85, IntAu&W 86, OxCAmL 83, SupFW, TwCYAW, WhoAm 74, -76, -78, -80, -82, -84, -86, -88, -90, -92, -94, WhoHr&F, WhoSciF, WhoUSWr 88, WhoWrEP 89, -92, WrDr 76, -80, -82, -84, -94*

Beaglehole, John Cawte 1901-1971 *CasWL, ChhPo, ConAu 33R, -P-2, DcLEL, DcNaB 1971, LongCTC, OxCCan SUP, OxCShps*

Beake, Lesley 1949- *DcChlFi*

Beal, George Charles 1918- *Au&Wr 71*

Bealer, Alex 1921-1980 *AuBYP 3*

Bealer, Alex Winkler 1921-1980 *AuBYP 2S, BioIn 11, –12, –13, ConAu 45, –97, –2NR, SmATA 8, –22N*

Beales, Valerie 1915- *SmATA 74*

Beals, Carleton 1893-1979 *AmAu&B, AuBYP 2, –3, Au&Wr 71, BioIn 1, –4, –5, –7, –11, –12, BlueB 76, ConAu 1R, –3NR, CurBio 41, DcLEL, EncAJ, IntAu&W 77, IntWW 74, –75, –76, –77, –78, –79, OxCAmL 65, –83, REnAL, ScF&FL 92, SmATA 12, TwCA, –SUP, WhAm 7, WhNAA, WhoAm 74, –76, –78, WhoWor 74, WrDr 76, –80*

Beals, Frank Lee 1881-1972 *AmAu&B, Au&Wr 71, BioIn 13, ConAu 5R, –103, SmATA 26N, WhAm 5, WhNAA*

Beaman, Joyce Proctor 1931- *ConAu 29R, IntAu&W 77, –89, WhoUSWr 88, WhoWrEP 89, –92, WrDr 76, –80, –82, –84, –86, –88, –90, –92, –94*

Beaman, S G Hulme 1886-1932 *BioIn 8, OxCChiL, TwCChW 83, –89, WhoChL*
Pseud./variant:
Hulme Beaman, S G

Beaman, S G Hulme 1887-1932 *BioIn 14*

Beame, Rona 1934- *BioIn 11, ConAu 45, SmATA 12*

Beamer, Charles 1942- *ConAu 121, ScF&FL 92, SmATA 43*

Beames, Margaret *DcChlFi*

Beaney, Jan *ConAu X, –35NR, SmATA X*
Main entry: Udall, Jan Beaney

Bear, Greg 1951- *ConAu 35NR, EncSF 93, IntAu&W 91, NewEScF, ScF&FL 92, ScFSB, SmATA 65, TwCSFW 86, –91, WrDr 86, –88, –90, –92*

Bear, Gregory Dale 1951- *WrDr 94*

Bear, John 1938- *BioIn 9, ConAu 73, –13NR, –29NR*

Beard, Adelia Belle 1857-1920 *ChhPo S1, DcNAA, DcWomA, OhA&B, WhAmArt 85, WomWWA 14*

Beard, Alice *DcWomA, WhAmArt 85*

Beard, Annie E S d1930 *DcNAA*

Beard, Charles A 1874-1948 *Benet 87, BenetAL 91, RAdv 13-3, RComAH, ThTwC 87, WorAlBi*

Beard, Charles Austin 1874-1946 *MorMA*

Beard, Charles Austin 1874-1948 *AmAu&B, AmPeW, BioIn 1, –2, –3, –4, –6, –7, –8, –9, –10, –11, –12, –13, –14, –15, –16, –17, ConAmA, ConAu 115, CurBio 41, –48, DcAmDH 80, –89, DcAmSR, DcLB 17, DcLEL, DcNAA, EncAB-H, EvLB, IndAu 1816, LongCTC, McGEWB, ObitOF 79, OxCAmH, OxCAmL 65, –83 PenC AM, REn, REnAL, SmATA 18, TwCA, –SUP, TwCLC 15, WebAB 74, –79, WebE&AL, WhAm 2, WorAl*

Beard, Daniel C 1850-1941 *BenetAL 91*

Beard, Daniel Carter 1850-1941 *Alli SUP, AmAu&B, AmLY, AuBYP 2S, BiD&SB, BioIn 1, –2, –3, –4, –6, –9, –10, –13, CarSB, ChhPo, CurBio 41, DcAmAu, DcNAA, IlrAm 1880, JBA 34, ObitOF 79, OhA&B, OxCAmL 65, REnAL, SmATA 22, TwCA, –SUP, WebAB 74, –79, WhAm 1, WhAmArt 85, WhNAA, WorAl, WorECar*

Beard, Daniel Carter 1859-1941 *AuBYP 3*

Beard, Lina d1933 *DcNAA, DcWomA, WhAm 1, WhAmArt 85, WhNAA, WomWWA 14*

Beard, William 1907- *AmAu&B, WhoAm 74, –76, –78, –80*

Bearden, Romare 1912-1988 *ConBlB 2, NewYTBS 88*

Bearden, Romare 1914- *BioIn 14, ConArt 89, DcCAA 88*

Bearden, Romare 1914-1988 *AfrAmAl 6, BioIn 15, –16, –17, ConAu 125, CurBio 88N, ModArCr 1, NegAl 89, SmATA 56N*

Bearden, Romare H 1914- *BlkAuII*

Bearden, Romare H 1914-1988 *BlkAuII 92, WhoBlA 90N*

Bearden, Romare Howard 1914- *AfroAA, AmArt, ASCAP 66, BioIn 8, –9, –10, –11, –12, –13, BlueB 76, ConArt 83, ConAu 102, CurBio 72, DcCAA 71, –77, DcCAr 81, InB&W 80, –85, NegAl 76, –83, OxCTwCA, PrintW 83, –85, SmATA 22, WhoAm 74, –80, –82, –84, –86, WhoAmA 73, –80, –82, –84, –86, WhoWor 74, WorArt 1950*

Bearden, Romare Howard 1914-1988 *WhAm 9*

Beardmore, George 1908-1979 *Au&Wr 71, BioIn 12, ConAu 69, –126, SmATA 20*

Pseud./variant:
Stokes, Cedric
Wolfenden, George

Beardsley, Aubrey Vincent 1872-1898 *AtlBL, Benet 87, BioIn 1, –2, –3, –6, –7, –8, –9, –10, –11, –12, –13, BritAu 19, ChhPo, –S2, DcBrBI, DcLEL, DcNaB S1, Dis&D, LongCEL, McGEWB, NewC, OxCArt, OxCEng 85, REn, WebE&AL, WorAl*

Bearman, Jane Ruth 1917- *BioIn 13, ConAu 105, SmATA 29, WhoAmA 80, –82, –84, WhoAmW 77*

Beatrice D'este *DcAmChF 1960*

Beattie, Jessie Louise 1896- *Au&Wr 71, BioIn 1, –8, –10, CanNov, CanWW 70, –79, –80, –81, –83, ConAu 5R, –2NR, –17NR, CreCan 2, IntAu&W 77, –82, –91, OxCCan, Profile 1, WhNAA, WhoCanL 85, WrDr 76, –80, –82, –84, –86, –88*

Beattie, Jessie Louise 1896-1985 *WhoCanL 87, –92*

Beatty, Elizabeth *ConAu X, IntAu&W 77X, SmATA X*
Main entry: Holloway, Teresa

Beatty, Hetty Burlingame 1907?-1971 *AuBYP 2, –3, BioIn 5, –6, –7, –8, –10, ConAu 1R, –103, IlsCB 1946, –1957, –1967, MorJA, SmATA 5, WhAmArt 85*

Beatty, Jerome, Jr. 1918- *AuBYP 2, –3, BioIn 8, –10, ConAu 9R, –3NR, ScF&FL 92, SmATA 5*

Beatty, John *AuBYP 3*

Beatty, John 1922-1975 *BioIn 7, –9, –10, ConAu 5R, –57, –4NR, DrAS 74H, SmATA 6, –25N, ThrBJA, TwCChW 78, –83, –89*

Beatty, John Louis 1922-1975 *DcAmChF 1960*

Beatty, Patricia 1922- *IntAu&W 91, SmATA 4AS, TwCChW 89, WrDr 86, –88, –90, –92*

Beatty, Patricia 1922-1991 *WrDr 94N*

Beatty, Patricia Robbins d1991 *NewYTBS 91*

Beatty, Patricia Robbins 1922- *AuBYP 2, –3, BioIn 7, –8, –9, ConAu 1R, –3NR, DcAmChF 1960, ForWC 70, OxCChiL, SmATA 1, –30, ThrBJA, TwCChW 78, –83, WrDr 80, –82, –84*

Beatty, Patricia Robbins 1922-1991 *ConAu 134, DcAmChF 1985, MajAI, SmATA 68, –73*

Pseud./variant:
Bartholomew, Jean

Beaty, Janice Janowski 1930- *ConAu 13R, ForWC 70*

Beaty, John Yocum 1884- *AuBYP 2, –3, BioIn 2, –7, WhAm 3*

Beaumont, Marie Leprince De 1711-1780 *OxCChiL*

Beausay, Florence E 1911- *IntAu&W 91, WrDr 86, –88, –90*

Beausay, Florence Edith 1911- *ConAu 21R, IntAu&W 77, WhoAmW 74, WrDr 76, –80, –82, –84*

Beaver, Barrington *Alli SUP*
Main entry: Kingston, William Henry Giles

Bebell, Mildred Hoyt 1909- *ConAu P-1*

Bebenroth, Charlotta M 1890- *OhA&B*

Bechstein, Ludwig 1801-1860 *AuBYP 2S, –3, BiD&SB, EvEuW, OxCChiL, OxCGer 76, –86*

Bechtel, Louise Seaman 1894-1985 *AmPB, BioIn 1, –9, –14, –15, ChhPo, –S1, ConAu 116, –P-2, SmATA 4, –43N*
Pseud./variant:
Seaman, Louise

Bechtold, Grace *ForWC 70*

Bechtold, Grace d1988 *BioIn 15, –16, NewYTBS 88*

Beck, Barbara L 1927- *BioIn 11, ConAu 17R, SmATA 12*

Beck, Calvin Thomas 1937- *ConAu 97*

Beck, Christopher *EncSF 93, WhoChL*

Beck, Helen L 1908- *ConAu 73*

Beck-Brandt, Katrin 1942- *BioIn 12, IlsCB 1967*

Becke, Louis 1850- *BbD, BiD&SB, BioIn 4, –7, Chambr 3*

Becke, Louis 1855-1913 *StaCVF*

Beckel, Graham 1913- *ConAu 1R*

Becker, Beril 1901- *AuBYP 2S, –3, BioIn 11, ConAu P-1, SmATA 11*

Becker, Charlotte *ChhPo, WhAmArt 85, WhoAmA 73, –78, –80, WhoAmW 74*

Becker, Edna M 1898- *WhNAA*

Becker, John Leonard 1901- *AuBYP 2, –3, BioIn 8, –11, ChhPo, –S2, ConAu P-1, SmATA 12*

Becker, Joyce 1936- *SmATA 39*

Becker, May Lamberton 1873-1958 *AmAu&B, BioIn 1, –4, –5, –14, ChhPo, –S1, ConAu 112, CurBio 41, –58, ObitOF 79, ObitT 1951, REnAL, SmATA 33, TwCA, –SUP, WhAm 3, WhNAA*

Becker, Paula Lee 1941- *ConAu 17R, ForWC 70, WhoAmW 74, –75, –93*

Becker, Ruby Wirt 1915- *ConAu 33R*

Beckett, Sheilah 1913- *BioIn 7, –14, ChhPo S1, SmATA 33*

Beckhard, Arthur J *AuBYP 2, –3, BioIn 8*

Beckhoff, Harry 1901-1979 *BioIn 1, IlrAm 1880, –D, WhAmArt 85*

Beckles Willson, Robina Elizabeth 1930- *Au&Wr 71, IntAu&W 91, WrDr 76, –80, –82, –84, –86, –88, –90*

Beckman, Delores *DcAmChF 1960*

Beckman, Delores 1914- *ConAu 121, IntAu&W 86, SmATA 51*

Beckman, Gunnel *TwCChW 89B*

Beckman, Gunnel 1910- *BioIn 10, ChlLR 25, ConAu 33R, –15NR, ConLC 26, FourBJA, MajAI, SmATA 6, –9AS, TwCChW 78B, –83B*

Beckman, Kaj
Main entry: Beckman, Karin

Beckman, Kaj 1913- *BioIn 5, –15, IlsCB 1946, SmATA X*

Beckman, Karin 1913- *SmATA 45*
Pseud./variant:
Beckman, Kaj

Beckman, Per 1913- *BioIn 5, –15, IlsCB 1946, SmATA 45*

Beckwith, Lillian
Main entry: Comber, Lillian

Beckwith, Lillian 1916- *ConAu X, IntAu&W 77, –82, –91, WrDr 76, –80, –82, –84, –86, –88, –90, –92, –94*

Beckwith, Yvonne 1936?- *ConAu 106, ForWC 70, WhoAmW 74*

Becky *BioIn 2, InB&W 80*
Main entry: Krehbiel, Rebecca Falconer

Beddall, Barbara Gould 1919- *ConAu 33R, IntAu&W 77, WhoAmW 75, –77, WrDr 76, –80, –82*

Beddington, Roy 1910- *BioIn 14, DcBrAr 1, IntAu&W 77, –89, –91, WhoArt 80, –82, –84, WrDr 76, –82, –84, –86, –88, –90*

Beddoe, Ellaruth *ConAu X*
Main entry: Elkins, Ella Ruth

Bede 673?-735 *Benet 87, BlmGEL, CamGLE, CyEd, DcBiPP, DcNaB, InSci, LuthC 75, OxCChiL, OxCEng 85*

Bede, Saint 673?-735 *CamGEL*

Bede, The Venerable 673-735 *BioIn 15*

Bedford, Annie North *ConAu X, SmATA 3*
Main entry: Watson, Jane Werner

Bedford, Francis Donkin 1864-1934 *BioIn 14*

Bedford, Francis Donkin 1864-1950 *BioIn 1, –8, ChhPo, –S1, –S2, ConICB, DcBrAr 2, DcBrBI, DcVicP 2, IlsCB 1744, OxCChiL, WhoChL*

Bedford, Francis Donkin 1864-1954 *DcVicP 2*

Bedford, Ruth *WomNov*

Bedford, Ruth 1882-1963 *AuWomWr, OxCAusL, SingR 1*

Bedoukian, Kerop 1907-1981 *BioIn 16, SmATA 53*

Bee, Clair 1900-1983 *AnObit 1983, AuBYP 2, BioIn 8, –9, ConAu 1R, –109*

Bee, Clair Francis 1896-1983 *BiDAmSp BK*

Bee, Clair Francis 1900-1983 *AuBYP 3*

Bee, Jay *SmATA 65*
Main entry: Brainerd, John Whiting

Bee, Joyce 1920- *BioIn 12, IlsCB 1967*

Beebe, Ann 1919- *BiDrLUS 70, ConAu 41R, WhoLibS 66*

Beebe, Burdetta Faye *AuBYP 2S, BioIn 9, ConAu 1R, ForWC 70, IntAu&W 77X, SmATA 1, WrDr 76, –80*
Main entry: Johnson, Burdetta Fay Beebe

Beebe, Burdetta Faye 1920- *AuBYP 3*

Beebe, William 1877-1962 *AmAu&B, AmLY, BenetAL 91, BioIn 1, –2, –4, –5, –6, –7, –8, –10, –12, –14, ConAmA, ConAmL, ConAu 73, CurBio 41, –62, DcAmB S7, DcLEL, EncAB-A 15, EvLB, ObitOF 79, OxCAmH,*

OxCAmL 65, -83, REnAL, SmATA 19, Str&VC, TwCA, -SUP, WebAB 74, -79, WhAm 4, WhNAA, WorAlBi

Beeby, Betty 1923- *BioIn 13, SmATA 25*

Beech, Linda *AuBYP 3*

Beech, Linda Mangelsdorf *AuBYP 2S, ForWC 70*

Beech, Webb *AuBYP 2S, -3, ConAu X, -40NR, SmATA 5*
Main entry: Butterworth, W E

Beeching, Jack *EngPo*

Beeching, Jack 1922- *BioIn 12, ConAu 21R, -13NR, ConSFA, EncSF 93, IntAu&W 86, -89, -91, ScF&FL 92, SmATA 14*
Pseud./variant:
Barbary, James

Beecroft, John William Richard 1902-1966 *AmAu&B, AuBYP 2, -3, BioIn 1, -3, -7, ConAu 5R, CurBio 54, -66, WhAm 4*

Beeding, Francis *CrtSuMy, CurBio 43, DcLEL, EncMys, EncSF 93, EvLB, LongCTC, NewC, SpyFic, TwCA, -SUP, TwCCr&M 80, -85, TwCWr, WhoSpyF*
Main entry: Palmer, John Leslie
Saunders, Hilary Aidan St. George

Beeding, Francis 1885-1944 *TwCCr&M 91*

Beeding, Francis 1898-1951 *TwCCr&M 91*

Beeks, Graydon 1919- *ConAu 65, ScF&FL 92*

Beeler, Janet *ConAu 127*

Beeler, Janet 1937- *SmATA X*
Main entry: Shaw, Janet

Beeler, Nelson Frederick 1910- *AuBYP 2, -3, BioIn 6, -7, ConAu 69, MorJA, SmATA 13*

Beer, Kathleen Costello 1926- *ConAu 25R, IntAu&W 77, WrDr 76, -80*

Beer, Richard *BioIn 8, IlsBYP, IlsCB 1957*

Beer, Richard 1928- *TwCPaSc*

Beers, Dorothy Sands 1917- *BioIn 11, ConAu 49, SmATA 9*

Beers, Lorna 1897- *BioIn 12, ConAu 49, SmATA 14*

Beers, V Gilbert 1928- *BioIn 11, -15, ConAu 49, -1NR, -16NR, -36NR, IntAu&W 89, -91, SmATA 9, WhoAm 86, -88, WhoMW 90*

Beery, Mary *WrDr 86, -88, -90, -92, -94*

Beery, Mary 1907- *ConAu 5R, ForWC 70, WrDr 76, -80, -82, -84*

Beetles, Peggy *ChhPo S1*

Beeton, Samuel Orchart 1831-1877 *Alli SUP, BioIn 1, -2, -11, -17, ChhPo S1, HsB&A, -SUP, OxCChiL, ScFEYrs, StaCVF*

Begay, Harrison 1917- *BioIn 4, -9, IlsBYP, WhAmArt 85*

Begley, Kathleen A 1948- *WhoAmW 91*

Begley, Kathleen Anne 1948- *BioIn 11, -12, ConAu 77, SmATA 21*

Behn, Harry 1898-1973 *AmPB, AnCL, ArizL, ArtsAmW 3, AuBYP 2, -3, BioIn 5, -6, -8, -9, -10, BkCL, ChhPo, -S1, -S2, ConAu 5R, -53, -5NR, DcAmChF 1960, DcLB 61, IlsCB 1946, -1957, -1967, MorBMP, MorJA, OxCChiL, SmATA 2, -34N, Str&VC, TwCChW 78, -83, -89, TwCYAW*

Behnke, Frances L *BioIn 11, ConAu 33R, SmATA 8*

Behnke, John 1945- *ConAu 69*

Behr, Joyce 1929- *BioIn 12, SmATA 15*

Behrens, June York 1925- *AuBYP 2, -3, BioIn 8, ConAu 17R, -8NR, -24NR, ForWC 70, SmATA 19, WhoAmW 75, -77*

Behrman, Carol H 1925- *ConAu 22NR, WhoWrEP 89*

Behrman, Carol Helen 1925- *BioIn 12, ConAu 61, -7NR, SmATA 14, WhoAmW 77, WhoWrEP 92*

Beiler, Edna 1923- *BioIn 17, ConAu 1R, -1NR, IndAu 1917, SmATA 61*

Beim, Jerrold 1910-1957 *AuBYP 2, BioIn 2, -4, -7, JBA 51, ObitOF 79*
Pseud./variant:
Anderson, Neil

Beim, Lorraine 1909-1951 *BioIn 2, JBA 51*

Beinicke, Steve 1956- *SmATA 69*

Beirne, Barbara 1933- *SmATA 71*

Beiser, Arthur 1931- *AuBYP 2, -3, BioIn 7, -13, ConAu 93, SmATA 22*

Beiser, Germaine 1931- *AuBYP 2, BioIn 11, SmATA 11*

Beisner, Monika *BioIn 16, SixBJA*

Beissel, Henry Eric 1929- *CanWW 89, ConAu 65, -10NR, ConPo 70, -75, IntAu&W 86, OxCCan SUP, WrDr 76, -80*

Beith, John Hay 1876-1952 *CmScLit*

Beith, John Hay, Sir 1876-1952 *BioIn 3, -4, Chambr 3, DcLEL, DcNaB 1951, EvLB, LongCTC, NewC, NotNAT B, ObitOF 79, ObitT 1951, REn, TwCA, -SUP*

Beitler, Ethel Jane 1906- *ConAu 5R, -2NR*

Beitler, Stanley 1924- *AuBYP 2, BioIn 7, ConAu 5R*

Beitler, Stanley Samuel 1924- *AuBYP 3*

Belair, Richard L 1934- *BioIn 15, SmATA 45*

Belaney, Archibald Stansfeld 1888-1938 *CanWr, ConAu 114, CreCan 1, DcLEL, LongCTC, OxCCan, OxCCanL, SmATA 24*
Pseud./variant:
Belaney, George Stansfeld
Grey Owl
Wa-Sha-Quon-Asin

Belaney, George Stansfeld
Main entry: Belaney, Archibald Stansfeld

Belden, Shirley *AuBYP 2, -3, BioIn 7*

Belden, Wilanne Schneider 1925- *BioIn 16, ConAu 23NR, ScF&FL 92, SmATA 56, WhoWrEP 89, -92*

Belfield, Eversley Michael Gallimore 1918- *Au&Wr 71, ConAu 25R, IntAu&W 82, WrDr 76, -80, -82, -84, -86*

Belfrage, Sally 1936- *BioIn 17, SmATA 65*

Belknap, B H *YABC 1*
Main entry: Ellis, Edward S

Bell, Adrian Hanbury 1901- *BioIn 4, -6, DcLEL, EvLB, IntAu&W 77, LongCTC, TwCA, -SUP, Who 74*

Bell, Anthea *ChhPo S1*

Bell, Catherine Douglas d1861 *Alli SUP, CarSB, DcEnL*

Bell, Clare 1952- *DcAmChF 1960*

Bell, Corydon Whitten 1894- *AuBYP 2, BioIn 3, -4, -5, -6, -8, -9, ChhPo, ConAu 5R, IlsBYP, IlsCB 1946, -1957, OhA&B, SmATA 3, ThrBJA*

Bell, Eileen 1907- *ConAu 33R, TwCPaSc*

Bell, Elizabeth Rose 1912- *ConAu 106*

Bell, Emerson *MajAI*

Bell, Emily Mary *ConAu X, SmATA X*
Main entry: Cason, Mabel Earp

Bell, Frank *ConAu 134, MajAI, SmATA 65, WrDr 94*
Main entry: Benson, Mildred Augustine Wirt

Bell, Frank 1904- *Who 88, -92*

Bell, Frederic 1928- *AuBYP 2S, -3*

Bell, Gail Winther 1936- *ChhPo S2, ConAu 41R, WhoAm 76*

Bell, Gertrude 1911- *AuBYP 2S, -3, BioIn 11, ConAu 13R, ForWC 70, SmATA 12*

Bell, Gina
Main entry: Iannone, Jeanne Koppel

Bell, Gina 1911- *ConAu X, SmATA 7*

Bell, Janet *AuBYP 3, ConAu X, SmATA X, WrDr 80*
Main entry: Clymer, Eleanor

Bell, John Keble 1875-1928 *ChhPo*

Bell, Joseph N 1921- *AuBYP 3*

Bell, Joseph Newton 1921- *AuBYP 2, ConAu 5R, IndAu 1917, WhoWest 74, -76*

Bell, Kensil 1907- *AuBYP 2, -3, BioIn 7*

Bell, Lettice *CarSB*

Bell, Louise Price *ConAu P-1*

Bell, Margaret Elizabeth 1898- *AmAu&B, AuBYP 2, -3, BioIn 2, -3, -6, -7, -9, ConAu 1R, -1NR, CurBio 52, MorJA, SmATA 2*

Bell, Neill 1946- *ConAu 118, SmATA 59*

Bell, Norman 1899- *BioIn 11, ConAu 61, SmATA 11*

Bell, Norman Andrew 1932- *WhoMW 90*

Bell, R S W 1871-1921 *OxCChiL*

Bell, Raymond M 1907- *WrDr 86, -88, -90, -92*

Bell, Raymond Martin 1907- *AmMWSc 73P, -76P, -82, -86, -89, -92, ConAu 29R, SmATA 13, WhoGen 81, WrDr 76, -80, -82, -84, -94*

Bell, Robert Stanley Warren 1871-1921 *BioIn 8, -13, ChhPo, ConAu 115, SmATA 27, StaCVF, WhoChL*

Bell, Thelma 1896- *AuBYP 3*

Bell, Thelma, and Corydon Whitten Bell *AuBYP 3*

Bell, Thelma Harrington 1896- *AuBYP 2, BioIn 3, -4, -5, -6, -8, -9, ChhPo, ConAu 1R, OhA&B, SmATA 3, ThrBJA*

Bell, Whitfield Jenks, Jr. 1914- *ConAu 105, DrAS 74H, -78H, -82H, WhoAm 74, -76, -78, -80, -82, -84, -86, -88, -90, -92, -94, WhoLibI 82*

Bellairs, John 1938- *BioIn 9, ConAu 21R, -8NR, -24NR, FifBJA, IntAu&W 82, -86, -89, -91, SmATA 2, WhoE 74, WrDr 76, -80, -82, -84, -86, -88, -90, -92*

Bellairs, John 1938-1991 *ConAu 133, DcAmChF 1985, MajAI, ScF&FL 92, SmATA 66, -68, WrDr 94N*

Beller, William Stern 1919- *ConAu 5R, WhoE 74, WhoFrS 84*

Bellingham, Brenda 1931- *BioIn 16, ConAu 123, IntAu&W 91, SmATA 51*

Belloc, Hilaire *IntvTCA 2*

Belloc, Hilaire 1870-1953 *Benet 87, BioIn 14, -15, -17, BlmGEL, CamGEL, CamGLE, DcLB 100, ModBrL S2, RAdv 13-1, -13-3, RfGEnL 91, ScFEYrs, TwCChW 89, WrChl*

Belloc, Hilaire Pierre Rene 1870-1953 *AnCL, AtlBL, AuBYP 2, BioIn 1, -2, -3, -4, -5, -6, -8, -9, -10, -11, -12, -13, BkC 5, CarSB, CasWL, CathA 1930, Chambr 3, ChhPo, -S1, -S2, CnE&AP, CnMWL, ConAu 106, CyWA 58, DcCathB, DcLB 19, DcLEL, EncWL 2, EvLB, FamPYP, GrBr, LongCEL, LongCTC, ModBrL, -S1, -S2, NewC, ObitOF 79, ObitT 1951, OxCChiL, OxCEng 67, -85, PenC ENG, RAdv 1, REn, TwCA, -SUP, TwCChW 78, -83, TwCLC 7, -18, TwCWr, WebE&AL, WhDW, WhAm 3, WhoChL, WhoLA, YABC 1*

Belloc, Joseph Hilaire Pierre 1870-1953 *AuBYP 3*

Bellows, Cathy *AuBYP 3*

Bellville, Cheryl Walsh 1944- *BioIn 16, IntAu&W 86, SmATA 49, -54*

Bell-Zano, Gina
Main entry: Iannone, Jeanne Koppel

Bell-Zano, Gina 1911- *ConAu X, SmATA 7*

Belpre, Pura *BioIn 14, InB&W 85*

Belpre, Pura 1899-1982 *AuBYP 2, -3, BioIn 7, -12, BkP, ConAu 73, -109, FourBJA, SmATA 16, -30N*

Belshaw, Michael 1928- *AmMWSc 73S, ConAu 21R*

Belson, Mary *OxCChiL*

Belting, Natalia Maree 1915- *AuBYP 2, -3, BioIn 7, -9, -10, ChhPo S2, ConAu 1R, -3NR, DrAS 74H, -78H, -82H, SmATA 6, ThrBJA*

Belton, John Raynor 1931- *BioIn 13, ConAu 69, SmATA 22*

Beltran, Alberto 1923- *BioIn 8, -15, IlsBYP, IlsCB 1957, SmATA 43, WhoAm 86, WhoGrA 62, -82, WhoSSW 73*

Beltran-Hernandez, Irene 1945- *SmATA 74*

Belvedere, Lee *ConAu X, IntAu&W 77X, -82X, SmATA 7, WrDr 76, -80, -82, -84*
Main entry: Grayland, Valerie Merle

Bemelmans, Ludwig d1963 *WhoAmA 86N*

Bemelmans, Ludwig 1898-1962 *AmAu&B, AmNov, AmPB, AuBYP 2, -3, Au&ICB, Benet 87, BenetAL 91, BioIn 1, -2, -3, -4, -5, -6, -7, -8, -10, -12, -14, -15, -17, Cald 1938, ChhPo, -S1, -S2, ChlLR 6, ChsFB I, CnDAL, ConAu 73, CurBio 41, -62, DcAmB S7, DcLB 22, DcLEL, EncWL, FamAIYP, IlsBYP, IlsCB 1744, -1946, -1957, LongCTC, MajAI, MorJA, Novels, ObitOF 79, OxCAmL 65, -83, OxCChiL, PenC AM, REn, REnAL, RfGAmL 87, SmATA 15, TwCA, -SUP, TwCChW 78, -83, -89, TwCWr, WhAm 4, WhoAmA 78N, -80N, -82N, WhoChL, WhoGrA 62, WorAlBi, WorAl, WrChl*

Bemelmans, Ludwig 1898-1963 *WhoAmA 89N, -91N*

Bemister, Margaret *OxCCan*

Benagh, Jim 1937- *AuBYP 2S, -3, ConAu 57, -9NR, MichAu 80*

Benander, Carl D 1941- *ConAu 141, SmATA 74*

Benarde, Melvin Albert 1923?- *AmMWSc 73P, -76P, -82, -86, -89, -92, ConAu 25R, WhoAm 82, -84, WhoE 74, -81, -83, WrDr 76, -80, -82, -84*

Benarde, Melvin Albert 1924- *WrDr 86, -88, -90, -92, -94*

Benarde, Melvin Albert 1925- *IntAu&W 89*

Benary, Margot *ConAu X, MajAI, SmATA X*
Main entry: Benary-Isbert, Margot

Benary-Isbert, Margot *BiGAW*

Benary-Isbert, Margot 1889-1979 *AnCL, AuBYP 2, -3, BioIn 6, -7, -9, -12, ChlLR 12, ConAu 5R, -4NR, ConLC 12, MajAI, MorJA, ScF&FL 92, SmATA 2, -21N*
Pseud./variant:
Benary, Margot

Benasutti, Marion *BioIn 17*

Benasutti, Marion 1908- *AmCath 80, BioIn 10, ConAu 21R, IntAu&W 77, SmATA 6, WrDr 76, -80, -82, -84, -86, -88, -90, -92*

Benasutti, Marion 1908-1992 *WrDr 94N*

Benchley, Nathaniel 1915-1981 *BenetAL 91, ScF&FL 92, TwCChW 89*

Benchley, Nathaniel Goddard 1915-1981 *AmAu&B, AnObit 1981, AuBYP 2S, -3, Au&Wr 71, BiE&WWA, BioIn 3, -4, -9, -10, -11, -12, -13, BlueB 76, CelR, ConAu 1R, -105, -2NR, -12NR, CurBio 53, -82N, DcAmChF 1960, FourBJA, IntAu&W 82, NewYTBS 81, NotNAT, SmATA 3, -25, -28N, TwCChW 78, -83, TwCYAW, WhAm 8, WhoAm 74, -76, -78, -80, WhoWor 74, WorAl, WorAu 1950, WrDr 76, -80, -82*

Benchley, Peter Bradford 1940- *AuNews 2, BioIn 9, -10, -11, -12, ConAu 17R, ConLC 4, -8, CurBio 76, IntAu&W 77, SmATA 3, WhoAm 76, -78, -80, -82, -84, -86, -88, -90, -92, -94, WhoEnt 92, WhoUSWr 88, WhoWrEP 89, -92, WorAl*

Benda, Wladyslaw Theodor 1873-1948 *PolBiDi*

Benda, Wladyslaw Theodore 1873-1948 *BioIn 1, ChhPo, IlrAm 1880, IlsCB 1744, WhAm 2, WhScrn 83*

Bender, Lucy Ellen 1942- *BioIn 13, ConAu 25R, SmATA 22*

Bendick, Jeanne 1919- *AmPB, AuBYP 2, -3, BioIn 2, -5, -6, -8, -9, BkP, ChlLR 5, ConAu 5R, -2NR, ForWC 70, IlsCB 1946, -1957, MajAI, MorJA, SmATA 2, -68, -4AS, WhoAmW 85*

Bendick, Robert L 1917- *AuBYP 2, BioIn 6, -8, -11, ConAu 61, IntMPA 75, -76, -78, -77, MorJA, NewYTET, SmATA 11*

Bendick, Robert Louis 1917- *AuBYP 3, WhoEnt 92*

Benedict, Dorothy Potter 1889-1979 *BioIn 11, -13, ConAu 93, -P-1, SmATA 11, -23N*

Benedict, Lois Trimble 1902-1967 *BioIn 11, ConAu P-2, SmATA 12*

Benedict, Rex 1920- *AuBYP 3, IntAu&W 91, TwCChW 89, WrDr 86, -88, -90, -92*

Benedict, Rex Arthur 1920- *AuBYP 2S, BioIn 11, ConAu 17R, IntAu&W 77, SmATA 8, TwCChW 78, -83, WhoE 74, WrDr 76, -80, -82, -84, -94*

Benedict, Stewart Hurd 1924- *BioIn 13, ConAu 13R, IntAu&W 77, SmATA 26, WhoE 74, -89*

Beneduce, Ann *BioIn 13, ForWC 70, WhoAmW 75*

Benenson, Lawrence A *AuBYP 2, -3, BioIn 8*

Benet, Laura 1884-1979 *AmAu&B, AuBYP 2, -3, BenetAL 91, BioIn 2, -8, -9, -10, -11, -13, -17, ChhPo, ConAu 9R, -85, -6NR, FemiCLE, JBA 51, REn, REnAL, ScF&FL 92, SmATA 3, -23N, WhAm 7, WhoAm 74, WhoAmW 74, WhoE 74*

Benet, Rosemary 1898?-1962 *BioIn 6, ChhPo, FamPYP, OxCChiL*

Benet, Stephen Vincent *IntvTCA 2*

Benet, Stephen Vincent 1898-1943 *AmAu&B, AnCL, AuBYP 2S, -3, Benet 87, BenetAL 91, BioIn 1, -2, -3, -4, -5, -6, -7, -10, -11, -12, -14, -15, -17, BkCL, CamGLE, CamHAL, CasWL, Chambr 3, ChhPo, -S1, -S2, CnDAL, CnE&AP, CnMWL, ConAmA, ConAmL, ConAu 104, CurBio 43, CyWA 58, DcLB 4, -48, -102, DcLEL, DcNAA, EncAB-A 29, EncSF 93, EncWL, -2, EvLB, FamPYP, HalFC 84, -88, LongCTC, McGEWB, ModAL, NewEScF, NewGrDA 86, NotNAT B, Novels, ObitOF 79, OxCAmH, OxCAmL 65, -83, OxCChiL, OxCEng 67, -85, PenC AM, RAdv 1, -13-1, REn, REnAL, RfGAmL 87, RfGShF, ShSCr 10, SixAP, Str&VC, SupFW, TwCA, -SUP, TwCLC 7, TwCRHW 90, TwCWr, WebAB 74, -79, WebE&AL, WhDW, WhAm 2, WhNAA, WhoHr&F, WhoTwCL, WorAlBi, WorAl, YABC 1*

Benet, Sula 1903?-1982 *AmMWSc 73S, -76P, AuBYP 2, BioIn 8, -12, -13, -14, ConAu 108, FifIDA, NewYTBS 82, SmATA 21, -33N*

Benet, Sula 1906-1982 *AuBYP 3*

Benet, William Rose 1886-1950 *AmAu&B, Benet 87, BenetAL 91, BioIn 1, -2, -3, -4, -10, -12, -15, CamGLE, CamHAL, ChhPo, -S1, -S2, CnDAL, ConAmA, ConAmL, ConAu 118, DcLB 45, DcLEL, LongCTC, ObitOF 79, OxCAmL 65, -83, OxCEng 67, PenC AM, REn, REnAL, RfGAmL 87,*

TwCA, –SUP, TwCLC 28, WebAB 74, –79, WhAm 3, WhNAA, WorAlBi, WorAl

Benezra, Barbara 1921- *BioIn 11, ConAu 13R, ForWC 70, SmATA 10*

Benford, Gregory *IntvTCA 2*

Benford, Gregory 1941- *ConAu 69, –12NR, –24NR, ConLC 52, DcLB Y82B, EncSF 93, IntAu&W 82, NewEScF, PostFic, RGTwCSF, ScF&FL 92, ScFSB, TwCSFW 86, –91, WhoSciF, WrDr 84, –86, –88, –90, –92*

Benford, Gregory Albert 1941- *WrDr 94*

Benford, Harry 1917- *AmMWSc 73P, –82, –86, –89, –92, IntAu&W 82*

Benford, Harry Bell 1917- *WhoAm 92, –94*

Benham, Leslie 1922- *ConAu 9R, SmATA 48*

Benham, Lois 1924- *ConAu 9R, SmATA 48*

Benham, Mary Lile 1914- *BioIn 16, CanWW 89, SmATA 55*

Benjamin, Nora *AuBYP 3, SmATA X*
Main entry: Kubie, Nora Gottheil Benjamin

Benjamin, Nora 1899- *BioIn 8, ConAu X, DcWomA, SmATA X, WhAmArt 85*

Benjamin, Nora 1899-1988 *BioIn 15, –16*

Bennett, Anna Elizabeth 1914- *ChhPo, ConAu 17R, IntAu&W 77, WhoUSWr 88, WhoWrEP 89, –92*

Bennett, Charles Moon 1899- *Au&Wr 71, EarABI SUP, IntAu&W 77, WrDr 76, –80*

Bennett, Deborah Elizabeth 1932- *Au&Wr 71*

Bennett, Dorothea *ConAu X, SmATA X*
Main entry: Young, Dorothea Bennett

Bennett, Ethel Hume 1881- *OxCCan, WhNAA*

Bennett, Eve *AuBYP 2, –3, BioIn 7*

Bennett, Fred 1877- *DcBrBI*

Bennett, Geoffrey M *ScF&FL 92*

Bennett, Geoffrey Martin 1909- *Au&Wr 71, ConAu 13R, IntAu&W 77, –82, Who 74, –82, –83, WhoSpyF, WrDr 76, –80, –82, –84*

Bennett, Jack 1934- *DcChlFi*

Bennett, Jay 1912- *Au&Arts 10, AuBYP 2S, –3, BioIn 10, –13, ConAu 69, –11NR, –42NR, ConLC 35, DcAmChF 1960, –1985, SixBJA, SmATA 27, –41, –4AS, TwCYAW, WhoAm 78, –80*

Bennett, Jill Crawford 1934- *BioIn 12, IlsCB 1967, SmATA 41*

Bennett, John 1865-1956 *AmAu&B, BenetAL 91, BioIn 1, –2, –4, –5, –6, –11, –14, –15, BlkAWP, CarSB, ChhPo, –S1, ConICB, DcAmAu, DcLB 42, IlsCB 1744, JBA 34, –51, ObitOF 79, OhA&B, OxCAmL 65, –83, OxCChiL, REnAL, WhAm 3, WhAmArt 85, YABC 1*

Bennett, Kay Curley 1922- *BioIn 9, ConAu 17R, ForWC 70*

Bennett, Lerone 1928- *BioIn 16, WhoBlA 85*

Bennett, Lerone, Jr. *IntvTCA 2*

Bennett, Lerone, Jr. 1928- *BlkAuII, –92, BlkWr 1, ConAu 25NR, ConBlB 5, EncTwCJ, InB&W 85, NegAl 89, WhoAm 86, –88, –90, –92, –94, WhoBlA 88, –90, –92, WhoUSWr 88, WhoWrEP 89, –92*

Bennett, Rachel *AuBYP 3, ConAu X, SmATA X*
Main entry: Hill, Margaret

Bennett, Rainey 1907- *BioIn 5, –8, –12, DcCAr 81, FourBJA, IlsBYP, IlsCB 1957, –1967, IndAu 1917, SmATA 15, WhAmArt 85, WhoAm 74, –76, –78, WhoAmA 78, –80, –82, –84, –86, –89, –91*

Bennett, Richard 1899-1971 *ArtsAmW 3, BioIn 1, –2, –5, –12, BlkAWP, IlsBYP, IlsCB 1744, –1946, JBA 51, SmATA 21, WhAmArt 85*

Bennett, Russell Hoadley 1896- *BioIn 6, –8, –13, SmATA 25, WhAm 8, WhoAm 74, –76, –78, –80, –82*

Bennett, Susan *IlsBYP*

Bennett, Susan Carroll 1953- *WhoAmW 91*

Benson, Edward Frederic 1867-1940 *BbD, BiD&SB, BioIn 2, –4, –17, Chambr 3, ConAu 114, CurBio 40, DcEnA A, DcLEL, DcNaB 1931, EncO&P 2, EvLB, LongCTC, ModBrL, NewC, Novels, OxCChiL, OxCEng 67, –85, PenC ENG, PenEncH, SupFW, TwCA, TwCCr&M 80, TwCWr*

Benson, Elizabeth P *BioIn 17*

Benson, Elizabeth P 1924- *SmATA 65*

Benson, Elizabeth Polk 1924- *WhoAmA 86, –89, –91*

Benson, Kathleen 1947- *ConAu 85, IntAu&W 82, –86, –89, SmATA 62*

Benson, Mildred Augustine Wirt 1905- *AuBYP 2, –3, BioIn 8, ConAu 134, ForWC 70, MajAI, OhA&B, SmATA 65, WrDr 94*
Pseud./variant:
Augustine, Mildred
Bell, Frank
Clark, Joan
Duncan, Julia K
Emerson, Alice B
Judd, Frances K
Palmer, Don
Thorndyke, Helen Louise
West, Dorothy
Wirt, Ann
Wirt, Mildred A

Benson, Mildred Wirt *ConAu 134, SmATA 65*

Benson, Sally 1900-1972 *AmAu&B, AmWomD, BenetAL 91, BiE&WWA, BioIn 1, –4, –9, –13, –14, CnDAL, ConAu 37R, –P-1, ConLC 17, CurBio 41, –72, FemiCLE, HalFC 84, –88, IntvTCA 2, NewYTBE 72, NotNAT B, ObitOF 79, OxCAmL 65, –83, REn, REnAL, SmATA 1, –27N, –35, TwCA SUP, WhAm 5, WomWMM, WorAl*
Pseud./variant:
Evarts, Esther

Benson, Virginia 1923- *ConAu 57*

Bent, Jennifer *BlkAuII 92*

Bentel, Pearl Bucklen 1901- *AuBYP 2, –3, BioIn 7, ConAu P-2*

Bentley, Judith 1945- *BioIn 15, ConAu 107, –23NR, SmATA 40, WhoWrEP 89*

Bentley, Judith McBride 1945- *WhoWrEP 92*

Bentley, Nicolas Clerihew 1907-1978 *Au&Wr 71, BioIn 1, –3, –5, –11, –12, –13, –14, BlueB 76, ChhPo, –S1, –S2, ConAu 65, –81, –11NR, DcNaB 1971, IlsCB 1744, IntAu&W 77, IntWW 74, –75, –76, –77, –78, –79N, LongCTC, NewC, SmATA 24N, Who 74, WhoWor 74, –78*

Bentley, Phyllis Eleanor 1894- *InWom SUP*

Bentley, Phyllis Eleanor 1894-1977 *Au&Wr 71, BioIn 1, –3, –4, –6, –10, –13, BlueB 76, ConAu 1R, –3NR, DcLEL, DcNaB 1971, EncMys, EvLB, IntAu&W 77, IntWW 74, –75, –76, –77, –78N, LongCTC, ModBrL, NewC, OxCEng 85, PenC ENG, RAdv 1, REn, SmATA 6, –25N, TwCA, –SUP, TwCCr&M 80, TwCWr, Who 74, WhoWor 74*

Bentley, Roy 1947- *ConAu 127, SmATA 46*

Benton, Patricia 1907- *ConAu 5R, IntAu&W 77, –82, –91, WhoAmW 77, –83, WhoWest 78, –80, –82, –84, WrDr 76, –80, –82, –84, –86, –88, –90*

Benton, Robert Douglas 1932- *AmAu&B, BioIn 1, –5, –8, –11, –12, ConAu 1R, –2NR, ConDr 73, –77A, –82A, DcLB 44, HalFC 84, IntMPA 75, –76, –78, –81, –82, –84, –86, –77, WhoAm 74, –82, –84, WhoE 74*

Benton, Thomas Hart 1889-1975 *AmAu&B, ArtsAmW 2, BenetAL 91, BioIn 1, –2, –3, –4, –5, –6, –7, –8, –9, –10, –11, –12, –13, –14, –15, –16, –17, BlueB 76N, BriEAA, CelR, ConAu 53, –93, CurBio 40, –75N, DcAmSR, DcCAA 71, –77, –88, EncAB-H, GrAmP, IlsCB 1744, –1946, IntDcAA 90, IntWW 74, –75N, McGEWB, MorMA, ObitOF 79, OxCAmH, OxCAmL 65, –83, OxCTwCA, OxDcArt, PhDcTCA 77, REn, REnAL, WebAB 74, –79, WhAm 6, WhAmArt 85, WhoAm 74, WhoAmA 73, –78N, –80N, –82N, –86N, –89N, –91N, WhoWor 74, WorAlBi, WorAl, WorArt 1950*

Berck, Judith 1960- *ConAu 142, SmATA 75*

Berckman, Evelyn Domenica 1900- *Au&Wr 71, BioIn 1, ConAmC 76, ConAu 1NR, EncMys, IntAu&W 77, WrDr 76*

Berdin, Richard *BioIn 1, –10*

Bere, Rennie Montague d1991 *Who 92N*

Bere, Rennie Montague 1907- *Au&Wr 71, ConAu 65, IntAu&W 77, Who 74, –82 –83, –85, –88, –90, WhoWor 78, WrDr 76, –80, –82, –84, –86, –88, –90, –92, –94*

Berelson, Howard 1940- *BioIn 10, IlsBYP, SmATA 5*

Berends, Polly B 1939- *SmATA 50*

Berends, Polly Berrien *BioIn 15, –16*

Berends, Polly Berrien 1939- *ConAu 108, SmATA 38*

Berenstain, Jan 1923- *BioIn 17, ChlLR 19, ConAu 36NR, SmATA 64*

Berenstain, Janice *AuBYP 3*

Berenstain, Janice 1923- *AmAu&B, AuBYP 2, BioIn 2, –8, –11, ConAu 25R, –14NR, FifBJA, MajAI, OxCChiL, SmATA 12, WhoAm 94, WorECar*

Berenstain, Michael 1951- *BioIn 15, ConAu 97, –14NR, –36NR, SmATA 45*

Berenstain, Stan 1923- *BioIn 16, –17, ChlLR 19, ConAu 36NR, SmATA 64*

Berenstain, Stanley 1923- *AmAu&B, AuBYP 2, -3, BioIn 2, -8, -11, ChhPo S1, ConAu 25R, -14NR, FifBJA, MajAI, OxCChiL, SmATA 12, WhoAm 94, WhoAmA 73, WorECar*

Berenzy, Alix 1957- *BioIn 17, ConAu 133, SmATA 65, WrDr 94*

Beresford, Elisabeth *BioIn 13, ConAu 102, IntAu&W 82, -89, -91, SingR 1, SmATA 25, TwCChW 78, -83, -89, TwCRHW 90, WrDr 80, -82, -84, -86, -88, -90, -92, -94*

Beresford, Marcus *ScF&FL 92*

Beresford, Marcus 1919- *AmAu&B, AmNov X, BioIn 2, ConAu 108*
Pseud./variant:
Brandel, Marc

Berg, Bjorn 1923- *FourBJA, SmATA 47*

Berg, Dave
Main entry: Berg, David

Berg, David 1920- *BioIn 13, ConAu 21R, -10NR, ConGrA 1, EncACom, IntAu&W 89, -91, SmATA 27, WhoAm 82, -84, -86, -88, -90, -92, -94, WhoUSWr 88, WhoWor 82, WhoWrEP 89, -92, WrDr 76, -80*
Pseud./variant:
Berg, Dave

Berg, Hans 1877- *WhoLA*

Berg, Jean Horton 1913- *AuBYP 3, IntAu&W 89, -91, WhoAm 86, WhoUSWr 88, WhoWrEP 89, -92*

Berg, Jean Horton Lutz *WhoAmW 87*

Berg, Jean Horton Lutz 1913- *AuBYP 2S, BioIn 10, ChhPo S1, ConAu 53, -4NR, ForWC 70, IntAu&W 77, SmATA 6, WhoAm 76, -78, -80, -82, -84, -88, -90, -92, -94, WhoAmW 74, -75, -77, -81, -83, -85, -89, -91, -93, WhoE 74, -89, -91, -93, WhoWor 93*

Berg, Joan *BioIn 8, ConAu X, IlsCB 1957, SmATA X*
Main entry: Victor, Joan Berg

Berg, Lasse 1943- *ConAu 73, -12NR, WhoWor 89*

Berg, Leila 1917- *TwCChW 89, WrDr 86, -88, -90, -92, -94*

Berg, Leila Rita 1917- *Au&Wr 71, ChlFicS, ConAu 101, IntAu&W 77, -82, -91, OxCChiL, TwCChW 78, -83, WrDr 82, -84*

Berg, Ron 1952- *SmATA 48*

Berg, Thomas 1914- *WhoAm 78, -80, -82, -84, -86, -88, -90, -92, -94, WhoSSW 84, -86, -88, WhoWor 82, -84, -87, -89*

Bergamini, David Howland 1928-1983 *BioIn 13, ConAu 1R, -110, -15NR, NewYTBS 83*

Bergaust, Erik 1925-1978 *AmAu&B, AuBYP 2, -3, BioIn 7, -12, ConAu 73, -77, -32NR, SmATA 20, WhAm 7, WhoAm 74, -76*

Berger, Barbara Helen 1945- *SixBJA, SmATA 77*

Berger, Fredericka *AuBYP 3*

Berger, Fredericka 1932- *ConAu 131, WrDr 94*

Berger, Gilda *ConAu 118, SmATA 42*

Berger, Gilda 1935- *ConAu 134, WrDr 94*

Berger, Josef 1903-1971 *AmAu&B, BioIn 9, -10, -11, -14, ConAu 5R, -33R, NewYTBE 71, SmATA 36*
Pseud./variant:
Digges, Jeremiah

Berger, Melvin 1927- *ChlLR 32*

Berger, Melvin H 1927- *AuBYP 2, -3, BioIn 10, ConAu 5R, -4NR, ConLC 12, FifBJA, MarqDCG 84, SmATA 5, -2AS, WhoAmM 83*

Berger, Phil *WhoEnt 92*

Berger, Phil 1942- *AuBYP 2S, -3, ConAu 61, -12NR, SmATA 62*

Berger, Terry 1933- *BioIn 11, ConAu 37R, IntAu&W 91, SmATA 8, WrDr 76, -80, -82, -84, -86, -88, -90*

Berger, William Merritt 1872- *ChhPo, ConICB, WhAmArt 85*

Bergere, Richard 1912- *WhAmArt 85, WhoAmA 73, -78*

Bergere, Thea *AuBYP 3*

Bergere, Thea Lindgren 1933- *AmAu&B, AuBYP 2*

Bergeron, Victor Jules 1902-1984 *AuBYP 3*

Bergeron, Victor Jules 1903-1984 *AuBYP 2S, BioIn 2, -4, -5, -7, -10, -11, -14, BioNews 74, BusPN, NewYTBS 84, WhAm 8, WhoAm 74, -76, -78, -82, -84, WhoWor 74*
Pseud./variant:
Trader Vic

Bergey, Alyce 1934- *BioIn 15, ConAu 5R, -7NR, ForWC 70, SmATA 45*

Bergman, Donna 1934- *SmATA 73*

Bergman, Roselyn J *ForWC 70*

Bergsoe, Jorgen Vilhelm 1835-1911 *BbD, BiD&SB, CasWL, EvEuW*

Bergstrom, Louise 1914- *ConAu 29R*

Berk, Phyllis Lavine *ForWC 70*

Berkebile, Fred D 1900-1978 *BioIn 13, ConAu 5R, -103, SmATA 26N*
Pseud./variant:
Donovan William
Ernest, William
Stauffer, Don

Berkeley, Anthony 1893-1970? *BioIn 4, -14, ConAu X, EncMys, LongCTC, Novels, TwCA, -SUP, TwCCr&M 80, -85, WorAlBi, WorAl*

Berkeley, Anthony 1893-1971 *CrtSuMy, DcLB 77, TwCCr&M 91*

Berkey, Barry Robert 1935- *BiDrAPA 89, BioIn 13, SmATA 24, WhoAm 80, WhoSSW 80*

Berkey, Helen L 1898- *ConAu P-2*

Berkman, Edward O 1914- *ConAu 61, -9NR*

Berkow, Ira 1940- *BioIn 10, ConAu 97, IntAu&W 82*

Berkow, Ira Harvey 1940- *WhoAm 86, -90, -94, WhoE 93*

Berkowitz, Freda Pastor 1910- *AuBYP 2, -3, BioIn 8, -11, ConAu P-1, SmATA 12*

Berliner, Don 1930- *ConAu 105, -21NR, IntAu&W 86, SmATA 33, WhoUSWr 88, WhoWrEP 89, -92*

Berliner, Franz 1930- *ConAu 29R, -12NR, -29NR, SmATA 13*

Berlitz, Charles L 1913- *SmATA 32*

Berman, Linda 1948- *ConAu 113, SmATA 38*

Berman, Paul *NewYTBS 86*

Berman, Paul 1949- *SmATA 66*

Berna, Paul *TwCChW 89B*

Berna, Paul 1910?- *AuBYP 2, -3, Au&Wr 71, BioIn 8, -9, -12, ChlLR 19, ConAu 73, OxCChiL, ScF&FL 92, SmATA 15, ThrBJA, TwCChW 78B, -83B*

Bernadette *ConAu X, -31NR, IntAu&W 77X, -82X, SmATA 4*
Main entry: Watts, Bernadette

Bernard, George I 1949- *SmATA 39*

Bernard, Jack F 1930- *ConAu 21R*

Bernard, Jacqueline 1921- *InWom SUP*

Bernard, Jacqueline 1921-1983 *AuBYP 2S, -3, BioIn 11, -13, ConAu 21R, -117, SmATA 8, -45N*

Bernards, Neal 1963- *SmATA 71*

Bernays, Anne *DrAPF 87, -89, -91, -93*

Bernays, Anne 1930- *ConAu X, DrAF 76, DrAPF 83, -85, ForWC 70, SmATA X, WhoAm 86, -88, WhoUSWr 88, WhoWrEP 89, -92*
Pseud./variant:
Kaplan, Anne Bernays

Bernays, Edward L 1891- *AmAu&B, BiDAmBL 83, BioIn 2, -4, -5, -7, -11, -13, -14, -15, -16, -17, ConAu 17R, CurBio 42, -60, EncAJ, EncTwCJ, EncWB, IntAu&W 77, REnAL, WhNAA, WhoAm 74, -76, -78, -80, -82, -84, -86, -88, -90, -92, -94, WhoAmJ 80, WhoE 81, -83, -85, -86, -89, -91, WhoWor 74, WhoWorJ 72, WrDr 76, -80, -82, -84, -86, -88, -90, -92, -94*

Berndt, Walter 1899-1979 *EncACom*

Berndt, Walter 1900-1979 *WhoAmA 86N, -89N, -91N*

Berndt, Walter 1905?-1979 *ArtCS, BioIn 12, WhoAmA 80N, -82N*

Berne, Eric 1910-1970 *AmAu&B, BioIn 7, -8, -9, -17, ConAu 5R, -25R, -4NR, MajTwCW, NewYTBE 70, WhAm 5*

Bernhardsen, Bris *AuBYP 3*
Main entry: Bernhardsen, Christian

Bernhardsen, Christian 1923- *AuBYP 2S, -3, ConAu 29R*
Pseud./variant:
Bernhardsen, Bris

Bernheim, Evelyne 1935- *ConAu 21R*

Bernheim, Marc 1924- *ConAu 21R*

Bernstein, Joanne E 1943- *ConAu 29NR*

Bernstein, Joanne Eckstein 1943- *ConAu 77, -13NR, SmATA 15*

Bernstein, Leonard d1990 *IntWW 91N LesBEnT 92, NewYTBS 92, Who 92N*

Bernstein, Leonard 1918- *AmAu&B, AmComp, AmSong, ASCAP 66, Baker 84, BiDD, BiE&WWA, BioIn 1, -2, -3, -4, -5, -6, -7, -8, -9, -10, -11, -12, -13, -14, -15, BlueB 76, CamGWoT, CelR, -90, CmpEPM, CompSN SUP, CpmDNM 82, ConAmC 76, -82, ConAu 1R, -2NR, -21NR, ConMus 2, ConTFT 3, CurBio 44, -60, DcCM, EncAB-H, EncMT, EncWT, FilmgC, HalFC 84, -88, IntAu&W 77, -82, IntWW 74, -75, -76, -77, -78, -79, -80, -81, -82, -83, -89, IntWWM 85, -90, LesBEnT, McGEWB, McGEWD 72, -84, NewCBMT, NewGrDA 86, NewOxM, NewYTBE 71, -72, NewYTBS 86, -87, NewYTET, NotNAT, OxCAmH, OxCAmL 65, -83, OxCAmT 84, OxCFilm, OxCMus, PenDiMP, -A, PenEncP, PlP&P, -A, RAdv 13-3, REn, REnAL, WebAB 74, -79, WhDW, Who 74, -82, -83, -85, -88, -90, WhoAm 74, -76, -78, -80, -82, -84, -86, -88, WhoAmJ 80, WhoAmM 83, WhoE 74, -81, -83, -85, -86, -89, WhoMus 72, WhoOp 76, WhoThe 72, -77, -81, WhoWor 74, -78, -80, -82, -84, -87, -89, WhoWorJ 72, -78, WorAlBi, WorAl, WorEFlm, WrDr 80, -82, -84, -86, -88, -90*

Bernstein, Leonard 1918-1990 *AnObit 1990, Baker 92, BenetAL 91, BioIn 16, -17, ConAu 132, ConCom 92, ConHero 2, CurBio 90N, JeAmHC, NewAmDM, NewYTBS 90, News 91, -91-1, OxCPMus, RComAH, WhAm 10, WhoAm 90, WhoE 91, WhoWor 91*

Bernstein, Margery 1933- *ConAu 57*

Bernstein, Ralph 1921- *AuBYP 2, -3, BioIn 7*

Bernstein, Theodore Menline 1904-1979 *BioIn 6, -11, -12, -13, ConAu 1R, -3NR, EncTwCJ, NewYTBE 72, SmATA 12, -27N, WhAm 7, WhJnl, WhNAA, WhoAm 74, -76, -78, WhoWorJ 72, -78*

Bernstein, Zena *ChhPo S1, IlsBYP*

Berquin, Arnaud 1749-1791 *CarSB, ChhPo, -S1, DcBiPP, OxCChiL, OxCFr*

Berrien, Edith Heal *AmWomPl*
Main entry: Heal, Edith

Berrien, Edith Heal 1903- *ConAu X, ForWC 70, SmATA 7, WhoAmW 85, -87, -89*

Berrill, Jacquelyn 1905- *AuBYP 2, -3, BioIn 7, -8, -11, ConAu 17R, IlsCB 1957, SmATA 12*

Berrill, Norman John 1903- *AmMWSc 73P, BlueB 76, CanWW 70, -80, -81, -83, -89, ConAu 17R, IntAu&W 82, -89, -91, IntWW 74, -79, -80, -81, -82, -83, -89, -91, Who 74, -82, -83, -85, -88, -92, WhoAm 86, -88, -90, -92, -94, WhoWor 74, WrDr 80, -82, -84, -86, -88, -90, -92, -94*

Berrill, Norman John, Prof 1903- *Who 90*

Berrington, John *ConAu X, DcLEL 1940, IntAu&W 91X, SmATA 6, WrDr 76, -80, -82, -84, -86*
Main entry: Brownjohn, Alan

Berrisford, Judith Mary *AuBYP 2, Au&Wr 71, BioIn 8, ConAu X, IntAu&W 77X, WrDr 76, -80*
Main entry: Lewis, Judith Mary

Berrisford, Judith Mary 1921- *AuBYP 3*

Berry, Barbara J 1937- *BioIn 10, ConAu 33R, SmATA 7, WrDr 76, -80*

Berry, Erick *AmPB, AuBYP 2, -3, ChhPo, ConAu X, ConICB, DcNAA, IlsCB 1946, JBA 34, -51, SmATA 2, -X*
Main entry: Best, Allena Champlin

Berry, Frederic Aroyce, Jr. 1906-1978 *ConAu 77*

Berry, James *BlkAuII 92, InB&W 85*

Berry, James 1924- *BlmGEL, CamGLE, WrDr 94*

Berry, James 1925- *ChlFicS, ChlLR 22, ConAu 135, ConPo 91, SmATA 67, TwCChW 89, WrDr 90, -92, -94*

Berry, James 1932- *AuBYP 2S, -3, BioIn 7, ConAu 21R*

Berry, Jane Cobb 1915?-1979 *SmATA 22N*

Berry, Joy *ConAu 134*

Berry, Joy 1944- *SmATA 58*

Berry, Joy Wilt *BioIn 15, SmATA 46*

Berry, Joy Wilt 1944- *BioIn 16, ConAu 134, WrDr 94*

Berry, Joyce Charlotte 1937- *WhoAm 92*

Berry, William David 1926- *AuBYP 3*

Berry, William David 1926-1979 *AuBYP 2, BioIn 8, -12, ConAu 73, IlsCB 1957, SmATA 14, WhoAmA 78, -80N, -82N, -86N, -89N, -91N*

Berson, Harold 1926- *BioIn 8, -9, ChhPo, ConAu 33R, FourBJA, IlsBYP, IlsCB 1957, -1967, SmATA 4*

Bertelli, Luigi 1858-1920 *CarSB*

Bertin, Leonard M 1918- *Au&Wr 71, ConAu 13R*

Bertol, Roland *AuBYP 2S, –3*

Bertolet, Paul *SmATA 73*
Main entry: McLaughlin, Frank

Berton, Pierre 1920- *Au&Wr 71, BioIn 5, –10, BlueB 76, CaW, CanWW 70, –79, –80, –81, –83, –89, CanWr, ConAu 1R, –2NR, CreCan 1, CurBio 91, DcLB 68, OxCCan, –SUP, OxCCanL, WhoAm 78, –80, –82, –84, –86, –88, –90, –92, –94, WhoCanL 85, –87, –92, WhoE 74, –75, –77, WhoWrEP 89, –92, WorAu 1975, WrDr 76, –80, –82, –84, –86, –88, –90, –92, –94*

Bertrand, Cecile 1953- *SmATA 76*

Berwick, Jean 1929- *ConAu 9R, SmATA X*
Pseud./variant:
Meyer, Jean Shepherd

Beskow, Elsa 1874-1953 *AnCL, AuBYP 2S, –3, BioIn 1, –2, –12, BkCL, ChhPo S2, ChlLR 17, ConAu 135, ConICB, DcWomA, IlsCB 1744, JBA 34, –51, OxCChiL, SmATA 20*

Beskow, Elsa Maartman 1874-1953 *MajAI*

Bess, Clayton 1944- *BioIn 16, –17, ConAu 129, SixBJA, SmATA X*
Main entry: Locke, Robert

Besser, Marianne *ForWC 70*

Best, Allena Champlin 1892- *AuBYP 3*

Best, Allena Champlin 1892-1974 *AuBYP 2, BioIn 1, –2, –5, –7, –9, –14, ConAu P-2, IlsCB 1744, –1946, JBA 34, –51, SmATA 2, –25N*
Pseud./variant:
Berry, Erick
Maxon, Anne

Best, Herbert 1894- *AuBYP 3, ScFSB*

Best, Herbert 1894-1980 *ScF&FL 92*

Best, Herbert 1894-1981 *AmAu&B, AmNov, AuBYP 2, BioIn 2, –8, –9, ConAu P-2, JBA 34, –51, SmATA 2, TwCChW 78, –83, –89, WrDr 80, –82, –84*

Bestall, Alfred 1892- *OxCChiL, TwCChW 83, WrDr 86*

Bestall, Alfred 1892-1986 *SmATA 48N, TwCChW 89*

Bestall, Alfred Edmeades 1892-1986 *BioIn 16*

Bester, Alfred *IntvTCA 2*

Bester, Alfred 1913- *AmAu&B, Benet 87, BioIn 11, –12, –13, –15, ConAu 13R, –12NR, ConSFA, DcLB 8, DcLEL 1940, IntAu&W 91, Novels, RGTwCSF, ScFSB, TwCSFW 86, WhoSciF, WrDr 76, –80, –82, –84, –86, –88*

Bester, Alfred 1913-1987 *AnObit 1987, BioIn 16, –17, ConAu 123, –36NR, EncSF 93, MajTwCW, NewEScF, ScF&FL 92, TwCSFW 91, WorAu 1980*

Beston, Henry 1888-1968 *AmAu&B, BenetAL 91, BioIn 1, –2, –4, –6, –7, –8, –10, –11, ConAu 25R, JBA 34, –51, ObitOF 79, OxCCan, REnAL, TwCA, –SUP, WhAm 5*
Pseud./variant:
Sheahan, Henry Beston

Betancourt, Jeanne 1941- *SmATA 43, –55*

Beth, Mary *ConAu X, SmATA X*
Main entry: Miller, Mary Beth

Bethancourt, T Ernesto *BioIn 16, ChlLR 3, ConAu X, FifBJA, SmATA 11*
Main entry: Paisley, Tom

Bethancourt, T Ernesto 1932- *ScF&FL 92*

Bethel, Dell 1929- *BioIn 16, ConAu 26NR, SmATA 52, WrDr 90, –92, –94*

Bethell, Jean 1922- *BioIn 11, ConAu 9R, –3NR, ScF&FL 92, SmATA 8*

Bethers, Ray 1902- *AuBYP 2, –3, Au&Wr 71, BioIn 7, –10, ConAu P-1, SmATA 6, WhAmArt 85, WhoArt 80, –82, –84*

Bethlen, T D *MajAI*

Bethune, J G *HsB&A, YABC 1*
Main entry: Ellis, Edward S

Bettelheim, Bruno 1903- *Benet 87, BioIn 5, –6, –8, –12, –13, BlueB 76, CelR 90, ConAu 23NR, IntAu&W 91, IntEnSS 79, IntWW 79, –80, –81, –82, –83, –89, OxCChiL, RAdv 13-5, ThTwC 87, WebAB 79, WhoAm 80, –82, –84, –88, WhoWor 80, –82, –84, –87, –89, WhoWorJ 78, WrDr 82, –84, –86, –88, –90*

Bettelheim, Bruno 1903-1990 *AnObit 1990, BenetAL 91, ConAu 131, ConLC 79, CurBio 90N, JeAmHC, MajTwCW, NewYTBS 90, News 90, –90-3, ScF&FL 92*

Bettenbender, John I d1988 *NewYTBS 88*

Bettenbender, John I 1921- *DrAS 74E, –78E, –82E, WhoAm 88*

Bettenbender, John I 1921-1988 *WhAm 9*

Betteridge, Anne *ConAu X, IntAu&W 82X, –91X, SmATA X, TwCRHW 90, WrDr 82, –84, –86, –88, –90, –92*
Main entry: Potter, Margaret

Betteridge, Anne 1926- *BioIn 14, WrDr 94*

Bettina *AuBYP 2, -3, ConAu X, DcWomA, IlsCB 1946, -1957, -1967, InWom SUP, MorJA, OxCChiL, REn, SmATA 1, TwCChW 83*
Main entry: Ehrlich, Bettina Bauer

Bettina 1903- *WrDr 86, -88, -90*

Bettina 1903-1985 *TwCChW 89*

Bettmann, Otto Ludwig 1903- *BiDAmJo, BiE&WWA, BioIn 1, -5, -6, -10, -12, -15, -16, ConAu 17R, CurBio 61, NotNAT, SmATA 46, WhoAm 74, -76, -78, -80, -82, -84, -86, -88, -90, -92, -94, WhoAmA 73, -78, -80, -82, -84, -86, -89, -91, WhoWor 74*

Betts, Ethel Franklin *ChhPo, -S1, DcWomA, IlrAm 1880, WhAmArt 85*

Betts, James *ConAu X, SmATA X*
Main entry: Haynes, Betsy

Betts, Victoria Bedford 1913- *WrDr 76, -80, -82, -84, -86, -88, -90*

Betz, Betty 1920- *AuBYP 2, -3, BioIn 1, -6, -7, -10, ConAu 1R, MorJA*

Betz, Eva Kelly 1897-1968 *BioIn 4, -11, BkC 5, ConAu P-1, SmATA 10*
Pseud./variant:
Peters, Caroline

Bevan, Tom 1868-1930? *BioIn 8, -12, WhoChL, YABC 2*
Pseud./variant:
Bamfylde, Walter

Bevans, Margaret *AuBYP 2, -3, BioIn 8*

Bevans, Michael H *AuBYP 2, -3, BioIn 7*

Bewick, John 1760?-1795 *Alli, CarSB, ChhPo S1, DcNaB, OxDcArt*

Bewick, Thomas 1753-1828 *Alli, BioIn 1, -2, -3, -4, -6, -8, -9, -10, -11, -12, BkIE, CamGLE, CarSB, CelCen, ChhPo, -S1, -S2, DcBiPP, DcBrBI, DcLEL, DcNaB, NewC, OxCArt, OxCChiL, OxCEng 85, OxDcArt, SmATA 16, Str&VC, WhDW, WhoChL*

Beyer, Audrey White 1916- *BioIn 11, ConAu 13R, DcAmChF 1960, ForWC 70, SmATA 9*

Beyer, Evelyn M 1907- *ConAu P-2*

Beyer, Paul J, III 1950- *SmATA 74*

Beynon, John *ConAu X, EncSF 93, ScF&FL 92, TwCSFW 86, WorAu 1950*

Bezencon, Jacqueline 1924- *SmATA 48*

Bhaktivedanta Swami, A C 1896-1977 *ConAu 73, -X*

Bhatia, Jamunadevi
Main entry: Bhatia, June

Bhatia, June *IntAu&W 91X, WhoCanL 92, WrDr 86, -88, -90, -92*

Bhatia, June 1919- *Au&Wr 71, BioIn 16, ConAu X, OxCCan SUP, WhoCanL 85, -87, WrDr 76, -80, -82, -84, -94*
Pseud./variant:
Bhatia, Jamunadevi
Edwards, June
Forrester, Helen

Bhatt, Kavery Ragunandan *DcChlFi*

Bhatty, Margaret R *DcChlFi*

Bial, Morrison David 1917- *BioIn 17, ConAu 61, SmATA 62, WhoAmJ 80, WhoE 75, WhoRel 92, WhoWorJ 72, -78*

Bial, Raymond 1948- *SmATA 76*

Bial, Raymond Steven 1948- *WhoUSWr 88, WhoWrEP 89, -92*

Bialer, Yehuda Leib 1896- *WhoWorJ 72, -78*

Bialk, Elisa *ConAu 131, SmATA 65*

Bialk, Elisa 1912- *AuBYP 2S, -3, BioIn 2, -3, -6, -9, ConAu X, CurBio 54, ForWC 70, MorJA, SmATA 1*
Pseud./variant:
Krautter, Elisa

Bialk, Elisa 1912-1990 *BioIn 16, -17, CurBio 90N*

Bianco, Margery *MajAI*

Bianco, Margery 1880-1944 *WomNov*

Bianco, Margery 1881-1944 *AuBYP 3*

Bianco, Margery Williams 1880-1944 *BioIn 14*

Bianco, Margery Williams 1881-1944 *AmAu&B, AnCL, AuBYP 2, BioIn 2, -8, BkCL, ChlLR 19, DcNAA, InWom SUP, JBA 34, -51, MajAI, NewC, OxCChiL, SmATA 15, Str&VC, TwCChW 78, -83, -89, WhAm 6, WhoChL, WrChl*
Pseud./variant:
Williams, Margery

Bianco, Pamela 1906- *AuBYP 2, -3, BioIn 1, -5, -8, -13, ChhPo, ConAu 85, ConICB, IlsCB 1744, -1946, JBA 34, -51, SmATA 28, WhoAmA 73, WhoAmW 74, -75*

Bianco, Pamela Ruby 1906- *WhoAmA 86*

Bianki, Vitali *AuBYP 3*

Bianki, Vitali 1894-1959 *AuBYP 2, BioIn 8*

Bibby, Cyril d1987 *Who 88N*

Bibby, Cyril 1914- *Au&Wr 71, ConAu 13R, –7NR, IntAu&W 77, –82, Who 74, –82, –83, –85, WrDr 76, –80, –82, –84, –86*

Bibby, Dause Leveridge 1911- *EncAB-A 31, IntYB 80, –81, –82, WhoAm 74, –76, –78, WhoFI 74*

Bibby, Violet 1908- *AuBYP 2S, –3, BioIn 13, ConAu 102, SmATA 24, TwCChW 78, –83, –89, WrDr 80, –82, –84, –86, –88, –90*

Bible, Charles 1937- *AfroAA, BioIn 16, BlkAuII, –92, ConAu 69, IlsBYP, InB&W 80, –85, SmATA 13*

Bice, Clare 1908-1976 *TwCChW 89*

Bice, Clare 1909-1976 *AuBYP 2, –3, BioIn 5, –7, –10, –13, CanWW 70, IlsCB 1946, Profile 1, SmATA 22, TwCChW 78, –83, WhoAm 74, –76, WhoAmA 73, –78, –80N, –82N, –86N, –89N, –91N, WhoArt 80, –82, –84*

Bickerstaff, Isaac *BenetAL 91, CamGEL, SmATA X*
Main entry: Swift, Jonathan

Bickerstaff, Isaac 1733-1808? *RfGEnL 91*

Bickerstaff, Isaac 1735-1812 *BioIn 17, DcIrB 88*

Bickerstaffe, Isaac John 1733-c. 1808 *IntDcT 2*

Bickham, Jack M 1930- *ConAu 23NR, IntAu&W 91, ScF&FL 92, TwCWW 91, WhoWrEP 89, WrDr 86, –88, –90, –92, –94*

Bickham, Jack Miles 1930- *AmAu&B, ConAu 5R, –8NR, EncFWF, EncSF 93, IntAu&W 82, SpyFic, WhoAm 74, WhoWrEP 92, WrDr 76, –80, –82, –84*

Biegel, Paul *TwCChW 89B*

Biegel, Paul 1925- *Au&Wr 71, BioIn 12, ChlLR 27, ConAu 77, –14NR, –32NR, IntAu&W 82, ScF&FL 92, SmATA 16, –18AS, TwCChW 78B, –83B, WhoWor 78, WrDr 76, –80, –82*

Biegel, Paul Johannes 1925- *ChlFicS, IntAu&W 86*

Bielawski, Joseph Gerald 1925- *IntAu&W 77, –82*

Bielski, Alison Joy Prosser 1925- *ConPo 70, IntAu&W 77, –89, –91, IntWWP 82, WrDr 76, –80*

Biemiller, Carl L 1912-1979 *BioIn 15, ConAu 121, ScF&FL 92*

Biemiller, Carl Ludwig 1912-1979 *AuBYP 2S, –3, BioIn 12, ConAu 106, SmATA 21N, –40*

Biemiller, Carl Ludwig, Jr. 1912-1979 *EncSF 93*

Biemiller, Ruth Cobbett 1914- *ConAu 37R, ForWC 70, WhoAmW 75, –77, WhoE 77*

Bienenfeld, Florence L 1929- *BioIn 15, ConAu 106, –23NR, SmATA 39*

Bierhorst, John 1936- *ConAu 28NR, SmATA 10AS, WhoE 86, WrDr 86, –88, –90, –92, –94*

Bierhorst, John W 1936- *AuBYP 2S, –3, BioIn 10, ConAu 33R, –13NR, FifBJA, IntAu&W 77, SmATA 6, WhoE 83, –85, WrDr 76, –80, –82, –84*

Biesterveld, Betty Parsons 1923- *ConAu 1R, –1NR*

Bigelow, Robert Sydney 1918- *AmMWSc 76P, Au&Wr 71, ConAu 102, FifIDA, WrDr 76, –80, –82, –84, –86, –88, –90*

Biggers, Earl Derr *Benet 87*

Biggers, Earl Derr 1884-1933 *AmAu&B, BenetAL 91, BioIn 11, –14, ChhPo S1, CmCal, ConAu 108, CorpD, CrtSuMy, DcNAA, EncMys, EvLB, FilmgC, HalFC 84, –88, NotNAT B, Novels, OhA&B, OxCAmL 65, –83, PenC AM, REn, REnAL, TwCA, TwCCr&M 80, –85, –91, TwCWr, WhAm 1, WhFla, WhNAA, WorAlBi, WorAl*

Biggers, John Thomas 1924- *AfroAA, ConAu 2NR, InB&W 80, –85, WhAmArt 85, WhoAmA 78, –80, –82, –84, –86, –89, –91*

Biggle, Lloyd, Jr. 1923- *ConAu 20NR, –35NR, EncSF 93, IntAu&W 91, NewEScF, RGTwCSF, ScFSB, SmATA 65, TwCSFW 86, –91, WrDr 86, –88, –90, –92, –94*

Biklen, Douglas Paul 1945- *ConAu 85, –15NR*

Bileck, Marvin 1920- *AmPB, BioIn 5, –8, FourBJA, IlsBYP, IlsCB 1946, –1957, SmATA 40, WhoAmA 73*

Bilibin, Ivan 1876-1942 *SmATA 61*

Bilibin, Ivan Iakolevich 1876-1942 *BioIn 17, WorECar*

Bill, Alfred Hoyt 1879-1964 *AmAu&B, BioIn 2, -6, -7, -15, ConAu 107, JBA 34, -51, MinnWr, SmATA 44, WhAm 4*

Billam, Rosemary 1952- *BioIn 17, ConAu 123, SmATA 61*

Billings, Charlene W *AuBYP 3*

Billings, Charlene W 1941- *ConAu 107, -24NR, SmATA 41*

Billings, Hammatt 1818-1874 *ArtsNiC, BiDAmAr, BioIn 13, MacEA, OxCChiL*

Billings, Henry 1901- *AmAu&B, BioIn 1, -5, -6, IlsCB 1946, MorJA, WhAmArt 85, WhoAmA 73, -78, -80, -82, -84, -86*

Billings, Henry 1901-1987 *WhoAmA 89N, -91N*

Billings, Peggy 1928- *ConAu 25R*

Billings, Peggy Marie 1928- *WhoAm 94, WhoAmW 91, -93*

Billington, Elizabeth T *ConAu 101, SmATA 43, -50*

Billout, Guy Rene 1941- *BioIn 11, ConAu 85, IntAu&W 82, SmATA 10*

Binder, Eando *AuBYP 3, EncSF 93, NewEScF, ScFSB*
Main entry: Binder, Otto Oscar

Binder, Eando 1911-1974 *TwCSFW 86, -91*

Binder, Otto O *EncSF 93*

Binder, Otto Oscar 1911-1974 *AuBYP 2, -3, BioIn 8, -10, ConAu 1R, -53, -3NR, ConSFA, NewEScF, WhoSciF*
Pseud./variant:
Binder, Eando
Giles, Gordon A

Binder, Pearl 1904- *Au&Wr 71, BioIn 1, -5, -11, ConAu X, IlsCB 1744, -1946*

Bindloss, Harold 1866-1945 *BioIn 1, -4, LongCTC, OxCCan, TwCA, -SUP, TwCWW 91, WhoLA*

Bingham, Caleb 1757-1817 *BenetAL 91, BioIn 15, CyEd, DcLB 42, OxCAmL 83*

Bingham, Evangeline M L 1899- *ConAu 65*
Pseud./variant:
Elliot, Geraldine

Bingley, David Ernest 1920- *ConAu 45, -2NR, -18NR, IntAu&W 77, -82, WrDr 88, -90*

Bingley, David Ernest 1920-1985 *ConAu 42NR, TwCWW 91*
Pseud./variant:
Roberts, John

Bingley, Margaret Jane 1947- *SmATA 72*
Pseud./variant:
Kirby, Margaret

Bingley, Thomas *Alli SUP, CarSB*

Binkley, Anne *ConAu X, SmATA X*
Main entry: Rand, Ann

Binks, Robert *ChhPo S2*

Binn, Mark A *IlsBYP*

Binns, Archie 1899-1971 *AmAu&B, AmNov, BenetAL 91, BioIn 2, -4, ConAu 73, -133, EncFWF, OxCAmL 65, -83, REnAL, TwCA, -SUP, WhAm 5, WhoPNW*

Binzen, Bill *AuBYP 2S, -3, BioIn 13, SmATA 24*

Birch, Cyril 1925- *ConAu 85, DrAS 74F, -78F, -82F*

Birch, Reginald Bathurst 1856-1943 *BioIn 2, -3, -5, -12, ChhPo, -S1, -S2, ConICB, CurBio 43, DcBrBI, IlrAm 1880, -A, ObitOF 79, OxCChiL, SmATA 19, WhAm 2, WhAmArt 85, WorECar*

Birchman, David 1949- *SmATA 72*

Bird, Alice *IlsBYP*

Bird, Anthony Cole 1917- *Au&Wr 71, ConAu 13R*

Bird, Caroline 1915- *BioIn 10, -11, -13, ConAu 17R, -11NR, CurBio 76, ForWC 70, IntAu&W 77, WhoAm 76, -78, -80, -82, -84, -86, -88, -90, -92, -94, WhoAmW 74, -75, -77, WhoE 75, WhoUSWr 88, WhoWor 89, -91, WhoWrEP 89, -92, WrDr 76, -80, -82, -84, -86, -88, -90, -92, -94*

Bird, Dorothy Maywood 1899- *ConAu P-1, WrDr 76, -80, -82, -84*

Bird, E J 1911- *SmATA 58*

Bird, Maria *BioIn 8, OxCChiL, WhoChL*

Bird, Marianne Clara 1954- *WhoAmW 87*

Bird, Patricia Amy 1941- *ConAu 61, -7NR, -22NR, WhoWrEP 89, -92*

Bird, Richard *OxCChiL, Who 92*

Bird, Traveller *AuBYP 2S, -3*

Birdseye, Tom *BioIn 17*

Birdseye, Tom 1951- *ConAu 133, SmATA 66, WrDr 94*

Birenbaum, Barbara 1941- *BioIn 17, ConAu 136, SmATA 65, WrDr 94*

Birley, Anthony R *ConAu 129*

Birley, Anthony Richard 1937- *Au&Wr 71*

Birmingham, Lloyd 1924- *BioIn 11, SmATA 12*

Birmingham, Lloyd P 1924- *BiDScF*

Biro, B *SmATA 67*
Main entry: Biro, Balint Stephen

Biro, Balint S 1921- *Au&Wr 71, BioIn 5, –8, –9, ConAu 25R, IlsBYP, IlsCB 1946, –1957, –1967, SmATA 1, TwCChW 78, WrDr 80*

Biro, Balint Stephen 1921- *ConAu 39NR, MajAI*
Pseud./variant:
Biro, B
Biro, Val

Biro, Val 1921- *BioIn 14, –17, ChlLR 28, ConAu X, IntAu&W 89, –91, OxCChiL, SmATA 13AS, TwCChW 83, –89, WhoArt 80, –82, –84, WhoWor 80, WrDr 82, –84, –86, –88, –90, –92, –94*

Biro, Val
Main entry: Biro, Balint Stephen

Birt, David 1936- *ConAu 73, –13NR, –35NR*

Birtles, Dora Toll 1903?- *DcChlFi*

Bischoff, David F 1951- *IntAu&W 91, NewEScF, ScFSB, TwCSFW 86, –91, WrDr 86, –88, –90, –92*

Bischoff, David Frederick 1951- *WrDr 94*

Bischoff, David Fredrick 1951- *ConAu 81, EncSF 93, WrDr 84*

Bischoff, Ilse Marthe 1903?- *AuBYP 2, –3, BioIn 1, –5, –6, –7, ChhPo, –S1, –S2, ConICB, IlsCB 1744, –1946, MorJA, WhAmArt 85*

Bischoff, Julia Bristol 1909-1970 *AuBYP 2, –3, BioIn 8, –11, ConAu P-2, SmATA 12*
Pseud./variant:
Arnoldy, Julie

Bisher, James Furman 1918- *ConAu 2NR, EncTwCJ, IntAu&W 89, –91, WhoAm 74, –76, –78, –80, –82, –84, –86, –88, –90, –92, –94, WhoSSW 73, –91, –93, WhoUSWr 88, WhoWrEP 89, –92*

Bishop, Bonnie 1943- *ConAu 103, SmATA 37*

Bishop, Claire *AuBYP 3*

Bishop, Claire Huchet *AmPB, AuBYP 2, BioIn 1, –2, –3, –7, –8, –14, BkP, CathA 1952, ConAu 73, –36NR, FamMS, JBA 51, OxCChiL, SmATA 14, TwCChW 78, –83, –89, WrDr 80, –82, –84, –86, –88, –90, –92*

Bishop, Claire Huchet 1898-1993 *WrDr 94N*

Bishop, Claire Huchet 1899?-1993 *ConAu 140, SmATA 74*

Bishop, Curtis 1912-1967 *AuBYP 3, DcAmChF 1960*

Bishop, Curtis Kent 1912-1967 *AuBYP 2, BioIn 7, –10, ConAu P-1, EncAB-A 39, SmATA 6*
Pseud./variant:
Brandon, Curt
Carroll, Curt

Bishop, Elizabeth *IntvTCA 2*

Bishop, Elizabeth 1911-1979 *AmAu&B, AmWr S1, ArtclWW 2, AuBYP 2S, –3, Au&Wr 71, Benet 87, BenetAL 91, BioAmW, BioIn 4, –7, –8, –10, –11, –12, –13, –14, –15, –16, –17, BlmGWL, BlueB 76, BroV, CamGLE, CamHAL, CelR, ChhPo, –S1, CnE&AP, ConAu 5R, –2BS, –26NR, ConLC 1, –4, –9, –15, –32, ConPo 70, –75, –80, ContDcW 89, CroCAP, CurBio 77, DcLB 5, DcLEL 1940, DrAP 75, EncWB, EncWL, –2, FemiCLE, FourBJA, InWom SUP, IntAu&W 77, IntDcWB, IntWW 74, –75, –76, –77, –78, –79, LiExTwC, MagSAmL, MajTwCW, MakMC, ModAL, –S1, –S2, ModAWP, ModAWWr, OxCAmL 65, –83, OxCEng 85, PenC AM, PoeCrit 3, RAdv 1, –13-1, REn, REnAL, RfGAmL 87, SmATA 24N, TwCA SUP, TwCWr, WebE&AL, WhAm 7, WhoAm 74, –76, –78, WhoAmW 74, –75, WhoE 74, WhoWor 74, WrDr 76, –80*

Bishop, Grace *AuBYP 2, –3, BioIn 8*

Bishop, Jack *AuBYP 2S, –3*
Main entry: Dorman, Michael L

Bishop, James Alonzo
Main entry: Bishop, Jim

Bishop, Jim *DrAPF 87, –89, –91, –93*

Bishop, Jim 1907- *AmAu&B, AuNews 1, –2, BioIn 3, –4, –8, –10, –11, –12, BioNews 74, CelR, ConAu 17R, CurBio 69, DrAP 75, EncTwCJ, REnAL, WhoAm 74, –76, –78, –80, –82, –84, –86, WhoSSW 73, –75, –76 WhoWor 74, –78, WorAlBi, WorAl*

Bishop, Jim 1907-1987 *AnObit 1987, CurBio 87N, NewYTBS 87, WhAm 9*

Pseud./variant:
Bishop, James Alonzo

Biskin, Miriam 1920- *ConAu 21R*

Biskin, Miriam Marcia Newell 1920- *WhoUSWr 88, WhoWrEP 89, –92*

Bisset, Donald 1910- *Au&Wr 71, BioIn 14, ConAu 33R, –13NR, IntAu&W 91, SmATA 7, TwCChW 78, –83, –89, WrDr 80, –82, –84, –86, –88, –90, –92, –94*

Bitter, Gary G 1940- *AmMWSc 86, –89, –92, ConAu 31NR*

Bitter, Gary Glen 1940- *AmMWSc 73P, –76P, –82, BioIn 13, ConAu 69, –14NR, LEduc 74, SmATA 22, WhoWest 74, –76*

Bixby, William 1920-1986 *ConAu 118, SmATA 47N*

Bixby, William Courtney 1920- *AmAu&B, AuBYP 2, BioIn 8, –10, ConAu 1R, SmATA 6, WhoAm 74*

Bixby, William Courtney 1920-1986 *AuBYP 3*

Bjerregaard-Jensen, Vilhelm Hans *SmATA X, WhoAm 84, –86, –88*
Main entry: Hillcourt, William

Bjoerk, Christina 1938- *ConAu 135, SmATA 67, WrDr 94*

Bjork, Christina *BioIn 17, ConAu 135*

Bjork, Christina 1938- *ChILR 22*

Bjorklund, Karna L *AuBYP 2S, –3*

Bjorklund, Lorence F 1913-1978 *BioIn 5, –8, –14, IlsBYP, IlsCB 1946, –1957, –1967, SmATA 32, –35, WhAmArt 85*

Black, Miss *CarSB, DcWomA*

Black, Algernon D d1993 *NewYTBS 93*

Black, Algernon David 1900- *BioIn 7, –10, –11, ConAu 1R, –2NR, SmATA 12*

Black, Algernon David 1900-1993 *ConAu 141, SmATA 76*

Black, Cyril E d1989 *NewYTBS 89*

Black, Cyril Edwin 1915- *AmAu&B, ConAu 1R, –3NR, DrAS 74H, –78H, –82H, WhoAm 74, –76, –78, –80, –82, –84, –86, –88, WhoE 74, WhoWor 74*

Black, Cyril Edwin 1915-1989 *BioIn 16, –17, ConAu 129, WhAm 10*

Black, Ian Stuart 1915- *Au&Wr 71, ConAu 6NR, ScF&FL 92*

Black, Irma Simonton 1906-1972 *AuBYP 2, –3, BioIn 7, –9, ConAu 1R, –37R, –6NR, NatCAB 58, SmATA 2, –25N*

Black, Ladbroke Lionel Day 1877-1940 *ChhPo S1*

Black, Mansell *ConAu X, SmATA X, TwCCr&M 80, –85, –91, WrDr 76, –80, –86, –88, –90, –92, –94*
Main entry: Trevor, Elleston

Black, Mansell 1920- *BioIn 14*

Black, Margaret K 1921- *ConAu 32NR*

Black, Margaret Katherine 1921- *Au&Wr 71, ConAu 29R, –14NR, IntAu&W 77, –82*
Pseud./variant:
Howorth, M K

Black, Susan Adams 1953- *ConAu 105, SmATA 40*

Blackburn, Claire *ConAu 30NR, SmATA X*
Main entry: Jacobs, Linda C

Blackburn, Edith H *AuBYP 2, –3, BioIn 8*

Blackburn, John Brewton 1952- *SmATA 15*

Blackburn, Joyce Knight 1920- *BioIn 13, ConAu 17R, IndAu 1917, SmATA 29, WhoAmW 74*

Blackerby, Alva W 1909-1959 *BioIn 5*

Blackett, Veronica Heath *WrDr 86, –88*

Blackett, Veronica Heath 1927- *Au&Wr 71, BioIn 11, ConAu 53, SmATA 12, WrDr 76, –80, –82, –84*
Pseud./variant:
Heath, Veronica

Blacklin, Malcolm *ConAu 31NR, IntAu&W 86X, –91X, MajAI, ScF&FL 92, SmATA 69, TwCYAW*
Main entry: Chambers, Aidan

Blackmore, Richard D 1825-1900 *CamGLE, RfGEnL 91*

Blackmore, Richard Doddridge 1825-1900 *Alli SUP, Benet 87, BbD, BiD&SB, BioIn 1, –2, –3, –4, –5, –10, –11, –12, –13, –16, BritAu 19, CelCen, Chambr 3, ChhPo, –S1, –S2, CyWA 58, DcBiA, DcEnA, –A, DcEnL, DcEuL, DcLEL, DcNaB S1, EvLB, JBA 34, MouLC 4, NewC, OxCEng 67, OxCLiW 86, PenC ENG, REn, TelT, WebE&AL*

Blackstock, Charity *Au&Wr 71, BioIn 14, ConAu X, –28NR, IntAu&W 91, ScF&FL 92, TwCCr&M 80, –85, –91, TwCRHW 90, TwCWr, WrDr 76, –80, –82, –84, –86, –88, –90, –92, –94*
Main entry: Torday, Ursula

Blackstone, Harry, Jr. 1934?- *BioIn 11, –12, ConAu 114, –X*

Blackstone, Harry Bouton, Jr. 1934- *WhoAm 86, –92, –94*

Blackton, Peter *ConAu X, SmATA X*
Main entry: Wilson, Lionel

Blackwood, Alan 1932- *SmATA 70*

Blackwood, Gary L 1945- *SmATA 72*

Blackwood, Paul Everett 1913- *AmMWSc 73P, ConAu 102, LEduc 74, WhoGov 77, –72, –75*

Blade, Alexander *MajAI*

Blades, Ann 1947- *BioIn 10, –12, CaW, CanWW 89, ChlLR 15, ConAu 77, –13NR, IlsCB 1967, OxCCan SUP, Profile 1, SmATA 16, –69, TwCChW 78, –83, –89, WhoAm 82, –84, –86, –88, –92, WhoCanL 85, –87, –92, WhoUSWr 88, WhoWrEP 89, –92, WrDr 80, –82, –84, –86, –88, –90, –92*

Blades, Ann Sager 1947- *MajAI, WrDr 94*

Bladow, Suzanne Wilson 1937- *ConAu 61, SmATA 14*

Blaine, John *AuBYP 3, BioIn 10, ConAu 131, –X, –29NR, SmATA 6, –65, –X*
Main entry: Goodwin, Harold Leland
Harkins, Philip

Blaine, John 1914-1990 *BioIn 16, –17, EncSF 93, ScF&FL 92*

Blaine, Margery Kay 1937- *AuBYP 2S, –3, BioIn 11, ConAu 61, SmATA 11*

Blair, Anne Denton 1914- *BioIn 15, SmATA 46*

Blair, Clay, Jr. 1925- *AmAu&B, AuNews 2, BioIn 8, –10, –11, IntWW 74*

Blair, Clay Drewry 1925- *WhoUSWr 88, WhoWrEP 89, –92, WrDr 94*

Blair, Culverson 1947- *BlkAuII 92*

Blair, Eric Arthur *RfGEnL 91*

Blair, Eric Arthur 1903-1950 *BioIn 1, –2, –3, –4, –5, –6, –7, –8, –9, –10, –11, DcEnL, DcNaB 1941, EvLB, GrBr, LongCTC, NewC, OxCEng 67, PenC ENG, REn, SmATA 29, WebE&AL*
Pseud./variant:
Orwell, George

Blair, Helen 1910- *BioIn 5, –13, IlsBYP, IlsCB 1946, SmATA 29, WhoAmA 73, –78, –80, –82, –84, –86, –89, –91*

Blair, Hunter *AuBYP 3*

Blair, Jay 1953- *SmATA 45*

Blair, Joan 1929- *BioIn 10*

Blair, Joane Ellen 1929- *WhoAmW 93*

Blair, Lucile *ConAu X*
Main entry: Yeakley, Marjory Hall

Blair, Lucille *AuBYP 3*

Blair, Mary Robinson 1911- *BioIn 4, –5, IlsCB 1946, PlP&P, WhAmArt 85*

Blair, Pauline Hunter *MajAI*

Blair, Ruth VanNess 1912- *AuBYP 2S, –3, BioIn 11, ConAu 21R, SmATA 12, WhoAmW 74, –81, WrDr 76, –80, –82, –84, –86, –88, –90, –92, –94*

Blair, Ruth Virginia VanNess 1912- *IntAu&W 89, WhoAmW 89, –93*

Blair, Shannon
Main entry: Kaye, Marilyn

Blair, Walter d1992 *NewYTBS 92*

Blair, Walter 1900- *AmAu&B, AuBYP 2, –3, BenetAL 91, BioIn 8, –11, ChhPo, ConAu 5R, –3NR, –18NR, DrAS 74E, –78E, –82E, IntAu&W 91, REnAL, SmATA 12, WhoAm 74, –76, –78, –80, WrDr 76, –80, –82, –84, –86, –88, –90*

Blair, Walter 1900-1992 *AnObit 1992, ConAu 139, SmATA 72*

Blaisdell, Elinore 1904- *BioIn 1, –5, IlsBYP, IlsCB 1744, –1946, WhAmArt 85*

Blake, Bud
Main entry: Blake, Julian Watson

Blake, Bud 1918- *ConAu 65, EncACom WhoAm 78, –80, –82, –84, –86, –88, –90, –92, –94*

Blake, C J *ChhPo, –S2, DcWomA*

Blake, Captain Wilton *WhoChL*

Blake, Julian Watson 1918- *ConAu 65*
Pseud./variant:
Blake, Bud

Blake, Olive *SmATA X*
Main entry: Supraner, Robyn

Blake, Quentin 1932- *ArtsCL, BioIn 6, –8, –11, –14, –15, –16, –17, ChhPo S1, ChlBIlD, ChlLR 31, ConAu 25R, –11NR, FifBJA, IlsBYP, IlsCB 1957, –1967, OxCChiL, SmATA 9, –52, WrDr 90, –92, –94*

Blake, Quentin Saxby 1932- *ConAu 37NR, MajAI*

Blake, Robert 1949- *SmATA 42*

Blake, Walker E *AuBYP 2S, ConAu X, –40NR, SmATA X*
Main entry: Butterworth, W E

Blake, William 1757-1827 *Alli, AnCL, AtlBL, AuBYP 2S, –3, Benet 87, BbD, BiDLA, BiD&SB, BioIn 1, –2, –3, –4, –5, –6, –7, –8, –9, –10, –11, –12, –13, –14, –15, –16, –17, BlmGEL, BkIE, BritAu 19, BritWr 3, CamGEL, CamGLE, CarSB, CasWL, CelCen, Chambr 2, ChhPo, –S1, –S2, ChrP, ClaDrA, CnDBLB 3, CnE&AP, CrtT 2, CyWA 58, DcBiPP, DcBrBI, DcEnA, –A, DcEnL, DcEuL, DcLB 93, DcLEL, DcNaB, Dis&D, EncO&P 1, –2, –3, EncPaPR 91, EvLB, FamPYP, IlEncMy, IntDcAA 90, LongCEL, LuthC 75, MagSWL, MajAI, McGEWB, MouLC 3, NewC, NinCLC 13, –37, OxCArt, OxCChiL, OxCEng 67, –85, OxCMus, OxDcArt, PenC ENG, PenEncH, RAdv 1, –13-1, RComWL, REn, RfGEnL 91, SmATA 30, Str&VC, WebE&AL, WhDW, WorAlBi, WorAl, WorLitC, WrChl, WrPh*

Blakeley, Phyllis 1922- *ConAu 61, OxCCan*

Blanc, Esther S 1913- *ConAu 131, WrDr 94*

Blanc, Esther Silverstein 1913- *BioIn 17, SmATA 66*

Blanc, Mel d1989 *LesBEnT 92*

Blanc, Mel 1908- *EncAFC, HalFC 88, IntMPA 86, –88*

Blanc, Mel 1908-1989 *AnObit 1989, BioIn 17, ConTFT 8, CurBio 89N, NewYTBS 89, News 89, SmATA 64, WhoCom, WorAlBi*

Blance, Ellen 1931- *ConAu 57, –7NR*

Blanchard, Amy Ella 1856-1926 *AmWomPl, BiDSA, BiD&SB, CarSB, ChhPo, –S1, –S2, DcAmAu, DcNAA, WhAm 1, WomWWA 14, WomNov*

Blanco, Richard L 1926- *SmATA 63*

Blanco, Richard Lidio 1926- *WhoHisp 94*

Blanco, Tomas 1900- *PueRA*

Bland, Edith 1858-1924 *ArtclWW 2, AuBYP 3, StaCVF, WomNov*

Bland, Edith Nesbit *AuBYP 2, BioIn 1, –3, –5, –6, –7, –8, –11, ChhPo, –S1, –S2, ConAu 137, EvLB, InWom SUP, JBA 34, MajAI, NewC, OxCChiL, TwCA, –SUP, YABC 1*
Main entry: Nesbit, E

Bland, Edith Nesbit 1858-1924 *BioIn 17*

Bland, Fabian *BlmGWL, ConAu 137, LongCTC, MajAI, YABC 1*
Main entry: Nesbit, E

Blandford, Percy William 1912- *AuBYP 2S, –3, Au&Wr 71, ConAu 9R, IntAu&W 77, –82, WhoWor 78, WrDr 76, –80*

Blane, Gertrude *ConAu X, SmATA X*
Main entry: Blumenthal, Gertrude

Blank, Clair 1915-1965 *BioIn 17, SmATA X*
Main entry: Blank, Clarissa Mabel

Blank, Clarissa Mabel 1915-1965 *SmATA 62*
Pseud./variant:
Blank, Clair

Blankenship, William D 1934- *ScF&FL 92*

Blankenship, William Douglas 1934- *ConAu 33R*

Blanton, Catherine 1907- *AuBYP 2, –3, BioIn 8, ConAu 1R*

Blanzaco, Andre C 1934- *ConAu 29R*

Blanzaco, Andre Charles 1934- *WhoE 81*

Blassingame, Wyatt Rainey 1909-1985 *AuBYP 2, –3, BioIn 8, –9, ConAu 1R, –114, –3NR, IntAu&W 77, –82, SmATA 1, –34, –41N, WhoHr&F, WhoSSW 76, WrDr 76, –80, –82, –84*
Pseud./variant:
Rainey, W B

Blathwayt, Jean 1918- *Au&Wr 71, ConAu 106, WrDr 76, –80, –82, –84, –86, –88, –90*

Blatter, Dorothy 1901- *ConAu P-1*

Blauer, Ettagale 1940- *ConAu 24NR, SmATA 49*
Pseud./variant:
Laure, Ettagale

Blaushild, Babette 1927- *ConAu 29R, WhoAmP 73*

Blechman, Robert O 1930- *BioIn 5, –12, –15, WorECar*

Bleeker, Sonia 1909-1971 *BioIn 2, -6, -9, BkP, ConAu X, ForWC 70, MorJA, SmATA 2, -26N*
Pseud./variant:
Zim, Sonia Bleeker

Blegvad, Erik 1923- *BioIn 5, -6, -8, -9, -12, ChhPo, ConAu 97, IlsBYP, IlsCB 1946, -1957, -1967, MajAI, OxCChiL, SmATA 14, -66, ThrBJA, WhoGrA 82*

Blegvad, Lenore 1926- *BioIn 9, -12, ConAu 69, -14NR, -31NR, SmATA 14, -66, ThrBJA*

Bleich, Alan R 1913- *BiDrAPH 79, ConAu 13R*

Bleier, Robert Patrick
Main entry: Bleier, Rocky

Bleier, Rocky *BioIn 15, -17*

Bleier, Rocky 1946- *BioIn 11, -12, ConAu 85, NewYTBS 74, -80*
Pseud./variant:
Bleier, Robert Patrick

Bleiler, Everette F 1920- *BioIn 11, ChhPo S2, WhoSciF*

Blessitt, Arthur 1940?- *BioIn 9, -11*

Bligh, William 1754-1817 *Alli, Benet 87, BiDLA, BioIn 2, -3, -4, -6, -7, -8, -9, -10, -11, -16, -17, CelCen, DcBiPP, DcNaB, McGEWB, NewC, OxCAusL, OxCShps, REn, WhDW, WorAlBi, WorAl*

Blinn, William *LesBEnT, -92, NewYTET*

Blinn, William 1937- *ConTFT 10*

Blish, James *IntvTCA 2*

Blish, James 1921-1975 *AmAu&B, Au&Wr 71, Benet 87, BenetAL 91, BioIn 10, -12, -13, -15, -17, ConAu 1R, -57, -3NR, ConNov 76, ConSFA, DcLB 8, EncSF 93, MajTwCW, NewEScF, Novels, ObitT 1971, RGTwCSF, ScF&FL 92, ScFSB, SmATA 66, TwCSFW 86, -91, WhoSciF, WorAlBi, WorAu 1950, WrDr 76*
Pseud./variant:
Atheling, William, Jr.
Laverty, Donald
Lyons, Marcus
MacDougal, John
Merlin, Arthur
Torley, Luke

Blishen, Edward 1920- *Au&Wr 71, BioIn 11, -15, -17, ChhPo, ChlFicS, ConAu 17R, -11NR, -27NR, IntAu&W 77, -89, -91, OxCChiL, ScF&FL 92, SmATA 8, -66, Who 82, -83, -85, -88, -90, -92, WrDr 76, -80, -82, -84, -86, -88, -90, -92, -94*

Bliss, Corinne Demas *DrAPF 87, -89, -91 -93*

Bliss, Corinne Demas 1947- *BioIn 15, ConAu 104, -28NR, DrAPF 83, -85, SmATA 37, WhoUSWr 88, WhoWrEP 89, -92*

Bliss, Michael 1941- *ConAu 103, -31NR, OxCCan SUP*

Bliss, Reginald *EncSF 93, MajTwCW, SmATA X*
Main entry: Wells, H G

Bliss, Ronald Gene 1942- *BioIn 11, ConAu 53, SmATA 12, WhoMW 78, WhoUSWr 88, WhoWrEP 89, -92*

Blitch, Fleming Lee 1933- *ConAu 9R, -X*

Blitzer, Charles 1927- *BioIn 16, WhoAm 74, -76, -78, -80, -82, -84, -88, -90, -92, -94, WhoGov 77, -72, -75*

Bliven, Bruce 1889-1977 *AmAu&B, AuBYP 2, Au&Wr 71, BioIn 4, -8, -11, -13, BlueB 76, ConAu 37R, -69, CurBio 41, -77N, DcLB 137, EncAJ, IntAu&W 77, IntWW 74, -75, -76, -77, -78N, NatCAB 62, ObitOF 79, TwCA, -SUP, WhAm 7, WhJnl, Who 74, WhoAm 74, -76, WhoWest 74, -76, WrDr 76*

Bliven, Bruce 1916- *IntAu&W 89, -91*

Bliven, Bruce, Jr. 1889-1977 *AuBYP 3*

Bliven, Bruce, Jr. 1916- *BioIn 9, ConAu 17R, -7NR, SmATA 2, WhoAm 74, -76, -78, -80, -82, -84, -86, -88, -90, -92, -94, WhoE 91, -93, WhoUSWr 88, WhoWor 78, -89, -91, WhoWrEP 89, -92*

Bliven, Naomi 1925- *ConAu 33R, WhoAm 74, -76, -78, -80, -82, -84, -86, -88, -90, -92, -94, WhoAmW 74*

Blixen, Karen *ArtclWW 2, CamGLE, DcScanL, GrFLW, RfGShF*

Blixen, Karen 1885-1962 *BioIn 12, -13 -16, -17, BlmGWL, ConAu 22NR, ContDcW 89, IntDcWB, MajTwCW, Novels, ObitT 1961, RAdv 13-2, SmATA 44*
Pseud./variant:
Andrezel, Pierre
B, Tania
Dinesen, Isak
Osceola

Blixen, Karen, Baroness *Benet 87*

Blixen, Karen, Baroness 1885-1962 *BioIn 14, -15*

Bloch, Lucienne 1909- *BioIn 1, -5, -11, IlsBYP, IlsCB 1744, -1946, SmATA 10, WhAmArt 85*

Bloch, Marie Halun 1910- *AuBYP 2, -3, Au&Wr 71, BioIn 7, -10, ConAu 1R, -4NR, -19NR, DcAmChF 1960, ForWC 70, FourBJA, IntAu&W 89, -91, SmATA 6, -9AS, TwCChW 78, WhoAmW 93, WrDr 76, -80, -82, -84, -86, -88, -90, -92, -94*

Bloch, Robert *DrAPF 87, -89, -91, -93, IntvTCA 2*

Bloch, Robert 1917- *AmAu&B, BioIn 7, -11, ConAu 5R, -5NR, ConLC 33, ConSFA, ConTFT 2, CrtSuMy, DcLB 44, DrAF 76, DrAPF 83, -85, EncMys, EncSF 93, FilmgC, HalFC 84, -88, IntAu&W 82, -86, -89, -91, IntMPA 75, -76, -78, -81, -82, -84, -86, -88, -92, -77, NewEScF, Novels, PenEncH, RGTwCSF, ScF&FL 92, ScFSB, SmATA 12, SupFW, TwCCr&M 80, -85, -91, TwCSFW 86, -91, WhoAm 82, -84, WhoHr&F, WhoSciF, WrDr 76, -80, -82, -84, -86, -88, -90, -92, -94*

Blochman, Lawrence G 1900-1975 *BioIn 10, -13, ConAu 53, -P-2, EncMys, SmATA 22, TwCCr&M 80, -85, -91, WhNAA, WhoWorJ 72, -78, WrDr 76, -80, -82, -84*

Blochman, Lawrence Goldtree 1900-1975 *BioIn 14*

Block, Eugene B 1890- *ConAu 5R, -2NR, WhoWorJ 72*

Block, Francesca Lia 1962- *ScF&FL 92, TwCYAW*

Block, Irvin 1917- *BioIn 11, ConAu 17R, SmATA 12*

Block, Seymour Stanton 1918- *AmMWSc 82, -86, -89, -92, WhoAm 78, -80, -82, -84, -94*

Blocksma, Mary *AuBYP 3, SmATA 44*

Blocksma, Mary 1942- *ConAu 130, WhoUSWr 88, WhoWrEP 89, -92, WrDr 94*

Blood, Charles Lewis 1929- *BioIn 13, ConAu 73, SmATA 28*

Bloom, Freddy 1914- *ConAu 101, IntAu&W 89, SmATA 37, WrDr 82, -84, -86, -88*

Bloom, Harold *AuBYP 3*

Bloom, Lloyd *SmATA 43*

Bloom, Lloyd 1947- *SixBJA*

Bloome, Enid P 1925- *AuBYP 2S, -3, ConAu 85*

Bloomfield, Diana *ChhPo*

Bloomfield, Michaela 1966- *SmATA 70*

Bloomfield, Robert 1766-1823 *Alli, BbD, BiDLA, BiD&SB, BioIn 1, -2, -8, -9, -12, -17, BritAu 19, CamGEL, CarSB, CasWL, Chambr 2, ChhPo, -S1, -S2, DcBiPP, DcEnL, DcLB 93, DcLEL, DcNaB, EvLB, NewC, OxCChiL, OxCEng 67, -85, OxCLiW 86, OxCMus, RfGEnL 91, WebE&AL*

Bloomfield, Robert 1766-1832 *CamGLE*

Bloomstein, Morris J 1928- *ConAu 25R*

Blos, Joan W 1928- *AuBYP 2S, -3, BioIn 12, -13, ChlLR 18, ConAu 101, -21NR, FifBJA, OxCChiL, SmATA 27, -33, -69, -11AS, TwCChW 83, -89, WhoAm 82, -84, -86, -88, -90, -92, -94, WhoAmW 81, -87, -89, -91, WhoE 86, WhoUSWr 88, WhoWrEP 89, -92*

Blos, Joan Winsor 1928- *DcAmChF 1960, MajAI, TwCYAW*

Blough, Glenn Orlando 1907- *AmAu&B, AuBYP 2, -3, BioIn 6, -8, -9, ConAu P-1, LEduc 74, MichAu 80, MorJA, SmATA 1, WhoAm 74, -76, -78, -80, -82, -84, -86, -88, -90, WhoUSWr 88, WhoWrEP 89, -92*

Blow, Michael *AuBYP 2S, -3*

Blow, Michael 1930- *ConAu 130, WrDr 94*

Blue, Rose *WhoAmW 87, -89, WhoE 86, -89*

Blue, Rose 1931- *AuBYP 2S, -3, ConAu 41R, -14NR, DcAmChF 1960, SmATA 5, WhoAmW 74, -75, -77, -81, -83, -85, -91, -93, WhoE 75, -77, -81, -83, -85*

Blue, Wallace *ConAu X*
Main entry: Kraenzel, Margaret

Blue, Zachary *SmATA 76, TwCYAW*
Main entry: Stine, Robert Lawrence

Blumberg, Leda *BioIn 16*

Blumberg, Leda 1956- *IntAu&W 89, SmATA 59, WhoUSWr 88, WhoWrEP 89, -92*

Blumberg, Rhoda 1917- *BioIn 14, -16, ChlLR 21, ConAu 65, -9NR, -26NR, MajAI, ScF&FL 92, SixBJA, SmATA 35, -70, WhoAmW 81, -83, WhoE 81, -83, -85, -86, -89, WrDr 92, -94*

Blumberg, Stanley 1921- *AmMWSc 73S, WhoSSW 82*

Blumberg, Stanley A 1912- *ConAu 136, WrDr 94*

Blume, Judy 1938- *ArtclWW 2, Au&Arts 3, AuBYP 2S, -3, BenetAL 91, BioIn 9, -10, -11, -12, -13, BlmGWL, CamGLE, ChlFicS, ChlLR 2, -15, ConAu 29R, -13NR,*

ConLC 12, –30, CurBio 80, DcLB 52, FemiCLE, FourBJA, HerW 84, IntAu&W 89, –91, MajTwCW, NewYTBS 82, OxCChiL, PiP, SmATA 2, –31, TwCChW 78, –83, –89, TwCYAW, WorAlBi, WorAl, WrDr 76, –80, –82, –84, –86, –88, –90, –92, –94

Blume, Judy Sussman 1938- *ConAu 37NR, MajAI*

Blume, Judy Sussman Kitchens 1938- *DcAmChF 1960*

Blumenfeld, Harold 1905?-1991 *BioIn 17, ConAu 133*

Blumenfeld, Harold 1908- *BioIn 6, ConAu 97, WhoWorJ 72, –78*

Blumenschein, Ernest Leonard 1874-1960 *BioIn 1, –2, –3, –5, –9, –11, –14, IlrAm 1880, –B, ObitOF 79, WhAm 4, WhAmArt 85, WhoAmA 80N, –82N, –86N, –89N, –91N*

Blumenthal, Gertrude 1907-1971 *BioIn 2, –9, –13, ConAu 104, SmATA 27N*
Pseud./variant:
Blane, Gertrude

Blumenthal, Lassor Agoos 1926- *ConAu 25R, WhoE 74*

Blumenthal, Shirley 1943- *SmATA 46*

Blunden, Godfrey 1906- *BioIn 1, OxCAusL*

Blunt, Don *ConAu X, IntAu&W 91X, TwCWW 91, WrDr 84, –86, –88, –90, –92*
Main entry: Booth, Edwin

Blunt, Don 1906- *WrDr 94*

Blust, Earl R *IlsBYP*

Blutig, Eduard *ConAu X, –30NR, MajAI, SmATA 70, –X, WrDr 80*
Main entry: Gorey, Edward St John

Bly, Janet Chester 1945- *SmATA 43*

Bly, Robert W 1957- *BioIn 16, SmATA 48*

Bly, Robert Wayne 1957- *ConAu 40NR*

Bly, Stephen A 1944- *BioIn 15, ConAu 121, SmATA 43*

Bly, Stephen Arthur 1944- *ConAu 40NR, WhoUSWr 88, WhoWrEP 89, –92*

Blyler, Allison Lee 1966- *SmATA 74*

Blyth, Harry 1852-1898 *Alli SUP, BioIn 8, EncMys, OxCChiL, WhoChL*

Blyton, Carey 1932- *BioIn 11, –12, ChhPo S2, CpmDNM 82, ConAu 49, IntWWM 85, –90, SmATA 9, WhoMus 72*

Blyton, Enid 1895-1968 *ContDcW 89*

Blyton, Enid 1897-1968 *BioIn 16, BlmGWL, CamGLE, ChlLR 31, ConAu 33NR, FemiCLE, TwCChW 89*

Blyton, Enid Mary 1897-1968 *AuBYP 3, InWom SUP, MajAI*

Blyton, Enid Mary 1898?-1968 *AuBYP 2, BioIn 1, –3, –7, –8, –10, –13, ChhPo, –S1, –S2, ConAu 25R, –77, DcNaB 1961, IntDcWB, LongCTC, ObitT 1961, OxCChiL, SmATA 25, TwCChW 78, –83, WhoChL*
Pseud./variant:
Pollock, Mary

Boardman, Fon W, Jr. 1911- *IntAu&W 91, WrDr 86, –88, –90, –92*

Boardman, Fon Wyman, Jr. 1911- *BioIn 10, ConAu 1R, –3NR, IntAu&W 82, SmATA 6, WhoE 91, WrDr 76, –80, –82, –84, –94*

Boardman, Gwenn R 1924- *BioIn 11, ConAu 45, –X, IntAu&W 77, SmATA 12, –X*
Main entry: Petersen, Gwenn Boardman

Boase, Wendy 1944- *BioIn 13, ConAu 105, SmATA 28*

Boatner, Mark Mayo, III 1921- *BioIn 13, ConAu 21R, SmATA 29*

Bobbe, Dorothie DeBear 1905-1975 *BioIn 9, –13, ConAu 57, –P-2, SmATA 1, –25N*

Bober, Harry d1988 *NewYTBS 88*

Bober, Harry 1915- *BioIn 7, WhoAm 84, –86*

Bober, Harry 1915-1988 *BioIn 16, ConAu 125, WhAm 9*

Bobri
Main entry: Bobritsky, Vladimir

Bobri, Vladimir
Main entry: Bobritsky, Vladimir

Bobritsky, Vladimir 1898- *BioIn 1, –5, –8, –14, –16, ForIl, IlrAm 1880, –D, IlsBYP, IlsCB 1744, –1946, –1957, SmATA 32, –47*
Pseud./variant:
Bobri
Bobri, Vladimir

Bocca, Geoffrey 1923-1983 *BioIn 3, –7, –13, ConAu 110, NewYTBS 83*

Boccaccio, Giovanni 1313-1375 *AtlBL, Benet 87, BbD, BiD&SB, BioIn 1, –4, –5, –6,*

-7, -8, -9, -11, -12, -13, -17, BlmGEL, CasWL, CyWA 58, DcBiA, DcBiPP, DcCathB, DcEnL, DcEuL, DcItL, Dis&D, EuAu, EuWr 2, EvEuW, GrFLW, LongCEL, LuthC 75, MagSWL, McGEWB, NewC, Novels, OxCEng 67, -85, PenC EUR, RAdv 13-2, RComWL, REn, ShSCr 10, WhDW, WorAlBi, WorAl

Bochak, Grayce 1956- *SmATA 76*

Bock, Hal
Main entry: Bock, Harold Irving

Bock, Harold Irving 1939- *BioIn 11, ConAu 29R, SmATA 10, WhoE 75, -77*
Pseud./variant:
Bock, Hal

Bock, Vera 1905- *BioIn 1, -5, -6, -8, ChhPo, -S1, -S2, ConICB, IlsBYP, IlsCB 1744, -1946, -1957, -1967, MorJA, WhAmArt 85, WhoAmA 73*

Bock, William Sauts-Netamux'we 1939- *BioIn 12, IlsBYP, IlsCB 1967, SmATA 14, WhoAmA 78, -80, -82, -84, -86, -89, -91*
Pseud./variant:
Netamuxwe

Bode, Carl *DrAPF 87, -89, -91, -93*

Bode, Carl d1993 *NewYTBS 93*

Bode, Carl 1911- *AmAu&B, Au&Wr 71, ConAu 1R, -3NR, -20NR, DrAP 75, DrAPF 83, -85, DrAS 74E, -78E, -82E, IntAu&W 77, -82, -86, -89, IntWWP 82, WhoAm 74, -76, -78, -80, -82, -84, -86, -88, -90, -92, WhoUSWr 88, WhoWor 74, -78, -80, -82, -84, -87, -89, WhoWrEP 89, -92, WrDr 76, -80, -82, -84, -86, -88, -90, -92*

Bode, Carl 1911-1993 *ConAu 140, WrDr 94N*

Bode, Janet 1943- *SmATA 60, TwCYAW*

Bodecker, N M d1988 *BioIn 15, -16, NewYTBS 88*

Bodecker, N M 1922- *IntAu&W 91, WrDr 86, -88*

Bodecker, N M 1922-1988 *ConAu 124, SixBJA, SmATA 54N, TwCChW 89*

Bodecker, Niels Mogens 1922-1988 *ConAu 40NR, MajAI, SmATA 73*

Bodecker, Nils Mogens 1922- *BioIn 5, -8, -11, -12, ChhPo S1, -S2, ConAu 49, -4NR, IlsBYP, IlsCB 1946, -1957, -1967, SmATA 8, TwCChW 78, -83, WrDr 76, -80, -82, -84*

Boden, Hilda *AuBYP 3*
Main entry: Bodenham, Hilda Morris

Bodenham, Hilda 1901- *AuBYP 3*

Bodenham, Hilda Morris 1901- *AuBYP 2S, ConAu 9R, -6NR, SmATA 13*
Pseud./variant:
Boden, Hilda
Welch, Pauline

Bodett, Tom 1955- *SmATA 70*

Bodie, Idella F 1925- *BioIn 11, ConAu 41R, SmATA 12*

Bodie, Idella Fallaw 1925- *WhoUSWr 88, WhoWrEP 89, -92*

Bodker, Cecil 1927- *ChlLR 23, DcScanL, EncCoWW, MajAI*

Bodker, Cecil Skaar 1927- *BioIn 12, CasWL, ConAu 73, -13NR, ConLC 21, FifBJA, IntAu&W 77, -82, SmATA 14*

Bodmer, Karl *DcVicP 2*

Bodmer, Karl 1809-1893 *ArtsNiC, BioIn 1, -3, -6, -7, -9, -11, -13, -14, -15, -17, BriEAA, ClaDrA, DcVicP 2, WhAm HS, WhNaAH*

Bodo, Peter T 1949- *ConAu 85*

Bodsworth, Fred *WhoCanL 87, -92*

Bodsworth, Fred 1918- *Au&Wr 71, BenetAL 91, CaW, CanWW 70, ConAu 1R, -3NR, ConNov 72, -76, -82, -86, -91, CreCan 2, DcLB 68, OxCCan, -SUP, OxCCanL, SmATA 27, WhoAm 94, WhoCanL 85, WrDr 76, -80, -82, -84, -86, -88, -90, -92*

Boeckman, Charles 1920- *AuBYP 2S, -3, BioIn 11, ConAu 13R, IntAu&W 86, -89, -91, SmATA 12*

Boegehold, Betty 1913-1985 *AuBYP 2, BioIn 8, ChhPo S1, ConAu 69, -115, -12NR, SmATA 42N*
Pseud./variant:
Doyle, Donovan

Boegehold, Betty Virginia 1913-1985 *AuBYP 3*

Boegehold, Betty Virginia Doyle *BioIn 14*

Boegehold, Betty Virginia Doyle 1913-1985 *BioIn 15*

Boeke, Kees 1884- *BioIn 3*

Boesch, Mark J 1917- *BioIn 11, ConAu 21R, SmATA 12, WhoPNW*

Boesen, Victor 1908- *AuBYP 2S, -3, BioIn 12, ConAu 37R, IndAu 1917, IntAu&W 77, SmATA 16, WhoWest 76, -78, -80, -82, -84*
Pseud./variant:
Hall, Jesse
Harald, Eric

Bogan, Louise 1897-1970 *AmAu&B, AmWr S3, ArtclWW 2, AuBYP 2, -3, Benet 87, BenetAL 91, BioAmW, BioIn 4, -8, -10, -12, -13, -14, -15, -17, BlmGWL, CamGLE, CamHAL, ChhPo, CnDAL, CnE&AP, ConAmA, ConAu 25R, -73, -33NR, ConLC 4, -46, ConPo 70, DcLB 45, DcLEL, EncWL, -2, FemiCLE, InWom SUP, MajTwCW, ModAL, -S1, -S2, ModAWWr, NewYTBE 70, NotAW MOD, ObitOF 79, OxCAmL 65, -83, PenC AM, RAdv 1, -13-1, REn, REnAL, RfGAmL 87, SixAP, TwCA, -SUP, TwCWr, WhAm 5*

Bogen, Constance *AuBYP 2S, -3*

Boggs, Ralph Steele 1901- *AnCL, AuBYP 2, -3, BioIn 8, -10, ConAu P-1, DcSpL, DrAS 74F, -78F, -82F, IndAu 1917, SmATA 7, WhNAA*

Bograd, Larry 1953- *AuBYP 3, ConAu 93, ConLC 35, SmATA 33*
Pseud./variant:
Barrol, Grady

Bohannan, Paul James 1920- *AmMWSc 73S, ConAu 9R, FifIDA, WhoAm 74, -86, -88, -90, -92, -94, WhoWest 87, -89, WhoWor 74, WrDr 76, -80*

Bohdal, Susi 1951- *BioIn 13, ConAu 97, SmATA 22*

Bohle, Bruce William 1918- *ConAu 21R, WhoAm 74, -80, -82, -84, -86, -88, -90, -92, -94, WhoUSWr 88, WhoWrEP 89, -92*

Bohlen, Nina 1931- *BioIn 16, SmATA 58, WhoAm 86, -88, -90, -92, -94, WhoAmA 86, -89, -91*

Bohner, Charles 1927- *ConAu 118, SmATA 62*

Bohner, Charles Henry 1927- *WhoAm 90, -92, -94*

Bohr, Theophilus *ConAu X*
Main entry: Thistle, Mel

Boissard, Janine 1932- *SmATA 59, TwCYAW*

Bojunga-Nunes, Lygia *TwCChW 89B*

Boker, Irving *IlsBYP*

Boland, Charles Michael 1917- *ConAu 9R*

Boland, Lillian C 1919- *ConAu 29R*

Bolden, Joseph *IlsBYP*

Bolden, Melvin Reed 1919- *WhoAmP 73, -75*

Boldrewood, Rolf
Main entry: Browne, Thomas Alexander

Boldrewood, Rolf 1826-1915 *Alli SUP, BiD&SB, CamGEL, CamGLE, CasWL, Chambr 3, ChhPo, DcLEL, EvLB, LongCTC, NewC, Novels, OxCAusL, OxCEng 67, PenC ENG, REn, RfGEnL 91, SingR 2, StaCVF, WebE&AL, WhDW*

Boles, Paul Darcy 1916-1984 *Au&Wr 71, BioIn 3, -4, -11, -13, -14, -15, ConAu 9R, -112, -4NR, CurBio 56, -84N, IndAu 1917, NewYTBS 84, SmATA 9, -38N, WhoSSW 73, -75, -76, -78, -80*

Bolian, Polly 1925- *BioIn 9, ConAu 33R, IlsBYP, SmATA 4*

Bolin, William Eugene 1940- *WhoRel 75*

Bollen, Roger 1941- *WhoAm 86, -88, -90, -92, -94*

Bollen, Roger 1942?- *ArtCS, AuNews 1, BioIn 10, -13, BioNews 74, SmATA 29, WhoAm 76, -78, -80, -82, -84*

Bolliger, Max 1929- *BioIn 10, ConAu 25R, FourBJA, IntAu&W 77, -82, SmATA 7*

Bolliger-Savelli, Antonella *IlsCB 1967*

Bolognese, Donald Alan 1934- *BioIn 8, -13, ChhPo S1, -S2, ConAu 97, FourBJA, IlsBYP, IlsCB 1957, -1967, MajAI, SmATA 24, -71*

Bolognese, Elaine Raphael 1933- *ConAu 97, FourBJA*
Pseud./variant:
Raphael, Elaine

Bolton, Carole 1926- *AuBYP 2S, -3, BioIn 10, ConAu 49, -1NR, ForWC 70, SmATA 6*

Bolton, Elizabeth *ConAu 32NR, SmATA X, WrDr 94*
Main entry: Johnston, Norma

Bolton, Evelyn *AuBYP 3, ConAu X, MajAI, SmATA X, TwCChW 83, -89, TwCYAW, WrDr 86, -88, -90, -92*
Main entry: Bunting, Anne Evelyn

Bolton, Evelyn 1928- *SmATA X, WrDr 94*

Bolton, Henry Carrington 1843-1903 *Alli SUP, BiD&SB, BiInAmS, ChhPo S1, DcAmAu, DcNAA, Str&VC, WhAm 1*

Bolton, Ivy May 1879- *AmWomPl, AuBYP 2, -3, BioIn 7*

Bolton, Sarah Knowles 1841-1916 *Alli SUP, AmAu, AmAu&B, BbD, BiD&SB, CarSB, ChhPo, -S1, -S2, DcAmAu, DcNAA, HarEnUS, OhA&B, WhAm 1, WomWWA 14*

Bomans, Godfried Jan Arnold 1913-1971 *ConAu P-2, WhoWor 74*

Bombard, Alain Louis 1924?- *BioIn 3, -9, -12*

Bonar, Veronica *ConAu 136, SmATA 68*
Main entry: Bailey, Donna Veronica Anne

Bond, B J
Main entry: Heneghan, James

Bond, Bruce 1939- *SmATA 61*

Bond, Felicia 1954- *ConAu 127, SixBJA, SmATA 49*

Bond, Geoffrey 1924- *Au&Wr 71, ConAu 29R*

Bond, Geoffrey 1924-1978 *ConAu 134*

Bond, Gladys Baker 1912- *ConAu 5R, -2NR, ForWC 70, SmATA 14, WhoAmW 74, -75, -77, WhoPNW, WhoWest 74, -76, -78*
Pseud./variant:
Mendel, Jo
Walker, Holly Beth

Bond, J Harvey *ConAu X, EncSF 93, SmATA X*
Main entry: Winterbotham, R R

Bond, Jean Carey *AuBYP 2S, -3, BlkAWP, BlkAuII, -92, ConAu 106*

Bond, Michael *IntAu&W 86, -89, -91, WrDr 86, -88, -90, -92*

Bond, Michael 1926- *AuBYP 2S, -3, Au&Wr 71, BioIn 8, -9, -10, -11, -15, BritCA, CamGLE, ChlLR 1, ConAu 5R, -4NR, -24NR, IntAu&W 77, -82, MorBMP, OxCChiL, SmATA 6, -58, -3AS, ThrBJA, TwCChW 78, -83, -89, Who 74, -82, -83, -85, -88, -90, -92, WhoChL, WrDr 76, -80, -82, -84*

Bond, Nancy 1945- *AuBYP 2S, -3, BioIn 13, ChlLR 11, ConAu 65, -9NR, -36NR, FifBJA, ScF&FL 92, SmATA 22, -13AS, TwCChW 83, -89, TwCYAW, WrDr 86, -88, -90, -92, -94*

Bond, Nancy Barbara 1945- *DcAmChF 1960, -1985, MajAI*

Bond, Raymond T 1893?-1981 *AmAu&B, BioIn 2, -12, ConAu 104, WhAm 8*

Bond, Ruskin 1934- *BioIn 12, ConAu 29R, -14NR, -31NR, DcLEL 1940, IntAu&W 77, -82, -86, -91, OxCChiL, SmATA 14, TwCChW 83, -89, WrDr 86, -88, -90, -92, -94*

Bond, Thomas Michael 1926- *ChlFicS, MajAI*

Bone, Stephen 1904-1958 *BioIn 5, -14, DcBrAr 1, DcNaB 1951, DcSeaP, IlsBYP, IlsCB 1946, LongCTC, ObitOF 79, ObitT 1951, TwCPaSc*

Bonehill, Captain Ralph *ConAu X, DcNAA, MajAI, WhAm 1*
Main entry: Stratemeyer, Edward L

Bonehill, Captain Ralph 1862-1930 *BioIn 15*

Bonehill, Ralph *SmATA 67*

Bonehill, Ralph 1862-1930 *BioIn 17*

Bonestell, Chesley *BioIn 14, -15, -16, -17*

Bonestell, Chesley 1888- *ArtsAmW 2, BioIn 11*

Bonestell, Chesley 1888-1986 *BiDScF, ConAu 119, EncSF 93, NewEScF, ScF&FL 92, SmATA 48N*

Bongar, Emmet Wald 1919- *ConAu 33R*

Bonham, Barbara Thomas 1926- *ConAu 17R, -7NR, SmATA 7, WrDr 76, -80*

Bonham, Frank 1914- *Au&Arts 1, AuBYP 2, -3, BioIn 8, -9, -10, ConAu 9R, -4NR, ConLC 12, DcAmChF 1960, EncFWF, IntAu&W 91, MorBMP, OxCChiL, SmATA 1, -49, -3AS, ThrBJA, TwCChW 78, -83, WrDr 80, -82, -84, -86, -88*

Bonham, Frank 1914-1988 *EncSF 93, ScF&FL 92, TwCChW 89, TwCWW 91*

Bonham, Frank 1914-1989 *ConAu 36NR, MajAI, SmATA 62, TwCYAW*

Boni, Margaret Bradford 1893?-1974 *AmAu&B, AuBYP 2S, -3, BioIn 10, ConAu 53*

Bonn, Patricia Carolyn 1948- *BioIn 15, SmATA 43*

Bonnell, Dorothy 1914- *AuBYP 3*

Bonnell, Dorothy Haworth 1914- *AuBYP 2S, ConAu 1R, -3NR, ForWC 70*

Bonner, Mary Graham 1890-1974 *AmAu&B, AuBYP 2, -3, BioIn 1, -2, -7, -10, -12, CanNov, CarSB, ChhPo, ConAu 49, -73, CurBio 50, ForWC 70, SmATA 19, WhAm 6, WhNAA*

Bonners, Susan *SmATA 48*

Bonners, Susan 1947- *SixBJA*

Bono, Philip 1921- *ConAu 101, WhoAm 74, -76, -78, -80, -82, -84, -86, -88, -90, -92,*

–94, WhoFI 74, –81, WhoWest 78, –80, –82, –84, –87, WhoWor 74, –82

Bonsall, Crosby 1921- *IntAu&W 91, TwCChW 89, WrDr 86, –88, –90, –92*

Bonsall, Crosby Barbara 1921- *BioIn 8, –9, –13, ConAu 73, IlsBYP, IlsCB 1957, –1967, SmATA 23, ThrBJA, TwCChW 78, –83, WrDr 80, –82, –84*
Pseud./variant:
Newell, Crosby

Bonsall, Crosby Newell 1921- *WrDr 94*

Bontemps, Arna 1902-1973 *AfrAmAl 6, BenetAL 91, BlkLC, BlkWr 1, BlkWrNE, CamGLE, CamHAL, ConAu 35NR, CyWA 89, DcLB 51, EarBlAP, MajTwCW, NegAl 89, TwCChW 89, WrChl*

Bontemps, Arna Wendell *IntvTCA 2*

Bontemps, Arna Wendell 1902-1973 *AmAu&B, AmNov, AnMV 1926, AuBYP 2, –3, Au&Wr 71, BioIn 1, –2, –7, –8, –9, –10, –12, –13, –14, –15, –16, –17, BlkAWP, BlkAuII, –92, BkCL, BroadAu, ChhPo S1, ChlLR 6, ConAu 1R, –41R, –4NR, ConLC 1, –18, ConPo 70, CurBio 46, –73, DcLB 48, EncAACR, InB&W 80, –85, JBA 51, ModBlW, MorBMP, NatCAB 61, NegAl 76, –83, NewYTBE 73, Novels, ObitOF 79, OxCAmL 65, –83, REnAL, SelBAAf, SelBAAu, SmATA 2, –24N, –44, SouBlCW, Str&VC, WebE&AL, WhAm 5, WhoAm 74, WhoBlA 75, WhoLibS 55, WhoWor 74*

Bontemps, Arnaud Wendell 1902-1973 *MajAI*

Bonzon, Paul Jacques 1908-1978 *AuBYP 2, –3, Au&Wr 71, BioIn 7, –13, ConAu 93, FourBJA, SmATA 22, WhoWor 74*

Boog Watson, Elspeth Janet 1900- *Au&Wr 71, ConAu P-1*

Booher, Dianna Daniels *BioIn 14*

Booher, Dianna Daniels 1948- *ConAu 103, IntAu&W 89, –91, SmATA 33, WhoFI 92, WhoSSW 86*

Booker, Simeon S 1918- *WhoBlA 85, –90, –92, –94*

Booker, Simeon Saunders 1918- *BioIn 10, ConAu 9R, InB&W 80, LivgBAA, SelBAAf, SelBAAu, WhoBlA 75, –77, –80, –85*

Booker, Simeon Saunders, Jr. 1918- *InB&W 85*

Bookman, Charlotte *ConAu X, –38NR, MajAI, SmATA X*
Main entry: Zolotow, Charlotte Shapiro

Boon, Emilie *AuBYP 3*

Boon, Emilie 1958- *ConAu 131*

Boon, Emilie Laetitia 1958- *WrDr 94*

Boone, Pat 1934- *AmAu&B, ASCAP 66, Baker 84, BioIn 4, –5, –9, –10, –11, –12, –13, CelR, –90, ConAu 1R, –2NR, CurBio 59 EncRk 88, FilmgC, HalFC 84, –88, IntMPA 75, –76, –78, –81, –82, –84, –86, –88, –92, –77, MotPP, MovMk, NewGrDA 86, OxCPMus, PenEncP, RkOn 74, RolSEnR 83, SmATA 7, WhoAm 74, –76, –78, –80, –82, –84, –86, –88, –92, –94, WhoEnt 92, WhoHol A, WhoRel 75, –77, WorAlBi, WorAl, WrDr 76, –80, –82, –84, –86, –88, –90, –92, –94*

Boone, Pat Charles Eugene 1934- *Baker 92*

Boone, Silas K *CarSB*

Boorer, Wendy 1931- *ConAu 57, –6NR*

Boorman, Linda 1940- *ConAu 121, SmATA 46*

Boorstin, Daniel J 1914- *BioIn 14, –15, –16, –17, ConAu 28NR, EncWB, IntAu&W 86, IntWW 89, –91, RAdv 13-3, SmATA 52 Who 88, –92, WhoAm 86, –88, –90, –92, –94, WhoUSWr 88, WhoWor 87, –89, –91, –93, WhoWrEP 89, –92, WorAlBi, WrDr 86, –88, –90, –92, –94*

Boorstin, Daniel J, Dr 1914- *Who 90*

Boorstin, Daniel Joseph 1914- *AmAu&B, AuNews 2, BioIn 6, –7, –8, –10, –11, –12, –13, BlueB 76, ConAu 1R, –1NR, CurBio 68, –84, DcLB 17, DcLEL 1940, DrAS 74H, –78H, –82H, IntAu&W 77, –82, –89, –91, IntWW 74, –75, –76, –77, –78, –79, –80, –81, –82, –83, OxCAmL 83, Who 82, –83, –85, WhoAm 74, –76, –78, –80, –82, –84, WhoAmJ 80, WhoAmP 85, –87, –89, –91, –93, WhoE 81, –83, –85, –86, WhoGov 77, –72, WhoLibI 82, WhoSSW 73, –75, –76, WhoWor 78, –80, –82, –84, WhoWorJ 72, –78, WorAl, WorAu 1950, WrDr 76, –80, –82, –84*

Booth, Edwin *ConAu 17R, –7NR, IntAu&W 91, TwCWW 91, WrDr 84, –86, –88, –90, –92*
Pseud./variant:
Blunt, Don

Booth, Edwin 1906- *WrDr 94*

Booth, Ernest Sheldon 1915-1984 *AmMWSc 73P, –76P, BioIn 15, ConAu 53, SmATA 43, WhoWest 74, –76, –78*

Booth, George *BiDrACP 79, BioIn 13*

Booth, Graham Charles 1935- *BioIn 8, IlsBYP, IlsCB 1957, –1967, SmATA 37*

Booth, Martin 1944- *ConAu 93, –2AS, ConPo 70, –75, –80, –85, IntAu&W 89, –91, WrDr 76, –80, –82, –84, –86, –88, –90, –92, –94*

Booth, Maud B 1865-1948 *BioAmW*

Booth, Maud Ballington 1865-1948 *BioIn 1, –3, –6, CarSB, DcAmAu, InWom SUP, NewC, ObitOF 79, WhAm 2, WomWWA 14, WomNov*

Booth, Patrick John 1929- *Au&Wr 71, ConAu P-1*

Booth, Rosemary Frances 1928- *ConAu 53, IntAu&W 77, WrDr 76, –80*
Pseud./variant:
Murray, Frances

Boothby, Guy Newell 1867-1905 *BioIn 2, BritAu 19, Chambr 3, DcNaB S2, EncMys, EvLB, LongCTC, WhoHr&F*

Boratynski, Antoni 1930- *IntAu&W 77*

Borden, Charles A 1912-1968 *AuBYP 2, –3, BioIn 8, ConAu 5R*

Borden, Louise 1949- *SmATA 68*

Borden, Louise Walker 1949- *ConAu 136, WrDr 94*

Borden, M *ConAu X*
Main entry: Saxon, Gladys Relyea

Bordier, Georgette 1924- *BioIn 12, SmATA 16*

Borea, Phyllis Gilbert 1924- *ConAu 29R, WhoAmW 75*

Borek, Ernest 1911- *AmMWSc 73P, –76P, ConAu 106*

Borek, Ernest 1911-1986 *BioIn 14, ConAu 118*

Boreman, Jean 1909- *ConAu P-2*

Boreman, Thomas *OxCChiL*

Borer, Mary Cathcart 1906- *Au&Wr 71, ConAu 9R, –4NR, IntAu&W 77, –82, –86, –89, WrDr 76, –80, –82, –84, –86, –88, –90, –92, –94*

Borg, Inga *AuBYP 3*

Borg, Inga 1925- *AuBYP 2, BioIn 8*

Borhegyi, Suzanne C Sims De *AuBYP 2*
Main entry: DeBorhegyi, Suzanne C Sims

Borhegyi, Suzanne Catherine Sims De 1926- *AuBYP 3*

Boring, Mel 1939- *ConAu 106, SmATA 35*

Borja, Corinne 1929- *BioIn 13, ConAu 97, IlsBYP, SmATA 22*

Borja, Robert 1923- *BioIn 13, ConAu 97, IlsBYP, SmATA 22*

Borland, Hal 1900- *TwCWW 91, WrDr 86*

Borland, Hal 1900-1978 *AmAu&B, Au&Wr 71, BenetAL 91, BioIn 4, –5, –6, –8, –10, –11, –17, ChhPo, ConAu 1R, –77, –6NR, ObitOF 79, REnAL, SmATA 5, –24N, WhAm 7, WhoAm 74, –76, –78, WhoWor 74, WorAu 1950, WrDr 84*
Pseud./variant:
West, Ward

Borland, Kathryn Kilby 1916- *BioIn 12, ConAu 53, –4NR, IndAu 1917, SmATA 16, WhoAm 74, –76, –78, –80, –82, –84, –86, –88, –90, –92, –94*
Pseud./variant:
Abbott, Alice
Land, Jane
Land, Ross

Born, Adolf 1930- *SmATA 49*

Bornschlegel, Ruth *IlsBYP*

Bornstein, Ruth 1927- *AuBYP 2S, –3, BioIn 12, ConAu 61, IlsCB 1967, SmATA 14*

Bornstein, Ruth Lercher 1927- *BioIn 16*

Borowitz, Eugene Bernard 1924- *ConAu 49, –1NR, WhoAmJ 80, WhoWorJ 72, –78*

Borski, Lucia Merecka 1903- *AnCL, BioIn 12, ConAu 73, SmATA 18, WhoLibS 66*

Borten, Helen Jacobson 1930- *AmPB, AuBYP 2, –3, BioIn 7, –8, –10, ChhPo S2, ConAu 5R, –3NR, ForWC 70, IlsCB 1957, –1967, SmATA 5, WrDr 76, –80*

Borton, Elizabeth *MajAI*

Borton, Elizabeth 1904- *ConAu X, NewbC 1966, SmATA 1, ThrBJA, WhoAmW 74*
Pseud./variant:
Borton DeTrevino, Elizabeth
DeTrevino, Elizabeth Borton
Trevino, Elizabeth Borton De

Borton DeTrevino, Elizabeth
Main entry: Borton, Elizabeth

Bortstein, Larry 1942- *BioIn 12, ConAu 33R, SmATA 16*

Bortz, Fred 1944- *ConAu 141, SmATA 74*

Bosco, Henri 1888-1976 *Benet 87, BioIn 7, –10, DcLB 72, ObitOF 79, OxCChiL*

Bosco, Jack *ConAu X, SmATA X*
Main entry: Holliday, Joseph

Boshell, Gordon 1908- *BioIn 12, ChhPo S2, ConAu 77, EngPo, IntAu&W 82, ScF&FL 92, SmATA 15*

Boshinski, Blanche 1922- *BioIn 11, ConAu 21R, SmATA 10*

Bossard, James Herbert Siward 1888-1960 *AmAu&B, BioIn 5, ObitOF 79, WhAm 3, WhNAA*

Bosschere, Jean De 1878?-1953 *BioIn 1, –8, –12, –14, ConAu 115, DcBrAr 2, IlsCB 1744, ScF&FL 92, TwCLC 19*
Pseud./variant:
DeBosschere, Jean

Bosse, Malcolm J *DrAPF 87, –89, –91, –93*

Bosse, Malcolm J 1932- *ScF&FL 92*

Bosse, Malcolm J 1933- *ConAu 106, DrAPF 83, –85, FifBJA, SmATA 35*

Bosse, Malcolm J 1934- *BioIn 14*

Bosse, Malcolm Joseph, Jr. *WhoAm 86, –88*

Bosse, Malcolm Joseph, Jr. 1926- *WhoAm 90, –92*

Bossom, Naomi 1933- *BioIn 14, ConAu 102, SmATA 35*

Bostelmann, Else 1882?-1961 *BioIn 1, –6, IlsCB 1744, WhAmArt 85*

Boston, L M 1892- *BioIn 15, WrDr 86, –88, –90*

Boston, L M 1892-1990 *BioIn 16*

Boston, L M 1892-1990 *BioIn 17, ScF&FL 92*

Boston, Lucy 1892- *ArtclWW 2, CamGLE, TwCChW 89*

Boston, Lucy 1892-1990 *AnObit 1990, BlmGWL, FemiCLE, NewYTBS 90*

Boston, Lucy M 1892- *Who 88, –90*

Boston, Lucy Maria 1892- *AnCL, AuBYP 2, –3, Au&Wr 71, BioIn 6, –7, –8, –9, –10, –11, –12, –13, –15, BritCA, ChlLR 3, ConAu 73, OxCChiL, PiP, SenS, SmATA 19, ThrBJA, TwCChW 78, –83, WhoChL, WrDr 76, –80, –82, –84*

Boston, Lucy Maria 1892-1990 *BioIn 16, –17, ConAu 131, SmATA 64*

Boston, Lucy Maria Wood 1892-1990 *MajAI, TwCYAW*

Boston, Lucy Marie 1892- *ChlFicS*

Boswell, Hazel 1882- *BioIn 1, –10, IlsCB 1744, OxCCan SUP, Profile 1*

Boswell, Hilda *ChhPo S2*

Boswell, James 1906-1971 *BioIn 8, –9, DcBrAr 1, –2, IlsCB 1957, TwCPaSc*

Bosworth, J Allan 1925- *AuBYP 2, –3, BioIn 8, –12, SmATA 19*

Bothwell, Jean d1977 *AuBYP 2, –3, BioIn 1, –2, –7, –9, ConAu 1R, –3NR, CurBio 46, JBA 51, SmATA 2*

Botkin, B A 1901-1975 *BenetAL 91, SmATA 40*

Botkin, Benjamin Albert 1901-1975 *AmAu&B, Au&Wr 71, BioIn 4, –10, ConAu 57, –P-1, DrAS 74E, REnAL, TwCA SUP, WhAm 6, WhoAm 74, WhoWorJ 72, –78*

Botkin, Benjamin Albert 1901-1987 *BioIn 15*

Botsford, Ward 1927- *SmATA 66*

Bottel, Helen *WrDr 88*

Bottel, Helen 1914- *BioIn 4, ConAu 25R, ForWC 70, WhoAmW 74, –75, –77, WhoWest 78, –82, WrDr 76, –80, –82, –84, –86, –90, –92, –94*

Bottel, Helen Alfea *WhoAm 92*

Botting, Douglas 1934- *ConAu 45, –1NR, –16NR, SmATA 43, WrDr 76, –80, –82, –84, –86, –88, –90, –92, –94*

Botting, Douglas Scott 1934- *ConAu 37NR*

Bottner, Barbara 1943- *AuBYP 2S, –3, BioIn 12, –16, ConAu 61, –8NR, –23NR, SixBJA, SmATA 14, WomWMM B*

Bottom, Raymond 1927- *ConAu 33R, MichAu 80*

Bouchard, Lois Kalb 1938- *AuBYP 2S, –3, ConAu 25R*

Boucher, Alan 1918- *Au&Wr 71, ConAu 5R, –9NR, –24NR*

Boudreau, Ingeborg 1943- *BiDrLUS 70*

Boudreau, Joseph 1934- *DrAS 74H*

Boughton, Richard 1954- *ConAu 142, SmATA 75*

Bouilly, Jean Nicolas 1763-1842 *BioIn 13, OxCChiL*

Boulet, Susan Seddon 1941- *BioIn 16, SmATA 50*

Boulle, Pierre Francois 1912- *Au&Wr 71, BioIn 5, –8, –10, –13, CasWL, ConAu 9R, Novels, REn, SmATA 22, TwCCr&M 80B, TwCWr, WhoSciF, WhoWor 74, WorAl, WorAu 1950*

Bour, Daniele 1939- *BioIn 17, SmATA 62*

Bourdeaux, Michael 1934- *Au&Wr 71, ConAu 33R, –14NR, WrDr 76, –80*

Bourdeaux, Michael Alan 1934- *IntAu&W 86, Who 92, WrDr 94*

Bourdon, David 1934- *SmATA 46, WhoAm 86, –90, –92, –94, WhoAmA 86, –89, –91, WhoUSWr 88, WhoWrEP 89, –92, WrDr 90, –92, –94*

Bourgeois, Florence 1904- *BioIn 1, IlsCB 1744*

Bourinot, John George 1837-1902 *BioIn 17, DcLB 99*

Bourinot, John George, Sir 1837-1902 *Alli SUP, BbtC, BritAu 19, DcNaB S2, DcNAA, OxCCan*

Bourliaguet, Leonce 1895-1965 *ConAu 102, FourBJA*

Bourne, Lesley *ConAu X, SmATA X, WrDr 84, –86, –88, –90*
Main entry: Marshall, Evelyn

Bourne, Miriam Anne 1931- *AuBYP 2S, –3, BioIn 12, ConAu 21R, –10NR, SmATA 16*

Bourne, Miriam Anne 1931-1989 *ConAu 129, SmATA 63*

Bourne, Peter *BioIn 3, ConAu X, EncMys*

Bourne, Russell 1928- *ConAu 133, IntAu&W 89, WhoAm 82, –84, –86, –88, –90, –92, –94, WrDr 94*

Bourne, William Oland *Alli SUP, CarSB, ChhPo, –S1, –S2, DcNAA*

Boutet DeMonvel, M 1850?-1913 *BioIn 14*

Boutet DeMonvel, Maurice 1850-1913 *AmPB, BioIn 1, –2, ChlLR 32, JBA 34, –51, OxCChiL, SmATA 30*
Pseud./variant:
Monvel, Maurice Boutet De

Bouton, Josephine *ChhPo*

Bouvet, Marie Marguerite 1865-1915 *AmAu, AmAu&B, BiD&SB, CarSB, DcAmAu, DcNAA, WhAm 1, WomWWA 14, WomNov*

Bova, Ben *IntvTCA 2*

Bova, Ben 1932- *ConAu 18AS, ConLC 45, IntAu&W 89, –91, MajTwCW, NewEScF, ScF&FL 92, ScFSB, SmATA 68, TwCSFW 86, –91, WrDr 86, –88, –90, –92*

Bova, Benjamin William 1932- *AuBYP 2S, –3, BioIn 10, –13, ChlLR 3, ConAu 5R, –11NR, ConSFA, DcLB Y81B, EncSF 93, FifBJA, IntAu&W 77, MajAI, Novels, RGTwCSF, SmATA 6, WhoAm 74, –76, –78, –82, –84, –90, –92, –94, WhoE 74, –75, –77, –89, WhoSciF, WhoWor 82, WrDr 76, –80, –82, –84, –94*

Bowden, Joan Chase 1925- *SmATA 38, –51*
Pseud./variant:
Bacon, Joan Chase
Godfrey, Jane
Graham, Charlotte
Kenny, Kathryn

Bowdler, Thomas 1754-1825 *BioIn 3, –6, –13, BlmGEL, CamGLE, DcBiPP, DcNaB, OxCChiL, OxCEng 85*

Bowen, Betty Morgan
Main entry: West, Betty

Bowen, Betty Morgan 1921- *AuBYP 2, –3, BioIn 8, –10, ConAu X, SmATA X*

Bowen, Catherine Drinker 1897-1973 *AmAu&B, BenetAL 91, BioIn 2, –4, –5, –6, –8, –10, ConAu 5R, –45, –15NR, CurBio 44, –73, InWom SUP, NatCAB 58, NewYTBE 73, ObitOF 79, OxCAmL 65, –83, RAdv 13-3, REn, REnAL, SmATA 7, TwCA SUP, WhAm 6, Who 74, WhoAm 74, WhoAmW 74, WhoGov 72, WhoWor 74*

Bowen, David *SmATA X*

Bowen, Elizabeth *IntvTCA 2*

Bowen, Elizabeth 1899-1973 *AuBYP 2, –3, Au&Wr 71, Benet 87, BioIn 1, –2, –3, –4, –5, –6, –7, –8, –9, –10, –11, –12, –13, –14, –15, –16, –17, BlmGEL, BlmGWL, BritWr S2, CamGEL, CamGLE, CasWL, CnDBLB 7, ConAu 41R, –35NR, –P-2, ConLC 1, –3, –6, –11, –15, –22, ConNov 72, ContDcW 89, CyWA 58, –89, DcIrL, DcIrW 1, DcLB 15, DcLEL, EncBrWW, EncWL, –2, EvLB, FemiCLE, IntDcWB, LongCTC, MagSWL, MajTwCW, ModBrL, –S1, –S2, ModIrL, NewC, NewYTBE 73, Novels, ObitOF 79, ObitT 1971, OxCEng 67, PenC ENG, PenEncH, RAdv 1, –13-1, REn, RfGEnL 91,*

ShSCr 3, ShSWr, SupFW, TwCA, –SUP, TwCWr, WebE&AL, WhAm 5, WhoHr&F, WhoTwCL, WorAlBi, WorAl

Bowen, Elizabeth Dorothea Cole 1899-1973 *GayLL*

Bowen, Ezra 1891-1945 *BioIn 1, WhAmArt 85*

Bowen, Irene *AuBYP 2, –3, BioIn 8, DcWomA*

Bowen, John *IntvTCA 2*

Bowen, John 1924- *Au&Wr 71, BioIn 7, –10, –13, CnThe, ConAu 1R, –2NR, ConDr 73, –77, –82, –88, ConNov 72, –76, –82, –86, –91, CroCD, DcLB 13, IntAu&W 82, NewC, REn, ScFSB, TwCWr, Who 74, –82, –83, –85, WhoThe 72, –77, –81, WhoWor 74, WorAu 1950, WrDr 76, –80, –82, –84, –86, –88, –90, –92*

Bowen, John Griffith 1924- *ConDr 93, EncSF 93, WrDr 94*

Bowen, Joshua David 1930- *AuBYP 2, –3, BioIn 8, –13, ConAu 105, SmATA 22*

Bowen, Marjorie *ScF&FL 92, TwCCr&M 91, WomNov*

Bowen, Marjorie 1886-1952 *BioIn 14, –15, DcLEL, EvLB, LongCTC, NewC, ObitT 1951, OxCEng 85, PenEncH, REn, TwCA, –SUP, TwCRHW 90, TwCWr, WhoHr&F, WhoLA*

Bowen, Marjorie 1888-1952 *FemiCLE*

Bowen, Olwen *BioIn 8, WhoChL*

Bowen, R Sydney 1900-1977 *SmATA 52*

Bowen, Richard Michael 1928- *ConAu 21R, WhoE 74, WrDr 76, –80, –82, –84*

Bowen, Robert Sidney 1900-1977 *AuBYP 3, BioIn 16, EncSF 93*

Bowen, Robert Sydney 1900-1977 *AuBYP 2, BioIn 8, –11, –12, ConAu 69, –73, –28NR, SmATA 21N*
Pseud./variant:
Richard, James Robert

Bower, B M *WomNov*

Bower, B M 1871-1940 *AmAu&B, BenetAL 91, DcNAA, EncFWF, FemiCLE, LongCTC, REnAL, TwCA, WhNAA*

Bower, B M 1874-1940 *ScFEYrs*

Bower, BM 1871-1940 *TwCWW 91*

Bowermaster, Jon 1954- *SmATA 77*

Bowers, Santha Rama Rau *ConAu 1R*
Main entry: Rau, Santha Rama

Bowes, Anne LaBastille *ConAu 57, –X*
Main entry: LaBastille, Anne

Bowie, Jim *ConAu X, DcAmChF 1960, IntAu&W 82X, –91X, MajAI, TwCWW 91, WrDr 76, –80, –82, –84, –86, –88*
Main entry: Norwood, Victor George Charles
Stratemeyer, Edward L

Bowie, Walter Russell 1882-1969 *AmAu&B, BioIn 2, –3, –8, ConAu 5R, –3NR, WhAm 5, WhNAA*

Bowker, John Westerdale 1935- *ConAu 25R, IntAu&W 91, Who 85, –88, –92, WrDr 76, –80, –82, –84, –86, –88, –90, –92, –94*

Bowker, John Westerdale, Prof 1935- *Who 90*

Bowkett, Stephen 1953- *ConAu 134, ScF&FL 92, SmATA 67, WrDr 94*
Pseud./variant:
Garou, Louis P

Bowler, Jan Brett *ConAu X, –41NR, MajAI, SmATA 71, –X*
Main entry: Brett, Jan

Bowles, D Richard 1910- *ConAu 33R*

Bowles, W M
Pseud./variant:
Cyclops

Bowman, Anne *Alli SUP, CarSB, ChhPo S1, DcEnL*

Bowman, Bruce 1938- *ConAu 65, WhoAmA 78, –80, –82, –84, –86, –89, –91, WhoWest 80, –82, –87, –89, –92, –94*

Bowman, Frederick H U 1894- *Alli SUP*

Bowman, James Cloyd 1880-1961 *AmAu&B, AnCL, AuBYP 2, –3, BioIn 2, –6, –8, –13, –14, ConAu 97, JBA 51, OhA&B, SmATA 23, Str&VC, WhAm 4, WhNAA*

Bowman, John S 1931- *ConAu 19NR*

Bowman, John Stewart 1931- *AuBYP 2S, –3, Au&Wr 71, BioIn 12, ConAu 9R, –5NR, –41NR, SmATA 16*

Bowman, Kathleen 1942- *ConAu 69, SmATA 40, –52*

Bowman, Marcelle 1914- *ConAu 25R*

Bowman, Robert Turnbull 1910- *ConAu 73*

Bowne, Eliza Soughgate 1783-1809 *CarSB*

Bowne, Eliza Southgate 1783-1809 *BlmGWL, InWom SUP*

Bowood, Richard *ConAu X*
Main entry: Daniell, Albert Scott

Bowring, John 1792-1872 *LuthC 75*

Bowring, John, Sir 1792-1872 *Alli, –SUP, BbD, BiD&SB, BioIn 6, –7, –8, –9, –10, BritAu 19, CarSB, CasWL, CelCen, Chambr 3, ChhPo, –S1, –S2, DcBiPP, DcEnL, DcLEL, DcNaB, EvLB, PoChrch*

Bowsfield, Hartwell *OxCCan SUP*

Boxer, Devorah *AuBYP 2, –3, BioIn 8*

Boyce, George A 1898- *BioIn 12, ConAu 53, SmATA 19*

Boyd, Candy Dawson *DcAmChF 1985*

Boyd, Candy Dawson 1946- *BioIn 16, BlkAull, –92, BlkWr 2, ConAu 138, SmATA 72, WhoBlA 90, –92*

Boyd, Frank *TwCCr&M 91*

Boyd, Frank 1893- *ConICB*

Boyd, James 1888-1944 *AmAu&B, BenetAL 91, BioIn 2, –3, –4, –5, –9, –11, –12, CnDAL, ConAmA, ConAmL, CurBio 44, CyWA 58, DcLB 9, DcLEL, DcNAA, DcNCBi 1, LongCTC, Novels, ObitOF 79, OxCAmL 65, –83, PenC AM, REnAL, RfGAmL 87, TwCA, –SUP, TwCRHW 90, WhAm 2, WhNAA*

Boyd, Jessie Edna 1899- *BiDrLUS 70, WhoLibS 55, –66*

Boyd, John *ConAu X, ConSFA, DcLB 8, WhoSciF, WrDr 76, –80, –82, –84*
Main entry: Upchurch, Boyd Bradfield

Boyd, John 1912- *BioIn 17, CamGLE, CamGWoT*

Boyd, John 1917-1989 *AnObit 1989, BioIn 16*

Boyd, John 1919- *EncSF 93, NewEScF, ScF&FL 92, ScFSB, TwCSFW 86, –91, WrDr 86, –88, –90, –92, –94*

Boyd, Lizi *AuBYP 3*

Boyd, Lorenz *AuBYP 2S, –3*

Boyd, Malcolm 1923- *AmAu&B, AuSpks, Au&Wr 71, BioIn 6, –7, –8, –10, –11, –15, BlueB 76, CelR, ConAu 5R, –11AS, –4NR, –26NR, CurBio 68, GayLL, IntAu&W 77, –82, –86, –89, WhoAm 74, –76, –78, –80, –82, –84, –86, –88, –90, –92, –94, WhoE 74, WhoRel 75, –77, –92, WhoUSWr 88, WhoWor 74, WhoWrEP 89, –92, WorAlBi, WorAl, WrDr 76, –80, –82, –84, –86, –88, –90, –92*

Boyd, Mildred 1921- *AuBYP 3*

Boyd, Mildred Worthy 1921- *AuBYP 2S, ConAu 17R, ForWC 70*

Boyd, Pauline *ConAu X, SmATA X*
Main entry: Schock, Pauline

Boyd, Selma *ConAu X, SmATA X*
Main entry: Acuff, Selma Boyd

Boyd, Waldo T 1918- *AuBYP 2S, –3, BioIn 12, ConAu 29R, –12NR, SmATA 18, WrDr 76, –80, –82, –84, –86, –88, –90, –92, –94*
Pseud./variant:
Andersen, Ted
Parker, Robert

Boyd, William Clouser 1903-1983 *AmMWSc 73P, –76P, AsBiEn, BiESc, BioIn 1, –13, ConAu 109, McGMS 80, NewYTBS 83, WhAm 8, WhoAm 74, –76, –78, –80, –82*

Boyer, Edward *AuBYP 3*

Boyer, Robert Ernst 1929- *AmMWSc 73P, –76P, –82, BioIn 12, –13, ConAu 41R, LEduc 74, SmATA 22, WhoAm 76, –78, –80, –82, –84, WhoFrS 84, WhoSSW 82*

Boyer, Sophia Ames 1907?-1972 *BioIn 9, ConAu 37R*

Boyes, Megan 1923- *Au&Wr 71, WrDr 76, –80, –82, –84, –86, –88, –90, –92, –94*

Boyesen, Hjalmar Hjorth 1848-1895 *Alli SUP, AmAu, AmAu&B, BenetAL 91, BbD, BiD&SB, BioIn 6, –12, –13, CarSB, ChhPo, –S1, DcAmAu, DcBiA, DcLB 12, –71, DcLEL, DcNAA, JBA 34, OhA&B, OxCAmL 65, –83, REnAL, WhAm HS*

Boyle, Ann 1916- *BioIn 11, ConAu 29R, –26NR, SmATA 10, WhoAmW 77, WrDr 76, –80, –82, –84, –86, –88, –90*

Boyle, Anna Marie 1926- *WhoAmW 93*

Boyle, Eleanor Vere 1825-1916 *BioIn 13, DcBrAr 2, DcWomA, SmATA 28*
Pseud./variant:
E V B

Boyle, Frederick 1814-1883? *ScFEYrs*

Boyle, Frederick 1841- *Alli SUP*

Boyle, Joyce 1901- *ConAu P-1*

Boyle, Kay *DrAPF 87, –89, –91, –93, IntvTCA 2*

Boyle, Kay 1902- *BioIn 15, –16, –17, BlmGWL, ConAu 29NR, ConLC 58, ConNov 86, –91, ConPo 91, DcLB 86, FemiCLE, InWom SUP, IntAu&W 89, –91, LiExTwC, MajTwCW, RfGAmL 87, Who 88, –90, –92, WhoAm 86, –88, –90, –92, WhoAmW 87, –89, –91, –93, WhoWrEP 89, –92, WrDr 86, –88, –90, –92, –94*

Boyle, Kay 1902-1992 *AnObit 1992, ConAu 140, NewYTBS 92, RfGShF*

Boyle, Kay 1903- *AmAu&B, AmNov, AmWomWr 92, ArtclWW 2, Benet 87, BenetAL 91, BioAmW, BioIn 1, –2, –4, –5, –8, –9, –11, –12, –13, –14, BlueB 76, CamGLE, CamHAL, CasWL, CnDAL, ConAmA, ConAu 13R, –1AS, ConLC 1, –5, –19, ConNov 72, –76, –82, ConPo 70, –75, –80, –85, CurBio 42, CyWA 89, DcLB 4, –9, –48, DcLEL, DrAF 76, DrAP 75, DrAPF 83, –85, EncWL, –2, ForWC 70, IntAu&W 77, IntWWP 82, LongCTC, ModAL, Novels, OxCAmL 65, –83, PenC AM, RAdv 1, REn, REnAL, ShSCr 5, ShSWr, TwCA, –SUP, Who 74, –82, –83, –85, WhoAm 74, –76, –78, –80, –82, –84, WhoAmW 74, –85, WhoTwCL, WhoUSWr 88, WhoWor 74, WrDr 76, –80, –82, –84*

Boyle, Kay 1903-1992 *CurBio 93N*

Boyle, Robert H 1928- *SmATA 65*

Boylston, Helen 1895-1984 *AuBYP 3*

Boylston, Helen Dore 1895- *FemiCLE*

Boylston, Helen Dore 1895-1984 *AuBYP 2, BioIn 2, –7, –8, –13, –14, –15, ConAu 73, –113, –21NR, CurBio 42, –84N, InWom SUP, JBA 51, MajAI, NewYTBS 84, OxCChiL, SmATA 23, –39N, TwCChW 78, –83, –89, WhoChL, WrDr 80, –82, –84*

Boynton, Sandra 1953- *ConAu 126, IntAu&W 91, SmATA 57*

Boynton, Sandra Keith 1953- *SmATA 38, WhoAm 82, –84, –86, –88*

Boyton, Neil *AuBYP 3*

Boyton, Neil 1884-1956 *AmAu&B, AuBYP 2, BioIn 1, –4, –8, BkC 1, CathA 1930, ObitOF 79, WhAm 3, WhNAA*

Boz *Benet 87, CamGLE, DcEnL, MajAI, NewC, OxCEng 67, –85, SmATA X, StaCVF*
Main entry: Dickens, Charles

Boze, Calvin *IlsBYP*

Bozzo, Frank 1937- *BioIn 12, IlsBYP, IlsCB 1967*

Brabourne, Edward H, Lord
Main entry: Knatchbull-Hugessen, E H

Brabourne, Edward H, Lord 1829-1893 *Alli SUP, BiD&SB, CelCen, OxCChiL, WhoChL*

Brace, Geoffrey 1930- *ConAu 69, –11NR*

Bracegirdle, Cyril 1920- *Au&Wr 71, ConAu 45, WrDr 76, –80*

Bracken, Anne *SingR 1*

Bracker, Charles Eugene 1895- *BioIn 1, IlsCB 1744, WhAmArt 85*

Bradbrooke, Joan *BioIn 8*

Bradbury, Bianca 1908- *AmAu&B, AuBYP 2, –3, BioIn 8, –9, ConAu 13R, –5NR, ForWC 70, FourBJA, SmATA 3*

Bradbury, Bianca 1908-1982 *BioIn 16, SmATA 56*
Pseud./variant:
Wyatt, Jane
Wyatt, Molly

Bradbury, Bianca Ryley 1908-1982 *ConAu 37NR, MajAI*

Bradbury, Parnell 1904- *Au&Wr 71, ConAu 13R, WrDr 76*

Bradbury, Peggy 1930- *ConAu 65*

Bradbury, Ray *ConSFF, DrAPF 87, –89, –91, –93, IntvTCA 2*

Bradbury, Ray 1920- *AmAu&B, AuNews 1, –2, Au&Wr 71, Benet 87, BenetAL 91, BioIn 2, –3, –4, –7, –8, –10, –11, –12, –13, –14, –15, –17, BioNews 74, BlueB 76, BroV, CamGEL, CamGLE, CamHAL, CasWL, CelR, –90, CmCal, CmMov, CnMWL, ConAu 1R –2NR, –30NR, ConLC 1, –3, –10, –15, –42, ConNov 72, –76, –82, –86, –91, ConSFA, ConTFT 10, CurBio 53, –82, CyWA 89, DcLB 2, –8, DrAF 76, DrAPF 83, –85, EncSF 93, FilmgC, HalFC 84, –88, IntAu&W 91, IntWW 89, –91, LongCTC, MagSAmL, MajTwCW, NewEScF, Novels, OxCAmL 65, –83, PenC AM, PenEncH, REn, REnAL, RGTwCSF, RfGShF, ScF&FL 92, ScFSB, SmATA 11, –64, SupFW, TwCA SUP, TwCCr&M 80, TwCSFW 86, –91, TwCWr, TwCYAW, WebAB 74, Who 74, WhoAm 74, WhoHr&F, WhoSciF, WhoWor 74, WorAlBi, WorEFlm, WorLitC, WrDr 76, –80, –82, –84, –86, –88, –90, –92*
Pseud./variant:
Banat, D R

Douglas, Leonard
Elliott, William
Spaulding, Douglas
Spaulding, Leonard
Sterling, Brett

Bradby, Godfrey Fox 1863-1947 *ChhPo, –S1, –S2, LongCTC*

Braddy, Nella 1894- *AuBYP 2, –3, BioIn 7, ChhPo S1*

Bradfield, Jolly Roger
Main entry: Bradfield, Roger

Bradfield, Margaret 1898- *WhAmArt 85*

Bradfield, Roger 1924- *AuBYP 2S, –3, ConAu 17R*
Pseud./variant:
Bradfield, Jolly Roger

Bradford, Adam, MD *AuBYP 2, ConAu X*
Main entry: Wassersug, Joseph David

Bradford, Adam M D *AuBYP 3*

Bradford, Ann 1917- *ConAu 116, SmATA 38, –56, WhoAmW 81, –83, –85*

Bradford, Barbara Taylor 1932?- *ArtclWW 2*

Bradford, Barbara Taylor 1933- *BestSel 89-1, BioIn 17, BlmGWL, ConAu 32NR, CurBio 91, EncTwCJ, IntWW 89, –91, MajTwCW, SmATA 66, TwCRHW 90, WhoAm 86, –88, WhoAmW 87, –89, WhoE 86, –89, WorAlBi, WrDr 90, –92, –94*

Bradford, Edwin Emmanuel 1860- *WhoLA*

Bradford, John Carroll 1924- *WhoAm 76, –78, –80, –82, –84, –86, –88, –90, –92, –94, WhoEnt 92*

Bradford, Karleen 1936- *BioIn 16, IntAu&W 86, –89, –91, SmATA 48, WhoCanL 87, –92*

Bradford, Lois J 1936- *ConAu 104, SmATA 36*

Bradford, Richard 1932- *BioIn 16, SmATA 59, TwCWW 91, WrDr 86, –88, –90, –92*

Bradford, Richard Roark 1932- *WrDr 94*

Bradford, William Castle 1910- *AmEA 74, AmMWSc 73S, –78S, ConAu 9R*

Bradley, Duane *AuBYP 2, BioIn 8, ConAu X, SmATA X*
Main entry: Sanborn, Duane

Bradley, Duane 1914- *AuBYP 3, DcAmChF 1960*

Bradley, Edward 1827-1889 *DcBiPP, DcNaB S1, OxCChiL, OxCEng 85, StaCVF*

Bradley, Edward 1941- *AfrAmBi*

Bradley, Ian Leonard 1925- *LEduc 74*

Bradley, Marion Z 1930- *BioAmW*

Bradley, Marion Zimmer *BioIn 14, –15, –17, DrAPF 87, –89*

Bradley, Marion Zimmer 1930- *ArtclWW 2, Au&Arts 9, BlmGWL, ConAu 10AS, –31NR, EncSF 93, MajTwCW, NewEScF, RGTwCSF, ScF&FL 92, ScFSB, TwCRHW 90, TwCSFW 86, –91, TwCYAW, WhoAm 86, –88, –90, –92, –94, WhoUSWr 88, WhoWest 87, –89, WhoWrEP 89, –92, WrDr 86, –88, –90, –92, –94*

Bradley, Virginia 1912- *BioIn 13, ConAu 61, –8NR, SmATA 23, WhoWest 80, –82, –84*

Bradley, William H 1868-1962 *BioIn 1, –3, –4, –6, –9, ChhPo, DcBrBI, IlsCB 1744*

Bradshaw, Percy Venner *BioIn 1, ChhPo, DcBrBI*

Bradshaw, Percy Venner 1877-1965 *EngPo*

Brady, Cyrus Townsend 1861-1920 *AmAu&B, AmLY, BenetAL 91, BiD&SB, CarSB, DcAmAu, DcNAA, HarEnUS, OhA&B, OxCAmL 65, –83, REn, REnAL, WhAm 1*

Brady, Esther Wood 1905- *ConAu 93, SmATA 31*
Pseud./variant:
Wood, Esther

Brady, Esther Wood 1905-1987 *ConAu 123, SmATA 53N*

Brady, Frank 1934- *ConAu 61, –9NR, IntAu&W 86, –91*

Brady, Irene 1943- *BioIn 9, –12, ConAu 33R, –20NR, IlsCB 1967, SixBJA, SmATA 4*

Brady, Lillian 1902- *BioIn 13, ConAu 105, SmATA 28*

Brady, Maxine L 1941- *AuBYP 2S, –3, ConAu 69*

Brady, Rita G *AuBYP 2, –3, BioIn 7*

Braenne, Berit 1918- *ConAu 21R*

Bragdon, Elspeth MacDuffie 1897- *BioIn 10, ConAu 5R, –5NR, SmATA 6*
Pseud./variant:
Elspeth

Bragdon, Lillian Jacot *AuBYP 2, -3, BioIn 7, -13, ConAu 73, SmATA 24*

Bragg, Charles 1931- *BioIn 12, IlsBYP, PrintW 85*

Bragg, Mabel Caroline 1870-1945 *BioIn 13, FourBJA, SmATA 24*
Pseud./variant:
Piper, Watty

Bragg, Michael 1948- *ConAu 128, SmATA 46*

Bragg, Ruth Gembicki 1943- *SmATA 77*

Brahm, Sumishta 1954- *BioIn 16, SmATA 58*

Brahs, Stuart John 1940- *ConAu 57*

Braider, Donald d1977 *WhoAmA 86N*

Braider, Donald 1923-1976 *BioIn 10, ConAu 65, -P-2, WhoAm 74, WhoAmA 78N, -80N, -82N, WrDr 76, -80, -82*

Braider, Donald 1923-1977 *WhoAmA 89N, -91N*

Brailsford, Frances *AuBYP 3, ConAu X, WrDr 76*
Main entry: Wosmek, Frances E

Braimah, Joseph Adam 1916- *ConAu 61*

Brainerd, John W 1918- *SmATA 65*

Brainerd, John Whiting 1918- *AmMWSc 73P, -76P, -82, -86, -89, ConAu 57*
Pseud./variant:
Bee, Jay

Braithwaite, Althea 1940- *BioIn 13, ConAu 97, -18NR, IntAu&W 82, OxCChiL, SmATA 23*
Pseud./variant:
Althea

Braithwaite, E R 1912- *CamGLE, ConNov 72, SelBAAf, WrDr 76, -80, -82*

Braithwaite, E R 1920- *BlkWr 1, ConAu 25NR*

Braithwaite, E R 1922- *WrDr 86, -88, -90, -92*

Braithwaite, Edward Richard 1922- *WrDr 94*

Braithwaite, Max 1911- *CaW, ConAu 93, CreCan 2, IntAu&W 86, OxCCan SUP, OxCCanL, WhoCanL 85, -87, -92*

Bram, Elizabeth 1948- *BioIn 14, ConAu 65, -9NR, SmATA 30, WhoUSWr 88, WhoWrEP 89, -92*

Bramble, Forbes 1939- *IntAu&W 82, WrDr 76, -80, -82, -84, -86, -88, -90*

Brancato, Robin F *BioIn 16, -17*

Brancato, Robin F 1936- *Au&Arts 9, ConAu 69, -11NR, ConLC 35, FifBJA, SmATA 23, -9AS*

Brancato, Robin Fidler 1936- *ChlLR 32, TwCYAW*

Brand, Christianna *ConAu 43NR*
Main entry: Lewis, Mary Christianna Milne

Brand, Christianna 1907?- *Au&Wr 71, BioIn 14, ChhPo, ConAu X, CrtSuMy, EncMys, InWom SUP, Novels, OxCChiL, TwCChW 78, -83, TwCCr&M 80, -85, WrDr 76, -80, -82, -84*

Brand, Christianna 1907-1988 *AnObit 1988, BioIn 16, -17, ScF&FL 92, SmATA X, TwCChW 89, TwCCr&M 91*

Brand, Christianna 1909- *WrDr 86, -88*

Brand, Max *AmAu&B, BenetAL 91, CmCal, ConAu X, CurBio 44, DcLEL, DcNAA, EncFWF, EncMys, FilmgC, HalFC 84, LongCTC, ObitOF 79, OxCAmL 83, REn, REnAL, TwCA, -SUP, TwCCr&M 80, WebAB 74, -79, WorAl*

Brand, Max 1891-1944 *ScFEYrs*

Brand, Max 1892-1944 *BioIn 14, -15, -16, EncSF 93, HalFC 88, NewEScF, ScF&FL 92, TwCWW 91, WorAlBi*

Brand, Oscar 1920- *AmAu&B, AuBYP 2, -3, Baker 84, -92, BioIn 6, -8, -14, BlueB 76, CanWW 70, -79, -80, -81, -83, -89, ConAu 1R, -4NR, ConTFT 1, CurBio 62, EncFCWM 69, -83, IntAu&W 77, -91, IntWWM 90, NatPD 77, -81, NotNAT, PenEncP, WhoAm 74, -76, -78, -80, -82, -84, -86, -88, -90, -92, -94, WhoEnt 92, WhoWor 74, WhoWorJ 72, -78, WrDr 76, -80, -82, -84, -86, -88, -90, -92, -94*

Brande, Ralph Thomas 1921- *ConAu 25R, WhoE 75, -83*

Brandel, Marc *AmAu&B, AmNov, Au&Wr 71, BioIn 2, ConAu X, IntAu&W 82*
Main entry: Beresford, Marcus

Brandel, Marc 1919- *ConAu 25NR, ScF&FL 92, SmATA 71*

Brandenberg, Aliki *BioIn 14, IntAu&W 86, -91*

Brandenberg, Aliki 1929- *WrDr 86, -88, -90, -94*

Brandenberg, Aliki Leacouras 1929- *AuBYP 3*

Brandenberg, Aliki Liacouras *WhoAmA 86, –89, –91*

Brandenberg, Aliki Liacouras 1929- *AuBYP 2, BioIn 8, –9, –12, –13, ChhPo S1, ConAu 1R, –4NR, –12NR, –30NR, IlsCB 1957, IntAu&W 77, –82, MajAI, SmATA 2, –35, –75, ThrBJA, WhoAmA 78, –80, –82, –84, WhoAmW 81, –83, WrDr 76, –80, –82, –84*
Pseud./variant:
Aliki

Brandenberg, Franz 1932- *AuBYP 3, BioIn 11, –14, ConAu 29R, –12NR, –30NR, FifBJA, IntAu&W 77, –91, MajAI, SmATA 8, –35, –75, WrDr 76, –80, –82, –84, –86, –88, –90, –92, –94*

Brandhorst, Carl Theodore 1898- *AmMWSc 73P, –76P, BioIn 13, ConAu P-2, SmATA 23*

Brandis, Marianne *WhoCanL 92*

Brandis, Marianne 1938- *DcChlFi, SmATA 59*

Brandon, Brumsic, Jr. 1927- *AfroAA, BioIn 11, ConAu 61, EncTwCJ, InB&W 80, –85, SmATA 9, WhoAm 78, –80, –82, –84, –86, –88, WhoBlA 75, –77, –80, –85, –88, –90, –92*

Brandon, Curt *AuBYP 2, –3, ConAu X, SmATA 6*
Main entry: Bishop, Curtis Kent

Brandon, John Gordon 1879-1941 *Alli, ConAu 112, TwCCr&M 80*

Brandon, William 1914- *ConAu 77, IndAu 1917*

Brandreth, Gyles 1948- *BioIn 9, –13, ConAu 65, IntAu&W 77, –91, SmATA 28, WrDr 76, –80, –82, –84, –86, –88, –90, –92*

Brandreth, Gyles Daubeney 1948- *WrDr 94*

Brandt, Catharine 1905- *ConAu 106, SmATA 40*

Brandt, Keith *ConAu X, SmATA X*

Brandt, Sue R 1916- *ConAu 25R, SmATA 59*

Brandwein, Paul Franz *AmMWSc 89*

Brandwein, Paul Franz 1912- *AmMWSc 76P, –82, –86, BioIn 1*

Brandys, Marian 1912- *ConAu 57, WhoWor 74*

Branfield, John 1931- *ConAu 33NR, TwCChW 89, WrDr 86, –88, –90, –92*

Branfield, John Charles 1931- *AuBYP 2S, –3, Au&Wr 71, BioIn 11, ConAu 41R, –14NR, IntAu&W 77, –82, –91, SmATA 11, TwCChW 83, WrDr 76, –80, –82, –84, –94*

Branham, Janet Lillian 1910- *WhoAmW 75, –77*

Branley, Franklyn M 1915- *AmMWSc 86, –89, –92, ChlLR 13, SmATA 68, –16AS*

Branley, Franklyn Mansfield 1915- *AmMWSc 73P, –76P, –82, AuBYP 2, –3, Au&Wr 71, BioIn 6, –7, –9, –17, BlueB 76, BkP, ConAu 33R, –14NR, –39NR, ConLC 21, MajAI, MorJA, REnAL, SmATA 4, WhoAm 74, –80*

Brann, Esther *AuBYP 2, –3, BioIn 2, –7, ConICB, JBA 34, –51, WhAmArt 85*

Branner, Martin Michael 1888-1970 *ArtCS, BioIn 8, –10, NewYTBE 70, WhAm 5*

Branner, Robert 1927-1973 *BioIn 10, NewYTBE 73, WhAm 6, WhoAm 74, WhoAmA 73, –78N, –80N, –82N, –86N, –89N, –91N*

Branscum, Robbie 1937- *BioIn 13, ConAu 61, –8NR, DcAmChF 1960, FifBJA, MajAI, SmATA 23, –72, –17AS, TwCYAW*

Bransom, Paul 1885-1979 *ArtsAmW 3, BioIn 1, –3, –5, –6, –12, –15, ChhPo, ConICB, IlrAm 1880, –B, IlsBYP, IlsCB 1744, –1946, MorJA, NatCAB 62, SmATA 43, WhAm 7, WhoAmA 73, –78, –80N, –82N, –86N, –89N, –91N, WorECar*

Branson, Margaret Stimmann 1922- *ConAu 49, IntAu&W 77, –82, WhoAmW 77, –93, WhoWest 74*

Brant, Irving Newton 1885-1976 *AmAu&B, BioIn 2, –4, –11, ConAu 9R, –69, EncTwCJ, REnAL, TwCA SUP, WhAm 7, WhoAm 74*

Brasch, Rudolph 1912- *Au&Wr 71, ConAu 21R, –8NR, –27NR, IntAu&W 91, WhoRel 92, WhoWor 74, WhoWorJ 72, –78, WrDr 76, –80, –82, –84, –86, –88, –90, –92, –94*

Brashler, William 1947- *BioIn 11, –13, ConAu 45, –2NR, WhoAm 90, –92, –94, WrDr 90, –92, –94*

Brasier, Virginia Rossmore 1910- *ConAu 61, Str&VC, WrDr 76*

Brathwaite, Errol Freeman 1924- *Au&Wr 71, ConAu 65, ConNov 72, –76, IntAu&W 82, –86, –89, –91, WrDr 76, –80*

Bratton, Helen 1899- *BioIn 9, ConAu P-2, SmATA 4*

Bratton, Karl H 1906- *AuBYP 3*

Bratton, Karl Henry 1906- *AuBYP 2, BioIn 7, WhoAm 74*

Braude, Michael 1936- *BioIn 10, –13, ConAu 17R, DrAPF 83, –85, SmATA 23, WhoFI 83, WhoMW 80, –82, –84, –86*

Brauer, Earle William 1918- *WhoE 74, –75, –77*

Braun *CarSB*

Braun, Kathy *AuBYP 2, –3, BioIn 8*

Braun, Saul M *AuBYP 2, –3, BioIn 8*

Braun, Wernher Von 1912-1977 *AsBiEn, AuBYP 2, –3, BiESc, CurBio 52, HisEWW, InSci, IntAu&W 77, IntWW 74, –75, –76, –78N, NewYTBE 70, WebAB 74, –79, WebAMB, WhDW*

Brautigan, Richard 1933?-1984 *AnObit 1984, Benet 87, ScF&FL 92*

Brautigan, Richard 1935- *ScFSB*

Brautigan, Richard 1935?-1984 *AmAu&B, AnObit 1984, BenetAL 91, BioIn 9, –10, –12, BlueB 76, CamGLE, CamHAL, CelR, CmCal, ConAu 53, –113, –34NR, ConLC 1, –3, –5, –9, –12, –34, –42, ConNov 72, –76, –82, ConPo 70, –75, –80, –85, CyWA 89, DcLB 5, –Y80A, –Y84N, DcLEL 1940, DrAF 76, DrAP 75, EncSF 93, IntAu&W 77, MagSAmL, MajTwCW, ModAL S1, NewYTBS 84, Novels, OxCAmL 83, PenC AM, PostFic, SmATA 56, WhAm 8, WhoAm 74, –76, –78, –80, –82, –84, WrDr 76, –80, –82, –84*

Braverman, Libbie Levin 1900- *OhA&B, WhoAmJ 80, WhoWorJ 72, –78*

Braverman, Robert Paul 1929- *WhoAm 74, –76*

Brawley, Benjamin 1882-1939 *BenetAL 91, BlkAuII, –92, BlkWr 1, BlkWrNE, ConAu 125, NegAl 89, SouBlCW*

Brawley, Benjamin Griffith 1882-1939 *AmAu&B, AmLY, BioIn 2, –3, –4, –5, –9, –16, BlkAWP, DcAmNB, DcNAA, InB&W 80, –85, REnAL, SelBAAf, SelBAAu, TwCA, –SUP, WhAm 1, WhNAA*

Brawley, Paul Leroy 1942- *BiDrLUS 70, MedPD, WhoLibS 66*

Bray, Warwick 1936- *ConAu 25R, –15NR*

Braymer, Marjorie Elizabeth 1911- *AnCL, BioIn 10, ConAu 1R, SmATA 6, WhoAm 74, –76, –78, –80, WhoAmW 74, WhoWest 74*

Brazil, Angela 1868-1947 *BioIn 1, –5, –8, –11, CamGLE, ConAu 112, DcLEL, DcNaB 1941, EvLB, InWom SUP, LongCTC, OxCChiL, TwCChW 78, –83, WhoChL, WhoLA*

Brazil, Angela 1869-1947 *BioIn 16, FemiCLE, TwCChW 89*

Breary, Nancy *TwCChW 83, –89*

Brecht, Bertolt 1898-1956 *AtlBL, Benet 87, BiGAW, BioIn 1, –2, –3, –4, –5, –6, –7, –8, –9, –10, –11, –12, –13, –14, –15, –16, –17, BlmGEL, CamGWoT, CasWL, ClDMEL 47, CnMD, CnMWL, CnThe, ConAu 104, –133, CroCD, CyWA 58, –89, DcFM, DcLB 56, –124, DcTwHis, DramC 3, EncWL, –2, EncWT, EuWr 11, EvEuW, FilmgC, GrFLW, HalFC 84, –88, IntDcT 2, LiExTwC, LongCTC, MagSWL, MajMD 1, MajTwCW, MakMC, McGEWD 72, –84, ModGL, ModWD, NotNAT A, –B, OxCAmT 84, OxCEng 67, –85, OxCFilm, OxCGer 76, –86, OxCPMus, OxCThe 67, –83, PenC EUR, RAdv 13-2, RComWL, REn, REnWD, ThTwC 87, TwCA, –SUP, TwCLC 1, –6, –13, –35, TwCWr, WhDW, WhAm HSA, WhoTwCL, WorAlBi, WorAl, WorEFlm, WorLitC, WrPh*

Brecht, Edith 1895-1975 *BioIn 10, –13, ConAu P-2, SmATA 6, –25N, WrDr 76*

Brecht, George 1925- *DcCAA 88*

Brecht, George 1926?- *BioIn 10, –11, ConArt 77, –83, –89, ConAu 106, ConDr 73, –77E, DcCAA 71, –77, NewGrDA 86, OxCTwCA, WhoAmA 78, –80, –82, –84, –86, –89, –91, WhoWor 74*

Breck, Vivian *AuBYP 3*
Main entry: Breckenfeld, Vivian Gurney

Breckenfeld, Vivian Gurney 1895- *AmAu&B, AuBYP 2, –3, BioIn 6, –8, –9, ConAu 5R, ForWC 70, MorJA, SmATA 1*
Pseud./variant:
Breck, Vivian

Breda, Tjalmar *BioIn 11, ConAu X, SmATA X*
Main entry: DeJong, David Cornel

Bredin, Thomas *OxCCan SUP*

Breeden, Kay 1939- *Au&Wr 71*

Breeden, Stanley 1938- *Au&Wr 71, ConAu 106, WrDr 76, –80, –82, –84, –86, –88, –90*

Breetveld, Jim Patrick 1925- *AuBYP 2 –3, BioIn 8, ConAu 1R, –2NR*

Breihan, Carl W 1916- *Au&Wr 71, ConAu 1R, –1NR*

Breinburg, Petronella 1927- *BioIn 16, BlkAuII, –92, ChlLR 31, IntAu&W 91, WrDr 86, –88, –90*

Breinburg, Petronella Alexandrina 1927- *BioIn 11, ConAu 53, SmATA 11, WrDr 76, –80*
Pseud./variant:
Ashey, Bella
Totham, Mary

Breisky, William J 1928- *BioIn 13, ConAu 53, SmATA 22*

Brelis, Nancy 1929- *ConAu 21R*

Brenda *OxCChiL*

Brennan, Dennis *AuBYP 2S, –3*

Brennan, Gale 1927- *BioIn 16, –17, ConAu 125, SmATA 64*

Brennan, Gale Patrick 1927- *SmATA 53*

Brennan, Joseph Gerard 1910- *AuBYP 2, –3, BioIn 8, ConAu 1R, –3NR, DrAS 74P, –78P, WhoAm 74, –76, –78, –80, –82, –84, –86, –88, –90, –92, –94*

Brennan, Joseph Lomas 1903- *BioIn 10, ConAu 5R, –2NR, IntAu&W 77, SmATA 6*
Pseud./variant:
Lomas, Steve

Brennan, Joseph Payne *ConSFF, DrAPF 87, –89*

Brennan, Joseph Payne 1918- *BioIn 15, ChhPo S1, ConAu 1R, –4NR, –19NR, DrAPF 83, –85, EncMys, IntAu&W 77, –82, –86, –89, –91, IntWWP 82, PenEncH, WhoE 77, –83, WhoHr&F, WhoUSWr 88, WhoWrEP 89, –92, WrDr 80, –82, –84, –86, –88, –90*

Brennan, Joseph Payne 1918-1990 *ScF&FL 92*

Brennan, Louis Arthur 1911-1983 *BioIn 3, –13, ConAu 17R, –109, NewYTBS 83, WhoE 74*

Brennan, Matthew J 1917- *ConAu 106, WhoAm 74, –76*

Brennan, Nicholas 1948- *AuBYP 3*

Brennan, Nicholas Stephen 1948- *AuBYP 2S, BioIn 10, IlsCB 1967*

Brennan, Tim *ConAu 131, IntAu&W 82X, SmATA 65, –X*
Main entry: Conroy, Jack

Brenner, Anita 1905-1974 *AmPB, AnCL, BioIn 10, ConAu 49, –53, NewYTBS 74, ObitOF 79, SmATA 56, TexWr*

Brenner, Barbara 1925- *AuBYP 3, ConAu 31NR, SmATA 14AS*

Brenner, Barbara Johnes 1925- *AuBYP 2, BioIn 8, –9, ConAu 9R, –12NR, DcAmChF 1985, ForWC 70, FourBJA, MajAI, SmATA 4, –42, –76, WhoUSWr 88, WhoWrEP 89, –92*

Brenner, Fred 1920- *FourBJA, IlsBYP, MajAI, SmATA 34, –36*

Brent, Charlton
Main entry: Emmett Brothers

Brent, Ernest
Main entry: Emmett Brothers

Brent, Hope 1935?-1984 *BioIn 15, SmATA 39N*

Brent, Stuart *AuBYP 2, –3, BioIn 6, –8, –12, ConAu 73, SmATA 14*

Brentano, Clemens Maria 1778-1842 *Benet 87, BioIn 7, –10, CelCen, NinCLC 1, OxCChiL*

Brent-Dyer, Elinor M 1894-1969 *TwCChW 89*

Brent-Dyer, Elinor Mary 1895-1969 *BioIn 8, ConAu 101, OxCChiL, TwCChW 78, –83, WhoChL*

Brereton, Frederick S 1872-1957 *BioIn 4, –8, ChhPo S1, OxCChiL, SixAP, WhoChL*

Breslin, Jimmy *ConAu 31NR, IntvTCA 2, MajTwCW*

Breslin, Jimmy 1929- *WhoAm 86, –88, –92, –94, WhoE 86, –89, –91, –93, WhoUSWr 88, WhoWrEP 89, –92, WorAlBi*

Breslin, Jimmy 1930- *AmAu&B, AuNews 1, BiDConC, BioIn 6, –7, –8, –10, –11, –13, CelR, –90, ConAu 73, ConLC 4, –43, CurBio 73, EncAJ, EncTwCJ, WhoAm 74, –76, –78, –80, –82, –84, WhoE 74, WhoWor 74, WorAl, WrDr 76, –80, –82, –84, –86, –88, –90, –92, –94*

Breslin, Theresa *SmATA 70*

Breslow, Maurice Allen 1935- *SmATA 72*

Breslow, Susan 1951- *SmATA 69*

Brett, Bernard 1925- *BioIn 12, –13, –14, ConAu 97, –17NR, IlsCB 1967, SmATA 22*

Brett, Dorothy 1883-1977 *BioIn 1, –3, –8, –10, –11, –16, –17, ConAu 73, DcBrAr 1, WhAm 7*

Brett, Dorothy 1883-1987 *TwCPaSc*

Brett, Edwin 1828-1895 *OxCChiL*

Brett, Edwin J 1828-1895 *BioIn 17*

Brett, Grace N 1900-1975 *ConAu 120*

Brett, Grace Neff 1900-1975 *ConAu 9R, SmATA 23, WhoAmW 75*

Brett, Harold M 1880?-1955 *BioIn 1, ChhPo, ConICB, IlrAm 1880, IlsCB 1744, WhAmArt 85*

Brett, Hawksley *ConAu X, SmATA X*

Brett, Jan *ChlBIlD*

Brett, Jan 1949- *BioIn 15, –16, ChlLR 27, ConAu 116, SixBJA, SmATA 42*
Pseud./variant:
Bowler, Jan Brett

Brett, Jan Churchill 1949- *ConAu 41NR, MajAI, SmATA 71*

Brett, Mary Elizabeth *Au&Wr 71, ConAu 9R, WhoArt 80, –82, –84, WrDr 76, –80, –82, –84, –86, –88*
Pseud./variant:
Brett, Molly

Brett, Molly
Main entry: Brett, Mary Elizabeth

Brevannes, Maurice 1904- *BioIn 5, IlsBYP, IlsCB 1946*

Brewer, Sally King 1947- *SmATA 33*

Brewster, Benjamin *AuBYP 2, –3, ConAu X, CurBio 41, IntAu&W 82X, –91X, SmATA 2, WrDr 76, –80, –82, –84, –86, –88, –90, –92*
Main entry: Elting, Mary
Folsom, Franklin Brewster

Brewster, Benjamin 1907- *WrDr 94*

Brewster, Patience *ChlBIlD*

Brewster, Patience 1952- *BioIn 16, ConAu 121, SmATA 51*

Brewton, John E 1898- *WhAm 10*

Brewton, John Edmund 1898- *BioIn 10, BkP, ChhPo, –S1, –S2, ConAu 5R, –3NR, SmATA 5*

Brewton, Sara W *BkP*

Brewton, Sara Westbrook d1976 *ConAu 122*

Brey, Charles *IlsBYP*

Briansky, Rita Prezament 1925- *WhoAmA 73, –80, –82, –84, –86, –89, –91, WhoAmW 74, –77, WhoWorJ 72*

Brick, John 1922-1973 *AmAu&B, AuBYP 2, –3, BioIn 3, –7, –10, –11, ConAu 45, –P-1, CurBio 53, –73, SmATA 10*

Brickdale, Eleanor Fortescue *InWom SUP*

Brickdale, Eleanor Fortescue 1871-1945 *BioIn 1, –14, ChhPo S1, ClaDrA, DcBrBI, DcVicP 2, DcWomA, IlsCB 1744, TwCPaSc*

Bridgers, Sue Ellen *DrAPF 87, –89, –91, –93*

Bridgers, Sue Ellen 1942- *Au&Arts 8, BioIn 13, –15, –16, ChlLR 18, ConAu 65, –11NR, –36NR, ConLC 26, DcAmChF 1960, –1985, DcLB 52, DrAPF 83, –85, FifBJA, MajAI, SmATA 22, –1AS, TwCChW 89, TwCYAW, WhoUSWr 88, WhoWrEP 89, –92, WrDr 90, –92*

Bridgers, Sue Ellen Hunsucker 1942- *WrDr 94*

Bridges, Laurie
Main entry: Bruck, Lorraine

Bridges, Robert Seymour 1844-1930 *Alli SUP, AnCL, AtlBL, BioIn 1, –2, –3, –4, –5, –5, –7, –9, –10, –11, –14, –16, BlmGEL, CasWL, ChhPo, –S1, –S2, CnE&AP, DcEnA, –A, DcLEL, DcNaB 1922, Dis&D, EncWL, EvLB, GrBr, LongCEL, LongCTC, ModBrL, NewC, OxCEng 67, OxCMus, PenC ENG, REn, TwCA, –SUP, TwCLC 1, TwCWr, WebE&AL, WhoTwCL*

Bridges, Thomas Charles 1868-1944 *BioIn 8, WhoChL*

Bridges, William Andrew 1901- *AuBYP 3*

Bridges, William Andrew 1901-1984 *AmAu&B, AuBYP 2, BioIn 7, –10, ConAu 33R, IndAu 1917, IntAu&W 77, SmATA 5, WhAm 8, WhoAm 74, –76, –78, –80, –82, WrDr 76, –80*

Bridgman, Elizabeth P 1921- *ConAu 73*

Bridgman, George Brandt 1864-1943 *ObitOF 79, WhAmArt 85*

Bridgman, George Brant 1864-1943 *BioIn 11*

Bridgman, Lewis Jesse 1857-1931 *CarSB, ChhPo, –S1, –S2, DcNAA, WhAm 1, WhAmArt 85*

Bridwell, Norman 1928- *BioIn 17, ConAu 20NR, SmATA 68*

Bridwell, Norman Ray 1928- *BioIn 9, ConAu 13R, IndAu 1917, IntAu&W 91,*

MajAI, SmATA 4, WhoE 83, –85, –86, –89, WrDr 76, –80, –82, –84, –86, –88, –90, –92, –94

Brier, Howard Maxwell 1903-1969 *AuBYP 2, –3, BioIn 2, –6, –7, –11, ConAu P-1, CurBio 51, MorJA, SmATA 8, WhoPNW*

Brierley 1958- *SmATA 59*

Briggs, Austin Eugene 1908-1973 *ArtCS, BioIn 2, –4, –7, –10, NewYTBE 73, WhAm 6, WhoAm 74, WhoAmA 73, –78N*

Briggs, Barbara *AuBYP 3*

Briggs, Barbara 1927- *AuBYP 2, BioIn 7, WhoAmW 83, –85*

Briggs, Carole S 1950- *SmATA 47*
Pseud./variant:
Ayres, Carole Briggs

Briggs, Jean 1925- *ConAu 93, WrDr 76, –80, –82, –84, –86, –88, –90*

Briggs, K M 1898-1980 *EncO&P 3, TwCChW 89*

Briggs, Katharine Mary 1898-1980 *ArtclWW 2, Au&Wr 71, BioIn 12, –13, ChhPo S2, ConAu 102, –12NR, EncO&P 2, FifBJA, IntAu&W 82, OxCChiL, SmATA 25N, TwCChW 83, WhoWor 78, WrDr 76, –80, –82*

Briggs, K M1898-1980 *ScF&FL 92*

Briggs, Mitchell Pirie 1892- *AmAu&B, WhAm 9*

Briggs, Peter 1921-1975 *BioIn 10, ConAu 57, –P-2, SmATA 31N, –39, WhoE 74*

Briggs, Raymond 1934- *CamGLE, ChlLR 10, SmATA 66, TwCChW 89, WrDr 86, –88, –90, –92*

Briggs, Raymond Redvers 1934- *ArtsCL, Au&Wr 71, BioIn 6, –8, –9, –10, –12, –13, BkP, ChhPo, –S1, –S2, ChlFicS, ChlLR 10, ConAu 73, EncSF 93, IlsBYP, IlsCB 1957, –1967, IntAu&W 89, –91, IntWW 89, –91, MajAI, OxCChiL, SmATA 23, ThrBJA, TwCChW 83, Who 82, –83, –85, –88, –90, –92, WhoChL, WrDr 82, –84, –94*

Briggs, Shirley Ann 1918- *ConAu 106, ForWC 70, WhoAm 78, –80, –82, –84, –86, –88, –90, –92, –94, WhoAmW 75, –77*

Brigham, Grace A *IlsBYP*

Bright, Robert d1988 *NewYTBS 88*

Bright, Robert 1902- *AmAu&B, AmNov, BioIn 2, –5, –6, –8, –13, ConAu 73, IlsBYP, IlsCB 1946, –1957, MorJA, SmATA 24, TwCChW 78, –83, WrDr 80, –82, –84, –86, –88*

Bright, Robert 1902-1988 *BioIn 16, –17, ConAu 127, SmATA 60, –63, TwCChW 89*
Pseud./variant:
Douglas, Michael

Bright, Sarah *SmATA 71*
Main entry: Shine, Deborah

Brightfield, Richard 1927- *BioIn 16, –17, ConAu 118, –35NR, ScF&FL 92, SmATA 53, –65*
Pseud./variant:
Brightfield, Rick

Brightfield, Rick *ConAu 35NR, ScF&FL 92, SmATA 65*

Brightfield, Rick 1927- *BioIn 16, –17*
Main entry: Brightfield, Richard

Brighton, Catherine 1943- *ConAu 130, SmATA 65, WrDr 94*

Brightwell, Leonard Robert 1889- *BioIn 1, –13, –14, IlsCB 1744, SmATA 29*

Brill, Marlene Targ 1945- *SmATA 77*
Pseud./variant:
Targ Brill, Marlene

Brimberg, Stanlee 1947- *BioIn 11, ConAu 49, SmATA 9, WrDr 76, –80, –82, –84*

Brimner, Larry Dane *AuBYP 3*

Brin, David *ScFSB*

Brin, David 1950- *BioIn 17, ConAu 24NR, IntAu&W 91, NewEScF, RGTwCSF, ScF&FL 92, SmATA 65, TwCSFW 91, WhoAm 86, –90, –92, WrDr 88, –90, –92, –94*

Brin, Ruth Firestone 1921- *ConAu 17R, –8NR, SmATA 22*

Brinckloe, Julie 1950- *BioIn 10, ConAu 65, IlsBYP, SmATA 13*

Brindel, June 1919- *AuBYP 3, ConAu 31NR*

Brindel, June Rachuy *DrAPF 87, –89, –91, –93*

Brindel, June Rachuy 1919- *AuBYP 2S, BioIn 10, ConAu 49, DrAPF 83, –85, IntWWP 82, ScF&FL 92, SmATA 7, WhoUSWr 88, WhoWrEP 89, –92*

Brindze, Ruth 1903- *AuBYP 2, BioIn 6, –8, –13, ConAu 73, MorJA, SmATA 23*

Brings, Lawrence Martin 1897- *BioIn 9, WhoAm 74, –76, –78, –80, –82, –84, –86, –88, –90, –92, –94, WhoMW 88*

Brink, Carol Ryrie 1895-1981 *AmAu&B, AmWomPl, AnObit 1981, AnCL, AuBYP 2, -3, Au&Wr 71, BioIn 1, -2, -3, -4, -6, -7, -8, -9, -10, -14, ChhPo S1, ChlLR 30, ConAu 1R, -104, -3NR, CurBio 46, FamMS, InWom SUP, IntAu&W 77, -82, JBA 51, MajAI, MinnWr, MorBMP, NewbMB 1922, OxCChiL, REnAL, SmATA 1, -27N, -31, Str&VC, TwCChW 78, -83, -89, TwCWW 91, WhAm 8, WhoAm 74, -76, -78, -80, WhoAmW 74, WhoPNW, WrChl, WrDr 76, -80, -82*

Brinkerhoff, Robert Moore 1880-1958 *ArtCS, BioIn 4, OhA&B, WhJnl, WhNAA*

Brinkman, Grover 1903- *ConAu 73*

Brinley, Bertrand R 1917- *ConAu 29R*

Brinsley, John *CyEd, DcNaB, OxCChiL*

Brinsmead, Hesba 1922- *AuWomWr, BlmGWL, SmATA 5AS, TwCChW 89*

Brinsmead, Hesba Fay 1922- *BioIn 12, -16, ChlFicS, ConAu 21R, -10NR, ConLC 21, DcChlFi, FourBJA, MajAI, OxCAusL, OxCChiL, SenS, SingR 2, SmATA 18, TwCChW 78, -83, WrDr 76, -80, -82, -84*
Pseud./variant:
Hungerford, Pixie

Brinton, Henry 1901-1977 *Au&Wr 71, ConAu 1R, -4NR, EncSF 93, ScF&FL 92*

Briquebec, John *ConAu X, SmATA X*
Main entry: Rowland-Entwistle, Theodore

Brisco, Patty *ConAu X, IntAu&W 86X, -91X, MajTwCW, SmATA X, TwCRHW 90, WrDr 84, -86, -88, -90, -92*
Main entry: Matthews, Clayton
Matthews, Patricia

Brisco, Patty 1927- *WrDr 94*

Briscoe, Ernest Edward 1882-1956 *DcBrAr 1, DcBrBI*

Briscoe, Jill 1935- *BioIn 16, SmATA 47, -56*

Brisley, Joyce Lankester 1896-1978 *Au&Wr 71, BioIn 12, -13, -14, ChhPo, -S1, ConAu 97, OxCChiL, SmATA 22, TwCChW 78, -83, -89, WrDr 76*

Brisson, Pat *BioIn 17*

Brisson, Pat 1951- *ConAu 134, SmATA 67, WrDr 94*

Brister, C W 1926- *ConAu 13R, -7NR, WhoRel 92*

Bristow, Joan *AuBYP 2S, -3*

Britt, Albert 1874-1969 *BioIn 6, -8, -11, -13, ConAu 103, SmATA 28N*

Britt, Dell 1934- *BioIn 9, ConAu 25R, SmATA 1*

Brittain, Bill *ConAu 30NR, DrAPF 87, -89, -91, -93, MajAI, SmATA 76, WrDr 86, -88, -90, -92*

Brittain, Bill 1930- *DcAmChF 1960, ScF&FL 92, SmATA 7AS, TwCChW 89*

Brittain, William 1930- *BioIn 14, ConAu 13NR, -30NR, DrAPF 83, -85, FifBJA, SmATA 36, TwCCr&M 80, -85, -91, WrDr 86, -88, -90, -92, -94*
Pseud./variant:
Knox, James

Brittain, William E *ScF&FL 92*

Brittain, William E 1930- *MajAI, SmATA 76*

Brittan, Charles Edward 1870- *BioIn 1, DcBrAr 1, IlsCB 1744*

Britten, Frank Curzon *ChhPo*

Brittingham, Geoffrey Hugh 1959- *SmATA 76*

Britton, Dorothy Guyver 1922- *ConAmC 76*

Britton, Kate
Main entry: Stegeman, Janet Allais

Britton, Louisa *ConAu X, SmATA X*
Main entry: McGuire, Leslie Sarah

Bro, Marguerite Harmon 1894- *AmWomPl*

Bro, Marguerite Harmon 1894-1977 *BioIn 2, -3, -6, -12, -13, ConAu 77, CurBio 52, MorJA, SmATA 19, -27N*

Broadhead, Helen Cross 1913- *ConAu 103, SmATA 25*
Pseud./variant:
Cross, Helen Reeder

Broadhurst, Alan Bagnall 1917- *Au&Wr 71, WrDr 76*

Brochmann, Elizabeth 1938- *BioIn 15, ConAu 112, DcChlFi, SmATA 41, WhoCanL 85, -87, -92*

Brock, Betty 1923- *AuBYP 3, WrDr 88, -90, -92*

Brock, Betty Carter 1923- *AuBYP 2S, BioIn 9, -10, ConAu 29R, SmATA 4, -7, WrDr 76, -80, -82, -84, -86, -94*

Brock, Charles E 1870-1938 *StaCVF*

Brock, Charles Edmond 1870-1938 *BioIn 14, –15*

Brock, Charles Edmund 1870-1938 *BioIn 2, –8, ChhPo, –S1, ClaDrA, DcBrAr 1, DcVicP 2, JBA 34, –51, OxCChiL, SmATA 32, –42, WhoChL*

Brock, Delia *SmATA 65, WrDr 94*
Main entry: Ephron, Delia

Brock, Emma Lillian 1886-1974 *AuBYP 2, –3, BioIn 1, –2, –5, –6, –7, –11, ChhPo, ConAu 5R, –103, ConICB, DcWomA, IlsCB 1744, –1946, JBA 34, –51, MinnWr, SmATA 8, Str&VC, WhAmArt 85, WhoPNW*

Brock, Henry Matthew 1875-1960 *BioIn 1, –2, –8, –14, –15, ChhPo, –S1, –S2, ClaDrA, DcBrAr 1, DcBrBI, IlsCB 1744, JBA 34, –51, OxCChiL, SmATA 42, WhoChL*

Brock, Stanley E 1936- *BioIn 9, ConAu 57*

Brock, Stuart *ConAu X, TwCWW 91*
Main entry: Trimble, Louis P

Brock, Virginia *AuBYP 2S, –3*

Brockett, Eleanor Hall 1913-1967 *BioIn 11, ConAu P-1, SmATA 10*

Brockman, C Frank 1902- *BioIn 13, ConAu 5R, SmATA 26*

Broderick, Dorothy M 1929- *AuBYP 2, –3, BiDrLUS 70, BioIn 8, –10, ConAu 13R, SmATA 5, WhoLibS 66*

Broderick, Francis L d1992 *NewYTBS 92*

Broderick, Francis Lyons 1922- *ConAu 101, DrAS 74H, –78H, –82H, WhoAm 74, –76, –78, –80, –82, –84, –86, –88, –90, WhoE 74*

Broderick, Francis Lyons 1922-1992 *ConAu 139*

Broderip, Frances Freeling 1830-1878 *DcNaB, OxCChiL*

Brodie, Sally *ConAu X, SmATA X*
Main entry: Cavin, Ruth

Brodin, Pierre Eugene 1909- *AuBYP 2S, –3, ConAu 85*

Brodsky, Beverly *DrAPF 87, –89*
Main entry: McDermott, Beverly Brodsky

Brodsky, Beverly 1941- *ConAu X, DrAPF 83, –85, FifBJA, IlsCB 1967*

Broekel, Rainer Lothar *AuBYP 3*

Broekel, Rainer Lothar 1923- *ConAu 3NR, –19NR, SmATA 38*

Broekel, Ray 1923- *AuBYP 3, BioIn 15*

Broger, Achim 1944- *BioIn 14, IntAu&W 77, –82, SmATA 31*

Brokamp, Marilyn 1920- *BioIn 11, ConAu 49, SmATA 10*
Pseud./variant:
Lynn, Mary

Bromhall, Winifred *BioIn 1, –5, –6, –13, –14, ChhPo, ConICB, IlsBYP, IlsCB 1744, –1946, MorJA, SmATA 26, WhAmArt 85*

Bromley, Dudley 1948- *BioIn 16, ScF&FL 92, SmATA 51*

Brommer, Gerald F 1927- *AmArt, ConAu 21NR, WhoAmA 86, –89, –91, WhoUSWr 88, WhoWrEP 89*

Brommer, Gerald Frederick 1927- *AmArt, BioIn 13, ConAu 105, SmATA 28, WhoAmA 78, –80, –82, –84, WhoWest 78, –84, –92, –94, WhoWrEP 92*

Brondfield, Jerome 1913- *BioIn 13, ConAu 73, IntMPA 75, –76, –78, –81, –82, –84, –86, –88, –92, –77, SmATA 22*

Bronin, Andrew 1947- *ConAu 45*

Bronowski, Jacob 1908-1974 *AmAu&B, AnCL, AuBYP 2S, –3, Benet 87, BioIn 2, –4, –5, –7, –10, –11, –12, –13, –14, –15, –16, BlueB 76N, ConAu 1R, –53, –3NR, DcLEL, DcNaB 1971, EngPo, InSci, IntWW 74, –75N, NewYTBS 74, ObitOF 79, ObitT 1971, RAdv 13-5, SmATA 55, ThTwC 87, WhAm 6, Who 74, WhoAm 74, WhoWor 74, WorAlBi, WorAl, WorAu 1950*

Bronson, Lynn *AuBYP 2, –3, ConAu X, MorJA, SmATA 4, –X, TwCChW 83, –89, WrDr 80, –82*
Main entry: Lampman, Evelyn Sibley

Bronson, Wilfrid Swancourt 1894-1985 *AmAu&B, AuBYP 2, –3, BioIn 1, –2, –5, –7, –15, ConAu 73, –116, IlsCB 1744, –1946, JBA 34, –51, SmATA 43N, Str&VC*

Bronte, Charlotte 1816-1855 *Alli, ArtclWW 2, AtlBL, BbD, BiD&SB, BioIn 1, –2, –3, –4, –5, –6, –7, –8, –9, –10, –11, –12, –13, –14, –15, –16, –17, BlmGEL, BlmGWL, BritAu 19, BritWr 5, CamGEL, CamGLE, CasWL, Chambr 3, ChhPo, –S1, –S2, CnDBLB 4, ContDcW 89, CrtT 3, CyWA 58, DcBiA, DcBiPP, DcEnA, –A, DcEnL, DcEuL, DcLB 21, DcLEL, DcNaB, DcWomA, Dis&D, EncBrWW, EvLB, FemiCLE, FilmgC, HalFC 84, –88, HerW, –84, HsB&A,*

InWom SUP, IntDcWB, LongCEL, MagSWL, McGEWB, MouLC 3, NinCLC 3, –8, –33, NotNAT B, Novels, OxCEng 67, –85, PenC ENG, PenEncH, RAdv 1, –13-1, RComWL, RfGEnL 91, StaCVF, WebE&AL, WhDW, WorAlBi, WorAl, WorLitC

Bronte, Emily Jane 1818-1848 *AtlBL, BbD, BiD&SB, BioIn 1, –2, –3, –4, –5, –6, –7, –8, –9, –10, –11, –12, –13, BritAu 19, CasWL, Chambr 3, ChhPo, –S1, –S2, CnE&AP, CrtT 3, CyWA 58, DcBiA, DcEnA, –A, DcEnL, DcEuL, DcLEL, DcNaB, DcWomA, Dis&D, EvLB, FilmgC, HerW, InWom SUP, LongCEL, McGEWB, MouLC 3, OxCEng 67, –85, PenC ENG, PenEncH, RAdv 1, –13-1, RComWL, WebE&AL, WorAl*

Brook, Judith 1926- *ConAu 122, SmATA 51, –59*

Brook, Judy 1926- *SmATA X, WrDr 90*

Brooke, L Leslie 1862-1940 *ChlLR 20, TwCChW 89*

Brooke, Leonard Leslie 1862-1940 *AnCL, BioIn 2, –5, –8, –12, –13, –14, ChhPo, –S1, ConICB, DcBrAr 1, DcBrBI, DcVicP 2, IlsBYP, JBA 34, –51, MajAI, OxCChiL, SmATA 17, Str&VC, TwCChW 78, –83, WhoChL*

Brooke-Haven, P *ConAu 33NR, MajTwCW, SmATA X*

Brookes, Kenneth 1897- *DcBrAr 1*

Brookins, Dana 1931- *BioIn 13, ConAu 69, ScF&FL 92, SmATA 28*

Brookins, Dana Martin 1931- *DcAmChF 1960*

Brooks, Amy d1931 *AmAu&B, AmLY, CarSB, DcNAA, DcWomA, WhAmArt 85, WhNAA, WomWWA 14, WomNov*

Brooks, Anita 1914- *AuBYP 2, –3, BioIn 8, –10, ConAu 17R, –X, SmATA 5*

Brooks, Anne *AuBYP 3*

Brooks, Anne Tedlock 1905- *AuBYP 2S, ConAu 1R, –1NR*
Pseud./variant:
Carter, Anne
Millburn, Cynthia

Brooks, Barbara *SmATA X*
Main entry: Simons, Barbara Brooks

Brooks, Bill 1939- *SmATA 59*

Brooks, Bruce *ScF&FL 92, SmATA 53*

Brooks, Bruce 1950- *Au&Arts 8, BioIn 16, –17, ChlLR 25, ConAu 137, DcAmChF 1985, MajAI, SixBJA, SmATA 72, TwCYAW*

Brooks, Bruce Delos 1950- *WhoAm 94*

Brooks, Charlotte K *AuBYP 3*

Brooks, Charlotte Kendrick *AuBYP 2, BioIn 13, ConBlAP 88, InB&W 80, –85, LivgBAA, SmATA 24, WhoBlA 77, –80, –85*

Brooks, Charlotte Kendrick 1918- *WhoBlA 88, –90, –92, –94*

Brooks, Edwy Searles 1889-1965 *BioIn 8, –14, EncMys, WhoChL*

Brooks, Elbridge S 1846-1902 *BenetAL 91*

Brooks, Elbridge Streeter 1846-1902 *Alli SUP, AmAu, AmAu&B, BbD, BiD&SB, BioIn 3, CarSB, ChhPo, DcAmAu, DcNAA, HarEnUS, JBA 34, REnAL, WhAm 1*

Brooks, George *MajAI*

Brooks, Gwendolyn *BioIn 14, –15, –16, –17, DrAPF 87, –89, –91, –93, IntvTCA 2, WhoBlA 85*

Brooks, Gwendolyn 1912- *NegAl 89*

Brooks, Gwendolyn 1917- *AfrAmW, AmAu&B, AmWr S3, ArtclWW 2, AuNews 1, Benet 87, BenetAL 91, BioAmW, BioIn 2, –4, –6, –7, –8, –9, –10, –11, –12, –13, BioNews 74, BlkAWP, BlkAuII, –92, BlkLC, BlkWr 1, BlmGWL, BlueB 76, BkCL, CamGLE, CamHAL, CasWL, CelR, –90, ChhPo, –S1, –S2, ChlLR 27, ConAu 1R, –1NR, –27NR, ConBlB 1, ConLC 1, –2, –4, –5, –15, –49, ConPo 70, –75, –80, –85, –91, ContDcW 89, CroCAP, CurBio 50, –77, CyWA 89, DcLB 5, –76, DcLEL 1940, DrAP 75, DrAPF 83, –85, EncAACR, EncAB-H, EncWB, EncWL 2, FemiCLE, FourBJA, HanAmWH, InWom SUP, IntAu&W 77, –89, –91, IntDcWB, IntWW 74, –75, –76, –77, –78, –79, –80, –81, –82, –83, –89, –91, LivgBAA, MajTwCW, ModAL, –S1, ModAWP, ModAWWr, ModBlW, NegAl 76, –83, NewCon, NotBlAW 92, OxCAmL 65, –83, PenC AM, PoeCrit 7, RAdv 1, –13-1, REnAL, RfGAmL 87, SmATA 6, TwCA SUP, WebAB 74, –79, WhoAm 74, –76, –78, –80, –82, –84, –86, –88, –90, –92, –94, WhoAmW 74, –75, –77, –81, –83, –85, –87, –89, –91, –93, WhoBlA 80, –85, WhoMW 86, –88, –90, –92, –93, WhoUSWr 88, WhoWor 74, –78, –80, –82, –84, –87, –89, WhoWrEP 89, –92, WorAlBi, WorLitC, WrDr 76, –80, –82, –84, –86, –88, –90, –92*

Brooks, Janice Young 1943- *ConAu 65, –9NR, –39NR*

Pseud./variant:
Singer, Amanda

Brooks, Jeremy 1926- *Au&Wr 71, BioIn 13, ConAu 5R, –7NR, ConNov 72, –76, DcLB 14, DcLEL 1940, IntAu&W 77, –82, –86, –91, OxCLiW 86, WrDr 76, –80, –82, –84, –86, –88, –90, –92, –94*

Brooks, Jerome 1931- *BioIn 13, ConAu 49, –2NR, SmATA 23, WhoMW 92*

Brooks, Lester 1924- *AuBYP 2S, –3, BioIn 10, ConAu 33R, –13NR, –42NR, SmATA 7*

Brooks, Lester James 1924- *IntAu&W 86*

Brooks, Martha *ConAu 136, SmATA 68, WhoCanL 92, WrDr 94*

Brooks, Maurice *BioIn 14, –15*

Brooks, Maurice 1900- *BioIn 13, SmATA 45, WhoAm 74*

Brooks, Noah 1830-1903 *Alli SUP, AmAu, AmAu&B, BenetAL 91, BbD, BiDAmJo, BiD&SB, BioIn 15, –16, CarSB, CmCal, DcAmAu, DcLB 42, DcNAA, JrnUS, JBA 34, OxCAmL 65, –83, OxCChiL, REnAL, WhAm 1, WhCiWar*

Brooks, Patricia K 1926- *IntAu&W 86*

Brooks, Patricia Kersten 1926- *ConAu 25R, WhoAmP 73, –75, –77, –81*

Brooks, Paul 1909- *ConAu 13R, –7NR, InB&W 80, IntAu&W 91, WhoAm 74, –76, –78, –80, WhoE 74, WrDr 80, –82, –84, –86, –88, –90, –92, –94*

Brooks, Phillips 1835-1893 *Alli SUP, AmAu&B, AnCL, BenetAL 91, BbD, BiD&SB, BioIn 2, –3, –5, –6, –9, –10, –11, Chambr 3, ChhPo, –S1, –S2, CyEd, DcAmAu, DcAmReB 2, DcNAA, HarEnUS, LuthC 75, McGEWB, OxCAmH, OxCAmL 65, –83, REnAL, WebAB 74, –79, WhAm HS*

Brooks, Polly Schoyer 1912- *BioIn 11, ConAu 1R, –17NR, SmATA 12*

Brooks, Ronald George 1948- *BioIn 12, ConAu 111, IlsCB 1967, SmATA 33*

Brooks, Sarah Warner 1822-1906 *AmAu&B, ChhPo S1, DcNAA, WhAm 1*

Brooks, Stewart Marshall 1923- *ConAu 17R, –9NR, WhoE 74*

Brooks, Terry *DrAPF 87, –89, –91, –93, ScFSB*

Brooks, Terry 1944- *BioIn 17, IntAu&W 86, ScF&FL 92, SmATA 60, TwCYAW, WhoAm 86, –94, WhoUSWr 88*

Brooks, Thomas 1925- *AuBYP 3*

Brooks, Thomas R 1925- *AuBYP 2S, ConAu 73, –34NR*

Brooks, Thomas Reed 1925- *WhoE 89*

Brooks, Van Wyck *IntvTCA 2*

Brooks, Van Wyck 1886-1963 *AmAu&B, AmLY, AmWr, AtlBL, Benet 87, BenetAL 91, BioIn 1, –2, –3, –4, –5, –6, –7, –8, –9, –11, –14, –15, –16, –17, CasWL, Chambr 3, CnDAL, ConAmA, ConAmL, ConAu 1R, ConLCrt 82, CurBio 41, –60, –63, DcLB 63, –103, DcLEL, EvLB, LongCTC, ModAL, MorMA, ObitOF 79, OxCAmL 65, PenC AM, RAdv 1, REn, REnAL, ScF&FL 92, TwCA, –SUP, TwCWr, WebE&AL, WhNAA, WorAlBi*

Brooks, Walter R 1886-1958 *ScF&FL 92, TwCChW 89*

Brooks, Walter Rollin 1886-1958 *AmAu&B, BioIn 2, –3, –5, –7, –12, ChhPo, ConAu 111, JBA 51, ObitOF 79, OxCChiL, SmATA 17, TwCChW 78, –83, WhAm 3, WhNAA*

Brooks-Hill, Helen 1908- *BioIn 16, SmATA 59*

Broome, Mary Anne, Lady 1831-1911 *Alli SUP, AuWomWr, CasWL, OxCAusL*

Broomfield, Robert 1930- *BioIn 8, –12, –14, IlsBYP, IlsCB 1957, –1967*

Brophy, Nannette 1963- *SmATA 73*

Brosnan, James Patrick 1929- *AuBYP 2S, –3, BioIn 5, –6, –7, –8, –10, –12, ConAu 1R, –3NR, CurBio 64, SmATA 14, WhoMW 74, –76*

Broster, Dorothy Kathleen 1877?-1950 *BioIn 2, –14, –15, –16, DcLEL, JBA 34, –51, OxCChiL, TwCWr, WhoLA, WomNov*

Brough, James 1918- *ConAu 111*

Broun, Emily *AmPeW, ConAu X, SmATA X*
Main entry: Sterne, Emma Gelders

Broun, Heywood C 1888-1939 *Ballpl 90*

Broun, Heywood Campbell 1886-1939 *BiDAmSp OS*

Broun, Heywood Campbell 1888-1939 *AmAu&B, AuBYP 2S, –3, BiDAmJo, BiDAmL, BioIn 1, –2, –3, –4, –5, –6, –10, –13, CathA 1930, ConAmA, CurBio 40, DcCathB,*

DcLEL, DcNAA, NotNAT B, OxCAmL 65, PlP&P, REn, REnAL, TwCA, –SUP, WebAB 74, WhAm 1, WorAl

Brow, Thea 1934- *BioIn 17, SmATA 60*

Browder, Walter Everett 1939- *ConAu 53*

Brower, Millicent *BioIn 11, ConAu 41R, –15NR, DrAPF 91, –93, SmATA 8*

Brower, Pauline 1929- *BioIn 13, ConAu 77, SmATA 22*

Browin, Frances Williams 1898- *AuBYP 2, –3, BioIn 8, –10, ConAu P-1, SmATA 5, WhoAmW 75*
Pseud./variant:
Williams, Frances B

Brown, Abbie Farwell 1871-1927 *AmWomPl, InWom SUP*

Brown, Abbie Farwell 1872?-1927 *AmAu&B, AmLY, AnCL, CarSB, ChhPo, –S1, –S2, DcAmAu, DcNAA, JBA 34, TwCA, –SUP, WhAm 1, WhNAA, WomWWA 14*

Brown, Alexis *ConAu X, SmATA X*
Main entry: Baumann, Amy Brown Beeching

Brown, Anne Ensign 1937- *BioIn 17, SmATA 61*

Brown, Beatrice Curtis *ChhPo, –S1, ConAu X*
Main entry: Curtis Brown, Beatrice

Brown, Beth *ASCAP 66, ConAu P-2*
Pseud./variant:
Retner, Beth A

Brown, Betty *ConAu X*
Main entry: Jones, Elizabeth Brown

Brown, Bill
Main entry: Brown, William L

Brown, Bill 1910-1964 *AuBYP 2, –3, BioIn 8, ConAu X, SmATA 5*

Brown, Bill, and Rosalie Moore Brown *AuBYP 3*

Brown, Billye Walker *ConAu X, SmATA X*
Main entry: Cutchen, Billye Walker

Brown, Bob
Main entry: Brown, Robert Joseph

Brown, Bob 1907- *ConAu X, SmATA X*

Brown, Buck 1936- *BioIn 15, SmATA 45, WhoAm 74, –76, WhoAmA 78, WhoBlA 75, –77, –80, –85, –90, –92, –94, WorECar*

Brown, Cassie 1919- *ArtclWW 2*

Brown, Cassie 1919-1986 *BioIn 16, ConAu 23NR, SmATA 55*

Brown, Claude *DrAPF 87, –89, –91, –93*

Brown, Claude 1927- *NegAl 89*

Brown, Claude 1937- *AfrAmAl 6, AmAu&B, Au&Arts 7, Benet 87, BenetAL 91, BioIn 7, –8, –16, –17, BlkAWP, BlkLC, BlkWr 1, CivR 74, ConAu 73, ConLC 30, CurBio 67, DrAF 76, InB&W 85, LivgBAA, SelBAAf, SelBAAu, WhoAm 74*

Brown, Conrad 1922- *AuBYP 2, –3, BioIn 8, SmATA 31*

Brown, Craig McFarland 1947- *SmATA 73*

Brown, Dale W 1926- *IntAu&W 91, WrDr 86, –88, –90, –92, –94*

Brown, Dale Weaver 1926- *ConAu 37R, DrAS 74P, –78P, –82P, WhoAm 74, –76, –78, –80, –82, –84, –86, –88, –90, –92, –94, WhoRel 75, –77, –92, WrDr 76, –80, –82, –84*

Brown, David *ConAu X, SmATA X*
Main entry: Myller, Rolf

Brown, Dee Alexander *BioIn 15, –16, –17*

Brown, Dee Alexander 1908- *ArtclWW 2, AuBYP 2S, –3, BiDrLUS 70, BioIn 10, –11, –12, ConAu 13R, DrAS 78H, –82H, SmATA 5, WhoAm 74, –76, –78, –80, –82, –84, –86, –88, –90, –92, –94, WhoLibS 66, WhoMW 74, WhoUSWr 88, WhoWest 94, WhoWrEP 89, –92, WrDr 76, –80*

Brown, Douglas 1907- *ConAu 25R, WrDr 76, –82, –84*

Brown, Drollene P 1939- *BioIn 16, ConAu 122, SmATA 53*

Brown, Duncan
Pseud./variant:
Nelson, T

Brown, Edna Adelaide 1875-1944 *AmAu&B, BioIn 2, DcNAA, JBA 34, –51, WhAm 2, WhNAA, WomNov*

Brown, Eleanor Frances 1908- *AuBYP 2, –3, BioIn 7, –9, ConAu 29R, SmATA 3, WhoLibS 55*

Brown, Elizabeth Myers 1915- *ConAu 107, SmATA 43, WhoAmW 74, –75, –77, –81, –83, –85, –87, WhoE 77, –81, –83, –85, –86, –89, WhoFI 81, –83, –85, WhoMW 80, –82, WhoWor 82, –84, –87, –89*

Brown, Fern G 1918- *ConAu 97, –17NR, –40NR, SmATA 34*

Brown, Fletch 1923- *BioIn 15, ConAu 116, SmATA 42*

Brown, Fornan 1901- *SmATA 71*
Pseud./variant:
Meeker, Richard

Brown, G W *DcVicP 2*

Brown, George Earl 1883-1964 *BioIn 11, ChhPo S1, ConAu 5R, SmATA 11*

Brown, George Mackay *BioIn 14, –16, –17*

Brown, George Mackay 1921- *BioIn 12, –13, BlueB 76, CamGLE, CmScLit, ConAu 6AS, –12NR, –37NR, ConLC 48, ConNov 82, –86, –91, ConPo 80, –85, –91, DcLB 14, –27, IntAu&W 82, –86, –89, IntWWP 82, MajTwCW, OxCEng 85, RfGEnL 91, ScF&FL 92, SmATA 35, Who 82, –83, –85, –88, –90, –92, WhoWor 80, WrDr 82, –84, –86, –88, –90, –92, –94*

Brown, George Williams 1894-1963 *BioIn 6, OxCCan SUP*

Brown, Helen, and Philip S Brown *AuBYP 3*

Brown, Helen Dawes 1857-1941 *Alli SUP, AmAu&B, CurBio 41, DcAmAu, DcNAA, WhAm 1, WhNAA, WomWWA 14, WomNov*

Brown, Helen E 1904?-1964 *AuBYP 2, BioIn 7, –8*

Brown, Huntley 1924- *AfroAA*

Brown, Ida Mae 1908- *ConAu P-2*

Brown, Irene Bennett 1932- *BioIn 9, ConAu 29R, –12NR, DcAmChF 1960, SmATA 3*

Brown, Irving *SmATA X, WebAB 79*
Main entry: Adams, William Taylor

Brown, Ivor John Carnegie 1891-1974 *Au&Wr 71, BiE&WWA, BioIn 2, –3, –4, –10, –13, ConAu 9R, –49, –12NR, DcLEL, EncWT, EvLB, IntAu&W 77, LongCTC, ModBrL, NewC, NewYTBS 74, ObitT 1971, OxCThe 67, PenC ENG, SmATA 5, –26N, TwCA SUP, WhAm 6, Who 74, WhoThe 72, WhoWor 74*

Brown, J J *OxCCan SUP*
Main entry: Brown, John J

Brown, Jamie 1945- *DcChlFi*

Brown, Jeannette Perkins 1887-1960 *BioIn 5, ChhPo*

Brown, Jeff *AuBYP 2, –3, BioIn 8, ChlFicS*

Brown, Jim 1935- *BlksAmF, DrBlPA 90*

Brown, Jim 1936- *BioIn 5, –6, –7, –8, –9, –10, –11, –14, –15, –16, –17, BioNews 74, CelR, –90, ConTFT 9, FilmgC, HalFC 84, –88, IntMPA 75, –76, –78, –81, –82, –84, –86, –88, –92, –77, MotPP, MovMk, NegAl 83, –89, NewYTBE 73, News 93-2, OxCCan SUP, WhoAm 74, –76, –78, –80, –82, –84, –86, –88, –92, –94, WhoBlA 75, –77, –80, –92, –94, WhoEnt 92, WhoHol A, WorAlBi, WorAl*

Brown, Joe David 1915-1976 *BioIn 2, –10, SmATA 44*

Brown, John 1810-1882 *Alli SUP, BiDLA, BiD&SB, BioIn 2, –7, –9, BritAu 19, CarSB, CasWL, CelCen, ChhPo, DcEnA, DcEnL, DcEuL, DcLEL, DcNaB, Dis&D, EvLB, NewC, OxCEng 67, –85, PenC ENG, REn*

Brown, John J 1916- *ConAu 13R*
Pseud./variant:
Brown, J J

Brown, John Mason 1900-1969 *AmAu&B, BenetAL 91, BiDSA, BiE&WWA, BioIn 1, –2, –3, –4, –5, –8, –9, –10, CamGWoT, CnDAL, ConAu 9R, –25R, CurBio 42, –69, EncAJ, LiHiK, LongCTC, NotNAT A, –B, ObitOF 79, OxCAmL 65, –83, OxCAmT 84, OxCThe 67, PenC AM, PlP&P, REnAL, TwCA, –SUP*

Brown, John Mason, Jr. 1900-1969 *DcAmB S8*

Brown, Joseph E 1929- *SmATA 51, –59*

Brown, Joseph Edward 1929- *ConAu 53, –6NR*

Brown, Judith Gwyn 1933- *AuBYP 2, –3, BioIn 8, –12, ChhPo S1, ConAu 93, –21NR, IlsCB 1957, –1967, SmATA 20, WhoAmA 78, –80, –82, –84, –86, –89, –91, WhoAmW 89*

Brown, Kay 1932- *BlkAuII 92*

Brown, Laurene Krasny *BioIn 16*

Brown, Laurene Krasny 1945- *SmATA 54*
Pseud./variant:
Meringoff, Laurene Krasny

Brown, LeRoy Chester 1908- *ConAu 13NR, –P-1, DrAS 74E, –78E, IndAu 1917*

Brown, Leslie Hilton 1917-1980 *Au&Wr 71, ConAu 7NR, IntAu&W 77, –82*

Brown, Lloyd Arnold 1907-1966 *AuBYP 2, –3, BioIn 4, –7, ConAu P-1, SmATA 36, WhAm 4*

Brown, M K *AuBYP 3*

Brown, Marc 1946- *ChlLR 29, ConAu 36NR, SmATA 53, TwCChW 89, WrDr 90, –92, –94*

Brown, Marc Tolon *BioIn 16, –17*

Brown, Marc Tolon 1946- *BioIn 11, ConAu 69, FifBJA, MajAI, SmATA 10*

Brown, Marcia 1918- *AmAu&B, AmPB, AnCL, ArtclWW 2, AuBYP 2, BioIn 3, -4, -5, -6, -7, -8, -10, -11, -12, -13, -15, -16, BkP, Cald 1938, ChhPo, -S2, ChlLR 12, ChsFB I, ConAu 41R, DcLB 61, FamAIYP, IlsBYP, IlsCB 1946, -1957, -1967, InWom SUP, MorJA, NewbC 1956, OxCChiL, SmATA 7, -47, TwCChW 89, WhoAm 74, -76, -78, -80, -82, -84, -86, -88, WhoAmW 74, -89, WrDr 90, -92, -94*

Brown, Marcia J 1918- *WhoAm 90, WhoAmW 91*

Brown, Marcia Joan 1918- *AuBYP 3, MajAI, WhoAm 92, -94*

Brown, Marel
Main entry: Brown, Margaret Elizabeth

Brown, Margaret Elizabeth 1899- *IntAu&W 77, WrDr 76, -80*
Pseud./variant:
Brown, Marel

Brown, Margaret Wise 1910-1952 *AmPB, ASCAP 66, AuBYP 2, -3, Au&ICB, BenetAL 91, BioIn 1, -2, -3, -4, -7, -9, -11, -12, -13, -14, -16, -17, ChhPo, -S1, ChlLR 10, ConAu 108, -136, DcLB 22, InWom SUP, JBA 51, MajAI, NotAW MOD, ObitOF 79, OxCChiL, REnAL, TwCChW 78, -83, -89, YABC 2*
Pseud./variant:
Hay, Timothy
MacDonald, Golden
Sage, Juniper

Brown, Margery *BioIn 10, BlkWr 1, ConAu 25R, -26NR, InWom SUP, SelBAAu, SmATA 5*

Brown, Margery Wheeler *BlkWr 2*

Brown, Marion Marsh 1908- *AuBYP 2, -3, BioIn 7, -10, ConAu 1R, -3NR, DrAS 74E, -78E, -82E, IntAu&W 77, SmATA 6*

Brown, Michael 1931- *ConAu 33R*

Brown, Myra Berry 1918- *AuBYP 2, -3, Au&Wr 71, BioIn 8, -10, ConAu 1R, -3NR, ForWC 70, SmATA 6*

Brown, Palmer 1919- *AmPB, BioIn 5, -8, ChhPo, ConAu 107, FifBJA, IlsBYP, IlsCB 1946, -1957, SmATA 36, TwCChW 83, -89, WrDr 86, -88, -90, -92, -94*

Brown, Pamela 1924- *IntAu&W 91, WrDr 86, -88*

Brown, Pamela 1924-1989 *AnObit 1989, ConAu 127, SmATA 61, TwCChW 89*

Brown, Pamela Beatrice 1924- *AuBYP 2, -3, Au&Wr 71, BioIn 7, -8, -10, ConAu 13R, IntMPA 75, -76, OxCChiL, SmATA 5, TelT, TwCChW 83, WhoChL, WrDr 84*

Brown, Pamela Beatrice 1924-1989 *BioIn 17*

Brown, Paul 1893- *AuBYP 3*

Brown, Paul 1893-1958 *AuBYP 2, BioIn 1, -2, -5, -7, BkCL, BritAS, IlrAm 1880, -D, IlsCB 1744, -1946, JBA 51, WhAmArt 85, WhoAmA 80N, -82N, -86N, -89N, -91N*

Brown, Philip S *AuBYP 2*

Brown, Ralph Adams 1908- *ConAu 33R, DrAS 74H, -78H, -82H, WrDr 76, -80, -82, -84, -86, -88, -90*

Brown, Raymond Bryan 1923-1977 *BioIn 11, ConAu 17R, -133, DrAS 74P, LEduc 74 WhoRel 75, -77*

Brown, Raymond Lamont 1939- *Au&Wr 71, ConAu 73, -X, IntAu&W 77, -82, WrDr 76, -80*

Brown, Regina *AuBYP 2, BioIn 8*

Brown, Regina Margaret *AuBYP 3*

Brown, Richard 1946- *SmATA 61*

Brown, Richard Christopher 1932- *WhoSSW 73*

Brown, Richard E 1946- *ConAu 130, WrDr 94*

Brown, Richard Eric 1946- *BioIn 12, IlsCB 1967*

Brown, Robert Joseph 1907- *BioIn 12, ConAu 13NR, -P-1, SmATA 14*
Pseud./variant:
Brown, Bob

Brown, Rosalie Moore 1910- *BioIn 8, -11, ConAu 5R, IntAu&W 82X, SmATA 9, WrDr 76, -80, -82, -84*
Pseud./variant:
Moore, Rosalie

Brown, Rose 1883-1952 *AmAu&B, BioIn 3*

Brown, Roswell *SmATA X*
Main entry: Webb, Jean Francis

Brown, Roswell 1910- *WrDr 94*

Brown, Roy 1921-1982 *Au&Wr 71, ConAu 65, -117, FourBJA, IntAu&W 82, OxCChiL, SmATA 39N, -51, TwCChW 78, -83, -89, WrDr 80, -82, -84*

Brown, Slater 1896- *AmAu&B*

Brown, Vinson 1912- *AuBYP 2, -3, BioIn 7, -12, ConAu 1R, -1NR, SmATA 19, WhoWest 74, -76, -78, WrDr 82, -84, -86, -88, -90, -92*

Brown, Vinson 1912-1991 *WrDr 94N*

Brown, Virginia Suggs 1924- *BioIn 16, BlkAWP, BlkAull, -92, ConAu 69, ForWC 70, LivgBAA*

Brown, Walter Reed 1929- *AmMWSc 73P, BioIn 12, ConAu 45, -2NR, SmATA 19*

Brown, Will *SmATA X*
Main entry: Ainsworth, William Harrison

Brown, William Allen 1934- *DrAS 78H, -82H*

Brown, William L 1910-1964 *AuBYP 2, BioIn 10, ConAu 1R, SmATA 5*
Pseud./variant:
Brown, Bill

Brown, William Louis *AuBYP 3*

Browne, Anthony 1946- *AuBYP 3, ChlLR 19, ConAu 97, -36NR, SixBJA, SmATA 44, -45, -61, TwCChW 89, WhoAm 92, WrDr 90, -92*

Browne, Anthony Edward Tudor 1946- *MajAI, WrDr 94*

Browne, Dik *ConAu 128, SmATA 67*
Main entry: Browne, Richard

Browne, Dik d1989 *NewYTBS 89*

Browne, Dik 1917- *AuNews 1, BioIn 10, -11, -15, ConGrA 1, EncTwCJ, SmATA X, WhoAm 76, -78, -80, -82, -84, -86, -88*

Browne, Dik 1917-1989 *AnObit 1989, BioIn 16, -17, EncACom, WhAm 10*

Browne, Frances 1816-1879 *Alli SUP, BioIn 1, -8, -17, BritAu 19, ChhPo, DcEnL, DcIrB 88, DcIrL, DcLEL, DcNaB MP, FamSYP, InWom SUP, JBA 34, OxCChiL, StaCVF, Str&VC, TelT, WhoChL*

Browne, Gordon Frederick 1858-1932 *BioIn 8, ChhPo, -S1, DcBrAr 1, DcBrBI, DcVicP 2, OxCChiL, WhAmArt 85, WhoChL*

Browne, Hablot K 1815-1880 *CamGLE*

Browne, Hablot Knight 1815-1882 *ArtsNiC, BioIn 1, -9, -11, -12, CelCen, ChhPo, -S1, -S2, DcBiPP, DcBrBI, DcNaB, DcVicP 2, HsB&A, NewC, OxCArt, OxCEng 85, OxDcArt, SmATA 21*
Pseud./variant:
Phiz

Browne, Hablot Knight 1815-1892 *DcVicP 2*

Browne, Hablot Knight 1851-1882 *BioIn 16*

Browne, Maggie *Alli SUP, TelT*
Main entry: Hamer, Margaret

Browne, Matthew *SmATA X*
Main entry: Rands, William Brighty

Browne, Michael Dennis *DrAPF 87, -89, -91, -93*

Browne, Michael Dennis 1940- *ChhPo S2, ConAu 29R, -15NR, ConPo 70, -75, -80, -85, -91, DcLB 40, DrAP 75, DrAPF 83, -85, WhoAm 78, -80, -82, -84, -86, -88, -90, -92, -94, WhoUSWr 88, WhoWrEP 89, -92, WrDr 76, -80, -82, -84, -86, -88, -90, -92, -94*

Browne, Reginald *WhoChL*

Browne, Richard 1917- *ConGrA 1, SmATA 38*
Pseud./variant:
Browne, Dik

Browne, Richard Arthur Allan 1917-1989 *SmATA 67*

Browne, Richard Arthur Allen 1917-1989 *ConAu 128*

Browne, Thomas Alexander *CamGEL, CamGLE, RfGEnL 91*

Browne, Thomas Alexander 1826-1915 *Alli SUP, BiD&SB, BioIn 2, -4, -8, -9, -10, BritAu 19, CarSB, CasWL, Chambr 3, DcLEL, EvLB, LongCTC, NewC, OxCAusL, OxCEng 67, PenC ENG, REn, SingR 2*
Pseud./variant:
Boldrewood, Rolf

Browne, Tom 1872-1910 *BioIn 8, DcBrAr 1, DcBrBI, DcVicP 2, WhoChL*

Browne, Vivian E 1929- *AfroAA, BioIn 14, InB&W 80, WhoAmA 78, -80, -82, -84, -86, -89, -91, WhoBlA 75, -77, -80, -85, -88, -90, -92, -94*

Brownell, Clifford Lee 1895- *BioIn 2, -6*

Brownell, James Garland 1933- *LEduc 74, WhoAm 74, -80, -82, -84, -86, -88, WhoUSWr 88, WhoWrEP 89, -92*

Browning, Colleen 1929- *BioIn 2, -3, -4, -12, -14, ChhPo S1, DcCAA 71, -77, -88, PrintW 85, WhoAm 74, -76, -78, WhoAmA 73, -78, -80, -82, -84, -86, -89, -91, WhoAmW 74, -75, -77, -83*

Browning, Elizabeth Barrett 1806?-1861 *Alli, -SUP, ArtclWW 2, AtlBL, Benet 87, BbD,*

BiD&SB, BioIn 1, –2, –3, –4, –5, –6, –7, –8, –9, –10, –11, –14, –15, –16, –17, BlmGEL, BlmGWL, BritAu 19, BritWr 4, CamGEL, CamGLE, CasWL, CelCen, Chambr 3, ChhPo, –S1, –S2, CnDBLB 4, CnE&AP, ContDcW 89, CrtT 3, CyWA 58, DcEnA A, DcEnL, DcEuL, DcLB 32, DcLEL, DcNaB, EncBrWW, EncPaPR 91, EvLB, HerW, –84, InWom SUP, IntDcWB, LongCEL, LuthC 75, MagSWL, McGEWB, MouLC 3, NewC, NinCLC 1, –16, OxCEng 67, –85, PenC ENG, PoeCrit 6, RAdv 1, –13-1, RComWL, REn, RfGEnL 91, WebE&AL, WhDW, WorAlBi, WorAl, WorLitC

Browning, Robert 1812-1889 *Alli, –SUP, AnCL, AtlBL, Benet 87, BiD&SB, BioIn 1, –2, –3, –4, –5, –6, –7, –8, –9, –10, –11, –12, –13, –14, –15, –16, –17, BlmGEL, BritAu 19, BritWr 4, CamGEL, CamGLE, CasWL, CelCen, Chambr 3, ChhPo, –S1, –S2, CnDBLB 4, CnE&AP, CnThe, CrtT 3, CyWA 58, DcBiPP, DcEnA, –A, DcEnL, DcEuL, DcLB 32, DcLEL, DcNaB C, –S1, Dis&D, EncO&P 1, –2, –3, EncPaPR 91, EncWT, EvLB, IlEncMy, LongCEL, LuthC 75, MagSWL, McGEWB, McGEWD 72, –84, MouLC 4, NewC, NinCLC 19, OxCChiL, OxCEng 67, –85, OxCMus, OxCThe 67, –83, PenC ENG, PlP&P, PoeCrit 2, RAdv 1, –13-1, RComWL, REn, REnWD, RfGEnL 91, Str&VC, WebE&AL, WhDW, WorAlBi, WorAl, YABC 1*

Browning, Robert Lynn 1924- *ConAu 85, –16NR, LEduc 74, WhoMW 82, –84, –86, –88, WhoRel 92*

Brownjohn, Alan *IntvTCA 2*

Brownjohn, Alan 1931- *Au&Wr 71, BioIn 10, –15, CamGLE, ChhPo S1, –S2, ConAu 25R, ConPo 70, –75, –80, –85, –91, DcLB 40, EngPo, IntAu&W 91, ScF&FL 92, SmATA 6, WhoWor 78, WrDr 76, –80, –82, –84, –86, –88, –90, –92*
Pseud./variant:
Berrington, John

Brownjohn, Alan Charles 1931- *EncSF 93, WrDr 94*

Brownjohn, John Nevil Maxwell *IntAu&W 86, –89, –91*

Brownjohn, John Nevil Maxwell 1929- *Au&Wr 71, IntAu&W 77, –82*

Brownlee, Walter 1930- *ConAu 57*

Brownlee, Walter D 1930- *SmATA 62*

Brownlow, Kevin 1938- *ConTFT 5, CurBio 92, HalFC 88, IntAu&W 89, –91, IntMPA 92, IntWW 89, –91, SmATA 65, Who 88, –90, –92, WorFDir 2, WrDr 86, –88, –90, –92, –94*

Brownmiller, Susan *BioIn 16, –17*

Brownmiller, Susan 1935- *BioIn 10, –11, –12, –13, CelR 90, ConAu 103, –35NR, CurBio 78, ForWC 70, InWom SUP, MajTwCW, WhoAm 78, –80, –84, WhoAmW 81, –83, –85, –91, –93, WhoUSWr 88, WhoWrEP 89, –92, WorAlBi, WorAl, WrDr 86, –88, –90, –92, –94*

Bruce, Dorita Fairlie 1885-1970 *BioIn 13 ChhPo S2, ConAu 107, OxCChiL, SmATA 27N, TwCChW 78, –83, –89*

Bruce, Harry 1934- *CaW, CanWW 80, –81, OxCCan SUP, OxCCanL*

Bruce, Mary 1927- *AuBYP 2S, –3, BioIn 9, ConAu 25R, SmATA 1*

Bruce, Mary Grant 1878-1958 *AuWomWr, BioIn 12, BlmGWL, CamGLE, FemiCLE, OxCAusL, OxCChiL, SingR 1, TwCChW 78, –83, –89*

Bruce, William Harry 1934- *SmATA 77*

Bruchac, Joseph 1942- *BioIn 15, IntAu&W 91, WrDr 86, –88, –90, –92, –94*

Bruchac, Joseph, III *DrAPF 87*

Bruchac, Joseph, III 1942- *ConAu 33R, –13NR, DrAF 76, DrAP 75, DrAPF 83, –85, SmATA 42, WrDr 76, –80, –82, –84*

Bruck, Lorraine *ScF&FL 92*

Bruck, Lorraine 1921- *BioIn 15, –16, SmATA 46, –55*
Pseud./variant:
Bridges, Laurie

Bruckner, Karl 1906- *EncSF 93, FourBJA, IntAu&W 77*

Bruemmer, Fred *BioIn 16*

Bruemmer, Fred 1929- *CanWW 89, IntAu&W 89, SmATA 47, WhoAm 86, –88, –90, –92, –94, WhoWrEP 89, –92, WrDr 86, –88, –90, –92, –94*

Bruere, Martha B 1879-1953 *BioIn 3, ChhPo, WhNAA, WomWWA 14*

Bruller, Jean *IntAu&W 86X, ScF&FL 92, Who 88, –90*

Bruller, Jean 1902- *ConAu 12NR, EvEuW, IlsCB 1744, IntAu&W 77X, –82X, IntWW 74, LongCTC, ModRL, REn, TwCA SUP, Who 74, –82, –83, –85, WhoWor 74*
Pseud./variant:
Vercors

Bruller, Jean 1902-1991 *BioIn 17, ConAu 134, NewYTBS 91*

Brumbaugh, Robert S 1918- *WrDr 86, –88, –90, –92*

Brumbaugh, Robert Sherrick 1918- *ConAu 5R, –3NR, DrAS 74P, –78P, –82P, WhoAm 74, –76, –78, –80, –82, –84, –86, –88, –90, –92, WhoUSWr 88, WhoWrEP 89, –92, WrDr 76, –80, –82, –84, –94*

Bruna, Dick *TwCChW 89B*

Bruna, Dick 1927- *BioIn 12, –14, –15, ChlLR 7, ConAu 112, –36NR, FifBJA, IlsCB 1967, MajAI, OxCChiL, SmATA 30, –43, –76, TwCChW 78B, –83B, Who 82, –83, –85, –88, –90, –92, WhoGrA 82*

Bruner, Richard Wallace 1926- *AuBYP 2S, –3, ConAu 49, NatPD 77, WhoUSWr 88, WhoWrEP 89, –92*

Brunetti, Cledo 1910-1971 *BioIn 1, ConAu P-2*

Brunhoff, Jean De *Benet 87, TwCChW 89B*

Brunhoff, Jean De 1899-1937 *AuBYP 2, –3, BioIn 1, –2, –5, –6, –7, –8, –13, ChlLR 4, ConAu 118, –137, IlsCB 1946, JBA 51, MajAI, OxCChiL, SmATA 24, TwCChW 78B, –83B, WhoChL, WorAlBi, WorAl, WorECar, WrChl*
Pseud./variant:
DeBrunhoff, Jean

Brunhoff, Laurent de *TwCChW 89B*

Brunhoff, Laurent De 1925- *AuBYP 2, –3, BioIn 5, –6, –7, –8, –10, –12, –13, –16, ChlLR 4, ConAu 73, IlsCB 1946, –1957, –1967, IntAu&W 82, MajAI, MorJA, NewYTBE 72, OxCChiL, SmATA 24, –71, TwCChW 78B, –83B, WhoChL, WorECar*
Pseud./variant:
DeBrunhoff, Laurent

Brunner, Fritz 1899- *IntAu&W 82*

Brunner, John *ConSFF, IntvTCA 2*

Brunner, John 1934- *Au&Wr 71, ConAu 1R, –8AS, –2NR, ConLC 8, –10, ConSFA, IntAu&W 82, MajTwCW, NewEScF, Novels, PostFic, RGTwCSF, ScF&FL 92, ScFSB, TwCSFW 86, –91, WhoSciF, WorAlBi, WorAu 1975, WrDr 76, –80, –82, –84, –86, –88, –90, –92*

Brunner, John K H 1934- *WrDr 94*

Brunner, John Kilian Houston 1934- *ConAu 37NR, EncSF 93*

Brussel-Smith, Bernard 1914- *BioIn 1, –3, –5, IlsBYP, IlsCB 1946, SmATA 58, WhoAm 74, –76, –78, –80, –82, –84, –86, –88, WhoAmA 78, –80, –82, –84, –86, –89, WhoE 86*

Brussel-Smith, Bernard 1914-1989 *WhAm 10, WhoAmA 91N*

Brustlein, Daniel 1904- *AmAu&B, BioIn 8, –15, IlsBYP, IlsCB 1957, SmATA 40, WhoAmA 78, –80, –82, –84, –86, –89, –91*
Pseud./variant:
Alain

Brustlein, Janice Tworkov *AuBYP 2, –3, BioIn 8, –15, ConAu 9R, SmATA 40*
Pseud./variant:
Janice

Bruton, Eric Moore *Au&Wr 71, ConAu 13R, –5NR, IntAu&W 77, –82, –86, WrDr 76, –80*

Bruton, Eric Moore 1915- *WhoWor 91, –93*

Bruton, J G 1914-1970 *BioIn 9, ConAu 9R*

Bruun, Bertel 1937- *Au&Wr 71, ConAu 45, IntAu&W 77, WhoE 77*

Bryan, Ashley 1923- *BlkAuII, –92*

Bryan, Ashley F 1923- *BioIn 12, BlkWr 1, –2, ChlLR 18, ConAu 107, –26NR, FifBJA, IlsCB 1967, MajAI, SelBAAf, SmATA 31, –72*

Bryan, Catherine 1907- *AnCL*
Pseud./variant:
Madden, Mabra

Bryan, Courtlandt Dixon Barnes *BioIn 16*

Bryan, Courtlandt Dixon Barnes 1936- *AmAu&B, ConAu 73, DrAF 76, WhoAm 74, –78, –80, –82, –84, –86, –88, –90, –92, –94, WhoE 74, WhoUSWr 88, WhoWrEP 89, –92*

Bryan, Dorothy M 1896?-1984 *BioIn 3, CathA 1952, ConAu 114, SmATA 39N*

Bryan, Joseph 1904- *AuBYP 3*

Bryan, Joseph, III d1993 *NewYTBS 93*

Bryan, Joseph, III 1904- *AmAu&B, AuBYP 2, ConAu 61, EncAI&E, REnAL, WhoAm 74, –76, –78, –84, –86, –88, –90, –92*

Bryant, Arthur 1899- *WrDr 86*

Bryant, Arthur, Sir 1899-1982? *Au&Wr 71, BioIn 3, –4, –7, –12, –13, BlueB 76, ConAu 105, –114, DcLEL, EvLB, InB&W 80, IntWW 74, –75, –76, –77, –78, –79, –80, –81, –82, –83, LongCTC, NewC, NewYTBS 82,*

–85, TwCA, –SUP, Who 74, –82, –83, –85, WhoWor 74, WrDr 76, –80, –82, –84

Bryant, Arthur, Sir 1899-1985 *AnObit 1985, BioIn 14, NewYTBS 85*

Bryant, Bernice 1908- *BioIn 2, –11, ConAu P-1, SmATA 11*

Bryant, Gertrude Thomson *AuBYP 2, –3, BioIn 8*

Bryant, Sara Cone 1873- *AmAu&B, WhAm 5, WomWWA 14*

Bryant, William Cullen 1794-1878 *Alli, –SUP, AmAu, AmAu&B, AmWr S1, AtlBL, Benet 87, BenetAL 91, BbD, BiDAmJo, BiD&SB, BioIn 1, –2, –3, –4, –5, –6, –7, –8, –9, –10, –11, –12, –14, –15, –16, CamGEL, CamGLE, CamHAL, CarSB, CasWL, CelCen, Chambr 3, ChhPo, –S1, –S2, CnDAL, CnE&AP, CrtT 3, CyAL, CyWA 58, DcAmAu, DcAmSR, DcBiPP, DcEnL, DcLB 3, –43, –59, DcLEL, DcNAA, EncAB-H, EncAJ, EvLB, HarEnUS, JrnUS, LuthC 75, McGEWB, MouLC 3, NewGrDA 86, NinCLC 6, OxCAmH, OxCAmL 65, –83, OxCEng 67, –85, PenC AM, PoChrch, RAdv 1, –13-1, REn, REnAL, RfGAmL 87, Str&VC, WebAB 74, –79, WebE&AL, WhAm HS, WhFla, WorAlBi, WorAl*

Brychta, Alex 1956- *BioIn 12, ConAu 103, –20NR, SmATA 21*

Bryson, Bernarda 1905?- *BioIn 4, –5, –8, –9, –11, ChhPo, ConAu 49, IlsBYP, IlsCB 1946, –1957, –1967, SmATA 9, ThrBJA*
Pseud./variant:
Shahn, Bernarda Bryson

Buba, Joy Flinsch 1904- *BioIn 5, –10, –15, IlsBYP, IlsCB 1946, SmATA 44, WhoAmA 73, –78, –80, –82, –84, –86, –89, –91*

Buban, Peter, Sr. 1920- *LEduc 74, WhoMW 76*

Bubley, Esther 1921- *ICPEnP A*

Buchan, Bryan 1945- *ConAu 107, ScF&FL 92, SmATA 36*

Buchan, John Tweedsmuir, Baron 1875-1940 *BioIn 1, –2, –3, –4, –5, –6, –7, –10, –11, –12, –13, CasWL, Chambr 3, ChhPo, –S1, –S2, CnMWL, ConAu 108, CorpD, CurBio 40, CyWA 58, DcLB 34, DcLEL, DcNaB 1931, EncMys, EncSoA, EvLB, FilmgC, HalFC 84, JBA 34, LongCTC, ModBrL, NewC, Novels, OxCCan, OxCCanL, OxCChiL, OxCEng 67, –85, PenC ENG, REn, TelT, TwCA, –SUP, TwCCr&M 80, –85, TwCWr, WebE&AL, WhDW, Who 83, –85, WhoHr&F, WhoSpyF, YABC 2*
Pseud./variant:
Tweedsmuir, Baron

Buchan, Stuart 1942-1987 *BioIn 15, –16, ConAu 123, NewYTBS 87, SmATA 54N*

Buchanan, William
Main entry: Buck, William Ray

Buchanan, William 1930- *AuBYP 2, –3, BioIn 8, ConAu X, WrDr 76, –80, –82, –84*

Buchanan-Brown, John 1929- *ConAu 102*

Buchheimer, Naomi Barnett
Main entry: Barnett, Naomi

Buchheimer, Naomi Barnett 1927- *ConAu 5R, –X, SmATA X*

Buchman, Dian Dincin *BiDrAPH 79, ConAu 61, –8NR*

Buchsbaum, Ralph 1907- *AmMWSc 73P, –76P, –82, –86, –89, –92, WhoAm 74, –76, –78, –80, –82, –84, –86, –88, –90, WhoOcn 78, WhoWest 87*

Buchwald, Ann *AuBYP 3*

Buchwald, Ann 1920- *ConAu 128*

Buchwald, Ann 1921?- *InWom SUP*

Buchwald, Ann McGarry *AuBYP 2S*

Buchwald, Art *BioIn 14, –15, –16, –17*

Buchwald, Art 1925- *AmAu&B, AuBYP 2S, –3, AuNews 1, BioIn 3, –4, –5, –6, –7, –8, –9, –10, –11, –12, –13, BioNews 74, BlueB 76, CelR, –90, ConAu 5R, –21NR, ConLC 33, CurBio 60, EncAHmr, EncAJ, EncTwCJ, IntAu&W 77, –82, –89, –91, IntWW 74, –75, –76, –77, –78, –79, –80, –81, –82, –83, –89, –91, JrnUS, MajTwCW, NewYTBE 72, PenC AM, SmATA 10, Who 74, –82, –83, –85, –88, –90, –92, WhoAm 74, –76, –78, –80, –82, –84, –86, –88, –90, –92, –94, WhoE 91, –93, WhoSSW 73, –75, –76, WhoUSWr 88, WhoWor 74, –78, –80, –82, –84, –87, –89, –91, –93, WhoWrEP 89, –92, WorAlBi, WorAl, WorAu 1950, WrDr 76, –80, –82, –84, –86, –88, –90, –92, –94*

Buchwald, Emilie *DrAPF 87, –89, –91, –93*

Buchwald, Emilie 1935- *BioIn 10, ConAu 49, –2NR, DrAPF 83, –85, SmATA 7*

Buck, Frank 1882?-1950 *AmAu&B, BioIn 1, –2, –4, CurBio 43, –50, FilmgC, HalFC 84, ObitOF 79, REnAL, WebAB 74, –79, WhAm 2, WhScrn 74, –83, –77, WhoHol B*

Buck, Frank 1884-1950 *BenetAL 91*

Buck, Frank 1888-1950 *HalFC 88*

Buck, Lewis A 1925- *ConAu 73, SmATA 18*

Buck, Margaret Waring 1910- *AuBYP 2, -3, BioIn 8, -9, ConAu 5R, IntAu&W 77, -82, SmATA 3, WrDr 76, -80, -82, -84, -86, -88, -90, -92, -94*

Buck, Pearl *IntvTCA 2*

Buck, Pearl 1892-1973 *ArtclWW 2, AuBYP 3, BenetAL 91, CamGEL, ConHero 2, FemiCLE, HalFC 88, LadLa 86, WorAlBi*

Buck, Pearl S 1892-1973 *AmAu&B, AmNov, AmWr S2, AuBYP 2, AuNews 1, Au&Wr 71, Benet 87, BiE&WWA, BioAmW, BioIn 1, -2, -3, -4, -5, -6, -7, -8, -9, -10, -11, -14, -15, -16, -17, BlmGWL, CamGLE, CamHAL, CasWL, CnDAL, ConAmA, ConAu 1R, -41R, -1NR, -34NR, ConLC 7, -11, -18, ConNov 72, ContDcW 89, CurBio 56, -73, CyWA 58, DcLB 9, -102, DcLEL, EncWL, EvLB, FilmgC, HerW, IntDcWB, LongCTC, MajTwCW, McGEWB, ModAL, MorMA, NewYTBE 73, NobelP, ObitT 1971, OxCAmL 65, PenC AM, REn, REnAL, RfGAmL 87, SmATA 1, -25, TwCA, -SUP, TwCRHW 90, TwCWr, WebAB 74, -79, WhAm 5, WhNAA, WhoAmW 74*
Pseud./variant:
Sedges, John

Buck, Pearl Sydenstricker 1892-1973 *InWom SUP*

Buck, William Ray *AuBYP 3*

Buck, William Ray 1930- *AuBYP 2, ConAu 1R, WrDr 76, -80, -82, -84*
Pseud./variant:
Buchanan, William

Buckels, Alec *BioIn 1, ChhPo, -S2, IlsCB 1744*

Buckeridge, Anthony 1912- *TwCChW 89, WrDr 86, -88, -90, -92, -94*

Buckeridge, Anthony Malcolm 1912- *BioIn 8, -10, ConAu 49, -2NR, IntAu&W 77, -91, OxCChiL, SmATA 6, TwCChW 78, -83, WhoChL, WrDr 80, -82, -84*

Buckholtz, Eileen 1949- *ScF&FL 92, SmATA 47, -54*
Pseud./variant:
Chase, Samantha
Howard, Alyssa
Lee, Amanda
York, Rebecca

Buckholtz, Eileen Garber 1949-
Pseud./variant:
Howard, Alyssa
Lee, Amanda
York, Rebecca

Buckingham, James William 1932- *Au&Wr 71, ConAu 29R*

Buckler, Ernest *IntvTCA 2*

Buckler, Ernest 1908- *CamGLE*

Buckler, Ernest 1908-1984 *BenetAL 91, CyWA 89, DcLB 68, SmATA 47, WhoCanL 87, -92*

Buckley, Arabella B 1840-1929 *OxCChiL*

Buckley, Francis Joseph 1928- *AmCath 80, ConAu 33R, -13NR, DrAS 74P, -78P, -82P, IntAu&W 77, -89, -91, WhoRel 75, -77, -92, WhoWest 87, -89, WrDr 76, -80, -82, -84, -86, -88, -90, -92, -94*

Buckley, Helen E 1918- *BioIn 9, ConAu 5R, -3NR, ForWC 70, SmATA 2*

Buckley, Jerome Hamilton 1917- *AmAu&B, CanWW 70, -79, -80, -81, -83, -89, ChhPo, ConAu 1R, -3NR, DrAS 74E, -78E, -82E, WhoAm 74, -76, -78, -80, -82, -84, -86, -88, -90, -92, -94, WhoWor 74*

Buckmaster, Henrietta
Main entry: Stephens, Henrietta Henkle

Buckmaster, Henrietta 1909-1983 *AmAu&B, AmNov, Au&Wr 71, ConAu X, CurBio 46, -83N, FemiCLE, InWom SUP, IntAu&W 77, NewYTBS 83, OhA&B, ScF&FL 92, SmATA 6, WhoAmW 77, WorAu 1950*

Buday, George *ConAu 132*

Buday, George 1907- *Au&Wr 71, ConAu X, DcBrAr 1, IntAu&W 77, Who 74, -82, -83, -85, -88, -90, WhoArt 80, -82, -84, WhoWor 78, -80, WrDr 76, -80, -82, -84, -86, -88, -90*

Budberg, Moura 1892?-1974 *BioIn 9, -10, ConAu 53, NewYTBS 74, ObitOF 79*

Budbill, David *DrAPF 87, -89, -91, -93*

Budbill, David 1940- *ConAu 73, ConPo 85, -91, DrAPF 83, -85, WrDr 86, -88, -90, -92, -94*

Budd, Lillian 1897- *AuBYP 2, -3, BioIn 7, -10, ConAu 1R, -4NR, IntAu&W 82, SmATA 7, WrDr 76, -80, -82, -84, -86, -88, -90*

Buddee, Paul Edgar 1913- *Au&Wr 71, ConAu 103, IntAu&W 77, -82, -86, -91, WhoWor 78, WrDr 76, -80, -82, -84, -86, -88, -90, -92, -94*

Budden, Maria Elizabeth 1780?-1832 *CarSB, OxCChiL*

Budlong, Ware T 1905-1967 *BioIn 8*

Buehnau, Ludwig *ConAu X, -36NR*
Main entry: Schreiber, Hermann Otto Ludwig

Buehr, Walter Franklin 1897-1971 *ArtsAmW 3, AuBYP 2, -3, BioIn 5, -7, -8, -9, ConAu 5R, -33R, -3NR, IlsCB 1946, -1957, SmATA 3, ThrBJA*

Buell, Ellen Lewis *AuBYP 2, -3, BioIn 8, ChhPo S1, ConAu 130, ForWC 70*

Buell, Ellen Lewis 1905-1989 *BioIn 16, -17, SmATA X*
Main entry: Cash, Ellen Lewis Buell

Buell, Harold G *AuBYP 3*

Buell, Harold George 1931- *AuBYP 2S, WhoAm 78, -80, -82, -84*

Buell, Lawrence 1939- *ConAu 49, DrAS 74E, -82E*

Buell, Lawrence Ingalls 1939- *WhoAm 88, -90, -92, -94*

Buell, Robert Kingery 1908-1971 *ConAu P-2*

Bufalari, Giuseppe 1927- *ConAu 25R, -16NR*

Bufano, Remo 1894-1948 *AuBYP 2, -3, BioIn 1, -2, -5, -8, NotNAT B, WhAmArt 85*

Buff, Conrad 1886-1975 *AuBYP 2, -3, BioIn 1, -2, -5, -6, -7, -8, -12, -14, BkCL, ConAu 135, IlsCB 1744, -1946, -1957, JBA 51, MajAI, SmATA 19, Str&VC, WhAm 7, WhAmArt 85, WhoAm 74, -76, -78, WhoAmA 78N, -80N, -82N, -86N, -89N, -91N, WhoWest 74*

Buff, Mary 1890-1970 *AuBYP 3, ConAu 135*

Buff, Mary E Marsh 1890-1970 *MajAI*

Buff, Mary Marsh 1890-1970 *AmAu&B, AuBYP 2, BioIn 2, -7, -14, BkCL, ConAu 116, JBA 51, SmATA 19, Str&VC, TwCChW 78, WhAm 8*

Buffett, Jimmy 1946- *BestSel 90-2, BioIn 14, ConAu 141, ConMus 4, PenEncP, SmATA 76, WhoAm 88, -90, -92, -94, WhoEnt 92*

Buffie, Margaret *DcChlFi*

Buffie, Margaret 1945- *SmATA 71*

Bugbee, Emma 1888?-1981 *AuBYP 2, -3, BioIn 7, -10, -12, -13, -15, BriB, ConAu 105, EncAJ, InWom SUP, NewYTBS 81, SmATA 29N*

Bulfinch, Thomas 1796-1867 *Alli, -SUP, AmAu, AmAu&B, Benet 87, BenetAL 91, BiD&SB, BioIn 3, -14, CarSB, ChhPo, DcAmAu, DcNAA, OxCAmL 65, -83, REn, REnAL, SmATA 35, WebAB 74, -79, WhAm HS*

Bull, Albert E *ChhPo*

Bull, Angela 1936- *ConAu 21R, -9NR, -24NR, IntAu&W 82, ScF&FL 92, SmATA 45, TwCChW 78, -83, -89, WrDr 80, -82, -84, -86, -88, -90, -92*

Bull, Angela Mary 1936- *WrDr 94*

Bull, Charles Livingston 1874-1932 *BioIn 11, ConICB, DcNAA, IlrAm 1880, -B, WhAm 1, WhAmArt 85, WorECar*

Bull, Johan 1893-1945 *CurBio 45, ObitOF 79, WhAmArt 85*

Bull, Norman John 1916- *Au&Wr 71, ConAu 93, -16NR, IntAu&W 77, SmATA 41, WrDr 76, -80, -82, -84, -86, -88, -90*

Bull, Peter 1912-1984 *AnObit 1984, BioIn 3, -7, -10, -13, -14, -15, ConAu 112, -11NR, ConTFT 1, HalFC 84, -88, IntAu&W 82, NewYTBS 84, SmATA 39N, WrDr 82, -84*

Bulla, Clyde 1914- *SmATA 6AS*

Bulla, Clyde Robert 1914- *AuBYP 2, -3, Au&ICB, BioIn 6, -7, -9, -15, -16, BkP, ConAu 5R, -3NR, -18NR, -40NR, DcAmChF 1960, IntAu&W 91, MajAI, MorJA, SmATA 2, -41, TwCChW 78, -83, -89, WhoAm 84, -86, -88, -90, -92, -94, WhoWest 74, -76, WrDr 80, -82, -84, -86, -88, -90, -92, -94*

Bullard, Marion d1950 *BioIn 2, ConICB*

Bullen, Frank T 1857-1915 *StaCVF*

Bullen, Frank Thomas 1857-1915 *BiD&SB, BioIn 5, -12, Chambr 3, CyWA 58, DcEnA A, DcNaB MP, EvLB, JBA 34, LongCTC, OxCShps, TwCA*

Bullen, N Ravenor H *ChhPo*

Bullivant, Cecil H 1882- *ScF&FL 92*

Bullivant, Cecil Henry 1882- *EncMys*

Bullock, Henry Morton 1902-1984 *EncWM, WhAm 8, WhoAm 74, -76, -78, -80, WhoWor 74*

Bullock, Kathleen Mary 1946- *SmATA 77*

Bullock, L G *AuBYP 2, –3, BioIn 8*

Bullock, W A C *Au&Wr 71*

Bullough, Donald Auberon 1928- *Au&Wr 71, IntAu&W 77, –82, Who 82, –83, –85, –88, –92*

Bullough, Donald Auberon, Prof 1928- *Who 90*

Bulsara, Cavas Nowshirwan 1927- *DcChlFi*

Bumstead, Kathleen Mary 1918- *ConAu 121*

Bumstead, Kathleen Mary 1918-1987 *SmATA 53*
Pseud./variant:
Morgan, Ellen

Bunce, William Harvey *AuBYP 3*

Bunce, William Harvey 1903- *AuBYP 2, BioIn 7, WhNAA*

Bundles, A'Lelia P *BioIn 17*

Bundles, A'Lelia Perry *InB&W 85*

Bundles, A'Lelia Perry 1952- *SmATA 76, WhoBlA 85, –88, –90, –92, –94*

Bunin, Catherine 1967- *ConAu 93, SmATA 30*

Bunin, Catherine 1968- *InB&W 85*

Bunin, Ivan Alekseevich 1870-1953 *BioIn 14, –15, HanRL*

Bunin, Ivan Alekseyevich 1870-1953 *Benet 87, BioIn 1, –2, –3, –4, –5, –8, –9, –12, –13, CasWL, ClDMEL 47, CnMWL, ConAu 104, CyWA 58, DcRusL, DcRusLS, EncWL, EvEuW, LongCTC, ModSL 1, OxCEng 85, PenC EUR, REn, TwCA, –SUP, TwCWr, WhDW, WhAm 3, WhoLA, WhoTwCL, WorAl*

Bunin, Ivan Alexeievich 1870-1953 *WhoNob, –90*

Bunin, Ivan Alexeyevitch 1870-1953 *LiExTwC*

Bunin, Sherry 1925- *ConAu 93, SmATA 30*

Buntain, Ruth Jaeger *AuBYP 2, –3, BioIn 8*

Bunting, A E *AuBYP 3, MajAI, SmATA X, TwCChW 89, WrDr 86, –88, –90, –92*
Main entry: Bunting, Anne Evelyn

Bunting, Anne Eve 1928- *BioIn 15, –16, –17*

Bunting, Anne Evelyn 1928- *AuBYP 2S, –3, BioIn 12, ConAu 53, –5NR, –19NR, DcAmChF 1985, MajAI, SmATA 18, TwCChW 83, TwCYAW, WhoAm 78, –80, –82, –84, –86, –88, –90, WhoUSWr 88, WhoWor 82, WhoWrEP 89, –92, WrDr 94*
Pseud./variant:
Bolton, Evelyn
Bunting, A E
Bunting, Eve

Bunting, Eve 1928- *Au&Arts 5, AuBYP 3, BioIn 15, –16, –17, ChlLR 28, ConAu X, FifBJA, ScF&FL 92, SmATA 64, –X, TwCChW 83, –89, WhoAm 84, –86, –88, WhoUSWr 88, WhoWrEP 89, –92, WrDr 86, –88, –90, –92*
Main entry: Bunting, Anne Evelyn

Bunting, Glenn 1957- *BioIn 13, SmATA 22*

Buntline, Ned *Alli SUP, AmAu, AmAu&B, Benet 87, BenetAL 91, BioIn 1, –2, –7, –9, DcAmAu, DcNAA, EncAJ, HsB&A, OhA&B, OxCAmH, OxCAmL 65, –83, OxCChiL, REn, REnAL, WebAB 74, –79, WhAm HS, WorAl*

Buntline, Ned 1823-1886 *WorAlBi*

Bunyan, John 1628-1688 *Alli, AtlBL, Benet 87, BbD, BiD&SB, BioIn 1, –2, –3, –4, –5, –6, –7, –8, –9, –10, –11, –12, –13, –14, –15, –16, BlmGEL, BritAu, CamGEL, CamGLE, CarSB, CasWL, Chambr 1, ChhPo, –S1, –S2, CnDBLB 2, CrtT 2, CroE&S, CyWA 58, DcBiPP, DcEnA, DcEnL, DcEuL, DcLB 39, DcLEL, DcNaB, Dis&D, EncSoB, EvLB, LitC 4, LongCEL, LuthC 75, MagSWL, McGEWB, MouLC 1, NewC, Novels, OxCChiL, OxCEng 67, –85, OxCMus, PenC ENG, RAdv 1, –13-1, RComWL, REn, RfGEnL 91, WebE&AL, WhDW, WorAlBi, WorAl, WorLitC, WrChl*

Burack, Abraham Saul 1908-1978 *AmAu&B, BioIn 4, –11, ConAu 9R, –77, –4NR, WhoE 75, WhoWorJ 72, –78*

Burack, Sylvia 1916- *ConAu 21R, –9NR, ForWC 70, SmATA 35, WhoAm 80, WhoAmW 77, WhoE 75*
Pseud./variant:
Kamerman, Sylvia E

Burack, Sylvia E Kamerman 1916- *WhoAm 92, –94, WhoAmW 87, WhoWrEP 89*

Buranelli, Marguerite *AuBYP 2S, –3*

Burbank, Addison 1895-1961 *ArtsAmW 3, BioIn 1, –5, –15, CathA 1930, IlsCB 1744, –1946, JBA 51, SmATA 37, WhAmArt 85*

Burch, Gladys 1899- *AuBYP 2, –3, BioIn 8*

Burch, Joann Johansen *ConAu 142, SmATA 75*

Burch, Robert 1925- *DcAmChF 1960, DcLB 52, TwCChW 89, WrDr 86, –88, –90, –92, –94*

Burch, Robert Joseph 1925- *AuBYP 2, -3, BioIn 7, -8, -9, -10, ConAu 5R, -2NR, -17NR, IntAu&W 82, MajAI, MorBMP, OxCChiL, SmATA 1, -74, ThrBJA, TwCChW 78, -83, TwCYAW, WhoAm 84, -86, -88, -90, -92, -94, WrDr 76, -80, -82, -84*

Burchard, Marshall *AuBYP 2S, -3*

Burchard, Peter 1921- *SmATA 13AS*

Burchard, Peter Duncan 1921- *AuBYP 2, -3, Au&Wr 71, BioIn 5, -8, -9, -10, ConAu 5R, -3NR, -18NR, -39NR, DcAmChF 1960, IlsCB 1946, -1957, -1967, IntAu&W 86, MajAI, SmATA 5, -74, ThrBJA, WhoAmA 78, -80, -82, -84, -86, -89, -91, WhoE 75, -77, -86, WhoWest 80*

Burchard, Sue 1937- *AuBYP 2S, -3, BioIn 13, ConAu 53, -4NR, -19NR, SmATA 22*

Burchardt, Nellie 1921- *BioIn 10, ConAu 21R, SmATA 7, WrDr 76, -80, -82, -84, -86*

Burchell, Mary *Au&Wr 71, WrDr 84, -86*

Burchell, Mary d1986 *TwCRHW 90*

Burchell, S C *AuBYP 2S, -3*

Burckmyer, Elizabeth *IlsBYP*

Burd, Clara Miller *ChhPo, -S2, ConICB, DcWomA, WhAmArt 85*

Burder, George 1752-1832 *DcBiPP, DcNaB, OxCChiL*

Burdick, Eugene 1918-1965 *AmAu&B, BioIn 5, -6, -7, -10, ConAu 5R, -25R, SmATA 22, TwCWr, WhAm 4, WhoSpyF, WorAl, WorAu 1950*

Burdick, Loraine 1929- *ConAu 57*

Burford, Eleanor *ConAu 140, -X, -28NR, EncMys, InWom SUP, IntAu&W 91X, Novels, SmATA 2, -74, TwCRHW 90, Who 74, -82, -83, -85, -88, -90, -92, WorAu 1950, WrDr 76, -84, -86, -88, -90, -92*
Main entry: Hibbert, Eleanor Burford

Burford, Eleanor 1906-1993 *WrDr 94N*

Burford, Lolah 1931- *BioIn 9, -14, ConAu 41R, TwCRHW 90, WrDr 76, -80, -82, -84, -86, -88, -90, -92, -94*

Burg, Marie 1905- *Au&Wr 71, IntAu&W 77, -82*

Burger, Carl Victor 1888-1967 *BioIn 8, -11, ConAu P-2, IlsCB 1957, SmATA 9*

Burger, John Robert 1942- *ConAu 81*

Burger, Nash K 1908- *ConAu P-2*

Burgess, Ann Marie *SmATA X*

Burgess, Ann Marie 1914-1988 *SmATA X*

Burgess, Anne Marie
Main entry: Gerson, Noel Bertram

Burgess, Anthony *DrAPF 87, -89, -91, -93 IntvTCA 2, MajTwCW*

Burgess, Anthony 1917- *AuNews 1, Au&Wr 71, Baker 84, -92, Benet 87, BioIn 7, -8, -9, -10, -12, -13, -15, -16, -17, BlmGEL, BlueB 76, BritWr S1, CamGEL, CamGLE, CasWL, CelR, -90, CnDBLB 8, ConAu 1R, -X, ConCom 92, ConLC 1, -2, -4, -5, -8, -10, -13, -15, -22, -40, -62, ConNov 72, -76, -82, -86, -91, ConSFA, CurBio 72, CyWA 89, DcLB 14, DcLEL 1940, DrAF 76, DrAPF 83, -85, EncSF 93, EncWB, EncWL, -2, HalFC 84, -88, IntAu&W 77, -86, -89, -91, IntWW 74, -75, -76, -77, -78, -79, -80, -81, -82, -83, -89, -91, IntWWM 90, LiExTwC, LongCTC, MagSWL, MakMC, MedPD, ModBrL, -S1, -S2, NewC, NewEScF, Novels, OxCEng 85, PenC ENG, RAdv 1, -13-1, RGTwCSF, RfGEnL 91, ScF&FL 92, ScFSB, TwCRHW 90, TwCSFW 86, -91, TwCWr, TwCYAW, WebE&AL, Who 74, -82, -83, -85, -88, -90, -92, WhoAm 76, -78, -80, -82, -84, -86, -88, -94, WhoSciF, WhoTwCL, WhoWor 74, -78, -80, -82, -84, -87, -89, -91, -93, WorAlBi, WorAl, WorAu 1950, WrDr 76, -80, -82, -84, -86, -88, -90, -92, -94*

Burgess, Anthony 1917-1993 *ConLC 81*

Burgess, Barbara Hood 1926- *SmATA 69*

Burgess, Christopher Victor 1921- *Au&Wr 71, ConAu 9R, IntAu&W 77*

Burgess, Em *SmATA X*
Main entry: Burgess, Mary Wyche

Burgess, Gelett *BioIn 14, -15, IntvTCA 2*

Burgess, Gelett 1866-1951 *AmAu&B, AmLY, AnMV 1926, BenetAL 91, BiD&SB, BioIn 1, -2, -3, -4, -5, ChhPo, -S1, CmCal, CnDAL, ConAmL, ConAu 113, ConICB, DcAmAu DcLB 11, EncAJ, EncMys, EvLB, IlsCB 1744, -1946, LongCTC, ObitOF 79, OxCAmL 65, -83, OxCChiL, REn, REnAL, ScFEYrs, -A, SmATA 30, -32, TwCA, -SUP, TwCCr&M 80, TwCWr, WebAB 74, -79, WhAm 3, WhAmArt 85, WhNAA*

Burgess, Mary Wyche 1916- *ConAu 61, SmATA 18*
Pseud./variant:
Burgess, Em

Burgess, Michael *AuBYP 3, ConAu 127, EncSF 93, ScF&FL 92, SmATA X*
Main entry: Gerson, Noel Bertram

Burgess, Michael 1914-1988 *SmATA X*

Burgess, Robert Forrest 1927- *AuBYP 2S, –3, BioIn 9, ConAu 25R, –11NR, SmATA 4*

Burgess, Thornton W 1874-1965 *BenetAL 91, BioIn 14*

Burgess, Thornton Waldo 1874-1965 *AmAu&B, AuBYP 2, –3, BioIn 1, –2, –4, –5, –7, –8, –12, –13, CarSB, ChhPo, ConAu 73, –41NR, DcAmB S7, DcLB 22, JBA 34, –51, MajAI, ObitOF 79, OxCAmL 65, –83, OxCChiL, REn, REnAL, SmATA 17, TwCChW 83, –89, WhAm 4, WhNAA, WhoChL*
Pseud./variant:
Thornton, W B

Burgess, Trevor *ConAu X, SmATA X, TwCCr&M 85, –91*
Main entry: Trevor, Elleston

Burglon, Nora 1896- *BioIn 2, –14, JBA 51*

Burgoyne, Leon E 1916- *AuBYP 2, –3, BioIn 7, MichAu 80*

Burgwyn, Mebane Holoman 1914- *BioIn 3, –4, –5, –10, ConAu 49, IntAu&W 77, SmATA 7*

Burian, Zdenek *ScF&FL 92*

Burian, Zdenek 1905- *WhoWor 74, –78*

Burke, Carl F 1917- *ConAu 25R*

Burke, David 1927- *BioIn 15, ConAu 23NR, SmATA 46*

Burke, Fred George 1926- *AmAu&B, AmMWSc 73S, ConAu 13R, LEduc 74, WhoAm 78, –80, –82, WhoE 74, –81, –83, –85, WhoGov 77, –75*

Burke, John *ConAu X, SmATA X*
Main entry: O'Connor, Richard

Burke, John Frederick 1922- *Au&Wr 71, ConAu 5R, IntAu&W 77, –82, –86, –89, –91, WhoHr&F*

Burke, Lynn *AuBYP 3*

Burke, Lynn 1943?- *AuBYP 2, BioIn 6, –7*

Burke, Ralph *MajAI*

Burke, Stanley 1923- *CaW, ConAu 101*

Burke, Thomas 1886?-1945 *BioIn 4, –14, ChhPo, –S1, –S2, ConAu 113, CurBio 45, EncMys, EngPo, EvLB, LongCTC, NewC, ObitOF 79, REn, TwCA, –SUP, TwCCr&M 80, –85, –91, WhoHr&F*

Burke, Tom *ConAu 73*

Burkert, Nancy Ekholm *BioIn 14*

Burkert, Nancy Ekholm 1933- *BioIn 8, –9, –11, ChhPo S1, IlsBYP, IlsCB 1957, –1967, MajAI, SmATA 24, –14AS, ThrBJA*

Burkett, Molly 1932- *ConAu 53, –9NR*

Burkholz, Herbert *DrAPF 87, –89, –91, –93*

Burkholz, Herbert 1932?- *Au&Wr 71, BioIn 8, –11, ConAu 25R, –11NR, –41NR, DrAPF 83, –85, ScF&FL 92, SpyFic*

Burland, Brian Berkeley 1931- *AuBYP 2, –3, BioIn 8, ConAu 13R, –7NR, DrAF 76, DrAPF 83, –85, IntAu&W 77, –86, –89, –91, SmATA 34, WhoAm 76, –78, –80, –84, –86, –88, –90, –92, –94, WhoE 75, WhoWest 94, WhoWor 78, –89, –91, –93, WrDr 76, –80, –82, –84*

Burland, Cottie Arthur 1905- *AuBYP 2, –3, Au&Wr 71, BioIn 8, –9, –10, ConAu 5R, EncO&P 1, FifIDA, IntAu&W 77, –82, SmATA 5, WhoArt 80, –82, –84N*

Burleigh, Robert 1936- *SmATA 55*

Burleson, Elizabeth *DcAmChF 1960*

Burlingame, Roger 1889-1967 *AmAu&B, AuBYP 2S, –3, BenetAL 91, BioIn 4, –5, –7, –9, ConAu 5R, REn, REnAL, SmATA 2, TwCA, –SUP, WhAm 4*

Burlingame, Virginia 1900- *ConAu P-2*
Pseud./variant:
Struble, Virginia

Burman, Alice Caddy 1896?-1977 *SmATA 24N*

Burman, Ben Lucien 1895-1984 *AmAu&B, AmNov, Au&Wr 71, BioIn 2, –3, –4, –10, –14, –15, ConAu 5R, –114, –8NR, IntAu&W 82, LiHiK, NewYTBS 84, OxCAmL 65, –83, REnAL, ScF&FL 92, SmATA 6, –40N, TwCA, –SUP, TwCChW 83, WhAm 8, WhNAA, WhoAm 74, –76, –78, –84, WhoWor 74, WrDr 76, –80, –82, –84*

Burman, Ben Lucien 1896-1984 *BenetAL 91, ConAu 32NR, TwCChW 89*

Burman, Caddy Alice
Main entry: Caddy, Alice

Burn, Barbara 1940- *ConAu 85, –17NR*

Burn, Doris 1923- *BioIn 8, –9, ConAu 29R, IlsCB 1957, SmATA 1, WhoPNW*

Burnes, Alan Jeffrey 1935- *AmMWSc 73S, -78S, WhoE 74, -75, -77, -81, WhoFI 83, WhoWor 80, -82*

Burness, Wallace B 1933- *ConAu 69, -21NR, WhoUSWr 88, WhoWrEP 89*

Burness, Wallace Binny 1933- *WhoWrEP 92*

Burnett, Avis 1937- *ConAu 41R*

Burnett, Carol 1933- *CelR 90, ConAu 127, ConTFT 8, CurBio 90, EncAFC, HalFC 88, InWom SUP, IntMPA 92, WhoAm 94, WhoCom, WorAlBi*

Burnett, Carol 1934?- *BiE&WWA, BioIn 5, -6, -8, -9, -10, -11, -12, -13, BioNews 74, BlueB 76, CelR, ConTFT 1, CurBio 62, EncMT, FilmgC, ForWC 70, HalFC 84, HerW 84, IntMPA 75, -76, -78, -81, -82, -84, -86, -77, NewYTBE 73, WhoAm 74, -76, -78, -80, -82, -84, WhoAmW 75, -81, -83, -85, WhoHol A, WhoThe 77, -81, WhoWor 74, WorAl*

Burnett, Carol 1936?- *ConMus 6, IntMPA 86, -88, WhoAm 86, -88, -90, -92, WhoAmW 89, -91, -93, WhoEnt 92*

Burnett, Constance 1893-1975 *AuBYP 3*

Burnett, Constance Buel 1893-1975 *AuBYP 2, BioIn 1, -8, -14, ConAu 5R, SmATA 36*

Burnett, Frances 1849-1924 *AuBYP 3, FemiCLE*

Burnett, Frances Eliza 1849-1924 *StaCVF*

Burnett, Frances Eliza Hodgson 1849-1924 *Alli SUP, AmAu&B, AmWomPl, AuBYP 2, BbD, BiDSA, BiD&SB, BioIn 1, -2, -7, -8, -10, -11, BlmGWL, CamGEL, CarSB, CelCen, Chambr 3, ChhPo, -S2, ConAmL, ConAu 108, -136, DcAmAu, DcBiA, DcLB 42, DcLEL, DcNaB MP, DcNAA, EvLB, FamSYP, HalFC 84, HerW, -84, InWom SUP, IntDcWB, JBA 34, LongCTC, MajAI, NotNAT B, NotWoAT, OxCAmL 65, -83, OxCChiL, OxCEng 67, -85, PenC AM, -ENG, PlP&P, REn, REnAL, TelT, TwCA, -SUP, TwCChW 78, -83, WhAm 1, WhoChL, WomWWA 14, WorAlBi, WorAl, YABC 2*

Burnett, Frances H 1849-1924 *BioAmW*

Burnett, Frances Hodgson *WomNov*

Burnett, Frances Hodgson 1849-1924 *ArtclWW 2, Benet 87, BenetAL 91, BioIn 14, -15, -16, -17, CamGLE, CamHAL, ChlLR 24, ContDcW 89, HalFC 88, OxCAmT 84, RfGAmL 87, RfGEnL 91, TwCChW 89, WrChl*

Burnett, Ruth 1919- *BiDrLUS 70, WhoLibS 66*

Burnett, Virgil *ChhPo S1*

Burnett, Whit 1899-1973 *AmAu&B, BenetAL 91, BioIn 4, -9, -10, -13, ConAu 41R, -P-2, CurBio 41, -73, DcLB 137, EncAJ, NewYTBE 73, ObitOF 79, REnAL, TwCA, -SUP, WhAm 5, WhoAm 74*

Burney, Anton *SmATA X*
Main entry: Hopkins, Kenneth

Burney, Eugenia 1913- *ConAu 29R*

Burnford, S D
Main entry: Burnford, Sheila

Burnford, Sheila 1918- *ArtclWW 2*

Burnford, Sheila 1918-1984 *AuBYP 2, -3, Au&Wr 71, BioIn 7, -9, -10, -11, -15, BlmGWL, BkCL, ChlLR 2, ConAu 1R, -112, -1NR, CreCan 2, DcChlFi, FemiCLE, FourBJA, OxCCan, OxCChiL, Profile 1, ScF&FL 92, SmATA 3, -38N, TwCChW 78, -83, -89, WhoCanL 85, -87, -92, WrDr 76, -80, -82, -84*
Pseud./variant:
Burnford, S D
Louisburgh, Sheila Burnford

Burnford, Sheila Philip Cochrane Every 1918-1984 *MajAI*

Burnham, John Hampden 1860-1940 *DcNAA, WhNAA*

Burnham, Sophy *WhoUSWr 88, WhoWrEP 89, -92*

Burnham, Sophy 1936- *BioIn 17, ConAu 38NR, IntAu&W 86, -89, -91, SmATA 65, WhoAm 94, WhoAmW 91, -93*

Burningham, Helen Oxenbury *ThrBJA*
Main entry: Oxenbury, Helen

Burningham, John 1936- *ConAu 36NR, IntAu&W 91, SmATA 59, TwCChW 89, WrDr 86, -88, -90, -92*

Burningham, John Mackintosh 1936- *Au&Wr 71, BioIn 7, -8, -9, -12, ChlLR 9, ConAu 73, IlsBYP, IlsCB 1957, -1967, IntAu&W 77, MajAI, OxCChiL, SmATA 16, ThrBJA, TwCChW 78, -83, Who 74, -82, -83, -85, -88, -90, -92, WhoChL, WrDr 80, -82, -84, -94*

Burns, Aubrey *TexWr*

Burns, Florence M 1905-1988 *BioIn 17, SmATA 61*

Burns, Irene *IlsBYP*

Burns, Joan Simpson 1927- *ConAu 65, ForWC 70, IntAu&W 77, –82, WhoE 83, –85, WrDr 76, –80, –82, –84, –86, –88, –90, –92, –94*

Burns, Marilyn *SmATA 33*

Burns, Olive Ann *BioIn 14, –17*

Burns, Olive Ann d1990 *NewYTBS 90*

Burns, Olive Ann 1924- *ConAu 120*

Burns, Olive Ann 1924-1990 *ConAu 132, –41NR, SmATA 65, TwCYAW*
Pseud./variant:
Larkin, Amy

Burns, Paul Clay 1923- *BioIn 10, ConAu 1R, –4NR, LEduc 74, SmATA 5*

Burns, Raymond 1924- *BioIn 11, SmATA 9*

Burns, Robert 1759-1796 *Alli, AtlBL, Benet 87, BiD&SB, BioIn 1, –2, –3, –4, –5, –6, –7, –8, –9, –10, –11, –12, –13, –14, –15, –16, –17, BlmGEL, BritAu, BritWr 3, CamGEL, CamGLE, CasWL, Chambr 2, ChhPo, –S1, –S2, CmScLit, CnDBLB 3, CnE&AP, CrtT 2, CyWA 58, DcBiPP, DcEnA, –A, DcEnL, DcEuL, DcLB 109, DcLEL, DcNaB, Dis&D, EvLB, FamAYP, LitC 3, LongCEL, MagSWL, McGEWB, MouLC 2, NewC, OxCEng 67, –85, OxCMus, PenC ENG, PoeCrit 6, RAdv 1, –13-1, RComWL, REn, RfGEnL 91, WebE&AL, WhDW, WorAlBi, WorAl, WorLitC*

Burns, Robert 1792-1866 *BiDrUSC 89*

Burns, William A 1909- *AuBYP 2S, BioIn 10, ConAu 11NR, –P-1, SmATA 5, Who 74, WhoAm 74, –76, –78, –80, –82, –84, –86, –88, –90, –92, –94, WhoWest 74*

Burns, William Aloysius 1909- *AuBYP 3*

Burow, Daniel Robert 1931- *ConAu 29R, –11NR, WhoMW 74, –76, WhoRel 75, –77*

Burr, Dan 1951- *SmATA 65*

Burr, Lonnie 1943- *SmATA 47*

Burr, Samuel Engle 1897-1987 *BioIn 15*

Burr, Samuel Engle, Jr. 1897- *WhoE 86, WhoSSW 73, –75, –76*

Burr, Samuel Engle, Jr. 1897-1987 *ConAu 124, WhAm 9*

Burrage, Alfred McLelland 1889-1956 *BioIn 15*

Burrell, Roy Eric Charles 1923- *SmATA 72*

Burris, Burmah *IlsBYP*

Burroughs, Edgar Rice *Benet 87*

Burroughs, Edgar Rice 1875-1950 *AmAu&B, AmLY, Au&Arts 11, BenetAL 91, BioIn 1, –2, –4, –6, –7, –8, –10, –12, –14, –15, –17, CamGLE, CmCal, ConAu 104, –132, DcLB 8, EncFWF, EncSF 93, EvLB, FilmgC, HalFC 84, –88, LongCTC, MajTwCW, NewEScF, Novels, ObitOF 79, OxCAmL 65, –83, OxCChiL, OxCEng 85, PenC AM, REn, REnAL, RGTwCSF, RfGAmL 87, ScF&FL 92, ScFSB, ScFEYrs, SmATA 41, TwCA, –SUP, TwCLC 2, –32, TwCSFW 86, –91, TwCWW 91, TwCWr, TwCYAW, WebAB 74, –79, WhAm 2, WhoHr&F, WhoSciF, WorAlBi, WorAl*

Burroughs, Jean Mitchell 1908- *BioIn 13, ConAu 65, SmATA 28*

Burroughs, John 1837-1921 *Alli SUP, AmAu, AmAu&B, AmLY, AnCL, Benet 87, BenetAL 91, BbD, BiD&SB, BioIn 1, –2, –3, –4, –5, –6, –7, –8, –9, –10, –11, –12, –13, –15, –16, –17, CarSB, Chambr 3, ChhPo, ConAmL, ConAu 109, DcAmAu, DcEnA A, DcLB 64, DcLEL, DcNAA, EvLB, InSci, JBA 34, McGEWB, OxCAmH, OxCAmL 65, –83, PenC AM, REn, REnAL, WebAB 74, –79, WhAm 1*

Burroughs, Margaret T G 1917- *WhoAmA 86, –89, –91*

Burroughs, Margaret Taylor *AuBYP 3*

Burroughs, Margaret Taylor 1917- *AfroAA, BioIn 2, –8, –11, –12, BlkAWP, BlkWr 1, ConAu 21R, –25NR, DcLB 41, InB&W 80, LivgBAA, NotBlAW 92, WhoAm 82, –84, WhoAmA 78, –80, –82, –84, WhoAmW 83, WhoBlA 75, –77, –80, –85, –88, –90, –92, –94*
Pseud./variant:
Taylor, Margaret

Burroughs, Margaret Taylor G 1917- *BioIn 16, BlkAuII, –92*

Burroughs, Margaret Taylor Goss 1917- *InB&W 85, WhoAmW 87, –89*

Burroughs, Polly 1925- *BioIn 9, ConAu 25R, SmATA 2*

Burrow, Diana Wynne *WrDr 86, –88*

Burrow, Diana Wynne 1934- *WrDr 76, –80, –82, –84*

Burrow, John W 1935- *ConAu 30NR*

Burrow, John Wyon 1935- *ConAu 21R, –12NR, IntWW 89, –91, Who 88, –92*

Burrow, John Wyon, Prof 1935- *Who 90*

Burroway, Janet *DrAPF 87, -89, -91, -93*

Burroway, Janet 1936- *AuBYP 3, ConAu 6AS, ConNov 86, -91, IntAu&W 89, WrDr 88, -90, -92*

Burroway, Janet G 1936- *WhoAm 92, -94, WhoSSW 91, -93*

Burroway, Janet Gay 1936- *AuBYP 2S, Au&Wr 71, BioIn 13, ConAu 21R, -12NR, ConNov 76, -82, DcLB 6, DrAPF 83, -85, DrAS 74E, -78E, -82E, IntAu&W 77, -91, SmATA 23, WhoUSWr 88, WhoWrEP 89, -92, WrDr 76, -80, -82, -84, -86, -94*

Burrows, Denys *SingR 1*

Burstein, Chaya M 1923- *BioIn 17, ConAu 126, SmATA 64*

Burstein, John 1949- *BioIn 10, ConAu 69, -21NR, SmATA 40, -54, WhoUSWr 88*
Pseud./variant:
Goodbody, Slim

Burt, Jesse Clifton 1921-1976 *BioIn 12, -15, ConAu 9R, -4NR, SmATA 20N, -46*

Burt, Mary Elizabeth 1850-1918 *Alli SUP, AmAu&B, AmLY, DcNAA, WhAm 1, WomWWA 14*

Burt, Nathaniel 1913- *AuBYP 2, -3, BioIn 3, -8, ConAu 17R, DrAS 74E, -78E, -82E, IntAu&W 89, WhoE 74, WhoUSWr 88, WhoWrEP 89, -92, WrDr 76, -80, -82, -84, -86, -88, -90, -92, -94*

Burt, Olive 1894- *AuBYP 3*

Burt, Olive F Wooley 1894- *AmWomPl*

Burt, Olive Wooley 1894- *InWom SUP*

Burt, Olive Woolley 1894- *AuBYP 2, BioIn 7, -9, ChhPo S2, ConAu 5R, -5NR, ForWC 70, IntAu&W 77, SmATA 4*

Burton, Elizabeth 1908- *AuBYP 2, -3, Au&Wr 71, BioIn 8, ConAu 65, -15NR, WrDr 82, -84, -86, -88, -90*

Burton, Hester 1913- *AuBYP 2S, -3, Au&Wr 71, BioIn 8, -9, -10, ChlLR 1, ConAu 9R, -10NR, IntAu&W 82, -86, -89, -91, OxCChiL, SmATA 7, -8AS, ThrBJA, TwCChW 78, -83, -89, WhoChL, WrDr 76, -80, -82, -84, -86, -88, -90, -92, -94*

Burton, Hester Wood-Hill 1913- *MajAI, SmATA 74, TwCYAW*

Burton, John Andrew 1944- *ConAu 65, -14NR, IntAu&W 91, WrDr 76, -80, -82, -84, -86, -88, -90, -92, -94*

Burton, Katherine 1880-1969 *FemiCLE*

Burton, Katherine 1887?-1969 *AuBYP 2, BioIn 1, -2, -8, BkC 3, CathA 1930, ConAu 77, EncAB-A 12, OhA&B*

Burton, Katherine 1890-1969 *AuBYP 3*

Burton, Leslie *ConAu X, SmATA X*
Main entry: McGuire, Leslie Sarah

Burton, Marilee Robin 1950- *BioIn 15, ConAu 121, SmATA 46*

Burton, Maurice 1898- *Au&Wr 71, BioIn 13, BlueB 76, ConAu 65, -9NR, -29NR, IntAu&W 77, -82, -86, -89, -91, SmATA 23, Who 74, -82, -83, -85, -88, -90, -92, WrDr 80, -82, -84, -86, -88, -90, -92, -94*

Burton, Maurice 1898-1992 *ConAu 139*

Burton, Philip 1904- *BiE&WWA, BioIn 7, -8, -10, ConAu 25R, NotNAT, -A*

Burton, Robert 1941- *Au&Wr 71, BioIn 13, ConAu 45, -1NR, -17NR, -29NR, SmATA 22, WhoSSW 82, -84*

Burton, Virginia Lee 1909-1968 *AmAu&B, AmPB, AnCL, ArtclWW 2, AuBYP 2, -3, Au&ICB, BioIn 1, -2, -4, -5, -7, -8, -9 -14, Cald 1938, ChlLR 11, ChsFB A, ConAu 25R, -P-1, CurBio 43, -68, DcLB 22, IlsBYP IlsCB 1744, -1946, -1957, -1967, InWom SUP, JBA 51, MajAI, OxCChiL, SmATA 2, TwCChW 78, -83, -89, WrChl*

Burton, William H 1890-1964 *BioIn 4, -11, ConAu 1R, -1NR, SmATA 11, WhAm 4*

Busby, Edith d1964 *AuBYP 2, -3, BioIn 7, ConAu 109, IndAu 1917, SmATA 29N*

Busby, F M 1921- *ConAu 65, -9NR, -24NR, IntAu&W 91, NewEScF, ScF&FL 92, ScFSB, TwCSFW 86, -91, WrDr 84, -86, -88, -90, -92*

Busby, Francis Marion 1921- *EncSF 93, WrDr 94*

Buscaglia, Felice Leonardo 1924-
Pseud./variant:
Buscaglia, Leo F

Buscaglia, Leo 1924- *BestSel 89-4, ConAu 30NR, SmATA 65, WhoAm 86, -88, WhoUSWr 88, WhoWrEP 89, WorAlBi*

Buscaglia, Leo F *ConAu 30NR, SmATA 65*
Main entry: Buscaglia, Felice Leonardo

Buscaglia, Leo F 1924- *WrDr 86, –88, –90, –92*

Buscaglia, Leo Felice 1924- *WrDr 94*

Busch, Phyllis S 1909- *ConAu 107, SmATA 30*

Busch, Wilhelm 1832-1908 *Benet 87, BiD&SB, BioIn 1, –2, –3, –7, –12, –13, –14, CasWL, ChhPo, –S1, –S2, ClDMEL 47, ConGrA 3, Dis&D, EuAu, EvEuW, OxCChiL, OxCGer 76, –86, PenC EUR, REn, WhDW*

Bush, Jim 1926- *ConAu 57*

Bush-Brown, Louise 1896?-1973 *AuBYP 2, –3, BioIn 4, –8, ConAu 49*

Bushmiller, Ernest Paul 1905-1982 *AnObit 1982, ArtCS, AuNews 1, BioIn 1, –10, –11, –13, ConAu 29R, –107, NewYTBS 82, SmATA 31N, WhAm 8, WhAmArt 85, WhoAm 74, –76, –78, –80, –82, WhoAmA 73, –80, –82, –84*

Buske, Morris Roger 1912- *ConAu 13R*

Busoni, Rafaello 1900-1962 *AmAu&B, AuBYP 2, –3, BioIn 1, –2, –3, –5, –6, –7, –8, –12, ConAu 117, IlsCB 1744, –1946, –1957, JBA 51, SmATA 16, WhAmArt 85*

Bussieres, Simone 1918- *BioIn 10, ConAu 53, IntAu&W 86, –89, Profile 1*

Butcher, Grace 1934- *ConAu 25R, DrAP 75, DrAPF 83, –85, –87, –89, –91, –93, InWom SUP, IntWWP 82, WhoMW 86, WhoUSWr 88, WhoWrEP 89, –92*

Butcher, Thomas Kennedy 1914- *Au&Wr 71, ConAu P-1, IntAu&W 77, WrDr 76, –80, –82, –84, –86, –88, –90, –92, –94*

Butler, Albert 1923- *ConAu 13R, –5NR*

Butler, Beverly 1932- *ScF&FL 92, SixBJA*

Butler, Beverly Kathleen 1932- *AuBYP 2, –3, BioIn 7, –10, ChhPo S2, ConAu 1R, –4NR, ForWC 70, SmATA 7*

Butler, David J 1946- *ConAu 69, WhoWest 80*

Butler, Dorothy 1925- *ConAu 133, IntAu&W 89, OxCChiL, SmATA 73, WrDr 84, –86, –88, –90, –92, –94*

Butler, Ellis Parker 1869-1937 *AmAu&B, BenetAL 91, ChhPo, DcNAA, EncMys, JBA 34, OxCAmL 65, –83, REnAL, ScFEYrs, TwCA, WhAm 1, WhNAA*

Butler, Gwendoline Williams 1922- *Au&Wr 71, ConAu 6NR, DcLEL 1940, IntAu&W 77, WrDr 76, –80*

Butler, Hal 1913- *AuBYP 2, –3, BioIn 8, ConAu 57, MichAu 80*

Butler, Horacio 1897- *BioIn 1, IlsCB 1744, OxCTwCA, PhDcTCA 77*

Butler, Kenneth C *OxCCan*

Butler, M Christina 1934- *SmATA 72*

Butler, Mildred Allen 1897- *AmWomPl, AuBYP 2S, –3, ConAu P-2, WhoPNW*

Butler, Octavia E 1947- *ArtclWW 2, BlkWr 1, ConAu 24NR, ConLC 38, FemiCLE, IntAu&W 91, MajTwCW, NewEScF, NotBlAW 92, ScF&FL 92, TwCSFW 86, –91, WhoBlA 85, –88, –90, –92, –94, WrDr 86, –88, –90, –92*

Butler, Octavia Estelle 1947- *BlkWr 2, ConAu 38NR, EncSF 93, TwCYAW, WhoAmW 89, –91, WhoWest 87*

Butler, Octavia Estelle 1948- *InB&W 85*

Butler, Stuart Thomas 1926-1982 *BioIn 11, –13, BlueB 76, ConAu 107, IntWWE, McGMS 80, WhoWor 74, –82, WrDr 80*

Butler, Suzanne 1919- *AuBYP 3, DcChlFi*

Butler, Suzanne Louise 1919- *AuBYP 2S, CreCan 2, SmATA X*
Main entry: Perreard, Suzanne Louise Butler

Butler, Walter C *ConAu X, EncFWF, EncMys, WebAB 74, –79*

Butler, William 1929- *AuBYP 2S, –3, Au&Wr 71, ConAu 107*

Butler, William Francis 1838-1910 *BiDIrW*

Butler, William Francis, Sir 1838-1910 *Alli SUP, BioIn 2, –8, BritAu 19, CelCen, Chambr 3, DcCathB, DcIrB 88, DcNaB S2, EncSoA, OxCCan*

Butters, Dorothy Gilman *ConAu 30NR, InWom SUP, IntAu&W 91X, ScF&FL 92, WhoAm 86, –88, WrDr 86, –88, –90, –92*

Butters, Dorothy Gilman 1923- *AmAu&B, AuBYP 2, –3, BioIn 14, ConAu 1R, –2NR, ForWC 70, SmATA 5, WhoAm 84, –90, –92, WrDr 82, –84, –94*
Pseud./variant:
Gilman, Dorothy

Butterworth, Emma Macalik 1928- *BioIn 15, ConAu 105, SmATA 43*

Butterworth, Hezekiah 1839-1905 *Alli SUP, AmAu, AmAu&B, BbD, BiD&SB, BioIn 15,*

CarSB, ChhPo, DcAmAu, DcLB 42, DcNAA, OxCChiL, WhAm 1

Butterworth, Oliver d1990 *NewYTBS 90*

Butterworth, Oliver 1915- *AuBYP 2S, -3, BioIn 9, ConAu 1R, DcAmChF 1960, FourBJA, IntAu&W 89, -91, OxCChiL, SmATA 1, TwCChW 83, -89, WhoAm 74, -76, -78, -80, WrDr 86, -88, -90, -92*

Butterworth, Oliver 1915-1990 *BioIn 17, ConAu 132, -37NR, MajAI, ScF&FL 92, SmATA 66, WhAm 10*

Butterworth, W E 1929- *AuBYP 2S, ConAu 1R, -2NR, -18NR, FifBJA, SmATA 5, WhoSSW 73, -75, -76*
Pseud./variant:
Beech, Webb
Blake, Walker E
Butterworth, William Edmund, III
Douglas, James McM
Scholefield, Edmund O
Williams, Patrick J

Butterworth, William E 1929- *ScF&FL 92*

Butterworth, William Edmund, III
Main entry: Butterworth, W E

Butterworth, William Edmund, III 1929- *AuBYP 3, ConAu 40NR*

Buttfield, Helen 1929- *ChhPo S1, ICPEnP A, MacBEP*

Button, Daniel *MedPD*

Buxton, Ralph *MajAI, SmATA 69*
Main entry: Silverstein, Alvin
Silverstein, Virginia B

Buzzati, Dino 1906-1972 *BioIn 2, -5, -9, -10, -13, -15, CnMD, ConAu 33R, ConLC 36, CroCD, DcItL, EncSF 93, EncWL, EncWT, IlsCB 1946, NewYTBE 72, ObitOF 79, PenC EUR, PenEncH, TwCSFW 86A, -91A, TwCWr, WhoTwCL, WorAu 1950*

Byard, Carole *BlkAuII, -92, InWom SUP*

Byard, Carole 1941- *BioIn 16, -17, SmATA 57*

Byard, Carole Marie 1941- *BioIn 11, WhoAmA 78, -80, -82, -84, -86, -89, -91*

Byars, Betsy 1928- *AuBYP 2, -3, BioIn 8, -9, -10, -12, -13, CamGLE, ChlFicS, ChlLR 1, -16, ConAu 33R, -18NR, -36NR, ConLC 35, DcLB 52, InWom SUP, IntAu&W 91, MajTwCW, MorBMP, NewbC 1966, OxCChiL, ScF&FL 92, SmATA 4, -46, -1AS, ThrBJA, TwCChW 78, -83, -89, TwCYAW, WrDr 80, -82, -84, -86, -88, -90, -92*

Byars, Betsy Cromer 1928- *DcAmChF 1960, -1985, MajAI, WrDr 94*

Bye, Beryl Joyce Rayment 1926- *Au&Wr 71, ConAu 61, WrDr 76, -80*

Byers, Irene 1906- *ConAu 9R, -3NR, WrDr 76, -80, -82, -84, -86, -88, -90*

Byfield, Barbara Ninde 1930- *BioIn 11, ConAu 1R, -4NR, IlsBYP, SmATA 8*

Byrd, Elizabeth 1912- *BioIn 14, ConAu 5NR, SmATA 34*

Byrd, Grady *IlsBYP*

Byrd, Robert 1942- *BioIn 9, IlsCB 1967, SmATA 33*

Byrne, Peter 1925- *ConAu 65*

Byrnes, Gene *EncACom*

Byrnes, Gene 1893-1974 *ArtCS, NewYTBS 74, WhAmArt 85*

Byron, George Gordon 1788-1824 *Benet 87, BioIn 16, -17, DcLB 96, PenEncH, WorAlBi*

Byron, George Gordon, Baron 1788-1824 *BioIn 15*

Byron, George Gordon, Lord 1788-1824 *BlmGEL, CamGEL, CamGLE, CamGWoT, CnDBLB 3*

Byron, George Gordon Noel 1788-1824 *RAdv 13-1*

Byron, George Gordon Noel, Baron 1788-1824 *CmScLit*

Byron, George Gordon Noel, Lord 1788-1824 *Alli, AtlBL, BbD, BiDLA, -SUP, BiD&SB, BioIn 1, -2, -3, -4, -5, -6, -7, -8, -9 -10, -11, -12, -13, BritAu 19, BritWr 4, CasWL, Chambr 3, ChhPo, -S1, -S2, CnE&AP, CnThe, CyWA 58, DcBiPP, DcEnA, DcEnL, DcEuL, DcLEL, DcNaB, Dis&D, EvLB, HsB&A, McGEWB, McGEWD 72, -84, NewC, NinCLC 2, -12, OxCEng 67, -85, OxCThe 67, -83, PenC ENG, RAdv 1, RComWL, REn, REnWD, WebE&AL, WhDW, WorAl*

C

C 3 3 *SmATA X*
Main entry: Wilde, Oscar

Cabassa, Victoria 1912- *ConAu 49*

Cabat, Erni *BioIn 16*

Cabat, Erni 1914- *SmATA 74*

Cable, Mary *DrAPF 87, –89*

Cable, Mary 1920- *BioIn 11, ConAu 25R, –11NR, –28NR, DrAF 76, DrAPF 83, –85, SmATA 9*

Cabot, John fl. 1497- *DcChlFi*

Cabral, O M
Main entry: Cabral, Olga

Cabral, Olga *DrAPF 93*

Cabral, Olga 1909- *BioIn 15, DrAPF 87, –89, –91, SmATA 46*
Pseud./variant:
Cabral, O M

Caddell, Foster 1921- *BioIn 8, WhoAmA 73, –78, –80, –82, –84, –86, –89, –91, WhoE 81, –83, –85, –86, –89, –91, –93, WhoWor 84, –87, –89, –91, –93*

Caddy, Alice 1896?-1977 *BioIn 5, –11, –12, –13, IlsCB 1946, NatCAB 59, SmATA X, WhAmArt 85*
Pseud./variant:
Burman, Caddy Alice

Cade, Toni *BlkAWP, BlkWr 1, –2, ConAu X, MajTwCW*
Main entry: Bambara, Toni Cade

Cade, Toni 1939- *WhoBlA 90, –92, –94*

Cadell, Elizabeth 1903- *Au&Wr 71, BioIn 2, –14, ConAu 57, –11NR, CurBio 51, FemiCLE, IntAu&W 91, TwCRHW 90, WrDr 76, –80, –82, –84, –86, –88, –90*
Pseud./variant:
Ainsworth, Harriet

Cadwallader, Sharon 1936- *BioIn 10, ConAu 49, –1NR, –17NR, SmATA 7*

Cady, Harrison 1877?-1970 *BioIn 1, –2, –3, –9, –12, ChhPo, –S1, ConAu 116, ForIl, IlsCB 1744, NewYTBE 70, OxCChiL, SmATA 19, WhAmArt 85, WhNAA*
Pseud./variant:
Cady, Walter Harrison

Cady, Walter Harrison
Main entry: Cady, Harrison

Caen, Herb *BioIn 14, –15, –16, NewYTBS 93*

Caen, Herb 1916- *AuBYP 2S, –3, AuNews 1, BioIn 1, –2, –4, –8, –10, CelR, –90, CmCal, ConAu 1R, –1NR, EncTwCJ, JrnUS, WhoAm 74, –76, –78, –80, –82, –84, –86, –88, –92, –94, WhoWest 89, –92, WhoWor 74*

Caffrey, Nancy *AuBYP 3*

Caffrey, Nancy 1928?-1960 *AuBYP 2, BioIn 5, –8*

Cagle, Malcolm W 1918- *BioIn 14*

Cagle, Malcolm Winfield 1918- *ConAu 108, SmATA 32, WhoAm 74*

Cahill, Susan Neunzig 1940- *BioIn 11, ConAu 37R*

Cahn, Rhoda 1922- *BioIn 15, ConAu 81, SmATA 37*

Cahn, William 1912-1976 *BioIn 11, –15, ConAu 21R, –69, SmATA 37*

Caidin, Martin 1927- *AmAu&B, AuNews 2, BioIn 6, –10, –11, –12, ConAu 1R, –2NR, ConSFA, EncSF 93, NewEScF, ScF&FL 92, ScFSB, TwCSFW 86, –91, WhoSciF, WrDr 84, –86, –88, –90, –92, –94*

Cailloux, Andre 1920- *CreCan 2, OxCCanL, OxCCanT*

Cain, Arthur Homer 1913- *AuBYP 2S, –3, BioIn 9, ConAu 1R, –4NR, SmATA 3*

Pseud./variant:
King, Arthur

Cain, Christopher *ConAu X, SmATA 8, WrDr 86*
Main entry: Fleming, Thomas James

Cain, Christopher 1927- *WrDr 94*

Caine, Geoffrey *ScF&FL 92, SmATA 66*
Main entry: Walker, Robert Wayne

Caines, Jeannette *AuBYP 3, BioIn 13, BlkAWP, ChlLR 24, SmATA 43*

Caines, Jeannette Franklin *BioIn 15*

Caines, Jeannette Franklin 1938- *BioIn 16, BlkAuII, -92, BlkWr 2*

Caird, Janet 1913- *Au&Wr 71, BioIn 14, ConAu 49, -2NR, IntAu&W 91, ScF&FL 92, TwCCr&M 80, TwCRHW 90, WrDr 76, -80, -82, -84, -86, -88, -90, -92*

Caird, Janet Hinshaw Kirkwood 1913- *WrDr 94*

Cairns, Trevor 1922- *BioIn 12, ConAu 33R, IntAu&W 77, -82, SmATA 14, WrDr 76, -80, -82, -84, -86*

Calahan, Harold Augustin 1889-1965 *BioIn 7, -8*

Calapai, Letterio *WhoAm 86, -88, -90, -92, -94, WhoAmA 86, -89, WhoMW 86*

Calapai, Letterio 1902- *WhoAmA 91*

Calapai, Letterio 1903- *BioIn 5, IlsCB 1946, WhAmArt 85, WhoAm 74, -76, -78, -80, -82, -84, WhoAmA 73, -78, -80, -82, -84, WhoMW 86*

Calapai, Letterio 1904- *BioIn 14*

Calde, Mark 1945- *ConAu 69*

Caldecott, Moyra 1927- *BioIn 13, ConAu 77, -13NR, -30NR, IntAu&W 86, -89, -91, ScF&FL 92, SmATA 22*

Caldecott, Randolph 1846-1886 *AnCL, BenetAL 91, BioIn 1, -2, -3, -4, -5, -8, -11, -12, -16, CamGLE, CarSB, CelCen, ChhPo, -S1, -S2, ChlLR 14, DcBrBI, DcNaB, DcVicP 2, IlsBYP, JBA 34, -51, OxCArt, OxCChiL, OxDcArt, SmATA 17, StaCVF, Str&VC, WhoChL*

Caldecott, Randolph J 1846-1886 *MajAI*

Calder, Lyn
Main entry: Calmenson, Stephanie

Calder-Marshall, Arthur 1908- *Au&Wr 71, BioIn 2, -10, BlueB 76, ConAu 61, ConNov 72, -76, -82, DcLEL, IntAu&W 77, Who 74, -82, -83, -85, -88, -90, -92, WorAu 1950, WrDr 76, -80, -82, -84, -86, -88, -90, -92, -94*

Calder-Marshall, Arthur 1908-1992 *ConAu 137*

Calderon, William Frank 1865-1943 *DcBrAr 1, DcBrBI, DcVicP 2, TwCPaSc*

Caldwell, Doreen Mary 1942- *SmATA 71*

Caldwell, Edward Sabiston 1928- *ConAu 55, WhoRel 75, -77, -92*

Caldwell, John Cope 1913- *AuBYP 2, -3, BioIn 7, -10, ConAu 21R, -13NR, SmATA 7*

Calhoun, Mary Huiskamp 1926- *AuBYP 2, -3, BioIn 7, -9, ConAu 5R, ForWC 70, SmATA 2, ThrBJA*
Pseud./variant:
Wilkins, Mary Huiskamp Calhoun

Calif, Ruth *BioIn 17*

Calif, Ruth 1922- *ConAu 134, SmATA 67, WrDr 94*

Calkins, Dick 1895-1962 *ArtCS, EncSF 93*

Calkins, Franklin *ConAu X*
Main entry: Stratemeyer, Edward L

Calkins, Franklin Welles 1857-1928 *AmAu&B, DcNAA, WhAm 1, WhNAA*

Call, Hughie Florence 1890-1969 *BioIn 9, ConAu 5R, SmATA 1, WhoPNW*

Callaghan, Morley *BioIn 16, -17, IntvTCA 2*

Callaghan, Morley d1990 *IntWW 91N, NewYTBS 90*

Callaghan, Morley 1903- *Benet 87, BenetAL 91, BioIn 1, -3, -4, -5, -6, -7, -9, -12, -13, BlueB 76, CamGLE, CanNov, CanWW 70, CanWr, CasWL, CathA 1930, ConAu 9R, ConLC 3, -41, ConNov 72, -76, -82, -86, CreCan 2, CyWA 89, DcLB 68, DcLEL, EncWL, -2, IntAu&W 77, -89, -91, IntWW 74, -75, -76, -77, -78, -79, -80, -81, -82, -83, -89, LongCTC, ModCmwL, NewC, Novels, OxCAmL 65, -83, OxCCan, -SUP, OxCCanL, PenC ENG, RAdv 13-1, REn, REnAL, TwCA, -SUP, TwCWr, WebE&AL, WhDW, Who 74, -82, -83, -85, -88, -90, WhoAm 74, WhoCanL 85, -87, WhoTwCL, WhoWor 84, WrDr 76, -80, -82, -84, -86, -88, -90*

Callaghan, Morley 1903-1990 *AnObit 1990, ConLC 65, LiExTwC, RfGEnL 91, WhoCanL 92*

Callaghan, Morley Edward 1903-1990 *RfGShF*

Callahan, Claire Wallis 1890- *AuBYP 2, -3, BioIn 8, ConAu 5R*
Pseud./variant:
Hartwell, Nancy

Callahan, Dorothy *AuBYP 2, BioIn 8*

Callahan, Dorothy 1934- *AuBYP 3*

Callahan, Dorothy M 1934- *BioIn 14, -15, ConAu 114, IntAu&W 86, SmATA 35, -39*

Callahan, Jack 1889-1954 *ArtCS, BioIn 3, EncACom*

Callahan, Philip Serna 1923- *AmMWSc 73P, -76P, -82, -86, -89, -92, AuBYP 2S, -3, BioIn 13, ConAu 102, SmATA 25*

Callan, Jamie *DrAPF 87, -89, -91, -93*

Callan, Jamie 1954- *BioIn 16, SmATA 59*

Callaway, Bernice 1923- *BioIn 16, ConAu 121, SmATA 48*

Callaway, Kathy *DrAPF 87, -89, -91, -93*

Callaway, Kathy 1943- *BioIn 14, ConAu 107, DrAPF 83, -85, SmATA 36*

Callaway, Kathy Jean 1943- *WhoWrEP 92*

Calle, Paul 1928- *BiDScF, BioIn 13, IlrAm 1880, WhoAmA 78, -80, -82, -84, -86, -89, -91*

Callen, Larry
Main entry: Callen, Lawrence Willard, Jr.

Callen, Larry 1927- *ConAu X, FifBJA, SmATA X*

Callen, Lawrence Willard, Jr. 1927- *BioIn 12, ConAu 73, -12NR, SmATA 19*
Pseud./variant:
Callen, Larry

Callenbach, Ernest *BioIn 16*

Callenbach, Ernest 1929- *ConAu 57, -6NR, -21NR, EncSF 93, IntAu&W 89, ScF&FL 92, TwCSFW 86, -91, WhoAm 84, -86, -88, -90, -92, -94, WhoUSWr 88, WhoWest 74, WhoWrEP 89, -92, WrDr 88, -90, -92, -94*

Callum, Myles 1934- *ConAu 9R, IntAu&W 89, -91, WhoAm 74, -76, -78, -80, -82, -84, -86, -88, -90, -92, -94, WhoEnt 92, WhoWor 78*

Calmenson, Stephanie *BioIn 15, -16*

Calmenson, Stephanie 1952- *ConAu 107, -24NR, ScF&FL 92, SmATA 37, -51*
Pseud./variant:
Calder, Lyn

Calvert, Elinor H *ConAu 5R*
Main entry: Lasell, Elinor H

Calvert, James *AuBYP 3*

Calvert, James Francis 1920- *AuBYP 2, BioIn 5, -6, -8, -14, NatCAB 63N, WhoAm 74, -76, -78, -80, -82, -84, -86, -88, -90, -92, -94, WhoFI 83, -85, WhoGov 72*

Calvert, John *ConAu X, -29NR, MajAI, SmATA X, TwCA SUP*
Main entry: Leaf, Munro

Calvert, Mary *ConAu 39NR, IntAu&W 91X, ScF&FL 92, WrDr 86, -88, -90, -92*

Calvert, Mary 1941- *ConAu 93, WrDr 76, -80, -82, -84, -94*

Calvert, Patricia 1931- *BioIn 15, -16, ConAu 105, -21NR, MajAI, SixBJA, SmATA 45, -69, -17AS, TwCYAW, WhoUSWr 88, WhoWrEP 89, -92*
Pseud./variant:
Freeman, Peter J

Calvert, Robert, Jr. 1922- *ConAu 25R*

Calvert, William Robinson 1882-1949 *BioIn 2*

Cam *BioIn 5, IlsCB 1946*
Main entry: Campbell, Barbara

Cameron, Ann *ChlFicS*

Cameron, Ann 1943- *AuBYP 3, BioIn 13, ConAu 101, DcAmChF 1985, SmATA 27*

Cameron, Barbara *SingR 2*

Cameron, Barbara Anne *ScF&FL 92*

Cameron, Edna M 1905- *BioIn 9, ConAu P-1, SmATA 3*

Cameron, Eleanor 1912- *AuBYP 2, -3, BioIn 6, -8, -9, -13, -15, -17, BlmGWL, ChhPo, ChlLR 1, ConAu 1R, -2NR, -22NR, DcLB 52, FemiCLE, IntAu&W 89, -91, MajTwCW, OxCChiL, ScF&FL 92, SmATA 1, -25, -10AS, ThrBJA, TwCChW 78, -83, -89, WrDr 80, -82, -84, -86, -88, -90, -92*

Cameron, Eleanor Butler 1912- *DcAmChF 1960, EncSF 93, WrDr 94*

Cameron, Eleanor Frances 1912- *MajAI, TwCYAW*

Cameron, Elizabeth *BioIn 11, –13, ConAu X, SmATA X*
Main entry: Nowell, Elizabeth Cameron

Cameron, Elizabeth Jane 1910-1976 *AuBYP 2S, –3, BioIn 14, ConAu 1R, –69, –1NR, SmATA 30N, –32, WrDr 76*
Pseud./variant:
Duncan, Jane
Sandison, Janet

Cameron, Ian *ConAu X, ConSFA, IntAu&W 77X, –82X, –91X, SmATA X, WrDr 76, –80, –82, –84, –86, –88, –90, –92*
Main entry: Payne, Donald Gordon

Cameron, Ian 1924- *BioIn 15, EncSF 93, ScF&FL 92, WrDr 94*

Cameron, John *ChhPo, –S1, DcBrAr 1*

Cameron, Katharine 1874-1965 *BioIn 1, –14, DcBrAr 1, DcBrBI, IlsCB 1744*

Cameron, Lucy Lyttleton 1781-1858 *DcNaB, OxCChiL*

Cameron, Polly 1928- *AuBYP 2, –3, BioIn 7, –8, –9, ChhPo, ConAu 17R, ForWC 70, FourBJA, IlsCB 1957, –1967, SmATA 2*

Cammaerts, Emile Leon 1878-1953 *BioIn 3, –4, –6, CarSB, ChhPo, –S1, –S2, DcLEL, EvEuW, LongCTC, TwCA SUP, WhoLA*

Cammaerts, Tita *CarSB*

Camp, Charles Lewis 1893-1975 *BioIn 10, –14, CmCal, ConAu 61, SmATA 31N, WhAm 6*

Camp, Fred V 1911- *ConAu 49*

Camp, Norma Cournow 1939- *ForWC 70*

Camp, Walter Chauncey 1859-1925 *AmAu&B, AmLY, BiDAmSp FB, BiD&SB, BioIn 2, –3, –5, –6, –9, –11, –12, ChhPo, DcAmAu, DcNAA, JBA 34, –51, OxCAmH, REnAL, WebAB 74, –79, WhAm 1, WhNAA, WhoFtbl 74, WorAl, YABC 1*

Campanella, Roy 1921- *Ballpl 90, BiDAmSp BB, BioIn 1, –2, –3, –4, –5, –6, –7, –8, –9, –10, –11, –13, –14, –15, –17, CelR, CurBio 53, InB&W 80, NegAl 76, –83, –89, WhoAm 74, –76, –78, WhoBlA 75, –77, –80, –85, WorAlBi, WorAl*

Campanella, Roy 1921-1993 *News 94-1*

Campanella, Roy, Sr. 1921- *InB&W 85, WhoBlA 88, –90, –92*

Campanella, Roy, Sr. 1921-1993 *WhoBlA 94N*

Campbell, Alistair 1925- *CamGLE, ChhPo S1, –S2, ConPo 70, –75, –80, –85, –91, IntWWP 82, RfGEnL 91, WrDr 76, –80, –82, –84, –86, –88, –90, –92*

Campbell, Alistair Te Ariki 1925- *WrDr 94*

Campbell, Andrea 1963- *BioIn 16, SmATA 50*

Campbell, Andrew C 1923- *AmMWSc 73F, ConAu 114*

Campbell, Angus *AnObit 1980, ConAu X, –30NR, IntAu&W 77X, –82X, NewYTBS 80*
Main entry: Chetwynd-Hayes, Ronald Henry Glynn

Campbell, Ann R 1925- *BioIn 11, ConAu 21R, SmATA 11*

Campbell, Archibald Bruce 1881-1966 *BioIn 2, –3, –7, ConAu P-1*

Campbell, Barbara *BioIn 16*

Campbell, Barbara 1913- *BioIn 5, IlsCB 1946*
Pseud./variant:
Cam

Campbell, Barbara 1929- *BlkAuII 92*

Campbell, Barbara 1939- *BlkAuII*

Campbell, Beatrice Murphy *BroadAu, ConAu 137, –X*
Main entry: Murphy, Beatrice M

Campbell, Beatrice Murphy 1908- *WhoBlA 90, –92, –94*

Campbell, Bruce *AuBYP 2, –3, BioIn 1[illegible], CpmDNM 82, ConAu X, –39NR, MorJA, SmATA 1, –X*
Main entry: Epstein, Samuel

Campbell, Bruce 1909- *Ballpl 90*

Campbell, Camilla 1905- *BioIn 13, ConAu P-2, SmATA 26*

Campbell, Elizabeth A *AuBYP 2, –3, BioIn 8*

Campbell, Hannah *ConAu 9R*

Campbell, Hope *WhoAmW 87*

Campbell, Hope 1925- *BioIn 12, ConAu 61, –10NR, ScF&FL 92, SmATA 20, WhoAmW 83, –85*
Pseud./variant:
Hughes, Virginia
Wallis, G McDonald
Wells, Helen

Campbell, Jane *BioIn 11, ConAu X, SmATA X, WhoUSWr 88, WhoWrEP 89, –92*
Main entry: Edwards, Jane Campbell

Campbell, Judith *IntAu&W 86X*
Main entry: Pares, Marion Stapylton

Campbell, Judith 1914- *ConAu X, IntAu&W 82X, –91, WrDr 76, –80, –82, –84, –86, –88, –90, –92, –94*

Campbell, Ken *BioIn 16*

Campbell, Ken 1941- *CamGWoT, ConAu 77, OxCThe 83, WhoThe 81*

Campbell, Kenneth Eugene, Jr. 1943- *WhoAm 94*

Campbell, M Rudolph *AuBYP 2S, –3*

Campbell, Malcolm, Sir 1885-1948 *BioIn 1, –2, –5, –8, –9, –12, –13, –14, CurBio 47, –49, DcNaB 1941, EncSoA, GrBr, ObitOF 79, WhDW*

Campbell, Margaret 1916- *ConAu 106, WrDr 80, –82, –84*

Campbell, Maria *IntvTCA 2*

Campbell, Maria 1940- *ArtclWW 2, BioIn 10, –13, BlmGWL, CaW, ConAu 102, FemiCLE, Profile 2, WhoCanL 85, –92*

Campbell, Marjorie Wilkins *CanWW 89*

Campbell, Marjorie Wilkins 1901- *CaW, CanWW 70, –80, –81, –83, ConAu 97, OxCCan, –SUP*

Campbell, Patricia J *BiDrAPA 89*

Campbell, Patricia J 1930- *BioIn 15, –17, ConAu 103, –35NR, SmATA 45*
Pseud./variant:
Campbell, Patty

Campbell, Patty
Main entry: Campbell, Patricia J

Campbell, Peter *AuBYP 2S, –3*

Campbell, Robert 1914- *CanWW 70, –79, –80*

Campbell, Robert 1927- *TwCCr&M 91, WrDr 92*

Campbell, Robert W *WhoAm 90*

Campbell, Robert Wright 1927- *BioIn 10, ConAu 57, –6NR, WrDr 94*

Campbell, Rod 1945- *BioIn 15, –16, SmATA 44, –51*

Campbell, Rosemae Wells 1909- *AuBYP 2, –3, BioIn 8, –9, ConAu 13R, –X, SmATA 1*

Campbell, Virginia 1914- *ArtclWW 2, BioIn 5, ChhPo, IlsBYP, IlsCB 1946*

Campbell, Wanda Jay *AuBYP 2, –3, BioIn 7*

Campbell, William Edward March 1893-1954 *AmAu&B, AmNov X, BioIn 2, –3, –4, –5, –12, ConAmA, ConAu 108, REn, REnAL, TwCA SUP*
Pseud./variant:
March, William

Campe, Joachim Heinrich 1746-1818 *BiD&SB, CarSB, CelCen, CyEd, DcBiPP, DcEuL, OxCChiL*

Campion, Nardi Reeder 1917- *AuBYP 2, –3, BioIn 7, ConAu 1R, –6NR, SmATA 22*

Campling, Elizabeth 1948- *BioIn 16, ConAu 123, SmATA 53, WrDr 90, –92, –94*

Camps, Luis 1928- *BioIn 17, SmATA 66*

Candell, Victor G 1903-1977 *BioIn 11, –12, –13, ConICB, DcCAA 71, –77, NatCAB 60, SmATA 24N, WhAm 7, WhAmArt 85, WhoAm 74, –76, WhoAmA 73, –78N, –80N, –82N*

Candy, Robert 1920- *AuBYP 2, –3, BioIn 5, –7, IlsCB 1946*

Caney, Steven 1941- *ConAu 104*

Canfield, Dorothea F *MajAI*

Canfield, Dorothea Frances *MajAI*

Canfield, Dorothy *BenetAL 91, ConAu 136, InWom SUP, MajAI, WomNov*
Main entry: Fisher, Dorothy Canfield

Canfield, Dorothy 1879-1958 *AmAu&B, AmNov, BioIn 1, –2, –3, –4, –11, –12, Chambr 3, CnDAL, ConAmA, ConAmL, ConAu X, DcBiA, DcLEL, JBA 34, LongCTC, NotAW MOD, OxCAmL 65, –83, REn, REnAL, TwCA, –SUP, WhNAA, YABC 1*

Canfield, Jane White 1897-1984 *BioIn 13, –14, –15, ConAu 109, –112, NewYTBS 84, SmATA 32, –38N, WhAm 9, WhoAmA 73, –78, WhoAmW 75*

Canfield, Kenneth French 1909- *ConAu P-1*

Caniff, Milton *BioIn 14*

Caniff, Milton 1907- *ArtCS, AuNews 1, BioIn 1, –2, –3, –4, –5, –8, –9, –10, CelR, ConAu 85, CurBio 44, OhA&B, REnAL,*

WebAB 74, WhoAm 74, WhoAmA 73, WhoE 74, WhoWor 74, WorAl

Caniff, Milton 1907-1988 *ConAu 125, ConGrA 3, EncACom, SmATA 58, WorAlBi*

Caniff, Milton Arthur 1907-1988 *BioIn 17*

Cannam, Peggie 1925- *AuBYP 2, -3, BioIn 8, ConAu 13R*

Cannan, Joanna 1896-1961 *FemiCLE*

Cannan, Joanna 1898-1961 *BioIn 4, -8, -14, ConAu X, LongCTC, OxCChiL, TwCA, -SUP, TwCChW 89, TwCCr&M 80, -85, -91, WhoChL*

Canning, John 1920- *IntAu&W 82, WhoWor 82*

Canning, Victor *BioIn 14*

Canning, Victor 1911- *Au&Wr 71, BioIn 10, ConAu 13R, -6NR, EncMys, HalFC 84, -88, IntAu&W 77, LongCTC, Novels, TwCCr&M 80, -85, Who 74, -82, -83, -85, WhoSpyF, WorAu 1950, WrDr 76, -80, -82, -84, -86*

Canning, Victor 1911-1986 *AnObit 1986, ConAu 118, EncSF 93, ScF&FL 92, SpyFic, TwCCr&M 91*

Cannon, Beth 1951- *ConAu 69*

Cannon, Bettie 1922- *ConAu 126, IntAu&W 91, SmATA 59*

Cannon, Cornelia James *BioIn 16*

Cannon, Cornelia James 1876-1969 *AmAu&B, BioIn 4, -8, -13, ConAu 109, JBA 34, SmATA 28, TwCA, -SUP, WhAm 5, WhNAA*

Cannon, Grant Groesbeck 1911-1969 *BioIn 8, ConAu 117, WhAm 5*

Cannon, Ravenna *ConAu X, SmATA X*
Main entry: Mayhar, Ardath

Cansdale, George 1909- *Au&Wr 71, BioIn 1, ConAu 9R, Who 74*

Cansdale, George Soper 1909- *Who 88, -90*

Cansdale, George Soper 1909-1993 *ConAu 142*

Canton, William 1845-1926 *DcNaB 1922, OxCChiL*

Cantwell, Mary *ConAu 140, ForWC 70, WhoAm 74, -76, -78, -80, -82, -84, -86, -88, -90, -92, -94, WhoAmW 81*

Canty, Mary *AuBYP 2S, -3*

Canusi, Jose *BioIn 11, ConAu X, IntWWP 82X, SmATA X, WrDr 76, -80, -82, -84*
Main entry: Barker, S Omar

Canziani, Estella Louisa Michaela 1887-1964 *BioIn 1, ChhPo S1, ClaDrA, DcBrAr 1, DcBrBI, DcWomA, IlsCB 1744, TwCPaSc*

Cape, Peter Irwin 1929- *IntAu&W 77, WrDr 76, -80, -82, -84*

Capizzi, Michael 1941- *ConAu 41R*

Caplin, Alfred Gerald 1909-1979 *BioIn 1, -2, -3, -4, -5, -6, -8, -9, -11, -12, ConAu 57, SmATA 21N, WebAB 74, -79, WhAmArt 85*
Pseud./variant:
Capp, Al

Capone, Hester 1727-1801 *Alli, BiD&SB, BioIn 1, -3, BritAu, CarSB, CasWL, Chambr 2, ChhPo, DcEnL, DcLEL, EvLB, NewC, WebE&AL*

Capp, Al
Main entry: Caplin, Alfred Gerald

Capp, Al 1909-1979 *AmAu&B, ArtCS, BenetAL 91, BioIn 1, -2, -3, -4, -5, -6, -8, -9, -11, -12, -15, -17, BlueB 76, CelR, ConAu X, CurBio 47, -80N, EncACom, EncAJ, IntWW 74, REnAL, SmATA 61, -X, WebAB 74, -79, WhDW, WhAm 7, WhAmArt 85, WhScrn 83, WhoAm 74, -76, WhoAmA 73, -78, -80N, -82N, -89N, -91N, WhoWor 74, WorAlBi, WorAl*

Cappel, Constance 1936- *BioIn 13, ConAu 10NR, SmATA 22, WhoAmW 91, -93, WhoWest 89, -92, -94, WhoWor 91, -93*
Pseud./variant:
Montgomery, Constance

Capps, Benjamin Franklin 1922- *BioIn 11, -12, ConAu 5R, -7NR, EncFWF, SmATA 9, WhoAm 74, -80, WrDr 76, -80*

Capps, Clifford Lucille Sheats 1902- *ConAu 37R*

Captain Kangaroo *ConAu X, ConTFT 4, SmATA X*
Main entry: Keeshan, Robert J

Captain Young of Yale *MajAI*

Caputo, Philip *BioIn 15, -17*

Caputo, Philip 1941- *BiDConC, ConAu 40NR, TwCYAW, WorAu 1980*

Caraker, Mary *EncSF 93, ScF&FL 92*

Caraker, Mary 1929- *SmATA 74*

Caras, Roger A *BioIn 15, -16*

Caras, Roger A 1928- *CurBio 88, WrDr 86, –88, –90, –92*

Caras, Roger Andrew 1928- *AmAu&B, BioIn 11, ConAu 1R, –5NR, IntAu&W 77, –82, –86, –89, –91, SmATA 12, WhoAm 74, –76, –78, –80, –82, –84, –86, –88, –90, –92, –94, WhoE 74, WhoWor 74, WhoWorJ 72, –78, WhoWrEP 89, –92, WrDr 76, –80, –94*
Pseud./variant:
Sarac, Roger

Caraway, Caren 1939- *BioIn 16, SmATA 57*

Carbonnier, Jeanne 1894-1974 *BioIn 9, –14, ConAu P-2, SmATA 3, –34N*

Card, Orson Scott *BioIn 17, IntvTCA 2*

Card, Orson Scott 1951- *Au&Arts 11, ConAu 27NR, ConLC 44, –47, –50, EncSF 93, IntAu&W 91, MajTwCW, NewEScF, RGTwCSF, ScF&FL 92, ScFSB, TwCSFW 86, –91, TwCYAW, WhoAm 90, –92, –94, WrDr 88, –90, –92, –94*

Carden, Priscilla *AuBYP 2, –3, BioIn 7*

Cardozo, Lois *AuBYP 3*

Cardozo, Lois S *AuBYP 2, ConAu 1R*
Main entry: Arquette, Lois S

Cardozo, Peter 1916- *ConAu 61*

Cardwell, Paul *AuBYP 2S, –3*

Care, Felicity *ConAu X, SmATA X*
Main entry: Coury, Louise Andree

Careless, James Maurice Stockford 1919- *BlueB 76, CanWW 70, –80, –81, –83, –89, DrAS 74H, OxCCan, –SUP, WhoAm 80, –82, –84, WhoCan 82*

Carew, Dorothy 1910?-1973 *BioIn 9, ConAu 41R, NewYTBE 73*

Carew, Jan 1925- *Benet 87, BenetAL 91, BioIn 14, –15, –16, FifCWr, IntAu&W 91, LiExTwC, SmATA 51, WrDr 88, –90, –92*

Carew, Jan R 1925- *ScF&FL 92*

Carew, Jan Rynveld 1925- *BlkAuII, –92, WhoAm 86, –88, –90, WhoMW 86, WrDr 86, –94*

Carew, Jan Rynveld Alwin 1925- *BioIn 9, CasWL, ConAu 77, ConNov 72, –76, IntAu&W 82, SmATA 40, WhoMW 84, –86, WrDr 76, –80, –82, –84*

Carey, Bonnie 1941- *BioIn 12, SmATA 18*

Carey, Ernestine Gilbreth *WrDr 86, –88, –90, –92, –94*

Carey, Ernestine Gilbreth 1908- *Au&Wr 71, BioIn 1, –2, –9, ConAu 5R, ConLC 17, CurBio 49, IntAu&W 77, SmATA 2, WhoAm 74, –76, –78, –80, –82, –84, –86, –88, –90, –92, –94, WhoAmW 74, –81, –83, –87, –89, –91, –93, WhoWor 74, –82, –87, –89, –91, WrDr 76, –80, –82, –84*

Carey, M V
Main entry: Carey, Mary Virginia

Carey, Mary Virginia 1925- *ConAu 81, –17NR, –38NR, IntAu&W 82, –86, SmATA 39, –44, WhoAmW 83, –85, –87, –89*
Pseud./variant:
Carey, M V

Carey, Valerie Scho 1949- *BioIn 17, ConAu 128, SmATA 60*

Carey, Winifred Rosen
Main entry: Rosen, Winifred

Carigiet, Alois 1902- *BioIn 5, –8, –9, –13, ConAu 73, IlsBYP, IlsCB 1946, –1957, –1967, SmATA 24, ThrBJA, WhoGrA 62, –82*

Carigiet, Alois 1902-1985 *BioIn 14, –16, ConAu 119, SmATA 47N*

Carini, Edward 1923- *BioIn 11, ConAu 61, SmATA 9*

Carkeet, David *DrAPF 87, –89, –91, –93*

Carkeet, David 1946- *ConAu 38NR, ScF&FL 92, SmATA 75, WhoMW 92, WrDr 86, –88, –90, –92, –94*

Carle, Eric *BioIn 16, –17, ChlBIlD*

Carle, Eric 1929- *BioIn 9, –12, –13, ChhPo S2, ChlLR 10, ConAu 25R, –10NR, –25NR, FourBJA, IlsBYP, IlsCB 1967, IntAu&W 77, –82, –91, MajAI, OxCChiL, SmATA 4, –65, –6AS, TwCChW 89, WhoE 74, –75, –77, –81, –83, –85, –86, –89, WrDr 90, –92, –94*

Carleton, Barbee Oliver 1917- *ConAu 21R, DcAmChF 1960, ScF&FL 92*

Carleton, Captain L C *HsB&A, YABC 1*
Main entry: Ellis, Edward S

Carleton, R Milton 1899- *AuBYP 2S, BioIn 1, ConAu 69*

Carleton, R Milton 1899-1986 *AuBYP 3, ConAu 120*

Carley, V Royal 1906-1976 *BioIn 12, ConAu P-2, SmATA 20N, WrDr 76, –80*

Carlisle, Clark *ConAu X, SmATA 3, TwCCr&M 85, –91*
Main entry: Holding, James

Carlisle, Clark, Jr. *AuBYP 3*

Carlisle, Olga Andreyev *BioIn 14*

Carlisle, Olga Andreyev 1930- *AuBYP 2S, –3, ConAu 13R, –7NR, IntAu&W 77, SmATA 35*

Carloni, Giancarlo *BioIn 8, IlsBYP, IlsCB 1957*

Carlsen, G Robert 1917- *BioIn 14, ConAu 17R, –8NR, –24NR, IntAu&W 77, SmATA 30, WrDr 76, –80, –82, –84, –86, –88, –90, –92*

Carlsen, George Robert 1917- *WrDr 94*

Carlsen, Ruth 1918- *AuBYP 3*

Carlsen, Ruth C 1918- *ConAu 24NR*

Carlsen, Ruth Christoffer 1918- *AuBYP 2S, BioIn 9, ConAu 17R, –8NR, IntAu&W 77, SmATA 2, WhoAmW 75, WrDr 76, –80, –82, –84, –86, –88*

Carlson, Al *IlsBYP*

Carlson, Bernice Wells 1910- *AuBYP 2, –3, BioIn 1, –7, ConAu 5R, –2NR, ForWC 70, IntAu&W 77, –82, MichAu 80, SmATA 8, WrDr 76, –80, –82, –84, –86, –88, –90, –92, –94*

Carlson, Carl Walter 1907- *AmMWSc 73P, ConAu 49*

Carlson, Dale 1935- *AuBYP 3, ScF&FL 92, WhoE 86*

Carlson, Dale Bick 1935- *AuBYP 2S, BioIn 9, ConAu 9R, –3NR, SmATA 1, WhoAm 88, –90, –92, –94, WhoAmW 77, –81, –83, –85, –87, –89, –91, –93, WhoE 74, –75, –77, –89, –91, WhoWor 84, –87, –89, –91*

Carlson, Daniel 1960- *BioIn 13, ConAu 105, SmATA 27*

Carlson, Daniel B *ScF&FL 92*

Carlson, Esther Elisabeth 1920- *AuBYP 2, –3, BioIn 1, –7, ConAu 5R*

Carlson, Nancy L 1953- *BioIn 15, –16, ConAu 110, SmATA 45, –56*

Carlson, Natalie 1906- *AuBYP 3, WrDr 86, –88*

Carlson, Natalie S 1906- *BenetAL 91*

Carlson, Natalie Savage *BioIn 14, –15*

Carlson, Natalie Savage 1906- *AmAu&B, AmCath 80, AnCL, ArtclWW 2, AuBYP 2, Au&ICB, Au&Wr 71, BioIn 6, –7, –9, –10, –17, ConAu 1R, –3NR, DcAmChF 1960, ForWC 70, InWom SUP, IntAu&W 77, MajAI, MorBMP, MorJA, OxCChiL, REnAL, SmATA 2, –68, –4AS, TwCChW 78, –83, –89, WhoAm 76, –78, –80, –82, –84, –86, –88 –90, –92, –94, WhoAmW 74, –81, WhoUSWr 88, WhoWrEP 89, –92, WrDr 76, –80, –90, –92, –94*

Carlson, Richard Stocks 1942- *ConAu 57*

Carlson, Vada F 1897- *AuBYP 2S, –3, BioIn 12, ConAu 21R, –10NR, –28NR, SmATA 16*
Pseud./variant:
Rose, Florella

Carlstrom, Nancy White *AuBYP 3*

Carlstrom, Nancy White 1948- *BioIn 16, ConAu 121, SixBJA, SmATA 48, –53*

Carlton, Keith *AuBYP 3*

Carlyle, Thomas 1795-1881 *Alli, –SUP, AtlBL, Benet 87, BbD, BiD&SB, BioIn 1, –2, –3, –4, –5, –6, –7, –8, –9, –10, –11, –12, –13, –14, –15, –16, –17, BlmGEL, BritAu 19, BritWr 4, CamGEL, CamGLE, CasWL, CelCen, Chambr 3, ChhPo, –S1, –S2, CmScLit, CnDBLB 3, CrtT 3, CyEd, CyWA 58, DcAmSR, DcBiPP, DcEnA, DcEnL, DcEuL, DcLB 55, DcLEL, DcNaB, Dis&D, EvLB, FamAYP, LongCEL, LuthC 75, McGEWB, MouLC 3, NewC, NinCLC 22, OxCEng 67, –85, OxCMus, PenC ENG, RAdv 1, –13-1, –13-3, RComWL, REn, RfGEnL 91, WebE&AL, WhDW, WorAlBi, WorAl, WrPh*

Carlyon, Richard *BioIn 16, ScF&FL 92 SmATA 55*

Carmer, Carl Lamson 1893-1976 *AmAu&B, AuBYP 2, –3, Au&Wr 71, BioIn 2, –3, –4, –7, –11, –14, –15, ChhPo, –S1, –S2, ConAu 5R, –69, –4NR, OxCAmL 65, –83, REn, REnAL, SmATA 30N, –37, Str&VC, TwCA, –SUP, WhAm 7, WhoAm 74, –76, WhoWor 74*

Carmer, Elizabeth 1904- *AuBYP 3*

Carmer, Elizabeth Black 1904- *AuBYP 2, BioIn 2, –5, –8, IlsCB 1946, SmATA 24, WhAmArt 85*

Carmichael, Carrie *BioIn 15, ConAu X, SmATA 40*
Main entry: Carmichael, Harriet

Carmichael, Harriet *ConAu 115, SmATA X*
Pseud./variant:
Carmichael, Carrie

Carmichael, Joel 1915- *AuBYP 2S, -3, ConAu 1R, -2NR, IntAu&W 91, WrDr 86, -88, -90, -92, -94*

Carmichael, William Edward 1922- *ConAu 37R, WrDr 76, -80, -82, -84*

Carnahan, Marjorie R *AuBYP 2, -3, BioIn 8*

Carnan, Thomas *OxCChiL*

Carney, Julia A 1823-1908 *OxCChiL*

Carney, Julia Abigail 1823-1908 *InWom SUP*

Carol, Bill J *AmAu&B, AuBYP 2S, BioIn 9, ConAu X, IntAu&W 91X, SmATA 3, WrDr 76, -80, -82, -84, -86, -88, -90, -92*
Main entry: Knott, William Cecil, Jr.

Carol, Bill J 1927- *BioIn 14, WrDr 94*

Carona, Philip 1925- *AuBYP 3*

Carona, Philip Ben 1925- *AuBYP 2, BioIn 8, ConAu 1R, -4NR, WhoSSW 82*

Caroselli, Remus F 1916- *BioIn 14*

Caroselli, Remus Francis 1916- *AmMWSc 82, -86, -89, -92, ConAu 97, DcAmChF 1960, SmATA 36*

Carpelan, Bo *EncSF 93*

Carpelan, Bo 1926- *BioIn 11, -14, ConAu 49, -2NR, -27NR, EncWL 2, IntAu&W 82, IntWWP 82, PenC EUR, ScF&FL 92, SmATA 8*

Carpelan, Bo Gustaf Berelsson 1926- *DcScanL*

Carpelan, Bo Gustaf Bertellsson 1926- *ConWorW 93*

Carpenter, Allan 1917- *BioIn 9, -17, BlueB 76, ConAu 9R, -3NR, IntAu&W 77, -89, -91, SmATA 3, WhoAm 78, -80, -82, -84, -86, -88, -90, -92, -94, WhoMW 84, WhoWor 82, WhoWrEP 89, -92, WrDr 76, -80, -82, -84, -86, -88, -90, -92, -94*

Carpenter, Angelica Shirley 1945- *SmATA 71*

Carpenter, Edmund Janes 1845-1924 *AmAu&B, AmLY, DcAmAu, DcNAA, OxCCan*

Carpenter, Edmund Snow 1922?- *AuBYP 2S, -3*

Carpenter, Frances 1890-1972 *AmAu&B, AuBYP 2, -3, Au&Wr 71, BioIn 6, -8, -9, -13, ConAu 5R, -37R, -4NR, ForWC 70, MorJA, SmATA 3, -27N*

Carpenter, Healy Evans *AuBYP 3*

Carpenter, Humphrey 1946- *ChlFicS*

Carpenter, John 1948- *Au&Arts 2, CelR 90, ConAu 134, ConTFT 8, EncSF 93, HalFC 88, IntMPA 86, -88, -92, NewEScF, SmATA 58, WorAlBi, WorFDir 2*

Carpenter, Margaret Haley d1985 *AmAu&B, ChhPo S1, ConAu 5R, -116, DrAS 74E, -78E, -82E, ForWC 70, IntAu&W 77, -82, IntWWP 82, WhoAmW 75, -77*

Carpenter, Mia 1933- *IlrAm 1880, -G*

Carpenter, Patricia 1920- *AmMWSc 73S, -78S, BioIn 11, ConAu 29R, SmATA 11, WhoAm 82, -84, WhoAmW 77, -91, WhoE 81, -83, -85, WhoFrS 84, WhoUSWr 88, WhoWrEP 89, -92*
Pseud./variant:
Evans, Patricia Healy

Carper, Jean Elinor 1932- *ConAu 17R, -7NR*

Carper, L Dean 1931- *ConAu 49*

Carpozi, George, Jr. 1920- *ConAu 13R, -11NR, ScF&FL 92*

Carr, Albert Z 1902-1971 *AmAu&B, BioIn 9, ConAu 1R, -33R, NewYTBE 71, WhAm 5*

Carr, Archie 1909- *AmMWSc 73P, ConAu 13R, WhoAm 74, WhoWor 74*

Carr, Archie 1909-1987 *ConAu 122*

Carr, Archie F 1909-1987 *WhAm 9*

Carr, Emily 1871-1945 *ArtclWW 2, ArtsAmW 2, BenetAL 91, BioIn 1, -2, -3, -5, -7, -8, -9, -10, -11, -12, -13, -14, -15, -16, -17, BlmGWL, CamGLE, ContDcW 89, CreCan 1, DcLB 68, DcNAA, DcWomA, FemiCLE, InWom SUP, IntDcWB, LongCTC, OxCArt, OxCCan, OxCCanL, OxDcArt, PhDcTCA 77, REnAL, TwCLC 32*

Carr, Gene 1881-1959 *ArtCS, BioIn 5, -6, ObitOF 79, REnAL, WhAm 3, WhAmArt 85*

Carr, Glyn *BioIn 8, ConAu X, SmATA X, TwCCr&M 80, -85, Who 82, -83, -85, -88, -90, -92, WrDr 82, -84*
Main entry: Styles, Frank Showell

Carr, Glyn 1908- *IntAu&W 91, OxCLiW 86, TwCCr&M 91, WrDr 86, -88, -90, -92, -94*

Carr, Harriett Helen 1899- *AuBYP 2, -3, Au&Wr 71, BioIn 6, -8, -9, ConAu P-1, DcAmChF 1960, ForWC 70, MichAu 80, MorJA, SmATA 3*

Carr, Jo Crisler 1926- *ConAu 21R, IntAu&W 91, WrDr 76, -80, -82, -84, -86, -88, -90*

Carr, Mary Jane 1899- *AmCath 80, AuBYP 2, –3, BioIn 2, –3, –7, –9, –14, BkC 1, CathA 1952, ChhPo S2, ConAu P-1, JBA 51, SmATA 2*

Carr, Mary Jane 1899-1988 *BioIn 16, ConAu 124, SmATA 55N*

Carr, Philippa *ConAu 140, –X, –28NR, InWom SUP, IntAu&W 77X, –91X, Novels, SmATA 74, TwCCr&M 85, –91, TwCRHW 90, Who 74, –82, –83, –85, –88, –90, –92, WrDr 76, –80, –82, –84, –86, –88, –90, –92*
Main entry: Hibbert, Eleanor Burford

Carr, Philippa 1906- *BioIn 14*

Carr, Philippa 1906-1993 *WrDr 94N*

Carr, Rachel *AuBYP 3*

Carr, Rachel E *AuBYP 2S*

Carr, Terry *IntvTCA 2*

Carr, Terry 1937- *ConAu 81, ConSFA, IntAu&W 91, ScFSB, TwCSFW 86, WhoSciF, WrDr 84, –86, –88*

Carr, Terry 1937-1987 *AnObit 1987, NewEScF, ScF&FL 92, TwCSFW 91*

Carr, Terry Gene 1937-1987 *EncSF 93*

Carrick, Carol *BioIn 17*

Carrick, Carol 1935- *BioIn 10, ConAu 45, –1NR, –17NR, FourBJA, SmATA 7, –63, –18AS*

Carrick, Carol Hatfield 1935- *ConAu 37NR, DcAmChF 1985, MajAI*

Carrick, Donald *BioIn 16, –17*

Carrick, Donald 1929- *BioIn 10, –12, ConAu 53, –5NR, –20NR, FourBJA, IlsBYP, IlsCB 1967, MichAu 80, SmATA 7*

Carrick, Donald 1929-1989 *SmATA 63*

Carrick, Donald F 1929-1989 *ConAu 37NR, MajAI*

Carrick, Malcolm 1945- *BioIn 13, ConAu 77, –14NR, IntAu&W 77, –82, –89, –91, SmATA 28, WrDr 76, –80, –82, –84, –86, –88, –90, –92, –94*

Carrick, Valery 1869-1948 *AnCL, BioIn 1, –2, ChhPo, ConICB, IlsCB 1744, JBA 34, –51*

Carrier, Lark 1947- *BioIn 16, SmATA 50, –71*

Carrighar, Sally *AnCL, BioIn 3, –13, ConAu 93, OhA&B, SmATA 24*

Carrillo, Lawrence W 1920- *WrDr 86, –88, –90, –92, –94*

Carrillo, Lawrence Wilbert, Jr. 1920- *ConAu 13R, LEduc 74, WrDr 76, –80, –82, –84*

Carrington, Molly *ConAu X*
Main entry: Matthews, C M

Carrington, Richard 1921- *Au&Wr 71, ConAu 9R*

Carris, Joan Davenport 1938- *BioIn 15, ConAu 106, –27NR, SmATA 42, –44*

Carrison, Daniel Jordan 1917- *ConAu 37R, WhoAmP 73, WhoGov 72, WhoSSW 76*

Carroll, Archer Latrobe 1894- *SmATA 7*

Carroll, Curt *AuBYP 2, –3, ConAu X, SmATA 6*
Main entry: Bishop, Curtis Kent

Carroll, Elizabeth *ConAu 135, SmATA X, WrDr 90, –92, –94*
Main entry: Barkin, Carol
James, Elizabeth

Carroll, Elizabeth 1944- *WrDr 94*

Carroll, Gladys Hasty 1904- *AmAu&B, AmNov, ArtclWW 2, Au&Wr 71, BenetAL 91, BioIn 2, –4, –6, BlueB 76, ConAu 1R, –5NR, DcLB 9, ForWC 70, InWom SUP, IntAu&W 89, OxCAmL 65, –83, REnAL, TwCA, –SUP, WhNAA, WhoAm 74, –76, –78, –80, –82, –84, –86, –88, –90, –92, –94, WhoAmW 74 WhoE 74, WhoWor 74, WrDr 76, –80, –82, –84, –86, –88, –90, –92, –94*

Carroll, John Millar 1925- *AmMWSc 73P, –82, –86, –89, –92, ConAu 5R, –8NR, WhoLibI 82, WhoMW 74*

Carroll, Joseph T 1935- *Au&Wr 71, ConAu 102*

Carroll, Latrobe 1894- *BioIn 1, –3, –4 –5, –6, –10, ConAu 1R, –3NR, MorJA, ScF&FL 92*

Carroll, Laura *ConAu X, SmATA X*
Main entry: Parr, Lucy

Carroll, Lewis *Alli SUP, AnCL, AtlBL, AuBYP 2, –3, BbD, BiD&SB, BioIn 1, –2, –3, –4, –5, –6, –7, –8, –9, –10, –11, –12 –13, BritAu 19, BritWr 5, CasWL, Chamb 3, ChhPo, –S1, –S2, ChlLR 2, ChrP, CnE&AP, CrtT 3, CyWA 58, DcEnA, DcEnL, DcEuL, DcLB 18, DcLEL, DcNaB S1, Dis&D, EvLB, FamAYP, FamPYP, FilmgC, HalFC 84, ICPEnP A, InSci, JBA 34, LongCEL MacBEP, MajAI, McGEWB, NewC, NewYTBE 71, NinCLC 2, Novels, OxCChiL, OxCEng 67, –85, PenC ENG, RAdv 1, REn,*

Str&VC, SupFW, TelT, TwCChW 78A, –83A, WebE&AL, WhDW, WhoChL, WorAl, YABC X
Main entry: Dodgson, Charles Lutwidge

Carroll, Lewis 1832-1898 *Benet 87, BioIn 14, –15, –16, –17, BlmGEL, CamGEL, CamGLE, ChlLR 18, CnDBLB 4, EncSF 93, HalFC 88, MagSWL, NewEScF, RAdv 13-1, RfGEnL 91, ScFSB, StaCVF, SupFW, TwCChW 89A, WorAlBi, WorLitC, WrChl*

Carroll, Raymond *BioIn 16, SmATA 47*

Carroll, Raymond 1924- *ConAu 126, IntAu&W 91*

Carroll, Ruth Robinson 1899- *BioIn 3, –4, –5, –6, –8, ConAu 1R, IlsBYP, IlsCB 1946, –1957, MorJA*

Carruth, Ella *AuBYP 3*

Carruth, Ella Kaiser *AmWomPl, AuBYP 2S*

Carruth, Estelle 1910- *ConAu 9R*

Carruth, Hayden *DrAPF 87, –89, –91, –93, IntvTCA 2*

Carruth, Hayden 1862-1932 *AmAu&B, AmLY, BioIn 10, CarSB, ChhPo, –S1, –S2, REnAL, ScFEYrs, WhAm 1*

Carruth, Hayden 1921- *BenetAL 91, BioIn 16, –17, ConAu 38NR, ConPo 91, CurBio 92, MajTwCW, RAdv 13-1, SmATA 47, WhoAm 86, –88, –90, –92, –94, WhoUSWr 88, WhoWrEP 89, –92, WrDr 86, –88, –90, –92, –94*

Carryl, Charles E 1841-1920 *BioIn 15*

Carryl, Charles Edward 1841?-1920 *AmAu, AmAu&B, AnCL, BenetAL 91, BiD&SB, CarSB, ChhPo, –S2, DcAmAu, DcLB 42, DcNAA, EvLB, JBA 34, OxCAmL 65, –83, OxCChiL, REn, REnAL, Str&VC, TwCA, WhAm 2*

Carse, Robert 1902-1971 *BioIn 9, –10, ConAu 1R, –29R, –1NR, NewYTBE 71, ObitOF 79, SmATA 5*

Carson, Captain James *ConAu X, –26NR*
Main entry: Stratemeyer, Edward L

Carson, John F 1920- *ScF&FL 92*

Carson, John Franklin 1920- *AuBYP 2, –3, BioIn 8, –9, ConAu 13R, IndAu 1917, MichAu 80, SmATA 1*

Carson, Josephine *DrAPF 87, –89, –91, –93*

Carson, Josephine 1919- *BioIn 4*

Carson, Julia Margaret 1899- *AuBYP 3*

Carson, Julia Margaret Hicks 1899- *AuBYP 2, BioIn 8, OhA&B*

Carson, Rachel L 1907-1964 *Benet 87*

Carson, Rachel Louise 1907-1964 *AmAu&B, AnCL, BioAmW, BioIn 2, –3, –4, –5, –6, –7, –8, –9, –10, –11, –12, –13, ConAu 77, –35NR, ConIsC 2, CurBio 51, –64, DcAmB S7, DcScB S2, EncAB-H, EvLB, HerW, –84, InSci, InWom SUP, IntDcWB, LongCTC, MajTwCW, McGEWB, NewYTBS 82, NotAW MOD, ObitOF 79, OxCAmL 65, –83, OxCEng 85, REn, SmATA 23, TwCA SUP, TwCWr, WebAB 74, –79, WhAm 4*

Carson, Robert *SmATA X*
Main entry: Somerlott, Robert

Carson, Rosalind *SmATA X*
Main entry: Chittenden, Elizabeth F

Carson, S M *ConAu X, SmATA X*
Main entry: Gorsline, Marie

Carswell, Evelyn Medicus 1919- *AuBYP 2, –3, BioIn 8, ConAu 57, LEduc 74, WhoAmW 77*

Carswell, Leslie *ConAu X*
Main entry: Stephens, Rosemary

Carter, Ad 1895-1957 *ArtCS*

Carter, Alden R *BioIn 17, DrAPF 89, –91, –93*

Carter, Alden R 1947- *ChlLR 22, ConAu 135, SmATA 67, –18AS*

Carter, Alden Richardson 1947- *TwCYAW, WrDr 94*

Carter, Angela *ConDr 88B, IntvTCA 2*

Carter, Angela 1940- *ArtclWW 2, BioIn 13, –14, –16, BlmGEL, CamGLE, ConAu 53, –12NR, –36NR, ConDr 82B, ConIsC 1, ConLC 5, –41, ConNov 82, –91, ContDcW 89, DcLB 14, DcLEL 1940, EncBrWW, FemiCLE, InWom SUP, IntAu&W 77, –89, –91, IntWW 89, –91, MajTwCW, Novels, OxCEng 85, RAdv 13-1, ScFSB, SmATA 66, TwCRHW 90, TwCSFW 86, –91, Who 88, –90, –92, WhoHr&F, WorAu 1980, WrDr 84, –86, –88, –90, –92*

Carter, Angela 1940-1992 *AnObit 1992, BioIn 17, BlmGWL, NewYTBS 92, RfGShF, ScF&FL 92*

Carter, Angela Olive 1940-1992 *ConAu 136, SmATA 70*

Carter, Angela Olive Stalker 1940-1992 *EncSF 93, WrDr 94N*

Carter, Anne *ConAu X*
Main entry: Brooks, Anne Tedlock

Carter, Anthony L *OxCCan SUP*

Carter, Avis Martin *WrDr 82*

Carter, Avis Morton *WrDr 76, –80*
Main entry: Allen, Kenneth Sydney

Carter, Avis Murton *ConAu 32NR*

Carter, Bruce *AuBYP 2, –3, BioIn 6, –12, ConAu X, IntAu&W 91X, OxCChiL, SmATA X, TwCChW 78, –83, Who 74, –82, –83, –85, –88, –90, –92, WrDr 80, –82, –84, –86, –88, –90, –92*
Main entry: Hough, Richard Alexander

Carter, Bruce 1922- *EncSF 93, ScF&FL 92, ScFSB, TwCChW 89, WrDr 94*

Carter, Bruce 1930- *WhoAmA 86, –89, –91*

Carter, Dorothy Sharp 1921- *BioIn 11, ConAu 49, IntAu&W 77, SmATA 8, WhoAmW 77*

Carter, Ernest Frank 1899- *Au&Wr 71*

Carter, Forrest d1979 *BioIn 14, –17*

Carter, Forrest 1925-1979 *TwCWW 91*

Carter, Forrest 1927?-1979 *BioIn 11, ConAu 107, EncFWF, SmATA 32*

Carter, Frances Tunnell *IntAu&W 91, WhoAm 92, –94, WhoSSW 88, WrDr 86, –88, –90, –92*

Carter, Frances Tunnell 1922- *AmMWSc 73S, –78S, ConAu 37R, IntAu&W 77, IntWWP 82, LEduc 74, WhoAmW 74, –75, –77, –83, WhoSSW 73, –78, –80, –82, –84, WrDr 76, –80, –82, –84*

Carter, Helene 1887-1960 *BioIn 1, –5, –6, –12, DcWomA, IlsCB 1744, –1946, MorJA, SmATA 15, WhoAmA 82N, –86N, –89N, –91N*

Carter, Hodding 1907-1972 *AmAu&B, AmNov, AuBYP 2, BioIn 1, –2, –3, –4, –5, –6, –8, –9, –11, –13, ConAu 33R, –P-1, CurBio 46, –72, EncAJ, EncSoH, EncTwCJ, NewYTBE 72, ObitOF 79, SmATA 2, –27N, TwCA SUP, WhAm 5, WhoSSW 73*

Carter, Hodding, Jr. 1907-1972 *DcLB 127, EncAACR*

Carter, James *AuBYP 3*

Carter, John T 1921- *WrDr 88, –90, –92*

Carter, John Thomas 1921- *AmMWSc 73S, –78S, ConAu 33R, LEduc 74, WhoAm 94, WhoSSW 73, –86, WrDr 76, –80, –82, –84, –86, –94*

Carter, Joseph 1912-1984 *ConAu 49, –112*

Carter, Katharine J 1905- *BioIn 9, ConAu 5R, SmATA 2*

Carter, Mary Kennedy 1934- *BioIn 16, BlkAuII, –92*

Carter, Nick *ConAu 127, –X, –29NR, –30NR, –35NR, –37NR, –39NR, CrtSuMy, EncSF 93, IntAu&W 91X, MajAI, OxCAmL 83, ScF&FL 92, SmATA 67, –X, SpyFic, TwCCr&M 80, –85, –91, WrDr 82, –84, –86, –88, –90, –92, –94*
Main entry: Granbeck, Marilyn
Lynds, Dennis
Stratemeyer, Edward L

Carter, Page *AuBYP 2S, –3*

Carter, Peter 1929- *BioIn 16, ConAu 69, IntAu&W 91, OxCChiL, SmATA 57, TwCChW 78, –83, –89, WrDr 80, –82, –84, –86, –88, –90, –92, –94*

Carter, Phyllis Ann *AuBYP 2, –3, ConAu X, SmATA 2, –X*
Main entry: Eberle, Irmengarde

Carter, Robert F 1930- *DrAS 74H, –78H, –82H*

Carter, Russell Gordon *IntvTCA 2*

Carter, Russell Gordon 1892-1957 *AmAu&B, WhAm 3, WhNAA*

Carter, Samuel 1904- *BioIn 15*

Carter, Samuel 1904-1988 *BioIn 16, –17*

Carter, Samuel, III 1904- *ConAu 57, SmATA 37, WrDr 80, –82, –84, –86, –88, –90*

Carter, Samuel, III 1904-1988 *ConAu 127, SmATA 60*

Carter, William E *BioIn 14*

Carter, William E 1926-1983 *AuBYP 3*

Carter, William Earl 1926?-1983 *AmMWSc 73S, –76P, AuBYP 2, BioIn 8, –9, ConAu 17R, –110, FifIDA, SmATA 1 –35N, WhoFla, WhoSSW 75, –76, –78*

Carter, William Hodding 1907-1972 *AuBYP 3*

Cartey, Wilfred d1992 *NewYTBS 92*

Cartey, Wilfred 1931- *BioIn 16, BlkAuII, –92, BlkWr 1, ConAu 25NR*

Cartey, Wilfred 1931-1992 *AnObit 1992, BioIn 17*

Cartey, Wilfred G *InB&W 85*

Cartey, Wilfred G O 1931- *WhoBlA 85, –88, –90, –92*

Cartey, Wilfred G O 1931-1992 *WhoBlA 94N*

Cartey, Wilfred George Onslow 1931- *ConAu 73, WhoAm 82, –84, –86, –88, –90, WhoBlA 80, –85, WhoWor 82*

Cartey, Wilfred George Onslow 1931-1992 *BlkWr 2, ConAu 137, WhAm 10*

Carthy, John Dennis 1923- *Au&Wr 71*

Cartlidge, Michelle 1950- *BioIn 15, –16, ConAu 93, SmATA 37, –49*

Cartner, William Carruthers 1910- *BioIn 11, ConAu 73, SmATA 11*

Carton, Lonnie Caming 1928- *ChhPo*

Cartwright, Reg *BioIn 17*

Cartwright, Reg 1938- *SmATA 64, TwCPaSc*

Cartwright, Sally 1923- *AuBYP 2S, –3, BioIn 11, ConAu 49, –2NR, SmATA 9*

Carty, Leo 1931- *AfroAA, BioIn 16, BlkAuII, –92, IlsBYP, IlsCB 1967*

Carus, Marianne 1928- *IntAu&W 86, –89, –91, LEduc 74, WhoAm 86, –88, –90, –92, –94, WhoAmW 87, –89, –91, –93*

Carver, John *ConAu X, SmATA X*
Main entry: Gardner, Richard M

Carver, Saxon Rowe 1905- *ConAu P-1*

Carwell, L'Ann *AuBYP 3, BlkWr 2, ConAu 38NR, MajAI, SmATA 73*
Main entry: McKissack, Patricia L'Ann Carwell

Cary *DcNaB, IlsBYP, SmATA X, Who 82, –83, –85, –88, –90, –92*
Main entry: Cary, Louis F

Cary, Alice 1820-1871 *Alli SUP, AmAu, AmAu&B, AmWomWr 92, ArtclWW 2, BenetAL 91, BbD, BiD&SB, BioAmW, BioIn 5, BlmGWL, CarSB, Chambr 3, ChhPo, –S1, CyAL, DcAmAu, DcNAA, EvLB, FemiCLE, InWom SUP, OhA&B, OxCAmL 65, –83, WebAB 74, –79, WhAm HS*

Cary, Barbara Knapp 1912?-1975 *BioIn 14, ConAu 61, SmATA 31N*

Cary, Louis F 1915- *BioIn 11, SmATA 9*
Pseud./variant:
Cary

Cary, Sturges Flagler 1913- *WhoAm 78, –80*

Caryl, Jean
Main entry: Kaplan, Jean Caryl Korn

Caryl, Jean 1926- *AuBYP 2, –3, BioIn 8, –11, ConAu X, SmATA X*

Casagrande, Louie B *AuBYP 3*

Case, Dianne 1955- *DcChlFi*

Case, Elinor 1914- *AuBYP 3*

Case, Elinor Rutt 1914- *AuBYP 2, BioIn 8, ConAu 1R*

Case, Geoffrey *ConAu 77*

Case, Marshal Taylor 1941- *BioIn 11, ConAu 57, SmATA 9, WhoE 75, –77, WhoSSW 78*

Case, Michael *ConAu X, SmATA 5*
Main entry: Howard, Robert West

Caseley, Judith *AuBYP 3*

Caseley, Judith 1951- *BioIn 16, ConAu 121, SmATA 53*

Casewit, Curtis 1922- *BioIn 9, ConAu 13R, –6NR, SmATA 4, WhoWest 76, –78*
Pseud./variant:
Green, D
Vernor, D
Werner, K

Casewit, Curtis W 1922- *ConAu 21NR*

Casewit, Curtis Werner 1922- *EncSF 93*

Casey, Brigid 1950- *BioIn 11, ConAu 49, –28NR, SmATA 9*

Casey, Denise *AuBYP 3*

Cash, Ellen Lewis Buell d1989 *NewYTBS 89*

Cash, Ellen Lewis Buell 1905-1989 *BioIn 16, –17, ConAu 130, SmATA 64*
Pseud./variant:
Buell, Ellen Lewis

Cashin, Edward L 1927- *ConAu 21R, –X, DrAS 74H*

Cashman, Tony *OxCCan SUP*

Casilla, Robert 1959- *SmATA 75*

Caskoden, Edwin *DcAmAu, DcNAA, WhAm 1*
Main entry: Major, Charles

Cason, Mabel Earp 1892-1965 *BioIn 11, ConAu P-1, SmATA 10*
Pseud./variant:
Bell, Emily Mary

Cass, Joan *AuBYP 3*

Cass, Joan E *ConAu 20NR, IntAu&W 91, WrDr 88, –90, –92*

Cass, Joan Evelyn *AuBYP 2, Au&Wr 71, BioIn 8, –9, ConAu 1R, –5NR, IntAu&W 77, SmATA 1, WrDr 76, –80, –82, –84, –86, –94*

Cass-Beggs, Barbara *OxCCan SUP*

Cass-Beggs, Barbara 1904- *BioIn 17, SmATA 62*

Cassedy, Sylvia 1930- *AuBYP 2S, BioIn 13, ChhPo S2, ConAu 105, –22NR, SmATA 27, WhoWrEP 89, –92, WrDr 90*

Cassedy, Sylvia 1930-1989 *AuBYP 3, BioIn 16, –17, ChlLR 26, DcAmChF 1985, ScF&FL 92, SixBJA, SmATA 61, –77, TwCChW 89, TwCYAW*

Cassel, Lili
Main entry: Wronker, Lili Cassel

Cassel, Lili 1924- *BioIn 4, –5, ChhPo, IlsCB 1946, SmATA X*

Cassell, Sylvia 1924- *ConAu 5R, ForWC 70, WhoAmW 74, –75, WhoMW 74*

Casselle, Corene Flowerette 1943- *BlkAWP*

Casserley, Anne *BioIn 2, JBA 34, –51*

Cassiday, Bruce 1920- *ConAu 1R, –4NR, –19NR, ScF&FL 92*

Cassidy, Vincent H 1923- *ConAu 21R, DrAS 74H, –78H, –82H*

Cassilis, Ina Leon *Alli SUP, AmWomPl*

Casson, Hugh Maxwell 1910- *BioIn 17, ConAu 20NR, –36NR, IntWW 91, SmATA 65*

Casson, Hugh Maxwell, Sir 1910- *IntWW 89*

Casson, Lionel 1914- *Au&Wr 71, ConAu 9R, –3NR, DrAS 74H, –78H, –82H*

Castaneda, Omar S 1954- *SmATA 71*

Castellanos, Jane 1913- *AuBYP 3*

Castellanos, Jane Mollie Robinson 1913- *AuBYP 2S, BioIn 11, ConAu 9R, SmATA 9*

Castellon, Federico 1914-1971 *BioIn 2, –5, –9, –16, DcCAA 71, –77, –88, GrAmP, IlsCB 1946, NewYTBE 71, SmATA 48, WhAmArt 85*

Castex, Pierre-Georges 1915- *IntAu&W 77, –82*

Castillo, Edmund Luis 1924- *AuBYP 2, –3, BioIn 8, –9, ConAu 29R, SmATA 1, WhoGov 77, –75, WhoSSW 75, –76, WrDr 76, –80, –82, –84*

Castle, Lee *ConAu X, SmATA X*
Main entry: Ogan, George F
Ogan, Margaret E

Castle, Lee d1990 *BioIn 17, NewYTBS 90*

Castle, Lee 1915- *PenEncP*

Castle, Paul *AuBYP 3, ConAu 139, –X, SmATA 73, –X*
Main entry: Howard, Vernon Linwood

Castlemon, Harry *Alli SUP, AmAu, AmAu&B, BenetAL 91, BiD&SB, BioIn 1, DcAmAu, DcNAA, OxCAmL 65, –83, OxCChiL, REnAL*
Main entry: Fosdick, Charles Austin

Castlemon, Harry 1842-1915 *BioIn 15*

Castor, Henry 1909- *AuBYP 2, –3, BioIn 8, ConAu 17R*

Castor, Pere *TwCChW 83B 89B*

Caswell, Helen 1923- *AuBYP 3*

Caswell, Helen Rayburn 1923- *AuBYP 2S, BioIn 11, ConAu 33R, OxCCan SUP, SmATA 12, WhoAmA 73, –78, –80, –82, –84, –86, –89, –91, WhoWest 84*

Catalano, Dominic 1956- *SmATA 76*

Catalanotto, Peter *ChlBIlD*

Catalanotto, Peter 1959- *SmATA 70*

Cate, Dick *ChlFicS*

Cate, Richard Edward Nelson 1932- *BioIn 13, ConAu 73, SmATA 28*

Cather, Carolyn *IlsBYP*

Cather, Willa S 1873-1947 *BioAmW*

Cather, Willa Sibert 1873?-1947 *AmAu&B, AmWr, ArtclWW 2, AtlBL, BioIn 1, –2, –3, –4, –5, –6, –7, –8, –9, –10, –11, –12, –13,*

CasWL, Chambr 3, ChhPo, –S1, CnDAL, ConAmA, ConAmL, ConAu 104, –128, CyWA 58, DcBiA, DcLB 9, –DS1, DcLEL, DcNAA, EncAB-H, EncFWF, EncWL, –2, EvLB, HerW, –84, InWom SUP, IntDcWB, JBA 34, LongCTC, MajTwCW, McGEWB, ModAL, –S1, –S2, MorMA, Novels, ObitOF 79, OxCAmH, OxCAmL 65, –83, OxCCan, OxCCanL, OxCEng 67, –85, PenC AM, RAdv 1, RComWL, REn, REnAL, SmATA 30, TwCA, –SUP, TwCLC 1, –11, TwCWr, WebAB 74, –79, WebE&AL, WhDW, WhAm 2, WhNAA, WhoTwCL, WomWWA 14, WomNov, WorAl

Cather, Willa Sibert 1876-1947 *DcAmImH*

Catherall, Arthur 1906- *AuBYP 3*

Catherall, Arthur 1906-1980 *AuBYP 2, Au&Wr 71, BioIn 8, –9, ConAu 5R, –38NR, IntAu&W 77, –82, MajAI, OxCChiL, SmATA 3, –74, TwCChW 78, –83, –89, WrDr 76, –80*
Pseud./variant:
Baltimore, J
Corby, Dan
Maine, Trevor
Peters, Linda
Ruthin, Margaret

Catherwood, Mary Hartwell 1847-1902 *Alli SUP, AmAu, AmAu&B, ArtclWW 2, BbD, BiD&SB, BioIn 1, –2, BlmGWL, DcAmAu, DcBiA, DcLB 78, DcLEL, DcNAA, InWom SUP, IndAu 1816, JBA 34, OhA&B, OxCAmL 65, REnAL, WhAm 1*

Cathon, Laura E 1908-1991 *BioIn 17*

Cathon, Laura Elizabeth 1908- *BiDrLUS 70, BioIn 13, ConAu 5R, ForWC 70, SmATA 27, WhoLibS 55, –66*

Catlin, George 1777?-1852 *NewGrDA 86*

Catlin, George 1796-1872 *Alli, –SUP, AmAu, AmAu&B, ArtsNiC, AtlBL, Benet 87, BenetAL 91, BbD, BiD&SB, BiInAmS, BioIn 1, –3, –4, –5, –6, –7, –9, –10, –11, –12, –13, –14, –15, –17, BriEAA, CasWL, DcAmAu, DcBiPP, DcEnL, DcLEL, DcNAA, EncAB-H, EvLB, HarEnUS, InSci, McGEWB, MemAm, OxCAmH, OxCAmL 65, –83, OxDcArt, REn, REnAL, WebAB 74, –79, WhAm HS, WhNaAH, WorAlBi, WorAl*

Catlin, Wynelle 1930- *ConAu 65, SmATA 13*

Catling, Patrick Skene 1925- *BioIn 6, ConAu 115, ScF&FL 92, WrDr 76, –80, –82, –84*

Catton, Bruce 1899-1978 *Alli SUP, AmAu&B, AuNews 1, Benet 87, BenetAL 91, BioIn 3, –4, –5, –6, –7, –8, –9, –10, –11, –12, –13, –15, –17, BioNews 74, BlueB 76, CelR, ConAu 5R, –81, –7NR, ConLC 35, CurBio 54, –78N, DcLB 17, DcLEL 1940, EncSoH, IntAu&W 77, IntWW 74, –75, –76, –77, –78, –79N, JrnUS, MichAu 80, ObitOF 79, OxCAmL 65, –83, PenC AM, RAdv 13-3, REn, REnAL, SmATA 2, –24N, TwCA SUP, WebAB 74, –79, WhAm 7, Who 74, WhoAm 74, –76, –78, WhoWor 74, –78, WorAlBi, WorAl, WrDr 76*

Catz, Max *ConAu X, SmATA X*
Main entry: Glaser, Milton

Caudell, Marian *BioIn 16*

Caudell, Marian 1930- *ConAu 121, SmATA 52*

Caudill, Rebecca 1899- *WrDr 86*

Caudill, Rebecca 1899-1985 *AmAu&B, AuBYP 2, –3, BioIn 2, –6, –7, –9, –10, –14, –15, ChhPo S1, ConAu 5R, –117, –2NR, CurBio 50, –86N, DcAmChF 1960, ForWC 70, LiHiK, MajAI, MorJA, SmATA 1, –44N, TwCChW 78, –83, –89, TwCYAW, WhAm 9, WhoAm 74, –76, –78, –80, –82, –84, WhoAmW 74, WrDr 76, –82, –84*

Cauley, Lorinda Bryan 1951- *BioIn 15, –16, ConAu 101, SixBJA, SmATA 43, –46*

Caulfield, Peggy F 1926- *ConAu 5R*

Caulfield, Peggy F 1926-1987 *BioIn 16, ConAu 123, SmATA 53N*

Cauman, Sam 1910-1971 *BioIn 9, ConAu P-2*

Cauman, Samuel 1910-1971 *BioIn 16, SmATA 48*

Causley, Charles *IntvTCA 2*

Causley, Charles 1917- *AuBYP 2, –3, Au&Wr 71, BioIn 8, –9, –10, –12, –14, –17, BlmGEL, BlueB 76, CamGLE, ChhPo, –S1, –S2, ChlLR 30, CnE&AP, ConAu 9R, –5NR, –35NR, ConLC 7, ConPo 70, –75, –80, –85, –91, DcLB 27, EngPo, IntAu&W 77, –82, –91, LongCTC, MajTwCW, NewC, OxCChiL, OxCEng 85, SmATA 3, –66, TwCChW 78, –83, –89, WebE&AL, WhDW, Who 74, WhoWor 74, WorAu 1950, WrDr 76, –80, –82, –84, –86, –88, –90, –92*

Causley, Charles Stanley 1917- *WrDr 94*

Cavallaro, Ann 1918- *BioIn 17, SmATA 62*
Pseud./variant:
Abelson, Ann

Cavallo, Diana *DrAPF 87, –89, –91, –93*

Cavallo, Diana 1931- *AmAu&B, BioIn 10, ConAu 1R, –2NR, DrAPF 83, –85, SmATA 7,*

WhoAm 74, –76, –78, –80, –82, –84, –86, –88, –90, WhoAmW 74, WhoE 74, WrDr 76, –80, –82, –84, –86, –88, –90, –92, –94

Cavanagh, Helen 1939- *BioIn 15, –16, ConAu 104, SmATA 37, –48*

Cavanah, Frances 1899-1982 *AuBYP 2, –3, BioIn 2, –3, –6, –7, –9, –14, ConAu 13R, –133, CurBio 54, ForWC 70, IndAu 1917, IntAu&W 77, MorJA, SmATA 1, –31, WhNAA, WhoAmW 74, –75, WhoSSW 73*

Cavanna, Betty 1909- *AuBYP 2, –3, Au&Wr 71, BioIn 2, –6, –7, –9, –14, –15, ConAu 9R, –6NR, ConLC 12, CurBio 50, DcAmChF 1960, IntAu&W 77, –82, –89, –91, MajAI, MorJA, SmATA 1, –30, –4AS, TwCChW 78, –83, –89, TwCYAW, WrDr 76, –80, –82, –84, –86, –88, –90, –92, –94*
Pseud./variant:
Allen, Betsy
Harrison, Elizabeth Cavanna
Headley, Elizabeth

Cave, Kathryn 1948- *SmATA 76*

Cavin, Ruth 1918- *BioIn 15, ConAu 61, –8NR, SmATA 38*
Pseud./variant:
Brodie, Sally
Soble, Jennie

Cavoukian, Raffi 1948- *ConAu 136, SmATA 68, WhoAm 94*
Pseud./variant:
Raffi

Cawley, Winifred 1915- *ConAu 69, IntAu&W 82, SmATA 13, TwCChW 78, –83, –89, WrDr 80, –82, –84, –86, –88, –90, –92, –94*

Caxton, Pisistratus *SmATA X*
Main entry: Lytton, Edward G E Lytton Bulwer-

Cazeau, Charles J 1931- *AmMWSc 86, –89, –92, BioIn 17, SmATA 65*

Cazeau, Charles Jay 1931- *AmMWSc 73P, –76P, –82, ConAu 104, WhoE 75, –77*

Cazet, Denys 1938- *BioIn 15, –16, ConAu 108, SmATA 41, –52, WrDr 90, –92, –94*

Cazzola, Gus 1934- *SmATA 73*

Cebulash, Mel 1937- *BioIn 11, ConAu 29R, –12NR, –30NR, IntAu&W 77, ScF&FL 92, SmATA 10, WhoE 75, WrDr 76, –80, –82, –84, –86, –88, –90, –92, –94*
Pseud./variant:
Farrell, Ben
Harlan, Glen
Jansen, Jared
Mara, Jeanette

Ceder, Georgiana Dorcas *AmAu&B, BioIn 2, –11, ConAu 1R, SmATA 10*
Pseud./variant:
Dor, Ana

Celender, Donald Dennis 1931- *WhoAm 80, WhoAmA 73, –78, –80, –82, –84, –86, –89*

Celestino, Martha Laing 1951- *BioIn 15, ConAu 107, SmATA 39*
Pseud./variant:
Laing, Martha

Cellini, Eva *IlsBYP*

Cellini, Joseph 1924- *BioIn 8, IlsBYP, IlsCB 1957, –1967, WhoAmA 80, –82, –84, –86, –89, –91*

C E M *SmATA 70*
Main entry: Martin, Charles E

Cerf, Bennett 1898-1971 *AuBYP 3, BenetAL 91, BioIn 15*

Cerf, Bennett A 1898-1971 *WorAlBi*

Cerf, Bennett Alfred 1898-1971 *AmAu&B, AuBYP 2, Au&Wr 71, BiE&WWA, BioIn 1, –2, –3, –4, –5, –6, –7, –8, –9, –10, –11, –12, –13, ConAu 29R, –P-2, CurBio 41, –58 –71, EncAHmr, NewYTBE 71, PlP&P, REn, REnAL, SmATA 7, WebAB 74, –79, WhAm 5, WorAl*

Cerf, Christopher *BioIn 14*

Cerf, Christopher 1941- *BioIn 9, ConAu 25R, ConSFA, ScF&FL 92, SmATA 2*

Cermak, Martin
Main entry: Duchacek, Ivo Duka

Cervantes, Miguel S De 1547-1616 *AtlBL, BbD, BiD&SB, BioIn 1, –2, –3, –4, –5 –6, –7, –8, –9, –10, –11, CasWL, ChhPo S2, CnThe, CyWA 58, DcBiA, DcEuL, DcSpL, EuAu, EvEuW, McGEWD 72, NewC, OxCEng 67, PenC EUR, RComWL, REn, REnWD*

Cervon, Jacqueline *ConAu X, SmATA X*
Main entry: Moussard, Jacqueline

Cetin, Frank Stanley 1921- *BioIn 9, ConAu 1R, SmATA 2*

Chabot, Cecile 1907- *CanWr, CreCan 1, OxCCan*

Chace, Isobel *TwCRHW 90*

Chace, Isobel 1934- *BioIn 14, WrDr 84, -86, -88, -90, -92, -94*

Chaconas, D J 1938- *AuBYP 2S, -3, ConAu 21R*

Chadwick, Doris *DcChlFi, SingR 1*

Chadwick, Lester *ConAu P-2, SmATA 1, -67*
Main entry: Stratemeyer, Edward L

Chafe, James Warren 1900- *CanWW 70, -80, -81, -83*

Chafetz, Henry 1916-1978 *AuBYP 2, -3, BioIn 7, -11, ConAu 1R, -73, -3NR*

Chaffee, Allen *AmAu&B, BioIn 9, ConAu P-1, SmATA 3, WhNAA, WrDr 76*

Chaffey, M Ella *OxCChiL*

Chaffin, Lillie 1925- *AuBYP 3*

Chaffin, Lillie D *DrAPF 87, -89, WhoWrEP 89, WrDr 86, -88, -90*

Chaffin, Lillie D 1925- *AuBYP 2S, BioIn 9, ConAu 33R, -13NR, DrAF 76, DrAPF 83, -85, ForWC 70, IntAu&W 77, -82, IntWWP 82, LiHiK, SmATA 4, WhoAmW 74, -75, WhoUSWr 88, WhoWrEP 92, WrDr 76, -82, -84*

Chaffin, Lillie Dorton 1925- *DcAmChF 1960*

Chai, Winberg 1932- *AmMWSc 73S, ConAu 5R, -9NR, WhoAm 82, -84, -86, -88, -90, -92, -94, WhoMW 80, -82, -84, -86, -88, WhoWest 89, -94, WhoWor 82, -87, -89, -91*

Chaikin, Miriam 1928- *BioIn 13, -16, ConAu 81, -14NR, ForWC 70, SixBJA, SmATA 24*

Chaillu, Paul Belloni Du
Main entry: DuChaillu, Paul Belloni

Chaillu, Paul Belloni Du 1835-1903 *BioIn 1, -10, -11, -13, CelCen, Chambr 3, DcEnL, JBA 34*

Challand, Helen J *AuBYP 3*

Challand, Helen J 1921- *ConAu 118, -121, SmATA 64*

Challans, Mary *AuBYP 3, InWom SUP, IntvTCA 2*

Challans, Mary 1905-1983 *BioIn 14, -16, ConAu 81, -111, DcNaB 1981, IntAu&W 77X, NewC, SmATA 23, -36N, Who 74, -82, -83, WorAu 1950, WrDr 76, -82, -84*
Pseud./variant:
Renault, Mary

Chalmers, Audrey 1899- *AuBYP 3*

Chalmers, Audrey 1899?-1957 *AuBYP 2, BioIn 1, -4, -5, -7, IlsCB 1744, -1946, WhAmArt 85*

Chalmers, John W 1910- *CaW, ConAu 93*

Chalmers, Mary 1927- *AuBYP 3, IntAu&W 89, SmATA 14AS, TwCChW 89, WrDr 86, -88, -90, -92*

Chalmers, Mary Eileen 1927- *AmPB, AuBYP 2, BioIn 5, -8, -9, -10, ChhPo, ConAu 5R, IlsCB 1946, -1957, -1967, OxCChiL, SmATA 6, ThrBJA, TwCChW 83, WhoAmA 80, -82, WrDr 94*

Chalmers, Mary Eilleen 1927- *IntAu&W 91*

Chalon, John *WrDr 76, -80, -82, -84*

Chamberlain, Christopher 1918- *ArtsCL, BioIn 6, -8, DcBrAr 1, IlsCB 1957, TwCPaSc*

Chamberlain, Elinor 1901- *AuBYP 2, -3, BioIn 8, ConAu P-1, ForWC 70, MichAu 80*

Chamberlain, Joseph Miles 1923- *AmMWSc 73P, -76P, -82, -86, -89, -92, ConAu 107, WhoAm 74, -76, -78, -80, -82, -84, -86, -88, -90, -92, -94, WhoMW 88, -90, -92, -93*

Chamberlain, Margaret 1954- *BioIn 15, SmATA 46*

Chamberlin, Eric Russell 1926- *Au&Wr 71, ConAu 97*

Chamberlin, Jo Hubbard *AuBYP 2, -3, BioIn 8*

Chamberlin, William Henry 1897-1969 *AmAu&B, BioIn 2, -4, -5, -8, DcLB 29, JrnUS, OxCAmL 65, OxCCan, REnAL, TwCA, -SUP, WhAm 5*

Chambers, Aidan 1934- *Au&Wr 71, BioIn 9, -16, ChhPo S2, ChlFicS, ConAu 25R, -12NR, -31NR, ConLC 35, IntAu&W 77, -82, -86, -89, -91, MajAI, OxCChiL, ScF&FL 92, SixBJA, SmATA 1, -69, -12AS, TwCChW 83, -89, TwCYAW, WrDr 84, -86, -88, -90, -92, -94*
Pseud./variant:
Blacklin, Malcolm

Chambers, Bradford 1922-1984 *AuBYP 2S, -3, BioIn 14, -15, ConAu 113, NewYTBS 84, SmATA 39N*

Chambers, C Bosseron 1883- *ConICB, WhAmArt 85*

Chambers, Catherine E *ConAu 32NR, SmATA X, WrDr 94*
Main entry: Johnston, Norma

Chambers, Edward James 1925- *AmEA 74, AmMWSc 73S, -78S, ConAu 17R, WhoAm 74, -76, -78*

Chambers, Henry Alban 1902- *WhoMus 72*

Chambers, John W 1933- *BioIn 15, -16, ConAu 124, SmATA 46, -57*

Chambers, Margaret Ada Eastwood 1911- *Au&Wr 71, BioIn 9, ConAu 9R, IntAu&W 77, SmATA 2*
Pseud./variant:
Chambers, Peggy

Chambers, Peggy
Main entry: Chambers, Margaret Ada Eastwood

Chambers, Robert W 1865-1933 *BenetAL 91, BioIn 15, PenEncH, ScF&FL 92, ScFEYrs, SupFW, TwCLC 41, TwCRHW 90*

Chambers, Robert Warner *AuBYP 3*

Chambers, Robert Warner 1924- *AmMWSc 73P, -76P, -82, AuBYP 2, BioIn 8, WhoAm 76, -78, -80, -82*

Chambers, Robert William 1865-1933 *AmAu&B, BbD, BiD&SB, CarSB, Chambr 3, ChhPo, -S2, DcAmAu, DcBiA, DcLEL, DcNAA, EncSF 93, OxCAmL 65, -83, REnAL, SupFW, TwCA, WhAmArt 85*

Champney, Elizabeth Williams 1850-1922 *AmAu&B, BbD, BiD&SB, CarSB, ChhPo, -S1, DcAmAu, DcNAA, OhA&B, WhAm 1, WomWWA 14*

Champney, Lizzie Williams 1850-1922 *ArtsNiC, OxCChiL*

Chan, Plato 1931 *BioIn 1, IlsCB 1744*

Chan, Plato X 1931- *BioIn 14*

Chance, John Newton *EncSF 93, ScF&FL 92*

Chance, John Newton 1911-1983 *AnObit 1983, BioIn 14, ConAu 102, -110, CrtSuMy, TwCCr&M 80, -85, -91, WrDr 82, -84*

Chance, Stephen *ConAu X, IntAu&W 77X, -82X, -86X, -91X, TwCChW 78, -83, -89, WrDr 80, -82, -84, -86, -88, -90, -92*
Main entry: Turner, Philip

Chance, Stephen 1925- *WrDr 94*

Chancellor, John 1900-1971 *Au&Wr 71, ConAu P-2*

Chandler, Anna Curtis 1890?-1969 *BioIn 8, ChhPo*

Chandler, Caroline Augusta 1906-1979 *AmAu&B, AmCath 80, AmMWSc 73S, -78S, AuBYP 2, -3, BiDrAPA 77, BioIn 1, -8, -13, BkC 4, CathA 1930, ConAu 17R, -93, SmATA 22N, -24, WhAm 7, WhoAm 74, -76, -78, -80, WhoAmW 74*

Chandler, David Leon *ConAu 49, -1NR, -16NR*

Chandler, David Leon 1937?- *ConAu 38NR*

Chandler, David Lewis 1926- *CanWW 80, -81, -83, WhoCan 80, -82, -84, WhoFI 83*

Chandler, David Porter 1933- *BioIn 13, ConAu 45, -29NR, SmATA 28*

Chandler, Edna Walker 1908-1982 *AuBYP 2, -3, BioIn 8, -11, -14, ConAu 1R, -108, -4NR, SmATA 11, -31N, WhoAmW 77*

Chandler, Linda S 1929- *BioIn 15, ConAu 106, -23NR, SmATA 39, WhoWrEP 89*

Chandler, Linda Smith 1929- *WhoWrEP 92*

Chandler, Robert 1953- *BioIn 15, ConAu 112, SmATA 40*

Chandler, Ruth Forbes 1894-1978 *AuBYP 2, -3, BioIn 7, -9, -13, ConAu 1R, -103, SmATA 2, -26N, WrDr 76*

Chandler, Thomas 1911- *AuBYP 2, -3, BioIn 8*

Chandler, Tony John 1928- *Au&Wr 71, IntAu&W 77, Who 74, -82, -83, -85, -88, -90, -92*

Chaneles, Sol 1926- *AmMWSc 73S, -78S, AuBYP 2S, -3, ConAu 41R*

Chaney, Jill 1932- *ConAu 25R, -11NR, TwCChW 83, -89, WrDr 76, -80, -82, -84, -86, -88, -90, -92, -94*
Pseud./variant:
Leeming, Jill

Chang, Isabelle C 1925- *WrDr 86, -88, -90*

Chang, Isabelle Chin 1924- *BiDrLUS 70, ConAu 21R, IntAu&W 77, -82, WhoAmW 74, WrDr 76, -80, -82, -84*

Chang, Margaret Scrogin 1941- *SmATA 71*

Chang, Raymond *SmATA 71*

Channel, A R *BioIn 9, ConAu X, -38NR, MajAI, SmATA 3, -74, TwCChW 83, -89*

Chaning-Renton, E M 1895- *WhoLA, WrDr 76*

Chanover, Hyman 1920- *BioIn 16, ConAu 49, –2NR, IntAu&W 77, WhoAmJ 80, WhoWorJ 72, –78*

Chant, Donald A 1928- *AmMWSc 86, –89, –92*

Chant, Donald Alfred 1928- *AmMWSc 82, CanWW 70, –80, –81, –83, ConAu 101, –18NR, WhoAm 80, –82, –84, –86, –88, –90, WhoCan 80, –82*

Chant, Eileen Joyce 1945- *ConAu 61*

Chapian, Marie 1938- *BioIn 13, ConAu 106, –22NR, SmATA 29*

Chapin, Alene Olsen Dalton d1986 *BioIn 16*

Chapin, Alene Olsen Dalton 1915?-1986 *ConAu 119, SmATA 47N*
Pseud./variant:
Dalton, Alene

Chapin, Henry 1893-1983 *AuBYP 2, –3, Au&Wr 71, BioIn 8, –11, –13, ConAu 93, –110*

Chapman, A H 1924- *ConAu 25R, –19NR*

Chapman, Abraham 1915- *ConAu 45, DrAS 74E*

Chapman, Allen *ConAu X, –P-2, SmATA 1, –67*
Main entry: Stratemeyer, Edward L

Chapman, Charles Henry 1879- *BioIn 14*

Chapman, Charles Henry 1879-1972 *BioIn 8, ObitT 1971, OxCChiL, WhoChL*

Chapman, Christine 1933- *ConAu 73, –12NR*

Chapman, Elizabeth 1919- *ConAu P-1, IntAu&W 77, –89, –91, SmATA 10, WrDr 76, –80, –84, –86, –88, –90, –92*

Chapman, Frank Michler 1864-1945 *AmAu&B, BioIn 1, –2, –3, –4, –7, –12, CurBio 46, DcAmAu, DcNAA, DcScB S2, InSci, JBA 34, ObitOF 79, REnAL, TwCA, –SUP, WebAB 74, –79, WhAm 2*

Chapman, Frederick Trench 1887-1983 *BioIn 1, –5, –13, ChhPo, IlrAm 1880, –D, IlsCB 1946*

Chapman, Gaynor 1935- *BioIn 14, SmATA 32*

Chapman, Graham 1941-1989 *WhoCom*

Chapman, Jean *AuWomWr, BioIn 14, ConAu 97, DcChlFi, SingR 2, SmATA 34*

Chapman, John Stanton Higham 1891-1972 *AmAu&B, AuBYP 2, –3, BioIn 2, –4, –7, –8, –13, ConAu 107, SmATA 27N, TwCA, –SUP, WhAm 6, WhNAA*
Pseud./variant:
Chapman, Maristan
Connell, Kirk
Ilsley, Dent
Selkirk, Jane

Chapman, Maristan *AmAu&B, AmNov, AuBYP 2, –3, BioIn 13, ConAu X, REnAL, SmATA X, TwCA, –SUP, WhNAA*
Main entry: Chapman, John Stanton Higham
Chapman, Mary Hamilton Illsley

Chapman, Mary Hamilton Illsley 1895- *AmAu&B, AmNov X, AuBYP 2, BioIn 2, –4, –7, –8, WhNAA, WhoAm 74*
Pseud./variant:
Chapman, Maristan
Selkirk, Jane

Chapman, Mary Ilsley *AuBYP 3*

Chapman, Mary Ilsley 1895- *WhAm 10*

Chapman, Peggy *IlsBYP*

Chapman, Sydney 1888-1970 *BiESc, BioIn 1, –2, –3, –4, –8, –9, ConAu 106, CurBio 57, –70, DcNaB 1961, DcScB S2, InSci, McGEWB, McGMS 80, NewYTBE 70, ObitOF 79, ObitT 1961, WhAm 8, WhoLA*

Chapman, Vera 1898- *BioIn 14, –16, ConAu 81, EncBrWW, ScF&FL 92, SmATA 33*
Pseud./variant:
Took, Belladonna

Chapman, Victoria L 1944- *ConAu 57*

Chapman, Walker *BioIn 15, –17, ConAu X, –36NR, DcLEL 1940, MajAI, MajTwCW, SmATA X, ThrBJA*
Main entry: Silverberg, Robert

Chapone, Hester 1727-1801 *BioIn 1, –3, CamGLE, ContDcW 89, DcBiPP, DcNaB, FemiCLE, IntDcWB. OxCChiL*

Chapone, Hester Mulso 1727-1801 *BlmGWL*

Chappell, Audrey 1954- *SmATA 72*

Chappell, Warren d1991 *NewYTBS 91*

Chappell, Warren 1904- *BioIn 1, –2, –3, –4, –5, –8, –9, –10, –12, ConAu 17R, –8NR, IlsBYP, IlsCB 1744, –1946, –1957, –1967, SmATA 6, –10AS, ThrBJA, WhAmArt 85, WhoAm 78, –80, –82, –84, –86, –88, –90, WhoAmA 73, –78, WhoGrA 62, WhoWor 84, –87, –89*

Chappell, Warren 1904-1991 *BioIn 17, ConAu 134, MajAI, SmATA 67, -68, WhAm 10*

Chardiet, Bernice Kroll 1927?- *BioIn 13, ConAu 103, ForWC 70, SmATA 27, WhoAmW 85, WhoE 83, -85*

Chardiet, Bernice Kroll 1930- *WhoAm 86, -88, -90, -92, -94, WhoAmW 87, -89, -91, WhoWor 87, -91, -93*

Charles, Donald *ConAu X, IlsBYP, SmATA X*
Main entry: Meighan, Donald Charles

Charles, Louis *ConAu X, MajAI, SmATA 67*
Main entry: Stratemeyer, Edward L

Charles, Nicholas *ThrBJA, WrDr 80, -82, -84, -86, -88, -90, -92*
Main entry: Kuskin, Karla Seidman

Charles, Nicholas 1932- *WrDr 94*

Charles, Nicholas J *ConAu 41NR, MajAI, SmATA 68*

Charles, Norma Mae 1940- *WhoCanL 85, -87, -92*

Charlesworth, Maria Louisa 1819-1880 *Alli SUP, BioIn 8, -16, DcEnL, DcNaB, InWom SUP, OxCChiL, StaCVF, WhoChL*

Charlie *InB&W 80*

Charlip, Remy *BioIn 17*

Charlip, Remy 1929- *AmPB, AuBYP 2, -3, BiDD, BioIn 5, -7, -8, -9, -13, ChhPo S1, ChlLR 8, ConAu 33R, IlsCB 1946, -1957, -1967, IntAu&W 91, MajAI, SmATA 4, -68, ThrBJA, WrDr 76, -80, -82, -84, -86, -88, -90, -92, -94*

Charlot, Jean 1898-1979 *AmPB, BioIn 1, -2, -3, -4, -5, -6, -8, -9, -10, -11, -12, -14, BriEAA, CathA 1952, ConAu 5R, -4NR, CurBio 45, -84N, GrAmP, IlsBYP, IlsCB 1744, -1946, -1957, -1967, MorJA, SmATA 8, -31N, WhAm 7, WhAmArt 85, WhoAm 74, -76, -78, -80, WhoAmA 73, -78, -80N, -82N, -86N, -89N, -91N, WhoWest 74, -76, -78, WrDr 76, -80*

Charlot, Martin 1944- *BioIn 17, ConAu 35NR, SmATA 64*

Charlot, Martin Day 1944- *AmArt*

Charlotte Elizabeth 1790-1846 *OxCChiL*

Charlson, David *ConAu X*
Main entry: Holmes, David Charles

Charlton, Michael Alan 1923- *BioIn 12, -14, IlsCB 1967, SmATA 34*

Charlwood, D E 1915- *ConAu 21R, -9NR, SingR 2, WrDr 76, -80, -82, -84, -86, -88, -90, -92*

Charlwood, Donald Ernest Cameron 1915- *WrDr 94*

Charmatz, Bill 1925- *BioIn 10, -15, ConAu 29R, ConGrA 2, SmATA 7, WhoAmA 82, -84, -86, -89, -91*

Charnas, Suzy M 1939- *SmATA 61*

Charnas, Suzy McKee *BioIn 17, DrAPF 87, -89, -91, -93, IntvTCA 2, PenEncH*

Charnas, Suzy McKee 1939- *ArtclWW 2, ConAu 39NR, EncSF 93, FemiCLE, IntAu&W 91, NewEScF, RGTwCSF, ScF&FL 92, ScFSB, TwCSFW 86, -91, WrDr 86, -88, -90, -92, -94*

Charnock, Joan 1903- *Au&Wr 71, ConAu P-2, WrDr 76*
Pseud./variant:
Thomson, Joan

Charosh, Mannis 1906- *BioIn 10, ConAu 29R, SmATA 5, WhoE 74*

Charry, Elias 1906- *ConAu 69, WhoWor 72, -78*

Charteris, Leslie d1993 *NewYTBS 93*

Charteris, Leslie 1907- *AmAu&B, Au&Wr 71, BioIn 1, -4, -9, -14, BlueB 76, ConAu 5R, -10NR, CorpD, CrtSuMy, DcLB 77, EncMys, EncSF 93, EvLB, FilmgC, HalFC 84, -88, IntAu&W 77, -82, -86, -89, -91, IntMPA 75, -76, -78, -81, -82, -84, -86, -88, -77 IntWW 74, -75, -76, -77, -78, -79, -80, -81, -82, -83, -89, -91, LongCTC, NewC, Novels, REn, REnAL, ScF&FL 92, TwCA, -SUP, TwCCr&M 80, -85, -91, TwCWr, Who 74, -82, -83, -85, -88, -90, -92, WhoAm 74, -76, -78, -80, -82, -84, -86, -88, -90, -92, WhoSSW 73, WhoSpyF, WrDr 76, -80, -82, -84, -86, -88, -90, -92*

Charteris, Leslie 1907-1993 *ConAu 141*

Chartier, Normand L 1945- *SmATA 66*

Charvat, William d1966 *DcLB Y92*

Charvat, William 1905- *ChhPo*

Chase, Alice *AuBYP 2S, -3, SmATA 77, -X*
Main entry: McHargue, Georgess

Chase, Alice Elizabeth 1906- *AuBYP 2S, -3, Au&Wr 71, BioIn 8, ConAu P-1, DrAS 74H,*

–78H, –82H, ForWC 70, WhAmArt 85, WhoAmA 73, –78, –80, –82, –84, –86, –89, –91

Chase, Edward Leigh 1884-1965 *BioIn 7, WhAmArt 85, WhoAmA 78N*

Chase, Emily *ConAu 136, SmATA 68, WrDr 94*
Main entry: Aks, Patricia
Sachs, Judith

Chase, Margaret Smith *AuBYP 3*

Chase, Mary 1907-1981 *AmWomD, AuBYP 3, BioIn 16, DramC 1, HalFC 88, ScF&FL 92, WorAlBi*

Chase, Mary Coyle 1907-1981 *AmAu&B, AuBYP 2, BenetAL 91, BiE&WWA, BioIn 1, –3, –4, –6, –7, –8, –10, CnDAL, CnMD, ConAu 77, ConDr 73, –77, –93, CurBio 45, DcLEL, EncWT, InWom SUP, LongCTC, McGEWD 72, –84, ModWD, NotNAT, NotWoAT, OxCAmL 65, –83, OxCAmT 84, PlP&P, REn, REnAL, SmATA 17, –29N, TwCA SUP, WhAm 8, WhoAm 74, –76, –78, WhoAmW 74, WhoThe 77, WorAl, WrDr 76, –80*

Chase, Mary Ellen 1887-1973 *AmAu&B, AmNov, ArtclWW 2, AuBYP 2, –3, Benet 87, BenetAL 91, BioAmW, BioIn 1, –2, –3, –4, –5, –7, –8, –10, –11, BlueB 76N, ChhPo, ConAmA, ConAu 41R, –P-1, ConLC 2, CurBio 40, –73, DcLEL, FemiCLE, FourBJA, InWom SUP, LongCTC, NewYTBE 73, Novels, ObitOF 79, OxCAmL 65, –83, PenC AM, REn, REnAL, SmATA 10, TwCA, –SUP, WhAm 5, WhNAA, Who 74, WhoAmW 74*

Chase, Powell *ChhPo*

Chase, Rhoda *ChhPo S2, ConICB*

Chase, Richard 1904- *AmAu&B, AnCL, AuBYP 2S, BioIn 4, –5, –6, BkCL, ChhPo S1, ConAu 61, MorJA, WhoAm 74, –76, –78, –80*

Chase, Richard 1904-1988 *AuBYP 3, BioIn 16, –17, ConAu 125, SmATA 56N, –64*

Chase, Samantha
Main entry: Buckholtz, Eileen

Chase, Stuart 1888- *BenetAL 91*

Chase, Stuart 1888-1985 *AmAu&B, AnObit 1985, BioIn 2, –3, –4, –14, –15, BlueB 76, ChhPo S2, ConAmA, ConAu 65, –117, CurBio 40, –86N, DcAmSR, DcLEL, Future, IntAu&W 77, –82, IntWW 74, –75, –76, –77, –78, –79, –80, –81, –82, –83, LongCTC, NewYTBS 85, OxCAmH, OxCAmL 65, –83, REn, REnAL, TwCA, –SUP, WebAB 74, –79, WhAm 9, WhNAA, Who 74, –82, –83, –85, WhoAm 74, –76, –78, WhoWor 74*

Chasek, Judith *AuBYP 2S, –3*

Chasins, Abram d1987 *NewYTBS 87*

Chasins, Abram 1903- *AmAu&B, ASCAP 66, AuBYP 2S, –3, Baker 84, BioIn 1, –2, –4, –5, –9, ConAmC 76, –82, ConAu 37R, –14NR, CurBio 60, IntWWM 85, –90, NewGrDA 86, OxCMus, WhAm 9, WhoAm 74, –76, WhoAmJ 80, WhoAmM 83, WhoMus 72, WhoWorJ 72, –78*

Chasins, Abram 1903-1987 *Baker 92, BioIn 15, ConAu 122, CurBio 87N, NewAmDM*

Chastain, Madye Lee 1908- *AmAu&B, BioIn 4, –5, –6, –9, ConAu 5R, CurBio 58, IlsCB 1946, MorJA, SmATA 4*

Chatelain, Clara De 1807-1876 *Alli SUP, CarSB, DcNaB, OxCChiL*

Chaucer, Geoffrey d1400 *BioIn 14, –15, –16, –17*

Chaucer, Geoffrey 1340?-1400? *Alli, AnCL, AtlBL, BbD, BiD&SB, BioIn 1, –2, –3, –4, –5, –6, –7, –8, –9, –10, –11, –12, –13, BlmGEL, BritAu, BritWr 1, CamGEL, CasWL, Chambr 1, ChhPo, –S1, –S2, CnDBLB 1, CnE&AP, CrtT 1, CyWA 58, DcBiPP, DcCathB, DcEnA, DcEnL, DcEuL, DcLEL, DcNaB, DcScB, Dis&D, EvLB, LitC 17, LongCEL, LuthC 75, McGEWB, MouLC 1, NewC, OxCChiL, OxCEng 67, –85, OxCMus, PenC ENG, PoLE, RAdv 1, –13-1, RComWL, REn, RfGEnL 91, WebE&AL, WhDW, WorAlBi, WorAl*

Chaucer, Geoffrey 1342?-1400 *WrPh*

Chaucer, Geoffrey 1343?-1400 *Benet 87, CamGLE, MagSWL*

Chauncy, Nan 1900-1970 *AuWomWr, AuBYP 3, BlmGWL, TwCChW 89*

Chauncy, Nan Cen Beryl Masterman 1900-1970 *DcChlFi*

Chauncy, Nan Masterman 1900-1970 *AuBYP 2, BioIn 8, –9, –10, ChlLR 6, ConAu 1R, –4NR, OxCAusL, OxCChiL, SingR 1, SmATA 6, ThrBJA, TwCChW 78, –83*

Chauncy, Nancen Beryl Masterman 1900-1970 *MajAI*

Chaundler, Christine 1887- *WomNov*

Chaundler, Christine 1887-1972 *Au&Wr 71, BioIn 8, –9, –13, ChhPo, –S1, –S2, ConAu P-2, OxCChiL, SmATA 1, –25N,*

TwCChW 83, –89, WhoChL
Pseud./variant:
Martin, Peter

Chavarie, Robert *OxCCan SUP*

Chaytor, Henry John 1871- *WhoLA*

Cheadle, Walter Butler 1835-1910 *BioIn 4, –7, –9, BritAu 19, DcNaB S2, OxCCan*

Chear, Abraham d1668 *OxCChiL*

Cheatham, Karyn Follis *DrAPF 87, –89, –91, –93*

Cheatham, Karyn Follis 1943- *ConAu 81*

Cheetham, Ann *ScF&FL 92, TwCChW 89*

Cheetham, Ann 1944- *WrDr 94*

Cheifetz, Dan *DrAPF 87, –89*

Cheifetz, Dan 1926- *ConAu 69, DrAF 76, DrAPF 83, –85*

Chekenian, Jane Gerard *ConAu X*
Main entry: Gerard, Jane

Chen, Anthony Young
Main entry: Chen, Tony

Chen, Tony 1929- *BioIn 9, –10, –12, ConAu 37R, –X, FifBJA, IlsCB 1967, IntAu&W 77, –82X, SmATA 6, WhoAmA 78, –80, –82, –84, –86, –89, WhoE 74, WrDr 76*
Pseud./variant:
Chen, Anthony Young

Chen, Tony Young 1929- *WhoAsA 94*

Chen, Yuan-tsung 1932- *SmATA 65*

Chenault, Nell *BioIn 9, ConAu X, SmATA 2*
Main entry: Smith, Linell Nash

Chenery, Janet 1923- *BioIn 13, ConAu 103, SmATA 25*

Cheney, Cora 1916- *AuBYP 2, –3, BioIn 8, –9, ConAu 1R, –4NR, SmATA 3*

Cheney, Richard Eugene 1921- *WhoAm 74, –76, –78, –84, –86, –88, –90, –92, –94, WhoE 74, –75, –93, WhoFI 74, –87, –89, –92, –94*

Cheney, Richard Eugene 1922- *WhoAmL 94*

Cheney, Sheldon Warren 1886-1980 *AmAu&B, Au&Wr 71, BiE&WWA, BioIn 4, –12, ConAu 102, NewYTBS 80, NotNAT, REnAL, TwCA, –SUP, WhAm 7, WhoAm 74, –76, –78, WhoAmA 73, –78, WhoWor 74*

Cheney, Ted
Main entry: Cheney, Theodore Albert Rees

Cheney, Theodore A Rees 1928- *IntAu&W 86*

Cheney, Theodore Albert 1928- *ConAu 23NR, WhoWrEP 89, –92*

Cheney, Theodore Albert Rees 1928- *BioIn 11, ConAu 61, –X, –8NR, IntAu&W 82, SmATA 11*
Pseud./variant:
Cheney, Ted

Cheng, Hou-Tien 1944- *ConAu 69*

Cheng, Judith 1955- *BioIn 14, SmATA 36*

Chermayeff, Ivan 1932- *AmGrD, AmPB, BioIn 8, –9, –10, –16, ChhPo, ConAu 97, ConDes 90, ConGrA 3, IlsCB 1957, SmATA 47, WhoAm 74, –76, –78, –80, –82, –84, –86, –88, –92, –94, WhoAmA 73, –78, –80, –82, –84, –86, –89, –91, WhoE 74 –75, –77, WhoEnt 92, WhoGrA 82*

Chernoff, Dorothy A *ConAu X, SmATA X*
Main entry: Ernst, John

Chernoff, Goldie Taub 1909- *BioIn 11, ConAu 33R, SmATA 10, WhoAmW 77*

Cherry, Carolyn Janice 1942- *TwCYAW*

Cherry, Lynne 1952- *SmATA 34*

Cherryh, Carolyn Janice *IntvTCA 2*

Cherryh, Carolyn Janice 1942- *TwCYAW*

Cherryholmes, Anne *AuBYP 2, –3, ConAu X, SmATA 8*
Main entry: Price, Olive

Chesher, Kim 1955- *ConAu 102, –19NR, IntAu&W 91, WrDr 76, –80, –82, –84, –86, –88, –90*

Chesler, Bernice *BioIn 16*

Chesler, Bernice 1932- *ConAu 25R, –16NR, SmATA 59*

Chesnutt, Charles W 1858-1932 *AfrAmW, BenetAL 91, BlkLC, BlkWr 1, CamGLE, CamHAL, ConAu 125, MajTwCW, WorAlBi*

Chesnutt, Charles Waddell *BioIn 15, –16*

Chesnutt, Charles Waddell 1858-1932 *BioIn 17, BlkAull, –92, DcLB 50, –78, DcNCBi 1, EncAACR, FifSWrB, InB&W 85, NegAl 89, RfGAmL 87, RfGShF, ShSCr 7, TwCLC 39*

Chess, Victoria 1939- *BioIn 14, –16, SixBJA*

Chess, Victoria Dickerson 1939- *BioIn 12, ChhPo S1, ConAu 107, IlsCB 1967, SmATA 33*

Chessare, Michele *BioIn 15, SmATA 42*

Chester, Michael 1928- *AuBYP 2, -3, BioIn 8, ConAu 1R, -1NR, ScF&FL 92*

Chesterfield, Philip D Stanhope, Earl Of 1694-1773 *Benet 87, BioIn 1, -2, -3, -5, -6, -8, -9, -10, -11, -14, CamGEL, CamGLE, DcBiPP, OxCChiL, OxCEng 85, RAdv 13-1*

Chesterton, Gilbert Keith 1874-1936 *AnCL, AtlBL, BioIn 1, -2, -3, -4, -5, -6, -7, -8, -9, -10, -11, -12, -13, -14, -15, -16, -17, BkC 6, BritWr 6, CasWL, CathA 1930, Chambr 3, ChhPo, -S1, -S2, ConAu 104, CorpD, DcBrBI, DcCathB, DcLB 10, -19, -34, DcLEL, DcNaB 1931, EncWL 2, EvLB, GrBr, HalFC 84, LongCEL, LuthC 75, MakMC, McGEWB, ModBrL S2, NotNAT B, Novels, OxCEng 67, -85, PenC ENG, ScFEYrs, SmATA 27, SpyFic, SupFW, TwCA, -SUP, TwCCr&M 80, -85, TwCLC 6, TwCWr, WhDW, WhoLA, WorAl*

Chestnutt, Charles W 1858-1932 *Benet 87, SouBlCW*

Chestnutt, Charles Waddell 1858-1932 *AmAu&B, AmLY, BioIn 2, -3, -4, -5, -6, -8, -9, -10, -11, BlkAWP, CasWL, CnDAL, CyWA 58, DcAmAu, DcNAA, ModBlW, OhA&B, OxCAmL 65, PenC AM, REn, REnAL, SelBAAu, TwCA, -SUP, WebAB 74, WhAm 1, WhNAA, WorAl*

Chetin, Helen 1922- *BioIn 10, ConAu 29R, -12NR, SmATA 6*

Chetwin, Grace *BioIn 16, ConAu 123, ScF&FL 92, SmATA 50, TwCYAW, WrDr 90, -92, -94*

Chetwynd-Hayes, Ronald Henry Glynn 1919- *ConAu 61, IntAu&W 82, WhoHr&F*
Pseud./variant:
Campbell, Angus

Chevalier, Christa 1937- *BioIn 14, ConAu 107, -24NR, SmATA 35*

Chew, Ruth 1920- *BioIn 10, -16, ConAu 41R, -14NR, -31NR, IntAu&W 82, ScF&FL 92, SixBJA, SmATA 7*
Pseud./variant:
Silver, Ruth

Cheyney, Peter 1896-1951 *BiDIrW, BioIn 2, -3, -14, ConAu 113, CrtSuMy, DcIrB 88, DcIrW 1, DcLEL, EncMys, EvLB, FilmgC, HalFC 84, -88, Novels, ObitOF 79, ObitT 1951, REn, TwCCr&M 80, -85, -91, TwCWr, WhoSpyF*

Chiang, Yee 1903-1977 *BioIn 1, -2, -3, -4, -5, -11, ConAu 65, -73, -15NR, DrAS 74F, IlsCB 1744, -1946, IntAu&W 77, IntWW 74, -75, -76, -77, -78N, LongCTC, TwCA SUP, WhAm 7, Who 74, WhoAm 74, -76, -78, WhoE 75*

Chickering, Marjorie *AuBYP 2S, -3*

Chicorel, Marietta S *WhoAm 86, -90, -92, WhoAmW 89, -91*

Chicorel, Marietta S 1924- *BiDrLUS 70, ConAu 85, IntAu&W 82, WhoAm 78, -80, -82, -84, WhoAmW 81, -83, WhoLibI 82, WhoLibS 66*

Chidsey, Donald Barr 1902-1981 *AmAu&B, AmNov, Au&Wr 71, BioIn 2, -4, -9, -13, ConAu 5R, -103, -2NR, REnAL, SmATA 3, -27N, TwCA SUP*

Chiefari, Janet D 1942- *SmATA 58*

Child, Mrs. *DcVicP 2, SmATA 67*
Main entry: Child, Lydia Maria

Child, Charles Jesse 1901- *BioIn 1, -6, ChhPo, IlsCB 1744*

Child, John 1922- *ConAu 93, WrDr 76, -80, -82, -84*

Child, L Maria *SmATA 67*
Main entry: Child, Lydia Maria

Child, Lydia M 1802-1880 *CamGLE, CamHAL*

Child, Lydia Maria 1802-1880 *Alli, -SUP, AmAu, AmAu&B, ArtclWW 2, BenetAL 91, BbD, BiD&SB, BioAmW, BioIn 1, -3, -4, -6, -7, -8, -9, -11, -12, -13, CarSB, CasWL, Chambr 3, ChhPo, -S1, -S2, ContDcW 89, CyAL, DcAmAu, DcAmSR, DcEnL, DcLB 1, -74, DcLEL, DcNAA, EncAB-H, EvLB, FemiCLE, HarEnUS, HerW, -84, IntDcWB, McGEWB, NinCLC 6, OxCAmH, OxCAmL 65, -83, OxCChiL, RComAH, REnAL, SmATA 67, Str&VC, WebAB 74, -79, WhAm HS, WhNaAH*
Pseud./variant:
Child, Mrs.
Child, L Maria

Child, Lydia Maria 1802-1888 *DcAmImH*

Child, Lydia Maria Frances 1802-1880 *InWom SUP*

Child, Lydia Maria Francis 1802-1880 *AmPeW, BioIn 15, -17, BlmGWL, HanAmWH, WhCiWar*

Child, Philip 1898-1978 *BenetAL 91, BioIn 16, DcLB 68, SmATA 47, TwCRHW 90*

Child, Richard Washburn 1881-1935 *AmAu&B, BioIn 16, DcAmDH 80, –89, DcCathB, DcNAA, EncMys, WhAm 1, WhNAA*

Childerhose, R J *OxCCan*

Childerhose, R J 1928- *ScF&FL 92*

Childers, Erskine 1905-1974 *BioIn 10, –11, BioNews 75, IntWW 74, NewYTBE 73, ObitT 1971, Who 74, WhoWor 74*

Children's Shepherd, The *SmATA X*
Main entry: Westphal, Arnold Carl

Childress, Alice *BlkWWr, DrAPF 87, –89, –91, –93, EarBlAP, WhoBlA 85*

Childress, Alice 1920- *AmWomD, ArtclWW 2, Au&Arts 8, AuBYP 2S, –3, BioIn 10, –12, –14, –15, –16, –17, BlkAWP, BlkAuII, –92, BlkLC, BlkWWr, BlkWr 1, BlkWrNE, BlmGWL, CamGWoT, ChlLR 14, ConAu 45, –3NR, –27NR, ConBlAP 88, ConDr 77, –82, –88, –93, ConLC 12, –15, ConTFT 10, DcAmChF 1960, DcLB 7, –38, DrAPF 83, –85, DrBlPA 90, DramC 4, FemiCLE, FifBJA, InB&W 80, –85, IntAu&W 91, IntDcT 2, LivgBAA, MajAI, MajTwCW, McGEWD 84, NegAl 83, –89, NotBlAW 92, NotNAT, NotWoAT, PlP&P A, SelBAAf, SelBAAu, SmATA 7, –48, TwCChW 89, TwCYAW, WhoAm 74, –76, –82, –84, –86, –88, –90, –92, –94, WhoAmW 74, WhoBlA 75, –77, –80, –85, –90, –92, WhoEnt 92, WorAu 1975, WrDr 80, –82, –84, –86, –88, –90, –92*

Childs, H Fay 1890-1971 *BioIn 9, –13, ConAu P-1, SmATA 1, –25N*

Childs, John Farnsworth *AuBYP 3*

Childs, John Farnsworth 1909- *AuBYP 2, BioIn 7, BlueB 76, IntYB 80, –81, –82, WhoAm 74, –76, –78, –80, –82, –84, –86, –88, –90, –92, –94, WhoFI 74, –92*

Childs, Maryanna 1910- *AmCath 80, ConAu 9R, DrAS 74E, –78E, –82E, WhoRel 75, WhoWrEP 89, –92*

Childs, Maryanna, Sister 1910- *WhoUSWr 88*

Chilton, Shirley Ray Shafer 1923- *ConAu 77, WhoAmW 75, –77*

Chimaera *ConAu X, MajAI, SmATA 2*
Main entry: Farjeon, Eleanor

Chin, Richard 1946- *BioIn 16, ConAu 121, SmATA 52*

Chinery, Michael 1938- *BioIn 13, ConAu 103, –20NR, IntAu&W 77, –91, SmATA 26, WhoAm 92, WrDr 76, –80, –82, –84, –86, –88, –90, –92, –94*

Chipperfield, Joseph E 1912-1976 *TwCChW 89*

Chipperfield, Joseph Eugene 1909?-1976 *AuBYP 2, Au&Wr 71, BioIn 6, –8, –9, ConAu 9R, –6NR, MorJA, OxCChiL, SmATA 2, TwCChW 78, –83, WrDr 80*
Pseud./variant:
Craig, John Eland

Chipperfield, Joseph Eugene 1912-1980? *AuBYP 3*

Chisholm, Matt *ConAu X, EncFWF, IntAu&W 82X, WrDr 84*
Main entry: Watts, Peter Christopher

Chisholm, Matt 1919-1983 *TwCWW 91*

Chislett, Gail 1948- *BioIn 16, SmATA 58*

Chitham, Edward 1932- *ConAu 103, –19NR, WrDr 76, –80, –82, –84, –86, –88, –90, –92, –94*

Chitham, Edward Harry Gordon 1932- *ConAu 41NR*

Chittenden, Elizabeth F 1903- *BioIn 11, ConAu 61, SmATA 9*
Pseud./variant:
Carson, Rosalind

Chittenden, Margaret 1933?- *BioIn 13, ConAu 53, –4NR, SmATA 28*

Chittenden, Margaret 1935- *ConAu 19NR, ScF&FL 92*

Chittum, Ida 1918- *AuBYP 2S, –3, BioIn 10, ConAu 37R, –14NR, SmATA 7, WrDr 76, –80, –82, –84, –86, –88, –90*

Chmielarz, Sharon 1940- *SmATA 72*

Choate, Florence *ConICB, DcWomA, WhAmArt 85*

Choate, Judith 1940- *BioIn 14, ConAu 105, SmATA 30*

Choi, Sook Nyul *SmATA 73*

Chonz, Selina *FourBJA*

Choquette, Adrienne 1915- *CanWr, CreCan 1, OxCCan*

Choquette, Adrienne 1915-1973 *BenetAL 91, DcLB 68*

Chorao, Ann McKay Sproat 1936- *MajAI*

Chorao, Kay 1936- *BioIn 11, –12, ConAu 49, –1NR, –19NR, FourBJA, IlsBYP, IlsCB 1967, SmATA 8, –69*

Choron, Jacques 1904-1972 *AuBYP 2, –3, BioIn 8, –9, ConAu 33R, –P-1, NewYTBE 72, WhoAm 74*

Chorpenning, Charlotte 1872-1955 *BioIn 15, –16, ConAu 114, OxCChiL, SmATA 37, TwCChW 78, –83, –89*

Chorpenning, Charlotte 1873- *InWom SUP*

Chorpenning, Charlotte Barrows 1873-1955 *AmWomPl*

Chrisman, Arthur Bowie 1889-1953 *AmAu&B, AnCL, AuBYP 2, –3, BenetAL 91, BioIn 2, –4, –7, –11, –14, JBA 34, –51, NewbMB 1922, ObitOF 79, OxCChiL, REnAL, TwCChW 83, –89, WhAm 3, YABC 1*

Christelow, Eileen 1943- *BioIn 14, –15, ConAu 111, SmATA 35, –38*

Christensen, Gardell Dano 1907- *AuBYP 2, –3, BioIn 5, –8, –9, ConAu 9R, IlsCB 1946, SmATA 1*

Christensen, Haaken 1886- *BioIn 5, IlsCB 1946*

Christensen, Yolanda Maria Ippolito 1943- *ConAu 57, –7NR, WhoAmW 77*

Christesen, Barbara 1940- *BioIn 15, ConAu 107, SmATA 40*

Christgau, Alice Erickson 1902- *ConAu P-2, SmATA 13*

Christian, Jill *ConAu X, IntAu&W 77X, –82X, WrDr 76, –80, –82, –84, –86*
Main entry: Dilcock, Noreen

Christian, Mary Blount 1933- *ArtclWW 2, AuBYP 3, BioIn 11, ConAu 45, –1NR, –17NR, IntAu&W 77, –91, SmATA 9, WhoAmW 83, WrDr 76, –80, –82, –84, –86, –88, –90, –92, –94*

Christian, Roy Cloberry 1914- *ConAu 93, IntAu&W 77, –82, –86, –89, –91, WrDr 76, –80, –82, –84, –86, –88, –90, –92, –94*

Christian, Samuel T *AuBYP 3*

Christian, Samuel Terry 1937- *AmMWSc 73P, –76P, –82, –86, –89, –92, AuBYP 2S*

Christie, Agatha *TwCRHW 90, WomNov*

Christie, Agatha 1890-1976 *Au&Arts 9, AuBYP 2, –3, AuNews 1, –2, Au&Wr 71, Benet 87, BiE&WWA, BioIn 1, –2, –4, –6, –7, –8, –9, –11, –12, –13, –17, BioNews 74, BlmGEL, BlmGWL, BlueB 76, BritWr S2, CamGLE, CasWL, CelR, CnDBLB 6, CnThe, ConAu 17R, –61, –10NR, ConDr 73, –77, ConLC 1, –6, –8, –12, –48, ConNov 72, –76, ContDcW 89, CrtSuMy, CurBio 40, –64, –76N, CyWA 89, DcLB 13, –77, DcLEL, EncBrWW, EncMys, EncWB, EncWT, EvLB, FemiCLE, FilmgC, HalFC 84, IntDcWB, IntWW 74, –75, –76N, LongCTC, MagSWL, MajTwCW, NewC, Novels, ObitOF 79, OxCEng 67, –85, PenC ENG, PenEncH, PlP&P, REn, RfGEnL 91, ScFEYrs, SmATA 36, TwCA, –SUP, TwCCr&M 80, –85, –91, TwCWr, WhAm 6, Who 74, WhoHr&F, WhoThe 72, –77, –81N, WhoWor 74, WorAlBi, WrDr 76*
Pseud./variant:
Mallowan, Agatha Christie

Christie, Agatha 1891-1976 *ArtclWW 2, BioIn 14, –15, –16, CamGWoT*

Christie, Agatha, Dame 1891-1976 *HalFC 88*

Christie, Agatha Mary Clarissa 1890-1976 *ConAu 37NR, ConDr 93, TwCYAW*

Christie, Ann Philippa *IntAu&W 82, –86, Who 82, –83, –85, –88, –90, –92, WrDr 76, –80*
Main entry: Pearce, Ann Philippa

Christie, Marie *SmATA X*
Main entry: Marie, Geraldine

Christie, Philippa *AuBYP 3*

Christie, Stephen *MarqDCG 84*

Christopher, John *ChlLR 2, ConAu X, –37NR, ConSFA, DcLEL 1940, FourBJA, LElec, MajAI, Novels, OxCChiL, SenS, SmATA X, TwCChW 78, –83, WhoSciF, WorAu 1950, WrDr 80, –82, –84*
Main entry: Youd, Samuel

Christopher, John 1922- *BioIn 14, –16, ChlFicS, EncSF 93, IntAu&W 89, –91, NewEScF, ScF&FL 92, ScFSB, TwCChW 89, TwCSFW 86, –91, TwCYAW, WrDr 86, –88, –90, –92, –94*

Christopher, Louise
Main entry: Hale, Arlene

Christopher, Matt 1917- *BioIn 16, ConAu 36NR, ScF&FL 92, SmATA 47, –9AS*

Christopher, Matthew F 1917- *AuBYP 2, –3, BioIn 8, –9, –10, ConAu 1R, –5NR, FifBJA, IntAu&W 77, –82, –82X, –86, –89, –91, MajAI, MorBMP, SmATA 2, WrDr 76, –80, –82, –84, –94*
Pseud./variant:
Martin, Frederick

Christopher, Matthew Frederick 1917- *WhoUSWr 88, WhoWrEP 89, –92*

Christopher, Milbourne *BioIn 14*

Christopher, Milbourne 1914-1984 *EncO&P 2S1, -3, EncPaPR 91, SmATA 46*

Christy, Howard Chandler d1952 *WhoAmA 86N*

Christy, Howard Chandler 1872-1952 *WhoAmA 89N, -91N*

Christy, Howard Chandler 1873?-1952 *AmAu&B, BioIn 1, -2, -3, -5, -11, -12, ChhPo, -S2, EncAB-A 25, EncAJ, IlrAm 1880, -B, IlsCB 1744, ObitOF 79, SmATA 21, WhAm 3, WhAmArt 85, WhoAmA 78N, -80N, -82N*

Chroman, Eleanor 1937- *ConAu 45*

Chrystie, Frances N 1904-1986 *SmATA 60*

Chrystie, Frances Nicholson 1904- *AuBYP 2, -3, BioIn 3, -7*

Chu, Daniel 1933- *BioIn 11, ConAu 13R, SmATA 11*

Chu, Samuel C 1929- *ConAu 69, DrAS 74H, -78H, -82H*

Chubb, Thomas Caldecot 1899-1972 *AmAu&B, Au&Wr 71, BenetAL 91, BioIn 9, ChhPo, -S1, -S2, ConAu 1R, -33R, -6NR, NewYTBE 72, REn, REnAL, WhAm 5, WhNAA*

Chukovsky, Kornei *TwCChW 89B*

Chukovsky, Kornei 1882-1969 *AuBYP 3*

Chukovsky, Kornei Ivanovich 1882-1969 *AmPB, AuBYP 2, BioIn 6, -7, -8, -9, -10, -11, CasWL, ChhPo S1, -S2, ConAu 5R, -25R, -4NR, -42NR, HanRL, MajAI, OxCChiL, PenC EUR, SmATA 5, -34, TwCChW 78B, -83B, WorAu 1950*

Church, Alfred John 1829-1912 *Alli SUP, AuBYP 2, -3, BioIn 2, -8, CarSB, ChhPo S2, JBA 34, -51, OxCChiL, TelT*

Church, Carol Bauer *AuBYP 2S, -3*

Church, Frederick Stuart 1842-1924 *ArtsEM, IlrAm 1880, OxCChiL, WhAmArt 85*

Church, Harrison Leon 1941- *DrAS 74E*

Church, Richard 1893-1972 *Au&Wr 71, BioIn 4, -6, -7, -8, -9, CamGLE, ChhPo, -S1, -S2, ConAu 1R, -33R, -3NR, ConNov 72, ConPo 70, DcLEL, EngPo, EvLB, LongCTC, ModBrL, MorJA, NewC, NewYTBE 72, Novels, ObitT 1971, OxCChiL, OxCEng 85, PenC ENG, REn, ScF&FL 92, SmATA 3, TwCA, -SUP, TwCChW 78, -83, -89, TwCWr, WhoChL*

Church, Ronald James H *Who 88, -92*

Church, Ronald James H, Prof *Who 90*

Church, Ronald James Harrison *Who 74, -82, -83, -85*

Churchill, E Richard 1937- *BioIn 11, ConAu 17R, -11NR, -30NR, SmATA 11, WrDr 76, -80, -82, -84, -86, -88, -90, -92, -94*

Churchill, Linda Rivers Ruler 1938- *ConAu 21R, -11NR, WhoAmW 74*

Churchill, Winston 1871-1947 *AmAu&B, AmLY, Benet 87, BenetAL 91, BbD, BiDSA, BiD&SB, BioIn 1, -2, -3, -4, -5, -6, -7, -8, -9, -10, -11, -12, CamGEL, CarSB, CasWL, Chambr 3, CnDAL, ConAmA, ConAmL, CyWA 58, DcAmAu, DcAmSR, DcBiA, DcLEL, DcNAA, EvLB, JBA 34, LongCTC, McGEWB, NotNAT B, Novels, ObitOF 79, OxCAmL 65, -83, OxCEng 67, -85, PenC AM, REn, REnAL, RfGAmL 87, TwCA SUP, TwCRHW 90, TwCWr, WebE&AL, WhAm 2, WhNAA*

Churne, William
Main entry: Paget, Francis Edward

Chute, B J *DrAPF 87*

Chute, B J 1913- *WrDr 86*

Chute, B J 1913-1987 *BioIn 15, -16, ConAu 123, SmATA 53N*

Chute, Beatrice Joy 1913- *AmAu&B, BioIn 1, -2, -6, -9, ConAu 1R, CurBio 50, IntAu&W 77, -82, MorJA, SmATA 2, WhoAmW 74, WrDr 76, -80*

Chute, Beatrice Joy 1913-1987 *BioIn 15, -16, NewYTBS 87*

Chute, Marchette 1909- *DcLB 103, IntAu&W 89, TwCChW 89, Who 88, -90, -92, WhoAm 86, -88, -90, -92, -94, WhoAmW 87, -89, -93, WhoUSWr 88, WhoWrEP 89, -92, WrDr 86, -88, -90, -92, -94*

Chute, Marchette G 1909- *BenetAL 91*

Chute, Marchette Gaylord 1909- *AmAu&B, AuBYP 2, -3, Au&Wr 71, BiE&WWA, BioIn 2, -3, -4, -5, -6, -7, -9, -17, EkCL, ChhPo, -S1, -S2, ConAu 1R, -5NR, CurBio 50, DrAS 74H, -78H, -82H, EvLB, IntAu&W 77, -82, MinnWr, MorJA, NotNAT, RAdv 1, REnAL, SmATA 1, TwCA SUP, TwCChW 78, -83, TwCYAW, Who 74, -82, -83, -85, WhoAm 74, -76, -78, -80, -82,*

–84, WhoAmW 74, –83, –85, WrDr 76, –80, –82, –84

Chwast, Jacqueline 1932- *BioIn 8, –10, ChhPo, –S2, ConAu 49, –5NR, FourBJA, IlsBYP, IlsCB 1957, –1967, SmATA 6*

Chwast, Seymour *BioIn 15, –17*

Chwast, Seymour 1931- *AmGrD, BioIn 9, –12, ConDes 84, –90, FourBJA, IlrAm 1880, IlsBYP, IlsCB 1967, SmATA 18, WhoAm 86, –88, –90, –92, –94, WhoAmA 78, –80, –82, –84, –86, –89, –91, WhoEnt 92, WhoGrA 82*

Ciancio, June 1920- *WhoAmA 82, –84, –86, –89, –91*

Ciardi, John *IntvTCA 2*

Ciardi, John 1916- *AmAu&B, AuBYP 2, BioIn 2, –4, –5, –6, –7, –8, –9, –12, –13, BlueB 76, BkCL, BkP, CasWL, CelR, ChhPo, –S1, –S2, CnDAL, ConAu 5R, –2AS, –5NR, ConLC 10, ConPo 70, –75, –80, –85, CurBio 67, DcLB 5, DrAP 75, DrAPF 83, –85, DrAS 74E, IntAu&W 91, ModAL, OxCAmL 65, –83, OxCChiL, PenC AM, RAdv 1, REn, REnAL, SmATA 1, Str&VC, ThrBJA, TwCA SUP, TwCChW 78, –83, WebAB 74, WebE&AL, WhoAm 74, –76, –78, –80, –82, –84, WhoE 74, WhoWor 74, WorAl, WrDr 76, –80, –82, –84, –86*

Ciardi, John 1916-1985 *Benet 87*

Ciardi, John 1916-1986 *AnObit 1986, AuBYP 3, BenetAL 91, BioIn 14, –15, –16, –17, ChlLR 19, ConAu 118, –33NR, ConLC 40, –44, CurBio 86N, DcLB Y86N, MajAI, MajTwCW, NewYTBS 86, SmATA 46N, –65, TwCChW 89, WhAm 9, WorAlBi*
Pseud./variant:
Anthony, John

Cimino, Maria *AuBYP 2S, –3, ChhPo*

Cingoli, Giulio *BioIn 8, IlsBYP, IlsCB 1957*

Cisneros, Sandra *BioIn 17, ConAu 131, DrAPF 87, –89, –91, HispWr, NewYTBS 93, WhoHisp 91*

Cisneros, Sandra 1954- *Au&Arts 9, ConLC 69, DcLB 122, IntvWPC, NotHsAW 93, TwCYAW, WhoHisp 92, –94*

Cisneros, Sandra 1955- *BlmGWL*

Citron, Samuel J 1908-1979 *BioIn 12, WhoWorJ 72, –78*

Claflin, Edward 1949- *AuBYP 2S, –3, ConAu 97*

Clagett, John 1916- *AmAu&B, AuBYP 2, –3, BioIn 3, –8, ConAu 5R, –6NR, DrAS 74E, LiHiK, ScF&FL 92*

Clagett, John Henry 1916- *EncSF 93*

Claiborne, Robert *BioIn 16, –17*

Claiborne, Robert d1990 *NewYTBS 90*

Claiborne, Robert 1919- *ConAu 29R, –12NR, –31NR, IntAu&W 77*

Claiborne, Robert 1919-1990 *ConAu 130*

Clair, Andree *BioIn 12, ConAu 29R, SmATA 19*

Clampett, Bob *BioIn 14, –15*
Main entry: Clampett, Robert

Clampett, Bob d1984 *LesBEnT 92*

Clampett, Bob 1914?-1984 *BioIn 10, –12, ConAu 112, ConGrA 1, HalFC 88, LesBEnT, SmATA 38N, –X, WhAm 8, WhoAm 80, –82*

Clampett, Robert 1914?-1984 *ConGrA 1, SmATA 44, WorECar*
Pseud./variant:
Clampett, Bob

Clancy, Joseph P 1928- *AuBYP 2S, –3, ConAu 101, –18NR, DrAS 74E, –78E, –82E*

Clancy, Joseph Patrick 1928- *OxCLiW 86*

Clancy, Joseph Patrick Thomas 1928- *IntAu&W 89, –91*

Clapp, Patricia 1912- *BioIn 9, –15, ConAu 25R, –10NR, –37NR, DcAmChF 1960, FifBJA, IntAu&W 82, –91, MajAI, OxCChiL, SmATA 4, –74, –4AS, TwCChW 78, –83, –89, TwCYAW, WhoE 83, WrDr 76, –80, –82, –84, –86, –88, –90, –92, –94*

Clare, Helen *AuBYP 2, –3, BioIn 8, –9, –11, ConAu X, EngPo, IntAu&W 77X, –82X, –86X, –91X, MajAI, SmATA 3, ThrBJA, TwCChW 83, –89, WhoChL, WrDr 80, –82, –84, –86, –88, –90, –92*
Main entry: Hunter Blair, Pauline

Clare, Helen 1921- *WrDr 94*

Clark, Alfred Edward 1873-1951 *WhAm 3*

Clark, Ann Nolan 1896- *AuBYP 3, BioIn 14, –15, DcLB 52, IntAu&W 91, MajAI, SmATA 16AS, TwCChW 89, WrDr 86, –88, –90*

Clark, Ann Nolan 1898?- *AmAu&B, AmCath 80, AmPB, AnCL, AuBYP 2, Au&ICB, BioIn 2, –3, –4, –6, –7, –9, –10, ChhPo, ChlLR 16, ConAu 5R, –2NR, JBA 51,*

MorBMP, NewbMB 1922, OxCChiL, SmATA 4, Str&VC, TwCChW 78, –83, WhAm 10, WhoAm 74, –76, –78, –80, –82, WhoAmW 74, WrDr 80, –82, –84

Clark, Bettina 1941- *WhoAmW 75, –77*

Clark, Billy C 1928- *ConAu 22NR*

Clark, Billy Curtis 1928- *BioIn 4, –8, ConAu 1R, LiHiK, WhoSSW 73*

Clark, Catherine Anthony 1892- *ArtclWW 2*

Clark, Catherine Anthony 1892-1977 *BlmGWL, ConAu P-1, CreCan 1, DcLB 68, OxCCanL, OxCChiL, ScF&FL 92, TwCChW 78, –83, –89*

Clark, Catherine Anthony Smith 1892-1970 *DcChlFi*

Clark, Champ 1923- *BioIn 16, ConAu 108, SmATA 47, WhoAm 74, –76, –78, –80, –82, –84, –86, –88, –90, WhoWrEP 89, –92*

Clark, David *ConAu X, IntAu&W 77X, SmATA X, TwCChW 83, –89, WrDr 76, –80, –82, –84, –86, –88, –90, –92*
Main entry: Hardcastle, Michael

Clark, David 1933- *WrDr 94*

Clark, David Allen *ConAu X, SmATA X*
Main entry: Ernst, John

Clark, Denis d1950? *AuBYP 2, –3, BioIn 7*

Clark, Dorothy Park 1899- *AmAu&B, AmNov X, BioIn 2, –4, ConAu 5R, CurBio 57*

Clark, Dorothy Park 1899-1983 *LiHiK*

Clark, Eleanor *BioIn 15, DrAPF 87, –89, –91, –93, IntAu&W 86, –89, WhoAm 86, –88, –90, –92, –94, WhoAmW 87, –89, –91, –93, WhoUSWr 88, WhoWrEP 89, –92*

Clark, Eleanor 1913- *AmAu&B, ArtclWW 2, BenetAL 91, BioIn 2, –4, –11, ConAu 9R, –41NR, ConLC 5, –19, ConNov 72, –76, –82, –86, –91, CurBio 78, DcLB 6, DcLEL 1940, DrAF 76, FemiCLE, InWom SUP, IntAu&W 77, –82, –91, OxCAmL 83, REnAL, TwCA SUP, WhoAm 74, –76, –78, –80, –82, –84, WrDr 76, –80, –82, –84, –86, –88, –90, –92*

Clark, Electa *AuBYP 3*

Clark, Electa 1910- *AuBYP 2S, ConAu 69, IndAu 1917*

Clark, Ella Elizabeth 1896- *ConAu 105, OxCCan, WhoPNW*

Clark, Emma Chichester 1955- *SmATA 69*

Clark, Eric 1911- *Au&Wr 71, ConAu 13R, –9NR, EngPo, WrDr 76, –80, –82, –84, –86, –88*

Clark, Frank 1922- *AuBYP 3*

Clark, Frank James 1922- *ASCAP 66, AuBYP 2, BioIn 8, ConAu 13R, –17NR, SmATA 18*

Clark, Frederick Stephen 1908- *ConAu 21R, IntAu&W 77, WrDr 76, –80*

Clark, Garel *AuBYP 3, ConAu 130, SmATA X*
Main entry: Garelick, May

Clark, H H *CarSB*

Clark, Howard *BioIn 12, ConAu X, WrDr 76, –80, –82, –84, –86*
Main entry: Haskin, Dorothy Clark

Clark, Imogen d1936 *AmAu&B, BiD&SB, CarSB, DcAmAu, DcNAA, WhAm 1, WhNAA, WomWWA 14, WomNov*

Clark, Joan *MajAI, SmATA 65*
Main entry: Benson, Mildred Augustine Wirt

Clark, Joan 1934- *BioIn 16, BlmGWL, DcChlFi, ScF&FL 92, SmATA 59*

Clark, Joan MacDonald 1934- *BioIn 13, ConAu 93, OxCCanL, Profile 2, WhoCanL 85, –87, –92*

Clark, Leonard *IntvTCA 2*

Clark, Leonard 1905-1981 *Au&Wr 71, BioIn 13, –14, ChhPo, –S1, –S2, ConAu 13R, –105, –7NR, ConPo 70, –75, –80, DcLEL 1940, EngPo, IntAu&W 77, –82, IntWWP 82, SmATA 29N, –30, TwCChW 78, –83, –89, Who 74, –82N, WhoWor 78, WrDr 76, –80, –82*

Clark, Leonard Hanley 1921- *WhoFI 89*

Clark, Lovell C 1918- *DrAS 74H, –82H, OxCCan SUP*

Clark, M R *ConAu 37NR, MajAI, SmATA 74*
Main entry: Clark, Mavis Thorpe

Clark, Margaret Goff 1913- *AuBYP 2, –3, BioIn 8, –11, ConAu 1R, –5NR, –20NR, –43NR, ForWC 70, SmATA 8, WhoAmW 75, –77, WhoUSWr 88, WhoWrEP 89, –92, WrDr 88, –90, –92*

Clark, Margery *BkCL*

Clark, Maria Louisa Guidish 1926- *ConAu 5R, ForWC 70, IntAu&W 82, WhoAmW 74, –75,*

–77, WrDr 76, –80, –82
Pseud./variant:
Clark, Mary Lou

Clark, Marjorie Agnes 1911- *Au&Wr 71, ConAu 33R, IntAu&W 77, WrDr 76*

Clark, Mary Higgins *BioIn 14, –15, –16, –17, SmATA 46, ThrtnMM, WhoAmW 87*

Clark, Mary Higgins 1929- *Au&Arts 10, CelR 90, ConAu 36NR, IntAu&W 89, –91, MajTwCW, TwCCr&M 91, TwCYAW, WhoAm 86, WhoUSWr 88, WhoWrEP 89, –92, WrDr 86, –88, –90, –92, –94*

Clark, Mary Higgins 1930?- *ArtclWW 2*

Clark, Mary Higgins 1931- *BestSel 89-4, WhoAm 88, –90, –92, –94, WhoAmW 89, –91, –93*

Clark, Mary Lou *ConAu X, IntAu&W 77X, –82X*
Main entry: Clark, Maria Louisa Guidish

Clark, Mavis Thorp *AuWomWr*

Clark, Mavis Thorpe *BioIn 16, IntAu&W 91, WrDr 86, –88, –90, –92*

Clark, Mavis Thorpe 1909- *ConAu 37NR, MajAI, SmATA 74, WrDr 94*
Pseud./variant:
Clark, M R

Clark, Mavis Thorpe 1912?- *BioIn 11, ChlLR 30, ConAu 57, –8NR, ConLC 12, FourBJA, OxCAusL, SingR 1, SmATA 8, –5AS, TwCChW 78, –83, –89, WrDr 80, –82, –84*
Pseud./variant:
Latham, Mavis

Clark, Merle *BioIn 12, ConAu X, IntAu&W 77X, SmATA X, WrDr 76, –80, –82, –84, –86, –88, –90, –92*
Main entry: Gessner, Lynne

Clark, Merle 1919- *WrDr 94*

Clark, Patricia 1929- *BioIn 11, ConAu 17R, SmATA 11*

Clark, Ronald W 1916-1987 *AnObit 1987, ScF&FL 92*

Clark, Ronald William *AuBYP 3, BioIn 16*

Clark, Ronald William 1916- *AuBYP 2, Au&Wr 71, BioIn 7, –9, ConAu 25R, ConSFA, SmATA 2*

Clark, Ronald William 1916-1987 *ConAu 122, EncSF 93, SmATA 52N*

Clark, Samuel 1810-1875 *DcNaB, OxCChiL*

Clark, Sue C 1935- *ConAu 41R*

Clark, Van D 1909- *BioIn 9, ConAu P-1, SmATA 2*

Clark, Virginia *AuBYP 3, ConAu X, SmATA 7*
Main entry: Gray, Patricia Clark

Clark, Walter VanTilburg *IntvTCA 2*

Clark, Walter VanTilburg 1909-1971 *AmAu&B, AmNov, BenetAL 91, BioIn 1, –2, –4, –5, –8, –9, –10, –11, –12, –13, –14, CmCal, CnDAL, ConAu 9R, –33R, ConLC 28, ConNov 72, –76, –82A, CyWA 58, –89, DcLB 9, DcLEL 1940, EncFWF, ModAL, NewYTBE 71, Novels, OxCAmL 65, –83, PenC AM, RAdv 1, REn, REnAL, RfGAmL 87, SmATA 8, TwCA SUP, TwCWW 91, WhAm 5, WorAlBi, WorAl*

Clarke, Arthur C *DrmM 2*

Clarke, Arthur C 1917- *Au&Arts 4, Benet 87, BioIn 15, –16, –17, CamGLE, CelR 90, ConAu 28NR, ConNov 86, –91, CyWA 89, EncO&P 2S1, –3, HalFC 88, IntAu&W 86, –89, LiExTwC, MagSWL, MajTwCW, NewEScF, RGTwCSF, ScF&FL 92, ScFSB, ShSCr 3, ShSWr, TwCSFW 86, –91, WorAlBi, WrDr 86, –88, –90, –92*

Clarke, Arthur Charles *IntvTCA 2*

Clarke, Arthur Charles 1917- *AuBYP 2, –3, Au&Wr 71, BioIn 3, –4, –6, –7, –8, –10, –11, –12, –13, –14, BlueB 76, CelR, ConAu 1R, –2NR, ConLC 1, –4, –13, –18, –35, ConNov 72, –76, –82, ConSFA, CurBio 66, DcLEL 1940, EncSF 93, EvLB, FourBJA, Future, HalFC 84, IntAu&W 77, –82, IntWW 74, –75, –76, –77, –78, –79, –80, –81, –82, –83, –89, –91, LongCTC, MajAI, NewC, Novels, OxCEng 85, RAdv 13-5, SmATA 13, –70, TwCA SUP, TwCWr, TwCYAW, WebE&AL, Who 74, –82, –83, –85, –88, –90, –92, WhoAm 86, –88, –92, –94, WhoSciF, WhoWor 74, –78, –82, –84, –87, –89, –91, –93, WorAl, WrDr 76, –80, –82, –84, –94*
Pseud./variant:
O'Brien, E G
Willis, Charles

Clarke, Arthur G 1887- *ConAu P-2*

Clarke, Caroline Cowles Richard 1842-1913 *CarSB*

Clarke, Clorinda 1917- *BioIn 10, ConAu 25R, SmATA 7, WhoAmW 74, WrDr 76, –80, –82, –84*

Clarke, Fred G d1964 *AuBYP 2S, –3*

Clarke, George Frederick 1883- *CanWW 70, CreCan 2, OxCCan*

Clarke, Harry 1889-1931 *BiDScF, BioIn 14, -15, DcIrB 88, PenEncH*

Clarke, Harry 1890-1931 *BioIn 12, -13, ConICB, DcBrAr 1, DcBrBI*

Clarke, J *SmATA 75*
Main entry: Clarke, Judith

Clarke, J Erskine *OxCChiL*

Clarke, J F Gates d1990 *NewYTBS 90*

Clarke, J F Gates 1905- *ConAu P-1*

Clarke, J F Gates 1905-1990 *ConAu 132*

Clarke, J F Gates 1905-1990 *BioIn 17*

Clarke, Joan 1921- *BioIn 13, -15, SmATA 27, -42, TwCChW 78, WrDr 76, -80, -82, -84*

Clarke, Joan B 1921- *ScF&FL 92*

Clarke, John *BioIn 4, -10, ConAu X, CyEd, DrAPF 83, -85, -87, -89, -91, -93, IntAu&W 77X, SmATA 5*
Main entry: Laughlin, Virginia Carli

Clarke, Judith 1943- *ConAu 142, SmATA 75*
Pseud./variant:
Clarke, J

Clarke, Machael *ConAu X*

Clarke, Marjorie E H *SingR 1*

Clarke, Mary Cowden *InWom SUP*

Clarke, Mary Cowden 1809-1898 *BioIn 1, -9, -16, BlmGWL, CelCen, DcBiPP, FemiCLE, OxCChiL, StaCVF*

Clarke, Mary Stetson 1911- *BioIn 10, ConAu 21R, -8NR, SmATA 5, WhoAmW 77, WhoE 83, -85, -86, -89, WrDr 76, -80, -82, -84, -86, -88, -90, -92, -94*

Clarke, Michael *ConAu X, SmATA 6, -X*
Main entry: Newlon, Clarke

Clarke, Mollie *ChhPo S1*

Clarke, Pauline *AnCL, AuBYP 2, Au&Wr 71, BioIn 6, -8, -9, -11, BritCA, ChhPo, ConAu X, IntAu&W 77, -82, -91X, OxCChiL, SmATA 3, ThrBJA, TwCChW 78, -83, WhoChL, WrDr 80, -82, -84*
Main entry: Hunter Blair, Pauline

Clarke, Pauline 1921- *AuBYP 3, ChlLR 28, EngPo, MajAI, ScF&FL 92, TwCChW 89, WrDr 86, -88, -90, -92, -94*

Clarke, Rebecca Sophia *InWom SUP*

Clarke, Rebecca Sophia 1833-1906 *Alli SUP, AmAu, AmAu&B, BiD&SB, BioIn 15, CarSB, ConAu 119, DcAmAu, DcLB 42, DcNAA, DcWomA, OxCChiL, WhAm 1, WomNov*

Clarke, Tom Eugene 1915- *ConAu 5R, WhoPNW*

Clark Latham, Mavis Thorpe 1912?- *DcChlFi*

Clarkson, E Margaret 1915- *ConAu 1R, -5NR, -20NR, IntAu&W 77, -89, SmATA 37, WrDr 76, -80, -82, -84, -86, -88, -90, -92, -94*

Clarkson, Ewan 1929- *BioIn 11, ConAu 25R, -17NR, IntAu&W 91, SmATA 9, TwCChW 78, WhoWor 78, WrDr 76, -80, -82, -84, -86, -88, -90, -92, -94*

Clarkson, Jan Nagel 1943- *ConAu 93, ForWC 70*

Clary, Jack T 1932- *ConAu 57*

Clason, Clyde B 1903- *BioIn 14, TwCCr&M 85, -91*

Clause, Frank *BioIn 6*

Clavel, Bernard 1923- *ConAu 45, -2NR, IntAu&W 77, -82, -89, IntWW 74, -75, -76, -77, -78, -79, -80, -81, -82, -83, -89, -91, WhoWor 74*

Clavel, Bernard Charles Henri 1923- *WhoWor 93*

Clavell, James *BioIn 15, -17, EncJap, IntAu&W 89, -91, Who 88, -90, -92*

Clavell, James 1922- *HalFC 88*

Clavell, James 1924- *AuBYP 3, Benet 87, CelR 90, IntWW 89, -91, WhoAm 86, -88, -90, -92, -94, WhoEnt 92, WorAlBi, WrDr 86, -88, -90, -92, -94*

Clavell, James 1925- *ConAu 26NR, CorNov 91, MajTwCW, ScF&FL 92*

Claveloux, Nicole *IlsBYP*

Claverie, Jean 1946- *BioIn 15, SmATA 38*

Clay, Charles 1906- *CreCan 1, OxCCan*

Clay, Patrice 1947- *BioIn 16, SmATA 47*

Clay, Wil 1938- *BlkAuII 92*

Claypool, Jane *ConAu X, SmATA X*
Main entry: Miner, Jane Claypool

Claypool, Jane 1933- *BioIn 15*

Clayton, Barbara *AuBYP 2S, -3, ConAu X*
Main entry: Pluff, Barbara Littlefield

Clayton, Lawrence Otto, Jr. 1945- *ConAu 142, SmATA 75*

Clayton, Thompson Bowker 1904- *ConAu 57*

Cleary, Beverly *BioIn 14, -15, -16, -17*

Cleary, Beverly 1916- *AmAu&B, Au&Arts 6, AuBYP 2, -3, Au&ICB, BioIn 6, -7, -8, -9, -10, -12, -13, ChlFicS, ChlLR 2, -8, ConAu 1R, -2NR, -19NR, -36NR, DcLB 52, IntAu&W 82, MajTwCW, MorBMP, MorJA, OxCChiL, SmATA 2, -43, TwCChW 78, -83, -89, WhoAm 74, WhoAmW 74, -77, WorAlBi, WrDr 76, -82, -84, -88, -90, -92, -94*

Cleary, Beverly Atlee Bunn 1916- *MajAI*

Cleary, Beverly Bunn 1916- *DcAmChF 1960, -1985*

Cleaver, Bill *BioIn 15, ConAu 38NR, MajAI*

Cleaver, Bill 1920- *TwCChW 89*

Cleaver, Bill 1920-1981 *BioIn 8, -13, ChlLR 6, ConAu 73, DcAmChF 1960, DcLB 52, FourBJA, OxCChiL, SmATA 22, -27N, SouSt, TwCChW 78, -83, TwCYAW*
Pseud./variant:
Cleaver, William

Cleaver, Carole 1934- *BioIn 10, ConAu 49, SmATA 6*

Cleaver, Carole Annamay 1934- *WhoE 93*

Cleaver, Eldridge *IntvTCA 2*

Cleaver, Eldridge 1935- *AmAu&B, BenetAL 91, BioIn 8, -9, -10, -11, -12, -14, -15, -16, -17, BlkAWP, BlkLC, BlkWr 1, CelR, CivR 74, CmCal, ConAu 21R, -16NR, ConLC 30, CurBio 70, DcLEL 1940, EncAACR, LiExTwC, LivgBAA, NegAl 76, -83, -89, PenC AM, SelBAAf, WebE&AL, WhoBlA 77, -80, -85, -88, -90, -92, WrDr 76, -80, -82, -84, -86, -88, -90, -92, -94*

Cleaver, Elizabeth 1939-1985 *BioIn 10, -13, -14, -15, ChlLR 13, ConAu 117, ConGrA 2, FourBJA, IlsCB 1967, OxCCan SUP, Profile 1, SmATA 23, -43N, WhoAmA 78, -80, -82, WhoCanL 85, -87, -92*

Cleaver, Hylton Reginald 1891-1961 *BioIn 8, ConAu 73, LongCTC, OxCChiL, SmATA 49, WhoChL*

Cleaver, Leroy Eldridge 1935- *TwCYAW*

Cleaver, Nancy *ConAu X*
Main entry: Mathews, Evelyn Craw

Cleaver, Vera *AuBYP 3, BioIn 15, -16*

Cleaver, Vera 1919- *AuBYP 2, BioIn 8, -13, ChlLR 6, ConAu 73, -38NR, DcAmChF 1960, DcLB 52, FourBJA, MajAI, OxCChiL, SmATA 22, SouSt, TwCChW 78, -83, -89, WrDr 84, -86, -88, -90, -92*

Cleaver, Vera 1919-1992 *SmATA 76, TwCYAW, WrDr 94N*

Cleaver, Vera 1919-1993 *Au&Arts 12*

Cleaver, William *AuBYP 2*
Main entry: Cleaver, Bill

Cleaver, William Joseph 1920-1981 *AuBYP 3, ConAu 38NR, MajAI*

Cleeve, Brian 1921- *Au&Wr 71, BioIn 14, ConAu 49, -1NR, -16NR, DcIrL, TwCCr&M 80, -85, -91, TwCRHW 90, WrDr 76, -82, -84, -86, -88, -90, -92*

Cleeve, Brian Talbot 1921- *WrDr 94*

Clegg, John 1909- *Au&Wr 71, ConAu 118, IntAu&W 89, -91, WrDr 76, -80, -82, -84, -86, -88, -90, -92, -94*

Cleishbotham, Jebediah *YABC X*

Cleishbotham, Jebediah
Main entry: Scott, Walter

Cleland, Mabel
Main entry: Widdemer, Mabel Cleland

Cleland, Mabel 1902-1964 *BioIn 10, ConAu X, SmATA 5*

Clemens, Samuel L *EncSF 93, ScF&FL 92*

Clemens, Samuel Langhorne *Benet 87, BenetAL 91, CamGEL, EncPaPR 91, RfGAmL 87, TwCSFW 86, -91*

Clemens, Samuel Langhorne 1835-1910 *Alli SUP, AmAu, AmAu&B, AnCL, ArizL, AuBYP 2, -3, BbD, BiDAmJo, BiDPara, BiDSA, BiD&SB, BioIn 1, -2, -3, -4, -5, -6, -7, -8, -9, -10, -11, -12, -13, -14, -15, -16, -17, CamHAL, CarSB, CasWL, CelCen, Chambr 3, ChhPo, -S1, CmCal, CnDAL, ConAu 104, -135, CyAL, DcAmAu, DcAmSR, DcBiPP, DcEnA, DcEnL, DcLB 12, -23, -64, -74, DcLEL, DcNAA, Dis&D, EncAB-H, EncAHmr, EncAJ, EncFWF, EncMys, EncO&P 1, -2, -3, EncSoH, EncWL, EvLB, FifSWrB, HarEnUS, JrnUS, JBA 34, LongCTC, MajAI, OxCAmH, OxCAmL 65, -83, OxCAusL, OxCChiL, OxCEng 67, -85, PenC AM, RAdv 13-1, RComWL, REn,*

REnAL, RealN, TwCA, WebAB 74, –79, WhAm 1, WhCiWar, YABC 2
Pseud./variant:
Mark Twain
Snodgrass, Thomas Jefferson
Twain, Mark

Clemens, Virginia Phelps 1941- *BioIn 14, ConAu 85, –15NR, SmATA 35*

Clement, Charles 1921- *BioIn 5, ChhPo S1, IlsCB 1946, WhoWest 74*

Clement, Charles Dave 1948- *WhoSSW 86*

Clement, Hal *AmAu&B, BioIn 12, –13, ConAu X, DcLB 8, IntvTCA 2, Novels, WrDr 84*
Main entry: Stubbs, Harry C

Clement, Hal 1922- *BioIn 17, ConAu 16AS, EncSF 93, IntAu&W 91, NewEScF, RGTwCSF, ScF&FL 92, ScFSB, TwCSFW 86, –91, WrDr 86, –88, –90, –92, –94*

Clement, Roland Charles 1912- *AmMWSc 73P, –76P, ConAu 49*

Clements, Bruce 1931- *AuBYP 2S, –3, BioIn 13, ConAu 53, –5NR, DcAmChF 1960, FifBJA, SmATA 27, TwCChW 83, –89, TwCYAW, WhoAm 92, –94, WrDr 86, –88, –90, –92, –94*

Clements, Frank *AuBYP 2, BioIn 8*

Clements, Frank A 1942- *AuBYP 3*

Clemons, Elizabeth *ConAu X, ForWC 70, SmATA X, WhoAmW 77, WhoWest 74*
Main entry: Nowell, Elizabeth Cameron

Clepper, Irene E *ConAu 53*

Clerk, N W *ConAu X, –33NR, MajAI, MajTwCW, SmATA X*
Main entry: Lewis, Clive Staples

Clery, Val 1924- *CanWW 89, ConAu 49, –3NR, ScF&FL 92*

Cleveland, Bob *ConAu X, SmATA X*

Cleveland, George d1985 *BioIn 15*

Cleveland, George 1903?-1985 *ConAu 116, SmATA 43N*

Cleven, Cathrine
Main entry: Cleven, Kathryn Seward

Cleven, Kathryn Seward *BioIn 9, ConAu 1R, ForWC 70, SmATA 2*
Pseud./variant:
Cleven, Cathrine

Clevin, Joergen 1920- *BioIn 10, ConAu 29R, SmATA 7*

Clewes, Dorothy 1907- *AuBYP 3, TwCChW 89, WrDr 86, –88, –90, –92*

Clewes, Dorothy Mary 1907- *AuBYP 2, Au&Wr 71, BioIn 8, –9, ConAu 5R, –3NR, OxCChiL, SmATA 1, TwCChW 78, –83, WrDr 80, –82, –84, –94*

Clifford, Carrie Williams *BlkAWP, SouBlCW*

Clifford, Carrie Williams 1862-1934 *HarlReB*

Clifford, Eth *AuBYP 2S, ConAu X, SmATA 3, WhoAmW 85*
Main entry: Rosenberg, Ethel

Clifford, Eth 1915- *AuBYP 3, BioIn 16, SixBJA, WhoAmW 87, –89*

Clifford, Harold B 1893- *BioIn 11, ConAu P-1, SmATA 10*
Pseud./variant:
Farnham, Burt

Clifford, Margaret Cort 1929- *BioIn 9, ConAu 25R, –23NR, ForWC 70, SmATA 1, WhoAmW 74, –75, –77, –91*
Pseud./variant:
Clifford, Peggy
Cort, M C

Clifford, Martin *ConAu X, –29NR, LongCTC, OxCChiL, OxCEng 85, SmATA X, TwCChW 83, –89, WhoChL*

Clifford, Mary Louise 1926- *AuBYP 3, IntAu&W 89, WrDr 86, –88, –90, –92, –94*

Clifford, Mary Louise Beneway 1926- *AuBYP 2S, BioIn 13, ConAu 5R, –3NR, IntAu&W 77, SmATA 23, WrDr 76, –82, –84*

Clifford, Peggy
Main entry: Clifford, Margaret Cort

Clifford, Peggy 1929- *ConAu X, SmATA 1*

Clifford, Rachel Mark *SmATA 72*
Main entry: Lewis, Brenda Ralph

Clifford, W K, Mrs *WomNov*

Clifford, W K, Mrs d1929 *Chambr 3, LongCTC, NotNAT B, OxCChiL, TelT*

Clifford, W K, Mrs 1853-1929 *StaCVF*

Clifton, Fred J d1984 *BioIn 16*

Clifton, Fred J 1935?-1984 *ConAu 114*

Clifton, Harry *ConAu X, –29NR, SmATA X*

Clifton, Lucille *DrAPF 87, –89, –91, –93*

Clifton, Lucille 1936- *ArtclWW 2, BenetAL 91, BioIn 10, –11, –12, –16, –17, BlkAWP, BlkAuII, –92, BlkLC, BlkWWr, BlkWr 1, BlmGWL, ChhPo S1, ChlLR 5, ConAu 49, –2NR, –24NR, ConLC 19, –66, ConPo 75, –80, –85, –91, DcLB 5, –41, DrAP 75, DrAPF 83, –85, FemiCLE, FifBJA, InWom SUP, MajTwCW, OxCChiL, SmATA 20, –69, TwCChW 78, –83, –89, WhoBlA 77, –80, –90, –92, WrDr 76, –80, –82, –84, –86, –88, –90, –92, –94*

Clifton, Thelma Lucille 1936- *MajAI*

Climo, Shirley 1928- *BioIn 14, –15, ConAu 107, –24NR, ScF&FL 92, SmATA 35, –39, –77*

Cline, C Terry, Jr. 1935- *BioIn 10, ConAu 61, –8NR, –25NR, ScF&FL 92*

Cline, Charles Terry, Jr. 1935- *EncSF 93*

Cline, Linda 1941- *ConAu 65, ScF&FL 92, WrDr 80, –82, –84*

Clinton, Dirk *MajAI*

Clinton, Jon *SmATA X*
Main entry: Prince, Jack Harvey

Clish, Marian 1946- *SmATA 43*
Pseud./variant:
Lee, Marian

Clithero, Myrtle E 1906- *ConAu P-2*
Pseud./variant:
Clithero, Sally

Clithero, Sally
Main entry: Clithero, Myrtle E

Clive, Clifford *ConAu X, –29NR, SmATA X*

Clokey, Art *BioIn 14, –16*

Clokey, Art 1921- *SmATA 59*

Cloudsley-Thompson, J L 1921- *ConAu 17R, –8NR, –23NR, SmATA 19, WrDr 80*

Clutesi, George 1909?- *BioIn 9, –10, OxCCan SUP, OxCCanL, Profile 1*

Clutha, Janet Paterson Frame *ScF&FL 92*
Main entry: Frame, Janet

Clutha, Janet Paterson Frame 1924- *ConAu 1R, –2NR, –36NR, MajTwCW*

Clymer, Eleanor 1906- *AuBYP 2, BioIn 7, –11, ConAu 61, –9NR, FourBJA, IntAu&W 82, –86, SmATA 9, –17AS, TwCChW 78, –83, –89, WhoAm 78, –80, –82, –84, –86, –88, –90, WhoWrEP 89, –92, WrDr 76, –80, –82, –84, –86, –88, –90, –92, –94*
Pseud./variant:
Bell, Janet
Kinsey, Elizabeth

Clymer, Eleanor Lowenton 1906- *AuBYP 3, DcAmChF 1960, IntAu&W 89, –91*

Clyne, Patricia Edwards *AuBYP 2S, –3, BioIn 14, SmATA 31*

Clyne, Patricia Edwards 1935- *WhoUSWr 88, WhoWrEP 89, –92*

Coakley, Mary Lewis *IntAu&W 86, –89, –91*

Coakley, Mary Lewis 1907- *BkC 6, ConAu P-1, ForWC 70, IntAu&W 77, –82, WhoAmW 75, WrDr 76, –80, –82, –84, –86, –88, –90, –92, –94*

Coalson, Glo 1946- *BioIn 13, ConAu 103, IlsBYP, IlsCB 1967, SmATA 26*

Coates, Anna 1958- *SmATA 73*
Pseud./variant:
Joseph, Anne
Scotti, Anna

Coates, Belle 1896- *BioIn 9, ConAu 5R, ForWC 70, SmATA 2*

Coates, Doreen Frances 1912- *Au&Wr 71, IntAu&W 77, –86, –89, WrDr 76, –80, –82, –84, –86*

Coates, Ruth Allison 1915- *BioIn 11, ConAu 57, SmATA 11, WhoAmW 77*

Coats, Alice M 1905- *Au&Wr 71, BioIn 1, –11, ConAu 53, IlsCB 1744, SmATA 11, WrDr 76*

Coats, Laura Jane *AuBYP 3*

Coatsworth, Elizabeth 1893- *BenetAL 91, WhoAm 86, WrDr 86*

Coatsworth, Elizabeth 1893-1986 *ConAu 120, ScF&FL 92, SmATA 49N, –56, TwCChW 89, WhAm 9*

Coatsworth, Elizabeth J d1986 *NewYTBS 86*

Coatsworth, Elizabeth Jane 1893- *AmAu&B, AmNov, AnCL, AuBYP 2, Au&ICB, BioIn 2, –4, –7, –8, –9, –10, –11, BkCL, ChhPo, –S1, –S2, ChlLR 2, ConAu 5R, –4NR, DcAmChF 1960, DcLB 22, FamMS, InWom SUP, JBA 34, –51, MorBMP, NewbMB 1922, OxCAmL 65, –83, OxCChiL, REnAL, SmATA 2, Str&VC, TwCA, –SUP, TwCChW 78, –83, WhoAm 74, –76, –78, –80, –82, –84, WhoAmW 74, WhoChL, WhoWor 74, WrDr 80, –82, –84*

Coatsworth, Elizabeth Jane 1893-1986 *AuBYP 3, BioIn 14, –15, –16, MajAI, TwCYAW*

Cobalt, Martin *ConAu 37NR, MajAI, ScF&FL 92, SmATA 68, TwCYAW*
Main entry: Mayne, William James Carter

Cobb, Alice 1909- *ConAu 5R, IndAu 1917*

Cobb, Geoffrey Belton 1892?-1971 *ConAu 104*

Cobb, Jane *SmATA X*

Cobb, Thomas 1854- *Alli, WhoLA*

Cobb, Thomas 1854-1932 *StaCVF*

Cobb, Vicki 1938- *AuBYP 2S, –3, BioIn 11, ChlLR 2, ConAu 33R, –14NR, FifBJA, IntAu&W 89, –91, MajAI, SmATA 8, –69, –6AS, WrDr 76, –80, –82, –84, –86, –88, –90, –92, –94*

Cobbett, Richard *ConAu X, IntAu&W 77X, –82X, –91X, SmATA X, WrDr 80, –82, –84, –86, –88, –90*
Main entry: Pluckrose, Henry

Cobbett, William 1762-1835 *Alli, AmWrBE, AtlBL, BbD, BbtC, BiDLA, –SUP, BiD&SB, BioIn 1, –2, –3, –4, –5, –6, –7, –8, –9, –10, –11, –12, –13, BlmGEL, BritAu 19, CamGEL, CarSB, CasWL, CelCen, Chambr 2, CnDAL, DcAmSR, DcBiPP, DcEnA, DcEnL, DcEuL, DcLB 43, DcLEL, DcNaB, –C, EncAJ, EvLB, HarEnUS, LongCEL, McGEWB, MouLC 3, NewC, OxCAmH, OxCAmL 65, –83, OxCEng 67, –85, OxCLaw, PenC ENG, REn, WebE&AL, WhDW, WhAm HS*

Cobbett, William 1763-1835 *BenetAL 91, BiDAmJo, BioIn 14, –15, –16, –17, CamGLE, DcCanB 6, DcLB 107, JrnUS, RAdv 13-3, RfGEnL 91*

Cober, Alan E 1935- *AmArt, BioIn 15, ConGrA 2, WhoAm 86, –88, –90, –92, –94, WhoAmA 86, –89, –91, WhoE 91*

Cober, Alan Edwin 1935- *AmArt, BioIn 7, –8, –9, –10, –11, –12, FourBJA, IlrAm 1880, –G, IlsBYP, IlsCB 1957, –1967, SmATA 7, WhoAmA 80, –82, –84, WhoGrA 82*

Cobham, Alan, Sir *ConAu X, –29NR, SmATA X*

Coblentz, Catherine Cate 1897-1951 *AnMV 1926, BioIn 2, –14, ChhPo, –S1, JBA 51*

Coblentz, Stanton A *DrAPF 87, –89*

Coblentz, Stanton A 1896- *ConAu 21NR*

Coblentz, Stanton A 1896-1982 *NewEScF, ScF&FL 92, ScFSB, TwCSFW 86, –91*

Coblentz, Stanton Arthur 1896- *AmAu&B, AnMV 1926, Au&Wr 71, BioIn 3, –5, –13, ChhPo, –S1, –S2, ConAu 5R, ConSFA, CurBio 54, DrAPF 83, –85, IntAu&W 77, –82, REnAL, WhAm 8, WhNAA, WhoAm 74, –76, –78, –80, –82, WhoSciF, WrDr 76, –80, –82, –84*

Coblentz, Stanton Arthur 1896-1982 *EncSF 93*

Coburn, Frederick Simpson 1871-1960 *BioIn 1, ChhPo, –S1, –S2, CreCan 2, IlsCB 1744*

Coburn, John Bowen 1914- *AmAu&B, AuBYP 2S, –3, ConAu 1R, –2NR, DrAS 74P, WhoAm 74, –76, –78, –80, –82, –84, –85, –88, –90, –92, –94, WhoE 81, –83, –85, –86, WhoRel 75, –77, –92*

Cocagnac, Augustin Maurice 1924- *BioIn 10, ConAu 25R, –17NR, SmATA 7*
Pseud./variant:
Warbler, J M

Cochran, Bobbye A 1949- *BioIn 11, SmATA 11*

Cochran, Hamilton 1898-1977 *AmAu&B, AmNov, Au&Wr 71, BioIn 2, –11, ConAu 1R, –73, –6NR, IntAu&W 77, WhAm 7, WhoAm 74, –76, WrDr 76*

Cochrane, Alfred Henry John 1865- *WhoLA*

Cochrane, Louise Morley 1918- *ConAu 9R*

Cockett, Mary *ConAu 19NR*

Cockett, Mary 1915- *Au&Wr 71, BioIn 9, ConAu 9R, –4NR, IntAu&W 77, –82, –91, OxCChiL, SmATA 3, TwCChW 78, –83, –89, WrDr 80, –82, –84, –86, –88, –90, –92, –94*

Cockling, Thelma *SingR 1*

Cockrell, Marian 1909- *AmAu&B, AmNov, BioIn 2, –14, ConAu P-2, TwCRHW 90, WrDr 84, –86, –88, –90, –92*

Cockrell, Marian Brown 1909- *WrDr 94*

Cocks, Myra *ConICB*

Cockton, Henry 1807-1853 *Alli, BioIn 8, BritAu 19, CamGLE, CelCen, Chambr 3, DcBiA, DcEnL, DcNaB, NewC, StaCVF, WhoChL*

CoConis, Ted *IlsBYP, IlsCB 1967*

CoConis, Ted 1927- *BiDScF*

Cody, Al *ConAu X, TwCWW 91, WrDr 84, –86*
Main entry: Joscelyn, Archie L

Cody, Iron Eyes *HalFC 88*

Cody, Iron Eyes 1915- *ConTFT 1, HalFC 84, MotPP, WhoAm 76, –78, –80, –82, –84, –86, –88, –92, WhoEnt 92, WhoHol A, WhoWor 82, –84, –87*

Coe, Douglas *AuBYP 2, –3, ConAu X, –39NR, OhA&B, SmATA 1, –X*
Main entry: Epstein, Beryl Williams
Epstein, Samuel

Coe, Lloyd 1899-1976 *BioIn 5, –11, –14, ConAu 69, IlsCB 1946, SmATA 30N, WhAmArt 85, WhoAmA 78N, –80N, –82N*

Coe, Lloyd 1899-1977 *WhoAmA 86N, –89N, –91N*

Coe, Miriam 1902- *IntAu&W 77, IntWWP 82, WhoAmW 74, –75, –77, –81, WhoArt 84, WhoSSW 73, –75, –76, –78, –80, –82, –84, –88, WrDr 76, –80, –82, –84*

Coe, Miriam M 1902- *WhoAm 90*

Coe, Richard N *BioIn 16*

Coe, Richard N 1923- *IntAu&W 91, WrDr 86, –88, –90*

Coe, Richard Nelson 1923- *ConAu 25R, –12NR, IntAu&W 77, WhoWest 87, WhoWor 78, WrDr 76, –82, –84*

Coen, Fabio 1918- *WhoAm 76*

Coen, Rena Neumann 1925- *ConAu 13R, ForWC 70, IntAu&W 91, SmATA 20, WhoAmW 75, –77, WrDr 76, –80, –82, –84, –86, –88, –90, –92, –94*

Coens, Mary Xavier, Sister 1918- *ConAu 21R, DrAS 74E, –78E, –82E, WhoAmW 74*

Coerr, Eleanor 1922- *AuBYP 3, BioIn 16, –17, SixBJA, SmATA 67*

Coerr, Eleanor Beatrice 1922- *AuBYP 2S, BioIn 9, ConAu 25R, IntAu&W 91, MajAI, SmATA 1, WhoAmW 77, –83, WrDr 76, –80, –82, –84, –86, –88, –90, –92, –94*
Pseud./variant:
Hicks, Eleanor B
Page, Eleanor

Coffey, Brian *ConAu 36NR, EncSF 93, LiExTwC, MajTwCW, ScF&FL 92, TwCCr&M 91, TwCYAW, WrDr 86, –88, –90, –92*

Coffey, Brian 1945- *BioIn 14, –15, –17, WrDr 94*

Coffey, Dairine 1933- *AuBYP 2S, –3, ChhPo S1, ConAu 21R*

Coffin, Charles Carleton 1823-1896 *Alli SUP, AmAu, AmAu&B, BenetAL 91, BbD, BiDAmJo, BiD&SB, BioIn 3, –16, CarSB, DcAmAu, DcNAA, EncAJ, HarEnUS, JrnUS, OxCAmL 65, –83, OxCChiL, REnAL, WhCiWar*

Coffin, Geoffrey *AuBYP 2, –3, ConAu X, EncMys, SmATA 3, –X, TwCCr&M 85, –91, WhoSpyF*
Main entry: Mason, Francis VanWyck

Coffin, Joseph 1899- *AuBYP 2S, ConAu 57*

Coffin, Jospeh 1899- *AuBYP 3*

Coffin, Robert P Tristram 1892-1955 *BenetAL 91, ConAu 123*

Coffin, Robert Peter Tristram 1892-1955 *AmAu&B, AnMV 1926, BioIn 1, –3, –4, –5, –6, –7, –8, –9, –11, –15, ChhPo, –S1, –S2, CnDAL, ConAmA, DcLB 45, DcLEL, LongCTC, ObitOF 79, OxCAmL 65, –83, PenC AM, REn, REnAL, Str&VC, TwCA, –SUP, WhAm 3, WhAmArt 85, WhNAA*

Coffman, Ramon Peyton 1896- *AmAu&B, Au&Wr 71, BioIn 9, ConAu P-2, IndAu 1917, SmATA 4, WhAm 10*
Pseud./variant:
Uncle Ray

Coggins, Herbert *AuBYP 2, –3, BioIn 8*

Coggins, Jack B *WrDr 86*

Coggins, Jack B 1914- *WrDr 88, –90, –92, –94*

Coggins, Jack Banham 1911- *AuBYP 2, BioIn 6, –7, –9, ConAu 5R, IntAu&W 77, MorJA, SmATA 2, WhoAm 74, –76, –78, –80, –82, –84, WhoAmA 82, –84, WrDr 76, –82, –84*

Coggins, Jack Banham 1914- *AuBYP 3, WhoAm 86, –88, –90, WhoAmA 86, –89, –91*

Coghill, Nevill Henry 1899-1980 *AnObit 1980, BioIn 12, BlueB 76, ConAu 13R, –102, –11NR, ConDr 73, –77D, IntAu&W 82, IntWW 74, –79, –80, NewC, OxCThe 83, REn, Who 74, WhoThe 77, –81, WrDr 76, –82*

Coghill, Nevill Henry Kendal Aylmer 1899-1980 *DcNaB 1971*

Cogswell, Coralie Norris 1930- *ConAu 13R, ForWC 70*
Pseud./variant:
Howard, Coralie

Cogswell, Frederick William 1917- *Au&Wr 71, CanWr, CasWL, ConAu 5R, ConPo 70, –75, CreCan 2, DrAS 74E, IntAu&W 89, OxCCan, –SUP, WhoAm 80, –82, –84, –86, –88, –90, –92, –94, WhoCanL 85, –87, –92, WhoWrEP 89, –92, WrDr 76, –80*

Cohan, Geoffrey *BioIn 9, –10, –11*

Coheleach, Guy Joseph *WhoAm 86, –88, –90, –92, –94, WhoAmA 86, –89, –91*

Coheleach, Guy Joseph 1932?- *BioIn 9, –10, –11, WhoAm 78, –80, –82, –84, WhoAmA 73, –78, –80, –82, –84, WhoE 75, –77, WhoWor 80, –82*

Cohen, Barbara 1932- *AuBYP 2S, –3, BioIn 11, ConAu 53, –4NR, –19NR, FifBJA, ScF&FL 92, SmATA 10, –7AS, TwCChW 89, WrDr 90, –92*

Cohen, Barbara 1932-1992 *AnObit 1992, ConAu 140, SmATA 74, –77*

Cohen, Barbara Kauder 1932-1992 *WrDr 94N*

Cohen, Caron Lee *AuBYP 3*

Cohen, Daniel 1936- *Au&Arts 7, AuBYP 2S, –3, BioIn 11, –15, –16, ChlLR 3, ConAu 45, –1NR, –20NR, IntAu&W 77, –82, –91, ScF&FL 92, SixBJA, SmATA 8, –4AS, WrDr 88, –90*

Cohen, Daniel E 1936- *MajAI, SmATA 70*

Cohen, Florence Chanock 1927- *ConAu 5R*

Cohen, Jene Barr *AuBYP 3*
Main entry: Barr, Jene

Cohen, Jene Barr 1900-1985 *BioIn 15, ConAu 115, –42NR, SmATA X*

Cohen, Joan Lebold 1932- *BioIn 9, ConAu 25R, –13NR, –30NR, MacBEP, SmATA 4, WhoAmA 78, –80, –82, –84, –86, –89, –91, WhoAmW 74, WhoE 86, –93*

Cohen, Joel H *AuBYP 2S, –3*

Cohen, Judith Louise Carter 1940- *WhoAmW 75, –77*

Cohen, Miriam 1926- *BioIn 13, ConAu 106, FifBJA, SmATA 29, –11AS, WhoAm 92, –94*

Cohen, Morton N 1921- *AuBYP 3, ConAu 28NR, ScF&FL 92, WrDr 86, –88, –92*

Cohen, Morton N 1922- *WrDr 90*

Cohen, Morton Norton 1921- *AuBYP 2S, Au&Wr 71, BioIn 12, ConAu 1R, –5NR, DrAS 74E, –78E, –82E, IntAu&W 77, –82, –89, –91, WrDr 76, –80, –82, –84, –94*
Pseud./variant:
Moreton, John

Cohen, Nora *SmATA 75*
Pseud./variant:
Tarlow, Nora

Cohen, Paul S 1945- *ConAu 123, SmATA 58*

Cohen, Peter Zachary 1931- *BioIn 9, ConAu 33R, –12NR, IntAu&W 82, SmATA 4, WhoMW 84, WrDr 76, –80, –82, –84, –86, –88, –90, –92, –94*

Cohen, Richard Murry 1938- *ConAu 103, –19NR*

Cohen, Robert Carl 1930- *AuBYP 2S, –3, BioIn 11, ConAu 57, SmATA 8*

Cohn, Angelo 1914- *BioIn 12, ConAu 5R, –4NR, IntAu&W 77, SmATA 19*

Cohn, Emma 1922- *BiDrLUS 70, WhoLibI 82, WhoLibS 66*

Cohn, Nik 1946- *AuBYP 2S, –3, Au&Wr 71, ConAu 102, ScF&FL 92*

Coit, Margaret Louise 1919- *AmAu&B, AuBYP 2, –3, Au&Wr 71, BioIn 2, –3, –4, –7, –9, ConAu 1R, –5NR, CurBio 51, DrAS 74H, ForWC 70, IntAu&W 77, OxCAmL 65, REnAL, SmATA 2, TwCA SUP, WhoAm 74, –76, –78, –80, –82, –84, –86, –88, –90 –92, –94, WhoAmW 74*

Coke, Desmond 1879-1940? *BioIn 8, OxCChiL, WhoChL, WhoLA*

Colabella, Vincent *IlsBYP*

Colbeck, Alfred *Alli SUP*

Colbeck, Maurice 1925- *Au&Wr 71, ConAu 13R, –5NR, –34NR, IntAu&W 77, –89, –91, WrDr 76, –80, –82, –84, –86, –88, –90, –92, –94*

Colbert, Anthony 1934- *BioIn 12, –14, IlsCB 1967, SmATA 15*

Colbert, Edwin H 1905- *WhoAm 86, –88*

Colbert, Edwin Harris 1905- *AmMWSc 73P, –76P, –82, –86, –89, –92, BioIn 2, –3, –7, –16, BlueB 76, ConAu 61, –8NR, CurBio 65, IntWW 74, –75, –76, –77, –78, –79, –80, –81, –82, –83, –89, –91, WhoAm 74, –76, –78, –80, –82, –84, –90, –92, –94, WhoFrS 84, WrDr 76, –82, –84, –86, –88, –90, –92, –94*

Colby, Carroll B 1904-1977 *BioIn 14*

Colby, Carroll Burleigh 1904-1977 *AuBYP 2, -3, BioIn 6, -7, -9, ConAu 1R, -6NR, IntAu&W 77, MorJA, SmATA 3, -35, WhAm 7, WhoAm 74, -76, -78*

Colby, Jean Poindexter 1907- *WrDr 92, -94*

Colby, Jean Poindexter 1909- *AuBYP 2S, -3, BioIn 2, ChhPo S1, ConAu 1R, -5NR, ForWC 70, IntAu&W 77, SmATA 23, WhoAmW 74, -75, WrDr 76, -80, -82, -84, -86, -88, -90*

Coldrey, Jennifer *AuBYP 3*

Coldrey, Jennifer 1940- *ConAu 121*

Coldsmith, Donald Charles 1926- *IntAu&W 86, WhoMW 74, -76, -78*

Cole, Ann 1937- *ConAu 65*

Cole, Annette *AuBYP 3, ConAu X, -30NR, SmATA X*
Main entry: Steiner, Barbara A

Cole, Babette *BioIn 17, TwCChW 89, WrDr 90, -94*

Cole, Babette 1949- *SmATA 61*

Cole, Brock 1938- *BioIn 16, ChlLR 18, ConAu 136, DcAmChF 1985, MajAI, SixBJA, SmATA 72, TwCYAW, WrDr 94*

Cole, Davis *AuBYP 2, -3, ConAu X, SmATA 2*
Main entry: Elting, Mary

Cole, Edward Bender 1923- *ConAu 107, WhoRel 75, -77*

Cole, Hannah 1954- *SmATA 74*

Cole, Henry 1808-1882 *BioIn 16*

Cole, Henry, Sir *OxDcArt*

Cole, Henry, Sir 1808-1882 *BioIn 2, -6, -14, CelCen, DcBiPP, DcNaB, DcVicP 2, MacEA, OxCChiL*

Cole, Jack *BioIn 12, ConAu X, SmATA X*
Main entry: Stewart, John

Cole, Jackson *ConAu X, EncFWF, SmATA X, TwCWW 91*
Main entry: Schisgall, Oscar

Cole, Jackson 1901-1986 *BioIn 15*

Cole, Jennifer *SmATA 70, -X*
Main entry: Stevens, Serita Deborah
Zach, Cheryl

Cole, Joanna *BioIn 15, -16*

Cole, Joanna 1944- *AuBYP 3, ChlLR 5, ConAu 115, -36NR, FifBJA, MajAI, ScF&FL 92, SmATA 37, -49*
Pseud./variant:
Cooke, Ann

Cole, Lois Dwight 1903?-1979 *AmAu&B, AuBYP 2, -3, BioIn 8, -11, -13, ConAu 1R, -104, -4NR, SmATA 10, -26N*
Pseud./variant:
Arnett, Caroline
Avery, Lynn
Dudley, Nancy
Dwight, Allan
Eliot, Anne

Cole, Margaret Alice *ConAu 9R, -6NR*

Cole, Michael 1947- *BioIn 16, SmATA 59*

Cole, Sheila R 1939- *ConAu 53, -4NR, SmATA 24, WrDr 76, -80, -82, -84, -86, -88, -90, -92, -94*

Cole, Stephen *ConAu X*
Main entry: Webbe, Gale D

Cole, Walter 1891- *BioIn 1, IlsCB 1744*

Cole, William *DrAPF 87, -89, -91, -93*

Cole, William 1919- *AuBYP 3, IntAu&W 91, SmATA 9AS, WrDr 86, -88, -90, -92, -94*

Cole, William Rossa 1919- *AuBYP 2, BioIn 8, -11, BkP, ChhPo, -S1, -S2, ConAu 9R, FourBJA, MajAI, SmATA 9, -71, WrDr 76*

Coleman, Francis 1913- *Au&Wr 71*

Coleman, Ken *BioIn 9, -13*

Coleman, Lester Laudy 1911- *WhoAm 80, -82, -84, -86, -88, -90, -92, -94*

Coleman, Lonnie *ConAu 39NR*

Coleman, Lonnie 1920-1982 *AmAu&B, AmNov, BiE&WWA, BioIn 2, -4, -5, -13, ConAu 77, -107, CurBio 58, -82N, NewYTBS 82, NotNAT*

Coleman, Pauline Hodgkinson *AuBYP 2, -3, BioIn 7*

Coleman, Ralph P d1968 *WhoAmA 86N*

Coleman, Ralph P 1892-1968 *WhoAmA 89N, -91N*

Coleman, Ralph Pallen 1892-1968 *BioIn 8, -12, IlrAm 1880, -D, WhAm 5, WhAmArt 85, WhoAmA 78N, -80N, -82N*

Coleman, Satis Narrona 1878-1961 *BioIn 5, WhAm 4, WhNAA*

Coleman, William L 1938- *BioIn 14, –16, ConAu 21NR, SmATA 34, –49*

Coleman, William V 1932- *ConAu 25NR*

Coleman, William Vincent 1932- *AmCath 80, ConAu 57, –9NR, IntAu&W 86*

Coleridge, Samuel Taylor 1772-1834 *Alli, AtlBL, Benet 87, BbD, BiDLA, BiDPsy, BiD&SB, BioIn 1, –2, –3, –4, –5, –6, –7, –8, –9, –10, –11, –12, –13, –14, –15, –16, –17, BlmGEL, BritAu 19, BritWr 4, CamGEL, CamGLE, CasWL, CelCen, Chambr 3, ChhPo, –S1, –S2, CnDBLB 3, CnE&AP, CrtT 2, CyWA 58, DcBiPP, DcEnA, DcEnL, DcEuL, DcLB 93, –107, DcLEL, DcNaB, –C, Dis&D, EncO&P 1, –2, –3, EncPaPR 91, EncWT, EvLB, LongCEL, LuthC 75, MagSWL, McGEWB, MouLC 3, NewC, NinCLC 9, NotNAT B, OxCEng 67, –85, OxCMus, OxCThe 67, –83, PenC ENG, PenEncH, RAdv 1, –13-1, RComWL, REn, RfGEnL 91, WebE&AL, WhDW, WorAlBi, WorAl, WorLitC, WrPh*

Coleridge, Samuel Taylor, Mrs *ArtclWW 2*

Coleridge, Sara 1802-1852 *Alli, BiD&SB, BioIn 10, –16, –17, BlmGWL, BritAu 19, CamGLE, CasWL, CelCen, Chambr 3, ChhPo, –S1, –S2, ContDcW 89, DcBiPP, DcEnL, DcLEL, DcNaB, EncBrWW, EvLB, FemiCLE, IntDcWB, NewC, NinCLC 31, OxCChiL, OxCEng 67, –85, StaCVF, Str&VC*

Coles, Robert Martin 1929- *AmAu&B, AuBYP 2S, –3, Au&Wr 71, BiDrAPA 77, BioIn 8, –9, –10, –11, –13, BlueB 76, CelR, ConAu 45, –3NR, CurBio 69, IntAu&W 89, IntWW 89, –91, MedPD, SmATA 23, WhoAm 74, –76, –82, –84, WhoE 83, WrDr 80, –82, –84*

Colin, Ann *MajAI*
Main entry: Ure, Jean

Collard, Derek 1936- *BioIn 12, –14, IlsBYP, IlsCB 1967*

Collett, Rosemary K 1931- *ConAu 69*

Collier, Basil 1908- *Au&Wr 71, ConAu 5R, –2NR*

Collier, Christopher 1930- *AuBYP 2S, –3, BioIn 11, –12, –14, –15, –16, ConAu 33R, –13NR, –33NR, ConLC 30, DcAmChF 1960, DrAS 74H, –78H, –82H, FifBJA, MajAI, SmATA 16, –70, TwCYAW, WhoE 75*

Collier, Edmund *AuBYP 2, –3, BioIn 7*

Collier, Ethel 1903- *AuBYP 2, –3, BioIn 8, –13, ConAu 65, SmATA 22*

Collier, Eugenia W 1928- *BlkAWP, ConAu 49, LivgBAA, SelBAAu, WhoBlA 77, –80, –85, –88, –90, –92, –94, WrDr 76, –80*

Collier, Eugenia Williams 1928- *BlkWr 2*

Collier, James L 1928- *ConAu 33NR*

Collier, James Lincoln 1928- *AuBYP 2S, –3, BioIn 7, –11, –14, –15, –16, ChlLR 3, ConAu 9R, –4NR, ConLC 30, DcAmChF 1960, FifBJA, MajAI, ScF&FL 92, SmATA 8, –70, TwCChW 89, TwCYAW, WrDr 90, –92, –94*
Pseud./variant:
Williams, Charles

Collier, Jane *ConAu 43NR, WhoUSWr 88, WhoWrEP 89, –92, WrDr 86, –88, –90, –92*
Main entry: Hampson, Zena

Collier, Jane 1926- *IntAu&W 82X, SmATA X, WrDr 82, –84*

Collier, John 1901-1980 *AnObit 1980, Benet 87, BioIn 2, –4, –11, –12, –14, –15, ConAu 97, –10NR, ConNov 72, –76, CyWA 89, DcLB 77, DcLEL, EncMys, FilmgC, HalFC 84, –88, LongCTC, NewC, NewYTBS 80, Novels, OxCEng 85, PenC AM, PenEncH, REn, REnAL, ScF&FL 92, ScFEYrs, SupFW, TwCA, –SUP, TwCCr&M 80, –85, –91, WrDr 76*

Collier, John Henry Noyes 1901-1980 *EncSF 93*

Collier, Peter *BioIn 14, NewYTBS 89*

Collier, Peter 1939- *BioIn 16, ConAu 65 IntAu&W 91, WrDr 84, –86, –88, –90, –92*

Collier, Peter Anthony 1939- *WrDr 94*

Collier, Steven 1942- *BioIn 17, SmATA 51*

Collier, Zena *DrAPF 87, –89, –91, –93*
Main entry: Hampson, Zena

Collier, Zena 1926- *BioIn 13, ConAu X, –3NR, –43NR, DrAPF 83, –85, IntAu&W 77X, –82X, SmATA 23, WhoAm 80, WhoAmW 81, WhoE 86, WhoUSWr 88, WhoWrEP 89, –92, WrDr 76, –80, –82, –84, –86, –88, –90, –92*

Collin, Hedvig *AuBYP 2, –3, BioIn 5, –8, ConICB, IlsCB 1946*

Collings, Ellsworth 1887- *AuBYP 2, –3, BioIn 7, ConAu 73, WhAm 8*

Collington, Peter *AuBYP 3, BioIn 16, –17*

Collington, Peter 1948- *ConAu 127, SmATA 59*

Collingwood, Harry *Alli SUP, WhoChL*

DcAmChF 1960, ForWC 70, MajAI, MorBMP, SmATA 1, –53, –14AS, ThrBJA, TwCChW 89, TwCYAW, WrDr 90, –92
Pseud./variant:
Crayder, Teresa

Colman, Hila Crayder *WrDr 94*

Colman, Morris 1899?-1981 *BioIn 12, –13, SmATA 25N*

Colman, Penny Morgan 1944- *SmATA 77*

Colman, Warren *BioIn 17*

Colman, Warren 1944- *SmATA 67*

Colman, Warren David 1944- *ConAu 136, WhoEnt 92, WrDr 94*

Colombo, John Robert 1936- *BioIn 15, –16, CanWW 80, –81, –83, –89, ConAu 25R, –11NR, ConPo 70, –75, –80, –85, –91, CreCan 2, DcLB 53, EncO&P 3, EncSF 93, IntAu&W 82, –86, –89, –91, IntWW 89, –91, IntWWP 82, OxCCan, –SUP, OxCCanL, ScF&FL 92, SmATA 50, WhoAm 80, –82, –84, –86, –88, –90, –92, –94, WhoCanL 85, –87, –92, WhoE 74, –83, WhoWrEP 89, –92, WrDr 76, –80, –82, –84, –86, –88, –90, –92, –94*

Colonius, Lillian 1911- *BioIn 9, ConAu 21R, SmATA 3*

Colorado, Antonio J 1903- *ConAu 32NR, HispWr*

Colorado, Antonio Julio
Main entry: Colorado Capella, Antonio Julio

Colorado, Antonio Julio 1903- *BioIn 13, SmATA 23*

Colorado Capella, Antonio J 1903- *ConAu 32NR*

Colorado Capella, Antonio Julio 1903- *ConAu 17R, PueRA*
Pseud./variant:
Colorado, Antonio Julio

Colt, Martin *AuBYP 2, –3, ConAu X, –39NR, SmATA 1, –X*
Main entry: Epstein, Samuel

Colton, Helen 1918- *ConAu 57, WhoAmW 74, –75*

Colton, Joel 1918- *ConAu 1R, –2NR, DrAS 74H, –78H, –82H, IntAu&W 77, –82, –86, –89, –91, WhoAm 74, –76, –78, –80, –82, –84, –86, –88, –90, –92, –94, WhoSSW 93, WhoWorJ 72, –78, WrDr 76, –80, –82, –84, –86, –88, –90, –92, –94*

Colum, Padraic *IntvTCA 2*

Colum, Padraic 1881-1972 *AmAu&B, AnCL, ASCAP 66, AuBYP 2, –3, Benet 87, BenetAL 91, BiDIrW, BioIn 1, –2, –3, –4, –5, –7, –8, –9, –10, –12, –13, –14, –17, BkC 3, CamGEL, CamGLE, CamGWoT, CarSB, CasWL, CathA 1930, ChhPo, –S1, –S2, CnMD, ConAu 33R, –73, –35NR, ConLC 28, ConPo 70, CyWA 89, DcIrB 88, DcIrL, DcIrW 1, DcLB 19, DcLEL, EncWL, EvLB, FamSYP, IntDcT 2, JBA 34, –51, LongCTC, MajAI, MajTwCW, McGEWB, McGEWD 72, –84, ModBrL, –S1, ModIrL, ModWD, NewC, NewYTBE 71, –72, NotNAT A, ObitT 1971, OxCChiL, OxCEng 85, OxCThe 67, –83, PenC ENG, RAdv 1, –13-1, REn, REnWD, RfGEnL 91, SmATA 15, Str&VC, TwCA, –SUP, TwCChW 78, –83, –89, TwCWr, WebE&AL, WhDW, WhAm 5, –7, WrChl*

Columella *MajAI, SmATA X*
Main entry: Moore, Clement Clarke

Colver, Alice Mary 1892- *AuBYP 3*

Colver, Alice Mary Ross 1892- *AmAu&B, AmNov, AuBYP 2, BioIn 2, –7, ConAu 69, WhNAA*

Colver, Anne 1908- *AmAu&B, AuBYP 2, –3, BioIn 7, –10, ConAu 45, –2NR, OhA&B, SmATA 7*
Pseud./variant:
Graff, Polly Anne Colver
Harris, Colver

Colwell, Eileen *ChlFicS, OxCChiL*

Colwell, Eileen 1904- *BioIn 6, –8, –9, ChhPo S1, ConAu 29R, –12NR, CurBio 63, SmATA 2, WhoChL*

Colwell, Robert 1931- *ConAu 33R*

Colwyn, Stewart *ConAu 127, SmATA X*
Main entry: Pepper, Frank S

Colyer, Penrose 1940- *ConAu 65, –14NR, –20NR*

Comay, Joan *ConAu 103, IntAu&W 77, –82, WrDr 80, –82, –84, –86, –88, –90*

Comber, Dorothy 1902- *SingR 2*

Comber, Lillian 1916- *Au&Wr 71, ConAu 9R, –3NR*
Pseud./variant:
Beckwith, Lillian

Combs, Joseph Franklin 1892- *WhoSSW 73, –75, –76, –78, –80, –82*

Combs, Robert *ConAu X, SmATA X*
Main entry: Murray, John

Comenius, Johann Amos 1592-1670? *BbD, BiD&SB, BioIn 1, –4, –7, –8, –9, –10, –12, CarSB, CasWL, ChhPo, –S1, CyEd, DcBiPP, DcEuL, Dis&D, EuAu, EvEuW, LuthC 75, OxCChiL, OxCEng 85, PenC EUR, Str&VC, WhDW, WorAl*

Comfort, Barbara 1916- *BioIn 5, IlsCB 1946, WhAmArt 85*

Comfort, Iris Tracy 1917- *ConAu 13R, –6NR, IntAu&W 77, –82, WhoAmW 83, WrDr 76, –80, –82, –84, –86, –88, –90*

Comfort, J L *AuBYP 3*

Comfort, Jane Levington *AuBYP 2, BioIn 8, ConAu X, SmATA 1*
Main entry: Sturtzel, Jane Levington

Comfort, Jane Levington 1903- *AuBYP 3*

Comfort, Mildred Houghton 1886- *BioIn 6, –9, –10, ConAu 9R, MinnWr, SmATA 3*

Comins, Ethel Mae 1901- *BioIn 11, ConAu 61, –8NR, SmATA 11, WhoAmW 74, –75, –77*

Comins, Jeremy 1933- *BioIn 13, ConAu 65, –14NR, SmATA 28*

Commager, Evan Carroll 1903?-1968 *BioIn 8*

Commager, Henry Steele 1902- *AmAu&B, AuBYP 2, –3, Benet 87, BenetAL 91, BioIn 1, –2, –4, –7, –10, –13, –16, –17, BioNews 74, BlueB 76, ChhPo S1, ConAu 21R, –26NR, CurBio 46, DcLB 17, DcLEL, DrAS 74H, –78H, –82H, EncWB, IntAu&W 77, IntWW 74, –75, –76, –77, –78, –79, –80, –81, –82, –83, –89, –91, MajTwCW, OxCAmH, OxCAmL 65, –83, PenC AM, RAdv 13-3, REn, REnAL, SmATA 23, TwCA SUP, WebAB 74, –79, WhAm 8, Who 74, –82, –83, –85, –88, –90, –92, WhoAm 74, –76, –78, –80, –82, –86, –88, –90, WhoE 74, WhoWor 74, WorAlBi, WorAl, WrDr 76, –80, –82, –84, –86, –88, –90, –92, –94*

Commins, Dorothy Berliner *AuBYP 2, –3, BioIn 8*

Commins, Dorothy Berliner d1991 *NewYTBS 91*

Commins, Saxe 1892?-1958 *AmAu&B, BioIn 5, ObitOF 79*

Commire, Anne *BioIn 15, ChhPo S2, ConAu 69, –21NR, ConTFT 1, NatPD 77, –81, WhoAm 80, –82, –84, –86, –88, –90, –92, –94, WhoAmW 81, WhoEnt 92, WhoUSWr 88, WhoWrEP 89, –92*

Comparetti, Alice 1907- *ConAu 37R, DrAS 74E*

Compere, Janet *IlsBYP*

Compton, Margaret *DcNAA*

Compton, Patricia A 1936- *ConAu 142, SmATA 75*

Comstock, Anna Botsford 1854-1930 *ArtsAmW 3, BioIn 1, –2, –3, –6, –9, –11, –15, –16, InSci, InWom SUP, WhAm 1, WhAmArt 85, WhNAA, WomWWA 14, WomSc*

Comte, The Great *SmATA X*

Comte, The Great
Main entry: Hawkesworth Eric William

Comus *SmATA X*
Main entry: Ballantyne, Robert Michael

Conan Doyle, Arthur
Main entry: Doyle, Arthur Conan, Arthur

Conan Doyle, Arthur 1859-1930 *CnDBLB 5, CorpD, EncMys, OxCEng 85, SmATA X*

Conan Doyle, Arthur, Sir 1859-1930 *GrBr*

Conant, Roger 1909- *AmMWSc 73P, –76P, –82, –86, –89, –92, ConAu 107*

Condit, Martha Olson 1913- *BiDrLUS 70, BioIn 13, ConAu 73, SmATA 28, WhoAmW 75, –77, –83, WhoLibI 82, WhoLibS 55, –66*

Condon, Richard Thomas 1915- *AmAu&B, Au&Wr 71, BioIn 2, –9, –10, –11, ConAu 1R, ConLC 4, –6, –8, –10, ConNov 72, –76, IntAu&W 77, IntWW 89, –91, ModAL, –S1, PenC AM, SpyFic, WhoAm 74, –76, –78, –88, –90, –92, –94, WhoEnt 92, WhoSpyF, WhoWor 74, –78, WorAu 1950, WrDr 76, –80*

Cone, Ferne Geller *IntAu&W 86*

Cone, Ferne Geller 1921- *BioIn 15, ConAu 107, SmATA 39, WhoAmW 91*

Cone, Molly 1918- *SmATA 11AS, WrDr 86, –88, –90*

Cone, Molly Lamken 1918- *AuBYP 2, –3, BioIn 7, –9, –13, ConAu 1R, –1NR, –16NR, –37NR, DcAmChF 1960, ForWC 70, IntAu&W 77, SmATA 1, –28, ThrBJA, WrDr 76, –82, –84*
Pseud./variant:
More, Caroline

Cone, Sydney M, Jr. 1904- *WhoAm 74*

Coney, Michael G 1932- *ScFSB, SmATA 61, TwCSFW 86, -91, WrDr 86, -88, -90, -92*

Coney, Michael Greatrex 1932- *EncSF 93, IntAu&W 91, WrDr 94*

Conford, Ellen *BioIn 16, -17*

Conford, Ellen 1942- *Au&Arts 10, AuBYP 2S, -3, BioIn 10, ChlLR 10, ConAu 33R, -13NR, -29NR, FifBJA, IntAu&W 91, MajAI, ScF&FL 92, SmATA 6, -68, TwCChW 83, -89, TwCYAW, WrDr 76, -80, -82, -84, -86, -88, -90, -92, -94*

Congdon, Tom 1931?- *BioIn 10*

Conger, Lesley *ConAu X, SmATA X, WhoWrEP 89, -92*
Main entry: Suttles, Shirley

Conger, Marion *AuBYP 3*

Conger, Marion 1915- *AuBYP 2, BioIn 8, IndAu 1917*

Conger, Marion 1915-1990 *ConAu 130*

Conklin, Gladys 1903- *AuBYP 3*

Conklin, Gladys Plemon 1903- *AuBYP 2, BiDrLUS 70, BioIn 8, -9, ConAu 1R, -4NR, ForWC 70, FourBJA, SmATA 2, WhoAmW 75, -77*

Conklin, Groff 1904-1968 *AmAu&B, BioIn 8, ConAu 1R, -3NR, ScFEYrs, WhoSciF*

Conklin, Paul *AuBYP 2S, -3, BioIn 14, -15, ConAu 111, -115, SmATA 33, -43*

Conkling, Fleur *AuBYP 2, -3, BioIn 7*

Conkling, Hilda 1910- *AmAu&B, AnCL, BenetAL 91, BioIn 1, -9, -13, BkCL, ChhPo, ConAmL, InWom SUP, REnAL, SmATA 23, Str&VC, TwCA, -SUP, WhNAA*

Conkling, Hilda 1910-1986 *BioIn 16*

Conlon-McKenna, Marita 1956- *SmATA 71*

Conly, Jane Leslie *AuBYP 3, EncSF 93, ScF&FL 92, TwCYAW*

Conly, Robert Leslie *AuBYP 3*

Conly, Robert Leslie 1918?-1973 *AuBYP 2S, ConAu 41R, -73, MajAI, SmATA 23*
Pseud./variant:
O'Brien, Robert C

Conn, Frances 1925- *AuBYP 3*

Conn, Frances Goldberg 1925- *AuBYP 2S, ConAu 33R*

Connell, Kirk *ConAu X, SmATA X*
Main entry: Chapman, John Stanton Higham

Connelly, John Peter 1926- *AmCath 80, WhoAm 84, WhoE 74, WhoFrS 84, WhoMW 74, -76, -78, -80, -82, -84*

Connelly, John Peter 1926-1986 *WhAm 9*

Connelly, Marc 1890-1980 *AnObit 1980, Benet 87, BenetAL 91, BioIn 1, -4, -5, -8, -10, -12, -13, -14, -15, BlueB 76, CamGLE, CamGWoT, CamHAL, ConAu 102, -30NR, CurBio 81N, CyWA 89, DcLB 7, -Y80A, EncAHmr, HalFC 84, -88, IntWW 79, -80, -81N, McGEWD 84, NewYTBS 80, OxCAmL 83, RfGAmL 87, SmATA 25N, WebAB 79, WhAm 7, WhScrn 83, Who 82N, WhoAm 80, WhoThe 81, WorAlBi, WrDr 82*

Connelly, Marc 1890-1981 *OxCAmT 84*

Connelly, Marcus Cook 1890-1980 *ConDr 93, IntDcT 2*

Conner, Patrick Reardon
Main entry: Conner, Rearden

Conner, Rearden 1907- *Au&Wr 71, BiDIrW, BlueB 76, ConAu 5R, DcIrW 1, IntAu&W 77, Who 74, -82, -83, -85, -88, -90, WrDr 76, -80, -82, -84, -86, -88, -90, -92, -94*
Pseud./variant:
Conner, Patrick Reardon

Connolly, Jerome Patrick 1931- *BioIn 8, -11, IlsBYP, IlsCB 1957, SmATA 8, WhoAmA 73, -78, -80, -82, -84, -86, -89, -91*

Connolly, Pat 1943- *SmATA 74*

Connolly, Peter 1935- *BioIn 16, IntAu&W 89, -91, SmATA 47, WrDr 86, -88, -90, -92, -94*

Connor, Chris *IlsCB 1967*

Connor, Chris 1927- *InWom SUP*

Connor, James *AuBYP 2S, -3*

Connor, Joyce Mary 1929- *ConAu X, -10NR, WrDr 76, -80, -82, -84*
Pseud./variant:
Marlow, Joyce

Connor, Ralph *BenetAL 91, CanWr, CasWL, Chambr 3, ChhPo, ConAu X, CreCan 1, DcBiA, DcLEL, DcNaB 1931, DcNAA, EvLB, LongCTC, LuthC 75, NewC, OxCAmL 65, -83, OxCCan, OxCCanL, OxCChiL, REnAL, TwCA, -SUP, TwCChW 78, TwCWr, WhNAA*
Main entry: Gordon, Charles William

Connor, Ralph 1860-1937 *BioIn 17, DcLB 92, TwCLC 31, TwCWW 91*

Conover, Chris *ChlBlD*

Conover, Chris 1950- *AuBYP 2S, -3, BioIn 12, -14, -16, ConAu 128, IlsCB 1967, SixBJA, SmATA 31*

Conquest, Owen *BioIn 8, -10, ConAu X, -29NR, LongCTC, SmATA X, WhoChL*

Conrad, Arthur S 1907- *BioIn 5, IlsCB 1946*

Conrad, Joseph *IntvTCA 2*

Conrad, Joseph 1856-1924 *ScFEYrs*

Conrad, Joseph 1857-1924 *AtlBL, Benet 87, BbD, BiD&SB, BioIn 1, -2, -3, -4, -5, -6, -7, -8, -9, -10, -11, -12, -13, -14, -15, -16, -17, BlmGEL, BritWr 6, CamGEL, CamGLE, CasWL, Chambr 3, CnDBLB 5, CnMD, CnMWL, ConAu 104, -131, CyWA 58, -89, DcEnA A, DcEuL, DcLB 10, -34, -98, DcLEL, DcNaB 1922, Dis&D, EncMys, EncSF 93, EncWL, -2, EvLB, FilmgC, GrBr, HalFC 84, -88, JBA 34, LiExTwC, LongCEL, LongCTC, MagSWL, MajTwCW, MakMC, McGEWB, ModBrL, -S1, -S2, ModWD, NewC, Novels, OxCAusL, OxCEng 67, -85, OxCShps, PenC ENG, PenEncH, RAdv 1, -13-1, RComWL, REn, RfGEnL 91, RfGShF, ShSCr 9, ShSWr, SmATA 27, SpyFic, TwCA, -SUP, TwCLC 1, -6, -13, -25, -43, TwCWr, WebE&AL, WhDW, WhoSpyF, WhoTwCL, WorAlBi, WorAl, WorLitC, WrPh*

Conrad, Pam 1947- *BioIn 16, -17, ChlLR 18, ConAu 121, -36NR, DcAmChF 1985, MajAI, ScF&FL 92, SixBJA, SmATA 49, -52, TwCYAW, WhoAm 92, -94, WrDr 90, -92, -94*

Conrad, Sybil 1921- *AuBYP 2, -3, BioIn 8, ConAu 21R*

Conroy, Jack 1898- *WhoAm 88*

Conroy, Jack 1898-1990 *WhAm 10*

Conroy, Jack 1899- *BenetAL 91, BioIn 15, CamHAL, EncAHmr, WhoAm 86, WhoUSWr 88, WhoWrEP 89*

Conroy, Jack 1899-1980 *AmAu&B, AmNov, BioIn 2, -10, -12, -13, BlueB 76, CamGLE, ConAu 5R, ConNov 72, -76, -82, DcLB Y81B, IntAu&W 77, -82, IntYB 80, -81, -82, Novels, OhA&B, OxCAmL 65, -83, SmATA 19, WhNAA, WhoAm 74, -76, -78, -80, -82, -84, WrDr 76, -80, -82, -84*
Pseud./variant:
Brennan, Tim
Conroy, John Wesley
Norcross, John

Conroy, Jack 1899-1990 *BioIn 16, -17*
Pseud./variant:
Morine, Hoder

Conroy, John Wesley 1899-1980
Main entry: Conroy, Jack

Conroy, John Wesley 1899-1990 *ConAu 131, IntAu&W 86, SmATA 65, WhoUSWr 88*

Conroy, Robert *AuBYP 3, ConAu X*
Main entry: Goldston, Robert Conroy

Conroy, Robert Warren 1938- *WhoAm 92*

Considine, Robert Bernard 1906-1975 *AmAu&B, AuNews 2, BiDAmJo, BioIn 1, -5, -7, -10, -11, CathA 1930, CelR, ConAu 61, -93, CurBio 47, -75N, EncAJ, EncTwCJ, REnAL, WhAm 6, WhoAm 74, WhoWor 74, WorAl*

Constant, Alberta 1908-1981 *AuBYP 3*

Constant, Alberta Wilson 1908-1981 *AuBYP 2S, BioIn 3, ConAu 1R, -109, -4NR, SmATA 22, -28N*

Constiner, Merle *WrDr 84, -86, -88, -90*

Contreras, Jerry *IlsBYP*

Converse, Florence 1871- *AmAu&B, AmWomPl, BiDSA, CarSB, ChhPo, -S1, -S2, DcAmAu, WhAm 6, WhNAA, WomWWA 14, WomNov*

Conway, Gordon *ConAu X, -29NR, SmATA X*

Conway, Helene *AuBYP 2, -3, BioIn 7*

Conway, Richard *BioIn 10*

Cook, Bernadine F 1924- *BioIn 11, MichAu 80, SmATA 11*

Cook, Fred J *BioIn 14*

Cook, Fred J 1911- *ConAu 23NR*

Cook, Fred James 1911- *AmAu&B, AuBYP 2, -3, BioIn 4, -5, -7, -9, ConAu 9R, -3NR, DcAmAu, EncAJ, EncTwCJ, SmATA 2, WhoAm 74, -76, -78, -80, -82, -84, -86, -88, -90, -92, -94, WhoWor 74*

Cook, George S 1920- *ConAu 49*

Cook, Gladys Emerson *WhoAmA 86N*

Cook, Gladys Emerson 1899- *AmAu&B, AuBYP 2, -3, BioIn 5, -8, ConAu 5R, DcWomA, ForWC 70, IlsCB 1946, WhAmArt 85, WhoAm 74, -76, -78, WhoAmA 73, -78, -89N, -91N, WhoAmW 74, -75, -77, WhoE 74, -75, -77*

Cook, Gladys Moon 1907- *ConAu 33R*

Cook, Howard Norton 1901- *WhoAmA 86N*

Cook, Howard Norton 1901-1980 *AmMWSc 82, AnObit 1980, BioIn 1, -2, -9, -12, DcCAA 71, -77, GrAmP, IlsCB 1744, NewYTBS 80, WhAm 7, WhAmArt 85, WhoAm 74, -80, WhoAmA 73, -80, -82N, -89N, -91N*

Cook, J Gordon 1916- *ConAu 9R*

Cook, John Estes *ThrBJA*

Cook, Joseph Jay 1924- *AuBYP 2, -3, BioIn 8, -11, ConAu 1R, -2NR, SmATA 8*

Cook, Lyn *BioIn 10, ConAu X, IntAu&W 77X, -82X, -86X, OxCCan SUP, Profile 1, SmATA X, TwCChW 78, WhoCanL 85, WrDr 76, -80, -82, -84, -86, -88, -90, -92*
Main entry: Waddell, Evelyn Margaret

Cook, Lyn 1918- *CanWW 89, IntAu&W 89, WhoCanL 87, -92, WrDr 94*

Cook, Marion Belden *AuBYP 2, -3, BioIn 8*

Cook, Marjorie 1920- *ConAu 81*

Cook, Olive Rambo 1892- *AuBYP 2, -3, BioIn 7, ConAu 13R*

Cook, Robert Carter 1898- *AmMWSc 73P, -76P, BioIn 7, WhAm 10, WhoAm 74*

Cook, Robert Carter 1898-1991 *BioIn 17*

Cook, Roy *MajAI*

Cook, Sherman R *AuBYP 2, -3, BioIn 8*

Cooke, Ann *ConAu X, -36NR, MajAI, SmATA X*
Main entry: Cole, Joanna

Cooke, Ann Marie 1936- *WhoAmW 75, -77*

Cooke, Barbara *AuBYP 3*
Main entry: Alexander, Anna Barbara Cooke

Cooke, Barbara 1913- *AuBYP 2, BioIn 7, ConAu 57*

Cooke, Charles *AuBYP 2S*

Cooke, Charles 1904?-1977 *AuBYP 3*

Cooke, David Coxe 1917- *AuBYP 2, -3, BioIn 8, -9, ConAu 1R, -2NR, SmATA 2*

Cooke, Donald E 1916-1985 *ScF&FL 92*

Cooke, Donald Ewin 1916-1985 *AuBYP 2, -3, BioIn 7, -9, -15, ConAu 1R, -117, -4NR, SmATA 2, -45N, WhAmArt 85, WhoAmA 73, -78, -80, WhoE 75, -77*

Cooke, Edith Helena *ChhPo S1*

Cooke, Jean 1927- *InWom SUP*

Cooke, Jean Isobel Esther 1929- *SmATA 74*

Cooke, John Estes *MajAI*

Cooke, Sarah Fabyan 1913?- *BioIn 1*
Pseud./variant:
Palfrey, Sarah

Cookson, Catherine *BioIn 14, -16, -17, InWom SUP*

Cookson, Catherine 1906- *Au&Wr 71, BioIn 8, -9, -10, -11, BlmGWL, ConAu 13R, -9NR, -28NR, FemiCLE, IntAu&W 89, -91, IntWW 89, -91, MajTwCW, Novels, ScF&FL 92, SmATA 9, TwCRHW 90, Who 83, -85, WrDr 76, -80, -82, -84, -86, -88, -90, -92*
Pseud./variant:
Marchant, Catherine
McMullen, Catherine

Cookson, Catherine Ann McMullen, Dame 1906- *WrDr 94*

Cooley, Lydia *IlsBYP*

Coolidge, Archibald Cary, Jr. 1928- *ConAu 37R, DrAS 74E, -78E, -82E*

Coolidge, Olivia Ensor 1908- *AuBYP 2, -3, BioIn 6, -7, -9, -14, BkCL, ConAu 5R, -2NR, DcAmChF 1960, IntAu&W 89, -91, MajAI, MorJA, SmATA 1, -26, TwCChW 78, WrDr 80*

Coolidge, Susan *Alli SUP, AmAu, AmAu&B, AmWomPl, BenetAL 91, BbD, BiD&SE, Chambr 3, ChhPo, -S2, ConAu X, DcAmAu, DcLEL, DcNAA, EvLB, InWom SUP, JBA 34, OhA&B, REnAL, TwCChW 78A, WhoChL, WomNov*
Main entry: Woolsey, Sarah C

Coolidge, Susan 1835-1905 *BioIn 15, TwCChW 89A*

Coomaraswamy, Ananda K d1947 *WhoAmA 86N*

Coomaraswamy, Ananda K 1877-1947 *WhoAmA 89N, -91N*

Coomaraswamy, Ananda Kentish 1877-1947 *BioIn 1, -2, -8, -10, -11, -12, ConAu 115, DcLEL, DcNAA, ObitOF 79, WhAm 2, WhAmArt 85, WhNAA, WhoAmA 78N, -80N, -82N*

Coombs, Charles I 1914- *ConAu 19NR, –36NR, SmATA 15AS*

Coombs, Charles Ira 1914- *AuBYP 2, –3, BioIn 7, –9, –15, ConAu 5R, –4NR, MajAI, SmATA 3, –43*
Pseud./variant:
Coombs, Chick

Coombs, Chick *AuBYP 3, ConAu 36NR, MajAI*
Main entry: Coombs, Charles Ira

Coombs, Patricia *WrDr 86, –88, –90, –92*

Coombs, Patricia 1926- *AuBYP 3, BioIn 8, –9, –12, –16, ConAu 1R, –1NR, FifBJA, IlsBYP, IlsCB 1957, –1967, IntAu&W 91, MajAI, OxCChiL, SmATA 3, –51, WrDr 76, –80, –82, –84, –94*

Coomer, Anne *AuBYP 2S, –3*

Coon, Martha Sutherland 1884- *ConAu P-2, WhoAmW 74, WrDr 76*

Cooney, Barbara *ChlBIlD*

Cooney, Barbara 1917- *AmAu&B, AuBYP 2, –3, BioIn 1, –5, –6, –7, –8, –10, –12, –14, –16, BkP, ChhPo, ChlLR 23, ConAu 5R, –3NR, –37NR, ForWC 70, IlsBYP, IlsCB 1744, –1946, –1957, –1967, MajAI, MorJA, NewbC 1956, SmATA 6, –59, Str&VC, WhoAm 74, –76, –78, –80, –82, –84, –86, –88, –90, –92, –94, WhoAmA 73, –78, –80, –82, –84, –86, WhoAmW 74, –81, –87, –89, –91, –93*

Cooney, Caroline B 1947- *Au&Arts 5, BioIn 15, –16, ConAu 97, –37NR, MajAI, ScF&FL 92, SmATA 41, –48*

Cooney, Nancy Evans 1932- *AuBYP 3, BioIn 15, ConAu 105, SmATA 42*

Cooney, Timothy J 1929- *BioIn 9, ConAu 107, WhoE 74*

Coontz, Otto 1946- *BioIn 14, ConAu 105, ScF&FL 92, SmATA 33*

Cooper, Alfred Benjamin 1863- *WhoLA*

Cooper, Edmund 1926- *ConAu 33R, ConSFA, IntAu&W 77, –82, WhoSciF, WhoSpyF, WrDr 76, –80, –82, –84, –86*

Cooper, Edmund 1926-1982 *ConAu 31NR, EncSF 93, NewEScF, ScF&FL 92, ScFSB, TwCSFW 86, –91*

Cooper, Elizabeth Keyser *BioIn 16, SmATA 47*

Cooper, Elizabeth Keyser 1910- *ConAu 1R, –1NR, FourBJA*

Cooper, Floyd Donald, II 1956- *BlkAuII 92*

Cooper, Frederic Taber 1864-1937 *AmAu&B, WhAm 1*

Cooper, George 1840-1927 *BioIn 1, BkCL, NewGrDA 86*

Cooper, Gordon 1932- *AuBYP 2S, –3, BioIn 13, ConAu 61, SmATA 23, TwCChW 78, –83, –89, WrDr 76, –82, –84*

Cooper, Harold E 1928- *AmMWSc 73P, –76P, ConAu 45*

Cooper, Henry S F, Jr. *SmATA 65*
Main entry: Cooper, Henry Spotswood

Cooper, Henry Spotswood 1933-
Pseud./variant:
Cooper, Henry S F, Jr.

Cooper, Henry Spotswood Fenimore, Jr. 1933- *SmATA 65*

Cooper, Henry St John *BioIn 14, ConAu X, MajTwCW, TwCRHW 90*

Cooper, Ilene *BioIn 17, SmATA 66*

Cooper, Ilene Linda 1948- *WhoAm 94*

Cooper, James A *ConAu X, –26NR*
Main entry: Stratemeyer, Edward L

Cooper, James Fenimore 1789-1851 *Alli, AmAu, AmAu&B, AmWr, AtlBL, AuBYP 2, –3, Benet 87, BenetAL 91, BbD, BiD&SB, BioIn 1, –2, –3, –4, –5, –6, –7, –8, –9, –10, –11, –12, –13, –14, –15, –16, –17, CamGEL, CamGLE, CamHAL, CasWL, CelCen, Chambr 3, CnDAL, CrtT 3, CyAL, CyWA 58, DcAmAu, DcBiA, DcBiPP, DcEnA, DcEnL, DcLB 3, DcLEL, DcNAA, EncAB-H, EncFWF, EncSF 93, EvLB, FilmgC, HalFC 84, –88, HarEnUS, HsB&A, MagSAmL, McGEWB, MemAm, MouLC 3, NinCLC 1, –27, Novels, OxCAmH, OxCAmL 65, –83, OxCChiL, OxCEng 67, –85, OxCShps, PenC AM, RAdv 1, –13-1, RComAH, RComWL, REn, REnAL, RfGAmL 87, ScFEYrs, SmATA 19, SpyFic, WebAB 74, –79, WebE&AL, WhDW, WhAm HS, WhNaAH, WhoChL, WhoSpyF, WorAlBi, WorAl, WrChl*

Cooper, Jamie Lee *ConAu 9R, IndAu 1917*

Cooper, John R *ConAu P-2, InB&W 80, SmATA 1*
Main entry: Stratemeyer, Edward L

Cooper, Joyce Elaine 1949- *WhoAmW 81, WhoBlA 75, –77, –80*

Cooper, Kay 1941- *BioIn 11, ConAu 45, –1NR, –16NR, –37NR, SmATA 11*

Cooper, Lee Pelham 1926- *AuBYP 2, –3, BioIn 8, –10, ConAu 5R, –4NR, SmATA 5, WrDr 76, –80, –82, –84, –86, –88, –90, –92, –94*

Cooper, Lester 1919-1985 *BioIn 14, –15, ConAu 108, –116, SmATA 32, –43N*

Cooper, Lettice 1897- *Au&Wr 71, BioIn 14, –16, ConAu 9R, –5NR, ConNov 72, –76, –82, –86, –91, FemiCLE, IntAu&W 77, –82, –86, –91, SmATA 35, TwCChW 78, –83, –89, TwCRHW 90, WrDr 76, –80, –82, –84, –86, –88, –90, –92, –94*

Cooper, M E *SmATA X*
Main entry: Davis, Maggie S

Cooper, M E 1936- *WrDr 94*

Cooper, Margaret *ChhPo S2*

Cooper, Marjorie L *ForWC 70*

Cooper, Mary d1761 *OxCChiL*

Cooper, Melrose *SmATA 76*
Main entry: Kroll, Virginia Louise

Cooper, Paul Fenimore 1900?-1970 *ConAu 104*

Cooper, Paulette 1944- *ConAu 37R, IntAu&W 77, WrDr 76, –80, –82, –84, –86, –88*

Cooper, Susan 1935- *AuBYP 3, BioIn 14, –16, –17, IntAu&W 91, ScF&FL 92, ScFSB, SmATA 64, –6AS, TwCChW 89, TwCSFW 91, WrDr 86, –88, –90, –92*

Cooper, Susan Mary 1935- *AuBYP 2S, Au&Wr 71, BioIn 9, –11, ChlLR 4, ConAu 29R, –15NR, –37NR, ConTFT 2, DcAmChF 1960, EncSF 93, FourBJA, IntAu&W 82, MajAI, OxCChiL, SmATA 4, TwCChW 78, –83, TwCYAW, WhoAm 80, –82, –84, –86, –88, WrDr 76, –80, –82, –84, –94*

Cooper, W D *CarSB*

Cooper, Wendy 1919- *Au&Wr 71, ConAu 13R, –6NR, IntAu&W 77, –82, WrDr 76, –80, –82, –84, –86, –88, –90, –92, –94*

Coopersmith, Harry 1903- *ASCAP 66, BioIn 2, ConAu P-2, WhoWorJ 72*

Coopersmith, Jerome 1925- *AuBYP 2S, –3, ConAu 73, WhoEnt 92*

Coopersmith, Stanley 1926- *AmMWSc 73S, –78S, ConAu 21R*

Coopersmith, Stanley 1926-1979 *ConAu 133*

Cope, Myron 1929- *ConAu 57, WhoE 77*

Copeland, Frances Virginia *AuBYP 2, –3, BioIn 7*

Copeland, Helen 1920- *BioIn 9, ConAu 25R, SmATA 4*

Copeland, Michael *SingR 2*
Main entry: Collins, Dale

Copeland, Paul W *AuBYP 3*

Copeland, Paul Worthington *AuBYP 2, BioIn 8, –13, ConAu 105, SmATA 23, WhoPNW*

Copley, Heather Pickering 1920?- *ArtsCL, BioIn 6, IlsCB 1957, SmATA 45*

Copp, Andrew James 1916- *ConAu 25R, WrDr 76, –80*

Coppard, Alfred Edgar *IntvTCA 2*

Coppard, Alfred Edgar 1878-1957 *BioIn 4, –8, –11, –15, ChhPo, –S1, –S2, DcLEL, DcNaB 1951, EvLB, LongCTC, ModBrL NewC, ObitOF 79, OxCEng 67, PenC ENG, REn, TwCA, –SUP, TwCWr, WhoChL, WhoTwCL, YABC 1*

Coppard, Audrey 1931- *ConAu 29R, –27NR, ScF&FL 92*

Coppel, Alfred 1921- *BioIn 14, ConAu 17R, –9AS, –10NR, ConSFA, DcLB Y83B, DrAF 76, DrAPF 83, –85, EncSF 93, ScF&FL 92, TwCSFW 86, –91, WhoAm 82, –84, –86, –88, –90, –92, –94, WhoSciF, WhoWest 74, WrDr 76, –80, –82, –84, –86, –88, –90, –92, –94*

Copping, Harold 1863-1932 *BioIn 14, ChhPo S2, DcBrAr 1, DcBrBI, DcVicP 2*

Coppock, Charles 1906- *AuBYP 2, –3, BioIn 8*

Cora Lee *SmATA 72*
Main entry: Anderson, Catherine Corley

Coralie *SmATA 72*
Main entry: Anderson, Catherine Corley

Corbalis, Judith *ChlFicS*

Corbett, Grahame *BioIn 14, –15, ConAu 116, SmATA 36, –43*

Corbett, Harry *BioIn 8, WhoChL*

Corbett, Harry 1918-1989 *AnObit 1989*

Corbett, James Edward 1875- *AuBYP 3*

Corbett, James Edward 1875-1955 *AuBYP 2, BioIn 1, –3, –4, –8, –12, CurBio 46, –55*

Corbett, Scott 1913- *AuBYP 2, -3, Au&Wr 71, BioIn 8, -9, -15, ChlLR 1, ConAu 1R, -1NR, -23NR, DcAmChF 1960, FourBJA, IntAu&W 77, -82, MajAI, ScF&FL 92, SmATA 2, -42, -2AS, TwCChW 78, -83, -89, WhoAm 80, -82, -84, -88, -90, WhoUSWr 88, WhoWrEP 89, WrDr 80, -82, -84, -86, -88, -90, -92, -94*

Corbett, W J *BioIn 15, -16*

Corbett, W J 1938- *ChlLR 19, ScF&FL 92, SmATA 44, -50, TwCChW 89, WrDr 90, -92*

Corbett, William Jesse 1938- *ConAu 137, MajAI, WrDr 94*

Corbett-Smith, A 1879- *WhoLA*

Corbin, John 1870-1959 *AmAu&B, BiD&SB, BioIn 5, CarSB, DcAmAu, NotNAT B, ObitOF 79, OxCAmT 84, WhAm 3, WhNAA*

Corbin, Sabra Lee *AuBYP 3, ConAu X, SmATA X*
Main entry: Malvern, Gladys

Corbin, William *AuBYP 3, ConAu 36NR*
Main entry: McGraw, William Corbin

Corbin, William 1916- *AuBYP 2, ConAu X, DcAmChF 1960, MorJA, SmATA 3*

Corby, Dan *ConAu X, -38NR, MajAI, SmATA 3, -74, TwCChW 83, -89, WrDr 76, -80, -82, -84*
Main entry: Catherall, Arthur

Corcoran, Barbara *DrAPF 87, -89, -91, -93*

Corcoran, Barbara 1911- *AuBYP 2S, BioIn 9, -15, ConAu 21R, -2AS, -11NR, -28NR, ConLC 17, DcAmChF 1960, DcLB 52, DrAPF 83, -85, FifBJA, IntAu&W 82, -86, SmATA 3, -77, TwCRHW 90, WrDr 76, -80, -82, -84, -86, -88, -90, -92, -94*
Pseud./variant:
Dixon, Paige
Hamilton, Gail

Corcoran, Barbara Asenath 1911- *WhoAm 92*

Corcoran, Brewer 1877- *WhAm 5, WhNAA*

Corcoran, Jean Kennedy 1926- *ConAu 1R, ForWC 70*

Corcos, Lucille 1908-1973 *AmAu&B, AuBYP 2, -3, BioIn 3, -5, -8, -10, -11, ChhPo, ConAu 21R, -134, IlsCB 1946, -1957, -1967, SmATA 10, WhAm 6, WhAmArt 85, WhoAm 74, WhoAmA 73, -78N, -80N, -82N, -86N, -89N, -91N, WhoAmW 74*

Cordell, Alexander *ConAu X, DcLEL 1940, SmATA 7, TwCChW 78, -83, WrDr 76, -80, -82, -84*
Main entry: Graber, Alexander

Cordell, Alexander 1914- *IntAu&W 89, -91, OxCLiW 86, TwCChW 89, TwCRHW 90, WrDr 86, -88, -90, -92, -94*

Corder, Eric *ConAu X*

Cordwell, Miriam 1908- *WhoAmW 74, -75, -77, WhoE 74, -81*

Cordwell, Miriam 1908-1986 *ConAu 120*

Coren, Alan 1938- *BioIn 14, ConAu 29NR, IntAu&W 89, IntWW 89, -91, OxCChiL, SmATA 32, Who 82, -83, -85, -88, -90, -92, WhoWor 80, WrDr 82, -84, -86, -88, -90, -92, -94*

Corey, Dorothy *BioIn 13, ConAu 69, -11NR, -26NR, SmATA 23*

Corey, Robert *IlsBYP*

Corfe, Thomas Howell 1928- *BioIn 13, ConAu 103, SmATA 27*
Pseud./variant:
Corfe, Tom

Corfe, Tom *Au&Wr 71, ConAu X, IntAu&W 77, SmATA X*
Main entry: Corfe, Thomas Howell

Corfield, Robin Bell 1952- *SmATA 74*

Corkery, Daniel 1878-1964 *BiDIrW, BioIn 1, -4, -10, CamGLE, CasWL, CathA 1930, DcIrB 88, DcIrL, DcIrW 1, ModIrL, NewC, TwCA SUP*

Corkran, Alice 1850-1916 *Alli SUP, ChhPo, -S1, OxCChiL, TelT*

Corkran, Alice 1856?-1916 *StaCVF*

Corlett, William 1938- *BioIn 15, ConAu 103, ConTFT 2, EncSF 93, IntAu&W 86, -91, ScF&FL 92, SmATA 39, -46, TwCChW 78, -83, -89, WrDr 80, -82, -84, -86, -88, -90, -92, -94*

Corley, Edwin Raymond 1931-1981 *BioIn 8, -12, ConAu 25R, -105, -12NR, WhoAm 74*

Cormack, M Grant 1913- *BioIn 11, ConAu 1R, SmATA 11*

Cormack, Maribelle 1902-1984 *AuBYP 3, ScF&FL 92*

Cormack, Maribelle B 1902- *AuBYP 2, BioIn 2, -7, JBA 51, SmATA 39*

Cormack, Maribelle B 1902-1984 *BioIn 15*

Cormier, Robert *BioIn 14, –15, –16, –17*

Cormier, Robert 1925- *Au&Arts 3, BroV, ChlLR 12, ConAu 23NR, DcAmChF 1960, DcLB 52, IntAu&W 91, MagSAmL, MajTwCW, ScF&FL 92, TwCChW 89, WrDr 86, –88, –90, –92, –94*

Cormier, Robert Edmund 1925- *BioIn 11, –12, –13, ConAu 1R, –5NR, ConLC 12, –30, DcAmChF 1985, FifBJA, IntAu&W 89, MajAI, OxCChiL, SmATA 10, –45, TwCChW 83, TwCYAW, WhoAm 82, –84, –86, –88, –90, –92, –94, WhoUSWr 88, WhoWrEP 89, –92, WrDr 84*
Pseud./variant:
Fitch, John, IV

Cornelius, Carol 1942- *BioIn 15, ConAu 115, SmATA 40*

Cornell, J *ConGrA 2, SmATA X*
Main entry: Cornell, Jeffrey

Cornell, James C, Jr. 1938- *BioIn 13, ConAu 69, –11NR, SmATA 27*

Cornell, Jean Gay 1920- *BioIn 13, ConAu 45, –1NR, SmATA 23, WhoAmW 77*

Cornell, Jeffrey 1945- *BioIn 11, SmATA 11*
Pseud./variant:
Cornell, J

Corner, Miss *CarSB*

Corner, Julia 1798-1875 *DcBiPP, DcNaB, OxCChiL*

Cornier, Vincent 1898- *EncMys*

Cornish, Sam 1935- *BioIn 16, –17, BlkAuII, –92, BlkWr 1, BlkWrNE, ConAu 24NR, ConPo 91, IntAu&W 91, WrDr 86, –88, –90, –92*

Cornish, Samuel James 1935?- *BioIn 13, BlkAWP, ConAu 41R, ConPo 70, –75, –80, –85, DcLB 41, DcLEL 1940, DrAP 75, InB&W 80, –85, LivgBAA, SelBAAf, SelBAAu, SmATA 23, WrDr 76, –82, –84, –94*

Cornwall, Ian W 1909- *ScF&FL 92*

Cornwall, Ian Wolfran 1909- *Au&Wr 71, BioIn 5, ConAu 9R, IntAu&W 77, Who 74, –82, –83, –85, –88, –90, –92*

Cornwall, Nellie *SmATA X*
Main entry: Sloggett, Nellie

Cornwell, David John Moore *BioIn 15, IntvTCA 2, WhoWor 91, WrDr 86, –88*

Cornwell, David John Moore 1931- *Au&Wr 71, BioIn 6, –7, –10, –11, –12, –13, –14, –16, –17, BlueB 76, ConAu 5R, ConLC 9, EncMys, IntAu&W 77, –89, –91, IntWW 74, –75, –76, –77, –78, –79, –80, –81, –82, –83, –89, –91, NewC, NewYTBS 74, SpyFic, Who 74, –82, –83, –85, –88, –90, –92, WhoAm 80, –82, –84, –90, –94, WhoSpyF, WhoWor 74, –78, –82, –84, –91, –93, WorAu 1950, WrDr 76, –82, –84*
Pseud./variant:
LeCarre, John

Corren, Grace *ConAu X, EncSF 93, IntAu&W 91X, ScF&FL 92, TwCSFW 86, –91, WrDr 84, –86, –88, –90, –92*
Main entry: Hoskins, Robert

Corren, Grace 1933- *WrDr 94*

Correy, Lee *BioIn 11, ConAu X, –30NR, EncSF 93, ScF&FL 92, SmATA X, TwCSFW 91, WrDr 84, –86, –88, –90, –92*
Main entry: Stine, George Harry

Correy, Lee 1928- *ScFSB, TwCSFW 86, WrDr 94*

Corrick, James A 1945- *SmATA 76, WhoWest 94*

Corrigan, Adeline 1909- *BiDrLUS 70, BioIn 13, ConAu 69, SmATA 23*

Corrigan, Barbara 1922- *BioIn 11, ChhPo, ConAu 57, SmATA 8*

Corrin, Sara
Pseud./variant:
Corrin, Stephen

Corrin, Sara 1918- *BioIn 16, ConAu 120, ScF&FL 92, SmATA 48*

Corrin, Stephen *BioIn 16, ConAu 121, ScF&FL 92, SmATA 48*
Main entry: Corrin, Sara

Corriveau, Monique 1927- *BioIn 10, ConAu 61, –12NR, OxCCan SUP, OxCCanL, Profile 1*

Corriveau, Monique 1927-1976 *ConAu 122*

Corson, Hazel W 1906- *ConAu 1R, –2NR*

Cort, M C
Main entry: Clifford, Margaret Cort

Cort, M C 1929- *ConAu X, SmATA 1*

Cortesi, Lawrence *ConAu X, WhoUSWr 88, WhoWrEP 89, –92*

Corwen, Leonard 1921- *ConAu 93, –15NR, IntAu&W 89, WhoE 91*

Corwin, Judith H 1946- *ConAu 32NR*

Corwin, Judith Hoffman 1946- *BioIn 11, ConAu 113, SmATA 10*

Corwin, June Atkin 1935- *BioIn 8, IlsCB 1957, -1967*

Cosby, Bill *BlkWr 1, ConAu 42NR, LesBEnT 92, NegAl 89, SmATA 66*

Cosby, Bill 1937- *AfrAmAl 6, BestSel 89-4, BioIn 6, -7, -8, -9, -10, -11, -12, -13, -14, -15, -16, -17, BioNews 74, BlksAmF, CelR, -90, CivR 74, ConAu 81, ConHero 1, ConTFT 3, -9, CurBio 67, -86, DrBlPA 90, EncAFC, EncJzS, FilmgC, HalFC 84, IntAu&W 91, IntMPA 75, -76, -78, -81, -82, -84, -86, -77, LesBEnT, NegAl 76, -83, NewYTET, WhoAm 74, -76, -78, -80, -82, -84, -86, -88, -90, -92, -94, WhoBlA 75, -77, WhoCom, WhoE 93, WhoEnt 92, WhoHol A, WhoUSWr 88, WhoWest 74, -76, -78, WhoWor 74, WhoWrEP 89, -92, WorAlBi, WorAl, WrDr 88, -90, -92*

Cosby, Bill 1938- *HalFC 88, IntMPA 86, -88, -92*

Cosby, William Henry 1937- *WhoBlA 85, -88, -90, -92, -94*

Cosby, William Henry, Jr. 1937- *AfrAmBi, BlkWr 1, -2, ConAu 27NR, InB&W 85, SmATA 66*

Cosgrave, Esta *BioIn 1*

Cosgrave, John O'Hara, II 1908-1968 *BioIn 1, -3, -5, -6, -8, -12, ConAu 1R, -1NR, IlsBYP, IlsCB 1744, -1946, -1957, -1967, MorJA, SmATA 21N, WhAm 5, WhAmArt 85*

Cosgrove, Edmund *OxCCan SUP*

Cosgrove, Margaret 1926- *AuBYP 2, -3, BioIn 8, -16, ConAu 9R, -6NR, FourBJA, IlsCB 1957, -1967, SmATA 47*

Cosgrove, Rachel *ConAu X, EncSF 93, IntAu&W 77X, -82X, -86X*
Main entry: Payes, Rachel Cosgrove

Cosgrove, Stephen E 1945- *AuNews 1, BioIn 10, ConAu 69, -22NR, SmATA 40, -53*

Coskey, Evelyn 1932- *AuBYP 2S, -3, BiDrLUS 70, BioIn 10, ConAu 41R, SmATA 7*

Cosner, Shaaron 1940- *BioIn 15, ConAu 116, -38NR, SmATA 43*

Cosner, Shaaron Louise 1940- *WhoWrEP 89*

Cossi, Olga *BioIn 17, IntAu&W 89, SmATA 67*

Cossi, Olga 1921- *ConAu 81*

Costabel, Eva Deutsch 1924- *BioIn 15, ConAu 125, SmATA 45*

Costain, Thomas B 1885-1965 *BioIn 14, TwCRHW 90*

Costain, Thomas Bertram 1885-1965 *AmAu&B, AmNov, AuBYP 2, -3, BioIn 2, -3, -4, -7, -8, -12, CanWr, ConAu 5R, -25R, ConLC 30, CreCan 2, CurBio 53, -65, DcAmB S7, DcLB 9, DcLEL, -1940, LongCTC, ObitOF 79, OxCAmL 65, -83, OxCCan, OxCCanL, REn, REnAL, TwCA SUP, TwCWr, WhAm 4, WhJnl, WorAl*

Costello, David F 1904- *WrDr 86, -88, -90*

Costello, David Francis 1904- *AmMWSc 73P, -76P, -82, -86, -89, BioIn 13, ConAu 33R, SmATA 23, WhoPNW, WrDr 76, -80, -82, -84*

Costello, Mary Cleophas, Sister 1905- *DrAS 74E*

Costley-White, Hope 1894- *Au&Wr 71, WrDr 76*

Cothern, Fayly H 1926- *ConAu 1R, ForWC 70, WrDr 76, -80, -82, -84*

Cothran, Jean 1910- *ConAu 93*

Cott, Jonathan *DrAPF 87, -89, -91, -93*

Cott, Jonathan 1942- *AuBYP 2S, -3, BioIn 13, ChhPo S2, ConAu 53, DrAPF 83, -85, IntAu&W 77, -82, IntWWP 82, ScF&FL 92, SmATA 23*

Cottam, Clarence 1899-1974 *BioIn 10, -12, -13, ConAu 97, InSci, NatCAB 58, NewYTBS 74, SmATA 25, WhAm 6, WhoAm 74, WhoWor 74*

Cotten, Nellie Wyllie 1908- *ConAu 1R*

Cotten, Sallie Sims Southall 1846-1929 *InWom SUP*

Cotten, Sallie Southall *BioIn 15*

Cotten, Sallie Southall 1846-1929 *BiDSA, BioIn 3, ChhPo, -S1, EncSoH, WhAm 1, WomWWA 14*

Cotten, Sallie Swepson Sims Southall 1846-1929 *DcNCBi 1*

Cottin, Sophie *OxCChiL*

Cottin, Sophie 1770-1807 *BioIn 17, BlmGWL, FrenWW*

Cottle, Thomas J 1937- *WrDr 86, -88, -90, -92, -94*

Cottle, Thomas Joseph 1937- *BbtC, ConAu 33R, –17NR, WhoE 77, –83, –85, –86, –89, WrDr 76, –82, –84*

Cottler, Joseph 1899- *BioIn 13, ConAu P-2, SmATA 22*

Cottman, Evans W 1901- *BioIn 7, IndAu 1917*

Cotton, Nathaniel 1705-1788 *Alli, BiDLA, BioIn 3, BritAu, CarSB, Chambr 2, ChhPo S1, –S2, DcBiPP, DcNaB, EvLB, NewC, OxCChiL*

Cottrell, Dorothy 1902-1957 *AuWomWr, BioIn 1, –2, –4, CurBio 55, –57, FemiCLE, OxCAusL, SingR 2*

Cottrell, Jack Warren 1938- *WhoRel 75, –77*

Cottrell, Leonard 1913-1974 *AuBYP 2, –3, Au&Wr 71, BioIn 8, –10, –13, BlueB 76N, ConAu 5R, –4NR, DcLEL 1940, FourBJA, IntAu&W 77, IntWW 74, –75, SmATA 24, TwCWr, WhAm 6, Who 74, WhoWor 74, WorAu 1950, WrDr 76*

Couch, Sir Arthur T Q
Main entry: Quiller-Couch, Arthur Thomas, Sir Arthur T Q

Couch, Arthur T Q, Sir *Alli SUP, ChhPo, DcNaB 1941, EvLB, JBA 34, OxCEng 67*

Couch, Arthur Thomas Quiller- 1863-1944 *BioIn 14, –15*

Couch, Helen F 1907- *ConAu P-2*

Couffer, Jack 1924- *Au&Wr 71, BioIn 7, ConAu 1R, –1NR, FilmgC, ScF&FL 92*

Coughlan, Margaret N 1925- *AuBYP 3*

Coughlan, Margaret Nourse 1925- *AuBYP 2S, BiDrLUS 70, ConAu 107, WhoLibS 55, –66*

Coughlan, Robert 1914- *AmAu&B, ConAu 65, IndAu 1917, WhoAm 78, –80, –82, –86, –88, –90, WhoUSWr 88, WhoWrEP 89, WrDr 76, –82, –84, –86, –88, –90, –92*

Counsel, June 1926- *ChlFicS, SmATA 70*

Counsilman, James E 1920- *ConAu 126*

Counsilman, James Edward 1920- *BiDAmSp BK, BioIn 10, –12, WhoAm 82, –84, –86, –88, –90, –92, –94*

Countryman, The *ConAu X, SmATA X*

Countryman, The
Main entry: Whitlock, Ralph

Counts, George S 1889-1974 *BioIn 14, –15, –16, DcAmImH, EncWB*

Counts, George Sylvester 1889-1974 *AmAu&B, Au&Wr 71, BiDAmL, BioIn 4, –8, –9, –10, –11, –13, ConAu 5R, –53, CurBio 41, –75N, NewYTBS 74, OxCAmH, TwCA SUP, WhAm 6, WhNAA, WhoAm 74*

Courlander, Harold 1908- *AnCL, AuBYP 2, –3, BioIn 6, –8, –10, –11, –14, –16, BkCL, ConAu 9R, –3NR, –18NR, –40NR, IndAu 1917, IntAu&W 77, –82, –86, –89, –91, MichAu 80, MorJA, ScF&FL 92, SmATA 6*

Cournos, Helen Sybil Norton 1894?-1959 *BioIn 5*

Cournos, John 1881-1966 *AmAu&B, BenetAL 91, BioIn 4, –7, –11, –15, ConAmL, ConAu P-2, DcLB 54, DcLEL, LongCTC, OxCAmL 65, –83, REnAL, TwCA, –SUP, WhoLA*

Courtis, Stuart Appleton 1874-1969 *BioIn 6, –13, ConAu 105, SmATA 29N, WhAm 5, WhNAA*

Courtney, Elizabeth *SingR 2*

Courtney, Grendoline *Au&Wr 71, ConAu P-1, WrDr 76, –80*

Coury, Louise Andree 1895?-1983 *BioIn 14, ConAu 109, SmATA 34N*
Pseud./variant:
Andree, Louise
Andrews, Laura
Auntie Deb
Auntie Louise
Care, Felicity
Mortimer, Mary H
Strange, Philippa

Cousins, Margaret 1905- *AmAu&B, AuBYP 2, –3, Au&Wr 71, BioIn 3, –6, –8, –9, ConAu 1R, –1NR, DcLB 137, EncTwCJ, ForWC 70, IntAu&W 77, –82, –89, –91 SmATA 2, TexWr, WhoAm 74, –76, –78, –80, –82, –84, –86, –88, –90, –92, –94, WhoAmW 74, WhoWor 74, WrDr 76, –80, –82, –84, –86, –88, –90, –92*
Pseud./variant:
Johns, Avery
Masters, William
Parrish, Mary

Cousteau, Jacques-Yves *LesBEnT 92*

Cousteau, Jacques-Yves 1910- *AmMWSc 89, –92, AnCL, AsBiEn, BiESc, BioIn 1, –2, –3, –4, –5, –6, –7, –8, –9, –10, –11, –12, –13, BioNews 74, CelR, ConAu 65, –15NR, ConLC 30, CurBio 76, DcFM, EncWB FilmgC, HalFC 84, –88, InSci, IntAu&W 77, –82, IntMPA 84, –86, –88, –92, IntWW 74, –75, –76, –77, –78, –79, –80, –81, –82, –83, –89, –91, MajTwCW, NewYTBE 72, NewYTBS 87, OxCFilm, OxCShps, REn,*

SmATA 38, WhDW, Who 74, –82, –83, –85, –88, –90, –92, WhoAm 80, –82, –84, –88, –90, –92, –94, WhoOcn 78, WhoWor 74, –78, –80, –82, –84, –87, –89, –91, –93, WorEFlm

Coutant, Helen *AuBYP 3*

Couture, Christin 1951- *SmATA 73*

Covarrubias, Miguel 1904-1957 *BioIn 1, –2, –3, –4, –5, –9, –12, –14, ConArt 83, CurBio 40, –57, EncLatA, IlsCB 1744, –1946, ObitOF 79, REnAL, WhDW, WhAm 3, WorECar*

Covici, Pascal, Jr. 1930- *ConAu 1R, DrAS 74E, –78E, –82E*

Coville, Bruce *BioIn 14*

Coville, Bruce 1950- *ConAu 97, –22NR, EncSF 93, ScF&FL 92, SmATA 32, –77, WhoWrEP 89, –92*

Covington, John *AuBYP 3*

Covington, John P *AuBYP 2S*

Cowan, Rachel *BioIn 10*

Cowden, Jeanne 1918- *ConAu 85*

Cowell, Cyril 1888- *ChhPo S2, ConAu P-2*

Cowell, Frank Richard 1897- *AuBYP 2, –3, Au&Wr 71, BioIn 8, ConAu 53, –8NR, IntAu&W 77, Who 74, WrDr 76, –80*

Cowen, Eve *ConAu X, –34NR, SmATA X*
Main entry: Werner, Herma

Cowen, Frances *Au&Wr 71, ConAu X, TwCCr&M 80, WrDr 76, –80, –82, –84*
Main entry: Munthe, Frances

Cowen, Frances 1915- *BioIn 14, IntAu&W 91, TwCRHW 90, WrDr 86, –88, –90, –92, –94*

Cowen, Ida 1898- *BioIn 17, SmATA 64*

Cowie, Evelyn Elizabeth *WrDr 86, –88, –90*

Cowie, Evelyn Elizabeth 1924- *Au&Wr 71, ConAu 13R, –9NR, IntAu&W 77, WrDr 76, –80, –82, –84*

Cowie, Leonard Wallace 1919- *Au&Wr 71, BioIn 9, ConAu 13R, –9NR, IntAu&W 77, –82, –89, –91, SmATA 4, WrDr 76, –80, –82, –84, –86, –88, –90, –92, –94*

Cowles, Fleur *BioIn 17, ConAu 24NR, IntAu&W 91, WhoAm 88, –90, –92, –94, WhoAmA 86, –89, –91, WrDr 86, –88, –90, –92, –94*

Cowles, Fleur 1910- *AmAu&B, AuNews 1, Au&Wr 71, BioIn 1, –2, –3, –8, –10, –11, BioNews 74, ConAu 9R, –4NR, CurBio 52, IntAu&W 77, WhoAm 74, WhoAmA 78, –80, –84, WhoWor 74, –80, WrDr 76, –80, –82, –84*

Cowles, Ginny 1924- *ConAu 57*

Cowles, Kathleen *ConAu X, SmATA X*
Main entry: Krull, Kathleen

Cowley, Cassia Joy Summers 1936- *DcChlFi*

Cowley, Joy 1936- *AuBYP 2S, –3, BioIn 9, ConAu 25R, –11NR, SmATA 4, TwCChW 89*

Cowley, Malcolm *IntvTCA 2*

Cowley, Malcolm d1989 *IntWW 89N*

Cowley, Malcolm 1898- *AmAu&B, AmWr S2, Au&Wr 71, Benet 87, BioIn 1, –2, –4, –6, –7, –10, –11, –12, –13, –14, –15, BlueB 76, CelR, ChhPo, CnDAL, ConAmA, ConAu 5R, –3NR, ConLCrt 77, –82, ConPo 70, –75, –80, –85, DcLB 4, –48, –Y81A, DcLEL, EncWL, –2, IntAu&W 77, –82, –86, –89, –91, IntWW 74, –75, –76, –77, –78, –79, –80, –81, –82, –83, IntWWP 82, ModAL, –S1, –S2, OxCAmL 65, –83, PenC AM, RAdv 1, –13-1, REn, REnAL, SixAP, TwCA, –SUP, WebAB 74, –79, WhNAA, WhoAm 74, –76, –78, –80, –82, –84, –86, –88, WhoE 83, –85, –86, –89, WhoWor 74, WrDr 76, –80, –82, –84, –86, –88*

Cowley, Malcolm 1898-1989 *AnObit 1989, BenetAL 91, BioIn 16, –17, ConAu 128, CurBio 89N, CyWA 89, DcLB Y89N, IntWW 89, LiExTwC, MajTwCW, NewYTBS 89, News 89-3, WhAm 10*

Cowlin, Dorothy *Au&Wr 71, ConAu X, IntAu&W 77X, –82X, WrDr 76, –80, –82, –84*
Main entry: Whalley, Dorothy

Cowlin, Dorothy 1911- *IntAu&W 91, WrDr 86, –88, –90*

Cowper, William 1731-1800 *Alli, AnCL, AtlBL, Benet 87, BbD, BiD&SB, BioIn 1, –2, –3, –4, –5, –6, –7, –8, –9, –11, –12, –13, –14, –15, –16, –17, BlmGEL, BritAu, BritWr 3, CamGEL, CamGLE, CarSB, CasWL, Chambr 2, ChhPo, –S1, –S2, CnE&AP, CrtT 2, CyEd, CyWA 58, DcBiPP, DcEnA, DcEnL, DcEuL, DcLB 104, –109, DcLEL, DcNaB, Dis&D, EvLB, LongCEL, LuthC 75, McGEWB, MouLC 2, NewC, NinCLC 8, OxCEng 67, –85, OxCMus, PenC ENG, PoChrch, RAdv 1, –13-1, REn, RfGEnL 91, WebE&AL, WhDW, WorAlBi, WorAl*

Cox, Anthony Berkeley 1893-1970? *BioIn 4, –14, EncMys, LongCTC, TwCA, –SUP*

Cox, Barry 1931- *BioIn 17, SmATA 62*

Cox, Clinton *SmATA 74*

Cox, David 1933- *BioIn 16, ConAu 119, SmATA 56*

Cox, Donald William 1921- *BioIn 13, ConAu 1R, -4NR, SmATA 23*

Cox, E Albert 1876-1955 *BioIn 1, DcBrAr 1, IlsCB 1744, TwCPaSc*

Cox, Edith Muriel *ConAu 102, WrDr 76, -80, -82, -84*
Pseud./variant:
Goaman, Muriel

Cox, Jack *Au&Wr 71, BioIn 8, ConAu X, SmATA X, WhoChL*
Main entry: Cox, John Roberts

Cox, John Roberts 1915-1981 *Au&Wr 71, BioIn 11, ConAu 29R, -14NR, IntAu&W 77, -82, SmATA 9, WhoWor 78*
Pseud./variant:
Cox, Jack
Havenhand, John
Roberts, David

Cox, Lee Sheridan 1916- *ConAu 25R, DrAS 74E, -78E, -82E, IndAu 1917*

Cox, Marion Monroe
Main entry: Monroe, Marion

Cox, Palmer 1840-1924 *Alli SUP, AmAu, AmAu&B, AuBYP 2S, -3, BenetAL 91, BbD, BiD&SB, BioIn 10, -13, -15, CarSB, ChhPo, -S1, -S2, ChlLR 24, CmCal, ConAu 111, DcAmAu, DcLB 42, DcNAA, JBA 34, OxCAmL 65, -83, OxCChiL, SmATA 24, TwCChW 83A, -89A, WhAm 1, WhAmArt 85, WorECar*

Cox, Victoria *ConAu X, SmATA X*
Main entry: Garretson, Victoria Diane

Cox, Victoria 1945- *BioIn 15*

Cox, Wally d1973 *LesBEnT 92*

Cox, Wally 1924-1973 *BioIn 2, -3, -4, -7, -9, -10, -13, ConAu 41R, CurBio 54, -73, EncAFC, FilmgC, HalFC 84, -88, LesBEnT, NewYTBE 73, NewYTET, NotNAT A, -B, ObitOF 79, SmATA 25, WhAm 5, WhScrn 83, -77, WhoCom, WhoHol B, WorAlBi, WorAl*

Cox, William R *SmATA 46*

Cox, William R 1901- *AuBYP 2, -3, BioIn 8, -14, ConAu 9R, -6NR, EncFWF, SmATA 31, TwCCr&M 85, WrDr 84, -86, -88, -90*
Pseud./variant:
Reeve, Joel

Cox, William R 1901-1988 *BioIn 15, -16, ConAu 126, NewYTBS 88, SmATA 57, TwCWW 91*
Pseud./variant:
d'Arcy, Willard
Frederic, Mike
Parkhill, John
Reeve, Joel
Robbins, Wayne
Spellman, Roger G
Ward, Jonas

Cox, William R 1901-1989 *TwCCr&M 91*

Coxe, George Harmon 1901-1984 *AmAu&B, BioIn 10, -14, ConAu 57, CrtSuMy, EncMys, Novels, REnAL, TwCCr&M 80, -85, -91, WhAm 8, WhoAm 74, -76, -78, -80, -82, WorAu 1950, WrDr 82, -84*

Coxe, Molly 1959- *SmATA 69*

Coxon, Michele 1950- *SmATA 76*

Coy, Harold 1902- *AuBYP 2, -3, BioIn 7, -9, ConAu 5R, -4NR, IntAu&W 77, SmATA 3, WrDr 76, -80, -82, -84*

Coyle, David Cushman 1887-1969 *ConAu 1R, -103, -15NR, WhAm 5*

Coyne, John 1940- *ConAu 93, -12NR*

Crabb, Edmund William 1912- *ConAu P-1, WrDr 76, -80, -82, -84, -86, -88 -90*

Crabtree, Judith 1928- *BioIn 17, ConAu 118, -42NR, SmATA 63*

Cradock, H C, Mrs *WhoChL*

Craft, K Y *SmATA 65*
Main entry: Craft, Kinuko Yamabe

Craft, Kinuko 1940- *BioIn 15, -17, SmATA 65*

Craft, Kinuko Yamabe 1940- *SmATA 65*
Pseud./variant:
Craft, K Y

Craft, Ruth *AuBYP 3, BioIn 14*

Craft, Ruth 1935- *AuBYP 2S, ConAu 110, -133, FifBJA, SmATA 31, WrDr 94*

Craig, A A *AuBYP 3, ConAu X, -34NR, EncSF 93, MajTwCW, SmATA X*
Main entry: Anderson, Poul

Craig, Alisa *ConAu X, -40NR, IntAu&W 91X, SmATA X, TwCCr&M 85, -91, TwCRHW 90, WrDr 84, -86, -88, -90, -92*
Main entry: MacLeod, Charlotte

Craig, Alisa 1922- *WrDr 94*

Craig, George *WhoAm 90, -92, -94*

Craig, George 1920- *Au&Wr 71*

Craig, Hazel Thompson 1904- *ConAu 1R*

Craig, Helen *AuBYP 3, BioIn 15, -16*

Craig, Helen 1934- *SmATA 46, -49*

Craig, Jean Teresa 1936- *ConAu 5R, LEduc 74, WrDr 76*

Craig, John 1921-1982 *TwCChW 89*

Craig, John Eland *AuBYP 3, ConAu X, SmATA 2, WrDr 80*
Main entry: Chipperfield, Joseph Eugene

Craig, John Ernest 1921-1982 *BioIn 10, -13, CaW, ConAu 101, OxCCan SUP, Profile 1, SmATA 23, TwCChW 78, -83, WhoAm 74, WrDr 82, -84*

Craig, M F *ConAu 133, SmATA 65*
Main entry: Craig, Mary Francis Shura

Craig, M Jean *AuBYP 3*

Craig, M Jean 1915- *AuBYP 2, BioIn 8, -12, ConAu 73, FourBJA, SmATA 17*

Craig, M S *ConAu 133, SmATA 65, WhoUSWr 88*
Main entry: Craig, Mary Francis Shura

Craig, Margaret Maze 1911-1964 *BioIn 6, -7, -11, ConAu 1R, MorJA, SmATA 9*

Craig, Mary
Main entry: Craig, Mary Francis Shura

Craig, Mary 1923- *WrDr 86, -88, -90*

Craig, Mary Francis *AuBYP 3*

Craig, Mary Francis 1923- *BioIn 9, -14, ConAu 1R, IntAu&W 77, -82, SmATA 6, ThrBJA, WhoAm 84, WhoAmW 74, -77, WrDr 76, -80*
Pseud./variant:
Shura, Mary Francis

Craig, Mary Francis 1923-1991 *BioIn 17*

Craig, Mary Francis Shura 1923- *SmATA 7AS, WhoAm 86, -88, -90, WhoUSWr 88, WhoWrEP 89, -92*

Craig, Mary Francis Shura 1923-1991 *WhAm 10*
Pseud./variant:
Craig, M F
Craig, M S
Craig, Mary
Craig, Mary S
Hill, Alexis
Hill, Meredith

Craig, Mary S *ConAu 133, -26NR, SmATA 65*
Main entry: Craig, Mary Francis Shura

Craig, Mary Shura 1923-1991 *BioIn 17, ConAu 133, SmATA 65*

Craigie, Dorothy M *ScF&FL 92*

Craigie, Dorothy M 1908- *BioIn 5, IlsCB 1946*

Craik, Mrs *CamGEL, RfGEnL 91*

Craik, Mrs 1826-1887 *Chambr 3, DcEnL, OxCEng 67, -85, TelT, WhoChL*

Craik, Dinah Maria *CamGLE*

Craik, Dinah Maria 1826-1887 *StaCVF*

Craik, Dinah Maria Mulock 1826-1887 *Alli SUP, AnCL, ArtclWW 2, BbD, BiD&SB, BioIn 1, -2, -3, -5, -8, -12, -14, -16, BlmGEL, BritAu 19, CarSB, CasWL, CelCen, ChhPo, -S1, -S2, DcEnA, -A, DcEuL, DcLB 35, DcLEL, DcNaB, EncBrWW, EvLB, FamSYP, HsB&A, InWom SUP, JBA 34, MajAI, NewC, OxCChiL, REn, SmATA 34, Str&VC*
Pseud./variant:
Mulock, Dinah Maria

Craik, Dinah Mulock 1826-1887 *BlmGWL, NinCLC 38*

Craik, Georgiana M *WomNov*

Craik, Georgiana M 1831?-1895 *StaCVF*

Craik, Georgiana Marion 1831-1895 *Alli SUP, BiD&SB, CarSB, Chambr 3, DcEnL, NewC*

Cram, L D 1898- *ArtsAmW 3, BioIn 5, IlsCB 1946*

Cramer, Kathryn 1943- *ConAu 25R*

Cramer, Richard Seldon 1928- *ConAu 29R, DrAS 74H, -78H, -82H, WhoWest 74, -76*

Crampton, Patricia Elizabeth 1925- *Au&Wr 71, ChhPo S1*

Cranch, Christopher Pearse 1813-1892 *ArtsNiC, BenetAL 91, BioIn 2, -3, -6, -8, -15, DcLB 42, OxCAmL 83, OxCChiL*

Crandall, Joy *ConAu 57*
Main entry: Martin, Joy

Crane, Alan 1901- *AuBYP 2, -3, BioIn 8, WhAmArt 85*

Crane, Barbara J 1934- *BioIn 14*

Crane, Barbara Joyce 1934- *SmATA 31, WhoAm 84, –86, –88, –90, –92, –94, WhoAmW 77, –85, –87, –89, WhoE 83, –85, –86, –89, WhoWrEP 89, –92*

Crane, Caroline 1930- *AuBYP 2S, –3, BioIn 11, ConAu 9R, –3NR, –19NR, –41NR, ForWC 70, ScF&FL 92, SmATA 11, WhoE 83, –85, –86, WrDr 76, –80, –82, –84, –86, –88, –90, –92*

Crane, Edna Temple *ConAu X*
Main entry: Eicher, Elizabeth

Crane, Florence *AuBYP 2, –3, BioIn 8*

Crane, Hart 1899-1932 *Benet 87, BenetAL 91, BioIn 1, –2, –3, –4, –5, –6, –7, –8, –9, –10, –11, –12, –13, –15, –16, –17, CamGEL, CamGLE, CamHAL, ConAu 104, –127, DcLB 4, –48, EncWL 2, LongCTC, MagSAmL, MajTwCW, McGEWB, ModAL, –S1, –S2, OhA&B, OxCAmH, OxCAmL 65, –83, OxCEng 67, –85, PenC AM, PoeCrit 3, RAdv 1, –13-1, REn, REnAL, RfGAmL 87, SixAP, Tw, TwCA, –SUP, TwCLC 2, –5, TwCWr, WebAB 74, –79, WebE&AL, WhDW, WhAm 1, WhoTwCL, WorAlBi, WorAl, WorLitC*

Crane, Irving *AuBYP 3*

Crane, Irving 1914?- *AuBYP 2, BioIn 8*

Crane, Lucy 1842-1882 *Alli SUP, ChhPo S1, DcNaB*

Crane, M A *SmATA X*
Main entry: Wartski, Maureen

Crane, Roy *BioIn 2, –11, –13, ObitOF 79, SmATA X, WhAmArt 85, WhoAmA 80N, –82N*

Crane, Roy 1901- *WhoAmA 86N*

Crane, Roy 1901-1977 *EncACom, WhoAmA 89N, –91N*

Crane, Royston Campbell 1901?-1977 *ArtCS, BioIn 2, –11, –13, EncTwCJ, SmATA 22N, WhAm 7, WhoAm 74, WhoAmA 73, –78, WhoWor 74*

Crane, Stephen *SourALJ*

Crane, Stephen 1871-1900 *AmAu, AmAu&B, AmWr, AtlBL, Benet 87, BenetAL 91, BbD, BiDAmJo, BiD&SB, BioIn 1, –2, –3, –4, –5, –6, –7, –8, –9, –10, –11, –12, –13, –14, –15, –16, –17, CamGEL, CamGLE, CamHAL, CasWL, Chambr 3, ChhPo, CnDAL, CnE&AP, ConAu 109, CrtT 3, CyWA 58, DcAmAu, DcLB 12, –54, –78, DcLEL, DcNAA, EncAB-H, EncAJ, EncFWF, EvLB, HalFC 84, –88, HarEnUS, JrnUS, LongCTC, MagSAmL, McGEWB, ModAL, Novels, OxCAmL 65, –83, OxCEng 67, –85, PenC AM, PenEncH, RAdv 1, –13-1, RComAH, RComWL, REn, REnAL, RealN, RfGAmL 87, RfGShF, ShSCr 7, ShSWr, TwCLC 11, –17, –32, WebAB 74, –79, WebE&AL, WhDW, WhAm 1, WhCiWar, WhFla, WorAlBi, WorLitC, YABC 2*
Pseud./variant:
Smith, Johnston

Crane, Stephen Townley 1871-1900 *ConAu 140*

Crane, Thomas 1843- *Alli SUP, CarSB, ChhPo*

Crane, Walter 1845-1915 *Alli SUP, ArtsNiC, BioIn 1, –2, –3, –8, –10, –12, –14, –15, –16, CamGLE, CarSB, CelCen, ChhPo, –S1, –S2, ClaDrA, DcBrAr 1, DcBrBI, DcNaB 1912, DcVicP 2, IlsBYP, JBA 34, –51, MacEA, MajAI, NewC, OxCArt, OxCChiL, OxCEng 85, OxDcArt, SmATA 18, StaCVF, Str&VC, WhoChL*

Crane, William D 1892- *BioIn 9, ConAu 5R, SmATA 1*

Cranfield, Ingrid 1945- *ConAu 141, SmATA 74*

Cranshaw, Stanley *MajAI*

Crary, Elizabeth Ann 1942- *SmATA 43, WhoWest 84*

Crary, Margaret Coleman 1906- *AuBYP 2, –3, BioIn 8, –11, ConAu 5R, ForWC 70, SmATA 9*

Craven, Carolyn *AuBYP 3*

Craven, Margaret 1901-1980 *BioIn 10, –12, ConAu 103, ConLC 17, WhAm 7, WhoAm 80, WrDr 76, –80, –82*

Craven, Thomas 1889-1969 *AmAu&B, AuBYP 2, –3, BioIn 8, –13, ConAu 97, CurBio 44, –69, ObitOF 79, REnAL, SmATA 22, TwCA, –SUP, WhAm 5*

Crawford, Char 1935- *ConAu 57*
Pseud./variant:
Johnson, Charlene

Crawford, Charles P 1945- *BioIn 13, ConAu 45, –24NR, SmATA 28*

Crawford, Deborah 1922- *BioIn 10, ConAu 49, IntAu&W 77, SmATA 6*

Crawford, Joanna 1941- *ConAu 9R*

Crawford, John E 1904-1971 *BioIn 9, ConAu P-2, SmATA 3*

Crawford, Mel 1925- *BioIn 14, –15, SmATA 33, –44, WhoAmA 78, –80, –82*

Crawford, Phyllis 1899- *BioIn 2, -9, -14, CurBio 40, JBA 51, SmATA 3, WhoLibS 55*
Pseud./variant:
Turner, Josie

Crawford, Thelmar Wyche 1905- *AuBYP 2, -3, BioIn 8, ConAu 1R*

Crawford, Will 1869-1944 *BioIn 7, ConICB, IlrAm 1880, -A, WhAmArt 85, WorECar*

Crawford, William 1929- *ConAu 1R, -4NR*

Crayder, Dorothy 1906- *AuBYP 2S, -3, BioIn 10, ConAu 33R, SmATA 7*

Crayder, Teresa *AuBYP 3, ConAu X, MajAI, SmATA 1, TwCChW 89, TwCYAW, WrDr 90, -92, -94*
Main entry: Colman, Hila

Crayon, Geoffrey *Alli, AmAu&B, BenetAL 91, CnDAL, DcEnL, OxCAmL 65, -83, OxCEng 67, -85, REn, REnAL, YABC X*
Main entry: Irving, Washington

Craz, Albert G 1926- *AuBYP 2, -3, BioIn 8, -13, ConAu 17R, -8NR, SmATA 24*

Creasey, John *CamGLE*

Creasey, John 1908-1973 *Au&Wr 71, BioIn 4, -5, -6, -7, -8, -9, -10, -14, -17, ConAu 5R, -41R, -8NR, ConLC 11, CorpD, CrtSuMy, CurBio 63, -73, DcLB 77, EncMys, EncSF 93, HalFC 84, -88, LongCTC, MajTwCW, NewYTBE 73, Novels, ObitT 1971, REn, ScF&FL 92, SpyFic, TwCCr&M 80, -85, -91, TwCSFW 91, TwCWr, WhAm 6, WhoSpyF, WorAlBi, WorAl, WorAu 1950*

Crecy, Jeanne *ConAu X, IntAu&W 77X, SmATA 5, WrDr 76, -80, -82, -84, -86, -88, -90, -92*
Main entry: Williams, Jeanne

Crecy, Jeanne 1930- *WrDr 94*

Credle, Ellis 1902- *AmPB, AuBYP 2, -3, BioIn 1, -2, -3, -4, -5, -7, -9, ConAu 13R, -9NR, IlsCB 1744, -1946, JBA 51, SmATA 1, Str&VC*

Creekmore, Raymond L 1905- *BioIn 5, IlsCB 1946, WhAmArt 85*

Creel, J Luke *BioIn 6, MinnWr*

Creighton, Helen *BioIn 10, ChhPo S1, OxCCan, -SUP*

Creighton, Helen 1899-1989 *BioIn 17, ConAu 130, SmATA 64*

Creighton, Luella Bruce 1901- *BioIn 2, -10, ConAu P-1, CreCan 2, OxCCan, -SUP, Profile 1*

Crespi, Pachita 1900- *AuBYP 3*

Crespi, Pachita 1900-1971 *AuBYP 2, BioIn 7, WhAmArt 85, WhoAmA 78N, -80N, -82N, -86N, -89N, -91N*

Cresswell, Helen 1934?- *AuBYP 2, -3, Au&Wr 71, BioIn 9, -16, ChlFicS, ChlLR 18, ConAu 17R, -8NR, -37NR, FourBJA, IntAu&W 77, -82, -89, -91, MajAI, OxCChiL, ScF&FL 92, SenS, SmATA 1, -48, TwCChW 78, -83, -89, Who 88, -90, -92, WrDr 76, -80, -82, -84*

Cresswell, Helen 1936- *WrDr 86, -88, -90, -92, -94*

Creswick, Paul 1866- *WhoLA*

Creswick, Paul 1866-1947 *StaCVF*

Cretan, Gladys 1921- *AuBYP 2S, -3, BioIn 9, ConAu 29R, SmATA 2, WhoAmW 74, -77*

Crew, Fleming H *AuBYP 3*

Crew, Fleming H 1882- *AmAu&B, BioIn 2, JBA 51, OhA&B*

Crew, Gary 1947- *ConAu 142, SmATA 75, TwCYAW*

Crew, Helen Coale 1866-1941 *AmAu&B, AmWomPl, BioIn 2, ChhPo, -S1, ConAu 121, JBA 34, -51, WomWWA 14, YABC 2*

Crew, Linda 1951- *ConAu 130, SmATA 71, TwCYAW, WrDr 94*

Crews, Donald *BioIn 14, -15, -16, -17, ChlBIlD*

Crews, Donald 1938- *BioIn 12, BlkAuII, -92, ChlLR 7, ConAu 108, FifBJA, IlsBYP, IlsCB 1967, MajAI, SmATA 30, -32, -76, WhoE 91*

Crichlow, Ernest 1914- *BioIn 16, BlkAuII, -92, InB&W 85, NegAl 89*

Crichlow, Ernest T 1914- *AfroAA, BioIn 8, FourBJA, IlsBYP, IlsCB 1957, -1967*

Crichton, John Michael 1942- *ConAu 40NR, TwCYAW, WrDr 94*

Crichton, Michael *IntMPA 86, -88*

Crichton, Michael 1942- *AmAu&B, Au&Arts 10, AuNews 2, Au&Wr 71, BioIn 8, -9, -10, -11, -12, -13, -14, -15, -16, -17, CelR, -90, ConAu 25R, -13NR, ConLC 2, -6,*

–54, ConNov 76, –82, ConTFT 5, CurBio 76, –93, CyWA 89, DcLB Y81B, EncSF 93, FilmgC, HalFC 84, –88, IntAu&W 89, –91, IntMPA 75, –76, –78, –81, –82, –84, –86, –92, –77, MajTwCW, NewEScF, NewYTBE 70, NewYTBS 81, Novels, ScF&FL 92, ScFSB, SmATA 9, TwCCr&M 80, –85, –91, TwCSFW 86, –91, WhoSciF, WorAlBi, WorAl, WorFDir 2, WrDr 76, –80, –82, –84, –86, –88, –90, –92
Pseud./variant:
Douglas, Michael
Hudson, Jefferey
Lange, John

Crimmins, James Curtis 1935- *WhoWest 89*

Crimmins, James Custis 1935- *ConAu 5R, –11NR*

Criner, Beatrice *AuBYP 3*

Criner, Beatrice Hall 1915- *AuBYP 2S, WhoAmW 75, –77, WhoSSW 78, –80, –82, –84*

Criner, Calvin *AuBYP 3*

Criner, Calvin L *AuBYP 2S*

Crisman, Ruth 1914- *SmATA 73*

Crispin, Edmund *Au&Wr 71, CamGLE, ConAu X, ConLC 22, ConSFA, CurBio 49, DcNaB 1971, EncMys, Novels, TwCCr&M 80, –85, WhoSciF, WorAl, WorAu 1950*
Main entry: Montgomery, Robert Bruce

Crispin, Edmund 1921-1978 *BioIn 14, CrtSuMy, DcLB 87, EncSF 93, TwCCr&M 91, WorAlBi*

Criss, Mildred 1890- *AuBYP 2, –3, BioIn 1, –7, BkC 3, CathA 1930*

Crist, Eda 1909- *AuBYP 2, –3, BioIn 8*

Crist, Richard Harrison 1909- *AuBYP 3*

Crockett, Davy *DcAmChF 1960*

Crockett, Lucy Herndon 1914- *BioIn 1, –3, –5, CurBio 53, IlsCB 1744, –1946*

Crockett, Samuel Rutherford 1860-1914 *BbD, BiD&SB, BioIn 3, –8, BritAu 19, CarSB, CasWL, Chambr 3, ChhPo, ConAu 116, DcBiA, DcEnA A, DcLEL, DcNaB 1912, EvLB, LongCTC, NewC, OxCChiL, OxCEng 85, PenC ENG, REn, TelT, TwCA, –SUP, TwCChW 78, –83, –89, WhoChL*

Crofford, Emily *BioIn 17*

Crofford, Emily 1927- *SmATA 61*

Crofut, Bill *SmATA X*

Crofut, William E, III 1934- *BioIn 13, ConAu 25R, SmATA 23, WhoE 74*

Crofut, William Elmer 1934- *WhoEnt 92*

Croker, T Crofton 1798-1854 *CamGLE, DcIrL, OxCChiL*

Croll, Carolyn 1945- *BioIn 16, ConAu 123 SmATA 52, –56*

Croman, Dorothy Young *ConAu X, IntAu&W 86X, SmATA X*
Main entry: Picard, Dorothy Young

Croman, Dorothy Young 1906- *BioIn 15*

Cromie, Alice 1914- *AuBYP 3*

Cromie, Alice Hamilton 1914- *AuBYP 2S ConAu 9R, –3NR, SmATA 24, WhoMW 74*
Pseud./variant:
Hamilton, Alice
Mort, Vivian

Cromie, William J 1930- *AuBYP 2S, BioIn 9, ConAu 13R, SmATA 4, WhoMW 84*

Cromie, William Joseph 1930- *AuBYP 3, WhoE 91, WhoMW 88*

Crommelynck, Landa *IlsBYP*

Crompton, Anne Eliot 1930- *AuBYP 2S, –3, ConAu 33R, –13NR, SmATA 23, –73*

Crompton, Frances Eliza 1866-1952 *OxCChiL, TelT*

Crompton, Richmal *ConAu X, DcNaB 1961, FilmgC, HalFC 84, LongCTC, NewC, Novels, ObitT 1961, OxCChiL, SmATA 5, TwCChW 78, –83, WhoChL, WhoHr&F*

Crompton, Richmal 1890-1969 *BioIn 14, –16, CamGLE, FemiCLE, GrBr, HalFC 88 TwCChW 89*

Cronbach, Abraham 1882-1965 *AmPeW, BioIn 5, –7, –11, ConAu 1R, IndAu 1917, OhA&B, SmATA 11, WhAm 4*

Crone, Ruth 1919- *AuBYP 2, –3, BioIn 9, ConAu 9R, ForWC 70, SmATA 4*

Cronin, A J 1896-1981 *AnObit 1981, Au&Wr 71, BioIn 1, –2, –3, –4, –6, –7, –8, BlueB 76, CasWL, CathA 1930, Chambr 3, ConAu 1R, –102, –5NR, ConLC 32, ConNov 76, CurBio 42, –81N, DcLEL, EncWL, EvLB, FilmgC, HalFC 84, LongCTC, ModBrL, NewC, NewYTBS 81, Novels, OxCEng 85, PenC ENG, RAdv 1, REn,*

SmATA 25N, –47, TwCA, –SUP, TwCWr, WhNAA, WrDr 76, –80, –82

Crook, Bette Jean 1921- *ConAu 73*
Pseud./variant:
Leslie, San

Crook, Beverly Courtney *BioIn 14, –15, ConAu 115, SmATA 35, –38*

Cropp, Ben 1936- *ConAu 33R, IntAu&W 77, WrDr 76, –80, –82, –84, –86*

Cros, Earl *SmATA X*
Main entry: Rose, Carl

Crosby, Alexander L 1906-1980 *AuBYP 2, –3, BioIn 7, –9, –10, –12, –13, ConAu 29R, –93, MorBMP, NewYTBS 80, SmATA 2, –23N*

Crosby, John *BioIn 14, IlsBYP*

Crosby, Percy 1891-1964 *AmAu&B, ArtCS, BioIn 7*

Crosby, Percy L 1891-1964 *EncACom*

Crosby, Phoebe *AuBYP 2, –3, BioIn 8*

Crosher, G R 1911- *ConAu 69, SmATA 14*
Pseud./variant:
Kesteven, G R

Cross, Anthony Glenn 1936- *ConAu 37R, IntAu&W 77, –89, –91, Who 88, –92, WhoWor 87, WrDr 76, –80, –82, –84, –86, –88, –90, –92, –94*

Cross, Anthony Glenn, Prof 1936- *Who 90*

Cross, Dennis *LElec*

Cross, Frank Bernard 1925- *AmMWSc 73P, –76P, –82, –86, –89, –92*

Cross, Gilbert B *ConAu 23NR*
Main entry: Winters, J C

Cross, Gilbert B 1939- *BioIn 16, –17, ScF&FL 92, SmATA 51, –60*
Pseud./variant:
Winters, J C
Winters, Jon

Cross, Gillian 1945- *BioIn 15, –16, ChlLR 28, ConAu 111, OxCChiL, ScF&FL 92, SixBJA, SmATA 38, TwCChW 83, –89, WrDr 86, –88, –90, –92*

Cross, Gillian Clare 1945- *ChlFicS, ConAu 38NR, MajAI, SmATA 71, TwCYAW, WrDr 94*

Cross, Helen Reeder *ConAu X, SmATA X*
Main entry: Broadhead, Helen Cross

Cross, John Keir 1914-1967 *AuBYP 2, –3, BioIn 8, ConAu 73, EncSF 93, TwCSFW 86, –91, WhoChL, WhoHr&F*
Pseud./variant:
MacFarlane, Stephen

Cross, Michael Sean 1938- *DrAS 74H, –82H*

Cross, Milton 1897-1975 *AmAu&B, BioIn 4, –9, –10, CelR, ConAu 53, CurBio 40, –75, NewYTBE 71, ObitOF 79, WhAm 6, WhScrn 77, WhoAm 74, WorAlBi*

Cross, Verda 1914- *ConAu 142, SmATA 75*

Cross, Wilbur L 1918- *WrDr 86, –88*

Cross, Wilbur Lucius 1918- *IntAu&W 89*

Cross, Wilbur Lucius, III 1918- *Au&Wr 71, BioIn 1, –2, –4, –8, –9, BlueB 76, ConAu 1R, –2NR, SmATA 2, WhoE 74, WrDr 76, –80, –82, –84*

Crosscup, Richard 1905- *AuBYP 2S, –3*

Crossley-Holland, Kevin *BioIn 15*

Crossley-Holland, Kevin 1941- *AuBYP 3, ConPo 91, TwCChW 89, WrDr 86, –88, –90, –92*

Crossley-Holland, Kevin John William 1941- *AuBYP 2S, BioIn 10, ChhPo S1, ChlFicS, ConAu 41R, ConPo 70, –75, –80, –85, DcLB 40, FourBJA, IntAu&W 77, –82, –86, –89, –91, IntWWP 82, MajAI, OxCChiL, SmATA 5, –74, TwCChW 78, –83, TwCYAW, Who 88, –90, –92, WrDr 76, –80, –82, –84, –94*

Crothers, Samuel McChord 1857-1927 *AmAu&B, BenetAL 91, BioIn 3, –5, –7, CarSB, ChhPo S2, ConAmL, DcAmAu, DcNAA, OxCAmL 65, –83, REnAL, TwCA, –SUP, WhAm 1, WhNAA*

Crouch, Marcus S 1913- *Au&Wr 71, BioIn 8, –9, ChhPo, –S2, ConAu 9R, –5NR, IntAu&W 77, OxCChiL, SmATA 4, WhoChL, WhoLib 54, –72, WrDr 76, –80, –82, –84, –86, –88, –90, –92, –94*

Crouch, Nathaniel 1632?-1725? *DcNaB, OxCChiL*

Crouse, Anna *AuBYP 2, –3, BioIn 8*

Crouse, Russel 1893-1966 *AmAu&B, AuBYP 2, BenetAL 91, BiE&WWA, BioIn 1, –2, –4, –5, –7, –8, –11, CamGWoT, CnDAL, CnThe, ConAu 25R, CurBio 41, –66, EncMT, EncWT, HalFC 84, –88, McGEWD 72, –84, ModWD, NewCBMT, NotNAT B, ObitOF 79, OhA&B, OxCAmL 65, –83, OxCAmT 84, OxCPMus,*

OxCThe 83, REn, REnAL, TwCA SUP, WhAm 4, WorAlBi, WorAl

Crouse, Russel M 1893-1966 *AuBYP 3*

Crouse, Russel McKinley 1893-1966 *DcAmB S8*

Crouse, William Harry 1907- *AmMWSc 73P, AuBYP 2, –3, BioIn 7, ConAu 5R, –6NR, IndAu 1917, WhoFI 83, WrDr 76*

Crout, George C 1917- *BioIn 11, ConAu 29R, –11NR, SmATA 11*

Crow, Bettina Lum *AuBYP 3*

Crow, Donna Fletcher 1941- *BioIn 15, ConAu 108, –25NR, SmATA 40, WhoUSWr 88*
Pseud./variant:
Paul, Elizabeth

Crowcroft, Peter 1922- *ScF&FL 92*

Crowcroft, Peter 1923- *ConAu 101*

Crowder, Michael 1934- *Au&Wr 71, ConAu 1R, –1NR, IntAu&W 77, –82, Who 82, –83, –85, –88, WhoWor 78, WrDr 76, –80, –82, –84, –86, –88*

Crowder, Michael 1934-1988 *AnObit 1988, BioIn 16, ConAu 126*

Crowe, Bettina Lum 1911- *AuBYP 2, Au&Wr 71, ConAu 9R, IntAu&W 77, –82, SmATA 6, WhoAm 74, WhoAmW 74, –75, WrDr 76, –80*
Pseud./variant:
Lum, Peter

Crowe, Jocelyn 1906- *BioIn 1, IlsCB 1744*

Crowe, John *ConAu X, IntAu&W 91X, SmATA X, TwCCr&M 80, –85, –91, WhoUSWr 88, WhoWrEP 89, –92, WrDr 82, –84, –86, –88, –90, –92*
Main entry: Lynds, Dennis

Crowe, John 1924- *BioIn 14, –15, –16, WrDr 94*

Crowe, Robert Lee 1937- *ConAu 69, WhoMW 80, –82, –84*

Crowell, Ann *AuBYP 2S, –3*

Crowell, Grace Noll 1877-1969 *AmAu&B, BioIn 4, –6, –7, –8, –14, BkCL, ChhPo, –S1, –S2, ConAu 107, InWom SUP, REnAL, SmATA 34, TexWr, WhAm 5, WhNAA*

Crowell, Pers 1910- *BioIn 3, –5, –6, –9, ConAu 29R, IlsBYP, IlsCB 1946, MorJA, SmATA 2, WhoPNW*

Crowell, Robert L 1909- *BioIn 17, SmATA 63*

Crowell, Robert Leland 1909- *WhoAm 86, –88, –90, WhoE 91*

Crowfield, Christopher *DcEnL, DcNAA, MajAI, OxCAmL 65, YABC 1*
Main entry: Stowe, Harriet Beecher

Crowley, Arthur McBlair 1945- *ConAu 107, SmATA 38*

Crowley, Christine 1922- *Au&Wr 71*

Crowley, John *BioIn 17*

Crowley, John 1942- *ConAu 43NR, ConLC 57, EncSF 93, NewEScF, ScF&FL 92, ScFSB, SmATA 65, TwCSFW 86, –91, WrDr 86, –88, –90, –92*

Crown, Abraham Wolf 1906- *Au&Wr 71*

Crownfield, Gertrude 1867-1945 *AmAu&B, AuBYP 2, –3, BioIn 2, –8, –11, ChhPo, –S1, CurBio 45, DcNAA, JBA 34, –51, ObitOF 79, OhA&B, WhAm 2, WhNAA, YABC 1*

Crownfield, Gertrude Frederica 1867-1945 *WomNov*

Crowther, Bosley d1981 *HalFC 88*

Crowther, Bosley 1905-1981 *AmAu&B, AnObit 1981, BioIn 4, –5, –8, –12, ConAu 65, –103, CurBio 57, –81N, EncTwCJ, HalFC 84, IntMPA 75, –76, –78, –81, –77, NewYTBS 81, WhAm 7, WhoWor 74, WorAlBi, WorAl*

Crowther, James Gerald 1899- *AuBYP 2, –3, BioIn 8, –12, ConAu 73, SmATA 14, WrDr 76, –80, –82, –84*

Cruickshank, Helen 1907- *AuBYP 2, –3, ConAu P-1, ForWC 70*

Cruikshank, George 1792-1878 *Alli, ArtsNiC, BioIn 1, –3, –10, –11, –12, –13, –16, BlmGEL, CamGLE, CarSB, CelCen, ChhPo, –S1, –S2, ClaDrA, DcBiPP, DcBrBI, DcNaB, DcVicP 2, Dis&D, IlsBYP, LongCEL, NewC, OxCArt, OxCChiL, OxCEng 85, OxDcArt, REn, SmATA 22, StaCVF, Str&VC, WhDW*

Crump, Fred H, Jr. 1931- *BioIn 11, ConAu 9R, –3NR, –19NR, –41NR, SmATA 11, –76*

Crump, Irving 1887-1979 *AmAu&B, AuBYP 2, BioIn 2, –8, ConAu 73, EncSF 93, JBA 34, –51, ScF&FL 92, SmATA 21N*

Crump, J Irving 1887-1979 *SmATA 57*

Crump, J Irving 1901-1979 *BioIn 16*

Crump, James Irving 1887-1979 *AuBYP 3*

Crunden, Reginald *ConAu X*

Crutcher, Chris 1946- *Au&Arts 9, BioIn 16, –17, ChlLR 28, ConAu 36NR, SmATA 52*

Crutcher, Christopher C 1946- *MajAI, TwCYAW, WhoUSWr 88*

Cruz, Nicky 1938- *BioIn 12, WhoRel 75*

Cruz, Ray 1933- *BioIn 10, –12, IlsBYP, IlsCB 1967, SmATA 6*

Cruz Martinez, Alejandro d1987 *SmATA 74*

Ctvrtek, Vaclav *TwCChW 89B*

Ctvrtek, Vaclav 1911-1976 *BioIn 13, ConAu 107, FourBJA, SmATA 27N, TwCChW 78B, –83B*

Cudlip, Pender, Mrs *DcEnL, WomNov*

Cudlip, Pender, Mrs 1838-1918 *StaCVF*

Cuffari, Richard 1925-1978 *BioIn 10, –13, –17, ChhPo S2, FifBJA, IlsBYP, IlsCB 1967, MajAI, SmATA 6, –25N, –66, WhoAmA 80, –82*

Cule, William Edward *ChhPo*

Cullen, Countee 1903-1946 *AfrAmAl 6, AmAu&B, AnCL, AnMV 1926, Benet 87, BenetAL 91, BioIn 1, –2, –3, –4, –6, –7, –8, –9, –10, –12, –13, –15, –16, –17, BlkAWP, BlkAull, –92, BlkLC, BlkWr 1, BlkWrNE, BroadAu, CamGLE, CamHAL, CasWL, ChhPo, –S1, ConAmA, ConAmL, ConAu 108, –124, CurBio 46, CyWA 89, DcAmNB, DcLB 4, –48, –51, DcLEL, DcNAA, EarBlAP, EncAACR, EncWL 2, FourBJA, InB&W 80, –85, LiExTwC, MajTwCW, ModAL, –S1, ModBlW, NegAl 76, –83, –89, ObitOF 79, OxCAmL 65, –83, PenC AM, RAdv 1, –13-1, REn, REnAL, RfGAmL 87, SelBAAf, SmATA 18, Tw, TwCA, –SUP, TwCLC 4, –37, WebE&AL, WhAm 2, WhNAA*

Cullen, Countee 1903-1949 *DrBlPA 90*

Culliford, Pierre 1928- *BioIn 15, ConAu 124, SmATA 40*

Culliford, Pierre 1928-1992 *AnObit 1992, ConAu 140, NewYTBS 92, SmATA 74*
Pseud./variant:
Peyo

Cullum, Albert *AuBYP 2S, –3*

Cullum, Ridgwell 1867-1943 *BioIn 4, EncFWF, EvLB, LongCTC, OxCCan, TwCA, –SUP*

Culp, Louanna McNary 1901-1965 *BioIn 9, ConAu P-1, SmATA 2*

Cumbaa, Stephen 1947- *SmATA 72*

Cumberlege, Vera G 1908- *ConAu 81*

Cumming, Primrose 1915- *TwCChW 89, WrDr 86, –88, –90, –92*

Cumming, Primrose Amy 1915- *Au&Wr 71, BioIn 13, ConAu 33R, OxCChiL, SmATA 24, TwCChW 83, WrDr 76, –80, –82, –84, –94*

Cumming, Robert 1945- *BioIn 17, SmATA 65*

Cummings, Betty Sue 1918- *BioIn 12, ConAu 73, –14NR, DcAmChF 1960, FifBJA, SmATA 15, –9AS, WhoUSWr 88, WhoWrEP 89, –92*

cummings, e e *AuBYP 3*

Cummings, E E 1894-1962 *AgeMat, AmAu&B, AmWr, AnCL, AtlBL, AuBYP 2, Benet 87, BenetAL 91, BioIn 1, –2, –3, –4, –5, –6, –7, –8, –9, –10, –11, –14, –15, –16, –17, CamGEL, CamGLE, CamHAL, CasWL, ChhPo, CnDAL, CnE&AP, CnMD, CnMWL, ConAmA, ConAmL, ConAu 73, –31NR, ConLC 1, –3, –8, –12, –15, –68, CyWA 58, DcAmB S7, DcLB 4, –48, DcLEL, EncWL, –2, EvLB, LiExTwC, LongCTC, MagSAmL, MajTwCW, McGEWD 72, –84, ModAL, –S1, –S2, ModWD, NewGrDA 86, ObitT 1961, OxCAmL 65, –83, OxCEng 67, –85, PenC AM, PoeCrit 5, RAdv 1, –13-1, RComAH, REn, REnAL, RfGAmL 87, SixAP, TwCA, –SUP, TwCWr, WebE&AL, WhAmArt 85, WhoTwCL, WorAlBi, WorAl, WorLitC*

Cummings, Edward Estlin 1894-1962 *AuBYP 3, BioIn 14, –15, –16, –17*

Cummings, Park 1902-1987 *SmATA 53N*

Cummings, Parke 1902- *AmAu&B, BioIn 9, ConAu P-1, SmATA 2, WhAm 9, WhoAm 74, –76, –78, –80, –82, –84, –86*

Cummings, Parke 1902-1987 *BioIn 15, –16, ConAu 123*

Cummings, Pat *ChlBIlD*

Cummings, Pat 1950- *BioIn 15, –16, ConAu 122, MajAI, SixBJA, SmATA 42, –13AS, WhoBlA 94*

Cummings, Pat Marie 1950- *BlkAull, –92, BlkWr 2, SmATA 71, WhoBlA 92*

Cummings, Ray 1887-1957 *BioIn 4, –6, –12, ConAu 113, –31NR, DcLB 8, EncSF 93, NewEScF, ScF&FL 92, ScFSB, ScFEYrs, TwCSFW 86, –91, WhoSciF*

Cummings, Richard *AuBYP 2, –3, BioIn 8, –13, ConAu X, SmATA X, WrDr 76, –80, –82*
Main entry: Gardner, Richard M

Cummings, Walter Thies 1933- *ConAu 1R*

Cummins, Maria S 1827-1866 *BioIn 15*

Cummins, Maria Susanna 1827-1866 *Alli SUP, AmAu, AmAu&B, BenetAL 91, BbD, BiD&SB, BioIn 8, –11, BlmGWL, CelCen, Chambr 3, ChhPo, DcAmAu, DcBiA, DcLB 42, DcLEL, DcNAA, EvLB, InWom SUP, OxCAmL 65, –83, OxCChiL, REn, REnAL, WhAm HS, WhoChL, YABC 1*

Cumpston, Astrid Kate Oatelaye *IlsBYP*
Main entry: Walford, Astrid

Cundall, Joseph 1818-1895 *Alli SUP, BioIn 11, –17, CarSB, DcLB 106, OxCChiL*

Cuneo, Cyrus C 1879-1916 *DcBrAr 1*

Cuneo, John Robert 1911- *ConAu 53, WhoE 83*

Cuneo, Terence Tenison 1907- *BioIn 1, –3, –11, –14, ClaDrA, DcBrAr 1, Who 74, –82, –83, –85, –88, –90, –92, WhoArt 80, –82, –84*

Cunliffe, Barrington Windsor 1939- *ConAu 53, –9NR, –24NR, IntAu&W 77, –82, –86, Who 74, –82, –83, –85, –88, –92, WhoWor 82, –84, WrDr 76, –80*

Cunliffe, Barrington Windsor, Prof 1939- *Who 90*

Cunliffe, John 1933- *TwCChW 89, WrDr 86, –88, –90, –92*

Cunliffe, John Arthur 1933- *Au&Wr 71, BioIn 11, ConAu 61, –11NR, IntAu&W 77, SmATA 11, TwCChW 83, WrDr 94*

Cunliffe, Marcus d1990 *NewYTBS 90*

Cunliffe, Marcus 1922- *AmAu&B, Au&Wr 71, BioIn 15, BlueB 76, ConAu 21R, –10NR, IntAu&W 91, SmATA 37, Who 74, WrDr 76, –82, –84, –86, –88, –90*

Cunliffe, Marcus 1922-1990 *AnObit 1990, BioIn 17, ConAu 132, SmATA 66*

Cunningham, Aline *ConAu 57, –9NR*

Cunningham, Captain Frank *ConAu X, SmATA X*
Main entry: Glick, Carl Cannon

Cunningham, Cathy *BioIn 13, ConAu X, ScF&FL 92, SmATA X, WrDr 86, –88, –90, –92*
Main entry: Cunningham, Chet

Cunningham, Cathy 1928- *WrDr 94*

Cunningham, Chet 1928- *BioIn 13, ConAu 49, –4NR, –19NR, IntAu&W 86, ScF&FL 92, SmATA 23, TwCWW 91, WrDr 84, –86, –88, –90, –92, –94*
Pseud./variant:
Cunningham, Cathy

Cunningham, Dale S 1932- *BioIn 11, ConAu 13R, –8NR, DrAS 74F, –78F, SmATA 11, WhoAm 76, WhoE 74, –75*

Cunningham, Dellwyn *ChhPo*

Cunningham, E V *AuBYP 2, –3, ConAu X, –33NR, ConNov 72, –76, –82, EncSF 93, IntAu&W 77X, Novels, SmATA 7, TwCCr&M 80, –85, WhoUSWr 88, WhoWrEP 89, –92, WrDr 76, –80, –82, –84, –86, –88, –90, –92*
Main entry: Fast, Howard

Cunningham, E V 1914- *CrtSuMy, TwCCr&M 91, WrDr 94*

Cunningham, Julia *BioIn 15*

Cunningham, Julia 1916- *AuBYP 3, ConAu 19NR, –36NR, SmATA 2AS, TwCChW 89*

Cunningham, Julia W 1916- *WrDr 86, –88, –90, –92*

Cunningham, Julia Woolfolk 1916- *AmAu&B, AuBYP 2, BioIn 7, –9, –10, –13, ConAu 9R, –4NR, ConLC 12, DcAmChF 1960, McjAI, MorBMP, SmATA 1, –26, –2AS, ThrBJA, TwCChW 78, –83, WhoAm 74, –76, –78, –80, –82, –84, –86, –88, –90, –92, –94, WhoAmW 74, WhoUSWr 88, WhoWrEP 89, –92, WrDr 80, –82, –84, –94*

Cunningham, Mary *AuBYP 2, –3*
Main entry: Pierce, Mary Cunningham

Cunningham, Virginia 1909- *AuBYP 2 –3, BioIn 7, –13, ConAu X, OhA&B, SmATA X*
Pseud./variant:
Holmgren, Virginia Cunningham

Cunningham, Walter *SingR 1*

Cunnington, Phillis 1887-1974 *Au&Wr 71, BiE&WWA, ConAu 53, WrDr 76, –80, –82, –84*

Curaie, Amicus
Main entry: Fuller, Edmund

Curiae, Amicus *AuBYP 3, SmATA X*

Curie, Eve 1904- *AmAu&B, AnCL, Au&Wr 71, BioIn 3, -6, -9, ConAu P-1, CurBio 40, InWom SUP, IntAu&W 77, IntWW 74, SmATA 1, Who 74, -83, -85, -88, -90, -92, WhoAm 74, -76, -78, -80, -82, -84, WhoAmW 74, -75, -81, -83, -85, -87, -89, -91, -93, WhoE 85, -86, WhoWor 74, -78, -80, -84, -87, -89, -91, -93*

Curley, Daniel *BioIn 16, -17, DrAPF 87*

Curley, Daniel d1988 *NewYTBS 89*

Curley, Daniel 1918- *BioIn 13, ConAu 3NR, -18NR, DrAPF 83, -85, IntAu&W 82, SmATA 23, WrDr 82, -84, -86, -88*

Curley, Daniel 1918-1988 *ConAu 127, SmATA 61*

Curren, Polly 1917- *ConAu 1R, -4NR*

Currier, Richard Leon 1940- *ConAu 57*

Currimbhoy, Nayana *AuBYP 3*

Curry, Ann Gabrielle 1934- *SmATA 72*

Curry, Jane L 1932- *ConAu 24NR, SmATA 52, -6AS*

Curry, Jane Louise 1932- *AuBYP 2, -3, BioIn 8, -9, -16, ChlLR 31, ConAu 17R, -7NR, DcAmChF 1960, FourBJA, IntAu&W 82, -89, -91, MajAI, ScF&FL 92, SmATA 1, TwCChW 78, -83, -89, WhoAm 82, -84, -90, -92, -94, WhoAmW 83, WhoUSWr 88, WhoWrEP 89, -92, WrDr 80, -82, -84*

Curry, Jennifer 1934- *ConAu 77*

Curry, John Steuart 1897-1946 *ArtsAmW 2, Benet 87, BioIn 1, -4, -5, -7, -10, -11, -13, BriEAA, CurBio 41, -46, DcCAA 71, -77, -88, GrAmP, IlsCB 1744, ObitOF 79, OxCAmL 65, OxCTwCA, OxDcArt, PhDcTCA 77, REn, REnAL, WhAm 2, WhAmArt 85*

Curry, Peggy Simson *DrAPF 87*

Curry, Peggy Simson 1911- *BioIn 4, -5, -11, ConAu 33R, -12NR, CurBio 58, DrAF 76, DrAPF 83, -85, SmATA 8, WrDr 84, -86*

Curry, Peggy Simson 1911-1987 *BioIn 16, ConAu 121, SmATA 50N, TwCWW 91*

Curtayne, Alice 1898- *Au&Wr 71, BioIn 1, BkC 6, CathA 1930, ConAu 53*

Curtin, Jeremiah 1840?-1906 *AmAu, AmAu&B, BenetAL 91, BiD&SB, BiInAmS, BioIn 7, DcAmAu, DcNAA, REnAL, WhAm 1*

Curtis, Alice Bertha *AuBYP 2, -3, BioIn 8*

Curtis, Alice Turner 1860-1958 *AmAu&B, AuBYP 2, -3, BioIn 8, CarSB, ChhPo, WhNAA, WomWWA 14*

Curtis, Anthony 1926- *ConAu 101, -18NR, -40NR, IntAu&W 77, -82, WrDr 76, -80, -82, -84, -86, -88, -90, -92, -94*

Curtis, Arnold 1917- *ConAu 29R, -12NR, -29NR*

Curtis, Arnold Bennett 1940- *WhoAm 92*

Curtis, Bruce *BioIn 14, -15, -16*

Curtis, Bruce 1944- *SmATA 30*

Curtis, Edward S 1868-1952 *AmAu&B, BioIn 3, -10, -11, -12, -13, -15, -17, ICPEnP, MacBEP, ObitOF 79, WhAm 4, WhAmArt 85*

Curtis, Edward Sheriff 1868-1952 *WhNaAH*

Curtis, Elizabeth *ArtsAmW 2, ConICB, DcWomA, WhAmArt 85*

Curtis, Patricia 1924- *BioIn 13, ConAu 69, -18NR, SmATA 23*

Curtis, Peter *AuBYP 2S, -3, BioIn 13, ConAu X, LongCTC, ScF&FL 92, SmATA 8, -X, TwCCr&M 80, TwCRHW 90, Who 74, -82, -83, WrDr 82, -84*
Main entry: Lofts, Norah

Curtis, Philip 1920- *ChlFicS, ScF&FL 92, SmATA 62*

Curtis, Richard 1937- *AuBYP 2S, -3, BioIn 13, ConAu 106, -25NR, ScF&FL 92, SmATA 29*
Pseud./variant:
Lilly, Ray
Richards, Curtis
Stultifer, Morton
Ward, Melanie

Curtis, Richard Alan 1937- *EncSF 93*

Curtis, Robert H *AuBYP 2S, -3*

Curtis, Rosemary Ann 1935- *AuBYP 2S, -3, ConAu 9R*

Curtis, Wade *ConAu 30NR, EncSF 93, IntAu&W 91X, SmATA X, WrDr 84, -86, -88, -90, -92*
Main entry: Pournelle, Jerry Eugene

Curtis, Wade 1933- *WrDr 94*

Curtis Brown, Beatrice *ConAu P-2*
Pseud./variant:
Brown, Beatrice Curtis

Curto, Josephine 1927- *ConAu 17R, WrDr 76, –80, –82, –84*

Curwood, James Oliver 1878-1927 *AmAu&B, BenetAL 91, BioIn 2, CreCan 1, DcNAA, EncFWF, LongCTC, MichAu 80, OxCAmL 65, –83, OxCCan, OxCCanL, REnAL, TwCA, –SUP, TwCWW 91, WhAm 1, WhNAA*

Cusack, Ellen Dymphna 1902- *Au&Wr 71, BioIn 11, BlueB 76, ConAu 9R, DcLEL, IntAu&W 77, –82, WhoWor 74, –78, –80, WrDr 76, –80*

Cusack, Margaret 1945- *AmArt, BioIn 15, –16, ConGrA 2, SmATA 58*

Cusack, Michael Joseph 1928- *ConAu 69, WhoAm 78, –80, –82, –90, –92*

Cushman, Doug 1953- *SmATA 65*

Cushman, Jerome *AuBYP 3*

Cushman, Jerome 1914- *AuBYP 2S, BiDrLUS 70, BioIn 9, ConAu 1R, SmATA 2, WhoAm 74, –76, –78, WhoLibS 55, –66, WhoWorJ 72, –78, WrDr 76, –80, –82, –84*

Cusick, Richie Tankersley 1952- *ConAu 134, ScF&FL 92, SmATA 67, TwCYAW, WrDr 94*

Cutchen, Billye Walker 1930- *ConAu 77, –13NR, SmATA 15, WhoSSW 84, –86*
Pseud./variant:
Brown, Billye Walker

Cutchins, Judy *AuBYP 3, BioIn 16*

Cutchins, Judy 1947- *ConAu 127, SmATA 59*

Cutforth, John Ashlin 1911- *Au&Wr 71, ConAu 9R*

Cutler, Ann *AuBYP 2, –3, BioIn 8*

Cutler, Ebbitt 1923- *AuBYP 3*

Cutler, Ivor *IntAu&W 91*

Cutler, Ivor 1923- *Au&Wr 71, BioIn 13, ConAu 5R, –9NR, ConPo 70, IntAu&W 77, –82, IntWWM 85, IntWWP 82, SmATA 24 Who 82, –83, –85, –88, –90, –92, WhoMus 72, WrDr 76, –80, –82, –84, –86, –88, –90, –92, –94*
Pseud./variant:
Knifesmith

Cutler, Jane 1936- *ConAu 142, SmATA 75 WhoUSWr 88, WhoWrEP 89, –92*

Cutler, Katherine Noble 1905- *ConAu 5R, –4NR*

Cutler, May Ebbitt 1923- *AuBYP 2S, BioIn 11, CanWW 89, ConAu 49, IntAu&W 77, SmATA 9, WhoAmW 77*

Cutler, Samuel *ConAu X, SmATA 5*
Main entry: Folsom, Franklin Brewster

Cutt, W Towrie 1898-1981 *BioIn 12, –13, ConAu 81, –115, OxCCan SUP, Profile 2, ScF&FL 92, SmATA 16, TwCChW 78, –83, –89, WrDr 76, –80, –82*

Cuyler, Margery Stuyvesant 1948- *ConAu 117, SmATA 39, WhoAmW 77, WhoLibI 82*
Pseud./variant:
Wallace, Daisy

Cuyler, Stephen *ConAu X, SmATA X*
Main entry: Bates, Barbara Snedeker

Cyclops
Main entry: Bowles, W M

Czaja, Michael 1911- *ConAu 57*

D

Dabcovich, Lydia *AuBYP 3, ConAu 124, SmATA 47, -58*

Dabcovich, Lydia 1935- *BioIn 16, SixBJA*

Dace, Letitia Skinner 1941- *DrAS 74E, -78E*

Dace, Wallace 1920- *ConAu 61, -34NR, DrAS 74E, -78E, -82E, NatPD 77, -81*

Dachs, David 1922-1980 *ConAu 69, -11NR*

Dadey, Debbie 1959- *SmATA 73*

Dagg, Anne Innis 1933- *AmMWSc 82, -86, -89, -92, CaW, ConAu 69, -11NR, -28NR*

Daggett, R M *Alli SUP*

Daglish, Eric Fitch 1892-1966 *BioIn 1, -4, -5, ConAu 102, ConICB, DcBrAr 1, IlsCB 1744, -1946, JBA 34, LongCTC, TwCA, -SUP*

Daglish, Eric Fitch 1894-1966 *BioIn 14*

Dahan, Andre *AuBYP 3*

Dahl, Borghild 1890-1984 *AuBYP 2, -3, BioIn 6, -8, -9, -10, -15, ConAu 1R, -2NR, MinnWr, SmATA 7, -37N, ThrBJA, WrDr 76, -80, -84*

Dahl, Georg 1905- *ConAu 85*

Dahl, Mary B *AuBYP 3*

Dahl, Mary Bartlett *AuBYP 2S*

Dahl, Roald *BioIn 15, -16, -17, DrAPF 87, -89, -91*

Dahl, Roald d1990 *IntWW 91N, Who 92N*

Dahl, Roald 1916- *AuBYP 2, -3, Au&Wr 71, Benet 87, BioIn 3, -5, -6, -8, -9, -10, -11, -12, -13, BioNews 74, CamGLE, ChlLR 1, -7, ConAu 1R, -6NR, -32NR, ConLC 1, -6, -18, ConNov 72, -76, -82, -86, ConTFT 6, DcLEL 1940, DrAF 76, HalFC 84, -88, IntAu&W 77, -82, -89, IntWW 82, -83, -89, MajTwCW, MorBMP, NewC, Novels, OxCChiL, PenEncH, PiP, RAdv 1, REn, REnAL, ScFSB, SmATA 1, -26, ThrBJA, TwCChW 78, -83, -89, TwCCr&M 80, Who 82, -83, -85, -88, -90, WhoAm 74, -76, -78, -80, -82, -84, -86, -88, -90, WhoHr&F, WhoSciF, WhoWor 74, -78, WorAlBi, WorAl, WorAu 1950, WrDr 76, -80, -82, -84, -86, -88, -90*

Dahl, Roald 1916-1990 *AnObit 1990, ChlFicS, ConAu 133, -37NR, EncSF 93, MajAI, NewYTBS 90, News 91, -91-2, ScF&FL 92, SmATA 65, -73, TwCYAW, WhAm 10*

Dahlberg, Charles C *BiDrAPA 89*

Dahlberg, Charles Clay *BioIn 11*

Dahlstedt, Marden 1921- *AuBYP 2S, -3, BioIn 11, ConAu 45, -1NR, SmATA 8, WrDr 76, -80, -82, -84*

Dain, Martin J 1924- *BioIn 14, ConAu 13R, SmATA 35*

Dakers, Elaine K *ScF&FL 92*

Dakers, Elaine Kidner 1905-1978 *ConAu 85, -30NR, LongCTC*
Pseud./variant:
Lane, Jane

Dal, Erik 1922- *Au&Wr 71, IntAu&W 77, -82, IntWW 89, -91, WhoWor 78, -93*

Dale, George E *ConAu 137, -36NR, MajAI, MajTwCW, SmATA 74*
Main entry: Asimov, Isaac

Dale, George E 1920-1992 *ConLC 76*

Dale, Jack *BioIn 11, ConAu X, IntAu&W 77X, SmATA X*
Main entry: Holliday, Joseph

Dale, Margaret J 1911- *BioIn 15*

Dale, Margaret J Miller 1911- *Au&Wr 71, ConAu 5R, -3NR, -19NR, IntAu&W 77, -82, SmATA 39*
Pseud./variant:
Miller, Margaret J

Dale, Margaret Jessy 1911- *IntAu&W 86, –89, –91*

Dale, Norman *AuBYP 2S, –3, ConAu X, SmATA X, TwCSFW 86, –91*
Main entry: Denny, Norman George

Dale, Norman 1901-1982 *BioIn 15*

Dale, Penny 1954- *SmATA 70*

Dale, Ruth Bluestone *AuBYP 2, –3, BioIn 8*

Daley, Arthur d1974 *Ballpl 90*

Daley, Arthur 1904-1974 *AmAu&B, BioIn 4, –10, ConAu 45, –P-2, CurBio 56, –74, NewYTBS 74, WhAm 6*

Dalgliesh, Alice 1893-1979 *AmAu&B, AmPB, AnCL, AuBYP 2, –3, BioIn 1, –2, –5, –6, –7, –12, –14, ChhPo, ConAu 73, JBA 34, –51, MajAI, SmATA 17, –21N, Str&VC, TwCChW 78, –83, –89, WhNAA, WrDr 80*

Dallas, Ruth *IntvTCA 2*

Dallas, Ruth 1919- *BlmGWL, ChhPo S2, ConAu 65, –10NR, ConPo 70, –75, –80, –85, –91, DcChlFi, DcLEL 1940, FemiCLE, IntAu&W 77, –82, –86, –91, IntWWP 82, LongCTC, TwCChW 78, –83, –89, WhoWor 80, WrDr 76, –80, –82, –84, –86, –88, –90, –92, –94*

Dalmas, John 1926- *EncSF 93, IntAu&W 91, ScF&FL 92, SmATA 76*
Main entry: Jones, John Robert

Dalmas, John 1936- *IntAu&W 89*

Dalton, Alene *BioIn 16, ChhPo*
Main entry: Chapin, Alene Olsen Dalton

Dalton, Anne 1948- *BioIn 12, –14, –15, IlsCB 1967, SmATA 40*

Dalton, Richard 1930- *ConAu 57*

Daly, Anne 1896- *ConAu P-2*

Daly, Carroll John 1889-1958 *AmAu&B, BioIn 4, –14, ConAu 112, CrtSuMy, EncMys, ScF&FL 92, TwCCr&M 80, –85, –91, WhAm 3, WhNAA*

Daly, Donald Francis 1928- *WhoFI 94*

Daly, Donald Fremont 1904- *ConAu 69, WhoWest 80, –82, –84*

Daly, Jim *ConAu X, MajAI*
Main entry: Stratemeyer, Edward L

Daly, Kathleen N *AuBYP 2S, –3, BioIn 15, ConAu 115, SmATA 37*

Daly, Maureen *BioIn 15, –16, IntAu&W 91, WrDr 86, –88, –90, –92*

Daly, Maureen 1921- *AmAu&B, AmNov, ArtclWW 2, Au&Arts 5, AuBYP 2, –3, BioIn 1, –2, –6, –7, –9, BkC 4, CathA 1930, ConAu X, –37NR, ConLC 17, CurBio 46, MajAI, MorJA, REnAL, SmATA 2, –1AS, TwCChW 78, –83, TwCYAW, WhoAmW 77, WrDr 80, –82, –84, –94*
Pseud./variant:
McGivern, Maureen Daly

Daly, Maureen 1922?- *TwCChW 89*

Daly, Nicholas 1946- *ConAu 111, –36NR, MajAI, SmATA 37, –76*
Pseud./variant:
Daly, Niki

Daly, Niki *BioIn 15, ConAu 36NR, MajAI, SmATA 76*
Main entry: Daly, Nicholas

Daly, Niki 1946- *BioIn 16, IntAu&W 89, –91, SixBJA*

Daly, Sheila John 1927?- *AuBYP 2, BioIn 2, –3, –8, CathA 1952*

Daly, Sheila John 1929- *AuBYP 3*

Daly, Thomas A 1871-1948 *BenetAL 91*

Daly, Thomas Augustine 1871-1948 *AmAu&B, AmLY, BioIn 1, –4, –5, –6, BkC 1, CathA 1930, ChhPo, –S2, CnDAL, ConAmL, DcCathB, DcNAA, FamPYP, OxCAmL 65, –83, REn, REnAL, TwCA, –SUP, WhAm 2, WhNAA*

Dalzell, Kathleen Elizabeth 1919- *IntAu&W 77, WrDr 76, –80, –82, –84*

D'Amato, Alex 1919- *AuBYP 2S, –3, BioIn 12, ConAu 81, –18NR, SmATA 20*

D'Amato, Janet 1925- *AuBYP 2S, –3, BioIn 11, ConAu 49, –18NR, SmATA 9*

D'Amato, Janet Potter *WhoAmA 86, –91*

Damjan, Mischa 1914- *AuBYP 2S, –3*

Damrell, Liz 1956- *SmATA 77*

Damrosch, Helen Therese *SmATA X, WhAmArt 85*
Main entry: Tee-Van, Helen Damrosch

Dana, Barbara 1940- *BioIn 13, ConAu 17R, –8NR, ForWC 70, SmATA 22*

Dana, Richard Henry 1815-1882 *BioIn 14, –15, –16, CamGEL, MorMA*

Dana, Richard Henry, Jr. 1815-1882
Alli, –SUP, AmAu, AmAu&B, Benet 87, BenetAL 91, BbD, BiD&SB, BioIn 1, –2, –3, –5, –6, –8, –9, –12, –13, CamGLE, CamHAL, CarSB, CasWL, Chambr 3, CivWDc, CmCal, CnDAL, CrtT 3, CyAL, CyWA 58, DcAmAu, DcAmSR, DcBiPP, DcEnL, DcLB 1, DcLEL, DcNAA, EncAB-H, EvLB, HarEnUS, McGEWB, MouLC 4, OxCAmH, OxCAmL 65, –83, OxCChiL, OxCEng 67, –85, OxCLaw, OxCShps, PenC AM, RAdv 13-3, REn, REnAL, RfGAmL 87, SmATA 26, WebAB 74, –79, WebE&AL, WhDW, WhAm HS, WhAmP, WorAlBi, WorAl

Danachair, Caoimhin O *SmATA X*
Main entry: Danaher, Kevin

Danaher, Kevin 1911-
Pseud./variant:
Danachair, Caoimhin O

Danaher, Kevin 1913- *BiDIrW, BioIn 13, ConAu 33R, SmATA 22, WrDr 80, –82, –84, –86, –88, –90, –92, –94*

D'Andrea, Bernard 1923- *BioIn 2, IlrAm 1880, –F*

D'Andrea, Kate *ConAu X, –30NR, SmATA X*
Main entry: Steiner, Barbara A

Dangerfield, Balfour *AuBYP 3, ConAu X, SmATA 2*
Main entry: McCloskey, Robert

Dangerfield, George 1904- *AmAu&B, BioIn 3, –10, ConAu 9R, CurBio 53, DrAS 74H, –78H, –82H, IntAu&W 82, OxCAmL 65, PoIre, WhoAm 74, –76, –78, –80, –82, –84, –86, WhoWest 74, –76, –78, –82, –84, WhoWor 74, WorAu 1950, WrDr 76*

Dangerfield, George 1904-1986 *AnObit 1986, BioIn 15, ConAu 121, CurBio 87N, NewYTBS 87, WhAm 9*

Daniel, Alan 1939- *BioIn 16, SmATA 53, –76*

Daniel, Anita 1893?-1978 *AuBYP 2, –3, BioIn 8, –11, –13, ConAu 77, ForWC 70, SmATA 23, –24N*
Pseud./variant:
Anita

Daniel, Anita 1902- *BiGAW*

Daniel, Anne *AuBYP 3, ConAu X, –30NR, SmATA X*
Main entry: Steiner, Barbara A

Daniel, Becky 1947- *BioIn 16, SmATA 56*
Pseud./variant:
Daniel, Rebecca 1947-

Daniel, Colin *ConAu 42NR, ScF&FL 92, TwCYAW*

Daniel, Colin 1938- *WrDr 94*

Daniel, Donna Lea 1944- *SmATA 76*

Daniel, Hawthorne 1890- *AmAu&B, Au&Wr 71, BioIn 2, –5, –11, ConAu 5R, IntAu&W 77, –82, JBA 34, –51, SmATA 8, WhAm 8, WhNAA, WhoAm 74, –76, –78, –80, –82, WhoWor 74, –80, WrDr 76*

Daniel, Milly Hawk *AuBYP 2S, –3*

Daniel, Rebecca 1947-
Main entry: Daniel, Becky

Daniel, Roland *WhoLA*

Daniel, Roland 1880-1969 *BioIn 14*

Daniell, Albert Scott 1906-1965 *ConAu 5R, –3NR, TwCChW 78*
Pseud./variant:
Bowood, Richard
Daniell, David Scott
Lewesdon, John

Daniell, David Scott
Main entry: Daniell, Albert Scott

Daniell, David Scott 1906-1965 *OxCChiL, TwCChW 83, –89*

Daniells, Roy 1902-1979 *Au&Wr 71, BioIn 12, CanWW 70, –80, CanWr, ConAu 57, ConPo 70, –80, CreCan 1, DcLB 68, OxCCan, –SUP, OxCCanL, WrDr 76, –82, –84*

Daniels, Guy *BioIn 16, –17*

Daniels, Guy 1919- *AuBYP 2S, –3, BioIn 10, –11, ChhPo S1, ConAu 21R, SmATA 11, WhoE 74*

Daniels, Guy 1919-1989 *ConAu 128, SmATA 62*

Daniels, Jonathan 1902-1981 *AuBYP 3, Benet 87, BenetAL 91, ConAu 29NR, JrnUS, ScF&FL 92*

Daniels, Jonathan Worth 1902-1981 *AmAu&B, AnObit 1981, AuBYP 2, Au&Wr 71, BioIn 2, –3, –4, –5, –7, –10, –12, –13, BlueB 76, CnDAL, ConAu 49, –105, CurBio 42, –82N, DcLB 127, DcNCBi 2, EncAACR, EncSoH, IntYB 80, –81, –82, NewYTBS 81, OxCAmL 65, –83, REn, REnAL, TwCA, –SUP, WhAm 8, WhoAm 74, –80, WhoAmP 73, WhoSSW 73, WhoWor 74, WrDr 80, –82*

Daniels, Leslie Noel, III 1943- *ConAu 65*

Danielsson, Bengt Emmerick 1921- *IntWW 89*

Danielsson, Bengt Emmerik 1921- *Au&Wr 71, FifIDA, IntAu&W 77, -82, -86, -89, IntWW 74, -75, -76, -77, -78, -79, -80, -81, -82, -83, -91, WhoWor 74, -78*

Danish, Barbara *DrAPF 87, -89, -91, -93*

Danish, Barbara 1948- *ConAu 57*

Dank, Gloria Rand 1955- *ScF&FL 92, SmATA 46, -56*

Dank, Leonard D 1929- *BioIn 15, WhoAmA 86, -89, -91*

Dank, Leonard Dewey 1929- *SmATA 44, WhoAm 90, -92, -94, WhoAmA 78, -80, -82, -84, WhoE 74, -75, -77, -81, -85, -86, -89, WhoWor 87, -89*

Dank, Milton 1920- *AmMWSc 82, -86, -89, -92, BioIn 14, ConAu 11NR, -28NR, ScF&FL 92, SmATA 31*

Dann, Colin Michael 1943- *ChlFicS*

Dann, Jack *BioIn 17, ConSFF, DrAPF 87, -89, -91, -93*

Dann, Jack 1945- *ConAu 49, -2NR, -30NR, DrAF 76, DrAPF 83, -85, IntAu&W 82, -89, -91, NewEScF, RGTwCSF, ScF&FL 92, TwCSFW 86, -91, WrDr 84, -86, -88, -90, -92, -94*

Dann, Jack 1949- *ScFSB*

Dann, Jack Mayo 1945- *EncSF 93*

Dann, Max 1955- *BioIn 17, ConAu 118, SmATA 62*

Dannay, Frederic *Benet 87, BenetAL 91, RfGAmL 87, TwCCr&M 91*

Dannay, Frederic 1905-1982 *AmAu&B, AnObit 1982, AuSpks, AuBYP 2, -3, BioIn 2, -3, -4, -8, -10, -11, -12, -13, -14, -17, ConAu 1R, -107, -1NR, -39NR, CurBio 40, -82N, DcLB 137, DcLEL, EncMys, EvLB, IntAu&W 77, IntWW 74, -75, -76, -77, -78, -79, -80, -81, -82, -83N, LongCTC, MajTwCW, NewYTBS 82, PenC AM, REn, TwCA, -SUP, TwCCr&M 80, -85, WebAB 74, -79, WhAm 8, Who 74, -82, -83N, WhoAm 74, -76, -78, -80, -82, WhoWor 74, WrDr 76, -80, -82*
Pseud./variant:
Nathan, Daniel
Queen, Ellery
Queen, Ellery, Jr.
Ross, Barnaby

Dannett, Sylvia Gwendolyn Liebowitz 1909- *ConAu 1R, -4NR, WhoAmW 74, -75, -77, WhoWorJ 72, -78*

Danska, Herbert 1927?- *BioIn 5, -8, ConAu 29R, IlsBYP, IlsCB 1946, -1957, -1967*

Dantzic, Cynthia Maris 1933- *ConAu 101, WhoAmA 84, -86, -89, -91, WhoAmW 74, -75, -77, WhoE 86, -91*

Danziger, Paula 1944- *Au&Arts 4, BioIn 14, -16, -17, ChlLR 20, ConAu 112, -115, -37NR, ConLC 21, FifBJA, MajAI, ScF&FL 92, SmATA 30, -36, -63, TwCChW 89, TwCYAW, WrDr 90, -92, -94*

Darby, Ada Claire 1883- *AuBYP 3*

Darby, Ada Claire 1883-1953 *AmAu&B, AuBYP 2, BioIn 3, -7, ObitOF 79, WhAm 3*

Darby, Gene Kegley 1921- *ConAu 5R, -2NR*

Darby, J N *AuBYP 3, ConAu X, SmATA X, WrDr 76, -80, -82, -84*
Main entry: Govan, Christine Noble

Darby, Jean 1921- *BioIn 17, SmATA 68*

Darby, Jean Kegley 1921- *ConAu 39NR, WhoWest 89*

Darby, Patricia *AuBYP 2, BioIn 12, ConAu 73, SmATA 14*

Darby, Ray 1912- *ASCAP 66, AuBYP 2, BioIn 8, -10, ConAu 17R, SmATA 7, WhoWest 74*

Darby, Raymond 1912- *AuBYP 3*

d'Arcy, Willard *SmATA X, TwCCr&M 91*
Main entry: Cox, William R

Dardig, Jill Carolyn 1948- *ConAu 69*

Dare, Eveline *SingR 2*

Dareff, Hal 1920- *AmAu&B, AuBYP 2, -3, BioIn 8, ConAu 65, WhoAm 74, -76, -78, -80, -82, -84, -86, -88, -90, -92, -94, WhoE 74, WhoUSWr 88, WhoWrEP 89, -92*
Pseud./variant:
Foley, Scott

Daringer, Helen Fern 1892- *BioIn 2, -6, -9, ConAu P-2, CurBio 51, MorJA, SmATA 1*

Darke, Marjorie 1929- *BioIn 12, ConAu 81, -15NR, -34NR, IntAu&W 82, ScF&FL 92, SmATA 16, TwCChW 78, -83, -89, Who 82, -83, -85, WrDr 80, -82, -84, -86, -88, -90, -92*

Darke, Marjorie Sheila 1929- *WrDr 94*

Darley, Felix Octavius Carr 1822-1888 *Alli SUP, AmAu&B, ArtsNiC, BenetAL 91, BiD&SB, BioIn 1, -2, -3, -7, -8, -9, -14, BriEAA, CarSB, ChhPo, -S1, DcAmAu, DcBiPP, DcNAA, EarABI, -SUP, HarEnUS, IlrAm 1880, OxCAmL 65, -83, OxCChiL, SmATA 35, WhAm HS, WhNaAH*

Darling, David J *BioIn 15, -17, SmATA 44*

Darling, David J 1953- *ConAu 138, SmATA 60*

Darling, Edward *BioIn 16*

Darling, Edward 1907-1974 *AmAu&B, BioIn 10, ConAu 49, -53, -3NR, WhAm 6, WhoAm 74*

Darling, Kathy
Main entry: Darling, Mary Kathleen

Darling, Kathy 1943- *BioIn 11, ConAu X, SmATA X*

Darling, Lois 1917- *AuBYP 3, IntAu&W 91, WrDr 86, -88, -90*

Darling, Lois MacIntyre d1989 *NewYTBS 89*

Darling, Lois MacIntyre 1917- *AmAu&B, AuBYP 2, BioIn 8, -9, ConAu 5R, -3NR, IlsCB 1957, -1967, SmATA 3, WhoAm 74, -76, -80, -82, -84, -86, -88, WhoAmW 74, WhoE 74, -83, -89, WrDr 76*

Darling, Lois MacIntyre 1917-1989 *BioIn 16, -17, ConAu 130, -38NR, MajAI, SmATA 64*

Darling, Louis 1916-1970 *AmAu&B, AuBYP 2, BioIn 5, -6, -8, -9, -13, ConAu 5R, -3NR, IlsCB 1946, -1957, -1967, MorJA, NewYTBE 70, SmATA 3, -23N, WhAm 5*

Darling, Louis, Jr. 1916-1970 *AuBYP 3, ConAu 38NR, MajAI*

Darling, Mary Kathleen 1943- *BioIn 11, ConAu 53, -4NR, SmATA 9*
Pseud./variant:
Darling, Kathy

Darling, Richard Lewis 1925- *AuBYP 2S, -3, BiDrLUS 70, ChhPo S1, ConAu 21R, LEduc 74, WhoAm 74, -76, -78, -80, -82, -84, -86, WhoE 74, WhoLibI 82, WhoLibS 66*

Darling, Sandra *BioIn 17, SmATA 67*
Main entry: Day, Alexandra

Darling, Sandra L Woodward 1941- *WhoAm 94*

Darlow, Denys 1921- *IntWWM 85, -90, WhoMus 72*

Darroll, Sally *SmATA 72*
Main entry: Odgers, Sally Farrell

Darrow, Whitney 1909- *AuBYP 3*

Darrow, Whitney, Jr. 1909- *AmAu&B, AuBYP 2S, BioIn 2, -5, ConAu 61, -14NR, CurBio 58, SmATA 13, WhAmArt 85, WhoAm 74, -76, -78, -80, -82, WhoAmA 73, -78, -80, -82, -84, -86, -89, -91, WhoWor 74, WorECar*

Darton, Frederick Joseph Harvey 1878-1936 *CarSB, ChhPo, OxCChiL*

Darwin, Beatrice *IlsBYP*

Darwin, Charles R 1809-1882 *WorAlBi*

Darwin, Charles Robert 1809-1882 *Alli, -SUP, AsBiEn, AtlBL, Benet 87, BbD, BiD&SB, BiESc, BioIn 1, -2, -3, -4, -5, -6, -7, -8, -9, -10, -11, -12, -13, -14, -15, -16, BlmGEL, BritAu 19, CamGEL, CarSB, CasWL, Chambr 3, CyWA 58, DcBiPP, DcEnA, -A, DcEnL, DcEuL, DcLEL, DcNaB, DcScB, Dis&D, EvLB, InSci, LongCEL, LuthC 75, McGEWB, MouLC 4, NewC, OxCEng 67, -85, OxCShps, PenC ENG, RAdv 13-5, RComWL, REn, WebE&AL, WhDW, WorAl*

Darwin, Elinor May d1954 *BioIn 1, -5, ChhPo, ConICB, IlsCB 1744, -1946*

Darwin, Len
Main entry: Darwin, Leonard

Darwin, Leonard 1916- *BioIn 13, IlsBYP, SmATA 24*
Pseud./variant:
Darwin, Len

Daryl, A J *Alli SUP*

Das, Kamala *IntvTCA 2*

Das, Kamala 1934- *ArtclWW 2, BioIn 10, -11, -12, BlmGWL, CasWL, ConAu 101, -27NR, ConPo 70, -75, -80, -85, -91, DcLEL 1940, FemiCLE, WrDr 76, -80, -82, -84, -86, -88, -90, -92, -94*

Dasent, George Webbe 1817-1896 *BioIn 17, SmATA 62, StaCVF*

Dasent, George Webbe, Sir 1817-1896 *Alli SUP, AnCL, BbD, BiD&SB, BioIn 8, -13, BritAu 19, CelCen, Chambr 3, DcBiPP, DcEnA, DcEnL, DcEuL, DcNaB S1, EvLB, NewC, OxCChiL, OxCEng 67, -85, SmATA 29, Str&VC, WhoChL*

Dasmann, Raymond F 1919- *WhoTech 84*

Dasmann, Raymond Frederic 1919- *BioIn 13, WhoTech 82*

Dasmann, Raymond Fredric 1919- *AmMWSc 73P, -76P, -82, -86, -89, -92, ConAu 5R, WhoAm 74, -76, -78, -80, -82, -84, -86, -88, -90, -92, -94, WhoWor 74*

Datta, Arup Kumar *DcChlFi*

D'Attilio, Anthony 1909- *IlsBYP, WhAmArt 85*

Daudet, Alphonse 1840-1897 *AtlBL, AuBYP 2S, -3, Benet 87, BbD, BiD&SB, BioIn 1, -2, -3, -4, -5, -6, -7, -10, -11, -15, CelCen, ChhPo, -S2, ClDMEL 47, CyWA 58, DcBiA, DcEuL, DcLB 123, Dis&D, EvEuW, GuFrLit 1, McGEWB, McGEWD 72, -84, NewC, NinCLC 1, NotNAT B, Novels, OxCEng 67, -85, OxCFr, OxCMus, PenC EUR, RComWL, REn, RfGShF, WhDW, WorAlBi, WorAl*

Dauer, Rosamond 1934- *BioIn 13, ConAu 65, -10NR, SmATA 23*

Daugherty, Charles Michael 1914- *AuBYP 2, -3, BioIn 5, -8, -12, ConAu 73, IlsCB 1946, SmATA 16, WhAmArt 85*

Daugherty, Harry R 1883- *BioIn 5, IlsCB 1946, WhAmArt 85*

Daugherty, James 1889-1974 *TwCChW 89*

Daugherty, James Henry 1887-1974 *BioIn 14, WrChl*

Daugherty, James Henry 1889-1974 *AmAu&B, AmLY, AmPB, AnCL, AuBYP 2, -3, BioIn 1, -2, -3, -4, -5, -7, -8, -10, BkP, ChhPo, -S1, ConAu 49, -73, CurBio 40, -74, IlsCB 1744, -1946, -1957, -1967, JBA 34, -51, MajAI, NewYTBS 74, NewbMB 1922, OxCChiL, SmATA 13, Str&VC, TwCChW 78, -83, WhAm 6, WhAmArt 85, WhoAm 74, WhoAmA 73, -78N*

Daugherty, James Henry 1898-1974 *WhoAmA 86N, -89N, -91N*

Daugherty, James Henry 1899-1974 *WhoAmA 80N, -82N*

Daugherty, Richard D 1922- *BioIn 14*

Daugherty, Richard Deo 1922- *AmMWSc 73S, -76P, ConAu 108, SmATA 35, WhoAm 74, -76, -78, -80*

Daugherty, Sonia Medwedeff d1971 *BioIn 13, ConAu 104, SmATA 27N*

D'Aulaire, Edgar Parin 1898- *AmAu&B, AmPB, AnCL, AuBYP 2, BioIn 12, BkCL, BkP, Cald 1938, ChhPo S2, ConAu 49, ConICB, CurBio 40, DcLB 22, IlsBYP, IlsCB 1744, -1946, -1957, -1967, JBA 34, -51, OxCChiL, SmATA 5, Str&VC, TwCChW 78, -83, WhoAm 74, -76, -78, -80, -82, -84, -86, WhoAmA 73, -78, -80, -82, -84, -86, WrDr 80, -82, -84, -86*
Pseud./variant:
Aulaire, Edgar Parin D'

D'Aulaire, Edgar Parin 1898-1986 *AuBYP 3, BioIn 14, -16, -17, ChlLR 21, ConAu 119, -29NR, MajAI, SmATA 47N, -66, TwCChW 89, WhoAmA 89N, -91N*

D'Aulaire, Ingri 1904-1980 *AuBYP 3, BioIn 14, -17, ChlLR 21, ConAu 29NR, SmATA 66*

D'Aulaire, Ingri Mortenson Parin 1904-1980 *AmAu&B, AmPB, AnCL, AuBYP 2, BioIn 12, -13, BkCL, BkP, Cald 1938, ChhPo S2, ConAu 49, -102, CurBio 40, DcLB 22, IlsBYP, IlsCB 1744, -1946, -1957, -1967, JBA 34, -51, MajAI, OxCChiL, SmATA 5, -24N, Str&VC, TwCChW 78, -83, WhAm 7, WhoAm 74, -76, -78, -80, WhoAmA 73, -78, -80, -82, -84, WrDr 80, -82*
Pseud./variant:
Aulaire, Ingri D'

d'Aulaire, Ingri Parin 1904- *TwCChW 89, WhoAmA 86*

D'Aulnoy, Marie d1705 *AuBYP 3*

D'Aulnoy, Marie C, Comtesse D'
Main entry: Aulnoy, Marie Catherine, Comtesse D'

D'Aulnoy, Marie Catherine, Comtesse 1650?-1705 *AuBYP 2S, OxCChiL, Str&VC, WhoChL*
Pseud./variant:
Aulnoy, Marie C, Comtesse

Davar, Ashok *ConAu 69*

Daveluy, Marie Claire 1880-1968 *CreCan 1*

Daveluy, Paule Cloutier 1919- *BioIn 10, -11, ConAu 9R, OxCCan SUP, Profile 1, SmATA 11*

Davenport, Marcia *IntvTCA 2*

Davenport, Marcia 1903- *AmAu&B, AmNov, AuBYP 2, -3, Baker 84, BenetAL 91, BioIn 1, -2, -3, -4, -5, -8, -14, -17, ConAu 9R, CurBio 44, DcLEL, InWom SUP, LongCTC, OxCAmL 65, -83, REn, REnAL, TwCA SUP, TwCRHW 90, WhoAm 74, -76, -78, -80, WhoAmW 74, WhoWor 74, WrDr 84 -86, -88, -90, -92*

Davenport, Marcia Gluck 1903- *WrDr 94*

Davenport, Spencer *ConAu X, -26NR*
Main entry: Stratemeyer, Edward L

Daves, Michael 1938- *AuBYP 2S, -3, ConAu 9R, SmATA 40*

Davey, Gilbert 1913- *Au&Wr 71, ConAu 12NR, -P-1, WrDr 76, -80, -82, -84*

Davey, John *ConAu X*
Main entry: Richey, David

Davey, John Edmund 1925- *AmMWSc 86, -92*

David, Alfred 1929- *ConAu 85, DrAS 74E, -78E, -82E, WhoMW 93*

David, Eugene *AuBYP 2, -3, BioIn 8*

David, Heather M 1937- *WrDr 86, -88, -90*

David, Heather MacKinnon 1937- *ConAu 37R, IntAu&W 77, WhoAmW 75, -77, WhoSSW 76, WrDr 76, -80, -82, -84*

David, Ismar *ChhPo S1*

David, Jonathan *ConAu X, SmATA 3*
Main entry: Ames, Lee Judah

Davidson, Alice Joyce 1932- *BioIn 15, -16, ConAu 115, SmATA 45, -54*

Davidson, Basil 1914- *AfSS 80, -81, -82, AmAu&B, Au&Wr 71, BioIn 10, ConAu 1R, -1NR, -17NR, IntAu&W 89, -91, IntWW 81, -82, -83, -89, -91, SmATA 13, Who 74, WhoWor 74, WorAu 1950, WrDr 76, -80, -82, -84, -86, -88, -90, -92, -94*

Davidson, Bill *AuBYP 2, -3, BioIn 8, -16, ConAu X*
Pseud./variant:
Davidson, William

Davidson, Bill 1918- *WhoEnt 92, WhoWest 89, -92, -94, WhoWor 91, -93*

Davidson, Gladys *ChhPo S1*

Davidson, Jessica 1915- *BioIn 10, ConAu 41R, -14NR, SmATA 5*

Davidson, Judith 1953- *BioIn 15, ConAu 116, SmATA 40*

Davidson, Margaret 1936- *AuBYP 2S, -3, BioIn 10, ConAu 25R, -17NR, SmATA 5*
Pseud./variant:
Davidson, Mickie

Davidson, Marion *ConAu X, SmATA X, WhoAmP 81, -83*
Main entry: Garis, Howard Roger

Davidson, Mary R 1885-1973 *BioIn 11, ConAu 5R, SmATA 9*

Davidson, Mary Richmond *AmWomPl*

Davidson, Mary S 1940- *BioIn 17, SmATA 61*

Davidson, Mickie *ConAu X*
Main entry: Davidson, Margaret

Davidson, Mildred 1935- *ConAu 93, IntAu&W 91, WrDr 76, -80, -82, -84, -86, -88, -90*

Davidson, R
Main entry: Davidson, Raymond

Davidson, Raymond *BioIn 15*

Davidson, Raymond 1926- *BioIn 14, SmATA 32*
Pseud./variant:
Davidson, R

Davidson, Rosalie *BioIn 17*

Davidson, Rosalie 1921- *BioIn 13, ConAu 69, SmATA 23*

Davidson, Sandra 1935- *AuBYP 2S, -3, ConAu 41R*

Davidson, T Whitfield 1876-1974 *BioIn 10, NewYTBS 74*

Davidson, William *AuBYP 3*
Main entry: Davidson, Bill

Davidson, William 1778-1857 *BiDrUSC 89, DcNCBi 2*

Davie, Helen Kay 1952- *SmATA 77*

Davies, Andrew 1936- *ConAu 105, FifBJA, IntAu&W 77, -82, -91, OxCChiL, ScF&FL 92, SmATA 27, TwCChW 83, -89, WrDr 86, -88, -90, -92*

Davies, Andrew Wynford 1936- *ChlFicS, WrDr 94*

Davies, Bettilu D 1942- *BioIn 14, ConAu 101, -18NR, SmATA 33*

Davies, Edward Hunter 1936- *ChlFicS*

Davies, Evelyn 1924- *ConAu 61, -8NR*

Davies, Hunter *Who 88, -90, -92, WrDr 86, -88, -90, -92*

Davies, Hunter 1936- *BioIn 15, -16, ConAu 12NR, IntAu&W 89, -91, SmATA 45, -55, Who 82, -83, -85, WrDr 82, -84, -94*
Pseud./variant:
Atticus

Davies, Joan *ScF&FL 92*

Davies, Joan 1934- *BioIn 16, ConAu 124, SmATA 47, -50*

Pseud./variant:
Lyngseth, Joan

Davies, Joan Howard 1934- *Au&Wr 71, WrDr 76, –80, –82, –84*
Pseud./variant:
Drake, Joan Howard

Davies, Leslie Purnell 1914- *BioIn 14, ConAu 21R, ConSFA, ScFSB, WrDr 80*

Davies, Peter *Who 88, –90, –92*

Davies, Peter 1897-1960 *DcLB 112*

Davies, Peter 1934- *WhoWor 87*

Davies, Peter 1937- *BioIn 10, –16, ConAu 53, Profile 1, SmATA 52*

Davies, Sumiko 1942- *ConAu 126, IntAu&W 91, SmATA 46*

Davies, Valentine 1905- *HalFC 88*

Davies, Valentine 1905-1961 *AmAu&B, AmNov, BioIn 2, –6, –8, HalFC 84, ObitOF 79, WhAm 4*

Davis, Arthur Kennard 1910- *ConAu P-1*

Davis, Arthur Kyle 1897-1972 *BioIn 10*

Davis, Barbara Steincrohn *SmATA X*
Main entry: Davis, Maggie S

Davis, Bette J 1923- *BioIn 12, ConAu 93, IlsBYP, SmATA 15*

Davis, Burke *DrAPF 87, IntAu&W 86X*

Davis, Burke 1913- *AmAu&B, AuBYP 2, –3, BioIn 3, –4, –5, –7, –9, ConAu 1R, –4NR, –25NR, SmATA 4, WhoAm 74, –76, –78, –80, –82, –88, WrDr 76, –80, –82, –84, –86, –88, –90, –92, –94*

Davis, Caroline E 1831- *Alli SUP, CarSB, DcAmAu*

Davis, Charles *BioIn 9*

Davis, Christopher *DrAPF 87, –89, –91, –93*

Davis, Christopher 1928- *AuBYP 2S, –3, Au&Wr 71, BioIn 10, ConAu 9R, –3NR, DrAF 76, DrAPF 83, –85, InB&W 80, SmATA 6, WhoUSWr 88, WhoWrEP 89, –92, WrDr 76, –80, –82, –84, –86, –88, –90, –92, –94*

Davis, Clive E 1914- *AuBYP 2, BioIn 8, ConAu 17R*

Davis, Clive Edward 1914- *AuBYP 3*

Davis, D Dwight 1908-1965 *BioIn 14, ConAu 111, DcScB S2, SmATA 33*

Davis, Daniel Sheldon 1936- *BioIn 11, ConAu 45, IntAu&W 77, SmATA 12, WhoE 77, –89*

Davis, David *Who 88, –90, –92*

Davis, David 1908- *OxCChiL, Who 82, –83, –85*

Davis, Delbert Dwight 1908-1965 *WhAm 4*

Davis, Dimitris 1905- *BioIn 8, IlsCB 1957*

Davis, Edith F 1893- *WhoAmW 75, –77*

Davis, Edwin Adams 1904- *ConAu P-2, DrAS 74H, –78H, WhoAm 74, –76, –78, –80, –82, –86, –88, WhoSSW 82, –84, –86, –88, WhoWor 78, –80, –82*

Davis, Elizabeth *AuBYP 3*

Davis, Emma *SmATA X*
Main entry: Davis, Maggie S

Davis, Frederick C 1902-1977 *AmAu&B, BioIn 14, ConAu 115, ScF&FL 92, TwCCr&M 80, –85, –91*

Davis, Frederick Clyde 1902-1977 *EncSF 93*

Davis, Gibbs 1953- *BioIn 15, ConAu 111, SmATA 41, –46*

Davis, Grania *EncSF 93*

Davis, Grania 1943- *BioIn 16, ConAu 85, –16NR, –39NR, ScF&FL 92, SmATA 50*
Pseud./variant:
Mama G

Davis, Harriet Eager 1892?-1974 *BioIn 1, –10, ConAu 49*

Davis, Hubert *NewYTBS 93*

Davis, Hubert 1904- *AuBYP 3*

Davis, Hubert J 1904- *AuBYP 2S, BioIn 14, ConAu 107, SmATA 31*

Davis, James Robert 1945- *ConAu 85, –16NR, –41NR, SmATA 32, WhoAm 82, –84, –86, –88, –90, –92, –94, WhoAmA 84, –86 –89, –91*
Pseud./variant:
Davis, Jim

Davis, Jenny 1953- *ConAu 128, SmATA 74, TwCYAW*

Davis, Jenny Schneider 1953- *DcAmChF 1985*

Davis, Jim
Main entry: Davis, James Robert

Davis, Julia *TwCRHW 90*

Davis, Julia 1900- *AmAu&B, BioIn 2, –6, –10, –14, ConAu 1R, –1NR, IntAu&W 82, JBA 51, SmATA 6, WhoAmW 74, –75, –77, WrDr 76, –80, –82, –84, –86, –88, –90*
Pseud./variant:
Adams, Julia Davis
Draco, F

Davis, Julia 1900?-1993 *ConAu 140, SmATA 75*

Davis, Kenneth S 1912- *ConAu 30NR*

Davis, Kenneth Sidney 1912- *WhoAm 86, –88, –90, –92, –94*

Davis, Kenneth Sydney 1912- *AmAu&B, AmNov, BioIn 2, ConAu 13R, IntAu&W 77*

Davis, Lavinia 1909- *AuBYP 3*

Davis, Lavinia Riker 1909-1961 *AmAu&B, AuBYP 2, BioIn 2, –6, –7, JBA 51, WhNAA*

Davis, Leslie *SmATA 72*
Main entry: Guccione, Leslie Davis

Davis, Lois Carlile
Main entry: Lamplugh, Lois

Davis, Lois Carlile 1921- *ConAu 13R*

Davis, Lou Ellen 1936- *AuBYP 2S, –3, ConAu 81*

Davis, Louise Littleton 1921- *BioIn 13, ConAu 103, SmATA 25*

Davis, Maggie S 1943- *BioIn 16, SmATA 57*
Pseud./variant:
Cooper, M E
Davis, Barbara Steincrohn
Davis, Emma

Davis, Marguerite 1889- *BioIn 1, –5, –14, ChhPo, –S2, ConICB, DcWomA, IlsCB 1744, –1946, SmATA 34, WhAmArt 85*

Davis, Marguerite Herr 1947- *WhoAmL 92*

Davis, Marilyn K 1928- *ConAu 5R, ForWC 70*

Davis, Marshall *BioIn 5, WhAmArt 85*

Davis, Marshall Earl 1931- *AmMWSc 86*

Davis, Mary Gould 1882- *AuBYP 3*

Davis, Mary Gould 1882-1956 *AmAu&B, AnCL, AuBYP 2, BioIn 2, –4, –8, –14, ChhPo, –S1, JBA 34, –51, WhAm 3*

Davis, Mary Lee 1935- *AuBYP 2S, –3, BioIn 11, ConAu 49, –4NR, IntAu&W 77, SmATA 9*

Davis, Mary Lillian 1928- *WhoAmP 85*

Davis, Mary Octavia 1901- *BioIn 10, ConAu P-2, SmATA 6, TexWr*
Pseud./variant:
Dutz

Davis, Nelle 1958- *SmATA 73*

Davis, Ossie *EarBlAP, NegAl 89, OxCAmT 84, WhoBlA 85*

Davis, Ossie 1917- *BenetAL 91, BioIn 14, –16, –17, BlkAull, –92, BlkWr 1, –2, BlksAmF, CamGWoT, CelR 90, ConAu 26NR, ConBlAP 88, ConDr 88, –93, ConTFT 9, DrBlPA 90, HalFC 88, InB&W 85, IntMPA 86, –88, –92, WhoAm 86, –88, –90, –92, –94, WhoBlA 88, –90, –92, WhoE 93, WhoEnt 92, WorAlBi, WrDr 86, –88, –90, –92*

Davis, Paxton 1925- *BioIn 12, ConAu 9R, –3NR, SmATA 16, WhoAm 90, –92, –94*

Davis, Phil d1964 *WhoAmA 86N, –89N, –91N*

Davis, Phil 1906-1964 *ArtCS, BioIn 1, –7, EncACom, WhoAmA 78N, –80N, –82N*

Davis, Reda *AuBYP 2, –3, BioIn 7*

Davis, Richard *ConAu 26NR, WrDr 86, –88, –90*

Davis, Richard 1945?- *Au&Wr 71, ConAu 53, –7NR, IntAu&W 77, ScF&FL 92, WhoHr&F, WrDr 76, –80, –82, –84*

Davis, Richard 1957- *WhoAmP 93*

Davis, Richard Harding *SourALJ*

Davis, Richard Harding 1864-1916 *AmAu&B, Benet 87, BenetAL 91, BbD, BiDAmJo, BiD&SB, BioIn 3, –4, –5, –6, –8, –9, –10, –12, –13, –14, –16, CamGLE, CamHAL, CarSB, CasWL, Chambr 3, CnDAL, ConAu 114, DcAmAu, DcAmDH 80, –89, DcBiA, DcEnA A, DcLB 12, –23, –78, –79, DcLEL, DcNAA, EncAJ, EncMys, EvLB, HarEnUS, JrnUS, JBA 34, LongCTC, McGEWB, MorMA, NotNAT B, Novels, OxCAmH, OxCAmL 65, –83, OxCAmT 84, PenC AM, REn, REnAL, RfGAmL 87, TwCA, –SUP, TwCLC 24, WebAB 74, –79, WebE&AL, WhAm 1, WorAlBi*

Davis, Richard Henry, Jr. *AmMWSc 89*

Davis, Robert 1881-1949 *AmAu&B, AnCL, BioIn 2, –11, CurBio 49, DcNAA, JBA 51, WhAm 6, YABC 1*

Davis, Roy Eugene 1931- *ConAu 9R*

Davis, Russell Gerard 1922- *BioIn 9, ConAu 5R, SmATA 3, WhoAm 74, –76, –78, –80*

Davis, Terry *TwCYAW*

Davis, Verne Theodore 1889-1973 *BioIn 10, ConAu 1R, SmATA 6*

Davis, William Stearns 1877-1930 *AmAu&B, CarSB, DcAmAu, DcNAA, JBA 34, OxCAmL 65, –83, TwCA, WhAm 1, WhNAA*

Davison, Frank Dalby *IntvTCA 2*

Davison, Frank Dalby 1893-1970 *AuLitCr, BioIn 4, –6, –9, –12, CasWL, ConAu 116, ConLC 15, DcChlFi, DcLEL, OxCAusL, OxCChiL, SingR 1, TwCWr*

Dawes, Robyn Mason 1936- *AmMWSc 73S, –78S, ConAu 37R, WhoAm 88, –90, –92, –94, WhoE 86, WhoWest 78, –84*

Dawlish, Peter
Main entry: Kerr, James Lennox

Dawlish, Peter 1899-1963 *ConAu X, OxCChiL, TwCChW 78, –83, –89*

Dawson, A J 1872?-1951 *BbD, BiD&SB, BioIn 8, NewC, OxCAusL, ScFEYrs, WhoChL*

Dawson, A J, Major 1872-1952 *StaCVF*

Dawson, Christopher Henry 1889- *WhAm 9*

Dawson, Christopher Henry 1889-1970 *BioIn 1, –4, –6, CathA 1930, ConAu 1R, –29R, ThTwC 87, TwCA SUP*

Dawson, Dagmar 1933- *SingR 2*

Dawson, Elmer A *ConAu P-2, SmATA 1, –67*
Main entry: Stratemeyer, Edward L

Dawson, Mary 1919- *BioIn 11, ChhPo S1, ConAu 21R, SmATA 11*

Dawson, Mitchell 1890- *AuBYP 3*

Dawson, Mitchell 1890-1956 *AuBYP 2, BioIn 2, –4, –8, WhAm 8*

Dawson, Peter *ConAu X, EncFWF, TwCWW 91*

Dawson, Thomas Rayner 1889-1951 *GolEC*

Day, A Grove 1904- *AmAu&B, BioIn 16, ConAu 21R, –8NR, –23NR, IntAu&W 89, –91, OxCAusL, ScF&FL 92, SmATA 59, WhNAA*

Day, Alexandra *BioIn 17, ChlLR 22, ConAu 136, SmATA 67, WrDr 94*
Pseud./variant:
Darling, Sandra

Day, Alexandra 1941- *WhoAm 94*

Day, Beth 1924- *AuBYP 3, BioIn 14, IntAu&W 86*

Day, Beth Feagles 1924- *AuBYP 2S, ChhPo S2, ConAu 9R, –3NR, –18NR, –40NR, ForWC 70, SmATA 33, WhoAmW 77*
Pseud./variant:
Feagles, Elizabeth

Day, Clarence Shepard, Jr. 1874-1935 *AmAu&B, BioIn 3, –4, –5, –6, ChhPo, –S1, ConAmA, CyWA 58, DcLEL, DcNAA, EncAHmr, EvLB, LongCTC, OxCAmL 65, PenC AM, REn, REnAL, TwCA, –SUP, TwCWr, WebAB 74, –79, WhAm 1, WorA*

Day, David 1947- *DcChlFi*

Day, Donald d1991 *NewYTBS 91*

Day, Donald 1899- *BioIn 3*

Day, Donald 1899-1991 *BioIn 17*

Day, Edward C 1932- *SmATA 72*

Day, Maurice 1892-1983 *BioIn 1, –13, CanICB, IlsCB 1744, SmATA 30*

Day, Maurice E 1892-1983 *BioIn 14*

Day, Thomas 1748-1789 *Alli, BbD, BiD&SB, BioIn 3, –5, –7, –8, –9, –11, –15, BritAu, CamGLE, CarSB, CasWL, Chambr 2, ChhPo, CyEd, CyWA 58, DcBiPP, DcEnA, DcEnL, DcEuL, DcLB 39, DcNaB, EvLB, LitC 1, NewC, OxCChiL, OxCEng 67, –85, PenC ENG, WhoChL, YABC 1*

Day Lewis, C *TwCCr&M 91*

Day Lewis, C 1904-1972 *Benet 87, BioIn 14, –17, CamGEL, CamGLE, ConAu 34NR, MajTwCW, ModBrL S2, RfGEnL 91, TwCChW 89*

Day-Lewis, Cecil 1904-1972 *Au&Wr 71, BioIn 3, –4, –5, –6, –8, –9, –10, –12, –13, –14, –17, BlmGEL, CasWL, ChhPo, –S1, CnE&AP, CnMWL, ConAu 33R, –P-1, ConLC 1, –6, –10, ConLCrt 77, –82, ConNov 72, ConPo 70, –75, CurBio 40, –69, –72, DcIrB 88, DcIrL, DcIrW 1, DcLB 15, –20, DcLEL, DcNaB 1971, EncMys, EncWL, –2, EngPo, GrBr, LongCEL, LongCTC, ModBrL, –S1, –S2, NewC, Novels, ObitOF 79, ObitT 1971, OxCChiL, OxCEng 67, –85, PenC ENG, RAdv 1, REn, TwCA, –SUP, TwCChW 78, –83, TwCCr&M 80, –85, TwCWr, WebE&AL, WhDW, WhAm 5, WhoTwCL*

Pseud./variant:
Lewis, Cecil Day

Day-Lewis, Cecil 1905-1972 *BiDIrW*

Dazey, Agnes *AuBYP 3*

Dazey, Agnes J *AuBYP 2S, BioIn 9, ConAu P-2, SmATA 2*
Pseud./variant:
Johnston, Agnes Christine

Dazey, Frank M *AuBYP 2S, -3, BioIn 9, ConAu P-2, SmATA 2*

Deacon, Eileen *ConAu X, SmATA X*
Main entry: Geipel, Eileen

Deacon, Richard *ConAu X, -32NR, IntAu&W 77X, -82X, -86X, SmATA X, WrDr 76, -80, -82, -84, -86, -88, -90, -92*
Main entry: McCormick, Donald

Deacon, Richard 1911- *WrDr 94*

Deadman, Ronald *IntAu&W 89, Who 88*

Deadman, Ronald 1919-1988? *BioIn 16, ConAu 125, SmATA 56N*

DeAmicis, Edmondo 1846-1908 *DcItL, OxCChiL*

Dean, Anabel 1915- *BioIn 11, ConAu 37R, -14NR, IntAu&W 77, SmATA 12, WhoAmW 83, WrDr 76, -80, -82, -84, -86, -88, -90, -92, -94*

Dean, Edith M 1915- *ConAu 111*

Dean, Elinor *ConAu 142, SmATA 75*
Main entry: McCann, Helen

Dean, Elizabeth Whetten 1868- *WomWWA 14*

Dean, Graham M 1904- *AuBYP 3*

Dean, Graham M 1904-1974 *AmAu&B, AuBYP 2, BioIn 8, WhAm 6, WhoAm 74*

Dean, Karen Strickler 1923- *BioIn 16, ConAu 26NR, SmATA 49*

Dean, Leigh *AuBYP 2S, -3*

Dean, Leon W 1889- *WhNAA*

Dean, Nell 1910- *AuBYP 3*

Dean, Nell Marr 1910- *AuBYP 2, BioIn 8, ConAu 21R, WhoAmW 77*
Pseud./variant:
Roberts, Virginia

Dean, Yetive H 1909- *ConAu P-1*

Deane, Fannie A *CarSB*

Deane, Norman *ConAu X, EncMys, LongCTC, MajTwCW, TwCCr&M 80, -85, -91, WhoSpyF*

Deane, Norman 1921- *AmMWSc 86, -89, -92*

Deane, Shirley Joan 1920- *AmAu&B, Au&Wr 71, ConAu 1R, -2NR, IntAu&W 77, WrDr 76, -80*

Deane, Vesey *WrDr 76*

De Angeli, Marguerite 1889- *AuBYP 3, InWom SUP, IntAu&W 91, WrDr 86, -88*

DeAngeli, Marguerite 1889-1987 *ConAu 122, SmATA 51N, TwCChW 89*

DeAngeli, Marguerite Lofft 1889- *AmAu&B, AuBYP 2, Au&ICB, AuNews 2, Au&Wr 71, BioIn 1, -2, -3, -4, -5, -7, -8, -9, -10, -11, -14, BkCL, ChhPo, -S1, ChlLR 1, ConAu 5R, -3NR, ConICB, CurBio 47, DcLB 22, DcWomA, FamMS, HerW, IlsCB 1744, -1946, -1957, -1967, JBA 51, MichAu 80, MorBMP, NewbMB 1922, OxCChiL, SmATA 1, -27, TwCChW 78, -83, WhAm 8, WhoAm 74, WhoAmA 73, WhoAmW 74, WrDr 80, -82, -84*
Pseud./variant:
Angeli, Marguerite De

DeAngeli, Marguerite Lofft 1889-1987 *BioIn 15, -16, MajAI*

DeArmand, Frances Ullmann 1904?-1984 *AuBYP 2, -3, BioIn 8, -11, ConAu 5R, -112, SmATA 10, -38N*

DeArmand, Frances Ullmann 1904?-1986 *BioIn 15*

Dearmin, Jennie Tarascou 1924- *ConAu 5R, ForWC 70, WhoAmW 74, -75, -77*

DeArmond, Dale Burlison 1914- *SmATA 70*

Deary, Terry 1946- *BioIn 15, -16, ConAu 110, SmATA 41, -51*

Deason, Hilary J 1903- *AmMWSc 73P, BiDrLUS 70, ConAu 73, WhoLibS 66*

Deaver, Julie Reece *BioIn 17*

Deaver, Julie Reece 1953- *ConAu 129, -37NR, SmATA 68, TwCYAW*

DeBanke, Cecile 1889-1965 *BioIn 11, ConAu P-1, LongCTC, SmATA 11*

DeBeck, Billy 1890-1942 *ArtCS, EncACom*

DeBlumenthal, Verra *CarSB*

DeBold, Richard Charles 1927- *AmMWSc 73S, –78S, ConAu 21R*

DeBono, Edward 1933- *BioIn 14, –15, –17, ConAu 43NR, IntAu&W 91, MajTwCW, SmATA 66, WrDr 86, –88, –90, –92*

DeBono, Edward Francis Charles 1933- *Au&Wr 71, BioIn 13, BlueB 76, ConAu 21R, IntAu&W 77, Who 74, –82, –83, –85, WrDr 76, –80, –94*

de Bono, Edward Francis Charles Publius 1933- *IntWW 89, –91, Who 88, –90, –92*

DeBorhegyi, Suzanne C Sims 1926- *AuBYP 2, BioIn 8, ConAu 5R, ForWC 70, WhoAmW 74*
Pseud./variant:
Borhegyi, Suzanne C Sims De

De Borhegyi, Suzanne Catherine Sims *AuBYP 3*

DeBos, Rene 1901- *BioIn 3, –5, –7, –9, –10, WrDr 80*

DeBosschere, Jean *ChhPo*
Main entry: Bosschere, Jean De

DeBosschere, Jean 1878-1953 *BioIn 14*

DeBrunhoff, Jean *ChsFB A, OxCChiL*
Main entry: Brunhoff, Jean De

DeBrunhoff, Laurent *Au&Wr 71, ConAu 73, IntAu&W 77, MorJA, OxCChiL, PiP*
Main entry: Brunhoff, Laurent De

De Brunhoff, Laurent 1925- *BioIn 16*

DeBruyn, Monica G 1952- *ConAu 65, SmATA 13*

De Camp, Catherine Crook *AuBYP 3*

DeCamp, Catherine Crook 1907- *BioIn 11, ConAu 21R, –9NR, –20NR, IntAu&W 77, –82, –91, ScF&FL 92, SmATA 12, WhoAmW 74, –75, –77, –83, WhoE 75, –77, WrDr 76, –80, –82, –84, –86, –88, –90, –92, –94*

DeCamp, L Sprague *IntvTCA 2*

DeCamp, L Sprague 1907- *AuBYP 2, BioIn 7, –8, –10, –11, –17, ConAu 1R, –1NR, –9NR, –20NR, ConSFA, DcLB 8, IntAu&W 77, –82, –89, –91, NewEScF, Novels, RGTwCSF, ScF&FL 92, ScFSB, SmATA 9, SupFW, TwCSFW 86, –91, WhoAm 78, –80, –82, –84, –86, –88, WhoHr&F, WhoSciF, WhoUSWr 88, WhoWrEP 89, WorAlBi, WorAl, WorAu 1950, WrDr 76, –80, –82, –84, –86, –88, –90, –92*
Pseud./variant:
Lyon, Lyman R
Wells, J Wellington

de Camp, L Strague 1907- *BenetAL 91*

De Camp, Lyon 1907- *AuBYP 3*

De Camp, Lyon Sprague 1907- *BioIn 17, EncSF 93, WhoAm 90, WhoWrEP 92, WrDr 94*

DeChatelain, Madame *OxCChiL*

Decker, Duane 1910-1964 *AuBYP 2, BioIn 2, –7, –10, ConAu 5R, SmATA 5*
Pseud./variant:
Wayne, Richard

Decker, Duane Walter 1910-1964 *AuBYP 3*

DeClements, Barthe 1920- *BioIn 14, –16, ChlLR 23, ConAu 105, –22NR, ScF&FL 92, SixBJA, SmATA 35, –71, WhoWrEP 89, –92*

DeConde, Alexander 1920- *AmAu&B, ConAu 5R, –6NR, DrAS 74H, –78H, –82H, WhoAm 74, –76, –78, –80, WhoWor 74*

de Conte, Sieur Louis *MajAI*

DeDiego, Julio 1900-1979 *BioIn 1, –2, –3, –6, –12, WhAmArt 85, WhScrn 83, WhoAmA 73, –78, –80N, –82N, –86N, –89N, –91N*

Dedmon, Emmett 1918-1983 *AmAu&B, AnObit 1983, Au&Wr 71, BioIn 13, BlueB 76, ConAu 9R, –110, –5NR, NewYTBS 83, WhAm 8, WhoAm 74, –76, –78, –80, –82, WhoFI 74, WhoMW 74, –76, WhoWor 74, WrDr 76, –80, –82, –84*

Dee, Ruby *BioIn 16, –17, BlkWr 1, NegAl 89, WhoAm 86, –90, –92, –94, WhoAmW 93, WhoBlA 90, –92, –94, WhoEnt 92*

Dee, Ruby 1923- *AfrAmAl 6, BlkAuIl 92, BlksAmF, CamGWoT, DrBlPA 90, HalFC 88, SmATA 77, WhoBlA 85, –88, WorAlBi*

Dee, Ruby 1924?- *BiE&WWA, BioIn 5, –6, –9, –10, –12, –13, BlkAWP, CelR, –90, ChhPo S2, CivR 74, ConAu X, ConBlAP 88, ConTFT 1, –9, CurBio 70, FilmgC, HalFC 84, InWom SUP, IntMPA 82, –84, –86, –88, –92, MotPP, MovMk, NegAl 76, –83, NewYTBE 70, NotBlAW 92, NotNAT, NotWoAT, WhoAm 74, –76, –78, –80, –82, –84, WhoAmW 74, –75, WhoBlA 75, –77, –80, –85, WhoHol A, WhoThe 72, –77, –81, WomWMM, WorAl*

Deedy, John Gerard 1923- *IntAu&W 89, –91*

Deedy, John Gerard, Jr. 1923- *AmCath 80, BioIn 13, ConAu 33R, SmATA 24, WhoAm 74, –80, –82, –84, –86, –88, –90, –92, –94, WhoE 74, WhoFI 74, WhoUSWr 88, WhoWrEP 89, –92*

Deegan, Paul Joseph 1937- *BioIn 15, –16, ConAu 102, SmATA 38, –48*
Pseud./variant:
O'Reilly, Sean

Deem, James Morgan 1950- *ConAu 142, SmATA 75*

Defoe, Daniel 1659-1731 *HalFC 88, WrChl*

Defoe, Daniel 1660?-1731 *Alli, AtlBL, Benet 87, BbD, BiD&SB, BioIn 1, –2, –3, –4, –5, –6, –7, –8, –9, –10, –11, –12, –13, BlmGEL, BritAu, BritWr 3, CamGEL, CamGLE, CarSB, CasWL, Chambr 2, ChhPo S1, CnDBLB 2, CrtT 2, CyEd, CyWA 58, DcBiA, DcBiPP, DcEnA, DcEnL, DcEuL, DcLB 39, –95, –101, DcLEL, DcNaB, –C, Dis&D, EncSF 93, EvLB, FilmgC, HalFC 84, HsB&A, LitC 1, LongCEL, LuthC 75, MagSWL, MajAI, McGEWB, MouLC 2, NewC, Novels, OxCChiL, OxCEng 67, –85, OxCShps, PenC ENG, RAdv 1, RComWL, REn, RfGEnL 91, ScFEYrs, SmATA 22, WebE&AL, WhDW, WhoChL, WhoHr&F, WorAlBi, WorAl, WorLitC*

Defoe, Daniel 1661?-1731 *BioIn 14, –15, –16, –17, RAdv 13-1*

Deford, Frank *BioIn 14, –15, –16*

Deford, Frank 1938- *BiDAmSp Sup, BioIn 10, –13, ConAu 33R, IntAu&W 89, –91, WhoAm 86, –88, –90, –92, –94, WhoEnt 92, WrDr 76, –80, –82, –84, –86, –88, –90, –92, –94*

DeForest, Charlotte B 1879-1971 *AuBYP 2S, –3, ConAu P-2, WhNAA, WomWWA 14*

DeFrance, Anthony *SmATA X*

DeGarza, Patricia *AuBYP 2S, –3*

Degen, Bruce *AuBYP 3, SmATA 47*

Degen, Bruce 1945- *BioIn 16, –17, ConAu 124, SixBJA, SmATA 57*

DeGenlis, Madame *OxCChiL*

Degens, T *FifBJA*

Degens, Tuti *DcAmChF 1960*

DeGering, Etta Fowler 1898- *AuBYP 2, –3, BioIn 8, –10, ConAu P-1, ForWC 70, SmATA 7*

DeGraft-Hanson, J O 1932- *OxCChiL, TwCChW 83, –89, WrDr 86, –88, –90, –92*

de Graft-Hanson, John Orleans 1932- *WrDr 94*

DeGrazia
Main entry: DeGrazia, Ettore

DeGrazia, Ettore 1909-1982 *BioIn 4, –6, –12, –13, –15, ConAu 61, –13NR, SmATA X, WhoAm 74, WhoAmA 73*
Pseud./variant:
DeGrazia
DeGrazia, Ted

De Grazia, Ettore Ted 1909-1982 *WhoAmA 91N*

DeGrazia, Ted
Main entry: DeGrazia, Ettore

DeGrazia, Ted 1909-1982 *BioIn 12, –13, ConAu X, SmATA 39*

DeGroat, Diane L 1947- *BioIn 12, ConAu 107, FifBJA, IlsCB 1967, SmATA 31, WhoAmA 78, –80, –82, –84, –86*

DeGroot, Lee *ChhPo S1*

DeGros, J H *AuBYP 2S, ConAu X*
Main entry: Villiard, Paul

De Grummond, Lena *AuBYP 3*

DeGrummond, Lena Young *AuBYP 2, BiDrLUS 70, BioIn 8, –10, ConAu 1R, –1NR, SmATA 6, WhoLibS 55*

De Grummond, Lena Young d1989 *BioIn 16, –17, SmATA 62*

Deguine, Jean-Claude 1943- *ConAu 81*

de Hamel, Joan 1924- *TwCChW 89, WrDr 86, –88, –90, –92*

DeHamel, Joan Littledale 1924- *ConAu 103, IntAu&W 82, –86, –89, TwCChW 83, WrDr 76, –80, –82, –84, –94*

De Hamel, Joan Littledale Pollock 1924- *DcChlFi*

DeHartog, Jan 1914- *AmAu&B, BiE&WWA, BioIn 16, CnMD, ConAu 1R, –1NR, ConLC 19, ConTFT 2, CurBio 70, IntAu&W 77, NotNAT, Novels, ScF&FL 92, WhoAm 74, –76, –78, –80, –82, –84, –86, –88, –92, –94, WhoWor 74, –78, –80, –82, –87, –89, –91, –93*
Pseud./variant:
Hartog, Jan De

De Haven, Tom 1949- *SmATA 72*

Dehn, Olive 1914- *ChhPo S1, ConAu 117, TwCChW 83, –89, WrDr 86, –88, –90, –92, –94*

Dehn, Paul 1912-1976 *Au&Wr 71, ChhPo, –S1, ConPo 70, –75, DcLEL, –1940, EngPo, FilmgC, HalFC 84, –88, IntMPA 75, –76, –77, LongCTC, OxCFilm, Who 74, WhoThe 72, –77, –81N, WrDr 76*

Deighton, Len 1929- *Au&Arts 6, BestSel 89-2, BioIn 6, –7, –9, –10, –12, –14, –17, CamGLE, CnDBLB 8, ConAu 9R, –33NR, ConLC 4, –7, –22, –46, ConNov 72, –76, –82, –86, –91, CorpD, CrtSuMy, CurBio 84, DcLB 87, DcLEL 1940, EncMys, EncSF 93, HalFC 84, –88, IntAu&W 77, –91, IntMPA 75, –76, –78, –77, IntWW 74, –75, –76, –77, –78, –79, –80, –81, –82, –83, –89, –91, MajTwCW, NewC, NewYTBS 81, Novels, ScF&FL 92, ScFSB, TwCCr&M 80, –85, –91, TwCWr, WhoAm 88, –90, –92, –94, WhoSpyF, WhoWor 74, –78, –80, –82, –84, –87, –89, –91, –93, WorAlBi, WorAl, WorAu 1950, WrDr 76, –80, –82, –84, –86, –88, –90, –92, –94*

Deiss, Joseph Jay 1915- *Au&Wr 71, BioIn 8, –11, ConAu 33R, –14NR, IntAu&W 77, –82, SmATA 12, WhoAm 74, –76, –78, –80, WhoWor 74, WrDr 76, –80, –82, –84, –86, –88, –90, –92, –94*

DeJong, David Cornel 1905-1967 *AmAu&B, AmNov, AuBYP 2, –3, BenetAL 91, BioIn 2, –4, –8, –9, –11, ConAu 5R, CurBio 44, –67, ObitOF 79, OxCAmL 65, –83, REn, REnAL, SmATA 10, TwCA, –SUP, WhAm 4A*
Pseud./variant:
Breda, Tjalmar

DeJong, Dola 1911- *AuBYP 2, –3, BioIn 7, –10, ConAu 5R, CurBio 47, DcAmChF 1960, MorJA, SmATA 7*

DeJong, Meindert d1991 *NewYTBS 91*

DeJong, Meindert 1906- *AnCL, AuBYP 2, –3, Au&ICB, Au&Wr 71, BioIn 2, –3, –4, –6, –7, –8, –9, –10, –14, –15, BkCL, CamGLE, CasWL, ChlFicS, ChlLR 1, ConAu 13R, CurBio 52, DcAmChF 1960, DcLB 52, FamMS, MichAu 80, MorBMP, MorJA, NewbMB 1922, OxCChiL, SenS, SmATA 2, TwCChW 78, –83, –89, WhAm 8, WhoAm 74, –76, –78, –80, –82, WrDr 80, –82, –84, –86, –88, –90, –92*

DeJong, Meindert 1906-1991 *AnObit 1991, BioIn 17, ConAu 134, –36NR, CurBio 91N, MajAI, SmATA 68, WrDr 94N*

Dejonge, Joanne E 1943- *BioIn 16, SmATA 56*

DeKay, James T 1930- *ConAu 25R, –10NR*

deKay, James Tertius 1930- *WhoE 91, WhoEnt 92*

de Kay, Ormonde 1923- *ConAu 29NR*

DeKay, Ormonde, Jr. 1923- *BioIn 10, ChhPo S2, ConAu 49, SmATA 7, WhoE 77, –81*

DeKiriline, Louise *ConAu X, SmATA X, WrDr 80*
Main entry: Lawrence, Louise DeKiriline

Dekker, Carl *AuBYP 3, ConAu X, IntAu&W 91X, SmATA X, TwCCr&M 85, –91, WhoUSWr 88, WhoWrEP 89, –92, WrDr 82, –84, –86, –88, –90, –92*
Main entry: Laffin, John
Lynds, Dennis

Dekle, Bernard 1905- *ConAu 17R*

DeKoven, Bernard 1941- *ConAu 85*
Pseud./variant:
DeKoven, Bernie

DeKoven, Bernie
Main entry: DeKoven, Bernard

Dekovic, Gene 1922- *ConAu 108, –26NR, WhoAm 74, –76, –78, –80*

DeKruif, Paul 1890-1971 *AmAu&B, BenetAL 91, BiE&WWA, BioIn 1, –2, –4, –6, –9, –10, –16, ConAu 9R, –29R, CurBio 42, –63, –71, JrnUS, JBA 34, LongCTC, OxCAmL 65, –83, REn, REnAL, SmATA 5, –50, TwCA, –SUP, WhAm 5, –8*
Pseud./variant:
Kruif, Paul De

DeLaboulaye, Edouard R L *JBA 34*
Main entry: Laboulaye, Edouard R L De

Delacre, Lulu 1957- *BioIn 14, SmATA 36*

DeLaCroix, Alice 1940- *ConAu 142, SmATA 75*

DeLaCroix, Robert *AuBYP 2, –3, BioIn 8*

DeLage, Ida 1918- *BioIn 11, ConAu 41R, –14NR, SmATA 11*

DeLaguna, Grace A 1878-1978 *BioIn 11, ConAu P-1, WomWWA 14*

DeLaIglesia, Maria Elena 1936- *ConAu 29R*

DeLaMare, Walter 1873-1956 *AnCL, AtlBL, AuBYP 2, Benet 87, BioIn 1, –2, –3, –4, –5, –6, –7, –8, –9, –10, –12, –13, –14, –15, BlmGEL, BkCL, CamGEL, CamGLE, CarSB, CasWL, Chambr 3, ChhPo, –S1, –S2, ChlLR 23, ChrP, CnDBLB 6, CnE&AP, CnMWL, ConAu 110, CyWA 58, DcLB 19, DcLEL, EncWL, –2, EngPo, EvLB, FamPYP, JBA 34, –51, LongCTC, ModBrL, NewC, Novels, ObitOF 79, ObitT 1951, OxCChiL, OxCEng 67, –85, PenC ENG, PenEncH, RAdv 1, –13-1, REn, RfGEnL 91, ShSCr 14,*

ShSWr, SmATA 16, Str&VC, SupFW, TelT, TwCA, –SUP, TwCChW 78, –83, –89, TwCLC 4, TwCWr, WebE&AL, WhDW, WhAm 3, WhoChL, WhoHr&F, WhoTwCL, WorAlBi, WorAl, WorLitC, WrChl
Pseud./variant:
LaMare, Walter De
Mare, Walter DeLa
Ramal, Walter

DeLaMare, Walter John *IntvTCA 2*

De La Mare, Walter John 1873-1956 *AuBYP 3, ConAu 137, GrBr, MajAI*

Delaney, Francis, Jr. 1931- *ConAu 57*

Delaney, Harry 1932- *BioIn 9, ConAu 25R, SmATA 3*

Delaney, Lolo M 1937- *ConAu 57*

Delaney, Ned 1951- *BioIn 13, ConAu 65, –X, SmATA 28*

Delano, Hugh 1933- *BioIn 12, ConAu 65, SmATA 20*

Delano, Isaac O 1904- *ConAu 25R*

Delap, Richard *MedPD*

De la Ramee, Louise 1839-1908 *BioIn 16*

DeLaRamee, Louise 1840-1908 *BioIn 1, –2, –3, –4, –5, –11, –12, –13, BritAu 19, CarSB, JBA 34, SmATA 20, TelT*
Pseud./variant:
LaRamee, Louise De
Ouida
Ramee, Louise DeLa

De la Roche, Mazo 1879-1961 *BenetAL 91, BioIn 14, –17, CamGLE, ConAu 30NR, DcLB 68, FemiCLE, RfGEnL 91, SmATA 64, TwCRHW 90*

DeLaRoche, Mazo 1885-1961 *BioIn 1, –4, –5, –6, –7, –9, –10, CanNov, CanWr, CasWL, Chambr 3, ConAmL, ConAu 85, CreCan 2, CyWA 58, DcLEL, EvLB, InWom SUP, JBA 34, LongCTC, NotNAT B, Novels, ObitOF 79, ObitT 1961, OxCAmL 65, OxCCan, OxCCanL, OxCEng 67, –85, PenC ENG, REn, REnAL, TwCA, –SUP, TwCWr, WhAm 4*

De La Roche Saint Andre, Anne 1950- *SmATA 75*
Pseud./variant:
Sara 1950-

DeLarrea, Victoria *IlsBYP*

De La Torre, Lillian *ConAu 142*
Main entry: McCue, Lillian Bueno

de la Torre, Lillian d1993 *NewYTBS 93*

DeLaTorre, Lillian 1902- *AmAu&B, AuBYP 2, –3, BioIn 1, –2, –3, –4, –7, –14, ConAu X, CrtSuMy, CurBio 49, EncMys, IntAu&W 89, –91, REnAL, TwCA SUP, TwCCr&M 80, –85, –91, WrDr 76, –80, –82, –84, –86, –88, –90, –92, –94*

De La Torre -Bueno, Lillian 1902-1993 *CurBio 93N*

Delaunay, Sonia Terk 1885- *BioIn 4, –5, –8, –10, –11, ConArt 77, CurBio 77, WhAm 9, WhoWor 74*

Delaune, Lynn *AuBYP 3, ConAu 21NR, WhoUSWr 88, WhoWrEP 89*

Delaune, Lynn DeGrummond *AuBYP 2, BioIn 8, –10, ConAu 1R, SmATA 7*

Delaurentis, Louise Budde *DrAPF 87, –89, –91, –93*

DeLaurentis, Louise Budde 1920- *BioIn 11, ConAu 5R, DrAPF 83, –85, ForWC 70, SmATA 12, WhoAmW 75, WhoUSWr 88, WhoWrEP 89, –92*

DelBarco, Lucy Salamanca *ConAu 17R, WhoAmW 74*
Pseud./variant:
Salamanca, Lucy

Del Barco, Lucy Salamanca d1989 *BioIn 17*

del Barco, Lucy Salamanca 1900?-1989 *ConAu 130, SmATA 64*

Delderfield, Eric R 1909- *WrDr 86, –88, –90, –92, –94*

Delderfield, Eric Raymond 1909- *Au&Wr 71, BioIn 12, ConAu 53, –4NR, IntAu&W 77, –82, –89, –91, SmATA 14, WrDr 76, –80, –82, –84*

Delderfield, Ronald Frederick 1912-1972 *Au&Wr 71, BioIn 2, –3, –8, –9, –10, –11, –12, –14, ConAu 37R, –73, DcLEL 1940, IntAu&W 77, SmATA 20, WhoChL*

Delear, Frank J 1914- *AuBYP 3, WrDr 86, –88, –90*

Delear, Frank Joseph 1914- *AuBYP 2S, ConAu 21R, –9NR, WhoE 75, WrDr 76, –80, –82, –84*

DeLeeuw, Adele 1899- *BioIn 14, IntAu&W 91, WrDr 86, –88*

De Leeuw, Adele 1899-1988 *BioIn 16, ConAu 125, SmATA 56N*

DeLeeuw, Adele Louise 1899- *AmAu&B, AuBYP 2, -3, BioIn 2, -7, -9, -12, ChhPo S1, ConAu 1R, -1NR, JBA 51, OhA&B, SmATA 1, -30, WhNAA, WhoAmW 74, -75, -77, WrDr 76, -80, -82, -84*
Pseud./variant:
Leeuw, Adele De

De Leeuw, Cateau 1903-1975 *AuBYP 3*

DeLeeuw, Cateau Wilhelmina 1903- *AuBYP 2, Au&Wr 71, BioIn 7, ConAu 1R, ForWC 70, IntAu&W 77, JBA 51, OhA&B, WhoAmA 73, WhoAmW 74, -75*
Pseud./variant:
Hamilton, Kay
Lyon, Jessica

Delessert, Etienne 1941- *BioIn 8, -11, -12, -13, -15, -16, ConAu 21R, -13NR, -37NR, IlsBYP, IlsCB 1967, MajAI, SixBJA, SmATA 27, -46, WhoGrA 82*

Delgado, Alan 1909- *Au&Wr 71, ConAu 9R, -5NR, WrDr 76, -80, -82, -84*

Dell, Draycot Montagu 1888- *ChhPo S1, -S2*

Delmar, Roy *BioIn 12, ConAu X, SmATA X*
Main entry: Wexler, Jerome

Deloria, Vine *BioIn 16, -17*

Deloria, Vine, Jr. 1933- *AmAu&B, AuSpks, BenetAL 91, BioIn 8, -9, -10, -11, -12, CamGLE, CamHAL, CivR 74, ConAu 53, -5NR, -20NR, ConHero 1, ConLC 21, CurBio 74, MajTwCW, SmATA 21, WhoAm 74, WorAu 1975*

DelRey, Lester *TwCSFW 86, -91*

del Rey, Lester d1993 *NewYTBS 93*

DelRey, Lester 1915- *AmAu&B, AuBYP 2, -3, BenetAL 91, BioIn 7, -9, -12, -13, -17, ConAu 65, -17NR, ConSFA, DcLB 8, EncSF 93, IntAu&W 89, -91, MajTwCW, NewEScF, Novels, RGTwCSF, ScF&FL 92, ScFSB, SmATA 22, ThrBJA, TwCSFW 86, -91, WhoAm 76, -78, -80, -82, -84, -86, -88, -90, -92, WhoSciF, WhoUSWr 88, WhoWrEP 89, -92, WorAlBi, WorAl, WrDr 84, -86, -88, -90, -92, -94*
Pseud./variant:
Rey, Lester Del
Saint John, Philip
VanLhin, Erik
Wright, Kenneth

del Rey, Lester 1915-1993 *ConAu 141, SmATA 76*
Pseud./variant:
Alvarez, John
Hall, Cameron
Henry, Marion
James, Philip
Kaempfert, Wade
Marion, Henry
McCann, Edson
Satterfield, Charles

Delton, Judy 1931- *Au&Arts 6, AuBYP 2S, BioIn 12, ConAu 57, -8NR, -25NR, DcAmChF 1985, FifBJA, SmATA 14, -77, -9AS*

DeLuca, Angelo Michael 1912- *ConAu 21R*

Delulio, John 1938- *BioIn 12, IlsBYP, SmATA 15*

DeLuna, Tony *IlsCB 1967*

Delving, Michael *AmAu&B, ConAu X, -39NR, IntAu&W 77X, MajAI, SmATA 3, -X, TwCCr&M 80, -85, WorAu 1950, WrDr 76*
Main entry: Williams, Jay

DeMare, Eric Samuel 1910- *Au&Wr 71, ConAu 9R, -6NR, IntAu&W 77, -89, -91*

Demaree, Doris Clore 1903- *BioIn 3, IndAu 1917*

Demarest, Chris L 1951- *BioIn 15, ConAu 109, SmATA 44, -45*

Demarest, Doug *ConAu X, SmATA 8*
Main entry: Barker, Will

DeMartelly, John Stockton 1903-1980 *BioIn 1, GrAmP, IlsCB 1744, WhAmArt 85, WhoAmA 78, -80, -82N, -86N, -89N, -91N*

Demas, Vida 1927- *BioIn 11, ConAu 49, SmATA 9*

DeMaupassant, Guy *EuAu, FilmgC, HalFC 84, ScF&FL 92, WhoHr&F*
Main entry: Maupassant, Guy De

De Maupassant, Guy 1850-1893 *HalFC 88*

DeMejo, Oscar 1911- *BioIn 14, -15, ConAu 111, IntAu&W 86, -89, -91, SmATA 40*

De Mejo, Oscar 1911-1992 *BioIn 17*

DeMessieres, Nicole 1930- *BioIn 15, ConAu 107, SmATA 39*

Demi *BioIn 15, -16, -17, ConAu 35NR, MajAI, SixBJA, SmATA 66*
Main entry: Hitz, Demi

Demijohn, Thom *MajAI*
Main entry: Disch, Thomas Michael

DeMille, James 1833?-1880 *Alli SUP, EbD, BiD&SB, BioIn 17, BritAu 19, CanWr CyAL,*

DcBiA, DcCanB 10, DcLB 99, DcLEL, DcNAA, EncSF 93, OxCAmL 65, OxCCan, OxCCanL, OxCChiL, ScFEYrs

Deming, Dorothy 1893- *AuBYP 2, -3, BioIn 7, CurBio 43*

Deming, Dorothy 1893-1972 *BioIn 16*

Deming, Edwin W 1860-1942 *BioIn 11, CurBio 42, ObitOF 79, WhAm 2*

Deming, Richard *ScF&FL 92*

Deming, Richard 1915- *AuBYP 3*

Deming, Richard 1915-1983 *AuBYP 2S, BioIn 13, -14, ConAu 9R, -3NR, IntAu&W 77, -82, SmATA 24, TwCCr&M 80, -85, -91, WrDr 76, -80, -82, -84*
Pseud./variant:
Franklin, Max
Moor, Emily

DeMiskey, Julian d1986 *WhoAmA 86N, -89N, -91N*

DeMiskey, Julian 1908-1976 *BioIn 8, -12, IlsCB 1957, -1967, WhoAmA 78, -80, -82, -84*

DeMorgan, Mary Augusta 1850-1907 *Alli SUP, OxCChiL, TelT*

DeMorgan, William Frend 1839-1917 *BioIn 3, -5, -7, -9, -12, CasWL, Chambr 3, CyWA 58, DcBiA, DcBrAr 1, DcBrBI, DcD&D, DcEuL, DcLEL, DcNaB 1912, EvLB, JBA 34, LongCTC, ModBrL, NewC, OxCEng 67, -85, PenC ENG, REn, TwCA, -SUP, TwCWr*

DeMuth, Flora Nash 1888- *BioIn 5, IlsCB 1946*

Demuth, Patricia Brennan 1948- *ConAu 118, SmATA 51*

Denetsosie, Hoke *AmPB*

Dengler, Sandy 1939- *BioIn 15, -16, ConAu 112, -30NR, IntAu&W 86, -89, -91, SmATA 40, -54*

Denholm, Therese Mary Zita White 1933- *ConAu 9R*
Pseud./variant:
White, Zita

Denison, Carol *AuBYP 2, -3, BioIn 7*

Denison, Muriel d1954 *AuBYP 3*

Denison, Muriel 1885-1954 *AuBYP 2, BioIn 3, -8, CreCan 1*

Denman, Frank *AuBYP 3*

Denman, Frank 1897?-1968 *AuBYP 2, BioIn 8*

Denmark, Harrison *EncSF 93, MajTwCW, SmATA X*
Main entry: Zelazny, Roger

Denney, Diana 1910- *BioIn 13, ConAu 104, SmATA 25*
Pseud./variant:
Gri
Ross, Diana

Dennis, C J
Main entry: Dennis, Clarence Michael James

Dennis, Clarence Michael James 1876-1938 *BioIn 2, -3, -7, -11, CamGLE, CasWL, ChhPo, DcLEL, EvLB, LongCTC, OxCAusL, OxCChiL, SingR 2, TwCWr*
Pseud./variant:
Dennis, C J

Dennis, Henry Charles 1918- *AmMWSc 73S, ConAu 41R, WhoFI 74, WhoWest 74, -76, -78*

Dennis, John Richard 1936- *LEduc 74*

Dennis, Landt 1937- *ConAu 65*

Dennis, Morgan 1891?-1960 *AmAu&B, AuBYP 2, -3, BioIn 1, -5, -6, -8, -12, IlsCB 1744, -1946, MorJA, SmATA 18, WhAmArt 85*

Dennis, Wesley 1903-1966 *AuBYP 2, -3, BioIn 1, -5, -6, -7, -8, -12, ConAu 135, IlsCB 1744, -1946, -1957, MajAI, MorJA, SmATA 18*

Dennison, George d1987 *NewYTBS 87*

Dennison, George 1925- *AmAu&B, BioIn 10, -13, ConAu 101, -6AS*

Dennison, George 1925-1987 *BioIn 15, -16, ConAu 123*

Dennison, Muriel *OxCChiL*

Denniston, Elinore 1900-1978 *BioIn 13, -14, ConAu 81, SmATA 24N*
Pseud./variant:
Foley, Rae

Denny, Norman George 1901-1982 *AuBYP 2S, -3, Au&Wr 71, ConAu 107, SmATA 43*
Pseud./variant:
Dale, Norman

Densen-Gerber, Judianne *BiDrAPA 89*

Densen-Gerber, Judianne 1934- *AuBYP 2S, -3, BiDrAPA 77, BioIn 9, -12, -13, ConAu 37R, CurBio 83, InWom SUP, NewYTBE 70, WhoAm 76, -78, -80, -82, -84, -88, -90,*

–92, –94, WhoAmL 83, –85, –87, –90, WhoAmW 74, –75, –77, –81, –83, WhoE 74, –77, –81, –83, –85, WrDr 76, –80, –82, –84, –86, –88, –90, –92, –94

Denslow, Sharon Phillips 1947- *BioIn 17, ConAu 136, SmATA 68, WrDr 94*

Denslow, W W 1856-1915 *ChlLR 15*

Denslow, William Wallace 1856-1915 *AmAu&B, AmPB, ArtsAmW 3, BioIn 9, –11, –12, ChhPo, –S1, –S2, DcNAA, FourBJA, OxCChiL, SmATA 16, WhAmArt 85*

Dent, Anthony Austen 1915- *Au&Wr 71, ConAu 25R, –15NR*

Denton, Kady MacDonald *BioIn 17, ConAu 134, SmATA 66, WrDr 94*

Denvir, Joan 1925- *ArtsCL, BioIn 6*

Denzel, Justin F 1917- *BioIn 15, ConAu 53, –4NR, SmATA 38, –46*

Denzel, Justin Francis 1917- *ConAu 42NR*

Denzer, Ann Wiseman *ConAu X, SmATA X*
Main entry: Wiseman, Ann

DeOsma, Lupe *AuBYP 2, –3, BioIn 8*

DePaola, Thomas Anthony 1934- *BioIn 8, –11, –16, –17, ConAu 49, –2NR, –37NR, IlsBYP, IlsCB 1957, –1967, MajAI, SmATA 11, –59, WhoAmA 78*
Pseud./variant:
DePaola, Tomie

dePaola, Tomie *ChlBIlD, ConAu 37NR, MajAI, SmATA X*
Main entry: DePaola, Thomas Anthony

DePaola, Tomie 1934- *BioIn 8, –11, –12, –14, –16, –17, ChlLR 4, –24, ConAu X, DcLB 61, FifBJA, IntAu&W 89, –91, OxCChiL, SmATA 15AS, –X, TwCChW 83, –89, WhoAmA 80, –82, –84, –86, –89, –91, WrDr 86, –88, –90, –92, –94*

deParrie, Paul 1949- *SmATA 74*

De Pauw, Linda 1940- *AuBYP 3*

DePauw, Linda Grant *InWom SUP*

DePauw, Linda Grant 1940- *AuBYP 2S, BioIn 13, ConAu 21R, –9NR, DrAS 74H, –78H, –82H, SmATA 24, WhoAm 84, –86, –88, –90, –92, –94, WhoAmW 83, –85, –87, –89, –91, WhoE 83, –85, –86*

Depew, Arthur M *ConAu 41R*

DePuy, Henry Walter 1820-1876 *Alli, BiD&SB, CarSB, DcAmAu, DcNAA*

DeRan, David 1946- *SmATA 76*

Derby, Pat 1942- *BioIn 10, ConAu 69*

DeRegniers, Beatrice 1914- *ArtclWW 2, SmATA 6AS*

De Regniers, Beatrice Schenk *BioIn 17*

DeRegniers, Beatrice Schenk 1914- *AmAu&B, AuBYP 2, –3, Au&Wr 71, BioIn 6, –7, –9, BkP, ChhPo, –S1, ConAu 13R, –6NR, –25NR, IndAu 1917, IntAu&W 89, –91, MorJA, OxCChiL, SmATA 2, –68, TwCChW 78, –83, –89, WhoAm 74, –76, –78, –80, –82, –84, –86, –88, –90, WhoAmW 74, WhoE 74, WrDr 76, –80, –82, –84, –86, –88, –90, –92, –94*

de Regniers, Beatrice Schenk Freedman 1914- *MajAI*
Pseud./variant:
Kitt, Tamara

Dereske, Jo 1947- *SmATA 72*

Derham, Arthur Morgan 1915- *WrDr 76, –80, –82, –84, –86, –88, –90, –92, –94*

Dering, Richard *Baker 84, –92*

Dering, Richard 1580?-1630 *NewAmDM*

Derleth, August 1909-1971 *AmAu&B, AmNov, AuBYP 2, Benet 87, BenetAL 91, BiDConC, BioIn 2, –3, –4, –6, –7, –8, –9, –10, BkC 6, ChhPo, –S2, CnDAL, ConAu 1R, –29R, –4NR, ConLC 31, ConNov 72, CrtSuMy, DcLB 9, DcLEL, EncMys, NewEScF, NewYTBE 71, Novels, OxCAmL 65, –83, REn, REnAL, ScF&FL 92, ScFSB, ScFEYrs, SmATA 5, SupFW, TwCA, –SUP, TwCCr&M 80, –85, –91, TwCRHW 90, TwCSFW 86, –91, WhAm 5, WhNAA, WhoSciF*
Pseud./variant:
Grendon, Stephen
Mason, Tally

Derleth, August W *IntvTCA 2*

Derleth, August W 1909-1971 *PenEncH*

Derleth, August William 1909-1971 *AuBYP 3, BioIn 14, –15, –17, EncSF 93, RGTwCSF*

Derman, Martha *ScF&FL 92*

Derman, Martha Winn *SmATA 74*

Derman, Sarah Audrey 1915- *BioIn 1[illegible], ConAu 1R, –17NR, SmATA 11*

DeRoin, Nancy 1934- *ConAu 65*

De Roo, Anne 1931- *IntAu&W 91, TwCChW 89, WrDr 86, –88, –90, –92*

DeRoo, Anne Louise 1931- *BioIn 13, ConAu 103, OxCChiL, SmATA 25, TwCChW 78, –83, WrDr 80, –82, –84, –94*

DeRopp, Robert S 1913- *Au&Wr 71, ConAu 17R*

deRosa, Dee *SmATA 70*

DeRosa, Peter 1932- *ConAu 21R, –9NR*

DeRossi, Claude 1942- *ConAu 53*

DeRoussan, Jacques
Main entry: Roussan, Jacques De

DeRoussan, Jacques 1929- *BioIn 14, ConAu 110, –123, Profile 1, SmATA 31*

Derrick, Thomas 1885-1954 *BioIn 1, ChhPo S1, DcBrAr 1, –2, IlsCB 1744, ObitT 1951*

Derrick, Thomas C 1885-1954 *BioIn 14*

Derry Down Derry *MajAI, SmATA X*
Main entry: Lear, Edward

Derwent, Lavinia *BioIn 12, ConAu 69, –27NR, IntAu&W 89, SmATA 14*

Desai, Anita 1937- *ArtclWW 2, Benet 87, BioIn 14, –16, –17, BlmGEL, BlmGWL, CamGLE, CasWL, ConAu 81, –33NR, ConLC 19, –37, ConNov 72, –76, –82, –86, –91, ContDcW 89, CyWA 89, DcChlFi, DcLEL 1940, FemiCLE, InWom SUP, IntAu&W 77, –82, –91, IntLitE, MajTwCW, Novels, OxCEng 85, RAdv 13-2, REn, SmATA 63, TwCChW 89, Who 88, –90, –92, WorAu 1975, WrDr 76, –80, –82, –84, –86, –88, –90, –92, –94*

DeSaint-Exupery, Antoine *ModRL, ObitOF 79, WhAm 2*
Main entry: Saint-Exupery, Antoine De

DeSaint-Exupery, Antoine 1900-1944 *BioIn 14, –15, –17*

DeSantis, Mary Allen 1930- *ConAu 9R*

Desbarats, Peter 1933- *BioIn 15, CanWW 79, –80, –81, –83, –89, ConAu 17R, –10NR, OxCCan, SmATA 39*

Desbarats, Peter Hullett 1933- *WhoAm 94*

DeSchanschieff, Juliet Dymoke *WrDr 86, –88*

DeSchanschieff, Juliet Dymoke 1919- *ConAu 106, WrDr 76, –80, –82, –84*

Deschin, Celia Spalter 1903- *ConAu 104, WhoAmW 74, –75*

DeSchweinitz, Karl 1887-1975 *AuBYP 2S, –3, BioIn 10, –14, ConAu 57, –61, NatCAB 63, ObitOF 79, WhAm 6*

DeSelincourt, Aubrey 1894-1962 *BioIn 6, –8, –12, ConAu 73, DcLEL, LongCTC, SmATA 14, WhoChL*

DeSeyn, Donna E 1933- *ConAu 21R, LEduc 74, WhoAmW 74, WhoE 83, WrDr 76, –80, –82, –84, –86, –88, –90*

DeShields, James Thomas 1891- *TexWr*

Deshpande, Chris 1950- *SmATA 69*

Desjarlais, John 1953- *SmATA 71*

DesJarlait, Patrick 1921-1972 *BioIn 9*

Deslys, Charles 1821-1885 *BiD&SB*

Desmond, Adrian J 1947- *BioIn 16, SmATA 51*

Desmond, Adrian John 1947- *ConAu 61, –8NR*

Desmond, Alice 1897- *AuBYP 3*

Desmond, Alice Curtis 1897- *AmAu&B, AuBYP 2, BioIn 7, –11, ConAu 1R, –2NR, DcWomA, SmATA 8, WhAm 10, WhAmArt 85, WhoAm 74, –76, –84, –86, –88, –90, WhoAmW 74, –75, –77, WhoE 74, –75, –77*

Desmond, J Patrick 1910- *ConAu 9R*

DeSola, Ralph 1908- *ConAu 53, IntAu&W 77, WhoAm 90, –92, –94, WhoWest 78, –80, –82, –84, –87, –89, –92, –94, WhoWor 91*

Desoutter, Denis Marcel 1919- *Au&Wr 71*

DesRivieres, Madeleine M *OxCCan SUP*

DeTerra, Rhoda Hoff 1901- *ConAu 1R*
Pseud./variant:
Hoff, Rhoda

DeTessier, Isabelle Emilie *DcVicP 2*

DeTessier, Isabelle Emily *DcVicP 2*
Pseud./variant:
Duval, Marie

Detine, Padre *ConAu X, –37NR, MajAI, SmATA 6*
Main entry: Olsen, Ib Spang

Detmold, Edward Julian 1883-1957 *DcVicP 2*

Detmold, Edward Julius 1883-1957 *BioIn 11, –12, –14, ChhPo S1, ClaDrA, ConICB, DcBrAr 1, –2, DcBrBI, DcVicP 2, TwCPaSc*

DeTrevino, Elizabeth Borton
Main entry: Borton, Elizabeth

DeTrevino, Elizabeth Borton 1904- *Au&ICB, BioIn 14, –16, ForWC 70, InWom SUP, IntAu&W 91, MorBMP, NewbC 1966, OxCChiL, TwCChW 78, –83, –89, WrDr 80*

Detwiler, Susan Dill 1956- *SmATA 58*

Detzer, Diane 1930- *ConSFA, EncSF 93*

Deucher, Sybil *BioIn 6, MorJA*

Deutsch, Babette 1895- *InWom SUP*

Deutsch, Babette 1895-1982 *AmAu&B, AnObit 1982, AnCL, Au&Wr 71, Benet 87, BenetAL 91, BioIn 4, –6, –9, –12, –13, –14, –15, BlueB 76, ChhPo, –S1, –S2, ConAmL, ConAu 1R, –108, –4NR, ConLC 18, ConPo 70, –75, –80, DcLB 45, DcLEL, DrAP 75, DrAS 74E, EvLB, FemiCLE, IntAu&W 77, –82, IntWW 74, –75, –76, –77, –78, –79, –80, –81, –82, –83N, IntWWP 82, LongCTC, MorJA, NewYTBS 82, Novels, OxCAmL 65, –83, PenC AM, RAdv 1, REn, REnAL, SmATA 1, –33N, TwCA, –SUP, TwCWr, WhAm 8, WhNAA, WhoAm 74, –76, –78, –80, WhoAmW 74, WhoWor 74, WhoWorJ 72, WrDr 76, –80, –82*

Deutsch, Helen *InWom SUP, IntMPA 86, –88, –92*

Deutsch, Helen d1992 *NewYTBS 92*

Deutsch, Helen 1906- *ConTFT 4, IntAu&W 86*

Deutsch, Helen 1906-1992 *AnObit 1992, BioIn 17, ConAu 137, SmATA 76*

DeValera, Sinead 1878-1975 *BiDIrW B*

DeValera, Sinead 1879?-1975 *BioIn 3, –10, CathA 1952, ConAu 53, SmATA 30N*

De Valera, Sinead Flanagan 1878-1975 *DcIrB 88*

Devaney, John 1926- *AuBYP 2S, –3, BioIn 11, ConAu 17R, –7NR, –23NR, SmATA 12*

Devaney, John Francis 1926- *WhoE 91*

DeVeaux, Alexis *DrAPF 87, –89, –91, –93*

DeVeaux, Alexis 1948- *BioIn 13, –14, –16, BlkAuII, –92, BlkWr 1, ConAu 65, –26NR, ConBlAP 88, DcLB 38, DrAF 76, DrAPF 83, –85, InB&W 80, –85, NatPD 77, WhoBlA 94*

Devereux, Frederick Leonard, Jr. 1914- *BioIn 8, –11, ConAu 49, –1NR, SmATA 9, WhoE 77, –81*

DeVeyrac, Robert 1901- *BioIn 1, IlsCB 1744*

DeVinck, Antoine 1924- *ConAu 53*

DeVitis, Angelo A 1925- *ConAu 107, DrAS 74E, –78E, –82E, IntAu&W 86, WhoAm 80*

Devlin, Dorothy Wende 1918- *MajAI, SmATA 74*

Devlin, Harry 1918- *BioIn 11, –15, ChhPo S2, ConAu 65, –8NR, –37NR, ConGrA 1, IlsBYP, IntAu&W 77, MajAI, SmATA 11, –74, WhoAmA 78, –80, –82, –84, –86, –89, –91, WhoArt 84*

Devlin, Thomas *AuBYP 3*

Devlin, Thomas J 1935- *AmMWSc 92*

Devlin, Thomas McKeown 1929- *AmMWSc 73P, –82, –86, –89, –92, AuBYP 2S, WhoAm 80, –82, –84, –86, –88, –90, –92, –94*

Devlin, Wende 1918- *BioIn 11, ConAu 61, –8NR, –37NR, IlsBYP, SmATA 11, WhoAmA 89, –91*

Devons, Sonia 1974- *SmATA 72*

Devore, Irven 1934- *BioIn 11, ConAu 21R, FifIDA, WhoAm 74, –76*

DeVries, John d1992 *NewYTBS 92*

DeVries, John 1915- *ASCAP 66*

De Vries, John 1915-1992 *BioIn 17*

DeVries, Leonard 1919- *Au&Wr 71, ChhPo S1, ConAu X*
Pseud./variant:
Vries, Leonard De

DeVries, Peter *BioIn 15, –17, DrAPF 87, –89, –91, –93, IntvTCA 2*

De Vries, Peter d1993 *NewYTBS 93*

DeVries, Peter 1910- *AmAu&B, Au&Wr 71, Benet 87, BenetAL 91, BiE&WWA, BioIn 4, –5, –6, –8, –10, –12, –13, BlueB 76, CelR, CnDAL, ConAu 17R, –41NR, ConLC 1 –2, –3, –7, –10, –28, –46, ConNov 72, –76, –82, –86, –91, ConTFT 1, CurBio 59, CyWA 89, DcLB 6, –Y82A, DcLEL 1940, DrAF 76, EncAHmr, EncWL, IntAu&W 77, –82, –89, –91, IntWW 74, –75, –76, –77, –78, –79, –80, –81, –82, –83, –89, –91, MajTwCW, ModAL, –S1, –S2, NotNAT, Novels, OxCAmL 65, –83, PenC AM, REnAL, Who 74, –82, –83, –85, –88, –90, –92, WhoAm 74, –76, –78, –80, –82, –84, –86, –88, –90, –92, –94, WhoTwCL, WhoUSWr 88, WhoWor 74,*

WhoWrEP 89, –92, WorAlBi, WorAu 1950, WrDr 76, –82, –84, –86, –88, –90, –92

De Vries, Peter 1910-1993 *ConAu 142*

DeWaard, Elliott John 1935- *BioIn 10, ConAu 49, SmATA 7*

Dewdney, Selwyn 1909-1979 *BioIn 12, –17, CanWW 70, ConAu 69, –27NR, CreCan 2, DcLB 68, OxCCan, SmATA 64*

DeWeese, Gene
Main entry: DeWeese, Thomas Eugene

De Weese, Gene 1934- *AuBYP 3, BioIn 15, EncSF 93, IntAu&W 91, ScF&FL 92, ScFSB, TwCSFW 86, –91, WrDr 84, –86, –88, –90, –92, –94*

De Weese, Jean *AuBYP 3, EncSF 93, ScF&FL 92, WrDr 86, –88, –90, –92*
Main entry: DeWeese, Thomas Eugene

DeWeese, Jean 1934- *WrDr 94*

DeWeese, Thomas E *ScF&FL 92*

De Weese, Thomas Eugene *AuBYP 3*

DeWeese, Thomas Eugene 1934- *ConAu 9NR, –24NR, SmATA 45, –46*
Pseud./variant:
DeWeese, Gene
DeWeese, Jean
Stratton, Thomas
Thomas, Victoria

Dewey, Ariane 1937- *BioIn 10, –12, ConAu 49, –3NR, FourBJA, IlsBYP, IlsCB 1967, SmATA 7, WhoWrEP 92*
Pseud./variant:
Aruego, Ariane

Dewey, Jennifer *BioIn 16, SmATA 48*

Dewey, Jennifer 1941- *ConAu 126, SmATA 58*

Dewey, Kenneth Francis 1940- *ConAu 112, SmATA 39, WhoAmA 73, –78*

DeWit, Dorothy May Knowles 1916-1980 *BioIn 13, ConAu 109, –113, SmATA 28N, –39, WhoLibI 82*

DeWitt, Cornelius Hugh 1905- *AmPB, BioIn 1, –5, ChhPo S1, IlsCB 1744, –1946, WhAmArt 85*

DeWitt, James *AuBYP 2, –3, BioIn 8, ConAu X*
Main entry: Lewis, Mildred D

Dewitt, Jamie *AuBYP 3*

Dewitz, Ludwig Richard Max 1916- *DrAS 74P, –78P, –82P*

Dexter, Patricia Egan *ConAu 81*

Deyneka, Anita 1943- *BioIn 13, ConAu 61, –11NR, –26NR, SmATA 24*

Deyrup, Astrith 1923- *AuBYP 3*

Deyrup, Astrith Johnson 1923- *AuBYP 2S, ConAu 65, SmATA 24*

D'Harnoncourt, Rene 1901-1968 *AmPB, BioIn 2, –3, –5, –6, –8, –12, CurBio 52, –68, DcAmB S8, IlsCB 1744, ObitOF 79, WhAm 5, WhAmArt 85*

Dhondy, Farrukh *BioIn 15, –17, ConDr 88C*

Dhondy, Farrukh 1944- *ConAu 132, MajAI, OxCChiL, SmATA 65, TwCChW 83, –89, TwCYAW, WrDr 86, –88, –90, –92, –94*

Dhotre, Damoo Gangaram 1902- *BioIn 2*

Diamond, Arthur 1957- *SmATA 76*

Diamond, Donna 1950- *BioIn 12, –14, ConAu 115, FifBJA, IlsCB 1967, MajAI, SmATA 30, –35, –69*

Diamond, Petra
Main entry: Sachs, Judith

Diamond, Rebecca
Main entry: Sachs, Judith

Dias, Earl Joseph 1916- *BioIn 15, ConAu 21R, DrAS 74E, –78E, –82E, SmATA 41, WhoE 75, –77, –81*

Dias, Ron 1937- *SmATA 71*

Diaz, Abby Morton 1821-1904 *CarSB, FemiCLE, HanAmWH, InWom SUP, OxCChiL*

Dibdin, Charles 1745-1814 *Alli, Baker 84, –92, BbD, BiDLA, –SUP, BiD&SB, BioIn 3, –4, –11, –12, –16, BritAu, CamGLE, CamGWoT, CasWL, CelCen, Chambr 2, ChhPo, –S1, –S2, DcBiPP, DcEnL, DcEuL, DcLEL, DcNaB, EvLB, NewAmDM, NewC, NewOxM, NotNAT A, –B, OxCEng 67, –85, OxCMus, OxCPMus, OxCShps, OxCThe 67, –83, PenDiMP A, RfGEnL 91, Str&VC, WhDW*

Dibdin, Henry Edward 1813-1866 *Baker 92*

Dibner, Bern d1988 *NewYTBS 88*

Dibner, Bern 1897- *BioIn 10, –11, –12, ConAu 107, LElec, WhAm 10, WhoAm 74, –76, –78, –80, WhoTech 82, –84*

Dibner, Bern 1897-1988 *BioIn 15, –16*

Di Certo, Joseph J 1933- *SmATA 60*

Dicey, Cluer *OxCChiL*

Dicey, William *OxCChiL*

Dick, Cappy *SmATA X*

Dick, Trella Lamson 1889-1974 *AuBYP 2, –3, BioIn 7, –11, ConAu 5R, SmATA 9*

Dickens, Charles 1812-1870 *Alli, –SUP, AtlBL, AuBYP 2, –3, Benet 87, BbD, BiD&SB, BioIn 1, –2, –3, –4, –5, –6, –7, –8, –9, –10, –11, –12, –13, –14, –15, –16, –17, BlmGEL, BritAu 19, BritWr 5, CamGEL, CamGLE, CamGWoT, CarSB, CasWL, CelCen, Chambr 3, ChhPo, –S1, –S2, CnDBLB 4, CrtSuMy, CrtT 3, CyEd, CyWA 58, DcAmSR, DcBiA, DcBiPP, DcEnA, –A, DcEnL, DcEuL, DcLB 21, –55, –70, DcLEL, Dis&D, EncMys, EncO&P 1, –2, –3, EncPaPR 91, EvLB, FamAYP, FilmgC, HalFC 84, –88, HsB&A, JBA 34, LongCEL, MagSWL, MouLC 3, NewC, NinCLC 3, –8, –18, –26, –37, NotNAT B, Novels, OxCAmH, OxCAmL 65, –83, OxCAusL, OxCChiL, OxCEng 67, OxCFilm, OxCMus, OxCThe 67, PenC AM, –ENG, PenEncH, PlP&P, RAdv 1, –13-1, RComWL, REn, RfGEnL 91, ScF&FL 92, SmATA 15, StaCVF, Str&VC, SupFW, TelT, TwCCr&M 80A, –85A, –91A, WebE&AL, WhDW, WhAm HS, WhoChL, WhoHr&F, WhoSpyF, WorAlBi, WorLitC, WrChl*
Pseud./variant:
Boz

Dickens, Charles 1837-1896 *StaCVF*

Dickens, Charles John Huffam 1812-1870 *MajAI, RfGShF*

Dickens, Charles John Huffham 1812-1870 *EncSF 93*

Dickens, Frank *ConAu X, SmATA X*
Main entry: Huline-Dickens, Frank William

Dickens, Frank William Huline- 1931- *BioIn 14*

Dickens, Monica 1915- *BioIn 16, BlmGWL, ConNov 86, –91, EncBrWW, FemiCLE, IntAu&W 91, ScF&FL 92, WrDr 86, –88, –90, –92*

Dickens, Monica 1915-1992 *AnObit 1992, NewYTBS 92*

Dickens, Monica Enid 1915- *AuBYP 2S, –3, Au&Wr 71, BioIn 1, –2, –3, –4, –5, –6, –7, –9, –10, –11, CathA 1930, ConAu 5R, ConNov 72, –76, DcLEL, EvLB, ForWC 70, InWom SUP, IntAu&W 77, –82, –89, IntWW 77, –78, –79, –80, –81, –82, –83, –89, –91, LongCTC, NewC, PenC ENG, REn, SmATA 4, TwCWr, Who 74, –82, –83, –85, –88, –90, –92, WhoAmW 74, –75, WorAu 1950, WrDr 76, –80, –94*

Dickens, Monica Enid 1915-1992 *ConAu 140, SmATA 74*

Dickerson, Grace Leslie 1911- *ConAu 5R, IndAu 1917, WhAmArt 85*

Dickerson, Roy Ernest 1886-1965 *BioIn 13, ConAu 103, SmATA 26N, WhAm 7*

Dickey, James *BioIn 14, –15, –16, –17, DrAPF 87, –89, –91, –93, IntvTCA 2*

Dickey, James 1923- *AmAu&B, AnCL, AuNews 1, –2, Benet 87, BenetAL 91, BioIn 8, –9, –10, –11, –12, –13, BlueB 76, BroV, CamGEL, CamGLE, CamHAL, CelR, –90, ConAu 9R, –2BS, –10NR, ConLC 1, –2, –4, –7, –10, –15, –47, ConPo 70, –75, –80, –85, –91, Conv 1, CroCAP, CurBio 68, DcLB 5, –DS7, –Y82A, DrAF 76, DrAP 75, DrAS 74E, –78E, –82E, EncWL, –2, FifSWrA, IntAu&W 77, IntWW 74, –75, –76, –77, –78, –79, –80, –81, –82, –83, –89, –91, IntWWP 82, MagSAmL, MajTwCW, ModAL, –S1, –S2, Novels, OxCAmL 65, –83, PenC AM, RAdv 1, –13-1, RfGAmL 87, WebAB 74, –79, WebE&AL, WhoAm 74, –76, –78, –80, –82, –84, –86, –88, –90, –92, –94, WhoSSW 73, –75, –76, WhoTwCL, WhoWor 74, –78, –80, –82, –84, –87, –89, –91, –93, WorAlBi, WorAl, WorAu 1950, WrDr 76, –80, –82, –84, –86, –88, –90, –92*

Dickey, James Lafayette 1923- *WrDr 94*

Dickey, Robert Livingston 1861-1944 *BioIn 2, ConICB, WhAmArt 85*

Dickie, Donalda James 1888- *CanWW 70, WhNAA*

Dickie, Edgar Primrose 1897- *Au&Wr 71, BlueB 76, ConAu P-1, IntAu&W 77, Who 74, –82, –83, –85, –88, WrDr 76, –80, –82, –84, –86*

Dickie, Edgar Primrose, Rev 1897- *Who 90*

Dickinson, Emily 1830-1866 *WorAlBi*

Dickinson, Emily 1830-1886 *AmAu, AmAu&B, AmWr, AnCL, ArtclWW 2, AtlBL, Benet 87, BenetAL 91, BiD&SB, BioAmW, BioIn 1, –2, –3, –4, –5, –6, –7, –8, –9, –10, –11, –12, –13, –14, –15, –16, –17, BlmGWL, CamGEL, CamGLE, CamHAL, CasWL, Chambr 3, ChhPo, –S1, –S2, CnDAL, CnE&AP, ContDcW 89, CrtT 3, CyWA 58, DcAmAu, DcLB 1, DcLEL, DcNAA, EncAB-H, EvLB, FemiCLE, HanAmWH, HerW, –84, IlEncMy, IntDcWB, MagSAmL, ModAL, –S1, ModAWWr, MorMA, NewGrDA 86, NewYTBE 73, NinCLC 21, OxCAmH, OxCAmL 65, –83, OxCEng 67, –85, PenC AM, PoeCrit 1, RAdv 1, –13-1, RComAH, RComWL, REn, REnAL, RealN,*

RfGAmL 87, SmATA 29, Str&VC, WebAB 74, –79, WebE&AL, WhDW, WhAm HS, WorAl, WorLitC, WrPh

Dickinson, Mary 1949- *BioIn 15, –16, ConAu 110, SmATA 41, –48*

Dickinson, Patric Thomas 1914- *Au&Wr 71, BioIn 7, ChhPo S1, –S2, ConAu 9R, –3NR, –43NR, ConPo 70, –75, DcLEL 1940, IntAu&W 77, –82, Who 74, –92, WrDr 76, –80*

Dickinson, Peter 1927- *Au&Arts 9, AuBYP 2S, –3, Au&Wr 71, BioIn 10, –14, –17, ChlFicS, ConAu 41R, –31NR, ConLC 12, –35, CrtSuMy, DcLB 87, EncMys, FourBJA, IntAu&W 77, –82, NewEScF, Novels, OxCChiL, ScF&FL 92, ScFSB, SmATA 5, –62, SouSt, TwCChW 78, –83, –89, TwCCr&M 80, –85, –91, TwCSFW 86, –91, WhoWor 74, WrDr 76, –80, –82, –84, –86, –88, –90, –92, –94*

Dickinson, Peter Malcolm 1927- *ChlLR 29, MajAI*

Dickinson, Peter Malcolm de Brissac 1927- *EncSF 93, TwCYAW*

Dickinson, Susan 1931- *BioIn 11, ConAu 57, SmATA 8*

Dickinson, William Croft 1897-1963 *BioIn 8, –15, ConAu 1R, PenEncH, SmATA 13, WhoChL*

Dickmeyer, Lowell A 1939- *BioIn 16, SmATA 51*

Dicks, Terrance 1935- *ChlFicS*

Dickson, Gordon R *IntvTCA 2*

Dickson, Gordon R 1923- *BioIn 17, NewEScF, RGTwCSF, ScF&FL 92, ScFSB, TwCSFW 86, –91*

Dickson, Gordon Rupert 1923- *BioIn 12, ConAu 9R, –6NR, ConSFA, DcLB 8, EncSF 93, IntAu&W 77, SmATA 77, WhoSciF, WorAl, WrDr 80*

Dickson, Helen *ConAu X, SmATA X*
Main entry: Reynolds, Helen M Greenwood Campbell

Dickson, Kwesi A 1929- *ConAu 134*

Dickson, Kwesi Abotsia 1929- *ConAu 109, IntAu&W 77, WhoWor 80, –82, WrDr 94*

Dickson, Marguerite 1873-1953 *AuBYP 2, –3, BioIn 2, –3, –6, –7, CurBio 52, –54, MorJA*

Dickson, Naida 1916- *BioIn 11, ConAu 37R, IntAu&W 77, –91, SmATA 8, WhoAmW 75, –77, WhoWest 80, –82, –84, WrDr 76, –80, –82, –84, –86, –88, –90*
Pseud./variant:
Richardson, Grace Lee

Diekmann, Miep 1925- *OxCChiL*

Dietrich, Wilson G 1916- *ConAu 25R*

Dietz, Betty Warner *AuBYP 2, –2S, –3, ConAu X*
Main entry: Dietz, Elisabeth H

Dietz, David Henry 1897-1984 *AmMWSc 73P, –76P, Au&Wr 71, BioIn 5, –11, BlueB 76, ConAu 1R, –114, –2NR, CurBio 40, IntAu&W 77, IntWW 74, –75, –76, –77, –78, OhA&B, REnAL, SmATA 10, –41N, WhAm 8, WhoAm 74, –76, –78, –80, WhoAmJ 80, WhoWorJ 72, –78*

Dietz, Elisabeth H 1908- *AuBYP 2S, BioIn 8, ConAu 29R, LEduc 74, WhoAmW 74, –75, –77*
Pseud./variant:
Dietz, Betty Warner

Dietz, Elizabeth H 1908- *AuBYP 3*

Dietz, Lew 1907- *AuBYP 2, –3, BioIn 8, –11, ConAu 5R, –3NR, SmATA 11, WhoAmP 73, –75, –77, WrDr 76, –80, –82, –84*

DiFiori, Lawrence *IlsBYP*

DiFranco, Anthony *DrAPF 87, –89, –91, –93*

DiFranco, Anthony 1945- *ConAu 118, DrAPF 85, SmATA 42*

Di Franco, Anthony M 1945- *WhoWrEP 92*

Digby, Anne 1935- *SmATA 72*

Digby, Desmond Ward 1933- *BioIn 12, IlsCB 1967, WhoOp 76*

Digges, Jeremiah *AmAu&B, ConAu X, SmATA X*
Main entry: Berger, Josef

Digges, Jeremiah 1903-1971 *BioIn 14*

Diggins, Julia E *AuBYP 2, –3, BioIn 8*

DiGirolamo, Vittorio 1928- *ConAu 45*

D'Ignazio, Fred 1949- *BioIn 14, –15, ConAu 110, ScF&FL 92, SmATA 35, –39, WhoSSW 84, –86*

DiGrazia, Thomas d1983 *BioIn 14, IlsBYP, IlsCB 1967, SmATA 32*

Pseud./variant:
Grazia, Thomas Di

Dilcock, Noreen 1907- *Au&Wr 71, ConAu 103, IntAu&W 77, -82, WrDr 76, -80, -82, -84, -86*
Pseud./variant:
Christian, Jill

Dillard, Annie *BioIn 14, -15, -16, -17, BlmGWL, DrAPF 87, -89, -91, -93, NewYTBS 92*

Dillard, Annie 1945- *ArtclWW 2, Au&Arts 6, BenetAL 91, BioIn 10, -11, -12, -13, BlueB 76, ConAu 49, -3NR, ConLC 9, -60, CurBio 83, CyWA 89, DcLB Y80B, DrAP 75, DrAPF 83, -85, FemiCLE, InWom SUP, IntAu&W 77, -82, -86, -89, IntWW 89, -91, MagSAmL, MajTwCW, OxCAmL 83, SmATA 10, WhoAm 76, -78, -80, -82, -84, -86, -88, -90, -92, -94, WhoAmW 81, -85, -87, -89, -91, -93, WhoUSWr 88, WhoWrEP 89, -92, WorAu 1975, WrDr 76, -80, -82, -84, -86, -88, -90, -92, -94*

Dillard, Polly Hargis 1916- *BioIn 13, ConAu 9R, -5NR, SmATA 24*

Dille, John M 1921?-1971 *ConAu 33R, NewYTBE 71*

Diller, Angela *AuBYP 3*

Diller, Angela 1877-1968 *AuBYP 2, Baker 84, -92, BioIn 4, -5, -7, -8, -12, InWom SUP, NewGrDA 86, NotAW MOD*

Diller, Corinne Boyd *BioIn 5*

Dillon, Barbara 1927- *BioIn 15, ConAu 110, -28NR, SmATA 39, -44*

Dillon, Corinne Boyd *BioIn 5, IlsBYP, IlsCB 1946*

Dillon, Diane *BioIn 14, -16, -17, InWom SUP*

Dillon, Diane 1933- *AuBYP 3, BiDScF, NewEScF, ScF&FL 92, SmATA 51*

Dillon, Diane Claire 1933- *MajAI*

Dillon, Diane Claire Sorber 1933- *AuBYP 2S, BioIn 11, -12, FifBJA, IlrAm 1880, IlsCB 1967, SmATA 15, WhoAm 78, -80, -82, -84, -90*

Dillon, Eilis 1920- *AuBYP 2, -3, Au&Wr 71, BiDIrW, BioIn 8, -9, -15, ChlLR 26, ConAu 9R, -3AS, -4NR, -38NR, ConLC 17, DcIrL, DcIrW 1, MajAI, OxCChiL, SmATA 2, -74, ThrBJA, TwCChW 78, -83, -89, WrDr 80, -82, -84, -86, -88, -90, -92, -94*
Pseud./variant:
O'Cuilleanain, Eilis Dillon

Dillon, Ellis 1920- *IntAu&W 91, TwCCYAW*

Dillon, Leo *BioIn 14*

Dillon, Leo 1933- *AuBYP 2S, -3, BiDScF, BioIn 11, -12, -16, -17, BlkAuII, -92, EncSF 93, FifBJA, IlrAm 1880, IlsCB 1967, InB&W 80, MajAI, NewEScF, ScF&FL 92, SmATA 15, -51*

Dillon, Sharon Saseen *BioIn 16*
Main entry: Saseen, Sharon Dillon

Dillon, Sharon Saseen 1949- *SmATA X*

Dilson, Jesse 1914- *BioIn 13, ConAu 25R, SmATA 24, WhoE 74, WrDr 76, -80, -82, -84*

Dimmitt, Richard Bertrand 1925- *ConAu 17R, WhoWest 74, -76, -78*

Dimmittz, Arthur Luther 1890?-1966 *BioIn 7*
Pseud./variant:
Allen, Don B

Dimmock, Frederick Hayden 1895-1955 *BioIn 8, OxCChiL, WhoChL*

Dimson, Theo Aeneas 1930- *BioIn 8, CanWW 70, -79, -80, -81, -83, IlsCB 1957, WhoAmA 73, -78, -80, -82, -84, -86, -89, -91, WhoGrA 62*

Dinan, Carolyn *BioIn 14, -16, ConAu 126, IntAu&W 91, SmATA 47, -59*

Dines, Glen 1925- *AuBYP 2, -3, BioIn 5, -8, -10, ConAu 9R, IlsCB 1946, -1957, -1967, SmATA 7*

Dinesen, Isak *BlmGWL, ConLC 29, ContDcW 89, EncWL 2, IntDcWB, MajTwCW, Novels, ObitOF 79, OxCEng 85, SmATA X, WorAl*
Main entry: Blixen, Karen

Dinesen, Isak 1885-1962 *ArtclWW 2, Benet 87, BioIn 14, -15, -16, -17, CamGLE, CyWA 89, DcAfHiB 86, DcScanL, EncCoWW, EuWr 10, FemiCLE, GrFLW, InWom SUP, LiExTwC, PenEncH, RAdv 13-2, RfGShF, ShSCr 7, ShSWr, WorAlBi, WrPh*

Dingle, Adrian 1911- *CanWW 70, WhoAmA 73*

Dinhofer, Alfred D 1930- *WrDr 76, -82, -84, -86, -88, -90, -92, -94*

Dinneen, Betty 1929- *BioIn 17, ConAu 57, -8NR, SmATA 61*
Pseud./variant:
Newark, Elizabeth 1929-

Dinnerstein, Harvey *BioIn 15, -16*

Dinnerstein, Harvey 1928- *BioIn 9, –13, ConAu 112, SmATA 42, WhoAm 82, –84, –86, –88, –90, –92, –94, WhoAmA 80, –82, –84, –86, –89, –91, WhoE 86*

Dinsdale, Mary *BioIn 14*

Dinsdale, Mary 1920- *ArtsCL, BioIn 6, –12, IlsCB 1967*

Dinsdale, Tim 1924- *BioIn 11, ConAu 1R, –2NR, SmATA 11, WrDr 76, –80, –82, –84, –86, –88*

Dinsdale, Tim 1924-1987 *ConAu 124*

Diole, Philippe Victor 1908- *ConAu 53, IntAu&W 77*

Diop, Birago d1989 *NewYTBS 89*

Diop, Birago 1906- *BioIn 14, BlkAuII, BlkWr 1, ConAu 125, DcAfHiB 86*

Diop, Birago 1906-1989 *AnObit 1989, BioIn 16, –17, BlkAuII 92, ConAu 130, MajTwCW, SmATA 64*

Diop, Birago Ismael 1906-1989 *BlkWr 2*
Pseud./variant:
Max
Provist, d'Alain

DiPreta, Tony *ArtCS*

Dirk *AuBYP 3*

Dirks, Rudolph d1968 *WhoAmA 86N, –89N, –91N*

Dirks, Rudolph 1877-1968 *ArtCS, BioIn 2, –4, –8, –14, –17, ConAu 106, EncACom, ObitOF 79, SmATA 31, WhAmArt 85, WhoAmA 78N, –80N, –82N*

Dirks, Wilhelmina 1916- *SmATA 59*
Pseud./variant:
Dirks, Willy 1916-

Dirks, Willy 1916- *BioIn 16, SmATA X*
Main entry: Dirks, Wilhelmina

Dirksen, Everett McKinley 1896-1969 *AuBYP 2S, –3, BiDrUSC 89, BioIn 2, –3, –4, –5, –6, –7, –8, –9, –10, –11, –12, –16, –17, CurBio 41, –57, –69, DcAmB S8, EncAB-H, EncWB, ObitOF 79, WebAB 74, –79, WhAm 5, WhAmP, WorAlBi, WorAl*

DiSalvo-Ryan, DyAnne 1954- *BioIn 16, SmATA 59*

Disch, Thomas M *BioIn 14, –15, –16, –17, DrAPF 87, –89, –91, –93*

Disch, Thomas M 1940- *BioIn 12, ChlLR 18, ConAu 21R, –4AS, –17NR, –36NR, ConLC 7, –36, ConPo 91, ConSFA, DcLB 8, DcLEL 1940, DrAPF 83, –85, IntAu&W 91, MajTwCW, NewEScF, PenEncH, RGTwCSF, ScF&FL 92, ScFSB, SmATA 54, –15AS, TwCSFW 86, –91, WhoAm 82, –84, –88, WhoE 74, WhoSciF, WorAu 1975, WrDr 84, –86, –88, –90, –92*

Disch, Thomas Michael 1940- *AuBYP 3, EncSF 93, MajAI, WhoAm 86, –90, –92, –94, WhoEnt 92, WrDr 94*
Pseud./variant:
Demijohn, Thom
Hargrave, Leonie
Knye, Cassandra

Diska, Pat *AuBYP 2S, –3*

Disney, Walt d1966 *LesBEnT 92*

Disney, Walt 1901-1966 *ArtCS, Benet 87, BenetAL 91, BioIn 1, –2, –3, –4, –5, –6, –7, –8, –9, –10, –11, –12, –13, –14, –15, –16, –17, ChhPo, –S1, –S2, CmCal, ConAu 107, ConHero 1, CurBio 40, –52, –67, DcFM, DcLB 22, FilmgC, HalFC 84, –88, LesBEnT, LongCTC, MakMC, NewYTET, ObitT 1961, OxCAmH, OxCAmL 65, –83, OxCChiL, OxCFilm, RAdv 13-3, RComAH, REn, REnAL, SmATA 27, –28, WebAB 74, –79, WhDW, WhoChL, WhoGrA 62, WhoHol B, WorAlBi, WorEFlm*
Pseud./variant:
Yensid, Retlaw

Disston, Harry 1899- *ConAu 41R, IntAu&W 77, WhAm 10, WhoAmP 73, –75, –77, –81, –83, –85, –87, –89, –91, WhoFI 87, –89, WhoSSW 73, –76, –78, –80, –82, –84, –86, –88, WhoWor 84, –87, –89, –91*

Disston, Harry 1899-1989 *BioIn 16*

Ditmars, Raymond Lee 1876-1942 *AmAu&B, AuBYP 2, –3, BioIn 2, –5, –7, CurBio 40, –42, DcNAA, InSci, JBA 34, –51, ObitOF 79, REnAL, TwCA, –SUP, WhAm 2, WhNAA*

Ditzel, Paul C 1926- *IntAu&W 89*

Ditzel, Paul Calvin 1926- *AuBYP 2S, –3, ConAu 41R, WhoWrEP 89, –92*

DiValentin, Maria Messuri 1911- *BioIn 10, ConAu 5R, –5NR, ForWC 70, SmATA 7, WhoE 74*

Divine, Arthur D 1904-1987 *ScF&FL 92*

Divine, Arthur Durham d1987 *Who 88N*

Divine, Arthur Durham 1904- *Au&Wr 71, BioIn 2, ConAu 103, DcLEL, IntAu&W 77, –82, –89, Who 74, –82, –83, –85*

Divine, Arthur Durham 1904-1987 *BioIn 16, ConAu 122, SmATA 52N*
Pseud./variant:
Divine, David
Rame, David

Divine, David
Main entry: Divine, Arthur Durham

Dix, Beulah M 1876-1970 *BioAmW*

Dix, Beulah Marie 1876- *WomNov*

Dix, Beulah Marie 1876-1970 *AmAu&B, AmWomPl, BioIn 2, –9, CarSB, DcAmAu, JBA 34, –51, OxCAmT 84, REnAL, WomWWA 14, WomWMM*

Dix, Harry 1912?-1968 *BioIn 8*

Dix, Maurice Buxton 1889-1957 *BioIn 1, CanNov*

Dixon, Ann R 1954- *SmATA 77*

Dixon, Conrad 1927- *IntAu&W 77, WrDr 76, –80, –82, –84*

Dixon, Dougal 1947- *BioIn 15, ConAu 107, –25NR, EncSF 93, IntAu&W 91, ScF&FL 92, SmATA 45, WrDr 84, –86, –88, –90, –92, –94*

Dixon, Franklin W *CarSB, ConAu 17R, –X, –37NR, EncMys, MajAI, OxCChiL, SmATA 1, –67, –X, WebAB 79*
Main entry: Adams, Harriet S
Stratemeyer, Edward L
Svenson, Andrew E

Dixon, Franklin W 1862-1930 *BioIn 15, –17*

Dixon, Jeanne *ScF&FL 92*

Dixon, Jeanne 1936- *BioIn 14, ConAu 105, SmATA 31*
Pseud./variant:
Harper, Mary Wood
Stone, Josephine Rector

Dixon, Marjorie 1887- *AuBYP 2, –3, BioIn 7, ConAu P-2*
Pseud./variant:
Mack, Marjorie

Dixon, Paige *AuBYP 2S, –3, ConAu X, –28NR, DrAPF 83, –85, –89, –91, –93, IntAu&W 82X, –86X, –91X, SmATA 77, WrDr 76, –80, –82, –84, –86, –88, –90, –92*
Main entry: Corcoran, Barbara

Dixon, Paige 1911- *BioIn 15, WrDr 94*

Dixon, Peter L 1931?- *BioIn 10, ConAu 45, –2NR, SmATA 6, WhoAm 74, –76, –78, –80, –82*

Dixon, Rachel 1952- *SmATA 74*

Dizenzo, Charles 1938- *BioIn 10, ConAu 25R, ConDr 73, –77, –82, –88, WrDr 76, –82, –84, –86, –88, –90, –92*

Dizenzo, Charles John 1938- *ConDr 93, WrDr 94*

Doan, Eleanor Lloyd *ConAu 1R, –1NR, IntAu&W 77, WhoAmW 75, –77, –81, WrDr 76, –80, –82, –84, –86, –88, –90, –92*

Doan, Eleanor Lloyd 1914- *WrDr 94*

Doane, Pelagie 1906-1966 *AuBYP 2, –3, BioIn 1, –5, –6, –7, –10, ChhPo, ConAu 1R, –6NR, IlsCB 1744, –1946, MorJA, SmATA 7, WhAmArt 85*
Pseud./variant:
Hoffner, Pelagie Doane

Dobbins, Dorothy Wyeth 1929- *ConAu 69*

Dobbins, Marybelle King 1900- *ConAu 41R, IndAu 1917*

Dobbs, Kildare R E *EngPo*

Dobbs, Kildare Robert 1923- *WhoCanL 87, –92*

Dobbs, Kildare Robert Eric 1923- *CaW, CanWW 70, –80, –81, –83, –89, CreCan 1, OxCCan, –SUP, WhoAm 74, WhoCanL 85*

Dobbs, Rose *AuBYP 2, –3, BioIn 8*

Dobell, Isabel Marian Barclay 1909- *BioIn 11, ConAu P-1, SmATA 11*
Pseud./variant:
Barclay, Isabel

Dobias, Frank 1902- *AmPB, BioIn 1, ConICB, IlsCB 1744*

Dobie, J Frank 1888-1964 *BenetAL 91, BioIn 14, –15, ConAu 6NR, DcAmB S7, EncFWF, ObitOF 79, OxCAmL 83, SmATA 43*

Dobkin, Alexander 1908-1975 *BioIn 5, –10, –14, ChhPo S1, ConAu 57, DcCAA 71, –77, –88, IlsCB 1946, SmATA 30N, WhAmArt 85, WhoAmA 73, –78N, –80N, –82N, –86N, –89N, –91N, WhoWorJ 72, –78*

Dobler, Lavinia Grace 1910- *BioIn 10, ConAu 1R, –2NR, ForWC 70, MorBMP, SmATA 6, WhoAmW 74, –75, –77, WhoLibS 55, –66*

Dobrin, Arnold 1928- *AuBYP 3*

Dobrin, Arnold Jack 1928- *AuBYP 2S, BioIn 7, –8, –9, ConAu 25R, IlsCB 1957, –1967, SmATA 4, WhoAmA 78, –80, WhoE 74*

Dobson, Julia *WrDr 88, –90, –92*

Dobson, Julia 1941- *BioIn 16, SmATA 48, WrDr 94*

Dobson, Rosemary *IntvTCA 2*

Dobson, Rosemary 1920- *ArtclWW 2, AuLitCr, AuWomWr, BlmGWL, CamGLE, ChhPo, ConAu 77, ConPo 70, –75, –80, –85, –91, DcLEL 1940, FemiCLE, InWom SUP, OxCAusL, RfGEnL 91, WhoTwCL, WrDr 76, –80, –82, –84, –86, –88, –90, –92, –94*

Dobuzhinskii, Mstislav Valerianovich 1875-1957 *BioIn 1, –2, –4, –5, IlsCB 1744, WorECar*

Dockery, Wallene T 1941- *BioIn 13, ConAu 105, –22NR, SmATA 27*

Docktor, Irv 1918- *BioIn 5, IlsCB 1946*

Doctor A *ConAu X, SmATA 8*
Main entry: Silverstein, Alvin

Doctor Seuss *AmPB, ConAu X, WhoAmA 78*
Main entry: Geisel, Theodor Seuss

Dodd, Ed d1991 *NewYTBS 91*

Dodd, Ed 1902- *EncACom, WhoAm 86, –88*

Dodd, Ed 1902-1991 *ConAu 134, SmATA 68*

Dodd, Ed Benton 1902- *BioIn 2, –5, –9, ConAu 25R, –73, SmATA 4, WhoAm 74, –76, WhoAmA 78*

Dodd, Edward Benton 1902-1991 *BioIn 17, WhAm 10*

Dodd, Lynley 1941- *BioIn 14, ConAu 107, –25NR, SmATA 35, TwCChW 89, WrDr 90*

Dodd, Lynley Stuart 1941- *BlmGWL*

Dodd, Wayne D 1930- *ConAu 33R, DrAP 75, DrAS 74E, –78E, –82E, IntAu&W 82, –86, IntWWP 82, WrDr 76, –80, –82, –84, –86, –88, –90, –92, –94*
Pseud./variant:
Wayne, Donald

Dodds, Andrew 1927- *ArtsCL, BioIn 6, –14, ChhPo, –S1, WhoArt 80, –82, –84, WhoWor 80*

Dodds, Dayle Ann 1952- *ConAu 142, SmATA 75*

Dodds, John W 1902- *WrDr 88*

Dodds, John Wendell 1902- *AuBYP 2S, –3, Au&Wr 71, BlueB 76, ConAu 5R, DrAS 74E, –78E, –82E, IntAu&W 77, –82, WhoAm 74, –76, –78, –80, WrDr 76, –80, –82, –84, –86*

Doderer, Klaus 1925- *OxCChiL*

Dodge, Bertha S 1902- *WrDr 88, –90, –92*

Dodge, Bertha Sanford 1902- *AuBYP 2, –3, BioIn 8, –11, ConAu 5R, –2NR, SmATA 8, WrDr 76, –80, –82, –84, –86, –94*

Dodge, Dick 1918?-1974 *BioIn 10, ConAu 49*

Dodge, Fremont *ConAu 37NR, SmATA 68*
Main entry: Grimes, Lee

Dodge, Gil *AuBYP 3*

Dodge, Langdon *ConAu 131, –X*
Main entry: Wolfson, Victor

Dodge, Mary 1831-1905 *AuBYP 3*

Dodge, Mary Elizabeth Mapes 1831?-1905 *Alli SUP, AmAu, AmAu&B, AuBYP 2, BbD, BiD&SB, BioIn 1, –2, –5, –6, –7, –8, –11, BlmGWL, CarSB, ChhPo, –S1, –S2, ConAu 109, –137, DcAmAu, DcBiA, DcLB 42, DcNAA, EncAJ, FamAYP, FamSYP, HerW, InWom SUP, JBA 34, MajAI, OxCAmL 65, –83, OxCChiL, REn, REnAL, SmATA 21, TwCChW 78, –83A, WebAB 74, –79, WhAm 1, WhoChL, WorAl*

Dodge, Mary Mapes 1830?-1905 *ArtclWW 2, BioIn 15, –17*

Dodge, Mary Mapes 1831-1905 *BenetAL 91, DcLB 79, TwCChW 89A, WorAlBi, WrChl*

Dodgson, Charles Lutwidge *CamGEL, CamGLE, RfGEnL 91*

Dodgson, Charles Lutwidge 1832-1898 *Alli SUP, AnCL, AtlBL, AuBYP 2, –3, BiD&SB, BioIn 1, –2, –3, –4, –5, –6, –7, –8, –9, –10, –11, –12, –13, –14, –15, –16, –17, BritAu 19, CarSB, CasWL, CelCen, Chambr 3, ChhPo, –S1, DcBrBI, DcEnA, –A, DcEnL, DcEuL, DcLEL, DcNaB S1, DcScB, Dis&D, EvLB, ICPEnP A, InSci, JBA 34, MacBEP, MajAI, MouLC 4, NewC, OxCChiL, OxCEng 67, –85, PenC ENG, RAdv 13-1, RComWL, REn, TelT, WhDW, WhoChL, YABC 2*
Pseud./variant:
Carroll, Lewis

Dodson, Kenneth M 1907- *BioIn 11, ConAu 1R, SmATA 11, WrDr 76, –80*

Dodson, Susan 1941- *BioIn 15, –16, ConAu 97, SmATA 40, –50*

Dodworth, Dorothy L *AuBYP 2, –3, BioIn 8*

Doerffler, Alfred 1884- *ConAu 1R*
Pseud./variant:
Ford, Fred

Doerksen, Nan 1934- *BioIn 16, ConAu 123, SmATA 50*

Doherty, Berlie *ChlLR 21*

Doherty, Berlie 1943- *ChlFicS, ConAu 131, MajAI, ScF&FL 92, SmATA 72, –16AS, TwCChW 89, TwCYAW, WrDr 92, –94*

Doherty, Charles Hugh 1913- *Au&Wr 71, BioIn 10, ConAu 9R, SmATA 6*

Doherty, G D 1927- *WhoSciF*

Doherty, Ivy R Duffy 1922- *ConAu 9R, –5NR*
Pseud./variant:
Hardwick, Sylvia

Doherty, John Stephen *AuBYP 2, –3, BioIn 7*

Dolan, Edward F 1924- *BioIn 14, –15*

Dolan, Edward F, Jr. 1924- *AuBYP 2S, ConAu 33R, SmATA 31, –45*

Dolan, Edward Francis 1924- *AuBYP 3, WhoAm 92, –94*

Dolan, Sean J 1958- *ConAu 141, SmATA 74*

Dolbier, Maurice 1912- *AmAu&B, AuBYP 2, –3, BioIn 4, –6, –7, –8, ConAu 65, CurBio 56, MorJA, WhoAm 74, –76, –78*

Dolce, J Ellen 1948- *SmATA 75*

Dolch, Edward W 1889-1961 *BioIn 16*

Dolch, Edward William 1889- *BioIn 4, WhNAA*

Dolch, Edward William 1889-1961 *SmATA 50*

Dolch, Marguerite P 1891-1978 *BioIn 16*

Dolch, Marguerite Pierce 1891-1978 *SmATA 50*

Dolezal, Carroll *IlsBYP*

Dolim, Mary Nuzum 1925- *AuBYP 2, –3, BioIn 8, ConAu 17R*

Dollar, Diane 1933- *BioIn 16, SmATA 57*

Dolson, Hildegarde 1908-1981 *BioIn 1, –10, –12, –14, ConAu 5R, –X, ForWC 70, SmATA 5, TwCCr&M 80, –85, WrDr 82, –84*

Domanska, Janina *AuBYP 2, –3, AuNews 1, BioIn 8, –9, –10, –12, –14, –15, –17, ChhPo S2, ConAu 17R, –11NR, IlsCB 1957, –1967, MajAI, SmATA 6, –68, ThrBJA, WhoAm 74, –76, –78, WhoAmA 78, –80, WhoAmW 74*
Pseud./variant:
Laskowski, Janina Domanska

Domanska, Janina 1912- *SmATA 18AS*

Dombrowski, Kathe Schonberger Von 1881- *BioIn 1, IlsCB 1744*

Dominguez, Angel 1953- *SmATA 76*

Dominguez, Angel De Jesus 1950- *WhoHisp 91, –94*

Domino, John *ConAu 139, –X, SmATA 72, –X*
Main entry: Averill, Esther Holden

Dominy, Eric Norman 1918- *Au&Wr 71, ConAu 9R, IntAu&W 89, WrDr 76, –80, –82, –84, –86, –88, –90, –92, –94*

Domjan, Joseph 1907- *AuBYP 2, –3, BioIn 5, –8, –13, ConAu 9R, –3NR, –24NR, SmATA 25, WhoAm 80, –82, –84, –86, –88, –90, –92, –94, WhoAmA 78, –80, –82, –84, –86, –89, –91*

Donahey, William 1883?-1970 *ArtCS, AuBYP 2, BioIn 2, –7, –8, ChhPo S2, OhA&B, WhAm 7, WhNAA*

Donahey, William 1884-1970 *AuBYP 3*

Donahoe, Bernard 1932- *ConAu 17R, DrAS 74H*

Donahoe, Bernard Francis 1932- *WhoMW 86, –92*

Donalds, Gordon *AuBYP 2, –3, ConAu X SmATA X, TwCWW 91, WrDr 76, –80, –82, –84, –86, –88, –90, –92*
Main entry: Shirreffs, Gordon Donald

Donalds, Gordon 1914- *WrDr 94*

Donaldson, Bryna *ConAu 136, SmATA 65*
Main entry: Stevens, Bryna

Donaldson, Frances 1907- *ConAu 12NR IntAu&W 91, WrDr 80, –82, –84, –86, –88, –90, –92, –94*

Donaldson, Gordon *BioIn 17*

Donaldson, Gordon 1913- *Au&Wr 71, ConAu 13R, –5NR, –22NR, IntAu&W 82, –91, SmATA 64, Who 74, –82, –83, –85, –88, –92, WhoWor 74, WrDr 76, –80, –82, –84, –86, –88, –90, –92, –94*

Donaldson, Gordon 1913-1993 *ConAu 141, SmATA 76*

Donaldson, Gordon, Prof 1913- *Who 90*

Donkin, Nance 1915- *AuWomWr, ConAu 103, -20NR, IntAu&W 91, SingR 1, TwCChW 78, -83, -89, WrDr 80, -82, -84, -86, -88, -90, -92*

Donkin, Nance Clare 1915- *ConAu 42NR*

Donna, Natalie 1934-1979 *AuBYP 2, -3, BioIn 8, -11, ConAu 9R, -6NR, ForWC 70, SmATA 9, WhoE 74, WrDr 76, -80, -82*

Donnelly, Elfie *TwCChW 83B, -89B*

Donovan, Dick *Alli SUP, EncMys, NewC, TwCCr&M 80, -85, WhoHr&F*

Donovan, Dick 1842-1934 *BioIn 14, -15, PenEncH, TwCCr&M 91*

Donovan, Frank 1906-1975 *SmATA 30N*

Donovan, Frank Robert 1906-1975 *AuBYP 2, -3, BioIn 8, -10, -14, ConAu 1R, -61, -6NR*

Donovan, John *BioIn 17*

Donovan, John d1992 *NewYTBS 92*

Donovan, John 1919- *IntAu&W 91*

Donovan, John 1928- *BioIn 13, ChlLR 3, ConAu 97, ConLC 35, DcAmChF 1960, FifBJA, OxCChiL, ScF&FL 92, SmATA 29, TwCChW 78, -83, -89, WrDr 84, -86, -88, -90, -92*

Donovan, John 1928-1992 *ConAu 137, MajAI, SmATA 72, TwCYAW, WrDr 94N*

Donovan, Robert John 1912- *AmAu&B, Au&Wr 71, BioIn 9, BlueB 76, ConAu 1R, -2NR, -18NR, -41NR, WhoAm 74, -76, -78, -80, -82, -84, -86, -88, -90, -92, -94, WhoWor 74*

Donovan, William *ConAu X, SmATA X*

Donovan William
Main entry: Berkebile, Fred D

Donze, Sara Lee 1925- *AuBYP 2S, -3, WhoLibI 82, WhoLibS 66*

Doob, Leonard W 1909- *IntWW 89, -91, WrDr 86, -88, -90, -92, -94*

Doob, Leonard William 1909- *AmAu&B, AmMWSc 73S, -78S, AuBYP 2S, -3, BioIn 11, BlueB 76, ConAu 5R, -2NR, IntWW 74, -75, -76, -77, -78, -79, -80, -81, -82, -83, SmATA 8, WhoAm 74, -76, -78, -80, -82, -84, -86, -88, -90, -92, -94, WhoWor 74, WrDr 76, -80, -82, -84*

Dooley, Norah 1953- *SmATA 74*

Doolittle, Jerome 1933- *ConAu 53, IntAu&W 77, -82*

Dor, Ana *ConAu X, SmATA X*
Main entry: Ceder, Georgiana Dorcas

Dorantes, Andres *DcAmChF 1960*

Doray, Maya 1922- *ConAu 45*

Dorcy, Mary Jean, Sister 1914- *AmCath 80, BkC 6, ConAu 9R, ForWC 70*

Dore, Gustave 1832-1882 *Benet 87*

Dore, Gustave 1832-1883 *AtlBL, BioIn 1, -3, -8, -9, -10, -11, -12, -13, -15, ChhPo, -S1, -S2, ConGrA 1, IlsBYP, IntDcAA 90, OxCArt, OxCChiL, OxCEng 85, OxCFr, OxDcArt, PlP&P, REn, SmATA 19, WhDW, WorECar*

Dore, Gustave 1833-1883 *PenEncH*

Doremus, Robert 1913- *BioIn 14, IlsBYP, SmATA 30*

Doren, Marion 1928- *ConAu 125, SmATA 57*

Doren, Marion Walker 1928- *BioIn 16, DcAmChF 1985*

Dorfman, Leon Monte 1922- *AmMWSc 73P, -76P, -82, -86, -89, -92, WhoAm 74, -76, -78, -80, -82, -84, -86, -88, -90, WhoAmJ 80*

Dorgan, Tad 1877-1929 *ArtCS, EncACom*

Dorian, Edith M 1900- *BioIn 10, ConAu P-1, ForWC 70, SmATA 5, WhoAmW 77*

Dorian, Harry *ConAu X, -29NR, SmATA X*

Dorian, Marguerite *BioIn 7, -10, ConAu 17R, SmATA 7*

Dorin, Patrick C 1939- *BioIn 16, ConAu 34NR, SmATA 52, -59*

Dorliae, Peter Gondro 1935- *ConAu 29R*

Dorling, Henry Taprell 1883-1968 *DcLEL, LongCTC, ObitT 1961, OxCShps, WhoSpyF*

Dorman, Michael 1932- *AuBYP 3*

Dorman, Michael L 1932- *AuBYP 2S, BioIn 10, ConAu 13R, IntAu&W 91, SmATA 7, WhoE 74, WrDr 76, -80, -82, -84, -86, -88, -90, -92, -94*
Pseud./variant:
Bishop, Jack

Dorman, N B 1927- *BioIn 15, ConAu 106, SmATA 39*

Dornberg, John Robert 1931- *AuBYP 2S, –3, ConAu 1R, –1NR, IntAu&W 77, –82, –91, WhoWor 89, WrDr 76, –80*

Dorning, Harold *ChhPo, –S2*

Dorris, Michael *BioIn 16, –17, NewYTBS 91*

Dorris, Michael 1945- *BestSel 90-1, TwCWW 91, WrDr 92*

Dorris, Michael A *SmATA 75*

Dorris, Michael Anthony 1945- *ConAu 19NR, SmATA 75, TwCYAW, WhoAm 86, –88, –90, –92, –94, WhoE 93, WrDr 94*

Dorset, Countess of *BiDEWW*

Dorset, Mrs *OxCChiL*

Dorset, Catherine Ann 1750?-1817? *BritAu 19, CarSB, ChhPo, –S1, DcNaB*

Dorset, Phyllis Flanders *WrDr 86*

Dorset, Phyllis Flanders 1924- *ConAu 25R, WhoAmW 83, WrDr 76, –80, –82, –84*

Dorson, Richard Mercer 1916-1981 *BioIn 12, –13, –14, ConAu 105, –106, DrAS 74H, –78H, NewYTBS 81, SmATA 30, WhAm 8, WhoAm 76, –78, WhoWor 78, –80*

Dorst, Tankred 1925- *CamGWoT, CnMD SUP, ConAu 41R, –30NR, CroCD, DcLB 75, –124, EncWT, IntAu&W 77, IntDcT 2, IntWW 83, –89, –91, McGEWD 72, –84, ModWD, OxCGer 76, –86, OxCThe 83*

Doskocilova, Hana 1936- *ConAu 61, –8NR, –23NR*

DosPassos, John *BioIn 14, –15, –16, –17, IntvTCA 2*

DosPassos, John 1896-1970 *AgeMat, AmAu&B, AmNov, AmWr, AtlBL, Au&Wr 71, Benet 87, BenetAL 91, BiE&WWA, BioIn 1, –2, –3, –4, –5, –6, –7, –8, –9, –10, –11, –12, –13, CamGEL, CamGLE, CamHAL, CasWL, Chambr 3, CnDAL, CnMD, ConAmA, ConAmL, ConAu 1R, –29R, –3NR, ConLC 1, –4, –8, –11, –25, CurBio 40, –70, CyWA 58, DcAmSR, DcCAr 81, DcLB 4, –9, –DS1, DcLEL, EncWL, –2, EvLB, LiExTwC, LongCTC, MagSAmL, MajTwCW, ModAL, –S1, –S2, ModWD, NewYTBE 70, Novels, ObitOF 79, OxCAmL 65, –83, OxCEng 67, PenC AM, RAdv 1, –13-1, REn, REnAL, RfGAmL 87, TwCA, –SUP, TwCWr, WebE&AL, WhDW, WhAm 5, WhNAA, WhoTwCL, WorAlBi, WorLitC, WrPh*
Pseud./variant:
Passos, John Dos

Doss, Helen 1918- *AuBYP 2, –3, BioIn 8, –12, ConAu 9R, –6NR, SmATA 20*

Doss, Margot *AuBYP 3*

Doss, Margot P 1920- *WrDr 90, –92*

Doss, Margot P 1922- *IntAu&W 91, WrDr 86, –88*

Doss, Margot Patterson 1920- *WrDr 94*

Doss, Margot Patterson 1922- *AuBYP 2S, BioIn 10, ConAu 29R, –12NR, SmATA 6, WhoAmW 75, –77, WrDr 76, –80, –82, –84*

DosSantos, Joyce Audy *ConAu 118, SmATA 42, –X*

DosSantos, Joyce Audy 1949- *BioIn 15, ConAu 136, WrDr 94*
Main entry: Zarins, Joyce Audy

Dostoevsky, Fyodor 1821-1881 *AtlBL, AuBYP 2S, –3, BbD, BiD&SB, BioIn 1, –2, –3, –4, –5, –6, –7, –8, –9, –10, –11, CasWL, ClDMEL 47, CyWA 58, DcEuL, DcRusL, EncWL, EuAu, EvEuW, GrFLW, McGEWB, NewC, NinCLC 33, OxCEng 67, PenC EUR, RComWL, REn*

Dotey, Clara *CarSB*

Dottig *SmATA X*
Main entry: Grider, Dorothy

Dotts, Maryann J 1933- *BioIn 14, ConAu 33R, –12NR, –30NR, IntAu&W 77, –82, SmATA 35, WhoAmW 83, WhoLibI 82, WhoRel 92, WrDr 76, –80, –82, –84, –86, –88, –90, –92, –94*

Doty, Jean Slaughter 1919- *AuBYP 3*

Doty, Jean Slaughter 1929- *AuBYP 2S, BioIn 13, ConAu 45, –2NR, SmATA 28*
Pseud./variant:
Slaughter, Jean

Doty, Roy 1922- *BioIn 13, ConAu 53, –8NR, IlsBYP, SmATA 28, WorECar*

Dotzenko, Grisha 1926?- *BioIn 2, IlsBYP*
Pseud./variant:
Grisha

Doubtfire, Dianne Joan 1918- *Au&Wr 71, BioIn 13, ConAu 1R, –1NR, –17NR, IntAu&W 77, –82, –86, –89, SmATA 29, WhoWor 78, WrDr 76, –80, –82, –84*

Douce, Francis *OxCChiL*

Douce, Francis 1757-1834 *CamGLE*

Dougherty, Charles 1922- *BioIn 12, SmATA 18*

Dougherty, Charles Edward 1921- *WhoSSW 86*

Dougherty, Joanna Foster *ConAu X*
Main entry: Foster, Joanna

Doughtie, Charles *AuBYP 2, -3, BioIn 8*

Doughty, Wayne Dyre 1929-1968 *IndAu 1917*

Douglas, Amanda Minnie 1831-1916 *InWom SUP*

Douglas, Amanda Minnie 1837?-1916 *Alli SUP, AmAu, AmAu&B, BbD, BiD&SB, BioIn 4, CarSB, ChhPo S1, -S2, DcAmAu, DcNAA, OxCChiL, WhAm 1, WomWWA 14, WomNov*

Douglas, Carole Nelson 1944- *SmATA 73*

Douglas, Emily Taft 1899- *AmPolW 80A, BiDrUSC 89, BioIn 2, -7, -10, -17, CurBio 45, InWom SUP*

Douglas, James McM *ConAu X, -40NR, SmATA 5*
Main entry: Butterworth, W E

Douglas, John Scott *AuBYP 3*

Douglas, John Scott 1905- *AuBYP 2, BioIn 8, WhNAA*

Douglas, Kathryn *AuBYP 2S, -3, BioIn 12, ConAu X, SmATA X*
Main entry: Ewing, Kathryn

Douglas, Leonard *SmATA X*
Main entry: Bradbury, Ray

Douglas, Marjory Stoneman *BioIn 15, -16, -17*

Douglas, Marjory Stoneman 1890- *AmAu&B, AuNews 2, BioIn 3, -11, ConAu 1R, -2NR, CurBio 53, ForWC 70, News 93-1, SmATA 10, WhAm 8*

Douglas, Michael *BioIn 14, -15, -16, -17, ConAu X, -40NR, ConTFT 5, MajTwCW, SmATA X, TwCChW 89, TwCCr&M 85, -91, TwCYAW, WrDr 76, -80, -82, -84, -86, -88, -90, -92, -94*
Main entry: Bright, Robert
Crichton, Michael

Douglas, William O 1898-1980 *Benet 87, BenetAL 91, BioIn 15, -17, ConAu 21NR, RComAH, WorAlBi*

Douglas, William Orville 1898-1980 *AmAu&B, AnObit 1980, AuBYP 2, -3, Au&Wr 71, BiDFedJ, BioIn 1, -2, -3, -4, -5, -6, -7, -8, -9, -10, -11, -12, -13, BlueB 76, CelR, ConAu 9R, -93, ConIsC 1, CurBio 41, -50, -80N, DcAmSR, DcLEL 1940, DcPol, DrAS 74P, -78P, EncAB-H, IntAu&W 77, IntWW 74, -75, -76, -77, -78, -79, McGEWB, MinnWr, NewYTBE 70, NewYTBS 80, OxCAmH, OxCAmL 65, -83, OxCLaw, REn, REnAL, TwCA SUP, WebAB 74, -79, WhAm 7, Who 74, WhoAm 74, -76, -78, -80, WhoAmL 78, WhoAmP 73, -75, -77, WhoGov 77, -72, -75, WhoPNW, WhoSSW 73, -75, WhoWest 74, -76, WhoWor 74, -78, WorAl, WrDr 76*

Douglass, Barbara 1930- *BioIn 15, ConAu 114, SmATA 40*

Douglass, Frederick c. 1817-1875 *AfrAmAl 6*

Douglass, Frederick 1817-1895 *Alli SUP, AmAu, AmAu&B, Benet 87, BbD, BiDAmJo, BiDAmL, BiDSA, BiD&SB, BioIn 1, -2, -3, -4, -5, -6, -7, -8, -9, -10, -11, -12, -13, -14, -15, -16, -17, BlkAWP, BlkLC, BlkWrNE, CamGLE, CamHAL, CelCen, Chambr 3, CivWDc, CyAG, DcAmAu, DcAmDH 80, -89, DcAmImH, DcAmNB, DcAmSR, DcBiPP, -A, DcLB 1, -43, -50, -79, DcNAA, EncAB-H, EncAJ, EncSoH, HarEnUS, InB&W 85, JrnUS, McGEWB, MemAm, NegAl 76, -89, NinCLC 7, OxCAmH, OxCAmL 65, -83, RAdv 13-3, REn, REnAL, SelBAAf, SelBAAu, SmATA 29, WebAB 74, -79, WebE&AL, WhAm HS, WhAmP, WhCiWar, WorAlBi, WorAl, WorLitC*

Douglass, Frederick 1818-1895 *AmWr S3, BenetAL 91, EncAACR, FifSWrB, RComAH, RfGAmL 87*

Douglass, Ralph 1895- *BioIn 1, -5, IlsCB 1744, -1946*

Douty, Esther 1911- *AuBYP 3*

Douty, Esther M 1911-1978 *AuBYP 2S, BioIn 11, -13, ConAu 5R, -85, -3NR, SmATA 8, -23N*

Dow, Emily R 1904- *BioIn 11, ConAu P-1, SmATA 10*

Dowd, J H *OxCChiL*

Dowd, Victor *IlsBYP*

Dowdell, Dorothy Karns 1910- *BioIn 11, ConAu 9R, -5NR, -20NR, ForWC 70, SmATA 12, WhoAmW 77*

Dowden, Anne Ophelia 1907- *SmATA 10AS, WhoE 91, WhoWest 94*

Dowden, Anne Ophelia Todd 1907- *AuBYP 2, -3, BioIn 8, -10, -12, ConAu 9R, -3NR, -18NR, FifBJA, IlsCB 1967, IntAu&W 91, SmATA 7, WhoAmA 73, -78, -80, -82, -84, -86, -89, -91, WhoAmW 83, WrDr 76, -80, -82, -84, -86, -88, -90, -92, -94*

Pseud./variant:
Todd, Anne Ophelia

Dowdey, Landon Gerald 1923- *BioIn 11, SmATA 11*

Dowds, Gertrude *AuBYP 2, -3, BioIn 8*

Dowdy, Mrs Regera *MajAI, SmATA 70*

Dowdy, Regera 1925- *WrDr 94*

Dowdy, Regera, Mrs *ConAu X, -30NR, SmATA X, WrDr 80, -82, -84*
Main entry: Gorey, Edward St John

Dowell, Jack 1908- *ConAu 57*

Dowling, Victor J 1906- *BioIn 5, IlsBYP, IlsCB 1946*

Downer, Marion 1892?-1971 *AuBYP 2, -3, BioIn 8, -9, -13, ConAu 33R, SmATA 25*

Downey, Fairfax D 1893-1990 *ConAu 131, SmATA 66*

Downey, Fairfax Davis 1893- *AmAu&B, ASCAP 66, AuBYP 2, -3, BioIn 1, -2, -8, -9, ChhPo, ConAu 1R, -1NR, CurBio 49, IntAu&W 82, -91, OxCCan, REnAL, SmATA 3, WhNAA, WhoAm 74, -76, -78, -80, WrDr 76, -80, -82, -84, -86, -88, -90*

Downey, Fairfax Davis 1893-1990 *WhAm 10*

Downey, Glanville 1908- *ConAu 1R, -1NR, DrAS 74H, -78H, -82H, WhoAm 74, -76, -78, -80*

Downey, Thomas *ChhPo*

Downey, Thomas J *BioIn 14*

Downie, John 1931- *AmMWSc 73P, -82, -86, -89, -92, ConAu 108, -26NR, OxCCan SUP, OxCCanL*

Downie, Mary Alice 1934- *BioIn 13, BlmGWL, CaW, CanWW 83, ConAu 25R, -10NR, -26NR, IntAu&W 82, OxCCan SUP, OxCCanL, Profile 2, SmATA 13, TwCChW 78, -83, -89, WhoCanL 85, -87, -92, WrDr 76, -80, -82, -84, -86, -88, -90, -92, -94*
Pseud./variant:
Hunter, Dawe

Downie, Mary Alice Dawe 1934- *CanWW 89, IntAu&W 86, -89, -91*

Downing, Brownie *SingR 2*

Downing, Warwick 1931- *ConAu 53*

Doyle, Arthur Conan 1859-1930 *AuBYP 3, BioIn 16, -17, BlmGEL, BritWr S2, ConAu 122, EncO&P 3, EncPaPR 91, EncSF 93, MagSWL, MajTwCW, NewEScF, PenEncH, RfGEnL 91, RfGShF, ScF&FL 92, ScFEYrs, ShSWr, SpyFic, StaCVF, TwCCr&M 91, TwCRHW 90, TwCSFW 86, -91, TwCYAW, WorAlBi, WorLitC*

Doyle, Arthur Conan 1859-1930
Pseud./variant:
Conan Doyle, Arthur

Doyle, Arthur Conan, Sir *IntvTCA 2*

Doyle, Arthur Conan, Sir 1859-1930 *Alli SUP, AtlBL, AuBYP 2, Benet 87, BbD, BiDPara, BiD&SB, BioIn 1, -2, -3, -4, -5, -6, -7, -8, -9, -10, -11, -12, -13, -14, -15, CamGEL, CamGLE, CarSB, CasWL, Chambr 3, ChhPo, -S1, CmScLit, ConAu 104, CrtSuMy, CyWA 58, DcBiA, DcEnA A, DcLB 18, -70, DcLEL, DcNaB 1922, Dis&D, EncMys, EncO&P 1, -2, EvLB, FilmgC, HalFC 84, -88, JBA 34, LongCEL, LongCTC, McGEWB, ModBrL, NewC, NotNAT B, Novels, OxCChiL, OxCEng 67, -85, PenC ENG, PlP&P, PoIre, RAdv 1, -13-1, REn, ScFSB, SmATA 24, TelT, TwCA, -SUP, TwCCr&M 80, -85, TwCLC 7, TwCWr, WebE&AL, WhDW, WhoChL, WhoHr&F, WhoSpyF, WhoTwCL, WorAl, WrChl*

Doyle, Brian 1930- *Au&Wr 71, ChhPo S1, ConAu 53, WhoCanL 85*

Doyle, Brian 1935- *ChlLR 22, ConAu 135, DcChlFi, MajAI, SmATA 67, -16AS, TwCChW 89, TwCYAW, WhoCanL 87, -92, WrDr 90, -92, -94*

Doyle, Donovan *AuBYP 3, ConAu X, SmATA X*
Main entry: Boegehold, Betty

Doyle, Janet *BioIn 8, ChhPo S1*

Doyle, Richard 1824-1883 *Alli SUP, ArtsNiC, BioIn 1, -10, -11, -12, -13, CamGLE, CelCen, ChhPo, -S1, -S2, ClaDrA, DcBiPP, DcBrBI, DcCathB, DcEuL, DcNaB, DcVicP 2, NewC, OxCArt, OxCChiL, OxCEng 85, OxDcArt, SmATA 21, StaCVF, WhDW WorECar*

Doyle, Robert Vaughn 1916- *ConAu 65*

Dozois, Gardner R 1947- *ConAu 108, -27NR, WhoSciF*

Dr A *ConAu 137, -36NR, MajAI, MajTwCW, SmATA 69, -74*
Main entry: Asimov, Isaac
Silverstein, Alvin
Silverstein, Virginia B

Dr A 1920-1992 *ConLC 76*

Drabble, Margaret *IntvTCA 2*

Drabble, Margaret 1939- *ArtclWW 2, Benet 87, BioIn 14, –15, –16, –17, BlmGEL, BlmGWL, CamGEL, CamGLE, CnDBLB 8, ConAu 35NR, ConLC 53, ConNov 86, –91, ContDcW 89, CyWA 89, EncBrWW, FemiCLE, InWom SUP, IntAu&W 89, –91, IntWW 89, –91, MagSWL, MajTwCW, ModBrL S2, RAdv 13-1, RfGEnL 91, SmATA 48, Who 88, –90, –92, WhoAm 86, –88, –90, –92, –94, WhoWor 87, –89, –91, –93, WorAlBi, WrDr 86, –88, –90, –92, –94*

Drackett, Phil 1922- *Au&Wr 71, BioIn 16, ConAu 9R, –3NR, IntAu&W 77, SmATA 53, WrDr 76, –82, –84, –86, –88, –90, –92, –94*
Pseud./variant:
King, Paul

Draco, F *ConAu 140, –X, IntAu&W 77X, SmATA 6, –75, WrDr 76, –80, –82, –84, –86, –88, –90*
Main entry: Davis, Julia

Dracup, Angela 1943- *ConAu 141, SmATA 74*
Pseud./variant:
Sibson, Caroline

Dragonwagon, Crescent *BioIn 15, –16, DrAPF 87, –89, –91, –93*

Dragonwagon, Crescent 1952- *BioIn 11, –13, ConAu 65, –12NR, –36NR, DrAPF 83, –85, IntAu&W 86, –89, –91, MajAI, SixBJA, SmATA 11, –41, –75, –14AS, WhoAm 90, –92, –94, WhoSSW 88*
Pseud./variant:
Parsons, Ellen

Drake, Frank *ConAu X, SmATA X*

Drake, Joan H *ConAu 24NR*

Drake, Joan Howard *Au&Wr 71, ConAu 13R, WrDr 76, –80*
Main entry: Davies, Joan Howard

Drake, Samuel Adams 1833-1905 *Alli, –SUP, AmAu, AmAu&B, BbD, BiD&SB, ChhPo S1, CyAL, DcAmAu, DcNAA, HarEnUS, WhAm 1*

Drake, Stan 1921- *ArtCS, EncACom*

Drake, Stanley Albert 1921- *WhoAm 92*

Dralle, Elizabeth Mary 1910- *ConAu 1R*

Draper, Cena C 1907- *WrDr 86, –88, –90*

Draper, Cena Christopher 1907- *ConAu 17R, –10NR, IntAu&W 77, WrDr 76, –80, –82, –84*

Draper, Hastings *ChhPo, ConAu X, IntAu&W 91X, WrDr 82, –84, –86, –88, –90, –92*
Main entry: Jeffries, Roderic

Draper, Hastings 1926- *WrDr 94*

Draper, Nancy *AuBYP 2, –3, BioIn 8*

Drapier, M B *SmATA X*
Main entry: Swift, Jonathan

Drawson, Blair 1943- *BioIn 12, ConAu 85, SmATA 17*

Drayton, Gigi 1877-1936 *ArtCS*

Dresang, Eliza Carolyn Timberlake 1941- *BiDrLUS 70, ConAu 69, SmATA 19*

Drescher, Henrik *ChlBIlD*

Drescher, Henrik 1955- *BioIn 16, –17, ChlLR 20, ConAu 135, MajAI, SixBJA, SmATA 67, WrDr 94*

Drescher, Joan E 1939- *BioIn 14, ConAu 106, SmATA 30, WhoAmW 85, –87, –89*

Drescher, Joan Elizabeth 1939- *AuBYP 3*

Dresser, Elizabeth *AuBYP 3*

Dresser, Lawrence *IlsBYP*

Dreves, Veronica R 1927-1986 *BioIn 16, ConAu 121, SmATA 50N*

Drew, Patricia Mary 1938- *BioIn 12, ConAu 77, SmATA 15*

Drew, Wayland *CaW, OxCCanL*

Drew, Wayland 1932- *EncSF 93, ScF&FL 92, TwCSFW 91*

Drewery, Mary 1918- *BioIn 10, ConAu 25R, IntAu&W 77, SmATA 6, WrDr 76, –80*

Drial, J E *ConAu X, SmATA X*
Main entry: Laird, Jean Elouise Rydeski

Driggs, Howard Roscoe 1873-1963 *AmAu&B, EncAB-A 34, WhAm 4, WhNAA*

Drimmer, Frederick *BioIn 17, SmATA 60*

Drimmer, Frederick 1916- *ConAu 23NR*

Drinkwater, John 1762-1844 *DcNaB*

Drinkwater, John 1882-1937 *Alli, Benet 87, BiDLA, BioIn 1, –2, –7, –9, –13, CamGLE, CamGWoT, CasWL, Chambr 3, ChhPo, –S1, –S2, CnMD, CnThe, ConAu 109, DcLB 10, –19, DcLEL, DcNaB 1931, EncWT, EvLB, JBA 34, LongCTC, McGEWD 72, –84, ModBrL, ModWD, NewC, NotNAT A, –B,*

OxCEng 67, –85, OxCMus, OxCThe 67, –83, PenC ENG, PlP&P, REn, RfGEnL 91, Str&VC, TwCA, –SUP, WebE&AL, WhoLA

Driscoll, Barry *BioIn 14, IlsCB 1957*

Driving Hawk, Virginia *BioIn 11, ConAu X*
Main entry: Sneve, Virginia Driving Hawk

Dr Mcloughlin *DcAmChF 1960*

Dr Seuss *BioIn 17, MajAI, SmATA 75*

Dr Seuss 1904-1991 *DcLB Y91N*

Drubert, John H 1925- *ConAu 45*

Druce, Kay *SingR 1*

Drucker, Malka 1945- *BioIn 13, –15, –16, ConAu 81, –14NR, –31NR, SmATA 29, –39*

Drummond, A H *AuBYP 2S, –3*
Pseud./variant:
Drummond, Lee

Drummond, John *TwCCr&M 85*

Drummond, Lee *AuBYP 2S, –3*
Main entry: Drummond, A H

Drummond, Maldwin Andrew Cyril 1932- *ConAu 73, –14NR, IntAu&W 89, Who 82, –83, –85, –88, –90, –92, WhoWor 80*

Drummond, V H 1911- *TwCChW 89, WrDr 86, –88, –90, –92*

Drummond, Violet Hilda 1911- *Au&Wr 71, BioIn 1, –5, –8, –9, –10, –12, –14, ConAu 13R, DcBrAr 2, IlsBYP, IlsCB 1946, –1957, –1967, OxCChiL, SmATA 6, ThrBJA, TwCChW 78, –83, WhoArt 80, –82, –84, WrDr 76, –80, –82, –84, –94*

Drummond, Walter *AuBYP 2, –3, ConAu X, –36NR, DcLEL 1940, MajAI, MajTwCW, SmATA X, ThrBJA*
Main entry: Silverberg, Robert

Druon, Maurice *TwCChW 89B*

Druon, Maurice 1918- *Benet 87, ScF&FL 92*

Druon, Maurice Samuel Roger Charles 1918- *Au&Wr 71, BioIn 10, CasWL, ConAu 13R, –12NR, EncWL, IntAu&W 77, –89, IntWW 74, –75, –76, –77, –78, –79, –80, –81, –82, –83, –89, –91, Novels, PenC EUR, REn, TwCChW 78B, –83B, Who 74, –82, –83, –85, –88, –90, –92, WhoWor 74, –78, WorAu 1950*

Drury, Clare Marie *ConAu X*
Main entry: Hoskyns-Abrahall, Clare

Drury, Keith Wesley 1945- *WhoRel 75*

Drury, Maxine Cole 1914- *ConAu 5R, ForWC 70, WrDr 76, –80, –82, –84, –86, –88, –90, –92, –94*

Drury, Roger W 1914- *AuBYP 2S, –3, BioIn 12, ConAu 65, SmATA 15*

Drury, Roger Wolcott 1914- *DcAmChF 1950*

Dr. X
Main entry: Nourse, Alan Edward

Dryden, Pamela *ConAu 32NR, SmATA X, WrDr 86, –88, –90, –92, –94*
Main entry: Johnston, Norma

Drysdale, William 1852-1901 *Alli SUP, BiDLA, BiD&SB, CarSB, DcAmAu, DcNAA, WhAm 1*

Duane, Diane *ArtclWW 2, IntvTCA 2, SmATA X, TwCSFW 86, –91, WrDr 88, –90, –92, –94*
Main entry: Duane-Smyth, Diane Elizabeth

Duane, Diane 1952- *BioIn 15, –16, ScF&FL 92, SmATA 46, TwCYAW*

Duane, Diane Elizabeth 1952- *ConAu 139, DcAmChF 1985*

Duane-Smyth, Diane 1952- *SmATA 58*

Duane-Smyth, Diane Elizabeth 1952-
Pseud./variant:
Duane, Diane

Dubanevich, Arlene 1950- *BioIn 16, ConAu 40NR, SmATA 56*

Dubelaar, Thea 1947- *BioIn 17, SmATA 60*

Dubkin, Lois 1911- *AuBYP 3*

Dubkin, Lois Knudson 1911- *AuBYP 2S, ConAu 5R*

DuBlane, Daphne *ConAu X, SmATA X*
Main entry: Groom, Arthur William

Dubois, Rochelle Holt *IntAu&W 86X*

DuBois, Rochelle Holt 1946- *ConAu 7NR, DrAPF 83, NatPD 81, SmATA X*
Pseud./variant:
Holt, Rochelle Lynn

Du Bois, Shirley Graham *AmWomPl, AuBYP 3, BiDAfM, BioIn 11, –12, –13, BlkAWP, ConAu 69, –77, CurBio 77N, InWom SUP, IndAu 1917, ObitOF 79, SmATA 24, WrDr 76*
Main entry: Graham, Shirley Lola

Du Bois, Shirley Graham 1904-1977 *NotBlAW 92*

DuBois, Shirley Graham 1906-1977 *BioIn 14, –16, –17, BlkWr 1, BlkWrNE, EarBlAP*

DuBois, Shirley Graham 1907-1977 *AmWomD, ArtclWW 2*

Du Bois, Theodora 1890- *AuBYP 3*

DuBois, Theodora 1890-1986 *ScF&FL 92*

Du Bois, Theodora Mc Cormick 1890- *AmWomPl*

DuBois, Theodora McCormick 1890- *AmAu&B, AuBYP 2, BioIn 3, –8, WhAm 8*

Du Bois, Theodora McCormick 1890-1986 *EncSF 93*

DuBois, William Edward Burghardt 1868-1963 *AfrAmAl 6, AmAu&B, AmPeW, AmWr S2, BiDAmJo, BiDSA, BioIn 1, –2, –3, –4, –5, –6, –7, –8, –9, –10, –11, –12, –13, –14, –15, –16, –17, BlkAWP, CamGEL, CasWL, ConAmL, ConAu 85, ConLC 1, –2, –13, CurBio 40, –63, DcAfHiB 86, DcAmAu, DcAmB S7, DcAmNB, DcAmSR, DcLB 47, DcLEL, DcTwHis, EncAACR, EncAB-H, EncAJ, EncSoH, HarEnUS, InB&W 80, –85, LongCTC, LuthC 75, NegAl 76, –83, Novels, ObitOF 79, ObitT 1961, OxCAmH, OxCAmL 65, –83, OxCEng 85, PenC AM, REn, REnAL, SelBAAf, SmATA 42, SouBlCW, TwCA, –SUP, WebAB 74, –79, WebE&AL, WhAm 4, WhAmP, WhJnl, WhNAA, WorAl*

du Bois, William Pene *MajAI, SmATA 68*

DuBois, William Pene 1916- *AmAu&B, AmPB, AuBYP 2, BioIn 1, –2, –4, –5, –7, –8, –9, –14, –16, –17, ChhPo S1, ChlLR 1, ConAu 5R, –17NR, DcAmChF 1960, DcLB 61, EncSF 93, IlsCB 1744, –1946, –1957, –1967, IntAu&W 91, JBA 51, NewbMB 1922, OxCChiL, SmATA 4, Str&VC, TwCChW 78, –83, –89, WhoAm 82, –84, –86, –88, WhoChL, WrDr 80, –82, –84, –86, –88, –90, –92*
Pseud./variant:
Pene DuBois, William

du Bois, William Pene 1916-1993 *WrDr 94N*

du Bois, William Sherman Pene *ConAu 41NR*

Du Bois, William Sherman Pene 1916- *AuBYP 3*

du Bois, William Sherman Pene 1916-1993 *ConAu 140, SmATA 74*

Dubos, Rene 1901-1982 *AmAu&B, AmMWSc 73P, AnObit 1982, CelR, ConAu 5R, –106, CurBio 52, –73, Future, IntEnSS 79, IntWW 74, NewYTBE 70, –71, NewYTBS 82, WebAB 74, WhoAm 74, WhoE 74, WhoWor 74, WrDr 82*

Dubos, Rene Jules 1901-1982 *BioIn 17, RAdv 13-5*

DuBose, LaRocque 1926- *BioIn 9, ConAu 21R, SmATA 2*

Dubrovin, Vivian *BioIn 17*

Dubrovin, Vivian 1931- *ConAu 57, –9NR, –40NR, SmATA 65*

Ducas, Dorothy 1905- *AuBYP 2, –3, BioIn 8, –10, ConAu 5R, ForWC 70, WhoAmW 74, –75, WhoE 74*

Ducas, Dorothy 1905-1987 *ConAu 27NR*

Duchacek, Ivo D d1988 *NewYTBS 88*

Duchacek, Ivo D 1913- *AmMWSc 73S, –78S, ConAu 1R, –1NR, IntAu&W 77, WrDr 76, –80, –82, –84, –86, –88*

Duchacek, Ivo D 1913-1988 *BioIn 15, –16, ConAu 124, SmATA 55N*

Duchacek, Ivo Duka 1913-1988
Pseud./variant:
Cermak, Martin
Duka, Ivo

Du Chaillu, Paul B 1835-1903 *BenetAL 91*

DuChaillu, Paul Belloni 1831-1903 *DcAfHiB 86*

DuChaillu, Paul Belloni 1835-1903 *Alli SUP, AmAu, AmAu&B, BbD, BiDSA, BiD&SB, BiInAmS, BioIn 1, –10, –11, –13, CarSB, Chambr 3, ConAu 112, DcAmAu, DcBiPP, DcEnL, DcNAA, HarEnUS, JBA 34, OxCAmL 65, –83, OxCChiL, REnAL, SmATA 26, WhAm 1*
Pseud./variant:
Chaillu, Paul Belloni Du

Duchesne, Janet 1930- *ArtsCL, BioIn 6, –8, –14, ConAu 111, IlsCB 1957, –1967, SmATA 32*

Duckett, Alfred 1917- *BlkAWP, ConAu 45*

Duckett, Alfred A *BioIn 14*

Duckham, Frederick, Baron 1933- *Au&Wr 71, ConAu 103, IntAu&W 77, –82, WrDr 76, –80, –82, –84, –90*

Ducornet, Erica 1943- *AuBYP 2S, –3, BioIn 10, ConAu 37R, –77, –14NR, –34NR, IntAu&W 82, –86, –89, SmATA 7*

Ducornet, Guy *AuBYP 2S, –3*

Ducornet, Rikki *AuBYP 3, ConAu 34NR, DrAPF 87, –89, –91, –93*

Ducornet, Rikki 1943- *IntAu&W 89, WhoCanL 87, –92*

Dudek, Louis 1918- *BenetAL 91, BioIn 12, CamGLE, CanWW 70, –80, –81, –83, –89, CanWr, CasWL, ConAu 45, –14AS, –1NR, ConLC 11, –19, ConPo 70, –75, –80, –85, –91, CreCan 2, DcLB 88, DcLEL, DrAS 74E, –82E, IntAu&W 91, OxCCan, –SUP, OxCCanL, WebE&AL, WhoAm 74, –80, WhoCanL 85, –87, –92, WrDr 76, –80, –82, –84, –86, –88, –90, –92, –94*

Duder, Tessa *DcChlFi*

Duder, Tessa 1940- *BlmGWL, IntAu&W 91, TwCChW 89, WrDr 90, –92, –94*

Dudley, Ernest 1908?- *Au&Wr 71, ConAu 13R*

Dudley, Geoffrey A 1917- *WrDr 86, –88, –90, –92*

Dudley, Geoffrey Arthur 1917- *Au&Wr 71, ConAu 13R, –6NR, IntAu&W 77, –82, –89, –91, WhoWor 78, WrDr 76, –80, –82, –84, –94*

Dudley, Martha Ward 1909?-1985 *BioIn 15, ConAu 117, SmATA 45N*

Dudley, Nancy *AuBYP 2, –3, ConAu X, SmATA X*
Main entry: Cole, Lois Dwight

Dudley, Robert *AuBYP 3, ConAu X, DcVicP 2, SmATA X*
Main entry: Baldwin, James

Dudley, Ruth Hubbell 1905- *BioIn 11, ConAu 61, SmATA 11, WhoWest 74, –76, –78*

Due, Linnea A 1948- *BioIn 17, SmATA 64*

Dueland, Joy V *BioIn 13, ConAu 106, SmATA 27*

Dufault, Joseph Ernest Nephtali *MajAI*

Dufek, George John 1903-1977 *BioIn 4, –11, BlueB 76, CurBio 57, IntWW 74, –75, –76, –77N, ObitOF 79, OxCShps, WhAm 7, WhoAm 74, –76, WhoSSW 73, WhoWor 74*

Duff, Annis *BioIn 5, ChhPo*

Duff, Annis 1904?-1986 *ConAu 120, SmATA 49N*

Duff, Annis J d1986 *BioIn 16*

Duff, Maggie
Main entry: Duff, Margaret K

Duff, Maggie 1916- *SixBJA*

Duff, Margaret K *BiDrLUS 70, BioIn 15, ConAu 37R, –14NR, SmATA 37, WhoAmW 85*
Pseud./variant:
Duff, Maggie

Duff, Margaret K 1916- *BioIn 16*

Duff, Margaret Kapp *WhoAmW 87*

Duffy, Michael Francis 1950- *WhoWor 89*

Dugan, James 1912-1967 *AnCL, BioIn 7, ConAu 5R, –4NR, ObitOF 79, WhAm 4*

Dugan, Michael Gray 1947- *BioIn 12, ConAu 77, OxCAusL, SmATA 15, WhoWor 80*

Dugdale, Vera A *AmMWSc 73P*

Duggan, Alfred Leo 1903-1964 *AnCL, AuBYP 2, –3, BioIn 3, –4, –6, –7, –8, –13, ConAu 73, FourBJA, LongCTC, ModBrL, SmATA 25, TwCA SUP, TwCWr*

Duggan, Mary M 1921- *ConAu 25R*

Duggan, Maurice *IntvTCA 2*

Duggan, Maurice 1922-1974 *RfGEnL 91, TwCChW 89*

Duggan, Maurice 1922-1975 *BioIn 14, –15*

Duggan, Maurice Noel 1922-1974 *DcChlFi, RfGShF*

Duggan, Maurice Noel 1922-1975 *BlueB 76N, CasWL, ConAu 53, –73, –17NR, ConNov 72, –76, DcLEL 1940, OxCChiL, SmATA 30N, –40, TwCChW 78, –83, WebE&AL, WorAu 1975*

Dugin, Andrej 1955- *SmATA 77*

Dugina, Olga 1964- *SmATA 77*

Dugo, Andre
Main entry: Szenes, Andre

Du Jardin, Rosamond 1902-1963 *AuBYP 3*

DuJardin, Rosamond Neal 1902-1963 *AmAu&B, AuBYP 2S, BenetAL 91, BioIn 2, –3, –6, –7, –9, ConAu 1R, –103, CurBio 53, InWom SUP, MorJA, REnAL, SmATA 2, WhAm 4*

Duka, Ivo
Main entry: Duchacek, Ivo Duka

Dukas, Paul-Abraham 1865-1935 *BioIn 2, –3, –4, –6, –8, OxCFr, OxCMus, WorAl*

Duke, Anita *WrDr 76, –80*

Duke, Kate *AuBYP 3*

Duke, Madelaine 1925- *Au&Wr 71, BioIn 14, ConAu 57, -9NR, ConSFA, IntAu&W 77, -82, -91, TwCCr&M 85, WrDr 76, -80, -82, -84, -86, -88, -90, -92*

Duke, Madelaine Elizabeth 1925- *EncSF 93, WrDr 94*

Dukert, Joseph M 1929- *WrDr 88, -90, -92*

Dukert, Joseph Michael 1929- *AuBYP 2, -3, BioIn 7, ConAu 5R, -3NR, IntAu&W 77, WhoAmP 77, -81, -83, -85, -87, -89, -91, -93, WhoE 83, WrDr 76, -80, -82, -84, -86, -94*

Dulac, Edmund 1882-1953 *BioIn 1, -2, -3, -8, -10, -11, -12, -14, CarSB, ChhPo, -S2, ConICB, DcBrAr 1, DcBrBI, DcNaB 1951, IlsCB 1744, JBA 51, ObitT 1951, OxCChiL, SmATA 19, TwCPaSc, WhoChL*

Dulack, Thomas 1935- *BioIn 8, ConAu 25R*

Dulieu, Jean *ConAu X, -31NR*
Main entry: VanOort, Jan

Dumas, Alexandre 1802-1870 *Benet 87, BioIn 15, -16, -17, CamGWoT, CrtSuMy, EuWr 6, GrFLW, GuFrLit 1, HalFC 88, PenEncH, RAdv 13-2, WorAlBi, WorLitC, WrChl*

Dumas, Alexandre, Pere 1802-1870 *AtlBL, BbD, BiD&SB, BioIn 1, -2, -3, -4, -5, -6, -7, -9, -10, -11, -12, -13, CarSB, CasWL, CelCen, CmCal, CnThe, CyWA 58, DcBiPP, DcEuL, Dis&D, EncWT, EuAu, EvEuW, FilmgC, HalFC 84, HsB&A, InB&W 80, -85, McGEWB, McGEWD 72, -84, NewC, NinCLC 11, NotNAT A, -B, Novels, OxCChiL, OxCEng 67, -85, OxCFr, OxCThe 67, -83, PenC EUR, PlP&P, RComWL, REn, REnWD, SmATA 18, WhDW, WhoChL, WhoHr&F, WorAl*

Dumas, Alexandre Davy de la Pailleterie 1802-1870 *DcLB 119*

Dumas, Frederic 1913- *ConAu 69*

Dumas, Gerald J 1930- *BlkAWP, ConAu 25R, DrAP 75*

Dumas, Gerald John 1930- *WhoEnt 92*

Dumas, Jacqueline 1946- *BioIn 16, ConAu 123, SmATA 55*

Dumas, Philippe 1940- *BioIn 16, SmATA 52*

DuMaurier, Daphne 1907- *ArtclWW 2, Au&Wr 71, Benet 87, BiE&WWA, BioIn 1, -2, -4, -5, -8, -9, -11, -13, -15, BlueB 76, CamGLE, ConAu 5R, -6NR, ConLC 6, -11, ConNov 72, -76, -82, -86, ContDcW 89, CrtSuMy, CurBio 40, CyWA 58, DcLEL, EncMys, EncWT, EvLB, FilmgC, HalFC 84, -88, InWom SUP, IntAu&W 77, -82, -86, -89, -91, IntWW 74, -75, -76, -77, -78, -79, -80, -81, -82, -83, LongCTC, ModBrL, NewC, NotNAT, Novels, OxCEng 85, OxCThe 67, PenC ENG, PenEncH, RAdv 1, REn, SmATA 27, TwCA, -SUP, TwCCr&M 80, -85, TwCWr, Who 74, -82, -83, -85, WhoAmW 74, -75, WhoHr&F, WhoWor 74, -78, WorAl, WrDr 76, -80, -82, -84, -86, -88*
Pseud./variant:
Maurier, Daphne Du

du Maurier, Daphne 1907-1989 *AnObit 1989, BioIn 16, -17, BlmGWL, ConAu 128, ConLC 59, CurBio 89N, EncSF 93, FemiCLE, MajTwCW, RfGEnL 91, RfGShF, ScF&FL 92, SmATA 60, TwCCr&M 91, TwCRHW 90, WorAlBi*

du Maurier, Daphne, Dame d1989 *IntWW 89N, NewYTBS 89, Who 90N*

DuMaurier, Daphne, Dame 1907- *BioIn 14, EncBrWW, IntWW 89, Who 88*

Dumbleton, Mike 1948- *SmATA 73*

Dumbrille, Dorothy Martha 1897?- *Au&Wr 71, BioIn 1, CanNov, CanWW 70, -79, CreCan 2, WrDr 76, -82, -84*

Dumm, Edwina d1990 *NewYTBS 90*

Dumm, Edwina 1893- *ArtCS, BioIn 5, DcWomA, WhAmArt 85*

Dumm, Edwina 1893-1990 *EncACom*

Dumpleton, John LeFevre 1924- *Au&Wr 71, ConAu 13R, IntAu&W 77*

Dunbar, Ernest 1927- *BioIn 9, ConAu 25R, InB&W 80, SelBAAf, SelBAAu, WhoE 74*

Dunbar, Joyce *AuBYP 3*

Dunbar, Joyce 1944- *SmATA 76*

Dunbar, Paul Laurence 1872-1906 *AfrAmAl 6, AfrAmW, AmAu, AmAu&B, AmWr S2, Benet 87, BenetAL 91, BiDAfM, BiD&SB, BioIn 1, -2, -3, -5, -6, -7, -8, -9, -10, -11, -12, -13, -14, -15, -16, -17, BlkAWP, BlkAull, -92, BlkLC, BlkWr 1, BkCL, CamGEL, CasWL, Chambr 3, ChhPo, -S1, -S2, CnDAL, ConAu 104, -124, CyWA 89, DcAmAu, DcAmNB, DcLB 50, -54, -78, DcNAA, Dis&D, EarBlAP, EncAACR, InB&W 80, -85, MagSAmL, McGEWB, ModBlW, NegAl 76, -83, -89, NewGrDA 86, OhA&B, OxCAmL 65, -83, OxCAmT 84,*

PenC AM, PoeCrit 5, RAdv 1, –13-1, REn, REnAL, RealN, RfGAmL 87, SelBAAf, SelBAAu, ShSCr 8, SmATA 34, TwCLC 2, –12, WebAB 74, –79, WebE&AL, WhAm 1, WhFla, WorLitC

Dunbar, Paul Lawrence 1872-1906 *WorAlBi, WorAl*

Dunbar, Robert E 1926- *BioIn 14, ConAu 34NR*

Dunbar, Robert Everett 1926- *ConAu 85, –15NR, SmATA 32, WhoE 77, –81, WhoFI 74, WhoMW 74*

Duncan, Alistair 1927- *ConAu 61*

Duncan, Ardinelle Bean 1913- *ConAu 1R, ForWC 70, WhoAmW 77, –81, WhoE 81, WhoSSW 84, –86, –88*

Duncan, David 1913- *AmAu&B, AmNov, Au&Wr 71, BioIn 2, –16, ConAu 5R, EncSF 93, HalFC 88, NewEScF, ScFSB, TwCSFW 86, –91, WhoPNW, WhoSciF, WrDr 84, –86, –88, –90, –92, –94*

Duncan, Denis Macdonald 1920- *Who 74, –82, –83, –85, –88, –92, WhoWor 78*

Duncan, Denis Macdonald, Rev 1920- *Who 90*

Duncan, Frances 1942- *BioIn 13, ConAu 97, –17NR, OxCCanL, Profile 2, SmATA 48, WhoCanL 85, –87*

Duncan, Frances Mary 1942- *BioIn 16*

Duncan, Gregory *AuBYP 3, ConAu X, SmATA 3*
Main entry: McClintock, Marshall

Duncan, Jane *AuBYP 2S, –3, Au&Wr 71, BioIn 10, –11, ConAu X, IntAu&W 77, SmATA X, TwCChW 83, Who 74*
Main entry: Cameron, Elizabeth Jane

Duncan, Jane 1910-1976 *CmScLit, FemiCLE, TwCChW 89*

Duncan, Julia K *AmNov X, ConAu 134, –P-2, MajAI, SmATA 1, –65, WrDr 94*
Main entry: Benson, Mildred Augustine Wirt
Stratemeyer, Edward L

Duncan, Leslie *InB&W 80*

Duncan, Lois *AuBYP 2, BioIn 8, ConAu X, ConLC 26, FifBJA, IntAu&W 82, SmATA 1, –2AS, TwCChW 83, WrDr 76, –80, –82, –84*
Main entry: Arquette, Lois S

Duncan, Lois 1934- *Au&Arts 4, AuBYP 3, BioIn 14, –15, –16, ChlLR 29, ConAu 2NR, –23NR, –36NR, DcAmChF 1960, –1985, IntAu&W 89, –91, MajAI, ScF&FL 92, SmATA 36, –75, –2AS, TwCChW 89, TwCYAW, WrDr 86, –88, –90, –92, –94*

Duncan, Norman 1871-1916 *AmAu&B, BenetAL 91, BioIn 2, –11, –17, CanWr, ConAu 117, CreCan 2, DcAmAu, DcLB 92, DcLEL, DcNAA, JBA 34, –51, OhA&B, OxCCan, OxCCanL, OxCChiL, REnAL, TwCChW 78, –83, –89, WhAm 1, YABC 1*

Duncan, Robert L *TwCCr&M 91*

Duncan, Robert L 1927- *ConAu 106, –2AS, ScF&FL 92, WrDr 82, –84, –86, –88, –90, –92*

Duncan, Robert Lipscomb 1927- *BioIn 14, –15, SpyFic, WrDr 94*

Duncan, Sylvia 1916- *Au&Wr 71*

Duncan, William Murdoch 1909- *Au&Wr 71, ConAu 13R*

Duncombe, Frances 1900- *BioIn 13, ConAu 25R, SmATA 25*

Dunham, Bertha Mabel *BioIn 1, –3, CaW, CanNov, CreCan 2, OxCCan, WhNAA*
Main entry: Dunham, Mabel

Dunham, Bertha Mabel 1881-1957 *DcChlFi, FemiCLE*

Dunham, John L 1939- *WhoBlA 85, –90, –92*

Dunham, John Lee 1939- *BioIn 9, ConAu 29R, WhoBlA 75, –77, –80, –85, WhoMW 74, –76, –78, –80*

Dunham, Katherine *BioIn 14, –15, –16, –17, IntWW 89, –91, NewYTBS 86, –91*

Dunham, Katherine 1909- *NotBlAW 92, WhoAm 94*

Dunham, Katherine 1910- *ArtclWW 2, ASCAP 66, BiDAfM, BiE&WWA, BioAmW, BioIn 1, –2, –3, –4, –5, –6, –8, –9, –10, –11, –12, –13, BlkAWP, BlkWr 1, ConAu 65, –17NR, ConBlB 4, CurBio 41, DrBlPA 90, HarlReB, HerW, –84, InB&W 85, InWom SUP, IntWW 74, –75, –76, –77, –78, –79, –80, –81, –82, –83, LivgBAA, NegAl 76, –83, –89, NotNAT, –A, OxCAmT 84, REnAL, SelBAAf, SelBAAu, WebAB 74, –79, WhoAm 74, –76, –78, WhoBlA 75, –77, –80, –85, –90, –92, –94, WhoE 74, WhoHol A, WhoThe 77, –81, WhoWor 74, WorAlBi, WorAl*

Dunham, Katherine 1912- *NotWoAT*

Dunham, Katherine 1919- *BlksAmF*

Dunham, Mabel 1881-1957 *CanNov, CanWr, ConAu 114, CreCan 2, OxCCan, TwCChW 78*
Pseud./variant:
Dunham, Bertha Mabel

Dunham, Montrew Goetz 1919- *ConAu 17R, IndAu 1917*

Dunlap, Hope 1880- *BioIn 1, ChhPo, ConICB, DcWomA, IlsCB 1744*

Dunlap, Lon *AuBYP 3*

Dunleavy, Janet Egleson 1928- *ConAu 57, –6NR, –21NR, DrAS 74E, –78E, –82E, WhoUSWr 88, WhoWrEP 89, –92*
Pseud./variant:
Egleson, Janet F
Frank, Janet

Dunlop, Agnes Mary Robertson d1982 *AuBYP 3*

Dunlop, Agnes Mary Robinson d1982 *AuBYP 2, Au&Wr 71, BioIn 6, –7, –8, –9, BlueB 76, ConAu 13R, –9NR, SmATA 3, Who 74, –82, WrDr 76, –80, –82*
Pseud./variant:
Kyle, Elisabeth
Ralston, Jan

Dunlop, Eileen 1938- *BioIn 13, –16, ConAu 73, –14NR, –32NR, ScF&FL 92, SixBJA, SmATA 24, –12AS, TwCChW 89, WhoWor 80, WrDr 80, –82, –84, –90, –92*

Dunlop, Eileen Rhona 1938- *MajAI, SmATA 76, TwCYAW, WrDr 94*

Dunn, Eleanor *WhoAmW 74, WhoMW 74*

Dunn, Harvey T d1952 *WhoAmA 86N*

Dunn, Harvey T 1884-1952 *BioIn 1, –3, –5, –8, –9, IlsCB 1744, SmATA 34, WhAm 3, WhAmArt 85, WhoAmA 78N, –80N, –82N, –89N, –91N*

Dunn, Hugh Patrick 1916- *ConAu 122, IntAu&W 91, WhoWor 80, WrDr 76, –80, –82, –84, –86, –88, –90, –92, –94*

Dunn, Joseph Allan Elphinstone 1872-1941 *AmAu&B, AmLY, CurBio 41, DcNAA, EncAB-A 13, WhAm 1*

Dunn, Judy *BioIn 10, ConAu X, SmATA 5*
Main entry: Spangenberg, Judith Dunn

Dunn, Marion Herndon 1920- *ConAu 29R*

Dunn, Marty *OxCCan SUP*

Dunn, Mary Lois 1930- *AuBYP 2S, –3, BiDrLUS 70, BioIn 10, ConAu 61, –12NR, DcAmChF 1960, SmATA 6, WhoLibS 66*

Dunn, Nell
Main entry: Sandford, Nell Mary

Dunn, Nell 1936- *BioIn 16, BlmGWL, ConAu X, ConDr 88, ConNov 76, –82, –86, –91, DcLEL 1940, EncBrWW, FemiCLE, InWom SUP, IntAu&W 91, Novels, OxCEng 85, WrDr 76, –80, –82, –84, –86, –88, –90, –92, –94*

Dunn, Nell Mary 1936- *ConDr 93*

Dunnahoo, Terry *IntAu&W 86*

Dunnahoo, Terry 1927- *BioIn 10, ConAu 41R, –14NR, –31NR, IntAu&W 77, –82, SmATA 7, WhoAm 74, –76, –78, –80, –82, –84, –86, –88, –90, –92, –94*

Dunne, J W 1875-1949 *EncO&P 2, –3, EncSF 93, OxCChiL, OxCEng 85*

Dunne, Jeanette 1952- *SmATA 72*

Dunne, Marie *MajAI*

Dunne, Mary 1914- *AuBYP 3*

Dunne, Mary Collins 1914- *AuBYP 2S, BioIn 11, ConAu 41R, –14NR, SmATA 11, WhoAmW 75, –77*
Pseud./variant:
Moore, Regina

Dunnett, Margaret Rosalind 1909-1977 *Au&Wr 71, ConAu 108, IntAu&W 77, SmATA 42, WrDr 76*

Dunning, Arthur Stephen 1924- *AuBYP 2S, –3, ChhPo S1, ConAu 25R, DrAS 74E, LEduc 74*

Dunnington, Tom *IlsBYP*

Dunrea, Olivier 1953- *BioIn 15, –16, SmATA 46, –59*

Dunsany, Edward J M Drax Plunkett, Baron 1878-1957 *Alli SUP, AtlBL, BioIn 1, –3, –4, –5, –9, –13, CamGEL, CasWL, ChhPo, –S1, –S2, CnMD, CnThe, ConAu 104, DcIrW 1, DcLB 10, DcLEL, EncMys, EvLB, JBA 34, LongCTC, McGEWD 72, ModBrL, ModWD, NewC, OxCEng 67, –85, OxCThe 67, –83, PenC ENG, REnWD, TwCA, –SUP, TwCLC 2, TwCWr*

Dunsany, Edward J M Drax Plunkett, Lord 1878-1957 *BiDIrW*

Dunsany, Edward John Moreton Drax P 1878-1957 *CamGWoT*

Dunsheath, Percy 1886- *Au&Wr 71, BioIn 10, ConAu 107, IntAu&W 77, IntWW 74, –75, –76, –77, –78, –79, Who 74*

Dunton, Mary Jane *ChhPo S1*

Dunton, Samuel Cady 1910-1975 *BioIn 10, -12, ConAu 61, NatCAB 60*

Duplaix, Georges *AmPB*
Pseud./variant:
Ariane
Nicole

Dupre, Catherine *Au&Wr 71, ConAu 25R, -16NR, IntAu&W 77, -91, WrDr 76, -80, -82, -84, -86, -88, -90*

Dupre, Catherine 1927- *IntAu&W 86*

Dupuy, R Ernest 1887-1975 *BioIn 10, ConAu 1R, -57, -6NR, ObitOF 79, WhAm 6, WhoWor 74*

Dupuy, Trevor Nevitt 1916- *AuBYP 2, -3, BioIn 8, -9, ConAu 1R, DrAS 74H, IntAu&W 77, SmATA 4, WhoAm 74, -76, -78, -80, -82, -84, -86, -88, -90, -92, -94, WhoWor 74, -84, -87, -89, WrDr 76, -80, -82, -84, -86*

Durack, Elizabeth 1916- *SingR 1, WhoWor 80, -82*

Durack, Mary 1913- *Au&Wr 71, BioIn 6, -9, ConAu 97, -17NR, FemiCLE, IntAu&W 77, -82, -86, -89, -91, OxCAusL, OxCChiL, SingR 1, TwCChW 78, -83, -89, Who 82, -83, -85, -92, WhoWor 78, WrDr 76, -80, -82, -84, -86, -88, -90, -92, -94*

Durack, Mary, Dame 1913- *AuWomWr, Who 88, -90*

Durand, Ruth Sawyer *AuBYP 3*

Durant, John 1902- *AmAu&B, AuBYP 2, -3, BioIn 7, -13, ConAu 9R, -5NR, SmATA 27, WhoAm 74, -76, -78, -80, -82, WhoSSW 73*

Duree, Barbara Joyce 1922- *BiDrLUS 70, BioIn 3, WhoLibI 82, WhoLibS 66*

Durell, Ann *AuBYP 3*

Durell, Ann 1930- *AuBYP 2, BioIn 8, -17, ConAu 136, SmATA 66, WhoAm 84, -86, -88, -90, -92, WrDr 94*

Durfee, David A 1929- *WrDr 86, -88, -90*

Durfee, David Arthur 1929- *ConAu 29R, IntAu&W 77, WhoE 75, WrDr 76, -80, -82, -84*

Durham, John *ConAu 31NR*

Durham, John 1925- *ConAu 107, DrAS 74E, -78E*

Durham, Mae *AnCL, BiDrLUS 70, ConAu 57*
Main entry: Roger, Mae Durham

Durham, Philip 1912-1977 *ConAu 9R, -7NR, DrAS 74E, -78E*

Durlacher, Ed *AuBYP 2, -3, BioIn 7*

Durr, Francoise *BioIn 9*

Durrant, Sheila 1945- *WrDr 76, -80, -82, -84*

Durrell, Donald Dewitt 1903- *ConAu 17R, -8NR, WhoAm 74, -76, -78, -80*

Durrell, Gerald Malcolm 1925- *AuBYP 2, -3, Au&Wr 71, BioIn 5, -8, -9, -10, -11, -12, -13, -14, -16, -17, ConAu 5R, DcLEL 1940, IntAu&W 77, -82, -89, -91, IntWW 74, -75, -76, -77, -78, -79, -80, -81, -82, -83, -89, LongCTC, NewC, REn, SmATA 8, TwCWr, Who 74, -82, -83, -85, -88, -90, -92, WhoAm 90, -92, -94, WhoWor 74, -78, -84, -87, -89, -91, -93, WorAu 1950, WrDr 76, -80*

DuSoe, Robert C 1892-1958 *BioIn 6, MorJA, WhNAA, YABC 2*

Dutta, Arup Kumar 1946- *DcChlFi*

Dutton, Geoffrey Piers Henry 1922- *Au&Wr 71, BioIn 6, -9, CasWL, ConAu 45, ConNov 72, -76, ConPo 70, -75, IntAu&W 77, -82, -89, -91, IntWW 89, -91, WhoWor 78, WrDr 76, -80*

Dutton, Maude Barrows 1880- *CarSB*

Dutton, William Sherman 1893- *WhNAA*

Dutz *ConAu X, SmATA 6*
Main entry: Davis, Mary Octavia

Duval, Katherine *SmATA X, WrDr 92*
Main entry: James, Elizabeth

Duval, Katherine 1945- *WrDr 94*

Duval, Marie
Main entry: DeTessier, Isabelle Emily

Duval, Paul *OxCCan SUP, OxCFr*

Duvall, Evelyn Millis 1906- *AmAu&B, AmMWSc 73S, -78S, BioIn 1, -11, ConAu 1R, -1NR, CurBio 47, ForWC 70, IntAu&W 89, -91, SmATA 9, WhoAm 76, -78, WhoAmW 74, WhoWor 74, WrDr 76, -80, -82, -84, -86, -88, -90, -92, -94*

Duvoisin, Louise *IntAu&W 77*
Main entry: Fatio, Louise

Duvoisin, Roger 1904-1980 *BioIn 14, –16, ChlLR 23, DcLB 61, TwCChW 89, WhoAmA 86N, –89N, –91N*

Duvoisin, Roger Antoine 1904-1980 *AmAu&B, AmPB, AnObit 1980, AuBYP 2, Au&ICB, Au&Wr 71, BioIn 1, –2, –3, –4, –5, –7, –8, –9, –10, –11, –12, –13, BkP, Cald 1938, ChhPo, –S1, –S2, ConAu 13R, –101, –11NR, FamAIYP, IlsBYP, IlsCB 1744, –1946, –1957, –1967, IntAu&W 77, –82, JBA 51, MajAI, NewYTBS 80, OxCChiL, SmATA 2, –23N, –30, Str&VC, TwCChW 78, –83, WhAm 9, WhAmArt 85, WhoAm 74, –76, –78, –80, WhoAmA 73, –78, –80, –82N, WhoChL, WhoGrA 62, WrDr 76, –80*

Duvoisin, Roger Antone 1904-1980 *AuBYP 3*

D'Vys, George Whitefield 1860-1941 *AmLY, CarSB, WhAm 1, WhNAA*

Dwiggins, Don 1913- *AuBYP 2S, –3, BioIn 9, ConAu 17R, –8NR, –23NR, SmATA 4*

Dwiggins, Don 1913-1988 *BioIn 17, ConAu 127, SmATA 60*

Dwiggins, William Addison 1880-1956 *AmAu&B, BioIn 1, –3, –4, –5, –15, –16, ConDes 84, EncAJ, IlsCB 1744, –1946, ObitOF 79, OhA&B, OxCAmL 65, REnAL, WhAm 3, WhAmArt 85, WhoAmA 80N, –82N, –86N, –89N, –91N*

Dwight, Allan *ConAu X, SmATA X*
Main entry: Cole, Lois Dwight

Dwyer, Bill *ArtCS*

Dwyer, Deanna *ConAu 36NR, MajTwCW, TwCCr&M 91, TwCYAW, WrDr 86, –88, –90, –92*

Dwyer, Deanna 1945- *WrDr 94*

Dwyer, K R *ConAu 36NR, EncSF 93, MajTwCW, TwCCr&M 91, TwCYAW, WrDr 86, –88, –90, –92*

Dwyer, K R 1945- *BioIn 14, –15, –17, WrDr 94*

Dwyer, Vera *SingR 1*

Dyck, Peter J 1914- *ConAu 142, SmATA 75*

Dyer, James Frederick 1934- *ConAu 102, IntAu&W 82, –86, –89, –91, SmATA 37, WrDr 76, –80, –82, –84*

Dyer, Thomas Allan 1947- *DcAmChF 1960*

Dyess, John Foster 1939- *SmATA 76*

Dygard, Thomas J 1931- *Au&Arts 7, AuBYP 3, BioIn 13, –16, ConAu 85, –15NR, SixBJA, SmATA 24, –15AS, WhoAm 86, WhoMW 84*

Dyke, Henry Van *Chambr 3, DrAPF 87, –93, JBA 34*
Main entry: VanDyke, Henry Jackson, Jr.

Dyke, John 1935- *ConAu 25R, –12NR, SmATA 35*

Dykes, James Grant 1920- *CanWW 70, –80, –81, –83, –89*

Dykes, James Joseph 1896-1976 *BiDAmSp BB, BioIn 1, –2, –5, –6, –10, NewYTBE 73*

Dykes, Jefferson Chenowth 1900- *ConAu 5R, WhoAm 74, –76, –78, –80, –82, –84, –86, –88, WhoE 89*

Dykes, Jefferson Chenowth 1900-1989 *BioIn 17, WhAm 10*

Dynely, James *AuBYP 3*

Dyson, Edward 1865-1931 *OxCAusL, SingR 2*

E

Eadington, Joan 1926- *ChlFicS*

Eagan, Andrea Boroff d1993 *NewYTBS 93*

Eagan, Andrea Boroff 1943- *ConAu 73*

Eagan, Andrea Boroff 1943-1993 *ConAu 140*

Eagar, Frances 1940- *BioIn 11, ConAu 61, SmATA 11*

Eagar, Frances 1940-1978 *BioIn 16, ConAu 120, SmATA 55N*

Eager, Edward 1911-1964 *AnCL, ASCAP 66, AuBYP 2, BioIn 6, –7, –8, –14, ChhPo, DcLB 22, MorJA, OxCChiL, SmATA 17, TwCChW 78, –83, –89, WhoChL*

Eager, Edward McMaken 1911-1964 *AuBYP 3, DcAmChF 1960, MajAI*

Eager, George B 1921- *SmATA 56*

Eagle, Ellen 1953- *SmATA 61*

Eagle, Mike 1942- *BioIn 11, SmATA 11*

Eagleson, John 1941- *ConAu 53*

Eames, Genevieve Torrey *AuBYP 2, –3, BioIn 7*

Earl, Lawrence 1915- *Au&Wr 71, ConAu 9R*

Earle, Alice Morse 1851-1911 *InWom SUP*

Earle, Alice Morse 1853?-1911 *AmAu&B, AuBYP 2S, –3, BenetAL 91, BbD, BiD&SB, BioIn 1, ChhPo S1, ConAu 117, DcAmAu, DcLEL, DcNAA, HarEnUS, OxCAmL 65, –83, REnAL, WhAm 1*

Earle, Eyvind 1916- *BioIn 5, –9, –13, IlsCB 1946, PrintW 83, –85*

Earle, Olive Lydia 1888- *Au&Wr 71, BioIn 5, –6, –8, –10, –12, ConAu 21R, DcWomA, IlsBYP, IlsCB 1946, –1957, –1967, IntAu&W 77, MorJA, SmATA 7*

Earle, Vana 1917- *BioIn 5, IlsCB 1946*

Earle, William *MajAI*
Main entry: Johns, William Earl

Early, Jon *MajAI*
Main entry: Johns, William Earl

Early, Margaret 1951- *SmATA 72*

Earnshaw, Brian 1929- *BioIn 12, ConAu 25R, –11NR, –27NR, EncSF 93, SmATA 17*

Earnshaw, Harold *ChhPo, DcBrBI*

Eastlake, William *DrAPF 87, –89, –91, –93*

Eastlake, William 1917- *AmAu&B, Au&Wr 71, BenetAL 91, BioIn 9, –10, –14, BlueB 76, ConAu 5R, –1AS, –5NR, ConLC 8, ConNov 72, –76, –82, –86, –91, DcLB 6, DrAF 76, DrAPF 83, –85, EncFWF, IntAu&W 82, ModAL S1, Novels, OxCAmL 65, –83, PenC AM, PostFic, REnAL, TwCWW 91, WhoAm 74, –80, –82, –84, WhoWor 74, WorAu 1950, WrDr 76, –80, –82, –84, –86, –88, –90, –92*

Eastlake, William Derry 1917- *WhoAm 92, WrDr 94*

Eastman, Addison John 1918- *ConAu 85, WhoRel 75*

Eastman, Charles A 1858-1939 *BenetAL 91*

Eastman, Charles Alexander 1858-1939 *AmAu&B, AmLY, BiNAW Sup, –SupB, BioIn 2, –3, –7, –8, –9, –11, –12, –13, –14, ConAmL, DcAmAu, InSci, JBA 34, –51, OxCAmL 65, –83, REnAL, WhAm 4, WhNaAH, YABC 1*

Eastman, P D 1909-1986 *BioIn 14, –15, ConAu 118, SmATA 46N*

Eastman, Philip D 1909- *AuBYP 2, BioIn 8, ConAu 107, IlsCB 1957, SmATA 33*

Eastman, Philip D 1909-1986 *BioIn 14, –15*

Eastman, Philip Dey 1909-1986 *AuBYP 3*

Easton, Robert 1915- *ConAu 13R, –14AS, –7NR, –27NR, EncFWF, TwCWW 91, WhoAm 84, –86, –88, –90, WhoWest 80, –82, –84, –87, –89, WhoWor 91, WrDr 76, –80, –82, –84, –86, –88, –90, –92, –94*

Eastwick, Ivy Ethel Olive *AuBYP 3*

Eastwick, Ivy Olive 1905- *AuBYP 2, BioIn 8, –9, BkCL, ChhPo, –S1, ConAu 5R, –2NR, SmATA 3, WrDr 76, –80, –82, –84*

Eaton, Anne T 1881-1971 *BioIn 14*

Eaton, Anne Thaxter 1881-1971 *AmAu&B, AmPB, BioIn 1, –9, ChhPo, –S1, ConAu 111, NewYTBE 71, SmATA 32*

Eaton, Evelyn *DrAPF 87*

Eaton, Evelyn 1902- *AmAu&B, AmNov, Au&Wr 71, BioIn 1, –2, –4, –5, –10, CanNov, CanWr, ConAu 53, DrAPF 83, –85, IntWWP 82, OxCCan, REnAL, TwCA SUP, TwCRHW 90*

Eaton, George L *AuBYP 2, –3, ConAu 131, –X, –37NR, IntAu&W 77X, SmATA 65, –X, WrDr 76, –80, –82, –84, –86, –88, –90*
Main entry: Verral, Charles Spain

Eaton, Janet *SmATA X*
Main entry: Givens, Janet Eaton

Eaton, Jeanette 1885-1968 *BioIn 14*

Eaton, Jeanette 1886-1968 *AmAu&B, AnCL, AuBYP 2S, –3, BioIn 2, –8, –13, ConAu 73, JBA 34, –51, MajAI, OhA&B, SmATA 24, Str&VC*

Eaton, John 1942- *IlsBYP*

Eaton, Tom 1940- *BioIn 13, ConAu 41R, –15NR, ConGrA 1, IlsBYP, SmATA 22, WhoAmA 91*

Eaton, Walter Prichard 1878-1957 *AmAu&B, BenetAL 91, BioIn 4, –8, CarSB, ChhPo, –S2, ConAmL, InSci, NotNAT B, ObitOF 79, OxCAmT 84, PlP&P, REnAL, TwCA, –SUP, WhAm 3, WhNAA*

Ebbutt, Phil *DcBrBI*

Ebel, Alex 1927- *BioIn 11, SmATA 11*

Eber, Dorothy Harley 1930- *SmATA 27*

Eberle, Irmengarde 1898-1979 *AmAu&B, AuBYP 2, –3, BioIn 1, –2, –7, –9, –13, BkCL, ConAu 1R, –85, –2NR, CurBio 46, JBA 51, SmATA 2, –23N, WhoAm 74, –76, –78, WhoAmW 74, –77, WhoWor 74*
Pseud./variant:
Allen, Allyn
Carter, Phyllis Ann

Eberstadt, Frederick *AuBYP 2, –3, BioIn 7, ChhPo*

Eberstadt, Frederick 1926- *WhoE 91, –93*

Eberstadt, Isabel 1933- *ConAu 126*

Eberstadt, Isabel 1934?- *AuBYP 2, –3, BioIn 7, ChhPo*

Eble, Diane 1956- *SmATA 74*
Pseud./variant:
Spence, Cynthia

Eby, Lois Christine 1908- *AuBYP 2, –3, BioIn 7, IndAu 1917*
Pseud./variant:
Lawson, Patrick

Eccles *SmATA X, Who 82, –83*
Main entry: Williams, Ferelith Eccles

Eccles, Frank 1923- *ConAu 103, WrDr 76, –80, –82, –84*

Eckblad, Edith Berven 1923- *ConAu 17R, ForWC 70, SmATA 23, WhoAmW 77, WrDr 76, –94*

Ecke, Wolfgang 1927-1983 *AuBYP 2S, –3, BioIn 15, ConAu 111, SmATA 37N*

Eckelberry, Don Richard 1921- *BioIn 10, WhoAm 74, –76, –78, WhoAmA 78, –80, –82, –84, –86, –89, –91*

Eckert, Allan W *BioIn 14*

Eckert, Allan W 1931- *AuBYP 2S, –3, BioIn 13, ConAu 13R, –14NR, ConLC 17, DcAmChF 1960, FourBJA, ScF&FL 92, SmATA 27, –29, WhoAm 74, –76, –78, –80, –82, –84, –86, –88, –90, –92, –94, WhoSSW 73*

Eckert, Allan Wesley 1931- *EncSF 93*

Eckert, Horst 1931- *BioIn 11, ConAu 37R, –38NR, MajAI, SmATA 8, –72*
Pseud./variant:
Janosch

Eckstein, Gustav 1890-1981 *AmAu&B, AnObit 1981, BioIn 1, –3, –4, –12, –13, ConAu 57, –104, CurBio 42, –81N, InSci, NewYTBS 81, OhA&B, TwCA SUP, WhAm 8, WhNAA*

Eckstrom, Jack Dennis *ConSFA*

Economakis, Olga *AuBYP 2, –3, BioIn 8*

Ed, Carl 1890-1959 *AmAu&B, ArtCS, BioIn 5, WhAm 3, WhoAmA 80N, –82N, –86N, –89N, –91N*

Eddings, Claire Neff *AuBYP 2S, –3*

Eddy, Daniel Clarke 1823-1896 *Alli, –SUP, AmAu&B, BiD&SB, BioIn 6, CarSB, DcAmAu, DcNAA, WhAm HS*

Ede, Janina 1937- *ArtsCL, BioIn 6, SmATA 33*

Edel, May Mandelbaum 1909-1964 *BioIn 6, –7*

Edell, Celeste *ConAu 1R, ForWC 70, SmATA 12*

Edelman, Elaine *BioIn 16, DrAPF 87, –89, –91, –93, IntAu&W 86, SmATA 50, WhoUSWr 88, WhoWrEP 89, –92*

Edelman, Lily 1915-1981 *AuBYP 2, –3, BioIn 7, –13, ConAu 61, –102, SmATA 22, WhoAmW 77, WhoWorJ 72*

Edelson, Edward 1932- *AuBYP 2S, –3, BioIn 16, ConAu 17R, –13NR, ScF&FL 92, SmATA 51, WhoAm 76, –78, –90, WhoE 74, –75, –77, –83, –85*

Eden, Dorothy 1912-1982 *AnObit 1982, BioIn 12, –14, ConAu 81, –106, TwCCr&M 80, TwCRHW 90, WrDr 76, –80, –82*

Edens, Cooper 1945- *BioIn 16, SmATA 49*

Edens, David, Bishop 1926- *AmMWSc 73S, ConAu 108, SmATA 39*

Edey, Maitland A d1992 *NewYTBS 92*

Edey, Maitland A 1910- *WrDr 90, –92*

Edey, Maitland A 1910-1992 *AnObit 1992*

Edey, Maitland Armstrong 1910- *BioIn 13, ConAu 57, –6NR, ConIsC 1, SmATA 25, WhoAm 82, –84, –86, –88, –90, WhoE 77*

Edey, Maitland Armstrong 1910-1992 *BioIn 17, ConAu 137, SmATA 71, WhAm 10, WrDr 94N*

Edgar, J G 1834-1864 *OxCChiL*

Edgar, Ken 1925- *ConAu 49, –27NR, ScF&FL 92*

Edgarton, S C, Miss 1819-1848 *CarSB*

Edgerton, Clyde 1944- *BioIn 16, ConAu 118, –134, ConLC 39, WrDr 92, –94*

Edgerton, Clyde Carlyle 1944- *TwCYAW*

Edgeworth, Maria 1757-1849 *OxCEng 85*

Edgeworth, Maria 1767-1849 *Alli, AtlBL, Benet 87, BbD, BiDIrW, BiDLA, BiD&SB, BioIn 1, –2, –3, –4, –5, –7, –8, –9, –10, –12, –13, –14, –16, –17, BlmGEL, BritAu 19, CamGEL, CamGLE, CarSB, CasWL, CelCen, Chambr 2, ChhPo, ContDcW 89, CrtT 2, CyEd, CyWA 58, DcBiA, DcBiPP, DcEnA, DcEnL, DcEuL, DcIrB 88, DcIrL, DcIrW 1, DcLEL, DcNaB, –C, EvLB, InWom SUP, IntDcWB, LongCEL, McGEWB, MouLC 3, NewC, NinCLC 1, Novels, OxCChiL, OxCEng 67, PenC ENG, PoIre, RAdv 1, –13-1, REn, SmATA 21, TelT, WebE&AL, WhDW, WhoChL*

Edgeworth, Maria 1768-1849 *ArtclWW 2, BlmGWL, DcBrAmW, DcLB 116, EncBrWW, FemiCLE, RfGEnL 91*

Edgun *BioIn 5, IlsBYP, IlsCB 1946*
Main entry: Wulff, Edgun Valdemar

Edison, Theodore *MajAI*

Edler, Tim 1948- *SmATA 56*

Edlin, Herbert Leeson 1913-1977 *Au&Wr 71, ConAu 61, –9NR, IntAu&W 77, WrDr 76, –80*

Edmonds, Harry 1891- *Au&Wr 71*

Edmonds, Harry 1891-1989 *ScF&FL 92*

Edmonds, Harry Moreton Southey 1891-1989 *EncSF 93*

Edmonds, I G 1917- *AuBYP 2S, –3, BioIn 11, ConAu 33R, –13NR, –30NR, SmATA 8*
Pseud./variant:
Gordon, Gary

Edmonds, Richard W *AuBYP 2, –3, BioIn 7*

Edmonds, Walter D 1903- *Benet 87, BenetAL 91, ScF&FL 92, SmATA 4AS, TwCChW 89, TwCRHW 90, WrDr 86, –88, –90, –92*

Edmonds, Walter Dumaux 1903- *AmAu&B, AmNov, AuBYP 2, –3, BioIn 1, –2, –4, –5, –6, –7, –9, –10, –12, –13, –14, –15, CnDAL, ConAmA, ConAu 5R, –2NR, ConLC 35, CurBio 42, CyWA 58, DcAmChF 1960, DcLB 9, DcLEL, IntAu&W 82, –91, MajAI, ModAL, MorBMP, MorJA, NewbMB 1922, Novels, OxCAmL 65, –83, OxCChiL, PenC AM, REn, REnAL, SmATA 1, –27, TwCA, –SUP, TwCChW 78, –83, WhoAm 74, –76, –78, –80, –82, –84, –86, –88, –90, –92, –94, WrDr 76, –80, –82, –84, –94*

Edmondson, Madeleine *AuBYP 2S, –3*

Edmund, Sean *BioIn 9, ConAu X, MajAI, SmATA 4, –68*
Main entry: Pringle, Laurence Patrick

Edsall, Marian 1920- *AuBYP 3, ConAu 27NR*

Edsall, Marian S 1920- *AuBYP 2S, BioIn 11, ConAu 49, SmATA 8, WhoAmW 77*

Edson, Gus 1901-1966 *AmAu&B, ArtCS, BioIn 7, EncAB-A 16, ObitOF 79, WhAm 4, WhAmArt 85*

Edwardes, Michael 1923- *Au&Wr 71, ConAu 57, -10NR*

Edwards, Al *ConAu X*
Main entry: Nourse, Alan Edward

Edwards, Alexander
Main entry: Fleischer, Leonore

Edwards, Anne 1927- *ArtclWW 2, Au&Wr 71, BioIn 5, -10, -11, -12, -13, -14, ConAu 61, -13NR, -33NR, IntAu&W 89, -91, ScF&FL 92, SmATA 35, TwCRHW 90, WrDr 76, -80, -82, -84, -86, -88, -90, -92, -94*

Edwards, Audrey 1947- *BioIn 14, -16, BlkAuII, -92, ConAu 81, InB&W 80, SmATA 31, -52*

Edwards, Audrey Marie 1947- *WhoBlA 94*

Edwards, Bertram *BioIn 11, ConAu X, SmATA X*
Main entry: Edwards, Herbert Charles

Edwards, Bronwen Elizabeth *ConAu X, SmATA X*
Main entry: Rose, Wendy

Edwards, Cecile Pepin 1916- *AuBYP 2, -3, BioIn 7, -13, ConAu 5R, SmATA 25, WhoE 89*

Edwards, David L 1929- *ConAu 29NR*

Edwards, David Lawrence 1929- *Au&Wr 71, ConAu 5R, -12NR, Who 74, -82, -83, -85, -88, -92*

Edwards, David Lawrence, Very Rev 1929- *Who 90*

Edwards, Don 1905-1963 *OxCAusL, SingR 1*

Edwards, Dorothy 1914-1982 *Au&Wr 71, BioIn 9, -14, ChlFicS, ConAu 25R, -107, -12NR, IntAu&W 77, OxCChiL, ScF&FL 92, SmATA 4, -31N, TwCChW 78, -83, -89, WrDr 76, -80, -82*

Edwards, George Wharton d1950 *WhoAmA 86N*

Edwards, George Wharton 1859?-1950 *Alli SUP, AmAu&B, AmLY, BbD, BiD&SB, BioIn 1, -2, ChhPo, -S2, DcAmAu, IlsCB 1744, ObitOF 79, WhAm 2, WhAmArt 85, WhNAA, WhoAmA 78, -80N, -82N*

Edwards, George Wharton 1869-1950 *WhoAmA 89N, -91N*

Edwards, Gunvor *BioIn 12, ConAu 107, IlsCB 1967, SmATA 32*

Edwards, Harvey 1929- *AuBYP 2S, -3, BioIn 10, ConAu 25R, SmATA 5, WrDr 76, -80, -82, -84, -86, -88, -90, -92, -94*

Edwards, Herbert Charles 1912- *Au&Wr 71, BioIn 11, ConAu 9R, SmATA 12*
Pseud./variant:
Edwards, Bertram

Edwards, Jane Campbell 1932- *BioIn 11, ConAu 13R, ForWC 70, SmATA 10*
Pseud./variant:
Campbell, Jane

Edwards, Julia *MajAI, SmATA 67*

Edwards, Julie *BioIn 16, ConAu X, ConTFT 7, SmATA X*
Main entry: Andrews, Julie
Stratemeyer, Edward L

Edwards, Julie Andrews *AuBYP 2S, -3, ConAu X, MorBMP, SmATA 7, Who 74, -88, -90, -92*

Edwards, June *ConAu X, IntAu&W 82X, -91X, WhoCanL 85, -87, -92, WrDr 76, -80, -82, -84, -86, -88, -90, -92, -94*
Main entry: Bhatia, June
Forrester, Helen

Edwards, Kate F 1877-1980 *ConAu 107, DcWomA, WhAm 7, WhAmArt 85, WhoAmA 73, WhoAmW 74, -75*

Edwards, Linda Strauss *SmATA 42*

Edwards, Linda Strauss 1948- *ConAu 126, SmATA 49*

Edwards, Lionel Dalhousie Robertson 1878-1966 *BioIn 1, -2, -5, -10, BritAS, ChhPo, ClaDrA, DcBrAr 1, DcBrBI, DcNaB 1961, IlsCB 1744, -1946, -1957*

Edwards, Lynne 1943- *ConAu 73*

Edwards, Margaret 1902- *BiDrLUS 70, ConAu P-2, WhoLibS 55, -66*

Edwards, Margaret 1902-1988 *ConAu 125, SmATA 56N*

Edwards, Margaret Royalty 1895- *BioIn 7, ChhPo S2*

Edwards, Michelle 1955- *SmATA 70*

Edwards, Monica 1912- *TwCChW 89, WrDr 86, -88, -90, -92, -94*

Edwards, Monica LeDoux Newton 1912- *Au&Wr 71, BioIn 8, -11, ConAu 9R, OxCChiL, SmATA 12, TwCChW 78, -83, WhoChL, WrDr 76, -80, -82, -84*

Edwards, Olwen *ConAu X, SmATA X*
Main entry: Gater, Dilys

Edwards, Page L, Jr. 1941- *SmATA 59*

Edwards, Page Lawrence, Jr. 1941- *IntAu&W 91, WhoAm 90, -92, -94*

Edwards, Pat *AuBYP 3*

Edwards, Peter William 1934- *BioIn 12, -14, IlsBYP, IlsCB 1967*

Edwards, R M *ConAu X*
Main entry: Edwards, Roselyn

Edwards, Roselyn 1929- *ConAu 25R*
Pseud./variant:
Alexander, Marge
Edwards, R M

Edwards, Sally 1929- *BioIn 10, ConAu 25R, SmATA 7*

Edwards, Samuel *ConAu 127, SmATA X*
Main entry: Gerson, Noel Bertram

Edy-Legrand *IlsCB 1946*
Main entry: Legrand, Edy

Eells, Elsie Spicer 1880-1963 *AmAu&B, WhAm 4*

Effinger, George Alec *ConSFF*

Effinger, George Alec 1947- *BioIn 12, ConAu 37R, -23NR, DcLB 8, EncSF 93, IntAu&W 91, NewEScF, ScF&FL 92, TwCSFW 86, -91, WhoE 75, -77, WhoSciF, WhoSSW 78, -80, -82, -84, -86, -88, WrDr 76, -80, -82, -84, -86, -88, -90, -92, -94*

Efron, Alexander 1897- *ConAu P-2*

Egan, E W 1922- *ConAu 21R, -9NR, SmATA 35*

Egan, Pierce 1772-1849 *BioIn 15*

Egan, Pierce 1814-1880 *Alli SUP, BbD, BiD&SB, CamGLE, Chambr 3, DcEnA, DcEnL, DcNaB, HsB&A, NewC, OxCEng 67, StaCVF*

Egermeier, Elsie E 1890- *ChhPo S1, ConAu 5R, WhNAA*

Egermeier, Elsie E 1890-1986 *BioIn 17, SmATA 65*

Eggenberger, David 1918- *BioIn 10, ConAu 9R, SmATA 6*

Eggenhofer, Nicholas 1897- *BioIn 9, -10, -11, IlsBYP*

Eggleston, Edward 1837-1902 *Alli SUP, AmAu, AmAu&B, BenetAL 91, BbD, BiD&SB, BioIn 1, -2, -5, -6, -12, -13, -15, CamGEL, CamGLE, CamHAL, CarSB, CasWL, Chambr 3, ChhPo, -S1, CnDAL, ConAu 111, CyAL, CyEd, CyWA 58, DcAmAu, DcBiA DcLB 12, DcNAA, DcRusL, EncWM, EvLB, HarEnUS, IndAu 1816, JBA 34, McGEWB, Novels, OxCAmH, OxCAmL 65, -83, OxCChiL, OxCEng 67, -85, PenC AM, REn, REnAL, RfGAmL 87, SmATA 27, WebAB 74, -79, WebE&AL, WhAm 1*

Egielski, Richard *BioIn 15, -16, ChlBIID*

Egielski, Richard 1952- *BioIn 11, -12, IlsCB 1967, MajAI, SixBJA, SmATA 11, -49, WhoAm 88, -92*

Egleson, Janet F *ConAu X*
Main entry: Dunleavy, Janet Egleson

Egner, Thorbjorn 1912- *IntAu&W 82, OxCChiL*

Egner, Thorbjorn 1912-1990? *BioIn 17*

Egoff, Sheila A 1918- *BiDrLUS 70, ConAu 116, -132, ScF&FL 92, WhoLibI 82, WrDr 94*

Egypt, Ophelia Settle 1903-1984 *BioIn 15, -16, BlkAuII, -92, ConAu 81, -112, LivgBAA, NotBlAW 92, SmATA 16, -38N*

Ehlert, Lois *ChlBIID*

Ehlert, Lois 1934- *AuBYP 3, BioIn 14, -17, ChlLR 28, SmATA 69*

Ehlert, Lois Jane 1934- *BioIn 8, -12, ConAu 137, IlsCB 1957, -1967, MajAI, SmATA 35*

Ehre, Edward d1990 *NewYTBS 90*

Ehre, Edward 1905- *ConAu 9R, WhoAm 76, -78, -80, -82, -84*

Ehre, Edward 1905-1990 *BioIn 16, -17*

Ehret, Walter 1918- *ASCAP 66*

Ehrhardt, Reinhold 1900- *ConAu 29R*

Ehrlich, Amy 1942- *BioIn 13, -17, ConAu 37R, -14NR, -32NR, SmATA 25, -65,*

TwCYAW, WhoAm 84, –86, –88, –90, –92, –94

Ehrlich, Arnold d1989 *NewYTBS 89*

Ehrlich, Arnold 1923- *ConAu 33R, WhoAm 74, –76, –78, –80*

Ehrlich, Arnold 1923-1989 *BioIn 16, ConAu 129*

Ehrlich, Bettina *TwCChW 89, WrDr 86, –88, –90, –92*

Ehrlich, Bettina 1903- *BioIn 14*

Ehrlich, Bettina Bauer 1903- *AuBYP 2, –3, BioIn 5, –6, –7, –8, –9, –12, ConAu P-1, IlsCB 1946, –1957, MorJA, OxCChiL, SmATA 1, TwCChW 83*
Pseud./variant:
Bettina

Eichenberg, Fritz d1990 *NewYTBS 90*

Eichenberg, Fritz 1901- *AnCL, BioIn 1, –3, –4, –5, –6, –8, –10, –11, –12, –13, –14, –16, ChhPo S2, ConAu 57, –6NR, ConGrA 3, GrAmP, IlsBYP, IlsCB 1744, –1946, –1957, –1967, MorJA, SmATA 9, –50, Str&VC, WhAmArt 85, WhoAm 74, –76, –78, –80, –82, –84, –86, –88, –90, WhoAmA 73, –78, –80, –82, –84, –86, –89, –91, WhoGrA 62, –82*

Eichenberg, Fritz 1901-1990 *BioIn 17, ConAu 133, MajAI, WhAm 10*

Eicher, Elizabeth *ConAu 17R*
Pseud./variant:
Crane, Edna Temple

Eichler, Margrit 1942- *AmMWSc 73S, –78S, BioIn 14, CanWW 89, ConAu 107, IntAu&W 86, –89, SmATA 35, WhoAmW 81*

Eichner, James A 1927- *BioIn 9, ConAu 13R, SmATA 4, WhoAmL 83*

Eicke, Edna *ChhPo, IlsBYP*

Eifert, Virginia Louise 1911-1966 *AuBYP 3*

Eifert, Virginia S 1911-1966 *ArtclWW 2*

Eifert, Virginia Snider 1911-1966 *AmAu&B, AuBYP 2, Au&Wr 71, BioIn 7, –9, ConAu 1R, –15NR, SmATA 2, WhAm 4*

Eige, Lillian 1915- *SmATA 65*

Eiloart, Mrs 1830- *DcEnL*

Eimerl, Sarel 1925- *ConAu 21R, WhoWest 74*

Einsel, Naiad 1927- *BioIn 5, –11, IlrAm 1880, SmATA 10*

Einsel, Walter 1926- *AuBYP 2, BioIn 5, –11, IlrAm 1880, SmATA 10*

Einstein, Charles 1926- *ConAu 65, –29NR, ConSFA, EncSF 93*

Einzig, Susan 1922- *ArtsCL, BioIn 6, –8, –14, –15, IlsCB 1957, SmATA 43, TwCPaSc*

Eipper, Paul 1891- *BioIn 2, JBA 34, –51*

Eiseman, Alberta 1925- *AuBYP 2S, –3, BioIn 12, ConAu 77, SmATA 15*

Eisenberg, Azriel 1903- *AuBYP 2, BioIn 7, –11, ConAu 49, –10NR, LEduc 74, SmATA 12, WhoAmJ 80, WhoWorJ 72, –78*

Eisenberg, Azriel Louis 1903- *AuBYP 3*

Eisenberg, Azriel Louis 1903-1985 *BioIn 14, –15*

Eisenberg, Lisa 1949- *BioIn 16, SmATA 50, –57*

Eisenberg, Phyllis Rose *IntAu&W 86X*

Eisenberg, Phyllis Rose 1924- *BioIn 15, ConAu 111, SmATA 41*

Eisenstat, Jane Sperry 1920- *ConAu 1R*
Pseud./variant:
Sperry, J E

Eisenstein, Judith Kaplan 1909- *ConAmC 76, WhoWorJ 72*

Eisgruber, Elsa *BioIn 1, ChhPo S1, IlsCB 1744*

Eisner, Vivienne
Main entry: Margolis, Vivienne

Eisner, Will 1917- *AmAu&B, BioIn 14, –15, –16, ConAu 108, ConGrA 1, EncACom, SmATA 31, WhoAm 74, –76, –78, –80, –82, –84, –86, –88, –90, –92, –94*
Pseud./variant:
Erwin, Will
Rensie, Willis

Eitzen, Allan 1928- *BioIn 11, IlsBYP, SmATA 9*

Eitzen, Ruth 1924- *BioIn 11, ConAu 41R, SmATA 9*

Eksell, Olle 1918- *BioIn 2, WhoGrA 62, –82*

Ekwensi, C O D *BlkWr 1, ConAu 42NR, MajTwCW, SmATA 66*
Main entry: Ekwensi, Cyprian

Ekwensi, Cyprian 1921- *AfSS 80, –81, –82, AfrA, Au&Wr 71, Benet 87, BioIn 9, –10, –14, –17, BlkLC, BlkWr 1, CamGLE, CasWL, ConAu 29R, –18NR, –42NR, ConLC 4,*

ConNov 72, –76, –82, –86, –91, CyWA 89, DcAfHiB 86, DcChlFi, DcLB 117, DcLEL 1940, EncWL, –2, InB&W 80, IntAu&W 77, –89, –91, IntWW 74, –75, –76, –77, –78, –79, –80, –81, –82, –83, –89, –91, IntvTCA 2, LongCTC, MajTwCW, McGEWB, ModBlW, OxCChiL, PenC CL, RAdv 13-2, RGAfL, RfGEnL 91, SmATA 66, TwCChW 78, –83, –89, TwCWr, WebE&AL, WhoTwCL, WhoWor 78, WorAu 1950, WrDr 76, –80, –82, –84, –86, –88, –90, –92, –94
Pseud./variant:
Ekwensi, C O D

Elam, Richard M 1920- *BioIn 11, ConAu 61, SmATA 9*

Elbert, Virginie Fowler 1912- *AuBYP 2S, –3, ConAu 61, –8NR, –35NR*

Elder, Michael Aiken 1931- *Au&Wr 71, ConAu 33R, IntAu&W 89, –91, WrDr 76, –80, –82, –84, –86, –88, –90, –92, –94*

Eldred, Vince 1924- *ConAu 69*

Eldridge, Mildred E 1909- *BioIn 5, ChhPo, ClaDrA, DcBrAr 1, IlsCB 1946, WhoArt 80, –82, –84*

Eleazar Ben Ya'ir *DcAmChF 1960*

Elegant, Robert Sampson 1928- *AmAu&B, BioIn 4, –7, –11, –12, BlueB 76, ConAu 1R, –1NR, IntAu&W 77, –82, –89, –91, WhoAm 74, –76, –78, –80, –82, –84, –86, –88, –90, –92, –94, WhoWest 74, –76, WhoWor 74, WrDr 76, –80, –82, –84*

Eleska, Elena *AmPB*

Elfman, Blossom 1925- *BioIn 11, ConAu 45, –2NR, –17NR, –39NR, ScF&FL 92, SmATA 8*

Elgin, Kathleen 1923- *BioIn 5, –8, –15, ConAu 25R, IlsBYP, IlsCB 1946, –1957, IntAu&W 77, SmATA 39, WhoAmW 74, –75, –77*

Elia *Benet 87, OxCEng 85, SmATA X*
Main entry: Lamb, Charles

Elias, Horace J 1910- *ConAu 16NR*

Eliot, Anne *ConAu X, SmATA X*
Main entry: Cole, Lois Dwight

Eliot, Dan *MajAI*

Eliot, Frances 1901- *BioIn 1, IlsCB 1744*

Eliot, George *NinCLC 41*
Main entry: Evans, Mary Ann

Eliot, George 1819-1880 *Alli SUP, ArtclWW 2, AtlBL, Benet 87, BbD, BiD&SB, BioIn 1, –2, –3, –4, –5, –6, –7, –8, –9, –10, –11, –12, –13, –14, –15, –16, –17, BlmGEL, BlmGWL, BritAu 19, BritWr 5, CamGEL, CamGLE, CasWL, CelCen, Chambr 3, ChhPo, –S2, CnDBLB 4, ContDcW 89, CrtT 3, CyWA 58, DcBiA, DcBiPP, DcEnA, –A, DcEnL, DcEuL, DcLB 21, –35, –55, DcLEL, Dis&D, EncBrWW, EncPaPR 91, EvLB, FemiCLE, HerW, –84, HsB&A, InWom SUP, IntDcWB, LongCEL, MagSWL, McGEWB, MouLC 3, NewC, NewOxM, NinCLC 4, –13, –23, Novels, OxCEng 67, –85, PenC ENG, RAdv 1, –13-1, RComWL, REn, RfGEnL 91, RfGShF, StaCVF, WebE&AL, WhDW, WorAlBi, WorAl, WorLitC, WrPh*

Eliot, George Fielding 1894-1971 *AmAu&B, BioIn 4, –9, –11, ConAu 29R, CurBio 40, –71, EncAJ, EncTwCJ, NewYTBE 71, REnAL, TwCA, –SUP, WhAm 5*

Eliot, Sonny 1926- *ConAu 81*

Eliot, T S *NewYTBS 88*

Eliot, T S 1888-1965 *AgeMat, AmAu&B, AmWr, AnCL, AtlBL, Benet 87, BenetAL 91, BiE&WWA, BioIn 1, –2, –3, –4, –5, –6, –7, –8, –9, –10, –11, –14, –15, –16, –17, BritWr 7, CamGEL, CamGLE, CamGWoT, CamHAL, CasWL, Chambr 3, ChhPo, –S1, –S2, CnDAL, CnE&AP, CnMD, CnMWL, CnThe, ConAmL, ConAu 5R, –25R, ConLC 1, –2, –3, –6, –9, –10, –13, –15, –24, –41, –57, ConLCrt 77, –82, CroCD, CurBio 62, –65, CyWA 58, –89, DcAmB S7, DcLB 7, –10, –45, –63, DcLEL, EncWL, –2, EvLB, HalFC 84, –88, LiExTwC, LongCTC, MagSAmL, MagSWL, MajMD 1, MajTwCW, McGEWD 72, ModAL, –S1, –S2, ModBrL, –S1, –S2, ModWD, NewC, NewGrDA 86, NobelP, NotNAT A, ObitOF 79, ObitT 1961, OxCAmH, OxCAmL 65, –83, OxCAmT 84, OxCChiL, OxCEng 67, –85, OxCThe 67, –83, PenC AM, –ENG, PlP&P, PoeCrit 5, RAdv 1, –13-1, –13-2, RComWL, REn, REnAL, REnWD, RfGAmL 87, RfGEnL 91, SixAP, ThTwC 87, TwCA, –SUP, TwCWr, WebAB 74, WebE&AL, WhAm 4, WhNAA, WhoChL, WhoTwCL, WorAlBi, WorAl, WorLitC, WrPh*

Eliot, Thomas Stearns 1888-1965 *ConAu 41NR, IntDcT 2*

Eliscu, Frank 1912- *BioIn 1, –11, ConAu 57, WhAmArt 85, WhoAm 74, –76, –78, –80, –82, –84, –92, –94, WhoAmA 73, –78, –80, –82, –84, –86, –89, –91, WhoWorJ 72, –78*

Elish, Dan 1960- *ConAu 136, SmATA 68, WrDr 94*

Elisofan, Eliot 1911-1973 *AmAu&B, BioIn 3, –4, –9, –10, ConAu 41R, CurBio 72,*

NewYTBE 73, SmATA 21N, WhAm 5, WhoAmA 73, –78N

Elkin, Benjamin 1911- *AuBYP 2, –3, Au&Wr 71, BioIn 7, –9, ConAu 1R, –4NR, FourBJA, IntAu&W 77, SmATA 3, WhoMW 74, WhoWorJ 72, –78, WrDr 76, –80, –82, –84, –86, –88, –90, –92, –94*

Elkins, Dov Peretz 1937- *AuBYP 2, –3, BioIn 8, –10, ConAu 29R, –12NR, –30NR, IntAu&W 89, –91, SmATA 5, WhoAmJ 80, WhoMW 92, WhoRel 92, WhoWorJ 78, WrDr 76, –80, –82, –84, –86, –88, –90, –92, –94*

Elkins, Ella Ruth 1929- *ConAu 25R*
Pseud./variant:
Beddoe, Ellaruth
Wren, Ellaruth

Elkon, Juliette
Main entry: Elkon-Hamelecourt, Juliette

Elkon-Hamelecourt, Juliette 1912- *ConAu 57*
Pseud./variant:
Elkon, Juliette

Ellacott, Samuel Ernest 1911- *BioIn 12, ConAu 5R, IntAu&W 82, SmATA 19, WrDr 80*

Elleman, Barbara *MedPD*

Ellen, Barbara 1938- *AuBYP 2, –3, BioIn 8, ConAu 5R*

Ellen, Jaye *ConAu 38NR, MajAI, TwCYAW*

Ellentuck, Shan *AuBYP 2S, –3*

Ellin, E M 1905- *ConAu P-2, OxCChiL, TwCChW 78, –83, –89, WrDr 80, –82, –84, –86*

Elliot, Geraldine *ConAu X*
Main entry: Bingham, Evangeline M L

Elliot, Ian 1925- *ConAu 69*

Elliot, John 1918- *WrDr 80, –82, –84*

Elliott, Don *MajAI*

Elliott, Elizabeth Shippen G *IlsCB 1744, WhAmArt 85, WomWWA 14*
Main entry: Green, Elizabeth Shippen

Elliott, Elizabeth Shippen Green *InWom SUP*

Elliott, Elizabeth Shippen Green 1871-1954 *BioIn 15*

Elliott, Gertrude *ChhPo*

Elliott, Harley *DrAPF 87, –89, –91, –93*

Elliott, Harley 1940- *ConAu 49, –4NR, DrAP 75, DrAPF 83, –85*

Elliott, Janice *BioIn 16*

Elliott, Janice 1931- *BioIn 13, ConAu 13R, –8NR, –29NR, ConLC 47, ConNov 91, DcLB 14, EncSF 93, FemiCLE, IntAu&W 82, –86, –89, –91, ScF&FL 92, WhoWor 78, WrDr 76, –80, –82, –84, –86, –88, –90, –92, –94*

Elliott, John H 1930- *IntAu&W 91*

Elliott, John Huxtable *BioIn 17*

Elliott, John Huxtable 1930- *ConAu 5R, –3NR, DrAS 74H, –78H, –82H, IntAu&W 82, –86, –89, IntWW 81, –82, –83, –91, Who 74, –82, –83, –85, –88, –92, WrDr 76, –80, –82, –84, –86, –88, –90, –92, –94*

Elliott, John Huxtable, Prof 1930- *IntWW 89, Who 90*

Elliott, Lesley 1905- *ConAu 77, –14NR*
Pseud./variant:
Gordon, Lesley

Elliott, Mary 1794?-1870 *Alli, CarSB, ChhPo, –S1, –S2, OxCChiL*

Elliott, Odette 1939- *ConAu 142, SmATA 75*

Elliott, Robert *ConAu X*
Main entry: Garfinkel, Bernard

Elliott, Roberta *ConAu 97, TwCChW 78, WrDr 80, –82, –84*

Elliott, Sarah McCarn 1930- *AuBYP 2S, –3, BioIn 12, ConAu 41R, SmATA 14*

Elliott, William *SmATA X*
Main entry: Bradbury, Ray

Ellis, Anyon *ConAu X, SmATA X*
Main entry: Rowland-Entwistle, Theodore

Ellis, Cuthbert Hamilton 1909- *Au&Wr 71, ConAu 13R*
Pseud./variant:
Ellis, Hamilton

Ellis, Edward S 1840-1916 *Alli SUP, AmAu, AmAu&B, BenetAL 91, BbD, BiD&SB, BioIn 8, –11, –15, CarSB, ConAu 122, DcAmAu, DcLB 42, DcNAA, HsB&A, NewEScF, OhA&B, OxCAmL 65, –83, OxCChiL, REnAL, ScFEYrs, WhAm 1, WhoChL, YABC 1*
Pseud./variant:
Belknap, B H
Bethune, J G
Carleton, Captain L C
Gordon, Colonel H R

Hawthorne, Captain R M
Jayne, Lieutenant R H
Lassalle, C E
Lisle, Seward D
Muller, Billex
Randolph, Lieutenant J H
Robins, Seelin
Rodman, Emerson
Wheeler, Captain

Ellis, Edward Sylvester 1840-1916 *EncSF 93*

Ellis, Ella 1928- *AuBYP 3*

Ellis, Ella T *WrDr 86, –88, –90, –92*

Ellis, Ella Thorp *DrAPF 87, –89, –91, –93*

Ellis, Ella Thorp 1928- *AuBYP 2S, BioIn 10, ConAu 49, –2NR, DrAPF 83, –85, FifBJA, IntAu&W 77, –82, –86, –89, –91, SmATA 7, –9AS, WhoAmW 77, WhoUSWr 88, WhoWrEP 89, –92, WrDr 76, –80, –82, –84, –94*

Ellis, Hamilton *IntAu&W 77*
Main entry: Ellis, Cuthbert Hamilton

Ellis, Harry Bearse 1921- *AmAu&B, AuBYP 2, –3, BioIn 8, –11, BlueB 76, ConAu 1R, –2NR, IntAu&W 77, –82, –89, SmATA 9, WhoAm 74, –76, –78, –80, –82, –84, –86, –88, –90, WhoWor 74, WrDr 76, –80, –82, –84, –86, –88, –90, –92, –94*

Ellis, Herbert *ConAu X, SmATA X*
Main entry: Wilson, Lionel

Ellis, James Hervey 1893-1978 *BioIn 9, –11*

Ellis, L Ethan 1898-1977 *BioIn 11, ConAu 5R, –4NR*

Ellis, Leo R 1909- *ConAu 9R*

Ellis, Mary Jackson 1916- *BioIn 6, ConAu 1R, –17NR, ForWC 70, MinnWr*

Ellis, Mary Leith 1921- *ConAu 21R, WhoAmW 74, WrDr 80, –82, –84*

Ellis, Melvin Richard 1912-1984 *BioIn 10, ConAu 13R, –113, SmATA 7, –39N*

Ellis, R Hobart, Jr. 1918-1972 *AmMWSc 73P, BioIn 9*

Ellis, Sarah *AuBYP 3*

Ellis, Sarah 1952- *ConAu 123, SmATA 68, TwCYAW*

Ellis, Veronica F 1950- *BlkAuII 92*

Ellison, Lucile Watkins d1979 *BioIn 16*

Ellison, Lucile Watkins 1907?-1979 *BioIn 13, ConAu 93, –109, SmATA 22N, –50*

Ellison, Ralph *BioIn 14, –15, –16, –17, DrAPF 87, –89, –91, –93, IntvTCA 2*

Ellison, Ralph 1914- *AfrAmW, AmWr S2, Benet 87, BenetAL 91, BlkLC, BlkWr 1, BlkWrNE, CamGEL, CamGLE, CamHAL, ConAu 24NR, ConLC 54, ConNov 86, –91, CurBio 93, CyWA 89, DcLB 76, EncAACR, FifSWrA, IntWW 89, –91, MagSAmL, MajTwCW, ModAL S2, NegAl 89, RAdv 13-1, RComAH, RfGAmL 87, WhoAm 86, –88, –90, WhoBlA 85, –88, WorAlBi, WorLitC, WrDr 86, –88, –90, –92*

Ellison, Ralph Waldo 1914- *TwCYAW, WrDr 94*

Ellison, Virginia Howell 1910- *AuBYP 2S, –3, BioIn 9, ConAu 33R, IntAu&W 91, SmATA 4, WrDr 76, –80, –82, –84, –86, –88, –90, –92, –94*
Pseud./variant:
Howell, Virginia Tier
Leong Gor Yung
Mapes, Mary A
Mussey, Virginia H
Soskin, V H

Ellsberg, Edward 1891- *AuBYP 3*

Ellsberg, Edward 1891-1983 *AmAu&B, AmNov, AuBYP 2, Au&Wr 71, BioIn 2, –3, –4, –6, –7, –8, –10, –13, –17, ConAu 5R, CurBio 42, –91N, JBA 34, –51, NewYTBS 83, REnAL, SmATA 7, TwCA, –SUP, WebAMB, WhAm 8, WhoAm 74, –76, –78, –80, –82*

Elman, Robert 1930- *ConAu 45, –3NR, WhoE 77, –85, –86, –89, –91, –93*

Elmer, Irene 1937- *AuBYP 2, –3, BioIn 8, ConAu 1R*

Elmore, Patricia *DrAPF 87, –89, –91, –93*

Elmore, Patricia 1933- *BioIn 14, –15, ConAu 114, DrAPF 83, –85, SmATA 35, –38*

Elrod, Jack *ArtCS*

Elsasser, Albert B 1918- *ConAu 22NR, WhoWrEP 89*

Elsasser, Albert Bertrand 1918- *AmMWSc 73S, –76P, ConAu 69, FifIDA, WhoWest 76, –78, –80, WhoWrEP 92*

Elson, William Harris 1856-1935 *DcNAA, WhAm 1*

Elspeth *ConAu X, SmATA 6*
Main entry: Bragdon, Elspeth MacDuffie

Elspeth, Davie 1919- *DcLB 139*

Elston, Allan Vaughan 1887-1976? *AmAu&B, Au&Wr 71, ConAu 1R, -3NR, EncFWF, IntAu&W 77, TwCWW 91, WrDr 76*

Elting, Mary 1906- *AuBYP 2, -3, BioIn 6, -8, -9, ConAu 9R, -4NR, -19NR, ForWC 70, MorJA, SmATA 2*
Pseud./variant:
Brewster, Benjamin
Cole, Davis
Gorham, Michael
Tatham, Campbell

Elwart, Joan Potter 1927- *BioIn 9, ConAu 25R, MichAu 80, SmATA 2*

Elwell, Felicia Rosemary *AuBYP 3*

Elwell, Felicia Rosemary 1912- *AuBYP 2, Au&Wr 71, BioIn 8*

Elwood, Ann 1931- *BioIn 16, ConAu 125, SmATA 52, -55, WrDr 90, -92, -94*

Elwood, Roger 1933- *EncSF 93, ScFEYrs*

Elwood, Roger 1943- *AuBYP 2S, -3, BioIn 16, ConAu 57, -10NR, ConSFA, ScF&FL 92, SmATA 58, WhoSciF*

Ely, George Herbert d1958 *BioIn 8, ObitT 1951*
Pseud./variant:
Strang, Herbert

Emberley, Barbara A 1932- *BioIn 9, -11, BkP, ChhPo, -S1, ChlLR 5, ConAu 5R, -5NR, SmATA 8, ThrBJA*

Emberley, Barbara Anne 1932- *MajAI, SmATA 70*

Emberley, Ed *BioIn 14*

Emberley, Ed 1931- *AuBYP 2, Au&ICB, BioIn 7, -8, -9, -11, -12, BkP, ChhPo, -S1, ChlLR 5, ConAu 5R, -5NR, -36NR, IlsBYP, IlsCB 1957, -1967, NewbC 1966, SmATA 8, ThrBJA*

Emberley, Edward Randolph 1931- *AuBYP 3, MajAI, SmATA 70*

Emberley, Michael 1960- *BioIn 14, ConAu 104, SmATA 34*

Embry, Margaret Jacob 1919-1975 *AuBYP 2S, -3, BioIn 10, ConAu 1R, -3NR, ForWC 70, SmATA 5*

Emecheta, Buchi *BioIn 14, -15, -16, -17*

Emecheta, Buchi 1941?- *InWom SUP*

Emecheta, Buchi 1944- *ArtclWW 2, BlkAuII, -92, BlkLC, BlkWr 1, CamGLE, ConAu 27NR, ConLC 48, ConNov 86, -91, ContDcW 89, FemiCLE, IntAu&W 89, -91, IntLitE, IntvWPC, LiExTwC, MajTwCW, RAdv 13-2, ScF&FL 92, SmATA 66, TwCChW 89, Who 88, -90, -92, WrDr 86, -88, -90, -92*

Emecheta, Buchi 1945- *BlmGWL*

Emerson, Alice B *AmAu&B, CarSB, ConAu 134, -P-2, MajAI, SmATA 1, -65, -67, WrDr 94*
Main entry: Benson, Mildred Augustine Wirt
Stratemeyer, Edward L

Emerson, Caroline Dwight 1891-1973 *AuBYP 2, -3, BioIn 7, ChhPo, ConAu 45, -P-1*

Emerson, Kathy Lynn *BioIn 17*

Emerson, Kathy Lynn 1947- *ConAu 127, SmATA 63, WhoUSWr 88, WhoWrEP 89, -92*
Pseud./variant:
Gorton, Kaitlyn

Emerson, Ralph Waldo 1803-1882 *Alli, -SUP, AmAu, AmAu&B, AmPeW, AmWr, AnCL, AtlBL, Benet 87, BenetAL 91, BbD, BiD&SB, BioIn 1, -2, -3, -4, -5, -6, -7, -8, -9, -10, -11, -12, -13, -14, -15, -16, -17, CamGEL, CamGLE, CamHAL, CasWL, CelCen, Chambr 3, ChhPo, -S1, CnDAL, CnE&AP, CrtT 3, CyAL, CyEd, CyWA 58, DcAmAu, DcAmReB 2, DcAmSR, DcBiPP, DcEnA, -A, DcEnL, DcLB 1, -59, -73, DcLEL, DcNAA, Dis&D, EncAB-H, EvLB, HarEnUS, LuthC 75, MagSAmL, McGEWB, MemAm, MouLC 4, NewGrDA 86, NinCLC 1, -38, OxCAmH, OxCAmL 65, -83, OxCEng 67, -85, PenC AM, RAdv 1, -13-1, RComAH, RComWL, REn, REnAL, RfGAmL 87, Str&VC, WebAB 74, -79, WebE&AL, WhDW, WhAm HS, WorAlBi, WorAl, WorLitC, WrPh*

Emerson, Ru 1944- *SmATA 70*

Emerson, Sybil 1895- *BioIn 1, IlsCB 1744, WhAmArt 85*

Emerson, William Keith 1925- *AmMWSc 73P, -76P, -82, -86, -89, -92, BioIn 13, ConAu 41R, SmATA 25, WhoAm 74, -76, -78, -80, -82, -84, -86, -88, -90, -92, WhoE 74, -93, WhoWor 74*

Emerson, Zack *TwCYAW*

Emery, Anne 1907- *AuBYP 2, BioIn 2, -3, -6, -7, -9, ConAu 1R, -2NR, CurBio 52, ForWC 70, MorJA, SmATA 1, -33*

Emery, Anne Eleanor McGuigan 1907- *AuBYP 3*

Emery, Russell Guy 1908- *AuBYP 2, –3, BioIn 7*

Emett, Rowland d1990 *Who 92N*

Emett, Rowland 1906- *BioIn 1, –3, –5, –7, –9, –11, –14, ConAu 102, IlsCB 1946, Who 74, –82, –83, –85, –88, –90, WhoArt 80, –82, –84, WhoGrA 62, –82, WorECar*

Emett, Rowland 1906-1990 *AnObit 1990, ConAu 133*

Emmens, Carol Ann 1944- *ConAu 106, SmATA 39*

Emmet, Eric Revell 1906- *Au&Wr 71, IntAu&W 77, –82, WhoWor 78, WrDr 76*

Emmett, Bruce 1949- *ConAu 57, ConGrA 1*

Emmett Brothers *OxCChiL*
Pseud./variant:
Brent, Charlton
Brent, Ernest
Lawrence, W E

Emmons, Della Gould 1890-1983 *BioIn 6, –15, ConAu 111, IntAu&W 77, MinnWr, SmATA 39N, WhoAmW 74, –75, WhoPNW*

Emrich, Duncan 1908-197-? *AuBYP 2SA, –3, BioIn 3, –4, –11, ChhPo S1, –S2, ConAu 61, –9NR, CurBio 55, SmATA 11, WhoAm 74*
Pseud./variant:
Macdonald, Blackie

Emrick, Harry Dale 1932- *WhoMW 74, –76*

Emslie, M L *ConAu X, SmATA X*
Main entry: Simpson, Myrtle Lillias

Endacott, Marie Violet 1915- *ConAu 9R*

Ende, Jean 1947- *ConAu 53*

Ende, Michael *BioIn 14, –15, –17*

Ende, Michael 1929- *ChlLR 14, ConAu 36NR, DcLB 75, ScF&FL 92, SmATA 61, WorAu 1980*

Ende, Michael 1930?- *BioIn 12, ConAu 118, –124, ConLC 31, OxCChiL, SmATA 42, TwCSFW 91A*

Ende, Michael Andreas Helmuth 1929- *MajAI*

Enderle, Judith 1941- *BioIn 15, ConAu 106, ScF&FL 92, SmATA 38*

Enderle, Judith Ross 1941- *WhoWrEP 89*

Enfield, Carrie
Main entry: Smith, Susan Vernon

Engdahl, Sylvia 1933- *ScFSB, TwCChW 89, TwCSFW 86, –91*

Engdahl, Sylvia L 1933- *WrDr 86, –88, –90, –92*

Engdahl, Sylvia Louise 1933- *AuBYP 2S, –3, BioIn 9, –14, –16, ChlLR 2, ConAu 29R, –14NR, DcAmChF 1960, EncSF 93, FourBJA, IntAu&W 77, MajAI, ScF&FL 92, SmATA 4, –5AS, TwCChW 78, –83, TwCYAW, WrDr 76, –80, –82, –84, –94*

Engebrecht, P A *DrAPF 87, –89, –91, –93*

Engebrecht, P A 1935- *ConAu 57*

Engel, Barbara Alpern 1943- *DrAS 78H, –82H*

Engel, Diana 1947- *SmATA 70*

Engel, Leonard 1916-1964 *AmAu&B, BioIn 7, EncSF 93*

Engel, Marian *InWom SUP, IntvTCA 2*

Engel, Marian 1933- *ArtclWW 2*

Engel, Marian 1933-1985 *BioIn 13, –15, BlmGWL, CamGLE, CaW, CanWW 70, –79, –80, –81, –83, ConAu 25R, –12NR, ConLC 36, ConNov 76, –82, DcLB 53, FemiCLE, OxCCan SUP, OxCCanL, Profile 2, WhAm 8, WhoAm 80, –82, –84, WhoCanL 85, –87, –92, WorAu 1975, WrDr 76, –80, –82, –84*

Engelhardt, Mary Veronice 1912- *WhoAmW 89, –91, WhoSSW 86*

Engelhardt, Mary Veronice, Sister 1912- *WhoAmW 75, –77, –83, WhoE 83, WrDr 76, –80*

Engelhart, Margaret S 1924- *ConAu 122, SmATA 59*

Engeman, John T 1901- *AuBYP 2, –3, BioIn 8*

England, George Allan 1877-1936 *AmAu&B, ChhPo, ConAu 112, DcNAA, EncSF 93, OxCCan, ScFSB, ScFEYrs, TwCSFW 85, –91, WhAm 1, WhNAA, WhoSciF*

England, George Allan 1877-1937 *NewEScF*

Engle, Eloise *IntAu&W 86X*

Engle, Eloise 1923- *BioIn 11, ConAu 1R, –2NR, ForWC 70, IntAu&W 77, –82X, SmATA 9, WhoAmW 81, WrDr 76, –82, –84, –86, –88, –90, –92, –94*

Englebardt, Stanley L 1925- *IntAu&W 82*

Englebert, Victor 1933- *BioIn 11, ConAu 57, SmATA 8*

Englefield, Cicely 1893- *BioIn 1, IlsCB 1744*

Engler, Larry 1949- *ConAu 53, WhoE 77*

English, James W 1915- *ConAu 21R, SmATA 37*

Engstrom, Ted Wilhelm 1916- *ConAu 65, –X*

Engvick, William *AuBYP 2, –3, BioIn 8, ChhPo*

Enos, Randall 1936- *BioIn 15, ConGrA 1, IlrAm 1880, WhoAm 86, –88, –90, –92, –94, WhoGrA 82*

Enright, D J 1920- *BioIn 14, –17, BlmGEL, BlueB 76, CamGLE, ConAu 1NR, ConLC 31, ConLCrt 82, ConPo 80, –85, –91, DcLB 27, EncWL 2, IntWWP 82, LiExTwC, ModBrL S2, Novels, OxCEng 85, SmATA 25, WrDr 82, –84, –86, –88, –90, –92*

Enright, Dennis Joseph 1920- *ConAu 42NR*

Enright, Elizabeth 1909-1968 *AmAu&B, AnCL, AuBYP 2, –3, BioIn 1, –2, –4, –5, –7, –8, –11, –14, BkCL, ChlLR 4, ConAu 25R, –61, CurBio 47, –68, DcAmChF 1960, DcLB 22, FamMS, IlsCB 1744, –1946, JBA 51, MajAI, NewbMB 1922, OxCChiL, SmATA 9, TwCChW 78, –83, –89, WhAm 5, WrChl*

Enright, Maginel Wright
Main entry: Barney, Maginel Wright

Enright, Maginel Wright 1881-1966 *IlrAm 1880, SmATA X, WhAmArt 85*

Ensign, Grayson Harter 1921- *WhoRel 75, –77*

Enys, Sarah L *SmATA X*
Main entry: Sloggett, Nellie

Ephron, Delia *BioIn 15, –16, –17*

Ephron, Delia 1944?- *ArtclWW 2, SmATA 50, –65, WrDr 90, –92, –94*
Pseud./variant:
Brock, Delia

Epler, Doris M 1928- *SmATA 73*

Epp, Margaret Agnes 1913- *BioIn 12, ConAu 9R, –3NR, IntAu&W 77, –89, –91, SmATA 20, WhoAmW 74, –75, WhoWest 74, –76, –78, WrDr 76, –80, –82, –84, –86, –88, –90, –92, –94*
Pseud./variant:
Goossen, Agnes

Eppenstein, Louise 1892-1987 *BioIn 16, ConAu 123, SmATA 54N*

Epple, Anne Orth 1927- *ConAu 33R, SmATA 20, WhoAmW 77, WrDr 76, –80, –82, –84, –86, –88, –90, –92, –94*

Epstein, Anne Merrick 1931- *SmATA 20*

Epstein, Beryl 1910- *ArtclWW 2, ChlLR 26, SmATA 17AS*

Epstein, Beryl M Williams 1910- *AuBYP 3, ConAu 39NR*

Epstein, Beryl Williams 1910- *AuBYP 2, BioIn 6, –7, –9, –13, –14, ConAu 5R, –2NR, –18NR, MorJA, OhA&B, SmATA 1, –31*
Pseud./variant:
Allen, Adam
Coe, Douglas
Williams, Beryl

Epstein, Connie C *BioIn 5*

Epstein, Edward Jay 1935- *BioIn 8, –11, ConAu 17R, –13NR, WhoWorJ 72, –78*

Epstein, June Sadie 1918- *ConAu 73, WhoWor 80, WrDr 76, –80*

Epstein, Morris 1921-1973 *BioIn 10, ConAu 45, –P-1, NewYTBE 73, WhoWorJ 72*

Epstein, Perle 1938- *AuBYP 3*

Epstein, Perle S 1938- *AuBYP 2S, ConAu 65, –9NR, SmATA 27*

Epstein, Sam 1909- *BioIn 14, ChlLR 26*

Epstein, Samuel 1909- *AuBYP 2, –3, BioIn 6, –7, –9, –13, ConAu 9R, –4NR, –18NR, –39NR, MorJA, SmATA 1, –31, –17AS, WhoWorJ 72, –78*
Pseud./variant:
Allen, Adam
Campbell, Bruce
Coe, Douglas
Colt, Martin
Strong, Charles

Erdman, Loula Grace d1976 *AuBYP 3, TwCWW 91*

Erdman, Loula Grace 1898-1976 *BioIn 15*

Erdman, Loula Grace 1905?-1976 *AmAu&B, AmNov, AuBYP 2, BioIn 2, –6, –7, –9, ConAu 5R, –10NR, DrAS 74E, EncFWF, ForWC 70, MorJA, SmATA 1, TexWr*

Erdoes, Richard 1912- *BioIn 1, –3, –8, –13, ConAu 77, IlsBYP, IlsCB 1957, SmATA 28, –33*

Erhard, Walter 1920- *BioIn 8, IlsCB 1957, SmATA 30*

Erickson, Charlotte Joan Rudolph *WhoAmW 75, –77*

Erickson, John R 1943- *SmATA 70*

Erickson, Phoebe *SmATA 59*

Erickson, Phoebe 1907- *AuBYP 2, –3, BioIn 5, –7, ConAu 1R, –3NR, IlsCB 1946*

Erickson, Russell E 1932- *AuBYP 2S, –3, BioIn 13, ConAu 93, SmATA 27*

Erickson, Sabra R 1912- *BioIn 14*

Erickson, Sabra Rollins 1912- *ConAu 5R, –5NR, SmATA 35, WhoAmW 77*
Pseud./variant:
Holbrook, Sabra

Ericson, Dick 1916- *WhoAmA 73, –78, –80*

Ericson, Walter *AuBYP 2, –3, ConAu X, –33NR, SmATA 7, TwCA SUP, TwCCr&M 85, –91*
Main entry: Fast, Howard

Erikson, Mel 1937- *IlsBYP, SmATA 31*

Erlanger, Baba *ConAu X, SmATA X*
Main entry: Trahey, Jane

Erlanger, Ellen 1950- *BioIn 16, ConAu 32NR, ScF&FL 92, SmATA 52*

Erlanger, Ellen Louise 1950- *ConAu 85, WhoAmW 81*

Erlich, Lillian 1910- *AuBYP 2, –3, BioIn 7, –11, ConAu 1R, –5NR, ForWC 70, SmATA 10*

Ernest, Brother 1897- *AuBYP 2, BioIn 1, –7, BkC 3, CathA 1930*

Ernest, CSC *AuBYP 3*

Ernest, William *ConAu X, SmATA X*
Main entry: Berkebile, Fred D

Ernst, Barbara 1945- *ConAu 65*

Ernst, John 1940- *ConAu 45, SmATA 39*
Pseud./variant:
Chernoff, Dorothy A
Clark, David Allen

Ernst, Kathryn 1942- *BioIn 13, ConAu 61, –12NR, SmATA 25, WhoAmW 75*

Ernst, Kathryn Fitzgerald 1942- *WhoAmW 87, WhoE 91, –93*

Ernst, Ken 1918-1985 *ArtCS, BioIn 8, –15, ConGrA 1, EncACom*

Ernst, Lisa Campbell 1957- *BioIn 15, –16, ConAu 114, SmATA 44, –55*

Errym, Malcolm J *HsB&A*

Errym, Malcolm J 1804-1882? *StaCVF*

Ervin, Janet Halliday 1923- *BioIn 9, ConAu 29R, ForWC 70, SmATA 4, WhoAmW 74, –75*

Erwin, Betty K *AuBYP 2S, –3, DcAmChF 1960*

Erwin, Will *ConAu X, ConGrA 1, SmATA X*
Main entry: Eisner, Will

Esbensen, Barbara J 1925- *SmATA 62*

Esbensen, Barbara Juster *BioIn 16, –17, DrAPF 83, –85, –87, –89, –91, –93, SmATA 53*

Esbensen, Barbara Juster 1925- *ConAu 134, WhoUSWr 88, WhoWrEP 89, –92, WrDr 94*

Eshelman, William Robert 1921- *BiDrLUS 70, BioIn 5, –8, DrLC 69, JrnUS, MedPD, WhoAm 74, –76, –78, –80, –82, –84, –88, –90, –92, –94, WhoE 74, WhoLibI 82, WhoLibS 55, –66, WhoWor 78*

Esherick, Joseph 1914- *AuBYP 2S, BioIn 13, –16, CmCal, MacEA, WhoAm 86, –90, –92, –94, WhoWest 89*

Esherick, Joseph W 1942- *AuBYP 3*

Eshmeyer, R E 1898- *BioIn 13, ConAu X SmATA 29*

Eshugbayi, Ezekiel Aderogba *AuBYP 2S, –3*

Eskenazi, Gerald 1936- *ConAu 61, –7NR, WhoAmJ 80*

Espeland, Pamela 1951- *BioIn 15, –16, ConAu 107, SmATA 38, –52, WrDr 90, –92*

Espeland, Pamela Lee 1951- *WrDr 94*

Espenshade, Edward Bowman 1910- *AuBYP 3*

Espenshade, Edward Bowman, Jr. 1910- *AmMWSc 73S, –82, –86, –89, –92, AuBYP 2S, BioIn 12, BlueB 76, ConAu 1R, MarqDCG 84, WhoAm 80, –82, –84, –86, –88, –90, –92, –94*

Espriella, Don Manuel Alvarez
Main entry: Southey, Robert

Espy, Willard R 1910- *BioIn 2, –11, ConAu 2NR, SmATA 38, WhoAm 80, –82, –84, –86, –88, WhoUSWr 88, WhoWor 80, –82, WhoWrEP 89, –92*

Espy, Willard Richard 1910- *WhoAm 90*

Espy, Willard Richardson 1910- *WhoAm 92, -94*

Essex, Rosamund Sibyl 1900- *Au&Wr 71, Who 74, -82, -83, -85*

Essrig, Harry 1912- *BioIn 17, ConAu 108, SmATA 66, WhoWorJ 72, -78*

Estep, Irene Compton *BioIn 10, ConAu 1R, SmATA 5*

Esterer, Arnulf K 1905- *AmMWSc 73P*

Esterl, Arnica 1933- *SmATA 77*

Estes, Eleanor d1988 *NewYTBS 88*

Estes, Eleanor 1906- *AmAu&B, AmNov, AnCL, AuBYP 2, -3, BioIn 1, -2, -4, -5, -7, -9, -10, -14, BkCL, ChlLR 2, ConAu 1R, -5NR, -20NR, CurBio 46, DcAmChF 1960, DcLB 22, IlsCB 1946, InWom SUP, JBA 51, MorBMP, NewbMB 1922, OxCChiL, REnAL, SenS, SmATA 4, -7, Str&VC, TwCChW 78, -83, WhoAm 74, -76, -78, -80, -82, -84, -86, -88, WhoAmW 74, -81, -83, -87, WrDr 80, -82, -84, -86, -88*

Estes, Eleanor 1906-1988 *BenetAL 91, BioIn 16, ConAu 126, CurBio 88N, ScF&FL 92, SmATA 56N, TwCChW 89, WhAm 9*

Estes, Eleanor Ruth 1906-1988 *MajAI*

Estes, Glenn *MedPD*

Estes, Sally C 1934- *MedPD, WhoLibS 66*

Estoril, Jean *AuBYP 2, -3, ConAu X, IntAu&W 77X, -82X, -91X, MajAI, OxCChiL, SmATA 5, -75, -X, TwCChW 83, -89, WrDr 76, -80, -82, -84, -86, -88, -90, -92*
Main entry: Allan, Mabel Esther

Estoril, Jean 1915- *WrDr 94*

Estrada, Doris 1923- *ConAu 17R, WhoAmW 77, WrDr 80, -82, -84, -86, -88*

Estrada, Pau 1961- *SmATA 74*

Etchemendy, Nancy 1952- *BioIn 15, ConAu 106, ScF&FL 92, SmATA 38*

Etchemendy, Nancy Elise Howell 1952- *WhoWest 94*

Etchemendy, Nancy Howell 1952- *IntAu&W 91*

Etchison, Birdie L 1937- *BioIn 15, ConAu 106, SmATA 38*
Pseud./variant:
Hunter, Leigh
Wood, Catherine

Etherington, Frank 1945- *BioIn 16, SmATA 58, WhoCanL 87, -92*

Etherton, P T 1879- *WhoLA*

Eton, Robert *ConAu 128, SmATA X, Who 88, WrDr 86, -88*
Main entry: Meynell, Laurence Walter

Ets, Marie Hall *DcAmImH*

Ets, Marie Hall 1893?- *AmPB, AnCL, AuBYP 2, -3, Au&ICB, Au&Wr 71, BioIn 1, -2, -5, -7, -8, -9, -10, -14, BkP, ChhPo, ConAu 1R, -4NR, DcLB 22, FamAIYP, ForWC 70, IlsBYP, IlsCB 1744, -1946, -1957, -1967, JBA 51, NewbC 1956, OxCChiL, SmATA 2, Str&VC, TwCChW 78, -83, -89, WhAm 8, WhAmArt 85, WhoAm 74, -76, -78, -80, -82, WhoAmA 73, -78, -80, -82, -84, WhoAmW 74, WrDr 76, -80, -82, -84, -86, -88, -90*

Ets, Marie Hall 1893-1984 *MajAI*

Ets, Marie Hall 1895- *InWom SUP*

Etter, Les 1904- *ConAu 25R*

Eubank, Nancy 1934- *ConAu 41R*

Eula, Joe *BioIn 11*

Euller, John E 1926- *ConAu 9R*

Eunson, Dale 1904- *AmAu&B, AmNov, BiE&WWA, BioIn 2, -10, ConAu 41R, IntAu&W 82, NotNAT, SmATA 5*

Eunson, Roby *AuBYP 2S, -3*

Eustis, Helen *BioIn 14*

Eustis, Helen 1916- *BioIn 3, -4, CrtSuMy, CurBio 55, EncMys, OhA&B, TwCCr&M 80, -85, -91, WrDr 82, -84, -86, -88, -90, -92*

Eustis, Helen White 1916- *WrDr 94*

Evanoff, Vlad 1916- *BioIn 16, ConAu 5R, -6NR, IntAu&W 77, SmATA 59, WrDr 76, -80, -82, -84, -86, -88, -90, -92, -94*

Evans, Anthony 1922- *Au&Wr 71*

Evans, C S *CarSB*

Evans, Constance May 1890- *ConAu 9R, IntAu&W 77, -82, WrDr 76, -80, -82*

Evans, E Estyn 1905- *ConAu 5R, -5NR, WrDr 80, -82, -84, -86, -88, -90*

Evans, E Estyn 1905-1989 *BioIn 17, ConAu 129*

Evans, Edmund 1826-1905 *BioIn 1, -8, CarSB, ChhPo, -S1, -S2, DcNaB S2, OxCChiL*

Evans, Edna 1913- *AuBYP 3*

Evans, Edna Hoffman 1913- *AuBYP 2, BioIn 7, ForWC 70*

Evans, Ernestine 1889-1967 *AmPB, BioIn 8, WhAm 4*

Evans, Eva 1905- *AuBYP 3*

Evans, Eva Knox 1905- *AuBYP 2, BioIn 6, -7, ConAu 73, MorJA, SmATA 27*

Evans, Evan *ConAu X*

Evans, Evan 1795-1855 *OxCLiW 86*

Evans, Evan 1925- *WhoTech 84, WhoWor 87, -89*

Evans, Greg 1947- *SmATA 73*

Evans, Gwyn 1899-1938 *ScF&FL 92*

Evans, Henry 1918- *BioIn 11, WhoAmA 73, -78, -80, -82, -84, -86, -89, -91*

Evans, Hubert 1892- *BioIn 12, -13, CaW, ConAu 103, OxCCan, OxCCanL, Profile 2, TwCChW 78, -83, WhoCanL 85, WrDr 80, -82, -84, -86*

Evans, Hubert 1892-1986 *BioIn 15, -16, -17, DcLB 92, TwCChW 89, WhoCanL 87, -92*

Evans, Hubert Reginald 1892-1986 *ConAu 119, SmATA 48N*

Evans, Idrisyn Oliver 1894- *ConAu 13R, ConSFA, EngPo, WhoSciF, WrDr 80, -82, -84*

Evans, Jay 1925- *ConAu 61*

Evans, Julia *AuBYP 3*

Evans, Julia 1913- *AuBYP 2, Au&Wr 71, ConAu 13R, IntAu&W 77, -82, -91, WrDr 76, -80, -82, -84, -86, -88, -90*
Pseud./variant:
Hobson, Polly

Evans, Katherine 1901-1964 *AuBYP 3*

Evans, Katherine Floyd 1901-1964 *AuBYP 2, BioIn 7, -8, -10, ConAu 5R, IlsCB 1957, SmATA 5*

Evans, Mari *AuBYP 3, BlkWWr, DrAPF 87, -89, -91, -93, NegAl 89, WhoAm 86, -88, -90, WhoBlA 85, -88, -92, WhoE 86, -89, WhoUSWr 88, WhoWrEP 89, -92, WrDr 86, -88, -90, -92*

Evans, Mari 1923- *AfrAmAl 6, AuBYP 2S, BioIn 10, -11, -16, BlkAWP, BlkWWr, BlkWr 1, BroadAu, ConAu 49, -2NR, -27NR, ConPo 75, -80, -85, -91, CroCAP, DcLB 41, DrAP 75, DrAPF 83, -85, FemiCLE, InWom SUP, LivgBAA, NegAl 76, -83, NotBlAW 92, SelBAAf, SelBAAu, SmATA 10, WhoAm 76, -78, -80, -82, -84, WhoBlA 75, -77, -80, -85, -90, WhoE 85, WrDr 76, -80, -82, -84*

Evans, Mari 1926- *BlkAuII, -92*

Evans, Mark *BioIn 12, ConAu 65, IntWWM 85, -90, SmATA 19, WhoAmM 83, WhoWest 80, WomWMM*

Evans, Mary Ann 1819-1880 *BiD&SB, BritAu 19, CarSB, DcLEL, EvLB, IntDcWB, NewC, OxCEng 67, -85, PenC ENG, RAdv 13-1, REn, WhDW*
Pseud./variant:
Eliot, George

Evans, Max 1925- *Au&Wr 71, ConAu 1R, -1NR, EncFWF, TwCWW 91, WrDr 84, -86, -88, -90*

Evans, Nancy 1950- *ConAu 34NR, SmATA 65, WhoAm 90, -92*

Evans, Patricia Healy *AuBYP 2, BioIn 8, ConAu X, SmATA X*
Main entry: Carpenter, Patricia

Evans, Patricia Healy 1920- *AuBYP 3*

Evans, Pauline Rush *AuBYP 2S, -3*

Evans, Shirlee 1931- *ConAu 61, SmATA 58*

Evansen, Virginia B *WrDr 86, -88, -90, -92*

Evansen, Virginia Besaw *WrDr 94*

Evansen, Virginia Besaw 1921- *ConAu 13R, WrDr 76, -80, -82, -84*

Evarts, Esther *SmATA X*
Main entry: Benson, Sally

Evarts, Hal G 1887-1934 *EncFWF*

Evarts, Hal G 1915- *AuBYP 3, DcAmChF 1960, WrDr 86, -88, -90*

Evarts, Hal G 1915-1989 *TwCWW 91*

Evarts, Hal G, Jr. 1915- *ScF&FL 92*

Evarts, Hal George, Jr. 1915- *AuBYP 2S, BioIn 10, ConAu 49, -2NR, EncFWF,*

SmATA 6, WhoWest 78, –80, –82, –84, –87, WrDr 84

Evatt, Harriet 1895- *BioIn 5, CurBio 59, ForWC 70, OhA&B, WhAmArt 85*

E V B *SmATA X*
Main entry: Boyle, Eleanor Vere

Evens, George Bramwell 1884-1943 *BioIn 8, WhoChL*
Pseud./variant:
Romany

Everett, Gail *AuBYP 3*
Main entry: Hale, Arlene

Everett, Michael *ChhPo S2*

Everett, Percy W 1870-1952 *BioIn 2, ObitOF 79*

Everett-Green, Evelyn *WomNov*

Everett-Green, Evelyn 1856-1932 *BioIn 8, CarSB, ConAu 114, FemiCLE, OxCChiL, TelT, TwCChW 78, –83A, –89A, WhoChL*
Pseud./variant:
Adair, Cecil
Green, Evelyn Everett
Ward, Evelyn

Everly, Jeannette 1908- *AuBYP 3*

Evernden, Margery 1916- *BioIn 10, ConAu 5R, ForWC 70, IntAu&W 77, SmATA 5, WrDr 76, –80, –82, –84, –86, –88, –90, –92*

Evernden, Margery Elizabeth 1916- *WhoWrEP 92*

Evernden, Margery Gulbransen 1916- *WrDr 94*

Evers, Alf 1905- *AuBYP 2, –3*

Evers, Helen *AuBYP 3*

Evers, Leonard Herbert 1926- *DcChlFi*

Eversley, David Edward Charles 1921- *Au&Wr 71, ConAu 1R, Who 74, –82, –83, –85, –88, –90, –92, WhoWor 87*
Pseud./variant:
Small, William

Eversole, Robyn Harbert 1971- *SmATA 74*

Everson, Dale Millar 1928- *ConAu 17R*

Everson, William K 1929- *IntMPA 86, –88, –92, ScF&FL 92*

Everson, William Keith 1929- *AuBYP 2, –3, BioIn 8, –10, ConAu 1R, –2NR, IntMPA 75, –76, –78, –81, –82, –84, –86, –77, WhoAm 74, –76*

Every, Philip Cochrane *AuBYP 3, WhoCanL 87, –92*

Evslin, Bernard d1993 *NewYTBS 93*

Evslin, Bernard 1922- *AuBYP 2S, –3, BioIn 13, –15, ConAu 21R, –9NR, ScF&FL 92, SmATA 28, –45*

Evslin, Bernard 1922-1993 *ConAu 142, SmATA 77*

Ewart, Claire 1958- *SmATA 76*

Ewart, William Dunlop 1923- *Au&Wr 71*

Ewen, David 1907- *AmAu&B, AuBYP 2, Au&Wr 71, Baker 84, BiE&WWA, BioIn 8, –9, –10, ConAu 1R, –2NR, IntAu&W 77, OxCAmT 84, REnAL, SmATA 4, WhoAm 74, –76, –78, –80, –82, –84, WhoMus 72, WhoSSW 73, WhoWor 74, WhoWorJ 72, –78, WrDr 76, –80, –82, –84, –86*

Ewen, David 1907-1985 *AuBYP 3, Baker 92, BioIn 14, –16, ConAu 118, NewGrDA 86, SmATA 47N, WhAm 9*

Ewen, Robert B 1940- *AmMWSc 73S, ConAu 37R, –15NR, WhoSSW 82, –93*

Ewers, John C 1909- *ConAu 22NR*

Ewers, John Canfield *BioIn 15*

Ewers, John Canfield 1909- *AmMWSc 73S, –76P, ConAu 17R, –7NR, FifIDA, IntAu&W 82, OxCCan, –SUP, WhoAm 74, –76, –78, –80, –82, –84, –86, –88, –90, –92, –94, WhoGov 77, –72, –75, WhoSSW 73, –75, –76, WhoWor 74, –78, –93*

Ewers, John Keith 1904- *BioIn 6, IntAu&W 77, SingR 1*

Ewing, Juliana Horatia 1841-1885 *BioIn 14, –16, –17, BlmGWL, CamGEL, EncBrWW, TwCChW 89A, WomNov, WrChl*

Ewing, Juliana Horatia, Mrs 1841-1885 *StaCVF*

Ewing, Juliana Horatia Gatty 1841-1885 *Alli SUP, BbD, BiD&SB, BioIn 2, –3, –7, –8, –12, BritAu 19, CarSB, CasWL, CelCen, ChhPo, –S1, –S2, DcLB 21, DcLEL, DcNaB, EvLB, FamSYP, JBA 34, NewC, OxCChiL, OxCEng 67, SmATA 16, Str&VC, TelT, TwCChW 78A, –83A, WhoChL*
Pseud./variant:
Gatty, Juliana Horatia

Ewing, Juliana Horatia Orr Gatty 1841-1885 *InWom SUP*

Ewing, Kathryn 1921- *AuBYP 2S, –3, BioIn 12, ConAu 61, –7NR, SmATA 20*

Pseud./variant:
Douglas, Kathryn

E-Yeh-Shure *AmPB*
Main entry: Abeita, Louise

Eyerly, Jeannette Hyde 1908- *AmCath 80, AuBYP 2S, BioIn 9, ConAu 1R, -4NR, -19NR, DcAmChF 1960, FifBJA, ForWC 70, SmATA 4, -10AS, TwCYAW, WhoAm 74, -76, -78, -80, -82, -84, -86, -88, WhoAmW 74, -75, -77*
Pseud./variant:
Griffith, Jeannette

Eyre, Dorothy *ConAu X, SmATA X*
Main entry: McGuire, Leslie Sarah

Eyre, Frank 1910- *OxCAusL, OxCChiL*

Eyre, Frank 1910-1988 *BioIn 17, SmATA 62*

Eyre, Katherine Wigmore 1901-1970 *AmAu&B, BioIn 2, -4, -6, -8, ConAu 104, CurBio 49, -57, MorJA, SmATA 26*

Eyvindson, Peter 1946- *BioIn 16, ConAu 124, SmATA 52*

Ezekiel, Nissim 1924- *BioIn 10, -11, CamGLE, CasWL, ConAu 61, ConLC 61, ConPo 70, -75, -80, -85, -91, DcLEL 1940, IntAu&W 82, -91, IntWWP 82, ModCmwL, REn, WebE&AL, WhoWorJ 72, WrDr 76, -80, -82, -84, -86, -88, -90, -92, -94*

Ezzell, Marilyn 1937- *BioIn 15, ConAu 109, SmATA 38, -42*

F

Fabe, Maxene 1943- *BioIn 12, ConAu 77, SmATA 15*

Fabell, Walter *AuBYP 2, BioIn 8*

Fabell, Walter C *AuBYP 3*

Faber, Doris 1924- *AuBYP 2, -3, BioIn 7, -9, ConAu 17R, -8NR, -30NR, ForWC 70, SmATA 3*

Faber, Harold 1919- *AuBYP 2, -3, BioIn 10, ConAu 13R, -8NR, -29NR, SmATA 5*

Fabian *AuBYP 3*

Fabre, Jean Henri 1823-1915 *AnCL, BiDPsy, BiESc, BioIn 1, -2, -3, -4, -5, -6, -8, -9, -11, -13, DcCathB, DcScB, Dis&D, InSci, JBA 34, -51, LongCTC, NamesHP, OxCFr, RAdv 13-5, REn, SmATA 22*

Fabre, Jean Henri Casimir 1823-1915 *BioIn 14, -17*

Fabres, Oscar 1895-1961 *WhoAmA 86N, -89N, -91N*

Fabres, Oscar 1900-1960 *BioIn 5, ChhPo S1, IlsBYP, IlsCB 1946*

Fabricius, Johan Wigmore 1899- *Au&Wr 71, BioIn 1, -3, -4, CasWL, ConAu 53, EvEuW, IlsCB 1744, IntAu&W 77, IntWW 74, -75, -76, -77, -78, TwCA, -SUP, WhoWor 74, -78*

Fabun, Don 1920- *ConAu 45, Future*

Facklam, Margery 1927- *AuBYP 3, ConAu 21NR, WhoUSWr 88, WhoWrEP 89*

Facklam, Margery Metz 1927- *AuBYP 2S, ConAu 5R, -6NR, SmATA 20, WhoWrEP 92*

Factor, June *AuBYP 3*

Fader, Shirley Sloan *WhoAm 86, -88, -90, -92, -94, WhoAmW 87, -89, -91, -93, WhoE 86, -89, -91, -93, WhoWor 91, -93*

Fader, Shirley Sloan 1931- *ConAu 77, -14NR, WhoAm 80, -82, -84, WhoAmW 75, -77, -81, -83, -85, WhoE 77, -81, -83, -85, WhoWor 80, -82*

Fadiman, Clifton *IntvTCA 2, WhoAm 86, -88, -90, -92, -94*

Fadiman, Clifton 1904- *AmAu&B, BioIn 3, -4, -9, -10, -11, CelR, ChhPo S2, ConAu 61, -9NR, CurBio 41, -55, EncAJ, IntAu&W 91, IntMPA 75, -76, -78, -81, -82, -84, -86, -88, -92, -77, RAdv 1, REnAL, SmATA 11, TwCA, -SUP, WebAB 74, WhoAm 74, -76, -78, -80, -82, -84, WhoWest 74, -76, -78, WhoWor 74, WorAlBi, WorAl, WrDr 86, -88, -90, -92, -94*

Fadiman, Edwin, Jr. 1925- *ConAu 29R*

Fago, Vincent 1915?- *BioIn 1*

Fahrmann, Willi *TwCChW 89B*

Fair, James R 1920- *AmMWSc 86, -89, -92, WhoTech 84*

Fair, James R, Jr. 1920- *ConAu 34NR*

Fair, James Rutherford, Jr. 1920- *AmMWSc 73P, -82, BioIn 11, ConAu 29R, WhoAm 80, -82, -84, -86, -88, -90, -92, -94, WhoFrS 84, WhoMW 74, -76, WhoTech 82, WhoWor 80, -82*

Fair, Sylvia 1933- *ConAu 69, SmATA 13*

Fairfax-Lucy, Brian 1898-1974 *AuBYP 2S, -3, BioIn 10, ConAu P-2, SmATA 6, -26N*

Fairley, Peter 1930- *ConAu 29R, -24NR, IntAu&W 77*

Fairlie, Gerard 1899-1983 *Au&Wr 71, BioIn 3, -14, ConAu 109, DcLB 77, EncMys, SmATA 34N, TwCCr&M 80, -85, -91, WhoSpyF, WrDr 82, -84*

Fairman, Joan Alexandra 1935- *BioIn 11, ConAu 33R, SmATA 10, WhoAmW 75, -77, WrDr 76, -82, -84, -86, -88, -90, -92, -94*

Fairman, Paul W 1909-1977 *ScF&FL 92*

Fairman, Paul W 1916-1977 *ConAu 114, ConSFA, EncSF 93, ScFSB, TwCSFW 86, –91, WhoSciF*

Faithfull, Gail 1936- *BioIn 11, ConAu 57, SmATA 8*
Pseud./variant:
Keller, Gail Faithfull

Falconer, James *ConAu X, IntAu&W 91X, SmATA X*
Main entry: Kirkup, James Falconer

Falconer, Pearl *ArtsCL, BioIn 6, –8, IlsCB 1957*

Falconer, Rebecca
Main entry: Krehbiel, Rebecca Falconer

Falk, Irving A 1921- *ConAu 21R*

Falk, Lee *ArtCS, BioIn 4, ConAu 133, NatPD 77, –81*

Falk, Lee 1924- *WrDr 94*

Falkner, John Meade 1858-1932 *BioIn 2, –8, –10, –15, CnMWL, DcLEL, DcNaB 1931, EvLB, LongCTC, OxCChiL, OxCEng 85, REn, WhDW, WhoChL, WorAu 1950*

Falkner, Leonard 1900-1977 *BioIn 11, ConAu 21R, OhA&B, SmATA 12, WhAm 7, WhNAA, WhoE 74*

Fall, Thomas *AuBYP 2, BioIn 8, –12, FourBJA, SmATA X*
Main entry: Snow, Donald Clifford

Fall, Thomas 1917- *AuBYP 3, DcAmChF 1960*

Fallow, Burnett *ChhPo*

Falls, Charles Buckles 1874-1959 *WhoAmA 86N, –89N, –91N*

Falls, Charles Buckles 1874-1960 *AmPB, AuBYP 2, –3, BioIn 1, –2, –5, –6, –8, –13, –15, ChhPo, –S2, ConAu 116, ConICB, IlrAm 1880, –B, IlsCB 1744, –1946, IndAu 1917, JBA 34, –51, SmATA 27, –38, WhAm 4, –5, WhAmArt 85, WhoAmA 80N, –82N, WorECar*

Falstein, Louis *DrAPF 91, –93*

Falstein, Louis 1909- *AmAu&B, ConAu 97, SmATA 37, WhoAm 74, –76, –78, –80, –82, –84, –86, –88, –90, WhoAmJ 80, WhoWorJ 72, –78*

Falter, John Philip 1910-1982 *BioIn 2, –9, –12, IlrAm 1880, –E, WhAmArt 85, WhoAmA 73, –78, –82, –84*

Fancourt, Mary St John 1898- *Au&Wr 71, WrDr 76*

Fanning, Leonard M 1888-1967 *BioIn 10, ConAu 5R, SmATA 5*

Faraday, Michael 1791-1867 *BiDPsy, BiESc, BioIn 1, –2, –3, –4, –5, –6, –7, –8, –9, –10, –11, –12, –13, –14, –15, –16, –17, CelCen, CyEd, DcBiPP, DcInv, DcNaB, Dis&D, EncO&P 2, –3, EncPaPR 91, InSci, OxCChiL, OxCEng 85, RAdv 13-5, WhDW, WorAlBi, WorAl*

Faralla, Dana 1909- *AmAu&B, AmNov, BioIn 2, –11, ConAu 49, IntAu&W 77, –82X, SmATA 9*
Pseud./variant:
Faralla, Dorothy W
Wilma, Dana

Faralla, Dorothy W
Main entry: Faralla, Dana

Farb, Peter 1929-1980 *AmAu&B, AnObit 1980, AuBYP 2S, –3, Au&Wr 71, BioIn 11, –12, –13, ConAu 13R, –97, –12NR, NewYTBS 80, SmATA 12, –22N, WhAm 7, WhoAm 74, –76, –78, –80, WhoE 74, WhoWor 74, –78, –80*

Farber, Joseph C 1903- *ConAu 33R*

Farber, Norma 1909- *WrDr 86*

Farber, Norma 1909-1984 *AuBYP 2S, –3, BioIn 12, –13, ConAu 102, –112, DcLB 61, FifBJA, MajAI, SmATA 25, –38N, –75, TwCChW 83, –89, WhoAm 80, –82, –84, WhoAmW 77, –81, –83*

Farge, Monique *SmATA X*
Main entry: Gree, Alain

Fargo, Lucille Foster 1880- *AuBYP 2, –3, BioIn 7, OhA&B*

Faris, John Thomson 1871-1949 *AmAu&B BioIn 1, –5, CarSB, DcNAA, ObitOF 79, WhAm 2, WhNAA*

Farjeon, Annabel 1919- *BiDD, BioIn 11, ConAu 53, SmATA 11*
Pseud./variant:
Jefferson, Sarah

Farjeon, Eleanor 1881-1965 *AnCL, ArtclWW 2, AuBYP 2, BioIn 2, –3, –4, –5, –6, –7, –8, –9, –11, –14, –15, –16, BkCL, CamGLE, CasWL, CathA 1952, ChhPo, –S1, –S2, ChlFicS, ConAu P-1, DcLEL, DcNaB 1961, EncBrWW, FamMS, FamPYP, FemiCLE, GrBr, HerW, InWom SUP, JBA 34, –51, LongCTC, McjAI, NewC, ObitT 1961, OxCChiL, OxCEng 85, ScF&FL 92, SmATA 2, Str&VC, TelT, TwCA, –SUP, TwCChW 78, –83, –89, TwCWr, WhoChL, WomNov, WrChl*

Pseud./variant:
Chimaera
Tomfool

Farjeon, Joan Jefferson 1913- *BioIn 5, IlsCB 1946*

Farjeon, Joseph Jefferson 1883-1955 *BioIn 3, –4, NewC, NotNAT B, ObitOF 79, ObitT 1951, TwCA, –SUP*

Farley, Carol
Main entry: McDole, Carol

Farley, Carol 1936- *AuBYP 2S, –3, BioIn 9, ConAu 10NR, –25NR, FifBJA, IntAu&W 77, –89, –91, MichAu 80, SmATA 4, WrDr 76, –80, –82, –84, –86, –88, –90, –92, –94*

Farley, Carol J Mcdole 1936- *DcAmChF 1960*

Farley, Harriet 1813-1907 *BlmGWL, HanAmWH, InWom SUP*

Farley, Harriet 1817-1907 *Alli, –SUP, AmAu, AmAu&B, BenetAL 91, BbD, BiD&SB, BioIn 12, CarSB, CyAL, DcAmAu, DcNAA, OxCAmL 65, –83, REnAL*

Farley, Walter d1989 *NewYTBS 89*

Farley, Walter 1915- *TwCChW 89*

Farley, Walter 1915-1989 *AnObit 1989, ConAu 29NR, ScF&FL 92*

Farley, Walter 1920- *AuBYP 2, –3, BioIn 1, –2, –7, –9, –10, ConAu 17R, –8NR, ConLC 17, CurBio 49, DcLB 22, JBA 51, MorBMP, OxCChiL, SmATA 2, –43, TwCChW 78, –83, WhoAm 74, WrDr 80, –82, –84, –86, –88, –90*

Farley, Walter Lorimer 1915-1989 *MajAI, TwCYAW*

Farley, Walter Lorimer 1922-1989 *WhAm 10*

Farlow, James Orville, Jr. 1951- *ConAu 142, SmATA 75*

Farman, Ella 1843-1907 *Alli SUP, AmAu&B, BiD&SB, CarSB, ChhPo, –S1, DcAmAu*

Farmer, Laurence 1895?-1976 *BioIn 10, ConAu 65*

Farmer, Penelope 1939- *AuBYP 2, –3, BioIn 7, –10, –11, BritCA, ChlLR 8, ConAu 13R, –9NR, FourBJA, IntAu&W 91, OxCChiL, ScF&FL 92, SmATA 39, –40, TwCChW 78, –83, –89, WrDr 76, –80, –82, –84, –86, –88, –90, –92, –94*

Farmer, Penelope Jane 1939- *ConAu 37NR, MajAI, TwCYAW*

Farmer, Peter 1950- *SmATA 38*

Farmer, Philip Jose *BioIn 15, –17, DrAPF 87, –89, –91, –93, IntvTCA 2*

Farmer, Philip Jose 1918- *AmAu&B, BioIn 7, –12, ConAu 1R, –4NR, –35NR, ConLC 1, –19, ConSFA, DcLB 8, DrAF 76, DrAPF 83, –85, EncSF 93, IndAu 1917, MajTwCW, NewEScF, Novels, RGTwCSF, ScF&FL 92, ScFSB, TwCSFW 86, –91, WhoAm 82, –84, –86, –88, WhoSciF, WhoUSWr 88, WhoWrEP 89, –92, WorAlBi, WorAl, WrDr 84, –86, –88, –90, –92, –94*

Farmer, Robert Allen 1938- *ConAu 21R*

Farmer, Wendell *AuBYP 2, –3*

Farnham, Burt *ConAu X, SmATA X*
Main entry: Clifford, Harold B

Farnol, Jeffrey 1878-1952 *BioIn 3, –4, –7, –10, DcNaB 1951, LongCTC, ObitT 1951, OxCChiL, OxCEng 85, TelT, TwCWr*

Farnsworth, Marjorie W 1921- *WhoTech 84*

Farnsworth, Marjorie Whyte 1921- *AmMWSc 73P, –76P, –82, –86, –89, –92, WhoTech 82*

Farnworth, Warren 1935- *ConAu 93, WrDr 76, –80*

Farquhar, Margaret C 1905- *ConAu 69, SmATA 13*

Farquharson, Alexander 1944- *SmATA 46*

Farquharson, Martha *Alli SUP, AmAu, AmAu&B, BiDSA, DcAmAu, DcNAA, InWom SUP, OhA&B, OxCAmL 65, –83, OxCChiL, SmATA X, WhoChL*
Main entry: Finley, Martha Farquharson

Farquharson, Martha 1828-1909 *BlmGWL*

Farr, Diana Pullein-Thompson *ConAu 13R, –7NR, IntAu&W 77*
Pseud./variant:
Pullein-Thompson, Diana
Thompson, Diana Pullein

Farr, Finis 1904-1982 *BioIn 11, –12, –14, ConAu 1R, –105, –1NR, IntAu&W 77, SmATA 10*

Farr, Finis King 1904- *SpyFic*

Farrant, Leda 1927- *ConAu 21R*

Farrar, F S d1955 *ObitOF 79, OxCCan*

Farrar, F W 1831-1903 *TwCChW 89A*

Farrar, Frederick William 1831-1903 *Alli SUP, BbD, BiD&SB, BioIn 3, –8, –9, BritAu 19, CasWL, Chambr 3, ChhPo, CyEd, DcBiPP, DcEnA, –A, DcEnL, EvLB, NewC, OxCChiL, OxCEng 85, PenC ENG, TelT, TwCChW 83A, WhoChL*

Farrar, Frederick William 1831-1905 *CamGLE*

Farrar, John Chipman 1896-1974 *AmAu&B, BioIn 3, –10, ChhPo, –S1, –S2, ConAu 53, –65, CurBio 54, –75N, NewYTBS 74, ObitOF 79, REnAL, Str&VC, WhAm 6, WhoAm 74*

Farrar, Richard Bartlett, Jr. 1939- *ConAu 65*

Farrar, Susan Clement 1917- *ConAu 101, SmATA 33*

Farre, Rowena *Au&Wr 71*

Farrell, Alan 1920- *Au&Wr 71, ConAu 13R*

Farrell, Anne A 1916- *ConAu 25R, WhoAmW 77*

Farrell, Ben *ConAu X, –30NR, IntAu&W 77X, SmATA X, WrDr 76, –80, –82, –84, –86, –88, –90, –92*
Main entry: Cebulash, Mel

Farrell, John Joseph 1934- *ConAu 110, WhoE 74*

Farrell, Sally *SmATA 72*
Main entry: Odgers, Sally Farrell

Farrington, Benjamin 1891-1974 *BioIn 12, SmATA 20N*

Farrington, Selwyn Kip, Jr. 1904-1983 *AmAu&B, AuBYP 2, –3, BioIn 7, –12, –13, ConAu 73, SmATA 20*

Farrow, G E 1862-1920? *TwCChW 89*

Farrow, George Edward 1866-1920? *BioIn 8, ChhPo, –S1, –S2, OxCChiL, TelT, TwCChW 83, WhoChL*

Farthing, Alison 1936- *ConAu 117, IntAu&W 77, SmATA 36, –45, WrDr 76, –80, –82, –84, –86, –88*

Fassler, Joan 1931- *BioIn 11, ConAu 61, SmATA 11, WhoAmW 77*

Fast, Howard *TwCCr&M 91*

Fast, Howard 1914- *AmAu&B, AmNov, AuBYP 2, Au&Wr 71, Benet 87, BenetAL 91, BioIn 2, –3, –4, –5, –7, –8, –9, –10, –11, –12, –13, –14, –17, BlueB 76, CamGLE, CamHAL, CnDAL, ConAu 1R, –1NR, –33NR, ConLC 23, ConNov 72, –76, –82, –86, –91, ConSFA, CurBio 43, –91, DcLB 9, DcLEL, EncFWF, HalFC 84, –88, IntAu&W 77, IntWW 74, –75, –76, –77, –78, –79, –80, –81, –82, –83, –89, –91, JeAmFiW, ModAL, NewEScF, NewYTBS 81, Novels, OxCAmL 65, PenC AM, REn, REnAL, ScF&FL 92, ScFSB, SmATA 7, TwCA SUP, TwCCr&M 80, –85, TwCRHW 90, TwCSFW 86, –91, TwCWW 91, TwCWr, WebE&AL, WhoAm 74, –76, –78, –80, –82, –84, –86, –88, WhoUSWr 88, WhoWor 74, –78, –80, –82, –84, –87, WhoWorJ 72, WhoWrEP 89, –92, WorAlBi, WorAl, WrDr 76, –80, –82, –84, –86, –88, –90, –92, –94*
Pseud./variant:
Cunningham, E V
Ericson, Walter

Fast, Howard Melvin 1914- *AuBYP 3, EncSF 93, TwCYAW, WhoAm 90, –92, –94, WhoE 93, WhoEnt 92*

Fatchen, Max 1920- *Au&Wr 71, BioIn 12 ConAu 25R, –11NR, –28NR, DcChlFi, OxCAusL, SingR 2, SmATA 20, TwCChW 78, –83, –89, WrDr 80, –82, –84, –86, –88, –90, –92, –94*

Father Xavier *ConAu 43NR, SmATA X*
Main entry: Hurwood, Bernhardt J

Fatigati, Evelyn DeBuhr 1948- *BioIn 13, ConAu 77, SmATA 24*

Fatio, Louise 1904- *ArtclWW 2, AuBYP 3, BioIn 6, –10, –11, BkP, ConAu 37R, IntAu&W 77X, –82, MorJA, SmATA 6, TwCChW 78, –83, –89, WrDr 76, –80, –82, –84, –86, –88, –90, –92, –94*
Pseud./variant:
Duvoisin, Louise

Faucher, Paul 1898-1967? *BioIn 10, OxCChiL*

Faulhaber, Martha 1926- *BioIn 10, ConAu 33R, SmATA 7*

Faulkner, Anne Irvin *AuBYP 3*

Faulkner, Anne Irvin 1906- *AuBYP 2, ConAu 1R, –2NR, ForWC 70, IntAu&W 77, SmATA 23*
Pseud./variant:
Faulkner, Nancy

Faulkner, Barry *WhoAmA 86N*

Faulkner, Barry 1881-1966 *BioIn 7, –10, –13, NatCAB 62, WhAm 4, WhAmArt 85, WhoAmA 78N, –80N, –82N, –89N, –91N*

Faulkner, Elsie 1905- *ConAu 65*

Faulkner, Georgene 1873- *AmAu&B, AuBYP 2, –3, BioIn 2, –8, WhAm 5, WhNAA, WomWWA 14*

Faulkner, John *IlsBYP*

Faulkner, John 1901-1963 *BioIn 2, -8, -9, ConAu 1NR*

Faulkner, Nancy
Main entry: Faulkner, Anne Irvin

Faulkner, Nancy 1906- *AuBYP 2, Au&Wr 71, BioIn 4, -7, -13, ConAu X, CurBio 56, DcAmChF 1960, FourBJA, IntAu&W 77X, SmATA X*

Faulkner, Nancy Irvin 1906- *AuBYP 3*

Faulkner, William *IntvTCA 2*

Faulkner, William 1897-1962 *AgeMat, AmAu&B, AmNov, AmWr, AtlBL, Au&Arts 7, AuNews 1, Benet 87, BenetAL 91, BioIn 1, -2, -3, -4, -5, -6, -7, -8, -9, -10, -11, -12, -13, -14, -15, -16, -17, BioNews 74, CamGEL, CamGLE, CamHAL, CasWL, Chambr 3, CnDAL, CnMD, CnMWL, ConAmA, ConAu 81, -33NR, ConLC 1, -3, -6, -8, -9, -11, -18, -28, -52, -68, CrtSuMy, CroCD, CurBio 51, -62, CyWA 58, -89, DcFM, DcLB 9, -11, -44, -102, -DS2, -Y86A, DcLEL, EncMys, EncWL, -2, FifSWrA, FilmgC, HalFC 84, -88, LongCTC, MagSAmL, MajTwCW, MakMC, McGEWB, MemAm, ModAL, -S1, -S2, ModWD, NobelP, NotNAT B, Novels, ObitOF 79, ObitT 1961, OxCAmH, OxCAmL 65, -83, OxCEng 67, OxCFilm, PenC AM, RAdv 1, -13-1, RComAH, RComWL, REn, REnAL, RfGAmL 87, RfGShF, ShSCr 1, ShSWr, TwCA, -SUP, TwCCr&M 80, -85, TwCWr, WebAB 74, WebE&AL, WhDW, WhAm 4, WhoTwCL, WorAlBi, WorEFlm, WorLitC, WrPh*

Faulkner, William 1897-1963 *PenEncH*

Faulknor, Cliff 1913- *IntAu&W 91, TwCChW 89, WhoCanL 87, WrDr 86, -88, -90, -92*

Faulknor, Clifford Vernon 1913- *BioIn 10, ConAu 17R, -8NR, OxCCan SUP, OxCChiL, Profile 1, TwCChW 78, -83, WhoCanL 85, WhoWest 74, -76, -78, WrDr 76, -80, -82, -84*

Fauset, Jessie 1882-1961 *ModAWWr*

Fauset, Jessie 1884?-1961 *BlkAull, -92*

Fauset, Jessie R 1882-1961 *CamGLE*

Fauset, Jessie Redmon 1882-1961 *BlmGWL*

Fauset, Jessie Redmond 1882-1961 *EncAACR*

Faust, Frederick *ScF&FL 92*

Faust, Frederick 1892-1944 *AmAu&B, BenetAL 91, BioIn 1, -3, -4, -8, -15, -16, ChhPo, CmCal, ConAu 108, CurBio 44, DcLEL, DcNAA, EncFWF, EncMys, LongCTC, ObitOF 79, REn, REnAL, TwCA, -SUP, TwCLC 49, WebAB 74, WhoHr&F*

Fava, Rita *BioIn 5, ChhPo, -S1, IlsCB 1946, -1957*
Main entry: Fegiz, Rita Fava

Faville, Barry *DcChlFi*

Fawcett, F Dubrez 1891-1968 *ConAu P-1*

Fax, Elton 1909- *AfrAmAl 6, BlkAull, NegAl 89*

Fax, Elton C 1909- *BlkAull 92, NegAl 89, WhoBlA 85, -88, -90, -92, -94*

Fax, Elton Clay 1909- *AfroAA, BioIn 10, -13, BlkWr 2, ConAu 13R, -15NR, IlsCB 1967, InB&W 80, -85, LivgBAA, SelBAAf, SmATA 25, WhoAm 76, -78, -80, -82, -84, -86, -88, -90, -92, WhoAmA 73, -78, -80, -82, -84, -86, -89, -91, WhoBlA 75, -77, -80, -85, WhoUSWr 88, WhoWor 78, WhoWrEP 89, -92*

Faxon, Lavinia *ConAu X, SmATA 74*
Main entry: Russ, Lavinia

Fay, Frederic L 1890- *ConAu P-2*

Feagles, Anita MacRae 1926- *AuBYP 2, BioIn 8, -11, ConAu 1R, -4NR, ForWC 70, FourBJA, SmATA 9*
Pseud./variant:
MacRae, Travis

Feagles, Anita MacRae 1927- *AuBYP 3*

Feagles, Elizabeth *ConAu X, -40NR, SmATA X*
Main entry: Day, Beth Feagles

Feague, Mildred H 1915- *ConAu 29R, SmATA 14*

Feaser, Daniel David 1920- *BioIn 8, IlsBYP, IlsCB 1957*

Fecher, Constance *ConAu 40NR, TwCRHW 90, WrDr 86, -88, -90, -92*

Fecher, Constance 1911- *AuBYP 2S, -3, Au&Wr 71, BioIn 10, -14, ConAu 49, -X, IntAu&W 77X, SmATA 7, WrDr 76, -80, -82, -84, -94*
Pseud./variant:
Heaven, Constance

Fedder, Ruth 1907- *AmMWSc 73S, ConAu 5R, -2NR, LEduc 74, WhoWest 74*

Feder, Harriet K 1928- *SmATA 73*

Feder, Paula 1935- *BioIn 13, ConAu 105, SmATA 26*

Feder, Raymond L 1920- *AmMWSc 73P, -82, -86, -89, -92*

Feder, Robert Arthur *AuBYP 3*

Feder, Robert Arthur 1909-1969 *ConAu 110, SmATA 35*
Pseud./variant:
Arthur, Robert

Fedor, Carol Zizmor 1937- *WhoAmW 75, -77*

Feelings, Muriel 1938- *BioIn 12, -16, BlkAWP, BlkAuIl, -92, BlkWr 1, ChILR 5, ConAu 93, FourBJA, InB&W 80, LivgBAA, SelBAAf, SelBAAu, SmATA 16*

Feelings, Muriel Grey 1938- *WhoBlA 94*

Feelings, Muriel L 1938- *SmATA 8AS*

Feelings, Muriel Lavita Gray 1938- *MajAI*

Feelings, Thomas 1933- *AfroAA, BioIn 8, -9, -11, BlkAuIl, -92, BlkWr 1, BkP, ConAu 49, -25NR, IlsBYP, IlsCB 1967, InB&W 80, -85, LivgBAA, MajAI, SelBAAu, SmATA 8, ThrBJA, WhoBlA 77, -80, -85, -88, -90, -92, -94, WhoE 77*
Pseud./variant:
Feelings, Tom

Feelings, Tom *BlkWr 1*
Main entry: Feelings, Thomas

Feelings, Tom 1933- *BioIn 12, ChILR 5, SelBAAf, SmATA 69*

Feerick, John David 1936- *ConAu 69, DrAS 82P, WhoAm 82, -84, -86, -88, WhoAmL 85, -87, -90, -92, -94*

Fegiz, Rita Fava 1932- *BioIn 8, IlsBYP, IlsCB 1957*
Pseud./variant:
Fava, Rita

Feher, Joseph 1908- *WhoAmA 73, -78, -80, -82, -84, -86*

Feher, Joseph 1908-1987 *WhoAmA 89N, -91N*

Fehler, Gene 1940- *SmATA 74*

Fehrenbach, Theodore Reed 1925- *ConAu 1R, IntAu&W 77, WhoSSW 73, -75, -76, WhoWor 78, WrDr 80*

Feibleman, Peter S 1930- *BenetAL 91, BioIn 4, ConAu 108, -110, OxCAmL 83, REnAL*

Feiffer, Jules *OxCAmT 84*

Feiffer, Jules 1929- *AmAu&B, ArtCS, Au&Arts 3, Au&Wr 71, Benet 87, BioIn 5, -6, -7, -8, -9, -10, -11, -12, -13, BlueB 76, CamGWoT, CelR, CnThe, ConAu 17R, -30NR, ConDr 73, -77, -82, -88, ConLC 2, -8, -64, ConTFT 1, CroCD, CurBio 61, DcLB 7, -44, DcLEL 1940, EncACom, EncAHmr, EncAJ, EncTwCJ, EncWT, FilmgC, HalFC 84, -88, IntAu&W 77, -89, -91, IntWW 74, -75, -76, -77, -78, -79, -80, -81, -82, -83, -89, -91, MajTwCW, McGEWD 72, -84, NatPD 81, NotNAT, SmATA 8, -61, WhoAm 74, -76, -78, -80, -82, -84, -86 -88, -90, -92, -94, WhoAmA 78, -80, -82, -84, -86, -89, -91, WhoAmJ 80, WhoE 86, -89, -91, -93, WhoEnt 92, WhoThe 72, -77, -81, WhoUSWr 88, WhoWor 74, -78, WhoWorJ 72, -78, WhoWrEP 89, -92, WorAlBi, WorAl, WrDr 76, -80, -82, -84, -86, -88, -90, -92, -94*

Feiffer, Jules Ralph 1929- *ConDr 93*

Feig, Barbara Krane 1937- *BioIn 14, ConAu 104, SmATA 34, WhoAmW 83, -89*

Feikema, Feike *BioIn 4, -6, -7, -10, -11, ConAu X, ConNov 82, IntAu&W 82X, -85X, OxCAmL 83, SmATA X, TwCWW 91, WrDr 82, -84, -86, -88, -90, -92*
Main entry: Manfred, Frederick Feikema

Feikema, Feike 1912- *WhoAm 94, WrDr 94*

Feil, Hila 1942- *BioIn 11, ConAu 37R, ScF&FL 92, SmATA 12*

Feilen, John *ConAu X, SmATA X*
Main entry: May, Julian

Feinberg, Barbara Jane 1938- *ConAu 22NR, SmATA 58, WhoWrEP 89, -92*
Pseud./variant:
Feinberg, Barbara Silberdick

Feinberg, Barbara Silberdick *BioIn 16, SmATA X*
Main entry: Feinberg, Barbara Jane

Feingold, S Norman *WrDr 86, -88, -90, -92, -94*

Feingold, S Norman 1914- *AmMWSc 73S, -78S, ConAu 13R, -13NR, -30NR, IntAu&W 89, LEduc 74, WhoAm 76, -78, -80, -82, -84, -86, -88, -90, -92, -94, WhoAmJ 80, WhoSSW 73, -75, -76, WhoWor 82, WhoWorJ 72, -78*

Feininger, Lyonel *EncACom*

Feininger, Lyonel 1871-1956 *ArtCS, AtlBL, BioIn 1, -2, -3, -4, -5, -11, -12, -13, -14, -17, ConArt 77, -83, CurBio 55, -56, DcCAA 71, -77, -88, IntDcAA 90, NatCAB 62, OxCArt, OxCGer 76, -86,*

OxCTwCA, OxDcArt, PhDcTCA 77, REn, WhAm 3

Feinman, Jeffrey 1943- *ConAu 65, –10NR, WhoE 83*

Feinman, Max L 1905- *AmMWSc 73P, –76P, –82, –86, –89, –92*

Feinstein, Alan Shawn 1931- *ConAu 25R, WhoAm 86, –88, –90, –92, –94, WhoE 74, –77, –81, –83, –85, –86, –89, WhoFI 87, –92*

Feis, Ruth 1892- *ConAu P-2*

Feist, Aubrey 1903- *Au&Wr 71, ConAu 41R*

Feld *IntAu&W 77X*
Main entry: Rosenfeld, Friedrich

Felder, Eleanor *AuBYP 2S, –3*

Feldman, Anne 1939- *BioIn 12, ConAu 73, SmATA 19*

Feldman, Herbert 1910- *ConAu 29R*

Feldman, Samuel Nathan 1931- *ConAu 25R*

Felix *SmATA X*
Main entry: Vincent, Felix

Felix Summerly *OxCChiL*

Felkin, Alfred Laurence 1856- *CarSB, WhoLA*

Felkin, Ellen Thorneycroft 1860-1929 *CarSB, DcNaB 1922, NewC, WhoLA, WomNov*

Feller, Bob
Main entry: Feller, Robert William Andrew

Feller, Robert William Andrew 1918- *AuBYP 2, –3, BiDAmSp BB, BioIn 1, –2, –3, –4, –5, –6, –7, –8, –9, –10, BioNews 74, CurBio 41, WebAB 74, –79, WhoAm 92, –94, WhoEnt 92, WhoWor 93, WorAl*
Pseud./variant:
Feller, Bob

Fellner, Rudolph *AuBYP 3*

Fellner, Rudolph 1913- *AuBYP 2, BioIn 8, WhoMus 72*

Fellows, Lawrence 1924- *ConAu 49*

Fellows, Muriel H *AuBYP 2, –3, BioIn 7, –11, ConAu 53, SmATA 10*

Felsen, Henry Gregor 1916- *AuBYP 2, –3, BioIn 2, –7, –9, ConAu 1R, –1NR, ConLC 17, JBA 51, SmATA 1, –2AS*
Pseud./variant:
Vicker, Angus

Felt, Sue 1924- *BioIn 2, –5, IlsCB 1946*

Felton, Bruce 1946- *ConAu 65*

Felton, Harold William 1902- *AuBYP 2, –3, BioIn 6, –8, –9, ChhPo S2, ConAu 1R, –1NR, MorJA, SmATA 1*

Felton, Ronald Oliver 1909-1982 *Au&Wr 71, BioIn 8, –9, ConAu 9R, –3NR, IntAu&W 77, OxCLiW 86, SmATA 3, WrDr 82*
Pseud./variant:
Welch, Ronald

Felts, Shirley 1934- *SmATA 33*

Fendell, Bob 1925- *ConAu 57*

Fenderson, Lewis H 1907-1983 *ConAu 106, –111, DrAS 74E, SmATA 37N, –47*

Fenelon, Francois de Pons de Salignac de la Mothe- 1651-1715 *GuFrLit 2*

Fenelon, Francois De Salignac DeLa Mothe 1651-1715 *WorAlBi*

Fenelon, Francois DeSalignac DeLa Mothe- 1651-1715 *Benet 87, BioIn 2, –4, –5, –7, –9, –10, –11, –14, CyEd, DcBiPP, DcCanB 1, DcCathB, Dis&D, EuWr 3, HarEnUS, IlEncMy, LuthC 75, OxCChiL, OxCEng 85, WhDW, WorAl*

Fenn, Eleanor, Lady 1743-1813 *CarSB, ChhPo, DcBrAmW, DcEnL, DcNaB, OxCChiL*

Fenn, George Manville 1831-1909 *Alli SUP, BbD, BiD&SB, BioIn 8, BritAu 19, Chambr 3, ChhPo, –S2, DcBiA, DcEnL, DcNaB S2, EvLB, HsB&A, NewC, NotNAT B, OxCChiL, StaCVF, TwCChW 83A, –89A, WhoChL*

Fennell, Hugh Wordsworth d1956
Pseud./variant:
Leonard, Henry

Fenner, Carol Elizabeth 1929- *BioIn 8, –10, –12, ConAu 5R, –3NR, IlsCB 1957, –1967, IntAu&W 77, –82, SmATA 7, WrDr 76, –80*
Pseud./variant:
Williams, Carol

Fenner, Phyllis R 1899-1982 *ScF&FL 92*

Fenner, Phyllis Reid 1899-1982 *AuBYP 2, –3, BioIn 3, –7, –9, –12, –13, ConAu 5R, –106, –2NR, ForWC 70, SmATA 1, –29N, WhoAmW 74, –75, –77, WhoLibS 66*

Fennimore, Stephen *DcChlFi, SingR 2*
Main entry: Collins, Dale

Fenten, Barbara D 1935- *BioIn 13, ConAu 53, –5NR, SmATA 26*

Fenten, D X 1932- *AuBYP 2S, -3, BioIn 9, ConAu 33R, -5NR, SmATA 4, WhoE 75, -77, WrDr 76, -80, -82, -84, -86, -88, -90, -94*

Fenton, Carroll Lane 1900-1969 *AmAu&B, AuBYP 2, -3, BioIn 6, -7, -8, -10, ConAu 1R, -29R, -6NR, MorJA, SmATA 5*

Fenton, Edward 1917- *AuBYP 2, -3, Au&Wr 71, BioIn 9, -10, ConAu 9R, -13NR, -34NR, DcAmChF 1960, IntAu&W 91, SmATA 7, ThrBJA, TwCChW 78, -83, -89, WrDr 80, -82, -84, -86, -88, -90, -92, -94*

Fenton, Edward 1917-1988 *ScF&FL 92*

Fenton, Mildred Adams 1899- *AuBYP 3, Au&Wr 71, BioIn 6, -7, ConAu 77, MorJA, SmATA 21*

Fenton, Sophia Harvati 1914- *ConAu 33R*

Fenwick, Charles Ghequiere 1880-1973 *AmPeW, BiDInt, BioIn 10, ConAu 41R, NewYTBE 73, OxCLaw, WhAm 5, -6*

Fenwick, Patti *SmATA X*
Main entry: Grider, Dorothy

Feola, Jose M 1926- *EncO&P 3*

Feola, Jose Maria 1926- *AmMWSc 82, -86, -89, -92, BiDPara, ConAu 69, EncO&P 1, -2, EncPaPR 91*

Feravolo, Rocco Vincent 1922- *AuBYP 2, -3, BioIn 7, -11, ConAu 1R, -1NR, SmATA 10*

Ferber, Edna *CamHAL, IntvTCA 2*

Ferber, Edna 1885-1968 *AmWomPl, BlmGWL, CyWA 89, DcLB 86, FemiCLE, HanAmWH, JeAmFiW, NotWoAT, RfGAmL 87, TwCRHW 90, TwCWW 91*

Ferber, Edna 1887-1968 *AmAu&B, AmNov, AmWomD, ArtclWW 2, AuNews 1, Benet 87, BenetAL 91, BiE&WWA, BioAmW, BioIn 1, -2, -3, -4, -5, -6, -8, -9, -10, -11, -12, -14, -16, -17, Chambr 3, CnDAL, CnMD, CnThe, ConAmA, ConAmL, ConAu 5R, -25R, ConLC 18, DcLB 9, -28, DcLEL, EncFWF, EncWL, EncWT, EvLB, FilmgC, HalFC 84, -88, InWom SUP, LongCTC, MajTwCW, McGEWB, McGEWD 72, -84, ModAL, ModWD, NatCAB 60, NotAW MOD, NotNAT A, -B, Novels, ObitOF 79, ObitT 1961, OxCAmL 65, -83, OxCAmT 84, OxCThe 67, -83, PenC AM, PlP&P, REn, REnAL, SmATA 7, TwCA, -SUP, TwCWr, WebAB 74, -79, WhAm 5, WhNAA, WisWr, WomNov, WorAlBi, WorAl*

Fergosi, Claudia 1946- *AuBYP 2S, ConAu 69*

Ferguson, Amos 1920- *BlkAuII 92*

Ferguson, Annabelle Evelyn 1923- *ConAu 102, WhoAmW 75, -77, WhoE 81*

Ferguson, Bob
Main entry: Ferguson, Robert Bruce

Ferguson, Cecil 1931- *SmATA 45, WhoBlA 75, -77, -80, -85, -90, -92, -94*

Ferguson, Charles W d1987 *NewYTBS 87*

Ferguson, Charles W 1901- *AmAu&B, ConAu 13R, REnAL, TexWr, WhoAm 74, -76*

Ferguson, Charles W 1901-1987 *ConAu 124, WhAm 9*

Ferguson, Evelyn C 1910- *WhoPNW, WrDr 76, -80*

Ferguson, Evelyn Cook 1910- *IntAu&W 86*

Ferguson, Robert Bruce 1927- *ConAu 69, SmATA 13*
Pseud./variant:
Ferguson, Bob

Ferguson, Robert D 1921- *ConAu 17R*

Ferguson, Sarah 1959- *BioIn 16, ConAu 135, News 90, -90-3, SmATA 66, WrDr 94*
Pseud./variant:
Sarah, Duchess of York

Ferguson, Walter W 1930- *BioIn 5, ConAu 107, IlsBYP, IlsCB 1946, SmATA 34*

Fergusson, Charles Bruce *OxCCan*

Fergusson, Erna 1888-1964 *AmAu&B, BioIn 3, -4, -7, -9, -10, ConAu P-1, CurBio 55, InWom SUP, SmATA 5, WhAm 8*

Ferman, Edward L *DrmM 2*

Ferman, Edward L 1937- *ConAu 106, ConSFA, ScF&FL 92, WhoAm 82, WhoSciF*

Ferman, Edward Lewis 1937- *EncSF 93*

Fermi, Laura Capon 1907- *InWom SUP*

Fermi, Laura Capon 1907-1977 *AmAu&B, AuBYP 2, -3, BioIn 3, -4, -5, -7, -10, -11, -13, BlueB 76, ConAu 1R, -6NR, CurBio 58, IntAu&W 77, SmATA 6, -28N, WhAm 7, WhoAm 74, -76, -78, WhoAmW 74, -75, WhoWor 74, WrDr 76, -80, -82, -84*

Fern, Eugene A 1919- *BioIn 11, ConAu 1R, -16NR, SmATA 10*

Fern, Eugene A 1919-1987 *BioIn 15, -16, ConAu 123, SmATA 54N*

Fernandes, Eugenie 1943- *SmATA 77*

Fernea, Elizabeth Warnock 1927- *BioIn 10, ConAu 13R, –12NR, –29NR, WhoSSW 86*

Ferns, Ronald George 1925- *BioIn 8, IlsCB 1957*

Ferrell, Nancy Warren 1932- *SmATA 70*

Ferrier, Lucy *ConAu X, –35NR, SmATA X*
Main entry: Penzler, Otto

Ferris, Helen Josephine 1890- *AmWomPl*

Ferris, Helen Josephine 1890-1969 *AmAu&B, AuBYP 2, –3, BioIn 2, –7, –8, –10, –12, ChhPo, ConAu 77, JBA 34, –51, REnAL, SmATA 21, WhAm 5, WhNAA*

Ferris, James Cody *AmNov X, ConAu X, –37NR, –P-2, MajAI, SmATA 1, –X*
Main entry: Stratemeyer, Edward L

Ferris, Jean 1939- *DcAmChF 1985, SmATA 50, –56*

Ferro, Walter *WhoAmA 86, –89, –91*

Ferro, Walter 1925- *BioIn 6, WhoAm 78, –80, –82, –84, –86, –88, –90, –92, –94, WhoAmA 73, –78, –80, –82, –84, WhoE 75, –77, –81, –83, –85, –86, WhoWor 80, –82, –84, –87*

Ferry, Charles 1927- *ConAu 97, –16NR, SmATA 43*

Fessenden, Katherine 1896?-1974 *BioIn 10, ConAu 53*

Fetz, Ingrid 1915- *BioIn 8, ChhPo S1, IlsBYP, IlsCB 1957, –1967, SmATA 30*

Feuerlicht, Roberta Strauss 1931- *ConAu 17R*

Feuerlicht, Roberta Strauss 1931-1991 *BioIn 17, ConAu 135, NewYTBS 91*

Feydy, Anne Lindbergh
Main entry: Sapieyevski, Anne Lindbergh

Feydy, Anne Lindbergh 1940- *AuBYP 2S, –3, BioIn 14, ConAu 111, –X, SmATA 32, –X*

Ffrench Blake, Robert Lofford Valentine 1913- *ConAu 61*

Fiammenghi, Gioia *BioIn 17*

Fiammenghi, Gioia 1929- *BioIn 5, –8, –11, –12, IlsBYP, IlsCB 1946, –1957, –1967, SmATA 9, –66*

Fiarotta, Noel 1944- *BioIn 12, ConAu 69, –X, SmATA 15*

Fiarotta, Phyllis 1942- *BioIn 12, ConAu 69, –X, SmATA 15*

Fichter, George S *AuBYP 3*

Fichter, George S 1922- *ConAu 23NR, IntAu&W 86, WrDr 86, –88, –90, –92*

Fichter, George S 1922-1993 *WrDr 94N*

Fichter, George Siebert 1922- *AuBYP 2S, BioIn 2, –10, ConAu 17R, –7NR, IntAu&W 82, SmATA 7, WhoSSW 73, –75, –76, WrDr 76, –80, –82, –84*
Pseud./variant:
Warner, Matt

Fidler, Kathleen 1899-1980 *Au&Wr 71, BioIn 9, –15, ConAu 25R, –117, –20NR, ScF&FL 92, SmATA 3, –45N, TwCChW 78, –83, –89, WrDr 76, –80, –82*

Fiedel, Roslyn *AuBYP 2S, –3*

Fiedler, Jean Feldman 1923- *BioIn 9, ConAu 29R, ForWC 70, SmATA 4, WhoAmW 74, –75*

Field, Adelaide Anderson 1916- *WhoAm 74, –76*

Field, E M, Mrs 1856-1940 *OxCChiL*

Field, Edward *DrAPF 87, –89, –91, –93*

Field, Edward 1924- *AmAu&B, BioIn 10, –11, ConAu 13R, –10NR, ConPo 70, –75, –80, –85, –91, CroCAP, DcLB 105, DcLEL 1940, DrAP 75, DrAPF 83, –85, IntAu&W 89, –91, SmATA 8, WhoUSWr 88, WhoWrEP 89, –92, WrDr 76, –80, –82, –84, –86, –88, –90, –92, –94*

Field, Elinor Whitney 1889-1980 *BioIn 13, ConAu 109, SmATA 28N*

Field, Eugene 1850-1895 *Alli SUP, AmAu, AmAu&B, ASCAP 66, AuBYP 2, –3, BenetAL 91, BbD, BiDAmJo, BiDSA, BiD&SB, BioIn 1, –2, –3, –4, –5, –6, –7, –8, –9, –10, –11, –12, –15, –16, CarSB, CasWL, Chambr 3, ChhPo, –S1, –S2, ChrP, CnDAL, DcAmAu, DcAmBC, DcLB 23, –42, –140, DcLEL, DcNAA, EncAHmr, EncAJ, EvLB, FamPYP, HarEnUS, JrnUS, JBA 34, MajAI, NinCLC 3, OxCAmL 65, –83, OxCChiL, OxCEng 67, –85, PenC AM, RAdv 1, –13-1, REn, REnAL, RfGAmL 87, SmATA 16, Str&VC, WebAB 74, –79, WhAm HS, WorAlBi, WorAl*

Field, Frances Fox 1913?-1977 *ConAu 69*
Pseud./variant:
Fox, Frances Margaret

Field, Gans T
Main entry: Wellman, Manly Wade

Field, Peter *TwCWW 91, WrDr 86, –88, –90*
Main entry: Hobson, Laura Zametkin

Field, Rachel 1894-1942 *AmAu&B, AnCL, AuBYP 2, BenetAL 91, BioIn 1, –2, –4, –6, –7, –12, –14, BlmGWL, BkCL, CarSB, ChhPo, –S1, –S2, ChlLR 21, CnDAL, ConAmA, ConAu 109, ConICB, CurBio 42, DcLB 9, –22, DcNAA, DcWomA, FamPYP, FilmgC, HalFC 84, –88, JBA 34, –51, LongCTC, NewbMB 1922, NotNAT B, OxCAmL 65, –83, OxCChiL, REnAL, SmATA 15, Str&VC, TwCA, –SUP, TwCChW 78, –83, –89, TwCRHW 90, TwCWr, WhAm 2, WorAlBi, WorAl*

Field, Rachel Lyman 1894-1942 *AmWomPl, AuBYP 3, ConAu 137, InWom SUP, MajAI, WrChl*

Fielder, Mildred 1913- *ConAu 13R, –10NR, ForWC 70, IntAu&W 89, –91, WhoAmW 81, WrDr 76, –80, –82, –84, –86, –88, –90, –92, –94*

Fielding, Lola 1930- *ArtsCL, BioIn 6*

Fielding, Sarah 1710-1768 *Alli, ArtclWW 2, BbD, BiD&SB, BioIn 3, –12, –15, –16, BlmGEL, BlmGWL, BritAu, CamGEL, CamGLE, CarSB, CasWL, Chambr 2, DcBiPP, DcBrAmW, DcEnA, DcEnL, DcEuL, DcLB 39, DcLEL, DcNaB, EncBrWW, EvLB, FemiCLE, InWom SUP, LitC 1, NewC, OxCChiL, OxCEng 67, –85, PenC ENG, RfGEnL 91*

Fife, Dale 1910- *AuBYP 2S, -3, BioIn 12, ConAu 85, –19NR, FourBJA, SmATA 18*

Figes, Eva *BioIn 15, –16, –17*

Figes, Eva 1932- *ArtclWW 2, Au&Wr 71, BioIn 12, –13, BlmGEL, BlmGWL, CamGLE, ConAu 53, –4NR, ConLC 31, ConNov 76, –82, –86, –91, ContDcW 89, DcLB 14, DcLEL 1940, EncBrWW, FemiCLE, InWom SUP, IntAu&W 77, –82, –86, –89, –91, IntDcWB, LiExTwC, Novels, OxCEng 85, WorAu 1980, WrDr 76, –80, –82, –84, –86, –88, –90, –92, –94*

Figueroa, John L *DrAPF 87*

Figueroa, John L 1936- *ConAu 65, DrAF 76, DrAPF 83, –85*

Figueroa, Pablo 1938- *BioIn 11, ConAu 61, HispWr, SmATA 9, WhoHisp 94*

Figuerola, Carmen *SingR 2*

Fijan, Carol 1918- *BioIn 11, ConAu 53, SmATA 12*

Fillmore, Parker Hoysted 1878-1944 *AmAu&B, BioIn 2, –11, DcNAA, JBA 34, –51, OhA&B, WhAm 2, YABC 1*

Filson, Floyd Vivian 1896- *AmAu&B, ConAu 61, WhoAm 74, –76*

Filstrup, Chris
Main entry: Filstrup, E Christian

Filstrup, E Christian 1942- *ConAu 113, SmATA 43, WhoAm 86, –88, –90, –92, –94, WhoLibI 82*
Pseud./variant:
Filstrup, Chris

Filstrup, Jane Merrill *SmATA X*
Main entry: Merrill, Jane

Filstrup, Janie *ConAu X, SmATA X*
Main entry: Merrill, Jane

Finch, Donald George 1937- *ConAu 53, WhoMW 78, –80, –82, –84, WhoWor 84, –87*

Finder, Martin *ConAu 137, –X, MajAI, SmATA X*
Main entry: Salzmann, Siegmund

Fine, Anne 1947- *BioIn 13, ChlFicS, ChlLR 25, ConAu 105, –38NR, IntAu&W 89, –91, MajAI, SmATA 29, –72, –15AS, TwCChW 83, –89, WhoAm 92, –94, WrDr 86, –88, –90, –92, –94*

Fineman, Morton *AuBYP 2S, –3*

Fineman, Morton A 1919- *AmMWSc 86*

Finger, Charles J 1861-1941 *ScFEYrs*

Finger, Charles J 1869-1941 *BenetAL 91 ConAu 119, TwCChW 89*

Finger, Charles Joseph 1869?-1941 *AmAu&B, AnCL, AuBYP 2, –3, BioIn 4, –6, –7, –14, –15, BkCL, CurBio 41, DcNAA, JBA 34, NewbMB 1922, OhA&B, REnAL, SmATA 42, TwCA, TwCChW 83, WebE&AL, WhAm 1*

Fink, Augusta 1916- *ConAu 33R, –13NR, IntAu&W 77, –82, WhoAmW 75, WrDr 76, –80, –82, –84, –86, –88, –90*

Fink, Sam 1916- *WhoAmA 73*

Fink, Samuel Donovan 1959- *WhoSSW 91*

Fink, Samuel Ira 1957- *WhoWest 94*

Fink, William Bertrand 1916- *BioIn 13, ConAu 41R, DrAS 74H, –78H, –82H, SmATA 22*

Finke, Blythe Foote 1922- *BioIn 13, ConAu 65, IntAu&W 82, SmATA 26, WhoAmW 91, WhoE 81, –83*

Finkel, George 1909-1975 *Au&Wr 71, BioIn 11, ConAu P-2, SingR 2, SmATA 8, TwCChW 78, –83, –89*
Pseud./variant:
Pennage, E M

Finkel, George Irvine 1909-1975 *DcChlFi*

Finkel, Lawrence S 1925- *ConAu 13R*

Finkelstein, Norman H 1941- *SmATA 73*

Finlay, Ian F 1924- *Au&Wr 71, WhoLib 72, WhoMus 72*

Finlay, Ian Hamilton 1925- *BioIn 10, –14, –15, –16, –17, BlmGEL, CamGLE, ChhPo S2, CmScLit, ConArt 77, –83, –89, ConAu 81, ConBrA 79, ConPo 70, –75, –80, –85, –91, DcLB 40, DcLEL 1940, IntAu&W 91, OxCEng 85, TwCPaSc, WebE&AL, WorAu 1950, WrDr 76, –80, –82, –84, –86, –88, –90, –92, –94*

Finlay, Winfred Lindsay Crawford 1910- *Au&Wr 71, ConAu 9R, TwCChW 78, WhoAmW 74, WhoWor 74, WrDr 76, –80*

Finlay, Winifred 1910- *BioIn 13, IntAu&W 82, ScF&FL 92, SmATA 23, TwCChW 83, –89, WrDr 82, –84, –86, –88, –90*

Finlayson, Ann 1925- *BioIn 11, ConAu 29R, SmATA 8*

Finley, Martha 1828-1909 *BioIn 15, ConAu 118, FemiCLE, TwCChW 89A, WomNov, WorAlBi*

Finley, Martha Farquaharson 1828-1909 *InWom SUP*

Finley, Martha Farquharson 1828-1909 *Alli SUP, AmAu, AmAu&B, BenetAL 91, BiDSA, BiD&SB, BioIn 2, –4, –8, –12, CarSB, CnDAL, DcAmAu, DcLB 42, DcNAA, IndAu 1816, OhA&B, OxCAmL 65, –83, OxCChiL, REnAL, SmATA 43, TwCChW 83A, WhAm 1, WhoChL, WorAl*
Pseud./variant:
Farquharson, Martha

Finnemore, Joseph 1860-1939 *BioIn 14, ClaDrA, DcBrAr 1, DcBrBI, DcVicP 2, TwCPaSc*

Finney, Gertrude Elva 1892- *AuBYP 2, –3, BioIn 4, –8, ConAu P-1, CurBio 57, ForWC 70, IndAu 1917, WhoPNW*

Finney, Shan 1944- *SmATA 65*

Finnin, Mary 1906- *AuWomWr, BlueB 76, ConAu 106, ConPo 70, IntWWP 82, OxCAusL, WhoWor 74, WrDr 76, –80, –82, –84*

Finocchiaro, Mary 1913- *ConAu 29R, –27NR, DrAS 74F, –78F, –82F, LEduc 74*

Finta, Alexander S 1881-1958 *ArtsAmW 2, BioIn 1, EncAB-A 11, IlsCB 1744, WhAm 3, WhAmArt 85, WhoAmA 80N, –82N*

Firdausi 935?-1020? *AnCL, BbD, BiD&SB, BioIn 4, CasWL, ChhPo S1, Dis&D, NewC, OxCEng 67, PenC CL, RComWL, REn, WhDW*

Firer, Ben Zion 1914- *BioIn 17, SmATA X*

Firer, Benzion 1914- *ConAu 131, SmATA 64*

Fireside, Bryna J 1932- *SmATA 73*

Firmin, Charlotte 1954- *BioIn 13, ConAu 106, –23NR, SmATA 29*

Firmin, Peter 1928- *BioIn 12, ConAu 81, –17NR, –40NR, SmATA 15, –58*

Fischbach, Julius 1894- *BioIn 11, ConAu 5R, –2NR, SmATA 10, WhoMW 74, –76, –78, –80, –82, –84*

Fischer, Ann A *IlsBYP*

Fischer, Anton Otto 1882-1962 *BioIn 1, –5, –6, –11, DcSeaP, IlrAm 1880, –C, IlsCB 1744, –1946, WhAm 4, WhAmArt 85, WorECar*

Fischer, Hans Erich 1909-1958 *BioIn 2, –3, –5, –6, –8, ChsFB I, IlsBYP, IlsCB 1946, –1957, MorJA*

Fischer-Nagel, Andreas 1951- *BioIn 16, ConAu 123, SmATA 56*

Fischer-Nagel, Heiderose 1956- *BioIn 16, ConAu 123, SmATA 56*

Fischler, Shirley *SmATA 66*

Fischler, Shirley Walton *ConAu 136, WrDr 94*

Fischler, Stan *ConAu 116, –128, SmATA 36, –66*

Fischtrom, Harvey *AuBYP 3*

Fischtrom, Harvey 1933-1974 *AuBYP 2S, ConAu 53, –P-2, ThrBJA*

Pseud./variant:
Zemach, Harve

Fischtrom, Margot Zemach *ThrBJA*
Pseud./variant:
Zemach, Margot
Main entry: Zemach, Margot

Fish, Byron 1908- *ConAu 45, WhoPNW*

Fish, Helen Dean 1890-1953 *AmAu&B, BioIn 3, ChhPo, ObitOF 79*

Fish, Richard G 1925- *WhoAmA 78, -80, -82, -84, -86, -89, -91*

Fishback, Margaret
Main entry: Antolini, Margaret Fishback

Fishback, Margaret 1904-1985 *BioIn 5, -6, -8, ConAu X, CurBio 85N, SmATA X*

Fisher, Aileen 1906- *IntAu&W 91, TwCChW 89, WrDr 86, -88, -90, -92*

Fisher, Aileen Lucia 1906- *AuBYP 2, -3, BioIn 6, -8, -9, -13, BkCL, BkP, ChhPo, -S1, -S2, ConAu 5R, -2NR, -17NR, -37NR, ForWC 70, MajAI, MorJA, SmATA 1, -25, -73, TwCChW 78, -83, WhoAmW 83, WrDr 80, -82, -84, -94*

Fisher, Anne Benson 1898-1967 *AmAu&B, AmNov, BioIn 2, WhAm 4, -5*

Fisher, Barbara 1940- *ConAu 104, -30NR, NatPD 81, SmATA 34, -44, WhoAmW 81*
Pseud./variant:
Perry, Barbara Fisher

Fisher, Barbara Turk 1940- *WhoAmW 93*

Fisher, Bud 1884-1954 *EncACom*

Fisher, Bud 1885-1954 *AmAu&B, ArtCS, BioIn 3, -6, -15, WebAB 74, -79, WhAm 3, WhAmArt 85, WhJnl*

Fisher, Clavin C 1912- *BioIn 13, ConAu 65, SmATA 24*

Fisher, Clay *AmAu&B, BenetAL 91, BioIn 13, ConAu 135, EncFWF, IntAu&W 91X, TwCWW 91, WrDr 84, -86, -88, -90, -92*
Main entry: Allen, Henry

Fisher, Clay 1912- *WrDr 94*

Fisher, David *AuBYP 2, -3, BioIn 8, -9*

Fisher, Dorothy Canfield *WomNov*

Fisher, Dorothy Canfield 1879-1958 *AmAu&B, AmNov X, ArtclWW 2, AuBYP 2S, -3, BenetAL 91, BioAmW, BioIn 1, -2, -3, -4, -5, -6, -9, -11, -17, CarSB, Chambr 3, ChhPo, -S1, -S2, CnDAL, ConAmA, ConAmL, ConAu 114, DcLB 9, -102, HerW, -84, InWom SUP, LongCTC, ModAL, NotAW MOD, ObitOF 79, OhA&B, OxCAmL 65, -83, OxCChiL, REn, REnAL, TwCA, -SUP, TwCChW 78, -83, -89, WebAB 74, -79, WhAm 3, WhNAA, WomWWA 14, YABC 1*
Pseud./variant:
Canfield, Dorothy

Fisher, Dorothy Frances Canfield 1879-1958 *ConAu 136, MajAI*

Fisher, Dudley 1890-1951 *ArtCS, BioIn 2, ObitOF 79, WorECar*

Fisher, Hammond Edward 1901?-1955 *AmAu&B, ArtCS, BioIn 3, -4, EncAJ, ObitOF 79, WhAmArt 85*

Fisher, Harvey Irvin *AmMWSc 86*

Fisher, Harvey Irvin 1916- *AmMWSc 73P, -76P, -82, ConAu 69, WhoAm 74, -76, -78, -80*

Fisher, James Maxwell McConnell 1912-1970 *Au&Wr 71, BioIn 5, -9, -14, DcNaB 1951, GrBr, NewYTBE 70, WhAm 5*

Fisher, John 1909- *Au&Wr 71, ConAu 81, SmATA 15*
Pseud./variant:
Piper, Roger

Fisher, Laura Harrison 1934- *BioIn 10, ConAu 13R, ForWC 70, SmATA 5*

Fisher, Leonard Everett *ChlBIlD*

Fisher, Leonard Everett 1924- *AuBYP 2, -3, BioIn 3, -5, -7, -8, -9, -10, -12, -14, -15, -16, ChlLR 18, ConAu 1R, -2NR, -37NR, DcLB 61, IlsCB 1946, -1957, -1967, IntAu&W 82, -86, -89, -91, MajAI, MorBMP, ScF&FL 92, SmATA 4, -34, -73, -1AS, ThrBJA, WhoAm 86, -88, -90, -92, WhoAmA 73, -78, -80, -82, -84, -86, -89, -91, WhoAmJ 80, WhoE 74, -85, -86, -89, WhoWorJ 72, -78, WrDr 76, -80, -82, -84, -86, -88, -90, -92, -94*

Fisher, Lois I 1948- *ConAu 113, SmATA 35, -38*

Fisher, Lois Jeannette 1909- *BioIn 2, ConAu 5R*

Fisher, M F K
Main entry: Fisher, Mary Frances Kennedy

Fisher, Margery 1913- *AuBYP 2, -3, Au&Wr 71, BioIn 8, -12, ChhPo, ConAu 73, IntAu&W 82, OxCChiL, SmATA 20, Who 82, -83, -85, WhoChL*

Fisher, Margery Turner 1913-1992 *ConAu 140, SmATA 74*

Fisher, Mary Frances 1908- *ArtclWW 2*

Fisher, Mary Frances Kennedy 1908- *BioIn 1, -2, -6, -9, -11, -12, -13, -15, -16, ConAu 77, ContDcW 89, CurBio 48, DrAF 76, InWom SUP*
Pseud./variant:
Fisher, M F K
Parrish, Mary Frances

Fisher, Mary Frances Kennedy 1908-1992 *BioIn 17*

Fisher, Olive M *OxCCan*

Fisher, Robert 1943- *ConAu 26NR, SmATA 47*

Fisher, Suzanne *SmATA 70*
Main entry: Staples, Suzanne Fisher

Fisher, Thomas Henry 1879-1962 *BioIn 8, -14*
Pseud./variant:
Henry, Thomas

Fishler, Mary 1920- *AuBYP 2S, -3, ConAu 5R, ForWC 70*

Fishlock, David Jocelyn 1932- *Au&Wr 71, IntAu&W 77, -86, -89, Who 85, -88, -92, WrDr 76, -80, -82, -84, -86, -88, -90, -92, -94*

Fishlock, David Jocelyn, Dr 1932- *Who 90*

Fishman, Isidore 1908- *Au&Wr 71*

Fishwick, Marshall William 1923- *AmMWSc 73S, ConAu 5R, -6NR*

Fisk, Nicholas 1923- *BioIn 13, -14, ChlFicS, ConAu 65, -11NR, -28NR, ConSFA, EncSF 93, IlsBYP, IntAu&W 91, OxCChiL, ScF&FL 92, ScFSB, SmATA 25, TwCChW 78, -83, -89, TwCSFW 86, -91, TwCYAW, WrDr 80, -82, -84, -86, -88, -90, -92, -94*

Fisk, Pauline 1948- *ConAu 136, ScF&FL 92, SmATA 66, WrDr 94*

Fitch, Bob 1938- *ConAu 21R*

Fitch, Clarke *AuBYP 2, -3, ConAmA, ConAu X, MajTwCW, SmATA X, TwCYAW*
Main entry: Sinclair, Upton Beall

Fitch, Clyde 1865-1909 *AmAu, AmAu&B, BenetAL 91, BioIn 1, -9, -12, -13, CamGWoT, CarSB, Chambr 3, CnDAL, CnMD, CnThe, ConAu 110, DcLEL, DcNAA, McGEWD 72, ModAL, ModWD, NotNAT A, -B, OxCAmL 65, -83, OxCAmT 84, OxCThe 83, PenC AM, PlP&P, REnAL, REnWD, RfGAmL 87, WhAm 1*

Fitch, Florence Mary 1875-1959 *AmAu&B, AuBYP 2, -3, BioIn 5, -6, -7, MorJA, ObitOF 79, OhA&B, WhAm 3, WomWWA 14*

Fitch, George Helgeson 1877-1915 *AmAu&B, CarSB, DcNAA, REnAL, WhAm 1*

Fitch, John, IV *BioIn 11, -12, -13, ConAu X, MajAI, SmATA X*
Main entry: Cormier, Robert Edmund

Fitchett, William Henry 1842-1928 *BioIn 2, Chambr 3, EncWM, OxCAusL*

Fitschen, Dale 1937- *BioIn 12, ConAu 77, SmATA 20*

Fitter, Richard Sidney Richmond 1913- *Au&Wr 71, ConAu 65, -11NR, IntAu&W 77, -82, -89, -91, Who 74, -82, -83, -85, -88, -90, -92, WrDr 76, -80*

Fitts, James Franklin 1840-1890 *AmAu&B, BiD&SB, CarSB, DcAmAu, DcNAA*

Fitzalan, Roger *ConAu X, DcLEL 1940, SmATA X, TwCCr&M 91, WrDr 76, -80, -82, -84, -94*
Main entry: Trevor, Elleston

Fitzalan, Roger 1920- *BioIn 14*

Fitzgerald, Captain Hugh *ConAu 133, -X, MajAI, SmATA X, ThrBJA*
Main entry: Baum, Lyman Frank

Fitzgerald, Cathleen 1932- *ConAu 33R, ForWC 70*

FitzGerald, Cathleen 1932-1987 *BioIn 16, ConAu 121, SmATA 50N*

Fitzgerald, Charles Patrick 1902- *Au&Wr 71, BioIn 7, ConAu 17R, IntAu&W 89, IntWW 89, -91, Who 74, -82, -83, -85, -88, -90, -92, WrDr 76, -82, -84, -86, -88, -90, -92, -94*

Fitzgerald, Ed 1898-1982 *BioIn 1, CurBio 47, -82N, NewYTBE 73, NewYTBS 82*

Fitzgerald, Edward Earl 1919- *AmAu&B, AuBYP 2, -3, BioIn 8, -12, ConAu 73, SmATA 20, WhoAm 74, -76, -78, -80, -82, -84, -86, -88, -90, -92, -94, WhoFI 74, WhoWor 78, -80, -82*

Fitzgerald, F A 1940- *SmATA 15*

Fitzgerald, John D 1906-1988 *TwCChW 89*

Fitzgerald, John D 1907- *AuBYP 2S, -3, BioIn 12, ChlLR 1, FifBJA, OxCChiL, SmATA 20, TwCChW 83, WrDr 86, -88*

Fitzgerald, John D 1907-1988 *BioIn 16, ConAu 126, SmATA 56N*

FitzGerald, John Daniel 1862-1922 *OxCAusL*

Fitzgerald, John David, Lord 1816-1889 *DcNaB S1, OxCLaw*

Fitzgerald, John Dennis 1907- *ConAu 93, DcAmChF 1960*

Fitzgerald, John Dennis 1907?-1988 *MajAI*

Fitzgerald, John Dillon 1897-1965 *BioIn 9*

Fitzgerald, Merni I 1955- *SmATA 53*

Fitzgerald, Merni Ingrassia 1955- *BioIn 16, ConAu 124*

Fitzgibbon, Constantine 1919- *ScFSB*

Fitzgibbon, Constantine 1919-1983 *AmAu&B, AnObit 1983, Au&Wr 71, BioIn 13, BlueB 76, ConAu 1R, –109, –2NR, DcIrL, DcNaB 1981, IntAu&W 77, –82, IntWW 74, –75, –76, –77, –78, –79, –80, –81, –82, –83, –83N, Novels, ScF&FL 92, TwCSFW 86, –91, Who 74, –82, –83, WhoWor 74, –78, WorAu 1950, WrDr 76, –80, –82, –84*

Fitzhardinge, Joan Margaret 1912- *AuBYP 2, –3, Au&Wr 71, BioIn 9, ConAu 13R, –6NR, –23NR, –36NR, IntAu&W 77, –82, MajAI, SmATA 2, –73, ThrBJA*
Pseud./variant:
Phipson, Joan

Fitzhugh, Louise 1928-1974 *AuBYP 2, –3, BioIn 8, –9, –10, –13, BlmGWL, ChlLR 1, ConAu 53, –34NR, –P-2, DcAmChF 1960, DcLB 52, NewYTBS 74, OxCChiL, SmATA 1, –24N, –45, ThrBJA, TwCChW 78, –83, –89*

Fitzhugh, Louise Perkins 1928-1974 *MajAI*

Fitzhugh, Percy Keese 1876-1950 *BioIn 17, ConAu 133, SmATA 65*
Pseud./variant:
Lloyd, Hugh

Fitzpatrick, Sir Percy
Main entry: Fitzpatrick, James Percy, Sir

Fitzpatrick, James Percy, Sir 1862-1931 *BioIn 2, –4, –8, –9, –11, Chambr 3, DcLEL, DcNaB 1931, EncSoA, OxCChiL, PenC ENG, TwCWr, WhoChL*
Pseud./variant:
Fitzpatrick, Sir Percy

Fitz-Randolph, Jane 1915- *SmATA 51*

Fitzsimmons, Robert *AuBYP 2, –3, BioIn 8, MedPD*

Fitzsimons, Raymund *ConAu 33R, WrDr 76, –82, –86, –88, –90*

Fitzsimons, Ruth Marie *AmMWSc 73S, ConAu 53, WhoAm 82, –84, –86, –88, WhoAmW 75, –77, WhoE 74, –75, –81, –83, –85, –86, –89*

Fitzsimons, Ruth Marie 1940-1989 *WhAm 10*

Fix, Philippe *AuBYP 2S, –3*

Flach, Vera 1895- *BioIn 9*

Flack, Marjorie 1897-1958 *AmAu&B, AmPB, AuBYP 2, –3, BioIn 1, –2, –5, –7, –12, ChhPo, ChlLR 28, ConAu 112, –136, IlsCB 1744, –1946, JBA 34, –51, MajAI, ObitOF 79, OxCChiL, Str&VC, TwCChW 78, –83, –89, WhAm 3, YABC 2*

Flack, Naomi John *ConAu 1NR, SmATA 35, –40*
Pseud./variant:
Sellers, Naomi John

Flack, Naomi John White *BioIn 14, –15*

Flaherty, Robert J 1884-1951 *BenetAL 91 WorFDir 1*

Flaherty, Robert Joseph 1884-1951 *AmAu&B, AuBYP 2S, –3, BiDFilm, BioIn 1, –2, –3, –5, –7, –9, –10, –11, –12, –14, –15, –16, ConAu 115, CurBio 49, –51, DcFM, EncAB-H, EncAJ, FilmgC, ICPEnP A, MacBEP, MovMk, ObitOF 79, OxCCan, OxCFilm, REn, WebAB 74, –79, WhAm 3, WomWMM, WorEFlm*

Flammonde, Paris *ConAu 17R, WhoUSWr 88, WhoWrEP 89, –92*

Flanagan, Geraldine Lux *AuBYP 2S, –3*

Flanders, Michael 1922-1975 *AuBYP 2, –3, Au&Wr 71, BiE&WWA, BioIn 5, –7, –8, –9, –10, BlueB 76N, CamGWoT, ChhPo, –S1, –S2, ConAu 5R, –57, –4NR, CurBio 70, –75N, IntWW 74, –75N, NotNAT B, ObitOF 79, ObitT 1971, OxCPMus, OxCThe 67, –83, WhAm 6, WhScrn 83, –77, Who 74, WhoHol C, WhoMus 72, WhoThe 72, WhoWor 74*

Flanders, Michael Henry 1922-1975 *DcNaB 1971*

Flash Flood *SmATA 6*
Main entry: Robinson, Jan M

Flaxman, Traudl 1942- *ConAu 25R*
Pseud./variant:
Traudl

Flayderman, Phillip C 1930-1969 *ConAu P-2*

Fleischer, Leonore 1932- *ScF&FL 92*

Fleischer, Leonore 1934?- *SmATA 47*
Pseud./variant:
Edwards, Alexander
Roote, Mike
Thomas, Allison

Fleischer, Max *EncACom*

Fleischer, Max 1889-1972 *ArtCS, BioIn 9, –11, –14, ConAu 109, DcFM, FilmgC, HalFC 84, –88, NewYTBE 72, ObitOF 79, OxCFilm, ScF&FL 92, SmATA 30, WorECar, WorEFlm*

Fleischhauer-Hardt, Helga 1936- *BioIn 14, ConAu 102, SmATA 30*

Fleischman, Albert Sid 1920- *IntAu&W 91*

Fleischman, Albert Sidney 1920- *AnCL, AuBYP 2, –3, BioIn 8, –11, –13, ChlLR 1, ConAu 1R, MajAI, SmATA 8, ThrBJA, TwCChW 78, WhoAm 82, –84, –86, –88, –90, –92, –94, WhoUSWr 88, WhoWrEP 89, –92, WrDr 80*
Pseud./variant:
Fleischman, Sid

Fleischman, Paul 1952- *Au&Arts 11, AuBYP 3, ChlLR 20, ConAu 113, –37NR, DcAmChF 1985, FifBJA, MajAI, ScF&FL 92, SmATA 32, –39, –72, TwCChW 89, TwCYAW, WhoAm 92, –94, WrDr 90, –92, –94*

Fleischman, Sid 1920- *BioIn 9, ChlLR 15, ConAu 5NR, DcAmChF 1960, –1985, OxCChiL, ScF&FL 92, SmATA 59, TwCChW 83, –89, WrDr 82, –84, –86, –88, –90, –92*

Fleischman, Sid
Main entry: Fleischman, Albert Sidney

Fleischmann, Glen Harvey 1909- *AuBYP 2S, –3, BioIn 2, ConAu 33R, WhoAm 74, –76, –78, –80, –82, –84, –86, WhoE 74, WhoWor 74, –78, –80, –82, –84*

Fleisher, Robbin 1951-1977 *BioIn 16, SmATA 49, –52*

Fleishman, Seymour 1918- *BioIn 5, –8, –14, –17, ConAu 111, –133, IlsBYP, IlsCB 1946, –1957, SmATA 32, –66, WrDr 94*

Fleissner, Else Mentz 1900- *DrAS 74F*

Fleming, Alice 1928- *AuBYP 3, IntAu&W 89, –91, WrDr 86, –88, –90, –92*

Fleming, Alice Carew Mulcahey 1928- *AuBYP 2, BioIn 8, –11, ConAu 1R, ForWC 70, SmATA 9, WhoAm 92, –94, WhoAmW 74, –75, –77, –83, –87, –89, –91, –93, WhoE 74, –81, WrDr 76, –80, –94*

Fleming, Elizabeth *AuBYP 2, BioIn 8, ChhPo, –S1, –S2, Str&VC*

Fleming, Elizabeth P 1888-1985 *AuBYP 3, BioIn 16, ConAu 119, SmATA 48N*

Fleming, Ian *IntvTCA 2*

Fleming, Ian 1908-1964 *AuBYP 2, –3, Benet 87, BioIn 5, –6, –7, –8, –10, –11, –14, –17, CamGLE, CnDBLB 7, ConAu 5R, ConLC 3, –30, CrtSuMy, CurBio 64, DcLB 87, EncMys, FifBJA, FilmgC, HalFC 84, LongCTC, MajTwCW, NewC, Novels, ObitT 1961, OxCChiL, PenC ENG, REn, RfGEnL 91, ScFSB, SmATA 9, TwCCr&M 80, –85, –91, TwCWr, WhAm 4, WhoSpyF, WorAlBi, WorAu 1950*
Pseud./variant:
Atticus

Fleming, Ian Lancaster 1908-1964 *EncSF 93, TwCYAW*

Fleming, Joan Margaret 1908-1980 *ConAu 81, –102*

Fleming, Ronald Lee 1941- *SmATA 56, WhoAm 86, –88, –90, –92, –94, WhoAmA 86, –89, –91, WhoE 86*

Fleming, Susan 1932- *ConAu 14NR, SmATA 32*

Fleming, Thomas J 1927- *BioIn 17*

Fleming, Thomas James 1927- *AmAu&B, AuBYP 2S, –3, BioIn 11, ConAu 5R, ConLC 37, SmATA 8, WhoAm 74, –76, –78, –80, –82, –84, –86, –88, –90, –92, –94, WhoUSWr 88, WhoWor 74, WhoWrEP 89, –92*
Pseud./variant:
Cain, Christopher
James, T F
Thomas, J F

Flender, Harold 1924- *AuBYP 2S, –3, ConAu 49, DrAF 76*

Flender, Harold 1924-1975 *ConAu 135*

Flesch, Yolande *WrDr 90*

Flesch, Yolande 1950- *ConAu 122*
Pseud./variant:
Greene, Yvonne

Flesch, Yolande Catarina 1950- *SmATA 55*

Fletcher, Adele 1898- *ConAu P-1, ForWC 70, WhNAA*

Fletcher, Alan Mark 1928- *AuBYP 2S, –3, ConAu 73, WrDr 76, –80, –82, –84, –86, –88*

Fletcher, Beale *AuBYP 2, –3, BioIn 7*

Fletcher, Charlie May *AuBYP 3*

Fletcher, Charlie May 1897-1977 *AuBYP 2, BioIn 9, -11, -12, ConAu 9R, SmATA 3*

Fletcher, Charlie May Hogue
Main entry: Simon, Charlie May

Fletcher, Colin 1922- *AuNews 1, BioIn 10, -12, -13, ConAu 13R, -11NR, IntAu&W 89, -91, SmATA 28, WhoAm 74, -76, -78, -80, -82, -84, -86, -88, -90, -92, -94, WrDr 76, -80, -82, -84, -86, -88, -90, -92, -94*

Fletcher, David
Main entry: Barber, D F

Fletcher, David 1940- *ConAu X, IntAu&W 82X, -91, WrDr 76, -80, -82, -84, -86, -88*

Fletcher, David 1940-1988 *TwCCr&M 91*

Fletcher, Frank *ArtCS, ChhPo S2*

Fletcher, Geoffrey Scowcroft *Who 88, -90, -92*

Fletcher, Geoffrey Scowcroft 1923- *ClaDrA, ConAu 103, DcBrAr 1, DcLEL 1940, IntAu&W 77, Who 74, -82, -83, -85*

Fletcher, Helen Jill 1911- *AuBYP 2, -3, BioIn 8, ConAu 9R, ForWC 70, SmATA 13*
Pseud./variant:
Lee, Carol
Morey, Charles

Fletcher, Jane A *SingR 1*

Fletcher, Jane Ada *DcChlFi*

Fletcher, Jane Ada 1871?-1956 *AuWomWr*

Fletcher, John Gould 1886-1950 *AmAu&B, AmLY, AnCL, Benet 87, BenetAL 91, BioIn 2, -3, -4, -5, -8, -11, -12, -15, -16, -17, CamGLE, CamHAL, CasWL, Chambr 3, ChhPo, CnDAL, ConAmA, ConAmL, ConAu 107, DcLB 4, -45, DcLEL, EncWL, EvLB, FifSWrA, LongCTC, ModAL, NewGrDA 86, ObitOF 79, OxCAmL 65, -83, PenC AM, REn, REnAL, RfGAmL 87, SixAP, TwCA, -SUP, TwCLC 35, WhAm 3, WhNAA*

Fletcher, Richard E 1917?-1983 *ConAu 109, SmATA 34N*
Pseud./variant:
Fletcher, Rick

Fletcher, Rick
Main entry: Fletcher, Richard E

Fletcher, Susan Clemens 1951- *SmATA 70*

Fletcher, W *CarSB, ChhPo S1*

Flettrich, Terry *WhoAmW 74*

Fleur, Anne 1901- *BioIn 5, IlsBYP, IlsCB 1946, SmATA 31*
Pseud./variant:
Sari

Flexner, James Thomas 1908- *AmAu&B, Au&Wr 71, BioIn 1, -11, -12, -14, ConAu 1R, -2NR, -37NR, IntAu&W 89, -91, IntWW 89, -91, NewYTBE 73, SmATA 9, WhAmArt 85, WhNAA, WhoAm 74, -76, -78, -80, -82, -84, -86, -88, -90, -92, -94, WhoAmA 73, -78, -80, -82, -84, -86, -89, -91, WhoE 74, WrDr 76, -80, -82, -84, -86, -88, -90, -92, -94*

Flint, David *OxCCan SUP*

Flint, Russ 1944- *SmATA 74*

Flint, Timothy 1780-1840 *Alli, AmAu, AmAu&B, BenetAL 91, BbD, BiDSA, BiD&SB, BioIn 1, -2, -3, -7, -8, -9, CnDAL, CyAL, DcAmAu, DcBiPP, DcEnL, DcLB 73, DcLEL, DcNAA, EncFWF, HarEnUS, OhA&B, OxCAmH, OxCAmL 65, -83, REnAL, WebAB 74, -79, WhAm HS*

Flitner, David Perkins, Jr. 1949- *BioIn 10, ConAu 45, -1NR, SmATA 7*

Floethe, Louise Lee 1913- *AuBYP 2, -3, BioIn 9, ConAu 1R, -2NR, ForWC 70, SmATA 4*

Floethe, Richard 1901- *BioIn 5, -6, -8, -9, -12, -14, ChhPo S2, ConAu 33R, IlsCB 1744, -1946, -1957, -1967, MorJA, SmATA 4, WhAmArt 85, WhoAmA 73, -78, -80, -82, -84, -86, -89*

Floethe, Richard 1901-1988 *WhoAmA 91N*

Floherty, John Joseph 1882-1964 *AmAu&B, AuBYP 2, -3, BioIn 2, -7, -13, JBA 51, SmATA 25, WhAm 4*

Flora, James 1914- *ConGrA 3, SmATA 6AS, TwCChW 89, WrDr 86, -88, -90, -92*

Flora, James Royer 1914- *AuBYP 2S, -3, BioIn 3, -5, -8, -9, ChsFB A, ConAu 5R, -3NR, IlsBYP, IlsCB 1946, -1957, -1967, IntAu&W 91, SmATA 1, -30, ThrBJA, TwCChW 78, -83, WhoAmA 78, -80, -82, -84, -86, -89, -91, WhoE 89, -93, WrDr 80, -82, -84, -94*

Floren, Lee 1910- *Au&Wr 71, ConAu 5R, -3NR, -18NR, IntAu&W 91, TwCWW 91, WhoPNW, WrDr 76, -80, -82, -84, -86, -88, -90*
Pseud./variant:
Nelson, Marguerite

Florence *IlsBYP*
Main entry: Wabbes, Maria

Flores, Joseph Alfonso 1941- *ChiSch*

Florian, Douglas 1950- *AuBYP 3, BioIn 12, ConAu 123, SixBJA, SmATA 19*

Flory, Jane 1917- *AuBYP 3*

Flory, Jane Trescott 1917- *AuBYP 2S, ConAu 9R, –3NR, SmATA 22*

Flory, Julia McCune 1882-1971 *BioIn 9, ConAu 29R, –P-2*

Flournoy, Valerie R 1952- *BlkAuII, –92*

Flournoy, Valerie Rose 1952- *WhoBlA 88, –90, –92, –94*

Flower, Desmond John Newman 1907- *Au&Wr 71, ChhPo, –S2, ConAu 9R, IntAu&W 82, –89, –91, IntYB 80, –81, –82, Who 74, –82, –83, –85, –88, –90, –92*

Flowerdew, Phyllis *BioIn 14, ConAu 103, IntAu&W 77X, –91, SmATA 33, WrDr 76, –80, –82, –84, –86, –88, –90, –92, –94*
Main entry: Kingsbury, Phyllis May

Floyd, Gareth 1940- *BioIn 12, ChhPo S1, IlsBYP, IlsCB 1967, SmATA 31, –62*

Fluchere, Henri Andre 1914- *ConAu 77, SmATA 40*

Flumiani, Carlo Maria 1911- *ConAu 13R, –9NR, WhNAA*

Flynn, Barbara *ConTFT 9*

Flynn, Barbara 1928- *BioIn 11, SmATA 9*

Flynn, Jackson *ConAu X, SmATA X, TwCWW 91, WrDr 76, –80, –82, –84, –86, –88, –90, –92*
Main entry: Shirreffs, Gordon Donald

Flynn, Jackson 1914- *WrDr 94*

Flynn, James J, III *BiDrACP 79*

Flynn, James Joseph 1911- *AuBYP 3*

Flynn, James Joseph 1911-1977 *AuBYP 2S, BioIn 11, ConAu 21R, DrAS 74H, –78H, WhoE 74*

Flynn, John A 1926- *WhoMW 74*

Flynn, John Aloysius 1900-1965 *BioIn 7, WhAm 4*

Flynn, John Bernard 1927- *AmMWSc 73P*

Flynn, Mary *SmATA X*
Main entry: Welsh, Mary Flynn

Flynn, Robert *DrAPF 87, –89, –91, –93*

Flynn, Robert 1932- *ConAu 29R, DrAF 76, DrAPF 83, –85, EncFWF, IntAu&W 91, TwCWW 91, WrDr 84, –86, –88, –90, –92*

Flynn, Robert Lopez 1932- *WrDr 94*

Fodor, Eugene d1991 *NewYTBS 91*

Fodor, Eugene 1905- *AmAu&B, BioIn 5, ConAu 21R, –14NR, WhoAm 74, –76, –78, –80, –82, –84, –86, –88, –90, WhoWor 74*

Fodor, Eugene 1905-1991 *AnObit 1991, BioIn 17, ConAu 133, WhAm 10*

Fodor, Eugene 1906?-1991 *News 91, –91-3*

Fodor, Ronald V 1944- *BioIn 13, ConAu 65, SmATA 25*

Fogelman, Phyllis Gensburg 1933- *ForWC 70*

Foley, Bernice Williams 1902- *BioIn 13, ConAu 29R, –12NR, ForWC 70, SmATA 28*

Foley, Daniel Joseph 1913- *AuBYP 2, –3, BioIn 8, ConAu 5R, –5NR, WhoE 74, –75*

Foley, June 1944- *ConAu 109, SmATA 44, TwCYAW*

Foley, Louise Munro 1933- *AuBYP 2S, –3, BioIn 15, –16, ConAu 37R, IntAu&W 77X, –91, ScF&FL 92, SmATA 40, –54, WrDr 76, –80, –82, –84, –86, –88, –90, –92*

Foley, Martha 1897-1977 *DcLB 137*

Foley, Rae
Main entry: Denniston, Elinore

Foley, Rae 1900-1978 *BioIn 13, –14, ConAu X, SmATA X, TwCCr&M 80, –85*

Foley, Scott *AuBYP 3, ConAu X*
Main entry: Dareff, Hal

Folkard, Charles James 1878-1963 *BioIn 1, –8, –13, ChhPo, –S1, ConAu 109, ConICB, DcBrAr 1, DcBrBI, IlsCB 1744, SmATA 28, WhoChL*

Follen, Eliza Lee 1787-1860 *Alli, AmAu, AmAu&B, BiD&SB, BioIn 3, –7, –12, ChhPo, –S1, –S2, DcAmAu, DcLB 1, DcNAA, FemPA, OxCAmH, OxCChiL, Str&VC, WhAm HS*

Follen, Eliza Lee Cabot 1787-1860 *InWom SUP*

Follett, Helen 1884?-1970 *AmAu&B, AuBYP 2, –3, BioIn 8, –13, SmATA 27N*

Follett, Robert J R 1928- *ConAu 23NR, WhoAmP 85, –87, –89, –91, –93*

Follett, Robert John Richard 1928- *ConAu 21R, –8NR, WhoAm 74, –76, –78, –80, –82, –84, –86, –88, –90, –92, –94, WhoAmP 83, WhoFI 85, WhoMW 84, –86, –90, –92, –93, WhoUSWr 88, WhoWrEP 89, –92*

Folsom, Franklin 1907- *AuBYP 3*

Folsom, Franklin Brewster 1907- *AuBYP 2, BioIn 8, –10, ConAu 1R, IntAu&W 82, –91, SmATA 5, WhoAm 80, –82, –84, –86, –88, –90, –92, –94, WrDr 76, –80, –82, –84, –86, –88, –90, –92, –94*
Pseud./variant:
Brewster, Benjamin
Cutler, Samuel
Gorham, Michael
Hopkins, Lyman
Nesbit, Troy

Folsom, Michael Brewster 1938- *AuBYP 2, –3, ConAu 112, SmATA 40*

FonEisen, Anthony T 1917- *ConAu 13R, DcAmChF 1960*

Fontana, Vincent J 1923- *AmMWSc 86, –89, –92*

Fontana, Vincent James 1923- *AmMWSc 73P, –76P, –82, ConAu 13R*

Fontane, Theodor 1819-1898 *Benet 87, BiD&SB, BioIn 1, –3, –5, –7, –11, –12, –13, –16, CasWL, ChhPo S2, ClDMEL 47, CyWA 58, DcLB 129, EncWT, EuAu, EuWr 6, EvEuW, GrFLW, McGEWB, NinCLC 26, Novels, OxCEng 85, OxCGer 76, –86, PenC EUR, RAdv 13-2, REn, WhDW, WorAlBi*

Fontenot, Mary Alice 1910- *BioIn 14, ConAu 37R, –14NR, –31NR, ForWC 70, IntAu&W 89, SmATA 34, WrDr 76, –80, –82, –84, –86, –88, –90, –92, –94*

Foon, Dennis 1951- *BioIn 17, ConAu 28NR, TwCChW 89, WhoCanL 87, –92, WrDr 90, –92, –94*

Fooner, Michael *AuBYP 2S, –3, BioIn 13, ConAu 81, SmATA 22*

Foote, Darby Mozelle 1942- *ConAu 61*

Foote, Samuel 1720?-1777 *Alli, AnCL, BiD&SB, BioIn 3, –9, –12, –14, –17, BritAu, CamGEL, CamGLE, CasWL, Chambr 2, ChhPo, DcBiPP, DcEnA, DcEnL, DcNaB, Dis&D, EncWT, EvLB, McGEWD 72, –84, MouLC 2, NewC, NotNAT A, –B, OxCEng 67, –85, OxCThe 67, –83, PenC ENG, REn, WebE&AL*

Foote, Samuel 1721-1777 *CamGWoT, DcLB 89, IntDcT 2, RfGEnL 91*

Foote, Timothy 1926- *SmATA 52*

Foote, Timothy Gilson 1926- *WhoAm 86, –92, –94*

Foote-Smith, Elizabeth *DrAPF 87, –89, –91, –93*

Foote-Smith, Elizabeth 1913- *BioIn 10, ConAu 69*

Foran, Mary Frances 1931- *Au&Wr 71*

Forberg, Ati 1925- *AuBYP 2, –3, BioIn 8 –13, ChhPo, –S1, –S2, ConAu X, FourBJA, IlsCB 1957, –1967, SmATA 22*

Forberg, Beate Gropius *AuBYP 3*

Forbes, Athol *NotNAT B*

Forbes, Bryan *ConDr 88A*

Forbes, Bryan 1926- *BioIn 7, –9, –10, –11, –13, –15, –16, BlueB 76, ConDr 82A, HalFC 84, –88, IntAu&W 82, –89, –91, IntMPA 81, –82, –84, –86, –88, –92, IntWW 79, –80, –81, –82, –83, –89, –91, SmATA 37, Who 82, –83, –85, –88, –90, –92, WhoAm 80, –82, –84, –86, –88, –90, –92, –94, WhoWor 82, –84, –87, –89, WorFDir 2, WrDr 82, –84, –86, –88, –90, –92, –94*

Forbes, Cabot L *AuBYP 3, ConAu X, SmATA X*
Main entry: Hoyt, Edwin Palmer, Jr.

Forbes, Colin *IntAu&W 91, TwCCr&M 91, WrDr 86, –88, –90, –92, –94*

Forbes, Colin 1923- *Au&Wr 71, ConAu X, WrDr 80, –82, –84*

Forbes, Colin 1928- *ConDes 90, Who 88, –90, –92*

Forbes, Elliot 1917- *Baker 84, –92, BlueB 76, ConAu 9R, DrAS 74H, –78H, –82H, IntWWM 85, –90, NewAmDM, NewGrDA 86, WhoAm 74, –76, –78, –80, –82, –84, –86, –88, –90, WhoAmM 83, WhoEnt 92*

Forbes, Esther *IntvTCA 2*

Forbes, Esther 1891-1967 *AmAu&B, AmNov, AnCL, AuBYP 2, BenetAL 91, BioIn 1, –2, –3, –4, –5, –6, –7, –8, –9, –11, –12, –14, ChhPo S2, ChlLR 27, ConAu 25R, –P-1, ConLC 12, CyWA 58, DcAmB S8, DcLB 22, DcLEL, FemiCLE, MajAI, MorJA, NewbMB 1922, NotAW MOD, ObitOF 79, OxCAmL 65, –83, OxCChiL, REn, REnAL, SmATA 2, TwCA, –SUP, TwCChW 78, –83, –89, TwCRHW 90, TwCYAW, WhAm 4*

Forbes, Esther 1894-1967 *AuBYP 3, InWom SUP*

Forbes, Graham B *ConAu P-2*
Main entry: Stratemeyer, Edward L

Forbes, Katherine d1956 *AuBYP 3*

Forbes, Kathryn
Main entry: McLean, Kathryn Anderson

Forbes, Kathryn 1909-1966 *AmAu&B, AmNov, BenetAL 91, CmCal, ConAu X, CurBio 44, –66, InWom SUP, ObitOF 79, REn, REnAL, SmATA X, WorAlBi, WorAl*

Forbus, Ina B *BioIn 5, ConAu 1R, ForWC 70, WrDr 76, –80, –82, –84, –86, –88, –90, –92, –94*

Ford, Albert Lee *ConAu X, MajAI*
Main entry: Stratemeyer, Edward L

Ford, Barbara *ConAu 112, –134, SmATA 34, –56, WrDr 94*

Ford, Bernette G 1950- *BlkAuIl 92*

Ford, Brian J 1939- *ConAu 34NR, IntAu&W 86, –89, SmATA 49*

Ford, Brian John 1939- *IntAu&W 91, WrDr 86, –88, –90, –92, –94*

Ford, Elbur *BlmGWL, ConAu 140, –X, –28NR, EncMys, InWom SUP, IntAu&W 91X, Novels, SmATA 74, TwCCr&M 85, –91, TwCRHW 90, Who 74, –82, –83, –85, –88, –90, –92, WrDr 76, –84, –86, –88, –90, –92*
Main entry: Hibbert, Eleanor Burford

Ford, Elbur 1906-1993 *WrDr 94N*

Ford, Ford Madox 1873-1939 *AtlBL, Benet 87, BioIn 1, –2, –4, –5, –6, –7, –8, –9, –11, –12, –13, –14, –15, –16, –17, BlmGEL, BritWr 6, CamGEL, CamGLE, CasWL, ChhPo, –S1, CnDBLB 6, CnMWL, ConAu 104, –132, CyWA 58, DcLB 34, –98, DcLEL, DcNaB 1931, EncSF 93, EncWL, –2, EvLB, GrBr, LiExTwC, LongCEL, LongCTC, MagSWL, MajTwCW, MakMC, McGEWB, ModBrL, –S1, –S2, NewC, Novels, OxCEng 67, –85, PenC ENG, RAdv 1, –13-1, REn, REnAL, RfGEnL 91, TwCA, –SUP, TwCLC 1, –15, –39, TwCRHW 90, TwCWr, WebE&AL, WhDW, WhAm 2, –4A, –HSA, WhoTwCL, WorAlBi, WorAl*

Ford, Fred *ConAu X*
Main entry: Doerffler, Alfred

Ford, Fred 1930- *AfrAmBi*

Ford, George *BioIn 12, ChhPo S2, ConAu 107, IlsCB 1967, SmATA 31*

Ford, George, Jr. 1936- *BlkAuIl, –92*

Ford, H J 1860-1941 *BioIn 14, OxCChiL*

Ford, Hilary *ConAu 37NR, MajAI, SmATA X, TwCChW 89, WrDr 82, –84, –86, –88, –90, –92*
Main entry: Youd, Samuel

Ford, Hilary 1922- *WrDr 94*

Ford, Hildegarde *ConAu X, SmATA X*
Main entry: Morrison, Velma Ford

Ford, Lauren 1891- *AuBYP 3*

Ford, Lauren 1891-1973 *AuBYP 2, BioIn 1, –2, –4, –5, –8, –10, –14, –17, DcWomA, IlsCB 1744, –1946, WhAmArt 85*

Ford, Lee 1936- *ConAu 25R*

Ford, Marcia *BioIn 10, ConAu X, SmATA 6*
Main entry: Radford, Ruby Lorraine

Ford, Mary Forker 1905-1973 *ConAu 9R, ForWC 70, IndAu 1917, WhAm 6*

Ford, Nancy K 1906-1961 *AuBYP 2, BioIn 8, –13, ConAu 109, SmATA 29N, WhAm 4*

Ford, Nancy Keffer 1906-1961 *AuBYP 3*

Ford, Paul Leicester 1865-1902 *Alli SUP, AmAu, AmAu&B, BenetAL 91, BbD, BiD&SB, BioIn 11, CarSB, Chambr 3, ChhPo S1, CnDAL, DcAmAu, DcAmBC, DcBiA, DcLEL, DcNAA, EvLB, HarEnUS, JBA 34, McGEWB, OxCAmL 65, –83, REn, REnAL, WebAB 74, –79, WhAm 1*

Ford, Peter 1936- *ConAu 126, IntAu&W 91, SmATA 59*

Foreman, Michael 1938- *BioIn 9, –11, –12, ChlLR 32, ConAu 21R, –10NR, –38NR, IlsCB 1967, IntAu&W 89, –91, MajAI, OxCChiL, SixBJA, SmATA 2, –73, TwCChW 78, –83, –89, Who 82, –83, –85, –88, –90, –92, WhoGrA 82, WrDr 80, –82, –84, –86, –88, –90, –92, –94*

Forer, Lois G 1914- *WhoAmL 85, –87*

Forer, Lois Goldstein 1914- *BioIn 3, ConAu 29R, WhoAm 74, –76, WhoAmL 78, WhoAmW 74, WhoE 74*

Forest, Antonia *BioIn 13, ConAu 103, OxCChiL, SmATA 29, TwCChW 78, –83, –89, WrDr 76, –80, –82, –84, –86, –88, –90, –92, –94*

Forester, Cecil Scott 1899-1966 *AmAu&B, BioIn 1, –2, –3, –4, –5, –7, –8, –9, ConAu 25R, –73, ConLC 35, CyWA 58,*

DcAmB S8, DcLEL, DcNaB 1961, EncMys, EvLB, HalFC 84, LongCTC, ModBrL, NewC, Novels, ObitOF 79, ObitT 1961, OxCChiL, OxCEng 85, OxCShps, RAdv 1, REn, REnAL, SmATA 13, TwCA, –SUP, TwCWr, WebE&AL, WhAm 4, WhoChL, WorAl

Forman, Brenda 1936- *AuBYP 2, –3, Au&Wr 71, BioIn 8, –9, ConAu 9R, –6NR, ForWC 70, SmATA 4, WhoAmW 75*

Forman, Harrison 1904-1978 *AmAu&B, AuBYP 2, –3, Au&Wr 71, BioIn 8, –11, BlueB 76, ConAu 5R, –77, IntAu&W 77, WhAm 7, WhoAm 74, –76, –78, WhoE 74, WhoWor 74, WrDr 76*

Forman, James D 1932- *ScF&FL 92*

Forman, James Douglas 1932- *AuBYP 3, ConAu 19NR, –42NR, DcAmChF 1960, EncSF 93, MajAI, SmATA 70, WhoE 91*

Forman, Joan *Au&Wr 71, ConAu 102, IntAu&W 82, –86, –89, –91, WrDr 76, –80, –82, –84, –86, –88, –90, –92, –94*

Forman, Leona S 1940- *ConAu 25R*

Forman, Werner *OxCCan SUP*

Forrest, Sybil *AuBYP 2, –3, BioIn 12, ConAu X, SmATA X*
Main entry: Markun, Patricia Maloney

Forrester, Charles Robert 1803-1850 *CarSB, DcNaB, NewC*

Forrester, Frank H *AuBYP 2, BioIn 7*

Forrester, Frank H d1986 *BioIn 16*

Forrester, Frank H 1919?-1986 *AuBYP 3, ConAu 119, SmATA 52N*

Forrester, Helen *BioIn 13, ConAu X, IntAu&W 86X, –91X, Profile 2, WhoCanL 85, –87, –92, WrDr 76, –80, –82, –84, –86, –88, –90, –92*
Main entry: Bhatia, June

Forrester, Helen 1919- *BioIn 16, BlmGWL, CanWW 89, FemiCLE, IntAu&W 89, –91, SmATA 48, WhoCanL 92, WrDr 94*
Pseud./variant:
Edwards, June
Rana, J

Forrester, Izola L 1878- *AmAu&B, CarSB*

Forrester, Izola Louise 1878- *WomNov*

Forrester, Marian *ConAu X, SmATA X*
Main entry: Schachtel, Roger

Forrester, Victoria 1940- *BioIn 14, –15, ConAu 108, –25NR, SmATA 35, –40*

Forsee, Aylesa *AuBYP 2S, –3, BioIn 9, ConAu 1R, –1NR, IntAu&W 77, –82, SmATA 1, WhoAm 74, –76, –78, –80, –82, –84, WhoAmW 74, –75, WhoFrS 84, WrDr 76, –80, –82, –84, –86*

Forsee, Aylesa d1986 *WhAm 9*

Forsey, Chris 1950- *SmATA 59*

Forshay-Lunsford, Cin *BioIn 17*

Forshay-Lunsford, Cin 1965- *ConAu 119, IntAu&W 89, –91, SmATA 60*

Forster, E M 1879-1970 *Au&Arts 2, Benet 87, BioIn 14, –15, –16, –17, BlmGEL, CamGEL, CamGLE, CnDBLB 6, ConLC 45, –77, CyWA 89, DcLB 98, –DS10, MagSWL, MajTwCW, ModBrL S2, NewEScF, RAdv 13-1, RfGEnL 91, ScFSB, ScFEYrs SmATA 57, SupFW, WorAlBi, WorLitC, WrPh*

Forster, Edward Morgan 1879-1970 *EncSF 93, GayLL*

Forster, F Blanche 1919- *BiDrLUS 70, BioIn 11, ConAu 61, SmATA 11, WhoMW 78*

Forsyth, Anne 1933- *ConAu 29R, –12NR, –29NR*

Forsyth, Frederick *IntWW 89, –91*

Forsyth, Frederick 1938- *BestSel 89-4, BioIn 9, –11, –12, –14, –15, CelR 90, ConAu 85, –38NR, ConLC 2, –5, –36, ConNov 82, –86, –91, CrtSuMy, CurBio 86, DcLB 87, EncSF 93, HalFC 84, –88, IntAu&W 91, MajTwCW, Novels, ScF&FL 92, SpyFic, TwCCr&M 80, –85, –91, WhoAm 74, –80, –90, –92, –94, WhoWor 84, –87, –89, –91, –93, WorAlBi, WorAl, WorAu 1975, WrDr 76, –80, –82, –84, –86, –88, –90, –92, –94*

Forsyth, Gloria *AuBYP 2, –3, BioIn 7*

Fort, John 1942- *ConAu 77*

Fort, Paul *ConAu 137, MajAI, SmATA X*
Main entry: Stockton, Francis Richard

Fortescue, John, Sir *OxCChiL*

Fortescue, John, Sir 1394?-1476? *CamGEL, CamGLE, RAdv 13-3*

Fortnum, Peggy 1919- *ArtsCL, BioIn 5, –6, –8, –11, –12, –13, –14, ChhPo, ConAu X, FourBJA, IlsBYP, IlsCB 1946, –1957, –1967, SmATA 26, WhoArt 80, –82, –84*

Fosburgh, Liza 1930- *AuBYP 3, ConAu 30NR, ScF&FL 92*

Fosdick, Charles Austin 1842-1915 *Alli SUP, AmAu, AmAu&B, BenetAL 91, BbD, BiD&SB, BioIn 1, –15, CarSB, ConAu 119, DcAmAu, DcLB 42, DcNAA, OxCAmL 65, –83, OxCChiL, REnAL, WhAm 1*
Pseud./variant:
Castlemon, Harry

Fosdick, Harry Emerson 1878-1969 *AmAu&B, AmPeW, AuBYP 2, –3, BenetAL 91, BioIn 1, –2, –3, –4, –6, –7, –8, –9, –10, –11, –14, –15, –16, –17, ConAu 25R, CurBio 40, –69, DcAmB S8, DcAmReB 2, LuthC 75, McGEWB, ObitOF 79, OxCAmH, REnAL, TwCA SUP, WebAB 74, –79, WhNAA, WorAlBi, WorAl*

Foss, William O 1918- *AuBYP 2, BioIn 8, ConAu 17R*

Foss, William Otto 1918- *AuBYP 3*

Foster, Alan Dean 1946- *SmATA 70*

Foster, Alfred Edye Manning *WhoLA*

Foster, Anne H 1875- *WhNAA*

Foster, Brad W 1955- *ConGrA 1, SmATA 34*

Foster, Celeste K *BioIn 6, MinnWr*

Foster, Doris VanLiew 1899- *BioIn 11, ConAu 1R, –102, SmATA 10, WrDr 76, –80*
Pseud./variant:
Foster VanLiew, Doris

Foster, Elizabeth 1905-1963 *AuBYP 2S, –3, BioIn 11, ConAu 1R, SmATA 10*

Foster, Elizabeth C 1902- *AuBYP 3*

Foster, Elizabeth Connell 1902- *AuBYP 2S, BioIn 11, ConAu 53, IntAu&W 77, SmATA 9, WhoAm 78, –80*

Foster, Elizabeth Vincent 1902- *BioIn 11, SmATA 12*

Foster, Ernest 1852- *Alli SUP*

Foster, Francis
Main entry: Foster, Reginald Francis

Foster, Francis 1896-1975 *ConAu 109, –X*

Foster, G Allen 1907-1969 *BioIn 8, –13, ConAu 9R, SmATA 26*

Foster, Genevieve 1893-1979 *AmAu&B, AnCL, AuBYP 2, –3, Au&ICB, BioIn 2, –5, –8, –9, –10, –12, –13, ChlLR 7, ConAu 5R, –4NR, DcLB 61, IlsCB 1946, –1957, –1967, JBA 51, MajAI, MorBMP, SmATA 2, –23N, WhoAmA 80N, –82N, –86N, –89N, –91N, WrDr 76, –80*

Foster, George Allen 1907-1969 *AuBYP 3*

Foster, George Allen 1927- *AuBYP 2, ConAu 9R*

Foster, Hal
Main entry: Foster, Harold Rudolf

Foster, Hal 1892-1982 *AnObit 1982, BioIn 11, ConAu X, EncACom, SmATA X, WhoAmA 80, –82, –86N, –89N, –91N*

Foster, Harold R 1892-1982 *BioIn 14, –15*

Foster, Harold Rudolf 1892-1982 *ArtCS, AuNews 2, BioIn 4, –5, –10, –11, –13, ConAu 107, EncAJ, NewYTBS 82, SmATA 31N, WhAm 8, WhoAmA 73*
Pseud./variant:
Foster, Hal

Foster, Joanna 1928- *AuBYP 2S, –3, ChhPo S1, ConAu 5R, –8NR, ForWC 70*
Pseud./variant:
Dougherty, Joanna Foster

Foster, John Thomas 1925- *AuBYP 2S, –3, BioIn 11, ConAu 33R, SmATA 8*

Foster, Laura Louise 1918- *AuBYP 2S, –3, BioIn 10, ConAu 17R, SmATA 6*

Foster, Leila Merrell 1929- *SmATA 73*

Foster, Lynne 1937- *SmATA 74*

Foster, Malcolm Burton 1931- *Au&Wr 71, CanWW 70, –79, –80, –81, –83, –89, DrAS 74E, –78E, –82E, WrDr 76, –80, –82, –84, –86, –88, –90, –92, –94*

Foster, Marcia Lane 1897- *BioIn 1, –5, DcBrAr 1, DcBrBI, DcWomA, IlsCB 1744, –1946, WhoArt 80, –82, –84*

Foster, Margaret Lesser 1899?-1979 *BioIn 12, SmATA 21N*

Foster, Marian Curtis 1909-1978 *AuBYP 2, –3, BioIn 3, –5, –8, –9, –13, ConAu 73, –85, IlsCB 1946, –1957, SmATA 23, ThrBJA*
Pseud./variant:
Mariana

Foster, Reginald Francis 1896-1975 *Au&Wr 71, ConAu 107, IntAu&W 77, Who 74*
Pseud./variant:
Foster, Francis

Foster, Sally *SmATA 58*

Foster VanLiew, Doris
Main entry: Foster, Doris VanLiew

Foulds, Elfrida Vipont 1902- *BioIn 2, –8, ConAu 53, –4NR, –38NR, IntAu&W 77, –82, –89, –91, MajAI, SmATA 52, WrDr 76, –80, –82, –84, –86, –88, –90, –92, –94*
Pseud./variant:
Vipont, Charles
Vipont, Elfrida

Fouque, Friedrich H, Freiherr DeLaMotte 1777-1843 *OxCGer 86*

Fouque, Friedrich H K 1777-1843 *BbD, BiD&SB, CarSB, CasWL, DcBiA, DcEuL, EuAu, EvEuW, HsB&A, NewC, OxCChiL, OxCEng 67, OxCGer 76, PenC EUR, REn, WhoChL*
Pseud./variant:
LaMotte Fouque, F H

Fouque, Friedrich H K DeLaMotte 1777-1843 *BioIn 5, –7, –8, CelCen*

Fouque, Friedrich Heinrich Karl La Motte- 1777-1843 *BioIn 17*

Fouque, Friedrich Heinrich Karl LaMotte- 1777-1843 *BioIn 15*

Fournier, Catharine 1908- *WhoAm 74, –76, WhoAmW 74*

Fourth Brother, The *SmATA X*
Main entry: Aung, Maung Htin

Fowke, Edith Margaret 1913- *IntAu&W 86, –89, –91, WrDr 86, –88, –90, –92, –94*

Fowke, Edith Margaret Fulton 1913- *BioIn 10, CaW, CanWW 70, –79, –80, –81, –83, –89, ChhPo S1, –S2, ConAu 37R, DrAS 74E, –82E, IntAu&W 82, OxCCan, –SUP, Profile 1, SmATA 14, WhoAm 80, –82, –84, –86, –88, –90, –92, –94, WhoAmW 75, –77, –81, –83, –85, –87, –89, –91, –93, WhoWrEP 89, –92, WrDr 76, –80, –82, –84*

Fowler, Elaine Wootten 1914- *ConAu 93, IntAu&W 89, WhoAm 82, –84, –86, –88, –90, –92*

Fowler, Ethel Louise *ChhPo S1, –S2*

Fowler, Francis George 1870-1918 *BioIn 17, DcLEL, LongCTC, OxCEng 85, TwCA, –SUP*

Fowler, Helen Marjorie 1910- *BioIn 3, SingR 1*

Fowler, Henry Watson 1858-1933 *Benet 87, BioIn 2, –3, –4, –7, –14, –17, CamGLE, DcLEL, DcNaB 1931, EncAJ, EvLB, GrBr, LongCTC, NewC, OxCEng 67, –85, PenC ENG, REn, TwCA, –SUP*

Fowler, Mark 1949- *ConAu 65*

Fowler, Mel 1921- *WhAm 9, WhoAmA 86, –89N, –91N, WhoSSW 86*

Fowler, Mel 1922- *AmArt, WhoAmA 78, –80, –82, –84, –86, –89, –91*

Fowler, Robert Howard 1926- *ConAu 73, WhoAm 74, –76, –78, –80, –82, –84, –86, –88, –90, –92, –94, WhoE 74, WhoFI 74, WhoWor 74*

Fowler, Thurley *DcChlFi*

Fowler, Virginie *AuBYP 3*

Fowles, John 1926- *AuSpks, AuBYP 2S, –3, Au&Wr 71, Benet 87, BioIn 7, –8, –10, –11, –12, –13, BlmGEL, BritWr S1, CamGLE, CelR, CnDBLB 8, ConAu 5R, –25NR, ConLC 1, –2, –3, –4, –6, –9, –10, –15, –33, ConNov 72, –76, –82, –86, –91, CurBio 77, CyWA 89, DcLB 14, DcLEL 1940, EncWB, EncWL, –2, HalFC 84, –88, IntAu&W 77, –89, –91, IntWW 74, –75, –76, –77, –78, –79, –80, –81, –82, –83, –89, –91, MagSWL, MajTwCW, ModBrL S1, –S2, NewC, NewYTBS 74, Novels, PostFic, RAdv 1, –13-1, RfGEnL 91, ScF&FL 92, SmATA 22, TwCRHW 90, TwCWr, WebE&AL, Who 82, –83, –85, –88, –90, –92, WhoAm 80, –82, –84, –86, –88, –90, –92, –94, WhoWor 74, –78, –80, –82, –84, –87, –89, –91, –93, WorAlBi, WorAl, WorAu 1950, WrDr 76, –80, –82, –84, –86, –88, –90, –92, –94, WrPa*

Fowles, John Robert 1926- *EncSF 93*

Fox, Aileen 1907- *Au&Wr 71, ConAu 5R –5NR, IntAu&W 91, SmATA 58, WrDr 76, –80, –82, –84, –86, –88, –90, –92, –94*

Fox, Charles Philip 1913- *BioIn 11, ConAu 1R, –1NR, IntAu&W 91, SmATA 12*

Fox, Dorothea M *AuBYP 2S, –3*

Fox, Dorothea Warren 1914- *ConAu 61*

Fox, Dorothy *AuBYP 2, –3, BioIn 8*

Fox, Eleanor *BioIn 11, ConAu X, SmATA X*
Main entry: Saint John, Wylly Folk

Fox, Fontaine Talbot, Jr. 1884-1964 *AmAu&B, ArtCS, BioIn 3, –7, –8, –11, –13, ChhPo, DcAmB S7, ObitOF 79, SmATA 23N, WhAm 4*

Fox, Frances Margaret
Main entry: Field, Frances Fox

Fox, Frances Margaret 1870-1959 *AmAu&B, MichAu 80, WhNAA, WomWWA 14*

Fox, Frances Margaret 1913?-1977 *BioIn 11, ConAu X*

Fox, Fred 1903?-1981 *BioIn 12, –13, ConAu 104, SmATA 27N*

Fox, Freeman *ConAu X, –29NR, SmATA X*

Fox, Geoffrey 1941- *SmATA 73*

Fox, George 1624-1690 *EncPaPR 91*

Fox, George 1624-1691 *Benet 87, BioIn 1, –2, –3, –4, –5, –6, –7, –8, –9, –10, –11, –12, –15, –17, BlmGEL, CamGEL, CamGLE, CyEd, DcAfL, DcAmReB 2, DcBiPP, DcNaB, Dis&D, EncO&P 2, –3, HarEnUS, IlEncMy, LuthC 75, OxCAmH, OxCAmL 83, OxCChiL, OxCEng 85, WhDW, WorAlBi, WorAl*

Fox, Grace *SmATA X*
Main entry: Anderson, Grace Fox

Fox, Henry *MedHR*

Fox, John, Jr. 1862?-1919 *AmAu&B, BbD, BiDSA, BiD&SB, BioIn 4, –8, –9, –10, –12, CarSB, CnDAL, ConAmL, ConAu 108, DcAmAu, DcBiA, DcLB 9, DcLEL, DcNAA, EvLB, OxCAmL 65, –83, REn, REnAL, TwCA, –SUP, TwCWr, WhAm 1*

Fox, John, Jr. 1863-1919 *BenetAL 91*

Fox, Larry *AuBYP 2S, –3, ConAu 106, SmATA 30*

Fox, Larry 1930- *WhoAm 86*

Fox, Lorraine 1922-1976 *BioIn 10, –11, –13, IlrAm 1880, –G, NatCAB 61, SmATA 11, –27N*

Fox, Mary Virginia 1919- *AuBYP 2, –3, BioIn 7, ConAu 29R, –12NR, SmATA 39, –44*

Fox, Mem
Main entry: Fox, Merrion Frances

Fox, Mem 1946- *AuBYP 3, BioIn 16, ChlLR 23, ConAu 127, IntAu&W 89, –91, MajAI, SixBJA*

Fox, Merrion Frances 1946- *ConAu 127, MajAI, SmATA 51*
Pseud./variant:
Fox, Mem

Fox, Michael Wilson 1937- *AmMWSc 73S, –76P, –78S, –82, –86, –89, –92, AuBYP 2S, –3, BioIn 11, –12, –13, ConAu 73, –14NR, CurBio 77, SmATA 15, WhoAm 78, –80, –82, –84, –86, –88, –90, –92, –94, WhoUSWr 88, WhoWor 82, WhoWrEP 89, –92, WrDr 76, –80*

Fox, Mona Alexis *WrDr 86, –88, –90, –92*

Fox, Mona Alexis 1915- *ArtclWW 2, Au&Wr 71, WrDr 76, –80, –82, –84*

Fox, Norman A 1911-1960 *BioIn 5, ConAu 114, EncFWF, TwCWW 91*

Fox, Paula *DrAPF 87, –89, –91, –93, InWom SUP*

Fox, Paula 1923- *ArtclWW 2, Au&Arts 3, AuBYP 2S, –3, BioIn 10, –11, –12, –13, CamGLE, ChlFicS, ChlLR 1, ConAu 73, –20NR, –36NR, ConLC 2, DcAmChF 1960, –1985, DcLB 52, DrAF 76, DrAPF 83, –85, FourBJA, IntAu&W 91, MajAI, MajTwCW, NewbC 1966, OxCAmL 83, OxCChiL, SenS, SmATA 17, –60, SouSt, TwCChW 78, –83, –89, TwCYAW, WhoAm 74, –76, –78, –80, –82, –84, –86, –88, –90, –92, –94, WhoAmW 87, –89, WhoE 75, –77, WorAu 1980, WrDr 76, –80, –82, –84, –86, –88, –90, –92, –94*

Fox, Petronella *SmATA X, WrDr 82, –84, –86, –88*
Main entry: Balogh, Penelope

Fox, Robert J 1927- *AmCath 80, ConAu 45, –1NR, –17NR, –40NR, CurBio 70, SmATA 33*

Fox, Sally Ingersoll 1925- *AmMWSc 73P, –76P, –82, –86, –89, –92*

Fox, Sonny 1925- *AuBYP 2S, –3, ConAu 41R*

Fox, William Wellington 1909- *AuBYP 2, –3, BioIn 7, ConAu 1R*

Foxton, Thomas 1695?-1740? *OxCChiL*

Fozdar, Jamshed K 1926- *ConAu 49*

Frace, Charles *IlsBYP*

Frace, Charles Lewis 1926- *WhoAmA 86, –91*

Fradin, Dennis Brindell 1945- *BioIn 13, ConAu 69, SmATA 29*

Fraelich, Richard Oddly 1924- *ConAu 5R*

Frahm, Anne Bayard Schwerdt 1927- *ConAu 9R, WhoAm 76, –78, WhoAmW 74*

Frame, Janet *ConAu 36NR, IntvTCA 2, MajTwCW*

Frame, Janet 1924- *ArtclWW 2, Benet 87, BioIn 10, –11, –13, BlmGEL, BlueB 76, CamGLE, CasWL, ConAu X, ConLC 2, –3, –6, –22, –66, ConNov 72, –76, –82, –86, –91, ConPo 75, –80, –85, ContDcW 89, CyWA 89, DcLEL 1940, EncWL 2, FarE&A 80, –81, FemiCLE, InWom SUP, IntAu&W 77, –89,*

-91, IntDcWB, IntLitE, IntWW 74, -75, -76, -77, -78, -79, -80, -81, -82, -83, -89, -91, LongCTC, ModCmwL, NewC, Novels, PenC ENG, RAdv 1, -13-1, RfGEnL 91, ScF&FL 92, TwCWr, WebE&AL, WorAu 1950, WrDr 76, -80, -82, -84, -86, -88, -90, -92, -94
Pseud./variant:
Clutha, Janet Paterson Frame

Frame, Janet Paterson 1924- *RfGShF*

Frame, Janet Patterson 1924- *EncSF 93*

Frame, Paul 1913- *BioIn 8, ConAu 111, IlsBYP, IlsCB 1957, -1967, SmATA 33*

Frame, Paul 1914- *SmATA 60*

Frances, Esteban 1914-1976 *BiDD, BioIn 2, -8, -11, IlsCB 1957, OxCTwCA*

Frances, Helen *DcChlFi*

Frances, Miss *ConAu X, SmATA X*

Frances, S D
Main entry: Janson, Hank

Franchere, Ruth Myers 1906- *ConAu 73, FourBJA, SmATA 18, WhoPNW*

Francis, Charles *AuBYP 3, ConAu 132, -X, SmATA 66, -X*
Main entry: Holme, Bryan

Francis, Dee *AuBYP 3, ConAu X, SmATA X*
Main entry: Haas, Dorothy F

Francis, Dorothy Brenner 1926- *BioIn 11, ConAu 21R, -9NR, -24NR, IntAu&W 91, ScF&FL 92, SmATA 10, WhoAmW 74, -75, WrDr 76, -80, -82, -84, -86, -88, -90, -92, -94*

Francis, Frank *ChhPo S2*

Francis, Helen Dannefer 1915- *ConAu 13R, ForWC 70, WhoAmW 75, -77, WrDr 76, -80, -82, -84, -86, -88*

Francis, Henry S 1925- *AuBYP 2, BioIn 8*

Francis, Henry S, Jr. 1925- *AuBYP 3*

Francis, Pamela 1926- *BioIn 11, ConAu 29R, SmATA 11, WrDr 76, -80, -82, -84*

Franco, Eloise 1910- *BioIn 17, SmATA 62*

Franco, Jean 1924- *ConAu 21R, -9NR, DrAS 74F, -78F, -82F, WhoAm 84, -86, -88*

Franco, Johan 1908- *Baker 84, BioIn 1, CpmDNM 82, ConAmC 76, -82, ConAu 97, DcCM, IntWWM 85, NewGrDA 86, WhoAm 74, -76, -78, -80, -82, -84, -86, -88, WhoAmM 83, WhoMus 72, WhoSSW 73, -75, -76*

Franco, Johan 1908-1988 *BioIn 17, SmATA 62, WhAm 9*

Franco, Johan Henri Gustav 1908-1988 *Baker 92*

Franco, Marjorie *ConAu 114, SmATA 38*

Francois, Andre 1915- *AmPB, Au&Wr 71, BioIn 5, -8, -9, -13, ChsFB I, ConArt 77, ConAu 93, ConDes 84, -90, IlsBYP, IlsCB 1946, -1957, -1967, SmATA 25, ThrBJA, WhoGrA 62, -82, WorECar*

Francoise *AmPB, AnCL, BioIn 1, -3, -5, -6, -8, -12, ConAu X, IlsBYP, IlsCB 1946, -1957, MorJA, SmATA X*
Main entry: Seignobosc, Francoise

Frandsen, Maude Linstrom 1908- *WhoAmW 74, WrDr 76, -80*

Frank, Anne 1929-1944 *Benet 87*

Frank, Anne 1929-1945 *Au&Arts 12, BioIn 2, -3, -4, -5, -7, -8, -10, -11, -12, -13, -14, -15, -16, -17, BlmGWL, ConAu 113, -133, ConHero 1, DcAmSR, EncWB, HerW, -84, HisEWW, InWom SUP, IntDcWB, MajTwCW, RAdv 13-3, REn, SmATA 42, TwCLC 17, TwCWr, WorAlBi, WorAl, WorLitC*

Frank, Anne 1930-1945 *ContDcW 89*

Frank, Annelies Marie 1929-1945 *TwCYAW*

Frank, Daniel B 1956- *SmATA 55*

Frank, Helene
Main entry: Vautier, Ghislaine

Frank, Janet *ConAu X*
Main entry: Dunleavy, Janet Egleson

Frank, Josette d1989 *NewYTBS 89*

Frank, Josette 1893- *AuBYP 2, -3, BioIn 8, -11, ChhPo, -S2, ConAu P-1, SmATA 10*

Frank, Josette 1893-1989 *BioIn 16, -17, ConAu 129, SmATA 63*

Frank, Mary 1933- *BioIn 6, -10, -11, -13, CenC, ConAmWS, DcCAA 71, -77, -88, InWom SUP, SmATA 34, WhoAm 76, -86, -88, -90, -92, -94, WhoAmA 73, -78, WhoE 85, -86, WorArt 1980*

Frank, Pat 1907-1964 *AmNov, BioIn 1, -2, -3, -5, -7, -17, ConAu 5R, NewEScF, RGTwCSF, ScFSB, TwCSFW 86, -91, WhAm 4, WhoSciF*

Frank, Pat Harry Hart 1907-1964 *EncSF 93*

Frank, R, Jr. *BioIn 13, ConAu X, SmATA X*
Main entry: Ross, Frank, Jr.

Frank, Rudolf *TwCChW 89B*

Frank, Rudolf 1886-1979 *ConAu 121*

Frank, Sidney R 1919- *WhoTech 84*

Frank, Sidney Raymond 1919- *AmMWSc 76P, –82, –86, –89, –92, WhoFrS 84, WhoOcn 78, WhoTech 82, WhoWest 74, –76, –78*

Frankau, Mary Evelyn Atkinson 1899- *BioIn 9, ConAu P-1, SmATA 4*
Pseud./variant:
Atkinson, Mary Evelyn

Frankel, Alona *BioIn 17*

Frankel, Alona 1937- *ConAu 135, SmATA 66, WrDr 94*

Frankel, Bernice *BioIn 11, ConAu 61, SmATA 9*

Frankel, Edward 1910- *AuBYP 2, –3, BioIn 8, –15, ConAu 85, LEduc 74, SmATA 44*

Frankel, Julie 1947- *ConAu 113, –36NR, SmATA 34, –40*

Frankenberg, Lloyd 1907-1975 *AmAu&B, BioIn 4, –10, ChhPo S1, ConAu 1R, –57, –6NR, ObitOF 79, REnAL, TwCA SUP, WhAm 6, WhoAm 74*

Frankenberg, Robert Clinton 1911- *BioIn 5, –8, –13, IlsBYP, IlsCB 1946, –1957, –1967, SmATA 22, WhoAmA 78, –80, –82, –84, –86, –89, –91*

Frankenstein, Alfred Victor 1906-1981 *AmAu&B, ConAu 1R, –104, –2NR, DrAS 74H, MedPD, WhAmArt 85, WhoAm 74, –76, –78, WhoAmA 73, –80, –82N, –86N, –89N, –91N, WhoMus 72, WhoWest 74, WhoWor 74*

Franklin, Benjamin 1706-1790 *Alli, AmAu, AmAu&B, AmWr, AmWrBE, AsBiEn, AtlBL, Baker 84, –92, Benet 87, BenetAL 91, BbD, BiDAmJo, BiDAmSp BK, BiDPsy, BiD&SB, BiDrUSC 89, BiESc, BiInAmS, BioIn 1, –2, –3, –4, –5, –6, –7, –8, –9, –10, –11, –12, –13, –14, –15, –16, –17, BriEAA, CamGEL, CamGLE, CamHAL, CasWL, Chambr 3, ChhPo, –S1, –S2, CnDAL, CrtT 3, CyAG, CyAL, CyEd, CyWA 58, DcAmAu, DcAmDH 80, –89, DcAmMeB, DcAmSR, DcBiPP, DcEnL, DcInv, DcLB 24, –43, –73, DcLEL, DcNAA, DcScB, Dis&D, EncAB-H, EncAI&E, EncAJ, EncAR, EncO&P 1S1, –2, –3, EvLB, GolEC, HarEnUS, InSci, JrnUS, MagSAmL, McGEWB, MemAm, MouLC 2, NamesHP, NewAmDM, NewC, NewGrDA 86, OxCAmH, OxCAmL 65, –83, OxCEng 67, –85, OxCMus, PenC AM, RAdv 13-3, –13-5, RComAH, RComWL, REn, REnAL, RfGAmL 87, WebAB 74, –79, WebE&AL, WhDW, WhAm HS, WhAmP, WhNaAH, WhoEc 81, –86, WorAlBi, WorAl*

Franklin, Cheryl J 1955- *SmATA 70*

Franklin, George Cory 1872- *BioIn 6, MorJA*

Franklin, Harold 1920- *ConAu 29R, SmATA 13*

Franklin, Harold L 1934- *ConAu 57*
Pseud./variant:
Alimayo, Chikuyo

Franklin, John 1786-1847 *BioIn 17, DcLB 99, Expl 93, WorAlBi*

Franklin, John, Sir 1786-1847 *Alli, BioIn 1, –2, –3, –4, –5, –6, –7, –8, –9, –11, –15, BritAu 19, DcBiPP, DcCanB 7, DcNaB, NewC, OxCAusL, OxCCan, OxCCanL, OxCEng 67, –85, OxCShps, WhDW*

Franklin, Josephine *CarSB*

Franklin, Lance *SmATA X*
Main entry: Lantz, Francess Lin

Franklin, Max *AuBYP 2S, –3, BioIn 13, ConAu X, IntAu&W 77X, –82X, SmATA X, TwCCr&M 80, –85, –91, WrDr 76, –80, –82, –84*
Main entry: Deming, Richard

Franklin, Max 1915-1983 *ScF&FL 92*

Franklin, Steve *BioIn 10, ConAu X, SmATA 6*
Main entry: Stevens, Franklin

Franzen, Lavern Gerhard 1926- *WhoAm 94, WhoRel 92*

Franzen, Lavern Gerhardt 1926- *ConAu 61, –7NR*

Franzen, Nils-Olof 1916- *BioIn 11, ConAu 29R, –25NR, IntAu&W 86, SmATA 10*

Frascino, Edward *ConAu 37NR, MajAI, SmATA 9AS*

Frascino, Edward 1938- *ConAu 111, –114, FifBJA, IlsBYP, IlsCB 1967, SmATA 33, –48*

Frasconi, Antonio 1919- *AmAu&B, AmPB, AnCL, AuBYP 2, –3, BioIn 2, –3, –4, –5, –6, –7, –8, –9, –10, –11, –13, BriEAA, ChsFB I, ConAu 1R, –1NR, CurBio 72, DcCAA 71, –77, –88, IlsCB 1946, –1957, –1967, MajAI, OxCTwCA, SmATA 6, –53, –11AS, ThrBJA, WhoAm 74, –76, –78, –80, –82, –84,*

WhoAmA 73, -78, -80, -82, -84, -89, -91, WhoE 74, -93, WhoGrA 62, -82, WhoWor 74

Fraser, Anthea *ConAu 25NR, TwCCr&M 91, WrDr 88, -90, -92, -94*

Fraser, Anthea 1930- *ConAu 65, -10NR, ScF&FL 92, WrDr 76, -80, -82, -84, -86*

Fraser, Antonia 1932- *BioIn 8, -10, -11, -12, -13, -14, -15, -16, -17, BlueB 76, CelR 90, ConAu 85, ConLC 32, CurBio 74, DcLEL 1940, EncBrWW, FemiCLE, IntAu&W 89, -91, IntWW 74, -75, -76, -77, -78, -79, -80, -81, -82, -83, -91, MajTwCW, NewYTBS 84, OxCEng 85, SmATA 32, TwCCr&M 80, -85, -91, Who 74, -82, -83, -85, -92, WhoAm 90, -92, -94, WhoAmW 74, WhoWor 74, -78, WorAlBi, WorAl, WrDr 76, -80, -82, -84, -86, -88, -90, -92, -94*

Fraser, Antonia, Lady 1932- *ArtclWW 2, Benet 87, CrtSuMy, EncWB, IntWW 89, ThrtnMM, Who 88, -90*

Fraser, Arvonne S 1925- *InWom SUP*

Fraser, Arvonne Skelton 1925- *ConAu 33R, WhoGov 77, WhoMW 90*

Fraser, B Kay 1941- *ConAu 69*

Fraser, Beatrice *AuBYP 2, -3, BioIn 7*

Fraser, Betty
Main entry: Fraser, Elizabeth Marr

Fraser, Betty 1928- *BioIn 8, -12, ChhPo S1, IlsBYP, IlsCB 1957, -1967, SmATA X*

Fraser, Carol Lucille 1930- *CreCan 2*

Fraser, Claude Lovat 1890-1921 *BioIn 2, -3, -9, -10, ChhPo, -S1, -S2, EncWT, JBA 51, OxCThe 67, -83*

Fraser, Conon 1930- *Au&Wr 71, ConAu P-1, IntAu&W 77, WrDr 76, -80, -82, -84, -86, -88, -90, -92, -94*

Fraser, Edith Emily Rose Oram 1903- *Au&Wr 71, ConAu P-1*

Fraser, Elizabeth Marr 1928- *BioIn 8, -12, SmATA 31*
Pseud./variant:
Fraser, Betty

Fraser, Eric 1902-1983 *BioIn 2, -5, -10, -14, -15, IlsCB 1946, SmATA 38, TwCPaSc*

Fraser, Ferrin *AuBYP 3*

Fraser, Ferrin 1903?-1969 *AuBYP 2, BioIn 7, -8*

Fraser, Frances *OxCCan SUP*

Fraser, Francis Charles 1903-1978 *BioIn 4 -12, Who 74*

Fraser, Kathleen *DrAPF 87, -89, -91, -93*

Fraser, Kathleen 1937- *ConAu 106, ConPo 70, -80, -85, -91, DrAP 75, DrAPF 83, -85, InWom SUP, WrDr 82, -84, -86, -88, -90, -92, -94*

Fraser, Kathleen Joy 1937- *WhoAm 92*

Fraser, Mary Ann 1959- *SmATA 76*

Fraser Darling, Frank 1903- *Au&Wr 71, BioIn 9, -12, BlueB 76, ConAu 61, IntWW 74, -75, -76, -77, -78, -79, Who 74, WrDr 80*

Fraser Darling, Frank, Sir *CmScLit*

Fraser Darling, Frank, Sir 1903-1979 *DcNaB 1971*

Frasier, Debra 1953- *SmATA 69*

Fraydas, Stan 1918- *ConAu 57*

Frazar, Douglas 1836-1896 *Alli SUP, CarSB, CivWDc, DcAmAu, DcNAA*

Frazer, Andrew *AuBYP 2, -3, ConAu X, IntAu&W 91X, TwCCr&M 85, -91, WrDr 76, -80*
Main entry: Lesser, Milton

Frazer, Andrew 1928- *WrDr 94*

Frazetta, Frank 1928- *BiDScF, EncACom, EncSF 93, NewEScF, PenEncH, ScF&FL 92, SmATA 58, WhoAm 86, -88, -90, -92, -94*
Pseud./variant:
Fritz

Frazier, Carl *AuBYP 2S, -3*

Frazier, Claude A 1920- *ConAu 32NR*

Frazier, Claude Albee 1920- *ConAu 29R, IntAu&W 77*

Frazier, Neta 1890- *AuBYP 3*

Frazier, Neta Lohnes d1990 *NewYTBS 90*

Frazier, Neta Lohnes 1890- *AuBYP 2, BioIn 7, -10, ConAu 1R, -1NR, ForWC 70, SmATA 7, WhoPNW, WrDr 76, -80, -82, -84*

Frazier, Neta Lohnes 1890-1990 *BioIn 16, -17, ConAu 131*

Frazier, Rosalie *AuBYP 2S, -3*

Freas, Lenwood *IlsBYP*

Frederic, Mike *IntAu&W 91X, SmATA X, WrDr 86, –88, –90*
Main entry: Cox, William R

Frederick, John *ConAu X, TwCWW 91*

Fredericks, Arnold *AmAu&B, AuBYP 2, –3, BioIn 8, DcNAA*
Main entry: Kummer, Frederic Arnold

Fredericks, Fred 1929- *ArtCS, EncACom*

Freed, Alvyn Mark 1913- *AmMWSc 73S, –78S, BioIn 13, ConAu 61, –8NR, SmATA 22, WhoWest 92, –94*

Freed, Ruth S *WhoE 86, –89*

Freed, Ruth Shelley 1922- *AmMWSc 73S, –76P, FifIDA*

Freed, Stanley Arthur 1927- *AmMWSc 73S, –76P, FifIDA, WhoAm 74, –76, –78, –80, –82, –84, –86, –88, –90, –92, –94*

Freedgood, Lillian 1911- *ConAu 13R*

Freedgood, Morton 1912?- *AuNews 1, BioIn 9, –10, ConAu 108, –128, EncMys, IntAu&W 91, WrDr 82, –84, –86, –88, –90*
Pseud./variant:
Godey, John

Freedman, Barnett 1901-1958 *BioIn 1, –4, –5, –14, DcBrAr 1, DcNaB 1951, IlsCB 1744, –1946, ObitOF 79, ObitT 1951, TwCPaSc*

Freedman, Benedict 1919- *AmAu&B, AmNov, BioIn 1, –2, –3, –13, ConAu 69, CurBio 47, SmATA 27, WhoAm 74, –76*

Freedman, Florence Bernstein 1908- *ChhPo S2, LEduc 74*

Freedman, Harold 1915- *SingR 1*

Freedman, Nancy 1920- *AmAu&B, AmNov, BioIn 1, –2, –3, –13, ConAu 45, –1NR, –19NR, CurBio 47, EncSF 93, ForWC 70, IntAu&W 86, ScFSB, SmATA 27, TwCSFW 86, WhoAm 74, WrDr 80, –82, –84, –86, –88, –90, –92, –94*

Freedman, Russell *BioIn 16*

Freedman, Russell 1929- *Au&Arts 4, AuBYP 2, –3, BioIn 8, –12, ChlLR 20, ConAu 17R, –7NR, –23NR, SixBJA, SmATA 16, –71, WhoE 74*

Freedman, Russell Bruce 1929- *MajAI, TwCYAW, WhoAm 92, –94*

Freehof, Solomon B 1892- *ConAu 93, WhoWorJ 72*

Freehof, Solomon B 1892-1990 *BioIn 16, –17, ConAu 131, NewYTBS 90*

Freehof, Solomon Bennett 1892- *WhAm 9*

Freeman, Anne Frances Huether 1936- *ForWC 70*
Pseud./variant:
Huether, Anne Frances

Freeman, Barbara C 1906- *ScF&FL 92, TwCChW 89, WrDr 86, –88, –90, –92*

Freeman, Barbara Constance 1906- *Au&Wr 71, BioIn 13, –14, ConAu 73, IntAu&W 77, SmATA 28, TwCChW 78, –83, WrDr 76, –80, –82, –84, –94*

Freeman, Bill *SmATA X*

Freeman, Bill 1938- *BioIn 13, DcChlFi, OxCCanL, Profile 2, TwCChW 89, WhoCanL 92, WrDr 90, –92, –94*
Main entry: Freeman, William Bradford

Freeman, Don 1908-1978 *AmPB, AuBYP 2, –3, BioIn 2, –3, –5, –6, –8, –11, –12, –14, BkP, ChlLR 30, ConAu 77, GrAmP, IlsCB 1946, –1957, –1967, MajAI, MorJA, SmATA 17, TwCChW 78, –83, –89, WhAmArt 85, WhoAmA 78N, –80N, –82N*

Freeman, Don 1909-1978 *WhoAmA 86N, –89N, –91N*

Freeman, Eugene 1906- *AuBYP 2, –3, BioIn 8, ConAu 41R, –26NR, DrAS 74P, –78P, –82P, WhoWest 76, –78, –80, –82, –84*

Freeman, Gillian *IntAu&W 86, IntvTCA 2*

Freeman, Gillian 1929- *Au&Wr 71, BioIn 10, ConAu 5R, –3NR, ConNov 72, –76, –82, –86, –91, DcLEL 1940, FemiCLE, IntAu&W 77, –82, –89, –91, WrDr 76, –80, –82, –84, –86, –88, –90, –92, –94*

Freeman, Godfrey *AuBYP 2, –3, BioIn 7*

Freeman, Ira Maximilian 1905- *AmAu&B, AmMWSc 73P, –76P, AuBYP 2, BioIn 6, –7, –12, ConAu 73, MorJA, SmATA 21*

Freeman, Ira Maximilian 1905-1987 *BioIn 16*

Freeman, Ira Maximillian 1905- *AuBYP 3*

Freeman, Jean Todd 1929- *ConAu 25R, IntAu&W 77*

Freeman, Lewis Ransome 1878- *AmAu&B, OxCCan, WhAm 6, WhNAA*

Freeman, Lucy 1916- *AmAu&B, BioIn 2, –3, –12, –13, ConAu 5R, –3NR, CurBio 53, ForWC 70, SmATA 24, WhoAm 74, –76, –78,*

–80, –82, –84, –86, –88, –90, WhoAmJ 80, WhoAmW 74, WhoWorJ 72, –78, WrDr 76, –80, –82, –84, –86, –88, –90, –92, –94

Freeman, Lydia 1907- *BioIn 6, MorJA*

Freeman, Madeline Austin *CaW, OxCCan SUP*

Freeman, Mae 1907- *AuBYP 3*

Freeman, Mae Blacker 1907- *BioIn 6, –8, –13, ConAu 73, MorJA, SmATA 25*

Freeman, Margaret 1893-1942 *BioIn 1, ChhPo, ConICB, DcWomA, IlsCB 1744, WhAmArt 85*

Freeman, Mary E Wilkins 1852-1930 *AmAu&B, AmLY, ArtclWW 2, BenetAL 91, BioAmW, BioIn 1, –4, –8, –9, –11, –12, –13, BlmGWL, CarSB, CasWL, ChhPo, –S1, –S2, CnDAL, ConAmL, ConAu 106, –X, DcAmAu, DcEnA A, DcLB 78, DcLEL, DcNAA, HarEnUS, LongCTC, ModAWWr, Novels, OxCAmL 65, –83, OxCEng 67, –85, PenC AM, REn, REnAL, RfGAmL 87, ShSWr, TwCA, WebAB 74, –79, WhAm 1, WhoHr&F, WomWWA 14*
Pseud./variant:
Wilkins, Mary Eleanor

Freeman, Mary Eleanor 1852-1930 *PenEncH, WomNov*

Freeman, Mary Eleanor Wilkin 1852-1930 *RfGShF*

Freeman, Mary Eleanor Wilkins 1852-1930 *AmWomPl, BioIn 14, –15, –17, CamGEL, EncAHmr, HanAmWH, InWom SUP*

Freeman, Nancy 1932- *SmATA 61*

Freeman, Peter J *MajAI, SmATA 69, –X, WhoUSWr 88, WhoWrEP 89, –92*
Main entry: Calvert, Patricia

Freeman, Sarah 1940- *ConAu 133, SmATA 66*

Freeman, Sarah Caroline 1940- *WrDr 94*

Freeman, Serge Herbert *AuBYP 3*

Freeman, Serge Herbert 1925- *AuBYP 2, BioIn 8*

Freeman, Terence Reginald 1909- *BioIn 5, IlsCB 1946*

Freeman, Tony *BioIn 15, ConAu 134, SmATA 44, WrDr 94*

Freeman, William Bradford 1938- *BioIn 16, SmATA 48, –58*
Pseud./variant:
Freeman, Bill

Fregosi, Claudia 1946- *AuBYP 3, BioIn 13, SmATA 24*

Freidel, Frank Burt, Jr. 1916- *AmAu&B, ConAu 1R, DrAS 74H, –78H, WhoAm 74, –80, –82, –84, –86, –88, –90, –92*

Fremantle, Anne 1910- *AmAu&B, BioIn 3, –4, –9, –12, BkC 5, CathA 1952, ConAu 13R, IntAu&W 91, LongCTC, REnAL, TwCA SUP, WrDr 80, –82, –84, –86, –88, –90*

French, Alice 1850-1934 *Alli SUP, AmAu, AmAu&B, AmLY, ArtclWW 2, BenetAL 91, BbD, BiDSA, BiD&SB, BioIn 6, –7, BlmGWL, CarSB, DcAmAu, DcLB 74, DcNAA, LongCTC, OxCAmL 65, –83, REn, REnAL, WhAm 1, WomNov*
Pseud./variant:
Thanet, Octave

French, Allen 1870-1946 *AmAu&B, BioIn 1, –2, –11, CarSB, ChhPo, ConAu 122, DcAmAu, JBA 34, –51, REnAL, WhAm 2, YABC 1*

French, Dorothy Kayser 1926- *AuBYP 2 –3, BioIn 8, –10, ConAu 9R, –3NR, ForWC 70, IntAu&W 77, –82, –86, SmATA 5, WhoAmW 77*

French, Fiona 1944- *BioIn 14, ConAu 40NR, IntAu&W 91, MajAI, SmATA 75, TwCChW 89, WrDr 86, –88, –90, –92, –94*

French, Fiona Mary 1944- *BioIn 10, –12, ConAu 29R, IlsCB 1967, IntAu&W 82, SmATA 6, TwCChW 78, –83, WrDr 80, –82, –84*

French, Kathryn *ConAu X, SmATA X*
Main entry: Mosesson, Gloria R

French, Marion Flood *AuBYP 3*

French, Marion Flood 1920- *AuBYP 2, BioIn 8, ConAu 33R, ForWC 70*

French, Michael 1944- *ScF&FL 92, SmATA 38, –49*

French, Michael Bruce 1954- *WhoFI 94*

French, Paul *AmAu&B, AuBYP 2, –3, BioIn 12, –13, ConAu 137, –X, –36NR, DcLEL 1940, EncSF 93, IntAu&W 91X, LongCTC, MajAI, MajTwCW, SmATA 74, –X, ThrBJA, TwCSFW 86, –91, TwCYAW*
Main entry: Asimov, Isaac

French, Paul 1920-1992 *ConLC 76*

French, Simon 1957- *ConAu 22NR, DcChlFi, TwCChW 89, TwCYAW, WrDr 90, –92, –94*

Freschet, Berniece Louise 1927- *AuBYP 2S, -3, ConAu 17R, ForWC 70, FourBJA*

Frese, Dolores Warwick 1936- *ConAu 5R, -9NR, DrAS 78E, -82E*
Pseud./variant:
Warwick, Dolores

Freuchen, Peter 1886-1957 *AuBYP 2, -3, BioIn 3, -4, -8, ConAu 114, ObitOF 79, ObitT 1951, PenC EUR, RAdv 13-3, TwCA, -SUP, WhAm 3*

Freund, Rudolf 1915-1969 *BioIn 1, -5, -6, -8, -13, IlsBYP, IlsCB 1744, -1946, SmATA 28*

Freund, Rudolf J 1937- *WhoTech 84*

Frewer, Glyn 1931- *AuBYP 2, -3, Au&Wr 71, BioIn 8, -11, ConAu 13R, -10NR, IntAu&W 82, SmATA 11, WrDr 76, -80, -82, -84, -86, -88, -90, -92*

Frewer, Glyn Mervyn Louis 1931- *WrDr 94*

Frey, Shaney *AuBYP 2, -3, BioIn 8*

Fribourg, Marjorie G 1920- *AuBYP 2, -3, BioIn 8, ConAu 1R, -4NR*

Frick, C H *ConAu X, IntAu&W 77X, -82X, SmATA 6, WrDr 76, -80, -82, -84, -86, -88, -90, -92*
Main entry: Irwin, Constance Frick

Frick, C H 1913- *WrDr 94*

Frick, Constance *BioIn 3, ConAu X, SmATA 6*
Main entry: Irwin, Constance Frick

Fried, John J 1940- *ConAu 33R, -12NR*

Friedland, Ronald Lloyd 1937-1975 *BioIn 10, ConAu 57, -P-2*
Pseud./variant:
Lloyd, Ronald

Friedlander, Joanne K 1930- *AuBYP 3*

Friedlander, Joanne Kohn 1930- *AuBYP 2S, BioIn 11, ConAu 61, SmATA 9, WhoMW 78*

Friedman, Estelle 1920- *AuBYP 3*

Friedman, Estelle Ehrenwald 1920- *AuBYP 2, BioIn 8, -10, ConAu 5R, ForWC 70, SmATA 7*

Friedman, Estelle Yudkin 1927- *WhoAmW 87*

Friedman, Eve Rosemary Tibber 1929- *Au&Wr 71, ConAu 5R*
Pseud./variant:
Tibber, Robert
Tibber, Rosemary

Friedman, Frieda 1905- *BioIn 6, -15, MorJA, SmATA 43*

Friedman, Ina 1926- *AuBYP 3*

Friedman, Ina R 1926- *AuBYP 2S, ConAu 53, SmATA 41, -49*

Friedman, Josephine Troth 1928- *ConAu 77*
Pseud./variant:
Friedman, Joy Troth

Friedman, Joy Troth
Main entry: Friedman, Josephine Troth

Friedman, Judi 1925- *AuNews 2, BioIn 11, ConAu 65*

Friedman, Judi 1935- *SmATA 59*

Friedman, Marvin 1930- *IlrAm 1880, -G, SmATA 33, -42, WhoAmA 78, -80, -82*

Friedman, Sara Ann 1935- *ConAu 77*

Friedrich, Otto Alva 1929- *AmAu&B, AmPB, ConAu 5R, -3NR, SmATA 33, WhoAm 74, -80, -82, -84, -86, -88, -90, WhoUSWr 88, WhoWrEP 89, -92*

Friedrich, Priscilla 1927- *AmPB, ConAu 113, SmATA 39*

Friend, John Albert Newton 1881-1966 *DcScB, WhoLA*

Friendlich, Dick
Main entry: Friendlich, Richard J

Friendlich, Dick 1909- *AuBYP 3, BioIn 8, -11, SmATA X*

Friendlich, Richard J *AuBYP 3*

Friendlich, Richard J 1909- *AuBYP 2, BioIn 8, -11, ConAu P-1, SmATA 11*
Pseud./variant:
Friendlich, Dick

Friermood, Elisabeth 1903- *AuBYP 3*

Friermood, Elisabeth H 1903- *WrDr 86, -88, -90, -92*

Friermood, Elisabeth Hamilton 1903- *AuBYP 2, BioIn 6, -8, -10, ConAu 1R, -1NR, ForWC 70, IndAu 1917, IntAu&W 89, -91, MorJA, SmATA 5, WrDr 76, -80, -82, -84*

Friermood, Elisabeth Hamilton 1903-1992 *WrDr 94N*

Friers, Rowel Boyd 1920- *BioIn 5, ClaDrA, DcBrAr 1, IlsCB 1946, WhoArt 80, -82, -84*

Friesel, Uwe 1939- *IntAu&W 82*

Friesner, Esther M 1951- *SmATA 71*

Friis, Babbis
Main entry: Friis-Baastad, Babbis Ellinor

Friis-Baastad, Babbis Ellinor 1921-1970 *AuBYP 2S, BioIn 9, –10, ConAu 17R, –134, ConLC 12, SmATA 7, ThrBJA*
Pseud./variant:
Baastad, Babbis Friis
Babbis, Eleanor
Friis, Babbis

Frimmer, Steven 1928- *AuBYP 2S, –3, ConAu 33R, SmATA 31*

Frisbee, Lucy Post *AuBYP 2, –3, BioIn 8*

Frisch, Otto Robert 1904- *AuBYP 3*

Frisch, Otto Robert 1904-1979 *AsBiEn, AuBYP 2, BiESc, BioIn 1, –8, –12, –13, –14, –16, –17, BlueB 76, ConAu 9R, DcNaB 1971, DcScB S2, EncWB, InSci, IntWW 74, –75, –76, –77, –78, –79, Who 74, WhoWor 74, WorAlBi, WorAl, WrDr 76, –80*

Frisch, Rose E *AuBYP 3, WhoTech 84*

Frisch, Rose Epstein 1918- *AmMWSc 82, –86, –89, –92, AuBYP 2S, WhoAm 92, –94, WhoAmW 91, –93, WhoE 93, WhoTech 82*

Friskey, Margaret 1901- *AuBYP 3*

Friskey, Margaret Richards 1901- *AuBYP 2, BioIn 2, –4, –8, –10, ConAu 5R, ForWC 70, SmATA 5*
Pseud./variant:
Sherman, Elizabeth

Friss-Baastad, Babbis Ellinor 1921- *AuBYP 3*

Frith, Henry 1840- *Alli SUP, CarSB, ChhPo S1, ScFEYrs*

Frith, Margaret *WhoAm 76, –78, –80, –82, –84, –86, –88, –94, WhoAmW 93*

Frith, Michael *IlsBYP*

Fritz *SmATA X*
Main entry: Frazetta, Frank

Fritz, Jean 1915- *AuBYP 3, ChlLR 14, DcLB 52, IntAu&W 91, ScF&FL 92, SmATA 2AS, TwCChW 89, TwCYAW, WrDr 86, –88, –90, –92, –94*

Fritz, Jean Guttery 1915- *AuBYP 2, BioIn 4, –7, –9, –10, –12, –13, ChhPo S2, ChlLR 2, ConAu 1R, –5NR, –16NR, –37NR, DcAmChF 1960, ForWC 70, MajAI, MorBMP, OxCChiL, SmATA 1, –29, –72, –2AS, ThrBJA, TwCChW 78, –83, WhoAm 84, –92, –94, WhoAmW 83, –89, –91, –93, WrDr 80, –82, –84*

Froboess, Harry 1899- *BioIn 3, ConAu P-2*

Froebel, Friedrich 1782-1852 *CyEd, DcBiPP, OxCChiL, WhDW*

Froebel, Friedrich Wilhelm 1782-1852 *WorAlBi*

Froehlich, Margaret Walden 1930- *BioIn 16, SmATA 56*

Frois, Jeanne 1953- *SmATA 73*

Froissart, Jean 1337?-1410? *AtlBL, Benet 87, BbD, BiD&SB, BioIn 1, –5, –7, –8, –9, –10, –12, –13, BlmGEL, CamGEL, CasWL, CyWA 58, DcBiPP, DcCathB, DcEuL, EvEuW, LongCEL, McGEWB, NewC, OxCChiL, OxCEng 67, –85, OxCFr, PenC EUR, REn, SmATA 28, WhDW, WhoChL*

Froissart, Jean 1338?-1410? *BioIn 15*

Frolov, Vadim *TwCChW 89B*

Frolov, Vadim 1913- *AuBYP 2S, –3, TwCChW 78B, –83B*

Froman, Elizabeth Hull 1920-1975 *BioIn 11, ConAu 53, –P-1, SmATA 10*

Froman, Robert 1917- *AuBYP 2, –3, BioIn 8, –11, ConAu 1R, –1NR, FourBJA, SmATA 8*

Fromm, Lilo 1928- *BioIn 13, ConAu 81, IlsBYP, IlsCB 1967, IntAu&W 82, SmATA 29*

Frommer, Harvey *BioIn 15*

Frommer, Harvey 1937- *ConAu 103, –26NR, IntAu&W 86, –89, –91, SmATA 41, WhoE 86, –89*

Front, Charles 1930- *BioIn 12, IlsCB 1967*

Frost, Arthur Burdett 1851-1928 *AmAu&B, AmPB, BioIn 2, –3, –4, –5, –12, ChhPo, –S1, –S2, DcAmAu, DcBrBI, DcNAA, IlrAm 1880, –A, MajAI, OxCAmL 65, –83, OxCChiL, OxCTwCA, REnAL, SmATA 19, Str&VC, WhAm 1, WhAmArt 85, WorECar*

Frost, C Vernon *EncMys*

Frost, Erica *BioIn 12, ConAu X, SmATA X*
Main entry: Supraner, Robyn

Frost, Frances Mary 1905-1959 *AmAu&B, AmNov, BioIn 2, –5, –6, BkCL, ChhPo, –S1, –S2, CurBio 50, –59, MorJA, REnAL, Str&VC, WhAm 3, WhNAA*

Frost, Lesley 1899?-1983 *BioIn 8, -12, -13, ConAu 21R, -110, SmATA 14, -34N*
Pseud./variant:
Ballantine, Lesley Frost

Frost, Robert *IntvTCA 2*

Frost, Robert 1874?-1963 *AmAu&B, AmLY, AmWr, AnCL, AtlBL, Benet 87, BenetAL 91, BioIn 1, -2, -3, -4, -5, -6, -7, -8, -9, -10, -11, -12, -13, -14, -15, -16, -17, CamGEL, CamGLE, CamHAL, CasWL, Chambr 3, ChhPo, -S1, -S2, CnDAL, CnE&AP, CnMWL, ConAmA, ConAmL, ConAu 33NR, ConLC 1, -3, -4, -9, -10, -13, -15, -26, CurBio 42, -63, CyWA 58, DcLB 54, -DS7, DcLEL, EncAB-H, EncWL, -2, EvLB, FamPYP, LongCTC, MagSAmL, MajTwCW, MakMC, MemAm, ModAL, -S1, -S2, NatCAB 58, NewGrDA 86, NewYTBE 72, NewYTBS 74, ObitOF 79, ObitT 1961, OxCAmH, OxCAmL 65, -83, OxCEng 67, PenC AM, PoeCrit 1, RAdv 1, -13-1, RComAH, RComWL, REn, REnAL, RfGAmL 87, SixAP, SmATA 14, Str&VC, Tw, TwCA, -SUP, TwCWr, WebAB 74, WebE&AL, WhDW, WhAm 4, WhNAA, WhoTwCL, WorAlBi, WorAl, WorLitC, WrPh*

Frost, Robert 1875-1963 *ModAL S2*

Frost, Thomas *ScF&FL 92*

Frost, Thomas 1821-1908 *Alli SUP, CarSB*

Frost, William Henry 1863-1904? *CarSB, DcNAA, WhAm 1*

Froud, Brian *BioIn 13, IlsCB 1967*

Fry, Charles Burgess 1872-1956 *BioIn 2, -4, -14, DcNaB 1951, GrBr, ObitOF 79*

Fry, Christopher 1907- *AuBYP 2, -3, Au&Wr 71, Benet 87, BiE&WWA, BioIn 2, -3, -4, -5, -6, -8, -9, -10, -13, BlmGEL, BlueB 76, CamGEL, CamGLE, CamGWoT, CasWL, CnMD, CnMWL, CnThe, ConAu 17R, -9NR, -30NR, ConDr 73, -77, -82, -88, -93, ConLC 2, -10, ConPo 70, -75, -80, -85, -91, CroCD, CurBio 51, CyWA 58, DcLB 13, DcLEL, EncWL, -2, EncWT, EngPo, EvLB, IntAu&W 89, -91, IntDcT 2, IntWW 74, -75, -76, -77, -78, -79, -80, -81, -82, -83, -89, -91, LongCTC, MajTwCW, McGEWD 72, -84, ModBrL, -S1, ModWD, NewC, NotNAT, -A, OxCAmT 84, OxCEng 67, -85, OxCThe 67, -83, PenC ENG, PlP&P, RAdv 13-2, REn, RfGEnL 91, SmATA 66, TwCA SUP, TwCWr, WebE&AL, Who 74, -82, -83, -85, -88, -90, -92, WhoThe 72, -77, -81, WhoWor 74, -78, WorAlBi, WorAl, WorEFlm, WrDr 76, -80, -82, -84, -86, -88, -90, -92, -94*

Fry, Edward B 1925- *WrDr 90, -92*

Fry, Edward Bernard 1925- *ConAu 5NR, SmATA 35*

Fry, Guy 1903- *ChhPo, WhoAm 74, -76, -78, -80, -82, -84, -86, WhoAmA 78*

Fry, Ronald William 1949- *ConAu 57, WrDr 80, -82, -84*

Fry, Rosalie K 1911- *SmATA 11AS, TwCChW 89, WrDr 86, -88, -90, -92*

Fry, Rosalie Kingsmill 1911- *AuBYP 2, -3, Au&Wr 71, BioIn 5, -8, -9, -14, ChhPo S1, ConAu 9R, IlsCB 1946, -1957, -1967, IntAu&W 77, -91, OxCLiW 86, SmATA 3, ThrBJA, TwCChW 78, -83, WrDr 76, -80, -82, -84*

Fry, Rosalie Kingsmill 1911-1992 *WrDr 94N*

Fryatt, Norma R *AuBYP 2, -3, BioIn 8, ConAu 57*

Frye, Dean *AuBYP 3*

Frye, Dean Carson 1932- *AuBYP 2, BioIn 8, DrAS 74E, -82E*

Frye, John 1910- *ConAu 49, -28NR*

Fryer, Judith 1939- *ConAu 69, DrAS 82E*

Fuchs, Erich 1916- *BioIn 10, ConAu 29R, FourBJA, SmATA 6*

Fuchs, Lucy 1935- *ConAu 30NR, SmATA 52, WrDr 90, -92, -94*

Fuchs, Lucy Ann 1935- *WhoSSW 93*

Fuchshuber, Annegert 1940- *AuBYP 2S, -3, BioIn 15, ConAu 112, SmATA 43*

Fufuka, Karama *ConAu X*
Main entry: Morgan, Sharon A

Fufuka, Karama 1951- *BioIn 16, BlkAuII, -92*

Fuge, Charles 1966- *SmATA 74*

Fuja, Abayomi *AuBYP 2S, -3*

Fujikawa, Gyo *BioIn 14*

Fujikawa, Gyo 1908- *BioIn 3, -8, -9, -15, ChlLR 25, ConAu 113, FourBJA, IlsBYP, IlsCB 1957, -1967, MajAI, SmATA 30, -39, -76, -16AS*

Fujimoto, Patricia *AuBYP 3*

Fujita, Tamao 1905- *BioIn 10, ConAu 37R, SmATA 7*

Fujiwara, Michiko 1946- *BioIn 12, ConAu 77, SmATA 15*
Pseud./variant:
Saito, Michiko

Fuka, Vladimir 1926-1977 *BioIn 11, -13, ConAu 104, SmATA 27N*

Fulford, Robert Marshall Blount 1932- *CanWW 70, -80, -81, -83, -89, OxCCan SUP*

Fulks, Bryan 1897- *AuBYP 2S, -3, ConAu 97*

Fullarton, Nan *SingR 1*

Fuller, Alice Cook *AmWomPl, AuBYP 2, -3, BioIn 8*

Fuller, Anna 1853-1916 *BiD&SB, CarSB, DcAmAu, DcNAA, FemiCLE, WhAm 1, WomWWA 14, WomNov*

Fuller, Catherine Leuthold 1916- *BioIn 11, ConAu 29R, SmATA 9*

Fuller, Edmund 1914- *AmAu&B, AuBYP 2, -3, BioIn 8, -10, -12, ChhPo S1, ConAu 77, ConNov 72, -76, DcLEL 1940, DrAS 74E, IntAu&W 77, SmATA 21, WorAu 1950, WrDr 76, -80, -82, -84, -86, -88, -90, -92, -94*
Pseud./variant:
Curaie, Amicus

Fuller, Iola *AmNov, BioIn 2, -7, -8, -9, ConAu X, ForWC 70, MichAu 80, REnAL, SmATA 3*
Main entry: McCoy, Iola Fuller

Fuller, J *OxCChiL*

Fuller, John G 1913-1990 *ConAu 133, ScF&FL 92, SmATA 65*

Fuller, John Grant 1913- *WhAm 10, WhoAm 86, -88, -90*

Fuller, John Grant 1913-1990 *BioIn 17*

Fuller, Lois Hamilton 1915- *AuBYP 2S, -3, BioIn 11, ConAu 1R, -29NR, SmATA 11*

Fuller, Margaret
Main entry: Ossoli, Sarah Margaret Marchesa D'

Fuller, Margaret 1810-1850 *AmWomWr 92, AmWr S2, ArtclWW 2, Benet 87, BenetAL 91, BioAmW, BioIn 14, -15, -16, -17, BlmGWL, BriB, CamGEL, CamGLE, CamHAL, Dis&D, EncAJ, FemiCLE, HanAmWH, HerW 84, InWom SUP, IntDcWB, JrnUS, NinCLC 5, OxCAmH, OxCAmL 83, OxCEng 85, PorAmW, RComAH, SmATA X, WebAB 79*

Fuller, Miriam Morris 1933- *BiDrLUS 70, ConAu 37R, WhoLibS 66*

Fuller, Ralph Briggs 1890-1963 *ArtCS, BioIn 2, -6*

Fuller, Raymond Tifft 1889- *AuBYP 3*

Fuller, Raymond Tifft 1889-1960 *AuBYP 2, BioIn 5, -8*

Fuller, Roy *IntvTCA 2*

Fuller, Roy 1912- *Benet 87, BlmGEL, CamGEL, CamGLE, ConAu 10AS, ConNov 86, -91, ConPo 91, EngPo, ModBrL S2, RAdv 13-1, RfGEnL 91, TwCChW 89, TwCCr&M 91, WrDr 86, -88, -90, -92*

Fuller, Roy 1912-1991 *AnObit 1991, ConAu 135*

Fuller, Roy Broadbent 1912- *Au&Wr 71, BioIn 4, -8, -10, -12, -13, -14, -17, BlueB 76, CasWL, ChhPo S1, -S2, CnE&AP, ConAu 5R, ConLC 4, -28, ConNov 72, -76, -82, ConPo 70, -75, -80, -85, DcLB 15 -20, EncWL 2, IntAu&W 89, -91, IntWW 74, -75, -76, -77, -78, -79, -80, -81, -82, -83, -89, -91, LongCTC, MakMC, ModBrL, -S1, -S2, NewC, Novels, OxCChiL, OxCEng 85, PenC ENG, RAdv 1, REn, TwCA SUP, TwCChW 78, -83, TwCCr&M 80, -85, TwCWr, WebE&AL, Who 74, -82, -83, -85, -88, -90, -92, WhoChL, WhoTwCL, WhoWor 74, -78, WrDr 76, -80, -82, -84*

Fuller, Roy Broadbent 1912-1991 *ConLC 70, WrDr 94N*

Fuller, S *OxCChiL*

Fuller, William Albert 1924- *AmMWSc 73P, -82, -86, -89, -92, ConAu 41R, WhoWest 74*

Fults, John Lee 1932- *ConAu 53, SmATA 33*

Funai, Mamoru 1932- *BioIn 15, SmATA 46*

Funai, Mamoru R 1932- *BioIn 8, ChhPo S1, IlsCB 1957, -1967*

Funderburk, Thomas R 1928- *ConAu 17R, IndAu 1917*

Fung, Paul 1897-1944 *ArtCS*

Funk, Peter V K 1921- *ConAu 21R, -13NR, WhoAm 94, WhoE 74*

Funk, Thompson 1911- *BioIn 10, ConAu 49, -2NR, IlsBYP, SmATA 7*
Pseud./variant:
Funk, Tom

Funk, Tom
Main entry: Funk, Thompson

Funke, Lewis B d1992 *NewYTBS 92*

Funke, Lewis B 1912- *AmAu&B, BiE&WWA, BioIn 11, ConAu 49, NotNAT, SmATA 11, WhoAm 74, –76, –80, –82, –84, –86, –88, WhoAmJ 80, WhoE 74, WhoWorJ 72, –78*

Funke, Lewis Bernard 1912- *WhoAm 90*

Furchgott, Terry 1948- *BioIn 13, ConAu 105, SmATA 29*

Furer, Howard Bernard 1934- *ConAu 33R, DrAS 74H, –78H, –82H*

Furlong, Monica 1930- *Au&Wr 71, ChlFicS, ConAu 117, FemiCLE, IntAu&W 89, ScF&FL 92, Who 83, –85, –88, –90, –92*

Furlong, Monica Mavis 1930- *TwCYAW*

Furnas, Clifford Cook 1900-1969 *AmAu&B, Au&Wr 71, BioIn 3, –4, –7, –8, –11, CurBio 56, –69, InSci, IndAu 1917, ObitOF 79, WhAm 5*

Furneaux, Rupert 1908- *ConAu 1R, –1NR*

Furness, Edna Lue 1906- *ConAu 37R, DrAS 74E, –78E, –82E, ForWC 70, IntAu&W 77, –82, WrDr 76, –80*

Furniss, Harry *DcVicP 2*

Furniss, Harry 1854-1925 *BioIn 8, –12, –13, –14, CelCen, ChhPo, –S1, –S2, DcBrAr 1, DcBrBI, DcIrB 88, DcNaB 1922, DcVicP 2, OxCChiL, WhScrn 83, –77, WhoChL, WorECar*

Furniss, Harry 1857-1925 *StaCVF*

Furniss, Tim 1948- *ConAu 29NR, SmATA 49*

Furnivall, Frederick James 1825-1910 *Alli SUP, BiD&SB, BioIn 12, –14, BritAu 19, CamGEL, CelCen, Chambr 3, ChhPo S1, –S2, CyEd, DcEnA, –A, DcEnL, DcLEL, DcNaB S2, EvLB, LongCTC, NewC, OxCEng 67, –85, REn*

Furrer, Juerg 1939- *ConAu 69*

Furukawa, Mel 1945?- *BioIn 10, IlsCB 1967*

Furukawa, Toshi 1924- *BioIn 13, ConAu 45, –2NR, SmATA 24*
Pseud./variant:
Kanzawa, Toshiko

Futcher, Jane P 1947- *SmATA 76*

Fyleman, Rose 1877-1957 *AmWomPl, AnCL, BioIn 2, –4, –5, –8, –12, BkCL, ChhPo, –S1, –S2, ConAu 111, EvLB, JBA 34, –51, LongCTC, ObitT 1951, OxCChiL, SmATA 21, Str&VC, TwCA, –SUP, TwCChW 78, –83, –89, WhoChL, WhoLA*

Fyleman, Rose Amy 1877-1957 *DcNaB 1951*

Fyson, J G *IntAu&W 86X*

Fyson, J G 1904- *BioIn 15, TwCChW 89, WrDr 86, –88, –90, –92*

Fyson, Jenny Grace 1904- *Au&Wr 71, ConAu P-2, IntAu&W 77, –82, –82X, –86, –89, –91, SmATA 42, TwCChW 78, –83, WrDr 80, –82, –84, –94*

G

Gaan, Margaret 1914- *IntAu&W 91, SmATA 65, WrDr 86, –88, –90, –92, –94*

Gabel, Margaret 1938- *BiDrLUS 70, ConAu 33R, WrDr 76, –80*

Gabhart, Ann *ScF&FL 92*

Gabhart, Ann 1947- *ConAu 142, SmATA 75*

Gabler, Mirko 1951- *SmATA 77*

Gabriel, Juri Evald 1940- *Au&Wr 71, IntAu&W 82, –86, –89, –91, WrDr 76, –80*

Gabrielson, Ira Noel 1889-1977 *AmMWSc 73P, BioIn 1, –3, –6, –11, –14, ConAu 73, –P-1, ObitOF 79, WhAm 7, WhoAm 74, –76, WhoWor 74*

Gackenbach, Dick 1927- *AuBYP 2S, –3, ConAu 115, –38NR, FifBJA, MajAI, SmATA 30, –48*

Gaddis, Vincent H 1913- *BioIn 14, IntAu&W 89*

Gaddis, Vincent Hayes 1913- *ConAu 13R, IntAu&W 77, SmATA 35, WrDr 76, –80, –82, –84, –86, –88, –90, –92, –94*

Gadler, Steve J 1905- *BioIn 14, ConAu 97, SmATA 36*

Gaeddert, Lou Ann 1931- *BioIn 12, BkP, ConAu 73, –13NR, –29NR, SmATA 20*

Gaer, Joseph 1897- *AmAu&B, AuBYP 2, –3, BioIn 2, –6, –8, –10, ConAu 9R, CurBio 51, MorJA, WhoAm 74, –76, WhoWorJ 72, –78*

Gaer, Joseph 1897-1969 *ConAu 122, ScF&FL 92*

Gaffney, Timothy R *AuBYP 3*

Gaffney, Timothy R 1951- *ConAu 137, SmATA 69*

Gag, Flavia 1907-1979 *AuBYP 2, –3, BioIn 1, –5, –6, –7, –13, ConAu 5R, –104, IlsCB 1744, –1946, MinnWr, MorJA, SmATA 24N*

Gag, Wanda 1893-1946 *AmAu&B, AmPB, AnCL, AuBYP 2, BenetAL 91, BioAmW, BioIn 1, –2, –4, –8, –10, –11, –14, ChhPo S2, ChlLR 4, ConAu 113, ConICB, CurBio 46, DcLB 22, DcNAA, DcWomA, FamAIYP, GrAmP, HerW, –84, IlsCB 1744, JBA 34, –51, ObitOF 79, OxCChiL, REnAL, TwCA, –SUP, TwCChW 78, –83, –89, WhAm 2, WhAmArt 85, WrChl, YABC 1*

Gag, Wanda Hazel 1893-1946 *AuBYP 3, ConAu 137, InWom SUP, MajAI*

Gagan, David P *OxCCan SUP*

Gage, Wilson *AuBYP 2, –3, ConAu 139, –X, DcAmChF 1960, MajAI, SmATA 3, –72, ThrBJA, TwCChW 89, WrDr 76, –80, –82, –84, –86, –88, –90, –92*
Main entry: Steele, Mary Quintard Govan

Gage, Wilson 1922- *WrDr 94*

Gagg, John Colton 1916- *Au&Wr 71*

Gagliardo, Ruth 1895?-1980 *AuBYP 2, BioIn 1, –7, –12, –13, –17, ConAu 104, SmATA 22N, WhoLibS 55*

Gagliardo, Ruth Garver 1895?-1980 *AuBYP 3*

Gagnier, Ed 1936- *ConAu 65*

Gagnon, Cecile 1936- *BioIn 16, IntAu&W 86, SmATA 58, WhoCanL 87, –92*

Gagnon, Maurice 1912- *CreCan 2, OxCCan SUP, WhoCanL 87, –92*

Gaidar, Arkady 1904-1941 *OxCChiL*

Gainer, Cindy 1962- *SmATA 74*

Gaines, Charles Kelsey 1854-1944? *AmAu&B, DcNAA, ScFEYrs, WhAm 2, WhNAA*

Gaines, Ernest J *DrAPF 87, –89, –91, –93, WhoAm 86, –88, –94, WhoUSWr 88, WhoWrEP 89, –92*

Gaines, Ernest J 1933- *AfrAmAl 6, AfrAmW, AuBYP 2S, –3, AuNews 1, Benet 87,*

BenetAL 91, BioIn 10, –11, –12, –14, –17, BlkAWP, BlkWr 1, BroV, CamGLE, CamHAL, CivR 74, CmCal, ConAu 9R, –6NR, –24NR, ConLC 3, –11, –18, ConNov 72, –76, –82, –86, –91, CyWA 89, DcLB 2, –33, –Y80A, DrAF 76, DrAPF 83, –85, FifSWrA, InB&W 80, IntAu&W 77, –82, LivgBAA, MajTwCW, ModAL S2, ModBlW, NegAl 76, –83, –89, OxCAmL 83, SelBAAf, SelBAAu, TwCRHW 90, WhoAm 74, –76, –78, –80, –82, –84, WhoBlA 75, –77, –80, –85, –88, –90, –92, WrDr 76, –80, –82, –84, –86, –88, –90, –92

Gaines, Ernest J K 1933- *InB&W 85*

Gaines, Ernest James 1933- *BlkWr 2, TwCYAW*

Gait, Robert I 1938- *AmMWSc 73P, –82*

Gait, Robert Irwin 1938- *AmMWSc 86, –89, –92*

Gaither, Bill *WhoAm 78, –80, –82, –84*

Gal, Laszlo 1933- *BioIn 13, –14, –16, Profile 2, SmATA 32, –52, WhoAm 82, –84, –86, –88, –90, –92*

Galantiere, Lewis 1895-1977 *AmAu&B, BioIn 11, WhAm 7, WhoAm 74, –76*

Galbraith, Jean 1906- *ConAu 37R, IntAu&W 77, WrDr 76, –80, –82, –84, –86, –88, –90, –92, –94*

Galdone, Paul *BioIn 14*

Galdone, Paul 1907?-1986 *ConAu 121, MajAI, SmATA 66*

Galdone, Paul 1914- *AuBYP 2, BioIn 5, –8, –9, –12, BkP, ChhPo, –S1, –S2, ConAu 73, –13NR, IlsCB 1946, –1957, –1967, OxCChiL, SmATA 17, ThrBJA*

Galdone, Paul 1914-1986 *AuBYP 3, BioIn 15, –16, –17, ChlBIID, ChlLR 16, SmATA 49N*

Gale, Elizabeth *WhNAA*

Gale, Zona *DrAPF 87, –89, –91, –93*

Gale, Zona 1874-1938 *AmAu&B, AmLY, AmPeW, AmWomD, AmWomPl, AnMV 1926, Benet 87, BenetAL 91, BioAmW, BioIn 4, –5, –6, –12, –15, –16, CamGLE, CamHAL, ChhPo, –S2, CnDAL, CnMD, ConAmA, ConAmL, ConAu 105, DcLB 9, –78, DcLEL, DcNAA, DrAPF 83, –85, EvLB, FemiCLE, InWom SUP, IntDcT 2, LongCTC, McGEWD 72, –84, ModWD, NotNAT A, –B, NotWoAT, Novels, OxCAmL 65, –83, OxCAmT 84, PenC AM, REn, REnAL, RfGAmL 87, ScFEYrs, TwCA, –SUP, TwCLC 7, TwCWr, WhAm 1, WhNAA, WisWr, WomWWA 14, WomNov*

Galinsky, Ellen 1942- *BioIn 13, ConAu 65, –9NR, SmATA 23*

Gall, Alice *AuBYP 3*

Gall, Alice Crew 1878-1949 *AmAu&B, AuBYP 2, BioIn 2, –7, JBA 51, OhA&B*

Gall, Morris 1907- *ConAu 45, DrAS 74H*

Gallagher, Thomas Michael 1918- *BioIn 3, ConAu 1R*

Gallant, Melvin 1933- *DrAS 74F*

Gallant, Roy A 1924- *ConAu 29NR, SmATA 68*

Gallant, Roy Arthur 1924- *AuBYP 2, –3, BioIn 8, –9, ChlLR 30, ConAu 5R, –4NR, ConLC 17, FifBJA, IntAu&W 91, MajAI, SmATA 4, WhoE 85, –86, WrDr 76, –80, –82, –84, –86, –88, –90, –92, –94*

Gallico, Paul 1897-1976 *AmAu&B, AmNov, AuSpks, AuBYP 2S, –3, AuNews 1, Au&Wr 71, BenetAL 91, BioIn 1, –2, –4, –6, –9, –10, –11, –12, BlueB 76, ConAu 5R, –69, –23NR, ConLC 2, ConNov 72, –76, CurBio 46, –76N, DcLB 9, DcLEL, EncAJ, EvLB, FilmgC, HalFC 84, –88, IntWW 74, NatCAB 59, Novels, ObitOF 79, OxCChiL, REnAL, ScF&FL 92, ScFSB, SmATA 13, TwCA SUP, TwCWr, WhAm 7, Who 74, WhoAm 74, WhoThe 81N, WhoWor 74, WorAl, WrDr 76*

Gallico, Paul 1898-1976 *Ballpl 90*

Gallico, Paul William 1897-1976 *EncSF 93, MajAI*

Gallienne, Eva Le *OxCThe 67, –83*
Main entry: LeGallienne, Eva

Gallob, Edward *AuBYP 2S, –3*

Galloway, Priscilla 1930- *IntAu&W 86, SmATA 66, WhoCanL 87, –92*
Pseud./variant:
Peebles, Anne

Gallu, Samuel 1918- *AuNews 2, BioIn 11, ConAu 85, FilmgC, HalFC 84, –88*

Gallup, Lucy A 1911- *BiDrLUS 70, WhoLibS 66*

Galster, Robert Miller 1928- *BioIn 8, IlsBYP, IlsCB 1957*

Galt, Thomas F, Jr. 1908- *WhoUSWr 88, WhoWrEP 89, –92*

Galt, Thomas Franklin, Jr. 1908- *BioIn 6, -10, ConAu 5R, MichAu 80, MorJA, SmATA 5*

Gamerman, Martha 1941- *BioIn 12, ConAu 77, SmATA 15*

Gammage, Allen Z 1917- *AmMWSc 73S, -78S, ConAu 5R, -11NR, WhoWest 76, -78*

Gammell, Stephen 1943- *BioIn 16, -17, ConAu 135, FifBJA, MajAI, SmATA 53, WrDr 94*

Gamoran, Mamie Goldsmith 1900- *ConAu 5R, ForWC 70, IntAu&W 77, -82, WhoAmW 74*

Gamow, George 1904-1968 *AmAu&B, AsBiEn, BiESc, BioIn 1, -2, -4, -8, -14, -17, ConAu 93, -102, CurBio 51, -68, DcAmB S8, DcScB, EncSF 93, EncWB, InSci, McGMS 80, ObitOF 79, RAdv 13-5, REnAL, TwCA SUP, WebAB 74, -79, WhAm 5, WorAlBi, WorAl*

Ganly, Helen 1940- *ConAu 125, SmATA 56*

Gann, Ernest K 1910- *BenetAL 91, HalFC 88, TwCRHW 90, WrDr 86, -88, -90, -92*

Gann, Ernest K 1910-1991 *ScF&FL 92*

Gann, Ernest Kellogg d1991 *NewYTBS 91*

Gann, Ernest Kellogg 1910- *AmAu&B, AmNov, AuNews 1, BioIn 2, -3, -4, -7, -8, -9, -10, -11, -12, -15, BlueB 76, ConAu 1R, -1NR, ConLC 23, HalFC 84, NewYTBS 81, Novels, OxCAmL 83, TwCWr, WhoAm 74, -76, -78, -80, -82, -84, -86, -88, -90, WhoEnt 92, WhoPNW, WhoUSWr 88, WhoWest 74, WhoWrEP 89, -92, WorAl, WorAu 1950, WrDr 76, -80, -82, -84*

Gann, Ernest Kellogg 1910-1991 *BioIn 17, ConAu 136, EncSF 93, WhAm 10, WrDr 94N*

Gannett, Ruth Chrisman 1896-1979 *BioIn 14*

Gannett, Ruth Chrisman Arens 1896-1979 *ArtsAmW 3, BioIn 5, -6, DcWomA, IlsCB 1946, MorJA, SmATA 33, WhAmArt 85*

Gannett, Ruth Stiles 1923- *AuBYP 2, -3, BioIn 7, -9, -14, BkCL, ConAu 21R, FourBJA, SmATA 3, TwCChW 78, -83, -89, WrDr 80, -82, -84, -86, -88, -90, -92, -94*

Gannon, Robert Haines 1931- *BioIn 11, ConAu 9R, -4NR, IntAu&W 86, -89, SmATA 8, WhoUSWr 88, WhoWrEP 89, -92*

Gano, Lila 1949- *SmATA 76*

Ganpat *BioIn 1*

Ganpat 1886-1951 *ScF&FL 92, ScFEYrs*

Gans, Carl 1923- *AmMWSc 73P, -76P, -82, -86, -89, -92, WhoAm 78, -80, -82, -84, -86, -88, -90, -92, -94, WhoFrS 84, WhoMW 84, -93*

Gans, Roma 1894- *AuBYP 2S, -3, BioIn 12, -15, -17, ConAu 77, -32NR, FifBJA, SmATA 45*

Gant, Elizabeth *AuBYP 2S, -3*

Gant, Jonathan *ConAu X, IntAu&W 91X, TwCWW 91, WrDr 84, -86, -88, -90*
Main entry: Adams, Clifton

Gant, Katherine *AuBYP 2S, -3*

Gant, Phyllis *BlmGWL*

Gant, Phyllis 1922- *ConAu 57*

Gantner, Susan 1939- *SmATA 63*

Gantos, Jack *ConAu X, FifBJA, SmATA X*
Main entry: Gantos, John, Jr.

Gantos, Jack 1951- *AuBYP 3, ChlLR 18*

Gantos, John, Jr. 1951- *AuBYP 2, BioIn 12, ConAu 65, -15NR, SmATA 20*
Pseud./variant:
Gantos, Jack

Gantos, John Bryan *AuBYP 3*

Gantry, Susan Nadler 1947- *ConAu 61*
Pseud./variant:
Nadler, Susan

Gantschev, Ivan *AuBYP 3*

Gantz, Charlotte Orr 1909- *ConAu 49*

Ganz, Yaffa 1938- *BioIn 16, -17, SmATA 52, -61*

Garbutt, Bernard 1900- *BioIn 5, -6, -11, -14, ConAu 110, IlsCB 1946, SmATA 31*

Gard, Janice *AmWomPl, AuBYP 3, IntAu&W 91X, MajAI, SmATA 68, TwCYAW, WrDr 86, -88, -90, -92*
Main entry: Latham, Jean Lee

Gard, Janice 1902- *WrDr 94*

Gard, Joyce *AuBYP 2*

Gard, Joyce 1911- *AuBYP 3, Au&Wr 71, BioIn 8, -11, -12, BritCA, ConAu 73, -X, IntAu&W 77, -82, -86, -89, OxCChiL, SmATA X, TwCChW 78, -83, -89, WrDr 80, -82, -84, -86, -88, -90, -92, -94*
Pseud./variant:
Reeves, Joyce

Gard, Robert E 1910- *OxCCanT*

Gard, Robert Edward 1910- *AuBYP 2, -3, BiE&WWA, BioIn 4, -8, -12, -13, ConAu 85, NotNAT, OxCCan, REnAL, SmATA 18, WhoAm 74, -76, -78, -80*

Gard, Robert Edward 1910-1992 *ConAu 140, SmATA 74*

Gard, Wayne 1899-1986 *BioIn 16, ConAu 120, SmATA 49N*

Gardam, Jane *BioIn 16*

Gardam, Jane 1928- *AuBYP 2S, -3, BioIn 13, ChlFicS, ChlLR 12, ConAu 49, -2NR, -18NR, -33NR, ConLC 43, DcLB 14, FifBJA, MajAI, MajTwCW, OxCChiL, ScF&FL 92, SmATA 28, -39, -76, -9AS, TwCChW 78, -83, -89, TwCYAW, WrDr 80, -82, -84, -86, -88, -90, -92, -94*

Garden, Nancy 1938- *AuBYP 2S, -3, BioIn 11, ConAu 33R, -13NR, -30NR, DrAPF 83, -85, FifBJA, IntAu&W 91, ScF&FL 92, SmATA 12, -77, -8AS, TwCYAW, WrDr 76, -80, -82, -84, -86, -88, -90, -92, -94*

Garden, Robert Hal 1937- *ConAu 69*

Gardiner, John Reynolds *AuBYP 3*

Gardiner, John Reynolds 1944- *BioIn 16, -17, ConAu 127, DcAmChF 1985, SixBJA, SmATA 64*

Gardner, Beau *AuBYP 3, SmATA 50*

Gardner, Beau 1941- *SixBJA*

Gardner, Dic *BioIn 8, -13, ConAu X, SmATA X*
Main entry: Gardner, Richard M

Gardner, Dic 1931- *AuBYP 3*

Gardner, Erle Stanley 1889-1970 *AmAu&B, Benet 87, BenetAL 91, BioIn 1, -2, -4, -5, -6, -7, -8, -9, -10, -11, -12, -13, -14, -17, CmCal, ConAu 5R, -25R, -13NR, CorpD, CrtSuMy, CurBio 44, -70, DcAmB S8, EncMys, EncSF 93, EvLB, FilmgC, HalFC 84, -88, LongCTC, MajTwCW, NatCAB 62, NewYTBE 70, Novels, ObitOF 79, ObitT 1961, OxCAmL 65, -83, PenC AM, REn, REnAL, RfGAmL 87, ScF&FL 92, ScFEYrs, TwCA, -SUP, TwCCr&M 80, -85, -91, TwCWr, WebAB 74, -79, WhAm 6, WhNAA, WorAlBi, WorAl*

Gardner, Gerald 1929- *ConAu 1R, -5NR, ScF&FL 92*

Gardner, Horace John 1896-1950 *BioIn 2, WhAm 3, WhJnl, WhNAA*

Gardner, Hugh 1910-1986 *BioIn 16, ConAu 120, SmATA 49N*

Gardner, Jeanne LeMonnier 1925- *BioIn 10, ConAu 17R, ForWC 70, SmATA 5, WhoAmW 74*

Gardner, John 1933-1982 *AuBYP 3, Benet 87, BenetAL 91, BioIn 14, -15, -17, CamGLE, CamHAL, ConNov 86A, CyWA 89, EncSF 93, MagSAmL, ModAL S2, PostFic, RAdv 13-1, RfGAmL 87, ScF&FL 92, ScFSB, ShSCr 7, WorAlBi, WrPh*

Gardner, John 1939-1988 *BioIn 16*

Gardner, John, Jr. 1933-1982 *ConAu 33NR, MajTwCW*

Gardner, John Champlin 1933-1982 *BioIn 14, -15, -17*

Gardner, John Champlin, Jr 1933-1982 *RfGShF*

Gardner, John Champlin, Jr. 1933-1982 *AnObit 1982, AuBYP 2S, AuNews 1, BioIn 7, -10, -11, -12, -13, ConAu 65, -107, ConLC 2, -3, -5, -7, -8, -10, -18, -28, ConNov 76, -82, Conv 1, CurBio 78, -82N, DcLB 2, -Y82A, DrAF 76, FifBJA, ModAL S1, -S2, NewYTBS 81, -82, -84, Novels, OxCAmL 83, RAdv 1, SmATA 31N, -40, WhAm 8, WhoAm 74, -76, -78, -80, -82, WrDr 76, -80, -82*

Gardner, John Edmund 1926- *WrDr 94*

Gardner, John Linton 1917- *Baker 92*

Gardner, Joseph L 1933- *ConAu 30NR*

Gardner, Joseph Lawrence 1933- *ConAu 29R, WhoAm 76, -78, -80, -82, -84, -86, -88, -90, -92, -94, WhoE 75, WhoUSWr 88, WhoWrEP 89, -92*

Gardner, Lillian Soskin 1907- *AuBYP 2, -3, BioIn 8*

Gardner, Martin 1914- *AmAu&B, AuBYP 2S, -3, BioIn 6, -10, -12, -13, ChhPo, -S1, -S2, ConAu 73, EncSF 93, ScF&FL 92, SmATA 16, WhoE 74, WhoSSW 91, -93, WorAu 1980*

Gardner, Richard A 1931- *AuBYP 3, ConAu 34NR, WrDr 86, -88, -90, -92, -94*

Gardner, Richard Alan 1931- *AuBYP 2S, BiDrAPA 77, ConAu 33R, SmATA 13, WhoAm 74, -76, -78, -80, -82, -84, -90, -92, -94, WhoE 77, WhoUSWr 88, WhoWor 78, WhoWrEP 89, -92, WrDr 76, -80, -82, -84*

Gardner, Richard M *AuBYP 3*

Gardner, Richard M 1931- *AmAu&B, AuBYP 2, ConAu 21R, –10NR, DrAPF 83, –85, SmATA 24, WrDr 76, –80, –82*
Pseud./variant:
Anderson, Clifford
Carver, John
Cummings, Richard
Gardner, Dic
Orth, Richard

Gardner, Robert 1929- *AuBYP 2S, –3, SmATA 43, WhoE 93*

Gardner, Sandra 1940- *SmATA 70*

Gardner, Sheldon 1934- *ConAu 104, SmATA 33*

Gardonyi, Geza 1863-1922 *BioIn 1, CasWL, ClDMEL 47, PenC EUR*

Garelick, May 1910- *AuBYP 2, –3, BioIn 8, –12, BkP, ConAu 73, SmATA 19*
Pseud./variant:
Clark, Garel

Garelick, May 1910-1989 *BioIn 16, –17, ConAu 130*

Garfield, Brian Wynne 1939- *BioIn 10, –14, ConAu 1R, WhoAm 74, –76, –78, –80, –82, –84, –86, –88, –90, –92, –94, WhoEnt 92, WhoSpyF, WhoUSWr 88, WhoWrEP 89, –92, WrDr 76, –80*
Pseud./variant:
O'Brian, Frank

Garfield, James B 1881-1984 *BioIn 10, –15, ConAu 112, SmATA 6, –38N*

Garfield, Leon 1921- *Au&Arts 8, AuBYP 2S, –3, Au&Wr 71, BioIn 8, –9, –10, CamGLE, ChlFicS, ChlLR 21, ConAu 17R, –38NR, –41NR, ConLC 12, FourBJA, IntAu&W 89, –91, MajAI, OxCChiL, PiP, ScF&FL 92, SenS, SmATA 1, –32, –76, SouSt, TwCChW 78, –83, –89, TwCYAW, Who 82, –83, –85, –88, –90, –92, WhoChL, WrDr 76, –80, –82, –84, –86, –88, –90, –92*

Garfinkel, Bernard 1929- *ConAu 25R*
Pseud./variant:
Allen, Robert
Elliott, Robert
Martin, Janet

Garis, Howard R 1873-1962 *BenetAL 91, BioIn 14, ConAu 27NR, ScF&FL 92, ScFEYrs*

Garis, Howard Roger 1873-1962 *AmAu&B, BioIn 1, –6, –7, –10, CarSB, ConAu 73, DcAmB S7, DcLB 22, EncSF 93, ObitOF 79, REnAL, SmATA 13, WhAm 4*
Pseud./variant:
Davidson, Marion

Garis, Lillian C 1873-1954 *BioIn 3, CarSB, OhA&B*

Garland, Hamlin 1860-1940 *AmAu&B, AmLY, AtlBL, Benet 87, BenetAL 91, BbD, BiDPara, BiD&SB, BioIn 1, –2, –3, –4, –5, –6, –8, –9, –10, –11, –12, –13, –14, CamGEL, CamGLE, CamHAL, CasWL, Chambr 3, ChhPo, CnDAL, ConAmA, ConAmL, ConAu 104, CurBio 40, CyWA 58, DcAmAu, DcAmSR, DcBiA, DcLB 12, –71, –78, DcLEL, DcNAA, EncFWF, EncO&P 1, –2, –3, EvLB, LongCTC, ModAL, NotNAT B, Novels, OxCAmL 65, –83, OxCCan, OxCEng 67 PenC AM, RAdv 1, –13-1, REn, REnAL, RfGAmL 87, Str&VC, TwCA, –SUP, TwCLC 3, TwCWW 91, WebAB 74, –79, WebE&AL, WhAm 1, WhNaAH, WhNAA, WisWr, WorAlBi, WorAl*

Garland, Rosemary *Au&Wr 71*

Garland, Sarah 1944- *SmATA 62*

Garland, Sherry 1948- *SmATA 73*
Pseud./variant:
Lawrence, Lynn

Garner, Alan 1934- *AuBYP 3, Au&Wr 71, BioIn 8, –9, –10, –11, –12, –16, –17, BritCA, CamGLE, CasWL, ChhPo S1, ChlFicS, ChlLR 20, ConAu 73, –15NR, ConLC 17, ConSFA, EncSF 93, IntAu&W 77, –82, –86, –89, –91, MajAI, MajTwCW, Novels, OxCChiL, OxCEng 85, PiP, ScFSB, SenS, SmATA 18, –69, SouSt, SupFW, TelT, ThrBJA, TwCChW 78, –83, –89, TwCYAW, Who 82, –83, –85, –88, –90, –92, WhoChL, WrDr 76, –80, –82, –84, –86, –88, –90, –92, –94*

Garner, Alan 1950- *ConAu 132*

Garner, Alan Francis 1950- *WrDr 94*

Garner, Claud W *AuBYP 3*

Garner, Claud Wilton 1891- *ConAu 9R*

Garner, Elvira 1895- *BioIn 1, IlsCB 1744*

Garnet, A H *MajAI, SmATA 72*

Garnett, Emmeline *AuBYP 3*

Garnett, Emmeline 1924- *AuBYP 2S*

Garnett, Eve *TwCChW 89*

Garnett, Eve d1991 *TwCYAW*

Garnett, Eve C R *AuBYP 2, –3, Au&Wr 71, BioIn 1, –5, –7, –8, –9, ConAu 1R, –2NR, DcBrAr 1, FifBJA, IlsCB 1744, –1946,*

IntAu&W 77, -82, -86, -89, -91, OxCChiL, SmATA 3, TwCChW 78, -83, WhoArt 80, -82, -84, WhoChL, WrDr 76, -80, -82, -84, -86, -88, -90, -92, -94

Garnett, Eve C R 1900-1991 *ConAu 134, SmATA 70*

Garnett, Henry 1905- *Au&Wr 71*

Garnett, Richard 1789-1850 *EncO&P 3*

Garnett, Richard 1835-1906 *Alli SUP, BbD, BiD&SB, BioIn 1, -15, -16, BritAu 19, CamGLE, CasWL, Chambr 3, ChhPo, -S1, DcEnA, -A, DcEnL, DcLEL, DcNaB S2, EncSF 93, EvLB, LongCTC, NewC, OxCEng 67, -85, PenC ENG, REn, SupFW*

Garnett, Richard 1923- *IntAu&W 91, WrDr 86, -88, -90, -92*

Garnett, Richard Duncan Carey 1923- *ConAu 5R, WrDr 76, -80, -82, -84, -94*

Garou, Louis P *ConAu 134, SmATA 67, WrDr 94*
Main entry: Bowkett, Stephen

Garraty, John A 1920- *ConAu 36NR*

Garraty, John Arthur 1920- *BioIn 10, -13, ConAu 1R, -2NR, DcLB 17, DrAS 74H, -78H, -82H, SmATA 23, WhoAm 74, -76, -78, -80, -88, -90, -92, WhoWor 74*

Garret, Maxwell R 1917- *BioIn 15, ConAu 106, SmATA 39, WhoWorJ 72, -78*

Garretson, Victoria Diane 1945- *BioIn 15, ConAu 108, SmATA 44*
Pseud./variant:
Cox, Victoria

Garrett, Helen 1895- *AuBYP 2, -3, BioIn 8, -9, -12, SmATA 21*

Garrett, Randall 1927- *ConSFA, ScFSB, ThrBJA, TwCSFW 86, WhoSciF, WrDr 84, -86, -88*

Garrett, Randall 1927-1987 *BioIn 17, ConAu 130, NewEScF, RGTwCSF, ScF&FL 92*

Garrett, Randall 1927-1988 *TwCSFW 91*

Garrett, Richard 1920- *ConAu 81, -16NR, -37NR, IntAu&W 82, -86, -91, WhoWor 80, WrDr 80, -82, -84, -86, -88, -90, -92, -94*

Garrigue, Sheila 1931- *AuBYP 2S, -3, BioIn 12, ConAu 69, SixBJA, SmATA 21*

Garrison, Barbara 1931- *BioIn 12, SmATA 19, WhoAmA 86, -89, -91*

Garrison, Christian 1942- *ConAu 65*

Garrison, Frederick *AuBYP 2, -3, ConAmA, ConAu X, MajTwCW, SmATA X, TwCYAW*
Main entry: Sinclair, Upton Beall

Garrison, Theodosia Pickering 1874-1944 *AmAu&B, AmWomPl, ChhPo, -S2, ConAmL, DcNAA, REnAL, Str&VC, WomWWA 14*

Garrison, Webb B 1919- *BioIn 13, ConAu 1R, -2NR, -18NR, SmATA 25*
Pseud./variant:
Webster, Gary

Garshin, Vsevolod Mikhailovich 1855-1888 *BbD, BiD&SB, BioIn 1, -7, -10, CasWL, ClDMEL 47, DcRusL, Dis&D, EuAu, EvEuW, HanRL, PenC EUR*

Garson, Eugenia *AuBYP 2S, -3, ChhPo S1*

Garst, Doris Shannon 1894?- *AuBYP 2, -3, BioIn 1, -2, -7, -9, ConAu 1R, CurBio 47, ForWC 70, JBA 51, SmATA 1*
Pseud./variant:
Garst, Shannon

Garst, Shannon *AuBYP 3*
Main entry: Garst, Doris Shannon

Garstang, James Gordon 1927- *ConAu 13R*

Garten, Jan *AuBYP 2, -3, BioIn 8*

Garthwaite, Marion 1893- *AuBYP 3*

Garthwaite, Marion Hook 1893- *AuBYP 2, BioIn 7, -10, ConAu 5R, IntAu&W 77, -82, SmATA 7, WhoAmW 75, -77*

Garthwaite, Wymond Bradbury 1895- *ChhPo, ConICB*

Gartland, Robert *AuBYP 3*

Gartland, Robert Aldrich 1927- *ConAu 17R*

Gartman, Louise 1920- *ConAu 17R*

Gartner, Chloe Maria 1916- *ConAu 1R, IntAu&W 77, -82, -86, -89, -91, WrDr 76, -80, -82, -84, -86, -88, -90, -92, -94*

Garton, Malinda D d1976 *BioIn 13, ConAu 103, SmATA 26N*

Gascoigne, Bamber 1935- *ConAu 28NR, IntAu&W 89, -91, SmATA 62, Who 88, -90, -92, WrDr 86, -88, -90, -92, -94*

Gasiorowicz, Cathy 1956?- *BioIn 10*

Gask, Lillian *CarSB*

Gaskell, Thomas F 1916- *ConAu 17R*

Gaskin, Catherine 1929- *AmAu&B, AuWomWr, Au&Wr 71, BioIn 4, ConAu 65, –10NR, DcLEL 1940, FemiCLE, InWom SUP, Novels, OxCAusL, TwCCr&M 80, TwCRHW 90, TwCWr, Who 74, –82, –83, –85, –88, –90, –92, WrDr 76, –80, –82, –84, –86, –88, –90, –92, –94*

Gasperini, Jim 1952- *BioIn 16, ConAu 122, ScF&FL 92, SmATA 49, –54, WrDr 90*

Gass, Irene *AuBYP 2, –3, BioIn 8*

Gaster, Theodor Herzl 1906- *DrAS 74P, –78P, –82P, WhoAm 74, –76, WhoWor 74, WhoWorJ 72, –78*

Gaster, Theodor Herzl 1906-1992 *BioIn 17, NewYTBS 92*

Gatcombe, George *DcBrBI*

Gatenby, Rosemary 1918- *ConAu 21R, –9NR*

Gater, Dilys 1944- *BioIn 15, ConAu 112, IntAu&W 86, SmATA 41*
Pseud./variant:
Edwards, Olwen
Holland, Lys
Owen, Dilys
Sinclair, Clover
Wright, Katrina
Young, Vivien

Gates, Doris 1901- *AnCL, AuBYP 2, –3, Au&ICB, BioIn 1, –2, –8, –9, –14, –15, –16, ConAu 1R, –1NR, DcAmChF 1960, DcLB 22, IntAu&W 91, JBA 51, SmATA 1, –34, –1AS, TwCChW 78, –83, WrDr 80, –82, –84, –86, –88*

Gates, Doris 1901-1987 *ConAu 124, MajAI, SmATA 54N, TwCChW 89*

Gates, Eleanor 1875-1951 *AmAu&B, AmWomD, BenetAL 91, BioIn 2, –12, CarSB, InWom SUP, NotNAT B, ObitOF 79, OxCChiL, REnAL, WhAm 3, WhNAA, WomWWA 14, WomNov, WomWMM*

Gates, Frieda 1933- *BioIn 13, ConAu 93, SmATA 26*

Gathorne-Hardy, Jonathan G 1933- *Au&Wr 71, BioIn 13, ConAu 104, –39NR, SmATA 26, TwCChW 78, WrDr 76, –80*

Gatland, Kenneth William 1924- *Au&Wr 71, WrDr 76, –80, –82, –84, –86, –88, –90, –92, –94*

Gatti, Attilio 1896- *AmAu&B, AuBYP 2, –3, BioIn 2, –8, JBA 51*

Gatti, Ellen *AuBYP 3*

Gatti, Ellen Morgan *AuBYP 2, BioIn 8*

Gatty, Horatia Katherine Frances 1846- *Alli SUP, CarSB, ChhPo, –S1*

Gatty, Juliana Horatia *DcCanB 11, DcEuL, NewC, SmATA X*
Main entry: Ewing, Juliana Horatia Gatty

Gatty, Margaret Scott 1807?-1873 *InWom SUP*

Gatty, Margaret Scott 1809-1873 *Alli SUP, BiD&SB, BioIn 2, –8, –13, CarSB, CelCen, ChhPo, –S1, –S2, DcBiPP, DcEnA, DcEnL, DcEuL, DcLEL, DcNaB, DcWomA, EvLB, NewC, OxCChiL, SmATA 27, TelT, WhoChL*

Gauch, Patricia Lee 1934- *AuBYP 3, BioIn 13, ConAu 57, –9NR, FifBJA, SmATA 26, WhoUSWr 88, WhoWrEP 89, –92*

Gaul, Albro T *AuBYP 2, –3, BioIn 7*

Gaul, Randy 1959- *BioIn 17, SmATA 63*

Gaulden, Ray 1914- *ConAu 17R, –8NR, TwCWW 91, WrDr 84, –86*

Gault, Clare S 1925- *ConAu 97, SmATA 36*

Gault, Frank 1926-1982 *ConAu 69, –11NR, SmATA 30, –36*

Gault, William Campbell 1910- *AuBYP 2, –3, BioIn 5, –7, –11, ConAu 49, –1NR, –16NR, –37NR, CrtSuMy, EncMys, IntAu&W 91, SmATA 8, TwCCr&M 80, –85, –91, WrDr 82, –84, –86, –88, –90, –92, –94*

Gaunt, Michael *ConAu X*
Main entry: Robertshaw, Denis

Gaver, Becky
Main entry: Gaver, Rebecca

Gaver, Rebecca 1952- *BioIn 12, SmATA 20*
Pseud./variant:
Gaver, Becky

Gavin, Jamila *ChlFicS*

Gay, Amelia *TwCChW 89, WrDr 86, –88, –90, –92*

Gay, Amelia 1905- *WrDr 94*

Gay, Francis *BioIn 13, ConAu X, SmATA X*
Main entry: Gee, H L

Gay, John *HalFC 88*

Gay, John 1685?-1732 *Alli, AtlBL, Baker 84, –92, Benet 87, BiD&SB, BioIn 1, –2, –3, –5, –6, –7, –9, –10, –12, –17, BlmGEL, BritAu, BritWr 3, CamGEL, CamGLE, CamGWoT, CarSB, CasWL, Chambr 2, ChhPo, –S1, –S2,*

CnE&AP, CnThe, CrtT 2, CyWA 58, DcEnA, –A, DcEnL, DcEuL, DcLB 84, –95, DcLEL, DcNaB, EncWT, EvLB, LongCEL, McGEWB, McGEWD 72, –84, MouLC 2, NewAmDM, NewC, NewOxM, NotNAT A, –B, OxCChiL, OxCEng 67, –85, OxCMus, OxCThe 67, –83, PenC ENG, PlP&P, –A, RAdv 13-2, REn, REnWD, RfGEnL 91, WebE&AL, WhDW, WorAlBi, WorAl

Gay, Kathlyn 1930- *AuBYP 3, ConAu 25NR, IntAu&W 89*

Gay, Kathlyn R 1930- *WrDr 86, –88, –90, –92, –94*

Gay, Kathlyn Ruth 1930- *IntAu&W 91, WhoMW 93*

Gay, Kathlyn Ruth McGarrahan 1930- *AuBYP 2S, BioIn 11, ConAu 21R, SmATA 9, WhoAmW 74, –75, WhoMW 84, WrDr 76, –80, –82, –84*

Gay, Marie-Louise 1952- *ChlLR 27, SmATA 68*

Gay, Peter 1923- *AmAu&B, BioIn 11, BlueB 76, ConAu 13R, –18NR, CurBio 86, DrAS 74H, –78H, –82H, IntAu&W 91, IntWW 89, –91, WhoAm 74, –76, –78, –80, –82, –84, –86, –88, –90, –92, –94, WhoE 74, WhoUSWr 88, WhoWor 74, WhoWrEP 89, –92, WorAu 1975, WrDr 80, –82, –84, –86, –88, –90, –92, –94*

Gay, Peter Jack 1923- *ConAu 41NR*

Gay, Zhenya 1906-1978 *AuBYP 2, –3, BioIn 1, –5, –6, –8, –12, BkCL, ChhPo, –S2, ConAu 73, IlsCB 1744, –1946, MorJA, SmATA 19, WhoAm 74, –76, –78, WhoAmW 74, –75*

Gay-Kelly, Doreen 1952- *ConAu 61*

Gayle, Addison 1932- *BioIn 16, BlkAuII, WhoAm 88, –90*

Gayle, Addison 1932-1991 *BioIn 17, BlkAuII 92, WhAm 10*

Gayle, Addison, Jr. d1991 *NewYTBS 91*

Gayle, Addison, Jr. 1932- *BlkWr 1, InB&W 85, NegAl 89, WhoBlA 85, –88, –90, –92*

Gayle, Addison, Jr. 1932-1991 *ConAu 135, WhoBlA 94N*

Geach, Patricia Sullivan 1916- *ConAu 29R*

Gear, Kathleen O'Neal 1954- *SmATA 71*

Gear, W Michael 1955- *SmATA 71*

Geary, Charles G 1911- *AmMWSc 73P*

Geary, Clifford N 1916- *BioIn 5, IlsBYP, IlsCB 1946*

Geary, Efton F 1940- *BlkAWP*

Gee, H L 1901-1977 *ConAu 103, SmATA 26N*
Pseud./variant:
Gay, Francis

Gee, Maurice *BioIn 15*

Gee, Maurice 1931- *CamGLE, ConAu 97, ConLC 29, ConNov 82, –86, –91, ScF&FL 92, ShSWr, SmATA 46, TwCChW 83, –89, WrDr 82, –84, –86, –88, –90, –92*

Gee, Maurice Gough 1931- *ChlFicS, DcChlFi, EncSF 93, WrDr 94*

Gee, Maurine H *AuBYP 2S, –3*

Geer, Charles 1922- *BioIn 5, –8, ConAu 108, IlsBYP, IlsCB 1946, –1957, –1967, SmATA 32, –42*

Gehr, Mary *BioIn 2, SmATA 32, WhoAm 82, –84, –86, –88, –90, –92, –94, WhoAmA 73, –78, –80, –82, –84, –86, –89, –91, WhoMW 74, –76*

Geipel, Eileen 1932- *BioIn 14, ConAu 107, SmATA 30*
Pseud./variant:
Deacon, Eileen

Geis, Darlene Stern *AuBYP 2, –3, BioIn 8, –10, ConAu 1R, –5NR, SmATA 7*
Pseud./variant:
Kelly, Ralph
London, Jane
Stevens, Peter

Geisel, Helen *AuBYP 3*

Geisel, Helen 1898-1967 *ConAu 107, SmATA 26*
Pseud./variant:
Palmer, Helen Marion

Geisel, Theodor Seuss *Benet 87, BenetAL 91, BioIn 17, IntvTCA 2, NewYTBS 87, TwCChW 89*

Geisel, Theodor Seuss 1904- *AmAu&B, AmPB, ASCAP 66, AuBYP 2, –3, Au&ICB, BioIn 1, –2, –3, –4, –5, –6, –7, –8, –9, –10, –11, –12, –13, –14, –15, –16, ChhPo, –S1, –S2, ChlLR 1, ChsFB A, ConAu 13R, –13NR, –32NR, ConGrA 3, CurBio 68, DcLB 61, FamAIYP, IlsCB 1744, –1946, –1957, IntAu&W 77, JrnUS, MajTwCW, NewYTET, REn, REnAL, SmATA 1, –28, TwCA, –SUP, TwCChW 78, –83, WebAB 74, –79, WhoAm 74, –76, –78, –80, –82, –84, –86, –88, –90, WhoAmA 78, –80, –82, –84, –86, –89, –91, WhoWest 74, –76, –78, –82,*

WhoWor 74, WorAlBi, WorECar
Pseud./variant:
Doctor Seuss
LeSieg, Theo
Seuss, Dr
Stone, Rosetta

Geisel, Theodor Seuss 1904-1991 *ConAu 135, ConLC 70, CurBio 91N, DcLB Y91N, MajAI, NewYTBS 91, SmATA 67, –75, WhAm 10*

Geisert, Arthur *ChlBIlD*

Geisert, Arthur 1941- *ConAu 120, SmATA 52, –56, WrDr 90, –92*

Geisert, Arthur Frederick 1941- *WrDr 94*

Geismar, Maxwell 1909-1979 *AmAu&B, Au&Wr 71, BenetAL 91, BioIn 1, –4, –8, ConAu 1R, –104, –33NR, ConLCrt 77, –82, IntAu&W 77, RAdv 1, REnAL, TwCA SUP, WhAm 7, WhoAm 74, WhoE 74, WhoWor 74, WhoWorJ 72, –78, WrDr 76, –80*

Gekiere, Madeleine *WhoAmA 86, –89, –91, WhoE 91*

Gekiere, Madeleine 1919- *BioIn 5, –8, –9, ChhPo, –S1, IlsBYP, IlsCB 1946, –1957, ThrBJA, WhoAm 80, –82, –84, WhoAmA 73, –78, –80, –82, –84*

Geldart, William 1936- *BioIn 12, SmATA 15, WhoArt 84*

Gelfand, Marilyn *AuBYP 3*

Gelinas, Paul J 1911- *BioIn 11, ConAu 41R, SmATA 10, WhoE 77*

Gelinas, Paul Joseph 1914- *WhoSSW 91*

Gell, Frank *AuBYP 2S, –3, ConAu 57, –X, –35NR*
Main entry: Kowet, Don

Geller, Allen 1941- *ConAu 25R*

Gellibrand, Emma *CarSB*

Gelman, Amy 1961- *SmATA 72*

Gelman, Jan 1963- *BioIn 16, SmATA 58*

Gelman, Rita Golden *ScF&FL 92*

Gelman, Rita Golden 1937- *ConAu 81, –16NR, SmATA 51, WhoAmW 91*
Pseud./variant:
Austin, R G

Gelman, Steve 1934- *AuBYP 2S, –3, BioIn 9, ConAu 25R, –16NR, SmATA 3, WhoE 74*

Gemme, Francis Robert 1934- *ConAu 21R, WhoE 74, –75*

Gemme, Leila Boyle 1942- *ConAu 81*

Gemmill, Jane Brown 1898- *ConAu 1R*

Gemming, Elizabeth 1932- *BioIn 11, ConAu 65, –9NR, SmATA 11*

Gendel, Evelyn W 1916?-1977 *ConAu 104, SmATA 27N*

Geng, Veronica *AuBYP 2S*

Geng, Veronica 1941- *AuBYP 3, ConAu 119, –124*

Genia *IlsBYP, IlsCB 1957*
Main entry: Wennerstrom, Genia Katherine

Genlis, S F D DeSaint-Aubin, Comtesse De 1746-1830 *OxCChiL*

Gennaro, Joseph F, Jr. 1924- *SmATA 53*

Gennaro, Joseph Francis 1924- *AmMWSc 86, –89, –92*

Gentle, Mary 1956- *EncSF 93, ScF&FL 92, ScFSB, SmATA 48, TwCSFW 86, –91, WrDr 88, –90, –92, –94*

Gentleman, David William 1930- *ArtsCL Au&Wr 71, BioIn 6, –10, ChhPo S1, ConAu 25R, IlsBYP, IlsCB 1967, IntAu&W 77, SmATA 7, Who 74, WhoGrA 62, –82, WrDr 76, –80*

Gentry, Byron Burk 1913- *ConAu 13R, WhoGov 77, –75*

Gentry, Helen 1897- *AmAu&B, AmPB, ForWC 70, WhAmArt 85*

George, Jean *MajAI*

George, Jean Craighead 1919- *AmAu&B, AnCL, Au&Arts 8, AuBYP 2, –3, Au&Wr 71, BioIn 5, –6, –7, –9, –10, –14, –15, –16, –17, ChLR 1, ConAu 5R, –25NR, ConLC 35, DcAmChF 1960, DcLB 52, IlsCB 1946, IntAu&W 77, –89, –91, MajAI, MorBMP, MorJA, NewbC 1966, OxCChiL, SmATA 2, –68, TwCChW 78, –83, –89, TwCYAW, WhoAm 82, –84, –86, –88, –90, –92, –94, WhoUSWr 88, WhoWrEP 89, –92, WrDr 80, –82, –84, –86, –88, –90, –92, –94*

George, John Lothar 1916- *AmAu&B, AmMWSc 73P, –76P, –82, –86, –89, –92, AnCL, AuBYP 2, –3, BiDLA, BioIn 7, –9, BkCL, ConAu 5R, SmATA 2*

George, Renee 1924- *BioIn 5, IlsCB 1946*

George, Sidney Charles 1898- *BioIn 11, ConAu 53, SmATA 11*

George, W Lloyd 1900?-1975 *BioIn 14, ConAu 53, SmATA 30N*

Georges, D V *AuBYP 3*

Georgiady, Nicholas Peter 1921- *LEduc 74*

Georgiou, Constantine 1927- *BioIn 10, ConAu 13R, SmATA 7*

Gerard, Jane *ConAu 1R*
Pseud./variant:
Chekenian, Jane Gerard

Gerard, Jean Ignace I 1803-1847 *BioIn 2, CelCen, OxCArt, SmATA 45, WorECar*
Pseud./variant:
Grandville, J J
Grandville, Jean Ignace I Gerard

Gerard, Jean Ignace Isidore 1803-1847 *BioIn 15*

Gerard, John 1545-1612 *CamGEL, CamGLE*

Geras, Adele 1944- *BioIn 13, ConAu 97, –19NR, SmATA 23, TwCChW 89, WrDr 90, –92*

Geras, Adele Daphne 1944- *ChlFicS, TwCYAW*

Geras, Adele Daphne Weston 1944- *WrDr 94*

Gerassi, John 1931- *AuBYP 2S, –3, ConAu 5R, –8NR, WrDr 92, –94*

Gerber, Merrill Joan *BioIn 17, DrAPF 87, –89, –91, –93*

Gerber, Merrill Joan 1938- *ConAu 26NR, SmATA 64, WrDr 92, –94*

Gerber, William 1908- *ConAu 37R, DrAS 74P, –78P, –82P, WhoAm 74, –76, –78, –80, –82, –84, –86, –88, –90, WhoAmJ 80, WhoWorJ 72, –78, WrDr 76, –80, –82, –84, –86, –88, –90, –92, –94*

Gerber, William Kenton 1954- *WhoAm 92*

Gerberg, Mort 1931- *SmATA 64*

Gerbers, Teresa 1933- *ConAu 53*

Gere, Charles March 1869-1957 *BioIn 1, –14, ClaDrA, DcBrAr 1, DcBrBI, DcNaB 1951, DcVicP 2, IlsCB 1744, ObitT 1951*

Gergely, Tibor 1900-1978 *AmPB, BioIn 1, –5, –11, –12, –14, –16, ConAu 106, –107, IlsBYP, IlsCB 1744, –1946, SmATA 20N, –54*

Gerhard, Mae *BioIn 5*

Gerhardt, Lillian Noreen 1932- *BiDrLUS 70, ForWC 70, WhoAm 76, –78, –80, –82, –84, –86, –88, –90, –92, –94, WhoAmW 75, –77, –87, –93, WhoE 74, –75, –77, WhoLibI 82, WhoLibS 66, WhoUSWr 88, WhoWrEP 89, –92*

Geringer, Laura 1948- *BioIn 13, ConAu 107, SmATA 29*

Gerler, William R 1917- *AuBYP 3, SmATA 47*

Gerler, William Robert 1917- *AuBYP 2S, ConAu 65*

Germar, Herb
Main entry: Germar, William H

Germar, William H 1911- *ConAu 21R*
Pseud./variant:
Germar, Herb

Gernstein, Mordicai *BioIn 14, ConAu 117, SmATA 36*

Gerrard, Jean 1933- *SmATA 51*

Gerrard, Roy 1935- *ChlBIlD, ChlLR 23, ConAu 110, SmATA 45, –47*

Gerrold, David 1944- *EncSF 93, IntAu&W 91, NewEScF, RGTwCSF, ScF&FL 92, ScFSB, SmATA 66, TwCSFW 86, –91, WrDr 86, –88, –90, –92, –94*

Gerry, Margarita Spalding 1870-1939 *AmWomPl*

Gerry, Margarita Spaulding 1870- *AmAu&B, CarSB, WhAm 5*

Gersh, Harry 1912- *BioIn 11, ConAu 1R, –1NR, WhoWorJ 72, –78*

Gerson, Corinne *BioIn 15, DrAPF 87, –89, –91, –93*

Gerson, Corinne 1927- *ConAu 93, –25NR, DrAPF 83, –85, SmATA 37*

Gerson, Corinne Schreibstein 1927- *DcAmChF 1960*

Gerson, Noel B 1914-1988 *BioIn 16, –17, NewYTBS 88, ScF&FL 92, SmATA 60*

Gerson, Noel Bertram 1914- *AmAu&B, AuBYP 2, –3, Au&Wr 71, BioIn 8, –13, ConAu 81, SmATA 22, WhoAm 74, –76, –78, –80, –82, –84, –86, –88, WhoE 74, –75, –77, –81, –83, –85, –86, –89, WhoUSWr 88, WhoWor 74, –78, –80, –82, –84, –87, –89, WhoWrEP 89, WrDr 76, –80*
Pseud./variant:
Burgess, Anne Marie
Burgess, Michael

Edwards, Samuel
Lewis, Paul
Phillips, Leon
Ross, Dana Fuller
Vaughan, Carter A

Gerson, Noel Bertram 1914-1988 *ConAu 127, WhAm 9*
Pseud./variant:
Porter, Donald Clayton

Gerson, Thomas Isaac 1906- *WhNAA*

Gerson, Virginia 1864?-1951 *Alli SUP, BioIn 1, -2, CarSB, ChhPo, -S1, IlsCB 1744*

Gerstein, Mordicai *AuBYP 3*

Gerstein, Mordicai 1935- *BioIn 16, ConAu 127, -36NR, MajAI, SixBJA, SmATA 47*

Gervasi, Frank H 1908-1990 *ConAu 130*

Gervasi, Frank Henry 1908- *AmAu&B, AuSpks, AuBYP 2S, -3, BioIn 2, -10, -11, ConAu 13R, -P-1, CurBio 42*

Gervasi, Frank Henry 1908-1990 *BioIn 16, -17*

Gervis, Ruth S 1894- *BioIn 1, IlsCB 1744*

Gesch, Roy George 1920- *ConAu 21R, IntAu&W 77, -89, WrDr 76, -80*

Gesner, Clark 1938- *ASCAP 66, ConAu 109, EncMT, NatPD 77, -81, SmATA 40*
Pseud./variant:
Gordon, John

Gesner, Elsie Miller *WhoUSWr 88, WhoWrEP 89, -92*

Gesner, Elsie Miller 1919- *ConAu 17R, ForWC 70, WrDr 76, -80, -82, -84*

Gessner, Lynne 1919- *ConAu 25R, -10NR, IntAu&W 77, SmATA 16, WrDr 76, -80, -82, -84, -86, -88, -90, -92, -94*
Pseud./variant:
Clark, Merle

Getzoff, Carole 1943- *ConAu 61*

Gevirtz, Eliezer 1950- *BioIn 16, ConAu 121, SmATA 49*

Gewe, Raddory *ConAu X, -30NR, MajAI, SmATA 70, -X*
Main entry: Gorey, Edward St John

Gezari, Temima Mintzowitz 1907- *WhoWorJ 72*

Gezi, Kalil I 1930- *ConAu 25R, -17NR*

Ghan, Linda R 1947- *SmATA 77*

Gherman, Beverly *BioIn 17*

Gherman, Beverly 1934- *ConAu 136, SmATA 68, WrDr 94*

Ghigna, Charles *DrAPF 87, -89, -91, -93 IntAu&W 89*

Ghigna, Charles 1946- *ChhPo S2, ConAu 77, DrAPF 83, -85, IntAu&W 82, -86, IntWWP 82, WhoUSWr 88, WhoWrEP 89, -92*

Ghikas, Panos 1923- *BioIn 1, -5, IlsCB 1946, WhoAmA 73*

Ghikas, Panos George *WhoAmA 86, -91*

Gianakoulis, Theodore *AuBYP 2, -3, BioIn 8*

Giannini, Enzo 1946- *BioIn 17, SmATA 68*

Gibbings, Robert John 1889-1958 *BiDIrW, BioIn 1, -4, -5, -6, CurBio 48, -58, DcBrAr 1, DcIrB 88, DcLEL, DcNaB 1951, EvLB, IlsCB 1744, -1946, LongCTC, ObitOF 79, ObitT 1951, OxCArt, TwCA SUP*

Gibbons, Faye 1938- *SmATA 65*

Gibbons, Gail 1944- *AuBYP 3, BioIn 13, ChlLR 8, ConAu 69, -12NR, MajAI, SixBJA, SmATA 23, -12AS*

Gibbons, Gail Gretchen 1944- *SmATA 72*

Gibbons, Orlando 1583-1625 *Alli, Baker 84, -92, BioIn 2, -4, -7, -8, DcBiPP, DcNaB, LuthC 75, NewAmDM, NewC, NewOxM, OxCEng 85, OxCMus, WhDW*

Gibbs, Alonzo 1915- *AuBYP 3, WrDr 86, -88, -90, -92*

Gibbs, Alonzo Lawrence 1915- *AuBYP 2, BioIn 8, -10, ConAu 5R, IntAu&W 82, -91, SmATA 5, WhoE 83, -85, -86, -89, WhoWor 84, -87, -89, WrDr 76, -80*

Gibbs, Alonzo Lawrence 1915-1992 *WrDr 94N*

Gibbs, Evelyn 1905- *BioIn 5, DcBrAr 1, IlsCB 1946, TwCPaSc, WhoArt 84*

Gibbs, May 1877-1969 *AuWomWr, BlmGWL, ConAu 104, FemiCLE, OxCAusL, OxCChiL, SingR 1, SmATA 27N, TwCChW 78, -83, -89*

Gibbs, Tony
Main entry: Gibbs, Wolcott, Jr.

Gibbs, Wolcott, Jr. 1935- *ConAu 85, SmATA 40*
Pseud./variant:
Gibbs, Tony

Gibbs-Smith, Charles Harvard 1909-1981 *Au&Wr 71, BlueB 76, ConAu 9R, –108, –4NR, IntAu&W 77, –82, IntWW 78, –79, –80, –81, –82N, Who 74, –82, –83N, WhoArt 80, –82, –84, WrDr 76, –80, –82, –84*

Giberne, Agnes 1845-1939 *FemiCLE, OxCChiL, StaCVF, WomNov*

Giblin, James Cross 1933- *AuBYP 3, ChlLR 29, ConAu 106, –24NR, MajAI, SixBJA, SmATA 33, –75, –12AS, WhoAm 92, –94*

Gibney, Somerville *Alli SUP, ChhPo, –S2*

Gibson, Andrew William 1949- *SmATA 72*

Gibson, Betty 1911- *SmATA 75*

Gibson, Charles E 1916- *IntAu&W 91, WrDr 86, –88, –90, –92*

Gibson, Charles Edmund 1916- *Au&Wr 71, ConAu 5R, IntAu&W 77, –89, WrDr 76, –80, –82, –84, –94*

Gibson, Gertrude Hevener 1906- *ConAu 5R*

Gibson, Gwen *ForWC 70*

Gibson, Josephine *AuBYP 3, ConAu X, IntAu&W 91X, SmATA 2, ThrBJA, WrDr 80, –82, –84, –86, –88, –90, –92*
Main entry: Joslin, Sesyle

Gibson, Josephine 1929- *WrDr 94*

Gibson, Katharine 1893- *AmAu&B, BioIn 2, JBA 51, OhA&B, Str&VC, WhAmArt 85*

Gibson, Truman K, Jr. 1912- *WhoAm 74, WhoBlA 75, –77, –80, –85, –90, –92, –94*

Gibson, Walter B 1897- *WrDr 86*

Gibson, Walter B 1897-1985 *ConAu 118, CrtSuMy, ScF&FL 92, TwCCr&M 91*

Gibson, Walter Brown 1897- *BioIn 7, ConAu 108, –110, EncMys, TwCCr&M 80, –85, WhJnl, WhNAA, WrDr 82, –84*

Gibson, Walter Brown 1897-1985 *EncSF 93*

Gibson, William *WhoAm 94*

Gibson, William 1914- *BenetAL 91, BiDConC, BiE&WWA, BioIn 3, –4, –5, –10, –12, –13, CamGWoT, CnMD, ConAu 9R, –9NR, ConDr 73, –77, –82, –88, –93, ConLC 23, ConTFT 2, CurBio 83, DcLB 7, DcLEL 1940, EncWT, IntAu&W 77, –91, MagSAmL, McGEWD 72, –84, ModAL, ModWD, NatPD 77, NotNAT, –A, OxCAmL 83, OxCAmT 84, PenC AM, PlP&P, REnAL, SmATA 66, WhoAm 74, –76, –78, –80, –82, –84, –86, –88, –90, –92, –94, WhoE 74, WhoThe 72, –77, –81, WhoWor 74, WorAlBi, WorAu 1950, WrDr 76, –80, –82, –84, –86, –88, –90, –92, –94*

Gibson, William 1948- *Au&Arts 12, BioIn 15, –17, ConAu 126, –133, ConLC 39, –63, IntAu&W 91, NewEScF, ScF&FL 92, TwCSFW 86, –91, WhoCanL 87, –92, WrDr 86, –88, –90, –92*

Gibson, William Ford 1948- *EncSF 93, TwCYAW, WrDr 94*

Gidal, Nachum *AuBYP 3*

Gidal, Nachum Tim *WhoWor 91*

Gidal, Nachum Tim 1909- *WhoWor 87, –93*

Gidal, Sonia 1922- *AuBYP 3*

Gidal, Sonia Epstein 1922- *AuBYP 2, Au&Wr 71, BioIn 8, –9, ConAu 5R, SmATA 2*

Gidal, Tim N 1909- *BioIn 8, –9, –10, –13, ConAu 5R, –14NR, –20NR, ConPhot 82, –88, ICPEnP A, MacBEP, SmATA 2*

Gidal, Tim Nachum *AuBYP 3*

Giegling, John Allan 1935- *BioIn 12, ConAu 29R, IntAu&W 77, SmATA 17, WrDr 76, –80, –82, –84*

Gielgud, Val Henry 1900-1981 *Au&Wr 71, BioIn 2, –7, –12, –14, BlueB 76, ConAu 9R, DcLEL, DcNaB 1981, EncMys, IntAu&W 77, IntWW 74, –75, –76, –77, –78, –79, –80, –81, –82N, NotNAT A, Who 74, –82, –83N, WhoLA, WhoWor 74, –78, WrDr 76, –80*

Gies, Frances 1915- *ConAu 25R, –9NR*

Gies, Joseph Cornelius 1916- *ConAu 5R*

Giesy, John Ulrich 1877-1947 *AmAu&B, BioIn 2, OhA&B, WhAm 2, WhoHr&F*

Gifaldi, David 1950- *SmATA 76*

Giff, Patricia Reilly *BioIn 15*

Giff, Patricia Reilly 1935- *AuBYP 3, ConAu 101, –18NR, –41NR, FifBJA, MajAI, SmATA 33, –70*

Giffen, Daniel H 1938- *ConAu 107, WhoE 74, WhoMW 74, –78, –80, –82, –84, –86*

Giffen, Daniel Harris 1938- *WhoAm 86, –88, –90, –92, –94, WhoMW 88, –90*

Gifford, Denis 1927- *ConAu 101, –18NR, IntAu&W 82, –91, ScF&FL 92, WhoArt 80,*

–82, –84, WhoWor 78, WorECar A, WrDr 76, –80, –82, –84, –86, –88, –90, –92, –94

Gifford, Griselda 1931- *BioIn 15, ConAu 107, –24NR, SmATA 42*
Pseud./variant:
Macdonald, Mary

Gifford, Thomas Eugene 1937- *ConAu 77*

Gift, Theo 1847-1923 *Alli SUP, BioIn 15, PenEncH, WhoHr&F*

Gikow, Louise *AuBYP 3, ScF&FL 92*

Gilbert, Alice *ChhPo S2*

Gilbert, Ann *SmATA X*
Main entry: Taylor, Ann

Gilbert, Ann 1782-1866 *FemiCLE*

Gilbert, Ellen *ChhPo S2*

Gilbert, Harriett 1948- *ConAu 9NR, SmATA 30, WrDr 82, –84, –86, –88, –90, –92, –94*

Gilbert, Helen Earle *AuBYP 3*

Gilbert, Helen Earle 1903?-1951 *AnMV 1926, AuBYP 2, BioIn 2, –8*

Gilbert, Joan 1931- *ConAu 21R, SmATA 10*

Gilbert, John Raphael 1926- *Au&Wr 71, ConAu 107, IntAu&W 82, –86, –89, –91, SmATA 36, WrDr 76, –80, –82, –84, –86, –88, –90, –92, –94*

Gilbert, Miriam *ConAu X, IntAu&W 77X, SmATA X, WhoAmW 74, –75, –77, WhoE 74, WrDr 76, –80, –82*
Main entry: Presberg, Miriam Goldstein

Gilbert, Nan *ConAu X, IntAu&W 77X, –82X, SmATA 2, WrDr 76, –80, –82, –84, –86, –88*
Main entry: Gilbertson, Mildred Geiger

Gilbert, Ruth Gallard Ainsworth *MajAI*
Main entry: Ainsworth, Ruth Gallard

Gilbert, Ruth Gallard Ainsworth 1908- *Au&Wr 71, ConAu 9R, –4NR*

Gilbert, Sara 1943- *AuBYP 2S, –3, BioIn 11, ConAu 57, –6NR, SmATA 11*

Gilbert, William S 1836-1911 *CamGLE, NewAmDM, WorAlBi*

Gilbert, William S, Sir 1836-1911 *Benet 87*

Gilbert, William Schwenck 1836-1911 *AuBYP 3, BioIn 14, –15, –17, BlmGEL, OxCAmT 84*
Pseud./variant:
Tomline, F Latour

Gilbert, William Schwenck, Sir 1836-1911 *Alli SUP, AtlBL, AuBYP 2S, Baker 84, BbD, BiD&SB, BioIn 1, –2, –3, –4, –5, –6, –7, –8, –9, –10, –11, –12, –13, BritAu 19, CamGWoT, CasWL, CelCen, Chambr 3, ChhPo, –S1, –S2, CnE&AP, CnThe, ConAu 104, CyWA 58, DcBrBI, DcEnA, –A, DcEnL, DcEuL, DcLEL, DcNaB S2, EvLB, HalFC 84, McGEWB, McGEWD 72, –84, ModWD, MouLC 4, NewC, NotNAT A, –B, OxCEng 67, –85, OxCThe 67, –83, PenC ENG, RAdv 13-2, REn, REnWD, SmATA 36, Str&VC, TwCLC 3, WebE&AL, WhDW, WhoTech 82, WorAl*
Pseud./variant:
B
Bab

Gilbert, William Schwenk, Sir 1836-1911 *CamGEL*

Gilbert, William Spencer 1927- *AmMWSc 86, –89, –92*

Gilberts, Helen Ilene 1909- *ConAu 29R, WrDr 76, –80, –82, –84*

Gilbertson, Mildred Geiger 1908- *BioIn 9, ConAu 5R, –2NR, ForWC 70, IntAu&W 77, –82, SmATA 2, WhoAmW 83, WrDr 76, –80*
Pseud./variant:
Gilbert, Nan
Mendel, Jo

Gilborn, Alice 1936- *ConAu 69*

Gilbreath, Alice 1921- *BioIn 11, ConAu 25R, –10NR, –25NR, SmATA 12*

Gilbreth, Frank Bunker, Jr. 1911- *AmAu&B, BioIn 1, –2, –9, ConAu 9R, ConLC 17, CurBio 49, SmATA 2, WhoAm 74, –76, –78, –80, –82, –84, –86, –88, –90, –92, –94, WhoSSW 73, WhoWor 74*

Gilchrist, Jan Spivey 1949- *BlkAuII 92, SmATA 72*

Gilden, Mel *AuBYP 3*

Gilden, Mel 1947- *ScF&FL 92*

Giles, Carl Howard 1935- *ConAu 29R, –39NR, WhoSSW 75, –91*

Giles, Gordon A *AuBYP 3, ConAu X, EncSF 93*
Main entry: Binder, Otto Oscar

Gilfond, Henry *BioIn 9, ConAu 21R, –9NR, –24NR, NatPD 77, –81, SmATA 2*

Gilge, Jeanette 1924- *BioIn 13, ConAu 61, SmATA 22*

Gili, Phillida 1944- *SmATA 70*

Gilkison, Grace *ConICB, DcWomA*

Gill, Bob 1931- *ConAu 1R, ConDes 84, -90, IlrAm G*

Gill, Derek L T 1919- *BioIn 11, ConAu 49, SmATA 9*

Gill, Elizabeth *WomWMM B*

Gill, Harold Bledsoe, Jr. 1933- *DrAS 78H, -82H*

Gill, Margery Jean 1925- *ArtsCL, BioIn 6, -8, ChhPo, -S1, FourBJA, IlsBYP, IlsCB 1957, -1967, SmATA 22*

Gill, Richard Cochran 1901- *AuBYP 3*

Gill, Richard Cochran 1901-1958 *AmAu&B, AuBYP 2, BioIn 7, WhAm 3*

Gill, Stephen *WhoCanL 92*

Gill, Stephen 1932- *IntAu&W 86, SmATA 63, WhoCanL 87*

Gillelan, George Howard 1917- *AuBYP 2, -3, BioIn 8, ConAu 1R*

Gillen, Mollie 1908- *ConAu 41R, IntAu&W 82*

Gillespie, John T 1928- *ConAu 31NR*

Gillespie, John Thomas 1928- *BiDrLUS 70, BioIn 9, ConAu 73, -13NR, LEduc 74, WhoAm 82, -84, -86, -88, -90, -92, -94, WhoE 89, WhoLibI 82, WhoLibS 66*

Gillett, Mary Bledsoe *BioIn 10, ConAu P-2, SmATA 7*

Gillette, Henry Sampson 1915- *BioIn 12, ConAu 5R, SmATA 14, WrDr 76, -80*

Gillham, Bill
Main entry: Gillham, William Edwin Charles

Gillham, Charles Edward 1898- *AnCL, BioIn 1*

Gillham, William Edwin Charles 1936- *SmATA 42*
Pseud./variant:
Gillham, Bill

Gilliam, Stan 1946- *SmATA 35, -39*

Gilliam, Terry 1940- *ConAu 141*

Gillies, Margaret 1803-1887 *ChhPo S1, ClaDrA, DcNaB, DcVicP 2, DcWomA*

Gilliland, Alexis Arnaldus 1931- *SmATA 72*

Gillon, Diana 1915- *Au&Wr 71, ConAu 13R, ConSFA*

Gillon, Meir Selig 1907- *Au&Wr 71, ConAu 13R, ConSFA*

Gillsater, Sven 1921- *Au&Wr 71, ConPhot 88*

Gillum, Helen L 1909- *ConAu 69*

Gilman, Dorothy *AuBYP 3*
Main entry: Butters, Dorothy Gilman

Gilman, Dorothy 1923- *Au&Wr 71, BioIn 7, -8, -10, -12, -14, ConAu X, -30NR, CrtSuMy, FemiCLE, InWom SUP, IntAu&W 91, ScF&FL 92, SmATA 5, SpyFic, TwCCr&M 80, -85, -91, WhoAm 78, -80, -82, -84, -86, -88, -90, -92, WorAlBi, WorAl, WrDr 82, -84, -86, -88, -90, -92, -94*

Gilman, Esther 1925- *BioIn 12, SmATA 15, WhoAmW 85, -87, -89, WhoWor 87, -89*

Gilman, Phoebe 1940- *SmATA 58*

Gilmer, Ann *ConAu X, -32NR*
Main entry: Ross, William Edward Daniel

Gilmore, David H *SingR 1*

Gilmore, Edith Spacil 1920- *ConAu 1R*

Gilmore, Horace Herman 1903- *AuBYP 2, -3, BioIn 8*

Gilmore, Iris 1900- *AuBYP 2, -3, BioIn 8, -13, ConAu 97, SmATA 22*

Gilmore, Mary 1864-1962 *FemiCLE*

Gilmore, Mary 1865-1962 *ArtclWW 2, BioIn 6, -8, -9, -12, -16, BlmGWL, CamGLE, CasWL, ConAu 114, DcLEL, LongCTC, ModCmwL, ObitT 1961, OxCAusL, RfGEnL 91, SingR 2, SmATA 49, TwCWr*

Gilmore, Mary, Dame 1865-1962 *AuWomWr*

Gilmore, Susan 1954- *SmATA 59*

Gilroy, Frank D *DrAPF 87, -89, -91, -93*

Gilroy, Frank D 1925- *BenetAL 91, CamGWoT, ConAu 32NR, ConDr 88, ConTFT 3, HalFC 88, IntAu&W 91, OxCAmT 84, WrDr 86, -88, -90, -92*

Gilroy, Frank Daniel 1925- *AmAu&B, BioIn 6, -7, -10, -12, -15, ConAu 81, ConDr 73, -77, -82, -93, ConLC 2, CroCD, CurBio 65, DcLB 7, DcLEL 1940, DrAF 76, HalFC 84, IntAu&W 82, McGEWD 72, -84, ModWD, NatPD 81, NotNAT, OxCAmL 65, -83, WhoAm 74, -76, -78, -80, -82, -84, -86,*

-88, -90, -92, -94, WhoE 74, WhoEnt 92, WhoThe 72, -77, -81, WhoWor 74, WrDr 76, -80, -82, -84, -94

Gilson, Barbara *EncSF 93, WhoChL, YABC X*
Main entry: Gilson, Charles James Louis

Gilson, Charles James Louis 1878-1943 *BioIn 8, WhoChL, WhoLA, YABC 2*
Pseud./variant:
Gilson, Barbara

Gilson, Jamie 1933- *AuBYP 3, BioIn 14, -15, -16, SixBJA*

Gilson, Jamie Marie 1933- *ConAu 111, SmATA 34, -37, WhoAmW 83, -85, -87, -89*

Gilstrap, Robert Lawrence 1933- *ConAu 9R, LEduc 74*

Gimpel, Herbert J 1915- *ConAu 17R*

Ginnings, Harriett W 1905- *ConAu X*
Pseud./variant:
Harriett

Ginsburg, Mirra *AuBYP 3, ConAu 28NR, IntAu&W 86, -89, -91, SixBJA*

Ginsburg, Mirra 1919- *AuBYP 2S, BioIn 10, ConAu 17R, -11NR, ConSFA, EncSF 93, IntAu&W 77, -82, ScF&FL 92, SmATA 6, WhoAmW 74, -75, -77*

Ginter, Maria 1922- *Au&Wr 71, ConAu 105, IntAu&W 86, WrDr 76, -80, -82, -84*

Giovanni, Nikki *DrAPF 87, -89, -91, -93, IntvTCA 2*

Giovanni, Nikki 1943- *ArtclWW 2, AuBYP 2S, -3, AuNews 1, Benet 87, BenetAL 91, BioIn 9, -10, -12, -13, BioNews 75, BlkAWP, BlkAuII, -92, BlkLC, BlkWWr, BlkWr 1, BlmGWL, BroadAu, CamGLE, CamHAL, CelR, -90, ChhPo S2, ChlLR 6, CivR 74, ConAu 29R, -6AS, -18NR, -41NR, ConLC 2, -4, -19, -64, ConPo 75, -80, -85, -91, CroCAP, CurBio 73, CyWA 89, DcLB 5, -41, DcLEL 1940, DrAP 75, DrAPF 83, -85, EncAACR, FemiCLE, FifBJA, InB&W 80, -85, InWom SUP, LivgBAA, MagSAmL, MajAI, MajTwCW, ModAWP, NegAl 76, -83, -89, NotBlAW 92, OxCAmL 83, RAdv 1, SelBAAf, SelBAAu, SmATA 24, TwCChW 78, TwCYAW, WhoAm 74, -76, -78, -80, -82, -84, -86, -88, -90, -92, -94, WhoAmW 81, -89, -91, -93, WhoBlA 75, -77, -80, -85, -88, -90, -92, WhoUSWr 88, WhoWrEP 89, -92, WrDr 76, -80, -82, -84, -86, -88, -90, -92*

Giovanni, Nikki Yolande C, Jr. 1943- *WrDr 94*

Giovanopoulos, Paul Arthur 1939- *BioIn 10, ChhPo S1, FourBJA, IlsBYP, SmATA 7, WhoE 74, -75, -77, -81, -83*

Gipson, Fred 1908-1973 *TwCChW 89, TwCWW 91*

Gipson, Frederick Benjamin 1903-1973 *BioIn 15*

Gipson, Frederick Benjamin 1908-1973 *AmAu&B, AuBYP 2, -3, BioIn 4, -5, -8, -9, -10, -12, -13, ConAu 1R, -45, -3NR, CurBio 57, EncFWF, MajAI, NewYTBE 73, ObitOF 79, SmATA 2, -24N, ThrBJA, TwCChW 78, -83, TwCYAW*

Girard, Linda Walvoord 1942- *SmATA 41, WhoAmW 91*

Girion, Barbara 1937- *BioIn 13, ConAu 85, -15NR, SmATA 26, -14AS*

Girion, Barbara 1938- *SixBJA*

Girvan, Helen 1891- *AuBYP 2, -3, BioIn 6, -7, ConAu 73, MorJA*

Girzone, Joseph F 1930- *BestSel 90-1, ConAu 130, ScF&FL 92, WrDr 92*

Girzone, Joseph Francis 1930- *SmATA 76, WrDr 94*

Gittings, Christine *Au&Wr 71, WrDr 76, -80, -82, -84*

Gittings, Jo Manton *AuBYP 3*

Gittings, Jo Manton 1919- *AuBYP 2, Au&Wr 71, BioIn 9, ConAu 5R, -3NR, SmATA 3*
Pseud./variant:
Manton, Jo

Gittings, Robert William Victor 1911- *Au&Wr 71, BioIn 10, ChhPo S2, ConAu 25R, ConPo 70, -75, IntAu&W 77, -82, OxCEng 85, SmATA 6, Who 74, WhoWor 74, WrDr 76, -80*

Gittings, Robert William Victor 1911-1992 *SmATA 70*

Giusti, George *WhAm 10, WhoAm 86, -90, WhoAmA 86, -89, -91, WhoE 86*

Giusti, George 1908- *BioIn 1, -2, -7, WhAmArt 85, WhoAm 74, -76, -78, -80, -82, -84, WhoAmA 73, -78, -80, -82, -84, WhoGrA 62, -82*

Givens, Janet Eaton 1932- *SmATA 60, WhoAmW 89, -91, -93, WhoE 86, -89, -91, -93*

Pseud./variant:
Eaton, Janet

Gladstone, Eve
Main entry: Werner, Herma

Gladstone, Gary 1935- *BioIn 11, ConAu 29R, SmATA 12*

Gladstone, Myron J 1923- *ConAu 53, SmATA 37, WhoAmA 78, -80, -82, -84*

Gladwin, William Zachary *BioIn 2, -13, ChhPo, ConAu X, DcAmAu, DcNAA, SmATA X, WhAm 1*
Main entry: Zollinger, Gulielma

Gladych, B Michael 1910- *ConAu 5R*

Glanckoff, Samuel 1894- *BioIn 1, ChhPo, ConICB, IlsCB 1744*

Glanville, Brian Lester *IntAu&W 91*

Glanville, Brian Lester 1931- *AuBYP 2S, -3, Au&Wr 71, BioIn 6, -10, -13, BlueB 76, ConAu 5R, -3NR, ConLC 6, ConNov 72, -76, -82, DcLB 15, DcLEL 1940, IntAu&W 77, -82, -86, NewC, Novels, SmATA 42, Who 74, -82, -83, -85, -88, -90, -92, WorAu 1950, WrDr 76, -80, -82, -84*

Glanzman, Louis S 1922- *BioIn 6, -8, IlrAm 1880, -F, IlsBYP, IlsCB 1957, -1967, SmATA 36*

Glaser, Dianne E 1937- *SmATA 50*

Glaser, Dianne Elizabeth 1937- *ConAu 77, SmATA 31*

Glaser, Milton *AmGrD*

Glaser, Milton 1929- *AmArt, AmGrD, BioIn 8, -9, -10, -11, -12, -13, ChhPo S2, ConAu 17R, -11NR, ConDes 84, -90, ConGrA 1, CurBio 80, EncTwCJ, FourBJA, IlrAm 1880, -G, IlsBYP, IlsCB 1957, -1967, SmATA 11, WhoAm 82, -84, -86, -88, -90, -92, -94, WhoAmA 78, -80, -82, -84, -86, -89, -91, WhoEnt 92, WhoGrA 82*
Pseud./variant:
Catz, Max

Glasgow, Ellen Anderson Gholson 1873-1945 *BioIn 14, -15, -17*

Glasgow, Ellen Anderson Gholson 1874-1945 *AmAu&B, AmWr, AtlBL, BiDSA, BiD&SB, BioIn 1, -2, -3, -4, -5, -6, -7, -8, -9, -10, -11, -12, -13, CasWL, Chambr 3, ChhPo, -S1, CnDAL, ConAmA, ConAmL, CurBio 46, CyWA 58, DcAmAu, DcBiA, DcLEL, DcNAA, EncSoH, EncWL, EvLB, InWom SUP, LongCTC, McGEWB, ModAL, OxCAmL 65, OxCEng 67, -85, PenC AM, RAdv 1, REn, REnAL, TwCA, -SUP, TwCLC 2, TwCWr, WebAB 74, -79, WebE&AL, WhAm 2, WhNAA, WomWWA 14, WomNov*

Glaspell, Susan 1882-1948 *AmAu&B, AmNov, AmWomD, AmWomWr 92, Benet 87, BenetAL 91, BioAmW, BioIn 1, -2, -4, -7, -12, -15, -16, -17, CamGLE, CamHAL, Chambr 3, CnDAL, CnMD, ConAmA, ConAmL, ConAu 110, DcLB 7, DcLEL, DcNAA, LongCTC, McGEWD 72, -84, ModWD, NotNAT B, Novels, OxCAmL 65, -83, OxCAmT 84, OxCThe 67, -83, PlP&P, REn, REnAL, RfGAmL 87, TwCA, -SUP, WhAm 2, WhNAA, WomWWA 14, YABC 2*

Glaspell, Susan Keating 1882?-1948 *IntDcT 2*

Glass, Andrew *ConAu 134, SixBJA, SmATA 46, WrDr 94*

Glass, Andrew James 1935- *WhoAm 92*

Glass, Malcolm *DrAPF 89, -91, -93*

Glass, Malcolm 1936- *ConAu 104, -20NR, DrAP 75*

Glass, Marvin *NewYTBS 74*

Glassman, Bruce 1961- *SmATA 76*

Glattauer, Ned *IlsBYP*

Glauber, Uta 1936- *BioIn 12, ConAu 29R, SmATA 17*

Glaus, Marlene Anne 1933- *ConAu 21R, WhoAmW 77, WrDr 76, -80*

Glazer, Tom 1914- *ASCAP 66, AuBYP 2S, -3, BioIn 11, ConAu 61, -8NR, EncFCWM 69, SmATA 9, WhoEnt 92*

Gleasner, Diana 1936- *BioIn 13, ConAu 65, -15NR, -33NR, IntAu&W 91, SmATA 29*

Gleasner, Diana Cottle 1936- *IntAu&W 86, WhoWrEP 92*

Gleason, Judith *DrAPF 87, -89, -91, -93*

Gleason, Judith 1929- *BioIn 8, -13, ConAu 61, -9NR, SmATA 24*

Gleeson, Joseph Michael 1861-1917 *ChhPo, -S2, EncAB-A 8, WhAm 1*

Gleeson, Libby 1950- *DcChlFi*

Gleick, Beth Youman *AuBYP 2, -3, BioIn 8*

Glemser, Bernard *ScF&FL 92*

Glemser, Bernard 1908- *Au&Wr 71*

Glemser, Bernard 1908-1990 *BioIn 16, –17, ConAu 131, NewYTBS 90*

Glendinning, Richard 1917- *BioIn 13, ConAu 21R, SmATA 24, WhoSSW 73, –75, –76*

Glendinning, Sally
Main entry: Glendinning, Sara W

Glendinning, Sara W 1913- *BioIn 13, ConAu 49, –2NR, SmATA 24*
Pseud./variant:
Glendinning, Sally

Glenn, John H, Jr. 1921- *AlmAP 88, –92, Who 88, –90, –92, WorAlBi*

Glenn, John Herschel, Jr. 1921- *AlmAP 78, –82, –84, AnCL, BiDrUSC 89, BioIn 5, –6, –7, –8, –9, –10, –11, –12, –13, BioNews 74, BlueB 76, CelR, CurBio 62, –76, IntWW 74, –75, –76, –77, –78, –79, –80, –81, –82, –83, –89, –91, NewYTBE 72, WebAB 74, –79, WebAMB, WhDW, Who 74, –82, –83, –85, WhoAm 74, –76, –78, –80, –82, –84, –86, –88, –90, –92, –94, WhoAmP 75, –77, –81, –83, –85, –87, –89, –91, –93, WhoGov 77, –75, WhoMW 76, –78, –80, –82, –84, –86, –88, –90, –92, –93, WhoSSW 73, WhoWor 74, –78, –80, –82, –84, –87, –89, –91, WorAl*

Glenn, Mel 1943- *ConAu 123, SmATA 45, –51, TwCYAW*

Gles, Margaret Breitmaier 1940- *ConAu 57, SmATA 22*

Glick, Carl Cannon 1890-1971 *AmAu&B, Au&Wr 71, BioIn 1, ConAu 5R, REnAL, SmATA 14, WhAm 5*
Pseud./variant:
Cunningham, Captain Frank
Holbrook, Peter

Glick, Virginia Kirkus *BioIn 13, ConAu 101, –P-2, SmATA 23N*
Main entry: Kirkus, Virginia

Gliewe, Unada G 1927- *BioIn 9, ConAu 29R, SmATA 3, WhoAmW 83, WrDr 76, –80, –82, –84, –86, –88, –90, –92, –94*
Pseud./variant:
Unada

Glines, Carroll Vane, Jr. 1920- *BioIn 12, ConAu 1R, –2NR, SmATA 19, WhoAm 76, –78, –80, –82, –84, –86, –88, –90, –92, –94, WhoE 81, WhoSSW 76, WhoWor 80, –82*

Gliori, Debi 1959- *SmATA 72*

Globe, Leah Ain 1900- *BioIn 15, ConAu 107, SmATA 41, WhoWorJ 72, –78*

Glovach, Linda 1947- *AuBYP 2S, –3, BioIn 10, ConAu 37R, –14NR, –31NR, SmATA 7, WrDr 76, –80, –82, –84, –86, –88, –90*

Glubok, Shirley *SmATA 7AS, WrDr 86*

Glubok, Shirley 1933- *AuBYP 2, –3, BioIn 8, –9, –10, –17, ChlLR 1, ConAu 5R, –4NR, ForWC 70, MorBMP, SmATA 6, –68, ThrBJA, WhoAmW 77, WhoE 74, WrDr 80, –82, –84*

Glubok, Shirley Astor *ConAu 43NR*

Glubok, Shirley Astor 1933- *MajAI*

Gluck, Felix 1923-1981 *TwCPaSc*

Gluck, Felix 1924?-1981 *BioIn 12, –13, ConAu 103, SmATA 25N*

Gluck, Herb 1925- *ConAu 45, –2NR, –31NR*

Glut, Donald F 1944- *ScF&FL 92, WhoEnt 92*

Glut, Donald Frank 1944- *ConAu 33R, –13NR, EncSF 93, IntAu&W 77, WrDr 76, –80*

Glyn, Anthony Leo Simon 1922- *Au&Wr 71, ConAu 53, DcLEL 1940, Who 74, WrDr 76, –80*

Glyn, Harrison
Pseud./variant:
Steffens, Arthur

Glynne-Jones, William 1907- *Au&Wr 71, BioIn 11, ConAu 5R, IntAu&W 77, SmATA 11*

Glynne-Jones, William 1907-1977 *OxCLiW 86*

Gnagey, Thomas David 1938- *ConAu 49, WhoMW 84*

Gnoli, Domenico, Count 1838-1915 *BioIn 1, CasWL, ClDMEL 47, IlsCB 1957*

Goaman, Muriel *Au&Wr 71, ConAu X, WrDr 76, –80, –82, –84, –86, –88, –90*
Main entry: Cox, Edith Muriel

Gobbato, Imero 1923- *BioIn 8, –12, –15, IlsBYP, IlsCB 1957, –1967, SmATA 39*

Gobhai, Mehlli *AuBYP 2S, –3, IlsCB 1967*

Goble, Dorothy *AuBYP 2S, –3, BioIn 13, ConAu 93, SmATA 26*

Goble, Paul *BioIn 14*

Goble, Paul 1933- *ALA 80, AuBYP 2S, –3, BioIn 12, –13, ChlLR 21, ConAu 93, –16NR, FourBJA, IlsCB 1967, MajAI, SmATA 25, –69, WhoAm 80, –82, –84, –86, –88, –90, –92, –94, WhoUSWr 88, WhoWrEP 89, –92*

Goble, Warwick d1943 *BioIn 1, –12, –14, –15, ChhPo S1, ConICB, DcBrAr 1, DcBrBI, DcVicP 2, IlsCB 1744, SmATA 46*

Gockel, Herman W 1906- *ConAu 1R, –1NR*

Goddard, Alice L *BioIn 1, –4, –7*

Godden, Margaret Rumer 1907- *MajAI*

Godden, Rumer 1907- *AnCL, AuSpks, Au&Arts 6, AuBYP 2, –3, Au&Wr 71, Benet 87, BioIn 2, –4, –6, –7, –8, –9, –10, –11, –14, –15, –16, –17, BlmGWL, BlueB 76, CamGLE, ChhPo, –S1, –S2, ChlLR 20, ConAu 5R, –4NR, –27NR, –36NR, ConLC 53, ConNov 72, –76, –82, –86, –91, CurBio 76, CyWA 89, DcLEL, EncBrWW, FamMS, FemiCLE, FilmgC, HalFC 84, –88, InWom SUP, IntAu&W 77X, –82, –89, –91, IntWW 74, –75, –76, –77, –78, –79, –80, –81, –82, –83, –89, –91, IntWWP 82X, LongCTC, ModBrL, MorJA, NewC, Novels, OxCChiL, PiP, RAdv 1, REn, SmATA 3, –36, –12AS, TwCA, –SUP, TwCChW 78, –83, –89, TwCRHW 90, TwCWr, Who 74, –82, –83, –85, –88, –90, –92, WhoAm 90, –92, –94, WhoAmW 74, –75, WhoChL, WhoWor 74, –78, WrDr 76, –80, –82, –84, –86, –88, –90, –92, –94*
Pseud./variant:
Haynes Dixon, Margaret Rumer

Godden, Rumer 1908- *NewYTBS 88*

Gode, Alexander
Main entry: Gode VonAesch, Alexander

Gode VonAesch, Alexander 1906-1970 *BioIn 12, ConAu P-1, NewYTBE 70, SmATA 14*
Pseud./variant:
Gode, Alexander

Godey, John *ConAu 128, –X, EncMys, IntAu&W 91X, Novels, TwCCr&M 80, –85, WrDr 82, –84, –86, –88, –90*
Main entry: Freedgood, Morton

Godey, John 1912- *TwCCr&M 91*

Godfrey, Jane *SmATA X*
Main entry: Bowden, Joan Chase

Godfrey, William *ConAu 37NR, MajAI, SmATA X, Who 92*
Main entry: Youd, Samuel

Godkin, Celia 1948- *BioIn 17, ConAu 133, SmATA 66*

Godkin, Celia Marilyn 1948- *WrDr 94*

Godoy Alcayaga, Lucila *BlmGWL*

Godoy Alcayaga, Lucila 1889-1957 *BioIn 1, –2, –3, –4, –5, –7, –8, –9, –10, –11, –12, –14, –15, –16, –17, BlkWr 2, ConAu 104, –131, CurBio 46, DcSpL, EncLatA, HispWr, MajTwCW, REn, WhoNob 90, WomWrSA*
Pseud./variant:
Mistral, Gabriela

Godwin, Edward Fell 1912- *BioIn 5, IlsCB 1946*

Godwin, Mary Jane 1766-1841 *BioIn 16, OxCChiL*

Godwin, Stephanie Mary *BioIn 5, IlsCB 1946*

Godwin, William *PenEncH*

Godwin, William 1756-1836 *Benet 87, BioIn 1, –2, –3, –5, –6, –7, –8, –9, –10, –11, –12, –13, –14, –15, –16, –17, BlmGEL, CamGEL, CamGLE, CelCen, CnDBLB 3, CrtSuMy, CyEd, DcAmSR, DcBiPP, DcLB 39, –104, DcNaB, NinCLC 14, Novels, OxCChiL, OxCEng 85, RfGEnL 91, ScFEYrs, TwCCr&M 80A, –85A, –91A, WhoEc 81, –86, WorAlBi, WorAl, WrPh P*

Goethe, Johann Wolfgang 1749-1832 *OxCGer 86*

Goethe, Johann Wolfgang Von 1749-1832 *AsBiEn, AtlBL, Baker 84, –92, Benet 87, BbD, BiDPsy, BiD&SB, BioIn 1, –2, –3, –4, –5, –6, –7, –8, –9, –10, –11, –12, –13, –14, –17, BlmGEL, CamGWoT, CasWL, CelCen, ChhPo, –S1, –S2, CnThe, CyEd, CyWA 58, DcBiA, DcBiPP, DcEnL, DcEuL, DcLB 94, DcScB, Dis&D, EncO&P 2, –3, EncPaPR 91, EncWT, EuAu, EuWr 5, EvEuW, GrFLW, InSci, IntDcT 2, LongCEL, LuthC 75, MagSWL, MajAI, McGEWB, McGEWD 72, –84, NamesHP, NewC, NinCLC 4, –22, –34, NotNAT B, Novels, OxCArt, OxCEng 67, –85, OxCFr, OxCGer 76, OxCThe 67, –83, OxDcArt, PenC EUR, PoeCrit 5, RAdv 13-2, RComWL, REn, REnWD, WhDW, WhoHr&F, WorAlBi, WorAl, WrPh*

Goettel, Elinor 1930- *BioIn 11, ConAu 29R, SmATA 12, WrDr 76, –80, –82, –84*

Goetz, Delia 1898- *AuBYP 2, –3, BioIn 2, –7, –13, ConAu 73, CurBio 49, SmATA 22*

Goetz, Lee Garrett 1932- *ConAu 25R*

Goff, Lloyd Lozes 1919- *WhoAmA 73, –78, –80, –82*

Goffe, Toni 1936- *SmATA 61*

Goffstein, Brooke *MajAI, SmATA 70*

Goffstein, M B *BioIn 17, ConAu 28NR, DcLB 61, SmATA 70*

Goffstein, Marilyn Brooke 1940- *AuBYP 2S, -3, BioIn 11, -12, ChlLR 3, ConAu 21R, FourBJA, IlsCB 1967, MajAI, SmATA 8, WhoAmW 75, -77*

Gohman, Fred Joseph 1918- *ConAu 5R*

Golann, Cecil Paige 1921- *BioIn 11, ConAu 33R, SmATA 11*

Golberg, Martha 1907- *AuBYP 3*

Golbin, Andree 1923- *SmATA 15, WhoAmA 78, -80, -82, -84, -86, -89, -91, WhoE 91*

Gold, Doris Bauman 1919- *ConAu 21R, -9NR, WhoAmJ 80, WhoUSWr 88, WhoWorJ 72, -78, WhoWrEP 89, -92*

Gold, Herbert *DrAPF 87, -89, -91, -93, IntvTCA 2*

Gold, Herbert 1924- *AmAu&B, Benet 87, BenetAL 91, BioIn 3, -4, -6, -7, -8, -9, -10, -13, -15, -16, -17, CamGLE, CamHAL, CmCal, ConAu 9R, -17NR, ConLC 4, -7, -42, ConNov 72, -76, -82, -86, -91, CurBio 55, DcLB 2, -Y81A, DcLEL 1940, DrAF 76, IntAu&W 77, JeAmFiW, MichAu 80, ModAL, Novels, OxCAmL 65, -83, PenC AM, RAdv 1, REnAL, TwCWr, WhoAm 74, -76, -78, -80, -82, -84, -86, -88, -90, WhoAmJ 80, WhoUSWr 88, WhoWor 74, WhoWorJ 72, -78, WhoWrEP 89, -92, WorAu 1950, WrDr 76, -80, -82, -84, -86, -88, -90, -92, -94*

Gold, Phyllis *BioIn 12, ConAu X, SmATA 21, WhoAmW 77*
Main entry: Goldberg, Phyllis

Gold, Robert S 1924- *SmATA 63*

Gold, Sharlya *BioIn 11, ConAu 61, -8NR, SmATA 9*

Goldberg, Herbert S 1926- *WhoMW 86, -88*

Goldberg, Herbert Sam 1926- *AmMWSc 73P, -76P, -82, -86, -89, -92, BioIn 13, ConAu 5R, SmATA 25, WhoMW 86*

Goldberg, Israel 1887-1964 *AmAu&B, BioIn 7*
Pseud./variant:
Learsi, Rufus

Goldberg, Lazer 1920- *LEduc 74*

Goldberg, Martha 1907- *AuBYP 2, BioIn 8*

Goldberg, Nathan 1924- *DrAS 74F, -78F, -82F*

Goldberg, Phyllis 1941- *ConAu 57*
Pseud./variant:
Gold, Phyllis

Goldberg, Reuben L 1883-1970 *AmAu&B, ArtCS, ArtsAmW 2, ASCAP 66, BioIn 1, -2, -5, -6, -7, -8, -9, -10, ConAu 5R, -9NR, CurBio 48, -71, EncAJ, NewYTBE 70, ObitOF 79, WebAB 74, WhAm 6, -7, WhNAA, WhScrn 77*
Pseud./variant:
Goldberg, Rube

Goldberg, Reuben Lucius 1883-1970 *DcAmB S8, EncTwCJ*

Goldberg, Rube
Main entry: Goldberg, Reuben L

Goldberg, Stan J 1939- *BioIn 13, ConAu 49, SmATA 26*

Goldberg, Susan 1948- *SmATA 71*

Goldemberg, Rose Leiman 1928- *ConAu 49, -2NR, ConTFT 1, NatPD 77, -81*
Pseud./variant:
Traven, Beatrice

Golden, Grace Blaisdell 1899-1966 *IndAu 1917*

Golden Gorse *Str&VC, WhoChL*

Goldenson, Robert M 1908- *WrDr 86, -88, -90, -92, -94*

Goldenson, Robert Myar 1908- *AmMWSc 73S, ConAu 29R, WhoAm 74, -76, -78, -80, -82, -84, -86, -88, -90, WrDr 76, -80, -82, -84*

Goldfeder, Cheryl *BioIn 11, ConAu 53, -X, MichAu 80, SmATA X*
Main entry: Pahz, Cheryl Suzanne

Goldfeder, James *ConAu 53, -X, SmATA X*
Main entry: Pahz, James Alon

Goldfeder, Jim *BioIn 11, ConAu X, SmATA X*
Main entry: Pahz, James Alon

Goldfrank, Helen Colodny 1912- *AuBYP 2, -3, ConAu 1R, -3NR, ForWC 70, SmATA 6, WhoE 83*
Pseud./variant:
Kay, Helen

Goldhurst, Richard 1927- *ConAu 57*

Goldin, Augusta Reider 1906- *ConAu 17R, ForWC 70, LEduc 74, SmATA 13, WhoAmW 74, -75, WrDr 76, -80*

Golding, Harry *CarSB, ChhPo S2*

Golding, Morton J 1925- *ConAu 21R*

Golding, William *IntvTCA 2*

Golding, William 1911- *Au&Arts 5, Benet 87, BioIn 6, -7, -8, -9, -10, -11, -12, -13, -14,*

–15, –16, –17, BlmGEL, BlueB 76, BritWr S1, CamGEL, CamGLE, CasWL, CelR 90, CnDBLB 7, CnMWL, ConAu 5R, –13NR, –33NR, ConLC 1, –2, –3, –8, –10, –17, –27, –58, ConNov 72, –76, –82, –86, –91, CurBio 64, CyWA 89, DcLB 15, –100, EncWL, –2, IntAu&W 89, –91, IntWW 74, –75, –76, –77, –78, –79, –80, –81, –82, –83, –91, LongCEL, LongCTC, MagSWL, MajTwCW, MakMC, ModBrL, –S1, –S2, ModWD, NewC, NewEScF, NobelP, Novels, OxCChiL, OxCEng 85, PenC ENG, RAdv 1, –13-1, REn, RfGEnL 91, ScF&FL 92, ScFSB, TwCRHW 90, TwCSFW 86, –91, TwCWr, WebE&AL, WhDW, Who 74, –82, –83, –85, –88, –92, WhoAm 80, –82, –84, WhoHr&F, WhoTwCL, WhoWor 74, –80, –82, –84, WorAlBi, WorAl, WorAu 1950, WrDr 76, –80, –82, –84, –86, –88, –90, –92

Golding, William 1911-1991 *WorLitC*

Golding, William 1911-1993 *ConLC 81*

Golding, William, Sir 1911- *IntWW 89, Who 90*

Golding, William Gerald 1911- *EncSF 93*

Golding, William Gerald 1911-1993 *ConAu 141, TwCYAW*

Golding, William Gerald, Sir 1911-1993 *WrDr 94N*

Goldman, Alex J 1917- *ConAu 49, SmATA 65, WhoAmJ 80, WhoRel 92, WhoWorJ 72, –78*

Goldman, Peter Louis 1933- *ConAu 21R, –8NR*

Goldman, Phyllis W 1927- *ConAu 29R*

Goldman, Susan 1939- *ConAu 65*

Goldman, William *ConDr 88A, DrAPF 87, –89, –93*

Goldman, William 1931- *AmAu&B, BiE&WWA, BioIn 11, –12, –13, –15, –17, BioNews 75, BlueB 76, ConAu 9R, –29NR, ConDr 73, –77A, –82A, ConLC 1, –48, ConNov 72, –76, –82, –86, –91, ConTFT 7, DcLB 44, DcLEL 1940, DrAF 76, FilmgC, HalFC 84, –88, IntMPA 78, –81, –82, –84, –86, –88, –92, IntWW 91, JeAmFiW, NotNAT, Novels, PenC AM, ScF&FL 92, WebE&AL, WhoAm 74, –76, –78, –80, –82, –84, –86, –88, –92, –94, WhoE 74, WhoWor 74, WorAlBi, WrDr 76, –80, –82, –84, –86, –88, –90, –92, –94*

Goldman, William 1932- *IntAu&W 91*

Goldner, Jameson Charles 1938- *WhoWest 74, –76, –80, –82, –84*

Goldreich, Gloria *DrAPF 83, –85, –87, –89, –91, –93*

Goldsborough, June 1923- *BioIn 12, SmATA 19*

Goldsmith, Howard *DrAPF 87, –89, –91, –93*

Goldsmith, Howard 1943- *BioIn 13, ConAu 101, –18NR, –21NR, –40NR, EncSF 93, ScF&FL 92, SmATA 24, WhoAm 86, –88, –90, WhoUSWr 88*
Pseud./variant:
Smith, Ward

Goldsmith, Howard 1945- *WhoAm 92, –94, WhoWrEP 89, –92*

Goldsmith, Ilse Sondra Weinberg 1933- *ConAu 37R*

Goldsmith, John Herman Thorburn d1987 *Who 88N*

Goldsmith, John Herman Thorburn 1903-1987 *BioIn 16, ConAu 122, SmATA 52N*
Pseud./variant:
Thorburn, John

Goldsmith, Maurice 1913- *Au&Wr 71*

Goldsmith, Oliver 1728?-1774 *Alli, AtlBL, BbD, BiDIrW, BiD&SB, BioIn 1, –2, –3, –4, –5, –6, –7, –8, –9, –10, –11, –12, –13, –14, –15, –17, BritAu, BritWr 3, CamGEL, CamGWoT, CarSB, CasWL, Chambr 2, ChhPo, –S1, –S2, CnE&AP, CnThe, CrtT 2, CyEd, CyWA 58, DcBiA, DcBiPP, DcEnA, –A, DcEnL, DcEuL, DcIrB 88, DcIrL, DcIrW 1, DcLB 39, DcLEL, DcNaB, –C, Dis&D, EncWT, EvLB, HsB&A, InSci, LitC 2, LongCEL, MagSWL, McGEWB, McGEWD 72, –84, MouLC 2, NewC, NotNAT A, –B, Novels, OxCChiL, OxCEng 67, –85, OxCMus, OxCThe 67, –83, PenC ENG, PlP&P, PoIre, RAdv 1, –13-1, –13-2, REn, REnWD, SmATA 26, WebE&AL, WhDW, WorAl, WorLitC*

Goldsmith, Oliver 1730-1774 *BlmGEL, CamGLE, CnDBLB 2, DcLB 89, –104, –109, IntDcT 2, RfGEnL 91, WorAlBi*

Goldsmith, Oliver 1731-1774 *Benet 87*

Goldsmith, Ruth M 1919- *SmATA 62*

Goldstein, Ernest A 1933- *SmATA 52*

Goldstein, Kenneth Michael 1940- *AmMWSc 73S, –78S, ConAu 33R, WhoE 75, –77, –86*

Goldstein, Margaret Ann 1939- *AmMWSc 82, –86, –89, –92, WhoAmW 77, –81*

Goldstein, Nathan 1927- *BioIn 12, ConAu 45, –1NR, –16NR, IlsBYP, SmATA 47, WhoAmA 78, –80, –82, –84, –86, –89, –91, WhoE 91*

Goldstein, Philip 1910- *AuBYP 2S, –3, BioIn 13, ConAu 53, SmATA 23*

Goldstein, Rhoda L *ConAu 30NR*

Goldstein, Rhoda Lois 1926- *AmMWSc 73S, –78S, ConAu 57, –X*

Goldstein, Rose B 1904- *WhoWorJ 72, –78*

Goldston, Robert Conroy 1927- *AmAu&B, AuBYP 2S, –3, Au&Wr 71, BioIn 10, ConAu 17R, FourBJA, SmATA 6, WhAm 8, WhoAm 74, –76, –78, –80, –82*
Pseud./variant:
Conroy, Robert
Stark, James

Goldszmit, Henryk 1878-1942 *BioIn 15, –16, –17, ConAu 133, SmATA 65*
Main entry: Korczak, Janusz

Goldwater, Daniel Leon 1922- *WhoAm 76*

Goll, Reinhold W 1897- *WrDr 86*

Goll, Reinhold Weimar 1897- *AuBYP 2, –3, BioIn 8, –13, ConAu 5R, SmATA 26, WrDr 76, –80, –82, –84*

Gollomb, Joseph 1881-1950 *AmAu&B, AnCL, AuBYP 2, –3, BenetAL 91, BioIn 2, –4, –7, JBA 34, –51, ObitOF 79, REnAL, TwCA, –SUP, WhAm 3*

Golombek, Harry 1911- *ConAu 103, GolEC, Who 74, –82, –83, –85, –88, –90, –92*

Gomi, Taro 1945- *AuBYP 3, SmATA 64*

Gompertz, M L G *BioIn 1*

Gondosch, Linda 1944- *BioIn 16, ConAu 127, ScF&FL 92, SmATA 58*

Gondosch, Linda Ann 1944- *WhoUSWr 88*

Gonne, Maud *ContDcW 89, DcIrB 88*

Gonne, Maud 1865?-1953 *FemiCLE*

Gonne, Maud 1866-1953 *ArtclWW 2, Benet 87, BioIn 1, –3, –7, –10, –11, –12, –16, –17, IntDcWB, NewC, REn*
Pseud./variant:
MacBride, Maud Gonne

Gonne, Maud Edith 1866-1953 *DcNaB MP*

Gonzales, Rodolfo Chena 1928- *BioIn 9, –10*

Gonzalez, Gloria 1940- *BioIn 13, ConAu 65, –24NR, NatPD 77, ScF&FL 92, SmATA 23*

Gonzalez, Xavier d1993 *NewYTBS 93*

Gonzalez, Xavier 1898- *ArtsAmW 2, BioIn 1, –2, –3, –5, DcCAA 71, –77, –88, HispAmA, IlsBYP, WhAmArt 85, WhoAm 74, –76, WhoAmA 73, –78, –80, –82, –84, –86, –89, –91, WhoHisp 91, –92, –94*

Good, Alice 1950- *SmATA 73*

Good, Paul 1929- *ConAu 85*

Good, Paul Joseph 1929- *WhoAm 90, –92*

Good, Stafford 1890- *ConICB*

Goodacre, Elizabeth Jane 1929- *Au&Wr 71, ConAu 102, IntAu&W 77, WrDr 76, –80, –82, –84, –86, –88, –90*

Goodall, John S 1908- *ChlLR 25, SmATA 66*

Goodall, John Strickland 1908- *BioIn 5, –9, ClaDrA, ConAu 33R, DcBrAr 1, FourBJA, IlsCB 1946, –1967, MajAI, SmATA 4, WhoArt 80, –82, –84*

Goodbody, Slim *SmATA X, WhoUSWr 88*
Main entry: Burstein, John

Goode, Diane *ChlBIlD*

Goode, Diane Capuozzo 1949- *BioIn 12, FifBJA, IlsCB 1967, SmATA 15*

Goode, John 1927- *Au&Wr 71, ConAu 103, IntAu&W 86, –89*

Goode, Ruth 1905- *ConAu 77*
Pseud./variant:
Rainer, Julia
Seinfel, Ruth

Goode, Stephen 1943- *SmATA 55*

Goode, Stephen Ray 1943- *ConAu 57, –105, –18NR, SmATA 40*

Goodenow, Earle *WhoE 89*

Goodenow, Earle 1913- *BioIn 5, IlsCB 1946, –1967, SmATA 40, WhAmArt 85*

Goodenow, Girard 1912- *BioIn 5, IlsBYP, IlsCB 1946*

Gooderham, Kent *OxCCan SUP*

Gooders, John *WrDr 86*

Gooders, John 1937- *Au&Wr 71, ConAu 57, –6NR, IntAu&W 77, –91, WhoWor 78, WrDr 76, –80, –82, –84, –88, –90, –92, –94*

Goodfellow, E J H 1843- *ChhPo, WhNAA*

Goodfellow, Thomas MacKey 1907- *BioIn 4, EncAB-A 31, WhoAm 74, –76, WhoFI 74, WhoSSW 73*

Goodheart, Barbara 1934- *ConAu 33R, WrDr 76, –80, –82, –84, –86, –88, –90*

Goodheart, Barbara Jean 1934- *WhoWrEP 92*

Goodin, Sallie Brown 1953- *SmATA 74*

Goodman, Deborah Lerme 1956- *BioIn 16, ConAu 121, ScF&FL 92, SmATA 49, –50*

Goodman, Elaine 1930- *AuBYP 2S, –3, BioIn 11, ConAu 37R, SmATA 9*

Goodman, Elaine Iris 1963- *WhoE 93*

Goodman, Elizabeth B 1912- *AuBYP 2S, –3, ConAu 25R*

Goodman, Joan E 1950- *BioIn 16*

Goodman, Joan Elizabeth 1950- *ConAu 126, IntAu&W 91, SmATA 50*

Goodman, Linda *WhoAm 94, WhoWor 87, –89, –91, –93*

Goodman, Linda 1933?- *BioIn 11, –12, CelR, WhoAm 74, –76, –78, –80, –82, WhoAmW 74, WhoWor 84*

Goodman, Nathan Gerson 1899-1953 *AmAu&B, BioIn 3, –4, REnAL, WhAm 3*

Goodman, Walter 1838- *DcVicP 2*

Goodman, Walter 1927- *AuBYP 2S, –3, BioIn 11, ConAu 9R, –7NR, SmATA 9, WhoAm 74, –76, –78, –80, –82, –84, –86, –88, –90, WhoAmJ 80, WhoE 74, WhoEnt 92, WhoUSWr 88, WhoWrEP 89, –92*

Goodrich, Samuel G 1793-1860 *ScFEYrs*

Goodrich, Samuel Griswold 1793-1860 *Alli, AmAu, AmAu&B, BenetAL 91, BbD, BbtC, BiD&SB, BioIn 1, –4, –8, –13, –15, –17, CarSB, ChhPo, –S1, –S2, CyAL, CyEd, DcAmAu, DcBiPP, DcEnL, DcLB 1, –42, –73, DcNAA, HarEnUS, OxCAmH, OxCAmL 65, –83, OxCChiL, REn, REnAL, SmATA 23, WebAB 74, –79, WhAm HS, WhoChL*
Pseud./variant:
Parley, Peter

Goodrum, John Cornelius 1918- *WhoFI 74*

Goodsell, Jane Neuberger 1921?-1988 *ConAu 126, SmATA 56N*

Goodspeed, Donald J 1919- *ConAu 5R, OxCCan SUP*

Goodwin, Hal *ConAu 131, –X, –29NR, ScF&FL 92, SmATA 65, –X*
Main entry: Goodwin, Harold Leland

Goodwin, Hal 1914-1990 *BioIn 16, –17*

Goodwin, Harold *EncAFC*

Goodwin, Harold 1917- *HalFC 88*

Goodwin, Harold 1919- *ConAu 57, IlsBYP*

Goodwin, Harold L 1914- *ConAu 29NR*

Goodwin, Harold L 1914-1990 *ConAu 131, SmATA 65*

Goodwin, Harold Leland 1914- *ConAu 1R, –2NR, SmATA 13, –51, WhoE 75, –77, WhoGov 77, –72, –75, WhoSSW 75*
Pseud./variant:
Blaine, John
Goodwin, Hal
Gordon, Hal
Savage, Blake

Goodwin, Harold Leland 1914-1990 *BioIn 16, –17*

Goodwin, Maud Wilder 1856-1935 *AmAu&B, BenetAL 91, BiD&SB, BioIn 12, CarSB, DcAmAu, DcNAA, REnAL, WhAm 1, WomWWA 14*

Goodyear, Robert Arthur Hanson 1877?-1948 *BioIn 8, WhoChL, WhoLA*

Goor, Nancy 1944- *BioIn 14, –15, ConAu 113, –32NR, SmATA 34, –39*

Goor, Ron 1940- *BioIn 14, –15, ConAu 113, –32NR, SmATA 34, –39*

Goor, Ronald Stephen 1940- *WhoAm 92, –94*

Goossen, Agnes *ConAu X, SmATA X*
Main entry: Epp, Margaret Agnes

Goossen, Irvy W 1924- *ConAu 37R*

Gordimer, Nadine *IntvTCA 2*

Gordimer, Nadine 1923- *ArtclWW 2, Benet 87, BioIn 14, –15, –16, –17, BlmGEL, BlmGWL, BritWr S2, CamGEL, CamGLE, ConAu 28NR, ConLC 51, –70, ConNov 86, –91, ContDcW 89, CyWA 89, DcLB Y91, EncWB, FemiCLE, InWom SUP, IntAu&W 89, –91, IntLitE, IntWW 89, –91, MagSWL, MajTwCW, NewYTBS 91, NobelP 91, RAdv 13-2, RfGEnL 91, ShSWr, TwCYAW, Who 88, –90, –92, WhoAm 94, WhoWor 87, –89, –91, –93, WorAlBi, WrDr 86, –88, –90, –92, –94*

Gordon, Bernard Ludwig 1931- *AmMWSc 73P, –76P, –82, –86, –89, –92, BioIn 13, ConAu 29R, DrLC 69, SmATA 27, WhoE 74, –81, –83*

Gordon, Charles W, the Rev 1860-1937 *StaCVF*

Gordon, Charles William 1860-1937 *BenetAL 91, BiD&SB, BioIn 1, –2, –11, –13, CanNov, CanWr, Chambr 3, ConAu 109, CreCan 1, DcLEL, DcNaB 1931, DcNAA, EvLB, LongCTC, LuthC 75, NewC, OxCAmL 65, OxCCan, OxCCanL, REnAL, TwCA, –SUP, WhNAA*
Pseud./variant:
Connor, Ralph

Gordon, Colonel H R *AmAu&B, YABC 1*
Main entry: Ellis, Edward S

Gordon, Cyrus H 1908- *Who 88, –92, WhoE 86*

Gordon, Cyrus H, Prof 1908- *Who 90*

Gordon, Cyrus Herzl 1908- *AuBYP 2S, –3, BioIn 6, BlueB 76, ConAu 1R, –5NR, CurBio 63, DrAS 78F, –82F, IntAu&W 77, –82, Who 74, –82, –83, –85, WhoAm 74, –76, –80, –82, –84, –86, –88, –90, –92, –94, WhoAmJ 80, WhoE 83, –89, WhoWor 74, –80, –82, WhoWorJ 72, –78, WrDr 76, –80, –82, –84, –86, –88, –90, –92, –94*

Gordon, Donald *BioIn 1, –2, ConAu X, EncSF 93, IntAu&W 91X, SmATA X, WrDr 76, –80, –82, –84, –86, –88, –90, –92*
Main entry: Payne, Donald Gordon

Gordon, Donald 1924- *WrDr 94*

Gordon, Donald 1929- *WrDr 90, –92*

Gordon, Donald Ramsay 1929- *WrDr 94*

Gordon, Dorothy 1893-1970 *AmAu&B, AuBYP 2, –3, BioIn 3, –4, –8, –9, –12, ChhPo S1, ConAu 73, CurBio 55, –70, ForWC 70, NewYTBE 70, SmATA 20, WhAm 5, WhoAm 74, WhoHol A*

Gordon, Elizabeth 1866-1922 *AmLY, CarSB, ChhPo, –S1, DcNAA, WhAm 1*

Gordon, Esther Saranga 1935- *BioIn 11, ConAu 53, –7NR, SmATA 10*

Gordon, Ethel E 1915- *WrDr 86, –88, –90, –92*

Gordon, Ethel Edison 1915- *BioIn 14, ConAu 53, TwCRHW 90, WrDr 76, –80, –82, –84, –94*

Gordon, Frederick *CarSB, ConAu 26NR, –P-2, SmATA 1*
Main entry: Stratemeyer, Edward L

Gordon, Gary *AuBYP 2S, –3, ConAu X, –30NR*
Main entry: Edmonds, I G

Gordon, George N 1926- *ConAu 1R, –5NR, IntAu&W 77, WrDr 76, –80, –82, –84, –86, –88, –90, –92, –94*

Gordon, Giles Alexander Esme 1940- *ConAu 41R, ConPo 70, –75, IntAu&W 77, –82, –86, –89, –91, IntWWP 82, Who 92, WrDr 76, –80*

Gordon, Gordon 1912- *AuBYP 2S, –3, Au&Wr 71, BioIn 7, –8, ConAu 5R, –7NR, EncMys, IndAu 1917*
Pseud./variant:
Gordons, The

Gordon, Hal *ConAu 131, –X, –29NR, SmATA 65, –X*
Main entry: Goodwin, Harold Leland

Gordon, Hal 1914-1990 *BioIn 16, –17*

Gordon, Jeffie Ross *ScF&FL 92, SmATA X, WhoWrEP 89, –92*
Main entry: Tessler, Stephanie Gordon

Gordon, John *ConAu X, SmATA X*
Main entry: Gesner, Clark

Gordon, John 1925- *ConAu 27NR, PenEncH, ScF&FL 92, TwCChW 89, WrDr 90, –92*

Gordon, John William 1925- *BioIn 10, ChlFicS, ConAu 25R, –103, –11NR, IntAu&W 91, SmATA 6, TwCChW 78, –83, WrDr 76, –86, –88, –94*

Gordon, Lesley *ConAu X*
Main entry: Elliott, Lesley

Gordon, Lew *AuBYP 2S, –3, ConAu X, IntAu&W 91X, SmATA X, TwCWW 91, WrDr 84, –86, –88, –90, –92*
Main entry: Baldwin, Gordon C

Gordon, Margaret Anna 1939- *BioIn 8, –11, –12, ChhPo S2, IlsBYP, IlsCB 1957, –1967, SmATA 9*

Gordon, Mildred 1905-1979 *TwCCr&M 91*

Gordon, Mildred 1912?-1979 *AuBYP 2S, –3, Au&Wr 71, BioIn 7, –8, –11, –13, –14, ConAu 5R, –85, –7NR, EncMys, SmATA 24N, TwCCr&M 80, –85, WhoAmW 74, –75*
Pseud./variant:
Gordons, The

Gordon, Patricia 1904- *AmAu&B, AuBYP 2S, –3*

Pseud./variant:
Howard, Joan

Gordon, Richard *Au&Wr 71, DcLEL 1940, IntAu&W 77, TwCWr, Who 74, -82, -83, -85, -88, -90, WrDr 80, -84*

Gordon, Richard 1921- *Who 92, WrDr 86, -88, -90, -92, -94*

Gordon, Robert Kay 1887- *CanWW 70*

Gordon, Selma *AuBYP 2S, -3, ConAu X, SmATA 3*
Main entry: Lanes, Selma Gordon

Gordon, Sheila 1927- *ChlLR 27, DcAmChF 1985*

Gordon, Shirley 1921- *ConAu 97, SmATA 41, -48*

Gordon, Sol 1923- *AmMWSc 73S, -78S, AuBYP 2S, -3, BioIn 11, ConAu 53, -4NR, ConLC 26, IntAu&W 77, LEduc 74, SmATA 11, WhoE 83*

Gordon, Stewart *AuBYP 2, -3, ConAu X, SmATA X, TwCWW 91, WrDr 76, -80, -82, -84, -86, -88, -90, -92*
Main entry: Shirreffs, Gordon Donald

Gordon, Stewart 1914- *WrDr 94*

Gordon, Sydney 1914- *Au&Wr 71, ConAu 29R, IntAu&W 82, WrDr 76, -80, -82, -84, -86, -88, -90*

Gordon, W J *Alli SUP, ChhPo*

Gordons *AuBYP 3*

Gordons 1906- *WrDr 94*

Gordons, The *ConAu X, SmATA X, TwCCr&M 85, -91, WrDr 82, -84, -86, -88, -90, -92*

Gordons, The
Main entry: Gordon, Gordon
Gordon, Mildred

Gore, Margaret 1919- *IntAu&W 77*

Gorelick, Molly Chernow 1920- *BioIn 11, ConAu 21R, SmATA 9, WhoAmW 74, -75, -77, -89*

Gorenstein, Shirley Slotkin 1928- *AmMWSc 92, ConAu 73, WhoAm 82, -84, -86, -88, -90, -92, -94, WhoAmW 75, -81, WhoE 89, -93*

Gorey, Edward *IntvTCA 2*

Gorey, Edward 1925- *BenetAL 91, BioIn 15, -16, ConAu 30NR, DcLB 61, PenEncH, WrDr 86, -88, -90, -92*

Gorey, Edward St. John 1925-
Pseud./variant:
Om
Ward, E D
Wryde, Dogear

Gorey, Edward St John 1925- *AmPB, BioIn 5, -8, -10, -11, -12, -13, ChhPo, -S1, ConAu 5R, Conv 1, CurBio 76, FourBJA, IlsBYP, IlsCB 1957, -1967, MajAI, NewYTBE 73, SmATA 27, -29, -70, WhoAm 78, -80, -82, -84, -86, -88, -90, -92, -94, WhoUSWr 88, WhoWrEP 89, -92, WrDr 80, -94*
Pseud./variant:
Blutig, Eduard
Dowdy, Regera, Mrs.
Gewe, Raddory
Grode, Redway
Mude, O
O Mude
Phypps, Hyacinthe
Pig, Edward
Weary, Ogdred
Wodge, Dreary

Gorham, Charles Orson 1911-1975 *AmAu&B, AmNov, BioIn 2, -10, -14, ConAu 1R, -61, -6NR, SmATA 36*

Gorham, Michael *AuBYP 2, -3, ConAu X, IntAu&W 82X, -91X, SmATA 5, WrDr 76, -80, -82, -84, -86, -88, -90, -92*
Main entry: Elting, Mary
Folsom, Franklin Brewster

Gorham, Michael 1907- *WrDr 94*

Gorman, James *AuBYP 3*

Gorman, James Carvill 1924- *WhoAm 92, -94*

Gorman, James Edward 1930- *WhoAmL 90*

Gorman, Terry *IlsBYP, IlsCB 1946*
Main entry: Powers, Richard M Gorman

Gormley, Beatrice 1942- *BioIn 14, -15, ConAu 113, ScF&FL 92, SmATA 35, -39*

Gorodetzky, Charles W *AuBYP 3*

Gorodetzky, Charles W 1937- *AmMWSc 86, -89, -92*

Gorodetzky, Charles William 1937- *AmMWSc 73P, -76P, -82, AuBYP 2S, WhoAm 80, -82, -84, -86, -88, -90, -92, -94, WhoSSW 75, -76, -78*

Gorog, Judith 1938- *BioIn 15, ConAu 114, ScF&FL 92, SmATA 39*

Gorog, Judith Katharine Allen 1938- *SmATA 75*

Gorsline, Douglas W d1985 *NewYTBS 85*

Gorsline, Douglas W 1913-1985 *BioIn 14, -15*

Gorsline, Douglas Warner 1913-1985
AmAu&B, BioIn 5, -7, -8, -11, ChhPo S1, ConAu 61, -116, -9NR, GrAmP, IlsBYP, IlsCB 1946, -1957, -1967, NewYTBS 85, SmATA 11, -43N, WhAmArt 85, WhoAm 74, WhoAmA 73, -78, -80, -82, -84, -86N, -89N, -91N

Gorsline, Marie 1928- *BioIn 13, ConAu 106, SmATA 28*
Pseud./variant:
Carson, S M
Gorsline, S M

Gorsline, S M *ConAu X, SmATA X*
Main entry: Gorsline, Marie

Gorton, Kaitlyn *ConAu 127, SmATA X, WhoUSWr 88, WhoWrEP 89, -92*
Main entry: Emerson, Kathy Lynn

Goryan, Sirak *ConAu X, -30NR, MajTwCW, SmATA X*
Main entry: Saroyan, William

Goscinny, Rene 1926-1977 *BioIn 10, -11, ConAu 113, -117, ObitOF 79, SmATA 39, -47*

Goshorn, Elizabeth 1953- *ConAu 61*

Goss, Clay 1946- *BlkAWP, ConAu 57, DrBlPA 90*

Goss, Clay 1947- *ConBlAP 88*

Goss, Clayton E 1946- *BlkWr 2*

Goss, Warren Lee 1835-1925 *Alli SUP, AmAu&B, AmLY, CarSB, DcAmAu, DcNAA, HarEnUS, WhAm 1, WhNAA*

Gosse, Edmund William, Sir 1849-1928
Alli SUP, BbD, BiD&SB, BioIn 1, -2, -3, -4, -5, -6, -7, -8, -9, -10, -11, -13, CamGEL, CarSB, CasWL, Chambr 3, ChhPo, -S1, -S2, CnMWL, DcEnA, -A, DcEnL, DcLEL, DcNaB 1922, EvLB, GrBr, LongCEL, LongCTC, ModBrL, NewC, NotNAT B, OxCEng 67, -85, PenC ENG, TwCA, -SUP, TwCWr, WebE&AL

Gossett, Margaret *AuBYP 2, -3, BioIn 8*

Gottlieb, Bill
Main entry: Gottlieb, William P

Gottlieb, Gerald 1923- *AuBYP 2, -3, BioIn 8, -10, ConAu 5R, SmATA 7*

Gottlieb, Robin 1928- *AuBYP 2, -3, BioIn 8, ConAu 1R, -2NR, ForWC 70*

Gottlieb, William P *AuBYP 2, BioIn 7, -13, ConAu 101, SmATA 24*
Pseud./variant:
Gottlieb, Bill

Gottlieb, William Paul 1917- *AuBYP 3*

Gottschalk, Alfred 1930- *DrAS 82P, LEduc 74, NewYTBE 71, WhoAm 74, -76, -78, -80, -82, -84, -86, -88, -90, -92, -94, WhoAmJ 80, WhoMW 80, -82, -84, -86, -88, -90, -92, -93, WhoRel 75, -77, -92, WhoWor 74, -80, -82, -84, -87, -89, -91, WhoWorJ 72, -78*

Goudey, Alice E 1898- *AuBYP 2, -3, BioIn 7, -9, ConAu 73, SmATA 20, ThrBJA*

Goudge, Elizabeth 1900-1984 *AuBYP 2, -3, Au&Wr 71, Benet 87, BioIn 1, -2, -3, -4, -8, -9, -10, -13, -14, -15, -16, BlueB 76, ChhPo, ConAu 5R, -112, -5NR, CurBio 40, -84N, EngPo, FemiCLE, InWom SUP, LongCTC, NewC, OxCChiL, REn, ScF&FL 92, SmATA 2, -38N, ThrBJA, TwCA, -SUP, TwCChW 78, -83, -89, TwCRHW 90, TwCWr, Who 74, -82, -83, WhoChL, WrDr 76, -80, -82, -84*

Goudge, Elizabeth de Beauchamp 1900-1984 *MajAI*

Goudsmit, Samuel Abraham 1902-1978
AmMWSc 73P, -76P, AsBiEn, BiESc, BioIn 3, -10, -11, -12, ConAu 81, CurBio 54, DcScB S2, InSci, IntAu&W 77, IntWW 74, -75, -76, -77, -78, -79N, McGMS 80, ObitOF 79, WhAm 7, WhoAm 74, -76, -78, WhoAtom 77, WhoWorJ 72, -78

Gough, Catherine 1931- *BioIn 13, ConAu 25R, -X, SmATA 24*
Pseud./variant:
Mulgan, Catherine

Gough, Irene *SingR 2*

Gough, Philip 1908- *BioIn 5, ChhPo, IlsCB 1946, -1967, SmATA 45*

Goulart, Frances Sheridan 1938- *ConAu 57, -7NR, -25NR, MichAu 80*

Goulart, Ron 1933- *BioIn 8, -10, ConAu 25R, -7NR, ConSFA, CrtSuMy, IntAu&W 82, NewEScF, ScF&FL 92, ScFSB, SmATA 6, TwCCr&M 80, -85, -91, TwCSFW 86, -91, WhoSciF, WhoUSWr 88, WhoWrEP 89, WrDr 82, -84, -86, -88, -90, -92*
Pseud./variant:
Lee, Howard
Robeson, Kenneth
Shawn, Frank S
Steffanson, Con

Goulart, Ronald Joseph 1933- *EncSF 93, WhoWrEP 92, WrDr 94*

Gould, Chester 1900- *EncTwCJ*

Gould, Chester 1900-1985 *AnObit 1985, ArtCS, Au&Arts 7, BioIn 1, -3, -4, -6, -9, -11, -14, -15, -16, -17, ConAu 77, -116, -30NR, ConGrA 1, ConNews 85-2, CurBio 71, -85N, EncACom, EncAJ, EncMys, NewYTBS 85, SmATA 43N, -49, WebAB 74, -79, WhAm 8, WhAmArt 85, WhoAm 74, -76, -78, -80, -82, -84, WhoAmA 78, -80, -82, WhoMW 74*

Gould, Deborah L *AuBYP 3*

Gould, Elizabeth Lincoln *AmWomPl*

Gould, Elizabeth Lincoln d1914 *CarSB, ChhPo, DcNAA, WhAm 1, WomWWA 14*

Gould, Elizabeth Lincoln 1873-1914 *WomNov*

Gould, George *AuBYP 2S, -3*

Gould, Jean R 1919- *ConAu 21NR, WrDr 86, -88, -90*

Gould, Jean Rosalind 1909-1993 *ConAu 142, SmATA 77*

Gould, Jean Rosalind 1919?- *AuBYP 2, -3, BioIn 7, -11, ConAu 5R, -3NR, IntAu&W 77, OhA&B, SmATA 11, WhoAm 74, -76, -78, -80, -82, -84, -86, -88, WhoAmW 74, WhoE 74, WhoUSWr 88, WhoWrEP 89, -92, WrDr 76, -80, -82, -84*

Gould, Lilian 1920- *BioIn 10, ConAu 49, -2NR, SmATA 6*

Gould, Marilyn 1928- *AuBYP 2S, -3, BioIn 12, SmATA 15, -76*

Gould, Marilyn A 1928- *WhoAmW 93*

Gould, Nathaniel 1857-1919 *BioIn 2, BritAS, CamGLE, DcLEL, DcNaB 1912, EvLB, OxCEng 67*

Gould, Toni S *AuBYP 2S, -3*

Goulding, Dorothy Jane 1923- *BioIn 10, ConAu 65, Profile 1*

Goulding, Francis Robert 1810-1881 *Alli, -SUP, AmAu&B, BenetAL 91, BiDSA, BiD&SB, CarSB, DcAmAu, DcNAA, REnAL, WhAm HS*

Goulet, John *DrAPF 89, -91, -93*

Goulet, John 1942- *ConAu 85*

Gourdie, Thomas 1913- *Au&Wr 71, ConAu 1R, -1NR, DcBrAr 1, WhoArt 80, -82, -84, WrDr 76, -80*

Govan, Christine 1898- *AuBYP 3*

Govan, Christine Noble 1898?- *AmNov, AuBYP 2, BioIn 2, -8, -11, ConAu 1R, -2NR, ForWC 70, SmATA 9, WrDr 76, -80, -82, -84*
Pseud./variant:
Allerton, Mary
Darby, J N

Gove, Doris 1944- *SmATA 72*

Govern, Elaine 1939- *BioIn 13, ConAu 53, SmATA 26*

Gowers, Ernest Arthur, Sir 1880-1966 *BioIn 7, -10, ChhPo, DcLEL 1940, DcNaB 1961, GrBr, LongCTC, NewC, WorAu 1950*

Graaf, Peter *MajAI*

Grabe, Andree Vilas 1914- *WhoAdv 72*

Graber, Alexander 1914- *BioIn 10, ConAu 1R, -1NR, SmATA 7*
Pseud./variant:
Cordell, Alexander

Graber, Richard Frederick 1927- *BioIn 13, ConAu 85, SmATA 26*

Grabianski, Janusz 1929-1976 *BioIn 8, -9, -11, -14, -15, ConAu 45, -2NR, IlsBYP, IlsCB 1957, -1967, SmATA 30N, -39, ThrBJA*

Graboff, Abner 1919- *BioIn 8, -14, ConAu 107, IlsBYP, IlsCB 1957, SmATA 35*

Grace, F *ConAu 111, SmATA 45*

Grace, Joseph *ConAu X*
Main entry: Hornby, John

Gracza, Margaret Young 1928- *BioIn 16, ConAu 13R, ForWC 70, SmATA 56*

Graeber, Charlotte Towner *BioIn 15, -16, ConAu 134, SmATA 44, -56, WrDr 94*

Graeme, Bruce *Au&Wr 71, ConAu X, EncMys, EncSF 93, IntAu&W 77, -82, TwCCr&M 80, -85, Who 74, -82, -83, WhoSpyF, WrDr 76, -80, -82*

Graeme, Bruce 1900-1982 *BioIn 14, CrtSuMy, ScF&FL 92, TwCCr&M 91*

Graeme, David *ConAu 77, -X, EncMys, TwCCr&M 80, -85, -91*

Graeme, Roderic *Au&Wr 71, ConAu X, EncMys, IntAu&W 91X, TwCCr&M 80, -85,*

–91, WrDr 82, –84, –86, –88, –90, –92
Main entry: Jeffries, Roderic

Graeme, Roderic 1926- *WrDr 94*

Graese, Judy 1940- *AmArt, WhoAmA 78, –80, –82, –84, –86, –89, –91*

Graff, Polly Anne Colver *ConAu X, SmATA 7*
Main entry: Colver, Anne

Graff, S Stewart 1908- *AuBYP 2, –3, BioIn 8, –11, ConAu 49, SmATA 9*

Grafton, Ann *ConAu X*
Main entry: Owens, Thelma

Graham, Ada *AuBYP 3*

Graham, Ada 1931- *BioIn 11, ConAu 29R, –4NR, IntAu&W 77, –82, –91, SmATA 11, WhoAmW 77, WrDr 76, –80, –82, –84, –86, –88, –90, –92, –94*

Graham, Al 1897- *AuBYP 2, –3, BioIn 7, ChhPo, –S1*

Graham, Alastair 1945- *ConAu 141, SmATA 74*

Graham, Alberta *AuBYP 3*

Graham, Alberta 1874?-1955 *AuBYP 2, BioIn 3, –4, –7*

Graham, Amanda *AuBYP 3*

Graham, Billy *ConAu 42NR, IntWW 89, –91, Who 88, –90, –92*
Main entry: Graham, William Franklin

Graham, Billy 1918- *BioIn 13, BioNews 74, BlueB 76, CelR, –90, ChhPo S1, ConAu X, ConHero 1, CurBio 51, –73, EncSoB SUP, IntWW 74, –75, –76, –77, –78, –79, –80, –81, –82, –83, McGEWB, News 92, –92-1, OxCAmH, RComAH, WebAB 74, –79, Who 74, –82, –83, –85, WhoAm 74, –76, –78, –92, –94, WhoRel 92, WrDr 80, –82, –84, –86, –88, –90, –92, –94*

Graham, Bob *AuBYP 3*

Graham, Bob 1936- *BioIn 14, –15, –16*

Graham, Bob 1942- *BioIn 17, ChlLR 31, SmATA 63, TwCChW 89, WrDr 90, –92, –94*

Graham, Brenda Knight 1942- *BioIn 14, ConAu 103, SmATA 32*

Graham, Charlotte *SmATA X*
Main entry: Bowden, Joan Chase

Graham, Clarence R 1907- *AuBYP 2, BiDrLUS 70, BioIn 2, –3, –7, CurBio 50, WhoAm 74, –76, –78, –80, WhoLibI 82, WhoSSW 73, –75, –76*

Graham, Clarence R 1907-1989 *BioIn 16*

Graham, Clarence Reginald 1907-1989 *AuBYP 3*

Graham, Edward Harrison 1902- *Au&Wr 71, BioIn 5, –7*

Graham, Edward Henry 1935- *WhoAmL 94*

Graham, Eleanor 1896-1984 *Au&Wr 71, BioIn 8, –12, –15, ChhPo, –S1, –S2, ConAu 73, –112, OxCChiL, SmATA 18, –38N, TwCChW 78, –83, –89, WhoChL, WrDr 80, –82, –84*

Graham, Frank 1894-1965 *AmAu&B, BioIn 7, WhAm 4*

Graham, Frank, Jr. 1925- *AuBYP 2, –3, BioIn 8, –11, ConAu 9R, –4NR, IntAu&W 91, WhoE 74, –75, WrDr 76, –80, –82, –84, –86, –88, –90, –92, –94*

Graham, Gail *DcAmChF 1960*

Graham, Harry 1874-1936 *TwCChW 89*

Graham, Harry Jocelyn Clive 1874-1936 *BioIn 8, ChhPo, –S1, –S2, CnMWL, EncMT, EvLB, LongCTC, NewC, NotNAT B, OxCChiL, TwCChW 83, WhoChL, WhoLA*

Graham, Helen Holland *AuBYP 2, –3, BioIn 8*

Graham, John 1926- *BioIn 11, ConAu 33R, DrAS 74E, –78E, –82E, SmATA 11, WrDr 76, –80, –82, –84, –86, –88, –90, –92, –94*

Graham, John 1933- *IntWWE*

Graham, Jory 1925-1983 *AnObit 1983, BioIn 11, –12, –13, ConAu 29R, –109, –13NR, WhoAmW 74, –75, –83, WhoMW 74*

Graham, Kennon *BioIn 13, ConAu X, SmATA X*
Main entry: Harrison, David Lee

Graham, Larry *SmATA X*
Main entry: Graham, Lawrence Otis

Graham, Lawrence 1962- *SmATA 63*

Graham, Lawrence Otis 1962-
Pseud./variant:
Graham, Larry

Graham, Lorenz d1989 *NewYTBS 89*

Graham, Lorenz 1902- *AuBYP 3, BlkAuII, BlkWr 1, ConAu 25NR, DcLB 76, SmATA 5AS, TwCChW 89, WrDr 86, –88, –90*

Graham, Lorenz 1902-1989 *BlkAuII 92, ConAu 129, SmATA 63*

Graham, Lorenz B 1902- *BioIn 15, ChlLR 10*

Graham, Lorenz B 1902-1989 *BioIn 16, -17*

Graham, Lorenz Bell 1902- *AuBYP 2S, BioIn 9, -10, BlkAWP, ChlLR 10, ConAu 9R, DcAmChF 1960, InB&W 80, -85, IntAu&W 77, LivgBAA, MorBMP, REnAL, SelBAAf, SelBAAu, SmATA 2, SouBlCW, ThrBJA, TwCChW 78, -83, WhoBlA 75, -77, -80, -85, -88, WrDr 80, -82, -84*

Graham, Lorenz Bell 1902-1989 *MajAI, SmATA 74, TwCYAW, WhoBlA 90N*

Graham, Margaret Bloy 1920- *AmPB, BioIn 5, -6, -8, -11, -14, IlsCB 1946, -1957, -1967, MorJA, SmATA 11, WhoAmA 78, -80, -82, -84, -86, -89*

Graham, Robert *ConAu X, CurBio 86, EncSF 93, ScF&FL 92, TwCSFW 86, -91, WrDr 80, -82, -84, -86, -88, -90, -92*
Main entry: Haldeman, Joe

Graham, Robin Lee 1949- *BioIn 8, -9, -10, -13, ConAu 49, SmATA 7*

Graham, Shirley *BlkWr 1, BlkWrNE, SmATA X*

Graham, Shirley 1896-1977 *DcLB 76*

Graham, Shirley 1906-1977 *BioIn 14, -16, -17*

Graham, Shirley 1907-1977 *AmWomPl, AuBYP 3, InB&W 85, InWom SUP, NegAl 89*

Graham, Shirley Lola 1906-1977 *BlkAuII, -92*

Graham, Shirley Lola 1907?-1977 *AmAu&B, AuBYP 2, BioIn 1, -4, -6, -8, -11, -12, -13, BlkAWP, BkCL, ConAu X, CurBio 46, -77N, InB&W 80, LivgBAA, MorJA, NegAl 83, SelBAAf, SelBAAu, Str&VC, TwCA SUP, WhAm 7, WhoAm 74, -76, WhoAmW 74, WhoBlA 75, -77*
Pseud./variant:
Dubois, Shirley Graham

Graham, William F 1918- *IntAu&W 91*

Graham, William Franklin *IntvTCA 2*

Graham, William Franklin 1918- *AmAu&B, BioIn 2, -3, -4, -5, -6, -7, -8, -9, -10, -11, -12, ChhPo S1, ConAu 9R, -20NR, -42NR, CurBio 51, -73, EncAB-H, EncSoH, IntAu&W 77, IntWW 74, -75, -76, -77, -78, -79, -80, -81, -82, -83, -89, -91, RAdv 13-4, WebAB 74, Who 74, -82, -83, -85, -88, -90, -92, WhoAm 74, -76, -78, -80, -82, -84, -86, -88, -90, -92, -94, WhoRel 75, -77, -92, WhoWor 74, -78, WorAl*
Pseud./variant:
Graham, Billy

Graham-Barber, Lynda *BioIn 15*

Graham-Barber, Lynda 1944- *ConAu 113, SmATA 42*

Graham-Cameron, M
Main entry: Graham-Cameron, Malcolm Gordon

Graham-Cameron, M G 1931- *ConAu 123, SmATA 53*

Graham-Cameron, Malcolm Gordon 1931- *SmATA 45*
Pseud./variant:
Graham-Cameron, M
Graham-Cameron, Mike

Graham-Cameron, Mike
Main entry: Graham-Cameron, Malcolm Gordon

Grahame, Kenneth 1859-1932 *AnCL, AtlBL, AuBYP 2, -3, Benet 87, BioIn 1, -2, -3, -5, -6, -7, -8, -9, -11, -12, -14, BkCL, CamGLE, CarSB, CasWL, Chambr 3, ChhPo, -S1, ChlLR 5, CmScLit, CnMWL, ConAu 108, -136, CyWA 58, DcLB 34, DcLEL, DcNaB 1931, EvLB, FamSYP, GrBr, JBA 34, LongCTC, MajAI, ModBrL, NewC, OxCChiL, OxCEng 67, -85, PenC ENG, REn, RfGEnL 91, ScF&FL 92, StaCVF, Str&VC, TelT, TwCA, -SUP, TwCChW 78, -83, -89, TwCWr, WhDW, WhoChL, WorAlBi, WorAl, WrChl, YABC 1*

Grainger, Francis Edward 1857-1924 *EncMys*

Gramatky, Hardie 1907-1979 *AmAu&B, AmPB, AnCL, AuBYP 2, -3, Au&ICB, AuNews 1, BioIn 1, -2, -5, -7, -8, -9, -10, -13, -14, BioNews 74, BlueB 76, BkP, ChlLR 22, ConAu 1R, -85, -3NR, DcLB 22, IlrAm 1880, -E, IlsCB 1744, -1946, -1957, -1967, JBA 51, MajAI, OxCChiL, SmATA 1, -23N, -30, Str&VC, TwCChW 78, -83, -89, WhAm 7, WhAmArt 85, WhoAm 74, -76, WhoAmA 73, -78, -80N, -82N, -86N, -89N, -91N, WhoWor 74, WorECar, WrDr 80*

Grambling, Lois G 1927- *SmATA 71*

Gramet, Charles *AuBYP 2, -3, BioIn 8, ConAu 1R*

Grammer, June Amos 1927- *BioIn 16, SmATA 58*

Granbeck, Marilyn 1927- *ConAu 77*
Pseud./variant:
Carter, Nick

Granberg, Wilber J 1906- *ConAu 5R*

Grand, Samuel 1912- *ConAu 107, SmATA 42, WhoAmJ 80, WhoWorJ 72, –78*

Granda, Julio *IlsBYP*

Grandville, J J *ConGrA 3*
Main entry: Gerard, Jean Ignace I

Grandville, J J 1803-1847 *OxCChiL, SmATA X*

Grandville, Jean Ignace I Gerard
Main entry: Gerard, Jean Ignace I

Grandville, Jean Ignace I Gerard 1803-1847 *DcBiPP, SmATA X*

Grange, Peter *ConAu X, ConNov 72, –76, –82, DcLEL 1940, IntAu&W 77X, –91X, SmATA 5, TwCRHW 90, WrDr 76, –80, –82, –84, –86, –88, –90, –92*
Main entry: Nicole, Christopher Robin

Grange, Peter 1930- *WrDr 94*

Granger, Helen *DcChlFi*

Granger, Margaret Jane *AuBYP 3*

Granger, Margaret Jane 1925?-1977 *BioIn 11, –13, ConAu 104, SmATA 27N*
Pseud./variant:
Granger, Peg
Granger, Peggy

Granger, Peg
Main entry: Granger, Margaret Jane

Granger, Peg 1925?-1977 *AuBYP 2S, –3*

Granger, Peggy
Main entry: Granger, Margaret Jane

Granick, Harry 1898- *ConAu 85, ConTFT 4, NatPD 77, –81*
Pseud./variant:
Taylor, Harry

Granstaff, Bill 1925- *BioIn 11, SmATA 10*

Grant, Alistair *Who 88, –90, –92*

Grant, Alistair 1925- *ArtsCL, BioIn 4, –6, DcBrAr 1, DcCAr 81, TwCPaSc*

Grant, Bruce 1893-1977 *AuBYP 2, –3, BioIn 2, –7, –10, –11, –13, ConAu 1R, –69, –6NR, SmATA 5, –25N*

Grant, Bruce 1925- *WrDr 86, –88, –90, –92*

Grant, Bruce Alexander 1925- *WrDr 94*

Grant, Cynthia D *DrAPF 87, –89, –91, –93*

Grant, Cynthia D 1950- *BioIn 14, ConAu 104, –20NR, –42NR, DrAPF 83, –85, SmATA 33, –77, TwCYAW*

Grant, Elizabeth Brubaker 1917- *WhoSSW 73*

Grant, Eva 1907- *AuBYP 2S, –3, BioIn 9, –10, ConAu 49, SmATA 7, WhoAmW 77*

Grant, Evva H 1913-1977 *BioIn 13, ConAu 104, –107, SmATA 27N, WhAm 7, WhoAm 80*

Grant, George Monro 1835-1902 *Alli SUP BenetAL 91, BbD, BbtC, BiD&SB, BioIn 12, –17, DcLB 99, DcLEL, DcNaB S2, DcNAA, OxCCan, OxCCanL*

Grant, Gordon Hope d1962 *WhoAmA 86N*

Grant, Gordon Hope 1875-1962 *AmAu&B, ArtsAmW 3, BioIn 1, –3, –5, –6, –13, ConAu 102, CurBio 53, –62, DcSeaP, GrAmP, IlrAm 1880, –C, IlsCB 1744, –1946, ObitOF 79, SmATA 25, WhAm 4, WhAmArt 85, WhoAmA 78N, –80N, –82N –89N, –91N, WorECar*

Grant, Gwen 1940- *BioIn 16, ConAu 22NR, ScF&FL 92, SmATA 47*

Grant, Gwendoline Ellen 1940- *ChlFicS*

Grant, J B 1940- *ConAu 57, –6NR, –28NR, WhoUSWr 88, WhoWrEP 89, –92*

Grant, Leigh 1947- *IlsBYP, SmATA 10*

Grant, Madeleine Parker 1895- *AuBYP 2, –3, BioIn 8, ConAu 73*

Grant, Matthew *AuBYP 3*

Grant, Matthew G *ConAu X, SmATA X*
Main entry: May, Julian

Grant, Maxwell *ConAu X, EncSF 93, IntAu&W 91X, ScF&FL 92, SmATA X, TwCCr&M 91, WrDr 86*
Main entry: Lynds, Dennis

Grant, Maxwell 1924- *WrDr 94*

Grant, Myrna 1934- *BioIn 12, ConAu 53, –4NR, SmATA 21*

Grant, Neil 1938- *BioIn 12, ConAu 33R, –15NR, –34NR, SmATA 14, WrDr 76, –80, –82, –84, –86, –88, –90, –92, –94*
Pseud./variant:
Mountfield, David

Grater, Michael 1923- *BioIn 16, SmATA 57*

Gravel, Fern *SmATA X*
Main entry: Hall, James Norman

Graves, Charles Parlin 1911-1972 *AuBYP 2, -3, BioIn 8, -9, ConAu 5R, -37R, -4NR, SmATA 4*
Pseud./variant:
Parlin, John

Graves, John 1920- *ConAu 13R, -9NR, DcLB Y83B, TwCWW 91, WrDr 92, -94*

Graves, John Alexander 1920- *WhoWrEP 92*

Graves, Richard H *DcChlFi*

Graves, Robert *IntvTCA 2*

Graves, Robert 1895- *BritWr 7, CamGEL, ModBrL S2, ScFSB*

Graves, Robert 1895-1985 *AnObit 1985, AnCL, AuBYP 2, -3, Au&Wr 71, Benet 87, BioIn 1, -2, -4, -5, -6, -7, -8, -9, -10, -11, -12, -13, -14, -15, -16, -17, BlmGEL, BlueB 76, BritWr 7, CamGLE, CasWL, Chambr 3, ChhPo, -S1, -S2, CnDBLB 6, CnE&AP, CnMWL, ConAu 5R, -117, -5NR, -36NR, ConLC 1, -2, -6, -11, -39, -45, ConLCrt 77, -82, ConNov 72, -76, -82, ConPo 70, -75, -80, -85, CurBio 78, -86N, CyWA 58, -89, DcLB 20, -100, -Y85N, DcLEL, EncWL, -2, EngPo, EvLB, IntAu&W 82, IntWW 74, -79, -80, -81, -82, -83, LiExTwC, LongCEL, LongCTC, MagSWL, MajTwCW, MakMC, ModBrL, -S1, -S2, NewC, NewYTBS 85, Novels, OxCChiL, OxCEng 67, -85, PenC ENG, PoeCrit 6, RAdv 1, -13-1, REn, RfGEnL 91, ScF&FL 92, SmATA 45, TwCA, -SUP, TwCRHW 90, TwCWr, WebE&AL, WhDW, WhAm 9, Who 74, -82, -83, -85, WhoTwCL, WhoWor 74, -82, -84, WorAlBi, WorAl, WrDr 76, -80, -82, -84, WrPh*

Graves, Robert Von Ranke 1895-1985 *EncSF 93*

Graves, Susan Bernard 1933- *ConAu 41R*

Graves, William *AuBYP 2S, -3*

Graves, William P E 1926- *WhoE 93*

Gray, A A, Miss *CarSB, ChhPo*

Gray, Alice *AuBYP 3*

Gray, Alice 1914- *AuBYP 2, BioIn 8, WhoAmW 74*

Gray, Anne 1931- *ConAu 65, -9NR*

Gray, Berkeley *EncMys*

Gray, Charles A 1938- *AmMWSc 73P, -82, -86, -89, -92, ConAu 17R, WrDr 76*

Gray, Charles Agustus 1938- *WhoAm 92, -94*

Gray, Clarence 1902-1957 *ArtCS*

Gray, Elizabeth Janet *AmAu&B, AnCL, AuBYP 2, ConAu X, CurBio 43, JBA 34, -51, MajAI, NewbMB 1922, SmATA 6, TwCChW 78, -83, -89, TwCYAW, WrDr 80, -82, -84, -86, -88, -90, -92*
Main entry: Vining, Elizabeth Gray

Gray, Elizabeth Janet 1902- *AuBYP 3, InWom SUP, OxCChiL, WrDr 94*

Gray, Genevieve S 1920- *BioIn 9, ConAu 33R, SmATA 4*
Pseud./variant:
Gray, Jenny

Gray, George Hugh 1922- *ConAu 17R, -7NR*
Pseud./variant:
Gray, Tony

Gray, Harold d1968 *WhoAmA 86N*

Gray, Harold 1894-1968 *AmAu&B, ArtCS, BenetAL 91, BioIn 7, -8, -10, -13, -14, -17, ConAu 107, EncACom, REnAL, SmATA 32, -33, WebAB 74, WhAm 5, WhAmArt 85, WhNAA, WhoAmA 78N, -80N, -82N, -89N, -91N*

Gray, Jenny *ConAu X, SmATA 4*
Main entry: Gray, Genevieve S

Gray, Lee Learner 1924- *AuBYP 2S, -3, ConAu 73*

Gray, Marian *ConAu X, SmATA X*
Main entry: Pierce, Edith Gray

Gray, Nicholas Stuart 1922-1981 *AnObit 1981, AuBYP 2S, -3, BioIn 9, -10, -13, ConAu 21R, -103, -11NR, IntAu&W 77, OxCChiL, PiP, ScF&FL 92, SmATA 4, -27N, TwCChW 78, -83, -89, WhScrn 83, WhoThe 72, -77, -81, WrDr 76, -80, -82*

Gray, Nigel 1941- *ConAu 85, SmATA 33*

Gray, Noel 1898-1983 *BioIn 16, SmATA 47*

Gray, Noel 1926- *DrAS 74H, -78H, -82H*

Gray, Patricia *AuBYP 3*

Gray, Patricia Clark *AuBYP 2, BioIn 8, -10, ConAu 29R, SmATA 7*
Pseud./variant:
Clark, Virginia

Gray, Patsey *AuBYP 3*

Gray, Robert *AuBYP 2S, -3*

Gray, Rockwell 1912- *WhoAm 74*

Gray, Tony *Au&Wr 71, ConAu X, DcIrW 1, WrDr 76, –80, –82, –84*
Main entry: Gray, George Hugh

Gray, Tony 1922- *BiDIrW, IntAu&W 91, WrDr 86, –88, –90, –92, –94*

Gray, William David 1916- *AmMWSc 86, –89, –92*

Gray, William Douglas 1941- *WhoAmL 92*

Gray, William Dudley 1912- *AmMWSc 76P, –82, IndAu 1917*

Graydon, William Murray 1864-1946 *CarSB*

Grayland, Valerie Merle *Au&Wr 71, BioIn 10, ConAu 9R, IntAu&W 77, –82, SmATA 7, WhoWor 78, WrDr 76, –80, –82*
Pseud./variant:
Belvedere, Lee
Subond, Valerie

Grayson, David *AmAu&B, AmLY X, AmPeW, BenetAL 91, ChhPo S2, ConAmL, CurBio 40, –46, DcLEL, DcNAA, EncAB-H, EvLB, LongCTC, OxCAmL 65, –83, REnAL, TwCA, –SUP, WebAB 74, –79, WhNAA*
Main entry: Baker, Ray Stannard

Grayson, David 1870-1946 *BioIn 15, –16, –17*

Grayson, Marion 1906-1976 *AuBYP 3*

Grayson, Marion F 1906-1976 *AuBYP 2, BioIn 8, ConAu 5R, –69, –4NR*

Grazia, Thomas Di *IlsBYP*
Main entry: DiGrazia, Thomas

Great Comte, The *ConAu X, SmATA X*

Great Comte, The
Main entry: Hawkesworth, Eric William

Greatorex, Wilfred *ConDr 88C, EncSF 93*

Greatorex, Wilfred 1921- *Au&Wr 71, ConAu 103, ConDr 73, –77C, –82C*

Greaves, Griselda *ChhPo S2*

Greaves, Margaret 1914- *AuBYP 2S, –3, Au&Wr 71, BioIn 10, ChlFicS, ConAu 25R, –18NR, IntAu&W 91, ScF&FL 92, SmATA 7, TwCChW 78, –83, –89, WrDr 76, –80, –82, –84, –86, –88, –90, –92, –94*

Greaves, Nick 1955- *SmATA 77*

Gree, Alain 1936- *BioIn 13, SmATA 28, WhoWor 82*
Pseud./variant:
Farge, Monique

Greeley, Andrew M 1928- *MajTwCW, ScF&FL 92, TwCCr&M 91, WorAlBi*

Greeley, Andrew Moran 1928- *AmCath 80, AmMWSc 73S, –78S, BioIn 9, –10, –11, –12, –13, ConAu 5R, –7NR, –43NR, ConLC 28, CurBio 72, EncSF 93, LEduc 74, NewYTBS 81, –82, –84, WhoAm 74, –76, –78, –80, –82, –84, –86, –88, –92, –94, WhoMW 90, –92, –93, WhoRel 77, –92, WhoUSWr 88, WhoWrEP 89, –92, WorAu 1975, WrDr 80*

Green, Adam *BenetAL 91, ConAu X, MajAI, REnAL, SmATA 2, –X*
Main entry: Weisgard, Leonard Joseph

Green, Anne Canevari *BioIn 17*

Green, Anne Canevari 1943- *SmATA 62*

Green, Barbara *AuBYP 2S, –3*

Green, D *ConAu X, SmATA 4*
Main entry: Casewit, Curtis

Green, D H 1922- *WrDr 90*

Green, Dennis Howard 1922- *WrDr 94*

Green, Elisabeth Sara 1940- *ConAu 42NR, WrDr 76, –80, –82, –84*

Green, Elizabeth Shippen *BioIn 3, ChhPo ClaDrA, ConICB, DcWomA, IlrAm 1880 –A, WhAmArt 85, WomWWA 14*
Pseud./variant:
Elliott, Elizabeth Shippen G

Green, Elizabeth Shippen 1871-1954 *BioIn 15, InWom SUP*

Green, Evelyn Everett *ConAu X, OxCChiL*
Main entry: Everett-Green, Evelyn

Green, Evelyn Everett 1856-1932 *InWom SUP, WomNov*

Green, Fitzhugh 1888-1947 *AmAu&B, BioIn 2, CarSB, DcNAA, ScFEYrs, WhAm 2, WhNAA*

Green, Hannah *BioIn 9, –12, –13, ConAu X, –32NR, DrAF 76, SmATA X, TwCYAW, WorAu 1975*
Main entry: Greenberg, Joanne Goldenberg

Green, Hannah 1932- *InWom SUP*

Green, Jane 1937- *AuBYP 2S, –3, BioIn 1?, ConAu 61, SmATA 9*

Green, Kathleen *AuBYP 2S, –3*

Green, Margaret 1926- *AuBYP 3*

Greene, Mrs *CarSB*

Greene, A C 1923- *BioIn 17, ConAu 37R, -14NR, IntAu&W 77, -91, WhoAm 74, -76, -78, -80, -82, WrDr 76, -80, -82, -84, -86, -88, -90, -92, -94*

Greene, Alma *OxCCan SUP*

Greene, Bette *DrAPF 87, -89, -91, -93*

Greene, Bette 1934- *Au&Arts 7, AuBYP 2S, -3, BioIn 11, -14, -15, -16, ChlLR 2, ConAu 53, -4NR, ConLC 30, DcAmChF 1960, FifBJA, MajAI, OxCChiL, SmATA 8, -16AS, TwCChW 78, -83, -89, TwCYAW, WhoAm 78, -80, -82, -84, -86, -88, WhoAmJ 80, WhoUSWr 88, WhoWrEP 89, -92, WrDr 76, -80, -82, -84, -86, -88, -90, -92, -94*

Greene, Carla 1916- *AuBYP 2, -3, BioIn 7, -9, ConAu 1R, -1NR, ForWC 70, IntAu&W 77, SmATA 1, -67, WhoAm 78, -80, -82, -84, -86, -88, -90, WhoUSWr 88, WhoWrEP 89, -92, WrDr 76, -80, -82, -84*

Greene, Carol *AuBYP 3, ConAu 134, SmATA 44, -66, WrDr 94*

Greene, Constance C 1924- *Au&Arts 7, AuBYP 2S, -3, BioIn 11, ConAu 61, -8NR, FourBJA, IntAu&W 91, SmATA 11, -11AS, TwCChW 78, -83, -89, WrDr 80, -82, -84, -86, -88, -90, -92*

Greene, Constance Clarke 1924- *ConAu 38NR, DcAmChF 1960, MajAI, SmATA 72, WrDr 94*

Greene, Ellin 1927- *AuBYP 2S, -3, BioIn 13, ConAu 77, IntAu&W 82, SmATA 23, WhoLibI 82, WhoLibS 66, WhoMW 86*

Greene, Frances Nimmo *AmAu&B, BiDSA, CarSB, WomWWA 14*

Greene, Frances Nimmo 1850-1921 *WomNov*

Greene, Graham *IntvTCA 2*

Greene, Graham d1991 *Who 92N*

Greene, Graham 1904- *AuBYP 2S, -3, AuNews 2, Au&Wr 71, Benet 87, BiE&WWA, BioIn 1, -2, -3, -4, -5, -6, -7, -8, -9, -10, -11, -12, -13, -14, -15, -16, BioNews 74, BlueB 76, BritWr S1, CamGEL, CamGLE, CamGWoT, CasWL, CathA 1930, CelR, ChhPo S2, CnMD, CnMWL, CnThe, ConAu 13R, ConDr 73, -77, -82, -88, ConLC 1, -3, -6, -9, -18, -27, -37, ConNov 72, -76, -82, -86, CorpD, CrtSuMy, CroCD, CurBio 69, CyWA 58, -89, DcLB 13, -15, -77, -100, -Y85A, EncMys, EncWL, -2, EncWT, FilmgC, HalFC 84, -88, IntAu&W 77, -89, IntWW 74, -75, -76, -77, -78, -79, -80, -81, -82, -83, -89, LiExTwC, LongCTC, MajTwCW, MakMC, McGEWB, McGEWD 72, -84, ModBrL, -S1, -S2, ModWD, NewC, NewYTBE 71, NewYTBS 85, NotNAT, -A, Novels, OxCChiL, OxCEng 67, -85, OxCFilm, OxCThe 67, -83, PenC ENG, PlP&P, RAdv 1, -13-1, REn, ShSWr, SmATA 20, SpyFic, TwCA, -SUP, TwCChW 78, TwCCr&M 80, -85, -91, TwCWr, WebE&AL, WhDW, Who 74, -82, -83, -85, -88, -90, WhoAm 80, -82, -84, -86, -88, -90, WhoChL, WhoSpyF, WhoThe 72, -77, -81, WhoTwCL, WhoWor 74, -78, -80, -82, -84, -87, -89, -91, WorAlBi, WorAl, WorEFlm, WrDr 76, -80, -82, -84, -86, -88, -90, WrPh*

Greene, Graham 1904-1991 *AnObit 1991, BioIn 17, CnDBLB 7, ConAu 133, -35NR, ConDr 93, ConLC 70, -72, CurBio 91N DcLB Y91N, IntWW 91, -91N, MagSWL, NewYTBS 91, News 91, RfGEnL 91, ScF&FL 92, WhAm 10, WorLitC*

Greene, Howard Rodger 1937- *ConAu 61 WhoE 77, -81*

Greene, Howard Roger 1937- *WhoE 93*

Greene, Hugh Carleton 1910- *WhoWor 87*

Greene, Hugh Carleton 1910-1987 *CurBio 87N*

Greene, Hugh Carleton, Sir d1987 *NewYTBS 87, Who 88N*

Greene, Hugh Carleton, Sir 1910- *BioIn 6, -7, ConAu 102, CurBio 63, IntAu&W 77, IntWW 74, -75, -76, -77, -78, Who 74, WhoAm 74, WhoWor 74, -84, WrDr 80*

Greene, Hugh Carleton, Sir 1910-1987 *WhAm 9*

Greene, Jacqueline Dembar 1946- *SmATA 76*

Greene, Laura 1935- *ConAu 107, -23NR, SmATA 38*

Greene, Lee Seifert 1905- *AmMWSc 73S, -78S, ConAu 13R, -5NR, WhoAm 74, -76, -78, -80, -82, -84, -86*

Greene, Lee Seifert 1905-1986 *WhAm 9*

Greene, Wade 1933- *AuBYP 2S, -3, BioIn 9, -11, SmATA 11*

Greene, Yvonne
Main entry: Flesch, Yolande

Greenebaum, Louise G *InWom SUP*

Greenebaum, Louise Guggenheim 1919- *ConAu 69*

Greener, Leslie 1900-1974 *DcChlFi*

Greenfeld, Howard *AuBYP 2S, –3, BioIn 10, –12, ConAu 81, –19NR, SmATA 19*

Greenfeld, Josh 1928- *SmATA 62, WhoEnt 92*

Greenfeld, Joshua Joseph 1928- *ConAu 140*

Greenfield, Eloise 1929- *ArtclWW 2, BioIn 10, –12, –16, –17, BlkAWP, BlkAuII, –92, BlkWr 1, –2, ChlLR 4, ConAu 49, –1NR, –19NR, DcAmChF 1960, FifBJA, InB&W 80, –85, IntAu&W 77, –82, LivgBAA, MajAI, SelBAAf, SelBAAu, SmATA 19, –61, –16AS, TwCChW 83, –89, WhoAm 92, WhoBlA 77, –80, –85, –88, –90, –92, WrDr 76, –80, –82, –84, –86, –88, –90, –92*

Greenfield, Jeff *LesBEnT 92*

Greenfield, Jeff 1943- *BioIn 8, –10, ConAu 37R, –24NR, EncTwCJ, WhoAm 94*

Greenhaus, Thelma Nurenberg *AuBYP 3*

Greenhaus, Thelma Nurenberg 1903-1984 *BioIn 15, ConAu 113, –42NR, SmATA 45*
Pseud./variant:
Nurenberg, Thelma

Greenhaus, Thelma Nurnberg 1903?-1984 *BioIn 14*

Greenhood, David 1895-1983 *BioIn 13, ConAu 1R, –109*
Pseud./variant:
Sawyer, Mark

Greenidge, Edwin *AuBYP 3*

Greenidge, Edwin 1929- *AuBYP 2S, LivgBAA*

Greening, Hamilton *ConAu X, –29NR, SmATA X*

Greenleaf, Barbara Kaye 1942- *BioIn 10, ConAu 29R, SmATA 6, WhoAmW 75, –77*

Greenleaf, Margery *AuBYP 2S, –3*

Greenleaf, Peter 1910- *ConAu 85, SmATA 33*

Greenlee, Sharon 1935- *SmATA 77*

Greenlee, William Purdy 1928- *DrAS 74P, –78P, –82P, WhoSSW 73*

Greenspan, Sophie 1906- *ConAu 97*

Greenspun, Adele Aron 1938- *SmATA 76*
Pseud./variant:
Schwarz, Adele Aron

Greenwald, Sheila *BioIn 8, –11, ChhPo, ConAu X, –39NR, FifBJA, IlsBYP, IlsCB 1957, SmATA 8*
Main entry: Green, Sheila Ellen

Greenwald, Sheila 1934- *AuBYP 3, TwCYAW*

Greenwald, Sheila Ellem 1934- *WhoE 91*

Greenwald, Sheila Ellen 1934- *WhoAm 94, WhoAmA 86*

Greenwood, Edward Alister 1930- *ConAu 29R, –12NR, –30NR*
Pseud./variant:
Greenwood, Ted

Greenwood, James 1832-1929 *Alli SUP, DcEnL, TelT*

Greenwood, Marianne Hederstrom 1926- *ConAu 9R*

Greenwood, Ted *ConAu 30NR*
Main entry: Greenwood, Edward Alister

Greenwood, Ted 1930- *BioIn 12, ConAu X, DcChlFi, FourBJA, IlsCB 1967, IntAu&W 91, OxCChiL, TwCChW 78, –83, –89, WrDr 80, –82, –84, –86, –88, –90, –92, –94*

Greer, Michael 1917- *CelR*

Greer, Richard *MajAI*

Greer, Terence 1929- *ArtsCL, BioIn 6*

Greet, W Cabell 1901-1972 *BioIn 9, NewYTBE 72*

Greey, Edward 1835-1888 *Alli SUP, BbD, BiD&SB, CarSB, DcAmAu, DcNAA*

Gregg, Charles T 1927- *BioIn 17, SmATA 65*

Gregg, Charles Thornton 1927- *AmMWSc 86, –89, –92, ConAu 40NR, WhoAm 90, –92, –94*

Gregg, Ernest *BlkAWP*

Gregg, James R 1914- *AmMWSc 73P, –76P, –82, –86, –89, –92, ConAu 21R*

Gregg, Martin *ConAu X, –28NR*

Gregg, Martin d1992 *NewYTBS 92*

Gregg, Mary Kirby 1817-1893 *CarSB*

Gregg, Walter Harold 1919- *BioIn 12, ConAu 73, SmATA 20*

Gregor, Arthur *DrAPF 87, –89, –91, –93*

Gregor, Arthur 1923- *BioIn 13, ConAu 25R, –10AS, –11NR, ConLC 9, ConPo 70, –75, –80, –85, –91, DrAP 75, IntAu&W 77, LiExTwC, SmATA 36, WhoAm 74, –76, –78, –80, –82, –84, –86, –88, –90, WhoAmJ 80, WhoE 83, WhoUSWr 88, WhoWrEP 89, –92,*

WorAu 1980, WrDr 76, –82, –84, –86, –88, –90, –92, –94

Gregor, Elmer Russell 1878-1954 *AmAu&B, BioIn 3, WhAm 3, WhNAA*

Gregori, Leon 1919- *BioIn 12, SmATA 15*

Gregorian, Joyce Ballou 1946- *BioIn 14, ConAu 107, –24NR, SmATA 30*

Gregorian, Joyce Ballou 1946-1991 *ScF&FL 92*

Gregorich, Barbara 1943- *ConAu 42NR, SmATA 66*

Gregorowski, Christopher 1940- *BioIn 14, ConAu 15NR, SmATA 30*

Gregory, Diana 1933- *ConAu 97, SmATA 42, –49*

Gregory, Dorothy Lake 1893- *BioIn 5, –9, DcWomA, WhAmArt 85*

Gregory, Horace 1898-1982 *AmAu&B, AnObit 1982, Benet 87, BenetAL 91, BioIn 4, –5, –9, –12, –13, –15, –17, CamGLE, CamHAL, ChhPo, –S1, –S2, CnDAL, ConAmA, ConAu 5R, –106, –3NR, –22NR, ConPo 70, –75, –80, DcLB 48, DcLEL, DrAP 75, IntWW 74, ModAL, NewYTBS 82, OxCAmL 65, –83, PenC AM, RAdv 1, REn, REnAL, RfGAmL 87, SixAP, TwCA, –SUP, WhoAm 74, WhoE 74, WhoWor 74, WrDr 76, –80, –82*

Gregory, James S 1912-1983 *ConAu 133*

Gregory, James Stothert 1912- *Au&Wr 71, ConAu 77, IntAu&W 82, WrDr 76, –80, –82, –84, –86, –88, –90*

Gregory, Jean *MajAI*
Main entry: Ure, Jean

Gregory, Kristiana 1951- *ConAu 141, SmATA 74*

Gregory, Peter Ronald 1947- *BioIn 12, IlsCB 1967*

Gregory, Stephan *ConAu X, IntAu&W 91X, WrDr 86, –88, –90, –92*
Main entry: Pendleton, Don

Gregory, Stephan 1927- *WrDr 94*

Gregory, Stephen *ConAu X, –35NR, SmATA X*
Main entry: Penzler, Otto

Greiner, James Duane 1933- *WhoWest 76, –78*

Greisman, Joan Ruth 1937- *ConAu 103, SmATA 31*

Gremmels, Marion Chapman 1924- *AuBYP 3*

Gremmels, Marion Louise Chapman 1924- *AuBYP 2S, ConAu 111, WhoAmW 74*

Gremmels, Marion Louise Chapman 1924-1987 *ConAu 142*

Grendon, Stephen *AuBYP 3, ConAu X, EncSF 93, SmATA 5*
Main entry: Derleth, August

Grenier, Mildred 1917- *ConAu 29R, –12NR*

Grenville, Pelham *ConAu 33NR, MajTwCW, SmATA X*

Gretz, Susanna 1937- *BioIn 10, ConAu 29R, –28NR, IlsCB 1967, SmATA 7*

Gretzer, John *BioIn 12, IlsBYP, SmATA 18*

Grey, Elizabeth *AuBYP 2, Au&Wr 71, ConAu X*
Main entry: Hogg, Beth

Grey, Elizabeth 1917- *AuBYP 3*

Grey, Elizabeth, Lady *InWom SUP*

Grey, Jerry 1926- *AmMWSc 73P, –82, –85, –89, –92, BioIn 11, ConAu 53, –5NR, –20NR, IntAu&W 89, IntWWE, SmATA 11, WhoAm 74, –76, –78, –80, –82, –84, –86, –88, –90, WhoE 74, –83, –91, WhoTech 82, –84, WhoWor 74, WrDr 82, –84, –86, –88, –90, –92, –94*

Grey, Vivian *ConAu 17R, ForWC 70*

Grey, Zane 1872-1939 *BioIn 14, –16, –17, CamGLE, CamHAL, ConAu 132, MajTwCW, RfGAmL 87, TwCWW 91*

Grey, Zane 1875?-1939 *AmAu&B, ArizL, Ballpl 90, Benet 87, BenetAL 91, BioIn 1, –2, –3, –4, –5, –6, –7, –8, –9, –10, –11, –12, –13, CmCal, ConAu 104, DcLB 9, DcLEL, DcNAA, EncFWF, EvLB, FilmgC, HalFC 84, –88, LongCTC, Novels, OhA&B, OxCAmL 65, –83, OxCAusL, PenC AM, REn, REnAL, TwCA, –SUP, TwCLC 6, TwCWr, WebAB 74, –79, WebE&AL, WhAm 1, WhNAA, WorAlBi, WorAl*

Grey, Zane 1950- *InB&W 85*

Grey Owl *BioIn 3, –6, –8, –9, –10, –11, –13, CanWr, ConAu X, CreCan 1, DcLEL, DcNAA, OxCCan, OxCCanL, OxCChiL, SmATA X, TwCChW 78, –83, WhoChL*
Main entry: Belaney, Archibald Stansfeld

Grey Owl 1888-1938 *BenetAL 91, BioIn 16, –17, ChlLR 32, DcLB 92, TwCChW 89*

Gri *BioIn 13, ConAu X, SmATA X*
Main entry: Denney, Diana

Gribble, Leonard Reginald 1908- *Au&Wr 71, ConAu 53, EncMys, IntAu&W 77, LongCTC, Who 74, –82, –83, –85*

Grice, Frederick 1910- *Au&Wr 71, BioIn 10, ConAu 9R, –3NR, IntAu&W 77, –82, SmATA 6, TwCChW 78, –83, WrDr 76, –80, –82, –84, –86*

Grice, Frederick 1910-1983 *TwCChW 89*

Grice, Mary *ChhPo S2*

Grider, Dorothy 1915- *BioIn 5, –14, ChhPo, IlsCB 1946, SmATA 31*
Pseud./variant:
Dottig
Fenwick, Patti

Gridley, Marion E 1906-1974 *AuBYP 3, BioIn 14*

Gridley, Marion Eleanor 1906-1974 *AuBYP 2S, BioIn 2, –13, ConAu 45, –103, ForWC 70, SmATA 26N, –35, WhAm 6, WhoAmW 75*

Grieder, Walter 1924- *BioIn 11, ConAu 41R, IntAu&W 77, SmATA 9*

Griego, Tony A 1955- *SmATA 77*

Grierson, Elizabeth Wilson d1943 *BioIn 2, ChhPo S2, JBA 34, –51*

Grierson, Francis 1848-1927 *AmAu&B, Au&Wr 71, BenetAL 91, BioIn 1, –5, –7, –16, DcNAA, OxCAmL 65, –83, REn, TwCA, –SUP*

Griese, Arnold Alfred 1921- *BioIn 11, ConAu 49, –1NR, LEduc 74, SmATA 9*

Grifalconi, Ann *ChlBIID*

Grifalconi, Ann 1929- *AuBYP 3, BioIn 8, –9, –12, BkP, ChhPo S1, ConAu 5R, –9NR, –35NR, ForWC 70, IlsBYP, IlsCB 1957, –1967, MajAI, SmATA 2, –66, –16AS, ThrBJA*

Griffen, Elizabeth *AuBYP 3*

Griffen, Elizabeth L *AuBYP 2S*

Griffin, Ella *AuBYP 2, –3, BioIn 8*

Griffin, Gillett Good 1928- *AuBYP 2, –3, BioIn 5, –7, –13, ChhPo, IlsCB 1946, SmATA 26*

Griffin, John Quely 1948- *ConAu 77*

Griffin, Judith Berry *AuBYP 2S, –3, BioIn 13, BlkAWP, BlkAull, –92, ConAu 108, SmATA 34*

Griffin, Peni R 1961- *ConAu 134, ScF&FL 92, SmATA 67*

Griffin, Peni Rae 1961- *WhoWrEP 89, –92, WrDr 94*

Griffin, Velma *AuBYP 2, –3, BioIn 8*

Griffis, William Elliot 1843-1928 *Alli SUP, AmAu, AmAu&B, AmLY, BbD, BiD&SB, BioIn 11, –16, CarSB, DcAmAu, DcNAA, EncAB-A 1, WhAm 1, WhNAA*

Griffith, Field *AuBYP 2S, –3*

Griffith, Helen V 1934- *ConAu 105, –22NR, SmATA 39, TwCChW 89, WhoWrEP 89, WrDr 90, –92*

Griffith, Helen Virginia 1934- *WhoWrEP 92, WrDr 94*

Griffith, Jeannette *ConAu X, SmATA 4*
Main entry: Eyerly, Jeannette Hyde

Griffiths, Aileen Esther *Au&Wr 71, WrDr 76*

Griffiths, Charles Tom Watson 1919- *Au&Wr 71, IntAu&W 77, WrDr 76, –80*

Griffiths, G D 1910-1973 *TwCChW 89*

Griffiths, Gordon Douglas 1910-1973 *Au&Wr 71, BioIn 12, ConAu P-2, SmATA 20N, TwCChW 78, –83*

Griffiths, Helen 1939- *AuBYP 2S, –3, BioIn 10, ConAu 17R, –7NR, –25NR, FourBJA, IntAu&W 82, –86, –89, –91, SmATA 5, –5AS, TwCChW 78, –83, –89, WrDr 80, –82, –84, –86, –88, –90, –92, –94*

Griffiths, Kitty Anna *ConAu 105*

Griffiths, Trevor 1935- *BioIn 10, –11, –12, –13, BlmGEL, CamGLE, CamGWoT, ConAu 97, ConDr 73, –77, –82, –88, –93, ConLC 13, –52, ConTFT 6, DcLB 13, DcLEL 1940, IntAu&W 77, –89, –91, IntDcT 2, IntWW 89, –91, McGEWD 84, Who 82, –83, –85, –88, –90, –92, WhoThe 77, –81, WrDr 76, –80, –82, –84, –86, –88, –90, –92, –94*

Griggs, Tamar 1941- *ConAu 77*

Grigson, Geoffrey 1905- *ModBrL S2, WrDr 86*

Grigson, Geoffrey 1905-1985 *AnObit 1985, AuBYP 3, BioIn 14, –17, CamGLE, ConAu 118, –20NR, –33NR, ConLC 39, EngPo, MajTwCW*

Grigson, Geoffrey Edward Harvey 1905- *AuBYP 2, Au&Wr 71, BioIn 2, –4, –8, ChhPo, –S1, –S2, ConAu 25R, ConLC 7,*

ConPo 70, –75, DcLEL, EvLB, IntAu&W 77, IntWW 74, –75, –76, –77, –78, LongCTC, ModBrL, –S1, NewC, OxCEng 85, PenC ENG, REn, TwCA SUP, Who 74, WhoTwCL, WhoWor 74, –78, WrDr 76, –80

Grigson, Geoffrey Edward Harvey 1905-1985 *DcNaB 1981*

Grigson, Jane 1928- *BioIn 13, ConAu 49, –1NR, –20NR, IntAu&W 77, –82, –86, –89, –91, SmATA 63, Who 82, –83, –85, –88, –90, WrDr 80, –82, –84, –86, –88, –90*

Grigson, Jane 1928-1990 *AnObit 1990, BioIn 16, –17, ConAu 131*

Grill, Nanette L 1935- *ConAu 65*

Grimes, Lee 1920- *BioIn 17, ConAu 37NR, SmATA 68*
Pseud./variant:
Dodge, Fremont

Grimes, Nikki *DrAPF 87, –89, –91, IntAu&W 86X*

Grimes, Nikki 1950- *BlkAWP, BlkAuII, –92, ConAu 77, DrAPF 83, –85, IntWWP 82X, WhoBlA 92, –94, WhoUSWr 88, WhoWrEP 89, –92*

Grimm, Cherry Barbara Lockett 1930- *ConAu 101, SmATA 43, WrDr 84*
Pseud./variant:
Wilder, Cherry

Grimm, Jacob 1785-1863 *BioIn 15, –16, –17, BlmGEL, DcLB 90, MagSWL, OxCGer 86, RAdv 13-2, WrChl*

Grimm, Jacob Ludwig Karl 1785-1863 *MajAI, RfGShF*

Grimm, Jakob Ludwig Karl 1785-1863 *AnCL, AtlBL, AuBYP 2, –3, BbD, BiD&SB, BioIn 1, –3, –6, –7, –8, –9, –12, –13, CarSB, CasWL, CelCen, ChhPo, DcBiPP, DcEuL, EuAu, EvEuW, FamSYP, FilmgC, NewC, NinCLC 3, OxCChiL, OxCEng 67, –85, OxCGer 76, PenC EUR, REn, SmATA 22, Str&VC, WhoChL, WorAl*

Grimm, Wilhelm 1786-1859 *BioIn 14, –15, –16, –17, BlmGEL, DcLB 90, HalFC 88, MagSWL, OxCGer 86, RAdv 13-2, WrChl*

Grimm, Wilhelm Karl 1786-1859 *AnCL, AtlBL, AuBYP 2, –3, BiD&SB, BioIn 1, –3, –6, –7, –8, –9, –12, –13, CarSB, CasWL, ChhPo, –S2, DcBiPP, DcEuL, EuAu, EvEuW, FamSYP, FilmgC, MajAI, McGEWB, NinCLC 3, OxCChiL, OxCEng 67, –85, OxCGer 76, PenC EUR, REn, RfGShF, SmATA 22, Str&VC, WorAl*

Grimm, William C 1907- *BioIn 12, ConAu 49, –34NR, SmATA 14*

Grimshaw, Mark *ConAu X*

Grimshaw, Nigel 1925- *BioIn 13, ConAu 101, –17NR, ScF&FL 92, SmATA 23*

Grimsley, Gordon *ConAu X, SmATA X*
Main entry: Groom, Arthur William

Gringhuis, Dirk *AuBYP 3, BioIn 10, –13, ConAu X, MichAu 80, SmATA X*
Main entry: Gringhuis, Richard H

Gringhuis, Richard H 1918-1974 *AuBYP 2, –3, BioIn 8, –10, –13, ConAu 1R, –5NR, MichAu 80, SmATA 6, –25N, WhoMW 74*
Pseud./variant:
Gringhuis, Dirk

Grinnell, David *AuBYP 2, –3, ConAu 135, –X, EncSF 93, SmATA 69, TwCSFW 86, –91*
Main entry: Wollheim, Donald Allen

Grinnell, George Bird 1849-1938 *AmAu&B, AmLY, BenetAL 91, BbD, BiD&SB, BioIn 2, –4, –9, –12, –14, –15, –16, –17, CarSB, DcAmAu, DcNAA, JBA 34, –51, OxCAmL 65, –83, REnAL, SmATA 16, Str&VC, WebAB 74, –79, WhAm 1, WhNaAH, WhNAA, WorAlBi*

Gripari, Pierre 1925- *ConAu 29R, –31NR, IntAu&W 77*

Gripe, Harald *IlsCB 1967*

Gripe, Maria *TwCChW 89B*

Gripe, Maria 1923- *ScF&FL 92*

Gripe, Maria K 1923- *AuBYP 3*

Gripe, Maria Kristina 1923- *AuBYP 2S, BioIn 9, ChlLR 5, ConAu 29R, –17NR, –39NR, IntAu&W 77, –82, MajAI, OxCChiL, SmATA 2, –74, ThrBJA, TwCChW 78B, –83B*

Grisdale, Alex *OxCCan SUP*

Grisha *BioIn 2, IlsBYP*
Main entry: Dotzenko, Grisha

Grishina Givago, Nadejda J *ConICB*

Grissom, Virgil I 1926-1967 *WorAlBi*

Grissom, Virgil Ivan 1926-1967 *BioIn 5, –6, –7, –8, –9, –10, –12, –13, CurBio 65, –67, DcAmB S8, WhAm 4, WorAl*

Griswold, Frances Irene Burge 1826-1900 *Alli SUP, AmAu&B, CarSB, ChhPo, DcAmAu, DcNAA*

Groch, Judith 1929- *AuBYP 2, -3, BioIn 8, -13, ConAu 9R, ForWC 70, SmATA 25*

Grode, Redway *ConAu X, -30NR, SmATA X*
Main entry: Gorey, Edward St John

Grodin, Adams John 1913- *BioIn 1, IlsCB 1744*

Groenhoff, Edwin L 1924- *ConAu 57*

Grohskopf, Bernice *DrAPF 87, -89, -91, WhoUSWr 88, WhoWrEP 89, -92, WrDr 86, -88, -90, -92, -94*

Grohskopf, Bernice 1921- *AuBYP 2S, -3, BioIn 10, ChhPo, ConAu 5R, -3NR, DrAPF 83, -85, ForWC 70, IntAu&W 77, -82, SmATA 7, WrDr 76, -80, -82, -84*

Grol, Lini R 1913- *ConAu 25NR*

Grol, Lini Richards 1913- *BioIn 11, ConAu 61, -8NR, SmATA 9*

Grollman, Earl Alan 1925- *BioIn 13, ConAu 21R, SmATA 22, WhoAmJ 80, WhoE 74, -75*

Gronowicz, Antoni *DrAPF 87, -89, -91, -93*

Gronowicz, Antoni c. 1912-1985 *PolBiDi*

Gronowicz, Antoni 1913-1985 *AmCath 80, AuBYP 2, -3, Au&Wr 71, BioIn 7, ConAu 25R, -117, DrAF 76, DrAP 75, DrAPF 83, -85, IntWWP 82, NatPD 81, WhAm 9, WhoAm 74, -76, -78, -80, -82, -84, WhoE 74, -75, WhoPolA, WhoWor 74, -82*

Groom, Arthur William 1898-1964 *BioIn 11, ConAu 1R, -1NR, SmATA 10*
Pseud./variant:
Adamson, Graham
Anderson, George
DuBlane, Daphne
Grimsley, Gordon
Pembury, Bill
Stanstead, John
Templar, Maurice
Toonder, Martin

Gropper, William 1897- *WhoAmA 86N*

Gropper, William 1897-1977 *AmAu&B, AmPB, Au&Wr 71, BioIn 1, -2, -5, -6, -8, -11, -12, -14, -17, BriEAA, ConAu 102, CurBio 40, -77N, DcCAA 71, -77, -88, GrAmP, IlsCB 1946, IntWW 74, -75, -76, -77N, ObitOF 79, OxCTwCA, OxDcArt, PhDcTCA 77, REnAL, WebAB 74, -79, WhAm 7, WhAmArt 85, Who 74, WhoAm 74, -76, WhoAmA 73, -78N, -80N, -82N, -89N, -91N, WhoWor 74, WhoWorJ 72, -78, WorArt 1950, WorECar*

Grose, Helen Mason 1880- *BioIn 1, DcWomA, IlsCB 1744, WhAmArt 85*

Groser, Horace George *Alli SUP, ChhPo S1, -S2*

Gross, Alan 1947- *ConAu 24NR, SmATA 43, -54, WhoE 83*

Gross, Ernie 1913- *ConAu 136, SmATA 67, WrDr 94*

Gross, Michael 1891?-1979 *BioIn 12, ConAu 97*

Gross, Milt 1895-1953 *AmAu&B, ArtCS, BenetAL 91, BioIn 3, DcLB 11, EncACom, ObitOF 79, REnAL, WhAm 3, WhAmArt 85*

Gross, Nathalie Friedland 1919- *WhoAdv 72*

Gross, Ruth Belov 1929- *AuBYP 2S, -3, BioIn 14, SmATA 33*

Gross, Sarah Chokla 1906-1976 *BioIn 11, -13, ConAu 61, -65, ForWC 70, SmATA 9, -26N, WhoAmW 77*

Gross, Stuart Diehl 1914- *ConAu 57, MichAu 80, WhoMW 78, -80, -82, -84*

Grosser, Morton 1931- *ConAu 97, -17NR, ScF&FL 92, SmATA 74, WhoWest 92, -94*

Grossinger, Tania 1937- *BioIn 10, ConAu 53, -4NR, IntAu&W 77, -86, WrDr 76, -80, -82, -84, -86, -88, -90, -92, -94*

Grossinger, Tania Seifer 1937- *WhoWrEP 92*

Grossman, Bill 1948- *SmATA 72*

Grossman, Mary Louise 1930- *ConAu 77*

Grossman, Nancy S 1940- *BioIn 8, -9, -10, -13, ConArt 77, -83, DcCAA 77, DcCAr 81, IlsBYP, IlsCB 1957, PrintW 83, -85, SmATA 29, WhoAm 82, -84, WhoAmA 73, -78, -80, -82, -84*

Grossman, Patricia 1951- *SmATA 73*

Grossman, Robert 1940- *BioIn 11, -12, SmATA 11*

Grossman, Ronald Philip 1934- *ConAu 21R, DrAS 74H, WhoMW 74*

Grossman, Ronald Phillip 1934- *DrAS 82H*

Grossman, Shelly 1928?-1975 *BioIn 10, ConAu 57*

Grosvenor, Donna Kerkam 1938- *ConAu 109, WhoAmW 74, -75, -77, WhoSSW 75, -76, -78*

Grote, William *AuBYP 2S, -3*

Groten, Dallas 1951- *BioIn 17, ConAu 38NR, SmATA 64*

Groth, John d1988 *NewYTBS 88*

Groth, John 1908- *BioIn 1, -4, -5, -9, -10, -12, ConAu 101, ConGrA 2, CurBio 43, IlrAm 1880, -E, SmATA 21, WhAmArt 85, WhoAm 74, -76, -78, -80, -82, -84, -86, -88, WhoAmA 73, -80, -82, -84*

Groth, John 1908-1988 *BioIn 15, -16, ConAu 125, CurBio 88N, SmATA 56N, WhAm 9*

Groulx, Lionel Adolph 1878-1967 *BioIn 1, -7, CanWr, CasWL, OxCCan, -SUP, OxCCanL*

Groulx, Lionel Adolphe 1878-1967 *BioIn 15*

Grousset, Paschal *EncSF 93*

Grousset, Paschal 1844-1909 *CarSB*

Grover, Eulalie Osgood 1873- *AuBYP 3*

Grover, Eulalie Osgood 1873-1958 *AmAu&B, AuBYP 2, BioIn 8, ChhPo, -S1, OhA&B, WhAm 5, WhNAA, WomWWA 14*

Grover, Wayne 1934- *SmATA 69*

Groves, Ernest Rutherford 1877-1946 *AmAu&B, BioIn 1, CurBio 43, -46, DcNAA, WhAm 2, WhNAA*

Groves, Georgina *ConAu X, SmATA X, WrDr 76, -80, -82, -84, -86, -88, -90, -92*
Main entry: Symons, Geraldine

Groves, Georgina 1909- *WrDr 94*

Groves, Paul 1930- *Au&Wr 71, ConAu 93, -17NR, ScF&FL 92*

Groves, Seli *SmATA 77*

Groves, William Ernest 1935- *AmMWSc 86*

Groves-Raines, Antony 1913- *AuBYP 2, BioIn 8, IlsCB 1957*

Groves-Raines, Ralph Gore Antony 1913- *AuBYP 3*

Gruber, Ruth *BioIn 1, -2, ConAu 25R, -12NR, ForWC 70, WhoWorJ 72, -78*
Pseud./variant:
Michaels, Ruth Gruber

Gruber, Terry 1953- *SmATA 66*

Gruelle, John Barton 1880-1938 *BioIn 14, ConAu 115, SmATA 32, -35*
Pseud./variant:
Gruelle, Johnny

Gruelle, Johnny
Main entry: Gruelle, John Barton

Gruelle, Johnny 1880-1938 *AmAu&B, ASCAP 66, BenetAL 91, BioIn 2, -10, ChhPo, ConAu X, DcLB 22, EncACom, OxCChiL, REnAL, SmATA X, TwCChW 83, -89, WorECar*

Gruenberg, Ben C 1875-1965 *BioIn 4, -7, ConAu P-1*

Gruenberg, Sidonie 1881-1974 *AuBYP 3*

Gruenberg, Sidonie Matsner 1881-1974 *AmAu&B, AuBYP 2, BioIn 2, -4, -7, -9, -10, ChhPo, ConAu 49, -P-1, CurBio 40, -74, InWom SUP, NewYTBS 74, NotAW MOD, SmATA 2, -27N, WhAm 6, WhNAA, WhoAmW 74*

Grumbine, E Evalyn 1881-1974
Pseud./variant:
McNally, E Evalyn Grumbine

Grumbine, E Evalyn 1900- *AuBYP 3*

Grummer, Arnold E 1923- *SmATA 49*

Grummer, Arnold Edward 1923- *IntAu&W 86*

Grund, Josef Carl 1920- *ConAu 73*

Grundtvig, Sven Hersleb *OxCChiL*

Grundtvig, Sven Hersleb 1824-1883 *CasWL, DcEuL*

Grunewalt, Pine *ConAu 134, SmATA 67, WrDr 94*
Main entry: Kunhardt, Edith

Gryski, Camilla *AuBYP 3*

Gryski, Camilla 1948- *BioIn 17, SmATA 72*

Guarcello, Giovanni *ChhPo*

Guarino, Dagmar *ConAu 136, SmATA 68, WrDr 94*
Main entry: Guarino, Deborah

Guarino, Deborah 1954- *BioIn 17, ConAu 136, SmATA 68*
Pseud./variant:
Guarino, Dagmar

Guay, Georgette 1952- *BioIn 16, ConAu 132, SmATA 54, WhoCanL 87, -92*

Guay, Georgette Marie Jeanne 1952- *WrDr 94*

Guccione, Leslie Davis 1946- *SmATA 72*
Pseud./variant:
Davis, Leslie

Guck, Dorothy 1913- *BioIn 13, ConAu 49, MichAu 80, SmATA 27*

Gudmundson, Shirley M *AuBYP 2, –3, BioIn 8*

Guerber, Helene Adeline 1859-1929 *AmLY, BiD&SB, DcAmAu, DcNAA, HarEnUS, WhAm 1, WhNAA, WomWWA 14*

Guess, Edward Preston 1925- *ConAu 73*
Pseud./variant:
Preston, Edward

Guest, Judith *DrAPF 87, –89, –91, –93*

Guest, Judith 1936?- *ArtclWW 2, Au&Arts 7, BioIn 10, –11, –12, ConAu 77, –15NR, ConLC 8, –30, DrAPF 83, –85, MajTwCW, MichAu 80, WrDr 80, –82, –84, –86, –88, –90, –92, –94*

Guggenheim, Hans 1924- *BioIn 8, IlsCB 1957*

Guggenmos, Josef 1922- *ConAu 81, IntAu&W 77, –82, OxCChiL*

Gugliotta, Bobette 1918- *BioIn 10, ConAu 41R, –14NR, –31NR, SmATA 7*

Guiberson, Brenda Z 1946- *SmATA 71*

Guild, Marion Felton *ChhPo S2*

Guillaume, Jeanette G Flierl 1899- *BioIn 11, ConAu 1R, SmATA 8*

Guillet, Edwin Clarence 1898-1975 *BioIn 10, CanWW 70, ConAu 107, OxCCan, Profile 1*

Guillot, Rene *TwCChW 89B*

Guillot, Rene 1900-1969 *AuBYP 2, –3, BioIn 6, –7, –8, –10, –11, ChlLR 22, ConAu 49, –39NR, MorJA, OxCChiL, SmATA 7, TwCChW 78B, –83B, WhoChL*

Guines, James Theodore 1932- *WhoGov 77, –72, –75*

Guinness, Bryan
Main entry: Moyne, Bryan Walter Guinness

Guinness, Bryan Walter *Au&Wr 71, BioIn 13, IntAu&W 77X, –82, IntWWP 82, Who 74, WrDr 76, –80*

Guinness, Bryan Walter 1905- *BiDIrW, IntAu&W 86, –89, –91*

Guirma, Frederic *BlkAuII, –92*

Guisewite, Cathy *BioIn 16, –17*

Guisewite, Cathy 1950- *Au&Arts 2, CurBio 89, EncACom, SmATA 57*

Guisewite, Cathy Lee 1950- *WhoAm 94*

Guiterman, Arthur 1871-1943 *AmAu&B, AmLY, BenetAL 91, BioIn 4, –5, –8, ChhPo, –S1, –S2, CnDAL, ConAu 120, CurBio 43, DcLB 11, DcNAA, EncAJ, EvLB, ObitOF 79, OxCAmL 65, –83, REn, REnAL, Str&VC, TwCA, –SUP, WhAm 2, WhNAA*

Guizot, Madam 1773-1827 *CarSB*

Guizot, Pauline 1773-1827 *BlmGWL*

Gulick, Bill
Main entry: Gulick, Grover C

Gulick, Grover C 1916- *ConAu 33R, –17NR, –39NR, EncFWF, WhoPNW*
Pseud./variant:
Gulick, Bill

Gulick, Peggy 1918- *AuBYP 2, –3, BioIn 8*

Gullahorn, Genevieve *AuBYP 2, –3, BioIn 7*

Gulley, Judie 1942- *BioIn 16, SmATA 58*

Gulliver, Lemuel *ConAu X, WrDr 76, –80*
Main entry: Hastings, Macdonald

Gumpertz, Bob 1925- *AuBYP 3*

Gumpertz, Robert 1925- *AuBYP 2S, ConAu 69*

Gundelfinger, John 1937- *IlrAm 1880, –G*

Gundelfinger, John 1937-1991 *BioIn 17*

Gundelfinger, John Andre 1937- *WhoAmA 86, –91*

Gundersheimer, Karen *BioIn 15, SmATA 44*

Gundersheimer, Karen 1939- *BioIn 16, ConAu 133, SixBJA, WrDr 94*

Gundrey, Elizabeth 1924- *BioIn 13, ConAu 13R, –6NR, SmATA 23*

Gunn, Aeneas, Mrs *WomNov*

Gunn, Aeneas, Mrs 1870-1961 *CamGLE, SingR 1*

Gunn, James E *IntvTCA 2*

Gunn, James E 1923- *ConAu 22NR, NewEScF, ScFSB, TwCSFW 86, –91, WrDr 86, –88, –90, –92*

Gunn, James Edwin 1923- *BioIn 12, ConAu 9R, –5NR, DcLB 8, DrAF 76, EncSF 93, IntAu&W 89, –91, SmATA 35,*

WhoMW 84, WhoSciF, WhoUSWr 88, WhoWrEP 89, –92, WrDr 76, –80, –82, –84, –94
Pseud./variant:
James, Edwin

Gunn, James Ewin 1923- *IntAu&W 86*

Gunn, Jeannie 1870-1961 *AuWomWr, BlmGWL, FemiCLE, OxCAusL, OxCChiL, SingR 1, WomNov*

Gunn, John *DcChlFi*

Gunning, Monica Olwen 1930- *ConAu 65*

Gunston, Bill *ConAu 42NR*
Main entry: Gunston, William Tudor

Gunston, Bill 1927- *IntAu&W 82, SmATA X, WrDr 82, –84, –86, –88, –90, –92, –94*

Gunston, David *Au&Wr 71*

Gunston, William Tudor 1927- *AuBYP 2S, –3, Au&Wr 71, BioIn 11, ConAu 49, –3NR, –19NR, –42NR, IntAu&W 77, –91, SmATA 9, WrDr 76, –80*
Pseud./variant:
Gunston, Bill

Gunterman, Bertha Lisette 1886?-1975 *BioIn 6, –10, –13, ConAu 104, SmATA 27N*

Gunther, John 1901-1970 *AmAu&B, AmNov, AuBYP 2, –3, Benet 87, BenetAL 91, BioIn 1, –2, –3, –4, –5, –6, –7, –8, –9, –16, –17, ConAu 9R, –25R, CurBio 41, –61, –70, DcAmB S8, EncAJ, EvLB, JrnUS, LongCTC, NewYTBE 70, ObitOF 79, ObitT 1961, OxCAmL 65, –83, PenC AM, RAdv 13-3, REn, REnAL, SmATA 2, TwCA, –SUP, WebAB 74, –79, WhAm 6, WorAlBi, WorAl*

Guralnik, David B 1920- *WhoAm 86, –88*

Guralnik, David Bernard 1920- *DrAS 74F, –78F, –82F, WhoAm 84, –90, WhoAmJ 80, WhoWorJ 72, –78*

Guravich, Dan 1918- *SmATA 74*

Guravich, Daniel 1918- *IntAu&W 86*

Gurko, Leo 1914- *BioIn 9, –11, –14, ConAu 5R, –5NR, DrAS 74E, –78E, –82E, SmATA 9, ThrBJA, WhoAm 74, –76*

Gurko, Miriam *BioIn 9, –11, ConAu 1R, SmATA 9, ThrBJA, WrDr 76, –80, –82, –84, –86, –88*

Gurko, Miriam d1988 *BioIn 16*

Gurko, Miriam 1910?-1988 *ConAu 126, SmATA 58*

Gurney, Gene 1924- *ConAu 5R, –9NR, SmATA 65*

Gurney, J Eric 1910- *AuBYP 2, –3, BioIn 8, ChhPo S2, ConAu 1R, –2NR, IntAu&W 77*

Gurney, James 1958- *BiDScF, EncSF 93, SmATA 76*

Gurney, John Steven 1962- *SmATA 75, WhoE 93*

Gurney, Nancy d1972 *AuBYP 3*

Gurney, Nancy Jack 1915?-1973 *AuBYP 2, BioIn 8, –10, ConAu 45*

Gurr, Robin Joy 1934- *SingR 2*

Gustafson, Anita 1942- *BioIn 15, ConAu 112, SmATA 45*

Gustafson, Elton T *AuBYP 2, –3, BioIn 8*

Gustafson, Marjorie *AuBYP 3*

Gustafson, Marjorie Lillian 1920- *AuBYP 2S, DrAS 74F, –82F, WhoAmW 77*

Gustafson, Sarah Regal *ConAu X, SmATA 1, WhoAmW 75*
Main entry: Riedman, Sarah Regal

Gustafson, Scott 1956- *BioIn 14, SmATA 34*

Gustaitis, Rasa 1934- *BioIn 8, ConAu 25R*

Gustkey, Earl 1940- *AuBYP 2S, –3, ConAu 57*

Guterman, Norbert 1900?-1984 *BioIn 14, ConAu 113, NewYTBS 84*

Guthrie, A B *DrAPF 87, –89, –91*

Guthrie, A B 1901- *HalFC 88*

Guthrie, A B 1901-1991 *BioIn 17*

Guthrie, A B, Jr. 1901- *Benet 87, ConAu 24NR, ConNov 86, CyWA 89, LiHiK, SmATA 62, WrDr 86, –88, –90*

Guthrie, A B, Jr. 1901-1991 *AnObit 1991, BenetAL 91, ConAu 134, CurBio 91N, NewYTBS 91, SmATA 67, TwCWW 91*

Guthrie, Alfred Bertram 1901- *BioIn 14, –15, –16*

Guthrie, Alfred Bertram 1901-1991 *BioIn 17*

Guthrie, Alfred Bertram, Jr. 1901- *AmAu&B, AmNov, BioIn 1, –2, –4, –5, –7, –8, –10, CmMov, CnDAL, ConAu 57, ConNov 72, –76, CurBio 50, CyWA 58, DcLEL, DrAF 76, IndAu 1917, IntAu&W 77, ModAL,*

OxCAmL 65, REnAL, TwCA SUP, WhoAm 74, –80, –82, –84, –86, –88, –90, WhoPNW, WhoWest 74, WhoWor 74, WrDr 76, –80

Guthrie, Alfred Bertram, Jr. 1901-1991 *ConLC 70, WhAm 10*

Guthrie, Anne 1890-1979 *AuBYP 2, –3, BioIn 7, –13, ConAu 5R, –134, SmATA 28*

Guthrie, Donna *AuBYP 3*

Guthrie, Donna W 1946- *SmATA 63*

Guthrie, Thomas Anstey 1856-1934 *Alli SUP, BiD&SB, BioIn 2, –4, –8, Chambr 3, ChhPo, –S1, –S2, ConAu 113, DcEnA A, DcLEL, DcNaB 1931, EvLB, LongCTC, NewC, OxCChiL, OxCEng 67, TelT, TwCA, –SUP, WhoChL, WhoHr&F*

Guthrie, Vee *ChhPo, –S2*

Gutman, Bill *AuBYP 2S, –3, ConAu 135, SmATA 43, –67, WrDr 94*

Gutman, Dan 1955- *ConAu 133, SmATA 77, WrDr 94*

Gutman, Naham 1899?-1981 *ConAu 102, SmATA 25N*

Gutmann, Bessie Pease 1876-1960 *SmATA 73*

Gutnik, Martin J 1942- *ConAu 49, –3NR*

Gutteridge, Donald George 1937- *CanWW 89, ConAu 65, ConPo 75, IntAu&W 82, –91, OxCCan SUP, WrDr 76, –80*

Guy, Anne W *ConAu 5R*

Guy, Rosa *DrAPF 89, –91, –93*

Guy, Rosa 1925?- *Au&Arts 4, BlmGWL, ConBlB 5, FemiCLE, SmATA 62*

Guy, Rosa 1928- *ArtclWW 2, BioIn 12, BlkAWP, BlkAull, –92, BlkWr 1, ChlLR 13, ConAu 17R, –14NR, –34NR, ConBlAP 88, ConLC 26, DcLB 33, FifBJA, IntAu&W 91, NotBlAW 92, OxCChiL, SmATA 14, TwCChW 78, –83, –89, WorAu 1980, WrDr 80, –82, –84, –86, –88, –90, –92*

Guy, Rosa Cuthbert 1925- *MajAI, TwCYAW*

Guy, Rosa Cuthbert 1928- *WrDr 94*

Guymer, Mary 1909- *BioIn 16, SmATA 50*

Gwynne, Fred d1993 *NewYTBS 93*

Gwynne, Fred 1926- *BioIn 11, –13, ConAu 113, ConTFT 2, –8, FilmgC, HalFC 84, –88, IlsBYP, IntMPA 84, –86, –88, –92, NotNAT, SmATA 27, –41, WhoAm 80, –82, –84, –86, –88, –90, –92, WhoCom, WhoEnt 92, WhoHol A, WhoThe 77, –81*

Gwynne, Frederick Hubbard 1926-1993 *ConAu 141, SmATA 75*

Gwynne, John Harold 1899- *AuBYP 2, –3, BioIn 8*

Gydal, Monica *TwCChW 78B, –83B, –89B*

H

Haack, Bruce C 1932- *ASCAP 66, ConAmC 76A, -82*

Haar, Jaap Ter *BioIn 10, FourBJA*
Main entry: Ter Haar, Jaap

Haar, Jaap Ter 1922- *ChlLR 15*

Haaren, John Henry 1855-1916 *CarSB, DcNAA*

Haas, Benjamin Leopold 1926-1977 *BioIn 11, ConAu 9R, -73, EncFWF, WrDr 80*

Haas, Carolyn Buhai 1926- *BioIn 15, ConAu 65, -9NR, IntAu&W 89, -91, SmATA 43, WhoAm 92, -94, WhoAmW 81, -83, -87, -89, -91, -93*

Haas, Dorothy *ScF&FL 92, SixBJA, SmATA 17AS*

Haas, Dorothy F *AuBYP 3, BioIn 15, -16, ConAu 5R, -3NR, -20NR, ForWC 70, SmATA 43, -46, WhoAmW 83*
Pseud./variant:
Francis, Dee

Haas, Dorothy Frances *DcAmChF 1985*

Haas, Irene 1929- *BioIn 5, -8, -9, -12, ChhPo S2, ConAu 97, IlsBYP, IlsCB 1946, -1957, -1967, SmATA 17, ThrBJA*

Haas, James E 1943- *BioIn 15, ConAu 61, -7NR, SmATA 40*

Haas, Kenneth Brooks, Sr. 1898- *ConAu 57, -6NR*

Haas, Kenneth Brooks, Jr. 1928- *AmMWSc 86, -89, -92*

Haas, Merle S d1985 *NewYTBS 85*

Haas, Merle S 1896?-1985 *ConAu 114, NewYTBS 85, SmATA 41N*

Habberton, John 1842-1921 *Alli SUP, AmAu, AmAu&B, BenetAL 91, BbD, BiD&SB, BioIn 8, -15, CarSB, CelCen, Chambr 3, DcAmAu, DcBiA, DcEnL, DcNAA, EncAHmr, EvLB, HarEnUS, OxCAmL 65, -83, OxCChiL, REnAL, WhAm 1, WhoChL*

Habberton, William *AuBYP 3*

Habberton, William 1899- *AuBYP 2, BioIn 8*

Habel, Norman Charles 1932- *ConAu 17R DrAS 74P*

Habenstreit, Barbara 1937- *AuBYP 2S, -3 BioIn 10, ConAu 29R, SmATA 5*

Haber, Heinz 1913- *AuBYP 2, -3, BioIn 3 -8, ConAu 73, CurBio 52, InSci*

Haber, Louis 1910- *BioIn 11, ConAu 29R, SmATA 12, WhoE 75*

Haber, Paul 1937- *BioIn 8, -9*

Habig, Marion A 1901-1984 *ConAu 20NR*

Habig, Marion Alphonse 1901- *WrDr 86*

Habig, Marion Alphonse 1901-1984 *AmCath 80, BioIn 1, BkC 2, CathA 1930, ConAu 5R, -114, -5NR, DrAS 74H, -78H, -82H, IntAu&W 77, WhoRel 75, -77, WrDr 76, -80, -82, -84*

Hack, Maria 1777-1844 *DcNaB, OxCChiL*

Hacker, Shyrle 1910- *ConAu 101*

Hacker, Tina 1946- *WhoAmW 81*

Hackett, Albert *ConDr 88A, OxCAmT 84*

Hackett, Albert 1900- *AmAu&B, AuBYP 2 -3, BenetAL 91, BiE&WWA, BioIn 4, -8, -11, -14, -15, CmMov, CurBio 56, DcLB 26, EncAFC, FilmgC, HalFC 84, -88, ModWD, NotNAT, OxCAmL 65, -83, REnAL, WhoAm 74, -76, -78, WorEFlm*

Hackett, Frances *AuBYP 2, -3, BioIn 8*

Hackett, Frances Goodrich 1891-1984 *BenetAL 91*

Hackett, John Winthrop 1910- *BioIn 16, –17, IntAu&W 91, IntWW 91, SmATA 65, Who 92*

Hackett, John Winthrop, Gen Sir 1910- *IntWW 89, Who 90*

Hackett, John Winthrop, Sir 1910- *BioIn 14, IntAu&W 89, Who 88*

Hackney, Frances *SingR 1*

Hacks, Peter 1928- *CamGWoT, CasWL, CnMD, ConFLW 84, ConWorW 93, CroCD, DcLB 124, EncWL, –2, EncWT, IntDcT 2, LiExTwC, MajMD 1, McGEWD 72, –84, ModGL, ModWD, OxCGer 76, –86, PenC EUR*

Hadath, Gunby 1880?-1954 *BioIn 8, OxCChiL*

Hadath, John Edward Gunby 1880?-1954 *BioIn 8, ChhPo, WhoChL, WhoLA*

Hader, Berta 1890?-1976 *AuBYP 3, ScF&FL 92*

Hader, Berta 1891-1976 *BioIn 14, TwCChW 89*

Hader, Berta Hoerner 1890?-1976 *AmAu&B, AmPB, ArtsAmW 2, AuBYP 2, Au&ICB, BioIn 1, –2, –4, –5, –7, –8, –10, –12, BkP, Cald 1938, ConAu 65, –73, ConICB, IlsBYP, IlsCB 1744, –1946, –1957, –1967, JBA 34, –51, OxCChiL, SmATA 16, Str&VC, TwCChW 78, –83, WhAm 6, –7, WhAmArt 85, WhoAm 74*

Hader, Berta Hoerner 1891-1976 *MajAI*

Hader, Elmer 1889-1973 *ScF&FL 92, TwCChW 89, WhoAmA 86N, –89N, –91N*

Hader, Elmer Stanley 1889-1973 *AmAu&B, AmPB, ArtsAmW 2, AuBYP 2, –3, Au&ICB, BioIn 1, –2, –4, –5, –7, –8, –12, –14, BkP, Cald 1938, ConAu 73, ConICB, IlsBYP, IlsCB 1744, –1946, –1957, –1967, JBA 34, –51, MajAI, OxCChiL, SmATA 16, Str&VC, TwCChW 78, –83, WhAm 7, WhAmArt 85, WhoAm 74, WhoAmA 73, –78N, –80N, –82N*

Hadfield, Alice M 1908- *ConAu 26NR*

Hadfield, Alice Mary 1908- *Au&Wr 71, ConAu 108, IntAu&W 77, –82*

Hadfield, Charles
Main entry: Hadfield, Ellis Charles Raymond

Hadfield, Ellis Charles Raymond 1909- *Au&Wr 71, ConAu 13R, IntAu&W 77, –82, Who 74*
Pseud./variant:
Hadfield, Charles

Hadithi, Mwenye *AuBYP 3, BioIn 17, ConAu 127, SmATA X*
Main entry: Hobson, Bruce

Hadley, Franklin *BioIn 11, ConAu X, EncSF 93, SmATA X*
Main entry: Winterbotham, R R

Hadley, Lee 1934- *BioIn 15, –16, ConAu 101, –19NR, –36NR, MajAI, SmATA 38, –47, –14AS*
Pseud./variant:
Irwin, Hadley

Hadley, Lee 1934- *TwCYAW*

Hadley, Leila 1925- *AuBYP 3*

Hadley, Leila 1926?- *AuBYP 2S, Au&Wr 71, BioIn 5, ConAu 41R, –14NR, WrDr 76, –80, –82, –84*

Hadley, Leila 1929- *IntAu&W 91, WrDr 86, –88, –90, –92*

Hadley, Leila E B 1929- *WrDr 94*

Hadley, Leila Eliott-Burton 1925- *WhoWor 93*

Haeffele, Deborah 1954- *SmATA 76*

Haertling, Peter 1933- *ConAu 22NR, MajAI, SmATA 66*

Hafner, Marylin 1925- *BioIn 10, –16, ChhPo S1, IlsBYP, SixBJA, SmATA 7*
Pseud./variant:
Reyna, Marylin De

Hagar, Alice 1894-1969 *AuBYP 3*

Hagbrink, Bodil 1936- *ConAu 104*

Hageman, Howard G d1992 *NewYTBS 92*

Hageman, Howard Garberich 1921- *ConAu 1R, –5NR, DrAS 74P, –78P, –82P, WhoAm 74, –76, –78, –80, –82, –84, –86, –88, –90, –92, WhoRel 75, –92, WhoWor 78*

Hageman, Howard Garberich 1921-1992 *ConAu 140*

Hager, Alice Rogers 1894-1969 *AmAu&B, AuBYP 2, BioIn 7, ConAu 5R, –103, SmATA 26N, WhAm 5, WhoSSW 73*

Haggard, Henry Rider *IntvTCA 2*

Haggard, Henry Rider 1856-1925 *BioIn 14, –15, –16, DcAfHiB 86, EncPaPR 91*

Haggard, Henry Rider, Sir 1856-1925 *Alli SUP, BbD, BiD&SB, BioIn 1, –2, –3, –5, –7, –8, –11, –12, –13, CamGLE, Chambr 3, CyWA 58, DcBiA, DcEnA A, DcEuL, DcLEL,*

DcNaB 1922, EncSoA, EvLB, FilmgC, LongCTC, ModBrL, NewC, OxCChiL, OxCEng 67, PenC ENG, REn, SmATA 16, TelT, TwCA, –SUP, WebE&AL, WhoChL, WhoHr&F

Haggerston, Scrope
Main entry: Richardson

Haggerty, James Joseph 1920- *BioIn 10, ConAu 41R, IntAu&W 77, SmATA 5, WhoAm 94, WhoE 81, –83, –85, –86, –91, –93, WhoSSW 73, –75, –76, WhoWor 84, –87, –89, –91, –93*

Hagon, Priscilla *ConAu X, IntAu&W 77X, –82X, –91X, MajAI, SmATA 5, –75, –X, TwCChW 83, –89, WrDr 76, –80, –82, –84, –86, –88, –90, –92*
Main entry: Allan, Mabel Esther

Hagon, Priscilla 1915- *WrDr 94*

Hague, Kathleen *SmATA 45*

Hague, Kathleen 1949- *BioIn 15, –16, ConAu 125, SmATA 49*

Hague, Michael *BioIn 14*

Hague, Michael 1948- *BioIn 16, ConAu 111, FifBJA, SmATA 32, –48*

Hague, Michael R 1948- *MajAI*

Hahn, Emily 1905- *AmAu&B, AuBYP 2, –3, BioIn 1, –2, –3, –4, –7, –8, –9, –11, –12, –13, –15, ConAu 1R, –11AS, –1NR, –27NR, CurBio 42, FemiCLE, IntAu&W 91, LongCTC, REnAL, SmATA 3, TwCA SUP, WhNAA, WhoAm 74, –76, –78, –80, –82, –84, –86, –88, –90, –94, WhoAmW 74, –75, –77, –83, –85, –93, WhoE 74, WhoWor 74, WrDr 80, –82, –84, –86, –88, –90, –92, –94*

Hahn, Hannelore *DrAPF 87, –89, –91, –93*

Hahn, Hannelore 1926- *BioIn 11, ConAu 5R, –3NR, DrAP 75, DrAPF 83, –85, SmATA 8, WhoAmW 75, –81*

Hahn, James 1947- *BioIn 11, ConAu 49, –2NR, –17NR, SmATA 9*

Hahn, Lynn 1949- *BioIn 11, ConAu 49, –2NR, –17NR, SmATA 9*

Hahn, Mary Downing 1937- *BioIn 15, –16, ConAu 122, DcAmChF 1985, MajAI, ScF&FL 92, SixBJA, SmATA 44, –50, –12AS, WhoAm 92, –94, WrDr 90, –92, –94*

Hahn, Phil 1932- *WhoAm 74, –76*

Haiblum, Isidore *DrAPF 87, –89, –91, –93*

Haiblum, Isidore 1935- *ConAu 53, –4NR, –19NR, DrAF 76, DrAPF 83, –85, EncSF 93, IntAu&W 91, ScF&FL 92, ScFSB, TwCSFW 86, –91, WrDr 84, –86, –88, –90, –92, –94*

Haig-Brown, Roderick *IntvTCA 2*

Haig-Brown, Roderick 1908- *BenetAL 91*

Haig-Brown, Roderick 1908-1976 *ChlLR 31, DcLB 88, TwCChW 89, TwCWW 91*

Haig-Brown, Roderick Langmere 1908-1976 *Au&Wr 71, BioIn 1, –2, –6, –11, –12, –13, CanNov, CanWW 70, CanWr, CasWL, ConAu 5R, –69, –4NR, –38NR, ConLC 21, CreCan 1, CurBio 50, DcChlFi, MajAI, OxCCan, OxCCanL, OxCChiL, REnAL, SmATA 12, TwCChW 78, –83, WhAm 7, WhoAm 74, WhoCan 73, WhoWest 74, –76, WrDr 76*

Haight, Anne Lyon 1895-1977 *BioIn 11, –14, ConAu 73, –P-2, SmATA 30N, WrDr 76, –80*

Haight, Gordon S d1985 *NewYTBS 85*

Haight, Gordon S 1901- *WrDr 86*

Haight, Gordon S 1901-1985 *AnObit 1985, ConAu 118, DcLB 103*

Haight, Gordon Sherman 1901-1985 *AmAu&B, BioIn 14, –17, BlueB 76, ChhPo S1, ConAu P-2, DrAS 74E, –78E, –82E, IntAu&W 77, –82, IntYB 80, –81, –82, NewYTBS 85, WhAm 9, Who 74, –82, –83, –85, WhoAm 74, –76, –78, WrDr 76, –80, –82, –84*

Haile, Ellen *Alli SUP, CarSB*

Hailey, Sheila 1927- *BioIn 11, ConAu 85*

Haines, Charles 1928- *AuBYP 2S, –3, ConAu 41R, DrAS 74E, IntAu&W 77, –82*

Haines, Francis 1899- *ConAu 5R*

Haines, Gail Kay 1943- *AuBYP 2S, –3, BioIn 11, ConAu 37R, –14NR, –31NR, IntAu&W 91, SmATA 11, WhoAmW 83, WhoWest 94, WrDr 76, –80, –82, –84, –86, –88, –90, –92, –94*

Haining, Peter 1940- *BioIn 12, –15, ConAu 45, –1NR, ConSFA, EncO&P 1S2, –2, –3, PenEncH, ScF&FL 92, ScFEYrs, SmATA 14, WhoHr&F, WhoSciF, WrDr 76*

Haining, Peter Alexander 1940- *WrDr 94*

Haislet, Edwin L 1908- *WhoMW 74, –76, –78*

Hakluyt, Richard 1522?-1616 *DcLB 136*

Hakluyt, Richard 1552?-1616 *Alli, AnCL, AtlBL, BenetAL 91, BiDSA, BiD&SB, BioIn 1, -3, -4, -5, -6, -8, -9, -11, BritAu, CamGEL, CamGLE, CasWL, Chambr 1, CroE&S, CyEd, CyWA 58, DcBiPP, DcEnA, DcEnL, DcEuL, DcLEL, DcNaB, DcScB, EvLB, HarEnUS, InSci, LongCEL, McGEWB, NewC, OxCAmH, OxCAmL 65, -83, OxCCan, OxCEng 67, -85, OxCShps, PenC ENG, RAdv 13-3, REn, REnAL, RfGEnL 91, WebE&AL, WhAm HS*

Hakluyt, Richard 1553-1616 *Benet 87, BlmGEL*

Halacy, Dan 1919- *SmATA 8AS*

Halacy, Daniel Stephen 1919- *BioIn 14*

Halacy, Daniel Stephen, Jr. 1919- *AuBYP 2, -3, BioIn 8, ConAu 5R, -9NR, FifBJA, SmATA 36*

Halam, Ann *EncSF 93, ScF&FL 92, TwCSFW 91, WrDr 92*

Halam, Ann 1952- *ChlFicS, TwCChW 89, TwCYAW, WrDr 90, -94*

Halas, John 1912- *ConAu 108, DcFM, FilmgC, HalFC 84, -88, IntMPA 75, -76, -78, -81, -82, -84, -86, -88, -77, OxCFilm, Who 82, -83, -85, -88, -90, -92, WhoGrA 62, WhoWor 80, WorECar, WorEFlm*

Haldane, J B S 1892-1964 *BioIn 16, CamGLE, ScF&FL 92, ScFSB, ThTwC 87, TwCChW 89, TwCSFW 86*

Haldane, John Burdon 1892-1964 *WorAlBi*

Haldane, John Burdon Sanderson 1892-1964 *BiESc, BioIn 4, -7, -8, -9, -12, -13, -14, -16, ConAu 101, CurBio 40, -65, DcLEL, DcNaB 1961, EncSF 93, EvLB, GrBr, InSci, LongCTC, McGMS 80, NewC, ObitOF 79, ObitT 1961, OxCChiL, OxCEng 67, -85, RAdv 13-5, TwCA, -SUP, TwCChW 78, -83, UFOEn, WhDW, WorAl*

Haldane, Roger John 1945- *BioIn 12, IlsCB 1967, SmATA 13*

Haldeman, Joe *ConSFF, DrAPF 87, -89, -91, -93, IntvTCA 2*

Haldeman, Joe 1943- *BioIn 12, ConAu 53, -6NR, ConLC 61, DcLB 8, DrmM 2, EncSF 93, NewEScF, RGTwCSF, ScF&FL 92, ScFSB, TwCSFW 86, -91, WrDr 80, -82, -84, -86, -88, -90, -92*
Pseud./variant:
Graham, Robert

Haldeman, Joe William 1943- *WrDr 94*

Hale, Arlene *AuBYP 3*
Pseud./variant:
Christopher, Louise

Hale, Arlene 1924- *AuBYP 2, BioIn 8, ConAu 1R, -1NR, WhoAmW 74, -75, -77*

Hale, Arlene 1924-1982 *BioIn 16, SmATA 49*
Pseud./variant:
Everett, Gail
Kirkland, Will
Williams, Lynn

Hale, Edward Everett 1822-1909 *Alli, -SUP, AmAu, AmAu&B, BenetAL 91, BbD, BiD&SB, BioIn 1, -2, -3, -4, -5, -7, -9, -12, -15, CarSB, Chambr 3, ChhPo, -S1, -S2, CnDAL, ConAu 119, CyAL, CyWA 58, DcAmAu, DcBiPP, DcEnL, DcLB 1, -42, -74, DcLEL, DcNAA, EncSF 93, EvLB, HarEnUS, JBA 34, LuthC 75, McGEWB, NewEScF, OxCAmH, OxCAmL 65, -83, OxCChiL, PenC AM, REn, REnAL, ScFEYrs, SmATA 16, WebAB 74, -79, WhAm 1*
Pseud./variant:
Ingham, Colonel Frederic

Hale, Glenn *ScF&FL 92, SmATA 66*
Main entry: Walker, Robert Wayne

Hale, Helen *AuBYP 2, -3, BioIn 11, ConAu X, SmATA X*
Main entry: Mulcahy, Lucille Burnett

Hale, Irina 1932- *BioIn 13, ConAu 105, SmATA 26*

Hale, Janet Campbell *DrAPF 93*

Hale, Janet Campbell 1947- *AuBYP 2S, -3, ConAu 49, DrAF 76*

Hale, John Rigby 1923- *Au&Wr 71, ConAu 102, -19NR, IntAu&W 77, IntWW 75, -76, -77, -78, -79, -80, -81, -82, -83, -91, Who 82, -83, -85, WhoWor 84, -87, -89, -91, -93*

Hale, John Rigby, Sir 1923- *IntWW 89*

Hale, Julian Anthony Stuart 1940- *ConAu 41R, IntAu&W 77*

Hale, Kathleen 1898- *Au&Wr 71, BioIn 5, -8, -12, -14, -17, ChhPo, ConAu 73, DcBrAr 1, DcWomA, IlsBYP, IlsCB 1946, -1957, -1967, IntAu&W 77, -82, -86, -89, -91, OxCChiL, SmATA 17, -66, TwCChW 78, -83, -89, TwCPaSc, Who 74, -82, -83, -85, -88, -90, -92, WhoChL, WrDr 80, -82, -84, -86, -88*

Hale, Linda 1929- *ConAu 5R, SmATA 6*

Hale, Lucretia P 1820-1900 *TwCChW 89A, WrChl*

Hale, Lucretia Peabody 1820-1900 *Alli SUP, AmAu, AmAu&B, BenetAL 91, BiD&SB, BioIn 1, –3, –4, –5, –8, –12, –13, –15, BlmGWL, CarSB, ChhPo S2, ConAu 122, –136, DcAmAu, DcLB 42, DcNAA, FamSYP, FemiCLE, JBA 34, MajAI, OxCAmH, OxCAmL 65, –83, OxCChiL, REnAL, SmATA 26, TwCChW 78A, –83A, WebAB 74, –79, WhAm 1, WhoChL*

Hale, Lucretia Peabody 1820-1920 *InWom SUP*

Hale, Nancy *DrAPF 87, –89, IntvTCA 2*

Hale, Nancy 1908- *BioIn 1, –2, –4, –7, –8, –12, –14, BlmGWL, ConNov 82, –86, DcLB Y80B, FemiCLE, IntAu&W 82, OxCAmL 83, SmATA 31, WhoAm 80, –82, –84, –86, –88, WhoUSWr 88, WrDr 82, –84, –86, –88*

Hale, Nancy 1908-1988 *BenetAL 91, BioIn 16, ConAu 126, CyWA 89, DcLB 86, –Y88N, NewYTBS 88, SmATA 57, WhAm 9*

Hale, Sarah Josepha *BioIn 14, –15, –16, –17*

Hale, Sarah Josepha 1788-1879 *ArtclWW 2, BioAmW, BioIn 1, –3, –5, –7, –10, –11, –12, –13, BlmGWL, ContDcW 89, DcLB 42, –73, EncAJ, FemiCLE, HanAmWH, HarEnUS, IntDcWB, OxCAmH, OxCAmL 83, OxCChiL, WebAB 79*

Hale, Sarah Josepha Buell 1788-1879 *BenetAL 91, BiDAmJo, InWom SUP, JrnUS*

Hale, William Harlan 1910-1974 *AmAu&B, BenetAL 91, BioIn 1, –10, –12, ConAu 49, –93, EncTwCJ, NatCAB 58, NewYTBS 74, REnAL, WhAm 6, WhoAm 74, WhoE 74*

Haley, Gail E *BioIn 14, –15*

Haley, Gail E 1939- *ChlLR 21, ConAu 35NR, IntAu&W 91, SmATA 13AS, WhoAmA 86, –89, –91, WrDr 86, –88, –90, –92*

Haley, Gail Einhart 1939- *BioIn 9, ConAu 21R, –14NR, IlsBYP, IlsCB 1967, MajAI, NewbC 1966, SmATA 28, –43, ThrBJA, TwCChW 78, WhoAm 74, –76, –78, –92, –94, WrDr 80, –82, –84, –94*

Haley, Neale *BioIn 16, SmATA 52*

Haliburton, Thomas Chandler 1796-1865 *Alli, –SUP, Benet 87, BenetAL 91, BbD, BbtC, BiD&SB, BioIn 3, –9, –11, –13, –15, –17, BritAu 19, CamGEL, CamGLE, CanWr, CasWL, CelCen, Chambr 3, DcBiPP, DcCanB 9, DcEnA, DcEnL, DcLB 11, –99, DcLEL, DcNaB, DcNAA, EncAHmr, EvLB, HarEnUS, NewC, NinCLC 15, OxCAmL 65, OxCCan, OxCEng 67, –85, PenC ENG, RAdv 13-1, REn, REnAL, RfGEnL 91, RfGShF, StaCVF, WebE&AL*

Halkin, Abraham S d1990 *NewYTBS 90*

Halkin, Abraham S 1903- *WhoWorJ 72, –78*

Halkin, Abraham S 1903-1990 *BioIn 16, –17, ConAu 131*

Halkin, Shimon d1987 *IntWW 89N*

Halkin, Shimon 1899- *BioIn 10, BlueB 76, CasWL, ConAu 53, IntAu&W 77, –82, IntWW 74, –75, –76, –77, –78, –79, –80, –81, –82, –83, MidE 80, –81, –82, WhoWorJ 72, –78, WrDr 76, –80*

Hall, Adam *ConAu X, DcLEL 1940, EncMys, IntAu&W 77X, Novels, ScF&FL 92, SmATA X, TwCCr&M 80, –85, Who 82, –83, –85, –88, –90, –92, WrDr 76, –80, –82, –84, –86, –88, –90, –92, –94*
Main entry: Trevor, Elleston

Hall, Adele 1910- *AuBYP 2, –3, BioIn 8, –10, ConAu 1R, SmATA 7*

Hall, Anna Gertrude 1882-1967 *BioIn 11, –14, ConAu P-1, SmATA 8, WhoLibS 55*

Hall, Anna Maria 1800-1881 *Alli, –SUP, BbD, BiDIrW, BiD&SB, BioIn 16, CamGLE, CarSB, DcBiPP, DcEnL, DcIrB 88, DcIrW 1, DcLEL, DcNaB, EvLB, FemiCLE, NewC, PoIre*
Pseud./variant:
Hall, Samuel Carter, Mrs.

Hall, Anna Maria Fielding 1800-1881 *BlmGWL, EncBrWW, InWom SUP*

Hall, Aylmer
Main entry: Hall, Norah E L

Hall, Aylmer 1914- *ConAu X, TwCChW 78, –83, –89, WrDr 80, –82, –84, –86, –88, –90, –92, –94*

Hall, Barbara 1960- *BioIn 17, ConAu 135, SmATA 68, TwCYAW, WrDr 94*

Hall, Borden *BioIn 6, –7, ConAu X, SmATA X*
Main entry: Yates, Raymond Francis

Hall, Brian P 1935- *BioIn 14, ConAu 61, –9NR, SmATA 31*

Hall, Cameron *ConAu 141, MajTwCW, SmATA 76*
Main entry: del Rey, Lester

Hall, Carolyn Vosburg 1927- *AuBYP 2S, –3, ConAu 61, MichAu 80*

Hall, Caryl *ConAu X, SmATA X*
Main entry: Hansen, Caryl

Hall, Charles Francis 1821-1871 *Alli SUP, BioIn 1, –5, –8, –9, –11, –12, –15, CelCen, DcAmAu, DcBiPP, DcCanB 10, DcNAA, Expl 93, HarEnUS, InSci, OhA&B, OxCCan, OxCShps, WhDW*

Hall, Donald Andrew 1928- *AmAu&B, AuBYP 2, BioIn 6, –8, –10, –12, –13, BlueB 76, ChhPo, –S1, CnE&AP, ConAu 5R, –2NR, ConLC 1, –13, –37, ConPo 70, –75, –80, –85, CurBio 84, DcLB 5, DrAF 76, DrAP 75, DrAPF 83, –85, FifBJA, NewYTBS 83, OxCAmL 65, –83, PenC AM, RAdv 1, REn, REnAL, SmATA 23, WhoAm 74, –76, –78, –80, –82, –84, WorAu 1950, WrDr 76, –80, –82, –84*

Hall, Donald Andrews, Jr. 1928- *AuBYP 3*

Hall, Douglas 1931- *BioIn 8, –12, –14, –15, IlsCB 1957, –1967, SmATA 43*

Hall, Douglas Kent *BioIn 14*

Hall, Douglas Kent 1938- *BioIn 9, ConAu 33R*

Hall, Elizabeth 1929- *AuBYP 2S, –3, ConAu 65, –14NR, –31NR, SmATA 77, WhoAm 76, –78, –92, –94, WhoAmW 81, –91*

Hall, Elvajean 1910- *AuBYP 2, –3, BiDrLUS 70, BioIn 7, –10, ConAu 13R, –8NR, DrLC 69, ForWC 70, SmATA 6, WhoAmW 74, –75, –77, –81, –83, –85, WhoE 74, –75, –77, WhoLibS 55, –66, WhoSSW 78, –80, –82, –84*

Hall, Esther Greenacre *AuBYP 2, –3, BioIn 7*

Hall, Geraldine Marion 1935- *ConAu 33R*

Hall, Gordon Langley *AuBYP 2, –3, Au&Wr 71, BioIn 8, –11, ConAu X*
Main entry: Simmons, Dawn Langley

Hall, H Tom 1932- *BioIn 15, ConGrA 1, IlrAm 1880*

Hall, J Tillman 1916- *ConAu 1R, –6NR, LEduc 74*

Hall, James Norman *TwCRHW 90*

Hall, James Norman 1887-1951 *AmAu&B, AmNov, AuBYP 2, –3, Benet 87, BenetAL 91, BioIn 1, –2, –3, –4, –5, –7, –8, –9, –12, ConAu 123, CyWA 58, DcLEL, JBA 34, ObitOF 79, OxCAmL 65, –83, OxCAusL, PenC AM, REn, REnAL, SmATA 21, TwCA, –SUP, TwCLC 23, WhAm 3, WhNAA*
Pseud./variant:
Gravel, Fern

Hall, Jennie 1875-1921 *AmLY, DcNAA, WhAm 1, WomWWA 14*

Hall, Jesse *AuBYP 2S, –3, ConAu X, SmATA X*
Main entry: Boesen, Victor

Hall, John A 1914- *WhoAmA 86, –89, –91*

Hall, John Alexander 1914- *CanWW 70, –80, –81, –83, –89, WhoAmA 73, –80, –82, –84*

Hall, Katy
Main entry: McMullan, Kate Hall

Hall, Kirsten Marie 1974- *ConAu 135, SmATA 67, WrDr 94*

Hall, Lynn 1937- *Au&Arts 4, AuBYP 2S, –3, BioIn 9, –15, –16, ConAu 21R, –9NR, –25NR, –37NR, DcAmChF 1960, FifBJA, IntAu&W 91, MajAI, ScF&FL 92, SmATA 2, –47, –4AS, TwCChW 83, –89, TwCYAW, WhoAm 92, WrDr 84, –86, –88, –90, –92, –94*

Hall, Malcolm 1945- *AuBYP 2S, –3, BioIn 10, ConAu 49, –4NR, SmATA 7*

Hall, Marjory *AuBYP 2, BioIn 4, –8, ConAu X, CurBio 57, IntAu&W 77X, –82X, SmATA X, WhoAmW 74, –75, –77, WhoE 74, WrDr 76, –80, –82, –84*
Main entry: Yeakley, Marjory Hall

Hall, Marjory 1908- *AuBYP 3, IntAu&W 91, WhoAm 92, WrDr 86, –88, –90, –92, –94*

Hall, Natalie Watson 1923- *BioIn 8, ConAu 5R, IlsCB 1957*

Hall, Norah E L 1914- *ConAu 97, WrDr 80, –82, –84*
Pseud./variant:
Hall, Aylmer

Hall, Pam 1951- *BioIn 13, Profile 2*

Hall, Ralph J 1891- *BioIn 9*

Hall, Richard *DcVicP 2*

Hall, Rosalys Haskell 1914- *AuBYP 2, –3, BioIn 6, –8, –10, ConAu 9R, ForWC 70, MorJA, SmATA 7*

Hall, Ruth 1858- *WomNov*

Hall, Ruth 1858-1934 *AmAu&B, BiD&SB, CarSB, ChhPo S1, DcAmAu, DcNAA, WhAm 4, WhNAA, WomWWA 14*

Hall, Samuel Carter, Mrs *Alli, BritAu 19, CarSB, Chambr 3, ChhPo, –S1, –S2, OxCChiL*
Main entry: Hall, Anna Maria

Hall, Susan *WhoAm 86, –88, –90, –92, –94*

Hall, Susan 1940- *ConAu 57, WhoAm 78, –80, –82, –84, WhoAmW 77, –81*

Hall, Valerie 1939- *IntAu&W 77*
Pseud./variant:
Pitt, Valerie

Hall, William Norman 1915-1974 *AuBYP 2, –3, BioIn 2, –8, –10, ConAu 53*

Hall, Willis *BioIn 17*

Hall, Willis 1929- *BioIn 10, CamGLE, CamGWoT, ChlFicS, CnMD, CnThe, ConAu 101, –36NR, ConDr 73, –77, –82, –88, –93, ConTFT 6, CroCD, DcLEL 1940, EncWT, FilmgC, HalFC 84, –88, IntAu&W 89, –91, LongCTC, MajTwCW, ModWD, OxCEng 85, OxCThe 83, PenC ENG, PlP&P, ScF&FL 92, SmATA 66, Who 74, –82, –83, –85, –88, –90, –92, WhoThe 72, –77, –81, WrDr 76, –80, –82, –84, –86, –88, –90, –92, –94*

Hallard, Peter *ConAu 38NR, MajAI, SmATA 74, TwCChW 89*

Hallard, Peter J *SmATA 3, TwCChW 83*

Hallas, Richard *ConAu 137, MajAI, SmATA X*
Main entry: Knight, Eric Mowbray

Hall-Clarke, James *ConAu X, SmATA X*
Main entry: Rowland-Entwistle, Theodore

Haller, Adolf 1897- *AuBYP 2, –3, BioIn 8*

Haller, Dorcas Woodbury 1946- *BioIn 15, SmATA 46*

Halliburton, Richard *BioIn 16*

Halliburton, Richard 1900-1939 *AmAu&B, BenetAL 91, BioIn 2, –5, –6, –7, CnDAL, ConAu 114, –135, DcNAA, EvLB, OxCAmL 65, –83, REnAL, TwCA, –SUP, WhAm 1, WhNAA*

Halliburton, Warren J 1924- *BioIn 12, BlkWr 1, –2, ConAu 33R, –24NR, LivgBAA, SelBAAf, SelBAAu, SmATA 19, WhoBlA 90, –92*

Halliday, E M 1913- *ConAu 1R*

Halliday, Michael *ConAu X, EncMys, LongCTC, MajTwCW, TwCCr&M 80, –85, –91, WhoSpyF*

Halliday, William R 1926- *BioIn 16, IntAu&W 86, SmATA 52, WrDr 90, –92*

Halliday, William Ross 1926- *WhoAm 86, –88, –90, –92, –94, WhoSSW 88, WhoWest 87, –89, –92, –94, WhoWor 87, –89, –91, –93, WrDr 94*

Hallin, Emily W *IntAu&W 91*

Hallin, Emily Watson *ConAu 26NR*

Hallin, Emily Watson 1919- *BioIn 10, ConAu 25R, –10NR, IntAu&W 77, SmATA 6, WhoAmW 81, WrDr 76, –80, –82, –84, –86, –88, –90, –92, –94*

Hallinan, P K 1944- *BioIn 15, ConAu 69, –11NR, SmATA 37, –39*

Halliwell, James Orchard 1820-1889 *Alli, CamGLE, CarSB, DcBiPP, DcEnA, DcNaB, OxCChiL, OxCEng 67, –85, Str&VC*

Halliwell-Phillips, James Orchard 1820-1889 *BioIn 1, OxCChiL*

Hallman, Ruth 1929- *BioIn 13, –15, ConAu 85, –15NR, SmATA 28, –43*

Hall-Quest, Edna Olga 1899-1986 *AuBYP 3*

Hall-Quest, Olga W 1899-1986 *BioIn 16, ConAu 118, SmATA 47N*

Hall-Quest, Olga Wilbourne 1899- *AuBYP 2, Au&Wr 71, BioIn 8, –11, ConAu 5R, ForWC 70, SmATA 11, WhoAm 74, –76, –78*

Hallstead, William F 1924- *ConAu 21NR*

Hallstead, William Finn 1924- *AuBYP 3*

Hallstead, William Finn, III *ScF&FL 92*

Hallstead, William Finn, III 1924- *AuBYP 2S, BioIn 11, ConAu 5R, –6NR, SmATA 11, WhoE 74, –75, –77, WhoUSWr 88, WhoWrEP 89, –92*

Hallward, Michael 1889- *BioIn 11, ConAu 49, SmATA 12*

Hallworth, Grace *ChlFicS*

Halmi, Robert 1924- *WhoAm 82, –84*

Halsell, Grace 1923- *AuBYP 2, –3, AuNews 1, BioIn 8, –10, ConAu 21R, –13NR, SmATA 13*

Halsell, Grace Eleanor 1923- *WhoAm 88, –90, –92*

Halsman, Philippe 1906-1979 *AmAu&B, AuBYP 2, –3, Au&Wr 71, BioIn 2, –4, –5, –7, –12, –13, ConAu 21R, –10NR, ConPhot 82, –88, CurBio 60, EncTwCJ, ICPEnP, WhAm 7, WhAmArt 85, WhoAm 76, –78, WhoAmA 80N, –82N, –86N, –89N, –91N, WhoWor 74*

Halsted, Anna Roosevelt 1906-1975 *BioIn 7, –10, –14, ConAu 61, ObitOF 79, SmATA 30N, WhoE 74*

Halter, Jon C 1941- *AuBYP 2S, –3, BioIn 13, ConAu 61, –13NR, MedPD, SmATA 22*

Halter, Jon Charles 1941- *WhoAm 90, –92, –94*

Halvorson, Marilyn 1948- *DcChlFi*

Ham, Olive Mary 1918- *Au&Wr 71, IntAu&W 77, WrDr 76, –80, –82, –84, –86, –88*

Hamada, Hirosuke 1893- *ConAu 45*

Hamalian, Leo 1920- *BioIn 15, ConAu 2NR, DrAS 82E, SmATA 41*

Hamann, Bente *AuBYP 2S, –3*

Hamberger, John F 1934- *BioIn 8, –12, ConAu 69, IlsBYP, IlsCB 1957, –1967, SmATA 14*

Hambleton, Jack *AuBYP 3*

Hambleton, Jack 1901-1961 *AuBYP 2, BioIn 8, CreCan 2*

Hamblin, Dora Jane 1920- *AuBYP 2, –3, BioIn 6, –14, ConAu 37R, ForWC 70, SmATA 36, WhoAmW 74*

Hamelt, Ova
Main entry: Lupoff, Richard Allen

Hamer, Margaret *TelT*
Pseud./variant:
Browne, Maggie

Hamer, Sam Hield 1869- *ChhPo, –S2*

Hamerstrom, Frances 1907- *AmMWSc 82, –86, –89, –92, BioIn 12, –13, ConAu 69, SmATA 24, WhoAmW 93, WhoMW 93*
Pseud./variant:
Windsor, Claire

Hamerton, Philip Gilbert *DcVicP 2*

Hamerton, Philip Gilbert 1834-1894 *Alli SUP, ArtsNiC, BbD, BiD&SB, BioIn 9, BritAu 19, CarSB, Chambr 3, ChhPo, –S1, ClaDrA, CyEd, DcBiA, DcEnL, DcNaB S1, DcVicP 2, EvLB, NewC, StaCVF*

Hamil, Thomas Arthur 1928- *AuBYP 2, –3, BioIn 8, –12, ConAu 73, SmATA 14*
Pseud./variant:
Hamil, Tom

Hamil, Tom
Main entry: Hamil, Thomas Arthur

Hamill, Ethel *ConAu X, IntAu&W 77X, SmATA X, TwCRHW 90, WrDr 76, –80, –82, –84, –86, –88, –90, –92*
Main entry: Webb, Jean Francis

Hamill, Ethel 1910- *BioIn 14, WrDr 94*

Hamilton, Alan 1943- *ConAu 36NR, SmATA 66*

Hamilton, Alice *SmATA X*
Main entry: Cromie, Alice Hamilton

Hamilton, Buzz *ConAu X*
Main entry: Hemming, Roy

Hamilton, Cecily 1872-1952 *LongCTC*

Hamilton, Charles 1876-1961 *CamGLE, ConAu 29NR*

Hamilton, Charles 1913- *AuBYP 2S, –3, BioIn 8, –10, –11, –12, –17, BlueB 76, ChhPo S2, ConAu 5R, –3NR, –20NR, CurBio 76, IntAu&W 91, SmATA 65, TwCChW 78, WrDr 80, –82, –84, –86, –88, –90, –92, –94*

Hamilton, Charles Harold St John 1875?-1961 *BioIn 3, –6, –7, –8, –10, –14, ConAu 73, DcNaB 1961, LongCTC, OxCChiL, OxCEng 67, –85, SmATA 13, TwCChW 83, WhoChL*

Hamilton, Charles Harold St John 1876-1961 *GrBr*

Hamilton, Clive *AuBYP 3, ConAu X, –33NR, CurBio 44, –64, EncSF 93, EvLB, LongCTC, MajAI, MajTwCW, NewC, SmATA X, TwCA SUP*
Main entry: Lewis, Clive Staples

Hamilton, Clive 1898-1963 *RAdv 13-1*

Hamilton, Diane *AuBYP 3*

Hamilton, Dorothy 1906-1983 *BioIn 11, –14, ConAu 33R, –110, SmATA 12, –35N, WhoAmW 77*

Hamilton, Edith 1865-1963 *ContDcW 89*

Hamilton, Edith 1867-1963 *AmAu&B, AmWomM, AmWomPl, AnCL, BenetAL 91, BioAmW, BioIn 3, –4, –5, –6, –7, –8, –9, –11, –12, ConAu 77, CurBio 63, DcAmB S7, EncAB-H, HerW, –84, InWom SUP, IntDcWB, NotAW MOD, ObitOF 79, RComAH, REn, REnAL, SmATA 20, TwCA, –SUP, WebAB 74, –79, WhAm 4, WhNAA*

Hamilton, Elizabeth 1906- *Au&Wr 71, BiDIrW, BioIn 3, –13, ConAu P-1, IntAu&W 82, SmATA 23, WrDr 76, –80, –82, –84, –86, –88, –90, –92, –94*

Hamilton, Franklin *MajAI*

Hamilton, Franklin W 1923- *WrDr 86, –88, –90*

Hamilton, Franklin Willard 1923- *ConAu 33R, DrAS 74E, –82E, MichAu 80, WrDr 76, –80, –82, –84*

Hamilton, Gail *ArtclWW 2, AuBYP 2S, –3, ConAu X, –28NR, DrAPF 89, –91, –93, SmATA 77, WrDr 90, –92*
Main entry: Corcoran, Barbara

Hamilton, Gail 1911- *BioIn 15, WrDr 94*

Hamilton, Kay *AuBYP 2, –3, ConAu X, IntAu&W 77X, OhA&B*
Main entry: DeLeeuw, Cateau Wilhelmina

Hamilton, Mary 1927- *BioIn 16, ConAu 123, SmATA 55, WrDr 90, –92*

Hamilton, Mary E 1927- *WrDr 94*

Hamilton, Mollie *IntAu&W 91X, MajTwCW, SmATA X, TwCRHW 90*
Main entry: Kaye, Mary Margaret

Hamilton, Morse 1943- *BioIn 14, ConAu 108, IntAu&W 86, –89, –91, SmATA 35*

Hamilton, Ralph *MajAI*

Hamilton, Robert W *ConAu X*
Main entry: Stratemeyer, Edward L

Hamilton, Russel *AuBYP 2, –3, BioIn 8*

Hamilton, Virginia 1926- *AuBYP 3*

Hamilton, Virginia 1936- *ArtclWW 2, Au&Arts 2, AuBYP 2, Au&ICB, AuNews 1, BioIn 9, –10, –11, –14, –15, –16, –17, BlkAWP, BlkWr 1, –2, BlmGWL, CamGLE, ChhPo S2, ChlLR 1, –11, ConAu 25R, –20NR, –37NR, ConLC 26, DcLB 33, –52, FourBJA, InB&W 80, MajAI, MajTwCW, MorBMP, NewbC 1966, NotBlAW 92, OxCChiL, ScF&FL 92, SmATA 4, –56, SouSt, TwCChW 78, –83, –89, WhoAm 76, –78, –80, –82, –84, –86, –88, –90, –92, –94, WhoAmW 74, –77, –81, –83, –85, –87, –89, –91, –93, WhoBlA 85, –88, –90, –92, WhoUSWr 88, WhoWrEP 89, –92, WrDr 80, –82, –84, –86, –88, –90, –92*

Hamilton, Virginia Esther 1933- *BlkAull, –92*

Hamilton, Virginia Esther 1936- *ChlFicS, DcAmChF 1960, –1985, EncSF 93, InB&W 85, TwCYAW, WrDr 94*

Hamilton-Paterson, James *AuBYP 3, BioIn 17*

Hamilton-Paterson, James 1941- *ConAu 137*

Hamilton-Paterson, James Lee *AuBYP 2S*

Hamlet, Ova *EncSF 93, TwCSFW 86, –91*

Hamlet, Ova 1935- *SmATA X*

Hamley, Dennis *ChlFicS*

Hamley, Dennis 1935- *BioIn 15, ConAu 57, –11NR, –26NR, ScF&FL 92, SmATA 39, –69*

Hamlin, V T 1900- *ArtCS*

Hamm, Jack 1916- *BioIn 2, ConAu 5R, –9NR*

Hammer, Charles *BioIn 16*

Hammer, Charles 1934- *SmATA 58*

Hammer, Jeanne-Ruth 1912- *ConAu 9R*

Hammer, Richard 1928- *BioIn 10, ConAu 25R, –11NR, SmATA 6, WhoEnt 92*

Hammerman, Gay M 1926- *BioIn 11, ConAu 33R, SmATA 9*

Hammett, Dashiell *DcLB Y91*

Hammett, Dashiell 1894-1961 *AgeMat, AmAu&B, AuNews 1, Benet 87, BenetAL 91, BioIn 2, –4, –5, –6, –7, –8, –10, –11, –12, –13, –14, –15, –17, BlmGEL, CamGEL, CamGLE, CamHAL, CasWL, CmCal, CrMov, CnDAL, CnMWL, ConAu 81, ConLC 3, –5, –10, –19, –47, CorpD, CrtSuMy, CyWA 58, –89, DcFM, DcLB DS6, DcLEL, EncAB-H, EncMys, EncWB, EvLB, FilmgC, HalFC 84, –88, LongCTC, MagSAmL, MajTwCW, ModAL, –S1, –S2, Novels, ObitOF 79, ObitT 1961, OxCAmL 65, –83, OxCEng 67, –85, OxCFilm, PenC AM, REn, REnAL, RfGAmL 87, ScFEYrs, ShSWr, TwCA, –SUP, TwCCr&M 80, –85, –91, TwCWr, WebAB 74, –79, WebE&AL, WhAm 4, WhoTwCL, WorAlBi, WorAl, WorEFlm*
Pseud./variant:
Hammett, Samuel Dashiell

Hammett, Samuel Dashiell
Main entry: Hammett, Dashiell

Hammid, Hella 1921- *MacBEP*

Hammond, Ralph *AuBYP 3, BioIn 16, DrAPF 93, WrDr 86, –88, –90, –92*
Main entry: Hammond Innes, Ralph

Hammond, Winifred 1899- *AuBYP 3*

Hammond, Winifred Graham 1899- *AuBYP 2S, ConAu 107, IndAu 1917, SmATA 29*

Hammond Innes, Ralph *ConNov 86, TwCCr&M 91*

Hammond Innes, Ralph 1913- *AuBYP 2, –3, Au&Wr 71, BioIn 3, –4, –5, –8, –10, –14, –16, BlueB 76, ConAu 5R, –4NR, –26NR, CurBio 54, IntAu&W 77, –82, –86, –89, –91,*

IntWW 75, –76, –77, –78, –79, –80, –81, –82, –83, –89, –91, LongCTC, Who 74, –82, –83, –85, –88, –90, –92, WhoWor 74, –78, –84, –87, –89, –91, –93, WrDr 76, –80, –82, –84, –86, –88, –90, –92, –94
Pseud./variant:
Hammond, Ralph

Hammontree, Marie Gertrude 1913- *ConAu 5R, ForWC 70, IndAu 1917, SmATA 13, WhoMW 74, WrDr 76, –80*

Hamori, Laszlo Dezso 1911- *ConAu 9R*

Hampden, John 1898- *Au&Wr 71, ConAu 109, Who 74*

Hample, Stoo 1926- *ChhPo*

Hampshire, Michael Allen *IlsBYP*

Hampson, Alfred Leete 1889?-1952 *BioIn 2, –3, ChhPo*

Hampson, Denman 1929- *SmATA 15*

Hampson, Frank 1917-1985 *EncSF 93*

Hampson, Frank 1918- *BioIn 14*

Hampson, Frank 1918-1985 *AnObit 1985, BiDScF, BioIn 15, DcNaB 1981, SmATA 46N*

Hampson, Zena 1926- *ConAu X, –19NR, IntAu&W 77, –82, WhoAm 80, WhoAmW 77*
Pseud./variant:
Collier, Jane
Collier, Zena
Shumsky, Zena Feldman

Hampton, Christopher Martin 1929- *ConAu 53, ConPo 75, DcLEL 1940, IntAu&W 77, –82, WrDr 76, –80, –86, –88*

Hamre, Leif *TwCChW 89B*

Hamre, Leif 1914- *Au&Wr 71, BioIn 10, ConAu 5R, –4NR, FourBJA, IntAu&W 82, –89, SmATA 5, TwCChW 78B, –83B, WrDr 76, –80, –82, –84, –86, –88, –90, –92, –94*

Hamsa, Bobbie 1944- *BioIn 15, –16, ConAu 106, SmATA 38, –52*

Hanaburgh, David Henry 1910- *WhoE 77*

Hanaford, Phebe Ann 1829-1921 *Alli SUP, AmAu&B, BbD, BiD&SB, CarSB, DcAmAu, HarEnUS, InWom SUP*

Hancock, Alice VanFossen 1890- *ConAu 1R*

Hancock, Lyn *IntAu&W 86X*

Hancock, Lyn 1938- *BioIn 9, –13, Profile 2, WhoCanL 85, –87, –92*

Hancock, Mary A 1923- *BioIn 14, ConAu 37R, SmATA 31*

Hancock, Ralph Lowell 1903- *AmAu&B, Au&Wr 71, ConAu P-1, IndAu 1917, IntAu&W 77, WhoAm 74, –76, –78, –80, –82, –84, –86*

Hancock, Ralph Lowell 1903-1987 *WhAm 9*

Hancock, Sibyl 1940- *BioIn 11, ConAu 49, –1NR, –16NR, SmATA 9*

Handel, Leo A *IntMPA 86, –88, –92*

Handel, Leo A 1941- *IntMPA 75, –76, –78, –81, –82, –84, –86, –77*

Handford, Martin *News 91, –91-3*

Handford, Martin 1956- *ChlLR 22, SmATA 64*

Handford, Martin John 1956- *ConAu 137, MajAI, WhoAm 94*

Handford, Nourma 1911- *AuWomWr, DcChlFi, OxCAusL, SingR 1*

Handforth, Thomas S 1897-1948 *AmAu&B, ArtsAmW 3, AuBYP 2, BioIn 1, –2, –4, –5, –7, Cald 1938, IlsBYP, IlsCB 1744, –1946, JBA 51, SmATA 42, WhAm 2, WhAmArt 85, WhoAmA 78N, –80N, –82N, –89N, –91N*

Handforth, Thomas Schofield 1897-1948 *AuBYP 3*

Handville, Robert T 1924- *BioIn 11, IlrAm 1880, –F, SmATA 45, WhoAm 84, WhoAmA 73, –78, –80, –82, –84, –86, –89, –91*

Handville, Robert Tompkins 1924- *WhoAm 86, –88, –90, –92*

Hane, Roger 1940-1975 *BioIn 10, SmATA 20N*

Hanes, Frank Borden *DrAPF 87, –89, –91, –93*

Hanes, Frank Borden 1920- *AmAu&B, BioIn 3, –4, ConAu 1R, –28NR, DrAPF 83, –85, WhoAm 76, –78, –80, –82, –84, –86, –88, –90, –92, –94, WhoSSW 73, –75, –76, WhoUSWr 88, WhoWor 82, WhoWrEP 89, –92, WrDr 76, –80, –82, –84, –86, –88, –90, –92, –94*

Haney, Erene Cheki *AuBYP 2S, –3*

Haney, Lynn 1941- *BioIn 13, ConAu 49, –1NR, ScF&FL 92, SmATA 23*

Hanff, Helene *ArtclWW 2, BioIn 11, –12, –13, –14, ConAu 5R, –3NR, NewYTBS 82, SmATA 11*

Hanff, Helene 1916- *Who 90, –92, WhoUSWr 88, WhoWrEP 89, –92, WrDr 90, –92, –94*

Hankey, William Lee 1869-1952 *BioIn 1, –6, –14, ChhPo S2, DcBrBI, IlsCB 1744*

Hankinson, Charles James 1866- *WhoLA*
Pseud./variant:
Holland, Clive

Hanley, Boniface 1924- *BioIn 17, SmATA 65*

Hanley, Boniface Francis 1924- *IntAu&W 86*

Hanlon, Emily *DrAPF 87, –89, –91, –93*

Hanlon, Emily 1945- *AuBYP 3, BioIn 12, –16, ConAu 77, ScF&FL 92, SixBJA, SmATA 15, WhoUSWr 88, WhoWrEP 89, –92*

Hann, Jacquie 1951- *BioIn 12, ConAu 73, –13NR, SmATA 19*

Hann, Judith 1942- *SmATA 77*

Hanna, Alfred Jackson 1893-1978 *ConAu 45, –2NR, DrAS 74H, –78H, WhAm 7, WhoAm 74, –76, –78, WhoWor 74*

Hanna, Archibald, Jr. 1916- *BiDrLUS 70, DrAS 74H, –78H, WhoAm 74, –76, –78, –80, –82, –84, –86, –88, –90, WhoLibS 55, –66*

Hanna, Bill
Main entry: Hanna, William

Hanna, Cheryl Irene 1951- *BlkAuII 92*

Hanna, Geneva R *AuBYP 3*

Hanna, Geneva R 1914- *AuBYP 2, BioIn 8*

Hanna, Jack *BioIn 16*

Hanna, Jack 1947- *WhoMW 86*

Hanna, Jack Bushnell 1947- *ConAu 141, SmATA 74, WhoAm 92*

Hanna, Kathryn Abbey 1896-1967 *EncAB-A 39, WhAm 5, WhFla*

Hanna, Nellie L 1908- *BioIn 16, SmATA 55*
Pseud./variant:
Nell

Hanna, Paul Robert 1902- *BioIn 11, –13, ConAu 45, LEduc 74, SmATA 9, WhoAm 76, –78, –80, –82, –84, –86, WhoWor 84, –87*

Hanna, William *IntMPA 86, –88*

Hanna, William 1910- *BioIn 16, ConTFT 8, SmATA 51*
Pseud./variant:
Hanna, Bill

Hanna, William 1911- *IntMPA 92*

Hannam, Charles 1925- *BioIn 16, SmATA 50, WhoWor 89*

Hannam, Charles Lewis 1925- *WrDr 94*

Hannele, Pirkko *SmATA 76*
Main entry: Vainio, Pirkko

Hannon, Leslie *OxCCan SUP*

Hannum, Sara *AuBYP 2, –3, BioIn 8, ChhPo S1*

Hano, Arnold 1922- *AuBYP 2, –3, BiDAmSp Sup, BioIn 8, –11, ConAu 9R, –5NR, SmATA 12, WhoWest 74, –76, –82*

Hansberry, Lorraine *OxCAmT 84*

Hansberry, Lorraine 1930-1965 *AfrAmW, AmAu&B, AmWomD, ArtclWW 2, AuNews 2, Benet 87, BenetAL 91, BiE&WWA, BioAmW, BioIn 5, –6, –7, –8, –9, –10, –12, –13, –14, –15, –16, –17, BlkAWP, BlkLC, BlkWr 1, BlmGWL, CamGLE, CamGWoT, CamHAL, CasWL, CnMD SUP, ConAu 25R, –109, –3BS, ConBlAP 88, ConBlB 6, ConDr 77F, –82E, –88E, ConLC 17, –62, ContDcW 89, CroCD, CurBio 59, –65, CyWA 89, DcLB 7, –38, DcLEL 1940, DrBlPA 90, DramC 2, EncWL 2, EncWT, FemiCLE, HalFC 84, –88, HanAmWH, HerW 84, IntDcWB, MagSAmL, MajTwCW, McGEWD 72, –84, ModAL S2, ModBlW, ModWD, NatCAB 60, NegAl 76, –83, –89, NewCon, NotAW MOD, NotBlAW 92, NotNAT B, NotWoAT, OxCAmL 83, PlP&P, –A, RAdv 13-2, REnAL, RfGAmL 87, SelBAAf, SelBAAu, WhAm 4, WorAlBi, WorAl, WorAu 1950*

Hansberry, Lorraine Vivian 1930-1965 *IntDcT 2*

Hansen, Caryl *BioIn 15*

Hansen, Caryl 1929- *ConAu 108, SmATA 39*
Pseud./variant:
Hall, Caryl

Hansen, Harry 1884-1977 *AmAu&B, AuBYP 2, –3, BioIn 1, –4, –8, –11, –17, ConAu 69, –73, CurBio 42, –91N, REnAL, TwCA, –SUP, WhAm 7, Who 74, WhoAm 74, –76, –78*

Hansen, Joyce *BioIn 15, –16*

Hansen, Joyce 1942- *ChlLR 21, ConAu 105, DcAmChF 1985, MajAI, SmATA 39, –46, –15AS, TwCChW 89, WrDr 90, –92, –94*

Hansen, Joyce Viola 1942- *BlkAuII 92, ConAu 43NR*

Hansen, Joyce W 1942- *BlkAuII*

Hansen, Mary Lewis 1933- *ConAu 17R*

Hansen, Ron *BioIn 16*

Hansen, Ron 1947- *AuBYP 3, ConNov 91, SmATA 56, TwCWW 91, WrDr 92, -94*

Hanser, Richard Frederick 1909-1981 *AuBYP 2S, -3, BioIn 12, -13, ConAu 5R, NewYTBS 81, SmATA 13, WhoAm 74, -76, -78, -80, -82, WhoWor 74*

Hanson, Charles Henry *Alli SUP, CarSB*

Hanson, Christilot 1947- *BioIn 7, CanWW 70, -80, -81, -83, -89*

Hanson, Harvey 1941- *ConAu 65*

Hanson, Joan 1938- *BioIn 11, ConAu 33R, -15NR, IntAu&W 91, SmATA 8, WrDr 76, -80, -82, -84, -86, -88, -90*

Hanson, Joseph E 1894?-1971 *BioIn 9, -13, ConAu 104, SmATA 27N*

Hanson, Michael James 1942- *ConAu 61, WrDr 76, -80, -82, -84, -86, -88*

Hansson, Gunilla 1939- *BioIn 17, SmATA 64*

Hapgood, Charles Hutchins 1904- *Au&Wr 71, ConAu 17R*

Hapgood, David 1926- *ConAu 13R, WrDr 76, -80, -82, -84, -86, -88, -90, -92, -94*

Hapgood, Elizabeth Reynolds 1894-1974 *BiE&WWA, BioIn 10, NewYTBS 74, NotNAT*

Harald, Eric *AuBYP 2S, -3, ConAu X, SmATA X*
Main entry: Boesen, Victor

Haraszty, Eszter *BioIn 4, -14*

Harcourt, Ellen Knowles 1890?-1984 *BioIn 13, -14, ConAu 111, SmATA 36N*

Hardcastle, Michael 1933- *BioIn 15, -16, ChlFicS, ConAu 25R, -12NR, IntAu&W 77, -89, -91, SmATA 38, -47, TwCChW 83, -89, WrDr 76, -80, -82, -84, -86, -88, -90, -92, -94*
Pseud./variant:
Clark, David

Harden, Oleta Elizabeth 1935- *ConAu 37R, IntAu&W 77, WhoAm 80, -82, -84, -90, -92, -94, WhoAmW 75, -77, WhoMW 78, -80, -82, -84, WrDr 76, -80*

Hardendorff, Jeanne B *ChhPo S2*

Harder, Eleanor 1925- *ConAu 37R*

Harder, Raymond Wymbs, Jr. *ConAu 85*

Harding, Charlotte 1873-1951 *BioIn 15, IlrAm 1880, -A, IlsCB 1744*

Harding, James 1929- *Au&Wr 71, ConAu 33R, -14NR, -32NR, IntAu&W 77, -89, -91, WrDr 76, -80, -82, -84, -86, -88, -90, -92, -94*

Harding, James Warren 1918- *WhoAm 92*

Harding, John Lee 1937- *DcChlFi*

Harding, Lee 1937- *BioIn 14, ConAu 106, IntAu&W 91, OxCAusL, ScF&FL 92, ScFSB, SmATA 31, -32, TwCChW 89, TwCSFW 86, -91, WrDr 84, -86, -88, -90, -92*
Pseud./variant:
Nye, Harold G

Harding, Lee John 1937- *EncSF 93, WrDr 94*

Harding, Robert 1897- *ChhPo S1*

Hardwick, Michael 1924- *Au&Wr 71, ConAu 49, -2NR, IntAu&W 77, -82, WrDr 76, -80, -82, -84, -86, -88, -90, -92, -94*

Hardwick, Michael 1924-1991 *ConAu 134*

Hardwick, Mollie *Au&Wr 71, BioIn 14, ConAu 49, -2NR, InWom SUP, IntAu&W 77, -82, -91, Novels, TwCRHW 90, Who 82, -83, -85, -88, -90, -92, WrDr 76, -80, -82, -84, -86, -88, -90, -92, -94*

Hardwick, Richard H 1923- *BioIn 11, ConAu 5R, -9NR, SmATA 12, WrDr 76, -80, -82, -84*
Pseud./variant:
Holmes, Rick

Hardwick, Sylvia *ConAu X*
Main entry: Doherty, Ivy R Duffy

Hardy, Alice Dale *ConAu 26NR, -P-2, SmATA 1, -67*
Main entry: Stratemeyer, Edward L

Hardy, David A 1936- *BiDScF, BioIn 11, ConAu 61, -8NR, IntAu&W 77, -82, ScF&FL 92, SmATA 9, WhoWor 84*

Hardy, David Andrews 1936- *EncSF 93, IntAu&W 86, -89*

Hardy, Jon 1958- *BioIn 16, ConAu 123, SmATA 53*

Hardy, Paul 1862- *BioIn 14, ChhPo, –S1, –S2, DcBrBI*

Hardy, Stuart *ConAu X, SmATA X*
Main entry: Schisgall, Oscar

Hardy, Thomas 1840-1928 *Alli SUP, AnCL, AtlBL, Benet 87, BbD, BiD&SB, BioIn 1, –2, –3, –4, –5, –6, –7, –8, –9, –10, –11, –12, –13, –14, –15, –16, –17, BlmGEL, BritAu 19, BritWr 6, CamGEL, CamGLE, CasWL, CelCen, Chambr 3, ChhPo, –S1, –S2, CnDBLB 5, CnE&AP, CnMWL, ConAu 104, –123, CrtT 3, CyWA 58, DcBiA, DcEnA, –A, DcEnL, DcEuL, DcLB 18, –19, DcLEL, DcNaB 1922, Dis&D, EncWL, –2, EvLB, FilmgC, GrBr, HalFC 84, –88, LongCEL, LongCTC, MagSWL, MajTwCW, McGEWB, ModBrL, –S1, –S2, ModWD, NewC, Novels, OxCChiL, OxCEng 67, –85, OxCMus, PenC ENG, PenEncH, PoeCrit 8, RAdv 1, –13-1, RComWL, REn, RfGEnL 91, ScF&FL 92, ShSCr 2, SmATA 25, TwCLC 4, –10, –18, –32, –48, TwCWr, WebE&AL, WhDW, WhoChL, WhoLA, WhoTwCL, WorAlBi, WorAl, WorLitC*

Hardy, William G 1895- *BioIn 14*

Hardy, William George 1895?- *Au&Wr 71, BioIn 1, CanNov, CanWW 70, CanWr, ConAu 5R, CreCan 1, DcLEL, DrAS 74F, –82F, IntAu&W 82, OxCCan, WhNAA, WrDr 76, –82*

Hare, Norma Q 1924- *BioIn 15, ConAu 101, SmATA 41, –46*

Hare, T Truxton 1878-1956 *BioIn 4, –6, CarSB, ObitOF 79, WhAm 6*

Harford, Henry *ConAu X, SmATA X*
Main entry: Hudson, William Henry

Hargens, Charles 1893- *ConICB, WhAmArt 85*

Hargis, Ed *ChhPo*

Hargis, John Edwin 1914- *BioIn 1, IlsCB 1744*

Hargrave, Leonie *AuBYP 3, ConAu 36NR, EncSF 93, MajAI, MajTwCW, WrDr 86, –88, –90, –92, –94*
Main entry: Disch, Thomas Michael

Hargrave, Sandra 1945- *SingR 2*

Hargreaves, Roger *BioIn 15, –16, OxCChiL*

Hargreaves, Roger 1935-1988 *AnObit 1988, ConAu 126, SmATA 56N*

Hargrove, James 1947- *ConAu 120, SmATA 50, –57*

Hargrove, Jim 1947- *BioIn 16, SmATA X*

Harington, Joy 1914- *Au&Wr 71, IntMPA 75, –76, –78, –81, –82, –84, –86, –88, –77, WrDr 76, –80, –82, –84, –86, –88, –90, –92*

Harington, Joy 1914-1991 *WrDr 94N*

Hark, Mildred *ConAu X, SmATA X*
Main entry: McQueen, Mildred Hark

Harkaway, Hal *ConAu X, MajAI*
Main entry: Stratemeyer, Edward L

Harker, Herbert *OxCCan SUP*

Harker, Ronald 1909- *ConAu 77*

Harkins, Philip 1912- *AuBYP 2, –3, BioIn 6, –7, –10, ConAu 29R, MorJA, SmATA 6*
Pseud./variant:
Blaine, John

Harlan, Elizabeth 1945- *BioIn 14, –15, ConAu 111, IntAu&W 86, –89, –91, SmATA 35, –41*

Harlan, Glen *ConAu X, –30NR, IntAu&W 77X, SmATA X, WrDr 76, –80, –82, –84, –86, –88, –90, –92*
Main entry: Cebulash, Mel

Harlan, Glen 1937- *WrDr 94*

Harlan, Judith 1949- *SmATA 74*

Harland, Henry 1861-1905 *Alli SUP, AmAu, AmAu&B, BenetAL 91, BbD, BiD&SB, BioIn 11, CamGEL, CamGLE, CamHAL, CarSB, Chambr 3, DcAmAu, DcBiA, DcCathB, DcEnA A, DcNaB S2, DcNAA, EvLB, LongCTC, Novels, OxCAmL 65, –83, OxCEng 67, –85, PenC AM, REnAL, StaCVF, WhAm 1*

Harland, Marion *Alli, –SUP, AmAu, AmAu&B, BenetAL 91, BiDSA, BiD&SB, BioIn 4, –12, ChhPo, DcAmAu, DcBiA, DcNAA, InWom SUP, OxCAmL 65, –83, REnAL, WomNov*
Main entry: Terhune, Mary Virginia

Harland, Marion 1830-1922 *FemiCLE*

Harley, Timothy *Alli SUP*

Harlow, Alvin Fay 1875- *AuBYP 3*

Harlow, Alvin Fay 1875-1963 *AmAu&B, AuBYP 2, BioIn 6, –8, ObitOF 79, WhAm 4, WhNAA*

Harman, Fred *EncACom*

Harman, Fred 1902?-1982 *BioIn 1, –11, –12, –14, –17, ConAu 106, NewYTBS 82, SmATA 30N, WhAmArt 85*

Harman, Hugh 1903-1982 *AnObit 1982, BioIn 13, –14, ConAu 108, HalFC 84, –88, SmATA 33N, WorECar*

Harmelink, Barbara *BioIn 11, ConAu 61, SmATA 9*

Harmer, Juliet *AuBYP 3*

Harmer, Mabel 1894- *BioIn 15, ConAu 9R, SmATA 45*

Harmon, Margaret 1906- *BioIn 12, ConAu 69, SmATA 20*

Harmon, William *DrAPF 87, –89, –91, –93*

Harmon, William 1938- *BioIn 17, ConAu 32NR, –35NR, ConLC 38, SmATA 65*

Harms, Valerie *DrAPF 87, –89, –91, –93*

Harms, Valerie 1940- *ConAu 49, –2NR, WhoAmW 77, WhoUSWr 88, WhoWrEP 89, –92, WomWMM B*

Harmsworth, Alfred Charles William 1865-1922 *BioIn 14, –16, DcBrBI, DcNaB 1922, GrBr, LongCTC, NewC, OxCChiL, OxCEng 85, WorAl*

Harnan, Terry 1920- *BioIn 11, ConAu 45, IntAu&W 77X, –82X, SmATA 12*
Pseud./variant:
Hull, Eric Traviss

Harnden, Ruth Peabody *AuBYP 2S, –3, ChhPo S2, ConAu 73, DcAmChF 1960*

Harner, Nevin Cowger 1901-1951 *BioIn 2, WhAm 3*

Harnett, Cynthia *BioIn 14*

Harnett, Cynthia 1893-1981 *TwCChW 89*

Harnett, Cynthia Mary 1893-1981 *AuBYP 2, –3, Au&Wr 71, BioIn 2, –5, –7, –8, –9, –10, ConAu 111, –P-1, IlsCB 1946, OxCChiL, SmATA 5, –32N, ThrBJA, TwCChW 78, –83, TwCYAW, WhoChL, WrDr 76, –80, –82*

Harper, Anita 1943- *BioIn 15, ConAu 114, SmATA 41*

Harper, Mary Wood *ConAu X, SmATA X*
Main entry: Dixon, Jeanne

Harper, Wilhelmina 1884-1973 *AmAu&B, AuBYP 2, –3, BioIn 7, –9, –13, ConAu P-1, SmATA 4, –26N, WhAm 6, WhNAA, WhoAmW 74, –75*

Harrah, Michael 1940- *BioIn 15, ConAu 115, SmATA 41*

Harrell, Janice 1945- *SmATA 70*

Harrell, Sara Gordon *BioIn 13, ConAu 105, SmATA X*
Main entry: Banks, Sara

Harrell, Sara Gordon 1938- *ScF&FL 92*

Harribance, Sean 1939- *BioIn 10, –11, BioNews 74*

Harries, Joan *IntAu&W 86X*

Harries, Joan 1922- *BioIn 15, ConAu 107, IntAu&W 89, SmATA 39*
Pseud./variant:
Katsarakis, Joan Harris

Harriett *ConAu 77, WhoAmW 75, –77, –81, WhoE 81, –83*
Main entry: Ginnings, Harriett W

Harrington, Alan *DrAPF 87, –89, –91, –93*

Harrington, Alan 1919- *AmAu&B, BioIn 3, ConAu 73, DrAF 76, EncSF 93, Novels, PenC AM, ScF&FL 92*

Harrington, Evelyn Davis *AuBYP 3*

Harrington, Lyn Davis 1911- *AuBYP 2, –3, BioIn 7, –10, CaW, ConAu 5R, OxCCan, –SUP, Profile 1, SmATA 5*

Harrington, Mark Raymond 1882-1971 *ConAu P-2, WhAm 5*

Harrington, Michael *BioIn 14, IntvTCA 2*

Harrington, Michael 1928- *AmAu&B, Benet 87, BenetAL 91, BiDAmL, BioIn 6, –8, –11, CelR, –90, ConAu 17R, –19NR, ConIsC 1, CurBio 69, –88, EncWB, NewYTBE 72, WhoAm 74, –76, –78, –80, –82, –84, –86, –88, WhoUSWr 88, WhoWrEP 89, WorAl, WorAu 1975, WrDr 80, –82, –84, –86, –88*

Harrington, Michael 1928-1989 *AmPeW, AnObit 1989, BioIn 16, ConAu 129, CurBio 89N, NewYTBS 89, RComAH, WhAm 10, WorAlBi*

Harris, Agnes *AuBYP 2S, –3*

Harris, Alan 1944- *SmATA 71*

Harris, Aurand 1915- *BioIn 15, ConAu 93, –16NR, –36NR, IntAu&W 82, –86, –89, –91, OxCChiL, SmATA 37, TwCChW 78, –83, –89, WhoAm 82, –84, –86, –88, –90, –92, –94, WhoEnt 92, WrDr 80, –82, –84, –86, –88, –90, –92, –94*

Harris, Benjamin d1720? *DcLB 42, –43, OxCChiL, WhDW*

Harris, Catherine
Main entry: Ainsworth, Catherine Harris

Harris, Christie 1907- *AuBYP 3, BlmGWL, DcLB 88, IntAu&W 91, SmATA 10AS, TwCChW 89, WhoCanL 87, -92, WrDr 86, -88, -90, -92*

Harris, Christie Irwin 1907- *ArtclWW 2, AuBYP 2S, BioIn 10, CaW, ConAu 5R, -6NR, ConLC 12, FourBJA, OxCCan SUP, OxCCanL, OxCChiL, Profile 1, SmATA 6, TwCChW 78, -83, WhoCanL 85, WrDr 80, -82, -84*

Harris, Christie Lucy Irwin 1907- *DcChlFi, MajAI, SmATA 74, WrDr 94*

Harris, Colver *AuBYP 3, ConAu X, OhA&B, SmATA 7*
Main entry: Colver, Anne

Harris, Dorothy Joan 1931- *BioIn 13, ConAu 45, -1NR, Profile 2, SmATA 13*

Harris, Gene Gray 1929- *ConAu 17R*

Harris, George Lawrence 1910- *AmMWSc 73S, -76P*

Harris, Geraldine 1951- *BioIn 16, ScF&FL 92, SmATA 54, TwCChW 89, WrDr 90, -92, -94*

Harris, Jacqueline L 1929- *BioIn 17, ConAu 126, SmATA 62*

Harris, Janet 1932-1979 *AuBYP 2S, -3, BioIn 9, -12, -13, ConAu 33R, -93, -28NR, ScF&FL 92, SmATA 4, -23N*

Harris, Joel Chandler *IntvTCA 2*

Harris, Joel Chandler 1848-1908 *Alli SUP, AmAu, AmAu&B, AnCL, AtlBL, AuBYP 2, -3, Benet 87, BenetAL 91, BbD, BiDAmJo, BiDSA, BiD&SB, BioIn 1, -2, -3, -4, -5, -6, -7, -8, -10, -11, -12, -13, -14, -15, -16, -17, CamGEL, CamGLE, CamHAL, CarSB, CasWL, Chambr 3, ChhPo, -S1, -S2, CnDAL, ConAu 104, -137, CyWA 58, DcAmAu, DcAmSR, DcBiA, DcCathB, DcEnA A, DcLB 11, -23, -42, -78, -91, DcLEL, DcNAA, EncAB-H, EncAHmr, EncAJ, EncSoH, EvLB, FamAYP, FifSWrB, HalFC 84, -88, HarEnUS, JrnUS, JBA 34, MajAI, McGEWB, MemAm, Novels, OxCAmL 65, -83, OxCChiL, OxCEng 67, -85, PenC AM, RAdv 1, -13-1, REn, REnAL, RfGAmL 87, RfGShF, Str&VC, TwCChW 78A, -83A, -89A, TwCLC 2, WebAB 74, -79, WebE&AL, WhDW, WhAm 1, WhoChL, WorAlBi, WorAl, WrChl, YABC 1*

Harris, John *AuBYP 3, TwCCr&M 91, WrDr 88, -90, -92*

Harris, John 1756-1846 *DcNaB, OxCChiL*

Harris, John 1916- *Au&Wr 71, BioIn 14, ConAu 93, IntAu&W 82, -86, -89, -91, WrDr 76, -80, -82, -84, -86*

Harris, John 1916-1991 *AnObit 1991, ConAu 134, ScF&FL 92, WrDr 94N*

Harris, John 1935- *AuBYP 2S*
Pseud./variant:
Hebden, Mark

Harris, John Roy 1915- *ConAu 5R*

Harris, John Wyndham Parkes Lucas Beynon 1903-1969 *BioIn 7, -8, -10, -14, -17, ConSFA, DcNaB 1961, LongCTC, REn, WorAu 1950*

Harris, Jonathan 1921- *BioIn 16, ConAu 121, SmATA 52, WrDr 90, -92, -94*

Harris, Julie *BioIn 16, -17, HalFC 88, IntMPA 86, -88, -92, NewYTBS 91*

Harris, Julie 1925- *AuBYP 2S, -3, BiDFilm, BiE&WWA, BioIn 2, -3, -4, -5, -6, -7, -9, -10, -11, -13, BioNews 74, CamGWoT, CelR, -90, ConAu 103, ConTFT 2, -8, CurBio 56, -77, EncWT, FilmgC, HalFC 84, -88, InWom SUP, IntMPA 75, -76, -78, -81, -82, -84, -86, -88, -92, -77, IntWW 79, -80, -81, -82, -83, -89, -91, MotPP, MovMk, NotNAT, NotWoAT, OxCAmT 84, OxCFilm, PlP&P A, WhoAm 74, -76, -78, -80, -82, -84, -86, -88, -90, -92, WhoAmW 74, -75, -81, -83, WhoEnt 92, WhoHol A, WhoThe 72, -77, -81, WhoWor 74, WorAlBi, WorAl*

Harris, Julie Ann 1925- *WhoAm 94*

Harris, Larry Vincent 1939- *SmATA 59*

Harris, Lavinia *ConAu X, -32NR, SmATA X, WrDr 86, -88, -90, -92*
Main entry: Johnston, Norma

Harris, Leon A, Jr. 1926- *ASCAP 66, AuBYP 2, -3, BioIn 8, -9, ConAu 9R, -3NR, SmATA 4, WhoAm 86, -88, -90, -92, -94, WhoAmA 73, -78, -80, -82, -84, -86, -89, -91, WhoSSW 82, -84*

Harris, Lorle K 1912- *ConAu 97, SmATA 22*

Harris, MacDonald *ConAu 142, -X, ConLC 9, WrDr 80, -82, -84*
Main entry: Heiney, Donald

Harris, MacDonald d1993 *NewYTBS 93*

Harris, Macdonald 1921- *EncSF 93, ScF&FL 92, WhoUSWr 88, WrDr 86, -88, -90, -92, -94*

Harris, Marilyn
Main entry: Springer, Marilyn Harris

Harris, Marilyn 1931- *ArtclWW 2, BioIn 16, ConAu X, DcAmChF 1960, IntAu&W 91, ScF&FL 92, TwCRHW 90, WrDr 84, –86, –88, –90, –92, –94*

Harris, Marion Rose 1925- *Au&Wr 71, ConAu 12NR, –30NR, –P-1, IntAu&W 77, –91, WrDr 76, –80, –82, –84, –86*

Harris, Mark Jonathan *DrAPF 91, –93*

Harris, Mark Jonathan 1941- *BioIn 14, ConAu 104, –21NR, DcAmChF 1960, SmATA 32, WhoUSWr 88, WhoWrEP 89, –92*

Harris, Mary K 1905-1966 *BioIn 3, CathA 1952, ConAu P-1, OxCChiL, TwCChW 78, –83, –89*

Harris, Norman Dyer *BioIn 2*

Harris, Ray *SingR 1*

Harris, Robie H *BioIn 16, SmATA 53*

Harris, Robin *SmATA 71*
Main entry: Shine, Deborah

Harris, Rosemary *AuBYP 3, BioIn 15, –16, ConAu 30NR, ConTFT 3*

Harris, Rosemary 1923- *BioIn 14, ChlLR 30, IntAu&W 91, ScF&FL 92, SmATA 7AS, TwCChW 89, TwCRHW 90, WrDr 86, –88, –90, –92*

Harris, Rosemary Jeanne 1923- *AuBYP 2S, Au&Wr 71, BiE&WWA, BioIn 9, ConAu 33R, –13NR, FourBJA, IntAu&W 77, –82, –89, OxCChiL, SmATA 4, TwCChW 78, –83, TwCCr&M 80, –85, Who 74, –82, –83, –85, –88, –90, –92, WrDr 76, –82, –84, –94*

Harris, Sherwood 1932- *BioIn 13, ConAu 97, SmATA 25*

Harris, Stephen LeRoy 1937- *ConAu 29R, DrAS 74E, –78E, –82E, WhoWest 74, –76, –92, –94*

Harris, Steven Michael 1957- *BioIn 16, ConAu 121, SmATA 55*

Harrison, C William *TwCWW 91*

Harrison, C William 1913- *AuBYP 2, BioIn 8, –14, ConAu 107, IndAu 1917, SmATA 35*
Pseud./variant:
Hickok, Will
Williams, Coe

Harrison, C William, Jr. 1913- *AuBYP 3*

Harrison, Cynthia Ellen 1946- *BiDrLUS 70, ConAu 57, DrAS 82H*

Harrison, David Lee 1937- *BioIn 13, ConAu 93, SmATA 26, WhoMW 84*
Pseud./variant:
Graham, Kennon

Harrison, Deloris 1938- *BioIn 11, ConAu 61, InB&W 80, SmATA 9*

Harrison, Edward Hardy 1926- *CanWW 89, ConAu 39NR, IntAu&W 89, –91, SmATA 56*
Pseud./variant:
Harrison, Ted

Harrison, Elizabeth Cavanna *ForWC 70, WrDr 76, –80, –82, –84*
Main entry: Cavanna, Betty

Harrison, Elizabeth Cavanna 1909- *ConAu 27NR*

Harrison, F Bayford *Alli SUP*

Harrison, George Russell 1898-1979 *AmMWSc 73P, –76P, BioIn 2, –3, –4, –12, ConAu 27NR, –P-2, McGMS 80, WhAm 7*

Harrison, Harry Max 1925- *AuBYP 2S, –3, BioIn 9, –11, ConAu 1R, ConSFA, SmATA 4, WhoSciF, WrDr 76, –80*

Harrison, Molly 1909- *Au&Wr 71, BioIn 15, ConAu 108, IntAu&W 77, SmATA 41, Who 74, –82, –83, –85, –88, –92*

Harrison, Molly, Mrs 1909- *Who 90*

Harrison, Sarah 1946- *BioIn 17, IntAu&W 86, –89, –91, SmATA 63, TwCRHW 90, WrDr 86, –88, –90, –92, –94*

Harrison, Ted
Main entry: Harrison, Edward Hardy

Harrison, William C 1919- *ConAu 25R*

Harron, Donald Hugh 1924- *BiE&WWA, CaW, CanWW 70, ConDr 73, NotNAT, WhoHol A, WrDr 76, –80*

Harsh, Fred T 1925- *SmATA 72*

Harshaw, Ruth Hetzel 1890-1968 *AuBYP 2, –3, BioIn 1, –2, –7, –8, ConAu 107, SmATA 27, WhNAA*

Harshman, Marc 1950- *SmATA 71*

Harshman, Terry Webb *AuBYP 3*

Harston, J Emmor 1864-1955 *WhNAA*

Harston, Ruth 1944- *ConAu 41R*

Hart, Bruce 1938- *BioIn 12, -15, -16, ConAu 107, SmATA 39, -57, WhoEnt 92*

Hart, Carole 1943- *BioIn 12, -15, -16, ConAu 107, SmATA 39, -57*

Hart, Carolyn G 1936- *ConAu 25NR, TwCCr&M 91, WrDr 92*

Hart, Carolyn Gimpel 1936- *ConAu 13R, ForWC 70, SmATA 74, WrDr 94*

Hart, Dick 1920- *ArtsCL, BioIn 5, -6, -14, IlsCB 1946*

Hart, Elizabeth Anna 1822-1886 *ChhPo S1, OxCChiL, TelT*

Hart, John Lewis
Main entry: Hart, Johnny

Hart, Johnny *BioIn 15*

Hart, Johnny 1931- *ArtCS, AuNews 1, BioNews 74, ConAu 49, -X, EncACom, IntAu&W 77*
Pseud./variant:
Hart, John Lewis

Hart, Patricia Warburton 1911- *BiDrLUS 70, WhoLibS 66*

Harte, Bret 1836?-1902 *AmAu, AmAu&B, AmWr S2, AtlBL, AuBYP 2, -3, Benet 87, BenetAL 91, BiD&SB, BioIn 1, -2, -3, -4, -5, -6, -7, -8, -9, -10, -11, -12, -13, -14, -15, -16, CamGEL, CamGLE, CamGWoT, CamHAL, CasWL, CmCal, CnDAL, ConAu 104, CrtT 3, CyWA 58, DcAmAu, DcAmSR, DcLB 12, -64, -74, -79, DcNAA, EncAHmr, EncFWF, HalFC 84, -88, MagSAmL, Novels, OxCAmH, OxCAmL 65, -83, OxCEng 85, PenC AM, RAdv 1, -13-1, REn, REnAL, RealN, RfGAmL 87, ShSCr 8, SmATA 26, TwCLC 1, -25, WebAB 74, -79, WebE&AL, WhDW, WhAm 1, WorAlBi, WorAl, WorLitC*

Hartelius, Margaret A *AuBYP 2S, -3*

Hartford, John *AuBYP 3*

Hartland, Edwin 1848-1927 *CarSB*

Hartley, Ellen Raphael 1915-1980 *BioIn 13, ConAu 4NR, IntAu&W 82, SmATA 23, WhoSSW 80, WrDr 82, -84*

Hartley, Fred Allan 1953- *BioIn 15*

Hartley, Fred Allan, III 1953- *ConAu 106, SmATA 41*

Hartley, William B 1913-1980 *BioIn 13, ConAu 4NR, SmATA 23*

Hartling, Peter 1933- *ChlLR 29*

Hartman, Evert *TwCChW 89B*

Hartman, Evert 1937- *BioIn 14, -15, ConAu 113, IntAu&W 86, SmATA 35, -38, TwCChW 83B*

Hartman, Gertrude 1876-1955 *AmAu&B, BioIn 2, -3, -4, JBA 51, ObitOF 79, WhAm 3*

Hartman, Jane E 1928- *BioIn 16, ConAu 22NR, SmATA 47, WhoWrEP 89*

Hartman, Jane Evangeline 1928- *WhoWrEP 92*

Hartman, Louis Francis 1901-1970 *BioIn 3, -9, -13, SmATA 22*

Hartmann, Helmut Henry 1931- *ConAu 105, WrDr 76, -80, -82, -84*

Hartog, Jan De *BioIn 2, -3, -4, -7, -8, -9, CasWL, EncWL, EncWT, IntAu&W 77, IntWW 74, -75, -76, -77, -78, -79, -80, -81, -82, -83, OxCThe 83, ScF&FL 92, TwCA SUP*
Main entry: DeHartog, Jan

Hartog, Jan de 1914- *BioIn 16, IntAu&W 89, IntWW 89, -91, LiExTwC*

Hartshorn, Ruth M 1928- *BioIn 11, SmATA 11*

Hartwell, Nancy *AuBYP 2, -3, ConAu X*
Main entry: Callahan, Claire Wallis

Hartwick, Harry *AmAu&B*

Harvey, Brett *BioIn 16, -17*

Harvey, Brett 1936- *ConAu 126, IntAu&W 91, SixBJA, SmATA 61*

Harvey, Edith 1908?-1972 *BioIn 13, ConAu 104, SmATA 27N*

Harvey, Roland 1945- *SmATA 71*

Harvey, Virginia Isham 1917- *ConAu 57*

Harwin, Brian *AuBYP 2, -3, ConAu X, SmATA X*
Main entry: Henderson, LeGrand

Harwood, David 1938- *Au&Wr 71, ConAu 104, IntAu&W 77, -91, WrDr 76, -80, -82, -84, -86, -88, -90, -92*

Harwood, Pearl Augusta 1903- *AuBYP 2S, -3, BioIn 11, ConAu 13R, SmATA 9*

Haseley, Dennis *BioIn 15, SmATA 44*

Haseley, Dennis 1950- *BioIn 16, SmATA 57*

Haskell, Arnold Lionel 1903-1981? *Au&Wr 71, BioIn 2, -3, -10, -12, BlueB 76, ConAu 5R, -102, -7NR, IntAu&W 77, IntWW 74, -75, -76, -77, -78, -79, -80, -81N, NewYTBS 80, SmATA 6, Who 74, WhoWor 74*

Haskell, Arnold Lionel David 1903-1980 *DcNaB 1971*

Haskell, Helen Eggleston 1871- *AmAu&B, BioIn 2, JBA 34, -51, WhAm 5*

Haskin, Dorothy C 1905- *WrDr 86*

Haskin, Dorothy Clark 1905- *ConAu 5R, ForWC 70, WhoAmW 74, -75, WhoRel 75, -77, WrDr 76, -80, -82, -84*
Pseud./variant:
Clark, Howard

Haskins, Ilma 1919- *ConAu 45*

Haskins, James 1941- *AuBYP 2S, -3, BioIn 11, -14, -15, -16, ChlLR 3, ConAu 33R, InB&W 80, IntAu&W 89, -91, LivgBAA, NegAl 76, -83, -89, SelBAAf, SelBAAu, SmATA 9, -69, WhoAm 90, -92, -94, WhoE 75, -91, WhoSSW 88, WrDr 76, -80*
Pseud./variant:
Haskins, Jim

Haskins, James S 1941- *BlkAuII, -92, BlkWr 1, ConAu 25NR, InB&W 85, MajAI, TwCYAW, WhoBlA 90, -92, -94*

Haskins, Jim *AuBYP 3, BlkWr 1, -2, MajAI, SmATA 69*
Main entry: Haskins, James

Haskins, Jim 1941- *SixBJA, SmATA 4AS, -X, WrDr 82, -84, -86, -88, -90, -92, -94*

Hasler, Eveline *EncCoWW*

Hasler, Eveline 1937- *ConAu 106*

Hasler, Joan 1931- *BioIn 13, ConAu 29R, SmATA 28*

Haslip, Joan 1912- *AuSpks, BioIn 9, -11, ConAu 107, IntAu&W 77, -89, -91, Who 74, -82, -83, -85, -88, -90, -92*

Hass, E A *AuBYP 3*

Hassall, Joan 1906- *BioIn 5, -14, -15, -16, ChhPo, -S1, -S2, DcBrAr 1, IlsCB 1946, SmATA 43, TwCPaSc, Who 74, -82, -83, -85, -88, WhoArt 80, -82, -84, WhoGrA 62, -82*

Hassall, Joan 1906-1988 *AnObit 1988, SmATA 56N*

Hassall, John 1868-1948 *BioIn 5, -14, ChhPo, -S1, ClaDrA, DcBrAr 1, DcBrBI, DcNaB 1941, DcVicP 2, LongCTC, TwCPaSc, WorECar*

Hassall, Mark William 1940- *ConAu 73, WhoWor 80*

Hasse, Henry L *ConSFA, WhoSciF*

Hasse, Henry L 1913-1977 *EncSF 93, ScF&FL 92*

Hasselriis, Else *BioIn 1, ConICB, IlsCB 1744*

Hassler, Jon *BioIn 17*

Hassler, Jon 1933- *BioIn 12, ConAu 73, -21NR, SmATA 19, WhoUSWr 88, WhoWrEP 89, WrDr 92*

Hassler, Jon Francis 1933- *WhoWrEP 92, WrDr 94*

Hastings, Beverly *ConAu 135, ScF&FL 92, SmATA X, WrDr 90, -92*
Main entry: Barkin, Carol
James, Elizabeth

Hastings, Beverly 1944- *WrDr 94*

Hastings, Beverly 1945- *WrDr 94*

Hastings, Graham *ConAu X, EncMys, IntAu&W 91X, TwCCr&M 85, -91, WrDr 82, -84, -86, -88, -90, -92*
Main entry: Jeffries, Roderic

Hastings, Graham 1926- *WrDr 94*

Hastings, Ian 1912- *BioIn 17, ConAu 45, SmATA 62*

Hastings, Macdonald *BioIn 14*

Hastings, Macdonald 1909-1982 *Au&Wr 71, BioIn 9, ConAu 53, -9NR, EncMys, IntAu&W 77, -82, TwCCr&M 80, -85, WrDr 76, -80, -82*
Pseud./variant:
Gulliver, Lemuel

Hastings, Paul G 1914- *ConAu 24NR*

Hastings, Paul Guiler 1914- *AmMWSc 73S, -78S, ConAu 1R, IndAu 1917, WhoAm 74, -76*

Hastings, Robert J *BioIn 15*

Hastings, Robert J 1924- *ConAu 122*

Hastings, Robert Jean 1924- *WhoRel 75, -92*

Haszard, Patricia Moyes 1923- *ConAu 29NR, SmATA X*
Main entry: Moyes, Patricia

Hatch, Alden 1898-1975 *AmAu&B, AuBYP 2, -3, Au&Wr 71, BioIn 8, -10, ConAu 57, -65, ObitOF 79, WhAm 6, WhoAm 74*

Hatch, Eric Stow 1901-1973 *AmAu&B, AmNov, BioIn 2, -4, -5, -7, -10, -11, ConAu 41R, NewYTBE 73, TwCA, -SUP*

Hatch, James Vernon 1928- *BiE&WWA, ConAu 41R, DrAS 74E, -78E, -82E, InB&W 85, NotNAT, SelBAAu*

Hatch, Mary Cottam 1912-1970 *AnCL, BiDrLUS 70, BioIn 3, -8, -13, ConAu 109, SmATA 28, Str&VC*

Hatch, Richard Warren 1898- *AmAu&B, BioIn 8, WhNAA, WhoChL*

Hatfield, William 1892-1969 *OxCAusL, SingR 1*

Hatfield, William Ernest Chapman 1892?- *DcChlFi*

Hathaway, Lulu 1903- *BiDrLUS 70, ConAu 13R, WhoLibS 66*

Hathorn, Libby 1943- *SmATA 74*

Hatlo, Jimmy 1898-1963 *BioIn 1, -2, -3, -6, -13, ConAu 93, DcAmB S7, EncACom, EncAJ, EncTwCJ, ObitOF 79, SmATA 23N, WhAmArt 85*

Hauff, Wilhelm *AuBYP 3*

Hauff, Wilhelm 1802-1827 *AuBYP 2, BiD&SB, BioIn 7, -8, -10, -17, CasWL, DcBiA, DcBiPP, DcLB 90, EuAu, EvEuW, OxCChiL, OxCGer 76, -86, PenC EUR, REn, SupFW, WhoChL, WhoHr&F*

Haufrecht, Herbert *AuBYP 3*

Haufrecht, Herbert 1909- *AuBYP 2S, BioIn 1, CpmDNM 82, ConAmC 76, -82, WhoEnt 92*

Haugaard, Erik 1923- *TwCChW 89, WrDr 86, -88, -90, -92*

Haugaard, Erik Christian 1923- *AuBYP 2, -3, BioIn 8, -9, -12, -17, ChlLR 11, ConAu 5R, -3NR, -38NR, DcAmChF 1960, -1985, IntAu&W 77, -82, -91, MajAI, SmATA 4, -68, -12AS, ThrBJA, TwCChW 78, -83, WrDr 76, -80, -82, -84, -94*

Haugen, Tormod 1945- *BioIn 17, ConAu 135, SmATA 66*

Haughey, Betty Ellen *AuBYP 2S, -3*

Haughton, James 1929- *CivR 74*

Haughton, Rosemary 1927- *AuBYP 2S, -3, Au&Wr 71, ConAu 5R, -35NR, WrDr 76, -80, -82, -84, -86, -88, -90, -92*

Haughton, Rosemary Elena Konradin 1927- *WrDr 94*

Hauman, Doris 1897?- *BioIn 5, IlsCB 1946, SmATA 32*

Hauman, Doris 1898- *BioIn 14*

Hauman, George 1890-1961 *BioIn 5, -14, IlsCB 1946, SmATA 32*

Haupt, Enid A *BioIn 15*

Haupt, Enid Annenberg 1906- *BioIn 5, ForWC 70, InWom SUP, NewYTBE 70, NewYTBS 82, WhoAmA 73, WhoAmW 74, -75*

Hauptly, Denis J 1945- *BioIn 16, ConAu 118, SmATA 57*

Hauptly, Denis James 1945- *WhoAmL 87*

Hauser, Hillary Rika 1944- *ConAu 69, -11NR, WhoWest 80, -82, -84, WhoWor 84*

Hauser, Margaret L 1909- *BioIn 11, ConAu P-1, SmATA 10*
Pseud./variant:
Head, Gay

Hausherr, Rosmarie *AuBYP 3*

Hausman, Gerald *DrAPF 87, -89, -91, -93*

Hausman, Gerald 1945- *ConAu 45, -2NR, -17NR, -38NR, DrAP 75, ScF&FL 92, SmATA 13*
Pseud./variant:
Hausman, Gerry

Hausman, Gerry
Main entry: Hausman, Gerald

Hausman, Leon Augustus 1888-1966 *BioIn 1, -2, -7, WhAm 4*

Hautzig, Deborah 1956- *BioIn 14, FifBJA, SmATA 31*

Hautzig, Esther 1930- *AuBYP 3, ChlLR 22, InWom SUP, IntAu&W 91, SmATA 15AS, TwCYAW, WrDr 86, -88, -90, -92, -94*

Hautzig, Esther Rudomin 1930- *AuBYP 2, BioIn 8, -9, -10, -11, -17, ConAu 1R, -5NR, -20NR, ForWC 70, HerW, -84, IntAu&W 77, -82, MajAI, MorBMP, OxCChiL, SmATA 4, -68, ThrBJA, WhoAmW 83, WrDr 76, -80, -82, -84*
Pseud./variant:
Rudomin, Esther

Havel, Jennifer *SmATA 74*
Main entry: Havill, Juanita

Havenhand, John *ConAu X, SmATA X*
Main entry: Cox, John Roberts

Haverstock, Mary Sayre 1932- *AuBYP 2S, -3, ConAu 81, WhoAmW 75*

Havighurst, Marion d1974 *AuBYP 3*

Havighurst, Marion 1894-1974 *ConAu 29NR*

Havighurst, Marion Boyd d1974 *AuBYP 2, BioIn 6, ConAu 49, -P-1, MorJA, OhA&B*

Havighurst, Marion Boyd 1899-1974 *BioIn 14*

Havighurst, Walter Edwin 1901- *AmAu&B, AmNov, AuBYP 2, -3, Au&Wr 71, BioIn 2, -4, -6, -7, -9, CnDAL, ConAu 1R, DrAS 74E, -78E, IntAu&W 77, MorJA, OhA&B, OxCAmL 65, REnAL, SmATA 1, TwCA SUP, WhoAm 74, -76, WhoWor 78, WrDr 76, -80*

Haviland, Virginia 1911- *AuBYP 2S, BiDrLUS 70, BioIn 10, ChhPo S1, -S2, ConAu 17R, -12NR, FourBJA, OxCChiL, SmATA 6, WhoAm 74, -76, -78, -80, -82, WhoAmW 74, -75, -77, WhoLibI 82, WhoLibS 55, -66, WhoSSW 73*

Haviland, Virginia 1911-1988 *AuBYP 3, BioIn 15, -16, ConAu 124, SmATA 54N, WhAm 9*

Havill, Juanita *AuBYP 3, DrAPF 87, -89, -91, -93*

Havill, Juanita 1949- *SmATA 74*
Pseud./variant:
Havel, Jennifer

Havrevold, Finn 1905- *AuBYP 2S, -3, ConAu 109, IntAu&W 77, -89, IntWW 74, -75, -76, -77, -78, -79, -80, -81, -82, -83, WhoWor 74, -78*

Hawes, Charles Boardman 1889-1923 *AmAu&B, AuBYP 2, -3, BenetAL 91, BioIn 4, -7, -14, DcNAA, JBA 34, NewbMB 1922, REnAL, TwCA, TwCChW 83, -89*

Hawes, Evelyn *AuNews 1, BioIn 10, ConAu 13R, ForWC 70, WhoAmW 77*

Hawes, Judy 1913- *AmPB, BioIn 9, ConAu 33R, SmATA 4, WrDr 76, -80, -82, -84, -86, -88, -90, -92, -94*

Hawes, Louise 1943- *BioIn 17, ScF&FL 92, SmATA 60*
Pseud./variant:
Suzanne, Jamie 1943-

Hawk, Virginia Driving *SmATA 8*
Main entry: Sneve, Virginia Driving Hawk

Hawke, David Freeman 1923- *ConAu 102, -18NR, DrAS 74H, -78H, -82H*

Hawkes, Hester 1900- *AuBYP 2, -3, BioIn 7*

Hawkesworth, Eric 1921- *AuBYP 3, WrDr 86, -88, -90, -92*

Hawkesworth, Eric William 1921- *AuBYP 2S, ConAu 29R, SmATA 13, WrDr 76, -80, -94*
Pseud./variant:
Great Comte, The

Hawkins, Anthony Hope, Sir *CamGLE*

Hawkins, Anthony Hope, Sir 1863-1933 *BbD, BiD&SB, BioIn 2, -4, -5, -8, -12, Chambr 3, DcEnA A, DcLEL, DcNaB 1931, EvLB, LongCTC, NewC, NotNAT B, OxCChiL, OxCEng 67, -85, REn, StaCVF, TelT, TwCA, -SUP, WhoChL*
Pseud./variant:
Hope, Anthony

Hawkins, Arthur 1903- *BioIn 12, ConAu 21R, -8NR, IlsBYP, SmATA 19, WhAmArt 85*

Hawkins, Arthur 1913- *Who 92*

Hawkins, Irene Beatrice 1906- *BioIn 5, -14, IlsCB 1946*

Hawkins, Laura *InWom SUP*

Hawkins, Laura 1951- *SmATA 74*

Hawkins, Quail *AuBYP 3*

Hawkins, Quail 1905- *AuBYP 2, BioIn 7, -10, ConAu 17R, SmATA 6*

Hawkins, Sheila 1905- *BioIn 1, -14, IlsCB 1744, SingR 1*

Hawkinson, John Samuel 1912- *AuBYP 2, -3, BioIn 8, -9, ConAu 21R, FourBJA, SmATA 4, WhoAm 74, -76, -78, WhoMW 74, -76, -78, WhoWor 78*

Hawkinson, Lucy 1924-1971 *AuBYP 2, -3, BioIn 8, -12, ConAu 103, SmATA 21*

Hawks, Francis Lister 1798-1866 *Alli, -SUP, AmAu, AmAu&B, BiDSA, BiD&SB, BioIn 11, CarSB, ChhPo, -S1, -S2, CyAL, DcAmAu, DcNAA, DcNCBi 3, HarEnUS, WhAm HS*

Hawley, Isabel Lockwood 1935- *ConAu 57, -7NR*

Hawley, Mabel C *ConAu 26NR, –P-2, SmATA 1, –67*
Main entry: Stratemeyer, Edward L

Hawthorne, Captain R M *HsB&A, YABC 1*
Main entry: Ellis, Edward S

Hawthorne, Hildegarde *AuBYP 3, ScF&FL 92, WomNov*

Hawthorne, Hildegarde 1871-1952 *AmAu&B, AuBYP 2, BenetAL 91, BioIn 2, –3, –7, –12, ChhPo, DcAmAu, JBA 34, –51, REnAL, WhAm 3, WhNAA, WomWWA 14*

Hawthorne, Jennie Crawley 1916- *ConAu P-1, WrDr 76, –80*

Hawthorne, Julian 1846-1934 *Alli SUP, AmAu&B, BenetAL 91, BbD, BiD&SB, BioIn 4, –7, –9, –15, –17, CarSB, CelCen, Chambr 3, ChhPo, –S2, DcAmAu, DcBiA, DcCathB, DcEnA, –A, DcEnL, DcNAA, EncMys, OxCAmL 65, –83, PenEncH, REnAL, ScFEYrs, –A, TwCA, TwCLC 25, WhAm 1, WhNAA, WhoHr&F*

Hawthorne, Nathaniel 1804-1864 *Alli, –SUP, AmAu, AmAu&B, AmWr, AtlBL, AuBYP 2S, –3, Benet 87, BenetAL 91, BbD, BiD&SB, BioIn 1, –2, –3, –4, –5, –6, –7, –8, –9, –10, –11, –12, –13, –14, –15, –16, –17, CamGEL, CamGLE, CamHAL, CarSB, CasWL, CelCen, Chambr 3, ChhPo S1, –S2, CnDAL, CrtT 3, CyAL, CyWA 58, DcAmAu, DcAmSR, DcBiA, DcBiPP, DcEnA, –A, DcEnL, DcLB 1, –74, DcLEL, DcNAA, Dis&D, EncAB-H, EncSF 93, EvLB, FamAYP, FilmgC, HalFC 84, –88, HarEnUS, LuthC 75, MagSAmL, McGEWB, MemAm, MouLC 3, NewEScF, NewGrDA 86, NinCLC 2, –10, –17, –23, –39, Novels, OxCAmH, OxCAmL 65, –83, OxCChiL, OxCEng 67, –85, PenC AM, PenEncH, RAdv 1, –13-1, RComAH, RComWL, REn, REnAL, RfGAmL 87, RfGShF, ScFSB, ScFEYrs, ShSCr 3, ShSWr, Str&VC, SupFW, WebAB 74, –79, WebE&AL, WhDW, WhAm HS, WhoChL, WhoHr&F, WorAlBi, WorAl, WorLitC, WrChl, WrPh, YABC 2*

Hawton, Hector 1901- *Au&Wr 71, ConAu 13R, EncSF 93, WrDr 76, –80, –82, –84*

Hay, Ian *Chambr 3, CmScLit, DcLEL, DcNaB 1951, EvLB, LongCTC, NewC, NotNAT B, ObitOF 79, ObitT 1951, OxCThe 67, –83, REn, TwCA, –SUP, TwCWr*

Hay, Ian 1876-1952 *CamGLE*

Hay, John 1915- *AmAu&B, ConAu 65, –9NR, IntWWP 82, SmATA 13, WhoAm 74, –76, –78, –80, –82, –92, –94*

Hay, Timothy *AuBYP 3, ConAu 136, –X, MajAI, ObitOF 79, YABC X*
Main entry: Brown, Margaret Wise

Hay, Timothy 1910-1952 *BioIn 14, –16, –17*

Hay, Will 1888-1949 *BioIn 1, –9, –12, CmMov, FilmgC, HalFC 84, –88, ObitOF 79, OxCFilm, WhoHol B, WorEFlm*

Haycock, Kate 1962- *SmATA 77*

Haycox, Ernest 1899-1950 *AmAu&B, BenetAL 91, BioIn 2, –4, –11, –14, EncFWF, ObitOF 79, REnAL, TwCA SUP, TwCWW 91, WhAm 3, WhNAA*

Haycraft, Howard *AuBYP 3*

Haycraft, Howard d1991 *NewYTBS 91*

Haycraft, Howard 1905- *AmAu&B, AuBYP 2, BiDrLUS 70, BioIn 3, –7, –8, –9, –10, ConAu 21R, CurBio 41, –54, EncMys, IntAu&W 77, –89, –91, IntWW 74, –75, –76, –77, –78, –79, –80, –81, –82, –83, –89, –91, IntYB 80, –81, –82, REnAL, SmATA 6, WhoAm 74, –76, –78, –80, WhoLibI 82, WhoLibS 55, –66*

Haycraft, Howard 1905-1991 *BioIn 17, ConAu 136, CurBio 92N, SmATA 70, WhAm 10*

Haycraft, Molly Costain 1911- *BioIn 10, ConAu 13R, SmATA 6*

Hayden, Gwendolen Lampshire 1904- *BioIn 14, SmATA 35, WhoAmW 74*

Hayden, Howard K 1930- *ConAu 17R*

Hayden, Robert C 1937- *BioIn 16, BlkWrNE, WrDr 86, –88*

Hayden, Robert C, Jr. 1937- *BioIn 13, BlkWr 1, ConAu 69, –24NR, SelBAAf, SelBAAu, SmATA 28, –47, WhoBlA 90, –92, –94, WrDr 76, –80, –82, –84*

Hayden, Robert E 1913-1980 *AfrAmAl 6, BenetAL 91, BlkWr 1, ConAu 24NR, Ear3lAP, EncAACR, MajTwCW, NegAl 89*

Hayden, Robert Earl *BioIn 14, –15*

Hayden, Robert Earl 1913-1980 *AmAu&B, AuBYP 2S, –3, BioIn 4, –10, –11, –12, –13, –17, BlkAWP, ChhPo S1, –S2, ConAu 97, ConLC 5, –9, ConPo 70, –75, Conv 1, CroCAP, DrAP 75, InB&W 80, –85, LivgBAA, ModBlW, NegAl 76, –83, NewYTBS 80, SelBAAf, SmATA 19, –26N, WhAm 7, WhoAm 80, WrDr 76, –80, –82*

Hayden, Torey L *BioIn 17*

Hayden, Torey L 1951- *ConAu 35NR, SmATA 65*

Haydon, Arthur Lincoln 1872- *ChhPo, –S1, –S2, OxCCan, WhoLA*

Haydon, Harold Emerson 1909- *CanWW 70, –80, –81, –83, –89, WhoAm 74, –80, –82, –84, –86, –88, –90, WhoAmA 73, –78*

Hayes, Carlton Joseph Huntley 1882-1964 *AmAu&B, AmLY, BioIn 1, –2, –4, –7, –11, –12, –16, CathA 1930, ConAu 1R, –3NR, CurBio 42, –64, DcAmB S7, LongCTC, REnAL, SmATA 11, TwCA SUP, WhAm 4, WhNAA*

Hayes, Clair W *CarSB*

Hayes, Daniel 1952- *SmATA 73*

Hayes, Florence 1895- *AuBYP 2, –3, BioIn 7*

Hayes, Geoffrey 1947- *BioIn 13, ConAu 65, –9NR, –25NR, SmATA 26*

Hayes, Hobe *AuBYP 3*

Hayes, John F 1904-1980 *BioIn 7, –11, –13, CanWW 70, –79, –80, ConAu P-1, CreCan 1, OxCChiL, Profile 2, SmATA 11, TwCChW 78, –83, –89, WrDr 80, –82, –84*

Hayes, John Francis 1904-1980 *DcChlFi*

Hayes, Nancy M *ChhPo, –S1, –S2*

Hayes, Sarah *AuBYP 3*

Hayes, Sheila 1937- *AuBYP 3, BioIn 16, ConAu 22NR, SmATA 50, –51, WhoWrEP 89, –92*

Hayes, Will *BioIn 10, ConAu 5R, SmATA 7*

Hayes, William 1913- *IntWW 89*

Hayes, William Dimitt 1913- *AuBYP 2, BioIn 8, –11, ConAu 5R, SmATA 8*

Hayes, William Dimitty 1913- *AuBYP 3*

Hayman, LeRoy 1916- *AuBYP 2S, –3, ConAu 85*

Haynes, Betsy 1935- *ConAu 57, –8NR, SmATA 37*
Pseud./variant:
Betts, James

Haynes, Betsy 1937- *BioIn 15, –16, ScF&FL 92, SmATA 48*

Haynes, Linda *SmATA X*
Main entry: Swinford, Betty June Wells

Haynes, Mary *BioIn 17, DrAPF 87, –89, –91, –93*

Haynes, Mary 1938- *ConAu 35NR, ScF&FL 92, SmATA 65*

Haynes, Max 1956- *SmATA 72*

Haynes, Nelma *AuBYP 2S, –3*

Haynes, Pat *ConAu X*

Haynes, Robert *IlsBYP*

Haynes-Dixon, Margaret Rumer *Who 88, –90, –92*
Main entry: Godden, Rumer

Haynes Dixon, Margaret Rumer 1907- *BlueB 76, IntAu&W 77, IntWWP 82, Who 74, –82, –83, –85*

Hays, Hobe *AuBYP 2, BioIn 8*

Hays, Hoffman Reynolds 1904-1980 *AmAu&B, AnObit 1980, BioIn 4, –12, –13, ConAu 81, –105, ConPo 70, –75, –80, DrAP 75, NewYTBS 80, SmATA 26, TwCA SUP, WhoE 75, –77, WrDr 76, –80, –82*

Hays, Wilma P 1909- *SmATA 3AS*

Hays, Wilma Pitchford 1909- *AuBYP 2, –3, BioIn 8, –9, –15, ConAu 1R, –5NR, ForWC 70, IntAu&W 77, –91, MajAI, SmATA 1, –28, ThrBJA, WhoAmW 74, –75, WrDr 76, –80, –82, –84, –86, –88, –90, –92, –94*

Hayward, Arthur Lawrence 1885-1939 *ArtCS, WhoLA*

Hayward, Charles Harold 1898- *Au&Wr 71, ConAu 9R, –7NR*

Hayward, Linda 1943- *BioIn 15, ConAu 112, SmATA 39*

Hayward, William Stephens *Alli SUP, EncSF 93*

Haywood, Carolyn d1990 *NewYTBS 90*

Haywood, Carolyn 1898- *AmAu&B, AuBYP 2, Au&ICB, BioIn 2, –7, –8, –9, –10, –13, ChhPo, ConAu 5R, –5NR, –20NR, ForWC 70, IntAu&W 91, JBA 51, MorBMP, OxCChiL, SmATA 1, –29, TwCChW 78, –83, –89, WhAmArt 85, WrDr 80, –82, –84, –86, –88, –90*

Haywood, Carolyn 1898-1990 *AuBYP 3, BioIn 16, –17, ChlLR 22, ConAu 130, MajAI, SmATA 64, –75*

Hazard, Paul 1878-1944 *BioIn 1, -3, -4, OxCChiL*

Hazel, Harry *Alli SUP, AmAu&B*

Hazeltine, Alice Isabel 1878- *AuBYP 3*

Hazeltine, Alice Isabel 1878-1959 *AuBYP 2, BioIn 5, -8, ChhPo, WhoLibS 55*

Hazelton, Elizabeth Baldwin *AuBYP 2S, -3*

Hazen, Barbara Shook 1930- *BioIn 13, -16, ConAu 105, -22NR, ScF&FL 92, SixBJA, SmATA 27, WhoAmW 91, WhoWrEP 89, -92*

Hazlett, Edward Everett 1892- *AuBYP 2, -3, BioIn 7*

Head, Ann *ConAu X*
Main entry: Morse, Anne Christensen

Head, Ann 1915- *TwCYAW*

Head, Gay *ConAu X, SmATA X*
Main entry: Hauser, Margaret L

Head, Lee 1931-1983 *BioIn 13, ConAu 65, -110*

Headington, Christopher 1930- *AuBYP 3, WrDr 86, -88, -90, -92*

Headington, Christopher John Magenis 1930- *AuBYP 2S, Baker 92, ConAu 106, IntWW 79, -80, -81, -82, -83, -89, -91, IntWWM 85, -90, WhoMus 72, WrDr 76, -80, -94*

Headley, Elizabeth *AuBYP 2, -3, BioIn 2, ConAu X, CurBio 50, MajAI, MorJA, SmATA 1, -X, TwCChW 83, -89, TwCYAW, WrDr 80*
Main entry: Cavanna, Betty

Headstrom, Birger Richard 1902- *AuBYP 3*

Headstrom, Richard 1902- *AuBYP 2, ConAu 77, -2NR, -13NR, SmATA 8, WrDr 80, -82, -84, -86, -88, -90, -92*

Headstrom, Richard Birger 1902- *WrDr 94*

Heady, Eleanor B 1917-1979 *ConAu 31NR*

Heady, Eleanor Butler 1917- *AuBYP 2S, -3, BioIn 10, -11, ConAu 41R, SmATA 7, -8, WhoAmW 75, WrDr 76, -80, -82, -84*

Heady, Harold F 1916- *ConAu 31NR, WhoTech 84, WrDr 86, -88, -90, -92*

Heady, Harold Franklin 1916- *AmMWSc 73P, -76P, -82, -86, -89, -92, ConAu 53, IntAu&W 89, WhoAm 74, -76, -78, -80, -82, -84, -86, -88, -90, WrDr 76, -80, -82, -84, -94*

Heafford, Philip Ernest 1906- *Au&Wr 71*

Heagy, William D 1964- *SmATA 76*

Heal, Edith 1903- *AmWomPl, BioIn 10, ConAu 1R, -2NR, SmATA 7, WhoE 74*
Pseud./variant:
Berrien, Edith Heal
Page, Eileen
Powers, Margaret

Healey, Brooks *BioIn 13, ConAu X, IntAu&W 82X, SmATA X, WhoWrEP 89, -92*
Main entry: Albert, Burton, Jr.

Healey, Larry 1927- *BioIn 15, ConAu 101, SmATA 42, -44*

Heaps, Willard Allison 1908- *AuBYP 2, -3, BioIn 8, -13, ConAu 85, SmATA 26, WhoLibS 55, -66*

Heard, J Norman 1922- *ConAu 9R, WhoLibS 55, -66*

Hearn, Emily
Main entry: Valleau, Emily

Hearn, Lafcadio 1850-1904 *Alli SUP, AmAu, AmAu&B, AnCL, AtlBL, Benet 87, BenetAL 91, BbD, BiDSA, BiD&SB, BioIn 1, -2, -3, -4, -5, -6, -8, -9, -10, -11, -12, -13, -14, -15, -16, -17, CamGEL, CamGLE, CamHAL, CasWL, Chambr 3, ChhPo, CnDAL, ConAu 105, CrtT 3, CyWA 58, DcAmAu, DcBiA, DcEuL, DcLB 12, -78, DcLEL, DcNAA, Dis&D, EncAB-H, EncJap, EncO&P 1, EvLB, McGEWB, ModAL, MorMA, NewC, Novels, OhA&B, OxCAmH, OxCAmL 65, -83, OxCEng 67, -85, PenC AM, -ENG, PenEncH, PoIre, RAdv 1, REn, REnAL, RfGAmL 87, ScF&FL 92, TwCLC 9, WebAB 74, -79, WhAm 1, WhoHr&F*

Hearne, Betsy 1942- *SixBJA*

Hearne, Betsy Gould *BioIn 15, -16*

Hearne, Betsy Gould 1942- *ConAu 114, -35NR, MedPD, ScF&FL 92, SmATA 38, WhoLibI 82*

Hearne, Samuel 1745-1792 *Alli, BenetAL 91, BbtC, BioIn 1, -2, -3, -5, -6, -8, -9, -12, -14, -17, DcBiPP, DcCanB 4, DcLB 99, DcLEL, DcNaB, Expl 93, OxCCan, OxCShps, WhDW, WhNaAH*

Hearon, Shelby *DrAPF 87, -89, -91, -93*

Hearon, Shelby 1931- *AuNews 2, BioIn 11, -12, -15, ConAu 25R, -11AS, -18NR, ConLC 63, WhoAm 94, WhoAmW 85, -87, -89, -93, WhoSSW 73, WhoUSWr 88, WhoWrEP 89, -92, WrDr 92, -94*

Heath, Charles D *Law&B 92*

Heath, Charles D 1941- *BioIn 15, ConAu 121, SmATA 46*

Heath, Ernest Dudley *BioIn 1, DcBrAr 1, DcBrBI, DcVicP 2, IlsCB 1744*

Heath, Monroe 1899-1966 *AmAu&B, ConAu P-1*

Heath, Royal Vale 1883- *WhNAA*

Heath, Veronica *ConAu X, SmATA X, WrDr 76, -80, -82, -84*
Main entry: Blackett, Veronica Heath

Heath, Veronica 1927- *WrDr 86, -88, -90, -92, -94*

Heath, William Ledbetter 1924- *BioIn 3*

Heaven, Constance *AuBYP 3, ConAu X, -2NR, -18NR, IntAu&W 77, SmATA 7, WrDr 76, -80, -82, -84*
Main entry: Fecher, Constance

Heaven, Constance 1911- *BioIn 14, ConAu 40NR, IntAu&W 91, TwCRHW 90, WrDr 86, -88, -90, -92, -94*

Heavilin, Jay *AuBYP 2S, -3*

Hebblethwaite, Peter *IntAu&W 89, -91*

Hebblethwaite, Peter 1930- *ConAu 69, Who 83, -85, -88, -90, -92, WhoWor 80, -87, WrDr 82, -84, -86, -88, -90, -92, -94*

Hebden, Mark *ConAu 134, -X, IntAu&W 82X, -86X, TwCCr&M 85, WrDr 76, -80, -82, -84, -86, -88, -90, -92*
Main entry: Harris, John

Hebden, Mark 1916- *BioIn 14, TwCCr&M 91*

Hebden, Mark 1916-1991 *WrDr 94N*

Hecht, George Joseph 1895-1980 *BioIn 1, -2, -12, -13, ConAu 97, CurBio 47, -80N, EncAB-A 28, EncTwCJ, NewYTBS 80, SmATA 22N, WhAm 7, WhJnl, WhNAA, WhoAm 78, -80, WhoAmJ 80, WhoWorJ 72*

Hecht, Henri Joseph 1922- *BioIn 11, ConAu 29R, SmATA 9*
Pseud./variant:
Maik, Henri

Hechtkopf, Henryk 1910- *BioIn 12, SmATA 17, WhoWorJ 72*

Heck, Bessie Holland 1911- *ConAu 5R, ForWC 70, SmATA 26*

Heckelmann, Charles N 1913- *ConAu 30NR, IntAu&W 89, -91, TwCWW 91, WrDr 86, -88, -90, -92*

Heckelmann, Charles Newman 1913- *ConAu 49, WhoAm 76, -78, -80, -82, -84, -86, -88, -90, -92, -94, WhoUSWr 88, WhoWrEP 89, -92, WrDr 84, -94*
Pseud./variant:
Lawton, Charles

Hedderwick, Mairi 1939- *BioIn 12, -14, ConAu 137, IlsCB 1967, MajAI, SmATA 30, -77, TwCChW 89, WrDr 90, -92, -94*

Heddle, Enid Moodie 1904- *AuWomWr, SingR 1*

Heddle, J F Moodie *SingR 2*

Hedges, Sidney George 1897-1974 *Au&Wr 71, BioIn 13, ChhPo, -S1, ConAu 9R, -4NR, SmATA 28, Who 74*

Hedges, Ursula M 1940- *ConAu 29R*

Hedgpeth, Joel Walker *AmMWSc 86*

Hedgpeth, Joel Walker 1911- *AmMWSc 73P, -76P, -82*

Heerwagen, Paul K 1895- *ConAu 29R, WrDr 76, -80, -82, -84, -86, -88, -90, -92*

Heerwagen, Paul K 1895-1992 *WrDr 94N*

Heffernan, John Baptist 1894- *WhAm 10*

Heffernan, John Baptist 1894-1974 *AmCath 80, DrAS 74H, WhoAm 74*

Heffron, Dorris 1944- *BioIn 17, ConAu 49, -36NR, SmATA 68, WhoCanL 85, -87, -92, WrDr 80, -82, -84, -86, -88, -90, -92, -94*

Hefley, James Carl 1930- *ConAu 13R, -7NR, WhoMW 93*

Hefter, Richard *BioIn 14*

Hefter, Richard 1942- *BioIn 13, ConAu 107, -23NR, SmATA 31*

Hegan, Alice Caldwell *InWom SUP, SmATA X*
Main entry: Rice, Alice Caldwell Hegan

Hegan, James Edward 1920- *BioIn 2, -4, -5, -8*

Hegarty, Reginald Beaton 1906-1973 *AuBYP 2, -3, BioIn 8, -9, -11, ConAu 41R, -P-1, SmATA 10*

Hegeler, Sten 1923- *Au&Wr 71, ConAu 107, IntAu&W 77, -82, -86, WhoWor 78, WrDr 76, -80, -82, -84, -86, -88, -90*

Hegner, Robert William 1880-1942 *BioIn 2, WhAm 2, WhNAA*

Heide, Florence 1919- *SmATA 6AS*

Heide, Florence Parry 1919- *AuBYP 2S, -3, BioIn 14, ChhPo S1, -S2, ConAu 93, -19NR, FourBJA, IntAu&W 89, -91, MajAI, SmATA 32, -69, TwCChW 83, -89, WhoWrEP 89, -92, WrDr 86, -88, -90, -92, -94*
Pseud./variant:
Allen, Alex B
McDonald, Jamie

Heiderstadt, Dorothy 1907- *AuBYP 2, -3, BiDrLUS 70, BioIn 7, -10, ConAu 1R, -1NR, ForWC 70, SmATA 6, WhoLibS 66*

Heilbroner, Joan 1922- *BioIn 17, SmATA 63*

Heilbroner, Joan Knapp 1922- *AuBYP 2S, -3, ConAu 1R*

Heilbrun, Lois Hussey d1987 *BioIn 15, -16, NewYTBS 87*

Heilbrun, Lois Hussey 1922?-1987 *ConAu 123, SmATA 54N*

Heilman, Grant 1919- *ConAu 53*

Heilman, Joan Rattner *BioIn 16, ConAu 21NR, IntAu&W 89, -91, SmATA 50, WhoUSWr 88, WhoWrEP 89, -92*

Heiman, Grover George 1920- *ConAu 5R, -6NR, IntAu&W 77, WhoAm 82, -84, WhoWor 84*

Heiman, Grover George, Jr. 1920- *WhoAm 86, -88, -90, -92, -94, WhoWor 87, -89*

Heimann, Susan 1940- *ConAu 33R*

Hein, Christoph *BioIn 16, TwCChW 89B*

Hein, Christoph 1944- *ConWorW 93, DcLB 124*

Hein, Lucille Eleanor 1915- *AuBYP 2S, -3, BioIn 12, ConAu 5R, -2NR, ForWC 70, IntAu&W 77, -89, SmATA 20, WhoAmW 83, WrDr 76, -80, -82, -84, -86, -88, -90, -92, -94*

Heine, Helme *BioIn 16, -17, TwCChW 83B, -89B*

Heine, Helme 1941- *ChlBIID, ChlLR 18, ConAu 135, MajAI, SixBJA, SmATA 67*

Heine, Robert Eugene 1916- *WhoFI 74*

Heinemann, George Alfred 1918- *BioIn 14, SmATA 31, WhoAm 80, -82, -84, -86, WhoEnt 92*

Heiney, Donald 1921- *ConAu 1R, -3NR, ConLC 9, DrAS 74E*
Pseud./variant:
Harris, MacDonald

Heiney, Donald W *ScF&FL 92*

Heiney, Donald William 1921-1993 *ConAu 142*

Heinlein, Robert A 1907- *AmAu&B, AuBYP 2, Au&Wr 71, Benet 87, BioIn 3, -4, -6, -7, -10, -11, -12, -13, CamGLE, ConAu 1R, -1NR, -20NR, ConLC 1, -3, -8, -26, ConNov 72, -76, -82, -86, ConSFA, CurBio 55, DcLB 8, DrAF 76, InSci, MorJA, NewYTBS 80, Novels, OxCAmL 83, OxCChiL, PenC AM, REnAL, ScFSB, SmATA 9, TwCA SUP, TwCChW 78, -83, TwCSFW 86, TwCWr, WebAB 74, -79, WebE&AL, WhoAm 74, -76, -78, -80, -82, -84, WhoSciF, WhoWor 78, -80, -82, -84, WorAl, WrDr 76, -80, -82, -84*
Pseud./variant:
MacDonald, Anson
Monroe, Lyle
Riverside, John
Saunders, Caleb

Heinlein, Robert A 1907-1988 *BenetAL 91, BioIn 15, -16, -17, ConAu 125, ConLC 55, CurBio 88N, CyWA 89, MagSAmL, MajTwCW, NewEScF, NewYTBS 88, RGTwCSF, ScF&FL 92, SmATA 56N, -69, TwCChW 89, TwCSFW 91*
Pseud./variant:
York, Simon

Heinlein, Robert Anson *IntvTCA 2*

Heinlein, Robert Anson 1907- *WhoAm 85, WhoUSWr 88, WhoWor 87*

Heinlein, Robert Anson 1907-1988 *AuBYP 3, EncSF 93, MajAI, TwCYAW, WhAm 9*

Heinlein, Robert Anthony 1953- *WhoSSW 91, -93*

Heinly, John *IlsBYP*

Heins, Ethel L 1918- *BiDrLUS 70, BioIn 10, ConAu 102, ForWC 70, MedPD, WhoAm 82, -84, -86, -88, -90, -92, -94, WhoAmW 81, -83, WhoLibI 82, WhoLibS 55, -66*

Heins, Paul 1909- *ConAu 69, SmATA 13, WhoE 74, -75, WhoLibI 82*

Heintze, Carl 1922- *BioIn 13, ConAu 57, SmATA 26*

Heinz, W C 1915- *ConAu 5R, -4NR, SmATA 26, WhoE 83, WrDr 76, -80, -82, -84, -86, -88, -90, -92*

Heinz, Wilfred Charles 1915- *WrDr 94*

Heinzen, Mildred *ConAu X, SmATA X*
Main entry: Masters, Mildred

Heit, Robert *AuBYP 2S, -3*

Heitzmann, William Ray 1948- *SmATA 73*
Pseud./variant:
Heitzmann, Wm Ray
Tolland, W R
Vincent, William R

Heitzmann, Wm Ray
Main entry: Heitzmann, William Ray

Held, Jacqueline 1936- *ConAu 73, -14NR*

Held, John, Jr. 1889-1958 *AmAu&B, ArtCS, ArtsAmW 3, BenetAL 91, BioIn 4, -5, -6, -7, -8, -9, ChhPo S1, EncAB-A 30, EncACom, EncAJ, IlrAm 1880, -C, ObitOF 79, OxCAmH, OxCAmL 65, -83, REnAL, WebAB 74, -79, WhAm 3, WhAmArt 85, WhoAmA 80N, -82N, -86N, -89N, -91N*

Helfman, Elizabeth 1911- *AuBYP 3*

Helfman, Elizabeth S 1911- *AuBYP 2, BioIn 8, -9, ConAu 5R, -5NR, ForWC 70, IntAu&W 91, SmATA 3, WhoE 83, WrDr 76, -80, -82, -84, -86, -88, -90, -92, -94*

Helfman, Elizabeth Seaver 1911- *IntAu&W 89*

Helfman, Harry 1910- *AuBYP 3*

Helfman, Harry Carmozin 1910- *AuBYP 2, BioIn 8, -9, ConAu 25R, SmATA 3, WhoE 74, WrDr 76, -80, -82, -84, -86, -88, -90*

Hellberg, Hans-Eric 1927- *BioIn 15, ConAu 101, -18NR, IntAu&W 77, -82, -86, -89, SmATA 38, WhoWor 78*

Heller, David 1922-1968 *BioIn 8, ConAu P-1*

Heller, Dean Fons 1924- *ConAu 9R, ForWC 70*

Heller, Joseph *BioIn 14, -15, -16, -17, DrAPF 87, -89, -91, -93, IntvTCA 2, NewYTBS 86*

Heller, Joseph 1923- *Benet 87, BenetAL 91, CamGEL, CamGLE, CamHAL, CelR 90, ConAu 42NR, ConDr 93, ConLC 63, ConNov 86, -91, CyWA 89, EncAHmr, HalFC 88, IntAu&W 89, -91, IntWW 89, -91, MagSAmL, MajTwCW, ModAL S2, RAdv 13-1, RfGAmL 87, ScF&FL 92, TwCYAW, WhoAm 86, -92, -94, WhoUSWr 88, WhoWrEP 89, -92, WorAlBi, WorLitC, WrDr 86, -88, -90, -92*

Heller, Linda *BioIn 15*

Heller, Linda 1944- *ConAu 108, SmATA 40, -46*

Heller, Ruth M 1924- *ConAu 130, SmATA 66*

Hellie, Ann 1925- *ConAu 77, -15NR, MichAu 80*

Hellman, Harold 1927- *AuBYP 2S, -3, BioIn 9, ConAu 25R, -10NR, IntAu&W 77, -82, SmATA 4, WhoE 89, WrDr 76, -80*

Helm, Everett 1913- *Baker 84, BioIn 1, -6, ConAmC 76, -82, ConAu 49, DcCM, IntAu&W 77, NewGrDA 86, WhoAm 74, -76*

Helm, Everett Burton 1913- *Baker 92*

Helm, Thomas 1919- *ConAu 5R, WhoSSW 73*

Helmer, Jean Cassels *IlsBYP*

Helmer, John 1946- *ConAu 41R*

Helms, Randel 1942- *ConAu 49, IntAu&W 91, ScF&FL 92, WhoAm 76, -78, -80, WrDr 76, -80, -82, -84, -86, -88, -90, -92, -94*

Helps, Racey 1913-1971 *AuBYP 2S, -3, BioIn 9, -13, ConAu 29R, -P-2, SmATA 2, -25N*

Helweg, Hans H 1917- *BioIn 5, -14, -16, ConAu 126, IlsCB 1946, -1967, SmATA 33, -50*

Hemans, Felicia Dorothea 1793-1835 *Benet 87, BlmGEL, CamGEL, CamGLE, OxCLiW 86*

Hemans, Felicia Dorothea Browne 1793-1835 *Alli, BbD, BiD&SB, BioIn 2, -6, -12, -15, -16, -17, BritAu 19, CarSB, CasWL, CelCen, ChhPo S2, DcBiPP, DcEnA, DcEnL, DcEuL, DcLEL, DcNaB, EncBrWW, EvLB, InWom SUP, NewC, OxCChiL, OxCEng 67, -85, PoChrch, REn, WebE&AL*

Hemery, David 1944- *BioIn 9, -11, WhoTr&F 73*

Hemmant, Lynette 1938- *SmATA 69*

Hemming, Roy 1928- *BioIn 11, ConAu 61, SmATA 11, WhoE 74*
Pseud./variant:
Hamilton, Buzz

Hemming, Roy G 1928- *WhoAm 86, -90, -92, -94*

Hemon, Louis 1880-1913 *Benet 87, BenetAL 91, BioIn 1, -5, -6, -17, CasWL, ClDMEL 47, CyWA 58, DcLB 92, LongCTC, OxCAmL 65, OxCCan, OxCCanL, OxCFr, PenC EUR, REn, REnAL, TwCA, -SUP*

Hemphill, Martha Locke 1904-1973 *BioIn 15, ConAu 37R, SmATA 37*

Hemphill, Paul 1930- *WrDr 90, –92*

Hemphill, Paul 1936- *AuBYP 3, BioIn 15, ConAu 29NR, DcLB Y87B*

Hemphill, Paul 1938- *WrDr 86, –88*

Hemphill, Paul James 1930- *WrDr 94*

Hemphill, Paul James 1936?- *AuBYP 2S, AuNews 2, BioIn 9, –10, –11, ConAu 49, WrDr 76, –80*

Hemschemeyer, Judith *DrAPF 87, –89, –91, –93*

Hemschemeyer, Judith 1935- *AuBYP 2S, –3, BioIn 13, ConAu 49, DrAP 75, DrAPF 83, –85, WhoUSWr 88, WhoWrEP 89, –92*

Hemyng, Bracebridge 1841-1901 *BioIn 8, –16, EncMys, HsB&A, StaCVF, WhoChL*

Hemyng, S Bracebridge 1841-1901 *OxCChiL*

Henbest, Nigel *BioIn 16*

Henbest, Nigel 1951- *ConAu 124, SmATA 52, –55, WrDr 90, –92, –94*

Henderley, Brooks *ConAu 26NR, –P-2, SmATA 1*
Main entry: Stratemeyer, Edward L

Henderlite, Rachel *InWom SUP*

Henderlite, Rachel 1905- *ConAu 1R, WhoAm 74, –76, –78, WhoAmW 74*

Hendershot, Judith *AuBYP 3*

Hendershot, Judith 1940- *BioIn 16, SixBJA*

Henderson, Dion 1921-1984 *BioIn 3, ConAu 9R, –114, –5NR*

Henderson, Gordon *BioIn 16, –17*

Henderson, Gordon 1950- *BioIn 16, SmATA 53*

Henderson, Harold Gould 1889-1974 *BioIn 10, ChhPo, –S1, ConAu 53, DrAS 74F, –78F, WhAm 6*

Henderson, Kathy *BioIn 16*

Henderson, Kathy 1949- *ConAu 123, SmATA 53, –55*

Henderson, Keith 1883- *BioIn 14*

Henderson, Keith 1883-1982 *BioIn 1, –9, ConAu 106, –107, DcBrAr 1, DcBrBI, IlsCB 1744, Who 74, –82, –83N, WhoArt 80*

Henderson, Le Grand 1905-1965 *AuBYP 3*

Henderson, LeGrand 1901-1965 *AuBYF 2, BioIn 1, –2, –5, –7, –8, –11, ConAu 5R, EncAB-A 38, IlsCB 1744, –1946, –1957, JBA 51, SmATA 9*
Pseud./variant:
Harwin, Brian
LeGrand

Henderson, Nancy Wallace 1916- *ConAu 97, IntAu&W 82, NatPD 77, SmATA 22*

Henderson, Richard 1924- *ConAu 13R, –5NR, –20NR, IntAu&W 77, –91, WrDr 76, –80, –82, –84, –86, –88, –90, –92, –94*

Henderson, Zenna *IntvTCA 2*

Henderson, Zenna 1917- *ArtclWW 2, BioIn 10, –12, BlmGWL, ConAu 1R, –1NR, ConSFA, DcLB 8, ForWC 70, SmATA 5, WhoSciF, WrDr 84, –86*

Henderson, Zenna 1917-1983 *ConAu 133, EncSF 93, NewEScF, RGTwCSF, ScF&FL 92, ScFSB, TwCSFW 86, –91*

Henderson, Zenna 1917-1989 *BioIn 17*

Hendin, David 1945- *ConAu 41R, IntAu&W 77, WhoAm 74, WorAl*

Hendin, David Bruce 1945- *EncTwCJ, WhoAm 90, –92, –94*

Hendrich, Paula Griffith 1928- *ConAu 1R, –1NR*

Hendrick, Joe *IlsBYP*

Hendrick, Thomas William 1909- *Au&Wr 71, WrDr 76, –80, –82, –84, –86, –88*

Hendricks, George David, Sr. 1913- *ConAu 5R, DrAS 74E, –78E, –82E, IntAu&W 91, WrDr 76, –80, –82, –84, –86, –88, –90, –92, –94*

Hendrickson, Walter B, Jr. 1936- *ScF&FL 92*

Hendrickson, Walter Brookfield, Jr. 1936- *BioIn 1, –2, –11, ConAu 1R, –1NR, IndAu 1917, SmATA 9, WhoMW 78, –80, –82, –84*

Hendry, Diana 1941- *BioIn 17, ConAu 136, SmATA 68, WrDr 94*

Hendry, James Findlay 1912- *ConAu 29R, DrAS 74F, EngPo, IntAu&W 82, OxCEng 85, PenC ENG, WhoCan 73, WrDr 76, –80, –82, –84, –86*

Hendryx, James B 1880-1963 *TwCWW 91*

Hendryx, James Beardsley 1880-1963 *AmAu&B, EncFWF, OhA&B, WhAm 4, WhNAA*

Heneghan, James 1930- *BioIn 16, ConAu 129, SmATA 53*
Pseud./variant:
Bond, B J

Heneghan, James Beyer 1935- *AmMWSc 86*

Heninger, S K, Jr. 1922- *ConAu 1R, –1NR*

Henkel, Stephen Charles 1933- *ConAu 37R, WhoE 75, WrDr 76, –80, –82, –84, –86*

Henkes, Kevin 1960- *AuBYP 3, BioIn 15, –16, ChlBIID, ChlLR 23, ConAu 114, –38NR, MajAI, SixBJA, SmATA 43, –76*

Henkle, Henrietta *AmAu&B, BioIn 1, –2, –10, –13, ConAu 69, CurBio 46, OhA&B*
Main entry: Stephens, Henrietta Henkle

Henle, Faye d1972 *BioIn 9, ConAu 37R, NewYTBE 72*

Henneberger, Robert G 1921- *BioIn 5, IlsBYP, IlsCB 1946*

Hennessey, Roger Anthony Sean 1937- *ConAu 29R*

Henning, Jean Maxine Oliver 1918- *IntWWP 82*

Henninger, Joseph *BioIn 11, –13*

Henri, Florette d1985 *NewYTBS 85*

Henri, Florette 1908-1985 *AmAu&B, BioIn 14, ConAu 73, –117, NewYTBS 85*

Henriod, Lorraine 1925- *AuBYP 2S, –3, BioIn 13, ConAu 45, SmATA 26*

Henry, Alexander 1739-1824 *Alli, BbtC, BioIn 1, –6, –17, DcAmAu, DcCanB 6, DcLB 99, DcLEL, DcNAA, OxCAmH, OxCCan, WhNaAH*

Henry, Joanne Landers 1927- *BioIn 10, ConAu 17R, IndAu 1917, SmATA 6*

Henry, Maeve *ScF&FL 92*

Henry, Maeve 1960- *ConAu 142, SmATA 75*

Henry, Marguerite *IntAu&W 86, SmATA 7AS, WhoAm 86, –88, –90, –92, –94, WhoUSWr 88, WhoWrEP 89, –92, WrDr 86, –88, –90, –92, –94*

Henry, Marguerite 1902- *AmAu&B, AuBYP 2, –3, Au&ICB, Au&Wr 71, BioIn 1, –2, –3, –4, –7, –8, –11, –12, –14, BkCL, ChlLR 4, ConAu 17R, –9NR, CurBio 47, DcLB 22, FamMS, InWom SUP, IntAu&W 77, –82, JBA 51, MajAI, NewbMB 1922, OxCChiL, SmATA 11, –69, TwCChW 78, –83, –89, WhoAm 74, –76, –78, –80, –82, –84, WhoAmW 74, –75, –77, WhoWor 74, WrDr 76, –80, –82, –84*

Henry, Marguerite Breithaupt 1902- *DcAmChF 1960*

Henry, Marie H *BioIn 17*

Henry, Marie H 1935- *SmATA 65*

Henry, Marion *ConAu 141, EncSF 93, MajTwCW, SmATA 76*
Main entry: del Rey, Lester

Henry, O *AmAu&B, AmWr S2, AtlBL, AuBYP 3, BiDSA, CamHAL, CasWL, Chambr 3, ChhPo, CnDAL, ConAu 131, –X, CyWA 58, DcAmSR, DcLEL, DcNAA, Dis&D, EncFWF, EncMys, EncWL, EvLB, FilmgC, HalFC 84, LongCTC, MajTwCW, McGEWB, ModAL, Novels, OxCAmL 65, –83, OxCEng 67, –85, PenC AM, RAdv 1, REn, REnAL, TwCA, –SUP, TwCLC 1, –19, TwCWr, WebAB 74, –79, WebE&AL, WhDW, WhAm 1, WhoTwCL, WorAl, YABC X*
Main entry: Porter, William Sydney

Henry, O 1862-1910 *AmWr S2, Benet 87, BenetAL 91, BioIn 14, –17, CamGLE, CrtSuMy, HalFC 88, RAdv 13-1, RfGAmL 87, RfGShF, ShSCr 5, ShSWr, TwCWW 91, WorAlBi, WorLitC*

Henry, Oliver
Main entry: Porter, William Sydney

Henry, Ralph B 1884?-1958 *BioIn 2, –5*

Henry, Robert Selph 1889-1970 *BioIn 10, –13, ConAu 1R, –103, –17NR, DcLB 17, NewYTBE 70, ObitOF 79, WhAm 5, WhNAA*

Henry, T E *ConAu X, SmATA X*
Main entry: Rowland-Entwistle, Theodore

Henry, Thomas *WhoChL*
Main entry: Fisher, Thomas Henry

Henry, Vera *ConAu P-2, MichAu 80, WrDr 76, –80, –82, –84*

Henry, Vera 1909?-1987 *ConAu 123*

Henry, Will *AmAu&B, AuBYP 2S, BenetAL 91, BioIn 13, ConAu 135, EncFWF, IntAu&W 91X, TwCWW 91, WrDr 84, –86, –88, –90, –92*
Main entry: Allen, Henry

Henry, Will 1912- *AuBYP 3, BioIn 15, –16, –17, WrDr 94*

Henschel, Georgie *BioIn 16, SmATA 56*

Henson, Clyde Eugene 1914- *ConAu 5R, DrAS 74E, -78E, -82E*

Henson, James Maury 1936- *ConAu 106, -124, SmATA 43, WhoAm 80, -82, -84, -86, -88, WorAl*
Pseud./variant:
Henson, Jim

Henson, James Maury 1936-1990 *ConAu 131, SmATA 65, WhAm 10*

Henson, Jim *BioIn 14, -15, -16, -17, ConAu 131, SmATA 65*
Main entry: Henson, James Maury

Henson, Jim 1936- *BioIn 11, -12, -13, CelR 90, ConAu X, ConTFT 1, HalFC 84, -88, IntMPA 81, -82, -84, -86, -88, LesBEnT, News 89-1, SmATA X*

Henson, Jim 1936-1990 *AnObit 1990, ConHero 2, ConTFT 11, CurBio 90N, LesBEnT 92, NewYTBS 90, News 90, WorAlBi*

Henson, Matthew A 1866-1955 *Expl 93, WorAlBi*

Henson, Matthew Alexander 1866-1955 *AfrAmAl 6, BioIn 1, -2, -3, -4, -6, -7, -8, -9, -10, -12, -13, -15, -16, -17, DcAmNB, InB&W 80, -85, ObitOF 79, WorAl*

Henson, Matthew Alexander 1867-1955 *BlksScM*

Henstra, Friso 1928- *BioIn 11, -12, FourBJA, IlsBYP, IlsCB 1967, SmATA 8, -73, -14AS, WhoGrA 82*

Hentoff, Nat *BioIn 14, -15, -16, -17, WrDr 86, -88, -90, -92*
Main entry: Hentoff, Nathan Irving

Hentoff, Nat 1925- *Au&Arts 4, BenetAL 91, ConAu 6AS, -25NR, CurBio 86, NewGrDA 86, SmATA 69, TwCChW 89*

Hentoff, Nat Irving 1925- *AuBYP 3*

Hentoff, Nathan Irving *WrDr 94*

Hentoff, Nathan Irving 1925- *AmAu&B, AuBYP 2, BioIn 7, -8, -9, -13, ChhPo S2, ChlLR 1, ConAu 1R, -5NR, ConLC 26, DcAmChF 1960, EncTwCJ, IntAu&W 77, MajAI, REnAL, SmATA 27, -42, ThrBJA, TwCChW 78, -83, TwCYAW, WhoAm 74, -80, -82, -84, -86, -88, -90, -92, -94, WhoE 74, -89, WhoUSWr 88, WhoWor 74, WhoWrEP 89, -92, WrDr 76, -80, -82, -84*
Pseud./variant:
Hentoff, Nat

Henty, G A 1832-1902 *BioIn 14, -16, CamGEL, CamGLE, SmATA 64, StaCVF, TwCChW 89A*

Henty, GA 1832-1902 *BioIn 17, RfGEnL 91*

Henty, George Alfred 1832-1902 *Alli SUP, BbD, BiD&SB, BioIn 2, -4, -8, -10, -11, -12, -13, -14, -16, -17, BritAu 19, CarSB, CasWL, Chambr 3, ConAu 112, DcBiPP, DcBrBI, DcLB 18, DcLEL, DcNaB S2, EvLB, JBA 34, LongCTC, NewC, Novels, OxCChiL, OxCEng 67, -85, OxCShps, PenC ENG, TelT, TwCChW 78A, -83A, WhoChL*

Henwood, James N J 1932- *ConAu 29R, DrAS 74H, -78H, -82H*

Hepburn, James Gordon 1922- *ConAu 85, -29NR, DrAS 74E, -82E, WhoAm 80*

Hepler, Loren George 1928- *AmMWSc 73P, -76P, -82, -86, -89, -92*

Heppenstall, Margit Strom 1913- *ConAu 21R*

Herald, Kathleen *ConAu X, -32NR, IntAu&W 86X, MajAI, SmATA X, ThrBJA, TwCChW 83, -89, TwCYAW*
Main entry: Peyton, Kathleen Wendy

Herald, Kathleen 1929- *BioIn 17, SmATA X, WrDr 94*

Herben, Beatrice Slayton *CarSB*

Herber, Harold L 1929- *ConAu 108, DrAS 74E, -82E, WhoAm 86, -88*

Herbert, Beth Ames *MedPD*

Herbert, Cecil *ConAu X, -29NR, SmATA X*

Herbert, Don *BioIn 14, -17, LesBEnT 92*

Herbert, Don 1917- *AuBYP 2, -3, BioIn 4, -8, -9, -11, ConAu 29R, -30NR, CurBio 56, LesBEnT, NewYTET, SmATA 2*
Pseud./variant:
Wizard, Mr

Herbert, Frank *BioIn 14, -15, -16, -17, EncSF 93*

Herbert, Frank d1986 *NewYTBS 86*

Herbert, Frank 1920- *ScFSB, WorAlBi, WrDr 86*

Herbert, Frank 1920-1986 *AnObit 1986, Benet 87, BenetAL 91, ConAu 118, ConLC 44, CyWA 89, MagSAmL, MajTwCW, NewEScF, RGTwCSF, ScF&FL 92, SmATA 47N, TwCSFW 86, -91*

Herbert, Frank Patrick *IntvTCA 2*

Herbert, Frank Patrick 1920- *AmAu&B, BioIn 10, -11, -12, -13, ConAu 53, -5NR, ConLC 12, -23, -35, ConSFA, DcLB 8, IntAu&W 77, Novels, SmATA 9, -37, WhoAm 74, -76, -78, -80, -82, -84, WhoSciF, WorAl, WrDr 76, -80, -82, -84*

Herbert, Frank Patrick 1920-1986 *ConAu 43NR, EncSF 93, TwCYAW, WhAm 9*

Herbert, Helen 1947- *BioIn 16*

Herbert, Helen Jean 1947- *SmATA 57*
Pseud./variant:
Howat, Jean

Herbert, Wally
Main entry: Herbert, Walter William

Herbert, Walter William 1934- *BioIn 13, ConAu 69, -15NR, IntWW 89, -91, SmATA 23, Who 74, -82, -83, -85, -88, -90, -92, WhoWor 74, -91*
Pseud./variant:
Herbert, Wally

Herbst, Judith 1947- *SmATA 74*

Herbst, Robert Leroy 1935- *BioIn 11, ConAu 61, WhoAm 78, -80, -82, -84, -86, -88, -90, -92, -94, WhoAmP 77, -81, -83, -85, -87, -89, -91, -93, WhoE 93, WhoGov 77, -75, WhoSSW 91*

Herda, D J 1948- *WhoMW 76*

Hereford, Robert A 1902- *AuBYP 2, -3, BioIn 8*

Herford, Oliver 1863-1935 *AmAu&B, AuBYP 2S, -3, BenetAL 91, BiD&SB, BioIn 2, -5, -8, CarSB, ChhPo, -S1, -S2, DcAmAu, DcNAA, EvLB, LongCTC, NewC, OxCAmL 65, -83, REnAL, TwCA, -SUP, WhAm 1, WhAmArt 85, WorECar*

Herge *BioIn 13, ChlLR 6, ConAu X, -31NR, IntAu&W 77X, -82X, SmATA X*
Main entry: Remi, Georges

Herge 1907-1983 *BioIn 14*

Herge, Henry Curtis, Sr. 1905- *WhoAm 94, WhoSSW 93*

Heriot, George 1759- *Alli, BbtC, BiDLA, OxCCan*

Heriot, George 1759-1839 *BioIn 14, DcCanB 7*

Heritage, Martin *EncMys*

Heriteau, Jacqueline 1925- *ConAu 45, -1NR, -16NR, -37NR, WhoAmW 83*

Herkimer, Lawrence Russell 1925?- *AuBYP 2S, -3, BioIn 6, -11, -13, ConAu 110, NewYTBE 72, SmATA 42*

Herlihy, Dirlie Anne 1935- *SmATA 73*

Herman, Charlotte 1937- *BioIn 12, ConAu 41R, -15NR, -34NR, SmATA 20*

Herman, George Richard 1925- *ConAu 5R, DrAS 74E, -78E, -82E, WhoWest 76, -78, -80, -82, WrDr 76, -80, -82, -84, -86, -88, -90, -92, -94*

Herman, Vic *WhoAmA 86, -89, -91*

Herman, Vic 1919- *BioIn 10, ConAu 107, WhAmArt 85, WhoAmA 73, -78, -80, -82, -84, WhoWest 74*

Hermanson, Dennis 1947- *BioIn 11, SmATA 10*

Hermes, Patricia 1936- *BioIn 14, -16, ConAu 104, -22NR, SixBJA, SmATA 31, TwCYAW*

Herndon, Venable 1927- *ConAu 109, -32NR, NatPD 77, -81, WhoAm 74*

Herold, Ann Bixby 1937- *SmATA 72*

Herold, J Christopher 1919-1964 *RAdv 13-3*

Herold, J Christopher 1919-1965 *BioIn 5, -7, CurBio 59, -65*

Heron, Frances Dunlap 1906- *BioIn 2*

Heroux, Denis *OxCCan SUP*

Herrera, Velino 1902-1973 *AmPB, BioIn 1, IlsCB 1744, WhAmArt 85*

Herrera, Velino Shije 1902- *BioIn 14*

Herrick, Jeanne Mellin *AuBYP 3*

Herrick, Robert 1591-1674 *Alli, AnCL, AtlBL, Benet 87, BbD, BiDRP&D, BiD&SB, BioIn 1, -2, -3, -4, -5, -6, -7, -10, -12, -14, -15, BlmGEL, BritAu, CamGEL, CamGLE, CasWL, Chambr 1, ChhPo, -S1, -S2, CnE&AP, CrtT 1, CroE&S, CyWA 58, DcBiPP, DcEnA, DcEnL, DcEuL, DcLB 126, DcLEL, DcNaB, Dis&D, EvLB, LitC 13, LongCEL, LongCTC, McGEWB, MouLC 1, NewC, OxCEng 67, -85, OxCMus, PenC ENG, RAdv 1, -13-1, REn, RfGEnL 91, WebE&AL, WhDW, WorAlBi, WorAl*

Herrick, Robert 1868-1938 *Benet 87, BenetAL 91, CamGEL, CamGLE, CamHAL, ConAu 119, DcLB 78, EncSF 93, RfGAmL 87*

Herriman, George 1880-1944 *ArtCS, BenetAL 91, BioIn 13, -14, -15, -17, ChhPo,*

EncACom, NewYTBS 86, ObitOF 79, REnAL, WebAB 74

Herriot, James *BioIn 9, -10, -11, -12, -15, -16, ConAu X, ConLC 12, IntAu&W 77, -91, IntWW 82, -83, SmATA X, Who 82, -83, -85, -88, -90, -92, WhoWor 84, WorAl, WorAu 1975, WrDr 76, -80, -82, -84, -86, -88, -90, -92*
Main entry: Wight, James Alfred

Herriot, James 1916- *Au&Arts 1, AuBYP 3, Benet 87, ConAu 40NR, CyWA 89, IntWW 89, -91, TwCYAW, WhoAm 94, WhoWor 87, -89, -91, -93, WorAlBi, WrDr 94*

Herrmann, Frank 1927- *ConAu 21R, -10NR*

Herrmanns, Ralph 1933- *AuBYP 2S, -3, BioIn 11, ConAu 9R, -3NR, -18NR, IntAu&W 77, -82, -89, -91, SmATA 11, WrDr 76, -80, -82, -84, -86, -88, -90, -92, -94*

Herron, Edward A 1912- *BioIn 9, ConAu 5R, SmATA 4*

Hersey, John *BioIn 16*

Hersey, John 1914- *Benet 87, BenetAL 91, BioIn 14, -15, -16, -17, CelR 90, ConAu 33NR, ConLC 40, ConNov 86, -91, CyWA 89, EncSF 93, EncTwCJ, HalFC 88, JrnUS, MajTwCW, NewEScF, ScFSB, SourALJ, TwCSFW 86, Who 88, -90, -92, WhoAm 86, -88, -90, -92, WhoUSWr 88, WhoWrEP 89, -92, WorAlBi, WrDr 86, -88, -90, -92*

Hersey, John 1914-1993 *ConLC 81*

Hersey, John Richard 1914- *AmAu&B, AmNov, BioIn 1, -2, -4, -5, -7, -8, -9, -10, -12, -13, BlueB 76, CasWL, CelR, CnDAL, ConAu 17R, ConLC 1, -2, -7, -9, ConNov 72, -76, -82, CurBio 44, CyWA 58, DcLB 6, DcLEL 1940, DrAF 76, DrAS 74E, -78E, -82E, EncAJ, HalFC 84, IntAu&W 77, -82, -89, -91, IntWW 74, -75, -76, -77, -78, -79, -80, -81, -82, -83, -89, -91, LongCTC, ModAL, Novels, OxCAmL 65, -83, PenC AM, RAdv 1, REn, REnAL, SmATA 25, TwCA SUP, WebAB 74, -79, Who 74, -82, -83, -85, WhoAm 74, -76, -78, -80, -82, -84, WhoE 74, WhoWor 74, -78, -80, -82, -84, WorAl, WrDr 76, -80, -82, -84*

Hersey, John Richard 1914-1993 *ConAu 140, CurBio 93N, SmATA 76*

Hershfield, Harry 1885-1974 *ArtCS, BioIn 10, ConAu 53, EncACom, NewYTBS 74, ObitOF 79, WhAmArt 85, WhScrn 83, -77*

Hershon, Robert *DrAPF 87, -89, -91, -93*

Hershon, Robert 1936- *ConAu 33R, -13NR, DrAP 75, DrAPF 83, -85, IntWWP 82*

Hersom, Kathleen 1911- *SmATA 73*

Herst, Herman, Jr. 1909- *BioIn 5, -9, ConAu 1R, -2NR, WhoAm 84, -86, -88, -90, -92, -94, WhoSSW 76, -78, -86*

Hertz, Grete Janus 1915- *BioIn 13, ConAu 101, SmATA 23*

Herz, Martin Florian 1917-1983 *BioIn 13, -17, BlueB 76, ConAu 21R, -111, -9NR, WhAm 8, WhoAm 74, -76, -78, -80, -82, WhoAmP 75, -77, WhoGov 77, -72, -75, WrDr 76, -80, -82, -84*

Herz, Peggy 1936- *ConAu 37R*
Pseud./variant:
Hudson, Peggy

Herzberg, Max J 1886-1958 *AmAu&B, BenetAL 91, BioIn 4, REnAL, WhAm 3 WhNAA*

Herzel, Catherine Williams 1908- *ConAu 5R, ForWC 70*

Herzig, Alison Cragin *AuBYP 3*

Herzka, Heinz 1935- *ConAu 37R*

Herzog, Arthur 1927- *ConAu 30NR, ScF&FL 92, WrDr 86, -88, -90, -92, -94*

Herzog, Arthur 1928- *ScFSB*

Herzog, Arthur, III 1927- *ConAu 17R, -9NR, EncSF 93, IntAu&W 77, WhoAm 76, -78, -80, -82, -84, -86, -88, -90, -92, -94, WhoE 74, WhoUSWr 88, WhoWrEP 89 -92, WrDr 76, -80, -82, -84*

Herzog, Emile Salomon Wilhelm *AuBYP 2, BioIn 8, ClDMEL 47, LongCTC, NewC TwCA, -SUP, WhDW*
Main entry: Maurois, Andre

Herzog, Emile Solomon Wilhelm *AuBYP 3*

Herzog, George 1901- *Baker 84, BioIn 13, BlueB 76, IntWW 74, -75, -76, -77, -78, -79, -80, -81, -82, -83, WhoAm 74*

Herzog, George 1901-1983 *Baker 92, NewGrDA 86*

Herzog, George 1901-1984 *BioIn 14*

Hess, Fjeril 1893- *AmAu&B, BioIn 2, JBA 34, -51*

Hess, Lilo 1916- *AmPB, AuBYP 2S, -3, BioIn 9, ConAu 33R, -12NR, FifBJA, SmATA 4*

Hesse, Hermann 1877-1962 *AtlBL, Benet 87, BioIn 1, -2, -3, -4, -5, -6, -7, -8, -9, -10, -11, -12, -13, -14, -15, -16, -17, CasWL, ClDMEL 47, ConAu 17R, -P-2, ConLC 1, -2, -3, -6, -11, -17, -25, -69, CurBio 62, CyWA 58, -89, DcLB 66, EncO&P 1, -2, -3, EncSF 93, EncWL, -2, EuWr 9, EvEuW, GrFLW, MagSWL, MajTwCW, MakMC, McGEWB, ModGL, NobelP, Novels, ObitOF 79, ObitT 1961, OxCEng 85, OxCGer 76, -86, PenC EUR, RAdv 13-2, RComWL, REn, ScF&FL 92, ScFSB, SmATA 50, TwCA, -SUP, TwCWr, WhDW, WhAm 4, WhoTwCL, WorAlBi, WorAl, WorLitC, WrPh*
Pseud./variant:
Lauscher, Hermann
Sinclair, Emil

Hesse, Karen 1952- *SmATA 74*

Hesselberg, Erik *AuBYP 2S, -3*

Hest, Amy *BioIn 16*

Hest, Amy 1950- *SmATA 55*

Hester, Kathleen B 1905- *ConAu P-2*

Hettlinger, Richard Frederick 1920- *ConAu 17R, -7NR, DrAS 74P, -78P, -82P*

Heuck, Sigrid *IlsBYP*

Heuer, John 1941- *ConAu 69, -14NR*

Heuer, John Michael 1941- *ConTFT 6*

Heuer, Kenneth John 1927- *ConAu 110, -30NR, SmATA 44, WhoAm 80, -82, -84, -86, -88, -90, -92, -94*

Heuman, William 1912- *WrDr 86*

Heuman, William 1912-1971 *AuBYP 2, -3, BioIn 7, -8, -12, ConAu 5R, -7NR, SmATA 21, TwCWW 91, WrDr 84*
Pseud./variant:
Kramer, George

Heward, Constance 1884-1968 *OxCChiL, TwCChW 83, -89*

Heward, May *ChhPo S1*

Heward, William Lee 1949- *ConAu 53, -4NR, MichAu 80, WhoFrS 84, WhoMW 84*

Hewes, Agnes 1874-1963 *AuBYP 3*

Hewes, Agnes Danforth 1874-1963 *AmAu&B, AuBYP 2, BioIn 2, -8, -14, ConAu 113, JBA 34, -51, SmATA 35*

Hewett, Anita 1918- *AuBYP 2, -3, BioIn 8, ConAu 21R, IntAu&W 77, -82, SmATA 13, TwCChW 78, -83, WhoWor 78, WrDr 76, -82, -84, -86, -88*

Hewett, Anita 1918-1989 *TwCChW 89*

Hewett, Joan *AuBYP 3*

Hewins, Caroline Maria 1846-1926 *BioIn 2, -3, -6, -15, HanAmWH, InWom SUP, OxCChiL*

Hewitt, Foster William 1903- *BioIn 8, CanWW 70, -80, -81, -83, WhoHcky 73*

Hewitt, Jean 1929- *Au&Wr 71*

Hewitt, Marsha 1948- *DcChlFi*

Hewitt, Philip Nigel 1945- *ConAu 81*

Hext, Harrington *ConAu X, EncSF 93, SmATA X, TwCCr&M 80, -85, -91*
Main entry: Phillpotts, Eden

Hext, Harrington 1862-1960 *ScFEYrs*

Hey, Nigel Stewart 1936- *BioIn 12, ConAu 33R, SmATA 20, WhoWest 92, -94, WhoWor 78, WrDr 76, -80*

Heyduck-Huth, Hilde 1929- *BioIn 11, ConAu 57, SmATA 8*

Heyer, Carol 1950- *ConAu 130, SmATA 74, WrDr 94*

Heyer, Georgette 1902-1974 *Au&Wr 71, Benet 87, BioIn 4, -10, -14, -16, -17, BlmGWL, ConAu 49, -93, CorpD, CrtSuMy, DcLB 77, DcLEL, DcNaB 1971, EncBrWW, EncMys, FemiCLE, InWom SUP, LongCTC, MajTwCW, NewC, NewYTBS 74, Novels, ObitOF 79, ObitT 1971, OxCChiL, OxCEng 85, REn, TwCA, -SUP, TwCCr&M 80, -85, -91, TwCRHW 90, TwCWr, WhAm 6, Who 74, WhoAm 74, WhoWor 74, WorAl*

Heyer, Marilee 1942- *BioIn 17, ConAu 125, SmATA 64*

Heyerdahl, Thor *BioIn 14, -15, -16, -17*

Heyerdahl, Thor 1914- *Au&Wr 71, BioIn 1, -2, -3, -4, -5, -6, -8, -9, -10, -11, -12, CelR, ConAu 5R, -5NR, -22NR, ConHero 2, ConLC 26, CurBio 47, -72, DcTwHis, InSci, IntAu&W 77, -82, -89, -91, IntWW 74, -75, -76, -77, -78, -79, -80, -81, -82, -83, -89, -91, LongCTC, MajTwCW, OxCShps, RAdv 13-3, SmATA 2, -52, TwCA SUP, TwCWr, UFOEn, WhDW, Who 74, -82, -83, -85, -88, -90, -92, WhoAm 80, -82, -84, -86, -88, WhoWor 74, -78, -82, -84, -87, -91, -93, WorAlBi, WorAl, WrDr 76, -80, -82, -84, -86, -88, -90, -92, -94*

Heyliger, William 1884- *AuBYP 3*

Heyliger, William 1884-1955 *AmAu&B, AuBYP 2, BioIn 1, –2, –3, –7, –11, CathA 1930, JBA 34, –51, REnAL, WhAm 7, YABC 1*
Pseud./variant:
Williams, Hawley

Heyman, Ken 1930- *BioIn 8, –14, –16, BlueB 76, ConAu 112, ICPEnP A, MacBEP, SmATA 34, WhoAm 74, –80, –82, WhoE 74*

Heyneman, Anne 1910?- *BioIn 1, –5, ChhPo, IlsCB 1744, –1946*

Heyward, DuBose 1885-1940 *AmAu&B, AmPB, ASCAP 66, Benet 87, BenetAL 91, BioIn 3, –4, –5, –8, –10, –12, –15, CamGLE, CamHAL, ChhPo, CnDAL, CnMD, ConAmA, ConAmL, ConAu 108, CurBio 40, CyWA 58, DcLB 7, –9, –45, DcLEL, DcNAA, EncSoH, EvLB, LongCTC, McGEWD 72, –84, ModAL, ModWD, NatCAB 60, NotNAT A, –B, Novels, OxCAmL 65, –83, OxCAmT 84, PenC AM, PlP&P, REn, REnAL, RfGAmL 87, SmATA 21, TwCA, –SUP, TwCWr, WebAB 74, –79, WhAm 1*

Heywood, Karen 1946- *BioIn 16, SmATA 48*

Hibbert, Christopher 1924- *Au&Wr 71, BioIn 9, BlueB 76, ConAu 1R, –2NR, IntAu&W 82, –86, –89, –91, LongCTC, OxCCan, SmATA 4, Who 74, –82, –83, –85, –88, –90, –92, WhoWor 80, WorAu 1975, WrDr 76, –80, –82, –84, –86, –88, –90, –92, –94*

Hibbert, Eleanor Alice 1906- *ArtclWW 2*

Hibbert, Eleanor Alice Burford *InWom SUP, WrDr 86, –88, –90, –92*

Hibbert, Eleanor Alice Burford 1906-1993 *ConAu 140, SmATA 74, WrDr 94N*

Hibbert, Eleanor Burford 1906- *BioIn 7, –9, –10, –11, ConAu 17R, –9NR, –28NR, ConLC 7, EncMys, IntAu&W 77, SmATA 2, Who 74, WorAu 1950, WrDr 76, –80*
Pseud./variant:
Burford, Eleanor
Carr, Philippa
Ford, Elbur
Holt, Victoria
Kellow, Kathleen
Plaidy, Jean
Tate, Ellalice

Hicken, Victor 1921- *ConAu 21R, DrAS 74H, –78H, –82H, WhoAm 74, –76, –78, –80, –82, –84, –86, –88, –90, WrDr 76, –80, –82, –84, –86, –88, –90, –92, –94*

Hickey, Madelyn Eastlund 1928- *WhoAmW 75, –77, WrDr 76*

Hickey, T Earl *ConSFA*

Hickman, Janet 1940- *BioIn 11, ConAu 65, –10NR, SmATA 12*

Hickman, Martha Whitmore *DrAPF 93*

Hickman, Martha Whitmore 1925- *BioIn 13, ConAu 25R, –10NR, –26NR, SmATA 26, WhoAmW 74, WhoWrEP 89, –92*

Hickok, Lorena A 1892?-1968 *AuBYP 2, –3, BioAmW, BioIn 7, –8, –10, –12, ConAu 73, EncAJ, NotAW MOD, SmATA 20*

Hickok, Lorena A 1893-1968 *ArtclWW 2, BiDAmJo, BioIn 16, –17*

Hickok, Will *AuBYP 3, ConAu X, SmATA X*
Main entry: Harrison, C William

Hicks, Clifford B 1920- *AuBYP 3, BioIn 16, ConAu 24NR, SmATA 50*

Hicks, Clifford Byron 1920- *AmAu&B, AuBYP 2, BioIn 7, ConAu 5R, –9NR, WhoAm 74, –76, –78, –80, –82, –84, –86, –88, –90, WhoUSWr 88, WhoWrEP 89, –92*

Hicks, Eleanor B *AuBYP 2S, –3, BioIn 9, –10, ConAu X, MajAI, SmATA 1, –67, WrDr 76, –80*
Main entry: Coerr, Eleanor Beatrice

Hicks, Harvey *ConAu X, MajAI, SmATA 67*
Main entry: Stratemeyer, Edward L

Hicks, Nancy 1946- *BioIn 9, InB&W 80, WhoBlA 80, –85*

Hicyilmaz, Gay 1947- *ConAu 133, SmATA 77, WrDr 94*

Hida, Keiko 1913- *ChhPo S1, IlsBYP*

Hieatt, Constance B 1928- *ConAu 23NR, WrDr 86, –88, –90, –92*

Hieatt, Constance Bartlett 1928- *BioIn 9, CanWW 89, ConAu 5R, –8NR, DrAS 74E, –78E, –82E, IntAu&W 77, –91, SmATA 4, WhoAm 82, –84, –86, –88, –90, –92, –94, WhoAmW 75, –83, –85, –87, –89, –91, –93, WhoWor 82, WhoWrEP 89, –92, WrDr 76, –80, –82, –84, –94*

Hiebert, Ray Eldon 1932- *AmAu&B, ConAu 17R, –7NR, DrAS 74E, –78E, SmATA 13, WhoAm 74, –76, –78, –80, –82, –84, –86, –88, –90, –92, –94, WhoE 74, –75, –77, –81, –83, –85, –86, WhoWor 82*

Hiebert, Susan *BioIn 13, Profile 2*

Higdon, Hal 1931- *AuBYP 2S, BioIn 9, -12, ConAu 9R, -3NR, IntAu&W 86, -91, SmATA 4, WhoMW 84, WrDr 76, -80, -82, -84, -86, -88, -90, -92, -94*
Pseud./variant:
Smith, Lafayette

Higginbottom, J Winslow 1945- *BioIn 13, SmATA 29*

Higgins, Charlotte M *Alli SUP, CarSB*

Higgins, Don 1928- *ArtsCL, BioIn 6, -14, ConAu 25R, -14NR*

Higgins, Helen Boyd 1892-1971 *IndAu 1917*

Higgins, Lewis R d1916
Pseud./variant:
Nugent, Frank

Higgins, Reynold Alleyne 1916- *ConAu 25R, IntAu&W 91, Who 74, -82, -83, -85, -88, -90, -92, WrDr 76, -80, -82, -84, -86, -88, -90, -92, -94*

Higgins, Reynold Alleyne 1916-1993 *ConAu 141*

Higginson, Thomas Wentworth 1823-1911 *Alli SUP, AmAu, AmAu&B, BenetAL 91, BbD, BiD&SB, BiInAmS, BioIn 3, -5, -6, -8, -9, -15, -16, -17, CamHAL, CasWL, Chambr 3, ChhPo, -S1, -S2, CnDAL, CyAL, DcAmAu, DcAmSR, DcLB 1, -64, DcLEL, DcNAA, HarEnUS, OxCAmL 65, -83, REn, REnAL, ScF&FL 92, TwCLC 36, WebAB 74, -79, WhAm 1, WhCiWar*

Higham, Charles 1931- *Au&Wr 71, BestSel 89-1, ConAu 33R, -17NR, ConPo 70, -75, -80, -85, DcLEL 1940, OxCAusL, ScF&FL 92, WhoE 75, -77, WrDr 76, -80, -82, -84, -86, -88, -90, -92, -94*

Higham, David 1949- *BioIn 16, ConAu 126, SmATA 50*

Higham, Jon Atlas *SmATA X*
Main entry: Higham, Jonathan Huw

Higham, Jonathan Huw 1960- *ConAu 127, SmATA 59*
Pseud./variant:
Higham, Jon Atlas

Highet, Helen *BioIn 13, ConAu X, -28NR, MajTwCW, SmATA X*
Main entry: MacInnes, Helen

Highet, Helen Clark *Who 88*

Highet, Helen MacInnes 1907-1985 *BioIn 17*

Highland, Harold Joseph *AmMWSc 86*

Highland, Harold Joseph 1917- *AmMWSc 73S, -76P, -82, WhoE 93*

Highsmith, Patricia *CamGLE, NewYTBS 88*

Highsmith, Patricia 1921- *ArtclWW 2, Au&Wr 71, BenetAL 91, BioIn 10, -12, -14, -15, -16, -17, BioNews 74, BlueB 76, ConAu 1R, -1NR, -20NR, ConLC 2, -4, -42, ConNov 72, -76, -82, -86, -91, CrtSuMy, CurBio 90, EncMys, FemiCLE, HalFC 84, -88, InWom SUP, IntAu&W 77, -82, -89, -91, IntWW 82, -83, -89, -91, MajTwCW, Novels, OxCEng 85, ScF&FL 92, TwCCr&M 80, -85, -91, Who 74, -82, -83, -85, -88, -90, -92, WhoHr&F, WhoTwCL, WhoWor 89, WorAlBi, WorAl, WorAu 1950, WrDr 76, -80, -82, -84, -86, -88, -90, -92*

Hightower, Florence 1916-1981 *TwCChW 89*

Hightower, Florence Cole 1916-1981 *AuBYP 2, -3, Au&Wr 71, BioIn 7, -9, -12, -13, ConAu 1R, -103, -35NR, DcAmChF 1960, SmATA 4, -27N, ThrBJA, TwCChW 78, -83*

Highwater, Jamake *BioIn 14, -15, -17, ConAu 7AS, DrAPF 87, -89, -91, -93, TwCChW 89, WhoAm 92, -94*

Highwater, Jamake 1942?- *Au&Arts 7, BenetAL 91, ChlLR 17, ConAu 10NR, -34NR, CyWA 89, DcAmChF 1985, DcLB 52, -Y85B, DrAPF 83, -85, FifBJA, IntAu&W 89, -91, OxCChiL, SmATA 30, -32, -69, TwCChW 83, WhoAm 80, -82, -84, -86, -88, -90, WhoAmA 80, -82, -84, -86, -89, -91, WhoE 81, -83, WhoUSWr 88, WhoWor 80, WhoWrEP 89, -92, WorAu 1980, WrDr 84, -86, -88, -90, -92, -94*
Pseud./variant:
Marks, J
Marks-Highwater, J

Highwater, Jamake Mamake 1942?- *MajAI*

Higson, Kit *BioIn 8, WhoChL*

Hildebrandt, Greg 1939- *Au&Arts 12, BiDScF, BioIn 12, -14, -16, ConAu 104, NewEScF, ScF&FL 92, SmATA 33, -55*

Hildebrandt, Tim 1939- *Au&Arts 12, BiDScF, BioIn 12, -14, -16, ConAu 111, -122, NewEScF, ScF&FL 92, SmATA 33, -55*

Hilder, Rowland 1905- *BioIn 1, -2, -8, -12, -14, -17, ChhPo S2, DcBrAr 1, IlsCB 1744, SmATA 36, TwCPaSc, Who 74, -82, -83, -85, -88, -90, -92, WhoArt 80, -82, -84, WhoChL*

Hilder, Rowland 1905-1993 *SmATA 77*

Hildick, E W 1925- *AuBYP 3, BioIn 17, MajAI, ScF&FL 92, ScFSB, SmATA 68, -6AS,*

TwCChW 89, WrDr 86, –88, –90, –92
Main entry: Hildick, Edmund Wallace

Hildick, Edmund Wallace 1925- *AuBYP 2S, Au&Wr 71, BioIn 8, –9, –17, ConAu 25R, IntAu&W 91, MajAI, OxCChiL, SmATA 2, TwCChW 78, –83, WhoChL, WrDr 80, –82, –84*
Pseud./variant:
Hildick, E W
Hildick, Wallace

Hildick, Emund Wallace 1925- *WrDr 94*

Hildick, Wallace *WrDr 92*
Main entry: Hildick, Edmund Wallace

Hildick, Wallace 1925- *SmATA 68*

Hildreth, Richard 1807-1865 *Alli, AmAu, AmAu&B, BenetAL 91, BbD, BiD&SB, BioIn 1, –14, –16, Chambr 3, CyAG, CyAL, DcAmAu, DcAmSR, DcBiPP, DcLB 1, –30, –59, DcLEL, DcNAA, EncABHB 6, HarEnUS, JrnUS, McGEWB, OxCAmH, OxCAmL 65, –83, REnAL, WhAm HS*

Hiles, Bartram 1872-1927 *DcBrAr 1*

Hilgartner, Beth 1957- *BioIn 16, ScF&FL 92, SmATA 58*

Hilken, Annie Kathleen 1902- *BioIn 5, IlsCB 1946*

Hill, Alexis *ConAu 133, SmATA 65, WrDr 86, –88, –90*
Main entry: Craig, Mary Francis Shura

Hill, Alfred Tuxbury 1908- *ConAu 21R, WhoAm 74*

Hill, David Charles 1936- *ConAu 17R, –11NR*

Hill, Deborah 1936- *ConAu 108*

Hill, Deirdre *DcChlFi*

Hill, Donna Marie *BiDrLUS 70, BioIn 13, ConAu 13R, –7NR, DrAPF 83, –85, SmATA 24, WhoAmW 77, –83, WhoLibS 55, –66*

Hill, Douglas 1935- *BioIn 15, –16, ScF&FL 92, ScFSB, SixBJA, TwCChW 89, WrDr 86, –88, –90, –92, –94*

Hill, Douglas Arthur 1935- *Au&Wr 71, BioIn 11, ChlFicS, ConAu 53, –4NR, ConPo 70, ConSFA, EncSF 93, IntAu&W 91, MacBEP, OxCCan SUP, SmATA 39, TwCYAW, WhoCanL 85, –87, –92, WrDr 76, –80, –82, –84*
Pseud./variant:
Hillman, Martin

Hill, Elizabeth Starr 1925- *AuBYP 2S, –3, BioIn 13, ConAu 17R, –31NR, ForWC 70, IntAu&W 77, –89, –91, SmATA 24, WrDr 76, –80, –82, –84, –86, –88, –90, –92, –94*

Hill, Eric *BioIn 16*

Hill, Eric 1927- *ChlLR 13, ConAu 134, MajAI, SixBJA, SmATA 53, –66, WrDr 94*

Hill, Fitzmaurice 1898- *DcChlFi, SingR 2*

Hill, Frank Ernest 1888-1969 *AuBYP 3*

Hill, Frank Ernest 1888-1970? *AmAu&B, AuBYP 2, BioIn 4, –8, ChhPo, ConAu 73, REnAL, TwCA, –SUP, WhAm 5*

Hill, George Canning 1825-1898 *Alli, –SUP, BiD&SB, CarSB, DcAmAu, DcNAA, HsB&A*

Hill, Grace Brooks *ConAu 26NR, –P-2, SmATA 1, –67*
Main entry: Stratemeyer, Edward L

Hill, Grace L 1865-1947 *BioAmW*

Hill, Grace Livingston *WomNov*

Hill, Grace Livingston 1865-1947 *AmAu&B, BenetAL 91, BioIn 1, –4, –14, –15, ChhPo, DcAmAu, DcNAA, InWom SUP, ObitOF 79, REnAL, TwCA, –SUP, TwCRHW 90, WhAm 2, WhNAA, YABC 2*
Pseud./variant:
Macdonald, Marcia

Hill, Headon *EncMys*

Hill, Headon 1857-1927 *StaCVF*

Hill, Helen d1942 *CurBio 42, DcNAA*

Hill, Helen M 1915- *ScF&FL 92*

Hill, Helen Morey 1915- *BioIn 13, SmATA 27*

Hill, Janet *AuBYP 3*

Hill, Janet 1930- *AuBYP 2S*

Hill, John *ConAu 36NR, EncSF 93, MajTwCW, ScF&FL 92, TwCSFW 86, –91, TwCYAW, WrDr 86, –88, –90, –92*

Hill, John 1945- *WrDr 94*

Hill, John Campbell 1888- *ConAu 37R, WrDr 76, –82, –84*

Hill, Johnson *ConAu 134, SmATA 67*
Main entry: Kunhardt, Edith

Hill, Kathleen L 1917- *CanWW 89*

Hill, Kathleen Louise 1917- *BioIn 9, –10, ConAu 9R, –3NR, OxCCan SUP, Profile 1, SmATA 4, WhoAm 74, –76, –78, –80, –82, –84, WhoAmW 74*

Hill, Kay Kathleen Louise 1917- *DcChlFi*

Hill, Kirkpatrick 1938- *SmATA 72*

Hill, L A 1918- *Au&Wr 71, ConAu 21R, WrDr 76, –80, –82*

Hill, Lorna 1902- *AuBYP 2, –3, Au&Wr 71, BioIn 7, –11, ConAu 14NR, –P-1, IntAu&W 77, SmATA 12, TwCChW 83, –89, WrDr 76, –80, –82, –84, –86, –88, –90*

Hill, Margaret 1915- *AuBYP 2, –3, BioIn 8, –14, ConAu 1R, –1NR, –16NR, SmATA 36*
Pseud./variant:
Bennett, Rachel
Hill, Meg
Thomas, Andrea

Hill, Meg
Main entry: Hill, Margaret

Hill, Meredith *ConAu 133, SmATA 65*
Main entry: Craig, Mary Francis Shura

Hill, Monica *ConAu X, SmATA 3*
Main entry: Watson, Jane Werner

Hill, Ralph Nading 1917- *AuBYP 2, –3, BioIn 8, ConAu 1R, –1NR*

Hill, Ralph Nading 1917-1987 *BioIn 15, –17, ConAu 124, NewYTBS 87, SmATA 65*

Hill, Reuben L d1985 *NewYTBS 85*

Hill, Reuben L 1912-1985 *BioIn 14, –15*

Hill, Reuben Lorenzo, Jr. 1912-1985 *AmMWSc 73S, NewYTBS 85, WhAm 9, WhoAm 74, –76, –78, –80, –82, –84, WhoWor 74, –82*

Hill, Robert W 1919-1982 *BioIn 14*

Hill, Robert White 1919-1982 *AuBYP 2, –3, BioIn 8, –11, –13, ConAu 9R, –107, SmATA 12, –31N, WhAm 8, WhoAm 76, –78, –80, –82*

Hill, Rowland 1744-1833 *CelCen, DcBiPP, DcNaB, –C, EncWM, OxCChiL*

Hill, Ruth A *BioIn 10, ConAu X, SmATA 6*
Main entry: Viguers, Ruth Hill

Hill, Ruth Livingston *BioIn 11, ConAu X, SmATA X*
Main entry: Munce, Ruth Hill

Hillcourt, William d1992 *NewYTBS 92*

Hillcourt, William 1900- *AmAu&B, AuBYP 2, –3, BioIn 7, –13, ConAu 93, MedPD, SmATA 27, WhoAm 74, –76, –78, –80, –82, –84, –86, –88, –90*
Pseud./variant:
Bjerregaard-Jensen, Vilhelm Hans

Hillcourt, William 1900-1992 *AnObit 1992, ConAu 139*

Hiller, Carl E *AuBYP 2S, –3*

Hiller, Ilo 1938- *BioIn 16, ConAu 121, SmATA 59*

Hillerman, Tony *BioIn 14, –16, –17, NewYTBS 89*

Hillerman, Tony 1925- *Au&Arts 6, BenetAL 91, BestSel 89-1, BioIn 8, –10, –12, ConAu 29R, –21NR, –42NR, ConLC 62, CrtSuMy, CurBio 92, EncFWF, IntAu&W 91, SmATA 6, TwCCr&M 80, –85, –91, TwCWW 91, TwCYAW, WhoAm 92, –94, WhoUSWr 88, WhoWest 92, –94, WhoWrEP 89, –92, WorAlBi, WrDr 82, –84, –86, –88, –90, –92*

Hillert, Margaret 1920- *AuNews 1, BioIn 10, –11, ConAu 49, –1NR, –17NR, –40NR, IntAu&W 86, –89, –91, IntWWP 82, MichAu 80, SmATA 8, WhoUSWr 88, WhoWrEP 89, –92*

Hilles, Helen 1905- *AuBYP 2, –3, BioIn 3, –8*

Hilliard, Noel 1929- *ConAu 9R, –7NR, ConLC 15, ConNov 72, –76, –82, –86, –91, IntAu&W 82, –91, WhoWor 80, WrDr 76, –80, –82, –84, –86, –88, –90, –92*

Hilliard, Noel Harvey 1929- *WrDr 94*

Hilliard, Robert L 1925- *ConAu 107, DrAS 74E, –78E, –82E, IntAu&W 86, –89, WhoGov 77, –72, –75*

Hillier, Caroline *AuBYP 3*

Hillier, Caroline 1931- *AuBYP 2S, IntAu&W 77, –89, WrDr 80, –82, –84, –86, –88*

Hillis, Dave 1945- *ConAu 57*

Hillman, Elizabeth 1942- *ConAu 142, SmATA 75*

Hillman, Martin *ConAu X, SmATA X, WhoCanL 85, –87, –92*
Main entry: Hill, Douglas Arthur

Hillman, May *AuBYP 2, –3, BioIn 8*
Main entry: Hipshman, May

Hillman, Priscilla 1940- *BioIn 15, –16, ConAu 108, SmATA 39, –48*

Hillocks, George, Jr. 1934- *ConAu 53, LEduc 74*

Hills, C A R 1955- *BioIn 15, ConAu 106, –23NR, SmATA 39*

Hills, Frances Elizabeth 1934- *WrDr 76, –80, –82*

Hills, Theodore Lewis 1925- *AmMWSc 73P, Au&Wr 71, ConAu 5R, OxCCan*

Hillyer, Virgil Mores 1875-1931 *AmAu&B, AuBYP 2, –3, BioIn 1, –2, –8, DcNAA, EncAB-A 5, JBA 34, –51, WhAm 1*

Hilton, Irene Pothus 1912- *BioIn 10, ConAu 1R, SmATA 7, WhoAmW 77*

Hilton, James 1900-1954 *Benet 87, BenetAL 91, BioIn 1, –2, –3, –4, –5, –14, CamGLE, ChhPo S1, ConAu 108, CurBio 42, –55, CyWA 58, DcLB 34, –77, DcLEL, DcNaB 1951, EncMys, EncSF 93, EvLB, FilmgC, HalFC 84, –88, LongCTC, ModBrL, NewC, NewEScF, NotNAT B, Novels, ObitOF 79, ObitT 1951, OxCEng 85, PenC ENG, REn, REnAL, ScFSB, SmATA 34, TwCA, –SUP, TwCCr&M 80, TwCLC 21, TwCWr, WhAm 3, WorAlBi, WorAl*
Pseud./variant:
Trevor, Glen

Hilton, John Buxton *BioIn 14*

Hilton, John Buxton 1921- *Au&Wr 71, ConAu 53, –5NR, IntAu&W 82, TwCCr&M 80, –85, WrDr 76, –80, –82, –84, –86, –88*
Pseud./variant:
Stanley, Warwick

Hilton, John Buxton 1921-1986 *TwCCr&M 91*

Hilton, Margaret Lynette 1946- *ConAu 136, SmATA 68*
Pseud./variant:
Hilton, Nette

Hilton, Nette *BioIn 17, ChlLR 25, ConAu 136, SmATA 68*
Main entry: Hilton, Margaret Lynette

Hilton, Ralph 1907- *BioIn 11, ConAu 29R, SmATA 8, WhoSSW 76, –78, –80, –82*

Hilton, Suzanne 1922- *AuBYP 2S, –3, BioIn 9, ConAu 29R, –12NR, –30NR, SmATA 4, WrDr 76, –80, –82, –84, –86, –88, –90, –92, –94*

Him, George 1900-1982 *BioIn 1, –3, –8, –14, BlueB 76, ConAu 106, ConDes 84, –90, IlsCB 1744, –1957, SmATA 30N, Who 74, –82, –83N, WhoGrA 62, –82, WhoWorJ 72, WrDr 80, –82*

Himler, Ann 1946- *BioIn 11, ConAu 53, SmATA 8*

Himler, Arnold Norbert 1937- *BioIn 11, ChhPo S2, ConAu 53, IlsBYP, IlsCB 1967, SmATA 6, WhoAmA 78*

Himler, Ronald *BioIn 16, ChlBIlD*

Himler, Ronald 1937- *SixBJA*

Himmelheber, Diana Martin 1938- *ConAu 17R*

Himmelman, John 1959- *AuBYP 3, BioIn 16, SmATA 47*

Hinckley, Helen *AuBYP 2, BioIn 8, –13, ConAu X, IntAu&W 77X, –82X, SmATA X, WrDr 76, –80, –82, –84*
Main entry: Jones, Helen Hinckley

Hinckley, Helen 1903- *AuBYP 3, IntAu&W 91, WrDr 86, –88, –90, –92, –94N*

Hind, Dolores 1931- *BioIn 16, ConAu 129, SmATA 49, –53*

Hind, Henry Youle 1823-1908 *Alli SUP, BbtC, BioIn 1, –12, DcLEL, DcNaB S2, DcNAA, OxCCan, OxCCanL*

Hinde, Cecilia Hamilton 1913- *Au&Wr 71*

Hindman, Jane Ferguson 1905- *BiDrLUS 70, ConAu 25R, –10NR, ForWC 70, MedPL, WhoAmW 74, –75*

Hinds, Bill 1950- *BioIn 10*

Hinds, E M *ConAu X*
Main entry: Hinds, Margery

Hinds, Margery *Au&Wr 71, ConAu 9R, OxCCan, WrDr 76, –80, –82, –84, –86, –88, –90*
Pseud./variant:
Hinds, E M

Hind Smith, Joan 1929- *CaW, WhoCanL 85*

Hine, Al 1915- *AuBYP 2, BioIn 8, –9, ChhPo, –S1, ConAu 1R, –2NR, ThrBJA*

Hine, Al 1915-1974 *ScF&FL 92*

Hine, Alfred Blakelee 1915- *AuBYP 3*

Hine, S J *AuBYP 3*

Hine, Sesyle Joslin *ConAu 13R, ThrBJA*
Main entry: Joslin, Sesyle

Hines, Anna G 1946- *ConAu 114, -36NR, SmATA 45, -51*

Hines, Anna Grossnickle 1946- *AuBYP 3, BioIn 15, -16, ScF&FL 92, SixBJA, SmATA 16AS, WhoAm 92, -94*

Hines, Bob *BioIn 4, IlsBYP*

Hines, Gary Roger 1944- *SmATA 74*

Hines, Ruth 1904- *BiDrLUS 70, WhoLibS 66*

Hingley, Ronald Francis 1920- *Au&Wr 71, ConAu 5R, IntAu&W 77, WorAu 1975*

Hinkins, Virginia *AuBYP 2, -3, BioIn 7*

Hinkle, Thomas C 1876-1949 *BenetAL 91*

Hinkle, Thomas Clark 1876-1949 *AmAu&B, AuBYP 2, -3, BioIn 1, -7, DcNAA, REnAL, WhAm 2*

Hinkson, H A 1865-1919 *BiDIrW, DcIrW 1, StaCVF*

Hinton, Charles Louis d1950 *WhoAmA 86N*

Hinton, Charles Louis 1869-1950 *BioIn 1, -2, ChhPo, -S2, IlsCB 1744, WhAm 3, WhAmArt 85, WhoAmA 78N, -80N, -82N, -89N, -91N*

Hinton, Nigel 1941- *ConAu 85*

Hinton, Phyllis *Au&Wr 71, IntAu&W 77*

Hinton, S E *BioIn 16, -17*

Hinton, S E 1948- *BenetAL 91, ChlLR 23, MagSAmL, WhoAm 86, -88, WrDr 86, -88, -90, -92*

Hinton, S E 1950- *Au&Arts 2, AuBYP 2S, -3, BioIn 8, -12, -13, ChlLR 3, ConAu 81, -32NR, ConLC 30, FourBJA, MajTwCW, OxCChiL, SmATA 19, -58, TwCChW 78, -83, -89, WhoAm 82, -84, WorAlBi, WrDr 80, -82, -84*

Hinton, Sam 1917- *BioIn 14, -15, ConAu 73, EncFCWM 69, -83, SmATA 43*

Hinton, Susan Eloise 1948- *WrDr 94*

Hinton, Susan Eloise 1950- *DcAmChF 1960, MajAI, TwCYAW*

Hintz, Martin 1945- *BioIn 15, -16, ConAu 12NR, -30NR, SmATA 39, -47*

Hintze, Naomi A 1909- *BioIn 8, -14, ConAu 45, -1NR, ScF&FL 92, TwCRHW 90, WrDr 76, -80, -82, -84, -86, -88, -90*

Hippel, Ursula Von *AuBYP 2, -3, BioIn 7*

Hippopotamus, Eugene H *AuBYP 2, -3, IntAu&W 91X, MajAI, SmATA 65, ThrBJA*
Main entry: Kraus, Robert

Hipshman, May 1919- *AuBYP 2, -3, BioIn 8*
Pseud./variant:
Hillman, May

Hirano, Cathy 1957- *BioIn 17, SmATA 68*

Hiraoka, Kimitake *Benet 87*

Hiraoka, Kimitake 1925-1970 *ConAu 29R, -97, ConLC 9, MajTwCW, WorAu 1950*
Pseud./variant:
Mishima, Yukio

Hirsch, Karen 1941- *BioIn 17, SmATA 61*

Hirsch, Phil 1926- *BioIn 14, ConAu 97, -102, SmATA 35*
Pseud./variant:
Peel, Norman Lemon
Vlasic, Bob

Hirsch, S Carl 1913- *AnCL, AuBYP 2S, -3, BioIn 9, ConAu 5R, -2NR, IntAu&W 77, SmATA 2, -7AS, ThrBJA, WrDr 76, -80, -82, -84, -86, -88, -90*

Hirsch, Thomas L 1931- *ConAu 49*

Hirschfeld, Burt 1923- *AuBYP 2S, -3, ConAu 111, -134, WrDr 94*

Hirschi, Ron *BioIn 16*

Hirschi, Ron 1948- *ConAu 120, SmATA 56*

Hirschmann, Linda 1941- *ConAu 106, SmATA 40*

Hirsh, Marilyn 1944- *AuBYP 3*

Hirsh, Marilyn 1944-1988 *BioIn 16, ConAu 126, SmATA 58*

Hirsh, Marilyn Joyce 1944- *AuBYP 2S, BioIn 9, -10, -12, ConAu 49, -1NR, -16NR, FifBJA, IlsCB 1967, SmATA 7*

Hirshberg, Albert Simon 1909-1973 *AuBYP 2, -3, BioIn 7, -9, ConAu 1R, -41R, -4NR, SmATA 38, WhAm 6, WhoE 74*

Hirst, Stephen Michael 1939- *ConAu 53*

Hiscock, Bruce *AuBYP 3*

Hiscock, Bruce 1940- *BioIn 16, ConAu 122, SmATA 57*

Hiser, Berniece T *AuBYP 3*

Hiser, Constance 1950- *SmATA 71*

Hiser, Iona Seibert 1901- *BioIn 9, ConAu 1R, –2NR, SmATA 4*

Hislop, Julia Rose Catherine 1962- *ConAu 141, SmATA 74*

Hiss, Anthony 1941- *BioIn 10, –11, ConAu 77*

Hissey, Jane *AuBYP 3*

Hissey, Jane 1952- *BioIn 16, ConAu 124, SmATA 58*

Hitchcock, Alfred *PenEncH*

Hitchcock, Alfred d1980 *LesBEnT 92*

Hitchcock, Alfred 1899-1980 *AnObit 1980, Au&Wr 71, BenetAL 91, BiDFilm, BioIn 1, –2, –3, –4, –5, –6, –7, –8, –9, –10, –11, –12, –13, –14, –15, –16, –17, BioNews 74, BlueB 76, CelR, CmCal, CmMov, ConAu 97, ConLC 16, ConTFT 1, CurBio 41, –60, –80N, DcFM, EncMys, FilmgC, HalFC 84, IntMPA 75, –76, –78, –77, IntWW 74, LesBEnT, MovMk, NewC, NewYTBE 72, NewYTBS 75, –80, NewYTET, OxCFilm, RAdv 13-3, REnAL, ScF&FL 92, SmATA 24N, –27, WebAB 74, WhDW, WhScrn 83, Who 74, WhoAm 74, WhoHr&F, WhoWest 74, WhoWor 74, WorAlBi, WorEFlm*

Hitchcock, Alfred, Sir 1899-1980 *Benet 87, HalFC 88, WorFDir 1*

Hitchcock, Patricia *AuBYP 2S, –3*

Hite, Sid 1954- *ConAu 142, SmATA 75*

Hitte, Kathryn *AuBYP 3*

Hitte, Kathryn 1919- *AuBYP 2, BioIn 8, –12, ConAu 21R, SmATA 16*

Hitz, Demi 1942- *BioIn 11, –15, –16, –17, ConAu 61, –8NR, –35NR, MajAI, SmATA 11, –66*
Pseud./variant:
Demi

Hnizdovsky, Jacques 1915-1985 *BioIn 5, –11, –14, IlsBYP, NewYTBS 85, SmATA 32, WhoAmA 73, –78, –80, –82, –84, –86N, –89N, –91N*

Ho, Minfong 1951- *BioIn 12, BlmGWL, ChlLR 28, ConAu 77, IntAu&W 82, SmATA 15, TwCYAW*

Hoag, Edwin 1926- *AuBYP 2, –3, BioIn 8, ConAu 13R, WrDr 82, –84, –86*

Hoagland, Edward *BioIn 16, –17, DrAFF 87, –89, –91, –93*

Hoagland, Edward 1932- *Benet 87, BenetAL 91, ConAu 31NR, ConNov 86 –91, CyWA 89, IntAu&W 86, IntWW 89, –91, SmATA 51, TwCWW 91, WhoAm 86, –88, –90, –92, –94, WhoUSWr 88, WhoWrEP 89, –92, WrDr 86, –88, –90, –92, –94*

Hoard, Edison 1934?- *BioIn 9*

Hoare, Robert J 1921-1975 *BioIn 15*

Hoare, Robert John 1921-1975 *Au&Wr 71, ConAu 9R, –6NR, SmATA 38, WrDr 76*
Pseud./variant:
King, Adam

Hoban, Julia *AuBYP 3*

Hoban, Lillian *MajAI, SmATA 69, WhoAmW 91, –93*

Hoban, Lillian 1925- *AmPB, AuBYP 2, –3, BioIn 8, –9, –12, –13, ChhPo S1, ConAu 69, –23NR, IlsCB 1957, –1967, SmATA 22, ThrBJA*

Hoban, Russell *BioIn 14, –15, –17*

Hoban, Russell 1925- *AuBYP 3, BenetAL 91, CamGLE, ConAu 23NR, ConNov 86, –91, DcAmChF 1960, DcLB 52, LiExTwC, MajTwCW, NewEScF, PostFic, ScF&FL 92, ScFSB, TwCChW 89, TwCSFW 86, –91, WrDr 86, –88, –90, –92, –94*

Hoban, Russell C 1925- *AmPB, AuBYP 2 BioIn 6, –8, –9, –10, –12, ChhPo S1, –S2, ChlLR 3, ConAu 5R, ConLC 7, –25, IlrAm G, Novels, OxCChiL, SmATA 1, –40, ThrBJA, TwCChW 78, –83, Who 82, –83, –85, WhoAm 82, –84, WorAu 1975, WrDr 76, –80, –82, –84*

Hoban, Russell Conwell 1925- *ChlFicS, ConAu 37NR, EncSF 93, IntAu&W 89, –91, IntWW 89, –91, MajAI, Who 88, –90, –92, WhoAm 86, –88, –90, –92, –94*

Hoban, Tana *AuBYP 2S, –3, BioIn 13, –15, ChlLR 13, ConAu 93, –23NR, FourBJA, MajAI, SmATA 22, –70, –12AS, WomWMM B*

Hoban, Walt 1890-1939 *ArtCS*

Hoban, Walter *EncACom*

Hobart, Billie 1935- *ConAu 49, WhoAmW 77, –81, –89, –93*

Hobart, Lois Elaine *AuBYP 2, –3, BioIn 6, –7, –10, ConAu 5R, ForWC 70, MinnWr, SmATA 7, WrDr 76, –80*

Hobbs, Will *BioIn 17, TwCYAW*

Hobbs, Will 1947- *SmATA 72*

Hoberman, Mary Ann *BioIn 14*

Hoberman, Mary Ann 1930- *AuBYP 2S, -3, BioIn 10, -16, BkCL, ChhPo S1, -S2, ChlLR 22, ConAu 41R, MajAI, SixBJA, SmATA 5, -72, -18AS, WhoAmW 87, -89, WhoE 93*

Hobley, Leonard Frank 1903- *Au&Wr 71, ConAu 13R, -5NR, WrDr 76, -80, -82, -84, -86, -88, -90*

Hobson, Bruce *AuBYP 3*

Hobson, Bruce 1950- *ConAu 127, SmATA 62*
Pseud./variant:
Hadithi, Mwenye

Hobson, Burton 1933- *BioIn 13, ConAu 5R, -2NR, SmATA 28, WhoAm 74*

Hobson, Burton Harold 1933- *WhoAm 86, -90*

Hobson, George Carey 1890-1945 *CasWL*

Hobson, Julius W 1922?-1977 *AuBYP 3, BlkWr 1*

Hobson, Julius Wilson 1922?-1977 *AuBYP 2S, BioIn 7, -8, -9, -11, CivR 74, ConAu 102, InB&W 80, LivgBAA, ObitOF 79*

Hobson, Laura Z 1900-1986 *AnObit 1986, BenetAL 91, ConAu 118, ConNov 86, CurBio 86N, JeAmFiW, NewYTBS 86, SmATA 52, WrDr 86*

Hobson, Laura Zametkin 1900- *AmAu&B, AmNov, Au&Wr 71, BioIn 1, -2, -3, -4, -6, -13, ConAu 17R, ConLC 7, -25, ConNov 72, -76, -82, CurBio 47, DcLB 28, DcLEL 1940, REn, REnAL, TwCA SUP, WhAm 9, WhoAm 74, -76, -78, -80, -82, -86, WhoAmW 74, -75, -77, -83, -85, WrDr 76, -80, -82, -84*
Pseud./variant:
Field, Peter

Hobson, Polly *AuBYP 2, BioIn 8, ConAu X, IntAu&W 77X, -82X, WrDr 76, -80, -82, -84, -86, -88, -90*
Main entry: Evans, Julia

Hobson, Polly 1913- *AuBYP 3*

Hobson, Samuel Bonnin 1888-1967 *CasWL*

Hochman, Sandra *DrAPF 87, -89, -91*

Hochman, Sandra 1936- *AmAu&B, BioIn 8, -12, ConAu 5R, ConLC 3, -8, ConPo 70, -75, -80, -85, -91, DcLB 5, DrAF 76, DrAP 75, InWom SUP, IntAu&W 91, NewYTBE 71, WhoAmW 74, -75, WhoE 74, WomWMM B, WrDr 76, -80, -82, -84, -86, -88, -90, -92, -94*

Hochman, Shirley Dean 1917- *ConAu 61*

Hochschild, Arlie Russell 1940- *BioIn 11, ConAu 57, SmATA 11*

Hochstein, Rolaine *ConAu 45, -23NR, DrAPF 83, -85, -87, -89, -91, -93*

Hockaby, Stephen *ConAu X, IntvTCA 2, SmATA X, WrDr 82, -84*
Main entry: Mitchell, Gladys

Hockenberry, Hope *ConAu X, SmATA X*
Main entry: Newell, Hope Hockenberry

Hocking, Silas 1850-1935 *OxCChiL*

Hocking, Silas K 1850-1935 *StaCVF*

Hodder, Edwin 1837?-1904 *Alli SUP, CarSB, ChhPo S1, DcEnL*

Hodeir, Andre 1921- *Baker 84, -92, ConAu 85, -15NR, -34NR, OxCPMus, WhoWor 74*

Hodge, Jane Aiken *BioIn 14*

Hodge, Jane Aiken 1917- *AuBYP 2, -3, Au&Wr 71, BioIn 8, ConAu 5R, -3NR, InWom SUP, IntAu&W 77, -82, -86, -91, Novels, TwCRHW 90, WrDr 76, -80, -82, -84, -86, -88, -90, -92, -94*

Hodge, Kenneth Raymond 1944- *WhoHcky 73*

Hodge, Paul W 1934- *WhoTech 84*

Hodge, Paul William 1934- *AmMWSc 82, -86, -89, -92, BioIn 11, ConAu 33R, -42NR, IntAu&W 89, -91, SmATA 12, WhoAm 80, -82, -84, -86, -88, -90, -92, -94, WhoTech 82, WrDr 80, -82, -84, -86, -88, -90, -92, -94*

Hodgell, P C *ScFSB*

Hodgell, P C 1951- *BioIn 15, ConAu 109, ScF&FL 92, SmATA 42*

Hodgell, Robert Overman 1922- *WhoAm 84, -86, -88, -90, -92, -94, WhoAmA 73, -80, -82, -84, -86, -89, -91*

Hodges, C Walter 1909- *BioIn 14, IntAu&W 86, -89, -91, TwCChW 89, Who 88, -90, -92, WrDr 86, -88, -90, -92*

Hodges, Carl G 1902-1964 *AuBYP 2, -3, BioIn 11, ConAu 5R, DcAmChF 1960, SmATA 10*

Hodges, Cyril Walter 1909- *AnCL, AuBYP 2, -3, Au&Wr 71, BioIn 1, -4, -5, -7, -8, -9, -12, -14, ChhPo S2, ConAu 13R, -5NR, IlsCB 1744, -1946, -1957, -1967, IntAu&W 77, -82, OxCChiL, SmATA 2, ThrBJA, TwCChW 78, -83, Who 74, -82, -83, -85, WhoArt 80, -82, -84, WhoChL, WrDr 80, -82, -84, -94*

Hodges, David *IlsBYP*

Hodges, Elizabeth Jamison *AuBYP 2, -3, BioIn 8, -9, ConAu 9R, ForWC 70, SmATA 1, WhoAmW 74*

Hodges, Margaret *BioIn 14*

Hodges, Margaret 1911- *AuBYP 3, IntAu&W 91, SmATA 9AS, WrDr 86, -88, -90, -92, -94*

Hodges, Margaret Moore 1911- *AuBYP 2S, BiDrLUS 70, BioIn 9, ConAu 1R, -2NR, -30NR, DrAS 74E, -78E, -82E, ForWC 70, FourBJA, IndAu 1917, IntAu&W 77, MajAI, SmATA 1, -33, -75, WhoAm 74, -76, -78, -80, -82, -84, -86, -88, -90, -92, -94, WhoAmW 74, -75, -77, -83, WrDr 76, -80*

Hodgetts, Blake Christopher 1967- *BioIn 15, ConAu 114, SmATA 43*

Hodgetts, James Frederick 1828-1906 *Alli SUP, DcNaB S2*

Hodgins, Bruce W 1931- *CanWW 89, ConAu 37R, DrAS 74H, -82H, OxCCan SUP*

Hodgins, Jack *IntvTCA 2*

Hodgins, Jack 1938- *BenetAL 91, CamGLE, CaW, ConAu 93, ConLC 23, ConNov 86, -91, DcLB 60, OxCCanL, WhoCanL 85, -87, -92, WrDr 92, -94*

Hodgins, Jack 1939- *BioIn 16, WrDr 88, -90*

Hodgson, Ralph 1871-1962 *AnCL, AtlBL, Benet 87, BioIn 4, -5, -6, -7, -12, -13, Chambr 3, ChhPo, -S1, -S2, CnE&AP, ConAu 102, DcLB 19, DcLEL, EvLB, LongCTC, ModBrL, NewC, ObitOF 79, ObitT 1961, OhA&B, OxCEng 67, PenC ENG, REn, RfGEnL 91, TwCA, -SUP, WhoTwCL*
Pseud./variant:
Yorick

Hoehling, Mary 1914- *AuBYP 2, -3, BioIn 7, ConAu 93*

Hoest, William 1926- *BioIn 8, ConAu 69*

Hoest, William 1926-1988 *EncACom*

Hoest, William P 1926- *ConAu 23NR*

Hoexter, Corinne K 1927- *BioIn 10, ConAu 49, -27NR, SmATA 6, WhoAmW 77*

Hofer, Jesse W 1910- *BioIn 10*

Hoff, Carol 1900- *BioIn 11, ConAu P-2, SmATA 11*

Hoff, Mary King 1956- *SmATA 74*

Hoff, P J *WhoAm 74, -76, -78*

Hoff, Rhoda *ChhPo S1*
Main entry: DeTerra, Rhoda Hoff

Hoff, Syd 1912- *AmAu&B, AuBYP 2, Au&Wr 71, BioIn 7, -8, -9, -11, -15, ChhPo S1, ConAu 5R, -4NR, ConGrA 1 EncACom, IlsCB 1957, -1967, IntAu&W 91, SmATA 9, -4AS, ThrBJA, TwCChW 78, -83, -89, WhAmArt 85, WhoAm 74, -76, -78, -82, -84, -86, -88, WhoSSW 84, WhoWor 74, WhoWorJ 72, -78, WorECar, WrDr 80, -82, -84, -86, -88, -90, -92*

Hoff, Sydney 1912- *AuBYP 3, ConAu 38NR, MajAI, SmATA 72, WhoAm 90, -92, -94, WrDr 94*

Hoffecker, Savin 1908- *AuBYP 2S, -3, ConAu 5R*

Hoffman, Edwin D *BioIn 16, ConAu 101, SmATA 49*

Hoffman, Franz 1814-1882 *CarSB*

Hoffman, Gail 1896- *ConAu 5R*

Hoffman, Gloria *AuBYP 2, -3, BioIn 8*

Hoffman, Gloria Levy 1933- *WhoFI 94*

Hoffman, Jo Ann S 1942- *ConAu 81*

Hoffman, Mary 1945- *BioIn 16, ConAu 13?, SmATA 59*

Hoffman, Mary Margaret 1945- *WrDr 94*

Hoffman, Paul *BioIn 16, ScF&FL 92*

Hoffman, Paul 1934-1984 *BioIn 13, ConAu 45, -112, -1NR, -28NR*

Hoffman, Phyllis M 1944- *ConAu 28NR*

Hoffman, Phyllis Miriam 1944- *BioIn 9, ConAu 29R, -12NR, SmATA 4, WhoAmW 74*

Hoffman, Rosekrans 1926- *BioIn 12, ConAu 15NR, SmATA 15*

Hoffmann, Christine *IlsBYP*

Hoffmann, E T A 1776-1822 *Benet 87, BioIn 14, -15, DcLB 90, EuWr 5, GrFLW, MagSWL, NewEScF, PenEncH, RAdv 13-2, ScFEYrs, ShSCr 13, ShSWr, SupFW, WrChl*

Hoffmann, Ernest Theodor Amadeus 1776-1822 *BiD&SB, BioIn 12, CyWA 58, EuAu, NewC, NewOxM, OxCChiL, OxCEng 67, OxCFr, OxCGer 76, RComWL, REn, SmATA 27, SupFW, WhoChL*

Hoffmann, Ernst Theodor Amadeus 1776-1822 *Baker 92, EncSF 93*

Hoffmann, Ernst Theodore Amadeus 1776-1822 *RfGShF*

Hoffmann, Felix 1911-1975 *BioIn 10, -11, ChhPo S1, ConAu 57, -P-2, IlsBYP, IlsCB 1946, -1957, -1967, SmATA 9, ThrBJA*

Hoffmann, Heinrich 1809-1894 *BiD&SB, BioIn 8, CarSB, ChhPo S1, DcEuL, EvEuW, OxCChiL, OxCEng 67, -85, WhoChL, WorECar, WrChl*

Hoffmann, Hilde 1927- *ConAu 25R, IlsBYP*

Hoffmann, Margaret Jones *AuBYP 3*

Hoffmann, Margaret Jones 1910- *AuBYP 2, BioIn 5, -7, ConAmC 76, ConAu 5R, -2NR, ForWC 70, SmATA 48, WrDr 76, -80*
Pseud./variant:
Hoffmann, Peggy 1910-

Hoffmann, Peggy 1910- *AuBYP 3, BioIn 16, WrDr 86, -88, -90, -92, -94*
Main entry: Hoffmann, Margaret Jones

Hoffmeister, Donald F 1916- *IntAu&W 91*

Hoffmeister, Donald Frederick 1916- *AmMWSc 73P, -76P, -82, -86, -89, -92, BlueB 76, ConAu 53, WhoAm 74, -76, -78, -80, -82, -84, -86, -88, -90, -92, -94, WrDr 76, -80, -82, -84, -86, -88, -90, -92, -94*

Hoffner, Pelagie Doane *AuBYP 2, -3*
Main entry: Doane, Pelagie

Hofland, Barbara 1770-1844 *DcBiPP, DcNaB, -C, DcWomA, FemiCLE, OxCChiL, StaCVF*
Pseud./variant:
Hofland, W H, Mrs.

Hofland, W H, Mrs.
Main entry: Hofland, Barbara

Hofland, W H, Mrs 1770-1844 *CarSB*

Hofman, David 1908- *Au&Wr 71*

Hofman, Ota *TwCChW 89B*

Hofman, Ota 1928- *IntAu&W 77, TwCChW 78B, -83B*

Hofsepian, Sylvia A 1932- *SmATA 74*

Hofsinde, Robert 1902-1973 *AuBYP 2, -3, BioIn 5, -7, -9, -10, -12, -17, ConAu 45, -73, IlsCB 1946, SmATA 21, ThrBJA*

Hogan, Bernice Harris 1929- *BioIn 11, ChhPo, ConAu 13R, -7NR, ForWC 70, SmATA 12*

Hogan, Inez 1895?- *AuBYP 2, -3, BioIn 1, -6, -7, -9, ConAu 1R, -1NR, IlsCB 1744, MorJA, SmATA 2, WhAmArt 85*

Hogarth, Jr *ConAu X, SmATA 6*

Hogarth, Burne 1911- *ArtCS, BioIn 15, -17, ConAu 93, ConGrA 1, EncACom, IntAu&W 82, SmATA 63, WhoAm 90, -92, -94, WhoAmA 80, -82, -84, -86, -89, -91, WhoE 81, WhoWest 87, -89, -92, -94, WhoWor 87, -89, -91, -93*

Hogarth, Grace 1905- *Au&Wr 71, TwCChW 78, -83, -89, WhoAmW 77, WrDr 80, -82, -84, -86, -88, -90, -92, -94*
Pseud./variant:
Weston, Allen

Hogarth, Jr.
Main entry: Kent, Rockwell

Hogarth, Paul *Who 88, -90, -92*

Hogarth, Paul 1917- *Au&Wr 71, BioIn 2, -4, -5, -6, -9, -14, -15, ConAu 49, -27NR, IntWW 89, -91, SmATA 41, TwCPaSc, Who 82, -83, -85, WhoGrA 62, -82, WhoWor 78*

Hogarth, William 1697-1764 *Alli, AtlBL, Benet 87, BioIn 1, -2, -3, -4, -5, -6, -7, -8, -9, -10, -11, -12, -13, -14, -15, -17, BlmGEL, BkIE, CamGLE, ChhPo, ClaDrA, ConGrA 2, DcBiPP, DcBrECP, DcNaB, Dis&D, IntDcAA 90, LongCEL, McGEWB, NewC, OxCArt, OxCEng 85, OxCMus, OxDcArt, PlP&P, REn, WhDW, WorAlBi, WorAl*

Hogben, Lancelot Thomas 1895-1975 *BioIn 1, -2, -4, -5, -10, -11, -12, -13, Chambr 3, ConAu 61, CurBio 41, DcNaB 1971, EvLB, InSci, IntWW 74, -75, -76N, LongCTC, NewC, TwCA, -SUP, WhAm 6, Who 74*

Hogeboom, Amy 1891- *AuBYP 2, -3, BioIn 8*

Hogg, Beth *AuBYP 3*

Hogg, Beth 1917- *AuBYP 2, BioIn 8, ConAu 5R, -X*
Pseud./variant:
Grey, Elizabeth

Hogg, Elizabeth *AuBYP 3*

Hogg, Garry 1902-1976 *Au&Wr 71, BioIn 8, –9, ConAu 21R, –10NR, SmATA 2, WhoChL, WrDr 76*

Hogner, Dorothy *AuBYP 3*

Hogner, Dorothy Childs *WrDr 86, –88, –90*

Hogner, Dorothy Childs 1904- *AmAu&B, AuBYP 2, BioIn 2, –7, –9, ConAu 33R, IntAu&W 77, JBA 51, OxCCan, SmATA 4, WhNAA, WhoAmW 81, WrDr 76, –80, –82, –84*

Hogner, Nils 1893-1970 *ArtsAmW 2, AuBYP 2, –3, BioIn 1, –2, –5, –7, –8, –9, –13, ConAu 77, IlsCB 1744, –1946, –1957, –1967, JBA 51, SmATA 25, WhAmArt 85*

Hogrogian, Nonny *BioIn 14, –15*

Hogrogian, Nonny 1932- *AuBYP 2, –3, BioIn 7, –8, –9, –10, –12, BkP, ChhPo S2, ChlLR 2, ConAu 45, –2NR, IlsBYP, IlsCB 1957, –1967, MajAI, NewbC 1966, OxCChiL, SmATA 7, –74, –1AS, ThrBJA, WhoAm 74, –76, –78, WhoAmA 78, WhoE 74*

Hoguet, Susan Ramsay 1945- *AuBYP 3, ConAu 119*

Hoh, Diane 1937- *BioIn 16, ConAu 120, ScF&FL 92, SmATA 48, –52*

Hohn, Hazel *ConAu 5R, ForWC 70, WrDr 82*

Hoke, Helen *ConAu 131*

Hoke, Helen 1903-1990 *BioIn 16, –17, NewYTBS 90, ScF&FL 92, SmATA 65*

Hoke, Helen L 1903- *AuBYP 2, –3, BioIn 8, ConAu 73, –43NR, SmATA 15*
Pseud./variant:
Sterling, Helen
Watts, Helen L Hoke

Hoke, John Lindsay 1925- *BioIn 10, ConAu 41R, SmATA 7*

Hokusai 1760-1849 *BioIn 2, –4, –5, –6, –7, –8, –9, –10, –11, –12, –13, –14, –15, –16, –17, EncJap, REn*

Holabird, Katharine *AuBYP 3, BioIn 17*

Holabird, Katharine 1948- *ConAu 121, SmATA 62*

Holbeach, Henry *SmATA X*
Main entry: Rands, William Brighty

Holberg, Richard A 1889-1942 *AuBYP 2, –3, BioIn 2, –8, JBA 51, WhAmArt 85*

Holberg, Ruth Langland 1889- *AuBYP 3, BioIn 1, –2, –8, –9, ConAu 5R, CurBio 49, DcWomA, JBA 51, SmATA 1, WhAmArt 85, WrDr 76, –80, –82, –84*

Holbrook, David Kenneth 1923- *Au&Wr 71, BioIn 7, –8, –10, ChhPo, –S1, ConAu 5R, ConNov 72, ConPo 70, –75, IntAu&W 82, –86, –89, –91, IntWWP 82, NewC, Who 82, –83, –85, –88, –90, –92, WhoWor 89, WorAu 1950, WrDr 76, –80*

Holbrook, Peter *ConAu X, SmATA X*
Main entry: Glick, Carl Cannon

Holbrook, Sabra *BioIn 1, ConAu X, CurBio 48, SmATA X*
Main entry: Erickson, Sabra Rollins

Holbrook, Sabra 1912- *BioIn 14*

Holbrook, Stewart H 1893-1964 *BenetAL 91*

Holbrook, Stewart Hall 1893-1964 *AmAu&B, AuBYP 2, –3, BioIn 2, –4, –5, –7, –8, –9, ConAu P-1, DcAmB S7, ObitOF 79, OxCAmL 65, –83, REnAL, SmATA 2, ThrBJA, TwCA SUP, WhAm 4, WhNAA, WhoPNW*

Holden, Elizabeth R *ScF&FL 92*

Holden, Elizabeth Rhoda *WrDr 86, –88, –90, –92*

Holden, Elizabeth Rhoda 1943- *ConAu 10NR, SmATA X*
Pseud./variant:
Lawrence, Louise

Holden, Matthew *ConAu X, IntAu&W 82X*
Main entry: Parkinson, Roger

Holden, Matthew, Jr. 1931- *AmMWSc 73S, –78S, ConAu 57, InB&W 80, LivgBAA, WhoAm 84, –86, –88, –90, WhoBlA 75, –77, –80, WhoMW 76, WhoSSW 91, WrDr 76, –80, –82, –84, –86, –88, –90, –92, –94*

Holden, Molly 1927- *WrDr 86*

Holden, Molly 1927-1981 *BioIn 15, –16, CamGLE, ConAu 25R, –133, ConPo 70, –75, –80, DcLB 40, EncBrWW, EngPo, WrDr 76, –80, –82, –84*

Holden, Raymond 1894-1972 *AuBYP 3, BenetAL 91*

Holden, Raymond Peckham 1894-1972 *AmAu&B, AuBYP 2, BioIn 4, –7, –9, ConAu 5R, –37R, NewYTBE 72, REnAL, TwCA, –SUP*

Holder, Glenn 1906- *AuBYP 2S, –3, ConAu 41R, DrAS 74E*

Holder, William G 1937- *AuBYP 2S, -3, ConAu 25R, -10NR*

Holding, Carlisle B 1849-1929 *Alli SUP, CarSB, OhA&B*

Holding, Elisabeth Sanxay 1889-1955 *AmAu&B, BioIn 3, -14, EncMys, TwCCr&M 80, -85, -91, WhAm 3, WhNAA*

Holding, James 1907- *AuBYP 2, -3, BioIn 8, -9, -14, ConAu 25R, SmATA 3, TwCCr&M 80, -85, -91*
Pseud./variant:
Carlisle, Clark
Queen, Ellery, Jr.

Holdren, John Paul 1944- *AmMWSc 73P, -76P, -82, -86, -89, -92, ConAu 33R, IntWWE, WhoAm 86, -88, -90, -92, -94, WhoFrS 84*

Holdsworth, William Curtis *IlsBYP*

Hole, Quentin 1923- *BioIn 12, IlsCB 1967*

Holiday, Henry 1839-1927 *BioIn 12, -13, ChhPo, -S2, DcBrAr 1, DcNaB 1922, DcVicP 2, OxCChiL*

Holiday, Jane *ChlFicS*

Holisher, Desider 1901-1972 *BioIn 9, -10, ConAu 37R, -P-2, SmATA 6, WhoWorJ 72*

Holl, Adelaide 1910- *AuBYP 3*

Holl, Adelaide Hinkle 1910?- *AmAu&B, AuBYP 2S, BioIn 11, ConAu 1R, -2NR, ForWC 70, SmATA 8, WhoAmW 74*

Holl, Kristi D 1951- *SmATA 51*

Holl, Kristi Diane 1951- *AuBYP 3*

Holland, Cecelia Anastasia 1943- *BioIn 7, -8, -9, -11, ConAu 17R, DrAF 76, WhoAm 74, WhoAmW 74, WrDr 76, -80*

Holland, Clive *Alli SUP, BiD&SB, WhoLA*
Main entry: Hankinson, Charles James

Holland, Clive 1866-1959 *StaCVF*

Holland, Deborah Katherine 1947- *ConAu 57, WhoAmW 77*

Holland, Isabelle *BioIn 14, -15, -16*

Holland, Isabelle 1920- *Au&Arts 11, AuBYP 2S, -3, BioIn 11, ConAu 21R, -10NR, -25NR, ConLC 21, DcAmChF 1960, FifBJA, IntAu&W 91, MajAI, OxCChiL, SmATA 8, -70, TwCChW 78, -83, -89, TwCRHW 90, WrDr 80, -82, -84, -86, -88, -90, -92, -94*

Holland, Isabelle Christian 1920- *WhoWor 93*

Holland, Janice d1962 *WhoAmA 86N*

Holland, Janice 1913-1962 *BioIn 5, -8, -12, ConAu 73, IlsBYP, IlsCB 1946, -1957, SmATA 18, WhAmArt 85, WhoAmA 78N, -80N, -82N, -89N, -91N*

Holland, John *AuBYP 2S, -3*

Holland, John Lewis 1919- *BioIn 12, ConAu 17NR, SmATA 20*

Holland, Joyce F 1921- *ConAu 5R*

Holland, Lynda H 1959- *SmATA 77*

Holland, Lys *ConAu X, SmATA X*
Main entry: Gater, Dilys

Holland, Marion 1908- *AuBYP 2, -3, BioIn 7, -10, ConAu 61, SmATA 6*

Holland, Marion 1908-1989 *BioIn 17, ConAu 128, SmATA 61*

Holland, Robert 1940- *ConAu 33R*

Holland, Rupert Sargent 1878-1952 *AmLY, BenetAL 91, BioIn 2, -3, ChhPo, JBA 34, -51, ObitOF 79, REnAL, WhAm 3, WhNAA*

Holland, Thomas 1908- *Au&Wr 71, BlueB 76, IntAu&W 77, Who 85, -88, -92, WrDr 76, -80, -82, -84*

Holland, Thomas, Rt Rev 1908- *Who 90*

Holland, Vicki *AuBYP 2S*

Holland, Viki *AuBYP 3*

Hollander, John *BioIn 15, -16, -17, DrAPF 87, -89, -91, -93, IntvTCA 2*

Hollander, John 1929- *AmAu&B, AuBYP 2, -3, BenetAL 91, BioIn 8, -10, -12, -13, CamGLE, CamHAL, ChhPo, -S1, ConAu 1R, -1NR, ConLC 2, -5, -8, ConPo 70, -75, -80, -85, -91, CurBio 91, DcLB 5, DcLEL 1940, DrAP 75, DrAS 74E, -78E, -82E, IntAu&W 77, -82, -86, -89, -91, IntWW 78, -79, -80, -81, -82, -83, -89, -91, IntWWP 82, ModAL S2, OxCAmL 65, -83, PenC AM, REnAL, SmATA 13, WhoAm 74, -76, -78, -80, -82, -84, -86, -88, -90, -92, -94, WhoE 74, WhoTwCL, WhoUSWr 88, WhoWrEP 89, -92, WorAu 1950, WrDr 76, -80, -82, -84, -86, -88, -90, -92, -94*

Hollander, Paul *AuBYP 2, -3, BioIn 8, ConAu 36NR, MajAI, MajTwCW*

Hollander, Phyllis *BioIn 15*

Hollander, Phyllis 1928- *AuBYP 2S, -3, ConAu 97, -18NR, SmATA 39*

Hollander, Zander *BioIn 17*

Hollander, Zander 1923- *AuBYP 2S, -3, ConAu 65, -18NR, SmATA 63*
Pseud./variant:
Peters, Alexander

Holldobler, Turid 1939- *BioIn 13, SmATA 26*

Holliday, Joe
Main entry: Holliday, Joseph

Holliday, Joseph 1910- *Au&Wr 71, BioIn 10, -11, ConAu P-2, IntAu&W 77, SmATA 11*
Pseud./variant:
Bosco, Jack
Dale, Jack
Holliday, Joe

Hollindale, Peter 1936- *ConAu 103, WrDr 76, -82, -84, -86, -88, -90, -92, -94*

Holling, Holling C 1900-1973 *BioIn 14, TwCChW 89*

Holling, Holling Clancy 1900-1973 *AmAu&B, AmPB, AuBYP 2, -3, Au&ICB, BioIn 1, -2, -3, -5, -7, -8, -12, -13, ConAu 106, IlsBYP, IlsCB 1946, -1957, JBA 51, MajAI, SmATA 15, -26N, Str&VC, TwCChW 78, -83*

Holling, Lucille Webster 1900- *BioIn 5, -8, IlsBYP, IlsCB 1946, -1957, JBA 51*

Hollings, F S *CarSB, ChhPo S2*

Hollingsworth, Alvin C 1930- *BioIn 15*

Hollingsworth, Alvin Carl 1928- *InB&W 85*

Hollingsworth, Alvin Carl 1930- *AfroAA, IlsBYP, SmATA 39, WhoAmA 73, -80, -82, -84, -86, -89, -91*

Hollis, James Russell 1940- *ConAu 41R, DrAS 74E*

Hollmann, Clide John 1896-1966 *ConAu 5R*

Holloway, Brenda Wilmar 1908- *Au&Wr 71, ConAu P-1*

Holloway, Charlotte Molyneux *CarSB*

Holloway, Teresa 1906- *BioIn 13, ConAu 17R, ForWC 70, IntAu&W 77, SmATA 26, WhoAmW 77, WhoSSW 73*
Pseud./variant:
Beatty, Elizabeth
McLeod, Margaret Vail

Holly, J Hunter *ConAu X, ConSFA, IntAu&W 77X, WhoSciF*
Main entry: Holly, Joan Carol

Holly, J Hunter 1932- *TwCSFW 86, WrDr 88, -90, -92, -94*

Holly, Joan C *TwCSFW 86*

Holly, Joan Carol 1932- *ConAu 1R, -1NR, IntAu&W 77*
Pseud./variant:
Holly, J Hunter

Holm, Anne *TwCChW 89B*

Holm, Anne 1922- *AnCL, BioIn 9, ConAu 17R, FourBJA, OxCChiL, ScF&FL 92, SmATA 1, -7AS, TwCChW 78B, -83B*

Holm, Else Anne Lise 1922- *MajAI, TwCYAW*

Holm, Hannebo *AuBYP 2, -3*

Holman, Bill d1987 *BioIn 15, NewYTBS 87*

Holman, Bill 1903- *ArtCS, BioIn 5*

Holman, Bill 1903-1987 *ConGrA 3, EncACom*

Holman, Felice 1919- *AuBYP 2, -3, BioIn 8, -10, ChhPo S2, ConAu 5R, -3NR, -18NR, -40NR, DcAmChF 1960, FourBJA, IntAu&W 77, -82, OxCChiL, SmATA 7, -17AS, TwCChW 78, -83, -89, TwCYAW, WhoAmW 75, -77, -83, WrDr 76, -80, -82, -84, -86, -88, -90, -92, -94*

Holme, Bryan d1990 *NewYTBS 90*

Holme, Bryan 1913- *AuBYP 2, -3, BioIn 8, -9, -13, ConAu 103, SmATA 26, WhoE 75*
Pseud./variant:
Francis, Charles

Holme, Bryan 1913-1990 *BioIn 17, ConAu 132, SmATA 66*

Holmes, Barbara Ware 1945- *ConAu 120, IntAu&W 89, SmATA 65, WhoUSWr 88, WhoWrEP 89, -92*

Holmes, David Charles 1919- *ConAu 9R, WhoE 81, -83*
Pseud./variant:
Charlson, David

Holmes, Efner Tudor 1949- *ConAu 65*

Holmes, John *ConAu 29NR, IntvTCA 2, SmATA X, WhoCanL 87, -92, WorAu 1980, WrDr 86, -88, -90, -92, -94*
Main entry: Souster, Holmes Raymond

Holmes, Marjorie Rose *IntAu&W 89, -91, WhoAm 86, -88, -90, -92, -94, WhoAmW 89,*

WhoUSWr 88, WhoWor 93, WhoWrEP 89, –92

Holmes, Marjorie Rose 1910- *AmAu&B, AmNov, AuBYP 2, –3, AuNews 1, Au&Wr 71, BioIn 2, –8, –10, ConAu 1R, –5NR, ForWC 70, IntAu&W 77, SmATA 43, WhoAm 78, –80, –82, –84, WhoAmW 74, –75, –77, WrDr 76, –80, –82, –84*

Holmes, Martha 1961- *SmATA 72*

Holmes, Martin 1905- *Au&Wr 71, ConAu 49, –1NR, IntAu&W 91, WrDr 80, –82, –84, –86, –88, –90, –92*

Holmes, Martin Rivington 1905- *WrDr 94*

Holmes, Oliver Wendell 1809-1894 *Alli, –SUP, AmAu, AmAu&B, AmWr S1, AsBiEn, AtlBL, BbD, BiD&SB, BiESc, BioIn 1, –2, –3, –4, –5, –6, –7, –8, –9, –10, –11, –12, –14, –16, CamGEL, CamGLE, CamHAL, CasWL, CelCen, Chambr 3, ChhPo, –S1, –S2, CnDAL, CrtT 3, CyAL, CyWA 58, DcAmAu, DcAmMeB, –84, DcAmSR, DcBiA, DcBiPP, DcEnA, DcEnL, DcLB 1, DcLEL, DcNAA, Dis&D, EncAB-H, EvLB, HarEnUS, InSci, McGEWB, MorMA, MouLC 4, NewGrDA 86, NinCLC 14, Novels, OxCAmH, OxCAmL 65, –83, OxCEng 67, –85, PenC AM, PoChrch, RAdv 1, –13-1, REn, REnAL, RfGAmL 87, ScFEYrs, SmATA 34, Str&VC, WebAB 74, –79, WebE&AL, WhDW, WhAm HS, WorAlBi, WorAl*

Holmes, Oliver Wendell 1809-1904 *EncPaPR 91*

Holmes, Oliver Wendell 1841-1935 *BioIn 14, –15, –16, –17, CamGEL, CamHAL, MemAm*

Holmes, Oliver Wendell, Sr. 1809-1894 *Benet 87, BenetAL 91*

Holmes, Oliver Wendell, Jr. 1841-1935 *Benet 87, BenetAL 91, RAdv 13-3, RComAH, ThTwC 87, WhCiWar, WorAlBi*

Holmes, Peggy 1898- *BioIn 17, ConAu 121, SmATA 60*
Pseud./variant:
Semloh

Holmes, Prescott *CarSB*

Holmes, Raymond *ConAu 29NR, WhoCanL 87, –92, WorAu 1980, WrDr 86, –88, –90, –92*
Main entry: Souster, Holmes Raymond

Holmes, Raymond 1921- *SmATA X, WrDr 94*

Holmes, Rick *ConAu X, SmATA X*
Main entry: Hardwick, Richard H

Holmes, William Kersley 1882- *ChhPo, –S1, –S2, ConAu P-1*

Holmgren, George Ellen *ConAu X, SmATA X*
Main entry: Holmgren, Helen Jean

Holmgren, George Ellen 1930- *BioIn 15*

Holmgren, Helen Jean 1930- *BioIn 15, ConAu 97, SmATA 45*
Pseud./variant:
Holmgren, George Ellen

Holmgren, Virginia Cunningham *AuBYP 3*
Main entry: Cunningham, Virginia

Holmgren, Virginia Cunningham 1909- *ConAu 107, OhA&B, SmATA 26*

Holmquist, Eve 1921- *BioIn 11, ConAu 53, IntAu&W 77, SmATA 11*

Holmstrand, Marie Juline 1908- *BioIn 6, ConAu 5R, MinnWr*

Holsaert, Eunice d1974 *AuBYP 2, –3, BioIn 8, –10, ConAu 53*

Holsinger, Jane Lumley *AuBYP 2, –3, BioIn 8, ConAu 17R, ForWC 70, WrDr 76*

Holst, Imogen Clare 1907-1984 *AnObit 1984, Baker 84, ConAu 112, DcNaB 1981, IntWWM 85, OxCMus, Who 82, –83*

Holt, Deloris Lenette *WhoBlA 75, –77, –80, –85, –88, –90, –92, –94*

Holt, John R *ScF&FL 92*

Holt, John Robert 1926- *ConAu 25R*
Pseud./variant:
Arre, John

Holt, Kaare
Main entry: Holt, Kare

Holt, Kare 1917- *CasWL, ConAu X, DcScanL, EncWL 2*
Pseud./variant:
Holt, Kaare

Holt, Margaret 1899-1963 *BioIn 14*

Holt, Margaret 1928- *WhoLib 54*

Holt, Margaret 1937- *AuBYP 2, –3, BioIn 9, ConAu 17R, SmATA 4*
Pseud./variant:
Parish, Margaret Holt

Holt, Margaret Van Vechten 1899-1963 *BioIn 6, –8, ConAu 111, SmATA 32*
Pseud./variant:
Holt, Rackham

Holt, Michael 1929- *ConAu 53, –5NR, IntAu&W 77, SmATA 13, WrDr 76, –80, –82, –84, –86, –88, –90, –92*

Holt, Michael Paul 1929- *WrDr 94*

Holt, Rackham
Main entry: Holt, Margaret Van Vechten

Holt, Rackham 1899-1963 *BioIn 6, ConAu X, CurBio 44, SmATA X, WhAm 4*

Holt, Richard *Who 85*

Holt, Rochelle Lynn *DrAPF 87, –89, –91, –93*
Main entry: DuBois, Rochelle Holt

Holt, Rochelle Lynn 1946- *ConAu X, DrAPF 85, IntAu&W 86, –89, –91, SmATA 41, WhoUSWr 88, WhoWrEP 89, –92*

Holt, Stephen *AuBYP 2, –3, ConAu X, IntAu&W 77X, SmATA X*
Main entry: Thompson, Harlan Howard

Holt, Stephen 1894-1987 *BioIn 16*

Holt, Thelma Jewett 1913- *ConAu 29R*

Holt, Victoria *AmAu&B, Au&Wr 71, Benet 87, BioIn 7, –9, –10, –11, BlmGWL, ConAu 140, –X, –28NR, CorpD, EncMys, InWom SUP, IntAu&W 77X, –91X, Novels, SmATA 2, –74, TwCCr&M 85, Who 74, –82, –83, –85, –88, –90, –92, WhoAm 74, –76, –78, –80, –82, –84, –86, –88, –90, –92, –94, WhoAmW 74, –75, –77, –81, –83, WhoUSWr 88, WhoWrEP 89, –92, WorAl, WorAu 1950, WrDr 76, –80, –82, –84*
Main entry: Hibbert, Eleanor Burford

Holt, Victoria 1906- *BestSel 90-4, BioIn 14, TwCCr&M 91, TwCRHW 90, WorAlBi, WrDr 86, –88, –90, –92*

Holt, Victoria 1906-1993 *WrDr 94N*

Holtan, Gene 1930- *BioIn 8*

Holton, Leonard *AuBYP 2, –3, ConAu X, EncMys, IntAu&W 77X, –82X, SmATA 2, –X, TwCCr&M 80, –85, WorAu 1950, WrDr 80, –82, –84*
Main entry: Wibberley, Leonard

Holton, Leonard 1915-1983 *CrtSuMy, TwCCr&M 91*

Holtze, Sally Holmes *BioIn 17*

Holtze, Sally Holmes 1952- *ConAu 123, SmATA 64*

Holtzman, Jerome 1926- *Ballpl 90, BioIn 16, SmATA 57, WhoAm 86, –88, –90, –92*

Holyer, Erna Maria 1925- *BioIn 13, ConAu 29R, –12NR, IntAu&W 77, –82, –89, –91, SmATA 22, WhoAmW 75, –77, –83, WhoUSWr 88, WhoWest 84, –87, WhoWor 84, –87, –89, WhoWrEP 89, –92, WrDr 76, –80*
Pseud./variant:
Holyer, Ernie

Holyer, Ernie *BioIn 13, ConAu X, IntAu&W 82X, SmATA X, WhoUSWr 88, WrDr 82, –84*
Main entry: Holyer, Erna Maria

Holyer, Ernie 1925- *WrDr 86, –88, –90, –92*

Holyer, Ernie M 1925- *WrDr 94*

Holz, Loretta 1943- *BioIn 12, ConAu 65, SmATA 17*

Holzman, Robert Stuart 1907- *AmAu&B, AmMWSc 73S, AuBYP 2S, –3, ConAu 1R, –2NR, DrAS 74H, –78H, WhoAm 74, –76, –78, –80, –82, –84, –86, –88, –90, –92, –94, WhoWor 78, –80, –82, –84, –87, –89, –91, –93*

Homar, Lorenzo 1913- *WhoAmA 73, –78, –80, –82, –84, –86, –89, –91, WhoGrA 62*

Home-Gall, Edward R 1899- *ScF&FL 92*

Home-Gall, Edward Reginald *EncSF 93*

Home-Gall, Edward Reginald 1899?- *OxCChiL*

Home-Gall, William Benjamin 1861-1936 *EncSF 93*

Homer *AtlBL, Benet 87, BbD, BiD&SB, BioIn 1, –2, –3, –4, –5, –6, –7, –10, –12 BlmGEL, CasWL, ChhPo, CyEd, CyWA 58, DcBiA, DcBiPP, DcEnL, DcEuL, Dis&D, GrFLW, LongCEL, LuthC 75, MagSWL, McGEWB, NewC, OxCClL 89, OxCEng 67, –85, OxCShps, PenC CL, PlP&P, RAdv 13-2, RComWL, WhDW, WorAlBi, WorAl*

Homer fl. c. 800BC- *EncSF 93*

Homer 1920-1971 *BioIn 14*

Homer, Winslow 1836-1910 *ArtsNiC, Benet 87, BioIn 1, –2, –3, –4, –5, –6, –7, –8, –9, –10, –11, –12, –13, –14, –15, –16, –17, CivWDc, DcSeaP, IntDcAA 90, MorMA, OxCAmH, OxCArt, OxCChiL, OxDcArt, RComAH, WebAB 79, WhDW, WhAmArt 85, WhCiWar, WhFla, WorAlBi, WorAl*

Homsher, Lola Mae 1913- *ConAu 1R, DrAS 74H, –78H, –82H, WhoWest 74, –76*

Homze, Alma C 1932- *BioIn 12, ConAu 29R, SmATA 17*

Homze, Edward L 1930- *ConAu 33R, DrAS 74H, -78H, -82H*

Homze, Edward Lee 1930- *WhoMW 93*

Honeycutt, Natalie *AuBYP 3*

Hong, Edna Hatlestad 1913- *ConAu 21R, -9NR, WhoAmW 75, -77*

Hong, Lily Toy 1958- *SmATA 76, WhoAsA 94*

Honig, Donald *DrAPF 87, -89, -91, -93*

Honig, Donald 1931- *Ballpl 90, BioIn 12, ConAu 17R, -9NR, -24NR, DrAF 76, DrAPF 83, -85, IntAu&W 77, SmATA 18*

Honness, Elizabeth 1904- *AuBYP 3*

Honness, Elizabeth H 1904- *AuBYP 2, BioIn 7, -9, ConAu 25R, SmATA 2, WhoAmW 74*

Honore, Paul 1885-1956 *ArtsEM, BioIn 1, -2, -3, -4, ChhPo, ConICB, IlsCB 1744, WhAm 3, WhAmArt 85*

Honour, Alan Edward 1918- *Au&Wr 71*

Hoobler, Dorothy *BioIn 13, ConAu 69, -11NR, -27NR, SmATA 28*

Hoobler, Thomas *BioIn 13, ConAu 69, -11NR, -27NR, SmATA 28*

Hoobler, Thomas 1942?- *ScF&FL 92*

Hoobler, Thomas 1944?- *EncSF 93*

Hood, Flora Mae 1898- *ConAu 5R, ForWC 70*

Hood, George W *ChhPo, ConICB*

Hood, George W d1949 *WhoAmA 86N*

Hood, George W 1869-1949 *WhoAmA 91N*

Hood, George W 1896-1949 *WhoAmA 89N*

Hood, Hugh John 1928- *IntAu&W 89, -91*

Hood, Hugh John Blagdon 1928- *Au&Wr 71, CanWW 70, CanWr, CasWL, ConAu 49, ConNov 72, -76, CreCan 1, IntAu&W 82, OxCCan, -SUP, WrDr 76, -80*

Hood, Joseph F 1925- *BioIn 9, ConAu 33R, SmATA 4*

Hood, Robert E 1926- *AuBYP 3*

Hood, Robert Eric 1926- *AuBYP 2S, BioIn 12, ConAu 21R, MedPD, SmATA 21, WhoAm 74, -76, -78, -80, WhoUSWr 88, WhoWrEP 89, -92*

Hood, Sarah *ConAu 32NR, SmATA X, TwCSFW 86*
Main entry: Killough, Lee

Hood, Thomas 1799-1845 *Alli, AnCL, AtlBL, Benet 87, BbD, BiD&SB, BioIn 1, -2, -3, -4, -6, -8, -9, -10, -12, -13, -15, -16, -17, BlmGEL, BritAS, BritAu 19, BritWr 4, CamGEL, CamGLE, CarSB, CasWL, CelCen, Chambr 3, ChhPo, -S1, -S2, CnE&AP, CrtT 2, DcBiPP, DcBrBI, DcEnA, DcEnL, DcEuL, DcLB 96, DcLEL, DcNaB, EvLB, LongCEL, MouLC 3, NewC, NinCLC 16, OxCEng 67, -85, PenC ENG, PenEncH, REn, RfGEnL 91, Str&VC, WebE&AL, WhDW*

Hood, Thomas 1835-1874 *Alli SUP, BiD&SB, BritAu 19, Chambr 3, ChhPo, -S1, -S2, DcEnL, DcNaB, EvLB, NewC, OxCEng 67, -85, TelT*

Hood, Tom 1835-1874 *DcBiPP, DcNaB, OxCChiL, StaCVF*

Hook, Frances A 1912- *BioIn 13, ConAu 105, SmATA 27, WhoAmA 80, -82, -84, -86*

Hook, Frances A 1912-1981 *WhoAmA 89N, -91N*

Hook, Martha 1936- *BioIn 13, ConAu 105, SmATA 27*

Hook, Martha Ann 1936- *WhoWrEP 89, -92*

Hook, Richard *BioIn 2*

Hooke, Hilda Mary *OxCCan*

Hooker, Brian 1880-1946 *ASCAP 66, BenetAL 91, BioIn 1, ChhPo, -S1, CmpEPM, DcNAA, EncMT, NotNAT B, ObitOF 79, OxCAmL 65, -83, OxCAmT 84, REn, REnAL, WhAm 2*

Hooker, Ruth *AuBYP 3*

Hooker, Ruth 1920- *AuBYP 2S, BioIn 12, ConAu 69, ScF&FL 92, SmATA 21*

Hooks, William H *BioIn 16*

Hooks, William H 1921- *BioIn 12, ConAu 81, -19NR, SixBJA, SmATA 16*

Hooks, William Harris 1921- *AuBYP 3*

Hoole, Charles 1610-1667 *CyEd, DcNaB, OxCChiL*

Hooper, Byrd *ConAu X, SmATA X*
Main entry: Saint Clair, Byrd Hooper

Hooper, Maureen Brett 1927- *SmATA 76*

Hooper, Meredith Jean 1939- *BioIn 13, ConAu 106, IntAu&W 77, SmATA 28, WrDr 76, –80, –82, –84, –86, –88, –90, –92, –94*

Hoopes, Lyn L 1953- *SmATA 49*

Hoopes, Lyn Littlefield 1953- *BioIn 15, –16, ConAu 120, IntAu&W 89, –91, SmATA 44*

Hoopes, Ned Edward 1932- *BioIn 12, ConAu 17R, DrAS 74E, –78E, –82E, SmATA 21, WrDr 76, –80*

Hoopes, Roy 1922- *AuBYP 2S, –3, BioIn 11, –14, ConAu 21R, –15NR, SmATA 11*

Hoople, Cheryl G *AuBYP 2S, –3, BioIn 14, ConAu 111, SmATA 32*

Hoover, F Louis 1913- *ConAu 41R*

Hoover, H M *IntAu&W 86X, ScFSB*

Hoover, H M 1935- *Au&Arts 11, BioIn 14, –15, –16, ConAu 22NR, –36NR, ScF&FL 92, SmATA 8AS, TwCChW 89, TwCSFW 86, –91, WhoWrEP 89, WrDr 86, –88, –90, –92*

Hoover, Helen 1910-1984 *Au&Wr 71, BioIn 9, –11, –14, –15, ConAu 21R, –113, ForWC 70, IntAu&W 77, –82, SmATA 12, –39N, WhAm 9, WhoAm 74, WhoAmW 77, WhoE 74, WrDr 76, –80, –82, –84*
Pseud./variant:
Price, Jennifer

Hoover, Helen Mary 1935- *ChlFicS, ConAu 105, EncSF 93, FifBJA, IntAu&W 86, –89, –91, MajAI, SmATA 33, –44, TwCYAW, WhoWrEP 92, WrDr 94*

Hope, Anthony
Main entry: Hawkins, Anthony Hope, Sir

Hope, Amanda *AuBYP 3*

Hope, Anthony *BiD&SB, Chambr 3, CyWA 58, DcBiA, DcEnA A, DcLEL, DcNaB 1931, EvLB, FilmgC, HalFC 84, IntvTCA 2, LongCTC, ModBrL, NewC, NotNAT B, Novels, OxCChiL, OxCEng 67, –85, PenC ENG, REn, TelT, TwCA, –SUP, TwCWr, WhoChL*

Hope, Anthony 1863-1933 *BioIn 14, CamGEL, CamGLE, HalFC 88, RfGEnL 91, TwCRHW 90*

Hope, Ascott Robert *Alli SUP, OxCChiL*

Hope, C E G 1900- *ConAu P-1*

Hope, Christopher 1944- *ConLC 52, ConNov 86, –91, LiExTwC, SmATA 62, Who 92, WorAu 1980, WrDr 88, –90, –92*

Hope, Christopher David Tully 1944- *WrDr 94*

Hope, Laura Lee *BenetAL 91, ConAu 17R –X, EncSF 93, InWom SUP, OxCChiL, REnAL, ScF&FL 92, SmATA 1, –67, –X, WebAB 79, WhoChL*
Main entry: Adams, Harriet S
Stratemeyer, Edward L

Hope, William Edward Stanton 1889-1961 *BioIn 5*

Hope-Simpson, Jacynth 1930- *IntAu&W 91, TwCChW 89, WrDr 86, –88, –90, –92*

Hope-Simpson, Jacynth Ann 1930- *Au&Wr 71, BioIn 11, ConAu 13R, –7NR, IntAu&W 82, SmATA 12, TwCChW 78, –83, WrDr 76, –80, –82, –84, –94*

Hopf, Alice *ScF&FL 92*

Hopf, Alice 1904- *AuBYP 3*

Hopf, Alice L 1904-1988 *ConAu 124, SmATA 55N*

Hopf, Alice Lightner 1904- *AuBYP 2S, BioIn 10, ConAu 17R, –9NR, ForWC 70, IntAu&W 77, –82, MichAu 80, SmATA 5, WhoAmW 77*

Hopf, Alice Lightner 1904-1988 *BioIn 15, –16*
Pseud./variant:
Lightner, A M

Hopkins, A T *AuBYP 2, –3, ConAu X, SmATA X*
Main entry: Turngren, Annette

Hopkins, Antony 1921- *Au&Wr 71, Baker 92, BioIn 13, BlueB 76, ConAu 101, –17NR, IntAu&W 77, –82, –89, –91, IntWW 76, –77, –78, –79, –80, –81, –82, –83, –89, –91, IntWWM 85, –90, NewOxM, OxCMus, PenDiMP A, Who 74, –82, –83, –85, –88, –90, –92, WhoMus 72, WrDr 76, –80, –82, –84, –86, –88, –90, –92, –94*

Hopkins, Clark 1895-1976 *AuBYP 2, –3, BioIn 8, –12, –14, ConAu 109, –129, DrAS 74F, NatCAB 59, SmATA 34N*
Pseud./variant:
Lee, Roy

Hopkins, Gerard Manley 1844-1889 *AnCL, AtlBL, Benet 87, BioIn 1, –2, –3, –4, –5, –6, –7, –8, –9, –10, –11, –12, –13, –14, –16, –17, BlmGEL, BritAu 19, BritWr 5, CamGEL, CamGLE, CasWL, Chambr 3, ChhPo, –S1, –S2, CnDBLB 5, CnE&AP, CnMWL, CrtT 3, CyWA 58, DcCathB, DcLB 35, –57, DcLEL, DcNaB MP, EvLB, IlEncMy, LongCEL, LongCTC, MagSWL, McGEWB, ModBrL, –S1, –S2, NewC, NinCLC 17, OxCEng 67, –85, OxCLiW 86, PenC ENG, RAdv 1, –13-1,*

RComWL, REn, RfGEnL 91, WebE&AL, WhDW, WhoTwCL, WorAlBi, WorAl, WorLitC, WrPh

Hopkins, Joseph G E 1909- *AmCath 80, BioIn 11, ConAu 1R, –5NR, DrAS 74H, –78H, –82H, SmATA 11, WhoAm 74, –76, –78*

Hopkins, Kenneth *ScF&FL 92*

Hopkins, Kenneth 1914- *EngPo*

Hopkins, Kenneth 1914-1988 *BioIn 16, –17, ConAu 125, SmATA 58*
Pseud./variant:
Adams, Christopher
Burney, Anton
Mannon, Warwick
Marsh, Paul
Marshall, Edmund
Meredith, Arnold

Hopkins, Lee Bennett 1938- *AuBYP 2S, –3, BioIn 9, –13, –14, –15, –16, –17, ChhPo S1, –S2, ConAu 25R, –29NR, FifBJA, IntAu&W 82, –91, MajAI, MedPD, ScF&FL 92, SmATA 3, –68, –4AS, WhoAm 92, –94, WhoBlA 75, –77, –80, WhoE 74, –75, –91, WrDr 76, –80, –82, –84, –86, –88, –90, –92, –94*

Hopkins, Lila *AuBYP 3*

Hopkins, Lyman *AuBYP 2, –3, ConAu X, IntAu&W 91X, SmATA 5, WrDr 76, –80, –82, –84, –86, –88, –90, –92*
Main entry: Folsom, Franklin Brewster

Hopkins, Lyman 1907- *WrDr 94*

Hopkins, Marjorie 1911- *AuBYP 2S, –3, BioIn 11, ConAu 21R, SmATA 9*

Hopkinson, Deborah 1952- *SmATA 76*

Hoppe, Joanne 1932- *BioIn 15, ConAu 81, SmATA 42*

Hoppe, Matthias 1952- *SmATA 76*

Hoppenstedt, Elbert M 1917- *ConAu 1R*

Hopper, Nancy J 1937- *BioIn 14, –15, ConAu 115, –38NR, SmATA 35, –38*

Hopper, Nancy Jane 1937- *WhoAmW 93, WhoMW 93*

Horder, Margaret L'Anson 1911- *BioIn 5, –12, IlsCB 1946, –1967, SingR 1, WhoAmW 74*

Horder, Mervyn 1910- *Au&Wr 71, ConAu 104, WrDr 76, –80, –82, –84, –86, –88, –90, –92, –94*

Horgan, Paul *DrAPF 87, –89, –91, –93, IntvTCA 2*

Horgan, Paul 1903- *AmAu&B, AmCath 80, AmNov, AuBYP 2, –3, Au&Wr 71, Benet 87, BenetAL 91, BiDConC, BioIn 1, –2, –3, –4, –5, –6, –7, –8, –9, –10, –13, –14, –15, –17, BlueB 76, CathA 1930, ChhPo, CnDAL, ConAu 13R, –9NR, –35NR, ConLC 9, –53, ConNov 72, –76, –82, –86, –91, CurBio 71, CyWA 89, DcLB 102, –Y85B, DcLEL, DrAF 76, DrAPF 83, –85, DrAS 74H, –78H, –82H, EncFWF, IlsCB 1744, IntAu&W 82, –91, IntWW 89, –91, MajTwCW, Novels, OxCAmL 65, –83, RAdv 13-3, REnAL, SmATA 13, TwCA SUP, TwCWW 91, WhNAA, WhoAm 74, –76, –78, –80, –82, –84, –86, –88, –90, –92, –94, WhoE 74, WhoGov 72, WhoWor 74, –78, –80, –82, –84, –87, –89, WrDr 76, –80, –82, –84, –86, –88, –90, –92, –94*

Horler, Sydney 1888-1954 *BioIn 3, –14, EncMys, EncSF 93, EvLB, LongCTC, ScF&FL 92, SpyFic, TwCCr&M 80, –85, –91, WhoHr&F, WhoSpyF*

Horn, Daniel d1991 *NewYTBS 91*

Horn, Daniel 1916- *AmMWSc 73S, WhoAm 74, –76, –78, WhoGov 77, –72, –75*

Horn, George F 1917- *ConAu 5R, –8NR*

Hornaday, William Temple 1854-1937 *Alli SUP, AmAu&B, AmLY, BiD&SB, BioIn 2, –4, –7, –9, ChhPo, DcAmAu, DcNAA, HarEnUS, InSci, IndAu 1816, JBA 34, OxCCan, REnAL, TwCA, –SUP, WhAm 1, WhFla, WhNAA*

Hornblow, Arthur 1865-1942 *CamGWoT*

Hornblow, Arthur 1893-1976 *BioIn 17*

Hornblow, Arthur, Jr. 1893-1976 *BioIn 11, –12, ConAu 65, FilmgC, HalFC 84, –88, IntMPA 75, –76, ObitOF 79, SmATA 15, WhAm 7, WhoAm 74, –76*

Hornblow, Leonora 1920- *AuBYP 2, –3, Au&Wr 71, BioIn 8, –12, ConAu 73, SmATA 18*

Hornby, John 1913- *Au&Wr 71, ConAu 9R*
Pseud./variant:
Grace, Joseph

Horne, Richard H 1803-1884 *Alli, –SUP, BbD, BiD&SB, BioIn 2, –6, –7, –8, –10, –13, BritAu 19, CarSB, CasWL, CelCen, Chambr 3, ChhPo, –S1, –S2, DcBiPP, DcEnA, DcEnL, DcEuL, DcLB 32, DcLEL, DcNaB, EvLB, JBA 34, NewC, OxCChiL, OxCEng 67, –85, SmATA 29*

Pseud./variant:
Mrs. Fairstar
O'Trigger, Lucius, Sir
Uzair, Salem Ben
Watts, Ephraim

Horne, Richard Henry 1803-1884 *BioIn 14, -16, CamGEL, CamGLE, EncSF 93*

Horner, Althea 1926- *BioIn 14, SmATA 36*

Horner, Althea Jane 1926- *WhoAm 90, WhoWest 94, WhoWor 93*

Horner, Dave 1934- *BioIn 11, ConAu 17R, SmATA 12*

Horner, John R *AuBYP 3, BioIn 14, -15, -16, -17*

Horner, John R 1946- *CurBio 92*

Horner, John Robert 1946- *WhoAm 92, -94, WhoWest 92, -94*

Hornik, Edith Lynn *ConAu 28NR*

Hornik, Edith Lynn 1930- *ConAu 61, -X*

Hornos, Axel 1907- *BioIn 12, ConAu P-2, SmATA 20*

Hornstein, Reuben Aaron 1912- *BioIn 17, CanWW 89, SmATA 64*

Hornung, Clarence Pearson 1899- *ConAu 17R, -9NR, WhAmArt 85, WhoAmA 73, -78, -80, -82, -84, -86, -89, -91*

Hornung, Ernest William 1866-1921 *BbD, BiD&SB, BioIn 1, -2, -14, Chambr 3, ConAu 108, CorpD, DcLEL, DcNaB MP, EncMys, EvLB, HalFC 84, LongCTC, NewC, Novels, OxCAusL, OxCChiL, OxCEng 85, REn, TelT, TwCA, -SUP, TwCCr&M 80, -85, TwCWr*

Horowitz, Anthony 1955- *ChlFicS*

Horowitz, Elinor Lander *ConAu 77*

Horrabin, James Francis 1884-1962 *BioIn 6, -8, DcBrAr 1, DcNaB 1961, NewC, WhoChL, WorECar*

Horrobin, David Frederick 1939- *AmMWSc 76P, -82, -86, -89, -92*

Horseman, Elaine 1925- *AuBYP 3*

Horseman, Elaine Hall 1925- *AuBYP 2S, ConAu 13R*

Horsfall, Magdalene 1884-1936 *CarSB*

Horsfall, Robert Bruce 1869-1948 *BioIn 1, -2, ChhPo, -S1, IlsCB 1744, WhNAA*

Horsley, Henry Sharpe *OxCChiL*

Horsley, Reginald Ernest 1863- *ChhPo*

Horton, Louise *DrAPF 87, -89, -91, -93*

Horton, Louise 1916- *ConAu 49, -2NR*

Horton, Louise Walthall 1916- *ConAu 40NR*

Horton, Madelyn Stacey 1962- *SmATA 77*

Horvath, Betty 1927- *AuBYP 3, WrDr 86, -88, -90, -92, -94*

Horvath, Betty F 1927- *AuBYP 2S, BioIn 9, ConAu 17R, ForWC 70, IntAu&W 82, MichAu 80, SmATA 4, WrDr 76, -80, -82, -84*

Horvath, Ferdinand Huszti 1891- *ArtsAmW 2, BioIn 1, ConICB, IlsCB 1744, WhAmArt 85*

Horvath, Joan *InWom SUP*

Horvath, Joan 1944- *BioIn 10, ConAu 81 WomWMM A*

Horwich, Frances 1908- *AuBYP 3*

Horwich, Frances R *IntMPA 86*

Horwich, Frances R 1908- *AmAu&B, AuBYP 2S, BioIn 3, -11, BlueB 76, ConAu P-1, CurBio 53, ForWC 70, IntMPA 76, -78, -81, -82, -84, -86, -77, SmATA 11, WhoAm 74, -76, WhoWorJ 72, -78*

Horwich, Frances Rappaport 1908- *InWom SUP*

Horwitz, Carrie Norris *CarSB*

Horwitz, Elinor Lander *AuBYP 2S, -3, BioIn 14, -15, ConAu 13NR, SmATA 33, -45*

Horwitz, Sylvia Laibman 1911- *ConAu 61*

Horwood, Harold *IntvTCA 2*

Horwood, Harold 1923- *CaW, ConAu 21R, -15AS, -9NR, -25NR, DcLB 60, IntAu&W 82, OxCCan SUP, OxCCanL, WhoCanL 85, -87, -92, WhoE 74*

Hosford, Dorothy 1900-1952 *AnCL, AuBYP 2S, -3, BioIn 3, -6, -13, BkCL, MorJA, SmATA 22, Str&VC*

Hosford, Jessie 1892- *BioIn 10, ConAu 41R, DcAmChF 1960, SmATA 5*

Hosford, Jessie Wiegand 1892- *InWom SUP*

Hosken, Clifford *TwCCr&M 80*

Hosken, Ernest Charles Heath 1875- *WhoLA*

Hosking, Eric 1909- *BioIn 3, –9, ConAu 17NR, ConPhot 82, –88, ICPEnP A, IntAu&W 77, –82, –86, MacBEP, Who 74, –82, –83, –85, –88, –90*

Hosking, Eric 1909-1991 *AnObit 1991*

Hoskins, Robert 1933- *ConAu 29R, EncSF 93, IntAu&W 91, NewEScF, ScF&FL 92, ScFSB, ScFEYrs, TwCSFW 86, –91, WrDr 84, –86, –88, –90, –92, –94*
Pseud./variant:
Corren, Grace

Hoskyns-Abrahall, Clare *Au&Wr 71, ConAu 29R, SmATA 13*
Pseud./variant:
Abrahall, Clare Hoskyns
Drury, Clare Marie

Hostetler, Marian 1932- *ConAu 65, –9NR, –24NR*

Houck, Carter 1924- *BioIn 13, ConAu 77, –14NR, SmATA 22*

Hough, Charlotte 1924- *BioIn 5, –11, ChhPo S2, ConAu 9R, –5NR, IlsCB 1946, IntAu&W 77, –89, –91, OxCChiL, SmATA 9, TwCChW 78, –83, –89, WrDr 76, –80, –82, –84, –86, –88, –90, –92, –94*

Hough, Emerson 1857-1923 *BenetAL 91, BioIn 8, –12, –14, ConAu 120, DcLB 9, EncFWF, OxCAmL 83, OxCChiL, TwCWW 91, WebAB 79*

Hough, Judy Taylor 1932- *ConAu 124, SmATA 51, –56, –63*
Pseud./variant:
Taylor, Judy

Hough, Richard *ScF&FL 92, TwCChW 89*

Hough, Richard 1922- *IntWW 91, WrDr 86, –88, –90, –92*

Hough, Richard Alexander 1922- *AuBYP 2, –3, Au&Wr 71, BioIn 7, –9, –12, ConAu 5R, –3NR, –18NR, IntAu&W 77, –82, –89, –91, SmATA 17, TwCChW 78, –83, Who 74, –82, –83, –85, –88, –90, –92, WrDr 82, –84, –94*
Pseud./variant:
Carter, Bruce

Houghton, Ellen *CarSB*

Houghton, Eric 1930- *AuBYP 2, –3, Au&Wr 71, BioIn 8, –10, ConAu 1R, –2NR, IntAu&W 77, –82, –91, ScF&FL 92, SmATA 7, WrDr 76, –80, –82, –84, –86, –88, –90, –92, –94*

Houlehen, Robert J 1918- *BioIn 12, ConAu 49, SmATA 18*

Houlihan, Raymond 1923- *BioIn 7*

Houlston, F *OxCChiL*

House, Boyce 1896-1961 *AmAu&B, BioIn 1, –6, WhAm 4*

House, Charles 1916- *AuBYP 2S, ConAu 25R*

House, Charles Albert 1916- *AuBYP 3*

Household, Geoffrey d1988 *NewYTBS 88*

Household, Geoffrey 1900- *AuBYP 2S, Au&Wr 71, BioIn 1, –4, –5, –8, –11, –12, –14, CamGLE, ConAu 77, ConLC 11, ConNov 72, –76, –82, –86, CrtSuMy, EncMys, LongCTC, NewC, Novels, OxCEng 85, SmATA 14, TwCA, –SUP, TwCCr&M 80, –85, Who 74, WhoChL, WhoSpyF, WhoWor 74, WrDr 76, –80, –82, –84, –86, –88*
Pseud./variant:
West, Edward

Household, Geoffrey 1900-1988 *AnObit 1988, BioIn 16, ConAu 126, DcLB 87, EncSF 93, ScF&FL 92, SmATA 59, TwCCr&M 91*

Houselander, Frances Caryll 1901-1954 *AuBYP 2S, BioIn 1, –3, –4, –6, –7, –8, –9, –10, –14, CathA 1930, ConAu 110, DcCathB, SmATA 31*

Houser, Allan C 1914- *AmPB, BioIn 1, –5, –8, –9, –10, –12, IlsBYP, IlsCB 1744, –1946, –1957, WhoAm 80, WhoAmA 78, –80, –82, –84, –86, –89, –91*

Houser, Norman W *AuBYP 2S, –3*

Housman, A E 1859-1936 *AnCL, AtlBL, Benet 87, BioIn 1, –2, –3, –4, –5, –8, –9, –10, –11, –14, –15, –16, –17, BlmGEL, BritWr 6, CamGEL, CamGLE, CnDBLB 5, CnE&AP, CnMWL, ConAu 104, –125, CyWA 58, DcLB 19, EncWL, –2, LongCEL, LongCTC, MagSWL, MajTwCW, ModBrL, –S1, –S2, OxCEng 85, PenC ENG, PoeCrit 2, RAdv 1, –13-1, RComWL, REn, RfGEnL 91, Str&VC, TwCLC 1, –10, TwCWr, WebE&AL, WhoTwCL, WorAlBi, WorAl*

Housman, Alfred Edward 1859-1936 *GayLL*

Housman, Clemence 1861-1955 *BioIn 15, –17, DcBrBI, ObitT 1951, PenEncH, WhoHr&F*

Housman, Clemence Annie 1861-1955 *BiDBrF 2*

Housman, Laurence 1865-1959 *AuBYP 2S, Benet 87, BiDBrF 2, BioIn 1, -3, -4, -5, -12, -13, -17, CamGEL, CamGLE, CamGWoT, Chambr 3, ChhPo, -S1, -S2, CnMD, ConAu 106, DcBrAr 1, DcBrBI, DcEnA A, DcLB 10, DcLEL, DcNaB 1951, EncSF 93, EvLB, IlsCB 1744, JBA 34, LongCTC, McGEWD 72, -84, ModBrL, ModWD, NewC, NotNAT A, -B, ObitOF 79, ObitT 1951, OxCChiL, OxCEng 67, -85, OxCThe 67, -83, PenC ENG, REn, RfGEnL 91, SmATA 25, StaCVF, TwCA, -SUP, TwCLC 7, WhAm 3, WhoHr&F, WhoLA*

Houston, Dick 1943- *SmATA 74*

Houston, James 1921- *DcChlFi*

Houston, James A 1921- *BioIn 14, -15, -16, CanWW 89, CurBio 87, IntAu&W 91, SmATA 17AS, TwCChW 89, WhoAmA 86, -89, -91, WrDr 86, -88, -90, -92*

Houston, James Archibald *IntvTCA 2*

Houston, James Archibald 1921- *AuBYP 2S, BioIn 8, -13, ChlLR 3, ConAu 65, -38NR, FourBJA, IlDcG, IlsCB 1957, -1967, MajAI, OxCCan SUP, OxCCanL, OxCChiL, Profile 2, SmATA 13, -74, TwCChW 78, -83, TwCYAW, WhoAm 82, -90, -92, -94, WhoCanL 85, WhoE 74, WhoEnt 92, WhoWor 82, WrDr 84, -94*

Houston, Joan 1928- *AuBYP 2, -3, BioIn 8, ConAu 17R*

Houston, W Robert 1928- *WrDr 86, -88, -90, -92, -94*

Houston, W Robert, Jr. 1928- *ConAu 5R, -3NR, -18NR, LEduc 74, WrDr 76, -80, -82, -84*

Houston, William Robert, Jr. 1928- *ConAu 40NR*

Houton, Kathleen *ConAu X, ScF&FL 92, SmATA X*
Main entry: Kilgore, Kathleen

Hovell, Lucille A *AuBYP 3*

Hovell, Lucille A 1916- *AuBYP 2, ConAu 5R*

Hovell, Lucy A 1916- *AuBYP 3*

Howard, Alan 1922- *BioIn 5, -8, -14, -15, ChhPo S1, -S2, IlsBYP, IlsCB 1946, -1957, SmATA 45*

Howard, Alice Woodbury *CarSB, OhA&B*

Howard, Alyssa
Main entry: Buckholtz, Eileen
Buckholtz, Eileen Garber

Howard, Barbara Peavy 1930- *ConAu 53, WhoRel 75*

Howard, Coralie *ChhPo, -S1, ConAu X*
Main entry: Cogswell, Coralie Norris

Howard, Edward Grenville George 1792?-1841 *Alli, BiD&SB, BioIn 8, BritAu 19, CasWL, Chambr 3, DcEnL, EvLB, OxCChiL, WhoChL*

Howard, Elizabeth *AuBYP 2, Au&Wr 71 ConAu X, CurBio 51, DcWomA, IntAu&W 77X, -82X, MichAu 80, MorJA, SmATA X, TexWr*
Main entry: Mizner, Elizabeth Howard

Howard, Elizabeth 1907- *AuBYP 3*

Howard, Elizabeth Fitzgerald *WhoBlA 85*

Howard, Elizabeth Fitzgerald 1927- *BlkAull 92, ConAu 128, SmATA 74, WhoBlA 88, -90, -92, -94*

Howard, Ellen 1943- *ConAu 130, DcAmChF 1985, SmATA 67, WrDr 92, -94*

Howard, Herbert *ChhPo*

Howard, Jane Temple 1935- *BioIn 7, -10 BioNews 74, ConAu 29R, WhoAm 76, -78, -80, -84, -86, -88, WhoUSWr 88, WhoWrEP 89, -92, WrDr 76, -80, -82, -84, -86*

Howard, Joan *AuBYP 2S*
Main entry: Gordon, Patricia

Howard, John *SmATA X*
Main entry: Stidworthy, John

Howard, Keble *NotNAT B*

Howard, Matthew V *BioIn 6, MinnWr*

Howard, Moses L 1928- *ConAu 109*

Howard, Moses Leon 1928- *BioIn 16, BlkAull, -92*

Howard, Prosper *ConAu X, -29NR, SmATA X*

Howard, Rob *IlsBYP*

Howard, Robert West 1908- *AmAu&B, Au&Wr 71, BioIn 10, ConAu 1R, -1NR, SmATA 5, WhoWor 74*
Pseud./variant:
Case, Michael

Howard, Thomas 1930- *ConAu 37R*

Howard, Vanessa 1955- *BlkAWP, BlkWr 2, InB&W 80*

Howard, Vernon Linwood 1918- *AuBYP 2, –3, BioIn 8, –15, ConAu 108, SmATA 40*
Pseud./variant:
Castle, Paul
Jordan, Don

Howard, Vernon Linwood 1918-1992 *SmATA 73*

Howard-Gibbon, Amelia Frances 1826-1874 *ChhPo S1*

Howarth, David 1912- *ConAu 25NR, WrDr 86, –88, –90, –92, –94*

Howarth, David 1912-1991 *ConAu 134, SmATA 68*

Howarth, David Armine d1991 *Who 92N*

Howarth, David Armine 1912- *BioIn 5, –10, ConAu 13R, IntAu&W 77, –89, –91, SmATA 6, Who 74, –82, –83, –85, –88, –90, WrDr 76, –80*

Howat, Jean *SmATA X*
Main entry: Herbert, Helen Jean

Howden, Marjorie *SingR 2*

Howe, Deborah 1946-1978 *BioIn 16, ConAu 105, ScF&FL 92, SixBJA, SmATA 29*

Howe, Fanny *BioIn 16, DrAPF 87, –89, –91, –93*

Howe, Fanny 1940- *BlmGWL, ConLC 47, SmATA 52, WhoAm 92, WrDr 90, –92, –94*

Howe, Gertrude Herrick 1902- *BioIn 5, IlsCB 1946, WhAmArt 85*

Howe, Irving *BioIn 14, –15, –16, –17*

Howe, Irving 1920- *AmAu&B, Benet 87, BenetAL 91, BioIn 3, –4, –10, –11, –12, –13, BlueB 76, ConAu 9R, –21NR, ConLCrt 77, –82, CurBio 78, CyWA 89, DcLB 67, DcLEL 1940, DrAS 74E, –78E, –82E, EncWL 2, JeAmHC, MajTwCW, ModAL, OxCAmL 83, RAdv 1, –13-1, REnAL, ScF&FL 92, TwCA SUP, WhoAm 74, –76, –78, –80, –82, –84, –86, –88, –90, –92, WhoAmJ 80, WhoRel 92, WhoUSWr 88, WhoWor 74, WhoWorJ 72, –78, WhoWrEP 89, –92, WorAlBi, WorAl, WrDr 80, –82, –84, –86, –88, –90, –92*

Howe, Irving 1920-1993 *ConAu 141*

Howe, James 1946- *AuBYP 3, BioIn 13, –15, –16, ChlFicS, ChlLR 9, ConAu 105, –22NR, IntAu&W 86, –89, –91, MajAI, ScF&FL 92, SixBJA, SmATA 29, –71, TwCChW 89, WrDr 90, –92, –94*

Howe, Jane Moore 1914- *IndAu 1917*

Howell, Francis Clark 1925- *AmMWSc 73S, –76P, –82, –86, –89, –92, IntWW 74, –75, –76, –77, –78, –79, –80, –81, –82, –83, –89, –91, WhoAm 74, –86, –88, –90, –92, –94*

Howell, Nancy 1938- *AmMWSc 73S, –78S, OxCCan SUP*

Howell, Pat 1947- *BioIn 12, SmATA 15*

Howell, S *ConAu X, SmATA X*
Main entry: Styles, Frank Showell

Howell, Virginia Tier *ConAu X, IntAu&W 91X, SmATA 4, WrDr 76, –80, –82, –84, –86, –88, –90, –92*
Main entry: Ellison, Virginia Howell

Howell, Virginia Tier 1910- *WrDr 94*

Howells, Mildred 1872- *ChhPo, DcWomA, WhAm 5, WhAmArt 85, WhNAA, WomWWA 14*

Howells, William D *ConAu 134*

Howells, William Dean *IntvTCA 2*

Howells, William Dean 1837-1920 *Alli SUP, AmAu, AmAu&B, AmWr, AtlBL, Benet 87, BenetAL 91, BbD, BiDAmJo, BiD&SB, BioIn 1, –2, –3, –4, –5, –6, –7, –8, –9, –10, –11, –12, –13, –14, –15, –16, –17, CamGEL, CamGLE, CamGWoT, CamHAL, CarSB, CasWL, CelCen, Chambr 3, ChhPo, –S1, –S2, CnDAL, ConAu 104, –134, CrtT 3, CyAL, CyWA 58, DcAmAu, DcAmSR, DcBiA, DcEnA, –A, DcEnL, DcLB 12, –64, –74, –79, DcLEL, DcNAA, EncAB-H, EncSF 93, EncWL, EvLB, HarEnUS, JrnUS, MagSAmL, McGEWB, McGEWD 72, –84, ModAL, –S1, ModWD, MorMA, NotNAT B, Novels, OhA&B, OxCAmH, OxCAmL 65, –83, OxCAmT 84, OxCChiL, OxCEng 67, –85, PenC AM, PlP&P, RAdv 1, –13-1, RComAH, RComWL, REn, REnAL, RealN, RfGAmL 87, ScFSB, ScFEYrs, TwCLC 7, –17, –41, TwCSFW 86, –91, WebAB 74, –79, WebE&AL, WhAm 1, WhAmArt 85, WorAlBi, WorAl*

Howes, Barbara *DrAPF 87, –89, –91, –93, IntvTCA 2*

Howes, Barbara 1914- *AmAu&B, ArtclWW 2, BenetAL 91, BioIn 10, –12, –15, ChhPo, ConAu 9R, –3AS, ConLC 15, ConPo 70, –75, –80, –85, –91, DcLEL 1940, DrAP 75, FemiCLE, ForWC 70, InWom SUP, IntAu&W 77, –82, –86, –89, –91, IntWWP 82, OxCAmL 83, PenC AM, REnAL, SmATA 5, WhoAm 74, –76, –78, –80, –82, –84, –86, –88, –90, WhoAmW 83, WhoUSWr 88,*

WhoWrEP 89, –92, WorAu 1950, WrDr 76, –80, –82, –84, –86, –88, –90, –92, –94

Howes, Edith 1874?-1954 *TwCChW 83, –89*

Howes, Edith Annie 1872-1954 *BlmGWL*

Howitt, Mary 1799-1888 *Alli, –SUP, BbD, BiD&SB, BioIn 3, –10, BritAu 19, CarSB, CasWL, ChhPo, –S1, –S2, DcEnA, DcEnL, DcEuL, DcLB 110, DcNaB, EvLB, FemiCLE, HsB&A, NewC, OxCChiL, StaCVF, TelT*

Howitt, William 1792-1879 *Alli, –SUP, BbD, BiD&SB, BioIn 3, –16, –17, BritAu 19, CarSB, CasWL, CelCen, Chambr 3, ChhPo, –S1, –S2, DcEnA, DcEnL, DcEuL, DcLB 110, DcNaB, EncO&P 1, –2, –3, EvLB, NewC, OxCAusL, OxCChiL, StaCVF*

Howker, Janni *BioIn 15, –16, SmATA 46*

Howker, Janni 1957- *Au&Arts 9, ChlLR 14, ConAu 137, MajAI, SixBJA, SmATA 72, –13AS, TwCChW 89, TwCYAW*

Howorth, M K *ConAu X, –32NR*
Main entry: Black, Margaret Katherine

Hoy, Linda 1946- *BioIn 17, ConAu 130, SmATA 65, TwCYAW, WrDr 94*

Hoy, Nina *ConAu 140, –X, SmATA 75, –X*
Main entry: Roth, Arthur J

Hoyland, Rosemary Jean 1929- *BioIn 5, IlsCB 1946*

Hoyle, Fred *BioIn 14, –15, –17*

Hoyle, Fred 1915- *AsBiEn, Au&Wr 71, BiESc, BioIn 4, –5, –6, –10, –12, –13, BlueB 76, ConAu 5R, –3NR, –29NR, ConNov 72, ConSFA, CurBio 60, DcLEL 1940, EncSF 93, InSci, IntAu&W 77, –91, IntWW 74, –75, –76, –77, –78, –79, –80, –81, –82, –83, –91, MajTwCW, McGMS 80, NewEScF, Novels, RGTwCSF, ScF&FL 92, ScFSB, ThTwC 87, TwCSFW 86, –91, TwCWr, Who 74, –82, –83, –85, –92, WhoSciF, WhoWor 74, –78, –82, WorAu 1950, WrDr 76, –80, –82, –84, –86, –88, –90, –92, –94*

Hoyle, Fred, Prof Sir 1915- *Who 90*

Hoyle, Fred, Sir 1915- *Benet 87, IntWW 89, Who 88, WhoWor 87*

Hoyle, Geoffrey 1941- *EncSF 93*

Hoyle, Geoffrey 1942- *Au&Wr 71, BioIn 12, ConAu 53, –6NR, –29NR, ConSFA, IntAu&W 77, –82, –91, NewEScF, ScF&FL 92, ScFSB, SmATA 18, TwCSFW 86, –91, WrDr 76, –80, –82, –84, –86, –88, –90, –92, –94*

Hoyt, Edwin P *DrAPF 87, –91, –93*

Hoyt, Edwin Palmer, Jr. 1923- *AuBYP 2, –3, BioIn 2, –8, –13, ConAu 1R, –1NR, SmATA 28*
Pseud./variant:
Forbes, Cabot L
Stuart, David

Hoyt, Erich 1950- *BioIn 17, CanWW 89, IntAu&W 89, –91, SmATA 65*

Hoyt, Mary Finch *WhoAm 86, –88, –90, –92, –94*

Hoyt, Mary Finch 1924?- *AmPolW 80E, AuBYP 2, –3, BioIn 8, –11, ConAu 107, WhoAm 78, –80, –82, –84, WhoAmW 8[illegible]*

Hoyt, Murray 1904- *ConAu 9R, IntAu&W 77, –82*

Hoyt, Olga 1922- *AuBYP 3*

Hoyt, Olga Gruhzit 1922- *AuBYP 2S, ConAu 25R, ScF&FL 92, SmATA 16, WhoAmW 74, –75, –77*

Hsiung, Shih-I d1991 *Who 92N*

Hsiung, Shih-I 1902- *BiE&WWA, FarE&A 81, IntAu&W 77, IntWW 74, –75, –76, –77, –78, –79, –80, –81, –82, –83, IntYB 80, –81, –82, Who 74, –82, –83, –85, –88, –90, WhoWor 78*

Hu, Chang-Tu 1921- *DrAS 74H, –78H, –82H, LEduc 74, WhoAm 84, –86, –88*

Hubbard, Freeman 1894- *ConAu 5R, WrDr 76, –82*

Hubbard, Margaret Ann *BioIn 1, –5, –6, BkC 4, CathA 1930, ConAu X, CurBio 58, MinnWr*
Main entry: Priley, Margaret Hubbard

Hubbard, Philip Maitland 1910- *Au&Wr 71, ConAu 85*

Hubbard, Philip Maitland 1910-1980 *BioIn 14*

Hubbard, Robert Hamilton 1916- *BlueB 76, CanWW 70, –80, –81, –83, –89, ConAu 1R, –21NR, DrAS 74H, –82H, IntAu&W 89, OxCCan SUP, WhoAm 74, –80, –82, –84, –86, –88, –90, –92, WhoAmA 73, –80, –82, –84, –86, –89, WhoArt 80, –82, –84, WhoWrEP 89, WrDr 76, –80, –82, –84, –86, –88, –90*

Hubbell, Harriet Weed 1909- *AuBYP 2, –3, BioIn 8, ConAu 5R*

Hubbell, Patricia *IntAu&W 86X*

Hubbell, Patricia 1928- *BioIn 11, BkCL, ChhPo S1, –S2, ConAu 17R, ForWC 70, IntAu&W 89, IntWWP 82X, SmATA 8*

Hubbell, Patricia Ann 1928- *WhoWrEP 89, –92*

Huber, Charlotte *Str&VC*

Huber, Miriam Blanton d1969 *AmAu&B, WhAm 5*

Hubka, Betty 1924- *ConAu 13R*

Hubler, Herbert Clark 1910- *AmMWSc 73P, –76P, BioIn 4, ConAu 85, LEduc 74, WhoMW 74, –76*

Hubley, Faith *LesBEnT 92*

Hubley, Faith 1924- *BioIn 10, ForWC 70, LesBEnT, SmATA 48, WomWMM, WorEFlm*

Hubley, Faith Elliot 1924- *BioIn 15*

Hubley, Faith Elliott 1924- *WhoAm 92, –94*

Hubley, John d1977 *LesBEnT 92*

Hubley, John 1914- *WhoAm 86*

Hubley, John 1914-1977 *BioIn 6, –11, –12, –13, –16, DcFM, FilmgC, HalFC 84, –88, LesBEnT, ObitOF 79, OxCFilm, SmATA 24N, –48, WhoAm 78, –80, –82, –84, WomWMM, WorECar, WorEFlm*

Huchet-Bishop, Claire *MajAI*

Huck, Charlotte S *AuBYP 3*

Huck, Charlotte Stephena 1922- *AuBYP 2S, WhoAmW 75, –77*

Huddy, Delia 1934- *ConAu 25R, –19NR, ScF&FL 92*

Hudson, Cheryl Willis 1948- *BlkAuII 92*

Hudson, Gossie Harold 1930- *ConAu 93, DrAS 74H, WhoBlA 75, –77, –80*

Hudson, James A 1924- *WrDr 86, –88*

Hudson, James Albert 1924- *ConAu 33R, WhoE 75, WrDr 76, –80, –82, –84*

Hudson, Jan 1954- *ConAu 136, DcChlFi, ScF&FL 92, WrDr 94*

Hudson, Jan 1954-1990 *BioIn 17, SmATA 77*

Hudson, Jefferey
Main entry: Crichton, Michael

Hudson, Jeffery *ConAu X, ConTFT 5, IntAu&W 82X, MajTwCW, SmATA X, TwCCr&M 85, TwCYAW, WrDr 76, –80*

Hudson, Kirsty 1911-
Pseud./variant:
McLeod, Kirsty

Hudson, Kirsty 1947- *BioIn 14, SmATA 32*

Hudson, Peggy *ConAu X, ForWC 70*
Main entry: Herz, Peggy

Hudson, Tom *ChhPo*

Hudson, Wade 1945- *BlkAuII 92*

Hudson, Wade 1946- *ConAu 142, SmATA 74*

Hudson, Wade 1948- *AfrAmAl 6*

Hudson, William Henry 1841-1922 *Alli SUP, AnCL, AtlBL, Benet 87, BioIn 1, –2, –3, –5, –6, –8, –9, –12, –13, –14, –15, –17, CarSB, CasWL, Chambr 3, ChhPo S1, –S2, ConAu 115, CyWA 58, DcBiA, DcEuL, DcLEL, DcNaB 1922, Dis&D, EncLatA, EvLB, GrBr, InSci, LongCTC, ModBrL, NewC, OxCEng 67, –85, PenC ENG, RAdv 1, –13-1, REn, ScFSB, SmATA 35, TwCA, –SUP, TwCWr, WebE&AL, WhDW*
Pseud./variant:
Harford, Henry

Hudson, Wilma Jones 1916- *ConAu 33R, IntAu&W 77, WhoAmW 75, –77, WhoLibI 82, WrDr 76, –80, –82, –84, –86, –88, –90, –92, –94*

Huerlimann, Bettina 1909-1983 *MajAI*

Hueston, Ethel 1887- *AmAu&B, AmNov, BioIn 2, CarSB, REnAL, WhAm 8, WomNov*

Huether, Anne Frances *ConAu X*
Main entry: Freeman, Anne Frances Huether

Huey, E G *AuBYP 3*

Huff, Afton W 1928- *ConAu 65*

Huff, Barbara A *AuBYP 3*

Huff, Barbara A 1929- *ConAu 135, SmATA 67, WrDr 94*

Huff, Betty Tracy *ConAu 25R, WrDr 76, –80, –82*

Huff, Roderick Remmele 1920- *AuBYP 2S, –3*

Huff, Tom E 1937?- *AuNews 2, BioIn 11*
Pseud./variant:
Marlow, Edwina

Huff, Vivian 1948- *BioIn 16, SmATA 59*

Huffaker, Clair 1926?-1990 *ConAu 131*

Huffaker, Clair 1927- *CmMov, ConAu 113, FilmgC, HalFC 84, –88, WhoAm 74, WorEFlm, WrDr 84*

Huffaker, Clair 1928- *WrDr 86, –88, –90*

Huffaker, Clair 1928-1990 *TwCWW 91*

Huffaker, Sandy 1943- *BioIn 11, SmATA 10*

Huffard, Grace Thompson 1892- *ChhPo, ConAu P-1, IndAu 1917*

Huffman, Tom 1935- *AmArt, BioIn 13, SmATA 24*

Huges, James Langston
Main entry: Hughes, Langston

Huggins, Alice Margaret 1891-1971 *ConAu P-1*

Huggins, Nathan I 1927- *SmATA 63*

Huggins, Nathan Irvin d1989 *NewYTBS 89*

Huggins, Nathan Irvin 1927- *BlkWr 1, BlkWrNE, ConAu 25NR, WhoAm 88, WhoBlA 85, –88, –90*

Huggins, Nathan Irvin 1927-1989 *BioIn 16, –17, ConAu 130, WhAm 10, WhoBlA 92N*

Hughes, Arthur 1830-1915 *OxDcArt*

Hughes, Arthur 1832-1915 *ArtsNiC, BioIn 1, –5, –6, –8, –14, –16, ChhPo, –S1, ClaDrA, DcBrAr 1, DcBrBI, DcNaB 1912, DcVicP 2, OxCArt, OxCChiL, StaCVF, WhoChL*

Hughes, Cledwyn *IntWW 91*

Hughes, Cledwyn 1920- *Au&Wr 71, ConAu 13R, IntAu&W 77, WrDr 76*

Hughes, Cledwyn 1920-1978 *ConAu 126, OxCLiW 86, ScF&FL 92*

Hughes, Cledwyn, Rt Hon *IntWW 89*

Hughes, D T *SmATA 77*
Main entry: Hughes, Dean

Hughes, Dean 1943- *AuBYP 3, BioIn 14, –16, ConAu 106, –22NR, SixBJA, SmATA 33, –77, TwCYAW, WhoWrEP 89, –92*
Pseud./variant:
Hughes, D T

Hughes, Fiona 1954- *Au&Wr 71, IntAu&W 77*

Hughes, James Langston 1902-1967 *DcAmB S8, GayLL, IntDcT 2*

Hughes, James Laughlin 1846-1935 *AmLY, ChhPo, DcNAA, WhNAA*

Hughes, James Mercer Langston 1902-1967 *MajAI, TwCYAW*

Hughes, James Wilfred 1934- *ConAu 77*

Hughes, Langston *DcAmImH, IntvTCA 2, OxCAmT 84*

Hughes, Langston 1902-1967 *AfrAmW, AgeMat, AmAu&B, AmWr S1, AnCL, ASCAP 66, Au&Arts 12, AuBYP 2, Benet 87, BenetAL 91, BiDAfM, BiE&WWA, BioIn 1, –2, –3, –4, –5, –6, –7, –8, –9, –10, –11, –12, –13, –14, –15, –16, –17, BlkAWP, BlkAuII, –92, BlkLC, BlkWr 1, BkCL, BroadAu, CamGLE, CamHAL, CasWL, ChhPo, –S1, –S2, ChlLR 17, CnDAL, CnMD, ConAmA, ConAu 1R, –25R, –1NR, –34NR, ConBlAP 88, ConBlB 4, ConHero 2, ConLC 1, –5, –10, –15, –35, ConPo 75 CroCD, CurBio 40, –67, CyWA 89, DcAmNB, DcLB 4, –7, –48, –51, –86, DcLEL, DrBlPA 90, DramC 3, EarBlAP, EncAACR, EncAB-H, EncJzS, EncWL, –2, EncWT, FourBJA, LiExTwC, LongCTC, MagSAmL, MajTwCW, McGEWB, McGEWD 72, –84, ModAL, –S1, –S2, ModBlW, ModWD, NegAl 76, –83, –89, NewGrDA 86, NotNAT A, –B, Novels, ObitOF 79, ObitT 1961, OxCAmL 65, –83, OxCEng 85, PenC AM, PoeCrit 1, RAdv 1, –13-1, RComAH, REn, REnAL, RfGAmL 87, SelBAAf, ShSCr 6, ShSWr, SixAP, SmATA 4, –33, Str&VC, TwCA, –SUP, WebAB 74, –79, WebE&AL, WhDW, WhAm 4, WhoTwCL, WorAlBi, WorAl, WorLitC, WrChl*
Pseud./variant:
Huges, James Langston

Hughes, Langston 1902-1969 *AuBYP 3*

Hughes, Libby *SmATA 71*

Hughes, Mary *CarSB, ChhPo, OxCChiL*

Hughes, Mary Louise 1910- *ConAu 29R*

Hughes, Matilda *ConAu X, –40NR, IntAu&W 91X, SmATA X, TwCRHW 90, WrDr 84, –86, –88, –90*
Main entry: MacLeod, Charlotte

Hughes, Matilda 1922- *WrDr 94*

Hughes, Monica *BioIn 16, ScFSB*

Hughes, Monica 1925- *BioIn 12, –13, BlmGWL, ChlLR 9, ConAu 77, –23NR, DcChlFi, EncSF 93, IntAu&W 86, –89, –91, OxCCanL, OxCChiL, Profile 2, ScF&FL 92, SixBJA, SmATA 15, –11AS, TwCChW 83, –89, TwCSFW 86, –91, WhoCanL 85, –87, –92, WrDr 84, –86, –88, –90, –92, –94*

Hughes, Monica Ince 1925- *MajAI, SmATA 70, TwCYAW*

Hughes, Patrick 1939- *ConArt 77, ConAu 61, ConBrA 79, DcCAr 81, TwCPaSc*

Hughes, Pennethorne 1907-1967 *ConAu P-2, EngPo*

Hughes, Peter 1921- *AuBYP 2S, –3*

Hughes, Peter James 1933- *WhoAm 92*

Hughes, Richard 1900-1976 *Benet 87, BlmGEL, CamGEL, CamGLE, MajTwCW, ModBrL S2, OxCLiW 86, RAdv 13-1, RfGEnL 91, ScFEYrs, TwCChW 89*

Hughes, Richard Arthur Warren 1900-1976 *Au&Wr 71, BioIn 4, –5, –6, –7, –8, –10, –11, –13, –14, –15, –17, CasWL, ChhPo, –S2, ConAu 5R, –65, –4NR, ConLC 1, –11, ConNov 72, –76, CyWA 58, DcLB 15, DcLEL, DcNaB 1971, EncWL, –2, EvLB, IntWW 74, –75, –76, –77N, LongCTC, ModBrL, –S1, –S2, NewC, OxCChiL, OxCEng 67, –85, PenC ENG, RAdv 1, REn, SmATA 8, –25N, TwCA, –SUP, TwCChW 78, –83, TwCWr, WhAm 7, Who 74, WhoChL, WhoLA, WhoTwCL, WhoWor 74, WrDr 76*

Hughes, Sam *ConAu X*
Main entry: Wilks, Brian

Hughes, Sara
Main entry: Saunders, Susan

Hughes, Shirley *BioIn 14, –17*

Hughes, Shirley 1927?- *BioIn 8, –12, ConAu 85, –24NR, FifBJA, IlsCB 1957, –1967, IntAu&W 91, MajAI, OxCChiL, SmATA 16, –70, TwCChW 78, –83, Who 85, –88, –90, –92, WrDr 76, –80, –82, –84, –86, –88, –90, –92, –94*

Hughes, Shirley 1929- *AuBYP 3, ChlFicS, ChlLR 15, TwCChW 89*

Hughes, Ted *IntvTCA 2*

Hughes, Ted 1930- *AuBYP 2S, –3, Benet 87, BioIn 7, –9, –10, –11, –12, –13, –14, –15, –16, –17, BlmGEL, BlueB 76, BritWr S1, CamGEL, CamGLE, CasWL, ChhPo, –S1, –S2, ChlFicS, ChlLR 3, CnE&AP, ConAu 1R, –1NR, –33NR, ConLC 2, –4, –9, –37, ConPo 70, –75, –80, –85, –91, DcLB 40, DcLEL 1940, EncSF 93, EncWB, EncWL, –2, EngPo, IntAu&W 77, –89, –91, IntWW 74, –75, –76, –77, –78, –79, –80, –81, –82, –83, –89, –91, LongCEL, LongCTC, MagSWL, MajAI, MajTwCW, MakMC, ModBrL, –S1, –S2, NewC, OxCChiL, OxCEng 85, PenC ENG, RAdv 1, –13-1, RfGEnL 91, ScF&FL 92, SmATA 27, –49, TwCChW 78, –83, –89, TwCWr, TwCYAW, WebE&AL, WhDW, Who 74, –82, –83, –85, –88, –90, –92, WhoAm 82, –84, –86, –88, –90, –92, –94, WhoTwCL, WhoWor 74, –78, –82, –84, –87, –89, –91, –93, WorAlBi, WorAl, WorAu 1950, WrDr 76, –80, –82, –84, –86, –88, –90, –92, –94*

Hughes, Thomas 1822-1896 *Alli SUP, BbD, BiD&SB, BioIn 3, –4, –5, –6, –8, –9, –12, –13, –14, –16, BritAu 19, CamGEL, CamGLE, CarSB, CasWL, Chambr 3, CyEd, CyWA 58, DcBiA, DcEnA, DcEnL, DcEuL, DcLB 18, DcLEL, DcNaB S1, EvLB, JBA 34, LongCEL, LuthC 75, MouLC 4, NewC, Novels, OxCChiL, OxCEng 67, –85, PenC ENG, REn, RfGEnL 91, SmATA 31, StaCVF, TelT, TwCChW 83A, –89A, WhoChL, WorAlBi, WorAl*
Pseud./variant:
Old Boy

Hughes, Virginia *ConAu X*
Main entry: Campbell, Hope

Hughes, Walter *AuBYP 3*

Hughes, Walter Llewellyn 1910- *Au&Wr 71, BioIn 8, –13, ConAu 1R, –1NR, IntAu&W 91, SmATA 26, WrDr 84*
Pseud./variant:
Walters, Hugh

Hughes, Zach *ConAu X, IntAu&W 77X, WrDr 76, –80, –82, –84, –86, –88, –90, –92*
Main entry: Zachary, Hugh

Hughes, Zach 1928- *EncSF 93, ScF&FL 92, ScFSB, TwCSFW 86, –91*

Hughey, Roberta 1942- *BioIn 17, SmATA 61*

Hugo, Victor *PenEncH*

Hugo, Victor 1802-1885 *Benet 87, BioIn 14, –15, –16, –17, CamGWoT, EncO&P 3, EuWr 6, GrFLW, GuFrLit 1, MagSWL, SmATA 47, WorAlBi, WorLitC*

Hugo, Victor Marie 1802-1885 *AtlBL, BbD, BiDFrPL, BiD&SB, BioIn 1, –2, –3, –4, –5, –6, –7, –8, –9, –10, –11, –12, –13, BlmGEL, CasWL, CelCen, ChhPo, –S1, –S2, ClaDrA, CnThe, CyWA 58, DcBiA, DcBiPP, DcEnL, DcEuL, DcLB 119, EncMys, EncO&P 1, EncPaPR 91, EncWT, EuAu, EvEuW, HsB&A, IntDcT 2, McGEWB, McGEWD 72, NewC, NinCLC 3, –10, –21, NotNAT A, –B, OxCEng 67, OxCFr, OxCMus, OxCThe 67, –83, PenC EUR, RAdv 13-2, RComWL, REn, REnWD, WhDW*

Hulick, Elizabeth *ChhPo S1*

Huline-Dickens, Frank William 1931- *BioIn 14, ConAu 107, SmATA 34*

Pseud./variant:
Dickens, Frank

Hull, Edna Mayne d1975 *AmAu&B, ConSFA, OxCCanL, WhoSciF*

Hull, Eleanor 1913- *BioIn 12, ConAu 9R, –4NR, –19NR, ForWC 70, IntAu&W 77, –91, SmATA 21, WhoAmW 77, WrDr 76, –80, –82, –84, –86, –88, –90, –92, –94*

Hull, Eric Traviss *ConAu X, IntAu&W 77X, –82X, SmATA X*
Main entry: Harnan, Terry

Hull, H Braxton *AmAu&B, ConAu X, SmATA X*
Main entry: Jacobs, Helen Hull

Hull, Jesse Redding
Main entry: Hull, Jessie Redding

Hull, Jessie Redding 1932- *SmATA 51*
Pseud./variant:
Hull, Jesse Redding

Hull, Katharine 1921-1977 *BioIn 13, ConAu 29R, OxCChiL, SmATA 23, TwCChW 83, –89*

Hull, Raymond 1919- *WrDr 86*

Hull, Raymond 1919-1985 *Au&Wr 71, ConAu 25R, –116, –11NR, WhoAm 74, WrDr 76, –80, –82, –84*

Hull, Raymond Whitford 1946- *WhoE 91, –93*

Hulme, Beaman S G *TwCChW 78*

Hulme, Joy N 1922- *SmATA 74*

Hulme, Kathryn C 1900-1981 *HalFC 88*

Hulme, Kathryn Cavarly 1900-1981 *AmAu&B, BioIn 4, –6, –8, –12, BkC 5, ConAu P-1, HalFC 84, NewYTBS 81, WhoAm 74, WhoAmW 74, –75, –77, WhoWor 74*

Hulme, William Edward 1920- *ConAu 13R, –5NR, DrAS 74P, –78P, –82P*

Hulme Beaman, S G *OxCChiL, TwCChW 83*
Main entry: Beaman, S G Hulme

Hulme Beaman, SG *TwCChW 89*

Hulsmann, Eva 1928- *BioIn 12, SmATA 16*

Hults, Dorothy Niebrugge 1898- *BioIn 10, ConAu P-1, SmATA 6, WhoLibS 55*

Humble, Richard 1945- *BioIn 17, ConAu 45, –2NR, –17NR, SmATA 60*

Hume, Fergus 1859-1932 *Alli SUP, BbD, BiD&SB, BioIn 2, –14, CamGLE, ConAu 109, DcLB 70, DcLEL, EncMys, LongCTC, NewC, NotNAT B, OxCAusL, ScF&FL 92, ScFEYrs, StaCVF, TwCA, –SUP, TwCCr&M 80, –85, –91, WhoHr&F*

Hume, Ferguson Wright 1859-1932 *EncSF 93*

Hume, Lotta Carswell *BioIn 10, ConAu P-1, SmATA 7*

Hume, Ruth 1922-1980 *AuBYP 3*

Hume, Ruth Fox 1922-1980 *AuBYP 2, BioIn 8, –13, ConAu 97, SmATA 22N, –26*
Pseud./variant:
Irving, Alexander

Hummel, Berta 1909-1946 *BioIn 1, –2, –3, –6, –15, –17, Entr, SmATA 43*
Pseud./variant:
Hummel, Maria Innocentia, Sister

Hummel, Lisl *BioIn 1, ChhPo, ConICB, IlsCB 1744*

Hummel, Maria Innocentia, Sister *SmATA X*
Main entry: Hummel, Berta

Hummell, Ruth Stevenson 1929- *ConAu 5R*

Humphreville, Frances Tibbetts 1909- *ConAu 9R*

Humphrey, F A, Mrs *CarSB*

Humphrey, Henry, III 1930- *BioIn 12, ConAu 77, SmATA 16*

Humphrey, Margo 1942- *BlkAuII 92*

Humphrey, William 1924- *AmAu&B, BenetAL 91, BioIn 4, –7, –8, –10, –11, CamGLE, CamHAL, ConAu 77, ConLC 45, ConNov 72, –76, –82, –86, –91, DcLB 6, DcLEL 1940, DrAF 76, Novels, OxCAmL 83, PenC AM, REnAL, TwCWW 91, WhoAm 74, WorAu 1950, WrDr 76, –80, –82, –84, –86, –88, –90, –92, –94*

Humphreys, Graham 1945- *BioIn 12, –14, IlsCB 1967, SmATA 32*

Humphreys, Martha 1943- *SmATA 71*

Humphreys, Mary Gay d1915 *DcNAA, OhA&B, WhAm 1, WomWWA 14, WomNov*

Humphries, Adelaide Morris 1898- *ConAu P-1, OhA&B*

Humphries, Helen Speirs Dickie 1915- *Au&Wr 71, ConAu P-1*

Humphries, Rolfe *IntvTCA 2*

Humphries, Rolfe 1894-1969 *AmAu&B, BenetAL 91, BioIn 4, -8, -12, -17, CnDAL, ConAu 5R, -25R, -3NR, ObitOF 79, OxCAmL 65, -83, OxCLiW 86, RAdv 1, REnAL, TwCA, -SUP, WhAm 5*

Humphrys, Leslie G *ScF&FL 92*

Humphrys, Leslie George 1921- *Au&Wr 71, ConAu 107, IntAu&W 77, -86, -89, WrDr 76, -80, -82, -84, -86, -88, -90, -92, -94*

Hungerford, Edward Buell 1900- *AuBYP 2, -3, BioIn 2, -7, ConAu 37R, DrAS 74E*

Hungerford, Harold Ralph 1928- *ConAu 33R, LEduc 74*

Hungerford, Pixie *BioIn 12, ConAu X, MajAI, SmATA X*
Main entry: Brinsmead, Hesba Fay

Hunkin, Tim 1950- *BioIn 16, SmATA 53*

Hunkin, Tim Mark Trelawney 1950- *WrDr 76, -80, -82, -84, -86, -88, -90, -92*

Hunkin, Timothy Mark Trelawney 1950- *WrDr 94*

Hunt, Angela Elwell 1957- *ConAu 142, SmATA 75*

Hunt, Bernice Kohn *AuBYP 3*
Main entry: Kohn, Bernice Herstein

Hunt, Bernice Kohn 1920- *IntAu&W 77, WhoAmW 83, WhoE 81, -83, WrDr 76, -80, -82, -84, -86, -88, -90, -92, -94*

Hunt, Clara Whitehill 1871-1958 *AmAu&B, BioIn 2, -4, JBA 34, -51, WhAm 3*

Hunt, Douglas 1918- *ConAu 13R*

Hunt, Earl Wilbur 1926- *ConAu 85, WhoMW 82*

Hunt, Francesca *IntAu&W 86X, TwCChW 89, WrDr 86, -88, -90, -92*

Hunt, Francesca 1920- *WrDr 94*

Hunt, Francis *ConAu 26NR, -P-2*
Main entry: Stratemeyer, Edward L

Hunt, George P d1991 *NewYTBS 91*

Hunt, George P 1918- *EncTwCJ*

Hunt, George Pinney 1918- *AuBYP 2, -3, BioIn 7, WhoAm 74, -76, -78, -80*

Hunt, George Pinney 1918-1991 *BioIn 17*

Hunt, Gladys M 1926- *ConAu 29R, -13NR, WhoAmW 83, -85, WrDr 76, -80, -82, -84, -86, -88, -90, -92, -94*

Hunt, Gladys Mae 1926- *WhoAmW 87*

Hunt, Helen *BenetAL 91, OxCAmL 83, OxCChiL*

Hunt, Henry George Bonavia 1847- *Alli SUP*

Hunt, Henry George Bonavia- 1847-1917 *DcNaB MP*

Hunt, Irene 1907- *AuBYP 2, -3, BioIn 7, -8, -9, -10, -11, -12, -14, -15, -17, ChlLR 1, ConAu 17R, -8NR, DcAmChF 1960, DcLB 52, IntAu&W 91, MajAI, MorBMP, NewbC 1966, OxCChiL, SmATA 2, ThrBJA, TwCChW 78, -83, -89, TwCYAW, WhoAm 74, WhoAmW 74, WrDr 80, -82, -84, -86, -88, -90, -92, -94*

Hunt, Joyce *BioIn 14*

Hunt, Joyce 1927- *ConAu 106, -22NR, IntAu&W 86, -89, -91, SmATA 31*

Hunt, Kari 1920- *AuBYP 2, -3, BioIn 8, ConAu 41R, WhoAmA 73, -78, -80, -82*

Hunt, Kyle *ConAu X, EncMys, LongCTC, MajTwCW, TwCCr&M 80, -85, -91*

Hunt, Lawrence J 1920- *DcAmChF 1960*

Hunt, Linda Lawrence 1940- *SmATA 39*
Pseud./variant:
Lawrence, Linda

Hunt, Mabel Leigh 1892-1971 *AmAu&B, AuBYP 2, -3, BioIn 2, -3, -7, -9, -12, -13, -14, ConAu 106, -P-1, CurBio 51, IndAu 1917, JBA 51, SmATA 1, -26N, TwCChW 78, -83, -89, WhAm 5*

Hunt, Marigold 1905- *BioIn 3, CathA 1952*

Hunt, Morton M 1920- *ConAu 21NR, WhoUSWr 88, WhoWrEP 89*

Hunt, Morton Magill 1920- *Au&Wr 71, BioIn 2, -13, ConAu 5R, SmATA 22, WhoE 81, -83, -85, -86, WhoWrEP 92*

Hunt, Nigel *SmATA X*
Main entry: Greenbank, Anthony Hunt

Hunt, Patricia 1922?-1983 *AuBYP 3*

Hunt, Patricia Joan *ConAu 21NR, WrDr 86, -88, -90, -92, -94*

Hunt, Patricia Joan 1922?-1983 *Au&Wr 71, ConAu 103, -109, IntAu&W 77, WrDr 76, -80, -82, -84*

Hunt, Peter 1945- *ConAu 32NR, SmATA 76, TwCChW 89, WrDr 90, -92*

Hunt, Peter Leonard 1945- *WrDr 94*

Hunt, Sam 1946- *ConPo 75, -80, -85, -91, IntAu&W 91, WrDr 76, -80, -82, -84, -86, -88, -90, -92, -94*

Hunter, Bernice Thurman 1922- *BioIn 15, ConAu 119, SmATA 45, WhoCanL 87, -92*

Hunter, Christine *ConAu X, IntAu&W 77X, WrDr 76, -80, -82, -84*
Main entry: Hunter, Maud Lily

Hunter, Christine 1910- *WrDr 86, -88*

Hunter, Clingham *SmATA X*
Main entry: Adams, William Taylor

Hunter, Dawe *BioIn 13, SmATA X*
Main entry: Downie, Mary Alice

Hunter, Edith Fisher 1919- *BioIn 14, ConAu 107, SmATA 31*

Hunter, Elizabeth *WrDr 84, -86, -88, -90, -92*

Hunter, Elizabeth 1934- *BioIn 14, TwCRHW 90, WrDr 94*

Hunter, Evan *DrAPF 87, -89, -91, TwCCr&M 91*

Hunter, Evan 1926- *AmAu&B, ASCAP 66, AuBYP 2, -3, Au&Wr 71, Benet 87, BenetAL 91, BioIn 4, -5, -8, -10, -12, -13, -14, -15, -17, BlueB 76, CamGLE, CamHAL, ConAu 5R, -5NR, -38NR, ConLC 11, -31, ConNov 72, -76, -82, -86, -91, CurBio 56, DcLB Y82B, DcLEL 1940, DrAF 76, DrAPF 83, -85, EncMys, EncSF 93, FilmgC, HalFC 84, -88, IntAu&W 77, -89, IntWW 74, -75, -76, -77, -78, -79, -80, -81, -82, -83, -89, -91, MajTwCW, Novels, PenC AM, REn, REnAL, ScF&FL 92, ScFSB, SmATA 25, TwCCr&M 80, -85, TwCSFW 86, -91, Who 82, -83, -85, -88, -90, -92, WhoAm 74, -76, -78, -80, -82, -84, -86, -88, -90, -92, -94, WhoE 74, WhoTwCL, WhoUSWr 88, WhoWor 74, WhoWrEP 89, -92, WorAlBi, WorAl, WorAu 1950, WorEFlm, WrDr 76, -80, -82, -84, -86, -88, -90, -92, -94*
Pseud./variant:
Collins, Hunt
Marsten, Richard
McBain, Ed

Hunter, Hilda 1921?- *AuBYP 2S, -3, Au&Wr 71, BioIn 10, ConAu 49, SmATA 7, WhoMus 72*

Hunter, James H 1890- *ConAu 85, IntAu&W 82*

Hunter, Jim 1939- *Au&Wr 71, ConAu 9R, -7NR, ConNov 72, -76, DcLB 14, DcLEL 1940, IntAu&W 77, SmATA 65, WrDr 76, -80, -82, -84, -86, -88, -90, -92, -94*

Hunter, Kristin *BioIn 14, DrAPF 87, -89, -91, -93, WhoUSWr 88, WhoWrEP 89, -92*

Hunter, Kristin 1931- *ArtclWW 2, AuBYP 2, -3, Au&ICB, AuNews 1, BenetAL 91, BioIn 10, -11, -13, -16, BlkAWP, BlkAull, -92, BlkWr 1, ChlLR 3, ConAu 13R, -13NR, ConLC 35, ConNov 72, -76, -82, -86, -91, DcLB 33, DrAF 76, DrAPF 83, -85, FemiCLE, ForWC 70, FourBJA, IntAu&W 77, -91, LivgBAA, OxCChiL, SmATA 12, -10AS, TwCChW 78, -83, -89, WhoAm 74, WhoBlA 75, WrDr 76, -80, -82, -84, -86, -88, -90, -92, -94*

Hunter, Kristin 1937- *WhoBlA 94*

Hunter, Kristin Eggleston 1931- *DcAmChF 1960, MajAI*

Hunter, Kristin Elaine 1931- *TwCYAW*

Hunter, Leigh *ConAu X, SmATA X*
Main entry: Etchison, Birdie L

Hunter, Maud Lily 1910- *Au&Wr 71, ConAu 9R, -4NR, IntAu&W 77*
Pseud./variant:
Hunter, Christine

Hunter, Maureen Mollie 1922- *TwCYAW*

Hunter, Mel *BioIn 15*

Hunter, Mel 1927- *ConAu 93, SmATA 39, WhoAmA 78, -80, -82, -84, -86, -89, -91, WhoE 81, -83*

Hunter, Mel 1929- *BiDScF, NewEScF*

Hunter, Mollie
Main entry: McIlwraith, Maureen Mollie Hunter

Hunter, Mollie 1922- *AuBYP 2, -3, BioIn 9, -11, -12, -14, -16, ChlLR 25, ConAu X, -37NR, ConLC 21, IntAu&W 77X, -89, -91, MajAI, OxCChiL, ScF&FL 92, SmATA 2, -54, -7AS, ThrBJA, TwCChW 78, -83, -89, WrDr 76, -80, -82, -84, -86, -88, -90, -92, -94*

Hunter, Norman 1899- *ScFSB, TwCChW 89, WrDr 86, -88, -90, -92*

Hunter, Norman George Lorimer 1899- *Au&Wr 71, BioIn 8, -13, ChhPo S2, ConAu 93, -15NR, EncSF 93, IntAu&W 77, -82, -86, -89, -91, OxCChiL, SmATA 26,*

TwCChW 78, –83, WhoChL, WrDr 76, –80, –82, –84, –94

Hunter Blair, Pauline *IntAu&W 86, –89, –91, TwCChW 89*

Hunter Blair, Pauline 1921- *ConAu 29R, SmATA 3, WhoAmW 77*
Pseud./variant:
Clare, Helen
Clarke, Pauline

Hunter Blair, Pauline Clarke 1921- *WhoAm 92, –94*

Huntington, Harriet Elizabeth 1909- *AmAu&B, AmPB, AuBYP 2, –3, BioIn 6, –7, –9, ConAu 5R, –5NR, MorJA, SmATA 1, WrDr 76, –80, –82, –84, –86*

Huntsberry, William Emery 1916- *BioIn 10, ConAu 1R, –2NR, DrAS 74E, –78E, –82E, SmATA 5*

Hurd, Clement 1908- *AmPB, AuBYP 2, BioIn 1, –5, –6, –7, –8, –9, –12, ChhPo S1, ConAu 29R, –9NR, IlsCB 1744, –1946, –1957, –1967, MorJA, SmATA 2*

Hurd, Clement 1908-1988 *AuBYP 3, BioIn 15, –16, –17, ConAu 124, –24NR, SmATA 54N, –64*

Hurd, Clement G 1908-1988 *MajAI*

Hurd, Edith 1910- *AuBYP 3, ConAu 24NR*

Hurd, Edith Thacher *IntAu&W 91, WrDr 86, –88, –90*

Hurd, Edith Thacher 1910- *AmPB, AuBYP 2, BioIn 6, –9, –17, ConAu 13R, ForWC 70, MajAI, MorJA, SmATA 2, –64, –13AS, WrDr 76, –80, –82, –84*
Pseud./variant:
Sage, Juniper
Thacher, Edith

Hurd, John Thacher 1949- *MajAI*

Hurd, Michael John 1928- *Au&Wr 71, ConAu 65, –12NR, IntAu&W 77, –82, –91, IntWWM 90, WhoMus 72, WhoWor 80, WrDr 76, –80, –82, –84, –86, –88, –90, –92, –94*

Hurd, Peter 1904- *AmArt, WhoAm 86, WhoAmA 86N, –89N, –91N*

Hurd, Peter 1904-1984 *AmArt, AnObit 1984, BioIn 1, –2, –4, –6, –7, –9, –10, –14, –17, ConICB, CurBio 57, –84N, IlsCB 1744, NewYTBS 84, WhAm 9, WhAmArt 85, WhoAm 74, –76, –78, –80, –82, –84, WhoAmA 73, –78, –80N, –82, –84, WhoWor 74*

Hurd, Thacher *BioIn 15, –16*

Hurd, Thacher 1949- *AuBYP 3, ConAu 106, –24NR, –36NR, SixBJA, SmATA 45, –46*

Hurlbut, Jesse Lyman 1843-1930 *Alli SUP, DcAmAu, DcNAA, EncWM, TwCA, WhAm 1*

Hurley, Leslie J 1911- *AuBYP 2, ConAu 49*

Hurley, Leslie John 1911- *AuBYP 3*

Hurley, Richard James 1906- *BiDrLUS 70, BioIn 1, DrLC 69, WhoLibS 55, –66*

Hurley, William James, Jr. 1924- *ConAu 9R, LEduc 74, WhoMW 92, –93, WhoWor 93*

Hurlimann, Bettina 1909-1983 *BioIn 9, –14, –15, ChhPo S1, ConAu X, SmATA 34N, –39, ThrBJA*

Hurlimann, Ruth 1939- *BioIn 12, –14, ConAu X, IlsCB 1967, SmATA 31, –32*

Hurmence, Belinda 1921- *BioIn 16, ChlLR 25, DcAmChF 1985, ScF&FL 92, SixBJA, SmATA 77*

Hurston, Zora Neale 1891-1960 *AfrAmW, AmWomWr 92, BenetAL 91, BlkWr 1, ConBlB 3, ConLC 61, DcLB 51, EarBlAP, FemiCLE, FifSWrA, HarlReB, MagSAmL, ModAWWr, NotBlAW 92, RComAH, ShSCr 4, TwCYAW*

Hurston, Zora Neale 1901?-1960 *AmWomPl, Benet 87, BioAmW, BlkLC, BlmGWL, ContDcW 89, DcLB 86, HanAmWH, InWom SUP, ModAL S2, RfGAmL 87, RfGShF*

Hurston, Zora Neale 1903-1960 *AfrAmAl 6, ArtclWW 2, CamGLE, CamHAL, CyWA 89, DrBlPA 90, EncWB, InB&W 85, MajTwCW, NegAl 89, SouBlCW*

Hurston, Zora Neale 1906-1960 *EncAACR*

Hurston, Zora Neale 1907-1960 *BioIn 14, –15, –16*

Hurt, Freda Mary Elizabeth 1911- *Au&Wr 71, ConAu 103, IntAu&W 77, WrDr 76, –80, –82, –84*

Hurwitz, Abraham B 1905-1981 *BioIn 12, ConAu 29R, –133, NewYTBS 81*

Hurwitz, Johanna *BioIn 15, –16, DrAPF 87, –89, –91, –93*

Hurwitz, Johanna 1937- *AuBYP 3, BioIn 12, ConAu 65, –10NR, –25NR, DrAPF 83, –85, MajAI, ScF&FL 92, SixBJA, SmATA 20, –71,*

–18AS, TwCChW 89, TwCYAW, WhoLibI 82, WhoUSWr 88, WhoWrEP 89, –92, WrDr 90, –92

Hurwitz, Johanna Frank 1937- *DcAmChF 1985, WrDr 94*

Hurwood, Bernhardt J *BioIn 15, –16*

Hurwood, Bernhardt J 1926- *BioIn 11, –13, ConAu 25R, SmATA 12*
Pseud./variant:
Father Xavier
Knight, Mallory T
Wilde, D Gunther
Xavier, Father

Hurwood, Bernhardt J 1926-1987 *ConAu 121, –43NR, NewYTBS 87, ScF&FL 92, SmATA 50*

Hurwood, Bernhardt Jackson 1926-1987 *EncSF 93*

Hutchens, Paul 1902-1977 *BioIn 2, –14, ConAu 61, SmATA 31*

Hutchings, Margaret 1918- *ConAu 9R, –3NR*

Hutchins, Carleen M 1911- *NewGrDA 86*

Hutchins, Carleen Maley *BioIn 15*

Hutchins, Carleen Maley 1911- *BioIn 6, –11, ConAu 17R, SmATA 9, WhoAmW 74, –93, WhoE 74*

Hutchins, Hazel J 1952- *BioIn 16, ConAu 123, SmATA 51, WrDr 90, –92, –94*

Hutchins, Pat *ChlBIID*

Hutchins, Pat 1942- *AmPB, AuBYP 3, BioIn 12, –14, –17, ChlFicS, ChlLR 20, ConAu 81, –15NR, –32NR, FourBJA, IlsBYP, IlsCB 1967, IntAu&W 91, MajAI, OxCChiL, SmATA 15, –70, –16AS, TwCChW 83, –89, WrDr 76, –80, –82, –84, –86, –88, –90, –92, –94*

Hutchins, Ross Elliott 1906- *AuBYP 3*

Hutchins, Ross Elliott 1906-1983 *AuBYP 2, BioIn 8, –9, ConAu 9R, –5NR, SmATA 4, ThrBJA, WhAm 8, WhoAm 74, –76, –78, –80*

Hutchinson, Veronica S 1895-1961 *BioIn 6, ChhPo S2, ConAu 111, OhA&B*

Hutchinson, W M L *AnCL*

Hutchinson, William M 1916- *IlsBYP, IlsCB 1957*

Hutchison, Chester Smith 1902- *AmMWSc 73P, ConAu P-2, WhoMW 74, –76*

Hutchison, Paula 1905- *BioIn 5, ChhPo, IlsBYP, IlsCB 1946*

Hutheesing, Krishna Nehru 1907-1967 *BioIn 2, –8*

Huthmacher, J Joseph 1929- *BioIn 10, ConAu 21R, DrAS 74H, –78H, –82H, IntAu&W 91, SmATA 5, WhoAm 78, WrDr 76, –80, –82, –84, –86, –88, –90*

Hutto, Nelson 1904- *BioIn 12, ConAu P-1, SmATA 20*

Hutton, Ann Hawkes 1909- *WhoAm 74, –78, –80, –82, –84, –86, –88, –90, –92, –94, WhoAmW 74, WhoGov 77, WhoWor 74, –80, –84, –87, –89*

Hutton, Clarke 1898- *BioIn 1, –5, –8, –12, –14, ConAu 107, DcBrAr 1, IlsCB 1744, –1946, –1957, –1967, WhoArt 80, –82, –84*

Hutton, Warwick *BioIn 16, ChlBIID*

Hutton, Warwick 1939- *BioIn 12, ConAu 9NR, SixBJA, SmATA 20, –17AS, WrDr 82, –84, –86, –88, –90, –92, –94*

Hutton, Warwick Blair 1939- *WhoAm 92*

Huxley, Aldous *IntvTCA 2*

Huxley, Aldous 1894-1963 *AmAu&B, AtBL, Au&Arts 11, Benet 87, BiDPara, BioIn 1, –2, –3, –4, –5, –6, –7, –8, –9, –10, –11, –12, –13, –14, –15, –16, –17, BlmGEL, BritWr 7, CamGEL, CamGLE, CasWL, Chambr 3 ChhPo, –S1, –S2, CmCal, CnDBLB 6, CnMD, CnMWL, ConAu 85, ConLC 1, –3, –4, –5, –8, –11, –18, –35, –79, CyWA 58, –89, DcAmB S7, DcLB 36, –100, DcLEL, DcNaB 1961, Dis&D, EncO&P 1, –2, –3, EncPaPR 91, EncSF 93, EncWL, –2, EvLB, HalFC 84, –88, IlEncMy, LongCEL, LongCTC, MagSWL, MajTwCW, MakMC, ModBrL, –S1, –S2, ModWD, NewC, NewEScF, NotNAT B, Novels, ObitOF 79, ObitT 1961, OxCEng 67, –85, PenC ENG, RAdv 1, –13-1, REn, RGTwCSF, RfGEnL 91, ScF&FL 92, ScFSB, SmATA 63, TwCA, –SUP, TwCSFW 86, –91, TwCWr, WebE&AL, WhDW, WhAm 4, WhoSciF, WhoTwCL, WorAlBi, WorAl, WorLitC, WrPh*

Huxley, Aldous Leonard 1894-1963 *TwCYAW*

Huxley, Elspeth 1907- *BioIn 14, –15, –16, –17, BlmGWL, ConAu 28NR, FemiCLE, SmATA 62, TwCCr&M 91, WrDr 86, –88, –90, –92*

Huxley, Elspeth Josceline 1907- *WrDr 94*

Huygen, Willibrord Joseph 1922- *ConAu 81*

Hyams, Joe 1923- *AmAu&B, BioIn 4, –10, ConAu 17R, –X, WhoAm 74, –76, –78, –80, –82, –84, –86, –88, –92, –94, WhoEnt 92, WhoUSWr 88, WhoWor 78, WhoWrEP 89, –92, WrDr 76, –80, –82, –84, –86, –88, –90, –92, –94*

Hyde, Dayton O 1925- *BioIn 15, –16, –17, WrDr 86, –88, –90, –92, –94*

Hyde, Dayton Ogden *AuBYP 3*

Hyde, Dayton Ogden 1925- *AuBYP 2S, BioIn 11, ConAu 25R, IntAu&W 77, –82, –91, MichAu 80, SmATA 9, WhoAm 74, –76, –78, –80, –82, –84, –86, WrDr 76, –80, –82, –84*
Pseud./variant:
Hyde, Hawk

Hyde, Hawk *ConAu X, SmATA X*
Main entry: Hyde, Dayton Ogden

Hyde, Laurence Evelyn 1914- *ConAu 17R, IntAu&W 77, TwCChW 78, WhoAm 84, –86, WhoAmA 73, –78, WrDr 76, –80, –82, –84*

Hyde, Margaret O 1917- *ChlLR 23, ConAu 36NR, SmATA 8AS*

Hyde, Margaret Oldroyd 1917- *AuBYP 2, –3, BioIn 8, –9, –15, ConAu 1R, –1NR, ConLC 21, MajAI, SmATA 1, –42, –76, ThrBJA*

Hyde, Michael 1908- *Au&Wr 71, IntAu&W 77, WrDr 76, –80, –82, –84, –86, –88, –90, –92, –94*

Hyde, Shelley *ConAu X, –36NR, EncSF 93, ScF&FL 92, SmATA X, TwCSFW 91*
Main entry: Reed, Kit

Hyde, Wayne Frederick 1922- *BioIn 10, ConAu 1R, SmATA 7*

Hyer, James Edgar 1923- *ConAu 77*

Hyland, Ann 1936- *WrDr 76, –80, –82, –84, –86, –88, –90*

Hylander, Clarence John 1897-1964 *AmAu&B, AuBYP 2, –3, BioIn 7, –9, –10, ConAu 5R, SmATA 7*

Hyman, Dick 1904- *ConAu 17R, –7NR*

Hyman, Frieda Clark 1913- *ConAu 5R, ForWC 70, WhoWorJ 72, –78*

Hyman, Helen Kandel 1920- *ConAu 105*

Hyman, Linda *AuBYP 3*

Hyman, Linda 1940- *AuBYP 2S, WhoAmA 82, –84, –86, –89, –91*

Hyman, Robin Philip 1931- *BioIn 11, ConAu 41R, –15NR, IntAu&W 77, SmATA 12, Who 82, –83, –85, –88, –90, –92, WhoWor 91*

Hyman, Trina Schart *BioIn 14, ChlBIID*

Hyman, Trina Schart 1939- *BioIn 8, –10, –12, –15, –16, ChhPo S1, –S2, ConAu 49, –2NR, –36NR, DcLB 61, FourBJA, HerW 84, IlsBYP, IlsCB 1957, –1967, MajAI, SmATA 7, –46, WhoAm 88, –90, WhoAmW 91*

Hymes, Lucia Manley 1907- *BioIn 10, ChhPo, –S1, ConAu 5R, SmATA 7*

Hynd, Alan 1904?-1974 *BioIn 10, ConAu 45*

Hyndman, Jane Andrews 1912-1978 *AuBYP 2, BioIn 6, –9, –11, –13, ConAu X, –5NR, SmATA 1, –23N, –46*
Pseud./variant:
Wyndham, Lee

Hyndman, Jane Andrews Lee 1912-1978 *BioIn 15*

Hyndman, Jane Lee *AuBYP 3*

Hyndman, Robert Utley 1906-1973 *BioIn 9, –12, ConAu 97, SmATA 18*
Pseud./variant:
Wyndham, Robert

Hyne, Charles John Cutcliffe Wright 1865?-1944 *BioIn 4, EncMys, EvLB, LongCTC, NewC, ObitOF 79, TwCA, –SUP, WhoLA*

I

Iannone, Jeanne Koppel *BioIn 10, SmATA 7*
Pseud./variant:
Bell, Gina
Bell-Zano, Gina

Ibbotson, Eva 1925- *ConAu 81, –15NR, –43NR, ScF&FL 92, SmATA 13, TwCRHW 90, WrDr 90, –92*

Ibbotson, Eva Maria Charlotte Michele Wiesner 1925- *WrDr 94*

Ibbotson, M C 1930- *BioIn 10, ConAu 25R, SmATA 5*

Icenhower, Joseph Bryan 1913- *AuBYP 2, –3, BioIn 8, ConAu 5R, –5NR*

Ichikawa, Satomi *BioIn 14, ConAu 116, SmATA 36*

Ichikawa, Satomi 1949- *BioIn 16, ConAu 126, IntAu&W 91, SmATA 47*

Icks, Robert J 1900- *AuBYP 2S, –3, ConAu 41R*

Idriess, Ion 1890-1979 *BioIn 1, –6, OxCAusL, SingR 1, TwCWr*

Idriess, Ion L 1890-1979 *TwCRHW 90*

Iger, Martin *AuBYP 3*

Iglauer, Edith 1917- *Au&Wr 71, CaW, ConAu 77, –X*

Igus, Toyomi 1953- *SmATA 76*

Ik, Kim Yong *AuBYP 2, –3, BioIn 8, DrAF 76, DrAPF 83, –85, –87, –89, –91, –93*

Ikeda, Daisaku 1928- *EncWB, IntWW 89, –91, SmATA 77*

Iles, Bert *ConAu 130, –X, WrDr 84, –86, –88, –90*
Main entry: Ross, Zola Helen

Iles, Bertha L *AmWomPl*

Ilin, M *AuBYP 2, –3, BioIn 2, –8, JBA 34, –51*
Main entry: Marshak, Ilia Iakovlevich

Illyn, Madeline Romano *MedPD*

Ilowite, Sheldon A 1931- *BioIn 13, ConAu 106, SmATA 27*

Ilsley, Dent *ConAu X, SmATA X*
Main entry: Chapman, John Stanton Higham

Ilsley, Velma E 1918- *WrDr 86, –88, –90, –92*

Ilsley, Velma Elizabeth 1918- *BioIn 5, –11, ConAu 9R, IlsBYP, IlsCB 1946, IntAu&W 89, SmATA 12, WrDr 76, –80, –82, –84, –94*

Imershein, Betsy 1953- *BioIn 17, SmATA 62*

Immel, Mary Blair 1930- *AuBYP 2, –3, BioIn 13, ConAu 13R, –6NR, ForWC 70, SmATA 28, WhoAmW 77, WhoUSWr 88, WhoWrEP 89, –92, WrDr 76, –80, –82, –84*

Impey, Rose 1947- *SmATA 69*

Ingalls, Leonard *AuBYP 2, –3, BioIn 8*

Ingamells, Rex 1913-1955 *Benet 87, BioIn 4, ObitOF 79, OxCAusL, SingR 1, TwCLC 35, TwCWr*

Ingelow, Jean 1820-1897 *Alli SUP, BbD, BiD&SB, BioIn 2, –3, –8, –9, –14, –16, BlmGWL, BritAu 19, CamGEL, CamGLE, CarSB, CasWL, Chambr 3, ChhPo, –S1, –S2, DcBiA, DcEnA, DcEnL, DcEuL, DcLB 35, DcLEL, DcNaB C, –S1, EncBrWW, EvLB, FemiCLE, InWom SUP, JBA 34, NewC, NinCLC 39, OxCChiL, OxCEng 67, –85, PenC ENG, SmATA 33, StaCVF, TelT, TwCChW 78A, –83A, –89A, WhoChL, WomNov*
Pseud./variant:
Orris

Ingersoll, Ernest 1852-1946 *Alli SUP, AmAu&B, AmLY, BenetAL 91, BbD, BiD&SB, BioIn 1, CarSB, ChhPo S1, DcAmAu, DcNAA, HarEnUS, REnAL, WhAm 2, WhNAA*

Ingham, Colonel Frederic *SmATA X*
Main entry: Hale, Edward Everett

Ingle, Lester 1908-1980 *AmMWSc 73P, WhAm 7, WhoAm 74, –76, –78*

Ingman, Nicholas 1948- *ConAu 134, SmATA 52, WrDr 90, –92, –94*

Ingraham, Erick *ChlBIlD*

Ingraham, Leonard W 1913- *BioIn 9, ConAu 25R, SmATA 4*

Ingraham, Prentiss 1843-1904 *AmAu&B, BenetAL 91, BiDSA, CarSB, DcAmAu, DcNAA, HsB&A, OxCAmH, OxCAmL 65, –83, REnAL, WebAB 74, –79, WebAMB, WhAm 1*

Ingram, Jerry Cleman 1941- *BioIn 10, WhoAmA 73, –78, –80, –82, –84, –86, –89*

Ingram, Tom 1924- *ChhPo, ConAu 49, –X*

Ingrams, Doreen Constance 1906- *Au&Wr 71, BioIn 12, ConAu 33R, IntAu&W 89, SmATA 20, WrDr 76, –80*

Innes, Brian 1928- *Au&Wr 71, ConAu 21R, –14NR, IntAu&W 77, –82, –86, –89, –91, WhoWor 78*

Innes, Hammond *AuBYP 3, IntWW 89, –91, IntvTCA 2, Who 88, –90, –92, WrDr 86, –88, –90, –92*

Innes, Hammond 1913- *BioIn 14, –16, ConNov 86, –91, TwCCr&M 91, WrDr 94*

Innis, Harold Adams 1894-1952 *BioIn 1, –3, –4, –11, –12, –14, –15, CanWr, DcLB 88, DcLEL, EncWB, ObitOF 79, OxCCan, OxCCanL, WhoEc 81, –86*

Inoue, Yukitoshi 1945- *ConAu 25R*
Pseud./variant:
Yuki

Inyart, Gene *AuBYP 3*
Main entry: Namovicz, Gene Inyart

Inyart, Gene 1927- *BioIn 10, ConAu X, IntAu&W 77X, SmATA 6*

Ionesco, Eugene *BioIn 14, –15, –17*

Ionesco, Eugene 1909?- *IntDcT 2*

Ionesco, Eugene 1912- *Benet 87, BiE&WWA, BioIn 5, –6, –7, –8, –9, –10, –11, –12, –13, CamGWoT, CasWL, CelR, –90, CnMD, CnMWL, CnThe, ConAu 9R, ConFLW 84, ConLC 1, –4, –6, –9, –11, –15, –41, ConTFT 4, ConWorW 93, CroCD, CurBio 59, CyWA 89, EncWL, –2, EncWT, EuWr 13, EvEuW, GrFLW, GuFrLit 1, IntAu&W 77, –82, –89, IntWW 74, –75, –76, –77, –78, –79, –80, –81, –82, –83, –89, –91, LiExTwC, LongCTC, MagSWL, MajMD 2, MajTwCW, MakMC, McGEWB, McGEWD 72, –84, ModFrL, ModRL, ModWD, NewYTBE 70, NotNAT, –A, OxCAmT 84, OxCEng 85, OxCThe 67, –83, PenC EUR, PlP&P, RAdv 13-2, RComWL, REn, REnWD, SmATA 7, TwCWr, WhDW, Who 74, –82, –85, –88, –90, –92, WhoAm 74, –76, –78, –80, –82, –84, –86, –88, –90, –92, –94, WhoEnt 92, WhoThe 72, –77, –81, WhoTwCL, WhoWor 74, –78, –82, –84, –87, –91, –93, WorAlBi, WorAl, WorAu 1950, WorLitC*

Ipcar, Dahlov 1917- *AuBYP 2, –3, BioIn 5, –8, –9, –12, –16, BkP, ChhPo S1, –S2, ConAu 17R, –9NR, IlsCB 1946, –1957, –1967, IntAu&W 77, –82, ScF&FL 92, SmATA 1, –49, –8AS, ThrBJA, WhAmArt 85, WhoAm 80, –82, –84, –86, –88, –90, –92, –94, WhoAmA 78, –80, –82, –84, –86, –89, –91, WhoAmW 74, –75, –77*

Ipcar, Dahlov Zorach 1917- *MajAI*

Ipsen, D C 1921- *ConAu 33R, IntAu&W 77, –82, WhoWest 78, –80, –82, WrDr 76, –80, –82, –84, –86, –88, –90, –92, –94*

Ireland, Arthur Joseph 1874- *WhoLA*

Ireson, Barbara *ChlFicS*

Ireson, Barbara 1927- *Au&Wr 71, ChhPo, –S1, ConAu 5R, –21NR, ScF&FL 92*

Irion, Ruth 1921- *ConAu 65*

Ironside, Jetske 1940- *BioIn 17, SmATA 60*
Pseud./variant:
Sybesma, Jetske 1940-
Yetska

Irsfeld, John H *DrAPF 89, –91, –93*

Irsfeld, John H 1937- *BioIn 15*

Irsfeld, John Henry *DrAPF 87*

Irsfeld, John Henry 1937- *ConAu 65, DrAPF 83, –85, DrAS 74E, –78E, –82E, IntAu&W 89, –91, WhoUSWr 88, WhoWest 92, –94, WhoWrEP 89, –92*

Irvin, Fred Maddox 1914- *SmATA 15, WhoAmA 78, –80, –82, –84, –86, –89, WhoWest 82, –84*

Irvine, Georgeanne 1955- *SmATA 72*

Irving, Alexander *SmATA X*
Main entry: Hume, Ruth Fox

Irving, Clifford Michael 1930- *AuNews 1, Au&Wr 71, BioIn 9, –10, –11, –13, BioNews 74, ConAu 1R, –2NR, NewYTBE 72, WrDr 76, –80*

Irving, Nancy *AuBYP 3*

Irving, Robert *IntAu&W 91X, MajAI*
Main entry: Adler, Irving

Irving, Robert 1913- *AmAu&B, Baker 84, BiDD, BioIn 9, –13, ConAu X, SmATA X, ThrBJA*

Irving, Washington 1783-1859 *Alli, AmAu, AmAu&B, AmWr, AtlBL, Benet 87, BenetAL 91, BbD, BiD&SB, BioIn 1, –2, –3, –4, –5, –6, –7, –8, –9, –10, –11, –12, –13, –14, –15, –16, CamGEL, CamGLE, CamHAL, CarSB, CasWL, CelCen, Chambr 3, ChhPo, –S2, CnDAL, CrtT 3, CyAL, CyWA 58, DcAmAu, DcAmDH 80, –89, DcBiA, DcBiPP, DcEnA, DcEnL, DcLB 3, –11, –30, –59, –73, –74, DcLEL, DcNAA, DcSpL, Dis&D, EncAB-H, EncAHmr, EncFWF, EvLB, FamAYP, HalFC 84, –88, HarEnUS, MagSAmL, McGEWB, MemAm, MouLC 3, NewGrDA 86, NinCLC 2, –19, NotNAT B, Novels, OxCAmH, OxCAmL 65, –83, OxCAmT 84, OxCCan, OxCChiL, OxCEng 67, –85, OxCThe 67, –83, PenC AM, PenEncH, PlP&P, RAdv 1, –13-1, REn, REnAL, RfGAmL 87, RfGShF, ScF&FL 92, ShSCr 2, ShSWr, SupFW, WebAB 74, –79, WebE&AL, WhDW, WhAm HS, WhoChL, WhoHr&F, WisWr, WorAlBi, WorAl, WorLitC, WrChl, YABC 2*
Pseud./variant:
Agapida, Fray Antonio
Crayon, Geoffrey
Knickerbocker, Diedrich
Langstaff, Launcelot
Oldstyle, Jonathan

Irving, William *AuBYP 3*

Irwin, Ann 1915- *ConAu 101, –19NR, –36NR, SmATA 38, –44, –14AS*

Irwin, Annabelle Bowen 1915- *MajAI, SixBJA*

Irwin, Constance Frick 1913- *BioIn 10, ConAu 1R, –5NR, ForWC 70, IndAu 1917, IntAu&W 77, –82, SmATA 6, WhoAmW 83, WrDr 76, –80*
Pseud./variant:
Frick, C H
Frick, Constance

Irwin, Grace *AuBYP 3*

Irwin, Grace 1907- *DcLB 68*

Irwin, Grace Lilian 1907- *AuBYP 2, Au&Wr 71, CanWW 70, –80, –81, –83, ConAu 17R, CreCan 2, IntAu&W 77, OxCCan, WhoAm 76, WhoAmW 74, –75, WhoCan 77, –80, –82, –84, WhoCanL 85, –87, WrDr 76, –80, –82, –84, –86, –88, –90, –92, –94*

Irwin, Grace Lillian 1907- *CanWW 89, FemiCLE*

Irwin, Hadley *ConAu X, –36NR, MajAI, SixBJA, SmATA 14AS, –X, TwCYAW*
Main entry: Hadley, Lee

Irwin, Inez Haynes 1873-1970 *AmAu&B, BenetAL 91, BioIn 4, –9, CarSB, ConAu 102, REnAL, TwCA, –SUP, WhAm 5, WhNAA*

Irwin, Keith Gordon 1885-1964 *BioIn 11, ConAu 5R, SmATA 11*

Irwin, Violet 1881- *AmAu&B, REnAL, WhNAA*

Irwin, Violet Mary 1881- *WomNov*

Irwin, Wallace Admah 1875-1959 *AmAu&B, BioIn 4, –5, ChhPo S1, –S2, CnDAL, ConAmL, DcAmAu, ObitOF 79, OxCAmL 65, REn, REnAL, Str&VC, TwCA, –SUP, WhAm 3, WhScrn 77*

Isaac, Joanne 1934- *BioIn 12, ChhPo S1, ConAu 25R, SmATA 21*

Isaacs, Jacob *ConAu 57, –X, SmATA X*
Main entry: Kranzler, George Gershon

Isadora, Rachel 1953?- *BioIn 12, ChlLR 7, ConAu 111, –137, FifBJA, MajAI, SmATA 32, –54*

Isen, Harold Bernard 1940- *WhoAmA 73*

Isenstein, K Harald 1898- *WhoWorJ 72*

Isham, Charlotte H 1912- *BioIn 12, ConAu 73, LEduc 74, SmATA 21, WhoAmW 75*

Ish-Kishor, Judith 1892-1972 *BioIn 11, ConAu 1R, –103, SmATA 11*

Ish-Kishor, Sulamith 1896-1977 *AuBYP 2, –3, BioIn 8, –11, –12, –14, ConAu 69, –73, DcAmChF 1960, FifBJA, SmATA 17, TwCChW 78, –83, –89, WhNAA*

Ishmael, Woodi 1914- *BioIn 1, –5, –14, IlsCB 1744, –1946, SmATA 31*

Ishmole, Jack 1924- *ConAu 49*

Israel, Charles E 1920- *WhoCanL 87*

Israel, Charles Edward 1920- *Au&Wr 71, CaW, CanWW 83, –89, CanWr, ConAu 1R, ConNov 72, –76, CreCan 1, DcLEL 1940 DrAF 76, IndAu 1917, IntAu&W 77, –86, OxCCan, WhoCanL 85, WrDr 76, –80*

Israel, Elaine 1945- *BioIn 11, ConAu 53, –9NR, SmATA 12*

Israel, Marion Louise 1882-1973 *BioIn 13, ConAu 1R, -103, SmATA 26N*

Issa *CasWL*

Issawi, Charles Philip 1916- *AmEA 74, AmMWSc 73S, -78S, Au&Wr 71, ConAu 5R, -4NR, -20NR, -42NR, MidE 80, -81, -82, WhoAm 74, -76, -78, -80, -82, -84, -86, -88, -90, -92, -94, WhoArab 81, WhoE 74, -83, WhoWor 80*

Issler, Anne Roller 1892- *ConAu 49, IndAu 1917, WrDr 76*

Italiano, Carlo 1920- *BioIn 13, Profile 2*

Iterson, S R Van *FourBJA*

Itse, Elizabeth Myers 1930- *ConAu 49, -1NR*

Ivan, Gustave *AuBYP 3*

Ivan, Gustave 1894-1964 *AuBYP 2, BioIn 7, -8*
Pseud./variant:
Tavo, Gus

Ivan, Martha Miller Pfaff 1909- *AuBYP 2, -3, ConAu P-2, ForWC 70, WhoAmW 74*
Pseud./variant:
Miller, Martha
Tavo, Gus

Ivanovsky, Elizabeth 1910- *BioIn 1, IlsCB 1744*

Iverson, Genie *WhoAmW 91*

Iverson, Genie 1942- *AuBYP 2S, -3, BioIn 16, ConAu 65, -9NR, SmATA 52*

Ivimey, John W *AuBYP 3*

Ivins, Florence Wyman *ChhPo, WhAmArt 85*

I W
Main entry: Watts, Isaac

Iwamatsu, Jun Altsushi 1908- *AuBYP 3*

Iwamatsu, Jun Atsushi 1908- *AuBYP 2, BioIn 7, -8, ConAu 73, MajAI, SmATA 14*
Pseud./variant:
Yashima, Taro

Iwasaki, Chihiro *TwCChW 89B*

Iwasaki, Chihiro 1918- *IlsCB 1967, TwCChW 78B, -83B*

Iwasaki, Chihiro 1918-1974 *ChlLR 18*

Izant, Grace Goulder 1893- *ConAu P-1*

Izenberg, Jerry *AuBYP 2S, -3*

Izenberg, Jerry 1930- *Ballpl 90*

J

Jablonski, Edward 1922- *AuBYP 2, -3, ConAu 1R, -2NR, -18NR, WhoAm 78, -80, -82, -84, -90, WhoE 75, -77, WhoWrEP 89, -92*

Jac, Lee *SmATA X*
Main entry: Morton, Lee Jack, Jr.

Jacberns, Raymond *CarSB*

Jacka, Martin 1943- *SmATA 72*

Jacker, Corinne *LesBEnT 92*

Jacker, Corinne 1933- *AuBYP 3, FemiCLE, WrDr 90, -92, -94*

Jacker, Corinne Litvin 1933- *AuBYP 2, ConAu 17R, ForWC 70, NatPD 77, WhoAm 80, -82, -84, -90, -92, -94, WhoAmW 74, -75, -81, -83, -85, WhoEnt 92, WhoWrEP 89, -92, WrDr 76, -80*

Jackman, Leslie 1919- *Au&Wr 71, ConAu 29R, -29NR*

Jackman, Sydney W 1925- *CanWW 89*

Jackman, Sydney Wayne 1925- *CanWW 80, -81, -83, ConAu 1R, -1NR, DrAS 74H, -82H, IntAu&W 82, OxCCan SUP, WrDr 76, -80, -82, -84, -90, -92, -94*

Jack Sheppard 1702- *OxCChiL*

Jackson, Ada Acraman *DcChlFi*

Jackson, Alison 1953- *SmATA 73*

Jackson, Anne 1896?-1984 *SmATA 37N, WhoLibS 66*

Jackson, Byron 1889-1949 *BioIn 1, ChhPo*

Jackson, C Paul 1902- *AuBYP 2, BioIn 7, -10, ConAu 5R, -6NR, MichAu 80, SmATA 6*
Pseud./variant:
Jackson, Caary Paul
Jackson, O B
Lochlons, Colin
Paulson, Jack

Jackson, Caary Paul
Main entry: Jackson, C Paul

Jackson, Caary Paul 1902- *AuBYP 3*

Jackson, Charles Reginald 1903-1968 *AmAu&B, AmNov, BioIn 1, -2, -3, -4, -5, -8, -9, CnDAL, ConAu 25R, CurBio 44, -68, CyWA 58, LongCTC, NotNAT B, OxCAmL 65, REn, REnAL, TwCA SUP, WhAm 5*

Jackson, Charlotte Cobden 1902- *ForWC 70*

Jackson, Charlotte E 1903?-1989 *BioIn 17, ConAu 128, SmATA 62*

Jackson, Donald 1919- *ConAu 17R, DrAS 74H, -82H*

Jackson, Edgar Newman 1910- *ConAu 77, WhoE 81, -83*

Jackson, Ellen B 1943- *SmATA 75*

Jackson, Genevieve Vaughan *IlsCB 1946*
Main entry: Vaughan-Jackson, Genevieve

Jackson, Geoffrey 1915- *BioIn 10, BlueB 76, ConAu 61, IntAu&W 77, -82, IntWW 74, -75, -76, -77, -78, -79, -80, -81, -82, -83, IntYB 80, -81, -82, NewYTBE 71, Who 74, -82, -83, -85, WhoWor 74, WrDr 76, -80, -82, -84*

Jackson, Geoffrey 1915-1987 *SmATA 53N*

Jackson, Guida M 1930- *SmATA 71*

Jackson, Helen Hunt 1830-1885 *BenetAL 91, BioAmW, BioIn 16, -17, FemiCLE, WhNaAH, WorAlBi*

Jackson, Helen Hunt 1831-1885 *Alli SUP, AmAu, AmAu&B, BbD, BiD&SB, BioIn 1, -2, -8, -10, -11, CarSB, CasWL, ChhPo, -S1, -S2, CmCal, CnDAL, DcAmAu, DcAmSR, DcBiA, DcLB 42, -47, DcLEL, DcNAA, EncAB-H, EncFWF, EvLB, IntDcWB, JBA 34, MouLC 4, OxCAmH, OxCAmL 65, -83, OxCChiL, REn, REnAL, Str&VC, WebAB 74, -79, WhAm HS, WorAl*

Jackson, Jacqueline 1928- *AuBYP 2S, -3, ConAu 45, DrAS 74E, FourBJA, ScF&FL 92, SmATA 65, WhoAm 74*

Jackson, Jacqueline Dougan 1928- *DcAmChF 1960*

Jackson, Jesse 1908-1983 *AuBYP 2, -3, BioIn 9, -11, -13, BlkAWP, BlkAuII 92, ChlLR 28, ConAu 25R, -109, ConLC 12, InB&W 80, LivgBAA, MajAI, OhA&B, SelBAAf, SelBAAu, SmATA 2, -29, -48N, TwCChW 78, -83, -89, WrDr 80, -82, -84*

Jackson, Kathryn 1907- *BioIn 1, ChhPo, -S1*

Jackson, LeRoy Freeman 1881- *ChhPo, WhAm 6*

Jackson, Mary Coleman *AuBYP 2, -3, BioIn 8*

Jackson, O B *AuBYP 2, -3, ConAu X, SmATA 6*
Main entry: Jackson, C Paul
Jackson, Orpha

Jackson, Orpha *AuBYP 2, -3, BioIn 8*
Pseud./variant:
Jackson, O B

Jackson, Robert Blake 1926- *AuBYP 2, -3, BioIn 7, -11, ConAu 5R, -6NR, SmATA 8, WhoLibS 55, -66*

Jackson, Rosemary Elizabeth 1917- *WrDr 76, -80, -82, -84, -90, -92, -94*

Jackson, Sally *AuBYP 3, ConAu X, SmATA X*
Main entry: Kellogg, Jean

Jackson, Shirley 1916-1965 *AmWomWr 92*

Jackson, Shirley 1919-1965 *AmAu&B, AmNov, Au&Arts 9, BenetAL 91, BioAmW, BioIn 1, -2, -3, -4, -6, -7, -8, -9, -10, -11, -16, BlmGWL, ConAu 1R, -25R, -4NR, ConLC 11, -60, ConNov 76, -82A, CyWA 89, DcLB 6, DcLEL 1940, EncSF 93, FemiCLE, LongCTC, ModAL, Novels, ObitOF 79, OxCAmL 65, -83, PenC AM, RAdv 1, REn, REnAL, ScF&FL 92, ShSCr 9, SmATA 2, SupFW, TwCA SUP, TwCCr&M 80, TwCRHW 90, WhAm 4, WhoHr&F, WorAlBi, WorAl, WorLitC*

Jackson, William Henry 1843-1942 *AmAu&B, BioIn 1, -5, -6, -7, -9, -10, -13, -16, BriEAA, DcNAA, ICPEnP, MacBEP, ObitOF 79, WhAm 2, WhAmArt 85, WhNaAH*

Jacob, Helen Pierce 1927- *ConAu 69, SmATA 21*

Jacob, Michelle *OxCCan SUP*

Jacobi, Kathy *SmATA 42*

Jacobs, Allan Duane 1934- *LEduc 74*

Jacobs, Beth *AuBYP 2, -3, BioIn 8*

Jacobs, Donald Martin 1937- *ConAu 110, DrAS 74H, -78H, -82H*

Jacobs, Flora Gill 1918- *AuBYP 2, -3, BioIn 8, -10, ConAu 1R, ForWC 70, SmATA 5, WhoAmW 75, WhoE 93*

Jacobs, Francine 1935- *ConAu 49, -1NR, -18NR, SmATA 42, -43*

Jacobs, Frank 1929- *AuBYP 2, -3, BioIn 8, ConAu 13R, -6NR, SmATA 30, WrDr 76, -80, -82, -84*

Jacobs, Helen Hull 1908- *AmAu&B, AuBYP 2, -3, Au&Wr 71, BiDAmSp OS, BioIn 1, -7, -8, -9, -11, -12, ConAu 9R, InWom SUP, IntAu&W 77, -82, SmATA 12, WhoAm 74, -76, -78, -80, -82, -84, -90, -92, -94, WhoAmW 74, WorAlBi, WorAl, WrDr 76, -80, -82, -84, -90, -92, -94*
Pseud./variant:
Hull, H Braxton

Jacobs, Howard 1908- *ConAu 65, WhoSSW 73*
Pseud./variant:
Bard Of Avondale

Jacobs, John Kedzie 1918- *ConAu 21R, WhoAm 74, -76, WhoSSW 73*

Jacobs, Joseph 1854-1916 *Alli SUP, AmAu&B, AnCL, BiD&SB, BioIn 1, -2, -3, -8, -13, -16, BritAu 19, CarSB, Chambr 3, ConAu 111, -136, DcAmAu, DcNAA, JBA 34, MajAI, OxCChiL, REnAL, SmATA 25, Str&VC, WhAm 1, WhoChL, WrChl*

Jacobs, Judy 1952- *SmATA 69*

Jacobs, Leland B d1992 *NewYTBS 92*

Jacobs, Leland B 1907-1992 *BioIn 17*

Jacobs, Leland Blair 1907- *AuBYP 2, -3, BioIn 5, -8, -12, ChhPo, -S1, -S2, ConAu 73, SmATA 20*

Jacobs, Leland Blair 1907-1992 *ConAu 137, SmATA 71*

Jacobs, Leslie *ChhPo*

Jacobs, Linda C 1943- *BioIn 12, SmATA 21*
Pseud./variant:
Austin, Tom
Blackburn, Claire

Jacobs, Lou 1921- *AuBYP 3*

Jacobs, Lou, Jr. 1921- *AuBYP 2S, BioIn 9, ConAu 21R, -9NR, IntAu&W 77, SmATA 2, WhoWest 74, -76, -78*

Jacobs, Louis 1920- *BioIn 7, ConAu 1R, -1NR, -17NR, -38NR, IntAu&W 77, -82, Who 92, WhoWorJ 78, WrDr 76, -80, -82, -84, -90, -92, -94*

Jacobs, Paul Samuel *DcAmChF 1985*

Jacobs, Shannon K 1947- *SmATA 77*

Jacobs, Susan 1940- *ConAu X, SmATA 30*
Pseud./variant:
Quinn, Susan

Jacobs, T C H 1899-1976 *Au&Wr 71, ConAu X, TwCCr&M 80, -85*

Jacobs, William Jay 1933- *BioIn 13, ConAu 57, -7NR, LEduc 74, SmATA 28*

Jacobs, William Wymark 1863-1943 *BbD, BiD&SB, BioIn 4, -5, -8, CasWL, Chambr 3, DcBiA, DcEnA A, DcLEL, DcNaB 1941, EncMys, EvLB, LongCTC, ModBrL, NewC, NotNAT B, OxCEng 67, OxCShps, PenC ENG, REn, TwCA, -SUP, TwCWr, WhoLA*

Jacobson, Daniel 1923- *AmMWSc 73S, -76P, AuBYP 2S, -3, BioIn 11, ConAu 53, MichAu 80, SmATA 12, WhoMW 78*

Jacobson, Ethel *ConAu 37R, WrDr 76, -80, -82, -84*

Jacobson, Morris Karl 1906- *BioIn 12, ConAu 45, -3NR, IntAu&W 77, SmATA 21*

Jacopetti, Alexandra 1939- *BioIn 12, ConAu 57, -X, SmATA 14*

Jacques, Brian 1939- *ChlLR 21, ConAu 127, ScF&FL 92, SmATA 62, TwCYAW*

Jacques, Robin 1920- *ArtsCL, BioIn 5, -6, -8, -9, ChhPo S1, IlsBYP, IlsCB 1946, -1957, -1967, MajAI, OxCChiL, SmATA 30, -32, -5AS, ThrBJA, Who 90, -92, WhoArt 80, -82, WhoChL*

Jaeger, Ellsworth 1898?-1962 *BioIn 6, -9, EncAB-A 34*

Jaffe, Leonard 1926- *WhoGov 72, -75, WhoWorJ 72, -78*

Jaffe, Rona *BioIn 17, IntAu&W 91, WrDr 90, -92, -94*

Jaffe, Rona 1932?- *AmAu&B, AuNews 1, BestSel 90-3, BioIn 5, -9, -10, -12, BioNews 75, ConAu 73, InWom SUP, MajTwCW, Novels, WhoAm 80, -82, -84, -90, -92, -94, WhoAmW 81, -83, -85, -91, -93, WhoWorJ 72, WhoWrEP 89, -92, WorAlBi, WrDr 76, -80, -82, -84*

Jaffee, Al 1921- *BioIn 17, ConAu 116, -135, SmATA 37, -66*

Jaffee, Allan 1921- *WrDr 94*

Jagendorf, Moritz 1888-1981 *AuBYP 3*

Jagendorf, Moritz A 1888-1981 *AnObit 1981, ConAu 102, SmATA 24N, WrDr 82*

Jagendorf, Moritz Adolf 1888-1981 *AnCL, AuBYP 2, BioIn 3, -6, -8, -9, -12, -13, ConAu 5R, CurBio 52, IntAu&W 82, MorJA, NewYTBS 81, SmATA 2, WhNAA, WhoAm 80, WrDr 76, -80*

Jagendorf, Moritz Adolph 1888- *WhAm 9*

Jahn, Michael *ScF&FL 92*

Jahn, Michael 1943- *ConAu X, SmATA 28*
Pseud./variant:
Jahn, Mike

Jahn, Mike
Main entry: Jahn, Michael

Jahn, Mike 1943- *BioIn 8, -13, ConAu X, EncSF 93, ScF&FL 92, SmATA X*

Jahoda, Gloria Adelaide Love 1926- *AuNews 1, BioIn 10, ConAu 1R, ForWC 70, WhoAmW 77, WrDr 76, -80*

Jahsmann, Allan Hart 1916- *BioIn 13, ConAu 106, SmATA 28, WhoRel 75, -77*

Jakes, John 1932- *AuBYP 3, BenetAL 91, BestSel 89-4, MajTwCW, NewEScF, ScF&FL 92, SmATA 62, TwCRHW 90, TwCSFW 91, TwCWW 91, WhoAm 90, -92, -94, WrDr 90, -92, -94*

Jakes, John W 1932- *AuBYP 2S, BioIn 11 ConAu 57, ConSFA, OxCCan SUP, WhoAm 78, WhoHr&F*
Pseud./variant:
Payne, Alan
Scotland, Jay

Jakes, John William 1932- *ConAu 43NR, EncSF 93, WhoAm 80, -82, -84, WhoWrEP 89, -92*
Pseud./variant:
Payne, Rachel Ann 1932-

Jakubowski, Charles *IlsBYP*

Jambor, Louis 1884-1954 *BioIn 3, EncAB-A 25, WhAmArt 85*

James, Alan 1943- *Au&Wr 71, IntAu&W 77, –82, –91, WrDr 76, –80, –82, –84, –90, –92, –94*

James, Andrew *ConAu X, DcLEL 1940, IntAu&W 82X, –91X, SmATA X*
Main entry: Kirkup, James Falconer

James, Bessie Rowland 1895-1974 *AmAu&B, BioIn 10, ConAu 107, WhNAA*

James, Captain Lew *MajAI*

James, Cy *ConAu X, EncFWF, IntAu&W 82X, TwCWW 91, WrDr 84*
Main entry: Watts, Peter Christopher

James, Dynely *ConAu X, –37NR, MajAI, SmATA 6, –68, ThrBJA, WrDr 76, –80, –82, –84*
Main entry: Mayne, William

James, Edwin *ConAu X, EncSF 93, SmATA X, WhoWrEP 89, –92*
Main entry: Gunn, James Edwin

James, Edwin 1923- *WrDr 94*

James, Elizabeth 1942- *AuBYP 3, SmATA 39, –45, –52, WrDr 90*
Pseud./variant:
Carroll, Elizabeth
Duval, Katherine
Hastings, Beverly
Lloyd, E James
Lloyd, James

James, Elizabeth 1945- *WrDr 92, –94*

James, Gilbert *BioIn 1, ChhPo, DcBrAr 2, DcBrBI, IlsCB 1744*

James, Harold L *IlsBYP*

James, Harry Clebourne 1896-1978 *BioIn 11, ConAu 5R, –4NR, SmATA 11, WhoWest 74*

James, Henry 1843-1916 *Alli SUP, AmAu, AmAu&B, AmWr, AtlBL, BbD, BiD&SB, BioIn 1, –2, –3, –4, –5, –6, –7, –8, –9, –10, –11, –12, –13, –16, –17, BlmGEL, BritWr 6, CasWL, CelCen, CnDAL, CnMD, CnMWL, CnThe, ConAu 104, –132, CrtT 3, CyWA 58, –89, DcAmAu, DcBiA, DcEnA, –A, DcEnL, DcEuL, DcLB 12, DcLEL, DcNaB 1912, DcNAA, Dis&D, EncAB-H, EncWL, –2, EncWT, EvLB, HalFC 84, –88, HarEnUS, JrnUS, LiExTwC, LongCEL, LongCTC, MagSAmL, MajTwCW, McGEWB, McGEWD 72, –84, ModAL, –S1, ModBrL, –S1, –S2, ModWD, NewC, NotNAT B, Novels, OxCAmH, OxCAmL 65, OxCEng 67, –85, OxCThe 67, –83, PenC AM, –ENG, RAdv 1, RComAH, RComWL, REn, REnAL, REnWD, RfGEnL 91, RfGShF, ScF&FL 92, ShSCr 8, SupFW, TwCLC 2, –11, –40, –47, TwCWr, WebAB 74, –79, WebE&AL, WhDW, WhAm 1, WhoHr&F, WhoTwCL, WorAlBi, WorAl, WorLitC, WrPh*

James, Henry, Jr. 1843-1916 *BenetAL 91*

James, Josephine *AmPeW, ConAu X, SmATA 6*
Main entry: Sterne, Emma Gelders

James, Leonard Frank 1904- *ConAu 49, IntAu&W 77, –82*

James, Marquis 1891-1955 *AmAu&B, BenetAL 91, BioIn 1, –2, –4, –6, JrnUS, OxCAmL 65, –83, REnAL, TwCA, –SUP, WhAm 3, WhNAA*

James, Mary *BioIn 17, MajAI, TwCYAW, WrDr 92*

James, Mary 1927- *WrDr 94*

James, Norma Wood *AuBYP 2, –3, BioIn 8*

James, Philip *ConAu 141, –38NR, EncSF 93, MajTwCW, ScF&FL 92, SmATA 76*
Main entry: del Rey, Lester

James, Robin 1953- *SmATA 50*

James, T F *SmATA 8*
Main entry: Fleming, Thomas James

James, Theodore, Jr. 1934- *ConAu 33R, WhoWrEP 89, –92, WrDr 76, –80, –82, –84, –90, –92, –94*

James, Will 1892-1942 *AuBYP 2, –3, BenetAL 91, BioIn 1, –2, –3, –4, –7, –8, –12, –13, –16, CurBio 42, DcNAA, EncFWF, JBA 34, –51, NewbMB 1922, OxCAmL 65, –83, OxCChiL, REnAL, SmATA 19, TwCA, –SUP, TwCChW 78, –83, –89, TwCWW 91, WhAm 2, WhAmArt 85, WhNAA*

James, William Roderick 1892-1942 *ConAu 137, MajAI*

Jameson, Anna Bronwell 1794-1860 *BlmGWL*

Jameson, Anna Brownell 1794-1860 *BioIn 16, –17, EncBrWW, FemiCLE*

Jameson, Anna Brownell Murphy 1794-1860 *Alli, BbtC, BiD&SB, BioIn 7, –11, BritAu 19, CanWr, Chambr 3, ChhPo S1, DcEnA, DcNaB, EvLB, InSci, InWom SUP, NewC, OxCCan, OxCEng 67, –85*

Jameson, Cynthia *AuBYP 2S, –3*

Jameson, Johnette H *AuBYP 2S, –3*

Jameson, Malcolm 1891-1945 *AuBYP 2, –3, BioIn 8, EncSF 93, NewEScF*

Jameson, Vic 1924- *ConAu 17R*

Jameson, Victor Loyd 1924- *WhoAm 90, -92, -94*

Jamison, Andrew 1948- *ConAu 29R*

Jamison, Cecilia Viets 1837?-1909 *Alli SUP, AmAu, AmAu&B, BiDSA, BiD&SB, BioIn 12, DcAmAu, DcNAA, DcWomA, WhAm 4*

Jance, J A
Main entry: Jance, Judith Ann

Jance, Judith Ann 1944- *SmATA 50*
Pseud./variant:
Jance, J A

Jane, Mary Childs 1909- *AuBYP 2, -3, BioIn 8, -10, ConAu 1R, -4NR, ForWC 70, SmATA 6*

Janeczka, Paul B 1945- *SmATA 53*

Janeczko, Paul B 1945- *Au&Arts 9, BioIn 16, SixBJA, SmATA 18AS, WhoWrEP 89*

Janeczko, Paul Bryan 1945- *TwCYAW, WhoWrEP 92*
Pseud./variant:
Wolny, P

Janes, Edward C 1908- *AuBYP 2, BioIn 8, -13, ConAu 93, SmATA 25*

Janes, Edward Clarence 1908- *AuBYP 3*

Janes, J Robert 1935- *SmATA 50*

Janeway, Elizabeth *DrAPF 89, -91, -93*

Janeway, Elizabeth 1913- *AmAu&B, AmNov, AuBYP 2, -3, AuNews 1, Au&Wr 71, BenetAL 91, BioIn 2, -3, -4, -8, -9, -10, -12, ChhPo, ConAu 45, -2NR, CurBio 44, DcLEL 1940, DrAF 76, DrAPF 83, -85, FemiCLE, REnAL, SmATA 19, TwCA SUP, WhoAm 74, WhoAmW 74, -75, -77, -81, -83, -85, WhoE 74, WhoWor 74, -78*

Janeway, Elizabeth Hall 1913- *DcAmChF 1960, WhoAmW 93*

Janeway, James 1636?-1674 *DcBiPP, DcNaB, OxCChiL*

Janger, Kathleen N 1940- *SmATA 66*

Janice *AuBYP 2, -3, ConAu X, SmATA X*
Main entry: Brustlein, Janice Tworkov

Janifer, Lawrence Mark 1933- *ConAu 9R*

Janiver, Thomas A 1849-1913 *CarSB*

Janosch *ConAu 38NR, MajAI, SmATA 72, TwCChW 89B*
Main entry: Eckert, Horst

Janosch 1931- *ChhPo S1, ChlLR 26, ConAu X, FourBJA, IlsBYP, IlsCB 1967, OxCChiL, SmATA 8, TwCChW 83B*

Jansen, Jared *ConAu X, -30NR, IntAu&W 77X, SmATA X, WrDr 82, -84, -90, -92*
Main entry: Cebulash, Mel

Jansen, Jared 1937- *WrDr 94*

Janson, Dora Jane 1916- *AuBYP 2, -3, BioIn 8, ConAu 106, SmATA 31*

Janson, Hank *ConAu X, EncSF 93, ScF&FL 92, WrDr 82, -84*
Pseud./variant:
Frances, S D
Williams, Richard

Janson, Horst Woldemar 1913-1982 *AuBYP 2, -3, BioIn 8, -10, -11, -13, ConAu 1R, DrAS 74H, -78H, -82H, SmATA 9, WhAm 8, WhoAm 74, -76, -78, -80, WhoAmA 73, -78, -80, -82, -91N, WhoArt 80, -82, -84, WhoWor 74, WrDr 76, -80, -82*

Jansson, Tove *TwCChW 89B*

Jansson, Tove 1914- *Au&Wr 71, BioIn 6, -8, -9, -12, BlmGWL, ChlLR 2, ConAu 17R, ConFLW 84, EncWL 2, IlsCB 1957, -1967, IntAu&W 77, -82, OxCChiL, ScF&FL 92, SmATA 3, -41, ThrBJA, TwCChW 78B, -83B, WhoChL, WhoWor 78, -80, -82, -84*

Jansson, Tove Maria 1914- *DcScanL*

Jansson, Tove Marika 1914- *ConWorW 93, MajAI, RfGShF*

Jantzen, Steven Lloyd 1941- *ConAu 77*

Janus, Grete *ConAu X, SmATA X*

Jaques, Faith 1923- *MajAI, SmATA 69*

Jaques, Faith Heather 1923- *BioIn 12, ChhPo, ConAu 103, IlsBYP, IlsCB 1967, OxCChiL, SmATA 21*

Jaques, Francis Lee 1887-1969 *ArtsAmW 3, BioIn 1, -2, -3, -5, -8, -10, -13, IlsCB 1946, SmATA 28, WhAm 5*

Jaquith, Priscilla 1908- *SmATA 51*

Jarman, Rosemary Hawley 1935- *BioIn 10, ConAu 49, -2NR, SmATA 7, TwCRHW 90, WrDr 90, -92*

Jarman, Rosemary Josephine Hawley Smith 1935- *WrDr 94*

Jarrell, Mary VonSchrader 1914- *BioIn 7, ConAu 77, SmATA 35*

Jarrell, Randall 1914-1965 *AmAu&B, AmWr, AnCL, AuBYP 2, -3, BenetAL 91, BioIn 3, -4, -5, -7, -8, -9, -10, -11, -12, -13, -16, -17, CasWL, ChhPo, -S1, ChlLR 6, CnDAL, CnE&AP, ConAu 5R, -25R, -6NR, -34NR, ConLC 1, -2, -6, -9, -13, ConLCrt 77, -82, ConPo 75, -80A, -85A, CroCAP, DcAmB S7, DcAmChF 1960, DcLB 48, -52, DcLEL 1940, DcNCBi 3, EncWL, -2, MajAI, MajTwCW, ModAL, -S1, -S2, Novels, ObitOF 79, OxCAmL 65, -83, OxCChiL, OxCEng 85, PenC AM, RAdv 1, REn, REnAL, SixAP, SmATA 7, ThrBJA, TwCA SUP, TwCChW 78, -83, -89, TwCWr, WebAB 74, -79, WebE&AL, WhAm 4, WhoAmA 78N, -80N, -82N, -91N, WhoTwCL, WorAlBi, WorAl*

Jarrett, Roxanne
Main entry: Werner, Herma

Jarvis, E K *MajAI*

Jasner, W K
Main entry: Watson, Jane Werner

Jaszi, Jean Yourd *AuBYP 2, -3, BioIn 8, BkCL, ChhPo*

Jauss, Anne Marie d1991 *NewYTBS 91*

Jauss, Anne Marie 1902?-1991 *ConAu 135, SmATA 69*

Jauss, Anne Marie 1907- *AuBYP 2, -3, BioIn 5, -8, -10, -11, ConAu 1R, -4NR, ForWC 70, FourBJA, IlsCB 1946, -1957, -1967, SmATA 10, WhoAmA 73, -78, -80, -82, -84, WrDr 76, -80, -82, -84, -90*

Jauss, Anne Marie 1907-1991 *BioIn 17*

Jaworski, Irene D *AuBYP 2, -3, BioIn 8*

Jayne, Caroline Furness 1873-1909 *WhAm 1*

Jayne, Lieutenant R H *AmAu&B, YABC 1*
Main entry: Ellis, Edward S

Jaynes, Clara *AuBYP 3*

Jaynes, Clare *AmAu&B, AmNov, AuBYP 2, BioIn 2, -3, -7, ConAu X, CurBio 54, SmATA X*
Main entry: Mayer, Jane Rothschild
Spiegel, Clara

Jaynes, Ruth 1899- *ConAu P-2, WhoAmW 77*

Jeake, Samuel, Jr. *AuBYP 3, ConAu X, MajTwCW, SmATA 3, -X*
Main entry: Aiken, Conrad Potter

Jeal, Tim 1945- *Au&Wr 71, ConAu 21R, -9NR, IntAu&W 77, -82, -91, WrDr 76, -80, -82, -84, -90, -92*

Jeanneret, Marsh d1990 *NewYTBS 90*

Jeanneret, Marsh 1917- *BlueB 76, CanWW 70, -80, -81, -83, -89, IntYB 80, -81, -82, OxCCanL, WhoAm 80, -82, -84, -90, WhoCan 73, -80, -82*

Jeanneret, Marsh 1917-1990 *BioIn 17, ConAu 132, WhAm 10*

Jefferds, Vincent H 1916- *BioIn 16, ConAu 127, SmATA 49, -59*

Jefferds, Vincent H 1916-1992 *BioIn 17*

Jefferds, Vincent Harris d1992 *NewYTBS 92*

Jefferds, Vincent Harris 1916-1992 *WhAm 10*

Jefferies, Richard 1838-1887 *ScFEYrs*

Jefferies, Richard 1848-1887 *BiD&SB, BioIn 1, -6, -7, -8, -9, -11, -12, -17, BlmGEL, BritAu 19, CarSB, CasWL, Chambr 3, DcEnA, DcEuL, DcLB 98, DcLEL, DcNaB, EvLB, IlEncMy, LongCEL, MouLC 4, NewC, Novels, OxCChiL, OxCEng 67, -85, PenC ENG, RAdv 1, REn, RfGEnL 91, ScF&FL 92, SmATA 16, StaCVF, TelT, TwCChW 83A, -89A, WebE&AL, WhoChL*

Jeffers, Harry Paul 1934- *AuBYP 2, -3*

Jeffers, Susan *ChlBIlD*

Jeffers, Susan 1942- *ChlLR 30, MajAI, SmATA 70*

Jeffers, Susan Jane 1942- *BioIn 12, FourBJA, IlsBYP, IlsCB 1967, SmATA 17*

Jefferson, Alan 1921- *ConAu 33R, -13NR, -29NR, IntAu&W 82, -91, WrDr 76, -80, -82, -84, -90, -92, -94*

Jefferson, Louise E 1907- *AfroAA, InB&W 80*

Jefferson, Robert Louis 1929- *IlsBYP*

Jefferson, Sarah *ConAu X, SmATA X*
Main entry: Farjeon, Annabel

Jefferys, Charles William 1869-1951 *BioIn 2, CreCan 2, WhAmArt 85, WhoAmA 80N, -82N, -91N*

Jeffrey, Adi-Kent Thomas 1916- *ConAu 37R, WhoE 75, -77, WrDr 76, -80, -82, -84*

Jeffries, Graham Montague 1900- *BioIn 3, ConAu 77, EncMys, IntAu&W 77X, -82X,*

Who 74, –82, –83, WhoSpyF, WhoWor 78, WrDr 80, –82

Jeffries, Roderic 1926- *AuBYP 2, –3, Au&Wr 71, BioIn 8, –9, ConAu 17R, –9NR, EncMys, SmATA 4, TwCCr&M 80, –85, –91, WrDr 82, –84, –90, –92, –94*
Pseud./variant:
Ashford, Jeffrey
Draper, Hastings
Graeme, Roderic
Hastings, Graham

Jellicoe, Ann *BioIn 16, Who 90, –92*

Jellicoe, Ann 1927- *BioIn 9, –10, –12, –13, BlmGEL, BlmGWL, BlueB 76, CnThe, ConAu 85, ConDr 73, –77, –82, ConLC 27, ConTFT 2, CroCD, DcLB 13, EncBrWW, EncWT, FemiCLE, IntAu&W 91, McGEWD 72, –84, ModWD, NewC, NotNAT, OxCEng 85, REnWD, TwCChW 78, –83, –89, TwCWr, Who 74, –82, –83, –85, WhoThe 77, –81, WorAu 1950, WrDr 76, –80, –82, –84, –90, –92, –94*

Jemne, Elsa Laubach 1888-1974 *ArtsAmW 3, BioIn 1, DcWomA, IlsCB 1744, WhAmArt 85*

Jenkins, Alan Charles 1914- *Au&Wr 71, ConAu 57, IntAu&W 77, –82, WrDr 76, –80*

Jenkins, Elizabeth *IntAu&W 91, IntWW 89, –91, Who 90, –92, WrDr 90, –92, –94*

Jenkins, Elizabeth 1905- *BioIn 5, –10, ConAu 73, –13NR, DcLEL, IntAu&W 77, IntWW 74, –75, –76, –77, –78, –79, –80, –81, –82, –83, Who 74, –82, –83, –85, WhoAm 74, –76, WhoAmW 74, WhoLibS 66, WorAu 1950, WrDr 80, –82, –84*

Jenkins, Ferguson 1943- *AfrAmBi, Ballpl 90, BioIn 8, –9, –10, –11, –13, –17, NewYTBE 71, WhoAm 74, –76, –80, –82, –84, WhoBlA 75, –77, –80, –85, –90, –92, –94, WorAlBi, WorAl*

Jenkins, Lyll Becerra De *DcAmChF 1985*

Jenkins, Marie M 1909- *AmMWSc 73P, –76P, –82, AuBYP 2S, BioIn 10, ConAu 41R, SmATA 7, WhoAmW 74, –75*
Pseud./variant:
Markins, W S
Scholastica, Mary, Sister

Jenkins, Marie Magdalen 1909- *AuBYP 3, BioIn 10*

Jenkins, Patrick 1955- *SmATA 72*

Jenkins, Raymond 1935- *Au&Wr 71, WrDr 76, –80*

Jenkins, William Atwell 1922- *BioIn 11, ConAu 61, DrAS 74E, –78E, –82E, SmATA 9, WhoAm 74, –76, –78, –80, –82, –84, –90, –92, –94, WhoMW 86*

Jenks, Tudor 1857-1922 *AmAu&B, AmLY, BenetAL 91, BiD&SB, CarSB, ChhPo, DcAmAu, DcNAA, REnAL, WhAm 1*

Jenkyns, Chris 1924- *BioIn 5, IlsBYP, IlsCB 1946, SmATA 51*

Jenner, H P *ChhPo*

Jeness, Aylette 1934- *ConAu 25R*

Jennings, Anne Heise *ChhPo S2, WhoAmW 77*

Jennings, Coleman A 1933- *SmATA 64*

Jennings, Coleman Alonzo 1933- *WhoAm 92, –94, WhoEnt 92*

Jennings, Elizabeth 1926- *Au&Wr 71, BioIn 3, –8, –10, –12, BlmGEL, BlmGWL, BlueB 76, ChhPo, –S1, –S2, ConAu 61, –8NR, ConLC 5, ConPo 70, –75, –80, –85, –91, DcLB 27, EncBrWW, EncWL 2, FemiCLE, InWom SUP, IntAu&W 91, IntWW 77, –78, –79, –80, –81, –82, –83, –89, –91, LongCTC, MajTwCW, ModBrL, –S1, –S2, NewC, OxCEng 85, PenC ENG, RAdv 1, SmATA 66, TwCWr, WebE&AL, Who 74, –82, –83, –85, –90 –92, WhoTwCL, WhoWor 78, –84, –91, –93, WorAu 1950, WrDr 76, –80, –82, –84, –90, –92*

Jennings, Elizabeth Joan 1926- *ConAu 39NR, WrDr 94*

Jennings, Gary *ScF&FL 92*

Jennings, Gary 1928- *AuBYP 2, –3, BioIn 8, –11, –12, ConAu 5R, –9NR, –29NR, SmATA 9, TwCRHW 90, WhoAmP 81*

Jennings, Gordon *AuBYP 2S, –3*

Jennings, Jerry 1935- *ConAu 53, –7NR*

Jennings, John Edward, Jr. 1906-1973 *AmAu&B, AmNov, AuBYP 2, –3, BenetAL 91, BioIn 2, –4, –8, –10, ConAu 45, –P-1, CurBio 49, REnAL, TwCA SUP, WhAm 6, WhoE 74*

Jennings, Michael 1931- *AuBYP 2S, –3, ConAu 69, WhoE 83, –85, WhoWor 84*

Jennings, Raymond Polson 1924- *ConAu 110, DrAS 74P, WhoRel 75, –77*

Jennings, Robert *ConAu X, –29NR, SmATA X*

Jennings, S M *ConAu X, SmATA 3, –X*
Main entry: Meyer, Jerome Sydney

Jennings, Thomas Joseph 1930- *AmMWSc 73P*

Jennison, C S *AuBYP 2, -3, BioIn 10, ConAu X, -38NR, MajAI, SmATA 6*
Main entry: Starbird, Kaye

Jennison, Christopher 1938- *ConAu 53*

Jennison, Keith Warren 1911- *AmAu&B, AuBYP 2, -3, BioIn 3, -4, -8, -12, ConAu 73, SmATA 14*

Jensen, David E *AuBYP 3*

Jensen, David Edward 1909- *AmMWSc 73P, -76P, -82, AuBYP 2, BioIn 8, WhoE 74, -75, -77, WhoFI 74*

Jensen, Julie M
Main entry: McDonald, Julie

Jensen, Julie M 1943- *BioIn 10, MedPD, WhoAm 84, WhoAmW 83, -85*

Jensen, Julie Mae 1943- *WhoAm 90*

Jensen, Niels 1927- *BioIn 13, ConAu 49, SmATA 25*

Jensen, Pauline Marie 1900- *ConAu P-2, ForWC 70*

Jensen, Virginia Allen 1927- *BioIn 11, ConAu 45, -1NR, SmATA 8*

Jeppson, J O
Main entry: Asimov, Janet Jeppson

Jeppson, J O 1926- *SmATA 46*

Jeram, Anita 1965- *SmATA 71*

Jeremiah, Edward John 1905-1967 *BioIn 7, ObitOF 79*

Jerome, Irene Elizabeth 1858-1945 *Alli SUP, ArtsAmW 2, CarSB, ChhPo, DcWomA*

Jerome, Jerome K 1859-1927 *BioIn 17, CamGWoT, DcLB 135, HalFC 88, RfGEnL 91, ScF&FL 92, ScFEYrs, StaCVF*

Jerome, Jerome Klapka 1859-1927 *Alli SUP, BbD, BiD&SB, BioIn 2, -5, -10, -12, -13, CasWL, Chambr 3, CyWA 58, DcBiA, DcEnA A, DcLB 10, -34, DcLEL, DcNaB 1922, EncWT, EvLB, HalFC 84, LongCTC, McGEWD 72, -84, ModBrL, ModWD, NewC, NotNAT A, -B, Novels, OxCEng 67, -85, OxCThe 67, -83, PenC ENG, REn, TwCA, TwCWr, WhDW*

Jerome, John 1932- *ConAu 45, -2NR, WrDr 92, -94*

Jerr, William A *AuBYP 2, -3, BioIn 7*

Jerrick, Stephen Joseph 1948- *BioIn 12, WhoAm 74, -76, -78, -80, -82*

Jersey, Countess Of 1849-1945 *BioIn 5, CarSB, DcNaB 1941*

Jeschke, Susan 1942- *BioIn 11, ConAu 77, FifBJA, IlsCB 1967, SmATA 27, -42*

Jessel, Camilla 1937- *BioIn 13, ConAu 104, SmATA 29*

Jessey, Cornelia *SmATA X*
Main entry: Sussman, Cornelia Silver

Jessey, Cornelia 1910- *AmAu&B, AmNov, BioIn 2, ConAu X*

Jessop, Gilbert Laird 1874-1955 *BioIn 1, -2, -3, -10, DcNaB 1951, ObitOF 79, ObitT 1951*

Jeter, Jacquelyn I 1935- *ConAu 25R*

Jewell, Nancy 1940- *ConAu 61, -7NR, SmATA 41*

Jewett, Eleanore Myers 1890-1967 *BioIn 6, -10, ChhPo, ConAu 5R, MorJA, SmATA 5*

Jewett, Sarah Orne 1849-1909 *Alli SUP, AmAu, AmAu&B, AmWomWr 92, AmWr, AtlBL, AuBYP 2, -3, BenetAL 91, BbD, BiD&SB, BioAmW, BioIn 1, -2, -3, -4, -5, -6, -7, -8, -9, -11, -12, -13, -16, -17, BlmGWL, CarSB, CasWL, Chambr 3, ChhPo, -S1, -S2, CnDAL, ConAu 108, -127, CrtT 3, CyWA 58, DcAmAu, DcBiA, DcLB 12, DcLEL, DcNAA, Dis&D, EvLB, FemiCLE, HanAmWH, HarEnUS, InWom SUP, IntDcWB, JBA 34, MagSAmL, McGEWB, ModAL, ModAWWr, Novels, OxCAmL 65, -83, OxCEng 67, -85, PenC AM, RAdv 1, REn, REnAL, ShSCr 6, SmATA 15, TwCLC 1, WebAB 74, -79, WebE&AL, WhAm 1, WorAlBi, WorAl*

Jezard, Alison 1919- *BioIn 16, ConAu 29R, SmATA 34, -57*

Jiler, John 1946- *ConAu 114, NatPD 81, SmATA 35, -42*

Jimenez, Juan Ramon *BioIn 16, -17*

Jimenez, Juan Ramon 1881-1958 *AnCL, AtlBL, BioIn 1, -2, -3, -4, -5, -6, -8, -9, -10, -11, CasWL, ClDMEL 47, CnMWL, ConAu 104, -131, CyWA 58, DcSpL, EncWL, -2, EvEuW, HispLC, HispWr, LiExTwC, MajTwCW, McGEWB, ModRL, ModSpP S, PenC EUR, REn, TwCLC 4, TwCWr, WhDW, WhAm 3, WhoNob 90, WhoTwCL, WorAlBi, WorAl, WorAu 1950*

Jobb, Jamie 1945- *BioIn 13, SmATA 29*
Pseud./variant:
Kabibble, Osh

Jobson, Patrick 1919- *BioIn 5, ClaDrA, IlsCB 1946, WhoArt 80, –82, –84*

Joerns, Consuelo *ConAu 111, –114, IlsBYP, SmATA 33, –44*

Johannis, Theodore B, Jr. 1914- *AmMWSc 73S, ConAu 33R*

Johansen, Margaret 1896- *AuBYP 3*

Johansen, Margaret Alison 1896- *AuBYP 2, BioIn 8, TexWr*

John, Elizabeth Beaman 1907- *ConAu 5R, –8NR, ForWC 70, IntAu&W 77, WrDr 76, –80*
Pseud./variant:
Saint John, Elizabeth

John, Hazel *WhoWest 74, WrDr 76, –80*

John, Joyce *SmATA 59*

John, Naomi *SmATA X*

Johns, Avery *AuBYP 3, ConAu X, SmATA 2, WrDr 76, –80, –82, –84, –90, –92*
Main entry: Cousins, Margaret

Johns, Avery 1905- *WrDr 94*

Johns, Captain W E
Main entry: Johns, William Earl

Johns, W E 1893-1968 *BioIn 16, ConAu 30NR, ScF&FL 92, SmATA 55, TwCChW 89, TwCSFW 91*

Johns, W E, Captain *MajAI*

Johns, William E *AmMWSc 92*

Johns, William Earl 1893-1968 *BioIn 8, –13, –16, DcNaB 1961, LongCTC, Novels, ObitT 1961, OxCChiL, TwCChW 78, –83, WhoChL*
Pseud./variant:
Earle, William
Early, Jon
Johns, Captain W E
William, Earle

Johns, William Earle 1893-1968 *EncSF 93, MajAI*

Johnson, A *MajAI, SmATA 72*
Main entry: Johnson, Annabell Jones

Johnson, A E *ConAu X, –37NR, IntAu&W 91X, MajAI, SmATA 2, –72, WrDr 80, –82, –84, –90, –92*
Main entry: Johnson, Annabel Jones
Johnson, Edgar Raymond

Johnson, Angela 1961- *SmATA 69*

Johnson, Angela 1962- *BlkAuII 92*

Johnson, Annabel *ConAu 37NR, MajAI SmATA 72*

Johnson, Annabel 1921- *AuBYP 3, ScF&FL 92, TwCChW 89, TwCYAW, WrDr 90, –92*

Johnson, Annabel Jones 1921- *AmAu&B, AuBYP 2, BioIn 4, –8, –9, ConAu 9R, DcAmChF 1960, SmATA 2, ThrBJA, TwCChW 78, –83, WrDr 80, –94*
Pseud./variant:
Johnson, A E

Johnson, Annabell Jones 1921- *MajAI, SmATA 72*
Pseud./variant:
Johnson, A

Johnson, Avery Fischer 1906- *BioIn 1, –5, IlsCB 1744, –1946, WhAmArt 85, WhoAm 74, –76, –78, –80, –82, –84, WhoAmA 73, –78, –80, –82, –84*

Johnson, Avery Fischer 1906-1990 *WhoAmA 91N*

Johnson, Bertha French 1906- *ConAu 41R*

Johnson, Bill *DcAmChF 1960*

Johnson, Burdetta Fay Beebe 1920- *ConAu 1R, IntAu&W 77, –82, WhoAmW 77, WhoWest 78*
Pseud./variant:
Beebe, Burdetta Faye

Johnson, Burdetta Faye *AuBYP 3*

Johnson, Burges 1877-1963 *AmAu&B, AmLY, BenetAL 91, ChhPo, –S1, –S2, REnAL, WhJnl, WhNAA, WhScrn 83, –77*

Johnson, Charlene *ConAu X*
Main entry: Crawford, Char

Johnson, Charlene Elizabeth 1933- *WhoAmW 93, WhoMW 93*

Johnson, Charles Frederick *AuBYP 2, –3, BioIn 8*

Johnson, Charles Raymond 1925- *BioIn 11, ConAu 65, SmATA 11, WhoAm 76, –78, –80, –82, –84, –90, WhoMW 74, –76*
Pseud./variant:
Johnson, Chuck

Johnson, Charlotte Buel 1918- *ConAu X, WhAm 8, WhoAm 74, –76, –78, –80, –82, WhoAmA 73, –78, –80, –82, WhoAmW 74*

Johnson, Charlotte Buel 1918-1982 *SmATA 46*

Johnson, Chuck *ConAu X, SmATA X*
Main entry: Johnson, Charles Raymond

Johnson, Corinne B *AuBYP 2S, -3*

Johnson, Crockett *AuBYP 3, MajAI*
Main entry: Leisk, David Johnson

Johnson, Crockett 1906-1975 *AmPB, AuBYP 2, Au&Wr 71, BioIn 1, -5, -8, -9, -10, BkP, ConAu X, CurBio 43, -84N, EncACom, IlsCB 1946, -1957, -1967, ObitOF 79, OxCChiL, SmATA 1, -X, ThrBJA, TwCChW 78, -83, -89, WhAm 6, WhoAmA 73, -78N, -80N*

Johnson, D William 1945- *BioIn 13, ConAu 97, SmATA 23*

Johnson, Daniel Shahid 1954- *SmATA 73*

Johnson, Dolores *BlkAuII 92*

Johnson, Dolores 1949- *SmATA 69*

Johnson, Doris 1922- *AuBYP 2S, -3*

Johnson, Dorothy M 1905-1984 *TwCWW 91*

Johnson, Dorothy Marie 1905-1984 *Au&Wr 71, BioIn 10, ConAu 5R, -114, -6NR, EncFWF, ForWC 70, SmATA 6, -40N, WhoPNW, WrDr 84*

Johnson, E Ned *AuBYP 3*

Johnson, Edgar 1901- *AmAu&B, AuBYP 2, BioIn 3, -4, -5, -7, -8, ConAu 9R, DcLB 103, DrAS 74E, -78E, NewYTBE 72, REnAL, TwCA SUP, WhoAm 74, -76, WhoWor 74*

Johnson, Edgar 1912- *TwCChW 89*

Johnson, Edgar 1912-1960 *AuBYP 3*

Johnson, Edgar Raymond 1912- *BioIn 9, ConAu 9R, DcAmChF 1960, SmATA 2, ThrBJA, TwCChW 78, -83*
Pseud./variant:
Johnson, A E

Johnson, Edgar Raymond 1912-1990 *MajAI, SmATA 72, TwCYAW*

Johnson, Elizabeth 1911-1984 *AuBYP 2S, -3, BioIn 2, -10, ConAu 1R, -117, -4NR, SmATA 7, -39N, WhoLibS 55*

Johnson, Emily Pauline 1861-1913 *BioIn 17, InWom SUP*

Johnson, Emily Pauline 1862-1913 *AmWomPl, BioIn 1, -7, -10, -11, -13, CreCan 2, WhNaAH*

Johnson, Enid 1892- *AuBYP 2, -3, BioIn 8, ConAu 73, JBA 34*

Johnson, Eric W 1918- *AuBYP 3, WrDr 90, -92*

Johnson, Eric Warner 1918- *AuBYP 2S, BioIn 11, ConAu 5R, -4NR, LEduc 74, SmATA 8, WhoE 75, -77, WrDr 76, -80, -82, -84, -94*

Johnson, Eugene Harper *BioIn 5, -8, IlsBYP, IlsCB 1946, -1957, InB&W 80, SmATA 44*
Pseud./variant:
Johnson, Harper

Johnson, Evelyne 1932- *BioIn 12, ConAu 69, SmATA 20*

Johnson, Fred *ArtCS*

Johnson, Fred d1982 *SmATA 63*

Johnson, Gaylord 1884- *BioIn 10, ConAu P-1, SmATA 7*

Johnson, George 1917- *ConAu 5R, IndAu 1917*

Johnson, George Metcalf 1885- *AmAu&B, WhNAA*

Johnson, Gerald W 1890-1980 *BenetAL 91*

Johnson, Gerald White 1890-1980 *AmAu&B, AnCL, AuBYP 2, -3, BioIn 2, -3, -4, -7, -9, -12, -13, CnDAL, ConAu 85, -97, DcLB 29, DcNCBi 3, EncAJ, EncSoH, JrnUS, NewYTBS 80, OxCAmL 65, -83, REnAL, SmATA 19, -28N, ThrBJA, TwCA SUP, WhAm 7, WhJnl, WhNAA, WhoAm 74, -76, -78, -80, WhoWor 74*

Johnson, Harper *SmATA X*
Main entry: Johnson, Eugene Harper

Johnson, Harriet 1908-1987 *SmATA 53N*

Johnson, Helen Lossing *AuBYP 3*

Johnson, Helen Louise Kendrick 1843-1917 *Alli SUP, AmAu, AmAu&B, BiD&SB, BioIn 12, CarSB, ChhPo S1, DcAmAu, DcNAA, WhAm 1, WomWWA 14*

Johnson, Helen Louise Kendrick 1844-1917 *InWom SUP*

Johnson, Herschel Lee 1948- *BlkAuII 92*

Johnson, Humphrey Wynne 1925-1976 *ConAu 61*

Johnson, James E 1927- *ConAu 77, DrAS 74H, -78H, -82H, WhoMW 92*

Johnson, James Edgar *Who 92*

Johnson, James Edgar, Air Vice-Marshal *Who 90*

Johnson, James Ralph 1922- *AuBYP 2, -3, BioIn 8, -9, ConAu 1R, -2NR, IntAu&W 77, -82, -91, SmATA 1, WhoAmA 78, -80, -82, -84, -91, WhoWest 78, -92, -94, WrDr 76, -80, -82, -84, -90, -92, -94*

Johnson, James Weldon 1871-1938 *AfrAmAl 6, AfrAmW, AmAu&B, AnCL, AnMV 1926, ASCAP 66, Baker 84, -92, BenetAL 91, BiDAfM, BioIn 1, -2, -4, -6, -7, -8, -9, -10, -12, -13, -16, -17, BlkAWP, BlkAull 92, BlkLC, CasWL, ChhPo, -S1, -S2, ChlLR 32, ConAmA, ConAmL, ConAu 104, CyWA 89, DcAfAmP, DcAmNB, DcAmSR, DcLEL, DcNAA, DrBlPA 90, EncAACR, EncAB-H, EncSoH, EncWL 2, FourBJA, InB&W 80, MajTwCW, McGEWB, ModAL S1, ModBlW, NegAl 76, -83, -89, NewAmDM, OxCAmH, OxCAmL 65, -83, OxCPMus, PenC AM, RAdv 1, RComAH, REn, REnAL, SelBAAf, SelBAAu, SixAP, SmATA X, TwCA, -SUP, TwCLC 3, -19, WebAB 74, -79, WebE&AL, WhAm 1, WhAmP, WhFla, WhNAA*
Pseud./variant:
Johnson, James William

Johnson, James William
Main entry: Johnson, James Weldon

Johnson, James William 1871-1938 *SmATA 31*

Johnson, Jane 1951- *SmATA 48*

Johnson, Jean *AuBYP 3*

Johnson, Jerry Mack 1927- *ConAu 53, -4NR*
Pseud./variant:
Mack, Jerry

Johnson, Joan J 1942- *SmATA 59, WrDr 90, -92, -94*

Johnson, John E 1929- *BioIn 8, ChhPo S1, ConAu 110, IlsBYP, IlsCB 1957, -1967, SmATA 34*

Johnson, Johnni 1922- *ConAu 13R*

Johnson, Joy Duvall 1932- *ConAu 110, WhoAmW 77, -91, -93*

Johnson, LaVerne B 1925- *ConAu 65, SmATA 13*

Johnson, Lissa H 1955- *SmATA 65*

Johnson, Lissa Halls 1955- *BioIn 17, ConAu 136, WrDr 94*

Johnson, Lois Smith 1894- *BioIn 10, ConAu P-1, SmATA 6*

Johnson, Lois Walfrid 1936- *ConAu 57, -6NR, SmATA 22, WhoWrEP 89, -92*

Johnson, Margaret *AmWomPl*

Johnson, Margaret 1860- *Alli SUP, AmAu&B, ChhPo, -S1, -S2, DcAmAu, DcWomA, WhAm 4, WhAmArt 85, WhNAA*

Johnson, Margaret 1926- *ConAu 37R*

Johnson, Margaret Sweet 1893-1964 *AuBYP 2, -3, BioIn 2, -8, ConAu 113, JBA 51, SmATA 35*

Johnson, Marilue Carolyn 1931- *ConAu 45, -1NR*
Pseud./variant:
Marilue

Johnson, Martha *AuBYP 3*

Johnson, Mary Frances K 1929?-1979 *ALA 80N, BioIn 13, ConAu 104, SmATA 27N*

Johnson, Maud Battle 1918?-1985 *SmATA 46N*

Johnson, Milton 1932- *AfroAA, BioIn 8, IlsCB 1957, -1967, InB&W 80, SmATA 31*

Johnson, Natalie *ConAu 30NR, SmATA X*
Main entry: Robison, Nancy L

Johnson, Neil 1954- *SmATA 73*

Johnson, Osa Helen 1894-1953 *AmAu&B, AuBYP 2, -3, BioIn 2, -3, -4, -6, -8, CurBio 40, -53, REnAL, WhAm 3, WhScrn 77, WomWMM*

Johnson, Osa Helen Leighty 1894-1953 *BioIn 16, InWom SUP*

Johnson, Owen McMahon 1878-1952 *AmAu&B, BioIn 1, -2, -4, ConAmL, DcAmAu, EncAB-A 15, EncMys, EncSF 93, ObitOF 79, OxCAmL 65, -83, OxCChiL, REnAL, TwCA, -SUP, WhAm 3*

Johnson, Pamela 1949- *SmATA 71*

Johnson, Pauline B *ConAu 1R, WhoAmA 73, -78*

Johnson, Peter 1930- *ConAu 65, Who 82, -83, -85, -92, WrDr 92*

Johnson, Peter, Sir 1930- *Who 90, WrDr 90*

Johnson, Peter Colpoys Paley, Sir 1930- *WrDr 94*

Johnson, Rebecca L 1956- *ConAu 136, SmATA 67, WrDr 94*

Johnson, Richard *ConAu 140, -X*
Main entry: Richey, David

Johnson, Richard 1573?-1659? *BioIn 3, DcNaB, OxCChiL, OxCEng 85*

Johnson, Richard 1734-1793 *CarSB, OxCChiL*

Johnson, Richard C 1919- *ConAu 33R*

Johnson, Richard Carl 1933- *WhoSSW 80, –82, –84*

Johnson, Richard Clayton 1930- *AmMWSc 82, –92, WhoAm 80, –82, –84, –90, –92, –94*

Johnson, Robert E *AuBYP 3*

Johnson, Robert E 1907- *AuBYP 2, BioIn 8, WhoFI 74*

Johnson, Robert E 1908?-1989 *ConAu 128*

Johnson, Robert Ivar 1933- *AmAu&B, AmMWSc 73P, –76P, ConAu 53, WhoAm 74, –76, –78, –80, –82, –84, –90, –92, WhoFI 74, WhoWor 74*

Johnson, Robert Underwood 1853-1937 *AmAu&B, AmLY, BenetAL 91, BbD, BiD&SB, BioIn 2, –4, –6, ChhPo, –S1, –S2, DcAmAu, DcNAA, HarEnUS, IndAu 1816, OxCAmL 65, –83, REn, REnAL, TwCA, –SUP, WhAm 1, WhNAA*

Johnson, Rossiter 1840-1931 *AmAu&B, BbD, BiD&SB, CarSB, ChhPo, –S1, DcAmAu, DcNAA, HarEnUS, OxCCan, REnAL, WhAm 1, WhNAA*

Johnson, Ryerson 1901- *AuBYP 2S, –3, ConAu 5R, –2NR, ScF&FL 92, SmATA 10*

Johnson, S Lawrence 1909-1978 *ConAu 29R, –12NR, IntAu&W 77, WrDr 76, –80*

Johnson, Scott 1952- *SmATA 76*

Johnson, Shirley King 1927- *BioIn 11, ConAu 9R, ForWC 70, SmATA 10, WrDr 76, –80, –82*

Johnson, Siddie Joe 1905-1977 *AuBYP 2, –3, BiDrLUS 70, BioIn 2, –7, –12, ChhPo S1, ConAu 106, JBA 51, SmATA 20N, TexWr, WhoLibS 55, –66*

Johnson, Spencer 1938?- *BioIn 13, ConAu 110, SmATA 38*

Johnson, Sylvia A *SmATA 52*

Johnson, William Martin 1862- *WhAm 4, WhAmArt 85*

Johnson, William R *ConAu 17R, –7NR, SmATA 38*

Johnson, William Weber 1909- *AmAu&B, AuBYP 2, –3, BioIn 8, –10, ConAu 17R, IntAu&W 77, –82, –91, SmATA 7, WhoAm 74, –76, WhoWest 74, –76, –78, WrDr 76, –80, –82, –84, –90, –92*

Johnson, William Weber 1909-1992 *ConAu 139, WrDr 94N*

Johnson, Winifred 1905- *ConAu 5R, ForWC 70*

Johnson Of Boone, Benj *MajAI*

Johnson Of Boone, Benj F *SmATA X*
Main entry: Riley, James Whitcomb

Johnston, Agnes Christine *AmWomPl, ConAu X, SmATA 2*
Main entry: Dazey, Agnes J

Johnston, Annie Fellows 1863-1931 *AmAu&B, AmWomPl, ArizL, BenetAL 91, BiDSA, BioIn 2, CarSB, ChhPo, ConAu 116, DcAmAu, DcLB 42, DcNAA, InWom SUP, IndAu 1816, JBA 34, LiHiK, OxCAmL 65, –83, OxCChiL, REnAL, SmATA 37, TwCA, –SUP, WhAm 1, WomWWA 14*

Johnston, Brenda A 1944- *ConAu 57*

Johnston, Charles Haven Ladd 1877-1943 *AmAu&B, AmLY, WhAm 2, WhNAA*

Johnston, Dorothy Grunbock 1915- *ConAu 5R, –5NR*

Johnston, Dorothy Grunbock 1915-1979 *BioIn 16*

Johnston, Dorothy Grunbock 1915-1987 *SmATA 54*

Johnston, Edith Constance Farrington 1890- *ArtsAmW 3, BioIn 1, –5, IlsCB 1744, –1946*

Johnston, Frederick Charles 1916- *AuBYP 2S, –3, WhoArt 80, –82, –84*

Johnston, Ginny *AuBYP 3*

Johnston, Ginny 1946- *BioIn 17, SmATA 60*

Johnston, H A S 1913-1967 *ConAu P-2, SmATA 14*
Pseud./variant:
Sturton, Hugh

Johnston, Janet 1944- *SmATA 71*

Johnston, Jennifer 1930- *BioIn 13, BlmGWL, ConAu 85, ConLC 7, ConNov 91, DcIrL, DcLB 14, EncBrWW, FemiCLE, InWom SUP, IntAu&W 91, Novels, Who 82, –83, –85, –90, –92, WorAu 1975, WrDr 90, –92, –94*

Johnston, Johanna 1914?-1982 *AuBYP 2, –3, BioIn 8, –11, –13, ConAu 57, –108, –7NR, FourBJA, SmATA 12, –33N*

Johnston, Laurie *AuBYP 2, –3, BioIn 8*

Johnston, Louisa Mae *AuBYP 3*

Johnston, Louisa Mae 1925- *AuBYP 2, BioIn 8*

Johnston, Mary 1870-1936 *AmAu&B, AmWomPl, BenetAL 91, BbD, BiDSA, BiD&SB, BioAmW, BioIn 4, –5, –6, –8, –12, BlmGWL, Chambr 3, ChhPo, CnDAL, ConAmL, ConAu 109, CyWA 58, DcAmAu, DcBiA, DcEnA A, DcLB 9, DcNAA, EncSoH, FemiCLE, InWom SUP, LongCTC, OxCAmL 65, –83, REn, REnAL, TwCA, TwCRHW 90, WhAm 1, WomWWA 14*

Johnston, Norma *BioIn 13, ConAu 105, –32NR, FifBJA, ScF&FL 92, SmATA 29, WrDr 84, –90, –92, –94*
Pseud./variant:
Bolton, Elizabeth
Chambers, Catherine E
Dryden, Pamela
Harris, Lavinia
Saint John, Nicole

Johnston, Portia *SmATA X*
Main entry: Takakjian, Portia

Johnston, Ralph E 1902- *AuBYP 2, –3, BioIn 8*

Johnston, Richard James Humphreys 1910- *AmAu&B, WhoAm 74, –76*

Johnston, Susan Taylor *AuBYP 3*

Johnston, Thomas 1945- *AuBYP 2S, –3, ConAu 104, ScF&FL 92*

Johnston, Tony 1942- *AuBYP 2S, –3, BioIn 11, ConAu 41R, SixBJA, SmATA 8*

Johnston, William 1924- *ConAu 85*

Johnston, William 1925- *IntAu&W 91, WrDr 90, –92*

Johnston, William Preston 1831-1899 *Alli SUP, AmAu, BiDSA, BiD&SB, BioIn 2, –3, ChhPo S2, CyEd, DcAmAu, DcNAA, HarEnUS, WhAm 1*

Johnstone, Anne G *IlsBYP*

Johnstone, Janet G *IlsBYP*

Johnstone, Kathleen Yerger 1906- *ConAu 9R, ForWC 70*

Jole, William *OxCChiL*

Jolly, Hugh Reginald 1918- *BlueB 76, ConAu 85, IntAu&W 77, Who 74, –82, –83, –85, WrDr 76, –80*

Jonas, Ann *ChlBIlD, SmATA 42*

Jonas, Ann 1932- *ChlLR 12, ConAu 136, MajAI, SmATA 50, WrDr 94*

Jonas, Arthur 1930- *ConAu 13R*

Jonas, Nita *ASCAP 66, ChhPo*

Jones, Adrienne 1915- *BioIn 10, ConAu 33R, –28NR, FifBJA, SmATA 7, –10AS, WhoAmW 77, WrDr 76, –80, –82, –84, –90, –92, –94*

Jones, Allan Frewin 1954- *TwCYAW*

Jones, Annabel
Main entry: Lewis, Mary Christianna Milne

Jones, Annabel 1907-1988 *ConAu X, –43NR, SmATA X, WrDr 82, –84*

Jones, Beryl Bailey *BioIn 5, IlsCB 1946*
Main entry: Bailey-Jones, Beryl

Jones, Betty Millsaps 1940- *SmATA 54*

Jones, C A *CarSB*

Jones, Candy d1990 *BioIn 16, –17, NewYTBS 90*

Jones, Candy 1925- *BioIn 6, ConAu 107, CurBio 61*

Jones, Candy 1925-1990 *ConAu 130, CurBio 90N*

Jones, Carol Ann 1942- *BioIn 8, IlsCB 1957*

Jones, Charles Martin 1912- *SmATA 53*
Pseud./variant:
Jones, Chuck

Jones, Charlotte Foltz 1945- *SmATA 77*

Jones, Christine 1937- *ConAu 61*

Jones, Chuck
Main entry: Jones, Charles Martin

Jones, Daisy Marvel 1906- *ConAu 17R, ForWC 70, IndAu 1917, LEduc 74, WhoWest 89*

Jones, David 1895-1974 *BioIn 4, –6, –8, –9, –10, –11, –12, –13, BlueB 76N, CasWL, ChhPo, –S2, CnDBLB 7, CnE&AP, CnMWL, ConAu 9R, –53, –28NR, ConLC 2, –4, –7, –13, ConPo 70, –75, DcBrAr 1, DcLB 20, –100, EncWL 2, LongCTC, MajTwCW, ModBrL, –S1, –S2, NewC, ObitOF 79, ObitT 1971, OxCEng 67, –85, OxCTwCA, PenC ENG, PhDcTCA 77, RAdv 1, REn, RfGEnL 91, TwCPaSc, TwCWr, WhAm 6, Who 74, WhoTwCL, WorAu 1950*

Jones, Diana Wynne 1934- *Au&Wr 71, BioIn 11, ChlFicS, ChlLR 23, ConAu 49, –4NR, ConLC 26, EncSF 93, FifBJA, IntAu&W 77, –91, MajAI, OxCChiL, ScF&FL 92, SmATA 9, –70, –7AS, TwCChW 78, –83, –89, TwCYAW, WhoAm 92, –94, WrDr 76, –80, –82, –84, –90, –92, –94*

Jones, Dorothy H 1919- *WhoLibS 55*

Jones, Dorothy Holder *ConAu 9R, ForWC 70*

Jones, Dorothy Holder 1925?-1991 *ConAu 134*

Jones, Douglas C 1924- *SmATA 52*

Jones, Edward H, Jr. 1922- *ConAu 13R*

Jones, Elizabeth Brown 1907- *ConAu 61, WhoAmW 83, –85, WhoMW 78, –80, –82, –84*
Pseud./variant:
Brown, Betty

Jones, Elizabeth Orton 1910- *AuBYP 2, –3, BioIn 1, –2, –4, –5, –7, –12, Cald 1938, ChhPo, –S1, ConAu 77, IlsBYP, IlsCB 1744, –1946, JBA 51, SmATA 18, Str&VC, WhAmArt 85, WhoAm 74, –76, –78, WhoAmA 73, –78, –80, –82, –84, WhoAmW 74*

Jones, Emrys 1920- *Au&Wr 71, BlueB 76, ConAu 17R, IntAu&W 82, Who 74, –82, –83, –85, –92, WrDr 76, –80, –82, –84, –90, –92, –94*

Jones, Emrys, Prof 1920- *Who 90*

Jones, Evan 1915- *AmAu&B, Au&Wr 71, BioIn 9, ConAu 9R, –6NR, SmATA 3*

Jones, Everett Le Roi 1934- *IntWW 89, –91*

Jones, Everett LeRoi 1934- *AmAu&B, BioIn 12, –13, CurBio 70, InB&W 80, IntAu&W 77, IntWW 74, –76, –78, –79, –80, –82, –83, MakMC, WorAu 1950*

Jones, Everett LeRoi
Main entry: Jones, LeRoi

Jones, Geraldine 1951- *SmATA 43*
Pseud./variant:
McCaughrean, Geraldine

Jones, Gillingham *ConAu X, –29NR, SmATA X*

Jones, Glyn *ScF&FL 92*

Jones, Glyn 1905- *Au&Wr 71, BioIn 10, –13, BlueB 76, CnMWL, ConAu 9R, –3NR, ConNov 72, –76, –82, –91, ConPo 70, –75, –80, –85, –91, DcLB 15, IntAu&W 77, –82, –91, ModBrL, WorAu 1950, WrDr 76, –80, –82, –84, –90, –92, –94*

Jones, Glyn 1908- *Who 92*

Jones, Glyn, Sir 1908- *Who 90*

Jones, Gwyn 1907- *Au&Wr 71, BioIn 11, –13, BlueB 76, CasWL, ConAu 117, ConNov 72, –76, –82, –91, DcLB 15, –139, IntAu&W 77, –82, –91, LongCTC, ModBrL, OxCCan, Who 74, –82, –83, –85, –92, WrDr 76, –80, –82, –84, –90, –92*

Jones, Gwyn, Prof 1907- *Who 90*

Jones, Gwyneth A *TwCChW 89, WrDr 90*

Jones, Gwyneth A 1952- *TwCSFW 91, WrDr 92, –94*

Jones, Harold 1904- *BioIn 1, –5, –8, –9, –12, ChhPo, ConAu 85, –15NR, DcBrAr 1, IlsBYP, IlsCB 1744, –1946, –1957, SmATA 14, ThrBJA, TwCPaSc, WhoArt 80, –82, –84, WhoChL*

Jones, Harold 1904-1992 *ConAu 139, SmATA 72*

Jones, Helen Hinckley *AuBYP 3*

Jones, Helen Hinckley 1903- *AuBYP 2, BioIn 4, –9, ChhPo S2, ConAu 5R, –5NR, IntAu&W 77, –82, SmATA 26, WhoAmW 75, WrDr 76, –80*
Pseud./variant:
Hinckley, Helen

Jones, Helen Louise 1903-1973 *BioIn 4, –9, –13, ConAu 104, SmATA 22N*

Jones, Hettie *DrAPF 89, –91, –93*

Jones, Hettie 1934- *AuBYP 2S, –3, BioIn 13, –16, ConAu 81, DrAPF 83, –85, SmATA 27, –42*

Jones, Hortense P 1918- *BioIn 11, ConAu 61, SmATA 9, WhoBlA 77*

Jones, Jessie Mae Orton 1887?-1983 *BioIn 2, ConAu 111, FifBJA, SmATA 37N*

Jones, John Beauchamp 1810-1866 *Alli, –SUP, AmAu, AmAu&B, BenetAL 91, BiDSA, BiD&SB, BioIn 4, –8, DcAmAu, DcLEL, DcNAA, OxCAmL 65, –83, REnAL, WhAm HS*

Jones, John Jay *CarSB*

Jones, John Robert 1926- *SmATA 76*
Pseud./variant:
Dalmas, John 1926-

Jones, Juanita Nuttall 1912- *AuBYP 2, –3, BioIn 8*

Jones, LeRoi *ConAu 38NR, ConDr 93, ConTFT 7, DrAPF 89, –91, –93, DrBlPA 90, IntDcT 2, MajTwCW*

Jones, LeRoi 1934- *BiDAfM, BioIn 7, –8, –9, –10, –11, –12, –13, –16, –17, BlueB 76, BroadAu, CasWL, ConAu 21R, ConDr 73, –77, –82, ConLC 1, –2, –10, ConNov 72, –76, –82, ConPo 70, –75, –80, –85, CroCAP, CroCD, DcLB DS8, DcLEL 1940, DrAPF 83, –85, EncAACR, EncWL, –SUP, EncWT, IntWW 75, –76, –77, –78, –79, –80, –81, –82, –83, LivgBAA, McGEWD 72, ModAL, –S1, ModWD, NotNAT, Novels, OxCAmL 65, –83, PenC AM, PlP&P A, RAdv 1, RComWL, SelBAAu, WebAB 74, –79, WebE&AL, WhoAm 74, –76, –78, –80, –82, –84, –90, –92, –94, WhoBlA 77, –80, –90, –92, –94, WhoTwCL, WhoWor 74, –78, WorAu 1950, WrDr 76, –80, –82, –84, –90, –92*
Pseud./variant:
Baraka, Imamu Amiri
Jones, Everett LeRoi

Jones, Lloid 1908- *AuBYP 2, –3, BioIn 8*

Jones, Lloyd E 1889-1958 *WhAm 3*

Jones, Louis C d1990 *NewYTBS 90*

Jones, Louis C 1908- *WhoAmA 91*

Jones, Louis C 1908-1990 *ConAu 133*

Jones, Louis Clark 1908- *ConAu 5R, DrAS 74H, –78H, –82H, WhoAm 74, –76, –78, WhoAmA 73, –78, –80, –82, –84, WhoE 74*

Jones, Louis Clark 1908-1990 *BioIn 17*

Jones, Marcia Thornton 1958- *SmATA 73*

Jones, Margaret Boone
Main entry: Zarif, Margaret Min'imah

Jones, Margaret Boone 1924-1983 *ConAu 25R, SmATA X*

Jones, Mary Alice 1898?-1980 *AuBYP 2, –3, BioIn 1, –2, –6, –7, –10, –12, ConAu 17R, EncWM, ForWC 70, MorJA, SmATA 6, WhoAmW 74, –75, –77*

Jones, Mary Voell 1933- *ConAu 21R, WhoAmW 74, WrDr 76, –80, –82, –84, –90, –92, –94*

Jones, McClure *ConAu 112, ScF&FL 92, SmATA 34*

Jones, Ossie Garfield 1884-1957 *BioIn 4*

Jones, Penelope 1938- *ConAu 81, –14NR, SmATA 31*

Jones, Peter 1921- *Au&Wr 71, ConAu 5R*

Jones, Raymond F 1915- *ConAu 106, ConSFA, EncSF 93, NewEScF, ScF&FL 92, TwCSFW 91, WhoSciF, WrDr 84, –90, –92, –94*

Jones, Rebecca C 1947- *ConAu 106, SmATA 33, WhoWrEP 89*

Jones, Rebecca Castaldi 1947- *WhoWrEP 92*

Jones, Richard 1926- *Au&Wr 71, BioIn 13, ConAu 49, –2NR, WrDr 76, –80, –82, –84, –90, –92, –94*

Jones, Richard C 1910- *BioIn 1, –5, IlsCB 1744, –1946*

Jones, Sanford W *SmATA X*
Main entry: Thorn, John

Jones, Terry 1942- *ConAu 35NR, ConTFT 7, HalFC 88, IntMPA 92, ScF&FL 92, SmATA 51, –67, Who 90, –92, WhoAm 90, –92, –94*

Jones, Terry 1942- *ConAu 141*
Pseud./variant:
Monty Python

Jones, Thomas Laird 1930- *WhoRel 75, –77*

Jones, Weyman 1928- *AuBYP 3, SmATA 11AS*

Jones, Weyman B 1928- *AuBYP 2, BioIn 8, –9, ConAu 17R, DcAmChF 1960, FourBJA, SmATA 4, WhoE 83*

Jones, Wilfred J 1888- *AmPB, BioIn 1, ConICB, IlsCB 1744, WhAmArt 85*

Jonk, Clarence 1906- *BioIn 11, ConAu 5R, IntAu&W 77, –82, SmATA 10*

Jonsson, Runer *TwCChW 89B*

Jonsson, Runer 1916- *IntAu&W 77, TwCChW 78B, –83B*

Joosse, Barbara M 1949- *SmATA 52*

Jordan, Don *AuBYP 3, BioIn 8, ConAu 139, –X, SmATA 73, –X*
Main entry: Howard, Vernon Linwood

Jordan, E L 1900- *SmATA 31*

Jordan, Elizabeth Garver 1865-1947 *InWom SUP*

Jordan, Elizabeth Garver 1867-1947 *AmAu&B, AmWomPl, BioIn 1, –4, –10, BkC 2, CarSB, CathA 1930, DcAmAu, DcNAA, REnAL, WhAm 2, WhNAA, WisWr, WomWWA 14*

Jordan, Emil Leopold 1900- *DrAS 74F, –78F, –82F*

Jordan, Hope Dahle 1905- *ConAu 77, –13NR, SmATA 15*

Jordan, Jael 1949- *SmATA 30*

Jordan, June *ChlLR 10, DrAPF 89, –91*

Jordan, June 1936- *AfrAmAl 6, AfrAmW, AuBYP 3, BenetAL 91, BlkAuII 92, BlmGWL, ConPo 91, DcAmChF 1960, FemiCLE, IntAu&W 91, MajAI, MajTwCW, NegAl 89, NotBlAW 92, TwCChW 89, TwCYAW, WrDr 90, –92*

Jordan, June M 1936- *WhoAm 90, –92, –94, WhoBlA 90, –92, –94*

Jordan, June Meyer 1936- *AuBYP 2S, BioIn 9, –12, –13, BlkAWP, ChhPo S1, –S2, ChlLR 10, ConAu 33R, ConLC 5, –11, –23, ConPo 80, –85, DcLB 38, DrAF 76, DrAP 75, DrAPF 83, –85, FourBJA, InB&W 80, InWom SUP, IntAu&W 77, IntWWP 82, LivgBAA, NegAl 83, OxCChiL, SelBAAf, SelBAAu, SmATA 4, TwCChW 78, –83, WhoAm 84, WhoAmW 75, –77, WhoBlA 77, –80, –85, WorAu 1975, WrDr 76, –80, –82, –84*
Pseud./variant:
Meyer, June

Jordan, Lee *ConAu 34NR, SmATA 66, WrDr 94*
Main entry: Scholefield, Alan

Jordan, Mildred A 1901- *AmAu&B, AmNov, BioIn 2, –4, –10, ConAu 25R, –P-2, CurBio 51, SmATA 5, TwCA SUP*

Jordan, Philip Dean 1940- *WhoRel 92*

Jordan, Philip Dillon 1903- *AuBYP 2, –3, BioIn 6, –8, ConAu 9R, DrAS 74H, –78H, IntAu&W 77, MinnWr, OhA&B, WhoAm 76, –78*

Jordan, Sherryl 1949- *SmATA 71*

Jorgensen, Mary Venn *AuBYP 3*

Jorgensen, Mary Venn 1908- *AuBYP 2, ConAu 1R, –1NR, SmATA 36*
Pseud./variant:
Adrian, Mary
Venn, Mary Eleanor

Jorgenson, Ivar *AuBYP 2, –3, BioIn 17, ConAu X, –36NR, DcLEL 1940, EncSF 93, MajAI, MajTwCW, SmATA X, ThrBJA, TwCSFW 91*
Main entry: Silverberg, Robert

J O Rocky, Jr.
Main entry: Maynes, J Oscar, Jr.

Joscelyn, Archie L 1899- *Au&Wr 71, ConAu 1R, –5NR, WhoPNW*
Pseud./variant:
Cody, Al
McKenna, Evelyn

Joseph, Alexander 1907-1976 *AmMWSc 73P, –76P, AuBYP 2, –3, BioIn 8, –11, ConAu 13R*

Joseph, Anne *SmATA 73*
Main entry: Coates, Anna

Joseph, Franz *ConAu X*
Main entry: Schnaubelt, Franz Joseph

Joseph, Franz 1914- *ScF&FL 92*

Joseph, James 1924- *SmATA 53*

Joseph, James Herz 1924- *ConAu 1R, IndAu 1917*
Pseud./variant:
Adams, Lowell
Alzada, Juan Sanchez
Perez, Walter

Joseph, Joan 1939- *ConAu 25R, –17NR, SmATA 34*

Joseph, Joseph M 1903-1979 *BioIn 13, SmATA 22*

Josephs, Anna Catherine *AuBYP 3*

Josh *MajAI*

Joshi, Niharika *DcChlFi*

Joslin, Sesyle 1929- *AuBYP 2, –3, Au&Wr 71, BioIn 8, –9, ConAu X, IntAu&W 91, SmATA 2, ThrBJA, TwCChW 78, WrDr 80, –82, –84, –90, –92, –94*
Pseud./variant:
Gibson, Josephine
Hine, Sesyle Joslin
Kirtland, G B

Jowett, Margaret 1921- *TwCChW 78, WrDr 80, –82, –84*

Joy, Charles Rhind 1885- *AuBYP 2, –3, BioIn 8, WhAm 7*

Joyce, Bill *SmATA 72*
Main entry: Joyce, William

Joyce, J Avery 1902-1987 *SmATA 50N*

Joyce, James 1882-1941 *AtlBL, AuBYP 2S, –3, BioIn 1, –2, –3, –4, –5, –6, –7, –8, –9, –10, –11, –12, –13, –16, –17, BlmGEL, BritWr 7, CasWL, Chambr 3, ChhPo, –S1, CnDBLB 6, CnMD, CnMWL, ConAu 104, CurBio 41,*

CyWA 58, –89, DcAmSR, DcIrL, DcIrW 1, DcLB 10, –19, –36, DcLEL, DcNaB 1941, Dis&D, EncWL, –2, EncWT, EvLB, LiExTwC, LongCEL, LongCTC, MagSWL, MajTwCW, MakMC, McGEWB, McGEWD 72, –84, ModBrL, –S1, –S2, ModWD, NewC, NewOxM, NotNAT B, Novels, ObitOF 79, OxCEng 67, –85, OxCMus, OxCThe 83, PenC ENG, PoIre, RAdv 1, RComWL, REn, RfGEnL 91, ShSCr 3, TwCA, –SUP, TwCLC 3, –8, –16, –35, –52, TwCWr, WebE&AL, WhDW, WhoTwCL, WorAlBi, WorAl, WorLitC, WrPh

Joyce, James Augustine 1882-1941 *DcIrB 88*

Joyce, James Augustine Aloysius 1882-1941 *RfGShF*

Joyce, James Avery 1902- *Au&Wr 71, BioIn 5, –11, ConAu 65, CurBio 59, IntAu&W 77, –82, SmATA 11, WhAm 9, WhoAm 74, –76, –82, –84, WhoWor 74, –78, –80, –82, –84*

Joyce, Jeremiah 1763-1816 *DcBiPP, DcNaB, OxCChiL*

Joyce, William 1957- *AuBYP 3, ChlBIlD, ChlLR 26, SixBJA, SmATA 72*
Pseud./variant:
Joyce, Bill

Joyce, William 1959?- *SmATA 46*

Joyner, Jerry 1938- *ConAu 107, IlsBYP, SmATA 34, WhoAm 78, –80*

Jucker, Sita 1921- *BioIn 10, ConAu 29R, –12NR, IlsBYP, IntAu&W 77, –82, SmATA 5*

Judah, Aaron 1923- *Au&Wr 71, ConAu 103, TwCChW 78, –83, –89, WrDr 80, –82, –84, –90, –92, –94*

Judd, Alfred *WhoLA*

Judd, Denis 1938- *ConAu 13NR, IntAu&W 82, –91, SmATA 33, WrDr 82, –84, –90, –92, –94*

Judd, Frances K *ConAu 134, –P-2, MajAI, SmATA 1, –65*
Main entry: Benson, Mildred Augustine Wirt
Stratemeyer, Edward L

Judd, William Wallace 1915- *AmMWSc 73P, –82, –92*

Judson, Clara 1879-1960 *AuBYP 3*

Judson, Clara Ingram 1879-1960 *AmAu&B, AuBYP 2, Au&ICB, BioIn 1, –2, –3, –5, –7, CarSB, ConAu 137, CurBio 48, IndAu 1816, JBA 51, MajAI, OxCCan, SmATA 27, –38, WhAm 4, WhJnl, WhNAA*

Judson, Edward Zane Carroll 1823?-1886 *Alli SUP, AmAu, AmAu&B, BioIn 1, –2, –7, –9, DcAmAu, DcNAA, EncAJ, HsB&A, OhA&B, OxCAmH, OxCAmL 65, –83, REn, REnAL, WebAB 74, –79, WhAm HS*

Judson, Harry Pratt 1849-1927 *Alli SUP, AmAu&B, BiD&SB, DcNAA, HarEnUS, WhAm 1*

Judson, Jeanne 1888?-1981 *BioIn 12*

Judy, Stephen N *TwCYAW*
Main entry: Tchudi, Stephen N

Jukes, Mavis *BioIn 16, SmATA 43*

Jukes, Mavis 1947- *ConAu 127, MajAI, SixBJA, SmATA 72, –12AS*

Julesberg, Elizabeth Rider Montgomery *AuBYP 3*

Julesberg, Elizabeth Rider Montgomery 1902-1985 *ConAu 42NR*

Julian, Nancy R *AuBYP 2, –3, BioIn 7*

Jullian, Philippe 1919-1977 *BioIn 5, –11, ConAu 73, IlsCB 1946*

Jumpp, Hugo *ConAu X, SmATA 4, –X, WhNAA*
Main entry: MacPeek, Walter G

Jupo, Frank J 1904- *AuBYP 2, –3, BioIn 5, –8, –10, ConAu 5R, –2NR, IlsCB 1946, SmATA 7, WrDr 76, –80, –82, –84*

Jurgensen, Barbara 1928- *ConAu 17R, ForWC 70, IntAu&W 77, –82, WhoAmW 75, –93, WhoMW 92, WhoRel 92, WrDr 76, –80, –82, –84*

Jurmain, Suzanne 1945- *SmATA 72*

Juster, Norton 1929- *AuBYP 2, –3, Au&Wr 71, BioIn 8, –9, ConAu 13R, –13NR, DcAmChF 1960, FourBJA, IntAu&W 91, MajAI, OxCChiL, SmATA 3, TwCChW 78, –83, –89, TwCYAW, WhoChL, WrDr 80, –82, –84, –90, –92, –94*

Justus, May 1898- *AmAu&B, AuBYP 2, –3, BioIn 2, –7, –9, ChhPo, –S1, –S2, ConAu 9R, ForWC 70, JBA 51, SmATA 1*

Juvenilia *SmATA X*
Main entry: Taylor, Ann

K

Kabdebo, Tamas
Main entry: Kabdebo, Thomas George

Kabdebo, Thomas George 1934- *BioIn 11, ConAu 53, SmATA 10, WhoLib 72, WrDr 76, -80, -82, -84*
Pseud./variant:
Kabdebo, Tamas

Kabibble, Osh *SmATA X*
Main entry: Jobb, Jamie

Kabotie, Fred 1900- *AmPB, BioIn 9, -11, ConAu 118, WhAmArt 85, WhoAm 74, -76, -78, -80, WhoAmA 78, -80, -82, -84, -86*

Kabotie, Fred 1900-1986 *BioIn 17*

Kadesch, Robert R 1922- *AmMWSc 73P, -76P, -82, -86, -89, -92, AuBYP 2S, -3, BioIn 14, ConAu 57, SmATA 31, WhoAm 74, -76, -78, -80, WhoTech 82, -84*

Kaempfert, Wade *ConAu 141, EncSF 93, MajTwCW, SmATA 76*
Main entry: del Rey, Lester

Kaestner, Erich
Main entry: Kastner, Erich

Kaestner, Erich d1974 *BioIn 10, -12, ConAu 49, -73, NewYTBS 74, ObitOF 79*

Kaestner, Erich 1899-1974 *ConAu 40NR, MajAI*

Kafka, Sherry 1937- *ConAu 21R*

Kahiga, Samuel 1940?- *AfrA*

Kahl, Jonathan D 1959- *SmATA 77*

Kahl, M P 1934- *BioIn 15, -16, ConAu 107, SmATA 37*

Kahl, Virginia 1919- *AuBYP 3, BioIn 15, -16, SmATA 48, TwCChW 89*

Kahl, Virginia C 1919- *WrDr 86*

Kahl, Virginia Caroline 1919- *AuBYP 2, BioIn 5, -6, -7, -8, BkP, ChhPo, -S1, ConAu 49, -2NR, IlsCB 1946, -1957, -1967, IntAu&W 77, MorJA, SmATA 38, TwCChW 78, -83, WhoAm 82, -84, WrDr 80, -84*

Kahler, Hugh M 1883-1969 *BenetAL 91*

Kahler, Hugh MacNair 1883-1969 *AmAu&B, BioIn 8, ConAu 102, REnAL, WhAm 5, WhNAA*

Kahn, Ely Jacques 1916- *BioIn 16*

Kahn, Ely Jacques, Jr. 1916- *AmAu&B, Au&Wr 71, BioIn 2, -4, -11, ConAu 65, TwCA SUP, WhoAm 74, -76, -78, -80, -82, -84, -86, -88, -90, -92, -94, WhoAmJ 80, WhoE 74, -93*

Kahn, Ismith 1925- *BioIn 9*

Kahn, Joan 1914- *AuBYP 2S, -3, BioIn 3, -8, ConAu 77, ScF&FL 92, SmATA 48, WhoAm 84*

Kahn, Roger *BioIn 14, -15, -16*

Kahn, Roger 1927- *AuBYP 2, -3, Ballpl 90, BiDAmSp Sup, BioIn 4, -8, -9, -10, -11, -12, -13, ConAu 25R, ConLC 30, Conv 3, SmATA 37, WhoAm 84, -86, -88, -90, -92, -94, WhoE 77, WhoUSWr 88, WhoWrEP 89, -92, WrDr 92, -94*

Kaiser, Ernest 1915- *BlkAWP, ConAu 49, -1NR, -16NR, InB&W 80, -85, LivgBAA, WhoBlA 75*

Kaizuki, Kiyonori 1950- *SmATA 72*

Kakacek, Gen *AuBYP 2, -3, BioIn 8*

Kakimoto, Kozo 1915- *BioIn 11, SmATA 11*

Kalashnikoff, Nicholas 1888-1961 *AmAu&B, BioIn 6, -12, -14, ConAu 73, MorJA, REnAL, SmATA 16*

Kalashnikoff, Nicholas S 1888-1961 *BenetAL 91*

Kalb, Jonah 1926- *AuBYP 2S, –3, BioIn 13, ConAu 53, –4NR, SmATA 23*

Kalb, S William 1897- *ConAu 33R, WhoWorJ 72, –78*

Kaler, James Otis 1848-1912 *Alli SUP, AmAu&B, BenetAL 91, BiD&SB, BioIn 2, –12, –15, CarSB, ConAu 120, DcAmAu, DcLB 42, DcNAA, JBA 34, –51, OxCAmL 65, –83, OxCChiL, SmATA 15, WhAm 1*
Pseud./variant:
Otis, James

Kalina, Sigmund 1911-1977 *AuBYP 2S, –3, ConAu 49, –3NR*

Kalish, Lionel 1931- *ChhPo S1, DcCAr 81*

Kalman, Bobbie 1947- *SmATA 63*

Kalman, Maira 1949?- *ChlLR 32*

Kalman, Rolf *OxCCan SUP*

Kalmenoff, Matthew 1905- *IlsBYP, WhAmArt 85*

Kalnay, Francis 1899- *AuBYP 2, –3, BioIn 8, –10, –14, BkCL, ConAu 49, SmATA 7*

Kalow, Gisela 1946- *BioIn 12, –14, ConAu 107, IlsCB 1967, SmATA 32*

Kalusky, Rebecca *AuBYP 2, –3, BioIn 8*

Kamen, Gloria 1923- *BioIn 11, ConAu 114, –35NR, IlsBYP, SmATA 9, WhoAmA 78, –80, –82, –84, –86, WhoE 86*

Kamerman, Sylvia E *ConAu X, SmATA X*
Main entry: Burack, Sylvia

Kamm, Herbert 1917- *ConAu 69, WhoAm 74, –76, –78, –80, –82, –84, –86, –88, –90, –92, –94, WhoMW 82, –84, WhoWest 94*

Kamm, Josephine 1905- *Au&Wr 71, BioIn 13, ConAu 9R, –5NR, OxCChiL, SmATA 24, TwCChW 78, –83, WrDr 76, –80, –82, –84, –90*

Kamm, Josephine 1905-1989 *TwCChW 89, TwCYAW*

Kamm, Josephine 1906- *WrDr 86, –88*

Kampen, Owen *IlsBYP*

Kandell, Alice S 1938- *BioIn 14, IntAu&W 91, WrDr 86, –88*

Kandell, Alice Susan 1938- *ConAu 33R, –13NR, IntAu&W 77, SmATA 35, WrDr 76, –80, –82, –84*

Kandoian, Ellen *AuBYP 3*

Kane, Basil G 1931- *ConAu 69, –24NR*

Kane, Bob *ArtCS, BioIn 16, EncMys, PrintW 85*

Kane, Bob 1916- *Au&Arts 8, EncACom*

Kane, George Francis 1948- *WhoAm 74*

Kane, Henry Bugbee 1902-1971 *AmPB, AuBYP 2, –3, BioIn 1, –5, –8, –9, –12, ChhPo, –S1, –S2, ConAu 73, IlsCB 1744, –1946, –1957, –1967, SmATA 14*

Kane, L A *SmATA X*
Main entry: Mannetti, Lisa

Kane, Paul 1810-1871 *Alli, ArtsEM, BbtC, BioIn 2, –3, –8, –9, –10, –11, –13, –16 DcCanB 10, DcNAA, OxCArt, OxCCan, OxCCanL, OxDcArt, WhNaAH*

Kane, Robert S 1925- *ConAu 9R, –7NR, –23NR*

Kane, Robert William 1910- *BioIn 5, –12, IlsCB 1946, SmATA 18, WhAmArt 85*

Kanetzke, Howard W 1932- *BioIn 15, ConAu 112, SmATA 38*

Kanetzke, Howard William 1932- *IntAu&W 86*

Kantor, MacKinlay 1904-1977 *AmAu&B, AmNov, AuSpks, AuBYP 2, –3, Benet 87, BenetAL 91, BioIn 1, –2, –3, –4, –7, –8, –9, –10, –11, –12, –16, –17, ChhPo S1, CnDAL, ConAmA, ConAu 61, –73, ConLC 7, ConNov 72, –76, ConSFA, DcLB 9, –102, DcLEL, EncFWF, EncMys, EncSF 93, FilmgC, HalFC 84, –88, IntAu&W 77, ModAL, Novels, ObitOF 79, OxCAmL 65, –83, PenC AM, REn, REnAL, ScFSB, TwCA, –SUP, TwCRHW 90, TwCWW 91, TwCWr, WhAm 7, WhScrn 83, WhoAm 74, –76, –78, WrDr 76*

Kantrowitz, Mildred *AuBYP 3*

Kanzawa, Toshiko *ConAu X, SmATA X*
Main entry: Furukawa, Toshi

Kaplan, Albert A *AuBYP 2, –3, BioIn 8*

Kaplan, Anne Bernays
Main entry: Bernays, Anne

Kaplan, Anne Bernays 1930- *ConAu 1R, –5NR, SmATA 32*

Kaplan, Arthur 1925- *ConAu 5R*

Kaplan, Bess 1927- *BioIn 13, DcChlFi, IntAu&W 82, SmATA 22, WhoCanL 85, –87, –92*

Kaplan, Boche 1926- *BioIn 12, -13, ConAu 21R, -10NR, IlsBYP, IlsCB 1967, SmATA 24*
Pseud./variant:
Roche, A K

Kaplan, Irma 1900- *BioIn 11, ConAu 29R, SmATA 10*

Kaplan, Jean Caryl Kom *AuBYP 3*

Kaplan, Jean Caryl Korn 1926- *BioIn 11, ConAu 5R, SmATA 10*
Pseud./variant:
Caryl, Jean

Kaplan, Margaret *AuBYP 2, -3, BioIn 8*

Kaplan, Philip 1916- *ConAu 13R*

Kaplan, Richard 1929- *ConAu 73, WhoAm 74, -76, -86, -92, -94*

Kaplan, Saul Howard 1938- *ConAu 25R*

Kaplow, Robert 1954- *SmATA 70*

Kapp, Paul *AuBYP 3*

Kapp, Paul 1907-1984 *ASCAP 66, AuBYP 2, BioIn 8, -13, ChhPo, -S1, -S2*

Karageorge, Michael *AuBYP 3, ConAu X, -34NR, EncSF 93, IntAu&W 82X, MajTwCW, SmATA X*
Main entry: Anderson, Poul

Karasz, Ilonka 1896-1981 *BioIn 1, -5, -12, -13, ChhPo, DcWomA, IlsBYP, IlsCB 1946, NewYTBS 81, SmATA 29N, WhAmArt 85*

Karasz, Mariska 1898-1960 *BioIn 2, -5, InWom SUP, WhoAmA 80N, -82N, -86N, -89N, -91N*

Karen, Ruth 1922- *AuBYP 2, -3, BioIn 8, -11, ConAu 17R, -11NR, SmATA 9, WhoAmW 74, -75, -83, -85, -87, WrDr 76, -80, -82, -84, -86, -88*

Karen, Ruth 1922-1987 *BioIn 15, -16, ConAu 123, SmATA 54N*

Kariuki, Elijah *TwCChW 89*

Kark, Nina Mary *AuBYP 3, ConAu 29NR, Who 88, -92*
Main entry: Bawden, Nina

Kark, Nina Mary 1925- *AuBYP 2S, ConAu 17R, -8NR, SmATA 4, Who 74, -82, -83, -85, WhoAmW 74*

Kark, Nina Mary, Mrs *Who 90*

Karl, Herb 1938- *SmATA 73*

Karl, Jean 1927- *AuBYP 3, BioIn 14, -16, SmATA 10AS*

Karl, Jean E 1927- *ScF&FL 92*

Karl, Jean Edna 1927- *AuBYP 2S, BioIn 11, ChhPo S1, ConAu 29R, -12NR, FifBJA, ForWC 70, SmATA 34, WhoAm 76, -78, -80, -82, -84, -86, -88, -90, WhoAmW 74, -75, WhoUSWr 88, WhoWrEP 89, -92*

Karlin, Bernie 1927- *BioIn 17, ConAu 136, SmATA 68, WrDr 94*

Karlin, Eugene 1918- *BioIn 7, -8, -11, IlsBYP, IlsCB 1957, SmATA 10, WhAmArt 85*

Karlin, Muriel Schoenbrun *ConAu 85, -X, WhoAmJ 80, WhoAmW 74, -77, WhoE 75, -77, -81*

Karlin, Nurit *BioIn 17, SmATA 63*

Karney, Beulah Mullen *ConAu 13R*

Karp, Naomi 1926- *AuBYP 3*

Karp, Naomi J 1926- *AuBYP 2S, ConAu 81, SmATA 16*

Karp, Walter *AuBYP 2S, -3, BioIn 16*

Karp, Walter d1989 *NewYTBS 89*

Karp, Walter 1934?-1989 *ConAu 129*

Kashiwagi, Isami 1925- *BioIn 5, -11, IlsBYP, IlsCB 1946, SmATA 10*

Kasper, Vancy *DcChlFi*

Kassem, Lou *BioIn 16, -17, SmATA 51*

Kassem, Lou 1931- *ConAu 128, ScF&FL 92, SmATA 62*

Kassil, Lev 1905- *TwCWr*

Kassil, Lev Abramovich 1905-1970 *DcRusLS, HanRL*

Kassirer, Norma *AuBYP 2, -3, BioIn 8*

Kastel, Warren *MajAI*

Kastner, Erich *TwCChW 89B*

Kastner, Erich 1899- *AuBYP 3*

Kastner, Erich 1899-1974 *AuBYP 2, BioIn 1, -5, -6, -7, -8, -9, -10, -12, -16, CasWL, ChlLR 4, ClDMEL 47, CnMD, CurBio 64, -74, DcLB 56, EncWL, -2, EncWT, EvEuW, HalFC 84, -88, IntWW 74, ModGL, ModWD, ObitT 1971, OxCChiL, OxCGer 76, -86, PenC EUR, ScF&FL 92, SmATA 14, ThrBJA,*

TwCChW 78B, -83B, WhDW, WhAm 6, Who 74, WhoChL, WhoWor 74, WorAu 1950, WrChl
Pseud./variant:
Kaestner, Erich

Kastner, Jill Marie 1964- *SmATA 70*

Kastner, Jonathan 1937- *ConAu 25R*

Kastner, Marianna 1940- *ConAu 25R*

Kasuya, Masahiro 1937- *BioIn 16, ConAu 29NR, SmATA 51*

Kasza, Keiko *AuBYP 3*

Katchamakoff, Atanas 1898- *ArtsAmW 2, BioIn 1, IlsCB 1744, WhAmArt 85*

Katchen, Carole 1944- *BioIn 10, -11, ConAu 61, SmATA 9*

Kathryn *ConAu X, SmATA X*
Main entry: Searle, Kathryn Adrienne

Katona, Robert 1949- *BioIn 12, SmATA 21*

Katsarakis, Joan Harries *ConAu X, SmATA X*

Katsarakis, Joan Harris
Main entry: Harries, Joan

Katz, Bobbi 1933- *BioIn 11, ChhPo S2, ConAu 37R, -16NR, -37NR, IntAu&W 91, SmATA 12, WrDr 76, -80, -82, -84, -86, -88, -90, -92, -94*

Katz, Fred 1938- *BioIn 10, ConAu 49, SmATA 6*

Katz, Herbert 1930- *AuBYP 3*

Katz, Herbert Melvin 1930- *AuBYP 2S, ConAu 103, WhoAm 74, -80, -82, -84*

Katz, Jacqueline Hunt *AuBYP 2S, -3*

Katz, Jane Bresler 1934- *ConAu 85, SmATA 33*

Katz, Jonathan *DrAPF 87, -89, -91*

Katz, Jonathan 1938- *ConAu 85, DrAPF 83, -85*

Katz, Jonathan Ned 1938- *GayLL*

Katz, Marjorie P *AuBYP 2S, ConAu X, SmATA X*
Main entry: Weiser, Marjorie P K

Katz, Marjorie P 1934- *AuBYP 3, BioIn 14*

Katz, Welwyn 1948- *TwCChW 89, WrDr 90, -92*

Katz, Welwyn Wilton *BioIn 17*

Katz, Welwyn Wilton 1948- *DcChlFi, ScF&FL 92, SmATA 62, WhoAm 92, WhoCanL 87, -92, WrDr 94*

Katz, William Loren 1927- *AuBYP 2S, -3, BioIn 11, BlueB 76, ConAu 21R, -9NR, IntAu&W 77, SmATA 13, WhoAm 74, -76, -78, -80, -82, -84, -86, -88, -90, -92, -94, WhoE 74, WhoUSWr 88, WhoWrEP 89, -92, WrDr 80, -82, -84, -86, -88, -90, -92, -94*

Kauffer, Edward McKnight 1890?-1954 *BioIn 14*

Kauffer, Edward McKnight 1891-1954 *ArtsAmW 3, BioIn 1, -3, -4, -8, -12, ConDes 84, DcBrAr 2, DcBrBI, IlsCB 1744, ObitOF 79*

Kaufman, Bel *ArtclWW 2, Au&Arts 4, BioIn 16, DrAPF 87, -89, -91, IntAu&W 89, -91, SmATA 57, WhoAm 86, -88, -90, -92, -94, WhoAmW 87, -89, WhoUSWr 88, WhoWrEP 89, -92, WrDr 86, -88, -90, -92, -94*

Kaufman, Bob 1925- *BioIn 13, BlkAWP, ConAu 41R, ConPo 70, DcLB 16, -41, DrAP 75, LivgBAA, PenC AM, RAdv 1*

Kaufman, Bob 1925-1986 *BlkWr 1, ConAu 118, -22NR, ConLC 49*

Kaufman, Joe 1911- *BioIn 2, -14, ConAu 107, SmATA 33, WhAmArt 85, WhoAmA 73, -78, -80, -82, -84, -86, -89, -91, WhoE 91, -93*

Kaufman, Mervyn Douglas 1932- *BioIn 9, ConAu 5R, SmATA 4, WhoAm 82, -84, -86, -88, -90, -92, -94*

Kaufmann, Angelika 1935- *BioIn 12, SmATA 15*

Kaufmann, Helen 1887- *AuBYP 3*

Kaufmann, Helen 1887-1978 *Baker 92*

Kaufmann, Helen L 1887- *AuBYP 2S, ConAu 5R, -7NR, WhAm 8, WhoMus 72*

Kaufmann, John 1931- *BioIn 8, -12, ConAu 81, IlsBYP, IlsCB 1957, -1967, SmATA 18*
Pseud./variant:
Swift, David

Kaufmann, John Henry 1934- *AmMWSc 85*

Kaula, Edna Mason 1906- *AuBYP 2, -3, BioIn 8, -11, ConAu 5R, SmATA 13*

Kaur, Simren 1940- *DcChlFi*

Kavaler, Lucy 1930- *AuBYP 2, –3, BioIn 8, –13, ConAu 57, –7NR, –22NR, SmATA 23, WhoWrEP 92*

Kavaler, Lucy Estrin 1930- *IntAu&W 91*

Kavalik, Vladimir 1928- *ConAu 25R*

Kavanagh, Patrick J 1931- *CamGLE*

Kavanagh, Patrick Joseph 1931- *BioIn 15, –17, EngPo*

Kavanagh, Patrick Joseph Gregory 1931- *Au&Wr 71, ConAu 81, ConPo 70, –75, DcLEL 1940, WrDr 76, –80*

Kavanaugh, Bill *ArtCS*

Kavanaugh, James J 1929?- *BioIn 8, ConAu 13R, WhoAm 74, –76, WrDr 80*

Kavet, Robert 1924- *ConAu 37R*

Kay, Gertrude Alice 1884-1939 *AmAu&B, ChhPo, ConICB, DcNAA, DcWomA, OhA&B, WhAm 1, WhAmArt 85, WhNAA*

Kay, Helen *AuBYP 3*
Main entry: Goldfrank, Helen Colodny

Kay, Helen 1912- *AuBYP 2, BioIn 7, –10, ConAu X, ForWC 70, SmATA 6, WhoAmW 75, –77, –91, –93, WhoE 85, –86, –89, –91, –93, WhoWor 89, –91, –93, WhoWrEP 92*

Kay, Kenneth 1915- *ConAu 9R, –6NR*

Kay, Mara *BioIn 11, ConAu 5R, –2NR, ForWC 70, IntAu&W 77, –82, –86, –89, –91, SmATA 13, WrDr 76, –80, –82, –84, –86, –88, –90*

Kay, Terence 1918- *ConAu 17R*
Pseud./variant:
Kay, Terry

Kay, Terry
Main entry: Kay, Terence

Kaye, Danny *BioIn 14, –15, –16*

Kaye, Danny d1987 *LesBEnT 92, Who 88N*

Kaye, Danny 1908?-1987 *HalFC 88*

Kaye, Danny 1913- *ConTFT 3, IntMPA 86, NewGrDA 86, OxCAmT 84, WhAm 9, WhoAm 86, WhoWor 87*

Kaye, Danny 1913-1987 *AnObit 1987, Baker 92, ConAu 121, ConNews 87-2, CurBio 87N, EncAFC, NewAmDM, NewYTBS 87, OxCPMus, PenEncP, SmATA 50N, WhoCom, WorAlBi*

Kaye, George 1911- *WhoAmA 73, –78, –80, –82, –84, –86, –89, –91, WhoE 85, –86, –89*

Kaye, Geraldine 1925- *ChlFicS, ConAu 22NR, IntAu&W 86, –89, –91, TwCChW 89, WhoWor 91, WrDr 86, –88, –90, –92, –94*

Kaye, Geraldine Hughesdon 1925- *Au&Wr 71, BioIn 11, ConAu 13R, –7NR, IntAu&W 77, –82, SmATA 10, TwCChW 78, –83, WhoWor 80, WrDr 76, –80, –82, –84*

Kaye, Judy *SmATA 71*
Main entry: Baer, Judy

Kaye, M M 1908- *BioIn 17, ConAu 24NR, IntAu&W 91, MajTwCW, SmATA 62, TwCRHW 90, WrDr 86, –92*

Kaye, M M 1909- *ScF&FL 92*

Kaye, Marilyn 1949- *AuBYP 3, BioIn 16, ConAu 24NR, ScF&FL 92, SmATA 56*
Pseud./variant:
Blair, Shannon

Kaye, Mary Margaret 1908- *WrDr 94*
Pseud./variant:
Hamilton, Mollie
Kaye, Mollie

Kaye, Mollie
Main entry: Kaye, Mary Margaret

Kaye, Mollie 1908- *MajTwCW, SmATA X*

Keach, Benjamin 1640-1704 *BioIn 16, DcBiPP, DcNaB, EncSoB, LuthC 75, OxCChiL*

Keane, Bil *EncACom*

Keane, Bil 1922- *BioIn 9, –14, –15, –16, ConAu 33R, –13NR, ConGrA 1, EncTwCJ, SmATA 4, WhoAm 78, –80, –82, –84, –86, –88, –90, –92, –94, WhoAmA 73, –78, –80, –82, –84, –86, –89, –91, WhoWest 76, –78*

Keary, Annie 1825-1879 *BbD, BiD&SB, BritAu 19, CamGEL, CamGLE, CasWL, CelCen, ChhPo, –S1, DcNaB, EvLB, FemiCLE, InWom SUP, OxCChiL, StaCVF, Str&VC, TelT*

Keating, Bern
Main entry: Keating, Leo Bernard

Keating, Bern 1915- *ConAu X, IntAu&W 91, SmATA X, WrDr 76, –80, –82, –84, –86, –88, –90, –92, –94*

Keating, Lawrence Alfred 1903-1966 *AuBYP 2, –3, BioIn 7, –13, ConAu 5R, SmATA 23*
Pseud./variant:
Bassett, John Keith
Thomas, H C

Keating, Leo Bernard 1915- *BioIn 11, ConAu 29R, SmATA 10*
Pseud./variant:
Keating, Bern

Keating, Norma *AuBYP 2, –3, BioIn 8*

Keats, Emma 1899?-1979? *ConAu 135, SmATA 68*
Pseud./variant:
Sanderson, Margaret Love

Keats, Ezra 1916-1983 *AuBYP 3*

Keats, Ezra Jack 1916- *WhoAmA 86N*

Keats, Ezra Jack 1916-1983 *AmPB, AnObit 1983, AuBYP 2, Au&ICB, AuNews 1, BioIn 5, –6, –7, –8, –9, –10, –12, –13, –14, –16, BioNews 74, BkP, ChhPo S1, –S2, ChlBIlD, ChlLR 1, ConAu 77, –109, DcLB 61, IlsBYP, IlsCB 1946, –1957, –1967, MajAI, MorJA, NewYTBS 83, NewbC 1956, OxCChiL, SmATA 14, –34N, –57, TwCChW 78, –83, –89, WhAm 8, WhoAm 74, –76, –78, –80, –82, WhoAmA 78, –80, –82, –84, –89N, –91N, WrDr 76, –80, –82, –84*

Keats, John *BioIn 15*

Keats, John 1795-1821 *Alli, AnCL, AtlBL, Benet 87, BiD&SB, BioIn 1, –2, –3, –4, –5, –6, –7, –8, –9, –10, –11, –12, –13, –14, –15, –16, –17, BlmGEL, BritAu 19, BritWr 4, CamGEL, CamGLE, CasWL, CelCen, Chambr 3, ChhPo, –S1, –S2, CnDBLB 3, CnE&AP, CrtT 2, CyWA 58, DcBiPP, DcEnA, DcEnL, DcEuL, DcLB 96, –110, DcLEL, DcNaB, Dis&D, EvLB, LongCEL, MagSWL, McGEWB, MouLC 2, NewC, NinCLC 8, OxCEng 67, –85, OxCMus, PenC ENG, PenEncH, PoeCrit 1, RAdv 1, –13-1, RComWL, REn, RfGEnL 91, Str&VC, WebE&AL, WhDW, WorAlBi, WorAl, WorLitC, WrPh*

Keats, Mark 1905- *ConAu 77*

Kedzie, Daniel P 1930- *WhoIns 93*

Kedzie, Daniel Peter 1930- *ConAu 17R, IntAu&W 77, WhoFI 83, WhoMW 92, WrDr 76, –80, –82, –84, –86, –88, –90*

Keefe, John Edwin 1942- *ConAu 107, DrAS 74F*

Keegan, Marcia 1943- *BioIn 11, ConAu 49, –32NR, ICPEnP A, IntAu&W 77, MacBEP, SmATA 9, WhoAmW 77*

Keel, Frank
Main entry: Keeler, Ronald F

Keeler, Katherine 1887- *AuBYP 2, BioIn 7, DcWomA*

Keeler, Ronald F 1913-1983 *BioIn 16, SmATA 47*
Pseud./variant:
Keel, Frank

Keely, Harry Harris 1904- *ConAu 65*

Keen, Martin L 1913- *AuBYP 3*

Keen, Martin Leon 1913- *AuBYP 2S, BioIn 9, ConAu 33R, SmATA 4, WhoE 75, WrDr 76, –80, –82, –84, –86, –88, –90*

Keenan, Deborah *DrAPF 87, –89, –91, –93*

Keenan, Deborah 1950- *ConAu 69, –11NR, –30NR, DrAPF 83, –85*

Keenan, Martha 1927- *ConAu 77*

Keene, Carolyn *AmAu&B, ConAu 134, –X, –37NR, EncMys, EncSF 93, InWom SUP, MajAI, OxCChiL, ScF&FL 92, SmATA 1, –65, –X, WebAB 74, –79*
Main entry: Adams, Harriet S
Stratemeyer, Edward L

Keenen, George *AuBYP 2S, –3*

Keeping, Charles 1924- *BioIn 14, –16, IntAu&W 91, WrDr 86, –88*

Keeping, Charles 1924-1988 *AnObit 1988, ConAu 125, ScF&FL 92, SmATA 56N, –69, TwCChW 89*

Keeping, Charles William James 1924- *ArtsCL, Au&Wr 71, BioIn 6, –8, –9, –10, –11, –12, BritCA, ConAu 21R, –11NR, IlsBYP, IlsCB 1957, –1967, OxCChiL, PiP, SmATA 9, ThrBJA, TwCChW 78, –83, Who 74, –82, –83, –85, –88, WrDr 82, –84*

Keeping, Charles William James 1924-1988 *ConAu 43NR, MajAI*

Keeshan, Robert J 1927- *BioIn 4, –5, –6, –7, –10, BioNews 74, ConAu 5R, –5NR, ConTFT 4, CurBio 65, IntMPA 75, –77, NewYTBE 72, SmATA 32, WebAB 74, –79, WhoAm 74, WhoWor 74*
Pseud./variant:
Captain Kangaroo

Keeton, Elizabeth B 1919- *ConAu 29R*

Kehret, Peg 1936- *SmATA 73*

Keigwin, Richard Prescott 1883- *ChhPo*

Keillor, Garrison *BioIn 14, –15, –16, –17, ConAu 36NR, DrAPF 87, –89, –91, –93, MajTwCW*

Keillor, Garrison 1942- *Au&Arts 2, BenetAL 91, BestSel 89-3, ConLC 40,*

DcLB Y87B, EncAHmr, IntAu&W 91, MagSAmL, SmATA 58, WhoCom, WorAlBi, WrDr 88, -90, -92

Keillor, Garrison Edward 1942- *WrDr 94*

Keir, Christine *ConAu X, SmATA 3*
Main entry: Popescu, Christine

Keith, Adolphus 1939- *BlkAWP*

Keith, Carlton *AuBYP 2, -3, ConAu 135, -X, -37NR, MajAI, SmATA 1, -69, WrDr 80, -82, -84, -86, -88, -90, -92*
Main entry: Robertson, Keith Carleton
Pseud./variant:
Robertson, Keith Charlton

Keith, Carlton 1914-1991 *WrDr 94N*

Keith, Eros 1942- *BioIn 16, ChhPo S2, ConAu 114, FourBJA, IlsBYP, IlsCB 1967, SmATA 52, WhoAmA 78, -80, -82, -84, -86, -89, -91*

Keith, Hal 1934- *BioIn 14, SmATA 36*

Keith, Harold 1903- *BioIn 14, IntAu&W 91, TwCChW 89, WrDr 86, -88, -90, -92*

Keith, Harold Verne 1903- *AmAu&B, AuBYP 2, -3, BioIn 4, -5, -6, -7, -9, -10, ConAu 5R, -2NR, CurBio 58, DcAmChF 1960, MajAI, MorBMP, MorJA, NewbC 1956, OxCChiL, SmATA 2, -74, TwCChW 78, -83, TwCYAW, WhNAA, WrDr 80, -82, -84, -94*

Keith, Robert *SmATA X*
Main entry: Applebaum, Stan

Keith-Lucas, Alan 1910- *ConAu 5R, -2NR, -20NR, -42NR, WhoAm 74, -76, -78, -80, WhoSSW 93*

Kelder, Diane 1934- *ConAu 25R, -18NR, -40NR*

Kelder, Diane M 1934- *WhoAmA 86, -91*

Keleinikov, Andrei 1924- *BioIn 17, SmATA 65*

Kelen, Emery 1896-1978 *AuBYP 2S, -3, BioIn 1, -2, -6, -11, -13, ConAu 9R, -103, IlsCB 1744, SmATA 13, -26N*

Kell, Joseph *MajTwCW, TwCYAW, Who 88, -90, -92, WrDr 86, -88, -90, -92*

Kell, Joseph 1917- *WrDr 94*

Kellaway, Frank 1922- *Au&Wr 71, ConAu 9R, DcChlFi, OxCAusL, SingR 1*

Kelleam, Joseph E 1913-1975 *BioIn 14, ScF&FL 92*

Kelleam, Joseph Everidge 1913-1975 *ConAu 107, ConSFA, EncSF 93, SmATA 31, WhoSSW 73, -76*

Kelleher, Victor 1939- *BioIn 16, ConAu 126, ConNov 91, IntAu&W 91, OxCAusL, ScF&FL 92, SmATA 52, TwCChW 83, -89, WrDr 86, -88, -90, -92*

Kelleher, Victor Michael Kitchener 1939- *DcChlFi, EncSF 93, SmATA 75, TwCYAW, WrDr 94*

Keller, Allan 1904?-1981 *BioIn 12, ConAu 29R, -29NR*

Keller, Beverly L *AuBYP 2S, -3, BioIn 11, SmATA 13*

Keller, Charles 1914- *BioIn 14*

Keller, Charles 1942- *AuBYP 2S, -3, BioIn 11, ConAu 49, -2NR, -43NR, SmATA 8*

Keller, Dick 1923- *SmATA 36*

Keller, Frances Ruth 1911- *AuBYP 2, -3*

Keller, Gail Faithfull *ConAu 57, SmATA 8*
Main entry: Faithfull, Gail

Keller, Helen Adams 1880-1968 *AmAu&B, AmPeW, BiDSA, BioAmW, BioIn 1, -2, -3, -4, -5, -6, -7, -8, -9, -10, -11, -12, ChhPo S1, CurBio 42, -68, DcAmB S8, DcLEL, EncAB-A 6, EncSoH, HarEnUS, HerW, InWom SUP, LongCTC, LuthC 75, MorMA, ObitOF 79, OxCAmL 65, REn, REnAL, WebAB 74, -79, WhDW, WhAm 5, WhNAA, WhoHol B, WomWWA 14*

Keller, Holly *AuBYP 3, BioIn 15, -16, ConAu 118, SmATA 42*

Keller, Holly 1942- *SmATA 76*

Keller, Irene 1927- *BioIn 14, ConAu 116, SmATA 36*

Keller, Mollie *SmATA 50*

Kellerhals-Stewart, Heather 1937- *BioIn 13, Profile 2, ScF&FL 92*

Kelley, Leo P 1928- *BioIn 14, ConAu 107, -24NR, IntAu&W 91, ScF&FL 92, ScFSB, SmATA 31, -32, TwCSFW 86, -91, TwCWW 91, WrDr 84, -86, -88, -90, -92*

Kelley, Leo Patrick 1928- *EncSF 93, WrDr 94*

Kelley, Reeve Spencer 1912- *AnCL*

Kelley, True Adelaide 1946- *ConAu 105, SmATA 39, -41*

Kellin, Sally Moffet 1932- *BioIn 11, ConAu 61, SmATA 9*

Kelling, Furn L 1914- *BioIn 15, ConAu 17R, SmATA 37*

Kellner, Esther 1909- *ConAu 13R, IndAu 1917*

Kellogg, Elijah 1813-1901 *Alli SUP, AmAu, AmAu&B, BenetAL 91, BiD&SB, BioIn 1, CarSB, DcAmAu, DcNAA, HarEnUS, OxCAmL 65, –83, OxCChiL, REnAL, WhAm HS*

Kellogg, Gene *AuBYP 3*
Main entry: Kellogg, Jean

Kellogg, Jean 1916-1978 *AuBYP 2, –3, BioIn 8, –11, ConAu 9R, –7NR, DrAS 74P, SmATA 10, WhoAmW 77, WhoRel 75*
Pseud./variant:
Jackson, Sally
Kellogg, Gene

Kellogg, Steven 1941- *AuBYP 3, BioIn 11, –12, –14, –16, ChlLR 6, ConAu 49, –1NR, DcLB 61, FourBJA, IlsBYP, IlsCB 1967, IntAu&W 91, SmATA 8, –57, TwCChW 89, WhoAm 92, –94, WrDr 76, –80, –82, –84, –86, –88, –90, –92, –94*

Kellogg, Steven Castle 1941- *MajAI*

Kellogg, Vernon Lyman 1867-1937 *AmAu&B, AmLY, BioIn 9, CarSB, DcAmAu, DcNAA, DcScB, InSci, WhAm 1, WhNAA*

Kellow, Kathleen *BlmGWL, ConAu 140, –X, –28NR, EncMys, InWom SUP, IntAu&W 91X, Novels, SmATA 2, –74, TwCRHW 90, Who 74, –82, –83, –85, –88, –90, –92, WorAu 1950, WrDr 76, –84, –86, –88, –90, –92*
Main entry: Hibbert, Eleanor Burford

Kelly, Eric 1884-1960 *TwCChW 89*

Kelly, Eric P 1884-1960 *BenetAL 91*

Kelly, Eric Philbrook 1884-1960 *AmAu&B, AnCL, AuBYP 2, –3, BioIn 2, –4, –5, –6, –7, –11, –14, ConAu 93, JBA 34, –51, MajAI, NewbMB 1922, OxCChiL, REnAL, TwCChW 78, –83, WhAm 3, WhNAA, YABC 1*

Kelly, Fiona *ConAu 142, SmATA 75*
Main entry: Welford, Sue

Kelly, Frank K 1914- *BioIn 1, –3, ConAu 1R, –1NR, –16NR, –39NR, ScF&FL 92, WhoSciF*

Kelly, Frank King 1914- *EncSF 93, WhoWest 89, –92, –94*

Kelly, George Anthony 1916- *AuBYP 2S, –3, BioIn 17, ConAu 43NR, DrAS 78P, WhoAm 80, –82, –84, –86, –88, –90, –92, –94, WhoE 74, WhoRel 92, WhoUSWr 88, WhoWrEP 89, –92*

Kelly, George W 1894- *ConAu 65, –9NR*

Kelly, James Edward 1855-1933 *ChhPo S1, HarEnUS, WhAm 1, WhAmArt 85*

Kelly, Jeff *ConAu 136, SmATA 65*

Kelly, Jeffrey *AuBYP 3*

Kelly, Jeffrey 1946- *BioIn 17, ConAu 136, SmATA 65, WrDr 94*

Kelly, Kathleen M 1964- *SmATA 71*

Kelly, Margaret Ricaud 1910- *WhoAmW 75, –77, –81, –83, –85, –87, WhoSSW 76, –78, –80, –82, –84, –86, WrDr 76, –80*

Kelly, Martha Rose 1914-1983 *BioIn 15, ConAu 69, SmATA 37*
Pseud./variant:
Kelly, Marty

Kelly, Marty
Main entry: Kelly, Martha Rose

Kelly, Myra 1875-1910 *AmAu&B, BioIn 1, –12, CarSB, DcAmAu, DcNAA, WhAm 2*

Kelly, Patricia Marie *WhoAmW 75, –77, –81*

Kelly, Ralph *ConAu X, SmATA 7*
Main entry: Geis, Darlene Stern

Kelly, Regina Z 1898- *BioIn 4, –10, ConAu 1R, –2NR, CurBio 56, ForWC 70, SmATA 5*

Kelly, Rosalie *ConAu 61, –11NR, SmATA 43*

Kelly, Walt 1913-1973 *AmAu&B, ArtCS, ASCAP 66, BenetAL 91, BioIn 1, –2, –3, –4, –6, –10, –12, CelR, ConAu 45, –73, CurBio 56, –73, EncACom, EncAJ, IlsBYP, NewYTBE 73, ObitOF 79, REnAL, SmATA 18, WhAm 6, WhoAm 74*

Kelsey, Alice 1896- *AuBYP 3*

Kelsey, Alice Geer 1896- *AnCL, AuBYP 2 Au&Wr 71, BioIn 6, –7, –9, ConAu 5R, ForWC 70, IntAu&W 77, MorJA, SmATA 1, WrDr 76, –80, –82, –84*

Kemp, Gene 1926- *BioIn 13, ChlFicS, ChlLR 29, ConAu 69, –12NR, IntAu&W 82, –91, MajAI, OxCChiL, SmATA 25, –75, TwCChW 83, –89, WrDr 76, –80, –82, –84, –86, –88, –90, –92, –94*

Kemp, Lysander 1920- *AmAu&B, ConAu 25, –1NR, WhoSSW 76*

Kempner, Mary Jean 1913-1969 *BioIn 8, -11, ConAu P-2, ObitOF 79, SmATA 10*

Kempton, Jean Welch 1914- *BioIn 11, ConAu 49, SmATA 10*
Pseud./variant:
Welch, Jean-Louise

Ken, Thomas 1637-1711 *BioIn 2, -3, -5, -6, CamGLE, DcBiPP, DcNaB, LuthC 75, OxCChiL, OxCEng 85*

Kenda, Margaret 1942- *SmATA 71*

Kendal, Wallis 1937- *BioIn 10, ConAu 107, Profile 1*

Kendall, Carol *BioIn 14*

Kendall, Carol 1917- *ConAu 25NR, IntAu&W 86, -89, -91, ScF&FL 92, SmATA 7AS, TwCChW 89, TwCYAW, WrDr 86, -88, -90, -92, -94*

Kendall, Carol Seeger 1917- *AuBYP 2, -3, BioIn 7, -9, -11, ConAu 5R, -7NR, DcAmChF 1960, ForWC 70, IntAu&W 77, -82, MajAI, OhA&B, OxCChiL, SmATA 11, -74, ThrBJA, TwCChW 78, -83, WrDr 80, -82, -84*

Kendall, Edward Augustus 1776?-1842 *Alli, BiDLA, CarSB, DcNaB, OxCChiL*

Kendall, Elaine 1929- *ConAu 17R*

Kendall, Lace *AmAu&B, ConAu X, SmATA 3, ThrBJA, WhoAm 74, -76, -78, WrDr 82, -84, -86, -88*
Main entry: Stoutenburg, Adrien

Kendall, Oswald *WhoLA*

Kendall, Sarita 1943- *IntAu&W 77*

Kendrew Family *OxCChiL*

Kendrick, Thomas Downing, Sir 1895- *ConAu 81, IntWW 74, -75, -76, -77, -78, -79, Who 74, WhoLib 54*

Kenealy, James P 1927- *BioIn 13, ConAu 93, SmATA 29, -52*
Pseud./variant:
Kenealy, Jim

Kenealy, Jim
Main entry: Kenealy, James P

Kenelski, Maurice *IlsBYP*

Kennard-Davis, Arthur 1910- *ConAu P-1*

Kennaway, Adrienne 1945- *BioIn 17, SmATA 60*

Kennedy, Brendan 1970- *BioIn 16, ConAu 123, SmATA 57*

Kennedy, Dana Forrest 1917- *SmATA 74*

Kennedy, David Michael 1941- *ConAu 29R, -13NR, DrAS 78H, -82H, IntAu&W 77, -82, -86, -89, -91, WhoAm 82, -84, -86, -88, -90, -92, -94, WhoWest 89, WrDr 76, -80, -82, -84, -86, -88, -90, -92, -94*

Kennedy, Dorothy M 1931- *BioIn 16, SmATA 53*

Kennedy, Dorothy Mintzlaff 1931- *ConAu 40NR*

Kennedy, Jerome Richard 1932- *DcAmChF 1985*

Kennedy, John F d1963 *NewYTBS 88*

Kennedy, John F 1917-1963 *BioIn 14, -15, -16, -17, RComAH, WorAlBi*

Kennedy, John Fitzgerald 1917-1963 *AmAu&B, AnCL, Benet 87, BenetAL 91, BiDrUSC 89, BiDrUSE 89, BioIn 1, -2, -3, -4, -5, -6, -7, -8, -9, -10, -11, -12, -13, ChhPo, ConAu 1R, -1NR, ConHero 1, CurBio 50, -61, -64, DcAmB S7, DcAmSR, DcPol, DcTwHis, EncAB-H, EncPaPR 91, EncSoH, MajTwCW, MakMC, McGEWB, NewYTBE 72, ObitOF 79, ObitT 1961, OxCAmH, OxCAmL 65, -83, RAdv 13-3, REn, REnAL, SmATA 11, WebAB 74, -79, WhDW, WhAm 4, WhAmP, WorAl*

Kennedy, Joseph 1929- *ConAu 1R, DcLEL 1940, IntWWP 82, SmATA 14*
Pseud./variant:
Kennedy, X J

Kennedy, Paul Edward 1929- *BioIn 8, IlsCB 1957, SmATA 33*

Kennedy, Richard 1910- *ArtsCL, BioIn 5, -6, -8, -11, -12, -14, ConAu 102, IlsBYP, IlsCB 1946, -1957, -1967, WhoArt 80, -82, -84*

Kennedy, Richard 1910-1989 *AnObit 1989, BioIn 17, ConAu 127, SmATA 60*

Kennedy, Richard 1932- *BioIn 13, -14, ConAu 57, -7NR, -26NR, FifBJA, ScF&FL 92, SmATA 22, TwCChW 83, -89, WhoAm 82, -84, WrDr 86, -88, -90, -92*

Kennedy, Richard Jerome 1932- *WrDr 94*

Kennedy, Robert 1938- *SmATA 63*

Kennedy, T A 1953- *ConAu 114, SmATA 35, -42*

Pseud./variant:
Vickery, Kate

Kennedy, William *DrAPF 87, –89, –91, –93*

Kennedy, William 1928- *Au&Arts 1, Benet 87, BenetAL 91, BiDConC, BioIn 14, –15, –16, –17, CelR 90, ConAu 31NR, ConLC 53, ConNov 86, –91, CyWA 89, MagSAmL, MajTwCW, PostFic, RAdv 13-1, ScF&FL 92, SmATA 57, WhoUSWr 88, WhoWrEP 89, –92, WorAlBi, WrDr 86, –88, –90, –92*

Kennedy, William Joseph 1928- *WrDr 94*

Kennedy, X 1929- *IntAu&W 82*

Kennedy, X J *BioIn 14, –16, ConAu 30NR, –40NR, DrAPF 87, –89, IntAu&W 86X, IntvTCA 2*
Main entry: Kennedy, Joseph

Kennedy, X J 1929- *AmAu&B, BiDConC, BioIn 10, –12, ChhPo, –S2, ChlLR 27, ConAu 9AS, –X, ConLC 8, –42, ConPo 70, –75, –80, –85, –91, DcLB 5, DcLEL 1940, DrAP 75, DrAPF 83, –85, –91, –93, IntWWP 82X, PenC AM, ScF&FL 92, SixBJA, SmATA X, TwCChW 89, WhoAm 74, –76, –80, –82, –84, –86, –88, –90, –92, –94, WhoUSWr 88, WhoWor 74, –93, WhoWrEP 89, –92, WorAu 1950, WrDr 76, –80, –82, –84, –86, –88, –90, –92, –94*

Kennell, Ruth Epperson 1893-1977 *BioIn 10, ConAu P-2, SmATA 6, –25N*

Kennemore, Tim 1957- *TwCChW 89, WrDr 90, –92, –94*

Kenny, Ellsworth Newcomb 1909-1971 *AuBYP 2, –3, BioIn 8, ConAu 5R, –103, SmATA 26N*
Pseud./variant:
Newcomb, Ellsworth

Kenny, Herbert A 1912- *WhoUSWr 88, WhoWrEP 89, –92*

Kenny, Herbert Andrew 1912- *AmCath 80, BioIn 11, ConAu 41R, SmATA 13, WhoAm 74, –76, –78, –80, –82, –84, –86, –88, -90, WhoE 74, –75*

Kenny, Hubert Alan 1900?-1969 *AuBYP 2, BioIn 8*

Kenny, Hugh 1909-1971 *AuBYP 3*

Kenny, Kathryn *ConAu X, SmATA X, WhoUSWr 88, WhoWrEP 89, –92*
Main entry: Bowden, Joan Chase
Krull, Kathleen
Sanderlin, Owenita
Stack, Nicolete Meredith

Kenny, Kathryn 1916- *WrDr 94*

Kenny, Kevin *ConAu X, SmATA X*
Main entry: Krull, Kathleen

Kenoyer, Natlee Peoples 1907- *ConAu 5R, –5NR, ForWC 70*

Kensington, Sarah 1949- *BioIn 12, IlsCB 1967*

Kent, Alexander *Au&Wr 71, BioIn 13, ConAu X, DcLEL 1940, IntAu&W 77, Novels, SmATA X, WrDr 76, –80, –82, –84, –86, –88, –90, –92*
Main entry: Reeman, Douglas Edward

Kent, Alexander 1924- *SmATA X, WrDr 94*

Kent, Arthur William Charles 1925- *Au&Wr 71, ConAu 102, IntAu&W 77, WrDr 76, –80*

Kent, David
Main entry: Lambert, David Compton

Kent, Deborah Ann 1948- *ConAu 103, SmATA 41, –47*

Kent, Jack *ConGrA 2*

Kent, Jack 1920- *AmAu&B, BioIn 12, –13, ConAu 85, –X, ConGrA 1, FifBJA, IlsCB 1967, SmATA X, WhoAm 74, WhoAmA 78, –80, –82, –84*

Kent, Jack 1920-1985 *BioIn 14, –15, EncACom, WhoAmA 86N, –89N, –91N*

Kent, John Wellington 1920-1985 *ConAu 117, –16NR, ConGrA 1, –2, SmATA 24, –45N, WhoSSW 84*

Kent, Louise 1886-1969 *AmAu&B, AmNov, AuBYP 2, –3, BioIn 2, –4, –8, ConAu 1R, –25R, JBA 51, REnAL, TwCA SUP, WhAm 5*
Pseud./variant:
Tempest, Teresa

Kent, Louise Andrews 1886-1969 *BenetAL 91*

Kent, Margaret 1894- *Au&Wr 71, BioIn 9, ConAu P-2, IntAu&W 77, SmATA 2*

Kent, Rockwell 1882-1971 *AmAu&B, BenetAL 91, BioIn 1, –2, –3, –4, –5, –7, –8, –9, –10, –11, –12, –13, –14, –17, BriEAA, ChhPo, ConAmA, ConArt 77, –83, ConAu 5R, –29R, –4NR, CurBio 42, –71, DcCAA 71, –77, –88, GrAmP, IlrAm 1880, –D, IlsBYP, IlsCB 1744, McGEWB, NatCAB 58, NewYTBE 71, ObitOF 79, OxCAmL 65, –83, OxCChiL, OxCTwCA, PhDcTCA 77, REnAL, SmATA 6, TwCA, –SUP, WebAB 74, –79 WhAm 5, WhAmArt 85, WhoAmA 78N, –80N, –82N, –86N, –89N, –91N, WorAlBi, WorAl*

Pseud./variant:
Hogarth, Jr.

Kent, Sherman d1986 *NewYTBS 86*

Kent, Sherman 1903- *AmMWSc 73S, BioIn 12, ConAu 53, SmATA 20*

Kent, Sherman 1903-1986 *BioIn 14, –15, –16, ConAu 118, EncAI&E, SmATA 47N, WhAm 9*

Kent, Zachary *AuBYP 3*

Kenward, James Macara 1908- *Au&Wr 71, BioIn 14, ConAu 5R, WrDr 76, –80*

Kenward, Jean 1920- *BioIn 15, ConAu 108, IntAu&W 89, –91, IntWWP 82X, SmATA 42, WrDr 82, –84, –86, –88, –90, –92, –94*

Kenworthy, Leonard Stout 1912- *BioIn 10, –11, ConAu 1R, –1NR, IndAu 1917, SmATA 6*

Kenyon, Ley 1913- *Au&Wr 71, BioIn 10, ConAu 13R, SmATA 6, WhoArt 80, –82, –84*

Kenyon, Raymond G 1922- *AuBYP 2, –3, BioIn 7*

Keogh, Brian 1931- *ArtsCL, BioIn 6*

Kepes, Gyorgy 1906- *AmAu&B, AmPB, Au&Wr 71, BioIn 1, –2, –5, –6, –9, –10, –11, –12, –13, ConAu 101, ConDes 84, –90, ConPhot 82, –88, CurBio 73, DcCAA 71, –77, –88, ICPEnP, MacBEP, OxCTwCA, WhoAm 74, –76, –78, –84, –94, WhoAmA 73, –78, –80, –82, –84, –86, –89, –91, WhoWor 84, –91, –93*

Kepes, Juliet 1919- *AmPB, AuBYP 2, BioIn 1, –2, –5, –8, –9, –11, –12, ChhPo, ChsFB I, ConAu 69, IlsCB 1946, –1957, –1967, SmATA 13, ThrBJA*

Kepes, Juliet Appleby 1919- *AuBYP 3*

Kepple, Ella Huff 1902- *ConAu P-2*

Keppler, Victor d1987 *NewYTBS 87*

Keppler, Victor 1904- *BioIn 4, –9, –13, ConPhot 82, –88, ICPEnP*

Keppler, Victor 1904-1987 *ConAu 124*

Ker, David 1842-1914 *Alli SUP, BbD, BiD&SB, ChhPo, DcAmAu, DcNAA, ScFEYrs*

Ker, John Bellenden 1765?-1842 *DcNaB, –C, OxCChiL*

Kerby, Mona 1951- *ConAu 142, SmATA 75*

Kerigan, Florence 1896- *BioIn 11, ChhPo, ConAu 29R, IntWWP 82, SmATA 12, WhNAA, WrDr 76, –80, –82, –84*
Pseud./variant:
Kerry, Frances

Kerman, Gertrude Lerner 1909- *ConAu 5R, ForWC 70, SmATA 21*

Kermond, Evelyn Carolyn Conway 1927- *Au&Wr 71, WrDr 76, –80*

Kerner, Ben *AuBYP 2, –3, BioIn 8*

Kerr, Donald Gordon Grady 1913-1976 *CanWW 70, ConAu 1R, DrAS 74H, OxCCan, WhoCan 73*

Kerr, George F 1869?-1953 *BioIn 3, WhAmArt 85*

Kerr, Illingworth H 1905- *CanWW 89*

Kerr, Illingworth Holey 1905?- *BioIn 11, CanWW 70, –80, –81, –83, CreCan 1*

Kerr, James Lennox 1899-1963 *ConAu 102, TwCChW 83, –89*
Pseud./variant:
Dawlish, Peter

Kerr, James Stolee 1928- *ConAu 17R*

Kerr, Jessica 1901- *AuBYP 2S, –3, BioIn 11, ConAu P-2, SmATA 13*

Kerr, Judith 1923- *AuBYP 2S, –3, BioIn 13, ConAu 93, FifBJA, IntAu&W 91, SmATA 24, TwCChW 78, –83, –89, WrDr 80, –82, –84, –86, –88, –90, –92*

Kerr, Laura 1904- *AuBYP 2, –3, BioIn 2, –7*

Kerr, M E *BioIn 15, –16, ConAu 37NR, MajAI, MajTwCW*
Main entry: Meaker, Marijane

Kerr, M E 1927- *Au&Arts 2, AuBYP 3, BioIn 17, ChlLR 29, DcAmChF 1960, SmATA X, TwCChW 89, TwCYAW, WrDr 90, –92, –94*

Kerr, M E 1932?- *AuBYP 2S, BioIn 10, ConAu X, ConLC 12, –35, FourBJA, IntAu&W 91, OxCChiL, SmATA 1AS, –X, TwCChW 78, –83, WrDr 80, –82, –84, –86, –88*

Kerr, Phyllis Forbes 1942- *SmATA 72*

Kerr, Tom 1950- *SmATA 77*

Kerrigan, Anthony d1991 *NewYTBS 91*

Kerrigan, Anthony 1918- *Au&Wr 71, ConAu 49, –11AS, –4NR, ConLC 4, –6, IntAu&W 77, LiExTwC, WhoAm 80, –82, –88,*

-90, -92, -94, WhoUSWr 88, WhoWor 78, WhoWrEP 89, WrDr 76, -80, -82, -84

Kerry, Frances *ConAu X, IntWWP 82X, SmATA X*
Main entry: Kerigan, Florence

Kerry, Lois *AuBYP 3, ConAu X, -36NR, IntAu&W 82X, MajAI, SmATA 1, -75, -X, TwCYAW*
Main entry: Arquette, Lois S

Kerry, Lois 1934- *WrDr 94*

Ker Wilson, Barbara *ScF&FL 92*

Ker Wilson, Barbara 1929- *Au&Wr 71, BioIn 12, ConAu 5R, -7NR, FourBJA, SmATA 20, -70, -18AS*
Pseud./variant:
Wilson, Barbara Ker

Kesey, Ken *BioIn 14, -15, -17, DrAPF 87, -89, -91, -93, IntvTCA 2*

Kesey, Ken 1935- *Benet 87, BenetAL 91, BroV, CamGLE, CamHAL, ConAu 22NR, ConLC 46, -64, ConNov 86, -91, CyWA 89, MagSAmL, MajTwCW, RAdv 13-1, SmATA 66, WhoAm 86, -88, -90, -92, -94, WhoWest 94, WorAlBi, WorLitC, WrDr 86, -88, -90, -92*

Kesey, Ken Elton 1935- *ConAu 38NR, TwCYAW, WrDr 94*

Kesler, Jay *BioIn 17*

Kesler, Jay 1935- *ConAu 61, -8NR, -26NR, SmATA 65, WhoRel 75*

Kessel, Joyce Karen 1937- *ConAu 105, SmATA 41*

Kessler, Ethel 1922- *AuBYP 3, ConAu 115, -121, FifBJA, SmATA 37, -44*

Kessler, Leonard P 1921- *AmPB, AuBYP 2, -3, BioIn 5, -8, -12, ChhPo, ConAu 77, FifBJA, IlsCB 1946, -1957, -1967, SmATA 14, WhoAmA 80, -82, -84*

Kesteven, G R *ConAu X, SmATA X*
Main entry: Crosher, G R

Kesteven, G R 1911- *EncSF 93, ScF&FL 92*

Ketcham, Hank
Main entry: Ketcham, Henry King

Ketcham, Hank 1920- *ArtCS, BioIn 3, -4, -5, -11, -13, -15, -17, ConAu X, CurBio 56, EncACom, EncAJ, SmATA X, WhoAmA 82, -84, -86*

Ketcham, Henry King 1920- *ConAu 105, EncTwCJ, SmATA 27, -28, WhoAm 80, -82, -84, -86, -88, -90, -92, -94, WhoAmA 80, -89, -91, WhoWest 94*
Pseud./variant:
Ketcham, Hank

Ketner, Mary Grace 1946- *SmATA 75*

Kettelkamp, Larry 1933- *AuBYP 3, BioIn 15, SmATA 3AS*

Kettelkamp, Larry Dale 1933- *AuBYP 2, BioIn 8, -9, ConAu 29R, ConLC 12, IlsCB 1957, -1967, IntAu&W 77, -91, SmATA 2, ThrBJA, WrDr 76, -80, -84, -86, -88, -90, -92, -94*

Ketteman, Helen 1945- *SmATA 73*

Kettle, Jocelyn Pamela 1934- *ConAu 25R*

Kevles, Bettyann 1938- *BioIn 13, ConAu 69, -11NR, -27NR, SmATA 23*

Kevles, Bettyann Holtzmann 1938- *WrDr 90, -94*

Key, Alexander 1904-1979 *AuBYP 3, ScF&FL 92, ScFSB, TwCSFW 86, -91*

Key, Alexander Hill 1904-1979 *AuBYP 2, BioIn 8, -11, -12, -13, ConAu 5R, -6NR, DcAmChF 1960, EncSF 93, IntAu&W 77, SmATA 8, -23N, WrDr 76, -80*

Keyes, Daniel *DrAPF 87, -89, -91, -93*

Keyes, Daniel 1927- *BenetAL 91, BioIn 7, -15, -17, ConAu 17R, -10NR, -26NR, ConSFA, DrAPF 83, -85, DrAS 74E, -78E, -82E, EncSF 93, IntAu&W 89, -91, NewEScF, Novels, RGTwCSF, ScFSB, SmATA 37, TwCSFW 86, -91, WhoAm 82, -84, -86, -88, -90, -92, -94, WhoMW 84, -92, WhoSciF, WhoUSWr 88, WhoWrEP 89, -92, WrDr 76, -80, -82, -84, -86, -88, -90, -92, -94*

Keyes, Fenton 1915- *AmMWSc 73S, -78S, BioIn 14, ConAu 107, SmATA 34, WhoAm 74, -76, -78, -80, -82, -84, -86, -88, -90, -92, -94*

Keyes, Nelson Beecher 1894- *AuBYP 3*

Keyes, Nelson Beecher 1894-1958 *AuBYP 2, BioIn 5, -8*

Keys, Ancel Benjamin 1904- *AmMWSc 73P, -76P, BioIn 5, -7, ConAu 61, CurBio 66, IntWW 74, WhoWor 74, WrDr 80*

Keyser, Marcia 1933- *BioIn 15, ConAu 116, SmATA 42*

Keyser, Sarah *ConAu X, SmATA X*
Main entry: McGuire, Leslie Sarah

Keyser, William R 1916- *ConAu 69*

Keyt, George *BioIn 2*

Keyt, George 1901- *BioIn 16*

Khalsa, Dayal Kaur *BioIn 16, –17*

Khalsa, Dayal Kaur 1943- *CanWW 89*

Khalsa, Dayal Kaur 1943-1989 *ChlLR 30, ConAu 137, MajAI, SmATA 62*

Khanshendel, Chiron *ConAu X, IntWWP 82X, SmATA X*
Main entry: Rose, Wendy

Khare, Narayan Bhaskar 1882- *ConAu P-1*
Pseud./variant:
Bapu

Kherdian, David *DrAPF 87, –89, –91, –93*

Kherdian, David 1931- *BioIn 12, –15, –17, ChlLR 24, ConAu 21R, –2AS, –39NR, ConLC 6, –9, DrAP 75, DrAPF 83, –85, FifBJA, IntAu&W 77, –91, MajAI, SmATA 16, –74, WhoAm 82, –84, –86, –88, –90, –92, –94, WhoWrEP 89, –92, WrDr 76, –80, –82, –84, –86, –88, –90, –92, –94*

Kibbe, Pat *BioIn 17, ConAu 125, SmATA 60*

Kidd, Kenneth E 1906- *AmMWSc 73S, CanWW 70, –80, –81, –83, –89, OxCCan*

Kidd, Ronald 1948- *BioIn 15, ConAu 116, –39NR, DcAmChF 1985, ScF&FL 92, SmATA 42*

Kidd, Ronald Alexander 1926- *Who 90*

Kiddell, John 1922- *Au&Wr 71, BioIn 9, ConAu 29R, SmATA 3*

Kiddell-Monroe, Joan 1908- *Au&Wr 71, BioIn 5, –8, ConAu P-1, IlsBYP, IlsCB 1946, –1957, SmATA 55, WhoChL*

Kiddell-Monroe, Joan 1908-1972 *BioIn 14, –16*

Kidder, Barbara 1933- *ConAu 41R*

Kidder, Jonathan Edward, Jr. 1922- *DrAS 74H, –78H, –82H, WhoWor 93*

Kiddle, Margaret Loch 1914-1958 *AuWomWr, SingR 1*

Kidwell, Carl 1910- *BioIn 15, IlsBYP, IndAu 1917, SmATA 43*

Kiefer, Irene 1926- *BioIn 12, ConAu 69, –11NR, SmATA 21*

Kielty, Bernardine *AuBYP 2, –3, BioIn 8, REnAL*
Main entry: Scherman, Bernardine Kielty

Kiene, Julia *AuBYP 2, –3, BioIn 8*

Kieran, John 1882-1981 *Ballpl 90*

Kieran, John 1892-1981 *AuBYP 3*

Kieran, John Francis 1892-1981 *AmAu&B, AuBYP 2S, BiDAmSp OS, BioIn 1, –2, –3, –4, –5, –7, –8, –9, –12, –13, CathA 1930, ChhPo S1, ConAu 101, –105, CurBio 40, NewYTBS 81, REn, REnAL, WhAm 8, WhoAm 74, –76, –78, WhoE 74*

Kieran, Margaret Ford *BioIn 3*

Kiesel, Stanley *DrAPF 87, –89, –91, –93*

Kiesel, Stanley 1925- *BioIn 14, ConAu 104, DrAPF 83, –85, SmATA 35*

Kihn, William Langdon 1898-1957 *BioIn 4, –9, WhAm 3, WhoAmA 80N, –82N, –86N, –89N, –91N*

Kijima, Hajime *ConAu X*
Main entry: Kojima, Shozo

Kikukawa, Cecily H 1919- *BioIn 14, –15, ConAu 113, SmATA 35, –44*

Kilbourn, William Morley 1926- *Au&Wr 71, BlueB 76, CaW, CanWW 70, –80, –81, –83, –89, ConAu 21R, DrAS 74H, –82H, OxCCan, –SUP, WhoCan 73, –80, –82, WhoE 74, WrDr 80*

Kilgore, Kathleen 1946- *BioIn 15, ConAu 109, –27NR, ScF&FL 92, SmATA 42*
Pseud./variant:
Houton, Kathleen

Kilian, Crawford 1941- *BioIn 14, CanWW 89, ConAu 105, –22NR, EncSF 93, ScF&FL 92, SmATA 35, TwCSFW 86, –91, WhoCanL 87, –92, WhoWest 92, WhoWrEP 89, –92, WrDr 86, –88, –90, –92, –94*

Killens, John Oliver *DrAPF 87*

Killens, John Oliver d1987 *NewYTBS 87, WhAm 9*

Killens, John Oliver 1916- *BioIn 14, BlkAWP, ConAu 77, –2AS, ConBlAP 88, ConLC 10, ConNov 72, –76, –82, –86, DcLB 33, DrAF 76, DrAPF 83, –85, InB&W 80, –85, IntAu&W 77, –91, LivgBAA, ModBlW, NegAl 76, –83, PenC AM, SelBAAf, SelBAAu, SouBlCW, WhoAm 74, –76, WhoBlA 75, –77, –80, –85, –88, WhoE 74, WrDr 76, –80, –82, –84, –86, –88*

Killens, John Oliver 1916-1987 *BenetAL 91, BioIn 15, -16, BlkWr 1, -2, ConAu 123, -26NR, DrBlPA 90, EncAACR, NegAl 89, WhoBlA 90N*

Killien, Christi 1956- *SmATA 73*

Killilea, Marie 1913- *BioIn 9, ConAu 5R, SmATA 2, WhoE 74*

Killingback, Julia *BioIn 17*

Killingback, Julia 1944- *SmATA 63*

Killough, Lee 1942- *BioIn 17, ConAu 32NR, IntAu&W 91, NewEScF, ScF&FL 92, ScFSB, SmATA 64, TwCSFW 86, -91, WrDr 86, -88, -90, -92*
Pseud./variant:
Hood, Sarah

Kilmer, Joyce 1886-1918 *AmAu&B, AmLY, ASCAP 66, Benet 87, BenetAL 91, BioIn 1, -5, -6, -7, -8, -15, ChhPo, -S2, CnDAL, ConAmL, ConAu 120, DcLB 45, DcLEL, DcNAA, LongCTC, OxCAmL 65, -83, REn, REnAL, Str&VC, TwCA, WebAB 74, -79, WebAMB, WhAm 1, WorAlBi, WorAl*

Kilner, Dorothy 1755-1836 *CarSB, ChhPo, DcBrAmW, OxCChiL*

Kilner, Mary Ann 1753-1831 *DcBrAmW, OxCChiL*

Kilreon, Beth *ConAu X, -38NR, SmATA 4*
Main entry: Walker, Barbara K

Kim, Yong-Ik *DcAmChF 1960*

Kim, Yong-Ik 1920- *ConAu 17R*

Kimball, Captain Kim
Main entry: Scribner, Kimball

Kimball, Dean 1912- *AuBYP 2S, -3, ConAu 69*

Kimball, Richard Laurance 1939- *ConAu 53, -7NR, IntAu&W 77, -82, LEduc 74, WhoWest 78*

Kimball, Yeffe 1914-1978 *BioIn 8, -9, -15, IlsCB 1957, SmATA 37, WhAm 7, WhAmArt 85, WhoAm 76, -78, WhoAmA 73, -78, -80N, -82N, -86N, -89N, -91N*

Kimberly, Gail *ConAu 81, ScF&FL 92*

Kimberly, Gail 1937- *EncSF 93*

Kimble, George Herbert Tinley 1908- *AmAu&B, Au&Wr 71, BioIn 2, -3, BlueB 76, ConAu 108, CurBio 52, InSci, IntYB 80, -81, -82, Who 74, WrDr 80*

Kimbrell, Grady 1933- *ConAu 33R*

Kimbrell, Grady Ned 1933- *WhoUSWr 88, WhoWest 89, -94, WhoWrEP 92*

Kimbrough, Emily 1898- *WhoAm 88, WhoAmW 89, WrDr 90*

Kimbrough, Emily 1898-1989 *WhAm 9*

Kimbrough, Emily 1899- *AmAu&B, Au&Wr 71, BioIn 1, -2, -3, -4, -9, -10, -12, BlueB 76, ConAu 17R, CurBio 44, InWom SUP, IndAu 1917, IntAu&W 91, OxCAmL 65, -83, REnAL, SmATA 2, WhoAm 74, -76, -78, -80, -82, -84, -86, WhoAmW 74, -83, -85, -87, WhoWor 74, WorAu 1950, WrDr 76, -80, -82, -84, -86, -88*

Kimbrough, Emily 1899-1989 *BenetAL 91, BioIn 16, -17, ConAu 127, CurBio 89N, SmATA 59*

Kimbrough, Richard Benito 1931- *ConAu 41R, WhoMW 76*

Kimenye, Barbara *IntAu&W 91, TwCChW 89, WrDr 86, -88, -90, -92, -94*

Kimenye, Barbara 1940?- *AfrA, BioIn 11 BlmGWL, ConAu 101, FemiCLE, OxCChiL, SelBAAf, TwCChW 78, -83, WrDr 80, -82, -84*

Kimmel, Eric A 1946- *WrDr 86, -88, -90, -92, -94*

Kimmel, Eric Alan 1946- *BioIn 11, ConAu 49, -3NR, IntAu&W 77, SmATA 13, WrDr 76, -80, -82, -84*

Kimmel, Margaret Mary *BioIn 14, -15*

Kimmel, Margaret Mary 1938- *ConAu 124, SmATA 33, -43, WhoLibS 66*

Kincaid, Jamaica *BioIn 14, -17, DrAPF 89, -91, -93*

Kincaid, Jamaica 1949?- *BenetAL 91, BlkLC, BlkWr 1, BlmGWL, ConAu 125, ConBlB 4, ConLC 43, -68, ConNov 86, -91, CurBio 91, CyWA 89, FemiCLE, FifCWr, IntAu&W 91, LiExTwC, NewYTBS 90, NotBlAW 92, TwCYAW, WhoAm 92, WhoAmW 93, WhoBlA 92, WorAu 1980, WrDr 88, -90, -92, -94*

Kindred, Wendy Good 1937- *BioIn 10, ConAu 37R, SmATA 7, WrDr 76, -80*

Kinert, Reed Charles 1912?- *AuBYP 2, -3 BioIn 7, IndAu 1917, WhAmArt 85*

Kines, Pat Decker 1937- *BioIn 11, ConAu 65, SmATA 12*

Pseud./variant:
Tapio, Pat Decker

King, Adam *ConAu X, SmATA X*
Main entry: Hoare, Robert John

King, Arthur *AuBYP 3*
Main entry: Cain, Arthur Homer

King, Arthur 1913- *ConAu X, SmATA 3*

King, Charles 1844-1933 *Alli SUP, AmAu&B, AmLY, ArizL, BiD&SB, BioIn 5, –8, CarSB, ConAu 122, DcAmAu, DcNAA, EncFWF, HarEnUS, OxCAmL 65, –83, TwCWW 91, WhAm 1, WhNaAH, WhNAA, WisWr*

King, Clive
Main entry: King, David Clive

King, Clive 1924- *BioIn 13, ConAu 104, IntAu&W 89, –91, OxCChiL, ScF&FL 92, SmATA 28, TwCChW 78, –83, –89, WrDr 82, –84, –86, –88, –90, –92*

King, Colin 1943- *SmATA 76*

King, Cynthia *DrAPF 87, –89, –91, –93*

King, Cynthia 1921- *DrAPF 83, –85, WhoLibI 82*

King, Cynthia 1925- *BioIn 10, ConAu 29R, –36NR, MichAu 80, ScF&FL 92, SmATA 7, WrDr 76, –80, –82, –84, –86, –88, –90, –92, –94*

King, David Clive 1924- *ChlFicS, WrDr 76, –80*
Pseud./variant:
King, Clive

King, Edith Louise Mary *ChhPo, Str&VC*

King, Frank L 1892-1958 *BioIn 5*

King, Frank O 1883-1969 *AmAu&B, ArtCS, BioIn 1, –2, –3, –8, –13, ChhPo S1, EncTwCJ, SmATA 22N, WhAm 5, WhAmArt 85, WhoAmA 78N, –89N, –91N*

King, Harold 1945- *ChhPo S2, ConAu 57, –7NR, ScF&FL 92, SpyFic*

King, Helen Hayes 1937?- *BlkAWP, ConAu 33R, LivgBAA, SelBAAu, WhoAm 76, –78, WhoBlA 75, –77, –80*

King, Hiram Burris 1890- *BioIn 10*

King, Larry L *BioIn 15, –17, ConDr 88D, IntvTCA 2*

King, Larry L 1929- *ConAu 24NR, ConTFT 10, IntAu&W 91, MajTwCW, SmATA 66, WhoAm 86, –88, –90, –92, –94, WhoE 89, –91, –93, WhoEnt 92, WrDr 86, –88, –90, –92, –94*

King, Maria Anna 1964- *SmATA 72*

King, Marian *AmAu&B, Au&Wr 71, BioIn 13, ConAu 5R, –2NR, ForWC 70, SmATA 23, WhoAm 74, –76, –78, –80, –82, –84, WhoAmW 74, –77, –81, WhoE 83, –85, WhoSSW 73, WrDr 76, –80, –82, –84, –86*

King, Marian d1986 *BioIn 16, WhAm 9*

King, Marian 1900?-1986 *ConAu 118, SmATA 47N*

King, Martha Bennett *AuBYP 2, –3, BioIn 7*

King, Martin *ConAu X, SmATA 14, –X*
Main entry: Marks, Stan

King, Martin Luther, Jr. 1929-1968 *BlkWr 2, EncAACR*

King, Mary Louise 1911- *ConAu 21R*

King, Patricia 1930- *ConAu 5R*

King, Paul
Main entry: Drackett, Phil

King, Reefe *SmATA 8*
Main entry: Barker, Albert W

King, Robin 1919- *BioIn 5, ConAu 5R, IlsCB 1946*

King, Ruth *ConICB, WhAmArt 85*

King, Ruth, Dame *Who 88*

King, Seth S *AuBYP 2, –3, BioIn 8, WhoE 74*

King, Stephen *DrmM 2, IntMPA 88, NewYTBS 88*

King, Stephen 1944- *WhoSSW 91, –93*

King, Stephen 1946- *HalFC 88, WrDr 86*

King, Stephen 1947- *Au&Arts 1, Benet 87, BenetAL 91, BestSel 90-1, BioIn 11, –12, –13, –14, –15, –16, –17, CelR 90, ConAu 61, –1NR, –30NR, ConLC 12, –26, –37, –61, ConTFT 8, CrtSuMy, CurBio 81, CyWA 89, DcLB Y80B, EncSF 93, HalFC 84, IntMPA 92, MagSAmL, MajTwCW, NewEScF, NewYTBS 81, Novels, PenEncH, ScF&FL 92, ScFSB, SmATA 9, –55, SupFW, TwCYAW, WhoAm 80, –82, –84, WhoHr&F, WorAlBi, WorAu 1980, WrDr 82, –84, –88, –90, –92, –94*
Pseud./variant:
Bachman, Richard

King, Tom 1730-1804 *OxCThe 83*

King, Tom 1946- *WhoSSW 93*

King, Tony 1947- *ConAu 109, SmATA 39*

King-Hall, Stephen 1893-1966 *BioIn 3, -7, -10, ChhPo S2, ConAu 5R, DcNaB 1961, LongCTC, WhoLA*

Kingman, Dong 1911- *BioIn 1, -2, -3, -4, -5, -6, -7, -8, -12, -13, -15, -16, -17, CelR, ConAu 112, CurBio 62, IlsCB 1946, IntMPA 75, -76, -78, -81, -82, -84, -86, -88, -92, -77, SmATA 44, WhoAm 74, -76, -78, -80, -82, -84, -86, -88, -90, -92, -94, WhoAmA 73, WhoAsA 94, WhoWest 94, WhoWor 74*

Kingman, Lee 1919- *AuBYP 2, BioIn 1, -6, -8, -9, -15, -17, ChhPo, -S1, ConAu 5R, ConLC 17, ForWC 70, IntAu&W 91, MorJA, SmATA 1, -67, -3AS, TwCChW 78, -83, -89, WrDr 76, -80, -82, -84, -86, -88, -90, -92*

Kingman, Mary Lee 1919- *AuBYP 3, DcAmChF 1960*

Kingsbury, Alison Mason 1898- *ChhPo, -S1, DcWomA, WhAmArt 85*

Kingsbury, Phyllis May *IntAu&W 77*
Pseud./variant:
Flowerdew, Phyllis

Kingsland, Leslie William 1912- *BioIn 11, ConAu 69, SmATA 13*

Kingsley, Charles 1819-1875 *Alli, -SUP, AnCL, AtlBL, AuBYP 2, -3, Benet 87, BbD, BiD&SB, BioIn 1, -2, -3, -4, -5, -6, -8, -9, -10, -11, -12, -14, -15, -16, BlmGEL, BritAS, BritAu 19, CamGEL, CamGLE, CarSB, CasWL, CelCen, Chambr 3, ChhPo, -S1, -S2, CrtT 3, CyEd, CyWA 58, DcAmSR, DcBiA, DcBiPP, DcBrBI, DcEnA, DcEnL, DcEuL, DcLB 21, -32, DcLEL, DcNaB, Dis&D, EvLB, FamPYP, JBA 34, LongCEL, LuthC 75, McGEWB, MouLC 3, NewC, NinCLC 35, Novels, OxCChiL, OxCEng 67, -85, PenC ENG, RAdv 1, -13-1, REn, RfGEnL 91, StaCVF, TelT, TwCChW 83A, -89A, WebE&AL, WhDW, WhoChL, WrChl, YABC 2*
Pseud./variant:
Lot, Parson

Kingsley, Emily Perl 1940- *BioIn 14, ConAu 107, SmATA 33, WhoAmW 93, WhoEnt 92*

Kingsley, Henry 1830-1876 *Alli SUP, BbD, BiD&SB, BioIn 2, -5, -9, -13, -14, BritAu 19, CamGEL, CamGLE, CarSB, CasWL, CelCen, Chambr 3, ChhPo S1, CyWA 58, DcBiA, DcBiPP, DcEnA, DcEnL, DcEuL, DcLB 21, DcLEL, DcNaB, -C, EvLB, HsB&A, NewC, OxCAusL, OxCEng 67, -85, PenC ENG, REn, RfGEnL 91, StaCVF WebE&AL*

King-Smith, Dick *IntAu&W 86X*

King-Smith, Dick 1922- *AuBYP 3, BioIn 15, -16, ChlFicS, ConAu 105, -22NR, IntAu&W 91, MajAI, ScF&FL 92, SixBJA, SmATA 38, -47, TwCChW 83, -89, WhoAm 84, -86, -88, -90, WrDr 86, -88, -90, -92, -94*

Kingston, Maxine Hong *BioIn 15, -16, -17, DrAPF 93, NewYTBS 89*

Kingston, Maxine Hong 1940- *AmWomWr 92, ArtclWW 2, Au&Arts 8, BenetAL 91, BlmGWL, ConLC 58, CurBio 90, CyWA 89, FemiCLE, HanAmWH, InWom SUP, IntAu&W 91, IntWW 91, MagSAmL, MajTwCW, ModAWWr, PostFic, SmATA 53, TwCWW 91, WhoAm 86, -88, -90, -92 -94, WhoAmW 87, -89, -91, -93, WrDr 88, -90, -92, -94*

Kingston, Maxine Ting Ting Hong 1940- *ConAu 38NR*

Kingston, William Henry Giles 1814-1880 *Alli, -SUP, BbD, BbtC, BiD&SB, BioIn 1, -8, BritAu 19, CarSB, CasWL, CelCen, Chambr 3, DcNaB, EvLB, OxCChiL, OxCEng 67, OxCShps, WhoChL*
Pseud./variant:
Beaver, Barrington

Kinney, C Cle 1915- *AuBYP 2S, BioIn 10, ConAu 9R, SmATA 6*

Kinney, Cle 1915- *AuBYP 3*

Kinney, Harrison 1921- *BioIn 11, ConAu 1R, SmATA 13*

Kinney, Jean 1912- *AuBYP 3*

Kinney, Jean Stout 1912- *AuBYP 2S, BioIn 11, ConAu 9R, ForWC 70, SmATA 12*

Kinser, Charleen *AuBYP 2S, -3*

Kinsey, Elizabeth *AuBYP 3, ConAu X, IntAu&W 86X, -91X, SmATA X, TwCChW 83, -89, WrDr 76, -80, -82, -84*
Main entry: Clymer, Eleanor

Kinsey, Elizabeth 1906- *WrDr 94*

Kinsey-Jones, Brian *ConAu X, IntAu&W 91X*
Main entry: Ball, Brian N

Kinsey-Warnock, Natalie 1956- *SmATA 7?*

Kinstler, Everett Raymond *BioIn 14*

Kinstler, Everett Raymond 1926- *ConAu 33R, ConGrA 3, WhoAm 74, -76, -78, -80, -82, -84, -86, -88, -90, -92, -94, WhoAmA 73, -78, -80, -82, -84, -86, -89, -91, WhoE 74, -75, -77, WhoWor 93*

Kinzel, Dorothy 1950- *SmATA 57*
Pseud./variant:
Kinzel, Dottie

Kinzel, Dottie
Main entry: Kinzel, Dorothy

Kinzel, Dottie 1950- *SmATA X*

Kiphuth, Robert John Herman 1890-1967 *BiDAmSp BK, BioIn 1, -4, -5, -6, -7, -8, -10, CurBio 57, -67, DcAmB S8, ObitOF 79*

Kipling, John Lockwood 1837-1911 *BioIn 12, -14, -15, ChhPo, DcBrBI, DcInB, NewC*

Kipling, Joseph Rudyard 1865-1936 *MajAI*

Kipling, Rudyard 1865-1936 *Alli SUP, AnCL, AtlBL, AuBYP 2, -3, Benet 87, BbD, BiD&SB, BioIn 1, -2, -3, -4, -5, -6, -7, -8, -9, -10, -11, -12, -13, -14, -15, -16, -17, BlmGEL, BritWr 6, CamGEL, CamGLE, CarSB, CasWL, Chambr 3, ChhPo, -S1, -S2, CmCal, CnDBLB 5, CnE&AP, CnMWL, ConAu 105, -120, -33NR, CrtT 3, CyWA 58, DcAmAu, DcBiA, DcBrBI, DcEnA, -A, DcEuL, DcInB, DcLB 19, -34, DcLEL, DcNaB 1931, Dis&D, EncPaPR 91, EncWL, -2, EvLB, FamAYP, FamSYP, FilmgC, GrBr, HalFC 84, -88, JBA 34, LongCEL, LongCTC, MagSWL, MajTwCW, ModBrL, -S1, -S2, NewC, NewEScF, NobelP, Novels, OxCAmL 65, -83, OxCCan, OxCChiL, OxCEng 67, -85, OxCMus, PenC ENG, PenEncH, PoeCrit 3, RAdv 1, -13-1, RComWL, REn, RfGEnL 91, ScF&FL 92, ScFSB, ScFEYrs, ShSCr 5, ShSWr, StaCVF, Str&VC, SupFW, TelT, TwCA, -SUP, TwCChW 78, -83, -89, TwCLC 8, -17, TwCSFW 86, -91, TwCWr, WebE&AL, WhDW, WhoChL, WhoHr&F, WhoLA, WhoTwCL, WorAlBi, WorAl, WorLitC, WrChl, YABC 2*

Kipniss, Robert 1931- *BioIn 15, ConGrA 2, DcCAA 71, -77, -88, IlsBYP, PrintW 85, WhoAm 80, -82, -84, -86, -88, -90, -92, -94, WhoAmA 73, -78, -80, -82, -84, -86, -89, -91, WhoE 91*

Kirby, Douglas James 1929- *Au&Wr 71, ChhPo S1, ConAu 25R*

Kirby, Elizabeth 1823-1873 *CarSB, DcNaB*

Kirby, Jean *AuBYP 2S, -3, ConAu X*
Main entry: McDonnell, Virginia Bleecker

Kirby, Margaret *SmATA 72*
Main entry: Bingley, Margaret Jane

Kirby, Susan Alice *AuBYP 3*

Kirby, Susan E 1949- *SmATA 62*
Pseud./variant:
Stephens, Suzanne 1949-

Kirby, William 1817-1906 *Alli SUP, BenetAL 91, BbtC, BiD&SB, BioIn 17, CanWr, CasWL, CreCan 2, DcLB 99, DcLEL, DcNAA, OxCAmL 65, OxCCan, -SUP, OxCCanL, REn, REnAL, StaCVF*

Kirk, Donald Robert 1935- *ConAu 57, WhoWest 78*

Kirk, Ellen Warner 1842-1928 *WomNov*

Kirk, Ellen Warner Olney 1842-1928 *Alli SUP, AmAu&B, BbD, BiD&SB, BioIn 12, CarSB, DcAmAu, DcBiA, DcNAA, WhAm 4, WomWWA 14*

Kirk, Maria Louise 1860?- *ChhPo S1, ConICB, DcWomA, WhAmArt 85*

Kirk, Rhina *AuBYP 2S, -3*

Kirk, Richard 1931- *ConAu 13R*

Kirk, Richard Ray 1877-1951 *BioIn 2, ChhPo S1, -S2, WhNAA*

Kirk, Ruth 1925- *AuBYP 3*

Kirk, Ruth Eleanor 1925- *AuBYP 2, BioIn 8, -10, ConAu 13R, ForWC 70, SmATA 5, WhoPNW*

Kirk, Thomas Hobson 1899- *Au&Wr 71, ConAu 21R, WrDr 76, -80, -82, -84*

Kirkland, Will
Main entry: Hale, Arlene

Kirkpatrick, Oliver Austin 1911- *BlkAull, ConAu 49, InB&W 80, LivgBAA*

Kirkpatrick, Oliver Austin 1911-1988 *BlkAull 92*

Kirkup, James Falconer 1927?- *Au&Wr 71, BioIn 4, -5, -8, -10, -11, ChhPo, -S2, ConAu 1R, ConLC 1, ConPo 70, -75, IntAu&W 77, IntWW 74, LongCTC, NewC, PenC ENG, REn, SmATA 12, Who 74, WhoWor 74, -82, -84, WorAu 1950, WrDr 76, -80*
Pseud./variant:
Falconer, James
James, Andrew

Kirkus, Virginia 1893-1980 *AmAu&B, AnObit 1980, BioIn 3, -12, -13, ConAu X, CurBio 41, -54, -80N, NewYTBS 80, SmATA X*

Pseud./variant:
Glick, Virginia Kirkus

Kirkwood, Ellen Swan 1904- *ConAu 25R*

Kirkwood, James 1930- *AuNews 2, Au&Wr 71, BioIn 11, –13, ConAu 1R, –6NR, ConLC 9, ConTFT 5, NatPD 77, –81, WhoAm 76, –78, –80, –82, –84, –86, –88, WhoThe 81, WrDr 80, –82, –84, –86, –88*

Kirkwood, James 1930-1989 *BioIn 16, –17, ConAu 128, –40NR, WhAm 10*

Kirmse, Marguerite 1885-1954 *BioIn 1, –3, –5, ConICB, DcWomA, IlsBYP, IlsCB 1744, –1946, WhAmArt 85*

Kirn, Ann Minette 1910- *AuBYP 2, –3, BioIn 8, ChhPo S1, ConAu 93, IlsCB 1957*

Kirsch, Paul John 1914- *ConAu 108, DrAS 74P, –78P, –82P, WhoRel 75, –77*

Kirst, Hans Hellmut d1989 *IntWW 89N*

Kirst, Hans Hellmut 1914- *AuSpks, BioIn 6, –8, –10, –11, CasWL, ConAu 104, DcLB 69, IntAu&W 77, –89, –91, IntWW 74, –75, –76, –77, –78, –79, –80, –81, –82, –83, ModGL, RAdv 13-2, TwCCr&M 80B, –85B, TwCWr, WhAm 9, WhoWor 74, –82, WorAu 1950*

Kirst, Hans Hellmut 1914-1989 *AnObit 1989, BioIn 16, ConAu 128, EncSF 93, ScF&FL 92, TwCCr&M 91B*

Kirst, Hans Helmut d1989 *NewYTBS 89*

Kirtland, G B *AuBYP 3, ConAu X, IntAu&W 91X, SmATA 2, ThrBJA, WrDr 80, –82, –84, –86, –88, –92*
Main entry: Joslin, Sesyle

Kirtland, G B 1929- *WrDr 90, –94*

Kiser, Martha Gwinn *AuBYP 2, –3, BioIn 2, –8*

Kish, Eleanor Mary 1924- *SmATA 73*
Pseud./variant:
Kish, Ely

Kish, Ely *SmATA 73*
Main entry: Kish, Eleanor Mary

Kishida, Eriko 1929- *BioIn 11, ConAu 53, –7NR, SmATA 12*

Kisinger, Grace Gelvin 1913-1960? *AuBYP 2, BioIn 8, –11, ConAu P-1, SmATA 10*

Kisinger, Grace Gelvin 1913-1965 *AuBYP 3*

Kissen, Fan 1904- *ConAu P-1*

Kissin, Eva H 1923- *BioIn 11, ConAu 29R, SmATA 10*

Kitamura, Satoshi 1956- *SmATA 62*

Kit Carson *WhNaAH*

Kit Carson 1809-1868 *OxCChiL*

Kitchen, Bert *ChlBIlD, SmATA 70*
Main entry: Kitchen, Herbert Thomas

Kitchen, Fred *ChhPo S2*

Kitchen, Herbert Thomas 1940- *SmATA 70*
Pseud./variant:
Kitchen, Bert

Kitchen, Herminie Broedel 1901-1973 *Au&Wr 71, BioIn 10, ConAu P-1*

Kitson, Harry Dexter 1886-1959 *BioIn 1, –2, –5, –9, CurBio 51, –59, InSci, IndAu 1816, ObitOF 79, WhAm 3, WhNAA*

Kitt, Tamara *IntAu&W 91X, MajAI, SmATA 68, TwCChW 83, –89, WrDr 82, –84, –86, –88, –90, –92, –94*
Main entry: de Regniers, Beatrice Schenk Freedman

Kittelsen, Theodor 1857-1914 *BioIn 3, –11, WorECar*

Kituomba *BlkWr 1, –2, MajAI, SmATA 67*
Main entry: Odaga, Asenath Bole

Kitzinger, Sheila 1929- *BioIn 16, ContDcW 89, SmATA 57, WrDr 86, –88, –90, –92, –94*

Kizer, Carolyn *BioIn 16, DrAPF 87, –89, –91, –93*

Kizer, Carolyn 1925- *ArtclWW 2, BenetAL 91, BioIn 10, –12, CamGLE, CamHAL, ConAu 65, –5AS, –24NR, ConLC 15, –39, ConPo 70, –75, –80, –85, –91, CroCAP, DcLB 5, DcLEL 1940, DrAP 75, DrAPF 83, –85, FemiCLE, InWom SUP, OxCAmL 83, PenC AM, WhoAm 82, –84, WorAu 1950, WrDr 76, –80, –82, –84, –86, –88, –90, –92, –94*

Kizer, Carolyn Ashley 1925- *WhoAm 92*

Kjelgaard, James A *ScF&FL 92*

Kjelgaard, James Arthur 1910-1959 *AuBYP 2, –3, BioIn 2, –3, –5, –7, –12, ConAu 109, –137, JBA 51, MajAI, SmATA 17, Str&VC, TwCChW 78*
Pseud./variant:
Kjelgaard, Jim

Kjelgaard, Jim *ConAu 137, EncSF 93, MajAI*
Main entry: Kjelgaard, James Arthur

Kjelgaard, Jim 1910-1959 *ConAu X, OxCChiL, ScF&FL 92, SmATA X, TwCChW 83, –89*

Klaasse, Piet *ChhPo S1*

Klagsbrun, Francine Lifton *ConAu 21R, ForWC 70, SmATA 36, WhoAmW 77, –81*

Klaits, Barrie 1944- *BioIn 16, ConAu 73, MichAu 80, SmATA 52*

Klaperman, Gilbert 1921- *BioIn 14, ConAu 49, SmATA 33, WhoAm 90, –92, –94, WhoAmJ 80, WhoRel 92, WhoWorJ 72, –78*

Klaperman, Libby Mindlin 1921-1982 *ConAu 9R, –107, SmATA 31N, –33*

Klass, Morton 1927- *AmMWSc 73S, –76P, AuBYP 2S, –3, BioIn 11, ConAu 1R, –5NR, FifIDA, SmATA 11, WhoAm 84, –86, –88, –90, –92, –94*

Klass, Sheila Solomon *BioIn 15, DrAPF 87, –89, –91, –93*

Klass, Sheila Solomon 1927- *ConAu 13NR, –37NR, DrAPF 83, –85, SmATA 45, WhoAmW 83, WhoUSWr 88, WhoWrEP 89, –92, WrDr 82, –84, –86, –88, –90, –92, –94*

Klause, Annette Curtis *BioIn 17, ScF&FL 92, TwCYAW*

Klause, Annette Curtis 1953- *WhoAm 92, –94*

Klausner, Abraham J 1915- *BioIn 1, ConAu 108, WhoAmJ 80, WhoE 75, WhoWorJ 72, –78*

Klaveness, Jan O'Donnell 1939- *DcAmChF 1960*

Klebe, Charles Eugene 1907- *BioIn 9, ConAu P-2, WhoAmA 73, –78*
Pseud./variant:
Klebe, Gene

Klebe, Gene
Main entry: Klebe, Charles Eugene

Kleberger, Ilse 1921- *BioIn 10, ConAu 41R, –15NR, –39NR, SmATA 5*

Kleeberg, Irene Cumming *BioIn 17*

Kleeberg, Irene Cumming 1932- *AuBYP 2S, –3, ConAu 61, –12NR, –35NR, SmATA 65*

Klein, Aaron E 1930- *AuBYP 2S, –3, BioIn 13, –15, ConAu 25R, –19NR, SmATA 28, –45*
Pseud./variant:
Little, A Edward

Klein, David d1988 *BioIn 15*

Klein, David 1919- *AmMWSc 73S, –78S, AuBYP 2, –3, BioIn 8, –9, –16, BlueB 76, ConAu 1R, –1NR, –18NR, –40NR, IntWW 74, –75, –76, –77, –78, –79, –80, –81, –82, –83, –89, –91, SmATA 59, WhoAm 74, –76, –78, –80, –82, –84, –86, –88, –90, –92, –94, WhoGov 72, –75, WhoWest 94, WhoWor 80, –82, –84, –87, –89, –91, –93*

Klein, David J *AuBYP 3*

Klein, Deana Tarson 1925- *AmMWSc 73P, –76P, –82, –86, –89, –92*

Klein, Gerda Weissmann 1924- *BioIn 15, ConAu 116, SmATA 44*

Klein, H Arthur *AuBYP 2, BioIn 11, ConAu 13R, SmATA 8*

Klein, Herbert Arthur *AuBYP 3*

Klein, Leonore 1916- *AuBYP 2, –3, BiDrLUS 70, BioIn 8, –10, ConAu 1R, –1NR, ForWC 70, SmATA 6, WhoLibS 66*

Klein, Mina C 1906-1979 *ConAu 133*

Klein, Mina Cooper 1906- *BioIn 11, ConAu 37R, IntAu&W 77, –82, SmATA 8*

Klein, Norma *DrAPF 87*

Klein, Norma d1989 *NewYTBS 89*

Klein, Norma 1938- *Au&Arts 2, AuBYP 2S, BioIn 10, –15, ChlLR 2, ConAu 41R, –15NR, ConLC 30, DcAmChF 1960, DrAF 76, DrAPF 83, –85, FifBJA, IntAu&W 77, –89, –91, OxCChiL, SmATA 7, –1AS, TwCChW 78, –83, WhoAm 84, –86, –88, WhoAmW 83, WhoUSWr 88, WhoWrEP 89, WrDr 80, –82, –84, –86, –88*

Klein, Norma 1938-1989 *AnObit 1989, AuBYP 3, BioIn 16, ChlLR 19, ConAu 128, –37NR, MajAI, SmATA 57, TwCChW 89, TwCYAW, WhAm 10*

Klein, Richard M 1923- *AmMWSc 73P, –76P, –82, –86, –89, –92, ConAu 108, –25NR*

Klein, Robin 1936- *AuWomWr, BioIn 15, –16, BlmGWL, ChlLR 21, ConAu 116, –40NR, DcChlFi, MajAI, ScF&FL 92, SmATA 45, –55, TwCChW 89, TwCYAW, WrDr 90, –92*

Klein, Robin McMaugh 1936- *WrDr 94*

Klein, Stanley 1930- *ConAu 57, WhoE 77*

Klein, Suzanne Marie 1940- *ConAu 57*

Klemin, Diana *AuBYP 2S, –3, BioIn 17, ChhPo S2, ConAu 49, SmATA 65*

Klemke, Werner 1917- *ArtsCL, BioIn 6, ConDes 84, -90, WhoGrA 62*

Klemm, Edward G 1910- *BioIn 14*

Klemm, Edward G, Jr. 1910- *ConAu 57, SmATA 30*

Klemm, Roberta K 1884- *BioIn 14, ConAu 61, IntAu&W 82, SmATA 30*

Kleven, Elisa 1958- *SmATA 76*
Pseud./variant:
Schneider, Elisa

Klever, Anita *AuBYP 2S, -3*

Klevin, Jill Ross 1935- *BioIn 15, ConAu 111, IntAu&W 86, -89, SmATA 38, -39*

Kliban, B 1935- *BioIn 11, -14, ConAu 106, SmATA 35, WhoAm 80, -82, -84, -86, -88*

Kliban, B 1935-1990 *AnObit 1990, BioIn 17, ConAu 132, NewYTBS 90, SmATA 66*

Kliban, Bernard 1935-1990 *WhAm 10*

Klimowicz, Barbara 1927- *AuBYP 2S, -3, BioIn 11, ConAu 21R, SmATA 10*

Kline, Morris d1992 *NewYTBS 92*

Kline, Morris 1908- *AmMWSc 73P, -76P, -82, -86, -89, -92, ConAu 5R, -2NR, IntAu&W 77, -82, WhoAm 74, -76, -78, WhoAmJ 80, WrDr 76, -80, -82, -84, -86, -88, -90, -92*

Kline, Morris 1908-1992 *ConAu 139, WhAm 10*

Kline, Nancy M 1937- *WhoLibI 82*

Kline, Nancy Mattoon 1937- *WhoE 91*

Kline, Nancy Meadors 1946- *ConAu 57*

Kline, Peter 1936- *ConAu 25R, WrDr 76, -80, -82, -84, -86, -88, -90, -92, -94*

Kline, Suzy 1943- *AuBYP 3, BioIn 16, -17, ConAu 120, SmATA 48, -67*

Klink, Johanna L 1918- *ChhPo S1, ConAu 61, -8NR*

Klopfer, Peter Hubert 1930- *AmMWSc 73P, -76P, -82, -86, -89, -92, ConAu 85, WhoSSW 75, -76*

Klose, Norma Cline 1936- *ConAu 17R*

Klots, Alexander Barrett 1903- *AmMWSc 73P, ConAu 107*

Klots, Alexander Barrett 1903-1989 *BioIn 16, -17, ConAu 128, SmATA 62*

Klots, Alexander Barrett, Dr d1989 *NewYTBS 89*

Kluetmeier, Heinz *BioIn 10*

Klug, Ron 1939- *BioIn 14, ConAu 107, -24NR, SmATA 31*

Klug, Ronald Allan 1939- *WhoWrEP 89, -92*

Kluwe, Mary Jean 1905-1975 *ConAu P-2*

Knapp, Edward *ConAu 134, SmATA 67, WrDr 94*
Main entry: Kunhardt, Edith

Knapp, J Augustus *ChhPo*

Knapp, Ron 1952- *ConAu 103, SmATA 34*

Knatchbull-Hugessen, E H 1829-1893 *BioIn 8, ChhPo, -S1, DcEnL, DcNaB S1, NewC, OxCChiL, TelT, WhoChL*
Pseud./variant:
Brabourne, Edward H, Lord

Knatchbull-Hugessen, Edward Hugessen 1829-1893 *Alli SUP*

Knauth, Percy 1914- *BioIn 10, -12, ConAu 57*

Knebel, Fletcher *DrAPF 87, -89, -91, -93*

Knebel, Fletcher d1993 *NewYTBS 93*

Knebel, Fletcher 1911- *BioIn 7, -10, -12, -14, -15, ConAu 3AS, -1NR, -36NR, ConNov 82, -86, -91, DrAPF 83, -85, IntAu&W 82, -86, -91, SmATA 36, WhoAm 80, -82, -84, -86, -88, -90, -92, WhoWest 94, WorAu 1975, WrDr 82, -84, -86, -88, -90, -92*

Knebel, Fletcher 1911-1992? *EncSF 93*

Knebel, Fletcher 1911-1993 *ConAu 140, SmATA 75, WrDr 94N*

Knerr, Harold 1883-1949 *ArtCS, BioIn 2, -4, -7*

Knerr, Harold H 1882-1949 *EncACom*

Knickerbocker, Diedrich *AmAu&B, CamGEL, DcEnL, DcNAA, EvLB, OxCAmL 65, OxCEng 67, -85, YABC X*
Main entry: Irving, Washington

Knifesmith *ConAu X, SmATA X*
Main entry: Cutler, Ivor

Kniffen, Fred Bowerman 1900- *AmMWSc 73S, -76P, ConAu 1R, FifIDA*

Knigge, Robert d1987 *BioIn 16*

Knigge, Robert 1921?-1987 *ConAu 121, SmATA 50N*

Knight, Anne Katherine 1946- *BioIn 12, IlsCB 1967, SmATA 34, WrDr 76, –80*

Knight, Arthur Lee *Alli SUP*

Knight, Bernard 1931- *Au&Wr 71, ConAu 49, –2NR, IntAu&W 91, OxCLiW 86, WrDr 76, –80, –82, –84, –86, –88, –90, –92, –94*

Knight, Bertram 1904- *Au&Wr 71, ConAu 103, IntAu&W 77, WrDr 76, –80, –82*

Knight, Charles Robert 1874-1953 *BioIn 1, –3, –4, –5, –12, –17, IlsCB 1946, WhAm 3, WhAmArt 85*

Knight, Charles W 1891- *ConAu P-1*

Knight, Clayton *EncACom*

Knight, Clayton 1891-1969 *AuBYP 2, –3, BioIn 1, –7, –8, ConAu P-1, IlrAm 1880, –D, WhAmArt 85*

Knight, Damon *IntvTCA 2*

Knight, Damon 1922- *BioIn 10, –11, ConAu 49, –10AS, –3NR, –17NR, –36NR, ConSFA, DcLB 8, NewEScF, Novels, RGTwCSF, ScF&FL 92, ScFSB, ScFEYrs, SmATA 9, TwCSFW 86, –91, WhoSciF, WorAu 1950, WrDr 76, –80, –82*

Knight, Damon Francis 1922- *EncSF 93*

Knight, David 1923- *ArtsCL, BioIn 6*

Knight, David 1923-1982 *BioIn 14*

Knight, David C 1925- *AuBYP 2, BioIn 8, –12, ConAu 73, SmATA 14*

Knight, David Carpenter 1925- *AuBYP 3*

Knight, Eric 1897-1943 *BenetAL 91, HalFC 88, LiExTwC, TwCChW 89*

Knight, Eric Mowbray 1897-1943 *AuBYP 2, –3, BioIn 1, –3, –4, –5, –7, –8, –12, CnDAL, ConAu 137, CurBio 42, –43, CyWA 58, FourBJA, HalFC 84, MajAI, OxCChiL, REn, REnAL, SmATA 18, TwCA, –SUP, TwCChW 83, WhAm 2, WhoChL, WorAl*
Pseud./variant:
Hallas, Richard

Knight, Francis Edgar 1905- *Au&Wr 71, BioIn 8, ConAu 73, SingR 2, SmATA 14, TwCChW 78, WhoChL, WrDr 80*
Pseud./variant:
Knight Frank
Salter, Cedric

Knight, Frank d1985 *BioIn 14*

Knight, Frank 1905- *BioIn 8, –12, IntAu&W 91, SmATA X, TwCChW 83, –89, WrDr 82, –84, –86, –88, –90, –92, –94*

Knight, Harold V 1907- *ConAu 21R*

Knight, Hilary 1926- *AuBYP 2, –3, BioIn 6, –8, –12, ChhPo, –S1, –S2, ConAu 73, FourBJA, IlsCB 1957, –1967, MajAI, SmATA 15, –69, WhoAmA 73, –78, –80, –82, –84*

Knight, Kathryn Lasky *MajAI, SmATA 69*
Main entry: Lasky, Kathryn

Knight, Mallory T *ConAu X, –43NR, SmATA X*
Main entry: Hurwood, Bernhardt J

Knight, Max *AuBYP 3*

Knight, Max d1993 *NewYTBS 93*

Knight, Max 1909- *AuBYP 2S, BioIn 8, ConAu 93, –40NR*

Knight, Max 1909-1993 *ConAu 142*

Knight, Maxwell 1900- *ConAu P-1*

Knight, Peter *AuBYP 2, –3, BioIn 8*

Knight, Ruth Adams 1898-1974 *AuBYP 2, –3, BioIn 3, –4, –6, –8, –12, ConAu 5R, –49, CurBio 43, –55, ForWC 70, MorJA, OhA&B, SmATA 20N*

Knight, Theodore O 1946- *SmATA 77*

Knight, Vick Ralph, Jr. 1928- *ConAu 45, –1NR, –16NR, –37NR, WhoWest 74, –76, –78*

Knight Frank
Main entry: Knight, Francis Edgar

Knightley, Phillip 1929- *ConAu 25R, WhoWor 74, WrDr 80, –82, –84, –86, –88, –90, –92*

Knightley, Phillip George 1929- *WrDr 94*

Knipe, Alden Arthur 1870-1950 *AmAu&B, AmLY, BioIn 2, JBA 34, –51, WhAm 4, WhNAA*

Knipe, Emilie Benson 1870-1958 *AmAu&B, AmLY, BioIn 2, –5, ChhPo, JBA 34, –51, WhAm 3, WhNAA*

Knoepfle, John *BioIn 17, DrAPF 87, –89, –91, –93*

Knoepfle, John 1923- *AuBYP 2S, -3, ConAu 13R, -12NR, -29NR, ConPo 70, -75, -80, -85, -91, DrAP 75, DrAPF 83, -85, DrAS 74E, SmATA 66, WhoUSWr 88, WhoWrEP 89, -92, WrDr 76, -80, -82, -84, -86, -88, -90, -92, -94*

Knoop, Faith Yingling 1896- *ConAu 97, IntAu&W 77*

Knopf, Mildred Oppenheimer 1898- *BioIn 2, WhoAmW 74*

Knott, William C 1927- *BioIn 14, ConAu 22NR, WhoWrEP 89, WrDr 86, -88, -90, -92*

Knott, William Cecil 1927- *AuBYP 3, WrDr 94*

Knott, William Cecil, Jr. *WhoWrEP 92*

Knott, William Cecil, Jr. 1927- *AmAu&B, AuBYP 2S, BioIn 9, ConAu 5R, -7NR, IntAu&W 91, SmATA 3, WrDr 76, -80, -82, -84*
Pseud./variant:
Carol, Bill J

Knotts, Howard Clayton 1922- *BioIn 12, -13, ConAu 69, -11NR, IlsCB 1967, SmATA 25*

Knowles, Anne *BioIn 15*

Knowles, Anne 1933- *ConAu 102, ScF&FL 92, SmATA 37, WrDr 82, -84, -86*

Knowles, John *DrAPF 87, -89, -91, -93*

Knowles, John 1926- *AmAu&B, Au&Arts 10, Au&Wr 71, Benet 87, BenetAL 91, BioIn 7, -10, -11, -17, BlueB 76, BroV, CasWL, ConAu 17R, -40NR, ConLC 1, -4, -10, -26, ConNov 72, -76, -82, -86, -91, CyWA 89, DcLB 6, DcLEL 1940, DrAF 76, DrAPF 83, -85, IntAu&W 77, -82, MagSAmL, MajTwCW, Novels, OxCAmL 83, RAdv 1, SmATA 8, TwCYAW, WhoAm 74, -76, -78, -80, -82, -84, -92, -94, WhoUSWr 88, WhoWor 74, WhoWrEP 89, -92, WorAlBi, WorAl, WorAu 1950, WrDr 76, -80, -82, -84, -86, -88, -90, -92, -94*

Knowles, Mabel Winifred 1875-1949 *BioIn 2, -14, ConAu 122, WhoLA, WomNov*

Knowlton, William Henry 1927- *ConAu 17R, IntAu&W 77, WrDr 76, -80, -82, -84*

Knox, Calvin M *AuBYP 2, -3, ConAu X, -36NR, DcLEL 1940, EncSF 93, MajAI, MajTwCW, SmATA X, ThrBJA, TwCSFW 86, -91*
Main entry: Silverberg, Robert

Knox, Calvin M 1935- *WrDr 94*

Knox, Eleanor Jessie 1909- *BioIn 14, SmATA 30*
Pseud./variant:
Shepard, Mary 1909-

Knox, James *ConAu X, -30NR, DrAPF 83, -85, -89, -91, -93, MajAI, SmATA 76, -X, TwCCr&M 91, WrDr 86, -88*
Main entry: Brittain, William

Knox, James 1807-1876 *BiDrUSC 89*

Knox, Jolyne 1937- *SmATA 76*

Knox, Mary Eleanor Jessie 1909- *MajAI, SmATA 59*

Knox, Olive Elsie *CanWW 70, -80, -81*

Knox, Rose Bell 1879- *AmAu&B, BioIn 2, -3, JBA 34, -51, WhNAA*

Knox, Thomas W 1835-1896 *BenetAL 91*

Knox, Thomas Wallace 1835-1896 *Alli SUP, AmAu, AmAu&B, BbD, BiD&SB, CarSB, DcAmAu, DcNAA, OxCChiL, REnAL, WhAm HS*

Knox-Johnston, Robin 1939- *Au&Wr 71, BioIn 8, ConAu 29R, -15NR, IntAu&W 77, -82, -86, -89, -91, Who 82, -83, -85, -88, -90, -92, WhoWor 78, WrDr 76, -80, -82, -84, -86, -88, -90, -92, -94*

Knudsen, James 1950- *ConAu 111, SmATA 42*

Knudsen, Margrethe June 1934- *WrDr 76, -80, -82, -84, -86, -88, -90, -92, -94*

Knudsen, Per Holm 1945- *IntAu&W 77*

Knudson, R R 1932- *IntAu&W 91, SixBJA, SmATA 18AS, TwCYAW, WrDr 88, -90, -92*

Knudson, R Rozanne 1932- *BioIn 16*

Knudson, Richard L 1930- *ConAu 104, -20NR, DrAS 82E, SmATA 34*

Knudson, Rozanne R 1932- *WrDr 86, -94*

Knudson, Rozanne Ruth 1932- *ConAu 33R, ForWC 70, SmATA 7, WhoAmW 74, WrDr 76, -80, -82, -84*

Knudson, R R *ConAu 35NR*

Knye, Cassandra *MajAI*
Main entry: Disch, Thomas Michael

Kobayashi, Masako Matsuno *AuBYP 3*

Kobayashi, Masako Matsuno 1935- *AuBYP 2, ConAu 5R, -13NR, -31NR*

Pseud./variant:
Matsuno, Masako

Kobrin, Janet 1942- *ConAu 57*

Koch, Charlotte *ConAu 85*
Pseud./variant:
Raymond, Charles

Koch, Claude *DrAPF 87, –89, –91, –93*

Koch, Claude 1918- *AmCath 80, BioIn 3, CathA 1952, ConAu 9R, DrAPF 85, DrAS 74E, –82E, IntAu&W 82, WrDr 76, –80, –82, –84*

Koch, Dorothy 1924- *AuBYP 3*

Koch, Dorothy Clarke 1924- *AuBYP 2, BioIn 7, –10, ConAu 5R, ForWC 70, SmATA 6*

Koch, Kenneth *DrAPF 87, –89, –91, –93, IntvTCA 2*

Koch, Kenneth 1925- *Benet 87, BenetAL 91, BioIn 17, CamGLE, CamHAL, ConAu 36NR, ConDr 88, –93, ConLC 44, ConPo 91, IntAu&W 91, RAdv 13-1, SmATA 65, WhoAm 90, –92, –94, WhoUSWr 88, WhoWrEP 89, –92, WrDr 86, –88, –90, –92, –94*

Koch, Raymond *ConAu 85*
Pseud./variant:
Raymond, Charles

Koch, Thomas J 1947- *ConAu 61*

Kochan, Lionel Edmund 1922- *Au&Wr 71*

Kochan, Miriam 1929- *ConAu 103, WrDr 80, –82, –84, –86, –88, –90, –92*

Kochan, Miriam Louise 1929- *WrDr 94*

Kock, Carl *AuBYP 2S, –3, BioIn 7*

Kocsis, James C 1936- *IlsBYP, IlsCB 1957, SmATA X*
Pseud./variant:
Paul, James

Koda-Callan, Elizabeth *BioIn 17*

Koda-Callan, Elizabeth 1944- *ConAu 136, SmATA 67, WhoAmW 87, –89, WrDr 94*

Koechlin, Patricia Rosemary
Main entry: Smythe, Patricia Rosemary

Koechlin, Patricia Rosemary 1928- *Who 74, –82, –83*

Koehn, Ilse *BioIn 14, ConAu 35NR*
Main entry: VanZwienen, Ilse Charlotte Koehn

Koehn, Ilse d1991 *NewYTBS 91*

Koehn, Ilse 1929- *BioIn 11, –13, FifBJA, HerW 84, SmATA X*

Koehn, Ilse 1929-1991 *BioIn 17*

Koenig, Laird *ConAu 32NR, PenEncH*

Koenig, Laird 1927- *BlkAWP, ConAu 29R, WhoAm 74*

Koering, Ursula 1921- *BioIn 5, –6, IlsBYP, IlsCB 1946, MorJA*

Koering, Ursula 1921-1976 *BioIn 17, SmATA 64*

Koerner, William Henry David 1878-1938 *SmATA 21, WhAm 1*

Koertge, Ron 1940- *Au&Arts 12*

Koertge, Ronald *BioIn 16, –17, DrAPF 87, –89, –91, –93*

Koertge, Ronald 1940- *ConAu 25NR, DcLB 105, SmATA 53, TwCYAW*

Koff, Richard M 1926- *BioIn 17, ScF&FL 92, SmATA 62, WhoTech 84, WrDr 86, –88, –90, –92, –94*

Koff, Richard Myram 1926- *WhoAm 86, –88, –90*

Koffler, Camilla d1955 *AuBYP 2, –3, BioIn 2, –3, –4, –6, –7*
Pseud./variant:
Ylla

Kogan, Deborah 1940- *BioIn 16, ConGrA 3, SmATA 50, WhoAmA 86, –89, –91, WhoE 86*
Pseud./variant:
Ray, Deborah Kogan 1940-

Kogan, Herman d1989 *NewYTBS 89*

Kogan, Herman 1914- *AuBYP 2S, –3, BioIn 11, ConAu 9R, –5NR, –20NR, WhoAm 74, –76, –78, –80, –82, –84, –86, –88, WhoMW 74, –76, –78, WhoWor 78, WhoWorJ 72*

Kogan, Herman 1914-1989 *BioIn 16, ConAu 128, WhAm 10*

Koger, Earl, Sr. *BlkAWP*

Kohl, Herbert 1937- *SmATA 47*

Kohl, Marguerite *AuBYP 2, –3, BioIn 8*

Kohl, MaryAnn F 1947- *SmATA 74*

Kohler, Julilly H 1915?-1976 *AmAu&B, BioIn 2, –11, ConAu 69, –77, OhA&B, SmATA 20N*

Kohn, Bernice Herstein 1920- *AuBYP 2, –3, BioIn 8, –9, ConAu 9R, SmATA 4, WrDr 76*
Pseud./variant:
Hunt, Bernice Kohn

Kohn, Eugene 1887-1977 *BioIn 11, –16, ConAu 69*

Kohner, Frederick 1905- *AmAu&B, Au&Wr 71, BioIn 11, ConAu 1R, –1NR, IntMPA 75, –76, –78, –81, –82, –84, –86, –77, SmATA 10, TwCWr*

Kohner, Frederick 1905-1986 *BioIn 16, ConAu 119, SmATA 48N*

Koidahl, Ilona 1924- *ConAu 97*

Koide, Tan 1938-1986 *BioIn 16, ConAu 132, SmATA 50*

Koike, Kay 1940- *SmATA 72*

Kojima, Shozo 1928- *ConAu 69*
Pseud./variant:
Kijima, Hajime

Kolatch, Alfred Jacob 1916- *ConAu 107, IntAu&W 86, WhoAm 78, –80, –82, –84, –86, –88, –90, –92, –94*

Kolba, Tamara *BioIn 13, SmATA 22, WhoAmA 80*
Pseud./variant:
Saint Tamara

Kolbrek, Loyal 1914- *ConAu 29R*

Koller, Earl L 1931- *WhoTech 84*

Koller, Earl Leonard 1931- *AmMWSc 73P, –76P, –82, –86, –89, –92*

Koller, Jackie French 1948- *SmATA 72*

Kolodny, Nancy J 1946- *SmATA 76*

Kolodny, Nancy Joan 1946- *WhoAmW 91*

Komaiko, Leah *AuBYP 3*

Komisar, Lucy 1942- *AuBYP 2S, –3, BioIn 11, ConAu 33R, ForWC 70, IntAu&W 86, –89, SmATA 9, WhoFI 94, WrDr 76, –80, –82, –84*

Komoda, Beverly 1939- *BioIn 13, ConAu 85, SmATA 25*

Komoda, Kiyo 1937- *BioIn 8, –11, IlsCB 1957, –1967, SmATA 9*

Komroff, Manuel 1890-1974 *AmAu&B, AmNov, AuBYP 2, –3, BenetAL 91, BioIn 2, –3, –4, –7, –9, –10, –12, CnDAL, ConAu 1R, –53, –4NR, DcLB 4, NewYTBS 74, ObitOF 79, OxCAmL 65, –83, REnAL, SmATA 2, –20N, TwCA, –SUP, WhAm 5, WhoAm 74, WhoWor 74, WrDr 76*

Konigsburg, E L *Au&Arts 3, BioIn 14, –15, –16, SmATA 48*

Konigsburg, E L 1930- *BioIn 17, DcLB 52, MajTwCW, TwCChW 89, WrDr 86, –88, –90, –92*

Konigsburg, Elaine L 1930- *AuBYP 3, WrDr 94*

Konigsburg, Elaine Lobl 1930- *AnCL, AuBYP 2, Au&ICB, BioIn 8, –9, –10, ChlLR 1, ConAu 21R, –17NR, –39NR, DcAmChF 1960, –1985, MajAI, MorBMP, NewbC 1966, OxCChiL, SmATA 4, SouSt, ThrBJA, TwCChW 78, –83, TwCYAW, WhoAm 74, –76, –78, –80, –82, –84, –85, –88, –90, –92, –94, WrDr 76, –80, –82, –84*

Koning, Hans
Main entry: Koningsberger, Hans

Koningsberger, Hans *DrAPF 89, –91, –93, IntAu&W 86X, WhoUSWr 88, WrDr 90, –92*

Koningsberger, Hans 1921- *AmAu&B, Au&Wr 71, BioIn 10, –17, BlueB 76, ConAu 1R, –2NR, DrAF 76, DrAPF 83, –85, SmATA 5, WhoAm 74, –76, –78, WhoWor 74, WorAu 1950, WrDr 76, –80*
Pseud./variant:
Koning, Hans

Koningsberger, Hans 1924- *WhoAm 90, –92, WrDr 94*

Konkle, Janet Everest 1917- *BioIn 11, ConAu 1R, ForWC 70, IntAu&W 77, MichAu 80, SmATA 12, WhoMW 74, WrDr 76, –80, –82, –84, –86, –88, –90, –92, –94*

Konwicki, Tadeusz *BioIn 14, –15, –17*

Konwicki, Tadeusz 1926- *Benet 87, BioIn 10, –12, –13, ConAu 101, –9AS, –39NR, ConFLW 84, ConLC 8, –28, –54, ConWorW 93, CyWA 89, DcFM, EncWL 2, IntWW 76, –77, –78, –79, –80, –81, –82, –83, –89, –91, MajTwCW, OxCFilm, RAdv 13-2, WhoWor 74, –82, –87, –89, –91, –93, WorAu 1980*

Koob, Theodora 1918- *AuBYP 2, –3, BioIn 8, ConAu 5R, SmATA 23*

Kooiker, Leonie
Main entry: Kooyker-Romijn, Johanna Maria

Koontz, Dean R *BestSel 90-2, PenEncH*

Koontz, Dean R 1945- *Au&Arts 9, BestSel 89-3, BioIn 17, ConAu 19NR, –36NR, ConLC 78, CrtSuMy, IntAu&W 91, MajTwCW, NewEScF, ScF&FL 92, ScFSB, TwCCr&M 91, TwCSFW 86, –91, TwCYAW, WrDr 86, –88, –90, –92*

Koontz, Dean Ray 1945- *EncSF 93, WhoAm 90, –92, –94, WrDr 94*

Koontz, Robin Michael *AuBYP 3*

Koontz, Robin Michal 1954- *ConAu 138, SmATA 70*

Kooyker-Romijn, Johanna Maria 1927- *BioIn 16, ConAu 34NR, SmATA 48*
Pseud./variant:
Kooiker, Leonie

Kopal, Zdenek d1993 *NewYTBS 93*

Kopal, Zdenek 1914- *AmMWSc 73P, –76P, –82, –86, –89, –92, BioIn 2, –8, –16, BlueB 76, ConAu 93, CurBio 69, IntAu&W 77, Who 74, –82, –83, –85, –88, –92, WhoWor 74, WrDr 80, –82, –84, –86, –88, –90, –92, –94*

Kopal, Zdenek 1914-1993 *ConAu 141*

Kopal, Zdenek, Prof 1914- *Who 90*

Kopper, Lisa 1950- *SmATA 51*

Korach, Mimi 1922- *BioIn 1, –11, SmATA 9*

Koralek, Jenny 1934- *SmATA 71*

Korczak, Janusz 1878-1942 *BioIn 15, –16, –17, ConAu 133, PolBiDi, SmATA 65*
Pseud./variant:
Goldszmit, Henryk 1878-1942

Koren, Edward 1935- *BioIn 10, –11, –12, ConAu 25R, –11NR, SmATA 5, WhoE 74*

Koren, Edward B 1935- *WhoAmA 86, –91*

Koren, Edward Benjamin 1935- *WhoAm 92, –94*

Korfker, Dena 1908- *ConAu 1R, –17NR, MichAu 80, WrDr 76, –80, –82, –84, –86, –88, –90, –92, –94*

Korinetz, Yuri *TwCChW 89B*

Korinetz, Yuri 1923- *BioIn 11, ChlLR 4, ConAu 61, –11NR, OxCChiL, SmATA 9, TwCChW 78B, –83B*

Korman, Gordon *BioIn 14, NewYTBS 85*

Korman, Gordon 1963- *Au&Arts 10, BioIn 13, –15, –16, ChlLR 25, ConAu 112, –34NR, IntAu&W 86, –89, NewYTBS 85, Profile 2, SmATA 41, –49, WhoCanL 85, –87, –92*

Korman, Gordon Richard 1963- *MajAI*

Korman, Justine 1958- *SmATA 70*

Korschunow, Irina 1925- *IntAu&W 77, –82*

Korson, George Gershon 1899-1967 *BioIn 7, –8, ChhPo S1, –S2, ObitOF 79*

Korte, Gene J 1950- *SmATA 74*

Korty, Carol 1937- *BioIn 12, ConAu 77, SmATA 15*

K O S 1881- *ConICB*

Koscielniak, Bruce *BioIn 17*

Koscielniak, Bruce 1947- *ConAu 134, SmATA 67, WrDr 94*

Koshland, Ellen 1947- *ConAu 33R, –13NR*

Kossin, Sandy 1926- *BioIn 8, –11, SmATA 10*

Kossoff, David 1919- *BlueB 76, ConAu 61, –35NR, FilmgC, HalFC 84, –88, IntAu&W 77, –82, –86, –89, –91, Who 74, –82, –83, –85, –88, –90, –92, WhoThe 72, –77, –81, WrDr 76, –80, –82, –84, –86, –88, –90, –92, –94*

Kostich, Dragos D 1921- *AuBYP 2, –3, BioIn 8, ConAu 5R, –10NR, DrAS 74H, –78H, –82H*

Kotker, Norman R 1931- *ConAu 25R, DrAF 76, IntAu&W 82, WhoAm 74, –80, –82, –84, WhoE 74, WrDr 76, –80, –82, –84, –86, –88, –90, –92, –94*

Kotker, Norman Richard 1931- *WhoAm 86, –88, –90, WhoUSWr 88, WhoWrEP 89, –92*

Kotowski, Joanne 1930- *ConAu 57, WhoAmW 77*

Kottler, Dorothy 1918- *ConAu 97*

Kotzwinkle, William *BioIn 14, –16, ScFSB*

Kotzwinkle, William 1938- *BioIn 13, ChlLR 6, ConAu 45, –3NR, ConLC 5, –35, EncSF 93, IntAu&W 91, MajAI, ScF&FL 92, SmATA 24, –70, TwCSFW 86, –91, WhoAm 82, –84, –86, –88, –90, –92, –94, WrDr 86, –88, –90, –92, –94*

Kouhi, Elizabeth 1917- *BioIn 16, ConAu 126, IntAu&W 91, SmATA 49, –54*

Koutoukas, H M
Main entry: Rivoli, Mario

Koutoukas, H M 1947- *BioIn 10, -11, ConDr 82, -88, -93, SmATA X, WhoAm 80, -82, WrDr 82*

Kouts, Anne 1945- *BioIn 11, ConAu 29R, SmATA 8*

Kovalik, Nada 1926- *AuBYP 2, -3, ConAu 25R*

Kovalski, Maryann *AuBYP 3*

Kovalski, Maryann 1951- *BioIn 16, CanWW 89, SmATA 58*

Kovel, Joel S 1936- *Au&Wr 71, BiDrAPA 77, ConAu 29R, -14NR, -32NR, IntAu&W 77, WrDr 76, -80*

Kowet, Don 1937- *AuBYP 2S, -3, ConAu 57, -10NR, -35NR*
Pseud./variant:
Gell, Frank

Kozelka, Paul 1909- *BiE&WWA, ConAu P-2, NotNAT*

Kraenzel, Margaret 1899- *ConAu 1R*
Pseud./variant:
Blue, Wallace

Krahn, Fernando 1935- *AmPB, AuBYP 2, -3, BioIn 12, -14, -16, ChhPo S1, ChlLR 3, ConAu 65, -11NR, FourBJA, IlsCB 1967, SmATA 31, -49, WhoGrA 82*

Kramer, Aaron *DrAPF 87, -89, -91, -93*

Kramer, Aaron 1921- *ConAu 21R, -12NR, DrAP 75, DrAPF 83, -85, DrAS 74E, -78E, -82E, IntAu&W 77, -82, -86, -89, -91, IntWWP 82, WhoAm 76, -78, -80, -82, -84, -88, -90, -92, -94, WhoE 74, -75, -77, WhoUSWr 88, WhoWorJ 72, -78, WhoWrEP 89, -92, WrDr 76, -80, -82, -84, -86, -88, -90, -92, -94*
Pseud./variant:
Spencer, Philip

Kramer, Anthony *SmATA 42*

Kramer, Edna Ernestine *ConAu 107, -X, WhoAmW 74, -75, -77*

Kramer, George *AuBYP 2, -3, BioIn 8, ConAu X, SmATA X, WrDr 84, -86*
Main entry: Heuman, William

Kramer, Nora *WhoAmW 87*

Kramer, Nora 1896?-1984 *AuBYP 2, -3, BioIn 8, -13, -14, -15, ConAu 107, -113, ForWC 70, ScF&FL 92, SmATA 26, -39N, WhoAmW 74, -75, -77, -81, -83, -85, WhoE 77, -81, -83, -85*

Kramer, Rita 1929- *ArtclWW 2, BioIn 13, ConAu 69, -31NR*

Kramer, Samuel Noah 1897- *AmAu&B, BioIn 15, ConAu 9R, DrAS 74H, WhoWorJ 72, -78*

Kramer, Samuel Noah 1897-1990 *BioIn 17, ConAu 133, NewYTBS 90*

Kramon, Florence 1920- *ConAu 25R*

Krantz, Hazel *WrDr 94*

Krantz, Hazel 1920- *BioIn 11, ConAu 1R, ForWC 70, SmATA 12, WrDr 76, -80, -82, -84, -86, -88, -90, -92*

Krantz, Hazel Newman *ConAu 40NR*

Krantz, Lucretia *AuBYP 2S, -3*

Kranyik, Robert Donald 1931- *LEduc 74, WhoAm 74, -80, -82, -84*

Kranzler, George G 1916- *WhoE 86*

Kranzler, George Gershon 1916- *AmMWSc 73S, -78S, BioIn 13, ConAu 57, -12NR, SmATA 28, WhoE 85*
Pseud./variant:
Isaacs, Jacob
Kranzler, Gershon

Kranzler, Gershon
Main entry: Kranzler, George Gershon

Krappe, Alexander Haggerty 1894-1947 *BioIn 1*

Krasilovsky, Phyllis 1926- *AuBYP 2, -3, BioIn 6, -7, -9, -15, -16, BkCL, ConAu 29R, -11NR, IntAu&W 91, MajAI, MorJA, OxCChiL, SmATA 1, -38, -5AS, TwCChW 78, -83, -89, WrDr 80, -82, -84, -86, -88, -90, -92, -94*

Kraske, Robert *ConAu 116, SmATA 36*

Krasne, Betty *SmATA 66, WhoAmW 93*
Main entry: Levine, Betty Krasne

Krauch, Velma 1916- *ConAu 37R, WhoAmW 77*

Krauch, Velma Ann 1916- *WhoAmW 91*

Kraus, George 1912- *IntWWM 90, WhoMus 72*

Kraus, Joanna Halpert 1937- *ConAu 104, -21NR, TwCChW 78, -83, -89, WhoE 91 WhoEnt 92, WhoUSWr 88, WhoWrEP 89,*

–92, WrDr 80, –82, –84, –86, –88, –90, –92, –94

Kraus, Richard Gordon 1923- *ConAu 13R, –11NR*

Kraus, Robert 1925- *AmAu&B, AuBYP 2, –3, BioIn 8, –9, –11, –12, –17, ConAu 33R, IlsCB 1957, –1967, IntAu&W 91, MajAI, SmATA 4, –65, –11AS, ThrBJA, TwCChW 78, –83, –89, WhoAm 74, –76, –78, –80, WhoE 74, WrDr 84, –86, –88, –90, –92, –94*
Pseud./variant:
Hippopotamus, Eugene H
Silly, E S
Tubby, I M

Krauss, Oscar *IlsBYP, IntMPA 75, –76, –78, –81, –82, –84, –86, –77*

Krauss, Ruth *BioIn 14, –15, DrAPF 87, –89, –91, –93*

Krauss, Ruth d1993 *NewYTBS 93*

Krauss, Ruth 1911- *AuBYP 3, ConDr 88, DcLB 52, IntAu&W 91, TwCChW 89, WrDr 86, –88, –90, –92, –94*

Krauss, Ruth Ida 1911?- *AmAu&B, AmPB, AuBYP 2, Au&ICB, Au&Wr 71, BioIn 6, –8, –9, –10, BkP, ChhPo, ConAu 1R, –1NR, –13NR, ConDr 73, –77, –82, –93, DrAP 75, DrAPF 83, –85, ForWC 70, IntWWP 82, MajAI, MorJA, OxCChiL, SmATA 1, –30, TwCChW 78, –83, WhoAm 74, –76, –78, –80, –82, –84, –86, –88, WrDr 76, –80, –82, –84*

Krauss, Ruth Ida 1911-1993 *ConAu 141, SmATA 75*

Krautter, Elisa *AuBYP 3, ConAu 1R, –1NR, CurBio 54, SmATA 1*
Main entry: Bialk, Elisa

Krautter, Elisa 1912?-1990 *ConAu 131, SmATA 65*

Krautter, Elisa Bialk 1912-1990 *BioIn 17*

Krauze, Andrzej 1947- *BioIn 15, SmATA 46*

Kravetz, Nathan 1921- *AmAu&B, ConAu 9R, LEduc 74, WhoAm 74, –76, –78, –80, –82, –84, WhoWor 82*

Krawitz, Ruth 1929- *ConAu 9R, ForWC 70*

Kredel, Fritz 1900-1973 *BioIn 1, –3, –5, –6, –8, –9, –12, ChhPo, ConAu 41R, IlsBYP, IlsCB 1744, –1946, –1957, –1967, MorJA, SmATA 17, WhAmArt 85, WhoAmA 73*

Kredenser, Gail 1936- *AuBYP 2S, –3, ConAu 21R*

Krehbiel, Rebecca Falconer 1919- *BioIn 2, ForWC 70*
Pseud./variant:
Becky
Falconer, Rebecca

Kreidolf, Ernst 1863-1956 *BioIn 4, OxCChiL*

Krementz, Jill *BioIn 15*

Krementz, Jill 1940- *AuBYP 3, AuNews 1, –2, BioIn 8, –10, –11, –12, –13, BioNews 75, ChlLR 5, ConAu 41R, –23NR, EncTwCJ, FifBJA, ICPEnP A, InWom SUP, MacBEP, MajAI, NewYTBS 82, SmATA 17, –71, –8AS, WhoAm 74, –76, –78, –80, –82, –84, –86, –88, –90, –92, –94, WhoAmW 74, –83, –85, –87, –89, –91, –93, WhoUSWr 88, WhoWrEP 89, –92*

Krensky, Stephen 1953- *BioIn 15, –16, ConAu 73, –13NR, ScF&FL 92, SixBJA, SmATA 41, –47*

Krentel, Mildred White 1921- *ConAu 5R*

Krents, Harold Eliot d1987 *NewYTBS 87*

Krents, Harold Eliot 1943- *BioIn 8, –9, ConAu 37R, WhoAmL 78*

Krents, Harold Eliot 1944-1987 *BioIn 15, ConAu 121*

Kresh, Paul 1919- *IntAu&W 86, –89, –91, SmATA 61, WhoAm 86, –88, –90, –92, –94, WhoEnt 92, WrDr 86, –88, –90, –92, –94*

Krevitsky, Nathan I 1914- *BioIn 7, ConAu 9R*

Krigstein, Bernard 1919- *AmArt, BioIn 15, ConGrA 2, WhoAmA 73, –78, –80, –82, –84, –86, –89, –91, WhoE 86, –91*

Krigstein, Bernard 1919-1990 *EncACom*

Kripke, Dorothy Karp *ConAu 17R, SmATA 30*

Kristof, Jane 1932- *BioIn 11, ConAu 29R, DrAS 74H, SmATA 8, WhoAmW 93, WhoWest 87*

Kristoffersen, Eva M 1901- *AuBYP 3*

Kristoffersen, Eva M 1901-1954 *AuBYP 2, BioIn 3, –4, –7*

Kroeber, Theodora Kracaw 1897- *AmAu&B, BioIn 9, ConAu 5R, ForWC 70, SmATA 1, WrDr 76*

Krog, Inge *TwCChW 78B*

Kroll, Francis Lynde 1904-1973 *BioIn 11, ConAu P-1, SmATA 10*

Kroll, Steven *BioIn 15, -17*

Kroll, Steven 1941- *AuBYP 2S, -3, BioIn 12, ConAu 65, -9NR, -25NR, -35NR, FifBJA, SmATA 19, -66, -7AS*

Kroll, Virginia Louise 1948- *SmATA 76*
Pseud./variant:
Cooper, Melrose

Kronenwetter, Michael 1943- *SmATA 62*

Kropp, Paul 1948- *ConAu 112, SmATA 34, -38, WhoCanL 85, -87, -92*

Kruess, James *AuBYP 3*

Kruess, James 1926- *ConAu 53, -5NR, MajAI, SmATA 8*
Pseud./variant:
Kruss, James
Polder, Markus
Ritter, Felix

Kruif, Paul De *CurBio 42, -63, NewYTBE 71*
Main entry: DeKruif, Paul

Krull, Kathleen 1952- *BioIn 15, -16, ConAu 106, SmATA 39, -52*
Pseud./variant:
Cowles, Kathleen
Kenny, Kathryn
Kenny, Kevin

Krum, Charlotte 1886- *AuBYP 2, -3, BioIn 7*

Krumgold, Joseph 1908-1980 *AnObit 1980, AuBYP 2, -3, BioIn 3, -4, -5, -6, -7, -8, -9, -12, -13, -16, ConAu 9R, -101, -7NR, ConLC 12, EncMys, FamMS, MorJA, NewbC 1956, NewbMB 1922, OxCChiL, SmATA 1, -23N, -48, TwCChW 78, -83, -89, WhAm 7, WrDr 80*

Krumgold, Joseph Quincy 1908-1980 *DcAmChF 1960, MajAI, TwCYAW*

Krummacher, Friedrich Adolf 1767-1845 *BiD&SB, CarSB, LuthC 75*

Krummacher, Friedrich Adolph 1768-1845 *DcBiPP*

Krupinski, Loretta 1940- *SmATA 67*

Krupp, E C *BioIn 16*

Krupp, E C 1944- *ConAu 21NR, SmATA 53*

Krupp, Robin Rector 1946- *BioIn 16, ConAu 135, SmATA 53, WrDr 94*

Krusch, Werner E 1927- *AuBYP 2, -3, BioIn 7, ConAu 5R*

Krush, Beth 1918- *BioIn 2, -5, -6, -8, -12, IlsBYP, IlsCB 1946, -1957, -1967, MajAI, MorJA, SmATA 18*

Krush, Joe 1918- *BioIn 2, -5, -6, -8, IlsBYP, IlsCB 1946, -1957, -1967, MajAI, MorJA, SmATA 18*

Kruss, James *TwCChW 89B*
Main entry: Kruess, James

Kruss, James 1926- *AuBYP 2, -3, BioIn 8, -9, -11, ChlLR 9, OxCChiL, ScF&FL 92, ThrBJA, TwCChW 78B, -83B*

Krutch, Joseph Wood 1893-1970 *AmAu&B, Au&Wr 71, Benet 87, BenetAL 91, BiE&WWA, BioIn 1, -3, -4, -5, -6, -8, -9, -12, -14, -15, -16, BlueB 76N, CnDAL, ConAmA, ConAmL, ConAu 1R, -25R, -4NR, ConLC 24, CurBio 59, -70, DcAmB S8, DcLB 63, DcLEL, EncWT, EvLB, InSci, NewYTBE 70, NotNAT B, ObitOF 79, OxCAmL 65, -83, OxCAmT 84, OxCThe 67, PenC AM, RAdv 13-5, REn, REnAL, ScF&FL 92, TwCA, -SUP, WebAB 74, -79, WhAm 5, WhJnl, WhNAA*

Krylov, Ivan Andreevich 1769-1844 *BioIn 1, -2, -7, -9, -10, CamGWoT, HanRL, NinCLC 1, OxCChiL, OxCEng 85, WhDW*

Krylov, Ivan Andreyevich 1769-1844 *Benet 87*

Krythe, Maymie Richardson *ConAu 17R*

Kubert, Joe 1926- *ArtCS, BioIn 15, ConGrA 1, EncACom*

Kubiak, Daniel James 1938- *WhoGov 77, -75*

Kubie, Nora Benjamin 1899-1988 *BioIn 15, -16, SmATA 59*

Kubie, Nora Gottheil Benjamin 1899- *AuBYP 2, -3, BioIn 8, ConAu 5R, SmATA 39, WhoAmW 74*
Pseud./variant:
Benjamin, Nora

Kubinyi, Kalman 1906- *BioIn 1, ConICB, IlsCB 1744, WhAmArt 85*

Kubinyi, Laszlo Kalman 1937- *BioIn 12, ChhPo S2, ConAu 85, IlsBYP, IlsCB 1967, SmATA 17*

Kublin, Hyman 1919- *AuBYP 2S, -3, ConAu 9R, DrAS 74H, -78H, -82H, WhoE 75, WhoWorJ 72, -78*

Kudian, Mischa *Au&Wr 71, ConAu 107, IntAu&W 77, -82, -86, -89, -91, WrDr 76, -80, -82, -84, -86, -88, -90, -92, -94*

Kuehner, Louis C *AuBYP 2S, -3*

Kugelmass, Joseph Alvin 1910-1972 *AmAu&B, AuBYP 2, -3, BioIn 8, -9, ConAu 5R, -33R, WhNAA, WhoAm 74, -76*

Kuh, Charlotte d1985 *BioIn 15*

Kuh, Charlotte 1892?-1985 *AmPB, ConAu 115, SmATA 43N*

Kuhlman, Kathryn 1907-1976 *BioIn 17, EncO&P 3, EncPaPR 91*

Kuhlman, Kathryn 1910-1976 *BioAmW, BioIn 9, -10, -11, BioNews 74, ConAu 57, -65, -12NR, CurBio 74, -76N, EncO&P 1, -2, NewYTBE 72, ObitOF 79, WhAm 6, -7, WhoAm 74, WhoRel 75, WorAlBi, WorAl, WrDr 76, -80, -82*

Kuhn, Bob 1920- *BioIn 13, WhoAmA 78, -80, -82, -84, -86, -89, -91*

Kuhn, Doris d1969 *AuBYP 3*

Kuhn, Doris 1900?-1969 *AuBYP 2S, BioIn 8*

Kuhn, Ferdinand 1905-1978 *AmAu&B, BioIn 11, ConAu 5R, -81, -36NR, IntWW 74, -75, -76, -77, -78, -79N, WhAm 7, WhoAm 74, -76, -78*

Kuijer, Guus *TwCChW 83B, -89B*

Kujoth, Jean 1935-1975 *AuBYP 3*

Kujoth, Jean Spealman 1935-1975 *AuBYP 2S, BioIn 14, ConAu P-2, SmATA 30N, WhAm 6, WhoAmW 75*

Kuklin, Susan *AuBYP 3, BioIn 17*

Kuklin, Susan 1941- *ConAu 130, SmATA 63, WrDr 94*

Kula, Elsa *AuBYP 2S, -3, BioIn 4*

Kullman, Harry 1919-1982 *BioIn 14, ConAu 93, -39NR, FifBJA, SmATA 35*

Kumin, Maxine *DrAPF 87, -89, IntvTCA 2*

Kumin, Maxine 1925- *ArtclWW 2, AuBYP 3, BenetAL 91, BioIn 14, -17, BlmGWL, CamGLE, CamHAL, ConAu 8AS, -21NR, ConPo 91, FemiCLE, MajTwCW, ModAWP, WhoUSWr 88, WhoWrEP 89, -92, WorAlBi, WrDr 86, -88, -90, -92, -94*

Kumin, Maxine W *DrAPF 91, -93*

Kumin, Maxine Winokur 1925- *AmAu&B, AnCL, AuBYP 2, AuNews 2, BioIn 8, -10, -11, ChhPo S1, ConAu 1R, ConLC 5, -13, ConPo 75, DrAF 76, DrAP 75, ForWC 70, InWom SUP, IntAu&W 77, -86, -89, -91, SmATA 12, WhoAm 74, -76, -78, -80, -82, -84, -86, -88, -90, -92, -94, WhoAmW 74, -75, -77, -81, -83, -85, -87, -89, -91, -93, WorAl, WrDr 76, -80*

Kummer, Frederic Arnold 1873- *AuBYP 3*

Kummer, Frederic Arnold 1873-1943 *AmAu&B, AuBYP 2, BioIn 8, DcNAA, NotNAT B, ScF&FL 92, WhAm 2, WhAmArt 85, WhNAA*
Pseud./variant:
Fredericks, Arnold

Kumpa *SmATA X*
Main entry: Barberis, Juan Carlos

Kuner, M C 1922- *ConAu 41R*

Kunhappa, Murkot 1905- *ConAu 69*

Kunhardt, Dorothy 1901-1979 *InWom SUP, SmATA 53*

Kunhardt, Dorothy Meserve 1901-1979 *AmPB, AuBYP 2S, BioIn 12, -13, -16, -17, ConAu 93, -107, SmATA 22N*

Kunhardt, Edith 1937- *AuBYP 3, BioIn 16, -17, ConAu 134, SmATA 67, WrDr 94*
Pseud./variant:
Grunewalt, Pine
Hill, Johnson
Knapp, Edward
Smith, Jessie 1937-
Verr, Harry Coe

Kunhardt, Philip B 1928- *AuBYP 2S, BioIn 9, ConAu 85*

Kunhardt, Philip Bradish, Jr. 1928- *ConAu 37NR*

Kunhart, Dorothy 1901-1979 *AuBYP 3*

Kunhart, Philip B 1928- *AuBYP 3*

Kunitz, Stanley J 1905- *AmAu&B, Benet 87, BioIn 5, -8, -10, -12, -13, BlueB 76, CnE&AP, ConAu 41R, ConLC 6, -11, ConPo 70, -75, CurBio 43, -59, DrAP 75, DrAS 74E, -78E, IntAu&W 89, IntWW 74, -79, -80, -81, -82, -83, -89, -91, ModAL, -S1, OxCAmL 65, -83, PenC AM, RAdv 1, REn, REnAL, WebE&AL, WhoAm 74, -80, -82, -84, WhoTwCL, WhoWor 74, WhoWorJ 72, -78, WorAl, WorAu 1950, WrDr 76, -80*

Kunitz, Stanley Jasspon 1905- *WhoAm 86, -88, -90, -92, -94*

Kunjufu, Jawanza 1953- *SmATA 73*

Kunnas, Mauri *AuBYP 3*

Kunstler, Morton 1927- *BioIn 11, PrintW 83, -85, SmATA 10, WhoAmA 82, -84*
Pseud./variant:
Mutz

Kunstler, Morton 1931- *WhoAmA 86, -89, -91, WhoE 91*

Kunz, Roxane 1932- *ConAu 121, SmATA 53*

Kunz, Virginia B 1921- *ConAu 21R*

Kupferberg, Herbert 1918- *Baker 84, -92, BioIn 12, ConAu 29R, IntAu&W 91, SmATA 19, WhoAmJ 80, WhoE 75, WhoWorJ 72, -78, WrDr 76, -80, -82, -84, -86, -88, -90, -92, -94*

Kuratomi, Chizuko *TwCChW 89B*

Kuratomi, Chizuko 1934- *ChlLR 32*

Kuratomi, Chizuko 1939- *BioIn 11, ConAu 21R, -10NR, SmATA 12, TwCChW 78B, -83B*

Kurelek, William 1927-1977 *AuBYP 2S, -3, BioIn 6, -11, -12, -13, -15, ChlLR 2, ConArt 77, ConAu 49, -3NR, CreCan 1, FifBJA, IlsCB 1967, MajAI, SmATA 8, -27N, WhoAmA 73, -78, -80N, -82N, -86N, -89N, -91N, WrDr 80*

Kurian, George 1928- *SmATA 65*

Kurkul, Edward 1916- *ConAu 25R*

Kurland, Gerald 1942- *BioIn 11, ConAu 41R, -14NR, DrAS 74H, -78H, -82H, SmATA 13, WhoSSW 80*

Kurland, Michael 1938- *BioIn 16, IntAu&W 91, NewEScF, ScF&FL 92, ScFSB, SmATA 48, SpyFic, TwCSFW 86, -91, WrDr 86, -88, -90, -92*

Kurland, Michael Joseph 1938- *EncSF 93, WrDr 94*
Pseud./variant:
Plum, J

Kuropas, Myron Bohdon 1932- *ConAu 45, WhoGov 77, -75, WhoMW 76*

Kursh, Harry 1919- *ConAu 9R, WhoE 75*

Kurten, Bjoern 1924-1988 *SmATA 64*

Kurtis, Arlene Harris 1927- *ConAu 25R, WhoAmW 77*

Kurtz, Edwin Bernard, Jr. 1926- *AmMWSc 73P, -76P, -82, -86, -89, -92*

Kurtz, Katherine 1944- *ConAu 25NR, NewEScF, ScF&FL 92, ScFSB, TwCSFW 91, WrDr 86, -88, -90, -92, -94*

Kurtz, Katherine Irene 1944- *EncSF 93, SmATA 76*

Kurz, Ron *DrAPF 87, -89, -91, -93*

Kurz, Ron 1940- *ConAu 81, -14NR, DrAPF 83, -85, WhoUSWr 88, WhoWrEP 89, -92, WrDr 76, -80, -82, -84, -86, -88, -90, -92, -94*

Kusan, Ivan 1933- *AuBYP 2, -3, BioIn 7, ConAu 9R, -6NR*

Kushner, Donn 1927- *BioIn 16, ConAu 35NR, ScF&FL 92, SmATA 52, WhoCanL 87, -92, WrDr 90, -92, -94*

Kushner, Donn 1929- *DcChlFi*

Kushner, Jill Menkes 1951- *BioIn 17, SmATA 62*

Kuskin, Karla *BioIn 15, -17*

Kuskin, Karla 1932- *ConAu 22NR, IntAu&W 91, MajAI, SmATA 68, -3AS, TwCChW 89, WhoAm 86, -88, -90, -92, -94, WhoWrEP 89, -92, WrDr 86, -88, -90, -92, -94*

Kuskin, Karla Seidman 1932- *AmPB, AuBYP 2, -3, BioIn 7, -8, -9, -12, -13, ChhPo, -S1, ChlLR 4, ConAu 1R, -4NR, -41NR, ForWC 70, IlsCB 1957, -1967, SmATA 2, ThrBJA, TwCChW 78, -83, WhoAm 82, -84, WrDr 80, -82, -84*
Pseud./variant:
Charles, Nicholas

Kuslan, Louis Isaac 1922- *AmMWSc 73P, -76P, -82, -86, -89, -92, ConAu 45, -1NR, LEduc 74, WhoAm 74, -76, -78, -80, -82, -84, -86*

Kusnick, Barry A 1910- *ConAu 53, -37NR*

Kutcher, Ben 1895-1967 *ArtsAmW 2, BioIn 1, -5, ChhPo, ConICB, IlsCB 1744, -1946, WhAmArt 85*

Kutner, Luis I 1908- *WhoAm 74, -76*

Kuttner, Paul *DrAPF 87, -89, -91, -93*

Kuttner, Paul 1931- *BioIn 12, ConAu 77, -13NR, -30NR, DrAPF 83, -85, IntAu&W 89, SmATA 18, WhoUSWr 88, WhoWrEP 89, -92*

Kutzer, Ernst 1880- *ConICB*

Kuzma, Kay *BioIn 15*

Kuzma, Kay 1941- *ConAu 106, –23NR, SmATA 39*

Kvale, Velma R 1898- *BioIn 11, ConAu P-2, SmATA 8*

Kwolek, Constance *ConAu X, WrDr 76, –80, –82*
Main entry: Porcari, Constance Kwolek

Kyle, Anne D 1896- *BioIn 2, JBA 34, –51*

Kyle, Anne Dempster 1896-1966 *BioIn 14*

Kyle, Barbara A *MedPD*

Kyle, Elisabeth *AuBYP 3*
Main entry: Dunlop, Agnes Mary Robinson

Kyle, Elisabeth d1982 *AuBYP 2, BioIn 6, –7, –8, –9, BlueB 76, ConAu X, IntAu&W 77, MorJA, SmATA 3, TwCChW 78, –83, –89, Who 74, –82, –83N, WhoChL, WrDr 76, –80, –82*

Kyle, R C *MedPD*

Kyte, Kathy S 1946- *SmATA 44, –50*

Kytle, Ray *DrAPF 87, –89, –91, –93*

Kytle, Ray 1941- *BioIn 10, ConAu 29R, DrAPF 83, –85, ScF&FL 92*

L

Labastida, Aurora *BioIn 6*

LaBastille, Anne *BioIn 15*

LaBastille, Anne 1938- *BioIn 10, -11, -12, -13, ConAu 57, -8NR, WhoAmW 77, -81, -83*
Pseud./variant:
Bowes, Anne LaBastille

LaBorde, Rene *ConAu X*
Main entry: Neuffer, Irene LaBorde

Laboulaye, Edouard R L De 1811-1883 *BbD, BiD&SB, BioIn 2, -11, CarSB, DcBiA, HarEnUS, JBA 34, -51*
Pseud./variant:
DeLaboulaye, Edouard R L

LaBrecque, Claude X *ConAu 85*

Lacerte, Rolande *OxCCan SUP*

Lacey, Elizabeth A *AuBYP 3*

Lacey, Elizabeth A 1954- *ConAu 132, WrDr 94*

Lacher, Gisella Loeffler 1903?- *IlsCB 1744, WhAmArt 85*
Pseud./variant:
Loeffler, Gisella

Lackey, Mercedes R *ConSFF*

Lackey, Mercedes R 1950- *ConAu 126, IntAu&W 91, TwCYAW*

Lacklan, Carli 1907- *AuBYP 3*

Lacks, Cecilia 1945- *ConAu 69, WhoAmW 89*
Pseud./variant:
Lacks, Cissy

Lacks, Cissy
Main entry: Lacks, Cecilia

Lacy, Dan 1914- *BiDrLUS 70, BioIn 2, -3, -7, -11, ConAu 37R, CurBio 54, WhoAm 74, -80, -82, -84, WhoFI 74, WhoLibI 82, WhoLibS 55*

Lacy, Dan Mabry 1914- *WhoAm 86, -90*

Lacy, Leslie Alexander 1937- *BioIn 8, -10, BlkWrNE, ConAu 33R, InB&W 80, LivgBAA, SelBAAf, SelBAAu, SmATA 6, WhoBlA 77, -80, -85, -90, -92*

Lada, Josef *TwCChW 78B*

Ladd, Veronica *ConAu X, IntAu&W 86X, SmATA X*
Main entry: Miner, Jane Claypool

Ladd, Veronica 1933- *BioIn 15*

Lader, Lawrence 1919- *AmAu&B, BioIn 10, ConAu 1R, -2NR, SmATA 6, WhoAm 74, -76, -78, -80, -82, -84, -86, -88, -90, -92, -94, WhoE 74, WhoUSWr 88, WhoWrEP 89, -92*

LaDoux, Rita C 1951- *SmATA 74*

Lady, A *SmATA X*

Lady, A
Main entry: Taylor, Ann

Ladyman, Phyllis *AuBYP 2S, -3, Au&Wr 71, ConAu 103*

Lady Mears *ConAu X, SmATA X*
Main entry: Tempest, Margaret Mary

Lady Of Quality, A *ConAu X, MajAI, SmATA 1, -X, TwCA, -SUP*

Lady of Quality, A *ConAu 40NR*
Main entry: Bagnold, Enid

La Farge, John 1835-1910 *BenetAL 91, BioIn 1, -2, -3, -4, -7, -8, -9, -10, -14, -15, -16, -17, DcCathB, HarEnUS, OxCAmH, OxCAmL 83, OxCChiL, WebAB 79, WhAmArt 85, WorAlBi, WorAl*

LaFarge, John 1880-1963 *Benet 87, DcAmReB 2*

LaFarge, Oliver 1901-1963 *AmAu&B, AmNov, AuBYP 2, -3, Benet 87, BenetAL 91, BioIn 2, -3, -4, -5, -6, -7, -8, -9, -12, -17, CnDAL, ConAmA, ConAu 81, -30NR, CurBio 53, -63, CyWA 89, DcLB 9, DcLEL, EncFWF, LongCTC, Novels, ObitOF 79, OxCAmH,*

OxCAmL 65, –83, PenC AM, REn, REnAL, RfGAmL 87, SmATA 19, TwCA, –SUP, TwCWW 91, WhAm 4, WhNAA, WorAlBi

La Farge, Phyllis *AuBYP 3*

LaFarge, Phyllis 1933- *AuBYP 2, BioIn 8, –12, ConAu 73, SmATA 14, WhoAm 82, –84, WhoAmW 85, –87, –89*

Laffin, John 1922- *AuBYP 2, –3, Au&Wr 71, BioIn 8, –14, ConAu 53, –7NR, –23NR, IntAu&W 77, –82, –86, –89, –91, SmATA 31, WhoWor 74, –78, –80, –82, –84, WrDr 76, –80, –82, –84, –86, –88, –90, –92, –94*
Pseud./variant:
Dekker, Carl
Napier, Mark
Sabre, Dirk

LaFontaine, Jean De 1621-1695 *AnCL, AtlBL, Benet 87, BbD, BiD&SB, BioIn 1, –2, –3, –5, –7, –8, –9, –10, –12, –14, –15, CarSB, CasWL, ChhPo, –S1, –S2, CyWA 58, DcBiPP, DcCathB, DcEuL, Dis&D, EuAu, EuWr 3, EvEuW, GrFLW, GuFrLit 2, MajAI, McGEWB, NewC, OxCChiL, OxCEng 67, –85, OxCFr, PenC EUR, RAdv 13-2, RComWL, REn, SmATA 18, WhDW, WhoChL, WorAlBi, WorAl*

LaFountaine, George 1934- *ConAu 57, –7NR, –41NR, WrDr 76, –80, –82, –84, –86*

LaGallienne, Richard 1866-1947 *Alli SUP, AnCL, BbD, BiD&SB, BioIn 1, –4, –5, –7, Chambr 3, ChhPo, –S1, –S2, DcAmAu, DcEnA A, DcLB 4, DcLEL, EvLB, LongCTC, MouLC 4, NewC, OxCAmL 65, OxCEng 67, PenC ENG, TwCA, –SUP, WebE&AL, WhAm 2, WhNAA*

Lager, Claude *SmATA 74*
Main entry: Lapp, Christiane Germain

Lager, Marilyn 1939- *BioIn 16, ConAu 121, SmATA 52*

Lagercrantz, Rose 1947- *BioIn 15, ConAu 108, SmATA 39*

Lagerlof, Selma *TwCChW 89B*

Lagerlof, Selma 1858-1940 *Benet 87, BioIn 14, –15, ContDcW 89, GrFLW, LadLa 86, NobelP, RAdv 13-2, TwCLC 36, WorAlBi*

Lagerlof, Selma O Lovisa 1858-1940 *BioIn 1, –2, –4, –5, –6, –8, –9, –10, –11, –12, CarSB, CasWL, ChlLR 7, ClDMEL 47, CurBio 40, CyWA 58, Dis&D, EncWL, EvEuW, JBA 34, LongCTC, McGEWB, Novels, OxCChiL, OxCFilm, PenC EUR, REn, SmATA 15, TwCA, –SUP, TwCChW 78B, –83B, TwCLC 4, TwCWr, WhDW, WhoChL, WhoLA, WhoTwCL, WorAl*

Lagerlof, Selma Ottilia Lovisa 1858-1940 *BlmGWL, DcScanL*

Lagerlof, Selma Ottilian Lovisa 1858-1940 *WhoNob, –90*

Lagerlof, Selma Ottiliana Louisa 1858-1940 *WomNov*

Lagerlof, Selma Ottiniana Louisa 1858-1940 *InWom SUP*

LaGumina, Salvatore John 1928- *ConAu 77, DrAS 74H, –78H, –82H*

Laiken, Deirdre S 1948- *ConAu 104, SmATA 40, –48*

Laimgruber, Monika 1946- *BioIn 11, –12, IlsCB 1967, SmATA 11*

Laing, Frederick 1905- *BioIn 4, ConAu 105*

Laing, Martha *ConAu X, SmATA X*
Main entry: Celestino, Martha Laing

Laing, Ronald David d1989 *Who 90N*

Laing, Ronald David 1927?- *BioIn 8, –9, –10, –11, –12, –13, –14, –15, BlueB 76, CelR, CurBio 73, IntAu&W 82, –86, IntWW 79, –80, –81, –82, –83, –89, MakMC, NewYTBE 72, Who 74, –82, –83, –85, –88, WhoAm 74, –80, –82, –84, –86, –88, WhoWor 78, –84, –87, –89, WrDr 76, –80*

Laing, Ronald David 1927-1989 *BioIn 16, –17*

Laird, Charlton Grant 1901- *ConAu 13R, WhJnl*

Laird, Elizabeth 1943- *ConAu 128, SmATA 77*

Laird, Helene Reed 1905- *OhA&B*

Laird, Jean E 1930- *BioIn 15*

Laird, Jean Elouise Rydeski 1930- *AmCath 80, ConAu 9R, –6NR, ForWC 70, SmATA 38, WhoAmW 74, –75, –77, –81, –83, –85, –87, –89, –91, –93, WhoMW 74, –76, –78, –93*
Pseud./variant:
Drial, J E
McKeever, Marcia
Wakefield, Jean L

Laite, Gordon 1925- *BioIn 8, –14, IlsBYP, IlsCB 1957, –1967, SmATA 31*

Lake, Harriet
Main entry: Taylor, Paula Wright

Laklan, Carli
Main entry: Laughlin, Virginia Carli

Laklan, Carli 1907- *AuBYP 2S, BioIn 10, ConAu X, –1NR, DcAmChF 1960, ForWC 70, IntAu&W 77, SmATA 5*

Lakritz, Esther 1928- *ConAu 1R, ForWC 70, IntAu&W 86, –89, WrDr 76, –80, –82, –84, –86*

Laliberte, Norman 1925- *AmAu&B, BioIn 8, ConAu 104, WhoAm 74, –76, WhoAmA 73, –78, –80*

Lalicki, Barbara *BioIn 17, ConAu 119, SmATA 61*

LaMare, Walter De *EngPo, JBA 51, TwCA, –SUP*
Main entry: DeLaMare, Walter

Lamb, Beatrice Pitney 1904- *ConAu 5R, SmATA 21*

Lamb, Charles 1775-1834 *Alli, AtlBL, Benet 87, BbD, BiDLA, BiD&SB, BioIn 1, –2, –3, –4, –5, –6, –7, –8, –9, –10, –11, –12, –13, –14, –15, –16, –17, BlmGEL, BritAu 19, BritWr 4, CamGEL, CamGLE, CamGWoT, CarSB, CasWL, CelCen, Chambr 3, ChhPo, –S1, –S2, CnDBLB 3, CrtT 2, CyWA 58, DcBiPP, DcEnA, DcEnL, DcEuL, DcInB, DcLB 93, –107, DcLEL, DcNaB, Dis&D, EvLB, LongCEL, McGEWB, MouLC 3, NewC, NinCLC 10, NotNAT B, OxCAusL, OxCChiL, OxCEng 67, –85, OxCMus, OxCThe 67, –83, PenC ENG, RAdv 1, –13-1, RComWL, REn, RfGEnL 91, SmATA 17, TelT, WebE&AL, WhDW, WhoChL, WorAlBi, WorAl, WorLitC*
Pseud./variant:
Elia

Lamb, Charles 1893-1964 *DcIrB 88*

Lamb, Elizabeth Searle *DrAPF 87, –89, –91, –93*

Lamb, Elizabeth Searle 1917- *BioIn 14, ConAu 33R, DrAPF 83, –85, IntAu&W 82, –86, –89, –91, SmATA 31, WhoAmW 75, –77, WhoUSWr 88, WhoWrEP 89, –92, WrDr 76, –80, –82, –84, –86, –88, –90, –92, –94*

Lamb, Geoffrey *AuBYP 3*

Lamb, Geoffrey Frederick *AuBYP 2S, Au&Wr 71, BioIn 11, ConAu 53, IntAu&W 77, –82, –91, SmATA 10, WrDr 76, –80, –82, –84, –86, –88, –90, –92, –94*
Pseud./variant:
Balaam

Lamb, Harold 1892-1962 *AuBYP 3, BenetAL 91, BioIn 16, SmATA 53*

Lamb, Harold Albert 1892-1962 *AmAu&B, AuBYP 2, BioIn 1, –2, –3, –4, –6, –7, –9, ChhPo S2, JBA 34, –51, ObitOF 79, OxCAmL 65, REn, REnAL, TwCA, –SUP, WhAm 4, WhNAA*

Lamb, Harold M *BioIn 1*

Lamb, Hugh 1946- *BioIn 15, ConAu 49, –1NR, PenEncH, ScF&FL 92, WhoHr&F*

Lamb, Lynton Harold 1907- *ArtsCL, Au&Wr 71, BioIn 5, –6, –8, –11, BlueB 76, ConAu 1R, DcBrAr 1, IlsBYP, IlsCB 1946, –1957, SmATA 10, Who 74, WhoGrA 62*

Lamb, Lynton Harold 1907-1977 *DcNaB 1971*

Lamb, Mary Ann 1764-1847 *Alli, ArtclWW 2, BioIn 1, –2, –6, –8, –9, –10, –11, –12, BlmGEL, CarSB, ChhPo, –S2, DcEnA, DcEnL, DcLEL, DcNaB, Dis&D, EncBrWW, InWom SUP, NewC, OxCChiL, OxCEng 67, –85, SmATA 17, TelT, WhoChL*

Lamb, Robert 1941- *BioIn 11, ConAu 29R, –35NR, SmATA 13*

Lamb, Ruth S *ConAu 21NR*

Lamb, Ruth Stanton *ConAu 45, DrAS 74F, –78F, –82F, WhoAmW 74, –75, –77*

Lambert, David 1932- *BioIn 16, ConAu 122*

Lambert, David Compton 1932- *SmATA 49*
Pseud./variant:
Kent, David

Lambert, Janet 1895?-1973 *AuBYP 3*

Lambert, Janet Snyder 1894-1973 *AuBYP 2 BenetAL 91, BioIn 3, –7, –9, –13, ConAu 41R, CurBio 54, IndAu 1917, REnAL, SmATA 25, ThrBJA*

Lambert, Richard Stanton 1894-1981 *BiDPara, CanWW 70, OxCCan, –SUP, Who 74, –82, –83N*

Lambert, Saul 1928- *BioIn 13, ConAu 106, IlsBYP, SmATA 23*

Lambo, Don *IlsBYP*

Lamburn, Richmal Crompton 1890-1969 *BioIn 8, –9, –10, –14, –16, ConAu 9R, –25R, –P-1, DcNaB 1961, GrBr, LongCTC, NewC, OxCChiL, SmATA 5, WhoChL*

Lamm, Joyce 1933- *ConAu 57*

Lamond, Henry George 1885-1969 *BioIn 8, ConAu 25R, OxCAusL, SingR 1*

Lamont, Marianne *ConAu 57, –X, IntAu&W 77X, TwCRHW 90, WrDr 76, –80,*

–82, –84, –86, –88, –90
Main entry: Rundle, Anne

Lamorisse, Albert 1922-1970 *BioIn 6, –8, –9, –13, –16, ConAu 101, CurBio 63, –70, DcFM, FilmgC, FourBJA, HalFC 84, –88, NewYTBE 70, ObitOF 79, OxCFilm, SmATA 23, WhAm 5, WorEFlm, WorFDir 2*

LaMotte Fouque, F H
Main entry: Fouque, Friedrich H K

LaMotte Fouque, Friedrich H K 1777-1843 *BiD&SB, BioIn 5, –7, –8, CyWA 58, EuAu, OxCChiL, OxCEng 67, OxCFr*

La Motte-Fouque, Friedrich Heinrich Karl, Freiherr von 1777-1843 *BioIn 17*

Lamparski, Richard *ConAu 21R, WhoAm 76, –78, –80, –82, –84, –86, –88, –90, WhoUSWr 88, WhoWrEP 89, –92*

Lampell, Millard 1919- *AmAu&B, AmNov, BenetAL 91, BiE&WWA, BioIn 1, –2, ConAu 9R, EncFCWM 69, NotNAT, PlP&P, REnAL, WhoAm 74, WhoEnt 92*

Lampert, Emily 1951- *BioIn 16, ConAu 121, SmATA 49, –52*

Lamplugh, Lois 1921- *BioIn 12, ConAu X, –9NR, –24NR, IntAu&W 77, –82, SmATA 17, TwCChW 83, –89, WrDr 90, –92, –94*
Pseud./variant:
Davis, Lois Carlile

Lampman, Evelyn 1907-1980 *AuBYP 3*

Lampman, Evelyn Sibley 1907-1980 *AuBYP 2, BioIn 6, –7, –9, ConAu 13R, –101, –11NR, DcAmChF 1960, MorJA, NewYTBS 80, ScF&FL 92, SmATA 4, –23N, TwCChW 78, –83, –89, WhoAmW 74, –75, –77, WhoPNW, WrDr 80*
Pseud./variant:
Bronson, Lynn

Lamprey, Louise 1869-1951 *AmAu&B, BenetAL 91, BioIn 2, –12, CarSB, ChhPo, ConAu 117, JBA 34, –51, REnAL, WhAm 3, WhNAA, YABC 2*

Lampton, Christopher *BioIn 16, –17, ConAu 125, –37NR, SmATA 47, –67*

Lancaster, Bruce *IntvTCA 2*

Lancaster, Bruce 1896-1963 *AmAu&B, AmNov, BenetAL 91, BioIn 1, –2, –4, –6, –7, –11, ConAu P-1, ConLC 36, ObitOF 79, SmATA 9, TwCA, –SUP, WhAm 4*

Lancaster, Clay 1917- *ConAu 5R, –8NR*

Lancaster, Matthew d1983 *BioIn 15*

Lancaster, Matthew 1973?-1983 *ConAu 117, SmATA 45N*

Lancaster, Osbert 1908- *BioIn 3, –4, –5, –6, –7, –8, –12, BlueB 76, ConAu 105, CurBio 64, DcBrAr 1, IlsCB 1946, IntAu&W 77, IntWW 74, –75, –76, –77, –78, –79, –80, –81, –82, –83, LongCTC, NewC, PhDcTCA 77, TwCA SUP, WhDW, Who 74, –82, –83, –85, WhoGrA 62, –82, WhoWor 74, WorECar, WrDr 76, –82, –84, –86*

Lancaster, Osbert 1908-1986 *BioIn 14, –15, –16, –17, ConAu 119, ConGrA 3, CurBio 86N*

Lancaster, Osbert, Sir 1908-1986 *AnObit 1986, NewYTBS 86*

Lancaster, William Joseph Cosens 1851-1922 *Alli SUP, BiD&SB, BioIn 8, WhoChL*

Lancaster Brown, Peter 1927- *Au&Wr 71, ConAu 19NR, IntAu&W 77, –86, –89, –91, WrDr 76, –80, –82, –84, –86, –88, –90, –92, –94*

Lance, James Waldo 1926- *Au&Wr 71, BlueB 76, ConAu 65, IntWW 89, –91, WhoWor 78, –80, –82, –91, –93, WrDr 76, –80, –82, –84, –86, –88, –90, –92, –94*

Lance, Kathryn 1943- *ConAu 122, EncSF 93, ScF&FL 92, SmATA 76*
Pseud./variant:
Beach, Lynn

Land, Barbara Neblett 1923- *ConAu 81, IntAu&W 77, –82, SmATA 16*

Land, Jane *BioIn 1, ConAu X, MichAu 80, SmATA X, WrDr 84, –86, –88, –90, –92*
Main entry: Borland, Kathryn Kilby
Speicher, Helen Ross

Land, Jane 1916- *WrDr 94*

Land, Myrick 1922- *BioIn 3, ConAu 13R, –11NR, SmATA 15, WhoE 74*

Land, Ross *ConAu X, SmATA X, WrDr 84*
Main entry: Borland, Kathryn Kilby
Speicher, Helen Ross

Land, Ross 1916- *WrDr 94*

Landau, Elaine 1948- *AuBYP 2S, –3, BioIn 11, ConAu 53, –5NR, IntAu&W 77, SmATA 10, WhoAmW 77, –81*

Landau, Jacob 1917- *BioIn 4, –5, –7, –8, –12, –15, BlueB 76, CurBio 65, DcCAA 71, –77, –88, IlsBYP, IlsCB 1946, –1957, –1967, OxCTwCA, PrintW 83, –85, SmATA 38, WhoAm 74, –76, –78, –80, –82, –84, –86, –88, –90, –92, –94, WhoAmA 73, –78, –80,*

–82, –84, –86, –89, –91, WhoAmJ 80, WhoWor 74, WhoWorJ 72, –78

Landau, Lev Davidovich 1908-1968 *AsBiEn, BiESc, BioIn 5, –6, –7, –8, –11, –12, –13, –15, –16, –17, ConAu 113, CurBio 63, –68, DcScB, McGEWB, McGMS 80, ObitOF 79, ObitT 1961, WhDW, WhAm 5, WhoNob, –90, WorAl*

Landeck, Beatrice 1904- *AuBYP 2, –3, BioIn 7, –12, ConAu 73, LEduc 74, SmATA 15*

Landells, Ebenezer 1808-1860 *DcNaB, OxCChiL*

Lander, Ernest McPherson, Jr. 1915- *ConAu 1R, –4NR, DrAS 74H, –78H, –82H, IntAu&W 82, –86, WrDr 76, –80, –82, –84, –86, –88, –90, –92, –94*

Landin, Les 1923- *BioIn 9, ConAu 5R, SmATA 2*

Landis, J D 1942- *ConAu 126, SmATA 52, –60, WrDr 90, –92*

Landis, James David 1942- *WrDr 94*

Landis, Paul Henry 1901- *AmMWSc 73S, ConAu 5R, –5NR, IntAu&W 77*

Landon, Herman 1882-1960 *AmAu&B, BioIn 5*

Landon, Herman A 1882-1960 *ScFEYrs*

Landon, Lucinda 1950- *BioIn 16, ConAu 123, SmATA 51, –56, WrDr 90, –92, –94*

Landon, Margaret *EngPo*

Landon, Margaret 1903- *AmAu&B, BioIn 4, –16, ConAu P-1, CurBio 45, ForWC 70, PlP&P, SmATA 50, TwCA SUP*

Landon, Margaret 1903-1993 *NewYTBS 93*

Landry, Lionel 1919- *WhoAm 74, –76, –78, –80, –82, –84*

Landshoff, Ursula 1908- *BioIn 11, ConAu 29R, SmATA 13*

Lane, Carl Daniel 1899- *AmAu&B, AuBYP 2, –3, BioIn 2, –7, ConAu 105, CurBio 51*

Lane, Carolyn 1926- *AuBYP 2S, –3, BioIn 11, ConAu 29R, –12NR, ScF&FL 92, SmATA 10, WhoAmW 77, WhoE 81, WrDr 76, –80, –82, –84, –86, –88, –90, –92, –94*

Lane, Ferdinand Cole 1885- *AmAu&B, BioIn 4, TwCA SUP*

Lane, Jane *Au&Wr 71, ConAu X, –30NR, IntAu&W 77, LongCTC, TwCWr, Who 74, WrDr 76, –80*
Main entry: Dakers, Elaine Kidner

Lane, Jane 1905-1978 *EncSF 93, ScF&FL 92, TwCRHW 90*

Lane, Jerry *ConAu X, –37NR, MajAI, SmATA X*
Main entry: Martin, Patricia Miles

Lane, John 1932- *BioIn 12, ConAu 106, SmATA 15*

Lane, Margaret 1907- *BioIn 10, –15, –17, ConAu 13NR, –29NR, IntAu&W 89, –91, SmATA 38, –65, Who 82, –83, –85, –88, –90, –92*

Lane, Neola Tracy *AuBYP 2, –3, BioIn 7*

Lane, Rose Wilder *InWom SUP*

Lane, Rose Wilder 1886?-1968 *AmAu&B, AmWomPl, ArtclWW 2, AuBYP 2S, BioIn 4, –8, –10, –14, –17, ConAu 102, EncFWF, NotAW MOD, REnAL, SmATA 28, –29, TwCA, –SUP, TwCWW 91, WhAm 5, WhNAA*

Lane, Rose Wilder 1887-1968 *AuBYP 3*

Lane, Sheena Porter *ThrBJA*
Main entry: Porter, Sheena

Lanes, Selma 1929- *AuBYP 3*

Lanes, Selma Gordon 1929- *AuBYP 2S, BioIn 9, ConAu 25R, SmATA 3, WhoAm 88, –90, –92, WhoAmW 74, –75, –77, –81, –83, –85, –87, –89, WhoE 85, –86, –89*
Pseud./variant:
Gordon, Selma

Lang, Andrew 1844-1912 *Alli SUP, AnCL, AuBYP 2, –3, Benet 87, BbD, BiDPara, BiD&SB, BioIn 1, –2, –3, –5, –6, –7, –8, –10, –12, –15, –16, –17, BritAu 19, CamGEL, CamGLE, CarSB, CasWL, Chambr 3, ChhPo, –S1, –S2, CmScLit, ConAu 114, –137, DcBiA, DcEnA, –A, DcEuL, DcLB 98, DcLEL, DcNaB 1912, Dis&D, EncO&P 1, –2, –3, EncPaPR 91, EncSF 93, EvLB, JBA 34, LongCTC, MajAI, ModBrL, NewC, OxCChiL, OxCEng 67, –85, PenC ENG, REn, RfGEnL 91, ScFSB, ScFEYrs, SmATA 16, StaCVF, Str&VC, TelT, TwCChW 78A, –83A, –89A, TwCLC 16, WebE&AL, WhoChL, WhoHr&F, WrChl*
Pseud./variant:
Longway, A Hugh

Lang, Paul Henry 1901- *AmAu&B, Baker 84, –92, ConAu 103, IntWW 74, –75, –76, IntWWM 90, NewGrDA 86, OxCMus, REnAL, WhoMus 72*

Lang, Paul Henry 1901-1991 *BioIn 17, ConAu 135, NewYTBS 91*

Lang, Robert 1912- *BiDrLUS 70, ConAu 41R, DrAS 74H*

Lang, Susan S *BioIn 17*

Lang, Susan S 1950- *ConAu 136, SmATA 68, WrDr 94*

Lang, T T *MajAI*

Langbridge, Frederick 1849-1922 *Alli SUP, ChhPo, –S1, –S2, PoIre, StaCVF*

Langdon, Eustella *OxCCan SUP*

Lange, John *ConAu X, –40NR, ConTFT 5, DcBrECP, EncSF 93, IntAu&W 82X, –91X, MajTwCW, SmATA X, TwCCr&M 80, –85, –91, TwCSFW 86, –91, TwCYAW, WrDr 76, –80, –82, –84, –86, –88, –90, –92*
Main entry: Crichton, Michael

Lange, John 1942- *WrDr 94*

Lange, Suzanne 1945- *BioIn 10, ConAu 29R, SmATA 5*

Langhorne, Doctor 1735-1779 *CarSB*

Langley, Noel Aubrey 1911-1980 *AnObit 1980, Au&Wr 71, BioIn 2, –13, ConAu 13R, –102, DcLEL, EncSoA, EvLB, FilmgC, HalFC 84, IntAu&W 82, IntMPA 75, –76, –78, –81, –77, NotNAT, OxCChiL, SmATA 25N, TwCWr, Who 74, WhoHr&F*

Langner, Nola *ConAu 41NR*

Langner, Nola 1930- *BioIn 8, –11, –12, ConAu 37R, –15NR, IlsBYP, IlsCB 1957, –1967, SmATA 8, WhoAmA 78, –80, –82, –84, WhoAmW 77*

Langone, John 1929- *BioIn 15, ConAu 49, –1NR, SmATA 38, –46*

Langseth-Christensen, Lillian *BioIn 2, –16, –17, WhAmArt 85*

Langstaff, John 1920- *AuBYP 3*

Langstaff, John M 1920- *BioIn 17*

Langstaff, John Meredith 1920- *AmAu&B, AuBYP 2S, BioIn 9, –10, ChhPo S2, ChlLR 3, ConAu 1R, –4NR, MajAI, SmATA 6, –68, ThrBJA, WhoAm 74, –76, –78, –80, –82, –84, –86, –88, –90, –92, –94, WhoEnt 92, WhoMus 72*

Langstaff, Launcelot *Alli, BenetAL 91, DcEnL, YABC X*
Main entry: Irving, Washington

Langstaff, Nancy 1925- *ConAu 73, –12NR*

Langston, Jane 1922- *SmATA 68*

Langton, Jane *BioIn 14, –16, –17*

Langton, Jane 1922- *AuBYP 2, –3, BioIn 9, –13, ConAu 1R, –1NR, –18NR, FemiCLE, FifBJA, ForWC 70, IntAu&W 86, –91, OxCChiL, ScF&FL 92, SmATA 3, –5AS, TwCChW 78, –83, –89, TwCCr&M 85, –91, TwCYAW, WhoAmW 83, WrDr 76, –80, –82, –84, –86, –88, –90, –92, –94*

Langton, Jane Gillson 1922- *ConAu 40NR, DcAmChF 1960, MajAI*

Langworthy, John Luther *CarSB*

Lanham, Urless Norton 1918- *AmMWSc 73P, –76P, –82, –86, –89, –92, WhoAm 82, –84, –86, –88, –90, –92, –94, WhoWest 74, –76, –78, –80*

Lanier, Sidney 1842-1881 *Alli SUP, AmAu, AmAu&B, AmWr S1, AtlBL, Baker 84, Benet 87, BenetAL 91, BbD, BiDSA, BiD&SB, BioIn 1, –2, –3, –4, –5, –6, –8, –9, –10, –11, –12, –16, CamGEL, CamGLE, CamHAL, CarSB, CasWL, Chambr 3, ChhPo, –S1, –S2, CnDAL, CnE&AP, CrtT 3, CyWA 58, DcAmAu, DcEnA A, DcLB 64, DcLEL, DcNAA, Dis&D, EncSoH, EvLB, FifSWrB, HarEnUS, MajAI, McGEWB, MouLC 3, NewGrDA 86, NinCLC 6, OxCAmL 65, –83, OxCChiL, OxCEng 67, –85, PenC AM, RAdv 1, –13-1, REn, REnAL, RfGAmL 87, SmATA 18, WebAB 74, –79, WebE&AL, WhAm HS, WhCiWar, WhFla, WorAlBi, WorAl*

Lanier, Sidney Clopton 1842-1881 *Baker 92*

Lanier, Sterling E 1927- *AuBYP 2, –3, ConAu 118, IntAu&W 91, NewEScF, ScF&FL 92, ScFSB, TwCSFW 86, –91, WhoHr&F, WrDr 84, –86, –88, –90, –92*

Lanier, Sterling Edmund 1927- *EncSF 93, WrDr 94*

Lankes, Julius J 1884-1960 *AmAu&B, BioIn 1, –5, ChhPo, –S1, GrAmP, IlsCB 1744, WhAm 4, WhAmArt 85, WhoAmA 80N, –82N, –86N, –89N, –91N*

Lankford, Mary D 1932- *SmATA 77*

Lansing, Alfred 1921-1975 *BioIn 10, –14, ConAu 13R, –61, SmATA 35*

Lansing, Elisabeth 1911- *AuBYP 2, BioIn 7, ConAu 5R*

Lansing, Elizabeth Carleton 1911- *AuBYP 3*

Lansing, Karen E 1954- *SmATA 71*

Lansing, Marion Florence 1883- *AmAu&B, AmWomPl, BioIn 2, JBA 34, –51, WhAm 7, WhNAA, WhoAmW 72, WomWWA 14*

Lantz, Fran *ConAu 39NR, IntAu&W 86X*
Main entry: Lantz, Francess Lin

Lantz, Fran 1952- *ScF&FL 92, SmATA X*

Lantz, Francess Lin 1952- *BioIn 17, ConAu 39NR, IntAu&W 86, –89, SmATA 63*
Pseud./variant:
Franklin, Lance
Lantz, Fran
Suzanne, Jamie

Lantz, Paul 1908- *BioIn 1, –5, –15, IlsCB 1744, –1946, SmATA 45, WhAmArt 85*

Lantz, Walter 1900- *BioIn 9, –12, –15, ConAu 108, HalFC 84, –88, IntMPA 81, –82, –84, –86, –88, –92, SmATA 37, WhoAm 80, –82, –84, –86, –88, –90, –92, –94, WhoEnt 92, WorECar*

Lapage, Geoffrey 1888-1971 *Au&Wr 71, BioIn 9, ConAu P-1*

Lapidus, Elaine 1939- *ConAu 21R*
Pseud./variant:
Peters, Lane

LaPietra, Mary 1929- *ConAu 61*
Pseud./variant:
Patanne, Maria

Lapp, Christiane Germain 1948- *SmATA 74*
Pseud./variant:
Lager, Claude

Lapp, Eleanor J 1936- *AuBYP 2S, –3, BioIn 17, ConAu 69, SmATA 61*

Lapp, Ralph Eugene 1917- *AmAu&B, AmMWSc 73P, BioIn 3, –4, ConAu 81, CurBio 55, InSci, WhoAm 74, –76, WhoWor 74*

Lappin, Peter 1911- *BioIn 14, ConAu 57, –7NR, –25NR, SmATA 32*

Lapsley, Susan *AuBYP 2S, –3*

LaRamee, Louise De *BiD&SB, BritAu 19, CamGLE, DcEnA, JBA 34*
Main entry: DeLaRamee, Louise

Larcom, Lucy 1824?-1893 *Alli, –SUP, AmAu, AmAu&B, BenetAL 91, BiD&SB, BioAmW, BioIn 1, –3, –7, –9, –12, –13, –17, BlmGWL, Chambr 3, ChhPo, –S2, ChrP, DcAmAu, DcLEL, DcNAA, FemiCLE, HanAmWH, InWom SUP, OxCAmL 65, –83, REnAL, WhAm HS*

Lardner, Rex *AuBYP 3*

Lardner, Rex 1881-1941 *AmAu&B, AuBYP 2S, ObitOF 79, REnAL*

Lariviere, Marian *AuBYP 2S, –3*

Larkin, Amy *ConAu 132, –41NR, SmATA 65*
Main entry: Burns, Olive Ann

Larkin, Rochelle T 1935- *ConAu 33R, IntAu&W 77, WrDr 76, –80*

Larkin, Sarah *ConAu X, IntAu&W 77X*
Main entry: Loening, Sarah Larkin

Larkin, Sarah 1896-1988 *BioIn 15*

Laroche, Giles 1956- *SmATA 71*

Larom, Henry V 1903?-1975 *AuBYP 2, –3, BioIn 8, –14, ConAu 61, SmATA 30N*

Larralde, Elsa *AuBYP 2, –3, BioIn 1, –8*

Larranaga, Robert O 1940- *ConAu 49*

Larrea, Jean-Jacques 1960- *ConAu 45*

Larrecq, John M 1926-1980 *BioIn 15*

Larrecq, John Maurice 1926-1980 *BioIn 12 –13, IlsBYP, IlsCB 1967, SmATA 25N, –44*

Larrick, Nancy *BioIn 16, –17*

Larrick, Nancy 1910- *DcLB 61, IntAu&W 86, –89, –91, WhoAmW 93, WrDr 86, –88, –90, –92, –94*

Larrick, Nancy G 1910- *AuBYP 2, –3, BioIn 7, –9, –10, ChhPo, –S1, –S2, ConAu 1R, LEduc 74, MedPD, MorBMP, SmATA 4, WhoAmW 74, –75, –77, WrDr 76, –80*

Larris, Ann *AuBYP 2S, –3*

Larsen, Egon 1904- *Au&Wr 71, BioIn 12, ConAu 9R, –3NR, IntAu&W 77, –82, –86, –91, SmATA 14, WrDr 76, –82, –84, –86, –88, –90*

Larsen, Johannes 1867- *BioIn 5, IlsCB 1946*

Larsen, Peter 1933- *ConAu 29R, –22NR, WrDr 76, –80, –82, –84*

Larsen, Rebecca 1944- *BioIn 16, ConAu 122, SmATA 54*

Larsen, Ronald J 1948- *ConAu 41R*

Larsen, Suzanne Kesteloo 1930- *BioIn 8, IlsCB 1957*

Larson, Charles R *DrAPF 87, –89, –91, –93*

Larson, Charles Raymond 1938- *BioIn 11, ConAu 53, -4NR, ConLC 31, DrAPF 83, -85, DrAS 78E, -82E, IntAu&W 77*

Larson, Eve *ConAu X, SmATA X*
Main entry: Saint John, Wylly Folk

Larson, Gary *BioIn 14, -15, -16, -17, EncTwCJ*

Larson, Gary 1950- *Au&Arts 1, ConAu 118, CurBio 91, EncACom, SmATA 57, WhoAm 90, -92, -94, WorAlBi, WrDr 92, -94*

Larson, Jean Russell 1930- *AuBYP 2S, -3, ConAu 21R, DcAmChF 1960, WhoAmW 74, -75, -81*

Larson, Norita D 1944- *BioIn 13, ConAu 105, SmATA 29*

Larson, William Herbert 1938- *BioIn 11, ConAu 21R, SmATA 10, WhoMW 74, -76, -78*

Larsson, Carl 1853-1919 *BioIn 13, ConAu 115, OxCArt, OxCChiL, OxDcArt, SmATA 35*

Larue, Gerald Alexander 1916- *ConAu 21R, DrAS 74P, -78P, WhoRel 75, -77*

LaRue, Mabel Guinnip 1880-1971 *AmAu&B, ChhPo S1, WhAm 5, WhNAA*

LaSalle, Donald P 1933- *ConAu 29R, LEduc 74, WrDr 76, -80, -82, -84*

Laschever, Barnett D 1924- *AuBYP 2, -3, BioIn 8, ConAu 1R, -6NR*

Lasell, Elinor H *AuBYP 3*

Lasell, Elinor H 1929- *AuBYP 2, BioIn 8, -12, ConAu X, -7NR, IlsCB 1957, -1967, SmATA 19*
Pseud./variant:
Calvert, Elinor H
Lasell, Fen H

Lasell, Fen 1929- *AuBYP 3*

Lasell, Fen H *ConAu X, SmATA X*
Main entry: Lasell, Elinor H

Lasenby, Jack 1931- *BioIn 17, ConAu 130, SmATA 65, WrDr 94*

Lash, Joseph P 1909- *BioIn 9, -11, -14, ConAu 16NR, SmATA 43, WhoAm 80, -82, -84, -86, WrDr 82, -84, -86*

Lash, Joseph P 1909-1987 *AnObit 1987, BioIn 15, -16, ConAu 123, CurBio 87N, NewYTBS 87, WhAm 9*

Lasher, Faith Betty 1921- *BioIn 11, ConAu 37R, SmATA 12, WrDr 76, -80, -82*

Lasker, David 1950- *BioIn 15, ConAu 112, SmATA 38*

Lasker, David Raymond 1950- *IntAu&W 91*

Lasker, Joe *ConAu 38NR*

Lasker, Joe 1919- *SmATA 17AS, WhoAmA 86, -89, -91*

Lasker, Joseph L 1919- *BioIn 8, -11, ConAu 49, -1NR, FifBJA, IlsBYP, IlsCB 1957, -1967, SmATA 9, WhAmArt 85, WhoAm 74, -76, -78, -80, -82, -84, -86, -88, -90, -92, -94, WhoAmA 73, -78, -82, -84, WhoE 83*

Lasker, Joseph Leon 1919- *ConAu 38NR*

Laski, Marghanita *IntAu&W 86X*

Laski, Marghanita d1988 *NewYTBS 88*

Laski, Marghanita 1915- *InWom SUP, Who 88, WrDr 86, -88*

Laski, Marghanita 1915-1988 *AnObit 1988, BioIn 15, -16, ConAu 124, CurBio 88N, EncBrWW, EncSF 93, FemiCLE, ScF&FL 92, SmATA 55*
Pseud./variant:
Russell, Sarah

Laskin, Pamela L 1954- *ConAu 142, SmATA 75*

Laskowski, Janina Domanska *ThrBJA*
Main entry: Domanska, Janina

Laskowski, Jerzy 1919- *BioIn 9, ConAu 77, ThrBJA*

Lasky, Kathryn *BioIn 16, -17*

Lasky, Kathryn 1944- *BioIn 11, ChlLR 11, ConAu 69, -11NR, DcAmChF 1985, MajAI, ScF&FL 92, SixBJA, SmATA 13, -69, TwCYAW*
Pseud./variant:
Knight, Kathryn Lasky

Lassalle, C E *YABC 1*
Main entry: Ellis, Edward S

Lassiter, Mary *ConAu 131, SmATA X*

Lassiter, Mary 1945- *WrDr 94*

Lasson, Robert 1922- *AuBYP 2, -3, BioIn 8*

Lasswell, Fred *BioIn 15, EncACom*

Lasswell, Fred 1916- *ArtCS, BioIn 6, WhoAm 82, -84, -86, -88, -90*

Latham, Barbara 1896- *BioIn 1, -5, -12, DcWomA, IlsCB 1744, -1946, SmATA 16,*

WhAmArt 85, WhoAmA 73, –78, –80, –82, –84, –86, –89

Latham, Donald C 1932- *WhoAm 86*

Latham, Donald Crawford 1932- *AuBYP 2S, –3, ConAu 9R, LElec, WhoAm 84*

Latham, Frank B 1910- *AuBYP 2S, –3, BioIn 10, ConAu 49, SmATA 6*

Latham, Jean Lee 1902- *AmAu&B, AmWomPl, AuBYP 2, –3, AuNews 1, Au&Wr 71, BioIn 4, –6, –7, –8, –9, –10, –12, –14, –17, ConAu 5R, –7NR, ConLC 12, CurBio 56, IntAu&W 91, MajAI, MorBMP, MorJA, NewbC 1956, OxCChiL, SmATA 2, –68, Str&VC, TwCChW 78, –83, –89, TwCYAW, WhoAm 74, –76, –78, –80, –82, –84, –86, –88, –90, –92, –94, WhoAmW 74, WrDr 80, –82, –84, –86, –88, –90, –92, –94*
Pseud./variant:
Gard, Janice
Lee, Julian

Latham, Mavis *ConAu X, –37NR, MajAI, SmATA 8, –74, WrDr 82, –84, –86, –88, –90, –92*
Main entry: Clark, Mavis Thorpe

Latham, Mavis 1909- *WrDr 94*

Latham, Philip *AuBYP 2, –3, ConAu X, IntAu&W 77X, –82X, SmATA 8, WrDr 84*
Main entry: Richardson, Robert Shirley

Latham, Philip 1902- *ScFSB*

Latham, Philip 1902-1981 *EncSF 93, TwCSFW 86, –91*

Lathrop, Dorothy P 1891-1980 *BioIn 14*

Lathrop, Dorothy Pulis 1891- *WhAm 9*

Lathrop, Dorothy Pulis 1891-1980 *AmAu&B, AuBYP 2, –3, BioIn 1, –2, –4, –5, –7, –8, –12, –13, BkP, Cald 1938, ChhPo, –S1, ConAu 73, –102, ConICB, DcLB 22, DcWomA, IlsBYP, IlsCB 1744, –1946, –1957, JBA 34, –51, MajAI, SmATA 14, –24N, Str&VC, WhAmArt 85, WhoAmA 73, –78*

Lathrop, Francis *ConAu X, –40NR, MajTwCW, SmATA 73, –X*
Main entry: Leiber, Fritz

Latourette, Kenneth S 1884-1968 *RAdv 13-3*

Latourette, Kenneth Scott 1884-1968 *AmAu&B, BioIn 3, –4, –6, –8, ConAu P-2, CurBio 53, –69, DcAmB S8, DcAmReB 2, EncSoB SUP, LuthC 75, OhA&B, TwCA SUP, WhNAA*

Lattimore, Eleanor 1904- *WrDr 86*

Lattimore, Eleanor 1904-1986 *TwCChW 89*

Lattimore, Eleanor Frances 1904- *AmAu&B AuBYP 2, –3, BioIn 1, –2, –5, –7, –8, –10, ConAu 9R, –6NR, IlsCB 1744, –1946, –1957, JBA 34, –51, OxCChiL, SmATA 5, –7, TwCChW 78, –83, WrDr 80, –82, –84*

Lattimore, Eleanor Frances 1904-1986 *BioIn 16, ConAu 119, SmATA 48N*

Lattin, Harriet 1898- *AuBYP 3*

Lattin, Harriet Pratt 1898- *AuBYP 2, BioIn 7, ConAu 33R, WrDr 76, –80, –82, –84*

Lauber, Patricia 1924- *AuBYP 2, –3, BioIn 7, –9, –14, ChlLR 16, ConAu 9R, –6NR, –24NR, ForWC 70, SmATA 1, –33, ThrBJA*

Lauber, Patricia Grace 1924- *ConAu 38NR, MajAI, SmATA 75, WhoAmW 91*

Laugesen, Mary E 1906- *BioIn 10, ConAu P-2, SmATA 5*

Laughbaum, Steve 1945- *BioIn 11, SmATA 12*

Laughlin, Florence Young 1910- *BioIn 9, ConAu 9R, ForWC 70, SmATA 3, WrDr 76, –80*

Laughlin, Ruth *AuBYP 2, –3, BioIn 7*

Laughlin, Virginia Carli 1907- *ConAu 1R*
Pseud./variant:
Clarke, John
Laklan, Carli

Laumer, Keith *DrmM 2, IntvTCA 2*

Laumer, Keith 1925- *AmAu&B, BioIn 12, –15, –17, ConAu 9R, –7NR, ConSFA, DcLB 8, IntAu&W 91, NewEScF, RGTwCSF, ScF&FL 92, ScFSB, TwCSFW 86, –91, WhoSciF, WrDr 84, –86, –88, –90, –92*

Laune, Paul Sidney 1899- *ConAu 17R, WhAmArt 85*

Laure, Ettagale
Main entry: Blauer, Ettagale

Laure, Jason 1940- *BioIn 15, –16, ConAu 104, SmATA 44, –50*

Laurence *IlsBYP*

Laurence, Ester Hauser 1935- *BioIn 10, ConAu 29R, SmATA 7, WrDr 76, –80, –82, –84*

Laurence, Margaret *IntvTCA 2*

Laurence, Margaret d1987 *NewYTBS 87*

Laurence, Margaret 1926- *ArtclWW 2, Benet 87, BenetAL 91, ConNov 86, DcChlFi, DcLB 53, InWom SUP, RAdv 13-1, WhoAm 86, WhoAmW 87, WrDr 86*

Laurence, Margaret 1926-1986 *ContDcW 89*

Laurence, Margaret 1926-1987 *AnObit 1987, BioIn 15, –16, –17, BlmGEL, ConAu 121, –33NR, ConLC 50, –62, CyWA 89, EncWB, FemiCLE, IntLitE, MagSWL, MajTwCW, RfGEnL 91, ShSCr 7, SmATA 50N, TwCWW 91, WhAm 9, WhoCanL 87, –92*

Laurence, Margaret 1928-1987 *CamGLE*

Laurence, Margaret Wemyss 1926- *Au&Wr 71, BioIn 8, –10, –11, CaW, CanWW 70, CanWr, ConAu 5R, ConLC 3, –6, –13, ConNov 72, –76, CreCan 1, OxCCan, –SUP, WhoWor 74, WrDr 76, –80*

Laurie, Rona *ConAu 85, –15NR, –33NR, IntAu&W 77, –89, WhoWor 78, WrDr 76, –80, –82, –84, –86, –88, –90, –92*

Laurie, Rona 1916- *BioIn 16, IntAu&W 91, SmATA 55, WrDr 94*

Laurie, Rona 1926- *IntAu&W 86*

Laurin, Anne *ConAu X, SmATA X*
Main entry: McLaurin, Anne

Lauritzen, Jonreed 1902- *BioIn 3, –11, ConAu 5R, CurBio 52, SmATA 13, WrDr 76, –80, –82, –84*

Lauscher, Hermann
Main entry: Hesse, Hermann

Laut, Agnes C 1871-1936 *BenetAL 91*

Laut, Agnes Christina 1871-1936 *AmAu&B, BioIn 1, –2, –12, –17, CanNov, CanWr, DcAmAu, DcLB 92, DcNAA, JBA 34, –51, OxCCan, REnAL, WhAm 1, WhNAA, WomWWA 14, WomNov*

Laux, Dorothy 1920- *BioIn 16, ConAu 61, SmATA 49*

Lavallee, Barbara 1941- *SmATA 74*

Lavell, Edith *CarSB*

Lavelle, Sheila *ChlFicS*

Lavender, David 1910- *AuBYP 2, –3, BioIn 8, –11, CmCal, ConAu 1R, –2NR, –18NR, SmATA 64*

Lavender, David Sievert 1910- *ConAu 40NR*

Laverty, Donald *ConAu 36NR, EncSF 93, MajTwCW, SmATA 66*
Main entry: Blish, James

Lavin, Mary *IntvTCA 2*

Lavin, Mary 1912- *ArtclWW 2, AuBYP 2S, –3, Au&Wr 71, BiDConC, BiDIrW, BioIn 1, –4, –5, –10, –13, –16, –17, BlmGWL, CamGLE, CasWL, CathA 1930, ConAu 9R, –33NR, ConLC 4, –18, ConNov 72, –76, –82, –86, –91, ContDcW 89, DcIrL, DcIrW 1, DcLB 15, DcLEL 1940, EncBrWW, EvLB, FemiCLE, InWom SUP, IntAu&W 77, –89, –91, IntWW 89, –91, LongCTC, MajTwCW, ModBrL S1, –S2, ModIrL, NewC, RAdv 1, RfGEnL 91, ShSCr 4, ShSWr, TwCA SUP, Who 74, –82, –83, –85, –88, –90, –92, WhoWor 74, WrDr 76, –80, –82, –84, –86, –88, –90, –92, –94*

Lavine, David 1928- *AuBYP 2, –3, BioIn 8, –14, SmATA 31, WhoAmP 73, –77, –81, –83, WhoE 74, –75, –77, –81*

Lavine, David 1929- *WhoAmP 85, –87, –89, –91, –93*

Lavine, Sigmund Arnold 1908- *AuBYP 2, –3, BioIn 7, –9, ConAu 1R, –4NR, –19NR, SmATA 3, WhoE 75, –77, WrDr 76, –80, –82, –84, –86, –88, –90, –92, –94*

Laviolette, Emily A d1975 *BioIn 16*

Laviolette, Emily A 1923?-1975 *SmATA 49*

Law, Denis *BioIn 6*

Lawford, Paula Jane *ConAu 125, SmATA 53, –X*
Main entry: Martyr, Paula Jane

Lawlor, John *AuBYP 3*

Lawlor, John James 1918- *AuBYP 2S, BlueB 76, Who 82, –83, –85, –88, –92, WrDr 80, –82, –84, –86, –88, –90, –92, –94*

Lawlor, John James, Prof 1918- *Who 90*

Lawrence, Ann 1942- *BioIn 15, ConAu 104, SmATA 41, TwCChW 78, –83, WrDr 82, –84, –86, –88*

Lawrence, Ann 1942-1987 *BioIn 16, ScF&FL 92, SmATA 54N, TwCChW 89*

Lawrence, David Herbert 1885-1930 *ArtsAmW 3, AtlBL, BioIn 1, –2, –3, –4, –5, –6, –7, –8, –9, –10, –11, –12, –13, –14, –15, –16, –17, CasWL, Chambr 3, ChhPo, –S1, CnE&AP, CnMD, CnMWL, CnThe, CyWA 58, DcLEL, DcNaB 1922, Dis&D, EncWL, EncWT, EvLB, FilmgC, GrBr, LongCEL, LongCTC, MakMC, McGEWB, ModBrL, –S1,*

ModWD, NewC, NotNAT B, OxCAmL 65, OxCEng 67, PenC ENG, RAdv 1, RComWL, REn, REnAL, TwCA, –SUP, TwCLC 2, TwCPaSc, TwCWr, WebE&AL, WhoTwCL

Lawrence, Isabelle *AuBYP 2, –3, BioIn 2, –8, –13, ForWC 70, SmATA 29, WhoAmW 74*

Lawrence, J T *ConAu X, SmATA X*
Main entry: Rowland-Entwistle, Theodore

Lawrence, Jacob *BioIn 15, –16, NewYTBS 86*

Lawrence, Jacob 1917- *AfrAmAl 6, AfroAA, AmArt, AmPB, BioIn 1, –2, –3, –4, –5, –6, –7, –8, –9, –10, –11, –13, BlkAull, –92, BriEAA, ChhPo S1, ConBlB 4, CurBio 65, –88, DcCAA 71, –77, –88, FourBJA, IlsBYP, IlsCB 1967, InB&W 80, McGEWB, NegAl 76, –83, –89, NewYTBS 74, OxCTwCA, PhDcTCA 77, PrintW 83, –85, RComAH, WhAmArt 85, WhoAm 74, –76, –78, –80, –82, –84, –86, –88, –90, –92, –94, WhoAmA 73, –78, –80, –82, –84, –86, –89, –91, WhoBlA 75, –80, –85, WhoWest 87, –89, –92, –94, WhoWor 74, –82, –87, WorArt 1950*

Lawrence, James D *ScF&FL 92*

Lawrence, James D 1918- *AuBYP 3*

Lawrence, James Duncan 1918- *AuBYP 2S, ConAu 27NR*

Lawrence, Jerome 1915- *AmAu&B, ASCAP 66, BiE&WWA, BioIn 10, –17, BlueB 76, CamGWoT, ConAu 41R, ConDr 73, –77, –82, –88, –93, ConTFT 5, EncMT, IntAu&W 77, –91, ModWD, NatPD 81, NotNAT, OhA&B, OxCAmT 84, SmATA 65, WhoAm 74, –76, –78, –80, –82, –84, –86, –88, –90, –92, –94, WhoAmJ 80, WhoEnt 92, WhoThe 72, –77, –81, WhoWest 84, –87, –89, –92, –94, WhoWor 74, WhoWorJ 72, –78, WrDr 76, –80, –82, –84, –86, –88, –90, –92, –94*

Lawrence, John 1933- *BioIn 12, –14, ConAu 107, –24NR, IlsCB 1967, OxCChiL, SmATA 30, Who 85, –88, –90, –92*

Lawrence, Josephine *IntvTCA 2*

Lawrence, Josephine 1890-1978 *BenetAL 91, ScF&FL 92*

Lawrence, Josephine 1897?-1978 *AmAu&B, AmNov, BioIn 1, –2, –4, –11, –12, –13, ConAu 77, ObitOF 79, OxCAmL 65, –83, REn, REnAL, SmATA 24N, TwCA, –SUP, WhAm 7, WhNAA, WhoAm 74, –76, –78, WhoAmW 75, WhoE 74*

Lawrence, Linda *IntAu&W 86X, SmATA X*
Main entry: Hunt, Linda Lawrence

Lawrence, Louise *ConAu 38NR*
Main entry: Holden, Elizabeth Rhoda

Lawrence, Louise 1943- *BioIn 15, –16, ConAu 97, –X, EncSF 93, IntAu&W 91, ScF&FL 92, SixBJA, SmATA 38, TwCChW 83, –89, TwCYAW, WrDr 86, –88, –90, –92, –94*

Lawrence, Louise DeKiriline *AmMWSc 86*

Lawrence, Louise DeKiriline 1894- *AmMWSc 73P, –76P, –82, BioIn 11, ConAu 25R, SmATA 13, WrDr 76, –80*
Pseud./variant:
DeKiriline, Louise

Lawrence, Lynn *SmATA 73*
Main entry: Garland, Sherry

Lawrence, Mildred Elwood 1907- *AuBYP 2 –3, BioIn 3, –6, –8, –9, ConAu 1R, –5NR, CurBio 53, ForWC 70, MichAu 80, MorJA, SmATA 3, TwCChW 78, WhoAmW 74, –75*

Lawrence, R D 1921- *BioIn 16, SmATA 55*

Lawrence, Ronald Douglas 1921- *BioIn 10, ConAu 65, Profile 1*

Lawrence, Thomas *ConAu X*
Main entry: Roberts, Thom

Lawrence, W E
Main entry: Emmett Brothers

Lawson, Carol Antell 1946- *BioIn 12, –14, –15, IlsCB 1967, SmATA 42*

Lawson, Don *BioIn 16*

Lawson, Don 1917- *ConAu 26NR, SixBJA*

Lawson, Don 1917-1990 *ConAu 130*

Lawson, Donald Elmer 1917- *AuBYP 2, –3, BioIn 7, –11, ConAu 1R, LEduc 74, SmATA 9, WhoAm 74, –76, –78, –80, –82, –84, –86, –88, WhoMW 74, –76, –78, –80, –82, –84*

Lawson, Donald Elmer 1917-1990 *WhAm 10*

Lawson, Donna Roberta 1937- *ConAu 41R*

Lawson, James 1938- *ConAu 65, IntAu&W 91, WhoAdv 80, WrDr 80, –82, –84, –86, –88, –90, –92, –94*

Lawson, Joan 1906- *BioIn 16, SmATA 55*

Lawson, John *AuBYP 2, –3, DcAmChF 1960*

Lawson, Marie 1894-1956 *AuBYP 3*

Lawson, Marie Abrams 1894-1956 *AuBYP 2, BioIn 4, –5, –7, IlsCB 1946, JBA 51*

Lawson, Marion Tubbs 1896- *SmATA 22*

Lawson, Patrick *AuBYP 2, -3*
Main entry: Eby, Lois Christine

Lawson, Robert 1892-1957 *Alli, -SUP, AmAu&B, AmPB, AnCL, AuBYP 2, -3, Au&ICB, BioIn 1, -2, -3, -4, -5, -7, -8, -10, -12, -14, BkCL, Cald 1938, ChhPo, -S2, ChILR 2, ConAu 118, -137, CurBio 41, -57, DcLB 22, FamAIYP, ForIl, IlsBYP, IlsCB 1744, -1946, JBA 51, MajAI, NewbMB 1922, ObitOF 79, OxCChiL, Str&VC, TwCChW 78, -83, -89, WhAm 3, WhAmArt 85, WhoAmA 80N, -82N, -86N, -89N, -91N, WrChl, YABC 2*

Lawson, Ted *CurBio 43*

Lawton, Charles *ConAu X, -30NR, TwCWW 91, WhoAm 84, -86, -88, WhoUSWr 88, WhoWrEP 89, -92, WrDr 84, -86, -88, -90, -92*
Main entry: Heckelmann, Charles Newman

Lawton, Charles 1913- *WhoAm 90, -92, -94, WrDr 94*

Lawton, George 1900-1957 *BiDPara, BioIn 1, -4, EncO&P 1, -2, -3*

Lawyer, Annabel Glenn 1906?-1974 *ConAu 53*

Laxalt, Robert Peter 1923- *ConAu 13R, -38NR*

Laycock, George Edwin 1921- *AuBYP 2, -3, BioIn 8, -10, ConAu 5R, SmATA 5, WhoMW 74, -76*

Lazare, Gerald John 1927- *BioIn 8, IlsBYP, IlsCB 1957, SmATA 44*
Pseud./variant:
Lazare, Jerry

Lazare, Jerry
Main entry: Lazare, Gerald John

Lazarevich, Mila 1942- *BioIn 12, SmATA 17*

Lazarus, Keo Felker 1913- *AuBYP 2S, -3, ConAu 41R, IntAu&W 82, -89, SmATA 21, WhoUSWr 88, WhoWrEP 89, -92, WrDr 76, -80, -82, -84, -86, -88*

Lazarus, Mell *WhoAm 86, -88, -90, -92, -94*

Lazarus, Mell 1927- *ArtCS, BioIn 13, ConAu 17R, -11NR, ConGrA 3, WhoAm 80, -84*

Lea, Alec 1907- *BioIn 12, ConAu 73, SmATA 19, TwCChW 78, WrDr 80, -82, -84, -86, -88*
Pseud./variant:
Lea, Richard

Lea, Joan *MajAI*

Lea, John 1871- *ChhPo, -S1, -S2*

Lea, Richard *SmATA X*
Main entry: Lea, Alec

Leach, Aroline Beecher 1899- *ConAu 61*

Leach, Maria 1892-1977 *AuBYP 2, -3, BioIn 8, -11, -13, -15, ChhPo S2, ConAu 53, -69, FourBJA, SmATA 28, -39*

Leacock, Stephen Butler 1869-1944 *BioIn 1, -3, -4, -5, -8, -9, -11, -14, -15, -17, CamGEL, CreCan 2, DcNaB 1941, EncAHmr, ObitOF 79, OxCEng 85*

Leacroft, Helen Mabel 1919- *Au&Wr 71, BioIn 10, ConAu 5R, SmATA 6*

Leacroft, Richard V B 1914- *Au&Wr 71, BioIn 10, ConAu 5R, SmATA 6, WhoArt 80, -82, -84*

Leaf, Margaret P 1909?-1988 *ConAu 124, SmATA 55N*

Leaf, Munro 1905-1976 *AmAu&B, AmPB, AuBYP 2, -3, BenetAL 91, BioIn 2, -4, -7, -8, -11, -12, BkP, ChhPo S2, ChILR 25, ConAu 69, -73, -29NR, JBA 51, LongCTC, ObitOF 79, OxCChiL, REnAL, SmATA 20, TwCA, -SUP, TwCChW 78, -83, -89, WhAm 7, WhAmArt 85, WhoAm 74, -76, WhoAmA 78N, -80N, -82N, WhoChL*
Pseud./variant:
Calvert, John
Mun

Leaf, Munro 1906-1977 *WhoAmA 86N, -89N, -91N*

Leaf, Russell Charles 1935- *AmMWSc 73S, -78S, ConAu 21R*

Leaf, VaDonna Jean 1929- *BioIn 13, ConAu 57, SmATA 26*

Leaf, Wilbur Munro 1905-1976 *MajAI*

Leak, Zenolia *BioIn 9*

Leakey, Richard E *NewYTBS 90*

Leakey, Richard E 1944- *BioIn 14, -15, -16, -17, WorAlBi*

Leakey, Richard Erskine 1944- *WhoAm 86, -88, WhoWor 91, -93*

Leakey, Richard Erskine Frere 1944- *AfSS 80, -81, -82, BioIn 8, -10, -12, -13, ConAu 93, -18NR, IntWW 79, -80, -81, -82, -83, -89, -91, SmATA 42, Who 82, -83, -85, -88, -90,*

–92, WhoAm 82, –84, WhoWor 82, –84, –87, WorAl

Leamy, Edmund Stanislaus 1889-1962 *BioIn 6, ChhPo, –S1, Str&VC*

Leander, Ed *BioIn 13, ConAu X, SmATA X*
Main entry: Richelson, Geraldine

Leaney, Alfred Robert Clare 1909- *Au&Wr 71, ConAu 5R, –2NR, IntAu&W 77, –82, WrDr 76, –80, –82, –84, –86, –88, –90, –92, –94*

Lear, Edward 1812-1888 *AmPB, AnCL, AtlBL, AuBYP 2, –3, Benet 87, BiD&SB, BioIn 1, –2, –3, –4, –5, –6, –7, –8, –9, –10, –11, –12, –13, –14, –16, –17, BlmGEL, BritAu 19, BritWr 5, CamGEL, CamGLE, CarSB, CasWL, Chambr 3, ChhPo, –S1, –S2, ChlLR 1, ChrP, ClaDrA, CnE&AP, CrtT 3, DcBrBI, DcEnL, DcEuL, DcLB 32, DcLEL, DcNaB, –C, DcVicP 2, Dis&D, EvLB, FamAIYP, FamPYP, GrBIl, JBA 34, LongCEL, MajAI, McGEWB, MouLC 4, NewC, NinCLC 3, OxCArt, OxCChiL, OxCEng 67, –85, OxDcArt, PenC ENG, REn, RfGEnL 91, SmATA 18, Str&VC, TelT, TwCChW 78A, –83A, –89A, WebE&AL, WhDW, WhoChL, WorECar, WrChl*
Pseud./variant:
Derry Down Derry

Lear, Melva Gwendoline Bartlett 1917- *Au&Wr 71, ConAu 5R, SingR 1*

Learsi, Rufus *AmAu&B, WhAm 4*
Main entry: Goldberg, Israel

Leary, Lewis d1990 *NewYTBS 90*

Leary, Lewis 1906- *AmAu&B, Au&Wr 71, CnDAL, ConAu 1R, –4NR, DrAS 74E, –78E, –82E, REnAL, WhoAm 74, –76, –78, –80, –82, –84, –86, –88, WrDr 80, –82, –84, –86, –88, –90*

Leary, Lewis 1906-1990 *BenetAL 91, ConAu 131, WhAm 10*

Leary, Lewis Gaston 1906-1990 *BioIn 17*

Leasor, James *BioIn 14*

Leasor, James 1923- *Au&Wr 71, BioIn 16, ConAu 1R, –2NR, EngPo, HalFC 84, –88, IntAu&W 77, –82, –86, –89, –91, Novels, SmATA 54, TwCCr&M 80, –85, –91, Who 74, –82, –83, –85, –88, –90, –92, WhoSpyF, WrDr 82, –84, –86, –88, –90, –92*

Leatham, Moyra 1928- *BioIn 5, IlsCB 1946*

Leavitt, Hart Day 1909- *ConAu 13R*

Leavitt, Jerome Edward 1916- *AuBYP 2, –3, BioIn 7, –13, ConAu 1R, –1NR, –17NR, IntAu&W 77, LEduc 74, SmATA 23, WhoAm 76, –78, –80, –82, –84, –86, –88, –90, –92, –94*

LeBar, Frank M 1920- *AmMWSc 73S, FifIDA*

LeBar, Mary E 1910-1982 *BioIn 14, ConAu 25NR*

LeBar, Mary Evelyn 1910-1982 *ConAu 107, DrAS 74P, –78P, ForWC 70, LEduc 74, SmATA 35*

LeBaron, Grace 1845- *CarSB, DcNAA*

Lebedev, Vladimir Vasilievich 1891- *BioIn 1, IlsCB 1744, WhoGrA 62*

LeBlanc, Annette M 1965- *SmATA 68*

Leblanc, Georgette 1869-1941 *WomNov*

Leblanc, Georgette 1876?-1941 *BioIn 3, –1?, CurBio 41, NotNAT A, –B, ObitOF 79, OxCThe 83, WhScrn 83, WhoHol B*

LeBlanc, L 1913- *SmATA 54*

Leblanc, Maurice 1864-1941 *CasWL, ConAu 110, CorpD, CrtSuMy, CurBio 42, EncMys, EvEuW, LongCTC, ObitOF 79, OxCFr, ScFEYrs, TwCA, TwCCr&M 80B, –85B, –91B, TwCLC 49*

Lebrun, Claude 1929- *BioIn 17, ConAu 136, SmATA 66*

LeCain, Errol 1941- *BioIn 14*

Le Cain, Errol 1941-1989 *AnObit 1989, BioIn 16, –17, SixBJA, SmATA 60, –68*

LeCain, Errol John 1941- *Au&Wr 71, BioIn 10, ChhPo S2, ConAu 33R, –13NR, IlsCB 1967, SmATA 6*

Le Cain, Errol John 1941-1989 *ConAu 127, –42NR, MajAI*

le Carre, John *ConAu 33NR, IntAu&W 91X, IntWW 89, –91, IntvTCA 2, MajTwCW, NewYTBS 86, Who 88, –90, –92*
Main entry: Cornwell, David John Moore

LeCarre, John 1931- *Benet 87, BestSel 89-4, BioIn 14, –15, –16, –17, BlueB 76, BritWr S2, CamGLE, CelR 90, CnDBLB 8, ConAu X, ConLC 3, –5, –9, –15, –28, ConNov 72, –76, –82, –86, –91, CorpD, CrtSuMy, CurBio 74, CyWA 89, DcLB 87, DcLEL 1940, EncMys, HalFC 84, –88, IntAu&W 77X, IntWW 74, –75, –76, –77, –78, –79, –80, –81, –82, –83, MagSWL, NewC, NewYTBS 74, –80, –83, Novels, OxCEng 85, RfGEnL 91,*

TwCCr&M 80, -85, -91, TwCWr, Who 74, -82, -83, -85, WhoAm 84, -86, -88, -90, -92, -94, WhoSpyF, WhoWor 91, -93, WorAlBi, WorAl, WorAu 1950, WrDr 76, -80, -82, -84, -86, -88, -90, -92, -94

Leckie, Robert 1920- *AuBYP 2, -3, BioIn 8, ConAu 13R*
Pseud./variant:
Barlow, Roger
Porter, Mark

Leclerc, Felix 1914- *CasWL, CreCan 1, DcLB 60, OxCCan, -SUP, OxCCanL, WhoCanL 85, -87*

Leclerc, Felix 1914-1988 *BioIn 16, OxCCanT, WhoCanL 92*

Lecourt, Nancy Hoyt 1951- *SmATA 73*

Leder, Jane M 1945- *SmATA 61*

Leder, Jane Mersky *BioIn 16, -17*

Leder, Jane Mersky 1945- *SmATA 51*

Lederer, Chloe 1915- *ConAu 77*

Lederer, Muriel 1929- *BioIn 16, SmATA 48*

Lederer, William J 1912- *BioIn 17, SmATA 62*

Lederer, William Julius 1912- *AmAu&B, Au&Wr 71, BioIn 2, -5, -10, ConAu 1R, -5NR, SpyFic, WhoAm 74, -76, -78, -80, -82, -84, -86, -88, -90, -92, -94, WhoSpyF, WhoUSWr 88, WhoWor 74, WhoWrEP 89, -92, WorAl, WorAu 1950*

LeDoux, Harold *ArtCS*

Le Doux, Harold A *WhoHisp 92*

LeDoux, Harold Anthony 1926- *WhoAm 86, -92, -94*

Leduc, Ozias 1864-1955 *BioIn 3, -13, CreCan 1, OxDcArt*

Lee, Addison Earl 1914- *AmMWSc 73P, -76P, -82, -86, -89, -92, BioIn 10, -11, ConAu 9R, LEduc 74, WhoAm 74, -76, -78, -80, -82, -84, -86, -88, -90*

Lee, Amanda
Main entry: Buckholtz, Eileen
Buckholtz, Eileen Garber

Lee, Anne S *AmAu&B, AuBYP 2, -3*
Main entry: Murphy, Mabel Ansley

Lee, Benjamin 1921- *BioIn 13, ConAu 104, SmATA 27, TwCChW 78, WrDr 82, -84, -86, -88, -90*

Lee, Betsy 1949- *BioIn 15, ConAu 106, SmATA 37*

Lee, C *OxCChiL*

Lee, Carol *ConAu X, SmATA X*
Main entry: Fletcher, Helen Jill

Lee, Carvel 1910- *BioIn 6, ConAu P-1, ForWC 70, MinnWr*

Lee, Dennis *IntvTCA 2*

Lee, Dennis 1939- *Benet 87, BenetAL 91, BioIn 10, -15, CanWW 70, ChlLR 3, ConAu 25R, -11NR, -31NR, ConPo 70, -75, -80, -85, -91, DcLB 53, OxCCan SUP, OxCCanL, OxCChiL, Profile 1, SmATA 14, TwCChW 78, -83, -89, WhoCanL 85, -87, -92, WrDr 76, -80, -82, -84, -86, -88, -90, -92*

Lee, Dennis Beynon 1939- *MajAI, WrDr 94*

Lee, Doris Emrick 1905-1983 *BioIn 1, -3, -5, -7, -10, -13, -14, -15, -17, BriEAA, ConAu 110, CurBio 54, GrAmP, IlsCB 1946, SmATA 35N, -44, WhAmArt 85, WhoAm 74, -76, -78, WhoAmA 73, -78, -80, -82, WhoAmW 74*

Lee, Essie E 1920- *ConAu 49, -4NR*

Lee, Harper *BlmGWL, DrAPF 87, -89, -91, -93, InWom SUP, IntvTCA 2*

Lee, Harper 1926- *AmAu&B, Benet 87, BenetAL 91, BioIn 5, -6, -8, -10, -11, -12, -15, -17, ConAu 13R, ConLC 12, -60, CyWA 89, DcLB 6, DrAF 76, DrAPF 83, -85, MagSAmL, MajTwCW, NewCon, Novels, OxCAmL 65, -83, REnAL, SmATA 11, TwCWr, WhoSSW 75, -76, WorAlBi, WorAl, WorAu 1950, WorLitC*

Lee, Holme *Alli SUP, DcEnL, DcNaB S1, TelT*
Main entry: Parr, Harriet

Lee, Holme 1828-1900 *FemiCLE*

Lee, Howard *ConAu X, WrDr 86, -88, -90, -92*
Main entry: Goulart, Ron

Lee, Howard 1933- *WrDr 94*

Lee, John R 1923-1976 *ConAu 120*

Lee, John Robert 1923-1976 *BioIn 13, ConAu 57, MichAu 80, SmATA 27*

Lee, Julian *AuBYP 3, ConAu X, IntAu&W 91X, MajAI, SmATA 68, TwCChW 83, -89, TwCYAW, WrDr 82, -84, -86, -88, -90, -92*
Main entry: Latham, Jean Lee

Lee, Julian 1902- *WrDr 94*

Lee, Laurie *BioIn 14, –15, –17, IntvTCA 2, Who 88, –90, –92*

Lee, Laurie 1914- *Au&Wr 71, BioIn 5, –6, –7, –8, –9, –10, –11, BlueB 76, CamGLE, CasWL, ConAu 77, –33NR, ConPo 70, –75, –80, –85, –91, DcLB 27, DcLEL 1940, EngPo, IntAu&W 77, –82, –89, –91, IntWW 74, –75, –76, –77, –78, –79, –80, –81, –82, –83, –89, –91, LongCTC, MajTwCW, ModBrL, NewC, OxCEng 85, PenC ENG, RAdv 1, REn, RfGEnL 91, TwCWr, WhDW, Who 74, –82, –83, –85, WhoWor 74, –78, WorAu 1950, WrDr 76, –80, –82, –84, –86, –88, –90, –92, –94*

Lee, M *OxCChiL*

Lee, Manfred B *BenetAL 91, RfGAmL 87, TwCCr&M 91*

Lee, Manfred B 1905-1971 *AmAu&B, AuSpks, AuBYP 2, –3, Au&Wr 71, BioIn 2, –3, –4, –8, –9, –10, –11, –12, ConAu 1R, –29R, –2NR, CurBio 40, DcLEL, EncMys, EvLB, LongCTC, NewYTBE 71, ObitOF 79, ObitT 1971, PenC AM, REn, REnAL, TwCA, –SUP, TwCCr&M 80, –85, WebAB 74, –79, WhAm 5*
Pseud./variant:
Queen, Ellery
Queen, Ellery, Jr.
Ross, Barnaby

Lee, Manning De Villeneuve 1894- *WhAm 10*

Lee, Manning DeVilleneuve 1894-1980 *BioIn 1, –5, –6, –13, –15, ConAu 104, ConICB, IlrAm 1880, IlsBYP, IlsCB 1744, –1946, MorJA, SmATA 22N, –37, WhAmArt 85, WhoAm 74, –76, –78, WhoAmA 73, –78*

Lee, Marian *SmATA X, WomNov*
Main entry: Clish, Marian

Lee, Marian 1946- *BioIn 15*

Lee, Mary 1934- *AuBYP 3*

Lee, Mary 1949- *ConAu 29R*

Lee, Mary Price 1934- *AuBYP 2S, BioIn 11, ConAu 57, –9NR, –24NR, SmATA 8*

Lee, Mildred *InWom SUP*

Lee, Mildred 1908- *AuBYP 2S, –3, BioIn 9, –10, –11, ConAu X, DcAmChF 1960, ForWC 70, IntAu&W 91, SmATA 6, –12AS, ThrBJA, TwCChW 78, –83, –89, TwCYAW, WrDr 80, –82, –84, –86, –88, –90*
Pseud./variant:
Scudder, Mildred Lee

Lee, Nelle Harper 1926- *TwCYAW*

Lee, Norma E 1924- *AuBYP 2S, –3, ConAu 65*

Lee, R, Mrs *DcVicP 2*

Lee, R, Mrs 1791-1856 *Alli, CarSB*

Lee, Robert C 1931- *AuBYP 2S, –3, BioIn 12, ConAu 25R, –10NR, ScF&FL 92, SmATA 20*

Lee, Robert E *LesBEnT 92, OxCAmT 84*

Lee, Robert E 1912- *WhoAm 86, –88, –90*

Lee, Robert E 1918- *BenetAL 91, ConDr 88, ConTFT 4, IntAu&W 91, SmATA 65, WrDr 86, –88, –90, –92*

Lee, Robert E 1919- *WhoSSW 86, –88*

Lee, Robert Edwin 1918- *AmAu&B, ASCAP 66, BiE&WWA, BioIn 10, –17, BlueB 76, ConAu 45, –2NR, ConDr 73, –77, –82, –93, EncMT, IntAu&W 77, ModWD, NotNAT, OhA&B, REnAL, WhoAm 74, –76, –78, –80, –82, –84, –86, –88, –90, –92, –94, WhoEnt 92, WhoSSW 84, WhoThe 72, –77, –81, WhoWest 76, WhoWor 74, WrDr 76, –80, –82, –84, –94*

Lee, Robert Ellsworth, Sr. 1938- *WhoFI 94*

Lee, Robert J 1921- *BioIn 11, IlsBYP, SmATA 10, WhoAmA 73, –78, –80, –82, –84, –86, –89, –91*

Lee, Rohama *MedPD, WomWMM B*

Lee, Roy *AuBYP 2, –3, ConAu 129, –X, SmATA X*
Main entry: Hopkins, Clark

Lee, Roy 1895-1976 *BioIn 14*

Lee, Sally *AuBYP 3, BioIn 17*

Lee, Sally 1943- *ConAu 134, SmATA 67, WrDr 94*

Lee, Stan *BioIn 16*

Lee, Stan 1922- *Au&Arts 5, BioIn 9, –11, ConAu 108, –111, ConLC 17, CurBio 93, EncACom, EncSF 93, ScF&FL 92, WhoAm 80, –82, –84, –86, –88, –92, –94*

Lee, Susan Dye 1939- *ConAu 85*

Lee, Tammie *ConAu 127, SmATA X*
Main entry: Townsend, Thomas L

Lee, Tanith *BioIn 17*

Lee, Tanith 1947- *BioIn 11, ChlFicS, ConAu 37R, ConLC 46, EncSF 93, IntAu&W 77, –82, –91, NewEScF, ScF&FL 92, ScFSB, SmATA 8, SupFW,*

TwCChW 89, TwCSFW 86, –91, TwCYAW, WrDr 76, –80, –82, –84, –86, –88, –90, –92, –94

Lee, Tina *BioIn 6, MorJA*

Lee, Virginia 1927- *ConAu 9R, ForWC 70, WhoAmW 77*

Lee, Wayne C 1917- *ConAu 1R, –2NR, –17NR, –41NR, IntAu&W 77, –82, –91, TwCWW 91, WhoMW 84, –86, WhoWor 84, WrDr 76, –80, –82, –84, –86, –88, –90, –92*
Pseud./variant:
Sheldon, Lee

Lee, Wayne Cyril 1917- *WhoMW 86, –88, WhoWor 87, –89*

Leechman, John Douglas 1890- *AmMWSc 73S, CanWW 70, –80, OxCCan, WhNAA*

Leedy, Loreen 1959- *BioIn 16, ConAu 122, SmATA 50, –54*

Lee-Hostetler, Jeri 1940- *SmATA 63*
Pseud./variant:
Marsh, Jeri

Leekley, Thomas Briggs 1910- *AuBYP 2, –3, BioIn 8, –13, ConAu 5R, SmATA 23*

Leeming, Jill
Main entry: Chaney, Jill

Leeming, Jill 1932- *WrDr 76, –80, –82, –84*

Leeming, Jo Ann
Main entry: Leeming, Joseph

Leeming, Joseph 1897-1968 *AuBYP 2, –3, BioIn 2, –7, –13, ConAu 73, JBA 51, SmATA 26*
Pseud./variant:
Leeming, Jo Ann
Professor Zingara
Swift, Merlin
Zingara, Professor

Leemis, Ralph B 1954- *SmATA 72*

Leen, Nina *BioIn 4, ICPEnP A, InWom SUP*

Leeper, John Joseph *WrDr 76*

Leeson, Muriel 1920- *BioIn 16, SmATA 54*

Leeson, R A *MajAI, SmATA 76*
Main entry: Leeson, Robert Arthur

Leeson, Robert *BioIn 14, –15*

Leeson, Robert 1928- *ConAu 105, –22NR, IntAu&W 91, OxCChiL, ScF&FL 92, SmATA 42, TwCChW 78, –83, –89, WrDr 80, –82, –84, –86, –88, –90, –92*

Leeson, Robert, Jr. 1932- *WhoE 91*

Leeson, Robert Arthur 1928- *ChlFicS, EncSF 93, MajAI, SmATA 76, TwCYAW, WrDr 94*
Pseud./variant:
Leeson, R A

Leeuw, Adele De *JBA 51, WhNAA*
Main entry: DeLeeuw, Adele Louise

LeFanu, Joseph Sheridan 1814-1873 *Alli SUP, AtlBL, BbD, BiDIrW, BiD&SB, BioIn 2, –5, –9, –12, –14, –15, –16, BritAu 19, CasWL, Chambr 3, ChhPo, CrtSuMy, CyWA 58, DcEnA, DcEnL, DcEuL, DcIrB 88, DcIrL, DcIrW 1, DcLB 21, DcLEL, DcNaB, Dis&D, EncMys, EvLB, HsB&A, NewC, NinCLC 9, OxCEng 67, PenC ENG, PoIre, REn, ShSCr 14, WorAlBi, WorAl*

Lefebure, Molly *AuBYP 2S, –3, Au&Wr 71, ConAu 57, IntAu&W 91, WrDr 76, –80, –82, –84, –86, –88, –90, –92, –94*

LeFeuvre, Amy d1929 *CarSB, ConAu 111, OxCChiL, TwCChW 78, –83, –89, WomNov*

LeFevre, Felicite *WhoLA*

Leffland, Ella *BioIn 14, –16, –17*

Leffland, Ella 1931- *ConAu 35NR, SmATA 65, WrDr 92, –94*

Lefkowitz, R J 1942- *ConAu 45*

Lefler, Irene 1917- *BioIn 11, ConAu 45, –1NR, SmATA 12*

Lefler, Irene Whitney 1917- *WhoWrEP 89, –92*

Lefranc, Margaret *WhoAmA 86, –89, –91*

Lefranc, Margaret 1907- *WhAmArt 85, WhoAmA 78, –80, –82, –84*

Leftwich, Joseph *EngPo*

Leftwich, Joseph 1892-1983 *Au&Wr 71, ConAu 5R, –109*

Le Gallienne, Eva d1991 *Who 92N*

LeGallienne, Eva 1899- *AmAu&B, AuBYP 2, –3, Benet 87, BiE&WWA, BioIn 1, –2, –3, –4, –6, –7, –10, –11, –12, –13, –14, –15, –16, BlueB 76, CamGWoT, ConAu 45, ConTFT 1, CurBio 42, –55, EncWT, FamA&A, FemiCLE, HalFC 84, –88, InWom SUP, IntAu&W 77, –89, IntMPA 82, –84, –86, –88, IntWW 77, –78, –79, –80, –81, –82, –83, –89, –91, NewYTBS 81, –82, –84, NotNAT, –A, NotWoAT, OxCAmL 83, OxCAmT 84, OxCThe 67, –83, PlP&P, REn, REnAL, SmATA 9, WebAB 74, –79, Who 74, –82, –83,*

–85, –88, –90, WhoAm 74, –76, –78, –80, –82, –84, –86, –88, –90, WhoAmW 74, –83, –85, –87, –89, WhoHol A, WhoThe 72, –77, –81, WhoWor 74, WorAlBi, WorAl
Pseud./variant:
Gallienne, Eva Le

Le Gallienne, Eva 1899-1991 *AnObit 1991, BenetAL 91, BioIn 17, ConAu 134, ConTFT 10, CurBio 91N, NewYTBS 91, SmATA 68, WhAm 10*

Leger, Alexis Saint-Leger *NobelP*

Leger, Alexis Saint-Leger 1887-1975 *BioIn 1, –2, –3, –4, –5, –6, –8, –9, –10, –12, –17, CasWL, ClDMEL 47, ConAu 13R, –61, CurBio 61, –75N, EvEuW, IntWW 74, –75, –76N, MajTwCW, ObitOF 79, OxCFr, RAdv 13-2, REn, TwCA, –SUP*
Pseud./variant:
Perse, Saint-John

Leger, Alexis Saint-Leger 1889-1975 *BioIn 14, –15*

Leger, Alexis St-Leger *Benet 87*

Legg, Sarah Martha Ross Bruggeman d1982 *BioIn 15, SmATA 40N*

Leggett, Ann *BioIn 11*

LeGrand *AuBYP 2, –3, BkCL, ConAu X, IlsCB 1946, –1957, JBA 51, SmATA X*
Main entry: Henderson, LeGrand

Legrand, Edy 1893- *AmPB, BioIn 2, –3, –5, IlsCB 1946*
Pseud./variant:
Edy-Legrand

LeGuin, Ursula 1929- *ArtclWW 2, AuBYP 3, BioIn 15, –16, –17, BlmGWL, CamGLE, CamHAL, CelR 90, FemiCLE, IntAu&W 86, PostFic, WorAlBi*

Le Guin, Ursula K *ConSFF, DrAPF 87, –89, –91, –93, IntvTCA 2*

Le Guin, Ursula K 1929- *Au&Arts 9, AuBYP 2S, AuNews 1, Au&Wr 71, Benet 87, BenetAL 91, BioAmW, BioIn 9, –10, –14, –15, –16, –17, BioNews 74, BroV, ChlLR 3, ConAu 21R, –9NR, –32NR, ConLC 8, –13, –22, –45, –71, ConNov 76, –82, –86, –91, ConSFA, CurBio 83, CyWA 89, DcLB 8, –52, DrAF 76, DrAPF 83, –85, FourBJA, IntAu&W 77, –91, MagSAmL, MajTwCW, ModAL S2, NewEScF, Novels, OxCChiL, RGTwCSF, ScF&FL 92, ScFSB, ShSCr 12, ShSWr, SmATA 4, –52, SupFW, TwCChW 78, –83, –89, TwCSFW 86, –91, WhoAm 74, –76, –78, –80, –82, –84, WhoAmW 74, –81, –83, –85, WhoSciF, WrDr 76, –80, –82, –84, –86, –88, –90, –92*

Le Guin, Ursula Kroeber 1929- *ChlLR 28, DcAmChF 1960, EncSF 93, GayLL, InWom SUP, IntAu&W 89, IntWW 89, –91, MajAI, TwCYAW, WhoAm 86, –88, –90, –92, –94, WhoAmW 87, –89, –91, –93, WhoUSWr 88, WhoWrEP 89, –92*

Legum, Colin 1919- *Au&Wr 71, BioIn 11, ConAu 1R, –4NR, IntAu&W 77, –82, –91, SmATA 10, WhoWor 78, –80, –82, WrDr 76, –80, –82, –84, –86, –88, –90, –92, –94*

Lehane, Brendan 1936- *ConAu 21R, –10NR, –26NR*

Lehman, Celia 1928- *ConAu 49, –1NR*

Lehman, Emil 1907- *WhoAmJ 80, WhoRel 75, –77, WhoWorJ 78*

Lehmann, Linda 1906- *ConAu 85*

Lehn, Cornelia 1920- *BioIn 15, ConAu 29R, –12NR, SmATA 46, WhoRel 75, –77*

Lehr, Delores 1902- *BioIn 10, –11, ConAu 17R, SmATA 10*

Lehr, Norma 1930- *SmATA 71*

Lehr, Paul E 1918- *ConAu 65*

Lehrer, James 1934- *BioIn 7, –11, ConAu 109, –114, CurBio 87, JrnUS, WorAlBi, WrDr 88, –90, –92*

Lehrer, James Charles 1934- *ConAu 43NR*

Lehrman, Robert L 1921- *ConAu 5R, –7NR*

Leib, Amos Patten 1917- *ConAu 45, DrAS 74E*

Leib, Amos Patten 1917-1977 *ConAu 133*

Leibel, Bernard S 1914- *AmMWSc 73P*

Leiber, Fritz *DrAPF 87, –89, –91, –93, DrmM 2, IntvTCA 2*

Leiber, Fritz 1910- *BioIn 7, –12, –13, –15, ConAu 2NR, ConLC 25, ConNov 82, –86, –91, DcLB 8, DrAPF 83, –85, MajTwCW, NewEScF, Novels, PenEncH, ScFSB, SmATA 45, SupFW, TwCSFW 86, –91, WhoAm 82, –84, WhoUSWr 88, WhoWrEP 89, –92, WorAu 1975, WrDr 82, –84, –86, –88, –90, –92*
Pseud./variant:
Lathrop, Francis

Leiber, Fritz 1910-1992 *AnObit 1992, BioIn 17, ScF&FL 92*

Leiber, Fritz, Jr. d1992 *NewYTBS 92*

Leiber, Fritz, Jr. 1910- *RGTwCSF, WhoAm 90, –92*

Leiber, Fritz, Jr. 1910-1992 *WhAm 10*

Leiber, Fritz Reuter, Jr. 1910- *WrDr 94*

Leiber, Fritz Reuter, Jr. 1910-1992 *ConAu 139, –40NR, EncSF 93, SmATA 73*

Leibold, Jay 1957- *BioIn 16, ConAu 123, ScF&FL 92, SmATA 52, –57, WrDr 90, –92, –94*

Leichman, Seymour 1933- *BioIn 10, ConAu 25R, IlsBYP, SmATA 5, WhoAmA 73, WhoE 74*

Leigh, Felix *ChhPo, –S1, –S2*

Leigh, Frances *AuBYP 2S*

Leigh, Frances Butler 1838-1910 *InWom SUP*

Leigh, Franes *AuBYP 3*

Leigh, Percival 1813-1889 *BritAu 19, CarSB, DcNaB*

Leigh, Tom 1947- *SmATA 46*

Leigh-Pemberton, John 1911- *BioIn 14, ClaDrA, ConAu 108, DcBrAr 1, SmATA 35, Who 74, –82, –83, –85, –88, –90, –92, WhoArt 80, –82, –84*

Leight, Edward *IlsBYP*

Leighton, Clare Veronica Hope 1900?- *AmAu&B, BioIn 2, –3, –4, –5, –8, ChhPo, –S1, ClaDrA, ConAu 108, DcBrAr 1, GrAmP, IlsBYP, IlsCB 1946, –1957, –1967, LongCTC, SmATA 37, TwCA, –SUP, Who 74, –82, –83, –85, WhoAmA 73, –78, –80, –82, WhoAmW 83, WhoArt 80, –82, –84*

Leighton, Frances Spatz *BioIn 8, –12, ConAu 81, –30NR, ForWC 70, WhoAm 82, –84, –86, –88, –90, –92, –94, WhoUSWr 88, WhoWor 82, –84, –87, –89, –91, –93, WhoWrEP 89, –92*

Leighton, Margaret 1896- *AuBYP 3*

Leighton, Margaret 1896-1987 *ConAu 123, SmATA 52N*

Leighton, Margaret Carver 1896- *AmAu&B, AuBYP 2, Au&Wr 71, BioIn 3, –6, –8, –9, ConAu 9R, MorJA, OhA&B, SmATA 1, Str&VC, WhAm 9, WhoAm 74, –76, –78, –80, WhoAmW 74, –83, –85, –87, WrDr 76, –80, –82, –84, –86, –88*

Leighton, Margaret Carver 1896-1987 *BioIn 16*

Leighton, Marie Connor d1941 *BioIn 1, LongCTC, WhoLA*

Leighton, Robert 1858-1934 *StaCVF*

Leighton, Robert 1859-1934 *CarSB, LongCTC*

Leiner, Katherine *AuBYP 3*

Leiner, Katherine 1949- *ConAu 132, WrDr 94*

Leipold, L Edmond 1902- *BioIn 12, ConAu 69, SmATA 16*

Leisk, David Johnson 1906-1975 *AuBYP 2, –3, ConAu 9R, –57, CurBio 43, IlsCB 1946, –1957, MajAI, SmATA 1, –26N, –30, ThrBJA*
Pseud./variant:
Johnson, Crockett

Leister, Mary 1917- *BioIn 13, ConAu 65, –11NR, SmATA 29*

Leister, Mary McFarland 1917- *WhoUSWr 88, WhoWrEP 89, –92*

Leitch, Adelaide 1921- *BioIn 10, ConAu 101, OxCCan SUP, Profile 1, TwCChW 78, WhoCanL 85, WrDr 80, –82, –84, –86, –88, –90*

Leitch, Patricia 1933- *BioIn 11, ConAu 61, –9NR, ScF&FL 92, SmATA 11*

Leith, John Haddon 1919- *ConAu 5R, –3NR, DrAS 74P, –78P, –82P, WhoAm 80, –82, –84, –86, –88, –90, –92, –94, WhoRel 92, WhoSSW 76, –78*

Leithauser, Gladys Garner 1925- *ConAu 13R, –27NR, ForWC 70, MichAu 80*

Leland, Charles G 1824-1903 *ConAu 118*

Leland, Charles Godfrey *BenetAL 91*

Leland, Charles Godfrey 1824-1903 *Alli, –SUP, AmAu, AmAu&B, BbD, BiGAW, BiD&SB, BioIn 5, –6, –8, –9, –14, CasWL, CelCen, Chambr 3, ChhPo, –S1, –S2, CyAL, CyEd, DcAmAu, DcBiPP, DcEnA, –A, DcEnL, DcLB 11, DcNAA, EncO&P 1, –2, –3, EvLB, HarEnUS, OxCAmL 65, –83, OxCEng 67, PenC AM, REn, ScFEYrs, WhAm 1*

LeMair, H Willebeek 1889-1966 *ChhPo, DcBrBI, IlsCB 1744, SmATA 29*
Pseud./variant:
Saida

Lemaster, Leslie Jean *AuBYP 3*

LeMaster, Leslie Jean 1943- *ConAu 125*

Lembo, Diana L 1925- *BiDrLUS 70, ConAu 17R, DrLC 69, ForWC 70*

Pseud./variant:
Spirt, Diana Louise

Lemieux, Germain 1914- *CanWW 80, –81, –83, OxCCan SUP*

Lemieux, Germain, Rev 1914- *CanWW 89*

Lemke, Horst 1922- *BioIn 8, –15, ConAu 107, IlsBYP, IlsCB 1957, –1967, SmATA 38*

Lemme, Janet E 1941- *ConAu 29R*

Lemmon, Robert Stell 1885- *AuBYP 3*

Lemmon, Robert Stell 1885-1964 *AmAu&B, AuBYP 2, BioIn 6, –7, WhAm 4, –7*

Lemoine, Georges 1935- *IlsBYP, WhoGrA 82*

Lemon, Mark 1809-1870 *BioIn 7, –9, –16, CamGLE, CelCen, DcBiPP, DcNaB, OxCChiL, OxCEng 85, StaCVF*

LeMond, Alan 1938- *ConAu 61, –9NR, WhoAm 74, WrDr 80, –82, –84, –86, –88*

Lenanton, C *ConAu X, SmATA X, TwCRHW 90*
Main entry: Oman, Carola

Lenard, Alexander 1910-1972 *BioIn 5, –6, –9, –12, ConAu 5R, –4NR, SmATA 21N*

L'Engle, Madeleine 1918- *AmAu&B, AmNov, ArtclWW 2, Au&Arts 1, AuBYP 2, –3, AuNews 2, BenetAL 91, BioIn 2, –6, –7, –9, –10, –11, –12, –13, –14, –15, –16, –17, BlmGWL, BlueB 76, ChhPo, –S1, ChlLR 1, –14, ConAu 1R, –3NR, –21NR, ConLC 12, DcAmChF 1960, DcLB 52, EncSF 93, ForWC 70, IntAu&W 77, –86, –89, –91, MajTwCW, MorBMP, MorJA, NewEScF, NewbC 1956, OxCChiL, PiP, RGTwCSF, ScF&FL 92, ScFSB, SenS, SmATA 1, –27, –15AS, TwCChW 78, –83, –89, TwCSFW 86, –91, TwCYAW, WhoAm 74, –76, –78, –80, –82, –84, –86, –88, –90, –92, –94, WhoAmW 74, –75, –77, –81, –83, –85, –87, –89, –91, –93, WhoE 74, WhoUSWr 88, WhoWor 82, WhoWrEP 89, –92, WorAlBi, WrDr 76, –80, –82, –84, –86, –88, –90, –92, –94*

L'Engle, Madeleine Camp Franklin 1918- *ConAu 39NR, MajAI, SmATA 75*

Lengyel, Cornel Adam *DrAPF 87, –89, –91, –93*

Lengyel, Cornel Adam 1915- *BioIn 13, ConAu 1NR, –24NR, DrAPF 83, –85, DrAS 82E, IntWWP 82, SmATA 27, WhoAm 80, –82, –84, –86, –88, –90, –92, –94, WhoUSWr 88, WhoWest 94, WhoWrEP 89, –92*

Pseud./variant:
Adam, Cornel

Lengyel, Emil d1985 *NewYTBS 85*

Lengyel, Emil 1895-1985 *AmAu&B, AmMWSc 73S, BioIn 4, –9, –14, –15, ConAu 9R, –115, –3NR, CurBio 42, –85N, DrAS 74H, –78H, –82H, NewYTBS 85, REnAL, SmATA 3, –42N, TwCA, –SUP, WhAm 8, WhNAA, WhoAm 74, –76, –78, WhoWor 74*

Lennig, Arthur 1933- *ConAu 57, DrAS 74E, –78E*

Lens, Sidney *BioIn 15, –16*

Lens, Sidney d1986 *NewYTBS 86*

Lens, Sidney 1912- *AuBYP 2, BioIn 7, –11, ConAu 1R, –1NR, –17NR, SmATA 13, WhoAm 74, –76, –78, –80, –82, –84, WhoWor 74*

Lens, Sidney 1912-1986 *AuBYP 3, ConAu 119, SmATA 48N, WhAm 9*

Lenski, Lois 1893- *WhoAmA 86N, –89N, –91N*

Lenski, Lois 1893-1974 *AmAu&B, AmPB, AuBYP 2, –3, Au&ICB, Au&Wr 71, BenetAL 91, BioIn 1, –2, –3, –4, –5, –7, –8, –9, –10, –11, –12, –13, –14, BlmGWL, BkCL, BkP, CarSB, ChhPo, –S1, –S2, ChlLR 26, ConAu 53, –41NR, –P-1, ConICB, DcLB 22, DcWomA, FamAIYP, HerW, –84, IlsCB 1744, –1946, –1957, –1967, InWom SUP, JBA 34, –51, MajAI, NatCAB 63, NewYTBS 74, NewbMB 1922, OhA&B, OxCChiL, REnAL, SmATA 1, –26, TwCChW 78, –83, –89, WhAm 6, WhAmArt 85, WhNAA, Who 74, WhoAm 74, WhoAmA 73, –78N, –80N, –82N, WhoAmW 74*

Lent, Blair 1930- *AmPB, BioIn 8, –9, –10, –12, –14, BkP, ConAu 21R, –11NR, IlsBYP, IlsCB 1957, –1967, IntAu&W 91, MajAI, NewbC 1966, SmATA 2, ThrBJA, WhoAmA 73, –78, –80, –82, –84, –86, –89 –91, WhoE 74, WrDr 76, –80, –82, –84, –86, –88, –90, –92, –94*
Pseud./variant:
Small, Ernest

Lent, Henry Bolles 1901-1973 *AuBYP 2, –3 BioIn 1, –2, –7, –12, ConAu 73, JBA 34, –51, SmATA 17, Str&VC*

Leodhas, Sorche Nic *BioIn 9, ChhPo, –S1, –S2, ConAu X, SmATA X, ThrBJA*
Main entry: Alger, Leclaire Gowans

Leodhas, Sorche Nic 1898-1968 *BioIn 14*

Leokum, Arkady *BioIn 15*

Leokum, Arkady 1916?- *BioIn 4, ConAu 116, SmATA 45*

Leonard, A Byron 1904- *AuBYP 2, -3, BioIn 8*

Leonard, Alison 1944- *SmATA 70*
Pseud./variant:
Sharman, Alison

Leonard, Constance 1923- *BioIn 15, ConAu 49, -28NR, IntAu&W 86, -89, -91, SmATA 40, -42, WrDr 76, -80, -82, -84, -86, -88, -90, -92, -94*

Leonard, Henry
Main entry: Fennell, Hugh Wordsworth

Leonard, Jonathan N 1903-1975 *BioIn 10, ConAu 57, -61, SmATA 36, WhAm 6, WhoAm 74*

Leonard, Jonathan Norton 1903-1975 *BioIn 14*

Leonard, Laura 1923- *ConAu 142, SmATA 75*

Leonard, V A d1984 *BioIn 14*

Leonard, V A 1898- *ConAu 37R, -15NR*

Leong, Gor Yun *IntAu&W 91X*

Leong, Gor Yung *SmATA 4, WrDr 84*

Leong Gor Yung
Main entry: Ellison, Virginia Howell

Leopold, Aldo Starker *AmMWSc 86*

Leopold, Aldo Starker 1913-1983 *AmMWSc 73P, -76P, -82, BioIn 7, -12, -13, -14, WhAm 8, WhoAm 74, -82, WhoFrS 84*

Leopold, Celine 1936- *BioIn 12, IlsCB 1967*

Leopold, Luna Bergere 1915- *AmMWSc 73P, -76P, -82, -86, -89, -92, BioIn 5, -9, BlueB 76, ConAu 49, -31NR, IntWW 74, -75, -76, -77, -78, -79, -80, -81, -82, -83, -89, -91, McGMS 80, WhoAm 74, -76, -78, -80, -82, -84, -86, -88, -90, -92, -94, WhoFrS 84, WhoGov 72, WhoWest 94*

Leprince DeBeaumont, Madame *OxCChiL*

Le Prince de Beaumont, Jeanne-Marie 1711-1780 *EncCoWW*

Le Prince de Beaumont, Marie *BlmGWL*

Lerangis, Peter 1955- *SmATA 72*
Pseud./variant:
Singer, A L

Lerner, Aaron B 1920- *BioIn 14*

Lerner, Aaron Bunsen 1920- *AmMWSc 73P, -76P, -82, -86, -89, -92, ConAu 108, IntMed 80, SmATA 35, WhoAm 74, -76, -78, -80*

Lerner, Carol 1927- *BioIn 14, -16, ConAu 102, SixBJA, SmATA 33, -12AS*

Lerner, Gerda *WhoAmW 87*

Lerner, Gerda 1920- *ArtclWW 2, BioIn 17, ConAu 26NR, InWom SUP, SmATA 65, WhoAm 86, -88, -90, WhoUSWr 88, WhoWrEP 89, -92*

Lerner, Marguerite Rush *AmMWSc 86*

Lerner, Marguerite Rush 1924- *AmMWSc 76P, -82, AuBYP 2, -3, BioIn 8, -11, ConAu 13R, SmATA 11, WhoAmW 74, -75, -77*

Lerner, Marguerite Rush 1924-1987 *BioIn 16, ConAu 122, SmATA 51N*

Lerner, Sharon Ruth 1938-1982 *BioIn 11, -12, -13, ConAu 5R, -106, -3NR, ForWC 70, SmATA 11, -29N, WhoAmW 77*

Leroe, Ellen W 1949- *SmATA 51, -61*

Leroe, Ellen Whitney 1949- *ConAu 40NR*

LeRoi, David 1905- *Au&Wr 71, BlueB 76, ConAu 9R, -3NR, IntAu&W 77, WrDr 76, -80*

LeRoi, David 1915- *WrDr 86, -88, -90*

Leroux, Gaston 1868-1927 *BioIn 15, -17, CasWL, ConAu 108, -136, CrtSuMy, EncMys, EncSF 93, LongCTC, Novels, OxCFr, PenEncH, ScF&FL 92, ScFEYrs, SmATA 65, TwCA, TwCCr&M 80B, -85B, -91B, TwCLC 25, WhoHr&F, WorAlBi, WorAl*

LeRoy, Douglas 1943- *ConAu 49, -3NR, -18NR, IntAu&W 77*

LeRoy, Gen *BioIn 14, -16, ConAu 115, -134, SmATA 36, -52, WrDr 94*

Lerrigo, Marion Olive 1898-1968 *BioIn 8, -13, ConAu 109, SmATA 29N, WhAm 5*

LeSage, M 1668-1747 *CarSB*

LeShan, Eda J 1922- *AuBYP 2S, -3, BioIn 10, -12, ChlLR 6, ConAu 13R, -21NR, ForWC 70, IntAu&W 77, -82, NewYTBE 73, SmATA 21, WhoUSWr 88, WhoWrEP 89, WrDr 76, -80, -82, -84, -86, -88, -90, -92, -94*

Le Shan, Eda Joan 1922- *WhoWrEP 92*

LeSieg, Theo *AuBYP 2, -3, BioIn 14, -15, -16, -17, ConAu 135, -X, -32NR, ConGrA 3,*

MajAI, MajTwCW, SmATA 1, –67, –75, –X, TwCChW 83, –89, WrDr 90, –92
Main entry: Geisel, Theodor Seuss

Le Sieg, Theo 1904-1991 *WrDr 94N*

Lesko, George 1932- *ConAu 17R*

Leslau, Wolf 1906- *ConAu 104, DrAS 74F, –78F, WhoAm 74, –76, WhoAmJ 80, WhoWorJ 72, –78*

Leslie, Arthur Forbes 1902-1970 *ChhPo S2, WhScrn 77*

Leslie, Robert Franklin 1911- *Au&Wr 71, BioIn 10, ConAu 49, –28NR, IntAu&W 77, –91, SmATA 7, WrDr 76, –80, –82, –84, –86, –88, –90*

Leslie, San *ConAu X*
Main entry: Crook, Bette Jean

Leslie, Sarah *ConAu X, SmATA X*
Main entry: McGuire, Leslie Sarah

Leslie-Melville, Betty *AuBYP 3*

LeSouef, Albert S *SingR 1*

Lessac, Frane *BioIn 17*

Lessac, Frane 1954- *ConAu 127, IntAu&W 91, SmATA 61*

Lesser, Margaret 1899?-1979 *BioIn 12, –13, ConAu 93, SmATA 22N*

Lesser, Milton *ScF&FL 92, TwCCr&M 91, WrDr 90, –92*

Lesser, Milton 1928- *AuBYP 2, –3, BioIn 7, ConAu 13R, –X, ConSFA, EncSF 93, IntAu&W 91, ScFSB, TwCCr&M 80, –85, TwCSFW 86, –91, WhoSciF, WrDr 76, –80, –82, –84, –86, –88, –94*
Pseud./variant:
Frazer, Andrew
Marlowe, Stephen
Ridgway, Jason
Thames, C H

Lesser, Rika *BioIn 16, DrAPF 87, –89, –91, –93*

Lesser, Rika 1953- *ConAu 118, SmATA 53*

Lesser, Rika Ellen 1953- *WhoWrEP 92*

Lessin, Andrew *AuBYP 2, –3, BioIn 7*

Lessin, Andrew Richard 1942- *WhoAm 92, –94, WhoE 86, –91*

Lester, Alison 1952- *BioIn 16, ConAu 125, SmATA 50*

Lester, Helen *BioIn 15*

Lester, Helen 1936- *ConAu 38NR, SmATA 46*

Lester, Julius *BioIn 14, –15, –16*

Lester, Julius 1939- *Au&Arts 12, BlkAuII, –92, BlkWr 1, BlkWrNE, ConAu 23NR, ConBlAP 88, IntAu&W 91, NegAl 89, TwCChW 89, WhoBlA 90, –92, WrDr 86, –88, –90, –92*

Lester, Julius B 1939- *AmAu&B, AuBYP 2, –3, Au&ICB, BiDAfM, BioIn 11, BlkAWP, ChlLR 2, CivR 74, ConAu 17R, –8NR, FourBJA, InB&W 80, –85, LivgBAA, NegAl 76, –83, SelBAAf, SelBAAu, SmATA 12, TwCChW 83, WhoAm 74, –76, –78, –80, –82, –84, –86, –88, –90, –92, –94, WhoBlA 75, –77, –80, WhoE 75, –77, WhoUSWr 88, WhoWrEP 89, –92*

Lester, Julius Bernard 1939- *ConAu 43NR, EncAACR, MajAI, SmATA 74, TwCYAW*

L'Estrange, James d1947 *BioIn 8, WhoChL*
Pseud./variant:
Strang, Herbert

LeSueur, Meridel *BioIn 14, –17*

LeSueur, Meridel 1900- *AmWomWr 92, ArtclWW 2, BenetAL 91, BioIn 6, –10, –12, –13, BlmGWL, CamGLE, CamHAL, ConAu 49, –2NR, –30NR, FemiCLE, MinnWr, MorJA, SmATA 6, TwCWW 91, WhoAm 84, –86, –88, WorAu 1980*

Lethbridge, K G 1904- *Au&Wr 71, WrDr 76, –80, –82, –84, –86, –88*

Le Tord, Bijou 1945- *BioIn 16, ConAu 65, –31NR, SixBJA, SmATA 49*

Leuchtenburg, William Edward 1922- *AmAu&B, BlueB 76, ConAu 5R, –12NR, DrAS 74H, –78H, –82H, WhoAm 74, –76, –78, –80, –82, –84, –86, –88, WhoWor 74, –78, –80, –82*

Leutscher, Alfred George 1913- *Au&Wr 71 BioIn 13, ConAu 73, SmATA 23*

Levai, Blaise 1919- *BioIn 15, ConAu 108, SmATA 39, WhoRel 75*

Levenkron, Steven 1941- *TwCYAW*

Levenson, Dorothy 1927- *ConAu 9R*

Levenson, Jordan *WhoEnt 92, WhoFI 85, WhoUSWr 88, WhoWrEP 89, –92*

Levenson, Jordan 1936- *ConAu 57, –7NR, –23NR*

Levenson, Kathe Tanous *AuBYP 3*

Lever, Charles James 1806-1872 *Alli, –SUP, AtlBL, BbD, BiDIrW, BiD&SB, BioIn 5, –7, –8, –12, BlmGEL, BritAu 19, CamGEL, CarSB, CasWL, Chambr 3, ChhPo S1, CyWA 58, DcBiA, DcBiPP, DcEnA, DcEnL, DcEuL, DcIrB 88, DcIrL, DcIrW 1, DcLEL, DcNaB, Dis&D, EvLB, HsB&A, LongCEL, MouLC 3, NewC, OxCEng 67, PenC ENG, PoIre, REn, WebE&AL*

Levering, Robert 1919- *WhoAmA 73*

LeVert, John 1946- *BioIn 16, ConAu 122, SmATA 55*

Levetus, Celia *DcBrBI*

Levi, Herbert Walter 1921- *AmMWSc 73P, –76P, –82, –86, –89, –92, WhoAm 74, –76, –78, –80, –82, –84, –86, –88, –90, –92, –94, WhoAmJ 80, WhoE 74, –91, WhoWorJ 72, –78*

Levin, Betty 1927- *BioIn 12, –16, ConAu 65, –9NR, –25NR, IntAu&W 86, –89, ScF&FL 92, SixBJA, SmATA 19, –11AS, TwCChW 83, –89, WrDr 86, –88, –90, –92*

Levin, Betty Lowenthal 1927- *WrDr 94*

Levin, Ira *BioIn 14, –15, –17*

Levin, Ira 1929- *Benet 87, BenetAL 91, ConNov 86, –91, ConTFT 9, CurBio 91, EncSF 93, HalFC 88, MajTwCW, NewEScF, OxCAmT 84, PenEncH, ScF&FL 92, ScFSB, SmATA 66, TwCCr&M 91, TwCSFW 86, –91, WhoAm 86, –88, –90, –92, –94, WhoUSWr 88, WhoWrEP 89, –92, WorAlBi, WrDr 86, –88, –90, –92, –94*

Levin, Jane Whitbread 1914- *ConAu 106*

Levin, Kristine Cox 1944- *ConAu 65*

Levin, Marcia Obrasky 1918- *AuBYP 2, –3, BioIn 8, –11, ConAu 13R, ForWC 70, SmATA 13*
Pseud./variant:
Martin, Jeremy
Martin, Marcia

Levin, Meyer 1905-1981 *AmAu&B, AmNov, AnObit 1981, AuNews 1, Au&Wr 71, Benet 87, BenetAL 91, BiE&WWA, BioIn 2, –4, –7, –10, –12, –13, –14, –17, BioNews 74, CelR, CnMD, ConAu 9R, –104, –15NR, ConLC 7, ConNov 72, –76, –82, CurBio 40, –81N, DcAmSR, DcLB 9, –28, –Y81A, DcLEL, DrAPF 83, HalFC 84, –88, IntAu&W 77, –82, JeAmFiW, JeAmHC, ModAL, NewYTBS 81, NotNAT, Novels, OxCAmL 65, –83, PenC AM, REn, REnAL, ScF&FL 92, SmATA 21, –27N, TwCA, –SUP, WhAm 9, WhoAm 74, –76, –78, –80, WhoWorJ 72, –78, WorAl, WrDr 76, –80, –82*

Levine, Abby *BioIn 16*

Levine, Abby 1943- *ConAu 126, SmATA 52, –54*

Levine, Betty K 1933- *AuBYP 2S, –3, BioIn 17, ConAu 93, WhoAmW 77*

Levine, Betty Krasne 1933- *SmATA 66*
Pseud./variant:
Krasne, Betty

Levine, David 1926- *BioIn 8, –9, –10, –11, –12, –14, –15, ConAu 113, –116, CurBio 73, EncAJ, IlrAm 1880, IlsCB 1957, IntWW 89, –91, MedPD, SmATA 35, –43, WhoAm 78, –80, –82, –84, –86, –88, –90, –92, –94, WhoAmA 78, –80, –82, –84, –86, –89, –91, WhoGrA 82, WorArt 1950, WorECar*

Levine, Edna Simon d1992 *NewYTBS 92*

Levine, Edna Simon 1910- *BioIn 14, ConAu 85, SmATA 35, WhoE 81, –83*

Levine, Edna Simon 1910-1992 *BioIn 17*

Levine, Evan 1962- *SmATA 74, –77*

Levine, Israel E 1923- *AuBYP 2, –3, BioIn 11, ConAu 1R, IntAu&W 77, –82, –86, –89, SmATA 12, WhoAm 92, –94, WhoAmJ 80, WhoWorJ 72, –78, WrDr 76, –80, –82, –84, –86, –88, –90, –92, –94*

Levine, Joan Goldman *BioIn 11, ConAu 61, SmATA 11*

Levine, Joseph 1910- *AuBYP 2, –3, BioIn 8, –14, BkP, ConAu 108, SmATA 33, WhoAm 76*

Levine, Milton Isra 1902- *AmMWSc 73P, –76P, BioIn 10, ConAu 109, WhoAm 74, WhoAmJ 80*

Levine, Rhoda *AuBYP 2, –3, BioIn 8, –10, –12, ConAu 73, SmATA 14*

Levine, Rhoda J *IntWWM 90*

Levine, Sarah 1970- *BioIn 16, ConAu 125, SmATA 57*

Levine, Sarah Loewenberg *WhoAmW 93*

Levine, Sol *WhoE 89*

Levine, Sol 1914- *ConAu 9R, WhoWorJ 72, –78*

Levine, Sol 1914-1987 *ConAu 124*

Levine-Freidus, Gail *SmATA 65*
Main entry: Provost, Gail Levine

Levinger, Elma Ehrlich 1887- *AuBYP 3*

Levinger, Elma Ehrlich 1887-1958 *AmAu&B, AmWomPl, AuBYP 2, BioIn 4, -7, OhA&B, REnAL, WhAm 3, WhNAA*

Levinson, Nancy Smiler 1938- *BioIn 14, ConAu 107, -23NR, SmATA 33*

Levinson, Riki *BioIn 16, ConAu 121, -37NR, MajAI, SixBJA, SmATA 49, -52, WhoAmW 91*

Levit, Herschel 1912- *ConAu 111, WhAmArt 85, WhoAmA 73, -78, -80, -82, -84, -86, -89, WhoAmJ 80, WhoWorJ 72, -78*

Levit, Herschel 1912-1986 *WhoAmA 91N*

Levit, Rose 1922- *ConAu 73*

Levitin, Sonia 1934- *AuBYP 2S, -3, BioIn 9, -15, -16, -17, ConAu 29R, -14NR, -32NR, ConLC 17, DcAmChF 1960, FifBJA, SmATA 4, -68, -2AS, TwCChW 89, TwCYAW, WrDr 90, -92*

Levitin, Sonia Wolff 1934- *DcAmChF 1985, MajAI, WrDr 94*
Pseud./variant:
Wolff, Sonia

Levitt, Sidney 1947- *BioIn 17, SmATA 68*

Levoy, Myron *AuBYP 2S, -3, BioIn 15, -16, ConAu 93, -18NR, -40NR, DcAmChF 1960, FifBJA, SmATA 37, -49*

Levoy, Myron 1930- *TwCChW 89, TwCYAW, WhoAm 92, -94, WrDr 90, -92, -94*

Levy, Benjamin 1940- *WhoAm 90, -92, -94, WhoE 75, -77, -81, -83, -85, -86, -89, -93*

Levy, Constance 1931- *SmATA 73*

Levy, Elizabeth 1942- *AuBYP 2S, -3, BiDrAPH 79, BioIn 14, ConAu 77, -15NR, -34NR, FifBJA, IntAu&W 82, MajAI, ScF&FL 92, SmATA 31, -69, -18AS*

Levy, Howard S 1923- *ConAu 17R, -10NR, -25NR, DrAS 74F, -78F, -82F*

Levy, Jessica Ann 1962?- *BioIn 10*

Levy, Marilyn *BioIn 17*

Levy, Marilyn 1937- *ConAu 135, SmATA 67*

Levy, Nathan 1945- *BioIn 17, SmATA 63*

Lewees, John *ConAu 137, MajAI, SmATA X*
Main entry: Stockton, Francis Richard

Lewellen, John Bryan 1910-1956 *AuBYP 2, -3, BioIn 2, -4, -6, -7, EncAB-A 31, IndAu 1917, MorJA*

Lewesdon, John *ConAu X*
Main entry: Daniell, Albert Scott

Lewin, Betsy 1937- *BioIn 14, ConAu 104, SmATA 32*

Lewin, Esther 1922- *ConAu 61*

Lewin, Hugh 1939- *BioIn 15, ChlLR 9, ConAu 113, -38NR, MajAI, SmATA 40, -72*

Lewin, Ralph Arnold 1921- *AmMWSc 73P, -82, -86, -89, -92, IntWWP 82, WhoOcn 78*

Lewin, Ted 1935- *BioIn 12, ConAu 69, -25NR, IlsBYP, SmATA 21, -76*

Lewis, Alfred E 1912-1968 *AuBYP 2, -3, BioIn 8, -14, ConAu 111, SmATA 32*

Lewis, Alfred H 1857-1914 *BioIn 14, JrnUS*

Lewis, Alfred Henry 1857-1914 *ConAu 120, TwCWW 91*

Lewis, Alfred Henry 1858?-1914 *AmAu&B, AtlBL, AuBYP 2, BenetAL 91, BiD&SB, BioIn 12, Chambr 3, CnDAL, DcAmAu, DcLB 25, DcLEL, DcNAA, EncFWF, EncMys, OhA&B, OxCAmL 65, -83, REnAL, WhAm 1*

Lewis, Alice C 1936- *BioIn 15, SmATA 46*

Lewis, Alice Hudson 1895?-1971 *AuBYP 2, -3, BioIn 7, -13, ConAu 109, NewYTBE 71, SmATA 29N*

Lewis, Allen
Main entry: Lewis, Arthur Allen

Lewis, Allen 1873-1957 *BioIn 1, -3, -4, -5, WhAmArt 85, WhoAmA 80N, -82N, -86N, -89N, -91N*

Lewis, Angelo J 1839- *Alli SUP*

Lewis, Anne *IlsBYP*

Lewis, Anthony *Who 88, -90, -92*

Lewis, Anthony 1927- *BioIn 3, -4, -7, -9, -13, -16, BlueB 76, ConAu 9R, CurBio 55, EncAJ, EncTwCJ, IntAu&W 89, -91, JrnUS, SmATA 27, Who 74, -82, -83, -85, WhoAm 74, -76, -78, -80, -82, -84, -86, -88, -90, -92, -94, WhoWor 74, WorAlBi, WorAl*

Lewis, Arthur Allen 1873-1957 *GrAmP, IlsCB 1744, -1946*
Pseud./variant:
Lewis, Allen

Lewis, Barbara A 1943- *SmATA 73*

Lewis, Brenda Ralph 1932- *SmATA 72*
Pseud./variant:
Clifford, Rachel Mark

Lewis, C S 1898-1963 *Au&Arts 3, Benet 87, BioIn 14, –15, –16, –17, BlmGEL, CamGLE, CnDBLB 7, ConAu 33NR, ConLC 27, ConLCrt 82, CyWA 89, DcLB 15, –100, EncWL 2, MagSWL, MajTwCW, ModBrL S2, NewEScF, Novels, ObitT 1961, OxCChiL, RAdv 13-1, –13-4, RfGEnL 91, ScF&FL 92, ScFSB, SupFW, ThTwC 87, TwCChW 83, –89, TwCSFW 86, –91, TwCYAW, WorAlBi, WorAl, WorLitC, WrChl, WrPh*

Lewis, Cecil Day *Benet 87, EngPo, IntvTCA 2, RfGEnL 91*
Main entry: Day-Lewis, Cecil

Lewis, Cecil Day 1904-1972 *BioIn 2, CasWL, Chambr 3, ChhPo, ConAu X, ConLC 1, CurBio 40, –69, CyWA 58, DcLEL, DcNaB 1971, EncMys, EvLB, LongCEL, LongCTC, McGEWB, ModBrL, NewC, NewYTBE 72, ObitT 1971, OxCChiL, OxCEng 67, –85, PenC ENG, REn, TwCWr, WhoChL, WorAlBi, WorAl*

Lewis, Claude Aubrey 1934- *ConAu 9R, WhoAm 80, –82*

Lewis, Claudia 1907- *AuBYP 3*

Lewis, Claudia L 1907- *IntAu&W 91*

Lewis, Claudia Louise 1907- *AuBYP 2S, BioIn 10, ChhPo S2, ConAu 5R, ForWC 70, IntAu&W 77, –82, SmATA 5, WrDr 76, –80, –82, –84, –86, –88, –90, –92, –94*

Lewis, Clive Staples 1898-1963 *AnCL, AuBYP 2, –3, Au&ICB, BiDIrW, BioIn 1, –3, –4, –6, –7, –8, –9, –10, –11, –12, –13, –14, –15, –16, –17, CasWL, ChhPo S1, –S2, ChlLR 3, –27, ConAu 81, ConLC 1, –3, –6, ConLCrt 77, CurBio 44, –64, DcIrB 88, DcLEL, DcNaB 1961, EncSF 93, EncWB, EncWL, EngPo, EvLB, GrBr, LongCEL, LongCTC, LuthC 75, MajAI, MakMC, ModBrL, –S1, MorJA, NewC, OxCEng 67, –85, PenC ENG, RAdv 1, REn, SmATA 13, TelT, TwCA SUP, TwCChW 78, TwCWr, WebE&AL, WhDW, WhAm 4, WhoChL, WhoSciF*
Pseud./variant:
Clerk, N W
Hamilton, Clive

Lewis, E M *BioIn 12, ConAu 69, SmATA 20*
Pseud./variant:
Melwood, Mary

Lewis, Edward Van Vliet 1914- *WhoAm 90, –92*

Lewis, Edward Van Vliet 1914-1992 *WhAm 10*

Lewis, Edward VanVliet 1914- *WhoAm 74, –80, –82, –84, –86, –88*

Lewis, Elizabeth Foreman 1892- *AuBYP 3*

Lewis, Elizabeth Foreman 1892-1958 *AmAu&B, AuBYP 2, BioIn 2, –4, –5, –7, –14, ChhPo S1, ConAu 137, JBA 34, –51, MajAI, NewbMB 1922, ObitOF 79, TwCChW 83, –89, TwCYAW, WhAm 3, YABC 2*

Lewis, Francine *ConAu X, –37NR, IntAu&W 77X, –82X, –86X, MajAI, SmATA 2*
Main entry: Wells, Helen

Lewis, George Q 1916-1979 *BioIn 12, ConAu 21R, –135*

Lewis, Harry 1917- *ConAu 109, LEduc 74, WhoE 75, –77*

Lewis, Hilda 1896-1974 *Au&Wr 71, BioIn 5, –12, ConAu 49, –93, OxCChiL, ScF&FL 92, SmATA 20N, TwCChW 78, –83, –89*

Lewis, J Patrick 1942- *SmATA 69*

Lewis, Jack 1924- *WhoAm 86*

Lewis, Jack P *BioIn 17*

Lewis, Jack P 1919- *ConAu 34NR, SmATA 65*

Lewis, Jack Pearl 1919- *WrDr 86, –88, –90, –92, –94*

Lewis, Janet *DcVicP 2, DrAPF 87, –89, –91, –93, WhoUSWr 88, WhoWrEP 89, –92*

Lewis, Janet 1899- *AmAu&B, AmNov, ArtclWW 2, ASCAP 66, Au&Wr 71, BenetAL 91, BioIn 2, –4, –10, –12, –13, –17, ChhPo, –S1, CnDAL, ConAu X, –29NR, ConLC 41, ConNov 72, –76, –82, –86, –91, DcLB Y87B, DrAPF 83, –85, FemiCLE, ForWC 70, InWom SUP, IntAu&W 77, –89, –91, IntWWP 82, –82X, OxCAmL 65, –83, TwCA SUP, TwCRHW 90, TwCWW 91, WhoAm 74, –76, –78, WhoAmW 74, WrDr 76, –80, –82, –84, –86, –88, –90, –92, –94*
Pseud./variant:
Winters, Janet Lewis

Lewis, Jean 1924- *BioIn 17, ConAu 28NR, SmATA 61*

Lewis, Judith Mary *AuBYP 3*

Lewis, Judith Mary 1912- *ConAu 97, WrDr 76, –80, –82, –84, –86, –88*
Pseud./variant:
Berrisford, Judith Mary

Lewis, June E 1905- *ConAu P-2, WrDr 76, –80, –82, –84, –86, –88*

Lewis, Leon 1833-1920 *DcNAA, HsB&A, –SUP, ScFEYrs*

Lewis, Linda *BioIn 17*

Lewis, Linda 1946- *ConAu 135, SmATA 67*

Lewis, Linda Joy 1946- *WrDr 94*

Lewis, Lucia Z *ConAu X, ForWC 70, SmATA X*
Main entry: Anderson, Lucia

Lewis, Marjorie 1929- *BioIn 14, –15, ConAu 108, DrAS 82E, SmATA 35, –40, WhoUSWr 88, WhoWrEP 89, –92*

Lewis, Mary *BioIn 14*

Lewis, Mary 1907?-1988 *ConAu 125, –43NR, SmATA 56N, –64*

Lewis, Mary Christianna Milne 1907?- *ConAu 77, EncMys*
Pseud./variant:
Ashe, Mary Ann

Lewis, Mary Christianna Milne 1907-1988 *BioIn 16, –17*
Pseud./variant:
Brand, Christianna
Jones, Annabel
Roland, Mary
Thompson, China

Lewis, Matthew Gregory 1775-1818 *Alli, Benet 87, BbD, BiDLA, BiD&SB, BioIn 3, –5, –6, –8, –9, –12, –15, BlmGEL, BritAu 19, CasWL, CelCen, Chambr 2, ChhPo, –S1, –S2, CrtT 2, CyWA 58, DcBiA, DcBiPP, DcEnA, DcEnL, DcEuL, DcLB 39, DcLEL, DcNaB, –C, EncO&P 1, –2, –3, EvLB, McGEWB, MouLC 2, NewC, NinCLC 11, NotNAT B, OxCEng 67, OxCThe 67, –83, PenC ENG, PenEncH, REn, RfGEnL 91, WebE&AL, WhoHr&F, WorAlBi*

Lewis, Mervyn *AuBYP 3, IntAu&W 91X, WrDr 86, –88, –90, –92*

Lewis, Mervyn 1931- *WrDr 94*

Lewis, Mervyn Keith 1941- *WhoWor 93*

Lewis, Mildred *AuBYP 3*

Lewis, Mildred D 1912- *AuBYP 2, –3, BioIn 7, ConAu 13R*
Pseud./variant:
DeWitt, James

Lewis, Milton *AuBYP 2, –3, BioIn 7*

Lewis, Naomi *AuBYP 2S, –3, OxCChiL, SmATA 76, Who 90, –92*

Lewis, Paul *AuBYP 3, ConAu 127, SmATA X*
Main entry: Gerson, Noel Bertram

Lewis, Paul 1914-1988 *SmATA X*

Lewis, Richard *DrAPF 87, –89, –91, –93*

Lewis, Richard 1935- *AuBYP 2, –3, BioIn 8, –9, BkP, ChhPo S1, ConAu 9R, –5NR, DrAP 75, DrAPF 83, –85, OxCCan SUP, SmATA 3*

Lewis, Richard William 1933-1966 *AfroAA, BioIn 8, IlsCB 1957*

Lewis, Rob 1962- *SmATA 72*

Lewis, Roger *AuBYP 3*
Main entry: Zarchy, Harry

Lewis, Roger 1912- *AuBYP 2, BlueB 76, ConAu X, SmATA X, WhoAm 80*

Lewis, Roger 1912-1987 *BioIn 15, –16, CurBio 88N, ScF&FL 92, WhAm 9*

Lewis, Shari *BioIn 14, –17*

Lewis, Shari 1934- *AuBYP 2S, –3, BioIn 4, –5, –13, CelR 90, ConAu 19NR, ConTFT 3, CurBio 58, InWom SUP, News 93-1, SmATA 30, –35, WhoAm 74, –76, –78, –80, –82, –84, –86, –88, –90, –92, –94, WhoAmW 74, –83, WhoEnt 92, WorAlBi, WorAl*

Lewis, Stephen *AuBYP 3*

Lewis, Stephen 1949- *AuBYP 2S*

Lewis, Thomas P 1936- *BioIn 13, ConAu 29R, IntAu&W 91, SmATA 27, WhoBlA 75, –77, –80, –85, –90, –92, –94, WrDr 76, –80, –82, –84, –86, –88, –90, –92*

Lewis, Thomas Parker 1936- *WrDr 94*

Lewiton, Mina 1904-1970 *AuBYP 2, –3, BioIn 6, –8, –9, ConAu 29R, –P-2, MorJA, SmATA 2*
Pseud./variant:
Simon, Mina Lewiton

LeWitt, Jan 1907- *AuBYP 2, –3, BioIn 1, –2, –3, –5, –7, –14, ConDes 84, –90, IlsCB 1744, –1946, IntAu&W 77, IntWW 89, –91, IntWWP 82, OxCChiL, Who 74, –82, –83, –85, –88, –90, WhoGrA 62*

Lewittes, Mordecai Henry
Main entry: Lewittes, Morton Henry

Lewittes, Morton H 1911-1990 *BioIn 17, ConAu 133*

Lewittes, Morton Henry 1911- *ConAu 25R, LEduc 74, WhoE 75, -77, WhoWorJ 72*
Pseud./variant:
Lewittes, Mordecai Henry

Lewty, Marjorie 1906- *Au&Wr 71, BioIn 14, ConAu P-1, IntAu&W 91, TwCRHW 90, WrDr 76, -80, -82, -84, -86, -88, -90, -92, -94*

Lexau, Joan M *AuBYP 2, -3, BioIn 8, -9, -14, BkP, ConAu 17R, -11NR, DcAmChF 1960, FourBJA, IntAu&W 91, SmATA 1, -36, TwCChW 78, -83, -89, WrDr 80, -82, -84, -86, -88, -90, -92, -94*
Pseud./variant:
Nodset, Joan L
Seth, Marie

Ley, Willy 1906-1969 *AmAu&B, AsBiEn, AuBYP 2, -3, Au&Wr 71, BenetAL 91, BioIn 2, -3, -4, -7, -8, -9, -17, ConAu 9R, -25R, CurBio 41, -53, -69, DcAmB S8, EncSF 93, InSci, NewEScF, ObitOF 79, REnAL, SmATA 2, ThrBJA, TwCA SUP, WhAm 5, WhoSciF, WorAlBi, WorAl*
Pseud./variant:
Willey, Robert

Leyda, Jay d1988 *NewYTBS 88*

Leyda, Jay 1910- *AmAu&B, BioIn 10, ConAu 108, OxCFilm, WorAu 1950*

Leyda, Jay 1910-1988 *BioIn 15, -16, ConAu 124*

Leydenfrost, Robert *BioIn 3*

Leydon, Rita Floden 1949- *SmATA 21*

Leyland, Eric 1911- *BioIn 8, -15, SmATA 37, WhoChL*

Leyland, Malcolm Rex 1944- *Au&Wr 71*

Leyson, Burr Watkins 1898- *AuBYP 2, -3, BioIn 7*

Lezra, Grizzella Paull 1934- *ConAu 61*

L'Heureux, Willard Joseph 1918- *ConAu 5R*

L'Hommedieu, Dorothy 1885-1961 *AmAu&B, AuBYP 2, -3, BioIn 5, -7, -13, ConAu 109, SmATA 29N*

Liang, Yen 1908- *AmArch 70, BioIn 5, ConAu 5R, IlsCB 1946, WhoE 74*

Lias, Godfrey *ConAu 5R*

Libby, Bill *AuBYP 3*
Main entry: Libby, William M

Libby, Bill 1927-1984 *AuBYP 2S, BioIn 10, -14, -15, ConAu 25R, -10NR, SmATA 5, WrDr 76, -80, -82, -84*

Libby, William M 1927-1984 *AuBYP 3, ConAu 113, SmATA 39N*
Pseud./variant:
Libby, Bill

Liberman, Judith 1929- *ConAu 73*

Liberty, Gene 1924- *BioIn 9, ConAu 5R, -8NR, SmATA 3*

Lichello, Robert 1926- *AuBYP 2, -3, BioIn 7, ConAu 13R, WhoE 75, -77, -81*

Lichtenberg, Margaret Klee 1941- *WhoAm 76, -78, -80, -82, -84, -86, -88, -90, -92, -94*

Liddell, Kenneth 1912-1975 *SmATA 63*

Liddell, Mary 1891- *BioIn 1, IlsCB 1744*

Liddell Hart, Basil Henry 1895-1970 *BioIn 3, -4, -7, -8, -9, -17, ConAu 103, CurBio 40, -70, DcLEL, DcNaB 1961, EvLB, LongCTC, NewC, TwCA, -SUP*

Liddell Hart, Basil Henry, Sir 1895-1970 *BioIn 14, GrBr*

Lide, Alice *AuBYP 2, -3, BioIn 8*

Lidstone, John *AuBYP 3*

Lidstone, John 1929- *AuBYP 2S*

Lidstone, John Barrie Joseph 1929- *IntAu&W 86, -91*

Lieb, Frederick George 1888-1980 *AuBYP 2, -3, BiDAmSp OS, BioIn 7, -11, -12, WhJnl, WhNAA*

Lieberg, Owen S 1896-1973 *ConAu P-2*

Lieberman, E James 1934- *BioIn 17, ConAu 22NR, SmATA 62, WhoWrEP 89*

Lieberman, Edwin James 1934- *WhoWrEP 92*

Lieberman, Mark 1942- *ConAu 29R*

Liebers, Arthur 1913- *BioIn 11, ConAu 5R, -3NR, SmATA 12, WrDr 76, -80, -82, -84*

Liebers, Ruth 1910- *ConAu P-1, ForWC 70*

Lieblich, Irene 1923- *BioIn 13, SmATA 22*

Liebman, Arthur *ScFEYrs*

Liebman, Arthur 1926- *ConAu 57, -6NR, ScF&FL 92*

Liebman, Oscar 1919- *BioIn 5, IlsCB 1946*

Liers, Emil E 1890-1975 *BioIn 15*

Liers, Emil Ernest 1890-1975 *AuBYP 2, -3, BioIn 2, -8, BkCL, ConAu 107, SmATA 37*

Liestman, Vicki 1961- *SmATA 72*
Pseud./variant:
Revsbech, Vicki

Lietz, Gerald S 1918- *AuBYP 2, -3, BioIn 8, -11, SmATA 11*

Liffring, Joan Louise 1929- *ConAu 17R*

Lifton, Betty Jean *ConAu 27NR, IntAu&W 91, TwCChW 89, WhoAm 92*

Lifton, Betty Jean 1926- *AuBYP 2, -3, BioIn 8, -9, -10, ConAu 5R, -12NR, ForWC 70, HerW 84, SmATA 6, ThrBJA, TwCChW 78, -83, WrDr 80, -82, -84, -86, -88, -90, -92, -94*

Lifton, Betty Jean Kirschner 1926- *DcAmChF 1960*

Lifton, Robert Jay *AmMWSc 89, BiDrAPA 89*

Lifton, Robert Jay 1926- *AmMWSc 86, BioIn 15, -16, -17, ConAu 27NR, ConLC 67, SmATA 66, WhoAm 86, -88, -90, -92, -94, WhoUSWr 88, WhoWrEP 89, -92, WorAlBi, WrDr 86, -88, -90, -92, -94*

Liggett, Clayton Eugene 1930- *ConAu 29R, WhoWest 74, -76, -78, -80*

Liggett, Thomas 1918- *AmPeW, ConAu 5R, IntAu&W 77, WrDr 76, -80, -82, -84, -86, -88, -90, -92, -94*

Lightner, A M *AuBYP 2S, -3, BioIn 10, ConAu X, ConSFA, ConSFF, IntAu&W 77X, -82X, MichAu 80, SmATA 5*
Main entry: Hopf, Alice Lightner

Lightner, A M 1904-1988 *ScF&FL 92*

Lightner, Alice Martha 1904-1988 *EncSF 93*

Lignell, Lois 1911- *BioIn 5, -15, IlsCB 1946, SmATA 37*

Liley, Helen Margaret Irwin 1928- *BlueB 76, ConAu 25R*

Lillie, Amy Morris *AuBYP 3*

Lillie, Amy Morris 1883-1967 *AuBYP 2, BioIn 7, -8, EncAB-A 40*

Lillie, Lucy Cecil 1855-1908? *Alli SUP, AmAu&B, BbD, BiD&SB, CarSB, DcAmAu, DcNAA, WhAm 1, WomNov*

Lillington, Kenneth 1916- *BioIn 15, IntAu&W 91, ScF&FL 92, TwCChW 89, WrDr 88, -90, -92*

Lillington, Kenneth James 1916- *Au&Wr 71, ConAu 5R, -3NR, SmATA 39, TwCYAW, WrDr 76, -80, -82, -84, -86, -94*

Lilly, Charles *BioIn 14, -16, BlkAuII, -92, IlsBYP, SmATA 33*

Lilly, Ray *ConAu X, SmATA X*
Main entry: Curtis, Richard

Lim, John 1932- *BioIn 15, ConAu 116, PrintW 83, -85, SmATA 43*

Liman, Ellen 1936- *AuBYP 2S, -3, BioIn 13, ConAu 61, -13NR, SmATA 22*

Limburg, Peter R 1929- *IntAu&W 91, WrDr 86, -88, -90, -92, -94*

Limburg, Peter Richard 1929- *BioIn 11, ConAu 33R, IntAu&W 77, -82, SmATA 13, WhoE 75, WrDr 76, -80, -82, -84*

Lincoln, C Eric *IntvTCA 2*

Lincoln, C Eric 1924- *AmAu&B, AmMWSc 73S, -78S, BioIn 10, BlkWr 1, BlkWrNE, CivR 74, ConAu 1R, -1NR, -27NR, DrAS 74P, -78P, -82P, IntAu&W 82, LivgBAA, NegAl 89, SmATA 5, WhoAm 74, -76, -78, -80, -82, -84, -86, -88, WhoBlA 77, -80, -85, -88, -90, -92, -94 WhoRel 75, -77, WhoUSWr 88, WhoWor 74, WhoWrEP 89, WrDr 76, -80, -82, -84, -86, -88, -90, -92*

Lincoln, Charles Eric 1924- *BlkWr 2, WhoWrEP 92*

Lincoln, Victoria 1904-1981 *AmAu&B, AmNov, AmWomWr, BenetAL 91, BioIn 1, -2, -3, -4, ConAu 104, -P-1, ForWC 70, OhA&B, OxCAmL 65, -83, REnAL, TwCA SUP, WhAm 8, WhoAm 74, -76, -78, WhoAmW 74*

Lind, Levi Robert 1906- *ConAu 5R, DrAS 74F, -78F, -82F, IntAu&W 91, WhoAm 74, -76, -78, -80, -82, -84, -86, -88, -90, WrDr 76, -80, -82, -84, -86, -88, -90, -92, -94*

Linday, Ryllis Elizabeth Paine 1919- *ConAu 13R*

Lindbergh, Anne *BioIn 14, -16, ConAu X, SmATA X*
Main entry: Sapieyevski, Anne Lindbergh

Lindbergh, Anne 1906- *FemiCLE*

Lindsay, Norman 1879-1969 *Benet 87, BioIn 17, CamGLE, OxDcArt, RAdv 13-1, SmATA 67, TwCChW 89*

Lindsay, Norman Alfred William 1879-1969 *BioIn 1, -4, -6, -8, -9, -10, -11, ChhPo S2, ChlLR 8, ConAu 102, DcBrAr 1, DcBrBI, DcLEL, LongCTC, ModCmwL, Novels, OxCArt, OxCAusL, OxCChiL, PenC ENG, REn, SingR 1, TwCA, -SUP, TwCChW 78, -83, TwCWr, WhoChL, WorECar*

Lindsay, Vachel *IntvTCA 2*

Lindsay, Vachel 1879-1931 *AmAu&B, AmLY, AmWr S1, AnCL, AnMV 1926, AtlBL, Benet 87, BenetAL 91, BioIn 1, -2, -4, -5, -6, -7, -8, -9, -10, -11, -12, -14, -15, -16, -17, BkCL, CamGEL, CamHAL, CasWL, Chambr 3, ChhPo, -S2, CnDAL, CnE&AP, CnMWL, ConAmA, ConAmL, ConAu 114, -135, CyWA 58, DcLB 54, DcLEL, DcNAA, EncWL, -2, EvLB, FamPYP, LongCTC, McGEWB, ModAL, NewGrDA 86, OxCAmH, OxCAmL 65, -83, OxCEng 67, -85, PenC AM, RAdv 1, -13-1, REn, REnAL, RealN, RfGAmL 87, SixAP, SmATA 40, Str&VC, TwCA, -SUP, TwCLC 17, TwCWr, WebAB 74, -79, WebE&AL, WhDW, WhAm 1, WhNAA, WhoTwCL, WorAlBi, WorAl, WorLitC*
Pseud./variant:
Lindsay, Nicholas Vachel

Lindsay, Zaidee 1923- *ConAu 29R*

Line, David *ConAu 43NR, ScF&FL 92, WrDr 86, -88, -90, -92*

Line, David 1922- *TwCChW 89, WrDr 94*

Line, Les 1935- *ConAu 73, SmATA 27*

Lines, Kathleen *AuBYP 2S, -3, ChhPo, -S1, OxCChiL*

Lines, Kathleen 1902-1988 *AnObit 1988, BioIn 17, ScF&FL 92*

Lines, Kathleen Mary 1902-1988 *ConAu 127, SmATA 61*

Liney, John J 1912?-1982 *ArtCS, BioIn 12, WhAm 8, WhoAm 82*

Linfield, Esther *BioIn 15, ConAu 112, SmATA 40*

Ling, Jack 1930- *ConAu 25R*

Ling, Jack Chieh-Sheng *WhoSSW 93*

Ling, Jack Chieh-Sheng 1930- *WhoAsA 94*

Lingard, Joan *AuBYP 3, BioIn 16, TwCChW 89, WrDr 86, -88, -90, -92*

Lingard, Joan 1932- *AuBYP 2S, Au&Wr 71, BioIn 11, ConAu 41R, -18NR, -40NR, FifBJA, MajAI, OxCChiL, SmATA 8, -74, -5AS, TwCChW 78, -83, WrDr 76, -80, -82, -84*

Lingard, Joan Amelia *WrDr 94*

Lingard, Joan Amelia 1932- *TwCYAW*

Lingenfelter, Mary Rebecca 1893-1953 *BioIn 3, WhAm 3*

Link, Martin 1934- *BioIn 13, ConAu 106, SmATA 28*

Link, Ruth 1923- *ConAu 29R*

Linklater, Eric 1899-1974 *Au&Wr 71, Benet 87, BioIn 1, -3, -4, -8, -9, -10, BlueB 76N, CamGLE, CasWL, Chambr 3, ChhPo, -S1, -S2, CmScLit, CnMD, ConAu 53, -P-2, ConNov 72, DcLEL, EncWT, EvLB, IntWW 74, -75N, LongCTC, ModBrL, ModWD, NewC, NewYTBS 74, Novels, ObitOF 79, ObitT 1971, OxCChiL, OxCEng 85, PenC ENG, REn, RfGEnL 91, ScF&FL 92, ScFSB, TelT, TwCA, -SUP, TwCChW 78, -83, -89, TwCWr, WhAm 6, Who 74, WhoChL, WhoWor 74*

Linklater, Eric Robert Russell 1899-1974 *EncSF 93, RfGShF*

Links, Marty *BioIn 1*

Linn, Charle F 1930- *AuBYP 3*

Linn, Charles F 1930- *AuBYP 2S, ConAu 85*

Linneman, Robert Ernst 1928- *AmMWSc 73S, -78S, ConAu 29R, WhoE 74, -75*

Linscott, Robert Newton 1886-1964 *BioIn 7, WhAm 4*

Linton, Calvin Darlington 1914- *ConAu 13R, -5NR, DrAS 74E, -78E, -82E, LEduc 74, WhoAm 74, -76, -78, -80, -82, -84, WhoE 83, -85, -86, -89, WhoRel 75, -77, WhoSSW 75, -76, WhoWor 74, -78, -80, -82*

Linton, Ralph 1893-1953 *AmAu&B, BiDPsy, BioIn 3, -4, -5, -9, InSci, McGEWB, NamesHP, ObitOF 79, TwCA SUP, WebAB 74, -79, WhAm 3, WhNAA*

Lionni, Leo 1910- *AmAu&B, AmPB, AuBYP 2, -3, Au&ICB, BioIn 3, -5, -6, -7, -8, -9, -10, -11, -14, -16, -17, BkP, ChhPo S2, ChlBkID, ChlLR 7, ChsFB I, ConAu 53, ConDes 84, -90, DcCAr 81, DcLB 61, FamAIYP, IlsCB 1957, -1967, IntAu&W 91, OxCChiL, SmATA 8, ThrBJA, TwCChW 78, -83, -89, WhoAm 74, -76, -78, -80, -82, -90, -92, -94, WhoAmA 73, -78, -80, -82, -84, -86,*

-89, -91, WhoGrA 62, -82, WrDr 80, -82, -84, -86, -88, -90, -92, -94

Lionni, Leonard 1910- *ConAu 38NR, MajAI, SmATA 72*

Lipinsky DeOrlov, Lino Sigismondo 1908- *BioIn 8, -13, BlueB 76, IlsCB 1957, SmATA 22, WhoAm 74, -76, -78, -80, -82, -84, -86, -88, WhoAmA 73, -78, -80, -82, -84, WhoE 86, -89, WhoWor 74, -80, -82*

Lipinsky de Orlov, Lino Sigismondo 1908-1988 *BioIn 16, WhAm 9*

Lipkind, William 1904-1974 *AmPB, AuBYP 2, -3, BioIn 2, -6, -7, -10, -12, ConAu 53, -101, MorJA, NewYTBS 74, SmATA 15, TwCChW 78, -83, -89*
Pseud./variant:
Will

Lipman, David 1931- *AuBYP 2S, -3, BioIn 12, ConAu 21R, IntAu&W 77, -86, -89, -91, SmATA 21, WhoAm 74, -76, -78, -80, -82, -84, -86, -88, -90, -92, -94, WhoAmJ 80, WhoMW 74, -76, -84, -86, -90, -92, -93, WhoUSWr 88, WhoWor 78, WhoWrEP 89, -92, WrDr 76, -80, -82, -84, -86, -88, -90, -92, -94*

Lipman, Matthew 1923- *BioIn 12, ConAu 33R, -13NR, -32NR, DrAS 74P, -78P, -82P, IntAu&W 77, -86, -89, SmATA 14, WhoE 91, WrDr 76, -80, -82, -84, -86, -88, -90, -92, -94*

Lippard, Lucy R *DrAPF 87, -89, -91, -93*

Lippard, Lucy R 1937- *ConAu 20NR*

Lippard, Lucy Rowland 1937- *ConAu 25R, DrAPF 83, -85, IntAu&W 77, -82, WhoAm 84, WhoAmA 73, -78, -80, -82, -84, -86, -89, -91, WhoAmW 74, -75, WhoUSWr 88, WhoWrEP 89, -92*

Lippincott, Bertram d1985 *BioIn 14, -15*

Lippincott, Bertram 1898?-1985 *ConAu 115, SmATA 42N, WhAm 8*

Lippincott, Gary A 1953- *SmATA 73*

Lippincott, Joseph Wharton 1887-1976 *AmAu&B, AuBYP 2, -3, BioIn 1, -3, -4, -6, -7, -11, -12, ConAu 69, -73, CurBio 55, -77N, MorJA, ObitOF 79, OxCChiL, REnAL, SmATA 17, TwCChW 78, -83, -89, WhAm 7, WhNAA*

Lippincott, Sara Jane 1823-1904 *Alli, AmAu, AmAu&B, AmWomWr, BenetAL 91, BbD, BioIn 1, -10, BlmGWL, CarSB, CyAL, DcAmAu, DcBiPP, DcEnL, DcLB 43, DcNAA, EncAJ, FemPA, HarEnUS, OxCAmL 65, -83, WhAm 1*

Lippincott, Sara Jane Clarke 1823-1904 *BiDAmJo, BioIn 15, -16, ConAu 120, JrnUS*

Lippincott, Sarah L *WhoTech 84*

Lippincott, Sarah Lee 1920- *AmMWSc 82, -86, -89, -92, BioIn 13, SmATA 22, WhoAm 80, -82, -84, -86, -88, -90, -92, -94, WhoFrS 84, WhoTech 82*

Lippman, Peter J 1936- *BioIn 8, -14, ConAu 108, -26NR, IlsBYP, IlsCB 1957, -1967, SmATA 31*

Lipscomb, George Dewey 1898-1957 *BioIn 4*

Lipscomb, James 1926- *ConAu 85, WhoE 85*

Lipsey, Robert Edward 1926- *AmEA 74, AmMWSc 73S, -78S, ConAu 5R, -2NR, -18NR, -40NR, WhoAm 74, -76, -78, -80, -82, -84, -86, -88, -90, -92, -94, WhoE 93, WhoFI 87, -92*

Lipsyte, Robert *BioIn 16, -17*

Lipsyte, Robert 1938- *Au&Arts 7, AuBYP 2S, -3, BioIn 10, -13, ChlLR 23, ConAu 17R, -8NR, ConLC 21, DcAmChF 1960, FifBJA, SmATA 5, -68, TwCChW 89, WrDr 90, -92*

Lipsyte, Robert Michael 1938- *MajAI, TwCYAW, WrDr 94*

Lipton, Leonard 1940- *IntAu&W 77, -82, -82X, -86, WrDr 76, -80*

Lisker, Sonia 1933- *AuBYP 3*

Lisker, Sonia O 1933- *AuBYP 2S, BioIn 15, ConAu 49, -2NR, SmATA 44*

Lisle, Janet T 1947- *SmATA 59*

Lisle, Janet Taylor *SmATA 47*

Lisle, Janet Taylor 1947- *BioIn 16, DcAmChF 1985, ScF&FL 92, SixBJA, SmATA 14AS*

Lisle, Seward D *EncSF 93, YABC 1*
Main entry: Ellis, Edward S

Lisowski, Gabriel 1946- *BioIn 14, -16, ConAu 97, IlsBYP, SmATA 31, -47*

Liss, Howard 1922- *AuBYP 2, -3, BioIn 8, -9, ConAu 25R, -16NR, SmATA 4*

Lissim, Simon 1900-1981 *BioIn 2, -3, -5, -11, -12, -13, BlueB 76, ConAu 109, IlsCB 1946, NewYTBS 81, SmATA 28, WhAm 7, -8, WhAmArt 85, WhoAm 74, -76, -78, -80, -82,*

WhoAmA 73, –78, –80, –82N, –86N, –89N, –91N, WhoArt 80, –82N, WhoE 74, –75, –77, WhoWor 74, –78, –80

Lisson, Deborah 1941- *SmATA 71*

List, Ilka Katherine *BioIn 10, ConAu 37R, ForWC 70, SmATA 6, WrDr 80*
Main entry: Maidoff, Ilka List

Lister, Gladys *SingR 1*

Lister, Mary 1950- *ChlFicS*

Liston, Robert A 1927- *AuBYP 2, –3, BioIn 8, –10, ConAu 17R, –12NR, –30NR, SmATA 5*

Litchfield, Ada B 1916- *BioIn 10, ConAu 25R, –10NR, SmATA 5*

Litchfield, Ada Bassett 1916- *WhoUSWr 88, WhoWrEP 89, –92*

Litchfield, Mary Elizabeth 1854- *CarSB, WhAm 4, WomWWA 14*

Litowinsky, Olga Jean 1936- *BioIn 13, ConAu 81, DrAPF 83, –85, SmATA 26*

Littell, Robert *AuBYP 2S, –3*

Littell, Robert 1935- *BioIn 14, –16, ConLC 42, IntAu&W 91, ScF&FL 92, SpyFic, TwCCr&M 91, WrDr 86, –88, –90, –92, –94*

Litten, Frederic Nelson 1885- *AuBYP 3*

Litten, Frederic Nelson 1885-1951 *AmAu&B, AuBYP 2, BioIn 2, –8, WhAm 3, WhNAA*

Littke, Lael J 1929- *ConAu 85, –15NR, –33NR, SmATA 51*

Little, A Edward *SmATA X*
Main entry: Klein, Aaron E

Little, A Edward 1930- *BioIn 15*

Little, Flora Jean 1932- *ChlFicS, ConAu 42NR, DcChlFi, MajAI, TwCYAW*

Little, Jean 1932- *AuBYP 2, –3, BioIn 8, –9, –10, –12, –17, BlmGWL, CaW, ChhPo S2, ChlLR 4, ConAu 21R, FemiCLE, FourBJA, IntAu&W 91, OxCCan SUP, OxCCanL, Profile 1, SmATA 2, –68, –17AS, TwCChW 78, –83, –89, WhoAm 92, WhoCanL 85, –87, –92, WrDr 80, –82, –84, –86, –88, –90, –92*

Little, John D 1894- *ConAu 65*

Little, Lessie Jones 1906-1986 *BioIn 16, –17, BlkAull 92, ConAu 121, SmATA 50N, –60*

Little, Mary E 1912- *AuBYP 2, –3, BioIn 8, –13, ConAu 105, DcWomA, SmATA 28*

Little, Thomas Russell 1911- *Au&Wr 71, ConAu 13R*

Littledale, Freya *BioIn 9, ConAu 21R, –10NR, –25NR, IntAu&W 77, –82, SmATA 2, WhoAmW 77, WrDr 76, –80, –82, –84, –86, –88, –90, –92*

Littledale, Freya Lota *WrDr 94*

Littledale, Freya Lota Brown *WhoAmW 93*

Littledale, Freya Lota Brown 1929-1992 *SmATA 74*

Littledale, Harold 1927- *ConAu 5R, LEduc 74*

Litvinoff, Barnet 1917- *ConAu 17R*

Lively, Penelope 1933- *ArtclWW 2, AuBYP 2S, –3, Au&Wr 71, BioIn 10, –11, –13, –15, –16, –17, BlmGWL, CamGLE, ChhPo S2, ChlLR 7, ConAu 41R, –29NR, ConLC 32, –50, ConNov 91, DcLB 14, FemiCLE, FourBJA, InWom SUP, MajTwCW, Novels, OxCChiL, ScF&FL 92, SmATA 7, –60, SouSt, TwCChW 78, –83, –89, WrDr 76, –80, –82, –84, –86, –88, –90, –92, –94*

Lively, Penelope Margaret 1933- *ChlFicS, MajAI*

Livermore, Elaine *ChhPo S2*

Liversidge, Douglas 1913- *Au&Wr 71, BioIn 11, ConAu P-1, IntAu&W 77, –82, –86, –89, –91, SmATA 8, WrDr 76, –80*
Pseud./variant:
Liversidge, Henry Douglas

Liversidge, Henry Douglas
Main entry: Liversidge, Douglas

Livesay, John *AuBYP 2S, –3, DcSeaP*

Livesey, Claire Warner 1927- *ConAu 29R*

Livingston, Carole *IntAu&W 86X*

Livingston, Carole 1941- *BioIn 15, ConAu 105, SmATA 42, WhoE 81*
Pseud./variant:
Aphrodite, J

Livingston, Myra 1926- *AuBYP 3*

Livingston, Myra Cohn *BioIn 14, –15, –16, –17, DrAPF 87, –89, –91, –93*

Livingston, Myra Cohn 1926- *AmAu&B, AmWomWr, AnCL, AuBYP 2S, BioIn 10, BkCL, BkP, ChhPo, –S1, –S2, ChlLR 7, ConAu 1R, –1NR, –33NR, DcLB 61, FourBJA,*

IntAu&W 77, -82, -86, -89, -91, IntWWP 82, MajAI, SmATA 5, -68, -1AS, TwCChW 78, -83, -89, WhoAm 82, -84, -86, -88, -90, -92, -94, WhoAmW 75, -77, -83, -85, -87, -89, -91, -93, WhoUSWr 88, WhoWest 87, -89, -92, -94, WhoWor 82, WhoWrEP 89, -92, WrDr 80, -82, -84, -86, -88, -90, -92, -94

Livingston, Peter *AuBYP 2S, -3, BioIn 15*

Livingston, Richard R 1922- *BioIn 11, ConAu 45, SmATA 8*

Livo, Norma J 1929- *ConAu 123, SmATA 76*

Llerena Aguirre, Carlos Antonio 1952- *BioIn 12, ConAu 77, SmATA 19*

Llewellyn, Claire 1954- *SmATA 77*

Llewellyn, Richard
Main entry: Llewellyn Lloyd, Richard D V

Llewellyn, Richard 1906-1983 *AnObit 1983, BioIn 4, -5, -11, -13, -14, -15, ConAu X, ConLC 80, CurBio 84N, DcLB 15, HalFC 84, -88, IntAu&W 82X, NewYTBS 83, Novels, OxCLiW 86, SmATA X, WhAm 8, Who 82, -83, WorAlBi, WorAl, WrDr 82, -84*

Llewellyn, Richard 1907-1983 *CamGLE*

Llewellyn Lloyd, Richard D V 1906-1983 *BioIn 2, -4, -5, -11, ConAu 53, -111, -7NR, ConLC 7, CurBio 40, CyWA 58, DcLEL, EvLB, IntAu&W 77X, LongCTC, NewC, RAdv 1, REn, SmATA 11, -37N, TwCA, -SUP, TwCWr, Who 74, WhoWor 74, WrDr 76, -80*
Pseud./variant:
Llewellyn, Richard
Lloyd, Richard Llewellyn

Llewelyn, T Harcourt *ConAu X, -29NR, SmATA X*

Llewelyn Owens, Joan 1919- *Au&Wr 71, ConAu 36NR, WrDr 76, -80, -82, -84, -86, -88, -90, -92, -94*

Lloyd, E James *SmATA X*
Main entry: James, Elizabeth

Lloyd, Edward 1815-1890 *BioIn 17, DcLB 106, DcNaB, NewC, StaCVF*

Lloyd, Errol 1943- *BioIn 12, -13, -14, -16, -17, BlkAuII, -92, ConAu 101, IlsCB 1967, SmATA 22*

Lloyd, Everett 1881- *AmAu&B, TexWr, WhJnl, WhNAA*

Lloyd, Hugh *BioIn 17, ConAu 133, SmATA 65*
Main entry: Fitzhugh, Percy Keese

Lloyd, James *SmATA X, WrDr 92*
Main entry: James, Elizabeth

Lloyd, John Uri 1849-1936 *Alli SUP, AmAu&B, BiD&SB, BioIn 4, -15, DcAmAu, DcAmMeB 84, DcNAA, DcScB, EncSF 93, LiHiK, OhA&B, WhAm 1, WhNAA*

Lloyd, Marjorie 1909- *Au&Wr 71, ConAu 5R, -8NR, WrDr 76, -80, -82, -84, -86, -88, -90*

Lloyd, Mary Norris 1908-1993 *ConAu 140, SmATA 75*

Lloyd, Megan 1958- *SmATA 77*

Lloyd, Noel *ChhPo S2*

Lloyd, Norman 1909-1980 *AnObit 1980, ASCAP 66, AuBYP 2S, -3, Baker 84, -92, BioIn 12, -13, ConAmC 76, -82, ConAu 37R, -101, -28NR, DcCM, NewGrDA 86, NewYTBS 80, SmATA 23N, WhAm 7, -8, WhoAm 74, -76, -78, -80*

Lloyd, Norris 1908- *BioIn 11, ConAu 1R, -1NR, ForWC 70, SmATA 10*

Lloyd, Richard Llewellyn *DcLEL, EvLB, LongCEL, TwCA, -SUP, Who 74, WrDr 76, -80*
Main entry: Llewellyn Lloyd, Richard D V

Lloyd, Richard Llewellyn 1906-1983 *OxCLiW 86*

Lloyd, Ronald *ConAu X*
Main entry: Friedland, Ronald Lloyd

Lloyd Webber, Andrew 1948- *Au&Arts 1, Baker 92, BioIn 14, -15, -16, -17, CamGWoT, CelR 90, ConMus 6, ConTFT 6, IntWW 89, -91, IntWWM 90, NewAmDM, NewGrDA 86, News 89-1, OxCPMus, PenEncP, SmATA 56, Who 88, -90, -92, WhoAm 86, -88, -90, -92, -94, WhoEnt 92, WhoWor 87, -89, -91, -93, WorAlBi*

Lobb, Charlotte 1935- *ConAu 65, -15NR*

Lobdell, Helen 1919- *ConAu 9R*

Lobel, Anita *ChlBIlD*

Lobel, Anita 1934- *BioIn 8, -9, -10, -16, BkP, ChhPo S1, ConAu 53, -9NR, -33NR, IlsBYP, IlsCB 1957, -1967, IntAu&W 91, SmATA 6, -55, ThrBJA, TwCChW 78, -83, -89, WrDr 80, -82, -84, -86, -88, -90, -92, -94*

Lobel, Anita Kempler 1934- *MajAI*

Lobel, Arnold *BioIn 14, -15, -16*

Lobel, Arnold 1933- *DcLB 61, WrDr 86, -88*

Lobel, Arnold 1933-1987 *AnObit 1987, BenetAL 91, ChlBIlD, ConAu 33NR, NewYTBS 87, SmATA 54N, -55, TwCChW 89*

Lobel, Arnold Stark 1933- *AuBYP 2, AuNews 1, BioIn 7, -8, -9, -10, -12, BkP, ChhPo S2, ChlLR 5, ConAu 1R, -2NR, IlsCB 1957, -1967, OxCChiL, SmATA 6, ThrBJA, TwCChW 78, -83, WhoAm 78, -80, -82, -84, -86, WhoUSWr 88, WhoWrEP 89, WrDr 80, -82, -84*

Lobel, Arnold Stark 1933-1987 *AuBYP 3, ConAu 124, MajAI, WhAm 9*

Loberg, Mary Alice 1943- *ConAu 29R*

Lobley, Robert John 1934- *Au&Wr 71, ConAu 29R, WrDr 76, -80, -82*

Lobsenz, Amelia Freitag *AuBYP 2, -3, BioIn 7, -11, ConAu 13R, ForWC 70, SmATA 12*

Lobsenz, Norman Mitchell 1919- *AmAu&B, BioIn 10, ConAu 9R, -4NR, IntAu&W 86, SmATA 6*

Lochak, Michele 1936- *BioIn 15, ConAu 106, SmATA 39*

Locher, Dick
Main entry: Locher, Richard

Locher, Richard 1929- *ConAu 85, -16NR*
Pseud./variant:
Locher, Dick

Locher, Richard Earl 1929- *ConGrA 2, WhoAm 90, -92, -94*

Lochlons, Colin *AuBYP 3, ConAu X, MichAu 80, SmATA 6*
Main entry: Jackson, C Paul

Lock, Anton 1893- *ClaDrA, DcBrAr 1, WhoArt 80, -82*

Locke, Clinton W *ConAu 26NR, -P-2, SmATA 1*
Main entry: Stratemeyer, Edward L

Locke, Edith Raymond *InWom SUP*

Locke, Edith Raymond 1921- *WhoAm 74, -80, -82, WhoAmW 81, -83, -85, -87, -89, WhoE 74, WhoEnt 92*

Locke, Elsie 1912- *ConAu 26NR, TwCChW 89, WrDr 86, -88, -90, -92*

Locke, Elsie Violet 1912- *Au&Wr 71, BlmGWL, ConAu 25R, -11NR, IntAu&W 77, -82, -86, -89, -91, OxCChiL, TwCChW 78, -83, WrDr 76, -80, -82, -84, -94*

Locke, John 1632-1704 *Benet 87, BenetAL 91, BiDPsy, BiESc, BioIn 1, -2, -3, -4, -5, -6, -7, -8, -9, -10, -11, -12, -13, -14, -15, -16, -17, BlmGEL, CamGEL, CamGLE, CyEd, DcAmSR, DcBiPP, DcInv, DcLB 31A, -101, DcNaB, DcSoc, Dis&D, EncAR, HarEnUS, InSci, LitC 7, LuthC 75, NamesHP, OxCAmH, OxCChiL, OxCEng 85, OxCLaw, RAdv 13-3, -13-4, RfGEnL 91, WhDW, WhoEc 81, -86, WorAlBi, WorAl, WrPh P*

Locke, Lucie 1904- *BioIn 11, ConAu 53, IntAu&W 77X, IntWWP 82X, SmATA 10, WrDr 76*
Pseud./variant:
Price, Lucie Locke

Locke, Margo *IlsBYP*

Locke, Robert 1944- *ConAu 129, SmATA 63*
Pseud./variant:
Bess, Clayton

Locke, Vance *IlsBYP*

Locker, Thomas 1937- *AuBYP 3, BioIn 16, ChlLR 14, ConAu 128, MajAI, SixBJA, SmATA 59*

Lockley, Ronald M 1903- *ConAu 22NR*

Lockley, Ronald Mathias 1903- *Au&Wr 71, BioIn 12, ConAu 9R, -5NR, IntAu&W 77, -89, -91, OxCLiW 86, Who 74, -82, -83, -85, -88, -90, -92, WrDr 76, -80, -82, -84, -86, -88, -90, -92, -94*

Lockwood, Mary *ConAu X, SmATA X*
Main entry: Spelman, Mary

Lockwood, Myna *AuBYP 2, -3, BioIn 7*

Lodge, Bernard 1933- *BioIn 14, ConAu 107, SmATA 33*

Lodge, Maureen Roffey *SmATA X*
Main entry: Roffey, Maureen

Loeb, Jeff *AuBYP 3*

Loeb, Jeffrey 1946- *BioIn 16, ConAu 123, SmATA 57*

Loeb, Robert H, Jr. 1917- *BioIn 12, ConAu 29R, -12NR, SmATA 21*

Loebl, Suzanne *AuBYP 2S, -3, ConAu 69, WhoE 74*

Loeff, An Rutgers van der *TwCChW 89B*

Loeff, An Rutgers VanDer *TwCChW 78B, -83B*

Loeffler, Gisella *BioIn 1, WhAmArt 85*
Main entry: Lacher, Gisella Loeffler

Loefgren, Ulf 1931- *BioIn 9, ConAu 25R, -16NR, SmATA 3*
Pseud./variant:
Lofgren, Ulf

Loemker, Elmer *BioIn 5*

Loening, Sarah Larkin d1988 *NewYTBS 88*

Loening, Sarah Larkin 1896- *ConAu 45, -21NR, IntAu&W 82, WhoAmW 77, -89, WhoE 81, -83, -85, -86, -89, WhoUSWr 88, WhoWrEP 89*
Pseud./variant:
Larkin, Sarah

Loening, Sarah Larkin 1896-1988 *BioIn 15, ConAu 124*

Loeoef, Jan 1940- *ConAu 81*

Loeper, John J 1929- *WrDr 86, -88, -90, -92*

Loeper, John Joseph 1929- *BioIn 11, ConAu 29R, -12NR, IntAu&W 77, -82, -86, SmATA 10, WhoE 75, WrDr 76, -80, -82, -84, -94*
Pseud./variant:
Lowe, Jay, Jr.

Loescher, Ann Dull 1942- *ConAu 61, -9NR, SmATA 20*

Loescher, Gil 1945- *BioIn 12, ConAu 61, -9NR, SmATA 20*

Loescher, Gilburt Damian 1945- *WhoMW 93*

Loewenstein, Bernice *BioIn 15, IlsBYP, SmATA 40*

LoFaro, Jerry 1959- *SmATA 77*

Lofgren, Ulf *FourBJA*
Main entry: Loefgren, Ulf

Lofting, Hugh *EncSF 93, ScFSB*

Lofting, Hugh 1886-1947 *AmAu&B, AnCL, AuBYP 2, -3, BenetAL 91, BioIn 1, -2, -3, -4, -7, -8, -12, -14, CamGLE, ChhPo, -S1, ChlLR 19, ConAu 109, ConICB, DcLEL, DcNAA, EngPo, EvLB, FamMS, HalFC 84, -88, IlsCB 1744, JBA 34, -51, LongCTC, NewbMB 1922, OxCChiL, OxCEng 85, REn, REnAL, ScF&FL 92, SmATA 15, Str&VC, TelT, TwCA, -SUP, TwCChW 78, -83, -89, WhAm 2, WhAmArt 85, WhNAA, WhoChL, WorAlBi, WorAl, WrChl*

Lofting, Hugh John 1886-1947 *ConAu 137, MajAI*

Lofts, Nora 1904-1983 *AuBYP 3*

Lofts, Norah 1904-1983 *AuBYP 2S, AuNews 2, Au&Wr 71, BioIn 3, -4, -9, -10, -11, -13, -14, ConAu 5R, -110, -6NR, FemiCLE, IntAu&W 77, -82, LongCTC, Novels, ScF&FL 92, SmATA 8, -36N, TwCA, -SUP, TwCCr&M 80, TwCRHW 90, WhAm 8, WhNAA, Who 74, -82, -83, WhoAm 74, WhoAmW 74, -75, WrDr 76, -80, -82, -84*
Pseud./variant:
Astley, Juliet
Curtis, Peter

Logan, Elizabeth D 1914- *ConAu 61, WhAmArt 85*

Logan, John *CamGEL, DrAPF 87, IntvTCA 2*

Logan, John d1987 *NewYTBS 87, Who 88N*

Logan, John 1923- *AmAu&B, BiDConC, BioIn 10, -12, ConAu 77, ConLC 5, ConPo 70, -75, -80, -85, CroCAP, DcLB 5, DrAF 76, DrAP 75, DrAPF 83, -85, IntAu&W 77, OxCAmL 65, -83, PenC AM, RAdv 1, -13-1, WhoAm 82, -84, WorAu 1950, WrDr 76, -80, -82, -84, -86, -88*

Logan, John 1923-1987 *Benet 87, BenetAL 91, BioIn 15, ConAu 124*

Logan, John Arthur, Jr. 1923- *WhoAm 92, -94*

Logan, Rayford W 1897-1982 *BlkWr 1, BlkWrNE, ConAu 25NR, NegAl 89*

Logan, Rayford Whittingham 1897-1982 *AmAu&B, BioIn 5, -9, -13, ConAu 1R, -108, -1NR, DrAS 74H, -78H, EncAACR, InB&W 80, NegAl 76, -83, NewYTBS 82, SelBAAf, SelBAAu, WhAm 8, WhoAm 74, -76, -78, -80, -82, WhoBlA 75, WhoWor 74, -78, -80, -82*

Logan, Rayford Whittingham 1897-1984 *InB&W 85*

Logier, Eugene Bernard Shelley 1893?-1979 *BioIn 12, WrDr 76, -80*

Logsdon, Lois Irene *AuBYP 2, -3, BioIn 8*

Logsdon, Richard Henry 1912- *AuBYP 2, -3, BiDrLUS 70, BioIn 1, -8, ConAu 5R, -2NR, DrLC 69, WhoAm 74, -76, -78, -80, -82, -84, -86, -88, -90, -92, -94, WhoLibI 82, WhoLibS 55, -66, WhoWor 80, -82*

Logue, Christopher *IntvTCA 2*

Logue, Christopher 1926- *Au&Wr 71, BioIn 4, -10, -13, -14, CamGLE, ChhPo S2, CnMD, ConAu 9R, -3NR, -42NR, ConPo 70, -75, -80, -85, -91, DcLB 27, DcLEL 1940, EngPo, IntAu&W 77, -82, -91, IntWWP 82, ModBrL, ModWD, NewC, OxCEng 85, SmATA 23, Who 74, -82, -83, -85, -88, -90,*

–92, WorAu 1950, WrDr 76, –80, –82, –84, –86, –88, –90, –92
Pseud./variant:
Vicarion, Palmiro, Count

Loh, Jules 1931- *ConAu 33R*

Loh, Morag *AuBYP 3*

Loh, Morag 1935- *SmATA 73*

Lohre, M *MedPD*

Loisy, Jeanne 1913- *AuBYP 2, –3, BioIn 7*

Loken, Newton 1919- *BioIn 13, ConAu 1R, SmATA 26*

Lolli, Giorgio 1905-1979 *BioIn 11, –12, ConAu 1R, –85, –2NR*

Lomas, Derek 1933- *ConAu 29R*

Lomas, Peter Eric Samuel 1923- *ConAu 21R, WhoWor 87, WrDr 76, –80*

Lomas, Steve *ConAu X, IntAu&W 77X, SmATA 6*
Main entry: Brennan, Joseph Lomas

Lomask, Milton 1909- *AuBYP 2, –3, BioIn 8, –12, BkC 6, ConAu 1R, –1NR, DrAS 74H, SmATA 20*

Lomask, Milton 1909-1991 *ConAu 135*

Lomask, Milton Nachman 1909- *WhoAm 86, –92*

Lomax, Alan *EncRk 88*

Lomax, Alan 1915- *AmAu&B, Au&Wr 71, Baker 84, –92, BenetAL 91, BioIn 2, –4, –5, –14, –15, –17, BlueB 76, ConAu 1R, –1NR, CurBio 41, EncFCWM 69, –83, IntWW 74, –75, –76, –77, –78, –79, –80, –81, –82, –83, –89, –91, NewAmDM, NewGrDA 86, OxCPMus, PenEncP, REnAL, TexWr, TwCA SUP, WebAB 79, WhoAm 74, –76, –84, WhoWor 74*

Lomax, John A 1867-1948 *BenetAL 91*

Lomax, John Albert 1930- *ConAu 61*

Lomax, John Avery 1867-1948 *Baker 92*

Lomax, John Avery 1872?-1948 *AmAu&B, Baker 84, Benet 87, BiDSA, BioIn 1, –2, –3, –4, –5, ChhPo, CnDAL, DcNAA, EncFCWM 69, –83, ObitOF 79, OxCAmL 65, –83, OxCMus, REn, REnAL, Str&VC, TexWr, TwCA SUP, WebAB 74, –79, WhAm 2, WhNAA*

Lomax, John Avery 1875-1948 *BioIn 14, –15, –17*

London, Carolyn 1918- *ConAu 57*

London, Jack *IntvTCA 2, MajAI, MajTwCW*
Main entry: London, John Griffith

London, Jack 1876-1916 *AmAu&B, AmWr, AtlBL, AuBYP 2, –3, AuNews 2, Benet 87, BenetAL 91, BiD&SB, BioIn 1, –2, –3, –4, –5, –6, –7, –8, –9, –10, –11, –12, –13, –14, –15, –16, –17, CamGEL, CamGLE, CamHAL, CarSB, CasWL, Chambr 3, CmCal, CnDAL, ConAmL, ConAu X, CyWA 58, DcAmAu, DcAmSR, DcBiA, DcLB 8, –12, –78, DcLEL, DcNAA, Dis&D, EncAB-H, EncFWF, EncMys, EncPaPR 91, EncSF 93, EncWL, –2, FamAYP, FilmgC, HalFC 84, –88, JBA 34, LongCTC, MagSAmL, MakMC, McGEWB, ModAL, –S1, MorMA, NewEScF, NotNAT B, Novels, OxCAmH, OxCAmL 65, –83, OxCCan, OxCCanL, OxCChiL, OxCEng 67, PenC AM, PenEncH, RAdv 1, –13-1, RComAH, RComWL, REn, REnAL, RealN, RfGAmL 87, RfGShF, ScF&FL 92, ScFSB, ScFEYrs, ShSCr 4, ShSWr, SmATA 18, Str&VC, TwCA, –SUP, TwCLC 9, –15, –39, TwCSFW 86, –91, TwCWW 91, TwCWr, TwCYAW, WebAB 74, –79, WebE&AL, WhDW, WhAm 1, WhoHr&F, WhoTwCL, WorAlBi, WorAl, WorLitC, WrPh*

London, Jane *ConAu X, SmATA 7*
Main entry: Geis, Darlene Stern

London, John Griffith *AuBYP 3*

London, John Griffith 1876-1916 *ConAu 110, –119, MajAI, MajTwCW, SmATA X*
Pseud./variant:
London, Jack

London, Jonathan *DrAPF 87, –89, –91, –93*

London, Jonathan Paul 1947- *SmATA 74, WhoWrEP 92*
Pseud./variant:
Sherwood, Jonathan

London, Julius 1917- *AmMWSc 73P, –76P, –82, –86, –89, –92, ConAu 118, WhoTech 82, –84*

Lonergan, Joy 1909- *AuBYP 2, –3, BioIn 7, –11, ConAu 1R, SmATA 10*

Lonette, Reisie Dominee 1924- *BioIn 5, –8, IlsBYP, IlsCB 1946, –1957, SmATA 43*

Long, Earlene 1938- *BioIn 16, ConAu 126, SmATA 50*

Long, Earlene Roberta 1938- *WhoWrEP 92*

Long, Helen Beecher *ConAu 26NR, -P-2, SmATA 1*
Main entry: Stratemeyer, Edward L

Long, John Luther *BiGAW*

Long, John Luther 1861-1927 *AmAu&B, BenetAL 91, BiD&SB, BioIn 7, -10, -11, CarSB, CnDAL, DcAmAu, DcLEL, DcNAA, ModWD, NotNAT B, OxCAmL 65, -83, OxCAmT 84, OxCThe 67, -83, PlP&P, REnAL, WhAm 1*

Long, Judith Elaine 1953- *BioIn 12, ConAu 65, SmATA 20*
Pseud./variant:
Long, Judy

Long, Judy
Main entry: Long, Judith Elaine

Long, Kim 1949- *SmATA 69*

Long, Laura Mooney 1892-1967 *BioIn 13, ConAu 109, IndAu 1917, SmATA 29N*

Longeaux Y Vasquez, Enriqueta 1930- *ConAu 57*

Longfellow, Henry Wadsworth 1807-1882 *Alli, -SUP, AmAu, AmAu&B, AmWr, AnCL, AtlBL, AuBYP 2, -3, Benet 87, BenetAL 91, BbD, BiD&SB, BioIn 1, -2, -3, -4, -5, -6, -7, -8, -9, -10, -11, -12, -13, -14, -16, CamGEL, CamGLE, CamHAL, CasWL, CelCen, Chambr 3, ChhPo, -S1, -S2, CnDAL, CnE&AP, CrtT 3, CyAL, CyEd, CyWA 58, DcAmAu, DcAmSR, DcBiA, DcBiPP, DcEnA, DcEnL, DcLB 1, -59, DcLEL, DcNAA, DcSpL, EncAB-H, EvLB, FamAYP, FamPYP, HarEnUS, LuthC 75, MagSAmL, McGEWB, MemAm, MouLC 4, NewGrDA 86, NinCLC 2, OxCAmH, OxCAmL 65, -83, OxCCanL, OxCChiL, OxCEng 67, -85, PenC AM, RAdv 1, -13-1, RComAH, RComWL, REn, REnAL, RfGAmL 87, SmATA 19, Str&VC, WebAB 74, -79, WebE&AL, WhDW, WhAm HS, WhNaAH, WorAlBi, WorAl*

Longman, Harold S 1919- *BioIn 10, ConAu 25R, SmATA 5*

Longmate, Norman Richard 1925- *Au&Wr 71, ConAu 9R, -6NR, -28NR, IntAu&W 77, -82, -86, -89, -91, WhoWor 78, WrDr 76, -80, -82, -84, -86, -88, -90, -92, -94*

Longo, Lucas 1919- *ConAu 25R, WhoE 74, WrDr 76, -80, -82, -84, -86*

Longstreet, Stephen *ConDr 88D*

Longstreet, Stephen 1907- *AmAu&B, BenetAL 91, BiE&WWA, BioIn 4, ConAu 9R, -7NR, ConDr 73, -77D, -82D, FilmgC, HalFC 84, -88, IntAu&W 86, -89, -91, IntMPA 75, -76, -78, -81, -82, -84, -86, -88, -92, -77, NotNAT, Novels, REnAL, TwCA SUP, WhoAm 74, -76, -78, -80, -82, -84, -86, -88, -90, -92, -94, WhoAmA 73, -78, -80, -82, -84, -86, -89, -91, WhoEnt 92, WhoWest 92, -94, WhoWorJ 72, -78, WrDr 76, -80, -82, -84, -86, -88, -90, -92, -94*

Longstreth, Joseph 1920- *AuBYP 2, -3, BioIn 7, IndAu 1917*

Longstreth, Thomas Morris 1886- *AuBYP 3*

Longstreth, Thomas Morris 1886-1975 *AmAu&B, AuBYP 2, Au&Wr 71, BioIn 2, -6, -7, ConAu 5R, CurBio 50, MorJA, OxCCan, WhAm 7, WhoAm 74, -76*

Longsworth, Polly Ormsby 1933- *AuBYP 2, -3, BioIn 8, -13, ConAu 106, IntAu&W 86, SmATA 28*

Longtemps, Kenneth 1933- *BioIn 12, SmATA 17*

Longway, A Hugh *Alli SUP, ConAu 137, -X, EncSF 93, MajAI, SmATA X*
Main entry: Lang, Andrew

Loof, Jan 1940- *AuBYP 2S, -3*

Loomis, Frederic Brewster 1873-1937 *AmLY, DcNAA, WhAm 1, WhNAA*

Loomis, J Paul *AuBYP 2, -3, BioIn 7*

Loomis, Robert D *AuBYP 3*

Loomis, Robert Duane 1926- *AuBYP 2, BioIn 7, -10, -11, ConAu 17R, SmATA 5, WhoAm 84, -86, -88, -90, -92, -94*

Loon, Hendrik Willem Van *JBA 34, TwCA, -SUP*
Main entry: VanLoon, Hendrik Willem

Loots, Barbara Kunz 1946- *ConAu 57, WhoAmW 91*

Lopez, Barry *DrAPF 87, -89, -91, -93*

Lopez, Barry 1945- *Au&Arts 9, ScF&FL 92, SmATA 67*

Lopshire, Robert M 1927- *ConAu 30NR*

Lopshire, Robert Martin 1927- *AuBYP 2, -3, BioIn 8, -10, ChhPo, ConAu 5R, -8NR, SmATA 6*

Lorayne, Harry 1926- *ConAu 41R, IntAu&W 77*

Lord, Athena V *DcAmChF 1960*

Lord, Athena V 1932- *BioIn 15, ConAu 109, SmATA 39*

Lord, Beman 1924- *AuBYP 2, BioIn 8, –10, ConAu 33R, FourBJA, SmATA 5*

Lord, Beman 1924-1991 *BioIn 17, ConAu 135, ScF&FL 92, SmATA 69*

Lord, Bemen 1924- *AuBYP 3*

Lord, Bette Bao *BioIn 16*

Lord, Bette Bao 1938- *BestSel 90-3, ConAu 41NR, DcAmChF 1985, IntAu&W 89, –91, SixBJA, SmATA 58, WhoAmW 87, –89, –91, –93*

Lord, Douglas *ConAu 130, EngPo*

Lord, Douglas 1904- *BioIn 11, ConAu P-1, SmATA 12, WrDr 76, –80, –82, –84*

Lord, Eugene Hodgdon 1894- *ConAu 1R*

Lord, John Vernon 1939- *BioIn 12, –14, ConAu 53, IlsBYP, IntAu&W 77, SmATA 21, WrDr 76, –80, –82, –84, –86, –88, –90, –92, –94*

Lord, Nancy *ConAu X, –30NR, DrAPF 89, –91, –93, SmATA 2, ThrBJA, WrDr 80, –82, –84, –86, –88, –90, –92*
Main entry: Titus, Eve

Lord, Nancy 1922- *WrDr 94*

Lord, Patricia C 1927-1988 *BioIn 16, SmATA 58*

Lord, Walter 1917- *AmAu&B, ASCAP 66, BioIn 5, –9, –10, ConAu 1R, –5NR, –22NR, CurBio 72, EncAI&E, IntAu&W 77, –82, –86, –89, –91, REnAL, SmATA 3, WhoAm 74, –76, –78, –80, –82, –84, –86, –88, –90, –92, –94, WhoUSWr 88, WorAu 1950, WrDr 80, –82, –84, –86, –88, –90, –92, –94*

Loree, Kate 1920- *ConAu 21R*

Lorentowicz, Irena 1910- *BioIn 1, –5, IlsBYP, IlsCB 1744, –1946, WhoPolA*

Lorenz, Ellen Jane 1907- *ASCAP 66, ConAmC 76, –82, IntWWM 85, WhoAmM 83, WhoMW 84, WhoMus 72*

Lorenz, Lee *BioIn 15*

Lorenz, Lee 1932- *ConAu 124, SmATA 39*

Lorenz, Lee Sharp 1932- *WhoAm 90, –92, –94*

Lorenzini, Carlo *Benet 87*

Lorenzini, Carlo 1826-1890 *AnCL, AuBYP 2, –3, BioIn 1, –2, –3, –5, –7, –8, –13, CasWL, DcItL, EuAu, JBA 34, –51, MajAI, OxCChiL, SmATA 29, WhoChL*
Pseud./variant:
Collodi, Carlo

Lorenzo, Carol Lee 1939- *ConAu 53*

Lorimer, James 1942- *CaW, CanWW 80, –81, –83, –89, ConAu 123*

Lorimer, Janet 1941- *BioIn 17, SmATA 60*

Lorimer, Lawrence T 1941- *ConAu 57, –6NR*

Loring, Emilie d1951 *BenetAL 91, InWom SUP, TwCRHW 90*

Loring, Emilie 1864?-1951 *SmATA 51*

Loring, Emilie Baker *AmWomPl*
Pseud./variant:
Story, Josephine

Loring, Selden M *AuBYP 2, –3, BioIn 8*

Lorioux, Felix *BioIn 1, IlsCB 1744*

Lorraine, Walter Henry 1929- *BioIn 5, –8, –12, ChhPo, –S1, –S2, FourBJA, IlsBYP, IlsCB 1946, –1957, –1967, SmATA 16*

Loss, Joan 1933- *BioIn 11, SmATA 11*

Lossing, Benson John 1813-1891 *Alli, –SUP, AmAu, AmAu&B, BbD, BiD&SB, BioIn 2, –8, –11, –14, ChhPo, CyAL, DcAmAu, DcBiPP, DcLB 30, DcNAA, EarABI, –SUP, HarEnUS, WhAm HS*

Lot, Parson *DcEnL, OxCEng 67, –85, YABC X*
Main entry: Kingsley, Charles

Loth, David *AuBYP 3*

Lothrop, Harriet Mulford 1844-1924 *AuBYP 3, WomNov*

Lothrop, Harriet Mulford Stone 1844-1924 *Alli SUP, AmAu, AmAu&B, AmWomWr, AuBYP 2S, BbD, BiD&SB, BioIn 8, –9, –12, –15, BlmGWL, CarSB, ChhPo, CnDAL, DcAmAu, DcLB 42, DcNAA, OxCAmL 65, –83, OxCChiL, REnAL, SmATA 20, WomWWA 14, WorAl*
Pseud./variant:
Mulford, Harriet
Sidney, Margaret

Lottman, Eileen 1927- *ConAu 57, –12NR, –30NR, EncSF 93, ScF&FL 92, WhoE 89*

Lotz, Wolfgang 1912-1981 *BioIn 17, ConAu 34NR, SmATA 65*

Lougheed, Robert Elmer 1910-1982 *BioIn 4, -9, -11, IlrAm 1880, -E, WhAmArt 85, WhoAm 80, WhoAmA 80, -82*

Louie, Ai-Ling 1949- *BioIn 14, -15, ConAu 112, SmATA 34, -40, WhoAsA 94*

Louis, Ray Baldwin 1949- *ConAu 65*

Louisburgh, Sheila Burnford *ConAu X, SmATA X*
Main entry: Burnford, Sheila

Louria, Donald Bruce 1928- *AmMWSc 73P, -76P, -82, -86, -89, -92, BiDrACP 79, ConAu 107, WhoAm 82, WhoE 75, WhoWor 84*

Lourie, Dick *DrAPF 87, -89, -91, -93*

Lourie, Dick 1937- *ConAu 33R, DrAP 75, DrAPF 83, -85, WhoUSWr 88, WhoWrEP 89, -92*

Lourie, Helen *AuBYP 2S, -3, ConAu X, SmATA X*
Main entry: Storr, Catherine

Love, Adelaide 1889-1973 *ChhPo, -S1, -S2*

Love, Katherine Isabel 1907- *BioIn 9, ChhPo, SmATA 3*

Love, Sandra *DrAPF 87, -89, -91, -93*

Love, Sandra 1940- *BioIn 13, ConAu 69, -11NR, SmATA 26*

Love, Sandra Rae 1947- *WhoAmW 93*

Lovechild, Mrs *OxCChiL*

Lovejoy, Bahija Fattouhi 1914- *AuBYP 3*

Lovejoy, Behija Fattuhi 1914- *AuBYP 2, BioIn 8, ConAu 5R*

Lovelace, Delos Wheeler 1894-1967 *AmAu&B, AuBYP 2, -3, BioIn 4, -6, -7, -10, ConAu 5R, -25R, MinnWr, SmATA 7, TwCA, -SUP, WhAm 4, WhNAA*

Lovelace, Maud Hart 1892-1980 *AmAu&B, AuBYP 2, -3, Au&Wr 71, BioIn 2, -4, -5, -6, -7, -9, -11, ConAu 5R, -104, -39NR, JBA 51, MajAI, MinnWr, REnAL, SmATA 2, -23N, TwCA, -SUP, TwCChW 83, -89, WhNAA, WhoAmW 74*

Lovell, Ingraham
Main entry: Bacon, Josephine Dodge Daskam

Lover, Samuel 1796-1868 *CamGEL, CamGLE*

Lover, Samuel 1797-1868 *Alli, -SUP, Baker 84, -92, BbD, BiDIrW, BiD&SB, BioIn 5, -12, BritAu 19, CasWL, CelCen, Chambr 3, ChhPo, -S1, -S2, CyWA 58, DcBiA, DcBiPP, DcEnA, DcEnL, DcEuL, DcIrB 88, DcIrL, DcIrW 1, DcLEL, DcNaB, DcVicP 2, EvLB, HsB&A, NewC, NotNAT A, -B, OxCEng 67, -85, OxCMus, PenC ENG, PoIre, REn, RfGEnL 91, StaCVF, WebE&AL*

Loverseed, Amanda Jane 1965- *ConAu 142, SmATA 75*

Lovett, Margaret Rose 1915- *Au&Wr 71, BioIn 13, ConAu 61, SmATA 22, WrDr 76, -80, -82, -84*

Lovoos, Janice *AuBYP 2S, -3, BioIn 16*

Low, Alice 1926- *AuBYP 2S, -3, BioIn 11, -16, ConAu 61, -8NR, ScF&FL 92, SixBJA, SmATA 11, -76*

Low, Elizabeth Hammond 1898- *AuBYP 2, -3, BioIn 8, -10, ConAu P-2, SmATA 5*

Low, Joseph 1911- *AmPB, AuBYP 2, -3, BioIn 2, -3, -5, -7, -8, -9, -12, ChhPo, -S1, -S2, ConAu 85, -15NR, IlsCB 1946, -1957, -1967, MajAI, SmATA 14, ThrBJA, WhoAm 74, -76, -78, -80, -82, -84, -86, -88, -90, -92, -94, WhoAmA 73, -78, -80, -82, -84, -86, -89, -91, WhoE 91, WhoGrA 62, WhoSSW 91*

Lowbury, Edward 1913- *ChhPo S2, ConAu 29R, -12NR, -29NR, ConPo 70, -75, -80, -85, -91, EngPo, IntAu&W 77, -82, IntMed 80, IntWWP 82, WrDr 76, -80, -82, -84, -86, -88, -90, -92*

Lowbury, Edward Joseph Lister 1913- *WrDr 94*

Lowe, Jay, Jr. *ConAu X, SmATA X*
Main entry: Loeper, John Joseph

Lowell, Amy 1874-1925 *Alli SUP, AmAu&B, AmLY, AmWomWr, AmWr, ArtclWW 2, AtlBL, Benet 87, BenetAL 91, BioAmW, BioIn 1, -3, -5, -6, -7, -8, -9, -10, -11, -12, -15, -17, BlmGWL, CamGLE, CamHAL, CasWL, Chambr 3, ChhPo, -S1, CnDAL, CnE&AP, ConAmA, ConAmL, ConAu 104, DcAmBC, DcLB 54, -140, DcLEL, DcNAA, EncAB-H, EncPaPR 91, EncWL 2, EvLB, FemiCLE, IntDcWB, LongCTC, MakMC, McGEWB, ModAL, ModAWWr, NewGrDA 86, OxCAmL 65, -83, OxCEng 67, -85, PenC AM, RAdv 1, -13-1, REn, REnAL, RfGAmL 87, SixAP, Str&VC, TwCA, -SUP, TwCLC 1, -8, TwCWr, WebAB 74, -79, WebE&AL, WhDW, WhAm 1, WomWWA 14, WorAl*

Lowell, Amy Lawrence 1874-1925 *GayLL*

Lowell, James Russell 1819-1891 *Alli, –SUP, AmAu, AmAu&B, AmWr S1, AtlBL, Benet 87, BenetAL 91, BbD, BiD&SB, BioIn 1, –2, –3, –4, –5, –6, –7, –8, –9, –10, –11, –12, –14, –15, –16, –17, CamGEL, CamGLE, CamHAL, CasWL, CelCen, Chambr 3, ChhPo, –S1, –S2, CnDAL, CnE&AP, CrtT 3, CyAG, CyAL, CyEd, CyWA 58, DcAmAu, DcAmDH 80, –89, DcAmSR, DcBiPP, DcEnA, –A, DcEnL, DcLB 1, –11, –64, –79, DcLEL, DcNAA, DcSpL, Dis&D, EncAB-H, EncAHmr, EvLB, HarEnUS, McGEWB, MouLC 4, NewGrDA 86, NinCLC 2, OxCAmH, OxCAmL 65, –83, OxCEng 67, –85, PenC AM, RAdv 1, –13-1, REn, REnAL, RfGAmL 87, Str&VC, WebAB 74, –79, WebE&AL, WhAm HS, WorAlBi, WorAl*

Lowenfels, Walter 1897-1976 *AmAu&B, AuBYP 2S, –3, BioIn 11, –12, –16, BlueB 76, ConAu 1R, –65, –3NR, ConPo 70, –75, DcLB 4, DrAP 75, PenC AM, RAdv 1, WhAm 7, WhoAm 76, WrDr 76*

Lowenstein, Bernice *ChhPo S1*

Lowenstein, Dyno 1914- *BioIn 10, –11, ConAu 9R, SmATA 6*

Lower, Joseph A 1907- *ConAu 21R*

Lowery, Linda *ScF&FL 92*

Lowery, Linda 1949- *ConAu 141, SmATA 74*

Lowis, Geoffrey Lyttelton 1896- *Au&Wr 71, WrDr 76, –84, –86*

Lowitz, Anson C 1901?-1978 *BioIn 11, –12, ConAu 73, –81, SmATA 18*

Lowitz, Sadyebeth Heath 1901?-1969 *BioIn 8, ConAu 85, SmATA 17*

Lownsbery, Eloise 1888- *BioIn 1, –2, –14, CurBio 47, JBA 51*

Lowrey, Janette 1892- *AuBYP 3*

Lowrey, Janette Sebring 1892- *AmAu&B, AuBYP 2, BioIn 1, –7, –15, ChhPo, ConAu 13R, SmATA 43, TexWr*

Lowry, Henry Dawson 1869-1906 *ChhPo, –S1, DcNaB S2*

Lowry, Lois *BioIn 15, –17*

Lowry, Lois 1937- *Au&Arts 5, AuBYP 2S, –3, BioIn 13, ChlFicS, ChlLR 6, ConAu 69, –13NR, –43NR, DcLB 52, FifBJA, MajAI, SmATA 23, –70, –3AS, TwCChW 89, TwCYAW, WrDr 90, –92*

Lowry, Lois Hammersberg 1937- *DcAmChF 1960*

Lowry, Lois Hammersberg 1937- *DcAmChF 1985, WrDr 94*

Lowry, Peter 1953- *AuBYP 2S, –3, BioIn 10, ConAu 49, SmATA 7*

Lowther, George F 1913-1975 *BioIn 10, –14, ConAu 57, SmATA 30N*

Lozansky, Edward D 1941- *BioIn 15, –17, SmATA 62*

Lozansky, Edward Dmitry 1941- *WhoE 93*

Lozier, Herbert 1915- *BioIn 13, ConAu 49, SmATA 26*

Lubell, Cecil 1912- *AuBYP 2, –3, BioIn 7, –10, BkP, ConAu 9R, –4NR, FourBJA, SmATA 6*

Lubell, Winifred 1914- *AuBYP 3*

Lubell, Winifred Milius 1914- *AuBYP 2, BioIn 5, –7, –8, –10, BkP, ConAu 49, FourBJA, IlsCB 1946, –1957, –1967, SmATA 6*

Lubin, Leonard *MajAI*

Lubin, Leonard B 1943- *BioIn 15, –16, ConAu 115, –125, –38NR, IlsCB 1967, MajAI, SmATA 37, –45*

Lucas, Edward Verrall 1868-1938 *BioIn 2, –6, –8, –10, –12, –17, CarSB, Chambr 3, ChhPo, –S1, –S2, DcLEL, DcNaB 1931, EvLB, LongCTC, ModBrL, NewC, OxCChiL, OxCEng 67, –85, PenC ENG, REn, SmATA 20, Str&VC, TelT, TwCA, –SUP, TwCWr, WhoChL, WhoLA*

Lucas, Eileen 1956- *SmATA 76*

Lucas, George *BioIn 14, –15, –16, –17, LesBEnT 92, TwCSFW 86, –91*

Lucas, George 1944- *Au&Arts 1, CelR 90, ConAu 30NR, ConTFT 4, –11, EncSF 93, IntMPA 92, IntWW 89, –91, ScF&FL 92, ScFSB, SmATA 56, Who 92, WhoAm 86, WorFDir 2, WrDr 86*

Lucas, George 1945- *BenetAL 91, HalFC 88, IntMPA 86, –88, NewEScF*

Lucas, George, Jr. 1944- *WorAlBi*

Lucas, Jannette May 1885- *BioIn 2, JBA 51*

Lucas, Jerry 1940- *BioIn 4, –6, –7, –8, –9, –10, –14, ConAu 108, CurBio 72, NewYTBE 72 SmATA 33*

Lucas, John 1937- *ConAu 37R, –14NR, –32NR, IntAu&W 77, –82, WrDr 76, –80, –82, –84, –86, –88, –90, –92, –94*

Lucas, Mary Seymour 1912- *AnCL*

Lucas, Victoria *ConAu 34NR, InWom SUP, MajTwCW, TwCYAW*

Luce, Celia 1914- *BioIn 15, ConAu 61, SmATA 38*

Luce, Willard 1914- *BioIn 15, ConAu 61, SmATA 38, WhoWest 80, –82, –84*

Luckhardt, Mildred Corell 1898- *AuBYP 2S, –3, BioIn 10, ConAu 13R, ForWC 70, IntAu&W 77, –82, SmATA 5, WhoAmW 77*

Luckock, Elizabeth 1914- *AuBYP 2S, –3, ConAu 21R*

Ludden, Allen d1981 *LesBEnT 92*

Ludden, Allen 1918?-1981 *AnObit 1981, BioIn 12, –13, ConAu 104, LesBEnT, NewYTBS 81, SmATA 27N, WhScrn 83*

Ludel, Jacqueline 1945- *AmMWSc 86, –89, –92, BioIn 17, IntAu&W 86, –89, SmATA 64, WhoAmW 91*

Ludlow, Geoffrey *ConAu 128, SmATA X, WrDr 86, –88, –90, –92*
Main entry: Meynell, Laurence Walter

Ludlum, Mabel Cleland *ConAu X, SmATA 5*
Main entry: Widdemer, Mabel Cleland

Ludovici, Laurence James 1910- *ConAu 21R, –X, WrDr 80*

Ludovico *DcAmChF 1960*

Ludwig, Charles Shelton 1918- *ConAu 9R, –5NR, –20NR, –42NR, WhoRel 75, –77*

Ludwig, Helen *BioIn 14, IlsBYP, SmATA 33*

Ludwig, Lyndell 1923- *BioIn 17, ConAu 38NR, SmATA 63*

Lueders, Edward George 1923- *AuBYP 2S, –3, BioIn 12, ChhPo S1, ConAu 13R, DrAP 75, DrAS 74E, –78E, –82E, SmATA 14, WhoAm 74, –76, –78, –80, –82, –84, –86, –88, –90, –92, –94, WhoUSWr 88, WhoWrEP 89, –92*

Luenn, Nancy 1954- *BioIn 16, ConAu 39NR, ScF&FL 92, SmATA 51*

Lufkin, Raymond H 1897- *BioIn 1, –5, –15, IlsBYP, IlsCB 1744, –1946, SmATA 38*

Lugard, Flora Louisa Shaw
Main entry: Shaw, Flora Louisa

Lugard, Flora Louisa Shaw 1852-1929 *BioIn 1, –12, SmATA 21*

Lugeba, Bonnie 1929- *OxCChiL*

Luger, Harriett Mandelay 1914- *ConAu 45, –1NR, SmATA 23*

Luginbuhl, Edna *AuBYP 2S, –3*

Luhrmann, Winifred B 1934- *BioIn 11, ConAu 61, SmATA 11*

Luis, Earlene W 1929- *BioIn 11, ConAu 61, SmATA 11*

Lukas, J Anthony 1933- *AmAu&B, AuBYP 2S, –3, BioIn 9, –10, –11, –13, –14, –15, –17, BlueB 76, ConAu 49, –2NR, –19NR, CurBio 87, IntAu&W 91, MajTwCW, WhoAm 74, –76, –78, –80, –82, –84, –86, –88, –90, –92, –94, WhoE 86, –89, –91, WrDr 88, –90, –92*

Lukas, Jay Anthony 1933- *WrDr 94*

Lum, Peter *AnCL, AuBYP 2, BioIn 7, –8, –10, ConAu X, IntAu&W 77X, –82X, SmATA 6, WrDr 76, –80, –82, –84*
Main entry: Crowe, Bettina Lum

Lum, Peter 1911- *AuBYP 3*

Lumn, Peter *AuBYP 2, –3*

Lund, Doris Herold 1919- *BioIn 11, ChhPo S2, ConAu 17R, ForWC 70, IndAu 1917, IntAu&W 77, SmATA 12*

Lundbergh, Holger *AuBYP 2S, –3*

Lunn, Arnold 1888?-1974 *Au&Wr 71, BioIn 1, –2, –3, –4, –5, –8, –10, BkC 4, CathA 1930, ChhPo S2, ConAu 49, –81, NewYTBS 74, ObitOF 79, ObitT 1971, Who 74, WhoChL, WhoLA, WhoWor 74*

Lunn, Carolyn *BioIn 17*

Lunn, Carolyn 1960- *SmATA 67*

Lunn, Carolyn Kowalczyk 1960- *WrDr 94*

Lunn, Janet 1928- *BioIn 9, –10, CaW, ChlLR 18, ConAu 33R, –22NR, DcChlFi, OxCCan SUP, OxCCanL, Profile 1, ScF&FL 92, SixBJA, SmATA 4, –68, –12AS, TwCChW 89, WhoCanL 85, –87, –92, WhoWrEP 89, WrDr 90, –92*

Lunn, Janet Louise Swoboda 1928- *MajAI, WhoWrEP 92, WrDr 94*

Lunt, Elizabeth Graves 1922- *ConAu 33R*

Lupoff, Dick
Main entry: Lupoff, Richard Allen

Lupoff, Dick 1935- *SmATA X*

Lupoff, Richard A *IntvTCA 2*

Lupoff, Richard A 1935- *BioIn 17, ConAu 21R, -9NR, -25NR, ConSFA, NewEScF, ScF&FL 92, ScFSB, SmATA 60, TwCSFW 86, -91, WhoSciF, WrDr 84, -86, -88, -90, -92*

Lupoff, Richard Allen 1935- *EncSF 93, IntAu&W 91, WrDr 94*
Pseud./variant:
Hamelt, Ova
Lupoff, Dick
O'Donnell, Dick
Pascudniak, Pascal
Steele, Addison, II

Lurie, Alison *BioIn 14, -15, -17, DrAPF 87, -89, -91, -93, IntAu&W 89, -91, IntvTCA 2*

Lurie, Alison 1926- *ArtclWW 2, Benet 87, BenetAL 91, BlmGWL, CelR 90, ConLC 39, ConNov 86, -91, CurBio 86, CyWA 89, FemiCLE, InWom SUP, IntAu&W 86, IntWW 89, -91, MagSAmL, MajTwCW, ScF&FL 92, SmATA 46, Who 88, -92, WhoAm 86, -88, -90, -92, -94, WhoAmW 87, -89, -91, -93, WhoE 86, -89, WhoUSWr 88, WhoWrEP 89, -92, WorAlBi, WrDr 86, -88, -90, -92, -94*

Lurie, Alison, Prof 1926- *Who 90*

Lurie, Morris 1938- *DcChlFi, SmATA 72*

Lustig, Arnost *BioIn 16*

Lustig, Arnost 1926- *Au&Arts 3, BioIn 11, CasWL, ConAu 69, ConLC 56, ConWorW 93, EncWL 2, IntAu&W 77, -82, -89, -91, IntWW 74, -75, -76, -77, -78, -79, -80, -81, -82, -83, -89, -91, LiExTwC, ModSL 2, SmATA 56, TwCWr, WhoWor 74, -84, -87, -89, -91, -93*

Lustig, Loretta 1944- *BioIn 15, SmATA 46*

Lutgen, Kurt 1911- *AuBYP 2S, -3, IntAu&W 82*

Luther, Frank 1905- *NewGrDA 86*

Luther, Frank 1905-1980 *BioIn 1, -2, -12, -13, ConAu 102, NewYTBS 80, SmATA 25N, WhScrn 83*

Luther, Martin *TwCSFW 86*

Luther, Martin 1483-1546 *AnCL, Baker 84, -92, Benet 87, BbD, BiD&SB, BioIn 1, -2, -3, -4, -5, -6, -7, -8, -9, -10, -11, -12, -13, -14, -15, -16, -17, BlmGEL, CasWL, ChhPo, -S1, CyEd, DcBiPP, DcEuL, Dis&D, EncPaPR 91, EuAu, EuWr 2, EvEuW, GrFLW, LitC 9, LongCEL, LuthC 75, McGEWB, NewC, NewOxM, OxCEng 67, -85, OxCGer 76, -86, OxCMus, PenC EUR, PoChrch, RAdv 13-4, RComWL, REn, WhDW, WorAlBi, WorAl*

Luttrell, Guy L 1938- *BioIn 13, ConAu 97, SmATA 22*

Luttrell, Ida 1934- *BioIn 14, -15, ConAu 110, -27NR, SmATA 35, -40*

Lutyens, Mary *TwCRHW 90*

Lutyens, Mary 1908- *Au&Wr 71, BioIn 5, -14, ConAu 25R, IntAu&W 77, -82, -86, -89, -91, Who 74, -82, -83, -85, -88, -90, -92, WhoWor 74, WrDr 76, -80, -82, -84, -86, -88, -90, -92, -94*

Lutz, Frank Eugene 1879-1943 *BioIn 5, -7, -9, CurBio 44, DcNAA, InSci, ObitOF 79, WhAm 2*

Lutz, John *IntvTCA 2*

Lutz, John 1939- *BioIn 14, ConAu 65, -9NR, -24NR, ScF&FL 92, TwCCr&M 80, -85, -91, WrDr 82, -84, -86, -88, -90, -92*

Lutz, John Thomas 1939- *WrDr 94*

Lutzeier, Elizabeth 1952- *SmATA 72*

Lutzker, Edythe d1991 *NewYTBS 91*

Lutzker, Edythe 1904- *AmMWSc 76P, -82, -86, -89, -92, BioIn 10, ConAu 37R, DrAS 74H, -78H, -82H, IntAu&W 77, -82, -86, -89, SmATA 5, WhoAmW 77, -81, -83, -85, -87, -89, WhoE 85, -86, -89, WhoWor 87, -89, WrDr 76, -80, -82, -84, -86, -88, -90*

Lutzker, Edythe 1904-1991 *BioIn 17, ConAu 135*

Lux, Donald Gregory 1924- *LEduc 74*

Luzzati, Emanuele 1921- *BioIn 5, -8, -10, ConAu 29R, ConDes 84, -90, IlsCB 1957, -1967, SmATA 7, TwCChW 78, WhoOp 76, WhoWorJ 72, -78, WorECar*

Luzzatto, Paola 1938- *BioIn 15, SmATA 38*

Lyall, Dennis *IlsBYP*

Lydon, Michael 1942- *BioIn 10, -11, ConAu 85, SmATA 11*

Lydon, Michael Clery 1942- *WhoE 93*

Lyfick, Warren *BioIn 13, ConAu X, SmATA X*
Main entry: Reeves, Lawrence F

Lyford-Pike, Margaret Prudence 1911- *WrDr 76, -80*

Lyle, Katie Letcher *DrAPF 87, –89, –91, –93*

Lyle, Katie Letcher 1938- *BioIn 11, –16, ConAu 49, –29NR, DrAPF 83, –85, SmATA 8, TwCYAW*

Lyles, Vina Honish 1935- *ConAu 9R*

Lyman, Susan E 1906-1976 *AuBYP 3*

Lyman, Susan Elizabeth 1906?-1976 *AuBYP 2, BioIn 8, –11, ConAu 69*

Lynch, Lorenzo 1932- *BioIn 10, –16, BlkAuIl, –92, ConAu 29R, SmATA 7*

Lynch, Lorenzo A, Sr. *WhoBlA 94*

Lynch, Lorenzo A, Sr. 1932- *WhoBlA 85*

Lynch, Marietta 1947- *BioIn 13, ConAu 106, SmATA 29*

Lynch, Patricia *InWom SUP*

Lynch, Patricia 1898-1972 *BiDIrW, DcIrB 88, TwCChW 89*

Lynch, Patricia Nora 1898-1972 *Au&Wr 71, BioIn 3, –4, –6, –8, –10, –11, BkC 5, CathA 1952, ConAu P-1, DcIrL, DcIrW 1, OxCChiL, SmATA 9, TwCChW 78, –83, WhoChL*

Lynch, Patrick B 1927- *ConAu 9R*

Lyndon, Barre 1896-1972 *FilmgC, HalFC 84, –88*

Lynds, Dennis *DrAPF 87, –89, –91, –93, TwCCr&M 91*

Lynds, Dennis 1924- *Au&Wr 71, BioIn 14, –15, –16, ConAu 1R, –6NR, –22NR, DrAPF 83, –85, EncMys, EncSF 93, IntAu&W 86, –89, –91, ScF&FL 92, SmATA 37, –47, TwCCr&M 80, –85, WhoUSWr 88, WhoWrEP 89, –92, WrDr 82, –84, –86, –88, –90, –92, –94*
Pseud./variant:
Arden, William
Carter, Nick
Collins, Michael
Crowe, John
Dekker, Carl
Grant, Maxwell
Sadler, Mark

Lyngseth, Joan
Main entry: Davies, Joan

Lynn, Mary *ConAu X, SmATA X*
Main entry: Brokamp, Marilyn

Lynn, Patricia *AuBYP 2, –3, ConAu X, SmATA X*
Main entry: Watts, Mabel Pizzey

Lyon, Elinor 1921- *BioIn 10, ConAu 25R, IntAu&W 77X, SmATA 6, TwCChW 89, WrDr 76, –80, –82, –84, –86, –88, –90, –92, –94*
Pseud./variant:
Wright, Elinor Bruce

Lyon, George Ella *DrAPF 87, –89, –91, –93*

Lyon, George Ella 1949- *AuBYP 3, BioIn 17, ConAu 120, DcAmChF 1985, LiHiK, SmATA 68, WhoUSWr 88, WhoWrEP 89, –92*

Lyon, Jessica *AuBYP 2, –3, ConAu X, IntAu&W 77X, OhA&B*
Main entry: DeLeeuw, Cateau Wilhelmina

Lyon, Lyman R *AuBYP 3, ConAu X, EncSF 93, IntAu&W 91X, SmATA X*
Main entry: DeCamp, L Sprague

Lyons, Arthur *BioIn 14*

Lyons, Arthur 1946- *ConAu 29R, –12NR, –35NR, IntAu&W 91, TwCCr&M 85, –91, WrDr 86, –88, –90, –92, –94*

Lyons, Dorothy M 1907- *ConAu 24NR*

Lyons, Dorothy Marawee 1907- *AmAu&B, BioIn 9, ConAu 1R, ForWC 70, IntAu&W 82, –91, SmATA 3, WrDr 76, –80, –82, –84, –86, –88, –90, –92, –94*

Lyons, Grant *DrAPF 87, –89, –91, –93*

Lyons, Grant 1941- *BioIn 14, ConAu 41R, –15NR, DrAPF 83, –85, SmATA 30*

Lyons, John H d1986 *BioIn 15*

Lyons, John H 1919- *BiDAmL, WhoAm 76, –78, –80, –82, –84, –86, WhoE 81, –83, –85*

Lyons, John H 1919-1986 *WhAm 9*

Lyons, Marcus *MajTwCW, SmATA 66*
Main entry: Blish, James

Lystad, Mary 1928- *BioIn 11, ConAu 65, –10NR, –26NR, SmATA 11, WhoAmW 77*

Lystad, Mary Hanemann 1928- *WhoAm 90, –92, –94*

Lytle, Ruby 1917- *ConAu P-1, ForWC 70*

Lyttle, Richard B 1927- *AuBYP 2S, –3, BioIn 13, ConAu 33R, –13NR, SmATA 23*

Lytton, Edward G E Lytton Bulwer- 1803-1873 *Alli, –SUP, BiD&SB, BioIn 1, –2, –5, –9, –10,*

–11, –12, –13, BritAu 19, CasWL, CelCen, ChhPo, –S2, DcEnA, DcEuL, DcLEL, DcNaB, –C, Dis&D, EvLB, HsB&A, LongCEL, NewC, OxCEng 67, OxCThe 67, –83, PenC ENG, REn, SmATA 23, TelT
Pseud./variant:
Caxton, Pisistratus

Lytton, Edward George E Lytton Bulwer- 1803-1873 *OxCAmT 84*

Lytton, Edward George Earle Lytton Bulwer- 1803-1873 *BlmGEL*

M

Maar, Leonard 1927- *BioIn 14, ConAu 106, SmATA 30*

Maartens, Maretha 1945- *SmATA 73*

Maas, Julie *ChhPo S1, IlsBYP*

Maas, Selve *BioIn 12, ConAu 69, SmATA 14*

Mabery, D L 1953- *ConAu 121, SmATA 53*

Mabie, Hamilton Wright 1845?-1916 *Alli SUP, AmAu&B, AnCL, BenetAL 91, BbD, BiD&SB, CarSB, ChhPo, –S1, –S2, DcAmAu, DcLB 71, DcNAA, HarEnUS, OxCAmL 65, –83, REnAL, TwCA, –SUP, WhAm 1*

Mac *ConAu 128, –X, IntAu&W 82X, SmATA X*
Main entry: MacManus, Seumas

MacAgy, Douglas G 1913-1973 *AuBYP 2, –3, BioIn 7, –10, CanWW 70, ConAu 102, NewYTBE 73, WhAm 6, WhoAmA 73, –80N, –82N, WhoSSW 73*

Macagy, Douglas Guernsey *WhoAmA 86N*

Macagy, Douglas Guernsey 1913-1973 *WhoAmA 89N, –91N*

MacAodhagain, Eamon *ConAu X, SmATA X*

MacArthur, David Wilson 1903- *Au&Wr 71, ConAu 9R, Who 74, –82, WhoWor 78, WrDr 76, –80, –82*

MacArthur, Douglas, II 1909- *BioIn 3, –4, –11, BlueB 76, CurBio 54, DcAmDH 80, –89, IntWW 74, –75, –76, –77, –78, –79, –80, –81, –82, –83, –89, –91, IntYB 80, –81, –82, WhoAm 74, –76, WhoAmP 73, –75, –77, WhoE 91, WhoGov 72, WhoWor 74, –78*

Macarthur-Onslow, Annette 1933- *AuBYP 3*

MacArthur-Onslow, Annette Rosemary 1933- *AuBYP 2S, BioIn 12, –13, ConAu 102, IlsCB 1967, SmATA 26*

Macaulay, Doctor 1817-1902 *CarSB*

Macaulay, David 1945- *DcLB 61*

Macaulay, David 1946- *BestSel 89-2, ChlLR 14, ConAu 34NR, IntAu&W 91, ScF&FL 92, SmATA 46, WrDr 90, –92*

Macaulay, David Alexander 1946- *AuBYP 2S, BioIn 11, –12, –13, ChlLR 3, ConAu 53, –5NR, EncSF 93, FifBJA, IlsCB 1967, MajAI, SmATA 27, –72, WhoAm 82, –92, WhoAmA 80, –82, –84, –86, –91, WhoE 81, –83, WrDr 76, –80, –82, –84, –94*

Macauley, David Alexander 1946- *AuBYP 3, WhoAmA 89*

MacAvoy, R A 1949- *ScF&FL 92, TwCSFW 91*

MacAvoy, Roberta Ann 1949- *EncSF 93, TwCYAW*

MacBean, Dilla Whittemore 1895- *AuBYP 2, –3, BioIn 2, ConAu 5R, ForWC 70*

MacBeth, George *IntvTCA 2*

Macbeth, George 1932- *AuBYP 3, Benet 87, CamGLE, ConPo 91, EngPo, IntAu&W 91, MajTwCW, ModBrL S2, RAdv 13-1, WrDr 86, –88, –90, –92*

Macbeth, George 1932-1992 *AnObit 1992, ScF&FL 92*

MacBeth, George Mann 1932- *AuBYP 2S, BioIn 8, –9, –10, ChhPo S2, ConAu 25R, ConLC 2, –5, –9, ConPo 70, –75, –80, –85, DcLB 40, IntAu&W 82, ModBrL S1, –S2, OxCEng 85, RAdv 1, SmATA 4, Who 74, –82, –83, –85, –88, –90, –92, WorAu 1950, WrDr 76, –80, –82, –84, –94*

MacBeth, George Mann 1932-1992 *ConAu 136, SmATA 70*

MacBride, Maud Gonne *IlsCB 1744, ObitOF 79*
Main entry: Gonne, Maud

MacBride, Maud Gonne 1865-1953 *DcIrB 88*

MacBride, Maud Gonne 1866-1953 *BioIn 16, -17*

MacBride, Roger Lea 1929- *AuBYP 2S, -3, BioIn 11, ConAu 81, IntAu&W 77, WhoAmP 77, -81, -83, -85, -87, -89, -91, -93*

MacCann, Donnarae 1931- *BiDrLUS 70, ChhPo S2, ConAu 45, -1NR, WhoAmW 77*

MacClain, George *IlsBYP*

MacClintock, Dorcas 1932- *AuBYP 2S, -3, BioIn 11, ConAu 57, -6NR, SmATA 8, WhoAmA 78, -80, -82, -84, -86, -89, -91*

MacCloskey, Monro 1902- *ConAu 9R, -5NR*

Maccloud, Malcolm *DcAmChF 1960*

MacDonald, Alexander 1878-1917 *OxCAusL*

Macdonald, Alexander, Jr. 1936- *AmMWSc 86*

MacDonald, Amy 1951- *ConAu 135, SmATA 76, WrDr 94*
Pseud./variant:
Tremens, Del

MacDonald, Anne Elizabeth Campbell Bard 1908-1958 *MajAI*

MacDonald, Anson *AuBYP 2, -3, ConAu X, EncSF 93, MajAI, MajTwCW, SmATA 69, -X*
Main entry: Heinlein, Robert A

MacDonald, Betty *MajAI*

MacDonald, Betty 1908- *AuBYP 3*

MacDonald, Betty 1908-1958 *BenetAL 91, ConAu 136, FemiCLE*

MacDonald, Betty Heskett 1908-1958 *AmAu&B, AuBYP 2, BioIn 1, -2, -3, -4, -5, -7, -11, CurBio 46, -58, EvLB, LongCTC, REnAL, TwCA SUP, WhAm 3, YABC 1*

Macdonald, Blackie *ConAu X, SmATA X*
Main entry: Emrich, Duncan

Macdonald, Caroline 1948- *BlmGWL, DcChlFi, ScF&FL 92, TwCChW 89, WrDr 90, -92, -94*

Macdonald, Dwight 1906-1982 *AnObit 1982, Benet 87, BenetAL 91, BioIn 1, -4, -8, -10, -11, -13, -14, -15, ConAu 108, CurBio 83N, EncAJ, EncTwCJ, EncWB, JrnUS, NewYTBS 82, OxCAmL 83, RAdv 13-1, SmATA 29, -33N, WhAm 8, WhoAm 80, -82, WrDr 82, -84*

MacDonald, George 1824-1905 *Alli, -SUP, AuBYP 2, -3, Benet 87, BbD, BiD&SB, BioIn 1, -3, -4, -6, -7, -8, -9, -10, -11, -12, -13, -14, -15, -16, BritAu 19, CamGEL, CamGLE, CarSB, CasWL, Chambr 3, ChhPo, -S1, -S2, CmScLit, ConAu 106, -137, DcBiA, DcEnA, -A, DcEnL, DcEuL, DcLB 18, DcLEL, DcNaB S2, EncSF 93, EvLB, FamSYP, JBA 34, LongCTC, MajAI, NewC, Novels, OxCChiL, OxCEng 67, -85, PenC ENG, REn, RfGEnL 91, ScF&FL 92, ScFSB, SmATA 33, StaCVF, SupFW, TelT, TwCChW 78A, -83A, -89A, TwCLC 9, TwCSFW 91, WebE&AL, WhoChL, WhoHr&F, WrChl*

MacDonald, Golden *AmPB, AuBYP 2, -3, BioIn 14, -16, -17, ConAu 136, -X, JBA 51, MajAI, ObitOF 79, TwCChW 83, -89, YABC X*
Main entry: Brown, Margaret Wise

Macdonald, Grant Kenneth 1909- *BioIn 1, CanWW 70, -80, -81, -83, CreCan 1, WhoAmA 73*

MacDonald, Greville Matheson 1856- *BioIn 3, ChhPo, -S1, JBA 34*

MacDonald, James *IlsBYP*

Macdonald, Malcolm J Ross *ConAu X, IntAu&W 77X, WrDr 76*
Main entry: Ross Macdonald, Malcolm John

Macdonald, Marcia *AmAu&B, BioIn 12, DcNAA, TwCRHW 90, WhNAA, YABC X*
Main entry: Hill, Grace Livingston

Macdonald, Mary *ConAu X, SmATA X*
Main entry: Gifford, Griselda

MacDonald, Maryann 1947- *SmATA 72*

MacDonald, Roberta *ChhPo*

Macdonald, Shelagh 1937- *BioIn 13, ConAu 97, SmATA 25, WrDr 76, -80, -82, -84*

MacDonald, Suse *AuBYP 3*
Pseud./variant:
Oakes, Bill

Macdonald, Suse 1940- *BioIn 16, ConAu 125, SixBJA, SmATA 52, -54*

MacDonald, Thoreau 1901- *BioIn 1, -7, -10, CreCan 1, WhoAmA 73*

Macdonald, Zillah K 1885- *AuBYP 2, BioIn 7, -11, ConAu P-1, ForWC 70, SmATA 11, WhoAmW 75, -77*
Pseud./variant:
Zillah

MacDonald, Zillah Katherine 1885- *AmWomPl, AuBYP 3*

MacDonnell, Megan *SmATA 70*
Main entry: Stevens, Serita Deborah

MacDonough, Glen 1870-1924 *ASCAP 66, CarSB, CmpEPM, EncMT, NewCBMT, NotNAT B, OxCAmT 84*

MacDougal, John *ConAu 128, EncSF 93, MajTwCW, SmATA 66, TwCSFW 86, –91*
Main entry: Blish, James

MacDougall, Mary Katherine *IntAu&W 86, –89, WhoAmW 91, WhoRel 92, WhoWrEP 89, –92*

MacDougall, Mary Katherine Slate *ConAu 29R, –12NR, ForWC 70, WhoAmW 75, –77, WrDr 76, –80, –82, –84*

MacDougall, Ruth Doan *DrAPF 87, –89, –91, –93*

MacDougall, Ruth Doan 1939- *AmWomWr, ConAu 17R, –8NR, DrAPF 83, –85, ForWC 70, WhoAmW 74*

Mace, Elisabeth 1933- *BioIn 13, ConAu 77, –23NR, ScF&FL 92, SmATA 27, WrDr 80, –82, –84*

Mace, Jean 1815-1894 *BiD&SB, CarSB*

Mace, Katherine 1921- *AuBYP 2, –3, BioIn 7*

Mace, Varian 1938- *BioIn 16, SmATA 49*

Mace, Wynn *AuBYP 2, –3, BioIn 7*

MacEwan, John Walter Grant 1902- *BioIn 12, CanWW 70, –80, –81, –83, ConAu 41R, OxCCan SUP, WhoAm 74, WhoCan 73, WhoWor 74, WrDr 80*

MacEwan, John Walter Grant, Hon 1902- *CanWW 89*

MacEwen, Gwendolyn *ConDr 88B, IntvTCA 2*

MacEwen, Gwendolyn 1941- *ArtclWW 2, Benet 87, BioIn 15, CamGLE, ConAu 22NR, DcLB 53, SmATA 50, WhoCanL 87, WrDr 86, –88*

MacEwen, Gwendolyn 1941-1987 *AnObit 1987, BioIn 16, –17, ConAu 124, ConLC 55, FemiCLE, ScF&FL 92, SmATA 55N, WhoCanL 92, WorAu 1980*

MacFall, Russell Patterson 1903-1983 *ChhPo S2, ConAu 110, –P-1, IndAu 1917*

MacFarlan, Allan A 1892-1982 *AuBYP 2, –3, BioIn 7, –14, ConAu 107, SmATA 35*

MacFarlane, Iris 1922- *BioIn 11, SmATA 11*

MacFarlane, Stephen *AuBYP 3, ConAu X, EncSF 93, WhoChL*
Main entry: Cross, John Keir

MacGibbon, Jean 1913- *AuBYP 2S, –3, ConAu 97, IntAu&W 91, OxCChiL, TwCChW 78, –83, –89, WrDr 76, –80, –82, –84, –86, –88, –90, –92, –94*

MacGill, Harold 1877-1952 *ArtCS, BioIn 3, –5*

MacGregor, Ellen 1906-1954 *AuBYP 2, –3, BioIn 2, –3, –6, –7, –13, ConAu 111, –137, CurBio 54, MajAI, MorJA, OxCChiL, ScF&FL 92, SmATA 27, –39, TwCChW 78, –83, –89*

MacGregor, James Grierson 1905- *BioIn 8, ConAu 25R, –10NR, IntAu&W 91, OxCCan, –SUP, WrDr 76, –80, –82, –84, –86, –88, –90*

Macgregor, James Grierson 1934- *AmMWSc 86, –89, –92, WhoAm 86, –88, –90, –92, –94*

MacGregor-Hastie, Roy 1929- *AuBYP 3, ConAu 20NR*

MacGregor-Hastie, Roy Alasdhair Niall 1929- *AuBYP 2, BioIn 7, –8, –9, ConAu 1R, IntAu&W 89, –91, SmATA 3, WhoWor 80, –82, –87, –93, WrDr 76, –80*

Machetanz, Frederick 1908- *AmAu&B, BioIn 1, –5, –14, IlsBYP, IlsCB 1744, –1946, OhA&B, SmATA 34, WhoAmA 73*

Machetanz, Sara Burleson 1918- *ConAu 1R, ForWC 70*

Machin Goodall, Daphne *BioIn 15, ConAu 7NR, SmATA 37*

Machlis, Joseph 1906- *Au&Wr 71, Baker 84, –92, BioIn 13, ConAu 1R, –2NR, –22NR, IntWWM 90, NewGrDA 86, NewYTBS 82, WhoAmM 83, WhoEnt 92*

Maciel, Judi 1942- *ConAu 33R*
Pseud./variant:
Stewart, Judith Anne

MacInnes, Colin 1914-1976 *Benet 87, BioIn 8, –10, –13, –17, BlueB 76, CamGLE, ConAu 65, –69, –21NR, ConLC 4, –23, ConNov 72, –76, DcLB 14, DcLEL 1940, LongCTC, MajTwCW, ModBrL, –S1, Novels, ObitOF 79, OxCEng 85, PenC ENG, RAdv 1, RfGEnL 91, TwCRHW 90, Who 74, WhoWor 74, WorAu 1950, WrDr 76*

MacInnes, Helen d1985 *NewYTBS 85*

MacInnes, Helen 1907-1985 *AmAu&B, AnObit 1985, AuSpks, Au&Wr 71, Benet 87,*

BenetAL 91, BioIn 1, -2, -4, -7, -8, -10, -11, -12, -13, -14, -15, -17, BlueB 76, ConAu 1R, -117, -1NR, -28NR, ConLC 27, -39, ConNov 72, -76, CorpD, CrtSuMy, CurBio 67, -85N, DcLB 87, EncMys, FemiCLE, ForWC 70, IntAu&W 77, -82, IntWW 74, -75, -76, -77, -78, -79, -80, -81, -82, -83, MajTwCW, NewC, NewYTBS 85, Novels, REnAL, SmATA 22, -44N, TwCA SUP, TwCCr&M 80, -85, -91, WhAm 9, Who 74, WhoAm 74, -76, -78, -80, -82, -84, WhoAmW 74, -83, -85, WhoE 74, WhoSpyF, WhoWor 78, -80, -82, -84, WrDr 76, -80, -82, -84
Pseud./variant:
Highet, Helen

Macintyre, Elisabeth 1916- *AuWomWr, BioIn 1, -5, -12, ChhPo, ConAu 9R, -5NR, IlsBYP, IlsCB 1744, -1946, IntAu&W 77, OxCAusL, OxCChiL, SingR 1, SmATA 17, TwCChW 78, -83, -89, WrDr 80, -82, -84, -86, -88, -90, -92, -94*

Mack, Jerry *ConAu X*
Main entry: Johnson, Jerry Mack

Mack, John 1935- *BioIn 9*

Mack, Louise 1874-1935 *AuWomWr, BlmGWL, OxCAusL, OxCChiL, SingR 2*

Mack, Marjorie *AuBYP 3, ConAu X*
Main entry: Dixon, Marjorie

Mack, Stanley *BioIn 12, ConAu 85, FourBJA, IlsBYP, SmATA 17*

Mack, Stanley 1936- *EncACom*

Mackarness, Matilda 1826-1881 *CarSB*

Mackarness, Matilda Anne 1826-1881 *WomNov*

Mackay, Claire 1930- *ConAu 105, -22NR, DcChlFi, SmATA 40, TwCChW 89, WhoCanL 85, -87, -92, WhoWrEP 89, -92, WrDr 90, -92*

Mackay, Claire Bacchus 1930- *WrDr 94*

Mackay, Constance D'Arcy *AmWomPl*

Mackay, Constance D'Arcy d1966 *AmAu&B, BioIn 2, ChhPo, ConAu 102, JBA 34, -51, TwCChW 78, -83, -89, WhAm 4, WomWWA 14*

MacKay, David *AuBYP 2S, -3, ChhPo S1*

MacKay, Donald A *BioIn 5, IlsBYP*

MacKaye, Percy Wallace 1875-1956 *AmAu&B, AnMV 1926, BioIn 1, -2, -4, -12, Chambr 3, ChhPo, -S1, -S2, CnDAL, CnMD, CnThe, ConAmA, ConAmL, ConAu 113, DcLEL, EncWT, McGEWD 72, -84, ModAL, ModWD, NotNAT B, ObitOF 79, OxCAmL 65, -83, OxCThe 67, PlP&P, REn, REnAL, REnWD, SmATA 32, Str&VC, TwCA, -SUP, WhAm 3, WhNAA*

MacKellar, William 1914- *AuBYP 2, -3, BioIn 7, -9, ConAu 33R, -13NR, SmATA 4*

Macken, Walter 1915-1967 *AuBYP 2S, -3, BioIn 2, -4, -7, -10, -11, -13, -14, CnMD, ConAu 25R, -P-1, DcIrL, DcIrW 1, DcLB 13, ModIrL, NotNAT B, ObitOF 79, OxCChiL, SmATA 36, TwCChW 78, -83, -89, WhAm 4, WhScrn 83, -77, WhoHol B, WorAu 1950*

Macken, Walter 1916-1967 *BiDIrW, DcIrB 88*

Mackenzie, Alexander 1755?-1820 *BioIn 16, -17, WorAlBi*

Mackenzie, Alexander 1763-1820 *DcLB 99*

MacKenzie, Alexander 1764-1820 *BenetAL 91, Expl 93, WhNaAH*

Mackenzie, Alexander 1847-1935 *WorAlBi*

Mackenzie, Alexander, Sir 1755?-1820 *Alli, BbtC, BiDLA, BioIn 1, -4, -5, -6, -7, -8, -9, -10, -11, -15, BritAu 19, DcBiPP, DcCanB 5, DcLEL, DcNaB, HarEnUS, NewC, OxCAmH, OxCAmL 65, OxCCan, OxCCanL, OxCShps, REnAL, WhDW, WorAl*

Mackenzie, Alexander Campbell 1847-1935 *Baker 92*

MacKenzie, Christine Butchart 1917- *ConAu 13R*

Mackenzie, Compton *IntvTCA 2*

Mackenzie, Compton 1883-1972 *AuBYP 3, BioIn 16, -17, BlmGEL, DcLB 100, RfGEnL 91, ScFSB*

Mackenzie, Compton 1883-1973 *SpyFic*

Mackenzie, Compton, Sir 1883-1972 *AuBYP 2S, Au&Wr 71, Benet 87, BioIn 1, -2, -4, -6, -7, -8, -9, -10, -14, CamGLE, CasWL, CathA 1930, Chambr 3, ChhPo, -S1, -S2, ConAu 37R, -P-2, ConLC 18, ConNov 72, DcLB 34, DcLEL, DcNaB 1971, EncWL, EvLB, GrBr, HalFC 84, -88, LongCEL, LongCTC, ModBrL, NewC, NewYTBE 72, Novels, ObitOF 79, ObitT 1971, OxCEng 67, -85, PenC ENG, REn, TwCA, -SUP, TwCWr, WebE&AL, WhDW, WhAm 7, WhScrn 83, WhoChL, WhoLA, WhoSpyF, WhoTwCL*

Mackenzie, Compton, Sir 1883-1974 *CmScLit*

MacKenzie, Garry 1921- *BioIn 5, –8, IlsBYP, IlsCB 1946, –1957, SmATA 31*

MacKenzie, Jean 1928- *BioIn 13, ConAu 93, –103, OxCCan SUP, Profile 2, TwCChW 78, WrDr 80, –82, –84, –86, –88*

Mackenzie, Jeanette Brown *AuBYP 2, –3, BioIn 8*

MacKenzie, Jill Kelly 1947- *ConAu 142, SmATA 75*

Mackenzie, Kathleen Guy 1907- *Au&Wr 71, ConAu 5R, WrDr 76, –80*

Mackenzie, Midge *BioIn 10*

Mackenzie, Willard, Doctor *ConAu X*
Main entry: Stratemeyer, Edward L, Doctor

Mackenzie, William Lyon *DcChlFi*

Mackie, John 1862- *BbD, OxCCan*

Mackie, John 1862-1939 *StaCVF*

Mackie, Maron *SmATA X*

Mackie, Moron
Main entry: McNeely, Jeannette

Mackinlock, Duncan *ConAu X, WrDr 84*
Main entry: Watts, Peter Christopher

MacKinnon, Bernie 1957- *SmATA 69*

MacKinnon Groomer, Vera 1915- *SmATA 57*

MacKinstry, Elizabeth 1879-1956 *BioIn 1, –4, –6, –15, ChhPo, –S2, ConICB, IlsCB 1744, MorJA, SmATA 42, WhAmArt 85*

Mackler, Bernard 1934- *AmMWSc 73S, ConAu 21R, LEduc 74, WhoE 77*

Mackler, Tina *WhoAm 86, –88, –90, –92, –94*

Mackler, Tina 1919- *WhoAm 76, –78, –80, –82, –84, WhoAmW 75, –77*

MacKnight, Ninon 1908- *BioIn 5, IlsBYP, IlsCB 1946*
Pseud./variant:
Ninon

MacLachlan, Patricia *AuBYP 3, BioIn 15, ConAu 118, DcAmChF 1960, SmATA 42, TwCChW 89, WhoAmW 91, WrDr 90, –92, –94*

MacLachlan, Patricia 1938- *ChlLR 14, ConAu 136, DcAmChF 1985, MajAI, SixBJA, SmATA 62, WhoAm 94, WhoAmW 93*

MacLean, Alistair 1922- *AuBYP 2S, –3, BioIn 9, –10, –13, –14, BlueB 76, ConAu 57, ConLC 3, –13, DcLEL 1940, HalFC 84, IntAu&W 77, IntWW 74, –75, –76, –77, –78, –79, –80, –81, –82, –83, Novels, SmATA 23, TwCCr&M 80, –85, Who 74, –82, –83, –85, WhoAm 78, –80, –82, –84, –86, WhoSpyF, WhoWor 78, –80, –82, –84, –87, WorAlBi, WorAu 1950, WrDr 76, –80, –82, –84, –86*
Pseud./variant:
Stuart, Ian 1922-

MacLean, Alistair 1922-1987 *AnObit 1987, BioIn 15, –16, –17, ConAu 121, –28NR, ConLC 50, –63, CrtSuMy, EncSF 93, HalFC 88, MajTwCW, NewYTBS 87, SmATA 50N, TwCCr&M 91, TwCWW 91, WhAm 9*

MacLean, Hugh *OxCCan SUP*

MacLennan, Hugh *BioIn 15, –17, IntvTCA 2*

MacLennan, Hugh d1990 *IntWW 91N, NewYTBS 90, Who 92N*

MacLennan, Hugh 1907- *Au&Wr 71, Benet 87, BenetAL 91, BioIn 1, –3, –4, –9, –10, –11, –12, BlueB 76, CamGLE, CaW, CanNov, CanWW 70, –80, –81, –83, –89, CanWr, CasWL, ConAu 5R, ConLC 2, ConNov 72, –76, –82, –86, CreCan 2, CurBio 46, CyWA 89, DcLB 68, EncWL 2, –SUP, IntAu&W 82, –89, –91, IntWW 79, –80, –81, –82, –83, –89, LongCTC, MajTwCW, NewC, Novels, OxCAmL 65, OxCCan, –SUP, OxCCanL, PenC ENG, RAdv 1, REn, REnAL, TwCA SUP, TwCWr, WebE&AL, WhDW, Who 74, –82, –83, –85, –88, –90, WhoAm 74, –80, –82, –84, –88, –90, WhoCan 73, WhoCanL 85, –87, WhoWor 74, WrDr 76, –80, –82, –84, –86, –88, –90*

MacLennan, Hugh 1907-1990 *AnObit 1990, ConAu 33NR, CurBio 91N, MagSWL, RfGEnL 91, ScF&FL 92, WhAm 10, WhoCanL 92*

MacLeod, Beatrice 1910- *AuBYP 2, –3, BioIn 7, –11, ConAmTC, ConAu P-1, ForWC 70, SmATA 10, WhoAmW 77*

MacLeod, Charlotte 1922- *BioIn 13, –14, ConAu 21R, –18NR, –40NR, CrtSuMy, DcAmChF 1960, IntAu&W 91, ScF&FL 92, SmATA 28, TwCCr&M 85, –91, TwCRHW 90, WhoAmW 91, –93, WrDr 84, –86, –88, –90, –92*
Pseud./variant:
Craig, Alisa
Hughes, Matilda

MacLeod, Charlotte Matilda 1922- *WrDr 94*

MacLeod, Doug 1959- *BioIn 17, IntAu&W 86, SmATA 60*

MacLeod, Ellen Jane *IntAu&W 86, WrDr 86, -88, -90, -92, -94*

MacLeod, Ellen Jane 1916- *Au&Wr 71, BioIn 12, ConAu 5R, -3NR, IntAu&W 77, -89, SmATA 14, WrDr 76, -80, -82, -84*

MacLeod, Ellen Jane 1918- *IntAu&W 82, -91*
Pseud./variant:
Anderson, Ella

Macleod, Fiona *BbD, BiD&SB, BioIn 12, BritAu 19, CamGLE, CasWL, Chambr 3, ChhPo, -S2, CmScLit, DcBiA, DcEnA A, DcLEL, DcNaB S2, EvLB, LongCTC, NewC, OxCAusL, OxCEng 85, RfGEnL 91, StaCVF, SupFW*

Macleod, Fiona 1855-1905 *SupFW*

MacLeod, Fiona 1856-1905 *EncO&P 2S1, -3*

MacLeod, Jean S 1908- *WrDr 94*

MacLeod, Jean Sutherland 1908- *Au&Wr 71, ConAu 9R, -3NR, IntAu&W 77, -82, -86, -89, -91, TwCRHW 90, WrDr 84, -86, -88, -90, -92*

MacLeod, Mary d1914 *ChhPo, -S2*

MacMahan, Horace Arthur, Jr. 1928- *AmMWSc 73P, -76P, -82, -86, -89, -92, LEduc 74, WhoMW 76, -78*

MacMahan, Horace Arthur, Jr. 1928- *WhoTech 84*

MacMahon, Bryan Michael 1909- *Au&Wr 71, BiDIrW, BioIn 1, -3, CathA 1952, ConAu 41R, DcIrW 1, IntAu&W 77, -82, -91, WhoWor 78, -80, -82, WrDr 76, -80, -82, -84, -86, -88, -90, -92, -94*

MacManus, James *AuBYP 3, ConAu X, SmATA X*
Main entry: MacManus, Seumas

MacManus, Seumas 1861-1960 *BiDIrW*

MacManus, Seumas 1869-1960 *AmAu&B, AnCL, AuBYP 2, -3, BioIn 1, -2, -4, -5, -6, -8, -13, BkC 5, CathA 1930, ChhPo, -S1, -S2, ConAu 93, -102, DcCathB, DcIrL, DcIrW 1, JBA 34, NewC, PoIre, SmATA 25, TwCA, -SUP, WhAm 4, -5, WhNAA*
Pseud./variant:
Mac
MacManus, James

MacManus, Seumas 1870-1960 *StaCVF*

MacMaster, Eve B 1942- *SmATA 46*

MacMillan, Annabelle *ConAu X, SmATA 2*
Main entry: Quick, Annabelle

Macmillan, Cyrus *OxCCan, OxCCanL*

MacMillan, Keith 1920- *CreCan 1*

MacMillan, Keith Campbell 1920- *CanWW 89*

MacMillan, William 1890- *WhNAA*

Macnamara, Ellen 1924- *ConAu 103, WrDr 76, -80, -82, -84*

MacNeill, James A *OxCCan SUP*

MacNutt, William Stewart 1908- *CanWW 70, DrAS 74H, OxCCan*

MacPeek, Walter G 1902-1973 *AuBYP 2S, -3, BioIn 9, -13, ConAu 41R, -P-2, SmATA 4, -25N, WhNAA*
Pseud./variant:
Jumpp, Hugo

MacPherson, Captain Angus *ChhPo S2*

Macpherson, Jean Jay 1931- *CanWW 89, CanWr, ConAu 5R, ConPo 70, -75, CreCan 1, DrAS 74E, IntAu&W 86, OxCCan, -SUP, WrDr 76, -80*

MacPherson, Margaret 1908- *AuBYP 2, BioIn 7, -11, BritCA, ConAu 49, FourBJA, SmATA 9, -4AS, TwCChW 78, -83, -89, WrDr 82, -84, -86, -88, -90, -92, -94*

MacPherson, Margaret L *AuBYP 3*

MacPherson, Thomas George 1915-1976 *AuBYP 2, -3, BioIn 8, -10, -14, ConAu 1R, -4NR, SmATA 30N, WhAm 7, WhoAm 76*
Pseud./variant:
Parsons, Tom

MacQuoid, Percy 1852-1925 *CarSB, NotNAT B*

MacQuoid, Percy Thomas 1852-1925 *DcVicP 2*

Macrae, Hawk *SmATA 8*
Main entry: Barker, Albert W

MacRae, Marion *OxCCan SUP*

Macrae, Travis *AuBYP 3, ConAu X, SmATA X*
Main entry: Feagles, Anita MacRae

MacRaois, Cormac 1944- *SmATA 72*

Macrow, Brenda G Barton 1916- *ConAu 9R*

Macumber, Mari *ConAu X, SmATA 5*
Main entry: Sandoz, Mari

MacVicar, Angus *EncSF 93*

MacVicar, Angus 1908- *Au&Wr 71, BioIn 11, -13, -15, ConAu 13R, -10NR, -30NR, IntAu&W 77, -89, -91, TwCChW 78, -83,*

–89, WrDr 76, –80, –82, –84, –86, –88, –90, –92, –94

Macy, William Hussey 1826-1891 *Alli SUP, CarSB, DcNAA*

Madden, Daniel Michael 1916- *ConAu 65*

Madden, Don 1927- *BioIn 8, –9, ConAu 25R, IlsBYP, SmATA 3, WhoE 74*

Madden, Mabra *AnCL*
Main entry: Bryan, Catherine

Maddison, Angela Mary *WrDr 86, –88, –90, –92*

Maddison, Angela Mary 1923- *Au&Wr 71, BioIn 11, ConAu 53, IntAu&W 77, SmATA 10, WrDr 76, –80, –82, –84*
Pseud./variant:
Banner, Angela

Maddock, Reginald 1912- *AuBYP 3*

Maddock, Reginald Bertram 1912- *AuBYP 2S, Au&Wr 71, BioIn 12, ConAu 81, SmATA 15, TwCChW 78, WrDr 80*

Madenski, Melissa Ann 1949- *SmATA 77*

Madhubuti, Safisha 1935- *BlkAuII 92*

Madian, Jon 1941- *AuBYP 2, –3, BioIn 11, ConAu 61, SmATA 9*

Madison, Arnold 1937- *AuBYP 2S, –3, BioIn 10, ConAu 21R, –9NR, DcAmChF 1960, SmATA 6*

Madison, Steve *IlsBYP*

Madison, Winifred *BioIn 10, ConAu 37R, SmATA 5*

Madlee, Dorothy *EncSF 93*

Madlee, Dorothy 1917-1980 *AuBYP 2S, –3, ConAu 17R, –10NR, ForWC 70, ScF&FL 92*

Maestro, Betsy 1944- *AuBYP 2S, –3, BioIn 14, –16, ConAu 61, –8NR, SixBJA, SmATA 30*

Maestro, Betsy C 1944- *ConAu 23NR, –37NR, MajAI, SmATA 59*

Maestro, Giulio 1942- *AuBYP 3, BioIn 16, ConAu 23NR, –37NR, IntAu&W 91, MajAI, SixBJA, SmATA 59, WrDr 86, –88, –90, –92, –94*

Maestro, Giulio Marcello 1942- *AuBYP 2S, BioIn 11, ChhPo S2, ConAu 57, IlsBYP, IlsCB 1967, SmATA 8, WhoAmA 78, –80, –82, –84, WrDr 80*

Maeterlinck, Maurice 1862-1949 *AtlBL, Benet 87, BbD, BiD&SB, BioIn 1, –2, –3, –4, –5, –6, –8, –9, –10, –11, –12, –13, –15, –17, BlmGEL, CamGWoT, CasWL, ChhPo, ClDMEL 47, CnMD, CnThe, ConAu 104, –136, CyWA 58, Dis&D, EncO&P 1, –2, –3, EncPaPR 91, EncWL, –2, EncWT, EuWr 8, EvEuW, GrFLW, GuFrLit 1, HalFC 84, –88, IntDcT 2, LongCTC, MajMD 2, McGEWB, McGEWD 72, –84, ModFrL, ModRL, ModWD, NewC, NobelP, NotNAT A, –B, ObitOF 79, OxCAmT 84, OxCEng 67, –85, OxCFr, OxCThe 67, –83, PenC EUR, PlP&P, RComWL, REn, REnWD, SmATA 66, TwCA, –SUP, TwCLC 3, TwCWr, WhDW, WhAm 2, WhoLA, WhoNob, WhoTwCL, WorAlBi, WorAl*

Magagna, Anna Maria *ChhPo S1*

Magee, Wes 1939- *ConAu 23NR, ConPo 91, IntAu&W 86, –89, –91, SmATA 64, WrDr 86, –88, –90, –92, –94*

Mager, Charles Augustus 1878-1956 *ArtCS, BioIn 4*
Pseud./variant:
Mager, Gus Watso

Mager, Gus Watso
Main entry: Mager, Charles Augustus

Maggio, Rosalie 1943- *SmATA 69*

Magid, Ken *BioIn 17, ConAu 128, SmATA 65*

Magnin, Etienne Nicolas 1922- *AmMWSc 73P, –82, –86, –89, –92*

Magnus, Erica 1946- *SmATA 77*

Magnussen, Karen 1952- *BioIn 10, –11, BlueB 76, InWom SUP, NewYTBE 73*

Magnusson, Magnus 1929- *ConAu 105, –23NR, IntAu&W 77, –82, –89, –91, Who 82, –83, –85, –88, –90, –92, WhoWor 80, –82, –84, –87, –89, WrDr 80, –82, –84, –86, –88, –90, –92, –94*

Magnusson, Magnus 1954- *WhoWor 89, –91*

Magorian, James *DrAPF 87, –89, –91, –93*

Magorian, James 1942- *BioIn 14, ConAu 102, –18NR, –40NR, DrAPF 83, –85, IntAu&W 82, –86, –91, IntWWP 82, SmATA 32, WhoMW 84, –86, –88*

Magorian, Michelle *TwCChW 89*

Magorian, Michelle 1947- *BioIn 16, –17, ConAu 135, MajAI, SixBJA, SmATA 67, TwCYAW, WrDr 94*

Magoun, Francis Peabody, Jr. 1895-1979? *AmAu&B, BioIn 12, ConAu 107, WhAm 7, WhoAm 74, –76, –78, –80*

Magubane, Peter 1932- *BioIn 14, –16, BlkAuIl, –92, ConPhot 88, IlBBlP, InB&W 85*

Maguire, Anne *ConAu X, IntAu&W 82X, SmATA X*
Main entry: Nearing, Penny

Maguire, Gregory 1954- *BioIn 13, ConAu 81, SmATA 28, TwCChW 89, WrDr 92, –94*

Maguire, Gregory 1955- *ScF&FL 92*

Maguire, Jack 1945- *SmATA 74*

Mahapatra, Jayanta *BioIn 17*

Mahapatra, Jayanta 1928- *BioIn 11, CamGLE, ConAu 73, –9AS, –15NR, –33NR, ConLC 33, ConPo 85, –91, IntAu&W 86, IntWWP 82, WorAu 1980*

Maher, John Edward 1925- *AmEA 74, AmMWSc 73S, –78S, ConAu 17R, WhoE 77, –91, WhoFI 92, –94*

Maher, Ramona 1934- *BioIn 11, ConAu 21R, –9NR, DcAmChF 1960, SmATA 13*

Mahlmann, Lewis *AuBYP 2S, –3*

Mahlqvist, Stefan 1943- *BioIn 14, ConAu 107, SmATA 30*

Mahon, Julia C 1916- *AuBYP 2S, –3, BioIn 11, ConAu 61, SmATA 11*

Mahony, Bertha *AmPB, ChhPo, –S1*
Pseud./variant:
Miller, Bertha Mahony

Mahony, Elizabeth Winthrop *AuBYP 3, SmATA 76*

Mahony, Elizabeth Winthrop 1948- *BioIn 11, ConAu 41R, SmATA 8*
Pseud./variant:
Winthrop, Elizabeth

Mahood, Kenneth 1930- *BioIn 12, –13, –14, ConAu 103, IlsCB 1967, SmATA 24*

Mahy, Margaret 1936- *Au&Arts 8, AuBYP 2S, –3, BioIn 12, ChhPo S2, ChlFicS, ChlLR 7, ConAu 69, –13NR, –30NR, –38NR, DcChlFi, FemiCLE, FourBJA, IntAu&W 91, MajAI, OxCChiL, ScF&FL 92, SmATA 14, –69, TwCChW 78, –83, –89, TwCYAW, WhoAm 92, –94, WrDr 80, –82, –84, –86, –88, –90, –92, –94*

Maiden, Cecil 1902-1981 *BioIn 16, SmATA 52*

Maiden, Cecil Edward 1902- *ConAu 73*

Maidoff, Ilka List 1935- *ConAu 5R, SmATA 6*
Pseud./variant:
List, Ilka Katherine

Maik, Henri *ConAu X, SmATA X*
Main entry: Hecht, Henri Joseph

Mail, Audrey Maureen 1924- *WrDr 76, –80, –82, –84, –86, –88, –90, –92, –94*

Maillet, Andree 1921- *CanWr, CreCan 2, OxCCan, –SUP, OxCCanL, WhoCanL 85, –87, –92*

Maillet, Antonine 1923- *OxCCanT*

Maillet, Antonine 1929- *BenetAL 91, BioIn 15, –16, –17, BlmGWL, CamGWoT, CanWW 89, ConAu 115, –120, ConLC 54, ConWorW 93, DcLB 60, FemiCLE, IntDcT 2, OxCCan SUP, OxCCanL, ScF&FL 92, WhoAmW 93, WhoCanL 85, –87, –92, WhoWor 87*

Maine, Trevor *ConAu 38NR, MajAI, SmATA 74*
Main entry: Catherall, Arthur

Maiorano, Robert 1946- *BiDD, BioIn 9, –12, ConAu 116, SmATA 43*

Mais, Stuart Petre Brodie 1885-1975 *Au&Wr 71, BioIn 3, –4, ConAu 57, –69, DcLEL, EvLB, IntAu&W 77, LongCTC, NewC, TwCA, –SUP, Who 74, WhoLA*

Maitland, Antony Jasper 1935- *BioIn 6, –8, –12, –13, ConAu 101, FourBJA, IlsBYP, IlsCB 1957, –1967, OxCChiL, SmATA 25, WhoWor 74*

Maitland, Julia Charlotte *Alli, –SUP, CarSB*

Maizel, Clarice Matthews 1919- *ConAu 9R*

Majerus, Janet 1936- *ConAu 65*

Majima, Setsuko *ChhPo S1*

Major, Charles 1856-1913 *AmAu&B, BenetAL 91, BiD&SB, BioIn 2, CarSB, DcAmAu, DcBiA, DcLEL, DcNAA, IndAu 1816, LongCTC, NotNAT B, OxCAmL 65, –83, REnAL, Str&VC, TwCA, WhAm 1*
Pseud./variant:
Caskoden, Edwin

Major, Henriette 1933- *BioIn 10, ConAu 109, OxCCan SUP, Profile 1, WhoCanL 85, –87, –92*

Major, Kevin 1949- *ChlLR 11, ConAu 21NR, DcChlFi, DcLB 60, IntAu&W 89, –91, TwCChW 89, WhoCanL 87, –92, WrDr 86, –88, –90, –92, –94*

Major, Kevin G 1949- *BioIn 13, ConAu 97, ConLC 26, OxCCanL, Profile 2, SmATA 32, TwCChW 83, WhoAm 82, -84, WhoCanL 85*

Major, Kevin Gerald 1949- *CanWW 89, ConAu 38NR, MajAI, TwCYAW, WhoAm 86, -88, -90, -92, -94, WhoWrEP 89, -92*

Makerney, Edna Smith 1921- *ConAu 61*

Maki, John McGilvrey 1909- *AmMWSc 73S, ConAu 109, WhoE 93*

Makie, Pam 1943- *SmATA 37*

Makower, Addie 1906- *ConAu 65*

Malavie, M J 1920- *ConAu 29R*

Malcolm, Dan *MajAI*

Malcolmson, Anne 1910- *AuBYP 3*

Malcolmson, Anne Elizabeth 1910- *AnCL, AuBYP 2, BioIn 6, -8, ChhPo S2, ConAu X, MorJA, SmATA 1*
Pseud./variant:
VonStorch, Anne B

Malcolmson, David 1899- *BioIn 10, ConAu 5R, SmATA 6, WhoWest 76, -78*

Male, David Arthur 1928- *ConAu 57*

Mali, Jane Lawrence 1937- *BioIn 15, -16, ConAu 114, -36NR, SmATA 44, -51*

Malkus, Alida Wright 1899- *AuBYP 3*

Malkus, Alida Wright Sims 1899?- *AuBYP 2, Au&Wr 71, BioIn 2, -7, ConAu 5R, JBA 34, -51, OxCCan*

Mallan, Lloyd 1914- *ConAu 5R*

Mallett, Anne 1913- *ConAu 49*

Mallett, Jerry J 1939- *SmATA 76*

Mallinson, Mavis *SingR 1*

Malloch, Douglas 1877-1938 *AmAu&B, ChhPo, -S1, -S2, DcNAA, MichAu 80, Str&VC, WhAm 1, WhNAA*

Mallory, Clare *SingR 1*

Mallowan, Agatha Christie *ConAu X, -37NR, MajTwCW, SmATA X*
Main entry: Christie, Agatha

Malmberg, Carl 1904- *BioIn 11, ConAu 33R, SmATA 9*
Pseud./variant:
Trent, Timothy

Malmgren, Dallin 1949- *BioIn 17, ConAu 133, SmATA 65, WrDr 94*

Malo, John W 1911- *BioIn 11, ConAu 33R, -12NR, SmATA 4*

Malocsay, Zoltan 1946- *ConAu 81*

Malone, Mary *AuBYP 2, -3, BioIn 7, ConAu 1R, -2NR*

Malone, Ruth *TwCCr&M 91*

Malone, Ruth 1918- *ConAu 93*

Maloney, Pat *AuBYP 2, -3, ConAu X*
Main entry: Markun, Patricia Maloney

Malory, Thomas *BioIn 16, BlmGEL, RfGEnL 91*

Malory, Thomas d1470? *WorAlBi*

Malory, Thomas d1471 *LitC 11*

Malory, Thomas 1410?-1471 *CnDBLB 1, SmATA 59*

Malory, Thomas, Sir *RAdv 13-1*

Malory, Thomas, Sir d1471 *CamGEL, CamGLE*

Malory, Thomas, Sir 1408?-1471 *Benet 87*

Malory, Thomas, Sir 1410?-1471? *Alli, AnCL, AtlBL, BbD, BiD&SB, BioIn 2, -3, -4, -5, -6, -7, -9, -10, -11, -12, -13, BritAu, BritWr 1, CarSB, CasWL, Chambr 1, CrtT 1, CyWA 58, DcBiPP, DcCathB, DcEnA, DcEnL, DcEuL, DcLEL, DcNaB, Dis&D, EvLB, LongCEL, McGEWB, MouLC 1, NewC, OxCChiL, OxCEng 67, -85, PenC ENG, RAdv 1, RComWL, REn, SmATA 33, WebE&AL, WhDW, WorAl*

Malot, Hector Henri 1830-1907 *AuBYP 2, -3, BbD, BiD&SB, BioIn 7, DcBiA, Dis&D, EvEuW, OxCChiL, OxCFr*

Maltby, Peg *SingR 1*

Maltese, Michael 1908?-1981 *BioIn 12, -13, ConAu 103, SmATA 24N*

Malvern, Corinne d1956 *WhoAmA 86N, -89N, -91N*

Malvern, Corinne 1905-1956 *BioIn 4, -14, ConAu 115, IlsBYP, JBA 51, SmATA 34, WhAmArt 85, WhoAmA 80N, -82N*

Malvern, Gladys d1962 *AmAu&B, AuBYP 2, -3, BioIn 2, -3, -6, -7, -13, ConAu 73, JBA 51, SmATA 23*

Pseud./variant:
Corbin, Sabra Lee
VonKlopp, Vahrah

Malzberg, Barry 1939- *AuBYP 3, IntAu&W 91, ScFSB, WrDr 86, -88, -90, -92*

Malzberg, Barry N 1939- *AuBYP 2S, BioIn 12, -13, ConAu 61, -4AS, -16NR, ConLC 7, DcLB 8, IntAu&W 77, NewEScF, RGTwCSF, ScF&FL 92, TwCCr&M 91, TwCSFW 86, -91, WhoE 77, WhoSciF, WrDr 84*
Pseud./variant:
O'Donnell, K M

Malzberg, Barry Nathaniel 1939- *WrDr 94*

Malzberg, Barry Norman 1939- *EncSF 93*

Mama G
Main entry: Davis, Grania

Mamlok, Gwyneth Leaver 1925- *Au&Wr 71, ChhPo*

Mammen, Edward William 1907- *AuBYP 2, -3, BioIn 7, DrAS 74E*

Manchel, Frank 1935- *AuBYP 2S, -3, BioIn 11, ConAu 37R, -14NR, DrAS 74E, -78E, -82E, IntAu&W 82, -91, ScF&FL 92, SmATA 10, WhoE 75, WhoEnt 92, WrDr 76, -80, -82, -84, -86, -88, -90, -92, -94*

Manchester, Harland 1898-1977 *BioIn 11, -12, ConAu 1R, -73, NatCAB 60*

Manchester, William 1922- *BenetAL 91, BestSel 89-2, ConAu 31NR, IntAu&W 86, IntWW 89, -91, MajTwCW, SmATA 65, Who 88, -90, -92, WhoAm 86, -88, -90, -92, -94, WhoEnt 92, WhoUSWr 88, WhoWor 87, -89, WhoWrEP 89, -92, WorAlBi, WrDr 86, -88, -90, -92, -94*

Mandel, Ellen *MedPD*

Mandel, Morris 1911- *ConAu 5R, -6NR*

Mandel, Oscar *DrAPF 87, -89, -91, -93*

Mandel, Oscar 1926- *ConAu 1R, -2NR, -21NR, DrAF 76, DrAPF 83, -85, DrAS 74E, -78E, -82E, IntAu&W 77, -89, WhoAm 74, WhoUSWr 88, WhoWest 92, -94, WhoWrEP 89, -92, WrDr 76, -80, -82, -84, -86, -88, -90, -92, -94*

Mandel, Sally 1944- *SmATA 64*

Mandelkorn, Eugenia Miller *AuBYP 3*

Mandelkorn, Eugenia Miller 1916- *ConAu 9R*
Pseud./variant:
Miller, Eugenia

Mandell, Muriel 1921- *BioIn 17, ConAu 9R, SmATA 63*

Mandell, Phyllis Levy *MedPD*

Mander, Anica Vesel 1934- *BioIn 11, ConAu 61, -8NR*

Mandino, Og 1923- *BioIn 10, ConAu 103, ScF&FL 92, WhoAm 74, -76, -78, -80, -82, -86, -88, -90, -92, -94, WhoUSWr 88, WhoWor 82, WhoWrEP 89, -92*

Mandry, Kathy *AuBYP 2S, -3*

Manes, Stephen *DrAPF 87, -89, -91, -93*

Manes, Stephen 1949- *AuBYP 3, ConAu 97, DrAPF 83, -85, ScF&FL 92, SmATA 40, -42*
Pseud./variant:
Pemsteen, Hans
Stephensen, A M

Manes, Stephen, Mel 1949-
Pseud./variant:
Starr, Ward And Murch, Mel

Manes, Stephen, Ward 1949-
Pseud./variant:
Murch, Mel And Starr, Ward

Manfred, Frederick Feikema *DrAPF 89, -91, -93, IntvTCA 2*

Manfred, Frederick Feikema 1912- *BenetAL 91, BioIn 4, -6, -7, -10, -11, -14, ConAu 5NR, IntAu&W 82, -86, -89, -91, SmATA 30, WhoAm 80, -82, -84, -90, -92, -94, WhoUSWr 88, WhoWrEP 89, -92, WrDr 82, -84*
Pseud./variant:
Feikema, Feike

Mangin, Marie-France 1940- *BioIn 16, SmATA 59*

Mangione, Jerre *DrAPF 87, -89, -91, -93*

Mangione, Jerre 1909- *AmAu&B, AmNov, BenetAL 91, BioIn 1, -2, -10, -11, ConAu 13R, -16NR, ConNov 72, -76, -82 -86, -91, CurBio 43, DrAF 76, DrAPF 83, -85, DrAS 74E, -78E, -82E, IntAu&W 77 -82, REnAL, SmATA 6, WhoAm 74, -76, -80, -82, -84, WorAu 1975, WrDr 76, -80, -82, -84, -86, -88, -90, -92*

Mangione, Jerre Gerlando 1909- *WhoAm 92, WrDr 94*

Mango, Cyril Alexander 1928- *DrAS 74H, -78H, -82H, Who 74, -82, -83, -85, -88, -92*

Mango, Cyril Alexander, Prof 1928- *Who 90*

Mango, Karin N *AuBYP 3*

Mango, Karin N 1936- *BioIn 16, ConAu 123, SmATA 52, WrDr 90, -92, -94*

Mangurian, David 1938- *BioIn 12, ConAu 57, -10NR, SmATA 14*

Manheim, Ralph d1992 *NewYTBS 92*

Manheim, Ralph 1907- *BioIn 8, -14, ConAu 115*

Manheim, Ralph 1907-1992 *AnObit 1992*

Manicas, Peter Theodore 1934- *ConAu 53, DrAS 74P, -78P, -82P*

Maniscalco, Joseph 1926- *BioIn 11, ConAu 5R, -8NR, SmATA 10*

Maniscalco, Joseph Stephen 1936- *WhoAm 86, -90, WhoIns 93*

Mankowitz, Wolf 1924- *BioIn 4, -5, -6, -8, -10, -12, -13, BlueB 76, ConAu 5NR, ConDr 82, -88, ConNov 82, -86, -91, ConTFT 11, DcLB 15, HalFC 84, -88, IntAu&W 82, -89, -91, IntMPA 81, -82, -84, -86, -88, -92, IntWW 79, -80, -81, -82, -83, -89, -91, NewYTBS 80, Novels, OxCChiL, ScF&FL 92, Who 82, -83, -85, -88, -90, -92, WhoThe 81, WhoWor 82, WrDr 82, -84, -86, -88, -90, -92*

Manley, Deborah 1932- *BioIn 13, ConAu 105, -22NR, SmATA 28*

Manley, Ruth *DcChlFi*

Manley, Seon *BioIn 15*

Manley, Seon 1921- *AuBYP 2S, -3, BioIn 12, ChlLR 3, ConAu 85, ScF&FL 92, SmATA 15, -2AS*

Mann, Arthur d1993 *NewYTBS 93*

Mann, Arthur 1922- *BlueB 76, ConAu 109, DrAS 74H, -78H, -82H, WhoAm 74, -76, -78, -80, -82, -84, -86, -88, -90, -92, WhoUSWr 88, WhoWor 78, -80, -82, -84, -87, -89, -91, -93, WhoWrEP 89, -92*

Mann, Arthur 1922-1993 *ConAu 140*

Mann, Avery *AuBYP 3*

Mann, Peggy *ASCAP 66, BioIn 3, -10, ConAu 25R, -10NR, -27NR, -35NR, DrAPF 83, -85, -87, -89, -91, IntAu&W 77, -82, -91, SmATA 6, WhoAm 92, WhoAmW 91, WrDr 76, -80, -82, -84, -86, -88, -90, -92, -94*

Mann, Peggy d1990 *WhAm 10*

Manners, Alexandra *ConAu 57, -X, IntAu&W 77X, -82X, TwCRHW 90, WrDr 76, -80, -82, -84, -86, -88, -90*
Main entry: Rundle, Anne

Mannetti, Lisa 1953- *ConAu 125, SmATA 51, -57*
Pseud./variant:
Kane, L A

Mannheim, Grete 1909- *BioIn 11, ConAu 9R, SmATA 10*

Manniche, Lise 1943- *BioIn 14, ConAu 107, -25NR, SmATA 31*

Mannin, Ethel Edith 1900- *Au&Wr 71, BioIn 1, -4, -5, -9, -10, -11, ConAu 53, ConNov 76, DcLEL, EvLB, IntAu&W 77, IntWW 74, -75, -76, -77, -78, LongCTC, NewC, PenC ENG, REn, TwCA, -SUP, Who 74, WrDr 76, -80*

Mannin, Ethel Edith 1900-1978 *InWom SUP*

Mannin, Ethel Edith 1900-1984 *DcNaB 1981*

Manning, Jack 1920- *ConAu 69, ICPEnP A, WhoAm 86, -88, -90, -92, -94, WhoE 83, -85, -86, -89*

Manning, Rosemary 1911- *AuBYP 2, -3, Au&Wr 71, BioIn 8, -10, -11, ConAu 1R, -1NR, IntAu&W 77, -82, -91, OxCChiL, SmATA 10, TwCChW 78, -83, -89, WorAu 1950, WrDr 76, -80, -86, -88, -90, -92, -94*
Pseud./variant:
Voyle, Mary

Manning, Rosemary 1911-1988 *ConAu 25NR, FemiCLE*

Manning, Stanley Arthur 1921- *ConAu 110, IntAu&W 77, -82, WrDr 80*

Manning-Sanders, Ruth 1888-1988 *AnObit 1988, FemiCLE, ScF&FL 92, TwCChW 89*

Manning-Sanders, Ruth 1895- *AuBYP 2S, -3, BioIn 9, -12, ChhPo, ConAu 73, IntAu&W 91, OxCChiL, SmATA 15, ThrBJA, TwCChW 78, -83, WrDr 80, -82, -84, -86, -88*

Manning-Sanders, Ruth 1895-1988 *BioIn 16, ConAu 126, -41NR, MajAI, SmATA 57, -73*

Mannix, Daniel P *AuBYP 3*

Mannix, Daniel P 1911-1984 *ScF&FL 92*

Mannix, Daniel Pratt 1911- *AuBYP 2S, BioIn 1, -2*

Mannon, Warwick
Main entry: Hopkins, Kenneth

Mannon, Warwick 1914-1988 *ScF&FL 92, SmATA X*

Manny, Louise *OxCCan SUP*

Manson, Beverlie 1945- *ConAu 113, SmATA 44, -57*

Mant, Alicia Catherine 1788?-1869 *OxCChiL*

Mantel, S G *AuBYP 2, -3, BioIn 8*

Mantinband, Gerda B 1917- *SmATA 74*

Mantle, Winifred Langford 1911- *Au&Wr 71, ConAu 13R, IntAu&W 77, -82, WrDr 76, -80, -82, -84*

Manton, Jo *AuBYP 2, ConAu X, SmATA 3*
Main entry: Gittings, Jo Manton

Manton, Jo 1919- *AuBYP 3*

Manton, Peter *ConAu X, LongCTC, MajTwCW, TwCCr&M 80, -85, -91*

Manuel, Don Juan 1281- *AuBYP 3*

Manuel, Don Juan 1282-1347? *AuBYP 2S, BiD&SB, DcSpL*

Manus, Willard 1930- *ConAu 108, -28NR, ConTFT 1, IntAu&W 86, NatPD 81, WhoEnt 92*

Manushkin, Fran 1942- *ScF&FL 92, SmATA 54*

Manushkin, Frances 1942- *BioIn 10, ConAu 49, SmATA 7*

Mapes, Mary A *ConAu X, IntAu&W 77X, -91X, SmATA 4, WrDr 76, -80, -82, -84, -86, -88, -90, -92*
Main entry: Ellison, Virginia Howell

Mapes, Mary A 1910- *WrDr 94*

Maples, Evelyn Palmer 1919- *ConAu 5R, -2NR, -17NR, ForWC 70, WhoAmW 77, WrDr 76, -80, -82, -84, -86, -88, -90, -92, -94*

Mapp, Alf Johnson, Jr. 1925- *Au&Wr 71, BioIn 6, -11, ConAu 1R, -1NR, DrAS 74H, -78H, -82H, IntAu&W 77, -86, -91, WhoAm 74, -76, -78, -80, -82, -84, -86, -88, -90, -92, -94, WhoSSW 73, WhoUSWr 88, WhoWor 78, -84, -87, -89, -91, -93, WhoWrEP 89, -92, WrDr 76, -80, -82, -84, -86, -88, -90, -92, -94*

Mara, Barney *AuBYP 2S, -3, ConAu 140, -X, SmATA 75, -X*
Main entry: Roth, Arthur J

Mara, Jeanette *ConAu X, -30NR, IntAu&W 77X, SmATA X*
Main entry: Cebulash, Mel

Mara, Thalia 1911- *Au&Wr 71, ConAu 9R, ForWC 70, WhoAmW 74*

Marabella, Madeline *AuBYP 2, -3, BioIn 8*

Marais, Josef 1905-1978 *ASCAP 66, AuBYP 2, -3, Baker 84, -92, BioIn 1, -7, -11, -13, ConAmC 76A, -82, ConAu 77, EncFCWM 69, OxCPMus, SmATA 24N, WhAm 7, WhoAm 74, -76, WhoWor 74*

Marasmus, Seymour *SmATA X*
Main entry: Rivoli, Mario

Marbach, Ethel *SmATA 76*
Main entry: Pochocki, Ethel Frances

Marble, Harriet Clement 1903-1975 *ConAu 73*

Marcatante, John 1930- *ConAu 25R, -10NR, LEduc 74, WhoE 74*

Marcatante, John Joseph 1930- *WhoE 86, -91, -93*

Marceau, Marcel *BioIn 14, -15, -16, NewYTBS 93*

Marceau, Marcel 1923- *BiE&WWA, BioIn 4, -5, -7, -9, -10, -11, -12, BioNews 74, CamGWoT, CelR 90, ConAu 85, CurBio 57, EncWB, EncWT, IntWW 74, -75, -76, -77 -78, -79, -80, -81, -82, -83, -89, -91, NewYTBE 73, NotNAT, OxCThe 67, -83, Who 82, -83, -85, -88, -90, -92, WhoAm 74, -76, -78, -80, -82, -84, -86, -88, -90, -92, -94, WhoCom, WhoEnt 92, WhoHol A, WhoWor 74, -78, -80, -82, -84, -87, -89, -91, -93, WorAlBi, WorAl, WorEFlm*

Marcelin, Pierre 1908- *BioIn 4, CasWL, ConAu 106, DcAfL, EncWL 2, ModBlW, ModFrL, TwCA SUP*

Marcelino *ConAu X, SmATA X*
Main entry: Agnew, Edith J

Marcellino, Fred 1939- *BioIn 17, SmATA 68, WhoAm 92, -94*

Marcet, Jane 1769-1858 *BioIn 5, -9, ContDcW 89, DcBiPP, DcNaB, FemiCLE, InSci, InWom SUP, OxCChiL, WhoEc 81, -86*

March, Carl *MajAI*

March, William *AmAu&B, CnDAL, ConAmA, ConAu X, DcLB 9, LongCTC, ModAL, ObitOF 79, OxCAmL 65, -83, REn, REnAL, TwCA SUP*
Main entry: Campbell, William Edward March

March, William 1893-1954 *BenetAL 91, DcLB 86*

Marchant, Bessie *WomNov*

Marchant, Bessie 1862-1941 *BioIn 8, -12, FemiCLE, OxCChiL, TwCChW 83, -89, WhoChL, YABC 2*

Marchant, Catherine *BlmGWL, ConAu X, -28NR, IntAu&W 91X, MajTwCW, SmATA X, TwCRHW 90, Who 83, -85, -88, -90, -92, WrDr 76, -80, -82, -84, -86, -88, -90, -92*
Main entry: Cookson, Catherine

Marchant, Catherine 1906- *WrDr 94*

Marchant, John *OxCChiL*

Marchant, Rex Alan 1933- *ConAu 13R, WrDr 80, -82, -84*

Marcher, Marion Walden 1890- *BioIn 11, ConAu 1R, SmATA 10*

Marcus, Rebecca 1907- *AuBYP 3*

Marcus, Rebecca Brian 1907- *AuBYP 2, BioIn 7, -11, ConAu 5R, -1NR, SmATA 9, WrDr 76, -80, -82, -84*

Mare, Walter DeLa *Chambr 3, EngPo, JBA 34, -51, ObitT 1951, TwCA, -SUP*
Main entry: DeLaMare, Walter

Marek, George R d1987 *NewYTBS 87*

Marek, George R 1902- *AuBYP 3, NewGrDA 86*

Marek, George R 1902-1987 *ConAu 121*

Marek, George Richard 1902- *AuSpks, AuBYP 2S, BioIn 4, -5, -10, -11, ConAu 49, -1NR, WhoAm 74, -76, -78, -80, -82, -84, -86, WhoFI 74*

Marek, George Richard 1902-1987 *BioIn 15, WhAm 9*

Marek, Margot L 1934?-1987 *ConAu 123, SmATA 54N*

Margaret, Karla *ConAu X, SmATA X*
Main entry: Andersdatter, Karla M

Margenau, Henry 1901- *AmMWSc 73P, BioIn 1, BlueB 76, ConAu 37R, -14NR, IntAu&W 91, WhoAm 74, -76, -78, WhoWor 74, WrDr 80, -82, -84, -86, -88, -90*

Margolies, Marjorie 1942- *ConAu 65, -13NR, WhoAmW 81*

Margolis, Ellen 1934- *ConAu 1R, ForWC 70*

Margolis, Richard J 1929- *AuBYP 3, ConAu 25NR*

Margolis, Richard J 1929-1991 *ConAu 134, NewYTBS 91, SmATA 67*

Margolis, Richard Jules 1929- *AuBYP 2S, ChhPo S1, ConAu 29R, SmATA 4, WhoE 75, WhoWorJ 72, -78*

Margolis, Vivienne 1922- *BioIn 15, SmATA 46*
Pseud./variant:
Eisner, Vivienne

Mari, Enzo 1932- *BioIn 14, ConArt 77, ConDes 84, -90, OxCTwCA, PhDcTCA 77*

Mariana *AuBYP 3*
Main entry: Foster, Marian Curtis

Mariana 1909-1978 *AuBYP 2, BioIn 3, -5, -8, -9, -13, ConAu X, IlsCB 1946, -1957, -1967, SmATA X, ThrBJA*

Marie, Geraldine 1949- *BioIn 17, SmATA 61, WhoAmW 87, -89*
Pseud./variant:
Christie, Marie

Maril, Nadja 1954- *ConAu 85, -17NR, WhoAmW 81, -83*

Marilue *ConAu X, IntAu&W 77X*
Main entry: Johnson, Marilue Carolyn

Marino, Dorothy 1912- *AuBYP 3*

Marino, Dorothy Bronson 1912- *AuBYP 2, ConAu 73, IlsCB 1946, -1957, SmATA 14*

Marion, Henry *ConAu 141, MajTwCW, SmATA 76*
Main entry: del Rey, Lester

Mariotti, Marcello 1938- *ConAu 29R*

Maris, Ron *AuBYP 3, SmATA 45, -71*

Marisa *ConAu X*
Main entry: Nucera, Marisa Lonette

Mark, Herman F 1895- *IntWW 89, -91, WhoAm 86, -88*

Mark, Herman F 1895-1992 *AnObit 1992, NewYTBS 92*

Mark, Herman Francis 1895- *AmMWSc 73P, -76P, -82, -86, -89, -92, BioIn 1, -3, -5, -6, -7, -10, -12, -13, -14, -16, CurBio 61, InSci, IntWW 74, -75, -76, -77, -78, -79, -80, -81, -82, -83, McGMS 80, WhoAm 74, -76, -78, -80, -84, -90*

Mark, Herman Francis 1895-1992 *BioIn 17, CurBio 92N, WhAm 10*

Mark, Jan 1943- *AuBYP 3, BioIn 13, CamGLE, ChlLR 11, ConAu 93, -17NR, FifBJA, IntAu&W 82, -86, -91, OxCChiL, ScF&FL 92, SmATA 22, -69, TwCChW 83, -89, WrDr 82, -84, -86, -88, -90, -92*

Mark, Jan Marjorie 1943- *ChlFicS*

Mark, Janet Marjorie 1943- *MajAI, TwCYAW, WrDr 94*

Mark, Pauline 1913- *BioIn 8, -12, ConAu 17R, -7NR, ForWC 70, SmATA 14*
Pseud./variant:
Mark, Polly

Mark, Polly *BioIn 8, -12, ConAu X, SmATA X*
Main entry: Mark, Pauline

Mark, Steven Joseph 1913- *ConAu 17R, IntAu&W 77, LEduc 74, WrDr 76, -80, -82, -84*

Markam, Richard *CarSB*

Markandaya, Kamala *BioIn 6, -10, IntAu&W 86, -89, -91*

Markandaya, Kamala 1924- *ArtclWW 2, Au&Wr 71, Benet 87, BioIn 14, BlmGWL, CamGLE, CasWL, ConAu X, ConLC 8, -38, ConNov 72, -76, -82, -86, -91, DcOrL 2, EncWL 2, FemiCLE, IntLitE, LiExTwC, ModCmwL, OxCEng 85, REn, WebE&AL, WhoWor 74, WorAu 1950, WrDr 76, -80, -82, -84, -86, -88, -90, -92*
Pseud./variant:
Taylor, Kamala

Markandaya, Kamala Purnalya 1924- *WrDr 94*

Marker, Sherry 1941- *SmATA 76*
Pseud./variant:
Whitman, Alice

Markham, Marion M *DrAPF 87, -89, -91, -93*

Markham, Marion M 1929- *ConAu 129, SmATA 60, WhoAmW 91, WhoMW 86, -88, WhoUSWr 88, WhoWrEP 89, -92*

Markham, Mrs 1780-1837 *OxCChiL, OxCEng 85*

Markins, W S *AuBYP 2S, -3, ConAu X, SmATA 7*
Main entry: Jenkins, Marie M

Markle, Sandra L 1946- *ConAu 111, SmATA 41, -57*

Marko, Katherine D 1913- *BioIn 13, ConAu 29R, -15NR, SmATA 28, WrDr 76, -80, -82, -84, -86, -88, -90, -92*

Marko, Katherine Dolores 1913- *IntAu&W 86, -89, -91*

Markoe, Karen 1942- *ConAu 81*

Markoosie 1942- *BioIn 10, ChlLR 23, ConAu X, OxCChiL, Profile 1, TwCChW 78, -83, -89, WrDr 80, -82, -84, -86, -88, -90, -92, -94*

Marks, Alan 1957- *SmATA 77*

Marks, Burton 1930- *ConAu 107, SmATA 43, -47*

Marks, Edwin S 1926- *BioIn 11, WhoAm 74, -76, -78, -80, -82, -84, -90, -92, -94, WhoE 81, WhoFI 81*

Marks, Geoffrey 1906- *AuBYP 2S, -3, ConAu 33R*

Marks, Hannah K
Main entry: Trivelpiece, Laurel

Marks, J *ConAu X, -34NR, DrAPF 83, -85 -89, -91, -93, MajAI, SmATA X*
Main entry: Highwater, Jamake

Marks, James Macdonald 1921- *AuBYP 2S, -3, BioIn 11, ConAu 61, IntAu&W 77, -82, SmATA 13, WrDr 76, -80, -82, -84*

Marks, Laurie J 1957- *ConAu 135, ScF&FL 92, SmATA 68, WrDr 94*

Marks, Margaret L 1911?-1980 *BioIn 13, ConAu 101, SmATA 23N*

Marks, Mickey Klar 1914- *AuBYP 2, -3, BioIn 7, -8, -11, ConAu 1R, -6NR, SmATA 12*

Marks, Peter *AuBYP 3, ConAu X, -42NR, SmATA 77, -X*
Main entry: Smith, Robert Kimmel

Marks, Rita 1938- *SmATA 47*

Marks, Stan *ConAu 31NR*

Marks, Stan 1929- *ConAu 29R, -12NR, SmATA 14, WrDr 76, -80, -82, -84, -86, -88, -90, -92*
Pseud./variant:
King, Martin

Marks, Stanley 1929- *WrDr 94*

Marks-Highwater, J *MajAI, SmATA X*
Main entry: Highwater, Jamake

Mark Twain *AmAu&B, BenetAL 91, BiD&SB, CasWL, CmCal, CyAL, DcEnL, EncSoH, HarEnUS, OxCAmL 83, OxCEng 67, -85,*

RComWL, Str&VC
Main entry: Clemens, Samuel Langhorne

Mark Twain 1835-1910 *EncO&P 2, –3*

Markun, Patricia 1924- *AuBYP 3*

Markun, Patricia Maloney 1924- *AmCath 80, AuBYP 2, BioIn 7, ConAu 5R, –4NR, SmATA 15, WhoAm 74, –76, –78, –80, –82, –84, –86, –88, –90, WhoAmW 74, WhoUSWr 88, WhoWrEP 89, –92*
Pseud./variant:
Forrest, Sybil
Maloney, Pat
Marroquin, Patricio
O'Carroll, Ryan

Marlow, Edwina *BioIn 10, ConAu X*
Main entry: Huff, Tom E

Marlow, Joyce *Au&Wr 71, ConAu 65, –X, IntAu&W 82, WrDr 76, –80, –82, –84*
Main entry: Connor, Joyce Mary

Marlow, Joyce 1929- *IntAu&W 91, WrDr 86, –88, –90, –92, –94*

Marlowe, Amy Bell *ConAu 26NR, –P-2, SmATA 1, –67*
Main entry: Stratemeyer, Edward L

Marlowe, Stephen *AuBYP 2, –3, ConAu 13R, –6NR, EncSF 93, IntAu&W 91X, TwCCr&M 80, –85, WrDr 76, –80, –82, –84, –86, –88*
Main entry: Lesser, Milton

Marlowe, Stephen 1928- *IntAu&W 86, ScF&FL 92, TwCCr&M 91, WrDr 90, –92, –94*

Marmur, Jacland 1901- *BenetAL 91*

Marmur, Jacland 1901-1970 *AmAu&B, AmNov, BioIn 2, ConAu 9R, REnAL, WhAm 5, WhNAA, WhoWorJ 72, –78*

Marokvia, Artur 1909- *BioIn 5, –8, –14, IlsBYP, IlsCB 1946, –1957, –1967, SmATA 31*

Marokvia, Mireille 1918- *AuBYP 2, –3, BioIn 7, –10, ConAu 29R, SmATA 5*

Marquis, Don Robert Perry 1878-1937 *AmAu&B, AmLY, BiDSA, BioIn 1, –4, –5, –6, –8, –10, CnDAL, CnE&AP, ConAmA, ConAmL, DcNAA, LongCTC, ModAL, NotNAT A, OxCAmL 65, PenC AM, RAdv 1, REn, REnAL, Str&VC, TwCA, –SUP, TwCWr, WhAm 1, WhNAA*

Marquis, Helen *ChhPo S1*

Marr, John S 1940- *ScF&FL 92, SmATA 48*

Marr, John Stuart 1940- *ConAu 81*

Marran, Ray J *AuBYP 2, –3, BioIn 7*

Marric, J J *ConAu 135, –X, EncMys, LongCTC, MajTwCW, TwCCr&M 80, –85, –91, WhoSpyF, WorAu 1950*

Marric, J J 1927- *WrDr 94*

Marrin, Albert 1936- *ConAu 30NR, SmATA 43, –53*

Marriott, Alice Lee d1992 *NewYTBS 92*

Marriott, Alice Lee 1910- *AmAu&B, AnCL, AuBYP 2, –3, BioIn 2, –7, –8, –14, ConAu 57, CurBio 50, InSci, SmATA 31*

Marriott, Alice Lee 1910-1992 *BioIn 17, ConAu 137, SmATA 71*

Marriott, Pat 1920- *BioIn 8, ChhPo S2, IlsCB 1957, –1967, SmATA 35*

Marroquin, Patricia *AuBYP 3*

Marroquin, Patricia 1957- *WhoAmW 93, WhoHisp 91, –92, –94*

Marroquin, Patricio *AuBYP 2, ConAu X*
Main entry: Markun, Patricia Maloney

Marrow, Alfred J 1905-1978 *AmMWSc 73S, –78S, BioIn 11, –12, ConAu 77, –81, NatCAB 60, WhoWorJ 72, –78*

Marryat, Francis Samuel 1826-1855 *CarSB, EarABI SUP*

Marryat, Frederick 1792-1838 *ScFEYrs*

Marryat, Frederick 1792-1848 *Alli, AtlBL, Benet 87, BenetAL 91, BbD, BiD&SB, BioIn 1, –2, –3, –5, –6, –8, –10, –12, –14, –16, BlmGEL, BritAu 19, CamGEL, CamGLE, CarSB, CasWL, CelCen, Chambr 3, ChhPo, CyWA 58, DcBiA, DcBiPP, DcBrBI, DcCanB 7, DcEnA, DcEnL, DcLB 21, DcLEL, DcNaB, EvLB, HarEnUS, HsB&A, –SUP, LongCEL, NewC, NinCLC 3, Novels, OxCAmH, OxCAmL 65, –83, OxCCan, OxCChiL, OxCEng 67, –85, OxCShps, PenC ENG, RAdv 1, –13-1, REn, REnAL, RfGEnL 91, StaCVF, TelT, TwCChW 83A, –89A, WebE&AL, WhDW, WhoChL, WhoHr&F, WrChl*

Mars, Ethel 1876-1956? *ChhPo, –S1, DcWomA, WhAmArt 85*

Mars, Witold Tadeusz J 1912?- *BioIn 5, –8, –9, ConAu 25R, IlsBYP, IlsCB 1946, –1957, –1967, SmATA 3, WhoE 74, –77, –81*

Marsden, John 1950- *BioIn 17, ConAu 135, SmATA 66, TwCYAW, WrDr 94*

Marsh, Corinna *AuBYP 2, –3, BioIn 8, ChhPo*

Marsh, Corinna 1891-1990 *ConAu 132*

Marsh, Dave 1950- *ConAu 41NR, NewGrDA 86, SmATA 66*

Marsh, Irving T 1907-1982 *ConAu 9R, –107*

Marsh, J E *ConAu X, SmATA X*
Main entry: Marshall, Evelyn

Marsh, James 1946- *SmATA 73*

Marsh, Jean *ConAu X, IntAu&W 86X, SmATA X*
Main entry: Marshall, Evelyn

Marsh, Jean 1897- *IntAu&W 89, TwCRHW 90, WrDr 86, –88, –90*

Marsh, Jean 1934- *ConTFT 3, –11, IntMPA 92, WorAlBi*

Marsh, Jean 1935- *HalFC 88*

Marsh, Jean Lyndsey Torren 1934- *WhoAm 92*

Marsh, Jeri 1940- *ConAu 85, SmATA X*
Main entry: Lee-Hostetler, Jeri

Marsh, John *TwCRHW 90*

Marsh, John 1907- *Au&Wr 71, ConAu P-1, IntAu&W 77, –82, WrDr 76, –80, –82*

Marsh, Leonard George 1930- *ConAu 73, –13NR, Who 82, –83, –85, –88, –90, –92*

Marsh, Ngaio 1895-1982 *BlmGWL, CamGWoT, CrtSuMy, RfGEnL 91, TwCCr&M 91*

Marsh, Ngaio 1899-1982 *AuBYP 3, Benet 87, BioIn 16, –17, CamGLE, ConLC 53, DcLB 77, DcNaB 1981, EncBrWW, FemiCLE, MajTwCW, WorAlBi*

Marsh, Ngaio, Dame 1899-1982 *BioIn 14, InWom SUP*

Marsh, Ngaio Edith 1899-1982 *AuBYP 2, Au&Wr 71, BioIn 1, –4, –5, –7, –8, ConAu 9R, ConLC 7, ConNov 72, –76, CorpD, DcLEL, EncMys, EvLB, IntWW 74, –75, –76, –77, –78, LongCTC, NewC, OxCEng 67, –85, REn, TwCA, –SUP, TwCWr, Who 74, WhoAmW 75, WhoWor 74, WrDr 76, –80*

Marsh, Paul *SmATA X*
Main entry: Hopkins, Kenneth

Marsh, Reginald 1898-1954 *BioIn 1, –3, –4, –5, –9, –12, –13, –14, BriEAA, CurBio 41, –54, DcCAA 71, –77, –88, GrAmP, IlsBYP, IlsCB 1946, McGEWB, NatCAB 62, ObitOF 79, OxCAmH, OxCTwCA, OxDcArt, PhDcTCA 77, WebAB 74, –79, WhAm 3, WhAmArt 85, WhoAmA 78N, –80N, –82N, –86N, –89N, –91N, WorArt 1950*

Marsh, Susan 1914- *ConAu 9R, ForWC 70*

Marsh, Susan R 1914- *IntAu&W 86*

Marshak, Ilia IAkolevich 1895- *AuBYP 3*

Marshak, Ilia Iakovlevich 1895-1953 *AuBYP 2, BioIn 2, –8, JBA 34, –51*
Pseud./variant:
Ilin, M

Marshak, Samuil Yakovlevich 1887-1964 *BioIn 1, –7, CasWL, ChhPo, –S1, ConAu 111, DcRusLS, EvEuW, HanRL, ModWD, OxCChiL, PenC EUR*

Marshall, Alan 1902-1984 *Au&Wr 71, BioIn 6, –9, –12, ConAu 85, IntAu&W 77, OxCAusL, OxCChiL, WhoWor 78, –80, –82*

Marshall, Anthony Dryden 1924- *BioIn 12, BlueB 76, ConAu 29R, SmATA 18, WhoAm 74, –76, –78, WhoAmP 73, –75, –77, WhoGov 77, –72, –75, WhoWor 74*

Marshall, Archibald 1866-1934 *AuBYP 2S, –3, BioIn 15, EncMys, EncSF 93, LongCTC, NewC, ScFEYrs, TwCA*

Marshall, Catherine *AuBYP 3*

Marshall, Catherine 1914-1983 *AmWomWr, AuBYP 2, BioIn 3, –4, –5, –7, –9, –11, –12, –13, ConAu 17R, –109, –8NR, CurBio 55, –83N, IntAu&W 77, NewYTBS 83, SmATA 2, –34N, WhoAm 74, WorAl, WrDr 76, –80, –82, –84*

Marshall, Constance Kay 1918- *BioIn 5, –12, IlsBYP, IlsCB 1946, –1967*

Marshall, Daniel *IlsBYP*

Marshall, Dean 1900- *AuBYP 2, –3, BioIn 8*

Marshall, Douglas *AuBYP 3, ConAu X, SmATA 3*
Main entry: McClintock, Marshall

Marshall, Edmund *SmATA X*
Main entry: Hopkins, Kenneth

Marshall, Edward *ConAu 139, –38NR, MajAI, SmATA 75, TwCChW 83, –89, WrDr 86, –88, –90, –92, –94*
Main entry: Marshall, James Edward

Marshall, Emma 1830?-1899 *Alli SUP, BioIn 2, –10, CarSB, DcNaB S1, FemiCLE, InWom SUP, OxCChiL, StaCVF, WomNov*

Marshall, Evelyn 1897- *Au&Wr 71, BioIn 11, ConAu 5R, –2NR, –18NR, IntAu&W 86, –91, SmATA 11, WrDr 84*
Pseud./variant:
Bourne, Lesley
Marsh, J E
Marsh, Jean

Marshall, Garry *HalFC 88, LesBEnT 92*

Marshall, Garry 1934- *Au&Arts 3, CelR 90, ConTFT 6, CurBio 92, IntMPA 88, –92, SmATA 60, WhoAm 86, –88, –90, –92, –94, WhoEnt 92, WorAlBi*

Marshall, H E 1876- *OxCChiL*

Marshall, James *AuBYP 3*
Main entry: Rister, Claude

Marshall, James d1992 *NewYTBS 92*

Marshall, James 1942- *AuBYP 3, ChlBIID, ChlLR 21, DcLB 61, IntAu&W 91, SmATA 51, TwCChW 89, WrDr 86, –88, –90, –92*

Marshall, James 1942-1992 *AnObit 1992*

Marshall, James 1949- *IntWWM 90*

Marshall, James Edward 1942- *AuBYP 2S, BioIn 10, –12, ConAu 41R, –38NR, FourBJA, IlsCB 1967, MajAI, OxCChiL, SmATA 6, TwCChW 83, WhoAm 76, –78, –80, –82, WrDr 94*
Pseud./variant:
Marshall, Edward

Marshall, James Edward 1942-1992 *ConAu 139, SmATA 75, WhAm 10*

Marshall, James Vance *ConAu X, IntAu&W 77X, –82X, –86X, –91X, SmATA X, WrDr 86, –88, –90, –92*
Main entry: Payne, Donald Gordon

Marshall, James Vance 1924- *WrDr 94*

Marshall, Jeff *AuBYP 3, ConAu 41NR*

Marshall, Jim 1891-1956 *Str&VC*

Marshall, Joanne *ConAu 57, –X, IntAu&W 77X, –82X, TwCRHW 90, WrDr 76, –82, –84, –86, –88, –90*
Main entry: Rundle, Anne

Marshall, John *BioIn 9, DcVicP 2*

Marshall, John 1755-1835 *Benet 87, BiDrUSC 89, BiDrUSE 89, DcAmDH 89, MemAm, RComAH, WorAlBi*

Marshall, Kim *ConAu X, SmATA X*
Main entry: Marshall, Michael

Marshall, Michael 1948- *ConAu 3NR, SmATA 37*
Pseud./variant:
Marshall, Kim

Marshall, Norman Bertram 1915- *Who 74, –82, –83, –85, –88, –90, –92, WhoOcn 78*

Marshall, Percy *ConAu 31NR, SmATA X*
Main entry: Young, Percy Marshall

Marshall, Samuel Lyman Atwood 1900-1977 *AmAu&B, AuBYP 2, –3, BioIn 3, –5, –8, –10, –11, –12, ConAu 73, –81, CurBio 53, –78, SmATA 21, WhAm 7, WhoAm 74, –76, –78, WorAu 1950*

Marshall, Sybil Mary Edwards 1913- *ConAu 1R, –1NR*

Marsoli, Lisa Ann 1958- *BioIn 16, ConAu 120, SmATA 53*

Marsten, Richard *ConAu X, –38NR, EncSF 93, IntAu&W 91X, MajTwCW, SmATA X, TwCCr&M 91, TwCSFW 86, –91, WrDr 86, –88, –90, –92, –94*
Main entry: Hunter, Evan

Marston, Hope Irvin 1935- *BioIn 14, ConAu 101, SmATA 31*

Martchenko, Michael 1942- *BioIn 16, CanWW 89, SmATA 50*

Marteka, Vincent James, Jr. 1936- *ConAu 13R, WhoAm 80, –82, –84, –86, –88, –90, –92, –94, WhoUSWr 88, WhoWrEP 89, –92*

Martel, Jane G 1926- *ConAu 57*

Martel, Suzanne 1924- *BioIn 10, OxCCanL, Profile 1, WhoCanL 85, –87, –92*

Martignoni, Margaret E 1908?-1974 *BioIn 10, –13, ConAu 104, SmATA 27N, WhoLibS 55*

Martin, Alexander Campbell 1897- *AmMWSc 73P*

Martin, Alfred 1916- *ConAu 117, DrAS 74P, –78P, LEduc 74*

Martin, Ann M 1955- *ConAu 111, –32NR, ScF&FL 92, SmATA 41, –44, –70*
Pseud./variant:
Matthews, Ann

Martin, Ann Matthews 1955- *ChlLR 32, MajAI, WhoAm 94, WhoUSWr 88*

Martin, April *ConAu X*
Main entry: Sherrill, Dorothy

Martin, Bernard 1928-1982 *ConAu 53, –4NR, DrAS 74P, –78P, IntAu&W 77, WhAm 8, WhoAm 74, –76, –78, –80, –82, WhoRel 75, –77, WhoWor 78, WhoWorJ 72, –78*

Martin, Bill *MajAI*

Martin, Bill, Jr. *ConAu 130, –X, MajAI, SmATA X*
Main entry: Martin, William Ivan

Martin, Bill, Jr. 1916- *SixBJA, SmATA 67, WrDr 94*

Martin, Charles E 1910- *BlueB 76, ConAu X, SmATA 70, WhAmArt 85, WhoAm 74, –76, –78, –80, –82, –84, –86, –88, WhoAmA 73, –78, –80, –82, –84, –86, –89, –91, WhoE 74*
Pseud./variant:
C E M

Martin, Charles Morris 1891- *AuBYP 2, –3, BioIn 7*

Martin, Claire 1933- *SmATA 76*

Martin, David 1915- *Au&Wr 71, BioIn 6, ChhPo S2, ConAu 103, –24NR, DcChlFi, IntAu&W 91, OxCAusL, TwCChW 78, –83, –89, WrDr 76, –80, –82, –84, –86, –88, –90, –92, –94*

Martin, David Stone d1992 *NewYTBS 92*

Martin, David Stone 1913- *BioIn 2, –5, IlrAm 1880, –F, IlsBYP, IlsCB 1946, SmATA 39, WhAmArt 85, WhoAm 86, –88, –90, WhoGrA 62, –82*

Martin, David Stone 1913-1992 *AnObit 1992, WhAm 10*

Martin, Donald Franklin 1944- *ConAu 65*

Martin, Dorothy 1921- *ConAu 57, –6NR, SmATA 47*

Martin, Eugene *ConAu 26NR, –P-2, SmATA 1*
Main entry: Stratemeyer, Edward L

Martin, Eva M 1939- *ConAu 126, SmATA 65*

Martin, Frances M 1906- *ConAu 61, SmATA 36*

Martin, Frederick *ConAu X, SmATA 2*
Main entry: Christopher, Matthew F

Martin, Fredric *AuBYP 3, ConAu 36NR, MajAI, WrDr 86, –88, –90, –92*

Martin, Fredric 1917- *WrDr 94*

Martin, George 1926- *AuBYP 3, ConAu 21NR, ConMus 6, ConTFT 8, EncRk 88, OxCPMus, PenEncP, WhoAm 86, –88, WhoUSWr 88, WhoWrEP 89*

Martin, George 1929- *WhoMW 90*

Martin, George Madden 1866-1946 *AmAu&B, AmWomWr, BiDSA, BioIn 1, CarSB, ChhPo S1, DcAmAu, DcNAA, FemiCLE, InWom SUP, WhAm 2, WhNAA, WomWWA 14*

Martin, George Madden, Mrs 1866-1946 *LiHiK*

Martin, George Whitney 1926- *AmAu&B, AuBYP 2, Au&Wr 71, BioIn 7, ConAu 9R, IntAu&W 77, –82, –86, –89, IntWWM 85, –90, WhoAm 76, –92, –94, WrDr 76, –80, –82, –84, –86, –88, –90, –92, –94*

Martin, J P 1880-1966 *BioIn 8, OxCChiL, TwCChW 83, –89*

Martin, Janet *ConAu X*
Main entry: Garfinkel, Bernard

Martin, Janet 1927- *Who 90*

Martin, Jeremy *ConAu X, SmATA X*
Main entry: Levin, Marcia Obrasky

Martin, Jerome *AuBYP 3*

Martin, John Percival 1880?-1966 *BioIn 8, –12, ConAu 81, SmATA 15, WhoChL*

Martin, John Perry, Jr. *AmMWSc 86*

Martin, Joseph Plumb 1760-1850 *BioIn 7, –10, –11*

Martin, Joy 1922- *ConAu 57*
Pseud./variant:
Crandall, Joy

Martin, Judith *AuBYP 2, –3, BioIn 8, EncTwCJ*

Martin, Judith 1938- *ArtclWW 2, CelR 90, CurBio 86, JrnUS, WhoUSWr 88, WhoWrEP 89, –92, WorAlBi, WrDr 86, –88, –90, –92, –94*

Martin, Lynne 1923- *AuBYP 2S, –3, BioIn 12, ConAu 65, SmATA 21*

Martin, Marcia *AuBYP 3, ConAu X, SmATA X*
Main entry: Levin, Marcia Obrasky

Martin, Marjorie 1942- *ConAu 53, IntAu&W 77, –86, –89, –91, WrDr 76, –80 –82, –84, –86, –88, –90, –92, –94*

Martin, Mary Steichen *AmPB, ConAu X*

Martin, Moyra 1898-1950 *SingR 1*
Pseud./variant:
Morell, Musette

Martin, Nancy *ConAu X, SmATA X, WrDr 76, –80, –82, –84*
Main entry: Salmon, Annie Elizabeth

Martin, Patricia Miles *WrDr 86*

Martin, Patricia Miles 1899- *AuBYP 2, BioIn 7, –9, ConAu 1R, –2NR, ForWC 70, IntAu&W 77, OxCChiL, SmATA 1, –43, TwCChW 78, –83, WhoAmW 74, –75, WrDr 76, –80, –82, –84*
Pseud./variant:
Lane, Jerry
Miles, Miska
Miles, Patricia A

Martin, Patricia Miles 1899-1986 *AuBYP 3, ConAu 119, –37NR, MajAI, SmATA 48N, TwCChW 89*

Martin, Peter *ConAu X, SmATA X, Who 88, –90, –92, WrDr 86, –88, –90*
Main entry: Chaundler, Christine

Martin, Peter 1890- *EncSF 93*

Martin, Phyllis R *ConAu 130*

Martin, Phyllis Rodgers *IntAu&W 77, WrDr 94*

Martin, Ralph G 1920- *AuBYP 3*

Martin, Ralph Guy 1920- *AmAu&B, AuSpks, AuBYP 2, BioIn 8, –10, –11, BlueB 76, ConAu 5R, IntAu&W 77, –89, –91, WhoAm 74, –76, –78, –80, –82, –84, –86, –88, –90, –92, –94, WhoE 74, WhoUSWr 88, WhoWor 80, –82, –84, –87, WhoWrEP 89, –92, WrDr 76, –80*

Martin, Rene 1891-1977 *BioIn 12, –15, IlsBYP, SmATA 20N, –42*

Martin, Richard *ConAu X, LongCTC, MajTwCW*

Martin, Rupert Claude d1991 *Who 92N*

Martin, Rupert Claude 1905- *SmATA 31, Who 74, –82, –83, –85, –88, –90*

Martin, Sarah Catherine 1768-1826 *ChhPo, –S1, –S2*

Martin, Stefan 1936- *BioIn 8, –14, ChhPo S1, IlsBYP, IlsCB 1957, –1967, PrintW 83, –85, SmATA 32, WhoAmA 84, –89, –91*

Martin, Sylvia Parsons *AuBYP 2S, –3*

Martin, Vicky *ConAu X, IntAu&W 77X, SmATA X, WrDr 80*
Main entry: Storey, Victoria Carolyn

Martin, Webber *MajAI*

Martin, Wendy 1940- *ConAu 37R, DrAS 74E, –78E, –82E*

Martin, William 1801-1867 *DcNaB, OxCChiL, StaCVF*

Martin, William G *AuBYP 2S, –3*

Martin, William Ivan 1916- *BioIn 10, –15, –16, –17, ConAu 117, –130, MajAI, SmATA 40*
Pseud./variant:
Martin, Bill, Jr.

Martindale, Cyril Charlie 1879-1963 *BioIn 1, –6, –7, BkC 4, CarSB, CathA 1930, DcNaB 1961, LongCTC*

Martineau, Harriet 1802- *BenetAL 91*

Martineau, Harriet 1802-1876 *Alli, –SUP, ArtclWW 2, Benet 87, BbD, BiD&SB, BioIn 1, –2, –4, –5, –6, –8, –9, –10, –11, –12, –13, –14, –15, –16, –17, BlmGEL, BlmGWL, BritAu 19, CamGEL, CamGLE, CarSB, CasWL, CelCen, Chambr 3, ChhPo, ContDcW 89, DcBiA, DcBiPP, DcEnA, DcEnL, DcEuL, DcLB 21, –55, DcLEL, DcNaB, Dis&D, EncBrWW, EvLB, FemiCLE, InWom SUP, IntDcWB, JBA 34, McGEWB, MouLC 3, NewC, NinCLC 26, Novels, OxCAmH, OxCAmL 65, –83, OxCChiL, OxCEng 67, –85, PenC ENG, REn, RfGEnL 91, StaCVF, TelT, WebE&AL, WhAm HS, WhoChL, WhoEc 81, –86, YABC 2*

Martinez, John *IlsBYP*

Martini, Teri 1930- *AuBYP 2, –3, BioIn 7, –9, ConAu 5R, –2NR, ForWC 70, IntAu&W 91, SmATA 3, WhoAmW 74, –75, WrDr 76, –80, –82, –84, –86, –88, –90, –92, –94*

Martyr, Paula Jane 1960- *SmATA 57*
Pseud./variant:
Lawford, Paula Jane

Maruki, Toshi 1912- *BioIn 14, –16, ChlLR 19, SixBJA*

Marx, Robert F 1936- *AuBYP 2, BioIn 8, –11, –13, ConAu 9R, –6NR, SmATA 24, WrDr 80*

Marx, Robert Frank 1936- *AuBYP 3*

Marx, Samuel d1992 *NewYTBS 92*

Marx, Samuel 1902- *BioIn 15, ConAu 103, IntMPA 75, –76, –78, –81, –82, –84, –86, –88, –92, –77*

Marx, Samuel 1902-1992 *BioIn 17, ConAu 137*

Marx, Wesley 1934- *ConAu 21R, –12NR, IntAu&W 77, –82, WhoAm 74, –76, –78, –80, –82, –84*

Marxhausen, Joanne G 1935- *ConAu 37R*

Marzani, Carl 1912- *Au&Wr 71, BioIn 1, –11, ConAu 61, SmATA 12, WrDr 76, –80, –82, –84, –86, –88, –90, –92, –94*

Marzollo, Jean 1942- *BioIn 13, ConAu 81, –15NR, ScF&FL 92, SixBJA, SmATA 29, –77, –15AS*

Masani, Shakuntala *AuBYP 2, –3, BioIn 5, –7, ConAu 112, IlsCB 1946*

Maschwitz, Eric 1901-1969 *BioIn 4, –8, –9, EncMT, LongCTC, ObitT 1961, OxCPMus, WhoLA, WhoMus 72*

Masefield, John *IntvTCA 2*

Masefield, John 1878-1967 *AnCL, AuBYP 2, –3, Benet 87, BioIn 1, –2, –3, –4, –5, –6, –7, –8, –9, –10, –11, –12, –13, –14, –16, –17, BlmGEL, BritAS, CamGEL, CamGLE, CamGWoT, CasWL, Chambr 3, ChhPo, –S1, –S2, CnDBLB 5, CnE&AP, CnMD, CnMWL, ConAu 25R, –33NR, –P-2, ConLC 11, –47, DcLB 10, –19, DcLEL, DcNaB 1961, EncWL, –2, EngPo, EvLB, LongCEL, LongCTC, MajTwCW, McGEWD 72, –84, ModBrL, –S1, ModWD, NewC, NotNAT B, Novels, ObitOF 79, ObitT 1961, OxCChiL, OxCEng 67, –85, OxCShps, OxCThe 67, –83, PenC ENG, PlP&P, RAdv 1, –13-1, REn, RfGEnL 91, SmATA 19, Str&VC, TelT, TwCA, –SUP, TwCChW 78, –83, –89, TwCRHW 90, TwCWr, WebE&AL, WhDW, WhAm 4, WhoChL, WhoTwCL, WorAlBi, WorAl*

Masey, Mary Lou d1991 *NewYTBS 91*

Masey, Mary Lou 1932- *AuBYP 3*

Masey, Mary Lou 1932-1991 *BioIn 17, ConAu 134*

Masey, Mary Louise 1932- *AuBYP 2S, ConAu 21R, WhoAmW 74, –75*

Masha *ChhPo, –S1, ConAu X*
Main entry: Stern, Marie

Maskell, A E Anderson, Mrs *Alli SUP, CarSB*

Mason, Alfred Edward Woodley 1865-1948 *BbD, BiD&SB, BioIn 1, –3, –4, –5, –12, Chambr 3, DcLEL, DcNaB 1941, EncMys, EvLB, HalFC 84, LongCTC, McGEWD 72, –84, ModBrL, NewC, NotNAT B, Novels, ObitOF 79, OxCChiL, OxCEng 67, –85, PenC ENG, REn, SpyFic, TelT, TwCA, –SUP, TwCCr&M 80, –85, TwCWr, WhoSpyF*

Mason, Alpheus Thomas d1989 *NewYTBS 89*

Mason, Alpheus Thomas 1899- *AmAu&B, AmMWSc 73S, –78S, BlueB 76, ConAu 1R –32NR, IntAu&W 77, –82, IntYB 80, –81, –82, REnAL, WhoAm 74, –76, –78, –80, –82, –84, –86, –88, WhoE 74, WhoWor 74*

Mason, Alpheus Thomas 1899-1989 *BioIn 16, –17, ConAu 130, WhAm 10*

Mason, Bernard Sterling 1896-1953 *AmAu&B, BioIn 3, OhA&B, WhAm 3*

Mason, Betty 1930- *ConAu 37R*

Mason, Bobbie Ann *DrAPF 87, –89, –91, –93, NewYTBS 88*

Mason, Bobbie Ann 1940- *Au&Arts 5, BenetAL 91, BlmGWL, ConAu 31NR, ConLC 43, ConNov 91, CurBio 89, DcLB Y87B, IntAu&W 91, LiHiK, MajTwCW, ShSCr 4, TwCYAW, WhoAm 92, –94, WhoAmW 87, –89, –91, –93, WhoUSWr 88, WhoWrEP 89, –92, WorAu 1980, WrDr 90, –92, –94*

Mason, Bobbie Anne 1940- *ArtclWW 2*

Mason, Brian Harold 1917- *AmMWSc 73P, –76P, –82, –86, –89, –92, WhoAm 74, –76, –78, –80, –82, –84, –86, –88, –90, –92, –94, WhoGov 77, –72, –75, WhoSSW 73, WhoWor 74*

Mason, Douglas Rankine 1918- *Au&Wr 71, ConAu 49, –1NR, –17NR, ConSFA, EncSF 93, IntAu&W 77, –82, –89, –91, ScF&FL 92, TwCSFW 86, –91, WhoSciF, WhoWor 78, WrDr 76, –80, –82, –84, –86, –88, –90, –92, –94*

Mason, Edwin A 1905-1979 *BioIn 2, –12, ConAu P-2, SmATA 32N*

Mason, Francis Van Wyck *AuBYP 3*

Mason, Francis Van Wyck 1901-1978 *SpyFic*

Mason, Francis VanWyck 1901-1978 *AmAu&B, AmNov, AuBYP 2, Au&Wr 71, BioIn 9, –11, –13, –14, BlueB 76, ConAu 5R, –81, –8NR, ObitOF 79, REnAL, SmATA 3, –26N, TwCCr&M 80, –85, WhAm 7, WhoAm 74, WhoSpyF, WhoWor 74*
Pseud./variant:
Coffin, Geoffrey
Mason, Frank W 1901-1978
Mason, VanWyck
VanWyck, Mason F
Weaver, Ward

Mason, Frank W 1901-1978 *AuBYP 3, SpyFic*
Main entry: Mason, Francis VanWyck

Mason, George Champlin 1820-1894 *Alli, –SUP, AmAu&B, BiDAmAr, DcAmAu*

DcNAA, HarEnUS, MacEA
Pseud./variant:
O'Lincoln, Robert

Mason, George Frederick 1904- *AuBYP 2, -3, BioIn 5, -7, -8, -12, ConAu 73, IlsCB 1946, -1957, -1967, SmATA 14*

Mason, Herbert Molloy, Jr. 1927- *ConAu 13R, -6NR, WrDr 80*

Mason, Miriam Evangeline 1900-1973 *AmAu&B, AuBYP 2, -3, BioIn 6, -7, -9, -13, ConAu 1R, -103, -15NR, IndAu 1917, MorJA, SmATA 2, -26N, WhAm 6, WhoAmW 74*

Mason, Olive *SingR 1*

Mason, Philip *WrDr 86, -88*

Mason, Philip 1906- *Au&Wr 71, BlueB 76, ConAu 9R, -3NR, IntAu&W 77, -82, -89, -91, IntWW 74, -75, -76, -77, -78, -79, -80, -81, -82, -83, -89, -91, Who 74, -82, -83, -85, -88, -90, -92, WhoWor 74, -78, WrDr 76, -80, -82, -84, -90, -92, -94*

Mason, Tally *AuBYP 3, ConAu X, EncMys, EncSF 93, SmATA 5*
Main entry: Derleth, August

Mason, VanWyck *ConAu X, EncMys, WhoAm 74, -76, -78*
Main entry: Mason, Francis VanWyck

Mason, Zane Allen 1919- *DrAS 74H, -78H, -82H*

Mass, Nuri 1918- *AuWomWr, OxCAusL, SingR 1*

Massee, May 1881-1966 *AmPB, BioIn 1, -2, -4, -5, -7, -8, -12, InWom SUP, NotAW MOD, WhAm 4*

Masselink, Ben 1919- *ConAu 17R*

Masselman, George 1897-1971 *BioIn 12, ConAu 9R, SmATA 19*

Massey, Erika 1900- *ConAu 61*
Pseud./variant:
Zastrow, Erika

Massie, Diane Redfield *AuBYP 3*

Massie, Diane Redfield 1930- *AuBYP 2, BioIn 7, -8, -12, ChhPo, -S1, ConAu 81, IlsCB 1957, -1967, SmATA 16*

Massie, Robert Kinloch 1929- *AuSpks, BioIn 8, -10, -11, -12, ConAu 77, -14NR, -40NR, WhoAm 76, -78, -80, -82, -84, -86, -88, -90, -92, -94, WorAu 1975*

Massie, Suzanne *BioIn 10, NewYTBS 85, WhoAm 76, -78*

Massie, Suzanne 1931- *ConAu 142*

Massie, Suzanne Rohrbach 1931- *WhoE 91*

Masson, Michel 1800-1883 *CarSB*

Masterman, Dodie 1918- *BioIn 5, -14, IlsBYP, IlsCB 1946*

Masteroff, Joe *ConDr 88D*

Masteroff, Joe 1919- *AmAu&B, BiE&WWA, ConDr 73, -77D, -82D, NotNAT, WhoAm 74, -76, -78, -80, -82*

Masters, Elaine 1932- *ConAu 57*

Masters, Kelly Ray 1897- *AuBYP 2, -3, Au&Wr 71, BioIn 3, -7, -9, ConAu 1R, CurBio 53, SmATA 3*
Pseud./variant:
Ball, Zachary

Masters, Mildred 1932- *ConAu 110, SmATA 42*
Pseud./variant:
Heinzen, Mildred

Masters, Nicholas Arthur 1929- *AmMWSc 73S, ConAu 13R*

Masters, William *ConAu X, SmATA 2*
Main entry: Cousins, Margaret

Maston, Thomas Bufford 1897- *ConAu 5R, IntAu&W 82, WrDr 80, -82, -84*

Maston, Thomas Bufford 1897-1988 *BioIn 16, WhAm 10*

Masuda, Takeshi
Main entry: Aska, Warabe

Masur, Jenny 1948- *ConAu 65*

Matas, Carol 1949- *DcChlFi*

Matchette, Katharine E 1941- *ConAu 53, SmATA 38*

Mateaux, Clara L *Alli SUP, CarSB, ChhPo*

Mates, Rudolf 1881- *BioIn 1, IlsCB 1744*

Math, Irwin 1940- *BioIn 15, ConAu 112, SmATA 42, WhoE 83, -85, -86, -89*

Mathabane, Mark 1960- *Au&Arts 4, BlkWr 1, -2, ConAu 125, TwCYAW, WrDr 92*

Mather, Kirtley F 1888-1978 *BioIn 16, -17, ConAu 35NR, SmATA 65*

Mather, Kirtley Fletcher 1888-1978 *BioIn 2, -7, -12, ConAu 17R, CurBio 51, DcScB S2, InSci, IntAu&W 77, IntWW 74, -75, -76, -77, -78, -79N, McGMS 80, REnAL, WhAm 7, WhNAA, WhoAm 74, -76, -78*

Mathers, Michael 1945- *ConAu 65*

Mathers, Petra *ChlBIID*

Mathes, J C 1931- *ConAu 49*

Matheson, Richard 1926- *BioIn 12, -13, CmMov, ConAu 97, ConLC 37, ConSFA, ConTFT 1, -6, CyWA 89, DcLB 8, -44, FilmgC, HalFC 84, -88, IntAu&W 91, NewEScF, NewYTET, Novels, PenEncH, ScF&FL 92, ScFSB, SupFW, TwCSFW 86, -91, WhoHr&F, WhoSciF, WorEFlm, WrDr 84, -86, -88, -90, -92*

Matheson, Richard Burton 1926- *EncSF 93, WrDr 94*

Mathews, Eliza Kirkham d1802 *CarSB*

Mathews, Eliza Kirkham 1772-1802 *FemiCLE*

Mathews, Evelyn Craw 1906- *ConAu P-2*
Pseud./variant:
Cleaver, Nancy

Mathews, Ferdinand Schuyler 1854-1938 *AmLY, ChhPo S2, DcAmAu, DcNAA, WhAm 1, WhNAA*

Mathews, Janet 1914- *ConAu 115, SmATA 41*

Mathews, Joanna Hooe 1849-1901 *Alli SUP, CarSB, DcAmAu, DcNAA, WhAm 1*

Mathews, Louise *ConAu X, SmATA X*
Main entry: Tooke, Louise Mathews

Mathews, Marcia Mayfield *ConAu 9R, ForWC 70, WrDr 76, -80, -82, -84*

Mathews, Mitford M d1985 *NewYTBS 85*

Mathews, Mitford M 1891-1985 *BioIn 14*

Mathews, Mitford McLeod, Sr. 1891-1985 *AmAu&B, ConAu 115, NewYTBS 85, WhAm 8*

Mathews, Roy Palmer 1898- *WhoAmP 73*

Mathews, Sally *ChhPo S1, -S2*

Mathiesen, Egon 1907-1976 *BioIn 5, -8, -13, ConAu 109, IlsBYP, IlsCB 1946, -1957, SmATA 28N*

Mathieu, Joe
Main entry: Mathieu, Joseph

Mathieu, Joseph 1949-
Pseud./variant:
Mathieu, Joe

Mathieu, Joseph P 1949- *ConAu 117, -125 SmATA 36, -43*

Mathis, Sharon Bell *DrAPF 87, -89, -91, -93, InB&W 85*

Mathis, Sharon Bell 1937- *AuBYP 2S, -3, BioIn 10, -15, -16, BlkAWP, BlkAull, -92, BlkWr 1, -2, ChlLR 3, ConAu 41R, DcAmChF 1960, DcLB 33, DrAF 76, DrAP 75, DrAPF 83, -85, FourBJA, InB&W 80, LivgBAA, MajAI, OxCChiL, SelBAAf, SelBAAu, SmATA 7, -58, -3AS, TwCChW 78, -83, -89, TwCYAW, WhoAm 74, -76, -78, -80, -82, -84, -86, -88, -90, -92, -94, WhoAmW 74, WhoBlA 75, -77, -80, -85, -88, -90, -92, WhoUSWr 88, WhoWrEP 89, -92, WrDr 76, -80, -82, -84, -86, -88, -90, -92*

Matilda, Mackarness 1826-1881 *CarSB*

Matloff, Gregory 1945- *SmATA 73*

Matson, Emerson N 1926- *BioIn 11, ConAu 45, SmATA 12, WhoAdv 80, WrDr 76, -80, -82, -84*

Matsubara, Naoko 1937- *BioIn 7, ConGrA 3, WhoAmA 82, -84, -86, -89, -91*

Matsui, Tadashi 1926- *BioIn 10, -11, ConAu 41R, IntAu&W 77, SmATA 8*

Matsuno, Masako *AmPB, AuBYP 2, BioIn 8, -10, BkCL, ConAu X, -31NR, FourBJA, SmATA 6, WhoWor 80, WrDr 76, -80, -82*
Main entry: Kobayashi, Masako Matsuno

Matsuno, Masako 1935- *AuBYP 3*

Matsutani, Miyoko 1925?- *ConAu 69, WhoWor 82*

Mattam, Donald 1909- *ConAu 45*

Matte, L'Enc 1936- *BioIn 13, SmATA 22*

Mattheos, Elizabeth R *ForWC 70*

Matthew, Eunice S *AuBYP 2, -3*

Matthew, Jack 1911- *BioIn 5, IlsCB 1946*

Matthews, Ann *SmATA X*
Main entry: Martin, Ann M

Matthews, C M 1908- *ConAu 25R*
Pseud./variant:
Carrington, Molly

Matthews, Clayton 1918- *BioIn 11, ConAu 53, -9NR, -25NR, ScF&FL 92*
Pseud./variant:
Brisco, Patty

Matthews, Downs 1925- *SmATA 71*

Matthews, Ellen 1950- *BioIn 13, SmATA 28*

Matthews, Herbert L 1900-1977 *BioIn 14, -16, EncTwCJ, JrnUS*

Matthews, Herbert Lionel 1900-1977 *AmAu&B, AuBYP 2, -3, Au&Wr 71, BiDAmJo, BioIn 1, -4, -8, -9, -10, -11, -13, BlueB 76, ConAu 1R, -73, -2NR, CurBio 43, -77N, EncAJ, IntAu&W 77, IntWW 74, -75, -76, -77, -78N, ObitOF 79, REnAL, WhAm 7, WhoAm 74, -76, -78, WhoWor 74, WrDr 80, -82, -84*

Matthews, Jacklyn Meek *ConAu X, SmATA X*
Main entry: Meek, Jacklyn O'Hanlon

Matthews, Kenneth David, Jr. 1924- *WhoAm 74*

Matthews, Patricia 1927?- *ArtclWW 2, BioIn 11, -13, -14, -17, ConAu 29R, -9NR, -25NR, MajTwCW, ScF&FL 92, SmATA 28, TwCRHW 90, WrDr 84, -86, -88, -90, -92, -94*
Pseud./variant:
Brisco, Patty
Wylie, Laura

Matthews, Rupert O 1961- *ConAu 118*

Matthews, Rupert Oliver 1961- *AuBYP 3, IntAu&W 89*

Matthews, William H 1919- *AuBYP 3*

Matthews, William Henry, III 1919- *AmMWSc 73P, -76P, -82, -86, -89, -92, AuBYP 2S, BioIn 13, ConAu 9R, SmATA 28, -45, WhoSSW 75, -76, -78*

Matthias, Catherine 1945- *ConAu 110, SmATA 41*

Matthiesen, Thomas *AuBYP 2, -3*

Matthiessen, Peter *DrAPF 87, -89, -91, -93, NewYTBS 90*

Matthiessen, Peter 1927- *AmAu&B, Au&Arts 6, Au&Wr 71, Benet 87, BenetAL 91, BestSel 90-4, BioIn 6, -9, -10, -13, BlueB 76, ConAu 9R, -21NR, ConLC 5, -7, -11, -32, -64, ConNov 72, -76, -82, -86, -91, CurBio 75, CyWA 89, DcLB 6, DcLEL 1940, DrAF 76, IntAu&W 77, -91, IntWW 89, -91, MagSAmL, MajTwCW, OxCAmL 83, SmATA 27, WhoAm 74, -76, -78, -80, -82, -84, -86, -88, -90, -92, -94, WhoUSWr 88, WhoWor 74, WhoWrEP 89, -92, WorAu 1950, WrDr 76, -80, -82, -84, -86, -88, -90, -92, -94*

Mattingley, Christobel 1931- *BioIn 15, ChlLR 24, ConAu 97, -20NR, DcChlFi, SmATA 37, -18AS, TwCChW 78, -83, -89, WrDr 80, -82, -84, -86, -88, -90, -92*

Mattingley, Christobel Rosemary 1931- *MajAI, WrDr 94*

Matulay, Laszlo 1912- *BioIn 5, -15, IlsBYP, IlsCB 1946, SmATA 43*

Matulka, Jan 1890-1972 *BioIn 1, -9, -13, -14, DcCAA 71, -77, -88, GrAmP, IlsCB 1744, NewYTBE 72, OxCTwCA, SmATA 28, WhAmArt 85, WhoAmA 78N, -80N, -82N, -86N, -89N, -91N*

Matus, Greta 1938- *BioIn 11, ConAu 93, SmATA 12*

Maude, Aylmer 1858-1938 *BioIn 2, DcNaB 1931, LongCTC, NewC, OxCCan, REn, TwCA, -SUP, WhoLA*

Maugham, W S *ConAu 40NR, MajTwCW*

Maugham, W Somerset *MajTwCW*

Maugham, W Somerset 1874-1965 *Benet 87, BioIn 14, -15, -16, -17, CamGEL, CnDBLB 6, ConLC 67, CrtSuMy, CyWA 89, DcLB 77, -100, HalFC 88, LiExTwC, MagSWL, RAdv 13-1, RfGEnL 91, ShSCr 8, ShSWr, SmATA 54, StaCVF, TwCCr&M 91, WorAlBi, WorLitC*

Maugham, William Somerset 1874-1965 *ConAu 40NR, IntDcT 2, RfGShF*

Maughan, Joyce Bowen 1928- *IntAu&W 77, WhoAmW 81, WhoWest 78, -80, -82, -89, WrDr 76, -80, -82, -84, -86, -88, -90*

Maule, Hamilton Bee 1915- *AuBYP 2, -3, BioIn 7, -9, -10, ConAu 1R, -3NR, WhoAm 74, -76, -78, -80, -82, -84, WhoUSWr 88, WhoWrEP 89, -92*
Pseud./variant:
Maule, Tex

Maule, Tex *AuBYP 3*
Main entry: Maule, Hamilton Bee

Maupassant, Guy De 1850-1893 *AtlBL, Benet 87, BiD&SB, BioIn 1, -2, -3, -4, -5, -7, -8, -9, -10, -11, -12, -14, -15, ClDMEL 47, CrtSuMy, CyWA 58, DcEuL, DcLB 123, Dis&D, EncWT, EuAu, EuWr 7, GrFLW, GuFrLit 1, MagSWL, NewC, NinCLC 1, -42, Novels, OxCEng 67, -85, OxCFr, PenC EUR, PenEncH, RAdv 13-2, RComWL, REn, ScF&FL 92, ShSCr 1, ShSWr,*

SupFW, WhDW, WhoHr&F, WorAlBi, WorAl, WorLitC
Pseud./variant:
DeMaupassant, Guy

Maureen, Mary, Sister 1924- *BioIn 11, ConAu 21R*

Maurer, Werner 1933- *IlsBYP, WhoGrA 82*

Maurice, Furnley *DcLEL, OxCAusL, SingR 2, WhoLA*
Main entry: Wilmot, Frank

Maurice, Furnley 1881-1942 *CamGLE*

Maurier, Daphne Du *CurBio 40, InWom SUP, LongCTC, ScF&FL 92, TwCA, –SUP*
Main entry: DuMaurier, Daphne

Maurois, Andre *TwCChW 89B*

Maurois, Andre 1885-1967 *AtlBL, AuBYP 2, –3, Benet 87, BioIn 1, –2, –3, –4, –5, –7, –8, –9, –12, –16, –17, CasWL, ChhPo S2, ClDMEL 47, ConAu 25R, –P-2, DcLB 65, EncSF 93, EncWL, –2, EvEuW, LongCTC, MajTwCW, ModFrL, NewC, Novels, ObitOF 79, ObitT 1961, OxCChiL, OxCEng 67, –85, OxCFr, PenC EUR, RAdv 1, –13-1, REn, ScF&FL 92, ScFSB, ScFEYrs, TwCA, –SUP, TwCChW 78B, –83B, TwCSFW 86A, –91A, TwCWr, WhDW, WhAm 4, WhoHr&F, WhoLA, WhoTwCL, WorAlBi, WorAl*
Pseud./variant:
Herzog, Emile Salomon Wilhelm

Maury, Inez 1909- *ConAu 61*

Maury, Jean West *WhNAA*

Mauser, Patricia Rhoads 1943- *AuBYP 3, ConAu 106, –22NR, IntAu&W 86, SmATA 37*

Mauzey, Merritt 1898-1973 *BioIn 14*

Mauzey, Merritt 1898-1975? *ArtsAmW 3, BioIn 5, –12, ConAu 102, IlsBYP, IlsCB 1946, WhAmArt 85, WhoAmA 73*

Maves, Mary Carolyn 1916- *BioIn 11, ConAu 49, SmATA 10*

Maves, Paul Benjamin 1913- *BioIn 11, ConAu 45, –1NR, –17NR, DrAS 74P, –78P, LEduc 74, SmATA 10, WhoAm 74, –76, –78, –80, –82, –84, –86, –88, –90, –92, –94*

Mavor, William 1758-1837 *DcBiPP, OxCChiL*

Mawicke, Tran 1911- *BioIn 9, –12, SmATA 15, WhAmArt 85, WhoAmA 73, –78, –80, –82, –84, –86, –89*

Mawson, Colin Ashley 1908- *AmMWSc 73P*

Max *Benet 87, BlkWr 1, –2, ConAu 130, MajTwCW, SmATA X*
Main entry: Diop, Birago Ismael

Max, Peter 1937?- *AmArt, BioIn 8, –9, –10, –12, –15, BioNews 74, ConAu 116, CurBio 71, IlsBYP, News 93-2, PrintW 83, –85, SmATA 45, WhoAm 74, –76, –78, –80, –82, –84, –88, –90, –92, –94, WhoAmA 73, –78, –80, –82, –84, –86, –89, –91, WhoE 83*

Max, Peter 1939- *ConGrA 3*

Maxey, Betty *IlsBYP*

Maxey, Dale 1927- *BioIn 8, ChhPo S1, IlsCB 1957*

Maxon, Anne *ConAu X, SmATA 2, –X*
Main entry: Best, Allena Champlin

Maxon, Rex *ArtCS*

Maxon, Rex 1892-1973 *EncACom*

Maxwell, Allen 1915- *WhoSSW 73*

Maxwell, Allen Jay 1873-1946 *DcNCBi 4*

Maxwell, Arthur S 1896-1970 *BioIn 11, ConAu P-1, SmATA 11, WhAm 5, –6*

Maxwell, Edith 1923- *AuBYP 2S, –3, BioIn 10, ConAu 49, SmATA 7, WhoAmW 77*

Maxwell, Gavin 1914-1969 *AuBYP 2, –3, BioIn 7, –8, –9, –10, –14, –17, CamGLE, ConAu 5R, –25R, DcLEL 1940, DcNaB 1961, GrBr, LongCTC, MajTwCW, NewC, ObitOF 79, OxCEng 85, SmATA 65, TwCWr, WhAm 5, WorAu 1950*

Maxwell, Jack *ConAu X, EncSF 93*

Maxwell, William *DrAPF 87, –89, –91, –93, WrDr 86, –88, –90, –92*

Maxwell, William 1908- *AmAu&B, AmNov, AuBYP 2, –3, BioIn 2, –4, –7, –12, –13, ConAu 93, ConLC 19, ConNov 72, –76, –82, –86, –91, CurBio 49, DcLB Y80B, IntAu&W 77, OxCAmL 65, –83, REn, REnAL, TwCA SUP, WhoAm 74, –76, –78, –80, –82, –84, –86, –88, –90, –92, –94, WhoUSWr 88, WhoWor 74, WhoWrEP 89, –92, WrDr 76, –80, –82, –84, –86, –88, –90, –92, –94*

Maxwell, William 1916- *WrDr 94*

Maxwell-Hudson, Clare 1946- *ConAu 69*

Maxwell-Lefroy, Cecil Anthony 1907- *ConAu P-1*

May, Charles Paul 1920- *AuBYP 2, -3, BioIn 7, -8, -9, ConAu 1R, -5NR, IntAu&W 77, -82, SmATA 4*

May, Ernest R 1928- *ConAu 22NR, WrDr 92*

May, Ernest Richard 1928- *AmAu&B, ConAu 1R, -6NR, DrAS 74H, -78H, -82H, WhoAm 74, -76, -78, -80, -82, -84, -86, WhoUSWr 88, WhoWor 74, WhoWrEP 89, -92, WrDr 94*

May, Frederick 1891- *DcBrAr 2, Who 74*

May, Julian 1931- *AuBYP 2, -3, BioIn 11, ConAu 1R, -6NR, EncSF 93, IntAu&W 91, NewEScF, ScF&FL 92, SmATA 11, TwCSFW 86, -91, WrDr 88, -90, -92, -94*
Pseud./variant:
Feilen, John
Grant, Matthew G
Thorne, Ian

May, Julian 1932- *RGTwCSF, ScFSB*

May, Karl Friedrich 1842-1912 *BioIn 1, -7, -8, -10, -15, EncFWF, OxCChiL, WhNaAH*

May, Lewis Victor, Jr. 1927- *IlsCB 1946*

May, Lola June 1923- *WhoAmW 75*

May, Robert Lewis 1905-1976 *BioIn 1, -2, -5, -7, -11, -13, ChhPo, -S2, ConAu 104, NatCAB 61, SmATA 27N*

May, Robert S *ScF&FL 92*

May, Robert Stephen 1929- *ConAu 30NR, SmATA 46*
Pseud./variant:
May, Robin

May, Robin
Main entry: May, Robert Stephen

May, Sophie *WomNov*

May, Sophie 1833-1906 *InWom SUP, OxCChiL*

Mayall, R Newton 1904- *ConAu P-1*

Mayberry, Florence V Wilson *BioIn 11, ConAu 9R, SmATA 10*

Maybury, Richard J 1946- *SmATA 72*

Mayer, Albert Ignatius, Jr. 1906-1960 *BioIn 13, ConAu 109, OhA&B, SmATA 29N, WhAm 4, WhoLibI 82*

Mayer, Ann M 1938- *BioIn 12, ConAu 57, SmATA 14*

Mayer, Barbara 1939- *SmATA 77*

Mayer, Hannelore 1929- *IntAu&W 77, -82, -86*
Pseud./variant:
Valencak, Hannelore

Mayer, Jane 1903- *AuBYP 3*

Mayer, Jane Rothschild 1903- *AmAu&B, AmNov X, AuBYP 2, Au&Wr 71, BioIn 2, -3, -7, -15, ConAu 9R, CurBio 54, ForWC 70, SmATA 38, WhoAm 74, WhoAmJ 80, WhoAmW 74, WhoWorJ 72, -78*
Pseud./variant:
Jaynes, Clare

Mayer, Joseph 1887-1975 *AmMWSc 73S, WhAm 6, WhNAA, WhoAm 74*

Mayer, Marianna 1945?- *ArtclWW 2, AuBYP 3, BioIn 12, ConAu 93, FourBJA, SmATA 32*

Mayer, Mercer 1943- *AuBYP 3, BioIn 12, -14, -16, ChlLR 11, ConAu 85, -38NR, DcLB 61, FourBJA, IlsBYP, IlsCB 1967, MajAI, SmATA 16, -32, -73*

Mayerson, Charlotte Leon *ConAu 13R, ForWC 70, SmATA 36*

Mayerson, Evelyn Wilde 1934- *BioIn 16*

Mayerson, Evelyn Wilde 1935- *SmATA 55*

Mayfield, Sue 1963- *SmATA 72*

Mayhar, Ardath *ConSFF, ScFSB*

Mayhar, Ardath 1930- *BioIn 15, ConAu 103, -19NR, -42NR, EncSF 93, IntAu&W 86, -89, -91, ScF&FL 92, SmATA 38, TwCSFW 86, -91, WrDr 88, -90, -92*
Pseud./variant:
Cannon, Ravenna

Mayhar, Ardath Hurst 1930- *WrDr 94*

Mayhew, Henry 1812-1887 *Alli, -SUP, BiD&SB, BioIn 8, -9, -10, -13, -14, -15, -16, BritAu 19, CamGEL, CamGLE, CarSB, ChhPo, DcBiPP, DcEnA, DcEnL, DcLB 18, -55, DcLEL, DcNaB, NinCLC 31, NotNAT B, OxCEng 67, -85, PenC ENG, StaCVF, WebE&AL, WhDW*

Mayhew, Ralph *CarSB, ChhPo S2*

Maynard, Chris
Main entry: Maynard, Christopher

Maynard, Christopher 1949- *ConAu 118, IntAu&W 91, SmATA 43, WrDr 82, -84, -86, -88, -90*
Pseud./variant:
Maynard, Chris

Maynard, Fredelle Bruser *BioIn 17*

Maynard, Fredelle Bruser 1922- *CaW, ConAu 85, IntAu&W 89, –91, OxCCan SUP*

Maynard, Joyce 1953- *AuBYP 3, ConAu 129*

Maynard, Olga 1920- *ConAu 114, SmATA 40, WhoAmW 77, –81*

Mayne, William 1928- *AnCL, AuBYP 2, –3, BioIn 6, –7, –8, –9, –10, –17, CamGLE, ChlFicS, ChlLR 25, ConAu 9R, ConLC 12, DcLEL 1940, IntAu&W 82, –86, –89, –91, OxCChiL, ScF&FL 92, ScFSB, SenS, SmATA 6, –68, –11AS, SouSt, ThrBJA, TwCChW 78, –83, –89, Who 82, –83, –85, –88, –90, –92, WhoAm 74, –76, –78, –80, –82, –84, –90, –92, –94, WhoChL, WhoWor 74, WrDr 76, –80, –82, –84*
Pseud./variant:
James, Dynely

Mayne, William 1929- *WrDr 86, –88, –90, –92, –94*

Mayne, William James Carter 1928- *ConAu 37NR, EncSF 93, MajAI, TwCYAW*
Pseud./variant:
Cobalt, Martin
Molin, Charles

Maynes, Dr. J O Rocky
Main entry: Maynes, J Oscar, Jr.

Maynes, J Oscar 1929- *BioIn 15*

Maynes, J Oscar, Jr. 1929- *ConAu 115, LEduc 74, SmATA 38*
Pseud./variant:
J O Rocky, Jr.
Maynes, Dr. J O Rocky

Mayo, Edward Leslie 1904- *AnCL, ChhPo, ConPo 70, –75, DrAS 74E, WrDr 76, –80*

Mayo, Margaret 1935- *ConAu 107, SmATA 38*

Mayrocker, Friederike 1924- *BioIn 13, BlmGWL, DcLB 85, EncCoWW, IntAu&W 86, –89, –91, IntWWP 82, OxCGer 76, –86, WomWrGe*

Mays, Lewis Victor, Jr. 1927- *BioIn 5, –8, –10, ConAu 25R, FourBJA, IlsBYP, IlsCB 1957, –1967, SmATA 5, WhoAmA 78, WhoE 86, –91*
Pseud./variant:
Mays, Victor

Mays, Lucinda L 1924- *SmATA 49*

Mays, Victor
Main entry: Mays, Lewis Victor, Jr.

Mazer, Anne 1953- *ConAu 135, SmATA 67, WrDr 94*

Mazer, Harry *DrAPF 87, –89, –91, –93*

Mazer, Harry 1925- *Au&Arts 5, BioIn 14, –16, –17, ChlLR 16, ConAu 97, –32NR, FifBJA, MajAI, SmATA 31, –67, –11AS, TwCYAW*

Mazer, Norma Fox *DrAPF 87, –89, –91, –93*

Mazer, Norma Fox 1931- *Au&Arts 5, BioIn 15, –16, –17, ChlLR 23, ConAu 69, –12NR, –32NR, ConLC 26, DcAmChF 1960, –1985, DrAPF 83, –85, FifBJA, MajAI, ScF&FL 92, SmATA 24, –67, –1AS, TwCChW 89, TwCYAW, WhoAm 88, –90, –92, –94, WhoAmW 87, –89, WrDr 90, –92, –94*

Mazonowicz, Douglas 1920- *ConAu 57, PrintW 83, –85*

Mazurkiewicz, Albert J 1926- *ConAu 9R, –3NR, LEduc 74*

Mazurkiewicz, Albert Joseph 1926- *WhoE 91*

Mazza, Adriana 1928- *BioIn 12, ConAu 4NR, SmATA 19*
Pseud./variant:
Saviozzi, Adriana Mazza

Mazzio, Joann 1926- *SmATA 74*

McAfee, Annalena *AuBYP 3*

McAleavy, Henry 1912-1968 *ConAu P-2*

McAllister, Mariana Kennedy *AuBYP 2, –3, BioIn 8*

McBain, Ed *AuBYP 2, –3, Benet 87, BlueB 76, CamGLE, ConAu X, –38NR, ConNov 72, –76, –82, DcLEL 1940, DrAPF 83, –85, –89, –91, EncMys, EncSF 93, HalFC 84, IntAu&W 77X, –91X, IntWW 74, –75, –76, –77, –78, –79, –80, –81, –82, –83, –89, –91, MajTwCW, Novels, PenC AM, ScF&FL 92, SmATA X, TwCCr&M 80, –85, TwCWr, Who 82, –83, –85, –88, –90, –92, WhoAm 84, –86, –88, WhoUSWr 88, WhoWor 74, WhoWrEP 89, –92, WorAu 1950, WrDr 76, –80, –82, –84, –86, –88, –90, –92*
Main entry: Hunter, Evan

McBain, Ed 1926- *BioIn 14, –15, –17, CrtSuMy, HalFC 88, TwCCr&M 91, WhoAm 94, WrDr 94*

McBain, William Norseworthy 1918- *AmMWSc 73S, –78S*

McBratney, Sam *ChlFicS*

McBride, Mary Margaret 1899-1976 *AmAu&B, AmWomWr, AuBYP 2S, BioIn 1, –3, –4, –5, –9, –10, –11, ConAu 65, –69, CurBio 41, –54, –76N, EncTwCJ, InWom SUP, ObitOF 79, WhAm 7, WhoAm 74, –76, WhoAmW 74, WorAlBi, WorAl*

McBride, Mary Margaret 1900-1976 *AuBYP 3*

McBride, Will 1931- *BioIn 8, -10, ConPhot 82, -88, ICPEnP A*

McBurney, Laressa Cox *WhNAA*

McCabe, John C, III 1920- *WrDr 86, -88, -90, -92*

McCabe, John Charles, III 1920- *ConAu 1R, -1NR, DrAS 74E, -78E, -82E, IntAu&W 77, WhoAm 74, -76, -78, -80, -82, -84, -86, -88, -90, WhoMW 74, -76, -78, -84, WhoUSWr 88, WhoWor 78, WhoWrEP 89, -92, WrDr 76, -80, -82, -84, -94*

McCabe, Joseph E *WhCiWar*

McCabe, Joseph E 1912- *BlueB 76, ConAu 17R, IntAu&W 77, LEduc 74, WhoAm 74, -76, -78, WhoMW 74, -76, -78, WhoRel 92*

McCabe, Olivia *CarSB*

McCaffery, Janet 1936- *BioIn 12, IlsBYP, IlsCB 1967, SmATA 38*

McCaffrey, Anne *IntvTCA 2*

McCaffrey, Anne 1926- *ArtclWW 2, Au&Arts 6, BestSel 89-2, BlmGWL, ConAu 35NR, DcAmChF 1960, IntAu&W 86, -91, MajTwCW, NewEScF, RGTwCSF, ScF&FL 92, ScFSB, SmATA 70, -11AS, TwCChW 89, TwCSFW 86, -91, WrDr 86, -88, -90, -92*

McCaffrey, Anne Inez 1926- *AmWomWr, AuNews 2, BioIn 10, -11, -12, -13, ConAu 25R, -15NR, ConLC 17, ConSFA, DcLB 8, EncSF 93, FifBJA, IntAu&W 77, -82, MajAI, SmATA 8, TwCYAW, WhoAm 74, -76, -78, -80, -82, -84, -86, -88, -90, -92, -94, WhoAmW 74, WhoSciF, WrDr 76, -80, -82, -84, -94*

McCaffrey, Mary *SmATA X*
Main entry: Szudek, Agnes Susan Philomena

McCague, James 1909-1977 *ConAu 1R, -2NR*

McCahill, William P *AuBYP 3*

McCahill, William Paul 1916- *AmCath 80, AuBYP 2, BioIn 7, BlueB 76, WhoAm 74, -76, WhoGov 72, WhoSSW 73, WhoWor 74*

McCaig, Robert Jesse 1907- *AmCath 80, Au&Wr 71, BioIn 10, ConAu 1R, -1NR, EncFWF, WhoPNW, WrDr 76, -80, -82*

McCain, Murray David, Jr. 1926-1981 *BioIn 10, -12, -13, ChhPo S1, ConAu 1R, -105, -15NR, SmATA 7, -29N*

McCaleb, Walter Flavius 1873-1967 *AmAu&B, ConAu P-1, OhA&B, TexWr, WhAm 5*

McCalip, William C 1935?- *BioIn 9*

McCall, Edith S 1911- *BioIn 10, ConAu 5R, LEduc 74, SmATA 6, WhoAmW 75, -77, WhoMW 84, WrDr 76, -80*

McCall, Edith Sansom 1911- *AuBYP 3*

McCall, Virginia 1909- *AuBYP 3*

McCall, Virginia Nielsen 1909- *AuBYP 2S, BioIn 11, ConAu 1R, -1NR, -17NR, -39NR, ForWC 70, SmATA 13, WhoAmW 74, -75*
Pseud./variant:
Nielsen, Virginia

McCall Smith, Alexander 1948- *SmATA 73*

McCallum, Phyllis 1911- *BioIn 11, ConAu 53, -4NR, IntAu&W 77, -82, -86, -89, -91, SmATA 10, WhoAmW 77, WrDr 76, -82, -84, -86, -88, -90, -92*

McCann, Edson *ConAu 141, -37NR, EncSF 93, IntAu&W 91X, MajTwCW, SmATA 76, TwCSFW 86, WrDr 86, -88, -90, -92, -94*
Main entry: del Rey, Lester

McCann, Gerald 1916- *BioIn 5, IlsBYP, IlsCB 1946, SmATA 41*

McCann, Helen 1948- *ConAu 142, SmATA 75*
Pseud./variant:
Dean, Elinor

McCannon, Dindga 1947- *BlkAuII, -92*

McCannon, Dindga Fatima 1947- *AfroAA, BioIn 15, -16, ConAu 114, SmATA 41, WhoBlA 90, -92, -94*

McCarter, Neely D *WhoAm 94, WhoRel 92, WhoWest 89, -92*

McCarter, Neely Dixon 1929- *BioIn 16, ConAu 109, SmATA 47, WhoRel 75, -77*

McCarthy, Agnes 1933- *BioIn 9, ConAu 17R, SmATA 4, WhoAmW 77*

McCarthy, Colin John 1951- *SmATA 77*

McCarty, Rega Kramer 1904- *BioIn 11, ConAu 5R, ForWC 70, SmATA 10*

McCary, James Leslie 1919-1978 *ConAu 85*

McCaslin, Nellie 1914- *BioIn 11, -16, ConAu 33R, DrAS 74E, -78E, -82E, IntAu&W 77, -82, -86, -89, -91, NotWoAT, SmATA 12, WhoAmW 74, -75, -77,*

WhoEnt 92, WrDr 76, –80, –82, –84, –86, –88, –90, –92, –94

McCaughrean, Geraldine
Main entry: Jones, Geraldine

McCaughrean, Geraldine 1951- *BioIn 15, ChlFicS, ConAu 117, ScF&FL 92, SmATA X, TwCChW 89, TwCYAW*

McCaughren, Tom *ScF&FL 92*

McCaughren, Tom 1936- *SmATA 75, TwCChW 89, WrDr 90, –92, –94*

McCauley, Carole Spearin *DrAPF 87, –89, –91, –93*

McCauley, Carole Spearin 1939- *ConAu 57, –8NR, –25NR, DrAF 76, DrAP 75, DrAPF 83, –85, WhoAmW 81, WhoUSWr 88, WhoWrEP 89, –92*

McCaw, Mabel Niedermeyer 1899- *ConAu P-2*

McCay, Winsor 1869-1934 *ArtCS, BioIn 10, DcLB 22, EncACom, HalFC 84, SmATA 41, WorECar, WorEFlm*
Pseud./variant:
Silas

McCay, Winsor 1871-1934 *BioIn 14, –15, –17*

McCay, Winsor 1886-1934 *BenetAL 91, HalFC 88*

McClary, Jane Stevenson *AuBYP 3*

McClary, Jane Stevenson 1919- *ConAu 1R, –1NR, ForWC 70, WhoAmW 77*
Pseud./variant:
McIlvaine, Jane

McClary, Jane Stevenson 1919-1990 *BioIn 17, ConAu 130, SmATA 64*

McClary, Jane Stevenson McIlvaine 1919- *IntAu&W 89, –91*

McClelland, Hugh *OxCCan SUP*

McClintock, Barbara 1955- *SmATA 57*

McClintock, Francis Leopold 1819-1907 *BiDIrW, Expl 93*

McClintock, Francis Leopold, Sir 1819-1907 *BioIn 2, –11, BritAu 19, DcIrB 88, DcNaB S2, OxCCan, OxCShps*

McClintock, Marshall 1906-1967 *AuBYP 2, –3, BioIn 7, –9, ChhPo, ConAu P-1, SmATA 3*
Pseud./variant:
Duncan, Gregory
Marshall, Douglas
McClintock, Mike
Starret, William

McClintock, Mike
Main entry: McClintock, Marshall

McClintock, Theodore 1902-1971 *AuBYP 2, –3, BioIn 8, –9, –12, ConAu 33R, –73, SmATA 14*

McClinton, Leon 1933- *BioIn 11, ConAu 65, SmATA 11*

McCloskey, John Robert 1914- *MajAI*

McCloskey, Robert 1914- *AmAu&B, AmPB AnCL, AuBYP 2, –3, Au&ICB, BenetAL 91, BioIn 1, –2, –4, –5, –7, –8, –9, –10, –12, BkP, Cald 1938, ChlLR 7, ConAu 9R, CurBio 42, DcLB 22, FamAIYP, IlsBYP, IlsCB 1744, –1946, –1957, –1967, JBA 51, NewbC 1956, OhA&B, OxCChiL, REnAL, SmATA 2, –39, Str&VC, TwCChW 78, –83, –89, WhAm 5 WhoAm 74, –76, –78, –80, –82, –84, –86, –88, –90, –92, –94, WhoAmA 73, –78, –80, –82, –84, –86, WrDr 80, –82, –84, –86, –88, –90, –92, –94*
Pseud./variant:
Dangerfield, Balfour

McCloy, James F 1941- *SmATA 59*

McClung, Nellie Letitia 1873-1951 *ArtclWW 2, BlmGWL, DcLB 92, EncWB, WomNov*

McClung, Nellie Letitia Mooney 1873-1951 *BioIn 1, –2, –7, –8, –10, –11, –12, –17, CanNov, CanWr, ChhPo, CreCan 1, ObitOF 79, OxCCan, OxCCanL, OxCChiL, WhNAA*

McClung, Robert M 1916- *ChlLR 11, ConAu 21NR, SmATA 68, –15AS, WhoUSWr 88, WhoWrEP 89*

McClung, Robert Marhall 1916- *WhoWrEP 92*

McClung, Robert Marshall 1916- *AuBYP 2, –3, AuNews 2, BioIn 6, –7, –8, –9, –11, –12, ConAu 13R, –6NR, IlsCB 1957, –1967, IntAu&W 86, –89, MajAI, MorJA, SmATA 2, WhoE 75, –77, WrDr 76, –80, –82, –84, –86, –88, –90, –92, –94*

McClure, Darrell *EncACom*

McClure, Darrell 1903- *ArtCS*

McClure, Gillian Mary 1948- *BioIn 14, ConAu 103, IntAu&W 86, –91, SmATA 31, WrDr 76, –80, –82, –84, –86, –88, –90, –92, –94*

McCluskey, John A *DrAPF 91*

McCluskey, John A 1944- *BioIn 7, -14, BlkAWP, BlkWrNE, ConAu 57, -7NR, DcLB 33, InB&W 80, -85, SelBAAf, WhoBlA 85*

McCluskey, John A, Jr. *DrAPF 87, -89, -93*

McCluskey, John A, Jr. 1944- *WhoBlA 85, -88, -90, -92, -94*

McColvin, Lionel Roy 1896-1976 *AuBYP 3, BioIn 15*

McColvin, Lionel Roy 1896-1977 *AuBYP 2, Au&Wr 71, BioIn 2, -8, -11, Who 74, WhoLib 54*

McConnell, James Douglas R 1915- *ConAu 9R, -6NR, EncMys, SmATA 40, WrDr 76, -80*
Pseud./variant:
Rutherford, Douglas
Temple, Paul

McConnell, James Douglas Rutherford 1915- *ConAu 22NR*

McConnell, James Douglas Rutherford 1915-1988 *ConAu 125, SmATA 56N*

McConnell, Mickey *BioIn 4*

McCord, Anne 1942- *ConAu 109, IntAu&W 91, SmATA 41, WrDr 76, -80, -82, -84, -86, -88, -90*

McCord, David 1897- *AmAu&B, AnCL, AuBYP 3, BenetAL 91, BioIn 6, -9, -11, -12, -13, BkCL, BkP, ChhPo, -S1, -S2, ChlLR 9, ConAu 73, DcLB 61, IntAu&W 91, OxCAmL 65, -83, OxCChiL, REnAL, SmATA 18, Str&VC, ThrBJA, TwCChW 78, -83, -89, WhNAA, WhoAm 74, -76, -78, -80, -82, -84, -86, WhoWor 74, -78, -80, -82, WrDr 80, -82, -84, -86, -88, -90*

McCord, David Thompson Watson 1897- *ConAu 38NR, MajAI*

McCord, Jean 1924- *BioIn 14, ConAu 49, SmATA 34*

McCormick, Alma Heflin *AuBYP 3*

McCormick, Alma Heflin 1910- *AuBYP 2, BioIn 7, WhoAmW 83, -85, -87, -91, -93*

McCormick, Arthur David 1860-1943 *BioIn 1, -14, DcBrAr 1, DcBrBI, DcVicP 2, IlsCB 1744*

McCormick, Bill *AuBYP 2S, -3, Ballpl 90*

McCormick, Brooks *SmATA X*
Main entry: Adams, William Taylor

McCormick, Dell J 1892-1949 *BioIn 1, -12, SmATA 19*

McCormick, Donald 1911- *Au&Wr 71, BioIn 12, ConAu 73, -14NR, -32NR, IntAu&W 77, -86, SmATA 14, WrDr 76, -80, -82, -84, -86, -88, -90, -92*
Pseud./variant:
Deacon, Richard
McCormick, George Donald

McCormick, Edith Joan 1934- *SmATA 30, WhoLibI 82*

McCormick, George Donald
Main entry: McCormick, Donald

McCormick, Jack Sovern 1929-1979 *AmMWSc 73P, ConAu 9R, -85, IndAu 1917, WrDr 76, -80*

McCormick, Jo Mary 1918- *WhoAmA 73, -78, -80, -82, -84, -86, -89, WhoAmW 75, -77*

McCormick, Mona *ConAu 77, WhoLibI 82*

McCormick, Rose Matthew, Sister 1914- *ConAu 21R*

McCormick, Wilfred 1903- *AuBYP 2, -3, BioIn 7, ConAu 1R, -1NR, IndAu 1917, WhAm 8, WhoAm 74, -76, -78, -80, -82, WhoWest 82, WhoWor 78, -80, -82*

McCourt, Edward Alexander 1907-1972 *Au&Wr 71, BioIn 13, CanWr, CasWL, ConAu 9R, -103, ConNov 72, CreCan 2, OxCCan, -SUP, OxCCanL, SmATA 28N*

McCoy, Iola Fuller 1906- *BiDrLUS 70, ConAu 13R, MichAu 80, SmATA 3*
Pseud./variant:
Fuller, Iola

McCoy, Joseph Jerome 1917- *AuBYP 2, -3, BioIn 8, -11, ConAu 13R, SmATA 8*

McCoy, Joseph Jerome, Jr. 1917- *WhoUSWr 88, WhoWrEP 89, -92*

McCoy, Kathleen 1945- *ConAu 81, -22NR, WhoAmW 77, WhoWrEP 89*

Mc Coy, Kathleen Kathy 1945- *WhoWrEP 92*

McCoy, Lois 1941- *ConAu 22NR, SmATA 38*

McCracken, Glenn 1908- *ConAu 5R*

McCracken, Harold 1894- *AmAu&B, AuBYP 2, -3, BioIn 2, -7, -8, ConAu 107, CurBio 49, JBA 51, WhAm 8, WhoAm 74, -76, -78, -80, -82, WhoAmA 73, -78, -80, -82, -84, WhoWest 76, WhoWor 78*

McCrady, Lady 1951- *BioIn 12, SmATA 16*

McCrea, James 1920- *BioIn 6, -8, -9, ConAu 5R, -8NR, IlsCB 1957, -1967, SmATA 3*

McCrea, Mary *AuBYP 2S, -3*

McCrea, Ruth 1921- *BioIn 6, -8, -9, ConAu 5R, -8NR, IlsCB 1957, -1967, SmATA 3*

McCuaig, Ronald 1908- *ConAu 114, ConPo 70, -75, -80, OxCAusL, WrDr 76, -80, -82, -84*

McCue, Lillian Bueno *AuBYP 3, WrDr 86, -88, -90, -92*

McCue, Lillian Bueno 1902- *AuBYP 2, ConAu 1R, -2NR, WrDr 76, -80, -82, -84*
Pseud./variant:
DeLaTorre, Lillian

McCue, Lillian Bueno 1902-1993 *ConAu 142*

McCue, Lisa 1959- *SmATA 65*

McCue, Lisa Emiline 1959- *ConAu 136, WrDr 94*

McCullagh, Sheila K 1920- *WrDr 86, -88, -90, -92*

McCullagh, Sheila Kathleen 1920- *Au&Wr 71, ConAu 110, IntAu&W 89, -91, WrDr 76, -80, -82, -84, -94*

McCullers, Carson *IntvTCA 2*

McCullers, Carson 1917-1967 *AmAu&B, AmNov, AmWomD, AmWomWr 92, AmWr, ArtclWW 2, Benet 87, BenetAL 91, BiE&WWA, BioIn 2, -4, -5, -6, -7, -8, -9, -10, -11, -12, -13, -15, -16, -17, BlmGWL, CamGEL, CamGLE, CamHAL, CasWL, CnDAL, CnMD, CnMWL, ConAu 5R, -25R, -1BS, -3BS, -18NR, ConLC 1, -4, -10, -12, -48, ConNov 76, -82A, -86A, ContDcW 89, CurBio 40, -67, CyWA 58, -89, DcAmB S8, DcLB 2, -7, DcLEL 1940, EncSoH, EncWL, -2, EncWT, FemiCLE, FifSWrA, FilmgC, GayLL, HalFC 84, -88, HanAmWH, IntDcWB, LongCTC, MagSAmL, MajTwCW, McGEWD 72, -84, ModAL, -S1, -S2, ModAWWr, ModWD, NewCon, NotAW MOD, NotNAT B, NotWoAT, Novels, ObitOF 79, ObitT 1961, OxCAmL 65, -83, PenC AM, PlP&P, RAdv 1, -13-1, REn, REnAL, RfGAmL 87, ShSCr 9, ShSWr, SmATA 27, TwCA, -SUP, TwCWr, WebAB 74, WebE&AL, WhDW, WhAm 4, WhoTwCL, WorAlBi, WorAl, WorLitC, WrPh*

McCullers, Lula Carson 1917-1967 *RfGShF*

McCullers, Lula Carson Smith 1917-1967 *TwCYAW*

McCulley, Johnston 1883-1958 *AmAu&B, BenetAL 91, BioIn 5, ConAu 115, EncFWF, REnAL, ScFEYrs, TwCWW 91, WhAm 3, WhNAA*

McCulloch, Derek Ivor Breashur 1897-1967 *BioIn 8, -13, ChhPo S1, ConAu 109, ObitT 1961, SmATA 29N, WhoChL*

McCulloch, John Tyler *ConAu 132, MajTwCW, TwCYAW*

McCulloch, Sarah *MajAI*
Main entry: Ure, Jean

McCullough, David *NewYTBS 92*

McCullough, David 1933- *ConAu 31NR, CurBio 93, SmATA 62, WhoAm 86, -88, -90, -92, -94*

McCullough, Derek 1897-1967 *OxCChiL*

McCullough, Frances Monson 1938- *BioIn 11, ConAu 41R, ForWC 70, SmATA 8, WhoAm 76, WhoAmW 74, WhoUSWr 88, WhoWrEP 89, -92*

McCully, Emily Arnold *DrAPF 89, -91, -93, MajAI, SmATA 76*

McCully, Emily Arnold 1939- *AuBYP 3, BioIn 8, -10, ConAu X, DrAPF 83, -85, FourBJA, IlsBYP, IlsCB 1957, -1967, SmATA 5, -7AS, WhoAm 94, WhoUSWr 88, WhoWrEP 89, -92*
Main entry: Arnold, Emily

McCunn, Ruthanne Lum *BioIn 17*

McCunn, Ruthanne Lum 1946- *ConAu 119, -43NR, IntAu&W 89, -91, SmATA 63, WhoUSWr 88, WhoWrEP 89, -92*

McCurdy, Michael 1942- *BioIn 11, ConAu 69, -25NR, SmATA 13*

McCurdy, Michael Charles 1942- *WhoAmA 91*

McCutcheon, Elsie 1937- *BioIn 17, ConAu 133, SmATA 60*

McCutcheon, Elsie Mary Jackson 1937- *WrDr 94*

McDaniel, Becky B 1953- *SmATA 61*

McDaniel, Becky Bring 1953- *BioIn 17*

McDaniel, J W *IlsBYP*

McDaniel, Lurlene 1944- *SmATA 71*

McDearmon, Kay *AuBYP 2S, -3, BioIn 12, ConAu 69, -11NR, SmATA 20*

McDermott, Beverly 1941- *AuBYP 3*

McDermott, Beverly Brodsky 1941- *AuBYP 2S, BioIn 10, –11, ConAu 65, –16NR, IlsCB 1967, SmATA 11*
Pseud./variant:
Brodsky, Beverly

McDermott, Gerald *ChlBIlD*

McDermott, Gerald 1941- *AuBYP 3, AuNews 2, BioIn 10, –11, –12, ChlLR 9, ConAu 85, FifBJA, IlsBYP, IlsCB 1967, NewbC 1966, SmATA 16, WhoAmA 80, –82, –84, –86, –89, –91*

McDermott, Gerald Edward 1941- *MajAI, SmATA 74*

McDermott, Michael 1962- *SmATA 76*

McDole, Carol *AuBYP 3*

McDole, Carol 1936- *AuBYP 2S, BioIn 9, ConAu 21R, –X, MichAu 80, SmATA 4*
Pseud./variant:
Farley, Carol

McDonald, Archibald 1790-1853 *BbtC, BioIn 12, DcCanB 8, DcNAA, OxCCan*

McDonald, Barbara Guthrie *AuBYP 2, –3, BioIn 8*

McDonald, Forrest 1927- *AuBYP 2S, –3, BioIn 13, ConAu 9R, –5NR, DcLB 17, DrAS 74H, –78H, –82H, IntAu&W 77, –82, –91, IntWW 91, WhoAm 88, –90, –92, –94, WrDr 76, –80, –82, –84, –86, –88, –90, –92, –94*

McDonald, Gerald D 1905-1970 *BiDrLUS 70, BioIn 1, –6, –8, –9, ChhPo, ConAu P-1, OhA&B, SmATA 3, WhoLibS 55, –66*

McDonald, Jamie *ConAu X, MajAI, SmATA X, WhoWrEP 89, –92, WrDr 86, –88, –90, –92*
Main entry: Heide, Florence Parry

McDonald, Jamie 1919- *WrDr 94*

McDonald, Jill Masefield 1927-1982 *BioIn 11, –12, –13, ConAu 65, –105, –12NR, IlsCB 1967, SmATA 13, –29N*

McDonald, Julie *DrAPF 87, –89, –91, –93*

McDonald, Julie 1929- *ConAu 29R, –12NR, –43NR, DrAF 76, WhoAmW 77*
Pseud./variant:
Jensen, Julie M

Mc Donald, Julie J 1929- *WhoWrEP 92*

McDonald, Kendall 1927- *IntAu&W 77, –82*

McDonald, Lucile 1898- *AuBYP 3*

McDonald, Lucile Saunders 1898- *AuBYP 2, BioIn 7, –10, –11, ConAu 1R, –4NR, –18NR, ForWC 70, IntAu&W 77, –82, SmATA 10, WhoAmW 74, –75, –77, –81, WhoPNW*

McDonald, Mary Reynolds 1888- *ConAu P-1*

McDonald, Megan 1959- *ConAu 135, SmATA 67, WrDr 94*

McDonald, Ralph J *IlsBYP*

McDonnell, Christine 1949- *AuBYP 3, ConAu 107, –23NR, SixBJA, SmATA 34, WhoLibI 82*

McDonnell, Jinny *AuBYP 3*

McDonnell, Lois Eddy *WrDr 86, –88, –90, –92, –94*

McDonnell, Lois Eddy 1914- *BioIn 11, ConAu 5R, IntAu&W 77, SmATA 10, WrDr 76, –80, –82, –84*

McDonnell, Virginia 1917- *AuBYP 3*

McDonnell, Virginia Bleecker *WhoWor 89*

McDonnell, Virginia Bleecker 1917- *AuBYP 2S, ConAu 21R, –8NR, WhoAmW 75, –77, –81, –83, –85, WhoE 75, –77, –83, –85, WhoWor 84*
Pseud./variant:
Kirby, Jean

McDonough, Irma K 1924- *WhoAmW 74, WhoLibI 82*

McDonough, Yona Zeldis 1957- *SmATA 73*

McDougall, Walt 1858-1938 *ArtCS*

McDowell, Elizabeth Tibbals 1912- *ConAu 5R*

McElderry, Margaret K *AmPB, BioIn 1, –9, –10, –11, ForWC 70, WhoLibI 82*

McElfresh, Adeline 1918- *BioIn 14, ConAu 1R, IntAu&W 91, TwCRHW 90, WrDr 84, –86, –88, –90, –92*

McElrath, William N 1932- *BioIn 17, ConAu 77, –35NR, SmATA 65*

McElroy, Clifford D *AuBYP 3*

McElroy, Clifford D, Jr. *AuBYP 2S*

McEntee, Dorothy L 1902- *BioIn 5, IlsBYP, IlsCB 1946, SmATA 37, WhAmArt 85*

McEntee, Howard Garrett 1905- *AuBYP 2S, –3*

McEvedy, Colin 1930- *ConAu 97, IntAu&W 91, WrDr 76, -80, -82, -84, -86, -88, -90, -92*

McEvedy, Colin Peter 1930- *WrDr 94*

McEvoy, Bernard 1842-1932 *ChhPo, DcNAA, WhNAA*

McEwen, Robert 1926-1980 *BioIn 13, ConAu 101, SmATA 23N*

McFadden, Dorothy Loa 1902- *AuBYP 2, -3, BioIn 8, ConAu 17R*

McFadyen, Ella *DcChlFi, SingR 1*

McFadyen, Ella May 1891?- *AuWomWr*

McFall, Christie 1918- *BioIn 11, ConAu 5R, SmATA 12*

McFarlan, Donald M 1915- *BioIn 16, ConAu 65, -10NR, SmATA 59, WhoWor 80*

McFarland, Kenton D 1920- *AuBYP 2S, -3, BioIn 11, ConAu 61, SmATA 11*

McFarland, Marvin Wilks 1919-1985 *BioIn 6, ConAu 115, DrAS 74H, -78H, -82H, InSci, WhoAm 74, -76, -78, -80, -82, WhoGov 77, -72, -75, WhoLibS 55*

McFarland, Wilma *AuBYP 2, -3, BioIn 8*

McFarlane, Leslie 1902-1977 *BioIn 11, -14, CanWW 80, -81, ConAu 112, DcLB 88, OxCCanL, SmATA 31*

McFarlane, Leslie Charles 1902-1977 *ConAu 37NR, MajAI*

McFerran, Ann *ChhPo, -S1, ConAu X*
Main entry: Townsend, Doris McFerran

McGavran, Grace Winifred *AuBYP 2, -3, BioIn 7*

McGavran, Grace Winifred 1896- *AmWomPl*

McGaw, Jessie Brewer 1913- *BioIn 8, -11, ConAu 1R, DrAS 74F, -78F, -82F, ForWC 70, IlsCB 1957, SmATA 10, WhoAmW 74, -75, -77, -81, -83, -85, -87, -89, -91, WhoSSW 73, -75, -76, -78, -80, -82, WhoWor 84, -87, WrDr 76, -80, -82, -84*

McGee, Barbara J 1943- *BioIn 10, ChhPo S1, ConAu 25R, SmATA 6*

McGee, Dorothy Horton *AuBYP 3*

McGee, Dorothy Horton 1913- *AuBYP 2, BioIn 7, WhoAm 94, WhoAmW 74, -75, -77, -81, -83, -85, -87, -89, -91, -93, WhoE 74, -75, -77, -81, -83, -85, -86, -89, -91, -93, WhoFI 87, -89, -92, -94, WhoWor 84, -87, -89, -91, -93*

McGiffin, Lee 1908- *AuBYP 2S, -3, BioIn 9, ConAu P-1, ForWC 70, SmATA 1*

McGillicuddy, Mr *AuBYP 3*

McGillicuddy, Mr *ConAu X*
Main entry: Abisch, Roslyn Kroop

McGinley, Phyllis 1905-1978 *AmAu&B, AmCath 80, AmWomWr, ArtclWW 2, AuBYP 2, Au&Wr 71, Benet 87, BenetAL 91, BioAmW, BioIn 1, -2, -3, -4, -5, -6, -7, -8, -9, -10, -11, -13, -15, BlueB 76, BkP, CelR, ChhPo, -S1, -S2, CnE&AP, CnMWL, ConAu 9R, -77, -19NR, ConPo 70, -75, CurBio 41, -61, -78, -78N, DcLB 11, -48, EncAHmr, EvLB, FemiCLE, InWom SUP, IntAu&W 77, IntWW 74, -75, -76, -77, -78, JBA 51, LongCTC, ModAL, ObitOF 79, OxCAmL 65, -83, PenC AM, RAdv 1, REn, REnAL, SmATA 2, -24N, -44, TwCA SUP, TwCChW 78, -83, -89, TwCWr, WhAm 7, WhoAm 74, -76, -78, WhoAmW 74, -75, -77, WhoTwCL, WhoWor 74, WorAlBi, WorAl WrDr 76*

McGinley, Phyllis Louise 1905-1978 *AuBYP 3*

McGinn, Maureen Ann *ConAu 61*
Main entry: Sautel, Maureen Ann

McGinnis, Lila S 1924- *ConAu 93, SmATA 44*

McGivern, Maureen Daly *AuBYP 3, ConAu 9R, -37NR, MajAI*
Main entry: Daly, Maureen

McGough, Elizabeth 1934- *ConAu 107, SmATA 33*

McGough, Roger *CamGLE*

McGough, Roger 1937- *BioIn 15, ChlFicS, ConPo 91, IntAu&W 91, TwCChW 89, Who 88, -90, -92, WrDr 86, -88, -90, -92, -94*

McGovern, Ann *AuBYP 2, -3, BioIn 7, -11, BkP, ConAu 49, -2NR, FourBJA, IntAu&W 77, -82, SmATA 8*

McGovern, Ann 1930- *IntAu&W 89, -91, MajAI, SmATA 70, -17AS, WhoAmW 89*

McGowen, Thomas *ScF&FL 92*

McGowen, Thomas 1927- *AuBYP 2S, -3, BioIn 9, ConAu 21R, -8NR, -25NR, SmATA 2*

McGrady, Mike *AuBYP 3*

McGrady, Mike 1933- *BioIn 10, ConAu 49, –2NR, SmATA 6*

McGrath, Edward 1901- *DrAS 74E*

McGrath, Thomas *DrAPF 87, –89, –91, –93, IntvTCA 2*

McGrath, Thomas d1990 *NewYTBS 90*

McGrath, Thomas 1916- *ConLC 59, ConPo 91, MajTwCW, WhoAm 86, –88, –90, –92, WhoUSWr 88, WhoWrEP 89*

McGrath, Thomas 1916-1990 *BioIn 17, ConAu 132, –33NR, SmATA 66*

McGrath, Thomas M 1916- *WrDr 86, –88, –90*

McGrath, Thomas Matthew 1916- *AmAu&B, ConAu 9R, –6NR, ConLC 28, ConPo 70, –75, –80, –85, DrAP 75, IntAu&W 77, PenC AM, SmATA 41, WhoAm 74, –76, –78, –80, –82, –84, WrDr 76, –80, –82, –84*

McGraw, Elois Jarvis 1915- *SmATA 67*

McGraw, Eloise Jarvis *BioIn 14, –17*

McGraw, Eloise Jarvis 1915- *AmAu&B, ArtclWW 2, AuBYP 2, –3, BioIn 3, –4, –6, –7, –9, ConAu 5R, –4NR, –19NR, –36NR, CurBio 55, DcAmChF 1960, IntAu&W 82, –89, –91, MajAI, MorJA, ScF&FL 92, SmATA 1, –6AS, TwCChW 78, –83, –89, TwCYAW, WhoPNW, WrDr 80, –82, –84, –86, –88, –90, –92, –94*

McGraw, James 1913- *ConAu 1R*

McGraw, William Corbin 1916- *AuBYP 2, –3, BioIn 6, –8, –9, ConAu 29R, –36NR, MorJA, SmATA 3, WhoAm 76, –78*
Pseud./variant:
Corbin, William

McGregor, Craig 1933- *Au&Wr 71, BioIn 11, ConAu 21R, –13NR, OxCAusL, SmATA 8*

McGregor, Iona 1929- *Au&Wr 71, BioIn 13, ConAu 105, IntAu&W 91, SmATA 25, TwCChW 78, –83, –89, WrDr 82, –84, –86, –88, –90, –92, –94*

McGuffey, Alexander Hamilton 1816-1896 *BioIn 17, SmATA 60*

McGuffey, William Holmes 1800-1873 *AmAu, AmAu&B, Benet 87, BenetAL 91, BioIn 1, –2, –3, –4, –5, –6, –7, –8, –9, –10, –11, –13, –15, –17, ChhPo, –S1, –S2, CyEd, DcLB 42, DcLEL, DcNAA, EncAB-H, McGEWB, MemAm, OhA&B, OxCAmH, OxCAmL 65, –83, PenC AM, REn, REnAL, SmATA 60, WebAB 74, –79, WhAm HS, WorAlBi, WorAl*

McGuire, Edna 1899- *AuBYP 2, –3, BioIn 8, –11, ConAu 5R, –2NR, SmATA 13*

McGuire, Frances *AuBYP 2, –3, BioIn 7*

McGuire, James Dean 1936- *ConAu 21R*

McGuire, Leslie Sarah 1945- *SmATA 45, –52*
Pseud./variant:
Britton, Louisa
Burton, Leslie
Eyre, Dorothy
Keyser, Sarah
Leslie, Sarah
Robinson, Shari
Strong, David

McGurk, Slater *AuBYP 2S, –3, ConAu 140, –X, SmATA 75, –X*
Main entry: Roth, Arthur J

McHargue, Georgess *AuBYP 3, BioIn 16*

McHargue, Georgess 1941- *AuBYP 2S, BioIn 9, ChlLR 2, ConAu 25R, –24NR, FifBJA, ScF&FL 92, SmATA 4, –77, –5AS*
Pseud./variant:
Chase, Alice
Usher, Margo Scegge

McHugh, Elisabet 1941- *BioIn 15, –16, ConAu 113, –32NR, SmATA 44, –55*

McHugh, Mary 1928- *ConAu 85*

McIlhany, Sterling *AuBYP 3*

McIlhany, Sterling Fisher 1930- *AuBYP 2S, BioIn 8, WhoAm 74, –80, –82, WhoE 74, –81, WhoFI 74, –81, –83, –85, –87, –89, WhoWest 87, –89, WhoWor 74, –80, –82, –87, –89, –91*

McIlvaine, Jane *AuBYP 2, BioIn 7, ConAu 130, –X*
Main entry: McClary, Jane Stevenson

McIlvaine, Jane 1919- *AuBYP 3*

McIlvaine, Jane 1919-1990 *BioIn 17, SmATA X*

McIlwraith, Maureen Mollie Hunter *AuBYP 3, MajAI*

McIlwraith, Maureen Mollie Hunter 1922- *Au&Wr 71, BioIn 9, –11, –12, ConAu 29R, IntAu&W 77, SmATA 2, ThrBJA, WrDr 76, –80*
Pseud./variant:
Hunter, Mollie

McInerney, Judith W 1945- *ConAu 118, SmATA 49*

McInerney, Judith Whitelock 1945- *AuBYP 3, BioIn 15, –16, ScF&FL 92, SmATA 46*

McIntire, Alta 1890- *BioIn 2*

McIntosh, Clarence Fredric 1922- *DrAS 74H, –78H, –82H*

McIntosh, Clifton *AuBYP 3*

McIntosh, Frank 1901- *BioIn 1, ConICB, IlsCB 1744*

McIntyre, Kevin *IlsBYP*

McIntyre, Vonda N *BioIn 17, IntvTCA 2*

McIntyre, Vonda N 1948- *ArtclWW 2, BioIn 13, ConAu 81, –17NR, –34NR, ConLC 18, IntAu&W 82, MajTwCW, NewEScF, RGTwCSF, ScF&FL 92, ScFSB, TwCSFW 86, –91, WhoAm 80, –82, –84, WhoSciF, WrDr 84, –86, –88, –90, –92*

McIntyre, Vonda Neel 1948- *EncSF 93, TwCYAW, WhoAm 86, –88, –90, –92, –94, WhoUSWr 88, WhoWrEP 89, –92, WrDr 94*

McKaughan, Larry Scott 1941- *ConAu 142, SmATA 75*

McKay, Don 1932- *ConAu 33R*

McKay, Donald 1810-1880 *BioIn 17*

McKay, Donald 1895- *BioIn 5, –15, IlsCB 1946, SmATA 45*

McKay, Robert 1921- *AuBYP 3*

McKay, Robert W 1921- *AuBYP 2S, BioIn 12, ConAu 13R, –10NR, SmATA 15*

McKeag, Ernest L 1896- *Au&Wr 71, ConAu P-1*

McKeag, Ernest L 1896-1976 *ScF&FL 92*

McKeag, Ernest Lionel 1896-1976 *EncSF 93*

McKeay, Eileen *ConAu X*

McKee, David *AuBYP 3, TwCChW 89, WrDr 86, –88, –90, –92*

McKee, David 1935- *IlsBYP, OxCChiL, SmATA 70, TwCChW 78, –83, WrDr 80, –82, –84*

McKee, David John *WrDr 94*

McKee, David John 1935- *ConAu 137, MajAI*

McKee, John Dukes 1899- *BioIn 2, WhAmArt 85*

McKee, Rose d1971 *WhAm 5*

McKeever, Marcia *ConAu X, SmATA X*
Main entry: Laird, Jean Elouise Rydeski

McKelvey, Gertrude Della *AuBYP 2, –3, BioIn 7*

McKemy, Kay 1924- *ChhPo S2, ConAu 29R, WrDr 76, –80, –82, –84, –86, –88*

McKendrick, Melveena 1941- *BioIn 16, SmATA 55*

McKendrick, Melveena Christine 1941- *ConAu 37NR*

McKendry, John Joseph 1933-1975 *BioIn 10, ConAu 61, WhAm 6, WhoAm 74, WhoAmA 78N*

McKenna, Colleen O'Shaughnessy 1948- *SmATA 76*

McKenna, Evelyn *ConAu X, WrDr 84, –86*
Main entry: Joscelyn, Archie L

McKenny, Kenneth 1929- *Au&Wr 71, ConAu 69, WrDr 76, –80*

McKenny, Margaret *AuBYP 2, –3, BioIn 7, ConAu 73, WhoAmW 74*

McKenzie, Dorothy Clayton 1910-1981 *BioIn 13, SmATA 28N, WhoLibI 82*

McKenzie, Ruth *OxCCan SUP*

McKeown, Martha Ferguson 1903- *WhoPNW*

McKern, Sharon S 1941- *ConAu 37R*

McKie, Roy *ChhPo S1, –S2*

McKillip, Patricia *ScFSB*

McKillip, Patricia 1948- *BioIn 14, SupFW TwCChW 89, WrDr 90, –92*

McKillip, Patricia A 1948- *AuBYP 2S, –3, BioIn 17, ConAu 49, –4NR, –18NR, FifBJA, MajTwCW, ScF&FL 92, SmATA 30, TwCSFW 91*

McKillip, Patricia Anne 1948- *EncSF 93, TwCYAW, WrDr 94*

McKim, Audrey Margaret 1909- *BioIn 16 CaW, ConAu 1R, –4NR, IntAu&W 77, OxCCan SUP, SmATA 47*

McKinley, Jennifer Carolyn Robin 1952- *DcAmChF 1960, –1985, MajAI, TwCYAW, WrDr 94*

McKinley, Robin 1952- *Au&Arts 4, ChlLR 10, ConAu 107, –31NR, DcLB 52, FifBJA,*

ScF&FL 92, SmATA 32, -50, TwCChW 89, WhoAm 94, WrDr 90, -92

McKinnell, James 1953- *ConAu 61*

McKinney, Harris D *ConICB*

McKinney, Roland Joseph 1898- *AuBYP 2, -3, BioIn 7, WhAmArt 85*

McKinnon, Robert Scott 1937- *ConAu 37R*

McKissack, Fredrick 1939- *BlkAuII 92*

McKissack, Fredrick L 1939- *ConAu 120, SmATA 53*

McKissack, Fredrick Lemuel 1939- *SmATA 73*

McKissack, Patricia C 1944- *AuBYP 3, BioIn 16, -17, BlkAuII 92, ChlLR 23, ConAu 118, SmATA 51*

McKissack, Patricia L'Ann Carwell 1944- *BlkWr 2, ConAu 38NR, MajAI, SmATA 73*
Pseud./variant:
Carwell, L'Ann

Mckown, Robin *DcAmChF 1960*

McKown, Robin d1976 *AuBYP 3*

McKown, Robin 1907- *AuBYP 2, Au&Wr 71, BioIn 7, -9, -10, ConAu 1R, SmATA 6, ThrBJA, WhoE 75*

McLachlin, Steve *IlsBYP*

McLanathan, Richard 1916- *AuBYP 3, IntAu&W 89, -91, WhoAm 86, -88, -90, -92, -94, WhoAmA 86, WhoE 89, WhoUSWr 88, WhoWrEP 89, -92*

McLanathan, Richard Barton Kennedy 1916- *AuBYP 2S, ConAu 81, WhoAm 74, -76, -78, -80, WhoAmA 73, -78, -80, -82, -84, WhoWor 74, -78*

McLaughlin, Charles Bernard 1937- *ConAu 61*

McLaughlin, Frank *MedPD*

McLaughlin, Frank 1934- *SmATA 73*
Pseud./variant:
Bertolet, Paul

McLaughlin, Lorrie Bell 1924-1971 *ConAu 5R, TwCChW 78*

McLaughlin-Gill, Frances 1919- *WhoAmW 77, WomWMM B*

McLaurin, Anne 1953- *BioIn 13, ConAu 106, SmATA 27*
Pseud./variant:
Laurin, Anne

McLean, Allan Campbell 1922- *Au&Wr 71, BioIn 11, BritCA, ConAu 1R, -4NR, FourBJA, IntAu&W 77, -91, OxCChiL, TwCChW 78, -83, -89, WrDr 76, -80, -82, -84, -86, -88, -90, -92, -94*

McLean, Donald James 1905-1975 *Au&Wr 71, ConAu 1R, -4NR, OxCAusL, SingR 2*

McLean, J Sloan *ConAu 34NR, SmATA X, WrDr 86, -88, -90, -92*

McLean, J Sloan 1914- *WrDr 94*

McLean, Kathryn Anderson 1909-1966 *AmWomWr, BioIn 2, -7, -11, ConAu 25R, -P-2, SmATA 9*
Pseud./variant:
Forbes, Kathryn

McLean, Ruari *Who 88, -90, -92*

McLean, Ruari 1917- *BlueB 76, ChhPo, -S1, ConAu 21R, -10NR, IntAu&W 89, Who 74, -82, -83, -85, WrDr 76, -80, -82, -84, -86, -88, -90, -92*

McLeish, Kenneth 1940- *BioIn 14, ConAu 29R, -13NR, IntAu&W 77, -82, -86, -89, -91, SmATA 35, WrDr 76, -80, -82, -84, -86, -88, -90, -92, -94*

McLenighan, Valjean 1947- *BioIn 15, ConAu 108, SmATA 40, -46*

McLeod, Emilie Warren 1926-1982 *BioIn 13, ConAu 33R, -69, -108, SmATA 23, -31N, WhoAmW 75, WhoLibI 82*

McLeod, Kirsty *ConAu X, SmATA X*
Main entry: Hudson, Kirsty

McLeod, Kirsty 1947- *BioIn 14*

McLeod, Margaret Vail *ConAu X, SmATA X*
Main entry: Holloway, Teresa

McLerran, Alice 1933- *BioIn 17, ConAu 136, SmATA 68, WrDr 94*

McLerran, Alice Enderton 1933- *WhoAmW 91*

McLin, Ruth 1924- *ConAu 61*

McLintock, Gordon E 1903- *BioIn 3, CurBio 53, WhoE 74*

McLoughlin, John C *BioIn 16, ScFSB*

McLoughlin, John C 1949- *EncSF 93, ScF&FL 92, SmATA 47*

McMahan, Ian *SmATA 45*

McMahan, Ian 1940- *ScF&FL 92*

McManus, George 1884-1954 *ArtCS, ArtsAmW 2, BenetAL 91, BioIn 2, -3, -6, -15, EncACom, EncAJ, EncTwCJ, ObitOF 79, REnAL, WhAm 3, WhAmArt 85, WhScrn 83, -77*

McManus, Kay 1922- *Au&Wr 71, IntAu&W 86, -89, WrDr 76, -80, -82, -84, -86, -88, -90, -92, -94*

McManus, Patrick 1933- *SmATA 46*

McMeekin, Clark *AuBYP 3, LiHiK*
Main entry: McMeekin, Isabel McLennan

McMeekin, Isabel McLennan 1895- *AmAu&B, AmNov, AuBYP 2, -3, BioIn 2, -4, -6, -7, -9, ChhPo, ConAu 5R, CurBio 42, -57, MorJA, SmATA 3*
Pseud./variant:
McMeekin, Clark

McMillan, Bruce *MajAI, SmATA 70*

McMillan, Bruce 1947- *AuBYP 3, BioIn 13, ConAu 73, -13NR, -35NR, SixBJA, SmATA 22*

McMillan, Constance *WhoAmA 89, -91*

McMillan, Constance 1924- *WhoAmA 86*

McMillan, Constance 1949- *ConAu 85*

McMillan, Priscilla Johnson 1928- *ConAu 41R, ForWC 70*

McMillan, Terry *DrAPF 87, -89, -91, -93*

McMillan, Terry 1951- *ConBlB 4, ConLC 50, -61, CurBio 93, NewYTBS 92, News 93-2, TwCYAW, WhoAm 94, WrDr 92*

McMillan, Terry L 1951- *BlkWr 2, ConAu 140*

McMillen, Neil Raymond 1939- *ConAu 33R, DrAS 74H, -78H, -82H, IntAu&W 91, WrDr 76, -80, -82, -84, -86, -88, -90, -92, -94*

McMillen, Wheeler d1992 *NewYTBS 92*

McMillen, Wheeler 1893- *AmAu&B, AuBYP 2, -3, BioIn 2, -7, ConAu 33R, OhA&B, WhNAA, WhoAm 74, -76, -78, -80, -82, -84, -86, -88, -90, WhoSSW 73*

McMillen, Wheeler 1893-1992 *BioIn 17, WhAm 10, WhoAm 92*

McMorris, William B *MedPD*

McMullan, Frank 1907- *Au&Wr 71, BiE&WWA, ConAu 5R, NotNAT*

McMullan, James 1934- *BioIn 7, -8, -13, ConGrA 1, IlrAm 1880, IlsBYP, IlsCB 1957*

McMullan, Kate 1947- *ScF&FL 92, SmATA 48, -52*

McMullan, Kate Hall 1947- *ConAu 123*
Pseud./variant:
Hall, Katy

McMullen, Catherine *ConAu X, SmATA X*
Main entry: Cookson, Catherine

McMurtrey, Martin A 1921- *BioIn 12, ConAu 69, SmATA 21*

McNair, Kate *AuBYP 3*

McNair, Kate 1911- *AuBYP 2S, BioIn 9, ConAu 17R, IndAu 1917, SmATA 3, WrDr 76, -80, -82, -84, -86, -88, -90*

McNair, Sylvia 1924- *ConAu 121, SmATA 74*

McNair, William Allen *DcChlFi*

McNally, Andrew, Jr. *AuBYP 3*

McNally, E Evalyn Grumbine *AuBYP 2, -3, BioIn 7*
Main entry: Grumbine, E Evalyn

McNally, Tom 1923- *ConAu 85*

McNamara, Louise *AuBYP 3*

McNamara, Louise Greep *AuBYP 2S*

McNamara, Margaret Craig 1915-1981 *BioIn 11, NewYTBS 81, SmATA 24N*

McNamee, James 1904- *AuBYP 3*

McNamee, James Owen 1904- *AuBYP 2, Au&Wr 71, BioIn 8, ConAu 5R*

McNaught, Harry *BioIn 3, ConAu 106, IlsBYP, SmATA 32*

McNaughton, Colin 1951- *ConAu 112, SmATA 39*

McNeely, Jeannette 1918- *BioIn 13, ConAu 41R, SmATA 25*
Pseud./variant:
Mackie, Moron

McNeely, Marian Hurd 1877-1930 *BioIn 2, -14, ChhPo, DcNAA, JBA 34, -51, WhNAA*

McNeer, May Yonge 1902- *AmAu&B, AuBYP 2, -3, BioIn 2, -7, -9, -10, BkCL, BkP, ConAu 5R, JBA 34, -51, SmATA 1, Str&VC*
Pseud./variant:
Ward, Mary McNeer

McNeill, James 1925- *BioIn 10, Profile 1*

McNeill, James Charles 1916- *WhoWor 87*

McNeill, Janet *IntAu&W 86X*

McNeill, Janet 1907- *AuBYP 2S, -3, Au&Wr 71, BiDIrW, BioIn 9, BlmGWL, ConAu 9R, -X, DcIrL, DcIrW 1, FemiCLE, FourBJA, IntAu&W 77X, -82X, -91, OxCChiL, ScF&FL 92, SmATA 1, TwCChW 78, -83, -89, WrDr 76, -80, -82, -84, -86, -88, -90, -92, -94*
Pseud./variant:
Alexander, Janet

McNeilly, Wilfred Glassford 1921- *ConAu 29R*

McNeilly, Wilfred Glassford 1921-1983 *EncSF 93, ScF&FL 92*

McNickle, D'Arcy 1904-1977 *BenetAL 91, BioIn 9, -12, -13, CamGLE, CamHAL, ConAu 9R, -85, -5NR, ConIsC 1, EncFWF, IntAu&W 77, SmATA 22N, TwCWW 91, WhoPNW, WrDr 76, -80*

McNulty, Faith 1918- *BioIn 11, -12, ConAu 49, -1NR, -25NR, IntAu&W 91, SmATA 12, WrDr 76, -80, -82, -84, -86, -88, -90, -92, -94*

McPhail, David 1940- *AuBYP 3*

McPhail, David M *BioIn 14, -16*

McPhail, David M 1940- *ConAu 22NR, SmATA 47*

McPhail, David Michael 1940- *AuBYP 2S, BioIn 12, ConAu 85, -38NR, FifBJA, IlsCB 1967, MajAI, SmATA 32*

McPharlin, Paul d1948 *WhoAmA 86N*

McPharlin, Paul 1903-1948 *BioIn 1, -14, ConAu 110, SmATA 31, WhAmArt 85, WhoAmA 80N, -82N, -89N, -91N*

McPhedran, Marie 1904?- *AuBYP 2, -3, BioIn 7, CanWW 70*

McPhee, Richard B 1934- *ConAu 111, SmATA 41*

McPherson, James M 1936- *ConAu 31NR, IntWW 89, -91, MajTwCW*

McPherson, James Munro 1936- *BioIn 12, ConAu 9R, DrAS 74H, -78H, -82H, IntAu&W 77, -82, -86, -89, -91, SmATA 16, WhoAm 74, -76, -78, -80, -82, -84, -86, -88, -90, -92, -94, WrDr 76, -80, -82, -84, -86, -88, -90, -92, -94*

McQueen, Lucinda *SmATA 48*

McQueen, Lucinda 1950- *BioIn 16, SmATA 58*

McQueen, Mildred Hark 1908- *BioIn 11, ConAu P-1, SmATA 12*
Pseud./variant:
Hark, Mildred

McQueen, Noel *BioIn 2*

McRae, Russell 1934- *ConAu 129, DcChlFi, SmATA 63*

McShean, Gordon 1936- *BioIn 11, -15, ConAu 108, SmATA 41, WhoLibS 66, WhoWest 74, -76, -78, -80*

McSpadden, Joseph Walker 1874-1960 *AmAu&B, BioIn 5, REnAL, WhAm 4*

McSwigan, Marie 1907-1962 *AuBYP 2, -3, BioIn 3, -6, -7, -13, BkC 6, ConAu 73, CurBio 53, -62, MorJA, SmATA 24, WhNAA*

McTaggart, Fred 1939- *ConAu 65*

McVey, Ruth T 1930- *AmMWSc 73S, -78S, ConAu 109*

McVicker, Charles Taggart 1930- *SmATA 39, WhoAm 78, -80, -82, -84, -86, -88, -90, WhoAmA 80, -82, -84, -86, -91, WhoE 74*
Pseud./variant:
McVicker, Chuck

McVicker, Charles Taggert 1930- *WhoAmA 89*

McVicker, Chuck
Main entry: McVicker, Charles Taggart

McWebb, Elizabeth Upham *ChhPo, Str&VC*

McWhirter, Alan Ross 1925-1975 *ConAu 17R, -61, SmATA 31N*
Pseud./variant:
McWhirter, Ross

McWhirter, Millie *BioIn 8, ForWC 70*

McWhirter, Norris Dewar 1925- *Au&Wr 71, BioIn 8, -12, ConAu 13R, IntAu&W 86, -89, -91, IntWW 81, -82, -83, -89, -91, SmATA 37, Who 82, -83, -85, -88, -90, -92, WhoWor 84, -87, -89, -91, -93, WorAl*

McWhirter, Ross *BioIn 8, -10, ObitT 1971, SmATA 37, WorAl*
Main entry: McWhirter, Alan Ross

McWhirter, Ross 1925-1975 *BioIn 14, -15, DcNaB 1971, WorAlBi*

McWilliams, Karen 1943- *ConAu 133, SmATA 65, WrDr 94*

Mead, Margaret *IntvTCA 2*

Mead, Margaret 1901-1978 *AmAu&B, AmMWSc 73S, –78S, AmWomWr, AuBYP 2, –3, AuNews 1, Au&Wr 71, Benet 87, BenetAL 91, BioAmW, BioIn 2, –3, –4, –5, –6, –7, –8, –9, –10, –11, –12, –13, –14, –15, –16, –17, BioNews 74, BlueB 76, CelR, ConAu 1R, –81, –4NR, ConHero 1, ConIsC 1, ConLC 37, ContDcW 89, CurBio 40, –51, DcLEL, EncAB-H, EncPaPR 91, EvLB, FemiCLE, FifIDA, ForWC 70, HanAmWH, HerW, –84, InSci, InWom SUP, IntAu&W 77, IntDcWB, IntEnSS 79, IntWW 74, –75, –76, –77, –78, –79N, LongCTC, MajTwCW, MakMC, McGEWB, McGMS 80, NewYTBE 70, –72, ObitOF 79, OxCAmL 65, –83, PenC AM, PorAmW, RAdv 13-3, RComAH, REn, REnAL, SmATA 20N, ThTwC 87, TwCA, –SUP, WebAB 74, –79, WhDW, WhAm 7, WhNAA, Who 74, WhoAm 74, –76, –78, WhoAmW 74, WhoWor 74, –78, WorAlBi, WorAl, WrDr 76*

Mead, Russell *ConAu 30NR*

Mead, Russell 1935- *BioIn 11, ConAu 9R, SmATA 10, WrDr 76, –80, –82, –84*

Mead, Stella d1981 *BioIn 13, ConAu 103, SmATA 27N, Who 82N*

Meade, Edward *OxCCan*

Meade, Elizabeth Thomasina 1850-1915 *BiDIrW*

Meade, Elizabeth Thomasina 1854-1914 *Alli SUP, BioIn 8, –14, –15, Chambr 3, ChhPo S1, –S2, ConAu 112, DcIrW 1, EncMys, TelT, WhoChL*
Pseud./variant:
Meade, Lillie Thomas
Smith, Elizabeth Thomasina M

Meade, Ellen 1936- *BioIn 10, ConAu 41R, SmATA 5*

Meade, Ellen Patricia, Sister *WhoAmW 87*

Meade, L T *WomNov*

Meade, L T 1854-1915 *StaCVF*

Meade, Lillie Thomas
Main entry: Meade, Elizabeth Thomasina

Meade, L T 1854-1914 *BioIn 14, –15, FemiCLE, InWom SUP, OxCChiL, ScFEYrs, TwCChW 83A, –89A, TwCCr&M 80, –85, –91*

Meade, Marion 1934- *BioIn 13, ConAu 49, –1NR, SmATA 23*

Meader, Stephen W 1892-1977 *TwCChW 89*

Meader, Stephen Warren 1892- *AuBYP 3, BioIn 14*

Meader, Stephen Warren 1892-1977 *AmAu&B, AuBYP 2, BioIn 2, –7, –9, ConAu 5R, JBA 34, –51, OxCChiL, REnAL, SmATA 1, TwCChW 78, –83, WhAm 7, WhoAm 74, –76, –78, WrDr 80*

Meadmore, Susan
Main entry: Sallis, Susan Diana

Meadow, Charles T 1929- *AuBYP 3, IntAu&W 86, –89, WrDr 86, –88, –90, –92*

Meadow, Charles Troub 1929- *AmMWSc 73P, AuBYP 2S, BioIn 13, ConAu 29R, –15NR, SmATA 23, WhoGov 72, WhoLibI 82, WhoSSW 75, WrDr 76, –80, –82, –84*

Meadowcroft, Enid 1898-1966 *AuBYP 3*

Meadowcroft, Enid LaMonte 1898-1966 *AuBYP 2, BioIn 1, –2, –7, –9, ConAu X, CurBio 49, JBA 51, REnAL, SmATA 3*
Pseud./variant:
Wright, Enid Meadowcroft

Meaker, M J *ConAu 37NR, MajAI, MajTwCW, TwCYAW*
Main entry: Meaker, Marijane

Meaker, M J 1927- *SmATA X*

Meaker, Marijane *AuBYP 3, BioIn 17*

Meaker, Marijane 1927- *BioIn 12, ConAu 107, FourBJA, MajTwCW, SmATA 20, –61, WrDr 80, –82, –84*
Pseud./variant:
Aldrich, Ann
Kerr, M E
Meaker, M J
Packer, Vin

Meaker, Marijane Agnes 1927- *ConAu 37NR, MajAI, WhoAm 94*

Means, Elliott *WhoAmA 86N*

Means, Elliott 1904-1962 *BioIn 6, IlsBYP, WhAmArt 85, WhoAmA 78N*

Means, Elliott 1905-1962 *WhoAmA 89N, –91N*

Means, Florence Crannell 1891-1980 *AmAu&B, AmWomWr, AuBYP 2, –3, BioIn 1, –2, –7, –9, –12, –14, BkCL, ConAu 1R, –103, –37NR, ForWC 70, IntAu&W 77, –82, JBA 34, –51 MajAI, OxCChiL, SmATA 1, –25N, TwCChW 78, –83, –89, TwCYAW, WhAm 7, WhNAA, WhoAm 74, –76, –78, –80, WhoAmW 74, –75, –77, WhoWest 76, –78, WrDr 80, –82*

Means, Florence Crannell 1897- *AmWomPl*

Mearian, Judy Frank 1936- *BioIn 16, SmATA 49, WhoEnt 92*

Medary, Marjorie 1890- *BioIn 2, –12, ConAu 73, JBA 51, SmATA 14*

Meddaugh, Susan 1944- *BioIn 13, ConAu 106, SmATA 29*

Medearis, Angela Shelf 1956- *BlkAuII 92, SmATA 72*

Medearis, Mary 1915- *BioIn 10, ConAu 69, SmATA 5*

Mee, Arthur Henry 1875-1943 *BioIn 1, –5, –8, ChhPo, –S1, –S2, DcLEL, DcNaB 1941, EvLB, LongCTC, OxCChiL, WhoChL*

Mee, Charles L, Jr. 1938- *BiE&WWA, BioIn 11, –12, –13, ConAu 45, –3NR, SmATA 8, –72, WhoAm 88, –90, –92, –94*

Meek, Jacklyn O'Hanlon 1933- *BioIn 14, –16, ConAu 77, SmATA 34, –51*
Pseud./variant:
Matthews, Jacklyn Meek
O'Hanlon, Jacklyn

Meek, Joe *DcAmChF 1960*

Meek, Pauline Palmer 1917- *ConAu 106*

Meek, S P 1894-1972 *AmAu&B, BioIn 13, ConAu 1R, –103, ConSFA, NewEScF, ScFSB, SmATA 28N, TwCSFW 86, –91, WhNAA, WhoSciF*

Meek, Sterner St Paul 1894-1972 *EncSF 93*

Meeker, Howard William 1924- *WhoHcky 73*

Meeker, Oden 1919?-1976 *AuBYP 2, –3, BioIn 8, –10, –12, ConAu 65, –73, SmATA 14*

Meeker, Richard
Main entry: Brown, Fornan

Meeks, Esther K *AuBYP 3*

Meeks, Esther K 1909- *AuBYP 2, BioIn 2, –7*

Meeks, Esther MacBain 1921- *BioIn 9, ConAu 1R, IntAu&W 86, –89, –91, SmATA 1, WhoMW 84, WrDr 76, –80, –82, –84, –86, –88, –90, –92, –94*

Meggendorfer, Lothar *BioIn 14*

Meggendorfer, Lothar 1847-1925 *BioIn 13, ConAu 115, OxCChiL, SmATA 36, WorECar*

Mehdevi, Alexander Sinclair 1947- *BioIn 10, ConAu 49, SmATA 7*

Mehdevi, Anne Sinclair 1922?- *AmAu&B, AuBYP 2, BioIn 8, –10, –11, ConAu 5R, FourBJA, SmATA 8, WorAu 1950*

Mehdevi, Anne Sinclair 1947- *AuBYP 3*

Meher Baba 1894-1969 *BioIn 1, –8, –9, –10, –11, –12, –13, –14, –17, EncO&P 1, –2, –3*
Pseud./variant:
Baba, Meher

Meidell, Sherry 1951- *SmATA 73*

Meier, August 1923- *ConAu 9R, –3NR, DrAS 74H, –78H, –82H, WhoAm 74, –76, –78, –80, –82, –84, –86, –88, –90, –92, –94, WhoBlA 75, –77, –80, –85, –90, –92, –94, WhoMW 74, –76, –78, WhoUSWr 88, WhoWrEP 89, –92*

Meier, Minta 1906- *BioIn 16, SmATA 55*

Meighan, Donald Charles 1929- *BioIn 14, ConAu 107, –24NR, SmATA 30*
Pseud./variant:
Charles, Donald

Meigs, Cornelia 1884-1973 *InWom SUP, TwCChW 89, WrChl*

Meigs, Cornelia Lynde 1884-1972 *BioIn 14*

Meigs, Cornelia Lynde 1884-1973 *AmAu&B, AmWomPl, AmWomWr, AnCL, AuBYP 2, –3, BioIn 1, –2, –4, –7, –10, ChhPo, ConAu 9R, –45, ForWC 70, JBA 34, –51, MajAI, NewYTBE 73, NewbMB 1922, OxCChiL, REnAL, SmATA 6, Str&VC, TwCChW 78, –83, TwCYAW, WhAm 6, –7, WomNov*
Pseud./variant:
Aldon, Adair

Meigs, Elizabeth Bleecker 1923- *AuBYP 2, –3, BioIn 7*

Meigs, Mildred Plew 1894-1944 *BkCL, ChhPo, –S2*

Meilach, Dona Z 1926- *BioIn 14, ConAu 22NR, WhoWrEP 89*

Meilach, Dona Zweigoron *WhoAmW 89, WhoWest 87*

Meilach, Dona Zweigoron 1926- *AuBYP 2S, –3, ConAu 9R, –5NR, ForWC 70, SmATA 34, WhoAmA 78, WhoWest 80, –82, WhoWrEP 92*
Pseud./variant:
Stanli, Sue

Meillon, Claire *Au&Wr 71, SingR 1*

Melady, John 1938- *ConAu 122, SmATA 49*

Melancon, Claude *BioIn 4, OxCCan SUP*

Melbo, Irving Robert 1908- *AuBYP 2, -3, BioIn 6, -8, ConAu 49, WhoAm 74, -76, -78, -80, -82, -84, -86, -88, -90, -92, -94, WhoWor 74, -91, -93*

Melcher, Daniel d1985 *NewYTBS 85*

Melcher, Daniel 1912-1985 *BioIn 7, -9, -14, -15, -17, ConAu 116, NewYTBS 85, SmATA 43N, WhAm 9, WhoLibI 82, WhoLibS 66*

Melcher, Frederic Gershom 1879-1963 *BioIn 1, -4, -5, -6, -13, -15, DcAmB S7, ObitOF 79, SmATA 22N, WhJnl, WhoLibS 55*

Melcher, Marguerite Fellows 1879-1969 *BioIn 8, -11, ConAu 5R, SmATA 10*

Mele, Frank M 1935- *AuBYP 2S, -3, ConAu 53*

Mele, Frank Michael 1935- *AmMWSc 86, -89, -92*

Melendez, Francisco 1964- *SmATA 72*

Melick, Arden Davis 1940- *ConAu 106, WhoE 91, WhoUSWr 88, WhoWrEP 89, -92*

Melin, Grace Hathaway 1892-1973 *BioIn 11, ConAu 45, -P-2, SmATA 10*

Mellen, Joan 1941- *ConAu 65, -11NR, DrAS 74E, -78E, -82E, IntAu&W 77, -91, WhoAmW 81, WrDr 76, -80, -82, -84, -86, -88, -90, -92, -94*

Mellen, Peter *OxCCan SUP*

Mellersh, Harold Edward Leslie 1897- *Au&Wr 71, BioIn 11, ConAu 53, SmATA 10, WrDr 76, -80*

Mellin, Jeanne 1929- *AuBYP 2, -3, BioIn 7, ConAu 49, -24NR*

Melling, O R *DcChlFi*

Mellor, Kathleen *SingR 1*

Mellor, William Bancroft 1906- *AuBYP 2S, -3, ConAu 61*

Melton, David 1934- *AuBYP 2S, -3, ConAu 69, -22NR, IntAu&W 91, WrDr 80, -82, -84, -86, -88, -90*

Meltzer, Milton 1915- *Au&Arts 8, AuBYP 2S, -3, BioIn 9, -10, -15, -16, -17, ChlLR 13, ConAu 13R, -38NR, ConLC 26, DcLB 61, DrAS 74H, -78H, -82H, MajAI, MorBMP, SmATA 1, -50, -1AS, ThrBJA, TwCYAW, WhoAm 74, -76, -78, -80, -82, -84, -86, -88, -90, -92, -94, WhoUSWr 88, WhoWrEP 89, -92*

Melville, Anne *ConAu X, IntAu&W 82X, -85X, -91X, SmATA X, WrDr 82, -84, -86, -88, -90, -92*
Main entry: Potter, Margaret

Melville, Anne 1926- *TwCRHW 90, WrDr 94*

Melville, Herman 1819-1891 *Alli, -SUP, AmAu, AmAu&B, AmWr, AtlBL, Benet 87, BenetAL 91, BbD, BiD&SB, BioIn 1, -2, -3, -4, -5, -6, -7, -8, -9, -10, -11, -12, -13, -14, -15, -16, -17, CamGEL, CamGLE, CamHAL, CasWL, Chambr 3, ChhPo, -S2, CnDAL, CnE&AP, CrtT 3, CyAL, CyWA 58, DcAmAu, DcBiA, DcEnA, DcEnL, DcLB 3, -74, DcLEL, DcNAA, Dis&D, EncAB-H, EncSF 93, EvLB, InSci, LuthC 75, MagSAmL, McGEWB, MemAm, MouLC 4, NewGrDA 86, NinCLC 3, -12, -29, Novels, OxCAmH, OxCAmL 65, -83, OxCChiL, OxCEng 67, -85, OxCShps, PenC AM, PenEncH, RAdv 1, -13-1, RComAH, RComWL, REn, REnAL, RfGAmL 87, RfGShF, ShSCr 1, SmATA 59, WebAB 74, -79, WebE&AL, WhDW, WhAm HS, WorAlBi, WorAl, WorLitC, WrPh*

Melvin, A Gordon 1894- *ConAu 9R, IntAu&W 77, WhoE 81, -83, WrDr 80, -82, -84, -86, -88, -90*

Melwood, Mary *BioIn 12, ConAu X, IntAu&W 91, SmATA X, TwCChW 78, -83, -89, WrDr 82, -84, -86, -88, -90, -92*
Main entry: Lewis, E M

Melzack, Ronald 1929- *AmMWSc 73S, -78S -86, -89, -92, BioIn 10, CanWW 89, ConAu 41R, -15NR, IntAu&W 77, -86, -89, OxCCan SUP, SmATA 5, WhoAm 74, -76, -78, -80, -82, -84, -86, -88, -90, -92, -94, WrDr 76, -80, -82, -84, -86, -88, -90, -92, -94*

Memling, Carl 1918-1969 *AuBYP 2, -3, BioIn 7, -8, -10, ConAu 1R, -4NR, SmATA 6*

Mendel, Jo *BioIn 12, ConAu X, IntAu&W 77X, -82X, SmATA X, WrDr 76, -80, -82, -84, -86, -88*
Main entry: Bond, Gladys Baker
Gilbertson, Mildred Geiger

Mendez, Phil 1947- *BlkAull 92*

Mendez, Raymond A 1947- *SmATA 66*

Mendonca, Susan 1950- *BioIn 15, -16, ConAu 102, ScF&FL 92, SmATA 45*
Main entry: Smith, Susan Vernon

Mendoza, George 1934- *AuBYP 2S, -3, BioIn 9, -11, ConAu 73, SmATA 39, -41, -7AS, ThrBJA, WhoAm 88, -90, -92, -94, WhoHisp 91, -92, -94, WhoWor 93*

Meng, Heinz 1924- *AmMWSc 73P, –82, BioIn 11, ConAu 69, SmATA 13*

Meng, Heinz Karl 1924- *AmMWSc 86, –92, WhoE 93*

Meniru, Teresa *DcChlFi*

Menotti, Gian Carlo 1911- *AmComp, ASCAP 66, AuBYP 2S, –3, Baker 84, –92, Benet 87, BenetAL 91, BiDD, BiE&WWA, BioIn 1, –2, –3, –4, –5, –6, –7, –8, –9, –10, –11, –12, –13, –14, –15, –16, –17, BlueB 76, CelR, –90, ChhPo S2, CompSN SUP, ConAmC 76, –82, ConAu 104, ConCom 92, CurBio 47, DcCM, IntWW 74, –75, –76, –77, –78, –79, –80, –81, –82, –83, –89, –91, IntWWM 90, McGEWB, McGEWD 72, –84, NewAmDM, NewGrDA 86, NewOxM, NewYTBS 74, –85, NotNAT, OxCAmL 65, OxCMus, PenDiMP A, REn, REnAL, SmATA 29, WebAB 74, –79, WhDW, Who 74, –82, –83, –85, –88, –90, –92, WhoAm 74, –76, –78, –80, –82, –84, –86, –88, –92, –94, WhoAmM 83, WhoEnt 92, WhoMus 72, WhoOp 76, WhoWor 74, –78, –87, –89, –91, –93, WorAlBi, WorAl*

Menuhin, Yehudi 1916- *Baker 84, –92, BioIn 1, –2, –3, –4, –5, –6, –7, –8, –9, –10, –11, –12, –13, –14, –15, BlueB 76, CelR 90, CmCal, ConAu 2NR, IntWW 79, –80, –81, –82, –83, –91, IntWWM 85, –90, NewAmDM, NewYTBS 81, PenDiMP, SmATA 40, WebAB 79, Who 82, –83, –85, –92, WhoAm 80, –82, –84, –86, –88, –92, –94, WhoAmJ 80, WhoAmM 83, WhoEnt 92, WhoWor 80, –82, –84, –87, –89, –91, –93, WhoWorJ 78, WorAlBi, WorAl, WrDr 82, –84, –86, –88, –90, –92, –94*

Menuhin, Yehudi, Sir 1916- *IntWW 89, NewGrDA 86, Who 88, –90*

Menville, Douglas 1935- *ScF&FL 92, SmATA 64*

Menville, Douglas Alver 1935- *EncSF 93*

Menzel, Barbara J 1946- *SmATA 63*

Menzel, Roderick 1907- *IntAu&W 77*
Pseud./variant:
Parma, Clemens

Mercer, Charles d1988 *NewYTBS 88*

Mercer, Charles 1917- *WhoAm 86, –88, WhoUSWr 88, WhoWrEP 89*

Mercer, Charles 1917-1988 *ConAu 127, SmATA 61, WhAm 9*

Mercer, Charles E 1917-1988 *BioIn 16, –17, ScF&FL 92*

Mercer, Charles Edward 1917- *AmAu&B, AuBYP 2S, –3, BioIn 12, ConAu 1R, SmATA 16, WhoAm 74, –76, –78, WhoE 74*

Mercer, Diana *SingR 1*

Mercer, Jessie *AuBYP 2, –3, ConAu 1R, –2NR*
Pseud./variant:
Payzant, Jessie Mercer Knechtel
Shannon, Terry

Merchant, Eve *DcChlFi*

Mercier, Jean F *MedPD*

Meredith, Arnold *SmATA X*
Main entry: Hopkins, Kenneth

Meredith, David William *AuBYP 2, –3, ConAu X, SmATA 1, –X*
Main entry: Miers, Earl Schenck

Meredith, Hal *EncMys, WhoChL*

Meredith, Louisa Anne 1812-1895 *ArtclWW 2, BioIn 2, –12, DcWomA, FemiCLE, OxCAusL, OxCChiL*

Meredith, Nicolete *AuBYP 2, BioIn 7, ConAu X*
Main entry: Stack, Nicolete Meredith

Meredith, Nicolete 1896- *AuBYP 3*

Meredith, Robert 1923- *ConAu 5R*

Merida, Carlos 1891- *BioIn 2, –5, –9, CurBio 60, DcCAr 81, IlsBYP, IlsCB 1946, OxCTwCA, WhoAmA 73, –78, –80, WhoGrA 62*

Meringoff, Laurene Krasny
Main entry: Brown, Laurene Krasny

Meriwether, Louise *BlmGWL, DrAPF 87, –89, –91, –93, InWom SUP*

Meriwether, Louise 1923- *BioIn 14, –16, BlkAWP, BlkWr 1, ConAu 77, DcLB 33, DrAF 76, DrAPF 83, –85, LivgBAA, NotBlAW 92, SelBAAf, SelBAAu, SmATA 31, –52, WhoBlA 75, –77, –80, –85, –88, –90, –92, –94*

Meriwether, Louise M *InB&W 85*

Meriwether, Louise M 1923- *BlkAull, –92*

Merkling, Erica *IlsBYP*

Merlin, Arthur *MajTwCW, SmATA 66*
Main entry: Blish, James

Mero, Lee *ChhPo*

Merriam, Eve *DrAPF 87, –89, –91, WhoAm 86, –88, –90*

Merriam, Eve d1992 *NewYTBS 92, WhAm 10*

Merriam, Eve 1916- *AmAu&B, AmWomD, ArtclWW 2, AuBYP 2, –3, BioIn 1, –8, –9, –12, –13, BkP, ChhPo, –S1, –S2, ChlLR 14, ConAu 5R, –29NR, ConTFT 1, DcLB 61, DrAP 75, DrAPF 83, –85, ForWC 70, InWom SUP, OxCChiL, SmATA 3, –40, ThrBJA, TwCChW 78, –83, –89, WhoAm 74, –76, –78, –80, –82, –84, WhoAmW 74, –75, –77, –81, WhoE 74, WhoUSWr 88, WhoWrEP 89, –92, WrDr 80, –82, –84, –86, –88, –90, –92*

Merriam, Eve 1916-1992 *AnObit 1992, BioIn 17, ConAu 137, MajAI, ScF&FL 92, SmATA 73, TwCYAW, WrDr 94N*

Merrill, Dean 1943- *ConAu 61, –8NR, –27NR*

Merrill, Jane 1946- *SmATA 42*
Pseud./variant:
Filstrup, Jane Merrill
Filstrup, Janie
Merrill, Phil

Merrill, Jean 1923- *TwCChW 89, WrDr 86, –88, –90, –92*

Merrill, Jean Fairbanks 1923- *AuBYP 2, –3, BioIn 7, –9, –10, ConAu 1R, –4NR, –38NR, DcAmChF 1960, ForWC 70, IntAu&W 77, –82, –86, –89, –91, MajAI, MorBMP, SmATA 1, ThrBJA, TwCChW 78, –83, WhoAm 78, –80, –82, –84, –86, –88, –90, –92, –94, WhoAmW 74, –75, –77, –81, WhoE 74, WrDr 76, –82, –84, –94*

Merrill, Mary Ann 1930- *WhoAmW 74, –75, WhoSSW 75*

Merrill, Phil *ConAu X, SmATA X*
Main entry: Merrill, Jane

Merriman, Alex *MajAI*

Merriman, Henry Seton 1862-1903 *BiD&SB, CarSB, Chambr 3, DcEnA A, DcLEL, DcNaB S2, EvLB, LongCTC, NewC, OxCEng 67*

Merritt, Muriel 1905- *ConAu 69*

Merriweather, Magnus 1849?-1892? *CarSB, DcNAA*

Merry, Malcolm James *HsB&A*

Mersand, Joseph 1907- *AmAu&B, ConAu 1R, –1NR, DrAS 74E, –78E, WhNAA, WhoE 74, –75, –77, –81, WhoWorJ 78*

Mertins, Louis 1885-1973 *AmAu&B, ConAu 41R, Str&VC, WhAm 6, WhNAA*

Mertz, Barbara 1927- *ConAu 36NR, SmATA 49*

Mertz, Barbara G *TwCCr&M 91*

Mertz, Barbara Gross 1927- *Au&Wr 71, BioIn 11, ConAu 21R, DrAS 74H, IntAu&W 86, –89, TwCCr&M 80, –85, WrDr 76, –80, –82, –84*
Pseud./variant:
Michaels, Barbara
Peters, Elizabeth

Mertz, Barbara Louise Gross 1927- *WrDr 94*

Merwin, Decie 1894-1961 *BioIn 5, –6, –14, ChhPo, ConAu 111, IlsBYP, IlsCB 1946, SmATA 32*

Meryman, Hope Brooks 1931-1975 *WhoAmA 78N*

Mesches, Arnold 1923- *AmArt, WhoAmA 73, –78, –80, –82, –84, –86, –89, –91, WhoE 93*

Meserole, Harrison Talbot 1921- *DrAS 74E, –78E, –82E*

Meshorer, Yaakov *WhoWorJ 72, –78*

Messager, Charles 1882-1971 *BioIn 1, –4, ConAu 93, McGEWD 72, REn, REnWD*
Pseud./variant:
Vildrac, Charles Messager

Messenger, Charles 1941- *SmATA 59*

Messenger, Charles 1942- *ConAu 31NR*

Messer, Ronald Keith 1942- *ConAu 57*

Messick, Dale *EncACom*

Messick, Dale 1906- *ArtCS, BioIn 5, –6, –10, –16, –17, CurBio 61, EncTwCJ, InWom SUP, SmATA 48, –64, WhoAm 74, –76, –78, –80, –82, –84, WhoAmA 78, –80, –82, –84, –86, –89, –91, WhoAmW 81, –83*

Messick, Hank
Main entry: Messick, Henry Hicks

Messick, Henry Hicks 1922- *ConAu 45, –2NR, IntAu&W 77*
Pseud./variant:
Messick, Hank

Messmer, Otto d1983 *BioIn 15*

Messmer, Otto 1892?-1983 *AnObit 1983, BioIn 13, ConAu 111, EncACom, NewYTBS 83, SmATA 37, WorECar*

Metayer, Maurice *OxCCan SUP*

Metcalf, John 1938- *CamGLE, ConAu 113, ConLC 37, ConNov 86, -91, DcLB 60, IntWW 91, OxCCan SUP, OxCCanL, WhoCanL 85, -87, -92, WrDr 88, -90, -92*

Metcalf, John Wesley 1938- *WrDr 94*

Metcalf, Suzanne *ConAu 133, -X, MajAI, MajTwCW, SmATA X, ThrBJA*
Main entry: Baum, Lyman Frank

Metcalfe, Jane M *AuBYP 2, -3*

Metos, Thomas H 1932- *ConAu 93, LEduc 74, SmATA 37*

Metos, Thomas Harry 1932- *WhoWest 92, -94*

Metter, Bert 1927- *SmATA 56*

Metter, Bertram Milton 1927- *WhoAm 86, -92*

Metzl, Ervine 1899-1963 *BioIn 1, -4, -6, ChhPo, WhAmArt 85*

Metzler, Paul 1914- *ConAu 57, -6NR*

Meyer, Carolyn 1935- *AuBYP 2S, -3, BioIn 11, ConAu 49, -2NR, FifBJA, ScF&FL 92, SmATA 9, -9AS*

Meyer, Carolyn Mae 1935- *MajAI, SmATA 70, TwCYAW*

Meyer, Edith Patterson 1895- *AuBYP 2, -3, BioIn 1, -8, -10, ConAu 1R, -1NR, DcAmChF 1960, SmATA 5, WhoAmW 75, -77*

Meyer, Elizabeth Cooper 1958- *ConAu 69*

Meyer, Franklyn Edward 1932- *AuBYP 2, -3, BioIn 7, -11, ConAu 1R, SmATA 9, WrDr 76, -80, -82, -84, -86*

Meyer, Gerard P d1993 *NewYTBS 93*

Meyer, Gerard Previn *AuBYP 2, -3, BioIn 7*

Meyer, Howard Nicholas 1914- *BioIn 10, ConAu 13R, WhoAmJ 80, WhoAmL 78, WhoE 75, WhoWorJ 72, -78*

Meyer, Jean Shepherd *BioIn 11, SmATA 11*
Main entry: Berwick, Jean

Meyer, Jerome Sydney 1895-1975 *AuBYP 2, -3, Au&Wr 71, BioIn 7, -9, -10, -13, ConAu 1R, -57, -4NR, SmATA 3, -25N, WhoWorJ 72*
Pseud./variant:
Jennings, S M

Meyer, June *AuBYP 2S, -3, BlkAWP, BlkWr 1, -2, ConAu X, IntAu&W 77X, -91X, MajAI, MajTwCW, SelBAAu, SmATA 4, WrDr 76, -80, -82, -84, -86, -88, -90, -92*
Main entry: Jordan, June Meyer

Meyer, June 1936- *WrDr 94*

Meyer, Kathleen Allan 1918- *BioIn 15, -16, ConAu 123, SmATA 46, -51*

Meyer, Lewis 1913- *BioIn 6, -9*

Meyer, Louis A 1942- *BioIn 11, ConAu 37R, SmATA 12*

Meyer, Mabel H 1890?-1976 *BioIn 10, ConAu 61*

Meyer, Renate 1930- *BioIn 10, ConAu 53, SmATA 6*

Meyer, Susan E *BioIn 17*

Meyer, Susan E 1940- *ConAu 19NR, SmATA 64, WhoAm 86, -88, -90, -92, -94, WhoAmA 86, -89, -91, WhoE 86, WhoUSWr 88, WhoWrEP 89*

Meyer, Zoe 1888- *AmAu&B, WhAm 8*

Meyers, Joan 1927- *AuBYP 3*

Meyers, Joan Simpson 1927- *AuBYP 2, BioIn 8, ConAu 17R, -14NR*

Meyers, Robert William 1919-1970 *BioIn 5, -11, IlsBYP, IlsCB 1946, WhoAmA 73, -78N, -80N, -82N, -86N, -89N, -91N*

Meyers, Susan 1942- *AuBYP 2S, -3, BioIn 12, ConAu 21R, -13NR, SmATA 19, WrDr 76, -80, -82, -84*

Meynell, Laurence 1899- *BioIn 14, WrDr 86, -88*

Meynell, Laurence 1899-1989 *AnObit 1989, BioIn 17, ScF&FL 92, TwCChW 89, TwCCr&M 91*

Meynell, Laurence W d1989 *IntWW 89N*

Meynell, Laurence W 1899-1989 *IntWW 89*

Meynell, Laurence Walter d1989 *Who 90N*

Meynell, Laurence Walter 1899- *Au&Wr 71, BioIn 8, ConAu 81, -15NR, IntAu&W 77, -82, -89, IntWW 74, -75, -76, -77, -78, -79, -80, -81, -82, -83, OxCChiL, TwCChW 78, -83, TwCCr&M 80, -85, Who 74, -82, -83, -85, -88, WhoChL, WhoWor 74, WrDr 82, -84*
Pseud./variant:
Baxter, Valerie
Tring, A Stephen

Meynell, Laurence Walter 1899-1989 *ConAu 128, SmATA 61*

Pseud./variant:
Eton, Robert
Ludlow, Geoffrey

Meynier, Yvonne 1908- *AuBYP 2, –3, BioIn 8, –12, ConAu 73, SmATA 14*

Mezey, Robert *DrAPF 87, –89, –91, –93*

Mezey, Robert 1935- *AmAu&B, BioIn 10, ConAu 57, –7NR, ConPo 70, –75, –80, –85, –91, CroCAP, DrAP 75, DrAPF 83, –85, DrAS 74E, –78E, –82E, IntWWP 82, PenC AM, SmATA 33, WhoAm 94, WhoWest 92, –94, WrDr 76, –80, –82, –84, –86, –88, –90, –92, –94*

M'Fall, Frances Elizabeth 1862-1943 *CarSB*

Mian, Mary 1902- *BioIn 16, ScF&FL 92, SmATA 47*

Micale, Albert *WhoAmA 86, –89, –91*

Micale, Albert 1913- *BioIn 13, SmATA 22, WhoAmA 78, –80, –82, –84*

Michael, Manfred *ConAu X, ThrBJA*
Main entry: Winterfeld, Henry

Michaels, Barbara *BioIn 11, ConAu X, –36NR, IntAu&W 86X, TwCCr&M 80, –85, –91, WrDr 76, –80, –82, –84*
Main entry: Mertz, Barbara Gross

Michaels, Barbara 1927- *BestSel 90-4, ScF&FL 92, TwCRHW 90, WrDr 86, –88, –90, –92, –94*

Michaels, Joanne Louise *SmATA X*
Main entry: Teitelbaum, Michael

Michaels, Kristin *ConAu X, TwCWW 91, WrDr 80, –82, –84, –86, –88, –90, –92*
Main entry: Williams, Jeanne

Michaels, Kristin 1930- *WrDr 94*

Michaels, Neal *SmATA X*
Main entry: Teitelbaum, Michael

Michaels, Ruth Gruber *ConAu X*
Main entry: Gruber, Ruth

Michaels, Ski
Main entry: Pellowski, Michael J

Michaels, Steve 1955- *SmATA 71*

Michaels, William M 1917- *SmATA 77*

Michel, Anna 1943- *ConAu 85, SmATA 40, –49*

Michel, Sandra Seaton 1935- *ConAu 77*

Michelson, Florence B *ConAu P-2*

Michie, Allan Andrew 1915-1973 *AuBYP 2, –3, BioIn 8, –10, –12, ConAu 45, CurBio 42, –74, NatCAB 58, NewYTBE 73*

Micich, Paul *SmATA 74*

Mickey, Paul Albert 1937- *ConAu 49, –1NR, DrAS 74P, –78P, –82P, WhoRel 92, WhoSSW 91, –93*

Micklewright, Robert 1923- *ArtsCL, BioIn 6, –12, –14, IlsCB 1967*

Micklish, Rita 1931- *BioIn 11, ConAu 49, SmATA 12*

Micoleau, Tyler *IlsBYP*

Middleton, O E *IntAu&W 86X*

Middleton, O E 1925- *ConAu 81, ConNov 72, –76, –82, –86, –91, IntAu&W 77, –82, WrDr 76, –80, –82, –84, –86, –88, –90, –92*

Middleton, Osman Edward 1925- *WrDr 94*

Middleton, Osman Edward Gordon 1925- *RfGShF*

Miers, Earl Schenck 1910-1972 *AmAu&B, AuBYP 2, –3, BenetAL 91, BioIn 1, –2, –5, –7, –8, –9, –10, –13, ChhPo S2, ConAu 1R, –37R, –2NR, CurBio 49, –67, –73, NewYTBE 72, REnAL, SmATA 1, –26N, ThrBJA, WhAm 5, –7, WhoAm 74, –76*
Pseud./variant:
Meredith, David William

Mighels, Philip Verrill 1869-1911 *AmAu&B, DcNAA, ScFEYrs, WhAm 1*

Mikaelsen, Benjamin John 1952- *SmATA 73*

Miklowitz, Gloria 1927- *Au&Arts 6, AuBYP 3*

Miklowitz, Gloria D 1927- *AuBYP 2S, BioIn 9, –17, ConAu 25R, –10NR, –26NR, IntAu&W 82, –91, MajAI, ScF&FL 92, SixBJA, SmATA 4, –68, –17AS, TwCYAW, WhoAmW 81, WrDr 76, –80, –82, –84, –86, –88, –90, –92, –94*

Mikolaycak, Charles d1993 *NewYTBS 93*

Mikolaycak, Charles 1937- *BioIn 11, –12, –15, ChlBIID, ConAu 61, –8NR, –23NR, –38NR, FifBJA, IlsBYP, IlsCB 1967, MajAI, SmATA 9, –4AS, WhoE 81, –83, –85, –86, –89, WhoWor 87, –89, –91*

Mikolaycak, Charles 1937-1993 *ConAu 141, SmATA 75*

Mild, Warren 1922- *ConAu 21R, –8NR, DrAS 74E, SmATA 41, WhoRel 75*

Miles, Bebe 1924-1980 *ConAu 61, -9NR*

Miles, Betty *DrAPF 87, -89, -91, -93*

Miles, Betty 1928- *AuBYP 2, -3, BioIn 8, -11, ConAu 1R, -5NR, -20NR, FifBJA, ForWC 70, IntAu&W 91, SmATA 8, -9AS, TwCYAW, WrDr 76, -80, -82, -84, -86, -88, -90, -92, -94*

Miles, Cyril 1918- *WhoAmA 73, -78, -80, -82, -89, -91*

Miles, Mary Lillian 1908- *ConAu 13R*

Miles, Miska *AuBYP 2, -3, BioIn 14, ChhPo S2, ConAu X, -37NR, FourBJA, IntAu&W 77X, MajAI, OxCChiL, SmATA 1, -X, TwCChW 78, -83, -89, WrDr 76, -80, -82, -84, -86*
Main entry: Martin, Patricia Miles

Miles, Miska 1899-1986 *BioIn 15, -16*

Miles, Patricia 1930- *AuBYP 2S, -3, BioIn 13, ConAu 69, -11NR, SmATA 29*

Miles, Patricia A *ConAu 37NR, MajAI, SmATA X*
Main entry: Martin, Patricia Miles

Milgram, Gail Gleason *IntAu&W 86, -89*

Milgram, Gail Gleason 1942- *ConAu 29R, WhoAmW 75, -77, -83, WrDr 76, -80, -82, -84, -86, -88, -90, -92, -94*

Milgrom, Harry 1912- *AmMWSc 73P, -76P, AuBYP 2S, -3, BioIn 13, ConAu 1R, -3NR, LEduc 74, SmATA 25, WhoE 75, -77*

Milhous, Katherine 1894-1977 *AmAu&B, AuBYP 2, -3, Au&ICB, BioIn 1, -2, -4, -5, -7, -8, -12, -14, BkP, Cald 1938, ChhPo, ConAu 104, DcWomA, IlsBYP, IlsCB 1744, -1946, -1957, JBA 51, SmATA 15, Str&VC, TwCChW 78, WhAm 7, WhAmArt 85, WhoAm 74, -76, WhoAmA 78N, -80N, -82N, -86N, -89N, -91N, WhoAmW 74, WrDr 80, -82*

Militant *ConAu X, -35NR, MajTwCW, SmATA 8*
Main entry: Sandburg, Carl

Mill, Eleanor 1927- *IlsBYP, WhoAmA 78, -80*

Millais, Raoul 1901- *SmATA 77*

Millar, Barbara F 1924- *BioIn 11, ConAu 25R, SmATA 12, WhoAmW 74*

Millar, Harold Robert 1869-1939? *BioIn 8, ChhPo, DcBrBI, OxCChiL, WhoChL*

Millar, Jeff 1942- *BioIn 10, ConAu 69, -11NR*

Millar, Jeffery Lynn 1942- *WhoAm 86, -90, -94, WhoSSW 93*

Millar, Margaret 1915- *BenetAL 91, ConNov 86, -91, CrtSuMy, FemiCLE, InWom SUP, IntAu&W 91, SmATA 61, ThrtnMM, TwCCr&M 91, TwCRHW 90, WrDr 86, -88, -90, -92*

Millar, Margaret Ellis 1915- *WrDr 94*

Millard, C E *ChhPo S1*

Millard, Reed *AuBYP 2S, -3*

Millay, Edna St Vincent *IntvTCA 2*

Millay, Edna St Vincent 1892-1950 *AmAu&B, AmWomD, AmWomPl, AmWomWr, AmWr, ArtclWW 2, ASCAP 66, AtlBL, Benet 87, BenetAL 91, BioAmW, BioIn 1, -2, -3, -4, -5, -6, -8, -9, -10, -11, -12, -15, -16, -17, BlmGWL, CamGLE, CamHAL, CasWL, Chambr 3, ChhPo, -S1, -S2, CnDAL, CnE&AP, CnMD, CnMWL, ConAmA, ConAmL, ConAu 104, -130, ContDcW 89, CyWA 58, DcLB 45, DcLEL, EncWL, -2, EvLB, FemiCLE, GayLL, HanAmWH, HerW, -84, InWom SUP, IntDcWB, LongCTC, MajTwCW, McGEWB, McGEWD 72, -84, ModAL, ModAWWr, ModWD, NewGrDA 86, NotNAT B, NotWoAT, OxCAmL 65, -83, OxCEng 67, -85, PenC AM, PoeCrit 6, RAdv 1, -13-1, REn, REnAL, RfGAmL 87, SixAP, Str&VC, Tw, TwCA, -SUP, TwCLC 3, -4, -49, TwCWr, WebAB 74, -79, WhDW, WhAm 3, WhNAA, WorAlBi, WorAl*

Millburn, Cynthia *ConAu X*
Main entry: Brooks, Anne Tedlock

Millender, Dharathula 1920- *BlkAull, -92*

Millender, Dharathula H 1920- *BioIn 16, WhoBlA 85, -90, -92, -94*

Millender, Dharathula Hood 1920- *AuBYP 2S, ConAu 17R, IndAu 1917, SelBAAu, WhoAmW 74, WhoBlA 75, -77, -80, -85*

Miller, Albert G 1905-1982 *BioIn 14*

Miller, Albert Griffith 1905-1982 *BioIn 11, -12, -13, ConAu 1R, -107, -1NR, NewYTBS 82, SmATA 12, -31N*

Miller, Alice P *ConAu 26NR*

Miller, Alice Patricia McCarthy *Au&Wr 71, BioIn 13, ConAu 29R, ForWC 70, SmATA 22, WhoAmW 74, -75, -77, WhoE 74*

Miller, Allan *AuBYP 2S, -3*

Miller, Arthur *AmMWSc 86, DrAPF 87, -89, -91, -93, IntvTCA 2, NewYTBS 87*

Miller, Arthur 1915- *AmAu&B, AmNov, AmWr, AuNews 1, Au&Wr 71, Benet 87, BenetAL 91, BiE&WWA, BioIn 1, -2, -4, -5, -6, -7, -8, -9, -10, -11, -12, -13, BioNews 74, BlueB 76, CamGEL, CamGLE, CamGWoT, CamHAL, CasWL, CelR, -90, CnDAL, CnMD, CnMWL, CnThe, ConAu 1R, -3BS, -2NR, -30NR, ConDr 73, -77, -82, -88, -93, ConLC 1, -2, -6, -10, -15, -26, -47, ConTFT 1, CroCD, CurBio 47, -73, CyWA 58, -89, DcFM, DcLB 7, DcLEL 1940, DrAF 76, DramC 1, EncAB-H, EncWL, -2, EncWT, FilmgC, HalFC 84, -88, IntAu&W 77, -89, -91, IntDcT 2, IntMPA 84, -86, -88, -92, IntWW 74, -75, -76, -77, -78, -79, -80, -81, -82, -83, -89, -91, JeAmHC, LongCTC, MagSAmL, MajMD 1, MajTwCW, MakMC, McGEWB, McGEWD 72, -84, ModAL, -S1, -S2, ModWD, NatPD 77, -81, NewCon, NewYTBE 72, NotNAT, -A, OxCAmL 65, -83, OxCAmT 84, OxCEng 67, -85, OxCFilm, OxCThe 67, -83, PenC AM, PlP&P, RAdv 13-2, RComAH, RComWL, REn, REnAL, REnWD, RfGAmL 87, TwCA SUP, TwCWr, WebAB 74, -79, WebE&AL, WhDW, Who 74, -82, -83, -85, -88, -90, -92, WhoAm 74, -76, -78, -80, -82, -84, -86, -88, -90, -92, -94, WhoAmJ 80, WhoE 85, -86, -89, -91, WhoEnt 92, WhoThe 72, -77, -81, WhoTwCL, WhoUSWr 88, WhoWor 74, -78, -80, -82, -84, -87, -89, -93, WhoWorJ 72, -78, WhoWrEP 89, -92, WorAlBi, WorAl, WorEFlm, WorLitC, WrDr 76, -80, -82, -84, -86, -88, -90, -92, -94, WrPh*

Miller, Barry 1946- *ConAu 33R*

Miller, Bertha Mahony
Main entry: Mahony, Bertha

Miller, Charles A 1937- *ConAu 29R, WrDr 76, -80, -82, -84, -86, -88, -90, -92, -94*

Miller, Charles Francis 1918- *WhoFI 75, WhoSSW 75, -76*

Miller, Cincinnatus Heine 1841?-1913 *Alli SUP, AmAu, AmAu&B, BbD, BiD&SB, BioIn 1, -2, -3, -7, -8, CyAL, DcAmAu, DcNAA, EvLB, HarEnUS, IndAu 1816, MouLC 4, REnAL*
Pseud./variant:
Miller, Joaquin

Miller, Cincinnatus Hiner *BenetAL 91*

Miller, David William 1940- *ConAu 49, DrAS 74H, -78H, -82H, WhoAm 88, -90, -92, -94, WhoMW 74*

Miller, Deborah Uchill 1944- *SmATA 61*

Miller, Don 1923- *BioIn 16, BlkAuII, -92*

Miller, Don D 1923- *AfroAA, SmATA 15*

Miller, Donald George 1909- *AuBYP 2, -3, Au&Wr 71, BioIn 7, ConAu 5R, -4NR, DrAS 74P, -78P, -82P, IntAu&W 77, -82, -86, -89, -91, WrDr 76, -80, -82, -84, -86, -88, -90, -92, -94*

Miller, Doris R *ConAu X, SmATA X*
Main entry: Mosesson, Gloria R

Miller, Eddie
Main entry: Miller, Edward

Miller, Edna 1920- *SixBJA*

Miller, Edna Anita 1920- *AuBYP 2, -3, BioIn 8, -13, ConAu 106, -112, IlsCB 1957, SmATA 29*

Miller, Edward 1905-1974 *BioIn 11, ConAu P-2, SmATA 8*
Pseud./variant:
Miller, Eddie

Miller, Edwin Haviland 1918- *ConAu 110, DrAS 74E, -78E, -82E, WhoE 93*

Miller, Elizabeth 1933- *ConAu 117, SmATA 41*

Miller, Elizabeth Cleveland 1889-1936 *BioIn 2, JBA 34, -51, WhNAA*

Miller, Elizabeth Cleveland 1899-1936 *BioIn 14*

Miller, Elizabeth Kubota 1932- *BiDrLUS 70, ConAu 13R, WhoLibI 82*

Miller, Ethel Hull 1889-1962 *OhA&B, WhAm 4*

Miller, Eugene 1925- *ConAu 101, SmATA 33, WhoAm 74, -76, -78, -80, -82, -84, -86, -88, -90, -92, -94, WhoFI 74, -75, -81, -83, -85, -87, -89, -92, -94, WhoMW 74, -76, -78, -80, -82, -84, -86, -88, -90, -92, -93*

Miller, Eugenia *AuBYP 2, BioIn 8, ConAu X*
Main entry: Mandelkorn, Eugenia Miller

Miller, Eugenia 1916- *AuBYP 3*

Miller, Eugenia Porretta 1928- *WhoAmW 87*

Miller, Floyd C 1912- *ConAu 1R, -2NR, IndAu 1917*

Miller, Frances A 1937- *ConAu 123, SmATA 46, -52, TwCYAW, WrDr 90, -92, -94*

Miller, Frank *ArtCS*

Miller, Grambs *IlsBYP*

Miller, Harriet M 1831-1918 *AmWomPl*

Miller, Harriet Mann 1831-1918 *Alli SUP, AmAu, AmAu&B, AmLY, AmWomWr, BiD&SB, BiInAmS, BioIn 15, CarSB, ChhPo, –S1, DcAmAu, DcNAA, InWom SUP, OhA&B, WhAm 1, WomWWA 14*

Miller, Helen Knapp *AuBYP 3*
Main entry: Miller, Helen Markley

Miller, Helen Louise *AmWomPl, AuBYP 2, –3, BioIn 7*

Miller, Helen Markley *AuBYP 3*

Miller, Helen Markley 1899- *AmAu&B, AuBYP 2, BioIn 7, –10, ConAu 1R, –2NR, SmATA 5*
Pseud./variant:
Miller, Helen Knapp

Miller, Helen Topping 1884-1960 *AmAu&B, AmNov, AuBYP 2, –3, BioIn 2, –3, –5, –7, ConAu 109, DcNCBi 4, MichAu 80, ObitOF 79, SmATA 29N, WhAm 3, –4, WhNAA*

Miller, J P 1919- *ConAu 25R, IntMPA 76, –78, –81, –82, –84, –88, NewYTET, WhoWor 91*

Miller, J Peter *BiGAW*

Miller, J Philip 1937- *WhoAm 86*

Miller, Jane 1906- *ChhPo, –S1, WhoAmW 74*

Miller, Jane 1925-1989 *ConAu 34NR*

Miller, Jane Andrews 1952- *WhoAmW 93*

Miller, Jane Judith 1925- *BioIn 12, ConAu 77, IntAu&W 82, –86, SmATA 15*

Miller, Jay 1928- *ConAu 45*

Miller, Jay Alan 1928- *WhoMW 92, –93*

Miller, Jay Earl *WhoUSWr 88, WhoWrEP 92*

Miller, Jewel 1956- *SmATA 73*

Miller, Jim Wayne *DrAPF 87, –89, –91, –93, IntvTCA 2*

Miller, Jim Wayne 1936- *BioIn 17, ConAu 15AS, –20NR, IntAu&W 86, –89, –91, LiHiK, TwCYAW, WhoUSWr 88, WhoWrEP 89, –92, WrDr 86, –88, –90, –92, –94*

Miller, Joaquin *Alli SUP, AmAu, AmAu&B, BiD&SB, BioIn 1, –2, –3, –7, –8, –12, CasWL, CelCen, Chambr 3, ChhPo, –S1, CmCal, CnDAL, CrtT 3, CyAL, DcAmAu, DcEnA A, DcEnL, DcLEL, DcNAA, EvLB, HarEnUS, LongCTC, MarqDCG 84, McGEWB, NotNAT B, OxCAmL 65, –83, OxCAmT 84, OxCEng 67, PenC AM, REn, REnAL, Str&VC, WebAB 74, –79, WhAm 1, WhoTech 84, WorAl*
Main entry: Miller, Cincinnatus Heine

Miller, Joaquin 1837-1913 *Benet 87, BenetAL 91, BioIn 14, WorAlBi*

Miller, Joaquin 1839-1913 *CamGLE, CamGWoT, CamHAL, RfGAmL 87*

Miller, Joaquin 1841-1913 *CamGEL*

Miller, John *ConAu X, SmATA 3*
Main entry: Samachson, Joseph

Miller, John C d1991 *NewYTBS 91*

Miller, John Chester 1907- *ConAu 73, DrAS 74H, –78H, –82H*

Miller, J P 1919- *ConTFT 7, ScF&FL 92*

Miller, Katherine *AuBYP 2, –3, BioIn 8*

Miller, Katherine Browning *AmWomPl*

Miller, Lisa *AuBYP 2, –3, BioIn 8*

Miller, Louise Rolfe 1940- *SmATA 76*

Miller, M Hughes d1989 *NewYTBS 89*

Miller, M Hughes 1913- *WhoAm 74, –76, –78, –80, –82, –84, –86, –88, WhoUSWr 88, WhoWrEP 89*

Miller, M Hughes 1913-1989 *BioIn 16, ConAu 130, WhAm 10*

Miller, Madge 1918- *ConAu 117, –123, SmATA 63, TwCChW 78, –83, –89*

Miller, Margaret J *Au&Wr 71, ConAu X, IntAu&W 82X, –91X, SmATA X*
Main entry: Dale, Margaret J Miller

Miller, Marilyn Jean 1925- *BioIn 3, –8, IlsCB 1957, SmATA 33, WhoAmW 74, –75*

Miller, Mark *AuBYP 2, –3, BioIn 7*

Miller, Martha *AuBYP 2, –3, ConAu X*
Main entry: Ivan, Martha Miller Pfaff

Miller, Marvin *ConAu 133, SmATA 65, WrDr 94*

Miller, Mary *ConAu X*
Main entry: Northcott, Cecil

Miller, Mary Beth 1942- *BioIn 11, ConAu 61, SmATA 9*
Pseud./variant:
Beth, Mary

Miller, Mary Britton 1883-1975 *AmAu&B, AmNov X, AmWomWr, AuSpks, AuBYP 2, -3, BioIn 1, -2, -4, -7, -9, -11, BkCL, ChhPo, -S1, ConAu 1R, -57, -16NR, FemiCLE, InWom SUP, LongCTC, ObitOF 79, Str&VC, TwCA SUP, WhAm 6, WhoAmW 74*

Miller, Maryann 1943- *SmATA 73*

Miller, May *AmWomPl, BlkAWP, DrAP 75, DrAPF 87, -89, -91, -93, InWom SUP, SelBAAu, SouBlCW*

Miller, May 1899- *BioIn 17, ConAu 142, EarBlAP, FemiCLE, HarlReB, NotBlAW 92*

Miller, Mitchell 1947- *ChhPo S2, FourBJA, IlsBYP, IlsCB 1967, WhoAmA 73*

Miller, Natalie 1917-1976 *BioIn 14, ForWC 70, SmATA 35*

Miller, Nicole Puleo 1944- *ConAu 49*
Pseud./variant:
Puleo, Nicole

Miller, Orlo *ConAu 138*

Miller, Orlo 1911- *IntAu&W 89, -91, WrDr 76, -80, -82, -84, -86, -88, -90, -92*

Miller, Ruth White *ConAu X, SmATA X*
Main entry: White, Ruth C

Miller, Sandy *ConAu 38NR*

Miller, Sandy 1948- *ConAu X, SmATA 35, -41*

Miller, Shane 1907- *BioIn 8, ConAu P-2, IlsCB 1957*

Miller, Thomas 1807-1874 *Alli, -SUP, BiD&SB, BritAu 19, CarSB, Chambr 3, ChhPo, -S1, -S2, DcBiPP, DcEnL, DcLEL, DcNaB, EvLB, NewC, StaCVF*

Miller, Warren 1921-1966 *AmAu&B, BioIn 4, -5, -7, -10, BlkWr 2, ConAu 25R, EncSF 93, Novels, ObitOF 79, PenC AM, WorAu 1950*

Miller, William Alvin 1931- *ConAu 49, -1NR, -17NR, WhoMW 93, WhoRel 75, -77*

Milligan, Spike *BlueB 76, ConAu X, -33NR, DcIrL, EngPo, HalFC 84, IntWW 82, -83, MajTwCW, OxCChiL, SmATA X, WhoThe 81, WrDr 82, -84*
Main entry: Milligan, Terence Alan

Milligan, Spike 1918- *BioIn 15, -16, -17, ConTFT 6, EncSF 93, HalFC 88, IntAu&W 91, IntWW 89, -91, WhoCom, WrDr 86, -88, -90, -92, -94*

Milligan, Terence Alan 1918- *Au&Wr 71, BioIn 15, -16, -17, ChhPo S1, -S2, ConAu 9R, -4NR, -33NR, EncWT, FilmgC, IntAu&W 77, MajTwCW, SmATA 29, Who 74, -82, -83, -85, -88, -90, -92, WhoHol A, WhoThe 72, -77, WrDr 76, -80*
Pseud./variant:
Milligan, Spike

Milligan, Terence Alan P S 1918- *EngPo*

Millimaki, Robert H 1931- *ConAu 57*

Millington, Roger 1939- *ConAu 65, IntAu&W 77, WrDr 76, -80, -82, -84, -86, -88*

Millotte, Alfred George 1904- *ConAu P-1, SmATA 11, WrDr 76*

Mills, Annette 1894?-1955 *BioIn 3, -8, NotNAT B, ObitOF 79, ObitT 1951, WhoChL*

Mills, Claudia 1954- *ConAu 109, -27NR, IntAu&W 86, -89, -91, SmATA 41, -44*

Mills, Elaine Rosemary 1941- *SmATA 72*

Mills, James Spencer 1932- *AuSpks, WhoAm 74, -80, -82, -84, -86, -88, -90, -92, -94, WhoUSWr 88, WhoWrEP 89, WrDr 80*

Mills, John FitzMaurice 1917- *Au&Wr 71, ConAu 103, WhoArt 82, -84*

Mills, Yaroslava Surmach 1925- *BioIn 8, -14, IlsCB 1957, SmATA 35*
Pseud./variant:
Yaroslava

Millspaugh, Ben P 1936- *SmATA 77*

Millstead, Thomas Edward *BioIn 14, ConAu 106, SmATA 30*

Milman, Constance *CarSB*

Milne, A A
Main entry: Milne, Alan Alexander

Milne, A A 1882-1956 *Benet 87, BioIn 14, -15, -17, BlmGEL, CamGLE, CamGWoT, ChlLR 26, ConAu 133, CrtSuMy, DcLB 77, -100, MajTwCW, RfGEnL 91, TwCChW 89, TwCCr&M 91, WorAlBi, WrChl*

Milne, Alan Alexander *IntvTCA 2*

Milne, Alan Alexander 1882-1956 *AnCL, AuBYP 2, -3, BioIn 1, -2, -3, -4, -5, -6, -7, -8, -9, -10, -11, -12, -13, -14, -15, -17, BkCL, CarSB, CasWL, Chambr 3, ChhPo, -S1, -S2, ChlLR 1, CnMD, ConAu 104, DcLB 10, DcLEL, DcNaB 1951, EncMys, EngPo, EvLB, FamMS, FamPYP,*

GrBr, JBA 34, –51, LongCTC, MajAI, McGEWD 72, –84, ModBrL, ModWD, NewC, NotNAT B, ObitOF 79, ObitT 1951, OxCChiL, OxCEng 67, –85, PenC ENG, RAdv 1, REn, Str&VC, TelT, TwCA, –SUP, TwCChW 78, –83, TwCCr&M 80, –85, TwCLC 6, TwCWr, WhDW, WhAm 3, WhoChL, WhoLA, WorAl, YABC 1
Pseud./variant:
Milne, A A

Milne, Lorus J *ChlLR 22, SmATA 18AS, WhoTech 84, WrDr 86, –88, –90, –92*

Milne, Lorus Johnson *AmMWSc 86, –89, CanWW 89, WhoAm 86, –88, –90, WhoE 86, WrDr 94*

Milne, Lorus Johnson 1910- *AuBYP 3*

Milne, Lorus Johnson 1912- *AmAu&B, AmMWSc 73P, –76P, –82, –92, AuBYP 2, Au&Wr 71, BioIn 7, –10, CanWW 70, –79, –80, –81, –83, ConAu 33R, –14NR, IntAu&W 77, –82, SmATA 5, WhoAm 74, –76, –78, –80, –82, –84, WhoTech 82, WrDr 76, –80, –82, –84*

Milne, Margaret Joan 1914- *AuBYP 3*

Milne, Margery *AmMWSc 86, –89, –92, SmATA 18AS, WrDr 86, –88, –90, –92*

Milne, Margery J *ChlLR 22*

Milne, Margery Joan 1922- *WhoAmW 91*

Milne, Margery Joan Greene *WrDr 94*

Milne, Margery Joan Greene 1915- *AmAu&B, AmMWSc 73P, –76P, Au&Wr 71, BioIn 7, –10, ConAu 33R, ForWC 70, SmATA 5, WhoAmW 74, –75, –77, WhoE 74, WrDr 76, –80*

Milonas, Rolf *ConAu X, SmATA X*
Main entry: Myller, Rolf

Milord, Susan 1954- *SmATA 74*

Milotte, Alfred G d1989 *NewYTBS 89*

Milotte, Alfred G 1904-1989 *ConAu 128, SmATA 62*

Milotte, Alfred George 1904- *WrDr 86, –88, –90*

Milotte, Alfred George 1904-1989 *BioIn 16, –17*

Milsten, David Randolph 1903- *WhoAm 74, –76, –78, –80, –82, –84, –86, –88, –90, –92, –94, WhoAmJ 80, WhoAmL 78*

Milton, Hilary 1920- *BioIn 13, ConAu 57, –6NR, –21NR, ScF&FL 92, SmATA 23, WhoUSWr 88, WhoWrEP 89*

Milton, Hilary Herbert 1920- *WhoWrEP 92*

Milton, John R 1924- *IntAu&W 86, WrDr 86, –88, –90, –92, –94*

Milton, John Ronald *IntvTCA 2*

Milton, John Ronald 1924- *BioIn 13, ConAu 33R, DrAF 76, DrAP 75, DrAS 74E, –78E, –82E, EncFWF, IntAu&W 77, –82, IntWWP 82, SmATA 24, WhoAm 80, –82, –84, –86, –88, –90, –92, –94, WhoMW 76, –78, –80, –82, –84, WhoUSWr 88, WhoWrEP 89, –92, WrDr 80, –82, –84*

Milton, Joyce *DrAPF 87, –89, –91, –93*

Milton, Joyce 1946- *ConAu 106, ScF&FL 92, SmATA 41, –52, WrDr 90, –92, –94*

Milverton, Charles A *ConAu 35NR, SmATA X*
Main entry: Penzler, Otto

Mims, Sam 1887- *AuBYP 2, –3, BioIn 7*

Minale, Marcello 1938- *BioIn 8, ChhPo, ConAu 108, ConDes 84, –90, IlsBYP, IlsCB 1957, WhoGrA 82*

Minard, Rosemary *AuBYP 3*

Minard, Rosemary 1939- *SmATA 63*

Minarik, Else 1920- *TwCChW 89*

Minarik, Else H 1920- *IntAu&W 91, WrDr 86, –88, –90, –92*

Minarik, Else Holmelund 1920- *AuBYP 2, –3, BioIn 7, –9, –12, BkP, ChhPo, –S1, ConAu 73, MajAI, OxCChiL, SmATA 15, ThrBJA, TwCChW 78, –83, WhoAm 88, WhoAmW 83, –85, –87, –89, –91, –93, WrDr 80, –84, –94*

Mincieli, Rose Laura 1912- *ConAu 5R, –4NR, WhoLibS 55*
Pseud./variant:
Ross, Laura

Mindlin, Helen Mather-Smith *AuBYP 2S, –3*

Miner, Irene Sevrey 1906- *AuBYP 2, ConAu 5R*

Miner, Jack 1865?-1944 *BioIn 2, DcNAA, OxCCan, WhNAA*

Miner, Jane Claypool 1933- *BioIn 15, ConAu 106, –27NR, SmATA 37, –38*

Pseud./variant:
Claypool, Jane
Ladd, Veronica

Miner, Lewis S 1909- *BioIn 11, ConAu P-1, SmATA 11*

Miner, Opal Irene Sevrey 1906- *AuBYP 3*

Mines, Jeanette 1948- *ConAu 119, SmATA 61*

Mines, Jeanette Marie 1948- *WhoWrEP 89*
Pseud./variant:
Ryan, Jeanette Mines 1948-

Minhinnick, Jeanne *OxCCan SUP*

Minier, Nelson *BioIn 6, -8, -9, ConAu X, SmATA 3, ThrBJA*
Main entry: Stoutenburg, Adrien

Minja, Park *IlsBYP*

Minor, Wendell *ChlBIlD*

Minshull, Evelyn 1929- *ConAu 37R*

Minton, Robert 1918- *ConAu 57*

Mintonye, Grace *AuBYP 2, -3, BioIn 9, ChhPo S1, ConAu 25R, SmATA 4*

Mintz, Lorelie Miller *AuBYP 2S, -3*

Miranda, Anne 1954- *SmATA 71*

Mirsky, Jeannette 1903- *AmAu&B, BioIn 11, ConAu P-2, ForWC 70, SmATA 8, WhoAm 74, -76, -78, -80, -82, -84, WhoAmW 74*

Mirsky, Jeannette 1903-1987 *BioIn 15, -16, ConAu 122, SmATA 51N*

Mirsky, Reba Paeff 1902-1966 *AuBYP 2, BioIn 7, -9, ConAu 1R, SmATA 1*

Mirsky, Reva Paeff 1902-1966 *AuBYP 3*

Mishima, Yukio *Au&Wr 71, BiDJaL, BioIn 2, -5, -7, -8, -9, -10, -12, CasWL, CnMD, ConAu X, ConLC 2, -4, -6, -9, -27, DcOrL 1, EncWL, -2, EncWT, MajTwCW, ModWD, NewYTBE 70, Novels, ObitOF 79, PenC CL, RComWL, REn, WhDW, WhAm 5, WhScrn 83, WhoTwCL, WorAl, WorAu 1950*
Main entry: Hiraoka, Kimitake

Mishima, Yukio 1925-1970 *Benet 87, BiDExR, BioIn 14, -15, -17, CyWA 89, DramC 1, EncWB, GayLL, GrFLW, MagSWL, MajAI, RAdv 13-2, ShSCr 4, WorAlBi*

Miskovits, Christine 1939- *BioIn 11, ConAu 53, SmATA 10*

Miss Read *ConAu X*
Main entry: Saint, Dora Jessie

Mister Rogers *ConAu X, SmATA X*
Main entry: Rogers, Fred McFeely

Mistral, Gabriela *ConAu 131, HispWr, MajTwCW, WomWrSA*
Main entry: Godoy Alcayaga, Lucila

Mistral, Gabriela 1889-1957 *AtlBL, Benet 87, BenetAL 91, BioIn 14, -15, -16, -17, BlmGWL, CasWL, CathA 1930, ChhPo, ConAu X, CurBio 46, -57, DcCathB, DcSpL, EncLatA, EncWL, -2, HispLC, InWom SUP, LadLa 86, LatAmWr, McGEWB, NobelP, ObitOF 79, ObitT 1951, PenC AM, RAdv 13-2, REn, SpAmA, SpAmWW, TwCA SUP, TwCLC 2, TwCWr, WhDW, WhAm 3, WhoNob, -90, WhoTwCL, WorAlBi, WorAl*

Mitchell, Arthur A 1926- *ConAu 9R*

Mitchell, Barbara Anne 1939- *ConAu 25R, WhoAmW 74*

Mitchell, Clyde *MajAI*

Mitchell, Cynthia 1922- *BioIn 13, ConAu 10C, SmATA 29*

Mitchell, David John 1924- *IntAu&W 82, WrDr 80*

Mitchell, Donald 1925- *Au&Wr 71, Baker 84 ChhPo S1, -S2, ConAu 103, OxCMus, WhoMus 72*

Mitchell, Donald Charles Peter 1925- *Baker 92*

Mitchell, Donald Grant 1822-1908 *Alli, -SUP, AmAu, AmAu&B, BenetAL 91, BbD, BiD&SB, BioIn 11, -12, CarSB, Chambr 3, CnDAL, CyAL, DcAmAu, DcBiA, DcEnL, DcLB 1, DcLEL, DcNAA, EvLB, HarEnUS, OxCAmL 65, -83, REn, REnAL, RfGAmL 87, WhAm 1*

Mitchell, Elyne 1913- *AuWomWr, ConAu 21NR, ScF&FL 92, TwCChW 89, WrDr 86, -88, -90, -92*

Mitchell, Elyne Keith 1913- *BioIn 11, ConAu 53, -5NR, IntAu&W 89, -91, OxCAusL, OxCChiL, SingR 1, SmATA 10, TwCChW 78, -83, WrDr 76, -80, -82, -84*

Mitchell, Gladys *IntvTCA 2*

Mitchell, Gladys 1901- *InWom SUP*

Mitchell, Gladys 1901-1983 *AnObit 1983, ArtclWW 2, Au&Wr 71, BioIn 5, -14, -15, -16, BlmGWL, ConAu 9R, -110, -9NR, CrtSuMy, DcLB 77, EncMys, IntAu&W 77,*

–82, LongCTC, Novels, SmATA 35N, –46, TwCCr&M 80, –85, –91, Who 74, –82, –83, WrDr 76, –80, –82, –84
Pseud./variant:
Hockaby, Stephen
Torrie, Malcolm

Mitchell, Hutton *DcBrBI*

Mitchell, Isla *AuBYP 2, –3, BioIn 7*

Mitchell, James E 1926- *WhoAmA 73, –80, –82, –84, –86*

Mitchell, Jay *SmATA 72*
Main entry: Roberson, Jennifer

Mitchell, Jerry 1905?-1972 *BioIn 9, ConAu 33R*

Mitchell, Joyce Slayton 1933- *BioIn 15, ConAu 65, –15NR, SmATA 43, –46*

Mitchell, Kathy 1948- *SmATA 59*

Mitchell, Lucy Sprague *NewYTBS 87*

Mitchell, Lucy Sprague 1878-1967 *AmPB, AmWomM, BioAmW, BioIn 2, –3, –8, –9, –15, ChhPo, DcAmB S8, InWom SUP, NotAW MOD, WomWWA 14*

Mitchell, Margaret *CamGEL, CamGLE, CamHAL*

Mitchell, Margaret 1900-1945 *BlmGWL*

Mitchell, Margaret 1900-1949 *ArtclWW 2, Benet 87, BenetAL 91, BioAmW, BioIn 14, –15, –16, –17, ConAu 125, FemiCLE, FifSWrA, HalFC 88, MajTwCW, RfGAmL 87, TwCRHW 90, WorAlBi*

Mitchell, Margaret Munnerlyn 1900-1949 *TwCYAW*

Mitchell, Minnie Belle Alexander 1863- *BioIn 2, IndAu 1816, WomWWA 14*

Mitchell, Sibyl Elyne Keith Chauvel 1913- *DcChlFi*

Mitchell, William O 1914- *IntAu&W 91*

Mitchell, William Ormond *IntvTCA 2*

Mitchell, William Ormond 1914- *BioIn 3, –13, CaW, CanWW 70, –80, –81, –83, –89, CanWr, CasWL, ConAu 77, ConNov 72, –76, CreCan 1, OxCCan, TwCWr, WhoCanL 85, –92, WrDr 76, –80*

Mitchell, Yvonne 1925-1979 *Au&Wr 71, BioIn 4, –11, –13, ConAu 17R, –85, –10NR, DcLEL 1940, FilmgC, HalFC 84, –88, IntMPA 75, –76, –78, –77, NotNAT A, OxCFilm, SmATA 24N, WhScrn 83, Who 74, WhoHol A, WhoThe 72, –77, –81N, WrDr 76, –80*

Mitchison, Naomi 1897- *BioIn 15, –16, BlmGWL, CamGEL, CamGLE, CmScLit, ConNov 86, –91, ContDcW 89, EncBrWW, EngPo, FemiCLE, IntAu&W 89, –91, IntWW 89, –91, RfGShF, ScF&FL 92, ScFSB, TwCChW 89, TwCRHW 90, TwCSFW 86, –91, WrDr 86, –88, –90, –92*

Mitchison, Naomi, Lady 1897- *Benet 87*

Mitchison, Naomi Margaret 1897- *Au&Wr 71, BioIn 4, –8, –10, –12, –13, BlueB 76, CasWL, Chambr 3, ChhPo, –S2, ConAu 77, –15NR, ConNov 72, –76, –82, ConSFA, DcLEL, EncSF 93, EvLB, IntAu&W 77, –82, IntWW 74, –75, –76, –77, –78, –79, –80, –81, –82, –83, LongCTC, ModBrL, NewC, Novels, OxCChiL, OxCEng 85, PenC ENG, REn, SmATA 24, TwCA, –SUP, TwCChW 78, –83, Who 74, –82, –83, –85, –85S, –88, –90, –92, WhoChL, WhoLA, WhoSciF, WhoWor 74, WrDr 76, –80, –82, –84, –94*

Mitchison, Naomi Margaret Haldane 1897-1964 *InWom SUP*

Mitchnik, Helen 1901- *ConAu 117, SmATA 35, –41*

Mitford, Bertram d1914 *Alli SUP, CasWL, DcLEL, StaCVF*

Mitgang, Herbert 1920- *AmAu&B, BioIn 11, –12, ConAu 9R, –4NR, IntAu&W 77, MedPD, ScF&FL 92, WhoAm 74, –76, –78, –80, –82, –84, –86, –88, –90, –92, –94, WhoAmJ 80, WhoE 74, WhoUSWr 88, WhoWor 74, –80, WhoWorJ 72, WhoWrEP 89, –92, WrDr 76, –80, –82, –84, –86, –88, –90, –92, –94*

Mitgutsch, Ali 1935- *SmATA 76*

Mitson, Eileen N 1930- *ConAu 25R, WrDr 76, –80, –82, –84, –86, –88, –90, –92*

Mitson, Eileen Nora 1930- *IntAu&W 91, WrDr 94*

Mitsuhashi, Yoko *IlsBYP, SmATA 33, –45*

Mitsui, Eiichi *BioIn 8, IlsBYP, IlsCB 1957*

Mitton, Jacqueline 1948- *SmATA 66*

Mitton, Simon 1946- *SmATA 66*

Mix, Paul E 1934- *ConAu 45*

Miyazawa, Kenji 1896-1933 *BioIn 13, –17, EncWL 2*

Mizner, Elizabeth H *ScF&FL 92*

Mizner, Elizabeth Howard *AuBYP 3*

Mizner, Elizabeth Howard 1907- *AuBYP 2, BioIn 2, -13, ConAu 13R, CurBio 51, IntAu&W 77, -82, SmATA 27*
Pseud./variant:
Howard, Elizabeth

Mizumura, Kazue *AmPB, BioIn 8, -9, -12, ChhPo S2, ConAu 85, IlsBYP, IlsCB 1957, -1967, SmATA 18, ThrBJA*

Moat, John 1936- *Au&Wr 71, ConAu 33R, -13NR, -29NR, ConPo 70, -75, -80, -85, -91, IntAu&W 77, -82, -86, -89, -91, IntWWP 82, WrDr 76, -80, -82, -84, -86, -88, -90, -92, -94*

Moche, Dinah L 1936- *BioIn 15, SmATA 40, -44*

Mochi, Ugo 1889-1977 *BioIn 2, -10, SmATA 38, WhAmArt 85, WhoAmA 73, -78N, -80N, -82N, WhoE 74*

Mochi, Ugo 1894-1977 *WhoAmA 86N, -89N, -91N*

Mochi, Ugo 1897-1977 *BioIn 15*

Mocniak, George *IlsBYP*

Modell, Frank B 1917- *ConAu 116, -39NR, FifBJA, SmATA 36, -39, WorECar*

Modell, Walter 1907- *AmMWSc 73P, -76P, -82, -86, -89, -92, BiDrACP 79*

Moderow, Gertrude *Str&VC*

Modesitt, Jeanne *AuBYP 3*

Modrell, Dolores 1933- *SmATA 72*

Moe, Barbara 1937- *BioIn 12, ConAu 69, SmATA 20*

Moe, Christian H 1929- *WrDr 86, -88, -90, -92*

Moe, Christian Hollis 1929- *BiE&WWA, ConAu 41R, DrAS 74E, -82E, IntAu&W 82, NotNAT, WhoEnt 92, WrDr 82, -84, -94*

Moe, Jorgen Engebretsen *Benet 87*

Moe, Jorgen Engebretsen 1813?-1882 *BiD&SB, BioIn 1, -7, -8, CasWL, DcEuL, EuAu, EvEuW, WhoChL*

Moe, Louis Maria Niels Peder Halling 1859- *BioIn 1, ChhPo, ConICB, IlsCB 1744*

Moeri, Louise 1924- *BioIn 13, ConAu 65, -9NR, FifBJA, ScF&FL 92, SmATA 24, -10AS, TwCYAW*

Moeri, Louise Healy 1924- *DcAmChF 1960*

Moeschlin-Hammar, Elsa 1879- *BioIn 1, ConICB, IlsCB 1744*

Moffett, Martha 1934- *BioIn 11, ConAu 37R, SmATA 8, WhoAmW 77*

Moffett, Robert K *AuBYP 3*

Moffett, Robert Knight *AuBYP 2S*

Mofsie, Louis B 1936- *BioIn 9, IlsBYP, SmATA 33*

Mogridge, George 1787-1854 *DcBiPP, DcNaB, OxCChiL*

Mohan, Beverly 1918- *AuBYP 2S, -3, ConAu 5R*

Mohn, Peter B 1934- *BioIn 13, ConAu 106, SmATA 28*

Mohn, Viola Kohl 1914- *BioIn 11, SmATA 8*

Mohr, Nicholasa 1935- *AfroAA, Au&Arts 8, AuBYP 2S, -3, BiDHisL, BioIn 11, -16, -17, BlmGWL, ChlLR 22, ConAu 49, -1NR, -32NR, ConLC 12, FifBJA, HanAmWH, HispAmA, HispLC, HispWr, IntAu&W 77, NotHsAW 93, SmATA 8, WhoHisp 91, -92*

Mohr, Nicholasa 1938- *TwCYAW, WhoHisp 94*

Mohr, Nicholasa 1939- *SmATA 8AS*

Mohr, Nicholasa Golpe 1935- *DcAmChF 1960*

Molan, Dorothy Lennon 1911- *ConAu 9R, ForWC 70*

Molarsky, Osmond 1909- *BioIn 12, ConAu 25R, SmATA 16*

Moldafsky, Annie 1930- *ConAu 61, WhoAmW 81, WhoMW 84*

Moldon, Peter L 1937- *BioIn 16, ConAu 121, SmATA 49*

Moldon, Peter Leonard 1937- *IntAu&W 89, -91*

Mole, John 1941- *ConAu 101, -18NR, -41NR, ConPo 80, -85, -91, IntAu&W 82, IntWWP 82, SmATA 36, WrDr 82, -84, -86, -88, -90, -92*

Molesworth, M L S 1839-1921 *WrChl*

Molesworth, Mary L *ScF&FL 92*

Molesworth, Mary Louisa 1839-1921 *BioIn 15, -16, -17, BlmGEL, BlmGWL, CamGEL, CamGLE, DcNaB MP, FemiCLE, PenEncH, TwCChW 89A, WomNov*

Molesworth, Mary Louisa, Mrs 1839-1921
StaCVF

Molesworth, Mary Louisa Stewart 1839?-1921
Alli SUP, BbD, BiD&SB, BioIn 2, -3, -7, -8, BritAu 19, CarSB, Chambr 3, ChhPo, DcLEL, EvLB, FamSYP, JBA 34, LongCTC, NewC, OxCChiL, OxCEng 85, TelT, TwCChW 78A, -83A, WhoChL, WhoHr&F

Molesworth, Mary Louise Stewart 1839-1921
InWom SUP

Molin, Charles *ConAu 37NR, MajAI, SmATA 68*
Main entry: Mayne, William James Carter

Molloy, Anne Stearns 1907- *AuBYP 3*

Molloy, Anne Stearns Baker 1907- *AuBYP 2, BioIn 7, ConAu 13R, ForWC 70, SmATA 32*

Molloy, Paul George 1920?- *BioIn 6, -10, ChhPo S2, ConAu 1R, -17NR, SmATA 5, WhoAm 74, WhoMW 74*

Momaday, N Scott *DrAPF 87, -89, -91, -93*

Momaday, N Scott 1934- *AmAu&B, Au&Arts 11, BenetAL 91, BioIn 9, -10, -11, CamGLE, CamHAL, ChhPo S1, CmCal, ConAu 25R, -14NR, -34NR, ConLC 2, -19, ConNov 76, -82, -86, -91, CurBio 75, CyWA 89, DcLEL 1940, DrAF 76, DrAPF 83, -85, EncFWF, MagSAmL, MajTwCW, ModAL S2, OxCAmL 83, SmATA 30, -48, TwCWW 91, WorAu 1975, WrDr 76, -80, -82, -84, -86, -88, -90, -92*

Momaday, Natachee Scott *DcAmChF 1960*

Momaday, Navarre Scott 1934- *TwCYAW, WrDr 94*

Momiyama, Nanae *WhoAmA 86, -89, -91, WhoAmW 89, WhoE 86*

Momiyama, Nanae 1924- *WhoAmA 78, -80, -82, -84, WhoAmW 75, -77, -83*

Mommens, Norman 1922- *BioIn 5, IlsBYP, IlsCB 1946*

Moncrieff, R Hope *OxCChiL*

Moncure, Jane Belk 1926- *ConAu 9R, -6NR, IntAu&W 82, -86, -89, -91, SmATA 23, WhoAmW 83, -89*
Pseud./variant:
Wannamaker, Bruce

Mondale, Joan Adams 1930- *BioIn 10, -11, ConAu 41R, InWom SUP, WhoAm 78, -80, -82, -84, -86, -88, -90, -92, -94, WhoAmA 78, -80, -82, -84, -86, -89, -91, WhoAmW 77, -81, WhoE 77, -81, -83, -86, WhoMW 93*

Monheit, Albert 1923- *BiDrLUS 70, WhoE 89, WhoLibS 55, -66*

Monjo, F N 1924-1978 *AuBYP 3, TwCChW 89*

Monjo, Ferdinand N 1924-1978 *AuBYP 2S, BioIn 2, -11, -12, ChlLR 2, ConAu 81, FifBJA, OxCChiL, SmATA 16, TwCChW 78, -83, WrDr 80*

Monjo, Ferdinand Nicholas, III 1924-1978
ConAu 37NR, MajAI

Monk, Kathleen Doris 1927- *Au&Wr 71*

Monk, Marvin Randolph 1921- *BioIn 5, IlsBYP, IlsCB 1946*

Monka, Paul 1935- *ConAu 29R*

Monro, A *DcBrBI*

Monro, Harold Edward 1879-1932 *AnCL, BioIn 2, -7, -13, ChhPo, -S1, -S2, DcLEL, DcNaB 1931, EvLB, LongCTC, ModBrL, NewC, OxCEng 67, PenC ENG, REn, TwCA, -SUP, WebE&AL, WhoLA, WhoTwCL*

Monroe, Lyle *AuBYP 2, -3, ConAu X, EncSF 93, MajAI, MajTwCW, SmATA X*
Main entry: Heinlein, Robert A

Monroe, Lynn Lee 1935- *ConAu 53*

Monroe, Marion 1898-1983 *AnObit 1983, BioIn 13, -14, ConAu X, NewYTBS 83, SmATA 34N, WhAmArt 85*
Pseud./variant:
Cox, Marion Monroe

Monsell, Helen 1895-1971 *BioIn 13, ConAu P-1, SmATA 24*

Monsell, Helen Albee 1895- *AmWomPl*

Monsell, John Robert 1877- *BioIn 1, -14, ChhPo, -S1, IlsCB 1744*

Monsky, Mark B VonSommer 1941-
ConAu 65, WhoAm 82, -84, -86, WhoE 81, -83, -85, -86

Montague, Peter Gunn 1938- *ConAu 85, WhoE 81, WhoWest 74, -76, -78*

Montana, Bob 1920-1975 *BioIn 10, -12, EncACom, ObitOF 79, SmATA 21N, WhoAmA 80N, -82N, -86N, -89N, -91N*

Montgomerie, Norah 1913- *AuBYP 3*

Montgomerie, Norah Mary 1913- *AuBYP 2, BioIn 5, -7, -8, -13, -14, ChhPo, -S1, -S2, IlsCB 1946, -1957, SmATA 26*

Montgomery, Bruce *BioIn 1, -2, -10, ConAu 104, EncMys*
Main entry: Montgomery, Robert Bruce

Montgomery, Charlotte Baker 1910- *IntAu&W 77, -82*
Pseud./variant:
Baker, Charlotte

Montgomery, Constance *ConAu X, SmATA X*
Main entry: Cappel, Constance

Montgomery, Elizabeth *ConAu 42NR*

Montgomery, Elizabeth 1902-1985 *AuBYP 3*

Montgomery, Elizabeth Rider *ConAu 42NR*

Montgomery, Elizabeth Rider 1902- *BioIn 14*

Montgomery, Elizabeth Rider 1902-1985 *AuBYP 2, BioIn 2, -3, -7, -9, -15, ConAu 1R, -X, -3NR, CurBio 52, ForWC 70, IntAu&W 77, -82, SmATA 3, -34, -41N, WhoAmW 74, -75, -77, -81, WhoPNW*

Montgomery, Florence *OxCChiL*

Montgomery, Florence 1843-1923 *FemiCLE, WomNov*

Montgomery, Florence 1843-1934 *StaCVF*

Montgomery, John 1916- *Au&Wr 71, IntAu&W 77, -82, -86*

Montgomery, L M 1874-1942 *Au&Arts 12, Benet 87, BenetAL 91, BioIn 14, -15, -16, -17, CamGEL, CamGLE, FemiCLE, RfGEnL 91, ScF&FL 92, TwCChW 89, TwCRHW 90, WrChl*

Montgomery, Lucy Maud *WomNov*

Montgomery, Lucy Maud 1874-1942 *AmWomPl, ArtclWW 2, BioIn 1, -3, -4, -6, -7, -10, -11, -12, -14, -15, -16, -17, BlmGWL, CanWr, CarSB, CasWL, Chambr 3, ChhPo, -S1, -S2, ChlLR 8, ConAu 108, -137, CreCan 2, DcChlFi, DcLB 92, DcLEL, DcNAA, EvLB, JBA 34, LongCTC, MajAI, ObitOF 79, OxCAmL 65, OxCCan, OxCCanL, OxCChiL, REn, REnAL, TwCA, TwCChW 78, -83, TwCWr, WhNAA, YABC 1*

Montgomery, Raymond A 1936- *SmATA 39*
Pseud./variant:
Mountain, Robert

Montgomery, Robert Bruce 1921- *BioIn 1, -2, -10, WorAu 1950*
Pseud./variant:
Crispin, Edmund
Montgomery, Bruce

Montgomery, Ruth Shick *WhoAm 86, -88, -90, -92, -94, WhoUSWr 88, WhoWrEP 89, -92*

Montgomery, Ruth Shick 1912- *AmWomWr, AuNews 1, BioIn 1, -4, -9, -10, -15, ConAu 1R, -2NR, -17NR, CurBio 57, ForWC 70, IntAu&W 77, -82, WhoAm 74, -76, -78, -80, -82, -84, WhoAmW 75, -77, WhoWor 74, WrDr 76, -80*

Montgomery, Rutherford *WrDr 86*

Montgomery, Rutherford 1894-1985 *TwCChW 89, TwCWW 91*

Montgomery, Rutherford George 1894- *AmAu&B, AuBYP 2, -3, BioIn 6, -7, -9, ConAu 9R, DcAmChF 1960, MorJA, OxCChiL, SmATA 3, TwCChW 78, -83, WhNAA, WhoAm 74, -76, -78, WrDr 76, -80, -82, -84*
Pseud./variant:
Avery, Al
Proctor, Everitt

Montgomery, Rutherford George 1894-1985 *ScF&FL 92*

Montgomery, Rutherford George 1896- *BioIn 14, WhAm 10*

Montgomery, Vivian *ConAu 102, SmATA 36*

Montgomery, Walter *Alli SUP, CarSB*

Montresor, Beni *ChlBIlD*

Montresor, Beni 1926- *AuBYP 2, -3, BioIn 6, -7, -8, -9, -11, -12, -13, -14, -15, -17, BkP, ChhPo, ConAu 29R, -28NR, CurBio 67, IlsBYP, IlsCB 1957, -1967, IntWWM 90, MajAI, NewbC 1956, SmATA 3, -38, -4AS, ThrBJA, WhoOp 76, WhoWor 74*

Montross, Lynn 1895-1961 *AmAu&B, BioIn 5, ObitOF 79, WhNAA*

Monty Python *Au&Arts 7, ConAu 129, -35NR, HalFC 88, IntMPA 86, -88, -92, SmATA 67*

Monvel, Maurice Boutet De *AmPB, BioIn [illegible]*
Main entry: Boutet DeMonvel, Maurice

Monypenny, Kathleen *SingR 1*

Moodie, John Rockwell 1920- *WhoGov 72*

Moody, Anne 1940- *ArtclWW 2, BenetAL 91, BioIn 8, -9, -11, BlkWr 1, ConAu 65, EncAACR, HerW, -84, InB&W 80,*

InWom SUP, IntAu&W 77, LivgBAA, SelBAAf, SelBAAu, WhoBlA 90, –92, –94

Moody, Ralph Owen 1898- *AuBYP 2, –3, BioIn 2, –3, –4, –6, –7, –8, –9, ConAu P-1, CurBio 55, SmATA 1, WhoAm 74, –76, –78*

Moon, Carl d1948 *WhoAmA 86N*

Moon, Carl 1879-1948 *AmAu&B, AuBYP 2, –3, BioIn 1, –2, –5, –7, –13, ConAu 111, ConICB, DcNAA, IlsCB 1744, JBA 34, –51, OhA&B, SmATA 25, WhAm 2, WhAmArt 85, WhNAA, WhoAmA 78N, –80N, –82N, –89N, –91N*

Moon, Grace Purdie 1877?-1946 *AuBYP 3*

Moon, Grace Purdie 1877?-1947 *AmAu&B, ArtsAmW 2, AuBYP 2, BioIn 1, –2, –7, –13, –14, ChhPo, ConAu 113, DcNAA, DcWomA, IndAu 1917, JBA 34, –51, SmATA 25, WhAm 2, WhNAA*

Moon, Mary Leonore *WrDr 76*

Moon, Sheila 1910- *AuBYP 2S, –3, BioIn 10, ConAu 25R, SmATA 5*

Moon, Sheila Elizabeth 1910- *DcAmChF 1960*

Mooney, Elizabeth C 1918- *ConAu 61, –9NR*

Mooney, Elizabeth C 1918-1986 *ConAu 119, SmATA 48N*

Mooney, Elizabeth Comstock 1918-1986 *BioIn 16*

Moor, Emily *SmATA X, TwCCr&M 85, –91, WrDr 82, –84*
Main entry: Deming, Richard

Moorcock, Michael 1939- *BioIn 15, –16, –17, CamGLE, ConAu 45, –5AS, –2NR, –17NR, ConLC 5, –27, –58, ConNov 91, ConSFA, DcLB 14, IntAu&W 77, –91, IntvTCA 2, MajTwCW, NewEScF, Novels, OxCEng 85, RGTwCSF, ScF&FL 92, ScFSB, SupFW, TwCSFW 86, –91, WhoHr&F, WhoSciF, WorAu 1975, WrDr 76, –80, –82, –84, –86, –88, –90, –92*

Moorcock, Michael John 1939- *ConAu 38NR, EncSF 93, WrDr 94*

Moore, Anne Carroll 1871-1961 *AmAu&B, AmPB, AuBYP 2, –3, BioAmW, BioIn 1, –2, –3, –4, –5, –7, –9, –11, –12, –14, –15, ChhPo, –S2, ConAu 73, DcAmB S7, HerW, –84, InWom SUP, JBA 34, –51, NotAW MOD, OxCChiL, REnAL, SmATA 13, WhAm 4, WhNAA*

Moore, Barbara 1934- *BioIn 6, –11, ConAu 53, –X, IntAu&W 91, WhoAmW 74, WrDr 76, –80, –82, –84, –86, –88, –90, –92, –94*

Moore, Carman Leroy 1936- *BiDAfM, BioIn 10, BlkAuII, –92, ConAmC 76, –82, ConAu 61, DrBlPA 90, InB&W 80, –85, IntAu&W 77, –82, IntWWM 85, –90, LivgBAA, WhoAm 76, –78, –80, –82, –84, –86, –88, WhoAmM 83, WhoBlA 75, –77, –80, –85, –88, –90, –92, –94, WhoE 75, WrDr 76, –80*

Moore, Clement Clarke 1779-1863 *Alli, AmAu, AmAu&B, AnCL, BenetAL 91, BiD&SB, BioIn 2, –3, –4, –6, –9, –12, –15, –17, BkCL, CarSB, ChhPo, –S1, –S2, CnDAL, CyAL, DcAmAu, DcLB 42, DcLEL, DcNAA, EvLB, FamPYP, HarEnUS, MajAI, OxCAmL 65, –83, OxCChiL, REn, REnAL, SmATA 18, Str&VC, WebAB 74, –79, WhAm HS, WorAl*
Pseud./variant:
Columella

Moore, Clyde B 1886-1973 *AuBYP 2S, –3, ConAu 1R, –4NR, WhAm 6, WhNAA, WhoAm 74*

Moore, David William *AuBYP 3*

Moore, David William 1895-1954 *AuBYP 2, BioIn 7, OhA&B*

Moore, Don W d1986 *NewYTBS 86*

Moore, Don W 1905?-1986 *ConAu 119, SmATA 48N*

Moore, Dorothea d1933 *OxCChiL, TwCChW 83*

Moore, Dorothea 1881-1933 *ConAu 121, TwCChW 89*

Moore, Elizabeth *IntAu&W 91X, MedPD, WrDr 86, –88, –90*

Moore, Emily R 1948- *BlkAuII, –92*

Moore, Eva 1942- *AuBYP 2S, –3, BioIn 12, ConAu 45, SmATA 20*

Moore, Fenworth *ConAu 26NR, –P-2*
Main entry: Stratemeyer, Edward L

Moore, Frank Gardner 1865-1955 *BioIn 4, –13, NatCAB 61, WhAm 3, WhNAA*

Moore, Jack William 1941- *ConAu 112, SmATA 32, –46, WhoAm 80, –82, –84*

Moore, Janet Gaylord 1905- *BioIn 12, –14, ConAu 77, IlsBYP, SmATA 18*

Moore, Jessie Eleanor 1886- *ConAu P-1*

Moore, Jim 1946- *SmATA 42*

Moore, John A 1915- *ConAu 26NR, IntWW 89, –91, WrDr 86, –88, –90*

Moore, John Alexander 1915- *AmMWSc 73P, -76P, -82, -86, -89, -92, Au&Wr 71, BioIn 11, BlueB 76, ConAu 45, IntAu&W 82, IntWW 74, -75, -76, -77, -78, -79, -80, -81, -82, -83, McGMS 80, WhoAm 74, -76, -78, -80, -82, -84, WhoFrS 84, WrDr 76, -80, -82, -84*

Moore, John Newton 1920- *AmMWSc 73P, WhoAm 82, -84, -86, -88, -90, -92, -94, WhoMW 76, -78, -80*

Moore, John Travers 1908- *BioIn 11, ChhPo, -S1, ConAu 5R, -3NR, SmATA 12, WhoAm 74, -76, -78, -80, -82, -84, -86, -88, -90, -92, -94, WhoSSW 75, -76, WhoWor 80*

Moore, Lamont 1909- *AuBYP 2, -3, BioIn 7, -13, SmATA 29*

Moore, Lilian *AuBYP 2, -3, BioIn 7, BkP, ChhPo S1, ChlLR 15, ConAu 103, FourBJA*

Moore, Lilian 1909- *DcAmChF 1985, MajAI, SmATA 52*

Moore, Margaret Rumberger 1903- *BioIn 11, ConAu 9R, SmATA 12, WhoAmW 74, -75, -81, -83, WhoSSW 75, -76*

Moore, Marianne C 1887-1972 *BioAmW*

Moore, Marianne Craig 1887-1972 *AmAu&B, AmWomWr, AmWr, AnCL, AnMV 1926, BioIn 1, -2, -3, -4, -5, -6, -7, -8, -9, -10, -11, -12, -13, CasWL, ChhPo S2, CnDAL, CnE&AP, CnMWL, ConAmA, ConAmL, ConAu 1R, -33R, ConLC 1, -2, -4, -8, -10, -13, ConPo 70, CurBio 52, -68, -72, DcLEL, EncAB-H, EncWL, EvLB, ForWC 70, HanAmWH, InWom SUP, LongCTC, MakMC, McGEWB, ModAL, -S1, NewYTBE 72, NotAW MOD, ObitOF 79, OxCAmL 65, OxCEng 67, -85, PenC AM, RAdv 1, REn, REnAL, SixAP, SmATA 20, TwCA, -SUP, TwCWr, WebAB 74, -79, WebE&AL, WhAm 5, WhoTwCL, WorAl*

Moore, Marie Drury 1926- *ConAu 33R*

Moore, Mary Jane 1922- *WhoSSW 78*

Moore, Mona 1917- *ArtsCL, BioIn 6, DcBrAr 1, WhoArt 80, -82, -84*

Moore, Nancy *AuBYP 2, -3, BioIn 7*

Moore, Patrick 1923- *IntWW 89, RAdv 13-5, ScF&FL 92, ScFSB, SmATA 49, -8AS, TwCSFW 86, -91, WrDr 86, -88, -90, -92*

Moore, Patrick Alfred 1923- *AuBYP 2, -3, Au&Wr 71, BioIn 7, BlueB 76, ConAu 13R, -8NR, DcLEL 1940, EncSF 93, FourBJA, IntAu&W 77, -82, SmATA 39, Who 74, WhoSciF, WrDr 76, -80, -82, -84*

Moore, Patrick Alfred Caldwell- 1923- *Who 90, -92, WrDr 94*

Moore, Ray *EncACom*

Moore, Ray 1905?-1984 *ConAu 111, ConGrA 1, SmATA 37N*

Moore, Ray 1926- *Ballpl 90*

Moore, Regina *AuBYP 2S, -3, BioIn 11, ConAu X, SmATA X*
Main entry: Dunne, Mary Collins

Moore, Robert L, Jr. 1925- *AmAu&B, ArtCS, AuNews 1, BioIn 10, BioNews 74, CelR, ConAu 13R, WhoAm 74, -76, -78, -80, -82, -84*
Pseud./variant:
Moore, Robin

Moore, Robin
Main entry: Moore, Robert L, Jr.

Moore, Rosalie *DrAPF 87, -91, -93*

Moore, Rosalie 1910- *BioIn 11, ChhPo, -S2, ConAu 3NR, DrAP 75, DrAPF 83, -85, InWom SUP, IntAu&W 82, IntWWP 82, SmATA X, WhoUSWr 88, WhoWrEP 89, -92, WrDr 76, -80, -82, -84*
Main entry: Brown, Rosalie Moore

Moore, Roy Benjamin 1908- *LEduc 74*

Moore, Ruth d1989 *WhAm 9*

Moore, Ruth 1908- *AmAu&B, Au&Wr 71, BioIn 2, -3, -5, -13, ConAu 1R, -6NR, CurBio 54, ForWC 70, SmATA 23, WhoAm 74, -76, -78, -80, -82, -84, WhoAmW 74, -89, WhoWest 87*

Moore, Ruth 1908-1989 *ConAu 127*

Moore, Ruth Nulton 1923- *BioIn 15, ConAu 81, -15NR, IntAu&W 82, -86, -89, -91, SmATA 38*

Moore, S E *BioIn 13, ConAu 2NR, SmATA 23*

Moore, Tara 1950- *ConAu 38NR, SmATA 61*

Moore, Vardine 1906- *AuBYP 3*

Moore, Vardine Russell 1906- *AuBYP 2, BioIn 7, ConAu 41R, IndAu 1917*

Moore, Virginia *AuBYP 3*

Moore, Virginia Bradley 1932- *WhoE 93*

Moore, Virginia Dryden 1911- *ConAu 17R*

Moore, Wilfred George 1907- *Au&Wr 71, ConAu 9R, -4NR, IntAu&W 77, -86, -91, WrDr 76, -80, -82, -84, -86, -88*

Moore, Yvette 1958- *SmATA 70*

Moore-Betty, Maurice *BioIn 9*

Moore-Betty, Maurice d1988 *BioIn 16, NewYTBS 88*

Moorehead, Alan 1910-1983 *AnObit 1983, Au&Wr 71, Benet 87, BioIn 4, -6, -9, -13, -17, BlueB 76, ConAu 5R, -110, -6NR, FarE&A 80, -81, IntAu&W 77, IntWW 74, -75, -76, -77, -78, -79, -80, -81, -82, -83, LongCTC, NewC, NewYTBS 83, OxCAusL, REn, TwCA SUP, WhAm 8, Who 74, WhoWor 74, WrDr 76, -80, -82, -84*

Moorehead, Alan McCrae 1910-1983 *DcNaB 1981*

Moores, Dick
Main entry: Moores, Richard Arnold

Moores, Richard d1986 *NewYTBS 86*

Moores, Richard 1909- *ArtCS, ConAu 69*

Moores, Richard 1909-1986 *BioIn 14, -15, ConAu 119*

Moores, Richard Arnold 1909-1986 *SmATA 48N*
Pseud./variant:
Moores, Dick

Moorhead, Diana 1940- *ConAu 105, IntAu&W 77, -89, OxCChiL, TwCChW 78, -83, -89, WrDr 80, -82, -84, -86, -88, -90, -92, -94*

Moorsom, Sasha 1931- *AuBYP 2S, -3, ConAu 69, -14NR*

Moos, Malcolm Charles 1916-1982 *AmAu&B, AmMWSc 73S, BioIn 5, -8, -12, ConAu 37R, -105, CurBio 68, IntWW 74, -75, -76, -77, -78, LEduc 74, WhAm 8, WhoAm 74, -80, WhoMW 74, WhoWor 74*

Mooser, Stephen 1941- *BioIn 13, ConAu 15NR, ScF&FL 92, SmATA 28, -75*

Mora, Francisco 1922- *WhoAm 86, -88, -90, -92, -94, WhoAmA 78, -80, -82*

Moran, Connie *BioIn 2, IlsBYP*

Moran, Eugene Francis 1872- *AuBYP 3*

Moran, Eugene Francis 1872-1961 *AuBYP 2, BioIn 2, -3, -4, -5, -7, -9, DcAmB S7, WhAm 4*

Moran, James Sterling 1909- *BiE&WWA, BioIn 3, ConAu 9R, -12NR, NotNAT*

Moran, Tom 1943- *ConAu 29NR, SmATA 60*

Moray Williams, Ursula 1911- *ConAu 111, -26NR, IntAu&W 89, -91, MajAI, SmATA 73, -9AS, TwCChW 83, -89, WrDr 76, -80, -82, -84, -86, -88, -90, -92, -94*
Main entry: Williams, Ursula Moray

Mordvinoff, Nicolas 1911-1973 *AmPB, AuBYP 2, -3, BioIn 1, -2, -3, -4, -5, -6, -7, -8, -9, -12, -14, Cald 1938, ChsFB I, ConAu 41R, -73, IlsBYP, IlsCB 1744, -1946, -1957, MorJA, OxCChiL, SmATA 17, WhAm 6, WhoAmA 73, -78N, -80N, -82N, -86N, -89N, -91N, WhoE 74*
Pseud./variant:
Nicolas

More, Caroline *AuBYP 2, -3, BioIn 12, ConAu X, -37NR, SmATA X, ThrBJA, WrDr 76, -80, -82, -84, -86, -88, -90, -92*
Main entry: Cone, Molly Lamken
Strachan, Margaret Pitcairn

More, Hannah 1745-1833 *Alli, ArtclWW 2, AtlBL, Benet 87, BbD, BiDLA, BiD&SB, BioIn 1, -2, -3, -4, -5, -6, -9, -11, -12, -14, -16, -17, BlmGEL, BlmGWL, BritAu 19, CamGEL, CamGLE, CarSB, CasWL, CelCen, Chambr 2, ChhPo, -S1, -S2, CyEd, DcBiA, DcBiPP, DcBrAmW, DcEnA, DcEnL, DcEuL, DcLB 107, -109, -116, DcLEL, DcNaB, EncBrWW, EncWM, EvLB, FemiCLE, InWom SUP, IntDcWB, LongCEL, LuthC 75, NewC, NinCLC 27, NotNAT B, OxCChiL, OxCEng 67, -85, OxCMus, PenC ENG, REn, RfGEnL 91, WebE&AL*

More, Hannah 1745-1835 *ContDcW 89*

Morehead, Albert Hodges 1909-1966 *AmAu&B, ASCAP 66, BioIn 3, -4, -7, ConAu P-1, CurBio 55, -66, ObitOF 79, WhAm 4*

Morell, Musette *AuWomWr, OxCAusL, SingR 1*
Main entry: Martin, Moyra

Moremen, Grace E 1930- *ConAu 45, -1NR*

Morency, Pierre 1942- *DcLB 60, OxCCan SUP, OxCCanL, WhoCanL 85, -87, -92*

Moreno, Martin *ConAu X*
Main entry: Swartz, Harry

Morenus, Richard 1897- *AuBYP 2, -3, BioIn 7*

Moreton, John *AuBYP 2S, -3, ConAu X, -28NR, IntAu&W 91X, WrDr 76, -80, -82, -84, -86, -88, -90, -92*
Main entry: Cohen, Morton Norton

Moreton, John 1921- *WrDr 94*

Morey, Charles *ConAu X, SmATA X*
Main entry: Fletcher, Helen Jill

Morey, Jean Anne Wuerfel 1927- *WhoAmW 74*

Morey, Walt d1992 *NewYTBS 92*

Morey, Walt 1907- *AuBYP 3, ConAu 31NR, IntAu&W 91, SmATA 51, –9AS, TwCChW 89, WrDr 86, –88, –90, –92*

Morey, Walt 1907-1992 *AnObit 1992, BioIn 17*

Morey, Walter Nelson 1907- *AuBYP 2, Au&Wr 71, BioIn 8, –9, ConAu 29R, DcAmChF 1960, OxCChiL, SmATA 3, ThrBJA, TwCChW 78, –83, WhoAm 74, –80, –82, WhoPNW, WrDr 80, –82, –84*

Morey, Walter Nelson 1907-1992 *ConAu 136, MajAI, SmATA 70, WhAm 10, WrDr 94N*

Morgan, Alfred Powell 1889-1972 *AuBYP 2, –3, BioIn 6, –7, –9, ConAu 107, MorJA, SmATA 33, WhAm 5, WhNAA*

Morgan, Alfred Powell 1899-1972 *BioIn 14*
Pseud./variant:
Powell, A M

Morgan, Alison 1930- *OxCLiW 86, TwCChW 89*

Morgan, Alison 1959- *ConAu 137*

Morgan, Alison M 1930- *WrDr 86, –88, –90, –92, –94*

Morgan, Alison Mary 1930- *ConAu 49, –1NR, –18NR, IntAu&W 89, –91, OxCChiL, SmATA 30, TwCChW 78, –83, WrDr 76, –80, –82, –84*

Morgan, Allen *AuBYP 3*

Morgan, Allen 1908- *AuBYP 2S, WhoAm 76*

Morgan, Allen 1946- *WhoCanL 87, –92*

Morgan, Ann Haven 1882-1966 *BioIn 12, InWom SUP, NotAW MOD, WhAm 4*

Morgan, Ava *IlsBYP*

Morgan, Bryan Stanford 1923-1976 *AuBYP 2S, –3, Au&Wr 71, ConAu 5R, –8NR, –9NR, IntAu&W 77, WrDr 76, –80*

Morgan, Dale Lowell 1914-1971 *BioIn 16, CmCal, ConAu 104*

Morgan, Edmund Sears 1916- *AmAu&B, Au&Wr 71, BioIn 13, –15, BlueB 76, ConAu 9R, –4NR, DcLB 17, DrAS 74H, –78H, –82H, WhoAm 74, –76, –78, –80, –82, –84, –86, –88, –90, –92, –94*

Morgan, Ellen
Main entry: Bumstead, Kathleen Mary

Morgan, Geoffrey 1916- *AuBYP 2S, –3, ConAu 21R, SmATA 46*

Morgan, Helen 1921- *Au&Wr 71, BioIn 13, ConAu 57, SmATA 29, TwCChW 83, –89, WrDr 76, –80, –82, –84, –86, –88, –90, –92*
Pseud./variant:
Morgan, Helen Tudor
Morgan, Louise

Morgan, Helen Gertrude Louise 1921- *WrDr 94*

Morgan, Helen Tudor
Main entry: Morgan, Helen

Morgan, Henry 1825-1884 *Alli SUP, BioIn 13, CarSB, DcAmAu, DcNAA*

Morgan, Jacqui 1939?- *BioIn 10, –11, –12, ConGrA 1, WhoAm 86, –88, –90, –92, –94 WhoGrA 82, WhoWor 91, –93*

Morgan, James 1861-1955 *Alli, –SUP, AmAu&B, BioIn 3, –4, WhAm 3, WhNAA*

Morgan, Jane *ConAu X, SmATA X*

Morgan, Joe Leonard 1943- *BioIn 10, –11, WhoAm 74, –78, –80, –82, –84, WhoBlA 77, –80, –85*

Morgan, Leonore H 1908?- *BioIn 11, ConAu P-2, SmATA 8, WrDr 76, –80*

Morgan, Louise *SmATA X*
Main entry: Morgan, Helen

Morgan, Paul 1928- *ConAu 61, IntWWM 85, –90*

Morgan, Pierr 1952- *SmATA 77*

Morgan, Roy 1928- *BioIn 5, IlsBYP, IlsCB 1946*

Morgan, Sarah 1959- *SmATA 68*

Morgan, Sarah Nicola 1959- *ConAu 136, WrDr 94*

Morgan, Sharon A 1951- *ConAu 61, WhoBlA 85*
Pseud./variant:
Fufuka, Karama

Morgan, Sharon Antonia 1951- *WhoBlA 85, –88, –90*

Morgan, Shirley 1933- *BioIn 11, ConAu 37R, SmATA 10*

Morgan, Tom 1942- *ConAu 108, SmATA 42*

Morgan, Violet 1898- *OhA&B*

Morgenroth, Barbara *ConAu 117, SmATA 36*

Morgenstern, Christian 1871-1914 *BioIn 1, –7, CasWL, ChhPo, –S1, –S2, ClDMEL 47, CnMWL, ConAu 105, Dis&D, EncWL, –2, EuAu, EvEuW, ModGL, OxCGer 76, –86, PenC EUR, REn, TwCLC 8, WhoTwCL*

Moriarty, Tim 1923- *ConAu 61*

Moriarty, Timothy *ScF&FL 92*

Morice, Stella *DcChlFi*

Morin, Claude 1929- *BioIn 12, CanWW 80, –81, –83, IntYB 80, –81, –82, OxCCan SUP*

Morine, Hoder *ConAu 131, SmATA 65*
Main entry: Conroy, Jack

Morison, Samuel Eliot 1887-1976 *AmAu&B, AmWr S1, AuSpks, AuBYP 2, –3, Au&Wr 71, Benet 87, BenetAL 91, BioIn 2, –3, –4, –5, –6, –7, –8, –10, –11, –12, –13, –14, –16, BlueB 76, CelR, ConAu 1R, –65, –4NR, CurBio 51, –62, –76N, DcLB 17, DcLEL, DrAS 74H, EncAB-H, IntAu&W 77, IntWW 74, –75, –76, –77N, LongCTC, McGEWB, NatCAB 61, NewYTBE 71, ObitOF 79, OxCAmH, OxCAmL 65, –83, OxCCan SUP, OxCShps, PenC AM, RAdv 13-3, REn, REnAL, ThTwC 87, TwCA SUP, WebAB 74, –79, WebAMB, WhAm 6, –7, Who 74, WhoAm 74, –76, WhoWor 74, WorAlBi, WorAl, WrDr 76*

Morland, Nigel 1905- *Au&Wr 71, BioIn 14, ChhPo S1, ConAu 53, EncMys, IntAu&W 77, TwCCr&M 80, –85, WrDr 82, –84, –86*

Morland, Nigel 1905-1986 *ConAu 119, ScF&FL 92, TwCCr&M 91*

Morley, Christopher Darlington 1890-1957 *AmAu&B, AmNov, BioIn 1, –2, –3, –4, –5, –8, –9, –11, –12, –17, CarSB, CasWL, ChhPo, –S1, –S2, CnDAL, ConAmA, ConAmL, DcLEL, EvLB, LongCTC, ModAL, NotNAT B, OxCAmL 65, OxCEng 67, PenC AM, REn, REnAL, Str&VC, TwCA, –SUP, WhAm 3, WhNAA*

Morningstar, Mildred 1912- *BioIn 17, ConAu 127, SmATA 61*

Morpurgo, Michael 1943- *ChlFicS*

Morrah, Dave
Main entry: Morrah, David Wardlaw, Jr.

Morrah, David Wardlaw, Jr. 1914- *BioIn 4, –11, ConAu 1R, SmATA 10*

Morrah, David Wardlaw, Jr. 1914-1991 *ConAu 134*
Pseud./variant:
Morrah, Dave

Morressy, John 1930- *AuBYP 2S, –3, BioIn 7, –13, ConAu 21R, –8NR, –28NR, DrAF 76, DrAPF 87, –89, –91, –93, EncSF 93, IntAu&W 77, –86, –89, –91, NewEScF, ScF&FL 92, SmATA 23, TwCSFW 86, –91, WhoE 93, WhoUSWr 88, WhoWrEP 89, –92, WrDr 76, –80, –82, –84, –86, –88, –90, –92, –94*

Morrill, Leslie H 1934- *BioIn 16, IlsBYP, MajAI, SmATA 33, –48*

Morris, Ann *AuBYP 3*

Morris, Chris 1946- *ConAu 133, EncSF 93, ScF&FL 92*

Morris, Christopher Crosby 1946- *SmATA 66, WrDr 94*
Pseud./variant:
Prescott, Casey
Stryker, Daniel 1946-

Morris, Desmond *WhoAm 86, –88, –90, –92, –94*

Morris, Desmond 1928- *Au&Wr 71, BioIn 6, –8, –10, –11, –12, CelR, ConAu 45, –2NR, –18NR, CurBio 74, IntAu&W 77, –82, –86, –89, IntWW 74, MajTwCW, SmATA 14, TwCPaSc, Who 74, WhoAm 74, –76, –78, –80, –82, –84, WhoWor 74, WorAu 1975, WrDr 76, –80, –82, –84, –86, –88, –90, –92, –94*

Morris, Desmond John 1928- *ConAu 38NR*

Morris, Edita 1903- *AmAu&B, AmNov, Au&Wr 71, BioIn 2, –12, ConAu 1R, –1NR*

Morris, Greggory *AuBYP 2S, –3*

Morris, Janet 1946- *ConAu 35NR, SmATA 66*

Morris, Jean 1924- *ConAu 116, ScF&FL 92, TwCChW 83, –89, WrDr 90, –92*

Morris, John V *ChhPo*

Morris, Judy K 1936- *SmATA 61*

Morris, Loverne Lawton 1896- *ConAu 5R*

Morris, Mary 1913- *ConAu 53, WhoAm 74*

Morris, Mary 1913-1986 *ConAu 121*

Morris, Percy Amos 1899-1969 *WhAm 5*

Morris, Phyllis 1894-1982 *ConAu 106, WhoHol A, WhoThe 77, -81*

Morris, Phyllis Sutton 1931- *WhoMW 93*

Morris, Richard B 1904-1989 *ConAu 128, NewYTBS 89, WorAu 1980*

Morris, Richard Brandon 1904- *AmAu&B, AuBYP 2, -3, BioIn 7, -13, ConAu 49, -2NR, DcLB 17, DrAS 74H, -78H, -82H, WhoAm 74, -76, -78, -80, -82*

Morris, Richard Brandon 1904-1989 *BioIn 16, -17, WhAm 10*

Morris, Robert Ada 1933- *BioIn 10, ConAu 49, SmATA 7*

Morris, Ruth *ConAu X, WrDr 76, -80*
Main entry: Webb, Ruth Enid Borlase Morris

Morris, Terry Lesser 1914- *ConAu 9R, WhoAmW 75, -77, WhoE 74, -75, -77*

Morris, Terry Lesser 1914-1993 *ConAu 142*

Morris, William 1786-1858 *DcCanB 8*

Morris, William 1834-1896 *Alli SUP, AtlBL, Benet 87, BbD, BiD&SB, BioIn 1, -2, -3, -4, -5, -6, -7, -8, -9, -10, -11, -12, -13, -14, -15, -16, -17, BlmGEL, BritAu 19, BritWr 5, CamGEL, CamGLE, CasWL, CelCen, ChhPo, -S1, -S2, CnDBLB 4, CnE&AP, CrtT 3, DcAmSR, DcBiA, DcBrBI, DcD&D, DcEnA, -A, DcEnL, DcEuL, DcLB 18, -35, -57, DcNaB S1, EncSF 93, EncUrb, EvLB, LongCEL, MacEA, McGEWB, MouLC 4, NewC, NinCLC 4, Novels, OxCArt, OxCChiL, OxCEng 67, -85, OxDcArt, PenC ENG, RAdv 1, -13-1, RComWL, REn, RfGEnL 91, ScF&FL 92, ScFSB, ScFEYrs, StaCVF, Str&VC, SupFW, TwCSFW 86B, -91, WebE&AL, WhDW, WhoHr&F, WorAlBi, WorAl*

Morris, William 1913- *AmAu&B, BioIn 13, BlueB 76, ConAu 17R, -12NR, SmATA 29, WhoAm 74, -76, -78, -80, -82, -84, -86, -88, -90, -92, -94, WhoUSWr 88, WhoWrEP 89, -92*

Morris, Willie 1934- *AuSpks, AuBYP 2S, -3, AuNews 2, BioIn 7, -8, -9, -10, -11, -12, -13, BlueB 76, CelR, ConAu 17R, -13NR, CurBio 76, DcLB Y80B, DrAF 76, EncAJ, EncTwCJ, IntAu&W 77, -89, -91, IntWW 74, -75, -76, -77, -78, -79, -80, -81, -82, -83, -89, -91, WhoAm 74, -76, -78, -80, -82, -84, -86, -88, -90, -92, -94, WhoE 74, WhoWor 74, WorAl, WorAu 1975, WrDr 80, -82, -84, -86, -88, -90, -92, -94*

Morriseau, Norval 1932?- *BioIn 6, -11, -12, OxCCan*

Morrison, Bill 1935- *ConAu 115, -135, SmATA 37, -66*

Morrison, Carl V 1908- *BiDrAPA 77, ConAu 93*

Morrison, Dorothy Nafus *ConAu 61, -8NR, -24NR, ScF&FL 92, SmATA 29*

Morrison, Frank M 1914- *ConAu 37R*

Morrison, Gert W *ConAu X*
Main entry: Stratemeyer, Edward L

Morrison, Joan 1922- *ConAu 133, SmATA 65, WhoAmW 91, -93*

Morrison, Lillian 1917- *AnCL, BiDrLUS 70, BioIn 2, -9, BkP, ChhPo, -S1, -S2, ConAu 9R, -7NR, -22NR, DrAP 75, DrAPF 87, -89, -91, -93, SixBJA, SmATA 3, WhoLibI 82, WhoLibS 55, -66, WhoUSWr 88, WhoWrEP 89, -92*

Morrison, Lucile Phillips 1896- *SmATA 17, WhNAA, WhoAmW 77, -81, -83, -85, -87, WhoWest 74, -80, -82, -84*

Morrison, Martha A 1948- *SmATA 77*

Morrison, Philip *MedPD*

Morrison, Roberta *ConAu X, SmATA X, TwCRHW 90, WrDr 82, -84, -86, -88, -90, -92, -94*
Main entry: Webb, Jean Francis

Morrison, Sean *ChhPo S1*

Morrison, Theodore d1988 *NewYTBS 88*

Morrison, Theodore 1901- *AmAu&B, BioIn 3, -4, BlueB 76, ConAu 1R, -1NR, DrAS 74E, -78E, -82E, IntAu&W 91, OxCAmL 65, -83, REnAL, TwCA SUP, WhoAm 74, -76, -78, WrDr 76, -80, -82, -84, -86, -88, -90*

Morrison, Theodore 1901-1988 *BioIn 16, ConAu 127, WhAm 9*

Morrison, Toni *BlkWWr, DrAPF 87, -89, -91, -93, IntvTCA 2, NewYTBS 87, -88, WhoAm 86*

Morrison, Toni 1931- *AfrAmW, AmWomWr 92, AmWr S3, ArtclWW 2, Au&Arts 1, Benet 87, BenetAL 91, BioIn 14, -15, -16, -17, BlkLC, BlkWr 1, BlmGWL, BroV, CamGLE, CamHAL, CelR 90, ConAu 27NR, ConBlAP 88, ConBlB 2, ConHero 2, ConLC 55, ConNov 86, -91, ContDcW 89, CyWA 89, DcLB Y93, EncWB, FemiCLE, HanAmWH, InB&W 85, InWom SUP, IntWW 91, MagSAmL, MajTwCW, ModAL S2, ModAWWr, NegAl 89, NotBlAW 92, PostFic, RAdv 13-1, ScF&FL 92, SmATA 57,*

TwCYAW, WhoAm 88, –90, –92, –94, WhoAmW 89, –91, –93, WhoBlA 85, –88, –90, –92, WhoUSWr 88, WhoWrEP 89, –92, WorAlBi, WorLitC, WrDr 86, –88, –90, –92

Morrison, Velma Ford 1909- *ConAu 9R, SmATA 21*
Pseud./variant:
Ford, Hildegarde

Morrison, Wilbur H 1915- *WrDr 86, –88, –90, –92*

Morrison, Wilbur Howard 1915- *ConAu 1R, –1NR, IntAu&W 77, –91, SmATA 64, WrDr 76, –80, –82, –84, –94*

Morrison, William *ConAu X, SmATA 3*
Main entry: Samachson, Joseph

Morriss, Frank 1923- *AmCath 80, ConAu 5R, –3NR, IntAu&W 77, –82, –86, –91, WrDr 76, –80, –82, –84, –86, –88, –90, –92, –94*

Morriss, James E 1932- *AuBYP 3*

Morriss, James Edward 1932- *AuBYP 2S, BioIn 11, ConAu 57, SmATA 8, WhoE 77*

Morrow, Albert 1863-1927 *BioIn 14, DcBrAr 1*

Morrow, Barbara *IlsBYP*

Morrow, Betty *ConAu X, SmATA 3*
Main entry: Bacon, Elizabeth

Morrow, Elizabeth Reeve Cutter 1873-1955 *AmAu&B, AmPB, BioIn 3, –4, –11, ChhPo, CurBio 43, –55, OhA&B, REnAL, Str&VC*

Morrow, George 1869-1955 *BioIn 3, –14, ChhPo, –S1, ConICB, DcBrAr 1, DcBrBI, ObitT 1951*

Morrow, Honore Willsie 1880-1940 *AmAu&B, AmWomPl, BenetAL 91, CurBio 40, DcNAA, EncFWF, InWom SUP, OxCAmL 65, –83, REnAL, TwCA, TwCWW 91, WhAm 1, WisWr, WomNov*

Morrow, Suzanne Stark *AuBYP 2, –3, BioIn 8*

Morse, Anne Christensen 1915- *ConAu 1R*
Pseud./variant:
Head, Ann

Morse, Carol *AuBYP 3, ConAu X, CurBio 57, SmATA X, WrDr 76, –80, –82, –84, –86, –88, –90, –92, –94*
Main entry: Yeakley, Marjory Hall

Morse, David 1940- *ChhPo S2, ConAu 37R*

Morse, Dorothy B 1906-1979 *WhoAmA 86N, –89N, –91N*

Morse, Dorothy Bayley 1906-1979 *BioIn 5, –11, IlsBYP, IlsCB 1946, SmATA 24N, WhoAmA 80N, –82N*

Morse, Flo 1921- *BioIn 14, ConAu 106, SmATA 30*

Mort, Vivian *SmATA X*
Main entry: Cromie, Alice Hamilton

Mortelmans, Edward Eugene Louis 1915- *BioIn 12, IlsCB 1967*

Mortimer, Derek *WrDr 76, –80, –82, –84, –86, –88*

Mortimer, Favell Lee 1802-1878 *Alli SUP, BioIn 2, CarSB, ChhPo, –S1, –S2, DcNaB, OxCChiL*

Mortimer, Mary H *ConAu X, SmATA X*
Main entry: Coury, Louise Andree

Morton, Anthony *ConAu X, EncMys, LongCTC, MajTwCW, TwCCr&M 80, –85, –91, WhoSpyF, WorAu 1950*

Morton, Brenda *WrDr 76, –80, –82, –84, –86, –88, –90, –92, –94*

Morton, David *LiHiK*

Morton, David 1886-1957 *AmAu&B, AnMV 1926, BioIn 4, –5, ChhPo, –S1, REn, REnAL, Str&VC, WhAm 3, WhNAA*

Morton, Jane 1931- *SmATA 50*

Morton, Lee Jack 1928- *BioIn 14*

Morton, Lee Jack, Jr. 1928- *SmATA 32*
Pseud./variant:
Jac, Lee

Morton, Marian 1918?-1985 *IlsBYP*

Morton, Miriam 1918?-1985 *AuBYP 2S, –3, BioIn 11, ChhPo, –S1, –S2, ConAu 49, –117, –2NR, ScF&FL 92, SmATA 9, –46N, WhoAmW 77, –81, –83*

Morton, William Lewis 1908- *BioIn 5, CanWW 70, –80, ConAu P-1, DrAS 74H, –82H, OxCCan, –SUP, WhoCan 73, –80, WhoWor 74*

Morton-Sale, Isobel 1904- *BioIn 1, –5, –8, –14, ChhPo, IlsBYP, IlsCB 1744, –1946, WhoChL*
Pseud./variant:
Sale, Isobel Morton

Morton-Sale, John 1901- *BioIn 1, –5, –8, –14, –17, ChhPo, IlsBYP, IlsCB 1744, –1946, WhoChL*

Pseud./variant:
Sale, John Morton

Moscati, Sabatino 1922- *Au&Wr 71, ConAu 77, IntAu&W 77, –82, WhoWor 78*

Moscow, Alvin 1925- *AmAu&B, AuBYP 2, –3, BioIn 7, –9, ConAu 1R, –4NR, SmATA 3*

Moscow, Warren 1908- *BioIn 1, ConAu 21R, WhoAm 76, –78, –80, –82, –84, –86, –88, –90, –92, WhoE 74, –75, –77, WhoWorJ 72, –78*

Moscow, Warren 1908-1992 *NewYTBS 92, WhAm 10*

Mosel, Arlene 1921- *AuBYP 3*

Mosel, Arlene Tichy 1921- *AuBYP 2, BioIn 10, ConAu 49, FifBJA, SmATA 7*

Moseley, Elizabeth Robards *ForWC 70*

Moser, Barry *ChlBIlD*

Moser, Barry 1940- *MajAI, SixBJA, SmATA 56, –15AS, WhoAm 86, WhoAmA 86, –89, –91*

Moser, Don
Main entry: Moser, Donald Bruce

Moser, Donald Bruce 1932- *ConAu 106, SmATA 31, WhoAm 80, –82, –84, –86, –88, –90, –92, –94, WhoE 83, –85, –86, –89, –93, WhoUSWr 88, WhoWrEP 89, –92*
Pseud./variant:
Moser, Don

Moses, Anna Mary 1860-1961 *AuBYP 2, –3, BioIn 1, –2, –3, –4, –5, –6, –7, –8, –9, –10, –11, –12, ChhPo, ConAu 93, CurBio 49, –62, DcAmB S7, DcWomA, HerW, –84, NotAW MOD, ObitOF 79, ObitT 1961, OxCArt, PhDcTCA 77, REn, WebAB 74, –79, WhAm 4, WhAmArt 85, WhoAmA 80N, –82N*

Moses, Anna Mary Robertson 1860-1961 *BioIn 14, –15, –16, –17, InWom SUP, OxDcArt, WhoAmA 86N, –89N, –91N*

Mosesson, Gloria R 1924- *BioIn 13, ConAu 41R, ForWC 70, SmATA 24, WhoAmW 75, –77, WhoWorJ 72, –78*
Pseud./variant:
French, Kathryn
Miller, Doris R

Moskin, Marietta D 1928- *ConAu 73, –13NR, SmATA 23*

Moskof, Martin Stephen 1930- *BioIn 13, ConAu 29R, SmATA 27*

Mosley, Elizabeth Robards *AuBYP 2S, –3*

Mosley, Francis 1957- *SmATA 57*

Mosley, Zack d1993 *NewYTBS 93*

Mosley, Zack 1906- *ArtCS, BioIn 15, ConGrA 2, EncACom, WhAmArt 85, WhoAm 74, WhoAmA 73*

Mosley, Zack Terrell 1906- *WhoAm 92*

Moss, Don 1920- *BioIn 11, SmATA 11*

Moss, Elaine 1924- *SmATA 57*

Moss, Elaine Dora 1924- *Au&Wr 71, BioIn 14, SmATA 31, Who 88, –90, –92*

Moss, Franklin 1909- *SingR 2*

Moss, Geoffrey 1938- *BioIn 11, WhoAm 78 –80, –82, –84, –86, –88, –90*

Moss, Jeffrey *SmATA 73*

Moss, Marissa 1959- *SmATA 71*

Moss, Miriam 1955- *SmATA 76*

Moss, Nancy *ConAu X, WrDr 80, –82, –84, –86, –88, –90, –92, –94*
Main entry: Moss, Robert

Moss, Peter *IntAu&W 91, WrDr 86, –88, –90, –92*

Moss, Peter 1921- *Au&Wr 71, ConAu 49, –2NR, IntAu&W 77, –82, WrDr 76, –80, –82, –84*

Moss, Peter D *ScF&FL 92*

Moss, Robert 1903- *Au&Wr 71, ConAu P-1, IntAu&W 77, WrDr 80, –82, –84, –86, –88, –90, –92, –94*
Pseud./variant:
Moss, Nancy
Moss, Roberta

Moss, Roberta
Main entry: Moss, Robert

Mossiker, Frances 1906-1985 *ConAu 9R, –116*

Most, Bernard 1937- *ConAu 104, –27NR, SmATA 40, –48, WhoE 86*

Mostert, Noel 1929- *ConAu 105, IntAu&W 82, WrDr 76, –80, –82, –84*

Mother Goose *BioIn 10, ChrP, FamPYP, InWom SUP, OxCAmL 83*

Mothner, Ira S 1932- *ConAu 21R, WhoE 74*

Mott, Evelyn Clarke 1962- *SmATA 75*

Mott, Michael 1930- *Au&Wr 71, ConAu 5R, –7AS, –7NR, –29NR, ConLC 15, DcLEL 1940, DrAF 76, DrAP 75, DrAPF 87, –89, –91, –93, IntAu&W 77, –82*

Mott, Michael Charles Alston 1930- *WhoWrEP 92*

Motz, Lloyd 1909?- *AmMWSc 73P, –76P, –82, BioIn 12, ConAu 9R, –4NR, IntAu&W 77, –82, SmATA 20, WhoAm 74, –76, –78, –80, –82, –84, WhoAmJ 80, WhoWorJ 72, –78*

Motz, Lloyd 1910- *AmMWSc 86, –89, –92, WhoE 93*

Moulton, Louise C 1835-1908 *BioAmW*

Moulton, Louise Chandler 1835-1908 *AmWomWr, BiD&SB, BioIn 3, CarSB, Chambr 3, ChhPo, –S1, CyAL, InWom SUP, OxCAmL 65, –83, REnAL, WhAm 1*

Mountain, Robert *ConAu X, ScF&FL 92, SmATA X*
Main entry: Montgomery, Raymond A

Mountfield, David *BioIn 12, ConAu X, –34NR, SmATA X, WrDr 80, –82, –84, –86, –88, –90, –92*
Main entry: Grant, Neil

Mountfield, David 1938- *WrDr 94*

Moussard, Jacqueline 1924- *BioIn 13, ConAu 61, –8NR, SmATA 24*
Pseud./variant:
Cervon, Jacqueline

Mow, Anna Beahm 1893- *ConAu 9R, –3NR, IntAu&W 77, WhoAmW 75, –77, –81, –83, –85, WhoSSW 84, WhoWor 84, WrDr 76, –80, –82, –84, –86*

Mowat, Farley 1921- *Au&Arts 1, AuBYP 3, Benet 87, BenetAL 91, BioIn 14, –15, –16, –17, CamGLE, CanWW 89, ChlLR 20, ConAu 24NR, CurBio 86, DcLB 68, MagSWL, MajTwCW, SmATA 55, TwCChW 89, WhoCanL 87, –92, WrDr 86, –88, –90, –92*

Mowat, Farley McGill 1921- *AmAu&B, AuBYP 2, Au&Wr 71, BioIn 2, –4, –5, –7, –9, –10, –11, –12, –13, BlueB 76, CaW, CanWW 70, –79, –80, –81, –83, CanWr, CasWL, ConAu 1R, –4NR, ConLC 26, CreCan 2, DcChlFi, DcLEL 1940, IntAu&W 77, –82, –86, –89, –91, IntWW 74, –75, –76, –77, –78, –79, –80, –81, –82, –83, –89, –91, MajAI, OxCCan, –SUP, OxCCanL, OxCChiL, Profile 2, SmATA 3, ThrBJA, TwCChW 78, –83, TwCYAW, WhoAm 74, –76, –78, –80, –82, –84, –86, –88, –90, –92, –94, WhoCan 73, –75, –77, –80, –82, –84, WhoCanL 85, WhoE 74, WhoWor 82, –84, –87, –89, –91, –93, WhoWrEP 89, –92, WorAu 1950, WrDr 76, –80, –82, –84, –94*

Mowbray, John *WhoChL*

Mowery, Dee Dunsing *WrDr 76, –80, –82, –84, –86, –88*

Moy, Seong 1921- *BioIn 4, –8, DcCAA 71, –77, –88, IlsBYP, IlsCB 1957, WhoAm 74, –76, –78, –80, –82, –84, –86, WhoAmA 73, –78, –80, –82, –84, –86, –89, –91, WhoE 74*

Moyers, William 1916- *BioIn 5, –7, –11, ChhPo, IlsBYP, IlsCB 1946, WhoAmA 78, –82, –84, –86, –89, –91*

Moyers, William Taylor 1916- *WhoWest 94*

Moyes, Patricia 1923- *Au&Wr 71, BiE&WWA, ConAu 17R, –X, –29NR, CrtSuMy, EncMys, FemiCLE, InWom SUP, IntAu&W 89, Novels, SmATA 63, TwCCr&M 80, –85, –91, TwCYAW, WrDr 76, –80, –82, –84, –86, –88, –90, –92, –94*
Pseud./variant:
Haszard, Patricia Moyes 1923-

Moyler, Alan 1926- *SmATA 36*

Moyne, Bryan Walter Guinness 1905- *BioIn 10, –13, BlueB 76, IntAu&W 77, –82, IntWW 74, –78, –79, –80, –81, Who 74, WhoWor 74*
Pseud./variant:
Guinness, Bryan

Mozley, Charles 1915- *ArtsCL, BioIn 6, –8, ChhPo S2, IlsCB 1957, –1967, SmATA 32, –43, WhoGrA 62*

Mozley, Harriet d1852 *OxCChiL*

Mozley, Harriet 1803-1852 *FemiCLE*

Mrs Fairstar *SmATA X*
Main entry: Horne, Richard H

Muddock, Joyce Emerson Preston 1843-1934 *Alli SUP, EncMys, NewC*

Muddock, Joyce Emmerson 1842-1934 *BioIn 14, –15*

Mude, O *ConAu X, –30NR*
Main entry: Gorey, Edward St John

Mudie, Ian 1911-1976 *Au&Wr 71, BlueB 76, ChhPo S2, ConAu 25R, –135, ConPo 70, –75, –80, DcLEL, OxCAusL, WrDr 76, –80, –82, –84*

Muehl, Lois Baker 1920- *AuBYP 2, –3, ConAu 1R, –18NR, ForWC 70, IntAu&W 91, WhoAmW 75, –77, WrDr 76, –80, –82, –84, –86, –88, –90, –92, –94*

Mueller, Amelia 1911- *ConAu 57*

Mueller, Charles S 1929- *ConAu 13R, -5NR, -20NR*

Mueller, Hans Alexander 1888-1962 *BioIn 2, -3, -5, -6, IlsBYP, IlsCB 1946, WhAm 4*

Mueller, Joerg 1942- *BioIn 17, ConAu 136, SmATA 67*

Mueller, Robert Emmett 1925- *ConAu 1R, IntAu&W 86, -89, -91, WrDr 76, -80, -82, -84, -86, -88, -90, -92, -94*

Mueller, Virginia 1924- *BioIn 13, ConAu 65, -10NR, -27NR, SmATA 28*

Muenchen, Al 1917-1975 *ConAu 49, IlrAm 1880, -F*

Mugnaini, Joseph Anthony 1912- *BioIn 6, WhoAmA 73*

Muhlenweg, Fritz *AuBYP 3*

Muhlenweg, Fritz 1898-1961 *AuBYP 2, BioIn 8, OxCChiL*

Muhlhausen, John P 1940- *ConAu 61, WhoFI 83, WhoSSW 84*

Muhlhausen, John Praque 1940- *WhoSSW 86*

Muir, Augustus *WrDr 86, -88, -90*

Muir, Augustus d1989 *Who 90N*

Muir, Augustus 1892- *Au&Wr 71, BlueB 76, ConAu 13R, IntAu&W 77, -82, Who 74, -82, -85, -88, WrDr 76, -80, -82, -84*

Muir, Augustus 1893?-1989 *ConAu 128*

Muir, Edwin 1887-1959 *AnCL, AtlBL, Benet 87, BioIn 3, -4, -5, -6, -7, -8, -10, -11, -12, -13, -14, -17, BlmGEL, CamGEL, CamGLE, CasWL, ChhPo, -S1, CmScLit, CnE&AP, CnMWL, ConAu 104, ConLCrt 77, -82, DcLB 20, -100, DcLEL, DcNaB 1951, EncWL, -2, EngPo, EvLB, GrBr, LongCEL, LongCTC, ModBrL, -S1, -S2, NewC, ObitOF 79, ObitT 1951, OxCEng 67, -85, PenC ENG, RAdv 1, -13-1, RComWL, REn, RfGEnL 91, TwCA, -SUP, TwCLC 2, TwCWr, WebE&AL, WhDW, WhoTwCL*

Muir, Frank 1920- *BlueB 76, ConAu 29NR, IntAu&W 89, -91, OxCChiL, SmATA 30, Who 82, -83, -85, -88, -90, -92, WrDr 82, -84, -86, -88, -90, -92, -94*

Muir, Helen 1937- *ConAu 130, SmATA 65, WrDr 94*

Muir, John 1838-1914 *AmAu&B, Benet 87, BenetAL 91, BiD&SB, BiInAmS, BioIn 1, -2, -3, -4, -5, -6, -7, -8, -9, -10, -11, -12, -13, -14, -15, -16, -17, CmCal, DcAmAu, DcAmImH, DcLEL, DcNAA, EncPaPR 91, EvLB, HarEnUS, InSci, JBA 34, McGEWB, MorMA, OxCAmH, OxCAmL 65, -83, RAdv 13-5, REn, REnAL, TwCA, -SUP, TwCLC 28, WebAB 74, -79, WhAm 1, WisWr, WorAlBi, WorAl*

Muir, Percy 1894-1981 *OxCChiL*

Muir, Wardrop Openshaw 1878-1927 *MacBEP*

Muirden, James 1942- *Au&Wr 71*

Mujeeb, Muhammad 1902- *IntWW 74, -75 -76, -77, -78, -79, -80, WhoWor 74*

Mukerji, Dhan Gopal 1890-1936 *AnCL, AuBYP 2, -3, BioIn 4, -7, -14, -15, BkCL, ChlLR 10, ConAu 119, -136, JBA 34, LongCTC, MajAI, NewbMB 1922, OxCChiL, SmATA 40, TwCA, TwCChW 78, -83, -89, WhAm 1*

Mulac, Margaret Elizabeth 1912- *ConAu 5R, -2NR, ForWC 70, WhoAmW 74, -75, -77*

Mulcahy, Lucille Burnett *AuBYP 3*

Mulcahy, Lucille Burnett 1918- *AuBYP 2, BioIn 11, ConAu 5R, ForWC 70, SmATA 12*
Pseud./variant:
Hale, Helen

Mulford, Clarence E 1883-1956 *BenetAL 91, TwCWW 91*

Mulford, Clarence Edward 1883-1956 *AmAu&B, BioIn 2, -4, -17, EncFWF, EvLB, FilmgC, HalFC 84, LongCTC, ObitOF 79, OxCAmL 65, -83, REnAL, TwCA, -SUP, WhAm 3, WhNAA*

Mulford, Harriet *JBA 34*
Main entry: Lothrop, Harriet Mulford Stone

Mulford, Philippa Greene 1948- *BioIn 15, ConAu 116, SmATA 43, WhoAmW 91, WhoUSWr 88, WhoWrEP 89, -92*

Mulgan, Catherine
Main entry: Gough, Catherine

Mulgan, Catherine 1931- *ConAu 11NR, SmATA X*

Mulholland, John 1898-1970 *AmAu&B, BioIn 3, -8, ConAu 5R, REnAL, WhAm 5, WhNAA*

Muller, Billex *HsB&A, YABC 1*
Main entry: Ellis, Edward S

Muller, Charles G 1897- *WrDr 86, -88*

Muller, Charles George 1897- *ConAu 1R, -2NR, IntAu&W 77, -82, WhNAA, WrDr 76, -80, -82, -84*

Muller, Charles George 1897-1987 *BioIn 15*

Muller, Jorg *BioIn 16, -17, ConAu 136, SixBJA, SmATA 67, TwCChW 83B*

Muller, Jorg, and St, Jorg *TwCChW 89B*

Mullin, Willard 1902-1978 *Ballpl 90, BioIn 4, -9, -11, NewYTBE 71, ObitOF 79, WhAm 7, WhoAmA 80N, -82N, -86N, -89N, -91N*

Mullins, Edward S 1922- *BioIn 11, ConAu 17R, IlsBYP, SmATA 10*

Mullins, Patricia Ann 1952- *BioIn 12, IlsCB 1967*

Mullins, Vera Cooper 1903- *ConAu 61*

Mulock, Dinah Maria *Alli SUP, ArtclWW 2, BiD&SB, BioIn 1, -2, -3, -5, -8, -12, BritAu 19, Chambr 3, CyWA 58, DcBiA, DcEnA, DcLEL, DcNaB, EvLB, HsB&A, InWom SUP, JBA 34, MajAI, NewC, OxCChiL, OxCEng 67, -85, PoIre, REn, SmATA X, TelT, WhoChL*
Main entry: Craik, Dinah Maria Mulock

Mulock, Dinah Maria 1826-1887 *CamGEL, CamGLE, RfGEnL 91*

Mulready, William 1786-1863 *ArtsNiC, BioIn 1, -10, -12, -13, -15, -16, CelCen, ClaDrA, DcBiPP, DcIrB 88, DcNaB, DcVicP 2, Dis&D, OxCArt, OxCChiL, OxDcArt*

Mulvihill, William Patrick 1923- *BioIn 4, -11, ConAu 1R, SmATA 8, WhoE 74, -75*

Mun *ConAu 29NR, MajAI, SmATA X, TwCChW 89*
Main entry: Leaf, Munro

Munari, Bruno 1907- *AuBYP 2, -3, BioIn 5, -7, -8, -9, -12, -14, -15, ChlLR 9, ConArt 77, -83, -89, ConAu 73, -38NR, ConDes 84, -90, IlsCB 1946, -1957, -1967, MajAI, OxCTwCA, PhDcTCA 77, SmATA 15, ThrBJA, TwCChW 78B, WhoGrA 62*

Munce, Ruth Hill 1898- *BioIn 11, ConAu P-1, SmATA 12*
Pseud./variant:
Hill, Ruth Livingston

Munch, Theodore W 1919- *AmMWSc 73P, -76P, ConAu 57*

Mundy, Simon 1954- *ConAu 128, SmATA 64*

Mundy, Talbot Chetwynd 1879-1940 *AmAu&B, CurBio 40, DcNAA, REnAL, TwCA, -SUP, WhAm 1, WhoHr&F*

Munn, Charles Clark 1848-1917 *AmAu&B, BiD&SB, CarSB, DcAmAu, DcNAA, WhAm 1*

Munowitz, Ken 1935-1977 *BioIn 11, -12, SmATA 14, WhoAmA 78N, -80N, -82N*

Munowitz, Ken 1936-1978 *WhoAmA 86N, -89N, -91N*

Munoz, Rie *WhoAmA 86, -89, -91*

Munoz, Rie 1921- *WhoAmA 78, -80, -82, -84, WhoWest 74, -76, -78, -82*

Munoz, William 1949- *SmATA 42*

Munro, Alice 1931- *ArtclWW 2, AuNews 2, Benet 87, BenetAL 91, BioIn 11, -13, BlmGWL, CamGLE, CaW, CanWW 70, -79, -80, -81, -83, -89, ConAu 33R, -33NR, ConLC 6, -10, -19, -50, ConNov 72, -76, -82, -86, -91, CreCan 1, CurBio 90, CyWA 89, DcLB 53, DcLEL 1940, FemiCLE, InWom SUP, IntAu&W 77, -91, IntLitE, MagSWL, MajTwCW, OxCCan, -SUP, OxCCanL, RAdv 13-1, RfGEnL 91, ShSCr 3, SmATA 29, WhoAm 80, -82, -86, -88, -90, -92, -94, WhoAmW 83, -85, -89, -91, -93, WhoCanL 85, -87, -92, WhoWrEP 92, WorAlBi, WorAu 1980, WrDr 76, -80, -82, -84, -86, -88, -90, -92, -94*

Munro, David Aird 1923- *AmMWSc 73P, CanWW 70, -80, -81*

Munro, Eleanor Carroll 1928- *AuBYP 2, -3, BioIn 7, ConAu 1R, SmATA 37, WhoAmA 82, -84, WhoAmW 81, -83*

Munro, George Colin 1907- *AmMWSc 73P*

Munro, Roxie 1945- *AuBYP 3, BioIn 16, ChlBIlD, SixBJA, SmATA 58*

Munroe, Kirk 1850-1930 *Alli SUP, AmAu&B, BbD, BiDSA, BiD&SB, BioIn 15, CarSB, ConAu 123, DcAmAu, DcLB 42, DcNAA, JBA 34, OxCAmL 65, -83, OxCChiL, TwCA, WhAm 1, WhFla*

Munsch, Robert 1945- *BioIn 13, CanWW 89, ChlLR 19, ConAu 121, IntAu&W 89, -91, Profile 2, SmATA 48, -50, TwCChW 83, -89, WhoCanL 85, -87, -92, WrDr 86, -88, -90, -92, -94*

Munsch, Robert Norman 1945- *ConAu 37NR, MajAI*

Munsey, Frank A 1854-1925 *BenetAL 91, BioIn 14, -15, -16, -17, DcLB 91, JrnUS*

Munsey, Frank Andrew 1854-1925 *Alli SUP, AmAu&B, BiDAmBL 83, BiDAmJo, BioIn 3, -4, -9, CarSB, ConAu 116, DcAmAu, DcAmSR, DcLB 25, DcNAA, EncAB-H, EncAJ, EncSF 93, McGEWB, OxCAmH, REnAL, WebAB 74, -79, WhAm 1, WhJnl, -SUP*

Munshi, Shehnaaz *ConAu X*
Main entry: Skagen, Kiki

Munsinger, Lynn 1951- *SmATA 33*

Munson, Gorham Bert 1896-1969 *AmAu&B, AuBYP 2, -3, BenetAL 91, BioIn 4, -7, -8, CnDAL, ConAu P-1, ObitOF 79, OxCAmL 65, PenC AM, REnAL, TwCA, -SUP, WhAm 5*

Munson-Benson, Tunie 1946- *ConAu 77, SmATA 15*

Munsterhjelm, Erik 1905- *ConAu 49, OxCCan*

Munthe, Frances 1915- *ConAu 9R*
Pseud./variant:
Cowen, Frances

Munthe, Nelly 1947- *BioIn 16, SmATA 53*

Munves, James 1922- *ConAu 5R, -3NR, SmATA 30, WhoE 91*

Munz, Peter 1921- *ConAu 13R, IntAu&W 77, -82, -86, -89, -91, WhoWor 87, -89, WrDr 76, -80, -82, -84, -86, -88, -90, -92, -94*

Munzer, Martha 1899- *AuBYP 3*

Munzer, Martha E 1899- *AuBYP 2S, BioIn 9, ConAu 1R, -4NR, IntAu&W 77, -82, -86, -89, SmATA 4, WrDr 76, -80, -82, -84, -86, -88, -90, -92, -94*

Munzer, Martha Eiseman 1899- *WhoAmW 89*

Murai, Gensai 1863-1927 *BiDJaL, CarSB*

Murch, Mel And Starr, Ward *SmATA X*
Main entry: Manes, Stephen, Ward

Mure, Eleanor *ChhPo S1, TelT*

Mure, Geoffrey 1893- *TelT, Who 74*

Murfree, Mary N 1850-1922 *DcLB 74*

Murfree, Mary Noailles 1850-1922 *Alli SUP, AmAu, AmAu&B, AmWomWr, ArtclWW 2, Benet 87, BenetAL 91, BbD, BiDSA, BiD&SB, BioIn 1, -8, -9, -12, -13, BlmGWL, CarSB, Chambr 3, CnDAL, ConAu 122, DcAmAu, DcLB 12, DcLEL, DcNAA, EncSoH, FemiCLE, FifSWrB, HarEnUS, InWom SUP, OxCAmL 65, -83, REn, REnAL, RfGAmL 87, WhAm 1, WomWWA 14, WomNov*

Murillo, Bartolome Esteban *DcAmChF 1960*

Murphy, Barbara Beasley 1933- *BioIn 10, ConAu 41R, -20NR, DrAPF 83, -85, -87, -89, -91, -93, SmATA 5*

Murphy, Beatrice M 1908- *BlkAWP, BroadAu, ConAu 53, -9NR, DcLB 76, InB&W 80, LivgBAA, WhoBlA 75, -77, -80, -90, -92, -94*

Murphy, Beatrice M 1908-1992 *BlkWr 2, ConAu 137*
Pseud./variant:
Campbell, Beatrice Murphy

Murphy, Claire Rudolf 1951- *SmATA 76*

Murphy, E Jefferson 1926- *AuBYP 2S, -3, BioIn 9, ConAu 25R, SmATA 4, WrDr 76, -80, -82, -84, -86, -88, -90, -92, -94*
Pseud./variant:
Murphy, Pat

Murphy, Jill *IntAu&W 91*

Murphy, Jill 1949- *AuBYP 3, ConAu 105, MajAI, OxCChiL, SixBJA, SmATA 37, -70, TwCChW 83, -89, WrDr 86, -88, -90, -92*

Murphy, Jill Frances 1949- *WrDr 94*

Murphy, Jill Francis 1949- *ChlFicS*

Murphy, Jim 1947- *ConAu 111, SmATA 32, -37, -77*

Murphy, Jimmy 1891-1965 *ArtCS, BioIn 7, WhAm 4*

Murphy, Jimmy 1892-1965 *EncACom*

Murphy, Joseph E, Jr. 1930- *ConAu 133, SmATA 65, WrDr 94*

Murphy, Joseph Edward, Jr. 1930- *WhoAm 92, -94, WhoFI 92*

Murphy, Mabel Ansley 1870- *AmAu&B, AuBYP 2, -3, BioIn 7, WhAm 5*
Pseud./variant:
Lee, Anne S

Murphy, Pat *ConAu X, DrAPF 87, -89, -91, -93, IntAu&W 86X, SmATA 4*
Main entry: Murphy, E Jefferson

Murphy, Pat 1955- *ConAu 137, EncSF 93 IntAu&W 89, ScF&FL 92, TwCSFW 91*

Murphy, Richard *Law&B 92*

Murphy, Richard 1927- *Au&Wr 71, BiDIrW, BioIn 7, -10, -13, CamGLE, CasWL, ConAu 29R, ConLC 41, ConPo 70, -75, -80, -85, -91, DcIrL, DcIrW 1, DcLB 40,*

DcLEL 1940, EncWL 2, IntAu&W 86, –89, –91, ModBrL S1, –S2, ModIrL, NewC, OxCEng 85, WorAu 1950, WrDr 76, –80, –82, –84, –86, –88, –90, –92, –94

Murphy, Robert William 1902-1971 *AuBYP 2, –3, BioIn 8, –9, –11, ConAu 29R, –P-1, FourBJA, NewYTBE 71, SmATA 10*

Murphy, Shirley Rousseau 1928- *BioIn 14, –16, ConAu 21R, –13NR, –29NR, IntAu&W 91, MajAI, ScF&FL 92, SixBJA, SmATA 36, –71, –18AS, TwCChW 89, TwCYAW, WhoAmW 74, –75, –77, WrDr 76, –80, –82, –84, –86, –88, –90, –92, –94*

Murphy, Thomas Basil, Jr. 1935- *ConAu 69, –11NR*

Murray, Albert L 1916- *BioIn 9, BlkAWP, BlkWr 1, ConAu 49, –26NR, ConLC 73, DcLB 38, InB&W 80, LivgBAA, NegAl 83, SelBAAf, WhoAm 74, –84, –86, –88, –90, –92, –94, WhoBlA 75, –80, –85, –88, –90, –92, –94, WrDr 76, –80, –82, –84*

Murray, Don 1924- *AuBYP 3*

Murray, Donald M 1924- *AmAu&B, AuBYP 2, BioIn 8, ConAu 1R, –17NR, WhoAm 74, –76, –78*

Murray, Frances 1928- *ConAu X, IntAu&W 77X, –91, TwCRHW 90, WrDr 86, –88, –90, –92, –94*
Main entry: Booth, Rosemary Frances

Murray, Gladys Hall *AuBYP 2, –3, BioIn 8, WhoAmW 74*

Murray, John 1923- *ConAu 5R, –4NR, –19NR, SmATA 39*
Pseud./variant:
Combs, Robert

Murray, Marguerite 1917- *SmATA 63*

Murray, Marian *BioIn 10, ConAu 41R, SmATA 5*

Murray, Mary Verona, Sister 1909- *ConAu 17R*

Murray, Michele 1933-1974 *ArtclWW 2, AuBYP 2S, BioIn 10, –13, ConAu 49, NewYTBS 74, ObitOF 79, SmATA 7*

Murray, Michele 1934-1974 *InWom SUP*

Murray, Michele Freedman 1933-1974 *AuBYP 3*

Murray, Ossie 1938- *BioIn 12, –15, IlsCB 1967, SmATA 43*

Murray, Sonia Bennett 1936- *ConAu 65, WhoAmW 87, WhoSSW 84, –86, –88*

Murray, William Henry Harrison 1840-1904 *Alli SUP, AmAu&B, BbD, BiD&SB, BioIn 16, CarSB, DcAmAu, DcNAA, HarEnUS, WhAm 1*

Murrell, Elsie Kathleen Seth-Smith 1883- *ConAu P-1*
Pseud./variant:
Seth-Smith, Elsie K

Murschetz, Luis *BioIn 7*

Mursgrave, Florence 1902- *AuBYP 2, BioIn 7, –9, ConAu P-1, SmATA 3*

Musciano, Walter A *AuBYP 2, –3*

Musciano, Walter A 1922- *ConAu 121, IntAu&W 89*

Musgrave, Florence 1902- *AuBYP 3*

Musgrave, Susan 1951- *ArtclWW 2, BioIn 13, BlmGWL, CanWW 89, ConAu 69, ConLC 13, –54, ConPo 75, –80, –85, –91, FemiCLE, IntAu&W 86, –91, IntvTCA 2, OxCCan SUP, OxCCanL, Profile 2, WhoCanL 85, –87, –92, WrDr 76, –80, –82, –84, –86, –88, –90, –92, –94*

Musgrove, Margaret 1943- *AuBYP 3, BlkAuII, –92*

Musgrove, Margaret Wynkoop 1943- *AuBYP 2S, ConAu 65, SmATA 26, WhoBlA 90, –92, –94*

Mussey, Virginia H *ConAu X, IntAu&W 77X, SmATA 4, WrDr 76, –80*
Main entry: Ellison, Virginia Howell

Mussino, Attilio 1878-1954 *IlsBYP, WorECar*

Mutel, Cornelia F 1947- *SmATA 74*

Mutz *SmATA X*
Main entry: Kunstler, Morton

My *SmATA X*
Main entry: Barberis, Juan Carlos

Myers, Alpha Blanche 1912- *BiDrLUS 70, WhoAmW 77, WhoLibS 55, –66*

Myers, Arthur 1917?- *ConAu 17R, –7NR, IntAu&W 86, –89, SmATA 35*

Myers, Arthur B 1917- *WhoAm 90, –92, –94*

Myers, Bernice *BioIn 11, ConAu 61, –8NR, IlsBYP, SmATA 9*

Myers, Caroline Elizabeth Clark 1887-1980 *BioIn 12, –13, ConAu 29R, –134, SmATA 28,*

WhAm 7, WhoAm 80, WhoAmW 74, –75, –77, –81, WhoE 74, –75, –77

Myers, Elisabeth Perkins 1918- *AuBYP 2S, ConAu 5R, –3NR, ForWC 70, SmATA 36, WhoAmW 74, –75, –77, WrDr 76, –80, –82, –84, –86, –88, –90, –92, –94*

Myers, Elizabeth Perkins 1918- *AuBYP 3*

Myers, Gail Eldridge 1923- *ConAu 49, –1NR, DrAS 74E, –78E, –82E, LEduc 74, WhoAm 78, –80, –82, –84, –86, –88, –90, WhoSSW 82*

Myers, Garry Cleveland 1884-1971 *ConAu P-2, OhA&B, WhAm 5, WhNAA*

Myers, Hortense 1913- *BioIn 11, ConAu 1R, –2NR, ForWC 70, IndAu 1917, SmATA 10, WhoAmW 85, –87, WrDr 76, –80, –82, –84, –86, –88*

Myers, Hortense 1913-1987 *ConAu 123*

Myers, Lou *BioIn 11*

Myers, Madeline Neuberger 1896- *AuBYP 2, –3, BioIn 7*

Myers, Norman 1934- *ConAu 49, –1NR, –20NR, CurBio 93, WhoWor 89*

Myers, Robert Eugene 1924- *ConAu 77, WhoWest 80, –82, –87, –94, WhoWor 87, –89*

Myers, Robert John 1924- *ConAu 107, –27NR, ScF&FL 92, WhoAm 74, –76, –78, –80, –82, –84, WhoE 77, –81, WhoSSW 76*

Myers, Walter Dean 1937- *Au&Arts 4, AuBYP 2S, –3, BioIn 13, BlkAWP, BlkAull, –92, BlkLC, BlkWr 1, ChlLR 4, –16, ConAu 33R, –20NR, ConLC 35, DcAmChF 1960, –1985, DcLB 33, DrAPF 83, –85, –87, –89, –91, –93, FifBJA, LivgBAA MajAI, ScF&FL 92, SelBAAf, SelBAAu, SmATA 27, –41, –71, –2AS, TwCChW 89, TwCYAW, WhoAm 76, WhoBlA 90, –92, –94, WrDr 90, –92*
Pseud./variant:
Myers, Walter M

Myers, Walter M *BlkWr 1, ConAu 42NR, MajAI, SmATA 71, TwCChW 89, WrDr 90, –92*
Main entry: Myers, Walter Dean

Myles, Eugenie Louise 1905- *ConAu P-1*

Myller, Lois Westerdahl *ForWC 70*

Myller, Rolf 1926- *AmArch 70, AuBYP 2, –3, BioIn 7, –13, BkCL, ConAu 5R, –8NR, SmATA 27*
Pseud./variant:
Brown, David
Milonas, Rolf

Myra, Harold Lawrence 1939- *BioIn 15, ConAu 8NR, SmATA 42, –46, WhoAm 80, –82, –84, –86, –88, –90, –92, –94*

Myrick, Mildred *AuBYP 2S, –3*

Myron, Robert 1926- *AuBYP 2S, –3, ConAu 13R, DrAS 74H, –78H, –82H*

Myrus, Donald 1927- *AuBYP 2, BioIn 8, –13, ConAu 1R, –4NR, SmATA 23*

Myrus, Donald Richard 1927- *AuBYP 3*

N

Nabokov, Peter 1940- *ConAu 21R, -9NR, -27NR, WrDr 90, -92*

Nabokov, Peter Francis 1940- *WrDr 94*

Nadejen, Theodore *BioIn 1, ConICB, IlsCB 1744*

Nadel, Laurie 1948- *SmATA 74*

Nadler, Robert *ChhPo S2, IlsBYP*

Nadler, Susan *ConAu X*
Main entry: Gantry, Susan Nadler

Nagenda, John *IntvTCA 2*

Nagenda, John 1938- *AfrA, BioIn 9, BlkWr 2*

Nagle, Avery *AuBYP 3*

Nagy, Al *IlsBYP*

Nagy, Gil D 1933- *ConAu 25R*

Naidoo, Beverley *BioIn 17, DcChlFi*

Naidoo, Beverley 1943- *SmATA 63, TwCYAW*

Naidoo, Beverly *AuBYP 3*

Naidoo, Beverly 1943- *ChlLR 29*

Nailor, Gerald A 1917- *AmPB, BioIn 1, IlsCB 1744*

Naismith, James 1861-1939 *BiDAmSp BK, BioIn 1, -3, -4, -5, -9, -10, -16, ConAu 118, WebAB 74, -79, WhAm 1, WorAlBi, WorAl*

Nakae, Noriko 1940- *AuBYP 2S, -3, BioIn 16, ConAu 49, SmATA 59*
Pseud./variant:
Ueno, Noriko

Nakamoto, Hiroko *AuBYP 2S, -3*

Nakano, Dokuohtei 1929- *AuBYP 3*

Nakano, Hirotaka 1942- *ConAu 33R*

Nakatani, Chiyoko *TwCChW 89B*

Nakatani, Chiyoko 1930- *BioIn 12, -15, ConAu 77, IlsBYP, IlsCB 1967, IntAu&W 82, SmATA 40, TwCChW 78B, -83B*

Nakatani, Chiyoko 1930-1981 *BioIn 16, ChlLR 30, SmATA 55*

Namioka, Lensey 1929- *BioIn 13, ConAu 69, -11NR, -27NR, SmATA 27, TwCYAW*

Namioka, Lensey Chao *DcAmChF 1960*

Namovicz, Gene Inyart 1927- *AuBYP 3, ConAu 17R, IntAu&W 77, WhoE 74*
Pseud./variant:
Inyart, Gene

Nandakumar, Prema 1939- *ConAu 9R*

Nankivel, Claudine *IlsBYP*

Nanogak, Agnes *OxCCan SUP*

Nanogak, Agnes 1925- *BioIn 17, SmATA 61*

Napier, Mark *ConAu X, IntAu&W 91X, SmATA X, WrDr 76, -80, -82, -84, -86, -88, -90, -92*
Main entry: Laffin, John

Napier, Mark 1922- *WrDr 94*

Napora, Paul Edward 1939- *WrDr 76, -80, -82, -84*

Narahashi, Keiko *AuBYP 3, ChlBIID*

Narayan, R K 1906- *Benet 87, BioIn 14, -15, -16, -17, BlmGEL, ConAu 33NR, ConLC 47, ConNov 86, -91, CurBio 87, CyWA 89, IntLitE, MajTwCW, RAdv 13-2, RfGEnL 91, ScF&FL 92, ShSWr, SmATA 62, Who 88, -90, -92*

Narayan, R K 1907- *CamGLE, WrDr 86, -88, -90, -92*

Narayan, Rasipuram Krishnaswamy 1906- *RfGShF*

Narayan, Rasipuran Krishnaswami 1907- *WrDr 94*

Narramore, Clyde Maurice 1916- *WhoAm 78*

Nasaw, Jonathan Lewis 1947- *ConAu 61*

Nash, Bruce M 1947- *BioIn 14, ConAu 15NR, IntAu&W 82, SmATA 34*

Nash, Frederic Ogden 1902-1971 *MajAI*

Nash, Frediric Ogden 1902-1971 *AuBYP 3*

Nash, Linell *ChhPo, ConAu X, SmATA 2*
Main entry: Smith, Linell Nash

Nash, Mary 1925- *AuBYP 2, -3, BioIn 8, -15, ConAu 5R, SmATA 41*

Nash, Ogden 1902-1971 *AmAu&B, AnCL, ASCAP 66, AuBYP 2, Au&Wr 71, Benet 87, BenetAL 91, BiE&WWA, BioIn 1, -2, -3, -4, -5, -6, -7, -8, -9, -10, -12, -13, -15, -16, -17, BkCL, CamGLE, CamHAL, CasWL, ChhPo, -S1, -S2, CnDAL, CnE&AP, CnMWL, ConAmA, ConAu 29R, -34NR, -P-1, ConLC 23, ConPo 70, CurBio 41, -71, DcLB 11, DcLEL, EncAHmr, EncMT, EncWL, FourBJA, LongCTC, MajTwCW, ModAL, NewGrDA 86, NewYTBE 71, NotNAT B, ObitOF 79, ObitT 1971, OxCAmL 65, -83, OxCAmT 84, OxCChiL, OxCEng 85, PenC AM, RAdv 1, REn, REnAL, RfGAmL 87, SmATA 2, -46, TwCA, -SUP, TwCWr, WebAB 74, -79, WebE&AL, WhDW, WhAm 5, WhoTwCL, WorAlBi, WorAl*

Nason, Thomas W 1889-1971 *WhoAmA 86N, -89N, -91N*

Nason, Thomas Willoughby 1889-1971 *BioIn 9, ChhPo, GrAmP, WhAm 5, WhAmArt 85, WhoAmA 78N, -80N, -82N*

Nast, Elsa Ruth *ConAu X, SmATA 3*
Main entry: Watson, Jane Werner

Nast, Thomas 1840-1902 *ArtsNiC, Benet 87, BenetAL 91, BiDAmJo, BioIn 3, -4, -7, -8, -9, -10, -11, -12, -13, -14, -15, -16, ChhPo, CivWDc, ConAu 112, ConGrA 1, DcAmSR, EarABI, -SUP, EncAB-H, EncAJ, HarEnUS, IlrAm 1880, JrnUS, McGEWB, MemAm, OxCAmH, OxCAmL 65, -83, RComAH, REn, REnAL, SmATA 33, -51, WebAB 74, -79, WhDW, WhAm 1, WhAmArt 85, WhAmP, WhCiWar, WorAlBi, WorAl, WorECar*

Nastick, Sharon 1954- *BioIn 15, ConAu 114, SmATA 41*

Nathan, Adele *AmWomPl, AuBYP 2, BioIn 8, ConAu 73, ForWC 70, WhoAm 74*

Nathan, Adele 1900?-1986 *AuBYP 3, ConAu 119, SmATA 48N*

Nathan, Adele Gutman d1986 *BioIn 16*

Nathan, Daniel *AuBYP 2, -3, ConAu X, -39NR, IntAu&W 77X, LongCTC, MajTwCW, WrDr 76, -80, -82*
Main entry: Dannay, Frederic

Nathan, Dorothy Goldeen d1966 *BioIn 7, -12, ConAu 81, SmATA 15*

Nathan, Leonard Edward 1924- *ConAu 5R, -7NR, ConPo 70, -75, DrAP 75, DrAS 78E, -82E, WhoAm 74, -76, -78, -80, -82, -84, -86, -88, -90, -92, -94, WhoAmJ 80, WhoUSWr 88, WhoWest 92, -94, WhoWrEP 89, -92, WrDr 76, -80*

Nathan, Robert *IntvTCA 2*

Nathan, Robert 1894- *SupFW*

Nathan, Robert 1894-1985 *AmAu&B, AmNov, ASCAP 66, Au&Wr 71, BenetAL 91, BioIn 1, -2, -4, -5, -6, -8, -10, -12, -14, -15, BlueB 76, ChhPo, -S1, CnDAL, ConAmA, ConAmC 76A, -82, ConAmL, ConAu 13R, -116, -6NR, ConNov 72, -76, -82, DcLB 9, HalFC 88, IntAu&W 77, -82, IntWW 74, -75, -76, -77, -78, -79, -80, -81, -82, -83, JeAmFiW, LongCTC, NewYTBS 85, OxCAmL 65, -83, REn, REnAL, ScF&FL 92, SmATA 6, -43N, SupFW, TwCA, -SUP, WhAm 8, WhoAm 74, -76, -78, WhoAmJ 80, WhoWest 74, WhoWorJ 72, -78, WrDr 76, -80, -82, -84*

Nathan, Robert 1896-1985 *AnObit 1985*

Nathan, Robert Gruntal 1894-1985 *EncSF 93*

Nathanson, Laura Walther 1941- *ConAu 123, SmATA 57*
Pseud./variant:
Thorpe, J K

Nation, Bob *AuBYP 2S, -3*

Nation, Kay *AuBYP 2S, -3*

Nation, Terry *WhoSciF*

Nation, Terry 1930- *EncSF 93, ScF&FL 92 ScFSB*

Natti, Susanna 1948- *BioIn 14, SmATA 32*

Natusch, Sheila Ellen 1926- *IntAu&W 82, -86, -89, -91, WrDr 80*

Naughton, Bill *BioIn 17, ConAu 136, -36NR*

Naughton, Bill d1992 *NewYTBS 92*

Naughton, Bill 1910- *BiDIrW, BioIn 10, -13, CamGWoT, CnThe, ConAu 105, ConDr 73, -77, -82, -88, ConNov 72, -76, -82, -86, -91, CroCD, DcLB 13, DcLEL 1940, EncWT, IntAu&W 77, -91, MajTwCW, OxCChiL,*

REnWD, TwCChW 83, –89, WhoThe 72, –81, WrDr 76, –80, –82, –84, –86, –88, –90, –92

Naughton, Bill 1910-1992 *AnObit 1992, ConDr 93, WrDr 94N*

Nava, Julian 1927- *BioIn 10, –16, ChiSch, ConAu 61, DrAS 74H, –78H, –82H, HispAmA, HispWr, MexAmB, WhAm 8, WhoAm 82, WhoHisp 91, –92, –94, WhoWor 80, –82, –84*

Navarra, John Gabriel 1927- *AmMWSc 73P, –76P, –82, –86, –89, –92, AuBYP 2S, –3, BioIn 5, –11, ConAu 41R, IntAu&W 77, SmATA 8, WhoE 74*

Navarra, Toby *IlsBYP*

Naylor, John Francis 1937- *DrAS 74H, –78H, –82H*

Naylor, Penelope 1941- *BioIn 11, ConAu 37R, IlsBYP, SmATA 10*

Naylor, Phyllis *MajAI, SmATA 66*

Naylor, Phyllis 1933- *ConAu 24NR*

Naylor, Phyllis Reynolds *DrAPF 87, –89, –91, –93*

Naylor, Phyllis Reynolds 1933- *Au&Arts 4, AuBYP 2S, –3, BioIn 11, –16, –17, ChlLR 17, ConAu 21R, DcAmChF 1960, –1985, DrAPF 83, –85, FifBJA, IndAu 1917, IntAu&W 77, –82, MajAI, ScF&FL 92, SmATA 12, –66, –10AS, TwCChW 89, TwCYAW, WhoAm 92, –94, WhoAmW 74, –75, –87, WhoUSWr 88, WhoWrEP 89, –92, WrDr 76, –80, –82, –84, –86, –88, –90, –92, –94*

Nazaroff, Alexander I 1898- *AuBYP 2S, –3, ConAu 33R, SmATA 4*

Neal, Charles Dempsey 1908- *ConAu 5R, –5NR*

Neal, Harry Edward d1993 *NewYTBS 93*

Neal, Harry Edward 1906- *AuBYP 2, –3, BioIn 7, –10, ConAu 5R, –2NR, IntAu&W 77, –82, –86, –89, –91, SmATA 5, WhoAm 76, –78, –80, –82, –84, –86, –88, –90, WrDr 76, –80, –82, –84, –86, –88, –90, –92, –94*

Neal, Harry Edward 1906-1993 *ConAu 141, SmATA 76*

Neal, Jean *AuBYP 2S, –3*

Neal, Michael *SmATA X*
Main entry: Teitelbaum, Michael

Nearing, Penny 1916- *BioIn 15, –16, ConAu 81, IntAu&W 82, SmATA 42, –47*
Pseud./variant:
Maguire, Anne

Neatby, Leslie Hamilton 1902- *Au&Wr 71, ConAu 5R, –3NR, DrAS 74H, OxCCan, –SUP*

Neavles, Janet Talmadge 1919- *ConAu 5R*

Nebel, Gustave E *BioIn 14, –15, IlsBYP, SmATA 33, –45*
Pseud./variant:
Nebel, Mimouca

Nebel, Mimouca *SmATA X*
Main entry: Nebel, Gustave E

Nee, Kay Bonner *BioIn 11, ConAu 49, –2NR, –31NR, SmATA 10, WhoAmP 73, WhoAmW 77, WhoFI 83, –85, –87, WhoMW 80, –82, WhoUSWr 88, WhoWrEP 89, –92*

Needham, Violet 1876-1967 *ConAu 116, TwCChW 83, –89*

Needle, Jan 1943- *BioIn 14, ChlFicS, ConAu 106, –28NR, IntAu&W 86, –89, –91, OxCChiL, SmATA 30, TwCChW 83, –89, TwCYAW, WrDr 84, –86, –88, –90, –92, –94*

Needleman, Jacob 1934- *BioIn 10, ConAu 29R, –12NR, DrAS 74P, –78P, –82P, IntWW 91, ScF&FL 92, SmATA 6, WhoAm 94, WhoRel 75, –77, WrDr 92, –94*

Neely, Henry Milton 1877-1963 *BioIn 6, NotNAT B*

Neely, Kate J *CarSB*

Nef, Evelyn Stefansson *AuBYP 3*

Nef, Evelyn Stefansson 1913- *ConAu 49, –20NR, WhoAm 76, –78, –80, –82, –84, –86, –88, –90, –92, –94, WhoAmW 75, –77*
Pseud./variant:
Stefansson, Evelyn Baird

Neff, Harry Richard 1933- *ConAu 33R, WhoFI 94, WhoRel 77, WrDr 76, –80*

Negri, Rocco Antonio 1932- *BioIn 11, IlsBYP, IlsCB 1967, SmATA 12, WhoAmA 78, –80, –82, –84, –86, –89, –91, WhoE 81, –93*

Neidlinger, William Harold 1863-1924 *Baker 84, BioIn 1, CarSB, ChhPo, WhAm 1*

Neier, Aryeh 1937- *BioIn 16, SmATA 59, WhoAm 86, –88, –90, –92, –94, WhoUSWr 88, WhoWrEP 89, –92*

Neighbour, Ralph W 1906- *IntAu&W 91, WrDr 86, –88, –90, –92*

Neighbour, Ralph Webster, Sr. 1906- *ConAu 1R, –1NR, IntAu&W 77, WhoRel 92, WrDr 76, –80, –82, –84, –94*

Neigoff, Anne 1911- *BioIn 11, ConAu 41R, ForWC 70, SmATA 13, WhoAmW 74, WhoMW 74*

Neigoff, Mike 1920- *BioIn 11, ConAu 5R, –2NR, SmATA 13*

Neilan, Sarah *BioIn 14, ConAu 69, IntAu&W 86, –89, –91, TwCRHW 90, WrDr 82, –84, –86, –88, –90, –92, –94*

Neill, John Rea 1878-1943 *ChhPo S2, DcNAA*

Neilson, Frances Fullerton 1910- *AuBYP 2, –3, BioIn 4, –7, –12, ConAu 73, CurBio 55, SmATA 14*

Neimark, Anne E 1935- *ConAu 36NR*

Neimark, Anne Elizabeth Loeb 1935- *BioIn 9, ConAu 29R, –16NR, SmATA 4, WhoAmW 75*

Neimark, Paul G *AuBYP 3*

Neimark, Paul G 1934- *AuBYP 2S, BioIn 15, ConAu 115, –135, SmATA 37, WrDr 94*

Neinke, Peter *WrDr 76*

Neitzel, Shirley 1941- *SmATA 77*

Nell
Main entry: Hanna, Nellie L

Nelson, Alix Robin 1938- *ForWC 70, WhoAmW 75*

Nelson, Carl Ellis 1916- *LEduc 74, WhoAm 74*

Nelson, Cholmondeley M 1903- *AuBYP 2, –3, BioIn 7, ConAu 5R*

Nelson, Cordner 1918- *BioIn 13, –16, SmATA 29, –54, WhoWest 80, –82, WrDr 82, –84, –86, –88, –90, –92, –94*

Nelson, Drew 1952- *SmATA 77*

Nelson, Esther L 1928- *BioIn 11, ConAu 69, –11NR, –28NR, SmATA 13*

Nelson, Gertrude *WhAmArt 85*

Nelson, Lawrence E 1928-1977 *BioIn 13, ConAu 103, SmATA 28N, WhAm 7*

Nelson, Marg 1899- *AuBYP 3*

Nelson, Marg Raibley 1899- *AuBYP 2, ConAu 1R*

Nelson, Marguerite *ConAu X, IntAu&W 91X, WrDr 76, –80, –82, –84, –86, –88, –90*
Main entry: Floren, Lee

Nelson, Mary Carroll 1929- *ConAu 49, –1NR, –16NR, SmATA 23, WhoAmA 78, –80, –82, –84, –86, –89, –91, WhoAmW 85, –87, –89, –91, –93, WhoWest 80, –82, –84, –87, –89, –92, –94*

Nelson, O Terry 1941- *BioIn 17, SmATA 62*

Nelson, O T 1941- *ScF&FL 92*

Nelson, Peter N 1953- *SmATA 73*

Nelson, Richard K *BioIn 17*

Nelson, Richard K 1941- *ConAu 30NR, SmATA 65*

Nelson, Roy P 1923- *WrDr 88, –90, –92*

Nelson, Roy Paul 1923- *BioIn 16, ConAu 17R, –7NR, –22NR, DrAS 74E, –78E, –82E, SmATA 59, WhoWest 74, –76, –78, WhoWrEP 89, –92, WrDr 76, –80, –82, –84, –86, –94*

Nelson, T
Main entry: Brown, Duncan

Nelson, Theresa *AuBYP 3*

Nelson, Theresa 1948- *DcAmChF 1985*

Nephew, William *AuBYP 2, –3, BioIn 8*

Nerlove, Miriam 1959- *BioIn 16, ConAu 121, SmATA 49, –53*

Nerman, Einar 1888-1980 *BioIn 12, ConICB, IntWW 74, –75, –76, –77, –78, –79, –80, –81, –82, –83, WhoWor 74, –78*

Nesbit, E *AuBYP 3, WomNov*

Nesbit, E 1858-1924 *Alli SUP, AtlBL, AuBYP 2, BioIn 15, –16, CamGEL, CamGLE, CarSB, CasWL, ChhPo, ChlLR 3, ConAu 118, DcLEL, EvLB, FamSYP, FemiCLE, JBA 34, LongCTC, MorJA, NewC, OxCChiL, OxCEng 67, –85, PenC ENG, PenEncH, RfGEnL 91, ScF&FL 92, TelT, TwCA, –SUP, TwCChW 78, –83, –89, WhoChL, WhoHr&F, WrChl, YABC 1*
Pseud./variant:
Bland, Edith Nesbit
Bland, Fabian

Nesbit, Edith 1858-1924 *BlmGWL, ConAu 137, MajAI*

Nesbit, Troy *AuBYP 2, –3, ConAu X, IntAu&W 82X, –91X, SmATA 5, WrDr 76,*

–80, –82, –84, –86, –88, –90, –92
Main entry: Folsom, Franklin Brewster

Nesbit, Troy 1907- *WrDr 94*

Nesbitt, Esta 1918- *BioIn 8, IlsCB 1957*

Nesbitt, Rosemary Sinnett 1924- *ConAu 81, DrAS 78E, –82E, WhoAm 76, –78, –80, –88, –90, –92, –94, WhoAmW 74, –75, –77, WhoEnt 92*

Nesmith, Robert I 1891-1972 *ConAu 1R, –103, –15NR*

Nespojohn, Katherine Veronica 1912- *BioIn 10, ConAu 37R, SmATA 7*

Ness, Evaline *BioIn 14*

Ness, Evaline 1911- *AuBYP 2, BioIn 4, –6, –7, –8, –9, –13, BkP, ChhPo, –S1, –S2, ChlLR 6, ConAu 5R, –5NR, IlsBYP, IlsCB 1957, –1967, NewbC 1966, OxCChiL, SmATA 1, –26, –1AS, ThrBJA, TwCChW 78, –83, WhAm 9, WhoAm 74, –76, –78, –80, –82, –84, –86, WhoAmA 78, –80, –82, –84, –86N, –89N, –91N, WhoAmW 74, –75, WhoUSWr 88, WrDr 80, –82, –84, –86*

Ness, Evaline 1911-1986 *AuBYP 3, BioIn 15, –16, ConAu 120, DcLB 61, SmATA 49N, TwCChW 89*

Ness, Evaline Michelow 1911-1986 *ConAu 37NR, MajAI*

Nestor, William P 1947- *BioIn 16, ConAu 26NR, SmATA 49*

Netamuxwe *IlsBYP*
Main entry: Bock, William Sauts-Netamux'we

Netherwood, Anne 1940- *BioIn 8, IlsCB 1957*

Neuberger, Richard Lewis 1912-1960 *AmAu&B, BiDrUSC 89, BioIn 2, –3, –4, –5, –7, –11, CurBio 55, –60, ObitOF 79, WhAm 3A, –4, WhAmP*

Neufeld, John 1938- *Au&Arts 11, AuBYP 2, –3, BioIn 10, –15, ConAu 25R, –11NR, ConLC 17, SmATA 6, –3AS*

Neufeld, John Arthur 1938- *ConAu 37NR, DcAmChF 1960, MajAI, TwCYAW*

Neufeld, Rose 1924- *ConAu 29R*

Neuffer, Claude Henry 1911- *ConAu 41R, DrAS 74E, –78E, –82E*

Neuffer, Irene LaBorde 1919- *ConAu 61*
Pseud./variant:
LaBorde, Rene

Neumeyer, Peter F 1929- *BioIn 11, ConAu 33R, –30NR, DrAS 74E, –78E, –82E, IntAu&W 91, SmATA 13, WrDr 76, –80*

Neumeyer, Peter Florian 1929- *WhoWest 92, –94*

Neurath, Marie 1898- *Au&Wr 71, BioIn 9, ConAu 13R, SmATA 1, WhoArt 80, –82, –84*

Neusner, Jacob 1932- *BioIn 14, –15, ConAu 7NR, –22NR, DrAS 82P, IntAu&W 82, –86, –89, SmATA 38, WhoAm 82, –84, –86, –88, –90, –92, –94, WhoE 83, –85, –86, –89, WhoRel 92, WrDr 82, –84, –86, –88, –90, –92, –94*

Neville, Emily Cheney 1919- *AmWomWr, AuBYP 2, –3, BioIn 6, –7, –9, –10, –14, –15, BkCL, ConAu 5R, –3NR, –37NR, ConLC 12, DcAmChF 1960, ForWC 70, MajAI, MorBMP, NewbC 1956, OxCChiL, SmATA 1, –2AS, ThrBJA, TwCChW 78, –83, –89, TwCYAW, WhoAm 74, –76, –78, –80, –82, –84, –86, –88, –90, WhoAmW 74, –75, WhoUSWr 88, WhoWrEP 89, –92, WrDr 80, –82, –84, –86, –88, –90, –92, –94*

Neville, Mary *ConAu X, DcWomA, SmATA 2, WhAmArt 85*
Main entry: Woodrich, Mary Neville

Nevin, Evelyn C *IntAu&W 86X*

Nevin, Evelyn C 1910- *WrDr 86, –88, –90, –92, –94*

Nevin, Evelyn Cook 1910- *ConAu 17R, WhoAmW 75, –77, WrDr 76, –80, –82, –84*

Nevins, Albert J 1915- *AmCath 80, AuBYP 2, –3, BioIn 3, –7, –12, BkC 6, CathA 1952, ConAu 5R, –5NR, –19NR, –41NR, SmATA 20, WhoAm 74, –76, –78, –80, –82, –90, –92, –94, WhoRel 75, –77, WhoWor 78*

Nevins, Allan *IntvTCA 2*

Nevins, Allan 1890-1971 *AmAu&B, Benet 87, BenetAL 91, BioIn 1, –2, –4, –5, –8, –9, –10, –11, –13, ConAu 5R, –29R, –30NR, CurBio 68, –71, DcLB 17, EncAB-H, EncWB, LongCTC, NewYTBE 71, ObitOF 79, OxCAmH, OxCAmL 65, –83, PenC AM, RAdv 13-3, REn, REnAL, TwCA, –SUP, WebAB 74, –79, WhAm 5, –8, WorAlBi, WorAl*

Newark, Elizabeth 1929- *SmATA X*
Main entry: Dinneen, Betty

Newberry, Clare 1903-1970 *AuBYP 3*

Newberry, Clare Turlay 1903-1970 *AmPB, AuBYP 2, BioIn 1, –2, –5, –7, –8, –9, –14, ChhPo, –S1, ConAu P-2, IlsCB 1744, –1946,*

–1967, JBA 51, SmATA 1, –26N, TwCChW 78, WhAmArt 85, WhoAmA 78N, –80N, –82N, –86N, –89N, –91N

Newbery, Elizabeth *OxCChiL*

Newbery, Francis 1743-1818 *DcNaB, OxCChiL*

Newbery, John 1713-1767 *Alli, Benet 87, BenetAL 91, BioIn 3, –4, –7, –8, –9, –11, –12, BritAu, CamGLE, ChhPo, –S1, DcLEL, DcNaB, MajAI, NewC, OxCChiL, OxCEng 85, REn, REnAL, SmATA 20, WhoChL*
Pseud./variant:
Aesop, Abraham
Telescope, Tom

Newbery, Thomas *DcNaB, OxCChiL*

Newbolt, Henry John, Sir 1862-1938 *BioIn 2, –13, CarSB, Chambr 3, ChhPo, –S1, –S2, DcEnA A, DcLEL, DcNaB 1931, EvLB, LongCTC, ModBrL, NewC, OxCEng 67, –85, OxCShps, PenC ENG, REn, TwCA, –SUP*

Newby, P H 1918- *Benet 87, BioIn 3, –4, –9, –10, –17, BlueB 76, ConAu 5R, –32NR, ConLC 13, ConNov 82, –86, –91, CurBio 53, DcLB 15, MajTwCW, ModBrL S2, Novels, RfGEnL 91, ScF&FL 92, WrDr 76, –80, –82, –84, –86, –88, –90, –92*

Newby, Percy Howard 1918- *WrDr 94*

Newcomb, Covelle 1908- *AmAu&B, AuBYP 2, –3, BioIn 1, –2, –7, BkC 1, CathA 1930, ConAu P-2, JBA 51*

Newcomb, Ellsworth *ConAu X, SmATA X*
Main entry: Kenny, Ellsworth Newcomb

Newcomb, Franc Johnson 1887-1970 *AmWomWr, BioIn 12, ConAu 17R, InWom SUP*

Newcomb, Harvey 1803-1863 *Alli, CarSB, DcAmAu, DcNAA, WhAm HS*

Newcomb, Harvey Russell 1916- *AmMWSc 86*

Newcombe, Jack *AuBYP 2, –3, BioIn 8, –12, –14, –15, –16, –17, ConAu 113, –130, –42NR, SmATA 33, –45*

Newcombe, Jack 1923-1990 *NewYTBS 90*

Newell, Crosby *ConAu X, IlsBYP, IntAu&W 91X, SmATA X, ThrBJA, TwCChW 83, –89, WrDr 80, –82, –84, –86, –88, –90, –92*
Main entry: Bonsall, Crosby Barbara

Newell, Crosby 1921- *BioIn 14, WrDr 94*

Newell, Edythe W 1910- *BioIn 11, ConAu 65, SmATA 11*

Newell, Homer Edward 1915-1983 *AuBYP 3*

Newell, Homer Edward, Jr. 1915-1983 *AmMWSc 73P, AuBYP 2, BioIn 1, –3, –5, –6, –7, –11, –13, BlueB 76, ConAu 97, –110, CurBio 54, –83N, InSci, IntWW 74, –79, –80, –81, –82, –83, NewYTBS 83, WhAm 8, WhoAm 74, WhoGov 72*

Newell, Hope 1896-1965 *AuBYP 3*

Newell, Hope Hockenberry 1896-1965 *AmAu&B, AuBYP 2, BioIn 6, –7, –13, ConAu 73, MorJA, SmATA 24*
Pseud./variant:
Hockenberry, Hope

Newell, Peter 1862-1924 *AmAu&B, BioIn 15, CarSB, ChhPo, –S2, ConAu 122, DcAmAu, DcLB 42, DcNAA, IlrAm 1880, OxCAmL 65, –83, OxCChiL, WhAm 1, WhAmArt 85, WorECar*

Newfeld, Frank 1928- *BioIn 13, CanWW 79, –80, –81, –83, –89, ConAu 105, Profile 1, SmATA 26*

Newlon, Clarke *AuBYP 3*

Newlon, Clarke d1982 *BioIn 14*

Newlon, Clarke 1905?-1982 *AuBYP 2S, BioIn 10, ConAu 49, –108, –10NR, SmATA 6, –33N*
Pseud./variant:
Clarke, Michael

Newman, Bernard *AuBYP 2S*

Newman, Bernard 1897-1968 *AuBYP 3, BioIn 14, EncSF 93, TwCCr&M 91*

Newman, Daisy *BioIn 15, WrDr 86, –88, –90, –92, –94*

Newman, Daisy 1904- *AuBYP 2S, –3, BioIn 13, ConAu 37R, IntAu&W 86, –89, –91, SmATA 27, WrDr 76, –80, –82, –84*

Newman, Gerald 1939- *BioIn 15, ConAu 101, SmATA 42, –46*

Newman, Leslea 1955- *SmATA 71*

Newman, Matthew 1955- *BioIn 16, SmATA 56*

Newman, Robert d1988 *NewYTBS 88*

Newman, Robert 1909- *AuBYP 2, –3, BioIn 8, –9, ConAu 1R, –4NR, –19NR, SmATA 4, TwCChW 83, WrDr 86, –88*

Newman, Robert 1909-1988 *BioIn 16, –17, ConAu 127, ScF&FL 92, SixBJA, SmATA 60, TwCChW 89*

Newman, Robert Howard 1909- *DcAmChF 1960*

Newman, Shirlee Petkin 1924- *AuBYP 2S, -3, BioIn 11, ConAu 5R, ForWC 70, SmATA 10, WhoAmW 74, -75, -77, WhoE 74*

Newman, Thelma Rita 1925-1978 *BioIn 11, ConAu 13R, -81, -7NR, ForWC 70, LEduc 74*

Newsom, Carol 1948- *BioIn 15, SmATA 40*

Newsome, Arden J 1932- *AuBYP 2S, -3, ConAu 29R*
Pseud./variant:
Sebastian, Jeanne

Newton, David C *ConAu X, EncSF 93*

Newton, David E *BioIn 17*

Newton, David E 1933- *ConAu 135, SmATA 67*

Newton, David Edward *AmMWSc 89*

Newton, David Edward 1933- *AmMWSc 86, WrDr 94*

Newton, James R 1935- *BioIn 13, ConAu 101, SmATA 23*

Newton, Laura P *AuBYP 3*

Newton, Suzanne *DrAPF 87, -89, -91, -93*

Newton, Suzanne 1936- *AuBYP 2S, -3, BioIn 10, -16, ConAu 41R, -14NR, ConLC 35, DrAPF 83, -85, IntAu&W 77, -91, SixBJA, SmATA 5, -77, WhoAm 92, WrDr 76, -80, -82, -84, -86, -88, -90, -92, -94*

Newton White, Muriel E *OxCCan*

Ney, John *AuBYP 3*

Ney, John 1923- *AuBYP 2S, BioIn 14, -15, ConAu 115, DcAmChF 1960, FifBJA, SmATA 33, -43*

Neyhart, Louise Albright *AuBYP 2, -3, BioIn 2, -8, WhoAmW 77, WhoMW 76, -78*

Nguyen-Dinh-Hoa 1924- *ConAu 21R*

Nichol, B P *IntvTCA 2*

Nichol, B P 1944- *BioIn 15, CamGLE, DcLB 53, IntAu&W 91, WrDr 86, -88*

Nichol, B P 1944-1988 *BioIn 17, SmATA 66*

Nicholas, A X 1943- *BlkAWP*

Nicholls, Frederick Francis 1926- *Au&Wr 71, ConAu 5R, WrDr 76, -80, -82, -84*

Nicholls, Judith 1941- *BioIn 17, ConAu 121, SmATA 61*

Nichols, Beverley 1898-1983 *DcNaB 1981, ScF&FL 92, TwCCr&M 91*

Nichols, Beverley 1899?-1983 *AnObit 1983, Au&Wr 71, BioIn 1, -2, -3, -4, -6, -7, -8, -9, -10, -14, -15, ChhPo, -S1, ConAu 93, -110, -17NR, IntAu&W 77, IntWW 74, -75, -76, -77, -78, -79, -80, -81, -82, -83, LongCTC, ModBrL, NewC, OxCChiL, TwCA, -SUP, TwCChW 78, TwCCr&M 80, -85, TwCWr, WhAm 8, Who 74, -82, -83, WhoChL, WhoWor 74, WrDr 82, -84*

Nichols, Cecilia Fawn 1906- *BioIn 11, ConAu P-1, ForWC 70, SmATA 12*

Nichols, Dale 1904- *BioIn 1, ConAu P-2, GrAmP, IlsCB 1744, WhAmArt 85, WhoAm 74, -80, -82, WhoAmA 80, WhoWor 74*

Nichols, Janet 1952- *BioIn 17, ConAu 135, SmATA 67*

Nichols, Janet Louise 1952- *WrDr 94*

Nichols, Joanna Ruth 1948- *DcChlFi*

Nichols, Leigh *BioIn 17, ConAu 36NR, EncSF 93, MajTwCW, ScF&FL 92, TwCYAW, WrDr 86, -88, -90, -92*

Nichols, Leigh 1945- *WrDr 94*

Nichols, Marie C 1905- *BioIn 5, IlsBYP, IlsCB 1946*

Nichols, Nell B *AuBYP 3*

Nichols, Nell Beaubien *AuBYP 2S*

Nichols, Peter *ConAu 37NR, MajAI, SmATA X*
Main entry: Youd, Samuel

Nichols, Ruth 1948- *AuBYP 2S, -3, Au&Wr 71, BioIn 10, -12, -16, BlmGWL, ConAu 25R, -16NR, DcLB 60, FourBJA, OxCCan SUP, OxCCanL, OxCChiL, Profile 1, ScF&FL 92, SmATA 15, TwCChW 78, -83, -89, WhoCanL 85, -87, -92, WrDr 80, -82, -84, -86, -88, -90, -92, -94*

Nichols, Spencer B d1950 *WhoAmA 86N*

Nichols, Spencer B 1875-1950 *WhoAmA 89N, -91N*

Nichols, Spencer Baird 1875?-1950 *BioIn 1, -2, ChhPo, IlsCB 1744, ObitOF 79, WhAm 3, WhAmArt 85, WhoAmA 78N, -80N, -82N*

Nicholson, Geoffrey 1929- *Au&Wr 71, ConAu 5R, -8NR, IntAu&W 86, -89, -91,*

WrDr 76, –80, –82, –84, –86, –88, –90, –92, –94

Nicholson, Joyce Thorpe 1919- *Au&Wr 71, BioIn 14, ConAu 9R, –5NR, SingR 1, SmATA 35*

Nicholson, Shirley J 1925- *ConAu 29R, –26NR*

Nicholson, Shirley Jean 1925- *WhoRel 92*

Nicholson, Thomas D 1922- *WhoAmA 86, –89, –91*

Nicholson, Thomas D 1922-1991 *BioIn 17, NewYTBS 91*

Nicholson, Thomas Dominic 1922- *AmMWSc 73P, –76P, –82, –86, –89, –92, WhoAm 74, –76, –78, –80, –82, –84, –86, –88, –90, WhoE 74, –81, –85, –86, –89, WhoWor 82, –84*

Nicholson, Thomas Dominic 1922-1991 *WhAm 10*

Nicholson, William 1872-1949 *TwCChW 89, TwCPaSc*

Nicholson, William, Sir 1872-1949 *AmPB, BioIn 1, –2, –3, –5, –12, –13, –14, BritAS, ChhPo, –S2, ClaDrA, DcBrAr 1, DcBrBI, DcNaB 1941, DcVicP 2, IlsCB 1744, –1946, NotNAT B, OxCArt, OxCChiL, OxCTwCA, OxDcArt, TwCChW 83*

Nickel, Mildred Lucille 1912- *BiDrLUS 70, ConAu 108, LEduc 74, WhoAmW 74, –75, –77, WhoLibS 66*

Nickell, Joe 1944- *SmATA 73*

Nickelsburg, Janet 1893- *BioIn 11, ConAu 65, SmATA 11*

Nickerson, Betty 1922- *ConAu 77, SmATA X*
Pseud./variant:
Nickerson, Elizabeth

Nickerson, Elizabeth
Main entry: Nickerson, Betty

Nickerson, Elizabeth 1922- *SmATA 14*

Nickerson, Jan *AuBYP 2, –3, BioIn 7, ConAu 1R*

Nickl, Barbara 1939- *BioIn 16, –17*

Nickl, Barbara Elisabeth 1939- *SmATA 56*
Pseud./variant:
Schroeder, Binette

Nicklaus, Carol *BioIn 14, –17, IlsBYP, SmATA 33, –62*

Nickless, Will 1902- *BioIn 8, –14, –17, ConAu 81, IlsCB 1957*

Nickless, Will 1902-1979? *SmATA 66*

Nickson, Hilda 1912- *IntAu&W 77*
Pseud./variant:
Pressley, Hilda

Niclas, Yolla 1900- *ConAu 25R*

Nic Leodhas, Sorche *AuBYP 2, –3, ConAu 73, MajAI, ThrBJA*
Main entry: Alger, Leclaire Gowans

Nicol, Ann *ConAu X, SmATA X*
Main entry: Turnbull, Ann

Nicol, Eric P 1919- *CanWW 89, WhoCanL 87, –92*

Nicol, Eric Patrick 1919- *Au&Wr 71, CanWW 70, –80, –81, –83, CanWr, ConAu 49, CreCan 2, IntAu&W 82, –86, OxCCan SUP, WhoCan 73, –80, –82, WhoCanL 85, WhoWest 74, WhoWor 74*

Nicolas *AmPB, AuBYP 2, –3, BkP, ConAu X, DcCanB 3, DcNaB, IlsBYP, IlsCB 1946, –1957, –1967, OxCChiL, SmATA X*
Main entry: Mordvinoff, Nicolas

Nicolay, Helen 1866- *AuBYP 3*

Nicolay, Helen 1866-1954 *AmAu&B, AmLY, AuBYP 2, BioIn 2, –3, –7, –11, ConAu 12., DcWomA, JBA 34, –51, REnAL, WhAm 3, WhAmArt 85, WomWWA 14, YABC 1*

Nicole *AmPB, ContDcW 89, IntDcWB*
Main entry: Duplaix, Georges

Nicole, Christopher 1930- *ScF&FL 92, WrDr 92, –94*

Nicole, Christopher Robin 1930- *Au&Wr 71, BioIn 10, ConAu 13R, ConNov 72, –76, DcLEL 1940, IntAu&W 77, –82, –89, –91, SmATA 5, SpyFic, WhoSpyF, WhoWor 78, WrDr 76, –80*
Pseud./variant:
Grange, Peter
York, Andrew

Nicoll, Helen *TwCChW 83, WrDr 86, –88*

Nicoll, Helen 1937- *ConAu 122, TwCChW 89, WrDr 90, –92, –94*

Niebling, Richard F *ChhPo, –S1*

Niehuis, Charles C *AuBYP 2, –3, BioIn 7*

Nield, W A *CarSB*

Nielsen, Kay 1886-1957 *BioIn 1, –11, –12, –14, CarSB, ChlLR 16, ConICB, DcBrAr 2, DcBrBI, IlsCB 1744, SmATA 16*

Nielsen, Kay Rasmus 1886-1957 *MajAI*

Nielsen, Virginia *ConAu X, –39NR, SmATA X*
Main entry: McCall, Virginia Nielsen

Nielson, Nancy J 1951- *SmATA 77*

Nieritz, Gustav 1795-1876 *OxCChiL*

Nies, Judith 1941- *ConAu 77, WhoAmW 75*

Nightingale, Charles T 1878- *ChhPo, –S1, ConICB*

Nightingale, Charles Thrupp 1878- *BioIn 14*

Nightingale, Sandy 1953- *SmATA 76*

Niizaka, Kazuo 1943- *ConAu 77*

Nikola-lisa, W 1951- *SmATA 71*

Niland, Deborah *BioIn 17*

Niland, Deborah 1951- *BioIn 12, –13, ConAu 106, IlsCB 1967, OxCChiL, SmATA 27*

Niland, Kilmeny *SmATA 75*

Niland, Kilmeny 1951- *BioIn 12, IlsCB 1967, OxCChiL*

Nilsson, Ulf *AuBYP 3*

Nimeth, Albert James 1918-1984 *AmCath 80, ConAu 25R, –114*

Nimmo, Jenny 1942- *ConAu 108, ScF&FL 92, WrDr 76, –80, –82, –84*

Nimmo, Jenny 1944- *ChlFicS, TwCChW 89, WrDr 90, –92, –94*

Ninon *IlsBYP, IlsCB 1946*
Main entry: MacKnight, Ninon

Nisbet, Noel Laura 1887-1956 *BioIn 1, DcBrAr 1, DcWomA, IlsCB 1744*

Nisenson, Samuel *BioIn 8, IlsBYP*

Nishiyama, Hidetaka *BioIn 10*

Nissman, Blossom S 1928- *ConAu 19NR, WrDr 86, –88, –90, –92, –94*

Nissman, Blossom Snoyer 1928- *ConAu 37R, LEduc 74, WhoAmW 83, WhoE 89, WrDr 76, –80, –82, –84*

Nister, Ernest *OxCChiL*

Niven, Larry
Main entry: Niven, Laurence VanCott

Niven, Laurence Van Cott 1938- *MajTwCW, WhoAm 90, –92, –94, WhoWrEP 89, –92*

Niven, Laurence VanCott 1938- *BioIn 12, ConAu 21R, –14NR, ConLC 8, ConSFA, DrAF 76, ScF&FL 92, WhoAm 74, –76, –78, –80, –82, –84, –86, –88, WhoSciF, WhoUSWr 88, WorAlBi, WorAl, WrDr 80*
Pseud./variant:
Niven, Larry

Niverville, Louis De 1933- *CreCan 1*

Nivola, Claire A *IlsBYP*

Nixon, Hershell H 1923- *BioIn 15*

Nixon, Hershell Howard 1923- *SmATA 42*

Nixon, Joan 1927- *AuBYP 3*

Nixon, Joan Lowery 1927- *ArtclWW 2, AuBYP 2S, BioIn 11, –13, –15, –16, ChlLR 24, ConAu 9R, –7NR, –24NR, –38NR, DcAmChF 1960, –1985, FifBJA, MajAI, ScF&FL 92, SmATA 8, –44, –9AS, TwCChW 89, TwCYAW, WhoAm 90, –92, –94, WrDr 90, –92, –94*

Nixon, K *AuBYP 3, BioIn 12, SmATA X*
Main entry: Nixon, Kathleen Irene
Nixon, Kathleen Irene Blundell

Nixon, Kathleen Irene *AuBYP 3*

Nixon, Kathleen Irene 1894- *AuBYP 2, BioIn 7, –12, –14, –16, ConAu 73, SmATA 14, WhoWor 78*
Pseud./variant:
Nixon, K

Nixon, Kathleen Irene 1894-1988? *ConAu 126*

Nixon, Kathleen Irene Blundell 1894-1988? *SmATA 59*
Pseud./variant:
Nixon, K

Nizaka, Kazuo 1943- *ConAu 77*

Nketia, J H Kwabena 1921- *AfrA, ConAu 9R, –7NR, PenC CL, WhoAmM 83*

Nketia, Joseph Hansen Kwabena 1921- *Baker 92*

Noad, Frederick 1929- *ConAu 9R, –4NR*

Noble, Iris 1922- *AuBYP 2, BioIn 7, –10, ConAu 1R, –2NR, SmATA 5*

Noble, Iris 1922-1986 *AuBYP 3, BioIn 16, ConAu 120, SmATA 49N*

Noble, Margaret Elizabeth 1867-1911 *BioIn 3, –10*

Noble, Trinka Hakes *BioIn 15, –16, ConAu 116, SixBJA, SmATA 37*

Noda, Phyllis Ann 1945- *WhoAmW 77, –81, –83, WhoMW 80*

Nodset, Joan L *AuBYP 2, –3, BioIn 8, –9, ConAu X, SmATA 1, –X, TwCChW 83, –89, WrDr 80, –82, –84, –86, –88, –90, –92, –94*
Main entry: Lexau, Joan M

Nodset, Joan L 1913- *WrDr 94*

Noel, Hilda Bloxton, Jr. *ConAu X*
Main entry: Schroetter, Hilda Noel

Noel, Maurice *Alli SUP, CarSB*

Noel-Baker, Francis Edward 1920- *BlueB 76, Who 74, –82, –83, –85, –88, –92*

Noel-Baker, Francis Edward, Hon 1920- *Who 90*

Noel Hume, Ivor 1927- *BioIn 17, IntAu&W 91, SmATA 65, WhoAm 86, –88, –90, –92, –94, WrDr 86, –88, –90, –92, –94*

Noestlinger, Christine *ScF&FL 92*

Noestlinger, Christine 1936- *BioIn 17, ConAu 123, –38NR, MajAI, SmATA 64*

Noguere, Suzanne *DrAPF 89, –91, –93*

Noguere, Suzanne 1947- *BioIn 14, ConAu 107, SmATA 34*

Nohl, Frederick 1927- *ConAu 5R, –3NR, WrDr 76, –80, –82, –84*

Nolan, Dennis 1945- *BioIn 14, –15, ConAu 112, –32NR, SmATA 34, –42*

Nolan, Jeannette Covert 1897?-1974 *AmAu&B, AuBYP 2, –3, Au&Wr 71, BioIn 2, –7, –9, ConAu 5R, –53, –4NR, ForWC 70, IndAu 1917, JBA 51, SmATA 2, –27N, WhAm 6, WhoAm 74, WhoAmW 74, –75*
Pseud./variant:
Tucker, Caroline

Nolan, Paul T 1919- *BioIn 16, SmATA 48, WrDr 86, –88, –90, –92, –94*

Nolan, Paul Thomas 1919- *ConAu 5R, –2NR, DrAS 74E, –78E, –82E, WhoAm 74, –76, –78, –80, –82, –84, –86, –88, –90, –92, –94, WhoSSW 73, WhoUSWr 88, WhoWrEP 89, –92, WrDr 76, –80, –82, –84*

Nolan, William F *IntvTCA 2*

Nolan, William F 1928- *BioIn 14, –16, ConAu 16AS, IntAu&W 91, NewEScF, ScF&FL 92, ScFSB, TwCCr&M 91, TwCSFW 86, –91, WrDr 86, –88, –90, –92*

Nolan, William Francis 1928- *BioIn 9, –12, –13, ConAu 1R, –1NR, ConSFA, DcLB 8, EncMys, EncSF 93, SmATA 28, TwCCr&M 80, –85, WhoAm 80, –82, WhoSciF, WhoWest 74, WrDr 76, –80, –82, –84, –94*

Nolen, Barbara 1902- *ChhPo S2, ConAu 104, WhoAmW 74, –75, –77, WhoE 74, –75, –77*

Nolen, William A 1928- *BioIn 14*

Nolen, William A 1928-1986 *BioIn 15, –17, ConAu 121*

Nolen, William Anthony 1928- *AuSpks, BioIn 9, –10, –11, ConAu 77, –15NR, WhoAm 80, –82, –84, –86, WhoUSWr 88, WhoWrEP 89*

Nolen, William Anthony 1928-1986 *WhAm 9*

Noll, Sally *AuBYP 3*

Nolte, Elleta 1919- *ConAu 61*

Nolte, Judith *ForWC 70*

Nonnast, Marie 1924- *BioIn 4, –5, –8, IlsBYP, IlsCB 1946, –1957*

Noonan, Julia 1946- *BioIn 9, –12, ConAu 33R, IlsBYP, IlsCB 1967, SmATA 4, WhoAmW 77*

Noonan, Michael 1921- *Au&Wr 71, ConAu 21R, SingR 1, WrDr 76, –80, –82, –84*

Norcross, Grace 1899- *ConICB, DcWomA, WhAmArt 85*

Norcross, John *ConAu 131, IntAu&W 82X, –86X, SmATA 65, –X*
Main entry: Conroy, Jack

Nordberg, Robert B 1921- *ConAu 13R, LEduc 74*

Nordenskjold, Birgitta 1919- *BioIn 8, IlsCB 1957*

Nordhoff, Charles 1830-1901 *Alli, –SUP, AmAu, AmAu&B, BenetAL 91, BbD, BiD&SB, CarSB, CmCal, CnDAL, CyAL, DcAmAu, DcAmSR, DcNAA, HarEnUS, JrnUS, OhA&B, OxCAmL 65, –83, REnAL, WhAm 1*

Nordhoff, Charles 1887-1947 *TwCLC 23, TwCRHW 90*

Nordhoff, Charles Bernard 1887-1947 *AmAu&B, AmNov, AuBYP 2, –3, Benet 87,*

BenetAL 91, BioIn 1, -2, -4, -5, -7, -8, -12, -13, CnDAL, ConAu 108, CyWA 58, DcLB 9, DcLEL, DcNAA, JBA 34, LongCTC, Novels, ObitOF 79, OxCAmL 65, -83, OxCAusL, PenC AM, REn, REnAL, SmATA 23, TwCA, -SUP, WorAlBi, WorAl

Nordlicht, Lillian *BioIn 13, ConAu 105, SmATA 29*

Nordstrom, Ursula *AmAu&B, AmPB, AuBYP 2, BioIn 1, -8, -9, -12, ConAu 13R, ForWC 70, SmATA 3*

Nordstrom, Ursula d1988 *NewYTBS 88, WhAm 9*

Nordstrom, Ursula 1910-1988 *AuBYP 3, BioIn 16, ConAu 126, SmATA 57*

Nordstrom, Ursula Litchfield *DcAmChF 1960*

Nordtvedt, Matilda *BioIn 17*

Nordtvedt, Matilda 1926- *ConAu 124, SmATA 67*

Noren, Catherine Hanf 1938- *ConAu 65, MacBEP, WhoAmW 81*

Norfleet, Mary Crockett 1919- *ConAu 1R*

Norling, Ernest Ralph 1892- *ArtsAmW 2, AuBYP 2, -3, BioIn 7, WhAmArt 85, WhoPNW*

Norling, Josephine 1895- *AuBYP 3*

Norling, Josephine Stearns 1895- *AuBYP 2, BioIn 7, ConAu 1R, WhoPNW*

Norman, Charles 1904- *AmAu&B, AuBYP 2, -3, BioIn 4, -7, -15, -17, ChhPo S2, ConAu 107, DcLB 111, REnAL, SmATA 38, TwCA SUP, WhoAm 74, -76*

Norman, James
Main entry: Schmidt, James Norman

Norman, James 1912- *BioIn 14, ConAu X, DrAPF 83, -85, SmATA X, TwCCr&M 80, -85, WrDr 82, -84*

Norman, Lilith 1927- *AuWomWr, ConAu 45, -1NR, DcChlFi, OxCAusL, TwCChW 78, -83, -89, WrDr 80, -82, -84, -86, -88, -90, -92, -94*

Norman, Mary 1931- *BioIn 14, SmATA 36*

Norman, Mary Marshall 1937- *WhoAmW 93*

Norman, Steve *ConAu X, SmATA X*
Main entry: Pashko, Stanley

Norris, Faith Grigsby *AuBYP 2, -3, BioIn 7*

Norris, Gunilla B *AuBYP 3*

Norris, Gunilla B 1939- *AuBYP 2S, BioIn 12, ConAu 93, DrAPF 83, SmATA 20*

Norris, Len 1913- *Profile 2*

Norris, Louanne 1930- *ConAu 53, -20NR*

Norris, Margaret *Str&VC*

Norris, Margaret Boose 1956- *WhoE 86*

Norris, Marianna *AuBYP 2S, -3*

Norris, Phyllis Irene 1909- *Au&Wr 71, WrDr 76, -80, -82, -84, -86, -88, -90, -92, -94*

Norsworthy, James, Jr. *MedPD*

North, Andrew *AmAu&B, ConAu X, -31NR, CurBio 57, EncSF 93, IntAu&W 77X, MajAI, MajTwCW, SmATA 1, -X, TwCChW 83, -89, TwCSFW 86, -91, TwCYAW, WorAu 1950, WrDr 84, -86, -88, -90, -92*
Main entry: Norton, Alice Mary

North, Andrew 1912- *WrDr 94*

North, Anthony *ConAu 36NR, MajTwCW, TwCCr&M 91, TwCYAW*

North, Captain George *MajAI, YABC X*

North, Jessica *BioIn 4*

North, Jessica Nelson 1894-1988 *FemiCLE*

North, Joan 1920- *AuBYP 3*

North, Joan Marian 1920- *AuBYP 2S, Au&Wr 71, ConAu 13R, IntAu&W 77, -86, -89, SmATA 16, WrDr 76, -80, -82, -84, -86, -88, -90*

North, Robert *ConAu X, -30NR, SmATA X*
Main entry: Withers, Carl A

North, Sterling 1906-1974 *AmAu&B, AmNov, AuBYP 2, -3, Au&Wr 71, BenetAL 91, BioIn 2, -4, -6, -7, -9, -10, -13, -14, -15, BlueB 76N, ConAu 5R, -53, -40NR, CurBio 43, -75N, DcAmChF 1960, MajAI, NewYTBS 74, REnAL, SmATA 1, -26N, -45, ThrBJA, TwCA, -SUP, TwCChW 78, -83, -89, TwCYAW, WhAm 6, WhoAm 74, WhoE 74*

Northcliffe, Lord *OxCChiL*

Northcliffe, Viscount *DcIrB 88*

Northcliffe, Viscount 1865-1922 *GrBr*

Northcliffe, Alfred Harmsworth, Viscount 1865-1922 *BlmGEL*

Northcott, Cecil *Who 88*

Northcott, Cecil 1902- *Au&Wr 71, BlueB 76, ConAu 9R, Who 74, –82, –83, –85, WrDr 76, –80, –82, –84*
Pseud./variant:
Miller, Mary

Northcott, Cecil 1902-1987 *ConAu 124, SmATA 55N*
Pseud./variant:
Temple, Arthur

Northcroft, George J H 1868- *ChhPo S1, –S2*

Northmore, Elizabeth Florence 1906-1974 *ConAu P-2*
Pseud./variant:
Stucley, Elizabeth

Norton, Alden H 1903- *ConAu 101, ConSFA, WhoSciF*

Norton, Alden H 1903-1987 *ScF&FL 92*

Norton, Alice M *ScF&FL 92*

Norton, Alice Mary *InWom SUP*

Norton, Alice Mary 1912- *AmAu&B, AmWomWr, ArtclWW 2, AuBYP 2, –3, BioIn 4, –6, –9, –10, –12, –15, –17, ConAu 1R, –2NR, CurBio 57, OhA&B, SmATA 1, –43*
Pseud./variant:
North, Andrew
Norton, Andre
Norton, Andrew
Weston, Allen

Norton, Andre *AuBYP 3, DrmM 2, IntvTCA 2*
Main entry: Norton, Alice Mary

Norton, Andre 1912- *AuBYP 2, BioIn 15, –17, ConAu X, –31NR, ConLC 12, ConSFA, CurBio 57, DcLB 8, –52, EncSF 93, InWom SUP, IntAu&W 77, –91, MajAI, MajTwCW, MorJA, NewEScF, Novels, OhA&B, OxCChiL, RGTwCSF, ScF&FL 92, ScFSB, SenS, SmATA 1, –X, SupFW, TwCChW 78, –83, –89, TwCSFW 86, –91, TwCYAW, WhoHr&F, WhoSciF, WorAu 1950, WrDr 76, –80, –86, –88, –90, –92*

Norton, Andre Alice 1912- *WrDr 94*

Norton, Andrew *AuBYP 2, –3*
Main entry: Norton, Alice Mary

Norton, Browning *ConAu X, SmATA X*
Main entry: Norton, Frank R B

Norton, Charles Eliot 1827-1908 *Alli, –SUP, AmAu, AmAu&B, Benet 87, BenetAL 91, BbD, BiD&SB, BioIn 1, –3, –4, –5, –7, –8, –10, –11, –15, –16, CamGEL, CamGLE, CamHAL, CarSB, Chambr 3, ChhPo S1, CyAL, CyEd, DcAmAu, DcLB 1, –64, DcNAA, EncAB-H, EvLB, HarEnUS, LongCTC, OxCAmH, OxCAmL 65, –83, OxCEng 85, PenC AM, REn, WebAB 74, –79, WhAm 1, WhAmArt 85*

Norton, Frank R B 1909- *BioIn 11, ConAu 61, SmATA 10*
Pseud./variant:
Norton, Browning

Norton, Mary 1903- *AnCL, AuBYP 2, –3, Au&ICB, Au&Wr 71, BioIn 5, –6, –8, –9, –12, –16, BkCL, CamGLE, CasWL, ChlLR 6, ConAu 97, DcLEL 1940, FamMS, IntAu&W 89, –91, MajAI, OxCChiL, SmATA 18, –60, TelT, ThrBJA, TwCChW 78, –83, –89, Who 85, –88, –90, –92, WhoChL, WrDr 76, –80, –82, –84, –86, –88, –90, –92*

Norton, Mary 1903-1992 *AnObit 1992, BioIn 17, ConAu 139, NewYTBS 92, ScF&FL 92, SmATA 72, WrDr 94N*

Norton, Olive *WrDr 86, –88, –90*

Norton, Olive 1913- *Au&Wr 71, ConAu 9R, WrDr 84*
Pseud./variant:
Norway, Kate

Norway, Kate
Main entry: Norton, Olive

Norway, Kate 1913- *BioIn 14, ConAu X, IntAu&W 91, WrDr 84, –86, –88, –90*

Norway, Kate 1913-1973 *TwCRHW 90*

Norway, Nevil Shute 1899-1960 *BioIn 3, –4, –5, –7, –11, ConAu 93, –102, DcNaB 1951, EvLB, GrBr, InSci, LongCTC, NewC, ObitT 1951, RAdv 13-1, REn, TwCA, –SUP*
Pseud./variant:
Shute, Nevil

Norwood, Victor George Charles 1920- *ConAu 21R, –10NR, IntAu&W 91, WrDr 76, –80, –82, –84, –86, –88*
Pseud./variant:
Bowie, Jim

Nostlinger, Christine *TwCChW 89B*

Nostlinger, Christine 1936- *BioIn 15, BlmGWL, ChlLR 12, ConAu X, EncCoWW, FifBJA, ScF&FL 92, SmATA 37, TwCChW 78B, –83B, TwCYAW, WomWrGe*

Notkin, Jerome J 1926- *LEduc 74, WhoAmJ 80, WhoE 75, –77*

Notkin, Jerome Johannes 1926- *WhoE 93*

Nourse, Alan E 1928- *ConAu 21NR, IntAu&W 89, NewEScF, ScFSB, SmATA 48, TwCSFW 86, -91, WhoUSWr 88, WhoWrEP 89, WrDr 86, -88, -90, -92*

Nourse, Alan E 1928-1992 *ScF&FL 92*

Nourse, Alan Edward 1928- *AuBYP 2, -3, Au&Wr 71, BioIn 7, -12, -16, ConAu 1R, -3NR, ConSFA, DcLB 8, WhoE 89, WhoPNW, WhoSciF, WhoWrEP 92, WrDr 84*
Pseud./variant:
Dr. X
Edwards, Al

Nourse, Alan Edward 1928-1992 *EncSF 93, WrDr 94N*

Novak, Matt *AuBYP 3*

Novak, Matt 1962- *BioIn 16, -17, ConAu 125, SmATA 52, -60*

Novelli, Luca 1947- *BioIn 17, SmATA 61*

Nowell, Elizabeth Cameron *BioIn 11, ConAu X, -1NR, SmATA 12, WhoAmW 85*
Pseud./variant:
Cameron, Elizabeth
Clemons, Elizabeth
Robinson, Elizabeth Cameron

Nowell, Elizabeth Cameron Clemons *WhoAmW 87, -89, -91, -93, WhoWest 87*

Nowlan, Nora *AuBYP 2S, -3*

Nowlan, Phil 1888-1940 *ArtCS*

Nowlan, Philip *EncACom*

Nowlan, Philip Francis 1888-1940 *EncSF 93, TwCSFW 86*

Nowlan, Philip Francis 1888-1944 *ScF&FL 92*

Noyes, Alfred 1880-1958 *AuBYP 2S, -3, Benet 87, BioIn 1, -2, -3, -4, -5, -6, -13, -14, BkC 6, CamGLE, CathA 1930, Chambr 3, ChhPo, -S1, -S2, ConAu 104, DcCathB, DcLB 20, DcLEL, DcNaB 1951, EncSF 93, EngPo, EvLB, FamPYP, GrBr, LongCTC, ModBrL, NewC, ObitOF 79, ObitT 1951, OxCEng 67, -85, OxCShps, PenC ENG, REn, RfGEnL 91, TwCA, -SUP, TwCLC 7, TwCWr, WhAm 3, WhoHr&F, WhoLA*

Noyes, Nell Braly 1921- *ConAu 37R, IntAu&W 77, WrDr 76, -80*

Nucera, Marisa Lonette 1959- *ConAu 17R*
Pseud./variant:
Marisa

Nugent, Frances Roberts 1904-1964? *AuBYP 2, -3, BioIn 7, ConAu 5R*

Nugent, Frank
Main entry: Higgins, Lewis R

Nugent, Nicholas 1949- *SmATA 73*

Numeroff, Laura Joffe 1953- *BioIn 13, ConAu 106, SmATA 28*

Nunan, Desmond James 1927- *ConAu 17R, WhoE 74, -77*

Nunes, Lygia Bojunga 1932- *ConAu 142, SmATA 75*

Nunn, Jessie Alford *AuBYP 2S, -3*

Nura *IlsBYP, IlsCB 1946, WhAmArt 85*
Main entry: Ulreich, Nura Woodson

Nurenberg, Thelma *ConAu 42NR*
Main entry: Greenhaus, Thelma Nurenberg

Nurenberg, Thelma 1903-1984 *AuBYP 2, -3, BioIn 8, ConAu 69, -X, SmATA X*

Nurnberg, Maxwell 1897-1984 *BioIn 13, -14, ChhPo S2, ConAu 5R, -114, -2NR, NewYTBS 84, SmATA 27, -41N*

Nussbaumer, Paul Edmund 1934- *BioIn 8, -12, IlsCB 1957, -1967, SmATA 16, WhoWor 82*

Nuttall, Kenneth 1907- *ConAu 17R, WrDr 76*

Nwapa, Flora *IntWW 89, -91*

Nwapa, Flora 1931- *AfSS 82, ArtclWW 2, Benet 87, BioIn 14, BlmGWL, ContDcW 89, DcLB 125, FemiCLE, IntDcWB, IntWW 83, RAdv 13-2, TwCChW 83, -89, WrDr 86, -88, -90, -92, -94*

Nwapa, Flora, 1931 *BlkWr 2*

Nyberg, Everett Wayne Morgan 1944- *DcChlFi*

Nyce, Helene VonStrecker 1885-1969 *BioIn 12, SmATA 19*

Nyce, Vera 1862-1925 *BioIn 12, SmATA 19*

Nye, Douglas Charles 1945- *IntAu&W 77*

Nye, Harold G *EncSF 93, SmATA X, TwCSFW 86, -91, WrDr 84, -86, -88, -90, -92*
Main entry: Harding, Lee

Nye, Harold G 1937- *WrDr 94*

Nye, Robert 1939- *Au&Wr 71, BioIn 10, -13, -17, ConAu 33R, -29NR, ConLC 13, -42, ConNov 72, -76, -82, -86, -91, ConPo 70,*

–75, –80, –85, –91, DcLB 14, IntAu&W 82, –89, –91, IntWW 91, IntWWP 82, MajTwCW, Novels, OxCChiL, ScF&FL 92, SmATA 6, TwCChW 78, –83, –89, TwCRHW 90, Who 82, –83, –85, –88, –90, –92, WrDr 76, –80, –82, –84, –86, –88, –90, –92, –94

Nyman, Ingrid Vang 1916- *BioIn 5, IlsBYP, IlsCB 1946*

Nystrom, Carolyn *BioIn 17*

Nystrom, Carolyn 1940- *ConAu 37NR, IntAu&W 86, –89, SmATA 67*

O

Oakes, Bill
Main entry: MacDonald, Suse

Oakes, Vanya 1909-1983 *AuBYP 2, BiDrLUS 70, BioIn 7, –10, –15, ConAu 33R, –111, SmATA 6, –37N, WhoAmW 74, WhoWest 74, –76*
Pseud./variant:
Oakes, Virginia Armstrong

Oakes, Virginia Armstrong *AuBYP 3*
Main entry: Oakes, Vanya

Oakley, Don 1927- *BioIn 11, ConAu 29R, SmATA 8*

Oakley, Graham *OxCChiL*

Oakley, Graham 1919- *FifBJA*

Oakley, Graham 1929- *BioIn 11, –12, ChILR 7, ConAu 106, –38NR, IlsCB 1967, IntAu&W 91, MajAI, SmATA 30, TwCChW 83, –89, WrDr 84, –86, –88, –90, –92, –94*

Oakley, Helen 1906- *BioIn 11, ConAu 17R, ForWC 70, SmATA 10*

Oakley, Thornton 1881-1953 *BioIn 1, –3, –5, ChhPo S1, ConICB, IlrAm 1880, –B, IlsCB 1744, ObitOF 79, WhAm 3, WhAmArt 85*

Oana, Katherine D 1929- *BioIn 15, –16, SmATA 37, –53, WhoAmW 83*
Pseud./variant:
Oana, Kay D

Oana, Kay D
Main entry: Oana, Katherine D

Oates, Stephen B 1936- *BioIn 16, ConAu 26NR, IntAu&W 91, SmATA 59, WrDr 88, –90, –92*

Oates, Stephen Baery 1936- *BioIn 13, ConAu 9R, –4NR, DrAS 74H, –78H, –82H, IntAu&W 77, –82, WhoAm 74, –76, –78, –80, –82, –84, –86, –88, –90, –92, –94, WrDr 76, –80, –82, –84, –86, –94*

Obed, Ellen Bryan 1944- *SmATA 74*

Oberhansli, Trudi *ConAu X*
Main entry: Schlapbach-Oberhansli, Trudi

Oberle, Joseph 1958- *SmATA 69*

Oberreich, Robert L 1910- *IndAu 1917*

Obligado, Lilian 1931- *BioIn 15, –17, ConAu 134, SmATA 61*

Obligado, Lilian Isabel 1931- *BioIn 8, IlsCB 1957, –1967, SmATA 45, WrDr 94*

Obrant, Susan 1946- *BioIn 11, IlsBYP, SmATA 11*

O'Brian, Frank *ConAu X, EncFWF, IntAu&W 77X, –82X, TwCWW 91, WhoSpyF, WhoUSWr 88, WhoWrEP 89, –92, WrDr 76, –80, –82, –84, –86, –88, –90, –92*
Main entry: Garfield, Brian Wynne

O'Brian, Frank 1939- *WrDr 94*

O'Brian, William *ChhPo S1*

O'Brien, Anne Sibley 1952- *SmATA 48, –53*

O'Brien, E G *AuBYP 3, MajAI, SmATA 70*
Main entry: Clarke, Arthur Charles

O'Brien, Esse Forrester 1895?-1975 *ConAu 61, ForWC 70, SmATA 30N, TexWr*

O'Brien, John Sherman 1898-1938 *AuBYP 2, –3, BioIn 1, –6, –7, DcNAA, MorJA*

O'Brien, Katherine *DcChlFi*

O'Brien, Robert C *MajAI*
Main entry: Conly, Robert Leslie

O'Brien, Robert C 1918?-1973 *AuBYP 2S, –3, BioIn 9, –13, ChlFicS, ChILR 2, ConAu X, DcAmChF 1960, FourBJA, NewbC 1966, OxCChiL, SmATA X, TwCChW 78, –83, –89, TwCYAW*

O'Brien, Thomas C 1938- *BioIn 13, ConAu 106, LEduc 74, SmATA 29*

O'Carroll, Ryan *ConAu X, SmATA X*
Main entry: Markun, Patricia Maloney

O'Clery, Helen 1910- *AuBYP 2, -3, BiDIrW, BioIn 7, ConAu 9R*

O'Connell, Desmond Henry 1906-1973 *WhAm 5, WhoFI 74*

O'Connell, Margaret F 1935-1977 *BioIn 14, -16, SmATA 49*

O'Connell, Margaret Forster 1935-1977 *ConAu 73, SmATA 30N*

O'Connell, Peg *ConAu X, SmATA X*
Main entry: Ahern, Margaret McCrohan

O'Connor, Genevieve A 1914- *SmATA 75*

O'Connor, Jane 1947- *BioIn 16, ConAu 124, ScF&FL 92, SmATA 47, -59*

O'Connor, Karen 1938- *ConAu 28NR, SmATA 34*
Pseud./variant:
Sweeney, Karen O'Connor

O'Connor, Patrick *AuBYP 3, TwCChW 89, WrDr 86*
Main entry: Wibberley, Leonard

O'Connor, Patrick 1899- *AmCath 80, BioIn 3, BkC 3, ChhPo S1*

O'Connor, Patrick 1915-1983 *AuBYP 2, BioIn 9, ConAu X, EncMys, IntAu&W 77X, -82X, SmATA 2, -X, TwCChW 83, WrDr 80, -82, -84*

O'Connor, Richard 1915-1975 *AmAu&B, AuBYP 2S, -3, BioIn 10, -12, ConAu 57, -61, IndAu 1917, ObitOF 79, SmATA 21N, TwCCr&M 80, WhAm 6, WhoAm 74, WhoE 74*
Pseud./variant:
Archer, Frank
Burke, John
Wayland, Patrick

O'Cuilleanain, Eilis Dillon *ThrBJA*
Main entry: Dillon, Eilis

O'Cuilleanain, Eilis Dillon 1920- *BioIn 15*

Odaga, Asenath 1937- *BlkWr 1, ConAu 124*

Odaga, Asenath 1938- *BioIn 17, IntAu&W 91, OxCChiL, SmATA 67, TwCChW 83, -89, WrDr 86, -88, -90, -92*

Odaga, Asenath Bole 1938- *ConAu 43NR, MajAI, WrDr 94*
Pseud./variant:
Kituomba

O'Daniel, Janet *IntAu&W 91, WrDr 86, -88, -90, -92, -94*

O'Daniel, Janet 1921- *BioIn 13, ConAu 29R, SmATA 24, WrDr 76, -80, -82, -84*

O'Daniel, Therman B 1908- *BlkWr 1*

O'Daniel, Therman B 1908-1986 *BioIn 15, ConAu 133*

O'Daniel, Therman Benjamin 1908- *BlkAWP, ConAu 45, DrAS 74E, -78E, -82E, InB&W 80, LivgBAA, SelBAAf, SelBAAu, WhoBlA 77, -80, -85, -90*

O'Daniel, Therman Benjamin 1908-1986 *WhoBlA 92N*

Oddo, Genevieve Grillo 1917- *ForWC 70, WhoAmW 77*

O'Dea, Marjory Rachel 1928- *DcChlFi*

O'Dell, Scott 1897- *WrDr 86*

O'Dell, Scott 1898- *Au&Arts 3, ChlLR 16, IntAu&W 86, TwCChW 89, WhoAm 86, -88, WhoUSWr 88, WrDr 88, -90*

O'Dell, Scott 1898-1989 *AnObit 1989, BioIn 17, ConAu 129, -30NR, MajAI, NewYTBS 89, SmATA 60, TwCYAW, WhAm 10*

O'Dell, Scott 1903?- *AmAu&B, AmNov, AnCL, AuBYP 2, Au&ICB, BioIn 1, -2, -5, -6, -7, -9, -10, -11, -14, -15, BkCL, CamGLE, ChlLR 1, ConAu 61, -12NR, ConLC 30, DcAmChF 1960, DcLB 52, MorJA, NewbC 1956, OxCChiL, PiP, SenS, SmATA 12, Str&VC, TwCChW 78, -83, WhoAm 74, -76, -78, -80, -82, -84, WhoWor 74, -78, WrDr 80, -82, -84*

O'Dell, Scott 1903-1989 *AuBYP 3, BioIn 16, DcAmChF 1985*

Odenwald, Robert Paul 1899-1965 *AuBYP 2, -3, BioIn 7, -11, ConAu 1R, SmATA 11*

Odescalchi, Esther Kando 1938- *BiDrLUS 70, ConAu 69, WhoLibS 66*

Odgers, Sally Farrell 1957- *SmATA 72*
Pseud./variant:
Darroll, Sally
Farrell, Sally

O'Donnell, Dick 1935- *SmATA X*
Main entry: Lupoff, Richard Allen

O'Donnell, K M *AuBYP 2S, -3, ConAu X, EncSF 93, TwCSFW 86, -91, WrDr 84, -86, -88, -90, -92*
Main entry: Malzberg, Barry N

O'Donnell, K M 1939- *WrDr 94*

O'Donnell, Lillian Udvardy *ArtclWW 2*

O'Donnell, Lillian Udvardy 1926- *ConAu 5R, -3NR, -18NR*

O'Donnell, Peter *BioIn 14*

O'Donnell, Peter 1920- *DcLB 87, IntAu&W 91, ScF&FL 92, SpyFic, TwCCr&M 91, WrDr 86, -88, -90, -92, -94*

O'Donoghue, Bryan 1921- *ConAu 77*

Odor, Ruth Shannon 1926- *BioIn 15, ConAu 120, SmATA 44*

Oechsli, Kelly 1918- *BioIn 8, -10, ChhPo, -S2, ConAu 97, -16NR, IlsBYP, IlsCB 1957, -1967, SmATA 5, WhoAmA 78, -80, -82, -84, -86, -89, -91, WhoE 86, -91, -93*

Oetting, Rae *BioIn 6, MinnWr*

O'Faolain, Eileen *BiDIrW, DcIrW 1*

O'Faolain, Eileen 1902-1988 *TwCChW 89*

Ofek, Uriel 1926- *BioIn 14, ChlLR 28, ConAu 101, -18NR, SmATA 36, WhoWorJ 78*

Offit, Sidney *DrAPF 87, -89, -91, -93*

Offit, Sidney 1928- *AuBYP 2S, -3, BioIn 11, ConAu 1R, -1NR, DrAF 76, DrAPF 83, -85, SmATA 10, WhoAm 74, -76, -78, -80, -82, -84, -86, -88, -90, -92, -94, WhoE 74, -75, -77, WhoUSWr 88, WhoWor 84, -87, -89, WhoWrEP 89, -92, WrDr 76, -80, -82, -84*

Offord, Lenore 1905- *AuBYP 3, FemiCLE*

Offord, Lenore Glen 1905- *AmWomWr, AuBYP 2, BioIn 1, -7, -14, CathA 1930, ConAu 77, EncMys, ForWC 70, TwCCr&M 80, -85, -91, WhoAmW 74, -75, WhoWest 74, -76, WrDr 82, -84, -86, -88*

Offutt, Andrew J *IntAu&W 91, IntvTCA 2*

Offutt, Andrew J 1934- *ScF&FL 92, ScFSB, TwCSFW 86, -91, WrDr 86, -88, -90, -92*

Offutt, Andrew J 1937- *NewEScF*

Offutt, Andrew Jefferson 1934?- *ConAu 41R, -15NR, WrDr 84*

Offutt, Andrew Jefferson V 1937- *EncSF 93*

Offutt, Andrew Jefferson V 1934- *WrDr 94*

Ofosu-Appiah, L H 1920- *BioIn 11, ConAu 33R, SmATA 13*

Ogan, George F *AuBYP 3*

Ogan, George F 1912- *AuBYP 2S, BioIn 11, ConAu 9R, -4NR, SmATA 13*
Pseud./variant:
Castle, Lee
Ogan, M G

Ogan, M G *ConAu X, SmATA X*
Main entry: Ogan, George F
Ogan, Margaret E

Ogan, Margaret 1923-1979 *AuBYP 3*

Ogan, Margaret E 1923-1979 *AuBYP 2S, BioIn 11, ConAu 9R, -4NR, SmATA 13*
Pseud./variant:
Castle, Lee
Ogan, M G

Ogburn, Charlton 1911- *BioIn 15, IntAu&W 89, -91, WhoAm 86, -88, -90, -92, -94, WhoUSWr 88, WhoWrEP 89, -92, WrDr 86, -88, -90, -92, -94*

Ogburn, Charlton, Jr. 1911- *AmAu&B, Au&Wr 71, BioIn 9, ConAu 5R, -3NR, IntAu&W 82, SmATA 3, WhoAm 74, -76, -78, -80, -82, -84, WhoSSW 73, WrDr 80, -82, -84*

Ogden, Brian John 1936- *Au&Wr 71, IntAu&W 77, WrDr 76, -80, -82, -84, -86*

Ogden, Ruth 1853-1927 *Alli SUP, AmAu&B, CarSB, ChhPo, -S1, DcAmAu, DcNAA*

Ogg, Oscar 1908-1971 *BioIn 9, ConAu 33R, -P-1, NewYTBE 71, WhoAmA 78N, -80N, -82N, -86N, -89N, -91N, WhoGrA 62*

Ogilvie, Elisabeth 1917- *AmAu&B, AmNov, AuBYP 2, -3, BioIn 2, -4, -5, -8, -13, -14, -15, -17, ConAu 103, CurBio 51, SmATA 29, -40, TwCA SUP, TwCRHW 90, WhoAmW 77, WhoE 74, WrDr 84, -86, -88, -90, -92*

Ogilvie, Elisabeth May 1917- *WrDr 94*

Ogilvy, Gavin *MajAI*

Ogle, Lucille *AuBYP 2S, -3*

Ogle, Lucille 1904-1988 *BioIn 16*

Ogle, Lucille Edith 1904-1988 *SmATA 59*

O'Gorman, Ned *DrAPF 87, -89, -91, -93*

O'Gorman, Ned 1929?- *AmAu&B, BioIn 8, -10, ChhPo S2, ConAu 81, ConPo 70, -75, -80, -85, -91, DrAP 75, DrAPF 83, -85, IntAu&W 91, WhoAm 74, -76, -78, -80, -82, -84, WhoE 74, -77, WorAu 1950, WrDr 76, -80, -82, -84, -86, -88, -90, -92, -94*

O'Gorman, Ned 1931- *WhoAm 86, WhoUSWr 88, WhoWrEP 89, –92*

O'Grady, Standish James 1846-1928 *Alli SUP, BioIn 4, –9, CamGEL, CamGLE, CasWL, ConAu 104, DcIrB 88, DcIrW 1, EvLB, PenC ENG, PoIre, TwCA SUP*

O'Green, Jennifer *SmATA 72*

O'Green, Jennifer Roberson
Main entry: Roberson, Jennifer

O'Hagan, Caroline 1946- *BioIn 15, ConAu 111, SmATA 38*

O'Hanlon, Jacklyn *ConAu X, SmATA X*
Main entry: Meek, Jacklyn O'Hanlon

O'Hara, Mary *MajAI*
Main entry: Alsop, Mary O'Hara

O'Hara, Mary 1885- *HalFC 88*

O'Hara, Mary 1885-1980 *AmAu&B, AmNov, AnObit 1980, Benet 87, BenetAL 91, BioIn 14, CathA 1952, ConAu X, CurBio 44, –81N, HalFC 84, OxCChiL, REn, REnAL, SmATA 2, –X, TwCA SUP, TwCChW 78, –83, –89, TwCWW 91, WhAm 7, WhoAm 74, –76, –78, –80, WhoAmW 74, WorAl, WrDr 80, –82*

O'Harris, Pixie
Main entry: Pratt, Rhona Olive

O'Harris, Pixie 1903- *AuWomWr, IntAu&W 77X, –82X, OxCAusL, SingR 1*

O Henry *AuBYP 2S, DcAmSR, OxCAmL 83, OxCEng 85*
Main entry: Porter, William Sydney

Ohlsson, Ib 1935- *BioIn 8, –10, –12, ChhPo S1, –S2, IlsBYP, IlsCB 1957, –1967, SmATA 7*

Ohtomo, Yasuo 1946- *BioIn 15, SmATA 37*

O'Kane, Dick *AuBYP 2S, –3*

O'Keefe, Adelaide *OxCChiL*

O'Kelley, Mattie Lou *BioIn 14*

O'Kelley, Mattie Lou 1908- *BioIn 12, –13, ConAu 116, SmATA 36, WhoAmA 80, –82*

Okimoto, Jean Davies 1942- *BioIn 14, ConAu 97, –16NR, –37NR, SmATA 34, TwCYAW*

Okoro, Anezi *OxCChiL*

Okoro, Anezi 1929- *TwCChW 89, WrDr 90, –92, –94*

Okun, Milt 1923- *EncFCWM 69*

Okun, Milton H *BiDrAPA 89*

Olaizola, Jose Luis *TwCChW 89B*

Olatunji, Michael Babatunde *AuBYP 2, –2S, –3, BiDAfM, BioIn 8, –9, DrBlPA 90, InB&W 80*

Olatunji, Michael Babatunde 1927- *BioIn 14, InB&W 85*

Olcheski, Bill 1925- *ConAu 61, –8NR*

Olcott, Frances Jenkins 1872?-1963 *AmAu&B, AuBYP 2S, –3, BenetAL 91, BioIn 2, –6, –12, JBA 34, –51, REnAL, SmATA 19*

Olcott, Henry Steel 1832-1907 *Alli, –SUP, AmAu&B, BiDPara, BioIn 4, –8, –9, ConAu 118, DcAmReB 2, DcNAA, EncO&P 1, –2, –3, EncPaPR 91, OhA&B, WhAm 1, WorAlBi, WorAl*

Olcott, Virginia *AmAu&B, AmWomPl, BioIn 2, JBA 34, –51*

Old Boy *SmATA X*
Main entry: Hughes, Thomas

Old Boy, An
Main entry: Reed, Talbot Baines

Oldden, Richard *IlsBYP*

Olden, Sam *AuBYP 2, –3, BioIn 7*

Oldenburg, E William 1936-1974 *BioIn 14, ConAu 105, MichAu 80, SmATA 35*

Old Fag *ConAu X, SmATA X*

Oldfield, Margaret J 1932- *BioIn 16, SmATA 56*

Oldfield, Pamela 1931- *ScF&FL 92, TwCChW 89, TwCRHW 90, WrDr 90, –92, –94*

Oldham, June *SmATA 70*

Oldham, Mary 1944- *BioIn 17, ConAu 109, SmATA 65*

Oldrin, John 1901- *AuBYP 2, –3, BioIn 7*

Olds, Elizabeth d1991 *NewYTBS 91*

Olds, Elizabeth 1896?- *AfroAA, AmAu&B, ArtsAmW 3, AuBYP 2, –3, BioIn 5, –7, –8, –9, ConAu 5R, DcWomA, IlsCB 1946, –1957, SmATA 3, WhAmArt 85, WhoAm 74, –80, –82, –84, –86, –88, WhoAmA 73, –78, –80, –82, –84, –86, –89, WhoAmW 74*

Olds, Elizabeth 1896-1991 *BioIn 17, ConAu 133, SmATA 66, WhAm 10*

Olds, Helen 1895-1981 *AuBYP 3*

Olds, Helen Diehl 1895-1981 *AuBYP 2, BioIn 7, –11, ConAu 1R, –103, –3NR, ForWC 70, OhA&B, SmATA 9, –25N*

Oldstyle, Jonathan *AmAu&B, BenetAL 91, CnDAL, DcEnL, OxCAmL 65, –83, REn, YABC X*
Main entry: Irving, Washington

O'Leary, Brian T 1940- *WhoSpc, WhoTech 84*

O'Leary, Brian Todd 1940- *AmMWSc 73P, –76P, –82, –86, –89, –92, BioIn 9, –10, ConAu 33R, SmATA 6, WhoAm 74, –76, –78, –80, –82, WhoE 74, WhoTech 82, WrDr 76, –80*

O'Leary, Frank 1922- *AuBYP 2S, –3, ConAu 5R*

Oleksy, Walter 1930- *ConAu 45, –1NR, –17NR, SmATA 33*
Pseud./variant:
Olesky, Walter

Oleksy, Walter G 1930- *AuBYP 3, BioIn 14*

Olesker, J Bradford 1949- *BioIn 10, ScF&FL 92*

Olesky, Walter *SmATA X*
Main entry: Oleksy, Walter

Oleson, Claire *AuBYP 2S, –3*

Olfson, Lewy 1937- *ConAu 93, NatPD 77, ScF&FL 92*

O'Lincoln, Robert *Alli, –SUP, CarSB, DcNAA*
Main entry: Mason, George Champlin

Oliver, Burton *AuBYP 3*

Oliver, Jane *AuBYP 2, –3, Au&Wr 71, ChhPo, ConAu X*
Main entry: Rees, Helen Christina Easson

Oliver, Jane 1903-1970 *ScF&FL 92*

Oliver, John E 1933- *WrDr 86, –88, –90, –92*

Oliver, John Edward 1933- *AmMWSc 73S, –76P, –86, –89, –92, BioIn 12, ConAu 33R, IntAu&W 86, –91, SmATA 21, WhoMW 86, WrDr 76, –80, –82, –84, –94*

Oliver, Mark *ConAu X, IntAu&W 77X, –91X, WrDr 76, –80, –82, –84, –86, –88, –90, –92*
Main entry: Tyler-Whittle, Michael Sidney

Oliver, Mark 1927- *WrDr 94*

Oliver, Roland Anthony 1923- *Au&Wr 71, BlueB 76, ConAu 73, –12NR, IntAu&W 82, –86, –91, IntWW 74, –75, –76, –77, –78, Who 74, –82, –83, –85, –88, WhoWor 84, –87, –89, –91, WrDr 76, –80, –82, –84, –86, –88, –90, –92, –94*

Oliver, Rupert *AuBYP 3*

Oliver, Shirley Louise Dawkins 1958- *SmATA 74*

Oliver Optic *BioIn 13, OxCChiL*

Ollivant, Alfred 1874-1927 *BiD&SB, CarSB, JBA 34, LongCTC, NewC, REn, ScFEYrs, StaCVF, TwCA, TwCChW 83, –89*

Olmsted, Lorena Ann 1890- *BioIn 11, ConAu 29R, SmATA 13*

Olmsted, Robert W 1936- *WrDr 86, –88, –90, –92*

Olmsted, Robert Walsh 1936- *ConAu 41R, IntAu&W 86, WhoE 93, WhoMW 76, WhoUSWr 88, WhoWrEP 89, –92, WrDr 76, –80, –82, –84, –94*

Olney, Ross R 1929- *AuBYP 3, IntAu&W 91, WrDr 88, –90, –92*

Olney, Ross Robert 1929- *AuBYP 2, BioIn 11, ConAu 13R, –7NR, IntAu&W 77, –82, SmATA 13, WhoWest 76, –78, WrDr 76, –80, –82, –84, –86, –94*

Olschewski, Alfred Erich 1920- *BioIn 10, ConAu 41R, IntAu&W 77, SmATA 7*

Olsen, Einar Arthur 1917- *WhoAm 76, –78, –80, –82, –84, –86, –88*

Olsen, Einar Arthur 1917-1985 *WhAm 10*

Olsen, Ib Spang 1921- *BioIn 8, –9, –10, ConAu 49, –3NR, –37NR, IlsCB 1957, –1967, MajAI, OxCChiL, SmATA 6, ThrBJA*
Pseud./variant:
Detine, Padre
Spang Olsen, Ib

Olsen, Violet 1922- *SmATA 58*

Olsen, Violet 1922-1991 *ConAu 134*

Olsen, Violet Mae 1922- *IntAu&W 86*

Olson, Arielle North *BioIn 17*

Olson, Arielle North 1932- *ConAu 134, SmATA 67, WrDr 94*

Olson, David F 1938- *ConAu 49*

Olson, Eugene E *ScF&FL 92*

Olson, Eugene E 1936- *ConAu 33R, UFOEn*
Pseud./variant:
Steiger, Brad

Olson, Gene 1922- *AuBYP 2, –3, BioIn 7, ConAu 106, SmATA 32*

Olson, Helen Kronberg *BioIn 16, SmATA 48*

Olugebefola, Ademola *BioIn 14, WhoBlA 85, –88, –90*

Olugebefola, Ademola 1941- *AfroAA, AmArt, BioIn 12, BroadAu, IlsBYP, InB&W 80, SmATA 15, WhoAmA 78, –80, –82, –84, WhoBlA 75, –77, –80, –85, –92, –94, WhoE 75, –77, –86*

Om *SmATA 70*
Main entry: Gorey, Edward St. John

O'Malley, Mary Dolling 1889-1974 *BioIn 3, –4, –8, –14, –16, ConAu 65, LongCTC*

O'Malley, Patricia *AuBYP 2, –3, BioIn 7*

Oman, Carola 1897-1978 *Au&Wr 71, BioIn 10, –14, ConAu 5R, –4NR, EvLB, FemiCLE, LongCTC, OxCChiL, SmATA 35, TwCChW 78, TwCRHW 90, Who 74, WorAu 1950, WrDr 80*
Pseud./variant:
Lenanton, C

O'Meara, Walter d1989 *NewYTBS 89*

O'Meara, Walter 1897- *AmAu&B, Au&Wr 71, BioIn 1, –4, –5, –6, –10, ConAu 13R, CurBio 58, MinnWr, WhoAm 74*

O'Meara, Walter 1897-1989 *BioIn 16, –17, ConAu 129, CurBio 89N, ScF&FL 92*

O'Meara, Walter A 1897-1989 *SmATA 65*

O'Meara, Walter Andrew 1897-1989 *WhAm 10*

Ommanney, Francis Downes 1903-1980 *BioIn 7, –13, ConAu 13R, –101, –7NR, SmATA 23, WrDr 80, –82, –84*

O Mude *SmATA X*
Main entry: Gorey, Edward St John

Onadipe, Kola *ConAu 101, DcChlFi, OxCChiL, TwCChW 78, WrDr 82, –84*

Oncken, Clara *AuBYP 2, –3, BioIn 8*

Ondaatje, Christopher *BioIn 16*

Ondaatje, Christopher 1933- *ConAu 49, WhoAm 80, –82, –84, WrDr 76, –80, –82, –84*

Ondaatje, Michael *IntvTCA 2*

Ondaatje, Michael 1943- *BenetAL 91, BioIn 11, –13, –16, –17, CamGLE, CaW, CanWW 70, –79, –80, –81, –83, –89, ConAu 77, ConLC 29, –51, ConNov 91, ConPo 70, –75, –80, –85, –91, CurBio 93, DcLB 60, IntAu&W 82, –91, IntWW 89, –91, LiExTwC, OxCCan SUP, OxCCanL, RAdv 13-1, WhoAm 82, –84, –86, –88, –94, WhoCanL 85, –87, –92, WhoWrEP 89, WorAu 1975, WrDr 76, –80, –82, –84, –86, –88, –90, –92*

Oneal, Elizabeth 1934- *BioIn 14, –15, –16, ConAu 106, –28NR, IntAu&W 91, MajAI, SmATA 30, WrDr 86, –88, –90, –92, –94*
Pseud./variant:
Oneal, Zibby

Oneal, Zibby *ConAu 28NR, MajAI, WrDr 92*
Main entry: Oneal, Elizabeth

Oneal, Zibby 1934- *Au&Arts 5, BioIn 14, –15, –16, ChLR 13, ConAu X, ConLC 30, DcAmChF 1960, –1985, SixBJA, SmATA X, TwCChW 89, TwCYAW, WrDr 94*

O'Neill, David P 1918- *ConAu 17R*

O'Neill, Gerard K d1992 *NewYTBS 92*

O'Neill, Gerard K 1927- *ConAu 21NR, SmATA 65*

O'Neill, Gerard Kitchen 1927- *AmMWSc 86 –89, WhoAm 86, –88, WhoE 91, WhoWor 87, –91, WhoWrEP 92*

O'Neill, Gerard Kitchen 1927-1992 *ConAu 137, CurBio 92N, WhAm 10*

O'Neill, Hester 1908- *AuBYP 3, BioIn 7*

O'Neill, Judith 1930- *BioIn 14, ConAu 109, –26NR, SmATA 34, TwCChW 89, WrDr 90, –92*

O'Neill, Judith Beatrice 1930- *TwCYAW*

O'Neill, Judith Lyall 1930- *WrDr 94*

O'Neill, Mary d1990 *NewYTBS 90*

O'Neill, Mary 1908- *AuBYP 2, BioIn 7, –9, BkCL, ChhPo, ConAu 5R, ForWC 70, SmATA 2, ThrBJA*

O'Neill, Mary L 1908?-1990 *ConAu 130, SmATA 64*

O'Neill, Mary le Duc 1908-1990 *AuBYP 3, BioIn 16, –17*

O'Neill, Rose 1875-1944 *ObitOF 79, OxCChiL, WhAmArt 85*

O'Neill, Rose Cecil 1874-1944 *BioAmW*

Ongaro, Alberto 1925- *ConAu 25R*

Ono, Chiyo 1941- *ConAu 29R, –12NR*

Onslow, John 1906-1985 *BioIn 16, ConAu 118, SmATA 47N*

Oosterman, Gordon 1927- *ConAu 49, LEduc 74*

Opdycke, John Baker 1878-1956 *AmAu&B, BioIn 4, WhAm 3*

Opgenoorth, Winfried 1939- *BioIn 16, SmATA 50*

Opie, Iona *InWom SUP*

Opie, Iona 1923- *AnCL, Au&Wr 71, BioIn 9, –13, CamGLE, ChhPo, –S1, –S2, ConAu 61, IntAu&W 77, –91, NewYTBE 73, OxCChiL, SmATA 3, –63, –6AS, WrDr 76, –80, –82, –84, –86, –88, –90, –92, –94*

Opie, Peter d1982 *BioIn 17*

Opie, Peter 1918-1982 *AnObit 1982, AnCL, Au&Wr 71, BioIn 9, –13, CamGLE, ChhPo, –S1, –S2, ConAu 5R, –106, –2NR, IntAu&W 77, –82, NewYTBE 73, OxCChiL, OxCEng 85, SmATA 3, –28N, –63, Who 82, WrDr 76, –80, –82*

Opie, Peter Mason 1918-1982 *DcNaB 1981*

Oppenheim, Edward Phillips
Main entry: Partridge, Anthony

Oppenheim, Edward Phillips 1866-1946 *Alli SUP, BioIn 1, –4, –5, –14, CorpD, DcLEL, DcNaB 1941, EncMys, EvLB, LongCTC, NewC, ObitOF 79, REn, TwCA, –SUP, TwCWr, WhoLA*

Oppenheim, Joanne 1934- *BioIn 10, ConAu 21R, –9NR, –25NR, SmATA 5*

Oppenheim, Shulamith Levey 1930- *ConAu 73*

Oppenheimer, Joan L 1925- *BioIn 13, ConAu 37R, –17NR, IntAu&W 82, SmATA 28*

Oppenheimer, Lillian *AuBYP 2, –3, BioIn 8*

Oppenheimer, Lillian 1898- *InWom SUP*

Oppenheimer, Lillian V d1992 *NewYTBS 92*

Opper, Frederick Burr 1857-1937 *Alli SUP, AmAu&B, ArtCS, AuNews 1, BenetAL 91, BioIn 4, –6, –10, –12, –13, –15, ChhPo, DcNAA, EncACom, EncAJ, OhA&B, REnAL, WhAm 1, WhAmArt 85, WhJnl, WhNAA*

Optic, Oliver *AmAu, AmAu&B, BenetAL 91, BiD&SB, ChhPo, –S2, CnDAL, ConAu X, DcAmAu, DcEnL, DcNAA, MajAI, OxCAmL 65, –83, OxCChiL, REnAL, SmATA 67, –X, WebAB 74, –79, WhAm HS*
Main entry: Adams, William Taylor
Stratemeyer, Edward L

Optic, Oliver 1822-1897 *Benet 87, BioIn 15*

Oram, Hiawyn *BioIn 16*

Oram, Hiawyn 1946- *SmATA 56*

Orbaan, Albert F 1913- *BioIn 5, ConAu 5R, –8NR, IlsBYP, IlsCB 1946*

Orbach, Ruth Gary 1941- *ConAu 65, SmATA 21*

Orczy, Emmuska 1865-1947 *AuBYP 3, BioIn 16, InWom SUP, ScFEYrs*

Orczy, Emmuska, Baroness *WomNov*

Orczy, Emmuska, Baroness 1865- *DcVicP 2*

Orczy, Emmuska, Baroness 1865-1947 *ArtclWW 2, AuBYP 2, BioIn 1, –4, –5, –8, –14, –15, ConAu 104, –X, DcLEL, DcNaB 1941, DcVicP 2, EncMys, EvLB, LongCTC, NewC, NotNAT B, OxCChiL, REn, SmATA 40, TelT, TwCA, –SUP, TwCWr, WhoLA*

Ord, Marion *WrDr 76, –80, –82*

O'Reilly, Bernard *DcChlFi*

O'Reilly, John 1906- *AuBYP 2, –3, BioIn 1, –7*

O'Reilly, Sean
Main entry: Deegan, Paul Joseph

Orgel, Doris 1929- *AuBYP 2, –3, AuNews 1, BioIn 8, –10, ConAu 45, –2NR, DcAmChF 1960, FourBJA, IntAu&W 91, SmATA 7, TwCChW 78, –83, –89, TwCYAW, WrDr 84, –86, –88, –90, –92, –94*
Pseud./variant:
Adelberg, Doris

Orgill, Michael 1946- *ConAu 61*

Oriolo, Joe 1913-1985
Main entry: Oriolo, Joseph

Oriolo, Joseph 1913- *IntMPA 86*

Oriolo, Joseph 1913-1985 *SmATA 46N*
Pseud./variant:
Oriolo, Joe

Orleans, Ilo 1897-1962 *BioIn 6, –11, BkCL, ChhPo, –S1, –S2, ConAu 1R, –15NR, SmATA 10*

Orlev, Uri 1931- *BioIn 16, ChlLR 30, ConAu 34NR, SmATA 58, TwCYAW*

Orlob, Helen Seaburg 1908- *AuBYP 2S, -3, ConAu 5R, WhoPNW*

Ormai, Stella *SmATA 48, -57*

Ormerod, Jan 1946- *AuBYP 3, ChlBIID, ChlLR 20, ConAu 113, -35NR, SixBJA, SmATA 44, -55*

Ormerod, Janette Louise 1946- *MajAI, SmATA 70*

Ormes, Jackie
Main entry: Ormes, Zelda J

Ormes, Zelda J 1914-1986 *ConAu 118, SmATA 47N*
Pseud./variant:
Ormes, Jackie

Ormondroyd, Edward 1925- *AuBYP 2, -3, BioIn 8, -9, -12, ConAu 73, DcAmChF 1960, ScF&FL 92, SmATA 14, ThrBJA, TwCChW 78, -83, -89, WrDr 82, -84, -86, -88, -90, -92, -94*

Ormsby, Robert John 1936- *DrAS 74F*

Ormsby, Virginia H *BioIn 11, ConAu 9R, ForWC 70, SmATA 11*

Orr, Jack *AuBYP 2S, -3*

Orr, Katherine Shelley 1950- *SmATA 72*

Orr, Munro Scott 1874- *BioIn 1, IlsCB 1744*

Orr, Robert Thomas 1908- *AmMWSc 73P, -76P, -82, -86, -89, -92, ConAu 33R, WhoAm 74, -76, -78, -80, -82, -84, -86, -88, -90, WhoWest 74, -76*

Orr, William A *IlsBYP*

Orris *BlmGWL, SmATA X*
Main entry: Ingelow, Jean

Orrmont, Arthur 1922- *AuBYP 2S, -3, ConAu 1R, -4NR, -35NR, WhoE 77, WhoUSWr 88, WhoWrEP 89, -92*

Orth, Richard *ConAu X, ScF&FL 92, SmATA X*
Main entry: Gardner, Richard M

Ortiz, Victoria 1942- *ConAu 107*

Orton, Helen 1872- *AuBYP 3*

Orton, Helen Fuller 1872-1955 *AmAu&B, AuBYP 2, BioIn 2, -3, -4, -7, CarSB, ChhPo S2, CurBio 41, -55, JBA 34, -51, ObitOF 79, WhAm 3*

Orwell, George *ConAu 132, MajTwCW*
Main entry: Blair, Eric Arthur

Orwell, George 1903-1950 *AtlBL, Benet 87, BioIn 1, -2, -3, -4, -5, -6, -7, -8, -9, -10, -11, -12, -13, -14, -15, -17, BlmGEL, BritWr 7, CamGEL, CamGLE, CasWL, CnDBLB 7, CnMWL, ConAu X, CyWA 58, -89, DcAmSR, DcLB 15, -98, DcLEL, DcNaB 1941, DcTwHis, EncSF 93, EncWL, -2, EvLB, GrBr, HalFC 84, -88, LongCEL, LongCTC, MagSWL, MakMC, McGEWB, ModBrL, -S1, -S2, NewC, NewEScF, NewYTBE 72, Novels, ObitOF 79, OxCEng 67, -85, PenC ENG, RAdv 1, -13-1, REn, RGTwCSF, RfGEnL 91, ScF&FL 92, ScFSB, SmATA X, ThTwC 87, TwCA, -SUP, TwCLC 2, -6, -15, -31, -51, TwCSFW 86, -91, TwCWr, TwCYAW, WebE&AL, WhDW, WhAm 4, WhoSciF, WhoTwCL, WorAlBi, WorAl, WorLitC*

Orwin, Joanna *DcChlFi*

Osborn, Lois D 1915- *SmATA 61*

Osborn, Merton B 1908- *ConAu 25R*

Osborn, Robert Chesley 1904- *AmAu&B, BioIn 1, -3, -5, -7, -8, -12, ConAu 13R, CurBio 59, IlsBYP, IlsCB 1957, WhAmArt 85, WhoAm 74, -76, -78, -80, -82, -86, -88, -90, -92, -94, WhoAmA 73, -78, WhoE 86, -93, WhoGrA 62, -82*

Osborn, Yotty *OxCChiL*

Osborne, Charles 1927- *BioIn 16, ConAu 34NR, IntAu&W 89, -91, IntWWM 90, SmATA 59, Who 88, -90, -92, WrDr 86, -88, -90, -92, -94*

Osborne, Chester G 1915- *ConAu 35NR*

Osborne, Chester Gorham 1915- *BioIn 11, ConAu 21R, -9NR, IntAu&W 82, -86, IntWWM 85, SmATA 11, WhoE 74, -75, WrDr 76, -80, -82, -84*

Osborne, David *AuBYP 2, -3, ConAu X, -36NR, DcLEL 1940, EncSF 93, MajAI, MajTwCW, SmATA X, ThrBJA, TwCSFW 86, -91, WrDr 84*
Main entry: Silverberg, Robert

Osborne, Dorothy Gladys Yeo 1917- *Au&Wr 71, ConAu 9R, WrDr 76, -80*

Osborne, George *MajAI*

Osborne, John Franklin 1907- *BioIn 8, -9, ConAu 61, WhoAm 74, -76, -78*

Osborne, Juanita Tyree 1916- *ConAu 61, -8NR, -23NR*

Osborne, Leone Neal 1914- *BioIn 9, ConAu 21R, SmATA 2*

Osborne, Linda Barrett 1949- *ConAu 65*

Osborne, Mary Pope 1949- *BioIn 15, –16, ConAu 111, –29NR, IntAu&W 86, –89, –91, ScF&FL 92, SmATA 41, –55*

Osborne, Walter D 1918-1975 *BioIn 9, NewYTBE 72*

Osceola *IntDcWB, MajTwCW, SmATA X*
Main entry: Blixen, Karen

Osceola 1800?-1838 *BenetAL 91*

Osceola 1803?-1838 *WhNaAH*

Osceola 1804-1838 *BioIn 14, –16, –17*

Osgood, M A, Mrs *Alli SUP, CarSB*

Osgood, William E 1926- *AuBYP 2, BiDrLUS 70, BioIn 15, ConAu 33R, SmATA 37, WhoLibS 55, –66*

Osgood, William Edward 1926- *AuBYP 3*

O'Shea, Pat *WrDr 90*

O'Shea, Pat 1931- *AuBYP 3, ChlLR 18, ScF&FL 92, TwCChW 89, WrDr 92*

O'Shea, Pat Shiels 1931- *WrDr 94*

Osmond, Edward 1900- *AuBYP 2, –3, Au&Wr 71, BioIn 5, –7, –10, –11, –12, –14, ConAu P-1, IlsCB 1946, –1967, SmATA 10, WhoArt 80, –82, –84*

Osmond, Laurie *Au&Wr 71, WrDr 76, –80, –82, –84, –86, –88*

Ossoli, Sarah M Fuller, Marchesa D' 1810-1850 *BioIn 14, –16*

Ossoli, Sarah Margaret, Marchesa D' 1810-1850 *AmWomWr, BioIn 1, –2, –3, –4, –5, –6, –7, –8, –9, –10, –11, –12, –13, CelCen, DcAmSR, SmATA 25*

Ossoli, Sarah Margaret Marchesa D' 1810-1850
Pseud./variant:
Fuller, Margaret

Ostendorf, Lloyd 1921- *AuBYP 3, BioIn 17, SmATA 65*

Ostendorf, Lloyd, Jr. 1921- *AuBYP 2, BioIn 8, ConAu 1R, –6NR, WhoAmA 73, –78, –80, –82, –84, –86, –89, –91*

Osterritter, John F 1923- *AuBYP 3*

Osterritter, John Ferdinand *AmMWSc 86*

Osterritter, John Ferdinand 1923- *AmMWSc 73P, –76P, –82, AuBYP 2S, ConAu 45*

Ostman, Lempi 1899- *BioIn 1, IlsCB 1744*

Ostrom, John H 1928- *AmMWSc 73P, –76P, –82, WhoAm 74, –76, –78, –80, –82, –84, –86, –88, –90, –92, –94*

Ostrom, John Harold 1928- *AmMWSc 86, –89, –92*

Otchis, Ethel 1920- *ConAu 13R, ForWC 70*

Otfinoski, Steven 1949- *BioIn 16, ScF&FL 92, SmATA 56*

Otis, James
Main entry: Kaler, James Otis

Otis, James 1848-1912 *Alli SUP, AmAu&B, BiD&SB, BioIn 15, DcAmAu, DcNAA, JBA 34, –51, OxCAmL 65, –83, OxCChiL, ScFEYrs, SmATA X, TwCChW 83A, –89A*

O'Toole, Thomas 1941- *SmATA 71*

O'Trigger, Lucius, Sir *SmATA X*
Main entry: Horne, Richard H

Ott, Virginia 1917- *ConAu 77*

Ottesen, Thea Tauber 1913- *ConAu 5R*
Pseud./variant:
Bank-Jensen, Thea

Ottley, Reginald *AuBYP 2S, –3, Au&Wr 71, FourBJA, OxCChiL, SmATA 26, TwCChW 78, WrDr 80, –82, –84*

Ottley, Reginald 1909-1985 *ChlLR 16*

Ottley, Reginald Leslie *DcChlFi*

Ottley, Reginald Leslie 1909-1985 *ConAu 34NR, MajAI*

Otto, Margaret 1909-1976 *AuBYP 3*

Otto, Margaret Glover 1909-1976 *AuBYP 2, BioIn 7, –14, ConAu 61, SmATA 30N*

Otto, Svend 1916- *BioIn 16, –17, SmATA 67*
Main entry: Soerensen, Svend Otto

Oughton, Frederick 1923- *ConAu 1R, –29NR, WhoWor 87*

Oughton, Jerrie 1937- *SmATA 76*

Ouida *BbD, BiD&SB, BritAu 19, CasWL, CelCen, Chambr 3, CyWA 58, DcBiA, DcEnA, –A, DcEnL, DcEuL, DcLB 18, DcLEL, DcNaB S2, EvLB, HalFC 84, HsB&A, IntDcWB, JBA 34, LongCTC, NewC, Novels,*

OxCChiL, OxCEng 67, –85, PenC ENG, SmATA X, TelT, WomNov
Main entry: DeLaRamee, Louise

Ouida 1839-1908 *ArtclWW 2, BlmGEL, BlmGWL, CamGEL, CamGLE, ContDcW 89, FemiCLE, HalFC 88, InWom SUP, RfGEnL 91, StaCVF, TwCLC 43*

Oursler, Fulton *BioIn 16*

Oursler, Fulton 1893-1952 *AmAu&B, AuBYP 2, –3, BenetAL 91, BioIn 1, –2, –3, –4, –6, –7, –8, –14, –17, CathA 1930, ConAu 108, CurBio 42, –52, DcCathB, DcSpL, EncAJ, NotNAT B, REn, REnAL, TwCA SUP, TwCCr&M 80, –85, WhAm 3, WhNAA*

Ousley, Odille 1896- *BioIn 11, ConAu P-1, SmATA 10*

Outcault, Richard F 1863-1928 *EncACom*

Outcault, Richard Felton 1863-1928 *ArtCS, BioIn 3, –15, –16, EncAJ, JrnUS, WebAB 79, WhAmArt 85*

Outcault, Richard Fenton 1863-1928 *BiDAmJo*

Outhwaite, Ida Rentoul 1889-1960 *OxCAusL, OxCChiL*

Overholser, Wayne D 1906- *AmAu&B, Au&Wr 71, BioIn 14, –16, ConAu 5R, –2NR, –16NR, DcAmChF 1960, EncFWF, IntAu&W 86, –91, TwCWW 91, WrDr 84, –86, –88, –90, –92, –94*

Overman, Michael 1920- *Au&Wr 71, ConAu 108, WrDr 76, –80, –82, –84, –86, –88*

Overton, Jenny 1942- *Au&Wr 71, BioIn 14, –16, ConAu 57, IntAu&W 77, SmATA 36, –52, TwCChW 78, –83, –89, WrDr 76, –80, –82, –84, –86, –88, –90, –92*

Overton, Jenny Margaret Mary 1942- *WrDr 94*

Overton, Robert *Alli SUP, ChhPo S1*

Ovington, Ray *AuBYP 2, –3, BioIn 8*

Owen, Annie 1949- *SmATA 75*

Owen, Benjamin Evan 1918- *IntAu&W 77, WrDr 76, –80, –82, –84*

Owen, Betty M *ScF&FL 92*

Owen, Betty Meek 1913- *ForWC 70*

Owen, Caroline Dale *OhA&B, WhNAA, WomNov, YABC X*
Main entry: Snedeker, Caroline Dale Parke

Owen, Clifford *ConAu X, –29NR, SmATA X*

Owen, Dilys *ConAu X, IntAu&W 86X, SmATA X*
Main entry: Gater, Dilys

Owen, Evan 1918-1984 *BioIn 15, ConAu 109, SmATA 38*

Owen, Frank 1893-1968 *BioIn 8, EncAB-A 40, ScFEYrs*

Owen, Gareth 1936- *ChlLR 31, SmATA 14AS, TwCChW 89, WrDr 90, –92*

Owen, Harold 1897- *BioIn 9, ChhPo S1, ConAu 13R, ObitT 1971*

Owen, Russell *AuBYP 3*

Owen, Russell 1889-1952 *AmAu&B, AuBYP 2, BioIn 2, –3, –7, ObitOF 79, REnAL, WhAm 3*

Owen, Ruth 1885- *AuBYP 3*

Owen, Ruth Bryan *AmWomPl*

Owen, Ruth Bryan 1885-1954 *AmAu&B, AmPolW 80A, –80C, AmWomWr, AuBYP 2, BiDrUSC 89, BioIn 17, ChhPo S1, CurBio 44, –54, DcAmDH 80, –89, InWom SUP, WhAmP, WhFla*
Pseud./variant:
Rohde, Ruth Bryan Owen

Owen, Tom *ConAu X, IntAu&W 82X, WrDr 84*
Main entry: Watts, Peter Christopher

Owen, Wilfred 1912- *AmMWSc 73S, ConAu 37R, –36NR, WhoFI 92, –94*

Owen, Will 1869-1957 *BioIn 14, DcBrAr 1, DcBrBI, ObitT 1951*

Owens, Gail 1939- *BioIn 12, –16, IlsCB 1967, SixBJA, SmATA 54*

Owens, Joan Llewelyn 1919- *ConAu 13R*

Owens, Richard Meredith 1944- *ConAu 61, –37NR*

Owens, Thelma 1905- *ConAu 69*
Pseud./variant:
Grafton, Ann

Oxenbury, Helen 1938- *AuBYP 3, BioIn 9, –12, –14, –15, –17, ChhPo S2, ChlLR 22, ConAu 25R, –35NR, IlsBYP, IlsCB 1967, MajAI, OxCChiL, SmATA 3, –68, ThrBJA*
Pseud./variant:
Burningham, Helen Oxenbury

Oxenham, Elsie J d1960 *ConAu X, OxCChiL, TwCChW 78, –83, –89*

Oxley, James Macdonald 1855-1907 *BiD&SB, DcLEL, DcNAA, OxCCan, OxCCanL, OxCChiL*

Oz, Frank *BioIn 17*

Oz, Frank 1944- *ConTFT 7, IntMPA 92, SmATA 60, WhoAm 94*

Oz, Frank Richard *WhoAm 86*

Ozer, Jerome S 1927- *BioIn 16, SmATA 59*

Ozer, Jerome Stanley 1927- *WhoE 93*

Ozmon, Howard A, Jr. 1929- *ConAu 25R, LEduc 74*

P

Paasche, Carol L 1937- *ConAu 5R*

Pabke, Marie *Alli SUP, CarSB*

Pace, Mildred Mastin 1907- *AuBYP 2S, -3, BioIn 13, -15, ConAu 5R, -5NR, SmATA 29, -46*

Pachter, Hedwig d1988 *BioIn 17, SmATA 63*

Pack, Janet 1952- *SmATA 77*

Pack, Janet Elaine 1952- *WhoWrEP 89, -92*

Pack, Robert *DrAPF 87, -89, -91, -93, IntvTCA 2*

Pack, Robert 1929- *AmAu&B, AuBYP 2, -3, BenetAL 91, BioIn 8, -10, -12, -13, ChhPo, ConAu 1R, -3NR, ConLC 13, ConPo 70, -75, -80, -85, -91, DcLB 5, DrAP 75, DrAPF 83, -85, OxCAmL 83, PenC AM, REnAL, WorAu 1950, WrDr 76, -80, -82, -84, -86, -88, -90, -92, -94*

Pack, Robert M 1929- *WhoWrEP 92*

Packard, Andrew 1929- *ConAu 1R*

Packard, Edward 1931- *BioIn 16, ConAu 114, ScF&FL 92, SmATA 47*

Packard, Frank L 1877-1942 *ScFEYrs, TwCCr&M 91*

Packard, Frank Lucius 1877-1942 *AmAu&B, AmLY, BioIn 1, -14, CanNov, CanWr, CreCan 2, CurBio 42, DcLEL, DcNAA, EncMys, NewC, ObitOF 79, OxCCan, TwCA, -SUP, TwCCr&M 85, WhAm 2*

Packard, Pearl *OxCCan SUP*

Packer, Joy 1905-1977 *AuBYP 2, -3, Au&Wr 71, BioIn 2, -8, -10, BlmGWL, ConAu 1R, -3NR, DcLEL 1940, EncSoA, IntAu&W 77, TwCWr, Who 74, WrDr 76*

Packer, Vin *BioIn 12, -17, ConAu X, -37NR, MajAI, MajTwCW, SmATA X, TwCYAW*
Main entry: Meaker, Marijane

Packer, Vin 1927- *SmATA X*

Pad, Peter *MajAI*

Padgett, James *AfroAA*

Padgett, James A 1948- *WhoBlA 85, -90, -94*

Page, Eileen *ConAu X, SmATA 7*
Main entry: Heal, Edith

Page, Eleanor *AuBYP 2S, -3, ConAu X, IntAu&W 91X, MajAI, SmATA 1, -67, WhoAm 82, -84, -86, -88, -90, WhoAmW 74, -81, WhoMW 76, -78, -80*
Main entry: Coerr, Eleanor Beatrice

Page, Grover, Jr. 1918- *ConAu 17R*

Page, Lou 1912- *AuBYP 3*

Page, Lou Williams 1912- *AuBYP 2, BioIn 5, ConAu 5R, -5NR, SmATA 38*

Page, Robert Joseph Douglas 1940- *DrAS 74H, -82H*

Page, Thomas Nelson 1853-1922 *Alli SUP, AmAu, AmAu&B, AmLY, Benet 87, BenetAL 91, BbD, BiDSA, BiD&SB, BioIn 1, -3, -5, -6, -8, -9, -12, -13, -16, CamGEL, CamGLE, CamHAL, CarSB, CasWL, Chambr 3, ChhPo, CnDAL, ConAu 118, CyWA 58, DcAmAu, DcAmDH 80, -89, DcBiA, DcLB 12, -78, DcLEL, DcNAA, EncSoH, FifSWrB, HarEnUS, JBA 34, McGEWB, Novels, OxCAmL 65, -83, OxCChiL, PenC AM, REn, REnAL, RfGAmL 87, Str&VC, WebE&AL, WhAm 1*

Pagels, Elaine Hiesey *WhoAm 90, -92, -94, WhoRel 92*

Pagels, Elaine Hiesey 1943- *ConAu 45, -2NR, -24NR, DrAS 74P, -78P, -82P, WhoAm 80, -82, -84, -88, WhoAmW 77, -81, -83, -85, -87, -89, WhoRel 75, -77, WhoUSWr 88, WhoWrEP 89, -92*

Paget, Francis Edward 1806-1882 *Alli, -SUP, BiD&SB, BioIn 8, BritAu 19, DcNaB, OxCChiL, TelT, WhoChL*

Pseud./variant:
Churne, William

Paget, H M, Mrs *DcVicP 2*

Paget, Stephen 1855-1926 *DcNaB 1922*

Paget, Walter *ClaDrA, DcVicP 2*

Paget, Walter 1863-1935 *BioIn 14*

Paget-Fredericks, Joseph E P Rous-Marten 1903?-1963 *BioIn 14*

Paget-Fredericks, Joseph E P Rous-Marten 1905?-1963 *BioIn 5, ChhPo, ConICB, IlsBYP, IlsCB 1946, SmATA 30, Str&VC*

Pahl, Aleta *AuBYP 2S, –3*

Pahz, Cheryl Suzanne 1949- *BioIn 11, ConAu X, –8NR, MichAu 80, SmATA 11, WhoAmW 77*
Pseud./variant:
Goldfeder, Cheryl
Paz, Zan

Pahz, James Alon 1943- *BioIn 11, ConAu X, –8NR, IntAu&W 77, SmATA 11*
Pseud./variant:
Goldfeder, James
Goldfeder, Jim
Paz, A

Paice, Margaret 1920- *AuWomWr, BioIn 11, ConAu 29R, –20NR, IntAu&W 82, SingR 1, SmATA 10*

Paige, Harry W 1922- *BioIn 14, –15, ConAu 113, –32NR, SmATA 35, –41*

Pain, Allison George Odell *ChhPo*

Pain, Barry Eric Odell 1864-1928 *BbD, Chambr 3, ChhPo, DcEnA A, DcLEL, DcNaB 1922, EncMys, EvLB, LongCTC, NewC, OxCEng 67, REn, TwCA, WhoHr&F*

Paine, Albert B 1861-1937 *AuBYP 3*

Paine, Albert Bigelow 1861-1937 *AmAu&B, AuBYP 2S, BenetAL 91, BiD&SB, BioIn 4, CarSB, ChhPo, –S1, –S2, CnDAL, ConAu 108, DcAmAu, DcNAA, EncPaPR 91, EncSF 93, JBA 34, OxCAmL 65, –83, OxCChiL, REn, REnAL, ScFEYrs, TwCA, WhAm 1, WhNAA*

Paine, Ralph D 1871-1925 *BenetAL 91*

Paine, Ralph Delahaye 1871-1925 *AmAu&B, AmLY, BioIn 16, DcNAA, JBA 34, REnAL, TwCA, WhAm 1*

Paine, Roberta M 1925- *AuBYP 3*

Paine, Roberta Mary 1925- *AuBYP 2S, BioIn 11, ConAu 33R, SmATA 13, WhoAmW 75, –77*

Painter, Charlotte *DrAPF 87, –89, –91, InWom SUP, IntAu&W 86, –89, WhoUSWr 88, WhoWrEP 89, –92, WrDr 86, –88, –90, –92, –94*

Painter, Charlotte 1926- *BioIn 10, ConAu 1R, –3NR, DrAF 76, DrAPF 83, –85, ScF&FL 92, WhoAmW 75, WrDr 82, –84*

Painter, Sidney 1902-1960 *AmAu&B, BioIn 5, WhAm 3*

Paisley, Tom 1932- *BioIn 11, ConAu 61, –15NR, SmATA X, WhoEnt 92*
Pseud./variant:
Bethancourt, T Ernesto

Palazzo, Anthony D 1905-1970 *AuBYP 2, BioIn 5, –7, –8, –9, ChhPo, –S1, ConAu 5R, –29R, IlsCB 1946, –1957, –1967, SmATA 3, ThrBJA*

Palazzo, Tony 1905-1970 *AuBYP 3*

Palder, Edward L 1922- *BioIn 10, SmATA 5*

Palecek, Josef 1932- *BioIn 16, SmATA 56*

Paley, Alan L 1943- *ConAu 69, ScF&FL 92*

Palfrey, Sarah *AuBYP 2S, –3, BiDAmSp OS*
Main entry: Cooke, Sarah Fabyan

Palfrey, Sarah 1913?- *BioIn 14*

Palgrave, Francis Turner 1824-1897 *Alli, –SUP, BiD&SB, BioIn 2, –6, –9, –14, –16, BritAu 19, CamGEL, CamGLE, CasWL, CelCen, Chambr 3, ChhPo, –S1, –S2, DcBiPP, DcEnA, –A, DcEnL, DcEuL, DcLB 35, DcLEL, DcNaB S1, EvLB, NewC, OxCEng 67, –85, PenC ENG, REn, StaCVF, WebE&AL*

Palin, Michael 1943- *BioIn 17, ConAu 35NR, ConTFT 5, HalFC 88, IntMPA 88, –92, ScF&FL 92, SmATA 67, WhoCom, WrDr 92*
Pseud./variant:
Monty Python

Palin, Michael Edward 1943- *WrDr 94*

Palladini, David 1946- *BioIn 12, –14, –15, IlsCB 1967, SmATA 32, –40*

Palladini, David Mario 1946- *MajAI*

Pallas, Dorothy Constance 1933-1971 *Au&Wr 71, BioIn 9, ConAu 33R*

Pallas, Norvin 1918- *BioIn 13, ConAu 1R, –3NR, SmATA 23, WrDr 76, –80, –82, –84*

Pallenberg, Corrado 1912- *ConAu 13R*

Palliser, John 1807-1887 *Alli, BioIn 5, -8, DcBiPP, DcCanB 11, DcLEL, DcNaB, OxCCan*

Palliser, John 1817-1887 *Expl 93*

Pallister, John C 1891-1980 *BioIn 1, -5, -13, ConAu 103, SmATA 26N*

Palmer, Bernard 1914- *BioIn 13, ConAu 57, -7NR, -12NR, SmATA 26, TwCWW 91*
Pseud./variant:
Runyan, John

Palmer, Bruce Hamilton 1932- *AuBYP 2S, -3, ConAu 1R*

Palmer, C Everard 1930- *BioIn 16, BlkAuII, -92, BlkWr 1, OxCChiL, SelBAAf, TwCChW 83, -89, WrDr 82, -90, -92*

Palmer, Candida 1926- *BioIn 11, ConAu 61, SmATA 11*

Palmer, Cyril Everard 1930- *Au&Wr 71, BioIn 12, ConAu 41R, DcLEL 1940, InB&W 80, SmATA 14, TwCChW 78, WrDr 80, -84, -86, -88*

Palmer, Don *ConAu 134, MajAI, SmATA 65, WrDr 94*
Main entry: Benson, Mildred Augustine Wirt

Palmer, Edward Vance 1885-1959 *BioIn 5, CasWL, DcLEL*
Pseud./variant:
Palmer, Vance Edward

Palmer, Geoffrey *ChhPo S2*

Palmer, Hap 1942- *BioIn 17, ConAu 136, SmATA 68, WrDr 94*

Palmer, Heidi 1948- *BioIn 12, SmATA 15*

Palmer, Heidi Marie 1955- *WhoAmW 91*

Palmer, Helen G 1911- *SingR 1*

Palmer, Helen M *AmWomPl*

Palmer, Helen Marion
Main entry: Geisel, Helen

Palmer, Helen Marion 1898-1967 *AuBYP 2, -3, BioIn 8, -13, ConAu X, SmATA X*

Palmer, John Leslie *TwCCr&M 91*

Palmer, John Leslie 1885-1944 *BioIn 4, -14, CurBio 44, DcLEL, EncMys, EvLB, LongCTC, NewC, NotNAT B, ObitOF 79, TwCA, -SUP, TwCCr&M 80, -85, WhoSpyF*
Pseud./variant:
Beeding, Francis

Palmer, Juliette 1930- *BioIn 12, -14, ConAu 81, IlsBYP, IntAu&W 77, SmATA 15, WhoArt 82, -84, WrDr 76, -80, -82, -84, -86, -88, -90, -92, -94*

Palmer, Marjorie 1919- *ConAu 57*

Palmer, Raymond *AuBYP 2S, -3*

Palmer, Raymond A 1910-1977 *EncO&P 3 TwCSFW 86*

Palmer, Raymond A 1939- *WhoAm 92, -94*

Palmer, Robin 1911- *AuBYP 2, -3, BioIn 7 -15, ConAu 109, SmATA 43*

Palmer, Roy 1932- *ConAu 61, -8NR, -23NR*

Palmer, Vance Edward *BioIn 9, -10, -11, ChhPo, LongCTC, ModCmwL, PenC ENG, TwCWr*
Main entry: Palmer, Edward Vance

Palovic, Lora 1918- *AuBYP 2S, -3, ConAu 25R*

Paltenghi, Madeleine *ConAu X*
Main entry: Anderson, Madeleine Paltenghi

Paltrowitz, Donna 1950- *BioIn 16, -17, ConAu 119, ScF&FL 92, SmATA 50, -61*

Paltrowitz, Stuart 1946- *BioIn 16, -17, ConAu 118, ScF&FL 92, SmATA 50, -61*

Panati, Charles 1943- *BioIn 17, ScF&FL 92, SmATA 65*

Panesis, Nicholas 1913- *BioIn 1, IlsCB 1744*

Panetta, George 1915-1969 *AuBYP 2S, -3, BiE&WWA, BioIn 2, -8, -12, ConAu 81, NotNAT B, SmATA 15*

Pannell, Lucile *BioIn 1, -2*

Panova, V 1915- *AuBYP 3*

Panova, Vera 1905-1973 *EncCoWW, RAdv 13-2*

Panova, Vera Fedorovna 1905-1973 *BioIn 17, BlmGWL*

Panova, Vera Fyodorovna 1905-1973 *AuBYP 2S, Benet 87, BioIn 9, -10, CasWL, DcRusL, DcRusLS, EncWL, -2, EvEuW, HanRL, McGEWD 84, ModSL 1, ModWD, PenC EUR, REn, TwCWr, WorAu 1950*

Panowski, Eileen Thompson *AuBYP 3*

Panowski, Eileen Thompson 1920- *AuBYP 2, ConAu 5R, SmATA 49, WrDr 76, –80*
Pseud./variant:
Thompson, Eileen

Pansy *AmAu&B, AmLY X, BiD&SB, DcAmAu, DcNAA, InWom SUP, OhA&B, OxCAmL 65, –83, OxCChiL, WhAm 1, WomWWA 14, WomNov, YABC X*
Main entry: Alden, Isabella Macdonald

Pansy 1841-1930 *BioIn 15*

Pantell, Dora *ScF&FL 92*

Pantell, Dora 1915- *AuBYP 2S, ConAu 111, SmATA 39*

Pantell, Dora F *AuBYP 3*

Pantell, Dora F 1915- *BioIn 15*

Panter, Carol 1936- *AuBYP 2S, –3, BioIn 11, ConAu 49, SmATA 9*

Panting, Phyllis *ConAu X*

Panzarella, Andrew 1940- *ConAu 25R, WhoE 74*

Papajani, Janet *AuBYP 3*

Papas, William 1927- *BioIn 8, ConAu 25R, –12NR, IlsCB 1957, –1967, IntAu&W 91, SmATA 50, WrDr 76, –80, –82, –84, –86, –88, –90, –92, –94*

Papashvily, George 1898-1978 *AmAu&B, BioIn 4, –10, –11, –12, ConAu 77, –81, CurBio 45, –78N, REnAL, SmATA 17, TwCA SUP, WhoAmA 73, –78N, –80N, –82N, –86N, –89N, –91N*

Papashvily, Helen 1906- *AmAu&B, AmWomWr, BioIn 4, –10, –12, ConAu 81, CurBio 45, REnAL, SmATA 17, TwCA SUP*

Pape, Donna L 1930- *BioIn 9, SmATA 2*

Pape, Eric 1870-1938 *BioIn 3, ChhPo, ConICB, WhAm 1, WhAmArt 85*

Paperny, Myra 1932- *BioIn 13, –14, –16, ConAu 69, DcChlFi, OxCCanL, Profile 2, SmATA 33, –51, WhoCanL 85*

Papin, Joseph 1825-1862 *BbtC, DcCanB 9, IlsBYP*

Paradis, Adrian A 1912- *SmATA 67*

Paradis, Adrian Alexis 1912- *AuBYP 2, –3, BioIn 6, –7, –9, ConAu 1R, –3NR, –18NR, –40NR, IntAu&W 77, –86, –89, MorJA, SmATA 1, –8AS, WrDr 76, –80, –82, –84, –86, –88, –90, –92, –94*

Paradis, Marjorie Bartholomew *AmWomPl*

Paradis, Marjorie Bartholomew 1886?-1970 *AmAu&B, AuBYP 2, –3, BioIn 7, –9, –11, ConAu 29R, –73, SmATA 17, WhNAA*

Pardoe, M 1902- *OxCChiL, TwCChW 83, –89, WrDr 86, –88, –90, –92*

Pardoe, Margot Mary 1902- *WrDr 94*

Parenteau, Shirley 1935- *BioIn 15, –16, ScF&FL 92, SmATA 47*

Parenteau, Shirley Laurolyn 1935- *ConAu 85, –15NR, –33NR, SmATA 40, WhoAmW 77*

Pares, Marion Stapylton 1914- *Au&Wr 71, ConAu 17R, IntAu&W 82, –86*
Pseud./variant:
Campbell, Judith

Paris, Jeanne 1918- *ConAu 1R, WhoAm 74, –76, WhoAmA 73, WhoAmW 74, WhoE 74*

Paris, Jeanne C *WhoAmA 86, –91*

Paris, John 1912- *Who 74, –82, –83, –85*

Parish, James Robert *IntMPA 88, –92*

Parish, James Robert 1944- *ConAu 33R, –37NR, IntAu&W 82, WhoAm 74, –76, –78, –80, –82, –92, –94, WrDr 76, –80*

Parish, James Robert 1946- *ScF&FL 92*

Parish, Margaret Cecile *AuBYP 3*

Parish, Margaret Cecile 1927- *WhoAm 86, –88, WhoWor 87, –89*

Parish, Margaret Cecile 1927-1988 *ConAu 127, –38NR, MajAI, SmATA 73, WhAm 9*
Pseud./variant:
Parish, Peggy

Parish, Margaret Holt *AuBYP 2, WhoLibS 66*
Main entry: Holt, Margaret

Parish, Mary *AuBYP 3*

Parish, Peggy *ConAu 127, –38NR, IntAu&W 91, MajAI, SmATA 73, WrDr 86, –88*

Parish, Peggy d1988 *NewYTBS 88*

Parish, Peggy 1927- *AuBYP 2, BioIn 7, –12, ConAu 73, ForWC 70, FourBJA, OxCChiL, SmATA 17, TwCChW 78, –83, WrDr 80, –82, –84*

Parish, Peggy 1927-1988 *AuBYP 3, BioIn 16, ChlLR 22, SmATA 59, TwCChW 89*
Main entry: Parish, Margaret Cecile

Park, Barbara 1947- *AuBYP 3, ConAu 113, DcAmChF 1985, SixBJA, SmATA 35, –40*

Park, Bill *ConAu X, –39NR, SmATA X*
Main entry: Park, W B

Park, Ed 1930- *ConAu 73*

Park, Rosina Ruth 1922?- *DcChlFi*

Park, Rosina Ruth Lucia *ChlFicS, TwCYAW*

Park, Ruth *ArtclWW 2, Au&Wr 71, BioIn 3, –6, –13, –16, CathA 1952, ConAu 105, OxCAusL, OxCChiL, SingR 2, SixBJA, SmATA 25, TwCChW 78, –83, –89, TwCWr, WrDr 80, –82, –84, –86, –88, –90, –92*

Park, Ruth 1922- *FemiCLE*

Park, Ruth c. 1923- *BlmGWL, ScF&FL 92*

Park, Thomas Choonbai *AuBYP 3*

Park, Thomas Choonbai 1919- *AuBYP 2, BioIn 8, LEduc 74, WhoMW 82*

Park, W B 1936- *BioIn 13, –15, ConAu 97, –17NR, ConGrA 2, SmATA 22*
Pseud./variant:
Park, Bill

Park, William Bryan 1936- *ConAu 39NR*

Parke, Margaret Bittner *AuBYP 2, BioIn 7, WhoAmW 74, –75, –77*

Parke, Margaret Bittner 1901- *AuBYP 3*

Parker, Alfred Eustace *AuBYP 2, –3, BioIn 7*

Parker, Arthur C *EngPo*

Parker, Arthur C 1881-1955 *BioIn 16*

Parker, Arthur Caswell *BiNAW Sup*

Parker, Arthur Caswell 1881-1955 *AmAu&B, BenetAL 91, BiNAW Sup, –SupB, BioIn 3, –4, –11, –12, ConAu 115, ObitOF 79, REnAL, WhAm 3*

Parker, Bertha Morris 1890-1980 *AuBYP 2, –3, BioIn 6, –7, ConAu 5R, –102, –5NR, ForWC 70, MorJA, WhAm 7, WhoAm 74, –76, –78, WhoAmW 74, –75, –77*

Parker, Dorothy D 1927- *FourBJA*

Parker, Edgar 1925- *BioIn 8, –9, ChhPo, IlsCB 1957, ThrBJA*

Parker, Elinor Milnor 1906- *BioIn 9, ChhPo, ConAu 1R, –3NR, SmATA 3, WhoAm 74, –76, –78, –80, WhoAmW 81, –83, –85, –87, –89*

Parker, Eric 1870-1955 *BioIn 3, ChhPo, –S1, –S2, DcNaB 1951, ObitT 1951, StaCVF, WhoLA*

Parker, Eric R 1897?- *BioIn 8, WhoChL*

Parker, Fania M Pockrose *AuBYP 2, –3, BioIn 7*

Parker, Henry Webster 1822?-1903 *Alli, BiInAmS, CarSB, CyAL, DcAmAu, DcNAA, InSci*

Parker, James 1834- *Alli SUP*

Parker, John 1923- *BiDrLUS 70, ConAu 5R, –5NR, DrAS 74H, –78H, –82H, WhoLibS 55, –66*

Parker, Kate Langloh 1855-1940 *AnCL, OxCChiL*

Parker, Kay Peterson 1901- *BioIn 5, IlsCB 1946*

Parker, Kristy 1957- *BioIn 16, ConAu 126, SmATA 59*

Parker, Lewis *BioIn 13, Profile 2*

Parker, Lois M 1912- *ConAu 69, –11NR, SmATA 30*

Parker, Lois May 1912- *ConAu 39NR*

Parker, Margot M 1937- *ConAu 122, SmATA 52*

Parker, Mary Jessie 1948- *SmATA 71*

Parker, Nancy W 1930- *WrDr 88, –90, –92*

Parker, Nancy Winslow *BioIn 14, –17, ChlBIID*

Parker, Nancy Winslow 1930- *AuBYP 3, BioIn 11, –12, ConAu 49, –1NR, –22NR, ConGrA 3, FifBJA, IlsBYP, IlsCB 1967, IntAu&W 77, MajAI, SingR 2, SmATA 10, –69, WhoAm 84, –86, –88, –90, –92, –94, WhoAmA 78, –80, –82, –84, –86, –89, –91, WhoAmW 83, WhoUSWr 88, WhoWrEP 89, –92, WrDr 76, –80, –82, –84, –86, –94*

Parker, Richard 1915- *AuBYP 2, –3, BioIn 8, –12, ConAu 73, EncSF 93, IntAu&W 91, OxCChiL, SmATA 14, TwCChW 78, –83, –89, WrDr 76, –80, –82, –84, –86, –88, –90*

Parker, Robert *AuBYP 2S, –3, ConAu X, SmATA X*
Main entry: Boyd, Waldo T

Parker, Robert Andrew *ChlBIID*

Parker, Robert Andrew 1927- *BioIn 6, -7, -12, -14, ChhPo S2, DcCAA 71, -77, -88, FourBJA, IlrAm 1880, IlsBYP, IlsCB 1967, WhoAm 74, -76, -78, -80, -82, -84, -86, -88, -90, -92, -94, WhoAmA 73, -78, -80, -82, -84, -86, -89, -91*

Parker, Rosa Abbott *Alli, -SUP, CarSB, DcNAA*

Parker, W H 1912- *ConAu 33R, IntAu&W 89, WrDr 76, -80, -82, -84, -86, -88, -90, -92*

Parker, William Henry 1912- *WrDr 94*

Parkhill, John *SmATA X*
Main entry: Cox, William R

Parkinson, Cyril Northcote *NewYTBS 87*

Parkinson, Cyril Northcote 1909- *Au&Wr 71, BioIn 4, -5, -6, -7, -10, -11, -12, -15, BlueB 76, ConAu 5R, CurBio 60, IntAu&W 82, -89, -91, IntWW 74, -79, -80, -91, LongCTC, NewYTBE 71, RAdv 1, Who 74, -82, -83, -85, -88, -90, -92, WhoAm 74, -80, -82, -84, WhoWor 74, WorAu 1950, WrDr 76, -80, -82, -84, -86, -88, -90, -92*

Parkinson, Cyril Northcote 1909-1993 *WrDr 94N*

Parkinson, Ethelyn M 1906- *AuBYP 3*

Parkinson, Ethelyn Minerva 1906- *AuBYP 2S, BioIn 11, ConAu 49, -1NR, SmATA 11, WhoAm 74, -76, -78, -80, -82, -84, -86, -88, -90, -92, -94, WhoAmW 74*

Parkinson, Kathy 1954- *SmATA 71*

Parkinson, Roger 1939-1978 *Au&Wr 71, ConAu 106, IntAu&W 77*
Pseud./variant:
Holden, Matthew

Parkinson, Virginia *ChhPo S1*

Parkman, Francis 1823-1893 *Alli, -SUP, AmAu, AmAu&B, AmWr S2, AtlBL, Benet 87, BenetAL 91, BbD, BbtC, BiD&SB, BiInAmS, BioIn 1, -2, -3, -4, -5, -6, -7, -8, -9, -10, -11, -13, -14, -15, -16, -17, CamGEL, CamGLE, CamHAL, CasWL, Chambr 3, CyAL, CyWA 58, DcAmAu, DcCanB 12, DcLB 1, -30, DcLEL, DcNAA, Dis&D, EncAB-H, EncFWF, EvLB, HarEnUS, McGEWB, MemAm, MouLC 4, NinCLC 12, OxCAmH, OxCAmL 65, -83, OxCCan, OxCCanL, OxCEng 67, -85, PenC AM, RAdv 13-3, REn, REnAL, RfGAmL 87, WebAB 74, -79, WebE&AL, WhDW, WhAm HS, WhNaAH*

Parks, Aileen Wells 1901- *BioIn 7, ConAu 5R*

Parks, David 1944- *ConAu 25R, InB&W 80*

Parks, Edd Winfield 1906-1968 *AmAu&B, BioIn 7, -10, -11, ConAu 5R, ScF&FL 92, SmATA 10, WhAm 5*

Parks, Gordon *IntMPA 86, -88*

Parks, Gordon 1912- *AfrAmAl 6, AfroAA, AmArt, AmAu&B, AuNews 2, BiDAfM, BioIn 3, -4, -6, -7, -8, -9, -10, -11, -12, -13, BlkAWP, BlkLC, BlkWr 1, BlueB 76, CelR, ConAu 41R, -26NR, ConBlB 1, ConHero 2, ConLC 1, -16, ConPhot 82, -88, ConTFT 6, CurBio 68, -92, DcLB 33, DrBlPA 90, EncAJ, EncTwCJ, FilmgC, ICPEnP, InB&W 80, IntMPA 75, -76, -78, -81, -82, -84, -86, -92, -77, LivgBAA, MacBEP, NegAl 76, -83, -89, SelBAAf, SmATA 8, WhoAm 74, -80, -82, -84, WhoBlA 75, -80, -85, WhoE 74, WhoWor 74, -82, WrDr 76, -80, -82, -84, -86, -88, -90, -92*

Parks, Gordon 1925- *HalFC 88*

Parks, Gordon, Sr. 1912- *BlksAmF*

Parks, Gordon Alexander Buchanan 1912- *WrDr 94*

Parks, Lillian Rogers 1896?- *BioIn 5, -8, -11, InB&W 80*

Parks, Van Dyke 1943- *SmATA 62*

Parley, Peter *Alli, AmAu, AmAu&B, BenetAL 91, BiD&SB, BritAu 19, ChhPo, -S1, -S2, CyEd, DcAmAu, DcEnL, DcNaB, DcNAA, OxCAmH, OxCAmL 65, -83, OxCChiL, REn, REnAL, SmATA X, WebAB 74, -79, WhAm HS, WhoChL*
Main entry: Goodrich, Samuel Griswold

Parley, Peter 1793-1860 *BioIn 15, -17*

Parlin, John *AuBYP 2, -3, BioIn 8, -9, ConAu X, SmATA 4*
Main entry: Graves, Charles Parlin

Parma, Clemens *ConAu X, IntAu&W 77X, IntWWP 82X*
Main entry: Menzel, Roderick

Parnall, Peter *BioIn 14*

Parnall, Peter 1936- *BioIn 8, -9, -12, ChhPo S2, ConAu 81, IlsBYP, IlsCB 1957, -1967, MajAI, SmATA 16, -69, -11AS, ThrBJA, WhoAmA 78, -80, -82, -84, WhoE 81, -83*

Parr, Adolph Henry 1900- *AuBYP 2, -3, BioIn 8*

Parr, Harriet 1828-1900 *Alli, –SUP, BbD, DcEnL, DcNaB S1, InWom SUP, PoChrch, StaCVF, TelT*
Pseud./variant:
Lee, Holme

Parr, Letitia Evelyn 1906- *ConAu 103, SmATA 37, WrDr 76, –80, –82, –84, –86*

Parr, Lucy 1924- *BioIn 11, ConAu 29R, SmATA 10, WrDr 76*
Pseud./variant:
Carroll, Laura

Parrish, Anne 1760-1800 *InWom SUP*

Parrish, Anne 1888-1957 *AmAu&B, AmNov, BenetAL 91, BioIn 1, –2, –4, –5, –13, –14, CnDAL, ConAmL, ConAu 115, EvLB, IlsBYP, IlsCB 1744, –1946, InWom SUP, LongCTC, ObitOF 79, ObitT 1951, OxCAmL 65, –83, REnAL, SmATA 27, TwCA, –SUP, TwCChW 83, –89, TwCWr, WhAm 3, WhNAA*

Parrish, Mary *ConAu X, SmATA 2*
Main entry: Cousins, Margaret

Parrish, Mary Frances *ConAu 138, –X*
Main entry: Fisher, Mary Frances Kennedy

Parrish, Mary-Frances 1908-1992 *ConLC 76*

Parrish, Maxfield d1966 *WhoAmA 86N*

Parrish, Maxfield 1870-1966 *AmAu&B, BenetAL 91, BioIn 1, –2, –3, –5, –6, –7, –9, –10, –12, ChhPo, ConICB, CurBio 65, –66, DcAmB S8, DcBrBI, IlrAm 1880, –B, IlsBYP, IlsCB 1744, JBA 34, –51, OxCAmL 65, OxCChiL, REnAL, SmATA 14, WebAB 74, –79, WhAm 4, WhAmArt 85, WhoAmA 78N, –80N, –82N, –89N, –91N, WorAl, WorECar*

Parry, David Harold 1868-1950 *BioIn 8, WhoChL*

Parry, Edward Abbott, Sir 1863-1943 *OxCChiL*

Parry, Marian *DrAPF 87, –89, –91, –93*

Parry, Marian 1924- *BioIn 11, ConAu 41R, DrAPF 85, IntAu&W 82, PrintW 83, –85, SmATA 13, WhoAmA 78, –80, –82, –84, –86, –89, –91*

Parsons, Ellen *ConAu 36NR, MajAI, SmATA 75*
Main entry: Dragonwagon, Crescent

Parsons, Kitty *AmWomPl, ChhPo, –S1, ConAu 13R, IntAu&W 77, WhAmArt 85, WhNAA, WhoAmA 73, WrDr 76*

Parsons, Kitty d1976 *ConAu 120*

Parsons, Tom *ConAu X, SmATA X*
Main entry: MacPherson, Thomas George

Parsons, Virginia *IlsBYP*

Parsons, Virginia Mae 1942- *WhoAmW 91, –93*

Parsons, William E 1936- *AuBYP 3*

Parsons, William Edward, Jr. 1936- *AuBYP 2S, ConAu 21R*

Partch, Virgil *AuBYP 3*

Partch, Virgil 1916-1984 *AuBYP 2S, Au&Wr 71, BioIn 1, ConAu 108, –113, ConGrA 1, CurBio 46, –84N, NewYTBS 84, SmATA 39N, –45, WhoAm 74, –80, –82, –84, WhoAmA 73, –80, –82, –84, WorECar*
Pseud./variant:
Vip

Partch, Virgil Franklin 1916- *WhoAmA 86N, –91N*

Parton, Ethel 1862-1944 *AmAu&B, BenetAL 91, BioIn 2, –7, ChhPo, DcNAA, JBA 34, –51, REnAL, WomWWA 14*

Partridge, Anthony *ConAu X, EncMys, TwCCr&M 80, –85, –91*
Pseud./variant:
Oppenheim, Edward Phillips

Partridge, B W *AuBYP 3*

Partridge, Benjamin Waring, Jr. 1915- *BioIn 13, ConAu 25R, SmATA 28, WhoE 74, –75*

Partridge, Jenny 1947- *BioIn 15, –16, ConAu 109, –26NR, SmATA 37, –52, WrDr 90, –92*

Partridge, Jenny Lilian 1947- *WrDr 94*

Pascal, David *WhoAmA 86*

Pascal, David 1918- *BioIn 8, –12, ChhPo S1, ConAu 9R, IlsCB 1957, SmATA 14, WhoAm 74, –76, –78, –80, –82, –84, –86, –88, –90, –92, –94, WhoAmA 73, –78, –80, –82, –84, –89, –91, WhoE 74, WhoWor 91, –93*

Pascal, Francine 1937- *WhoAm 94*

Pascal, Francine 1938- *Au&Arts 1, BioIn 15, –16, ChlLR 25, ConAu 115, –123, –39NR FifBJA, IntAu&W 91, MajAI, ScF&FL 92 SmATA 37, –51, WrDr 90*

Paschal, Nancy *AuBYP 2, –3, ConAu X, ForWC 70, SmATA X*
Main entry: Trotter, Grace V

Pascudniak, Pascal 1935- *SmATA X*
Main entry: Lupoff, Richard Allen

Pashko, Stanley 1913- *BioIn 13, ConAu 97, SmATA 29*
Pseud./variant:
Norman, Steve
Robbins, Tony

Passos, John Dos *BioIn 10, CurBio 40, –70, PenC AM, TwCA, –SUP*
Main entry: DosPassos, John

Patanne, Maria *ConAu X*
Main entry: LaPietra, Mary

Patapoff, Elizabeth 1917- *ConAu 29R*

Patch, Edith Marion 1876-1954 *AmAu&B, AmLY, BioIn 2, –3, –4, –9, JBA 34, –51, WhAm 3, WhNAA, WomWWA 14, WomSc*

Patch, Edith Marion 1879-1954 *BioIn 15*

Patch, Olive 1839-1927 *Alli SUP, CarSB*

Patchett, Mary Elwyn 1897- *AuWomWr, AuBYP 3, IntAu&W 91, TwCChW 89, WrDr 86, –88, –90*

Patchett, Mary Elwyn Osborne 1897- *DcChlFi*

Patchett, Mary Osborne Elwyn 1897- *AuBYP 2, Au&Wr 71, BioIn 8, ConAu 5R, –3NR, IntAu&W 77, –82, OxCChiL, SingR 1, TwCChW 78, –83, WrDr 76, –80, –82, –84*

Pate, Billie 1932- *ConAu 61*

Patent, Dorothy Hinshaw *BioIn 16*

Patent, Dorothy Hinshaw 1940- *AuBYP 2S, –3, ChlLR 19, ConAu 61, –9NR, –24NR, MajAI, SixBJA, SmATA 22, –69, –13AS, WhoAm 94, WhoWest 87*

Paterson, Andrew B 1864-1941 *AuBYP 3*

Paterson, Andrew Barton 1864-1941 *AuBYP 2S, Benet 87, BioIn 2, –4, –7, –8, –9, –10, –14, CasWL, Chambr 3, ChhPo, –S2, DcLEL, LongCTC, McGEWB, PenC ENG, RfGEnL 91, WebE&AL*

Paterson, Diane *AuBYP 3*

Paterson, Diane 1946- *AuBYP 2S, BioIn 12, ConAu 101, IlsCB 1967, SixBJA, SmATA 33, –59*

Paterson, Katherine 1932- *Au&Arts 1, AuBYP 2SA, –3, BioIn 11, –12, ChlFicS, ChlLR 7, ConAu 21R, –28NR, ConLC 12, –30, DcLB 52, FemiCLE, FifBJA, MajTwCW, OxCChiL, SmATA 13, –53, TwCChW 83, –89, WrDr 84, –86, –88, –90, –92*

Paterson, Katherine Womeldorf 1932- *DcAmChF 1960, –1985, MajAI, TwCYAW, WrDr 94*

Patmore, Coventry 1823-1896 *Benet 87, CamGLE, DcLB 35, –98, OxCChiL, RfGEnL 91, WhDW*

Patmore, Coventry Kersey Dighton 1823-1896 *BioIn 17, BlmGEL*

Paton, Alan *BioIn 14, IntvTCA 2*

Paton, Alan 1903- *AuBYP 3, Benet 87, CamGLE, ConAu 22NR, ConNov 86, IntAu&W 91, RAdv 13-2, Who 88, WrDr 86, –88*

Paton, Alan 1903-1988 *AnObit 1988, BritWr S2, ConAu 125, ConLC 55, CurBio 88N, IntLitE, MagSWL, MajTwCW, News 88-3, RfGEnL 91, SmATA 56N, WorAlBi, WorLitC*

Paton, Alan 1913-1988 *NewYTBS 88*

Paton, Alan Stewart 1903- *AfSS 80, –81, –82, AuBYP 2, Au&Wr 71, BioIn 2, –3, –4, –5, –7, –8, –11, CamGEL, CasWL, ConAu P-1, ConLC 4, –10, ConNov 72, –76, CurBio 52, CyWA 58, DcAfHiB 86, DcLEL 1940, EncSoA, EncWL, IntAu&W 77, –82, –86, –89, IntWW 74, –75, –76, –77, –78, –79, –80, –81, –82, –83, LongCTC, McGEWB, ModCmwL, NewC, PenC ENG, PlP&P, REn, SmATA 11, TwCA SUP, TwCWr, WebE&AL, Who 74, WhoTwCL, WhoWor 74, –84, –87, WorAl, WrDr 76, –80*

Paton, James *CarSB*

Paton, Jane Elizabeth 1934- *Au&Wr 71, BioIn 14, ChhPo, –S1, IlsBYP, IlsCB 1957, –1967, SmATA 35*

Paton Walsh, Gillian 1937- *Au&Wr 71, BioIn 9, ConAu 38NR, MajAI, SmATA 4, SouSt, TwCChW 78, WhoAmW 74, WrDr 76, –80*
Pseud./variant:
Paton Walsh, Jill
Walsh, Gillian Paton
Walsh, Jill Paton

Paton Walsh, Gillian 1939- *SmATA 72*

Paton Walsh, Jill *ConAu 38NR, MajAI, SmATA 72*
Main entry: Paton Walsh, Gillian

Paton Walsh, Jill 1937- *Au&Arts 11, BioIn 9, –15, –16, IntAu&W 91, OxCChiL, ScF&FL 92, SmATA 3AS, TwCChW 83, –89, TwCYAW, Who 90, –92, WhoAm 92, –94, WrDr 82, –84, –86, –88, –90, –92, –94*

Patrick, Douglas Arthur 1905- *CanWW 83, ConAu 17R, WhoE 74, –81, –83*

Patron, Susan 1948- *SmATA 76*

Patten, Brian 1946- *BioIn 10, –13, ConAu 25R, –43NR, ConPo 70, –75, –80, –85, –91, IntAu&W 77, –82, –86, –89, –91, IntWWP 82, OxCChiL, OxCEng 85, ScF&FL 92, SmATA 29, TwCChW 78, –83, –89, Who 82, –83, –85, –88, –90, –92, WrDr 76, –80, –82, –84, –86, –88, –90, –92*

Patten, Lewis B 1915-1981 *ConAu 21NR, TwCWW 91*

Patten, Lewis Byford 1915-1981 *BioIn 12, ConAu 25R, –103, DcAmChF 1960, EncFWF, WhAm 7, WhoAm 74, –76, –78, –80, WhoWest 74, –76, –78*

Patten, William Gilbert 1866-1945 *AmAu&B, BenetAL 91, CarSB, CnDAL, HsB&A, OxCAmL 65, –83, REnAL*
Pseud./variant:
Standish, Burt L

Patterson, Charles 1935- *ConAu 41NR, SmATA 59*

Patterson, Charles 1941- *ConBlAP 88*

Patterson, E Palmer 1927- *DrAS 82H, OxCCan SUP*

Patterson, Emma L 1904- *ConAu P-2, WhoLibS 55*

Patterson, Emma L 1904-1984 *ConAu 135*

Patterson, Francine *AuBYP 3*

Patterson, Franklin 1916- *ConAu 45, WhoAm 74*

Patterson, Geoffrey 1943- *BioIn 15, –16, ConAu 103, SmATA 44, –54*

Patterson, Letha Lemon 1913- *ConAu 5R*

Patterson, Lillie G *AuBYP 2, –3, BioIn 7, –12, BlkAuII, –92, ConAu 73, InB&W 80, SmATA 14*

Patterson, Nancy Ruth 1944- *SmATA 72*

Patterson, Russell 1894-1977 *ArtCS, BioIn 11, EncACom, IlrAm 1880, –C, ObitOF 79, WhAm 7, WhAmArt 85, WhoAm 74, –76*

Patterson, Samuel White 1883-1975 *AmAu&B, BioIn 10, ChhPo, ConAu 61, –P-2, DrAS 74H, WhAm 6, WhNAA*

Patterson, Ward L 1933- *ConAu 23NR*

Patterson, Ward Lamont 1933- *ConAu 57, –8NR, WhoMW 78*

Pattison, Darcy S 1954- *SmATA 72*

Patton, Alva Rae *AmMWSc 89*

Patton, Alva Rae 1908- *AmMWSc 76P, –82 –86, ConAu 5R*

Patton, Frances Gray 1906- *AmAu&B, AmWomWr, Au&Wr 71, BenetAL 91, BioIn 3, –4, –5, CnDAL, ConAu 101, ConNov 72, –76, CurBio 55, DcLEL 1940, InWom SUP, REnAL, WrDr 76, –80, –82, –84*

Paul, Aileen *WhoUSWr 88, WhoWrEP 89, –92*

Paul, Aileen 1917- *AuBYP 2S, –3, BioIn 11, ConAu 41R, –19NR, SmATA 12, WhoWest 82*

Paul, Ann Whitford 1941- *SmATA 76*

Paul, Anthony 1941- *ConAu 77*

Paul, David 1934-1988 *ConAu 125, SmATA 56N*

Paul, Elizabeth *ConAu X, SmATA X*
Main entry: Crow, Donna Fletcher

Paul, Grace 1908- *ConAu 17R, WhoAmW 77, –83, –85, –87, –89, WhoMW 90, –92, –93, WhoSSW 78, –80, –82, WhoWor 84, –87, –89, –91, WrDr 76, –80, –82, –84, –86, –88*

Paul, James
Main entry: Kocsis, James C

Paul, James 1936- *BioIn 8, –13, IlsBYP, SmATA 23*

Paul, Robert *SmATA X*
Main entry: Roberts, John G

Paulden, Sydney 1932- *ConAu 29R, –12NR WrDr 76, –80, –82, –84*

Pauli, Hertha Ernestine 1909-1973 *AmAu&B, AuBYP 2, –3, BioIn 1, –4, –7, –9, –13, BkC 5, CathA 1930, ConAu 1R, –41R, –2NR, ForWC 70, NewYTBE 73, SmATA 3, –26N, WhAm 5, WhoAmW 74, WhoE 74*

Paull, Grace A 1898- *AuBYP 2, –3, BioIn 1 –2, –5, –7, –13, DcWomA, IlsCB 1744, –1946, JBA 51, SmATA 24*

Paull, Harry Major 1854-1934 *ChhPo S1, NotNAT B*

Paull, Mary Anna *Alli SUP, CarSB*

Paull, Minnie E 1859-1895 *CarSB, ChhPo, DcNAA*

Paulsen, Brendan Patrick *AuBYP 3*

Paulsen, Gary 1939- *Au&Arts 2, AuBYP 3, BioIn 13, ChlLR 19, ConAu 73, -30NR, DcAmChF 1985, MajAI, ScF&FL 92, SixBJA, SmATA 22, -50, -54, TwCChW 89, TwCWW 91, TwCYAW, WrDr 90, -92, -94*

Paulson, Jack *AuBYP 3, ConAu X, MichAu 80, SmATA 6*
Main entry: Jackson, C Paul

Paulsson, Bjoern K 1932- *ConAu 61*

Pausacker, Jenny 1948- *SmATA 72*

Pausewang, Gudrun *TwCChW 89B*

Pausewang, Gudrun 1928- *ScF&FL 92*

Paustovsky, Konstantin Georgievich 1892-1968 *BioIn 6, -7, -8, -9, -10, -11, CasWL, ConAu 25R, EncWL 2, HanRL, ObitOF 79, PenC EUR, TwCWr, WhAm 5, WorAu 1950*

Paustovsky, Konstantin Georgiyevich 1892-1968 *Benet 87, DcRusLS*

Pavel, Frances K 1907- *BioIn 11, ConAu 21R, SmATA 10*

Paxton, Tom 1937- *SmATA 70*

Payes, Rachel Cosgrove 1922- *ConAu 49, -1NR, -16NR, IntAu&W 77, -82, -86, -89*
Pseud./variant:
Arch, E L
Cosgrove, Rachel

Payne, Alan *ConAu X, -43NR, MajTwCW, NewYTBE 73, WrDr 82, -84, -86, -88, -90, -92*
Main entry: Jakes, John W

Payne, Alan 1932- *SmATA X, WrDr 94*

Payne, Alma Smith *AuBYP 2, -3, BioIn 8, ConAu X, ForWC 70*
Main entry: Ralston, Alma

Payne, Bernal C 1941- *BioIn 17*

Payne, Bernal C, Jr. 1941- *ScF&FL 92, SmATA 60*

Payne, Donald Gordon *ScF&FL 92*

Payne, Donald Gordon 1924- *Au&Wr 71, BioIn 15, ConAu 13R, -9NR, -24NR, IntAu&W 77, -82, -86, -89, -91, SmATA 37, WrDr 76, -82, -84, -86, -88, -90, -92, -94*
Pseud./variant:
Cameron, Ian
Gordon, Donald
Marshall, James Vance

Payne, Emmy *AuBYP 2, -3, ConAu X, SmATA X*
Main entry: West, Emily

Payne, Joan Balfour 1923-1973 *BioIn 5, -8, ConAu 41R, IlsBYP, IlsCB 1946, -1957, -1967*

Payne, Rachel Ann 1932- *SmATA X*
Main entry: Jakes, John William

Payne, Sherry Neuwirth *AuBYP 3*

Payne, Stephen *AmAu&B*

Payson, Dale 1943- *BioIn 11, ConAu 49, -3NR, IlsBYP, SmATA 9*

Payzant, Charles *BioIn 12, IlsBYP, SmATA 18*

Payzant, Jessie Mercer Knechtel *SmATA X*
Main entry: Mercer, Jessie

Paz, A *ConAu X, SmATA X*
Main entry: Pahz, James Alon

Paz, Zan *ConAu X, SmATA X*
Main entry: Pahz, Cheryl Suzanne

Peabody, Josephine Preston 1874-1922 *AmAu&B, AmWomPl, AmWomWr, BenetAL 91, BiD&SB, BioIn 16, CarSB, ChhPo, -S1, CnDAL, ConAmL, DcAmAu, DcNAA, EvLB, InWom SUP, LongCTC, ModWD, NotWoAT, OxCAmL 65, -83, OxCAmT 84, REnAL, TwCA, WhAm 1, WomWWA 14*

Peach, Lawrence DuGarde 1890-1974 *Au&Wr 71, ConAu 101, DcLEL, LongCTC, Who 74*

Peacock, Lucy 1785-1816 *DcBrAmW*

Peacock, Lucy 1786-1815 *Alli, BiDLA, CarSB, DcNaB*

Peacock, Thomas Love 1785-1866 *Benet 87, BioIn 1, -2, -3, -4, -5, -6, -7, -8, -9, -10, -12, -13, -16, -17, BlmGEL, BritWr 4, CamGEL, CamGLE, CelCen, DcBiPP, DcInB, DcLB 96, -116, DcNaB, NinCLC 22, Novels, OxCChiL, OxCEng 85, OxCLiW 86, RAdv 13-1, RfGEnL 91, RfGShF, WhDW*

Peacocke, Isabel Maud *WomNov*

Peacocke, Isabel Maud 1881-1973 *BlmGWL, ConAu 116, TwCChW 83, -89*

Peake, Margaret Lilian 1924- *IntAu&W 77, -82*

Peake, Mervyn Laurence 1911-1968 *BioIn 14, -15, -17, GrBr*

Peake, Mervyn Lawrence 1911-1968 *BiDScF, BioIn 1, -5, -8, -9, -10, -11, -12, -13, ChhPo, -S1, -S2, ConAu 5R, -25R, -3NR, ConLC 7, ConNov 76, DcBrAr 2, DcLB 15, DcLEL 1940, DcNaB 1961, IlsCB 1946, -1967, LongCTC, MakMC, ModBrL S2, Novels, ObitOF 79, OxCChiL, OxCEng 85, OxCTwCA, REn, SmATA 23, WhoChL, WhoHr&F, WorAu 1950*

Peake, Miriam Morrison 1901- *ConAu 57*

Peale, Norman Vincent *BioIn 14, -16, -17*

Peale, Norman Vincent 1898- *AmAu&B, AuBYP 2, -3, AuNews 1, Au&Wr 71, BenetAL 91, BioIn 1, -2, -3, -4, -5, -7, -8, -10, -11, -12, -13, BioNews 74, CelR, ConAu 81, -29NR, CurBio 46, -74, EncTwCJ, EncWB, MajTwCW, OhA&B, REnAL, SmATA 20, WebAB 74, -79, WhoAm 74, -76, -78, -80, -82, -84, -86, -88, -90, -92, -94, WhoE 86, -89, -91, -93, WhoRel 77, -92, WhoWor 74, -78, -80, -82, -84, -87, -89, -91, -93, WorAlBi, WorAl, WrDr 76, -80, -82, -84, -86, -88, -90, -92, -94*

Peale, Norman Vincent 1898-1993 *NewYTBS 93*

Pearce, Ann Philippa *ChlFicS, IntAu&W 86, -89, -91, MajAI, SmATA 67, Who 88, -90, -92*

Pearce, Ann Philippa 1920- *Au&Wr 71, BioIn 5, -6, -7, -8, -9, CasWL, ConAu X, DcLEL 1940, IntAu&W 82, -82X, OxCChiL, Who 82, -83, -85, WhoAm 74, WhoAmW 74, -75, WhoChL, WrDr 76, -80, -82, -84*
Pseud./variant:
Christie, Ann Philippa
Pearce, Philippa

Pearce, Frances *DcChlFi*

Pearce, Philippa *AuBYP 2, -3, ChlLR 9, ConAu 5R, -X, ConLC 21, EncSF 93, IntAu&W 86X, ScFSB, SenS, SmATA 1, ThrBJA, TwCChW 78, -83, -89, Who 82, -83, -85, -88, -90, -92, WhoWor 74, WrDr 86, -88, -90, -92*
Main entry: Pearce, Ann Philippa

Pearce, Philippa 1920- *ArtclWW 2, BioIn 16, -17, CamGLE, MajAI, ScF&FL 92, SmATA 67*

Pearce, Philippa 1921- *FemiCLE*

Pearce, W E 1907- *AmMWSc 73P*

Pearcy, G Etzel 1905-1980 *ConAu 1R, -3NR*

Peare, Catherine Owens 1911- *AuBYP 2, -3, Au&Wr 71, BioIn 5, -6, -7, -11, ConAu 5R, CurBio 59, MorJA, SmATA 9*

Pearl, Hal 1914?-1975 *BioIn 10, ConAu 61*

Pearl, Jack
Main entry: Pearl, Jacques Bain

Pearl, Jacques B *ScF&FL 92*

Pearl, Jacques Bain 1923- *ConAu 5R, -23NR*
Pseud./variant:
Pearl, Jack

Pearl, Richard Maxwell 1913- *AuBYP 3*

Pearl, Richard Maxwell 1913-1980 *AmMWSc 73P, -76P, AuBYP 2, BioIn 7, -12, ConAu 9R, -3NR, WhAm 7, WhoAm 76, -78, -80, WhoWor 80*

Pearlman, Moshe 1911- *ConAu 5R, -X, WhoWor 74, WhoWorJ 72, WrDr 76, -80, -82, -84, -86, -88, -90, -92, -94*

Pears, Charles 1873-1958 *BioIn 1, -4, -14, ChhPo, ClaDrA, ConAu 114, DcBrAr 1, DcBrBI, DcSeaP, DcVicP 2, IlsCB 1744, OxCShps, SmATA 30*

Pearse, Alfred d1933 *DcVicP 2*

Pearse, Alfred 1854?-1933 *DcBrAr 1, -2, DcBrBI, DcVicP 2*

Pearse, Alfred 1856-1933 *BiDScF, BioIn 12*

Pearse, Susan Beatrice *BioIn 1, ConICB, DcWomA, IlsCB 1744*

Pearse, Susan Beatrice 1878-1980 *BioIn 14*

Pearson, Benjamin Harold 1893- *ConAu 65, EncWM*

Pearson, Edmund Lester 1880-1937 *AmAu&B, BenetAL 91, BioIn 4, CarSB, DcNAA, LongCTC, OxCAmL 65, REnAL, TwCA, WhAm 1, WhNAA*

Pearson, Gayle *AuBYP 3*

Pearson, Gayle 1947- *BioIn 16, ConAu 122, SmATA 53, WrDr 90, -92, -94*

Pearson, Kit 1947- *ChlLR 26, ScF&FL 92, SmATA 77, TwCYAW, WhoCanL 92*

Pearson, Kit Kathleen 1947- *DcChlFi*

Pearson, Margaret M *SingR 1*

Pearson, Norman Holmes 1909-1975 *AmAu&B, BioIn 10, -15, ConAu 61, -P-1, DcAmBC DrAS 74E, EncAI&E, WhAm 6, WhoAm 74, -76, WhoGov 72, -75, WhoWor 74, WrDr 76*

Pearson, Susan 1946- *AuBYP 2S, -3, BioIn 13, ConAu 65, -14NR, SmATA 27, -39*

Pearson, Tracey Campbell 1956- *SmATA 64*

Peary, Josephine Diebitsch 1863-1895 *AmAu&B, BioIn 4, –6, CarSB, DcAmAu, REnAL, WhAm 3, WhNAA, WomWWA 14*

Pease, Howard 1894- *WhAm 10*

Pease, Howard 1894-1974 *AmAu&B, AuBYP 2, –3, BenetAL 91, BioIn 1, –2, –7, –9, –10, –13, ConAu 5R, –106, JBA 34, –51, MajAI, REnAL, SmATA 2, –25N, TwCChW 78, –83, –89, WhoAm 74, –76*

Pease, Josephine Van Dolzen *AuBYP 3*

Pease, Josephine VanDolzen *AuBYP 2, BioIn 2, –7, ChhPo, –S1*

Pease, Lucius Curtis 1869-1963 *ArtCS, ArtsAmW 3, BioIn 1, –2, –6, CurBio 49, –63, REnAL, WhJnl, WorECar*
Pseud./variant:
Pease, Lute

Pease, Lute
Main entry: Pease, Lucius Curtis

Peattie, Donald Culross 1898-1964 *AmAu&B, AuBYP 2, –3, BenetAL 91, BioIn 2, –3, –4, –7, –16, ConAmA, ConAu 102, CurBio 40, –65, DcAmB S7, DcLEL, InSci, OxCAmL 65, –83, REnAL, TwCA, –SUP, WhAm 4, WhNAA*

Peattie, Louise Redfield 1900-1965 *AmAu&B, AmWomWr, BioIn 4, –16, TwCA, –SUP, WhAm 4, WhNAA*

Peavy, Linda *DrAPF 87, –89, –91, –93*

Peavy, Linda 1943- *ConAu 31NR, SmATA 54, WhoUSWr 88, WhoWrEP 89, –92*

Peck, Anne Merriman 1884- *AmAu&B, ArtsAmW 3, AuBYP 2, –3, BioIn 1, –2, –5, –8, –12, ChhPo, –S1, ConAu 77, DcWomA, IlsCB 1744, –1946, JBA 34, –51, SmATA 18, WhAmArt 85*

Peck, Clara Elsene 1883- *ConICB, DcWomA, IlrAm 1880, –B, WhAmArt 85*

Peck, George Wilbur 1840-1916 *AmAu, AmAu&B, BenetAL 91, BbD, BiD&SB, BioIn 5, –8, –15, CarSB, CnDAL, ConAu 115, DcAmAu, DcLB 23, –42, DcNAA, JrnUS, OxCAmL 65, –83, OxCChiL, PenC AM, REn, REnAL, WhAm 1, WhAmP, WhoChL, WisWr*

Peck, Helen Estelle 1910- *ConAu 5R, ForWC 70*

Peck, Ira 1922- *ConAu 77, ScF&FL 92*

Peck, Ralph H 1926- *ConAu 22NR*

Peck, Ralph Harold-Henry *ConAu 69*

Peck, Richard *DrAPF 87, –89, –91, –93*

Peck, Richard 1934- *Au&Arts 1, BioIn 12, –13, ChhPo S2, ChlLR 15, ConAu 85, –19NR, ConLC 21, DcAmChF 1960, –1985, DrAF 76, DrAP 75, DrAPF 83, –85, FifBJA, IntAu&W 82, –89, –91, OxCChiL, ScF&FL 92, SmATA 18, –55, –2AS, TwCChW 78, –83, –89, WhoAm 80, –82, –84, WrDr 80, –82, –84, –86, –88, –90, –92*

Peck, Richard Wayne 1934- *ConAu 38NR, MajAI, TwCYAW, WrDr 94*

Peck, Robert Newton *IntAu&W 91, WrDr 86, –88, –90, –92*

Peck, Robert Newton 1928- *Au&Arts 3, AuBYP 2S, –3, BioIn 12, –15, –16, –17, ConAu 81, –31NR, ConLC 17, FifBJA, MajAI, SmATA 21, –62, –1AS, TwCChW 78, –83, –89, TwCYAW, WrDr 80, –82, –84, –94*

Peck, Robert Newton, III 1928- *DcAmChF 1960*

Peckham, Howard Henry 1910- *AmAu&B, BioIn 3, ChhPo, ConAu 9R, DrAS 74H, –78H, –82H, WhoAm 74, –76, –78, –80, –82, –84, –86, –88, –90, –92, –94, WhoLibS 55*

Peckham, Richard *AuBYP 3, BenetAL 91*

Peckinpah, Betty *AuBYP 2, –3, BioIn 8*

Pecznick, Ira *BioIn 11*

Peddie, Tom *ChhPo*

Pedersen, Elsa Kienitz 1915- *AuBYP 2, –3, BioIn 8, ConAu 1R, –2NR, ForWC 70*

Pedersen, Kent Alden 1931- *WhoWest 74, –80, –82*

Pedersen, Thelma Jean Jorgenson *WhoAmW 93, WhoWest 87*

Pedersen, Thelma Jean Jorgenson 1934- *ConAu 57, WhoWest 84*

Pedley, Ethel C *OxCAusL, OxCChiL, SingR 1*

Peebles, Anne *IntAu&W 86X, SmATA 66*
Main entry: Galloway, Priscilla

Peek, Merle 1938- *AuBYP 3, BioIn 15, ConAu 105, –22NR, SmATA 39*

Peel, Bruce Braden 1916- *BiDrLUS 70, BlueB 76, CanWW 70, –80, –81, –83, –89, ConAu 17R, IntAu&W 82, –86, –89, IntYB 80, –81, –82, WhoAm 74, –80, –82, –84, –86, WhoLibI 82, WhoLibS 55, –66, WhoWest 74,*

WhoWor 74, WrDr 76, -82, -84, -86, -88, -90, -92, -94

Peel, H M 1930- *ConAu 9R, -4NR, WrDr 76, -80, -82, -84, -86, -88, -90, -92*

Peel, Hazel Mary 1930- *WrDr 94*

Peel, Norman Lemon *ConAu X, SmATA X*
Main entry: Hirsch, Phil

Peeples, Edwin A 1915- *BioIn 10, ConAu 9R, IntAu&W 77, SmATA 6, WhoE 83, -85, WhoFI 74, WrDr 76, -80*

Peeples, Edwin A, Jr. 1915- *ScF&FL 92*

Peeples, Edwin Augustus 1915- *WhoE 86, -89, -93, WhoFI 94*

Peet, Bill *ConAu 38NR, MajAI*
Main entry: Peet, William Bartlett

Peet, Bill 1915- *ChlLR 12, IntAu&W 91, OxCChiL, SmATA X, TwCChW 83, -89, WrDr 82, -84, -86, -88, -90, -92, -94*

Peet, Creighton 1899-1977 *AuBYP 2, -3, BioIn 7, -11, ConAu 69, -106, SmATA 30*

Peet, Creighton B 1899-1977 *BioIn 14*

Peet, William Bartlett 1915- *AmPB, AuBYP 2, -3, Au&Wr 71, BioIn 7, -8, -9, -12, -13, ChhPo, -S1, ChsFB A, ConAu 17R, -38NR, IlsCB 1957, -1967, IndAu 1917, MajAI, SmATA 2, -41, ThrBJA, TwCChW 78, WrDr 76, -80*
Pseud./variant:
Peet, Bill

Pei, Mario Andrew 1901-1978 *AmAu&B, AmCath 80, BiDInt, BioIn 3, -4, -8, -9, -11, -12, ConAu 5R, -77, -5NR, CurBio 68, -78N, DrAS 74F, NatCAB 60, REnAL, TwCA SUP, WhAm 7, WhoAm 74, -76, -78, WhoWor 74, WrDr 76*

Peirce, Waldo 1884- *WhoAmA 86N*

Peirce, Waldo 1884-1970 *BioIn 1, -2, -4, -8, -9, -10, -13, CurBio 44, -70, DcCAA 71, -77, -88, IlsCB 1744, SmATA 28, WhAm 5, WhAmArt 85, WhoAmA 78N, -80N, -82N, -89N, -91N*

Pekarsky, Mel 1934- *BioIn 16, PrintW 85, WhoAmA 78, -80, -82, -84, -86, -89, -91*

Pekarsky, Melvin Hirsch 1934- *WhoAm 92, -94*

Pelaez, Jill Fletcher 1924- *BioIn 11, ConAu 33R, SmATA 12, WrDr 76, -80, -82, -84*

Pelavin, Cheryl 1946- *ConAu 106*

Pelham, David 1938- *SmATA 70*

Pelletier, Ingrid 1912- *ConAu 29R*

Pellowski, Anne 1933- *ALA 80, AuBYP 2S, -3, BiDConC, BiDrLUS 70, BioIn 12, ChhPo S1, ConAu 21R, -9NR, FifBJA, SmATA 20, WhoAmW 74, -75, WhoLibI 82*

Pellowski, Anne R 1933- *WhoAm 92*

Pellowski, Anne Rose 1933- *WhoAm 94*

Pellowski, Michael J 1949- *SmATA 48*
Pseud./variant:
Michaels, Ski

Pels, Gertrude Jaeckel *AuBYP 2, -3, BioIn 7*

Pelta, Kathy 1928- *BioIn 12, ConAu 85, SmATA 18*

Peltier, Leslie C 1900-1980 *AmMWSc 73P, -76P, BioIn 1, -2, -7, -11, -12, -15, -17, ConAu 17R, SmATA 13*

Peltz, George A *CarSB*

Pemberton, Max 1863-1950 *ConAu 120, EncSF 93, ScFEYrs, StaCVF*

Pemberton, Max, Sir 1863-1950 *BbD, BiD&SB, BioIn 2, -8, Chambr 3, DcBiA, DcEnA A, DcLB 70, EncMys, EvLB, LongCTC, NewC, NotNAT B, ObitOF 79, TwCCr&M 80, WhoChL, WhoLA*

Pembury, Bill *ConAu X, SmATA X*
Main entry: Groom, Arthur William

Pemsteen, Hans *SmATA X*
Main entry: Manes, Stephen

Pendennis, Arthur, Esq *SmATA X*
Main entry: Thackeray, William Makepeace

Pender, Lydia 1907- *AuWomWr, BioIn 17, IntAu&W 86, -89, -91, SmATA 61, WrDr 86, -88, -90, -92*

Pender, Lydia Kathleen 1907- *WrDr 94*

Pender, Lydia Podger 1907- *AuBYP 2, -3, BioIn 7, -9, ConAu 5R, -2NR, IntAu&W 77, SingR 1, SmATA 3, WrDr 76, -80*

Pendery, Rosemary Schmitz *BioIn 10, ConAu 53, SmATA 7*

Pendexter, Hugh 1875-1940 *AmAu&B, BenetAL 91, REnAL, ScFEYrs A, TwCWW 91, WhAm 1, WhNAA*

Pendle, Alexy 1943- *BioIn 12, -13, IlsCB 1967, SmATA 29*

Pendle, George 1906-1977 *Au&Wr 71, BioIn 13, ConAu 5R, -103, IntAu&W 77, SmATA 28N*

Pendleton, Don *ConAu 127, ScF&FL 92, WhoUSWr 88, WhoWrEP 89, -92*

Pendleton, Don 1927- *BioIn 14, ConAu 33R, IntAu&W 91, Novels, ScF&FL 92, TwCCr&M 80, -85, -91, WhoMW 74, -76, -78, -80, WrDr 82, -84, -86, -88, -90, -92*
Pseud./variant:
Gregory, Stephan

Pendleton, Donald Eugene 1927- *EncSF 93, WrDr 94*

Pendleton, Louis 1861-1939 *AmAu&B, BbD, BiDSA, BiD&SB, CarSB, DcAmAu, DcNAA, WhAm 1, WhNAA*

Pendower, Jacques 1899-1976 *Au&Wr 71, BioIn 14, ConAu 9R, SpyFic, TwCCr&M 80, -85, WrDr 76*

Pene DuBois, William *AmPB, IlsCB 1967*
Main entry: DuBois, William Pene

Pene du Bois, William 1916- *BioIn 16, -17, SmATA 68*

Pene du Bois, William Sherman 1916- *MajAI*

Pene du Bois, William Sherman 1916-1993 *ConAu 41NR*

Penfield, Thomas 1903- *ConAu 5R*

Penn, Ruth Bonn *AuBYP 2S, -3, ConAu X, SmATA 3*
Main entry: Rosenberg, Ethel

Pennage, E M *ConAu X, SmATA 8*
Main entry: Finkel, George

Penner, Fred 1946- *ConMus 10, SmATA 67*

Penner, Fred Ralph Cornelius 1946- *ConAu 136, WrDr 94*

Penner, Lucille Recht *AuBYP 3*

Penney, Grace Jackson 1904- *AnCL, BioIn 14, ConAu 5R, SmATA 35*

Penney, Ian 1960- *SmATA 76*

Penney, Richard L 1935- *AmMWSc 73P*

Pennington, Eunice 1923- *BiDrLUS 70, BioIn 13, ConAu 57, ForWC 70, SmATA 27, WhoMW 74*

Pennington, Howard 1923- *ConAu 49*

Pennington, Lillian Boyer 1904- *BioIn 15, SmATA 45, WhoAmW 75, -77, -81*

Penrose, Elizabeth 1780-1837 *DcNaB, OxCChiL*

Penrose, Gordon 1925- *BioIn 17, ConAu 127, SmATA 66*

Penrose, Margaret *ConAu P-2*
Main entry: Stratemeyer, Edward L

Penzler, Otto 1942- *BioIn 13, -15, ConAu 81, -35NR, SmATA 38, WhoE 85*
Pseud./variant:
Adler, Irene
Ferrier, Lucy
Gregory, Stephen
Milverton, Charles A

Pepe, Phil 1935- *ConAu 25R, -18NR, SmATA 20*

Peppe, Rodney 1934- *BioIn 14, SmATA 10AS, WrDr 86, -88, -90, -92*

Peppe, Rodney Darrell 1934- *BioIn 9, -12, ChhPo S2, ConAu 33R, FifBJA, IlsCB 1967, IntAu&W 77, -86, -89, -91, MajAI, SmATA 4, -74, WrDr 76, -80, -82, -84, -94*

Pepper, Curtis G 1920- *ConAu 21R, -10NR*

Pepper, Frank S 1910-1988 *BioIn 17, ConAu 127, ScF&FL 92, SmATA 61*
Pseud./variant:
Colwyn, Stewart

Peppler, Alice Stolper 1934- *ConAu 53, IntAu&W 82X, WhoAmW 77, -81, -83, WhoFI 81, -83, WhoMW 84, -86, -88, WhoWor 82*

Perales, Alonso M *BioIn 11*

Perard, Victor S 1867-1957 *WhoAmA 86N, -89N, -91N*

Perard, Victor Semon 1870-1957 *BioIn 1, -4, IlsCB 1744, ObitOF 79, WhAm 3, WhAmArt 85, WhoAmA 80N, -82N*

Perceval, Don 1908- *BioIn 5, -6, IlsBYP, IlsCB 1946*

Percival, John 1927- *ConAu 33R*

Percival, Thomas 1740-1804 *Alli, BioIn 2, -9, CarSB, DcBiPP, DcNaB*

Percy, Charles H 1919- *BioIn 14, -16, WorAlBi*

Percy, Charles Harting 1919- *AlmAP 78, -82, -84, AuBYP 2S, -3, BiDrUSC 89, BioIn 2, -3,*

–5, –6, –7, –8, –9, –10, –11, –12, BioNews 74, BlueB 76, CelR, ConAu 65, CurBio 59, –77, IntWW 74, –75, –76, –77, –78, –79, –80, –81, –82, –83, –89, –91, NatCAB 63N, PolsAm 84, WhoAm 74, –76, –78, –80, –82, –84, –86, –88, –90, –92, –94, WhoAmP 73, –75, –77, –81, –83, –85, –87, –89, –91, –93, WhoGov 77, –72, –75, WhoMW 74, –76, –78, –80, –82, –84, WhoWor 74, –78, –80, –82, –84, WorAl

Percy, Charles Henry *BlmGWL, ConAu 133, –X, –37NR, MajAI, SmATA 4, –65*
Main entry: Smith, Dodie
Smith, Dorothy Gladys

Percy, Rachel 1930- *BioIn 17, SmATA 63*

Pere Castor *OxCChiL*

Perera, Thomas B 1938- *WhoE 93*

Perera, Thomas Biddle 1938- *AmMWSc 73S, –78S, BioIn 11, ConAu 37R, –21NR, SmATA 13, WhoFrS 84, WhoWrEP 89, –92*

Peretz, Don 1922- *AmMWSc 73S, –78S, ConAu 9R, –4NR, –19NR, –41NR, IntAu&W 77, –82, WhoAmJ 80, WhoWorJ 72, –78*

Perez, Walter
Main entry: Joseph, James Herz

Perkins, Al 1904-1975 *BioIn 14, ChhPo S1, ConAu 57, –107, SmATA 30*

Perkins, Alan J 1953- *WhoAm 94*

Perkins, Charles Elliott 1881-1943 *WhAm 2*

Perkins, Lucy Fitch 1865-1937 *AmAu&B, AmWomWr, BenetAL 91, BioAmW, BioIn 1, –2, –4, CarSB, ChhPo, –S2, ConAu 122, –137, ConICB, DcNAA, InWom SUP, IndAu 1816, JBA 34, –51, MajAI, OxCAmL 65, –83, OxCChiL, REnAL, SmATA 72, TwCChW 78, –83, –89, WhAm 1, WhAmArt 85, WhNAA, WomWWA 14*

Perkins, Marlin 1905-1986 *AnObit 1986, BioIn 15, –16, ConAu 119, SmATA 48N*

Perkins, Nancy *ChhPo S2*

Perkins, Newton Stephens 1925- *ConAu 49*
Pseud./variant:
Perkins, Steve

Perkins, R Marlin 1905-1986 *AuBYP 3, CurBio 86N, NewYTBS 86, WhAm 9*

Perkins, Richard Marlin 1905- *AmMWSc 73P, AuBYP 2, BioIn 2, –3, –6, –7, ConAu 77, CurBio 51, InSci, SmATA 21, WebAB 74, –79, WhoAm 74, –76, –78, –84*

Perkins, Steve
Main entry: Perkins, Newton Stephens

Perkins, Terry William 1936- *WhoAm 74, –80, –82, –84, –86, –88*

Perkins, Wilma Lord 1897-1976 *BioIn 11, BlueB 76, ConAu 104, WhAm 7, WhoAm 74*

Perl, Lila *AuBYP 2, –3, BioIn 8, –10, ConAu 33R, SixBJA, SmATA 6, –72*

Perl, Susan 1922-1983 *BioIn 8, –12, –13, –14, ChhPo, –S2, ConAu 17R, –110, –11NR, IlsBYP, IlsCB 1957, –1967, SmATA 22, –34N, WhoE 74*

Perlman, Raymond 1923- *WhoAm 82, –84, –86, –88, –90, WhoAmA 73, –78, –80, –82, –84, –86*

Perlmutter, O William 1920-1975 *AuBYP 2S, BioIn 11, BlueB 76, ConAu 57, SmATA 8*

Perlmutter, William *AuBYP 3*

Perlmutter, William 1920-1975 *ScF&FL 92*

Perowne, Barry *ConAu X, EncMys, TwCCr&M 80, –85, WrDr 82, –84, –86*

Perowne, Barry 1908- *BioIn 14*

Perowne, Barry 1908-1985 *TwCCr&M 91*

Perowne, Stewart Henry d1989 *IntWW 89N, Who 90N*

Perowne, Stewart Henry 1901- *Au&Wr 71, BlueB 76, ConAu 1R, –3NR, IntAu&W 77, IntWW 74, –75, –76, –77, –78, –79, –80, –81, –82, –83, –89, MidE 80, –81, –82, Who 74, –82, –83, –85, –88, WhoWor 74, –78, WrDr 76, –80*

Perowne, Stewart Henry 1901-1989 *ConAu 128*

Perrault, Charles 1628-1703 *AnCL, AuBYP 2S, –3, Benet 87, BbD, BiD&SB, BioIn 1, –2, –3, –5, –7, –8, –12, –13, –16, BlmGEL, CarSB, CasWL, ChhPo, DcBiPP, DcCathB, DcEuL, EuAu, EvEuW, GuFrLit 2, LitC 2, LongCEL, MajAI, NewC, Novels, OxCChiL, OxCEng 67, –85, OxCFr, PenC EUR, REn, SmATA 25, Str&VC, WhDW, WhoChL, WorAlBi, WrCal*

Perreard, Suzanne Louise Butler *AuBYP 3*

Perreard, Suzanne Louise Butler 1919-
BioIn 13, SmATA 29
Pseud./variant:
Butler, Suzanne Louise

Perret, Gene 1937- *SmATA 76*

Perrin, Blanche Chenery 1894-1973 *BioIn 9, -10, ConAu 5R, -41R*

Perrine, Mary 1913- *AuBYP 2S, -3, BioIn 9, ConAu 25R, SmATA 2*

Perrins, Lesley 1953- *BioIn 16, ConAu 123, SmATA 56*

Perrott, Jennifer *BioIn 9, IlsBYP*

Perry, Barbara Fisher *ConAu X, -30NR, SmATA X*
Main entry: Fisher, Barbara

Perry, Bill 1905- *ArtCS*

Perry, George 1935- *ConAu 103, -26NR, IntAu&W 77, -82, WrDr 82, -84, -86, -88, -90, -92, -94*

Perry, John *WhoAmP 85*

Perry, John 1914- *AuBYP 2, -3, BioIn 8, ConAu 5R, -6NR, WhoGov 72*

Perry, Nora 1831-1896 *Alli SUP, AmAu, AmAu&B, BenetAL 91, BbD, BiD&SB, CarSB, ChhPo, -S1, -S2, DcAmAu, DcNAA, InWom SUP, REnAL, WhAm HS*

Perry, Patricia 1949- *BioIn 14, ConAu 106, SmATA 30*

Perry, Phyllis J 1933- *BioIn 17, SmATA 60*

Perry, Phyllis Jean 1933- *WhoWest 87*

Perry, Richard *ConAu 41R*

Perry, Richard 1944- *BioIn 16, BlkWr 1, WhoBlA 90, -92, -94*

Perry, Ritchie 1942- *ChlFicS*

Perry, Roger 1933- *BioIn 13, ConAu 77, -14NR, ConTFT 1, SmATA 27*

Perry, Shauneille 1929- *DrBlPA 90*

Perry, Shauneille 1930- *BlkAWP, ConAu 113, ConBlAP 88, InB&W 80, NewYTBE 71*

Perry, Steve 1947- *EncSF 93, ScF&FL 92, SmATA 76*

Perse, Saint-John *AnCL, CnMWL, ConAu X, ConLC 4, -11, CyWA 58, EncWL, EvEuW, GrFLW, IntWW 74, -75, MajTwCW, McGEWB, ModRL, PenC EUR, REn, TwCWr, WhAm 6, WhoTwCL, WhoWor 74*
Main entry: Leger, Alexis Saint-Leger

Perse, Saint-John 1887-1975 *BioIn 17, EuWr 10, NobelP*

Perse, Saint-John 1889-1975 *BioIn 14, -15*

Perse, St-John *ConAu 43NR*

Perse, St-John 1887-1975 *Benet 87, ConLC 46, WorAlBi*

Pershall, Mary K 1951- *SmATA 70*

Pershing, Marie *ConAu X, SmATA X*
Main entry: Schultz, Pearle Henriksen

Perske, Robert 1927- *BioIn 16, SmATA 57*

Person, William Thomas 1900- *AuBYP 2, -3, BioIn 7*

Pesek, Ludek 1919- *ConAu 29R, EncSF 93, ScF&FL 92*

Peter *MajAI*

Peter, John Desmond 1921- *Au&Wr 71, CaW, CanWW 83, ConAu 1R, CreCan 2, DrAS 74E, -78E, OxCCan SUP*

Peterkin, Julia 1880-1961 *AmAu&B, ArtclWW 2, BenetAL 91, BioAmW, BioIn 4, -6, -8, -11, -12, -13, CnDAL, ConAmA, ConLC 31, DcLB 9, FemiCLE, LongCTC, NatCAB 62, OxCAmL 65, -83, REn, REnAL, TwCA, -SUP, WhAm 4*

Peterkin, Julia Mood 1880-1961 *AmWomPl*

Peter Parley *HarEnUS, OxCAmL 83, OxCChiL*

Peters, Alexander
Main entry: Hollander, Zander

Peters, Alexander 1923- *ConAu X, SmATA X*

Peters, Arthur Anderson 1913-1979 *BioIn 2, -6, -12, ConAu 93*

Peters, Caroline *ConAu X, SmATA X*
Main entry: Betz, Eva Kelly

Peters, David 1954- *SmATA 72*

Peters, Donald Leslie 1925- *ConAu 21R, IntAu&W 77, WhoWest 74, -76*

Peters, Elizabeth *ConAu 36NR, ScF&FL 92, TwCRHW 90, WrDr 86, -88, -90, -92*
Main entry: Mertz, Barbara Gross

Peters, Elizabeth 1927- *BioIn 14, -15, -16, ConAu X, CrtSuMy, TwCCr&M 80, -85, -91, WrDr 76, -80, -82, -84, -94*

Peters, Ken 1929- *ConAu 17R*

Peters, Lane *ConAu X*
Main entry: Lapidus, Elaine

Peters, Linda *ConAu 38NR, MajAI, SmATA 74*
Main entry: Catherall, Arthur

Peters, Lisa Westberg 1951- *ConAu 141, SmATA 74*

Peters, Margaret Evelyn 1936- *ConAu 53*

Peters, Maureen *ScF&FL 92*

Peters, Maureen 1935- *Au&Wr 71, BioIn 14, ConAu 33R, IntAu&W 77, –91, TwCRHW 90, WrDr 76, –80, –82, –84, –86, –88, –90, –92, –94*

Peters, S H *ConAu 131, –X, MajTwCW, YABC X*
Main entry: Porter, William Sydney

Petersen, David *AuBYP 3*

Petersen, David 1946- *SmATA 62*

Petersen, Gwenn Boardman 1924- *BioIn 17, SmATA 61*
Pseud./variant:
Boardman, Gwenn R

Petersen, P J 1941- *BioIn 15, –16, ConAu 112, –30NR, IntAu&W 86, –89, –91, SixBJA, SmATA 43, –48*

Petersen, Peter James 1941- *MajAI, TwCYAW*

Petersham, Maud 1889-1971 *AmAu&B, AmPB, AnCL, AuBYP 2, BioIn 1, –2, –4, –5, –7, –8, –9, –12, –14, BkP, Cald 1938, ChhPo, –S1, ChlLR 24, ConAu 33R, –73, ConICB, DcLB 22, IlsBYP, IlsCB 1744, –1946, –1957, –1967, JBA 34, –51, OxCChiL, REnAL, SmATA 17, Str&VC, TwCChW 78, –83, –89, WhoAmA 73*

Petersham, Maud 1890-1971 *AuBYP 3, ConAu 29NR*

Petersham, Maud Fuller 1890-1971 *MajAI*

Petersham, Miska 1888-1959 *WhoAmA 86N, –89N, –91N*

Petersham, Miska 1888-1960 *AuBYP 3, BenetAL 91, BioIn 14, ChlLR 24, ConAu 29NR, MajAI, TwCChW 89*

Petersham, Miska 1889-1960 *AmAu&B, AmPB, AnCL, AuBYP 2, BioIn 1, –2, –4, –5, –7, –12, BkP, Cald 1938, ChhPo, –S1, ConAu 73, ConICB, DcLB 22, IlsBYP, IlsCB 1744, –1946, JBA 34, –51, OxCChiL, SmATA 17, Str&VC, TwCChW 78, –83, WhAmArt 85, WhoAmA 80N, –82N*

Peterson, Betty Ferguson 1917- *BioIn 8, IlsCB 1957*

Peterson, Charles Emil 1906- *BioIn 12, WhoAm 76, –78, –80, –82, –84, –86, –90, –92, –94*

Peterson, Charles Eric 1914- *WhoWest 87, –89, –92, –94*

Peterson, Esther Allen 1934- *BioIn 14, ConAu 16NR, SmATA 35*
Pseud./variant:
Allen, Ruth

Peterson, Florence 1894- *OhA&B*

Peterson, Hans 1922- *AuBYP 2S, –3, BioIn 11, ConAu 49, –1NR, FourBJA, IntAu&W 77, –82, SmATA 8*

Peterson, Harold L 1922- *AuBYP 3*

Peterson, Harold Leslie 1922-1978 *AuBYP 2S, BioIn 2, –11, ConAu 1R, –4NR, DrAS 74H, SmATA 8, WhoSSW 76, WrDr 76*

Peterson, Helen Stone 1910- *BioIn 11, ConAu 37R, SmATA 8, WhoAmW 77, WrDr 76, –80, –82, –84, –86, –88, –90*

Peterson, James *AuBYP 2, –3, ConAu X*
Main entry: Zeiger, Henry Anthony

Peterson, Jeanne Whitehouse *ConAu X, SmATA X*
Main entry: Whitehouse, Jeanne

Peterson, John Lawrence 1924- *AuBYP 2S –3*

Peterson, Len 1917- *CanWr, CreCan 1, DcLB 88, OxCCan SUP, OxCCanL, OxCCanT*

Peterson, Lenka 1925- *ConTFT 5*

Peterson, Lorraine 1940- *BioIn 15, –16, ConAu 113, SmATA 44, –56*

Peterson, Ottis 1907- *ConAu 21R*

Peterson, Roger Tory *AmMWSc 86, NewYTBS 93*

Peterson, Roger Tory 1908- *AmArt, AmAu&B, AmMWSc 76P, –82, BenetAL 91, BioIn 4 –5, –6, –7, –8, –10, –11, –12, –14, –15, BlueB 76, CelR, ConAu 1R, –1NR, CurBio 59, InSci, IntAu&W 77, –82, IntWW 74, –75, –76, –77, –78, –79, –80, –81, –82, –83, –89, –91, NewYTBS 74, –80, REnAL, TwCA SUP, WebAB 74, –79, WhAmArt 85, WhoAm 74, –76, –78, –80, –82, –84, –86, –88, –90, –92, –94, WhoAmA 78, –80, –82, –84, –86, –89, –91, WhoWor 74*

Peterson, Russell Francis *AuBYP 2, –3, BioIn 7, –8, IlsCB 1957*

Petie, Haris *BioIn 11, ConAu X, IlsBYP, SmATA 10*
Main entry: Petty, Roberta

Petrich, Patricia Barrett 1942- *ConAu 61*

Petrides, Heidrun 1944- *BioIn 8, -12, IlsCB 1957, SmATA 19*

Petrie, Catherine 1947- *BioIn 15, -16, ConAu 109, SmATA 41, -52, WrDr 90*

Petroski, Catherine *BioIn 16, DrAPF 87, -89, -91, -93*

Petroski, Catherine 1939- *ConAu 22NR, IntAu&W 86, -89, -91, SmATA 48, WhoUSWr 88, WhoWrEP 89, -92*

Petrovich, Michael Boro *BioIn 15, -17*

Petrovich, Michael Boro 1922- *ConAu 108, DrAS 74H, -78H, -82H, SmATA 40, WhoAm 84, -86, -88*

Petrovskaya, Kyra 1918- *ConAu 1R, -X, SmATA 8*
Pseud./variant:
Wayne, Kyra Petrovskaya

Petruccio, Steven James 1961- *SmATA 67*

Petry, Ann *DrAPF 87, -89, -91, -93, WhoBlA 85*

Petry, Ann 1908- *AfrAmAl 6, BenetAL 91, BlkAuII, -92, BlkWr 1, BlmGWL, ChlLR 12, ConAu 6AS, ConNov 86, -91, DcLB 76, IntAu&W 86, MajTwCW, TwCChW 89, WhoBlA 90, -92, WhoUSWr 88, WhoWrEP 89, -92, WrDr 86, -88, -90, -92*

Petry, Ann 1911- *ArtclWW 2, BlkWrNE, FemiCLE, NegAl 89, NotBlAW 92*

Petry, Ann 1912- *AfrAmW, InWom SUP*

Petry, Ann Lane 1908- *AmWomWr 92, DcAmChF 1960, HarlReB, MajAI, WrDr 94*

Petry, Ann Lane 1911- *BioIn 16, -17, InB&W 85*

Petry, Ann Lane 1912?- *AmAu&B, AmNov, AmWomWr, AnCL, AuBYP 2, -3, BioIn 1, -2, -3, -4, -6, -7, -9, -10, BlkAWP, ConAu 5R, -4NR, ConLC 1, -7, -18, ConNov 72, -76, -82, CurBio 46, DcLEL 1940, DrAP 75, DrAPF 83, -85, InB&W 80, IntAu&W 77, -82, LivgBAA, NegAl 76, -83, OxCAmL 83, OxCChiL, REn, REnAL, SelBAAf, SelBAAu, SmATA 5, ThrBJA, TwCA SUP, TwCChW 78, -83, WhoAmW 74, WhoBlA 77, -80, -85, WrDr 76, -80, -82, -84*

Pettit, Florence H *AuBYP 3*

Pettit, Florence Harvey *AuBYP 2S*

Pettit, Mary P *AuBYP 2, -3, BioIn 8*

Petty, Roberta 1915- *ConAu 61, -10NR*
Pseud./variant:
Petie, Haris

Pevear, Richard *AuBYP 3, DrAPF 87, -91, -93*

Pevsner, Nikolaus 1902-1983 *BioIn 17, MajTwCW*

Pevsner, Nikolaus, Sir 1902-1983 *AnObit 1983, Au&Wr 71, BioIn 7, -8, -10, -11, -13, -14, -15, ConAu 9R, -110, -7NR, DcLEL, IntAu&W 82, IntWW 74, -75, -76, -77, -78, -79, -80, -81, -82, -83, LongCTC, NewYTBS 83, OxDcArt, Who 74, -82, -83, WhoArt 80, -82, -84N, WhoWor 74, WorAu 1950, WrDr 76, -80, -82, -84*

Pevsner, Stella *BioIn 11, -12, -16, ConAu 57, -27NR, FifBJA, SmATA 8, -77, -14AS*

Peyo *ConAu 140, SmATA 74, -X*
Main entry: Culliford Pierre

Peyo 1928- *BioIn 15*

Peyton, K M *ConAu 32NR, IntAu&W 91X, MajAI*
Main entry: Peyton, Kathleen Wendy

Peyton, K M 1929- *AuBYP 3, BioIn 17, CamGLE, ChlFicS, IntAu&W 82X, OxCChiL, ScF&FL 92, SmATA 17AS, -X, TwCChW 83, -89, TwCYAW, WrDr 82, -84, -86, -88, -90, -92, -94*

Peyton, Karen 1897-1960? *ConAu P-1*

Peyton, Kathleen 1929- *SmATA 62*

Peyton, Kathleen Wendy *AuBYP 3*

Peyton, Kathleen Wendy 1929- *AuBYP 2, Au&Wr 71, BioIn 9, -10, -11, -12, -17, BritCA, ChlLR 3, ConAu 69, -32NR, IntAu&W 77, -82, -86, -89, -91, MajAI, PiP, ScF&FL 92, SenS, SmATA 15, SouSt, ThrBJA, TwCChW 78, Who 83, -85, -88, -90, -92, WrDr 76, -80*
Pseud./variant:
Herald, Kathleen
Peyton, K M

Pfadt, Robert E 1915- *AmMWSc 86, -89, -92*

Pfadt, Robert Edward 1915- *AmMWSc 73P, -76P, -82, ConAu 73, WhoWest 74, -76*

Pfanner, Louise 1955- *BioIn 17, SmATA 68*

Pfeffer, Susan Beth 1948- *Au&Arts 12, BioIn 9, -16, ChlLR 11, ConAu 29R, -31NR,*

DcAmChF 1985, IntAu&W 91, SixBJA, SmATA 4, –17AS, WhoAmW 75, –77, WhoE 77, –81, WrDr 76, –80, –82, –84, –86, –88, –90

Pfeifer, Lillian E 1907- *Au&Wr 71, OxCCan SUP*

Pfeiffer, John Edward 1914- *ConAu 101, FifIDA, WhoAm 74, –76, –78, –80, –82, –84, –86, –88, –90, –92, –94*

Pfister, Marcus *AuBYP 3*

Phares, Ross 1908- *ConAu P-1*

Phelan, Joseph A *IlsBYP*

Phelan, Josephine *AuBYP 3*

Phelan, Josephine 1905- *AuBYP 2, BioIn 4, –7, –10, –14, BkC 5, CanWW 70, –79, IntAu&W 77, OxCCan, –SUP, Profile 1, SmATA 30, WrDr 76, –80, –82, –84*

Phelan, Mary Kay 1914- *AuBYP 2S, –3, BioIn 9, ConAu 1R, –4NR, ForWC 70, IntAu&W 77, –82, –91, SmATA 3, WhoAmW 74, –75, –77, –81, WhoMW 74, –76, WrDr 76, –80, –82, –84, –86, –88, –90, –92, –94*

Phelan, Terry Wolfe 1941- *BioIn 16, SmATA 56*

Phelps, Elizabeth S 1815-1852 *BioAmW*

Phelps, Elizabeth Stuart *AmWomPl, WomNov*

Phelps, Elizabeth Stuart 1815-1852 *Alli, AmAu, AmAu&B, AmWomWr, ArtclWW 2, BlmGWL, CarSB, Chambr 3, CyAL, DcAmAu, DcNAA, OxCAmL 65, REnAL*

Phelps, Elizabeth Stuart 1844-1910 *HanAmWH*

Phelps, Elizabeth Stuart 1844-1911 *BioIn 17, DcLB 74, FemiCLE*

Phelps, Elizabeth Stuart Ward 1844-1911 *Alli, –SUP, AmAu, AmAu&B, ArtclWW 2, BbD, BiD&SB, BioIn 2, –9, CarSB, ChhPo, –S1, CyAL, DcAmAu, DcBiA, DcEnL, DcLEL, DcNAA, OxCChiL*
Pseud./variant:
Ward, Elizabeth Stuart P

Phelps, Ethel Johnston 1914- *BioIn 14, ConAu 106, SmATA 35*

Phelps, Margaret *AuBYP 2, –3, BioIn 8*

Phelps Ward, Elizabeth Stuart 1844-1911 *BlmGWL*

Philbrook, Clem 1917- *AuBYP 2, –3, BioIn 13, ConAu 104, SmATA 24*

Philip of Spain, IV *DcAmChF 1960*

Philipson, Morris H 1926- *AmAu&B, ConAu 1R, –4NR, WhoAm 74, –76, –78, WhoFI 74*

Philipson, Susan Sacher 1934- *ChhPo, ConAu 9R*

Phillips, Barbara 1936- *WhoBlA 77, –80, –85, –90, –92, –94*

Phillips, Betty Lou *SmATA X, WhoAm 94, WhoAmW 91, –93, WhoWest 92, –94, WhoWor 91, –93*
Main entry: Phillips, Elizabeth Louise

Phillips, Bob 1940- *ConAu 69*

Phillips, Elizabeth Louise *SmATA 48, –58, WhoAmW 87, –89, WhoWest 89, WhoWor 87, –89*
Pseud./variant:
Phillips, Betty Lou

Phillips, Ethel Calvert d1947 *AmAu&B, BioIn 1, –2, DcNAA, JBA 34, –51, WhAm 2, WhNAA*

Phillips, Irving W 1905- *WhoAmA 86, –89, –91*

Phillips, Irving W 1908?- *BioIn 11, ConAu 55, SmATA 11, WhoAmA 73, –78, –80, –82, –84*
Pseud./variant:
Sabuso

Phillips, Jack *ConAu X, –35NR, MajAI, MajTwCW, SmATA 8*
Main entry: Sandburg, Carl

Phillips, Jo McKeeby *NewYTBS 74*

Phillips, Julien Lind 1945- *ConAu 77*

Phillips, Leon *ConAu 127, –X, SmATA X*
Main entry: Gerson, Noel Bertram

Phillips, Leon 1914-1988 *SmATA X*

Phillips, Leonard Ellis, Jr. 1943- *WhoE 93*

Phillips, Loretta 1893- *BioIn 11, ConAu P-1, SmATA 10*

Phillips, Louis *DrAPF 87, –89, –91, –93*

Phillips, Louis 1942- *BioIn 11, ConAu 49, –3NR, –20NR, DrAPF 83, –85, IntAu&W 82, NatPD 77, –81, SmATA 8*

Phillips, Louis James 1942- *WhoWrEP 92*

Phillips, Marie Tello 1874-1962 *AmAu&B, AnMV 1926, BioIn 6, ChhPo S1, WhAm 5, WhNAA*

Phillips, Mary Geisler 1881-1964 *AuBYP 2, -3, BioIn 1, -7, -11, CarSB, ConAu 5R, SmATA 10, WhNAA*

Phillips, Mary Walker 1923- *BriEAA, InWom SUP*

Phillips, Maurice Jack 1914-1976 *ConAu 5R, -103*

Phillips, Michael Joseph *DrAPF 87, -89, -91, -93*

Phillips, Michael Joseph 1937- *ConAu 49, -3NR, -18NR, DrAP 75, DrAPF 83, -85, IntAu&W 77, -91, IntWWP 82, WhoMW 76, -78, -80, WhoUSWr 88, WhoWrEP 89, -92, WrDr 76, -80, -82, -84, -86, -88, -90, -92, -94*

Phillips, Mildred *AuBYP 3*

Phillips, Mildred E 1928- *AmMWSc 86, -92*

Phillips, Prentice 1894- *BioIn 11, ConAu P-1, SmATA 10*

Phillips, Robert A J 1922- *IntAu&W 86*

Phillips, Robert Arthur Joseph 1922- *OxCCan SUP, WrDr 76, -80*

Phillips, Rog 1909-1965 *EncSF 93, ScFSB, TwCSFW 86, -91, WhoSciF*

Phillips, Walter Joseph 1884-1963 *BioIn 1, ClaDrA, CreCan 1, DcBrAr 2*

Phillpotts, Eden 1862-1960 *BbD, BiD&SB, BioIn 2, -4, -5, -8, -13, -14, -15, CamGLE, CarSB, Chambr 3, ChhPo, -S1, -S2, ConAu 93, -102, CrtSuMy, DcBiA, DcEnA A, DcLB 10, -70, -135, DcLEL, DcNaB 1951, EncMys, EncSF 93, EncWT, EngPo, EvLB, InWom SUP, LongCTC, ModBrL, NewC, NotNAT B, ObitOF 79, ObitT 1951, OxCChiL, OxCEng 85, OxCThe 67, -83, PenEncH, REn, ScF&FL 92, ScFSB, ScFEYrs, SmATA 24, StaCVF, SupFW, TwCA, -SUP, TwCCr&M 80, -85, -91, TwCWr, WhAm 4, WhoChL, WhoHr&F, WhoLA*
Pseud./variant:
Hext, Harrington

Phin 1863-1940 *SmATA X*
Main entry: Thayer, Ernest Lawrence

Phipps, William E 1930- *ConAu 30NR*

Phipps, William Eugene 1930- *ConAu 29R, -12NR, DrAS 74P, -78P, -82P, IntAu&W 86, WhoRel 75, -77, -92, WhoSSW 86, WrDr 76, -80, -82, -84, -86, -88, -90, -92, -94*

Phipson, Joan *AuBYP 3, ConAu 36NR, MajAI, SmATA 73*
Main entry: Fitzhardinge, Joan Margaret

Phipson, Joan 1912- *AuWomWr, AuBYP 2, BioIn 9, -15, ChlLR 5, ConAu X, IntAu&W 77X, -82X, -91, OxCAusL, OxCChiL, ScF&FL 92, SingR 1, SmATA 2, -3AS, ThrBJA, TwCChW 78, -83, -89, WhoAm 74, WhoAmW 74, WhoWor 74, WrDr 76, -80, -82, -84, -86, -88, -90, -92, -94*

Phipson, Joan Margaret 1912- *TwCYAW*

Phipson, Joan Margaret Fitzhardinge 1912- *DcChlFi*

Phiz *BioIn 1, -9, -11, -12, CamGLE, CelCen, ChhPo, DcBrBI, DcNaB, DcVicP 2, LongCEL, NewC, OxCArt, OxCEng 85, OxDcArt, REn, SmATA X*
Main entry: Browne, Hablot Knight

Phiz 1815-1882 *Benet 87, BlmGEL, StaCVF*

Phiz 1851-1882 *BioIn 16*

Phleger, Fred B 1909- *AmMWSc 86, -89, -92, AuBYP 3, BioIn 14, ConAu 21NR, WhoWrEP 89, -92*

Phleger, Frederick B 1909- *AmMWSc 73P, -82, AuBYP 2, BioIn 7, ConAu 1R, SmATA 34, WhoAm 74, WhoWor 74*

Phleger, Marjorie Temple d1986 *BioIn 16*

Phleger, Marjorie Temple 1908?-1986 *ConAu 118, SmATA 47N*

Phleger, Marjorie Temple 1909- *BioIn 9, ConAu 9R, ForWC 70, SmATA 1*

Phypps, Hyacinthe *SmATA X*
Main entry: Gorey, Edward St John

Piaget, Jean 1896-1980 *AnObit 1980, Benet 87, BiDPsy, BioIn 4, -5, -7, -8, -9, -10, -11, -12, -13, -14, -15, -17, ConAu 101, -31NR, CurBio 80N, DcTwHis, GuPsyc, InSci, IntEnSS 79, IntWW 79, -80, -81N, MajTwCW, MakMC, McGMS 80, NewYTBS 80, RAdv 13-3, SmATA 23N, ThTwC 87, WhDW, WhAm 7, WhoWor 80, WorAlBi, WorAl*

Piatti, Celestino 1922- *AuBYP 2, -3, BioIn 8, -9, -12, -13, -17, ChhPo S1, ChsFB I, ConAu 73, IlsCB 1957, -1967, SmATA 16, ThrBJA, WhoGrA 62, -82*

Picard, Barbara Leonie 1917- *AuBYP 2, –3, Au&Wr 71, BioIn 7, –9, –11, BritCA, ConAu 5R, –2NR, IntAu&W 77, –82, –86, –89, –91, MajAI, OxCChiL, SmATA 2, –10AS, ThrBJA, TwCChW 78, –83, –89, WrDr 76, –80, –82, –84, –86, –88, –90, –92, –94*

Picard, Dorothy Young 1906- *ConAu 45*
Pseud./variant:
Croman, Dorothy Young

Piccard, Joan Russell *ConAu 29R*

Picchio, Carlo *TwCChW 83B, –89B*

Pick, Robert 1898-1978 *BioIn 3, –11, ConAu 17R, –77, –8NR*

Pickard, Charles 1932- *BioIn 14, IlsBYP, SmATA 36*

Pickard, Dorothea Wilgus 1902- *ConAu 21R*

Picker, Ingrid 1932- *ConAu 25R*

Pickering, Edgar *CarSB*

Pickering, James Sayre 1897-1969 *BioIn 8, –13, –14, ConAu 1R, –103, –16NR, SmATA 28N, –36*

Pickering, Wilhelmina *TelT*
Main entry: Stirling, Anna Maria D Wilhelmina

Pickett, Carla 1944- *ConAu 37R*

Pickthall, Marjorie L C 1883-1922 *BenetAL 91*

Pickthall, Marjorie Lowry Christie 1883-1922 *BioIn 1, –17, CanNov, CanWr, Chambr 3, ChhPo, –S1, –S2, ConAu 107, CreCan 1, DcLEL, DcNAA, LongCTC, OxCCan, REnAL, TwCA, –SUP, WomNov*

Pienkowski, Jan *BioIn 14*

Pienkowski, Jan 1936- *BioIn 16, ScF&FL 92, SmATA 58*

Pienkowski, Jan Michal 1936- *BioIn 10, –12, ChlLR 6, ConAu 65, –11NR, –38NR, FourBJA, IlsCB 1967, MajAI, OxCChiL, SmATA 6, Who 82, –83, –85, –88, –90, –92*

Pier, Arthur Stanwood 1874-1966 *AmAu&B, AmLY, BenetAL 91, BiD&SB, BioIn 2, –7, –9, –10, CarSB, ChhPo, ConAu 25R, DcAmAu, JBA 34, –51, REnAL, WhAm 4, WhNAA*

Pierce, Edith Gray 1893-1977 *BioIn 15, ConAu 61, SmATA 45*
Pseud./variant:
Gray, Marian

Pierce, Frank Richardson 1887- *AmAu&B*

Pierce, Katherine *ConAu X, SmATA X*
Main entry: Saint John, Wylly Folk

Pierce, Mary Cunningham 1908- *AuBYP 2, –3, BioIn 8*
Pseud./variant:
Cunningham, Mary

Pierce, Meredith Ann *PenEncH*

Pierce, Meredith Ann 1958- *BioIn 16, –17, ChlLR 20, ConAu 26NR, IntAu&W 86, –89 –91, MajAI, ScF&FL 92, SixBJA, SmATA 48, –67, TwCChW 89, TwCYAW, WrDr 90, –92, –94*

Pierce, Meredith Ann 1959- *DcAmChF 1960*

Pierce, Philip Nason *AuBYP 2, –3, BioIn 7*

Pierce, Robert Fletcher Young 1852- *WhAm 4, WhNAA*

Pierce, Ruth Ireland *WrDr 86, –88*

Pierce, Ruth Ireland 1936- *BioIn 10, ConAu 29R, SmATA 5, WrDr 76, –80, –82, –84*

Pierce, Tamora 1954- *BioIn 16, ConAu 118, ScF&FL 92, SmATA 49, –51, TwCYAW*

Pierik, Robert 1921- *BioIn 11, ConAu 37R, SmATA 13*

Pierson, Clara Dillingham *CarSB*

Pierson, Sherleigh G *AuBYP 2, –3, BioIn 8*

Pig, Edward *ConAu X, –30NR, MajAI, SmATA 70, –X*
Main entry: Gorey, Edward St John

Piggott, Juliet *AuBYP 2S, –3*

Pike, Christopher *BioIn 17, ChlLR 29, ConAu 136, EncSF 93, ScF&FL 92, SmATA 68, TwCYAW, WrDr 94*

Pike, E Royston 1896- *BioIn 13, ConAu 9R, SmATA 22, WrDr 80*

Pike, E Royston 1896-1980 *BioIn 16, ConAu 125, SmATA 56N*

Pike, Morton *WhoChL*

Pike, Norman 1901- *ConAu P-2*

Pilarski, Laura P 1926- *WrDr 86, –88, –90, –92, –94*

Pilarski, Laura Patricia 1926- *AmCath 80, BioIn 11, ConAu 29R, IntAu&W 77, SmATA 13, WhoAmW 75, –77, WrDr 76, –80, –82, –84*

Pilgrim, Anne *AuBYP 2, -3, BioIn 10, ConAu X, IntAu&W 77X, -82X, -91X, MajAI, SmATA 5, -75, -X, TwCChW 83, -89, WrDr 76, -80, -82, -84, -86, -88, -90, -92*
Main entry: Allan, Mabel Esther

Pilgrim, Anne 1915- *WrDr 94*

Pilkey, Dav 1966- *BioIn 17, ConAu 136, SmATA 68, WrDr 94*

Pilkington, Francis Meredyth 1907- *BioIn 9, ConAu P-2, SmATA 4, WrDr 76, -80, -82, -84, -86, -88, -90*

Pilkington, Mary 1766-1839 *DcBrAmW, DcNaB, FemiCLE, OxCChiL*

Pilkington, Roger Windle 1915- *AuBYP 2, -3, Au&Wr 71, BioIn 7, -11, ConAu 1R, IntAu&W 77, -82, -89, -91, SmATA 10, Who 74, -82, -83, -85, -88, -92, WhoWor 80, WrDr 76, -80, -82, -84, -86, -88, -90, -92, -94*

Pilkington, Roger Windle, Dr 1915- *Who 90*

Pilling, Ann 1944- *ChlFicS, TwCChW 89, WrDr 90, -92, -94*

Pilss-Samek, Hannelore 1924- *IntAu&W 77*

Pimlott, Douglas Humphreys 1920- *AmMWSc 73P, -76P, -82*

Pinchard, Elizabeth *DcBrAmW, FemiCLE, OxCChiL*

Pinchot, David d1983 *BioIn 14*

Pinchot, David 1914?-1983 *ConAu 109, SmATA 34N*

Pincus, Harriet 1938- *AmPB, BioIn 12, -13, ConAu 102, FourBJA, IlsBYP, IlsCB 1967, SmATA 27*

Pine, Tillie Schloss 1896- *AuBYP 2, -3, BioIn 8, -11, BkP, ConAu 69, SmATA 13*

Pines, Maya *Au&Wr 71, ConAu 13R, WrDr 76, -80, -82, -84, -86, -88, -90*

Pinkerton, Kathrene Sutherland 1887-1967 *AuBYP 2, -3, BioIn 1, -3, -7, -8, -13, ConAu 1R, -103, CurBio 40, -67, SmATA 26N, WhAm 4A*

Pinkney, Brian *ChlBIlD*

Pinkney, Brian 1961- *BlkAuII 92*

Pinkney, J Brian *SmATA 74*

Pinkney, Jerry 1939- *AfroAA, BioIn 8, -12, -14, -15, -16, -17, BlkAuII, -92, ChlBIlD, IlrAm 1880, IlsCB 1957, -1967, InB&W 80, MajAI, SixBJA, SmATA 32, -41, -71, -12AS, WhoAm 94, WhoAmA 86, -89, -91, WhoBlA 90, -92, -94, WhoE 91*

Pinkney, Jerry Brian 1961- *SmATA 74*

Pinkwater, Daniel M 1941- *ScF&FL 92*

Pinkwater, Daniel Manus 1941- *Au&Arts 1, AuBYP 2S, BioIn 11, -15, -17, ChlLR 4, ConAu 29R, -12NR, -38NR, ConLC 35, EncSF 93, FifBJA, IntAu&W 77, MajAI, SmATA 8, -46, -76, -3AS, TwCChW 89, TwCSFW 91, TwCYAW, WhoAm 86, -88, -90, -92, WhoE 75, WrDr 90, -92, -94*
Pseud./variant:
Pinkwater, Manus

Pinkwater, Manus *ConAu 38NR, MajAI, SmATA 76, TwCChW 89, WrDr 90, -92*
Main entry: Pinkwater, Daniel Manus

Pinkwater, Manus 1941- *AuBYP 3, BioIn 15, -17*

Pinner, Joma *ConAu X, -34NR, SmATA X*
Main entry: Werner, Herma

Pinney, Roy 1911- *ConAu 5R, -6NR*

Pinson, William M, Jr. 1934- *WrDr 86, -88, -90, -92*

Pinson, William Meredith 1934- *WhoRel 92, WhoSSW 91, -93*

Pinson, William Meredith, Jr. 1934- *ConAu 17R, -9NR, DrAS 74P, -78P, -82P, IntAu&W 77, -89, WhoAm 82, WhoRel 75, -77, WhoSSW 73, -84, WhoWor 82, WrDr 76, -82, -84, -94*

Pinto, Jacqueline 1927- *Au&Wr 71, WrDr 76, -80, -82, -84, -86, -88, -90, -92, -94*

Pinto, Ralph *IlsBYP*

Pintoff, Ernest 1931- *BioIn 6, -7, ConAu 17R, DcFM, FilmgC, HalFC 84, -88, OxCFilm, WhoAm 78, -80, -82, -84, -86, -88, WorECar, WorEFlm*

Pioneer *ConAu X, SmATA X*
Main entry: Yates, Raymond Francis

Piowaty, Kim Kennelly 1957- *BioIn 16, SmATA 49*

Piper, Roger *ConAu X, SmATA X*
Main entry: Fisher, John

Piper, Watty *ChhPo, -S2, ConAu 137, DcLB 22, MajAI, SmATA X*
Main entry: Bragg, Mabel Caroline

Pippen, Christie *AuBYP 3*

Pippet, Gabriel Joseph 1880- *BioIn 1, –14, ChhPo S1, IlsCB 1744*

Pirani, Leila *SingR 1*

Pirmantgen, Patricia H 1933- *ConAu 45, WhoAmW 77*

Pirner, Connie White 1955- *SmATA 72*

Piro, Richard 1934- *BioIn 10, ConAu 49, SmATA 7*

Pirsig, Robert M 1928- *BenetAL 91, ConLC 73, CyWA 89, MajTwCW*

Pirsig, Robert Maynard 1928- *BioIn 10, –13, ConAu 42NR, SmATA 39, WhoAm 80, –82, –84, –86, –88, –90, –92, –94, WhoUSWr 88, WhoWrEP 89, –92*

Pissarro, Lucien 1863-1944 *BioIn 1, –2, –3, –5, –6, –8, –9, –11, –14, ClaDrA, DcBrAr 1, DcBrBI, DcNaB 1941, DcVicP 2, GrBr, IlsCB 1744, –1946, OxCArt, OxCTwCA, OxDcArt, PhDcTCA 77, TwCPaSc*

Pistorius, Anna *AuBYP 2, –3, BioIn 2, –7*

Pitcher, Robert Walter 1918- *AmMWSc 73S, –78S, ConAu 29R, LEduc 74, WhoMW 74, –76, –78*

Pitkin, Dorothy 1899?-1972 *BioIn 9, ConAu 37R*

Pitman, James 1901- *IntAu&W 91, WrDr 86, –88*

Pitman, James 1901-1985 *DcNaB 1981, SmATA 46N*

Pitman, James, Sir 1901-1985 *AnObit 1985, BioIn 15*

Pitrone, Jean 1920- *AuBYP 3*

Pitrone, Jean Maddern 1920- *AuBYP 2S, BioIn 9, ConAu 17R, –8NR, ForWC 70, SmATA 4, WhoAmW 74, –75, –83, –91, WhoMW 84, WrDr 76, –80, –82, –84, –86, –88, –90, –92, –94*

Pitseolak *WhoAm 86*

Pitseolak 1902?- *BioIn 10, –12, –13, OxCCan SUP, WhoGrA 82*

Pitt, Sarah *Alli SUP, CarSB*

Pitt, Valerie
Main entry: Hall, Valerie

Pitt, Valerie 1939- *IntAu&W 77X, –82*

Pittenger, William Norman 1905- *AmAu&B, Au&Wr 71, ConAu 1R, DrAS 74P, –78P, –82P, IntAu&W 77, –82, WhoAm 74, –76, WhoWor 74, WrDr 76, –80*

Pittman, Helena Clare 1945- *SmATA 71*

Pitz, Henry Clarence 1895-1976 *AmAu&B, BioIn 1, –2, –3, –4, –5, –6, –8, –9, –11, –12, –13, ChhPo, –S1, ConAu 9R, –69, –9NR, ConICB, ForIl, IlrAm 1880, –E, IlsBYP, IlsCB 1744, –1946, –1957, –1967, IntAu&W 77, MorJA, OxCChiL, SmATA 4, –24N, WhAm 7, WhAmArt 85, WhoAm 74, –76, WhoAmA 73, –78N, –80N, –82N, –86N, –89N, –91N, WrDr 76, –80*

Piussi-Campbell, Judy *IlsBYP*

Pizer, Abigail *AuBYP 3*

Pizer, Vernon 1918- *AuBYP 2, –3, BioIn 7, –12, ConAu 1R, –4NR, SmATA 21, WrDr 76, –80, –82, –84, –86, –88, –90, –92, –94*

Place, Marian T 1910- *ConAu 20NR*

Place, Marian Templeton 1910- *AuBYP 2, –3, BioIn 7, –9, ConAu 1R, –5NR, IndAu 1917, SmATA 3, WhoAmW 74, WhoPNW*
Pseud./variant:
White, Dale
Whitinger, R D

Place, Robin Mary 1926- *SmATA 71*

Plagemann, Bentz 1913- *AmAu&B, AmNov, AuBYP 2S, –3, BioIn 2, –3, –14, ConAu 1R, –4NR, IntAu&W 91, WrDr 84, –86, –88, –90*

Plagemann, Bentz 1913-1991 *BioIn 17, ConAu 134*

Plaidy, Jean *Au&Wr 71, BioIn 7, –9, –10, –11, ConAu 140, –X, –28NR, ConLC 7, IntAu&W 77X, –91X, Novels, SmATA 2, –74, TwCRHW 90, TwCWr, Who 74, –82, –83, –85, –88, –90, –92, WorAu 1950, WrDr 76, –80, –82, –84, –86, –88, –90, –92*
Main entry: Hibbert, Eleanor Burford

Plaidy, Jean 1906- *BioIn 14, BlmGWL, FemiCLE, InWom SUP*

Plaidy, Jean 1906-1993 *WrDr 94N*

Plain, Belva *BioIn 17, DrAPF 87, –89, –91, –93*

Plain, Belva 1918- *IntAu&W 91, WrDr 86, –88, –90, –92, –94*

Plain, Belva 1919- *BestSel 89-4, ConAu 29NR, SmATA 62*

Plaine, Alfred R 1898?-1981 *BioIn 12, -13, ConAu 105, SmATA 29N*

Planche, James Robinson 1795-1880 *CamGWoT*

Planche, James Robinson 1796-1880 *Alli, -SUP, BbD, BiD&SB, BioIn 8, -12, -16, BritAu 19, CamGLE, CarSB, CasWL, CelCen, Chambr 3, ChhPo, -S1, DcBiPP, DcEnA, DcEnL, DcEuL, DcNaB, EncWT, EvLB, IntDcT 2, NewC, NinCLC 42, NotNAT A, -B, OxCChiL, OxCEng 67, -85, OxCThe 67, -83, REn, RfGEnL 91, TelT*

Plant, John 1914- *ArtsCL, BioIn 6*

Plasencia, Peter P *IlsBYP*

Plate, Robert 1918- *AuBYP 2, -3, BioIn 7, ConAu 17R, WrDr 76, -80, -82, -84*

Plate, Thomas 1944- *ConAu 69, -23NR*

Plate, Thomas Gordon 1944- *WhoAm 92, WhoWest 92, -94*

Platero, Dillon 1926- *BioIn 9*

Plath, Sylvia *BioIn 14, -15, -16, -17, IntvTCA 2*

Plath, Sylvia d1963 *NewYTBS 88*

Plath, Sylvia 1932-1963 *AmAu&B, AmWomWr, AmWr S1, ArtclWW 2, AuBYP 2S, -3, Benet 87, BenetAL 91, BioAmW, BioIn 7, -8, -9, -10, -11, -12, -13, BlmGEL, BlmGWL, CamGEL, CamGLE, CamHAL, CasWL, ChhPo S1, ConAu 34NR, -P-2, ConLC 1, -2, -3, -5, -9, -11, -17, -51, -62, ConPo 75, -80A, -85A, ContDcW 89, CroCAP, CyWA 89, DcAmB S7, DcLB 5, -6, DcLEL 1940, DcNaB MP, EncWB, EncWL, -2, FemiCLE, HanAmWH, InWom SUP, IntDcWB, LongCEL, LongCTC, MagSAmL, MajTwCW, MakMC, ModAL S1, -S2, ModAWP, ModAWWr, NewCon, NewYTBS 74, NotAW MOD, Novels, OxCAmL 65, -83, OxCEng 85, PenC AM, PoeCrit 1, RAdv 1, -13-1, RfGAmL 87, TwCWr, TwCYAW, WebE&AL, WhDW, WhAm 4, WhoTwCL, WorAlBi, WorAl, WorAu 1950, WorLitC, WrPh*

Platt, Charles 1944- *ConAu 21R, ConSFA, IntAu&W 91, NewEScF, ScFSB, TwCSFW 86, -91, WhoSciF, WrDr 84, -86, -88, -90, -92, -94*

Platt, Charles 1945- *ConAu 24NR, ScF&FL 92*

Platt, Charles Michael 1945- *EncSF 93*

Platt, Kin 1911- *Au&Arts 11, AuBYP 2S, -3, BioIn 8, -12, -16, ConAu 17R, -11NR, ConLC 26, DcAmChF 1960, FifBJA, ScF&FL 92, SmATA 21, -17AS, WhoAm 74*

Platt, Rutherford Hayes 1894-1975 *BioIn 10, ConAu 61, OhA&B, WhAm 6*

Pleck, Joseph H 1946- *ConAu 23NR*

Pleck, Joseph Healy 1946- *AmMWSc 78S, ConAu 57, -7NR, WhoFrS 84*

Pletsch, Oskar 1830-1888 *CarSB, ChhPo S2*

Plimpton, George Ames 1927- *AuNews 1, BioIn 4, -6, -7, -8, -9, -10, -11, CelR, ConAu 21R, CurBio 69, EncTwCJ, IntWW 91, NewYTBE 70, SmATA 10, WebAB 74, -79, WhoAm 74, -80, -82, -84, -86, -88, -90, -92, -94, WhoE 91, -93, WhoHol A, WhoUSWr 88, WhoWor 74, WhoWrEP 89, -92, WrDr 80*

Plimpton, Ruth Talbot 1916- *ConAu 13R*

Pliss, Louise *AuBYP 2, -3, BioIn 7*

Plomer, William Charles Franklin 1903-1973 *ConAu 34NR, MajTwCW*

Plomer, William Charles Franklyn 1903-1973 *Au&Wr 71, BioIn 4, -8, -10, -13, BlkAWP, CamGEL, CasWL, Chambr 3, ChhPo, -S2, CnE&AP, ConAu P-2, ConLC 4, -8, ConNov 72, ConPo 70, -75, DcLB 20, DcLEL, DcNaB 1971, EncSoA, EncWL, -2, EvLB, IntAu&W 77, -82, LongCTC, ModBrL, -S1, ModCmwL, NewC, Novels, ObitT 1971, OxCEng 85, PenC ENG, REn, SmATA 24, TwCA, -SUP, TwCWr, WebE&AL, WhDW, WhoTwCL, WhoWor 74*

Plotz, Helen 1913- *BioIn 15, -16, SixBJA*

Plotz, Helen Ratnoff 1913- *ChhPo, -S1, ConAu 9R, -8NR, SmATA 38*

Plowden, Alison 1931- *ConAu 33R, -15NR, IntAu&W 91, WrDr 76, -80, -82, -84, -86, -88, -90, -92*

Plowden, Alison Margaret Chichele 1931- *WrDr 94*

Plowden, David 1932- *BioIn 11, ConAu 33R, ConPhot 82, -88, ICPEnP A, MacBEP, SmATA 52, WhoAm 94, WhoAmA 86, -89, -91, WrDr 90, -92, -94*

Plowhead, Ruth Gipson 1877-1967 *AmAu&B, BioIn 15, SmATA 43, WhAm 6*

Plowitz, Kurt M 1912?-1969 *BioIn 8*

Plowman, Stephanie 1922- *BioIn 10, ConAu 53, -5NR, OxCChiL, SmATA 6,*

TwCChW 78, –83, –89, WrDr 76, –80, –82, –84, –86, –88, –90, –92, –94

Pluche, Noel-Antoine 1688-1761 *CarSB, DcScB, OxCFr*

Pluckrose, Henry 1931- *BioIn 11, ConAu 33R, IntAu&W 91, SmATA 13, WrDr 80, –82, –84, –86, –88, –90*
Pseud./variant:
Cobbett, Richard

Pluff, Barbara 1926- *AuBYP 3*

Pluff, Barbara Littlefield 1926- *AuBYP 2S, ConAu 5R*
Pseud./variant:
Clayton, Barbara

Plum, J *ConAu 33NR, MajTwCW, SmATA X*
Main entry: Kurland, Michael Joseph

Plumb, Charles P 1900?-1982 *BioIn 13, ConAu 105, SmATA 29N*

Plume, Ilse *BioIn 15, FifBJA, SmATA 43*

Plummer, Beverly Jeanette 1918- *ConAu 29R, WhoAmW 75, WrDr 76, –80, –82, –84*

Plummer, Margaret 1911- *BioIn 9, ConAu P-2, SmATA 2*

Plummer, William Kirtman *IlsBYP*

Plympton, Almira George 1852-1939 *Alli SUP, AmAu&B, CarSB, ChhPo, DcAmAu, DcNAA, WomWWA 14, WomNov*

Pocci, Franz, Graf Von 1807-1876 *Baker 84, –92, BiD&SB, ChhPo S1, OxCGer 76, –86*

Pochocki, Ethel Frances 1925- *SmATA 76*
Pseud./variant:
Marbach, Ethel

Pocklington, Geoffrey Richard 1879- *ChhPo S1, –S2*

Pocock, Guy Noel 1880- *ChhPo, –S1*

Pocock, Roger 1865-1941 *BioIn 8, OxCCan, OxCCanL, ScFEYrs, TwCWW 91, WhoLA*

Podendorf, Illa E 1903?-1983 *BioIn 12, ConAu 81, –110, ForWC 70, SmATA 18, –35N*

Poe, Charlsie 1909- *ConAu P-2*

Poe, Edgar Allan 1809-1849 *Alli, AmAu, AmAu&B, AmWr, AnCL, AtlBL, Benet 87, BenetAL 91, BbD, BiDSA, BiD&SB, BioIn 1, –2, –3, –4, –5, –6, –7, –8, –9, –10, –11, –12, –13, –14, –15, –16, –17, BlmGEL, CamGEL, CamGLE, CamHAL, CasWL, CelCen, Chambr 3, ChhPo, –S1, –S2, CnDAL, CnE&AP, CrtSuMy, CrtT 3, CyAL, CyWA 58, DcAmAu, DcBiA, DcBiPP, DcEnA, DcEnL, DcLB 3, –59, –73, –74, DcLEL, DcNAA, Dis&D, EncAB-H, EncAJ, EncMys, EncSF 93, EncSoH, EvLB, FifSWrB, FilmgC, HalFC 84, –88, HarEnUS, MagSAmL, McGEWB, MemAm, MorMA, MouLC 3, NewEScF, NewGrDA 86, NinCLC 1, –16, Novels, OxCAmH, OxCAmL 65, –83, OxCAmT 84, OxCEng 67, –85, PenC AM, PenEncH, PoeCrit 1, RAdv 1, –13-1, RComAH, RComWL, REn, REnAL, RfGAmL 87, RfGShF, ScF&FL 92, ScFSB, ScFEYrs, ShSCr 1, ShSWr, SmATA 23, SpyFic, Str&VC, SupFW, TwCCr&M 80A, –85A, –91A, WebAB 74, –79, WebE&AL, WhDW, WhAm HS, WhoHr&F, WhoSciF, WorAlBi, WorAl, WorLitC*

Poe, Edgar Allan 1871-1961 *BiDAmSp FB*

Pogany, William Andrew 1882-1955 *ArtsAmW 2, IlrAm 1880, SmATA 44, WhAmArt 85*
Pseud./variant:
Pogany, Willy

Pogany, Willy
Main entry: Pogany, William Andrew

Pogany, Willy 1882-1955 *BioIn 1, –2, –3, –4, –6, –12, –14, –15, ChhPo, –S1, –S2, ConICB, IlsBYP, IlsCB 1744, JBA 34, –51, NotNAT B, ObitOF 79, OxCChiL, REn, SmATA 30, WhAm 3*

Pohl, Frederik *DrAPF 87, –89, –91, –93, IntvTCA 2*

Pohl, Frederik 1919- *Benet 87, BioIn 10, –11, –12, –13, –14, –15, –17, ConAu 61, –1AS, –11NR, –37NR, ConLC 18, ConNov 72, –76, –82, –86, –91, ConSFA, CyWA 89, DcLB 8, DrAF 76, DrAPF 83, –85, EncSF 93, Future, IntAu&W 77, –82, –91, MajTwCW, NewEScF, Novels, PenC AM, RGTwCSF, ScF&FL 92, ScFSB, SmATA 24, TwCSFW 86, –91, WhoAm 74, –76, –78, –80, –86, –88, –90, –92, –94, WhoSciF, WhoUSWr 88, WhoWrEP 89, –92, WorAlBi, WorAl, WorAu 1950, WrDr 76, –80, –82, –84, –86, –88, –90, –92, –94*

Pohlmann, Lillian 1902- *AuBYP 2, –3, BioIn 8, –11, ConAu 9R, ForWC 70, SmATA 11, WrDr 76, –80, –82, –84*

Pohrt, Tom *SmATA 67*

Poignant, Axel 1906- *BioIn 14, OxCAusL*

Poindexter, David 1929- *ConAu 29R*

Poindexter, Marian Jean 1929- *ConAu 29R*

Pointon, Robert *BlmGWL, ConAu X, IntAu&W 77X, -82X, SmATA X*
Main entry: Rooke, Daphne Marie

Pointon, Robert 1914- *WrDr 94*

Pola *ConAu X, -29NR, SmATA X*
Main entry: Watson, Pauline

Polacco, Patricia *ChlBlID*

Polacco, Patricia 1944- *SmATA 74*

Poland, Marguerite 1950- *TwCChW 89, WrDr 90, -92, -94*

Polatnick, Florence T 1923- *BioIn 10, ConAu 29R, SmATA 5*

Polder, Markus *ConAu X, IntAu&W 77X, -82X, MajAI, SmATA 8*
Main entry: Kruess, James

Pole, James T *AuBYP 2S, -3*

Polese, Carolyn 1947- *BioIn 16, ConAu 127, DcAmChF 1985, SmATA 58*

Polese, Marcia Ann 1949- *ConAu 65*

Polette, Nancy 1930- *BioIn 15, ConAu 6NR, -21NR, SmATA 42, WhoUSWr 88, WhoWrEP 89*

Polette, Nancy Jane 1930- *WhoWrEP 92*

Polgreen, John *IlsBYP, WhAmArt 85*

Polhamus, Jean Burt 1928- *BioIn 12, ConAu 103, SmATA 21*

Policoff, Stephen Phillip 1948- *SmATA 77*

Polikoff, Barbara Garland 1929- *SmATA 77*

Polisar, Barry Louis 1954- *SmATA 77, WhoE 93*

Politi, Leo 1908- *AmPB, AuBYP 2, -3, Au&ICB, BioIn 1, -2, -3, -4, -5, -7, -8, -9, -12, -14, -16, BkP, Cald 1938, CathA 1952, ChlLR 29, ConAu 17R, -13NR, IlsBYP, IlsCB 1744, -1946, -1957, -1967, JBA 51, MajAI, OxCChiL, SmATA 1, -47, Str&VC, TwCChW 78, WhAmArt 85, WrDr 80, -82, -84, -86, -88, -90*

Polk, Dora 1923- *ConAu 49*

Polking, Kirk 1925- *BioIn 10, ConAu 29R, -12NR, -30NR, ForWC 70, IntAu&W 89, SmATA 5, WhoMW 74, -76, -78, -84, WhoUSWr 88, WhoWrEP 89, -92, WrDr 76, -80, -82, -84, -86, -88, -90, -92, -94*

Pollack, Cecelia 1909- *ConAu 29R, LEduc 74*

Pollack, Merrill S 1924- *BioIn 3, ConAu 5R*

Pollack, Merrill S 1924-1988 *ConAu 124, SmATA 55N*

Pollack, Pamela D *MedPD, WhoLibI 82*

Pollack, Peter 1911-1978 *BioIn 11, ConAu 77, -81, ICPEnP, MacBEP, WhoAmA 73, -78, -80N, -82N, -86N, -89N, -91N*

Pollack, Reginald Murray 1924- *BioIn 8, -12, ConAu 37R, DcCAA 71, -77, IlsCB 1957, -1967, WhoAm 74, -76, -78, -80, -82, -84, -86, -88, -90, -92, -94, WhoAmA 73, -78, -80, -82, -84, -86, -89, -91, WhoWor 74, WrDr 76, -80*

Pollak, Felix *DrAPF 87, IntvTCA 2*

Pollak, Felix 1909- *BiDrLUS 70, BioIn 9, ConAu 25R, -10NR, DrAP 75, DrAPF 83, -85, IntAu&W 89, WhoLibS 55, -66, WhoMW 74, -76, -78, WhoUSWr 88, WhoWrEP 89, -92, WrDr 76, -80, -82, -84*

Polland, Barbara K 1939- *BioIn 15*

Polland, Barbara Kay 1939- *ConAu 73, SmATA 44*

Polland, Madeleine A 1918- *BioIn 17, IntAu&W 91, SmATA 68, -8AS, TwCChW 89, TwCRHW 90, WrDr 88, -90, -92*

Polland, Madeleine Angela 1918- *IntAu&W 86, WrDr 94*

Polland, Madeleine Angela Cahill 1918- *AuBYP 2, -3, BioIn 7, -9, -10, ConAu 5R, -3NR, -37NR, MajAI, SmATA 6, ThrBJA, TwCChW 78, -83, WrDr 80, -82, -84*
Pseud./variant:
Adrian, Frances

Pollard, Alfred *CarSB*

Pollard, Jack 1926- *ConAu 29R, -30NR*

Polley, Judith Anne 1938- *IntAu&W 86, -89, -91, WrDr 80, -82, -84, -86, -88, -90, -92, -94*

Pollinger, Gerald J *AuBYP 3*

Pollinger, Gerald J 1925- *AuBYP 2S, Au&Wr 71*

Pollock, Bruce 1945- *BioIn 15, ConAu 23NR, SmATA 46*

Pollock, Bruce 1951- *WhoAmA 86*

Pollock, Dean 1897- *WhoPNW*

Pollock, George 1938- *ConAu 61*

Pollock, Mary *AuBYP 3, ConAu X, –33NR, MajAI, SmATA X, TwCChW 83, –89*
Main entry: Blyton, Enid Mary

Pollock, Penny 1935- *BioIn 15, ConAu 101, SmATA 42, –44*

Pollowitz, Melinda Kilborn 1944- *BioIn 13, ConAu 77, –13NR, SmATA 26*

Polmar, Norman 1938- *Au&Wr 71, ConAu 49*

Polner, Murray *BioIn 17*

Polner, Murray 1928- *ConAu 23NR, SmATA 64*

Polo, Eddie 1875-1961 *BioIn 17, MotPP, WhScrn 74, –83, –77, WhoHol B*

Polonsky, Arthur 1925- *BioIn 1, –14, SmATA 34, WhoAm 80, –82, –84, –86, –88, –90, –92, –94, WhoAmA 73, –78, –80, –82, –84, –86, –89, –91, WhoAmJ 80, WhoE 93, WhoWorJ 72, –78*

Polseno, Jo *BioIn 12, ConAu 81, IlsBYP, SmATA 17*

Polushkin, Maria *AuBYP 2S, –3, BioIn 16, SixBJA*

Polykoff, Shirley *BioIn 7, –8, –10, –14, ForWC 70, InWom SUP, WhoAmW 74, WhoE 74, –75, WhoFI 74, –75*

Pomerantz, Charlotte *BioIn 16*

Pomerantz, Charlotte 1930- *AuBYP 2S, –3, BioIn 12, ConAu 85, –16NR, –38NR, SixBJA, SmATA 20, WhoAm 78, –80, –82, –84, –86, WhoUSWr 88, WhoWrEP 89, –92*

Pomeroy, Pete *AuBYP 2S, –3, ConAu 140, –X, SmATA 75, –X*
Main entry: Roth, Arthur J

Pomeroy, Wardell Baxter 1913- *AmMWSc 73S, –78S, BioIn 10, ConAu 1R, –1NR, CurBio 74, IndAu 1917, WhoAm 74, –76, –78, –80, –82, –84, –86*

Pomminville, Louise 1940- *BioIn 13, Profile 2*

Pond, Alonzo William 1894- *AmMWSc 73S, –76P, BioIn 10, ConAu 1R, –1NR, SmATA 5, WhoAm 74, –76, –78, –80, –82, –84, –86*

Pond, Alonzo William 1894-1986 *WhAm 9*

Pond, Grace Isabelle 1910- *Au&Wr 71, ConAu 13R, IntAu&W 77, –82, WrDr 76, –80*

Pond, John Hamilton 1923- *WhoFI 74, –75*

Pond, Seymour Gates 1896- *AuBYP 2, –3, BioIn 8*

Ponsot, Marie Birmingham 1922- *ConAu 9R, ForWC 70*

Pont, Clarice Holt 1907- *ConAu 5R*

Pontiflet, Ted *IlBBlP*

Pontiflet, Ted 1932- *BioIn 14, ConAu 105, SmATA 32*

Pool, Eugene 1943- *ConAu 85*

Pool, Eugene Hillhouse 1943- *WhoE 89*

Poole, Frederick King 1934- *BioIn 9, ConAu 25R*

Poole, Gray 1906- *AuBYP 3*

Poole, Gray Johnson 1906- *AuBYP 2, –2S, BioIn 7, –9, ConAu 5R, –6NR, SmATA 1*

Poole, Josephine *IntAu&W 86X*

Poole, Josephine 1933- *Au&Wr 71, BioIn 10, –15, ConAu 21R, –10NR, ConLC 17, IntAu&W 77, ScF&FL 92, SmATA 5, –2AS, TwCChW 78, –83, –89, WrDr 76, –80, –82, –84, –86, –88, –90, –92, –94*

Poole, Lynn 1910-1969 *AuBYP 3*

Poole, Lynn D 1910-1969 *AmAu&B, AuBYP 2, –2S, BioIn 3, –6, –7, –8, –9, ConAu 5R, CurBio 54, –69, MorJA, SmATA 1, WhAm 5*

Poole, Peggy 1925- *BioIn 15, ConAu 107, –24NR, SmATA 39*
Pseud./variant:
Roche, Terry

Poole, Peter Andrews *AmMWSc 73S, ConAu 113*

Pooley, Sarah *AuBYP 3*

Poortvliet, Marien *ScF&FL 92, SmATA 65, –X*
Main entry: Poortvliet, Rien

Poortvliet, Rien *BioIn 15, –16, –17*

Poortvliet, Rien 1932- *ConAu 136, SmATA 65*
Pseud./variant:
Poortvliet, Marien

Poortvliet, Rien 1933?- *BioIn 12, ScF&FL 92, SmATA 37*

Pope, Clifford Hillhouse 1899-1974 *AmAu&B, AmMWSc 73P, AuBYP 2, –3, Au&Wr 71, BioIn 7, ConAu 1R, –103, WhAm 6, WhoAm 74*

Pope, Elizabeth Marie 1917- *AuBYP 2S, –3, BioIn 14, –15, ConAu 49, DcAmChF 1960,*

DrAS 74E, –78E, –82E, FifBJA, ScF&FL 92, SmATA 36, –38

Pope, Joyce *AuBYP 3*

Pope, Ray 1924- *IntAu&W 91, WrDr 86, –88, –90*

Pope, Ray 1924-1979 *ConAu 29R, WrDr 80, –82, –84*

Popescu, Christine 1930- *ConAu 13R, –7NR, –20NR, IntAu&W 77, –82, –86*
Pseud./variant:
Keir, Christine
Pullein-Thompson, Christine
Thompson, Christine Pullein

Popescu, Julian John Hunter 1928- *Au&Wr 71, ConAu 1R, –1NR*

Popham, Estelle I 1906- *ConAu 1R, –5NR, ForWC 70, WhoAm 74*

Popham, Hugh 1920- *Au&Wr 71, ConAu 5R, –6NR, DcLEL 1940, EngPo, IntAu&W 91, IntWWP 82, WrDr 76, –80, –82, –84, –86, –88, –90, –92, –94*

Poploff, Michelle 1956- *ConAu 135, SmATA 67, WrDr 94*

Poppel, Hans 1942- *SmATA 71*

Poppleton, Marjorie 1895- *Au&Wr 71, BlueB 76, ConAu P-1, WrDr 76, –80*

Porcari, Constance Kwolek 1933- *ConAu 33R*
Pseud./variant:
Kwolek, Constance

Porchat, J J 1800-1864 *Alli, CarSB*

Portal, Colette 1936- *BioIn 8, –10, ConAu 53, FourBJA, IlsCB 1957, –1967, SmATA 6, WhoGrA 82*

Porte, Barbara Ann *AuBYP 3, BioIn 15, –16, DrAPF 85, –87, –89, –91, –93, SmATA 45, –57*
Pseud./variant:
Porte-Thomas, Barbara Ann

Porte, Barbara Ann 1943- *BioIn 16, SixBJA*

Porteous, Richard S 1897- *SingR 1*

Porter, Admiral *CarSB*

Porter, A P 1945- *SmATA 68*

Porter, Anthony Peyton 1945- *ConAu 136*

Porter, Donald Clayton 1914-1988 *ConAu 127, SmATA X*
Main entry: Gerson, Noel Bertram

Porter, Eleanor H *Benet 87*

Porter, Eleanor H 1868-1920 *BenetAL 91, BioIn 14, TwCChW 89, TwCRHW 90*

Porter, Eleanor Hodgman 1868-1920 *AmAu&B, AmLY, AmWomPl, AmWomWr, BioIn 1, –3, –8, CarSB, ConAu 108, DcLB 9, DcLEL, DcNAA, EvLB, InWom SUP, LongCTC, OxCAmL 65, –83, OxCChiL, REn, REnAL, TwCA, –SUP, TwCChW 83, TwCWr, WhAm 1, WhoChL*

Porter, Ella Blodwen *AuBYP 2, –3, BioIn 7, ForWC 70*

Porter, Gene Stratton 1862-1924 *InWom SUP*

Porter, Gene Stratton 1863-1924 *Benet 87, BenetAL 91, BioIn 14, –15, –17, TwCChW 89, TwCLC 21, TwCRHW 90*

Porter, Gene Stratton 1868-1924 *AmAu&B, AmLY, BioIn 1, –2, –5, –8, –9, –10, CarSB, ChhPo, CnDAL, ConAu 112, DcLEL, DcNAA, EvLB, HalFC 84, IndAu 1816, LongCTC, Novels, OxCAmL 65, –83, OxCChiL, PenC AM, REn, REnAL, TwCA, –SUP, TwCChW 78, –83, TwCWr, WebAB 74, –79, WhAm 1, WhoChL, WomWWA 14*

Porter, Gene Stratton 1886-1924 *HalFC 88*

Porter, George *IlsBYP*

Porter, George 1920- *IntAu&W 91*

Porter, Horace 1863- *CarSB*

Porter, Jane 1776-1850 *Alli, ArtclWW 2, BbD, BiDLA, BiD&SB, BioIn 1, –5, –16, BritAu 19, CamGEL, CamGLE, CarSB, CelCen, Chambr 2, CmScLit, CyWA 58, DcBiA, DcBiPP, DcEnA, DcEnL, DcEuL, DcLB 116, DcLEL, DcNaB, EncBrWW, EvLB, FemiCLE, HsB&A, InWom SUP, NewC, OxCEng 67, –85, REn*

Porter, Janice Lee 1953- *SmATA 68*

Porter, Jean Macdonald 1906- *BioIn 5, IlsBYP, IlsCB 1946*

Porter, Katherine Ann 1951- *WhoMW 92*

Porter, Katherine Anne *IntvTCA 2*

Porter, Katherine Anne 1890- *WorAlBi*

Porter, Katherine Anne 1890-1980 *AmAu&B, AmWomWr, AmWr, AnObit 1980, ArtclWW 2, AuNews 2, Benet 87, BenetAL 91, BiDConC, BioAmW, BioIn 1, –3, –4, –5, –6, –7, –8, –9, –10, –11, –12, –13, –14, –15, –16, –17, BlmGWL, BlueB 76, CamGEL, CamGLE, CamHAL, CasWL, CelR, CnDAL, CnMWL,*

ConAmA, ConAu 1R, –101, –1NR, ConLC 1, –3, –7, –10, –13, –15, –27, ConNov 72, –76, ContDcW 89, CurBio 40, –63, –80N, CyWA 58, –89, DcLB 4, –9, –102, –Y80A, DcLEL, DrAF 76, EncFWF, EncSoH, EncWL, –2, EvLB, FemiCLE, FifSWrA, ForWC 70, HalFC 84, –88, InWom SUP, IntAu&W 77, IntDcWB, IntWW 74, –76, –77, –78, –79, –80, –81N, LongCTC, MagSAmL, MajTwCW, MakMC, McGEWB, ModAL, –S1, –S2, ModAWWr, NewYTBE 70, NewYTBS 80, Novels, OxCAmL 65, –83, OxCEng 67, –85, PenC AM, RAdv 1, REn, REnAL, RfGAmL 87, RfGShF, ShSCr 4, ShSWr, SmATA 23N, –39, TwCA, –SUP, TwCWW 91, TwCWr, WebAB 74, –79, WebE&AL, WhDW, WhAm 7, Who 74, WhoAm 74, –76, –78, –80, WhoAmW 74, –75, –77, –81, WhoE 74, WhoTwCL, WhoWor 74, –78, WorAl, WrDr 76, –80

Porter, Katherine Anne 1894-1980 *AmWomWr 92, RAdv 13-1*

Porter, Kathryn *SmATA X*
Main entry: Swinford, Betty June Wells

Porter, Mark *AuBYP 3, ConAu X*
Main entry: Leckie, Robert

Porter, Sheena 1935- *BioIn 7, –9, –13, ConAu 81, IntAu&W 82, OxCChiL, SmATA 24, –10AS, ThrBJA, TwCChW 78, –83, –89, WrDr 80, –82, –84, –86, –88, –90, –92, –94*
Pseud./variant:
Lane, Sheena Porter

Porter, Sue 1951- *SmATA 76*

Porter, William Sidney 1862-1910 *CamHAL*

Porter, William Sydney *Benet 87, BenetAL 91, RfGAmL 87*

Porter, William Sydney 1862-1910 *AmAu&B, AtlBL, AuBYP 2S, –3, BioIn 1, –2, –3, –4, –5, –6, –7, –8, –9, –10, –11, –12, –13, –14, –17, CasWL, CnDAL, ConAu 104, –131, DcLB 12, –78, –79, DcLEL, DcNAA, Dis&D, EncFWF, EncMys, EncSoH, EvLB, FifSWrA, LongCTC, MajTwCW, OhA&B, OxCAmL 65, –83, OxCEng 67, –85, PenC AM, RAdv 13-1, REn, REnAL, RealN, TwCA, –SUP, WebAB 74, –79, WebE&AL, YABC 2*
Pseud./variant:
Henry, O
Henry, Oliver
O Henry
Peters, S H

Porter, William Syndey *RfGShF*

Porte-Thomas, Barbara Ann *BioIn 16, SmATA X*
Main entry: Porte, Barbara Ann

Portinari, Candido 1903-1962 *BioIn 1, –3, –4, –6, ConArt 83, CurBio 40, –62, EncLatA, IlsCB 1744, McGEWB, ObitOF 79, OxCArt, OxCTwCA, OxDcArt, PhDcTCA 77, WhAm 4, WorArt 1950*

Portisch, Hugo 1927- *ConAu 21R, –36NR, WhoWor 74*

Portteus, Eleanora Marie Manthei d1983 *SmATA 36N*

Portteus, Eleanora Marie Manthei d1986 *BioIn 14*

Posell, Elsa Z *AuBYP 3, ConAu 20NR*

Posell, Elsa Zeigerman *AuBYP 2S, BioIn 9, ConAu 1R, –4NR, SmATA 3, WhoAmW 74*

Posey, Anita E *ChhPo S1*

Posey, Sam 1944?- *BioIn 8, –9, –10, –11, ConAu 93*

Posner, Richard *DrAPF 87, –89, –91, –93*

Posner, Richard 1944- *ConAu 53, –5NR, –20NR, IntAu&W 77, –91, ScF&FL 92, WrDr 76, –80, –82, –84, –86, –88, –90, –92, –94*

Post, Elizabeth Lindley 1920- *ConAu 49, WhoAm 76, –78, –80, –82, –84, –86, –88, –90, –92, WhoAmW 74, –75*

Post, Henry 1948- *ConAu 61*
Pseud./variant:
Spot, Ryhen

Posten, Margaret L 1915- *BioIn 11, ConAu 29R, SmATA 10*

Postma, Lidia 1952- *ConAu 101*

Poston, Martha Lee *AuBYP 2, –3, BioIn 7*

Potok, Chaim *DrAPF 87, –89, –91, –93*

Potok, Chaim 1929- *AmAu&B, AuSpks, AuNews 1, –2, Au&Wr 71, Benet 87, BenetAL 91, BioIn 7, –10, –11, –13, –14, –15, –16, –17, BioNews 74, ConAu 17R, –19NR, –35NR, ConLC 2, –7, –26, ConNov 86, –91, CurBio 83, CyWA 89, DcLB 28, DrAF 76 DrAPF 83, –85, IntAu&W 77, –86, JeAmFiW, JeAmHC, MagSAmL, MajTwCW, Novels, SmATA 33, TwCYAW, WhoAm 74, –76, –78, –80, –82, –84, –86, –88, –90, –92, –94, WhoAmJ 80, WhoE 74, –86, WhoUSWr 88, WhoWor 74, WhoWorJ 72, –78, WhoWrEP 89, –92, WorAlBi, WorAl, WorAu 1975, WrDr 76, –80, –82, –84, –86, –88, –90, –92, –94*

Pott, Charles L *DcBrBI, DcVicP 2*

Pott, William H *CarSB*

Pottebaum, Gerald A 1934- *ConAu 9R, –5NR*

Potter, Beatrix 1858-1954 *ArtclWW 2*

Potter, Beatrix 1861-1943 *ContDcW 89*

Potter, Beatrix 1866-1943 *AnCL, AuBYP 2, Benet 87, BioIn 1, –2, –3, –4, –5, –6, –7, –8, –9, –10, –11, –12, –13, –14, –15, –16, –17, CarSB, CasWL, ChhPo, –S1, –S2, ChlLR 1, –19, ConAu 108, CurBio 44, DcBrAr 1, DcLEL, DcNaB 1941, DcWomA, EncBrWW, EvLB, FamAIYP, FemiCLE, GrBr, HerW, –84, InWom SUP, IntDcWB, JBA 34, –51, LongCTC, NewC, NewYTBS 88, ObitOF 79, OxCChiL, OxCEng 67, –85, PenC ENG, REn, Str&VC, TelT, TwCChW 78, –83, –89, WhDW, WhoChL, WorAlBi, WorAl, WrChl, YABC 1*

Potter, Bronson *AuBYP 2S, –3, DcAmChF 1960*

Potter, Edna *ConICB*

Potter, F Scarlet 1834- *OxCChiL*

Potter, Helen Beatrix 1866-1943 *AuBYP 3, CamGLE, DcVicP 2, MajAI, TwCPaSc*

Potter, Margaret *IntAu&W 86, WomNov*

Potter, Margaret 1926- *Au&Wr 71, BioIn 12, ConAu 13R, –6NR, –21NR, IntAu&W 77, –82, –91, SmATA 21, WhoWor 78, WrDr 76, –80, –82, –84, –86, –88, –90, –92*
Pseud./variant:
Betteridge, Anne
Melville, Anne

Potter, Margaret Newman 1926- *WrDr 94*

Potter, Marian 1915- *AuBYP 3, BioIn 11, ConAu 49, –1NR, SmATA 9, WhoAmW 77, –81*

Potter, Miriam Clark 1886-1965 *AmAu&B, AuBYP 2, –3, BioIn 7, –9, ChhPo, ConAu 5R, SmATA 3, WhNAA*

Potter, Robert Ducharme 1905-1978 *AmMWSc 73P, AuBYP 2, –3, BioIn 7, –11, ConAu 77, WhoE 74*

Potter, Stephen 1900-1969 *AuBYP 2, –3, BioIn 2, –3, –4, –5, –8, –9, –13, –17, ConAu 25R, –101, DcLEL, EvLB, LongCTC, MajTwCW, ModBrL, NewC, ObitOF 79, ObitT 1961, PenC ENG, RAdv 1, REn, TwCA SUP, WhDW, WhAm 5*

Potter, Stephen Meredith 1900-1969 *BioIn 14*

Potts, Arthur, Mrs *CarSB*

Pough, Frederick H 1906- *WhoTech 84*

Pough, Frederick Harvey 1906- *AmMWSc 73P, –76P, –82, –86, –89, –92, AuBYP 2, –3, BioIn 2, –7, ConAu 81, WhoAm 74, –76, –78, –80, –82, –84, –86, –88, –90, –92, –94, WhoTech 82, WhoWest 82, –92, –94*

Pough, Frederick Harvey 1942- *AmMWSc 86, –89, –92*

Pough, Richard Hooper *BioIn 14*

Pough, Richard Hooper 1904- *AmMWSc 73P, –76P, –82, –86, –89, –92, BioIn 3, –9, News 89-1, WhoAm 74, –76, –78, –80, –82, –84, –86, –88, –90, –92, WhoE 89*

Poulet, Virginia Maniglier *AuBYP 3*

Poulin, Stephane 1961- *ChlLR 28*

Poulsson, Emilie 1853-1939 *AmAu&B, BioIn 2, CarSB, JBA 34, –51, WhNAA*

Pournelle, Jerry Eugene 1933- *AmMWSc 73S, BioIn 13, ConAu 77, DrAF 76, DrAPF 83, –85, EncSF 93, Novels, SmATA 26, WhoAm 88, –90, –92, –94, WhoWest 74, –87, –89, –92, –94, WrDr 84*
Pseud./variant:
Curtis, Wade

Powell, A M *ConAu X, SmATA X*
Main entry: Morgan, Alfred Powell

Powell, Ann 1951- *BioIn 13, Profile 2, SmATA 51*

Powell, David 1925- *ChhPo S1, ConAu 142, WhoLib 72*

Powell, E Sandy 1947- *SmATA 72*

Powell, Fern 1942- *ConAu 25R*

Powell, Lawrence Clark 1906- *AmAu&B, BiDrLUS 70, BioIn 2, –3, –5, –7, –8, –10, –13, –15, –16, ChhPo, CmCal, ConAu 21R, –8NR, –25NR, CurBio 60, OxCAmL 83, ScF&FL 92, WhoAm 74, –76, WhoLibI 82, WhoLibS 55, –66, WorAu 1950*

Powell, Lesley Cameron 1924- *DcChlFi*

Powell, Meredith 1936- *ConAu 37R*

Powell, Richard Stillman *AmAu&B, DcNAA, SmATA X*
Main entry: Barbour, Ralph Henry

Powell, William Stevens 1919- *BiDrLUS 70, ConAu 69, DrAS 74H, –78H, –82H*

Power, Effie Louise 1873- *AuBYP 2, BioIn 7, OhA&B*

Power, Effie Louise 1873-1969 *AuBYP 3, BioIn 15*

Power, Jules 1921- *IndAu 1917, WhoAm 74, -76, -78, -80, -82, -84, -86, -88, -90, -92, -94, WhoEnt 92*

Power, Margaret 1950- *ConAu 127*

Power, Margaret M *SmATA 75*

Power, Phyllis M *SingR 1*

Power, Rhoda 1890-1957 *OxCChiL, TwCChW 78, -83, -89*

Powers, Anne 1913- *AmAu&B, AmCath 80, Au&Wr 71, BioIn 6, -11, ConAu X, ForWC 70, IntAu&W 77X, -82, -86, MinnWr, SmATA X, WhoAm 74, -76, -78, -80, -82, -84, -86, WhoAmW 74, -75, WhoUSWr 88, WrDr 76, -80, -82, -84, -86, -88, -90, -92*
Pseud./variant:
Schwartz, Anne Powers

Powers, Anne 1913-1987 *WhAm 9, WrDr 94N*

Powers, Bill 1931- *ConAu 77, SmATA 31, -52, WrDr 90, -92*

Powers, David Guy 1911-1967 *BioIn 8, ConAu P-2, EncAB-A 40*

Powers, Margaret *ConAu X, NewYTBE 72, SmATA 7*
Main entry: Heal, Edith

Powers, Richard M 1921- *BiDScF, BioIn 15, EncSF 93, NewEScF, PenEncH*

Powers, Richard M Gorman 1921- *BioIn 5, -8, ConAu 21R, IlrAm 1880, -G, IlsBYP, IlsCB 1946, -1957, -1967*
Pseud./variant:
Gorman, Terry

Powers, William K 1934- *ConAu 25R, OxCCan SUP*

Power-Waters, Alma Shelley 1896-1983 *ConAu 1R, -18NR*

Powledge, Fred 1935- *ConAu 21R, -9NR, -27NR, SmATA 37, WhoE 74, WrDr 76, -80, -82, -84, -86, -88, -90, -92, -94*

Powledge, Fred Arlius 1935- *WhoE 93*

Powling, Chris 1943- *ChlFicS, ConAu 121, TwCChW 89, WrDr 90, -92, -94*

Pownall, Marjorie Evelyn Sheridan *DcChlFi, SingR 1*

Poynter, Margaret 1927- *BioIn 13, ConAu 93, -16NR, -36NR, SmATA 27*

Praeger, Rosamond 1867-1954 *BioIn 14, EngPo, TwCChW 89*

Prager, Arthur *ConAu 12NR, SmATA 44*

Prago, Albert 1911- *ChiSch, ConAu 29R, IntAu&W 77, -82*

Prance, June E *WhoUSWr 88, WhoWrEP 89, -92*

Prance, June Elizabeth 1929- *ConAu 69, WhoAmW 81, -83*

Pratchett, Terry 1948- *ChlFicS*

Prater, Ernest *DcBrBI, DcVicP 2*

Prater, John *AuBYP 3*

Prater, John 1947- *SmATA 72*

Prather, Ray *BlkAuII, -92*

Pratt, Davis *AuBYP 2S, -3*

Pratt, Edwin John 1882-1964 *BioIn 14, -17*

Pratt, Edwin John 1883-1964 *BioIn 1, -3, -4, -5, -6, -7, -9, -11, CanWr, CasWL, ChhPo, -S1, ConAu 93, CreCan 2, DcLEL, EvLB, LongCTC, NewC, ObitOF 79, OxCCan, -SUP, OxCEng 67, PenC ENG, REn, REnAL, TwCA SUP, WebE&AL, WhDW, WhNAA*

Pratt, Fletcher 1897-1956 *AmAu&B, AuBYP 2, BioIn 1, -2, -4, -6, -7, ConAu 113, CurBio 42, -56, NewEScF, Novels, ObitOF 79, REnAL, ScF&FL 92, ScFSB, SupFW, TwCA SUP, TwCSFW 86, -91, WhAm 3, WhNAA, WhoHr&F, WhoSciF*

Pratt, John 1931- *Au&Wr 71, ConAu 1R, -2NR*
Pseud./variant:
Winton, John

Pratt, John L 1906-1968 *AuBYP 3*

Pratt, John Lowell 1906-1968 *AuBYP 2S, BioIn 8, ConAu 1R, -3NR, WhAm 5*

Pratt, Laura Maria Loring *Alli SUP, CarSB, ChhPo S2*

Pratt, Murray Fletcher 1897-1956 *AuBYP 3*

Pratt, Rhona Olive 1903- *IntAu&W 77, -82*
Pseud./variant:
O'Harris, Pixie

Pratt, Viola Leone 1892- *WrDr 76, -80, -82, -84*

Prebble, John Edward Curtis 1915- *Au&Wr 71, BioIn 5, ConAu 5R, -3NR, DcLEL 1940,*

IntAu&W 77, –82, Who 74, –82, –83, –85, WrDr 76, –80

Preiss, Byron *BioIn 15, –16, ConAu 69, –14NR, SmATA 42, –47*

Preiss, Byron 1953- *ScF&FL 92*

Preiss, Byron Cary 1953- *EncSF 93*

Prelutsky, Jack *AuBYP 2S, –3, BioIn 13, –15, –16, –17, ChhPo S1, –S2, ConAu 93, FifBJA, SmATA 22, TwCChW 83*

Prelutsky, Jack 1940- *ChlLR 13, ConAu 38NR, DcLB 61, IntAu&W 91, MajAI, SmATA 66, TwCChW 89, WhoAm 92, WrDr 86, –88, –90, –92, –94*

Prentiss, Elizabeth P 1818-1878 *BioAmW*

Prentiss, Elizabeth Payson 1818-1878 *Alli SUP, AmAu&B, AmWomWr, BenetAL 91, BbD, BiD&SB, BioIn 5, –12, CarSB, ChhPo, –S1, DcAmAu, DcBiA, DcNAA, InWom SUP, OxCAmL 65, –83, OxCChiL, PoChrch, WhAm HS*

Presberg, Miriam Goldstein 1919-1978 *BioIn 15, ConAu 1R, –3NR, ForWC 70, SmATA 38, WhoWorJ 72, WrDr 76, –80*
Pseud./variant:
Gilbert, Miriam

Prescott, Casey *ConAu 133, SmATA 66, WrDr 94*
Main entry: Morris, Christopher Crosby

Prescott, Gerald W 1899-1988 *BioIn 16*

Prescott, Gerald Webber 1899- *AmMWSc 73P, –76P, Au&Wr 71, WrDr 76, –80*

Prescott, Orville 1906- *AmAu&B, AuSpks, AuBYP 2, –3, BioIn 4, –8, –11, ConAu 41R, CurBio 57, REnAL, WhoAm 74, –76, –78, –80, –82, –84, –86, –88, –90*

Pressley, Hilda *IntAu&W 77X*
Main entry: Nickson, Hilda

Preston, Alice Bolam 1889-1958 *BioIn 1, DcWomA, IlsCB 1744, WhAmArt 85, WhoAmA 80N, –82N, –86N, –89N, –91N*

Preston, Carol *AuBYP 2S, –3*

Preston, Edna Mitchell *AuBYP 2S, –3, ChhPo S2, ConAu 111, SmATA 40*

Preston, Edward *ConAu X*
Main entry: Guess, Edward Preston

Preston, Lillian Elvira 1918- *BioIn 16, ConAu 108, DrAS 74E, –78E, SmATA 47*

Preussler, Otfried *TwCChW 89B*

Preussler, Otfried 1923- *AuBYP 2, –3, BioIn 8, –13, ConAu 77, ConLC 17, FourBJA, IntAu&W 77, OxCChiL, ScF&FL 92, SmATA 24, TwCChW 78B, –83B*

Prevert, Jacques *BioIn 14*

Prevert, Jacques 1900-1977 *Benet 87, BioIn 2, –10, –11, –12, –17, CasWL, CnMWL, ConAu 69, –77, –29NR, ConLC 15, DcFM, EncWL, –2, EvEuW, FilmgC, GuFrLit 1, HalFC 84, –88, IntAu&W 77, IntWW 76, –77N, MajTwCW, ModFrL, ObitOF 79, OxCFilm, OxCFr, PenC EUR, REn, SmATA 30N, TwCWr, WorAu 1950, WorEFlm*

Price, Beverley Joan 1931- *Au&Wr 71, ConAu 106, –24NR, WrDr 76, –80*

Price, Christine Hilda 1928-1980 *AuBYP 2, –3, Au&Wr 71, BioIn 5, –6, –7, –8, –9, –12, –13, ChhPo S1, ConAu 5R, –93, –4NR, IlsCB 1946, –1957, –1967, MorJA, SmATA 3, –23N, WhoAmW 74, –75, –77, WrDr 76, –80*

Price, Derek John DeSolla 1922-1983 *AmMWSc 73S, –78S, BioIn 11, –13, ConAu 1R, WhoAm 74, –76, –78, WhoE 74, WhoWor 74, WhoWorJ 78, WrDr 76, –80*

Price, Edith Ballinger 1897- *AmAu&B, BioIn 2, ChhPo, DcWomA, JBA 34, –51, WhAmArt 85, WhNAA*

Price, Eugenia 1916- *AmAu&B, BestSel 89-4, BioIn 4, –5, –12, ConAu 5R, –2NR, –18NR, IntAu&W 91, WhoSSW 75, –76*

Price, Evadne 1896- *BioIn 14*

Price, Evadne 1896-1985 *AnObit 1985, Au&Wr 71, ConAu 116, OxCChiL, TwCChW 83, –89, TwCRHW 90*

Price, Garrett 1896-1979 *ArtsAmW 3, BioIn 8, –11, –13, ChhPo, ConAu 85, IlrAm 1880, –D, IlsBYP, IlsCB 1957, SmATA 22N, WhAmArt 85, WhoAmA 80N, –82N, WorECar*

Price, Garrett 1897-1979 *WhoAmA 86N, –89N, –91N*

Price, Harold 1912- *BioIn 5, IlsBYP, IlsCB 1946*

Price, Harold A 1893-1990 *BioIn 17*

Price, Hattie Longstreet 1891- *BioIn 1, ConICB, DcWomA, IlsCB 1744*

Price, Jennifer *ConAu X, IntAu&W 91X, SmATA X, WrDr 76, –80, –82, –84*
Main entry: Hoover, Helen

Price, Jonathan *DrAPF 87, –89, –91, –93*

Price, Jonathan 1941- *BioIn 15, ConAu 19NR, SmATA 46*

Price, Leo 1941- *ConAu 77*

Price, Lillian L *CarSB*

Price, Lucie Locke *ConAu X, SmATA X, WrDr 76*
Main entry: Locke, Lucie

Price, Luxor *ConICB*

Price, Margaret E *WhoAmA 86N*

Price, Margaret E 1888- *WhoAmA 89N, –91N*

Price, Margaret Evans 1888-1973 *AmAu&B, BioIn 1, –10, –13, ConAu 109, DcWomA, IlsCB 1744, SmATA 28, WhAm 8, WhAmArt 85, WhNAA, WhoAmA 78N, –80N, –82N*

Price, Norman Mills d1951 *WhoAmA 86N*

Price, Norman Mills 1877-1951 *BioIn 1, –2, –5, IlrAm 1880, –B, IlsBYP, IlsCB 1744, –1946, WhoAmA 78N, –80N, –82N, –89N, –91N*

Price, Olive 1903- *AuBYP 2, BioIn 7, –11, ConAu 41R, SmATA 8*
Pseud./variant:
Cherryholmes, Anne
West, Barbara

Price, Olive M *AmWomPl*

Price, Olive M 1903- *AuBYP 3*

Price, Roger 1920- *IntMPA 86, –88*

Price, Roger 1921- *ConAu 9R, IntMPA 75, –76, –78, –81, –82, –84, –86, –77*

Price, Roger Taylor 1921- *EncSF 93*

Price, Steven D 1940- *ConAu 49, –1NR, –16NR*

Price, Steven David 1940- *ConAu 37NR*

Price, Susan 1955- *BioIn 13, ChlFicS, ConAu 105, IntAu&W 91, ScF&FL 92, SmATA 25, TwCChW 78, –83, –89, WrDr 76, –80, –82, –84, –86, –88, –90, –92, –94*

Price, Willadene 1914- *AuBYP 3*

Price, Willadene Anton 1914- *AuBYP 2, ConAu 5R, ForWC 70*

Price, Willard 1887- *WhAm 9*

Price, Willard 1887-1963 *BioIn 15, –16*

Price, Willard 1887-1983 *SmATA 48, TwCChW 89*

Price, Willard De Mille 1887- *AuBYP 3*

Price, Willard DeMille 1887- *AmAu&B, AuBYP 2, Au&Wr 71, BioIn 2, –8, BlueB 76, ConAu 1R, –1NR, IntAu&W 77, IntWW 74, –75, –76, –77, –78, –79, –80, –81, –82, –83, SmATA 38, TwCChW 83, WhNAA, Who 74, –82, –83, –85N, WhoAm 74, –76, WhoWor 74, WrDr 80, –82, –84*

Prichard, Katharine Susannah *WomNov*

Prichard, Katharine Susannah 1883-1969 *AuWomWr, Benet 87, BlmGWL, ConAu 33NR, ConLC 46, FemiCLE, MajTwCW, RfGEnL 91, RfGShF, SmATA 66*

Prichard, Katharine Susannah 1884-1969 *ArtclWW 2, BioIn 4, –6, –8, –9, –10, –11, –12, –17, CasWL, ConAu P-1, DcLEL, EvLB, NewC, Novels, OxCAusL, PenC ENG, REn, TwCWr, WhoLA, WorAu 1950*

Prichard, Katharine Susannah 1884-1972 *InWom SUP*

Priddy, Frances Rosaleen 1931- *AuBYP 2, –3, BioIn 8, ConAu 1R*

Prideaux, Tom d1993 *NewYTBS 93*

Prideaux, Tom 1908- *BiE&WWA, BioIn 6, –15, ChhPo, ConAu 108, NotNAT, SmATA 37*

Prideaux, Tom 1908-1993 *ConAu 141, SmATA 76*

Priest, Christopher *BioIn 17, DrmM 2*

Priest, Christopher 1943- *BioIn 13, ConAu 33R, DcLB 14, IntAu&W 82, –86, –91, NewEScF, Novels, RGTwCSF, ScF&FL 92, ScFSB, TwCSFW 86, –91, WhoSciF, WrDr 76, –80, –82, –84, –86, –88, –90, –92*

Priest, Christopher McKenzie 1943- *EncSF 93, WrDr 94*

Priestley, Harold Edford 1901- *Au&Wr 71, ConAu 73, IntAu&W 77, –82*

Priestley, J B 1894- *BritWr 7, ScFSB, WorAlBi*

Priestley, J B 1894-1984 *AnObit 1984, Benet 87, BiE&WWA, BioIn 1, –2, –3, –4, –5, –6, –7, –9, –10, –11, –14, –15, –17, BlmGEL, BlueB 76, BritWr 7, CamGEL, CamGLE, CamGWoT, CnDBLB 6, CnThe, ConAu 9R, –113, –33NR, ConDr 73, –77, –82, ConLC 2, –5, –9, –34, ConNov 72, –76, –82, CrtSuMy, CroCD, CurBio 76, –84N, CyWA 58, –89, DcLB 10, –34, –77, –100, –139, –Y84N, EncMys, EncWB, EncWL 2, HalFC 84, –88,*

IntMPA 75, -76, -78, -81, -82, -77, LongCTC, MajTwCW, McGEWD 72, -84, ModBrL, -S1, -S2, ModWD, NewC, NewEScF, NewYTBS 74, -84, NotNAT, Novels, OxCEng 85, OxCThe 83, PenC ENG, PlP&P, RAdv 13-2, REn, REnWD, RfGEnL 91, ScF&FL 92, TwCCr&M 80, -85, -91, TwCSFW 86, -91, TwCWr, WebE&AL, WhoThe 72, -77, -81, WhoTwCL, WorAl, WorEFlm, WrDr 76, -80, -82, -84

Priestley, J B, Mrs *Who 88, -90, -92*

Priestley, John Boynton 1894-1983 *ConDr 93*

Priestley, John Boynton 1894-1984 *EncSF 93, IntDcT 2*

Priestley, Lee Shore 1904- *AuBYP 2, BioIn 8, ConAu 5R, -2NR, SmATA 27, WhoAmW 87, WhoWest 74*

Priestly, Lee Shore 1904- *AuBYP 3*

Prieto, Mariana *IntAu&W 86X*

Prieto, Mariana 1912- *AuBYP 3*

Prieto, Mariana Beeching 1912- *AuBYP 2, Au&ICB, BioIn 7, -11, BkP, ConAu 5R, -5NR, ForWC 70, IntAu&W 91, SmATA 8, WhoAmW 75, WrDr 76, -80, -82, -84, -86, -88, -90*

Priley, Margaret Hubbard 1909- *ConAu 1R*
Pseud./variant:
Hubbard, Margaret Ann

Primavera, Elise 1954- *BioIn 15, -16, SixBJA, SmATA 48, -58*

Prime, Cecil T 1909- *AuBYP 2S, ConAu 49*

Prime, Cecil T 1909-1979 *AuBYP 3*

Prime, Derek James 1931- *Au&Wr 71, ConAu 108, IntAu&W 77, -86, -89, SmATA 34, WhoWor 78, WrDr 76, -80, -82, -84, -86, -88, -90, -92, -94*

Primrose, Jean Logan 1917- *BioIn 8, ChhPo S1, DcBrAr 1, IlsCB 1957*

Prince, Alison 1931- *BioIn 13, -14, ConAu 29R, -26NR, ScF&FL 92, SmATA 28, TwCChW 89, WhoArt 80, -82, -84, WrDr 90, -92, -94*

Prince, Jack Harvey 1908- *BioIn 12, SmATA 17*
Pseud./variant:
Aquillo, Don
Clinton, Jon
Wardell, Dean

Prince, Leonora E *IlsBYP*

Pringle, Laurence *MajAI*

Pringle, Laurence 1935- *SmATA 6AS*

Pringle, Laurence P 1935- *AuBYP 3, SmATA 68*

Pringle, Laurence Patrick 1935- *AuBYP 2S, BioIn 9, ChlLR 4, ConAu 29R, -14NR, FourBJA, MajAI, SmATA 4, WhoAm 92, -94, WhoE 75, -77*
Pseud./variant:
Edmund, Sean

Pringle, Patrick 1917- *Au&Wr 71*

Priolo, Pauline Pizzo 1907- *ConAu 1R*

Pritchett, Elaine H 1920- *BioIn 14*

Pritchett, Elaine Hillyer 1920- *ConAu 108, ForWC 70, SmATA 36*

Prochazka, Jan *TwCChW 89B*

Prochazka, Jan d1971 *AuBYP 3*

Prochazka, Jan 1929?-1971 *AuBYP 2S, BioIn 9, NewYTBE 71, TwCChW 78B, -83B*

Prochazkova, Iva 1953- *BioIn 17, ConAu 135, SmATA 68*

Procter, Adelaide Ann 1825-1864 *Alli, BbD, BiD&SB, BioIn 6, BritAu 19, CarSB, CasWL, Chambr 3, ChhPo, -S1, -S2, DcBiPP, DcCathB, DcEnA, DcEnL, DcEuL, DcLB 32, DcNaB, EvLB, NewC, OxCEng 67*

Procter, Adelaide Anne 1825-1864 *BioIn 14, -16, CamGLE, InWom SUP*

Proctor, Everitt *AuBYP 2, -3, ConAu X, SmATA 3, TwCChW 83, -89, WrDr 76, -80, -82, -84, -86*
Main entry: Montgomery, Rutherford George

Proctor, John *DcBrBI, DcVicP 2, WorECar*
Pseud./variant:
Puck

Proctor, Samuel D 1921- *ConAu 118, -133*

Proctor, Samuel DeWitt 1921- *BioIn 5, InB&W 80, LEduc 74, LivgBAA, NegAl 76, -83, -89, NewYTBE 72, WhoAm 74, -76, -78, -80, -82, -84, -86, -88, WhoBlA 75, -77, -80, -85, -88, -90, -92, -94, WhoE 75, -77, WhoRel 75, -77, -92, WhoWor 80, -82, WrDr 94*

Professor Zingara *SmATA X*
Main entry: Leeming, Joseph

Prohaska, Ray 1901-1981 *BioIn 1, IlrAm 1880, –E, WhAmArt 85, WhoAmA 73, –78, –80, –82N, –86N, –89N, –91N*

Prohias, Antonio 1921- *ConAu 104*

Prokofiev, Serge 1891-1953 *AnCL, AtlBL, BiDD, BioIn 1, –2, –3, –4, –5, –6, –7, –8, –9, –11, CompSN SUP, CurBio 41, –53, DcCM, DcFM, NewAmDM, OxCFilm, RAdv 13-3, REn, WhAm 3, WorAl, WorEFlm*

Prokofiev, Sergei Sergeievich 1891-1953 *Baker 92*

Pronzini, Bill 1934- *IntAu&W 86*

Pronzini, Bill 1943- *ConAu 49, –1NR, –14NR, –32NR, CrtSuMy, EncSF 93, ScF&FL 92, TwCCr&M 80, –85, –91, TwCWW 91, WrDr 82, –84, –86, –88, –90, –92, –94*

Prose, Francine 1947- *BioIn 10, –16, –17, ConAu 109, –112, ConLC 45, IntAu&W 86, ScF&FL 92, WorAu 1980, WrDr 90, –92, –94*

Proudeit, Isabel 1898- *AuBYP 3*

Proudfit, Isabel 1898- *AuBYP 2, BioIn 6, –7, MorJA*

Proujan, Carl 1929- *ConAu 81, WhoAm 74, –76, –78, –80, –82, –84, WhoE 74, –75, –77, –91*

Prout, Geoffrey 1894- *ChhPo S2*

Provensen, Alice
Pseud./variant:
Provensen, Martin

Provensen, Alice 1918- *BioIn 5, –8, –9, –11, –12, ChhPo, –S2, ChlLR 11, ConAu 53, –5NR, IlsBYP, IlsCB 1946, –1957, –1967, MajAI, SmATA 9, –70, ThrBJA, WhoAmW 77, WhoChL, WhoE 74, WhoGrA 82*

Provensen, Alice Rose Twitchell *WhoAm 86, –90, –92, –94*

Provensen, Martin 1916- *BioIn 5, –8, –9, –11, –12, ChlLR 11, ConAu 53, –5NR, IlsBYP, IlsCB 1946, –1957, –1967, SmATA 9, ThrBJA, WhoChL, WhoGrA 62, –82*

Provensen, Martin 1916-1987 *BioIn 15, –16, ConAu 122, ConGrA 3, NewYTBS 87, SmATA 51N*
Main entry: Provensen, Alice

Provensen, Martin Elias 1916-1987 *MajAI, SmATA 70*

Provist, D'Alain *BlkWr 1, –2, ConAu 130, MajTwCW, SmATA X*
Main entry: Diop, Birago Ismael

Provost, Gail Levine *BioIn 17*

Provost, Gail Levine 1944- *ConAu 127, SmATA 65*
Pseud./variant:
Levine-Freidus, Gail

Provost, Gary 1944- *BioIn 17, ConAu 133, SmATA 66*

Provost, Gary Richard 1944- *WrDr 94*

Proysen, Alf *AuBYP 2S, –3, ConAu 136, OxCChiL, TwCChW 78B, –83B, –89B*

Proysen, Alf 1914-1970 *BioIn 17, ChlLR 24, DcScanL, SmATA 67*

Prud'hommeaux, Rene *AuBYP 2, –3, BioIn 7*

Pruitt, William O 1922- *IntAu&W 91, WrDr 86, –88, –90, –92, –94*

Pruitt, William O, Jr. 1922- *AmMWSc 92, ConAu 21R, WrDr 76, –80, –82, –84*

Prusina, Katica 1935- *ConAu 69*

Pruszynska, Aniela 1888- *IlsCB 1744*

Pryce, Dick *MedPD*

Pryor, Ainslie *AuBYP 3*

Pryor, Bonnie *AuBYP 3*

Pryor, Bonnie 1942- *SmATA 69*

Pryor, Bonnie H 1942- *ConAu 130, WrDr 94*

Pryor, Helen Brenton 1897-1972 *BioIn 9, –11, ConAu P-2, SmATA 4*

Pucci, Albert John 1920- *BioIn 15, SmATA 44, WhoAm 74*

Puck
Main entry: Proctor, John

Pudney, John 1909-1977 *EngPo, TwCChW 89*

Pudney, John Sleigh 1909-1977 *Au&Wr 71, BioIn 8, –10, –12, –13, BlueB 76, ChhPo, –S1, –S2, ConAu 9R, –77, –5NR, ConNov 72, –76, ConPo 70, –75, DcNaB 1971, IntAu&W 77, IntMPA 75, –76, –78, –77, IntWW 74, –75, –76, –77, –78N, LongCTC, ModBrL, NewC, OxCChiL, PenC ENG, SmATA 24, TwCChW 78, –83, Who 74, WhoChL, WhoWor 74, WorAu 1950, WrDr 76*

Pugh, Ellen 1920- *AuBYP 3*

Pugh, Ellen Tiffany 1920- *AuBYP 2S, BiDrLUS 70, ConAu 49, SmATA 7, WhoAmW 74, –75, WhoLibS 55*

Pugh, Mabel 1891- *BioIn 3, ChhPo, ConICB, DcWomA, WhAmArt 85*

Puleo, Nicole *ConAu X*
Main entry: Miller, Nicole Puleo

Pullein-Thompson, Christine *Au&Wr 71, BioIn 9, ConAu X, IntAu&W 77X, –86X, OxCChiL, SmATA 3, TwCChW 83, WhoChL, WrDr 76, –80, –82, –84*
Main entry: Popescu, Christine

Pullein-Thompson, Christine 1930- *IntAu&W 89, –91, TwCChW 89, WrDr 86, –88, –90, –92, –94*

Pullein-Thompson, Diana *Au&Wr 71, BioIn 9, ConAu X, IntAu&W 77, –86X, OxCChiL, SmATA 3, TwCChW 83, WhoChL, WrDr 76, –80, –82, –84, –86, –88, –90, –92, –94*
Main entry: Farr, Diana Pullein-Thompson

Pullein-Thompson, Diana 1930- *TwCChW 89*

Pullein-Thompson, Josephine *ConAu 20NR, TwCChW 89, WrDr 86, –88, –90, –92*

Pullein-Thompson, Josephine M W *Au&Wr 71, BioIn 9, ConAu 5R, –7NR, IntAu&W 77, –82, OxCChiL, SmATA 3, TwCChW 83, WhoChL, WrDr 76, –80, –82, –84*
Pseud./variant:
Thompson, Josephine P

Pullein-Thompson, Josephine M Wedderburn *IntAu&W 86*

Pullein-Thompson, Josephine Mary Wedderburn *ConAu 43NR*

Pullman, Philip 1946- *BioIn 16, –17, ChlLR 20, ConAu 127, ScF&FL 92, SixBJA, SmATA 65, –17AS*

Pullman, Philip N 1946- *MajAI, TwCYAW*

Pulver, Robin 1945- *SmATA 76, WhoWrEP 92*

Pumphrey, George Henry 1912- *Au&Wr 71, ConAu 13R, IntAu&W 77, WrDr 76, –80, –82, –84, –86*
Pseud./variant:
Pumphrey, H George

Pumphrey, H George
Main entry: Pumphrey, George Henry

Pundt, Helen Marie *AuBYP 2, –3, BioIn 8, ConAu 5R, ForWC 70*

Puner, Helen W 1915- *BioIn 15, ConAu 5R, –2NR, SmATA 37*

Puner, Helen W 1915-1989 *BioIn 16, –17, ConAu 129, SmATA 63*

Puner, Helen Walker d1989 *NewYTBS 89*

Punshon, Ernest Robinson 1872-1956 *EncMys*

Purcell, John Wallace *AuBYP 2, –3, BioIn 8*

Purdy, Captain Jim *AuBYP 3*

Purdy, Carol *AuBYP 3*

Purdy, Carol 1943- *ConAu 136, SmATA 66, WrDr 94*

Purdy, Claire Lee 1906- *AuBYP 2, –3, BioIn 7, WhNAA*

Purdy, Susan Gold 1939- *AuBYP 2, –3, BioIn 8, –11, ChhPo, –S1, ConAu 13R, –10NR, ForWC 70, IlsCB 1957, SmATA 8, WhoAmW 74, –75, –77, WhoE 77*

Purnell, Idella 1901- *AnMV 1926, ChhPo, –S1, ConAu 61, WhNAA*
Pseud./variant:
Stone, Idella Purnell
Stone, Ikey

Purscell, Phyllis 1934- *BioIn 10, ConAu 25R, SmATA 7*

Pursell, Weimer *IlsBYP*

Purtill, Richard L 1931- *BioIn 16, ConAu 29NR, SmATA 53, WrDr 86, –88, –90, –92, –94*

Purton, Rowland William Crisby 1925- *Au&Wr 71, ConAu 53, –4NR, IntAu&W 77, WhoWor 78, WrDr 76, –80, –82, –84*

Pushker, Gloria Teles 1927- *ConAu 142, SmATA 75*

Pushkin, Aleksandr Sergeevich 1799-1837 *BioIn 14, –15, –16, –17, CamGWoT, HanRL*

Pushkin, Aleksandr Sergeyevich 1799-1837 *AtlBL, Benet 87, BbD, BiD&SB, BioIn 1, –2, –3, –4, –5, –6, –7, –8, –9, –10, –11, –12, –13, CasWL, ChhPo S1, CnThe, CyWA 58, DcBiA, DcEuL, DcRusL, EuAu, EvEuW, McGEWD 72, –84, NewC, OxCEng 67, OxCThe 67, PenC EUR, RComWL, REn, REnWD, WhDW*

Pushkin, Alexander 1799-1837 *EuWr 5, GrFLW, MagSWL, NinCLC 27, SmATA 61, WorAlBi, WorLitC*

Pushkin, Alexander Sergeyevich 1799-1837 *InB&W 85, IntDcT 2, OxCChiL, OxCEng 85, OxCThe 83, WorAl*

Putnam, Alice 1916- *BioIn 17, SmATA 61*

Putnam, Alice Harvey Whiting 1841-1919 *InWom SUP*

Putnam, Arthur Lee *SmATA X*
Main entry: Alger, Horatio

Putnam, David Binney 1913- *CarSB*

Putnam, David Binney 1913-1992 *BioIn 17*

Putnam, David Binney, Sr. d1992 *NewYTBS 92*

Putnam, Peter B 1920- *BioIn 14*

Putnam, Peter Brock 1920- *BioIn 4, IntAu&W 82, SmATA 30, WhoAm 74, -76, -78, -80, -82, -84, -86, -88, -90, -92, -94*

Putnam, Samuel 1892-1950 *AmAu&B, BenetAL 91, BioIn 1, -2, -4, -7, -8, -12, DcLB 4, ObitOF 79, REnAL, TwCA SUP*

Puzo, Mario *DrAPF 87, -89, -91, -93*

Puzo, Mario 1920- *AmAu&B, Benet 87, BenetAL 91, BiDConC, BioIn 3, -9, -10, -11, -13, -14, -15, -17, CelR, ConAu 65, -4NR, -42NR, ConLC 1, -2, -6, -36, ConNov 72, -76, -82, -86, -91, ConTFT 10, CurBio 75, DcLB 6, DcLEL 1940, DrAF 76, DrAPF 83, -85, HalFC 84, -88, IntAu&W 77, MajTwCW, Novels, ScF&FL 92, WhoAm 74, -76, -78, -80, -82, -84, -86, -88, -92, -94, WhoUSWr 88, WhoWor 87, -89, -91, -93, WhoWrEP 89, -92, WorAlBi, WorAl, WrDr 76, -80, -82, -84, -86, -88, -90, -92*

Pye, David 1932- *ConAu 25R*

Pye, Virginia 1901- *BioIn 8, TwCChW 78, -83, -89, WhoChL, WrDr 80, -82, -84, -86, -88, -90*

Pyk, Ann Phillips 1937- *ConAu 77*

Pyk, Jan *IlsBYP*

Pyke, Helen Godfrey 1941- *ConAu 29R*

Pyle, Howard 1853-1911 *Alli SUP, AmAu, AmAu&B, AnCL, AuBYP 2, -3, BenetAL 91, BbD, BiD&SB, BioIn 1, -2, -3, -5, -7, -8, -10, -12, -13, -14, -15, CamGLE, CarSB, ChhPo, -S1, -S2, ChILR 22, ClaDrA, ConAu 109, -137, ConGrA 2, DcAmAu, DcBrBI, DcLB 42, DcLEL, DcNAA, FamSYP, HarEnUS, IlrAm 1880, -A, IlsBYP, JBA 34, MajAI, OxCAmL 65, -83, OxCChiL, REnAL, SmATA 16, TwCChW 78A, -83A, -89A, TwCYAW, WebAB 74, -79, WhAm 1, WhAmArt 85, WhoChL, WrChl*

Pyle, Katharine 1863-1938 *AmAu&B, AnCL, BioIn 2, -17, ChhPo, -S1, DcAmAu, DcNAA, DcWomA, JBA 34, -51, SmATA 66, WhAm 1, WhAmArt 85, WhNAA, WomWWA 14*

Pym, T *OxCChiL*

Pyne, Mable Mandeville 1903-1969 *AuBYP 2, -3, BioIn 1, -5, -7, -11, ConAu 1R, -103 IlsCB 1744, -1946, SmATA 9*

Pyrnelle, Louise-Clarke 1850-1907 *BioIn 15*

Pyrnelle, Louise Clarke 1852-1907 *AmAu&B, DcLB 42*

Q

Quackenbush, Robert 1929- *SmATA 7AS*

Quackenbush, Robert M 1929- *ScF&FL 92*

Quackenbush, Robert Mead 1929- *AuBYP 3, BioIn 7, –8, –10, ChhPo S2, ConAu 45, –2NR, –17NR, –38NR, FourBJA, IlsBYP, IlsCB 1957, –1967, MajAI, SmATA 7, –70, WhoAm 94, WhoE 75, –91, –93*

Quaife, Milo Milton 1880-1959 *AmAu&B, BioIn 5, ConAu 114, MichAu 80, REnAL, WhAm 3, WhNAA, WisWr*

Quammen, David 1948- *BiDConC, BioIn 9, –10, ConAu 29R, –28NR, SmATA 7*

Quarles, Benjamin 1905- *BlkAuII 92*

Quarles, Benjamin A 1904- *WhoBlA 90, –92, –94*

Quarles, Benjamin Arthur 1904- *AmAu&B, BioIn 5, –6, –9, –11, ConAu 1R, DrAS 74H, –78H, LivgBAA, SelBAAf, SmATA 12, WhoAm 74, WhoBlA 75, –80, –85, WhoE 74, WhoWor 74*

Quarrie, Bruce 1947- *ConAu 103, WrDr 76, –80, –82, –84, –90, –92, –94*

Quayle, Eric 1921- *Au&Wr 71, ChhPo S1, –S2, ConAu 21R, –36NR, IntAu&W 82, WrDr 76, –80, –82, –84, –90, –92, –94*

Queen, Ellery *AmAu&B, AuSpks, AuBYP 2, BenetAL 91, BioIn 2, –3, –4, –8, –9, –10, –11, –12, –13, CelR, ConAu X, –32NR, –39NR, ConLC 3, –11, CorpD, CrtSuMy, CurBio 40, DcLEL, EncMys, EvLB, IntAu&W 77X, IntWW 74, –75, –76, –77, –78, –79, –80, –81, –82, LongCTC, MajTwCW, Novels, OxCAmL 65, –83, PenC AM, REn, REnAL, ScF&FL 92, TwCA, –SUP, TwCCr&M 80, –85, –91, TwCWr, WebAB 74, –79, Who 74, –82, WorAlBi, WorAl, WrDr 76, –80, –82, –84, –90*
Main entry: Dannay, Frederic
Lee, Manfred B

Queen, Ellery, Jr. *AuBYP 2, –3, BioIn 9, ConAu X, –39NR, SmATA 3*
Main entry: Dannay, Frederic
Holding, James
Lee, Manfred B

Quennell, Charles Henry Bourne 1872-1935 *BioIn 6, DcBrBI, LongCTC, MorJA, TwCA, –SUP*

Quennell, Marjorie 1884-1972 *BioIn 4, –6, –13, DcBrAr 1, DcLEL, DcWomA, EvLB, JBA 34, LongCTC, MorJA, SmATA 29, TwCA, –SUP*

Quennell, Peter C d1993 *NewYTBS 93*

Quennell, Peter Courtney 1905- *Au&Wr 71, BioIn 4, –5, –11, ChhPo S2, ConPo 70, DcLEL, EvLB, IntAu&W 77, IntWW 74, –75, –76, –77, –78, LongCTC, ModBrL, NewC, PenC ENG, RAdv 1, REn, TwCA, –SUP, TwCWr, Who 74, WrDr 76, –80*

Quibell, Agatha Hunt 1921- *Au&Wr 71, IntAu&W 77, –82, WrDr 76, –80, –82, –84*

Quick, Annabelle 1922- *BioIn 9, ConAu 21R, SmATA 2, WhoAmW 74, –75, –77, WhoFI 74*
Pseud./variant:
MacMillan, Annabelle

Quigg, Jane d1986 *SmATA 49N*

Quigley, John 1927- *Au&Wr 71, ConAu 17R, IntAu&W 77, WrDr 76, –80, –82, –84*

Quilici, Folco 1930- *ConAu 105, WhoWor 82*

Quiller-Couch, Arthur Thomas, Sir 1863-1944 *BbD, BiD&SB, BioIn 1, –4, –5, –12, CasWL, Chambr 3, ChhPo, –S1, –S2, CurBio 44, DcBiA, DcEnA, –A, DcLEL, DcNaB 1941, EvLB, JBA 34, LongCTC, ModBrL, NewC, Novels, ObitOF 79, OxCChiL, OxCEng 67, –85, PenC ENG, RAdv 1, REn, SupFW, TwCA, –SUP, TwCWr, WhAm 2, WhoHr&F*
Pseud./variant:
Couch, Sir Arthur T Q

Quiller-Couch, Lilian M *ChhPo*

Quimby, George Irving 1913- *AmMWSc 73S, BlueB 76, ConAu 57, –34NR, FifIDA,*

MichAu 80, WhoAm 74, –80, –82, –84, –90, –92, –94, WhoWest 74, –82, –84, –92, WhoWor 74, –80, –82, –84, –91, –93, WrDr 80

Quimby, Myrtle 1891- *ConAu P-2*

Quin, Tarella d1934 *OxCAusL, SingR 1*

Quin-Harkin, Janet 1941- *Au&Arts 6, BioIn 12, ConAu 81, –15NR, –33NR, IntAu&W 82, SmATA 18*

Quinlan, Patricia *AuBYP 3*

Quinn, Elisabeth 1881-1962 *BioIn 13, SmATA 22*
Pseud./variant:
Adams, Dale
Quinn, Vernon
Vequin, Capini

Quinn, John Paul 1943- *ConAu 33R*

Quinn, Patrick 1950- *SmATA 73*

Quinn, Susan *AmWomPl*
Main entry: Jacobs, Susan

Quinn, Susan 1940- *ConAu 103, SmATA X*

Quinn, Susan 1942- *WhoAmL 90*

Quinn, Vernon *SmATA X*
Main entry: Quinn, Elisabeth

Quinn, Vernon 1881-1962 *AmAu&B, BioIn 5, –13, WhAm 6*

Quinn, Zdenka 1942- *ConAu 33R*

Quintanilla, Luis 1900?- *AmAu&B, BioIn 1, –2, –3, CurBio 40, IlsBYP, IlsCB 1946, IntWW 74, –75, –76, –77, IntYB 80, –81, –82, WhAmArt 85, WhNAA, WhoWor 74*

Quinton, Leslie *OxCCan SUP, WhoCanL 85*

Quirk, Leslie W 1882- *AmAu&B, CarSB, WhAm 7, WhNAA, WisWr*

Quirk, Thomas Charles, Jr. 1922- *WhoAmA 73, –78, –80, –82, –84, –91*

Quittenton, Richard Martin Howard 1833-1914 *BioIn 8*

Quixley, Jim 1931- *SmATA 56*

Quiz, Roland *Alli, BioIn 8, WhoChL*

R

Ra, Carol F 1939- *SmATA 76*

Ra, Carol Fae 1939- *WhoWrEP 89, –92*

Raab, Robert Allen 1924- *ConAu 29R*

Rabalais, Maria 1921- *ConAu 61*

Rabe, Berniece Louise 1928- *BioIn 10, ConAu 49, –1NR, FifBJA, IntAu&W 82, –86, –89, –91, SmATA 7, –77, –10AS, WhoUSWr 88, WhoWrEP 89, –92, WrDr 80, –82, –84, –86, –88, –90, –92, –94*

Rabe, Olive d1968 *AuBYP 3*

Rabe, Olive H 1887-1968 *AuBYP 2, BioIn 11, ConAu P-2, SmATA 13*

Rabinovitz, Rubin 1938- *ConAu 21R, DrAS 74E, –78E, –82E, IntAu&W 86, WrDr 76, –82, –84, –86, –88, –90, –92, –94*

Rabinowich, Ellen 1946- *BioIn 13, ConAu 106, SmATA 29*

Rabinowitz, Sandy 1954- *BioIn 15, –16, ConAu 103, SmATA 39, –52, WrDr 90*

Rabinowitz, Sholem
Main entry: Rabinowitz, Solomon J

Rabinowitz, Solomon J 1859-1916 *AmAu&B, BenetAL 91, BioIn 1, –2, –3, –4, –5, –6, –7, –8, –9, –10, –11, LongCTC, McGEWD 72, REn, REnAL, REnWD, TwCA, –SUP*
Pseud./variant:
Aleichem, Sholem
Rabinowitz, Sholem

Raboff, Ernest Lloyd *AuBYP 2S, –3, SmATA 37*

Raboy, Mac 1914-1967 *ArtCS, BioIn 8, WhAmArt 85*

Raboy, Mac 1916-1967 *EncACom*

Rachleff, Owen Spencer 1934- *ConAu 21R, –14NR, –40NR, ScF&FL 92, WhoAm 76, –78, –80, –82, –84, –86, –88, –90, –92, –94, WhoE 74, –75, –77, WhoEnt 92*

Rachlin, Carol K 1919- *BioIn 17, SmATA 64*

Rachlin, Harvey 1951- *BioIn 16, ConAu 26NR, SmATA 47, WhoAm 94, WhoUSWr 88, WhoWrEP 89, –92*

Rachlin, Nahid 1944- *ConAu 17AS, DrAPF 87, –89, –91, –93, SmATA 64, WhoUSWr 88, WhoWrEP 89, –92*

Rachlis, Eugene d1986 *NewYTBS 86*

Rachlis, Eugene 1920- *ConAu 5R*

Rachlis, Eugene 1920-1986 *BioIn 15, –16, ConAu 121, SmATA 50N*

Racina, Thom 1946- *ConAu 73, –12NR, –29NR, ScF&FL 92, WhoAm 88, –90, –92, –94, WhoEnt 92, WhoWest 80, –82, –84, –87, –89, –92, –94*

Rackham, Arthur 1867-1939 *BioIn 1, –2, –3, –5, –8, –9, –10, –12, –14, –15, –17, CamGLE, CarSB, ChhPo, –S1, –S2, ClaDrA, ConICB, DcBrAr 1, DcBrBI, DcNaB 1931, DcVicP 2, JBA 34, –51, LongCTC, MajAI, OxCChiL, OxCEng 85, OxDcArt, PenEncH, SmATA 15, StaCVF, Str&VC, TwCPaSc, WhoChL*

Raddall, Thomas Head 1903- *Au&Wr 71, BioIn 1, –2, –3, –4, –11, –13, BlueB 76, CanNov, CanWW 70, –80, –81, –83, –89, CanWr, CasWL, ConAu 1R, –28NR, ConNov 72, –76, –82, –86, –91, CreCan 1, CurBio 51, DcLEL, IntAu&W 82, –86, IntvTCA 2, OxCCan, –SUP, TwCRHW 90, TwCWr, WhoCan 73, –80, –82, WhoCanL 85, –87, –92, WrDr 76, –80, –82, –84, –86, –88, –90, –92, –94*

Radford, Ruby Lorraine 1891-1971 *BioIn 10, ConAu 1R, –4NR, ForWC 70, SmATA 6*
Pseud./variant:
Bailey, Matilda
Ford, Marcia

Radiguet, Raymond 1903-1923 *AtlBL, Benet 87, BioIn 1, –2, –3, –4, –7, –8, –9, –10, –11, –16, CasWL, ClDMEL 47, CnMWL, DcLB 65, EncWL, –2, EvEuW, GuFrLit 1,*

ModFrL, ModRL, OxCFr, RAdv 13-2, REn, TwCA, –SUP, TwCLC 29

Radin, Ruth Yaffe 1938- *AuBYP 3, BioIn 16, ConAu 124, SmATA 52, –56, WrDr 90, –92, –94*

Radlauer, David 1952- *BioIn 13, ConAu 106, SmATA 28*

Radlauer, David G 1954- *WhoAmL 94*

Radlauer, Edward 1921- *AuBYP 2, –3, BioIn 12, ConAu 69, –13NR, –30NR, SmATA 15*

Radlauer, Ruth Shaw 1926- *BioIn 12, ConAu 81, –13NR, –30NR, SmATA 15*

Radley, Gail 1951- *BioIn 13, ConAu 16NR, SmATA 25*

Rae, Gwynedd 1892-1977 *BioIn 8, –15, ConAu 65, OxCChiL, SmATA 37, TwCChW 78, –83, –89, WhoChL, WrDr 80*

Rae, John *BioIn 17*

Rae, John 1882-1963 *AmAu&B, BioIn 1, –6, ChhPo, –S1, IlsCB 1744, WhAm 4, WhAmArt 85, WhNAA*

Rae, John 1931- *Who 92*

Rae, John Malcolm 1931- *ConAu 1R, –4NR, IntAu&W 77, –82, –86, –89, –91, Who 74, –82, –83, –85, –88, –90, WhoWor 78, WrDr 76, –80, –82, –84, –86, –88, –90, –92, –94*

Raebeck, Lois 1921- *BioIn 10, ConAu 13R, ForWC 70, SmATA 5*

Raef, Laura C *ConAu 29R, –11NR*

Raffi *BioIn 15, –16, –17, CelR 90, ConAu 136, ConMus 8, ConNews 88-1, SixBJA, SmATA 68, WhoAm 94, WrDr 94*

Raffi 1948-
Main entry: Cavoukian, Raffi

Raftery, Gerald 1905- *ChhPo S1, ConAu P-1, SmATA 11*

Ragland, Phillda 1940- *AfroAA, BioIn 8, IlBBlP, InB&W 80*

Ragozin, Zenaide Alexeievna 1835?-1924 *Alli SUP, BiD&SB, CarSB, DcAmAu, DcInB, DcNAA, WhAm 5*

Rahmas, D Steve 1944- *WhoAmL 78*

Rahn, Joan Elma 1929- *AmMWSc 73P, –76P, –82, –86, –89, –92, BioIn 13, –16, ConAu 37R, –13NR, SixBJA, SmATA 27, WhoFrS 84, WhoMW 84*

Raible, Alton Robert 1918- *BioIn 8, IlsBYP, IlsCB 1957, –1967, SmATA 35*

Raiff, Stan 1930- *BioIn 11, ConAu 61, SmATA 11*

Raikes, Robert 1735-1811 *BioIn 1, –3, –5, –6, –10, –14, –16, CyEd, DcBiPP, DcNaB, EncWM, LuthC 75, OxCChiL, WhDW, WorAlBi, WorAl*

Raine, William MacLeod 1871-1954 *AmAu&B, AmLY, BenetAL 91, BioIn 3, –4, EncFWF, EvLB, ObitOF 79, REnAL, TwCA, –SUP, TwCWW 91, WhAm 3, WhNAA*

Rainer, Julia *ConAu X*
Main entry: Goode, Ruth

Rainey, W 1852-1936 *Alli SUP, ChhPo S1*

Rainey, W B *AuBYP 3, ConAu X, SmATA X*
Main entry: Blassingame, Wyatt Rainey

Rainey, William 1852-1936 *BioIn 14*

Rainwater, Clarence Elmer 1884-1925 *DcNAA, WhAm 1*

Ralston, Alma *ConAu 17R, –11NR*
Pseud./variant:
Payne, Alma Smith

Ralston, Jan *AuBYP 2, –3, ConAu X, SmATA 3, WrDr 80, –82*
Main entry: Dunlop, Agnes Mary Robinson

Ramakrishna 1836-1886 *BioIn 15, –17*

Ramakrishna, Sri 1836-1886 *EncO&P 3*

Ramakrishna, Swami 1836-1886 *BioIn 4, –5, –7, –8, –9, –10, –11*

Ramal, Walter *AuBYP 3, ConAu 137, –X, EvLB, LongCTC, MajAI, SmATA X*
Main entry: DeLaMare, Walter

Rama Rau, Santha 1923- *AmAu&B, BiE&WWA, BioIn 2, –5, –7, –10, ConAu X, CurBio 45, –59, IntAu&W 89, –91, IntWW 89, –91, LiExTwC, NewC, Who 92, WhoAmW 74, WhoWor 74, WorAu 1950*
Main entry: Rau, Santha Rama

Rame, David
Main entry: Divine, Arthur Durham

Ramee, Louise DeLa *BiD&SB, BioIn 1, –2, –3, –11, –13, BritAu 19, Chambr 3, DcEuL, EvLB*
Main entry: DeLaRamee, Louise

Ramee, Louise DeLa 1839-1908 *BioIn 16*

Ramirez, Carolyn Hulmes 1933- *ConAu 5R, -2NR*

Rampling, Anne *BioIn 17, ConAu 36NR, TwCYAW, WrDr 90, -92*

Rampling, Anne 1941- *BioIn 15, -16, WrDr 94*

Ramsay, William McDowell 1922- *ConAu 13R, -12NR, WhoSSW 75, -76, -93*

Ramsay, WIlliam Morrill 1955- *WhoE 91, -93, WhoSSW 88*

Rana, J
Main entry: Forrester, Helen

Ranadive, Gail 1944- *BioIn 11, ConAu 53, SmATA 10*

Rand, Addison 1896- *AuBYP 2, -3, BioIn 7*

Rand, Ann *AuBYP 2, -3, BioIn 7, -14, ChhPo, ConAu 106, SmATA 30, ThrBJA*
Pseud./variant:
Binkley, Anne

Rand, Ayn 1905-1982 *ArtclWW 2, Au&Arts 10, Benet 87, BenetAL 91, BioAmW, BioIn 14, -15, -16, -17, BlmGWL, CamGLE, CamHAL, ConAu 27NR, ConLC 79, EncSF 93, InWom SUP, IntvTCA 2, MajTwCW, NewEScF, OxCAmT 84, ScF&FL 92, ScFSB, TwCSFW 86, -91, TwCYAW, WorAlBi, WorLitC, WrPh*

Rand, Paul 1914- *AmPB, AuBYP 2, -3, BioIn 1, -3, -5, -7, -8, -9, -10, -12, -14, -16, BlueB 76, ConAu 21R, ConDes 84, -90, ConGrA 3, IlsCB 1946, -1957, SmATA 6, ThrBJA, WhAmArt 85, WhoAm 74, -76, -78, -80, -82, -84, -94, WhoAmA 73, -78, -80, -82, -84, -86, -89, -91, WhoE 91, WhoGrA 62, -82*

Rand, Ted *BioIn 16, ChlBIlD*

Rand, Ted 1915- *SixBJA*

Randal, Judith Ellen 1929- *WhoAm 74, -76, -78*

Randall, Blossom E *AuBYP 2, -3, BioIn 7*

Randall, Christine *IlsBYP*

Randall, Florence Engel 1917- *AuBYP 2S, -3, BioIn 10, -14, -16, BlkAWP, ConAu 41R, IntAu&W 77, ScF&FL 92, SixBJA, SmATA 5, TwCRHW 90, WhoAmW 77, -81, WrDr 84, -86, -88, -90, -92, -94*

Randall, Homer *CarSB*

Randall, Janet *AuBYP 2, -3, BioIn 7, -9, ConAu X, IntAu&W 77X, -82X, PoIre, SmATA 3, WrDr 76, -80, -82, -84, -86, -88, -90, -92, -94*
Main entry: Young, Janet Randall
Young, Robert W

Randall, Kenneth Charles *AuBYP 2, -3, BioIn 7*

Randall, Mary *AuBYP 3*

Randall, Robert *AuBYP 2, -3, BioIn 15, -17, ConAu 130, -X, -36NR, DcLEL 1940, EncSF 93, MajAI, MajTwCW, OxCCan, SmATA X, ThrBJA, TwCSFW 86, -91, WrDr 84, -86, -88, -90, -92*
Main entry: Silverberg, Robert

Randall, Robert 1927- *WrDr 94*

Randall, Ruth Elaine Painter 1892-1971 *AmAu&B, AuBYP 2, -3, Au&Wr 71, BioIn 4, -7, -8, -9, ConAu 1R, CurBio 57, SmATA 3, WhAm 5*

Randolph, Ellen *ConAu X, -32NR*
Main entry: Ross, William Edward Daniel

Randolph, Lieutenant J H *HsB&A, YABC 1*
Main entry: Ellis, Edward S

Rands, William Brighty 1823-1882 *Alli, -SUP, BioIn 12, BritAu 19, ChhPo, -S1, -S2, DcEnL, DcLEL, DcNaB, NewC, OxCChiL, OxCEng 67, -85, SmATA 17, TelT*
Pseud./variant:
Browne, Matthew
Holbeach, Henry
Talker, T

Raney, Ken 1953- *BioIn 15, ConGrA 2, SmATA 74*

Raney, Ken William, III 1953- *WhoMW 93*

Ranger, Ken *ConAu X, MajTwCW*

Rankin, Louise S 1897?-1951 *BioIn 2, -6, MorJA*

Rankin, Louise Spieker 1897-1951 *BioIn 14*

Rankin, Robert H *AuBYP 3*

Rankin, Robert Harry 1909- *AuBYP 2S, WhNAA*

Rankin, Robert Harry 1909-1990 *ConAu 131*

Ranney, Agnes V 1916- *BioIn 10, ConAu 5R, SmATA 6*
Pseud./variant:
Reeves, Ruth Ellen

Ransohoff, Doris *AuBYP 2, -3, BioIn 7*

Ransom, Candice F 1952- *BioIn 16, ConAu 121, SmATA 49, -52, WrDr 90, -92, -94*

Ransome, Arthur 1884-1967 *Benet 87, BioIn 14, -15, CamGLE, ConAu 30NR, ScFEYrs, TwCChW 89, WrChl*

Ransome, Arthur Michell 1884-1967 *Alli SUP, AuBYP 2, -3, BioIn 2, -3, -4, -7, -8, -11, -13, CarSB, CasWL, ChhPo, -S1, ChlFicS, ChlLR 8, ConAu 73, DcLEL, DcNaB 1961, EvLB, GrBr, JBA 34, -51, LongCTC, MajAI, NewC, Novels, ObitT 1961, OxCChiL, OxCEng 85, OxCShps, PenC ENG, REn, SmATA 22, TelT, TwCA, -SUP, TwCChW 78, -83, WhoChL, WhoLA*

Ransome, James 1961- *BlkAull 92*

Ransome, James E 1961- *SmATA 76*

Ranucci, Renato 1921- *AuBYP 2, -3, BioIn 7*
Pseud./variant:
Rascel, Renato

Rapaport, Stella F *BioIn 11, ConAu 1R, SmATA 10*

Raphael, Elaine
Main entry: Bolognese, Elaine Raphael

Raphael, Elaine 1933- *BioIn 13, ConAu X, SmATA 23*

Raposo, Joe 1938?- *BioIn 10*

Raposo, Joseph G d1989 *NewYTBS 89*

Raposo, Joseph G 1937-1989 *BioIn 16, -17*

Raposo, Joseph Guilherme 1938- *WhoAm 86, -88*

Raposo, Joseph Guilherme 1938-1989 *ConAu 127, SmATA 61, WhAm 9*

Rappaport, Eva 1924- *BioIn 10, ConAu 29R, SmATA 6*

Rarick, Carrie 1911- *BioIn 15, ConAu 115, SmATA 41*

Rascel, Renato *AuBYP 2, -3, BioIn 7*
Main entry: Ranucci, Renato

Rasch, Sunna Cooper 1925- *ConAu 105, WhoE 74*

Raskin, Edith Lefkowitz 1908- *AuBYP 2S, -3, BioIn 11, ConAu 9R, -3NR, ForWC 70, SmATA 9*

Raskin, Ellen 1925?-1984 *DcAmChF 1960*

Raskin, Ellen 1928- *WhoAm 86, WhoUSWr 88, WhoWrEP 89*

Raskin, Ellen 1928-1984 *ALA 80, AmPB, BioIn 8, -9, -10, -12, -14, -15, BkP, ChhPo, -S1, -S2, ChlLR 1, -12, ConAu 21R, -113, -37NR, DcLB 52, IlsBYP, IlsCB 1957, -1967, MajAI, OxCChiL, SmATA 2, -38, ThrBJA, TwCChW 78, -83, -89, TwCYAW WhAm 9, WhoAm 80, -82, -84, WhoAmA 80, -82, -84, WrDr 80, -82, -84*

Raskin, Joseph 1897-1982 *BioIn 11, -12, -13, ConAu 33R, -105, -13NR, SmATA 12, -29N, WhAmArt 85, WhoAmJ 80, WhoWorJ 72, -78*

Rasky, Frank 1922- *CanWW 89*

Rasky, Frank 1923- *ConAu 107, OxCCan SUP*

Rasmussen, Knud Johan Victor 1879-1933 *BioIn 5, -11, -14, ConAu 113, InSci, OxCCan, OxCShps, PenC EUR, REn, SmATA 34*

Raspe, Rudolf Erich 1737-1794 *BioIn 2, -3, -4, -5, -8, CarSB, CasWL, Chambr 2, DcEuL, DcNaB, DcScB, EvEuW, EvLB, HsB&A, OxCGer 76, -86, ScFEYrs*

Rasp-Nuri, Grace 1899- *IntAu&W 77*

Rasporich, Anthony Walter 1940- *DrAS 74H, -82H, WhoAm 88, -90, -92, -94, WhoWest 92, -94*

Raswan, Carl Reinhard 1893-1966 *BioIn 7, -10*

Ratcliffe, E *ChhPo*

Ratcliffe, E Jane 1917- *WrDr 86, -90, -94*

Ratcliffe, Mary Joan 1925- *IntAu&W 82, WrDr 76, -80*

Rathbone, St George 1854-1928 *CarSB, DcAmAu*

Rathjen, Carl Henry 1909- *BioIn 11, ConAu 5R, -2NR, EncSF 93, IntAu&W 77, -82, SmATA 11*
Pseud./variant:
Russell, Charlotte

Rattner, David S 1916- *ConAu 69*

Rattray, Simon *ConAu X, DcLEL 1940, IntAu&W 77X, SmATA X, TwCCr&M 80, -85, -91, WrDr 76, -80, -82, -84, -86, -88, -90, -92, -94*
Main entry: Trevor, Elleston

Rattray, Simon 1920- *BioIn 14*

Ratz de Tagyos, Paul 1958- *SmATA 76*

Rau, Margaret 1913- *BioIn 11, ChILR 8, ConAu 61, -8NR, IntAu&W 82, SmATA 9*

Rau, Santha Rama *InWom SUP, IntWW 91, Who 92*

Rau, Santha Rama 1923- *BioIn 2, -5, -7, -10, BlmGWL, CelR, CurBio 45, -59, DcLEL 1940, FarE&A 80, -81, IntWW 74, -75, -76, -77, -78, -79, -80, -81, -82, -83, -89, ModCmwL, PenC ENG, TwCWr, Who 74, -82, -83, -85, -88, -90, WhoAm 76, WhoWor 74*
Pseud./variant:
Bowers, Santha Rama Rau
Rama Rau, Santha

Rauch, Constance 1937- *BioIn 10, ConAu 57*

Rauch, Mabel Thompson 1888-1972 *BioIn 13, ConAu 103, SmATA 26N*

Raucher, Herman 1928- *BioIn 11, ConAu 29R, -29NR, ConTFT 1, IntMPA 86, -88, -92, Novels, ScF&FL 92, SmATA 8, WhoAm 80, -82, -84, -86, -88, -90, -92, -94, WhoE 77, -81, -83, -91, WhoEnt 92, WrDr 76, -80, -82, -84, -86, -88, -90, -92, -94*

Raverat, Gwendolen Mary 1885-1957 *BioIn 1, -3, -4, -5, ChhPo, DcBrAr 1, DcNaB 1951, DcWomA, IlsBYP, IlsCB 1744, -1946, LongCTC*

Ravielli, Anthony 1916- *AuBYP 2, -3, Au&Wr 71, BioIn 5, -7, -8, -9, ConAu 29R, -11NR, IlsCB 1946, -1957, -1967, SmATA 3, ThrBJA, WhoE 74*

Ravilious, Robin 1944- *SmATA 77*

Rawding, F W 1930- *BioIn 16, SmATA 55*

Rawlings, Marjorie Kinnan *IntvTCA 2*

Rawlings, Marjorie Kinnan 1896-1953 *AmAu&B, AmNov, AmWomWr, ArtclWW 2, Benet 87, BenetAL 91, BioAmW, BioIn 1, -2, -3, -4, -5, -7, -8, -9, -10, -11, -14, -15, -16, -17, BlmGWL, CnDAL, ConAu 104, -137, CurBio 42, -54, CyWA 58, DcLB 9, -22, -102, DcLEL, EvLB, FifSWrA, LongCTC, MajAI, ModAL, NotAW MOD, Novels, ObitOF 79, OxCAmL 65, -83, OxCChiL, PenC AM, REn, REnAL, RfGAmL 87, ThrBJA, TwCA, -SUP, TwCChW 78, -83, -89, TwCLC 4, TwCWr, TwCYAW, WhAm 3, WrChl, YABC 1*

Rawlings, Marjorie Kinnan 1898-1953 *InWom SUP*

Rawlins, Margaret Grace *ChhPo S2*

Rawls, Wilson 1913- *AuBYP 3, BioIn 16*

Rawls, Wilson 1913-1984 *SixBJA*

Rawls, Woodrow Wilson 1913- *AuBYP 2S, AuNews 1, BioIn 10, -13, BioNews 74, ConAu 1R, -5NR, IntAu&W 77, -82, -82X, SmATA 22*

Rawlyk, George A *BioIn 17*

Rawlyk, George Alexander 1935- *CanWW 89, ConAu 26NR, SmATA 64, WhoWor 87*

Ray, Anna Chapin 1865-1945 *AmAu&B, BioIn 1, CarSB, DcAmAu, WhAm 2, WomWWA 14, WomNov*

Ray, Carl 1943- *BioIn 10, Profile 1*

Ray, Carl 1943-1978 *BioIn 17, SmATA 63*

Ray, Deborah 1940- *BioIn 11, ConAu 57, -X, ConGrA 3, IlsBYP, SmATA 8, WhoAmA 78, -80, -82, -84, -86, -89, -91*

Ray, Deborah Kogan 1940- *BioIn 16, SixBJA*
Main entry: Kogan, Deborah

Ray, Deborah Kogan 1941- *WhoWrEP 89, -92*

Ray, Delia 1963- *SmATA 70*

Ray, Irene *ConAu X, IntAu&W 77X, -82X, -86X, SmATA 1*
Main entry: Sutton, Margaret Beebe

Ray, Jane 1960- *SmATA 72*

Ray, JoAnne 1935- *BioIn 11, ConAu 61, SmATA 9*

Ray, Mary 1932- *TwCChW 89, WrDr 86, -88, -90, -92*

Ray, Mary E 1911- *WhoBlA 85, -88, -90, -92, -94*

Ray, Mary Eva Pedder 1932- *Au&Wr 71, BioIn 9, ConAu 29R, -12NR, IntAu&W 77, -82, -86, OxCChiL, SmATA 2, TwCChW 78, -83, WrDr 76, -80, -82, -84, -94*

Ray, Ophelia *AuBYP 2, -3, BioIn 8*

Ray, Ralph 1920-1952 *BioIn 2, -5, IlsBYP, IlsCB 1946*

Ray, Rena *CarSB*

Ray, Willis Eugene 1929- *LEduc 74*

Rayevsky, Robert *ChlBIlD*

Raymond, Alexander Gillespie 1909-1956 *ArtCS, BioIn 1, -2, -4, EncAJ, ObitOF 79, WhAmArt 85*

Raymond, Charles *ConAu X*
Main entry: Koch, Charlotte
Koch, Raymond

Raymond, James Crossley 1917-1981 *BioIn 12, –13, ConAu 105, NewYTBS 81, SmATA 29N*

Raymond, John *AuBYP 3*

Raymond, John Francis 1925- *AuBYP 2, BioIn 8, WhoSSW 73*

Raymond, Margaret Thomsen *AuBYP 3*

Raymond, Margaret Thomsen 1900- *AuBYP 2, BioIn 1, –2, –7*

Raymond, Robert *AuBYP 3, BioIn 11, ConAu X, SmATA X*

Raymond, Rossiter Worthington 1840-1918 *Alli, –SUP, AmAu&B, BiInAmS, CarSB, ChhPo, –S1, DcAmAu, DcNAA, OhA&B, WhAm 1*

Rayner, Gordon 1935- *CreCan 1, DcCAr 81, OxCTwCA, PrintW 83, –85, WhoAmA 80, –82, –84, –86, –89, –91*

Rayner, Mary 1933- *BioIn 14, ConAu 29NR, TwCChW 89, WrDr 86, –88, –90, –92*

Rayner, Mary Yoma 1933- *BioIn 12, –13, ConAu 69, –12NR, FifBJA, IlsCB 1967, IntAu&W 89, –91, SmATA 22, TwCChW 83*

Rayner, Mary Yoma Grigson 1933- *WrDr 94*

Rayner, William 1929- *Au&Wr 71, BioIn 14, –16, ConAu 77, ScF&FL 92, SmATA 36, –55, TwCChW 78, TwCWW 91, WrDr 80, –82, –84, –86, –88, –90, –92, –94*

Raynes, John 1929- *ArtsCL, BioIn 6, IlsBYP*

Raynor, Dorka *BioIn 13, ConAu 106, SmATA 28*

Rayson, Steven 1932- *BioIn 14, ConAu 106, SmATA 30, WrDr 76, –80, –82, –84*

Razzell, Arthur George 1925- *AuBYP 2S, Au&Wr 71, BioIn 11, SmATA 11, WrDr 76, –80, –82, –84*

Razzell, Mary 1930- *DcChlFi*

Razzi, James 1931- *BioIn 11, ConAu 53, –5NR, ScF&FL 92, SmATA 10*

Read, Brian 1927- *Au&Wr 71, ConAu 108, IntAu&W 77, –82, WrDr 76, –80, –82, –84, –86, –88, –90, –92, –94*

Read, Charles Anderson 1841-1878 *BiDIrW, DcIrB 88, DcIrL, DcIrW 1, DcNaB, PoIre, StaCVF*

Read, Elfreida 1920- *AuBYP 2S, –3, Au&Wr 71, BioIn 9, ConAu 21R, –9NR, –25NR, IntAu&W 77, SmATA 2, WhoCanL 85, –87, –92, WrDr 76, –80, –82, –84, –86, –88, –90, –92, –94*

Read, Herbert Edward *IntvTCA 2*

Read, Herbert Edward 1893-1968 *BioIn 17*

Read, Herbert Edward, Sir 1893-1968 *BioIn 1, –3, –4, –6, –7, –8, –9, –10, –14, CasWL, ChhPo, –S1, CnE&AP, ConAu 25R, ConLC 4, CurBio 62, –68, DcLEL, DcNaB 1961, EncWL, EvLB, GrBr, LongCTC, ModBrL, –S1, NewC, OxCEng 67, –85, PenC ENG, RAdv 1, REn, TwCA, –SUP, TwCWr, WhAm 5, WhoLA, WhoTwCL*

Read, Miss *Benet 87, BioIn 5, –10, –15, DcLEL 1940, IntAu&W 77X, –82X, –86X, –91X, Novels, SmATA X, Who 88, WorAu 1950, WrDr 80, –84, –86, –88, –94*
Main entry: Saint, Dora Jessie

Read, Piers Paul 1941- *Au&Wr 71, BioIn 10, –12, –13, ConAu 21R, –38NR, ConDr 73, –77B, ConLC 4, –10, –25, ConNov 76, –82, –86, –91, DcLB 14, DcLEL 1940, IntAu&W 77, –82, –86, –89, –91, IntWW 89, –91, Novels, ScF&FL 92, SmATA 21, Who 74, –82, –83, –85, –88, –90, –92, WhoAm 82, –84, –86, –88, –90, –92, –94, WrDr 76, –80, –82, –84, –86, –88, –90, –92, –94*

Read, Ritchard 1914- *ConAu 57*

Reade, Deborah 1949- *SmATA 69*

Reader, Dennis 1929- *SmATA 71*

Reader, Sarah *ChhPo S2*

Reading, Val
Pseud./variant:
Val

Ready, Kirk L 1943- *BioIn 15, ConAu 114, SmATA 39*

Reaney, James 1926- *BenetAL 91, BioIn 15, CamGLE, CamGWoT, CanWW 89, ConAu 42NR, ConDr 88, ConPo 91, DcLB 68, IntvTCA 2, OxCCanT, RfGEnL 91, TwCChW 89, WrDr 86, –88, –90, –92*

Reaney, James Crerar 1926- *Au&Wr 71, BioIn 8, –10, –11, CanWW 70, –79, –80, –81, –83, CanWr, CasWL, ChhPo S1, CnThe, ConAu 41R, –15AS, ConDr 73, –77, –82, –93, ConLC 13, ConPo 70, –75, –80, –85, CreCan 1, DcLEL 1940, DrAS 74E, –78E,*

–82E, IntAu&W 82, –86, IntDcT 2, McGEWD 72, –84, ModCmwL, OxCCan, –SUP, OxCCanL, OxCThe 83, PenC ENG, REnAL, REnWD, SmATA 43, TwCChW 78, –83, WebE&AL, WhoAm 80, –82, –84, –86, –88, –92, –94, WhoCanL 85, –87, –92, WhoMW 80, –82, WrDr 76, –80, –82, –84, –94

Rearden, Jim 1925- *ConAu 65, –40NR*

Reardon, Mary A *WhoAmA 73, –78, –80, –82, –84, –86, –89, –91*

Reardon, Mary Agnes 1912- *WhoE 86, –91, –93*

Reaver, Chap 1935- *ConAu 137, SmATA 69*

Reaver, Chap 1935-1993 *ConAu 142, SmATA 77, TwCYAW*

Reboul, Antoine *AuBYP 2S, –3*

Rechnitzer, Ferdinand Edsted 1894- *AuBYP 2, –3, BioIn 7*

Reck, Alma Kehoe 1901- *AuBYP 2, –3, BioIn 7, ConAu 1R, ForWC 70, IndAu 1917*

Reck, Franklin Mering 1896-1965 *BioIn 7, –14, ConAu 109, SmATA 30, WhAm 4, WhNAA*

Redding, Robert Hull 1919- *AuBYP 2S, –3, BioIn 9, ConAu 21R, –11NR, –28NR, IntAu&W 82, SmATA 2*

Redekopp, Elsa *BioIn 17, ConAu 127, SmATA 61*

Redford, Lora Bryning *AuBYP 2, –3, BioIn 8*

Redman, Ben Ray 1896-1961 *AmAu&B, AnMV 1926, Au&Wr 71, BenetAL 91, BioIn 6, ConAu 93, DcAmB S7, NotNAT B, REnAL, WhAm 4*

Redman, Lister Appleton 1933- *Au&Wr 71, IntAu&W 77, WrDr 76, –80, –82, –84, –86, –88, –90, –92, –94*

Redsky, James *OxCCan SUP*

Redway, Ralph *ConAu X, –29NR, LongCTC, SmATA X, WhoChL*

Redway, Ridley *ConAu X, –29NR, SmATA X*

Reed, A W 1908-1979 *ConAu 9R, –4NR, OxCAusL, WrDr 76, –80*

Reed, Betty Jane 1921- *BioIn 9, ConAu 29R, SmATA 4*

Reed, Elizabeth Liggett 1895- *ConAu 77*

Reed, Elizabeth Liggett 1895-1978 *ConAu 133*

Reed, Gwendolyn E 1932- *AuBYP 3*

Reed, Gwendolyn Elizabeth 1932- *AuBYP 2, BioIn 8, –10, –12, ChhPo S1, ConAu 25R, SmATA 21, WhoAmW 74, –75*

Reed, Harrison Merrick, Jr. 1898- *ConAu 1R, –134*

Reed, Henry d1986 *Who 88N*

Reed, Henry 1808-1854 *BioIn 16, DcLB 59*

Reed, Henry 1914- *Au&Wr 71, BioIn 14, CnE&AP, ConAu 104, ConPo 70, –75, –80, –85, DcLB 27, EngPo, IntAu&W 89, LongCTC, OxCEng 85, REn, Who 74, –82, –83, –85, WorAu 1950, WrDr 76, –82, –84, –86*

Reed, Henry 1914-1986 *AnObit 1986, CamGLE, ConAu 121*

Reed, Henry Clay 1899-1972 *BioIn 9, ConAu 111, WhAm 5*

Reed, Henry Hope 1808-1854 *AmAu&B, ChhPo, –S2, ConDr 73, CyAL, DcAmAu, DcNAA, EvLB, WhAm HS*

Reed, Ivy Kellerman 1877- *ChhPo, WhAm 5, WomWWA 14*

Reed, Ivy Kellerman 1877-1968 *ScF&FL 92*

Reed, Kit *ConAu 36NR, DrAPF 87, –89, –91, DrmM 2, TwCSFW 86, WhoAm 86, –88, –90, WhoEnt 92, WhoWrEP 89, –92, WrDr 94*
Main entry: Reed, Lillian Craig

Reed, Kit 1932- *BioIn 14, ConAu 16NR, EncSF 93, NewEScF, ScF&FL 92, ScFSB, SmATA 34, WhoAm 80, –82, –84, WrDr 82, –84, –86, –88, –90, –92*
Pseud./variant:
Hyde, Shelley

Reed, Lillian Craig 1932- *AmAu&B, Au&Wr 71, BioIn 14, ConAu 1R, –1NR, WhoAm 74, –76, –78, WhoAmW 74, WhoUSWr 88, WrDr 76, –80*
Pseud./variant:
Reed, Kit

Reed, Mary 1880?-1960 *AmAu&B, BioIn 5*

Reed, Mathilda Newman 1905- *ConAu 1R*

Reed, Philip G 1908- *BioIn 1, –6, –8, –9, –13, –14, ChhPo, IlsBYP, IlsCB 1744, –1957, SmATA 29, ThrBJA, WhoMW 74, –76, –78, –80, –82*

Reed, Stanley William 1911- *Au&Wr 71, BlueB 76, Who 74, -82, -83, -85, -88, -90, -92, WhoWor 74, WrDr 76*

Reed, Talbot Baines 1852-1893 *Alli SUP, BioIn 8, CamGEL, CamGLE, CasWL, ChhPo S2, DcNaB, EvLB, LongCTC, OxCChiL, StaCVF, TelT, TwCChW 78A, -83A, -89A, WhoChL*
Pseud./variant:
Old Boy, An

Reed, Thomas 1947- *BioIn 14, ConAu 103, SmATA 34*

Reed, Veronica *IlsBYP, IlsCB 1946*
Main entry: Sherman, Theresa

Reed, William Leonard 1910- *Baker 84, -92, IntWWM 85, -90, WhoMus 72*

Reed, William Maxwell 1871-1962 *BioIn 2, -12, JBA 51, SmATA 15*

Reeder, Carolyn *DcAmChF 1985*

Reeder, Carolyn 1937- *BioIn 17, ConAu 135, SmATA 66, WrDr 94*

Reeder, Colin Dawson 1938- *ConAu 141, SmATA 74*

Reeder, Colonel Red
Main entry: Reeder, Russell P, Jr.

Reeder, Red *AuBYP 3*

Reeder, Russell P, Jr. 1902- *AuBYP 2, BioIn 7, -9, ConAu 1R, -5NR, SmATA 4*
Pseud./variant:
Reeder, Colonel Red

Reeder, Russell Potter 1902- *AuBYP 3*

Reef, Catherine 1951- *SmATA 73*

Reely, Mary Katharine 1881- *AmWomPl, AuBYP 2, -3, BioIn 1, -5, -7*

Reeman, Douglas Edward 1924?- *Au&Wr 71, BioIn 13, ConAu 1R, -3NR, DcLEL 1940, IntAu&W 77, -89, -91, SmATA 28, -63, WrDr 76, -80*
Pseud./variant:
Kent, Alexander

Rees, David *BioIn 16*

Rees, David 1936- *BioIn 14, -16, SmATA 69, -5AS, TwCChW 89, WrDr 90, -92*

Rees, David, Prof 1918- *Who 90*

Rees, David Bartlett 1936- *ConAu 105, FifBJA, IntAu&W 82, -86, MajAI, OxCChiL, SmATA 36, TwCChW 83, WrDr 82, -84, -86, -88, -94*

Rees, David Bartlett 1936-1993 *ConAu 141, GayLL, SmATA 76*

Rees, Ennis 1925- *AuBYP 2, -3, BioIn 8, -9, -15, ChhPo S1, ConAu 1R, -2NR, DrAP 75, DrAPF 83, -85, -87, -89, -91, -93, DrAS 74E, -78E, -82E, IntAu&W 77, -82, IntWWP 82, SmATA 3*

Rees, George Leslie Clarke 1905- *DcChlFi*

Rees, Helen Christina Easson 1903-1970 *AuBYP 2, -3, BioIn 8, ConAu 5R*
Pseud./variant:
Oliver, Jane

Rees, Jean Anglin Sinclair 1912- *Au&Wr 71, ConAu 1R, -1NR*

Rees, Leslie 1905- *Au&Wr 71, BlueB 76, ConAu 104, -26NR, IntAu&W 77, -82, IntYB 80, -81, -82, OxCAusL, OxCChiL, SingR 1, TwCChW 78, -83, -89, WrDr 80, -82, -84, -86, -88, -90, -92*

Rees, Mary *AuBYP 3*

Reese, Bob 1938- *BioIn 16, -17, SmATA X*
Main entry: Reese, Robert A

Reese, Carolyn Johnson 1938- *BioIn 17, ConAu 30NR, SmATA 64*

Reese, John Henry *AuBYP 2, -3, BioIn 7*

Reese, Lizette Woodworth 1856-1935 *Alli SUP, AmAu&B, AmWomWr, AnCL, ArtclWW 2, BenetAL 91, BiDSA, BiD&SB, BioIn 1, -4, -8, -11, -15, ChhPo, -S2, CnDAL, ConAmA, ConAmL, DcAmAu, DcLB 54, DcLEL, DcNAA, FemiCLE, InWom SUP, LongCTC, OxCAmL 65, -83, REn, REnAL, TwCA, -SUP, WhAm 1, -2*

Reese, M M 1910- *ConAu 9R, -3NR, WrDr 84*

Reese, M M 1910-1987 *ConAu 123*

Reese, Robert A 1938- *SmATA 53, -60*
Pseud./variant:
Reese, Bob

Reese, Terence 1913- *BioIn 16, ConAu 109, -30NR, SmATA 59, Who 74, -83, -85*

Reeser, Michael *AuBYP 3*

Reesink, Maryke 1919- *ConAu 25R*

Reeve, Joel *AuBYP 3, ConAu X, IntAu&W 91X, SmATA X, WrDr 84, -86, -88, -90*
Main entry: Cox, William R
Cox, William R

Reeves, Faye Couch 1953- *SmATA 76*

Reeves, James 1909-1978 *AnCL, AuBYP 2, -3, Au&Wr 71, BioIn 7, -8, -9, -10, -12, BlueB 76, BkCL, CamGLE, ChhPo, -S1, -S2, ConAu 5R, ConPo 70, -75, DcLEL 1940, EngPo, IntAu&W 77, OxCChiL, PenC ENG, SmATA 15, ThrBJA, TwCChW 78, -83, -89, Who 74, WhoChL, WhoTwCL, WorAu 1950, WrDr 76*

Reeves, Joyce *AuBYP 3, BioIn 12, ConAu 12NR, IntAu&W 82X, -86X, SmATA 17, WrDr 82, -94*
Main entry: Gard, Joyce

Reeves, Lawrence F 1926- *BioIn 13, ConAu 105, SmATA 29, WhoLibS 55*
Pseud./variant:
Lyfick, Warren
Seever, R

Reeves, Marjorie E 1905- *ConAu 20NR, WrDr 86, -88, -90, -92, -94*

Reeves, Marjorie Ethel 1905- *Au&Wr 71, ConAu 13R, -42NR, IntAu&W 77, -82, -86, -89, IntWW 89, -91, Who 74, -82, -83, -85, -88, -90, -92, WhoWor 78, WrDr 76, -80, -82, -84*

Reeves, Martha Emilie 1941- *ConAu 65*

Reeves, Ruth Ellen *ConAu X, DrAS 74E, SmATA 6*
Main entry: Ranney, Agnes V

Regan, Dian Curtis *ScF&FL 92*

Regan, Dian Curtis 1950- *ConAu 142, SmATA 75*

Regehr, Lydia 1903- *BioIn 15, ConAu 45, SmATA 37*

Reggiani, Renee 1925- *BioIn 12, ConAu 85, -36NR, IntAu&W 77, SmATA 18, TwCChW 78B*

Regli, Adolph Casper 1896- *AuBYP 2, -3, BioIn 7*

Rehm, Karl M 1935- *SmATA 72*

Reichert, Edwin C 1909-1988 *BioIn 16, ConAu 126, SmATA 57*

Reid, Alastair 1926- *AuBYP 2, -3, BioIn 3, -8, -10, -11, -12, -14, -15, ChhPo, -S1, -S2, ConAu 5R, -3NR, ConPo 70, -75, -80, -85, -91, DcLB 27, IntAu&W 77, -89, SmATA 46, WorAu 1950, WrDr 76, -80, -82, -84, -86, -88, -90, -92, -94*

Reid, Barbara 1922- *BioIn 12, ConAu 25R, -12NR, DrAPF 87, -89, -91, -93, SmATA 21*

Reid, Barbara 1957- *ChlBIlD*

Reid, Bill *IlsBYP*

Reid, Desmond *ConAu X, -28NR, -38NR, EncSF 93, MajTwCW*

Reid, Desmond 1939- *WrDr 94*

Reid, Desmond 1945- *BlkAuII 92*

Reid, Dorothy M d1974 *BioIn 10, -13, ConAu 109, OxCCan, -SUP, Profile 1, SmATA 29*

Reid, Dorothy-Marie 1937- *WhoAmW 91*

Reid, Eugenie Chazal 1924- *BioIn 11, ConAu 13R, ForWC 70, SmATA 12*

Reid, George Kell 1918- *AmMWSc 73P, -76P, -82, -86, -89, -92, WhoAm 92, -94*

Reid, J H Stewart *OxCCan*

Reid, James *BioIn 14*

Reid, James 1907- *ChhPo, -S2, ConICB*

Reid, John Calvin *BioIn 12, ConAu 25R, -11NR, SmATA 21*

Reid, John Calvin 1901- *ScF&FL 92*

Reid, Mayne 1818-1883 *Alli, -SUP, AmAu&B, BenetAL 91, BbD, BiD&SB, BioIn 8, -9, -13, -14, BritAu 19, CamGEL, CamHAL, CarSB, CelCen, Chambr 3, DcAmAu, DcBiPP, DcEnL, DcIrL, DcLB 21, EvLB, HsB&A, NewC, Novels, OxCAmL 65, -83, OxCChiL, PenC AM, REn, REnAL, SmATA 24, WhoChL*
Pseud./variant:
Beach, Charles

Reid, Mayne, Captain 1818-1883 *StaCVF*

Reid, Meta Mayne *WrDr 86, -88, -90, -92, -94*

Reid, Meta Mayne 1905- *Au&Wr 71, BioIn 14, -16, ConAu 13R, IntAu&W 77X, -82X, SmATA 36, -58, TwCChW 78, -83, -89, WrDr 76, -80, -82, -84*

Reid, Stephen 1873-1948 *BioIn 1, -14, ChhPo, -S1, ClaDrA, DcBrAr 1, DcBrBI, DcVicP 2, IlsCB 1744*

Reid, Victor S *BioIn 14*

Reid, Victor Stafford 1913- *BioIn 9, DcAfL, IntAu&W 89, -91, WrDr 76, -80*

Reid Banks, Lynne *AuBYP 3, ConNov 86, TwCChW 89, Who 88, -90, -92*

Reid Banks, Lynne 1929- *Au&Arts 6, BioIn 13, -16, -17, ChlLR 24, ConAu 6NR, -22NR, -38NR, ConNov 82, EncBrWW, MajAI, SmATA 22, -75, TwCChW 83, TwCYAW, WrDr 82, -84, -86, -88, -90, -92, -94*
Pseud./variant:
Banks, Lynne Reid

Reidel, Marlene 1923- *OxCChiL*

Reidy, John Patrick 1930- *ConAu 17R*

Reiff, Stephanie Ann 1948- *BioIn 13, -16, ConAu 93, SmATA 28, -47*

Reig, June Wilson 1933- *ConAu 105, SmATA 30, WhoAm 82, -84, -86, -88, -90, -92, -94, WhoEnt 92*

Reigot, Betty Polisar 1924- *BioIn 15, -16, ConAu 111, SmATA 41, -55*

Reiley, Catherine Conway *AuBYP 2, -3, BioIn 7*

Reilly, Robert Thomas 1922- *ConAu 5R, -2NR, DrAS 78E, -82E, IntAu&W 77, -82, -86, WhoMW 92, WrDr 76, -80, -82, -84, -86, -88, -90, -92, -94*

Reilly, William K *ConAu X*

Reinach, Jacquelyn 1930- *ASCAP 66, BioIn 13, ConAu 105, -22NR, SmATA 28, WhoAmW 77, WhoWrEP 89*

Reinach, Jacquelyn Krasne 1930- *WhoWrEP 92*

Reincheld, Bill 1946- *ConAu 57*

Reinecke, Esther E *BioIn 6, MinnWr*

Reiner, William B 1910-1976 *BioIn 14, -15, BlueB 76, ConAu 45, -61, -3NR, LEduc 74, SmATA 30N, -46, WrDr 80*

Reinfeld, Fred 1910-1964 *AuBYP 2, -3, BioIn 6, -7, -9, ConAu P-1, GolEC, ObitOF 79, SmATA 3*
Pseud./variant:
Young, Edward

Reingold, Carmel Berman *AuBYP 2S, -3*

Reiniger, Lotte *InWom SUP*

Reiniger, Lotte 1899-1981 *AnObit 1981, BioIn 5, -11, -14, -15, ConAu 108, ContDcW 89, DcFM, FilmgC, HalFC 84, -88, IlsCB 1946, IntDcWB, OxCChiL, OxCFilm, SmATA 33N, -40, WomWMM, -B, WorECar, WorEFlm*

Reis, Mary Elizabeth Barrett *WhoAmW 77, WhoE 74*

Reisgies, Teresa Maria 1966- *SmATA 74*

Reiss, Johanna 1932- *AuBYP 3, BioIn 14, -15, ChlLR 19*

Reiss, Johanna DeLeeuw 1932- *AuBYP 2S, BioIn 10, -11, -12, ConAu 85, FifBJA, HerW, -84, SmATA 18, TwCChW 78B*

Reiss, John J *AuBYP 2S, -3, BioIn 13, ConAu 106, IlsCB 1967, SmATA 23*

Reiss, Kathryn *ScF&FL 92*

Reiss, Kathryn 1957- *SmATA 76*

Reiss, Marilyn Leitner *AuBYP 2S, -3*

Reit, Seymour 1918- *AuBYP 3*

Reit, Seymour V *AuBYP 2S, SmATA 21*
Pseud./variant:
Reit, Sy

Reit, Seymour V 1918- *ScF&FL 92*

Reit, Sy
Main entry: Reit, Seymour V

Reitci, Rita Krohne *AuBYP 3*

Reitici, Rita Krohne 1930- *ConAu 5R*
Pseud./variant:
Ritchie, Rita

Relf, Patricia 1954- *SmATA 71*

Remarque, Erich Maria 1898?-1970 *AmAu&B, Benet 87, BenetAL 91, BiGAW, BioIn 1, -3, -4, -5, -9, -13, -14, -15, -16, -17, CasWL, ClDMEL 47, ConAu 29R, -77, ConLC 21, CyWA 58, DcLB 56, Dis&D, EncWL, -2, EvEuW, FilmgC, HalFC 84, -88, LiExTwC, LongCTC, MajTwCW, McGEWB, ModGL, NewYTBE 70, NotNAT B, Novels, ObitOF 79, ObitT 1961, OxCEng 67, -85, OxCGer 76, -86, PenC EUR, RAdv 13-2, REn, REnAL, TwCA, -SUP, TwCWr, WhAm 5, WhScrn 83, -77, WhoTwCL, WorAlBi, WorAl*

Rembadi, Gemma Mongiardini 1856- *CarSB*

Remi, Georges 1907-1983 *AnObit 1983, BioIn 11, -13, -14, ConAu 69, -109, -31NR, IntAu&W 77, -82, NewYTBS 83, SmATA 13, -32, -32N*
Pseud./variant:
Herge

Remington, Barbara *ChhPo S1*

Remington, Ella-Carrie 1914- *ConAu 69*
Pseud./variant:
Alden, Carella

Remington, Frederic 1861-1909 *AmAu, AmAu&B, AtlBL, Benet 87, BenetAL 91, BioIn 1, -2, -3, -4, -5, -6, -7, -8, -9, -10, -11, -12, -13, -14, -15, -16, -17, ClaDrA, CnDAL, ConAu 108, DcAmAu, DcLB 12, DcLEL, DcNAA, EncAB-H, EncFWF, McGEWB, MemAm, OxCAmH, OxCAmL 65, -83, OxDcArt, REn, REnAL, SmATA 41, WebAB 74, -79, WhAm 1, WhCiWar, WhNaAH, WhoFtbl 74, WorAlBi, WorAl*

Remini, Robert V 1921- *ConAu 20NR*

Remini, Robert Vincent 1921- *ConAu 9R, -3NR, DrAS 74H, -78H, -82H, IntAu&W 77, WhoAm 74, -76, -78, -80, -82, -84, -86, -88, -90, -92, -94*

Remkiewicz, Frank 1939- *SmATA 77*

Rempel, John I *OxCCan*

Renaud, Bernadette 1945- *BioIn 17, ConAu 134, IntAu&W 86, SmATA 66, WhoCanL 87, -92*

Renaud, Bernadette Marie Elise 1945- *WhoAm 94*

Renault, Mary 1905-1983 *AnObit 1983, ArtclWW 2, AuBYP 2, -3, Au&Wr 71, Benet 87, BioIn 5, -6, -8, -9, -10, -11, -13, -14, -16, BlmGWL, BlueB 76, CamGEL, CamGLE, ConAu X, ConLC 3, -11, -17, ConNov 72, -76, -82, CurBio 59, -84N, CyWA 89, DcLB Y83N, DcNaB 1981, EncBrWW, EncSoA, FemiCLE, GayLL, InWom SUP, IntAu&W 77, IntWW 74, -75, -76, -77, -78, -79, -80, -81, -82, -83, IntvTCA 2, LongCTC, ModBrL S1, -S2, ModCmwL, NewC, NewYTBS 83, Novels, OxCEng 85, RAdv 1, REn, RfGEnL 91, SmATA X, TwCRHW 90, TwCWr, WhAm 8, Who 74, -82, -83, -85N, WhoWor 74, -78, WorAlBi, WorAl, WorAu 1950, WrDr 76, -80, -82, -84*
Main entry: Challans, Mary

Rendell, Joan *Au&Wr 71, BioIn 13, ConAu 61, -7NR, -23NR, IntAu&W 77, -86, -89, SmATA 28, WrDr 76, -80, -82, -84, -86, -88, -90, -92, -94*

Rendina, Laura Cooper 1902- *AuBYP 2, -3, BioIn 6, -7, -11, ConAu 9R, MorJA, SmATA 10*

Renich, Jill 1916- *ConAu 25R, MichAu 80*

Renick, Marion 1905- *AuBYP 3*

Renick, Marion Lewis 1905- *AuBYP 2, BioIn 6, -7, -9, ConAu 1R, MorJA, OhA&B, SmATA 1*

Renken, Aleda 1907- *BioIn 13, ConAu 21R, -12NR, SmATA 27*

Renlie, Frank H 1936- *BioIn 11, SmATA 11*

Renner, Beverly Hollett 1929- *ConAu 85*

Rennert, Richard Scott 1956- *ConAu 135, SmATA 67*
Pseud./variant:
Scott, Richard

Rensie, Willis *ConAu X, ConGrA 1, SmATA X*
Main entry: Eisner, Will

Renstrom, Moiselle *ChhPo S1*

Renton, Cam *ConAu X, WrDr 80, -82, -84, -86, -88*
Main entry: Armstrong, Richard

Renvoize, Jean 1930- *Au&Wr 71, BioIn 10, ConAu 41R, SmATA 5*

Resciniti, Angelo G 1952- *SmATA 75*

Resnick, Michael D *ScF&FL 92*

Resnick, Michael D 1942- *ConAu 107, -24NR, EncSF 93, ScFSB, SmATA 38*
Pseud./variant:
Resnick, Mike

Resnick, Mike
Main entry: Resnick, Michael D

Resnick, Seymour 1920- *AuBYP 2, -3, BioIn 8, -13, ConAu 73, DrAS 74F, -78F, -82F, SmATA 23*

Ressler, Theodore Whitson *AuBYP 3*

Ressler, Theodore Whitson 1926- *AuBYP 2, BioIn 8, WhoE 77*

Ressner, Philip 1922- *AuBYP 2, -3, BioIn 8, ConAu 13R*

Rethi, Lili 1894-1969 *BioIn 8, DcWomA, IlsBYP, WhAmArt 85*

Retla, Robert *AuBYP 3, ConAu X, SmATA X*
Main entry: Alter, Robert Edmond

Retner, Beth A *ConAu X*
Main entry: Brown, Beth

Rettig, Jack Louis 1925- *AmMWSc 73S, -78S, ConAu 57*

Reuter, Bjarne 1950- *BioIn 17, ConAu 137, SmATA 68*

Reuter, Bjarne 1959- *TwCChW 89B*

Reuter, Carol 1931- *BioIn 9, ConAu 21R, SmATA 2*

Revena 1927- *SmATA X*
Main entry: Wright, Betty Ren

Revsbech, Vicki *SmATA 72*
Main entry: Liestman, Vicki

Rey, Hans Augusto 1898-1977 *AmPB, AuBYP 2, -3, Au&ICB, BioIn 1, -2, -5, -7, -8, -9, -10, -11, -12, -13, -14, -16, BkP, ChlLR 5, ChsFB A, ConAu 5R, -73, -6NR, DcLB 22, FamAIYP, IlsCB 1744, -1946, -1957, -1967, JBA 51, MajAI, OxCChiL, SmATA 1, -26, -69, TwCChW 78, -83, -89, WhAmArt 85, WhoAmA 73, -78, -80, -82N*
Pseud./variant:
Uncle Gus

Rey, Lester del *ScF&FL 92, ThrBJA*
Main entry: DelRey, Lester

Rey, Margaret Elizabeth 1906- *AuBYP 3, IntAu&W 89*

Rey, Margret 1906- *AmPB, AuBYP 2, Au&ICB, BioIn 7, -15, -16, BkP, ChlLR 5, ConAu 105, SmATA 26, TwCChW 78, -83, -89, WrDr 84, -86, -88, -90, -92, -94*

Rey, Margret Elisabeth 1906- *ConAu 38NR, MajAI*

Reyher, Becky
Main entry: Reyher, Rebecca Hourwich

Reyher, Rebecca Hourwich 1897- *BioIn 12, SmATA 18, WhoAmW 75, -77, -81, -83, -85, -87*
Pseud./variant:
Reyher, Becky

Reyher, Rebecca Hourwich 1897-1987 *BioIn 15, -16, ConAu 121, SmATA 50N*

Reyna, Marylin De *IlsBYP*
Main entry: Hafner, Marylin

Reynolds, Barbara Leonard 1915- *AuBYP 2S, -3, OhA&B*

Reynolds, Christopher 1911- *Au&Wr 71, ConAu 104*

Reynolds, Dallas McC *ScF&FL 92*

Reynolds, Dallas McCord 1917- *BioIn 12, ConAu 5R, -9NR*
Pseud./variant:
Reynolds, Mack

Reynolds, Dickson *ConAu X, SmATA X*
Main entry: Reynolds, Helen M Greenwood Campbell

Reynolds, Frank 1876-1953 *BioIn 1, -3, -14, ClaDrA, DcBrAr 1, DcBrBI, IlsCB 1744, ObitT 1951, TwCPaSc, WorECar*

Reynolds, George W M 1814-1879 *PenEncH*

Reynolds, George William Macarthur 1814-1879 *Alli, BioIn 2, -14, -15, -16, BritAu 19, DcLEL, DcNaB*

Reynolds, Helen M Greenwood Campbell 1884-1969 *BioIn 13, ConAu 5R, -103, SmATA 26N, WhNAA*
Pseud./variant:
Dickson, Helen
Reynolds, Dickson

Reynolds, John *ConAu X, IntAu&W 86X, SmATA X, WrDr 86, -88, -90, -92, -94*
Main entry: Whitlock, Ralph

Reynolds, Mack *AuBYP 2S, -3, ConAu X, ConSFA, WhoSciF*
Main entry: Reynolds, Dallas McCord

Reynolds, Mack 1917-1983 *EncSF 93, NewEScF, ScF&FL 92, ScFSB, TwCSFW 86, -91*

Reynolds, Madge *ConAu X, IntAu&W 86X, SmATA X, WrDr 82, -84, -86, -88, -90, -92, -94*
Main entry: Whitlock, Ralph

Reynolds, Malvina 1900-1978 *ASCAP 66, BioIn 6, -8, -10, -11, -13, -14, -15, CmCal, ConAu 105, -114, EncFCWM 69, -83, InWom SUP, NewGrDA 86, PenEncP, SmATA 24N, -44, WhAm 7, WhoAm 74, -76, -78, WhoAmW 74, WhoWest 74, WhoWor 74*

Reynolds, Marjorie Harris 1903- *AuBYP 2, -3, BioIn 8, ConAu 5R*

Reynolds, Pamela 1923- *BioIn 14, ConAu 103, SmATA 34*

Reynolds, Quentin James 1902-1965 *AmAu&B, AuBYP 2, -3, BiDAmJo, BioIn 2, -3, -4, -6, -7, -8, -16, ConAu 73, CurBio 41, -65, DcAmB S7, LongCTC, REnAL, TwCA SUP*

Reynolds, Warwick 1880-1926 *BioIn 14, DcBrAr 1, DcBrBI, DcVicP 2*

Rhine, Richard *MajAI, SmATA 69*
Main entry: Silverstein, Alvin
Silverstein, Virginia B

Rhinehart, Susan Oneacre 1938- *ConAu 1R, WrDr 76, -80, -82, -84, -86, -88, -90, -92, -94*

Rhoads, Dorothy Mary 1895- *AuBYP 2, -3, BioIn 7, ConAu P-2*

Rhodes, Bennie Loran 1927- *ConAu 108, SmATA 35, WhoRel 75*

Rhodes, Clifford Oswald 1911- *Au&Wr 71, ConAu 65, IntAu&W 77, Who 74, –82, –83, –85, WrDr 76, –82, –84, –86*

Rhodes, Clifford Oswald 1911-1985 *ConAu 118*

Rhodes, Evan H 1929- *ConAu 57, –10NR*

Rhodes, Frank Harold Trevor 1926- *AmMWSc 73P, –76P, –82, –86, –89, –92, BioIn 11, –15, ConAu 107, IntWW 83, –89, –91, SmATA 37, WhoAm 74, –76, –78, –80, –82, –84, –86, –88, –90, –92, –94, WhoE 81, –83, –85, –86, –89, –91, –93, WhoWor 80, –89, –91, –93*

Rhodin, Eric Nolan 1916- *ConAu 1R, –3NR*

Rhue, Morton *ConAu X, MajAI, SmATA 71, –X, WhoUSWr 88, WhoWrEP 89, –92, WrDr 90, –92, –94*
Main entry: Strasser, Todd

Rhyne, Nancy 1926- *BioIn 17, ConAu 133, SmATA 66, WrDr 94*

Rhys, Megan *BioIn 10, SmATA 5*
Main entry: Williams, Jeanne

Ribalow, Harold U 1919- *WrDr 86, –88*

Ribalow, Harold U 1919-1982 *BioIn 13, ConAu 5R, –108, –2NR, NewYTBS 82, WhoAmJ 80, WhoWorJ 72, –78, WrDr 76, –80, –82, –84*

Ribbons, Ian 1924- *BioIn 5, –8, –14, –15, ConAu 108, FourBJA, IlsBYP, IlsCB 1946, –1957, –1967, SmATA 30, –37, –3AS*

Ricciuti, Edward R 1938- *BioIn 11, ConAu 41R, IntAu&W 77, SmATA 10*

Rice, Alice Caldwell 1870-1942 *WomNov*

Rice, Alice Caldwell Hegan 1870-1942 *AmAu&B, AmLY, AmWomWr, BiDSA, BioIn 1, CarSB, ChhPo, CnDAL, ConAmL, CurBio 42, DcAmAu, DcBiA, DcNAA, EvLB, InWom SUP, LongCTC, ObitOF 79, OxCAmL 65, –83, OxCChiL, REn, REnAL, TwCA, –SUP, TwCChW 83, TwCWr, WhAm 1, WhNAA, WomWWA 14*
Pseud./variant:
Hegan, Alice Caldwell

Rice, Alice Hegan 1870-1942 *BenetAL 91, BioIn 17, LiHiK, SmATA 63, TwCChW 89*

Rice, Anne *DrAPF 87, –89, –91, –93, NewYTBS 90*

Rice, Anne 1941- *Au&Arts 9, BenetAL 91, BestSel 89-2, BioIn 15, –16, –17, BlmGWL, ConAu 36NR, ConLC 41, CurBio 91, FemiCLE, PenEncH, ScF&FL 92, TwCYAW, WhoAm 92, –94, WhoAmW 91, –93, WhoWrEP 92, WrDr 86, –88, –90, –92, –94*

Rice, Charles D 1910-1971 *AuBYP 2, BioIn 7, –9, –13, ConAu 104, NewYTBE 71, SmATA 27N*

Rice, Charles Duane 1910-1971 *AuBYP 3*

Rice, Dale R 1948- *ConAu 116, SmATA 42*

Rice, David Talbot 1903-1972 *Au&Wr 71, BioIn 9, –10, ConAu 9R, –5NR, LongCTC*

Rice, Dorothy 1916- *BiDrLUS 70, WhoLibS 66*

Rice, Edward E 1918- *AuBYP 2S, –3, BestSel 90-4, BioIn 15, –16, ConAu 49, –1NR, SmATA 42, –47*

Rice, Elizabeth 1913- *BioIn 9, ConAu 21R, ForWC 70, IlsBYP, SmATA 2*

Rice, Esme *DcChlFi*

Rice, Eve 1951- *AuBYP 3, BioIn 14, –16*

Rice, Eve Hart 1951- *AuBYP 2S, BioIn 12, ConAu 53, –4NR, FifBJA, IlsCB 1967, SmATA 34*

Rice, Inez 1907- *AuBYP 2, –3, BioIn 8, –11, ConAu 29R, SmATA 13*

Rice, James 1934- *BioIn 13, ConAu 61, –8NR, SmATA 22*

Rice, Ruth Little 1884-1927 *WomNov*

Rice, Ruth Little Mason 1884-1927 *AnMV 1926, DcNAA, WhNAA*

Rice, Tamara Talbot 1904- *AuBYP 2S, –3, ConAu 111*

Rich, Barbara *ConAu 36NR, EncSF 93, MajTwCW, WrDr 76, –80, –82*
Main entry: Rinkoff, Barbara Jean

Rich, Elaine Sommers 1926- *AuBYP 2, –3, BioIn 8, –10, ConAu 17R, –9NR, –24NR, IndAu 1917, IntAu&W 86, –89, –91, SmATA 6, WhoAmW 91, WhoMW 90, WhoRel 92, WrDr 76, –80, –82, –84, –86, –88, –90, –92, –94*

Rich, Gibson 1936- *ConAu 57*

Rich, Josephine 1912- *AuBYP 3*

Rich, Josephine Bouchard 1912- *AuBYP 2, BioIn 7, –11, ConAu 5R, SmATA 10*

Rich, Louise 1903- *AuBYP 3*

Rich, Louise Dickinson d1991 *NewYTBS 91*

Rich, Louise Dickinson 1903- *AmAu&B, AmWomWr, AuBYP 2, BenetAL 91, BioIn 1, –2, –3, –4, –7, –16, ConAu 73, CurBio 43, DcAmChF 1960, REnAL, SmATA 54, TwCA SUP*

Rich, Louise Dickinson 1903-1991 *BioIn 17, ConAu 134, CurBio 91N, SmATA 67*

Rich, Mark J 1948- *BioIn 16, SmATA 53*

Richard, Adrienne 1921- *AuBYP 2S, –3, BioIn 10, ConAu 29R, DcAmChF 1960, FifBJA, SmATA 5, –9AS, WrDr 76, –80, –82, –84, –86, –88, –90, –92, –94*

Richard, James Robert *AuBYP 3, ConAu X, –28NR*
Main entry: Bowen, Robert Sydney

Richards, Arlene Kramer 1935- *ConAu 65, –11NR, LEduc 74, WhoAmW 75, –83*

Richards, Carl Edward, Jr. 1933- *ConAu 45, –24NR*

Richards, Christine-Louise 1910- *IntAu&W 77, WhoAmW 74, –75, –77, –81, –83, –85, –87, –89, –91, WhoE 74, –75, –77, –81, –83, WhoEnt 92, WhoFI 81, –83, WhoWor 80, –82, WrDr 76, –80, –82, –84, –86, –88, –90, –92, –94*

Richards, Curtis *ScF&FL 92, SmATA X*
Main entry: Curtis, Richard

Richards, Dorothy *CarSB*

Richards, Frank *CamGLE, ConAu X, –29NR, DcVicP 2, LongCTC, Novels, OxCChiL, SmATA X, TwCChW 78, –83, WhoChL*

Richards, Frank 1875-1961 *BioIn 14*

Richards, Frank 1876-1961 *GrBr, TwCChW 89*

Richards, George Mather 1880- *BioIn 1, ChhPo, IlsCB 1744, WhAmArt 85*

Richards, Hilda *ConAu X, –29NR, LongCTC, SmATA X, TwCChW 83, –89, WhoChL*

Richards, Jack *AuBYP 3*

Richards, Jack 1918- *AuBYP 2S, BioIn 13, OxCCan SUP, Profile 2*

Richards, Jane 1934- *ConAu 33R*

Richards, John Paul *IlsBYP*

Richards, Kay *ConAu X, SmATA X*
Main entry: Baker, Susan

Richards, Laura Elizabeth 1850-1943 *Alli SUP, AmAu&B, AmLY, AmWomWr, AnCL, ArtclWW 2, BenetAL 91, BiD&SB, BioIn 2, –4, –6, –11, BkCL, CarSB, ChhPo, –S1, –S2, ChrP, CnDAL, ConAu 120, CurBio 43, DcAmAu, DcLB 42, DcNAA, FamPYP, FemiCLE, JBA 34, ObitOF 79, OxCAmL 65, –83, OxCChiL, REnAL, Str&VC, TwCA, –SUP, TwCChW 78, –83, –89, WebAB 79, WhAm 2, WhNAA, WomWWA 14, WomNov, WorAl, WrChl, YABC 1*

Richards, Laura Elizabeth Howe 1850-1943 *AmWomPl, BioIn 15, ConAu 137, MajAI*

Richards, Laura Elizabeth Howe Ward 1850-1943 *InWom SUP*

Richards, Lawrence O 1931- *ConAu 20NR, –42NR*

Richards, Lawrence Oscar 1931- *ConAu 29R, WhoRel 75, WhoWest 74, –76*

Richards, Norman 1932- *AuBYP 2S, –3, BioIn 16, ConAu 112, –31NR, SmATA 48*

Richards, R C W 1923- *ConAu 10NR, –26NR, SmATA 43, –59*
Pseud./variant:
Saddler, Allen
Saddler, K Allen

Richards, Ruth *AuBYP 2S, –3*

Richards, Walter 1907-1988 *SmATA 56N*

Richards, Walter A d1988 *BioIn 15*

Richards, Walter A 1907-1988 *BioIn 16*

Richards, William Carey 1818-1892 *Alli, –SUP, BiDSA, BioIn 11, CarSB, ChhPo, DcAmAu, DcLB 73, DcNAA*

Richardson *BioIn 15, Who 90, –92*
Pseud./variant:
Haggerston, Scrope

Richardson, Arleta 1923- *ConAu 93, –16NR, –36NR*

Richardson, Baron 1910- *IntWW 89, –91, Who 88, –90, –92, WrDr 86, –88, –90, –92, –94*

Richardson, Carol 1932- *BioIn 16, SmATA 58*

Richardson, Dorothy 1922- *IntAu&W 86, –89, WrDr 76, –80, –82, –84*

Richardson, Flavia *WhoHr&F*

Richardson, Frank Howard *AuBYP 3*

Richardson, Frank Howard 1882-1970
AmAu&B, AuBYP 2S, BioIn 9, -13, ConAu 104, SmATA 27N, WhAm 6, WhNAA

Richardson, Frederick 1862-1937 *ChhPo, ConICB, WhAm 1, WhAmArt 85*

Richardson, Gladwell *BioIn 15*

Richardson, Gladwell 1903- *ArizL*

Richardson, Gladwell 1903-1980 *ConAu 123*

Richardson, Gladwell 1904-1980 *TwCWW 91*

Richardson, Grace Lee *ConAu X, IntAu&W 77X, SmATA 8*
Main entry: Dickson, Naida

Richardson, Jean *BioIn 16, ConAu 127, ScF&FL 92, SmATA 59*

Richardson, Judith Benet 1941- *SmATA 77*

Richardson, Midge Turk 1930- *ConAu 33R, EncTwCJ, IntAu&W 82, -86, -89, -91, WhoAm 78, -80, -82, -84, -86, -88, -90, -92, -94, WhoAmW 81, -83, -85, -89, -91, WhoE 91, -93, WhoUSWr 88, WhoWrEP 89, -92, WrDr 82, -84, -86, -88, -90, -92, -94*
Pseud./variant:
Turk, Midge

Richardson, Robert S *EncSF 93, TwCSFW 86, -91*

Richardson, Robert S 1902-1981 *ScF&FL 92*

Richardson, Robert Shirley 1902-
AmMWSc 73P, BioIn 8, -11, ConAu 49, IntAu&W 77, -82, SmATA 8
Pseud./variant:
Latham, Philip

Richardson, Samuel 1689-1761 *Benet 87, BioIn 1, -2, -3, -5, -7, -8, -9, -10, -12, -13, -14, -15, BlmGEL, BlmGWL, BritWr 3, CamGEL, CamGLE, CnDBLB 2, DcBiPP, DcLB 39, DcNaB, -C, LitC 1, MagSWL, Novels, OxCChiL, OxCEng 85, OxCGer 86, RAdv 13-1, RfGEnL 91, WhDW, WorAlBi, WorAl, WorLitC*

Richardson, Willis 1889-1977 *BioIn 15, -17, BlkWr 1, ConAu 124, DcLB 51, DrBlPA 90, EarBlAP, InB&W 85, NegAl 89, SmATA 60, SouBlCW*

Richason, Benjamin Franklin, Jr. 1922-
AmMWSc 73P, -76P, -86, -89, -92, BioIn 11, ConAu 41R, WhoAm 74

Richason, Benjamin Franklin, Jr. 1922-1988
BioIn 16

Richelson, Geraldine 1922- *BioIn 13, ConAu 106, ScF&FL 92, SmATA 29*
Pseud./variant:
Leander, Ed

Richey, David 1939- *ConAu 57, -10NR*
Pseud./variant:
Davey, John
Johnson, Richard

Richey, Dorothy Hilliard *ConAu 9R, -6NR, ForWC 70, WhoAmW 74, -75, -77, -81, WhoSSW 76*

Richler, Mordecai 1931- *AuNews 1, Au&Wr 71, Benet 87, BenetAL 91, BioIn 9, -10, -11, -12, -13, -14, -15, -16, -17, BioNews 75, BlueB 76, CamGLE, CaW, CanWW 70, -79, -80, -81, -83, -89, CanWr, CasWL, ChlLR 17, ConAu 65, -31NR, ConLC 3, -5, -9, -13, -18, -46, -70, ConNov 72, -76, -82, -86, -91, CreCan 1, CurBio 75, CyWA 89, DcChlFi, DcLB 53, DcLEL 1940, EncAHmr, EncWL, -2, HalFC 84, -88, IntAu&W 77, -86, -89, -91, IntWW 74, -75, -76, -77, -78, -79, -80, -81, -82, -83, -89, -91, IntvTCA 2, LiExTwC, MagSWL, MajAI, MajTwCW, ModCmwL, Novels, OxCCan, -SUP, OxCCanL, PenC ENG, RAdv 13-1, REnAL, RfGEnL 91, SmATA 27, -44, TwCWr, WebE&AL, Who 74, -82, -83, -85, -88, -90, -92, WhoAm 76, -78, -80, -82, -84, -86, -88, -90, -92, -94, WhoCanL 85, -87, -92, WhoTwCL, WhoWor 74, -78, -80, -82, -84, -87, -89, -91, -93, WhoWrEP 89, -92, WorAlBi, WorAl, WorAu 1950, WrDr 76, -80, -82, -84, -86, -88, -90, -92, -94*

Richmond, Grace *TwCRHW 90*

Richmond, Grace 1866-1959 *AmAu&B, BioIn 5, CarSB, EvLB, TwCA, WhAm 3, WomWWA 14*

Richmond, Grace Louise Smith 1866-1959
AmWomPl

Richmond, Julius B 1916- *AuBYP 3, IntWW 89, -91*

Richmond, Julius Benjamin 1916-
AmMWSc 73P, -76P, -82, -86, -89, -92, AuBYP 2S, BiDrAPA 77, ConAu 29R, WhoAm 74, -76, -78, -80, -82, -84, -86, -88, -90, -92, -94, WhoAmP 77, -81, WhoE 74, WhoFrS 84

Richmond, Legh 1772-1827 *Alli, BbD, BiDLA, BiD&SB, CarSB, ChhPo S2, DcBiPP, DcEnL, DcNaB, -C, OxCEng 67, -85*

Richmond, Leonard d1965 *ArtsAmW 3, BioIn 2, -5, DcBrAr 1*

Richmond, Robert P 1914- *WrDr 86, -88, -90, -92, -94*

Richmond, Robert Price 1914- *ConAu 21R, WhoE 74, -75, -77, WrDr 76, -80, -82, -84*

Richmond, Robin 1951- *ConAu 142, SmATA 75, TwCPaSc*

Richoux, Patricia 1927- *BioIn 10, ConAu 25R, SmATA 7*

Richter, Alice 1941- *BioIn 14, ConAu 105, SmATA 30*

Richter, Conrad 1890-1968 *AuBYP 3, Benet 87, BenetAL 91, BioIn 14, -16, -17, ConAu 23NR, MagSAmL, MajTwCW, RfGAmL 87, TwCWW 91*

Richter, Conrad Michael 1890-1968 *AmAu&B, AmNov, AuBYP 2S, BioIn 1, -2, -3, -4, -5, -7, -8, -9, CnDAL, ConAu 5R, -25R, CurBio 51, -68, CyWA 58, DcAmB S8, DcLEL, McGEWB, ModAL, OxCAmL 65, PenC AM, RAdv 1, REn, REnAL, SmATA 3, TwCA, -SUP, TwCYAW, WhAm 5, WhNAA*

Richter, Dorothy 1906- *ConAu 29R*

Richter, Ed *AuBYP 2S, -3*

Richter, Hans Peter *TwCChW 89B*

Richter, Hans Peter 1925- *BioIn 9, -10, ChlLR 21, ConAu 45, -2NR, FourBJA, IntAu&W 77, -82, -86, -89, -91, MajAI, OxCChiL, SmATA 6, -11AS, TwCChW 78B, -83B, TwCYAW, WhoWor 78*

Richter, Mischa *AuBYP 3*

Richter, Mischa 1910?- *AuBYP 2S, BioIn 1, WhAmArt 85, WorECar*

Rickard, Graham 1949- *SmATA 71*

Ricker, John *OxCCan SUP*

Rickert, Corinne Holt *ConAu X*
Main entry: Sawyer, Corinne Holt

Rico, Don 1917-1985 *ConAu 81, -115, -28NR, ScF&FL 92, SmATA 43N*

Riddell, Chris *AuBYP 3*

Riddle, Maxwell 1907- *AuBYP 2S, -3, ConAu 5R, -3NR, WhoMW 74, -76, -78, -80, -82, -84, -86, -88, -90, -92, WhoUSWr 88, WhoWor 84, -87, -89, -91, -93*

Riddle, Tohby 1965- *SmATA 74*

Rideing, William Henry 1853-1918 *Alli SUP, AmAu, AmAu&B, AmLY, BiD&SB, CarSB, DcAmAu, DcNAA, HarEnUS, WhAm 1*

Rider, John Russell 1923- *ConAu 25R, DrAS 74E, -78E, -82E, WhoMW 74, -76, -90*

Ridge, Antonia 1895-1981 *TwCChW 89*

Ridge, Antonia Florence 1895-1981 *Au&Wr 71, BioIn 10, -13, ChhPo S1, ConAu 9R, -104, IntAu&W 77, -82, OxCChiL, SmATA 7, -27N, TwCChW 78, -83, WrDr 76, -80, -82*

Ridge, Martin 1923- *BioIn 15, ConAu 121, DrAS 74H, -78H, -82H, SmATA 43, WhoAm 78, -80, -82, -84, -86, -88, -90, WhoWest 92, -94*

Ridge, William Pett 1859-1930 *DcLB 135*

Ridge, William Pett 1860?-1930 *BiD&SB, Chambr 3, DcLEL, EvLB, LongCTC, NewC*

Ridgway, Jason *AuBYP 2, -3, ConAu X, IntAu&W 91X, TwCCr&M 91, WrDr 94*
Main entry: Lesser, Milton

Ridgway, John M 1938- *ConAu 25R, IntAu&W 77, WrDr 76, -80*

Ridle, Julia Brown 1923- *ConAu 1R*

Ridley, Anthony 1933- *Au&Wr 71, ConAu 107, IntAu&W 77, -82, WrDr 76, -80, -82, -84, -86, -88, -90*

Ridley, Nat, Jr. *ConAu 26NR, -P-2*
Main entry: Stratemeyer, Edward L

Ridlon, Marci 1942- *BioIn 13, SmATA 22*
Main entry: Balterman, Marcia Ridlon

Ridout, Albert K 1905- *ConAu P-2*

Ridout, Ronald 1916- *Au&Wr 71, ConAu 103, -20NR, IntAu&W 77, -86, -89, -91, WrDr 76, -80, -82, -84, -86, -88, -90, -92, -94*

Ridpath, Ian William 1947- *ConAu 77*

Riedesel, C Alan 1930- *ConAu 25R, LEduc 74*

Riedman, Sarah Regal 1902- *AuBYP 2, -3, BioIn 8, -9, ConAu 1R, -1NR, -37NR, ForWC 70, SmATA 1*
Pseud./variant:
Gustafson, Sarah Regal

Rieger, Shay 1929- *ConAu 29R*

Rienow, Leona Train 1903?-1983 *AuBYP 2, -3, BioIn 8, -13, ConAu 111, ScF&FL 92, WhoAmW 74, -75, -77, WhoE 74*

Rieseberg, Harry E 1892- *BioIn 9, ConAu 5R*

Riesenberg, Felix, Jr. 1913-1962 *AuBYP 2, BioIn 4, -7, -13, ConAu 101, CurBio 57, SmATA 23*

Riesenberg, Felix, Jr. 1913-1962 *AuBYP 3*

Riessen, Clare
Main entry: Riessen, Martin Clare

Riessen, Martin Clare 1941- *AuBYP 2S, -3, ConAu 41R*
Pseud./variant:
Riessen, Clare

Rietveld, Jane 1913- *AuBYP 2, -3, BioIn 2, -8*

Rieu, E V 1887-1972 *BioIn 14, -15, SmATA 46, TwCChW 89*

Rieu, Emile Victor 1887-1972 *AnCL, AuBYP 2, -3, BioIn 7, -9, -10, -13, -14, -15, ChhPo, -S1, ConAu 1R, -103, -15NR, DcNaB 1971, ObitT 1971, OxCEng 85, SmATA 26N, TwCChW 83*

Rifkin, Lillian *AuBYP 2, -3, BioIn 7*

Riggio, Anita *AuBYP 3*

Riggio, Anita 1952- *SmATA 73*

Riggs, Ida Berry *AuBYP 2, -3, BioIn 8*

Riggs, Sidney Noyes 1892-1975 *BioIn 13, ConAu 103, SmATA 28N*

Rigney, Francis J 1882- *WhAmArt 85*

Rigoni, Orlando Joseph 1897?- *ConAu 13R, IntAu&W 77, WrDr 76, -80*
Pseud./variant:
Wesley, James

Riha, Bohumil 1907- *IntWW 83*

Riis, Jacob A *SourALJ*

Riis, Jacob A 1849-1914 *BenetAL 91, BiDAmJo, BioIn 15, -16, WorAlBi*

Riis, Jacob August 1849-1914 *AmAu&B, BbD, BiD&SB, BioIn 1, -3, -6, -7, -8, -9, -10, -13, ConAu 113, DcAmAu, DcAmImH, DcAmMeB 84, DcAmSR, DcNAA, EncAB-H, EncAJ, HarEnUS, ICPEnP, MacBEP, McGEWB, OxCAmL 65, -83, REn, REnAL, WebAB 74, -79, WhAm 1, WhAmArt 85, WorAl*

Riis, Jacob Augustus 1849-1914 *JrnUS*

Rikhoff, Jean 1928- *AuBYP 2S, -3, BioIn 11, ConAu 61, DrAPF 83, -85, IntAu&W 82, SmATA 9*

Rikki *AuBYP 3, ConAu 34NR, IntAu&W 86X, WhoCanL 87, -92*

Rikon, Irving 1931- *ConAu 29R*

Riley, Dick 1946- *ConAu 101, ScF&FL 92, WrDr 80, -82, -84, -86, -88, -90, -92, -94*

Riley, James Whitcomb 1849-1916 *Alli SUP, AmAu, AmAu&B, ASCAP 66, Benet 87, BenetAL 91, BbD, BiD&SB, BioIn 1, -2, -3, -4, -5, -6, -7, -8, -9, -10, -11, -12, -13, -14, -15, BlkAWP, CamGEL, CamGLE, CamHAL, CarSB, CasWL, Chambr 3, ChhPo, -S1, -S2, ChrP, CnDAL, ConAu 118, -137, DcAmAu, DcEnA A, DcLEL, DcNAA, EncAHmr, EvLB, FamPYP, IndAu 1816, JBA 34, LongCTC, MajAI, McGEWB, OxCAmL 65, -83, OxCChiL, PenC AM, RAdv 1, -13-1, REn, REnAL, RfGAmL 87, SmATA 17, Str&VC, TwCLC 51, WebAB 74, -79, WhAm 1, WhFla, WorAlBi, WorAl*
Pseud./variant:
Johnson Of Boone, Benj F

Riley, Jocelyn *BioIn 16, -17, DrAPF 87, -89, -91, -93*

Riley, Jocelyn 1949- *ConAu 39NR, SmATA 50, -60*

Riley, Louise 1904-1957 *BioIn 4, -5, DcChlFi, TwCChW 78*

Riley, Tex *ConAu X, MajTwCW*

Rimanelli, Giose 1926- *OxCCan, WorAu 1975*

Rinaldi, Ann 1934- *BioIn 16, SmATA 50, -51, TwCYAW*

Rinard, Judith E 1947- *BioIn 15*

Rinard, Judith Ellen 1947- *ConAu 97, IntAu&W 82, SmATA 44*

Rinehart, Mary Roberts *IntvTCA 2*

Rinehart, Mary Roberts 1876-1956 *Benet 87*

Rinehart, Mary Roberts 1876-1958 *AmAu&B, AmNov, AmWomD, AmWomPl, AmWomWr, ArtclWW 2, BenetAL 91, BioAmW, BioIn 1, -2, -3, -4, -5, -11, -14, -16, ConAmL, ConAu 108, CorpD, CrtSuMy, DcBiA, DcLEL, EncAB-A 2, EncMys, EvLB, HalFC 84, -88, InWom SUP, LongCTC, ModWD, NotAW MOD, NotNAT B, Novels, ObitOF 79, ObitT 1951, OxCAmL 65, -83, OxCAmT 84, PenC AM, REn, REnAL, RfGAmL 87, ScF&FL 92, TwCA, -SUP, TwCCr&M 80, -85, -91, TwCLC 52, TwCRHW 90, TwCWr, WebAB 74, -79, WhAm 3, WhNAA, WomWWA 14, WorAlBi, WorAl*

Ringgold, Faith 1930- *BioIn 14, –16, –17, BlkAuII 92, ConBlB 4, EncWB, InWom SUP, NegAl 89, SmATA 71, WhoAm 92, –94, WhoAmA 91, WhoBlA 85, –88, –90, –92, –94, WhoE 86, WorArt 1980*

Ringgold, Faith 1934- *ChlLR 30, ContDcW 89, WhoAmA 86, –89*

Ringi, Kjell Arne Sorensen 1939- *BioIn 11, ConAu 45, –1NR, FourBJA, IlsBYP, SmATA 12*
Pseud./variant:
S-Ringi, Kjell

Ringwood, Gwen Pharis *ArtclWW 2*

Ringwood, Gwen Pharis 1910- *BenetAL 91*

Ringwood, Gwen Pharis 1910-1984 *BioIn 11, BlmGWL, CamGLE, CamGWoT, ConAu 112, ConLC 48, CreCan 2, DcLB 88, OxCCan, OxCCanL, OxCCanT, WhAm 8, WhoAm 80, –82, WhoCanL 87*

Ringwood, Gwendolyn Margaret Pharis 1910-1984 *IntDcT 2*

Rink, Paul 1912- *AuBYP 2, –3, BioIn 7*

Rinker, Rosalind Beatrice 1906- *ConAu 5R, –5NR*

Rinkoff, Barbara 1923-1975 *DcAmChF 1960*

Rinkoff, Barbara Jean 1923-1975 *AuBYP 2, –3, BioIn 8, –9, –10, –13, ConAu 57, –P-2, MorBMP, SmATA 4, –27N, WhAm 6, WhoAmW 75, WrDr 76*
Pseud./variant:
Rich, Barbara

Riordan, James 1936- *BioIn 13, ConAu 69, –11NR, SmATA 28, WrDr 82, –84, –86, –88, –90, –92*

Riordan, James William 1936- *WrDr 94*

Rios, Juan Antonio 1888-1946 *BioIn 1, –16, CurBio 42, –46, EncLatA, ObitOF 79, WhAm 2*

Rios, Tere *ConAu X, ForWC 70, SmATA 2*
Main entry: Versace, Marie Teresa Rios

Ripley, Elizabeth 1906-1969 *AuBYP 3*

Ripley, Elizabeth Blake 1906-1969 *AuBYP 2, BioIn 4, –5, –7, –8, –10, ChhPo S2, ConAu 1R, –3NR, CurBio 58, SmATA 5*

Ripley, S Dillon 1913- *AmMWSc 73P, BioIn 2, –7, –9, –10, –11, BlueB 76, CelR, ConAu 57, CurBio 66, IntAu&W 77, –82, –86, IntWW 74, –75, –76, –77, –78, –79, –80, –81, –82, –83, –89, –91, WhoGov 72, WhoSSW 73*

Ripper, Charles L 1929- *BioIn 8, –9, ConAu 1R, –1NR, IlsBYP, IlsCB 1946, –1957, SmATA 3*

Riq *ConAu 135, MajAI, SmATA 66*
Main entry: Atwater, Richard Tupper

Riser, Wayne H 1909- *AmMWSc 73P, –76P, BioIn 4, ConAu P-1*

Riskind, Mary *AuBYP 3*

Riskind, Mary 1944- *BioIn 17, ConAu 26NR, SmATA 60*

Rissman, Art
Main entry: Sussman, Susan

Rissman, Susan
Main entry: Sussman, Susan

Rist Arnold, Elisabeth 1950- *ConAu 65*

Rister, Claude
Pseud./variant:
Marshall, James

Riswold, Gilbert *BioIn 8, –12, ChhPo S2, IlsBYP, IlsCB 1957, –1967*

Ritchie, Anne Isabella Thackeray, Lady 1837-1919 *Alli SUP, ArtclWW 2, BbD, BiD&SB, BioIn 1, –3, –4, –8, –11, –12, –13, BritAu 19, CarSB, ChhPo S2, DcEnA, –A, EvLB, LongCTC, NewC, OxCEng 67, –85, REn*

Ritchie, Barbara Gibbons *AuBYP 3*

Ritchie, Barbara Gibbons 1943- *AuBYP 2, BiDrLUS 70, BioIn 8, –12, ConAu 73, SmATA 14*

Ritchie, Cicero Theodore 1914- *ConAu 9R, IntAu&W 82, WrDr 76, –80*

Ritchie, Jean 1922- *ASCAP 66, BioIn 5, –8, –14, –16, ConMus 4, CurBio 59, EncFCWM 69, InWom SUP, NewAmDM, NewGrDA 86, PenEncP*

Ritchie, Paul 1923- *ConAu 21R, EncSF 93, ScF&FL 92, ScFSB*

Ritchie, Rita *AuBYP 2, BioIn 6, ConAu X*
Main entry: Reitici, Rita Krohne

Ritchie, Rita 1930- *AuBYP 3, ScF&FL 92*

Ritchie, Trekkie 1902- *BioIn 5, –14, ChhPo, –S1, –S2, DcBrAr 1, IlsBYP, IlsCB 1946*

Ritson, Joseph 1752-1803 *BioIn 3, DcBiPP, DcNaB, OxCChiL, OxCEng 85*

Ritson, Joseph 1753-1803 *CamGLE*

Rittenhouse, Mignon 1904- *ConAu 41R, WhoAmW 74, -75, -77, -81*

Ritter, Felix *ConAu X, IntAu&W 77X*
Main entry: Kruess, James

Ritter, Lawrence S *BioIn 16*

Ritter, Lawrence S 1922- *ConAu 22NR, SmATA 58, WhoE 89*

Ritts, Paul 1920?-1980 *BioIn 12, -13, ConAu 102, NewYTBS 80, SmATA 25N, WhScrn 83*

Rivera, Carlos 1916- *BioIn 3, WhoSSW 73*

Rivera, Edith *AuBYP 2S, -3, BioIn 9*

Rivera, Geraldo *BioIn 15, -16, -17, LesBEnT 92*

Rivera, Geraldo 1943- *AuBYP 3, CelR 90, ConAu 32NR, ConTFT 6, EncTwCJ, HispAmA, HispWr, IntMPA 86, -88, -92, News 89-1, SmATA 54, WhoAm 90, -92, -94, WhoEnt 92*

Rivera, Geraldo Miguel 1943- *AuBYP 2S, BioIn 9, -10, -12, -13, ConAu 108, CurBio 75, EncAJ, IntMPA 78, -81, -82, -84, -86, LesBEnT, NewYTBE 71, NewYTET, SmATA 28, WhoAm 76, -78, -80, -82, -84, WhoE 74, -75, WhoHisp 91, -92, -94*

Riverside, John *AuBYP 2, -3, ConAu X, EncSF 93, MajAI, MajTwCW, SmATA 69, -X*
Main entry: Heinlein, Robert A

Riviere, William Alexander 1916- *ConAu 5R, -8NR*

Rivkin, Ann 1920- *BioIn 15, ConAu 112, SmATA 41*

Rivoli, Mario 1943- *BioIn 8, -11, IlsBYP, IlsCB 1957, SmATA 10, WhoAmA 78, -80, -82, -84*
Pseud./variant:
Koutoukas, H M
Marasmus, Seymour

Riwkin-Brick, Anna 1908-1970 *AuBYP 2, -3, BioIn 5, -7*

Roach, Marilynne K 1946- *BioIn 11, ConAu 57, -12NR, ScF&FL 92, SmATA 9*

Roach, Portia *SmATA X*
Main entry: Takakjian, Portia

Robb, Dodi *OxCCan, WomWMM*

Robbins, Chandler S 1918- *WhoE 86, -89*

Robbins, Chandler Seymour 1918- *AmMWSc 73P, -76P, -82, -86, -89, -92, WhoAm 90, -92, -94, WhoE 83, -85, WhoWor 84*

Robbins, Frank 1917- *ArtCS, BioIn 14, -15, ConAu 109, EncACom, IlsBYP, SmATA 42, WhoAmA 73, -78, -80N, -82N, -86N, -89N, -91N*

Robbins, Ken *BioIn 16, -17, SmATA 53*

Robbins, Leonard H 1877-1947 *BenetAL 91*

Robbins, Leonard Harman 1877-1947 *BioIn 1, ChhPo, -S2, DcNAA, REnAL, WhAm 2*

Robbins, Raleigh *ConAu X, -29NR, SmATA X*

Robbins, Ruth 1917?- *AuBYP 2, -3, BioIn 8, -9, -12, ConAu 73, IlsCB 1957, -1967, SmATA 14, ThrBJA*

Robbins, Tony *ConAu X, SmATA X*
Main entry: Pashko, Stanley

Robbins, Wayne *SmATA X, TwCCr&M 91*
Main entry: Cox, William R

Roberson, Jennifer 1953- *SmATA 72*
Pseud./variant:
Mitchell, Jay
O'Green, Jennifer Roberson

Roberson, John R 1930- *BioIn 16, ConAu 129, SmATA 53*

Roberson, John Royster 1930- *WhoE 91*

Roberson, Peter 1907- *ArtsCL, BioIn 6*

Robertiello, Richard C *BioIn 15*

Robertiello, Richard C 1923- *BiDrAPA 89, WrDr 86, -88, -90, -92, -94*

Robertiello, Richard Candela 1923- *BiDrAPA 77, ConAu 9R, -3NR, IntAu&W 77, -86, -89, WhoE 77, -81, -91, WrDr 76, -80, -82, -84*

Roberts, Bruce 1930- *BioIn 15, -16, SmATA 47*

Roberts, Bruce Stuart 1930- *ConAu 9R, -6NR, ICPEnP A, MacBEP, SmATA 39*

Roberts, Catherine Christopher 1905- *AuBYP 2, -3, BioIn 8*

Roberts, Charles G 1860-1943 *RAdv 13-1*

Roberts, Charles G D 1860-1943 *BenetAL 91, BioIn 15, DcLB 92, TwCChW 89*

Roberts, Charles G D, Sir 1860-1943 *Benet 87, CamGLE*

Roberts, Charles G D 1860-1943 *BioIn 17, RfGEnL 91*

Roberts, Charles George Douglas 1860-1943 *EncSF 93, RfGShF*

Roberts, Charles George Douglas, Sir 1860-1943 *Alli SUP, BbD, BiD&SB, BioIn 1, -4, -5, -9, -10, -13, CanNov, CanWr, Chambr 3, ChhPo, -S1, -S2, ConAmL, ConAu 105, CreCan 2, CurBio 44, DcAmAu, DcBiA, DcNAA, EvLB, JBA 34, LongCTC, ObitOF 79, OxCAmL 65, -83, OxCCan, OxCCanL, OxCChiL, OxCEng 67, PenC ENG, REn, REnAL, SmATA 29, TwCA, -SUP, TwCChW 78, -83, TwCLC 8, WebE&AL, WhAm 3*

Roberts, David *ConAu X, SmATA X*
Main entry: Cox, John Roberts

Roberts, Doreen 1922- *BioIn 8, -12, -14, ConAu 108, IlsCB 1957, -1967*

Roberts, Elizabeth Madox *BlmGWL*

Roberts, Elizabeth Madox 1881-1941 *BioAmW, BioIn 14, -15, -17, DcLB 54, -102, FemiCLE, FifSWrA, LiHiK, RfGAmL 87, TwCChW 89, TwCWW 91, WrChl*

Roberts, Elizabeth Madox 1886-1941 *AmAu&B, AmWomWr, AnCL, ArtclWW 2, Benet 87, BenetAL 91, BioIn 4, -5, -6, -7, -8, -12, -13, BkCL, ChhPo, -S1, CnDAL, ConAmA, ConAmL, ConAu 111, CurBio 41, CyWA 58, DcLB 9, DcLEL, DcNAA, EncSoH, EncWL, InWom SUP, LongCTC, ModAL, Novels, ObitOF 79, OxCAmL 65, -83, OxCChiL, PenC AM, REn, REnAL, SmATA 27, -33, Str&VC, TwCA, -SUP, TwCChW 78, -83, WebAB 74, -79, WhAm 1*

Roberts, Elliott B 1899- *ConAu 1R, WrDr 76, -80, -82, -84*

Roberts, Elliott B 1899-1988 *ConAu 126*

Roberts, Eric B 1914- *Au&Wr 71, ConAu 5R, WrDr 76, -80*

Roberts, Jack 1894- *BioIn 1, IlsCB 1744*

Roberts, Jim *ConAu X, SmATA X*
Main entry: Bates, Barbara Snedeker

Roberts, John *ConAu X, -42NR, EncSF 93, IntAu&W 91X, TwCWW 91, WrDr 88, -90*
Main entry: Bingley, David Ernest

Roberts, John G 1913- *BioIn 13, ConAu 49, SmATA 27*
Pseud./variant:
Paul, Robert

Roberts, John Morris 1928- *Au&Wr 71, ConAu 85, IntAu&W 77, -82, -86, -91, IntWW 89, -91, Who 74, -82, -83, -85, -88, -92, WrDr 76, -80, -82, -84, -86, -88, -90, -92, -94*

Roberts, John Morris, Dr 1928- *Who 90*

Roberts, Kenneth Lewis 1885-1957 *AmAu&B, AmNov, BioIn 1, -2, -4, -5, -7, -12, CasWL, CnDAL, ConAmA, DcAmAu, DcLEL, EvLE, LongCTC, ModAL, ObitOF 79, OxCAmL 65, OxCCan, PenC AM, REn, REnAL, TwCA, -SUP, TwCWr, WhNAA, WorAl*

Roberts, Margaret 1833- *OxCChiL*

Roberts, Margaret 1833-1919 *FemiCLE, WomNov*

Roberts, Nancy 1924- *AuBYP 3, BioIn 16*

Roberts, Nancy 1938- *WhoAm 94*

Roberts, Nancy Correll *WhoAm 92*

Roberts, Nancy Correll 1924- *AuBYP 2S, BioIn 13, ConAu 9R, -6NR, ForWC 70, SmATA 28, -52, WhoAmW 75, -77, WrDr 90, -92, -94*

Roberts, Paul Henley 1891- *BioIn 2, -7*

Roberts, Terence *ConAu X, EncSF 93, SmATA 6*
Main entry: Sanderson, Ivan T

Roberts, Theodore Goodrich 1877-1953 *BenetAL 91*

Roberts, Theodore Goodridge 1877-1953 *BioIn 1, -3, -7, -17, CanNov, CanWr, ChhPo, -S1, -S2, CreCan 1, DcLB 92, DcLEL, OxCCan, OxCCanL, REnAL*

Roberts, Thom 1940- *ConAu 81, -15NR*
Pseud./variant:
Lawrence, Thomas

Roberts, Virginia *AuBYP 3, ConAu X*
Main entry: Dean, Nell Marr

Roberts, Willo David 1928- *IntAu&W 91*

Roberts, Willo Davis *BioIn 14*

Roberts, Willo Davis 1928- *AuBYP 3, ConAu 49, -3NR, -19NR, DcAmChF 1960, -1985, FifBJA, IntAu&W 86, MajAI, MichAu 80, ScF&FL 92, SmATA 21, -70, -8AS, TwCCr&M 85, -91, TwCRHW 90, TwCYAW, WrDr 76, -80, -82, -84, -86, -88, -90, -92, -94*

Robertshaw, Denis 1911- *ConAu 65*
Pseud./variant:
Gaunt, Michael

Robertson, Barbara Anne 1931- *BioIn 11, ConAu 25R, IntAu&W 77, -91, OxCCan SUP, SmATA 12, WhoAmW 74, WrDr 76, -80, -82, -84, -86, -88, -90, -92, -94*

Robertson, Colin 1906- *Au&Wr 71, ConAu 9R, IntAu&W 77*

Robertson, Don 1929- *BioIn 11, -15, ConAu 9R, -7NR, -23NR, SmATA 8*

Robertson, Dorothy Lewis 1912- *AuBYP 2S, -3, BioIn 11, ConAu 25R, SmATA 12*

Robertson, Ellis *MajAI*

Robertson, Frank C 1890-1969 *BenetAL 91, TwCWW 91*

Robertson, Frank Chester 1890-1969 *AmAu&B, BioIn 2, ConAu 1R, -4NR, REnAL, WhAm 8, WhNAA, WhoPNW*

Robertson, G E *ChhPo S1, -S2*

Robertson, James Logie 1846-1922 *Alli SUP, ChhPo S1, -S2*

Robertson, Janet 1935- *BioIn 17, SmATA 68*

Robertson, Janet E 1935- *ConAu 137*

Robertson, Jennifer Sinclair 1942- *BioIn 11, ConAu 53, -5NR, SmATA 12*

Robertson, John Ross 1841-1918 *Alli SUP, BioIn 9, -11, DcNAA, OxCCan*

Robertson, Keith 1914- *AuBYP 3, TwCChW 89, WrDr 86, -88, -90, -92*

Robertson, Keith 1914-1991 *BioIn 17, ConAu 135, SmATA 15AS*

Robertson, Keith Carleton 1914- *AuBYP 2, Au&Wr 71, BioIn 6, -7, -9, -10, ConAu 9R, MorBMP, MorJA, OxCChiL, SmATA 1, TwCChW 78, -83, WrDr 80, -82, -84*
Pseud./variant:
Keith, Carlton

Robertson, Keith Carlton d1991 *NewYTBS 91*

Robertson, Keith Carlton 1914- *DcAmChF 1960*

Robertson, Keith Carlton 1914-1991 *ConAu 37NR, MajAI, SmATA 69, TwCYAW, WrDr 94N*

Robertson, Keith Charlton
Main entry: Keith, Carlton

Robertson, Mary E 1937- *WhoUSWr 88, WhoWrEP 89, -92*

Robertson, Mary Elsie *DrAPF 87, -89, -91, -93*

Robertson, Mary Elsie 1937- *BioIn 13, ConAu 81, -15NR, -33NR*

Robertson, Robert 1934- *AmMWSc 76P, -82, -86, -89, -92, WhoAm 76, -78, -80, -82, -84*

Robertson, Stephen *SmATA 66*
Main entry: Walker, Robert Wayne

Robertus, Polly M 1948- *SmATA 73*

Robeson, Kenneth *ConAu X, CorpD, EncSF 93, NewEScF, ScF&FL 92, TwCCr&M 91, TwCSFW 86, -91, WrDr 86, -88, -90, -92*
Main entry: Goulart, Ron

Robeson, Kenneth 1933- *WrDr 94*

Robinet, Harriette Gillem 1931- *BioIn 13, -16, -17, BlkAuII, -92, ConAu 69, -42NR, SmATA 27, WhoBlA 90, -92*

Robins, Joan *AuBYP 3*

Robins, John Daniel 1884-1952 *CanWr, CreCan 2, OxCCan*

Robins, Patricia Denise 1921- *Au&Wr 71, WrDr 76, -80*

Robins, Seelin *HsB&A, YABC 1*
Main entry: Ellis, Edward S

Robinson, Adjai 1932- *BioIn 11, -16, BlkAuII, -92, ConAu 45, InB&W 80, SmATA 8*

Robinson, Alice Merritt 1920-1983 *ConAu 108, -109, WhoAmW 75, -77*

Robinson, Aminah Brenda Lynn 1940- *ConAmWS, SmATA 77, WhoMW 93*

Robinson, Anthony *DrAPF 87, -89, -91, -93*

Robinson, Anthony 1931- *AmAu&B, ConAu 1R, -1NR*

Robinson, Barbara Webb 1927- *AuBYP 2, -3, BioIn 8, -11, ConAu 1R, -30NR, FifBJA, SmATA 8*

Robinson, Barry James 1938- *ChhPo S1, ConAu 25R, WhoE 74, -81, -83, -85, -86, -89*

Robinson, Ben Carl 1890- *OhA&B*

Robinson, Boardman d1952 *WhoAmA 86N*

Robinson, Boardman 1876-1952 *AmAu&B, ArtsAmW 3, BioIn 1, -3, -12, BriEAA, ChhPo, CurBio 41, -52, DcCAA 71, -77, -88, EncAJ, IlsCB 1744, ObitOF 79, WhAm 3, WhAmArt 85, WhoAmA 78N, -80N, -82N, -89N, -91N, WorECar*

Robinson, C A, Jr. 1900-1965 *ConAu 4NR, SmATA 36*

Robinson, Chaille Howard Payne *ConAu 13R*
Pseud./variant:
Robinson, Kathleen

Robinson, Charles 1870-1937 *BioIn 8, -11, -12, -14, ChhPo, -S1, -S2, DcBrAr 1, DcBrBI, DcVicP 2, OxCChiL, SmATA 17, WhoChL*

Robinson, Charles 1931- *BioIn 10, -12, -16, ConAu 49, -2NR, IlsBYP, IlsCB 1967, SixBJA, SmATA 6*

Robinson, Charles Alexander 1900-1965 *AuBYP 3, BioIn 14*

Robinson, Charles Alexander, Jr. 1900-1965 *AmAu&B, AuBYP 2, BioIn 1, -3, -7, ConAu 1R, WhAm 4*

Robinson, David 1929- *AmMWSc 73P, -76P, -82, -86, -89, -92*

Robinson, Dorothy W 1929- *BioIn 16, SmATA 54*

Robinson, Dorothy Washington 1929- *BlkAuII 92*

Robinson, Earl d1991 *NewYTBS 91*

Robinson, Earl 1910- *ASCAP 66, Baker 84, BioIn 1, -8, ConAmC 76, -82, ConAu 45, -2NR, EncFCWM 69, NewAmDM, NewGrDA 86, WhoAm 74, WhoWest 74*

Robinson, Earl 1910-1991 *AnObit 1991, ConAu 135, News 92, -92-1*

Robinson, Earl Hawley 1910-1991 *Baker 92, ConAu 43NR*

Robinson, Edith 1858- *Alli SUP, AmAu&B, BiD&SB, CarSB, DcAmAu, DcNAA, WhAm 4, WomWWA 14*

Robinson, Elizabeth Cameron *ConAu 1R*
Main entry: Nowell, Elizabeth Cameron

Robinson, Florine 1920- *LivgBAA, WrDr 76, -80, -82, -84, -86, -88*

Robinson, Frank M 1926- *BioIn 11, ConAu 49, -3NR, -19NR, NewEScF, ScF&FL 92, ScFSB, TwCSFW 86, -91, WhoSciF, WrDr 84, -86, -88, -90, -92*

Robinson, Frank Malcolm 1926- *EncSF 93, WhoWest 87, WrDr 94*

Robinson, Helen Caister 1899- *CaW, ConAu 93, -16NR*

Robinson, Irene Bowen 1891- *AfroAA, ArtsAmW 2, BioIn 1, -2, -5, DcWomA, IlsBYP, IlsCB 1744, -1946, JBA 51, WhAmArt 85*

Robinson, Jan M 1933- *AuBYP 2S, -3, BioIn 10, ConAu 61, SmATA 6*
Pseud./variant:
Flash Flood

Robinson, Jean O 1934- *AuBYP 2S, -3, BioIn 10, ConAu 29R, SmATA 7*

Robinson, Jerry 1922- *BioIn 14, ConAu 112, EncACom, IlsBYP, SmATA 34*

Robinson, Joan G *WrDr 86, -88*

Robinson, Joan G 1910- *AuBYP 2S, -3, Au&Wr 71, BioIn 8, -9, -10, -14, ConAu 5R, -5NR, IntAu&W 77X, -82X, OxCChiL, SmATA 7, TwCChW 78, -83, WhoChL, WrDr 80, -82, -84*
Pseud./variant:
Thomas, Joan Gale

Robinson, Joan G 1910-1988 *TwCChW 89*

Robinson, John Lewis 1918- *AmMWSc 73S, BioIn 9, BlueB 76, CanWW 70, WhoAm 74, -80, -82, -84, -86, -88, -90, -92, -94, WhoCan 73, -80, -82, WrDr 84, -86, -88*

Robinson, Katherine Prentis Woodroofe 1939- *LEduc 74, WhoAm 74, -80, -82, -84, -86, WhoAmW 87, WhoUSWr 88, WhoWrEP 89, -92*

Robinson, Kathleen *ConAu X*
Main entry: Robinson, Chaille Howard Payne

Robinson, Lloyd *AuBYP 2S, -3, ConAu 36NR, MajAI, MajTwCW, Who 88, -90, -92*

Robinson, Louie *AuBYP 3, BioIn 16*

Robinson, Louie, Jr. 1926- *AuBYP 2S, BlkAuII, -92, ConAu 107, LivgBAA, WhoBlA 75, -77, -80, -85, -88, -90, -92, -94*

Robinson, Mabel Louise 1874-1962 *AmAu&B, AmNov, BioIn 1, -2, -6, -7, -14, ConAu 113, DcLB 22, JBA 51, WhAm 4, WhNAA*

Robinson, Marileta 1942- *BioIn 14, ConAu 101, SmATA 32*

Robinson, Martha
Main entry: Alexander, Martha Kathleen

Robinson, Matt 1937- *ConAu 45, ConBlAP 88, DrBlPA 90, WhoBlA 75, –77, –80, –94*

Robinson, Maudie Millian Oller 1914- *BioIn 11, ConAu 61, –8NR, SmATA 11*

Robinson, Maurice Richard 1895-1982 *BioIn 4, –5, –6, –9, –12, –13, ConAu 106, EncTwCJ, NewYTBS 82, SmATA 29N, WhAm 8, WhJnl, WhoAm 80, –82, WhoFI 81*

Robinson, Nancy K 1942- *AuBYP 3, BioIn 14, ConAu 106, –24NR, SmATA 31, –32*

Robinson, Paul 1898?-1974 *ArtCS, BioIn 10*

Robinson, Ray 1920- *AuBYP 2, –3, BioIn 7, ConAu 77, SmATA 23*

Robinson, Ray 1920-1989 *WorAlBi*

Robinson, Richard 1945- *BioIn 10, ConAu 57, –13NR*

Robinson, Robert Shirley 1902- *AuBYP 3*

Robinson, Roland 1912- *AuBYP 3, ConPo 91, IntAu&W 91, WrDr 86, –88, –90, –92*

Robinson, Roland Edward 1912- *AuBYP 2S, BioIn 11, ConPo 70, –75, IntAu&W 82, IntWWP 82, WrDr 76, –80, –94*

Robinson, Rowland Evans 1833-1900 *Alli SUP, AmAu, AmAu&B, BenetAL 91, BioIn 13, CarSB, CnDAL, DcAmAu, DcLEL, DcNAA, OxCAmL 65, –83, REnAL, WhAm 1*

Robinson, Shari *ConAu X, SmATA X*
Main entry: McGuire, Leslie Sarah

Robinson, Sondra Till 1931- *ConAu 53, –7NR*

Robinson, Spider *BioIn 17, CanWW 89*

Robinson, Spider 1948- *ConAu 65, –11NR, EncSF 93, IntAu&W 82, –91, NewEScF, OxCCanL, RGTwCSF, ScF&FL 92, ScFSB, TwCSFW 86, –91, TwCYAW, WhoCanL 85, –87, –92, WrDr 84, –86, –88, –90, –92, –94*

Robinson, Stuart 1936- *BiE&WWA*

Robinson, Thomas Heath 1869-1950 *BioIn 1, –8, –12, –14, DcBrBI, IlsCB 1744, SmATA 17, WhoChL*

Robinson, Thomas Pendleton 1878- *AuBYP 3*

Robinson, Thomas Pendleton 1878-1954 *AuBYP 2, BioIn 2, –3, –4, –8, BkCL, ChhPo, –S1, JBA 51, Str&VC*

Robinson, Timothy Michael 1934- *Au&Wr 71, WrDr 76, –80, –82*

Robinson, Tom D *AuBYP 2S, –3*

Robinson, Veronica *AuBYP 3*

Robinson, Veronica 1926- *AuBYP 2S, BioIn 14, ConAu 105, SmATA 30*

Robinson, W Heath 1872-1944 *OxCChiL*

Robinson, W W 1891- *JBA 51, Str&VC*

Robinson, William Heath 1872-1944 *BioIn 1, –5, –8, –10, –12, –14, ChhPo, –S1, –S2, ConICB, CurBio 44, DcBrAr 1, DcBrBI, DcNaB 1941, GrBr, SmATA 17, TwCPaSc, WhoChL*

Robinson, William Wheeler 1918- *ConAu 5R, –3NR, –18NR, WhoAm 76, –78, –80, –82, –84, –86, –88, –90, –92, –94, WhoE 89, WhoUSWr 88, WhoWrEP 89, –92*

Robison, Bonnie 1924- *BioIn 11, ConAu 57, SmATA 12*

Robison, Deborah *AuBYP 3*

Robison, Mabel Otis 1891- *BioIn 6, ConAu P-1, MinnWr*

Robison, Nancy L 1934- *ConAu 93, –30NR, SmATA 32*
Pseud./variant:
Johnson, Natalie

Robottom, John Carlisle 1934- *Au&Wr 71, BioIn 10, ConAu 29R, SmATA 7, WrDr 76, –80*

Rocca, Guido 1928-1961 *AuBYP 2S, –3*

Roche, A K *AuBYP 3, ConAu X, SmATA X*
Main entry: Abisch, Roslyn Kroop
Kaplan, Boche

Roche, Arthur Somers 1883-1935 *AmAu&B, BioIn 3, DcNAA, TwCA, WhAm 1*

Roche, P K *BioIn 14, ConAu 112, SmATA 34*

Roche, P K 1935- *BioIn 16*

Roche, P K 1935- *SmATA 57*

Roche, Regina Maria 1764?-1834 *ArtclWW 2*

Roche, Regina Maria 1764?-1845 *Alli, BbD, BiDLA, BiD&SB, BioIn 16, BritAu 19, CarSB, DcBiA, DcBiPP, DcBrAmW, DcNaB, –C, FemiCLE, NewC*

Roche, Regina Mary 1764-1845 *BiDIrW*

Roche, Terry *ConAu X, IntWWP 82X, SmATA X*
Main entry: Poole, Peggy

Roche, Terry 1925- *BioIn 15*

Rock, Gail *AuBYP 2S, -3, BioIn 14, ConAu 111, SmATA 32*

Rocker, Fermin 1907- *BioIn 8, -15, IlsCB 1957, SmATA 40*

Rockne, Knute Kenneth 1888-1931 *BiDAmSp FB, BioIn 1, -2, -3, -4, -5, -6, -7, -8, -9, -10, -11, -12, DcCathB, IndAu 1917, McGEWB, OxCAmH, WebAB 74, -79, WhAm 1, WhoFtbl 74*

Rockowitz, Murray 1920- *ConAu 25R, WhoE 74*

Rockwell, Anne 1934- *AuBYP 3, BioIn 12, ConAu 21R, -22NR, FifBJA, IlsBYP, IlsCB 1967, SmATA 33, TwCChW 89, WhoAm 92, WrDr 90, -92*

Rockwell, Anne F 1934- *MajAI, SmATA 71*

Rockwell, Anne Foote 1934- *WrDr 94*

Rockwell, Gail *BioIn 14*

Rockwell, Gail 1894-1978 *BioIn 12, BlueB 76, ChhPo S1, ConAu 65, -109, FifBJA, IlrAm C, IlsBYP, IlsCB 1967, ObitOF 79, SmATA 33, -36, WebAB 79*

Rockwell, Harlow *BioIn 14, ConAu 22NR*

Rockwell, Harlow 1910-1988 *BioIn 16, ConAu 125, SmATA 56N*

Rockwell, Norman 1894-1978 *Benet 87, BenetAL 91, BioIn 1, -2, -3, -4, -5, -6, -7, -9, -10, -11, -12, -13, -14, -15, -16, CelR, ChhPo S2, ConAu 81, CurBio 45, EncAJ, ForIl, IlrAm 1880, IlsBYP, IlsCB 1744, NewYTBE 71, PrintW 83, -85, REn, REnAL, SmATA 23, WebAB 74, WhAm 7, WhoAm 74, -76, -78, WhoAmA 73, -78, -80N, -82N, -86N, -89N, -91N, WhoGrA 62, WhoWor 74, WorAlBi, WorAl*

Rockwell, Thomas 1933- *BioIn 10, -14, ChhPo S1, ChlLR 6, ConAu 29R, FifBJA, IntAu&W 77, MajAI, SmATA 7, -70, WrDr 76, -80, -82, -84, -86, -88, -90, -92, -94*

Rockwood, Joyce 1947- *BioIn 15, ConAu 57, -6NR, DcAmChF 1960, SmATA 39*

Rockwood, Roy *ConAu 37NR, -P-2, EncSF 93, HsB&A, MajAI, ScF&FL 92, ScFEYrs, SmATA 1, -67, -X*
Main entry: Stratemeyer, Edward L

Rodari, Gianni *TwCChW 89B*

Rodari, Gianni 1920- *OxCChiL, TwCChW 78B, -83B*

Rodari, Gianni 1920-1980 *ChlLR 24*

Rodd, Kathleen Tennant 1912-1988 *ConAu 124, SmATA 55N, -57*
Pseud./variant:
Tennant, Kylie

Rodd, Kylie 1912- *AuBYP 3*

Rodd, Kylie Tennant 1912- *AuBYP 2S, ConAu 5R, -5NR*

Rodd, Kylie Tennant 1912-1988 *ConAu 26NR, MajTwCW*
Pseud./variant:
Tennant, Kylie

Rodda, Emily 1948?- *ChlLR 32, ScF&FL 92*

Rodda, Emily Jennifer Rowe 1948- *DcChlFi*

Roddenberry, Eugene Wesley 1921- *ConAu 110, ScF&FL 92, SmATA 45, WhoAm 80, -82, -84, -86, -88, -90*

Roddenberry, Eugene Wesley 1921-1991 *ConAu 135, -37NR, NewYTBS 91, WhAm 10*
Pseud./variant:
Roddenberry, Gene

Roddenberry, Gene d1991 *LesBEnT 92*

Roddenberry, Gene 1921- *Au&Arts 5, BioIn 14, -15, -16, ConAu 135, -X, -37NR, ConLC 17, ConTFT 3, HalFC 84, IntMPA 84, -86, -88, -92, LesBEnT, NewEScF, SmATA X*

Roddenberry, Gene 1921-1991 *AnObit 1991, BioIn 17, ConLC 70, ConTFT 10, EncSF 93, News 92, -92-2, ScF&FL 92, SmATA 69*
Main entry: Roddenberry, Eugene Wesley

Roddy, Lee 1921- *BioIn 16, ConAu 123, SmATA 57, WrDr 90, -92, -94*
Pseud./variant:
Banner, Rachel

Rodenas, Paula *SmATA 73*

Rodgers, Frank 1944- *SmATA 69*

Rodgers, Mary 1931- *ASCAP 66, AuBYP 2S, BiE&WWA, BioIn 5, -11, ChlLR 20, ConAmC 76, -82, ConAu 49, -8NR, ConLC 12, DcAmChF 1960, EncMT, FifBJA, IntAu&W 77, -91, MajAI, NewAmDM, NotNAT, ScF&FL 92, SmATA 8, TwCChW 78, -83, -89, WhoAm 78, -80, -82, -84, -86, -88, -92, WhoAmW 74, -75, WhoEnt 92, WhoThe 81, WrDr 80, -82, -84, -86, -88, -90, -92, -94*

Rodman, Bella 1903- *AuBYP 2S, -3, ConAu P-2*

Rodman, Emerson *HsB&A, YABC 1*
Main entry: Ellis, Edward S

Rodman, Eric *MajAI*

Rodman, Maia *BioIn 14, -15, ConAu X, -41NR, DrAPF 83, -85, -89, -91, ForWC 70, MajAI, SmATA 1, -X, TwCChW 83, -89*
Main entry: Wojciechowska, Maia

Rodman, Oliver H P *AuBYP 3*

Rodman, Selden 1909- *AmAu&B, AuBYP 2S, BenetAL 91, BioIn 4, -11, ChhPo, -S1, ConAu 5R, -5NR, -25NR, OxCAmL 65, -83, REn, REnAL, SmATA 9, TwCA SUP, WhoAm 74, -76, -78, WhoAmA 73, -78, -80, -82, -84, -86, -89, -91, WhoWor 74*

Rodman, Seldon 1909- *AuBYP 3*

Rodowsky, Colby 1932- *ConAu 23NR, ScF&FL 92, SixBJA, SmATA 77*

Rodowsky, Colby F 1932- *BioIn 16, ConAu 69, SmATA 21*

Roe, Edward Payson 1838-1888 *Alli SUP, AmAu, AmAu&B, BbD, BiD&SB, BioIn 13, CarSB, Chambr 3, DcAmAu, DcLEL, DcNAA, OxCAmL 65, REnAL, WhAm HS*

Roe, Harry Mason *ConAu 26NR, -P-2*
Main entry: Stratemeyer, Edward L

Roedder, Kathleen 1920- *BiDrLUS 70*

Roehrig, Catharine H 1949- *ConAu 134, SmATA 67, WrDr 94*

Roethke, Theodore 1908-1963 *AmAu&B, AmWr, AnCL, AtlBL, Benet 87, BenetAL 91, BioIn 3, -4, -6, -7, -8, -9, -10, -11, -12, -13, -14, -15, -16, -17, CamGEL, CamGLE, CamHAL, CasWL, ChhPo, -S1, -S2, CnDAL, CnE&AP, ConAu 81, -2BS, ConLC 1, -3, -8, -11, -19, -46, ConPo 75, -80A, -85A, CroCAP, DcAmB S7, DcLB 5, DcLEL 1940, EncWL, -2, IntvTCA 2, LongCTC, MagSAmL, MajTwCW, MakMC, McGEWB, MichAu 80, ModAL, -S1, -S2, NewCon, NewGrDA 86, ObitOF 79, ObitT 1961, OxCAmL 65, -83, OxCEng 85, PenC AM, RAdv 1, -13-1, REn, REnAL, RfGAmL 87, TwCA SUP, TwCWr, WebAB 74, -79, WebE&AL, WhDW, WhAm 4, WhoPNW, WhoTwCL, WorAlBi, WorAl, WrPh*

Roever, J M *AuBYP 3*

Roever, J M 1935- *AuBYP 2S, ConAu 105, IlsBYP, SmATA 26*

Rofes, Eric Edward 1954- *BioIn 16, SmATA 52, WrDr 90, -92, -94*

Roffey, Maureen 1936- *BioIn 12, -14, ConAu 108, IlsCB 1967, SmATA 33*
Pseud./variant:
Lodge, Maureen Roffey

Rogasky, Barbara 1933- *ConAu 130, TwCYAW, WrDr 94*

Roger, Mae Durham *ConAu 57*
Pseud./variant:
Durham, Mae

Rogers, Alan 1933- *ConAu 28NR*

Rogers, Alan 1937- *BioIn 9, ConAu 25R, -18NR, SmATA 2*

Rogers, Bertha *ChhPo, DrAPF 89, -91, -93*

Rogers, Carol *IlsBYP*

Rogers, Cedric 1915- *AuBYP 2, -3, BioIn 7, ConAu 1NR*

Rogers, Cyril H 1907- *ConAu 20NR*

Rogers, Cyril Harold 1907- *Au&Wr 71, ConAu 9R, -5NR, WrDr 76, -80, -82, -84*

Rogers, Dale Evans 1912- *AmAu&B, BioIn 3, -4, -9, -10, -14, -15, ConAu 103, CurBio 56, InWom SUP, WhoAm 76, -78, -80, -82*

Rogers, Emma 1951- *SmATA 74*

Rogers, Frances 1888-1974 *BioIn 11, ConAu 5R, MichAu 80, SmATA 10*

Rogers, Fred Baker 1926- *AmMWSc 73P, -76P, -82, -86, -89, -92, BiDrACP 79, ConAu 109, WhoAm 74, -76, -78, -80, -82, -84, -86, -88, -90, -92, -94*

Rogers, Fred McFeely 1928- *ASCAP 66, BioIn 8, -9, -11, -13, ConAu 107, CurBio 71, IntMPA 81, -82, -84, -86, NewYTBS 83, SmATA 33, WhoAm 74, -80, -82, -84, -86, -88, -90, -92, -94, WhoE 74, -75, -77, -93, WhoEnt 92*
Pseud./variant:
Mister Rogers

Rogers, Isabel Wood 1924- *DrAS 74P, -78P, -82P, WhoAm 90, -92, -94, WhoAmW 91, -93, WhoRel 75, -77, -92*

Rogers, James Tracy 1921- *ConAu 45, WhoE 75, -77*

Rogers, Jean 1919- *BioIn 16, SmATA 47, -55*

Rogers, Joe *ChhPo S2*

Rogers, Julia Ellen 1866- *AmAu&B, WhAm 4, WomWWA 14*

Rogers, Mary 1931- *AuBYP 3*

Rogers, Matilda 1894-1976 *BioIn 10, -14, ConAu P-2, SmATA 5, -34N*

Rogers, Pamela 1927- *AuBYP 2S, -3, BioIn 11, ConAu 49, -4NR, SmATA 9, WrDr 80, -82, -84, -86, -88, -90, -92, -94*

Rogers, Paul *AuBYP 3*

Rogers, Paul 1950- *BioIn 16, ConAu 123, SmATA 54*

Rogers, Robert *ConAu X, -29NR, SmATA X*

Rogers, William Barton 1804-1882 *BbtC, BiInAmS, BioIn 3, CyEd, InSci*

Rogers, William Garland 1896-1978 *AmAu&B, AuBYP 2, -3, BioIn 1, -8, -11, -13, ConAu 9R, -77, IntAu&W 77, SmATA 23, WrDr 76*

Rohde, Ruth Bryan Owen *AmAu&B, BioIn 3, -4, -7, -10, CurBio 44, -54, DcAmDH 80, NotAW MOD, ObitOF 79*
Main entry: Owen, Ruth Bryan

Rohde, Ruth Bryan Owen 1885-1954 *BioIn 16, DcAmDH 89, EncWB*

Rohmer, Harriet *BioIn 16*

Rohmer, Harriet 1938- *SmATA 56*

Rohmer, Sax *BioIn 1, -4, -5, -6, -9, -13, -14, -15, ConAu X, CorpD, EncMys, EncO&P 3, EvLB, HalFC 84, LongCTC, NewC, NotNAT B, Novels, ObitOF 79, PenC ENG, SupFW, TwCA, -SUP, TwCCr&M 80, -85, TwCWr, WhoHr&F, WhoLA, WhoSpyF, WorAl*

Rohmer, Sax 1883-1959 *CrtSuMy, DcLB 70, EncSF 93, NewEScF, PenEncH, ScF&FL 92, ScFEYrs, SpyFic, SupFW, TwCCr&M 91, TwCLC 28, WorAlBi*

Rohmer, Sax 1886-1959 *HalFC 88*

Rojan
Main entry: Rojankovsky, Feodor Stepanovich

Rojankovsky, Feodor 1891-1970 *AuBYP 3*

Rojankovsky, Feodor Stepanovich 1891-1970 *AmPB, AuBYP 2, BioIn 1, -2, -4, -5, -7, -8, -9, -12, -14, BkP, Cald 1938, ChhPo, -S1, ConAu 77, IlsBYP, IlsCB 1744, -1946, -1957, -1967, JBA 51, NewYTBE 70, NewbC 1956, SmATA 21, WhAm 5, WhoAmA 78N, -80N, -82N, -86N, -89N, -91N, WhoChL*
Pseud./variant:
Rojan

Rokeby-Thomas, Anna Elma 1911- *BioIn 12, ConAu 77, IntAu&W 82, -86, SmATA 15*

Roland, Albert 1925- *BioIn 11, ConAu 61, SmATA 11, WhoGov 77*

Roland, Betty 1903- *AuWomWr, BioIn 12, BlmGWL, ConAu 103, DcChlFi, FemiCLE, IntAu&W 77, OxCAusL, SingR 2, WrDr 76, -82, -84*

Roland, Mary *ConAu X, -43NR, SmATA X, WrDr 82, -84, -86, -88*
Main entry: Lewis, Mary Christianna Milne

Roland Smith, Gordon 1931- *ConAu 102, WrDr 76, -80, -82, -84, -86, -88, -90, -92, -94*

Rolerson, Darrell A 1946- *BioIn 11, ConAu 49, SmATA 8*

Rolfsrud, Erling Nicolai 1912- *ConAu 65*

Roll, Winifred 1909- *BioIn 10, ConAu 49, SmATA 6*

Rollins, Charlemae 1897-1979 *AuBYP 3, BioIn 16, -17, BlkAuII, -92, BlkWr 1, HanAmWH*

Rollins, Charlemae Hill 1897-1979 *ALA 80N, AuBYP 2, BioIn 2, -3, -7, -9, -10, BlkAWP, BlkWr 1, ChhPo S1, ConAu 9R, -104, ForWC 70, InB&W 80, -85, LivgBAA, MorBMP, NotBlAW 92, SelBAAf, SelBAAu, SmATA 3, -26N, WhoAm 76*

Rollo, Vera Foster 1924- *ConAu 81, WhoAmW 83, WhoE 75, -77, WrDr 76, -80, -82, -84, -86, -88, -90, -92, -94*

Rollock, Barbara T *WhoBlA 92*

Rollock, Barbara T d1992 *WhoBlA 94N*

Rollock, Barbara T 1924- *BioIn 17, SmATA 64*

Rolls, Eric Charles 1923- *Au&Wr 71, ConAu 33R, -13NR, ConPo 70, IntAu&W 82, -86, -89, -91, IntWWP 82, OxCAusL, WrDr 76, -80, -82, -84, -86, -88, -90, -92, -94*

Rolt-Wheeler, Francis W 1876-1960 *AmLY, BioIn 2, JBA 34, -51, WhAm 4, WhNAA, WhoLA*
Pseud./variant:
Wheeler, Francis W Rolt

Rolvaag, Ole E 1876-1931 *DcAmImH, DcScanL*

Rolvaag, Ole Edvart 1876-1931 *AmAu&B, Benet 87, BenetAL 91, BioIn 2, -5, -9, -10, -12, -14, -16, CasWL, CnDAL, ConAmA, CyWA 58, DcLEL, DcNAA, EncWL, EvLB, LongCTC, McGEWB, ModAL, OxCAmL 65, PenC AM, RAdv 13-2, REn, REnAL, TwCA, -SUP, TwCWr, WebAB 74, -79, WebE&AL, WhAm 1, WhNAA*

Romano, Clare 1922- *BioIn 2, ConAu 41R, -24NR, ForWC 70, PrintW 83, -85, WhoAmA 73*
Main entry: Ross, Clare Romano

Romano, Clare Camille *WhoAmA 91*

Romano, Louis G 1921- *BioIn 14, ConAu 17R, -8NR, LEduc 74, SmATA 35, WrDr 76, -80*

Romano, Louis George 1921- *IntAu&W 86*

Romany *WhoChL*
Main entry: Evens, George Bramwell

Rombauer, Irma S 1877-1962 *BioIn 2, -3, -6, CurBio 53, -62, ObitOF 79, WorAlBi, WorAl*

Rome, Anthony *AuBYP 3, ConAu 30NR, IntAu&W 91X, TwCCr&M 91, WrDr 86, -88, -90, -92, -94*

Ronan, Colin Alistair 1920- *Au&Wr 71, ConAu 5R, -6NR, IntAu&W 77, -82, -86, WrDr 76, -80, -82, -84, -86, -88, -90, -92, -94*

Rongen, Bjoern 1906- *BioIn 11, ConAu P-2, SmATA 10*

Rongione, Louis Anthony 1912- *AmCath 80, BiDrLUS 70, ConAu 57, WhoAm 74, -76, -78, -80, WhoLibS 66*

Ronksley, William *OxCChiL*

Ronne, Finn 1899-1980 *AmMWSc 73S, -76P, AnObit 1980, BioIn 1, -4, -8, -12, ConAu 1R, -97, -1NR, CurBio 48, -80N, InSci, NewYTBS 80, WhAm 7, WhoAm 74, -76, -78, WhoWor 74*

Rood, Ronald N 1920- *BioIn 11, ConAu 21R, SmATA 12*

Rook, Elizabeth Jane 1844- *ChhPo*

Rooke, Daphne 1914- *AuBYP 3, BlmGWL, ConNov 86, -91, WrDr 86, -88, -90, -92*

Rooke, Daphne Marie 1914- *AuBYP 2, Au&Wr 71, BioIn 2, -7, -10, -11, ConAu 53, ConNov 72, -76, IntAu&W 77, -82, -86, -89, SmATA 12, TwCWr, Who 74, -82, -83, -85, -88, -90, -92, WorAu 1950, WrDr 76, -80, -94*
Pseud./variant:
Pointon, Robert

Rooke, Patrick John 1925- *Au&Wr 71*

Roop, Connie
Main entry: Roop, Constance Betzer

Roop, Constance Betzer 1951- *ConAu 122, SmATA 49, -54*

Roop, Constance Betzer 1951-
Pseud./variant:
Roop, Connie

Roop, Peter 1951- *BioIn 16, ConAu 122, SmATA 49, -54, WrDr 90, -92, -94*

Roos, Ann *AuBYP 2, -3, BioIn 6, -7, MorJA*

Roos, Audrey Kelley 1912-1982 *BioIn 14, ConAu 108*

Roos, Stephen 1945- *AuBYP 3, BioIn 15, -16, ConAu 112, -31NR, SixBJA, SmATA 41, -47, -77*

Roos, William 1911- *TwCCr&M 85, -91, WrDr 82, -84, -86, -88, -90, -92, -94*

Roose-Evans, James *BioIn 17*

Roose-Evans, James 1927- *ConAu 29R, -35NR, OxCChiL, OxCLiW 86, SmATA 65, TwCChW 78, -83, -89, WhoThe 72, -77, -81, WrDr 76, -80, -82, -84, -86, -88, -90, -92, -94*

Roosevelt, Anna Eleanor *InWom SUP*

Roosevelt, Anna Eleanor 1884-1962 *AuBYP 3, BiDInt, DcAmDH 89*

Roosevelt, Eleanor 1884-1962 *AmAu&B, AmPeW, AuBYP 2, Benet 87, BenetAL 91, BioIn 1, -2, -3, -4, -5, -6, -7, -8, -9, -10, -11, -12, -13, -14, -15, -16, -17, BioNews 74, ConHero 1, ContDcW 89, CurBio 40, -49, -63, DcAmB S7, DcTwHis, EncAACR, FemiCLE, HanAmWH, HerW, -84, InWom SUP, IntDcWB, JrnUS, LongCTC, MemAm, ObitOF 79, ObitT 1961, OxCAmH, OxCAmL 65, -83, PorAmW, RAdv 13-3, RComAH, REn, REnAL, SmATA 50, WebAB 74, -79, WorAlBi*

Roosevelt, Wyn *CarSB*

Root, Frederick Stanley 1853-1906 *CarSB, DcNAA, WhAm 1*

Root, Phyllis *AuBYP 3, SmATA 48*

Root, Phyllis 1949- *BioIn 16, ConAu 123, SmATA 55, WrDr 90, -92, -94*

Root, Shelton L 1923-1986 *BioIn 16*

Root, Shelton L, Jr. 1923-1986 *SmATA 51N*

Root, Vernon Metcalf 1923- *DrAS 74E, -78E, -82P, WhoSSW 75, -76*

Root, Waverley Lewis 1903-1982 *AmAu&B, BioIn 12, -13, -15, ConAu 25R, CurBio 43, -83N, DcLB 4, IntAu&W 82, WhAm 8, WhoAm 74, WrDr 76, -80*

Roote, Mike
Main entry: Fleischer, Leonore

Roper, Laura Wood *AuBYP 3, BioIn 14*

Roper, Laura Wood 1911- *ConAu 57, SmATA 34, WhoAm 76, -78, WrDr 76, -80, -82, -84, -86, -88, -90, -92, -94*
Pseud./variant:
Wood, Laura Newbold

Roquelaure, A N *ConAu 36NR, ScF&FL 92, TwCYAW, WrDr 90, -92*

Roquelaure, A N 1941- *BioIn 17, WrDr 94*

Roscoe, D T 1934- *BioIn 15, ConAu 113, SmATA 42*

Roscoe, William 1753-1831 *Alli, BbD, BiDLA, BiD&SB, BlmGEL, BritAu 19, CasWL, CelCen, Chambr 2, ChhPo, -S1, -S2, DcBiPP, DcEnL, DcEuL, DcLEL, DcNaB, EvLB, NewC, OxCChiL, OxCEng 67, -85, TelT*

Rose, Anna P *BioIn 8, ConAu X, ObitOF 79, SmATA X*
Main entry: Wright, Anna Rose

Rose, Anne *BioIn 11, ConAu 49, -2NR, SmATA 8*

Rose, Barbara *BioIn 10, -15, InWom SUP*

Rose, Barbara 1937- *WhoAmA 86, -89, -91*

Rose, Carl 1903-1971 *BioIn 9, -14, ChhPo, ConAu 29R, NewYTBE 71, SmATA 31, WorECar*
Pseud./variant:
Cros, Earl

Rose, Deborah Lee 1955- *SmATA 71*

Rose, Elizabeth 1933- *BioIn 17, SmATA 68*

Rose, Elizabeth Jane 1933- *BioIn 5, -9, -13, ConAu 5R, SmATA 28, ThrBJA*

Rose, Florella *AuBYP 2S, -3, BioIn 12, ConAu X, -28NR, SmATA X*
Main entry: Carlson, Vada F

Rose, Gerald 1935- *BioIn 5, -8, -9, -14, -17, ChhPo S2, ConAu 65, -9NR, IlsBYP, IlsCB 1957, -1967, SmATA 30, -68, ThrBJA*

Rose, Gerald Hembdon Seymour 1935- *ConAu 42NR*

Rose, Nancy A 1934- *WrDr 94*
Main entry: Sweetland, Nancy Ann

Rose, Nancy Ann 1934- *ConAu 37R, WhoAmW 75, WrDr 76, -80*

Rose, Richard 1933- *Au&Wr 71, ConAu 21R, -10NR, -27NR, IntAu&W 77, -82, -86, -89, -91, IntWW 89, -91, ScF&FL 92, Who 74, -82, -83, -85, -88, -90, -92, WhoWor 80, -91, WrDr 76, -80, -82, -84, -86, -88, -90, -92, -94*

Rose, Wendy *DrAPF 87, -89, -91, -93*

Rose, Wendy 1948- *BioIn 11, ConAu 53, -5NR, DrAP 75, FemiCLE, InWom SUP, SmATA 12*
Pseud./variant:
Edwards, Bronwen Elizabeth
Khanshendel, Chiron

Rose, Wendy Bronwen Elizabeth 1948- *WhoWrEP 92*

Roseberry, Cecil R 1902- *ConAu 21R*

Roselli, Luciana *AuBYP 2, -3, BioIn 8*

Roseman, Kenneth David 1939- *SmATA 52, WrDr 90, -92, -94*

Rosen, Lillian 1928- *BioIn 17, SmATA 63*

Rosen, Michael *BioIn 15, -16*

Rosen, Michael 1946- *Au&Wr 71, ConAu 25R, -15NR, -32NR, DcLEL 1940, OxCChiL, SmATA 40, -48, TwCChW 83, -89, WrDr 86, -88, -90, -92*

Rosen, Michael Wayne 1946- *WrDr 94*

Rosen, Ruth Chier 1925- *WhoAmW 75, -77*

Rosen, Sidney 1916- *AmMWSc 73P, -76P, -82, -86, -89, -92, BioIn 9, ConAu 9R, IntAu&W 77, -82, -86, -89, LEduc 74, SmATA 1, WhoMW 90, WrDr 76, -80, -82, -84, -86, -88, -90, -92, -94*

Rosen, Winifred 1943- *BioIn 11, ConAu 29R, -32NR, SmATA 8*
Pseud./variant:
Carey, Winifred Rosen

Rosenbach, A S W 1876-1952 *BenetAL 91, DcAmBC, DcLB 140, ObitT 1951, OxCAmL 83, OxCChiL*

Rosenbaum, Eileen 1936- *AuBYP 2S, -3, ConAu 21R*

Rosenbaum, Jean 1927- *ConAu 17R, WhoWest 92, -94*

Rosenbaum, Maurice 1907- *ConAu 17R, SmATA 6*

Rosenberg, Amye 1950- *SmATA 74*

Rosenberg, Arthur D 1939- *AmEA 74, ConAu 61*

Rosenberg, Arthur Donald 1939- *WhoE 93*

Rosenberg, Dorothy 1906- *BioIn 15, ConAu 2NR, -18NR, SmATA 40*

Rosenberg, Ethel *AuBYP 3*

Rosenberg, Ethel 1915- *ConAu 29R, -16NR, SmATA 3, WhoAmW 77*
Pseud./variant:
Clifford, Eth
Penn, Ruth Bonn

Rosenberg, Ethel 1915-1953 *BioAmW, BioIn 17, ContDcW 89, WorAlBi*

Rosenberg, Ethel 1916-1953 *BioIn 15, -16*

Rosenberg, Jane 1949- *BioIn 16, ConAu 121, IntAu&W 89, SmATA 58, WhoAmA 86, -89, -91*

Rosenberg, Liz *BioIn 16, DrAPF 87, -89, -91, -93, NewYTBS 92*

Rosenberg, Liz 1958- *ConAu 142, SmATA 75*

Rosenberg, Maxine B 1939- *BioIn 16, SmATA 47, -55*

Rosenberg, Maxine Berta 1939- *AuBYP 3, ConAu 41NR*

Rosenberg, Nancy 1931- *AuBYP 3, ConAu 22NR*

Rosenberg, Nancy Sherman 1931- *AmAu&B, AuBYP 2S, ConAu 1R, -5NR, ForWC 70, SmATA 4, WhoAm 74, -76, -78, -80, -82, -84, -86, -88, WhoAmW 74, WhoE 74, WhoUSWr 88, WhoWrEP 89, -92*
Pseud./variant:
Sherman, Nancy

Rosenberg, Sharon 1942- *BioIn 11, ConAu 57, -10NR, SmATA 8*

Rosenblatt, Arthur S 1938- *BioIn 15, -17, ConAu 134, SmATA 45, -68, WrDr 94*

Rosenblatt, Suzanne Maris 1937- *ConAu 69, WhoAmA 78, -80, -82, -84, -86, -89, -91, WhoMW 78, -80*

Rosenbloom, Joseph R 1928- *ConAu 57, DrAS 82H, SmATA 21, WhoWorJ 78, WrDr 80, -82, -84, -86, -88, -90, -92, -94*

Rosenblum, Marc J 1936- *AmMWSc 73S, ConAu 29R*

Rosenblum, Marc Joseph 1936- *WhoAmL 94*

Rosenblum, Richard 1928- *BioIn 11, ConAu 65, -9NR, IlsBYP, SmATA 11*

Rosenburg, John M 1918- *AuBYP 2, -3, BioIn 7, -10, ConAu 21R, SmATA 6*

Rosendall, Betty 1916- *ConAu 49*

Rosenfeld, Friedrich 1902- *IntAu&W 77*
Pseud./variant:
Feld

Rosenfeld, Sam 1920- *AuBYP 2S, -3, ConAu 9R*

Rosenfield, James Alexander 1943- *ConAu 49*

Rosenthal, Harold 1914- *BioIn 2, -14, ConAu 111, SmATA 35, WhoAmJ 80, WhoE 75, -77, WhoWorJ 72, -78*

Rosenthal, Jules M 1924- *ConAu 17R*

Rosenthal, M L *DrAPF 87, -89, -93*

Rosenthal, M L 1917- *BioIn 16, ConAu 6AS, ConPo 91, DrAPF 91, SmATA 59, WhoWrEP 89, -92, WrDr 86, -88, -90, -92*

Rosenthal, Macha Louis 1917- *WrDr 94*

Rosenthal, Mark A 1946- *SmATA 64*

Roser, Wiltrud *AuBYP 2S, -3*

Rosmond, Babette 1921?- *AmAu&B, AmNov, BioIn 2, ConAu 5R, -6NR, ForWC 70, WhoAmW 74, -75, -77, WhoE 74, -75, -77*

Rosner, Joseph 1914- *ConAu 57*

Rosner, Lynn 1944- *ConAu 61, WhoWest 78*

Rosoman, Leonard 1913- *ArtsCL, BioIn 4, -6, -14, ConBrA 79, DcBrAr 1, TwCPaSc, Who 74, WhoArt 80, -82, -84, WhoGrA 82*

Ross, Alan *ConAu X, SmATA X*
Main entry: Warwick, Alan Ross

Ross, Alan 1921- *EngPo*

Ross, Alan 1922- *Au&Wr 71, BioIn 4, –10, BlueB 76, ChhPo, ConAu 9R, –6NR, –21NR, ConPo 70, –75, –80, –85, –91, DcLEL 1940, IntAu&W 77, –82, –86, –89, –91, LongCTC, ModBrL, NewC, TwCA SUP, Who 74, –82, –83, –85, –88, –90, –92, WrDr 76, –80, –82, –84, –86, –88, –90, –92, –94*

Ross, Alex 1909- *BioIn 2, –9, –13, IlrAm 1880, –F, SmATA 29, WhAmArt 85, WhoAm 74*

Ross, Alexander 1783-1856 *AmAu, AmAu&B, BenetAL 91, BbtC, BioIn 2, DcCanB 8, DcNaB, DcNAA, HarEnUS, OxCAmL 65, –83, OxCCan, REnAL, WhNaAH*

Ross, Alexander 1908- *WhAm 10, WhoAm 86, –88, –90, WhoAmA 86, –89, –91*

Ross, Anne 1925- *Au&Wr 71*

Ross, Arnold Ephraim 1906- *AmMWSc 73P, –76P, BioIn 15*

Ross, Barnaby *AmAu&B, AuBYP 2, –3, BenetAL 91, ConAu X, –39NR, CurBio 40, DcLEL, EncMys, EvLB, IntAu&W 77X, LongCTC, MajTwCW, PenC AM, REnAL, TwCA, –SUP, TwCCr&M 91, WebAB 74, –79, WrDr 76, –80, –82*
Main entry: Dannay, Frederic
Lee, Manfred B

Ross, Charles H 1842?-1897 *StaCVF*

Ross, Charles Henry 1842-1897 *Alli, –SUP, ChhPo, –S2, DcBrBI, HsB&A, –SUP*

Ross, Clare 1922- *SmATA 48*

Ross, Clare Romano 1922- *BioIn 8, –12, –16, ChhPo, –S1, IlsCB 1957, –1967*
Pseud./variant:
Romano, Clare

Ross, Dan *ConAu X, –32NR*
Main entry: Ross, William Edward Daniel

Ross, Dan 1912- *ScF&FL 92*

Ross, Dana 1912- *WrDr 94*

Ross, Dana Fuller *ConAu 127, SmATA X*
Main entry: Gerson, Noel Bertram

Ross, Dave *AuBYP 3, IntAu&W 86X*

Ross, Dave 1949- *BioIn 14, ConAu X, SmATA 32*
Main entry: Ross, David

Ross, David 1896-1975 *BioIn 10, –12, –16, ChhPo S2, ConAu 61, –65, SmATA 20N, –49, WhAm 6, WhScrn 83, –77, WhoAm 74, WhoHol C*

Ross, David 1949- *AuBYP 3, BioIn 16, –17, ConAu 111*
Pseud./variant:
Ross, Dave

Ross, Diana
Main entry: Denney, Diana

Ross, Diana 1910- *ConAu X, OxCChiL, SmATA X, TwCChW 78, –83, –89, WrDr 80, –82, –84, –86, –88, –90*

Ross, Eulalie Steinmetz 1910- *BiDrLUS 70, ConAu 17R, WhoLibS 55*
Pseud./variant:
Steinmetz, Eulalie

Ross, Eulalie Steinmetz 1910-1975 *ConAu 134*

Ross, Frances Aileen 1909- *ConAu P-1*

Ross, Frank *AuBYP 3*

Ross, Frank, Jr. 1914- *AuBYP 2S, ChhPo S1, ConAu 93, –16NR, SmATA 28*
Pseud./variant:
Frank, R, Jr.

Ross, Ishbel 1895-1975 *BiDAmJo, BioIn 15, BriB*

Ross, Ishbel 1897-1975 *AmAu&B, AmNov, AuSpks, BioIn 2, –10, –11, –16, ConAu 61 –93, ForWC 70, InWom SUP*

Ross, John *BiNAW Sup*

Ross, John 1921- *BioIn 8, –12, –15, ConAu 108, IlsBYP, IlsCB 1957, –1967, SmATA 45, WhoAmA 73*

Ross, Judy 1942- *BioIn 16, SmATA 54*

Ross, Judy Thompson 1942- *IntAu&W 89*

Ross, Laura *AuBYP 2S, –3, ConAu X*
Main entry: Mincieli, Rose Laura

Ross, Leonard Q *AmAu&B, BenetAL 91, ConAu X, CurBio 42, IntAu&W 77X, –82X, –91X, LongCTC, OxCAmL 65, –83, PenC AM, REnAL, TwCA, –SUP, Who 74, –82, –83, –85, –88, –90, –92, WhoAm 84, –86, –88, WrDr 76, –80, –82, –84, –86, –88, –90, –92*
Main entry: Rosten, Leo Calvin

Ross, Leonard Q 1908- *WhoAm 92, –94, WrDr 94*

Ross, Lillian Hammer 1925- *SmATA 72*

Ross, Mabel Irene Hughes 1909- *ConAu 81*

Ross, Nancy Wilson *WhoAm 86*

Ross, Nancy Wilson d1986 *NewYTBS 86, WhAm 9*

Ross, Nancy Wilson 1905?-1986 *BioIn 14, –15*

Ross, Nancy Wilson 1907?- *AmAu&B, AmNov, BioIn 1, –2, –3, –4, ConAu 97, CurBio 52, DrAPF 83, –85, TwCA SUP, WhoAm 74, –78, –80, –82, –84, WhoAmW 74*

Ross, Nancy Wilson 1907-1986 *CurBio 86N*

Ross, Nancy Wilson 1910-1986 *ConAu 118*

Ross, Pat *BioIn 15, –16, InWom SUP*

Ross, Pat 1943- *AuBYP 3, ConAu 128, SmATA 48, –53*

Ross, Patricia 1899- *AuBYP 3*

Ross, Patricia Fent 1899- *AnCL, AuBYP 2, BioIn 8*

Ross, Ramon Royal 1930- *BioIn 17, SmATA 62*

Ross, Tony 1938- *BioIn 12, –14, –16, –17, ConAu 77, –35NR, IntAu&W 82, MajAI, OxCChiL, SixBJA, SmATA 17, –65, TwCChW 89, WrDr 90, –92, –94*

Ross, Wilda 1915- *AuBYP 2S, –3, BioIn 15, –16, ConAu 85, SmATA 39, –51, WrDr 76, –80, –82, –84, –86, –88*

Ross, William Edward Daniel 1912- *ConAu 81, IntAu&W 86, WhoRel 75, –77, WrDr 80*
Pseud./variant:
Gilmer, Ann
Randolph, Ellen
Ross, Dan

Ross, Zola Helen d1989 *BioIn 16*

Ross, Zola Helen 1912- *AuBYP 2, –3, BioIn 7, ConAu 53, WhoAmW 85, –87, WhoPNW*
Pseud./variant:
Arre, Helen
Iles, Bert

Ross, Zola Helen 1912-1989 *ConAu 130*

Rossel, Seymour 1945- *BioIn 13, ConAu 53, –5NR, –21NR, SmATA 28, WrDr 76, –80, –82, –84, –86, –88, –90, –92*

Rossel, Seymour H 1945- *WrDr 94*

Rosselli, Colette 1916- *BioIn 8, ChhPo, IlsCB 1957*

Rossel-Waugh, C C *ConAu X, SmATA X*
Main entry: Waugh, Carol-Lynn Rossel

Rossetti, Christina 1830-1894 *BlmGWL, CamGLE, ContDcW 89, EncBrWW, FemiCLE, PenEncH, PoeCrit 7, RAdv 13-1, RfGEnL 91, WorLitC, WrChl*

Rossetti, Christina Georgina 1830-1894
Pseud./variant:
Alleyn, Ellen

Rossetti, Christina Georgina 1830-1894 *Alli, –SUP, AnCL, ArtclWW 2, AtlBL, Benet 87, BbD, BiD&SB, BioIn 1, –2, –3, –4, –5, –6, –7, –8, –9, –10, –11, –12, –13, –14, –15, –16, BlmGEL, BritAu 19, CamGEL, CarSB, CasWL, CelCen, Chambr 3, ChhPo, –S1, –S2, ChrP, CnE&AP, CrtT 3, CyWA 58, DcBiPP, DcEnA, –A, DcEnL, DcEuL, DcLEL, DcNaB, EvLB, FamPYP, InWom SUP, JBA 34, LongCEL, MajAI, McGEWB, MouLC 4, NewC, NinCLC 2, OxCChiL, OxCEng 67, –85, PenC ENG, RAdv 1, REn, SmATA 20, Str&VC, WebE&AL, WomNov*

Rossi, Mario 1916- *ConAu 5R, –8NR*

Rossiter, Ian *ConAu X*
Main entry: Ross Williamson, Hugh

Ross Macdonald, Malcolm John 1932- *Au&Wr 71, ConAu 65, –13NR, IntAu&W 82, –89, –91, WrDr 76, –80*
Pseud./variant:
Macdonald, Malcolm J Ross

Rossman, George Parker 1919- *ConAu 69, DrAS 78P, –82P*

Ross Williamson, Hugh 1901-1978 *Au&Wr 71, BioIn 4, ConAu 17R, –8NR, IntAu&W 77, IntWW 74, –75, –76, –77, –78N, LongCTC, Who 74*
Pseud./variant:
Rossiter, Ian

Rostand, Edmond Eugene Alexis 1868-1918 *AtlBL, BiD&SB, BioIn 1, –5, –11, CasWL, ClDMEL 47, CnMD, CnThe, CyWA 58, EncWL, EncWT, EvEuW, LongCTC, McGEWD 72, ModFrL, ModRL, ModWD, NewC, NotNAT B, OxCEng 67, OxCFr, OxCThe 67, –83, PenC EUR, REn, REnWD, TwCA, –SUP*

Rosten, Leo C 1908- *EncTwCJ, IntAu&W 89, –91, Who 88, –90, –92*

Rosten, Leo Calvin 1908- *AmAu&B, Au&Wr 71, BenetAL 91, BioIn 4, –5, –8, –13, –15, ConAu 5R, –6NR, ConNov 72, –76, CurBio 42, EncAJ, IntAu&W 77, OxCAmL 65, PenC AM, REn, REnAL, TwCA, –SUP, WhNAA, Who 74, –82, –83, –85, WhoAm 74, –76, –78, –80, –82, –84, –86, –88, –90, –92, –94, WhoAmJ 80, WhoEnt 92, WhoWor 74, WhoWorJ 72, –78, WrDr 76, –80*

Pseud./variant:
Ross, Leonard Q

Rostkowski, Margaret I 1945- *BioIn 15, –16, ConAu 127, DcAmChF 1985, SixBJA, SmATA 59, TwCYAW*

Roth, Arnold 1929- *AuBYP 2S, –3, BioIn 12, ConAu 21R, IlsBYP, SmATA 21, WhoE 74, –75, –77, WorECar*

Roth, Arthur d1993 *NewYTBS 93*

Roth, Arthur 1920- *ConAu 1R*

Roth, Arthur 1921- *ScF&FL 92*

Roth, Arthur 1925- *SmATA 11AS*

Roth, Arthur J *DrAPF 87, –89, –91, –93*

Roth, Arthur J 1925- *AuBYP 2S, –3, BioIn 13, –15, ConAu 53, –7NR, DrAF 76, SmATA 28, –43*
Pseud./variant:
Hoy, Nina
Mara, Barney
McGurk, Slater
Pomeroy, Pete

Roth, Arthur Joseph 1925-1993 *ConAu 140, SmATA 75*

Roth, Bernhard A *AuBYP 2S, –3*

Roth, Charles E 1934- *ConAu 111, –30NR*

Roth, Charles Edmund 1934- *IntAu&W 86*

Roth, David 1940- *BioIn 14, ConAu 106, SmATA 36*

Roth, Harold *BioIn 16, SmATA 49*

Roth, June Doris Spiewak 1926- *ConAu 9R, –5NR, ForWC 70, IntAu&W 82, –86, –89, WhoAm 80, –82, –84, –86, –88, –90, –92, –94, WhoAmW 81, –83, WhoE 74, –81, –83, WhoUSWr 88, WhoWor 80, WhoWrEP 89, WrDr 76, –80, –82, –84*

Roth, Mark Joseph 1941- *ConAu 77*

Roth, Mary Jane 1913- *ConAu 21R, WhoAmW 74, WhoMW 74, –76*

Rothberg, Abraham 1922- *AmAu&B, BioIn 16, ConAu 33R, SmATA 59, WhoAm 74, –76, –78, –80, –82, –84, –86, –88, –90, –92, –94, WhoAmJ 80, WhoUSWr 88, WhoWrEP 89, –92*

Rothenberg, Lillian 1922- *ConAu 9R*

Rothery, Agnes Edwards 1888- *AmWomPl, AuBYP 3*

Rothery, Agnes Edwards 1888-1954 *AmAu&B, AmLY, AuBYP 2, BioIn 1, –2, –3, –7, CathA 1952, CurBio 46, –54, WhNAA*

Rothery, Guy Cadogan 1863- *WhoLA*

Rothkopf, Carol Zeman 1929- *BioIn 9, ConAu 25R, SmATA 4, WhoAmW 74, –75*

Rothman, Joel 1938- *BioIn 10, ConAu 37R, SmATA 7, WrDr 76, –80, –82, –84, –86, –88, –90, –92, –94*

Rothman, Milton A *EncSF 93*

Rothman, Milton A 1919- *AmMWSc 73P, –76P, –82, –86, –89, –92, ConAu 41R*

Rothweiler, Paul R 1931- *WrDr 86, –88, –90, –92, –94*

Rothweiler, Paul Roger 1931- *ConAu 65, –10NR, IntAu&W 82, WhoE 81, –83, –85, –86, WrDr 80, –82, –84*

Rotner, Shelley 1951- *SmATA 76*

Rottensteiner, Franz 1942- *ConAu 81, –15NR, –33NR, EncSF 93, ScF&FL 92, WhoSciF*

Roucek, Joseph S 1902- *AmMWSc 73S, ConAu 9R, –32NR, IntAu&W 77*

Roueche, Berton 1911- *AmAu&B, Au&Wr 71, BenetAL 91, BioIn 5, –13, –15, ConAu 1R, –1NR, CurBio 59, DrAF 76, DrAPF 83, –85, –87, –89, –91, –93, EncAJ, EncTwCJ, REnAL, SmATA 28, WhoAm 74, –76, –78, –80, –82, –84, –86, –88, –90, –92, –94, WhoUSWr 88, WhoWor 74, WhoWrEP 89, –92, WorAu 1975, WrDr 90, –92, –94*

Roughsey, Dick *BioIn 14*

Roughsey, Dick 1921?- *BioIn 12, ConAu 109, IlsCB 1967, OxCAusL, OxCChiL, SmATA 35, TwCChW 83, WrDr 86, –88*

Roughsey, Dick 1924-1985 *TwCChW 89*

Rounds, Glen 1906- *AuBYP 3, BenetAL 91, ChlBIID, ConAu 22NR, TwCChW 89, WrDr 86, –88, –90, –92*

Rounds, Glen H 1906- *AmPB, AuBYP 2, BioIn 1, –2, –3, –5, –7, –8, –10, –11, –12, ChhPo S1, –S2, ConAu 53, –7NR, IlsCB 1744, –1946, –1957, –1967, JBA 51, OxCChiL, REnAL, SmATA 8, TwCChW 78, –83, WhAmArt 85, WrDr 80, –82, –84*

Rounds, Glen Harold 1906- *MajAI, SmATA 70, WrDr 94*

Rountree, Harry 1878-1950 *BiDScF, BioIn 1, –8, –14, ChhPo S1, –S2, DcBrAr 1, DcBrBI, IlsCB 1744, WhoChL, WorECar*

Rourke, Constance M 1885-1941 *Benet 87, BenetAL 91, BioAmW*

Rourke, Constance Mayfield 1885-1941 *AmAu&B, AmWomWr, AnCL, ArtclWW 2, BioIn 1, –6, –11, –12, –14, CnDAL, ConAmA, CurBio 41, DcNAA, InWom SUP, ModAL, MorJA, OhA&B, OxCAmL 65, PenC AM, REn, REnAL, TwCA, –SUP, WhAm 1, YABC 1*

Rouse, Parke Shepherd, Jr. 1915- *ConAu 17R, IntAu&W 82, WhoSSW 73, WrDr 76, –80, –82, –84, –86, –88, –90, –92, –94*

Rouse, William Henry Denham 1863-1950 *BioIn 2, –5, DcInB, DcNaB 1941, WhoLA*

Roussan, Jacques De 1929- *BioIn 10, OxCCan SUP*
Pseud./variant:
DeRoussan, Jacques

Routh, Jonathan *BioIn 3, ConAu 110, WrDr 76, –80, –82, –84*

Routledge, Edmund 1843-1899 *Alli, –SUP, ChhPo, –S1, –S2, HsB&A*

Routledge, George 1812-1888 *DcLB 106, DcNaB, OxCChiL, StaCVF*

Rouverol, Jean *ConAu X*

Rouverol, Jean 1916- *WhoEnt 92*

Roux, Georges 1914- *ConAu 17R*

Rowan, Deirdre *ConAu X, IntAu&W 77X, WrDr 76, –80, –82, –84, –86, –88, –90, –92, –94*
Main entry: Williams, Jeanne

Rowand, Phyllis *BioIn 5, IlsBYP, IlsCB 1946*

Rowe, Dorothy 1898- *BioIn 2, JBA 34, –51*

Rowe, Dorothy E d1989 *BioIn 16*

Rowe, Dorothy Isdell 1929- *WhoAmW 89*

Rowe, Jeanne A 1938- *ConAu 29R*

Rowe, Richard 1828-1879 *BioIn 2, DcNaB, OxCAusL, OxCChiL*

Rowe, Richard Brian 1933- *Who 88, –90*

Rowe, Richard Edwin 1944- *WhoAmL 94*

Rowe, Richard Lloyd 1926- *WhoAm 92*

Rowe, Viola Carson 1903-1969 *AuBYP 2, –3, BioIn 7, –13, ConAu 1R, –103, SmATA 26N*

Rowe, W Bayless *Law&B 92*

Rowe, W G *EngPo*

Rowe, William 1942- *ConAu 131*

Rowe, William Neil 1942- *WrDr 94*

Rowland, Florence 1900- *AuBYP 3*

Rowland, Florence Wightman 1900- *AuBYP 2S, BioIn 11, ConAu 5R, –5NR, SmATA 8*

Rowland-Entwistle, Theodore 1925- *BioIn 14, ConAu 107, –24NR, IntAu&W 77, –86, –89, –91, SmATA 31*
Pseud./variant:
Briquebec, John
Ellis, Anyon
Hall-Clarke, James
Henry, T E
Lawrence, J T

Rowley, Peter 1934- *ConAu 65*

Rowling, Marjorie Alice 1900- *Au&Wr 71, ConAu 5R, IntAu&W 77, WrDr 76, –80, –82, –84*

Rowsome, Frank Howard, Jr. 1914-1983 *AmAu&B, ConAu 112, SmATA 36, WhoGov 77, –75, WhoSSW 73*

Roxborough, Henry Hall 1891- *Au&Wr 71, ConAu 5R*

Roy, Cal *ChhPo*

Roy, Jacqueline 1954- *BlkWr 2, SmATA 74*

Roy, Jessie H *ConBlAP 88*

Roy, Jessie H 1895- *WhoBlA 85, –90*

Roy, Jessie H 1895-1986 *WhoBlA 92N*

Roy, Jessie Hailstalk 1895-1986 *BioIn 16, ConAu 121, SmATA 51N*

Roy, Liam *ConAu X, SmATA 2*
Main entry: Scarry, Patricia

Roy, Michael 1913-1976 *BioIn 10, ConAu 61, –65, –10NR*

Roy, Ron 1940- *BioIn 14, –15, ConAu 114, SmATA 35, –40*

Roy, Thomas Albert *DcChlFi*

Royds, Caroline 1953- *BioIn 16, ConAu 123, SmATA 55*

Royston, Olive 1904- *ConAu 102, WrDr 76, –80, –82, –84*

Rozek, Evalyn Robillard 1941- *ConAu 61*

Rubel, Nicole 1953- *BioIn 12, ConAu 125, FifBJA, SmATA 18*

Rubenstein, Gillian *DcChlFi*

Rubenstone, Jessie 1912- *ConAu 69*

Rubicam, Harry Cogswell 1902- *AuBYP 3*

Rubicam, Harry Cogswell, Jr. 1902- *AuBYP 2, BioIn 7, ConAu P-2*

Rubin, Arnold Perry 1946- *ConAu 69, WhoE 81*

Rubin, Eva Johanna 1925- *BioIn 8, –15, ChhPo S1, IlsCB 1957, SmATA 38*

Rubin, Mark *DrAPF 87, –89, –91, –93*

Rubin, Mark 1946- *ConAu 53, –9NR*

Rubin, Mark Stephen 1946- *WhoWor 93*

Rubin, Robert *AuBYP 2S, –3*

Rubin, Theodore I 1923- *BiDrAPA 89, WrDr 86, –88, –90, –92, –94*

Rubin, Theodore Isaac 1923- *AmAu&B, AuNews 1, BiDrAPA 77, BioIn 7, –9, –10, –12, BioNews 74, ConAu 108, –110, CurBio 80, WhoAm 74, –76, –78, –80, –82, –84, –86, –88, –90, –92, –94, WhoWor 74, WrDr 76, –80, –82, –84*

Rubinstein, Gillian 1942- *BioIn 17, EncSF 93, ScF&FL 92, SmATA 68, TwCChW 89, WrDr 90, –92*

Rubinstein, Gillian Margaret 1942- *ConAu 136, TwCYAW*

Rubinstein, Gillian Margaret Hanson 1942- *WrDr 94*

Rubinstein, Robert E 1943- *BioIn 16, SmATA 49*

Rublowsky, John M 1928- *AuBYP 3, SmATA 62*

Rublowsky, John Martin 1928- *AuBYP 2S, ConAu 17R, WhoE 74*

Ruby, Lois 1942- *BioIn 14, –16, ConAu 97, SixBJA, SmATA 34, –35*

Ruby, Lois F 1942- *ConAu 39NR, TwCYAW*

Ruchlis, Hyman d1992 *NewYTBS 92*

Ruchlis, Hyman 1913- *AuBYP 2, –3, BioIn 7, –9, ConAu 1R, SmATA 3*

Ruchlis, Hyman 1913-1992 *SmATA 72*

Ruckman, Ivy 1931- *BioIn 15, –16, ConAu 111, –30NR, SixBJA, SmATA 37*

Ruck-Pauquet, Gina *AuBYP 3*

Ruck-Pauquet, Gina 1931- *AuBYP 2S, BioIn 15, ConAu 116, –122, SmATA 37, –40*

Rudeen, Kenneth *BioIn 10, –14, ConAu 11?, SmATA 36*

Rudin, Ellen *BioIn 6*

Rudley, Stephen 1946- *BioIn 14, ConAu 1C6, SmATA 30*

Rudman, Jack 1912- *WhoAm 76, –78, WhoE 83, –85, WhoFI 74, –75, –81, WhoWor 82*

Rudolph, L C 1921- *BiDrLUS 70, ConAu 5R, –2NR, WhoLibI 82*

Rudolph, Marguerita 1908- *AuBYP 2, –3, BioIn 8, –12, ChhPo S2, ConAu 33R, –13NR, LEduc 74, SmATA 21*

Rudomin, Esther *AuBYP 3, ConAu X, MajAI, SmATA 4, –68, WrDr 76, –80, –82, –84, –86, –88, –90, –92*
Main entry: Hautzig, Esther Rudomin

Rudomin, Esther 1930- *WrDr 94*

Rudwick, Elliott 1927- *AmMWSc 78S, DrAS 74H*

Rue, Leonard Lee *BioIn 15*

Rue, Leonard Lee 1926- *AuBYP 3*

Rue, Leonard Lee, III 1926- *AuBYP 2S, BioIn 12, ConAu 1R, –1NR, IntAu&W 77, –82, –86, SmATA 37, WrDr 76, –80, –82, –84, –86, –88, –90, –92, –94*

Ruedi, Norma Paul *ConAu X, SmATA X*
Main entry: Ainsworth, Norma Paul Rueci

Ruffell, Ann 1941- *BioIn 14, ConAu 107, –23NR, ScF&FL 92, SmATA 30*

Ruffins, Reynold 1930- *BioIn 15, –16, BlkAuII, –92, ConAu 112, FifBJA, MajAI, SmATA 41*

Ruffins, Reynolds 1930- *WhoBlA 94*

Ruffo, Vinnie 1928- *ConAu 25R, WhoAmW 77*

Rugh, Belle Dorman 1908- *AuBYP 2, -3, Au&Wr 71, BioIn 7, -9, ConAu P-1, ForWC 70, ThrBJA*

Rugoff, Milton 1913- *DrAS 82E, SmATA 30, WhoAm 80, -82, -84, -86, -88, -90, WhoUSWr 88*

Ruhen, Olaf 1911- *Au&Wr 71, BioIn 6, -12, ConAu 1R, -5NR, -20NR, IntAu&W 77, -82, -86, OxCAusL, SingR 2, SmATA 17, WrDr 76, -80, -82, -84, -86, -88, -90, -92, -94*

Ruiz, Ramon Eduardo *BioIn 16*

Ruiz, Ramon Eduardo 1921- *ChiSch, ConAu 25R, -11NR, -30NR, DrAS 74H, -78H, -82H, HispAmA, HispWr, MexAmB, WhoAm 74, -76, -78, -80, -82, -84, -86, -88, -90, -92, -94, WhoHisp 91, -92, -94*

Rukeyser, Muriel 1913- *BenetAL 91, IntvTCA 2*

Rukeyser, Muriel 1913-1980 *AmAu&B, AmWomWr, AnObit 1980, ArtclWW 2, AuBYP 2, -3, Benet 87, BioIn 4, -7, -8, -10, -11, -12, -13, -14, -15, -17, BlmGWL, BlueB 76, CamGLE, CamHAL, CasWL, ChhPo, -S1, CnDAL, ConAu 5R, -93, -26NR, ConLC 6, -10, -15, -27, ConPo 70, -75, -80, ContDcW 89, CurBio 43, -80N, DcLB 48, DcLEL, DrAP 75, DrAS 74E, -78E, FemiCLE, ForWC 70, HanAmWH, InWom SUP, IntDcWB, IntWW 78, -79, IntWWP 82, MajTwCW, ModAL, -S1, -S2, NewYTBS 80, OxCAmL 65, -83, PenC AM, RAdv 1, REn, REnAL, RfGAmL 87, SixAP, SmATA 22N, TwCA, -SUP, TwCWr, WebE&AL, WhAm 7, WhoAm 74, -76, -78, -80, WhoAmW 74, -83, WhoWor 74, WorAlBi, WorAl, WrDr 76, -80*

Rukeyser, Muriel 1914-1980 *ModAWP*

Rumbelow, Donald 1940- *ConAu 49, WrDr 80, -82, -84*

Rumsey, Marian 1928- *BioIn 12, ConAu 21R, SmATA 16, Str&VC*

Rundle, Anne *Au&Wr 71, BioIn 14, ConAu 57, -12NR, IntAu&W 77, -82, -91, ScF&FL 92, TwCRHW 90, WrDr 76, -80, -82, -84, -86, -88, -90*
Pseud./variant:
Lamont, Marianne
Manners, Alexandra
Marshall, Joanne
Sanders, Jeanne

Runnerstroem, Bengt Arne 1944- *SmATA 75*

Runyan, John *ConAu X, SmATA X*
Main entry: Palmer, Bernard

Runyon, Catherine 1947- *BioIn 17, ConAu 61, SmATA 62*

Ruoff, A LaVonne Brown 1930- *SmATA 76, WhoMW 93*

Rus, Vladimir 1931- *ConAu 17R, IntAu&W 77*

Rush, Alison 1951- *BioIn 15, ConAu 115, ScF&FL 92, SmATA 41*

Rush, Anne Kent 1945- *ConAu 61, -8NR, WhoAmW 83*

Rush, Peter 1937- *BioIn 14, ConAu 111, SmATA 32*

Rush, Philip 1908- *Au&Wr 71, ConAu 104, ConTFT 5, IntAu&W 77, -82, TwCChW 78, -83, -89, WrDr 76, -80, -82, -84, -86, -88, -90, -92, -94*

Rush, William Marshall 1887-1950 *AuBYP 2, -3, BioIn 2, -7*

Rushmore, Arthur *AmPB*

Rushmore, Helen 1898- *AuBYP 2, -3, BioIn 3, -8, -9, ConAu 25R, SmATA 3*

Rushmore, Robert 1926- *BioIn 11, -15, -16, ConAu 25R, DrAF 76, SmATA 8*

Rushmore, Robert 1926-1986 *ConAu 120, SmATA 49N*

Rushton, William 1937- *IntAu&W 91, WrDr 76, -80, -82, -84, -86, -88, -90, -92*

Rushton, William George 1937- *WrDr 94*

Rushton, William James, III 1929- *WhoIns 93*

Ruskin, Ariane 1935- *AuBYP 2, -3, BioIn 8, -10, ConAu 13R, -X, SmATA 7*
Main entry: Batterberry, Ariane Ruskin

Ruskin, John 1819-1900 *Alli, -SUP, ArtsNiC, AtlBL, Benet 87, BbD, BiD&SB, BioIn 1, -2, -3, -4, -5, -6, -7, -8, -9, -10, -11, -12, -13, -14, -15, -16, -17, BlmGEL, BriEAA, BritAu 19, BritWr 5, CamGEL, CamGLE, CarSB, CasWL, CelCen, Chambr 3, ChhPo, -S1, -S2, ClaDrA, CnDBLB 4, ConAu 114, -129, CrtT 3, CyEd, CyWA 58, DcAmSR, DcBiPP, DcBrBI, DcEnA, -A, DcEnL, DcEuL, DcLB 55, DcLEL, DcNaB S1, DcVicP 2, Dis&D, EncO&P 1, -2, -3, EncPaPR 91, EncUrb, EvLB, FamSYP, LongCEL, MacEA, MagSWL, McGEWB, MouLC 4, NewC, OxCArt, OxCChiL, OxCEng 67, -85, OxDcArt, PenC ENG, RComWL, REn, RfGEnL 91, SmATA 24, StaCVF, TelT, TwCLC 20, WebE&AL, WhDW, WhoChL, WorAlBi, WorAl, WrChl*

Russ, Lavinia 1904- *AuBYP 2S, -3, BioIn 9, ConAu 25R*
Pseud./variant:
Faxon, Lavinia

Russ, Lavinia 1904-1992 *BioIn 17, SmATA 74*

Russ, Lavinia Faxon 1904-1992 *ConAu 137*

Russell, Andy d1992 *BioIn 17, NewYTBS 92*

Russell, Andy 1915- *BioIn 9, ConAu 21R, -10NR, -26NR*

Russell, Charlotte *ConAu X, IntAu&W 82X, SmATA X*
Main entry: Rathjen, Carl Henry

Russell, Don 1899- *ConAu 1R, -1NR, WrDr 76, -80, -82, -84*

Russell, Don 1899-1986 *BioIn 16, ConAu 118, SmATA 47N*

Russell, Francis 1910- *Au&Wr 71, ConAu 25R, IntAu&W 77, -86, -89, -91, WhoAm 74, -76, -78, -80, -82, -84, -86, -88, WhoUSWr 88, WhoWrEP 89, WrDr 76, -80, -82, -84, -86, -88, -90*

Russell, Francis 1910-1989 *BioIn 16, ConAu 128, NewYTBS 89, WhAm 10*

Russell, Franklin 1926- *AuBYP 3, WrDr 86, -88, -90, -92*

Russell, Franklin Alexander 1926- *AmAu&B, AuBYP 2, Au&Wr 71, BioIn 8, -11, ConAu 17R, OxCCan, SmATA 11, WhoAm 74, -76, -78, -80, -82, WrDr 76, -80, -94*

Russell, Helen Ross *AmMWSc 86*

Russell, Helen Ross 1915- *AmMWSc 73P, -76P, -82, BioIn 11, ConAu 33R, SmATA 8, WhoAmW 75, WhoUSWr 88, WhoWrEP 89, -92, WrDr 76, -80, -82, -84, -86, -88, -90, -92, -94*

Russell, Ivy Ethel 1909- *Au&Wr 71, ChhPo S1, ConAu 5R*

Russell, James 1933- *SmATA 53*
Pseud./variant:
Russell, Jim

Russell, Jim 1933- *BioIn 12, -14, -16, IlsCB 1967*
Main entry: Russell, James

Russell, John *BioIn 14*

Russell, John 1919- *Au&Wr 71, BioIn 14, -17, ConAu 13R, -34NR, IntAu&W 77, -91, IntWW 89, -91, Who 74, -82, -83, -85, -88, -90, -92, WhoAm 78, -80, -82, -84, -86, -88, -90, WhoArt 80, -82, -84, WhoE 75, WorAu 1975, WrDr 86, -88, -90, -92, -94*

Russell, Loris Shano 1904- *AmMWSc 73P, -82, -86, -89, -92, BioIn 5, CanWW 70, -80, -81, -83, -89, McGMS 80, OxCCan SUP, WhoAm 80, WhoWor 80*

Russell, M A B *OxCChiL*

Russell, Patrick *ConAu X, SmATA 4*
Main entry: Sammis, John

Russell, Paul 1942- *BioIn 16, -17, SmATA 57*

Russell, Robert W 1924- *ConAu 34NR*

Russell, Robert William 1924- *ConAu 1R, DrAS 78E, -82E, WhoAm 84*

Russell, Sarah
Main entry: Laski, Marghanita

Russell, Solveig Paulson 1904- *AuBYP 2, -3, BioIn 7, -9, ConAu 1R, -5NR, SmATA 3, WhoPNW*

Russell, William Clark 1844-1911 *Alli SUP, BbD, BiD&SB, BioIn 5, -8, -15, BritAu 19, Chambr 3, CyWA 58, DcBiA, DcEnA, -A, DcLEL, DcNaB S2, EncMys, EvLB, NewC, NotNAT B, OxCEng 67, OxCShps, REn, WhoChL*

Russell Taylor, Elizabeth 1930- *ConAu 81, WrDr 80*

Russo, Marisabina *AuBYP 3, BioIn 16, ChlBIID*

Russo, Susan 1947- *BioIn 14, ConAu 106, SmATA 30*

Russon, Mary Georgina 1937- *BioIn 8, -14, IlsCB 1957*

Rust, Doris *Au&Wr 71, ConAu 13R*

Rutgers VanDerLoeff-Basenau, An Maria 1910- *ConAu 9R, -7NR, OxCChiL, SmATA 22*

Ruth, Babe
Main entry: Ruth, George Herman

Ruth, George Herman 1895-1948 *BioIn 1, -2, -3, -4, -5, -6, -7, -8, -9, -10, -11, -12, -13, -14, -15, -16, -17, BioNews 74, ConAu 116, CurBio 44, -48, DcCathB, NewYTBE 73, WebAB 79, WhScrn 77, WhoHol B, WorAlBi, WorAl*
Pseud./variant:
Ruth, Babe

Ruth, George Herman, Jr. 1895-1948 *BiDAmSp BB*

Ruth, Rod 1912- *BiDScF, BioIn 11, IlsBYP, SmATA 9*

Ruth, Rod 1912-1987 *EncSF 93*

Rutherford, Douglas *Au&Wr 71, ConAu X, SmATA X, TwCCr&M 80, -85, WrDr 76, -80, -82, -84, -86, -88, -90*
Main entry: McConnell, James Douglas R

Rutherford, Douglas 1915- *BioIn 14*

Rutherford, Douglas 1915-1988 *TwCCr&M 91*

Rutherford, Meg 1932- *BioIn 14, ConAu 29R, SmATA 34*

Ruthin, Margaret *BioIn 9, ConAu 38NR, MajAI, SmATA 4, -74, TwCChW 83, -89*
Main entry: Catherall, Arthur

Rutledge, Archibald Hamilton 1883-1973 *AmAu&B, AmLY, BiDSA, BioIn 10, BioNews 74, ChhPo, -S1, -S2, ConAu 5R, -45, REnAL, WhAm 6, WhNAA*

Rutstrum, Calvin 1895-1982 *BioIn 6, -12, ConAu 1R, -106, -1NR, IndAu 1917, IntAu&W 77, MinnWr*

Rutz, Viola Larkin 1932- *BioIn 11, ConAu 21R, SmATA 12*

Ruxton, George Augustus Frederick 1820-1848 *Alli, BioIn 2, -7, -10, EncFWF, OxCAmL 65, REnAL*

Ruzic, Neil P 1930- *ConAu 39NR*

Ruzic, Neil Pierce 1930- *ConAu 17R, -8NR, Future, IntAu&W 77, WhoAm 74, -76, -78, -80, -82, -84, -86, -88, -90, -92, -94, WhoFI 74, WhoUSWr 88, WhoWor 74, WhoWrEP 89, -92*

Ruzicka, Rudolph 1883-1978 *BioIn 1, -3, -5, -6, -8, -11, -13, -14, -15, ConAu 81, GrAmP, IlsBYP, IlsCB 1744, -1946, SmATA 24N, WhAm 7, WhAmArt 85, WhoAm 74, -76, -78, WhoAmA 78, -80N, -82N, -86N, -89N, -91N*

Ryan, Betsy
Main entry: Ryan, Elizabeth

Ryan, Cheli Duran *AuBYP 2S, -3, BioIn 12, ConAu 102, FifBJA, SmATA 20*

Ryan, Elizabeth *WhoAmA 91*

Ryan, Elizabeth 1943- *BioIn 14, ConAu 61, -7NR, SmATA 30*
Pseud./variant:
Ryan, Betsy

Ryan, Elizabeth Anne 1943- *WhoAmW 93*

Ryan, Jeanette Mines 1948- *SmATA X*
Main entry: Mines, Jeanette Marie

Ryan, John Gerald Christopher 1921- *Au&Wr 71, BioIn 12, -13, ConAu 49, -1NR, -16NR, IlsCB 1967, IntAu&W 77, -86, -89, -91, OxCChiL, SmATA 22, WhoArt 80, -82, -84, WrDr 76, -80, -82, -84*

Ryan, Mary E *BioIn 17*

Ryan, Mary E 1953- *SmATA 61*

Ryan, Mary Elizabeth *DrAPF 87, -89, -91, -93*

Ryan, Mary Elizabeth 1953- *WhoUSWr 88, WhoWest 94, WhoWrEP 89, -92*

Ryan, Peter Charles 1939- *BioIn 12, ConAu 61, SmATA 15*

Ryan, Tom Kreusch 1926?- *BioIn 11, WhoAm 80, -82, -84, -86, -88, -90, -92, -94*

Ryback, Eric 1952- *ConAu 37R*

Rybolt, Thomas R *BioIn 17*

Rybolt, Thomas R 1954- *SmATA 62*

Rydberg, Ernest E 1901- *BioIn 12, ConAu 13R, SmATA 21, WrDr 76, -80*

Rydberg, Lou 1908- *BioIn 13, SmATA 27*

Rydberg, Louisa Hampton 1908- *ConAu 69*

Rydell, Wendell
Main entry: Rydell, Wendy

Rydell, Wendy 1927- *BioIn 9, ConAu 33R, IntAu&W 77, -82, SmATA 4, WhoAmW 77, WrDr 76, -80, -82, -84, -86, -88, -90, -92, -94*
Pseud./variant:
Rydell, Wendell

Ryden, Hope *AuBYP 3, InWom SUP, WrDr 92, -94*

Ryden, Hope Elaine *BioIn 10, -11, ConAu 33R, ForWC 70, SmATA 8, WhoE 74, WomWMM A, -B*

Ryder, Joanne *BioIn 14, -16, -17, ConAu 112, SmATA 34*

Ryder, Joanne 1946- *ConAu 133, SixBJA, SmATA 65*

Ryder, Joanne Rose 1946- *MajAI, WrDr 94*

Rye, Anthony *ConAu 37NR, MajAI, SmATA X*
Main entry: Youd, Samuel

Ryland, Lee *ConAu X*
Main entry: Arlandson, Leone

Rylant, Cynthia 1954- *Au&Arts 10, AuBYP 3, BioIn 15, –16, ChlLR 15, ConAu 136, DcAmChF 1985, MajAI, SixBJA, SmATA 44, –76, –13AS, TwCChW 89, TwCYAW, WhoAm 94, WrDr 90, –92, –94*

Rymer, Alta May 1925- *BioIn 14, ConAu 49, –1NR, SmATA 34*

Rymer, James Malcolm *HsB&A, WhoHr&F*

Rymer, James Malcolm 1814-1881 *BioIn 15, PenEncH*

Rymer, James Malcolm 1814-1884 *ScF&FL 92*

S

S, Svend Otto *ConAu 132, SmATA 67*
Main entry: Soerensen, Svend Otto

S, Svend Otto 1916- *OxCChiL, SixBJA, WrDr 94*

Saal, Jocelyn
Main entry: Sachs, Judith

Sabatini, Rafael 1875-1950 *BioIn 2, -4, -11, -14, DcBiA, DcLEL, DcNaB MP, EvLB, FilmgC, HalFC 84, -88, LongCTC, NewC, NotNAT B, ObitOF 79, REn, TwCA, -SUP, TwCLC 47, TwCRHW 90, TwCWr, WhAm 2, WhoSpyF*

Saberhagen, Fred *IntvTCA 2, PenEncH*

Saberhagen, Fred 1930- *BioIn 12, -15, -17, ConAu 7NR, -27NR, -33NR, DcLB 8, MajTwCW, NewEScF, RGTwCSF, ScF&FL 92, ScFSB, SmATA 37, TwCSFW 86, -91, WrDr 84, -86, -88, -90, -92*

Saberhagen, Fred Thomas 1930- *WrDr 94*

Saberhagen, Frederick Thomas 1930- *EncSF 93*

Sabin, Edwin L 1870-1952 *ScF&FL 92, ScFEYrs*

Sabin, Edwin Legrand 1870-1952 *AmAu&B, AmLY, BioIn 2, -12, ChhPo S2, DcAmAu, JBA 34, -51, REnAL, WhAm 5, WhNAA, YABC 2*

Sabin, Francene *BioIn 13, ConAu 69, -11NR, SmATA 27*

Sabin, Louis 1930- *BioIn 13, ConAu 69, -11NR, SmATA 27, WhoE 91*

Sabre, Dirk *ConAu X, IntAu&W 91X, SmATA X, WrDr 76, -80, -82, -84, -86, -88, -90, -92*
Main entry: Laffin, John

Sabre, Dirk 1922- *WrDr 94*

Sabuso *SmATA X*
Main entry: Phillips, Irving W

Sachar, Abram Leon 1899- *BioIn 2, -5, -8, ConAu 97, CurBio 49, DrAS 74H, -82H, LEduc 74, WhNAA, WhoAm 74, -80, -82, -84, -86, -88, -90, -92, -94, WhoAmJ 80, WhoE 85, WhoWorJ 72, -78*

Sachar, Abram Leon 1899-1993 *ConAu 142*

Sachar, Louis 1954- *AuBYP 3, BioIn 16, -17, ChlLR 28, ConAu 81, -15NR, -33NR, SmATA 50, -63*

Sachs, Elizabeth-Ann 1946- *SmATA 48*

Sachs, Judith 1947- *BioIn 16, ConAu 122, SmATA 51, -52, WrDr 90, -92, -94*
Pseud./variant:
Chase, Emily
Diamond, Petra
Diamond, Rebecca
Saal, Jocelyn
Sarasin, Jennifer
Saxon, Antonia

Sachs, Marilyn 1927- *Au&Arts 2, BioIn 15, -16, -17, IntAu&W 86, -89, -91, SmATA 52, -68, -2AS, TwCChW 89, WrDr 86, -88, -90, -92*

Sachs, Marilyn Stickle 1927- *AmWomWr, BioIn 9, ChlLR 2, ConAu 17R, -13NR, ConLC 35, DcAmChF 1960, -1985, FourBJA, IntAu&W 77, -82, MajAI, OxCChiL, SmATA 3, -2AS, TwCChW 78, -83, TwCYAW, WhoAm 92, -94, WhoAmW 75, WrDr 76, -80, -82, -84, -94*

Sack, John 1930- *ConAu 21R, -14NR, WhoE 74, WhoEnt 92*

Sackett, Samuel John 1928- *BioIn 11, ConAu 1R, SmATA 12, WrDr 80, -82, -84*

Sackson, Sid 1920- *BioIn 12, ConAu 69, -12NR, SmATA 16*

Saddler, Allen *ConAu X, IntAu&W 82X, -86X, SmATA X*
Main entry: Richards, R C W

Saddler, Allen 1923- *BioIn 15, -16, IntAu&W 91, WrDr 86, -88, -90, -92, -94*

Saddler, K Allen *ConAu X, IntAu&W 91X, SmATA X*
Main entry: Richards, R C W

Sader, Lillian *IlsBYP*

Sadie, Stanley John 1930- *Au&Wr 71, BioIn 12, ConAu 17R, IntAu&W 77, –89, IntWW 79, –80, –81, –82, –83, –89, –91, SmATA 14, Who 74, WhoMus 72, WhoWor 84, –87, –89, –91, –93, WrDr 76, –80, –82*

Sadler, Arthur Lindsay 1882- *ConAu 5R*

Sadler, Catherine Edwards *BioIn 15, SmATA 45*

Sadler, Catherine Edwards 1952- *BioIn 17, SmATA 60*

Sadler, Glenn Edward 1935- *ChhPo S1, –S2, ConAu 97, DrAS 74E, –78E, –82E, WhoE 93, WhoWest 78, –80*

Sadler, Mark *ConAu X, IntAu&W 91X, SmATA X, TwCCr&M 80, –85, –91, WhoUSWr 88, WhoWrEP 89, –92, WrDr 82, –84, –86, –88, –90, –92*
Main entry: Lynds, Dennis

Sadler, Mark 1924- *BioIn 15, –16, WrDr 94*

Sadler, S Whitechurch d1890 *Alli SUP*

Sagan, Carl 1934- *AmMWSc 73P, –76P, –82, –86, –89, –92, AsBiEn, Au&Arts 2, BioIn 6, –8, –10, –11, –12, –13, –14, –15, –16, –17, ConAu 25R, –11NR, –36NR, ConHero 1, ConIsC 2, ConLC 30, CurBio 70, EncSF 93, IntWW 76, –77, –78, –79, –80, –81, MajTwCW, NewEScF, NewYTBS 85, RAdv 13-5, ScF&FL 92, SmATA 58, UFOEn, WhoAm 74, WhoE 74, WorAlBi, WorAl, WorAu 1975, WrDr 76, –80, –82, –84, –86, –88, –90, –92, –94*

Sagarin, Edward 1913- *AmMWSc 73S, –78S, ConAu 5R, –4NR*

Sagarin, Edward 1913-1986 *BioIn 15, GayLL, ScF&FL 92*

Sagarin, Mary 1903- *ConAu 81*

Sage, Juniper *AmPB, AuBYP 3, ConAu 136, –X, MajAI, ObitOF 79, SmATA 2, –X, YABC X*
Main entry: Brown, Margaret Wise
Hurd, Edith Thacher

Sage, Michael *AuBYP 2S, –3*

Sagsoorian, Paul 1923- *BioIn 11, IlsBYP, SmATA 12*

Saida *SmATA X*
Main entry: LeMair, H Willebeek

Saidman, Anne 1952- *ConAu 142, SmATA 75*

Saint, Dora Jessie 1913- *Au&Wr 71, BioIn 5, –10, –11, –15, –16, ConAu 13R, –7NR, –22NR, IntAu&W 77, –82, –86, –89, –91, SmATA 10, Who 88, –90, –92, WhoWor 78 –91, WorAu 1950, WrDr 76, –80, –82, –84*
Pseud./variant:
Miss Read
Read, Miss

Saint Aubyn, Giles Rowan 1925- *Au&Wr 71, ConAu 5R, IntAu&W 82, WrDr 76, –80*

Saint Briavels, James *SmATA 1*
Main entry: Wood, James Playsted

Saint Clair, Byrd Hooper 1905-1976 *SmATA 28N*
Pseud./variant:
Hooper, Byrd

Saint-Exupery, Antoine de *TwCChW 89B*

Saint-Exupery, Antoine De 1900-1944 *AnCL, AtlBL, Benet 87, BioIn 1, –2, –3, –4, –5, –7, –9, –10, –11, –12, –13, –14, –15, –17, CasWL, ChlLR 10, ClDMEL 47, CnMWL, ConAu 108, –132, CurBio 40, –45, CyWA 58, DcLB 72, EncSF 93, EncWL, –2, EuWr 12, EvEuW, FourBJA, GuFrLit 1, HalFC 84, –88, InSci, LiExTwC, LongCTC, MajTwCW, McGEWB, ModFrL, ModRL, Novels, OxCChiL, OxCEng 85, OxCFr, PenC EUR RAdv 13-2, REn, SmATA 20, TwCA, –SUP, TwCChW 78B, –83B, TwCLC 2, TwCWr, WhDW, WhoTwCL, WorAlBi*
Pseud./variant:
DeSaint-Exupery, Antoine

Saint-Exupery, Antoine Jean Baptiste Marie Roger de 1900-1944 *MajAI*

Saint George, Judith 1931- *BioIn 11, ConAu 69, –14NR, SmATA 13*

Saint John, Elizabeth *ConAu X*
Main entry: John, Elizabeth Beaman

Saint John, Judith 1914- *ChhPo, –S1, –S2, OxCChiL*

Saint John, Nicole *ConAu X, SmATA X*
Main entry: Johnston, Norma

Saint John, Patricia Mary 1919- *Au&Wr 71, ConAu 5R, –3NR, WrDr 76, –80, –82, –84*

Saint John, Percy Bolingbroke 1821-1889 *Alli, –SUP, BbD, BiD&SB, DcEnL, DcNaB, HsB&A*

Saint John, Philip *AuBYP 2, BioIn 7, ConAu X, SmATA X*
Main entry: DelRey, Lester

Saint John, Primus 1939- *BlkAWP, ConAu 113, DrAP 75, DrAPF 83, –85*

Saint John, Robert 1902- *AmAu&B, Au&Wr 71, BioIn 1, –3, –4, –5, BlueB 76, ConAu 1R, –5NR, CurBio 42, EncAJ, IntAu&W 82, WhoAm 74, –76, –78, –80, –82, –84, WhoWor 74, –82, WrDr 76, –80, –82, –84*

Saint John, Wylly Folk 1908-1985 *AuBYP 2S, BioIn 11, ConAu 21R, –117, ForWC 70, IntAu&W 77, –82, SmATA 10, –45N, WhoAmW 74, –75, –77, –81, WhoSSW 75, –76, –78, –80, –82, WrDr 76, –80, –82, –84*
Pseud./variant:
Fox, Eleanor
Larson, Eve
Pierce, Katherine
Vincent, Mary Keith
Williams, Michael

Saint Myer, Ned *ConAu X*
Main entry: Stratemeyer, Edward L

Saintsbury, Noel, Jr. 1884- *CarSB*

Saint Tamara *SmATA X*
Main entry: Kolba, Tamara

Saito, Michiko *AuBYP 2S, ConAu X, SmATA X*
Main entry: Fujiwara, Michiko

Saito, Michiko 1946- *AuBYP 3*

Sakers, Don 1958- *SmATA 72*

Sakharnov, S 1923- *ConAu 133, SmATA 65*
Main entry: Sakharnov, Svyatoslav

Sakharnov, Svyatoslav 1923- *BioIn 17, ConAu 133, SmATA 65*
Pseud./variant:
Sakharnov, S 1923-

Sala, George Augustus 1828-1895 *BenetAL 91, StaCVF*

Sala, George Augustus 1828-1896 *ScFEYrs*

Sala, George Augustus Henry 1828-1895 *Alli, –SUP, BbD, BiD&SB, BritAu 19, CasWL, CelCen, Chambr 3, ChhPo, DcBiPP, DcBrBI, DcCathB, DcEnA, –A, DcEnL, DcEuL, DcLEL, DcNaB, EvLB, HarEnUS, NewC, OxCAusL, OxCEng 67, –85, REn, REnAL*

Sala, George Augustus Henry 1828-1896 *BioIn 16*

Salai, Andrea *DcAmChF 1960*

Salamanca, Lucy *ConAu 130, –X*
Main entry: DelBarco, Lucy Salamanca

Salamanca, Lucy d1989 *BioIn 17*

Salamanca, Lucy 1900?-1989 *SmATA X*

Salassi, Otto R *BioIn 15*

Salassi, Otto R d1993 *NewYTBS 93*

Salassi, Otto R 1939- *BioIn 16, ConAu 106, SixBJA, SmATA 38*

Salassi, Otto Russell 1939-1993 *ConAu 142, SmATA 77*

Saldutti, Denise 1953- *BioIn 15, SmATA 39*

Sale, Isobel Morton *ChhPo, IlsCB 1946*
Main entry: Morton-Sale, Isobel

Sale, Isobel Morton- 1904- *BioIn 14*

Sale, J Kirkpatrick
Main entry: Sale, Kirkpatrick

Sale, John Morton *IlsCB 1946*
Main entry: Morton-Sale, John

Sale, Kirkpatrick *BioIn 17*

Sale, Kirkpatrick 1937- *ConAu 13R, –10NR, ConLC 68, IntAu&W 82, –91, WhoAm 92, –94, WrDr 88, –90, –92, –94*
Pseud./variant:
Sale, J Kirkpatrick

Sale-Barker, Mrs *CarSB*

Sales, Grover 1919- *ConAmTC, ConAu 65, WhoWest 87*

Saletan, Alberta L 1917- *WrDr 76, –80, –82, –84*

Salinger, J D *DrAPF 87, –93, IntvTCA 2*

Salinger, J D 1919- *AmAu&B, AmWr, Au&Arts 2, Au&Wr 71, Benet 87, BenetAL 91, BioIn 2, –4, –5, –6, –7, –8, –9, –10, –11, –14, –15, –16, –17, BlueB 76, CamGEL, CamGLE, CamHAL, CasWL, CelR, –90, ChlLR 18, CnMWL, ConAu 5R, ConLC 1, –3, –8, –12, –56, ConNov 72, –76, –82, –86, –91, CyWA 89, DcLB 2, –102, DrAF 76, DrAPF 83, –85, –89, –91, EncWL, –2, IntAu&W 77, –91, IntWW 74, –75, –76, –77, –78, –79, –80, –81, –82, –83, –89, –91, LongCTC, MagSAmL, MajTwCW, ModAL, –S1, NewCon, Novels, OxCAmL 65, –83, OxCChiL, OxCEng 85, PenC AM, RAdv 1, –13-1, REn, REnAL, RfGAmL 87, ShSCr 2, SmATA 67, TwCA SUP, TwCWr, WebE&AL, WhoTwCL, WorAlBi, WorAl, WorLitC, WrDr 76, –80, –82, –84, –86, –88, –90, –92*

Salinger, Jerome David 1919- *ConAu 39NR, MajAI, TwCYAW, WrDr 94*

Salisbury, Graham 1944- *SmATA 76*

Salkey, Andrew 1928- *BioIn 9, -12, -14, -16, BlkAuII, -92, BlkWr 1, CamGLE, CasWL, ChhPo S2, ConAu 5R, -13NR, -27NR, ConNov 72, -76, -82, -86, -91, FifCWr, IntAu&W 77, -91, LiExTwC, LongCTC, Novels, OxCChiL, PenC ENG, RAdv 13-2, SelBAAf, SmATA 35, TwCChW 78, -83, -89, WebE&AL, WrDr 76, -80, -82, -84, -86, -88, -90, -92*

Sallis, Susan 1929- *BioIn 16, SmATA 55, TwCRHW 90*

Sallis, Susan Diana
Pseud./variant:
Meadmore, Susan

Salmon, Annie Elizabeth 1899- *Au&Wr 71, BioIn 11, ConAu 69, -12NR, SmATA 13, WrDr 76, -80, -82, -84*
Pseud./variant:
Ashley, Elizabeth
Martin, Nancy

Salmon, Edward *OxCChiL*

Salten, Felix *AuBYP 2, -3, BioIn 1, -4, -5, -8, -13, ClDMEL 47, ConAu 137, -X, CurBio 45, CyWA 58, LongCTC, MajAI, ObitOF 79, OxCChiL, OxCGer 76, SmATA X, TwCA, -SUP, TwCChW 78B, -83B, -89B, WhAm 2, WhoChL*
Main entry: Salzmann, Siegmund

Salten, Felix 1869-1945 *WrChl*

Salten, Felix 1869-1947 *OxCGer 86*

Salter, Cedric *Au&Wr 71, BioIn 12, ConAu X, SmATA X, WrDr 80, -82, -84, -86, -88, -90, -92*
Main entry: Knight, Francis Edgar

Salter-Mathieson, Nigel Cedric Stephen 1932- *ConAu 1R*

Saltman, Judith 1947- *ConAu 126, IntAu&W 91, SmATA 64, WhoCanL 92*

Saltzberg, Barney *AuBYP 3*

Salvadori, Mario G 1907- *BioIn 8, -10, -13, ConAu 108, SmATA 40, WhoAm 80*

Salvadori, Mario George 1907- *BioIn 15*

Salwi, Dilip M 1952- *DcChlFi*

Salzer, L E *ConAu X, SmATA X*
Main entry: Wilson, Lionel

Salzman, Marian 1959- *SmATA 77*

Salzman, Marian Lynn 1959- *WhoAmW 87*

Salzman, Siegmund 1869-1945 *AuBYP 3*

Salzman, Yuri *BioIn 15, SmATA 42*

Salzmann, C G 1744-1811 *CarSB, OxCChiL*

Salzmann, Siegmund 1869-1945 *AuBYP 2, ConAu 108, -137, MajAI, SmATA 25*
Pseud./variant:
Finder, Martin
Salten, Felix

Samachson, Dorothy 1914- *AuBYP 2, -3, BioIn 7, -9, ConAu 9R, ForWC 70, SmATA 3*

Samachson, Joseph 1906- *AmMWSc 73P, AuBYP 2, -3, BioIn 7, -9, ConAu 17R, SmATA 3*
Pseud./variant:
Miller, John
Morrison, William

Samachson, Joseph 1906-1980 *BioIn 16, ConAu 122, EncSF 93, ScF&FL 92, SmATA 52N*
Pseud./variant:
Sterling, Brett

Sammis, John 1942- *BioIn 9, ConAu 29R, SmATA 4*
Pseud./variant:
Russell, Patrick

Sampson, Emma Keats Speed 1868-1947 *SmATA 68*
Pseud./variant:
Sanderson, Margaret Love
Van Dyne, Edith

Sampson, Emma Speed 1868-1947 *AmAu&B, BioIn 1, -3, -17, ConAu 135, DcNAA, LiHiK, ObitOF 79, WhAm 2, WhAmArt 85, WhNAA*

Sampson, Fay *ChlFicS*

Sampson, Fay 1935- *BioIn 15, ConAu 101, -18NR, ScF&FL 92, SmATA 40, -42*

Sampson, Fay Elizabeth 1935- *ConAu 40NR*

Samson, Anne Stringer 1933- *BioIn 9, ConAu 25R, SmATA 2, WhoAmW 74*

Samson, Joan 1937-1976 *BioIn 11, ConAu 73, ScF&FL 92, SmATA 13, WrDr 76*

Samstag, Nicholas 1903-1968 *AuBYP 2, -3, BioIn 8, ConAu 5R, -25R*

Samton, Sheila White *AuBYP 3*

Samuel, Helen Jo 1909- *SingR 1*

Samuels, Barbara *AuBYP 3*

Samuels, Charles 1902-1982 *BioIn 11, –12, ConAu 1R, –106, –5NR, SmATA 12*

Samuels, Cynthia K *AuBYP 3, BioIn 16*

Samuels, Cynthia K 1946- *ConAu 135*

Samuels, Cynthia Kalish 1946- *WhoAm 94, WhoAmW 89, –91, –93, WhoEnt 92, WrDr 94*

Samuels, Gertrude *AuBYP 2, –3, BioIn 7, –12, ConAu 9R, –6NR, ForWC 70, NatPD 77, –81, SmATA 17, WhoAmW 75, –77, –81, WhoWorJ 72, –78*

Sanborn, Duane *AuBYP 3*

Sanborn, Duane 1914- *AuBYP 2, BioIn 15, ConAu 1R, –1NR, SmATA 38*
Pseud./variant:
Bradley, Duane

Sancha, Sheila 1924- *BioIn 15, ConAu 69, –11NR, SmATA 38*

Sanchez, Carlos 1908- *BioIn 1, ChhPo, ConICB, IlsCB 1744*

Sanchez, Sonia *DrAPF 87, –89, –91, –93*

Sanchez, Sonia 1934- *ArtclWW 2, BenetAL 91, BioIn 10, –13, –17, BlkAWP, BlkLC, BlkWWr, BlkWr 1, –2, BlkWrNE, BlmGWL, BroadAu, ChlLR 18, ConAu 33R, –24NR, ConBlAP 88, ConLC 5, ConPo 75, –80, –85, –91, CroCAP, CyWA 89, DcLB 41, –DS8, DrAP 75, DrBlPA 90, FemiCLE, InB&W 80, LivgBAA, MajAI, MajTwCW, NegAl 76, –83, –89, NotBlAW 92, SelBAAf, SelBAAu, SmATA 22, WhoBlA 80, –85, WrDr 76, –80, –82, –84, –86, –88, –90, –92*

Sanchez-Silva, Jose Maria *TwCChW 89B*

Sanchez-Silva, Jose Maria 1911- *BioIn 9, –12, ChlLR 12, ConAu 73, MajAI, SmATA 16, ThrBJA, TwCChW 78B, –83B*

Sand, George X *AuBYP 2S, –3, BioIn 15, ConAu 13R, SmATA 45, WhoUSWr 88, WhoWrEP 89, –92*

Sandak, Cass R 1950- *BioIn 15, –16, ConAu 108, SmATA 37, –51*

Sandberg, Harold W 1902- *BioIn 6, MinnWr*

Sandberg, Inger 1930- *BioIn 9, –12, ConAu 65, –11NR, –26NR, OxCChiL, SmATA 15, ThrBJA, TwCChW 78B*

Sandberg, Karl C 1931- *BioIn 14, ConAu 49, DrAS 74F, –78F, –82F, SmATA 35, WhoAm 74, –76, –78, –80*

Sandberg, Lasse Eric Mathias 1924- *OxCChiL*

Sandberg, Lasse Erik Mathias 1924- *BioIn 8, –9, –12, IlsBYP, IlsCB 1957, –1967, SmATA 15, ThrBJA, TwCChW 78B*

Sandberg, Margaret M 1919- *ConAu 61*

Sandburg, Carl *IntvTCA 2*

Sandburg, Carl 1878-1967 *AmAu&B, AmWr, AnCL, ASCAP 66, AtlBL, AuBYP 2, –3, Benet 87, BenetAL 91, BioIn 1, –2, –3, –4, –5, –6, –7, –8, –9, –10, –11, –12, –13, –14, –15, –16, –17, CamGEL, CamGLE, CamHAL, CasWL, Chambr 3, ChhPo, –S1, –S2, CnDAL, CnE&AP, CnMWL, ConAmA, ConAmL, ConAu 5R, –25R, –35NR, ConLC 1, –4, –10, –15, –35, CurBio 40, –63, –67, CyWA 58, DcLB 17, –54, DcLEL, EncAB-H, EncAJ, EncFCWM 69, EncWL, –2, EvLB, FamPYP, LongCTC, MagSAmL, MajTwCW, MakMC, ModAL, –S1, –S2, MorMA, NewGrDA 86, ObitOF 79, ObitT 1961, OxCAmH, OxCAmL 65, –83, OxCChiL, OxCEng 67, OxCMus, PenC AM, PoeCrit 2, RAdv 1, –13-1, –13-3, REn, REnAL, RealN, RfGAmL 87, SixAP, SmATA 8, Str&VC, TwCA, –SUP, TwCWr, WebAB 74, –79, WebE&AL, WhDW, WhAm 4, WhoTwCL, WisWr, WorAlBi, WorAl, WorLitC, WrChl*
Pseud./variant:
Militant
Phillips, Jack

Sandburg, Carl August 1878-1967 *MajAI*

Sandburg, Charles *AuBYP 3, ConAu 35NR, MajAI, MajTwCW*

Sandburg, Helga *BioIn 16, IntAu&W 91*

Sandburg, Helga 1918- *AuBYP 2, –3, BioIn 4, –8, –9, –11, BlueB 76, ConAu 1R, –5NR, ConPo 70, ForWC 70, IntAu&W 82, –86, IntWWP 82, MichAu 80, SmATA 3, –10AS, ThrBJA, WhoAm 74, –76, –78, –80, –82, –84, –86, –88, –90, –92, –94, WhoAmW 74, –75, –77, WhoUSWr 88, WhoWrEP 89, –92, WrDr 80, –82, –84, –86, –88, –90, –92, –94*

Sanderlin, George 1915- *BioIn 9, ConAu 13R, DrAS 74E, IntAu&W 77, –82, –89, SmATA 4, WhoUSWr 88, WhoWrEP 89, –92, WrDr 76, –80, –82, –84, –86, –88, –90, –92, –94*

Sanderlin, Owenita 1916- *BioIn 11, ConAu 17R, –7NR, SmATA 11, WrDr 76, –80, –82, –84, –86, –88, –90, –92, –94*
Pseud./variant:
Kenny, Kathryn

Sanderlin, Owenita Harrah 1916- *WhoWrEP 92*

Sanders, Byrne Hope 1902- *CanWW 70, –80, –81, ConAu X, OxCCan*

Pseud./variant:
Sperry, Byrne Hope

Sanders, Jack Thomas 1935- *ConAu 37R, DrAS 74P, –78P, –82P, WhoAm 84, –86, –88, –90, –92, –94, WhoRel 75, –77, –92, WhoWest 74, –76*

Sanders, Jeanne *ConAu 57, –X, WrDr 76, –80, –82, –84, –86, –88, –90*
Pseud./variant:
Rundle, Anne

Sanders, Lawrence 1920- *AuSpks, BestSel 89-4, BioIn 8, –11, –12, –14, –16, –17, ConAu 81, –33NR, ConLC 41, CrtSuMy, CurBio 89, EncSF 93, IntAu&W 77, –91, MajTwCW, Novels, ScF&FL 92, ScFSB, TwCCr&M 80, –85, –91, WhoAm 80, –82, –84, –86, –88, –90, –92, –94, WhoUSWr 88, WhoWrEP 89, –92, WorAlBi, WorAl, WrDr 82, –84, –86, –88, –90, –92, –94*

Sanders, Scott R 1945- *BioIn 17, SmATA 56*

Sanders, Scott Russell *DrAPF 87, –89, –91, –93*

Sanders, Scott Russell 1945- *ConAu 35NR, EncSF 93, ScF&FL 92, WhoUSWr 88, WhoWrEP 89, –92*

Sanders, Sol 1926- *ConAu 49, –2NR*

Sanders, Sylvia 1931- *WhoAmP 75, –77*

Sanders, Winston P *AuBYP 2S, –3, ConAu X, –34NR, EncSF 93, IntAu&W 82X, –86X, MajTwCW, SmATA X*
Main entry: Anderson, Poul

Sanderson, Irma 1912- *BioIn 17, ConAu 135, SmATA 66, WrDr 94*

Sanderson, Ivan T *EncSF 93*

Sanderson, Ivan T 1911-1973 *AmAu&B, AmMWSc 73P, –76P, AuBYP 2, BioIn 1, –4, –5, –7, –9, –10, –11, ConAu 37R, –41R, EncO&P 1S1, –2, –3, IlsCB 1744, –1946, InSci, NewYTBE 73, REnAL, SmATA 6, TwCA, –SUP, UFOEn*
Pseud./variant:
Roberts, Terence

Sanderson, Ivan Terence 1911-1973 *AuBYP 3*

Sanderson, Margaret Love *ConAu 135, SmATA 68*
Main entry: Keats, Emma
Sampson, Emma Keats Speed

Sanderson, Ruth L 1951- *BioIn 12, IlsCB 1967, SmATA 41*

Sandford, Nell Mary 1936- *ConAu 81, WrDr 76, –80*
Pseud./variant:
Dunn, Nell

Sandham, Elizabeth *Alli, BiDLA, CarSB, OxCChiL*

Sandin, Joan 1942- *BioIn 11, –12, –16, IlsBYP, IlsCB 1967, SixBJA, SmATA 12*

Sandison, Janet *AuBYP 3, CmScLit, ConAu X, SmATA X*
Main entry: Cameron, Elizabeth Jane

Sandman Lilius, Irmelin *ScF&FL 92, TwCChW 83B, –89B*

Sandoz, Edouard 1918-1970 *BioIn 5, –9, IlsBYP, IlsCB 1946*

Sandoz, Mari *IntvTCA 2*

Sandoz, Mari 1896-1966 *AmAu&B, AmWomWr, AuBYP 2, Benet 87, BioAmW, BioIn 3, –4, –5, –7, –9, –10, –12, –14, –17, CnDAL, ConAu 1R, –25R, –17NR, ConLC 28, CyWA 89, DcAmB S8, DcLB 9, EncFWF, FemiCLE, HanAmWH, InWom SUP, MajTwCW, NotAW MOD, ObitOF 79, OxCAmL 65, –83, REn, REnAL, SmATA 5, ThrBJA, TwCA, –SUP, TwCWW 91, WhAm 4, WhNAA*
Pseud./variant:
Macumber, Mari

Sandoz, Mari 1901-1966 *ArtclWW 2, BenetAL 91*

Sandoz, Mari Susette 1901-1966 *DcAmChF 1960*

Sandoz, Marie 1901-1966 *AuBYP 3*

Sandstrom, George F *IlsBYP*

Sandstrom, Marita *IlsBYP*

Sanfield, Steve *AuBYP 3, DrAPF 87, –89, –91, –93*

Sanfield, Steve 1937- *ConAu 124, WhoUSWr 88, WhoWrEP 89, –92*

Sanford, Agnes 1897- *ConAu 17R*

Sanford, Agnes 1897-1976 *SmATA 61*

Sanford, Agnes Mary White 1897-1976 *BioIn 17*

Sanford, Doris 1937- *SmATA 69*

Sanford, Mary Bouchier *OxCCan, WomNcv*

Sanger, Frances Ella *AuBYP 2, –3, BioIn 7*

Sanger, Marjory Bartlett 1920- *AuBYP 2S, -3, BioIn 11, ConAu 37R, IntAu&W 86, -91, SmATA 8, WrDr 76, -80, -82, -84, -86, -88, -90, -92, -94*

Sankey, Alice 1910- *BioIn 13, ConAu 61, SmATA 27*

Sansom, Clive 1910- *EngPo*

Sansom, Clive 1910-1981 *ConAu 104, OxCAusL, OxCChiL, WrDr 82, -84*

San Souci, Robert D 1946- *ConAu 108, ScF&FL 92, SmATA 40*

Santalo, Lois *AuBYP 2, -3, BioIn 8*

Santee, Ross 1888- *BenetAL 91*

Santee, Ross 1888?-1965 *AmAu&B, ArizL, BioIn 2, -3, -4, -7, -8, ConAu 108, EncFWF, ObitOF 79, REnAL, TwCA SUP, TwCWW 91, WhAmArt 85*

Santee, Ross 1889- *BioIn 14*

Santesson, Hans Stefan 1914?-1975 *BioIn 10, -14, ConAu 57, -93, ConSFA, EncSF 93, SmATA 30N*

Santos, Helen *IntAu&W 86X, TwCChW 89*

Sapieha, Christine *IlsBYP*

Sapieyevski, Anne L *ScF&FL 92*

Sapieyevski, Anne Lindbergh *AuBYP 3*

Sapieyevski, Anne Lindbergh 1940- *ConAu 113, -115, SmATA 35*
Pseud./variant:
Feydy, Anne Lindbergh
Lindbergh, Anne

Sapper 1887-1937 *HalFC 88*

Sapper 1888-1937 *BioIn 14, CrtSuMy, EncSF 93, HalFC 84, Novels, OxCChiL, OxCEng 85, ScF&FL 92, ScFEYrs, TwCCr&M 80, -85, -91, TwCLC 44*

Sara 1925- *WrDr 86*

Sara 1950- *SmATA 75*
Main entry: De La Roche Saint Andre, Anne

Sara, Dorothy 1897?-1976 *ConAu 69, ForWC 70, WhoAmW 75, -77*

Sarac, Roger *ConAu X, ConSFA, IntAu&W 91X, SmATA X*
Main entry: Caras, Roger Andrew

Sarac, Roger 1928- *EncSF 93*

Sarah, Duchess Of York 1959- *BioIn 14, -15, -16, -17, ConAu 135, CurBio 87, SmATA 66, WrDr 94*
Main entry: Ferguson, Sarah

Sarasin, Jennifer
Main entry: Sachs, Judith

Sarasy, Phyllis Powell 1930- *AuBYP 2, -3, BioIn 7, ConAu 13R*

Sarg, Tony 1880-1942 *AmAu&B, BioIn 1, -2, -11, ChhPo, -S1, -S2, ConICB, CurBio 42, DcBrBI, DcNAA, IlrAm 1880, -C, JBA 34, -51, ObitOF 79, OxCChiL, REnAL, WhAm 2, WhAmArt 85, WorECar, YABC 1*

Sargent, George Etell 1808?-1883 *Alli, -SUP, CarSB, ChhPo S1*

Sargent, John Singer 1856-1925 *ArtsAmW 3, ArtsNiC, AtlBL, Benet 87, BioIn 1, -2, -3, -4, -6, -7, -9, -10, -11, -12, -13, -14, -15, -16, ChhPo, -S1, ClaDrA, DcBrAr 1, DcNaB 1922, DcVicP 2, EncAB-H, HarEnUS, IntDcAA 90, LongCTC, MorMA, OxCAmH, OxCAmL 65, OxCArt, OxDcArt, PhDcTCA 77, RComAH, REn, REnAL, TwCPaSc, WebAB 74, -79, WhDW, WhAm 1, WhAmArt 85, WorAlBi, WorAl*

Sargent, Maud Elizabeth *ChhPo, -S1, -S2, PoIre*

Sargent, Pamela *BioIn 16, DrAPF 87, -89, -91, -93*

Sargent, Pamela 1948- *BioIn 12, -13, ConAu 61, -18AS, -8NR, DcLB 8, DrAF 76, DrAPF 83, -85, EncSF 93, IntAu&W 91, NewEScF, ScF&FL 92, ScFSB, SixBJA, SmATA 29, TwCChW 89, TwCSFW 86, -91, TwCYAW, WhoAm 94, WhoAmW 89, -91, WhoE 93, WrDr 84, -86, -88, -90, -92*

Sargent, Robert Edward 1933- *BioIn 8, -9, ConAu 21R, IlsCB 1957, SmATA 2, WhoAm 82, -84, -86*

Sargent, Sarah 1937- *BioIn 15, -16, ConAu 106, ScF&FL 92, SixBJA, SmATA 41, -44*

Sargent, Shirley *BioIn 17*

Sargent, Shirley 1927- *AuBYP 2, -3, BioIn 7, -11, ConAu 1R, -2NR, ForWC 70, SmATA 11*

Sari *IlsBYP, IlsCB 1946, SmATA X*
Main entry: Fleur, Anne

Sari 1901- *BioIn 14*

Saris, Anthony 1924- *BioIn 5, IlrAm 1880, -G, WhoGrA 82*

Saris, Anthony Simiers 1924- *WhoAm 86*

Sarnoff, Jane 1937- *AuBYP 2S, -3, BioIn 11, ConAu 53, -9NR, FifBJA, SmATA 10*

Sarnoff, Paul 1918- *BioIn 12, ConAu 5R, -2NR, -18NR, -40NR, WhoE 89, -91, -93*

Saroyan, William *IntvTCA 2*

Saroyan, William 1908- *WorAlBi*

Saroyan, William 1908-1981 *AmAu&B, AmNov, AnObit 1981, Au&Wr 71, Benet 87, BenetAL 91, BiE&WWA, BioIn 1, -2, -3, -4, -5, -6, -7, -8, -9, -10, -11, -12, -13, -14, -15, -17, BlueB 76, CamGLE, CamGWoT, CamHAL, CasWL, CelR, CmCal, CnDAL, CnMD, CnMWL, CnThe, ConAmA, ConAu 5R, -103, -30NR, ConDr 73, -77, -93, ConLC 1, -8, -10, -29, -56, ConNov 72, -76, CurBio 40, -72, -81N, CyWA 58, -89, DcLB 7, -9, -86, -Y81A, DcLEL, DrAF 76, EncWL, -2, EncWT, EvLB, FilmgC, HalFC 84, -88, IntAu&W 77, IntDcT 2, IntWW 74, -75, -77, -78, -79, -80, -81, -81N, LongCTC, MagSAmL, MajTwCW, McGEWB, McGEWD 72, -84, ModAL, -S1, ModWD, NewYTBE 72, NewYTBS 81, NotNAT, -A, Novels, OxCAmL 65, -83, OxCAmT 84, OxCThe 67, -83, PenC AM, PlP&P, RAdv 1, -13-2, REn, REnAL, REnWD, RfGAmL 87, RfGShF, SmATA 23, -24N, TwCA, -SUP, TwCWr, WebAB 74, -79, WebE&AL, WhAm 7, Who 74, -82N, WhoAm 74, -76, -78, -80, WhoThe 72, -77, -81, WhoTwCL, WhoWor 74, WorAl, WorLitC, WrDr 76, -80, -82*
Pseud./variant:
Goryan, Sirak

Sarton, Eleanore Marie
Main entry: Sarton, May

Sarton, May *DrAPF 87, -89, -91, -93, IntvTCA 2*

Sarton, May 1912- *AmAu&B, AmWomWr, ArtclWW 2, Benet 87, BenetAL 91, BioAmW, BioIn 4, -5, -8, -10, -11, -12, -13, -14, -15, -16, -17, BlmGWL, BlueB 76, CamGLE, CamHAL, ConAu 1R, -1NR, -34NR, ConLC 4, -49, ConNov 72, -76, -82, -86, -91, ConPo 70, -75, -80, -85, -91, CurBio 82, CyWA 89, DcLB 48, -Y81B, DrAF 76, DrAP 75, DrAPF 83, -85, DrAS 74E, -78E, -82E, EncWL 2, FemiCLE, InWom SUP, IntAu&W 77, -86, -91, MajTwCW, ModAL, -S1, -S2, NewYTBS 83, Novels, OxCAmL 65, -83, PenC AM, RAdv 1, REnAL, SmATA 36, TwCA SUP, WhoAm 74, -76, -78, -80, -82, -90, -92, WhoAmW 81, -83, -85, -87, -89, -91, -93, WhoWor 74, WrDr 76, -80, -82, -84, -86, -88, -90, -92, -94*
Pseud./variant:
Sarton, Eleanore Marie

Sasaki, Tazu 1932- *AuBYP 2S, -3, ConAu 25R, -10NR*

Saseen, Sharon Dillon 1949- *SmATA 59*
Pseud./variant:
Dillon, Sharon Saseen

Saseen, Sharon Louise 1949- *WhoSSW 91, -93*

Sasek, Miroslav 1916-1980 *Au&Wr 71, BioIn 8, -9, -12, -13, BkP, ChlLR 4, ConAu 73, -101, IlsCB 1957, -1967, SmATA 16, -23N, ThrBJA*

Satchwell, John *BioIn 16, SmATA 49*

Satterfield, Charles *ConAu 141, -37NR, EncSF 93, MajTwCW, SmATA 76*
Main entry: del Rey, Lester

Sattler, Helen Roney *BioIn 16*

Sattler, Helen Roney 1921- *AuBYP 2S, -3, BioIn 9, ChlLR 24, ConAu 33R, -14NR, -31NR, SixBJA, SmATA 4, WhoUSWr 88, WhoWrEP 89, -92*

Sattler, Helen Roney 1921-1992 *SmATA 74*

Sauer, Julia 1891-1983 *TwCChW 89*

Sauer, Julia L 1891-1983 *ScF&FL 92*

Sauer, Julia Lina 1891-1983 *BioIn 6, -13, -14, ConAu 81, MorJA, SmATA 32, -36N, TwCChW 83, WhoLibS 55*

Saul, Wendy 1946- *BioIn 15, ConAu 114, SmATA 42*

Saunders, Allen 1899- *ArtCS, ConAu 69*

Saunders, Allen 1899-1986 *BioIn 14, ConAu 118, EncACom, NewYTBS 86*

Saunders, Blanche 1906-1964 *AuBYP 2, -3, Au&Wr 71, BioIn 2, -7, ConAu P-1*

Saunders, Caleb *AuBYP 2, -3, ConAu X, EncSF 93, MajAI, MajTwCW, SmATA 69, -X*
Main entry: Heinlein, Robert A

Saunders, Hilary Aidan St. George 1898-1951
Pseud./variant:
Beeding, Francis

Saunders, Hilary Aidan St George 1898-1951 *BioIn 1, -2, -3, -4, -14, CathA 1930, ConAu 121, CurBio 43, -52, DcLEL, EncMys, EvLB, LongCTC, NewC, ObitOF 79, TwCA, -SUP, TwCCr&M 80, -85*

Saunders, Hilary Aiden St George *TwCCr&M 91*

Saunders, Jean 1932- *ConAu 102, –19NR, IntAu&W 82, –86, TwCRHW 90, WrDr 76, –80, –82, –84, –86, –88, –90, –92, –94*

Saunders, Keith 1910- *BioIn 11, ConAu 57, SmATA 12*

Saunders, Margaret Marshall 1861-1947 *BiD&SB, BioIn 1, –4, –17, BlmGWL, CanNov, CanWr, CarSB, DcAmAu, DcLB 92, DcNAA, FemiCLE, JBA 34, ObitOF 79, OxCAmL 65, OxCCan, TwCA, –SUP, WhAm 2, WhNAA, WomWWA 14, WomNov*
Pseud./variant:
Saunders, Marshall

Saunders, Marshall *WomNov*
Main entry: Saunders, Margaret Marshall

Saunders, Marshall 1861-1947 *OxCCanL, OxCChiL*

Saunders, Rubie 1929- *BioIn 12, ConAu 49, ForWC 70, SmATA 21*

Saunders, Rubie Agnes 1929- *WhoAm 86, –90, –94, WhoAmW 93*

Saunders, Susan 1945- *ConAu 106, SmATA 41, –46*
Pseud./variant:
Hughes, Sara

Sauro, Regina Calderone 1924- *ConAu 9R, ForWC 70*

Sautel, Maureen Ann 1951- *ConAu 61*
Pseud./variant:
McGinn, Maureen Ann

Sauter, Edwin Charles Scott, Jr. 1930- *ConAu 13R*

Sauvage, Sylvain 1888- *BioIn 1, IlsCB 1744*

Sauvain, Philip Arthur 1933- *ConAu 104, –21NR, IntAu&W 77, –91, WrDr 76, –80, –82, –84, –86, –88, –90, –92, –94*

Savage, Blake *ConAu 131, –X, –29NR, EncSF 93, SmATA 65, –X*
Main entry: Goodwin, Harold Leland

Savage, Blake 1914-1990 *BioIn 16, –17*

Savage, Deborah *DcAmChF 1985*

Savage, Deborah 1955- *SmATA 76*

Savage, Katharine James 1905-1989 *BioIn 17, ConAu 128, SmATA 61*

Savage, Katharine James Sanford 1905- *Au&Wr 71, ConAu 13R, FourBJA*

Savage, Steele 1900- *BioIn 5, IlsBYP, IlsCB 1946*

Savery, Constance 1897- *AuBYP 3*

Savery, Constance Winifred 1897- *AuBYP 2, Au&Wr 71, BioIn 1, –2, –7, –9, ConAu 9R, CurBio 48, IntAu&W 77, –86, –91, JBA 51, SmATA 1, WrDr 76, –80, –82, –84, –86, –88, –90, –92, –94*

Saville, Malcolm 1901-1982 *AnObit 1982, BioIn 8, –13, –14, ChhPo S1, ConAu 101, –107, IntAu&W 82, OxCChiL, ScF&FL 92, SmATA 23, –31N, TelT, TwCChW 78, –83, –89, Who 74, –82, –83N, WhoChL, WrDr 76, –80, –82*

Saviozzi, Adriana Mazza *BioIn 8, ConAu 1R, IlsCB 1957, SmATA X*
Main entry: Mazza, Adriana

Savitt, Sam *IntAu&W 91, WhoAmA 86, –89, –91, WrDr 86, –88, –90, –92, –94*

Savitt, Sam 1917- *AuBYP 2, –3, BioIn 7, –11, ConAu 1R, –1NR, –17NR, IntAu&W 77, SmATA 8, WhoAmA 78, –80, –82, –84, WhoAmJ 80, WhoE 77, WrDr 76, –80, –82, –84*

Savitz, Harriet May 1933- *AuBYP 2S, –3, BioIn 10, ConAu 41R, –14NR, –32NR, FifBJA, MajAI, SmATA 5, –72, –9AS, TwCYAW, WhoAmW 81, –83, WhoE 83, –85, –86, –89*

Savoldi, Gloria Root *AuBYP 2, –3, BioIn 8*

Sawicki, Norma Jean *AuBYP 3*

Sawyer, Corinne Holt 1924- *ConAu 17R, DrAS 74E, –82E, WhoAmW 75, –83, WhoUSWr 88, WhoWrEP 89, –92, WrDr 76, –80, –82, –84, –86, –88*
Pseud./variant:
Rickert, Corinne Holt

Sawyer, Frederick Donald 1947- *SmATA 72*

Sawyer, Mark *ConAu X*
Main entry: Greenhood, David

Sawyer, Ruth 1880-1970 *AmAu&B, AmLY, AmWomPl, AmWomWr, AnCL, AuBYP 2, –3, BioAmW, BioIn 2, –4, –6, –7, –8, –9, –11, –12, –14, BkCL, CarSB, ChhPo, ConAu 73, –37NR, DcLB 22, HerW, InWom SUP, JBA 51, MajAI, NewbMB 1922, NotAW MOD, OxCChiL, SmATA 17, TwCA, –SUP, TwCChW 78, –83, –89, WhAm 5, WhNAA, WomNov, WrChl*

Saxby, H M
Main entry: Saxby, Henry Maurice

Saxby, Henry Maurice 1924- *SmATA 71*
Pseud./variant:
Saxby, H M

Saxby, Jessie Margaret 1842-1940 *StaCVF, WomNov*

Saxby, Jessie Margaret Edmondston 1842- *ChhPo, –S1, –S2, WhoLA*

Saxe, John Godfrey 1816-1887 *Alli, –SUP, AmAu, AmAu&B, AnCL, AuBYP 2, –3, BenetAL 91, BbD, BiD&SB, BioIn 7, –13, Chambr 3, ChhPo, –S1, –S2, CnDAL, CyAL, DcAmAu, DcEnL, DcLEL, DcNAA, HarEnUS, OxCAmL 65, –83, REnAL, WhAm HS*

Saxon, Antonia
Main entry: Sachs, Judith

Saxon, Gladys Relyea *ConAu 5R*
Pseud./variant:
Borden, M
Seyton, Marion

Say, Allen 1937- *BioIn 13, –16, –17, ChlBIlD, ChlLR 22, ConAu 29R, –30NR, MajAI, SixBJA, SmATA 28, –69, WhoAsA 94*

Sayers, Charles Marshall 1892- *AuBYP 2, –3, BioIn 7*

Sayers, Dorothy L 1893-1957 *Benet 87, BioIn 14, –16, –17, BlmGEL, BlmGWL, CamGLE, CnDBLB 6, ConAu 119, ContDcW 89, CrtSuMy, CyWA 89, DcLB 77, –100, EncBrWW, HalFC 88, MagSWL, MajTwCW, ModBrL S2, RfGEnL 91, ShSWr, TwCCr&M 91, WorAlBi*

Sayers, Dorothy Leigh 1893-1957 *ArtclWW 2, BioIn 2, –4, –8, –10, –11, –12, –13, CasWL, Chambr 3, CnMD, ConAu 104, CorpD, DcLB 10, –36, DcLEL, DcNaB 1951, EncMys, EncWL, EngPo, EvLB, GrBr, HalFC 84, IntDcWB, LongCTC, ModBrL, –S1, –S2, ModWD, NewC, NotNAT B, Novels, ObitOF 79, ObitT 1951, OxCEng 67, –85, PenC ENG, REn, TwCA, –SUP, TwCCr&M 80, –85, TwCLC 2, –15, TwCWr, WhAm 3, WhoHr&F, WorAl*

Sayers, Frances Clarke 1897- *AuBYP 2, BioIn 2, –7, –9, –10, –15, ChhPo, –S2, ConAu 17R, JBA 51, SmATA 3, WhoLibS 66, WhoWest 74*

Sayers, Frances Clarke 1897-1989 *AuBYP 3, BioIn 16, –17, ConAu 129, SmATA 62*

Sayler, Harry Lincoln 1863-1913 *AmAu&B, BioIn 2, CarSB, DcNAA, IndAu 1816, OhA&B*

Sayles, E B 1892- *ConAu P-2*
Pseud./variant:
Sayles, Ted

Sayles, Ted
Main entry: Sayles, E B

Sayre, Anne 1923- *ConAu 61*

Sayre, Woodrow Wilson *BioIn 7*

Saywell, John Tupper 1929- *CanWW 70, –80, –81, –83, –89, ConAu 13R, DrAS 74H, –82H, OxCCan, –SUP*

Sazer, Nina 1949- *BioIn 11, ConAu 69, SmATA 13*

Scabrini, Janet 1953- *BioIn 11, SmATA 13*

Scagnetti, Jack 1924- *AuBYP 2S, –3, BioIn 10, ConAu 49, –4NR, IntAu&W 86, –89, MichAu 80, SmATA 7*

Scagnetti, Jack James 1924- *WhoEnt 92, WhoWrEP 92*

Scalabrini, Rita *OxCCan SUP*

Scalzo, Joe 1941- *ConAu 49*

Scamell, Ragnhild 1940- *SmATA 77*

Scanlon, Marion Stephany d1977 *BioIn 6, –11, ConAu 5R, ForWC 70, MichAu 80, MinnWr, SmATA 11, WrDr 76, –80*

Scannell, Vernon *BioIn 14, –16, IntvTCA 2*

Scannell, Vernon 1922- *CamGLE, ConAu 24NR, ConLC 49, ConPo 91, EngPo, IntAu&W 89, –91, IntWW 89, –91, SmATA 59, TwCChW 89, Who 88, –90, –92, WrDr 86, –88, –90, –92, –94*

Scarborough, Alma May C 1913- *ConAu 5R*

Scarf, Maggie 1932- *ArtclWW 2, BioIn 10, –12, –15, ConAu 29R, –22NR, IntAu&W 91, SmATA 5, WhoWrEP 89, –92, WrDr 84, –86, –88, –90, –92, –94*

Scargall, Jeanne *CaW*

Scarlett, Susan *MajAI*
Main entry: Streatfeild, Mary Noel

Scarry, Huck *ConAu 130, SmATA X*
Main entry: Scarry, Richard, Jr.

Scarry, Huck 1953- *BioIn 14, WrDr 94*

Scarry, Patricia 1924- *AuBYP 2S, –3, BioIn 9, ConAu 17R, SmATA 2*
Pseud./variant:
Roy, Liam

Scarry, Richard 1919- *AuBYP 2, -3, BioIn 8, -9, -10, -12, -14, -16, ChlLR 3, ConAu 17R, -18NR, DcLB 61, FamAIYP, IlsCB 1957, -1967, IntAu&W 77, -82, -86, -91, OxCChiL, PiP, SmATA 2, -35, ThrBJA, TwCChW 78, -83, -89, WrDr 76, -80, -82, -84, -86, -88, -90, -92, -94*

Scarry, Richard, Jr. 1953- *SmATA 35*
Pseud./variant:
Scarry, Huck

Scarry, Richard McClure 1919- *ConAu 39NR, MajAI, SmATA 75*

Schaaf, Martha Eckert 1911- *ConAu 1R, -1NR, IndAu 1917*

Schachner, Erwin *IlsBYP*

Schachtel, Roger 1949- *BioIn 15, ConAu 106, SmATA 38*
Pseud./variant:
Forrester, Marian

Schaefer, Charles E 1933- *ChhPo S2, ConAu 37R*

Schaefer, Jack 1907- *IntMPA 86, TwCChW 89*

Schaefer, Jack 1907-1991 *AnObit 1991, ConAu 133, NewYTBS 91, ScF&FL 92, SmATA 65, -66, TwCWW 91*

Schaefer, Jack Warner 1907- *AmAu&B, AuBYP 2, -3, Au&Wr 71, BioIn 5, -8, -9, -11, -14, ConAu 17R, -15NR, DcAmChF 1960, IntMPA 75, -76, -78, -77, OhA&B, SmATA 3, ThrBJA, TwCChW 78, WhoAm 74, -76, -78, -80, -82, -84, -86, -88, -90, WhoWest 74*

Schaefer, Jack Warner 1907-1991 *BioIn 17, WhAm 10*

Schaeffer, Elizabeth 1939- *ConAu 45*

Schaeffer, Mead 1898-1980 *BioIn 1, -2, -12, IlrAm 1880, -D, IlsCB 1744, SmATA 21, WhAmArt 85*

Schaeffer, Susan Fromberg *BioIn 14, -16, -17, DrAPF 87, -89, -91, -93*

Schaeffer, Susan Fromberg 1941- *AmWomWr, ArtclWW 2, BioIn 10, ConAu 49, -18NR, ConLC 6, -11, -22, ConNov 86, -91, DcLB 28, DrAF 76, DrAP 75, DrAPF 83, -85, DrAS 74E, -78E, -82E, IntAu&W 77, -82, IntWWP 82, JeAmFiW, MajTwCW, ScF&FL 92, WhoAmW 81, -83, -85, -87, -89, -91, -93, WhoUSWr 88, WhoWrEP 89, -92, WorAu 1980, WrDr 76, -80, -82, -84, -86, -88, -90, -92, -94*

Schaeren, Beatrix 1941- *ConAu 29R*

Schafer, Edward H *BioIn 15, -17*

Schafer, Edward Hetzel 1913- *ConAu 1R, -1NR, DrAS 74F, -78F, -82F, IntAu&W 77, -82, -86, -89, -91, WhAm 10, WhoAm 80, -82, -84, -86, -88, -90, WhoUSWr 88, WhoWrEP 89, -92, WrDr 76, -80, -82, -84*

Schaff, Louise E *AuBYP 2S, -3*

Schaleben-Lewis, Joy 1938- *WhoAmW 77, -81*

Schaller, George B *BioIn 14*

Schaller, George B 1933- *AuBYP 2S, -3, ConAu 5R, -9NR, CurBio 85, FifIDA, SmATA 30, WhoAm 84, WrDr 88, -90, -92*

Schaller, George Beals 1933- *IntWW 91, WhoAm 86, -88, -90, -92, -94, WhoUSWr 88, WhoWrEP 89, -92, WrDr 94*

Schami, Rafik *TwCChW 89B*

Schanzer, Ros *SmATA 77*
Main entry: Schanzer, Rosalyn

Schanzer, Rosalyn 1942- *SmATA 77*
Pseud./variant:
Schanzer, Ros
Schanzer, Roz

Schanzer, Rosalyn Good 1942- *WhoSSW 93*

Schanzer, Roz *SmATA 77*
Main entry: Schanzer, Rosalyn

Scharbach, John Alexander 1909- *DrAS 74E, WhoPNW*

Scharl, Josef 1896-1954 *BioIn 1, -3, -4, IlsCB 1744, -1946, ObitOF 79, PhDcTCA 77, WhAm 3, WhAmArt 85*

Scharper, Philip J d1985 *BioIn 14, NewYTBS 85*

Scharper, Philip Jenkins 1919-1985 *AmAu&B, AmCath 80, NewYTBS 85, WhAm 8, WhoAm 78, -80*

Schary, Dore 1905-1980 *AmAu&B, AnObit 1980, BenetAL 91, BiDFilm, BiE&WWA, BioIn 1, -2, -3, -4, -5, -6, -9, -10, -12, -17, BlueB 76, ConAu 1R, -101, -1NR, ConDr 73, -77, -93, CurBio 48, -80N, DcFM, FilmgC, HalFC 84, -88, IntMPA 75, -76, -78, -81, -82, -77, ModWD, NatPD 77, NewYTBE 70, NewYTBS 80, NotNAT, OxCFilm, REnAL, WhAm 7, WhoAm 74, -76, -78, -80, WhoAmJ 80, WhoE 74, -75, -77, -81, WhoThe 72, -77, -81, WhoWor 74, -78, -80, WhoWorJ 72, -78, WorAlBi, WorAl, WorAu 1950, WorEFlm, WrDr 76, -80*

Schatell, Brian *BioIn 16, –17, ConAu 124, SmATA 47, –66*

Schatzki, Walter 1899- *BioIn 14, SmATA 31*

Schau, Michael 1945- *ConAu 85*

Scheader, Catherine 1932- *ConAu 85*

Schealer, John Milton 1920- *AuBYP 2, –3, BioIn 7, ConAu 5R*

Schechter, Ben 1935- *AuBYP 3*

Schechter, Betty Goodstein 1921- *AuBYP 2, –3, BioIn 8, –10, ConAu 5R, FourBJA, SmATA 5*

Schecter, William 1934- *ConAu 21R*

Scheele, William Earl 1920- *AuBYP 2, –3, BioIn 5, –7, –8, –9, IlsCB 1946, –1957, ThrBJA, WhoAm 74, –76, –78*

Scheer, George F 1917- *AuBYP 2S, –3, BioIn 10, –11, ConAu 13R*

Scheer, Julian 1926- *AuBYP 3*

Scheer, Julian Weisel 1926- *AmAu&B, AuBYP 2, BioIn 8, –11, ConAu 49, SmATA 8, WhoAm 74, –76, –78, –80, –82, –84, –86, –90, –92, –94, WhoFI 83, –85, –92, WhoGov 72, WhoWor 82*

Scheffer, Victor B 1906- *AmMWSc 86, –89, –92, IntAu&W 86, –91, WrDr 86, –88, –90, –92*

Scheffer, Victor Blanchard 1906- *BioIn 10, ConAu 29R, –11NR, SmATA 6, WhoAm 74, –76, WrDr 80, –82, –84, –94*

Scheffrin-Falk, Gladys 1928- *SmATA 76*

Scheib, Ida *AuBYP 2, –3, BioIn 7*

Scheier, Michael 1943- *BioIn 14, –15, ConAu 115, –36NR, SmATA 36, –40*

Schein, Clarence Jacob *AmMWSc 86*

Schein, Clarence Jacob 1918- *AmMWSc 73P, –76P, –82, ConAu 65, WhoE 75, –77, WhoWorJ 72, –78*

Schell, Mildred 1922- *BioIn 15, ConAu 113, SmATA 41*

Schell, Orville H 1940- *AuBYP 2S, –3, BioIn 11, –12, –13, ConAu 25R, SmATA 10*

Schell, Orville Hickok 1940- *IntAu&W 91*

Schell, Orville Hickok, III 1940- *IntAu&W 86*

Scheller, Melanie *BioIn 17*

Scheller, Melanie 1953- *SmATA 77*

Schellie, Don 1932- *BioIn 13, ConAu 101, SmATA 29*

Schemm, Mildred Walker 1905- *ConAu 1R, –1NR, DrAS 74E, SmATA 21, WhoAm 74, –76*
Pseud./variant:
Walker, Mildred

Schenker, Dona 1947- *BioIn 17, ConAu 135, SmATA 68, WrDr 94*

Scher, Paula *AuBYP 3*

Scher, Paula 1948- *AuBYP 2S, BioIn 16, ConAu 115, SmATA 47*

Scher, Paula Joan 1948- *WhoAm 92, –94*

Schere, Monroe 1913- *ConAu 85*

Scherf, Margaret 1908-1979 *AuBYP 3, BioIn 14, TwCCr&M 91*

Scherf, Margaret Louise 1908- *AmAu&B, AuBYP 2S, Au&Wr 71, BioIn 11, ConAu 5R, EncMys, SmATA 10, WhoAmW 74, –75, –77, WhoPNW, WhoWest 74, –76*

Scherf, Margaret Louise 1908-1979 *DcAmChF 1960*

Scherman, Bernardine Kielty 1890?-1973 *BioIn 10, ConAu 45, ForWC 70, WhoE 74*
Pseud./variant:
Kielty, Bernardine

Scherman, Katharine 1915- *AuBYP 2, –3, BioIn 4, –7, ConAu 5R, –11NR, –27NR*

Schermer, Judith 1941- *ConAu 106, SmATA 30*

Schertle, Alice 1941- *AuBYP 3, BioIn 14, ConAu 107, –23NR, SmATA 36*

Schertle, Alice Marguerite 1941- *WhoAm 92*

Schick, Alice 1946- *AuBYP 2S, –3, BioIn 13, ConAu 81, –15NR, SmATA 27*

Schick, Eleanor 1942- *AuBYP 2S, –3, BioIn 8, –11, –12, ChhPo S2, ConAu 49, –4NR, –19NR, –41NR, FifBJA, IlsCB 1957, –1967, IntAu&W 77, SmATA 9*

Schick, Joel 1945- *BioIn 12, –14, ConAu 107, IlsCB 1967, SmATA 30, –31*

Schickel, Richard *BioIn 17*

Schickel, Richard 1933- *AuNews 1, BioIn 10, BioNews 74, ConAu 1R, –1NR, –34NR, ConTFT 10, IntAu&W 91, IntWW 89, –91,*

WhoAm 74, –76, –78, –80, –82, –84, –86, –88, –92, –94, WhoE 74, WhoEnt 92, WhoUSWr 88, WhoWrEP 89, –92, WorAu 1980, WrDr 76, –80, –82, –84, –86, –88, –90, –92

Schickel, Richard Warren 1933- *WrDr 94*

Schields, Gretchen 1948- *SmATA 75*

Schiesel, Jane *AuBYP 2S, –3*

Schiff, Kenneth Roy 1942- *BioIn 10, ConAu 49, SmATA 7*

Schiffer, Donald 1919?-1964 *BioIn 7*

Schiffer, Robert L *AuBYP 2S, –3*

Schiffer, Selma *AuBYP 2S, –3*

Schiller, Andrew 1919- *BioIn 12, ConAu 41R, DrAS 74F, –78F, –82F, SmATA 21*

Schiller, Barbara 1928- *AuBYP 2, –3, BioIn 8, –12, ConAu 17R, SmATA 21*

Schiller, Justin G 1943- *BioIn 14, ConAu 110, SmATA 31*

Schiller, Justin Galland 1943- *WhoE 86*

Schilling, Betty 1925- *ConAu 106, IlsBYP*

Schimel, John L *BiDrAPA 89*

Schimel, John L d1991 *NewYTBS 92*

Schimel, John L 1916- *BiDrAPA 77, ConAu 25R, WhoE 91*

Schimel, John L 1916-1991 *BioIn 17*

Schindel, John 1955- *SmATA 77*

Schindelman, Joseph 1923- *BioIn 8, –9, –14, –17, ChhPo, IlsBYP, IlsCB 1957, –1967, SmATA 32, –67, ThrBJA*

Schindler, S D *BioIn 16, SmATA 50*

Schindler, Steven D 1952- *SmATA 75*

Schisgall, Oscar 1901-1984 *BioIn 11, –13, ConAu 53, –112, –9NR, SmATA 12, –38N*
Pseud./variant:
Cole, Jackson
Hardy, Stuart

Schisgall, Oscar 1901-1986 *BioIn 15*

Schlapbach-Oberhansli, Trudi 1944- *ConAu 21R*
Pseud./variant:
Oberhansli, Trudi

Schlee, Ann 1934- *BioIn 14, –15, ConAu 101, –29NR, ConLC 35, FifBJA, ScF&FL 92, SmATA 36, –44, TwCChW 78, –83, –89, WrDr 80, –82, –84, –86, –88, –90, –92, –94*

Schleichert, Elizabeth 1945- *SmATA 77*

Schlein, Miriam *IntAu&W 91, TwCChW 89, WhoAmW 87, –89, –91, –93, WrDr 86, –88, –90, –92, –94*

Schlein, Miriam 1926- *AmPB, AuBYP 2, –3, BioIn 5, –6, –7, –9, ConAu 1R, –2NR, CurBio 59, MorJA, SmATA 2, TwCChW 78, –83, WhoAmW 83, –85, WrDr 80, –82, –84*
Pseud./variant:
Stanhope, Lavinia
Weiss, Miriam

Schlesinger, Arthur M 1917- *BioIn 15, –17*

Schlesinger, Arthur M, Jr. 1917- *BenetAL 91, ConAu 28NR, MajTwCW, RAdv 13-3, SmATA 61, WorAlBi*

Schlesinger, Arthur Meier, Jr. 1917- *EncAI&E, EncWB, WhoAm 92, –94, WhoWor 93*

Schlichting, Harold E 1915- *AuBYP 3*

Schlichting, Harold Eugene 1926- *IntAu&W 86, –89*

Schlichting, Harold Eugene, Jr. 1926- *AmMWSc 73P, –76P, –82, –86, –89, –92, AuBYP 2S, ConAu 112*

Schlichting, Mary Southworth *AuBYP 2S, –3*

Schloat, G Warren, Jr. 1914- *BioIn 9, ConAu 21R, SmATA 4*

Schloss, Ezekiel 1912- *WhoAm 78, WhoWorJ 78*

Schloss, Ezekiel 1912-1987 *BioIn 16*

Schmandt-Besserat, Denise 1933- *ConAu 69, –20NR, –42NR, DrAS 78H, –82H, FifIDA, WhoAm 82, –84, –86, –90, –92, –94, WhoAmA 78, –80, –82, –84, –86, –89, –91, WhoFrS 84*

Schmid, Christoph Von *BiGAW*

Schmid, Christoph Von 1768-1854? *DcCathB, OxCChiL, OxCGer 86*

Schmid, Eleonore 1939- *ConAu 53, FourBJA, IntAu&W 77, SmATA 12*

Schmiderer, Dorothy 1940- *BioIn 12, ChhPo S2, ConAu 85, SmATA 19*

Schmidt, Annie M G 1911- *BioIn 16, –17, ChlLR 22, ConAu 135, EncCoWW, SmATA 67*

Schmidt, Diane 1953- *SmATA 70*

Schmidt, Harvey Lester 1929- *ASCAP 66, BiE&WWA, BioIn 5, -9, -10, -12, BioNews 74, BlueB 76, EncMT, IlrAm 1880, -G, NewCBMT, NotNAT, WhoAm 74, -80, -82, WhoAmA 80, -82, WhoThe 81*

Schmidt, James Norman 1912- *BioIn 12, -14, ConAu 1R, -1NR, DrAS 74E, -78E, -82E, SmATA 21*
Pseud./variant:
Norman, James

Schmidt, Karl Patterson 1890-1957 *BioIn 4, -8, DcScB S2*

Schmidt, Lynette 1952- *SmATA 76*

Schmitt, Gladys *IntvTCA 2*

Schmitt, Gladys 1909-1972 *AmAu&B, AmNov, AmWomWr, Au&Wr 71, BenetAL 91, BioIn 1, -2, -3, -4, -9, -12, ConAu 1R, -37R, -2NR, CurBio 43, -72, NewYTBE 72, ObitOF 79, OxCAmL 65, -83, REnAL, TwCA SUP, WhAm 5, WhoAmW 74*

Schmitt, Marshall L 1919- *ConAu 13R*

Schmitz, Dennis Mathew 1937- *ConAu 29R, ConPo 70, -75, -80, -85, DrAP 75, DrAPF 83, -85, IntAu&W 82, IntWWP 82, WhoAm 80, -82, -84, -86, -88, -90, -92, -94, WhoWest 92, -94, WrDr 76, -80, -82, -84*

Schmitz, James H *IntvTCA 2*

Schmitz, James H 1911- *BioIn 12, -17, ConAu 103, ConSFA, DcLB 8, TwCSFW 86, -91, WhoSciF, WrDr 84, -86, -88*

Schmitz, James H 1911-1981 *RGTwCSF, ScF&FL 92*

Schmitz, James Henry 1911-1981 *EncSF 93*

Schmitz, Joseph William 1905-1966 *ConAu 5R, WhAm 4*

Schnabel, Martha 1926- *BioIn 9*

Schnaubelt, Franz Joseph 1914- *ConAu 65*
Pseud./variant:
Joseph, Franz

Schneider, Elisa *SmATA 76*
Main entry: Kleven, Elisa

Schneider, Herman 1905- *AmPB, AuBYP 2, -3, Au&Wr 71, BioIn 6, -7, -10, ConAu 29R, -16NR, IntAu&W 77, -82, MorJA, SmATA 7*

Schneider, Laurie *ConAu X, SmATA X*
Main entry: Adams, Laurie

Schneider, Leo 1916- *ConAu 5R*

Schneider, Nina *DrAPF 87, -89, -91, -93*

Schneider, Nina 1913- *AmPB, AuBYP 2, -3 Au&Wr 71, BioIn 6, -7, -9, ConAu 29R, -15NR, DrAPF 83, -85, MorJA, SmATA 2*

Schneider, Pierre 1925?- *BioIn 8*

Schneider, Rex 1937- *BioIn 15, ConAu 122, SmATA 44*

Schnirel, James R 1931- *ConAu 69, SmATA 14*

Schnurre, Wolfdietrich 1920- *DcLB 69, IntAu&W 89, -91, IntWW 89, OxCGer 86, WhoWor 87, -89, -91*

Schnurre, Wolfdietrich 1920-1989 *AnObit 1989, BioIn 17, ConAu 129, SmATA 63*

Schock, Pauline 1928- *ConAu 111, SmATA 45*
Pseud./variant:
Boyd, Pauline

Schoen, Barbara 1924- *BioIn 11, ConAu 21R, IntAu&W 77, -86, -91, SmATA 13, WrDr 76, -80, -82, -84, -86, -88, -90*

Schoen, Barbara Taylor 1924- *WhoE 93*

Schoen, Barbara Taylor 1924-1993 *ConAu 142*

Schoen, Juliet P 1923- *ConAu 69*

Schoenherr, John *ChlBIlD*

Schoenherr, John 1935- *BiDScF, BioIn 15, -16, -17, SmATA 66, -13AS, WhoAm 90, WhoAmA 89, -91*

Schoenherr, John Carl 1935- *BioIn 8, ConAu 136, FourBJA, IlsBYP, IlsCB 1957, -1967, MajAI, SmATA 37, WhoAm 92, -94, WhoAmA 78, -80, -82, -84, -86, WhoE 74, WrDr 94*

Schoffelmayer, Victor H *BioIn 2, TexWr*

Scholastica, Mary, Sister *ConAu X, SmATA 7*
Main entry: Jenkins, Marie M

Scholefield, A T *ConAu 34NR, SmATA 66*
Main entry: Scholefield, Alan

Scholefield, Alan 1931- *BioIn 17, ConAu 34NR, IntAu&W 86, -91, SmATA 66, WrDr 86, -88, -90, -92*
Pseud./variant:
Jordan, Lee
Scholefield, A T

Scholefield, Alan A T 1931- *WrDr 94*

Scholefield, Edmund O *ConAu X, -40NR, SmATA 5*
Main entry: Butterworth, W E

Scholes, Percy Alfred 1877-1958 *Baker 84, BioIn 4, -5, -14, DcNaB 1951, GrBr, LongCTC, NewOxM, ObitOF 79, OxCMus, TwCA SUP, WhoLA*

Scholey, Arthur 1932- *BioIn 13, ConAu 93, IntAu&W 86, -89, -91, SmATA 28, WrDr 82, -84, -86, -88, -90, -92*

Scholey, Arthur Edward 1932- *WrDr 94*

Scholz, Catherine Hammersley 1915- *WhoAmW 77, WhoE 74, -81*

Scholz, Jackson d1986 *NewYTBS 86*

Scholz, Jackson 1897-1986 *BioIn 15, -16, SmATA 49N*

Scholz, Jackson Volney 1897- *AuBYP 2, BioIn 6, -8, -13, ConAu 5R, MorJA, WhoTr&F 73*

Scholz, Jackson Volney 1897-1986 *AuBYP 3, BiDAmSp OS, ConAu 120*

Schomburg, Alex 1905- *BiDScF, EncACom, EncSF 93, NewEScF, ScF&FL 92, WhoSciF*

Schonberg, Harold C *AuBYP 3, BioIn 15, -16*

Schonberg, Harold C 1915- *AmAu&B, AuBYP 2S, Baker 84, BioIn 5, -8, -12, BlueB 76, ConAu 112, IntAu&W 77, -91, IntWW 74, -75, -76, -77, -78, -79, -80, -81, -82, -83, -89, -91, NewGrDA 86, NewYTBS 81, OxCMus, WhoAm 74, -76, -78, -80, -82, -84, -86, -88, WhoAmM 83, WhoE 74, WhoWor 74, WrDr 80, -82, -84, -86, -88, -90, -92*

Schonberg, Harold Charles 1915- *Baker 92, IntWWM 90, WhoAm 90, -92, -94, WhoEnt 92, WrDr 94*

Schonborg, Virginia 1913- *ConAu 77*

Schone, Virginia *BioIn 13, ConAu 97, SmATA 22*

Schongut, Emanuel *BioIn 14, IlsBYP, SmATA 36*

Schongut, Emanuel 1936- *BioIn 16, SmATA 52*

Schoolcraft, Henry Rowe 1793-1864 *Alli, AmAu, AmAu&B, Benet 87, BenetAL 91, BbD, BiD&SB, BiInAmS, BioIn 1, -3, -4, -8, -9, -13, -16, CelCen, CyAL, DcAmAu, DcBiPP, DcNAA, DcScB, EncAB-H, HarEnUS, InSci, McGEWB, MichAu 80, OxCAmH, OxCAmL 65, -83, OxCCan, REn, REnAL, WebAB 74, -79, WhAm HS, WhNaAH*

Schoolland, Marian M 1902- *ConAu 5R, -2NR, WrDr 76, -80, -82, -84*

Schoonover, Frank Earle 1877-1972 *ArtsAmW 2, BioIn 1, -6, -7, -11, -13, ConAu 106, ConICB, IlrAm 1880, -B, IlsCB 1744, MorJA, SmATA 24, WhAm 5, WhAmArt 85*

Schoor, Gene 1921- *AuBYP 2, -3, BioIn 7, -9, ConAu 29R, -29NR, SmATA 3*

Schosberg, Paul Alan 1938- *ConAu 13R, WhoAm 94, WhoAmJ 80, WhoAmP 73, -75, -77, WhoFI 83, -85, WhoGov 72*
Pseud./variant:
Allyn, Paul

Schraff, Anne E 1939- *AuBYP 2S, BioIn 13, ConAu 49, -1NR, -17NR, ScF&FL 92, SmATA 27*

Schraff, Anne Elaine 1939- *AuBYP 3, ConAu 39NR*

Schramm, Ulrik 1912- *BioIn 8, IlsCB 1957*

Schrank, Joseph 1900-1984 *AuBYP 2, -3, BioIn 8, -13, -14, -15, ConAu 5R, -112, -20NR, IntAu&W 77, NatPD 77, NewYTBS 84, SmATA 38N, WrDr 76, -80*

Schranz, Karl 1938- *BioIn 8, -9, CurBio 71, WhoWor 74*

Schreiber, Elizabeth Anne 1947- *BioIn 11, ConAu 69, SmATA 13*

Schreiber, Georges 1904-1977 *AmAu&B, BioIn 2, -5, -13, -14, ConAu 109, CurBio 43, GrAmP, IlsBYP, IlsCB 1946, PrintW 83, -85, SmATA 29, WhAmArt 85, WhoAm 74, -76, WhoAmA 73, -78N, -80N, -82N, -86N, -89N, -91N, WhoWorJ 72, -78*

Schreiber, Hermann O L 1920- *IntAu&W 91, WrDr 86, -88*

Schreiber, Hermann Otto Ludwig 1920- *Au&Wr 71, ConAu 25R, IntAu&W 77, -86, WrDr 76, -80, -82, -84*
Pseud./variant:
Bassermann, Lujo
Buehnau, Ludwig

Schreiber, Ralph W *BioIn 15, -16*

Schreiber, Ralph Walter *AmMWSc 89*

Schreiber, Ralph Walter 1942- *AmMWSc 76P, -82, -86, BioIn 11, ConAu 69, SmATA 13*

Schreiner, Samuel Agnew, Jr. 1921- *SmATA 70*

Schreiter, Rick 1936- *BioIn 8, ChhPo S1, ConAu 21R, IlsBYP, IlsCB 1957*

Schreivogel, Paul A *BioIn 16*

Schreivogel, Paul A 1930- *ConAu 25R*

Schroeder, Alan 1961- *BioIn 17, ConAu 133, SmATA 66, WrDr 94*

Schroeder, Binette
Main entry: Nickl, Barbara Elisabeth

Schroeder, Mary 1903- *ConAu 73, WhoAmW 75*

Schroeder, Ted 1931-1973 *BioIn 10, –12, SmATA 20N*

Schroetter, Hilda Noel 1917- *ConAu 29R, WhoSSW 73*
Pseud./variant:
Noel, Hilda Bloxton, Jr.

Schubert, Delwyn George 1919- *ConAu 9R, LEduc 74*

Schubert, Dieter 1947- *BioIn 17, ConAu 28NR, SmATA 62*

Schubert-Gabrys, Ingrid 1953- *ConAu 28NR, SmATA 62*

Schuberth, Christopher J 1933- *ConAu 25R*

Schucker, James *IlsBYP*

Schuett, Stacey 1960- *SmATA 75*

Schule, Clifford H *BioIn 5, IlsBYP, IlsCB 1946*

Schulke, Flip *BioIn 15, –16*

Schulke, Flip 1930- *SmATA 57*

Schull, Joseph 1910-1980 *OxCCanT*

Schull, Joseph 1916?-1980 *CanWr, ConAu 53, –8NR, CreCan 2, DcLEL, OxCCan, –SUP, WhNAA, WrDr 76, –80*

Schulman, Janet 1933- *BioIn 13, ConAu 101, SmATA 22*

Schulman, Janet Carol 1933- *WhoAm 86, –90, –92*

Schulman, L M 1934- *BioIn 11, ConAu 33R, –12NR, SmATA 13*

Schulte, Elaine L 1934- *BioIn 14, ConAu 28NR*

Schulte, Elaine Louise
Main entry: Young, Elaine L

Schulte, Elaine Louise 1934- *ConAu 73, –12NR, SmATA 36*
Pseud./variant:
Young, Elaine L

Schultz, Barbara 1923- *ConAu 21R*

Schultz, Gwendolyn M *AmMWSc 73P, ConAu 65, SmATA 21, WhoAmW 77, WhoMW 74*

Schultz, Harry Pershing 1918- *AmMWSc 73P, –76P, –82, –86, –89, –92, WhoAm 74, –84*

Schultz, James Willard 1859-1947 *AmAu&B, AuBYP 2, –3, BioIn 2, –7, –8, –11, –12, –15, –16, ConAu 121, JBA 34, –51, WhAm 2, WhNaAH, WhNAA, YABC 1*

Schultz, Pearle Henriksen 1918- *BioIn 12, ConAu 49, –1NR, SmATA 21*
Pseud./variant:
Pershing, Marie

Schultze, Bunny 1866-1939 *ArtCS, BenetAL 91, REnAL*

Schulz, Charles M *BioIn 14, –15, –16, –17, LesBEnT 92*

Schulz, Charles M 1922- *EncTwCJ, JrnUS, WorAlBi*

Schulz, Charles Monroe 1922- *AmAu&B, ArtCS, AuBYP 2, –3, BioIn 4, –5, –6, –7, –8, –9, –10, –11, –12, CelR, ConAu 9R, –6NR, ConLC 12, CurBio 60, EncAJ, IntWW 78, –79, –80, –81, –82, –83, –89, –91, LesBEnT, MinnWr, NewYTET, SmATA 10, ThrBJA, WebAB 79, WhoAm 74, –76, –78, –80, –82, –84, –86, –88, –90, –92, –94, WhoAmA 73, –78, –80, –82, –84, –86, –89, –91, WhoEnt 92, WhoWor 74, –84, –87, –89, –93, WorAl, WrDr 76, –80*

Schulz, Florence 1908- *ConAu P-2*

Schuman, Benjamin N 1923- *ConAu 17R*

Schumann, Elizabeth Creighton 1907- *ConAu P-1*

Schuon, Karl A 1913-1984 *BioIn 14*

Schuon, Karl Albert 1913-1984 *AuBYP 2, –3, BioIn 7, ConAu 13R, –114, WhoSSW 73*

Schur, Maxine *ConAu 129*

Schur, Maxine 1948- *BioIn 16, SmATA 49, –53*

Schurfranz, Vivian 1925- *BioIn 11, ConAu 61, SmATA 13*

Schurr, Cathleen *BioIn 16, ConAu 9R, InWom SUP*

Schuster, Edgar Howard 1930- *DrAS 74E*

Schutzer, A I 1922- *BioIn 11, ConAu 25R, SmATA 13*

Schuyler, Pamela R 1948- *BioIn 14, ConAu 106, SmATA 30*

Schuyler, Remington 1884-1955 *ArtsAmW 2, BioIn 1, –5, IlsBYP, IlsCB 1744, –1946, WhAmArt 85*

Schwabe, Randolph 1885-1948 *BioIn 1, –5, –14, DcBrAr 1, DcBrBI, DcNaB 1941, IlsCB 1744, TwCPaSc, WhoLA*

Schwalberg, Carol 1930- *ConAu 69, IntAu&W 89*

Schwalje, Earl G 1921- *AuBYP 2, –3, BioIn 7*

Schwalje, Marjory C *AuBYP 2, –3, BioIn 7*

Schwandt, Stephen *BioIn 17*

Schwandt, Stephen 1947- *ConAu 126, IntAu&W 91, SmATA 61*

Schwark, Mary Beth 1954- *BioIn 16, SmATA 51*

Schwartz, Alvin d1992 *NewYTBS 92*

Schwartz, Alvin 1927- *AuBYP 2S, –3, BioIn 9, –15, –16, ChlLR 3, ConAu 13R, –7NR, –24NR, FifBJA, SmATA 4, –56, WhoE 75, –77*

Schwartz, Alvin 1927-1992 *AnObit 1992, BioIn 17, ConAu 137, MajAI, SmATA 71, WhAm 10*

Schwartz, Amy *BioIn 14, ChlBIID*

Schwartz, Amy 1954- *BioIn 15, –16, –17, ChlLR 25, ConAu 110, –29NR, SixBJA, SmATA 41, –47, –18AS*

Schwartz, Anne Powers *BioIn 11, ConAu 1R, –1NR, IntAu&W 77, SmATA 10*
Main entry: Powers, Anne

Schwartz, Carol 1954- *SmATA 77*

Schwartz, Charles Walsh 1914- *AuBYP 2, –3, BioIn 7, –11, ConAu 13R, SmATA 8*

Schwartz, Daniel Bennet 1929- *BioIn 13, IlrAm 1880, –G, SmATA 29, WhoAm 74, WhoE 74, WhoGrA 82*

Schwartz, Daniel Bennett 1929- *WhoAm 86, –88, –90, –92, –94*

Schwartz, David M *BioIn 16*

Schwartz, David M 1951- *ConAu 118, SixBJA, SmATA 59*

Schwartz, Elizabeth Reeder 1912- *AmMWSc 73P, –76P, AuBYP 2, –3, BioIn 7, –11, ConAu 13R, SmATA 8*

Schwartz, George I 1908-1974 *BioIn 6, –10*

Schwartz, Joel L *DrAPF 89, –91, –93*

Schwartz, Joel L 1940- *BioIn 16, ConAu 121, SmATA 51, –54*

Schwartz, Joel Louis 1940- *BiDrAPA 89*

Schwartz, Julius 1907- *AuBYP 2, –3, BioIn 7, –15, ConAu 109, SmATA 45*

Schwartz, Lieselotte *ChhPo S2*

Schwartz, Perry 1942- *ConAu 142, SmATA 75*

Schwartz, Sheila R *WrDr 86, –88, –90, –92, –94*

Schwartz, Sheila Ruth 1929- *BioIn 13, ConAu 25R, –11NR, DrAS 74E, –78E, –82E, LEduc 74, SmATA 27, WrDr 76, –80, –82, –84*

Schwartz, Stephen 1948?- *BioIn 9, –12, –15, CelR, –90, ConAu 85, ConTFT 5, EncMT, NotNAT, OxCPMus, SmATA 19, WhoThe 77*

Schwarz, Adele Aron *SmATA 76*
Main entry: Greenspun, Adele Aron

Schwarz, Herbert T *CaW*

Schwatka, Frederick 1849-1892 *Alli SUP, AmAu, AmAu&B, BbD, BiD&SB, BiInAmS, BioIn 7, –15, DcAmAu, DcCanB 12, DcNAA, HarEnUS, OxCCan, OxCShps, WhAm HS, WhoPolA*

Schwebell, Gertrude C *ConAu 9R, WhoE 74*

Schwebell, Gertrude Clorius 1910- *BiGAW*

Schweitzer, Byrd Baylor *AuBYP 3, MajAI, SmATA 69*

Schweitzer, Byrd Baylor 1924- *AuBYP 2, BioIn 8, ChhPo, ConAu X*
Pseud./variant:
Baylor, Byrd

Schweitzer, Iris *BioIn 14, –16, ConAu 117, SmATA 36, –59*

Schweninger, Ann R 1951- *BioIn 13, ConAu 107, SmATA 29, WhoAmA 82, –84*

Schweninger, Ann Rozzelle 1951- *WhoAmA 86, –89, –91*

Schwerin, Doris *BioIn 17, DrAPF 87, –89, –91, –93*

Schwerin, Doris 1922- *ScF&FL 92, SmATA 64, WhoUSWr 88, WhoWrEP 89, –92*

Schwiebert, Ernest George 1895- *ConAu P-1, DrAS 74H, –78H, IntAu&W 77, OhA&B*

Scieszka, Jon 1954- *BioIn 17, ChlLR 27, ConAu 135, SmATA 68, WrDr 94*

Scioscia, Mary 1926- *BioIn 17, SmATA 63*

Scism, Carol K 1931- *ConAu 41R*

Scobey, Joan 1927- *ConAu 57, –7NR*

Scofield, Penrod 1933- *BioIn 17, SmATA 62*

Scoggin, Margaret C 1905-1968 *BioIn 1, –2, –3, –8, –13, CurBio 52, –68, SmATA 28, –47*

Scoggin, Margaret Clara 1905-1968 *BioIn 15, –16*

Scoltock, Jack 1942- *SmATA 72*
Pseud./variant:
Zebra, A

Scoppettone, Sandra 1936- *Au&Arts 11, AuBYP 3, BioIn 15, –16, DcAmChF 1985, GayLL, TwCYAW*

Scoppettone, Sandra Valerie 1936- *AuBYP 2S, BioIn 11, ConAu 5R, ConLC 26, FifBJA, NatPD 77, –81, SmATA 9, WhoAm 80, –82, –84, WhoUSWr 88, WhoWrEP 89, –92*

Scorer, Richard Seger 1919- *ConAu 77*

Scortia, Thomas N 1926- *BioIn 11, –17, ConAu 1R, –6NR, RGTwCSF, ScFSB, TwCSFW 86, WhoSciF, WrDr 84, –86*

Scortia, Thomas N 1926-1976 *TwCSFW 91*

Scortia, Thomas N 1926-1986 *ConAu 119, NewEScF, ScF&FL 92*

Scortia, Thomas Nicholas 1926-1986 *EncSF 93*

Scotland, Jay *AuBYP 2S, –3, ConAu X, –43NR, IntAu&W 82X, MajTwCW, TwCRHW 90, WrDr 82, –84, –86, –88, –90, –92*
Main entry: Jakes, John W

Scotland, Jay 1932- *SmATA X, WrDr 94*

Scott, Alastair
Main entry: Allen, Kenneth Sydney

Scott, Alex 1882- *SingR 1*

Scott, Ann *TwCChW 89*

Scott, Ann 1926- *AuBYP 3*

Scott, Ann Herbert 1926- *AuBYP 2S, BioIn 13, –16, BkP, ConAu 21R, FourBJA, SmATA 29, –56*

Scott, Barbara Ann *BioIn 16, –17*

Scott, Barbara Ann 1928- *BioIn 1, –2, –3, –8, –10, –11, CanWW 70, CurBio 48, InWom SUP*

Scott, Bill *ConAu 132*

Scott, Bill d1985 *BioIn 14, –15, NewYTBS 85*

Scott, Bill 1920?-1985 *SmATA 46N*

Scott, Bill 1923- *DcChlFi, IntAu&W 91, ScF&FL 92, TwCChW 83, –89, WrDr 86, –88, –90, –92, –94*

Scott, Bruce Martin 1933- *WhoE 74*

Scott, Cora Annett *AuBYP 3*

Scott, Cora Annett 1931- *AuBYP 2, BioIn 11, ConAu 17R, SmATA 11*
Pseud./variant:
Annett, Cora

Scott, Dan *ConAu X, –P-2, IntAu&W 77X, SmATA X*
Main entry: Barker, S Omar
Stratemeyer, Edward L

Scott, Elaine 1940- *ArtclWW 2, BioIn 13, –14, ConAu 105, –21NR, SmATA 36*

Scott, Eric *DcAmChF 1960*

Scott, Evelyn 1893- *ArtclWW 2*

Scott, Evelyn 1893-1963 *AmAu&B, AmWomPl, AmWomWr, BenetAL 91, BioAmW, BioIn 4, –9, –10, –12, –13, –14, –15, –16, –17, CnDAL, ConAmA, ConAmL, ConAu 104, –112, ConLC 43, DcLB 9, –48, DcLEL, FemiCLE, OxCAmL 65, –83, REnAL, TwCA, –SUP, TwCRHW 90, WhNAA*

Scott, Francis Reginald 1899-1985 *BioIn 5, –14, –15, –16, CreCan 1, EncWB, IntWWP 82, WhoCanL 85, WrDr 80*

Scott, Fraser *BioIn 10*

Scott, Harold Richard 1887- *BioIn 2, –5, ConAu 5R*

Scott, Harold Richard 1887-1969 *DcNaB MP*

Scott, J Irving Elias 1901- *BioIn 10, ConAu 73, WhoBlA 75, –80, –85, –90*

Scott, J Irving Elias 1901-1981 *WhoBlA 92N*

Scott, Jack Denton *SmATA 14AS*

Scott, Jack Denton 1915- *AuBYP 3, BioIn 8, –10, –14, –16, ChlLR 20, ConAu 108, MajAI, SixBJA, SmATA 31*

Scott, Jane 1931- *BioIn 16, SmATA 55*

Scott, John 1912-1976 *AmAu&B, Au&Wr 71, BioIn 11, –12, –17, ConAu 5R, –69, –6NR, IntAu&W 77, SmATA 14, WhAm 7, WhoAm 74*

Scott, John Anthony 1916- *AuBYP 2S, –3, BioIn 6, –13, ConAu 9R, –6NR, –23NR, DrAS 74H, –78H, –82H, IntAu&W 77, –86, –89, SmATA 23, WrDr 76, –80, –82, –84, –86, –88, –90, –92, –94*
Pseud./variant:
Scott, Tony

Scott, John M 1913- *BioIn 11, ConAu 65, –10NR, –25NR, SmATA 12*

Scott, Joseph *AuBYP 3*

Scott, Joseph 1917- *AuBYP 2S, ConAu 57*

Scott, Judith Unger 1916- *ConAu 5R, ForWC 70*

Scott, Lenore *AuBYP 2S, –3, ForWC 70*

Scott, Michael 1789-1835 *BioIn 5, –9, CelCen, CmScLit, DcBiPP, DcNaB, OxCChiL, OxCEng 85, OxCShps*

Scott, Natalie Anderson 1906- *AmAu&B, AmNov, BenetAL 91, BioIn 1, –2, ConAu P-2, REnAL, WhoAmW 74*

Scott, Reginald Thomas Maitland 1882- *AmAu&B, WhNAA*

Scott, Richard *ConAu 135, SmATA 67*
Main entry: Rennert, Richard Scott

Scott, Robert F *BiDrAPA 89*

Scott, Robert F 1868-1912 *WorAlBi*

Scott, Robert Falcon 1868-1912 *AnCL, AsBiEn, BioIn 1, –2, –3, –4, –5, –6, –7, –8, –9, –10, –11, –12, –13, –14, –15, –17, ConAu 115, DcNaB 1912, Expl 93, InSci, McGEWB, NewC, OxCEng 67, –85, OxCShps, RAdv 13-3, REn, WhDW, WorAl*

Scott, Robert Lee 1908- *AuBYP 3, BioIn 17*

Scott, Robert Lee, Jr. 1908- *WhoAm 88, –90, –92, –94*

Scott, Sally Elisabeth 1948- *AuBYP 3*

Scott, Sally Elizabeth 1948- *SmATA 44*

Scott, Sally Fisher 1909-1978 *BioIn 15, ConAu 116, SmATA 43*

Scott, Tom *BioIn 16*

Scott, Tom 1918- *Au&Wr 71, BioIn 14, ChhPo S2, CmScLit, ConAu 9R, ConPo 70, –75, –80, –85, –91, DcLB 27, EngPo, IntAu&W 77, –91, WrDr 76, –80, –82, –84, –86, –88, –90, –92, –94*

Scott, Tony *IntMPA 84, –86, –88, –92, SmATA X*
Main entry: Scott, John Anthony

Scott, Walter 1771-1832 *BioIn 17, BlmGEL, CnDBLB 3, DcLB 93, –107, –116, EncPaPR 91, MagSWL, PenEncH, RfGEnL 91, RfGShF, ScF&FL 92, WorAlBi, WorLitC*
Pseud./variant:
Cleishbotham, Jebediah

Scott, Walter, Sir 1771-1832 *Alli, AnCL, AtlBL, Benet 87, BbD, BiDLA, –SUP, BiD&SB, BioIn 1, –2, –3, –4, –5, –6, –7, –8, –9, –10, –11, –12, –13, –14, –15, BritAu 19, BritWr 4, CamGEL, CamGLE, CarSB, CasWL, CelCen, Chambr 3, ChhPo, –S1, –S2, CmScLit, CnE&AP, CrtT 2, CyWA 58, DcBiA, DcBiPP, DcEnA, –A, DcEnL, DcEuL, DcLEL, DcNaB, Dis&D, EvLB, FamAYP, HalFC 84, –88, HsB&A, LongCEL, LuthC 75, McGEWB, MouLC 3, NewC, NinCLC 15, Novels, OxCChiL, OxCEng 67, –85, OxCMus, OxCThe 83, PenC ENG, PlP&P, PoChrch, RAdv 1, –13-1, RComWL, REn, Str&VC, SupFW, WebE&AL, WhDW, WhoChL, WhoHr&F, WorAl, YABC 2*

Scott, Warwick *ConAu X, DcLEL 1940, EncSF 93, IntAu&W 77X, SmATA X, TwCCr&M 80, –85, –91, WrDr 76, –80, –82, –84, –86, –88, –90, –92, –94*
Main entry: Trevor, Elleston

Scott, Warwick 1920- *BioIn 14*

Scott, William Beverley 1917- *AmMWSc 73P, –82, –86, –89, –92, WhoAm 84, –86, –90, –92, –94, WhoE 74*

Scott, William Beverly 1917- *WhoAm 88*

Scotti, Anna *SmATA 73*
Main entry: Coates, Anna

Scott Moncrieff, Martha Christian 1897- *ConAu 61, IntAu&W 82*

Scovel, Myra *DrAPF 87, –89, –91*

Scovel, Myra 1905- *ConAu 5R, –2NR, DrAPF 83, –85, ForWC 70, IntAu&W 77, –82, IntWWP 82, WrDr 76, –80, –82, –84*

Scoville, Samuel, Jr. 1872-1950 *AmAu&B, BioIn 2, ChhPo, JBA 34, –51, REnAL, WhAm 3, WhNAA*

Scribner, Charles, Jr. *BioIn 14, –16*

Scribner, Charles, Jr. 1921- *AmAu&B, BioIn 11, BlueB 76, CelR, ConAu 69, IntAu&W 82, IntWW 74, –75, –76, –77, –78, –79, –80, –81, –82, –83, –89, –91, SmATA 13, WhoAm 74, –76, –78, –80, –82, –84, –86, –88, –90, –92, –94, WhoFI 74, WhoWor 74*

Scribner, Joanne L 1949- *BioIn 14, SmATA 33*

Scribner, Kimball 1917- *SmATA 63*
Pseud./variant:
Kimball, Captain Kim

Scribner, Kimball J 1917- *BioIn 17*

Scrimsher, Lila Gravatt 1897-1974 *AuBYP 2, –3, BioIn 7, –13, ConAu 1R, –103, SmATA 28N*

Scudder, Horace E 1838-1902 *BenetAL 91, ConAu 119*

Scudder, Horace Elisha 1838-1902 *Alli, –SUP, AmAu, AmAu&B, BbD, BiD&SB, BioIn 1, –2, –3, –15, CarSB, ChhPo, DcAmAu, DcLB 42, –71, DcNAA, HarEnUS, JBA 34, OxCAmL 65, –83, OxCChiL, REn, REnAL, WhAm 1*

Scudder, Mildred Lee *ConAu 9R, ThrBJA*
Main entry: Lee, Mildred

Scull, Florence Doughty 1905- *ConAu P-1, IntAu&W 77, WhoAmW 75, WrDr 76, –80, –82, –84*

Scull, Marie-Louise 1943-1993 *SmATA 77*

Scull, Marie-Louise Walter 1943- *WhoEnt 92*

Scuro, Vincent 1951- *BioIn 12, ConAu 53, –5NR, –40NR, SmATA 21*

Seaborg, Glenn T 1912- *IntWW 89, –91, NobelP, WorAlBi*

Seaborg, Glenn Theodore 1912- *AmMWSc 73P, –76P, –82, –86, –89, –92, AsBiEn, BiESc, BioIn 1, –2, –3, –4, –5, –6, –7, –9, –10, –11, –12, –14, –15, BlueB 76, CmCal, ConAu 49, –2NR, CurBio 48, –61, EncWB, Future, InSci, IntAu&W 77, IntWW 74, –75, –76, –77, –78, –79, –80, –81, –82, –83, McGMS 80, NewYTBE 70, OxCAmH, WebAB 74, –79, Who 74, –82, –83, –85, –88, –90, –92, WhoAm 74, –76, –78, –80, –82, –84, –86, –88, –90, –92, –94, WhoAmP 73, –75, –77, WhoFrS 84, WhoNob, –90, WhoWest 78, –80, –82, –84, –87, –89, –92, –94, WhoWor 74, –78, –80, –82, –84, –87, –89, –91, –93, WorAl*

Seabrook, William B 1886-1945 *BioIn 17*

Seabrook, William Buehler 1886-1945 *AmAu&B, BioIn 4, –7, –12, ConAu 107, CurBio 40, –45, DcLB 4, DcNAA, ObitOF 79, REnAL, TwCA, –SUP, WhAm 2, WhNAA, WhoHr&F*

Seabrooke, Brenda 1941- *BioIn 14, ConAu 107, SmATA 30*

Sealey, Leonard George William 1923- *Au&Wr 71, IntAu&W 77, –86, –89, –91, WhoE 81, WrDr 76, –80*

Seaman, Augusta 1879-1950 *AuBYP 3, WomNov*

Seaman, Augusta Huiell 1879-1950 *AmAu&B, AuBYP 2, BenetAL 91, BioIn 2, –7, –14, ChhPo, ConAu 110, InWom SUP, JBA 34, –51, REnAL, SmATA 31, WhAm 3, WhNAA*

Seaman, David M *AuBYP 2, –3, BioIn 7*

Seaman, Donald 1922- *ConAu 114, Novels, WhoSpyF*

Seaman, Donald Peter 1922- *SpyFic*

Seaman, Louise *AmPB*
Main entry: Bechtel, Louise Seaman

Seaman, Mary Lott *ConICB*

Seamands, Ruth 1916- *BioIn 11, ConAu 45, SmATA 9*

Seamer, H St John *ChhPo*

Searcy, Margaret Z 1926- *SmATA 54*

Searcy, Margaret Zehmer 1926- *BioIn 15, –16, ConAu 81, SmATA 39*

Searight, Mary W 1918- *ConAu 29R, SmATA 17, WhoAmW 77*

Searle, Kathryn Adrienne 1942- *BioIn 11, ConAu 29R, SmATA 10*
Pseud./variant:
Kathryn

Searle, Ronald 1920- *Au&Wr 71, BioIn 1, –2, –4, –5, –6, –12, –14, –15, –17, BlueB 76, ChhPo S2, ConAu 9R, –25NR, DcBrAr 1, IlsBYP, IlsCB 1946, IntAu&W 91, IntWW 74, –75, –76, –77, –78, –79, –80, –81, –82, –83, –89, –91, NewC, OxCChiL, OxCTwCA, SmATA 42, TwCPaSc, WhDW, Who 74, –82, –83, –85, WhoAm 74, –76, –78, –80, –82, –84, –86, –88, –90, –92, –94, WhoArt 80, –82, –84, WhoGrA 62, –82, WhoWor 74, –82, –84, –87, –89, WorECar, WrDr 76, –80, –82, –84, –86, –88, –90, –92*

Searle, Ronald William Fordham 1920- *MajAI, SmATA 70, WrDr 94*

Sears, Paul Bigelow 1891- *AmAu&B, BiESc, BioIn 3, -4, -5, -7, -13, BlueB 76, ConAu 17R, CurBio 60, InSci, IntWW 74, -75, -76, -77, -78, -79, -80, -81, -82, -83, McGMS 80, OhA&B, WhAm 9, WhoAm 74, -76, -78, -80*

Sears, Paul M 1920- *ConAu 1R*

Sears, Stephen W 1932- *BioIn 9, ConAu 33R, SmATA 4*

Seawell, Molly Elliot 1860-1916 *AmAu&B, AmWomPl, AmWomWr, BiDSA, BiD&SB, CarSB, DcAmAu, DcBiA, DcNAA, TwCA, WhAm 1, WomWWA 14, WomNov*

Sebastian, Jeanne *AuBYP 2S, -3, ConAu X*
Main entry: Newsome, Arden J

Sebastian, Lee *BioIn 15, -17, ConAu X, -36NR, DcLEL 1940, MajAI, MajTwCW, SmATA X, ThrBJA, WrDr 84, -86, -88, -90, -92*
Main entry: Silverberg, Robert

Sebastian, Lee 1935- *WrDr 94*

Sebestyen, Igen *MajAI, SmATA X*
Main entry: Sebestyen, Ouida

Sebestyen, Ouida 1923- *DcAmChF 1960*

Sebestyen, Ouida 1924- *Au&Arts 8, BioIn 15, -16, ChlLR 17, ConAu 107, -40NR, ConLC 30, FifBJA, IntAu&W 91, MajAI, SmATA 39, -10AS, TwCChW 89, TwCYAW, WhoAmW 89, WrDr 82, -84, -86, -88, -90, -92, -94*
Pseud./variant:
Sebestyen, Igen

Sechrist, Elizabeth 1903- *AuBYP 3*

Sechrist, Elizabeth Hough 1902-1991 *ScF&FL 92*

Sechrist, Elizabeth Hough 1903- *AmAu&B, AuBYP 2, BioIn 7, -9, ChhPo, ConAu 5R, SmATA 2, WhoAm 74, -76, -78, WhoAmW 74, -75, -77*

Secunda, Sheldon 1929- *ASCAP 66*

Sedges, John *AmPeW, ConAu X, -34NR, MajTwCW, SmATA 1, -X, WebAB 74, -79*
Main entry: Buck, Pearl S

Sedgwick, Catherine Maria 1789-1867 *Alli, ArtclWW 2, BenetAL 91, BioIn 4, -10, -11, CarSB, ChhPo, DcEnL, DcLEL, DcNAA, HarEnUS*

See, Ruth Douglas 1910- *ConAu 1R, -1NR, -35NR, ForWC 70*

Seed, Cecile Eugenie 1930- *BioIn 11, ConAu 21R, -10NR, -26NR, IntAu&W 86, -91, SmATA 8, TwCChW 78, WrDr 76, -80*
Pseud./variant:
Seed, Jenny

Seed, Jenny *IntAu&W 86X*
Main entry: Seed, Cecile Eugenie

Seed, Jenny 1930- *BioIn 11, ConAu X, TwCChW 83, -89, WrDr 82, -84, -86, -88, -90, -92, -94*

Seed, Sheila Turner 1937?-1979 *BioIn 13, SmATA 23N*
Pseud./variant:
Turner, Sheila R

Seed, Suzanne *AuBYP 3, InWom SUP*

Seed, Suzanne Liddell 1940- *AuBYP 2S, WhoAmA 82, -84, -86, -89, -91, WhoAmW 77, -81*

Seeger, Elizabeth 1889-1973 *BioIn 10, -12, -14, ConAu 45, SmATA 20N*

Seeger, Pete *BioIn 14, -15, -16, -17*

Seeger, Pete 1919- *Baker 84, BioIn 6, -7, -8, -10, -11, -12, -13, BioNews 74, BlueB 76, CelR, -90, CmpEPM, ConAu 69, -33NR, ConHero 2, ConMus 4, CurBio 63, EncFCWM 69, -83, EncRk 88, EncWB, NewAmDM, NewGrDA 86, OxCPMus, PenEncP, RolSEnR 83, SmATA 13, WebAB 74, -79, WhoAm 74, -76, -78, -80, -82, -84, -86, -88, -90, -92, -94, WhoEnt 92, WhoHol A, WhoWor 74, WorAlBi, WorAl*

Seeger, Peter 1919- *Baker 92*

Seeger, Ruth Porter 1901-1953 *AuBYP 3*

Seeger, Ruth Porter Crawford 1901-1953 *AuBYP 2, BioIn 1, -3, -7, -10, -12, ChhPo, DcCM*

Seegers, Kathleen Walker 1915- *ConAu 21R*

Seeley, Laura L 1958- *SmATA 71*

Seeman, Bernard 1911- *Au&Wr 71, ConAu 21R, WhoE 74, -75, -77, -81, -83, -85, -86, -89, -91, WhoFI 74, -75, -81, -83, -85, -87, -89, WhoWor 82*

Seeman, Bernard 1911-1990 *WhAm 10*

Seever, R *ConAu X, SmATA X*
Main entry: Reeves, Lawrence F

Sefton, Catherine *ChlFicS, ConAu X, –34NR, IntAu&W 91X, SmATA X, TwCChW 83, –89, WrDr 92*
Main entry: Waddell, Martin

Sefton, Catherine 1941- *ScF&FL 92, WrDr 86, –88, –90, –94*

Segal, Abraham 1911?-1977 *BioIn 11, ConAu 69*

Segal, Erich 1937- *AmAu&B, ASCAP 66, AuSpks, BestSel 89-1, BioIn 8, –9, –10, –11, –14, –15, –17, BlueB 76, CelR, ConAu 25R, –20NR, –36NR, ConLC 3, –10, ConTFT 1, CurBio 71, DcLB Y86B, DrAS 74F, –78F, –82F, HalFC 84, –88, IntAu&W 82, –91, MajTwCW, NewYTBE 71, Novels, Who 85, –88, –92, WhoAm 74, –76, –78, –80, –82, –84, –86, –88, –92, –94, WhoE 74, WhoHol A, WhoUSWr 88, WhoWor 80, –82, –84, WhoWorJ 72, –78, WhoWrEP 89, –92, WorAl, WrDr 76, –80, –82, –84, –86, –88, –90, –92, –94*

Segal, Erich, Prof 1937- *Who 90*

Segal, Joyce 1940- *BioIn 14, ConAu 101, SmATA 35*

Segal, Lore *DrAPF 87, –89, –91, –93, InWom SUP*

Segal, Lore 1928- *IntAu&W 91, LiExTwC, SmATA 66, –11AS, WhoAm 86, –88, –90, –92, –94, WhoAmW 87, WhoUSWr 88, WhoWrEP 89, –92, WorAu 1980, WrDr 86, –88, –90, –92, –94*

Segal, Lore Groszmann *BioIn 16, –17*

Segal, Lore Groszmann 1928- *AmAu&B, AuBYP 2S, BioIn 9, ConAu 13R, DrAF 76, FourBJA, IntAu&W 77, SmATA 4, WhoAm 74, –76, –78, WrDr 76, –80*

Segal, S S 1919- *ConAu 25R, WrDr 76, –80, –82, –84, –86, –88, –90, –92*

Segal, Stanley Solomon 1919- *WrDr 94*

Segar, E C 1894-1938 *EncACom, SmATA 61*

Segar, Elzie Crisler 1894-1938 *BioIn 17*

Segar, Elzie Crisler 1895-1938 *ArtCS, DcNAA, WebAB 74, –79*

Segawa, Yasuo 1932- *BioIn 16*

Segawa, Yasuo 1933- *FourBJA, IlsBYP*

Segovia, Andres d1987 *Who 88N*

Segovia, Andres 1893- *BioIn 14, NewYTBS 86, WhoWor 87*

Segovia, Andres 1893-1987 *AnObit 1987, Baker 92, BioIn 15, –16, ConAu 122, ConMus 6, ConNews 87-3, CurBio 87N, NewAmDM, NewYTBS 87, PenDiMP, SmATA 52N*

Segovia, Andres 1894- *WhoAm 86*

Segovia, Andres 1894-1987 *WhAm 9, WorAlBi*

Segraves, Kelly L 1942- *ScF&FL 92*

Segraves, Kelly Lee 1942- *ConAu 61, –13NR, WhoWest 78, –80*

Segun, Mabel D 1930- *TwCChW 89, WrDr 90, –92*

Segun, Mabel Dorothy 1930- *DcChlFi*

Segun, Mabel Dorothy Aig-Imoukhuede 1930- *WrDr 94*

Segur, Sophie Rostopchine, Comtesse De 1799-1874 *BioIn 11, –17, CarSB, DcCathB, FrenWW, InWom SUP, OxCChiL, OxCFr*

Seide, Diane 1930- *ConAu 73, –14NR, –31NR*
Pseud./variant:
Seidner, Diane

Seidelman, James Edward 1926- *AuBYP 2, –3, BioIn 10, ChhPo S1, ConAu 25R, SmATA 6*

Seiden, Art *BioIn 15, SmATA 42*

Seiden, Arthur *WhoAmA 91*

Seidler, Ann 1925- *ConAu 25R, IntAu&W 91, WrDr 76, –80, –82, –84, –86, –88, –90, –92, –94*

Seidler, Tor *BioIn 15*

Seidler, Tor 1952- *BioIn 16, ConAu 123, SixBJA, SmATA 46, –52, WrDr 90, –92, –94*

Seidman, Laurence Ivan 1925- *BioIn 12, ConAu 77, SmATA 15*

Seidner, Diane *ConAu X, –31NR*
Main entry: Seide, Diane

Seigel, Kalman 1917- *BioIn 11, ConAu 25R SmATA 12, WhoE 74*

Seignobosc, Francoise 1900-1961 *AmPB, AnCL, BioIn 1, –3, –5, –6, –8, –12, ConAu 73, IlsBYP, IlsCB 1744, –1946, –1957, MorJA, SmATA 21, WhAm 4*
Pseud./variant:
Francoise

Seinfel, Ruth *ConAu X*
Main entry: Goode, Ruth

Seitz, Jacqueline 1931- *SmATA 50*

Seitz, Patricia *IlsBYP*

Seixas, Judith S 1922- *AuBYP 3, BioIn 12, ConAu 85, SmATA 17*

Sejima, Yoshimasa 1913- *BioIn 11, ConAu 33R, SmATA 8*

Selberg, Ingrid 1950- *BioIn 17, SmATA 68*

Selberg, Ingrid Maria 1950- *ConAu 136, WhoWor 89, -91, WrDr 94*

Selby, John Allen 1897-1980 *AmAu&B, AmNov, Au&Wr 71, BioIn 2, -12, ConAu 1R, WhAm 7, WhoAm 74*

Selden, George *AuBYP 3, ConAu 130, -37NR, MajAI, SmATA 73*
Main entry: Thompson, George Selden

Selden, George 1929- *AuBYP 2, BioIn 14, -15, ChlLR 8, ConAu X, DcAmChF 1960, DcLB 52, FourBJA, IntAu&W 91, MorBMP, OxCChiL, SmATA 4, TwCChW 78, -83, -89, WrDr 80, -82, -84, -86, -88, -90*

Selden, George 1929-1989 *BioIn 16, -17, ScF&FL 92, SmATA X*

Selden, Neil R 1931- *BioIn 17, ScF&FL 92, SmATA 61*

Selden, Neil Roy 1931- *IntAu&W 86*
Pseud./variant:
Aaron, Anna 1931-

Selden, Samuel 1899-1979 *AuBYP 2, -3, BiE&WWA, BioIn 7, ConAu 1R, -3NR, DrAS 74E, NotNAT, WhoAm 74*

Seldon Truss, Leslie 1892- *Au&Wr 71, ConAu 5R, IntAu&W 89, -91, Who 74, -82, -83, -85, -88, -90*
Pseud./variant:
Truss, Leslie Seldon

Self, Margaret Cabell 1902- *AmAu&B, AuBYP 2, -3, BioIn 7, -13, ConAu 5R, -3NR, IntAu&W 77, -82, -91, OhA&B, SmATA 24, WhoAm 74, -76, -78, -80, -82, WhoAmW 74, WhoSSW 73, -75, -76, WrDr 76, -80, -82, -84, -86, -88, -90*

Selig, Sylvie 1942- *BioIn 11, -12, IlsBYP, IlsCB 1967, SmATA 13*

Seligman, Dorothy Halle *AuBYP 2S, -3*

Seligsohn, Isaac J 1924- *WhoAdv 72*

Seligsohn, Nancy 1929- *WhoAmW 75, -77*

Selkirk, Jane *AmAu&B, AuBYP 2, -3, ConAu X, SmATA X, TwCA SUP, WhoAm 74, -76, -78*
Main entry: Chapman, John Stanton Higham Chapman, Mary Hamilton Illsley

Sellar, Gordon *BioIn 9, OxCCan*

Sellers, Naomi John *SmATA X*
Main entry: Flack, Naomi John

Sellew, Catharine Freeman 1922- *AuBYP 2, -3, BioIn 7*

Selman, LaRue W 1927- *BioIn 16, SmATA 55*

Selsam, Millicent 1912- *AuBYP 3*

Selsam, Millicent Ellis 1912- *AmPB, AnCL, AuBYP 2, BioIn 6, -7, -9, BkP, ChlLR 1, ConAu 9R, -5NR, -38NR, IntAu&W 77, MajAI, MorJA, SmATA 1, -29*

Seltzer, Charles Alden 1875-1942 *AmAu&B, AmLY, DcNAA, EncFWF, OhA&B, TwCA, TwCWW 91, WhAm 1*

Seltzer, Meyer 1932- *BioIn 12, SmATA 17*

Seltzer, Richard *BioIn 15, DrAPF 87, -89, -91, -93*

Seltzer, Richard 1946- *ConAu 105, SmATA 41*

Selvin, David F 1913- *ConAu 25R*

Selway, Martina 1940- *SmATA 74*

Semloh 1898- *SmATA X*
Main entry: Holmes, Peggy

Senarens, Luis P 1863-1969 *NewEScF*

Senarens, Luis P 1865-1939 *TwCSFW 86, -91*

Senarens, Luis Philip 1863?-1939? *AmAu&B, BenetAL 91, BioIn 7, -12, CurBio 40, DcNAA, EncSF 93, REnAL, WhoSciF*

Senarens, Luis Philip 1865-1939 *ScFSB*

Sendak, Jack *AuBYP 2, -3, BioIn 8, -13, ConAu 77, SmATA 28*

Sendak, Maurice *BioIn 14, -15, -16, -17, ConDr 88D*

Sendak, Maurice 1928- *AmAu&B, AmPB, ArtsCL, AuBYP 2, -3, Au&ICB, BenetAL 91, BioIn 5, -6, -7, -8, -9, -10, -11, -12, -13, BkP, CamGLE, ChhPo, -S1, -S2, ChlLR 1, -17, ChsFB A, ConAu 5R, -11NR, CurBio 68, -89, DcLB 61, FamAIYP, IlrAm 1880, IlsBYP, IlsCB 1946, -1957, -1967, MajTwCW, MorJA, NewYTBE 70, -73, NewYTBS 80, NewbC 1956, OxCAmL 83, OxCChiL, PiP,*

SmATA 1, –27, Str&VC, TwCChW 78, –83, –89, Who 85, WhoAm 74, –80, –82, –84, WhoAmA 80, –82, –84, WhoGrA 82, WorAlBi, WorAl, WrDr 76, –80, –82, –84, –86, –88, –90, –92, –94

Sendak, Maurice Bernard 1928- *ConAu 39NR, MajAI*

Sender, Ruth M 1926- *SmATA 62*

Sender, Ruth Minsky *BioIn 16*

Sender, Ruth Minsky 1926- *BioIn 17*

Sendler, David A 1938- *WhoUSWr 88, WhoWrEP 89, –92*

Sendler, David Alan 1938- *ConAu 65, WhoAm 80, –84, –86, –88, –90*

Sengler, Johanna 1924- *BioIn 12, SmATA 18*

Sengupta, Abhijit *DcChlFi*

Sengupta, Poile Ambika 1948- *DcChlFi*

Senior, Margaret *SingR 1*

Senn, Steve 1950- *BioIn 16, –17, ScF&FL 92, SmATA 48, –60*

Sentman, George Armor *AuBYP 2, –3, BioIn 7*

Serage, Nancy 1924- *BioIn 11, ConAu 65, SmATA 10*

Serebriakoff, Alexandre 1907-1975 *BioIn 1, IlsCB 1744*

Seredy, Kate 1896-1975 *AuBYP 3, InWom SUP, WrChl*

Seredy, Kate 1899?-1975 *AmWomWr, AnCL, AuBYP 2, Au&ICB, BioIn 1, –2, –4, –5, –7, –8, –9, –10, –13, –14, BkCL, ChhPo, ChlLR 10, ConAu 5R, –57, CurBio 40, –75N, DcLB 22, IlsCB 1744, –1946, JBA 51, MajAI, NewbMB 1922, OxCChiL, SmATA 1, –24N, Str&VC, TwCChW 78, –83, –89, WhoAmA 73*

Serif, Med 1924- *ConAu 17R*

Serling, Rod *PenEncH*

Serling, Rod d1975 *LesBEnT 92*

Serling, Rod 1924-1975 *AmAu&B, AuNews 1, BenetAL 91, BioIn 4, –5, –6, –7, –10, –14, –16, CelR, ConAu 57, –65, ConDr 73, ConLC 30, CurBio 59, –75N, DcLB 26, EncO&P 1S2, –2, –3, EncSF 93, FilmgC, HalFC 84, –88, IntMPA 75, –76, LesBEnT, NewEScF, NewYTET, ObitOF 79, REnAL, ScF&FL 92, ScFSB, TwCSFW 86, –91, WhAm 6, WhScrn 83, –77, WhoAm 74, WhoSciF, WhoWor 74, WorAlBi, WorAl, WorEFlm*

Seroff, Victor I 1902-1979 *Au&Wr 71, BioIn 11, –13, ConAu 25R, –85, SmATA 12, –26N, WhoMus 72*

Serraillier, Ian 1912- *BioIn 15, EngPo, IntAu&W 91, SmATA 3AS, TwCChW 89, WrDr 86, –88, –90, –92*

Serraillier, Ian Lucien 1912- *Au&Wr 71, BioIn 9, ChhPo, –S1, –S2, ChlLR 2, ConAu 1R, –1NR, IntAu&W 86, –89, MajAI, OxCChiL, SmATA 1, –73, ThrBJA, TwCChW 78, –83, TwCYAW, WrDr 76, –80, –82, –84, –94*

Servello, Joe 1932- *BioIn 11, –12, IlsCB 1957, SmATA 10*

Serventy, Vincent Noel *Au&Wr 71, ConAu 65, IntAu&W 77, –82, WrDr 76, –80, –82, –84, –86, –88, –90, –92*

Serventy, Vincent Noel 1926- *WrDr 94*

Service, Pamela 1945- *TwCYAW*

Service, Pamela F *BioIn 17*

Service, Pamela F 1945- *ConAu 120, EncSF 93, ScF&FL 92, SmATA 64*

Service, Pamela Floy 1945- *WhoMW 86*

Service, Robert W 1874-1958 *AuBYP 3, Benet 87, BenetAL 91, BioIn 15, –17, NewEScF, RAdv 13-1, ScFEYrs, WorAlBi, WorLitC*

Service, Robert W 1876-1958 *CamGLE*

Service, Robert William 1874?-1958 *AuBYP 2S, BioIn 1, –2, –3, –4, –5, –11, –12, CanNov, CanWr, CasWL, Chambr 3, ChhPo, –S1, –S2, CnDAL, CnE&AP, ConAu 115, –140, CreCan 1, DcLEL, DcNaB 1951, EncSF 93, EvLB, LongCTC, NewC, ObitOF 79, ObitT 1951, OxCAmL 65, OxCCan, OxCCanL, OxCEng 85, PenC ENG, REn, REnAL, SmATA 20, TwCA, –SUP, TwCLC 15, TwCWr, WebE&AL, WhAm 3, WhNAA, WhoLA, WorAl*

Service, Robert William 1876-1958 *CamGEL*

Serwadda, William Moses 1931- *BioIn 13, –16, BlkAuII, –92, SmATA 27*

Serwer, Blanche L 1910- *BioIn 11, ConAu 65, SmATA 10*

Sesshu 1420-1506 *Benet 87, BioIn 4, REn*

Sesshu Toyo 1420-1506 *EncJap*

Seth, Marie *ScF&FL 92, SmATA X*
Main entry: Lexau, Joan M

Seth, Ronald 1911-1985 *AuBYP 2, -3, Au&Wr 71, ConAu 106, -115, SpyFic, WhoSpyF*

Seth-Smith, Elsie K *ConAu X*
Main entry: Murrell, Elsie Kathleen Seth-Smith

Seton, Anya *BioIn 14, IntAu&W 86, -89, -91, TwCRHW 90, Who 88, -90, WhoAm 86, WrDr 86, -88, -90*

Seton, Anya d1990 *BioIn 17, NewYTBS 90, WhAm 10, Who 92N*

Seton, Anya 1904?- *FemiCLE*

Seton, Anya 1904-1990 *AnObit 1990, ConAu 133, CurBio 91N, ScF&FL 92, SmATA 66*

Seton, Anya 1916- *AmAu&B, AmNov, AmWomWr, Au&Wr 71, Benet 87, BioIn 2, -3, -4, -6, -9, ConAu 17R, CurBio 53, EncFWF, IntAu&W 77, -82, LongCTC, Novels, OxCAmL 65, -83, PenC AM, REn, REnAL, SmATA 3, TwCA SUP, Who 74, -82, -83, -85, WhoAm 74, -76, -78, -80, -82, -84, WhoAmW 83, WhoWor 74, WorAl, WrDr 76, -80, -82, -84*

Seton, Anya 1916-1990 *BenetAL 91*

Seton, Ernest Thompson 1860-1946 *AmAu&B, AmLY, Benet 87, BenetAL 91, BioIn 1, -2, -3, -4, -5, -8, -10, -11, -12, -14, -15, -17, CamGEL, CamGLE, CanWr, CarSB, Chambr 3, ChhPo, -S1, ConAmL, ConAu 109, CreCan 2, CurBio 43, -48, DcBrAr 1, DcBrBI, DcLB 92, DcLEL, DcNAA, DcVicP 2, EncSoH, EncWB, EvLB, HarEnUS, IlsCB 1744, InSci, JBA 34, LongCTC, ObitOF 79, OxCAmL 65, -83, OxCCan, OxCCanL, OxCChiL, REn, REnAL, SmATA 18, TelT, TwCA, -SUP, TwCChW 78, -83, -89, TwCLC 31, TwCWr, WhAm 2, WhAmArt 85, WhNaAH, WhNAA, WhoChL*

Settle, Mary Lee *BioIn 14, -15, -16, -17, DrAPF 87, -89, -91*

Settle, Mary Lee 1918- *ArtclWW 2, BioIn 3, -5, -7, -10, -12, ConAu 1AS, ConLC 19, -61, CurBio 59, CyWA 89, DcLB 6, DrAPF 83, -85, FemiCLE, NewYTBS 80, WhoAm 80, -82, -84, -88, -90, -92, -94, WhoAmW 81, -83, -85, -87, -89, -91, -93, WhoUSWr 88, WorAu 1950, WrDr 92, -94*

Setton, Kenneth M 1914- *AmAu&B, BioIn 4, ConAu 9R, -3NR, -18NR, -39NR, DrAS 74H, -78H, -82H, WhoAm 74, -76, -78, -80, -82, -84, -86, -88, -90, -92, -94, WhoWor 80, -84, -87, -89, -91, -93*

Setzekorn, William David 1935- *ConAu 65, WhoWest 74, -76, -78, -80, -82*

Seuling, Barbara 1937- *AuBYP 3, BioIn 11, ConAu 61, -8NR, -26NR, SmATA 10*

Seuss, Dr *AmAu&B, AmPB, AuBYP 2, -3, BioIn 14, -15, -16, -17, BkP, ChhPo, -S1 ChlLR 9, ConAu X, -135, -32NR, ConGrA 3, IlsCB 1946, -1957, -1967, MajTwCW, MorJA, OxCChiL, PiP, REn, REnAL, SmATA 1, -X, -67, -75, Str&VC, TwCA, -SUP, TwCChW 78, -83, WhoAm 74, -76, -78, -80, -84, -86, -88, WhoChL, WorECar, WrDr 76, -80, -82, -84, WhAm 10*

Seuss, Dr 1904- *Benet 87, BenetAL 91, CamGLE, CelR 90, TwCChW 89, WrDr 86, -88, -90, -92*
Main entry: Geisel, Theodor Seuss

Seuss, Dr 1904-1991 *AnObit 1991, WrDr 94N*

Severin, Mark 1906- *BioIn 5, -14, ChhPo S2, ClaDrA, ConAu 107, IlsBYP, IlsCB 1946, WhoGrA 62, WhoWor 74*

Severn, David *AuBYP 2, -3, BioIn 7, -12, BlueB 76, ConAu X, IntAu&W 77X, -82X, OxCChiL, SmATA X, TwCChW 78, -83, Who 74, -82, -83, -85, -88, -90, -92, WrDr 76, -80, -82, -84, -86, -88, -90, -92*
Main entry: Unwin, David Storr

Severn, David 1918- *BioIn 14, ScFSB, TwCChW 89, WrDr 94*

Severn, Sue 1918- *AuBYP 2, -3, BioIn 7, ConAu 5R, ForWC 70*

Severn, William Irving 1914- *AuBYP 2, -3, BioIn 7, -9, ConAu 1R, -1NR, -16NR, -36NR, SmATA 1*

Severy, Richard 1944- *ChlFicS*

Sewall, Marcia *AuBYP 3, ChlBIID*

Sewall, Marcia 1935- *BioIn 15, MajAI, SmATA 69*

Sewall, Marcia Osgood 1935- *BioIn 12, ConAu 45, -1NR, -18NR, FifBJA, IlsCB 1967, SmATA 37*

Seward, Prudence Eaton 1926- *BioIn 12, -14, DcBrAr 1, IlsBYP, IlsCB 1967, SmATA 16, WhoArt 80, -82*

Sewell, Anna *Benet 87*

Sewell, Anna 1820-1878 *ArtclWW 2, BioIn 1, -2, -4, -8, -9, -13, -16, BlmGEL, BlmGWL, BritAu 19, CamGEL, CamGLE, CarSB, CasWL, ChlLR 17, DcLEL, DcNaB, EncBrWW, EvLB, FemiCLE, JBA 34, MajAI, NewC, OxCChiL, OxCEng 67, -85, REn, SmATA 24, StaCVF, TelT, TwCChW 78A, -83A, -89A, WhoChL, WrChl*

Sewell, Elizabeth *BioIn 14, DrAPF 87, -89, -91, -93*

Sewell, Elizabeth 1919- *AmWomWr, BioIn 3, -10, CathA 1952, ConAu 49, DrAF 76, DrAP 75, IntAu&W 77, IntWWP 82, TelT, WhoAm 94, WhoAmW 75, -91, WhoUSWr 88, WhoWrEP 89, -92, WorAu 1950*

Sewell, Elizabeth Missing 1815-1906 *ArtclWW 2, BioIn 16, DcBiPP, DcNaB S2, InWom SUP, OxCChiL, StaCVF*

Sewell, Helen 1896-1957 *ConAu 123, TwCChW 89*

Sewell, Helen Moore 1896-1957 *AmAu&B, AmPB, AuBYP 2, -3, BioIn 1, -2, -3, -4, -5, -7, -14, -15, ChhPo, -S2, ConAu 137, ConICB, MajAI, TwCChW 78, -83, WhAmArt 85, WhoAmA 80N, -82N*

Sewell, Helen Moore 1897-1957 *WhoAmA 86N, -89N, -91N*

Sexton, Anne Harvey 1928-1974 *AmAu&B, BioIn 7, -9, -10, -11, CasWL, ChhPo S1, ConAu 1R, -53, ConLC 2, -4, -6, -8, -10, ConPo 70, -75, CroCAP, DcLEL 1940, DrAS 74E, -78E, ForWC 70, MakMC, ModAL, -S1, NewYTBS 74, PenC AM, RAdv 1, SmATA 10, WebE&AL, WhAm 6, WhoAm 74, WhoAmW 74, -75, WhoE 74, WhoTwCL, WorAu 1950*

Sexton, Irwin 1921- *WhoAm 74, -76, -78, -80, -82, -84, -88, WhoSSW 73, -76, -78, -82, -84, -86*

Seyfert, Ella Maie *AuBYP 2, -3, BioIn 7*

Seymour, Alta Halverson *BioIn 2, -11, ConAu P-1, SmATA 10*

Seymour, Alta Halverson 1893- *AmWomPl*

Seymour, Brenda Meredith *ChhPo S2*

Seymour, Flora Warren 1888-1948 *AmAu&B, BioIn 2, CurBio 42, OhA&B, WhAm 2, WhNAA*

Seymour, Mary *Alli SUP, CarSB*

Seyton, Marion *ConAu X*
Main entry: Saxon, Gladys Relyea

Sgroi, Peter Philip 1936- *ConAu 57*

Sgroi, Suzanne Mary 1943- *ConAu 108, WhoAmW 77*

Shachtman, Tom 1942- *BioIn 16, SmATA 49*

Shackleton, C C *ConAu X, -28NR, EncSF 93, MajTwCW, SmATA X*
Main entry: Aldiss, Brian Wilson

Shactman, Tom *AuBYP 3*

Shafer, Robert Eugene 1925- *BioIn 11, BlueB 76, ConAu 57, -10NR, DrAS 74E, -78E, -82E, LEduc 74, SmATA 9, WhoAm 82, -84, -86, -88, -90, WhoWest 74, -76, -78, -80, WrDr 80*

Shafer, Robert Eugene 1936- *WhoWest 92*

Shaff, Albert Laverne 1937- *ConAu 29R*

Shaffer, Paul Raymond 1910- *AmMWSc 73P, -76P, WhoAm 74*

Shaftner, Dorothy 1918- *ConAu 25R*

Shah, Amina 1918- *ConAu 49*

Shahan, Sherry *AuBYP 3*

Shahan, Sherry Jean 1949- *WhoAmW 93*

Shahar, David 1926- *CasWL, ConAu 65, IntAu&W 89, IntWW 83, -89, -91, RAdv 13-2, WhoWorJ 72, -78*

Shahn, Ben 1898-1969 *AtlBL, Benet 87, BioIn 1, -2, -3, -4, -5, -6, -7, -8, -9, -10, -12, -13, -14, -17, BriEAA, ChhPo S1, ConArt 77, -83, -89, ConAu 121, ConPhot 82, -88, CurBio 54, -69, DcCAA 71, -77, -88, EncAB-H, ICPEnP A, IlsCB 1957, -1967, IntDcAA 90, MacBEP, McGEWB, ObitOF 79, ObitT 1961, OxCAmL 65, -83, OxCArt, OxCTwCA, OxDcArt, PhDcTCA 77, PrintW 83, -85, REn, SmATA 21N, WhAm 5, WhAmArt 85, WhoAmA 78N, -80N, -82N, -86N, -89N, -91N, WhoGrA 62, WorAlBi, WorAl, WorArt 1950*

Shahn, Bernarda Bryson *ConAu 49, SmATA X, WhoE 83*
Main entry: Bryson, Bernarda

Shahn, Bernarda Bryson 1903- *BioIn 14, WhoAmA 86, -89, -91*

Shakespeare, William *OxCGer 86*

Shakespeare, William 1564-1616 *Alli, AnCL, AtlBL, Benet 87, BbD, BiDRP&D, BiD&SB,*

BioIn 1, –2, –3, –4, –5, –6, –7, –8, –9, –10, –11, –12, –13, –14, –15, –16, –17, BlmGEL, BritAu, BritWr 1, CamGEL, CamGLE, CamGWoT, CarSB, CasWL, Chambr 1, –2, –3, ChhPo, –S1, –S2, CnDBLB 1, CnE&AP, CnThe, CrtT 1, CroE&S, CyWA 58, DcBiPP, DcEnA, –A, DcEnL, DcEuL, DcLB 62, DcLEL, DcNaB, Dis&D, EncPaPR 91, EncWT, EvLB, FamAYP, FilmgC, HalFC 84, –88, IntDcT 2, LongCEL, LuthC 75, MagSWL, McGEWB, McGEWD 72, –84, MouLC 1, NewC, NotNAT A, –B, OxCAmT 84, OxCEng 67, –85, OxCFilm, OxCFr, OxCGer 76, OxCThe 67, –83, PenC ENG, PlP&P, –A, RComWL, REn, REnWD, RfGEnL 91, WebE&AL, WhDW, WorAlBi, WorAl, WorLitC

Shane, Harold Gray d1993 *NewYTBS 93*

Shane, Harold Gray 1914- *BioIn 14, –15, –17, ConAu 9R, –3NR, –21NR, Future, LEduc 74, SmATA 36, WhoAm 74, –76, –78, –80, –82, –84, –86, –88, –90, WhoMW 92*

Shane, Harold Gray 1914-1993 *ConAu 141, SmATA 76*

Shange, Ntozake *BioIn 14, –15, –16, –17, DrAPF 87, –89, –91, –93, WrDr 86, –88, –90, –92*

Shange, Ntozake 1948- *AfrAmW, AmWomD, ArtclWW 2, Au&Arts 9, BenetAL 91, BlkLC, BlkWr 1, BlmGWL, CamGWoT, ConAu 3BS, –27NR, ConBlAP 88, ConDr 88, –93, ConLC 38, –74, ConPo 91, ConTFT 5, CyWA 89, DrBlPA 90, DramC 3, FemiCLE, InB&W 85, InWom SUP, IntDcT 2, MagSAmL, MajTwCW, NegAl 89, NotBlAW 92, NotWoAT, TwCYAW, WhoAm 86, –88, –90, –92, –94, WhoBlA 85, –88, –90, –92, WhoUSWr 88, WhoWrEP 89, –92, WrDr 94*

Shange, Ntozake 1949- *HanAmWH*

Shankar, Ravi *AuBYP 3, BioIn 14*

Shankar, Ravi 1920- *AuBYP 2S, Baker 84, –92, BioIn 6, –7, –8, –9, –11, –13, CelR, ConMus 9, CurBio 68, EncRk 88, FarE&A 80, –81, IntWW 74, –75, –76, –77, –78, –79, –80, –81, –82, –83, –89, –91, IntWWM 90, NewAmDM, NewGrDA 86, PenDiMP, PenEncP, Who 92, WhoHol A, WhoMus 72, WhoWor 74, –84, –87, –89, –91, –93, WorAl, WorEFlm*

Shankar, Ravi, Pandit 1920- *Who 90*

Shanks, Ann Zane *WhoAm 86, –88, –90, WhoAmW 91, –93, WhoE 91, WhoEnt 92*

Shanks, Ann Zane Kushner *BioIn 11, ConAu 53, SmATA 10, WhoAm 80, –82, –84, WhoAmW 74, –75, –77, WomWMM B*

Shannon, George 1952- *BioIn 14, –16, ConAu 106, –23NR, SixBJA, SmATA 35*

Shannon, Jacqueline *BioIn 17, SmATA 63*

Shannon, Monica d1965 *BioIn 14, TwCChW 89*

Shannon, Monica 1905?-1965 *AmAu&B, AmWomWr, AuBYP 2, –3, BioIn 2, –4, –7, –13, ChhPo, ConAu 109, JBA 51, NewbMB 1922, SmATA 28, Str&VC, TwCChW 78, –83*

Shannon, Terry *AuBYP 2, –3, BioIn 7, –12, ConAu X, SmATA 21*
Main entry: Mercer, Jessie

Shapiro, Irwin 1911- *AuBYP 3*

Shapiro, Irwin 1911-1981 *AuBYP 2, BioIn 2, –7, –14, ChhPo S1, ConAu 81, JBA 51, SmATA 32*

Shapiro, Karl Jay 1913- *AmAu&B, AnCL, BioIn 1, –4, –5, –7, –8, –10, –11, –12, –15, –16, –17, CasWL, CelR, ChhPo, –S2, CnDAL, CnE&AP, ConAu 1R, ConLC 4, –8, ConLCrt 77, ConPo 70, –75, CroCAP, CurBio 44, DcLEL, DrAF 76, DrAP 75, DrAS 74E, –78E, –82E, EncWL, EvLB, IntAu&W 77, –89, IntWW 74, –75, –76, –77, –78, –79, –80, –81, –82, –83, –89, –91, ModAL, –S1, OxCAmL 65, PenC AM, RAdv 1, REn, REnAL, SixAP, TwCA SUP, TwCWr, WebAB 74, –79, WebE&AL, WhoAm 74, –76, –78, –80, –82, –84, –86, –88, –90, –92, –94, WhoTwCL, WhoWest 74, WhoWor 74, WhoWorJ 72, –78, WorAl, WrDr 76, –80*

Shapiro, Milton J 1926- *AuBYP 2, –3, BioIn 7, –14, ConAu 81, SmATA 32*

Shapiro, Rebecca *AuBYP 2, –3, BioIn 8*

Shapiro, William E 1934- *ConAu 25R, –20NR*

Shapp, Charles M 1906- *ConAu 57*

Shapp, Charles M 1906-1989 *BioIn 16, –17, ConAu 127, SmATA 61*

Shapp, Martha Glauber 1910- *BioIn 9, ConAu 1R, –2NR, ForWC 70, SmATA 3, WhoAm 74, –76, –78, –80, –82, –84, –86, –88, –90, WhoAmW 74*

Sharfman, Amalie *AuBYP 2, –3, BioIn 7, –12, ConAu 73, SmATA 14*

Sharma, Partap 1939- *BioIn 12, ConAu 77, –14NR, IntAu&W 82, SmATA 15*

Sharman, Alison *SmATA 70*
Main entry: Leonard, Alison

Sharmat, Marjorie Weinman 1928- *AuBYP 2S, -3, BioIn 9, -14, ConAu 25R, -12NR, -39NR, FifBJA, IntAu&W 77, -82, -86, -91, MajAI, SmATA 4, -33, -74, TwCChW 78, -83, -89, WrDr 76, -80, -82, -84, -86, -88, -90, -92, -94*
Pseud./variant:
Andrews, Wendy

Sharmat, Mitchell 1927- *BioIn 14, -16, ConAu 104, ScF&FL 92, SixBJA, SmATA 33*

Sharoff, Victor *AuBYP 2, -3*

Sharp, Adda Mai *AuBYP 2, -3, BioIn 7*

Sharp, Dallas Lore 1870-1929 *AmAu&B, ConAmL, DcAmAu, DcNAA, JBA 34, REnAL, TwCA, WhAm 1*

Sharp, Edith Lambert 1917- *CanWW 70, -79, -80, ConAu 5R, DcChlFi, OxCCanL, OxCChiL, TwCChW 78, WrDr 80, -82, -84*

Sharp, Margery *IntAu&W 89, IntWW 89, Who 88, -90, WhoWor 87, -89, -91*

Sharp, Margery d1991 *IntWW 91N, Who 92N*

Sharp, Margery 1905- *AuBYP 2, -3, Au&Wr 71, BioIn 1, -2, -4, -8, -9, -13, -16, BlueB 76, ConAu 21R, -18NR, ConNov 72, -76, -82, -86, DcLEL, EncBrWW, EvLB, IntAu&W 77, IntWW 74, -75, -76, -77, -78, -79, -80, -81, -82, -83, LongCTC, NewC, OxCChiL, RAdv 1, REn, SmATA 1, -29, ThrBJA, TwCA, -SUP, TwCChW 78, -83, -89, Who 74, -82, -83, -85, WhoAmW 74, WhoWor 74, -84, WrDr 76, -80, -82, -84, -86, -88, -90*

Sharp, Margery 1905-1991 *BioIn 17, ChlLR 27, ConAu 134, MajAI, ScF&FL 92, SmATA 67*

Sharp, William 1855-1905 *Alli SUP, AnCL, BbD, BiD&SB, BioIn 12, -16, BritAu 19, CamGLE, CasWL, ChhPo, -S1, -S2, CmScLit, DcBiA, DcEnA, -A, DcLEL, DcNaB S2, Dis&D, EvLB, LongCTC, NewC, OxCAusL, OxCEng 67, -85, PenC ENG, RfGEnL 91, StaCVF, TwCLC 39*

Sharp, William 1900-1961 *BioIn 1, -2, -3, -5, -6, -14, IlsBYP, IlsCB 1744, -1946, WhAmArt 85, WhoAmA 80N, -82N, -86N, -89N, -91N*

Sharp, Zerna A 1889-1981 *AnObit 1981, BioIn 12, -13, ConAu 104, NewYTBS 81, SmATA 27N*

Sharpe, Caroline *IlsBYP*

Sharpe, Mitchell Raymond 1924- *Au&Wr 71, BioIn 11, ConAu 29R, SmATA 12, WhoSSW 75, -76, -93, WrDr 76, -80, -82, -84*

Sharpe, Stella Gentry *AmPB*

Sharpe, Susan 1946- *SmATA 71*

Shattuck, Roger *IntvTCA 2*

Shattuck, Roger 1923- *SmATA 64, WrDr 86, -88, -90, -92, -94*

Shaw, Arnold d1989 *NewYTBS 89*

Shaw, Arnold 1909- *ASCAP 66, AuBYP 2S, -3, Baker 84, BioIn 3, -9, CpmDNM 82, ConAmC 76, -82, ConAu 1R, -1NR, IntWWM 85, -90, NewGrDA 86, SmATA 4, WhoAm 74, -76, -78, -80, -82, -84, -86, -88, WhoAmM 83, WhoE 74, WhoUSWr 88, WhoWest 87, WhoWor 78, WhoWrEP 89*

Shaw, Arnold 1909-1989 *Baker 92, ConAu 129, ScF&FL 92, SmATA 63, WhAm 10*

Shaw, Charles Green 1892-1974 *AmAu&B, AmPB, BioIn 10, -11, ConAu P-1, DcCAA 71, -77, IlsBYP, SmATA 13, WhAm 6, WhAmArt 85, WhoAm 74, WhoAmA 73, -78N, -80N, -82N, -86N, -89N, -91N*

Shaw, Edward Richard 1850-1903 *Alli SUP, BiInAmS, CarSB, CyEd, DcNAA, WhAm 1*

Shaw, Evelyn 1927- *AmMWSc 73P, -76P, BioIn 7, -13, SmATA 28*

Shaw, Flora L 1851-1929 *StaCVF*

Shaw, Flora Louisa 1852-1929 *Alli SUP, BioIn 1, -12, BritAu 19, JBA 34, NewC, OxCChiL, SmATA X, TelT*
Pseud./variant:
Lugard, Flora Louisa Shaw

Shaw, Frank H 1878- *BioIn 1, -5*

Shaw, James Byrnie 1866-1948 *AmLY, IndAu 1816, WhAm 2, WhNAA*

Shaw, Janet *DrAPF 87*

Shaw, Janet 1937- *ConAu 127, SmATA 61, WhoUSWr 88, WhoWrEP 89, -92*
Pseud./variant:
Beeler, Janet
Shaw, Janet Beeler

Shaw, Janet Beeler *ConAu 127, DrAPF 89, -91, -93*

Shaw, Janet Beeler 1937- *BioIn 17, SmATA X*
Main entry: Shaw, Janet

Shaw, John Mackay 1897-1984 *BiDrLUS 70, ChhPo, -S1, -S2, ConAu 29R, -13NR, IntAu&W 77, WhoLibS 66, WrDr 76, -80, -82, -84*

Shaw, Kerry *NatPD 77*

Shaw, Margaret 1940- *SmATA 68*

Shaw, Margaret Mason 1904- *Au&Wr 71*

Shaw, Nancy 1946- *SmATA 71*

Shaw, Ray *BioIn 1, -10, ConAu 33R, ForWC 70, IntAu&W 82, SmATA 7, WhoAmW 74, -75, WrDr 76, -80, -82, -84*

Shaw, Reeves 1886-1952 *BioIn 2*

Shaw, Richard *DrAPF 87, -89, -91, -93*

Shaw, Richard 1923- *BioIn 11, ChhPo S2, ConAu 37R, DrAP 75, SmATA 12, WrDr 76, -80, -82, -84, -86, -88*

Shaw, Ronald Erwin 1923- *ConAu 17R, DrAS 74H, -78H, -82H, IntAu&W 77, -82, WrDr 76, -80, -82, -84*

Shaw, Wayne Eugene 1932- *ConAu 53, DrAS 78E, -82E, WhoMW 78, -80, -92*

Shawn, Frank S *ConAu X, EncSF 93, TwCSFW 86, -91, WrDr 82, -84, -86, -88, -90, -92*
Main entry: Goulart, Ron

Shawn, Frank S 1933- *WrDr 94*

Shay, Arthur 1922- *BioIn 9, ConAu 33R, SmATA 4, WhoAm 74, -76, -78, WhoMW 74, -76*

Shay, Frank 1888-1954 *AmAu&B, BenetAL 91, BioIn 2, -3, ChhPo S1, -S2, CurBio 52, -54, ObitOF 79, REnAL, Str&VC, WhAm 3, WhNAA*

Shay, Lacey *ConAu 41NR, SmATA X*
Main entry: Shebar, Sharon Sigmond

Shay, Myrtle Quick 1889- *ForWC 70*

Shea, George 1940- *BioIn 15, -16, ConAu 108, ScF&FL 92, SmATA 42, -54*

Shea, Pegi Deitz 1960- *SmATA 77*

Shead, Isobel Ann *SingR 1*

Sheahan, Henry Beston *AmAu&B, JBA 34, -51, WhAm 8*
Main entry: Beston, Henry

Shealy, C Norman 1932- *ConAu 57, -7NR*

Shearer, John 1947- *AuBYP 2S, -3, BioIn 13, -15, -16, BlkAuII, -92, ConAu 125, SmATA 27, -43*

Shearer, Ted d1992 *NewYTBS 92*

Shearer, Ted 1919- *BioIn 15, SmATA 43*

Shebar, Sharon Sigmond 1945- *BioIn 14, ConAu 103, -19NR, -41NR, SmATA 36*
Pseud./variant:
Shay, Lacey

Shecter, Ben *WrDr 86, -88, -92, -94*

Shecter, Ben 1935- *AuBYP 2, BioIn 8, -9, -12, ChhPo S1, ConAu 81, IlsCB 1957, -1967, ScF&FL 92, SmATA 16, ThrBJA, WrDr 76, -80, -82, -84*

Shedd, Charlie W 1915- *BioIn 2, -10, ConAu 17R*

Sheean, Vincent 1899-1975 *AmAu&B, AmNov, AuBYP 2S, -3, BenetAL 91, BioIn 1, -2, -3, -4, -5, -10, -14, -16, CnDAL, ConAmA, ConAu 61, CurBio 41, -75N, EncAJ, IntAu&W 77, NewYTBS 74, ObitOF 79, OxCAmL 65, -83, REn, REnAL, TwCA, -SUP*

Sheed, Wilfrid John Joseph 1930- *BioIn 8, -10, -11, ConAu 65, ConLC 2, -4, -10, ConNov 72, -76, DrAF 76, IntAu&W 89, -91, IntWW 89, -91, ModAL S1, NewC, WhoAm 74, -80, -82, -86, -88, -90, -92, -94, WorAu 1950, WrDr 76, -80*

Sheedy, Alexandra Elizabeth 1962- *BioIn 10, -12, ConAu 85, SmATA 19, -39*
Pseud./variant:
Sheedy, Ally

Sheedy, Ally *BioIn 14, -15, -17, HalFC 88, NewYTBS 86*
Main entry: Sheedy, Alexandra Elizabeth

Sheedy, Ally 1962- *BioIn 13, ConTFT 2, -6, IntMPA 86, -88, -92, News 89-1, SmATA X, WhoAm 92, -94, WhoAmW 91, -93, WhoEnt 92, WorAlBi*

Sheehan, Ethna 1908- *AuBYP 2, -3, BioIn 8, -11, ConAu 61, SmATA 9, WhoLibS 55*

Sheehan, George Augustine 1918- *BioIn 11, ConAu 73*

Sheehan, Patty 1945- *SmATA 77*

Shefelman, Janice 1930- *SmATA 58*

Shefelman, Janice Jordan 1930- *BioIn 16, ConAu 120*

Shefelman, Tom 1927- *BioIn 16, SmATA 58*

Sheffe, Norman *OxCCan SUP*

Sheffer, H R
Main entry: Abels, Harriette Sheffer

Sheffield, Janet N 1926- *BioIn 13, ConAu 65, SmATA 26*

Shefter, Harry 1910- *ConAu 9R*

Shefts, Joelle *BioIn 16, SmATA 49*

Shekerjian, Haig *IlsBYP*

Shekerjian, Regina Tor *AuBYP 3, BioIn 12, ChhPo S2, IlsBYP, SmATA 16*
Pseud./variant:
Tor, Regina

Shelby, Brit 1949- *ConAu 73*

Sheldon, Ann *ConAu P-2, OxCChiL, SmATA 1, -67*
Main entry: Stratemeyer, Edward L

Sheldon, Ann 1936- *WrDr 94*

Sheldon, Aure 1917-1976 *BioIn 11, ConAu 61, SmATA 12*

Sheldon, Lee *ConAu X, -41NR, ConSFA, IntAu&W 91X, WrDr 76, -80, -82, -84, -86, -88, -90, -92*
Main entry: Lee, Wayne C

Sheldon, Lee 1917- *EncSF 93, WrDr 94*

Sheldon, Muriel *AuBYP 3*

Sheldon, Muriel 1926- *BioIn 15, ConAu 101, -18NR, SmATA 39, -45*
Pseud./variant:
Batherman, Muriel

Sheldon, Walter J 1917- *AuBYP 2, -3, AuNews 1, BioIn 3, -10, ConAu 25R, -10NR*
Pseud./variant:
Walters, Shelly

Sheldon, Walter J 1917-1979? *ScF&FL 92*

Sheldon, Walter James 1917- *IntAu&W 86*

Sheldon, William D 1915- *ScF&FL 92*

Sheldon, William Denley 1915- *ConAu 17R, WhoAm 74, -76*

Shellabarger, Samuel 1888-1954 *AmAu&B, AmNov, BenetAL 91, BioIn 1, -2, -3, -4, -7, -14, CnDAL, CurBio 45, -54, ObitOF 79, OhA&B, REn, REnAL, TwCA SUP, TwCRHW 90, WhAm 3*

Shelley, Frances *SmATA X*
Main entry: Wees, Frances Shelley

Shelley, Mary Wollstonecraft 1797-1851 *ArtclWW 2, Benet 87, BioIn 15, -16, -17, BlmGEL, BlmGWL, CnDBLB 3, DcLB 110, -116, EncBrWW, EncSF 93, HalFC 88, NewEScF, PenEncH, RAdv 13-1, ScF&FL 92, WorAlBi*

Shelley, Mary Wollstonecraft Godwin 1797-1851 *Alli, AtlBL, BbD, BiD&SB, BioIn 1, -2, -3, -4, -5, -7, -8, -9, -10, -11, -12, -13, BritAu 19, CasWL, Chambr 3, ChhPo, -S1, ContDcW 89, CyWA 58, DcBiA, DcBiPP, DcEnA, DcEnL, DcEuL, DcLEL, DcNaB, EncMys, EvLB, FilmgC, HalFC 84, HerW, -84, InWom SUP, IntDcWB, MouLC 3, NewC, NinCLC 14, OxCEng 67, -85, PenC ENG, RAdv 1, REn, SmATA 29, WebE&AL, WhDW, WhoHr&F, WhoSciF, WorAl, WorLitC*

Shelley, Noreen *WrDr 86, -88*

Shelley, Noreen 1920- *ConAu 104, OxCChiL, SingR 1, TwCChW 78, -83, WrDr 80, -82, -84*

Shelley, Noreen Walker 1920- *DcChlFi*

Shelton, William Roy 1919- *AuBYP 2S, -3 AuNews 1, BioIn 2, -10, ConAu 5R, -11NR, IntAu&W 77, -82, -86, SmATA 5, WhoSSW 76, -78*

Shemin, Margaretha 1928- *BioIn 9, ConAu 13R, SmATA 4*

Shemin, Margaretha Hoeneveld 1928- *DcAmChF 1960*

Shenton, Edward 1895-1977 *AmAu&B, BioIn 1, -2, -5, -15, IlrAm 1880, -E, IlsBYP, IlsCB 1744, -1946, SmATA 45, WhAmArt 85*

Shepard, Aaron 1950- *ConAu 142, SmATA 75*

Shepard, Ernest H 1879-1976 *BioIn 14*

Shepard, Ernest Howard 1879-1976 *Au&Wr 71, BioIn 1, -4, -5, -6, -8, -9, -10, -11, -12, -13, ChhPo, -S1, -S2, ChlLR 27, ConAu 9R, -65, -23NR, ConICB, DcBrA 1, -2, DcBrBI, DcNaB 1971, DcVicP 2, GrBr, IlsBYP, IlsCB 1744, -1946, -1957, -1967, MajAI, MorJA, OxCChiL, REn, SmATA 3, -24N, -33, Who 74, WhoChL*

Shepard, Mary *MajAI, SmATA X*

Shepard, Mary 1909-
Main entry: Knox, Eleanor Jessie

Shepard, Mary Eleanor 1909- *BioIn 5, -8, -14, -16, IlsBYP, IlsCB 1946, -1957, -1967, WhoChL*

Shephard, Esther 1891-1975 *BioIn 1, –10, –13, ConAu 57, –P-2, DrAS 74E, SmATA 5, –26N*

Shepherd, Catherine 1912-1976 *AuWomWr, OxCAusL, SingR 2*

Shepherd, Elizabeth *AuBYP 2S, –3, BioIn 9, ConAu 33R, SmATA 4*

Shepherd, James Affleck 1867-1946? *BioIn 1, –14, DcBrBI, IlsCB 1744*

Shepherd, Walter Bradley 1904- *Au&Wr 71, ConAu 105*

Shepherd, William Robert 1871-1934 *DcAmAu, DcNAA, HarEnUS, WhAm 1*

Sheppard, Harold Lloyd 1922- *AmMWSc 73S, ConAu 45, –1NR, WhoSSW 76, –91*

Sheppard, Raymond 1913-1958 *BioIn 5, –14, ClaDrA, DcBrAr 1, IlsCB 1946*

Sheppard, Sally 1917- *ConAu 69*

Sheppard-Jones, Elisabeth Maia 1920- *Au&Wr 71, ConAu 13R, WrDr 76, –80*

Sherburne, Zoa 1912- *BioIn 16, SmATA 18AS*

Sherburne, Zoa Lillian Morin 1912- *AuBYP 2, BioIn 8, –9, ConAu 1R, ForWC 70, FourBJA, SmATA 3, WhoPNW*

Sherburne, Zoa Morin 1912- *AuBYP 3, ConAu 37NR, EncSF 93, MajAI, TwCYAW*

Sherer, Mary Louise 1901- *ConAu 101*

Sheret, Rene 1933- *ConAu 29R, WhoWest 74*

Sheridan, James Edward 1922- *ConAu 21R, DrAS 74H, –78H, –82H, WhoAm 74, –76, –78, –80, –82, –84, –86, –88, –90, –92, –94, WhoMW 84*

Sherin, Ray 1926- *BioIn 8, IlsCB 1957*

Sherlock, A B *ChhPo*

Sherlock, Patti *SmATA 71*

Sherlock, Philip 1902- *BlkAuII 92, Who 92, WrDr 86, –88, –90*

Sherlock, Philip, Sir 1902- *BlkAuII, Who 88, –90*

Sherlock, Philip Manderson 1902- *AuBYP 3, BioIn 16*

Sherlock, Philip Manderson, Sir 1902- *AnCL, AuBYP 2, Au&Wr 71, BioIn 7, –9, ConAu 5R, –6NR, ConPo 70, DcAfL, IntAu&W 77, Who 74, WhoWor 74, WrDr 80*

Sherman, Allan 1924-1973 *ASCAP 66, AuBYP 2, –3, BioIn 6, –7, –8, –9, –10, ChhPo S1, ConAu 45, –101, CurBio 66, –74, NewYTBE 73, ObitOF 79, RkOn 74, WhAm 6, WhoCom, WorAl*

Sherman, D R 1934- *BioIn 13, –16, ConAu 13R, –8NR, SmATA 29, –48*

Sherman, Diane 1928- *BioIn 11, ConAu 9R, –5NR, SmATA 12*

Sherman, Elizabeth *AuBYP 2, –3, ConAu X, SmATA 5*
Main entry: Friskey, Margaret Richards

Sherman, Emalene 1920- *ConAu 21R*

Sherman, Frank Dempster 1860-1916 *Alli SUP, AmAu, AmAu&B, BenetAL 91, BbD, BiD&SB, BioIn 13, ChhPo, –S1, ChrP, CnDAL, DcAmAu, DcNAA, OxCAmL 65, –83, REn, REnAL, WhAm 1*

Sherman, Harold M 1898-1987 *ScF&FL 92*

Sherman, Harold Morrow 1898- *BiDPara, BioIn 15, ConAu 77, EncO&P 1, –2, SmATA 37, WhNAA, WhoSSW 73, –75, –76*

Sherman, Harold Morrow 1898-1987 *EncSF 93*

Sherman, Ingrid Kugelmann 1919- *IntAu&W 77, WhoAmM 83, WhoE 74, WrDr 76, –80*

Sherman, Jane 1908- *BioIn 10, ConAu 73, –12NR*

Sherman, Josepha *ConAu 127, ScF&FL 92, SmATA 75*

Sherman, Nancy *AuBYP 2S, –3, ConAu X, SmATA 4*
Main entry: Rosenberg, Nancy Sherman

Sherman, Theresa 1916- *BioIn 5, IlsBYP, IlsCB 1946*
Pseud./variant:
Reed, Veronica

Sherrard, Philip 1922- *Au&Wr 71, ConAu 13R, –7NR*

Sherriff, Robert Cedric 1896-1975 *Au&Wr 71, BiE&WWA, BioIn 2, –4, –5, –8, –10, –13, –14, Chambr 3, CnMD, CnThe, ConAu 61, –85, ConDr 73, CroCD, CyWA 58, DcLEL, DcNaB 1971, EncWT, EvLB, GrBr, IntMPA 75, IntWW 74, –75, –76N, LongCTC, McGEWD 72, ModBrL, ModWD, NewC, NotNAT A, –B, OxCEng 67, OxCThe 67, PenC ENG, REn, TwCA, –SUP, TwCWr, Who 74, WhoThe 72, WhoWor 74*

Sherrill, Dorothy 1901- *AmPB, ConAu 69*
Pseud./variant:
Martin, April

Sherrington, Richard Wallace *WrDr 76*

Sherrod, Jane *ConAu X, SmATA 4, –X*
Main entry: Singer, Jane Sherrod

Sherrod, Jane 1917-1985 *BioIn 15*

Sherry, Sylvia *AuBYP 3, IntAu&W 86X, –91, TwCChW 89, WrDr 86, –88, –90, –92, –94*

Sherry, Sylvia 1932- *AuBYP 2S, Au&Wr 71, BioIn 11, ConAu 49, –34NR, SmATA 8, TwCChW 78, –83, WrDr 76, –80, –82, –84*

Sherwan, Earl 1917- *BioIn 9, ConAu 5R, SmATA 3*

Sherwood, Mrs 1775-1851 *CarSB*

Sherwood, Debbie *ConAu 25R, WhoAmW 74, –75, WrDr 76, –80, –82, –84*

Sherwood, Jonathan *SmATA 74*
Main entry: London, Jonathan Paul

Sherwood, Mary Martha 1775-1851 *Alli, ArtclWW 2, BiD&SB, BioIn 1, –8, –10, BritAu 19, CamGLE, CarSB, CasWL, Chambr 3, DcBiPP, DcBrAmW, DcEnL, DcEuL, DcInB, DcNaB, EvLB, FemiCLE, NewC, OxCChiL, OxCEng 67, –85, WhoChL*

Sherwood, Merriam 1892-1961 *AnCL, BioIn 5*

Shetty, Sharat 1940- *ConAu 73*

Shevey, Sandra *WomWMM B*

Shick, Eleanor 1942- *SmATA 9*

Shideler, Ross *AuBYP 2S, –3*

Shiefman, Vicky *DrAPF 87, –89, –91, –93*

Shiefman, Vicky 1942- *BioIn 13, ConAu 57, DrAPF 83, –85, MichAu 80, SmATA 22*

Shiel, Matthew Phipps 1865-1947 *BbD, BioIn 1, –4, –7, –12, –14, –15, DcLEL, EncMys, LongCTC, NewC, ObitOF 79, TwCA, –SUP, WhoLA*

Shields, Brenda Desmond 1914- *BioIn 15, ConAu 5R, SmATA 37*

Shields, Charles 1944- *BioIn 11, SmATA 10*

Shields, Karena *AuBYP 2, –3, BioIn 7*

Shields, Rita *AuBYP 2, –3, BioIn 7*

Shiels, Barbara 1943- *SmATA X*
Main entry: Adams, Barbara Johnston

Shigley, Forrest Dwight 1930- *ConAu 1R, IndAu 1917*

Shikes, Ralph E 1912-1992 *BioIn 17, ConAu 137, NewYTBS 92*

Shikes, Ralph Edmund 1912- *ConAu 29R, –12NR, IntAu&W 77, –82, WrDr 76, –80, –82, –84, –86, –88, –90, –92*

Shikes, Ralph Edmund 1912-1992 *WrDr 94N*

Shillabeer, Mary Eleanor 1904- *BioIn 8, IlsCB 1957*

Shillaber, Benjamin Pendleton 1814-1890 *EncAHmr*

Shillaber, Benjamin Penhallow 1814-1890 *Alli, –SUP, AmAu, AmAu&B, BenetAL 91, BbD, BiD&SB, BioIn 1, –9, –11, –13, –15, CarSB, ChhPo, –S2, CnDAL, DcAmAu, DcEnL, DcLB 1, DcLEL, DcNAA, HarEnUS, OxCAmL 65, –83, REnAL, WhAm HS*

Shilstone, Arthur 1923?- *BioIn 5, IlsBYP*

Shimer, John Asa 1913- *AmMWSc 73P, –76P*

Shimin, Symeon 1902- *BioIn 5, –8, –9, –11, BkP, ChhPo S1, –S2, ConAu 81, IlsBYP, IlsCB 1946, –1957, –1967, MajAI, SmATA 13, ThrBJA, WhAmArt 85*

Shine, Deborah 1932- *SmATA 71*
Pseud./variant:
Adams, Edith
Bright, Sarah
Harris, Robin
Slier, Debby

Shinn, Everett 1876-1953 *BioIn 1, –2, –3, –4, –5, –6, –10, –12, –14, BriEAA, ChhPo, –S2, CurBio 51, –53, DcCAA 71, –77, –88, IlrAm 1880, –A, IlsBYP, IlsCB 1744, –1946, ObitOF 79, OxCTwCA, OxDcArt, PhDcTCA 77, SmATA 21, WhAm 3, WhAmArt 85, WhoAmA 78N, –80N, –82N, –86N, –89N, –91N*

Shipley, Joseph T d1988 *NewYTBS 88*

Shipley, Joseph T 1893- *WhoAm 86*

Shipley, Joseph T 1893-1988 *ConAu 125, ConTFT 6, WhAm 9*

Shipley, Joseph Twadell 1893- *AmAu&B, AnMV 1926, BioIn 2, BlueB 76, ChhPo, –S1, ConAmTC, ConAu 13R, –9NR, IntAu&W 82, –86, NotNAT, REnAL, WhJnl, WhNAA, WhoAm 74, –76, –78, –80, –82, –84,*

WhoThe 77, –81, WrDr 76, –80, –82, –84, –86, –88

Shipley, Joseph Twadell 1893-1988 *BioIn 15, –16*

Shipley, Nan 1904- *BioIn 10, ConAu 9R, OxCCan SUP, Profile 1*

Shippen, Katherine Binney 1892-1980 *AnCL, AuBYP 2, –3, BioIn 2, –3, –6, –7, –9, –12, –13, –14, ConAu 5R, –93, CurBio 54, MorJA, SmATA 1, –23N, Str&VC*

Shipton, Eric Earle 1907-1977 *Au&Wr 71, BioIn 8, –11, ConAu 65, DcNaB 1971, IntAu&W 77, SmATA 10, Who 74*

Shirer, William L *BioIn 14, –15, –16, –17, NewYTBS 90*

Shirer, William L 1904- *Benet 87, EncWB, IntAu&W 86, –91, MajTwCW, NewYTBS 86, WorAlBi, WrDr 86, –88, –90, –92*

Shirer, William L 1904-1993 *NewYTBS 93*

Shirer, William Lawrence 1904- *AmAu&B, AuBYP 2, –3, Au&Wr 71, BiDAmJo, BioIn 1, –2, –3, –4, –6, –7, –8, –11, –12, –13, BlueB 76, ConAu 9R, –7NR, CurBio 41, –62, DcLB 4, EncAJ, EncTwCJ, IntAu&W 77, –82, –89, IntWW 74, –75, –76, –77, –78, –79, –80, –81, –82, –83, –89, –91, JrnUS, OxCAmL 65, –83, REn, REnAL, SmATA 45, TwCA SUP, WebAB 74, –79, Who 74, –82, –83, –85, –88, –90, –92, WhoAm 74, –76, –78, –80, –82, –84, –86, –88, –90, –92, –94, WhoUSWr 88, WhoWor 74, –78, WhoWrEP 89, –92, WorAl, WrDr 76, –80, –82, –84, –94*

Shirk, Jeanette Campbell 1898- *AuBYP 2, BioIn 7, ChhPo, –S1*

Shirk, Jeannette Campbell 1898- *AuBYP 3*

Shirley, Jean 1919- *SmATA 70*

Shirreffs, Gordon D *BioIn 15*

Shirreffs, Gordon D 1914- *BioIn 16, ConAu 21NR, TwCWW 91*

Shirreffs, Gordon Donald 1914- *AuBYP 2, –3, BioIn 7, –11, ConAu 13R, –6NR, EncFWF, IntAu&W 91, SmATA 11, WrDr 76, –80, –82, –84, –86, –88, –90, –92, –94*
Pseud./variant:
Donalds, Gordon
Flynn, Jackson
Gordon, Stewart

Shirts, Morris A 1922- *BioIn 17, ConAu 73, LEduc 74, SmATA 63*

Shirvanian, Rose *ChhPo*

Shissler, Barbara Johnson *ConAu 28NR*

Shissler, Barbara Johnson 1931- *ConAu 29R, WhoAmW 74, –75*

Shoberg, Lore 1949- *ConAu 33R*

Shockley, Robert Joseph 1921- *LEduc 74*

Shoemaker, Hurst Hugh 1907- *AmMWSc 73P, –76P, IndAu 1917*

Shoemaker, J W, Mrs *DcNAA*

Shoesmith, Kathleen A 1938- *IntAu&W 91, TwCRHW 90, WrDr 86, –88, –90, –92, –94*

Shoesmith, Kathleen Anne 1938- *Au&Wr 71, ConAu 49, –1NR, –17NR, IntAu&W 77, –82, WrDr 76, –80, –82, –84*

Sholokhov, Mikhail A 1905-1984 *AuBYP 3*

Sholokhov, Mikhail Aleksandrovich 1905-1984 *AuBYP 2S, Benet 87, BioIn 1, –4, –5, –6, –7, –9, –10, –11, –12, –13, –14, –15, –17, CasWL, ClDMEL 47, CnMWL, ConLC 7, CurBio 42, –60, –84N, CyWA 58, DcRusL, DcRusLS, EncWL, EvEuW, HanRL, IntAu&W 77, IntWW 74, –75, –76, –77, –78, –79, –80, –81, –82, –83, LongCTC, MakMC, McGEWB, ModSL 1, NewYTBS 84, OxCEng 85, PenC EUR, REn, SmATA 36N, TwCA, –SUP, TwCWr, Who 74, –82, –83, –85N, WhoTwCL, WhoWor 74, –82, WorAl*

Shor, Pekay 1923- *ConAu 45*

Shore, June Lewis *AuBYP 2S, –3, AuNews 1, BioIn 10, –14, ConAu 105, SmATA 30*

Shore, Robert 1924- *BioIn 5, –8, –15, IlrAm 1880, –G, IlsBYP, IlsCB 1957, SmATA 39*

Shore, Wilma 1913- *ConAu 13R, ForWC 70*

Short, Alison 1920- *ConAu 61*

Short, Lester Le Roy 1933- *AmMWSc 92*

Short, Lester Leroy 1933- *AmMWSc 89*

Short, Lester LeRoy, Jr. 1933- *AmMWSc 73P, –76P, –82, –86, WhoE 75*

Short, Michael 1937- *BioIn 17, ConAu 42NR, IntWWM 90, SmATA 65*

Short, Robert L 1932- *ScF&FL 92*

Short, Robert Lester 1932- *ConAu 77, WhoMW 74, –76*

Short, Roger *SmATA X*
Main entry: Arkin, Alan

Shortall, Leonard W *BioIn 5, –8, ConAu 81, IlsBYP, IlsCB 1946, –1957, –1967, SmATA 19*

Shorter, Bani *AuBYP 2, –3, BioIn 7*

Shortt, Terence M *BioIn 15*

Shortt, Terence Michael 1911- *BioIn 11, ConAu 77*

Shostak, Jerome 1913- *ConAu 17R, –7NR, WhoE 75, –77*

Shotwell, Louisa R 1902- *TwCChW 89, WrDr 86, –88, –90*

Shotwell, Louisa Rossiter 1902- *AuBYP 2S, –3, BioIn 3, –9, –10, ConAu 1R, –4NR, DcAmChF 1960, MorBMP, OxCChiL, SmATA 3, ThrBJA, TwCChW 78, –83, WrDr 76, –80, –82, –84*

Showalter, Jean *AuBYP 3*

Showalter, Jean B *AuBYP 2S, BioIn 11, ConAu 21R, SmATA 12*

Showell, Ellen Harvey 1934- *BioIn 14, ConAu 85, SmATA 33*

Showers, Paul 1910- *SmATA 7AS*

Showers, Paul C 1910- *AmPB, BioIn 12, ChlLR 6, ConAu 1R, –4NR, –38NR, FourBJA, MajAI, MichAu 80, SmATA 21*

Shreve, Susan 1939- *AuBYP 3, SixBJA*

Shreve, Susan R 1939- *WrDr 88, –90, –92*

Shreve, Susan Richards *BioIn 15, –16, DrAPF 87, –89, –91, –93*

Shreve, Susan Richards 1939- *ConAu 5AS, –5NR, –38NR, ConLC 23, DcAmChF 1985, DrAPF 83, –85, IntWW 91, MajAI, ScF&FL 92, SmATA 41, –46, WhoAm 88, –90, –92, –94, WhoAmW 87, –89, –91, –93, WhoUSWr 88, WrDr 82, –84, –86, –94*

Shriver, Donald Woods, Jr. 1927- *ConAu 45, –1NR, DrAS 74P, –78P, –82P, WhoAm 80, –82, –84, –86, –88, –90, –92, –94, WhoE 81, –83, WhoRel 75, –92*

Shriver, Jean Adair 1932- *ConAu 142, SmATA 75*

Shtainmets, Leon *BioIn 12, –14, ConAu 105, IlsCB 1967, SmATA 32*

Shub, Elizabeth *AuBYP 2S, –3, BioIn 10, –17, ChhPo S2, ConAu 41R, –15NR, FifBJA, SmATA 5*

Shubert, Reinold 1905- *IntAu&W 77*

Shulevitz, Uri *ChlBIID*

Shulevitz, Uri 1935- *AuBYP 2, –3, BioIn 8, –9, –12, –14, –16, BkP, ChhPo S1, ChlLR 5, ConAu 9R, –3NR, DcLB 61, IlsBYP, IlsCB 1957, –1967, IntAu&W 77, –82, MajAI, NewbC 1966, SmATA 3, –50, ThrBJA, WhoAm 74, –76, –78, –80, –82, –84, –86, –88, –90, –92, –94, WhoUSWr 88, WhoWrEP 89, –92*

Shull, Margaret Anne Wyse 1940- *ConAu 77*

Shulman, Alix Kates *DrAPF 87, –89, –91, –93*

Shulman, Alix Kates 1932- *BioIn 10, –13, ConAu 29R, –43NR, ConLC 2, –10, DrAF 76, DrAPF 83, –85, JeAmFiW, SmATA 7, WhoAmW 74, –75, WorAu 1975*

Shulman, Irving 1913- *AmAu&B, AmNov, Au&Wr 71, BioIn 2, –4, –11, ConAu 1R, –6NR, CurBio 56, SmATA 13, WhoAm 74, –76, –78, –80, –82, –84, –88, –90, –92, WhoE 74, WhoUSWr 88, WhoWorJ 72, –78, WhoWrEP 89, –92, WrDr 76, –80, –82, –84, –86, –88, –90, –92, –94*

Shulman, Max *DrAPF 87, –89, –91*

Shulman, Max 1919- *IntMPA 86, –88, WhoAm 86, –88, WhoUSWr 88*

Shulman, Max 1919-1988 *BioIn 16, ConAu 126, CurBio 88N, NewYTBS 88, SmATA 59, WhAm 9*

Shulman, Milton *Who 88, –90, –92*

Shulman, Milton 1913- *Au&Wr 71, BlueB 76, ConAu 103, IntAu&W 77, Who 74, WhoThe 72, –77, –81, WrDr 76, –80, –82, –84, –86, –88, –90, –92, –94*

Shultz, Gladys Denny 1895- *ConAu 49, WhoWest 78, –80*

Shultz, Gladys Denny 1895-1984 *BioIn 14*

Shultz, James Willard 1859- *ArizL*

Shumsky, Zena Feldman
Main entry: Hampson, Zena

Shumsky, Zena Feldman 1926- *ConAu 1R, SmATA X, WrDr 76, –80, –82, –84*

Shura, Mary Francis *BioIn 9, –10, –12, ConAu 133, –X, ForWC 70, IntAu&W 77X, –82X, –86X, SmATA 6, –65, ThrBJA, WhoUSWr 88, WhoWrEP 89, –92, WrDr 76, –80, –86, –88, –90*
Main entry: Craig, Mary Francis

Shura, Mary Francis 1923- *AuBYP 3*

Pseud./variant:
Siegel, Helen

Siegmeister, Elie 1909- *AmAu&B, AmComp, ASCAP 66, AuBYP 2, -3, Au&Wr 71, Baker 84, BiE&WWA, BioIn 1, -2, -7, -8, -9, -11, -14, -16, BlueB 76, CompSN SUP, ConAmC 76, -82, ConAu 1R, -1NR, DcCM, IntWWM 85, -90, NewGrDA 86, NewOxM, NotNAT, OxCMus, WhoAm 74, -76, -78, -80, -82, -84, -86, -88, -90, WhoAmJ 80, WhoAmM 83, WhoE 83, -85, WhoWorJ 72, WrDr 76, -80, -82, -84*

Siegmeister, Elie 1909-1991 *Baker 92, BioIn 17, ConAu 133, NewAmDM, NewYTBS 91, WhAm 10*

Sievers, Harry Joseph 1920-1977 *AmCath 80, BioIn 11, ConAu 25R, -73, DrAS 74H, LEduc 74, WhAm 7, WhoAm 74, -76, -78*

Sigourney, Lydia H 1791-1865 *BioAmW, DcLB 73*

Sigourney, Lydia Howard 1791-1865 *BioIn 15, FemiCLE*

Sigourney, Lydia Howard Huntley 1791-1865 *Alli, AmAu, AmAu&B, AmPeW, AmWomWr, BenetAL 91, BbD, BiD&SB, BioIn 3, -4, -7, -9, -11, -12, -13, CarSB, CasWL, CelCen, Chambr 3, ChhPo, -S1, -S2, CnDAL, CyAL, CyEd, DcAmAu, DcEnL, DcLB 42, DcLEL, DcNAA, EvLB, FemPA, HarEnUS, InWom SUP, NewGrDA 86, OxCAmL 65, -83, PoChrch, REnAL, WebAB 74, -79, WhAm HS*

Sigourney, Lydia Huntley 1791-1865 *BlmGWL*

Siks, Geraldine Brain 1912?- *BiE&WWA, BioIn 16, ConAu 25R, DrAS 74E, -78E, -82E, IntAu&W 82, -86, NotNAT, NotWoAT*

Silas *ConGrA 1, SmATA X*
Main entry: McCay, Winsor

Silber, Irwin 1925- *ConAu 9R, EncFCWM 69, WhoWest 94*

Silcock, Sara Lesley 1947- *BioIn 11, -12, ChhPo S2, IlsCB 1967, SmATA 12*

Sill, Cathryn 1953- *SmATA 74*

Sill, John 1947- *SmATA 74*

Silliman, Leland 1906- *AuBYP 2, -3, BioIn 7*

Sillitoe, Alan *BioIn 15, -16, IntAu&W 86, -89, IntvTCA 2*

Sillitoe, Alan 1928- *Benet 87, BlmGEL, CamGLE, CnDBLB 8, ConAu 26NR, ConLC 57, ConNov 86, -91, ConPo 91, CyWA 89, EncSF 93, HalFC 88, IntAu&W 91, IntWW 89, -91, MajTwCW, ModBrL S2, RAdv 13-1, RfGEnL 91, ScFSB, SmATA 61, Who 88, -90, -92, WhoWor 87, -89, -91, -93, WorAlBi, WrDr 86, -88, -90, -92, -94*

Silly, E S *MajAI, SmATA 65*
Main entry: Kraus, Robert

Silman, Roberta *DrAPF 87, -89, -91, -93*

Silman, Roberta 1934- *BioIn 14, ConAu 101, DcLB 28, DrAPF 83, -85, IntAu&W 82, -86, -89, -91, WrDr 90, -92, -94*

Silman, Roberta Karpel 1934- *DcAmChF 1960*

Silsbe, Brenda 1953- *SmATA 73*

Silvaroli, Nicholas Joseph 1930- *ConAu 29R, -12NR, LEduc 74, WhoAm 90, WhoWest 74, -76*

Silver, Ruth *ConAu X, -31NR, SmATA 7*
Main entry: Chew, Ruth

Silver, Samuel Manuel 1912- *ConAu 21R, -11NR, WhoAm 74, -76, -78, -80, -82, -84, -86, -88, -90, -92, -94, WhoAmJ 80, WhoE 74, -75, -77, WhoRel 75, -92, WhoWorJ 72, -78*

Silverberg, Robert *BioIn 15, -17, IntvTCA 2, WhoAm 86, -88, -90, WhoUSWr 88, WhoWest 89, WhoWrEP 89, -92*

Silverberg, Robert 1935- *AmAu&B, AuBYP 2, -3, BenetAL 91, BioIn 7, -9, -11, -12, -13, ConAu 1R, -3AS, -1NR, -20NR, -36NR, ConLC 7, ConSFA, DcLB 8, DcLEL 1940, EncSF 93, IntAu&W 82, -91, MajAI, MajTwCW, NewEScF, Novels, RGTwCSF, ScF&FL 92, SmATA 13, ThrBJA, TwCSFW 86, -91, WhoAm 74, -76, -78, -80, -82, -84, -92, -94, WhoSciF, WhoWest 92, -94, WorAlBi, WorAl, WrDr 84, -86, -88, -90, -92, -94*
Pseud./variant:
Chapman, Walker
Drummond, Walter
Jorgenson, Ivar
Knox, Calvin M
Osborne, David
Randall, Robert
Sebastian, Lee

Silverberg, Robert 1936- *ScFSB*

Silverman, Al 1926- *AuSpks, AuBYP 2, -3, BioIn 7, -10, -11, ConAu 9R, WhoAm 74, -76, -78, -80, -82, -84, -86, -88, -90, -92, -94, WhoUSWr 88, WhoWrEP 89, -92*

Silverman, Burton Philip 1928- *AmArt, BioIn 8, -9, IlsBYP, IlsCB 1957, WhoAm 78, -80, -82, -84, -90, -92, -94, WhoAmA 73,*

–78, –80, –82, –84, –86, –89, –91, WhoE 75, –77, –91

Silverman, Hillel E 1924- *WhoRel 92, WrDr 86, –88, –90*

Silverman, Hillel Emanuel 1924- *ConAu 21R, –11NR, IntAu&W 77, WhoRel 75, –77, WhoWorJ 78, WrDr 76, –80, –82, –84*

Silverman, Melvin Frank 1931-1966 *BioIn 7, –8, –10, –11, ConAu 5R, IlsBYP, IlsCB 1957, SmATA 9*

Silverman, Morris 1894-1972 *AmAu&B, BioIn 9, –16, ConAu 33R, WhAm 5, WhoWorJ 72, –78*

Silverman, William Bertram 1913- *ConAu 49, WhoMW 74, –76, WhoRel 75, –77, WhoWorJ 72, –78*

Silvers, Robert B *MedPD*

Silvers, Vicki 1941- *ConAu 93, WhoUSWr 88, WhoWrEP 89, WrDr 76, –80*

Silverstein, Alvin 1933- *AuBYP 2S, –3, BioIn 11, ChlLR 25, ConAu 49, –2NR, ConLC 17, FifBJA, IntAu&W 77, –82, MajAI, SmATA 8, –69, WhoE 91, –93*
Pseud./variant:
Buxton, Ralph
Doctor A
Dr. A
Rhine, Richard

Silverstein, Robert Alan 1959- *SmATA 77*

Silverstein, Shel *BioIn 14, –16*

Silverstein, Shel 1932- *BioIn 6, –10, –11, ChlLR 5, ConAu 107, EncFCWM 83, FifBJA, IntAu&W 91, NewYTBS 81, PenEncP, SmATA 27, –33, TwCChW 83, –89, WrDr 86, –88, –90, –92*
Pseud./variant:
Uncle Shelby

Silverstein, Shelby 1932- *MajAI, WhoAm 92, WrDr 94*

Silverstein, Virginia 1937- *AuBYP 3*

Silverstein, Virginia B 1937- *ChlLR 25, SmATA 69*
Pseud./variant:
Buxton, Ralph
Dr. A
Rhine, Richard

Silverstein, Virginia Barbara 1937- *WhoE 91, –93*

Silverstein, Virginia Barbara Opshelor 1937- *AuBYP 2S, BioIn 11, ConAu 49, –2NR, ConLC 17, FifBJA, IntAu&W 77, –82, MajAI, SmATA 8*

Silverthorne, Elizabeth 1930- *BioIn 14, SmATA 35*

Simak, Clifford D 1904- *BenetAL 91, IntAu&W 91, NewEScF, RGTwCSF, ScFSB, TwCSFW 86, WrDr 86, –88*

Simak, Clifford D 1904-1988 *AnObit 1988, BioIn 15, –16, –17, ConAu 125, –35NR, ConLC 55, MajTwCW, ScF&FL 92, SmATA 56N, TwCSFW 91, WhAm 9*

Simak, Clifford Donald *IntvTCA 2*

Simak, Clifford Donald d1988 *NewYTBS 88*

Simak, Clifford Donald 1904- *BioIn 6, –7, –10, –12, ConAu 1R, –1NR, ConLC 1, ConSFA, DcLB 8, DcLEL 1940, IntAu&W 77, MinnWr, Novels, WhoAm 82, –84, WhoSciF, WorAu 1950, WrDr 84*

Simak, Clifford Donald 1904-1988 *EncSF 93*

Simbari, Nicola 1927- *AuBYP 2, –3, BioIn 5, –7, –10, ConAu 1R, –1NR, PrintW 83, –85, WhoGrA 62*

Simister, Florence Parker 1913- *ConAu 5R, –2NR, ForWC 70, WrDr 76, –80, –82*

Simmel, Johannes Mario 1924- *Au&Wr 71, BioIn 13, ConAu 81, DcLB 69, IntAu&W 77, –82, WhoWor 74, –78*

Simmonds, Posy *ChlLR 23*

Simmonds, Posy 1945- *Who 88, –90, –92*

Simmons, Anthony *IntMPA 92, WrDr 86, –88*

Simmons, Anthony 1922- *Au&Wr 71, ConAu 103, FilmgC, IntAu&W 86, –89, WorEFlm, WrDr 76, –80, –82, –84*

Simmons, Anthony 1924?- *HalFC 88*

Simmons, Dawn Langley *AuBYP 3*

Simmons, Dawn Langley 1937- *ConAu 29R, NewYTBS 74*
Pseud./variant:
Hall, Gordon Langley

Simmons, Ellie *AuBYP 2S, –3*

Simmons, Patricia A 1930- *ConAu 93*

Simmons, Paul D 1936- *ConAu 31NR*

Simmons, Paul Dewayne 1936- *ConAu 45, DrAS 74P, –78P, –82P, WhoRel 75, –77, –92*

Simon, Charlie May 1897- *AuBYP 3, WhAm 10*

Simon, Charlie May 1897-1977 *AmAu&B, AuBYP 2, BioIn 1, –2, –3, –7, –11, –12, ConAu X, CurBio 46, JBA 51, NatCAB 60, SmATA 3, WhoAm 76, –78, WhoAmW 74*
Pseud./variant:
Fletcher, Charlie May Hogue

Simon, Edith 1917- *Au&Wr 71, BioIn 3, –10, ConAu 13R, CurBio 54, WorAu 1950, WrDr 76, –80, –82, –84, –86, –88, –90, –92, –94*

Simon, George Thomas 1912- *BioIn 8, ConAu 25R, –17NR, IntAu&W 77, –82, WhoAm 74, –76, –78, –80, –82, –84*

Simon, Henry W 1901-1970 *AuBYP 3*

Simon, Henry William 1901-1970 *AmAu&B, AuBYP 2S, BioIn 9, ConAu 5R, –29R, –4NR, WhAm 5*

Simon, Hilda Rita 1921- *AuBYP 2, –3, BioIn 8, –13, ConAu 77, FourBJA, IlsCB 1957, –1967, SmATA 28*

Simon, Howard 1903-1979 *BioIn 1, –5, –6, –8, –9, –12, –14, ChhPo, ConAu 33R, IlsBYP, IlsCB 1744, –1946, –1957, –1967, MorJA, SmATA 21N, –32, WhoAmA 73, –78, –80N, –82N, –86N, –89N, –91N*

Simon, John Oliver *ConSFF, DrAP 75, DrAPF 87, –89, –91, –93*

Simon, John Oliver 1942- *WhoUSWr 88, WhoWrEP 89, –92*

Simon, Joseph Henry 1913- *BioIn 10, ConAu 29R, SmATA 7, WhoE 75, –77*

Simon, Martin P 1903-1969 *BioIn 11, ConAu P-1, LuthC 75, SmATA 12*

Simon, Mina Lewiton *AuBYP 3, ChhPo, ConAu X, ForWC 70, SmATA 2*
Main entry: Lewiton, Mina

Simon, Norma 1927- *AuBYP 2, –3, BioIn 7, –9, ConAu 5R, –6NR, –21NR, ForWC 70, SmATA 3, –68, WhoAmW 77*

Simon, Norma Bernice 1927- *WhoAmW 91*

Simon, Norma Feldstein 1927- *MajAI*

Simon, Paul 1928- *AlmAP 78, –82, –84, –88, –92, AuBYP 2S, –3, BioIn 2, –13, –14, –15, –16, ChgDr 89, –91, ConAu 81, EncWB, IntAu&W 89, IntWW 89, –91, PolsAm 84, WhoAm 74, –76, –78, –80, –82, –84, –86, –88, –90, –92, –94, WhoAmP 73, –75, –77, –81, –83, –85, –87, –89, –91, –93, WhoGov 77, –72, –75, WhoMW 74, –76, –78, –80, –82, –84, –86, –88, –90, –92, –93, WhoUSWr 88, WhoWor 87, –89, –91, WhoWrEP 89, –92*

Simon, Ruth Corabel 1918- *AuBYP 2, –3, BioIn 7*

Simon, Seymour 1931- *AuBYP 2S, BioIn 9, ChlLR 9, ConAu 25R, –11NR, –29NR, FifBJA, MajAI, ScF&FL 92, SmATA 4, –73, WrDr 76, –80, –82, –84, –86, –88, –90, –92, –94*

Simon, Shirley 1921- *BioIn 11, ConAu 5R, –1NR, –16NR, ForWC 70, SmATA 11, WhoAmW 77*

Simon, Solomon 1895-1970 *BioIn 15, ConAu 104, SmATA 40, WhoWorJ 72*

Simon, Tony 1921- *AmAu&B, ConAu 5R*

Simonetta, Linda 1948- *BioIn 12, ConAu 77, SmATA 14*

Simonetta, Sam 1936- *BioIn 12, ConAu 77, SmATA 14*

Simons, Barbara B 1934- *BioIn 15*

Simons, Barbara Brooks 1934- *ConAu 108, SmATA 41, WhoAmW 74, –75*
Pseud./variant:
Brooks, Barbara

Simons, Robin 1951- *ConAu 65*

Simonson, Mary Jane *ConAu X*
Main entry: Wheeler, Mary Jane

Simont, Marc *BioIn 14*

Simont, Marc 1915- *AmAu&B, AmPB, AuBYP 2, –3, BioIn 4, –5, –6, –7, –8, –11 BkP, Cald 1938, ChhPo S1, –S2, ConAu 61, –38NR, IlsBYP, IlsCB 1946, –1957, –1967, MajAI, MorJA, NewbC 1956, SmATA 9, –73, WhoAm 74, –76, –78, –80, –82, –84, –86, –88, –90, –92, –94, WhoAmA 73, –78, –80, –82*

Simpich, Frederick, Jr. 1911-1975 *ConAu 57, –61, WhoAm 74, –76*

Simpson, Colin 1908- *WrDr 86, –88, –90*

Simpson, Colin 1908-1983 *Au&Wr 71, BioIn 6, –12, ConAu 53, –5NR, IntAu&W 77, –82, OxCAusL, SmATA 14, WrDr 76, –80, –82, –84*

Simpson, Dorothy *BioIn 14*

Simpson, Dorothy 1933- *BioIn 17, ConAu 107, –30NR, IntAu&W 91, MajTwCW, TwCCr&M 85, –91, WrDr 86, –88, –90, –92, –94*

Simpson, Harriette
Main entry: Arnow, Harriette Louisa Simpson

Simpson, Jean 1925- *WrDr 76, –80*

Simpson, Margaret 1935- *AmMWSc 73P, –76P, –82, –86, –89, –92*

Simpson, Maxwell Stewart 1896- *BioIn 1, –6, IlsCB 1744, WhAmArt 85, WhoAmA 73, WhoE 75, –77*

Simpson, Myrtle Lillias 1931- *Au&Wr 71, BioIn 12, ConAu 21R, InWom SUP, IntAu&W 86, –89, SmATA 14, WrDr 76, –80, –82, –84, –86, –88, –90, –92, –94*
Pseud./variant:
Emslie, M L

Sims, Agnes 1910- *WhoAmA 73, –78, –80*

Sims, Blanche L *SmATA 75*

Sims, Carolyn 1940- *WhoAm 76*

Sims, George R 1847-1922 *DcLB 70, StaCVF*

Sims, George Robert 1847-1922 *Alli SUP, BbD, BiD&SB, BioIn 1, –14, BritAu 19, Chambr 3, ChhPo, –S1, –S2, DcLB 35, –135, DcNaB MP, EncMys, EvLB, LongCTC, NewC, NotNAT B*

Sims, Lydel *AuBYP 2, –3, BioIn 8*

Sims, Naomi R 1949- *BioIn 8, –9, –10, ConAu 69, SelBAAf, WhoAm 80, –82, WhoBlA 75, –80, –85, –88, –90, –92, –94*

Simundsson, Elva 1950- *BioIn 17, SmATA 63*

Sinclair, Catherine 1800-1864 *Alli, BiD&SB, BioIn 3, –8, –16, BlmGWL, BritAu 19, CmScLit, DcEnL, DcNaB, FemiCLE, InWom SUP, NewC, OxCChiL, OxCEng 67, –85, StaCVF, TelT, WhoChL*

Sinclair, Clover *ConAu X, SmATA X*
Main entry: Gater, Dilys

Sinclair, Emil
Main entry: Hesse, Hermann

Sinclair, Harold Augustus 1907-1966 *AmAu&B, AmNov, BioIn 2, –4, –7, ConAu 5R, REnAL, TwCA, –SUP, WhAm 4*

Sinclair, Jeff 1958- *SmATA 77*

Sinclair, Olga Ellen 1923- *Au&Wr 71, ConAu 61, IntAu&W 77, –86, –89, –91, WrDr 76, –80, –82, –84, –86*

Sinclair, Upton *IntvTCA 2*

Sinclair, Upton 1878-1968 *AgeMat, Benet 87, BenetAL 91, BioIn 14, –15, –16, –17, CamGLE, CamHAL, ConLC 63, DcAmImH, EncO&P 3, EncPaPR 91, MajTwCW, RAdv 13-1, RfGAmL 87, ScFSB, ScFEYrs, TwCSFW 86, –91, WorAlBi, WorLitC*

Sinclair, Upton Beall 1878-1968 *AmAu&B, AmNov, AuBYP 2, –3, BiDPara, BioIn 1, –2, –4, –5, –6, –8, –9, –10, –11, –12, CasWL, Chambr 3, ChhPo S1, CnDAL, ConAmA, ConAmL, ConAu 5R, –25R, ConLC 1, –11, CurBio 62, –69, CyWA 58, DcAmAu, DcLEL, EncAB-H, EncO&P 1, EncSF 93, EncWL, EvLB, JrnUS, LongCTC, ModAL, MorMA, OxCAmL 65, OxCEng 67, –85, OxCFilm, PenC AM, RAdv 1, REn, REnAL, SmATA 9, SpyFic, TwCA, –SUP, TwCWr, TwCYAW, WebAB 74, –79, WebE&AL, WhDW, WhNAA, WhoTwCL, WorAl, WorEFlm*
Pseud./variant:
Fitch, Clarke
Garrison, Frederick
Stirling, Arthur

Sinclair, Upton Beall, Jr. 1878-1968 *BiDAmJo, DcAmB S8*

Singer, A L *SmATA 72*
Main entry: Lerangis, Peter

Singer, Amanda *ConAu X, –39NR*
Main entry: Brooks, Janice Young

Singer, Arthur 1917- *BioIn 14*

Singer, Arthur 1917-1990 *BioIn 16, –17, SmATA 64*

Singer, Arthur B d1990 *NewYTBS 90*

Singer, Arthur B 1917- *BioNews 75, WhoAmA 78, –80, –82, –84, –86, –89*

Singer, Arthur B 1917-1990 *WhoAmA 91N*

Singer, David *AuBYP 3*

Singer, David Lin 1937- *AuBYP 2S, ConAu 73*

Singer, Isaac *ConAu 134, –39NR, MajAI, MajTwCW, SmATA 68*

Singer, Isaac Bashevis *IntvTCA 2*

Singer, Isaac Bashevis d1991 *NobelP 91N, Who 92N*

Singer, Isaac Bashevis 1904- *AmAu&B, AmWr, AnCL, AuSpks, AuBYP 2, –3, AuNews 1, –2, Au&Wr 71, Benet 87, BenetAL 91, BioIn 6, –7, –8, –9, –10, –11, –12, –13, –14, –15, –16, BlueB 76, CasWL, CelR, ChlLR 1, ConAu 1R, –1NR, ConLC 1, –3, –6, –9, –11, –15, –23, –38, ConNov 72, –76, –82, –86, CurBio 69, CyWA 89, DcLB 6, –28, –52, DrAF 76,*

EncWL, -2, IntAu&W 77, -89, -91, IntWW 74, -75, -76, -77, -78, -79, -80, -81, -82, -83, -89, -91, LiExTwC, MajTwCW, McGEWB, ModAL S1, -S2, MorBMP, NewCon, NewYTBE 70, -72, NobelP, Novels, OxCAmL 83, OxCChiL, OxCEng 85, PenC AM, PenEncH, RfGAmL 87, ShSCr 3, ShSWr, SmATA 3, -27, ThrBJA, TwCChW 78, -83, -89, TwCWr, WebAB 74, -79, WebE&AL, Who 82, -83, -85, -88, -90, WhoAm 74, -76, -78, -80, -82, -84, -86, -88, -90, WhoAmJ 80, WhoE 74, -81, -83, -85, -86, -89, -91, WhoNob, -90, WhoTwCL, WhoUSWr 88, WhoWor 74, -78, -80, -82, -84, -87, -89, -91, WhoWrEP 89, WorAlBi, WorAl, WorAu 1950, WrDr 76, -80, -82, -84, -86, -88, -90, -92, WrPh
Pseud./variant:
Bashevis, Isaac
Warshofsky, Isaac

Singer, Isaac Bashevis 1904-1991 *AnObit 1991, BioIn 17, ConAu 134, -39NR, ConLC 69, -70, CurBio 91N, DcLB Y91N, JeAmHC, MagSWL, MajAI, NewYTBS 91, News 92, -92-1, PolBiDi, ScF&FL 92, SmATA 68, WhAm 10, WorLitC*

Singer, Jane Sherrod 1917-1985 *BioIn 15, ConAu 25R, -115, -17NR, ForWC 70, SmATA 4, -42N, WhoAmW 74, -75, -77, WhoWest 74, -76, -78*
Pseud./variant:
Sherrod, Jane

Singer, Julia 1917- *BioIn 13, ConAu 65, SmATA 28*

Singer, Kurt D 1911- *BioIn 15*

Singer, Kurt Deutsch 1911- *AmAu&B, Au&Wr 71, BioIn 3, ConAu 49, -2NR, CurBio 54, IntAu&W 89, -91, SmATA 38, WhoAm 74, -76, -78, -80, -82, -84, -86, -88, -90, -92, -94, WhoFI 87, -89, WhoHr&F, WhoUSWr 88, WhoWest 74, -76, -78, -94, WhoWor 74, WhoWrEP 89, -92*

Singer, Marilyn 1948- *AuBYP 3, BioIn 15, -16, ConAu 65, -9NR, -39NR, MajAI, ScF&FL 92, SixBJA, SmATA 38, -48, -13AS, TwCYAW*

Singer, Samuel L 1911- *WhoAm 86, -88*

Singer, Samuel Loewenberg 1911- *ConAu 65, WhoAm 74, -76, -78, -80, -82, -84, -90, -92, -94*

Singer, Susan 1941- *BioIn 11, ConAu 61, SmATA 9*

Singmaster, Elsie *BiGAW*

Singmaster, Elsie 1879-1958 *AmAu&B, AmNov, AmWomWr, BenetAL 91, BioIn 2, -4, -5, -12, -14, ChhPo, ConAmL, ConAu 110, CyWA 58, DcLB 9, InWom SUP, JBA 34, LuthC 75, ObitOF 79, OxCAmL 65, -83, REnAL, TwCA, -SUP, WhAm 3, WhNAA, WomWWA 14, WomNov*

Sinha, Nilima *DcChlFi*

Sinha, Sarojini 1922- *DcChlFi*

Sinykin, Sheri Cooper 1950- *SmATA 72*

Sirof, Harriet Toby 1930- *ConAu 104, DrAPF 83, -85, IntAu&W 89, -91, SmATA 37, WhoAmW 85, -87, -89, WhoUSWr 88, WhoWrEP 89, -92*

Sirois, Allen L 1950- *SmATA 76*

Sirois, Allen Louis 1950- *WhoE 93*

Sis, Peter *BioIn 16, ChlBIID*

Sis, Peter 1949- *ConAu 128, SixBJA, SmATA 67*

Sisson, Rosemary Anne 1923- *Au&Wr 71, BioIn 11, ConAu 13R, -12NR, -29NR, IntAu&W 89, -91, SmATA 11, TwCRHW 90, Who 85, -88, -90, -92, WrDr 76, -80, -82, -84, -86, -88, -90, -92, -94*

Sitomer, Harry 1903- *BioIn 14, ConAu 101, SmATA 31*

Sitomer, Mindel 1903- *BioIn 14, ConAu 101 SmATA 31*

Sitwell, Edith *IntvTCA 2*

Sitwell, Edith 1877-1964 *ContDcW 89*

Sitwell, Edith 1887-1964 *AnCL, ArtclWW 2, AtlBL, Benet 87, BioIn 1, -2, -3, -4, -5, -6, -7, -8, -9, -10, -11, -12, -13, -16, -17, BlmGEL, BlmGWL, BritWr 7, CamGLE, CasWL, Chambr 3, ChhPo, -S1, -S2, ClDMEL 47, CnDBLB 7, CnMWL, ConAu 9R, -35NR, ConLC 2, -9, -67, DcLB 20, DcLEL, DcNaB 1961, EncWL, -2, EvLB, FemiCLE, IntDcWB, LongCEL, LongCTC, MajTwCW, MakMC, McGEWB, ModBrL, -S1, -S2, NewC, ObitT 1961, OxCEng 67, -85, OxCMus, PenC ENG, PoeCrit 3, RAdv 1, -13-1, REn, RfGEnL 91, TwCA, -SUP, TwCWr, WebE&AL, WhDW, WhAm 4, WhoTwCL, WorAlBi, WorAl*

Sitwell, Edith 1887-1965 *CamGEL*

Sitwell, Edith, Dame 1887-1964 *BioIn 14, EncBrWW, EngPo, InWom SUP*

Sive, Helen R 1951- *BioIn 14, ConAu 107, SmATA 30*

Sivulich, Sandra Stroner 1941- *AuBYP 2S, -3, BioIn 11, ConAu 61, SmATA 9*

Sjoberg, Leif 1925- *ConAu 65, DrAS 74F, -78F, -82F*

Sjoberg, Leif T 1925- *IntAu&W 89*

Sjowall, Maj 1935- *Benet 87, BioIn 9, -10, ConAu 65, ConLC 7, CrtSuMy, EncMys, NewYTBE 71, Novels, TwCCr&M 85B, WorAlBi, WorAl*

Skaar, Grace Brown 1903- *AmPB, ConAu 69*

Skagen, Kiki 1943- *ConAu 37R, -X*
Pseud./variant:
Munshi, Shehnaaz

Skarmeta, Antonio *BioIn 16*

Skarmeta, Antonio 1940- *ConAu 131, ConWorW 93, HispWr, LiExTwC, RAdv 13-2, SmATA 57, SpAmA*

Skeel, Dorothy June *ConAu 61, -8NR, LEduc 74, WhoAmW 74, -75, WhoSSW 82*

Skelly, James R *AuBYP 3*

Skelly, James R 1927- *AuBYP 2S, BioIn 12, SmATA 17*

Skelton, Charles L *BioIn 11, Str&VC*

Skelton, Red *LesBEnT 92*

Skelton, Red 1910- *HalFC 88, WorAlBi*

Skelton, Red 1913- *AuBYP 2S, -3, BioIn 1, -2, -3, -4, -5, -6, -7, -10, -11, -12, -16, CelR, CmMov, ConAu 104, ConTFT 8, CurBio 47, EncAFC, FilmgC, HalFC 84, IntAu&W 82X, IntMPA 75, -76, -78, -81, -82, -84, -86, -88, -92, -77, LesBEnT, MotPP, MovMk, NewYTET, WhoAm 76, -78, -80, -82, -88, -90, -92, -94, WhoCom, WhoEnt 92, WhoHol A, WorAl*

Skelton, Robin *BioIn 14, -15, -16, DrAPF 87, -89, -91, -93*

Skelton, Robin 1925- *AuNews 2, Au&Wr 71, BioIn 10, -11, CaW, CanWW 70, -79, -80, -81, -83, -89, ChhPo S1, CnE&AP, ConAu 5R, -5AS, -28NR, ConLC 13, ConPo 70, -75, -80, -85, -91, DcLB 27, -53, DcLEL 1940, DrAP 75, DrAPF 83, -85, DrAS 74E, -78E, -82E, EngPo, IntAu&W 77, -82, -89, -91, IntWWP 82, OxCCan SUP, OxCCanL, ScF&FL 92, Who 74, -82, -83, -85, -88, -92, WhoAmA 78, -80, -82, WhoCanL 85, -87, -92, WhoWest 74, -76, WorAu 1950, WrDr 76, -82, -84, -86, -88, -90, -92, -94*

Skelton, Robin, Prof 1925- *Who 90*

Skiles, Jacqueline Dean 1937- *ConAu 108, WhoAmW 77, -81*

Skinner, Constance Lindsay 1877-1939 *AmWomPl, DcLB 92, InWom SUP*

Skinner, Constance Lindsay 1879-1939 *BenetAL 91, WomNov*

Skinner, Constance Lindsay 1882?-1939 *AmAu&B, AmWomWr, BioIn 1, -4, -6, -11, -12, -17, CanNov, ChhPo, DcLEL, DcNAA, JBA 34, MorJA, OxCAmL 65, -83, OxCCan, Str&VC, TwCA, -SUP, WhAm 1, WhNAA, YABC 1*

Skinner, Cornelia Otis 1901-1979 *AmAu&B, AmWomD, AmWomPl, AmWomWr, ArtclWW 2, Au&Wr 71, Benet 87, BenetAL 91, BiE&WWA, BioIn 1, -2, -3, -4, -5, -7, -9, -12, -13, -16, BlueB 76, CamGWoT, CelR, ChhPo, ConAu 17R, CurBio 42, -64, DcLEL, EncWT, EvLB, FemiCLE, FilmgC, HalFC 84, -88, InWom SUP, IntAu&W 77, IntWW 74, -75, -76, -77, -78, -79N, LongCTC, NatCAB 62, NotNAT, -A, NotWoAT, OxCAmL 65, -83, OxCAmT 84, OxCThe 67, PenC AM, REn, REnAL, SmATA 2, TwCA SUP, TwCWr, WhScrn 83, Who 74, WhoAm 74, -76, -78, WhoAmW 74, WhoHol A, WhoThe 72, -77, -81N, WhoWor 74, -78, -80, WorAlBi, WorAl, WrDr 76, -80*

Skinner, Elliott P 1924- *WhoBlA 92, -94*

Skinner, Elliott Percival 1924- *AmMWSc 73S, -76P, ConAu 13R, FifIDA, InB&W 80, NegAl 76, -83, -89A, WhoBlA 77, -80*

Skipper, G C 1939- *BioIn 15, ConAu 77, -14NR, SmATA 38, -46, WhoE 86*

Skipper, Mervyn 1886-1958? *OxCAusL, SingR 1*

Skofield, James *AuBYP 3, BioIn 15, SmATA 44*

Skold, Betty Westrom 1923- *BioIn 15, ConAu 112, SmATA 41*

Skolnik, Peter L 1944- *ConAu 57*

Skorpen, Liesel Moak 1935- *BioIn 9, ConAu 25R, SmATA 3*

Skulicz, Matthew V 1944- *ConAu 37R*

Skurzynski, Gloria 1930- *BioIn 11, ConAu 33R, -13NR, -30NR, DcAmChF 1960, -1985, FifBJA, SmATA 8, -9AS*

Skurzynski, Gloria Joan 1930- *SmATA 74*

Slackman, Charles B 1934- *BioIn 11, ChhPo, SmATA 12, WhoAm 86*

Slade, Gurney d1956 *OxCAusL*

Slade, Richard 1910-1971 *Au&Wr 71, BioIn 11, ConAu P-2, SmATA 9*

Sladen, Kathleen 1904- *ConAu 69*

Slate, Joseph 1928- *BioIn 15, ConAu 110, SmATA 38*

Slate, Joseph Frank 1928- *WhoAmA 91*

Slater, James Derrick 1929- *SmATA 58*
Pseud./variant:
Slater, Jim

Slater, Jim *SmATA X*

Slater, Jim 1929- *BioIn 14, -16, BlueB 76, ConAu 112, ScF&FL 92, SmATA 34*
Main entry: Slater, James Derrick

Slater, Mary Louise 1923- *ConAu 29R*

Slater, Patrick *OxCCan, OxCCanL*

Slater, Patrick 1880-1951 *DcLB 68*

Slaughter, Jane Mundy 1905?- *ConAu 73, WhoAmW 81, -83, -85, -87, -89, -91, WhoSSW 82, -84, WhoWor 84, -87, -89*

Slaughter, Jean *AuBYP 2S, -3, ConAu X, SmATA X*
Main entry: Doty, Jean Slaughter

Slavin, Bill 1959- *SmATA 76*

S L C *MajAI*

Sleator, William *BioIn 15, -16, -17*

Sleator, William 1945- *Au&Arts 5, BioIn 9, ChlLR 29, ConAu 29R, FifBJA, ScF&FL 92, SmATA 3, -68, TwCChW 89, WrDr 90, -92*

Sleator, William Warner, III 1945- *DcAmChF 1985, EncSF 93, MajAI, TwCYAW, WrDr 94*

Sleigh, Barbara 1906-1982 *BioIn 14, ScF&FL 92, TwCChW 89*

Sleigh, Barbara DeRiemer 1906-1982 *Au&Wr 71, BioIn 8, -9, ConAu 13R, -106, -6NR, IntAu&W 77, OxCChiL, SmATA 3, -30N, TwCChW 78, -83, WhoChL, WrDr 76, -80, -82*

Slepian, Jan 1921- *BioIn 15, -16, DcAmChF 1960, FifBJA, SmATA 45, -51, -8AS*

Slepian, Janice B 1921- *ConAu 136, MajAI, TwCYAW, WrDr 94*

Slicer, Margaret O 1920- *BioIn 9, ConAu 25R, SmATA 4*

Slier, Debby *SmATA 71*
Main entry: Shine, Deborah

Sloan, Carolyn 1937- *BioIn 16, ConAu 127, ScF&FL 92, SmATA 58*

Sloan, Carolyn June 1937- *WhoAmW 87*

Sloan, Irving J 1924- *ConAu 17R, -7NR*

Sloan, William J 1927- *BioIn 16*

Sloan, William James 1927- *BiDrLUS 70, WhoLibI 82, WhoLibS 55*

Sloane, Carolyn *AuBYP 3*

Sloane, Eric *BioIn 14, -15, -16, -17*

Sloane, Eric 1905-1985 *NewYTBS 85*

Sloane, Eric 1910- *AmArt*

Sloane, Eric 1910?-1985 *AmArt, AmAu&B, AnObit 1985, BioIn 8, -9, -10, -11, ConAu 108, -115, CurBio 72, -85N, IlsCB 1957, NewYTBS 85, SmATA 42N, -52, WhAm 8, WhAmArt 85, WhoAm 74, -76, -78, WhoAmA 73, -78, -80, -82, -86N, -89N, -91N*

Sloane, William 1906-1974 *PenEncH*

Sloane, William, III 1906-1974 *AmAu&B, BioIn 1, -2, BlueB 76, ConAu 53, WhAm 6, WhoAm 74, WhoE 74, -75, WhoFI 74*

Sloane, William M 1906-1974 *TwCSFW 91*

Sloat, Teri 1948- *SmATA 70*

Slobodkin, Florence Gersh 1905- *BioIn 10, ConAu 1R, SmATA 5*

Slobodkin, Louis 1903-1975 *AmAu&B, AuBYP 2, -3, BenetAL 91, BioIn 1, -2, -4, -5, -7, -8, -9, -10, -13, -14, BkCL, BkP, Cald 1938, ChhPo, ConAu 13R, -57, CurBio 57, -75N, IlsBYP, IlsCB 1744, -1946, -1957, -1967, JBA 51, MajAI, ObitOF 79, OxCChiL, REnAL, SmATA 1, -26, TwCChW 78, -83, -89, WhAm 6, WhAmArt 85, WhoAm 74, WhoAmA 73, -78N, -80N, -82N, -86N, -89N, -91N, WhoWorJ 72, -78*

Slobodkina, Esphyr 1908- *AmPB, AuBYP 2, BioIn 5, -7, -9, ChhPo, ConAu 1R, -1NR, ForWC 70, IlsCB 1946, SmATA 1, -8AS, ThrBJA, TwCChW 78, -83, -89, WhoAmA 86, -89, -91, WrDr 80, -82, -84, -86, -88, -90, -92, -94*

Slobodkina, Esphyr 1909- *AuBYP 3*

Slocum, Rosalie 1906- *BioIn 1, IlsCB 1744*

Sloggett, Nellie 1851-1923 *BioIn 2, –15, SmATA 44*
Pseud./variant:
Cornwall, Nellie
Enys, Sarah L
Tregarthen, Enys

Sloss, Lesley Lord 1965- *SmATA 72*

Slote, Alfred *TwCChW 89, WrDr 90, –92*

Slote, Alfred 1926- *AuBYP 2S, –3, BioIn 11, –13, ChlLR 4, DcAmChF 1960, FifBJA, MajAI, ScF&FL 92, SmATA 8, –72, WrDr 94*

Sluman, Norma *OxCCan, –SUP*

Small, Austin J d1929 *ScFEYrs*

Small, Austin J 1894-1929 *BioIn 15, EncSF 93, PenEncH, ScF&FL 92*

Small, David 1945- *BioIn 15, –16, ScF&FL 92, SixBJA, SmATA 46, –50*

Small, Ernest *ConAu X, IntAu&W 91X, MajAI, SmATA 2, ThrBJA, WrDr 76, –80, –82, –84, –86, –88, –90, –92*
Main entry: Lent, Blair

Small, Ernest 1930- *WrDr 94*

Small, Terry 1942- *ConAu 142, SmATA 75*

Small, William *ConAu X*
Main entry: Eversley, David Edward Charles

Smalley, Janet *WhoAmA 86N*

Smalley, Janet 1893- *WhoAmA 89N, –91N*

Smalley, Janet 1893-1964? *ConICB, WhAmArt 85, WhoAmA 78N, –80N, –82N*

Smalls-Hector, Irene 1950- *SmATA 73*

Smallwood, Norah 1909-1984 *AnObit 1984*

Smallwood, Norah 1910?-1984 *AnObit 1984, BioIn 15, ConAu 114, SmATA 41N*

Smallwood, Norah Evelyn 1909-1984 *DcNaB 1981*

Smaridge, Norah 1903- *AuBYP 2, –3, BioIn 8, –10, ConAu 37R, SmATA 6*

Smart, Christopher 1722-1771 *Benet 87, BioIn 1, –2, –3, –4, –5, –6, –7, –8, –10, –12, –13, –14, –15, –17, BlmGEL, CamGEL, CamGLE, DcBiPP, DcLB 109, DcNaB, –C, Dis&D, LitC 3, OxCChiL, OxCEng 85, OxCLiW 86, RAdv 13-1, RfGEnL 91*

Smedley, Francis Edward 1818-1864 *Alli, CamGEL, CamGLE, CarSB, CasWL, CelCen, Chambr 3, ChhPo, DcBiPP, DcEnL, DcEuL, DcLEL, DcNaB, EvLB, NewC, OxCEng 67, –85*

Smee, David Charles 1937- *BioIn 12, –14, IlsCB 1967*

Smee, Nicola 1948- *SmATA 76*

Smiley, Lavinia 1919- *BioIn 5, –14, IlsCB 1946*

Smiley, Virginia Kester 1923- *BioIn 9, ConAu 29R, –12NR, –28NR, SmATA 2, WhoUSWr 88, WhoWrEP 89, –92*

Smith, Agnes *AuBYP 2, –3, BioIn 7, WhoAm 74, –76, –78, –80, –82, –84, –86, –88, –90, –92, WhoAmW 74*

Smith, Al d1986 *BioIn 15, NewYTBS 86*

Smith, Al 1902- *ArtCS, BioIn 5*

Smith, Al 1902-1986 *ConGrA 3*

Smith, Alison 1932- *DcAmChF 1960*

Smith, Alvin 1933- *AfroAA, BioIn 8, –10, IlsBYP, IlsCB 1957, –1967, InB&W 80, WhoAmA 73, –78, WhoBlA 77, –80, –85, –90, –92, –94*

Smith, Anne Warren 1938- *BioIn 14, –15, ConAu 111, SmATA 34, –41*

Smith, Barry Edward Jervis 1943- *SmATA 75*

Smith, Beatrice Lieb 1862-1942 *WhScrn 74, –83, –77*

Smith, Beatrice S *BioIn 11, ConAu 57, –10NR, SmATA 12*

Smith, Ben Arwood 1916- *Au&Wr 71, ConAu 1R*

Smith, Betsy Covington 1937- *BioIn 15, –16, ConAu 111, SmATA 43, –55*

Smith, Betty *Benet 87*

Smith, Betty 1896-1972 *AmAu&B, AmNov, BiDConC, BioIn 1, –2, –3, –4, –5, –9, –10, –13, –16, CnDAL, ConAu 5R, –33R, ConLC 19, CurBio 43, –72, CyWA 58, DcLB Y82B, DcLEL 1940, FemiCLE, LongCTC, NewYTBE 72, NotNAT B, ObitOF 79, OxCAmL 65, PenC AM, REn, REnAL, SmATA 6, TwCA SUP, WhAm 5*

Smith, Bradford 1909-1964 *AmAu&B, BioIn 2, –3, –7, –10, ChhPo, ConAu 1R, –16NR, ObitOF 79, SmATA 5, WhAm 4*

Smith, C Fox 1882-1954 *TwCChW 83, –89*

Smith, C W *DrAPF 87, –89, –91, –93*

Smith, C W 1940- *BioIn 14, –15, ConAu 61*

Smith, Caesar *ConAu X, DcLEL 1940, EncMys, IntAu&W 77X, SmATA X, TwCCr&M 85, –91, WrDr 76, –80, –82, –84, –86, –88, –90, –92, –94*
Main entry: Trevor, Elleston

Smith, Caesar 1920- *BioIn 14*

Smith, Catherine Collier 1929- *ConAu 29R, WhoAmW 75*
Pseud./variant:
Smith, Kay

Smith, Charlotte *BioIn 16*

Smith, Charlotte 1749-1806 *BioIn 2, –3, –10, –12, –15, –16, CamGEL, CamGLE, DcBiPP, DcBrAmW, DcLB 39, –109, DcNaB, –C, FemiCLE, NinCLC 23, Novels, OxCChiL, OxCEng 85, RfGEnL 91*

Smith, Cicely Fox d1954 *WomNov*

Smith, Cicely Fox 1882-1954 *ChhPo, TwCChW 78, WhoLA*

Smith, Datus Clifford, Jr. 1907- *AuBYP 2S, BioIn 7, –11, ConAu P-1, SmATA 13, WhoAm 74, –76, –78, –80, –82, –84, –86, –88, –90, –92, –94, WhoWor 74*

Smith, David E 1860-1944 *DcAmBC*

Smith, David E 1939- *WrDr 94*

Smith, David Eugene 1860-1944 *AmAu&B, DcAmAu, DcNAA, ObitOF 79, REnAL, WhAm 2, WhNAA*

Smith, Deborah *AuBYP 3*

Smith, Dodie *ConAu 133, –37NR, InWom SUP, MajAI, SmATA 65, WrDr 86, –88, –90*

Smith, Dodie d1990 *IntWW 91N, Who 92N*

Smith, Dodie 1896- *Au&Wr 71, BiE&WWA, BioIn 4, –9, –10, –11, –12, –13, –15, BlmGWL, BlueB 76, Chambr 3, ConAu 33R, ConDr 77, –82, –88, DcLB 10, DcLEL, FemiCLE, IntAu&W 77, –82, –89, –91, IntWW 74, –75, –76, –77, –78, –79, –80, –81, –82, –83, –89, LongCTC, McGEWD 72, –84, NewC, NotNAT, OxCChiL, PlP&P, REn, SmATA 4, TwCChW 83, –89, Who 74, –82, –83, –85, –88, –90, WhoThe 72, –77, –81, WhoWor 74, –78, WorAu 1950, WrDr 76, –80, –82, –84*
Main entry: Smith, Dorothy Gladys

Smith, Dodie 1896-1990 *AnObit 1990, BioIn 17, ConDr 93, ScF&FL 92*

Smith, Don *AuBYP 3*

Smith, Donald G 1927- *AuBYP 2, –3, ConAu 13R*

Smith, Donald Taylor 1906- *ConAu 49, IntAu&W 77*

Smith, Doris Buchanan *BioIn 15*

Smith, Doris Buchanan 1934- *AuBYP 2S, BioIn 13, ConAu 69, –11NR, DcAmChF 1960, –1985, DcLB 52, FifBJA, MajAI, ScF&FL 92, SmATA 28, –75, –10AS, TwCChW 89, TwCYAW, WrDr 90, –92, –94*

Smith, Dorothy Blakey *OxCCan SUP*

Smith, Dorothy Gladys 1896-1990 *ConAu 133, –37NR, MajAI, SmATA 65*
Pseud./variant:
Anthony, C L
Percy, Charles Henry
Smith, Dodie

Smith, Dorothy Stafford 1905- *BioIn 10, ConAu 21R, SmATA 6*
Pseud./variant:
Smith, Sarah Stafford

Smith, Dorothy Valentine 1908- *ConAu 29R*

Smith, E Boyd 1860-1943 *AmPB, CarSB, ConICB, WhAm 5, YABC 1*
Pseud./variant:
Smith, Elmer Boyd

Smith, E Brooks 1917- *BioIn 15, ConAu 5R, SmATA 40*

Smith, E T *OxCChiL*

Smith, E Toulmin *DcVicP 2*

Smith, Elizabeth Oakes 1806-1893 *ArtclWW 2, BenetAL 91, BioAmW*

Smith, Elizabeth Oakes P 1806-1893 *Alli, AmAu, AmAu&B, AmWomWr, BiD&SB, BioIn 3, –6, –11, –12, ChhPo, –S2, CnDAL, CyAL, DcAmAu, DcNAA, FemPA, HsB&A, OxCAmL 65, –83, REnAL, WhAm HS*

Smith, Elizabeth Oakes Prince 1806-1893 *InWom SUP*

Smith, Elizabeth Thomasina 1854-1914 *WomNov*

Smith, Elizabeth Thomasina M *Alli SUP, CarSB, EncMys*
Main entry: Meade, Elizabeth Thomasina

Smith, Elmer Boyd *AmAu&B, BioIn 11*
Main entry: Smith, E Boyd

Smith, Elva S 1871-1965 *BioIn 14*

Smith, Elva Sophronia 1871-1965 *ConAu 107, SmATA 31, WhAm 5, WhNAA*

Smith, Emma 1923- *AuBYP 2, -3, BioIn 8, -14, -16, ConAu 73, ConNov 72, -76, -82, -86, -91, DcLEL 1940, IntAu&W 77, -82, -86, -89, -91, LongCTC, SmATA 36, -52, TwCChW 78, -83, -89, Who 74, -82, -83, -85, -88, -90, -92, WrDr 76, -80, -82, -84, -86, -88, -90, -92, -94*

Smith, Eunice Young 1902- *AuBYP 2, BioIn 2, -7, -10, ConAu P-1, ForWC 70, IndAu 1917, SmATA 5, WhoAmW 74, -75, -77*

Smith, Frances C 1904- *BioIn 9, ConAu 1R, -1NR, ForWC 70, SmATA 3, WhoAmW 74, -75, WhoWest 78, -80*
Pseud./variant:
Smith, Jean

Smith, Francis Hopkinson 1838-1915 *Alli SUP, AmAu, AmAu&B, BbD, BiDSA, BiD&SB, BioIn 8, -11, -13, CarSB, Chambr 3, ChhPo, -S2, CnDAL, DcAmAu, DcBiA, DcLEL, DcNAA, HarEnUS, OxCAmL 65, -83, REnAL, WhAm 1, WhAmArt 85*

Smith, Fredrika Shumway 1877-1968 *AuBYP 2, -3, BioIn 8, -10, -14, ConAu 109, SmATA 30*

Smith, Garry 1933- *AuBYP 2S, ConAu 5R*

Smith, Gary 1933- *AuBYP 3*

Smith, Gary, and Vesta Smith *AuBYP 3*

Smith, Gary R 1932- *BioIn 12, ConAu 69, LEduc 74, SmATA 14*

Smith, Gene 1929- *ConAu 81*

Smith, George Harmon 1920- *BioIn 10, ConAu 49, SmATA 5*

Smith, George O 1911- *TwCSFW 86, -91*

Smith, George O 1911-1981 *ConAu 28NR, NewEScF, ScF&FL 92*

Smith, George O 1911-1982 *ScFSB*

Smith, George Oliver 1911-1981 *BioIn 12, ConAu 97, -103, DcLB 8, EncSF 93, NewYTBS 81, WhoSciF, WrDr 84*

Smith, Guy N *PenEncH*

Smith, Guy N 1939- *ScF&FL 92, WhoHr&F*

Smith, H Allen 1907-1976 *AmAu&B, AuNews 1, Benet 87, BenetAL 91, CelR, ChhPo, ConAu 5R, -65, -5NR, CurBio 42, DcLB 11, -29, EncAHmr, LongCTC, ObitOF 79, REn, REnAL, SmATA 20N, TwCA SUP, WhoAm 74, -76, WhoE 74, WrDr 76*

Smith, H Arthur 1848-1922 *EncPaPR 91*

Smith, Harriet Lummis d1947 *AmAu&B, BioIn 1, DcNAA, ObitOF 79, WhAm 2, WomWWA 14*

Smith, Harry Allen 1907-1976 *EncSF 93*

Smith, Helen C 1903- *WrDr 86, -88*

Smith, Helen Catharine 1903- *ChhPo S1, WhoAmW 74, -75, -77, -81, -83, -85, -87, -89, -91, WhoMW 74, -76, -78, WhoWor 84, -87, -89, WrDr 76, -82, -84*

Smith, Helen Zenna *WrDr 86, -88*

Smith, Helen Zenna 1896- *BioIn 14*

Smith, Helen Zenna 1896-1985 *ConAu X*

Smith, Hobart Muir 1912- *AmMWSc 73P, -76P, -82, -86, -89, -92, ConAu 65, -9NR, IntAu&W 77, -82, WhoAm 74, -76, -78, -80, -82, WrDr 76, -80, -82, -84, -86, -88, -90, -92, -94*

Smith, Howard E, Jr. 1927- *ConAu 21NR, WrDr 86, -88, -90, -92, -94*

Smith, Howard Everett, Jr. 1927- *BioIn 11, ConAu 25R, IntAu&W 77, -86, -91, SmATA 12, WrDr 76, -80, -82, -84*

Smith, Howard G *AuBYP 2S, -3*

Smith, Howard K *LesBEnT 92*

Smith, Howard K 1914- *AmAu&B, BioIn 6, -8, -10, -11, -16, BioNews 74, BlueB 76, CelR, ConAu 45, -2NR, CurBio 43, -76, EncAJ, EncTwCJ, IntAu&W 77, -82, -89, IntMPA 75, -76, -78, -81, -82, -84, -86, -88, -92, -77, IntWW 74, -75, -76, -77, -78, -79, -80, -81, -82, -83, LesBEnT, WhoAm 74, -76, -78, -80, -82, WhoSSW 73, -75, -76, WhoWor 74, -78, WorAlBi, WorAl, WrDr 76, -80, -82, -84, -86, -88, -90*

Smith, Howard Kingsbury 1914- *BiDAmJo, JrnUS*

Smith, Hugh Letcher 1921- *AuBYP 3*

Smith, Hugh Letcher 1921-1968 *AuBYP 2S, ChhPo S1, ConAu P-2, SmATA 5*

Smith, Imogene Henderson 1922- *AuBYP 2, -3, BioIn 8, -11, ConAu 5R, SmATA 12*

Smith, Irene 1900- *WrDr 76, -80, -82*

Smith, Irene 1903- *AuBYP 2, -3, BioIn 7, ConAu 73*

Smith, Jacqueline B 1937- *BioIn 15, SmATA 39*

Smith, James K *OxCCan SUP*

Smith, Jan *AuBYP 3*

Smith, Janet Buchanan Adam *ChhPo, -S2, LongCTC, Who 74*
Main entry: Adam Smith, Janet Buchanan

Smith, Janice Lee *AuBYP 3*

Smith, Janice Lee 1949- *BioIn 16, SmATA 54*

Smith, Jean *ConAu X, SmATA 3*
Main entry: Smith, Frances C

Smith, Jean Pajot 1945- *BioIn 11, ConAu 53, InB&W 80, SmATA 10*

Smith, Jessie *ConAu 134, SmATA 67*

Smith, Jessie 1937- *WrDr 94*
Main entry: Kunhardt, Edith

Smith, Jessie W 1863-1935 *BioAmW*

Smith, Jessie Wilcox 1863-1935 *AuBYP 3, InWom SUP*

Smith, Jessie Willcox 1863-1935 *AuBYP 2, BioIn 2, -8, -11, -12, -13, -14, -15, ChhPo, -S1, -S2, ConICB, DcNAA, DcWomA, IlrAm 1880, -A, JBA 34, -51, MajAI, OxCChiL, SmATA 21, WhAm 1, WhAmArt 85, WomWWA 14*

Smith, Jim *BioIn 16*

Smith, Jim 1920- *BioIn 14, -17, ConAu 115, SmATA 36, -61*

Smith, Joan 1933- *BioIn 15, -16, SmATA 46, -54*

Smith, John *AuBYP 3, BioIn 16*

Smith, John 1924- *AuBYP 2S, Au&Wr 71, ConAu 103, ConPo 70, -75, -80, -85, -91, EngPo, IntAu&W 91, WhoAm 92, WrDr 76, -80, -86, -88, -90, -92, -94*

Smith, Johnston *AmAu, BenetAL 91, ConAu 140, -X, DcNAA, REnAL, YABC X*
Main entry: Crane, Stephen

Smith, Joseph A 1936- *SmATA 73*

Smith, Katherine E *BioIn 16*

Smith, Katherine E 1954- *WhoE 93*

Smith, Katherine Eunice Young 1902- *AuBYP 3*

Smith, Kay *BioIn 14, ConAu X*
Main entry: Smith, Catherine Collier

Smith, Kenneth Danforth 1902- *ConAu 45, WhoAm 74, -76, -78*

Smith, Kenneth Homan 1928- *AmMWSc 73S, -78S*

Smith, L H 1872- *WhNAA*

Smith, L Herman 1911- *DrLC 69*

Smith, Lacey Baldwin 1922- *AmAu&B, ConAu 5R, -6NR, DrAS 74H, -78H, -82H, IntAu&W 91, WhoAm 74, -76, -78, -80, -82, -90, -92, WrDr 76, -80, -82, -84, -86, -88, -90, -92, -94*

Smith, Lafayette *AuBYP 2S, -3, ConAu X, SmATA 4*
Main entry: Higdon, Hal

Smith, Lane *ChlBIID*

Smith, Lane 1959- *SmATA 76*

Smith, Lawrence Beall 1909- *BioIn 8, ChhPo, IlsBYP, IlsCB 1957, WhoAm 94, WhoAmA 78, -80, -82, -84, -86, -89, -91*

Smith, Lee *DrAF 76, IlsCB 1957, SmATA X*
Main entry: Albion, Lee Smith

Smith, Lendon 1921- *SmATA 64*

Smith, Lendon H 1921- *BioIn 17*

Smith, LeRoi 1934- *AuBYP 3*

Smith, LeRoi Tex 1934- *AuBYP 2S, ConAu 29R, WhoWest 74*

Smith, Lillian H 1887-1983 *BioIn 14, -17*

Smith, Lillian Helena 1887-1983 *BioIn 3, -13, ConAu 111, OxCChiL, SmATA 32N*

Smith, Linell 1932- *AuBYP 3*

Smith, Linell Nash 1932- *AuBYP 2S, BioIn 9, ConAu 5R, SmATA 2*
Pseud./variant:
Chenault, Nell
Nash, Linell

Smith, Lucia B 1943- *BioIn 14, ConAu 108, SmATA 30*

Smith, Lynwood S 1928- *AmMWSc 73P, –76P, –82, –86, –89, –92*

Smith, Lynwood Stephen 1928- *WhoAm 94, WhoWest 87, –89, –92, –94*

Smith, Margaret Chase 1897- *AmPolW 80, –80A, AmWomM, AuBYP 2S, –3, BiDrUSC 89, BioAmW, BioIn 1, –2, –3, –4, –5, –6, –7, –8, –9, –10, –11, –15, –16, –17, BlueB 76, CelR, ConAu 73, ContDcW 89, CurBio 45, –62, EncWB, HerW, –84, InWom SUP, IntDcWB, IntWW 74, –75, –76, –77, –78, –79, –80, –81, –82, –83, –89, –91, NewYTBE 70, –72, WhoAm 74, –76, –78, –80, –82, WhoAmP 73, –75, –77, –81, –83, –85, –87, –89, –91, –93, WhoAmW 75, –77, –81, –83, WhoE 74, –75, –77, WhoGov 72, –75, WhoWor 78, –80, –82, WorAlBi, WorAl*

Smith, Marion Hagens 1913- *BioIn 11, ConAu 17R, SmATA 12*

Smith, Marion Jaques 1899- *BioIn 11, ConAu 69, –11NR, SmATA 13*

Smith, Mary 1918- *Au&Wr 71, IntAu&W 77, –82, WrDr 76, –80*

Smith, Mary Ellen *BioIn 11, ConAu 69, ForWC 70, SmATA 10, WhoFI 75*
Pseud./variant:
Smith, Mike

Smith, Mary Prudence Wells 1840-1930 *Alli SUP, AmAu&B, AmLY, CarSB, DcAmAu, DcNAA, OhA&B, TwCA, WhAm 1, WhNAA, WomWWA 14*

Smith, Mike *ConAu X, SmATA X*
Main entry: Smith, Mary Ellen

Smith, Moishe 1929- *PrintW 83, –85, WhoAm 82, –84, –86, –88, –90, –92, –94, WhoAmA 73, –78, –80, –82, –84, –86, –89, –91, WhoWest 94*

Smith, Moyne Rice *AuBYP 2, –3, BioIn 7*

Smith, Nancy Covert 1935- *BioIn 11, ConAu 57, –10NR, SmATA 12*

Smith, Ned *IlsBYP*

Smith, Neville 1897- *SingR 2*

Smith, Nila Banton *WrDr 86*

Smith, Nila Banton d1976 *BioIn 5, –11, ConAu 21R, IntAu&W 77, LEduc 74, WhoAmW 74, –75, –77, WhoWest 74, –76, WrDr 76, –80, –82, –84*

Smith, Nila Banton 1890-1976 *ConAu 120*

Smith, Nora Archibald *AmWomPl, InWom SUP*

Smith, Nora Archibald 1859?-1924 *AuBYP 3*

Smith, Nora Archibald 1859?-1934 *AmAu&B, AmLY, AuBYP 2S, BenetAL 91, ChhPo, –S1, –S2, DcAmAu, DcNAA, JBA 34, REnAL, WhAm 1, WomWWA 14, WomNov*

Smith, Norman David 1923- *Au&Wr 71, IntAu&W 82, WrDr 76, –80, –82, –84, –86, –88*

Smith, Norman Dwight 1941- *AmMWSc 86*

Smith, Norman F 1920- *BioIn 10, ConAu 29R, SmATA 5, –70*

Smith, Patrick D *DrAPF 87, –89, –91*

Smith, Patrick D 1927- *WhoSSW 91, –93, WhoUSWr 88*

Smith, Patrick Davis 1927- *ConAu 77, WhoUSWr 88, WhoWrEP 89, –92*

Smith, Pauline C 1908- *ConAu 29R, SmATA 27*

Smith, Philip Hardy 1931- *WhoAmP 73, –81, –83, –85, –87, –89, –91, –93*

Smith, Philip Henry 1842- *Alli SUP, DcAmAu, DcNAA*

Smith, Philip M 1927- *AuBYP 2, –3, BioIn 8*

Smith, Philip Matusak 1953- *WhoSSW 88*

Smith, Philip Meek 1932- *WhoAm 86*

Smith, Philip Warren 1936- *SmATA 46*

Smith, Ralph Lee 1927- *AmAu&B, AuBYP 2, –3, BioIn 8, ConAu 1R, –1NR, IntWWM 90, WhoAm 74, –76, –78, –80, –82, –84, –86, –88, –90, –92, –94, WhoWor 82, –84, WrDr 76, –80, –82, –84, –86, –88, –90, –92, –94*

Smith, Richard 1931- *BioIn 7, –10, ConArt 77, –83, –89, ConBrA 79, DcCAr 81, IntWW 74, –75, –76, –77, –78, –79, –80, –81, –82, –83, –89, –91, OxCTwCA, PhDcTCA 77, PrintW 83, –85, WhoWor 82, –84, –87, –89, –91, –93*

Smith, Richard Harris 1946- *ConAu 41R*

Smith, Richard James 1947- *AmMWSc 82, –86, –89, –92*

Smith, Richard Jay 1930- *WhoAm 74, –80, –82, –84, –86, –88, WhoE 74, –85, –86, WhoUSWr 88, WhoWrEP 89, –92*

Smith, Richard Shirley *ChhPo S1*

Smith, Robert Gene 1945- *WhoMW 90*

Smith, Robert Gillen 1913- *ConAu 42NR, WhoWor 74*

Smith, Robert K 1930- *AuBYP 3*

Smith, Robert Kimmel 1930- *AuBYP 2S, BioIn 11, –13, –16, ConAu 61, –8NR, –42NR, NatPD 81, SixBJA, SmATA 12, –77, WhoAm 92, –94, WhoE 81*
Pseud./variant:
Marks, Peter

Smith, Robert Paul *BioIn 14*

Smith, Robert Paul 1915-1977 *AmAu&B, AmNov, AuBYP 2, –3, BiE&WWA, BioIn 2, –5, –8, –10, –11, –16, ChhPo, ConAu 69, –73, CurBio 58, NotNAT, SmATA 30N, –52, WhAm 7, WhoAm 74, –76, WorAu 1950*

Smith, Robert Paul 1942- *AmMWSc 86*

Smith, Robert W 1926- *AuBYP 3*

Smith, Robert William 1926- *AuBYP 2S, ConAu 13R*

Smith, Ruth Leslie 1902- *BioIn 9, ConAu P-2, SmATA 2*

Smith, Sally Liberman 1929- *BioIn 3, ConAu 21R, –11NR*

Smith, Samantha *BioIn 14, –15, –16*

Smith, Samantha d1985 *NewYTBS 85*

Smith, Samantha 1972-1985 *BioIn 13, ConAu 117, NewYTBS 85, SmATA 45N*

Smith, Sandra Lee 1945- *ConAu 142, SmATA 75*

Smith, Sarah *BlmGWL, InWom SUP*

Smith, Sarah 1832-1911 *BioIn 16, Chambr 3, ConAu 112, DcLEL, DcNaB S2, NewC, OxCChiL, TelT, WomNov*
Pseud./variant:
Stretton, Hesba

Smith, Sarah Bixby- 1871-1935 *BioIn 17*

Smith, Sarah Louisa P Hickman 1811-1832 *Alli, AmAu&B, ChhPo, DcAmAu, DcNAA, FemPA, OhA&B*

Smith, Sarah Stafford *ConAu X, SmATA 6*
Main entry: Smith, Dorothy Stafford

Smith, Sidney 1877-1935 *AmAu&B, ArtCS, DcNAA, EncACom, WhAm 1, WhAmArt 85*

Smith, Stan 1946- *BioIn 8, –9, –10, CelR, ConAu 85, NewYTBE 73*

Smith, Susan Carlton 1923- *BioIn 11, SmATA 12, WhoAmA 78, –80, –82, –84, –86, –89, –91*

Smith, Susan Mathias 1950- *BioIn 14, –15, ConAu 114, SmATA 35, –43*

Smith, Susan Vernon 1950- *ConAu 19NR, SmATA 48, WhoAmW 89*
Pseud./variant:
Enfield, Carrie
Mendonca, Susan
Vernon, Rosemary

Smith, Theresa Kalab *AuBYP 2S, –3*

Smith, Ursula 1934- *BioIn 16, SmATA 54*

Smith, Vesta 1933- *AuBYP 2S, ConAu 5R*

Smith, Vian 1920- *AuBYP 3*

Smith, Vian 1920-1969 *AuBYP 2S, BioIn 11, ConAu 1R, –3NR, SmATA 11, TwCChW 83, –89*

Smith, Vincent D 1929- *AmArt, BioIn 14, WhoAmA 86, –89, –91, WhoBlA 85, –88, –90, –92, –94*

Smith, Vincent DaCosta 1929- *AfroAA, AmArt, InB&W 80, –85, WhoAm 80, –82, –84, –86, –88, –90, –92, –94, WhoAmA 78, –80, –82, –84, WhoBlA 75, –77, –80, –85*

Smith, Vivian Brian 1933- *ConAu 61, ConPo 70, –75, IntAu&W 82, –86, –91, IntWWP 82, WrDr 76, –80*

Smith, W Eugene 1918?-1978 *BioIn 1, –4, –6, –7, –9, –10, –11, –12, –13, –14, –15, –16, BriEAA, ConAu 81, ConPhot 82, –88, ICPEnP, MacBEP, NewYTBS 74, –85, ObitOF 79, WhAmArt 85, WhoAm 76*

Smith, Wanda VanHoy 1926- *BioIn 17, ConAu 133, SmATA 65, WrDr 94*

Smith, Ward *ConAu X, –40NR, SmATA X, WhoUSWr 88, WhoWrEP 89, –92*
Main entry: Goldsmith, Howard

Smith, William Arthur 1918- *BioIn 1, –2, –3, –4, –5, –11, ChhPo, IlrAm 1880, –F, IlsBYP, IlsCB 1744, –1946, SmATA 10, WhAmArt 85, WhoAm 74, –76, –78, –80, –82, –84, –86, –88, WhoAmA 73, –78, –80, –82, –84, –86, –89, –91N, WhoE 74, WhoWor 74, –80, –89*

Smith, William Arthur 1918-1989 *WhAm 10*

Smith, William Eugene 1918-1978 *ConAu 142*

Smith, William Jay *DrAPF 87, –89, –91, –93*

Smith, William Jay 1918- *AuBYP 2S, –3, BenetAL 91, BioIn 6, –8, –9, –10, –11, –12, –17, BkCL, ChhPo, –S1, –S2, ConAu 5R, ConLC 6, ConPo 70, –75, –80, –85, –91, CurBio 74, DcLB 5, DcLEL 1940, DrAP 75, DrAS 74E, –78E, FifBJA, IntAu&W 77, MajAI, OxCAmL 83, PenC AM, SmATA 2, –68, TwCChW 78, –83, –89, WhoAm 74, –76, –78, –80, –82, –84, –86, –88, –90, –92, –94, WhoUSWr 88, WhoWrEP 89, –92, WorAu 1950, WrDr 76, –80, –82, –84, –86, –88, –90, –92, –94*

Smith, Winsome 1935- *BioIn 15, ConAu 115, SmATA 45*

Smith, Z Z *ConAu X, IntAu&W 77X, –82X, –91X, SmATA X, WhoUSWr 88, WhoWrEP 89*
Main entry: Westheimer, David

Smith, Z Z *WhoWrEP 92*

Smithies, Richard H R 1936- *ConAu 21R*

Smits, Teo
Main entry: Smits, Theodore Richard

Smits, Theodore Richard 1905- *BioIn 13, ConAu 77, SmATA 28, –45, WhoAm 74, –76, –78, –80, –82, –84, –86, –88, –90*
Pseud./variant:
Smits, Teo

Smothers, Ethel Footman 1944- *SmATA 76*

Smucker, Barbara 1915- *BlmGWL, ChlLR 10, ConAu 23NR, WhoCanL 87, –92*

Smucker, Barbara Claasen 1915- *BioIn 13, ChlLR 10, ConAu 106, OxCCanL, Profile 2, SmATA 29, WhoCanL 85*

Smucker, Barbara Claassen 1915- *DcChlFi, MajAI, SmATA 76, –11AS, TwCChW 83, –89, WhoAm 82, –84, –86, –88, –90, –92, –94, WrDr 86, –88, –90, –92, –94*

Smyth, John, Sir 1893-1983 *Au&Wr 71, BioIn 5, BlueB 76, ConAu 61, –109, –11NR, Who 74, –82, –83, WrDr 76, –80, –82, –84*

Smythe, Ernest *DcBrBI*

Smythe, J Louis 1880- *BioIn 8, WhoChL*

Smythe, Patricia Rosemary 1928- *Au&Wr 71, BioIn 4, Who 74, –82, –83, –85*
Pseud./variant:
Koechlin, Patricia Rosemary

Smythe, Patricia Rosemary K *Who 88, –90, –92*

Snedeker, Caroline Dale 1871- *AuBYP 3*

Snedeker, Caroline Dale 1871-1956 *BioIn 14, TwCChW 89, WomNov*

Snedeker, Caroline Dale Parke 1871-1956 *AmAu&B, AmWomWr, AnCL, AuBYP 2, BioIn 1, –2, –4, –8, –12, IndAu 1816, JBA 34, –51, OhA&B, TwCChW 78, –83, WhAm 3, WhNAA, WomWWA 14, YABC 2*
Pseud./variant:
Owen, Caroline Dale

Snell, Nigel 1936- *BioIn 15, –16, ConAu 111, SmATA 40, –57*

Snell, Roy Judson 1878- *AmAu&B, WhAm 6, WhNAA*

Snellgrove, L E 1928- *BioIn 16, ConAu 23NR, SmATA 53*

Sneve, Virginia Driving Hawk 1933- *BioIn 11, ChlLR 2, ConAu 49, –3NR, SmATA 8*
Pseud./variant:
Driving Hawk, Virginia
Hawk, Virginia Driving

Sneve, Virginia Drwing Hawk 1933- *InWom SUP*

Sniff, Mr *AuBYP 3*

Sniff, Mr *ConAu X, SmATA X*
Main entry: Abisch, Roslyn Kroop

Snodgrass, Mary Ellen *BioIn 16*

Snodgrass, Mary Ellen 1944- *ConAu 142, SmATA 75, WhoAmW 91*

Snodgrass, Quentin Curtius *MajAI*

Snodgrass, Thomas Jefferson *AuBYP 3, ConAu 135, –X, MajAI, YABC X*
Main entry: Clemens, Samuel Langhorne

Snook, Barbara Lilian 1913-1976 *Au&Wr 71, ConAu 109, SmATA 34, WrDr 76, –80, –82, –84*

Snow, Donald Clifford *AuBYP 3*

Snow, Donald Clifford 1917- *AuBYP 2, BioIn 12, ConAu 85, FourBJA, SmATA 16*

Pseud./variant:
Fall, Thomas

Snow, Dorothea J 1909- *BioIn 11, ConAu 1R, –3NR, –27NR, SmATA 9*

Snow, Dorothy Mary Barter 1897- *Au&Wr 71, ConAu P-1, WrDr 76*

Snow, Edward Rowe 1902-1982 *Au&Wr 71, BioIn 1, –5, BlueB 76, ConAu 9R, –106, –6NR, CurBio 58*

Snow, Kathleen Mary 1918- *BiDrLUS 70, WhoLibS 66*

Snow, Lee Erlin 1924- *WhoAmA 78, –80, –82, –84, –86, –89, –91, WhoWest 92, –94*

Snow, Richard F *BioIn 15, –16*

Snow, Richard F 1947- *ConAu 106, SmATA 37, –52, WrDr 90, –92*

Snow, Richard Folger 1947- *DcAmChF 1960, WrDr 94*

Snyder, Anne 1922- *BioIn 9, ConAu 37R, –14NR, SmATA 4, WrDr 76, –80, –82, –84, –86, –88, –90, –92, –94*

Snyder, Carol 1941- *BioIn 14, ConAu 85, SmATA 35*

Snyder, Diane *AuBYP 3*

Snyder, Diane Carsillo 1960- *WhoSSW 93*

Snyder, Dick *AuBYP 2, –3, BioIn 8*

Snyder, Gerald S 1933- *BioIn 14, –16, ConAu 61, –12NR, SmATA 34, –48*

Snyder, Jerome 1916-1976 *BioIn 8, –10, –11, –12, ConAu 65, ConDes 84, –90, IlsBYP, IlsCB 1957, –1967, ObitOF 79, SmATA 20N, WhAmArt 85, WhoGrA 62*

Snyder, Louis L d1993 *NewYTBS 93*

Snyder, Louis L 1907- *ConAu 34NR, WrDr 86, –88, –90, –92, –94*

Snyder, Louis Leo 1907- *AuBYP 2, –3, BioIn 8, BlueB 76, ConAu 1R, –2NR, DrAS 74H, –78H, –82H, IntAu&W 77, –91, WhoAm 74, –76, –78, –84, –86, –88, –90, –92, –94, WhoE 74, WhoWor 74, –89, –93, WrDr 76, –80, –82, –84*

Snyder, Zilpha K 1927- *ScF&FL 92*

Snyder, Zilpha Keatley *BioIn 14, –15, –16*

Snyder, Zilpha Keatley 1927- *AmWomWr, AuBYP 2, –3, BioIn 8, –9, –10, –13, ChlLR 31, ConAu 9R, –38NR, ConLC 17, DcAmChF 1960, IntAu&W 89, –91, MajAI, MorBMP, OxCChiL, SmATA 1, –28, –75, –2AS, ThrBJA, TwCChW 78, –83, –89, TwCYAW, WhoAm 82, –84, WhoUSWr 88, WhoWrEP 89, –92, WrDr 80, –82, –84, –85, –88, –90, –92, –94*

Snyderman, Reuven Kenneth 1922- *BioIn 10, ConAu 29R, SmATA 5, WhoAm 78, –80, –82, –84, –86, –88, –90, –92, –94, WhoE 74, –75, –77*

Sobel, Robert 1931- *ConAu 5R, –8NR, –31NR, DrAS 74H, –78H, –82H, WhoE 91*

Sobin, Gustaf 1935- *ConAu 115, –38NR, ConPo 91, IntAu&W 91, WrDr 88, –90, –92, –94*

Soble, Jennie *ConAu X, SmATA X*
Main entry: Cavin, Ruth

Sobol, Donald J 1924- *AuBYP 2, –3, BioIn 8, –9, –14, ChlLR 4, ConAu 1R, –1NR, –18NR, –38NR, DcAmChF 1960, FourBJA, IntAu&W 89, –91, MajAI, ScF&FL 92, SmATA 1, –31, –73, TwCChW 78, –83, –89, WhoAm 78, –80, –82, –84, –86, –88, WhoAmJ 80, WhoUSWr 88, WhoWor 80, –82, –84, –87, WrDr 84, –86, –88, –90, –92, –94*

Sobol, Harriet Langsam 1936- *BioIn 14, –16 ConAu 61, –8NR, SmATA 34, –47*

Sobol, Ken 1938- *WrDr 76, –80, –82, –84, –86, –88, –90, –92, –94*

Sobol, Rose 1931- *ConAu 101, SmATA 76*

Sockman, Ralph Washington 1889-1970 *AmAu&B, BioIn 1, –2, –3, –6, –9, –10, –17, ConAu 5R, CurBio 46, –70, DcAmReB 2, EncWM, LuthC 75, NewYTBE 70, ObitOF 79, OhA&B, WhAm 5, WhNAA*

Soderhjelm, Kai 1918- *IntAu&W 77*

Soderlind, Arthur Edwin 1920- *BioIn 12, ConAu 69, SmATA 14, WhoE 81*

Soerensen, Svend Otto 1916- *ConAu 132, SmATA 67*
Pseud./variant:
Otto, Svend
S, Svend Otto
Sorensen, Svend Otto
S Svend, Otto

Sofia *IlsBYP, IlsCB 1946, –1957*
Main entry: Zeiger, Sophia

Softly, Barbara 1924- *TwCChW 89, WrDr 86, –88, –90, –92*

Softly, Barbara Charmian 1924- *WrDr 94*

Softly, Barbara Charmian Frewan 1924- *Au&Wr 71, BioIn 11, ConAu 5R, SmATA 12, TwCChW 78, -83, WrDr 76, -80, -82, -84*

Soglow, Otto *EncACom*

Soglow, Otto 1900-1973 *EncTwCJ*

Soglow, Otto 1900-1975 *AmAu&B, ArtCS, BenetAL 91, BioIn 3, -10, -14, ChhPo, ConAu 57, -93, CurBio 40, -75N, NatCAB 63, ObitOF 79, REnAL, SmATA 30N, WhAm 6, WhAmArt 85, WhoAm 74, WhoAmA 78N, -80N, -82N, -86N, -89N, -91N*

Sohl, Frederic John 1916- *BioIn 11, ConAu 21R, SmATA 10, WrDr 76, -80, -82, -84*

Sohn, David Albert 1929- *ConAu 9R, -6NR, IndAu 1917, WhoMW 74, -76*

Sokol, Bill
Main entry: Sokol, William

Sokol, William 1923?- *AuBYP 2, -3, BioIn 8, ChhPo, ChsFB I, IlsCB 1957, -1967, SmATA 37, WhoGrA 62*
Pseud./variant:
Sokol, Bill

Sokolov, Kirill 1930- *BioIn 12, -14, SmATA 34*

Solbert, Romaine G 1925- *BioIn 5, -8, -9, -12, ChhPo S2, ConAu 29R, IlsBYP, IlsCB 1946, -1957, -1967, SmATA 2*
Pseud./variant:
Solbert, Ronni G

Solbert, Ronni G
Main entry: Solbert, Romaine G

Soldati, Mario *TwCChW 89B*

Soldati, Mario 1906- *Au&Wr 71, BioIn 4, -5, -10, -15, ConAu 108, ConFLW 84, ConWorW 93, CurBio 58, DcFM, DcItL, EncWL, -2, FilmgC, HalFC 84, -88, IntAu&W 77, -89, IntMPA 75, -76, -78, -81, -82, -84, -86, -88, -77, IntWW 74, -75, -76, -77, -78, -79, -80, -81, -82, -83, LiExTwC, ModRL, OxCFilm, PenC EUR, REn, RfGShF, ScF&FL 92, ScFSB, TwCChW 78B, -83B, TwCWr, WhoWor 74, WorAu 1950, WorEFlm, WorFDir 1*

Solem, Alan 1931- *AmMWSc 73P, -76P, -82, ConAu 57*

Solley, Charles Marion, Jr. 1925- *AmMWSc 73S, -78S, ConAu 1R*

Solomon, Joan *BioIn 15, -16, SmATA 51*

Solomon, Joan 1930?- *ConAu 109, -28NR, SmATA 40*

Solomon, Louis *AuBYP 2, -3, BioIn 8*

Solomons, Ikey, Jr., Esq *SmATA X*
Main entry: Thackeray, William Makepeace

Solonevich, George 1915- *BioIn 12, SmATA 15*

Solot, Mary Lynn 1939- *AuBYP 2S, -3, BioIn 11, ConAu 49, SmATA 12*

Soltes, Avraham 1917-1983 *BioIn 13, NewYTBS 83, WhoWorJ 72, -78*

Somerlott, Robert 1928- *BioIn 17, ScF&FL 92, SmATA 62*
Pseud./variant:
Carson, Robert

Somerset, David *DcChlFi*

Somerville, Elizabeth *Alli, BiDLA, CarSB*

Somerville, James Hugh Miller 1922- *ConAu 9R, WrDr 80, -82, -84, -86, -88, -90, -92, -94*

Somerville, Lee 1915- *ConAu 69*

Sommer, Elyse 1929- *AuBYP 2S, -3, BioIn 10, ConAu 49, -2NR, SmATA 7*

Sommer, Joellen 1957- *ConAu 45*

Sommer, Robert 1929- *AmMWSc 73S, BiDPara, BioIn 10, -11, ConAu 9R, -3NR, -18NR, EncO&P 1, -2, -3, SmATA 12*

Sommer, Robert B 1947- *WhoAmL 94*

Sommer-Bodenburg, Angela *BioIn 17, TwCChW 89B*

Sommer-Bodenburg, Angela 1948- *ConAu 132, ScF&FL 92, SmATA 63*

Sommerfelt, Aimee *TwCChW 89B*

Sommerfelt, Aimee 1892- *AuBYP 3*

Sommerfelt, Aimee 1892-1975 *AuBYP 2, BioIn 8, -9, -10, ConAu 37R, OxCChiL, SmATA 5, ThrBJA, TwCChW 78B, -83B*

Sommerschield, Rose *IlsBYP*

Soni, Welthy H *AuBYP 2, -3, BioIn 8*

Sonnabend, Roger Philip 1925- *BioIn 8, WhoAm 74, -76, -78, -80, -86, -88, -90, -92, -94, WhoE 74, WhoFI 94, WhoSSW 84, WhoWorJ 72, -78*

Sonneborn, Ruth A 1899-1974 *BioIn 9, –10, –13, BkP, ConAu 49, –P-2, SmATA 4, –27N*

Sonnenmark, Laura A 1958- *SmATA 73*

Sootin, Harry *AuBYP 2, –3, BioIn 7*

Soper, Eileen A 1905-1990? *ConAu 131*

Soper, Eileen Alice 1905- *Au&Wr 71, BioIn 1, –5, –14, ConAu 9R, DcBrAr 1, IlsBYP, IlsCB 1744, –1946, WhoArt 80, –82, –84, WrDr 76, –80, –82, –84*

Soper, George 1870-1942 *BioIn 14, DcBrAr 1, DcBrBI, DcVicP 2*

Sopko, Eugen 1949- *BioIn 16, SmATA 58*

Sorden, L G 1898- *ConAu 1R, –1NR*

Sorel, Edward 1929- *BioIn 5, –8, –12, –15, –16, –17, ConAu 9R, –33NR, ConGrA 1, EncSF 93, IlrAm 1880, IlsBYP, IlsCB 1957, SmATA 37, –65, WhoAm 74, –76, –78, –80, –82, –84, –86, –88, –90, –92, –94, WhoAmA 78, –80, –82, –84, –86, –89, –91, WhoE 74, WhoGrA 82, WhoWor 74, WorECar*

Sorell, Walter 1905- *BiGAW, BioIn 14, –15, ConAu 21R, WhoE 74*

Sorensen, Henri 1950- *SmATA 77*

Sorensen, Svend Otto *ConAu 132, OxCChiL, SmATA 67*
Main entry: Soerensen, Svend Otto

Sorensen, Svend Otto 1916- *BioIn 16, –17*

Sorensen, Virginia 1912- *AmAu&B, AmNov, ArtclWW 2, AuBYP 2, –3, Au&Wr 71, BenetAL 91, BioIn 2, –4, –6, –7, –9, –10, ConAu 13R, –22NR, CurBio 50, DcAmChF 1960, EncFWF, MorBMP, MorJA, NewbC 1956, OxCAmL 83, OxCChiL, SmATA 2, TwCA SUP, TwCChW 78, –83, –89, TwCWW 91, WhAm 10, WhoAm 74, –76, –78, –80, –82, –84, –86, –88, –90, WhoAmW 74, WhoWor 74, WrDr 76, –80, –82, –84, –86, –88, –90, –92*

Sorensen, Virginia 1912-1991 *ConAu 139, MajAI, SmATA 72, –15AS, WrDr 94N*

Sorenson, Jane 1926- *SmATA 63*

Sorley, Walker Kathrine *AuBYP 3*

Sorley Walker, Kathrine *Au&Wr 71, ConAu 5R, –6NR, IntAu&W 77, –82, –86, –89, SmATA 41, WrDr 76, –80, –82, –84, –86, –88, –90, –92, –94*

Sorrell, Alan 1904-1974 *Au&Wr 71, BioIn 4, ConAu 93, DcBrAr 1, –2, TwCPaSc, Who 74*

Sorrells, Dorothy C *ConAu 9R*

Sorrentino, Joseph Nicholas 1937- *BioIn 7, –10, –11, ConAu 49, –3NR, SmATA 6, WhoWest 78*

Sortor, June Elizabeth 1939- *BioIn 11, ConAu 61, SmATA 12*
Pseud./variant:
Sortor, Toni

Sortor, Toni
Main entry: Sortor, June Elizabeth

Soskin, V H *ConAu X, IntAu&W 91X, SmATA 4, WrDr 76, –80, –82, –84, –86, –88, –90, –92*
Main entry: Ellison, Virginia Howell

Soskin, V H 1910- *WrDr 94*

Soto, Gary *BioIn 16, –17, DrAPF 87, –89, –91, –93*

Soto, Gary 1952- *Au&Arts 10, ChiLit, ConAu 119, –125, ConPo 91, DcLB 82, HispAmA, HispWr, MexAmB, TwCYAW, WhoAm 92, WhoHisp 91, –92, WhoWest 87, WrDr 86, –88, –90, –92, –94*

Sotomayor, Antonio 1902?- *BioIn 1, –5, –1[illegible], ConAu 73, IlsBYP, IlsCB 1946, IntWW 74, –75, –76, –77, –78, –79, –80, –81, –82, –83, SmATA 11, WhoWest 74, –76, –78, WhoWor 74, –78*

Sotomayor, Antonio 1904- *IntWW 89, –91*

Soudley, Henry *ConAu X, SmATA 1*
Main entry: Wood, James Playsted

Soule, Gardner 1913- *AuBYP 3, IntAu&W 89, –91*

Soule, Gardner Bosworth 1913- *AuBYP 2S, BioIn 12, ConAu 5R, –2NR, SmATA 14, WhoAm 80, –82, –84, –86, –88, –90, –92, –94*

Soule, Jean Conder 1919- *BioIn 11, ConAu 5R, ForWC 70, SmATA 10*

Souster, Holmes Raymond 1921- *SmATA 63*
Pseud./variant:
Holmes, John
Holmes, Raymond
Souster, Raymond

Souster, Raymond *IntvTCA 2*
Main entry: Souster, Holmes Raymond

Souster, Raymond 1921- *Benet 87, BenetAL 91, BioIn 14, –15, –17, CamGLE, CanWW 89, ConAu 14AS, –29NR, ConPo 91, DcLB 88, IntAu&W 91, RfGEnL 91, WhoCanL 87, –92, WorAu 1980, WrDr 86, –88, –90, –92, –94*

Soutar, Andrew 1879-1941 *ChhPo S2, NewC, NotNAT B, ObitOF 79*

Southall, Ivan 1921- *AuBYP 3, BioIn 15, -17, CamGLE, SmATA 68, -3AS, TwCChW 89, WrDr 86, -88, -90, -92*

Southall, Ivan Francis 1921- *AuBYP 2, Au&Wr 71, BioIn 6, -8, -9, -10, ChlFicS, ChlLR 2, ConAu 9R, -7NR, DcChlFi, IntAu&W 86, -89, -91, IntWW 89, -91, MajAI, OxCAusL, OxCChiL, SenS, SingR 1, SmATA 3, SouSt, ThrBJA, TwCChW 78, -83, TwCYAW, WhoAm 92, -94, WhoWor 74, -87, -89, -91, WrDr 76, -80, -82, -84, -94*

Southard, Helen Elizabeth Fairbairn 1906- *ConAu 5R, ForWC 70, WhoAmW 83, -85, -91*

Southey, Robert 1774-1843 *Alli, AtlBL, Benet 87, BbD, BiDLA, BiD&SB, BioIn 1, -2, -3, -5, -6, -7, -8, -9, -10, -11, -12, -13, -16, -17, BlmGEL, BritAu 19, BritWr 4, CamGEL, CamGLE, CasWL, CelCen, Chambr 3, ChhPo, -S1, -S2, CnE&AP, CrtT 2, CyWA 58, DcBiPP, DcEnA, -A, DcEnL, DcEuL, DcLB 93, -107, DcLEL, DcNaB, Dis&D, EvLB, LongCEL, MouLC 3, NewC, NinCLC 8, OxCChiL, OxCEng 67, -85, PenC ENG, PoLE, REn, RfGEnL 91, SmATA 54, WebE&AL, WhDW, WhoChL*
Pseud./variant:
Espriella, Don Manuel Alvarez

Southgate, Vera *Au&Wr 71, BioIn 16, ConAu 109, SmATA 54, WrDr 76, -80, -82, -84, -86, -88, -90*

Southworth, John VanDuyn 1904- *Au&Wr 71, BlueB 76, ConAu 5R, -6NR, IntAu&W 77, WhNAA, WhoAm 74, -76, -78, WrDr 80*

Southworth, John VanDuyn 1904-1986 *ConAu 118*

Sowerby, Amy Millicent 1878-1967 *BioIn 1, ChhPo S1, ConICB, DcBrAr 1, DcWomA, IlsCB 1744, Who 74*

Sowers, Phyllis *AuBYP 2, -3, BioIn 8*

Sowter, Nita *SmATA 69*

Soya, Kiyoshi *AuBYP 3*

Spache, George D 1909- *WrDr 86, -88, -90, -92, -94*

Spache, George Daniel 1909- *AmMWSc 73S, AuBYP 2, -3, BioIn 8, ConAu 5R, -6NR, IntAu&W 77, -89, -91, WrDr 76, -80, -82, -84*

Spanfeller, James John 1930- *BioIn 8, ChhPo S1, -S2, FourBJA, IlrAm 1880, IlsCB 1957, -1967, MajAI, SmATA 19, WhoAm 78, -80, -82, -86, -88, WhoGrA 82*

Spanfeller, James John, Jr. 1956- *WhoE 89*

Spanfeller, Jim *MajAI*

Spanfeller, Jim 1930- *SmATA 8AS*

Spangenberg, Judith Dunn 1942- *BioIn 10, ConAu 29R, -12NR, SmATA 5*
Pseud./variant:
Dunn, Judy

Spangler, Earl 1920- *BioIn 6, ConAu 5R, -5NR, DrAS 74H, -78H, -82H, LEduc 74, MinnWr, WhoMW 74, -76*

Spang Olsen, Ib *ThrBJA*
Main entry: Olsen, Ib Spang

Spar, Jerome 1918- *AmMWSc 73P, -76P, -82, -86, -89, -92, BioIn 11, ConAu 25R, SmATA 10, WhoAm 82, WhoE 81, -83*

Spark, Muriel *BioIn 15, -16, -17, ConNov 86, IntvTCA 2, WrDr 86, -88, -90, -92*

Spark, Muriel 1917- *ContDcW 89*

Spark, Muriel 1918- *ArtclWW 2, Benet 87, BlmGEL, BlmGWL, BritWr S1, CamGEL, CamGLE, CnDBLB 7, ConAu 36NR, ConLC 40, ConNov 91, ConPo 91, CyWA 89, DcLB 139, EncBrWW, FemiCLE, HalFC 88, LiExTwC, MagSWL, MajTwCW, ModBrL S2, RAdv 13-1, RfGEnL 91, ScF&FL 92, ShSCr 10, WorAlBi*

Spark, Muriel Sarah 1918- *TwCYAW, WrDr 94*

Sparks, Beatrice Mathews 1918- *BioIn 13, -15, ConAu 97, SmATA 28, -44*

Sparks, James Calvin, Jr. 1925- *AuBYP 2S, WhoE 74*

Sparks, Mary W 1920- *SmATA 15*

Spaulding, Douglas *ConAu 30NR, ConTFT 10, MajTwCW, SmATA X*
Main entry: Bradbury, Ray

Spaulding, Leonard *ConAu 30NR, IntAu&W 91X, MajTwCW, SmATA X*
Main entry: Bradbury, Ray

Spaull, Hebe 1893- *Au&Wr 71, ConAu 9R*

Speare, Elizabeth George *BioIn 14, -16*

Speare, Elizabeth George 1908- *AmAu&B, AmWomWr, AuBYP 2, -3, Au&Wr 71, BioIn 5, -6, -7, -10, -17, ChlLR 8, ConAu 1R, CurBio 59, DcAmChF 1960, ForWC 70, IntAu&W 77, -82, MajAI,*

MorBMP, MorJA, NewbC 1956, OxCChiL, SmATA 5, –62, TwCChW 78, –83, –89, TwCYAW, WhoAm 74, –76, –78, –80, –82, –84, –86, –88, –90, –92, –94, WhoAmW 74, –93, WrDr 76, –80, –82, –84, –86, –88, –90, –92, –94

Spearing, Judith 1922- *BioIn 11, ConAu 49, –3NR, ScF&FL 92, SmATA 9*

Specking, Inez 1890-1960? *AmAu&B, BioIn 1, –11, BkC 1, CathA 1930, ConAu 5R, SmATA 11, WhNAA*

Speckter, Otto 1807-1871 *BioIn 9, CarSB, ChhPo, DcBiPP, OxCChiL*

Spector, Robert D 1922- *WrDr 86, –88, –90, –92*

Spector, Robert Donald 1922- *ConAu 13R, DrAS 74E, –78E, –82E, ScF&FL 92, WhoAm 74, –76, –78, –80, –82, –84, –86, –88, –90, WhoAmJ 80, WhoE 75, –77, WhoUSWr 88, WhoWrEP 89, –92, WrDr 76, –80, –82, –84, –94*

Spector, Robert Melvyn 1926- *DrAS 74H, –78H, –82H, WhoAmL 78*

Spector, Shushannah 1903- *ConAu 9R*

Speed, Lancelot 1860-1931 *BioIn 14, ChhPo, –S2, DcBrAr 1, DcBrBI, DcVicP 2, WorECar*

Speed, Nell *ConAu 135*

Speed, Nell 1878-1913 *BioIn 17, ConAu 135, SmATA 68*

Speevack, Yetta *AuBYP 2, –3, BioIn 8*

Speicher, Helen Ross 1915- *BioIn 11, ConAu 5R, –4NR, ForWC 70, IndAu 1917, SmATA 8, WrDr 84, –86, –88, –90*
Pseud./variant:
Abbott, Alice
Land, Jane
Land, Ross

Speiser, Jean *ConAu 69*

Spellman, John Willard 1934- *BioIn 12, CanWW 89, ConAu 13R, DrAS 74H, –78H, –82H, SmATA 14*

Spellman, Roger G *IntAu&W 91X, SmATA X, TwCWW 91, WrDr 86, –88, –90*
Main entry: Cox, William R

Spelman, Mary 1934- *BioIn 13, ConAu 77, –13NR, SmATA 28*
Pseud./variant:
Lockwood, Mary
Towne, Mary

Spence, Cynthia *SmATA 74*
Main entry: Eble, Diane

Spence, Eleanor 1928- *AuWomWr, ChlLR 26, TwCChW 89, WrDr 86, –88, –90, –92, –94*

Spence, Eleanor Rachel 1927?- *DcChlFi*

Spence, Eleanor Rachel 1928- *Au&Wr 71, BioIn 12, ConAu 49, –3NR, IntAu&W 82, OxCChiL, SingR 1, SmATA 21, TwCChW 78, –83, TwCYAW, WrDr 76, –80, –82, –84*

Spence, Geraldine 1931- *ArtsCL, BioIn 6, –8, –12, –14, –16, IlsCB 1957, –1967, SmATA 47*

Spence, Lewis 1874-1955 *BioIn 3, –4, CmScLit, ConAu 115, EncO&P 2, –3, ObitOF 79, ObitT 1951, TwCA SUP, WhoLA*

Spencer, Ann 1918- *BioIn 11, ConAu 29R, SmATA 10*

Spencer, Cornelia *AmAu&B, AmNov, AuBYP 2, –3, ConAu X, JBA 51, SmATA 5*
Main entry: Yaukey, Grace Sydenstricker

Spencer, Donald D 1931- *BioIn 15, ConAu 108, SmATA 41*

Spencer, Elizabeth *BioIn 14, –16, –17, CanWW 89, DrAPF 87, –89, –91, –93, IntAu&W 86, –91, IntWW 89, –91, WhoAm 86, WhoAmW 87, WhoCanL 87*

Spencer, Elizabeth 1921- *AmAu&B, AmNov, AmWomWr, ArtclWW 2, Au&Wr 71, BenetAL 91, BioAmW, BioIn 2, –4, –8, –12, –13, BlmGWL, BlueB 76, CamGLE, CamHAL, ConAu 13R, –32NR, ConLC 22, ConNov 72, –76, –82, –86, –91, DcLB 6, DcLEL 1940 DrAF 76, FemiCLE, FifSWrA, ForWC 70, InWom SUP, IntAu&W 77, –82, MajTwCW, Novels, OxCAmL 83, OxCCanL, PenC AM, RAdv 1, REnAL, SmATA 14, TwCA SUP, WhoAm 74, –76, –80, –82, –84, –88, –90, –92, –94, WhoAmW 89, –91, –93, WhoWor 74, WrDr 76, –80, –82, –84, –86, –88, –90, –92, –94*

Spencer, Leonard G *MajAI*

Spencer, Lila 1928- *AuBYP 2S, ForWC 70, WhoAmW 75*

Spencer, Philip *IntAu&W 82X, –86X*
Main entry: Kramer, Aaron

Spencer, William 1922- *AuBYP 2, –3, BioIn 8, –11, ConAu 17R, –8NR, –23NR, DrAS 74H, –78H, IntAu&W 77, –82, –86, –89, –91, IntMed 80, SmATA 9, WhoFla, WrDr 76, –80, –82, –84, –86, –88, –90, –92, –94*

Spencer, William A 1922- *WhoAm 92*

Spencer, Zane A 1935- *BioIn 14, MichAu 80, SmATA 35*

Spender, Stephen *IntvTCA 2*

Spender, Stephen 1909- *AuBYP 2S, -3, Au&Wr 71, Benet 87, BioIn 1, -2, -3, -4, -5, -8, -9, -10, -11, -12, -13, -14, -15, -16, -17, BlmGEL, BlueB 76, BritWr S2, CamGEL, CasWL, Chambr 3, ChhPo, -S2, CnDBLB 7, CnE&AP, CnMD, CnMWL, ConAu 9R, -31NR, ConLC 1, -2, -5, -10, -41, ConLCrt 77, -82, ConPo 70, -75, -80, -85, -91, CurBio 40, -77, CyWA 58, -89, DcLB 20, DcLEL, EncWL, -2, EvLB, IntAu&W 77, -91, IntWW 74, -75, -76, -77, -78, -79, -80, -81, -82, -83, -91, LongCEL, LongCTC, MajTwCW, ModBrL, -S1, -S2, ModWD, NewC, OxCEng 67, PenC ENG, RAdv 1, -13-1, REn, RfGEnL 91, TwCA, -SUP, TwCWr, WebE&AL, WhDW, Who 74, -82, -83, -85, -92, WhoAm 76, WhoTwCL, WhoWor 74, -78, -80, -82, WorAlBi, WrDr 76, -80, -82, -84, -86, -88, -90, -92*

Spender, Stephen, Sir 1909- *CamGLE, EngPo, IntWW 89, Who 88, -90*

Spender, Stephen Harold 1909- *GayLL*

Sperling, Dan 1949- *BioIn 17, SmATA 65*

Sperling, Daniel Lee 1949- *IntAu&W 86*

Sperry, Armstrong 1897-1976 *TwCChW 89*

Sperry, Armstrong W 1897-1976 *AmPB, AnCL, AuBYP 2, -3, BioIn 1, -2, -4, -5, -7, -9, -10, -13, -14, ConAu 107, -P-1, CurBio 41, IlsCB 1744, -1946, JBA 51, MajAI, NewbMB 1922, OxCChiL, SmATA 1, -27N, Str&VC, TwCChW 78, -83*

Sperry, Byrne Hope *ConAu 69*
Main entry: Sanders, Byrne Hope

Sperry, J E *ConAu X*
Main entry: Eisenstat, Jane Sperry

Sperry, Margaret 1905?- *ConAu 37R, IntAu&W 77, -82, WrDr 76, -80, -82, -84*

Sperry, Margaret 1908- *WrDr 86*

Sperry, Raymond, Jr. *ConAu 26NR, -P-2, SmATA 1*
Main entry: Stratemeyer, Edward L

Speyer, Leonora 1872-1955 *BenetAL 91*

Speyer, Leonora 1872-1956 *AmAu&B, AnCL, BioIn 4, -10, ChhPo, -S1, CnDAL, DcLEL, OxCAmL 65, -83, REn, REnAL, TwCA, -SUP, WhAm 3, WhNAA*

Speyer, Leonora von Stosch 1872-1956 *AmWomPl*

Spicer, Dorothy Gladys *AmWomPl, AuBYP 3*

Spicer, Dorothy Gladys d1975 *AuBYP 2, BioIn 8, ConAu 1R, -4NR, ForWC 70, SmATA 32*

Spiegel, Clara *AuBYP 3*

Spiegel, Clara 1904- *AmAu&B, AmNov X, AuBYP 2, Au&Wr 71, BioIn 2, -3, ConAu X, CurBio 54*
Pseud./variant:
Jaynes, Clare

Spiegelman, Art *BioIn 15, -16*

Spiegelman, Art 1948- *Au&Arts 10, ConAu 125, ConGrA 3, ConLC 76, EncACom, TwCYAW, WhoAm 92, -94*

Spiegelman, Judith M *BioIn 10, ConAu 21R, SmATA 5*

Spielberg, Steven *LesBEnT 92, NewYTBS 92*

Spielberg, Steven 1946- *HalFC 88, NewEScF*

Spielberg, Steven 1947- *Au&Arts 8, BenetAL 91, BioIn 10, -11, -12, -13, -14, -15, -16, -17, CelR 90, ConAu 32NR, ConHero 1, ConLC 20, ConTFT 1, -10, EncSF 93, HalFC 84, IntMPA 81, -82, -84, -86, -88, -92, IntWW 83, -89, -91, NewYTBS 82, News 93, ScF&FL 92, ScFSB, SmATA 32, Who 88, -90, -92, WhoAm 80, -82, -84, -86, -88, -90, -92, -94, WhoEnt 92, WorAlBi, WorFDir 2*

Spielberg, Steven 1948- *PenEncH*

Spielmann, Mabel Henrietta 1862-1938 *CarSB, ChhPo S2, WhoLA, WomNov*

Spier, Peter *BioIn 14*

Spier, Peter 1927- *BioIn 16, DcLB 61, SmATA 54*

Spier, Peter Edward 1927- *AuBYP 2SA, -3, BioIn 5, -8, -9, -10, -12, BkP, ChhPo S1, -S2, ChlLR 5, ConAu 5R, -41NR, IlsBYP, IlsCB 1946, -1957, -1967, MajAI, SmATA 4, ThrBJA, WhoAm 74, -76, -78, -80, -82, -84, -86, -88, -90, -94, WhoAmA 78, -80, -82, -84, -86, -89, -91*

Spilhaus, Athelstan 1911- *AmMWSc 73P, BioIn 5, -7, -8, -11, BlueB 76, ConAu 17R, -31NR, CurBio 65, Future, IntWW 74, SmATA 13, WhoAm 74, -76, -78, -80, -82, -84, -86, -88, -90, -92, -94, WhoFI 74, WhoGov 72, -75, WhoSSW 73, -75, -76,*

WhoWor 74, WrDr 76, –82, –84, –86, –88, –90, –92, –94

Spilka, Arnold 1917- *AuBYP 2, –3, BioIn 8, –9, –10, ChhPo S1, –S2, ConAu 49, IlsCB 1957, –1967, SmATA 6, ThrBJA*

Spillane, Frank Morrison 1918- *ConAu 28NR, IntAu&W 91, MajTwCW, SmATA 66, SpyFic*
Pseud./variant:
Spillane, Mickey

Spillane, Mickey *ConAu 28NR, IntvTCA 2, MajTwCW, SmATA 66, WhoUSWr 88, WhoWrEP 89, –92*

Spillane, Mickey 1918- *Benet 87, BenetAL 91, BioIn 14, –15, –17, CelR 90, CrtSuMy, HalFC 88, SpyFic, TwCCr&M 91, WhoAm 86, –88, –90, –92, –94, WorAlBi, WrDr 86, –88, –90, –92, –94*
Main entry: Spillane, Frank Morrison

Spinelli, Eileen *DrAPF 87, –89, –91, –93*

Spinelli, Eileen 1942- *BioIn 15, ConAu 107, SmATA 38*

Spinelli, Jerry 1941- *Au&Arts 11, BioIn 15, –16, –17, ChlLR 26, ConAu 111, –30NR, MajAI, SixBJA, SmATA 39, –71, TwCYAW, WhoAm 92, –94*

Spink, Reginald 1905- *Au&Wr 71, BioIn 11, ConAu 53, –4NR, –19NR, IntAu&W 77, –82, –86, –89, SmATA 11, WrDr 76, –80, –82, –84, –86, –88, –90, –92, –94*

Spink, Reginald William 1905- *ConAu 41NR*

Spinka, Penina Keen 1945- *SmATA 72*

Spinner, Stephanie 1943- *BioIn 15, ChhPo S2, ConAu 45, –32NR, ScF&FL 92, SmATA 38*

Spinossimus *ConAu X, –31NR, SmATA X, WrDr 76, –80*
Main entry: White, William, Jr.

Spires, Elizabeth 1952- *SmATA 71*

Spiro, Jack D 1933- *ConAu 9R, –6NR*

Spirt, Diana Louise
Main entry: Lembo, Diana L

Spirt, Diana Louise 1925- *ConAu 17R, WhoLibI 82*

Spitzing, Gunter 1931- *IntAu&W 77, –82, WhoWor 78, –80, –82, –87*

Spivak, Gayatri Chakravorty 1941- *BlmGWL*

Spivak, Gayatri Chakravorty 1942- *ConAu 110, DrAS 78E, –82E*

Splaver, Sarah *WhoAmW 93, WhoSSW 91, –93*

Splaver, Sarah 1921- *AuBYP 2S, –3, BioIn 13, ConAu 85, SmATA 28, WhoAmW 74, –75, –77, –81, WhoE 74, –75, –77, –81, WhoWorJ 72, –78*

Spohn, David 1948- *SmATA 72*

Spollen, Christopher 1952- *BioIn 11, SmATA 12*

Spot, Ryhen *ConAu X*
Main entry: Post, Henry

Sprague, Gretchen 1926- *AuBYP 2, –3, BioIn 8, –13, ConAu 13R, SmATA 27*

Sprague, Gretchen Burnham 1926- *DcAmChF 1960*

Sprague, Rosemary 1922?- *AmWomWr, AuBYP 2, –3, BioIn 8, ConAu 17R, DrAS 74E, –78E, –82E, OhA&B, WhoAmW 74*

Sprigge, Elizabeth Miriam Squire 1900-1974 *Au&Wr 71, BiE&WWA, BioIn 4, –11, ConAu 13R, NotNAT, SmATA 10, TwCA, –SUP, Who 74*

Spring, Howard 1889-1965 *BioIn 1, –4, –7, –8, –9, –13, ConAu P-1, CurBio 41, –65, DcLEL, DcNaB 1961, EvLB, HalFC 84, –88, LongCTC, NewC, Novels, ObitOF 79, ObitT 1961, OxCChiL, OxCEng 85, OxCLiW 86, PenC ENG, REn, SmATA 28, TwCA, –SUP, TwCWr, WhAm 4, WhoChL*

Spring, Ira Lou 1918- *ConAu 57, –7NR*

Spring, Norma 1917- *ConAu 61*

Spring, Robert Walton 1918- *ConAu 57, –7NR*

Springer, L Elsinore 1911- *ConAu 69*

Springer, Marilyn Harris 1931- *ConAu 21R, –9NR, SmATA 47*
Pseud./variant:
Harris, Marilyn

Springer, Nancy *BioIn 17, ConSFF, DrAPF 87, –89, –91, –93, ScFSB*

Springer, Nancy 1948- *ConAu 41NR, IntAu&W 89, –91, ScF&FL 92, SmATA 65, TwCSFW 91*

Springstubb, Tricia *DrAPF 87, –89, –91, –93*

Springstubb, Tricia 1950- *BioIn 15, –16, ConAu 105, –21NR, DrAPF 83, –85, SixBJA, SmATA 40, –46*

Sproule, Anna *AuBYP 3*

Sproule, Michael *AuBYP 3*

Sprunt, Alexander, Jr. 1898-1973 *BioIn 1, -9, ConAu 37R, EncAB-A 21, WhAm 5*

Spurling, Jack 1871-1933 *DcBrAr 1, DcVicP 2*

Spykman, E C 1896-1965 *TwCChW 89*

Spykman, Elizabeth C 1896-1965 *BioIn 6, -7, -11, ConAu 101, MorJA, SmATA 10, TwCChW 78, -83*

Spykman, Elizabeth Choate 1896-1965 *DcAmChF 1960*

Spyri, Johanna *Benet 87*

Spyri, Johanna 1827-1901 *AuBYP 3, BlmGWL, ChlLR 13, EncCoWW, WrChl*

Spyri, Johanna 1829-1901 *OxCGer 86*

Spyri, Johanna Heusser 1827?-1901 *AnCL, AuBYP 2, BioIn 1, -2, -3, -4, -7, -8, -12, CarSB, ConAu 137, InWom SUP, JBA 34, -51, MajAI, OxCChiL, OxCGer 76, SmATA 19, WhoChL*

Squire, Elizabeth Daniels 1919- *ConAu 13R*

Squire, Maud Hunt 1873-1955? *ChhPo, -S1, DcWomA*

Squire, Roger *AuBYP 2S*

Squires, James Duane 1904-1981 *AmAu&B, Au&Wr 71, BlueB 76, ConAu 5R, DrAS 74H, -78H, IntAu&W 77, WhAm 8, Who 74, -82N, WhoAm 74, -76, -78, -80, -82, WhoAmP 73, WhoGov 77, -75, WrDr 76, -80, -82*

Squires, Phil *ConAu X, IntAu&W 77X, IntWWP 82X, SmATA X, WrDr 76, -80, -82, -84*
Main entry: Barker, S Omar

S-Ringi, Kjell *ConAu X, SmATA X*
Main entry: Ringi, Kjell Arne Sorensen

Srivastava, Jane Jonas *BioIn 15, SmATA 37*

Srivastava, Jane Jonas 1941- *ConAu 119*

S Svend, Otto
Main entry: Soerensen, Svend Otto

Stables, William Gordon 1840-1910 *Alli SUP, BioIn 8, BritAu 19, ChhPo, -S1, EvLB, NewC, OxCChiL, WhoChL*

Stack, Nicolete *AuBYP 3*

Stack, Nicolete Meredith 1896- *AuBYP 2, ConAu 13R, ForWC 70, WhoMW 74*
Pseud./variant:
Kenny, Kathryn
Meredith, Nicolete

Stacpoole, Henry De Vere 1863-1951 *DcIrB 88, StaCVF*

Stacpoole, Henry DeVere 1863-1951 *BiDIrW, BioIn 2, -3, CamGLE, ChhPo S2, DcIrW 1, DcNaB 1951, EvLB, ObitOF 79, PoIre, TwCWr*

Stacy, Donald L 1925- *ConAu 29R, PrintW 83, -85, WhoAmA 78, -80, -82, -84, -86, -89, -91*

Stadtler, Bea 1921- *BioIn 12, ConAu 65, IntAu&W 86, SmATA 17*

Stadtler, Beatrice 1921- *IntAu&W 91*

Stadtler, Beatrice Horwitz 1921- *WhoAm 92, -94*

Staebler, Edna *CaW, ConAu 101, WrDr 76, -80, -82, -84*

Stafford, Ellen *OxCCan*

Stafford, Jean *IntvTCA 2*

Stafford, Jean 1915-1979 *AmAu&B, AmNov, AmWomWr, -92, ArtclWW 2, Benet 87, BenetAL 91, BioAmW, BioIn 2, -3, -4, -7, -11, -12, -13, -14, -15, -16, -17, BlmGWL, BlueB 76, CamGLE, CamHAL, CnDAL, ConAu 1R, -85, -3NR, ConLC 4, -7, -19, -68, ConNov 72, -76, CurBio 51, CyWA 89, DcLB 2, DcLEL 1940, DrAF 76, EncWL, FemiCLE, InWom SUP, IntAu&W 77, MajTwCW, ModAL, NewYTBS 84, Novels, OxCAmL 65, -83, PenC AM, RAdv 1, REn, REnAL, RfGAmL 87, RfGShF, ShSWr, SmATA 22N, TwCA SUP, TwCWW 91, WhAm 7, WhoAm 74, -76, -78, WhoAmW 74, WhoE 74, WhoTwCL, WhoWor 74, WorAlBi, WorAl, WrDr 76, -80*

Stagg, James 1918- *Au&Wr 71*

Stahl, Ben 1910- *BioIn 1, -2, -7, -8, -10, -11, -12, ConAu 29R, IlsBYP, IlsCB 1957, -1967, SmATA 5, WhAm 9, WhAmArt 85, WhoAm 74, -76, -78, -80, -82, -84, -86, WhoAmA 73, -78, -80, -82, -84, -86, WhoSSW 73, -75, -76, WhoWor 80, -82*

Stahl, Ben 1910-1987 *BioIn 15, -16, ConAu 123, NewYTBS 87, ScF&FL 92, SmATA 54N*

Stahl, Hilda 1938- *BioIn 16, ConAu 40NR, SmATA 48*

Stahl, Hilda 1938-1993 *ConAu 142, SmATA 77*

Stahl, Hilda Ann 1938- *IntAu&W 89*

Stahl, L C *CarSB*

Stair, Gobin 1912- *BioIn 10, -14, SmATA 35, WhoAm 74, -76, -78, -80, -82, -84, -86, -88, -90, -92, -94, WhoRel 75*

Stalder, Valerie *BioIn 13, ConAu 41R, SmATA 27*

Stall, Dorothy *AuBYP 2, -3, BioIn 8*

Stallybrass, Oliver George Weatherhead 1925- *Au&Wr 71, ConAu 29R*

Stamaty, Mark Alan *BioIn 15*

Stamaty, Mark Alan 1947- *BioIn 11, -12, ConAu 61, -15NR, EncACom, IlsCB 1967, SmATA 12, WhoAm 86, -88, -90, WhoGrA 82*

Stambler, Irwin 1924- *AuBYP 2, -3, BioIn 8, -10, ConAu 5R, -2NR, IntAu&W 89, -91, SmATA 5, WhoUSWr 88, WhoWrEP 89, -92, WrDr 76, -80, -82, -84, -86, -88, -90, -92, -94*

Stanbury, David 1933- *Au&Wr 71, ConAu 104*

Standish, Burt L *AmAu&B, BenetAL 91, CurBio 45, DcNAA, ObitOF 79, OxCAmL 65, -83, REnAL, TwCA, -SUP, WebAB 74, -79*
Main entry: Patten, William Gilbert

Standish, Burt L 1866-1945 *Ballpl 90*

Standon, Anna 1929- *ConAu 17R*

Standon, Edward Cyril 1929- *BioIn 8, -12, -14, IlsBYP, IlsCB 1957, -1967*

Standring, Heather 1928- *ArtsCL, BioIn 6*

Stanek, Lou Willett *BioIn 17*

Stanek, Lou Willett 1931- *SmATA 63*

Stanek, Muriel *BioIn 14*

Stanek, Muriel 1915- *ConAu 112, SmATA 34*

Stanev, Emilian 1907- *AuBYP 2S, CasWL, ConAu X*

Stanev, Emilian 1907-1979 *AuBYP 3*

Stanford, Donald Kent 1918- *BioIn 1, ConAu 53, WrDr 80, -82, -84*

Stanford, Ernest Elwood 1888- *WhAm 9*

Stanford, Ernest Elwood 1888-1966 *WhNAA*

Stang, Judit 1921-1977 *BioIn 13, ConAu 5R, -8NR, SmATA 29*
Pseud./variant:
Stang, Judy
Varga, Judy

Stang, Judy
Main entry: Stang, Judit

Stangl, Jean *BioIn 17*

Stangl, Jean 1928- *SmATA 67*

Stanhope, Eric *ConAu X, -29NR, SmATA X*

Stanhope, Lavinia *WrDr 80*
Main entry: Schlein, Miriam

Staniforth, John William 1863-1927 *OxCChiL*

Stankevich, Boris 1928- *BioIn 9, ConAu 21R, SmATA 2*

Stanley, Diana 1909- *BioIn 5, -8, DcBrAr 1, IlsBYP, IlsCB 1946, SmATA 30, WhoChL*

Stanley, Diane *ChlBIlD*

Stanley, Diane 1943- *BioIn 14, -15, -16, ConAu 112, -32NR, IntAu&W 86, SixBJA, SmATA 32, -37, -15AS, WrDr 90, -92, -94*
Pseud./variant:
Zuromskis, Diane

Stanley, George Edward 1942- *BioIn 16, ConAu 39NR, SmATA 53*
Pseud./variant:
Symons, Stuart

Stanley, George Francis Gillman 1907- *Au&Wr 71, BioIn 4, CanWW 70, -80, -81, -83, -89, ConAu 41R, -15NR, DrAS 74H, OxCCan, -SUP, WhoAm 86, -88, WhoCan 73, -80, -82, WhoE 83, -85, -86, -89*

Stanley, George Francis Gilman 1907- *DrAS 82H*

Stanley, Henry M 1841-1904 *BenetAL 91, BioIn 14, -16, -17, WorAlBi*

Stanley, Henry Morton 1841?-1904 *DcAfHiB 86, EncPaPR 91, Expl 93, OxCLiW 86, WhCiWar*

Stanley, Henry Morton, Sir 1841-1904 *Alli SUP, AmAu&B, Benet 87, BbD, BiD&SB, BioIn 1, -2, -3, -4, -5, -6, -7, -8, -9, -10, -11, -12, BritAu 19, CamGEL, CamGLE, CarSB, Chambr 3, DcAmAu, DcBrBI, DcEnA, -A, DcNaB S2, EvLB, HarEnUS McGEWB, OxCAmH, OxCAmL 65, -83, OxCEng 67, -85, RAdv 13-3, REn, REnAL, WebAB 74, -79, WhDW, WhAm 1, WorAl*

Stanley, Robert *ConAu X, -29NR, SmATA X*

Stanley, Warwick *ConAu X, WrDr 76, –80*
Main entry: Hilton, John Buxton

Stanley-Brown, Rudolph *ConICB*

Stanley-Wrench, Margaret 1916- *Au&Wr 71, ConAu 9R*

Stanley Wrench, Margaret 1916-1974 *FemiCLE*

Stanli, Sue *ConAu X, SmATA X*
Main entry: Meilach, Dona Zweigoron

Stannard, Russell *ScF&FL 92*

Stanovich, Betty Jo 1954- *BioIn 16, ConAu 118, SmATA 51*

Stansky, Peter David Lyman 1932- *BioIn 12, ConAu 17R, DrAS 74H, –82H, IntAu&W 91, WhoAm 80, –82, –84, –86, –88, –90, –92, –94, WrDr 76, –80*

Stanstead, John *ConAu X, SmATA X*
Main entry: Groom, Arthur William

Stanton, Rosamond *AuBYP 3*

Stanton, Schuyler *ConAu X, ThrBJA, TwCA, –SUP*
Main entry: Baum, Lyman Frank

Stanton-Hope, W E *BioIn 8*

Stapler, Harry 1919- *ConAu 61, –13NR, WhoMW 74*

Stapler, Harry Bascom 1919- *WhoSSW 86*

Staples, Suzanne Fisher 1945- *ConAu 132, SmATA 70, TwCYAW, WrDr 94*
Pseud./variant:
Fisher, Suzanne

Stapleton, Marjorie 1932- *BioIn 13, ConAu 106, SmATA 28*

Stapp, Arthur Donald 1906-1972 *AuBYP 2, –3, BioIn 6, –8, –9, ConAu 1R, –33R, –2NR, MorJA, SmATA 4*

Starbird, Kaye 1916- *AuBYP 2, –3, BioIn 10, ChhPo, –S1, ConAu 17R, –38NR, MajAI, SmATA 6*
Pseud./variant:
Jennison, C S

Stark, James *AuBYP 2S, –3, ConAu X, SmATA 6*
Main entry: Goldston, Robert Conroy

Stark, John H 1914- *ConAu 49*

Starkey, Marion L 1901- *BioIn 11, ConAu 1R, –1NR, ForWC 70, SmATA 13, WrDr 76, –80, –82, –84*

Starkie, Walter Fitzwilliam 1894- *BlueB 76*

Starkie, Walter Fitzwilliam 1894-1976 *Au&Wr 71, BiDIrW, BioIn 1, –4, –6, –7, –11, –17, CarSB, CathA 1930, ConAu 69, –77, CurBio 64, –77N, DcIrB 88, IntAu&W 77, IntWW 74, LongCTC, NewC, TwCA, –SUP, WhAm 7, Who 74, WhoAm 74, –76, WhoMus 72*

Starr, Leonard 1925- *ArtCS, EncACom, WhoAm 82, –84, –86, –88*

Starr, Ward And Murch, Mel *SmATA X*
Main entry: Manes, Stephen, Mel

Starret, William *ConAu X, SmATA 3*
Main entry: McClintock, Marshall

Starrett, Charles Vincent Emerson 1886-1974 *AmAu&B, AuBYP 2, BioIn 4, –7, –8, –10, ChhPo, –S2, ConAu 45, –73, DcLEL, EncMys, NewYTBS 74, REn, REnAL, TwCA, –SUP, WhNAA*

Starrett, Vincent 1886-1974 *AuBYP 3, BenetAL 91, BioIn 14, ConAu 31NR, CrtSuMy, ScF&FL 92, TwCCr&M 91*

Stashin, Leo *NewYTBE 73*

Stasiak, Krystyna *BioIn 16, SmATA 49*

St Aubyn, Giles R 1925- *IntAu&W 89*

Staudacher, Rosemarian V 1918- *IntAu&W 86*

Staudacher, Rosemarian Valentiner 1918- *ConAu 5R, ForWC 70, IntAu&W 77, –82, WrDr 76, –80, –82, –84*

Stauffer, Don *ConAu X, SmATA X*
Main entry: Berkebile, Fred D

Stauffer, Dwight G *AuBYP 2S, –3*

Staunton, Schuyler *ConAu 133, EncSF 93, MajAI, MajTwCW, SmATA X, WebAB 79*
Main entry: Baum, Lyman Frank

Steadman, Ralph Idris 1936- *BioIn 8, –10, –12, –13, ChhPo S2, ConAu 107, IntWW 89, –91, SmATA 32, Who 82, –83, –85, –88, –90, –92, WhoChL, WhoGrA 82, WorECar*

Steahly, Vivian Eugenia Emrick 1915- *ConAu 61, DrAS 74E, –78E, –82E, IntAu&W 82, –86, –89, WhoAmW 74, –75, –77, –81, –83, WhoMW 74, –76, –78*

Stearn, Jess *ConAu 97, EncSF 93, ScF&FL 92, WrDr 76, –80, –82, –84, –86, –88, –90, –92, –94*

Stearns, John Newton 1829-1895 *Alli, AmAu&B, CarSB, ChhPo, –S1, DcNAA, WhAm HS*

Stearns, Monroe 1913- *WrDr 86, –88*

Stearns, Monroe 1913-1987 *BioIn 15, –16, ConAu 124, SmATA 55N*

Stearns, Monroe Mather 1913- *AuBYP 2S, –3, BioIn 10, ConAu 5R, SmATA 5, WrDr 80*

Stearns, Pamela Fujimoto 1935- *ConAu 65*

Stebbins, George S *CarSB*

Steckler, Arthur 1921-1985 *BioIn 17, SmATA 65*

Steedman, Marguerite Couturier 1908- *AuBYP 2S, –3, ConAu 1R, –1NR*

Steegmuller, Francis *DrAPF 87, –89, –91, –93*

Steegmuller, Francis 1906- *AmAu&B, Au&Wr 71, Benet 87, BenetAL 91, BioIn 2, –4, –12, –17, ChhPo, ConAu 49, –2NR, ConNov 72, –76, DcLB 111, DrAPF 83, –85, IntAu&W 77, –82, –86, –89, –91, NewYTBS 80, OxCAmL 83, REnAL, TwCA SUP, Who 74, –82, –83, –85, –88, –90, –92, WhoAm 74, –76, –78, –80, –82, –84, –86, –88, –90, –92, –94, WrDr 76, –80, –82, –84, –86, –88, –90, –92, –94*

Steel, Danielle *BestSel 90-4, BioIn 14, –15, –16, –17, ConAu 19NR, WrDr 86*

Steel, Danielle 1947?- *ArtclWW 2, BestSel 89-1, ConAu 36NR, CurBio 89, MajTwCW, SmATA 66, TwCRHW 90, WorAlBi, WrDr 88, –90, –92, –94*

Steel, Danielle 1948- *CelR 90*

Steel, Danielle 1950- *IntWW 91*

Steel, Flora Annie 1847-1929 *BbD, BiD&SB, BioIn 13, CarSB, Chambr 3, ConAu 116, DcBiA, DcInB, DcNaB 1922, EncBrWW, FemiCLE, LongCTC, NewC, OxCChiL, OxCEng 67, REn, Str&VC, TwCA, WomNov*

Steel, Flora Annie, Mrs 1847-1929 *StaCVF*

Steel, Flora Annie Webster 1847-1929 *BioIn 16, InWom SUP*

Steele, Addison, II 1935- *SmATA X*
Main entry: Lupoff, Richard Allen

Steele, Chester K *ConAu X, –26NR*
Main entry: Stratemeyer, Edward L

Steele, George Peabody 1924- *ConAu 1R, WhoE 89, –91, –93, WhoFI 81, –83, –85, –87, –89, –92, –94, WhoWor 80, –82, –84, –87 –89, –91, –93, WrDr 80*

Steele, Mary *DcChlFi*

Steele, Mary Q 1922- *BioIn 14, –16, ConAu 22NR, IntAu&W 91, SmATA 51, TwCChW 89, WrDr 86, –88, –90, –92*

Steele, Mary Q 1922-1992 *ScF&FL 92*

Steele, Mary Quintar 1922- *ArtclWW 2*

Steele, Mary Quintard 1922- *AuBYP 3, WrDr 94*

Steele, Mary Quintard Govan 1922- *AuBYP 2, BioIn 8, –9, –11, ConAu 1R, –6NR, DcAmChF 1960, MajAI, SmATA 3, ThrBJA, TwCChW 78, –83, WrDr 76, –80, –82, –84*
Pseud./variant:
Gage, Wilson

Steele, Mary Quintard Govan 1922-1992 *ConAu 139, SmATA 72*

Steele, Max *DrAPF 87, –89, –91, –93*

Steele, Max 1922- *AmAu&B, BioIn 11, –12 ConAu 25R, DcLB Y80B, DrAF 76, IntAu&W 82, SmATA 10, WhoSSW 73, –75, –76, WrDr 76, –80, –82, –84, –86, –88, –90, –92*

Steele, William O 1917-1979 *SmATA 51, TwCChW 89, TwCWW 91*

Steele, William Owen 1917- *BioIn 14, –16*

Steele, William Owen 1917-1979 *AmAu&B AuBYP 2, –3, Au&Wr 71, BioIn 6, –8, –9, –12, –13, BlueB 76, BkCL, ConAu 5R, –2NR, IntAu&W 77, MajAI, MorJA, OxCChiL, SmATA 1, –27N, TwCChW 78, –83, WhAm 7, WhoAm 74, –76, –78, WrDr 76, –80*

Steelsmith, Shari 1962- *SmATA 72*

Stefanik, Alfred T 1939- *BioIn 16, SmATA 55*

Stefansson, Evelyn Baird *AuBYP 2, BioIn 8, ConAu 49*
Main entry: Nef, Evelyn Stefansson

Stefansson, Evelyn Baird 1913- *AuBYP 3*

Stefansson, Thorsteinn 1912- *ConAu 77, –29NR, IntAu&W 77, –82, –86, –89, WhoWor 80*

Stefansson, Vilhjalmur 1879-1962 *AmAu&B, BenetAL 91, BioIn 1, -2, -3, -4, -5, -6, -7, -8, -11, -12, -15, -16, -17, CurBio 42, -62, DcAmB S7, DcAmBC, DcLEL, Dis&D, Expl 93, InSci, ObitOF 79, ObitT 1961, OxCAmL 65, -83, OxCCan, OxCShps, RAdv 13-3, REnAL, TwCA, -SUP, WebAB 79, WhNAA, WorAlBi, WorAl*

Steffan, Alice Kennedy 1907- *ConAu 5R, WhoPNW*
Pseud./variant:
Steffan, Jack

Steffan, Jack
Main entry: Steffan, Alice Kennedy

Steffanson, Con *ConAu X, EncSF 93, TwCSFW 86, -91, WrDr 82, -84, -86, -88, -90, -92*
Main entry: Goulart, Ron

Steffanson, Con 1933- *WrDr 94*

Steffen, Randy 1917?-1977 *BioIn 11*

Steffens, Arthur
Main entry: Glyn, Harrison

Steffens, Bradley 1955- *SmATA 77*

Steffens, Lincoln *SourALJ*

Steffens, Lincoln 1866-1936 *AmAu&B, Benet 87, BenetAL 91, BioIn 1, -2, -3, -4, -5, -6, -8, -9, -10, -11, -12, -13, -15, -16, CmCal, ConAu 117, CyWA 89, DcAmSR, EncAJ, JrnUS, LongCTC, McGEWB, MemAm, ModAL, OxCAmH, OxCAmL 65, -83, PenC AM, REn, REnAL, TwCA, -SUP, TwCLC 20, WebAB 74, -79, WebE&AL, WhAm 1, WorAlBi, WorAl*

Steffens, Lincoln 1886-1936 *DcAmImH*

Stefferud, Alfred Daniel 1903- *AuBYP 2, -3, BioIn 8, ConAu P-1, IntYB 80, -81, WhoAm 74, -76, -78, WhoE 74, -75*

Stegeman, Janet A 1923- *BioIn 16*

Stegeman, Janet Allais 1923- *ConAu 128, SmATA 49, -53*
Pseud./variant:
Britton, Kate

Steichen, Paula 1943- *ChhPo S1, ConAu 25R*

Steig, William 1907- *AmAu&B, AmPB, AuBYP 2, AuNews 1, BenetAL 91, BioIn 8, -9, -10, -12, -13, -14, -15, -16, -17, CelR, ChlLR 2, -15, ConAu 77, -21NR, CurBio 44, DcAmChF 1960, DcLB 61, EncTwCJ, IlsBYP, IlsCB 1967, MajAI, NewYTBE 72, NewbC 1966, OxCChiL, REnAL, SmATA 18, -70, ThrBJA, TwCChW 78, -83, -89, WhoAm 74, -76, -78, -80, -82, -84, -86, -88, -90, -92, -94, WhoAmA 73, -78, -80, -82, -84, -86, -89, WhoE 74, WhoGrA 82, WhoWor 74, WorECar, WrDr 80, -82, -84, -86, -88, -90, -92, -94*

Steig, William H 1907- *AuBYP 3*

Steiger, Brad *ConAu X, EncO&P 1S1*
Main entry: Olson, Eugene E

Steiger, Brad 1936- *ConAu 21NR, EncO&P 3, ScF&FL 92*

Stein, Evaleen 1863-1923 *AmAu&B, AmLY, BioIn 2, ChhPo, DcAmAu, DcNAA, IndAu 1816, JBA 34, -51, WhAm 1, WomWWA 14*

Stein, Gertrude *IntvTCA 2*

Stein, Gertrude 1874-1946 *AmAu&B, AmPB, AmWomD, AmWomPl, AmWomWr, -92, AmWr, ArtclWW 2, AtlBL, Benet 87, BenetAL 91, BioAmW, BioIn 1, -2, -3, -4, -5, -6, -7, -8, -9, -10, -11, -12, -13, -14, -15, -17, BlmGWL, CamGEL, CamGLE, CamHAL, CasWL, Chambr 3, ChhPo S1, CmCal, CnDAL, CnE&AP, CnMD, CnMWL, ConAmA, ConAmL, ConAu 104, -132, ContDcW 89, CurBio 46, CyWA 89, DcLB 4, -54, -86, DcLEL, DcNAA, EncAB-H, EncAB-A 6, EncWL, -2, EncWT, EvLB, FemiCLE, GayLL, HanAmWH, HerW, -84, InWom SUP, IntDcWB, LiExTwC, LongCTC, MajTwCW, MakMC, McGEWB, ModAL, -S1, -S2, ModAWWr, ModWD, MorMA, NewGrDA 86, NotNAT A, -B, NotWoAT, Novels, ObitOF 79, OxCAmH, OxCAmL 65, -83, OxCAmT 84, OxCChiL, OxCEng 67, -85, PenC AM, RAdv 1, -13-1, RComAH, RComWL, REn, REnAL, RfGAmL 87, SixAP, Tw, TwCA, -SUP, TwCLC 1, -6, -28, -48, TwCWr, WebAB 74, -79, WebE&AL, WhDW, WhAm 2, WhAmArt 85, WhNAA, WhoAmW 74, WhoTwCL, WomNov, WorAlBi, WorAl, WorLitC*

Stein, Harry 1938- *ConAu 61, -120*

Stein, Harve 1904- *BioIn 5, -14, IlsBYP, IlsCB 1946, SmATA 30, WhoAmA 73, -78, -80, -82, -84, -86, -89, -91*

Stein, Meyer Lewis 1920- *AmMWSc 73S, AuBYP 2, -3, BioIn 8, -10, ConAu 17R, DrAS 74E, -78E, -82E, SmATA 6, WhoE 74*

Stein, Mini *ASCAP 66, BioIn 9, ConAu 29R, SmATA 2*

Stein, R Conrad 1937- *BioIn 14, ConAu 41R, -22NR, SmATA 31*

Stein, Sara Bonnett *BioIn 14, SmATA 34*

Stein, Susan M 1942- *ConAu 37R, -14NR*

Stein, Walter 1924- *ConAu 25R, IntAu&W 77, -82, WhoAmA 73, -78, -80, -82, -84, WhoWorJ 72, -78, WrDr 76, -80, -82, -84*

Stein, Wendy 1951- *SmATA 77*

Steinbach, Alexander Alan 1894-1978 *BioIn 11, ConAu 85, WhoWorJ 72*

Steinbeck, John *IntvTCA 2, SourALJ*

Steinbeck, John 1902-1968 *AgeMat, AmAu&B, AmNov, AmWr, Au&Arts 12, AuBYP 2S, -3, Benet 87, BenetAL 91, BiE&WWA, BioIn 1, -2, -3, -4, -5, -6, -7, -8, -9, -10, -11, -12, -13, -14, -15, -16, -17, CamGEL, CamGLE, CamGWoT, CamHAL, CasWL, CmCal, CnDAL, CnMD, CnMWL, CnThe, ConAmA, ConAu 1R, -25R, -1NR, -35NR, ConLC 1, -5, -9, -13, -21, -45, -75, CurBio 40, -63, -69, CyWA 58, -89, DcAmSR, DcLB 7, -9, -DS2, DcLEL, EncAB-H, EncFWF, EncWL, -2, EncWT, EvLB, FilmgC, HalFC 84, -88, LongCTC, MagSAmL, MajTwCW, MakMC, McGEWD 72, -84, ModAL, -S2, ModWD, NatCAB 61, NobelP, NotNAT B, Novels, ObitOF 79, ObitT 1961, OxCAmH, OxCAmL 65, -83, OxCAmT 84, OxCEng 67, OxCFilm, OxCThe 67, PenC AM, RAdv 1, -13-1, RComAH, RComWL, REn, REnAL, RfGAmL 87, ScF&FL 92, ShSCr 11, ShSWr, SmATA 9, TwCA, -SUP, TwCRHW 90, TwCWW 91, TwCWr, WebAB 74, WebE&AL, WhDW, WhAm 5, WhoTwCL, WorAlBi, WorLitC*

Steinbeck, John Ernst 1902-1968 *RfGShF, TwCYAW*

Steinberg, Alfred 1917- *AuBYP 2, -3, BioIn 8, -11, ConAu 5R, -9NR, SmATA 9*

Steinberg, David Joel 1937- *ConAu 25R, DrAS 74H, -78H, -82H, WhoAm 88, -90, -92, -94, WhoE 91*

Steinberg, David Michael *IlsBYP*

Steinberg, Fannie 1899- *BioIn 15, ConAu 115, SmATA 43*

Steinberg, Fred Jay 1933- *BioIn 9, ConAu 37R, SmATA 4, WhoE 75, WrDr 76, -80*

Steinberg, Phillip Orso 1921- *BioIn 6, -14, ConAu 5R, -2NR, MinnWr, SmATA 34*

Steinberg, Rafael 1927- *BioIn 15, ConAu 61, -9NR, SmATA 45, WhoAm 74, WhoAmJ 80, WhoE 74*

Steinberg, Saul *BioIn 15, WhoAmA 86*

Steinberg, Saul 1914- *AmArt, AmAu&B, Benet 87, BenetAL 91, BioIn 1, -2, -3, -4, -5, -7, -8, -9, -11, -12, -13, -17, CelR, ConArt 77, -83, -89, CurBio 57, DcCAA 71, -77, -88, EncAI&E, IntWW 74, -75, -76, -77, -78, -79, -80, -81, -82, -83, -89, -91, OxCAmL 65, -83, OxCTwCA, PhDcTCA 77, REn, SmATA 67, WebAB 74, -79, WhAmArt 85, WhoAm 74, -76, -78, -80, -82, -84, -86, -88, -90, -92, -94, WhoAmA 78, -80, -82, -84, -89, -91, WhoGrA 62, WhoWor 74, WorArt 1950, WorECar*

Steiner, Barbara A 1934- *BioIn 11, ConAu 73, -13NR, -30NR, SmATA 13, -13AS*
Pseud./variant:
Cole, Annette
D'Andrea, Kate
Daniel, Anne

Steiner, Barbara Annette 1934- *AuBYP 3, WhoUSWr 88, WhoWrEP 89, -92*

Steiner, Charlotte 1900-1981 *AuBYP 2, -3, BioIn 8, -15, SmATA 45*

Steiner, George *IntvTCA 2*

Steiner, George 1929- *Benet 87, BioIn 14, -16, -17, CamGLE, ConAu 31NR, CyWA 89, DcLB 67, IntAu&W 89, -91, IntWW 89, -91, MajTwCW, RAdv 13-1, SmATA 62, Who 88, -92, WhoAm 86, -88, -90, -92, -94, WhoWor 87, -93, WrDr 86, -88, -90, -92, -94*

Steiner, George, Prof 1929- *Who 90*

Steiner, Jorg *BioIn 14, -15*

Steiner, Jorg 1930- *SmATA 35*

Steiner, Rudolf 1861-1925 *BioIn 2, -4, -5, -9, -10, -11, -12, -13, -14, -15, -17, ConAu 107, EncO&P 1, -2, -3, EncPaPR 91, LongCTC, LuthC 75, MacEA, MakMC, OxCGer 76, -86, ThTwC 87, TwCLC 13*

Steiner, Shari 1941- *ConAu 73*

Steiner, Shari Yvonne 1941- *WhoAmW 93*

Steiner, Stan *BioIn 15, -16, WhoAm 86*

Steiner, Stan d1987 *NewYTBS 87, WhAm 9*

Steiner, Stan 1925- *ChiSch, ConAu 45, -1NR, -16NR, IntAu&W 77, SmATA 14, WhoAm 74, -76, -78, -80, -82, -84, WrDr 80, -82, -84, -86, -88*

Steiner, Stan 1925-1987 *ConAu 121, SmATA 50N*

Steiner, Stanley 1925-1987 *ConAu 39NR*

Steiner-Prag, Hugo 1880-1945 *BioIn 3, -14, SmATA 32, WhAmArt 85*

Steinmetz, Eulalie *ConAu 134, -X*
Main entry: Ross, Eulalie Steinmetz

Stensoboel, Ottar 1930- *ConAu 69*

Stenzel, Al *MedPD*

Step, Edward 1855-1931 *Alli SUP, LongCTC*

Stephen, David 1910- *Au&Wr 71, ConAu 106, ScF&FL 92*

Stephens, Alice Barber 1858-1932 *BioIn 15, -17, ChhPo, ConICB, IlrAm 1880, -A, InWom SUP, SmATA 66, WhAm 1, WhAmArt 85, WomWWA 14*

Stephens, Charles Asbury 1844-1931 *Alli SUP, AmAu&B, BiD&SB, BioIn 8, -11, -15, CarSB, ChhPo, -S1, DcAmAu, DcLB 42, DcNAA, OxCChiL, WhAm 1*

Stephens, Henrietta Henkle 1909-1983 *ConAu 9R, -109, -6NR*
Pseud./variant:
Buckmaster, Henrietta
Henkle, Henrietta

Stephens, Henry Louis 1824-1882 *Alli, ChhPo S1, -S2, DcNAA, EarABI, -SUP, WorECar*

Stephens, James 1880-1950 *DcIrB 88, ModBrL S2, ModIrL, RfGEnL 91*

Stephens, James 1882-1950 *AnCL, AuBYP 2S, -3, Benet 87, BiDIrW, BioIn 1, -2, -3, -4, -5, -6, -7, -10, -11, -12, -13, -14, CamGEL, CamGLE, CarSB, CasWL, Chambr 3, ChhPo, -S1, -S2, CnE&AP, ConAu 104, CyWA 58, DcIrL, DcIrW 1, DcLB 19, DcLEL, DcNaB 1941, EncWL, -2, EvLB, LongCTC, McGEWB, ModBrL, -S1, -S2, NewC, Novels, OxCEng 67, -85, PenC ENG, PoIre, RAdv 1, REn, ScF&FL 92, Str&VC, SupFW, TwCA, -SUP, TwCLC 4, TwCWr, WhDW, WhAm 3*

Stephens, Mary Jo 1935- *BioIn 11, ConAu 37R, SmATA 8*

Stephens, Peggy *AuBYP 2S, -3*

Stephens, Peter John *AuBYP 2, -3, BioIn 8*

Stephens, Rosemary *DrAPF 87, -89, -91, -93*

Stephens, Rosemary 1924- *ConAu 77, DrAF 76, DrAP 75, IntAu&W 77*
Pseud./variant:
Carswell, Leslie

Stephens, Suzanne 1949- *SmATA X*
Main entry: Kirby, Susan E

Stephens, William M 1925- *AuBYP 2S, -3, BioIn 12, ConAu 57, SmATA 21*

Stephensen, A M *SmATA X*
Main entry: Manes, Stephen

Stephenson, Marjorie *ChhPo S1*

Stepp, Ann *AuBYP 3*

Stepp, Ann 1935- *AuBYP 2S, BioIn 13, ConAu 106, SmATA 29*

Stepto, Michele 1946- *BioIn 17, ConAu 128, SmATA 61*

Steptoe, John d1989 *NewYTBS 89*

Steptoe, John 1950- *AuBYP 3, BlkAuII, BlkWr 1, ChlLR 12, ConAu 26NR, WrDr 86, -88, -90*

Steptoe, John 1950-1989 *AnObit 1989, BioIn 16, -17, BlkAuII 92, ChlBIID, ConAu 129, SmATA 63, TwCChW 89*

Steptoe, John Lewis 1950- *AfroAA, BioIn 8, -11, -12, BlkAWP, BlkWrNE A, ChlLR 2, ConAu 49, -3NR, FourBJA, IlsBYP, IlsCB 1967, InB&W 80, LivgBAA, OxCChiL, SelBAAf, SelBAAu, SmATA 8, TwCChW 78, -83, WhoAm 74, -76, WhoBlA 90, WrDr 82, -84*

Steptoe, John Lewis 1950-1989 *MajAI, WhoBlA 92N*

Sterling, Brett *EncSF 93, TwCSFW 86, -91*

Sterling, Brett 1906-1980
Main entry: Samachson, Joseph

Sterling, Brett 1920- *SmATA X*
Main entry: Bradbury, Ray

Sterling, Chandler Winfield 1911- *BioIn 9, ConAu 21R, IntAu&W 77, -82, WhoAm 74, -76, -78, -80, -82, WrDr 76, -80*

Sterling, Chandler Winfield 1911-1984 *WhAm 9*

Sterling, Christopher Hastings 1943- *AmMWSc 73S, -78S*

Sterling, Dorothy 1913- *AuBYP 2, -3, BioIn 5, -8, -9, -10, -15, BkCL, ChlLR 1, ConAu 9R, -5NR, -28NR, ForWC 70, MajAI, MorBMP, SmATA 1, -2AS, ThrBJA*

Sterling, Helen *AuBYP 2, -3, ConAu 131, -X, -43NR, DcVicP 2, SmATA 65, -X*
Main entry: Hoke, Helen L

Sterling, Philip d1989 *NewYTBS 89*

Sterling, Philip 1907- *BioIn 11, ConAu 49, SmATA 8*

Sterling, Philip 1907-1989 *BioIn 16, –17, ConAu 129, SmATA 63*

Sterman, Betsy *AuBYP 3*

Sterman, Betsy 1927- *ScF&FL 92*

Sterman, Samuel *AuBYP 3*

Sterman, Samuel 1918- *AmMWSc 86, –89, –92, ScF&FL 92*

Stern, Catherine 1894-1973 *AuBYP 2S, –3, BioIn 9, –11, –12, ConAu 37R, NotAW MOD*

Stern, Catherine Brieger 1894-1973 *InWom SUP*

Stern, Ellen Norman *IntAu&W 86X*

Stern, Ellen Norman 1927- *BioIn 13, ConAu 37R, –14NR, IntAu&W 86, –89, –91, SmATA 26, WrDr 76, –80, –82, –84, –86, –88, –90, –92, –94*

Stern, Judith M 1951- *ConAu 142, SmATA 75*

Stern, Madeleine 1912- *AuBYP 3*

Stern, Madeleine B 1912- *ConAu 22NR, DcLB 111, –140, IntAu&W 86, WrDr 86, –88, –90, –92*

Stern, Madeleine Bettina 1912- *AuBYP 2, BioIn 8, –10, –12, –17, ChhPo, ConAu 17R, –7NR, DrAS 78E, –82E, ForWC 70, IntAu&W 77, –82, –91, SmATA 14, WhoAm 84, –86, –88, –90, –92, –94, WhoAmJ 80, WhoAmW 74, –75, –77, –83, WhoE 74, –77, WhoUSWr 88, WhoWorJ 72, –78, WhoWrEP 89, –92, WrDr 76, –80, –82, –84*

Stern, Marie 1909- *BioIn 1, ConAu 45, IlsCB 1744*
Pseud./variant:
Masha

Stern, Philip Van Doren 1900-1984 *BenetAL 91, ScF&FL 92*

Stern, Philip VanDoren 1900-1984 *AmAu&B, AmNov, AuBYP 2S, –3, Au&Wr 71, BioIn 2, –4, –11, –14, –15, ConAu 5R, –113, –6NR, DrAS 74H, –78H, NewYTBS 84, REnAL, SmATA 13, –39N, TwCA SUP, WhAm 8, WhNAA, WhoAm 74, –76, –78, –80, –82*
Pseud./variant:
Storme, Peter

Stern, Simon 1943- *BioIn 12, –14, ChhPo S2, IlsCB 1967, SmATA 15*

Sterne, Emma Gelders 1894- *WhAm 10*

Sterne, Emma Gelders 1894-1971 *AmAu&B, AmPeW, BioIn 4, –6, –10, ConAu 5R, –5NR, MorJA, SmATA 6, TwCA, –SUP*
Pseud./variant:
Broun, Emily
James, Josephine

Sterrett, Cliff *EncACom*

Sterrett, Cliff d1964 *WhoAmA 86N*

Sterrett, Cliff 1883-1964 *ArtCS, BioIn 7, WhAm 7, WhAmArt 85, WhoAmA 78N, –80N, –82N, –89N, –91N*

Sterrett, Virginia Frances 1900- *ConICB*

Steurt, Marjorie Rankin 1888- *BioIn 11, ConAu 13R, SmATA 10, WrDr 76, –80*

Stevens, Alden Gifford 1886- *AuBYP 2, –3, BioIn 8*

Stevens, Beatrice 1876-1947 *ChhPo, ConICB, WhAm 2, WhAmArt 85*

Stevens, Beatrice M *AmWomPl*

Stevens, Bryna *BioIn 17*

Stevens, Bryna 1924- *ConAu 136, SmATA 65, WrDr 94*
Pseud./variant:
Donaldson, Bryna

Stevens, Carla 1928- *AuBYP 3*

Stevens, Carla McBride 1928- *AuBYP 2, BioIn 8, –11, ConAu 69, –12NR, SmATA 13, WhoAmW 74, –75, –77*

Stevens, David Kilburn 1860-1946 *AmAu&B, ASCAP 66, ChhPo, –S2, DcNAA, WhAm 2, WhNAA*

Stevens, Fae Hewston
Main entry: Stevens, Frances Isted

Stevens, Frances Isted 1907- *Au&Wr 71, ConAu P-1, SingR 2*
Pseud./variant:
Stevens, Fae Hewston

Stevens, Franklin 1933- *BioIn 10, ConAu 29R, SmATA 6*
Pseud./variant:
Franklin, Steve

Stevens, Gwendolyn Ruth 1944- *ConAu 104, SmATA 33, WhoAmW 83, –85, –87, WhoFrS 84*

Stevens, James Floyd 1892-1971 *AmAu&B, AmNov, BioIn 1, -2, -4, -5, -9, CnDAL, ConAmL, ConAu 33R, CyWA 58, OxCAmL 65, REnAL, TwCA, -SUP, WhAm 5*

Stevens, Janet 1953- *SixBJA*

Stevens, Kathleen 1936- *BioIn 16, ConAu 39NR, SmATA 49*

Stevens, Leonard A *BioIn 17*

Stevens, Leonard A 1920- *ConAu 17R, -12NR, SmATA 67*

Stevens, Lucile V 1899- *BioIn 16, SmATA 59*

Stevens, Lucile Vernon 1899- *ConAu 61*

Stevens, Lucy Beatrice 1876-1947 *BioIn 1, DcWomA, IlsCB 1744*

Stevens, Mary E 1920-1966 *BioIn 5, -7, -8, IlsBYP, IlsCB 1946, -1957*

Stevens, Patricia Bunning 1931- *BioIn 13, ConAu 53, SmATA 27*

Stevens, Peter *ConAu X, SmATA 7*
Main entry: Geis, Darlene Stern

Stevens, Serita Deborah 1949- *SmATA 70*
Pseud./variant:
Cole, Jennifer
MacDonnell, Megan
Stevens, Shira

Stevens, Shira *SmATA 70*
Main entry: Stevens, Serita Deborah

Stevens, Sylvester Kirby 1904-1974 *AmAu&B, BioIn 7, -8, -12, ConAu 45, -P-1, NatCAB 58, WhoAm 74, WhoE 74*

Stevens, William Oliver 1878- *AuBYP 3*

Stevens, William Oliver 1878-1955 *AmAu&B, AmLY, AuBYP 2, BiDPara, BioIn 3, -8, ChhPo, EncAB-A 26, EncO&P 1, -2, -3, WhAm 3, WhAmArt 85, WhNAA*

Stevenson, Anna 1905- *BioIn 11, SmATA 12*

Stevenson, Arthur Lionel *CanWW 70, WhNAA*
Main entry: Stevenson, Lionel

Stevenson, Augusta *AmWomPl*

Stevenson, Augusta 1869?-1976 *AuBYP 2, -3, BioIn 2, -6, -7, -9, -13, ConAu 1R, -65, IndAu 1816, MorJA, SmATA 2, -26N*

Stevenson, Burton E 1872-1962 *BenetAL 91*

Stevenson, Burton Egbert 1872-1962 *AmAu&B, BiD&SB, BioIn 4, -6, -13, ChhPo, -S2, ConAu 102, DcAmAu, EvLB, ObitOF 79, OhA&B, REn, REnAL, SmATA 25, TwCA, -SUP, WhAm 4, WhJnl, WhNAA*

Stevenson, Drew 1947- *BioIn 17, ScF&FL 92, SmATA 60*

Stevenson, Florence *BioIn 8, -9, -14, ConAu 97, -16NR, IntAu&W 86, -91, ScF&FL 92, TwCRHW 90, WrDr 84, -86, -88, -90, -92, -94*

Stevenson, Gloria 1945- *ConAu 61*

Stevenson, James *MajAI*

Stevenson, James 1813-1894 *DcCanB 12*

Stevenson, James 1929- *AuBYP 2S, -3, BioIn 8, -12, -14, -15, -17, ChlLR 17, ConAu 115, FifBJA, IlsCB 1967, SmATA 34, -42, -71, TwCChW 89, WrDr 90, -92, -94*

Stevenson, Janet 1913- *AuBYP 2S, -3, BioIn 4, -11, ConAu 13R, -29NR, ForWC 70, SmATA 8*

Stevenson, Lionel 1902-1973 *AmAu&B, Au&Wr 71, BioIn 10, -12, ConAu 45, -103, NatCAB 58, NewYTBE 73, OxCCan, Str&VC, WhAm 6, WhoSSW 73*
Pseud./variant:
Stevenson, Arthur Lionel

Stevenson, Mabel Rose 1875-1953 *ChhPo S1, -S2, Str&VC*

Stevenson, Orlando John 1869- *AuBYP 3*

Stevenson, Orlando John 1869-1950 *AuBYP 2S, BioIn 2, OxCCan*

Stevenson, Robert Lloyd 1951- *WhoSSW 86*

Stevenson, Robert Louis 1850-1894 *Alli SUP, AnCL, AtlBL, AuBYP 2, -3, Benet 87, BenetAL 91, BbD, BiD&SB, BioIn 1, -2, -3, -4, -5, -6, -7, -8, -9, -10, -11, -12, -13, -14, -15, -16, -17, BritAu 19, BritWr 5, CamGEL, CamGLE, CarSB, CasWL, Chambr 3, ChhPo, -S1, -S2, ChlLR 10, -11, ChrP, CmCal, CmScLit, CnDBLB 5, CrtSuMy, CrtT 3, CyWA 58, DcBiA, DcBrBI, DcEnA, -A, DcEuL, DcLB 18, -57, DcLEL, DcNaB, -C, Dis&D, EncMys, EncPaPR 91, EvLB, FamAYP, FamPYP, FilmgC, HalFC 84, -88, JBA 34, MagSWL, McGEWB, MouLC 4, NewC, NewEScF, NinCLC 5, -14, Novels, OxCAmL 65, -83, OxCAusL, OxCChiL, OxCEng 67, OxCMus, PenC ENG, PenEncH, RAdv 1, -13-1, REn, REnAL, RfGEnL 91, RfGShF, ScF&FL 92, ScFSB, ShSCr 11, ShSWr, StaCVF, Str&VC, SupFW, TelT, TwCChW 78A, -83A, -89A, WebE&AL, WhDW, WhoChL, WhoHr&F, WorAlBi, WorLitC, WrChl, YABC 2*

Stewart, Ramona 1922- *AuSpks, BioIn 8, –9, –11, ConAu 1R, –6NR, ForWC 70, InWom SUP, ScF&FL 92*

Stewart, Robert Neil 1891-1972 *BioIn 10, ConAu 9R, SmATA 7*

Stewart, Ruth Ann 1942- *BlkAuII 92*

Stewart, Scott *SmATA X*
Main entry: Zaffo, George J

Stewart, W P 1924- *BioIn 16, SmATA 53*

Stewart, Walter Bingham 1913- *ConAu 85, –16NR, WhoSSW 73, –78, –80, –82, –84*

Stewig, John Warren 1937- *BioIn 13, ConAu 14NR, –32NR, SmATA 26, WhoMW 84*

St George, Judith 1931- *Au&Arts 7, BioIn 16, ScF&FL 92, SixBJA, SmATA 12AS, WrDr 86, –88, –90, –92, –94*

Stidworthy, John 1943- *Au&Wr 71, SmATA 63*
Pseud./variant:
Howard, John

Stiles, Martha Bennet *WhoUSWr 88*

Stiles, Martha Bennett *BioIn 10, ConAu 37R, DcAmChF 1960, DrAPF 83, –85, –87, –89, –91, –93, IntAu&W 82, MichAu 80, SmATA 6, WhoAmW 75, WhoWrEP 89, –92*

Stiles, Martha Bennett 1933- *IntAu&W 89, LiHiK*

Stiles, Norman B 1942- *ConAu 114, SmATA 36, WhoAm 80*

Still, C Henry 1920- *ConAu 9R, WhoWest 74, –76, –78*

Still, James *DrAPF 87, –89, –91, –93, IntvTCA 2*

Still, James 1906- *AmAu&B, AuBYP 3, BenetAL 91, BioIn 4, –5, –6, –8, –12, –13, ConAu 65, –17AS, –10NR, –26NR, ConLC 49, CyWA 58, DcLB 9, DrAF 76, DrAS 74E, IntAu&W 77, –82, LiHiK, REn, REnAL, SmATA 29, TwCA, –SUP*

Stillerman, Robbie 1947- *BioIn 11, SmATA 12*

Stilley, Frank 1918- *BioIn 13, ConAu 61, SmATA 29*

Stillman, Myra Stephens 1915- *AuBYP 2, –3, BioIn 8, ConAu 5R, –6NR, ForWC 70*

Stillman, Richard J 1917- *ConAu 34NR, WrDr 90, –92*

Stillman, Richard Joseph 1917- *AmEA 74, AmMWSc 73S, ConAu 37R, –14NR, InB&W 80, IntAu&W 77, –82, –86, –91, WrDr 76, –80, –82, –84, –86, –88, –94*

Stilwell, Alison 1921- *BioIn 5, IlsCB 1946*

Stine, George Harry 1928- *AuBYP 2, –3, BioIn 8, –11, –17, ConAu 65, IntAu&W 91, SmATA 10, WhoAm 82, –84, –86, –88, –90, –92, –94, WhoWest 80, –82, –92, –94*
Pseud./variant:
Correy, Lee

Stine, Jovial Bob *ConAu X, ScF&FL 92, SmATA 76, –X*
Main entry: Stine, Robert Lawrence

Stine, Jovial Bob 1943- *BioIn 14, –15*

Stine, R L 1943- *ConAu 22NR, WhoWrEP 89*

Stine, R L 1943- *ScF&FL 92*

Stine, Robert L 1943- *BioIn 14, –15*

Stine, Robert Lawrence 1943- *ConAu 105, SmATA 31, –76, TwCYAW, WhoWrEP 92*
Pseud./variant:
Affabee, Eric
Blue, Zachary
Stine, Jovial Bob

Stinetorf, Louise A 1900- *BioIn 11, ConAu 9R, ForWC 70, SmATA 10*

Stirling, Anna Maria D Wilhelmina 1865-1965 *BioIn 5, ConAu P-1, LongCTC, TelT*
Pseud./variant:
Pickering, Wilhelmina

Stirling, Anna Maria Diana Wilhelmina 1865-1965 *WomNov*

Stirling, Arthur *ConAmA, ConAu X, MajTwCW, OxCAmL 65, –83, SmATA X, TwCYAW*
Main entry: Sinclair, Upton Beall

Stirling, Ian 1941- *SmATA 77*

Stirling, Lilla 1902- *AuBYP 2, –3, BioIn 8, ConAu 107*

Stirling, Monica 1916-1983 *AuBYP 2S, –3, ConAu 81, –111, ConNov 72, –76, –82, DcLEL 1940, IntAu&W 77, –82, WrDr 76, –80, –82, –84*

Stirling, Nora B *WrDr 86*

Stirling, Nora B 1900- *WrDr 88, –90*

Stirling, Nora Bramley 1900- *AuBYP 3*

Stirling, Nora Bromley 1900- *AuBYP 2, BioIn 8, –9, ConAu 5R, –3NR, SmATA 3, WrDr 76, –80, –82, –84*

Stirnweis, Shannon 1931- *BioIn 11, IlrAm 1880, IlsBYP, SmATA 10, WhoAmA 89, –91*

St John, Nicole *ConAu 32NR, ScF&FL 92, SmATA 7AS, TwCRHW 90, WrDr 86, –88, –90, –92, –94*

St John, Patricia Mary 1919- *EngPo, IntAu&W 89, WrDr 86, –88, –90, –92, –94*

St John, Patricia Mary 1919-1993 *ConAu 142*

St John, Philip *AuBYP 3, ConAu 141, EncSF 93, MajTwCW, SmATA 76, TwCSFW 86, –91, WrDr 86, –88, –90, –92*

St John, Philip 1915- *WrDr 94*

St John, Primus *DrAPF 87, –89, –91, –93*

St John, Primus 1939- *BlkWr 1, WhoBlA 90, –92, –94*

St John, Robert 1902- *WrDr 86, –88, –90, –92, –94*

St John, Wylly Folk 1908- *DcAmChF 1960, WrDr 86*

St John, Wylly Folk 1908-1985 *AuBYP 3, BioIn 15*

St Meyer, Ned *MajAI*

Stobart, Ralph *IlsBYP*

Stobbs, William *BioIn 14*

Stobbs, William 1914- *ArtsCL, BioIn 5, –6, –8, –9, –12, ChhPo, –S2, ConAu 81, IlsBYP, IlsCB 1946, –1957, –1967, OxCChiL, SmATA 17, ThrBJA, WhoChL*

Stock, Carolmarie 1951- *SmATA 75*

Stock, Catherine 1952- *ConAu 119, SmATA 65*

Stock, Catherine Julia 1952- *IntAu&W 91*

Stock, Ralph 1881- *CarSB, OxCAusL*

Stockham, Peter 1928- *BioIn 16, SmATA 57*

Stockham, Peter Alan 1928- *IntAu&W 86*

Stockton, Francis R *ScF&FL 92*

Stockton, Francis R 1834-1902 *BenetAL 91*

Stockton, Francis Richard *AuBYP 3*

Stockton, Francis Richard 1834-1902 *ConAu 108, –137, MajAI, SmATA 44, WhAmArt 85*
Pseud./variant:
Fort, Paul
Lewees, John
Stockton, Frank Richard

Stockton, Frank R *Benet 87, ConAu 137, MajAI*

Stockton, Frank R 1834-1902 *CrtSuMy, CyWA 89, DcLB 74, NewEScF, ScF&FL 92, ScFSB, SupFW, TwCChW 89A, TwCLC 47, TwCSFW 86, –91, WrChl*

Stockton, Frank Richard
Main entry: Stockton, Francis Richard

Stockton, Frank Richard 1834-1902 *Alli, AmAu, AmAu&B, AuBYP 2, –3, BbD, BiD&SB, BioIn 1, –5, –6, –8, –12, –13, CarSB, CnDAL, ConAu X, CyAL, DcLB 42, DcLEL, EncMys, EncSF 93, EvLB, FamSYP, JBA 34, OxCAmL 65, –83, OxCChiL, OxCEng 67, RAdv 1, REn, SmATA 32, –X, SupFW, TwCChW 78A, –83A, WebAB 74*

Stoddard, Edward George 1923- *AuBYP 2, –3, BioIn 8, –11, ConAu 9R, SmATA 10, WhoE 75, –77*

Stoddard, Hope 1900- *AuBYP 2, –3, BioIn 8, –10, ConAu 49, SmATA 6*

Stoddard, Sandol *AuBYP 3*
Main entry: Warburg, Sandol Stoddard

Stoddard, Sandol 1927- *ConAu 8NR, FourBJA, SmATA X, WhoAmW 91, –93*

Stoddard, William Osborn 1835-1925 *Alli SUP, AmAu, AmAu&B, BenetAL 91, BiD&SB, BioIn 3, CarSB, ChhPo, DcAmAu, DcNAA, HarEnUS, OxCAmL 65, –83, OxCChiL, REnAL, WhAm 1*

Stoddart, Isabella *CarSB*

Stohlman, Martha Lou Lemmon 1913- *ConAu 65*

Stoiko, Michael 1919- *BioIn 12, ConAu 9R SmATA 14*

Stoker, Abraham *ScF&FL 92*

Stoker, Abraham 1847-1912 *BiDIrW, ConAu 105, DcIrB 88, DcNaB MP, SmATA 29*
Pseud./variant:
Stoker, Bram

Stoker, Bram
Main entry: Stoker, Abraham

Stoker, Bram 1847-1912 *Alli SUP, Benet 87, BioIn 5, –6, –8, –10, –11, –12, –13, –14, –15, –16, –17, CamGLE, CnDBLB 5, ConAu X, CyWA 58, DcIrL, DcLB 36, –70, DcLEL, EncMys, EncO&P 1, –2, –3, EvLB, FilmgC, HalFC 84, –88, LongCTC, NewEScF, NotNAT B, Novels, OxCEng 85, PenC ENG, PenEncH, REn, RfGEnL 91, ScF&FL 92, SmATA X, StaCVF, SupFW, TwCA, –SUP, TwCCr&M 80, TwCLC 8, WhDW, WhoChL, WhoHr&F, WorAlBi, WorAl, WorLitC*

Stokes, Cedric *BioIn 12, SmATA X*
Main entry: Beardmore, George

Stokes, Jack 1923- *BioIn 11, ConAu 29R, SmATA 13*

Stokes, Olivia Pearl 1916- *BioIn 14, ConAu 37R, InB&W 80, SmATA 32*

Stokes, William Forest 1931- *WhoUSWr 88, WhoWrEP 89, –92*

Stokes, William Forrest 1931- *WhoAm 76, –78, –80, –82, –84, –86, –88, –90*

Stokley, James 1900- *AmAu&B, AmMWSc 86, –89, –92, WhJnl, WhoAm 74, –76, –78*

Stoliar, Joan *WhoAmW 77*

Stolper, Joel *BioIn 1, IlsCB 1744*

Stolz, Mary 1920- *Au&Arts 8, AuBYP 3, BioIn 14, –15, –16, InWom SUP, IntAu&W 91, ScF&FL 92, SmATA 3AS, TwCChW 89, TwCYAW, WrDr 86, –88, –90, –92*

Stolz, Mary Slattery 1920- *AmAu&B, AuBYP 2, AuNews 1, Au&Wr 71, BenetAL 91, BioIn 3, –6, –7, –10, –11, –13, BioNews 74, ConAu 5R, –13NR, –41NR, ConLC 12, CurBio 53, DcAmChF 1960, –1985, ForWC 70, MajAI, MorBMP, MorJA, OxCChiL, REnAL, SmATA 10, –71, TwCChW 78, –83, WhoAm 74, –76, –78, –80, –82, WhoAmW 74, WhoE 74, WrDr 80, –82, –84*

Stonaker, Frances Benson *AuBYP 2S, –3*

Stone, A Harris *AuBYP 2S, –3*

Stone, Alan *ConAu P-2, SmATA 1, –2, –X*
Main entry: Stratemeyer, Edward L
Svenson, Andrew E

Stone, David K 1922- *BioIn 11, ChhPo S2, ConAu 85, IlsBYP, SmATA 9*

Stone, David Karl 1922- *BiDScF, WhoSSW 93*

Stone, Elaine Murray 1922- *ConAu 17NR, –38NR, IntAu&W 77, –82, WhoAmW 74, –75, –77, –81, –83, –89, WrDr 76, –80, –82, –84*

Stone, Eugenia 1879-1971 *BioIn 10, ConAu 9R, SmATA 7*

Stone, George K *AuBYP 2, –3, BioIn 8*

Stone, Helen 1904- *BioIn 1, –3, –5, –6, –8, –10, –14, ChhPo, –S2, ConAu 25R, ForWC 70, IlsBYP, IlsCB 1744, –1946, –1957, MorJA, SmATA 6*

Stone, Idella Purnell *ConAu X*
Main entry: Purnell, Idella

Stone, Idella Purnell 1901-1982 *ScF&FL 92*

Stone, Ikey *ConAu X*
Main entry: Purnell, Idella

Stone, Irving *NewYTBS 85*

Stone, Irving 1903- *AmAu&B, AmNov, AuNews 1, Au&Wr 71, Benet 87, BioIn 2, –4, –5, –6, –7, –8, –9, –10, –12, –14, –15, BlueB 76, CelR, CmCal, ConAu 1R, –3AS, –1NR, –23NR, ConLC 7, ConNov 72, –76, –82, –86, CurBio 67, DrAS 74E, –78E, –82E, HalFC 84, –88, IntAu&W 77, –89, –91, IntWW 74, –75, –76, –77, –78, –79, –80, –81, –82, –83, –89, LongCTC, Novels, OxCAmL 83, PenC AM, REn, REnAL, SmATA 3, TwCA, –SUP, TwCWr, WhNAA, WhoAm 74, –76, –78, –80, –82, –84, –86, –88, WhoAmJ 80, WhoWor 74, –78, WhoWorJ 72, –78, WorAl, WrDr 76, –80, –82, –84, –86, –88, –90*

Stone, Irving 1903-1989 *AnObit 1989, BenetAL 91, BioIn 16, –17, ConAu 129, CurBio 89N, CyWA 89, MajTwCW, NewYTBS 89, News 90, –90-2, SmATA 64, TwCRHW 90, WhAm 10, WorAlBi*

Stone, James Champion 1916- *ConAu 17R, WhoWest 74, –76*

Stone, Jon 1931- *BioIn 15, ConAu 107, SmATA 39, WhoEnt 92*

Stone, Josephine Rector *ConAu X, SmATA X*
Main entry: Dixon, Jeanne

Stone, Josephine Rector 1936- *ScF&FL 92*

Stone, Leslie F *ConSFA*

Stone, Leslie F 1905-1991 *ScF&FL 92*

Stone, Leslie Frances 1905-c. 1987 *EncSF 93*

Stone, Lynn M *AuBYP 3*

Stone, Peter *ConDr 88D*

Stone, Peter 1930- *BioIn 15, -17, HalFC 88, IntAu&W 91, IntMPA 86, -88, SmATA 65, WhoAm 90, -92, -94, WhoE 93, WhoEnt 92*

Stone, Ralph A 1934- *ConAu 37R, WrDr 76, -80*

Stone, Raymond *CarSB, ConAu 26NR, -P-2, SmATA 1*
Main entry: Stratemeyer, Edward L

Stone, Richard A *ConAu X*
Main entry: Stratemeyer, Edward L

Stone, Rosetta *ConAu 135, -32NR, ConGrA 3, MajAI, MajTwCW, SmATA 67, -75, TwCChW 89*
Main entry: Geisel, Theodor Seuss

Stoneham, Charles Thurley 1895- *BioIn 4*

Stonehouse, Bernard 1926- *Au&Wr 71, BioIn 11, ConAu 49, -2NR, -19NR, IntAu&W 77, -82, SmATA 13, WrDr 76, -80, -82, -84, -86, -88, -90, -92, -94*

Stoneman, Elvyn Arthur 1919- *AmMWSc 73S, ConAu 17R*

Stones, Cyril Anthony 1934- *SmATA 72*

Stones, Rosemary *BioIn 15, OxCChiL*

Stong, Phil 1899-1957 *BenetAL 91, TwCChW 89*

Stong, Philip Duffield 1899-1957 *AmAu&B, AmNov, AuBYP 2, -3, BioIn 1, -2, -4, -5, -6, -7, -14, CnDAL, ConAmA, CyWA 58, EncSF 93, MorJA, ObitOF 79, OxCAmL 65, -83, OxCChiL, REnAL, SmATA 32, Str&VC, TwCA, -SUP, TwCChW 78, -83, WhAm 3*

Storch, Anne B *AuBYP 3*

Storey, Margaret 1926- *BioIn 11, ConAu 49, -1NR, ScF&FL 92, SmATA 9, TwCChW 78, -83, -89, WrDr 80, -82, -84, -86, -88, -90, -92, -94*

Storey, Robert Gerald 1893-1981 *BioIn 2, -3, -4, -5, -7, BlueB 76, CurBio 53, IntWW 74, -75, -76, -77, -78, -79, -80, -81N, WhAm 7, WhoAm 74, -76, -78, -80, WhoSSW 73, WhoWor 74, -78*

Storey, Victoria Carolyn 1945- *BioIn 12, ConAu 33R, IntAu&W 77, SmATA 16*
Pseud./variant:
Martin, Vicky

Storm, Theodor 1817-1888 *AuBYP 3, Benet 87, DcLB 129, EuWr 6*

Storm, Theodor Woldsen 1817-1888 *AuBYP 2S, BbD, BiD&SB, BioIn 1, -3, -4, -7, -9, CasWL, ClDMEL 47, DcEuL, EuAu, EvEuW, McGEWB, OxCGer 76, -86, PenC EUR, REn*

Stormcrow *SmATA 75*
Main entry: Talifero, Gerald

Storme, Peter *AuBYP 2S, -3, ConAu X, SmATA X*
Main entry: Stern, Philip VanDoren

Storr, Catherine 1913- *AuBYP 2S, -3, Au&Wr 71, BioIn 11, ConAu 13R, -23NR, EncSF 93, IntAu&W 91, OxCChiL, ScF&FL 92, SmATA 9, TwCChW 78, -83, -89, WrDr 76, -80, -82, -84, -86, -88, -90, -92, -94*
Pseud./variant:
Adler, Irene
Lourie, Helen

Storry, George Richard 1913- *Au&Wr 71*

Story, Jack Trevor 1917- *ConAu 29R, DcLEL 1940, IntAu&W 77, -91, ScFSB, WrDr 76, -80, -82, -84, -86, -88, -90, -92*

Story, Jack Trevor 1917-1991 *AnObit 1991, ConAu 136, EncSF 93, ScF&FL 92, WrDr 94N*

Story, Josephine
Main entry: Loring, Emilie Baker

Story, Norah *OxCCan SUP*

Stott, Dorothy M 1958- *BioIn 17, ConAu 134, SmATA 67, WrDr 94*
Pseud./variant:
Stott, Dot

Stott, Dot *ConAu 134, SmATA 67, WrDr 94*
Main entry: Stott, Dorothy M

Stoutenburg, Adrien 1916- *AmAu&B, AuBYP 2, -3, Au&Wr 71, BioIn 6, -8, -9, ChhPo S2, ConAu 5R, ConPo 70, -75, -80, DrAP 75, ForWC 70, MinnWr, SmATA 3, ThrBJA, WhoAm 74, -76, -78, -80, -82, WhoAmW 74, WhoWest 74, WrDr 76, -80, -82, -84, -86*
Pseud./variant:
Arden, Barbi
Kendall, Lace
Minier, Nelson

Stoutenburg, Adrien 1916-1982 *ScF&FL 92*

Stover, Allan C 1938- *BioIn 12, ConAu 69, -12NR, SmATA 14*

Stover, Jo Ann 1931- *ConAu 37R, IlsBYP*

Stover, Marjorie Filley 1914- *BioIn 11, ConAu 45, -31NR, SmATA 9*

Stow, Julian Randolph 1935- *DcChlFi*

Stowe, Harriet Beecher 1811-1896 *Alli, –SUP, AmAu, AmAu&B, AmWr S1, ArtclWW 2, AtlBL, AuBYP 2S, –3, Benet 87, BenetAL 91, BibAL 8, BbD, BiD&SB, BioAmW, BioIn 1, –2, –3, –4, –5, –6, –7, –8, –9, –10, –11, –14, –15, –16, –17, BlmGWL, CamGEL, CamGLE, CamHAL, CarSB, CasWL, CelCen, Chambr 3, ChhPo, –S1, –S2, CivWDc, CnDAL, ContDcW 89, CrtT 3, CyAL, CyWA 58, DcAmAu, DcAmSR, DcBiA, DcEnA, DcEnL, DcLB 1, –12, –42, –74, DcLEL, DcNAA, DcWomA, EncAB-H, EncPaPR 91, EvLB, FilmgC, HalFC 84, –88, HanAmWH, HerW, –84, IntDcWB, JBA 34, LiHiK, MagSAmL, MemAm, MouLC 4, NewGrDA 86, NinCLC 3, NotNAT B, Novels, OhA&B, OxCAmH, OxCAmL 65, –83, OxCChiL, OxCEng 67, PenC AM, PlP&P, RAdv 1, –13-1, RComAH, REn, REnAL, RealN, RfGAmL 87, WebAB 74, WebE&AL, WhDW, WhAm HS, WhAmP, WhCiWar, WhFla, WhoChL, WorAlBi, WorAl, WorLitC, YABC 1*
Pseud./variant:
Crowfield, Christopher

Stowe, Harriet Elizabeth Beecher 1811-1896 *MajAI*

Stowe, Leland 1899- *BiDAmJo, BioIn 16, –17, EncTwCJ, IntAu&W 89, –91, IntWW 89, –91, JrnUS, SmATA 60, WhoAm 86, –88, –90, –92, –94*

Stowell, Gordon William 1898- *Au&Wr 71*

Stowers, Carlton 1942- *ConAu 81, –14NR, –31NR*

Stowers, Carlton Eugene 1942- *WhoAm 92, –94*

Strachan, Ian 1938- *ChlFicS*

Strachan, Margaret Pitcairn 1908- *BioIn 12, ConAu 5R, SmATA 14, WhoPNW, WrDr 76, –80, –82, –84*
Pseud./variant:
More, Caroline

Strachey, Constance, Baroness *ChhPo, –S2*

Strain, Frances Bruce 1892-1975 *AmAu&B, ConAu P-2, OhA&B*

Strainchamps, Ethel Reed 1912- *BioIn 7, ConAu 53*

Strait, Treva Adams 1909- *BioIn 14, ConAu 97, IntAu&W 82, SmATA 35*

Strand, Mark *DrAPF 87, –89, –91, –93, IntvTCA 2*

Strand, Mark 1934- *Benet 87, BenetAL 91, BioIn 9, –10, –11, –12, –13, –15, –17, ConAu 40NR, ConLC 18, –41, –71, ConPo 80, –85, –91, DcLB 5, DrAPF 83, –85, DrAS 82E, IntAu&W 86, ModAL S2, OxCAmL 83, RAdv 13-1, SmATA 41, WhoAm 80, –82, –84, –86, –88, –90, –92, –94, WhoUSWr 88, WhoWest 94, WhoWrEP 89, –92, WrDr 82, –84, –86, –88, –90, –92, –94*

Strang, Herbert *ChhPo S1, –S2, LongCTC, OxCChiL, TwCChW 83, –89, WhoChL*
Main entry: Ely, George Herbert
L'Estrange, James

Strang, Ruth May 1895-1971 *BioIn 5, –9, –12, ConAu 1R, –2NR, CurBio 60, –71, InWom SUP, NewYTBE 71, NotAW MOD*

Strange, Philippa *ConAu X, SmATA X*
Main entry: Coury, Louise Andree

Stranger, Joyce *ConAu X, IntAu&W 77, –86, –86X, –89, –91, OxCChiL, SmATA X, TwCChW 78, –83, –89, WrDr 80, –82, –84, –86, –88, –90, –92, –94*
Main entry: Wilson, Joyce Muriel

Strasser, Todd *DrAPF 87, –89, –91, –93*

Strasser, Todd 1950- *Au&Arts 2, BioIn 11, –13, –15, –16, ChlLR 11, ConAu 117, –123, DcAmChF 1985, MajAI, ScF&FL 92, SixBJA, SmATA 41, –45, –71, WhoUSWr 88, WhoWrEP 89, –92, WrDr 90, –92, –94*
Pseud./variant:
Rhue, Morton

Stratemeyer, Edward L 1862-1930 *AmAu&B, Benet 87, BiD&SB, BioIn 9, –11, CarSB, ConAu 27NR, –P-2, DcAmAu, DcLB 42, DcNAA, EncMys, HarEnUS, HsB&A, MajAI, OxCAmL 65, –83, REn, REnAL, ScF&FL 92, SmATA 1, –67, WebAB 74, –79, WhAm 1, WorAl*
Pseud./variant:
Abbott, Manager Henry
Adams, Harrison
Alger, Horatio, Jr.
Appleton, Victor
Appleton, Victor, II
Barnum, Richard
Bartlett, Philip A
Barton, May Hollis
Beach, Charles Amory
Bonehill, Captain Ralph
Bowie, Jim
Calkins, Franklin
Carson, Captain James
Carter, Nick
Chadwick, Lester
Chapman, Allen
Charles, Louis
Cooper, James A
Cooper, John R
Daly, Jim
Davenport, Spencer

Dawson, Elmer A
Dixon, Franklin W
Duncan, Julia K
Edwards, Julie
Emerson, Alice B
Ferris, James Cody
Forbes, Graham B
Ford, Albert Lee
Gordon, Frederick
Hamilton, Robert W
Hardy, Alice Dale
Harkaway, Hal
Hawley, Mabel C
Henderley, Brooks
Hicks, Harvey
Hill, Grace Brooks
Hope, Laura Lee
Hunt, Francis
Judd, Frances K
Keene, Carolyn
Locke, Clinton W
Long, Helen Beecher
Marlowe, Amy Bell
Martin, Eugene
Moore, Fenworth
Morrison, Gert W
Optic, Oliver
Penrose, Margaret
Ridley, Nat, Jr.
Rockwood, Roy
Roe, Harry Mason
Saint Myer, Ned
Scott, Dan
Sheldon, Ann
Sperry, Raymond, Jr.
Steele, Chester K
Stone, Alan
Stone, Raymond
Stone, Richard A
Strayer, E Ward
Thorndyke, Helen Louise
Warner, Frank A
Webster, Frank V
West, Jerry
Wheeler, Janet D
White, Ramy Allison
Winfield, Arthur M
Winfield, Edna
Woods, Nat
Young, Clarence

Stratemeyer, Edward L, Doctor 1862-1930
Pseud./variant:
Mackenzie, Willard, Doctor

Stratford, Philip 1927- *BioIn 16, CanWW 70, –79, –80, –81, –83, –89, ConAu 9R, –5NR, DrAS 74E, –82E, OxCCan SUP, SmATA 47, WhoCanL 85, –87, –92*

Stratton, Helen *BioIn 14, ChhPo, DcBrBI*

Stratton, Lucille *AuBYP 3*

Stratton, Thomas *AuBYP 3, ConAu X, EncSF 93, SmATA X, TwCSFW 86, –91, WrDr 86, –88, –90, –92*
Main entry: DeWeese, Thomas Eugene

Stratton, Thomas 1934- *WrDr 94*

Stratton, William David 1896- *AuBYP 2, –3, BioIn 8, ConAu P-1*

Stratton-Porter, Gene *AmWomWr, BenetAL 91, DcLEL, DcNAA, InWom SUP, OxCAmL 65, –83, SmATA 15, WebAB 74, –79, WomWWA 14, WomNov*

Stratton-Porter, Gene 1863-1924 *BioAmW, BioIn 14, –15, –17, FemiCLE, MajAI*

Stratton-Porter, Geneva Grace 1863-1924 *ConAu 137*

Straub, Peter *BioIn 14, –15, –16, –17, IntvTCA 2, ScFSB*

Straub, Peter 1943- *BestSel 89-1, BioIn 12, –13, ConAu 85, –28NR, ConLC 28, CurBio 89, DcLB Y84B, MajTwCW, PenEncH, ScF&FL 92, WrDr 80, –82, –84 –86, –88, –90, –92*

Straub, Peter Francis 1943- *WrDr 94*

Straus, Jacqueline Harris *AuBYP 2, –3, BioIn 8*

Strauss, Bertram Wiley 1901- *ConAu 13R*

Strauss, Gwen 1963- *SmATA 77*

Strauss, Joyce 1936- *BioIn 16, SmATA 53*

Strauss, Susan Elizabeth 1954- *ConAu 142, SmATA 75*

Strayer, E Ward *ConAu X, MajAI, SmATA 67*
Main entry: Stratemeyer, Edward L

Streano, Vince 1945- *BioIn 12, ConAu 53, SmATA 20*

Streatfeild, Mary Noel 1897-1986 *MajAI*
Pseud./variant:
Scarlett, Susan

Streatfeild, Noel 1895- *IntAu&W 86, WrDr 86*

Streatfeild, Noel 1895-1986 *AnObit 1986, AuBYP 3, BioIn 15, –16, CamGLE, ChlLR 17, ConAu 120, –31NR, FemiCLE, TwCChW 89*

Streatfeild, Noel 1897- *AuBYP 2, BioIn 2, –3, –6, –7, –8, –9, –12, ChhPo S2, ConAu 81, ConLC 21, IntAu&W 77, JBA 51, LongCTC, OxCChiL, OxCEng 85, SmATA 20, TelT, TwCChW 78, –83, Who 74, –82, –83, –85, WhoChL, WrDr 76, –80, –82, –84*

Streatfeild, Noel 1897-1985 *SmATA 48N*

Street, Alicia 1911- *ConAu 5R*

Street, James *IntvTCA 2*

Street, James 1903-1954 *AmAu&B, AmNov, BenetAL 91, BioIn 1, –2, –3, –4, –5, CnDAL, CurBio 46, –54, REnAL, TwCA SUP*

Street, Julia Montgomery *IntAu&W 91*

Street, Julia Montgomery 1898- *BioIn 4, –5, –11, ConAu 5R, –2NR, ForWC 70, SmATA 11, WhoAmW 75, –77, –83, –87, WhoUSWr 88, WhoWrEP 89, –92, WrDr 76, –80, –82, –84, –86, –88, –90, –92, –94*

Street, Thomas Watson 1916- *WhoAm 74, –76, –78, WhoRel 75, –77*

Streeter, Floyd Benjamin 1888- *WhNAA*

Streeter, James *ConAu 61, IntAu&W 77*

Stren, Patti 1949- *BioIn 15, ChlLR 5, ConAu 117, –124, SmATA 41, WhoCanL 85, –87, –92*

Strete, Craig Kee 1950- *ConAu 114, SmATA 44*

Stretton, Barbara 1936- *BioIn 14, –15, ConAu 116, SmATA 35, –43*

Stretton, Barbara Humphrey 1936- *ConAu 39NR*

Stretton, Hesba *Alli, –SUP, BiGAW, Chambr 3, ConAu X, DcEnL, DcLEL, DcNaB S2, LongCTC, NewC, OxCChiL, OxCEng 85, TelT, TwCChW 78A, –83A, WomNov*
Main entry: Smith, Sarah

Stretton, Hesba 1832-1911 *BioIn 16, FemiCLE, InWom SUP, StaCVF, TwCChW 89A*

Stretton, Hesba Sarah 1832-1911 *BlmGWL*

Strickland, Agnes 1796?-1874 *Alli, –SUP, BbD, BiD&SB, BioIn 2, –16, BritAu 19, CamGEL, CamGLE, CarSB, CelCen, Chambr 3, ChhPo, –S1, –S2, DcBiPP, DcEnL, DcEuL, DcNaB, EvLB, FemiCLE, InWom SUP, NewC, OxCChiL, OxCEng 67, PenC ENG, REn*

Strickland, Agnes, Miss 1796-1874 *StaCVF*

Strickland, Joshua 1896- *ConAu 81*

Strickland, Samuel 1804?-1867 *Alli, BbtC, BioIn 8, –17, DcCanB 9, DcLB 99, DcNaB, DcNAA, OxCCan*

Strieber, Whitley 1945- *DcAmChF 1985*

Striker, Susan 1942- *BioIn 17, SmATA 63*

Stringer, Arthur John Arbuthnott 1874-1950 *AmAu&B, BiD&SB, BioIn 1, –2, –4, –17, CanNov, CanWr, CasWL, ChhPo, –S2, CreCan 2, DcAmAu, DcLEL, EncMys, OxCCan, REn, TwCA, –SUP, WhAm 3*

Stringer, Ruth M Pearson 1905- *ConAu 5R*

Strong, Charles *AuBYP 2, –3, ConAu X, –39NR, SmATA 1, –X*
Main entry: Epstein, Samuel

Strong, Charles S *TwCWW 91*

Strong, Charles Stanley 1906- *AuBYP 3*

Strong, Charles Stanley 1906-1962 *AmAu&B, AuBYP 2, BioIn 3, –6, –8, CathA 1952, WhAm 4, WhNAA*

Strong, David *ConAu X, SmATA X*
Main entry: McGuire, Leslie Sarah

Strong, Harrington *AmAu&B, ConAu X, WhNAA*

Strong, J J *ConAu X, SmATA X*

Strong, Jeremy 1949- *BioIn 14, ConAu 108, SmATA 36*
Pseud./variant:
Strong J J

Strong, L A G 1896-1958 *CamGLE, RfGEnL 91, TwCChW 89*

Strong, Leonard Alfred George 1896-1958 *BiDIrW, BioIn 4, –5, –6, CasWL, ChhPo, –S1, –S2, CyWA 58, DcIrL, DcLEL, DcNaB 1951, EngPo, EvLB, LongCTC, ModBrL, NewC, Novels, ObitOF 79, ObitT 1951, OxCEng 85, PenC ENG, REn, TwCA, –SUP, TwCChW 78, –83, TwCWr, WhoLA*

Strong, Pat *AuBYP 3, IntAu&W 91X, WrDr 86, –88, –90, –92*

Strong, Pat 1922- *WrDr 94*

Strong, Patricia Arlene 1949- *WhoAmW 93*

Strong, Stacie 1965- *ConAu 141, SmATA 74*

Strong J J
Main entry: Strong, Jeremy

Strother, Elsie W 1912- *ConAu 65*

Strousse, Flora G 1897?-1974 *BioIn 10, ConAu 49*

Stroyer, Poul 1923- *BioIn 11, ConAu 77, IntAu&W 77, –82, SmATA 13*

Struble, Steve *AuBYP 3*

Struble, Virginia *ConAu X*
Main entry: Burlingame, Virginia

Strutton, William H *ScF&FL 92*

Strutton, William Harold 1918- *Au&Wr 71, ConAu 77, WrDr 76, –80*

Stryker, Daniel *EncSF 93, ScF&FL 92, SmATA 66*

Stryker, Daniel 1946- *WrDr 94*
Main entry: Morris, Christopher Crosby

St Tamara *WhoAmA 86, –89, WhoAmW 89, –91*

St Tamara 1950- *WhoAmW 87*

Stuart, Colin *BioIn 8*

Stuart, David *AuBYP 3, BioIn 16, ConAu X, SmATA X*
Main entry: Hoyt, Edwin Palmer, Jr.

Stuart, Donald
Main entry: Verner, Gerald

Stuart, Esme *Alli SUP, BbD, BiD&SB, WomNov*

Stuart, Esme 1851-1934 *FemiCLE*

Stuart, Forbes *WrDr 86, –88*

Stuart, Forbes 1924- *BioIn 11, ConAu 69, IntAu&W 77, –82, SmATA 13, WrDr 76, –80, –82, –84, –90*

Stuart, Gene *AuBYP 2S, –3*

Stuart, George E *AuBYP 2S, –3*

Stuart, Hilton Jesse 1907- *DcAmChF 1960*

Stuart, Ian *AuBYP 2S, –3, ConAu 57, –28NR, DcLEL 1940, EncSF 93, MajTwCW, SmATA X, TwCCr&M 80, –85, –91, WhoSpyF, WorAu 1950, WrDr 76, –80, –82, –84, –86*

Stuart, Ian 1922?- *BioIn 14*
Main entry: MacLean, Alistair

Stuart, Ian 1922-1987 *BioIn 15, –16, –17*

Stuart, Jesse Hilton 1907-1984 *AmAu&B, AmNov, AnObit 1984, AuBYP 2S, –3, Au&Wr 71, BioIn 1, –2, –3, –4, –5, –6, –8, –9, –10, –11, –12, –13, BlueB 76, ChhPo, –S1, ConAu 5R, –112, ConLC 1, –8, –11, –34, ConNov 72, –76, –82, CurBio 40, –84N, CyWA 58, DcLB 9, –48, –Y84N, IntAu&W 77, IntWW 74, –75, –76, –77, –78, –79, –80, –81, –82, –83, NewYTBS 84, OxCAmL 65, –83, RAdv 1, REn, REnAL, SixAP, SmATA 2, –36N, TwCA SUP, TwCWr, WhAm 8, WhoAm 74, –76, –78, –80, –82, WhoSSW 73, –75, –76, WhoWor 74, –78, WrDr 76, –80, –82, –84*

Stuart, Morna 1905- *Au&Wr 71*

Stuart, Ronald
Main entry: Verner, Gerald

Stuart, Sheila *Au&Wr 71, ChhPo S2, ConAu X, SmATA X*
Main entry: Baker, Mary Gladys Steel

Stuart-Clark, Christopher *BioIn 14*

Stuart-Clark, Christopher 1940- *ConAu 107, –24NR, SmATA 32*

Stubbs, Harry C *IntvTCA 2*

Stubbs, Harry C 1922- *AmAu&B, BioIn 12, –13, ConAu 13R, –7NR, –26NR, WrDr 84*
Pseud./variant:
Clement, Hal

Stubbs, Harry Clement *ScF&FL 92, WrDr 86, –88, –90, –92*

Stubbs, Harry Clement 1922- *BioIn 17, WrDr 94*

Stubbs, Joanna 1940- *BioIn 12, –14, –16, IlsCB 1967, SmATA 53*

Stubenrauch, Robert *AuBYP 2S, –3*

Stubis, Talivaldis 1926- *BioIn 10, ChhPo S1, IlsBYP, SmATA 5*

Stubley, Trevor Hugh 1932- *BioIn 12, –13, IlsCB 1967, SmATA 22, WhoArt 80, –82, –84*

Stucky, Naomi R 1922- *SmATA 72*

Stucley, Elizabeth
Main entry: Northmore, Elizabeth Florence

Stucley, Elizabeth 1906-1974 *ConAu X, OxCChiL, TwCChW 78, –83, –89*

Studdy, George E 1878-1948 *OxCChiL*

Studdy, George Ernest 1878-1948 *BioIn 14*

Stultifer, Morton *ConAu X, SmATA X*
Main entry: Curtis, Richard

Stump, Sarain *DrAP 75*

Sture-Vasa, Mary *AmWomWr, BioIn 1, –2, –3, –4, –7, CathA 1952, CurBio 44, InWom SUP, MajAI, SmATA 2, –X, TwCA SUP*
Main entry: Alsop, Mary O'Hara

Sturges, Patricia P 1930- *ConAu 69*

Sturtevant, Wallis Hall *ConICB, WhAmArt 85*

Sturton, Hugh *ConAu X, SmATA X*
Main entry: Johnston, H A S

Sturtzel, Howard A 1894- *BioIn 6, –9, ConAu 1R, –6NR, SmATA 1*
Pseud./variant:
Annixter, Paul

Sturtzel, Jane L *AuBYP 3*

Sturtzel, Jane Levington 1903- *BioIn 9, ConAu 1R, –6NR, MichAu 80, SmATA 1*
Pseud./variant:
Annixter, Jane
Comfort, Jane Levington

Styles, Frank Showell *WrDr 86, –88, –90, –92*

Styles, Frank Showell 1908- *AuBYP 2, Au&Wr 71, BioIn 8, –11, ConAu 1R, IntAu&W 82, OxCLiW 86, SmATA 10, Who 82, –83, –85, –88, –90, –92, WrDr 82, –84, –94*
Pseud./variant:
Carr, Glyn
Howell, S
Styles, Showell

Styles, Showell *TwCCr&M 91, Who 88, –90, –92*
Main entry: Styles, Frank Showell

Styles, Showell 1908- *AuBYP 3, BioIn 14, ConAu 21NR, IntAu&W 89, –91, WrDr 94*

Styron, Rose 1928- *ConAu 17R*

Styron, Rose Burgunder 1928- *WhoAmW 93*

Suba, Susanne *AmArt, WhoAmA 86, –89, –91*

Suba, Susanne 1913- *BioIn 1, –5, –6, –8, –9, –12, ChhPo S2, ConAu 29R, ForWC 70, IlsBYP, IlsCB 1744, –1946, –1957, –1967, MorJA, SmATA 4, WhAmArt 85, WhoAmA 73, –78, –80, –82, –84*

Sublette, Clifford MacClellan 1887-1939 *AmAu&B, BioIn 2, JBA 34, –51, WhAm 8*

Subond, Valerie *ConAu X, IntAu&W 77X, –82X, SmATA 7, WrDr 76, –80, –82, –84, –86, –88, –90*
Main entry: Grayland, Valerie Merle

Such, Peter 1939- *BioIn 16, CaW, DcLB 60, OxCCan SUP, OxCCanL, WhoCanL 85, –87, –92*

Sudbery, Rodie 1943- *BioIn 15, ConAu 104, IntAu&W 77, ScF&FL 92, SmATA 42, TwCChW 78, –83, –89, WrDr 76, –80, –82, –84, –86, –88, –90, –92, –94*

Suddaby, Donald 1900-1964 *TwCChW 89*

Suddaby, Donald 1901?-1964 *BioIn 8, LongCTC, OxCChiL, TwCChW 78, –83, WhoChL*

Suddon, Alan *OxCCan SUP*

Sufrin, Mark 1925- *SmATA 76*

Sugarman, Daniel Arthur 1931- *AmMWSc 73S, ConAu 21R*

Sugarman, Joan G 1917- *SmATA 64*

Sugarman, Tracy 1921- *BioIn 15, ConAu 21R, IlrAm 1880, –F, SmATA 37*

Suggs, Robert Carl 1932- *AuBYP 2, –3, BioIn 6, –8, ConAu 9R*

Sugimoto, Etsu Inagaki 1874-1950 *BioIn 2, –4, –6, JBA 34, TwCA, –SUP*

Sugita, Yutaka *BioIn 14*

Sugita, Yutaka 1930- *BioIn 12, ConAu 115, IlsCB 1967, IntAu&W 86, SmATA 36, WhoGrA 82*

Suhl, Yuri d1986 *NewYTBS 86*

Suhl, Yuri 1908- *AuBYP 2S, –3, BioIn 11, ChlLR 2, ConAu 45, –2NR, SmATA 8, –1AS, WhoWorJ 72, –78*

Suhl, Yuri 1908-1986 *BioIn 15, –16, ConAu 121, SmATA 50N*

Suhl, Yuri Menachem 1908-1986 *ConAu 38NR, MajAI*

Suid, Murray 1942- *BioIn 13, ConAu 97, –30NR, SmATA 27*

Suid, Roberta *MedPD*

Sujata, Anagarita 1948- *ConAu 65*

Sullivan, Aloysius Michael 1896-1980 *AmCath 80, AnCL, BioIn 1, –3, –12, BkC 3, CathA 1930, ChhPo, –S1, –S2, ConAu P-2, CurBio 53, REnAL, WhAm 7*

Sullivan, Arthur S 1842-1900 *NewAmDM*

Sullivan, Arthur Seymour 1842-1900 *AuBYP 3*

Sullivan, Arthur Seymour, Sir 1842-1900 *Alli, AtlBL, AuBYP 2S, Baker 84, BioIn 1, –2, –3, –4, –5, –6, –7, –8, –9, –10, –11, –12, –13, CelCen, DcNaB S1, Dis&D, EncWT, FilmgC, LuthC 75, McGEWB, NewC, NotNAT A, –B, OxCMus, REn, REnWD*

Sullivan, George E 1927- *WrDr 90, –92*

Sullivan, George Edmund 1932- *WhoAm 86, –88, –90, –92, –94, WhoWor 87, –89*

Sullivan, George Edward 1927- *AuBYP 2, –3, BioIn 8, –9, –12, ConAu 13R, IntAu&W 89, SmATA 4, WhoAm 84, –86, –88, –90, –92, –94, WrDr 76, –80, –82, –84, –86, –88, –94*

Sullivan, James Frank 1853-1936 *CarSB, DcBrAr 2, DcBrBI*

Sullivan, Mary Ann 1954- *BioIn 17, ConAu 125, SmATA 63*

Sullivan, Mary W 1907- *BioIn 11, ConAu 73, –12NR, ScF&FL 92, SmATA 13, WhoAmW 81, –83*

Sullivan, Mary Wilson 1907- *IntAu&W 91*

Sullivan, Navin 1929- *Au&Wr 71, ConAu 5R*

Sullivan, Pat 1887-1933 *ArtCS, ConAu X, HalFC 84, –88, WhAmArt 85, WorECar, WorEFlm*

Sullivan, Peggy Anne 1929- *BiDrLUS 70, BioIn 6, ConAu 29R, WhoAm 94, WhoAmW 93, WhoLibI 82, WhoLibS 55*

Sullivan, Thomas Joseph *WhoAmP 93*

Sullivan, Thomas Joseph 1947- *WhoAmP 85, –87, –89, –91*

Sullivan, Thomas Joseph, Jr. 1947- *ConAu 81, IntAu&W 82, SmATA 16*
Pseud./variant:
Sullivan, Tom

Sullivan, Tom *ScF&FL 92*
Main entry: Sullivan, Thomas Joseph, Jr.

Sullivan, Tom 1947- *BioIn 10, –11, –12, –17, ConTFT 2, IntAu&W 82X, SmATA X, WhoEnt 92*

Sullivan, Tom 1950- *BioIn 14*

Sullivan, Walter 1906- *ConAu 13R*

Sullivan, Walter 1918- *JrnUS, WrDr 86, –88, –90, –92*

Sullivan, Walter Seagar 1918- *WhoAm 86, –88, WhoUSWr 88*

Sullivan, Walter Seagar, Jr. 1918- *EncTwCJ*

Sullivan, Walter Seager 1918- *AmAu&B, AmMWSc 73P, –82, –86, –89, –92, BioIn 6, –10, –12, –13, BlueB 76, ConAu 1R, –2NR, IntAu&W 82, –89, –91, IntWW 74, –79, –80, –81, –82, –83, –89, –91, WhoAm 74, –80, –82, –84, –90, –92, –94, WhoWor 74, WhoWrEP 89, –92, WrDr 76, –94*

Sully, Francois 1927-1971 *AuBYP 2S, –3, BioIn 9, ConAu 29R, –P-2*

Sulzberger, Cyrus Leo 1912- *Au&Wr 71, BioIn 3, –4, –7, –8, –9, –10, –11, CelR, ConAu 53, CurBio 44, IntWW 74, –79, –80, –81, –82, –83, –89, –91, REnAL, WhoAm 74, –80, –82, –84, –86, –90, –92, –94, WhoWor 74, –89, WrDr 80*

Sulzberger, Cyrus Leo 1942- *WhoAm 88*

Sumichrast, Jozef *BioIn 15*

Sumichrast, Jozef 1948- *BioIn 13, ConGrA 1, SmATA 29, WhoAm 86, –88, –90, –92, –94, WhoGrA 82*

Summerlin, Sam 1928- *ConAu 45, –34NR, WhoAm 74, –76, –78, –80, –84, –86, WhoE 74, –75, WhoUSWr 88, WhoWrEP 89, –92*

Summerly, Felix *OxCChiL*

Summers, Essie *IntAu&W 86X*

Summers, Essie 1912- *BioIn 10, –14, BlmGWL, ConAu X, IntAu&W 91, TwCRHW 90, WrDr 84, –86, –88, –90, –92, –94*

Summers, James 1910- *AuBYP 3*

Summers, James L 1910- *AuBYP 2, BioIn 6, –8, –13, ConAu 13R, MorJA, SmATA 28*

Summers, James L 1910-1973 *BioIn 16, SmATA 57*

Summers, JoAn 1943- *ConAu 106*

Summers, William Francis 1919- *AmMWSc 73S*

Sumner, Aurea 1913- *IntAu&W 86, WrDr 76, –80, –82, –84, –86, –88, –90, –92*

Sundell, Abner *AuBYP 2S, –3*

Sunderlin, Sylvia Sweetman 1911- *BioIn 13, ConAu 73, ForWC 70, SmATA 28, WhoAmW 75*

Sung, Betty Lee *InWom SUP*

Sung, Betty Lee 1924- *AmMWSc 78S, BioIn 13, ConAu 25R, –10NR, SmATA 26, WhoAsA 94*

Super, Arthur Saul 1908- *Au&Wr 71, WhoWorJ 72, –78*

Suponov, Michael 1923- *ConAu 65*

Supraner, Robyn *DrAPF 87, –89, –91, –93*

Supraner, Robyn 1930- *BioIn 12, ConAu 69, –26NR, DrAPF 85, SmATA 20*
Pseud./variant:
Blake, Olive
Frost, Erica
Warren, Elizabeth

Supree, Burton 1941- *ConAu 65*

Supree, Burton 1941-1992 *BioIn 17, SmATA 73*

Surany, Anico *AuBYP 2, –3, BioIn 8*

Surge, Frank 1931- *BioIn 11, ConAu 69, SmATA 13*

Surplus, Robert W 1923- *ConAu 5R, LEduc 74, WhoSSW 91, –93, WrDr 80, –82, –84*

Surrey, Philip Henry 1910- *BioIn 7, CanWW 81, –83, –89, CreCan 2, DcCAr 81, WhoAm 80, –82, –84, –86, –88, –90, –92, –94, WhoAmA 73, –80, –82, –84, –86, –89*

Surrey, Philip Henry 1910-1990 *WhoAmA 91N*

Susac, Andrew 1929- *BioIn 10, ConAu 49, SmATA 5*

Suschitzky, Wolfgang *MacBEP*

Suschitzky, Wolfgang 1912- *IntWW 91*

Suskind, Richard 1925- *ConAu 13R, –9NR, NewYTBE 72*

Sussman, Cornelia *BioIn 16*

Sussman, Cornelia 1914- *SmATA 59*

Sussman, Cornelia Silver 1914- *ConAu 5R, –13NR*
Pseud./variant:
Jessey, Cornelia

Sussman, Irving 1908- *BioIn 16, SmATA 59*

Sussman, Susan *WhoUSWr 88, WhoWrEP 89, –92*

Sussman, Susan 1942- *BioIn 16, ConAu 30NR, SmATA 48*
Pseud./variant:
Rissman, Art
Rissman, Susan

Sutal, Louis *OxCCan SUP*

Sutal, Louis 1939- *WhoCanL 87*

Sutcliff, Rosemary *BioIn 14*

Sutcliff, Rosemary 1920- *AuBYP 2, –3, Au&Wr 71, BioIn 5, –6, –7, –8, –10, –11, –15, –16, BlmGWL, BlueB 76, BritCA, CamGLE, CasWL, ChhPo, ChlLR 1, ConAu 5R, –37NR, ConLC 26, DcBrAr 1, DcLEL 1940, HerW, InWom SUP, IntAu&W 77, –82, –86, –89, –91, MajAI, MorJA, OxCChiL, OxCEng 85, PiP, SenS, SmATA 6, –44, TelT, TwCChW 78, –83, –89, Who 74, –82, –83, –85, –88, –90, –92, WhoAmW 74, WhoChL, WhoWor 74, WrDr 76, –80, –82, –84, –86, –88, –90, –92*

Sutcliff, Rosemary 1920-1992 *Au&Arts 10, BioIn 17, ConAu 139, ScF&FL 92, SmATA 73, TwCYAW, WrDr 94N*

Sutherland, Efua 1924- *BlkAuII, –92, BlkWr 1, BlmGWL, ConDr 88, FemiCLE, InWom SUP, IntDcT 2, WrDr 86, –88, –90, –92*

Sutherland, Efua Theodora *IntvTCA 2*

Sutherland, Efua Theodora 1924- *AfrA, BioIn 9, –10, –13, –14, –16, BlkAWP, CamGWoT, ConAu 105, ConDr 73, –77, –82, –93, DcLEL 1940, InB&W 80, McGEWD 84, OxCThe 83, RGAfL, SelBAAf, SmATA 25, TwCChW 78, –83, WhoWor 74, WomWMM, WrDr 76, –80, –82, –84, –94*

Sutherland, Efua Theodora Morgue 1924- *DcLB 117*

Sutherland, Margaret 1941- *BioIn 12, BlmGWL, ConAu 77, –14NR, FemiCLE, IntAu&W 77, –86, –89, –91, SmATA 15, WrDr 76, –80, –82, –84, –86, –88, –90, –92, –94*

Sutherland, Zena 1915- *AuBYP 3, BioIn 15*

Sutherland, Zena B 1915- *AuBYP 2S, BiDrLUS 70, ConAu 102, MedPD, SmATA 37, WhoAmW 85, WhoLibI 82, WhoLibS 66*

Sutherland, Zena Bailey 1915- *WhoAmW 87, –89*

Sutphen, Judith Ann 1944?- *BioIn 9*

Suttles, Shirley 1922- *BioIn 12, SmATA 21*
Pseud./variant:
Conger, Lesley

Suttles, Shirley Janet 1922- *WhoWrEP 89, –92*

Sutton, Ann 1923- *AuBYP 2, BioIn 8, ConAu 5R, –10NR, SmATA 31*

Sutton, Ann Livesay 1923- *BioIn 14*

Sutton, Anne C 1921- *WhoAmP 89*

Sutton, Eve 1906- *ConAu 65, –10NR, IntAu&W 82X, OxCChiL, SmATA 26, TwCChW 78, –83, –89, WrDr 80, –82, –84, –86, –88, –90, –92*

Sutton, Evelyn Mary 1906- *WrDr 94*

Sutton, Evelyn Mary Breakell 1906- *DcChlFi*

Sutton, Felix 1910?- *AuBYP 2, -3, BioIn 8, -14, ConAu 77, SmATA 31*

Sutton, Jane 1950- *BioIn 15, -16, SmATA 43, -52, WrDr 90, -92, -94*

Sutton, Jean *AuBYP 3*

Sutton, Jean 1916- *ConSFA, TwCSFW 86, -91, WrDr 84, -86, -88, -90*

Sutton, Jean 1917- *EncSF 93*

Sutton, Jeff 1913-1979 *AuBYP 3, ScF&FL 92, ScFSB, TwCSFW 86, -91*

Sutton, Jefferson H 1913- *AuBYP 2S, ConAu 21R, ConSFA, WhoSciF*

Sutton, Jefferson Howard 1913-1979 *EncSF 93*

Sutton, Larry M 1931- *BioIn 13, ConAu 14NR, SmATA 29*

Sutton, Margaret Beebe 1903- *AuBYP 2, -3, BioIn 8, -9, ConAu 1R, ForWC 70, IntAu&W 77, SmATA 1*
Pseud./variant:
Ray, Irene

Sutton, Myron Daniel 1925- *AuBYP 2, -3, BioIn 8, -14, ConAu 107, SmATA 31*

Sutton, Myron Daniel, and Ann Sutton *AuBYP 3*

Sutton-Smith, Brian 1924- *AmMWSc 73S, -78S, ConAu 29R, -17NR*

Suzanne, Jamie 1943- *SmATA X*
Main entry: Hawes, Louise

Suzanne, Jamie 1952- *SmATA X*
Main entry: Lantz, Francess Lin

Svenson, Andrew E 1910-1975 *BioIn 9, -10, -13, ConAu 5R, -61, -27NR, ObitOF 79, SmATA 2, -26N, WhoE 74*
Pseud./variant:
Dixon, Franklin W
Stone, Alan
West, Jerry

Swados, Elizabeth *BioIn 17*

Swados, Elizabeth 1951- *AmWomD, BioIn 11, -12, -13, CelR 90, ConAu 97, ConLC 12, InWom SUP, NewGrDA 86, WhoThe 81*

Swados, Harvey *BioIn 14, -15*

Swados, Harvey 1920-1972 *AmAu&B, AuBYP 2S, -3, BenetAL 91, BioIn 5, -6, -9, -10, ConAu 5R, -37R, -6NR, ConLC 5, ConNov 72, DcLB 2, DcLEL 1940, JeAmFiW, ModAL, NewYTBE 72, OxCAmL 65, -83, PenC AM, REnAL, WhAm 5, WorAu 1950*

Swaim, Joseph Carter 1904- *BioIn 1*

Swaim, Joseph Carter, Jr. 1934- *WhoAm 88, -90, -92, -94, WhoAmL 90, -92, -94*

Swain, Suzan Noguchi 1916- *BioIn 8, ConAu 5R, IlsCB 1957, SmATA 21*

Swainson, Donald 1938- *ConAu 109, -30NR, DrAS 82H, OxCCan SUP*

Swan, Susan 1944- *BioIn 13, SmATA 22*

Swank, Roy Laver 1909- *AmMWSc 73P, -76P, -82, -86, -89, -92, WhoAm 74, -76, -78, -80, -82, -84, -86, -88, -90, -92, -94, WhoWest 94, WhoWor 74, -78, -93*

Swann, Peter Charles 1921- *CanWW 70, -79, -80, -81, -83, -89, ConAu 5R, IntAu&W 77, -82, WhoWor 74*

Swanson, Anne *AuBYP 2, -3, BioIn 8*

Swanson, Arlene Collyer 1913- *AuBYP 2, -3, BioIn 8, ConAu 5R*

Swanson, Gloria Borseth 1927- *ConAu 77*

Swanson, June 1931- *SmATA 76*

Swanson, Neil H 1896-1983 *BenetAL 91, BioIn 15, TwCRHW 90*

Swanson, Neil Harmon 1896-1983 *AmAu&B, AmNov, AuBYP 2, -3, BioIn 2, -4, -8, -13, ConAu 109, NewYTBS 83, REnAL, TwCA, -SUP*

Swarthout, Glendon *DrAPF 87, -89, -91, -93*

Swarthout, Glendon d1992 *NewYTBS 92*

Swarthout, Glendon 1918- *AuBYP 2, -3, BenetAL 91, BioIn 4, -11, ConAu 1R, -1NR, ConLC 35, ConNov 72, -76, -82, -86, -91, DrAPF 83, -85, EncFWF, FourBJA, IntAu&W 77, -91, MagSAmL, MichAu 80, Novels, SmATA 26, TwCWW 91, WhoWest 74, WrDr 76, -80, -82, -84, -86, -88, -90, -92*

Swarthout, Glendon 1918-1992 *AnObit 1992, WrDr 94N*

Swarthout, Glendon Fred 1918- *DcAmChF 1960*

Swarthout, Glendon Fred 1918-1992 *ConAu 139, TwCYAW*

Swarthout, Kathryn 1919- *AuBYP 2, -3, BioIn 10, ConAu 41R, DcAmChF 1960, FourBJA, MichAu 80, SmATA 7*

Swartz, Harry 1911- *AmMWSc 73P, -76P, -82, -86, -89, -92, ConAu 57, -6NR, MichAu 80, WhoE 89, WhoSSW 75, -76, -78, -80, -82, WhoWorJ 72, -78*
Pseud./variant:
Moreno, Martin
Valcoe, H Felix

Swayne, Sam 1907- *BioIn 16, SmATA 53*

Swayne, Zoa 1905- *BioIn 16, SmATA 53*

Swayne, Zoa Lourana 1905- *BioIn 5, IlsBYP, IlsCB 1946*

Swayze, Beulah Garland 1907- *ConAu 5R*

Swayze, Fred *OxCCan SUP*

Sweat, Lynn *IlsBYP*

Sweat, Lynn 1934- *BioIn 16, SmATA 57*

Swede, George 1940- *BioIn 17, CanWW 89, ConAu 32NR, IntAu&W 86, -91, SmATA 67, WhoCanL 87, -92*

Sweeney, James Bartholomew 1910- *BioIn 12, ConAu 29R, -12NR, SmATA 21, WhoSSW 75*

Sweeney, Joyce 1955- *BioIn 17, ConAu 35NR, ScF&FL 92, SmATA 65, -68*

Sweeney, Joyce Kay 1955- *WhoAmW 87*

Sweeney, Karen O'Connor *BioIn 14, ConAu 28NR, SmATA X*
Main entry: O'Connor, Karen

Sweet, Ozzie *BioIn 11*

Sweet, Ozzie 1918- *BioIn 16, -17, SixBJA*

Sweet, Sophie *CarSB*

Sweetland, Nancy Ann 1934- *BioIn 16, SmATA 48*
Pseud./variant:
Rose, Nancy A

Sweetser, Mary 1894- *ConAu 41R, ForWC 70*

Sweney, Frederic 1912- *BioIn 8, IlsBYP, IlsCB 1957, WhoAmA 73*

Swenson, Allan Armstrong 1933- *BioIn 12, ConAu 77, SmATA 21*

Swenson, May *DrAPF 87, -89*

Swenson, May d1989 *NewYTBS 89*

Swenson, May 1919- *AmAu&B, AmWomWr, AnCL, ArtclWW 2, AuBYP 2S, -3, Benet 87, BioIn 8, -9, -10, -12, -14, -15, ChhPo S1, -S2, ConAu 5R, ConLC 4, ConPo 70, -75, -80, -85, CroCAP, DcLB 5, DcLEL 1940, DrAP 75, FemiCLE, InWom SUP, IntWWP 82, ModAL S2, PenC AM, RAdv 1, SmATA 15, WhoAm 74, -76, -78, -80, -82, -84, -86, -88, WhoAmW 74, -75, -77, -81, -85, -87, -89, WhoUSWr 88, WhoWor 74, WhoWrEP 89, WorAu 1950, WrDr 76, -80, -82, -84, -86, -88, -90*

Swenson, May 1919-1989 *AnObit 1989, BenetAL 91, BioIn 16, -17, ConAu 130, -36NR, ConLC 61, MajTwCW*

Swenson, Peggye 1933- *ConAu 73*

Swetenham, Violet Hilda *WrDr 76, -80*

Swetenham, Violet Hilda 1911- *IntAu&W 89, -91*

Swettenham, John Alexander 1920- *Au&Wr 71, OxCCan SUP*

Swezey, Kenneth M 1905?-1972 *BioIn 9, ConAu 33R*

Swift, David *ConAu X, SmATA X*
Main entry: Kaufmann, John

Swift, Edd 1943- *ConAu 37R*

Swift, Helen Miller 1914- *AuBYP 2, -3, BioIn 8, ConAu 1R*

Swift, Hildegarde 1890?-1977 *AuBYP 3*

Swift, Hildegarde Hoyt d1977 *BioIn 14*

Swift, Hildegarde Hoyt 1890?-1977 *AuBYP 2, BioIn 2, -7, -11, ChhPo S2, ConAu 69, JBA 51, SmATA 20N*

Swift, Jonathan 1667-1745 *Alli, AtlBL, Benet 87, BbD, BiDIrW, BiD&SB, BioIn 1, -2, -3, -4, -5, -6, -7, -8, -9, -10, -11, -12, -13, -14, -15, -16, -17, BlmGEL, BritAu, BritWr 3, CamGLE, CarSB, CasWL, Chambr 2, ChhPo, -S1, CnDBLB 2, CnE&AP, CrtT 2, CyWA 58, DcBiA, DcBiPP, DcEnA, -A, DcEnL, DcEuL, DcIrB 88, DcIrL, DcIrW 1, DcLB 39, -95, -101, DcLEL, DcNaB, Dis&D, EncSF 93, EvLB, HalFC 84, -88, HsB&A, LitC 1, LongCEL, LuthC 75, MagSWL, McGEWB, MouLC 2, NewC, NewEScF, Novels, OxCChiL, OxCEng 67, -85, OxCMus, PenC ENG, PoIre, RAdv 1, RComWL, REn, RfGEnL 91, ScFSB, ScFEYrs, SmATA 19, UFOEn, WebE&AL, WhDW, WhoChL, WorAlBi, WorAl, WorLitC, WrChl, WrPh*
Pseud./variant:
Bickerstaff, Isaac

Drapier, M B
Waystaff, Simon

Swift, Jonathan 1667-1754 *CamGEL*

Swift, Merlin *AuBYP 3, ConAu X, SmATA X*
Main entry: Leeming, Joseph

Swiger, Elinor Porter *InWom SUP*

Swiger, Elinor Porter 1927- *AuBYP 2S, –3, BioIn 11, ConAu 37R, SmATA 8, WhoAmL 83, –90, WhoAmW 75, –77, –91, –93*

Swinburne, Algernon Charles 1837-1909 *Alli, –SUP, AtlBL, Benet 87, BbD, BiD&SB, BioIn 1, –2, –3, –5, –6, –7, –8, –9, –10, –11, –12, –13, –14, –16, –17, BlmGEL, BritAu 19, BritWr 5, CamGEL, CamGLE, CarSB, CasWL, CelCen, Chambr 3, ChhPo, –S1, –S2, CnDBLB 4, CnE&AP, ConAu 105, –140, CrtT 3, CyWA 58, DcBiPP, DcEnA, –A, DcEnL, DcEuL, DcLEL, DcNaB S2, Dis&D, EvLB, LongCEL, MagSWL, McGEWB, MouLC 4, NewC, NotNAT B, OxCEng 67, –85, PenC ENG, RAdv 1, RComWL, REn, RfGEnL 91, TwCLC 8, WebE&AL, WhDW, WorAlBi, WorAl*

Swinburne, Laurence 1924- *BioIn 11, ConAu 61, –15NR, SmATA 9*

Swindells, Robert 1939- *ConAu 21NR, SmATA 14AS, TwCChW 89, WrDr 90, –92*

Swindells, Robert E 1939- *BioIn 14, –16, ConAu 97, ScF&FL 92, SmATA 34, –50*

Swindells, Robert Edward 1939- *ChlFicS, MajAI, TwCYAW, WrDr 94*

Swindler, William F 1913- *WrDr 86*

Swindler, William Findley 1913-1984 *Au&Wr 71, ConAu 13R, –112, DrAS 74P, –78P, –82P, WhAm 8, WhoAm 74, –76, –78, –80, –82, –84, WhoAmL 78, WrDr 76, –80, –82, –84*

Swinford, Betty 1927- *BioIn 16, SmATA 58*

Swinford, Betty June Wells 1927- *ConAu 5R, ForWC 70, IndAu 1917*
Pseud./variant:
Haynes, Linda
Porter, Kathryn
Swinford, Bob
Wells, June

Swinford, Bob *SmATA X*
Main entry: Swinford, Betty June Wells

Swinnerton, A R 1912- *AuBYP 3*

Swinnerton, James Guilford 1875?-1974 *ArtCS, BioIn 6, –9, –10, CmCal, ConAu 93, NewYTBS 74, ObitOF 79, WhAm 6, WhoAmA 78N*

Swinton, William Elgin 1900- *AmMWSc 73P, AuBYP 2, –3, Au&Wr 71, BioIn 8, CanWW 70, –79, –80, –81, –83, –89, ConAu 13R, WhoAm 82, –84, –86, –88, –90, WhoWor 82, –89*

Switzer, Ellen 1923- *ConAu 45, –2NR, SmATA 48*

Switzer, Ellen Eichenwald 1923- *BioIn 16*

Swortzell, Lowell Stanley 1930- *ConAu 49, DrAS 74E, –82E, LEduc 74, WhoEnt 92*

Sybesma, Jetske 1940- *SmATA X*
Main entry: Ironside, Jetske

Sydney, Frank *ConAu X, SmATA X*
Main entry: Warwick, Alan Ross

Syers, William Edward 1914- *BioIn 10, ConAu 1R, –4NR, IntAu&W 86, WrDr 80*

Syers, William Edward 1926- *WhoWest 87, –89, –92, WhoWor 87*

Sykes, Jo *AuBYP 3*

Sykes, Jo 1928- *AuBYP 2, BioIn 8, WhoPNW*

Sykes, Pamela *AuBYP 3*

Sykes, Pamela 1927- *AuBYP 2S, Au&Wr 71*

Sylvester, Natalie G 1922- *ConAu 97, SmATA 22*

Syme, Ronald 1910- *TwCChW 89, WrDr 86, –88, –90, –92*

Syme, Ronald 1913?- *AuBYP 2, –3, Au&Wr 71, BioIn 6, –8, –9, ConAu 9R, –6NR, MorJA SmATA 2, TwCChW 78, –83, WrDr 80, –82, –84*

Symes, R F *SmATA 77*

Symington, Fraser *OxCCan SUP*

Symonds, Francis Addington 1893- *Au&Wr 71*

Symonds, John *EncO&P 1, TwCChW 78, –83, WrDr 86, –88, –90, –92, –94*

Symonds, John 1914- *EncO&P 3, TwCChW 89*

Symons, Arthur 1865-1945 *Alli SUP, AtlBL, Benet 87, BiD&SB, BioIn 2, –4, –5, –6, –8, –10, –11, –13, –15, –16, –17, CamGEL, CamGLE, CasWL, Chambr 3, ChhPo S1, –S2, CnE&AP, ConAu 107, CurBio 45, DcEnA A, DcLB 19, DcLEL, Dis&D, EvLB, LongCTC, ModBrL, NewC, NotNAT B, ObitOF 79,*

OxCEng 67, PenC ENG, REn, RfGEnL 91, TwCA, –SUP, TwCLC 11, TwCWr, WebE&AL

Symons, Geraldine 1909- *BioIn 14, ConAu 85, OxCChiL, ScF&FL 92, SmATA 33, TwCChW 78, –83, –89, WrDr 76, –80, –82, –84, –86, –88, –90, –92, –94*
Pseud./variant:
Groves, Georgina

Symons, Robert David 1898-1973 *Au&Wr 71, BioIn 10, CanWW 70, ConAu 41R, OxCCan SUP*

Symons, Stuart
Main entry: Stanley, George Edward

Synge, Ursula 1930- *BioIn 11, ConAu 49, –1NR, IntAu&W 77, SmATA 9, WrDr 76, –80, –82, –84, –86, –88, –90, –92, –94*

Sypher, Lucy Johnston 1907- *BioIn 10, ConAu 45, –2NR, SmATA 7, WrDr 76, –80, –82, –84, –86, –88, –90*

Syred, Celia Mary 1911- *ConAu 29R, DcChlFi, SingR 2*

Syvertsen, Edythe 1921- *ConAu 73*

Szasz, Suzanne Shorr 1915- *AuBYP 3*

Szasz, Suzanne Shorr 1919- *AuBYP 2, BioIn 8, –11, –13, ConAu 5R, SmATA 13*

Szasz, Thomas Stephen 1920- *AmAu&B, AmMWSc 73S, –82, –86, –89, –92, BioIn 9, –10, –12, –13, –15, ConAu 17R, CurBio 75, IntAu&W 82, –86, –89, –91, IntWW 79, –80, –81, –82, –83, –89, –91, MakMC, NewYTBE 71, WhoAm 74, –80, –82, –84, –86, –88, –90, –92, –94, WhoE 91, WhoWor 74, WorAu 1975, WrDr 76, –80, –82, –84, –86, –88, –90, –92, –94*

Sze, Mai-Mai *AuBYP 2, –3, BioIn 7*

Sze, Mai-Mai d1992 *NewYTBS 92*

Szekeres, Cyndy 1933- *BioIn 10, –12, –17, ConAu 137, IlsBYP, IlsCB 1967, MajAI, SmATA 5, –60, –13AS*

Szenes, Andre 1895-1957 *BioIn 4, –6*
Pseud./variant:
Dugo, Andre

Szolnoki, Rose Namath 1912- *BioIn 8, –10*

Szudek, Agnes Susan Philomena *SmATA 49, –57*
Pseud./variant:
McCaffrey, Mary

Szulc, Tad *BioIn 15*

Szulc, Tad 1926- *AmAu&B, BioIn 10, –13, ConAu 9R, –4NR, –23NR, EncTwCJ, SmATA 26, SpyFic, WhoAm 74, –76, –78, –80, –82, –84, –86, –88, –90, –92, –94, WhoWor 74, –80, –84, –87, –89, WhoWrEP 89, –92, WrDr 76, –80, –82, –84, –86, –88, –90, –92, –94*

Szyk, Arthur d1951 *WhoAmA 86N*

Szyk, Arthur 1894-1951 *BioIn 1, –2, –3, –5, –16, ChhPo, CurBio 46, –51, IlsBYP, IlsCB 1946, ObitOF 79, PolBiDi, WhAm 3, WhAmArt 85, WhoAmA 78N, –80N, –82N, –89N, –91N, WorECar*

T

Taback, Simms 1932- *BioIn 14, –15, ChhPo S1, ConAu 115, SmATA 36, –40, WhoAmA 78, –80, –82, –84, –86, –89, –91*

Tabart, Benjamin *OxCChiL*

Taber, Gladys Bagg 1899-1980 *AmAu&B, AmNov, AmWomWr, Au&Wr 71, BioIn 1, –2, –3, –5, –10, –12, –13, –15, ConAu 5R, –97, –4NR, CurBio 52, –80N, ForWC 70, NewYTBS 80, SmATA 22N, WhAm 7, –8, WhoAm 74, –78, –80, WhoAmW 74, WrDr 80*

Tabrah, Ruth M 1921- *WhoAmP 85*

Tabrah, Ruth Milander 1921- *ConAu 13R, –10NR, –28NR, ForWC 70, IntAu&W 77, –82, LEduc 74, SmATA 14, WhoAmP 81, –83, WhoAmW 74, –75*

Tadjo, Veronique 1955- *BlkAuII 92*

Taffrail *DcLEL, LongCTC, TwCWr, WhoSpyF*

Tafuri, Nancy 1946- *AuBYP 3*

Tafuri, Nancy *BioIn 15, –16, ChlBIID*

Tafuri, Nancy 1946- *ConAu 118, MajAI, SixBJA, SmATA 39, –75, –14AS*

Tague, Lola F 1902-1962 *IndAu 1917*

Taha, Karen Terry 1942- *SmATA 71*

Tailfeathers, Gerald 1925- *BioIn 9*

Tait, Agnes 1894?-1981 *BioIn 5, –11, ChhPo, DcWomA, IlsBYP, IlsCB 1946, WhAmArt 85*

Tait, Douglas William Campbell 1944- *BioIn 11, –12, –13, IlsBYP, IlsCB 1967, Profile 2, SmATA 12*

Tait, George E 1910- *IntAu&W 86*

Tait, George Edward 1910- *Au&Wr 71, CanWW 70, –79, –80, –81, –83, –89, ConAu 5R, LEduc 74, WrDr 76, –80, –82, –84, –86, –88, –90, –92, –94*

Takakjian, Portia 1930- *SmATA 15*
Pseud./variant:
Johnston, Portia
Roach, Portia
Wiesner, Portia

Takashima, Shizuye 1928- *BioIn 6, –11, –13, ConAu 45, ConGrA 3, CreCan 2, HerW, –84, InWom SUP, OxCCan SUP, Profile 2, SmATA 13*

Talbert, Ansel Edward 1912-1987 *ConAu 124*

Talbert, Ansel Edward McLaurine d1987 *BioIn 15*

Talbert, Ansel Edward McLaurine 1912- *AuBYP 2, BioIn 5, –8, WhoAm 74, –76, –80, –82, –84, –86, WhoSSW 73*

Talbert, Ansel Edward McLaurine 1912-1987 *WhAm 9*

Talbert, Ansel Edward McLaurine 1915- *AuBYP 3*

Talbert, Marc 1953- *BioIn 17, ConAu 136, SmATA 68, WrDr 94*

Talbot, Charlene Joy 1924- *WrDr 86, –88, –90*

Talbot, Charlene Joy 1928- *AuBYP 2S, –3, BioIn 11, ConAu 17R, –8NR, ForWC 70, SmATA 10, WrDr 76, –80, –82, –84*

Talbot, Charles Remington 1851-1891 *Alli SUP, AmAu&B, BiD&SB, CarSB, ChhPo, DcAmAu, DcNAA*

Talbot, Ethel *EngPo, OxCChiL, TwCChW 83, –89*

Talbot, Toby 1928- *AuBYP 2S, –3, BioIn 12, ConAu 21R, –29NR, SmATA 14, WomWMM B*

Talbot, Winifred Winter 1894-1970 *BioIn 5, MinnWr, WhAm 5*

Talifero, Gerald 1950- *SmATA 75*
Pseud./variant:
Stormcrow

Talker, T *SmATA X*
Main entry: Rands, William Brighty

Tallant, Robert 1909-1957 *AmAu&B, AmNov, AuBYP 2, –3, BenetAL 91, BioIn 2, –3, –4, –8, CurBio 53, –57, ObitOF 79, REnAL, TwCA SUP*

Tallcott, Emogene *BioIn 11, ConAu 29R, SmATA 10*

Tallis, Robyn *ConAu 142, ScF&FL 92, SmATA 75*
Main entry: Zambreno, Mary Frances

Tallon, Robert 1935- *AuBYP 3*

Tallon, Robert 1940- *AuBYP 2S, BioIn 13, ConAu 9R, –8NR, SmATA 28, –43*

Talmadge, Marian *AuBYP 2, –3, BioIn 8, –12, SmATA 14*

Talwick, Maria *BioIn 10*

Tamar, Erika 1934- *BioIn 17, SmATA 62*

Tamarin, Alfred H 1913-1980 *BioIn 10, –11, –12, ConAu 29R, –102, –4NR, FifBJA, IntMPA 75, –76, –78, –77, MorBMP, NewYTBS 80, SmATA 13, WrDr 80*

Tamburine, Jean 1930- *AuBYP 2, –3, BioIn 7, –8, –11, ChhPo S1, ConAu 9R, ForWC 70, SmATA 12, WhoAmA 78, –80, –82, –84, –86, –89, –91, WhoAmW 74*

Tames, Richard 1946- *SmATA 67*

Tames, Richard Lawrence 1946- *IntAu&W 91, WrDr 88, –94*

Tamminga, Frederick William 1934- *BioIn 17, ConAu 135, ScF&FL 92, SmATA 66, WrDr 94*
Pseud./variant:
Willius, T F

Tammuz, Benjamin d1989 *NewYTBS 89*

Tammuz, Benjamin 1919- *CasWL, ConAu 85, IntAu&W 82, WhoWor 74, WhoWorJ 72, –78*

Tammuz, Benjamin 1919-1989 *BioIn 16, –17, ConAu 129, –36NR, SmATA 63*

Tamulaitis, Vytas 1913- *ConAu 17R*

Tan, Amy *BioIn 16, –17, DrAPF 91, –93*

Tan, Amy 1952- *AmWomWr 92, Au&Arts 9, BestSel 89-3, BlmGWL, ConAu 136, ConLC 59, CurBio 92, IntAu&W 91, SmATA 75, TwCYAW, WrDr 94*

Tanaka, Beatrice 1932- *ConAu 115, SmATA 76*

Tang, You-Shan 1946- *SmATA 53*

Tangye, Derek Alan Trevithick 1912- *Au&Wr 71, IntAu&W 77*

Tannehill, Ivan Ray 1890- *AuBYP 3*

Tannehill, Ivan Ray 1890-1959 *AuBYP 2, BioIn 8, OhA&B*

Tannen, Mary 1943- *BioIn 15, ConAu 105, IntAu&W 86, –89, ScF&FL 92, SmATA 37*

Tannenbaum, Beulah Goldstein 1916- *AuBYP 2, –3, BioIn 9, ConAu 5R, –7NR, ForWC 70, SmATA 3*

Tannenbaum, D Leb 1948- *BioIn 15, ConAu 115, SmATA 42*

Tanner, James M 1920- *Au&Wr 71, ConAu 13R, –5NR, IntMed 80*

Tanner, Jane 1946- *SmATA 74*

Tanner, Louise *AuBYP 3*

Tanner, Louise S 1922- *AuBYP 2S, BioIn 11, ConAu 69, SmATA 9*

Tanobe, Miyuki 1937- *BioIn 13, ConAu 69, SmATA 23*

Tanous, Helen Nicol 1917- *AuBYP 2, –3, BioIn 8*

Tanyzer, Harold Joseph 1929- *ConAu 9R*

Tapio, Pat Decker *ConAu X, SmATA X*
Main entry: Kines, Pat Decker

Tapley, Caroline *AuBYP 3*

Tapley, Caroline 1934- *AuBYP 2S, ConAu 97*

Taplinger, Richard Jacques 1911-1973 *BioIn 9, ConAu 41R, WhAm 5*

Tapp, Kathy Kennedy 1949- *AuBYP 3, BioIn 16, ConAu 39NR, ScF&FL 92, SmATA 50*

Tappan, Eva March 1854-1930 *AmAu&B, AmLY, AmWomWr, BiD&SB, BioIn 15, CarSB, ChhPo, –S1, DcAmAu, DcNAA, JBA 34, REnAL, TwCA, WhAm 1, WhNAA, WomWWA 14, WomNov*

Tappan, Eva March 1854-1950 *InWom SUP*

Tardiff, Olive 1916- *ConAu 73*

Targ Brill, Marlene *SmATA 77*
Main entry: Brill, Marlene Targ

Tarkington, Booth 1869-1946 *AmAu&B, AtlBL, Benet 87, BenetAL 91, BbD, BiD&SB, BioIn 1, -2, -3, -4, -5, -6, -8, -10, -11, -12, -13, -14, -16, -17, CamGLE, CamGWoT, CamHAL, CarSB, CasWL, Chambr 3, ChhPo S2, CnDAL, ConAmA, ConAmL, ConAu 110, CurBio 46, CyWA 58, DcAmAu, DcBiA, DcLB 9, -102, DcLEL, DcNAA, EncAB-A 15, EvLB, FilmgC, HalFC 84, -88, IndAu 1816, JBA 34, LongCTC, McGEWB, McGEWD 72, -84, ModAL, ModWD, MorMA, NotNAT B, Novels, ObitOF 79, OxCAmL 65, -83, OxCAmT 84, OxCChiL, OxCEng 67, -85, OxCThe 67, -83, PenC AM, PlP&P, REn, REnAL, RfGAmL 87, SmATA 17, TwCA, -SUP, TwCChW 89, TwCLC 9, TwCWr, WebAB 74, -79, WebE&AL, WhAm 2, WhAmArt 85, WhNAA, WhoChL, WorAlBi, WorAl*
Pseud./variant:
Tarkington, Newton Booth

Tarkington, Newton Booth
Main entry: Tarkington, Booth

Tarlow, Nora *SmATA 75*
Main entry: Cohen, Nora

Tarnawsky, Patricia Warren 1936- *ConAu 45, ForWC 70*
Pseud./variant:
Warren, Patricia Nell

Tarr, Judith *BioIn 17*

Tarr, Judith 1955- *ConAu 120, ScF&FL 92, SmATA 64, TwCSFW 91*

Tarrant, Margaret W 1888-1959 *BioIn 14, ChhPo, -S1, -S2, ConICB, DcBrAr 1, DcWomA*

Tarry, Ellen *WhoBlA 85*

Tarry, Ellen 1906- *AmPB, AuBYP 2, -3, BioIn 3, -8, -9, -12, -16, -17, BlkAWP, BlkAull, -92, BlkWr 1, BkP, ChlLR 26, ConAu 73, HarlReB, InB&W 80, -85, LivgBAA, NegAl 76, -83, -89, NotBlAW 92, SelBAAf, SelBAAu, SmATA 16, -16AS, SouBlCW, WhoBlA 77, -80, -85, -90, -92, -94*

Tarshis, Barry *AuBYP 2S, -3*

Tarshis, Jerome 1936- *BioIn 11, ConAu 61, MedPD, SmATA 9, WhoAmA 78, -80, -82, -84, -86, -89, -91*

Tarsky, Sue 1946- *BioIn 15, ConAu 112, -31NR, SmATA 41*

Tashjian, Virginia A 1921- *AnCL, AuBYP 2S, -3, BiDrLUS 70, BioIn 9, ConAu 29R, FifBJA, ForWC 70, SmATA 3, WhoAmW 75, WhoLibI 82, WhoLibS 55*

Tashlin, Frank 1913-1972 *BiDFilm, BioIn 9, -15, -16, CmMov, ConAu 110, -113, DcFM, DcLB 44, EncAFC, FilmgC, HalFC 84, -88, NewYTBE 72, ObitOF 79, OxCFilm, WhAm 5, WorECar, WorEFlm, WorFDir 2*

Tasker, James 1908- *BioIn 11, ConAu 49, SmATA 9*

Tate, Carole *ChhPo S2*

Tate, Eleanora E *DrAPF 89, -91, -93*

Tate, Eleanora E 1948- *BioIn 15, -16, BroadAu, ConAu 105, -25NR, SmATA 38*

Tate, Eleanora Elaine 1948- *BlkAull, -92, BlkWr 2, TwCYAW, WhoBlA 90, -92, -94*

Tate, Elizabeth *AuBYP 2, -3, BioIn 8*

Tate, Elizabeth 1948- *TwCPaSc*

Tate, Ellalice *Au&Wr 71, BlmGWL, ConAu 140, -X, -28NR, EncMys, IntAu&W 91X, Novels, SmATA 2, -74, TwCRHW 90, Who 74, -82, -83, -85, -88, -90, -92, WorAu 1950, WrDr 76, -84, -85, -88, -90, -92*
Main entry: Hibbert, Eleanor Burford

Tate, Ellalice 1906- *BioIn 14*

Tate, Ellalice 1906-1993 *WrDr 94N*

Tate, Joan 1922- *BioIn 11, ConAu 49, -1NR, IntAu&W 77, -91, OxCChiL, SmATA 9, TwCChW 78, -83, -89, WrDr 76, -80, -82, -84, -86, -88, -90, -92, -94*

Tate, Nahum 1652-1715 *Alli, AnCL, Benet 87, BiDIrW, BioIn 3, -9, -12, BlmGEL, BritAu, CamGLE, CamGWoT, CasWL, Chambr 2, ChhPo, DcBiPP, DcEnA, DcEnL, DcEuL, DcIrB 88, DcIrL, DcIrW 1, DcLEL, DcNaB, EvLB, IntDcT 2, LuthC 75, NewC, NotNAT B, OxCEng 67, -85, OxCMus, OxCThe 67, -83, PenC ENG, PlP&P, PoChrch, PoIre, PoLE, REn, RfGEnL 91*

Tatham, Campbell *AuBYP 2, -3, ConAu X MorJA, SmATA 2*
Main entry: Elting, Mary

Tattersall, Muriel Joyce 1931- *Au&Wr 71, ConAu P-1, WrDr 76, -80, -82, -84*
Pseud./variant:
Waud, Elizabeth

Taves, Isabella 1915- *BioIn 13, ConAu 21R, -8NR, SmATA 27, WhoAmW 74, -75*

Tavo, Gus *AuBYP 2, -3, ConAu X*
Main entry: Ivan, Gustave
Ivan, Martha Miller Pfaff

Taylor, Sybil *BioIn 1, IlsCB 1744*

Taylor, Allan M *ChhPo, –S2*

Taylor, Andrew John Robert 1951- *SmATA 70*
Pseud./variant:
Taylor, John Robert

Taylor, Ann *Who 92*

Taylor, Ann 1782-1866 *Alli, BioIn 8, –14, –15, –16, BlmGEL, BlmGWL, BritAu 19, CarSB, ChhPo, –S1, –S2, ChrP, DcBiPP, DcEnL, DcEuL, DcNaB, EncBrWW, EvLB, FamPYP, InWom SUP, NewC, OxCChiL, OxCEng 67, SmATA 35, –41, Str&VC, TelT, WhoChL*
Pseud./variant:
Gilbert, Ann
Juvenilia
Lady, A

Taylor, Arthur *AuBYP 2, –3, BioIn 8*

Taylor, Audilee Boyd 1931- *BioIn 16, SmATA 59*

Taylor, Barbara J 1927- *BioIn 11, ConAu 53, SmATA 10*

Taylor, Bernard 1937- *ConAu 69, WhoHr&F*

Taylor, Carl 1937- *AuBYP 2, –3, BioIn 12, SmATA 14*

Taylor, Cora 1936- *ConAu 124, ScF&FL 92, SmATA 64, WhoCanL 87, –92*

Taylor, Cora Lorraine 1936- *DcChlFi*

Taylor, David 1900-1965 *BioIn 7, –11, ConAu 1R, EncAB-A 36, SmATA 10*

Taylor, Dawson 1916- *ASCAP 66, ConAu 13R, –25NR, MichAu 80*

Taylor, Duncan 1912- *Au&Wr 71, ConAu 25R*

Taylor, Edgar 1793-1839 *Alli, ChhPo, DcNaB, –C, Str&VC*

Taylor, Elizabeth 1912- *ArtclWW 2*

Taylor, Elizabeth 1912-1975 *Au&Wr 71, Benet 87, BioIn 1, –3, –4, –11, –15, –16, –17, BlmGWL, BlueB 76, –76N, CamGLE, ConAu 13R, –9NR, ConLC 2, –4, –29, ConNov 72, –76, ContDcW 89, DcLB 139, DcLEL 1940, EncBrWW, FemiCLE, LongCTC, MajTwCW, NewC, Novels, ObitT 1971, OxCEng 85, RAdv 1, RfGEnL 91, ShSWr, SmATA 13, TwCA SUP, TwCWr, Who 74, WhoAmW 74, WhoWor 74, WrDr 76*

Taylor, Ethel Stoddard 1895?-1975 *BioIn 10, ConAu 57*

Taylor, Florance Walton *BioIn 11, ConAu 37R, SmATA 9*

Taylor, Florence M 1892- *BioIn 11, ConAu 13R, SmATA 9*

Taylor, George Boardman 1832-1907 *Alli, –SUP, BiDSA, CarSB, DcAmAu, DcNAA, EncSoB, WhAm 1*

Taylor, Gordon Rattray *BioIn 14*

Taylor, Gordon Rattray 1911-1981 *Au&Wr 71, ConAu 85, –105, EncO&P 3, Future, IntAu&W 77, Who 74, –82, –83N*

Taylor, Gordon Richard 1925- *WhoLib 54*

Taylor, Harry *ConAu X, ConTFT 4*
Main entry: Granick, Harry

Taylor, Helen L *Alli SUP*

Taylor, Herb d1987 *NewYTBS 87*

Taylor, Herb 1942- *BioIn 13, ConAu 97, MacBEP, SmATA 22*

Taylor, Herb 1942-1987 *BioIn 15, –16, ConAu 123, SmATA 54N*

Taylor, Isaac 1759-1829 *Alli, BiDLA, BiD&SB, BkIE, BritAu 19, CarSB, ChhPo, –S1, DcBiPP, DcEuL, DcNaB, OxCChiL*

Taylor, Jane 1783-1824 *Alli, ArtclWW 2, BioIn 2, –6, –8, –13, –15, –16, BlmGEL, BlmGWL, CarSB, ChhPo, –S1, ChrP, DcBiPP, DcEnL, DcEuL, DcNaB, EncBrWW, EvLB, FamPYP, FemiCLE, InWom SUP, OxCChiL, OxCEng 67, –85, PoChrch, SmATA 35, –41, Str&VC, TelT, WhoChL*

Taylor, Jefferys 1792-1853 *Alli, BritAu 19, CarSB, ChhPo, –S1, DcNaB, OxCChiL*

Taylor, Jerry Duncan 1938- *AmMWSc 86, –89, –92, BioIn 16, SmATA 47, WhoAm 94, WhoSSW 91, –93*

Taylor, John G 1931- *Au&Wr 71, ConAu 29R, Who 82, –83, –85, WrDr 80*

Taylor, John Gerald 1931- *IntAu&W 86, –91, Who 88, –92*

Taylor, John Gerald, Prof 1931- *Who 90*

Taylor, John Robert *SmATA 70*
Main entry: Taylor, Andrew John Robert

Taylor, Judy 1932- *IntAu&W 89, –91, SmATA X, Who 88, –90, –92*
Main entry: Hough, Judy Taylor

Taylor, Kamala *BioIn 6, –10, ConAu 77, WorAu 1950*
Main entry: Markandaya, Kamala

Taylor, Kenneth Nathaniel 1917- *AuNews 2, Au&Wr 71, BioIn 9, –10, –11, –12, –13, ConAu 17R, –8NR, SmATA 26, WhoAm 74, –76, –78, –80, –82, –84, –86, –88, –90, –92, –94, WhoFI 85, WhoRel 75, –77*

Taylor, L B, Jr. 1932- *BioIn 13, ConAu 11NR, –26NR, SmATA 27*

Taylor, Louise Todd 1939- *BioIn 16, SmATA 47, WhoSSW 91, –93*

Taylor, Margaret *AuBYP 2, BioIn 8, BlkWr 1, ConAu X*
Main entry: Burroughs, Margaret Taylor

Taylor, Margaret 1917- *AuBYP 3, WhoBlA 90, –92, –94*

Taylor, Margaret Alexander 1926- *WhoAmW 93*

Taylor, Mark *AuBYP 3*

Taylor, Mark 1927- *AuBYP 2S, BioIn 13, ConAu 108, SmATA 28, –32, WhoAm 94, WhoWest 89*

Taylor, Mildred D *ArtclWW 2, AuBYP 2S, –3, BioIn 11, –12, –14, BlkWr 1, ChlLR 9, ConAu 85, –25NR, ConLC 21, DcAmChF 1960, –1985, FifBJA, InB&W 80, –85, IntAu&W 91, OxCChiL, SelBAAf, SelBAAu, SmATA 15, TwCChW 83, WhoAm 92, WrDr 86, –88, –90, –92*

Taylor, Mildred D 1943- *Au&Arts 10, BlkAuII, –92, BlkWr 2, DcLB 52, MajAI, SmATA 70, –5AS, TwCChW 89, TwCYAW, WhoBlA 90, –92*

Taylor, Paula 1942- *BioIn 14, –16, ConAu 111, –122, SmATA 33*

Taylor, Paula Wright 1942- *SmATA 48*
Pseud./variant:
Lake, Harriet

Taylor, Rebe Prestwich 1911- *Au&Wr 71, ConAu 13R, WhoLib 54*

Taylor, Robert Lewis 1912- *AmAu&B, Au&Wr 71, BenetAL 91, BioIn 1, –2, –5, –7, –8, –10, –11, BlueB 76, ConAu 1R, –3NR, ConNov 72, –76, CurBio 59, EncFWF, EncSF 93, IntAu&W 77, OxCAmL 65, –83, REnAL, SmATA 10, TwCWW 91, WhoAm 74, –76, –78, –80, –82, –84, –86, –88, WhoE 74, –75, –77, WhoWor 74, –78, –80, –82, –84, –89, WhoWrEP 89, –92, WorAu 1950, WrDr 76, –80, –82, –84, –86, –88, –90, –92, –94*

Taylor, Sydney 1904-1978 *TwCChW 89*

Taylor, Sydney Brenner 1904?-1978 *AuBYP 2, –3, BioIn 6, –8, –9, –10, –11, –13, BkCL, ConAu 5R, –77, –4NR, IntAu&W 77, MajAI, MorBMP, MorJA, SmATA 1, –26N, –28, TwCChW 78, –83, WrDr 76*

Taylor, Theodore *DrAPF 87, –89, –91, –93*

Taylor, Theodore 1921- *Au&Arts 2, AuBYP 2S, BioIn 10, –15, –16, ChlLR 30, ConAu 21R, –9NR, –25NR, –38NR, DcAmChF 1960, FourBJA, IntAu&W 77, MajAI, OxCChiL, SmATA 5, –54, –4AS, TwCChW 78, –83, –89, TwCYAW, WhoAm 74, –80, –82, –84, WrDr 76, –80, –82, –84, –86, –88, –90, –92, –94*

Taylor, Theodore 1924- *AuBYP 3*

Taylor, William *DcChlFi, DcVicP 2*

Taylor, William 1938- *TwCChW 89, WrDr 90, –92, –94*

Tazewell, Charles 1900-1972 *BioIn 9, –10, ConAu 37R, NewYTBE 72, ObitOF 79, SmATA 74*

Tchudi, Stephen N 1942- *AuBYP 3, BioIn 16, ConAu 22NR, SmATA 55, TwCYAW*
Pseud./variant:
Judy, Stephen N

Tchudi, Susan J *AuBYP 3*

Teague, Bob *BlkWr 2, EncTwCJ*
Main entry: Teague, Robert

Teague, Bob 1929- *ConAu X, NegAl 76, –83, –89, SmATA X*

Teague, Donald 1897- *ArtsAmW 3, BioIn 1, –2, –11, –13, ConICB, ForIl, IlrAm 1880, –C, IlsCB 1744, WhAmArt 85, WhoAm 74, –76, –78, –80, –82, –84, –86, –88, –90, WhoAmA 73, –78, –80, –82, –84, –86, –89, –91, WhoWest 74, WhoWor 80*

Teague, Donald 1897-1991 *WhAm 10*

Teague, Kathleen 1937- *ConAu 97, IntAu&W 82*

Teague, Mark 1963- *BioIn 17, SmATA 68*

Teague, Mark Christopher 1963- *ConAu 136, WrDr 94*

Teague, Robert *AuBYP 3*

Teague, Robert 1929- *AuBYP 2S, BioIn 8, BlkAWP, BlkWr 2, ConAu 106, InB&W 80, LivgBAA, ScF&FL 92, SelBAAu, SmATA 31, –32, WhoBlA 80, –85, –90, –92*

Pseud./variant:
Teague, Bob

Teal, Val 1903- *AmAu&B, AmNov, BioIn 1, -2, -11, ConAu 61, SmATA 10*

Teale, Edwin Way 1899-1980 *AmAu&B, AnObit 1980, AuBYP 2, -3, Au&Wr 71, BenetAL 91, BioIn 1, -2, -3, -4, -5, -6, -7, -8, -9, -10, -12, -13, -15, ConAu 1R, -102, -2NR, CurBio 61, -81N, InSci, NewYTBS 80, OxCAmL 83, REnAL, SmATA 7, -25N, Str&VC, ThrBJA, TwCA SUP, WhAm 7, WhNAA, WhoAm 74, -76, -78, -80, WhoWor 74, WrDr 76, -82, -84*

Teasdale, Sara 1884-1933 *AmAu&B, AmWomPl, AmWomWr, AnCL, AnMV 1926, ArtclWW 2, Benet 87, BenetAL 91, BiDSA, BioAmW, BioIn 4, -5, -8, -11, -12, -14, -15, -16, BlmGWL, BkCL, CasWL, ChhPo, -S1, -S2, CnDAL, ConAmA, ConAmL, ConAu 104, DcLB 45, DcLEL, DcNAA, EvLB, FemiCLE, GayLL, InWom SUP, LongCTC, OxCAmL 65, -83, RAdv 1, REn, REnAL, RfGAmL 87, SixAP, SmATA 32, Str&VC, TwCA, -SUP, TwCLC 4, TwCWr, WebAB 74, -79, WhAm 1, -7, WhNAA, WomWWA 14, WorAlBi, WorAl*

Tebbel, John 1912- *AmAu&B, BioIn 3, -13, ConAu 85, -29NR, CurBio 53, DrAS 74E, IntAu&W 89, -91, SmATA 26, WhoAm 74, -76, -78, -80, -82, -84, -86, -88, -90, -92, -94, WhoUSWr 88, WhoWrEP 89, -92*

Techter, David 1932- *BiDPara, EncO&P 1, -2, -3*

Tee-Van, Helen Damrosch 1893-1976 *BioIn 11, -13, ConAu 49, -65, DcWomA, IlsBYP, SmATA 10, -27N, WhAmArt 85, WhoAmA 73, -78N, -80N, -82N, -86N, -89N, -91N*
Pseud./variant:
Damrosch, Helen Therese

Tegner, Bruce 1928- *ConAu 61, -8NR*

Tegner, Bruce 1928-1985 *BioIn 17, SmATA 62*

Teitelbaum, Michael 1953- *BioIn 16, ConAu 121, SmATA 59*
Pseud./variant:
Michaels, Joanne Louise
Michaels, Neal
Neal, Michael
Watson, B S

Tejima 1931- *ChlLR 20*

Tejima, Keizaburo *AuBYP 3*

Teleki, Geza 1943- *BioIn 15, ConAu 3NR, -19NR, SmATA 45*

Telemaque, Eleanor Wong *DrAPF 87, -89, -91, -93*

Telemaque, Eleanor Wong 1933- *WhoWrEP 92*

Telemaque, Eleanor Wong 1934- *BioIn 15, ConAu 104, DrAPF 83, -85, SmATA 43*

Telescope, Tom *MajAI, SmATA X*
Main entry: Newbery, John

Teltsch, Kathleen *AuBYP 2S, -3, WhoAm 76, -78*

Temkin, Sara Anne Schlossberg 1913- *AuBYP 2, -3, BiDrLUS 70, BioIn 8, -13, ConAu 1R, ForWC 70, SmATA 26, WhoLibI 82, WhoLibS 66*

Temko, Florence *AuBYP 3, ConAu 37NR, IntAu&W 86*

Temko, Florence 1927- *AuBYP 2S, BioIn 11, ConAu 49, -1NR, -17NR, IntAu&W 77, -82, SmATA 13*

Tempest, Margaret Mary 1892-1982 *Au&Wr 71, BioIn 14, ChhPo, ConAu 108, DcBrAr 1, DcWomA, SmATA 33N, Who 74, -83N*
Pseud./variant:
Lady Mears

Tempest, Teresa *AuBYP 2*
Main entry: Kent, Louise

Tempest, Theresa *AuBYP 3*

Templar, Maurice *ConAu X, SmATA X*
Main entry: Groom, Arthur William

Temple, Arthur
Main entry: Northcott, Cecil

Temple, Herbert 1919- *AfroAA, BioIn 15, InB&W 80, SmATA 45, WhoBlA 75, -77, -80, -85, -88, -90, -92, -94*

Temple, Nigel Longdale 1926- *ChhPo S2, ConAu 29R, WrDr 76, -80*

Temple, Paul *ConAu X, IntAu&W 91X, SmATA X, TwCCr&M 85, -91*
Main entry: McConnell, James Douglas R

Tenenbaum, Samuel 1902- *AmMWSc 73S*

Tenggren, Gustaf Adolf 1896-1970 *AmPB, BioIn 1, -4, -5, -6, -8, IlsBYP, IlsCB 1744, -1946, -1967, MorJA, SmATA 18, -26N, WhAm 6, WhAmArt 85*

Tennant, Kylie 1912- *AuWomWr, AuBYP 2S, -3, Au&Wr 71, Benet 87, BioIn 1, -6, -10, -15, BlueB 76, CamGLE, CasWL, ConAu X, ConNov 72, -76, -82, -86, DcLEL, EvLB, IntAu&W 77, -82, -86, -89, -91, IntvTCA 2, MajTwCW, OxCAusL, REn, SingR 1, SmATA 6, -X, TwCWr, WhoWor 74,*

WorAu 1950, WrDr 76, -80, -82, -84, -86, -88

Tennant, Kylie 1912-1988 *AnObit 1988, AuLitCr, BioIn 16, -17, BlmGWL, DcChlFi, FemiCLE, RfGEnL 91*
Main entry: Rodd, Kathleen Tennant
Rodd, Kylie Tennant

Tennant, Veronica 1946- *BiDD, BioIn 9, -11, -14, -16, CanWW 80, -81, -83, ConAu 103, SmATA 36, WhoAm 80, -82, -84*

Tennant, Veronica 1947- *CanWW 89, WhoAm 86, -88, -92, -94, WhoEnt 92*

Tenneshaw, S M *MajAI*

Tenney, Sanborn, Mrs 1836- *Alli, CarSB*

Tenniel, John 1820-1914 *BioIn 16, -17, MajAI, SmATA 74, StaCVF*

Tenniel, John, Sir 1820-1914 *Alli, ArtsNiC, Benet 87, BioIn 1, -2, -3, -8, -9, -11, -12, -13, CamGLE, CelCen, ChhPo, -S1, -S2, ChlLR 18, ClaDrA, ConAu 111, DcBiPP, DcBrBI, DcNaB 1912, DcVicP 2, IlsBYP, JBA 34, -51, LongCTC, NewC, OxCArt, OxCChiL, OxCEng 85, OxDcArt, REn, SmATA 27, Str&VC, WhDW, WhoChL, WorECar*

Tennissen, Anthony Cornelius *AmMWSc 89*

Tennissen, Anthony Cornelius 1920- *AmMWSc 86*

Tennissen, Anthony Cornelius 1920-1982 *AmMWSc 73P, -76P, -82, ConAu 114*

Tennyson, Alfred 1809-1892 *Alli, -SUP, AnCL, AtlBL, AuBYP 2, -3, Benet 87, BbD, BiD&SB, BioIn 1, -2, -3, -4, -5, -6, -7, -8, -9, -10, -11, -12, -13, -16, -17, BlmGEL, BritAu 19, BritWr 4, CasWL, CelCen, Chambr 3, ChhPo, -S1, -S2, CnE&AP, CnThe, CrtT 3, CyWA 58, DcBiPP, DcEnA, -A, DcEnL, DcEuL, DcLB 32, DcLEL, DcNaB, Dis&D, EncPaPR 91, EvLB, IlEncMy, LongCEL, LuthC 75, MagSWL, McGEWB, McGEWD 72, MouLC 4, NewC, NinCLC 30, NotNAT B, OxCEng 67, -85, OxCMus, OxCThe 67, -83, PenC ENG, PenEncH, PoLE, RAdv 1, RComWL, REn, REnWD, RfGEnL 91, Str&VC, WebE&AL, WhDW, WorAlBi, WorAl, WorLitC*

Tennyson, Alfred, Lord 1809-1892 *CamGEL, CamGWoT, CnDBLB 4*

Tenpas, Margaret 1923- *ConAu 85*

Tensen, Ruth Marjorie *AuBYP 3, WrDr 86, -88, -90*

Tensen, Ruth Marjorie 1905- *AuBYP 2, BioIn 7, ConAu 5R, ForWC 70, WrDr 76, -80, -82, -84*

Terban, Marvin *AuBYP 3, SmATA 45*

Terban, Marvin 1940- *SmATA 54*

Ter Haar, Jaap 1922- *ConAu 37R, SmATA 6*
Pseud./variant:
Haar, Jaap Ter

Terhune, Albert Payson 1872-1942 *AmAu&B, AmLY, AuBYP 2, -3, BenetAL 91, BiD&SB, BioIn 2, -5, -7, -8, -9, -11, -12, ChhPo, CnDAL, ConAu 111, -136, CurBio 42, DcAmAu, DcLB 9, DcNAA, EvLB, JBA 34, MajAI, ObitOF 79, OxCAmL 65, -83, OxCChiL, REnAL, SmATA 15, TwCA, -SUP, TwCChW 83, -89, WebAB 74, -79, WhAm 2, WhNAA, WorAlBi, WorAl*

Terhune, Mary Virginia 1830?-1922 *Alli, -SUP, AmAu, AmAu&B, AmWomWr, BenetAL 91, BbD, BiDSA, BiD&SB, BioIn 4, -12, CarSB, ChhPo, CnDAL, CyAL, DcAmAu, DcNAA, InWom SUP, LivgFWS, OxCAmL 65, -83, REnAL, WhAm 1, WomWWA 14, WomNov*
Pseud./variant:
Harland, Marion

Terkel, Studs *IntAu&W 91, MajTwCW, NewYTBS 92, WrDr 86, -88, -90, -92*

Terkel, Studs 1912- *AmAu&B, AuNews 1, BenetAL 91, BioIn 7, -10, -11, -14, -16, -17, CelR 90, ConAu 57, -X, ConLC 38, CurBio 74, EncAJ, OxCAmL 83, WhoAm 74, -90, -92, -94, WhoMW 74, -76, -92, -93, WorAlBi, WrDr 76, -82, -84*

Terkel, Studs Louis 1912- *WrDr 94*

Terkel, Susan N 1948- *SmATA 59*

Terkel, Susan Neiburg 1948- *BioIn 16, ConAu 38NR, IntAu&W 89, WhoAm 92, -94*

Terlouw, Jan 1931- *BioIn 14, ConAu 108, OxCChiL, ScF&FL 92, SmATA 30, WhoEIO 82, WhoWor 82*

Terlouw, Jan-Cornelis 1931- *IntWW 89*

Terraine, John Alfred 1921- *Au&Wr 71, ConAu 5R, IntAu&W 89, -91, IntWW 79, -80, -81, -82, -83, -89, -91, Who 74, -82, -83, -85, -88, -90, -92, WhoWor 84, -87, -89, -91, -93, WrDr 76, -80, -82, -84, -86, -88, -90, -92, -94*

Terrell, John Upton d1988 *NewYTBS 88*

Terrell, John Upton 1900- *AmAu&B, AmNov, AuBYP 2, -3, BioIn 2, -8, ConAu 29R, OxCCan SUP, WhoWest 74*

Terrell, John Upton 1900-1988 *BioIn 16, -17, ConAu 127, SmATA 60*

Terres, John Kenneth 1905- *AmAu&B, AmMWSc 73P, -76P, Au&Wr 71, BioIn 5, ConAu 5R, -5NR, WhoAm 74, -76, -78, -80, -82, -84, WhoWor 78*

Terrien, Samuel 1911- *DrAS 74P, -78P, -82P, WhoAm 74*

Terris, Susan *DrAPF 87, -89, -91, -93*

Terris, Susan 1937- *AuBYP 2S, BioIn 9, ConAu 29R, -12NR, DrAPF 83, -85, FifBJA, IntAu&W 77, -82, -89, -91, SmATA 3, -77, WhoAmW 75, WhoWrEP 89, -92, WrDr 76, -80, -82, -84, -86, -88, -90, -92, -94*

Terry, Luther L 1911-1985 *BioIn 14, -15, NewYTBS 85*

Terry, Luther Leonidas 1911-1985 *AmMWSc 73P, -76P, -82, BiDrACP 79, BiDrAPH 79, BioIn 5, -6, -11, BlueB 76, ConAu 115, -P-2, CurBio 61, -85N, InSci, IntWW 74, -75, -76, -77, -78, -79, -80, -81, -82, -83, NewYTBS 85, SmATA 11, -42N, WhAm 8, WhoAm 74, -76, -78, -80, -82, -84, WhoE 85, WhoWor 82*

Terry, Walter d1991 *Who 92N*

Terry, Walter 1913-1982 *AmAu&B, AnObit 1982, AuBYP 2, -3, BioIn 8, -12, -13, ConAu 21R, -107, -10NR, MedPD, NewYTBS 82, SmATA 14, WhAm 8, WhoAm 74, -76, -78, -80, -82*

Terzian, James P 1915- *AuBYP 2S, -3, BioIn 12, ConAu 13R, SmATA 14*

Tessendorf, K C *AuBYP 3*

Tessendorf, Kenneth Charles 1925- *ConAu 142, SmATA 75*

Tessler, Stephanie Gordon 1940- *BioIn 17, ConAu 124, SmATA 64*
Pseud./variant:
Gordon, Jeffie Ross

Tester, Sylvia Root 1939- *BioIn 15, -17, ConAu 8NR, SmATA 37, -64*

Tether, Graham 1950- *ConAu 57, -6NR, SmATA 36, -46*

Tetlow, George 1934- *SingR 2*

Teuffel, Blanche Willis Von 1847-1898 *BiD&SB, CarSB, DcAmAu, DcNAA, WomNov*

Thacher, Alida McKay 1951- *ConAu 69, -11NR*

Thacher, Edith *AmPB*
Main entry: Hurd, Edith Thacher

Thacher, Mary McGrath 1933- *BioIn 11, SmATA 9*

Thackeray, William Makepeace 1811-1863 *Alli, ArtsNiC, AtlBL, Benet 87, BbD, BiD&SB, BioIn 1, -2, -3, -4, -5, -6, -7, -8, -9, -10, -11, -12, -13, -14, -15, -16, BlmGEL, BritAu 19, BritWr 5, CamGEL, CamGLE, CarSB, CasWL, CelCen, Chambr 3, ChhPo, -S1, -S2, CnDBLB 4, CrtT 3, CyWA 58, DcBiA, DcBiPP, DcBrBI, DcEnA, -A, DcEnL, DcEuL, DcInB, DcLB 21, DcLEL, DcNaB, Dis&D, EncO&P 2, -3, EncPaPR 91, EvLB, FamSYP, HsB&A, LongCEL, MagSWL, McGEWB, MouLC 3, NewC, NinCLC 5, -14, -22, Novels, OxCAmL 65, -83, OxCChiL, OxCEng 67, -85, PenC ENG, RAdv 1, RComWL, REn, RfGEnL 91, ScF&FL 92, SmATA 23, StaCVF, TelT, WebE&AL, WhDW, WhoChL, WorAlBi, WorAl, WorLitC*
Pseud./variant:
Pendennis, Arthur, Esq.
Solomons, Ikey, Jr., Esq
Titmarsh, Michael Angelo

Thackray, Derek Vincent 1926- *ConAu 103, WrDr 76, -80, -82, -84, -86, -88, -90*

Thaler, Michael C 1936- *ConAu 124, SmATA 47, -56*
Pseud./variant:
Thaler, Mike

Thaler, Mike *AuBYP 3*
Main entry: Thaler, Michael C

Thaler, Shmuel 1958- *SmATA 72*

Thalmann, Rita Renee Line 1926- *ConAu 53, -4NR, -19NR*

Thamer, Katie *BioIn 15, SmATA 42, -76*
Main entry: Treherne, Katie Thamer

Thames, C H *AuBYP 2, -3, ConAu X, IntAu&W 91X, WrDr 82, -84, -86, -88, -90, -92*
Main entry: Lesser, Milton

Thames, C H 1928- *WrDr 94*

Thames, Christopher H *EncSF 93*

Thane, Adele 1904- *AuBYP 2S, -3, BiE&WWA, ConAu 25R*

Thane, Elswyth 1900- *AmAu&B, AmNov, AmWomWr, Au&Wr 71, BenetAL 91, BioIn 2, -11, -14, ConAu 5R, ForWC 70, InWom SUP,*

REnAL, SmATA 32, TwCRHW 90, WhoAm 74, –78, WhoAmW 74, WhoE 74, WrDr 84

Thane, Elswyth 1900-1984 *ScF&FL 92*

Thanet, Octave *Alli SUP, AmAu, AmAu&B, AmLY X, BenetAL 91, BiD&SB, BioIn 6, –7, BlmGWL, DcAmAu, DcNAA, LongCTC, OxCAmL 65, –83, REn, WomNov*
Main entry: French, Alice

Thanet, Octave 1850-1934 *BioAmW, InWom SUP*

Tharp, Louise Hall 1898- *AmAu&B, AuBYP 2, –3, Au&Wr 71, BioIn 2, –3, –4, –6, –8, –9, –10, ChhPo, ConAu 1R, –33NR, CurBio 55, ForWC 70, MorJA, RAdv 1, SmATA 3, WhoAm 74, WorAu 1950*

Thatcher, Alice Dora 1912- *WrDr 86, –88, –90*

Thatcher, Alice Dora Fickling 1912- *Au&Wr 71, ConAu 13R, WrDr 76, –80, –82, –84*

Thatcher, Joan Claire 1934- *WhoRel 75, –77, WhoWest 74, –76, –78*

Thaxter, Celia L 1835-1894 *BioAmW*

Thaxter, Celia Laighton 1835?-1894 *Alli SUP, AmAu, AmAu&B, AmWomWr, ArtclWW 2, BibAL 8, BbD, BiD&SB, BioIn 1, –2, –6, –14, –15, –16, –17, BlmGWL, Chambr 3, ChhPo, –S2, ChrP, CyAL, DcAmAu, DcLEL, DcNAA, InWom SUP, OxCAmL 65, REnAL, WhAm HS*

Thayer, Emma 1842-1908 *ArtsAmW 3, BiD&SB, CarSB, DcAmAu, DcNAA, DcWomA, WhAm 1, WhAmArt 85, WomNov*

Thayer, Ernest Lawrence 1863-1940 *AuBYP 2, –3, BioIn 1, –6, –8, –17, ChhPo, –S1, ConAu 119, CurBio 40, EvLB, SmATA 60, WhAm 1*
Pseud./variant:
Phin

Thayer, Jane *AuBYP 2, –3, BioIn 6, –7, –9, ConAu X, MorJA, SmATA 3, WhoAm 84, –86, –88, WhoAmW 89*
Main entry: Woolley, Catherine

Thayer, Jane 1904- *WhoAm 90, –92, –94, WhoAmW 91, –93, WhoWor 93*

Thayer, Marjorie *BioIn 4, ConAu 116, SmATA 37*

Thayer, Marjorie 1908-1992 *SmATA 74*

Thayer, Peter *ConAu X, SmATA X, ThrBJA*
Main entry: Ames, Rose Wyler

Thayer, William Makepeace 1820-1898 *Alli, –SUP, AmAu&B, BbD, BiD&SB, CarSB, DcAmAu, DcNAA, HarEnUS, WhAm HS*

Thayne, Emma Lou *DrAPF 87*

Thayne, Emma Lou 1924- *ConAu 65, DrAPF 83, –85*

Thayne, Emma Lou W *DrAPF 89, –91, –93*

Thayne, Emma Lou Warner 1924- *WhoUSWr 88, WhoWrEP 89, –92*

Thayne, Mirla Greenwood 1907- *ConAu 21R*

Theiner, George *BioIn 16*

Theiner, George d1988 *NewYTBS 88*

Theiner, George 1927- *ConAu 29R*

Theiner, George 1927-1988 *ConAu 27NR*

Theiss, Lewis Edwin *AuBYP 3*

Theiss, Lewis Edwin 1878-1963 *AmAu&B, AuBYP 2, BioIn 6, –8, WhAm 4, WhJnl, WhNAA*

Thelwell, Norman 1923- *BioIn 12, –14, –15, ConAu 5R, –4NR, DcLEL 1940, IntAu&W 89, –91, SmATA 14, TwCPaSc, Who 74, –82, –83, –85, –88, –90, –92, WhoArt 80, –82, –84*

Themerson, Stefan 1910- *Au&Wr 71, ConAu 65, –9NR, –28NR, IntAu&W 77, –86, –89, WrDr 76, –80, –82, –84, –86, –88*

Themerson, Stefan 1910-1988 *AnObit 1988, BioIn 17, ConAu 126, EncSF 93, ScF&FL 92, SmATA 65*

Theriault, Yves *BioIn 14*

Theriault, Yves d1983 *WhoCanL 92*

Theriault, Yves 1915-1983 *BenetAL 91, BioIn 10, –15, –17, CaW, CanWW 70, –79, –80, –81, –83, CanWr, CasWL, ConAu 102, ConLC 79, CreCan 1, DcLB 88, Novels, OxCCan, –SUP, OxCCanL, OxCCanT, PenC ENG, Profile 1, REnAL, WhoCanL 85, –87*

Theroux, Alexander Louis *DrAPF 87, –89 –91, –93*

Theroux, Alexander Louis 1939- *BiDConC, BioIn 11, ConAu 85, ConLC 2, DrAF 76, DrAPF 83, –85*

Theroux, Paul *DrAPF 87, –89, –91, IntvTCA 2, LiExTwC*

Theroux, Paul 1941- *Benet 87, BenetAL 91, BestSel 89-4, BiDConC, BioIn 11, –12, –13, CamGLE, ConAu 20NR, ConLC 15, –28, –46, ConNov 82, –86, –91, CyWA 89, DrAPF 83, –85, EncWB, IntAu&W 82, –89, –91, MajTwCW, ModAL S2, Novels, OxCAmL 83, ScF&FL 92, SmATA 44, Who 82, –83, –85, WhoAm 80, –82, –84, WorAlBi, WorAl, WrDr 82, –84, –86, –88, –90, –92, –94*

Theroux, Paul Edward 1941- *EncSF 93*

Thesman, Jean *ScF&FL 92, SmATA 74*

The Tjong Khing 1933- *SmATA 76*

Thieda, Shirley Ann 1943- *BioIn 11, ConAu 69, SmATA 13*

Thiele, Colin 1920- *Au&Wr 71, BioIn 12, –15, ChILR 27, ConAu 29R, –12NR, –28NR, ConLC 17, ConPo 70, –75, DcChlFi, FifBJA, OxCAusL, OxCChiL, SingR 1, SmATA 14, –2AS, TwCChW 78, –83, –89, WrDr 76, –80, –82, –84, –86, –88, –90, –92*

Thiele, Colin Milton 1920- *MajAI, SmATA 72, TwCYAW, WrDr 94*

Thiele, Margaret Rossiter 1901- *ConAu 21R, WrDr 76, –80, –82, –84*

Thiry, Joan 1926- *BioIn 15, ConAu 121, SmATA 45*

Thistle, Mel 1914- *ConAu 53, WrDr 76, –80, –82, –84*
Pseud./variant:
Bohr, Theophilus

Thistle, Melville William 1914- *IntAu&W 86*

Thistlethwaite, Miles 1945- *BioIn 11, SmATA 12*

Thoburn, Tina *AuBYP 2S, –3*

Thoby-Marcelin, Philippe 1904-1975 *BioIn 4, –10, BlkWr 1, CasWL, ConAu 61, –125, DcAfL, DcCLAA, EncWL 2, ModBlW, ModFrL, SelBAAf, TwCA SUP*

Thollander, Earl Gustave 1922- *BioIn 8, –13, ConAu 101, –18NR, IlsBYP, IlsCB 1957, SmATA 22, WhoAmA 78, –80, –82, –84*

Thomas, Allison
Main entry: Fleischer, Leonore

Thomas, Andrea *AuBYP 3, ConAu X, SmATA X*
Main entry: Hill, Margaret

Thomas, Annie *Alli, –SUP, CelCen, DcEnL, HsB&A, WomNov*

Thomas, Annie 1838-1918 *FemiCLE*

Thomas, Arline d1989 *NewYTBS 89*

Thomas, Arline 1913- *ConAu 49, NewYTBE 71*

Thomas, Arline 1913-1989 *BioIn 16, ConAu 128*

Thomas, Art 1952- *BioIn 15, –16, ConAu 105, SmATA 38, –48*

Thomas, Benjamin Platt 1902-1956 *AuBYP 2, –3, BioIn 3, –4, –7, –8, ObitOF 79*

Thomas, Beth Eileen Wood 1916- *WhoAm 80, –82, –84, –86, –88, –90, –92, –94, WhoAmW 77, –87, –89, –91*

Thomas, Bill 1934- *ConAu 61, –8NR, IntAu&W 82, WhoMW 78, –80*

Thomas, David St John 1929- *Au&Wr 71, ConAu 112, –30NR, IntAu&W 82, –86, WhoAm 80, –82, –84, –86, –88, WrDr 76, –82, –84, –86, –88, –90, –92, –94*

Thomas, David Stanley 1946- *WhoWest 89*

Thomas, Dawn C *BlkAuIl, –92*

Thomas, Dylan *IntvTCA 2*

Thomas, Dylan 1914-1953 *AnCL, AtlBL, Benet 87, BioIn 1, –2, –3, –4, –5, –6, –7, –8, –9, –10, –11, –12, –13, –14, –15, –16, –17, BritWr S1, CamGEL, CamGLE, CamGWoT, CasWL, ChhPo, –S1, –S2, CnDBLB 7, CnE&AP, CnMD, CnMWL, ConAu 104, –120, ConPo 75, CyWA 58, DcLB 13, –20, –139, DcLEL, EncWL, –2, EncWT, EngPo, EvLB, HalFC 84, –88, LongCTC, MagSWL, MajTwCW, McGEWD 72, –84, ModBrL, –S1, –S2, ModWD, NewC, NotNAT B, Novels, ObitOF 79, ObitT 1951, OxCEng 67, OxCLiW 86, PenC ENG, PlP&P, PoeCrit 2, RAdv 1, –13-1, RComWL, REn, RfGEnL 91, ShSCr 3, SmATA 60, TwCA, –SUP, TwCLC 1, –8, –45, TwCWr, WebE&AL, WhDW, WhAm 4, –HSA, WhoTwCL, WorAlBi, WorAl, WorLitC*

Thomas, Dylan Marlais 1914-1953 *RfGShF*

Thomas, Edward 1878-1917 *AnCL, AtlBL, Benet 87, BioIn 3, –4, –5, –6, –8, –9, –10, –11, –12, –13, –14, –15, –16, –17, CamGEL, CamGLE, ChhPo, –S1, –S2, CnE&AP, CnMWL, ConAu 106, DcLB 19, –98, DcLEL, EncWL 2, LongCTC, ModBrL, –S1, –S2, NewC, OxCEng 67, –85, OxCLiW 86, PenC ENG, REn, RfGEnL 91, TwCA, –SUP, TwCLC 10, TwCWr, WebE&AL, WhDW, WhoTwCL*

Thomas, Estelle Webb 1899- *ArizL, ConAu 21R, IntAu&W 77, SmATA 26, WrDr 76, –80, –82, –84*

Thomas, Glen *IlsBYP*

Thomas, H C *AuBYP 2, –3, ConAu X, SmATA X*
Main entry: Keating, Lawrence Alfred

Thomas, Henry 1886-1970 *BioIn 9, ConAu 29R, NewYTBE 70, WhNAA*

Thomas, Ianthe 1951- *BioIn 15, –16, BlkAuII, –92, ChlLR 8, SmATA 42*

Thomas, Isaiah 1749-1831 *BenetAL 91, BiDAmJo, DcAmBC, NewAmDM, NewGrDA 86*

Thomas, Isaiah 1750-1831 *AmWrBE, BioIn 1, –2, –3, –7, –10, –15, –16, –17, DcLB 43, –73, EncAJ, HarEnUS, JrnUS, OxCAmH, OxCAmL 83, OxCChiL, WebAB 79*

Thomas, J F *ConAu X, SmATA 8*
Main entry: Fleming, Thomas James

Thomas, Jane Resh 1936- *AuBYP 3, BioIn 15, ConAu 106, –24NR, ScF&FL 92, SmATA 38*

Thomas, Joan Gale *AuBYP 2S, –3, ConAu X, IntAu&W 77X, –82X, SmATA 7, TwCChW 83, –89, WrDr 80, –82, –84, –86, –88*
Main entry: Robinson, Joan G

Thomas, John 1890- *ConAu 49, IntAu&W 77*

Thomas, Joyce Carol *DrAPF 87, –89, –91, –93*

Thomas, Joyce Carol 1938- *BioIn 13, BlkAWP, BlkAuII, –92, BlkWr 1, –2, ChlLR 19, ConAu 113, –116, ConBlAP 88, ConLC 35, DcLB 33, DrAPF 83, –85, FemiCLE, MajAI, MajTwCW, ScF&FL 92, SmATA 40, –7AS, TwCYAW, WhoAm 88, WhoAmW 87, –89, WhoBlA 75, –77, –80, –85, –88, –90, –92, WhoUSWr 88, WhoWrEP 89, –92*

Thomas, Kathleen *AuBYP 3*

Thomas, Lowell Jackson 1892- *AmAu&B, AuBYP 2, AuNews 1, –2, Au&Wr 71, BioIn 1, –2, –3, –4, –5, –7, –8, –10, –11, BioNews 74, CelR, ConAu 45, CurBio 40, –52, FilmgC, IntMPA 75, –77, JBA 34, NewYTBE 70, OhA&B, OxCCan, REnAL, TwCA, –SUP, WebAB 74, –79, WhNAA, Who 74, WhoAm 74, WhoHol A, WorAl, WrDr 80*

Thomas, Lowell Jackson 1892-1981 *AuBYP 3, BiDAmJo*

Thomas, Lowell Jackson, Jr. 1923- *AmAu&B, AuBYP 2, –3, BioIn 8, –10, –11, ConAu 85, SmATA 15, WhoAm 74, –76, –78, WhoAmP 73, –75, –77, WhoGov 77, –75, WhoHol A, WhoWest 74, –76, –78*

Thomas, May *SingR 1*

Thomas, Patricia 1934- *AuBYP 3*

Thomas, Patricia J 1934- *AuBYP 2S, ConAu 37R, SmATA 51*

Thomas, Ronald Stuart 1913- *BioIn 6, –10, –12, –14, –15, –17, BlueB 76, CasWL, ChhPo, –S1, –S2, CnE&AP, ConLC 6, –13, ConPo 70, –75, IntAu&W 89, –91, IntWW 74, –79, –80, –81, –82, –83, –89, –91, LongCTC, ModBrL, –S1, NewC, OxCLiW 86, PenC ENG, TwCWr, WebE&AL, Who 74, –82, –83, –85, –88, –92, WhoTwCL, WhoWor 74, WorAu 1950, WrDr 76, –80*

Thomas, Ronald Stuart 1915- *EngPo*

Thomas, Ronald Stuart, Rev 1913- *Who 90*

Thomas, Ruth *AuBYP 2, –3, BioIn 8, ChlFicS*

Thomas, Vernon 1934- *SmATA 56*

Thomas, Victoria *ConAu 127, SmATA X, WrDr 86, –88, –90, –92*
Main entry: DeWeese, Thomas Eugene

Thomas, Victoria 1934- *WrDr 94*

Thomas, W Jenkyn *CarSB*

Thomas, William 1906- *ConAu 73*

Thompson, Blanche Jennings 1887- *AmWomPl, AuBYP 2S, –3, BioIn 1, BkC 1, BkP, CathA 1930, ChhPo, –S1, ConAu 5R*

Thompson, Brenda 1935- *ConAu 106, SmATA 34, Who 74, –82, –83, –85, –88, –90, WrDr 76, –80, –82, –84, –86, –88, –90*

Thompson, Charles K *SingR 1*

Thompson, China *ConAu X, –43NR, TwCCr&M 85, –91, WrDr 82, –84, –86, –88*
Main entry: Lewis, Mary Christianna Milne

Thompson, China 1907-1988 *SmATA X*

Thompson, Christine Pullein *SmATA 3*
Main entry: Popescu, Christine

Thompson, Corrie 1887- *ConAu 61*

Thompson, Daniel Pierce 1795-1868 *Alli, AmAu, AmAu&B, BenetAL 91, BibAL 8, BioIn 5, CarSB, CnDAL, CyAL, CyWA 58 DcAmAu, DcBiA, DcLEL, DcNAA, HarEnUS, OxCAmL 65, –83, OxCChiL, REn, REnAL, WhAm HS*

Thompson, D'Arcy Wentworth 1829-1902 *Alli, ChhPo, –S1, DcNaB S2, TelT*

Thompson, David Hiram 1897- *WhNAA*

Thompson, David Hugh 1941- *BioIn 12, SmATA 17*

Thompson, Diana Pullein *SmATA 3*
Main entry: Farr, Diana Pullein-Thompson

Thompson, Donnis 1928- *AuBYP 3*

Thompson, Donnis Stark 1928- *AuBYP 2S, ConAu 21R*

Thompson, Eileen
Main entry: Panowski, Eileen Thompson

Thompson, Eileen 1920- *AuBYP 2, -3, BioIn 8, ConAu X, ForWC 70, WrDr 76, -80, -82, -84*

Thompson, Eileen Panowski 1920- *DcAmChF 1960*

Thompson, Frances C 1906- *ConAu P-1*

Thompson, George S *ScF&FL 92*

Thompson, George Selden d1989 *NewYTBS 89*

Thompson, George Selden 1929- *AuBYP 2, BioIn 8, -9, -10, ConAu 5R, -21NR, SmATA 4, WrDr 80, -82, -84*
Pseud./variant:
Selden, George

Thompson, George Selden 1929-1989 *AuBYP 3, ConAu 130, -37NR, MajAI, SmATA 63, -73*

Thompson, Gordon Vallins Elliot 1920- *Au&Wr 71*

Thompson, Harlan 1894-1987 *BioIn 16, ConAu 123, ScF&FL 92, SmATA 53N*

Thompson, Harlan H 1894- *AuBYP 3*

Thompson, Harlan Howard 1894- *AuBYP 2, BioIn 7, -11, ConAu P-1, IntAu&W 77, SmATA 10, Str&VC, WhoWest 78, -80, -82*
Pseud./variant:
Holt, Stephen

Thompson, Harwood 1894- *ConAu 65*

Thompson, Hilary 1943- *ConAu 127, SmATA 49, -56*

Thompson, Hildegard 1901- *AuBYP 3*

Thompson, Hildegard Steerstedter 1901- *AuBYP 2, BioIn 8, ConAu 17R, IndAu 1917, IntAu&W 77, WrDr 76, -80*

Thompson, Josephine P *SmATA 3*
Main entry: Pullein-Thompson, Josephine M W

Thompson, Joyce Blaikie 1920- *Au&Wr 71, WrDr 76, -80*

Thompson, Julian F 1927- *Au&Arts 9, BioIn 15, -16, ChlLR 24, ConAu 111, -30NR, ScF&FL 92, SmATA 40, -55, -13AS*

Thompson, Julian Francis 1927- *IntAu&W 86, MajAI*

Thompson, Kay *AuBYP 3*

Thompson, Kay 1911?- *InWom SUP*

Thompson, Kay 1912- *AmAu&B, ASCAP 66, BioIn 1, -3, -4, -5, -8, -9, -12, CelR, ChhPo, ChlLR 22, CmpEPM, ConAu 85, CurBio 59, FourBJA, MajAI, MotPP, SmATA 16, WhoAm 74, -76, WhoAmW 74, WhoHol A, WorAl*

Thompson, Mary 1886- *AuBYP 3*

Thompson, Mary Wolfe 1886- *AmAu&B, AuBYP 2, BioIn 2, -8, CurBio 50, WhAm 7*

Thompson, Maurice 1844-1901 *AmAu, AmAu&B, BenetAL 91, BbD, BiDSA, BiD&SB, BioIn 2, -3, -7, -8, CarSB, ChhPo, -S1, CnDAL, DcAmAu, DcLB 71, -74, DcLEL, DcNAA, InSci, OxCAmL 65, -83, REnAL, WhAm 1*

Thompson, Mozelle 1927-1970 *AfroAA, IlsBYP, InB&W 80*

Thompson, N D 1927- *WrDr 76, -80, -82*

Thompson, Paul Devries 1939- *AmMWSc 73P, -82, -86, -89, -92, WhoFI 94*

Thompson, Philip Duncan *AmMWSc 89*

Thompson, Philip Duncan 1922- *AmMWSc 73P, -76P, -82, -86, IndAu 1917, WhoAm 74, -76, -78, WhoWor 78*

Thompson, Ralph *BioIn 5, IlsBYP, IlsCB 1946*

Thompson, Ruth Plumly 1891?-1976 *AmAu&B, BioIn 8, ChhPo, ConAu 113, -134, DcLB 22, SmATA 66, WhAm 7, WhoAm 74, -76, WhoAmW 74, WhoChL*
Pseud./variant:
Baum, L Frank

Thompson, Ruth Plumly 1893-1976 *BioIn 14, -17*

Thompson, Stephen *Alli, WhoBlA 94*

Thompson, Stith 1885-1976 *AmAu&B, AnCL, Au&Wr 71, BioIn 10, -11, -12, -16, ConAu 5R, -61, -5NR, FifIDA, IndAu 1917, OxCCan, SmATA 20N, -57, WhAm 6*

Thompson, Vivian L 1911- *IntAu&W 86, -89, -91, WrDr 86, -88, -90, -92, -94*

Thompson, Vivian Laubach 1911- *AuBYP 2, -3, BioIn 8, -9, ConAu 1R, -1NR, ForWC 70, IntAu&W 77, -82, SmATA 3, WhoAmW 74, -75, WrDr 76, -80, -82, -84*

Thompson, William E, Jr. 1923- *ConAu 13R*

Thoms, William John 1803-1885 *BioIn 11, CelCen, DcBiPP, DcNaB, OxCChiL, OxCEng 85*

Thomson, Arline K 1912- *BioIn 5, IlsBYP*

Thomson, Arthur, Sir 1861-1933 *InSci, LongCTC*

Thomson, Christine Campbell 1897- *BioIn 2, -15, PenEncH, WhoHr&F*

Thomson, Christine Campbell 1897-1985 *ScF&FL 92, ScFEYrs*

Thomson, David 1914- *Au&Wr 71, BioIn 10, -11, ConAu 107, IntAu&W 86, -91, SmATA 40, WrDr 76, -80, -82, -84, -86, -88*

Thomson, David 1914-1988 *BioIn 15, -16, ConAu 124, -24NR, SmATA 55N*

Thomson, Edward William 1849-1924 *AmAu&B, BiD&SB, BioIn 12, -17, CanWr, ChhPo, CreCan 2, DcAmAu, DcLB 92, DcLEL, DcNAA, OxCCan, OxCCanL, REnAL, TwCA*

Thomson, Hugh 1860-1920 *BioIn 14, ChhPo, -S1, -S2, DcBrAr 1, DcBrBI, DcIrB 88, DcNaB 1912, DcVicP 2*

Thomson, Joan *ConAu X, IntAu&W 77X*
Main entry: Charnock, Joan

Thomson, Karline 1912- *IlsCB 1946*

Thomson, Pat *AuBYP 3*

Thomson, Pat 1939- *SmATA 77*

Thomson, Peggy 1922- *ConAu 85, SixBJA, SmATA 31*

Thomson, Peter 1913- *AuBYP 2, -3, BioIn 8, ConAu 5R*

Thorburn, John
Main entry: Goldsmith, John Herman Thorburn

Thordarson, Bruce M *OxCCan SUP*

Thoreau, Henry David 1817-1862 *Alli, AmAu, AmAu&B, AmWr, AnCL, AtlBL, Benet 87, BenetAL 91, BibAL 8, BbD, BbtC, BiD&SB, BioIn 1, -2, -3, -4, -5, -6, -7, -8, -9, -10, -11, -12, -13, -14, -15, -16, -17, CamGEL, CamGLE, CamHAL, CasWL, CelCen, Chambr 3, ChhPo, CnDAL, CnE&AP, CrtT 3, CyAL, CyWA 58, DcAmAu, DcAmSR, DcEnA, DcLB 1, DcLEL, DcNAA, Dis&D, EncAB-H, EvLB, HarEnUS, IlEncMy, InSci, MagSAmL, McGEWB, MemAm, MouLC 3, NewGrDA 86, NinCLC 7, -21, OxCAmH, OxCAmL 65, -83, OxCCan, OxCEng 67, -85, PenC AM, RAdv 1, -13-1, RComAH, RComWL, REn, REnAL, RfGAmL 87, WebAB 74, -79, WebE&AL, WhAm HS, WorAlBi, WorAl, WorLitC, WrPh*

Thorn, Ismay *OxCChiL*

Thorn, John 1947- *ConAu 97, -17NR, SmATA 59*
Pseud./variant:
Jones, Sanford W

Thorndike, Susan 1944- *ConAu 41R*

Thorndyke, Helen Louise *ConAu 134, -P-2 MajAI, SmATA 1, -65, -67*
Main entry: Benson, Mildred Augustine Wirt
Stratemeyer, Edward L

Thorndyke, Helen Louise 1905- *WrDr 94*

Thorne, Diana 1894- *AmAu&B, BioIn 1, -5, DcWomA, IlsBYP, IlsCB 1744, -1946, WhAmArt 85*

Thorne, Ian *ConAu X, EncSF 93, ScF&FL 92, SmATA X*
Main entry: May, Julian

Thorne-Thomsen, Gudrun 1873-1956 *BioIn 2, -4, JBA 34, -51*

Thornhill, Jan 1955- *SmATA 77*

Thornton, Edward *WhoChL*

Thornton, Hall *MajAI*

Thornton, W B *ConAu 41NR, MajAI, SmATA X*
Main entry: Burgess, Thornton Waldo

Thornycroft, Rosalind 1891- *BioIn 1, -14, ChhPo, IlsCB 1744*

Thorpe, E G 1916- *BioIn 12, ConAu 9R, IntAu&W 77, SmATA 21, WrDr 80, -82, -84*

Thorpe, J K *SmATA X*
Main entry: Nathanson, Laura Walther

Thorsen, Harry D, Jr. 1913- *WhoAm 74, -76, WrDr 76, -80, -82, -84*

Thorvall, Kerstin 1925- *BioIn 11, ConAu 17R, -13NR, SmATA 13*

Thrasher, Crystal 1921- *BioIn 13, –16, ConAu 61, –8NR, SixBJA, SmATA 27*

Threadgall, Colin 1941- *SmATA 77*

Throckmorton, Peter d1990 *NewYTBS 90*

Throckmorton, Peter 1928- *AuBYP 2, –3, BioIn 8, –9, ConAu 17R*

Throckmorton, Peter 1928-1990 *AnObit 1990, BioIn 16, –17, ConAu 131*

Throneburg, James *AuBYP 2, –3, BioIn 8, ConAu 5R*

Thum, Gladys 1920- *BioIn 13, ConAu 41R, SmATA 26*

Thum, Gladys Ethel 1920- *IntAu&W 86*

Thum, Marcella *AuBYP 2S, –3, BioIn 9, –13, ConAu 9R, –6NR, –21NR, DcAmChF 1960, IntAu&W 77, –86, –89, –91, SmATA 3, –28, TwCRHW 90, WrDr 76, –80, –82, –84, –86, –88, –90, –92*

Thum, Marcella 1924- *WrDr 94*

Thundercloud, Katherine *ConAu X, SmATA X*
Main entry: Witt, Shirley Hill

Thurber, James *IntvTCA 2, OxCAmT 84*

Thurber, James 1894-1961 *AgeMat, AmAu&B, AmWr S1, AnCL, AtlBL, AuBYP 2, –3, Ballpl 90, Benet 87, BenetAL 91, BioIn 1, –2, –3, –4, –5, –6, –7, –8, –9, –10, –11, –12, –13, –14, –15, –16, –17, BkCL, CamGEL, CamGLE, CamHAL, CasWL, CnDAL, CnMWL, ConAmA, ConAu 73, –17NR, ConLC 5, –11, –25, CurBio 40, –60, –62, CyWA 58, –89, DcLB 4, –11, –22, –102, DcLEL, EncTwCJ, EncWL, EvLB, FilmgC, HalFC 84, –88, LongCTC, MajTwCW, McGEWD 72, –84, ModAL, MorJA, NotNAT A, –B, Novels, ObitOF 79, ObitT 1961, OhA&B, OxCAmL 65, –83, OxCChiL, OxCEng 67, PenC AM, RAdv 1, –13-1, REn, REnAL, RfGAmL 87, ShSCr 1, SmATA 13, SupFW, TwCA, –SUP, TwCChW 78, –83, –89, TwCWr, WebAB 74, WebE&AL, WhAm 4, WhoGrA 62, WhoTwCL, WorAlBi*

Thurber, James Grover 1894-1961 *ConAu 39NR, MajAI, RfGShF*

Thurman, Judith *DrAPF 87, –89, –91, –93*

Thurman, Judith 1946- *ArtclWW 2, BioIn 13, –14, –16, ConAu 49, –1NR, DrAP 75, DrAPF 83, –85, SixBJA, SmATA 33, WhoAmW 87, –89*

Thurman, Mark 1948- *ConAu 131, SmATA 63, WhoCanL 87, –92*

Thurman, Mark Gordon Ian 1948- *WrDr 94*

Thurman, Wallace 1902-1934 *AmAu&B, BenetAL 91, BioIn 10, –15, BlkAWP, BlkLC, BlkWr 1, ConAu 104, –124, CyWA 89, DcAmNB, DrBlPA 90, EarBlAP, InB&W 80, –85, ModBlW, NegAl 76, –83, –89, REnAL, SelBAAf, SelBAAu, TwCLC 6*

Thwaite, Ann 1932- *TwCChW 89, WrDr 86, –88, –90, –92*

Thwaite, Ann Barbara 1932- *Au&Wr 71, BioIn 12, ConAu 5R, IntAu&W 77, –82, OxCChiL, SmATA 14, TwCChW 78, –83, Who 92, WrDr 76, –80, –82, –84, –94*

Thwaite, Ann Barbara Harrop 1932- *ConAu 41NR*

Tibber, Robert *ConAu X, IntAu&W 82X, –86X, WrDr 76, –80, –82, –84, –86, –88, –90, –92*
Main entry: Friedman, Eve Rosemary Tibber

Tibber, Robert 1929- *WrDr 94*

Tibber, Rosemary *ConAu X, WrDr 80, –82, –84, –86, –88, –90, –92*
Main entry: Friedman, Eve Rosemary Tibber

Tibber, Rosemary 1929- *WrDr 94*

Tibbets, Albert B 1888- *AuBYP 2S, –3, ConAu 5R*

Tibble, Anne 1912-1980 *Au&Wr 71, BioIn 12, ChhPo S2, ConAu 9R, –102, –10NR, IntAu&W 77, –82, WrDr 80*

Tibble, John William 1901- *ChhPo*

Tibo, Gilles *BioIn 17*

Tibo, Gilles 1951- *ConAu 136, SmATA 67*

Tiburzi, Bonnie *BioIn 15*

Tiburzi, Bonnie 1948- *BioIn 17, ConAu 136, SmATA 65, WrDr 94*

Tice, George A 1938- *ConPhot 88*

Tice, George Andrew 1938- *BioIn 10, –13, ConAu 61, –12NR, ConPhot 82, ICPEnP A, MacBEP, PrintW 85, WhoAm 80, –82, –84, –86, –88, –90, –92, –94, WhoAmA 78, –80, –82, –84, –86, –89, –91, WhoE 93*

Ticheburn, Cheviot *SmATA X*
Main entry: Ainsworth, William Harrison

Tichenor, Tom 1923- *AuBYP 2S, –3, BiE&WWA, BioIn 12, ConAu 29R, NotNAT,*

SmATA 14, WrDr 76, –80, –82, –84, –86, –88, –90

Tichy, William 1924- *ConAu 107, SmATA 31*

Tickle, Phyllis 1934- *ConAu 65*

Tickle, Phyllis A 1934- *IntAu&W 86, –91*

Tickle, Phyllis Alexander *DrAPF 93*

Tickle, Phyllis Alexander 1934- *WhoSSW 93*

Tidd, Robert Frederick 1924- *AmMWSc 73P, –76P, –82*

Tiegreen, Alan F 1935- *BioIn 14, FifBJA, SmATA 36, WhoAmA 82, –84, –86, –89, –91*

Tierney, Frank M 1930- *BioIn 16, SmATA 54*

Tietjens, Eunice 1884-1944 *AmAu&B, AmWomWr, BenetAL 91, BioAmW, BioIn 4, ChhPo, –S1, –S2, ConAmL, CurBio 44, DcLB 54, DcLEL, DcNAA, FemiCLE, InWom SUP, JBA 34, OxCAmL 65, –83, REn, REnAL, TwCA, –SUP, WhAm 2, WhNAA*

Tietjens, Eunice Hammond 1884-1944 *AmWomPl*

Tiffault, Benette W 1955- *SmATA 77*

Tilly, Nancy 1935- *ConAu 120, SmATA 62*

Tilly, Nancy McFadden *DrAPF 91, –93*

Tiltman, Hugh Hessell 1897-1976 *BioIn 11, ConAu 69, NewYTBS 76, Who 74*

Tilton, Madonna Elaine 1929- *ConAu 114, –36NR, IntAu&W 86, SmATA 41*
Pseud./variant:
Tilton, Rafael

Tilton, Rafael *ConAu X, –36NR, IntAu&W 86X, SmATA X*
Main entry: Tilton, Madonna Elaine

Tilton, Rafael 1929- *BioIn 15, WhoUSWr 88, WhoWrEP 89, –92*

Tilton, Rafael, Sister *WhoUSWr 88*

Tilton, Rafael, Sister 1929- *IntAu&W 89*

Timmins, William Frederick *BioIn 11, SmATA 10, WhoAmA 73, –78, –80, –82, –84, –86, –89, WhoWest 84*

Timoney, Francis 1938- *ConAu 61, IntAu&W 82*

Tinbergen, Niko d1988 *NobelP 91N*

Tinbergen, Niko 1907- *BioIn 14, –15, IntAu&W 86, NobelP*

Tinbergen, Niko 1907-1988 *BioIn 16, –17, ConAu 127, CurBio 89N, SmATA 60*

Tinbergen, Nikolaas d1988 *IntWW 89N*

Tinbergen, Nikolaas 1907- *AmMWSc 89, –92, Au&Wr 71, BiESc, BioIn 10, –11, –12, BlueB 76, IntEnSS 79, IntWW 74, –79, –80, –81, –82, –83, MakMC, McGMS 80, NewYTBE 73, RAdv 13-3, –13-5, Who 74, –82, –83, –85, –88, WhoAm 74, –88, WhoNob, WhoWor 74, –80, –82, –84, –87, –89, WorAl, WrDr 80, –88*

Tinbergen, Nikolaas 1907-1988 *AnObit 1988, NewYTBS 88, WhAm 9, WhoNob 90, WorAlBi*

Tinbergen, Nikolaas, Prof d1988 *Who 90N*

Tindale, Norman B 1900- *DcChlFi*

Tindall, Gillian 1938- *Au&Wr 71, ConAu 21R, –11NR, ConLC 7, ConNov 72, –76, –82, –86, –91, EncBrWW, IntAu&W 77, Who 82, –83, –85, WorAu 1980, WrDr 76, –80, –82, –84, –86, –88, –90, –92*

Tindall, Gillian Elizabeth 1938- *WrDr 94*

Tiner, John Hudson 1944- *ConAu 101, –18NR, –40NR, SmATA 32*

Tinkelman, Murray 1933- *AmArt, BiDScF, BioIn 9, –11, IlrAm 1880, IlsCB 1967, SmATA 12*

Tinkle, Lon 1906-1980 *AmAu&B, BioIn 14, ConAu 104, SmATA 36, WhoSSW 73, –75, –76*

Tippett, James S 1885-1958 *ConAu 135, SmATA 66*

Tippett, James Sterling 1885-1956 *BioIn 17*

Tippett, James Sterling 1885-1958 *AnCL, BioIn 3, –4, –7, BkCL, ChhPo, Str&VC*

Tippette, Giles 1934- *ConAu 37NR, TwCWW 91*

Tippette, Giles 1936- *ConAu 65, –17NR, WrDr 84, –86, –88, –90, –92, –94*

Titcomb, Margaret 1891- *ConAu 5R, –5NR, ForWC 70, WhoLibS 55*

Titherington, Jeanne *AuBYP 3*

Titherington, Jeanne 1951- *SixBJA*

Titler, Dale Milton 1926- *AuBYP 2S, –3, BioIn 13, ConAu 81, SmATA 28, –35*

Titmarsh, Michael Angelo *CamGEL, OxCEng 85, SmATA X*
Main entry: Thackeray, William Makepeace

Tittle, Yelberton A 1926- *BioIn 4, –5, –6, –7, –8, –9, –10, –11, CurBio 64, NewYTBE 70, WhoFtbl 74*

Tittle, Yelberton Abraham 1926- *BioIn 15, –17*

Tittle, Yelberton Abraham, Jr. 1926- *BiDAmSp FB*

Titus, Eve 1922- *AuBYP 2, –3, BioIn 8, –9, ConAu 29R, –30NR, OxCChiL, SmATA 2, ThrBJA, TwCChW 78, –83, –89, WrDr 80, –82, –84, –86, –88, –90, –92, –94*
Pseud./variant:
Lord, Nancy

Tobias, Tobi 1938- *BioIn 10, ChlLR 4, ConAu 29R, –16NR, SmATA 5*

Tocci, Salvatore *AuBYP 3*

Todaro, John *AuBYP 2, –3, BioIn 8*

Todd, Alden 1918- *ConAu 1R, –6NR, DrAS 74H, –82H, IntAu&W 77, –89, WhoE 74, –75*

Todd, Anne Ophelia *AuBYP 2, –3, ConAu X, SmATA 7, WhAmArt 85*
Main entry: Dowden, Anne Ophelia Todd

Todd, Barbara Euphan 1890?-1976 *Au&Wr 71, BioIn 8, ChhPo, –S1, –S2, ConAu 104, OxCChiL, TwCChW 78, –83, –89, WhoChL*

Todd, Barbara K 1917- *BioIn 11, ConAu 61, SmATA 10*

Todd, H E 1908- *IntAu&W 91, WrDr 86, –88*

Todd, H E 1908-1988 *TwCChW 89*

Todd, Herbert Eatton 1908- *Au&Wr 71, BioIn 11, ConAu 12NR, –P-1, IntAu&W 77, OxCChiL, SmATA 11, TwCChW 78, –83, WrDr 76, –80, –82, –84*

Todd, Herbert Eatton 1908-1988 *ConAu 30NR*

Todd, Karen Rohne Pritchett 1936- *AmMWSc 73S, ConAu 111, LEduc 74*

Todd, Leonard 1940- *AmMWSc 76P, –82, –86, –89, –92, ConAu 65*

Todd, Loreto 1942- *BioIn 14, ConAu 107, SmATA 30*

Todd, Malcolm 1939- *ConAu 101, Who 88, –92*

Todd, Malcolm, Prof 1939- *Who 90*

Todd, Mary Fidelis *AuBYP 2, –3, BioIn 7*

Todd, Ronald Dean 1934- *LEduc 74*

Todd, Ruthven 1914- *AuBYP 2, –3, BioIn 4, –6, –7, ChhPo, –S2, CmScLit, ConAu 81, ConPo 70, –75, LongCTC, ModBrL, MorJA, TwCA SUP, WrDr 76*

Todd, Ruthven 1914-1978 *EncSF 93, EngPo, ScF&FL 92*

Toepfer, Ray Grant 1923- *ConAu 21R*

Tofte, Arthur 1902-1980 *ConAu 73, –103, IntAu&W 77, ScF&FL 92*

Tofte, Arthur R 1902-1980 *EncSF 93*

Tolan, Stephanie S *DrAPF 87, –89, –91, –93*

Tolan, Stephanie S 1942- *BioIn 15, –16, ConAu 77, –15NR, –34NR, DcAmChF 1985, DrAPF 83, –85, SixBJA, SmATA 38*

Toland, John Willard 1912- *AmAu&B, Au&Wr 71, BioIn 10, BlueB 76, ConAu 1R, –6NR, SmATA 38, WhoAm 74, –76, –78, –80, –82, –84, –86, –88, –90, –92, –94, WhoEnt 92, WhoUSWr 88, WhoWor 80, –82, –84, –87, –89, –91, –93, WhoWrEP 89, –92, WorAu 1950, WrDr 76, –80, –82, –84*

Tolchin, Martin 1928- *ConAu 120, WhoAm 84, –86, –88, –90, –92, –94, WhoE 74, –75, WhoUSWr 88, WhoWrEP 89, –92*

Tolchin, Susan Popper 1944- *ForWC 70*

Tolford, Joshua 1909- *BioIn 5, IlsBYP, IlsCB 1946*

Tolkien, J R R *IntvTCA 2*
Main entry: Tolkien, John Ronald Reuel

Tolkien, J R R 1892-1973 *AuBYP 3, Benet 87, BioIn 14, –16, BlmGEL, BritWr S2, CamGEL, CamGLE, CnDBLB 6, ConAu 36NR, ConLC 38, CyWA 89, HalFC 88, MagSWL, MajTwCW, ModBrL S2, RAdv 13-1, ScFSB, SupFW, TwCChW 89, TwCSFW 86B, –91, WorAlBi, WrChl*

Tolkien, John Ronald Reuel 1892-1973 *AnCL, Au&Arts 10, AuBYP 2, AuNews 1, Au&Wr 71, BioIn 3, –4, –6, –7, –8, –9, –10, –11, –12, –13, –14, –16, –17, CasWL, CelR, ChhPo, –S1, –S2, CnMWL, ConAu 45, –P-2, ConLC 1, –2, –3, –12, ConNov 72, –76, CurBio 57, –67, –73, DcLB 15, DcLEL, DcNaB 1971, EncSF 93, EncWL, –2, GrBr, HalFC 84, LongCTC, MajAI, MakMC, ModBrL, –S1, –S2, MorJA, NewC, NewYTBE 73, Novels, ObitOF 79, ObitT 1971, OxCChiL, OxCEng 67, –85, PenC ENG, RAdv 1, REn, SmATA 2, –24N,*

–32, SupFW, TelT, TwCChW 78, –83, TwCWr, TwCYAW, WebE&AL, WhDW, WhAm 6, WhoChL, WhoTwCL, WhoWor 74, WorAl, WorAu 1950
Pseud./variant:
Tolkien, J R R

Tolland, W R *SmATA 73*
Main entry: Heitzmann, William Ray

Tolles, Martha *WhoUSWr 88, WhoWrEP 89, –92*

Tolles, Martha 1921- *BioIn 11, ConAu 49, SmATA 8, –76*

Tolliver, Ruby C *DrAPF 87, –89, –91, –93*

Tolliver, Ruby C 1922- *BioIn 15, –16, ConAu 111, DrAPF 85, SmATA 41, –55*

Tolliver, Ruby Changos 1922- *IntAu&W 86*

Tolmie, Kenneth Donald 1941- *BioIn 12, –13, CanWW 83, –89, ConAu 69, Profile 2, SmATA 15, WhoAm 80, –82, –84, –86, –88, –90, –92, –94, WhoAmA 78, –80, –82, –84, –86, –89, –91, WhoE 81*

Tolstoi, Aleksei Nikolaevich 1882?-1945 *BioIn 1, –2, –4, –7, ClDMEL 47, ConAu X, CurBio 45, EncWL, McGEWD 72, ModSL 1, ModWD, PenC EUR, REn*

Tolstoi, Aleksei Nikolaevich 1883-1945 *CamGWoT, HanRL*

Tolstoi, Leo 1828-1910 *OxCChiL, OxCThe 83, SmATA 26, WhDW, WorAl*

Tolstoy, Serge *AuBYP 2, –3, BioIn 7*

Tomalin, Miles 1903- *Au&Wr 71, WrDr 76, –80, –82, –84*

Tomalin, Ruth *Au&Wr 71, BioIn 13, ConAu 13R, –13NR, –29NR, DcLEL 1940, EngPo, FemiCLE, IntAu&W 77, –82, –86, –89, –91, ScF&FL 92, SmATA 29, TwCChW 78, –83, –89, WrDr 76, –80, –82, –84, –86, –88, –90, –92, –94*

Tomerlin, John *AuBYP 3*

Tomerlin, John 1930- *AuBYP 2S*

Tomes, Margot Ladd *WhoAmA 86, –89, –91*

Tomes, Margot Ladd 1917- *BioIn 8, –13, ChhPo S1, –S2, FifBJA, IlsBYP, IlsCB 1957, –1967, SmATA 27, –36, WhoAmA 78, –80, –82, –84*

Tomes, Margot Ladd 1917-1991 *MajAI, SmATA 69, –70*

Tomey, Ingrid 1943- *SmATA 77*

Tomfool *ConAu X, MajAI, SmATA 2*
Main entry: Farjeon, Eleanor

Tomkins, Calvin 1925- *BioIn 2, –17, ConAu 13R, –8NR, WhoAm 84, –86, –88, –90, –92, –94, WhoAmA 78, –80, –82, –84, –86, –89, –91, WhoE 86, WhoUSWr 88, WhoWrEP 89, –92, WorAu 1980, WrDr 76 –80, –82, –84, –86, –88, –90, –92, –94*

Tomkins, Jasper *ConAu X, SmATA X*
Main entry: Batey, Tom

Tomkins, Jasper 1946- *BioIn 15, –16, WrDr 90, –92, –94*

Tomline, F Latour
Main entry: Gilbert, William Schwenck

Tomline, F Latour *SmATA X*

Tomlinson, Everett Titsworth 1859-1931 *AmAu&B, BiD&SB, CarSB, DcAmAu, DcNAA, REnAL, WhAm 1, WhNAA*

Tomlinson, Jill 1931- *WrDr 86*

Tomlinson, Jill 1931-1976 *Au&Wr 71, BioIn 9, –13, ConAu P-2, SmATA 3, –24N, WrDr 76, –80, –82, –84*

Tomlinson, Paul Greene 1888- *AmAu&B, CarSB, WhAm 8, WhNAA*

Tomlinson, Reginald Robert 1885-1979? *BioIn 13, ClaDrA, ConAu 104, DcBrAr 1, SmATA 27N, WhoArt 80N*

Tompert, Ann 1918- *BioIn 12, –16, ConAu 69, –11NR, MichAu 80, SixBJA, SmATA 14*

Tompkins, Alan 1907- *WhAmArt 85, WhoAmA 73, –78, –80, –82, –84, –86, –89, –91, WhoE 75, –91*

Tompkins, Jane 1898- *AuBYP 2, –3, BioIn 7*

Tompkins, Walker A 1909- *WrDr 86, –88*

Tompkins, Walker A 1909-1988 *ScF&FL 92*

Tompkins, Walker A 1909-1990? *TwCWW 91*

Tompkins, Walker Allison 1909- *AuBYP 2, –3, ConAu 5R, WhoWest 84*

Toner, Raymond John 1908- *BioIn 11, ConAu 5R, SmATA 10*

Tong, Gary S 1942- *ConAu 135, SmATA 66, WrDr 94*

Tonkin, Humphrey 1939- *ConAu 41R, –16NR, –38NR, DrAS 74E, LEduc 74*

Tonkin, Humphrey Richard 1939- *WhoAm 86, -90, -94*

Tonks, Rosemary *BioIn 8, -13, ConNov 72, -76, ConPo 70, -75, -80, -85, DcLB 14, DcLEL 1940, WrDr 76, -80, -82, -84, -86*

Tonn, Martin H 1921- *ConAu 5R, LEduc 74, WrDr 76, -80*

Tonn, Martin Helmuth 1921- *WhoMW 92*

Tonn, Maryjane Hooper 1927- *WhoAmW 74, -77*

Took, Belladonna *SmATA X*
Main entry: Chapman, Vera

Tooke, Louise Mathews 1950- *ConAu 105, SmATA 38*
Pseud./variant:
Mathews, Louise

Toonder, Martin *ConAu X, SmATA X*
Main entry: Groom, Arthur William

Toor, Frances 1890-1956 *BioIn 4, ObitOF 79*

Toothaker, Roy Eugene 1928- *BioIn 12, ConAu 65, SmATA 18*

Tooze, Ruth 1892- *AuBYP 3*

Tooze, Ruth 1892-1972 *AuBYP 2, BioIn 7, -9, ConAu 5R, ForWC 70, SmATA 4*

Topelius, Zachris 1818-1898 *OxCChiL*

Topolski, Feliks d1989 *Who 90N*

Topolski, Feliks 1907- *BioIn 1, -4, -5, -7, -11, -14, BlueB 76, ConAu 112, DcBrAr 1, IlsBYP, IlsCB 1946, IntWW 74, -75, -76, -77, -78, -79, -80, -81, -82, -83, -89, OxCArt, OxCTwCA, OxDcArt, PhDcTCA 77, PolBiDi, Who 74, -82, -83, -85, -88, WhoArt 80, -82, -84, WhoGrA 62, -82, WhoWor 74, -82, WorArt 1950*

Topolski, Feliks 1907-1989 *AnObit 1989, BioIn 16, NewYTBS 89, TwCPaSc, WhAm 10*

Toppin, Edgar Allan 1928- *ConAu 21R, DrAS 74H, -78H, -82H, InB&W 80, LivgBAA, SelBAAf, SelBAAu, WhoBlA 75, -77, -80, -85, -90, -92, -94*

Topping, Anne Marie *Au&Wr 71, ConAu 25R*

Topping, Audrey R 1928- *BioIn 9, ConAu 41R, SmATA 14*

Tor, Regina *AuBYP 2, -3, BioIn 7, SmATA X*
Main entry: Shekerjian, Regina Tor

Torbert, Floyd James 1922- *BioIn 13, ConAu 105, SmATA 22*

Torbet, Laura 1942- *ConAu 69, -16NR, WhoAmW 81, -83, -85, -87, WhoE 85, -86, -89, WhoWor 84*

Torday, Ursula *ScF&FL 92, TwCRHW 90, WrDr 86, -88, -90, -92*

Torday, Ursula 1888- *Au&Wr 71, ConAu 97, -28NR, TwCWr, WrDr 76, -80, -82, -84*
Pseud./variant:
Allardyce, Paula
Blackstock, Charity

Torga, Miguel *ConAu 141, TwCChW 89B*

Torga, Miguel 1907- *BioIn 4, CasWL, ConFLW 84, ConWorW 93, EncWL, -2, EvEuW, ModSpP P, OxCThe 83, PenC EUR, RfGShF, TwCChW 78B, -83B, TwCWr, WhoTwCL*

Torgersen, Don Arthur 1934- *BioIn 15, -16, ConAu 111, SmATA 41, -55*

Torley, Luke *MajTwCW, SmATA 66*
Main entry: Blish, James

Torok, Lou 1927- *BioIn 10, ConAu 49*

Torrey, Helen 1901- *BioIn 5, IlsBYP, IlsCB 1946*

Torrey, Marjorie 1899- *BioIn 5, -6, -14, ChhPo S1, IlsBYP, IlsCB 1946, MorJA*

Torrie, Malcolm *ConAu X, IntAu&W 82X, IntvTCA 2, SmATA X, TwCCr&M 80, -85, -91, Who 82, -83*
Main entry: Mitchell, Gladys

Toschik, Larry 1922- *BioIn 5, IlsBYP, IlsCB 1946, WhoAmA 78, -80, -82, -84, -86, -89, -91*

Toth, Marian Davies *WhoAmW 81, -83, -85, WhoE 81, WhoWor 84, -87*

Totham, Mary *ConAu X, IntAu&W 77X, SmATA X*
Main entry: Breinburg, Petronella Alexandrina

Toto, Joe *IlsBYP*

Tottle, John *AuBYP 2, -3, BioIn 7*

Tournier, Michel *BioIn 14, -16, -17, TwCChW 89B*

Tournier, Michel 1924- *BioIn 10, -13, ConAu 49, -3NR, -36NR, ConFLW 84, ConLC 6, -23, -36, CurBio 90, CyWA 89, DcLB 83, EncWL, -2, GuFrLit 1, IntAu&W 77, -82, IntWW 74, -75, -76, -77,*

-78, -79, -80, -81, -82, -83, -89, -91, MajTwCW, ModFrL, PostFic, RAdv 13-2, SmATA 23, TwCChW 78B, -83B, WhoWor 84, -87, -89, -91, -93, WorAu 1975

Tournier, Michel Edouard 1924- *ConWorW 93, GayLL*

Tournier, Paul 1898- *BioIn 7, -9, ConAu 81*

Tournier, Paul 1898-1986 *ConAu 120, -29NR*

Tourtel, Mary *BioIn 8, ChhPo S1, OxCChiL, TwCChW 83, WhoChL*

Tourtel, Mary 1874-1948 *TwCChW 89*

Tousey, Sanford *AuBYP 3*

Tousey, Sanford d1961 *AuBYP 2, BioIn 2, -5, -6, -7, JBA 51*

Touster, Irwin *AuBYP 3*

Touster, Irwin 1921- *AuBYP 2S*

Tovey, Doreen Evelyn 1918- *Au&Wr 71, ConAu 104*

Towne, Bonnie *AuBYP 3*

Towne, Mary *AuBYP 2S, ConAu X, SmATA X*
Main entry: Spelman, Mary

Towne, Mary 1934- *AuBYP 3, ScF&FL 92*

Towns, Elmer L 1932- *ConAu 45, -2NR*

Townsend, Doris Ann McFerran 1914- *ForWC 70, WhoAmW 75, WhoE 74, -75*

Townsend, Doris McFerran 1914- *ConAu 19NR*
Pseud./variant:
McFerran, Ann

Townsend, J David 1888- *ConAu 5R*

Townsend, Janet *AuBYP 3*

Townsend, Janet 1925- *AuBYP 2S, ConAu 107*

Townsend, John Rowe 1922- *Au&Arts 11, AuBYP 2S, -3, Au&Wr 71, BioIn 9, -10, ChhPo S2, ChlFicS, ChlLR 2, ConAu 37R, -41NR, DcLEL 1940, EncSF 93, EngPo, FourBJA, IntAu&W 77, -82, -86, -91, MajAI, OxCChiL, PiP, ScF&FL 92, ScFSB, SmATA 4, -68, -2AS, SouSt, TwCChW 78, -83, -89, TwCYAW, WhoWor 74, -84, WrDr 76, -80, -82, -84, -86, -88, -90, -92*

Townsend, Lee d1965 *WhoAmA 86N*

Townsend, Lee 1895-1965 *BioIn 5, -7, ChhPo S1, IlsBYP, IlsCB 1946, WhAmArt 85, WhoAmA 78N, -80N, -82N, -89N, -91N*

Townsend, Richard F *IlsBYP*

Townsend, Sue 1945- *BlmGWL, FemiCLE*

Townsend, Sue 1946- *ConAu 119, -127, ConDr 88, -93, ConLC 61, ConTFT 10, IntAu&W 91, IntWW 91, MajTwCW, SmATA 48, -55, TwCYAW, WrDr 88, -90, -92, -94*

Townsend, Thomas L 1944- *ConAu 127, SmATA 59*
Pseud./variant:
Lee, Tammie
Townsend, Tom

Townsend, Tom *ConAu 127, ScF&FL 92, SmATA X*
Main entry: Townsend, Thomas L

Townson, Hazel 1928- *ChlFicS*

Towry, M H *Alli SUP, CarSB*

Toye, Clive 1933?- *BioIn 12, SmATA 30*

Toye, William Eldred 1926- *BioIn 13, CanWW 83, -89, ConAu 1R, -4NR, OxCCan, -SUP, OxCCanL, Profile 2, SmATA 8, WhoCanL 85*

Tozer, Katharine 1905?- *TwCChW 83, -89*

Tozer, Kathleen *OxCChiL*

Trace, Arther Storrey, Jr. 1922- *ConAu 1R, -20NR, DrAS 74E, -78E, -82E, LEduc 74*

Tracey, Hugh 1903-1977 *ConAu 77, -P-2*

Trachsel, Myrtle Jamison *AmAu&B, AuBYP 2, -3, BioIn 7, WhNAA*

Trader Vic *AuBYP 2S, -3, ConAu X*
Main entry: Bergeron, Victor Jules

Trager, Helen G 1910- *ConAu 69*

Traherne, Michael *ConAu 132, -X, -38NR, IntAu&W 77X, -82X, SmATA 6, -66*
Main entry: Watkins-Pitchford, Denys James

Trahey, Jane *InWom SUP*

Trahey, Jane 1923- *AmWomM, BioIn 8, -14, ConAu 17R, -17NR, ForWC 70, SmATA 36, WhoAmW 74, -75, -81, WhoE 74, WhoFI 74*
Pseud./variant:
Erlanger, Baba

Traill, Catharine Parr *DcCanB 12*

Traill, Catharine Parr 1802-1899 *Alli, -SUP BbD, BbtC, BiD&SB, BioIn 7, -8, -9, BritAu 19, CamGLE, CanWr, DcLB 99,*

DcLEL, DcNAA, FemiCLE, NinCLC 31, OxCCan, OxCCanL, OxCChiL, REn, REnAL

Traill, Catharine Parr Strickland 1802-1899 *BioIn 17*

Train, Arthur Cheney *IntvTCA 2*

Train, Arthur Cheney 1875-1945 *AmAu&B, BioIn 1, -4, -14, CarSB, CurBio 46, DcNAA, EncMys, ObitOF 79, OxCAmL 65, REn, REnAL, TwCA, -SUP, WhAm 2, WhNAA*

Tranter, Nigel 1909- *AuBYP 2, -3, Au&Wr 71, BioIn 8, -14, CmScLit, ConAu 9R, -5NR, -20NR, IntAu&W 77, -82, -89, Novels, TwCRHW 90, Who 74, -82, -83, -85, WhoSpyF, WrDr 76, -80, -82, -84, -86, -88, -90, -92*

Tranter, Nigel Godwin 1909- *WrDr 94*

Trapp, Maria Augusta 1905-1987 *CurBio 87N*

Trapp, Maria Augusta Von 1905- *AmAu&B, BioIn 3, -6, -7, -8, -9, -10, -12, -13, CathA 1952, CurBio 68, InWom SUP, SmATA 16, WhoAm 74, -76, -78, -80, -82, -84, -86, WhoAmW 74, WhoE 74, WhoWor 74, WorAl*
Pseud./variant:
VonTrapp, Maria Augusta

Trapp, Maria Augusta Von 1905-1987 *NewYTBS 87*

Traudl *ConAu X*
Main entry: Flaxman, Traudl

Travaglini, Barbara Carlson 1925- *WhoAmW 74, -75, -77, -81, -83, -85, -87, WhoE 81, WhoFI 81, -83*

Traven, B d1969 *Benet 87, BenetAL 91, MajTwCW, OxCGer 86*

Traven, B 1882?-1969? *DcLB 56, HalFC 88, RfGAmL 87, ScF&FL 92*

Traven, B 1890?-1969 *AmAu&B, BioIn 1, -2, -4, -5, -6, -7, -8, -9, -11, -12, -13, ConAu 25R, -P-2, ConLC 8, -11, DcLB 9, DcMexL, EncFWF, EncWL, -2, HalFC 84, ObitOF 79, OxCAmL 65, -83, OxCEng 85, OxCGer 76, REnAL, TwCA, -SUP, WebE&AL, WhAm 5*

Traven, Beatrice *ConAu X*
Main entry: Goldemberg, Rose Leiman

Travers, P L 1906- *Benet 87, CamGLE, ConAu 30NR, FemiCLE, ScF&FL 92, SmATA 54, -2AS, TwCChW 89, WrDr 86, -88, -90, -92*

Travers, Pamela 1906- *AuBYP 3*

Travers, Pamela L 1906- *BioIn 15, -16*

Travers, Pamela Lyndon *IntvTCA 2*

Travers, Pamela Lyndon 1899- *MajAI*

Travers, Pamela Lyndon 1906- *AnCL, ArtclWW 2, AuWomWr, AuBYP 2, BioIn 1, -2, -3, -4, -6, -7, -8, -9, -10, -11, -13, ChlLR 2, ConAu 33R, FamMS, JBA 51, LongCTC, MorBMP, NewC, OxCChiL, REn, SmATA 4, -2AS, TelT, TwCA, -SUP, TwCChW 78, -83, WhoChL, WhoWor 74, WrDr 80, -82, -84, -94*

Travis, Buck *DcAmChF 1960*

Travis, Dempsey J 1920- *WhoBlA 88, -90, -92, -94, WrDr 90, -92*

Travis, Dempsey Jerome 1920- *BioIn 9, -10, -13, ConAu 85, -15NR, InB&W 80, -85, WhoAm 74, -80, -82, -84, -86, -88, -90, -92, -94, WhoBlA 75, -77, -80, -85, WhoFI 74, -77, -81, -85, WhoMW 74, -78, -80, -82, -84, WhoWor 74*

Treadgold, Mary 1910- *Au&Wr 71, BioIn 8, -16, ConAu 13R, IntAu&W 89, -91, OxCChiL, SmATA 49, TwCChW 78, -83, -89, WhoChL, WrDr 76, -80, -82, -84, -86, -88, -90, -92, -94*

Treadway, Ruby Peeples *AuBYP 2S, -3*

Trease, Geoffrey *Who 88, -90, -92*

Trease, Geoffrey 1909- *AuBYP 2, -3, BioIn 6, -7, -8, -9, -10, -17, ConAu 5R, -7NR, -22NR, DcLEL, IntAu&W 86, -89, -91, MorJA, OxCChiL, SmATA 2, -60, -6AS, TelT, TwCChW 78, -83, -89, Who 74, -82, -83, -85, WhoChL, WrDr 76, -80, -82, -84, -86, -88, -90, -92*

Trease, Robert Geoffrey 1909- *ConAu 38NR, MajAI, TwCYAW, WrDr 94*

Treat, Lawrence 1903- *CrtSuMy, IntAu&W 89, -91, SmATA 59, TwCCr&M 91, WhoAm 86, -88, -90, -92, -94, WhoUSWr 88, WhoWrEP 89, -92, WrDr 86, -88, -90, -92, -94*

Treat, Roger L *AuBYP 3*

Treat, Roger L 1905- *AuBYP 2, BioIn 7*

Trebing, Harry M 1926- *ConAu 31NR*

Trebing, Harry Martin 1926- *AmEA 74, AmMWSc 73S, -78S, ConAu 29R, WhoMW 74, -76*

Tredez, Alain 1926?- *BioIn 8, -9, -12, ConAu 85, IlsCB 1957, SmATA 17, ThrBJA*

Pseud./variant:
Trez, Alain

Tredez, Denise 1930- *BioIn 9, ConAu 5R, -8NR, SmATA 50, ThrBJA*
Pseud./variant:
Trez, Denise

Treece, Henry 1911?-1966 *AuBYP 2, -3, BioIn 4, -6, -7, -8, -9, CamGLE, ConAu 1R, -25R, -6NR, DcLEL, EvLB, LongCTC, ModBrL, MorJA, NewC, ObitOF 79, OxCChiL, OxCEng 85, PenC ENG, REn, SmATA 2, TwCA SUP, TwCChW 78, -83, -89, TwCRHW 90, TwCWr, TwCYAW, WhoChL*

Treece, Henry 1912-1966 *Benet 87, EngPo, MajAI*

Treffinger, Carolyn Elizabeth 1891- *OhA&B*

Tregarthen, Enys *BioIn 2, SmATA X*
Main entry: Sloggett, Nellie

Tregaskis, Richard 1916-1973 *AmAu&B, AuBYP 2, Au&Wr 71, BioIn 7, -9, -10, -12, -13, BlueB 76, ConAu 1R, -45, -2NR, CurBio 73, EncAJ, NatCAB 59, NewYTBE 73, ObitOF 79, SmATA 3, -26N, WhAm 6, WhoAm 74, WhoWor 74*

Tregaskis, Richard William 1916-1973 *AuBYP 3*

Tregear, Thomas R 1897- *ConAu 21R, WrDr 76, -80, -82, -84, -86, -88, -90*

Treherne, Katie Thamer 1955- *SmATA 76*
Pseud./variant:
Thamer, Katie

Treichler, Jessie 1906?-1972 *AuBYP 3*

Treichler, Jessie C 1906?-1972 *AuBYP 2, BioIn 7, ConAu 37R*

Trelease, Allen W 1928- *AuBYP 3*

Trelease, Allen William 1928- *AuBYP 2S, ConAu 108, DrAS 74H, -78H, -82H, WhoAm 74, -76, -78, -80, -82, -84, -86, -88, -90, -92, -94*

Trell, Max 1900- *BioIn 12, ConAu 41R, SmATA 14*

Tremain, Ruthven 1922- *BioIn 12, ConAu 85, SmATA 17*

Tremblay, Gilberte *OxCCan SUP*

Tremble, Freda B 1894- *ConAu 73*

Tremellan, Wilfred
Main entry: Webber, Stawford

Tremens, Del *ConAu 135, SmATA 76, WrDr 94*
Main entry: MacDonald, Amy

Trent, Robbie 1894- *AuBYP 2, -3, BioIn 7, -13, ConAu P-1, SmATA 26*

Trent, Timothy *ConAu X, SmATA X*
Main entry: Malmberg, Carl

Treseder, Terry Walton 1956- *SmATA 68*

Tresilian, Cecil Stuart 1891- *BioIn 1, -5, -8, -14, IlsBYP, IlsCB 1744, -1946, -1957, SmATA 40*

Tresselt, Alvin 1916- *AmPB, AuBYP 2, BioIn 6, -7, -10, BkP, ChlLR 30, ConAu 49, -1NR, IntAu&W 91, MajAI, MorJA, SmATA 7, TwCChW 78, -83, -89, WrDr 80, -82, -84, -86, -88, -90, -92, -94*

Tresselt, Alvin R 1916- *AuBYP 3*

Trevelyan, Julian O 1910-1988 *ConAu 126*

Trevelyan, Julian Otto 1910- *Au&Wr 71, BioIn 4, -6, BlueB 76, ConArt 77, ConAu 9R, DcBrAr 1, Who 74, -82, -83, -85, -88, WrDr 76, -80*

Trevelyan, Pauline 1905- *BioIn 1, ChhPo, IlsCB 1744*

Trevino, Elizabeth Borton De
Main entry: Borton, Elizabeth

Trevino, Elizabeth Borton De 1904- *AuBYP 2, BioIn 7, -8, -9, -10, -11, -14, ConAu 17R, -9NR, DcAmChF 1960, MajAI, NewbC 1956, SmATA 1, -29, -5AS, ThrBJA, WhoAm 74 -76, -78, -80, -82, WhoAmW 74, WhoSSW 73, -75, -76*

Trevino, Elizabeth de 1904- *AuBYP 3, IntAu&W 89, -91*

Trevor, Elleston *IntAu&W 89, TwCCr&M 91, Who 88, -90, -92, WhoWor 87, WrDr 86, -88, -90, -92, -94*

Trevor, Elleston 1920- *Au&Wr 71, BioIn 13, -14, ConAu 5R, CrtSuMy, DcLEL 1940, EncMys, EncSF 93, IntAu&W 77, Novels, ScF&FL 92, ScFSB, SmATA 28, SpyFic, TwCChW 78, TwCCr&M 80, -85, Who 74, -82, -83, -85, WhoAm 74, -76, -78, -80, -82, WhoWor 74, -82, -84, WrDr 76, -80, -82, -84*
Pseud./variant:
Black, Mansell
Burgess, Trevor
Fitzalan, Roger
Hall, Adam
Rattray, Simon
Scott, Warwick
Smith, Caesar

Trevor, Glen *ConAu X, SmATA X, TwCCr&M 80*
Main entry: Hilton, James

Trevor, Meriol 1919- *Au&Wr 71, BioIn 11, ConAu 1R, -1NR, -16NR, IntAu&W 77, -82, -89, -91, IntWWP 82, ScF&FL 92, SmATA 10, TwCChW 78, -83, -89, Who 74, -82, -83, -85, -88, -90, -92, WhoAmW 74, -75, WhoWor 74, WrDr 76, -80, -82, -84, -86, -88, -90, -92*

Trez, Alain *IlsCB 1957, SmATA X, ThrBJA*
Main entry: Tredez, Alain

Trez, Denise *ConAu X, ThrBJA*
Main entry: Tredez, Denise

Trier, Walter 1890-1951 *BioIn 1, -2, -3, -5, -12, -14, IlsBYP, IlsCB 1744, -1946, WorECar*

Triggs, Tony D 1946- *SmATA 70*

Trigoboff, Joseph *DrAPF 87, -89, -91*

Trigoboff, Joseph 1947- *ConAu 81, DrAPF 83, -85*

Trimble, Joe *AuBYP 2, -3, BioIn 7*

Trimble, Louis P 1917- *ConAu 13R, -6NR, ConSFA, DrAS 74F, -78F, -82F, WhNAA, WhoPNW*
Pseud./variant:
Brock, Stuart

Trimby, Elisa 1948- *BioIn 12, -14, -15, -16, ConAu 122, IlsCB 1967, SmATA 40, -47*

Trimmer, Ellen 1915- *ConAu 9R, WhoAmW 77, WrDr 76, -80, -82, -84, -86, -88, -90*

Trimmer, Sarah Kirby 1741-1810 *Alli, BioIn 3, -5, -8, -9, -16, BritAu, CarSB, CasWL, CyEd, DcBiPP, DcEnL, DcLEL, DcNaB, IntDcWB, OxCChiL, OxCEng 67, -85*

Trimmer, Sarah Kirby 1741-1811 *EncBrWW*

Tring, A Stephen *ConAu 128, -X, OxCChiL, TwCChW 83, -89, Who 74, -82, -83, -85, -88, WrDr 82, -84, -86, -88*
Main entry: Meynell, Laurence Walter

Tring, A Stephen 1899-1989 *SmATA X*

Tripp, Eleanor B 1936- *BioIn 9, ConAu 29R, SmATA 4*

Tripp, Paul 1911- *AuBYP 3*

Tripp, Paul 1916?- *ASCAP 66, AuBYP 2S, BioIn 1, -11, ConAu 21R, ConTFT 2, SmATA 8, WhoAm 84, -86, -88, -90, -92, WhoE 74, -75, -77, -81, -83, -85, -86, -89, WhoEnt 92, WhoHol A*

Tripp, Wallace Whitney 1940- *BioIn 12, ChhPo S2, ConAu 106, FifBJA, IlsBYP, IlsCB 1967, SmATA 31, WhoAmA 78*

Trippett, Frank 1926- *ConAu 21R*

Trivas, Irene *AuBYP 3*

Trivelpiece, Laurel *DrAPF 87, -89, -91, -93*

Trivelpiece, Laurel 1926- *BioIn 15, -16, ConAu 123, SmATA 46, -56, WrDr 90, -92, -94*
Pseud./variant:
Marks, Hannah K

Trivett, Daphne 1940- *BioIn 13, ConAu 97, SmATA 22*

Trnka, Jiri 1910-1969 *HalFC 88*

Trnka, Jiri 1912-1969 *BioIn 7, -8, -9, -14, -15, ConAu 111, DcFM, FilmgC, HalFC 84, IlsCB 1957, -1967, MajAI, OxCFilm, SmATA 32, -43, ThrBJA, WhoGrA 62, WorECar, WorEFlm*

Trollope, Anthony 1815-1882 *Benet 87, BenetAL 91, BioIn 1, -2, -3, -4, -5, -6, -7, -8, -9, -10, -11, -12, -13, -14, -15, -16, -17, BlmGEL, BritWr 5, CamGEL, CamGLE, CelCen, CnDBLB 4, DcBiPP, DcLB 21, -57, DcNaB, Dis&D, EncSF 93, MagSWL, NinCLC 6, -33, Novels, OxCAusL, OxCEng 85, RAdv 13-1, RfGEnL 91, RfGShF, ScFSB, ScFEYrs, SmATA 22, StaCVF, WhDW, WorAlBi, WorAl, WorLitC, WrPh*

Troop, Miriam 1917- *ConAu 13R*

Tropp, Martin 1945- *ConAu 65, ScF&FL 92*

Trost, Lucille Wood 1938- *BioIn 11, ConAu 61, -9NR, SmATA 12*

Trott, Susan 1937- *ConAu 97*

Trotta, John 1936- *ConAu 45*

Trotter, Grace V 1900- *AuBYP 2, BioIn 7, -11, ConAu 1R, -1NR, SmATA 10*
Pseud./variant:
Paschal, Nancy

Trotter, Grace Violet 1900- *AuBYP 3*

Troughton, Joanna Margaret 1947- *BioIn 12, ConAu 109, IlsCB 1967, SmATA 37*

Trowbridge, John Townsend 1827-1916 *Alli, -SUP, AmAu, AmAu&B, BenetAL 91, BibAL 8, BbD, BiD&SB, BioIn 1, -2, -5, CarSB, ChhPo, -S1, CyAL, CyWA 58,*

DcAmAu, DcBiA, DcEnL, DcLEL, DcNAA, HarEnUS, OxCAmL 65, –83, OxCChiL, REnAL, WhAm 1

Trowbridge, Leslie W 1920- *AuBYP 3*

Trowbridge, Leslie Walter 1920- *AmMWSc 73P, –76P, –82, –86, –92, AuBYP 2S, ConAu 77, –13NR*

Troy, Carol 1945?- *BioIn 11, –12*

Troy, Hugh 1906-1964 *BioIn 1, –5, –7, –8, –13, –14, IlsBYP, IlsCB 1744, –1946, –1957*

Troy, Una *BiDIrW, IntAu&W 86, –89, WrDr 86, –88, –90, –92*

Troy, Una 1910- *WrDr 94*

Troy, Una 1913- *Au&Wr 71, ConAu 1R, –3NR, DcIrW 1, WrDr 76, –80, –82, –84*

Troyer, Johannes 1902-1969 *BioIn 3, –5, –8, –15, ChhPo, IlsBYP, IlsCB 1946, –1957, SmATA 40*

Trudeau, G B
Main entry: Trudeau, Garretson Beekman

Trudeau, Garretson Beckman 1948- *BioIn 10, –11, ConAu 81, SmATA 35*

Trudeau, Garretson Beekman 1948-
Pseud./variant:
Trudeau, G B
Trudeau, Garry B

Trudeau, Garry B *ConAu 31NR*
Main entry: Trudeau, Garretson Beekman

Trudeau, Garry B 1948- *BioIn 14, –15, –17, ConLC 12, IntWW 89, –91, WhoAm 80, –82, –84, –86, –88, –90, –92, –94, WhoAmA 84, –86, –89, –91, WhoE 91, –93, WhoUSWr 88, WhoWrEP 89, –92, WrDr 76, –80*

Trueman, Stuart *OxCCan*

Truesdell, Susan G *SmATA 45*

Trumbo, Dalton 1905-1976 *Benet 87, BenetAL 91, BioIn 14, –16, –17, HalFC 88, LiExTwC, TwCYAW*

Trump, Fred L 1924- *ConAu 13R*

Trupin, James E 1940- *ConAu 37R*

Truse, Kenneth 1946- *ConAu 105*

Trusler, John 1735-1820 *Alli, BiDLA, –SUP, CarSB, DcBiPP, DcNaB*

Truss, Jan 1925- *BioIn 13, CanWW 89, ConAu 102, DcChlFi, Profile 2, SmATA 35, TwCChW 83, –89, WhoCanL 85, –87, –92 WrDr 86, –88*

Truss, Leslie S *Who 88, –90*

Truss, Leslie Seldon *Who 74, –82, –83, –85*
Main entry: Seldon Truss, Leslie

Tsinajinnie, Andrew 1918- *BioIn 4, –9*

Tsireh, Awa *AmPB*

Tubb, E C 1919- *ConAu 101, –21NR, ConSFA, IntAu&W 86, –89, –91, NewEScF, ScF&FL 92, ScFSB, TwCSFW 86, –91, TwCWW 91, WhoSciF, WrDr 84, –86, –88, –90, –92*

Tubb, Edwin Charles 1919- *EncSF 93, WrDr 94*

Tubby, I M *MajAI, SmATA 65*
Main entry: Kraus, Robert

Tuck, Raphael 1821-1900 *OxCChiL*

Tucker, Caroline *AuBYP 2, –3, ConAu X, SmATA 2, –X*
Main entry: Nolan, Jeannette Covert

Tucker, Charlotte Maria 1821-1893 *Alli, –SUP, BioIn 8, –16, BritAu 19, CarSB, ChhPo S1, –S2, DcInB, DcNaB, FemiCLE, LuthC 75, NewC, OxCChiL, StaCVF, WhoChL, WomNov*
Pseud./variant:
A L O E

Tucker, Charlotte Maria 1825-1893 *InWom SUP*

Tucker, Ernest Edward 1916-1969 *AuBYP 2, –3, BioIn 7, –8, ConAu 61*

Tucker, Nicholas 1936- *ChhPo S2, ConAu 65, –11NR*

Tudor, Bethany *AuBYP 2, –3, BioIn 8*

Tudor, Tasha *WrDr 86*

Tudor, Tasha 1915- *AmAu&B, AuBYP 2, –3, BioIn 1, –2, –5, –7, –8, –11, –12, ChhPo, ChlLR 13, ConAu 81, HerW 84, IlsCB 1744, –1946, –1957, –1967, JBA 51, MajAI, OxCChiL, SmATA 20, –69, TwCChW 78, WhAmArt 85, WhoAmA 73, –78, –80, WhoAmW 74, WrDr 80, –82, –84, –88, –90, –92, –94*

Tuer, A W 1838-1900 *OxCChiL*

Tuer, Andrew White 1838-1900 *Alli SUP, CarSB, ChhPo, –S1, DcNaB S1*

Tuerk, Hanne 1951- *SmATA 71*

Tuffs, J Elsden 1922- *ConAu 5R*

Tufts, Anne *AuBYP 2, –3, BioIn 7*

Tufts, Georgia *AuBYP 2, –3, BioIn 7*

Tufty, Barbara *InWom SUP*

Tufty, Barbara 1923- *ConAu 37R, WhoAmW 77, WrDr 76, –80, –82, –84, –86, –88, –90, –92, –94*

Tulloch, Richard George 1949- *SmATA 76*

Tully, John 1923- *BioIn 12, ConAu 69, –12NR, –28NR, ScF&FL 92, SmATA 14*

Tunbo, Frances G *DcAmChF 1985*

Tung, Shih-Tsin 1900- *ConAu 5R*

Tunis, Edwin Burdett 1897-1973 *AuBYP 2, –3, BioIn 5, –6, –8, –9, –10, –13, ChlLR 2, ConAu 5R, –45, –7NR, IlsCB 1946, –1957, –1967, MajAI, MorJA, SmATA 1, –24N, –28, WhAmArt 85, WhoAmA 73, –78N, –80N, –82N*

Tunis, John R 1889-1975 *BenetAL 91, BioIn 14, –15, TwCChW 89*

Tunis, John Robert 1889-1975 *AuBYP 3*

Tunis, John Roberts 1889-1975 *AuBYP 2, Au&ICB, BioIn 4, –6, –7, –8, –10, –12, ConAu 57, –61, ConLC 12, DcAmChF 1960, DcLB 22, MajAI, MorJA, NatCAB 58, ObitOF 79, OxCChiL, REnAL, SmATA 30, –37, TwCA, –SUP, TwCChW 78, –83, TwCYAW*

Tunnicliffe, C F 1901-1979 *BioIn 14, –17, SmATA 62*

Tunnicliffe, Charles Frederick 1901- *BioIn 5, –12, ClaDrA, DcBrAr 1, IlsBYP, IlsCB 1946, Who 74, WhoArt 80N*

Tunnicliffe, Charles Frederick 1901-1979 *BioIn 14, –17, DcNaB 1971*

Turk, Midge *BioIn 9, ConAu X, WrDr 76, –80, –82, –84, –86, –88*
Main entry: Richardson, Midge Turk

Turk, Midge 1930- *WrDr 94*

Turkle, Brinton 1915- *TwCChW 89, WrDr 86, –88, –90, –92, –94*

Turkle, Brinton Cassaday 1915- *BioIn 8, –9, –10, –12, –14, BkP, ChhPo S2, ConAu 25R, FamAIYP, IlsBYP, IlsCB 1957, –1967, OxCChiL, SmATA 2, ThrBJA, TwCChW 78, –83, WrDr 80, –82, –84*

Turlington, Bayly 1919- *BioIn 10, ConAu 29R, DrAS 74F, SmATA 5, WhoAm 74, –76*

Turlington, Bayly 1919-1977 *ConAu 122, SmATA 52N*

Turnage, Anne Shaw 1927- *ConAu 77*

Turnage, Maclyn Neil 1927- *ConAu 77*

Turnbull, Agnes Sligh 1888-1982 *AmAu&B, AmNov, AmWomWr, AnObit 1982, AuBYP 2, –3, Au&Wr 71, BenetAL 91, BioIn 2, –4, –5, –7, ConAu 1R, –105, –2NR, InWom SUP, NewYTBS 82, REnAL, SmATA 14, TwCA, –SUP, WhNAA, WhoAm 74, –76, –78, –80, –82, WhoAmW 74*

Turnbull, Ann 1943- *BioIn 12, ConAu 65, ScF&FL 92, SmATA 18*
Pseud./variant:
Nicol, Ann

Turnbull, Bob 1936- *BioIn 10, ConAu 37R, –14NR*

Turner, Alice Kennedy *IntAu&W 86, WhoAm 86, –88*

Turner, Alice Kennedy 1940- *BioIn 11, ConAu 53, SmATA 10, WhoAm 76, –78, –80, –82, –84*

Turner, Ann *EncO&P 3*

Turner, Ann 1945- *SixBJA*

Turner, Ann W 1945- *ConAu 69, –14NR, –31NR, ScF&FL 92, SmATA 14*

Turner, Ann Warren 1945- *AuBYP 3, SmATA 77*

Turner, Bonnie 1932- *ConAu 142, SmATA 75*

Turner, Edward Reuben Arthur 1924- *ConAu 81*

Turner, Elizabeth 1775?-1846 *Alli, BritAu 19, ChhPo, –S1, OxCChiL, TelT, YABC 2*

Turner, Eloise Fain 1906- *AuBYP 2, –3, BioIn 8, ConAu 5R*

Turner, Ernest Sackville 1909- *Au&Wr 71, BioIn 10, IntAu&W 77, –82, –86, –89, WorAu 1950, WrDr 76*

Turner, Ethel 1872-1958 *AuWomWr, BlmGWL, CamGLE, FemiCLE, TwCChW 89*

Turner, Ethel Sybil *WomNov*

Turner, Ethel Sybil 1872-1958 *BioIn 4, –12, CarSB, Chambr 3, ChhPo S1, –S2,*

ConAu 111, DcLEL, OxCAusL, OxCChiL, SingR 1, –2, TwCChW 78, –83

Turner, Gerry *AuBYP 2S, –3*

Turner, Glennette Tilley 1933- *BlkAuIl 92, SmATA 71*

Turner, Gwenda 1947- *BioIn 16, ConAu 118, –42NR, SmATA 59*

Turner, John Freeland 1942- *BioIn 11, WhoAm 90, WhoAmP 73, –75, –77, –81, –83, –85, –87, –89, –91, –93, WhoWest 84, –87, –89, –92, –94*

Turner, Josie *SmATA 3*
Main entry: Crawford, Phyllis

Turner, Morris Nolten 1923- *BioIn 6, –7, –9, ConAu 29R, WhoBlA 75, –77, –80, WhoWest 74, –78, –80*

Turner, Nancy Byrd 1880- *AmAu&B, BioIn 1, BkCL, ChhPo, –S2, Str&VC, WhAm 6, WhNAA*

Turner, Philip 1925- *Au&Wr 71, BioIn 7, –11, ConAu 25R, –11NR, –27NR, FourBJA, OxCChiL, SmATA 11, –6AS, TwCChW 78, –83, –89, WrDr 80, –82, –84, –86, –88, –90, –92*
Pseud./variant:
Chance, Stephen

Turner, Philip William 1925- *WrDr 94*

Turner, Robyn 1947- *SmATA 77*

Turner, Sheila R *SmATA X*
Main entry: Seed, Sheila Turner

Turngren, Annette 1902?-1980 *AuBYP 2, –3, BioIn 6, –7, –12, –13, ConAu 9R, –101, MinnWr, MorJA, SmATA 23N*
Pseud./variant:
Hopkins, A T

Turngren, Ellen d1964 *AuBYP 2, –3, BioIn 6, –7, –9, ConAu 5R, MinnWr, SmATA 3*

Turska, Krystyna Zofia 1933- *BioIn 12, –13, ChhPo S1, ConAu 106, IlsCB 1967, SmATA 27, –31*

Tusa, Tricia 1960- *SmATA 72*

Tusan, Stan 1936- *BioIn 13, ConAu 105, SmATA 22*

Tusiani, Joseph 1924- *AmAu&B, AmCath 80, AuBYP 2, –3, BioIn 8, –15, BkC 6, ChhPo S2, ConAu 9R, –5NR, –20NR, –43NR, DrAS 74F, –82F, IntAu&W 77, –82, –86, –89, –91, SmATA 45, WhoAm 74, –76, –78, –80, –82, –84, –86, –88, WhoUSWr 88, WhoWrEP 89, –92*

Tuska, George *ArtCS*

Tuska, George 1916- *EncACom*

Tute, Warren 1914- *Au&Wr 71, ConAu 1R, –1NR, IntAu&W 77, –82, Novels, Who 82, –83, –85, WrDr 76, –80, –82, –84, –86, –88, –90*

Tuthill, Louisa Caroline 1798-1879 *Alli, AmWomWr, CarSB, ChhPo S1, CyAL, DcAmAu, DcNAA*

Tuthill, Louisa Caroline Huggins 1798?-1879 *InWom SUP*

Tutt, Kay Cunningham *AuBYP 2, –3, BioIn 8*

Tuttle, Wilbur C 1883- *ConAu P-2, WhAm 7, WhoPNW*

Tutton, Barbara 1914- *Au&Wr 71, WrDr 76, –80, –82, –84, –86, –88, –90*

Twain, Mark *AuBYP 3, CamHAL, ConAu 135, DcLB Y92, MajAI, NewYTBS 88, OxCAmT 84, SourALJ, WhCiWar*
Main entry: Clemens, Samuel Langhorne

Twain, Mark 1835-1910 *Alli, –SUP, AmAu, AmAu&B, AmWr, AtlBL, AuBYP 2, Benet 87, BenetAL 91, BiDPara, BiDSA, BiD&SB, BioIn 14, –15, –17, CamGEL, CamGLE, CasWL, CelCen, Chambr 3, CmCal, CnDAL, ConAu X, CrtSuMy, CrtT 3, CyWA 58, –89, DcAmAu, DcAmSR, DcBiPP, DcEnA, –A, DcEnL, DcLB 11, DcLEL, DcNAA, Dis&D, EncAB-H, EncFWF, EncMys, EncPaPR 91, EncSF 93, EncSoA, EncSoH, EncWL, EvLB, FamAYP, FilmgC, HalFC 84, –88, HarEnUS, JBA 34, MagSAmL, McGEWB, MemAm, ModAL, –S1, NewEScF, NewGrDA 86, NotNAT B, Novels, OxCAmH, OxCAmL 65, –83, OxCAusL, OxCChiL, OxCEng 67, –85, OxCMus, PenC AM, RAdv 1, –13-1, RComAH, RComWL, REn, REnAL, RfGAmL 87, RfGShF, ScF&FL 92, ScFSB, ScFEYrs, ShSCr 6, ShSWr, SupFW, TwCChW 78A, –83A, –89A, TwCLC 6, –12, –19, –36, –48, TwCSFW 86, –91, TwCYAW, WebAB 74, –79, WebE&AL, WhDW, WhoChL, WhoTwCL, WorAlBi, WorAl, WorLitC, WrChl, YABC X*

Tweedie, Michael Willmer Forbes 1907- *Au&Wr 71*

Tweedsmuir, Baron *ScF&FL 92*
Main entry: Buchan, John Tweedsmuir, Baron

Tweedsmuir, Baron 1875-1940 *BioIn 15, DcLEL, DcNaB 1931, EncMys, EvLB, GrBr, NewC, TwCA, –SUP, YABC X*

Tweedsmuir, Baron 1911- *Who 88, –90, –92*

Tweton, D Jerome 1933- *BioIn 16, DrAS 74H, –78H, –82H, SmATA 48*

Twidle, Arthur 1865-1936 *DcBrAr 2, DcBrBI*

Twiname, Eric 1942?-1980 *ConAu 102*

Tworkov, Jack 1900-1982 *AnObit 1982, BioIn 3, –5, –6, –7, –10, –13, –14, –16, BriEAA, ConArt 77, –83, –89, ConAu 107, CurBio 64, –82N, DcCAA 71, –77, –88, DcCAr 81, NewYTBS 82, OxCTwCA, OxDcArt, PhDcTCA 77, PrintW 83, –85, SmATA 31N, –47, WhAm 8, WhAmArt 85, WhoAm 74, –76, –78, –80, –82, WhoAmA 73, –78, –80, –82, –86N, –89N, –91N, WhoAmJ 80, WhoWor 74, WhoWorJ 72, –78, WorArt 1950*

Tyler, Anne *DrAPF 87, –89, –91, –93, IntvTCA 2*

Tyler, Anne 1941- *AmWomWr, ArtclWW 2, BenetAL 91, BestSel 89-1, BioIn 10, –11, –12, –13, –15, –16, –17, BlmGWL, ConAu 9R, –33NR, ConLC 7, –11, –18, –28, –44, –59, ConNov 72, –76, –82, –86, –91, CurBio 81, CyWA 89, DcLB 6, –Y82A, DcLEL 1940, DrAF 76, DrAPF 83, –85, FemiCLE, FifSWrA, InWom SUP, IntAu&W 77, –91, IntWW 91, MagSAmL, MajTwCW, ModAL S2, ModAWWr, OxCAmL 83, SmATA 7, TwCYAW, WhoAm 76, –78, –80, –82, –84, –86, –88, –90, –92, –94, WhoAmW 74, –75, –81, –83, –85, –87, –89, –91, –93, WhoE 74, –75, –77, WhoUSWr 88, WhoWrEP 89, –92, WrDr 76, –80, –82, –84, –86, –88, –90, –92, –94*

Tyler, Linda *ConAu 136, SmATA 65*
Main entry: Tyler, Linda Wagner

Tyler, Linda Wagner 1952- *BioIn 17, ConAu 136, SmATA 65, WrDr 94*
Pseud./variant:
Tyler, Linda

Tyler, Vicki 1952- *ConAu 121, SmATA 64*

Tyler, William Royall 1910- *BlueB 76, ConAu 37R, IntWW 74, –75, –76, –77, –78, –79, –80, –81, –82, –83, IntYB 80, –81, –82, WhoAm 74, –76, –78, WhoAmP 73, –75, –77, –81, –83, –85, –87, –89, –91, –93, WrDr 80, –82, –84*

Tyler-Whittle, Michael Sidney 1927- *Au&Wr 71, ConAu 5R, –4NR, WrDr 76, –80*
Pseud./variant:
Oliver, Mark
Whittle, Tyler

Tyll, Al *AuBYP 3*

Tyll, Al 1932- *AuBYP 2S*

Tyner, Clara L *OxCCan*

Tyrwhitt, Janice 1928- *CaW, ConAu 97*

Tytler, Ann Fraser *OxCChiL*

U

Ubell, Earl 1926- *BioIn 5, –9, ConAu 37R, SmATA 4, WhoAm 74, –76, –78, –80, –82, –84, –86, –88, –90, –92, –94, WhoUSWr 88, WhoWrEP 89, –92*

Uchida, Yoshiko *BioIn 14, –15, –16, –17, DrAPF 87, –89, –91, –93*

Uchida, Yoshiko d1992 *NewYTBS 92*

Uchida, Yoshiko 1921- *AuBYP 2, –3, BioIn 6, –7, –9, BkCL, ChlLR 6, ConAu 13R, –6NR, –22NR, DrAPF 83, –85, MajTwCW, MorJA, SmATA 1, –53, –1AS, TwCChW 78, –83, –89, WrDr 80, –82, –84, –86, –88, –90, –92*

Uchida, Yoshiko 1921-1992 *AnObit 1992, ConAu 139, MajAI, SmATA 72, WrDr 94N*

Udall, Jan Beaney 1938- *BioIn 11, ConAu 65, –35NR, SmATA 10*
Pseud./variant:
Beaney, Jan

Uden, Grant 1910- *AuBYP 2S, –3, BioIn 13, ConAu 102, FourBJA, SmATA 26*

Udry, Janice 1928- *AuBYP 3, WrDr 86, –88, –90, –92*

Udry, Janice May 1928- *AmPB, AuBYP 2, BioIn 7, –9, BkP, ConAu 5R, –6NR, SmATA 4, ThrBJA, TwCChW 78, WrDr 80, –94*

Ueno, Noriko *AuBYP 2S, –3, ConAu X, SmATA X*
Main entry: Nakae, Noriko

Ueno, Noriko 1940- *BioIn 16*

Uhl, Melvin John 1915- *ConAu 5R, –34NR*

Ulam, S M 1909-1984 *ConAu 34NR, SmATA 51*

Ulanoff, Stanley M 1922- *ConAu 23NR, IntAu&W 86, –89*

Ulanoff, Stanley Melvin 1922- *AmMWSc 73S, –78S, ConAu 17R, –7NR, IntAu&W 77, –82, WhoE 74, –75, –77*

Ullman, James Ramsey 1907-1971 *AmAu&B, AuBYP 2, –3, Au&Wr 71, BenetAL 91, BioIn 1, –2, –4, –7, –9, –10, –11, –14, ConAu 1R, –29R, –3NR, CurBio 45, –71, FourBJA, LongCTC, NewYTBE 71, ObitOF 79, REn, REnAL, SmATA 7, TwCA SUP, WhAm 5, WhNAA*

Ullyot, Marianne Williams 1940- *WhoMW 78, –80*

Ulm, Robert 1934-1977 *BioIn 12, SmATA 17*

Ulmer, Louise 1943- *BioIn 16, SmATA 53*

Ulreich, Nura Woodson 1899-1950 *BioIn 1, –2, –5, IlsBYP, IlsCB 1744, –1946, WhAmArt 85, WhoAmA 78N, –80N, –82N, –86N, –89N, –91N*
Pseud./variant:
Nura

Ulrich, Betty Garton 1919- *ConAu 29R, IntAu&W 86, –89, –91, WrDr 76, –80, –82, –84*

Ulrich, Homer 1906- *AmAu&B, AuBYP 2, –3, Au&Wr 71, Baker 84, –92, BioIn 7, ConAu 5R, –2NR, DrAS 74H, –78H, –82H, IntWWM 85, LEduc 74, WhoAm 74, –76, WhoAmM 83, WhoUSWr 88*

Ulrich, Homer 1906-1987 *ConAu 124, –36NR*

Ulyatt, Kenneth 1920- *BioIn 12, ConAu 61, –8NR, SmATA 14*

Umphelby, Fanny 1788-1852 *DcNaB, OxCChiL*

Unada *ConAu X, SmATA 3, WrDr 76, –80, –82, –84, –86, –88, –90, –92*
Main entry: Gliewe, Unada G

Unada 1927- *WrDr 94*

Uncle Gus *ConAu X, MajAI, SmATA 1, –69, –X*
Main entry: Rey, Hans Augusto

Uncle Mac *ConAu X, SmATA X*

Uncle Ray *AmAu&B, ConAu X, SmATA 4*
Main entry: Coffman, Ramon Peyton

Uncle Shelby *ConAu X, MajAI, SmATA X, WrDr 94*
Main entry: Silverstein, Shel

Underhill, Alice Mertie 1900-1971 *BioIn 11, ConAu 1R, -103, SmATA 10*

Underhill, Liz 1936- *SmATA 49*

Underhill, Liz 1948- *BioIn 16, ConAu 121, SmATA 53, TwCPaSc*

Underhill, Ruth M 1884-1984 *BioIn 14, -15*

Underhill, Ruth Murray 1884-1984 *AmAu&B, Au&Wr 71, BioIn 3, -7, BlueB 76, ConAu 1R, -114, -3NR, -39NR, CurBio 54, -84N, FifIDA, InSci, InWom SUP, IntAu&W 77, OxCCan SUP, WhAm 7, WhoAm 76, WhoWor 78, WrDr 76, -80*

Underwood, Betty 1921- *AuBYP 3*

Underwood, Leon 1890-1975 *BioIn 1, -6, -10, -16, ClaDrA, ConICB, DcBrAr 1, -2, DcNaB 1971, IlsCB 1744, ObitT 1971, OxCTwCA, OxDcArt, TwCPaSc, WhAmArt 85, Who 74*

Underwood, Leon 1890-1977 *BioIn 14*

Underwood, Mary Betty Anderson 1921- *AuBYP 2S, ConAu 37R, DcAmChF 1960, WhoAmW 81*

Undset, Sigrid 1882-1949 *AtlBL, AuBYP 2, -3, Benet 87, BioIn 1, -2, -3, -4, -5, -7, -8, -9, -10, -11, -12, -14, -15, -17, BlmGWL, CasWL, CathA 1930, ClDMEL 47, ConAu 104, -129, ContDcW 89, CurBio 40, -49, CyWA 58, DcCathB, DcScanL, EncCoWW, EncWL, -2, EuWr 9, EvEuW, GrFLW, InWom SUP, LadLa 86, LiExTwC, LongCTC, MajTwCW, McGEWB, NobelP, Novels, ObitOF 79, OxCEng 67, PenC EUR, RAdv 13-2, REn, TwCA, -SUP, TwCLC 3, TwCWr, WhAm 2, WhoNob, -90, WorAlBi, WorAl, WorLitC*

Unger, Harlow G 1931- *ConAu 142, SmATA 75*

Unger, Jim 1937- *SmATA 67*

Unger, Marvin H 1936- *ConAu 29R*

Ungerer, Jean Thomas
Main entry: Ungerer, Tomi

Ungerer, Jean Thomas 1931- *MajAI, SmATA 33*

Ungerer, Jean Tomi 1931- *WhoAm 86, -88, WhoUSWr 88, WhoWrEP 89, -92*

Ungerer, Tomi 1931- *AmAu&B, AmPB, AuBYP 2, -3, Au&Wr 71, BioIn 5, -7, -8, -9, -10, -11, -12, -13, -14, -16, BkP, ChhPo, ChlLR 3, ConAu 41R, FamAIYP, IlsCB 1957, -1967, IntAu&W 77, MajAI, NewYTBS 81, OxCChiL, SmATA 5, -X, ThrBJA, TwCChW 78, -83, -89, Who 90, -92, WhoAm 74, WhoGrA 62, -82*
Pseud./variant:
Ungerer, Jean Thomas

Ungermann, Arne 1902- *BioIn 5, ChhPo S2, IlsBYP, IlsCB 1946, WhoGrA 62, WorECar*

Ungermann, Kenneth Armistead 1916- *ConAu 9R*

Unkelbach, Kurt 1913- *AuBYP 2S, -3, BioIn 9, ConAu 21R, -8NR, SmATA 4, WhoE 74*

Unnerstad, Edith *TwCChW 89B*

Unnerstad, Edith 1900- *AuBYP 3*

Unnerstad, Edith Totterman 1900- *AuBYP 2, Au&Wr 71, BioIn 7, -9, ConAu 5R, -6NR, SmATA 3, ThrBJA, TwCChW 78B, -83B*

Unrau, Ruth 1922- *BioIn 11, ConAu 61, SmATA 9*

Unstead, Robert J 1915-1988 *SmATA 56N*

Unstead, Robert John 1915- *Au&Wr 71, BioIn 11, BlueB 76, ConAu 9R, -7NR, DcLEL 1940, IntAu&W 77, -82, -86, -89, -91, OxCChiL, SmATA 12, Who 74, -82, -83, -85, -88, WrDr 76, -80, -82, -84, -86, -88*

Unsworth, Walter 1928- *BioIn 9, ConAu 29R, IntAu&W 86, -89, SmATA 4*

Unterecker, John *DrAPF 87*

Unterecker, John 1922- *AuBYP 3*

Unterecker, John 1922-1989 *ConAu 127, -34NR*

Unterecker, John E 1922- *AmAu&B, AuBYP 2, Au&Wr 71, BioIn 8, ConAu 17R, DrAP 75, DrAS 74E, -82E, IntAu&W 82, IntWWP 82, WhoAm 74, -80, -82, -84, WrDr 76, -80, -82, -84, -86, -88*

Unterecker, John Eugene 1922- *WhoAm 86, -88, WhoUSWr 88, WhoWrEP 89*

Unterecker, John Eugene 1922-1989 *BioIn 16, WhAm 9*

Untermeyer, Bryna Ivens 1909- *ConAu 77, -3NR, -31NR*

Untermeyer, Bryna Ivens 1909-1985 *BioIn 17, SmATA 61*

Untermeyer, Louis 1885-1977 *AmAu&B, AmLY, AnCL, AnMV 1926, AuBYP 2, –3, Au&Wr 71, Benet 87, BenetAL 91, BioIn 1, –4, –5, –6, –7, –8, –9, –11, –13, –14, –15, BlueB 76, CelR, Chambr 3, ChhPo, –S1, –S2, CnDAL, ConAmA, ConAmL, ConAu 5R, –73, –31NR, ConPo 70, –75, CurBio 67, –78, –78N, DcLEL, EvLB, IntAu&W 77, IntWW 74, –75, –76, –77, –78N, IntWWP 82, LongCTC, ObitOF 79, OxCAmL 65, –83, REn, REnAL, SmATA 2, –26N, –37, TwCA, –SUP, TwCWr, WhAm 7, WhNAA, Who 74, WhoAm 74, –76, WhoWorJ 72, –78, WorAlBi, WorAl, WrDr 76*

Unthank, Luisa-Teresa 1924- *Au&Wr 71, ConAu 33R, DrAS 74E, WhoAmW 77, WrDr 76, –80*
Pseud./variant:
Unthank, Tessa Brown

Unthank, Tessa Brown
Main entry: Unthank, Luisa-Teresa

Unwin, David Storr 1918- *AuBYP 2, –3, Au&Wr 71, BioIn 7, –12, –14, BlueB 76, ConAu 9R, –6NR, IntAu&W 77, –82, OxCChiL, SmATA 14, Who 74, –82, –83, –85, –88, –90, –92, WrDr 76, –80, –82, –84*
Pseud./variant:
Severn, David

Unwin, Nora S 1907-1982 *ConAu 120, SmATA 49N*

Unwin, Nora Spicer d1982 *WhoAmA 86N, –89N, –91N*

Unwin, Nora Spicer 1907-1982 *AmAu&B, AuBYP 2, –3, BioIn 1, –2, –5, –6, –8, –9, –12, –14, –16, –17, ChhPo, –S1, –S2, ConAu 21R, DcBrAr 1, IlsCB 1744, –1946, –1957, –1967, MorJA, OxCChiL, SmATA 3, Str&VC, TwCChW 78, Who 74, –82, –83N, WhoAm 74, –76, –78, WhoAmA 73, –78, –80, –82, WhoAmW 74, WhoArt 80, –82, –84N, WrDr 80, –82*

Upchurch, Boyd Bradfield 1919- *BioIn 8, –12, ConAu 25R, WrDr 76, –80, –82, –84*
Pseud./variant:
Boyd, John

Updike, John *BioIn 14, –15, –16, –17, DrAPF 87, –89, –91, –93, IntvTCA 2*

Updike, John 1932- *AmAu&B, AmWr, AnCL, AuBYP 2, –3, Au&Wr 71, Benet 87, BenetAL 91, BioIn 5, –6, –7, –8, –9, –10, –11, –12, –13, BlueB 76, BroV, CamGEL, CamGLE, CamHAL, CasWL, CelR, –90, ChhPo, ConAu 1R, –1BS, –4NR, –33NR, ConLC 1, –2, –3, –5, –7, –9, –13, –15, –23, –34, –43, –70, ConNov 72, –76, –82, –86, –91, ConPo 70, –75, –80, –85, –91, CurBio 66, –84, CyWA 89, DcLB 2, –5, –DS3, –Y80A, –Y82A, DrAF 76, DrAPF 83, –85, EncAB-H, EncWL, –2, IntAu&W 77, IntWW 74, MagSAmL, MajTwCW, MakMC, ModAL, –S1, –S2, NewYTBS 89, Novels, OxCAmL 65, –83, PenC AM, RAdv 1, –13-1, REn, REnAL, RfGAmL 87, ScF&FL 92, ShSCr 13, ShSWr, TwCWr, WebAB 74, WebE&AL, Who 74, WhoAm 74, WhoTwCL, WhoWor 74, WorAlBi, WorAu 1950, WorLitC, WrDr 76, –80, –82, –84, –86, –88, –90, –92, WrPh*

Updike, John Hoyer 1932- *EncSF 93, WrDr 94*

Upington, Marion *AuBYP 2, –3, BioIn 8*

Upton, Bertha 1849-1912 *ChhPo, ConAu 121, TwCChW 78, –83, –89*

Upton, Florence K 1873-1922 *BioIn 8, ChhPo, –S2, DcBrAr 1, DcBrBI, DcWomA, LongCTC, OxCChiL, WhAmArt 85, WhoChL*

Upton, Florence Kate 1873-1922 *BioIn 14*

Ure, Jean 1943- *AuBYP 3, BioIn 16, ChlFicS, ConAu 125, MajAI, SixBJA, SmATA 48, –14AS, TwCChW 89, TwCYAW, WrDr 90, –92, –94*
Pseud./variant:
Colin, Ann
Gregory, Jean
McCulloch, Sarah

Uris, Leon 1924- *Benet 87, BestSel 89-2, BioIn 16, –17, CelR 90, ConNov 86, –91, CyWA 89, JeAmFiW, MajTwCW, SmATA 49, SpyFic, WhoAm 86, –88, –92, –94, WhoRel 92, WhoUSWr 88, WhoWrEP 89, –92, WorAlBi, WrDr 86, –88, –90, –92*

Uris, Leon Marcus 1924- *ConAu 40NR, WrDr 94*

Urmston, Mary 1891- *BioIn 6, MorJA*

Uroff, Margaret Dickie 1935- *ConAu 93, DrAS 78E*

Urwin, George Glencarin 1916- *Au&Wr 71*

Uschold, Maud E *AnMV 1926, ChhPo, Str&VC*

Usher, Margo Scegge *AuBYP 2S, –3, ConAu X, SmATA 4*
Main entry: McHargue, Georgess

Usher, Margo Scegge 1949- *SmATA 77*

Usherwood, Stephen Dean 1907- *Au&Wr 71, ConAu 5R, –3NR, –19NR, –41NR, IntAu&W 77, –86, –89, WrDr 76, –80*

Uston, Ken *BioIn 15, –17*

Uston, Ken 1935-1987 *ConAu 123, SmATA 65*

Uttley, Alice Jane
Main entry: Uttley, Alison

Uttley, Alice Jane 1884-1976 *AuBYP 3, BioIn 13, ConAu 7NR, DcNaB 1971, SmATA 26N*

Uttley, Alison 1884-1976 *AuBYP 2, –3, Au&Wr 71, BioIn 3, –8, –9, –10, –12, –14, –16, BlmGWL, CamGLE, ChhPo, ConAu 53, –65, –X, DcLEL, FemiCLE, LongCTC, OxCChiL, OxCEng 85, SmATA 3, –X, TelT, TwCChW 78, –83, –89, Who 74, WhoChL, WrDr 76*
Pseud./variant:
Uttley, Alice Jane

Utz, Lois 1932- *BioIn 10, ConAu 25R, SmATA 5, WhoAm 80, –82, WhoAmW 77*

Utz, Lois 1932-1986 *BioIn 16, ConAu 121, SmATA 50N*

Uzair, Salem Ben *SmATA X*
Main entry: Horne, Richard H

V

Vachell, Horace Annesley 1861-1955 *BbD, BiD&SB, BioIn 1, -2, -3, -4, CmCal, ConAu 120, DcAmAu, DcLEL, DcNaB 1951, EncMys, EvLB, LongCTC, ModBrL, NewC, NotNAT B, ObitOF 79, ObitT 1951, OxCChiL, REn, TwCA, -SUP, TwCWr, WhoLA*

Vaeth, J Gordon 1921- *ConAu 5R, SmATA 17*

Vainio, Pirkko 1957- *SmATA 76*
Pseud./variant:
Hannele, Pirkko

Vaizey, George de Horne, Mrs 1857- *TwCRHW 90*

Vaizey, George DeHorne, Mrs *WomNov*

Vaizey, George DeHorne, Mrs 1860-1916 *OxCChiL*

Vaizey, John 1929-1984 *Au&Wr 71, BioIn 6, -7, -10, -14, ConAu 5R, -113, -4NR, CurBio 64, DcLEL 1940, IntAu&W 77, -82, IntWW 74, -75, -76, Who 74, WhoWor 74, WrDr 76, -80, -82, -84*

Vaizey, John Ernest 1929-1984 *DcNaB 1981*

Val
Main entry: Reading, Val

Val Baker, Denys *AuBYP 3*

Val Baker, Denys 1917- *AuBYP 2, BioIn 8, -13, -14, -15*

Valcoe, H Felix *ConAu X*
Main entry: Swartz, Harry

Valen, Felice *AuBYP 3*

Valen, Nanine 1950- *BioIn 12, ConAu 65, SmATA 21*

Valencak, Hannelore *IntAu&W 86X*
Main entry: Mayer, Hannelore

Valencak, Hannelore 1929- *BioIn 15, ConAu X, IntAu&W 77X, -82X, -89, -91, SmATA 42*

Valens, Amy 1946- *SmATA 70*

Valens, Evans G 1920- *AuBYP 3*

Valens, Evans Gladstone 1920- *WhoAm 86, -88, -90, -92, -94*

Valens, Evans Gladstone, Jr. 1920- *AuBYP 2, BioIn 7, -9, ChhPo S2, ConAu 5R, -14NR, SmATA 1, WhoAm 80, -82, -84, WhoWest 76, -78*

Valentine, James Cheyne 1935- *ConAu 45*
Pseud./variant:
Valentine, Tom

Valentine, Johnny *SmATA 72*

Valentine, L B *OxCChiL*

Valentine, Tom
Main entry: Valentine, James Cheyne

Valleau, Emily 1925- *SmATA 51*
Pseud./variant:
Hearn, Emily

Valli *IlsBYP*
Main entry: VanDeBovencamp, Valli

Valpy, Judith *ChhPo S1, IlsBYP*

Valpy, Judith 1940- *BioIn 14*

VanAbbe, Salaman 1883?-1955 *BioIn 2, -3 -5, IlsBYP, IlsCB 1946, SmATA 18*

Vanall, Emilie *AuBYP 3*

VanAllsburg, Chris *BioIn 14, -15, -16, -17, NewYTBS 89*

Van Allsburg, Chris 1949- *AuBYP 3, ChlLR 5, -13, ConAu 113, -117, -38NR, DcLB 61, FifBJA, MajAI, ScF&FL 92, SmATA 37, -53, TwCChW 89, WhoAm 84, -86, -88, -90, -92, -94*

VanAnrooy, Francine 1924- *BioIn 9, ConAu 21R, SmATA 2*
Pseud./variant:
Anrooy, Frans Van

VanCamp, J Lloyd 1898- *CanWW 70*

Vance, Eleanor Graham 1908- *BioIn 11, ConAu 9R, ForWC 70, SmATA 11, WhoAmW 74, -75, WrDr 76, -80, -82, -84, -86, -88*

Vance, F T *CarSB*

Vance, Gerald *MajAI*

Vance, Marguerite 1889-1965 *AmAu&B, AuBYP 2, -3, BioIn 2, -6, -7, -13, ConAu 109, CurBio 51, -65, MorJA, OhA&B, SmATA 29*

VanCleave, Janice 1942- *ConAu 142, SmATA 75*

VanCoevering, Jack
Main entry: VanCoevering, Jan Adrian

Van Coevering, Jack 1900- *AuBYP 3*

Van Coevering, Jan Adrian *AuBYP 3*

VanCoevering, Jan Adrian 1900- *AuBYP 2, BioIn 7, ConAu P-1*
Pseud./variant:
VanCoevering, Jack

VanDeBovencamp, Valli *IlsBYP*
Pseud./variant:
Valli

Vandegrift, Margaret *Alli SUP, AmAu&B, BiD&SB, BioIn 12, CarSB, ChhPo, -S2, DcAmAu, DcNAA, WhAm 1, WomWWA 14, WomNov*

Vandenburg, Mary Lou 1943- *BioIn 12, ConAu 73, SmATA 17, WhoAmW 91, WhoE 93*

Vanderboom, Mae M *AuBYP 2, -3, BioIn 8, -12, SmATA 14*

Vandercook, Margaret 1876- *AmAu&B, CarSB, WhNAA*

Vander Els, Betty 1936- *BioIn 16, -17, SixBJA, SmATA 63*

VanDerHaas, Henrietta *AuBYP 2, -3, BioIn 8*

VanDerHorst, Brian 1944- *ConAu 41R*

VanDerPost, Laurens Jan 1906- *Au&Wr 71, BioIn 4, -8, -9, -10, CasWL, ConAu 5R, ConLC 5, ConNov 72, -76, DcLEL, IntAu&W 77, -89, -91, IntWW 74, -79, -80, -81, -82, -83, -91, LongCTC, ModCmwL, OxCEng 85, PenC ENG, REn, TwCWr, Who 74, WhoAm 74, WhoWor 74, WorAu 1950, WrDr 76, -80*

Van Der Post, Laurens Jan, Sir 1906- *IntWW 89*

Van Dersal, William R 1907-1990 *ConAu 131*

VanDersal, William Richard 1907- *AmMWSc 73P, -76P, ConAu 77, IntAu&W 82, WhoGov 72*

Vanderveen, Bart H *ConAu X*

VanDerVeer, Judy 1912-1982 *BioIn 9, -13, -14, ChhPo, -S1, ConAu 33R, -108, SmATA 4, -33N, WhNAA*

VanDerVeldt, James A 1893?-1977 *AuBYP 2, -3, BioIn 3, -7, CathA 1952, ConAu 73*

Vande Velde, Vivian 1951- *SmATA 62*

Vandivert, Rita 1905- *BioIn 12, ConAu 5R, -6NR, SmATA 21, WhoE 74*

Vandivert, William Wilson 1912- *BioIn 6, CurBio 63, WhoAm 74*

VanDoren, Margaret 1917- *BioIn 1, IlsCB 1744*

VanDruten, John William 1901-1957 *BioIn 1, -3, -4, -5, Chambr 3, CnMD, CnThe, CurBio 44, -58, DcLEL, EncWT, FilmgC, LongCTC, McGEWD 72, ModAL, ModBrL, ModWD, NewC, NotNAT A, -B, OxCAmL 65, OxCThe 67, PenC AM, PlP&P, REn, REnAL, TwCA, -SUP, TwCLC 2, TwCWr, WhAm 3*

VanDuyn, Janet 1910- *BioIn 12, ConAu 69, SmATA 18*

VanDyke, Henry Jackson, Jr. 1852-1933 *Alli SUP, AmAu&B, BbD, BiD&SB, BioIn 1, -2, -5, -6, -11, Chambr 3, ChhPo, -S1, -S2, ConAmL, DcAmAu, DcNAA, EvLB, JBA 34, LongCTC, REnAL, Str&VC, TwCA, -SUP, WhAm 1, WhNAA*
Pseud./variant:
Dyke, Henry Van

VanDyne, Edith *AmAu&B, AuBYP 2, -3, ConAu 133, -135, -X, DcNAA, EncSF 93, MajAI, MajTwCW, SmATA 68, -X, ThrBJA, TwCChW 83, WebAB 74, -79*
Main entry: Baum, Lyman Frank
Sampson, Emma Keats Speed

VanEssen, William 1910- *Au&Wr 71, IntAu&W 82, WrDr 76, -80*

VanEveren, Jay *BioIn 1, ConICB, IlsCB 1744, WhAmArt 85*

VanGelder, Richard George 1928- *AmMWSc 73P, -76P, -82, -86, -89, -92, AuBYP 2S, -3, ConAu 73, WhoAm 74, -76, -78, -80, -82, -84, -86, -88, -90, WhoWor 74*

VanHaasteren, Joan *MedPD*

VanHomrigh, Clay M R *AuBYP 2S, -3*

Van Hook, Beverly Hennen *AuBYP 3*

VanHorn, Grace *AuBYP 2, -3, BioIn 7*

VanHorn, William 1939- *BioIn 15, ConAu 115, SmATA 43*

VanIterson, S R *BioIn 13, ConAu 102, SmATA 26*

Van Kampen, Vlasta 1943- *BioIn 16, SmATA 54*

VanLawick, Hugo 1937- *AuBYP 2S, -3, ConAu 85, WrDr 76, -80, -82, -84, -86, -88, -90, -92, -94*

Van Leeuwen, Jean *AuBYP 3*

VanLeeuwen, Jean 1937- *BioIn 10, ConAu 25R, -11NR, -28NR, FifBJA, SmATA 6, -8AS, WhoAmW 74, -75*

van Lhin, Erik *ConAu 141, -X, EncSF 93, IntAu&W 91X, MajTwCW, ScF&FL 92, SmATA 76, -X, TwCSFW 86, WrDr 86, -88*
Main entry: DelRey, Lester

Van Lhin, Erik 1915- *WrDr 94*

VanLoon, Hendrik Willem *IntvTCA 2*

VanLoon, Hendrik Willem 1882-1944 *AmAu&B, AnCL, AuBYP 2, -3, Benet 87, BenetAL 91, BioIn 1, -2, -3, -4, -7, -8, -9, -12, -14, ChhPo S2, ConAmA, ConAmL, ConAu 117, CurBio 44, DcLEL, DcNAA, JBA 34, LongCTC, NewbMB 1922, ObitOF 79, OxCAmL 65, -83, OxCChiL, REn, REnAL, SmATA 18, TwCA, -SUP, WhAm 2, WhAmArt 85, WhNAA, WrChl*
Pseud./variant:
Loon, Hendrik Willem Van

VanOort, Jan 1921- *ConAu 29R, -31NR*
Pseud./variant:
Dulieu, Jean

VanOrden, M D 1921- *AuBYP 2S, -3, BioIn 9, ConAu 37R, SmATA 4, WhoOcn 78*

VanRensselaer, Alexander 1892-1962 *AuBYP 2, -3, BioIn 6, -8, -12, ConAu 73, SmATA 14*

Van Riper, Guernsey 1909- *AuBYP 3*

VanRiper, Guernsey, Jr. 1909- *AuBYP 2S, BioIn 9, ConAu 5R, -6NR, IndAu 1917, SmATA 3, WhoMW 84, -86, -88, -90, -92, -93, WrDr 76, -80, -82, -84, -86, -88, -90, -92, -94*

VanRjndt, Philippe 1950- *BioIn 11, CanWW 89, ConAu 65, -14NR, ScF&FL 92, WrDr 80, -82, -84, -86, -88, -90, -92, -94*

VanSantvoord, George 1891-1975 *BioIn 3, -10*

VanSchaick, George Gray 1861-1924 *CarSB, DcNAA*

VanScott, Glory *BlkAWP, ConBlAP 88, DrBlPA 90*

Vansittart, Peter 1920- *Au&Wr 71, BioIn 10, -14, CamGLE, ConAu 1R, -3NR, ConLC 42, ConNov 86, -91, DcLEL 1940, EncSF 93, IntAu&W 77, -82, -86, -89, -91, OxCEng 85, ScF&FL 92, ScFSB, TwCRHW 90, WhoAm 74, -76, -78, -80, -82, -84, -86, -88, -90, -92, -94, WhoWor 74, WorAu 1950, WrDr 76, -80, -82, -84, -86, -88, -90, -92, -94*

Van Steenwyk, Elizabeth 1928- *AuBYP 3, BioIn 14*

VanSteenwyk, Elizabeth Ann 1928- *AuBYP 2S, ConAu 101, -18NR, -40NR, SmATA 34*

VanStockum, Hilda 1908- *AuBYP 2, -3, BioIn 1, -2, -5, -7, -8, -10, -12, -14, BkC 2, CathA 1930, ChhPo, ConAu 9R, -5NR, DcAmChF 1960, IlsCB 1744, -1946, -1957, -1967, JBA 51, OxCChiL, SmATA 5, TwCChW 78, -83, -89, WhAmArt 85, WrDr 80, -82, -84, -86, -88, -90, -92, -94*

VanSwearingen, Earl Cornelius 1904- *WhoSSW 73, -75, -76, -78*

VanTuyl, Barbara 1940- *BioIn 11, ConAu 53, SmATA 11*

van Vogt, Alfred E 1912- *CanWW 89*

VanVogt, Alfred Elton *IntvTCA 2*

VanVogt, Alfred Elton 1912?- *AmAu&B, AmNov, Au&Wr 71, BioIn 2, -4, -7, -10, -12, -15, -17, CanWW 70, -80, -81, -83, CnMWL, ConAu 21R, ConLC 1, ConSFA, IntAu&W 77, -82, -86, REnAL, SmATA 14, TwCA SUP, WhoAm 82, -84, -86, -88, -90, -92, -94, WhoSciF, WhoUSWr 88, WhoWest 78, -80, -82, WorAl*

VanWoerkom, Dorothy 1924- *ArtclWW 2, AuBYP 3, ConAu 26NR*

VanWoerkom, Dorothy O'Brien 1924- *AuBYP 2S, BioIn 12, -13, ConAu 57, -11NR, FifBJA, IntAu&W 82, SmATA 21, WhoAm 78, -80, -82, -84, -86, -88, -90, WhoUSWr 88, WhoWrEP 89, -92*

VanWormer, Joe
Main entry: VanWormer, Joseph Edward

VanWormer, Joseph Edward 1913- *ConAu 9R, -5NR, IntAu&W 77, SmATA 35, WhoPNW*
Pseud./variant:
VanWormer, Joe

VanWyck, Mason F
Main entry: Mason, Francis VanWyck

VanWyck Mason, F *SmATA X*

VanZwienen, Ilse Charlotte Koehn 1929- *SmATA 34*
Pseud./variant:
Koehn, Ilse

Van Zwienen, Ilse Charlotte Koehn 1929-1991 *ConAu 35NR, SmATA 67*

VanZwienin, Ilse Charlotte Koehn 1929- *BioIn 13, SmATA 28*

Varga, Judy *ConAu X, SmATA X*
Main entry: Stang, Judit

Varley, Dimitry V 1906- *BioIn 11, ConAu P-1, SmATA 10, WrDr 76, -80, -82, -84*

Varley, Susan 1961- *SmATA 63*

Varner, Velma V 1916-1972 *AmPB, BioIn 5, -9, ConAu 37R, ForWC 70*

Varney, Joyce *BioIn 7*

Vasiliu, Mircea 1920- *BioIn 3, -5, -8, -9, ChhPo S2, ConAu 21R, IlsBYP, IlsCB 1946, -1957, -1967, SmATA 2, WhoE 74, -75, -77*

Vasils, Albert 1915- *WhoAmA 78, -80N, -82N, WhoMW 78*

Vasquez, Joseph Cruz 1917- *BioIn 9, WhoGov 72*

Vass, George 1927- *BioIn 14, -16, ConAu 37R, SmATA 31, -57*

Vaughan, Anne 1913- *BioIn 1, -5, IlsBYP, IlsCB 1744, -1946*

Vaughan, Carter A *ConAu 127, SmATA X*
Main entry: Gerson, Noel Bertram

Vaughan, Carter A 1914-1988 *SmATA X*

Vaughan, Harold Cecil 1923- *BioIn 12, ConAu 29R, SmATA 14, WhoE 75*

Vaughan, Marcia 1951- *BioIn 17, SmATA 60*

Vaughan, Sam S 1928- *ConAu 13R, SmATA 14*

Vaughan-Jackson, Genevieve 1913- *BioIn 5, ForWC 70, IlsBYP, IlsCB 1946*
Pseud./variant:
Jackson, Genevieve Vaughan

Vaughn, Ruth 1935- *BioIn 12, ConAu 41R, -15NR, SmATA 14, WhoAmW 77, WhoWor 89*

Vautier, Ghislaine 1932- *BioIn 16, SmATA 53*
Pseud./variant:
Frank, Helene

Vavra, Robert James 1935- *BioIn 11, -15, ConAu 25R, -25NR, SmATA 8*

Vebell, Edward 1921- *BioIn 6*

Vecsey, George 1939- *BioIn 11, ConAu 61, SmATA 9*

Vecsey, George Spencer 1939- *WhoAm 92, -94*

Vedral, Joyce L *BioIn 17*

Vedral, Joyce L 1943- *SmATA 65*

Vedral, Joyce Lauretta 1943- *ConAu 41NR*

Veglahn, Nancy Crary 1937- *AuBYP 2, -3, BioIn 8, -10, ConAu 17R, SmATA 5*

Velazquez, Diego Rodriguez de Silva *DcAmChF 1960*

Velthuijs, Max *IlsCB 1967*

Velthuijs, Max 1923- *BioIn 16, SmATA 53*

Venable, Alan 1944- *BioIn 11, ConAu 45, SmATA 8*

Venn, Mary Eleanor *AuBYP 2, BioIn 8, SmATA X*
Main entry: Jorgensen, Mary Venn

Venn, Mary Eleanor 1908- *AuBYP 3*

Ventura, Piero *BioIn 15, -17*

Ventura, Piero 1937- *ChlLR 16, ConAu 103, IlsBYP, SmATA 43, -61*

Ventura, Piero Luigi 1937- *ConAu 39NR, MajAI*

Venturo, Betty Lou *ScF&FL 92*

Venturo, Betty Lou Baker *AuBYP 3*
Main entry: Baker, Betty

Venturo, Betty Lou Baker 1928- *AuBYP 2, ConAu 1R, ThrBJA*

Vequin, Capini *SmATA X*
Main entry: Quinn, Elisabeth

VerBeck, Frank 1858-1933 *DcNAA, WhNAA*

Vercors *ConAu 134*
Main entry: Bruller, Jean

Vercors d1991 *Who 92N*

Vercors 1902- *Benet 87, BioIn 1, -3, -4, CasWL, ClDMEL 47, ConAu X, EncWL 2, EvEuW, HisEWW, IntAu&W 82, IntWW 74, -79, -80, -81, -82, -83, -89, -91, LongCTC, ModRL, NewEScF, REn, ScFSB, TwCA SUP, TwCSFW 86A, TwCWr, Who 74, -82, -83, -85, -88, -90, WhoWor 74*

Vercors 1902-1991 *AnObit 1991, BioIn 17, EncSF 93, ScF&FL 92, TwCSFW 91A*

Verdick, Mary 1923- *ConAu 1R, -4NR*

verDorn, Bethea Stewart 1952- *SmATA 76*

Vergara, William C 1923- *WhoTech 84*

Vergara, William Charles 1923- *AmMWSc 73P, -82, -86, -89, -92, ConAu 1R, WhoE 77, WhoTech 82*

Verite, Marcelle 1904- *IntAu&W 77*

Vermeer, Jackie *AuBYP 2S, -3*

Vermes, Hal G *AuBYP 3*

Vermes, Hal G d1965 *AuBYP 2, BioIn 7*

Vermes, Jean C 1907- *AuBYP 2, BioIn 8, ConAu 106*

Vermes, Jean Campbell Pattison 1907- *AuBYP 3*

Verne, Jules 1828-1905 *AtlBL, AuBYP 2, -3, Benet 87, BbD, BiD&SB, BioIn 1, -2, -3, -4, -5, -6, -7, -8, -9, -10, -11, -12, -13, -14, -17, CarSB, CasWL, CelCen, ConAu 110, -131, CyWA 58, DcBiA, DcBiPP, DcCathB, DcEnL, DcEuL, DcLB 123, Dis&D, EuAu, EvEuW, FilmgC, GuFrLit 1, HalFC 84, -88, JBA 34, -51, LongCEL, LongCTC, MagSWL, McGEWB, NewC, NewEScF, Novels, OxCChiL, OxCEng 67, -85, OxCFr, OxCShps, PenC EUR, REn, ScF&FL 92, ScFSB, ScFEYrs, SmATA 21, TwCLC 6, -52, TwCSFW 86A, -91A, WhDW, WhoChL, WhoSciF, WorAlBi, WorAl, WrChl*

Verne, Jules, and Michel Verne *ScFEYrs*

Verne, Jules, and Gr, Paschal *ScFEYrs*

Verne, Jules Gabriel 1828-1905 *EncSF 93, MajAI*

Verner, Gerald 1896-1980 *ScF&FL 92, TwCCr&M 91*

Verner, Gerald 1897?-1980 *BioIn 13, ConAu 102, SmATA 25N, WhoSpyF*

Pseud./variant:
Stuart, Donald
Stuart, Ronald

Verney, John 1910- *BioIn 14*

Verney, John 1913- *AuBYP 3, TwCChW 89, TwCPaSc, Who 92, WrDr 86, -88, -90, -92, -94*

Verney, John 1913-1993 *ConAu 140, SmATA 75*

Verney, John, Sir 1913- *AuBYP 2, Au&Wr 71, BioIn 8, -12, ChhPo S2, ConAu 65, DcBrAr 1, IlsCB 1957, -1967, OxCChiL, SmATA 14, TwCChW 78, -83, Who 74, -82, -83, -85, -88, -90, WrDr 80, -82, -84*

Vernon, Louise A 1914- *ConAu 53, SmATA 14*

Vernon, Rosemary
Main entry: Smith, Susan Vernon

Vernor, D *ConAu X, SmATA 4*
Main entry: Casewit, Curtis

Verr, Harry Coe *ConAu 134, SmATA 67, WrDr 94*
Main entry: Kunhardt, Edith

Verral, Charles Spain d1990 *NewYTBS 90*

Verral, Charles Spain 1904- *AuBYP 2, -3, BioIn 7, -11, ConAu 16NR, -P-1, IntAu&W 77, SmATA 11, WhoE 75, -77, -81, -83, -85, -86, -89, WhoWor 89, -91, WrDr 76, -80, -82, -84, -86, -88, -90*
Pseud./variant:
Eaton, George L

Verral, Charles Spain 1904-1990 *BioIn 16, -17, ConAu 131, -37NR, SmATA 65*

Verrone, Robert J 1935?-1984 *BioIn 14, -15, ConAu 113, SmATA 39N*

Versace, Marie Teresa Rios 1917- *BioIn 9, ConAu 17R, SmATA 2*
Pseud./variant:
Rios, Tere

Vesey, A *BioIn 17*

Vesey, A 1939- *ConAu 127, SmATA 62*

Vesey, Paul *BlkWr 1, IntAu&W 86X*
Main entry: Allen, Samuel Washington

Vesey, Paul 1917- *BioIn 11, BlkAWP, ConAu X, InB&W 80, IntAu&W 82X, IntWWP 82X, SmATA X, WrDr 80, -82, -84, -86, -88, -90, -92, -94*

Vesey-Fitzgerald, Brian Seymour 1900-1981 *Au&Wr 71, BioIn 2, BlueB 76, BritAS,*

ConAu 104, -105, IntAu&W 77, IntWW 74, -75, -76, -77, Who 74, WhoWor 74, WrDr 76, -80

Vessel, Matthew F *AmMWSc 86*

Vessel, Matthew F 1912- *AmMWSc 73P, -76P, -82, ConAu 108, LEduc 74*

Vestal, Edith Ballard 1884-1970 *ConAu P-2*

Vestal, Herman B *IlsBYP*

Vestly, Anne-Cath *TwCChW 89B*

Vestly, Anne-Cath 1920- *BlmGWL*

Vestly, Anne Catharina 1920- *BioIn 12, ConAu 85, -18NR, IntAu&W 77, -82, SmATA 14, TwCChW 78B, -83B*

Vetter, Carole 1939- *ConAu 25R*

Vevers, Gwynne 1916- *BioIn 15*

Vevers, Gwynne 1916-1988 *BioIn 16, ConAu 126, SmATA 57*

Vevers, Henry Gwynne 1916- *Au&Wr 71, BioIn 15, ConAu 113, IntAu&W 77, SmATA 45*

Vevers, Henry Gwynne 1916-1988 *BioIn 16*

Viator, Vacuus *SmATA X*

Vicar, Henry *AuBYP 3*

Vicarion, Palmiro, Count *ConAu X, IntAu&W 91X, SmATA X, WrDr 82*
Main entry: Logue, Christopher

Vicker, Angus *AuBYP 2, -3, ConAu X, SmATA 1*
Main entry: Felsen, Henry Gregor

Vickers, Roy C 1888?-1965 *TwCCr&M 91*

Vickers, Roy C 1889?-1965 *Au&Wr 71, EncMys, TwCCr&M 80, -85*

Vickery, Kate *ConAu X, SmATA X*
Main entry: Kennedy, T A

Victor, Edward 1914- *BioIn 9, ConAu 1R, -3NR, IntAu&W 86, LEduc 74, SmATA 3, WrDr 76, -80, -82, -84, -86, -88, -90, -92, -94*

Victor, J *DcVicP 2*

Victor, Joan Berg 1937- *BioIn 8, -14, ConAu 105, IlsBYP, IlsCB 1957, -1967, SmATA 30*
Pseud./variant:
Berg, Joan

Viereck, Ellen 1928- *AuBYP 3*

Viereck, Ellen K 1928- *AuBYP 2, BioIn 7, ConAu 53, SmATA 14*

Viereck, Phillip R 1925- *AuBYP 2, -3, BioIn 7, -9, ConAu 5R, DcAmChF 1960, SmATA 3, WhoE 74, -75, -77, WrDr 76, -80*

Viertel, Janet d1992 *NewYTBS 92*

Viertel, Janet 1915- *BioIn 11, ConAu 53, SmATA 10*

Vigna, Judith 1936- *AuBYP 3, BioIn 12, ConAu 77, -13NR, -29NR, SmATA 15*

Vignes, Jacques 1921- *BioIn 3*

Viguers, Ruth 1903-1971 *AuBYP 3*

Viguers, Ruth Hill 1903-1971 *AuBYP 2, BiDrLUS 70, BioIn 8, -9, -10, ChhPo, -S1, ConAu 29R, -P-1, SmATA 6, WhAm 5, WhoLibS 55, -66*
Pseud./variant:
Hill, Ruth A

Viksten, Albert 1889- *AuBYP 2, -3, BioIn 7*

Vildrac, Charles Messager
Main entry: Messager, Charles

Vildrac, Charles Messager 1882-1971 *CasWL, ClDMEL 47, CnMD, ConAu X, EvEuW, McGEWD 72, -84, ModFrL, ModWD, OxCChiL, OxCFr, OxCThe 83, REn, REnWD*

Villasenor, David V 1913- *ConAu 13R*

Villiard, Paul 1910-1974 *AuBYP 2S, -3, BioIn 10, -12, -16, ConAu 53, -10NR, -P-2, SmATA 20N, -51*
Pseud./variant:
DeGros, J H

Villiers, Alan 1903- *DcChlFi*

Villiers, Alan John 1903- *AuBYP 3*

Villiers, Alan John Murray 1903-1982 *AuBYP 2, Au&Wr 71, BioIn 1, -4, -7, -10, -11, -13, BlueB 76, ConAu 1R, DcLEL, EvLB, IntWW 74, -79, -80, -81, -82N, LongCTC, OxCShps, SingR 1, SmATA 10, TwCA, -SUP, TwCWr, WhNAA, Who 74, -82, -83N, WhoAm 74, WhoWor 74, WrDr 80*

Vimar, A 1851-1916 *CarSB*

Vincent, Eric Douglas 1953- *SmATA 40*

Vincent, Felix 1946- *BioIn 15, ConAu 118, SmATA 41*
Pseud./variant:
Felix

Vincent, Gabrielle *ChlLR 13, ConAu 126, IntAu&W 91, MajAI, SixBJA, SmATA 61, TwCChW 83B, -89B*

Vincent, Joan *ConAu 21R*

Vincent, Mary Keith *ConAu X, SmATA X*
Main entry: Saint John, Wylly Folk

Vincent, W R *SmATA 73*

Vincent, William R
Main entry: Heitzmann, William Ray

Vineberg, Ethel 1902- *ConAu 85, OxCCan SUP*

Vinge, Joan Carol Dennison *TwCYAW*

Vinge, Joan Carol Dennison 1948- *EncSF 93, WrDr 94*

Vinge, Joan D *IntvTCA 2*

Vinge, Joan D 1948- *BioIn 14, -17, ConAu 93, ConLC 30, DrmM 2, IntAu&W 91, NewEScF, RGTwCSF, ScF&FL 92, SmATA 36, TwCSFW 86, -91, WrDr 84, -86, -88, -90, -92*

Vining, Elizabeth Gray *AuBYP 3*

Vining, Elizabeth Gray 1902- *AmAu&B, AmWomWr, AuBYP 2, BioIn 1, -2, -3, -4, -5, -7, -10, -11, -14, ConAu 5R, -7NR, EncJap, JBA 51, MajAI, SmATA 6, TwCChW 78, -83, -89, TwCYAW, WhoAm 74, -76, -78, -80, -82, -84, -86, -88, -90, -92, -94, WhoAmW 74, -75, WrDr 80, -82, -84, -86, -88, -90, -92, -94*
Pseud./variant:
Gray, Elizabeth Janet

Vining, Elizabeth Janet Gray 1902- *DcAmChF 1960*

Vins, Georgi Petrovich 1928- *BioIn 10, -11*

Vinson, Kathryn
Main entry: Williams, Kathryn Vinson

Vinson, Kathryn 1911- *BioIn 12, ConAu 5R, IntAu&W 77X, SmATA 21, WrDr 76, -80, -82, -84, -86, -88, -90, -92, -94*

Vinton, Iris *AmWomPl, AuBYP 2, BioIn 7, -13, ConAu 77, ForWC 70, SmATA 24*

Vinton, Iris d1988 *AuBYP 3, BioIn 15, -16, NewYTBS 88*

Vinton, Iris 1906?-1988 *ConAu 124, SmATA 55N*

Viorst, Judith *ArtclWW 2, AuBYP 2S, -3, BioIn 9, -10, -11, -12, -15, -16, ChlLR 3, ConAu 49, -2NR, DcLB 52, FourBJA, InWom SUP, SmATA 7, TwCChW 78, -83, WhoSSW 73, -75, -76, WrDr 80, -82, -84, -86, -88, -90, -92*

Viorst, Judith 1931- *BenetAL 91, BestSel 90-1, ConAu 26NR, IntAu&W 86, MajAI, SmATA 70, TwCChW 89, WrDr 94*

Viorst, Judith Stahl 1931- *WhoAm 92*

Vip *AuBYP 2S, -3, ConAu X, ConGrA 1, SmATA X, WorECar*
Main entry: Partch, Virgil

Vip 1916-1984 *BioIn 14, -15*

Vipont, Charles *ConAu X, -38NR, IntAu&W 77X, -82X, MajAI, WhoChL, WrDr 76, -80, -82, -84, -86, -88, -90, -92*
Main entry: Foulds, Elfrida Vipont

Vipont, Elfrida *Au&Wr 71, BioIn 2, -8, ChhPo S1, ConAu X, -38NR, IntAu&W 77X, -82X, MajAI, OxCChiL, TwCChW 78, -83, WhoChL, WrDr 76, -80, -82, -84, -86, -88*
Main entry: Foulds, Elfrida Vipont

Vipont, Elfrida 1902- *BioIn 16, TwCChW 89*

Virgines, George E 1920- *ConAu 25R, -12NR, -28NR*

Viscott, David S 1938- *BioIn 15, -17, ConAu 26NR, SmATA 65, WrDr 86, -88, -90, -92*

Viscott, David Steven 1938- *AuNews 1, BiDrAPA 77, BioIn 9, -10, ConAu 29R, IntAu&W 77, WrDr 76, -80, -82, -84, -94*

Visser, W F H 1900-1968 *BioIn 11, ConAu P-2, SmATA 10*

Vitray, Laura *BioIn 10*

Vittengl, Moran John 1928- *AuBYP 2, BioIn 7, ConAu 5R*

Vittengl, Morgan John 1928- *AuBYP 3*

Vivas, Julie *ChlBIlD*

Vivelo, Jackie *BioIn 17*
Main entry: Vivelo, Jacqueline Jean

Vivelo, Jackie 1943- *ScF&FL 92, SmATA X*

Vivelo, Jacqueline Jean 1943- *SmATA 63, WhoE 91, -93, WhoMW 93, WhoWor 93*
Pseud./variant:
Vivelo, Jackie

Vivian, Frederick d1968 *AuBYP 2S, -3*

Vivier, Colette 1898- *FourBJA*

Vizenor, Gerald Robert *DrAPF 87, –89, –91, –93*

Vizenor, Gerald Robert 1934- *BioIn 14, –17, ConAu 13R, –5NR, –21NR, DrAP 75, DrAPF 83, –85, WhoWest 89, –92, –94*

Vlahos, Olivia 1924- *BioIn 14, ConAu 21R, SmATA 31*

Vlasic, Bob *ConAu X, SmATA X*
Main entry: Hirsch, Phil

Voake, Charlotte *AuBYP 3*

Vo-Dinh, Mai 1933- *AmArt, BioIn 12, ConAu 77, –13NR, –29NR, ConGrA 2, PrintW 83, –85, SmATA 16, WhoAmA 78, –80, –82, –84, –86, –89, –91*

Vogel, Carole Garbuny 1951- *SmATA 70*

Vogel, Helen Wolff 1918- *ConAu 17R, ForWC 70*

Vogel, Ilse-Margret 1918- *BioIn 12, ChhPo, ConAu 13R, –7NR, SmATA 14*

Vogel, John H, Jr. 1950- *BioIn 12, ConAu 77, SmATA 18*

Vogel, Ray *AuBYP 3*

Vogel, Ray 1943- *AuBYP 2S, WhoWor 74*

Vogelsinger, Hubert 1938- *ConAu 25R, WhoE 74, –75, –77*

Vogt, Esther Loewen 1915- *ConAu 17R, –7NR, ForWC 70, IntAu&W 77, –82, –86, SmATA 14, WhoAmW 74, –75*

Vogt, Gregory *SmATA 45*

Vogt, Marie Bollinger 1921- *BioIn 15, ConAu 57, SmATA 45*

Voight, Virginia Frances 1909- *AuBYP 2, –3, BioIn 6, –8, –11, ConAu 5R, –2NR, –18NR, MorJA, SmATA 8*

Voigt, Cynthia 1942- *ArtclWW 2, Au&Arts 3, AuBYP 3, BioIn 13, ChlLR 13, ConAu 106, –18NR, –37NR, –40NR, ConLC 30, DcAmChF 1960, –1985, FifBJA, MajAI, ScF&FL 92, SmATA 33, –48, TwCChW 89, TwCYAW, WhoAm 84, –86, –88, –92, –94, WhoAmW 89, –91, –93, WhoUSWr 88, WhoWrEP 89, –92, WrDr 86, –88, –90, –92, –94*

Voigt, Erna 1925- *BioIn 14, SmATA 35*
Pseud./variant:
Voigt-Rother, Erna

Voigt-Rother, Erna
Main entry: Voigt, Erna

Voils, Jessie Wiley 1900- *ConAu P-2, WhNAA, WhoAmW 74, –75*

Vojtech, Anna 1946- *BioIn 15, SmATA 42*

Volgyes, Ivan 1936- *AmMWSc 73S, –78S, ConAu 104, –20NR*

Volk, Vic 1906- *BioIn 1*

Volpe, Robert 1942- *BioIn 10, –11, WhoAmA 78, –80, –82, –84, –86, –89, –91*

VonAlmedingen, Martha Edith *ConAu X, SmATA 3*
Main entry: Almedingen, E M

VonArnim, Achim *OxCChiL*

VonDaniken, Erich 1935- *AuBYP 2S, –3, AuNews 1, BioIn 10, –11, –12, BioNews 75, ConAu 37R, ConLC 30, CurBio 76, EncO&P 1S1, –2, –3, EncSF 93, IntAu&W 77, UFOEn, WhoSciF, WhoWor 82, –84, WorAl*

VonDumzene, Anneliese Freifrau *ConICB*
Pseud./variant:
VonLewinski, Anneliese

VonHagen, Christine *AuBYP 2, –3, BioIn 7*

VonHagen, Victor Wolfgang 1908- *AmAu&B, AuBYP 2, –3, Au&Wr 71, BioIn 3, –4, –5, –8, –13, ConAu 105, CurBio 42, IntAu&W 77, REnAL, SmATA 29, TwCA SUP, Who 74, –82, –83, –85, WhoAm 74, –76, –78, WhoWor 74, WrDr 76, –80, –82, –84, –86*

Von Hippel, Gertrud *AuBYP 3*

VonHippel, Ursula *BioIn 7*

VonHirsch, Andrew 1934- *ConAu 81, –14NR, WhoE 89*

VonHoffman, Nicholas 1929- *AmAu&B, BioIn 8, –10, CelR, –90, ConAu 81, –34NR, EncAJ, EncTwCJ, IntAu&W 82, WhoAm 74, –76, –78, –80, –82, –84, –86, –88, –90, –92, –94, WhoE 89, –91, –93, WhoSSW 73, –75, –76, WrDr 90, –92, –94*

Von Klopp, Vahrah *AuBYP 3, ConAu 73, SmATA X*
Main entry: Malvern, Gladys

VonLewinski, Anneliese
Main entry: VonDumzene, Anneliese Freifrau

VonLewinski, Anneliese Freifrau *ConICB*

Vonnegut, Kurt *DrAPF 87, –89, –91, –93*

Vonnegut, Kurt 1922- *AmWr S2, Au&Arts 6, BenetAL 91, BestSel 90-4, BioIn 14, -15, -16, -17, IntAu&W 89, -91, ModAL S2, PostFic, ScF&FL 92, ScFSB*

Vonnegut, Kurt, Jr. *IntvTCA 2*

Vonnegut, Kurt, Jr. 1922- *Benet 87, BroV, CamGEL, CamGLE, CamHAL, ConAu 25NR, ConDr 93, ConLC 40, -60, ConNov 86, -91, ConTFT 6, CurBio 91, CyWA 89, EncSF 93, IntWW 89, -91, MagSAmL, MajTwCW, NewEScF, RAdv 13-1, RGTwCSF, RfGAmL 87, ShSCr 8, SpyFic, TwCSFW 86, -91, TwCYAW, Who 88, -90, -92, WhoAm 86, -88, -90, -92, -94, WhoE 91, -93, WhoEnt 92, WhoUSWr 88, WhoWor 87, -89, -91, -93, WhoWrEP 89, -92, WorAlBi, WorLitC, WrDr 86, -88, -90, -92, -94*

VonSchmidt, Eric 1931- *AuBYP 2, -3, BioIn 8, -14, -16, ChhPo, ConAu 17R, -13NR, IlsCB 1957, -1967, SmATA 36, -50, WhoAmA 89, -91*

VonStorch, Anne B *BioIn 9, ConAu P-2, SmATA 1*
Main entry: Malcolmson, Anne Elizabeth

VonTrapp, Maria Augusta
Main entry: Trapp, Maria Augusta Von

VonTrapp, Maria Augusta 1905- *AmCath 80, ConAu 81*

VonTrapp, Maria Augusta 1905-1987 *ConAu 122*

Vorspan, Albert 1924- *ConAu 21R, -13NR, WhoAm 78, WhoAmJ 80, WhoWorJ 72, -78*

Vorwald, Alan *AuBYP 2, -3, BioIn 8*

Vos, Ida 1931- *SmATA 69*

Vosburgh, John R 1911- *BioIn 5*

Vosburgh, Leonard 1912- *BioIn 12, IlsBYP, SmATA 15*

Voss, Carl Hermann 1910- *AmAu&B, BlueB 76, ConAu 21R, -10NR, IntAu&W 77, -82, -86, -89, WhoAm 74, -76, -78, -80, -82, -84, -86, -88, -90, -94, WhoRel 92, WhoWor 80*

Voss, George Lewis 1922- *ConAu 57, WhoWest 78*

Voute, Kathleen 1892- *BioIn 5, DcWomA, IlsBYP, IlsCB 1946, WhAmArt 85*

Vox, Maximilien *BioIn 1, IlsCB 1744*

Voyle, Mary *AuBYP 2, -3, ConAu X, DcLEL 1940, IntAu&W 77X, -82X, -91X, SmATA X, WorAu 1950*
Main entry: Manning, Rosemary

Vreeland, Herbert Harold, III 1920- *AmMWSc 73S, -78S*

Vries, Leonard De
Main entry: DeVries, Leonard

Vries, Leonard De 1919- *AuBYP 2S, -3, ConAu 113*

Vroman, Mary Elizabeth d1967 *BioIn 14*

Vroman, Mary Elizabeth 1923-1967 *BioIn 7, BlkAWP, BlkWr 1, ConAu 109, -125, ConBlAP 88, DcAfL, DcLB 33, InB&W 80, SelBAAf, SelBAAu*

Vugteveen, Verna Aardema *AuBYP 3*

Vugteveen, Verna Aardema 1911- *ConAu 39NR*

Vuilleumier, Marion 1918- *ConAu 81, ForWC 70*

Vuong, Lynette 1938- *SmATA 60*

Vuong, Lynette Dryer 1938- *WhoWrEP 89*

Vuong, Lynette Dyer 1938- *BioIn 17, IntAu&W 89*

W

Waaland, J Robert 1943- *AmMWSc 73P*

Wabbes, Maria *IlsBYP*
Pseud./variant:
Florence

Waber, Bernard 1924- *AmPB, AuBYP 2, –3, BioIn 7, –8, –9, –10, –12, ConAu 1R, –2NR, –38NR, IlsCB 1957, –1967, MajAI, SmATA 40, –47, ThrBJA, TwCChW 78, –83, –89, WrDr 80, –82, –84, –86, –88, –90, –92, –94*

Wachter, Oralee *BioIn 16, –17*

Wachter, Oralee 1935- *ConAu 122, SmATA 61, WrDr 90, –92*

Wachter, Oralee Roberts 1935- *SmATA 51, WrDr 94*

Wacker, Charles H *AuBYP 3*

Wacker, Charles H, Jr. 1925- *AuBYP 2S, ConAu 73*

Wackerbarth, Marjorie *BioIn 6, ConAu P-1, MinnWr*

Waddell, Evelyn Margaret 1918- *BioIn 11, ConAu 53, IntAu&W 77, –82, –86, –89, –91, SmATA 10, WrDr 76, –80, –82, –84, –86, –88, –90, –92*
Pseud./variant:
Cook, Lyn

Waddell, Helen Jane 1889-1965 *AnCL, BiDIrW, BioIn 7, –9, –14, –15, –16, –17, Chambr 3, ChhPo S2, DcIrW 1, DcLEL, DcNaB 1961, EncBrWW, EvLB, GrBr, LongCTC, NewC, OxCEng 85, REn, TwCA, –SUP, TwCWr*

Waddell, Martin *ScF&FL 92*

Waddell, Martin 1941- *ChlFicS, ChlLR 31, ConAu 113, –34NR, IntAu&W 86, –89, –91, SmATA 43, –15AS, TwCChW 83, –89, WrDr 92, –94*
Pseud./variant:
Sefton, Catherine

Wade, Mary Hazelton Blanchard 1860-1936 *AmAu&B, AmLY, AmWomPl, CarSB, DcAmAu, DcNAA, WhAm 1, WhNAA, WomWWA 14*

Wade, Theodore E, Jr. 1936- *SmATA 37*

Wade, Theodore Everett, Jr. 1936- *WhoUSWr 88, WhoWest 87, WhoWrEP 89, –92*

Wadowski-Bak, Alice *IlsBYP*

Wadsworth, Wallace Carter 1894-1933 *BioIn 1, IndAu 1917, Str&VC*

Wagenheim, Kal 1935- *BioIn 12, ConAu 29R, –26NR, SmATA 21*

Wagenknecht, Edward 1900- *AmAu&B, BioIn 4, –17, BlueB 76, ConAu 1R, –6NR, –22NR, DcLB 103, DrAS 74E, –78E, –82E, IntAu&W 77, –82, –86, –89, –91, REn, REnAL, ScF&FL 92, TwCA SUP, WhoAm 74, –76, –78, –80, –82, –84, –86, –88, –90, –92, –94, WrDr 76, –80, –82, –84, –86, –88, –90, –92, –94*

Wagenvoord, James 1937- *ConAu 41R*

Wagner, Frederick 1928- *AuBYP 2, –3, BioIn 7, ConAu 5R*

Wagner, Frederick Reese 1928- *WhoAm 90*

Wagner, Glenn A *AuBYP 2, –3, BioIn 7, MedPD*

Wagner, Jane *AuBYP 2S, –3, ConAu 109, DcAmChF 1960, LesBEnT, SmATA 33, WhoLibS 66*

Wagner, Jane 1935- *ConAu 42NR, ConTFT 6, IntMPA 88, –92*

Wagner, Jenny *OxCChiL, TwCChW 89, WrDr 90, –92, –94*

Wagner, John Philip 1943- *WhoAmA 73, –78, WhoWest 76, –78*

Wagner, Ken 1911- *ConAu 37R*

Wagner, Margaret D 1949- *ConAu 5R, ForWC 70, WhoAmW 75*

Wagner, Sharon Blythe 1936- *BioIn 9, ConAu 25R, –10NR, IntAu&W 77, –91, SmATA 4, WhoAmW 74, –75, WrDr 76, –80, –82, –84, –86, –88, –90, –92, –94*

Wagner, Walter 1927?-1983? *ConAu 109*

Wagoner, David *DrAPF 87, –89, –91, –93*

Wagoner, David 1926- *AmAu&B, BenetAL 91, BioIn 3, –10, –12, ConAu 1R, –3AS, –2NR, ConLC 3, –5, –15, ConNov 72, –76, –82, –86, –91, ConPo 70, –75, –80, –85, –91, CroCAP, DcLB 5, DrAF 76, DrAP 75, DrAPF 83, –85, DrAS 74E, –82E, OxCAmL 83, SmATA 14, TwCWW 91, WhoAm 80, –82, –84, WhoPNW, WorAu 1950, WrDr 76, –82, –84, –86, –88, –90, –92*

Wagoner, David Russell 1926- *WrDr 94*

Wagoner, Jean Brown 1896- *IndAu 1917*

Wahl, Jan 1933- *AuBYP 2, –3, BioIn 8, –9, –14, –15, ConAu 25R, –12NR, IntAu&W 91, SmATA 2, –34, –3AS, ThrBJA, TwCChW 78, –83, –89, WrDr 80, –82, –84, –86, –88, –90, –92, –94*

Wahl, Jan Boyer 1933- *ConAu 38NR, MajAI, SmATA 73*

Wahl, Robert 1948- *ConAu 49, –1NR*

Wahloo, Per *Benet 87*

Wahloo, Per 1926-1975 *BioIn 9, –10, ConAu 57, –61, ConLC 7, EncMys, EncSF 93, InWom SUP, NewYTBE 71, Novels, ObitOF 79, ScF&FL 92, ScFSB, TwCCr&M 80B, –85B, –91B, WorAlBi, WorAl*

Wahloo, Per, and Maj Sjowall *TwCCr&M 91B*

Waide, Jan 1952- *BioIn 13, ConAu 105, SmATA 29*

Wain, Louis 1860-1939 *BioIn 14, –16, TwCPaSc*

Wain, Louis 1861?-1939 *BioIn 2, –8, –9, ChhPo, –S1, –S2, WhoChL*

Wainscott, John Milton 1910-1981 *BioIn 16, SmATA 53*

Waite, Helen Elmira 1903-1967 *BioIn 7, ConAu 1R*

Waite, P B 1922- *SmATA 64*

Waite, Peter B 1922- *CanWW 89*

Waite, Peter Busby 1922- *BioIn 17, BlueB 76, CanWW 70, –80, –81, –83, ConAu 9R, DrAS 74H, –82H, IntAu&W 91, OxCCan, –SUP, WhoAm 80, WhoWor 80, WrDr 80*

Waitley, Douglas 1927- *ConAu 9NR, SmATA 30*

Wakefield, Connis LaVon 1948- *ConAu 65*

Wakefield, Jean L *ConAu X, SmATA X*
Main entry: Laird, Jean Elouise Rydeski

Wakefield, Priscilla 1750?-1832 *Alli, BiDLA, BioIn 16, BritAu 19, CarSB, DcBiPP, DcNaB, OxCChiL*

Wakefield, Priscilla 1751-1832 *DcBrAmW, FemiCLE*

Wakefield, S A *OxCChiL*

Wakeman, Marion Freeman 1891-1953 *BioIn 5, DcWomA, IlsBYP, IlsCB 1946*

Wakin, Edward 1927- *ConAu 5R, –2NR, –17NR, SmATA 37, WhoE 74, WhoUSWr 88, WhoWrEP 89, –92*

Walck, Henry Z 1908?-1984 *BioIn 1, –14, –15, ConAu 114, SmATA 40N*

Walcott, Fred George 1894- *ConAu 37R, DrAS 74E, –78E, WhoMW 76*

Walcutt, Charles C 1908-1989 *BioIn 16*

Walcutt, Charles Child 1908- *ConAu 1R, –3NR, DrAS 74E, –78E, –82E, WrDr 76, –80, –82, –84, –86, –88, –90*

Walcutt, Charles Child 1908-1989 *ConAu 128*

Wald, Carol 1935- *BioIn 10, –13, ConAu 65, ConGrA 3, WhoAmA 91*

Waldeck, Jo Besse McElveen *BioIn 2, JBA 51*

Waldeck, Theodore J 1894- *AuBYP 2, –3, BioIn 2, –8, JBA 51*

Walden, Amelia Elizabeth *TwCYAW, WhoAm 86, –88, –90, –92, –94, WhoAmW 87, WhoWor 87, –89*

Walden, Amelia Elizabeth 1909- *AuBYP 2, –3, BioIn 4, –6, –7, –9, ConAu 1R, –2NR, CurBio 56, ForWC 70, IntAu&W 77, –82, MorJA, SmATA 3, WhoAm 74, –76, –78, –80, –82, –84, WhoAmW 74, –75, –77, –83, –85, WhoE 74, –77, WhoWor 74, –78, –80, –82, –84, WrDr 76, –80, –82, –84*

Walden, Howard T, II 1897-1981 *ConAu 45, –103, IntAu&W 77*

Waldherr, Kris 1963- *SmATA 76*

Waldman, Bruce 1949- *BioIn 12, SmATA 15*

Waldman, Frank 1919- *AuBYP 2, -3, BioIn 7*
Pseud./variant:
Webster, Joe

Waldman, Frank 1919-1990 *ScF&FL 92*

Waldman, Neil 1947- *ConAu 128, SmATA 51*

Waldron, Ann Wood 1924- *ConAu 13R, -7NR, SmATA 16, WhoAm 74, -76*

Waldrop, W Earl 1910- *ConAu 5R*

Waley, Alison 1901- *ArtclWW 2, BioIn 13*

Walford, Astrid 1907- *BioIn 5, ChhPo, IlsBYP, IlsCB 1946*
Pseud./variant:
Cumpston, Astrid Kate Oatelaye

Walker, Alice *DrAPF 87, -89, -91, -93*

Walker, Alice 1944- *AfrAmAl 6, AfrAmW, AmWomWr, -92, AmWr S3, ArtclWW 2, AuSpks, Au&Arts 3, Benet 87, BenetAL 91, BestSel 89-4, BioIn 11, -13, BlkAWP, BlkAull, -92, BlkLC, BlkWWr, BlkWr 1, BlkWrNE, BlmGWL, BroV, BroadAu, CamGLE, CamHAL, CelR 90, ConAu 37R, -9NR, -27NR, ConBlB 1, ConHero 1, ConLC 5, -6, -9, -19, -27, -46, -58, ConNov 86, -91, CurBio 84, CyWA 89, DcLB 6, -33, DrAF 76, DrAP 75, DrAPF 83, -85, EncAACR, EncSF 93, EncWB, FemiCLE, HanAmWH, InB&W 80, InWom SUP, IntAu&W 82, IntDcWB, LivgBAA, MagSAmL, MajTwCW, ModAL S2, ModAWWr, ModBlW, NegAl 76, -83, -89, NewYTBS 83, NotBlAW 92, OxCAmL 83, PostFic, RfGAmL 87, ScF&FL 92, SelBAAf, ShSCr 5, SmATA 31, WhoAm 74, -76, -78, -84, WhoAmW 74, WhoBlA 75, -77, -80, -85, -88, WorAlBi, WorAu 1975, WrDr 86, -88, -90, -92*

Walker, Alice Malsenior 1944- *BlkWr 2, TwCYAW*

Walker, Barbara Jeanne Kerlin 1921- *ConAu 38NR*

Walker, Barbara K 1921- *AuBYP 2S, BioIn 9, ConAu 33R, -16NR, SmATA 4*
Pseud./variant:
Kilreon, Beth

Walker, Barbara M 1928- *SmATA 57*

Walker, Barbara Muhs 1928- *BioIn 16*

Walker, Braz 1934-1983 *BioIn 15, ConAu 69, SmATA 45*

Walker, Charles 1911- *ConAu 17R, WrDr 76, -80, -82, -84, -86, -88*

Walker, Charles W *IlsBYP*

Walker, David 1911- *IntAu&W 91, TwCChW 89, WhoCanL 87, WrDr 86, -88, -90, -92*

Walker, David 1911-1992 *ScF&FL 92*

Walker, David G 1926- *SmATA 60*

Walker, David Harry 1911- *BenetAL 91, BioIn 6, -10, -11, CanWW 70, -79, -80, -81, -83, -89, CanWr, CasWL, ConAu 1R, -1NR, ConNov 72, -76, DcLEL 1940, IntAu&W 77, -82, LongCTC, OxCCan, -SUP, OxCCanL, OxCChiL, Profile 1, REnAL, SmATA 8, TwCChW 78, -83, Who 74, -82, -83, -85, -88, -92, WhoAm 76, -78, -80, -82, -84, -86, -88, -90, WhoCan 73, -75, -77, -80, -82, -84, WhoCanL 85, -92, WhoWor 80, WorAu 1950, WrDr 76, -80, -82, -84*

Walker, David Harry 1911-1992 *AnObit 1992, ConAu 137, EncSF 93, SmATA 71, WhAm 10, WrDr 94N*

Walker, David Harry, Major 1911- *Who 90*

Walker, Diana 1925- *AuBYP 2S, -3, BioIn 11, -13, ConAu 49, -4NR, Profile 2, SmATA 9*

Walker, Dugald Stewart 1888?-1937 *ChhPo, -S1, -S2, ConICB, DcNAA, WhAm 1, WhAmArt 85*

Walker, Frank 1930- *ConAu 69, SmATA 36*

Walker, Gil 1927- *BioIn 6*

Walker, Greta 1927- *ConAu 77*

Walker, Holly Beth *ConAu X, SmATA X*
Main entry: Bond, Gladys Baker

Walker, James Perkins 1829-1868 *Alli, AmAu&B, BioIn 4, CarSB, DcAmAu, DcNAA*

Walker, Kathrine Sorley *AuBYP 2, -3, BioIn 8, -15, EngPo*

Walker, Lou Ann 1952- *ConAu 126, IntAu&W 91, SmATA 53, -66, WhoUSWr 88, WhoWrEP 89, -92*

Walker, Louise Jean 1891-1976 *BioIn 14, ConAu 110, MichAu 80, SmATA 35N*

Walker, Mary Alexander *DrAPF 87, -89, -91, -93*

Walker, Mary Alexander 1927- *ConAu 104, DrAPF 83, -85, IntAu&W 89, -91, ScF&FL 92, SmATA 61, WhoAmW 85, -87*

Walker, Mildred *AmAu&B, AmNov, Au&Wr 71, BioIn 1, -2, -4, ConAu X, CurBio 47, InB&W 80, MichAu 80, REnAL, SmATA X, TwCA SUP, WhoAm 74, -76, WhoAmW 74, -75, WrDr 76, -80, -82, -84*
Main entry: Schemm, Mildred Walker

Walker, Mildred 1905- *BenetAL 91*

Walker, Mort 1923- *BioIn 2, -8, -11, ConAu 49, -3NR, -25NR, ConGrA 2, EncACom, EncTwCJ, SmATA 8, WhoAm 74, -76, -78, -80, -82, -84, -86, -88, -90, -92, -94, WhoAmA 73, -78, -80, -82, -84, -86, -89, -91, WhoE 74, WhoWor 74*

Walker, Nedda *BioIn 5, IlsBYP, IlsCB 1946*

Walker, Pamela *DrAPF 87, -89, -91, -93*

Walker, Pamela 1948- *BioIn 13, DrAPF 83, -85, SmATA 24, WhoUSWr 88, WhoWrEP 89, -92*

Walker, Richard L *WhoAmP 93*

Walker, Richard Louis 1922- *AmMWSc 73S, -78S, BioIn 13, ConAu 9R, -7NR, IntAu&W 77, -82, WhoAm 74, -76, -78, -80, -82, -84, -86, -88, -90, -92, -94, WhoWor 82, -84, -87*

Walker, Robert H 1924- *ConAu 23NR*

Walker, Robert Harris 1924- *ConAu 13R, -7NR, DrAS 74E, -78E, -82H, WhoAm 80, -82, -84, -86, -88, -90, -92, -94, WhoWor 93*

Walker, Robert W 1948- *ConAu 23NR, ScF&FL 92, SmATA 66*

Walker, Robert Wayne 1948- *IntAu&W 86, -89, -91, WhoUSWr 88, WhoWrEP 89, -92*
Pseud./variant:
Caine, Geoffrey
Hale, Glenn
Robertson, Stephen

Walker, Stephen J 1951- *BioIn 11, SmATA 12*

Walker, Stuart 1880?-1941 *ConAu 120, TwCChW 89*

Walker, Stuart 1887-1941 *HalFC 88*

Walker, Stuart 1888?-1941 *AmAu&B, ArtsAmW 3, BenetAL 91, BioIn 3, ChhPo S2, ConAmL, CurBio 41, DcNAA, FilmgC, HalFC 84, LiHiK, NotNAT B, ObitOF 79, OxCAmT 84, REnAL, TwCChW 78, -83, WhAm 1, WhNAA*

Walker, W H *DcBrBI, OxCAusL*

Walker, W H 1827-1895 *ScFEYrs*

Walkey, Samuel 1871?-1950? *BioIn 8, WhoChL*

Wall, Charles *Alli, CarSB*

Wall, Dorothy 1894- *AuWomWr*

Wall, Dorothy 1894-1942 *OxCAusL, OxCChiL, TwCChW 83, -89*

Wall, Gertrude Wallace *AuBYP 2, -3, BioIn 7*

Wallace, Barbara Brooks *ConAu 28NR, SmATA 17AS, WrDr 86, -88, -90, -92, -94*

Wallace, Barbara Brooks 1922- *BioIn 9, ConAu 29R, -11NR, IntAu&W 77, SixBJA, SmATA 4, WhoAmW 77, -81, WrDr 76, -80, -82, -84*

Wallace, Beverly Dobrin 1921- *BioIn 12, ConAu 101, SmATA 19*

Wallace, Bill
Main entry: Wallace, William Keith

Wallace, Bill 1947- *SmATA 47*

Wallace, Bryan Edgar *Au&Wr 71*

Wallace, Daisy *ConAu X, SmATA X*
Main entry: Cuyler, Margery Stuyvesant

Wallace, Dillon 1863-1939 *AmAu&B, AmLY, BenetAL 91, BioIn 2, -3, CarSB, DcNAA, JBA 34, -51, OxCCan, REnAL, WhAm 1, WhNAA*

Wallace, Edgar *IntvTCA 2*

Wallace, Edgar 1875-1932 *Benet 87, BioIn 2, -7, -8, -10, -14, CamGWoT, CasWL, ConAu 115, CrtSuMy, DcLB 70, DcLEL, DcNaB 1931, EncMys, EncSF 93, EncSoA EvLB, FilmgC, GrBr, HalFC 84, -88, LongCTC, ModBrL, NewC, Novels, OxCEng 67, -85, OxCThe 67, PenC ENG, REn, RfGEnL 91, ScF&FL 92, ScFSB, ScFEYrs, TwCA, -SUP, TwCCr&M 80, -85, -91, TwCSFW 86, -91, TwCWr, WhoSpyF, WhoTwCL, WorAlBi, WorAl*

Wallace, Ian 1950- *CanWW 89, ConAu 25NR, -38NR, MajAI, SixBJA, SmATA 53, -56, TwCChW 89, WhoCanL 87, -92, WrDr 90, -92, -94*

Wallace, John Adam 1915- *AuBYP 2, -3, BioIn 7, -9, ConAu 5R, SmATA 3*

Wallace, Lewis 1827-1905 *Alli SUP, AmAu AmAu&B, BibAL 8, BbD, BiD&SB, BioIn 1, -2, -3, -5, -6, -7, -12, CarSB, CasWL, Chambr 3, ChhPo, CivWDc, CnDAL, CyWA 58, DcAmAu, DcAmDH 80, -89, DcBiA, DcEnA A, DcLEL, DcNAA, EncAB-H,*

EvLB, HarEnUS, IndAu 1816, JBA 34, McGEWB, NotNAT B, OxCAmL 65, PenC AM, RAdv 1, -13-1, REn, REnAL, WebAB 74, -79, WebAMB, WhAm 1, WhCiWar

Wallace, M Imelda, Sister 1884- *BioIn 1, BkC 4*

Wallace, May Nickerson 1902- *AuBYP 2, -3, BioIn 7*

Wallace, Nigel *ConAu X, -29NR, SmATA X*

Wallace, Robert *DrAPF 87, -89, -91, -93*

Wallace, Robert 1932- *SmATA 47, WhoUSWr 88, WhoWrEP 89, -92*

Wallace, Robert A 1932- *SmATA 37*

Wallace, William Keith 1947- *ConAu 124, SmATA 53*
Pseud./variant:
Wallace, Bill

Wallace, William N 1924- *ConAu 13R*

Wallace, William Stewart 1884-1970 *BioIn 4, -9, ConAu 116, DcLEL, OxCCan, WhNAA, WhoLibS 55*

Wallace-Brodeur, Ruth 1941- *BioIn 15, -16, ConAu 107, SmATA 41, -51*

Wallas, Ada Radford d1934 *CarSB, ChhPo*

Waller, Leslie 1923- *AmAu&B, AmNov, AuBYP 2S, -3, Au&Wr 71, BioIn 2, -6, -12, ConAu 1R, -2NR, ScF&FL 92, SmATA 20, WrDr 84, -86, -88, -90, -92, -94*

Wallerstedt, Don *IlsBYP*

Wallhauser, Henry T 1930- *ConAu 29R*

Wallis, Diz 1949- *SmATA 77*

Wallis, G McDonald *ConAu X, ConSFA, ScF&FL 92, SmATA X*
Main entry: Campbell, Hope

Wallis, George C *ScFEYrs, WhoSciF*

Wallis, George C 1871-1956 *EncSF 93, ScF&FL 92*

Wallis, George C and Wallis B *ScFEYrs*

Wallis, Geraldine June McDonald 1925- *EncSF 93*

Wallner, Alexandra 1946- *ConAu 73, -13NR, SmATA 41, -51*

Wallner, John C 1945- *MajAI, SmATA 51*

Wallner, John Charles 1945- *BioIn 11, -12, FifBJA, IlsCB 1967, SmATA 10*

Wallower, Lucille 1910- *AuBYP 2, -3, BiDrLUS 70, BioIn 7, -11, ConAu 21R, -9NR, IntAu&W 77, -82, -89, SmATA 11, WhoAmW 74, -75, WrDr 76, -80, -82, -84, -86, -88, -90, -92, -94*

Walmsley, Leo 1892-1966 *BioIn 4, -8, CamGLE, ConAu P-1, DcLEL, LongCTC, NewC, TwCA, -SUP, TwCWr*

Walpole, Hugh Seymour, Sir 1884-1941 *BioIn 1, -2, -3, -4, -5, -6, -7, -8, -9, -10, CasWL, Chambr 3, ChhPo S2, ConAu 104, CurBio 41, CyWA 58, DcBiA, DcLB 34, DcLEL, DcNaB 1941, Dis&D, EvLB, FilmgC, GrBr, HalFC 84, LongCTC, ModBrL, NewC, NotNAT B, Novels, ObitOF 79, OxCChiL, OxCEng 67, -85, PenC ENG, REn, TwCA, -SUP, TwCLC 5, TwCWr, WebE&AL, WhScrn 74, -83, -77, WhoChL, WhoHol B, WhoHr&F, WhoLA, WhoTwCL, WorEFlm*

Walser, Richard 1908- *BioIn 3, -4, -5, ChhPo, ConAu 5R, -2NR, DrAS 74E, -78E, -82E*

Walsh, Ann 1942- *SmATA 62*

Walsh, Chad *DrAPF 87, -89, -91, -93*

Walsh, Chad 1914- *AmAu&B, Au&Wr 71, BioIn 2, -4, -6, -10, ConAu 1R, -6NR, ConPo 70, -75, -80, -85, -91, CurBio 62, DrAP 75, DrAPF 83, -85, DrAS 74E, -78E, -82E, WhoAm 74, -76, -78, WorAu 1950, WrDr 76, -80, -82, -84, -86, -88, -90, -92*

Walsh, Chad 1914-1991 *BioIn 17, ConAu 133, CurBio 91N, NewYTBS 91, ScF&FL 92, WrDr 94N*

Walsh, Ellen Stoll *ChlBIID*

Walsh, Ellen Stoll 1942- *BioIn 16, SmATA 49*

Walsh, Frances Waggener *AuBYP 2, -3, BioIn 7, ChhPo*

Walsh, George Ethelbert 1865-1941 *AmAu&B, AmLY, CurBio 41, WhAm 1*

Walsh, George Johnston 1889-1981 *BioIn 16, SmATA 53*

Walsh, Gillian Paton
Main entry: Paton Walsh, Gillian

Walsh, Gillian Paton 1937- *ConAu 37R*

Walsh, Jill P *Who 90, -92*

Walsh, Jill Paton *ScF&FL 92, SmATA 72, TwCChW 89*
Main entry: Paton Walsh, Gillian

Walsh, Jill Paton 1937- *AuBYP 2S, BioIn 15, –16, CamGLE, ChlFicS, ChlLR 2, ConAu X, ConLC 35, FourBJA, OxCChiL, SmATA 4, TwCChW 83*

Walsh, Jill Paton 1939- *AuBYP 3*

Walsh, John Evangelist 1927- *ConAu 85, IntAu&W 82, –86, –89, –91, ScF&FL 92*

Walsh, Richard John 1886-1960 *AmAu&B, AuBYP 2, –3, BioIn 1, –5, –7, ObitOF 79, WhAm 4*

Walsh, William B 1920- *AuBYP 3*

Walsh, William Bertalan *BioIn 16*

Walsh, William Bertalan 1920- *AmCath 80, AuBYP 2S, BioIn 6, ConAu 49, –4NR, CurBio 62, WhoAm 74, –76, –78, –80, –82, –84, –86, –88, –90, –92, WhoWor 78, –80*

Walter, Frances *IlsBYP*

Walter, Frances V 1923- *SmATA 71*

Walter, Marion *AuBYP 2S, –3*

Walter, Mildred 1922- *BlkAuII, –92*

Walter, Mildred Pitts *AuBYP 2S, –3, BioIn 15, SmATA 45, TwCChW 89, WhoBlA 94, WrDr 90, –92*

Walter, Mildred Pitts d1992 *WrDr 94N*

Walter, Mildred Pitts 1922- *BioIn 16, BlkWr 2, ChlLR 15, ConAu 138, DcAmChF 1985, MajAI, SixBJA, SmATA 69, –12AS, TwCYAW*

Walter, Nina Willis 1900- *AmWomPl, ChhPo S2, ConAu 5R, ForWC 70, WrDr 76, –80, –82, –84*

Walter, Villiam Christian *MajAI, YABC 1*
Main entry: Andersen, Hans Christian

Walters, Audrey 1929- *BioIn 12, IlsBYP, SmATA 18*

Walters, Helen B d1987 *ConAu 121, –133, SmATA 50N*

Walters, Hugh *AuBYP 2, ConAu X, ConSFA, SmATA X, WrDr 84*
Main entry: Hughes, Walter Llewellyn

Walters, Hugh 1910- *AuBYP 3, EncSF 93, ScF&FL 92, ScFSB, TwCSFW 86, –91, WrDr 86, –88, –90, –92*

Walters, Hugh 1910-1993 *WrDr 94N*

Walters, Marguerite *AuBYP 2, –3, BioIn 7*

Walters, Shelly *AuNews 1, ConAu X*
Main entry: Sheldon, Walter J

Walters, Thomas N *DrAPF 87, –89, –91, –93*

Walters, Thomas N 1935- *ConAu 65, DrAP 75, DrAPF 83, –85*

Waltham, Antony Clive 1942- *ConAu 65, –10NR, –26NR, IntAu&W 77, –82, WrDr 76, –80*

Walther, Thomas A 1950- *ConAu 107, SmATA 31*
Pseud./variant:
Walther, Tom

Walther, Tom
Main entry: Walther, Thomas A

Waltner, Elma 1912- *AuBYP 2, –3, BioIn 7, –15, ConAu 17R, ForWC 70, SmATA 40*

Waltner, Willard *AuBYP 2, BioIn 7, SmATA 40*

Waltner, Willard 1909- *AuBYP 3*

Waltner, Willard H 1909- *BioIn 15*

Walton, Bryce 1918- *ConAu 21R, WhoSciF*

Walton, Bryce 1918-1988 *EncSF 93, ScF&FL 92*

Walton, Cecile 1891-1956 *BioIn 1, –14, ChhPo, ClaDrA, DcBrAr 1, DcWomA, IlsCB 1744*

Walton, Darwin McBeth 1926- *BlkAuII 92*

Walton, Elizabeth Cheatham *ConAu 5R, ForWC 70, WrDr 76, –80, –82, –84*

Walton, Izaak 1593-1683 *Alli, AtlBL, Benet 87, BbD, BiDRP&D, BiD&SB, BioIn 1, –2, –3, –4, –5, –7. –12, –13, –16, –17, BritAu, CamGEL, CamGLE, CarSB, Chambr 1, CnDBLB 1, CroE&S, CyWA 58, DcEnA, DcEnL, DcEuL, DcLEL, DcNaB, –C, DcScB, EvLB, LongCEL, McGEWB, NewC, OxCEng 67, –85, OxCMus, PenC ENG, REn, RfGEnL 91, WebE&AL, WorAlBi, WorAl*

Walton, Octavius Frank, Mrs 1849-1939 *BioIn 8, OxCChiL, TwCChW 83A, WhoChL*

Walton, O F, Mrs 1850-1939 *TwCChW 89A*

Walton, Richard J 1928- *WrDr 86, –88, –90, –92*

Walton, Richard John 1928- *BioIn 9, ConAu 25R, IntAu&W 77, OxCCan SUP, SmATA 4, WrDr 76, –80, –82, –84, –94*

Walton, Tony *WhoEnt 92*

Walton, Tony 1934- *BiE&WWA, BioIn 12, –13, ConTFT 4, HalFC 84, –88, NotNAT, WhoAm 92, WhoThe 77, –81*

Waltrip, Lela 1904- *BioIn 11, BkCL, ConAu 5R, ForWC 70, SmATA 9*

Waltrip, Mildred 1911- *IlsBYP, SmATA 37, WhAmArt 85*

Waltrip, Rufus 1898- *BioIn 11, BkCL, ConAu 5R, SmATA 9*

Walworth, Jane *IlsBYP*

Walworth, Nancy Zinsser 1917- *ConAu 5R, –3NR, SmATA 14*

Wand, John William Charles 1885- *Au&Wr 71, BioIn 7, BlueB 76, IntWW 74, –75, Who 74*

Wangboje, Solomon Irein *AfroAA*

Wangerin, Walter, Jr. 1944- *ConAu 108, ScF&FL 92, SmATA 37, –45, TwCYAW*

Wangerin, Walter J 1944- *ConAu 34NR*

Waniek, Marilyn 1946- *SmATA 60*

Waniek, Marilyn Nelson *DrAPF 87, –89, –93*

Waniek, Marilyn Nelson 1946- *WhoAmW 93*

Wannamaker, Bruce *ConAu X, SmATA X*
Main entry: Moncure, Jane Belk

Warbler, J M *ConAu X, SmATA 7*
Main entry: Cocagnac, Augustin Maurice

Warburg, Sandol Stoddard 1927- *AuBYP 2, –3, BioIn 8, BkP, ChhPo S1, ConAu 5R, –X, ForWC 70, SmATA 14*
Pseud./variant:
Stoddard, Sandol

Ward, Arthur Sarsfield *BioIn 14, –15, ScF&FL 92*

Ward, Arthur Sarsfield 1883?-1959 *EncMys, EvLB, LongCTC, ObitOF 79, ObitT 1951, PenC ENG*

Ward, Charles Forbes, Jr. 1904- *WhoAm 76*

Ward, Colin 1924- *ConAu 57*

Ward, Don 1911- *ConAu 17R*

Ward, E D *MajAI, SmATA 70*
Main entry: Gorey, Edward St. John

Ward, Elizabeth Honor 1926- *Au&Wr 71, ConAu 9R, IntAu&W 77, WrDr 76, –80, –82, –84, –86, –88, –90, –92, –94*

Ward, Elizabeth Stuart 1844-1911 *WomNov*

Ward, Elizabeth Stuart P
Main entry: Phelps, Elizabeth Stuart Ward

Ward, Elizabeth Stuart Phelps *ArtclWW 2*

Ward, Elizabeth Stuart Phelps 1844-1911 *Alli SUP, AmAu, AmAu&B, AmWomPl, AmWomWr, BenetAL 91, BibAL 8, BiD&SB, BioIn 2, –9, –12, –17, ChhPo, CnDAL, DcAmAu, DcLEL, DcNAA, InWom SUP, OxCAmL 65, –83, OxCChiL, REnAL*

Ward, Evelyn *ConAu X, WhoChL*
Main entry: Everett-Green, Evelyn

Ward, Evelyn Svec *WhoAmA 86*

Ward, Helen 1962- *SmATA 72*

Ward, Herman Matthew 1914- *ChhPo, ConAu 5R, –2NR, –18NR, –39NR, DrAS 74E, –78E, –82E*

Ward, Jay d1989 *LesBEnT 92, NewYTBS 89*

Ward, Jay 1920-1989 *AnObit 1989, ConTFT 8, SmATA 63*

Ward, John *Who 88, –90, –92*

Ward, John 1917- *BioIn 5, ConBrA 79, IlsBYP, IlsCB 1946, SmATA 42, TwCPaSc, Who 74*

Ward, John C 1963- *BlkAuII 92*

Ward, Jonas *IntAu&W 91X, SmATA X, TwCWW 91, WrDr 86, –88, –90, –92*
Main entry: Cox, William R

Ward, Lynd Kendall 1905-1985 *AmAu&B, AuBYP 2, –3, Au&ICB, BioIn 1, –2, –3, –4, –5, –6, –7, –8, –9, –10, –12, –14, –15, BkP, Cald 1938, ChhPo, –S2, ConAu 17R, –116, ConGrA 1, ConICB, DcLB 22, FourBJA, GrAmP, IlrAm 1880, –E, IlsBYP, IlsCB 1744, –1946, –1957, –1967, JBA 34, –51, MajAI, NewYTBS 85, SmATA 2, –36, –42N, Str&VC, WhAm 8, WhAmArt 85, WhoAm 74, –76, –78, –80, –84, WhoAmA 73, –78, –80, –82, –84, WrDr 76, –80, –82, –84*

Ward, Martha Eads 1921- *BiDrLUS 70, BioIn 10, ConAu 17R, SmATA 5, WhoAmW 74, –75, WhoLibS 55*

Ward, Mary Augusta 1851-1920 *Alli SUP, BioIn 1, –2, –9, –10, –12, –13, CamGLE, CarSB, DcBiA, DcEnA, –A, DcLEL, DcNaB 1912, EvLB, FemiCLE, OxCEng 67, –85, TwCA, –SUP, WomNov*

Ward, Mary Augusta Arnold *InWom SUP*

Ward, Mary Augusta Arnold 1851-1920
BioIn 16, –17, EncBrWW

Ward, Mary McNeer
Main entry: McNeer, May Yonge

Ward, May McNeer *Au&ICB*

Ward, Melanie *ConAu X, SmATA X*
Main entry: Curtis, Richard

Ward, Nanda Weedon 1932- *AuBYP 2, –3, BioIn 7*

Ward, Norman 1918- *AmMWSc 73S, BlueB 76, CaW, CanWW 70, –80, –81, –83, –89, ConAu 41R, IntAu&W 82, OxCCan SUP, WhoAm 74, –80, –82, –84, –86, –88, –90, WhoCanL 85, –87, –92, WrDr 76, –80, –82, –84, –86, –88, –90, –92, –94*

Ward, Ralph T 1927- *AuBYP 2S, ConAu 49*

Ward, Tom *MajAI*

Ward, William Gates 1929- *ConAu 21R, WhoMW 74, –76, –78, –80*

Wardell, Dean *SmATA X*
Main entry: Prince, Jack Harvey

Wardell, Phyl 1909- *ConAu P-1, TwCChW 89, WrDr 90, –92*

Wardell, Phyllis Robinson 1909- *WrDr 94*

Ward-Thomas, Evelyn Bridget Patricia
InWom SUP

Ward-Thomas, Evelyn Bridget Patricia S 1928- *ConAu 26NR*

Ward-Thomas, Evelyn Bridget Stephens 1928- *Au&Wr 71, ConAu 9R, –5NR, WrDr 82, –84*
Pseud./variant:
Anthony, Evelyn

Ware, Gilbert 1933- *ConAu 65, WhoBlA 75, –77, –80, –88, –90, –92, –94*

Ware, Jean 1914- *ConAu P-1, WrDr 76, –80, –82, –84, –86, –88, –90, –92, –94*

Ware, Leon Vernon 1909- *AuBYP 2, BioIn 7, –9, ConAu 1R, DcAmChF 1960, SmATA 4*

Ware, Leon Vernon 1909-1976 *AuBYP 3*

Warmke, Roman Francis 1929- *ConAu 17R, –9NR, LEduc 74, WhoMW 74, –76*

Warne, Frederick 1825- *DcLB 106*

Warne, Frederick 1825-1901 *DcNaB S2, OxCChiL*

Warner, Anna B 1827-1915 *BioAmW*

Warner, Anna Bartlett 1820-1915 *InWom SUP*

Warner, Anna Bartlett 1824-1915 *BibAL 8*

Warner, Anna Bartlett 1827?-1915 *Alli, –SUP, AmAu, AmAu&B, AmWomWr, BenetAL 91, BiD&SB, BioIn 6, –12, BlmGWL, CarSB, ChhPo, –S1, –S2, CyAL, DcAmAu, DcEnL, DcLEL, DcNAA, REnAL, WhAm 1, WomWWA 14, WomNov*

Warner, Edythe Records 1916- *BioIn 8, ConAu 5R, IlsCB 1957*

Warner, Edythe Records 1916-1980
ConAu 134

Warner, Frank A *ConAu 26NR, –P-2, SmATA 1, –67*
Main entry: Stratemeyer, Edward L

Warner, Gary 1936- *ConAu 21R*

Warner, Gertrude Chandler *AmWomPl*

Warner, Gertrude Chandler 1890-1979
AmAu&B, AuBYP 2, –3, BioIn 7, –11, ConAu 1R, –3NR, ForWC 70, SmATA 9, –73, WhAm 7, WhNAA, WhoAmW 75

Warner, John F 1929- *ConAu 142, SmATA 75*

Warner, Lucille Schulberg *BioIn 14, ConAu 69, –11NR, SmATA 30*

Warner, Matt *AuBYP 2S, ConAu X, WrDr 80, –82, –84, –86, –88, –90, –92*
Main entry: Fichter, George Siebert

Warner, Matt 1922- *AuBYP 3*

Warner, Matt 1922-1993 *WrDr 94N*

Warner, Oliver 1903-1976 *Au&Wr 71, BioIn 13, ConAu 1R, –69, –3NR, DcLEL 1940, IntAu&W 77, LongCTC, OxCCan SUP, SmATA 29, Who 74*

Warner, Peter 1939- *BioIn 8, IlsCB 1957*

Warner, Priscilla Mary 1905- *BioIn 5, IlsCB 1946*

Warner, Rex *IntvTCA 2*

Warner, Rex 1905- *Benet 87, BioIn 1, –4, –7, –8, –13, BlmGEL, BlueB 76, ChhPo, –S1, ConNov 72, –76, –82, –86, ConPo 70, –75, –80, –85, DcLB 15, DcLEL, EngPo, IntAu&W 77, IntWW 74, –75, –76, –77, –78, –79, –80, –81, –82, –83, LongCTC, ModBrL, NewC, Novels, OxCEng 85, PenC ENG, REn, TwCA, –SUP, TwCWr, WebE&AL, Who 74,*

–82, –83, –85, WhoAm 74, WhoWor 74, WrDr 76, –80, –82, –84, –86

Warner, Rex 1905-1986 *AnObit 1986, BioIn 15, CamGLE, ConAu 119, ConLC 45, EncSF 93, NewYTBS 86, RfGEnL 91, ScF&FL 92, TwCRHW 90*

Warner, Susan 1819-1885 *NinCLC 31, TwCChW 89A*

Warner, Susan B 1819-1885 *BioAmW, CamGLE, CamHAL*

Warner, Susan Bogert 1819-1885 *Alli, –SUP, AmAu, AmAu&B, AmWomWr, ArtclWW 2, BenetAL 91, BibAL 8, BbD, BiD&SB, BioIn 1, –4, –8, –12, BlmGWL, CarSB, Chambr 3, ChhPo, –S1, –S2, CyAL, DcAmAu, DcBiA, DcEnL, DcLB 3, –42, DcLEL, DcNAA, EvLB, FemiCLE, InWom SUP, OxCAmL 65, –83, OxCChiL, REnAL, WhAm HS, WhoChL*
Pseud./variant:
Wetherell, Elizabeth

Warner, Wayne Earl 1933- *ConAu 49, –3NR, WhoRel 77*

Warren, Betsy *ConAu X, SmATA X*
Main entry: Warren, Elizabeth Avery

Warren, Billy *AuBYP 3, SmATA X*
Main entry: Warren, William Stephen

Warren, Cathy *AuBYP 3, SmATA 46*

Warren, Cathy 1951- *SmATA 62*

Warren, Elizabeth *BiDEWW, BioIn 12, ConAu X, SmATA X*
Main entry: Supraner, Robyn

Warren, Elizabeth Avery 1916- *ConAu 5R, –8NR, ForWC 70, SmATA 38, –46*
Pseud./variant:
Warren, Betsy

Warren, Fred *AuBYP 2S, –3*

Warren, Fred Franklin 1922- *WhoBlA 85, –90, –94*

Warren, George A *CarSB*

Warren, Joyce Williams 1935- *Au&Wr 71, BioIn 12, ConAu 77, SmATA 18*

Warren, Leslie 1897- *WhNAA*

Warren, Mary Crowninshield *CarSB*

Warren, Mary Phraner 1929- *AuBYP 2S, –3, BioIn 11, ConAu 53, –5NR, SmATA 10*

Warren, Maude Lavinia 1875-1934 *WomNov*

Warren, Maude Lavinia Radford 1875-1934 *AmAu&B, CarSB, DcNAA, WhAm 1, WomWWA 14*

Warren, Nathan Boughton 1815?-1898 *Alli, CarSB, CyAL, DcAmAu, DcNAA*

Warren, Patricia Nell
Main entry: Tarnawsky, Patricia Warren

Warren, Patricia Nell 1936- *ConAu 1NR, GayLL, ScF&FL 92, WhoAmW 75*

Warren, Robert Penn *DrAPF 87, –89, IntvTCA 2*

Warren, Robert Penn d1989 *Who 90N*

Warren, Robert Penn 1905- *AmAu&B, AmNov, AmWr, AuNews 1, Au&Wr 71, Benet 87, BioIn 2, –3, –4, –5, –6, –7, –8, –9, –10, –11, –12, –13, –14, –15, BlueB 76, BroV, CamGEL, CamGLE, CamHAL, CasWL, CnDAL, CnE&AP, CnMD, ConAmA, ConAu 13R, –10NR, ConLC 1, –4, –6, –8, –10, –13, –18, –39, –53, ConLCrt 77, –82, ConNov 72, –76, –82, –86, ConPo 70, –75, –80, –85, Conv 1, CurBio 70, CyWA 58, –89, DcLB 2, –48, –Y80A, DcLEL, DrAF 76, DrAP 75, DrAPF 83, –85, EncSoH, EncWL, –2, EvLB, FifSWrA, FilmgC, HalFC 84, –88, IntAu&W 77, –82, –86, –89, IntWW 74, –75, –76, –77, –78, –79, –80, –81, –82, –83, –89, IntWWP 82, LiHiK, LongCTC, McGEWB, ModAL, –S1, –S2, ModWD, Novels, OxCAmL 65, –83, OxCEng 85, PenC AM, RAdv 1, –13-1, RComWL, REn, REnAL, RfGAmL 87, SixAP, SmATA 46, TwCA, –SUP, WebAB 74, –79, WebE&AL, WhDW, WhNAA, Who 74, –82, –83, –85, –88, WhoAm 74, –76, –78, –80, –82, –84, –86, –88, WhoTwCL, WhoUSWr 88, WhoWor 74, –80, –82, –84, –87, –89, WhoWrEP 89, WorAl, WrDr 76, –80, –82, –84, –86, –88*

Warren, Robert Penn 1905-1989 *AnObit 1989, BenetAL 91, BioIn 16, –17, ConAu 129, ConLC 59, CurBio 89N, DcLB Y89N, MagSAmL, MajTwCW, NewYTBS 89, News 90, –90-1, RfGShF, ShSCr 4, SmATA 63, TwCRHW 90, WorAlBi, WorLitC, WrDr 90, WrPh*

Warren, William Stephen 1882-1968 *AuBYP 2, –3, BioIn 7, –11, ConAu P-2, SmATA 9*
Pseud./variant:
Warren, Billy

Warrick, Patricia S 1925- *BioIn 14, ScF&FL 92*

Warrick, Patricia Scott 1925- *ConAu 61, –8NR, –25NR, DrAS 82E, EncSF 93, SmATA 35, WhoMW 78, –80, –82*

Warriner, John d1987 *NewYTBS 87*

Warriner, John 1907?-1987 *ConAu 123, SmATA 53N*

Warring, Ronald Horace 1920- *Au&Wr 71*

Warsh *ConAu X, SmATA X*
Main entry: Warshaw, Jerry

Warshaw, Jerry 1929- *ConAu 37R, -14NR, SmATA 30*
Pseud./variant:
Warsh

Warshofsky, Fred 1931- *BioIn 13, ConAu 9R, SmATA 24, WhoE 74, WhoEnt 92*

Warshofsky, Isaac *ConAu 134, -X, -39NR, IntAu&W 91X, MajAI, MajTwCW, SmATA 3, -68, -X*
Main entry: Singer, Isaac Bashevis

Wartski, Maureen 1940- *SmATA 37, -50*
Pseud./variant:
Crane, M A

Wartski, Maureen Ann Crane 1940- *DcAmChF 1960, TwCYAW*

Wartski, Maureen Crane 1940- *BioIn 15, -16*

Warwick, Alan R 1900-1973 *BioIn 15*

Warwick, Alan Ross 1900-1973 *ConAu 112, SmATA 42*
Pseud./variant:
Ross, Alan
Sidney, Frank
Sydney, Frank

Warwick, Dolores *ConAu X*
Main entry: Frese, Dolores Warwick

Wa-Sha-Quon-Asin *ConAu X, SmATA X*
Main entry: Belaney, Archibald Stansfeld

Washburn, Bradford 1910- *ConAu 49, -3NR, DcCAr 81, ICPEnP A, MacBEP, SmATA 38*

Washburn, Jan 1926- *SmATA 63*

Washburne, Heluiz Chandler 1892-1970 *AmAu&B, AuBYP 2, -3, Au&Wr 71, BioIn 7, -11, ConAu 104, -P-1, MichAu 80, OhA&B, SmATA 10, -26N, WhAm 5, WhNAA*

Washington, Booker T *DcAmImH*

Washington, Booker T 1856-1915 *BenetAL 91, BioIn 14, -15, -16, -17, BlkLC, BlkWr 1, CamGEL, CamGLE, CamHAL, ConAu 125, ConBlB 4, ConHero 2, FifSWrB, RAdv 13-3, RComAH, RfGAmL 87, WorAlBi*

Washington, Booker T 1859-1915 *MemAm*

Washington, Booker Taliaferro 1856-1915 *AfrAmAl 6, AmAu&B, BiDSA, BiD&SB, BioIn 1, -2, -3, -4, -5, -6, -7, -8, -9, -10, -11, -12, -13, BlkAWP, CasWL, Chambr 3, ConAu 114, CyAG, DcAmAu, DcAmNB, DcAmSR, DcLEL, DcNAA, EncAACR, EncAB-H, EncSoH, HarEnUS, InB&W 80, -85, LongCTC, LuthC 75, McGEWB, NegAl 76, -83, -89, OxCAmH, OxCAmL 65, -83, OxCEng 67, -85, PenC AM, REn, REnAL, SelBAAf, SelBAAu, SmATA 28, TwCLC 10, WebAB 74, -79, WebE&AL, WhAm 1, WorAl*

Wasserman, Burton 1929- *AmArt, ConAu 53, PrintW 83, -85, WhoAmA 73, -78, -80, -82, -84, -86, -89, -91, WhoE 74, -75, -77, -91*

Wasserman, Selma 1929- *ConAu 5R*

Wassersug, Joseph David 1912- *AuBYP 2, -3, BioIn 7, ConAu 17R, WhoWorJ 72, -78*
Pseud./variant:
Bradford, Adam, M.D.

Wasson, Valentina P 1901-1958 *BioIn 5, ObitOF 79*

Watanabe, Shigeo *TwCChW 89B*

Watanabe, Shigeo 1928- *BioIn 14, -15, -16, ChlLR 8, ConAu 112, MajAI, SixBJA, SmATA 32, -39, TwCChW 83B*

Waterfall, Beth Lien 1929- *ForWC 70*

Waterhouse, Charles Howard 1924- *ConAu 29R, WhoAmA 80, -82, -84, -86, -89, -91*

Waters, Ethel 1896- *BlksAmF*

Waters, Ethel 1896?-1977 *Baker 84, -92, BiDAfM, BiDJaz, BiE&WWA, BioIn 2, -3, -4, -6, -8, -9, -10, -11, -12, -13, -16, -17, CamGWoT, CelR, CmpEPM, ConAu 73, -81, CurBio 41, -51, -77N, DrBlPA 90, EncJzS, EncMT, EncWT, FamA&A, FilmgC, HalFC 84, -88, InB&W 80, IntMPA 75, -76, -77, MotPP, MovMk, NegAl 76, -83, NewAmDM, NewGrDA 86, NotBlAW 92, NotNAT, -A, ObitOF 79, OxCPMus, OxCThe 67, -83, PlP&P, WebAB 74, -79, WhScrn 83, WhoAm 74, -76, WhoAmW 75, WhoBlA 75, WhoHol A, WhoJazz 72, WhoRel 77, WhoThe 77, -81N, WorAl*

Waters, Ethel 1900?-1976 *NotWoAT*

Waters, Ethel 1900-1977 *AfrAmAl 6, BioAmW, HanAmWH, InWom SUP, NegAl 89, OxCAmT 84, PenEncP, WorAlBi*

Waters, John F 1930- *AuBYP 3, ConAu 23NR, WrDr 88, -90, -92*

Waters, John Frederick 1930- *AuBYP 2S, BioIn 9, ConAu 37R, IntAu&W 77, –82, –86, –89, –91, SmATA 4, WhoE 75, –77, WrDr 76, –80, –82, –84, –86, –94*

Waters, Sheila *IlsBYP*

Waters, Tony 1958- *ConAu 142, SmATA 75*

Waterston, Elizabeth 1922- *ConAu 69, DrAS 74E, –82E*

Waterton, Betty 1923- *ConAu 111, –28NR, SmATA 34, –37, WhoCanL 87, –92*

Watkin, Lawrence Edward 1901- *BioIn 4, ConAu 81, IntAu&W 82, TwCA, –SUP, WhoAm 74, –76, –78, –80, –82, WhoWor 80*

Watkin, Lawrence Edward 1901-1981 *ScF&FL 92*

Watkins, Peter 1934- *SmATA 66*

Watkins, William John *DrAPF 89, –91, –93*

Watkins, William John 1942- *ScF&FL 92, WhoUSWr 88, WhoWrEP 89, –92, WrDr 90*

Watkins, William Jon *ConSFF, DrAPF 87, ScF&FL 92*

Watkins, William Jon 1942- *ConAu 41R, DrAPF 83, –85, EncSF 93, ScFSB, TwCSFW 86, –91, WrDr 84, –86, –88*

Watkins, Yoko Kawashima *DcAmChF 1985*

Watkins-Pitchford, D J 1905- *BioIn 14, –15, SmATA 4AS, TwCChW 89, WrDr 86, –88, –90*

Watkins-Pitchford, Denys James 1905- *Au&Wr 71, BioIn 2, –5, –8, –9, –10, –12, ChhPo S1, ConAu 9R, –4NR, DcBrAr 2, IlsCB 1946, IntAu&W 77, –82, –89, –91, OxCChiL, SmATA 6, ThrBJA, TwCChW 78, –83, Who 82, –83, –85, –88, –90, WhoChL, WrDr 76, –80, –82, –84*
Pseud./variant:
Traherne, Michael

Watkins-Pitchford, Denys James 1905-1990 *ConAu 132, –38NR, SmATA 66*
Pseud./variant:
B B

Watkins-Pitchford, D J 1905-1990 *BioIn 17*

Watling, James 1933- *SmATA 67*

Watney, John Basil *IntAu&W 89, –91, WrDr 86, –88, –90*

Watney, John Basil 1915- *Au&Wr 71, ConAu 9R, –5NR, WrDr 76, –80, –82, –84*

Watson, Aldren A 1917- *WhoAmA 86, –89, –91*

Watson, Aldren Auld 1917- *BioIn 1, –5, –8, –12, –14, –15, ChhPo, –S2, ConAu 81, –4NR, –39NR, ForIl, IlsBYP, IlsCB 1744, –1946, –1957, –1967, SmATA 36, –42, WhAmArt 85, WhoAmA 73, –78, –80, –82, –84*

Watson, Amy Zakrzewski 1965- *SmATA 76*

Watson, B S *SmATA X*
Main entry: Teitelbaum, Michael

Watson, Clyde 1947- *ConAu 39NR, MajAI, SmATA 68, TwCChW 89, WrDr 86, –88, –90, –92, –94*

Watson, Clyde Dingman 1947- *AuBYP 2S, –3, BioIn 10, ChhPo S2, ChlLR 3, ConAu 49, –4NR, FourBJA, OxCChiL, SmATA 5, TwCChW 78, –83, WrDr 76, –80, –82, –84*

Watson, Elliot Lovegood Grant 1885-1970 *BioIn 1, ConAu P-1*

Watson, Emily *AuBYP 2, BioIn 7, –10*

Watson, H B Marriott *EncSF 93*

Watson, H B Marriott 1863-1921 *Alli SUP, CarSB, Chambr 3, LongCTC, NewC, StaCVF*

Watson, Helen Orr 1892-1978 *AmAu&B, AuBYP 2, –3, BioIn 7, ConAu 5R, –77, ForWC 70, SmATA 24N*

Watson, Henry Clay 1831-1869 *Alli, AmAu&B, BbD, BiDSA, BiD&SB, CarSB, ChhPo, DcAmAu, DcNAA, HarEnUS, WhAm HS*

Watson, Howard N 1929- *AfroAA, IlsBYP, WhoAmA 84, –86, –91*

Watson, Ina *SingR 1*

Watson, James 1936- *Au&Wr 71, BioIn 11, ConAu 53, –4NR, IntAu&W 82, –86, –89, –91, SmATA 10, TwCChW 89, WrDr 76, –80, –82, –84, –86, –88, –90, –92, –94*

Watson, Jane 1915- *AuBYP 3*

Watson, Jane Werner 1915- *AuBYP 2S, BioIn 9, –16, ConAu 5R, –8NR, ScF&FL 92, SmATA 3, –54*
Pseud./variant:
Bedford, Annie North
Hill, Monica
Jasner, W K
Nast, Elsa Ruth
Werner, Elsa Jane
Werner, Jane

Watson, Julia *WrDr 88*

Watson, Julia 1943- *Au&Wr 71, ConAu 41R, –15NR, IntAu&W 77, –82, –86, WrDr 76, –80, –82, –84, –86*

Watson, Lyall 1939- *ConAu 57, –8NR, –24NR, DcCAr 81, EncO&P 1S1, –2, –3, IntAu&W 89, –91, IntWW 89, –91, WrDr 76, –80, –82, –84, –86, –88, –90, –92, –94*

Watson, Nancy Dingham *WrDr 86, –88*

Watson, Nancy Dingman *AuBYP 2S, –3, BioIn 14, ConAu 49, –4NR, DrAPF 83, –85, –87, –89, –91, –93, IntAu&W 77, –82, SmATA 32, WhoAmW 77, –81, WrDr 80, –82, –84, –90*

Watson, Pauline 1925- *BioIn 12, ConAu 69, –11NR, –29NR, SmATA 14, WhoAmW 81*
Pseud./variant:
Pola

Watson, Richard F *MajAI*

Watson, Richard Jesse *ChlBIID*

Watson, Richard Jesse 1951- *SmATA 62*

Watson, Sally 1924- *AuBYP 2S, –3, BioIn 9, ConAu 5R, –3NR, FourBJA, IntAu&W 77, –82, SmATA 3*

Watson, Sally Lou 1924- *DcAmChF 1960, TwCYAW*

Watson, Sara Ruth 1907- *AuBYP 2, –3, BioIn 7, ConAu 37R, DrAS 74E, –78E, –82E, IntAu&W 77, –82*

Watson, Sara Ruth, and Emily Watson *AuBYP 3*

Watson, Wendy 1942- *BioIn 10, –12, ChhPo S1, –S2, ConAu 49, –4NR, FourBJA, IlsBYP, IlsCB 1967, SmATA 5, WhoAmA 78*

Watson, Wendy McLeod 1942- *ConAu 39NR, MajAI, SmATA 74*

Watson, William 1858-1935 *RfGEnL 91*

Watson, William, Sir 1858-1935 *Alli SUP, AnCL, BbD, BiD&SB, BioIn 2, –8, –13, CamGLE, Chambr 3, ChhPo, –S1, –S2, DcEnA, –A, DcLEL, DcNaB 1931, EvLB, LongCTC, ModBrL, NewC, OxCEng 67, –85, PenC ENG, TwCA, –SUP*

Watson Taylor, Elizabeth 1915- *SmATA 41*

Watt, Ruth 1919- *ConAu 57, WhoWest 78*

Watt, Thomas 1935- *Au&Wr 71, BioIn 9, ConAu 37R, SmATA 4, WrDr 76, –80*

Wattenberg, Ben J 1933- *BioIn 8, BlueB 76, ConAu 57, –33NR, CurBio 85, JrnUS, WhoAm 76, –78, –80, –82, –84, –86, –88, –90, –92, WhoE 89, WhoUSWr 88, WhoWrEP 89, –92, WrDr 80, –82, –84, –86, –88, –90, –92, –94*

Watterson, Bill *WhoAm 90*

Watterson, Bill 1958- *Au&Arts 9, ConAu 134, EncACom, News 90, –90-3, SmATA 66, WhoAm 92, –94, WrDr 94*

Watt-Evans, Lawrence *ConAu 32NR*

Watt-Evans, Lawrence 1954- *EncSF 93, IntAu&W 89, –91, ScF&FL 92, SmATA 75*

Watts, Alan James 1925- *Au&Wr 71, WrDr 76, –80, –82, –84, –86*

Watts, Bernadette 1942- *BioIn 9, –12, ChhPo S1, ConAu 29R, –31NR, IlsBYP, IlsCB 1967, SmATA 4*
Pseud./variant:
Bernadette

Watts, Ephraim *SmATA X*
Main entry: Horne, Richard H

Watts, Franklin 1904-1978 *SmATA 46*

Watts, Franklin Mowry 1904-1978 *Au&Wr 71, BioIn 8, –11, –12, –15, ConAu P-2, SmATA 21N, WhAm 7, WhoAm 74*

Watts, Helen L Hoke 1903-1990 *ConAu 131, –43NR, SmATA 65*
Main entry: Hoke, Helen L

Watts, Irene N 1931- *SmATA 56, WhoCanL 87, –92*

Watts, Irene Naemi 1931- *IntAu&W 86*

Watts, Isaac 1674-1748 *Alli, –SUP, AnCL, Benet 87, BbD, BiD&SB, BioIn 1, –2, –3, –4, –6, –7, –8, –10, –16, –17, BlmGEL, BritAu, CamGEL, CamGLE, CarSB, CasWL, Chambr 2, ChhPo, –S1, –S2, CnE&AP, DcBiPP, DcEnA, DcEnL, DcEuL, DcLB 95, DcLEL, DcNaB, EncWM, EvLB, LongCEL, LuthC 75, NewC, OxCChiL, OxCEng 67, –85, OxCMus, PenC ENG, PoChrch, REn, SmATA 52, Str&VC, WebE&AL*
Pseud./variant:
I W

Watts, Isaac 1675-1748 *RfGEnL 91*

Watts, James K M 1955- *SmATA 59*

Watts, John Francis 1926- *Au&Wr 71, ConAu 25R, IntAu&W 77, –82, Who 82, –83, –85, –88, –90, –92, WrDr 76, –80, –82, –84, –86, –88, –90, –92, –94*

Watts, K G O *AuBYP 2S, -3*

Watts, Mabel Pizzey 1906- *AuBYP 2, -3, BioIn 8, -11, ChhPo S1, ConAu 1R, -3NR, ForWC 70, IntAu&W 77, SmATA 11, WhoAm 78, WhoAmW 75, -77, WrDr 76, -80*
Pseud./variant:
Lynn, Patricia

Watts, May Theilgaard 1893-1975 *ConAu 41R, WhAm 6, WhoAm 74, WrDr 76*

Watts, May Thielgaard 1893-1975 *BioIn 13*

Watts, Peter Christopher 1919- *ConAu 69, -12NR, EncFWF, IntAu&W 82*
Pseud./variant:
Chisholm, Matt
James, Cy
Mackinlock, Duncan
Owen, Tom

Waud, Elizabeth *ConAu X*
Main entry: Tattersall, Muriel Joyce

Waud, Elizabeth 1931- *WrDr 82*

Waugh, Carol-Lynn Rossel 1947- *BioIn 15, ConAu 107, ScF&FL 92, SmATA 41, WhoAmW 85, -87, -89, -91*
Pseud./variant:
Rossel-Waugh, C C

Waugh, Dorothy *WrDr 86, -88, -90, -92, -94*

Waugh, Dorothy 1896- *AmPB, Au&Wr 71, BioIn 1, -5, -11, ConAu 1R, -1NR, IlsCB 1744, -1946, IntAu&W 77, SmATA 11, WhNAA, WrDr 76, -80, -82, -84*

Wax, Wendy A 1963- *SmATA 73*

Way, Margaret *BioIn 14, TwCRHW 90, WrDr 84, -86, -88, -90, -92, -94*

Wayland, April Halprin *AuBYP 3*

Wayland, Patrick
Main entry: O'Connor, Richard

Wayland, Patrick 1915-1975 *ConAu X, SmATA X, TwCCr&M 80*

Wayman, Vivenne 1926- *WrDr 76, -80*

Wayne, Donald *WrDr 86, -88, -90, -92*
Main entry: Dodd, Wayne D

Wayne, Donald 1913- *WhoAm 80, -82, -84, WrDr 76, -80, -82, -84*

Wayne, Donald 1930- *ConAu X, IntAu&W 82X, WrDr 94*

Wayne, Jenifer 1917-1982 *Au&Wr 71, BioIn 12, -14, ConAu 105, -108, SmATA 32, TwCChW 78, -83, -89*

Wayne, Kyra Petrovskaya
Main entry: Petrovskaya, Kyra

Wayne, Kyra Petrovskaya 1918- *BioIn 11, ConAu X, -4NR, SmATA 8, WhoAmW 87, -89, -91, WhoWest 76, -80, -82, -87, -89, -92, -94, WhoWor 87, -89*

Wayne, Richard *AuBYP 2, -3, ConAu X, SmATA 5*
Main entry: Decker, Duane

Waystaff, Simon *SmATA X*
Main entry: Swift, Jonathan

Weafer, Elizabeth 1924- *BioIn 4, -5, CurBio 58*

Weale, Anne *WrDr 90, -92*

Weale, Anne 1929- *Au&Wr 71, IntAu&W 77*

Weales, Gerald 1925- *AmAu&B, BiE&WWA, BioIn 11, ConAmTC, ConAu 5R, -3NR, DrAS 74E, -78E, -82E, IndAu 1917, SmATA 11, WrDr 80, -82, -84, -86, -88, -90, -92, -94*

Weart, Edith Lucie 1898?-1977 *AuBYP 2, -3, BioIn 7, ConAu 69*

Weart, Spencer R 1942- *AmMWSc 82, ConAu 25R, -29NR, DrAS 82H, WhoWest 74, WrDr 90, -92*

Weart, Spencer Richard 1942- *AmMWSc 86, -89, -92, WhoE 91, WrDr 94*

Weary, Ogdred *ConAu X, -30NR, MajAI, SmATA 70, -X, WrDr 80, -82, -84, -86, -88, -90, -92*
Main entry: Gorey, Edward St John

Weary, Ogdred 1925- *WrDr 94*

Weatherbee, Donald Emery 1932- *AmMWSc 73S, -78S, WhoAm 80, -82, -84, -86, -88, -90, -92, -94*

Weatherby, Meredith 1915- *WhoAm 78, -80, -82, -84*

Weaver, Emily Poynton 1865-1943 *DcNAA, OxCCan, WomNov*

Weaver, Harriet E 1908- *ConAu 5R*

Weaver, Harriett E 1908- *BioIn 17, SmATA 65*

Weaver, Jack 1925- *BioIn 5, IlsBYP, IlsCB 1946*

Weaver, John Downing 1912- *AmAu&B, AmNov, AuBYP 2, -3, BioIn 2, -7, ConAu 9R, -4NR*

Weaver, John L 1928- *WhoAmP 93*

Weaver, John L 1949- *ConAu 112, SmATA 42*

Weaver, John Lockerbie 1936- *WhoSSW 91*

Weaver, Robert G *DrAPF 87, -89, -91, -93*

Weaver, Robert Glenn 1920- *DrAPF 83, -85, DrAS 74E, -78E, -82E, IlsBYP*

Weaver, Ward *AmNov X, AuBYP 2, -3, ConAu X, SmATA 3, -X, TwCRHW 90, WhoSpyF*
Main entry: Mason, Francis VanWyck

Webb, Cecil S *AuBYP 2, -3, BioIn 3, -8*

Webb, Christopher *ConAu X, EncMys, IntAu&W 77X, -82X, SmATA 2, -X, TwCChW 83, -89, WrDr 80, -82, -84, -86*
Main entry: Wibberley, Leonard

Webb, Clifford Cyril 1895-1972 *AuBYP 2, -3, BioIn 1, -2, -5, -8, ChhPo S1, ClaDrA, DcBrAr 1, IlsCB 1744, -1946, -1957*

Webb, Francoise *IlsBYP*

Webb, Jean Francis 1910- *ConAu 5R, -6NR, -21NR, IntAu&W 77, SmATA 35, TwCRHW 90, WrDr 76, -80, -82, -84, -86, -88, -90, -92, -94*
Pseud./variant:
Brown, Roswell
Hamill, Ethel
Morrison, Roberta

Webb, Kaye *BioIn 9, OxCChiL, Who 82, -83, -85, -88, -90, -92*

Webb, Kaye 1914- *SmATA 60*

Webb, Margot 1934- *ConAu 134, SmATA 67, WrDr 94*

Webb, Marion St John 1890-1930 *BioIn 8, ChhPo S1, -S2, OxCChiL, WhoChL, WhoLA*

Webb, Mildred *WomWMM*

Webb, Nancy 1915- *ConAu 1R, -21NR*

Webb, Robert N *AuBYP 2, -3, BioIn 8*

Webb, Ruth Enid Borlase Morris 1926- *Au&Wr 71, ConAu 9R, WrDr 76, -80*
Pseud./variant:
Morris, Ruth

Webb, Sharon *DrAPF 87, -89, -91, -93, ScFSB*

Webb, Sharon 1936- *ConAu 113, -32NR, DrAPF 83, -85, ScF&FL 92, SmATA 41, TwCSFW 86, -91, WrDr 88, -90, -92, -94*

Webb, Sharon Lynn 1936- *EncSF 93*

Webb, Walter Prescott 1888-1963 *AmAu&B, BenetAL 91, BioIn 3, -4, -5, -6, -7, -8, -9, -10, -11, -13, -14, -16, ConAu 113, DcAmB S7, DcLB 17, EncAB-A 36, ObitOF 79, OxCAmL 65, -83, REnAL, TexWr, WhAm 4*

Webbe, Gale D 1909- *ConAu 5R*
Pseud./variant:
Cole, Stephen

Webber, Irma Eleanor Schmidt 1904- *AmMWSc 73P, -76P, AmPB, BioIn 1, -5, -12, ConAu 69, IlsBYP, IlsCB 1744, -1946, SmATA 14*

Webber, Stawford
Pseud./variant:
Tremellan, Wilfred

Weber, Alfons 1921- *AmMWSc 73P, -82, BioIn 11, ConAu 29R, SmATA 8, WhoAm 74, -80*

Weber, Alice *CarSB*

Weber, Bruce 1942- *SmATA 73*

Weber, Debora 1955- *SmATA 58*

Weber, Judith E 1938- *SmATA 64*

Weber, Lenora 1895-1971 *AuBYP 3*

Weber, Lenora Mattingly 1895-1971 *AmAu&B, AuBYP 2, BioIn 2, -6, -8, -9, BkC 3, ConAu 29R, -P-1, ConLC 12, MorJA, SmATA 2, -26N*

Weber, Walter Alois 1906- *BioIn 1, IlsCB 1744*

Weber, William J 1927- *ConAu 25NR*

Weber, William John 1927- *BioIn 12, ConAu 69, SmATA 14*

Webster, Alice *BioIn 8, DcNAA, SmATA 17*
Main entry: Webster, Jean

Webster, David 1930- *AuBYP 2S, -3, BioIn 11, ConAu 29R, SmATA 11*

Webster, Frank V *CarSB, ConAu P-2, ScFEYrs, SmATA 1, -67*
Main entry: Stratemeyer, Edward L

Webster, Gary *ConAu X, SmATA X*
Main entry: Garrison, Webb B

Webster, James 1925-1981 *BioIn 12, –13, ConAu 73, –104, –29NR, IntAu&W 77, SmATA 17, –27N*

Webster, Jean *OxCAmT 84, WomNov*

Webster, Jean 1876-1915 *SmATA X*

Webster, Jean 1876-1916 *AmAu&B, AmWomPl, AmWomWr, BenetAL 91, BioIn 8, –12, –14, BlmGWL, CarSB, ChhPo, CnDAL, ConAu X, DcNAA, EvLB, InWom SUP, JBA 34, LongCTC, NotNAT B, OxCAmL 65, –83, OxCChiL, REn, REnAL, SmATA X, TwCA, TwCChW 83, –89, TwCRHW 90, TwCWr, WhAm 1, WhoChL, WomWWA 14*
Pseud./variant:
Webster, Alice

Webster, Joe *AuBYP 2, –3*
Main entry: Waldman, Frank

Webster, Noah 1758-1843 *AmWrBE, Benet 87, BenetAL 91, BiDAmJo, BiInAmS, BioIn 1, –2, –3, –4, –5, –6, –7, –8, –9, –10, –11, –12, –13, –14, –15, –16, –17, CelCen, CyEd, DcAmMeB, –84, DcBiPP, DcInv, DcLB 37, –42, –43, –73, Dis&D, HarEnUS, JrnUS, MemAm, NinCLC 30, OxCAmH, OxCAmL 83, OxCChiL, OxCEng 85, WebAB 79, WhDW, WorAlBi, WorAl*

Webster, Thomas Bertram Lonsdale 1905-1974 *ConAu 105, –107, Who 74*

Webster, Vera R *AuBYP 3*

Wechsberg, Joseph 1907- *BiGAW*

Wechsberg, Joseph 1907-1983 *AmAu&B, Au&Wr 71, BenetAL 91, BioIn 1, –3, –4, –9, –10, –12, –13, BlueB 76, ConAu 105, –109, –34NR, CurBio 55, –83N, EncAJ, EncTwCJ, NewYTBS 83, OxCAmL 65, –83, REnAL, WhAm 8, WhoAm 74, –76, –78, –80, –82, WhoMus 72, WhoWor 74, WrDr 80, –82, –84*

Wechsler, Herman J 1904-1976 *BioIn 10, –12, ConAu 61, –65, SmATA 20N, WhoAmA 73*

Wechter, Nell Wise 1913- *BioIn 5, –17, ConAu 57, SmATA 60, WhoAmW 77, –81, WhoSSW 78*

Wechter, Nell Wise 1913-1989 *ScF&FL 92*

Weck, Thomas L 1942- *ConAu 128, SmATA 62*

Weck, Thomas Lincoln 1942- *WhoE 89*

Weddle, Ethel Harshbarger 1897- *AuBYP 2, –3, BiDrLUS 70, BioIn 8, –11, ConAu 9R, –4NR, ForWC 70, SmATA 11*

Weddle, Ferris 1922- *ConAu 17R, WhoWest 74*

Wedel, Leonard E 1909- *ConAu 21R*

Wedgwood, Cicely Veronica 1910- *BioIn 4, –16, –17, DcLEL, EncWB, IntAu&W 77, IntWW 74, –75, –78, –83, LongCTC, ModBrL, REn, Who 74, –82, –83, –85, –92, WhoAm 74, WhoWor 74, –78, WrDr 76, –80*

Wedgwood, Cicely Veronica, Dame 1910- *IntWW 89, Who 88, –90*

Weeks, Thelma E 1921- *ConAu 57, WhoWest 84*

Weeks, Thelma Evans 1921- *WhoWest 89*

Weems, John Edward 1924- *ConAu 1R, –4NR, –19NR, IntAu&W 77, –82, WhoSSW 75, –76, –78, –80, –82, –84, –86, –88, –91, –93, WhoWor 91, –93, WrDr 76, –80, –82, –84, –86, –88, –90, –92, –94*

Weems, Mason Locke 1759-1825 *AmWrBE, Benet 87, BenetAL 91, BioIn 3, –4, –5, –6, –10, –12, –13, –14, –15, –16, DcLB 30, –37, –42, EncAR, EncSoH, HarEnUS, MemAm, OxCAmH, OxCAmL 83, WebAB 79*

Wees, Frances Shelley 1902- *AuBYP 3*

Wees, Frances Shelley 1902-1982 *AuBYP 2, BioIn 8, –13, –16, CanWW 70, –79, –80, –81, –83, CanWr, ConAu 5R, –3NR, ForWC 70, IntAu&W 77, –82, SmATA 58*
Pseud./variant:
Shelley, Frances

Weevers, Peter 1944- *SmATA 59*

Wegen, Ron *SmATA 44*

Wegner, Fritz 1924- *BioIn 5, –12, ChhPo S2, IlsBYP, IlsCB 1946, –1967, SmATA 20, WhoArt 80, –82, –84*

Wegner, Kenneth Walter 1932- *AmMWSc 73S, LEduc 74*

Wehen, Joy De Weese 1926- *AuBYP 3*

Wehen, Joy Deweese- *BioIn 14*

Wehen, Joy DeWeese 1936- *AuBYP 2, BioIn 8, ConAu 5R, –3NR, WrDr 76, –80, –82, –84, –86, –88, –90, –92, –94*

Weidhorn, Manfred 1931- *BioIn 17, SmATA 60*

Weigle, Marta *WhoAmW 87, –89, –91, –93*

Weigle, Marta 1944- *ConAu 69, –11NR, –26NR*

Weihs, Erika 1917- *BioIn 12, ConAu 93, SmATA 15, WhoAmA 89, –91, WhoE 93*

Weik, Mary Hays 1878-1979 *AuBYP 3*

Weik, Mary Hays 1898-1979 *AuBYP 2S, BioIn 9, –10, –12, –13, –14, ConAu 21R, –93, IndAu 1917, MorBMP, SmATA 3, –23N, WhAm 7, WhoAm 74, –76*

Weil, Ann Yezner 1908-1969 *BioIn 11, ConAu 5R, –103, IndAu 1917, SmATA 9, WhAm 5*

Weil, Lisl *WhoAmA 86, –89, –91, WhoE 91, –93*

Weil, Lisl 1910- *BioIn 4, –5, –8, –10, ConAu 49, –2NR, CurBio 58, FourBJA, IlsBYP, IlsCB 1946, –1957, –1967, SmATA 7, WhoAm 74, –76, –78, –80, –82, –84, WhoAmA 78, –80, –82, –84*

Weilerstein, Sadie Rose 1894- *BioIn 9, ConAu 5R, SmATA 3, WhoWorJ 72*

Weilerstein, Sadie Rose 1894-1993 *ConAu 141, SmATA 75*

Weinbaum, Eleanor Perlstein *WhoSSW 86, –91, WhoWrEP 89, –92*

Weinbaum, Eleanor Perlstein 1900- *IntAu&W 77, –82, IntWWP 82, WhoAmW 77, –81, –83, WhoSSW 80, –82, –84*

Weinberg, Larry
Main entry: Weinberg, Lawrence E

Weinberg, Lawrence *WhoAm 86, WhoWest 87, –89*

Weinberg, Lawrence E *ScF&FL 92, SmATA 48*
Pseud./variant:
Weinberg, Larry

Weinberger, Betty Kiralfy 1932- *ConAu 65*

Weiner, Sandra 1922- *AuBYP 2S, –3, BioIn 9, –12, ConAu 49, SmATA 14*

Weingarten, Violet 1915-1976 *ArtclWW 2, BioIn 9, –11, –13, ConAu 9R, –65, –7NR, ForWC 70, ObitOF 79, SmATA 3, –27N*

Weingartner, Charles 1922- *BioIn 10, ConAu 49, DrAS 74E, –78E, –82E, Future, LEduc 74, SmATA 5*

Weingast, David E 1912- *AuBYP 2, BioIn 8, ConAu 5R*

Weingast, David Elliott 1912- *AuBYP 3*

Weinheimer, George *IlsBYP*

Weinkauf, Mary Stanley 1938- *DrAS 74E, –78E, –82E, WhoMW 74*

Weinstein, Nina 1951- *SmATA 73*

Weinstock, Herbert 1905-1971 *AmAu&B, AuBYP 2, –3, Baker 84, –92, BioIn 8, –9, ConAu 1R, –33R, –2NR, NewGrDA 86, NewYTBE 71, WhAm 5*

Weir, Bob 1947- *RkOn 85, SmATA 76*

Weir, Harrison 1824-1906 *CelCen, DcBiPP, OxCChiL*

Weir, Harrison William 1824-1906 *DcVicP 2*

Weir, LaVada *BioIn 9, ConAu 21R, –9NR, SmATA 2, WrDr 76, –80, –82, –84, –86, –88*

Weir, Rosemary 1905- *AuBYP 2, –3, Au&Wr 71, BioIn 8, –12, ConAu 13R, –10NR, SmATA 21, TwCChW 78, –83, –89, WrDr 80, –82, –84, –86, –88, –90, –92, –94*

Weir, Wendy 1949- *SmATA 76*

Weis, Margaret 1948- *ConAu 111, –34NR, ScF&FL 92, SmATA 38*
Pseud./variant:
Baldwin, Margaret

Weisberg, Joseph S *AuBYP 3*

Weisberg, Joseph Simpson 1937- *AmMWSc 73P, –76P, –82, –86, –89, –92, AuBYP 2S, ConAu 107, IntAu&W 86, WhoE 75, –77, –93, WhoFrS 84*

Weisberger, Bernard A 1922- *BioIn 12, ConAu 5R, –7NR, DrAS 74H, –78H, –82H SmATA 21*

Weiser, Marjorie P K 1934- *BioIn 14, ConAu 103, SmATA 33*
Pseud./variant:
Katz, Marjorie P

Weiser, Marjorie Phillis Katz *AuBYP 3*

Weisgard, Leonard Joseph 1916- *AmPB, AuBYP 2, –3, BioIn 1, –2, –4, –5, –7, –8, –9, BkP, Cald 1938, ChhPo, –S1, ConAu 9R, IlsBYP, IlsCB 1744, –1946, –1957, –1967, JBA 51, MajAI, REnAL, SmATA 2, –30, WhAmArt 85, WhoAmA 73, –78, –80, –82*
Pseud./variant:
Green, Adam

Weisheit, Eldon 1933- *ConAu 29R, –14NR, WhoRel 77*

Weiss, Adelle 1920- *BioIn 12, ConAu 81, SmATA 18*

Weiss, Ann E 1943- *ConAu 45, –1NR, –11NR, –28NR, SixBJA, SmATA 30, –69, –13AS*

Weiss, Ann Edwards 1943- *MajAI*

Weiss, Carol *AuBYP 2S*

Weiss, David Ansel *AuBYP 2S*

Weiss, David Ansel 1909- *AuBYP 3*

Weiss, David Ansel 1922- *WhoFI 87, –92*

Weiss, Edna *AuBYP 2S, –3, ConAu 41R, –X*
Main entry: Barth, Edna

Weiss, Elizabeth S 1944- *ConAu 61, –11NR*

Weiss, Ellen 1953- *ConAu 113, ScF&FL 92, SmATA 44*

Weiss, Emil 1896-1965 *BioIn 8, IlsBYP, IlsCB 1957*

Weiss, Harvey 1922- *AuBYP 2, –3, BioIn 5, –8, –9, –13, ChlLR 4, ConAu 5R, –6NR, –38NR, IlsCB 1946, –1957, –1967, MajAI, SmATA 1, –27, –76, ThrBJA, WhoAmA 73, –78, –80, –82, –84, –86, –89, –91, WhoE 75, –77, –91*

Weiss, Jaqueline Shachter *BioIn 17*

Weiss, Jaqueline Shachter 1926- *ConAu 119, IntAu&W 89, SmATA 65*

Weiss, Leatie 1928- *BioIn 16, ConAu 65, SmATA 50, WhoAmW 81*

Weiss, M Herbert 1882-1944 *BioIn 2, EncAB-A 19*

Weiss, Malcolm Earl 1928- *BioIn 9, ConAu 25R, –11NR, SmATA 3, WhoE 74, –75, –77*

Weiss, Miriam *ConAu X, SmATA 2, WhoWorJ 72*
Main entry: Schlein, Miriam

Weiss, Nicki 1954- *ConAu 108, –26NR, SixBJA, SmATA 33*

Weiss, Nicki Monica Jane 1954- *WhoAmW 93*

Weiss, Peter *AuBYP 2S*

Weiss, Peter 1916-1982 *AnObit 1982, AuBYP 3, Benet 87, BioIn 7, –8, –10, –12, –13, CamGWoT, CasWL, CnThe, ConAu 45, –106, –3NR, ConLC 3, –15, –51, CroCD, CurBio 68, –82N, CyWA 89, DcLB 69, –124, EncWL, –2, EncWT, GrFLW, IntAu&W 77, IntWW 74, –75, –76, –77, –78, –79, –80, –81, –82, –82N, LiExTwC, MajMD 1, McGEWD 72, –84, ModGL, ModWD, NewYTBS 82, NotNAT, –A, OxCFilm, OxCGer 76, –86, OxCThe 83, PenC EUR, PlP&P, –A, RAdv 13-2, REnWD, TwCWr, Who 74, –82, WhoThe 72, –77, –81, WhoWor 74, WorAlBi, WorAl, WorAu 1950, WorEFlm*

Weiss, Peter, and Carol Weiss *AuBYP 3*

Weiss, Peter Ulrich 1916-1982 *IntDcT 2*

Weiss, Renee 1923- *AuBYP 3*

Weiss, Renee Karol 1923- *AuBYP 2S, BioIn 10, ConAu 41R, IntAu&W 91, SmATA 5, WhoAm 94, WhoAmW 74, –75*

Weissenborn, Hellmuth 1898-1982 *BioIn 14, ConAu 107, DcCAr 81, SmATA 31N, WhoArt 80, –82, –84N*

Weitz, Joseph Leonard 1922- *AmMWSc 73P, –76P, –82, –86, –89, –92*

Weitzman, Alan 1933- *ConAu 29R, WhoAmJ 80*

Wekesser, Carol A 1963- *SmATA 76*

Welber, Robert *AuBYP 2S, –3, BioIn 13, ConAu 104, SmATA 26*

Welch, Amanda Jane 1945- *SmATA 75*

Welch, Ann Courtenay 1917- *IntAu&W 86, –89, WrDr 86, –88, –90, –92, –94*

Welch, Ann Courtenay Edmonds 1917- *Au&Wr 71, ConAu 9R, –3NR, –18NR, IntAu&W 82, WrDr 76, –80, –82, –84*

Welch, D'Alte A 1907-1970 *DcAmBC*

Welch, D'Alte Aldridge 1907-1970 *BioIn 13, ConAu 104, OxCChiL, SmATA 27N*

Welch, Jean-Louise *ConAu X, SmATA X*
Main entry: Kempton, Jean Welch

Welch, June Rayfield 1927- *ConAu 41R, WhoAm 76, WhoAmL 90, WhoSSW 86*

Welch, Martha McKeen 1914- *BioIn 15, ConAu 114, SmATA 45, WhoAmW 77*

Welch, Mary Scott *IntAu&W 86*

Welch, Mary-Scott 1919- *WhoAmW 91, WhoE 93*

Welch, Mary Scott Stewart *ConAu 104, IntAu&W 82, WhoAmW 74, –75, –77, –83, –85, WhoE 81, –83, –85, WhoWor 84*

Welch, Pauline *AuBYP 2S, –3, ConAu X, SmATA X*
Main entry: Bodenham, Hilda Morris

Welch, Ronald
Main entry: Felton, Ronald Oliver

Welch, Ronald 1909-1982 *ConAu X, OxCChiL, OxCLiW 86, SmATA 3, TwCChW 78, –83, –89, WhoChL, WrDr 82*

Welcher, Rosalind 1922- *ConAu 45, –25NR, ForWC 70, WhoAmW 74, WhoE 85, –86, –89, WrDr 76, –80, –82, –84, –86, –88, –90, –92, –94*

Weldon, Martin 1913- *AuBYP 3*

Weldon, Martin 1913-1966 *AuBYP 2, BioIn 7, –8*

Welford, Sue 1942- *ConAu 142, SmATA 75*
Pseud./variant:
Kelly, Fiona

Weller, George Anthony 1907- *AmAu&B, BlueB 76, ConAu 65, REnAL, SmATA 31, WhNAA, WhoAm 74, –80, –82, –84, –86, WhoWor 84, –87, WrDr 76, –80, –82, –84, –86, –88, –90*
Pseud./variant:
Wharf, Michael

Welles, Samuel P 1907- *WrDr 88, –90, –92*

Welles, Samuel Paul 1907- *AmMWSc 76P, –82, –86, –89, –92, BlueB 76, WhoAm 74, –76, –78, WrDr 76, –80, –82, –84, –86, –94*

Welles, Winifred *EngPo*

Welles, Winifred 1893-1939 *AmAu&B, AnMV 1926, BenetAL 91, BioIn 1, –13, BkCL, ChhPo, –S1, ConAmA, ConAu 112, REnAL, SmATA 27, Str&VC*

Wellington, Monica 1957- *ConAu 136, SmATA 67, WrDr 94*

Wellman, Alice 1900- *SmATA 36*

Wellman, Alice 1900-1984 *SmATA 51*

Wellman, Henry Q 1945- *ConAu 37R*

Wellman, Manly Wade 1903- *AuBYP 2, BioIn 3, –4, –5, –6, –8, –10, ConAu 1R, –6NR, –16NR, ConSFA, CurBio 55, EncMys, IntAu&W 91, MorJA, SmATA 6, SupFW, TwCSFW 86, WhoHr&F, WhoSciF, WrDr 84, –86, –88*

Wellman, Manly Wade 1903-1986 *BioIn 15, –16, ConAu 118, ConLC 49, EncSF 93, ScF&FL 92, ScFEYrs, SmATA 47N, TwCSFW 91*
Pseud./variant:
Field, Gans T

Wellman, Manly Wade 1905- *PenEncH*

Wellman, Manly Wade 1905-1986 *AuBYP 3*

Wellman, Paul I 1898-1966 *BenetAL 91, TwCWW 91*

Wellman, Paul Iselin 1898-1966 *AmAu&B, AmNov, AuBYP 2, –3, Au&Wr 71, BioIn 1, –2, –4, –7, –8, –9, ConAu 1R, –25R, –16NR, CurBio 49, EncFWF, ObitOF 79, REn, REnAL, SmATA 3, TwCA SUP, WhAm 4*

Wells, Ann *SingR 2*

Wells, Carolyn 1862-1942 *DcAmBC, InWom SUP, TwCLC 35, WomNov*

Wells, Carolyn 1869?-1942 *AmAu&B, AmLY, AmWomPl, AmWomWr, BenetAL 91, BiD&SB, BioIn 13, –14, –15, CarSB, ChhPo, –S1, –S2, ConAu 113, CurBio 42, DcAmAu, DcLB 11, DcNAA, EncAHmr, EncMys, EvLB, REn, REnAL, TwCA, TwCCr&M 80, –85, –91, TwCWr, WhAm 2, WhNAA, WomWWA 14*

Wells, Evelyn *ConAu 53*

Wells, H G 1866-1946 *Benet 87, BioIn 14, –15, –16, –17, BlmGEL, BritWr 6, CamGEL, CamGLE, CnDBLB 6, ConAu 110, –121, DcLB 34, –70, EncUrb, EncWL 2, HalFC 84, –88, MagSWL, MajTwCW, ModBrL S2, NewEScF, Novels, OxCChiL, OxCEng 85 PenEncH, RAdv 13-1, RGTwCSF, RfGEnL 91, ScFSB, ScFEYrs, –A, ShSCr 6, SmATA 20, StaCVF, SupFW, TwCLC 6, –12, –19, TwCSFW 86, –91, WhScrn 83, WorAlBi, WorAl, WorLitC, WrChl*
Pseud./variant:
Bliss, Reginald

Wells, H G 1886-1946 *ScF&FL 92*

Wells, Helen *ConAu X*
Main entry: Campbell, Hope

Wells, Helen 1910- *AuBYP 2, BioIn 8, –9, ConAu 29R, ForWC 70, IntAu&W 82, SmATA 2, WhoAmW 74, –75, WrDr 76, –80, –82, –84*
Pseud./variant:
Lewis, Francine

Wells, Helen 1910-1986 *ConAu 37NR, IntAu&W 86, MajAI, SmATA 49*

Wells, Helen 1910-1988 *BioIn 16*

Wells, Helen 1915- *WrDr 86, –88*

Wells, Helen Frances 1910- *AuBYP 3*

Wells, Herbert George *IntvTCA 2*

Wells, Herbert George 1866-1946 *AtlBL, BbD, BiDInt, BiD&SB, BioIn 1, –2, –3, –4, –5, –6, –7, –8, –9, –10, –11, –12, –13, –14, –15, –16, –17, CasWL, Chambr 3, CnMWL, CurBio 46, CyWA 58, DcAmSR, DcBiA, DcEnA A, DcLEL, DcNaB 1941, EncMys, EncSF 93, EncWL, EvLB, FilmgC, GrBr, LongCEL, LongCTC, MakMC, McGEWB, ModBrL, –S1,*

NewC, NotNAT B, ObitOF 79, OxCEng 67, PenC ENG, PlP&P, RAdv 1, RComWL, REn, RfGShF, SmATA 20, TwCA, –SUP, TwCWr, TwCYAW, WebE&AL, WhDW, WhAm 2, WhScrn 74, –77, WhoHol B, WhoHr&F, WhoLA, WhoSciF, WhoTwCL

Wells, J Wellington *ConAu X, IntAu&W 91X, SmATA X*
Main entry: DeCamp, L Sprague

Wells, June *SmATA X*
Main entry: Swinford, Betty June Wells

Wells, Lorraine Rosemary Siplon 1930- *DrAS 74E, WhoAmW 74, –77, WhoMW 74*

Wells, Maie Lounsbury *AuBYP 2, –3, BioIn 8*

Wells, Peter 1912- *BioIn 1, CurBio 42, IlsCB 1744*

Wells, Reuben Field 1880-1938 *DcNAA*

Wells, Rhea 1891- *AmAu&B, BioIn 1, –2, ConICB, IlsCB 1744, JBA 34, –51, WhAmArt 85*

Wells, Robert L 1913- *AuBYP 2, –3, BioIn 7*

Wells, Robert W 1918- *ConAu 49, –2NR*

Wells, Rosemary 1943- *BioIn 12, ChhPo S1, –S2, ChlLR 16, ConAu 85, DcAmChF 1960, –1985, FourBJA, IlsBYP, IlsCB 1967, MajAI, ScF&FL 92, SmATA 18, –69, –1AS, TwCChW 83, –89, TwCYAW, WhoAm 92, WrDr 86, –88, –90, –92, –94*

Wels, Byron G 1924- *BioIn 11, ConAu 61, –8NR, SmATA 9*

Welsh, Mary Flynn 1910?-1984 *BioIn 15, ConAu 112, SmATA 38N*
Pseud./variant:
Flynn, Mary

Weltner, Linda R 1938- *ConAu 105, SmATA 38*

Welty, Eudora *DrAPF 87, –89, –91, –93, IntvTCA 2, Who 88, –90, –92, WhoAm 86, –88, –90, –92, –94, WhoAmW 87, –89, –91, –93, WhoUSWr 88, WhoWor 87, –89, –91, –93, WhoWrEP 89, –92*

Welty, Eudora 1909- *AmAu&B, AmNov, AmWomWr, –92, AmWr, ArtclWW 2, Benet 87, BenetAL 91, BioAmW, BioIn 1, –2, –3, –4, –5, –6, –7, –8, –9, –10, –11, –12, –13, –14, –15, –16, –17, BlmGWL, BlueB 76, CamGLE, CamHAL, CasWL, CelR, ChhPo, CnDAL, ConAu 9R, –1BS, –32NR, ConLC 1, –2, –5, –22, –33, ConNov 72, –76, –82, –86, –91, ContDcW 89, Conv 3, CurBio 42, –75, CyWA 58, –89, DcLB 102, –Y87A, DcLEL 1940, DrAF 76, DrAPF 83, –85, EncSoH, EncWL, –2, FemiCLE, FifSWrA, ICPEnP A, InWom SUP, IntAu&W 77, –89, –91, IntDcWB, IntWW 74, –75, –76, –77, –78, –79, –80, –81, –82, –83, –89, –91, LongCTC, MacBEP, MagSAmL, MajTwCW, ModAL, –S1, –S2, ModAWWr, NewCon, NewYTBS 80, –83, Novels, OxCAmL 65, –83, PenC AM, PenEncH, RAdv 1, –13-1, REn, REnAL, RfGAmL 87, ShSCr 1, ShSWr, TwCA SUP, WebAB 74, –79, WebE&AL, WhDW, Who 74, –82, –83, –85, WhoAm 74, –76, –78, –80, –82, –84, WhoAmW 81, –83, –85, WhoSSW 76, –78, WhoTwCL, WhoWor 74, –78, –80, –82, –84, WorAlBi, WorAl, WorLitC, WrDr 76, –80, –82, –84, –86, –88, –90, –92, –94*

Welty, Eudora Alice 1909- *RfGShF*

Welty, S F
Main entry: Welty, Susan F

Welty, Susan F 1905- *BioIn 11, ConAu P-2, SmATA 9*
Pseud./variant:
Welty, S F

Wende, Philip 1939- *ConAu 29R, IlsBYP*

Wendelin, Rudolph 1910- *BioIn 13, SmATA 23*

Wender, Dorothea 1934- *ConAu 45, –24NR, DrAS 74F*

Wendt, Lloyd *AuBYP 3*

Wendt, Lloyd 1908- *AuBYP 2S, ConAu 102, –25NR, EncTwCJ, WhoAm 74, –76, –78, –80, –82, –84, –86, –88, –90, –92, –94, WhoMW 74, –76, –78, WhoUSWr 88, WhoWrEP 89, –92*

Wennerstrom, Genia Katherine 1930- *BioIn 8, IlsBYP, IlsCB 1957*
Pseud./variant:
Genia

Wenning, Elisabeth *AuBYP 3*

Wenning, Elizabeth *AuBYP 2, BioIn 7*

Went, Frits Warmolt *AmMWSc 89*

Went, Frits Warmolt 1903- *AmMWSc 76P, –82, –86, BlueB 76, IntWW 74, –75, –76, –77, –78, –79, –80, –81, –82, –83, McGMS 80*

Wentworth, Charles *HsB&A*

Wentz, Robert William, Jr. 1932- *WhoAm 74, –76, WhoGov 75*

Werenskiold, Erik 1855-1938 *BioIn 4, –11, OxCArt, OxDcArt, PhDcTCA 77*

Wernecke, Herbert Henry 1895- *AuBYP 2, –3, BioIn 8, ConAu 5R*

Werner, Elsa Jane
Main entry: Watson, Jane Werner

Werner, Herma 1926- *BioIn 15, –16, ConAu 85, –15NR, –34NR, SmATA 41, –47*
Pseud./variant:
Cowen, Eve
Gladstone, Eve
Jarrett, Roxanne
Pinner, Joma

Werner, Jane *ChhPo, ConAu X, SmATA 3*
Main entry: Watson, Jane Werner

Werner, K *ConAu X, SmATA 4*
Main entry: Casewit, Curtis

Werner, Pat *AuBYP 2, –3, BioIn 8*

Werner, Victor Emile 1894- *ConAu 29R, WrDr 76, –80, –82, –84*

Werner, Vivian *AuBYP 3*

Werner, Vivian 1921- *AuBYP 2S, ConAu 105*

Wernick, Robert 1918- *ConAu 97*

Wersba, Barbara 1932- *ArtclWW 2, Au&Arts 2, AuBYP 2, –3, BioIn 8, –9, –11, ChlLR 3, ConAu 29R, –16NR, –38NR, ConLC 30, DcAmChF 1960, DcLB 52, MajAI, OxCChiL, SmATA 1, –58, –2AS, ThrBJA, TwCChW 78, –83, –89, TwCYAW, WrDr 80, –82, –84, –86, –88, –90, –92, –94*

Werstein, Irving 1914?-1971 *AuBYP 2, –3, BioIn 7, –9, –12, ConAu 29R, –73, FourBJA, NewYTBE 71, SmATA 14*

Wertenbaker, Lael Tucker *ConTFT 9*

Wertenbaker, Lael Tucker 1909- *Au&Wr 71, BioIn 16, ConAu 5R, ForWC 70, IntAu&W 77, –82, WhoAmW 75, WhoE 74, WrDr 76, –80, –82, –84, –86, –88, –90, –92, –94*

Werth, Kurt 1896- *BioIn 5, –6, –8, –12, ChhPo, –S1, –S2, ConAu 81, IlsBYP, IlsCB 1946, –1957, –1967, MorJA, SmATA 20, WhoAmA 73, –78, –80, –82*

Wesley, Alison
Main entry: Barnes, Michael

Wesley, James *ConAu X, IntAu&W 77X, –82X, WrDr 76, –80, –82, –84, –86, –88, –90*
Main entry: Rigoni, Orlando Joseph

Wesley, Mary *BioIn 17*

Wesley, Mary 1912- *ConAu 49, ConNov 91, FemiCLE, IntAu&W 91, MajTwCW, SmATA 66, WrDr 90, –92, –94*

West, Anna 1938- *ConAu 106, SmATA 40*

West, Anthony 1914- *AmAu&B, Au&Wr 71, BioIn 2, –4, –13, ConAu 45, –3NR, –19NR, ConNov 72, –76, –82, –86, DcLB 15, LongCTC, ModBrL, NewC, REn, TwCA SUP, WhoAm 74, WhoWor 74, WrDr 76, –80, –82, –84, –86, –88*

West, Anthony 1914-1987 *AnObit 1987, Benet 87, BenetAL 91, ConAu 124, ConLC 50, EncSF 93, NewYTBS 87, ScF&FL 92*

West, Barbara *ConAu X, SmATA 8*
Main entry: Price, Olive

West, Betty *AuBYP 3*

West, Betty 1921- *AuBYP 2, Au&Wr 71, BioIn 11, ConAu 5R, –7NR, SmATA 11*
Pseud./variant:
Bowen, Betty Morgan

West, Bruce 1951- *SmATA 63*

West, C P *ConAu 33NR, MajTwCW, SmATA X*

West, Dorothy *ConAu 134, MajAI, SmATA 65, WrDr 94*
Main entry: Benson, Mildred Augustine Wirt

West, Edward *BioIn 12, SmATA X*
Main entry: Household, Geoffrey

West, Emily 1919- *AuBYP 2, –3, BioIn 8, ConAu 109, SmATA 38*
Pseud./variant:
Payne, Emmy
West, Emmy

West, Emmy
Main entry: West, Emily

West, Fred 1918- *ConAu 5R*

West, James *AuBYP 2, –3, ConAu X, –30NR, SmATA X*
Main entry: Withers, Carl A

West, Jerry *CmCal, ConAu X, SmATA 2, –X, WhoAm 80, WorAl*
Main entry: Stratemeyer, Edward L
Svenson, Andrew E

West, Jessamyn *IntvTCA 2*

West, Jessamyn d1984 *BioIn 14, –15, –16, –17*

West, Jessamyn 1902-1984 *AmWomWr, AnObit 1984, BenetAL 91, BioIn 2, –3, –4, –5, –8, –9, –10, –11, –12, –13, CmCal, ConAu 112, –27NR, ConLC 17, ConNov 82,*

CurBio 84N, CyWA 89, DcLB 6, –Y84N, DrAPF 83, –85, EncFWF, FemiCLE, InWom SUP, MajTwCW, NewYTBS 84, OxCAmL 83, ScF&FL 92, SmATA 37N, TwCRHW 90, TwCWW 91, WhAm 8, WhoAm 80, –82, WhoAmW 81, –83, WrDr 82, –84

West, Jessamyn 1907-1984 *ArtclWW 2, BioAmW*

West, Joyce *ConAu 106, OxCChiL, TwCChW 78, –83, WrDr 80, –82, –84, –86, –88*

West, Joyce d1985 *TwCChW 89*

West, Marvin 1879-1917 *CarSB, DcNAA*

West, Mary Jessamyn 1902-1984 *EncSF 93, TwCYAW*

West, Owen *ConAu 36NR, EncSF 93, MajTwCW, ScF&FL 92, TwCYAW, WrDr 86, –88, –90, –92*

West, Owen 1945- *WrDr 94*

West, Paul *DrAPF 87, –89, –91, –93, IntvTCA 2*

West, Paul 1930- *AmAu&B, BenetAL 91, BioIn 10, –13, ChhPo, ConAu 13R, –7AS, –22NR, ConLC 7, ConLCrt 77, –82, ConNov 72, –76, –82, –86, –91, CyWA 89, DcLB 14, DrAF 76, DrAPF 83, –85, DrAS 74E, EngPo, IntAu&W 77, –82, –86, ScF&FL 92, WorAu 1950, WrDr 76, –80, –82, –84, –86, –88, –90, –92, –94*

West, Wallace 1900- *ConSFA, ScFSB, ScFEYrs, TwCSFW 86, WrDr 84, –86, –88, –90*

West, Wallace 1900-1980 *NewEScF, ScF&FL 92*

West, Wallace George 1900-1980 *EncSF 93*

West, Walter Richard 1912- *BioIn 5, –9, IlsBYP, IlsCB 1946, WhAmArt 85*

West, Ward *AmAu&B, ConAu X, SmATA 5, –X, TwCWW 91, WorAu 1950, WrDr 84, –86, –88*
Main entry: Borland, Hal

Westall, Robert *DcVicP 2*

Westall, Robert d1993 *NewYTBS 93*

Westall, Robert 1929- *ChlLR 13, ScF&FL 92, SmATA 69, –2AS, TwCChW 89, WrDr 86, –88, –90, –92*

Westall, Robert 1929-1993 *WrDr 94N*

Westall, Robert Atkinson 1929- *BioIn 13, ChlFicS, ConAu 69, –18NR, ConLC 17, DcVicP 2, EncSF 93, FifBJA, IntAu&W 77, –82, –91, MajAI, OxCChiL, SmATA 23, –2AS, TwCChW 78, –83, Who 90, –92, WrDr 80, –82, –84*

Westall, Robert Atkinson 1929-1993 *ConAu 141, SmATA 75, TwCYAW*

Westcott, Alvin Milton 1930- *LEduc 74*

Westcott, Jan Vlachos 1912- *AmAu&B, AmNov, BioIn 2, ConAu 1R, –2NR*

Westcott, Nadine *AuBYP 3*

Westcott, Nadine Bernard 1949- *BioIn 16, SixBJA*

Westerberg, Christine 1950- *BioIn 13, ConAu 61, SmATA 29*

Westerman, Percy 1876-1959 *TwCChW 89*

Westerman, Percy F *EncSF 93*

Westerman, Percy F 1876-1959 *ScF&FL 92*

Westerman, Percy Francis 1876-1960? *BioIn 5, –8, ConAu 110, OxCChiL, TwCChW 78, –83, WhoChL*

Westervelt, Virginia Veeder 1914- *BioIn 11, ConAu 61, –10NR, IntAu&W 77, SmATA 10, WhoAmW 74, –75*

Westheimer, David *DrAPF 87, –89, –91, –93*

Westheimer, David 1917- *AmAu&B, AmNov, Au&Wr 71, BioIn 2, –12, ConAu 1R, –2NR, DrAPF 83, –85, IntAu&W 77, –89, –91, SmATA 14, WhoUSWr 88, WhoWrEP 89, –92, WrDr 76, –80, –82, –84, –86, –88, –90, –92, –94*
Pseud./variant:
Smith, Z Z

Westmacott, Bernard 1887- *ConICB*

Westmacott, Mary *AuBYP 3, ConAu X, –37NR, EncMys, EvLB, InWom SUP, LongCTC, MajTwCW, SmATA X, TwCA SUP, WrDr 76*

Westmacott, Mary 1890-1976 *TwCRHW 90*

Westman, Barbara *ConAu 105, SmATA 70*

Westman, Paul 1956- *ConAu 106, SmATA 39*

Westman, Wesley Charles 1936- *AmMWSc 73S, –78S, ConAu 29R*

Westmoreland, Lesley *SingR 2*

Westmoreland, William C 1914- *SmATA 63, WorAlBi*

Westmoreland, William Childs 1914- *EncWB, IntWW 91*

Westmoreland, William Childs, Gen 1914- *IntWW 89*

Weston, Allen *ConAu X, -31NR, MajAI, MajTwCW, SmATA X, WrDr 82, -84, -86, -88, -90, -92*
Main entry: Hogarth, Grace
Norton, Alice Mary

Weston, Allen 1905- *WrDr 94*

Weston, Henry Griggs, Jr. 1922- *AmMWSc 73P, -76P, -82, -86, -89*

Weston, John 1932- *BioIn 12, ConAu 17R, SmATA 21*

Weston, Martha 1947- *ConAu 129, SmATA 53*

Westover, Russ 1886-1966 *EncACom*

Westover, Russ 1896-1966 *ArtCS, BioIn 7*

Westphal, Arnold Carl *BioIn 14*

Westphal, Arnold Carl 1897- *SmATA 57, WhoRel 92*
Pseud./variant:
Children's Shepherd, The

Westphal, Barbara Osborne 1907- *ConAu P-1, WhoAmW 74, -75*

Westphal, Clarence 1904- *ConAu P-2*

Westwood, Gwen 1915- *ConAu 25R, -19NR, TwCRHW 90, WrDr 76, -80, -82, -84, -86, -88, -90, -92, -94*

Westwood, Jennifer 1940- *BioIn 11, ConAu 65, -X, -29NR, SmATA 10, WhoWor 80*

Wetherell, Elizabeth *Alli, AmAu, AmAu&B, BenetAL 91, BiD&SB, BlmGWL, Chambr 3, ChhPo S1, DcAmAu, DcEnL, EvLB, InWom SUP, OxCAmL 65, -83, OxCChiL, REnAL, WhAm HS, WhoChL*
Main entry: Warner, Susan Bogert

Wetterer, Margaret K *AuBYP 2S, -3*

Wettlaufer, George 1935- *ConAu 57*

Wettlaufer, Nancy 1939- *ConAu 57*

Wexler, Jerome 1923- *ConAu 73, SmATA 14*
Pseud./variant:
Delmar, Roy

Weygant, Noemi *AuBYP 3*

Weygant, Noemi, Sister *AuBYP 2, ConAu 45, -2NR, MorBMP*

Weyman, Stanley J 1855-1928 *StaCVF*

Weyman, Stanley John 1855-1928 *BbD, BiD&SB, BioIn 6, CamGEL, CarSB, Chambr 3, DcBiA, DcLEL, DcNaB 1922, EvLB, LongCTC, NewC, OxCChiL, OxCEng 67, -85, TelT, TwCA*

Weyn, Suzanne 1955- *ScF&FL 92, SmATA 63*

Whalen, Philip 1923- *AmAu&B, BenetAL 91, BioIn 8, -11, -13, ConAu 9R, -5NR, -39NR, ConLC 6, -29, ConPo 70, -75, -80, -85, -91, DcLB 16, DcLEL 1940, DrAF 76, DrAP 75, OxCAmL 83, PenC AM, RAdv 1, WrDr 76, -80, -82, -84, -86, -88, -90, -92*

Whalen, Philip Glenn 1923- *WrDr 94*

Whalley, Dorothy 1911- *ConAu P-1, IntAu&W 77, -82*
Pseud./variant:
Cowlin, Dorothy

Whalley, Joyce Irene *WrDr 86, -88, -90, -92, -94*

Whalley, Joyce Irene 1923- *SmATA 61*

Wharf, Michael *SmATA X*
Main entry: Weller, George Anthony

Wharmby, Margot *ConAu 24NR, SmATA 63*

Wheatcroft, John Stewart 1925- *ConAu 37R, DrAS 74E, -82E, WhoAm 74, -80, -82, -84, -86, -88, -90, WhoUSWr 88, WhoWrEP 89, -92, WrDr 76, -80, -82, -84, -86, -88, -90, -92, -94*

Wheatley, Arabelle 1921- *BioIn 12, SmATA 16*

Wheatley, Nadia 1949- *AuWomWr, BlmGWL, DcChlFi, TwCChW 89*

Wheelan, Ed 1888- *ArtCS*

Wheelan, Ed 1888-1966 *EncACom*

Wheeler, Benson 1905- *WhNAA*

Wheeler, Captain *Alli, HsB&A, -SUP, YABC 1*
Main entry: Ellis, Edward S

Wheeler, Cindy 1955- *ConAu 110, -31NR, SmATA 40, -49*

Wheeler, Francis W Rolt *JBA 34, -51*
Main entry: Rolt-Wheeler, Francis W

Wheeler, Harvey 1918- *AmMWSc 73S, BioIn 6, ConAu 45, -1NR, -17NR, WhoAmP 73*

Wheeler, Janet D *CarSB, ConAu 26NR, –P-2, SmATA 1*
Main entry: Stratemeyer, Edward L

Wheeler, Keith 1911- *BioIn 6, ConAu 5R, –7NR*

Wheeler, Mary Jane *ConAu 29R*
Pseud./variant:
Simonson, Mary Jane

Wheeler, Molly 1920- *ConAu 29R, WrDr 76, –80, –82, –84, –86, –88*

Wheeler, Opal 1898- *BioIn 6, –13, ChhPo S1, –S2, MorJA, SmATA 23*

Wheeler, Paul 1934- *Au&Wr 71, ConAu 25R*

Wheeler, Penny Estes 1943- *ConAu 33R, WrDr 76, –80, –82, –84, –86, –88, –90, –92, –94*

Wheeler, Post 1869- *AuBYP 3*

Wheeler, Post 1869-1956 *AmAu&B, AmLY, AnCL, AuBYP 2, BioIn 4, –5, –7, DcAmAu, ObitOF 79, REnAL, WhAm 3, WhNAA*

Wheeler, Post 1869-1957 *BenetAL 91*

Wheeler, Ruth Carr 1899- *ConAu 5R, ForWC 70*

Wheeler, Sessions S *AuBYP 3*

Wheeler, Sessions S 1911- *ConAu 25NR*

Wheeler, Sessions Samuel 1911- *AuBYP 2, BioIn 8, ConAu 17R, IntAu&W 77, WhoAm 78, –80, –82, –84, –86, –88, –90, –92, WhoWor 80, –91, –93*

Wheelhouse, M V *BioIn 1, ConICB, IlsCB 1744*

Wheeling, Lynn *AuBYP 2, –3, BioIn 8*

Wheelock, John Hall 1886-1978 *AmAu&B, AmLY, AnMV 1926, Au&Wr 71, BenetAL 91, BioIn 4, –5, –9, –10, –11, –15, BlueB 76, ChhPo, –S1, –S2, CnDAL, ConAmA, ConAmL, ConAu 13R, –77, –14NR, ConPo 70, –75, DcLB 45, DcLEL, DrAP 75, IntAu&W 77, IntWW 74, –75, –76, –77, –78N, ModAL, ObitOF 79, OxCAmL 65, –83, RAdv 1, REn, REnAL, TwCA, –SUP, WhAm 7, WhNAA, WhoAm 74, –76, –78, WhoWor 74, WrDr 76*

Wheelright, John Tyler 1856-1925 *CarSB*

Wheelwright, Jere Hungerford *AuBYP 3*

Wheelwright, Jere Hungerford, Jr. 1905?-1961 *AmAu&B, AuBYP 2, BioIn 2, –3, –5, –6, –8, CurBio 52, –61*

Whelan, Elizabeth M 1943- *AmMWSc 86, –89, –92, ConAu 24NR*

Whelan, Elizabeth Murphy 1943- *AmMWSc 82, BiDrAPH 79, ConAu 57, –8NR, SmATA 14, WhoFrS 84*

Whempner, Verna Huber *BioIn 6, MinnWr*

Whipple, A B C 1918-
Pseud./variant:
Whipple, Cal

Whipple, Addison Beecher Colvin 1918- *BioIn 17, ConAu 125, SmATA 64*

Whipple, Cal *SmATA X*
Main entry: Whipple, A B C

Whipple, Chandler 1905- *ConAu 25R, WhoE 74*

Whistler, Reginald John 1905-1944 *BioIn 14, DcNaB 1941, SmATA 30*
Pseud./variant:
Whistler, Rex

Whistler, Rex *SmATA X*
Main entry: Whistler, Reginald John

Whistler, Rex 1905-1944 *BioIn 14, –15, OxDcArt, TwCPaSc*

Whistler, Theresa 1927- *BioIn 5, IlsCB 1946*

Whitaker, David 1930- *ConAu 21R, ConSFA*

Whitaker, David 1930-1980 *ConAu 134, ScF&FL 92*

Whitaker, Evelyn *CarSB*

Whitaker, George O *AuBYP 2, –3, BioIn 8*

Whitcomb, Jan 1906-1988 *SmATA 56N*

Whitcomb, Jon 1906- *BioIn 2, –3, –7, –11, ConAu P-1, IlrAm 1880, –E, SmATA 10, WhAmArt 85, WhoAm 74, –76, –78, WhoAmA 73, –78, –80, –82*

Whitcomb, Jon 1906-1988 *BioIn 15, –16, ConAu 125*

White, Alan *Au&Wr 71, ConAu 45, –3NR, DcLEL 1940, WrDr 76, –82, –84, –86, –88*

White, Alice Violet 1922- *Au&Wr 71, ConAu 61, –13NR*

White, Alicen *ConAu 77, ScF&FL 92*

White, Anne Hitchcock 1902-1970 *BioIn 14, ConAu 108, FourBJA, SmATA 33*

White, Anne Terry 1896- *AmWomWr, AuBYP 2, -3, BioIn 6, -7, -9, ConAu 9R, MorJA, SmATA 2*

White, Anne Terry 1896-1980 *ConAu 135*

White, Antonia 1889-1930 *BlmGWL*

White, Antonia 1899- *InWom SUP*

White, Antonia 1899-1980 *AnObit 1980, ArtclWW 2, Au&Wr 71, Benet 87, BioIn 3, -4, -7, -10, -12, -13, -16, BkC 5, CamGLE, CathA 1952, ConAu 97, -104, ConNov 72, -76, EncBrWW, FemiCLE, IntAu&W 77, LongCTC, NewC, OxCEng 85, REn, Who 74, WorAu 1950, WrDr 76, -80*

White, Bessie 1892- *AuBYP 2, -3, BioIn 7*

White, Bessie 1892?-1986 *ConAu 121, SmATA 50N*

White, Dale *AuBYP 2, -3, ConAu X, SmATA 3*
Main entry: Place, Marian Templeton

White, David Omar 1927- *ConAu 17R, IlsBYP*

White, Dori 1919- *BioIn 11, ConAu 37R, SmATA 10*

White, E B
Main entry: White, Elwyn Brooks

White, E B 1899-1985 *AnObit 1985, Benet 87, BenetAL 91, BioIn 14, -15, -16, -17, ChlLR 21, ConLC 39, EncAHmr, EncTwCJ, EncWB, MajTwCW, NewYTBS 85, RAdv 13-1, RfGAmL 87, TwCChW 89, WorAlBi*

White, Edgar B 1947- *BlkAWP, BlkAuII, -92, ConAu 61, ConBlAP 88, DcLB 38, DrBlPA 90, LivgBAA, NatPD 77, PlP&P A*

White, Edward Lucas 1866-1934 *AmAu&B, BenetAL 91, BiDSA, BioIn 10, -15, DcNAA, JBA 34, OxCAmL 65, -83, PenEncH, REn, REnAL, ScFEYrs, TwCA, WhAm 1, WhNAA, WhoHr&F*

White, Eliza Orne 1856-1947 *AmAu&B, AmLY, AmWomWr, BbD, BiD&SB, BioIn 2, -3, -12, CarSB, DcAmAu, DcNAA, InWom SUP, JBA 34, -51, TwCChW 78, -83, -89, WhAm 2, WomWWA 14, WomNov, YABC 2*

White, Ellen Emerson *ScF&FL 92, TwCYAW*

White, Elwyn B 1899-1985 *CamGLE*

White, Elwyn Brooks *IntvTCA 2*

White, Elwyn Brooks 1899-1985 *AmAu&B, AmPeW, AmWr S1, AuBYP 2, -3, Au&ICB, AuNews 2, BioIn 1, -3, -4, -5, -6, -7, -8, -9, -10, -11, -12, -13, -14, -15, -16, -17, BlueB 76, BkCL, CamHAL, CelR, ChhPo, -S1, -S2, ChlLR 1, CnDAL, ConAu 13R, -116, -16NR, -37NR, ConLC 10, CurBio 60, -85N, DcAmChF 1960, DcLB 11, -22, DcLEL, EncAJ, EvLB, FamMS, IntAu&W 77, IntWW 74, -75, -76, -77, -78, -79, -80, -81, -82, -83, JrnUS, LongCTC, MajAI, ModAL, MorBMP, MorJA, NewYTBS 80, -85, OxCAmH, OxCAmL 65, -83, OxCChiL, PenC AM, PiP, RAdv 1, REn, REnAL, SmATA 2, -29, -44N, TwCA, -SUP, TwCChW 78, -83, TwCWr, WebAB 74, -79, WhAm 10, Who 74, -82, -83, -85, WhoAm 74, -76, -78, -80, -82, -84, WhoChL, WhoWor 74, -84, WorAl, WrDr 76, -80, -82, -84*
Pseud./variant:
White, E B

White, Florence *AuBYP 3*

White, Florence M 1910- *ConAu 41R, IntAu&W 77, SmATA 14*

White, JoAnn 1941- *ConAu 53*

White, John S 1847-1922 *Alli SUP, DcAmAu, DcNAA*

White, Jon Manchip *DrAPF 87, -89, -91, -93, WhoUSWr 88, WhoWrEP 89, -92*

White, Jon Manchip 1924- *ConAu 13R, -4AS, -15NR, -32NR, ConNov 72, -76, -82, ConPo 70, DcLEL 1940, DrAF 76, DrAPF 83, -85, DrAS 74E, -78E, -82E, IntAu&W 77, -82, -86, -91, IntWWP 82, ScF&FL 92, TwCCr&M 80, -85, -91, WhoWor 78, WrDr 76, -80, -82, -84, -86, -88, -90, -92, -94*

White, Laurence B, Jr. 1935- *BioIn 11, ConAu 65, -9NR, -24NR, SmATA 10*

White, Martin *Who 92*

White, Martin 1943- *SmATA 51*

White, Mary *CarSB*

White, Nancy Bean 1922- *AuBYP 2, -3, BioIn 8, ConAu 13R, ForWC 70*

White, Osmar Egmont Dorkin 1909- *ConAu 105*

White, Patrick Cecil Telfer 1924- *ConAu 85, DrAS 74H, -78H, -82H, IntAu&W 82*

White, Paul Hamilton Hume 1910- *Au&Wr 71, BioIn 3, -4, -7, -8, ConAu 5R, -7NR, -23NR*

White, Pauline *AuBYP 2, -3, BioIn 7*

White, Percival 1887-1970 *AuBYP 2, –3, BioIn 7, –8, ConAu 1R, –2NR, SmATA 20N, WhAm 5*

White, Ramy Allison *CarSB, ConAu 26NR, –P-2, SmATA 1, –67*
Main entry: Stratemeyer, Edward L

White, Reginald James 1905-1971 *ConAu 104, –108*

White, Robb 1909- *AmAu&B, AuBYP 2, –3, BioIn 2, –3, –7, –9, ChlLR 3, ConAu 1R, –1NR, DcAmChF 1960, JBA 51, SmATA 1, –1AS, TwCYAW, WhNAA, WhoAm 74, –76, –78, –80, –82, –84, –86, –88, –90, –92, –94*

White, Ruth C 1942- *ConAu 111, DcAmChF 1985, SmATA 39*
Pseud./variant:
Miller, Ruth White

White, Stewart Edward 1863-1946 *ScFEYrs*

White, Stewart Edward 1873-1946 *AmAu&B, ArizL, BenetAL 91, BiDPara, BioIn 1, –4, –17, CarSB, CmCal, CnDAL, ConAmA, ConAmL, CurBio 46, DcAmAu, DcLEL, DcNAA, EncFWF, EncO&P 1, –2, –3, EncSF 93, LongCTC, ObitOF 79, OxCAmL 65, –83, REnAL, TwCA, –SUP, TwCWW 91, WhAm 2, WhNAA, WhoSpyF*

White, Stewart Edward & Adams, Samuel H *ScFEYrs*

White, T H *IntvTCA 2*
Main entry: White, Terence Hanbury

White, T H 1906-1964 *Benet 87, BioIn 15, CamGLE, LiExTwC, RAdv 13-1, RfGEnL 91, ScF&FL 92, SupFW, TwCChW 89, TwCRHW 90, WorAlBi*

White, Terence Hanbury 1906-1964 *BioIn 4, –5, –6, –7, –8, –10, –11, –12, –13, –15, CasWL, CnMWL, ConAu 73, –37NR, ConLC 30, DcIrL, DcLEL, DcNaB MP, EncSF 93, EngPo, LongCTC, MajAI, ModBrL, Novels, ObitOF 79, OxCChiL, OxCEng 67, –85, PenC ENG, RAdv 1, REn, SmATA 12, SupFW, TelT, TwCA, –SUP, TwCChW 78, –83, TwCWr, TwCYAW, WhDW, WhAm 4, WhoChL, WhoHr&F, WorAl*
Pseud./variant:
Aston, James
White, T H

White, Theodore Edwin 1938- *ConAu 21R, –12NR, ConSFA, WhoSciF*

White, Thomas *OxCChiL*

White, Thomas 1943- *WhoAm 94, WhoE 91, –93*

White, Thomas Allan 1942- *WhoMW 88*

White, Timothy 1952- *SmATA 60*

White, William 1910- *AmAu&B, BlueB 76, ConAu 21R, –29NR, DrAS 74E, –78E, –82E, IntAu&W 77, –82, –86, –89, MichAu 80, WhoAm 74, –76, –78, –80, –82, –84, WrDr 76, –80, –82, –84, –86, –88, –90, –92, –94*

White, William 1934- *InB&W 85, WhoBlA 88, –90*

White, William, Jr. 1934- *ConAu 37R, –14NR, –31NR, DrAS 74H, –78H, –82H, IntAu&W 77, –82, MarqDCG 84, SmATA 16, WhoE 81, –83, –85, WrDr 76, –80, –82, –84, –86, –88, –90, –92, –94*
Pseud./variant:
Spinossimus

White, Zita *ConAu X, SingR 1*
Main entry: Denholm, Therese Mary Zita White

Whitebead, Baida *IlsBYP*

Whitechurch, Victor L 1868-1933 *DcLB 70, ScFEYrs*

Whitechurch, Victor Lorenzo 1868-1933 *ChhPo, –S1, ConAu 116, EncMys, TwCCr&M 80, WhoLA*

Whiteford, Andrew H 1913- *ConAu 26NR*

Whiteford, Andrew Hunter 1913- *AmMWSc 73S, –76P, ConAu 45, FifIDA, WhoAm 74, –76, –78, –82, –84, –86, –88, –90, –92, –94*

Whitehead, Don F 1908-1981 *AmAu&B, BioIn 3, –5, –9, ConAu 9R, –102, CurBio 53, SmATA 4, WhoAm 74, –76, –78*

Whitehead, Robert John 1928- *ChhPo S1, ConAu 37R, –13NR, IndAu 1917, LEduc 74*

Whitehead, Ruth *AuBYP 2S, –3*

Whitehill, Dorothy *CarSB*

Whitehouse, Arch *ConAu X, SmATA X*
Main entry: Whitehouse, Arthur George

Whitehouse, Arch 1895-1979 *AuBYP 3*

Whitehouse, Arthur George 1895-1979 *AuBYP 3*
Pseud./variant:
Whitehouse, Arch

Whitehouse, Arthur George Joseph 1895-1979 *AuBYP 2, BioIn 7, –8, –12, –13, ConAu 5R, –4NR, SmATA 14, –23N*

Whitehouse, Elizabeth S 1893-1968 *BioIn 14, ConAu P-1, SmATA 35*

Whitehouse, Jeanne 1939- *BioIn 13, ConAu 103, SmATA 29*
Pseud./variant:
Peterson, Jeanne Whitehouse

Whitelaw, Nancy 1933- *SmATA 76*

Whitelaw, Nancy Eaton 1933- *WhoUSWr 88, WhoWrEP 89, -92*

Whitinger, R D *AuBYP 2, -3, ConAu X, SmATA 3*
Main entry: Place, Marian Templeton

Whitley, Mary A 1951- *SmATA 62*

Whitley, Mary Ann 1951- *WhoUSWr 88, WhoWrEP 89, -92*

Whitlock, Herbert Percy 1868-1948 *AmAu&B, BioIn 1, -2, DcNAA, InSci, WhAm 2*

Whitlock, Judith *SingR 2*

Whitlock, Pamela *TwCChW 89*

Whitlock, Pamela 1920-1982 *ChhPo, ConAu 107, OxCChiL, SmATA 31N*

Whitlock, Pamela 1921?-1982 *BioIn 14*

Whitlock, Ralph 1914- *Au&Wr 71, ConAu 101, -20NR, IntAu&W 77, -82, -86, -89, SmATA 35, WrDr 76, -80, -82, -84, -86, -88, -90, -92, -94*
Pseud./variant:
Countryman, The
Reynolds, John
Reynolds, Madge

Whitman, Alice *SmATA 76*
Main entry: Marker, Sherry

Whitman, Edmund Spurr 1900- *ConAu 17R, WhoAm 74, -76, -78*

Whitman, Walt 1819-1892 *Alli, -SUP, AmAu, AmAu&B, AmWr, AnCL, AtlBL, Benet 87, BenetAL 91, BbD, BiDAmJo, BiD&SB, BioIn 1, -2, -3, -4, -5, -6, -7, -8, -9, -10, -11, -12, -13, -14, -15, -16, -17, CamGEL, CamGLE, CamHAL, CasWL, CelCen, Chambr 3, ChhPo, -S1, CnDAL, CnE&AP, CrtT 3, CyWA 58, DcAmAu, DcAmSR, DcEnA, -A, DcEnL, DcLB 3, -64, DcLEL, DcNAA, Dis&D, EncAB-H, EvLB, HarEnUS, IlEncMy, JrnUS, MagSAmL, McGEWB, MemAm, MouLC 4, NewGrDA 86, NinCLC 4, -31, OxCAmH, OxCAmL 65, -83, OxCAusL, OxCCan, OxCEng 67, -85, PenC AM, PoeCrit 3, RAdv 1, -13-1, RComAH, RComWL, REn, REnAL, RfGAmL 87, SmATA 20, Str&VC, WebAB 74, -79, WebE&AL, WhDW, WhCiWar, WorAlBi, WorAl, WorLitC, WrPh*

Whitney, Adeline Dutton 1824-1906 *WomNcv*

Whitney, Adeline Dutton Train 1824-1906 *Alli, -SUP, AmAu, AmAu&B, AmWomWr, BbD, BiD&SB, BioIn 3, CarSB, ChhPo, -S1, CyAL, DcAmAu, DcNAA, HanAmWH, InWom SUP, OxCChiL, WhAm 1*

Whitney, Alex 1922- *ConAu 53, SmATA 14*

Whitney, Charles Allen 1929- *AmMWSc 73P, -76P, -82, -86, -89, -92, ConAu 81, WhoAm 74, -76, -78, -80, -82, -84, -86, -88, -90, -92, -94, WhoE 75, -77, WhoGov 77, -75*

Whitney, David C 1921- *SmATA 48*

Whitney, David Charles 1921- *BioIn 13, ConAu 9R, -5NR, DrAS 74H, -78H, SmATA 29, WhoAm 74, -76, -78, -80, -82, -84, -86, WhoUSWr 88, WhoWor 78*

Whitney, Elinor 1889- *AmAu&B, BioIn 2, -14, ChhPo, -S1, JBA 34, -51*

Whitney, George D 1918- *ConAu 93*

Whitney, Leon Fradley 1894-1973 *AmAu&B, AuBYP 2, -3, BioIn 7, ConAu 5R, -5NR, WhAm 6, WhNAA, WhoAm 74*

Whitney, Phyllis A *ThrtnMM*

Whitney, Phyllis A 1903- *BestSel 90-3, ConAu 25NR, ConLC 42, CrtSuMy, IntAu&W 91, ScF&FL 92, TwCChW 89, TwCCr&M 91, TwCRHW 90, WrDr 86, -88, -90, -92*

Whitney, Phyllis Ayame 1903- *AmAu&B, AmWomWr, AuBYP 2, -3, AuNews 2, BioIn 1, -2, -7, -9, -11, -12, ConAu 1R, -3NR, -38NR, CurBio 48, DcAmChF 1960, EncMys, ForWC 70, InWom SUP, JBA 51, MajAI, Novels, SmATA 1, -30, TwCChW 78, -83, TwCCr&M 80, -85, TwCYAW, WhoAm 76, -78, -80, -82, -84, -86, -88, -90, -92, -94, WhoAmW 74, -75, -89, -91, -93, WorAl, WrDr 76, -80, -82, -84, -94*

Whitney, Sharon 1937- *SmATA 63*

Whitney, Thomas P *AuBYP 3*

Whitney, Thomas Porter 1917- *AuBYP 2S, BioIn 10, -13, ConAu 104, SmATA 25, WhoAm 74, -76, WhoE 74, -75, -77, -81, -83, -85, -86, -89, -91, -93, WhoWor 74, -78, -80, -82, -84, -89, -91, -93*

Whitridge, Arnold d1989 *NewYTBS 89*

Whitridge, Arnold 1891- *AmAu&B, Au&Wr 71, ConAu 9R, DrAS 74H, WhoAm 74, –76, –78*

Whitridge, Arnold 1891-1989 *BioIn 16, ConAu 127, WhAm 9*

Whittaker, Otto 1916- *ConAu 25R*

Whittam, Geoffrey William 1916- *BioIn 5, IlsBYP, IlsCB 1946*

Whittemore, Constance *ConICB*

Whittier, John Greenleaf 1807-1892 *Alli, –SUP, AmAu, AmAu&B, AmPeW, AmWr S1, AnCL, AtlBL, Benet 87, BenetAL 91, BbD, BiD&SB, BioIn 1, –2, –3, –4, –5, –6, –7, –8, –9, –10, –11, –12, –13, –15, –16, CamGEL, CamGLE, CamHAL, CarSB, CasWL, CelCen, Chambr 3, ChhPo, –S1, –S2, CnDAL, CrtT 3, CyAL, CyWA 58, DcAmAu, DcAmSR, DcBiPP, DcEnA, DcEnL, DcLB 1, DcLEL, DcNAA, Dis&D, EncAB-H, EvLB, HarEnUS, McGEWB, MouLC 4, NewGrDA 86, NinCLC 8, OxCAmH, OxCAmL 65, –83, OxCChiL, OxCEng 67, –85, PenC AM, RAdv 1, –13-1, REn, REnAL, RfGAmL 87, Str&VC, WebAB 74, –79, WebE&AL, WhDW, WhAm HS, WhCiWar, WorAlBi, WorAl*

Whittingham, Richard 1939- *ConAu 37R, –36NR*

Whittington, Mary Kathrine 1941- *SmATA 75*

Whittle, Tyler *ConAu X, IntAu&W 77X, –86X, –91X, WrDr 76, –80, –82, –84, –86, –88, –90, –92*
Main entry: Tyler-Whittle, Michael Sidney

Whittle, Tyler 1927- *WrDr 94*

Whittlesey, Susan 1938- *AuBYP 2S, –3, ConAu 29R*

Whymper, Edward 1840-1911 *Alli, BbD, BiD&SB, BioIn 1, –4, –5, –7, –8, –9, –13, BritAu 19, Chambr 3, DcBiPP, DcNaB S2, EvLB, InSci, OxCEng 67, WhDW*

Whyte, Mal 1933- *SmATA 62*

Whyte, Ron *ConTFT 6*

Whyte, Ron d1989 *NewYTBS 89*

Whyte, Ron 1942?-1989 *ConAu 129, –132, SmATA 63*

Whyte, Ronald M 1942- *WhoWest 94*

Whyte-Melville, George John 1821-1878 *BbD, BiD&SB, BioIn 1, –2, –5, BritAS, BritAu 19, CamGEL, CelCen, Chambr 3, ChhPo, –S2, CmScLit, CyWA 58, DcEnA, –A, DcLEL, DcNaB, EvLB, NewC, OxCEng 67, –85, REn, StaCVF, WebE&AL*

Wibbelsman, Charles J 1945- *ConAu 128, SmATA 59*

Wibberley, Leonard *TwCCr&M 91*

Wibberley, Leonard 1915- *ScFSB, WrDr 86*

Wibberley, Leonard 1915-1983 *AnObit 1983, AuBYP 2, –3, BioIn 5, –6, –7, –9, –10, –13, –14, –15, ChhPo, ChlLR 3, ConAu 5R, –3NR, DcAmChF 1960, EncMys, MorJA, NewYTBS 83, OxCChiL, REn, ScF&FL 92, SmATA 2, –36N, –45, TwCChW 78, –83, –89, TwCCr&M 80, –85, TwCSFW 86, WorAu 1950, WrDr 80, –82, –84*
Pseud./variant:
Holton, Leonard
O'Connor, Patrick
Webb, Christopher

Wibberley, Leonard Patrick O'Connor 1915-1983 *EncSF 93*

Wiberg, Harald Albin 1908- *BioIn 8, IlsCB 1957, –1967, SmATA 40*

Wicker, Ireene *AuBYP 3*

Wicker, Ireene 1900-1987 *BioIn 15, –16*

Wicker, Ireene 1905- *AuBYP 2S, BioIn 1, –2, –8, –11, CmpEPM, ConAu 69, CurBio 43, ForWC 70, InWom SUP, WhoAm 74, –76, –78, –80, –82, WhoAmW 74, –75, –77, WhoE 74, –75, –77, WhoWor 74, –78, –82*

Wicker, Ireene 1905?-1987 *ConAu 124, CurBio 88N, SmATA 55N*

Wickers, David 1944- *ConAu 77*

Widdemer, Mabel 1902-1964 *AuBYP 3*

Widdemer, Mabel Cleland 1902-1964 *AuBYP 2, BioIn 7, –8, –10, ConAu 5R, SmATA 5, WhAm 4*
Pseud./variant:
Cleland, Mabel
Ludlum, Mabel Cleland

Widder, Robert B 1923- *WrDr 76, –80, –82, –84*

Widell, Helene 1912- *ConAu 37R, OxCCan SUP, WrDr 76, –80, –82, –84*

Widerberg, Siv 1931- *AuBYP 2S, –3, BioIn 11, ConAu 53, SmATA 10*

Widmer, Eleanor Rackow 1925- *ConAu 17R, WrDr 76, –80, –82, –84*

Wieler, Diana Jean 1961- *DcChlFi*

Wier, Ester 1910- *AuBYP 2, -3, BioIn 6, -7, -9, ConAu 9R, DcLB 52, SmATA 3, ThrBJA, TwCChW 78, -83, -89, WrDr 84, -86, -88, -90, -92*

Wier, Ester Alberti 1910- *DcAmChF 1960, WrDr 94*

Wiese, Kurt 1887-1974 *AmAu&B, AmPB, AuBYP 2, -3, BenetAL 91, BioIn 1, -2, -4, -5, -7, -8, -9, -10, -13, -14, ChhPo, ConAu 9R, -49, ConICB, IlsCB 1744, -1946, -1957, -1967, JBA 34, -51, MajAI, OxCChiL, REnAL, SmATA 3, -24N, -36, TwCChW 78, WhAmArt 85*

Wiesel, Elie *DrAPF 87, -89, -91, -93*

Wiesel, Elie 1928- *Au&Arts 7, Benet 87, BenetAL 91, BioIn 14, -15, -16, -17, ConAu 4AS, ConHero 1, CurBio 86, CyWA 89, DcLB 83, -Y87B, EncWB, InWom SUP, IntAu&W 89, -91, IntWW 89, -91, JeAmHC, LiExTwC, MagSWL, MajTwCW, NobelP, RAdv 13-2, SmATA 56, Who 88, -90, -92, WhoAm 86, -88, -90, -92, -94, WhoE 86, -89, -91, -93, WhoNob 90, WhoRel 92, WhoUSWr 88, WhoWor 89, -91, -93, WhoWrEP 89, -92, WorAlBi, WrDr 86, -88, -90, -92, -94*

Wiesel, Eliezer 1928- *ConAu 40NR, ConWorW 93, TwCYAW*

Wiesner, David *AuBYP 3, ChlBIlD*

Wiesner, David 1956- *SmATA 72*

Wiesner, Portia *SmATA X*
Main entry: Takakjian, Portia

Wiesner, William 1899- *BioIn 5, -8, -10, ChhPo, ConAu 41R, IlsBYP, IlsCB 1946, -1957, -1967, SmATA 5*

Wiest, Claire Johnson 1930- *WhoAmW 77, -81*

Wiggin, Kate Douglas *WomNov*

Wiggin, Kate Douglas 1856-1923 *Alli SUP, AmAu&B, AmWomWr, AuBYP 2S, -3, BenetAL 91, BbD, BiD&SB, BioAmW, BioIn 1, -2, -3, -4, -6, -8, -10, -11, -12, CamGLE, CarSB, Chambr 3, ChhPo, -S1, -S2, CmCal, CnDAL, ConAmL, ConAu 111, DcAmAu, DcLB 42, DcLEL, DcNAA, EvLB, FamAYP, FamSYP, FemiCLE, HerW, -84, JBA 34, LongCTC, OxCAmL 65, -83, OxCChiL, REn, REnAL, TwCA, -SUP, TwCChW 78, -83, -89, WebAB 74, -79, WhAm 1, WhoChL, WomWWA 14, WorAlBi, WorAl, WrChl, YABC 1*

Wiggin, Kate Douglas Smith 1856-1923 *InWom SUP*

Wiggin, Kate Douglas Smith 1856-1923 *AmWomPl, BioIn 15, ConAu 137, MajAI*

Wiggin, Maurice 1912- *Au&Wr 71, BioIn 8, -9, ConAu 9R, -5NR*

Wiggins, Archibald Raymond 1893- *WrDr 76*

Wigginton, Eliot 1943?- *AuNews 1, BioIn 10, -12, BioNews 74, ConAu 101*

Wight, James Alfred *AuBYP 3*

Wight, James Alfred 1916- *ConAu 77, SmATA 44, -55, Who 82, -83, -85, -88, -90, -92, WhoAm 94, WhoWor 91, -93, WrDr 76, -80, -82, -84*
Pseud./variant:
Herriot, James

Wightman, Francis P *BiDSA, CarSB, WhAmArt 85*

Wighton, Rosemary Neville 1925- *ConAu 9R*

Wignell, Edel 1936- *SmATA 69*

Wikland, Ilon 1930- *BioIn 8, -14, ConAu 111, FourBJA, IlsCB 1957, -1967, SmATA 32*

Wilber, Donald Newton 1907- *AuBYP 2, -3, BioIn 7, -14, -15, ConAu 5R, -2NR, IntAu&W 77, -82, SmATA 35, WhoE 75, -77, WrDr 76, -80, -82, -84, -86, -88, -90, -92, -94*

Wilberforce, Samuel 1805-1873 *BioIn 1, -4, -7, -9, -12, -16, CelCen, DcBiPP, DcNaB, OxCChiL*

Wilbur, C Keith 1923- *BioIn 13, ConAu 25R, -11NR, -28NR, SmATA 27*

Wilbur, Richard P 1921- *AuBYP 3*

Wilbur, Richard Purdy 1921- *AmAu&B, AuBYP 2S, Au&Wr 71, BiE&WWA, BioIn 3, -4, -7, -8, -9, -10, -11, CasWL, ChhPo S1, -S2, CnDAL, CnE&AP, CnMWL, ConAu 1R, ConLC 3, -6, -9, ConPo 70, -75, CroCAP, CurBio 66, DcLEL 1940, DrAF 76, DrAP 75, DrAS 74E, -78E, -82E, EncWL, IntAu&W 77, IntWW 74, -75, -76, -77, -78, ModAL, -S1, NotNAT, OxCAmL 65, OxCEng 85, PenC AM, PlP&P, RAdv 1, REn, REnAL, SmATA 9, TwCA SUP, TwCWr, WebE&AL, WhoAm 74, -76, -78, -80, -82, -84, -86, -88, -90, -92, -94, WhoE 74, -93, WhoEnt 92, WhoThe 72, -77, WhoTwCL, WhoUSWr 88, WhoWor 74, WhoWrEP 89, -92, WorAl, WrDr 76, -80*

Wilburn, Kathy 1948- *SmATA 68*

Wilcox, Charlotte 1948- *SmATA 72*

Wilcox, Daniel 1941- *ConAu 53*

Wilcox, Don *AuBYP 2, –3*

Wilcox, Don 1905- *EncSF 93, NewEScF*

Wilcox, R Turner 1888-1970 *BiE&WWA, BioIn 9, –14, ConAu 5R, –29R, SmATA 36*

Wild, Jocelyn 1941- *BioIn 14, –15, ConAu 116, SmATA 46*

Wild, Robin 1936- *ConAu 116, SmATA 46*

Wilde, D Gunther *ConAu X, –43NR, SmATA X*
Main entry: Hurwood, Bernhardt J

Wilde, Nicholas *ChlFicS*

Wilde, Oscar 1854?-1900 *Alli SUP, AtlBL, Benet 87, BbD, BiD&SB, BioIn 1, –2, –3, –4, –5, –6, –7, –8, –9, –10, –11, –12, –13, –14, –15, –16, –17, BritAu 19, BritWr 5, CamGEL, CamGLE, CamGWoT, CarSB, CasWL, Chambr 3, ChhPo, –S2, CnDBLB 5, CnE&AP, CnMD, CnThe, ConAu 104, –119, CrtT 3, CyWA 58, DcAmSR, DcBiA, DcEnA A, DcEuL, DcIrL, DcLB 10, –19, –34, –57, DcLEL, Dis&D, EncWL, EncWT, EvLB, FilmgC, HalFC 84, –88, LongCTC, MagSWL, MajMD 1, McGEWD 72, –84, ModWD, MouLC 4, NewC, NotNAT A, –B, OxCAmT 84, OxCEng 67, OxCFilm, OxCFr, OxCThe 67, PenC ENG, PenEncH, PlP&P, PoIre, RAdv 1, –13-1, –13-2, RComWL, REn, REnWD, RfGEnL 91, RfGShF, ScF&FL 92, ShSCr 11, SmATA 24, StaCVF, SupFW, TelT, TwCLC 1, –8, –23, –41, WebE&AL, WhDW, WhoChL, WhoHr&F, WorAlBi, WorLitC, WrChl*
Pseud./variant:
C 3 3

Wilde, Oscar Fingal O'Flahertie Wills 1854?-1900 *GayLL, IntDcT 2*

Wilder, Alec 1907-1980 *AnObit 1980, AuBYP 2, –3, Baker 84, –92, BiE&WWA, BioIn 1, –8, –9, –10, –12, –16, –17, CmpEPM, CpmDNM 81, ConAmC 76, –82, ConAu X, CurBio 80, –81N, DcCM, NewAmDM, NewGrDA 86, NewYTBS 80, NotNAT A, OxCPMus, PenEncP, WhAm 7, –8, WhoAm 74, –76, –78, –82, WhoHol A, WhoWor 74*

Wilder, Alexander Lafayette Chew *AuBYP 3*

Wilder, Cherry *ConAu X, SmATA X, WrDr 84*
Main entry: Grimm, Cherry Barbara Lockett

Wilder, Cherry 1930- *BioIn 15, EncSF 93, IntAu&W 89, –91, ScF&FL 92, ScFSB, TwCSFW 86, –91, WrDr 86, –88, –90, –92, –94*

Wilder, Laura 1867-1957 *AuBYP 3, ChlFicS, FemiCLE*

Wilder, Laura Elizabeth Ingalls 1867-1957 *ConAu 137, MajAI*

Wilder, Laura Ingalls 1867-1957 *AmWomWr, AnCL, ArtclWW 2, AuBYP 2, BenetAL 91, BioAmW, BioIn 1, –2, –3, –4, –5, –7, –8, –9, –10, –11, –14, –15, –16, –17, BlmGWL, BkCL, CamGLE, CasWL, ChhPo S1, ChlLR 2, ConAu 111, CurBio 48, –57, DcLB 22, EncFWF, FamMS, HerW, –84, InWom SUP, JBA 51, NotAW MOD, ObitOF 79, OxCAmL 83, OxCChiL, REnAL, SmATA 15, –29, Str&VC, TwCChW 78, –83, –89, TwCWW 91, WhAm 3, WhoChL, WorAlBi, WrChl*

Wilder, Thornton *IntvTCA 2*

Wilder, Thornton 1897-1975 *AmAu&B, AmNov, AmWr, AuNews 2, Au&Wr 71, Benet 87, BenetAL 91, BiE&WWA, BioIn 1, –2, –3, –4, –5, –6, –7, –8, –9, –10, –11, –13, –14, –15, –16, –17, BlueB 76, CamGEL, CamGLE, CamHAL, CasWL, CelR, Chambr 3, CnDAL, CnMD, CnMWL, CnThe, ConAmA, ConAmL, ConAu 13R, –61, ConDr 73, –77, ConLC 1, –5, –6, –10, –15, –35, ConNov 72, CroCD, CurBio 43, –71, –76N, CyWA 58, –89, DcLB 4, –7, –9, DcLEL, DramC 1, EncAB-H, EncWL, –2, EvLB, FilmgC, HalFC 84, –88, IntWW 74, LongCTC, MagSAmL, MajMD 1, MajTwCW, McGEWD 84, MemAm, ModAL, –S1, –S2, ModWD, NotNAT A, –B, Novels, ObitOF 79, ObitT 1971, OxCAmL 65, –83, OxCAmT 84, OxCEng 67, OxCThe 67, PenC AM, PiP, PlP&P, RAdv 1, –13-1, –13-2, RComWL, REn, REnAL, REnWD, RfGAmL 87, TwCA, –SUP, TwCRHW 90, TwCWr, WebAB 74, WebE&AL, WhDW, WhAm 6, WhNAA, Who 74, WhoAm 74, WhoTwCL, WhoWor 74, WisWr, WorAlBi, WorEFlm, WorLitC, WrDr 76, WrPh*

Wilder, Thornton Niven 1897-1975 *ConAu 40NR, ConDr 93, IntDcT 2*

Wildsmith, Brian 1930- *AuBYP 3, ConAu 35NR, MajAI, SmATA 69, –5AS*

Wildsmith, Brian Lawrence 1930- *ArtsCL, Au&ICB, BioIn 6, –8, –9, –11, –12, BkP, BritCA, ChhPo, –S1, ChlLR 2, ConAu 85, IlsBYP, IlsCB 1957, –1967, IntAu&W 89, –91, OxCChiL, SmATA 16, ThrBJA, Who 74, –82, –83, –85, –88, –90, –92, WhoChL*

Wiley, Farida A d1986 *NewYTBS 86*

Wiley, Farida A 1887?-1986 *ConAu 121*

Wiley, Farida Anna 1887- *OhA&B*

Wiley, Karla 1918- *AuBYP 3*

Wiley, Karla H 1918- *AuBYP 2, BioIn 8, ConAu 61*

Wilford, John Noble 1933- *AuBYP 3, IntAu&W 86, -89, -91, WrDr 92*

Wilford, John Noble, Jr. 1933- *AuBYP 2S, ConAu 29R, -15NR, IntAu&W 77, -82, WhoAm 80, -82, -84, -86, -88, -90, -92, -94, WhoE 74, -85, -86, WrDr 94*

Wilhelm, Hans 1945- *ConAu 119, SmATA 58*

Wilhelm, Stephen Roger 1905-1967 *AmAu&B, BioIn 9, WhAm 4*

Wilk, Max *DrAPF 87, -89, -91, -93*

Wilk, Max 1920- *BioIn 10, ConAu 1R, -1NR, -16NR, -37NR, DrAPF 83, -85, WhoUSWr 88, WhoWrEP 89, -92*

Wilkerson, David Ray 1931- *Au&Wr 71, ConAu 41R*

Wilkes, Marilyn Z *AuBYP 3, ScF&FL 92*

Wilkie, Katharine E 1904-1980 *ConAu 125*

Wilkie, Katharine Elliot 1904-1980 *AuBYP 2, BioIn 7, ConAu 21R, ForWC 70, SmATA 31*

Wilkie, Katharine Elliott 1904- *BioIn 14*

Wilkie, Katharine Elliott 1904-1980 *AuBYP 3*

Wilkin, Eloise 1904- *SmATA 49*

Wilkin, Eloise 1904-1987 *ConAu 124, SmATA 54N*

Wilkin, Eloise Burns 1904- *BioIn 1, -5, IlsBYP, IlsCB 1744, -1946*

Wilkin, Eloise Burns 1904-1987 *BioIn 16, MajAI*

Wilkins, Frances *AuBYP 3*

Wilkins, Frances 1923- *AuBYP 2S, BioIn 12, ConAu 73, SmATA 14*

Wilkins, Hugh Percival 1896- *AuBYP 3*

Wilkins, Hugh Percival 1896-1960 *AuBYP 2, BioIn 5, -7*

Wilkins, Marilyn 1926- *ConAu 105, SmATA 30*
Pseud./variant:
Wilkins, Marne

Wilkins, Marne *ConAu X, SmATA X*
Main entry: Wilkins, Marilyn

Wilkins, Mary E *BenetAL 91, WomNov*

Wilkins, Mary Eleanor *Alli SUP, AmAu&B, AmLY X, BbD, BiD&SB, CasWL, Chambr 3, ChhPo, DcAmAu, DcEnA A, DcNAA, HarEnUS, OxCAmL 65, -83, REn, REnAL, TwCA, -SUP, WebAB 74, -79*
Main entry: Freeman, Mary E Wilkins

Wilkins, Mary H *AuBYP 3*

Wilkins, Mary Huiskamp Calhoun
Main entry: Calhoun, Mary Huiskamp

Wilkins, Mary Huiskamp Calhoun 1926- *ConAu 2NR, -18NR, TarBJA, WhoAmW 77*

Wilkins, William Vaughan 1890-1959 *BioIn 4, -5, -8, LongCTC, TwCA SUP, WhAm 3, WhoChL*

Wilkinson, Anne 1910-1961 *ArtclWW 2, BenetAL 91, BlmGWL, CamGLE, CanWr, CreCan 2, DcLB 88, DcLEL 1940, FemiCLE, OxCCan, -SUP, OxCCanL, RfGEnL 91, TwCChW 78*

Wilkinson, Barry 1923- *BioIn 12, FourBJA, IlsCB 1967, SmATA 32, -50*

Wilkinson, Brenda 1946- *BioIn 12, BlkAWP, BlkAull, -92, BlkWr 1, -2, ChlLR 20, ConAu 69, -26NR, DcAmChF 1960, FifBJA, InB&W 80, SmATA 14, TwCYAW, WhoBlA 90, -92*

Wilkinson, Burke
Main entry: Wilkinson, John Burke

Wilkinson, Burke 1913- *AuBYP 2, -3, BioIn 8, ConAu 9R, SmATA 4, WrDr 76, -82, -84, -86, -88, -90, -92*

Wilkinson, Charlotte Jefferson *ConAu 69*

Wilkinson, Douglas *OxCCan, -SUP*

Wilkinson, John Burke 1913- *AmAu&B, Au&Wr 71, BioIn 9, BlueB 76, IntAu&W 82, WhoAm 74, -80, -82, -84, -86, -88, -90, -92, -94, WhoWor 74, -80, -82, WrDr 80*
Pseud./variant:
Wilkinson, Burke

Wilkinson, Marguerite Ogden 1883-1928 *AnCL, ChhPo, -S1, ConAmL, DcNAA, REnAL, TwCA, WhAm 1, WhNAA, WomNov*

Wilkinson, Marguerite Ogden Bigelow 1883-1928 *AmWomPl*

Wilkinson, Sylvia *DrAPF 87, -89, -91, -93*

Wilkinson, Sylvia 1940- *ArtclWW 2, BioIn 7, -9, -10, DrAPF 83, -85, SmATA 39, WrDr 82, -84*

Wilkinson, Sylvia J 1940- *SmATA 56, WrDr 86, -88, -90, -92, -94*

Wilkinson, T W *ChhPo*

Wilkinson, Tom *DcBrBI*

Wilkon, Jozef 1930- *BioIn 8, -14, ConAu 107, IlsBYP, IlsCB 1957, MajAI, SmATA 31, -71*

Wilks, Brian 1933- *ConAu 69*
Pseud./variant:
Hughes, Sam

Wilks, Michael Thomas 1947- *ConAu 110, IntAu&W 86, SmATA 44*
Pseud./variant:
Wilks, Mike

Wilks, Mike
Main entry: Wilks, Michael Thomas

Will *ConAu X, SmATA X, TwCChW 83, -89*
Main entry: Lipkind, William

Will And Nicolas *OxCChiL*

Willard, Barbara 1909- *IntAu&W 91, SmATA 5AS, TwCChW 89, WrDr 86, -88, -90, -92, -94*

Willard, Barbara Mary 1909- *Au&Wr 71, BioIn 11, -12, BritCA, ChlLR 2, ConAu 81, -15NR, FourBJA, MajAI, OxCChiL, SmATA 17, -74, TwCChW 78, -83, TwCYAW, WrDr 76, -82, -84*

Willard, Charlotte 1914-1977 *BioIn 11, ConAu 73, -81, WhAm 7, WhoAm 74, -76, -78, WhoAmA 73, -78, WhoAmW 74*

Willard, Frank *DcVicP 2*

Willard, Frank d1958 *WhoAmA 86N*

Willard, Frank 1893-1958 *ArtCS, ArtsAmW 2, BioIn 1, -3, -4, -5, -6, DcVicP 2, EncACom, EncAJ, WhAm 3, -4, WhAmArt 85, WhoAmA 80N, -82N*

Willard, Mildred Wilds 1911- *ConAu 21R, SmATA 14, WrDr 76, -80*

Willard, Mildred Wilds 1911-1978 *ConAu 135, ScF&FL 92*

Willard, Nancy *DrAPF 87, -89, -91, -93*

Willard, Nancy 1936- *AmAu&B, ArtclWW 2, AuBYP 3, BioIn 12, -13, ChlLR 5, ConAu 10NR, -39NR, ConLC 7, -37, ConPo 75, -80, -85, -91, DcAmChF 1960, DcLB 5, -52, DrAP 75, DrAPF 83, -85, FifBJA, InWom SUP, MajAI, MajTwCW, ScF&FL 92, SmATA 30, -37, -71, TwCChW 83, -89, WhoAmW 77, WrDr 76, -80, -82, -84, -86, -88*

Willcox, Isobel 1907- *BioIn 15, ConAu 111, IntAu&W 86, SmATA 42*

Willcox, Sandra *IlsBYP*

Willetts, Ronald Frederick 1915- *ConAu 5R, EngPo, IntAu&W 82, IntWWP 82, WrDr 80, -82, -84, -86, -88, -90, -92, -94*

Willey, Margaret *DrAPF 87, -89, -91, -93*

Willey, Margaret 1950- *ConAu 40NR, TwCYAW*

Willey, Robert *AuBYP 2, -3, ConAu X, EncSF 93, SmATA 2*
Main entry: Ley, Willy

Willhoite, Michael A 1946- *SmATA 71*

William, Earle
Main entry: Johns, William Earl

Williams, Alan 1935- *IntWWE, Novels, SpyFic, WhoSpyF, WrDr 80, -82, -84, -86, -88, -90, -92, -94*

Williams, Barbara 1925- *AuBYP 2S, -3, BioIn 11, -13, ConAu 49, -1NR, -17NR, SixBJA, SmATA 11, -16AS, Who 74*

Williams, Barbara 1937- *SmATA 62*
Pseud./variant:
Wilson, Barbara

Williams, Barry 1932- *ConAu 29R, WrDr 76, -80, -82, -84, -86, -88, -90, -92, -94*

Williams, Bert 1930- *BioIn 10, Profile 1, WrDr 76, -82, -84, -86, -88, -90, -92*

Williams, Bert Nolan 1930- *WrDr 94*

Williams, Beryl *ConAu X, -39NR, InB&W 80, OhA&B, SmATA X*
Main entry: Epstein, Beryl Williams

Williams, Billy 1938- *Ballpl 90, BioIn 8, -9, -10, -11, WhoAm 74, -76, WhoBlA 75*

Williams, Brad 1918- *ConAu 1R, -1NR*

Williams, Brian 1943- *SmATA 54*

Williams, Byron 1934- *ConAu 29R*

Williams, Carol *WrDr 76, -80, -82, -84*
Main entry: Fenner, Carol Elizabeth

Williams, Charles *AuBYP 3, ConAu X, -33NR, MajAI, SmATA 8, -70*
Main entry: Collier, James Lincoln

Williams, Clayton Wheat 1895- *WhoSSW 73*

Williams, Clayton Wheat, Jr. *BioIn 15, –16, –17*

Williams, Clyde C 1881-1974 *AuBYP 2S, –3, BioIn 10, –11, –13, ConAu P-2, IntAu&W 77, SmATA 8, –27N*
Pseud./variant:
Williams, Slim

Williams, Coe *AuBYP 3, ConAu X, SmATA X, TwCWW 91*
Main entry: Harrison, C William

Williams, Dorian 1914- *Au&Wr 71, BioIn 9, –12, ConAu 9R, –3NR, IntAu&W 77, Who 74, –82, –83, –85*

Williams, Dorian 1914-1985 *AnObit 1985*

Williams, E Neville 1917- *ConAu 9R*

Williams, Edgar *AuBYP 2, –3, BioIn 7*

Williams, Edward G *DrAPF 87, –89, –91, –93*

Williams, Edward G 1929- *AuBYP 2S, –3, BlkAWP, ConAu 29R, ConBlAP 88, DrAF 76, DrAPF 83, –85, WhoUSWr 88, WhoWrEP 89, –92*

Williams, Effie M *WhNAA*

Williams, Eric Ernest 1911-1983 *AuBYP 2, –3, Au&Wr 71, BioIn 7, –12, BioNews 75, ConAu 9R, –111, CurBio 66, DcLEL 1940, DcNaB 1981, IntAu&W 77, –82, SmATA 14, –38N, Who 74, –82, –83, –85N, WrDr 76, –80, –82, –84*

Williams, Ferelith Eccles 1920- *BioIn 13, ConAu 105, SmATA 22*
Pseud./variant:
Eccles

Williams, Frances B *ConAu X, SmATA 5*
Main entry: Browin, Frances Williams

Williams, Garth 1912- *ConAu 134, SmATA 66, –7AS*

Williams, Garth Montgomery 1912- *AmAu&B, AmPB, AuBYP 2, –3, BenetAL 91, BioIn 1, –5, –6, –7, –8, –11, –12, ChhPo, –S1, DcLB 22, IlsCB 1967, MajAI, MorJA, REnAL, SmATA 18, Str&VC, WhAmArt 85, WhoAm 74, –76, –78, –80, –82, –84, –86, –88, –90, –92, –94, WhoAmA 73, –78, –80, –82, WrDr 94*

Williams, George W *Who 88, –90, –92*

Williams, George Walton 1922- *ConAu 9R, DrAS 74E, –78E, –82E, WhoAm 82, –84, –86, –88, –90, –92, –94, WhoSSW 93*

Williams, Gurney 1941- *BioIn 17*

Williams, Gurney, III 1941- *ConAu 69, –30NR*

Williams, Guy R 1920- *ConAu 31NR, WrDr 86, –88, –90, –92*

Williams, Guy Richard 1920- *Au&Wr 71, BioIn 11, ConAu 13R, DcBrAr 1, IntAu&W 77, –82, –86, –91, SmATA 11, WhoArt 80, –82, –84, WrDr 76, –82, –84*

Williams, Guy Richard Owen 1920- *WrDr 94*

Williams, Hawley *YABC 1*
Main entry: Heyliger, William

Williams, Helen 1948- *SmATA 77*

Williams, Herbert Darkin 1802- *ChhPo S1, –S2*

Williams, J R
Main entry: Williams, Jeanne

Williams, J Walker *ConAu 33NR, MajTwCW, SmATA X*

Williams, Jay *ScFSB*

Williams, Jay 1914-1978 *AuBYP 2S, –3, BioIn 4, –7, –9, –10, –11, –13, –15, ChlLR 8, ConAu 1R, –81, –2NR, –39NR, CurBio 55, –78, –78N, FourBJA, IntAu&W 77, MajAI, NatCAB 61, ObitOF 79, ScF&FL 92, SmATA 3, –24N, –41, TwCChW 78, –83, –89, TwCCr&M 80, –85, WhScrn 83, WorAu 1950, WrDr 76*
Pseud./variant:
Delving, Michael

Williams, Jay 1924-1978 *DcAmChF 1960*

Williams, Jeanne *DcAmChF 1960*

Williams, Jeanne 1930- *BioIn 10, ConAu 25R, IntAu&W 77, –91, ScF&FL 92, SmATA 5, TwCWW 91, WrDr 76, –80, –82, –84, –86, –88, –90, –92, –94*
Pseud./variant:
Crecy, Jeanne
Michaels, Kristin
Rhys, Megan
Rowan, Deirdre
Williams, J R

Williams, Jenny 1939- *BioIn 8, ChhPo S1, ConAu 112, IlsCB 1957, –1967, SmATA 60*

Williams, Jerome 1926- *AmMWSc 73P, –76P, –82, –86, –89, –92, ConAu 49, –1NR, WhoE 74, –75, –77*

Williams, Joel *AuBYP 3*

Williams, John A *DrAPF 87, –89, –91, –93*

Williams, John A 1925- *Benet 87, BenetAL 91, BlkLC, BlkWr 1, ConAu 26NR, ConBlAP 88,*

ConNov 86, -91, CyWA 89, IntAu&W 91, ModAL S2, NegAl 89, ScF&FL 92, ScFSB, TwCSFW 86, -91, WhoAm 86, -88, -90, -92, -94, WhoUSWr 88, WhoWrEP 89, -92, WrDr 86, -88, -90, -92

Williams, John Alfred 1925- *AmAu&B, AuSpks, Au&Wr 71, BioIn 8, -9, -10, -11, -12, BlkAWP, BlkWr 2, ConAu 53, -3AS, -6NR, ConLC 5, -13, ConNov 72, -76, -82, DcLB 2, -33, DrAF 76, EncSF 93, InB&W 80, -85, LivgBAA, ModAL S2, ModBlW, NegAl 76, -83, OxCAmL 83, PenC AM, RAdv 1, SelBAAf, SelBAAu, WhoAm 74, -76, -78, -80, -82, -84, WhoBlA 80, -85, -88, -90, -92, -94, WorAu 1950, WrDr 76, -80, -82, -84*

Williams, Karen Lynn 1952- *ConAu 133, SmATA 66, WrDr 94*

Williams, Kathryn Vinson 1911- *ForWC 70, IntAu&W 77, WhoAmW 75, -77, WrDr 76, -80, -82, -84*
Pseud./variant:
Vinson, Kathryn

Williams, Kit 1946?- *BioIn 12, -13, -15, ChlLR 4, ConAu 107, NewYTBS 80, -81, ScF&FL 92, SmATA 44, TwCPaSc, WrDr 82, -84*

Williams, Leslie 1941- *ConAu 107, SmATA 42*

Williams, Linda *AuBYP 3*

Williams, Linda 1948- *SmATA 59*

Williams, Louise Bonino d1984 *BioIn 15*

Williams, Louise Bonino 1904?-1984 *ConAu 114, SmATA 39N*

Williams, Lynn *AuBYP 3*
Main entry: Hale, Arlene

Williams, Marcia Dorothy 1945- *SmATA 71*

Williams, Margery *AmWomPl, JBA 34, MajAI, TwCChW 83, -89, WomNov*
Main entry: Bianco, Margery Williams

Williams, Margery 1880-1944 *BioIn 14*

Williams, Martin d1992 *NewYTBS 92*

Williams, Martin 1924- *ConAu 49, IntWWM 85, -90, NewGrDA 86, WhoAm 74, -76, -78, -80, -82, -84*

Williams, Martin 1924-1992 *AnObit 1992, ConAu 137*

Williams, Maureen 1951- *BioIn 11, ConAu 85, SmATA 12*

Williams, Michael *ConAu X, SmATA X*
Main entry: Saint John, Wylly Folk

Williams, Patrick J *ConAu X, -40NR, SmATA 5*
Main entry: Butterworth, W E

Williams, Richard
Main entry: Janson, Hank

Williams, Richard Lippincott 1910-
ConAu 101, WhoAm 74, -76, -78, -80, -82, -84, -86, -88

Williams, Ruth C *DcChlFi, SingR 1*

Williams, Selma R 1925- *BioIn 12, ConAu 49, -1NR, SmATA 14*

Williams, Sheron 1955- *SmATA 77*

Williams, Slim *AuBYP 2S, -3, BioIn 4, -13, ConAu X, SmATA 8, -X*
Main entry: Williams, Clyde C

Williams, Suzanne Bullock 1953- *SmATA 71*

Williams, T Harry
Main entry: Williams, Thomas Harry

Williams, Ted
Main entry: Williams, Theodore Samuel

Williams, Theodore Samuel 1918-
BiDAmSp BB, BioIn 1, -2, -3, -4, -5, -6, -7, -8, -9, -10, -11, CelR, CurBio 47, NewYTBE 70, NewYTBS 74, WebAB 74, -79, WhoAm 76, -78, WhoHol A, WhoSSW 73
Pseud./variant:
Williams, Ted

Williams, Thomas Harry 1909- *AmAu&B, BioIn 2, -8, ConAu 1R, DrAS 74H, EncSoH, WhoAm 74, -76, -78, WhoSSW 73, -75, -76*
Pseud./variant:
Williams, T Harry

Williams, Ursula Moray *IntAu&W 86X, SmATA 73, TwCChW 89, WrDr 86, -88, -90, -92*

Williams, Ursula Moray 1911- *AuBYP 2S, Au&Wr 71, BioIn 8, -9, -14, ConAu 13R, -X, -10NR, FourBJA, IntAu&W 77, -82, -86, OxCChiL, ScF&FL 92, SmATA 3, TwCChW 78, -83, WhoChL, WrDr 76, -80, -82, -84*
Pseud./variant:
Moray Williams, Ursula 1911-

Williams, Valentine 1883-1946 *BioIn 1, -4, -14, CathA 1930, ConAu 111, DcLB 77, EncMys, LongCTC, NewC, ObitOF 79, TwCA, -SUP, TwCCr&M 80, -85, -91, WhoLA, WhoSpyF*

Williams, Vera B *TwCChW 89*

Williams, Vera B 1927- *AuBYP 3, ChILR 9, ConAu 123, –38NR, FifBJA, MajAI, SmATA 33, –53, WrDr 92, –94*

Williams, William Lloyd 1902?- *SingR 2*

Williams-Ellis, Amabel 1894-1984 *AnObit 1984, Au&Wr 71, BioIn 4, –13, –15, ConAu 105, –114, EvLB, FemiCLE, IntAu&W 77, –82, IntWW 74, –75, –76, –77, LongCTC, OxCLiW 86, REn, ScF&FL 92, SmATA 29, –41N, TwCA, –SUP, TwCWr, Who 74, –82, –83, –85N*

Williams-Garcia, Rita *TwCYAW*

Williamson, Henry 1895-1977 *Au&Wr 71, BioIn 1, –4, –5, –8, –11, –12, –13, –14, –15, –17, BlueB 76, CamGEL, CamGLE, CasWL, ConAu 73, –81, –36NR, ConNov 72, –76, DcLEL, DcNaB 1971, EvLB, IntAu&W 77, IntWW 74, –75, –76, –77, –78N, LongCTC, MajTwCW, ModBrL, –S2, NewC, Novels, OxCChiL, OxCEng 85, REn, RfGEnL 91, SmATA 30N, –37, TwCA, –SUP, TwCChW 83, –89, TwCWr, WhDW, Who 74, WhoChL, WhoWor 74, WrDr 76*

Williamson, Henry 1897-1977 *Benet 87, ModBrL S2*

Williamson, Henry Darvall 1907- *ConAu 65*

Williamson, Jack
Main entry: Williamson, John Stewart

Williamson, Jane 1920- *LEduc 74*

Williamson, Joanne Small 1926- *AuBYP 2, –3, BioIn 8, –9, ConAu 13R, DcAmChF 1960, ForWC 70, SmATA 3, ThrBJA*

Williamson, John Stewart 1908- *AmAu&B, BioIn 7, ConAu 17R, –23NR, ConSFA, DrAS 74E, –78E, –82E, WhNAA, WhoSciF, WhoWest 74, –76, WorAl, WrDr 76, –80*
Pseud./variant:
Williamson, Jack

Williamson, Margaret 1924- *AuBYP 2, –3, BioIn 7*

Williamson, Margaret Louise 1939- *WhoMW 90*

Williamson, Stanford Winfield 1916-1968 *BioIn 8, ConAu 5R*

Willis, Anthony Armstrong 1897-1976 *BioIn 3, ConAu 69, IntAu&W 77, Who 74*

Willis, Charles *AuBYP 3, ConAu 28NR, EncSF 93, MajAI, MajTwCW, SmATA 70*
Main entry: Clarke, Arthur Charles

Willis, Corinne Denneny *AuBYP 2S, ConAu 21R*

Willis, Corrine *AuBYP 3*

Willis, Irene *DrAPF 91, –93*

Willis, Irene 1929- *ConAu 65, –10NR*

Willis, Jeanne 1959- *ConAu 128, SmATA 61*

Willis, Priscilla D *AuBYP 2, –3, BioIn 7*

Willis, Robert J *AuBYP 2, –3, BioIn 7*

Willis, Ted *Who 88, –90, –92*

Willis, Ted d1992 *NewYTBS 92*

Willis, Ted 1918- *ConAu 9R, –7NR, –23NR ConDr 77, –82, –88, –93, ConTFT 7, HalFC 84, –88, IntAu&W 77, –82, IntMPA 75, –76, –78, –81, –82, –84, –86, –88, –92, –77, Novels, TwCCr&M 80, –85, –91, TwCWr, Who 74, –82, –83, –85, WhoSpyF, WhoThe 72, –77, –81, WrDr 76, –80, –82, –84, –86, –88, –90, –92*

Willis, Ted 1918-1992 *AnObit 1992, ConAu 140, ConTFT 11*

Willis, Val *AuBYP 3*

Willis, Val 1946- *ConAu 130, WrDr 92, –94*

Willius, T F *SmATA 66*
Main entry: Tamminga, Frederick William

Willmott, Frank 1948- *DcChlFi*

Willock, Ruth *Au&Wr 71, ConAu 13R*

Willoughby, Elaine Macmann 1926- *ConAu 101*

Wills, Jonathan 1947- *ConAu 69*

Willson, Dixie *AuBYP 2, –3, BioIn 7, ChhPo*

Willson, Robina Beckles 1930- *BioIn 13, ConAu 5NR, SmATA 27*

Wilma, Dana *BioIn 11, ConAu 49, IntAu&W 77X, –82X, SmATA X*
Main entry: Faralla, Dana

Wilmot, Frank 1881-1942 *BioIn 2, –4, –9, DcLEL, SingR 2, WhoLA*
Pseud./variant:
Maurice, Furnley

Wilms, Barbara 1941- *ConAu 57*

Wilms, Denise M *MedPD*

Wilson, Augusta Jane 1835-1909 *WomNov*

Wilson, Augusta Jane Evans *InWom SUP*

Wilson, Augusta Jane Evans 1835-1909 *BioIn 2, -3, -4, -5, -8, -15, -17, DcLB 42, EncSoH, FifSWrB*

Wilson, Barbara *SmATA X*
Main entry: Williams, Barbara

Wilson, Barbara Ker *SmATA 70*
Main entry: Ker Wilson, Barbara

Wilson, Barbara Ker 1929- *ConAu X, ScF&FL 92, SingR 2, TwCChW 78, -83, -89, WrDr 76, -80, -82, -84, -86, -88, -90, -92, -94*

Wilson, Beth *AuBYP 3, BlkAuIl, -92*

Wilson, Beth P *AuBYP 2S, BioIn 11, ConAu 49, -1NR, InB&W 80, SmATA 8, WhoAmW 77*

Wilson, Beth Pierre *InB&W 85*

Wilson, Budge 1927- *BioIn 16, ConAu 121, IntAu&W 91, SmATA 55, WhoCanL 92*
Pseud./variant:
Wilson, Marjorie

Wilson, Carter 1941- *AuBYP 2S, -3, BioIn 7, -10, ConAu 17R, IntAu&W 77, -91, SmATA 6, WrDr 76, -80, -82, -84, -86, -88, -90, -92, -94*

Wilson, Charles *InB&W 85*

Wilson, Charles 1932- *AmMWSc 73P, ConAu 65*

Wilson, Charles Banks 1918- *BioIn 5, -14, -15, -16, -17, ConGrA 2, IlsBYP, IlsCB 1946, PrintW 83, -85, WhAmArt 85, WhoAm 78, -80, -82, -84, -86, -88, -90, -92, -94, WhoAmA 73, -78, -80, -82, -84, -86, -89, -91*

Wilson, Charles Morrow 1905-1977 *AmAu&B, AuBYP 2, -3, Au&Wr 71, BioIn 4, -8, -14, ConAu 5R, -4NR, IntAu&W 77, REnAL, SmATA 30, TwCA SUP, WhoAm 74, -76, -78, WrDr 76, -80*

Wilson, Christopher B 1910?-1985 *BioIn 15, SmATA 46N*

Wilson, Colin 1931- *Au&Wr 71, Benet 87, BioIn 4, -5, -6, -8, -9, -10, -13, BlmGEL, BlueB 76, CamGLE, CasWL, ConAu 1R, -5AS, -1NR, -22NR, -33NR, ConLC 3, ConNov 72, -76, -82, -86, -91, CurBio 63, DcLB 14, EncO&P 1S1, -2, -3, IntAu&W 77, -82, IntWW 74, LongCTC, MajTwCW, ModBrL, -S1, NewC, NewEScF, Novels, PenEncH, RAdv 1, REn, ScF&FL 92, ScFSB, TwCCr&M 80, -85, -91, TwCSFW 86, TwCWr, Who 74, WhoHr&F, WhoWor 74, -78, WorAu 1950, WrDr 76, -80, -82, -84, -86, -88, -90, -92*

Wilson, Colin 1932- *RAdv 13-1*

Wilson, Colin Henry 1931- *EncSF 93, WrDr 94*

Wilson, Dagmar 1916- *BioIn 6, -9, -11, -14, ChhPo S2, InWom SUP, SmATA 31, WhoAmW 74, -75*

Wilson, David Henry 1937- *ChlFicS, ConAu 113, -32NR, IntAu&W 89, ScF&FL 92, WhoAm 92, WrDr 76, -80, -82, -84, -86, -88, -90, -92, -94*

Wilson, Derek Alan 1935- *IntAu&W 77, -82, -86*

Wilson, Dorothy Clarke 1904- *AmAu&B, AmNov, AmWomPl, Au&Wr 71, BioIn 2, ConAu 1R, -6NR, CurBio 51, ForWC 70, IntAu&W 77, -82, -86, -89, -91, SmATA 16, WhoAm 74, -76, -78, -80, -82, -84, -86, -88, -90, -92, -94, WhoAmW 74, WrDr 76, -80, -82, -84, -86, -88, -90, -92, -94*

Wilson, Edward A 1886-1970 *BioIn 15*

Wilson, Edward Arthur 1886-1970 *BioIn 1, -3, -4, -5, -9, ChhPo, -S1, -S2, ConAu 116, IlrAm 1880, -B, IlsBYP, IlsCB 1744, -1946, SmATA 38, WhAm 5, -7, WhAmArt 85*

Wilson, Eleanore Hubbard *AuBYP 2, -3, BioIn 7*

Wilson, Ellen Janet d1976 *AuBYP 2S, -3, BioIn 11, -13, ConAu 49, -103, SmATA 9, -26N*

Wilson, Eric 1940- *BioIn 13, ConAu 101, -20NR, Profile 2, ScF&FL 92, SmATA 32, -34, WhoCanL 85, -87, -92*

Wilson, Erica *ConAu 53, -7NR, -23NR, NewYTBE 71, SmATA 51*

Wilson, Erle 1898- *Au&Wr 71, ConAu 5R, OxCAusL, SingR 1*

Wilson, Forrest 1918- *AmArch 70, BioIn 13, ConAu 53, -7NR, SmATA 27, WhoE 85A, WhoMW 74*

Wilson, Forrest Russell 1918- *WhoAm 88*

Wilson, Gahan 1930- *BiDScF, BioIn 12, -13, ConAu 25R, -19NR, ConGrA 2, IlsBYP, PrintW 83, -85, ScF&FL 92, SmATA 27, -35, WhoAm 78, -80, -82, -84, -86, -88, -92, -94, WhoHr&F, WorECar*

Wilson, Gahan 1935- *PenEncH*

Wilson, Gina 1943- *ConAu 106, IntAu&W 86, –91, SmATA 34, –36, TwCChW 83, –89, WrDr 86, –88, –90, –92, –94*

Wilson, Granville 1912- *Au&Wr 71, BioIn 12, ConAu 69, –11NR, ScF&FL 92, SmATA 14*

Wilson, Hazel 1898- *AuBYP 2, –3, BioIn 9, ConAu 1R, –6NR, SmATA 3, WrDr 76, –80, –82, –84, –86, –88*

Wilson, Hazel Hutchins 1898-1992 *ConAu 139, SmATA 73*

Wilson, Holly *AuBYP 2, –3, BioIn 7, MichAu 80*

Wilson, J Christy 1891-1973 *WhAm 6, WhoAm 74*

Wilson, Jacqueline 1945- *ConAu 38NR, IntAu&W 91, SmATA 52, –61, TwCChW 89, WrDr 86, –88, –90, –92*

Wilson, Jacqueline Aitken 1945- *WrDr 94*

Wilson, Jeanne 1920- *ConAu 69, –12NR*

Wilson, John 1922- *AfroAA, BioIn 9, –11, –13, IlsBYP, InB&W 80, NegAl 76, –83, –89, SmATA 22, WhoAm 74, –76, –78, –80, –82, –84, –86, –88, –90, –92, –94, WhoAmA 78, –80, –82, –84, –86, –89, –91, WhoBlA 75, –77, –80, –85, –88, –90, –92, –94, WhoE 86, –89*

Wilson, John Park 1867-1932 *WhoAm 74*

Wilson, John Rowan 1919- *Au&Wr 71, BioIn 5*

Wilson, Johnniece Marshall 1944- *BlkAuII 92, ConAu 142, SmATA 75*

Wilson, Joyce Muriel *BioIn 12, ConAu 17R, –12NR, SmATA 21, WrDr 80, –82, –84*
Pseud./variant:
Stranger, Joyce

Wilson, Joyce Muriel 1921- *IntAu&W 91*

Wilson, Julia 1927- *BkP, ConAu 21R*

Wilson, Katharine M 1895- *IntAu&W 82, WrDr 76, –80, –82*

Wilson, Keith 1929- *ConAu 121, Profile 2*

Wilson, Kenneth Lee 1916- *ConAu 29R, WhoAm 74, –76, –78, WhoRel 75, –77*

Wilson, Lionel 1924- *ConAu 105, SmATA 31, –33*
Pseud./variant:
Blackton, Peter
Ellis, Herbert
Salzer, L E

Wilson, Marjorie *SmATA 51*
Main entry: Wilson, Budge

Wilson, Maurice *ChhPo*

Wilson, Maurice 1914- *SmATA 46*

Wilson, Maurice Charles John 1914- *BioIn 14*

Wilson, Mitchell 1913-1973 *AmAu&B, AmNov, Au&Wr 71, BenetAL 91, BioIn 2, –5, –6, –9, ConAu 1R, –41R, –31NR, ConNov 72, DcLEL 1940, IntAu&W 77, NewYTBE 72, –73, ObitOF 79, OxCAmL 65, –83*

Wilson, Peggy *BioIn 8, ChhPo S1, IlsBYP, IlsCB 1957*

Wilson, Ron 1941- *ConAu 112, SmATA 38*

Wilson, Ruth *AuBYP 3*

Wilson, Ruth 1899- *AuBYP 2, BioIn 7*

Wilson, Sarah *Alli SUP, CarSB, ChhPo, –S1*

Wilson, Sarah 1934- *ConAu 127, SmATA 50*

Wilson, Tom 1931- *ConAu 106, SmATA 30, –33, WhoAm 80, –82, –84, –86, –88, –92, –94, WhoAmA 86, –89, –91*

Wilson, W Harmon 1905- *ConAu 37R*

Wilson, Walt 1939- *ConAu 69, SmATA 14*

Wilton, Elizabeth M 1937- *ConAu 69, SingR 2, SmATA 14*

Wilton, Hal *ConAu 127*

Wilton, Hal 1910-1988 *SmATA X*

Wiltrout, Dorothea Armstrong 1898- *IndAu 1917*

Wilwerding, Walter Joseph 1891-1966 *BioIn 1, –6, –11, ConAu P-1, IlsCB 1744, MinnWr, SmATA 9, WhAm 4, WhAmArt 85*

Wimmer, Helmut Karl 1925- *BioIn 8, IlsCB 1957*

Wimmer, Mike 1961- *SmATA 70*

Winborn, Marsha Lynn 1947- *SmATA 75*

Winchester, Clarence 1895-1981 *ChhPo S1, ConAu 104, EngPo, IntAu&W 77, Who 74, –82N*

Winchester, James Hugh 1917-1985 *AmAu&B, BioIn 15, ConAu 17R, –117, SmATA 30, –45N, WhoAm 74, –76, –78, –80, –82, –84, WhoWor 78*

Winchester, M E *Alli SUP, CarSB*

Winder, Blanche *ChhPo, –S1, –S2*

Winder, Viola Hitti *AuBYP 2, –3, BioIn 8*

Winders, Gertrude Hecker 1897- *BioIn 9, ConAu 1R, –6NR, ForWC 70, IndAu 1917, SmATA 3*

Windham, Basil *ConAu X, –33NR, MajTwCW, SmATA X*

Windham, Kathryn Tucker 1918- *ConAu 69, –11NR, SmATA 14*

Windolph, F Lyman 1889- *AmAu&B, ConAu 41R*

Windrow, Martin *ConAu 134*

Windrow, Martin 1944- *SmATA 68*

Windrow, Martin Clive 1944- *WrDr 94*

Windsor, Claire *SmATA X*
Main entry: Hamerstrom, Frances

Windsor, Patricia 1938- *ConAu 49, –4NR, –19NR, –42NR, DcAmChF 1985, FifBJA, IntAu&W 91, ScF&FL 92, SmATA 30, WhoAm 88, –90, –92, –94, WhoAmW 83, WrDr 80, –82, –84, –86, –88, –90, –92*

Windsor, Patricia Frances 1938- *TwCYAW*

Windsor-Richards, Arthur Bedlington 1904- *Au&Wr 71, ConAu P-1, WrDr 76*

Winer, Richard 1929- *ConAu 73, –12NR*

Winfield, Arthur M *BenetAL 91, ConAu X, DcNAA, MajAI, REn, REnAL, SmATA 67, WebAB 74, –79, WhAm 1*
Main entry: Stratemeyer, Edward L

Winfield, Arthur M 1862-1930 *BioIn 15, –17*

Winfield, Edna *ConAu X, MajAI*
Main entry: Stratemeyer, Edward L

Winfield, Julia *SmATA 77*
Main entry: Armstrong, Jennifer

Wing, Helen *ChhPo*

Wingate, Gifford Wendell 1925- *ConAu 65, DrAS 74E, –78E, –82E*

Wingate, John 1920- *Au&Wr 71, ConAu 77, –24NR, WrDr 76, –80, –82, –84, –86, –88, –90, –92*

Wingate, John Allan 1920- *WrDr 94*

Winkler, Rolf 1884- *ConICB*

Winks, Robin W 1930- *SmATA 61, Who 88, –90, –92, WrDr 92*

Winks, Robin William *WhoE 89*

Winks, Robin William 1930- *ConAu 30NR, WhoAm 90, –92, –94*

Winks, Robin William Evert 1930- *WrDr 94*

Winn, Charles S 1932- *ConAu 69, –23NR*

Winn, Chris 1952- *ConAu 117, SmATA 42*

Winn, Janet B *DrAPF 87, –89, –91, –93*

Winn, Janet Bruce 1928- *BioIn 15, ConAu 105, DrAPF 83, –85, SmATA 43*

Winn, Marie *AuBYP 3*

Winn, Marie 1936- *AuBYP 2S, BioIn 13, ConAu 111, SmATA 38*

Winnick, Karen B B 1946- *SmATA 51*

Winnick, Karen Beth Binkoff 1946- *ConAu 73*

Winokur, Joan Gelman 1935- *ConAu 41R*

Winship, Florence Sarah *WhAmArt 85, WhoAmA 73, –78, –80, –82*

Winslow, Eugene 1919- *WhoBlA 77, –80, –85, –88, –90, –92, –94*

Winsor, Robert *AuBYP 2S, –3*

Winston, Clara 1921-1983 *BioIn 13, –14, –15, –16, ConAu 113, NewYTBS 83, SmATA 39N, –54, WhoAmW 81, –83*

Winston, Richard 1917-1979 *AuBYP 2S, –3, BioIn 12, –14, –16, ConAu 25R, –93, NewYTBS 80, SmATA 54, WhAm 8, WhoAm 80*

Winter, Charles A 1902- *AmMWSc 73P*

Winter, Elmer Louis 1912- *BioIn 7, –9, BlueB 76, ConAu 13R, IntYB 80, –81, –82, WhoAm 74, –76, –78, –80, WhoFI 74, –85, WhoMW 88, –92, WhoWorJ 78, WrDr 80, –82, –84*

Winter, Ginny Linville 1925- *AuBYP 2, –3, BioIn 7, ConAu 1R, –1NR, ForWC 70, IndAu 1917*

Winter, Jeanette *AuBYP 3*

Winter, Klaus 1928- *ConAu 29R, WhoGrA 62, –82*

Winter, Milo Kendall 1888-1956 *BioIn 1, -4, -5, -12, ChhPo S2, ConICB, IlsBYP, IlsCB 1744, -1946, ObitOF 79, SmATA 21*

Winter, Paula 1929- *SixBJA*

Winter, Paula Cecelia 1929- *BioIn 12, IlsCB 1967, SmATA 48, WhoAm 80, -82, -84, -86*

Winter, R R *ConAu X, SmATA X*
Main entry: Winterbotham, R R

Winter, William John 1912- *AuBYP 2, -3, BioIn 7*

Winterbotham, R R 1904-1971 *BioIn 11, ConAu 1R, -103, SmATA 10*
Pseud./variant:
Addy, Ted
Bond, J Harvey
Hadley, Franklin
Winter, R R

Winterfeld, Henry 1901- *BioIn 9, ConAu 77, SmATA 55, ThrBJA*
Pseud./variant:
Michael, Manfred

Winterfeld, Henry 1901-1990 *ScF&FL 92*

Winters, J C
Main entry: Cross, Gilbert B

Winters, J C 1939- *SmATA X*
Pseud./variant:
Cross, Gilbert B

Winters, Janet Lewis *ConAu 29NR, -P-1, DrAF 76, DrAP 75, InWom SUP, IntAu&W 77, IntWWP 82, WhoAm 74, -76, -78, WrDr 76, -80*
Main entry: Lewis, Janet

Winters, Janet Lewis 1899- *WhoUSWr 88, WhoWrEP 89, -92*

Winters, Jon *SmATA X*
Main entry: Cross, Gilbert B

Winters, Nina 1944- *SmATA 62*

Winters, Yvor 1900-1968 *AmAu&B, AmWr S2, AnCL, AtlBL, Benet 87, BenetAL 91, BioIn 1, -4, -5, -8, -10, -11, -12, -13, -15, -17, CamGLE, CamHAL, CnDAL, CnE&AP, ConAmA, ConAu 25R, -P-1, ConLC 4, -8, -32, ConLCrt 77, -82, DcLB 48, DcLEL, EncWL, -2, LongCTC, MajTwCW, ModAL S1, -S2, ObitOF 79, OxCAmL 65, -83, OxCEng 85, PenC AM, RAdv 1, REn, REnAL, RfGAmL 87, SixAP, TwCA, -SUP, TwCWr, WebE&AL, WhAm 4A, WhoTwCL*

Winterton, Gayle *SmATA X*
Main entry: Adams, William Taylor

Winthrop, Elizabeth *DrAPF 87, -89, -91, -93, WhoUSWr 88*
Main entry: Mahony, Elizabeth Winthrop

Winthrop, Elizabeth 1948- *AuBYP 3, ConAu X, DrAPF 83, -85, FifBJA, ScF&FL 92, SmATA 8, -76*

Winton, Ian Kenneth 1960- *SmATA 76*

Winton, John *ConAu X, IntAu&W 91X*
Main entry: Pratt, John

Wintterle, John 1927- *ConAu 29R, DrAS 74H, WhoWest 74*

Winwar, Frances 1900- *AmAu&B, AmWomWr, AuBYP 2, -3, Au&Wr 71, BioIn 2, -4, -7, InWom SUP, OxCAmL 65, -83, REn, REnAL, TwCA, -SUP, WhoAm 74, -76, -78, -80, -82, -84, WhoAmW 74*

Winwar, Frances 1900-1985 *WhAm 9*

Wirt, Ann *ConAu 134, MajAI, SmATA 65, WrDr 94*
Main entry: Benson, Mildred Augustine Wirt

Wirt, Mildred 1905- *AuBYP 3*

Wirt, Mildred A *AmAu&B, AuBYP 2, BioIn 7, CarSB, ConAu 134, MajAI, SmATA 65, WrDr 94*
Main entry: Benson, Mildred Augustine Wirt

Wirtenberg, Patricia Z 1932- *BioIn 11, ConAu 61, SmATA 10*

Wirth, Beverly 1938- *ConAu 118, SmATA 63*

Wirths, Claudine G 1926- *ConAu 126, IntAu&W 91, SmATA 64*

Wirths, Claudine Gibson 1926- *WhoAmW 89, WhoUSWr 88, WhoWrEP 89, -92*

Wisbeski, Dorothy G 1929- *ConAu 9R*

Wise, Daniel 1813-1898 *Alli, -SUP, AmAu&B, BiD&SB, CarSB, DcAmAu, DcNAA, WhAm HS*

Wise, William 1923- *AuBYP 2, -3, BioIn 7 -9, ChhPo, ConAu 13R, -6NR, SmATA 4*

Wise, Winifred E *AuBYP 3, WrDr 86, -88*

Wise, Winifred E 1906- *AuBYP 2, BioIn 7, -9, ConAu 25R, ForWC 70, SmATA 2, WrDr 76, -80, -82, -84*

Wiseman, Ann 1926- *ConAu 65, -9NR, SmATA 31*
Pseud./variant:
Denzer, Ann Wiseman

Wiseman, Bernard 1922- *AuBYP 2S, -3, BioIn 9, ConAu 5R, IntAu&W 77, SmATA 4, WhoE 75, -77, WhoSSW 78, -80, -82, -84, WrDr 76, -80, -82, -84, -86, -88, -90, -92, -94*

Wiseman, David 1916- *ConAu 109, -30NR, FifBJA, IntAu&W 86, -89, -91, ScF&FL 92, SmATA 40, -43*

Wiser, Guy Brown 1895- *ArtsAmW 2, ChhPo, WhAmArt 85*

Wishinsky, Frieda 1948- *SmATA 70*

Wiskur, Darrell *IlsBYP*

Wisler, G Clifton 1950- *BioIn 15, -16, ConAu 129, ScF&FL 92, SmATA 46, -58, TwCWW 91, WrDr 86, -88, -90, -92*

Wisler, Gary Clifton *DcAmChF 1960*

Wisler, Gary Clifton 1950- *WrDr 94*

Wismer, Donald 1946- *ConAu 28NR, SmATA 59*

Wisner, Bill
Main entry: Wisner, William L

Wisner, William L 1914?-1983 *AuBYP 2, -3, BioIn 8, -13, ConAu 110, -111, SmATA 42*
Pseud./variant:
Wisner, Bill

Wissmann, Ruth H *AuBYP 3*

Wissmann, Ruth Helen Leslie 1914- *AuBYP 2, BioIn 7, ConAu 5R, IntAu&W 77, WhoAmW 75*

Wister, Owen *Benet 87, OxCAmT 84*

Wister, Owen 1860-1938 *Alli SUP, AmAu&B, AmLY, ArizL, BenetAL 91, BiD&SB, BioIn 1, -3, -4, -5, -7, -9, -10, -12, -13, -14, -16, -17, CamGEL, CamGLE, CamHAL, CarSB, CasWL, Chambr 3, ChhPo, -S2, CnDAL, ConAmA, ConAmL, ConAu 108, CyWA 58, DcAmAu, DcLB 9, -78, DcLEL, DcNAA, EncAB-H, EncFWF, HalFC 84, -88, HarEnUS, LongCTC, MemAm, Novels, OxCAmL 65, -83, PenC AM, RAdv 1, -13-1, REn, REnAL, RfGAmL 87, SmATA 62, TwCA, -SUP, TwCLC 21, TwCWW 91, WebAB 74, -79, WebE&AL, WhAm 1, WhNAA, WorAlBi*

Wister, Owen 1869-1938 *WorAl*

Witham, Ross 1917- *ConAu 105, SmATA 37*

Witheridge, Elizabeth P *AuBYP 3*

Witheridge, Elizabeth P 1907- *AuBYP 2S, BioIn 6, ConAu 97, IntAu&W 82, MinnWr*

Withers, Carl 1900-1970 *AuBYP 3*

Withers, Carl A 1900-1970 *AnCL, AuBYP 2, BioIn 7, -12, ConAu 73, -30NR, SmATA 14*
Pseud./variant:
North, Robert
West, James

Witherspoon, Gary Jay 1943- *AmMWSc 73S*

Witker, Jim *AuBYP 2, -3, BioIn 8*

Witt, Shirley Hill 1934- *AmMWSc 73S, -76P, ConAu 53, -5NR, FifIDA, SmATA 17, WhoAmW 77, -81, WhoWest 80, -82, -84*
Pseud./variant:
Thundercloud, Katherine

Wittanen, Etolin 1907- *BioIn 16, SmATA 55*

Witte, Betty J *AuBYP 2, -3, BioIn 8*

Wittels, Harriet Joan 1938- *BioIn 14, ConAu 107, SmATA 31*

Wittenbach, Henry August 1900- *WrDr 76, -80, -82, -84, -86, -88, -90*

Wittman, Sally 1941- *ConAu 107, SmATA 30*

Witton, Dorothy *AuBYP 2, -3, BioIn 7, ConAu 73, MichAu 80*

Witty, Paul A 1898-1976 *BioIn 14, -16, SmATA 50*

Witty, Paul Andrew 1898-1976 *AuBYP 2, -3, BioIn 4, -7, -9, -10, ConAu 65, -73, IndAu 1917, SmATA 30N, WhAm 6, WhoAm 74, -76*

Wizard, Mr *SmATA 2*
Main entry: Herbert, Don

Wodehouse, Pelham Grenville *IntvTCA 2*

Wodehouse, Pelham Grenville 1881-1975 *AmAu&B, ASCAP 66, AuNews 2, Au&Wr 71, BiE&WWA, BioIn 1, -2, -3, -4, -5, -6, -7, -8, -9, -10, -11, -12, -13, -14, -16, -17, BlueB 76N, CasWL, CelR, Chambr 3, CmpEPM, ConAu 45, -57, -3NR, ConDr 73, ConLC 2, -5, -22, ConNov 72, -76, CurBio 71, -75N, DcLB 34, DcLEL, EncMT, EncWL, -2, EncWT, EvLB, GrBr, HalFC 84, IntWW 74, -75N, LongCTC, MakMC, McGEWD 72, -84, ModBrL, -S1, -S2, NewC, NewCBMT, NotNAT A, Novels, ObitOF 79, OxCChiL, OxCEng 67, -85, OxCThe 83, PenC ENG, PlP&P, RAdv 1, REn, SmATA 22, TwCA, -SUP, TwCWr, WebE&AL, WhDW, WhAm 6, Who 74, WhoAm 74, WhoChL, WhoTwCL, WhoWor 74, WorAl*

Wodehouse, Pelham Grenville, Sir 1881-1975 *DcNaB 1971*

Wodge, Dreary *ConAu X, –30NR, SmATA X*
Main entry: Gorey, Edward St John

Wohlberg, Meg d1990 *NewYTBS 90*

Wohlberg, Meg 1905- *BioIn 8, –15, ChhPo S1, IlsCB 1957, SmATA 41, WhAmArt 85*

Wohlberg, Meg 1905-1990 *BioIn 17, ConAu 133, SmATA 66*

Wohlrabe, Raymond A 1900-1977 *AuBYP 3*

Wohlrabe, Raymond Adolph 1900-1977 *AuBYP 2, BioIn 7, –9, ConAu 1R, –3NR, SmATA 4, WhoPNW, WhoWest 74, WrDr 76, –80, –82, –84*

Wojciechowska, Maia *DrAPF 87, –89, –91, –93*

Wojciechowska, Maia 1927- *AmAu&B, AmCath 80, Au&Arts 8, AuBYP 2, –3, Au&ICB, BioIn 7, –8, –9, –10, –11, –13, –14, –15, ChlLR 1, ConAu 9R, –4NR, ConLC 26, CurBio 76, DrAPF 83, –85, HerW, –84, MorBMP, NewbC 1956, OxCChiL, PiP, SmATA 1, –28, –1AS, ThrBJA, TwCChW 78, –83, –89, WhoAm 74, WhoUSWr 88, WhoWrEP 89, WrDr 80, –82, –84, –86, –88, –90, –92*
Pseud./variant:
Rodman, Maia

Wojciechowska, Maia Rodman 1927- *WhoWrEP 92*

Wojciechowska, Maia Teresa 1927- *ConAu 41NR, MajAI, TwCYAW*

Wojciechowska Rodman, Maia 1927- *DcAmChF 1960*

Wolberg, Lewis R d1988 *NewYTBS 88*

Wolberg, Lewis Robert 1905- *BiDrAPA 77, ConAu 45, –2NR, –19NR, WhoAm 74, –76, –78, –80, –82, –84, –86, WhoWor 80*

Wolberg, Lewis Robert 1905-1988 *BioIn 15, ConAu 124, WhAm 9*

Wolcott, Carolyn Muller *AuBYP 2, –3, BioIn 7*

Wolcott, Elizabeth Tyler 1892-1951 *BioIn 2, ConICB, DcWomA*

Wolcott, John *AuBYP 3*

Wolcott, Leonard Thompson *AuBYP 2, –3, ConAu 13R, –11NR, –28NR, DrAS 74P, –78P, –82P, IntAu&W 77, –91, WrDr 76, –80, –82, –84, –86, –88, –90, –92, –94*

Wolcott, Patty 1929- *BioIn 12, ConAu 57, IntAu&W 77, –82, SmATA 14, WrDr 76, –80, –82, –84, –86, –88, –90, –92, –94*

Wold, Allen L 1943- *ConAu 22NR, EncSF 93, SmATA 64*

Wold, Allen Lester 1943- *IntAu&W 86, WhoSSW 91*

Wold, Jo Anne 1938- *ConAu 61, SmATA 30, WhoAmW 81, –83*

Wolde, Gunilla *TwCChW 78B*

Woldin, Beth Weiner 1955- *BioIn 14, ConAu 102, SmATA 34*

Wolf, Arnold Jacob 1924- *ConAu 29R, WhoAmJ 80, WhoRel 77, –92, WhoWorJ 78*

Wolf, Bernard 1930- *ConAu 115, FifBJA, SmATA 37*

Wolf, Stephanie Grauman 1932- *DrAS 82H, WhoE 86*

Wolfe, Art 1952- *SmATA 76*

Wolfe, Burton H 1932- *WrDr 86, –88, –90, –92, –94*

Wolfe, Burton Harold 1932- *BioIn 10, ConAu 25R, DcAmSR, IntAu&W 77, –82, SmATA 5, WhoWest 74, –76, –78, WrDr 76, –80, –82, –84*

Wolfe, Gene Rodman 1931- *ConAu 57, DrAF 76*

Wolfe, Humbert 1885-1940 *AnCL, BioIn 2, ChhPo, –S1, –S2, CurBio 40, DcLEL, DcNaB 1931, EngPo, EvLB, LongCTC, ModBrL, NewC, NotNAT B, PenC ENG, REn, Str&VC, TwCA, –SUP, TwCWr, WhoLA*

Wolfe, Josephine Brace 1917- *ConAu 5R, WhoAmW 74, –75*

Wolfe, Louis 1905- *AuBYP 2, –3, BioIn 7, –11, ConAu 5R, –3NR, EncSF 93, SmATA 8*

Wolfe, Louis 1905-1985 *ScF&FL 92*

Wolfe, Rinna 1925- *BioIn 15, ConAu 105, SmATA 38*

Wolfenden, George *SmATA X*
Main entry: Beardmore, George

Wolfert, Jerry *AuBYP 2, –3*

Wolff, Alexander 1957- *SmATA 63*

Wolff, Ashley *AuBYP 3, ChlBIlD*

Wolff, Ashley 1956- *ConAu 118, SixBJA, SmATA 50*

Wolff, Diane 1945- *ConAu 77, SmATA 27*

Wolff, Janet Loeb *WhoAm 86, -88, WhoAmW 87*

Wolff, Janet Loeb 1924- *ConAu 5R, ForWC 70, WhoAm 80, -82, -84, WhoAmW 74, -81, -85, WhoFI 74*

Wolff, Leslie 1912- *Au&Wr 71, WrDr 76, -80, -82*

Wolff, Robert Jay 1905- *WrDr 86*

Wolff, Robert Jay 1905-1977 *BioIn 11, BlueB 76, ConAu 25R, -73, DcCAA 71, -77, IntAu&W 77, ObitOF 79, SmATA 10, WhAm 7, WhAmArt 85, WhoAm 74, -76, -78, WhoAmA 73, -78N, -80N, -82N, WrDr 76, -80, -82, -84*

Wolff, Robert Jay 1905-1978 *WhoAmA 86N, -89N, -91N*

Wolff, Ruth 1909?-1972 *BioIn 9, ConAu 37R*

Wolff, Sonia *ConAu 32NR, MajAI, SmATA 68, WrDr 90, -92, -94*
Main entry: Levitin, Sonia Wolff

Wolff, Virginia Euwer 1937- *DcAmChF 1985, TwCYAW*

Wolfson, Evelyn *AuBYP 3*

Wolfson, Evelyn 1937- *SmATA 62*

Wolfson, Victor d1990 *NewYTBS 90*

Wolfson, Victor 1910- *BiE&WWA, BioIn 1, -4, ConAu 33R, NotNAT, TwCA SUP, WhoWorJ 72, -78*
Pseud./variant:
Dodge, Langdon

Wolfson, Victor 1910-1990 *BioIn 16, -17, ConAu 131*

Wolitzer, Hilma *BioIn 14, DrAPF 87, -89, -91, -93*

Wolitzer, Hilma 1930?- *ArtclWW 2, BioIn 11, ConAu 65, -18NR, -40NR, ConLC 17, DrAF 76, DrAPF 83, -85, FifBJA, SmATA 31, TwCYAW, WhoAm 82, -84, -86, -88, -94, WhoUSWr 88, WhoWrEP 89, -92, WrDr 76, -80, -82, -84, -86, -88, -90, -92, -94*

Wolkoff, Judie *ConAu 115, SmATA 37*

Wolkstein, Diane *DrAPF 87, -89, -91, -93, WhoUSWr 88, WhoWrEP 89, -92*

Wolkstein, Diane 1942- *BioIn 10, ConAu 37R, -14NR, -32NR, DrAPF 85, FifBJA, IntAu&W 89, SmATA 7, WhoAmW 75, WhoE 93*

Wollheim, Donald A *DrmM 2*

Wollheim, Donald A 1914- *ConAu 19NR, NewEScF, ScFSB, ScFEYrs, TwCSFW 86, WrDr 86, -88, -90*

Wollheim, Donald A 1914-1990 *BioIn 17, ConAu 135, ScF&FL 92, TwCSFW 91*

Wollheim, Donald Allen 1914- *AuBYP 2, -3, BioIn 7, ConAu 1R, -1NR, ConSFA, WhoAm 78, -80, -82, -84, -86, -88, WhoE 74, -75, -77, WhoHr&F, WhoSciF, WhoUSWr 88, WhoWor 80, WhoWrEP 89, WrDr 76, -80, -82, -84*
Pseud./variant:
Grinnell, David

Wollheim, Donald Allen 1914-1990 *EncSF 93, SmATA 69*

Wollstonecraft, Mary *InWom SUP*

Wollstonecraft, Mary 1759-1797 *ArtclWW 2, Benet 87, BioIn 1, -2, -3, -7, -8, -9, -10, -11, -12, -13, -14, -15, -16, -17, BlmGEL, BlmGWL, CamGEL, CamGLE, CelCen, CnDBLB 3, ContDcW 89, CyEd, DcBrAmW, DcLB 39, -104, DcNaB, Dis&D, EncBrWW, FemiCLE, HerW 84, IntDcWB, LitC 5, OxCChiL, OxCEng 85, RfGEnL 91, WorAlBi*

Wolman, Baron 1937- *BioIn 10*

Wolny, P
Main entry: Janeczko, Paul Bryan

Wolseley, Roland E 1904- *ConAu 39NR, WrDr 86, -88, -90, -92, -94*

Wolseley, Roland Edgar 1904- *BioIn 2, ConAu 1R, -1NR, -17NR, DrAS 74E, -78E, -82E, IntAu&W 77, -82, WhNAA, WhoAm 74, -76, -78, WrDr 76, -80, -82, -84*

Wolters, Richard A 1920- *BioIn 8, -12, -14, ConAu 3NR, -18NR, SmATA 35, WrDr 82, -84, -86, -88, -90, -92, -94*

Wondriska, William Allen 1931- *AuBYP 2, -3, BioIn 8, -9, -10, ConAu 1R, IlsCB 1957, -1967, SmATA 6, ThrBJA*

Wong, Jade Snow *BioIn 16*

Wong, Jade Snow 1919- *BlmGWL*

Wong, Jade Snow 1922- *ArtclWW 2, BenetAL 91, BioIn 2, -4, -10, -13, ConAu 109, ConLC 17, WhoAsA 94*

Wong, Jeanyee 1920- *BioIn 2, –3, –5, –8, IlsBYP, IlsCB 1946*

Wong, Ovid K *AuBYP 3*

Wong, Ovid K 1946- *WhoAsA 94*

Wonsetler, John Charles 1900- *BioIn 1, –5, IlsBYP, IlsCB 1744, –1946, WhAmArt 85*

Wood, Anne 1937- *BioIn 17, SmATA 64*

Wood, Audrey *AuBYP 3, ConAu 137, MajAI, SmATA 44, –50*

Wood, Audrey d1985 *NewYTBS 85*

Wood, Audrey 1905-1985 *AnObit 1985, BioIn 16, ConAu 118, NotWoAT*

Wood, Audrey 1948- *ChlLR 26, SixBJA*

Wood, Catherine *ConAu X, SmATA X*
Main entry: Etchison, Birdie L

Wood, Clement 1888-1950 *AmAu&B, AnMV 1926, ASCAP 66, Benet 87, BioIn 2, –4, ChhPo, –S1, –S2, ObitOF 79, REn, REnAL, TwCA, –SUP, WhAm 3, WhNAA*

Wood, David 1944- *ConAu 97, IntAu&W 82, IntWWM 90, OxCChiL, TwCChW 83, –89, TwCPaSc, Who 82, –83, –85, –88, –90, –92, WhoThe 81, WrDr 84, –86, –88, –90, –92, –94*

Wood, Don *ChlBIlD*

Wood, Don 1945- *ChlLR 26, ConAu 136, MajAI, SixBJA, SmATA 44, –50*

Wood, Dorothy Carrico *AuBYP 2, –3*

Wood, Edgar Allardyce 1907- *BioIn 12, ConAu 77, IntAu&W 82, –89, –91, SmATA 14, WrDr 80, –82, –84*
Pseud./variant:
Wood, Kerry

Wood, Eric *ChhPo S2*

Wood, Esther
Main entry: Brady, Esther Wood

Wood, Esther 1905- *BioIn 2, ConAu X, JBA 51, OhA&B, SmATA X*

Wood, Frances Elizabeth *ConAu 107, SmATA 34*

Wood, Harrie 1902- *BioIn 1, ConICB, IlsCB 1744, WhAmArt 85*

Wood, Irene 1943- *MedPD, WhoLibI 82*

Wood, J G *DcWomA*

Wood, James Playsted 1905- *AmAu&B, AuBYP 2, –3, Au&Wr 71, BioIn 8, –9, ChhPo S2, ConAu 9R, –3NR, FourBJA, IntAu&W 77, –82, SmATA 1, WhAm 8, WhoAm 74, –76, –78, –80, –82, WrDr 76, –80, –82, –84*
Pseud./variant:
Saint Briavels, James
Soudley, Henry

Wood, John George 1827-1889 *Alli, –SUP, BiDLA, BiD&SB, BioIn 16, CarSB, CelCen, DcBiPP, DcEnL, DcNaB, EvLB, InSci*

Wood, Joyce 1928- *ConAu 25R*

Wood, Kenneth 1922- *ConAu 69, –11NR, –26NR*

Wood, Kenneth Arthur 1926- *WhoWest 94, WhoWor 93*

Wood, Kerry *IntAu&W 91X*
Main entry: Wood, Edgar Allardyce

Wood, Kerry 1907- *BioIn 10, –12, ConAu X, DcChlFi, IntAu&W 82X, OxCCan SUP, OxCChiL, Profile 1, SmATA X, TwCChW 78, –83, –89, WrDr 80, –82, –84, –86, –88, –90, –92, –94*

Wood, Laura Newbold *AuBYP 2, BioIn 7, ConAu 57, IntAu&W 77X, SmATA X, WrDr 76, –80, –82, –84, –86, –88, –90, –92*
Main entry: Roper, Laura Wood

Wood, Laura Newbold 1911- *AuBYP 3, WrDr 94*

Wood, Lawson 1878-1957 *BioIn 1, –14, DcBrAr 1, DcBrBI, IlsCB 1744*

Wood, Leslie 1920- *BioIn 5, IlsBYP, IlsCB 1946*

Wood, Linda C 1945- *SmATA 59*

Wood, Linda Carol 1945- *IntAu&W 86*

Wood, Lorna 1913- *Au&Wr 71, BioIn 8, ConAu 69, OxCChiL, TwCChW 78, –83, –89, WhoChL, WrDr 76, –80, –82, –84, –86, –88, –90*

Wood, Nancy 1936- *BioIn 10, ConAu 21R –9NR, MacBEP, SmATA 6*

Wood, Owen 1929- *SmATA 64*

Wood, Paul W 1922- *ConAu 61*

Wood, Peter 1930- *ConAu 93*

Wood, Phyllis Anderson 1923- *AuBYP 2S, –3, BioIn 14, ConAu 37R, –14NR, IntAu&W 77,*

SmATA 30, -33, WrDr 76, -80, -82, -84, -86, -88, -90, -92, -94

Wood, Ray *ChhPo*

Wood, Robert Henry 1923- *Au&Wr 71, WrDr 76, -80, -82, -84, -86*

Wood, Robert Williams 1869?-1955 *BiESc, BioIn 2, -4, -6, -8, -12, ChhPo, -S1, DcScB, InSci, ObitOF 79, OxCAmH, WhAm 3, WhNAA*

Wood, Ruth C *AuBYP 2S, -3, ConAu 37R*

Wood, Samuel Andrew 1890- *EncSF 93*

Wood, Stanley L *DcVicP 2*

Wood, Stanley L 1866-1928 *BioIn 14, DcBrAr 2, DcBrBI, DcVicP 2*

Wood, Stanley Llewellyn 1866-1928 *BiDScF*

Wood, Theodore 1862- *Alli SUP, CarSB*

Wood, Wallace 1927-1981 *AnObit 1981, BioIn 14, ConAu 108, ScF&FL 92, SmATA 33N*

Woodard, Carol 1929- *BioIn 12, ConAu 73, SmATA 14, WhoAm 82, -84, WhoAmW 81, -83, -85*

Woodard, Carol Jane 1929- *WhoAm 86, -90, -94, WhoAmW 93*

Woodberry, Joan 1921- *AuBYP 3*

Woodberry, Joan Merle 1921- *AuBYP 2S, Au&Wr 71, ConAu 9R, DcChlFi, SingR 1, WrDr 76, -80, -82, -84, -86, -88, -90*

Woodbridge, Frederick James Eugene 1867-1940 *AmAu&B, BioIn 2, -4, CurBio 40, DcNAA, REnAL, WebAB 74, -79, WhAm 1*

Woodburn, John Henry 1914- *AuBYP 2S, -3, BioIn 11, ConAu 1R, -4NR, LEduc 74, SmATA 11*

Woodbury, David O *AuBYP 3*

Woodbury, David O 1896-1981 *ScF&FL 92*

Woodbury, David Oakes 1896- *AuBYP 2S*

Woodbury, David Oakes 1896-1981 *BioIn 17, EncSF 93, SmATA 62*

Woodcock, George *ConDr 88B*

Woodcock, George 1912- *Au&Wr 71, Benet 87, BenetAL 91, BioIn 13, -16, BlueB 76, CaW, CanWW 70, -79, -80, -81, -83, -89, CanWr, CasWL, ConAu 1R, -6AS, -1NR, ConDr 82B, ConPo 70, -75, -80, -85, -91, CurBio 64, DcLB 88, DcLEL 1940, EngPo, IntAu&W 77, -82, -89, -91, IntWW 79, -80, -81, -82, -83, -89, -91, ModBrL, OxCCan, -SUP, OxCCanL, ScF&FL 92, Who 74, -82, -83, -85, -88, -92, WhoAm 74, -76, -78, -80, -82, -84, -86, -88, -90, -92, -94, WhoCanL 85, -87, -92, WhoWest 92, -94, WhoWor 84, -87, -89, -91, -93, WhoWrEP 89, -92, WrDr 76, -80, -82, -84, -86, -88, -90, -92, -94*

Woodcock, George, Dr 1912- *Who 90*

Wooden, John 1910- *BioIn 6, -9, -10, -11, CelR, CmCal, CurBio 76, IndAu 1917, NewYTBE 72, -73, WorAlBi*

Wooden, John Robert 1910- *WhoAm 92, WhoWest 94*

Woodford, Cecile *WrDr 86, -88, -90*

Woodford, Cecile 1913- *WrDr 76, -80, -82, -84*

Woodford, Peggy 1937- *BioIn 13, ConAu 104, IntAu&W 91, SmATA 25, WrDr 80, -82, -84, -86, -88, -90, -92, -94*

Woodgate, Mildred Violet *Au&Wr 71, ConAu 9R, WrDr 76*

Woodgate, Mildred Violet 1904- *WomNov*

Woodhouse, Barbara d1988 *NewYTBS 88*

Woodhouse, Barbara 1910- *InWom SUP*

Woodhouse, Barbara 1910-1988 *AnObit 1988, ConAu 126, -30NR, CurBio 88N, SmATA 63*

Woodhouse, Martin Charlton 1932- *AuSpks, Au&Wr 71, BioIn 7, -11, ConAu 21R, WrDr 80*

Wooding, Sharon *ConAu 136, SmATA 66*

Wooding, Sharon 1943- *BioIn 17*

Wooding, Sharon L 1943- *SmATA 66*

Wooding, Sharon Louise 1943- *ConAu 136, WhoE 89, WrDr 94*

Woodling, Eugene R 1922- *BioIn 3, -4, -6*

Woodman, Allen *DrAPF 87, -89, -91, -93*

Woodman, Allen 1954- *IntAu&W 86, SmATA 76, WhoUSWr 88, WhoWrEP 89, -92*

Woodress, James 1916- *ConAu 5R, -3NR, DrAS 74E, -78E, -82E, IntAu&W 91,*

WhoAm 74, –80, –82, –84, WrDr 80, –82, –84, –86, –88, –90, –92

Woodress, James Leslie, Jr. 1916- *WhoAm 92, WrDr 94*

Woodrich, Mary Neville 1915- *BioIn 9, ConAu 25R, SmATA 2*
Pseud./variant:
Neville, Mary

Woodroffe, Paul Vincent 1875- *DcVicP 2*

Woodroffe, Paul Vincent 1875-1945? *BioIn 1, –12, ChhPo, –S2, DcBrBI, DcVicP 2, IlsCB 1744*

Woodroffe, Paul Vincent 1875-1954 *BioIn 14*

Woodruff, Anne Helena 1850- *AmAu&B, CarSB, ChhPo S1, DcNAA, WhAm 4, WomWWA 14*

Woodruff, Elvira 1951- *SmATA 70*

Woods, George d1988 *NewYTBS 88*

Woods, George 1926-1988 *SmATA 57*

Woods, George A 1926- *AuBYP 2S, –3, ConAu 29R, SmATA 30*

Woods, George A 1926-1988 *BioIn 16, ConAu 126*

Woods, George Allan 1926- *DcAmChF 1960*

Woods, Geraldine 1948- *ConAu 97, SmATA 42, –56*

Woods, Harold 1945- *ConAu 97, SmATA 42, –56*

Woods, Kate Tannatt 1838-1910 *Alli SUP, AmAu&B, BiD&SB, CarSB, ChhPo, –S2, DcAmAu, DcNAA, WhAm 1*

Woods, Katherine Irvin 1886-1968 *AmAu&B, BioIn 8, WhAm 7, WhNAA*

Woods, Loren Paul 1913- *AmMWSc 73P, –76P*

Woods, Margaret 1921- *BioIn 9, ConAu 21R, SmATA 2*

Woods, Margaret Staeger 1911- *ConAu 81, LEduc 74, WhoAmW 74, –75*

Woods, Nat *ConAu X, MajAI*
Main entry: Stratemeyer, Edward L

Woodson, Carter G 1875-1950 *AfrAmAl 6, BlkWrNE, ConBlB 2, NegAl 89, RComAH, WorAlBi*

Woodson, Carter Godwin 1875-1950 *BenetAL 91, BioIn 14, –15, –16, –17, ConAu 141, EncAACR, InB&W 85*

Woodson, Carter Goodwin 1875-1950 *BlkAull, –92*

Woodson, Jack
Main entry: Woodson, John Waddie, Jr.

Woodson, Jacqueline 1964- *BlkAull 92*

Woodson, John Waddie, Jr. 1913- *BioIn 11, SmATA 10*
Pseud./variant:
Woodson, Jack

Woodville, Richard Caton 1856-1927 *BioIn 14, ClaDrA, DcBrAr 1, DcVicP 2*

Woodward, Alice Bolingbroke *DcVicP 2*

Woodward, Alice Bolingbroke 1862- *BioIn 1, ChhPo, –S1, –S2, ConICB, DcBrBI, DcVicP 2, DcWomA, IlsBYP, IlsCB 1744, InWom SUP*

Woodward, Alice Bolingbroke 1862-1911 *BioIn 14*

Woodward, C Vann 1908- *BioIn 8, –13, –14, –15, –16, –17, BlueB 76, ConAu 5R, –2NR, –17NR, CurBio 86, DcLB 17, IntAu&W 77, –82, IntWW 80, –81, –82, –83, –89, –91, RAdv 13-3, ThTwC 87 Who 74, –82, –83, –85, –88, –90, –92, WhoAm 76, –80, –82, –88, –92, –94, WhoE 85, –86, –89, WhoUSWr 88, WhoWor 74, –80, –82, –87, WhoWrEP 89, WrDr 80, –82, –84, –86, –88, –90, –92*

Woodward, Cleveland 1900- *BioIn 11, SmATA 10, WhoAm 74, WhoAmA 73, –86*

Woodward, Cleveland 1900-1986 *BioIn 16, SmATA 48N*

Woodward, Comer Vann 1908- *WhoWrEP 92, WrDr 94*

Woodward, Hildegard 1898- *AuBYP 2, –3, BioIn 1, –5, –7, –14, ConAu 5R, DcWomA, ForWC 70, IlsCB 1744, –1946*

Woodward, Ian 1941- *IntAu&W 77, –82, WhoWor 78*

Woodward, Lucy Berton *OxCCan SUP*

Woodworth, Francis Channing 1812-1859 *Alli, AmAu&B, CarSB, ChhPo, –S1, DcNAA*

Woody, Regina Llewellyn 1894- *AuBYP 3*

Woody, Regina Llewellyn Jones 1894- *AuBYP 2, BioIn 6, –7, –9, ConAu 5R,*

ForWC 70, MorJA, SmATA 3, WhoAmW 74, WhoE 74, WrDr 76, –80

Wooldridge, Rhoda 1906- *AuBYP 2, BioIn 8, –13, ConAu 77, SmATA 22*

Wooldridge, Rhode 1906- *AuBYP 3*

Woolgar, Jack 1894- *ConAu 17R*

Woolheim, Donald Allen 1914- *BioIn 7*

Woolley, Catherine 1904- *AuBYP 2, –3, Au&Wr 71, BioIn 6, –7, –9, ConAu 1R, –6NR, ForWC 70, MorJA, SmATA 3, WhoAm 78, –80, –82, –84, –86, –88, –90, –92, –94, WhoAmW 74, –75, –77, –81, –83, –85, –87, –89, –91, –93, WhoE 75, –77, WhoWor 93*
Pseud./variant:
Thayer, Jane

Woolley, Horace A *ChhPo*

Woolsey, Janette 1904- *AuBYP 2, –3, BioIn 7, –9, ConAu 1R, –2NR, ForWC 70, SmATA 3, WhoLibS 55*

Woolsey, Janette 1904-1989 *ScF&FL 92*

Woolsey, Sarah C 1835?-1905 *Alli SUP, AmAu, AmAu&B, AmWomWr, BiD&SB, BioIn 5, –8, CarSB, Chambr 3, ChhPo, ConAu 115, DcAmAu, DcLB 42, DcLEL, DcNAA, EvLB, JBA 34, OhA&B, OxCChiL, REnAL, WhAm 1, WhoChL*
Pseud./variant:
Coolidge, Susan

Woolsey, Sarah Chauncey 1835-1905 *AmWomPl, BenetAL 91, InWom SUP, WomNov*

Woolsey, Sarah Chauncy 1835-1905 *BioIn 15*

Worcester, Donald E 1915- *ConAu 19NR, WrDr 86, –88, –90, –92, –94*

Worcester, Donald Emmet 1915- *AmAu&B, AuBYP 2, –3, BioIn 7, –12, –16, BlueB 76, ConAu 1R, –4NR, DrAS 74H, –78H, –82H, IntAu&W 77, –82, SmATA 18, WhoAm 74, –76, –78, –80, –82, –84, –86, –88, –90, –92, –94, WhoSSW 73, –91, –93, WhoWor 78, WrDr 76, –80, –82, –84*

Worcester, Gurdon Saltonstall 1897- *ConAu P-1, DcAmChF 1960*

Worde, Wynkyn De d1534? *Benet 87, BioIn 10, CamGEL, CamGLE, DcBiPP, DcNaB, OxCChiL, OxCLaw*

Worden, Alfred Merrill 1932- *BioIn 9, –10, BlueB 76, ConAu 101, IntWW 74, –75, –76, –77, NewYTBE 71, WhoAm 74, –76, –78, –80, –82, –84, –86, –88, –90, –92, –94, WhoSSW 73, WhoWest 76, –78*

Wordsworth, William 1770-1850 *Alli, AnCL, AtlBL, Benet 87, BbD, BiDLA, BiD&SB, BioIn 1, –2, –3, –4, –5, –6, –7, –8, –9, –10, –11, –12, –13, –14, –15, –16, –17, BlmGEL, BritAu 19, BritWr 4, CamGEL, CamGLE, CasWL, CelCen, Chambr 3, ChhPo, –S1, –S2, CnDBLB 3, CnE&AP, CrtT 2, CyEd, CyWA 58, DcBiPP, DcEnA, DcEnL, DcEuL, DcLB 93, –107, DcLEL, DcNaB, Dis&D, EvLB, IlEncMy, LongCEL, LuthC 75, MagSWL, McGEWB, MouLC 3, NewC, NinCLC 12, –38, OxCEng 67, –85, OxCMus, PenC ENG, PoeCrit 4, PoLE, RAdv 1, –13-1, RComWL, REn, RfGEnL 91, Str&VC, WebE&AL, WhDW, WorAlBi, WorAl, WorLitC, WrPh*

Work, Virginia 1946- *ConAu 113, SmATA 45, –57*

Worline, Bonnie Bess 1914- *AuBYP 2, –3, BioIn 7, –12, ConAu 69, SmATA 14*

Worm, Piet 1909- *Au&Wr 71, BioIn 5, ConAu 81, IlsBYP, IlsCB 1946*

Wormser, Richard Edward 1908- *ConSFA, DcAmChF 1960, IntMPA 75, –76, –78, –77*

Wormser, Sophie 1897- *BioIn 13, ConAu 65, SmATA 22*

Worrell, Estelle *AuBYP 3*

Worrell, Estelle Ansley 1929- *AuBYP 2S*

Worstell, Emma Vietor *ChhPo*

Worth, Kathryn 1898- *AuBYP 2, –3, BioIn 2, –3, –4, –5, –8, ChhPo, JBA 51*

Worth, Richard *SmATA 46*

Worth, Richard 1945- *IntAu&W 86, SmATA 59*

Worth, Valerie *BioIn 11, ChhPo S2, ConAu X, FifBJA, SmATA 8*
Main entry: Bahlke, Valerie Worth

Worth, Valerie 1933- *ChlLR 21, MajAI, ScF&FL 92, SmATA 70, TwCChW 89*

Worthington, Arthur Mason 1852-1916 *Alli SUP*

Worthington, Phoebe 1910- *BioIn 16, SmATA 52*

Worthington, R *CarSB*

Worthylake, Mary Moore 1904- *ConAu 1R, –4NR, ForWC 70, WhoPNW, WhoWrEP 89, –92*

Wortis, Avi *TwCChW 89*

Wortis, Avi 1937- *BioIn 12, –15, –16, ConAu 69, –12NR, –42NR, MajAI, SmATA 14, WhoAm 92, –94*
Pseud./variant:
Avi 1937-

Worton, Stanley Nelson 1923- *ConAu 57, DrAS 74H, –78H, –82H*

Wosmek, Frances 1917- *AuBYP 3, ConAu 26NR, DcAmChF 1960*

Wosmek, Frances E 1917- *BioIn 13, ConAu 29R, –11NR, SmATA 29, WrDr 80, –82, –84*
Pseud./variant:
Brailsford, Frances

Woychuk, Denis 1953- *SmATA 71*

Wrede, Patricia C 1953- *Au&Arts 8, BioIn 17, ConAu 134, ScF&FL 92, SmATA 67*

Wrede, Patricia Collins 1953- *TwCYAW, WhoAmW 93, WhoMW 93, WhoUSWr 88, WhoWrEP 89, WrDr 94*

Wren, Ellaruth *ConAu X*
Main entry: Elkins, Ella Ruth

Wren, Percival Christopher 1875-1941 *DcNaB MP*

Wren, Percival Christopher 1885-1941 *BioIn 1, –14, ConAu 123, CurBio 42, DcLEL, EvLB, LongCTC, NewC, ObitOF 79, OxCEng 67, PenC ENG, REn, TwCA, TwCWr*

Wriggins, Sally Hovey 1922- *ConAu 97, SmATA 17*

Wright, Anna Rose 1890-1968 *BioIn 2, –3, –8, –14, ConAu 109, CurBio 52, SmATA 35*
Pseud./variant:
Rose, Anna P

Wright, Betty Ren *AuBYP 3, BioIn 16, –17, DcAmChF 1960, SmATA 48*

Wright, Betty Ren 1927- *ScF&FL 92, SixBJA, SmATA 63*
Pseud./variant:
Revena 1927-

Wright, Blanche Fisher *ChhPo, –S1*

Wright, Bruce Stanley 1912-1975 *AmMWSc 73P, ConAu P-2*

Wright, Cliff 1963- *SmATA 76*

Wright, Dare 1926?- *AuBYP 2, –3, BioIn 6, –7, –12, ConAu 93, SmATA 21*

Wright, David K 1943- *SmATA 73*

Wright, Elinor Bruce *Au&Wr 71, IntAu&W 77*
Main entry: Lyon, Elinor

Wright, Enid Meadowcroft *AuBYP 2, –3, ConAu P-2, SmATA 3*
Main entry: Meadowcroft, Enid LaMonte

Wright, Esmond 1915- *Au&Wr 71, BioIn 11, BlueB 76, ConAu 1R, –6NR, IntAu&W 77, –82, –91, SmATA 10, Who 74, –82, –83, –85, –88, –92, WhoWor 80, –87, WrDr 76, –80, –82, –84, –86, –88, –90, –92, –94*

Wright, Esmond, Prof 1915- *Who 90*

Wright, Frances 1897- *AuBYP 3*

Wright, Frances Fitzpatrick 1897- *AuBYP 2, BioIn 8, –11, ConAu P-1, SmATA 10*

Wright, Gordon 1902?- *BioIn 11*

Wright, Gordon 1912- *WhoAm 86*

Wright, Helen *ScF&FL 92*

Wright, Helen 1914- *AmAu&B, BioIn 4, ConAu 9R, CurBio 56, InSci, WhoAm 74, –76, –78, –80, –82, –84, –86, –88, –90, WhoAmW 74*

Wright, Henrietta Christian d1899 *Alli SUP, AmAu&B, BiD&SB, CarSB, ChhPo, DcAmAu, DcNAA, HarEnUS*

Wright, J B *SmATA 77*
Main entry: Barkan, Joanne

Wright, John Stafford 1905- *Au&Wr 71, ConAu 57, WhoWor 78, WrDr 76, –80, –82, –84, –86*

Wright, Judith Arundel 1915- *AnCL, BioIn 8, –9, –10, –11, BlueB 76, CamGEL, CasWL, ChhPo, CnMWL, ConAu 13R, ConLC 11, ConPo 70, –75, DcLEL 1940, FarE&A 80, –81, IntAu&W 77, –82, IntWW 74, –75, –76, –77, –78, –79, –80, –81, –82, –83, –89, –91, LongCTC, ModCmwL, PenC ENG, SingR 1, SmATA 14, TwCWr, WebE&AL, Who 74, WhoTwCL, WhoWor 74, WorAu 1950, WrDr 76, –80, –82, –84, –86, –88, –90, –92, –94*

Wright, Katrina *ConAu X, SmATA X*
Main entry: Gater, Dilys

Wright, Kenneth *AuBYP 3, ConAu 141, –X, EncSF 93, IntAu&W 91X, MajTwCW, SmATA 76, –X, TwCSFW 86, –91, Who 82, –83, –85, WrDr 84, –86, –88, –90, –92*
Main entry: DelRey, Lester

Wright, Kenneth 1915- *WrDr 94*

Wright, Kit 1944- *TwCChW 89*

Wright, Louis B 1899-1984 *BenetAL 91, BioIn 14*

Wright, Louis Booker 1899-1984 *AmAu&B, AnObit 1984, Au&Wr 71, BiE&WWA, BioIn 1, -2, -3, -8, -13, BlueB 76, ChhPo S1, ConAu 1R, -112, -1NR, CurBio 50, -84N, DcLB 17, DrAS 74H, -78H, -82H, IntAu&W 77, -82, IntWW 74, -75, -76, -77, -78, -79, -80, -81, -82, -83, NotNAT, REnAL, WhAm 8, Who 74, -82, -83, -85N, WhoAm 74, -76, -78, -80, -82, WrDr 76, -80, -82, -84*

Wright, Mabel Osgood 1859-1934 *AmAu&B, AmLY, AmWomWr, BiD&SB, CarSB, DcAmAu, DcNAA, InWom SUP, ScF&FL 92, WhAm 1*

Wright, Mary Patricia 1932- *IntAu&W 82, -86, -89, -91*

Wright, Mildred Whatley *AuBYP 2S, -3*

Wright, Nancy Means *BioIn 15, ConAu 104, DrAPF 83, -85, -87, -89, -91, -93, IntAu&W 82, -89, -91, SmATA 38, WhoUSWr 88, WhoWrEP 89, -92*

Wright, Nathan, Jr. 1923- *BioIn 9, BlkAWP, BlkWrNE, ConAu 37R, DrAS 74H, InB&W 80, -85, LivgBAA, NegAl 76, -83, -89, SelBAAf, SelBAAu, WhoBlA 75, -77, -80, WhoE 74, -75, -77*

Wright, Patricia 1932- *ConAu 65, -10NR, -26NR, WrDr 80, -82, -84, -86, -88, -90, -92*

Wright, Richard 1908-1960 *AfrAmAl 6, AfrAmW, AgeMat, Au&Arts 5, Benet 87, BenetAL 91, BioIn 14, -15, -16, -17, BlkLC, BlkWr 1, CamGEL, CamGLE, CamHAL, ConLC 48, -74, CyWA 89, DcLB 76, -102, DrBlPA 90, EncAACR, FifSWrA, LiExTwC, MagSAmL, MajTwCW, ModAL S2, NegAl 89, RAdv 13-1, RComAH, RfGAmL 87, ShSCr 2, SouBlCW, WorAlBi, WorLitC, WrPh*

Wright, Richard 1909-1960 *EarBlAP*

Wright, Richard 1944- *BioIn 15, ConGrA 2, WhoAmP 85, -87, -89, -91, -93*

Wright, Richard B 1937- *CanWW 83, -89, ConAu 85, ConLC 6, DcLB 53, IntAu&W 82, OxCCan SUP, WhoAm 80, -82, -84, WhoCanL 85, -87, -92, WorAu 1975*

Wright, Richard Nathaniel 1908-1960 *RfGShF, TwCYAW*

Wright, Robert H 1906- *AmMWSc 73P, -76P, -82, BioIn 10, ConAu 17R, SmATA 6*

Wright, Robert Hamilton *AmMWSc 86*

Wright, Wendell William 1893-1961 *BioIn 6, IndAu 1917*

Wright, Wynna *ConICB*

Wrightfrierson *SmATA X*
Main entry: Wright-Frierson, Virginia

Wright-Frierson, Virginia 1949- *BioIn 16, SmATA 58*
Pseud./variant:
Wrightfrierson

Wrightson, Alice Patricia 1921- *ChlFicS, DcChlFi, MajAI, TwCYAW, WrDr 94*

Wrightson, Patricia 1921- *AuWomWr, Au&Arts 5, AuBYP 2, -3, BioIn 8, -11, -15, -17, BlmGWL, CamGLE, ChlLR 4, -14, ConAu 45, -3NR, -19NR, -36NR, FourBJA, OxCAusL, OxCChiL, ScF&FL 92, SenS, SingR 1, SmATA 8, -66, -4AS, SouSt, TwCChW 78, -83, -89, WrDr 80, -82, -84, -86, -88, -90, -92*

Wrigley, Denis *ChhPo S1, -S2*

Wronker, Lili Cassel 1924- *BioIn 8, -11, IlsBYP, IlsCB 1957, SmATA 10*
Pseud./variant:
Cassel, Lili

Wroth, Lawrence Counselman 1884-1970 *AmAu&B, BioIn 1, -9, -10, ConAu 29R, NewYTBE 70, OxCAmL 65, REnAL, WhNAA*

Wryde, Dogear *MajAI, SmATA 70*
Main entry: Gorey, Edward St. John

Wulff, Edgun Valdemar 1913- *BioIn 5, IlsBYP, IlsCB 1946*
Pseud./variant:
Edgun

Wulff, Lee 1905- *ConAu 61, IntAu&W 89*

Wulff, Lee 1905-1991 *AnObit 1991, BioIn 17, ConAu 134, NewYTBS 91*

Wulffson, Don L 1943- *ConAu 102, -19NR, -42NR, SmATA 32*

Wunder, George 1912- *ArtCS, BioIn 1, -9*

Wunder, George 1912-1987 *EncACom*

Wunder, George S d1987 *NewYTBS 87*

Wunsch, Josephine 1914- *AuBYP 3, ConAu 34NR, SmATA 64*

Wunsch, Josephine M 1914- *IntAu&W 91, WrDr 86, -88, -90, -92, -94*

Wunsch, Josephine McLean 1914- *AuBYP 2, BioIn 8, ConAu 1R, ForWC 70, MichAu 80, WhoMW 84, WrDr 76, –80, –82, –84*

Wuorio, Eva-Lis *AuBYP 3*

Wuorio, Eva-Lis 1918- *AuBYP 2S, BioIn 9, –13, –14, ConAu 77, –40NR, CreCan 1, DcChlFi, ScF&FL 92, SmATA 28, –34, ThrBJA*

Wyatt, Edgar *AuBYP 2, –3, BioIn 7*

Wyatt, Geraldine 1907- *AuBYP 2, –3, BioIn 7*

Wyatt, Isabel *AuBYP 2, –3, BioIn 7*

Wyatt, Jane *MajAI*
Main entry: Bradbury, Bianca

Wyatt, Molly
Main entry: Bradbury, Bianca

Wyatt-Brown, Bertram 1932- *ConAu 25R, –21NR, DrAS 74H, –78H, –82H, WhoAm 76, –78, –80, –82, –84, –86, –88, –90, –92, –94, WhoUSWr 88, WhoWrEP 89, –92*

Wyckoff, James M 1918- *AuBYP 2, –3, BioIn 8, ConAu 17R, –39NR*

Wyeth, Betsy James 1921- *BioIn 15, SmATA 41, WhoE 86*

Wyeth, Newell Convers 1882-1944 *OxDcArt*

Wyeth, Newell Convers 1882-1945 *AmAu&B, ArtsAmW 3, BioIn 1, –2, –4, –5, –7, –8, –9, –10, –12, –13, –15, –17, ChhPo, –S2, ConICB, CurBio 45, ForIl, IlrAm 1880, –B, IlsBYP, JBA 34, –51, MajAI, ObitOF 79, OxCAmH, OxCChiL, REnAL, SmATA 17, WebAB 74, –79, WhAm 2, WhAmArt 85*

Wyler, Rose *AuBYP 2, BioIn 7, –9, –12, BkP, ConAu 93, SmATA 18, ThrBJA*
Main entry: Ames, Rose Wyler

Wyler, Rose 1909- *AuBYP 3*

Wylie, Betty Jane *ConAu 21NR, SmATA 48, WhoCanL 87, –92*

Wylie, Betty Jane 1931- *BioIn 16, CanWW 89, OxCCanT*

Wylie, Elinor Hoyt 1885-1928 *AmAu&B, AmWomWr, AmWr S1, AnCL, AtlBL, BioAmW, BioIn 1, –5, –8, –11, –14, –15, CasWL, Chambr 3, ChhPo, –S1, –S2, CnDAL, CnE&AP, ConAmA, ConAmL, CyWA 58, DcLEL, DcNAA, EvLB, LongCTC, ModAL, –S1, OxCAmL 65, OxCEng 67, PenC AM, RAdv 1, REn, REnAL, SixAP, Str&VC, TwCA, –SUP, TwCWr, WebAB 74, –79, WhAm 1*

Wylie, Laura *IntAu&W 91X, MajTwCW, ScF&FL 92, SmATA X, TwCRHW 90, WrDr 84, –86, –88, –90, –92*
Main entry: Matthews, Patricia

Wylie, Laura 1927- *WrDr 94*

Wyman, Andrea *ConAu 142, SmATA 75*

Wymark, Olwen *BioIn 10, ConAu 104, ConDr 73, –77, –82, IntvTCA 2, TwCChW 78, –83, WrDr 76, –80, –82, –84, –86, –88, –90, –92*

Wymark, Olwen 1929- *FemiCLE*

Wymark, Olwen 1932- *ConDr 88, TwCChW 89*

Wymark, Olwen Margaret *WrDr 94*

Wymark, Olwen Margaret 1932- *ConDr 93*

Wymer, Norman 1911- *AuBYP 2, –3, Au&Wr 71, BioIn 7, –13, ConAu 104, SmATA 25, WrDr 76, –80, –82, –84*

Wynants, Miche 1934- *BioIn 8, –14, IlsCB 1957, –1967, SmATA 31*

Wyndham, John 1903- *WorAlBi*

Wyndham, John 1903-1969 *Benet 87, BioIn 14, –17, CamGLE, ConAu X, ConLC 19, DcLEL 1940, DcNaB 1961, EncSF 93, FilmgC, HalFC 84, –88, LngCTC, NewEScF, Novels, ObitOF 79, OxCEng 85, REn, RGTwCSF, ScF&FL 92, ScFSB, TwCSFW 86, –91, TwCWr, WebE&AL, WhoSciF, WorAl, WorAu 1950*

Wyndham, Lee *AuBYP 2, ConAu 5R, –X, ForWC 70, IntAu&W 77, –82, MorJA, SmATA 1, –X, TwCChW 78, WhoE 74, WrDr 76*
Main entry: Hyndman, Jane Andrews

Wyndham, Lee 1912-1978 *AuBYP 3, BioIn 15*

Wyndham, Robert *AuBYP 2S, BioIn 9, –12, ChhPo S1, ConAu 41R, –X, SmATA X*
Main entry: Hyndman, Robert Utley

Wyndham, Robert 1906?-1973 *AuBYP 3*

Wynne, Annette 1885- *ChhPo, –S1, –S2, Str&VC*

Wynne, John Huddlestone 1743-1788 *Alf, CarSB, ChhPo, DcBiPP, DcNaB, PoIre*

Wynne, May *TwCChW 83, WhoLA, WomNov*

Wynne, May 1875- *TwCChW 89*

X-Y

Xavier, Father *ConAu X, SmATA X*
Main entry: Hurwood, Bernhardt J

Ximenes, Ben Cueller, Jr. 1911- *ConAu 5R*

Yadin, Yigael 1917-1984 *AnObit 1984, BioIn 14, –16, SmATA 55*

Yaffe, Alan *ConAu X, –38NR, IntAu&W 86X, MajAI, SmATA X*
Main entry: Yorinks, Arthur

Yakovetic 1952- *BioIn 16, SmATA 59*

Yakovetic, Joe 1952- *SmATA X*

Yalon, Reuven 1935- *WhoAmJ 80, WhoWorJ 72, –78*

Yamaguchi, John Tohr 1932- *ConAu 17R, ThrBJA*

Yamaguchi, Marianne Illenberger 1936- *BioIn 8, –9, –10, ConAu 29R, IlsBYP, IlsCB 1957, SmATA 7, ThrBJA*

Yang, Jay 1941- *BioIn 11, ConDes 84, IlsBYP, SmATA 12*

Yang, Jay 1946- *ConDes 90*

Yang, Mingyi 1943- *SmATA 72*

Yap, Weda 1894- *BioIn 5, IlsBYP, IlsCB 1946*

Yarbro, Chelsea Quinn *PenEncH*

Yarbro, Chelsea Quinn 1942- *BioIn 14, ConAu 65, –9NR, –25NR, DcAmChF 1985, EncSF 93, IntAu&W 91, NewEScF, ScF&FL 92, ScFSB, TwCRHW 90, TwCSFW 86, –91, WrDr 84, –86, –88, –90, –92, –94*

Yarbrough, Camille *ConBlAP 88*

Yarbrough, Camille 1938- *BlkWr 1, –2, ChlLR 29, ConAu 125*

Yarbrough, Camille 1948- *BioIn 16, BlkAuII, –92*

Yarbrough, Ira 1910?-1983 *BioIn 14, ConAu 110, SmATA 35N*

Yarmolinsky, Avrahm 1890-1975 *AmAu&B, Au&Wr 71, BioIn 3, –4, –8, –10, ConAu 5R, –61, –7NR, DrAS 74F, TwCA, –SUP, WhAm 6, WhNAA, WhoAm 74, WhoLibS 55, WhoWor 74, WhoWorJ 72, –78, WrDr 76*

Yaroslava
Main entry: Mills, Yaroslava Surmach

Yaroslava 1925- *BioIn 14, IlsCB 1957, –1967, SmATA X*

Yashima, Taro *AmPB, AuBYP 3, BioIn 1, –3, –5, –6, –7, –8, –12, BkP, ChhPo S2, ChlLR 4, ChsFB I, ConAu X, IlsBYP, IlsCB 1946, –1957, –1967, MajAI, MorJA, SmATA X, TwCChW 83, WorECar*
Main entry: Iwamatsu, Jun Atsushi

Yashima, Taro 1908- *BioIn 14, TwCChW 89, WrDr 86, –88, –90, –92, –94*

Yates, Brock W 1933- *WhoAm 94*

Yates, Brock Wendel 1933- *AuBYP 2, –3, BioIn 7, –9, ConAu 9R*

Yates, Elizabeth 1905- *AmAu&B, AmNov, AmWomWr, AuBYP 2, –3, Au&ICB, Au&Wr 71, BenetAL 91, BioIn 1, –2, –3, –4, –5, –7, –9, –10, –12, –14, –17, ChhPo, ConAu 13R, –6NR, –21NR, CurBio 48, HerW 84, InWom SUP, IntAu&W 77, –91, JBA 51, MajAI, MorBMP, NewbMB 1922, OxCChiL, REnAL, SmATA 4, –68, –6AS, TwCA SUP, TwCChW 78, –83, –89, TwCYAW, WhoAm 74, –76, –78, –80, –82, –84, –86, –88, –90, WhoAmW 74, WrDr 80, –82, –84, –86, –88, –90, –92, –94*

Yates, Janelle Kaye 1957- *SmATA 77*

Yates, John 1939- *SmATA 74*

Yates, Raymond F 1895-1966 *BioIn 14*

Yates, Raymond Francis 1895-1966 *AuBYP 2, –3, Au&Wr 71, BioIn 6, –7, ConAu 110, EncAB-A 38, MorJA, SmATA 31, WhAm 4*

WhNAA
Pseud./variant:
Hall, Borden
Pioneer

Yaukey, Grace Sydenstricker 1899- *AmAu&B, AmNov X, AuBYP 2, –3, BioIn 2, –8, –10, ConAu 1R, –1NR, JBA 51, SmATA 5*
Pseud./variant:
Spencer, Cornelia

Yeakley, M H *AuBYP 3*

Yeakley, Marjory Hall 1908- *ConAu 1R, –2NR, CurBio 57, IntAu&W 77, –82, SmATA 21*
Pseud./variant:
Blair, Lucile
Hall, Marjory
Morse, Carol

Yeatman, Linda 1938- *BioIn 15, ConAu 117, SmATA 42*

Yeats, Jack Butler 1871-1957 *AtlBL, BiDIrW, BioIn 1, –2, –4, –5, –6, –7, –8, –9, –12, –14, –17, CarSB, ChhPo, CnMD, ConArt 77, –83, DcBrAr 1, DcBrBI, DcIrB 88, DcIrL, DcIrW 1, DcNaB 1951, IlsCB 1744, –1946, NewC, ObitT 1951, OxCEng 85, OxDcArt, PhDcTCA 77, TwCPaSc, WorArt 1950*

Yeats, William Butler 1865-1939 *Alli SUP, AnCL, ArizL, Benet 87, BbD, BiDIrW, BiD&SB, BioIn 1, –2, –3, –4, –5, –6, –7, –8, –9, –10, –11, –12, –13, –14, –15, –16, –17, BritWr 6, CamGEL, CamGLE, CamGWoT, CasWL, Chambr 3, ChhPo, –S1, –S2, CnDBLB 5, CnE&AP, CnMD, CnMWL, CnThe, ConAu 104, –127, CyWA 58, DcEnA, –A, DcIrB 88, DcIrL, DcIrW 1, DcLB 10, –19, –98, DcLEL, DcNaB 1931, Dis&D, EncPaPR 91, EncWL, –2, EncWT, EvLB, GrBr, IntvTCA 2, LongCTC, MagSWL, MajMD 1, MajTwCW, MakMC, McGEWB, McGEWD 72, –84, ModBrL, –S1, –S2, ModIrL, ModWD, NewC, NobelP, NotNAT A, –B, OxCEng 67, –85, OxCThe 67, –83, PenC ENG, PenEncH, PlP&P, PoIre, RAdv 1, –13-1, –13-2, RComWL, REn, REnWD, RfGEnL 91, TwCA, –SUP, TwCLC 1, –11, –18, –31, TwCWr, WebE&AL, WhDW, WhoNob, –90, WhoTwCL, WorAlBi, WorAl, WorLitC, WrPh*

Yee, Paul 1956- *ConAu 135, DcChlFi, SmATA 67*

Yee, Paul R 1956- *WrDr 94*

Yefremov, Ivan 1907- *WhoSciF*

Yefremov, Ivan 1907-1972 *TwCSFW 86A, –91A*

Yefremov, Ivan Antonovich 1907-1972 *EncSF 93*

Yektai, Niki *AuBYP 3*

Yensid, Retlaw *ConAu X, SmATA X*
Main entry: Disney, Walt

Yeo, Wilma 1918- *BioIn 13, ConAu 25R, SmATA 24*

Yeoman, John 1934- *Au&Wr 71, BioIn 13, ConAu 106, SmATA 28*

Yep, Laurence *BioIn 14, –15, –16, –17*

Yep, Laurence 1948- *Au&Arts 5, ChlLR 17, DcLB 52, NewEScF, ScF&FL 92, ScFSB, TwCChW 89, TwCSFW 86, –91, WrDr 86, –88, –90, –92*

Yep, Laurence Michael 1948- *BioIn 10, ChlLR 3, ConAu 49, –1NR, ConLC 35, DcAmChF 1960, EncSF 93, FifBJA, MajAI, SmATA 7, –69, TwCChW 83, TwCYAW, WhoAm 78, –80, –82, –84, –86, –88, –90, –92, –94, WhoWest 94, WrDr 84, –94*

Yepsen, Roger B *BioIn 16*

Yepsen, Roger B, Jr. 1947- *ConAu 35NR, SmATA 59*

Yerby, Frank G 1916- *BlkWr 1, MajTwCW*

Yerby, Frank Garvin 1916- *AmAu&B, AmNov, Au&Wr 71, BioIn 1, –2, –3, –4, –5, –7, –9, BlkAWP, CivR 74, ConAu 9R, –16NR, ConLC 1, –22, ConNov 72, CurBio 46, EncSoH, InB&W 80, –85, IntAu&W 77, –89, –91, IntWW 74, –79, –80, –81, –82, –83, –89, –91, LivgBAA, LongCTC, PenC AM, SelBAAu, TwCA SUP, WebAB 74, –79, Who 74, –82, –83, –85, –88, –90, –92, WhoAm 74, –76, –78, WhoBlA 75, –77, –90, –92, WorAl, WrDr 76, –80*

Yerby, Frank Garvin 1916-1991 *ConAu 136, WhoBlA 94N*

Yerian, Cameron John *BioIn 12, ConAu 73, MichAu 80, SmATA 21*

Yerian, Margaret A *BioIn 12, ConAu 73, MichAu 80, SmATA 21*

Yerkow, Charles *AuBYP 3*

Yerkow, Charles 1912- *AuBYP 2S*

Yetska *SmATA X*
Main entry: Ironside, Jetske

Yezback, Steven A 1943- *AuBYP 2, –3*

Yezzo, Domoinick 1947- *ConAu 53*

Ylla *AmPB, AuBYP 3, ICPEnP A, MorJA*
Main entry: Koffler, Camilla

Yocom, Charles Frederick *AmMWSc 89*

Yocom, Charles Frederick 1914- *AmMWSc 73P, –76P, –82, –86, ConAu 17R, –7NR, WhoWest 82, –84*

Yolen, Jane *BioIn 14, ConSFF*

Yolen, Jane 1939- *Au&Arts 4, AuBYP 3, ConAu 29NR, DcLB 52, EncSF 93, IntAu&W 89, –91, ScF&FL 92, ScFSB, TwCChW 89, TwCSFW 91, WhoWrEP 89, WrDr 86, –88, –90, –92, –94*

Yolen, Jane H 1939- *AuBYP 2, BioIn 8, –9, –13, ChhPo S2, ChlLR 4, ConAu 13R, –11NR, ForWC 70, FourBJA, SmATA 4, –40, –1AS, TwCChW 78, –83, WhoAm 78, –80, –82, –84, WhoAmW 83, WrDr 80, –82, –84*

Yolen, Jane Hyatt 1939- *DcAmChF 1985, MajAI, SmATA 75, TwCYAW, WhoAm 86, –88, –90, –92, –94, WhoWrEP 92*

Yonge, Charlotte 1823-1901 *BlmGWL, ContDcW 89, FemiCLE, RfGEnL 91, TwCChW 89A, TwCLC 48*

Yonge, Charlotte M 1823-1901 *CamGEL, CamGLE*

Yonge, Charlotte Mary 1823-1901 *Alli, –SUP, ArtclWW 2, BbD, BiD&SB, BioIn 1, –3, –6, –8, –9, –12, –13, –16, BlmGEL, BritAu 19, CarSB, CasWL, CelCen, Chambr 3, ChhPo S1, ConAu 109, DcBiA, DcBiPP, DcEnA, –A, DcEnL, DcEuL, DcLB 18, DcLEL, DcNaB S2, Dis&D, EncBrWW, EvLB, FamSYP, InWom SUP, IntDcWB, JBA 34, LongCEL, NewC, Novels, OxCChiL, OxCEng 67, –85, PenC ENG, REn, SmATA 17, StaCVF, TelT, TwCChW 78A, –83A, WhoChL, WomNov, WrChl*

Yoo, Grace S
Main entry: Yoo, Young Hyun

Yoo, Young Hyun 1927- *BiDrLUS 70, ConAu 41R, IntAu&W 77, –82, WhoSSW 73, –82, –84, WhoWor 84, –87, –89*
Pseud./variant:
Yoo, Grace S

Yorick *OhA&B*
Main entry: Hodgson, Ralph

Yorinks, Arthur 1953- *BioIn 14, –16, –17, ChlLR 20, ConAu 106, –38NR, IntAu&W 86, MajAI, SixBJA, SmATA 33, –49*
Pseud./variant:
Yaffe, Alan

York, Andrew *ConAu X, ConNov 72, –76, –82, DcLEL 1940, IntAu&W 77X, –82X, –91X, SmATA 5, TwCCr&M 80, –85, WhoSpyF, WrDr 76, –80, –82, –84, –86, –88, –90, –92*
Main entry: Nicole, Christopher Robin

York, Andrew 1930- *BioIn 14, TwCCr&M 91, WrDr 94*

York, Carol 1928- *AuBYP 3*

York, Carol Beach 1928- *AuBYP 2S, BioIn 10, ConAu 1R, –6NR, FifBJA, ForWC 70, ScF&FL 92, SmATA 6, –77*

York, Jeremy *ConAu X, EncMys, LongCTC, MajTwCW, TwCCr&M 80, –85, –91, WhoSpyF*

York, Rebecca
Main entry: Buckholtz, Eileen
Buckholtz, Eileen Garber

York, Simon *AuBYP 3, MajAI, MajTwCW, SmATA 69*
Main entry: Heinlein, Robert A

Yorke, Ritchie Ian 1944- *ConAu 77, IntAu&W 77, WrDr 76, –80, –82, –84, –86, –88, –90, –92, –94*

Yoshida, Toshi 1911- *SmATA 77*

Yost, Edna 1889-1971 *AuBYP 2, –3, BioIn 1, –7, –13, ConAu 1R, –103, SmATA 26N*

Youd, Christopher Samuel 1922- *MajAI*

Youd, Samuel 1922- *BioIn 10, ConAu 77, SmATA 30, –47, –6AS, WorAu 1950*
Pseud./variant:
Christopher, John
Ford, Hilary
Godfrey, William
Nichols, Peter
Rye, Anthony

Young, Andrew Sturgeon Nash 1924- *BioIn 16, BlkAull, –92, InB&W 80, –85, LivgBAA, WhoBlA 75, –77*

Young, Astrid *OxCCan SUP*

Young, Bernice Elizabeth 1931- *AuBYP 2S, –3, BioIn 16, BlkAull, –92, ConAu 37R, SelBAAf, SelBAAu, WhoAmW 75, –77, WrDr 76, –80, –82, –84, –86, –88, –90*

Young, Bob *BioIn 7, ConAu X, SmATA 3*
Main entry: Young, Robert W

Young, Chesley Virginia 1919- *WrDr 86, –88, –90, –92*

Young, Chesley Virginia Barnes 1919- *ASCAP 66, ConAu 33R, IntAu&W 77, WhoAmW 74, –75, –77, –81, WhoE 74, –75, –77, –81, WrDr 76, –80, –82, –84, –94*

Young, Chic *ArtCS, BioIn 1, –3, –9, ConAu X, NewYTBE 73, ObitOF 79, WebAB 74, –79, WhAm 5, –6, WhoAm 74, WhoAmA 78N, –80N, –82N*
Main entry: Young, Murat Bernard Chic

Young, Chic 1901- *WhoAmA 86N*

Young, Chic 1901-1973 *EncACom, EncTwCJ, WhoAmA 89N, –91N*

Young, Chip *OxCCan SUP*

Young, Clarence *ConAu P-2, MajAI, SmATA 1, –67, WebAB 74*
Main entry: Stratemeyer, Edward L

Young, Delbert A 1907-1975 *ConAu 105, OxCCan SUP, TwCChW 78*

Young, Desmond 1892-1966 *BioIn 6, –7, WhScrn 83, –77, WhoHol B*

Young, Dorothea Bennett 1924- *BioIn 14, ConAu 13R, –13NR, SmATA 31*
Pseud./variant:
Bennett, Dorothea

Young, Ed *ChlBIlD*

Young, Ed 1931- *BioIn 9, –11, ChhPo S1, ChlLR 27, ConAu 116, –130, IlsBYP, IlsCB 1967, SmATA 10, ThrBJA*

Young, Ed Tse-chun 1931- *MajAI, SmATA 74, WrDr 94*

Young, Edward *AuBYP 2, –3, ConAu X, SmATA 3*
Main entry: Reinfeld, Fred

Young, Egerton Ryerson 1840-1909 *DcLEL, DcNAA, EncWM, OxCCan, OxCCanL, OxCChiL*

Young, Elaine L *ConAu X, –28NR, SmATA X*
Main entry: Schulte, Elaine Louise

Young, Eleanor R 1918- *WrDr 86, –88*

Young, Eleanor Robbins 1918- *ConAu 37R, IntAu&W 82, WhoAmW 75, –77, –81, WrDr 76, –80, –82, –84*

Young, Ella 1867?-1956 *AmWomWr, AnCL, AuBYP 2, –3, BioIn 2, –4, –7, –14, ChhPo, –S1, –S2, JBA 34, –51, ObitOF 79, ScF&FL 92, TwCA, –SUP*

Young, Ernest 1869- *CarSB*

Young, Evelyn *AmPB*

Young, Frederica *AuBYP 2, –3, BioIn 8*

Young, Jan *AuBYP 3, WrDr 86, –88, –90, –92*

Young, Jan 1919- *WrDr 94*

Young, Janet Randall *AuBYP 3*

Young, Janet Randall 1919- *AuBYP 2, BioIn 7, –9, ConAu 5R, –5NR, ForWC 70, IntAu&W 77, –82, SmATA 3, WhoAmW 75, WrDr 76, –80, –82, –84, –86, –88, –90, –92, –94*
Pseud./variant:
Randall, Janet

Young, John Richard *AuBYP 2, –3, BioIn 7*

Young, Judy Elaine Dockrey 1949- *SmATA 72*

Young, Lois 1911-1981 *AuBYP 3*

Young, Lois Horton 1911-1981 *AuBYP 2S, ConAu 9R, SmATA 26*

Young, Louise B 1919- *SmATA 64, WrDr 86, –88, –90, –92, –94*

Young, Louise Buchwalter 1919- *ConAu 25R, –10NR, IntAu&W 77, WhoMW 84, WrDr 76, –80, –82, –84*

Young, Margaret B 1922- *BioIn 16, BlkAuII, –92*

Young, Margaret Buckner *WhoAm 92, –94, WhoAmW 89, –91, –93, WhoBlA 85, –88, –90, –92, –94, WhoE 86, –89, –91, –93, WhoWor 87, –89, –91*

Young, Margaret Buckner 1922- *BioIn 9, BkP, ConAu 21R, InB&W 80, –85, SelBAAf, SelBAAu, SmATA 2, WhoAmW 74, –75, –83, WhoBlA 75, –77, –80, –85, WhoE 74, –75, –77, –81, –85*

Young, Marjabelle *AuBYP 2S, –3*

Young, Miriam 1913-1974 *AuBYP 2, –3, BioIn 7, –10, ConAu 37R, –53, NewYTBS 74, SmATA 7, WrDr 76, –80*

Young, Morris N 1909- *WrDr 86, –88, –90, –92, –94*

Young, Morris Nathan 1909- *AmMWSc 73P, –76P, –82, –86, –89, –92, BioIn 8, ConAu 33R, WhoE 77, WrDr 76, –80, –82, –84*

Young, Murat Bernard Chic 1901-1973 *ConAu 41R, WebAB 74, –79*
Pseud./variant:
Young, Chic

Young, Noela 1930- *BioIn 12, IlsCB 1967*

Young, Patrick *AuBYP 3, IntAu&W 86X*

Young, Patrick 1937- *AuBYP 2, BioIn 8, -11, -13, ConAu 69, SmATA 22, WhoAm 92, -94*

Young, Percy M 1912- *BioIn 14, ConAu 31NR*

Young, Percy Marshall 1912- *AuBYP 2, -3, Au&Wr 71, Baker 84, -92, BioIn 8, ConAu 13R, IntWWM 90, OxCMus, SmATA 31, WhoMus 72*
Pseud./variant:
Marshall, Percy

Young, Richard Alan 1946- *SmATA 72*

Young, Robert W 1916-1969 *AuBYP 2, BioIn 8, -9, ConAu 5R, -5NR, SmATA 3*
Pseud./variant:
Randall, Janet
Young, Bob

Young, Robert William 1916-1969 *AuBYP 3*

Young, Ruth *BioIn 17*

Young, Ruth 1946- *ConAu 136, SmATA 67, WrDr 94*

Young, Scott A 1918- *ConAu 20NR*

Young, Scott Alexander 1918- *BioIn 10, CaW, CanWW 79, -80, -81, -83, -89, ConAu 9R, -5NR, IntAu&W 91, OxCCan, -SUP, SmATA 5, TwCChW 78, WhoAm 74, -76, -78, -80, -82, -84, -86, -88, -90, -92, -94, WrDr 80*

Young, Stanley 1906-1975 *AuBYP 3, BioIn 14*

Young, Virginia Brady *DrAPF 87, -89, -91, -93, WhoE 89*

Young, Virginia Brady 1918- *WhoUSWr 88, WhoWrEP 89, -92*

Young, Virginia Brady 1921- *ConAu 61, DrAP 75, DrAPF 83, -85, IntAu&W 82*

Young, Vivien *ConAu X, SmATA X*
Main entry: Gater, Dilys

Youngs, Betty 1934-1985 *BioIn 12, -15, -16, ConAu 117, IlsCB 1967, SmATA 42N, -53*

Youngs, Betty F 1928- *WrDr 86, -88, -90, -92, -94*

Youngs, Betty Ferrell 1928- *ConAu 33R, WhoAmW 75, -77, -81, WrDr 76, -82, -84*

Younkin, Paula 1942- *SmATA 77*

Yount, John Thomas 1927- *WhoSSW 75*

Yount, Lisa 1944- *ConAu 141, SmATA 74*

Yudell, Lynn D 1943- *ConAu 29R*

Yuditskaya, Tatyana 1964- *SmATA 75*

Yue, Charlotte *AuBYP 3*

Yue, David *AuBYP 3*

Yuill, Phyllis Jean 1941- *ConAu 65*

Yuki *ConAu X*
Main entry: Inoue, Yukitoshi

Yukich, Joseph E *AmMWSc 92*

Yukio, Takeda 1927- *WhoWor 93*

Yurchenco, Henrietta 1916- *AuBYP 2S, ConAu 37R, ForWC 70, WhoAm 74*

Yurchenco, Henrietta Weiss 1916- *WhoAm 86, -90, -92, -94*

Yurchenko, Henrietta 1916- *AuBYP 3*

Z

Zabransky, Adolf 1909- *BioIn 8, IlsCB 1957, WhoGrA 62*

Zach, Cheryl 1947- *BioIn 16, SmATA 51, –58*
Pseud./variant:
Cole, Jennifer

Zacharis, John C 1936- *ConAu 73*

Zachary, Hugh *EncSF 93, ScF&FL 92, TwCSFW 91*

Zachary, Hugh 1928- *ConAu 21R, –13NR, IntAu&W 77, –91, WhoSSW 73, –75, –76, WrDr 76, –80, –82, –84, –90, –92, –94*
Pseud./variant:
Hughes, Zach

Zacks, Irene *AuBYP 2, –3, BioIn 8*

Zaffo, George J d1984 *AmPB, AuBYP 2, –3, BioIn 7, SmATA 42*
Pseud./variant:
Stewart, Scott

Zagoren, Ruby 1922-1974 *AuBYP 2, –3, ConAu P-1, ForWC 70, WhoAmW 74*

Zaid, Barry 1938- *SmATA 51*

Zaidenberg, Arthur 1908?- *AmAu&B, AuBYP 2, –2S, BioIn 7, ConAu 108, SmATA 34, WhoAm 74, –76, –78, –80, –82, –84, WhoAmA 78, –80, –82*
Pseud./variant:
Azaid

Zaidenberg, Arthur 1908?-1990 *AuBYP 3, BioIn 16, –17, ConAu 131, SmATA 66*
Pseud./variant:
Azaid

Zalben, Jane Breskin *DrAPF 89, –91, –93, WrDr 90, –92*

Zalben, Jane Breskin 1950- *BioIn 10, ConAu 49, –4NR, DrAPF 83, –85, FifBJA, SmATA 7, TwCYAW, WhoWrEP 89, –92, WrDr 76, –80, –82, –84*

Zallinger, Jean Day 1918- *BioIn 8, –12, IlsBYP, IlsCB 1957, –1967, SmATA 14, WhoAmA 78, –80, –82, –84, –91*

Zallinger, Peter Franz 1943- *SmATA 49*

Zambreno, Mary Frances 1954- *ConAu 142, ScF&FL 92, SmATA 75*
Pseud./variant:
Tallis, Robyn

Zander, Hans 1905- *WhoMus 72*

Zanger, Jack 1926?-1970 *BioIn 8*

Zappler, Lisbeth 1930- *AuBYP 2S, –3, BioIn 11, ConAu 49, –4NR, SmATA 10*

Zapun, Simone *AuBYP 2S, –3*

Zarchy, Harry 1912- *AuBYP 2, –3, BioIn 6, –7, ConAu 1R, –2NR, MorJA, SmATA 34*
Pseud./variant:
Lewis, Roger

Zarem, Lewis *AuBYP 2, –3, BioIn 7, EncSF 93*

Zarif, Margaret Min'imah d1983 *MichAu 80, SmATA 33*
Pseud./variant:
Jones, Margaret Boone

Zaring, Jane 1936- *BioIn 16, ConAu 108, SmATA 40, –51*

Zarins, Joyce Audy 1949- *BioIn 16, ConAu 136, SmATA 57, WrDr 94*
Pseud./variant:
Dos Santos, Joyce Audy 1949-

Zaslavsky, Claudia 1917- *ConAu 1NR, SmATA 36*

Zastrow, Erika *ConAu X*
Main entry: Massey, Erika

Zaturenska, Marya 1902-1982 *AmWomWr, AnObit 1982, BenetAL 91, BioIn 4, –11, –12, –17, ChhPo, CnDAL, ConAu 13R, –105, ConLC 6, –11, ConPo 70, –75, –80, DrAP 75, FemiCLE, ForWC 70, InWom SUP, NewYTBS 82, OxCAmL 65, –83, PenC AM,*

REn, REnAL, SixAP, TwCA, –SUP, WhAm 8, WhoAm 74, –76, –78, –80, WhoAmW 74, –75, –77, WhoPolA, WrDr 76, –80, –82

Zebra, A *SmATA 72*
Main entry: Scoltock, Jack

Zebrowski, George *DrAPF 89, –91, –93*

Zebrowski, George 1945- *BioIn 12, –17, ConAu 41R, –30NR, DcLB 8, DrAF 76, EncSF 93, NewEScF, ScF&FL 92, SmATA 67, TwCSFW 91, WrDr 84, –90, –92, –94*

Zechlin, Ruth Hedwig Conradine 1899- *Au&Wr 71*

Zeck, Gerald Anthony 1939- *ConAu 114, SmATA 40*
Pseud./variant:
Zeck, Gerry
Zupa, G Anthony

Zeck, Gerry
Main entry: Zeck, Gerald Anthony

Zed, Dr *SmATA 66*

Zei, Alki *AuBYP 3, TwCChW 89B*

Zei, Alki 1925- *BlmGWL*

Zei, Alki 1928- *AuBYP 2, BioIn 13, ChlLR 6, ConAu 77, FourBJA, SmATA 24, TwCChW 78B, –83B*

Zeiger, Henry Anthony 1930- *AuBYP 2, –3, ConAu 9R*
Pseud./variant:
Peterson, James

Zeiger, Sophia 1926- *BioIn 5, –8, IlsBYP, IlsCB 1946, –1957*
Pseud./variant:
Sofia

Zelazny, Roger *BioIn 16, –17, ConSFF, DrAPF 89, –91, –93*

Zelazny, Roger 1937- *Au&Arts 7, BioIn 12, –13, ConLC 21, DcLB 8, DrAPF 83, –85, IntAu&W 82, MajTwCW, NewEScF, Novels, RGTwCSF, ScF&FL 92, SmATA 39, –57, SupFW, TwCSFW 91, WhoAm 82, –84, WorAlBi, WorAl, WrDr 82, –84, –90, –92*
Pseud./variant:
Denmark, Harrison

Zelazny, Roger Joseph 1937- *EncSF 93*

Zelazny, Roger Joseph Christopher 1937- *WrDr 94*

Zelinsky, Paul O *AuBYP 3, BioIn 16, –17, ChlBIlD, SmATA 33*

Zelinsky, Paul O 1953- *ConAu 38NR, MajAI, SixBJA, SmATA 49, WhoAm 94*

Zellan, Audrey Penn 1950- *ConAu 77, –X, SmATA 22*

Zemach, Harve *AmAu&B, AmPB, AuBYP 2, BioIn 9, –10, ConAu X, SmATA 3, ThrBJA, WhAm 7, WhoAm 74, –76, –78*
Main entry: Fischtrom, Harvey

Zemach, Harve 1933-1974 *AuBYP 3*

Zemach, Kaethe 1958- *ConAu 57, –8NR, SmATA 39, –49*

Zemach, Margot *BioIn 16, –17*
Main entry: Fischtrom, Margot Zemach

Zemach, Margot 1931- *AmPB, BioIn 8, –9, –10, –11, –12, ConAu 97, HerW 84, IlsBYP, IlsCB 1957, –1967, NewbC 1966, OxCChiL, SmATA 21, ThrBJA, WhoAm 74, –76, –78, –80, –82, –84, WhoAmW 74*
Pseud./variant:
Fischtrom, Margot Zemach

Zemach, Margot 1931-1989 *AnObit 1989, ChlBIlD, ConAu 128, –38NR, MajAI, NewYTBS 89, SmATA 59, –70, WhAm 10*

Zens, Patricia Martin 1926-1972 *SmATA 50*

Zeoli, William Judson 1932- *BioIn 10, WhoAm 76, –78, WhoMW 74, –76, –78, –82, WhoRel 75, –77, WhoWor 78*

Zerman, Melvyn Bernard 1930- *SmATA 46*

Zettner, Pat 1940- *SmATA 70*

Zidel, Paul 1936- *DcLB 52*

Ziefert, Harriet *AuBYP 3*

Ziegler, Jack 1942- *BioIn 17, SmATA 60, WhoAm 90*

Ziegler, Jack Denmore 1942- *WhoAm 94*

Ziegler, Ursina *AuBYP 2, –3*

Ziel, Ron 1939- *ConAu 21R*

Ziemer, Edna Ericka Wilson 1899- *WhoAmW 74*

Ziemer, Gregor Athalwin 1899- *BioIn 1, ConAu P-1, CurBio 42, WhoAm 76, –78*

Ziemian, Joseph 1922-1971 *ConAu 65*

Ziemienski, Dennis 1947- *BioIn 11, SmATA 10*

Zillah *ConAu X, IntWWP 82X, SmATA X, WhNAA*
Main entry: Macdonald, Zillah K

Zim, Herbert S 1909- *WrDr 90, -92*

Zim, Herbert Spencer 1909- *AmAu&B, AmPB, AuBYP 2, -3, Au&Wr 71, BioIn 2, -3, -4, -7, -9, BlueB 76, BkP, ChlLR 2, ConAu 13R, -17NR, CurBio 56, JBA 51, MajAI, SmATA 1, -30, -2AS, WhoAm 74, -76, -78, -80, -82, -84, -90, -92, -94, WrDr 80, -82, -84, -94*

Zim, Sonia Bleeker *ConAu 1R, -33R, -3NR, SmATA X*
Main entry: Bleeker, Sonia

Zimelman, Nathan *AuBYP 2, -3, BioIn 17, SmATA 37*

Zimelman, Nathan 1921- *ConAu 133, SmATA 65, WrDr 94*

Zimmer, Dirk *BioIn 16, -17*

Zimmer, Dirk 1943- *SixBJA, SmATA 65*

Zimmerman, Eleanor 1916- *ConAu 61*

Zimmerman, Naoma 1914- *BioIn 2, -11, ConAu 1R, ForWC 70, SmATA 10, WhoAmW 77, WrDr 76, -80, -82, -84, -90, -92, -94*

Zimmerman, Paul Lionel 1932- *ConAu 25R, -10NR*

Zimmerman, Velma E 1902- *ConAu 29R*

Zimmermann, Arnold E 1909- *SmATA 58*

Zimmy *MajAI*

Zimnik, Reiner *TwCChW 89B*

Zimnik, Reiner 1930- *AuBYP 2S, -3, BioIn 5, -8, -9, -10, ChlLR 3, ChsFB I, ConAu 77, IlsBYP, IlsCB 1946, -1957, -1967, OxCChiL, SmATA 36, ThrBJA, TwCChW 78B, -83B, WhoGrA 82, WorECar*

Zindel, Bonnie 1943- *ConAu 105, -31NR, IntAu&W 91, SmATA 34, WhoAmW 85, WhoEnt 92*

Zindel, Paul *BioIn 16, -17*

Zindel, Paul 1936- *AuBYP 2, -3, BenetAL 91, BioIn 9, -10, -11, -12, CamGWoT, CelR, ChlLR 3, CnThe, ConAu 73, -31NR, ConDr 73, -77, -82, -93, ConLC 6, -26, CurBio 73, DcAmChF 1960, DcLB 7, DcLEL 1940, FifBJA, IntAu&W 91, MagSAmL, MajAI, MajTwCW, McGEWD 72, -84, NatPD 77, -81, NotNAT, OxCAmL 83, OxCChiL, SmATA 16, -58, TwCChW 78, -83, -89, TwCYAW, WhoAm 74, -76, -78, -80, -82, -84, -90, -92, -94, WhoThe 72, -77, -81, WhoWrEP 89, -92, WorAlBi, WorAl, WrDr 76, -80, -82, -84, -90, -92, -94*

Ziner, Florence Feenie Katz 1921- *AuBYP 2, BioIn 7, -10, ConAu 1R, ForWC 70, SmATA 5*

Ziner, Florence Katz 1921- *AuBYP 3*

Zingara, Professor *ConAu 73*
Main entry: Leeming, Joseph

Zinkin, Taya 1918- *ConAu 1R, IntAu&W 77, -82, WrDr 76, -80, -82, -84, -90, -92, -94*

Zinkoff, Dave *AuBYP 2, -3, BioIn 7*

Zinsser, Hans 1878-1940 *AmAu&B, BenetAL 91, BioIn 1, -2, -3, -4, -5, -7, -9, -10, CurBio 40, DcAmMeB 84, DcNAA, DcScB, InSci, LongCTC, REnAL, TwCA, -SUP, WebAB 74, -79, WhAm 1*

Zinsser, William Knowlton 1922- *AmAu&B, BioIn 5, -6, -13, ConAu 17R, DcLEL 1940, WhoAm 74, -76, -78, -80, -82, -84, -90, -92, -94*

Zion, Eugene 1913-1975 *AmPB, AuBYP 2, Au&Wr 71, BioIn 6, -7, -10, ConAu 61, -81, MorJA, SmATA 18, TwCChW 78, WhoE 75, WrDr 76*
Pseud./variant:
Zion, Gene

Zion, Gene
Main entry: Zion, Eugene

Zion, Gene 1913-1975 *AuBYP 3, BioIn 12, OxCChiL, TwCChW 83, -89*

Zipes, Jack David 1937- *ConAu 65, DrAS 74H, -78F, -82F, WhoMW 92*

Zirbes, Laura *AuBYP 3*

Zirbes, Laura 1884- *AuBYP 2, BioIn 7*

Zistel, Era *ConAu 25R, -41NR*

Zollinger, Gulielma 1856-1917 *BioIn 2, -13, ChhPo, ConAu 109, DcAmAu, DcNAA, JBA 34, -51, SmATA 27, WhAm 1*
Pseud./variant:
Gladwin, William Zachary

Zolotow, Charlotte 1915- *AuBYP 3, BioIn 17, DcLB 52, IntAu&W 91, TwCChW 89, WrDr 90, -92, -94*

Zolotow, Charlotte Shapiro 1915- *AmPB, AmWomWr, AuBYP 2, BioIn 6, -7, -9, -10, -13, BkP, ChlLR 2, ConAu 5R, -3NR, -18NR, -38NR, ForWC 70, IntAu&W 77, MajAI,*

MichAu 80, MorJA, OxCChiL, PiP, SmATA 1, –35, TwCChW 78, –83, WhoAm 76, –78, –80, –82, –84, –90, –92, –94, WhoAmW 74, –75, –77, –81, –83, –85, –91, –93, WhoWrEP 89, –92, WrDr 76, –80, –82, –84
Pseud./variant:
Bookman, Charlotte

Zonia, Dhimitri 1921- *AmArt, BioIn 12, SmATA 20, WhoAmA 78, –80, –82, –84, –91, WhoMW 78, –84*

Zubrowski, Bernard 1939- *ConAu 104, SmATA 35*

Zudeck, Darryl 1961- *SmATA 61*

Zudeck, Darryl S 1961- *BioIn 17*

Zuelke, Ruth Evelyn 1924- *ConAu 13R, ForWC 70*

Zulli, Floyd, Jr. 1922-1980 *BioIn 4, –5, –12, ConAu 37R, –108, CurBio 58, –81N, DrAS 74F, –78F, WhoE 75*

Zumwalt, Eva 1936- *ConAu 65, –9NR*

Zupa, G Anthony *ConAu X, SmATA X*
Main entry: Zeck, Gerald Anthony

Zurhorst, Charles 1913- *BioIn 11, ConAu 45, –1NR, SmATA 12*
Pseud./variant:
Stewart, Charles

Zuromskis, Diane *ConAu X, –32NR, SmATA X*
Main entry: Stanley, Diane

Zvirin, Stephanie *MedPD*

Zweifel, Frances W 1931- *ConAu 73, –12NR, SmATA 14*

Zwerger, Lisbeth *BioIn 16, –17*

Zwerger, Lisbeth 1954- *MajAI, SixBJA, SmATA 66, –13AS*

Zwilgmeyer, Dikken 1853-1913 *EncCoWW*

Zwilgmeyer, Dikken 1859-1913 *BioIn 2, JBA 34, –51*

Zwinger, Ann 1925- *SmATA 46*

KEY TO SOURCE CODES

BlkAWP Black American Writers Past and Present
BlkAuIl Black Authors and Illustrators of Children's Books
BlkLC Black Literature Criticism
BlkWWr Black Women Writers (1950-1980)
BlkWr Black Writers
BlkWrNE Black Writers in New England
BlksAmF Blacks in American Films and Television
BlksScM Blacks in Science and Medicine
BlmGEL The Bloomsbury Guide to English Literature
BlmGWL The Bloomsbury Guide to Women's Literature
BlueB The Blue Book
BkC The Book of Catholic Authors
BkCL A Book of Children's Literature
BkIE Book Illustrators in Eighteenth-Century England
BkP Books Are by People
BriB Brilliant Bylines
BriEAA The Britannica Encyclopedia of American Art
BritAS British and American Sporting Authors: Their Writings and Biographies
BritAu British Authors before 1800
BritCA British Children's Authors
BritWr British Writers
BroV Broadening Views, 1968-1988
BroadAu Broadside Authors and Artists
BusPN Business People in the News
Cald Caldecott Medal Books: 1938-1957
CamGEL The Cambridge Guide to English Literature
CamGLE The Cambridge Guide to Literature in English
CamGWoT The Cambridge Guide to World Theatre
CamHAL The Cambridge Handbook of American Literature
CaW Canada Writes!
CanNov Canadian Novelists, 1920-1945
CanWW Canadian Who's Who
CanWr Canadian Writers
CarSB The Carolyn Sherwin Bailey Historical Collection of Children's Books
CasWL Cassell's Encyclopaedia of World Literature
CathA Catholic Authors
CelCen Celebrities of the Century
CelR Celebrity Register
CenC A Century of Ceramics in the United States, 1878-1978
Chambr Chambers's Cyclopaedia of English Literature
ChiLit Chicano Literature: A Reference Guide
ChiSch Chicano Scholars and Writers
ChhPo Childhood in Poetry
ChlBIID Children's Book Illustration and Design
ChlFicS Children's Fiction Sourcebook
ChlLR Children's Literature Review
ChrP The Children's Poets
ChsFB The Child's First Books
CivR Civil Rights: A Current Guide to the People, Organizations, and Events
CivWDc The Civil War Dictionary
ClaDrA The Classified Directory of Artists' Signatures, Symbols, & Monograms
ClDMEL Columbia Dictionary of Modern European Literature
CmCal A Companion to California
CmMov A Companion to the Movies: From 1903 to the Present Day
CmScLit Companion to Scottish Literature
CmpEPM The Complete Encyclopedia of Popular Music and Jazz, 1900-1950
CompSN Composers since 1900
CpmDNM Composium Directory of New Music
CnDAL Concise Dictionary of American Literature
CnDBLB Concise Dictionary of British Literary Biography
CnE&AP The Concise Encyclopedia of English and American Poets and Poetry
CnMD The Concise Encyclopedia of Modern Drama
CnMWL The Concise Encyclopedia of Modern World Literature
CnThe A Concise Encyclopedia of the Theatre
CngDr Congressional Directory
ConAmA Contemporary American Authors
ConAmC Contemporary American Composers
ConAmL Contemporary American Literature
ConAmTC Contemporary American Theater Critics
ConAmWS Contemporary American Women Sculptors
ConArt Contemporary Artists
ConAu Contemporary Authors
ConBlAP Contemporary Black American Playwrights and Their Plays
ConBlB Contemporary Black Biography
ConBrA Contemporary British Artists
ConCom Contemporary Composers
ConDes Contemporary Designers
ConDr Contemporary Dramatists
ConFLW Contemporary Foreign Language Writers
ConGAN Contemporary Gay American Novelists
ConGrA Contemporary Graphic Artists
ConHero Contemporary Heroes and Heroines
ConICB Contemporary Illustrators of Children's Books
ConIsC Contemporary Issues Criticism
ConLC Contemporary Literary Criticism
ConLCrt Contemporary Literary Critics
ConMus Contemporary Musicians
ConNews Contemporary Newsmakers
ConNov Contemporary Novelists
ConPhot Contemporary Photographers
ConPo Contemporary Poets
ConSFA Contemporary Science Fiction Authors
ConSFF Contemporary Science Fiction, Fantasy, and Horror Poetry
ConTFT Contemporary Theatre, Film, and Television
ConWorW Contemporary World Writers
ContDcW The Continuum Dictionary of Women's Biography
Conv Conversations
CorpD Corpus Delicti of Mystery Fiction
CreCan Creative Canada
CrtSuMy Critical Survey of Mystery and Detective Fiction
CrtT The Critical Temper
CroCAP Crowell's Handbook of Contemporary American Poetry
CroCD Crowell's Handbook of Contemporary Drama
CroE&S Crowell's Handbook of Elizabethan & Stuart Literature
CurBio Current Biography Yearbook
CyAG Cyclopedia of American Government
CyAL Cyclopaedia of American Literature
CyEd A Cyclopedia of Education
CyWA Cyclopedia of World Authors
DcAfHiB Dictionary of African Historical Biography
DcAfAmP Dictionary of Afro-American Performers
DcAfL Dictionary of Afro-Latin American Civilization
DcAmAu A Dictionary of American Authors
DcAmB Dictionary of American Biography
DcAmBC Dictionary of American Book Collectors
DcAmChF Dictionary of American Children's Fiction
DcAmDH Dictionary of American Diplomatic History
DcAmImH Dictionary of American Immigration History
DcAmMeB Dictionary of American Medical Biography
DcAmNB Dictionary of American Negro Biography
DcAmReB Dictionary of American Religious Biography
DcAmSR A Dictionary of American Social Reform
DcBiA A Dictionary of Biographies of Authors Represented in the Authors Digest Series
DcBiPP A Dictionary of Biography, Past and Present
DcBrAmW A Dictionary of British and American Women Writers, 1660-1800
DcBrAr Dictionary of British Artists Working 1900-1950

DcBrBI	The Dictionary of British Book Illustrators and Caricaturists, 1800-1914
DcBrECP	The Dictionary of British Eighteenth Century Painters in Oils and Crayons
DcCanB	Dictionary of Canadian Biography
DcCathB	Dictionary of Catholic Biography
DcChlFi	Dictionary of Children's Fiction from Australia, Canada, India, New Zealand, and Selected African Countries
DcCAA	Dictionary of Contemporary American Artists
DcCAr	Dictionary of Contemporary Artists
DcCLAA	A Dictionary of Contemporary Latin American Authors
DcCM	Dictionary of Contemporary Music
DcD&D	Dictionary of Design & Decoration
DcEnA	A Dictionary of English Authors, Biographical and Bibliographical
DcEnL	Dictionary of English Literature
DcEuL	A Dictionary of European Literature
DcFM	Dictionary of Film Makers
DcInB	Dictionary of Indian Biography
DcInv	Dictionary of Inventions & Discoveries
DcIrB	A Dictionary of Irish Biography
DcIrL	Dictionary of Irish Literature
DcIrW	Dictionary of Irish Writers
DcItL	Dictionary of Italian Literature
DcLB	Dictionary of Literary Biography
DcLEL	A Dictionary of Literature in the English Language
DcMexL	Dictionary of Mexican Literature
DcNaB	The Dictionary of National Biography
DcNAA	A Dictionary of North American Authors Deceased before 1950
DcNCBi	Dictionary of North Carolina Biography
DcOrL	Dictionary of Oriental Literatures
DcPol	A Dictionary of Politics
DcRusL	Dictionary of Russian Literature
DcRusLS	Dictionary of Russian Literature since 1917
DcScanL	Dictionary of Scandinavian Literature
DcScB	Dictionary of Scientific Biography
DcSeaP	Dictionary of Sea Painters
DcSoc	A Dictionary of Sociology
DcSpL	Dictionary of Spanish Literature
DcTwHis	Dictionary of Twentieth-Century History, 1914-1990
DcVicP	The Dictionary of Victorian Painters
DcWomA	Dictionary of Women Artists
DrAF	A Directory of American Fiction Writers
DrAP	A Directory of American Poets
DrAPF	A Directory of American Poets and Fiction Writers
DrAS	Directory of American Scholars
DrBlPA	Directory of Blacks in the Performing Arts
DrLC	Directory of Library Consultants
Dis&D	Disease and Destiny
DramC	Drama Criticism
DrmM	Dream Makers
EarABI	Early American Book Illustrators and Wood Engravers, 1670-1870
EarBlAP	Early Black American Playwrights and Dramatic Writers
EncAACR	Encyclopedia of African-American Civil Rights
EncAB-H	Encyclopedia of American Biography
EncAB-A	Encyclopedia of American Biography
EncABHB	Encyclopedia of American Business History and Biography
EncACom	The Encyclopedia of American Comics
EncAFC	Encyclopedia of American Film Comedy
EncAHmr	Encyclopedia of American Humorists
EncAI&E	The Encyclopedia of American Intelligence and Espionage
EncAJ	The Encyclopedia of American Journalism
EncAR	Encyclopedia of the American Revolution
EncBrWW	An Encyclopedia of British Women Writers
EncCoWW	An Encyclopedia of Continental Women Writers
EncFCWM	The Encyclopedia of Folk, Country & Western Music
EncFWF	Encyclopedia of Frontier and Western Fiction
EncJap	Encyclopedia of Japan
EncJzS	Encyclopedia of Jazz in the Seventies
EncLatA	Encyclopedia of Latin America
EncMT	Encyclopaedia of the Musical Theatre
EncMys	Encyclopedia of Mystery and Detection
EncO&P	Encyclopedia of Occultism & Parapsychology
EncPaPR	The Encyclopedia of Parapsychology and Psychical Research
EncRk	Encyclopedia of Rock
EncSF	The Encyclopedia of Science Fiction
EncSoA	Encyclopaedia of Southern Africa
EncSoB	Encyclopedia of Southern Baptists
EncSoH	The Encyclopedia of Southern History
EncTwCJ	Encyclopedia of Twentieth-Century Journalists
EncUrb	Encyclopedia of Urban Planning
EncWB	Encyclopedia of World Biography: 20th Century Supplement
EncWL	Encyclopedia of World Literature in the 20th Century
EncWM	The Encyclopedia of World Methodism
EncWT	The Encyclopedia of World Theater
EngPo	English Poetry of the Second World War
Entr	Entrepreneurs
EuAu	European Authors, 1000-1900
EuWr	European Writers
EvEuW	Everyman's Dictionary of European Writers
EvLB	Everyman's Dictionary of Literary Biography, English and American
Expl	Explorers and Discoverers of the World
FamA&A	Famous Actors and Actresses on the American Stage
FamAIYP	Famous Author-Illustrators for Young People
FamAYP	Famous Authors for Young People
FamMS	Famous Modern Storytellers for Young People
FamPYP	Famous Poets for Young People
FamSYP	Famous Storytellers for Young People
FarE&A	The Far East and Australasia
FemPA	The Female Poets of America
FemiCLE	The Feminist Companion to Literature in English
FifBJA	Fifth Book of Junior Authors & Illustrators
FifIDA	Fifth International Directory of Anthropologists
FifCWr	Fifty Caribbean Writers
FifSWrB	Fifty Southern Writers before 1900
FifSWrA	Fifty Southern Writers after 1900
FilmgC	The Filmgoer's Companion
ForWC	Foremost Women in Communications
ForIl	Forty Illustrators and How They Work
FourBJA	Fourth Book of Junior Authors & Illustrators
FrenWW	French Women Writers
Future	The Future
GayLL	Gay & Lesbian Literature
GolEC	Golombek's Encyclopedia of Chess
GrAmP	Great American Prints, 1900-1950
GrBIl	The Great Bird Illustrators and Their Art, 1730-1930
GrBr	Great Britons
GrFLW	Great Foreign Language Writers
GuFrLit	Guide to French Literature
GuPsyc	A Guide to Psychologists and Their Concepts
HalFC	Halliwell's Filmgoer's Companion
HanAmWH	Handbook of American Women's History
HanRL	Handbook of Russian Literature
HarlReB	Harlem Renaissance and Beyond
HarEnUS	Harper's Encyclopaedia of United States History: From 458 A.D. to 1915
HerW	Her Way

(Continued on back endleaf)

OxCChiL	The Oxford Companion to Children's Literature
OxCClL	The Oxford Companion to Classical Literature
OxCEng	The Oxford Companion to English Literature
OxCFilm	The Oxford Companion to Film
OxCFr	The Oxford Companion to French Literature
OxCGer	The Oxford Companion to German Literature
OxCLaw	The Oxford Companion to Law
OxCLiW	The Oxford Companion to the Literature of Wales
OxCMus	The Oxford Companion to Music
OxCPMus	The Oxford Companion to Popular Music
OxCShps	The Oxford Companion to Ships and the Sea
OxCThe	The Oxford Companion to the Theatre
OxCTwCA	The Oxford Companion to Twentieth-Century Art
OxDcArt	The Oxford Dictionary of Art
PenC	The Penguin Companion to World Literature
PenDiMP	The Penguin Dictionary of Musical Performers
PenEncH	The Penguin Encyclopedia of Horror and the Supernatural
PenEncP	The Penguin Encyclopedia of Popular Music
PhDcTCA	Phaidon Dictionary of Twentieth-Century Art
PiP	The Pied Pipers
PlP&P	Plays, Players, and Playwrights
PoeCrit	Poetry Criticism
PoChrch	The Poets of the Church
PoIre	The Poets of Ireland
PoLE	The Poets Laureate of England
PolBiDi	Polish Biographical Dictionary
PolsAm	Politics in America
PorAmW	Portraits of American Women
PostFic	Postmodern Fiction
PrintW	The Printworld Directory of Contemporary Prints & Prices
Profile	Profiles
PueRA	Puerto Rican Authors
RAdv	The Reader's Adviser
RComAH	The Reader's Companion to American History
RComWL	The Reader's Companion to World Literature
REn	The Reader's Encyclopedia
REnAL	The Reader's Encyclopedia of American Literature
REnWD	The Reader's Encyclopedia of World Drama
RGAfL	A Reader's Guide to African Literature
RGTwCSF	Reader's Guide to Twentieth-Century Science Fiction
RealN	Realism, Naturalism, and Local Color, 1865-1917
RfGAmL	Reference Guide to American Literature
RfGEnL	Reference Guide to English Literature
RfGShF	Reference Guide to Short Fiction
RkOn	Rock On
RolSEnR	The Rolling Stone Encyclopedia of Rock & Roll
ScF&FL	Science Fiction & Fantasy Literature, 1975-1991
ScFSB	The Science Fiction Source Book
ScFEYrs	Science Fiction: The Early Years
SelBAAf	Selected Black American, African, and Caribbean Authors
SelBAAu	Selected Black American Authors
SenS	A Sense of Story
ShSCr	Short Story Criticism
ShSWr	Short Story Writers & Their Work
SingR	Singing Roads
SixBJA	Sixth Book of Junior Authors & Illustrators
SixAP	Sixty American Poets, 1896-1944
SmATA	Something about the Author
SouSt	A Sounding of Storytellers
SourALJ	A Sourcebook of American Literary Journalism
SouBlCW	Southern Black Creative Writers, 1829-1953
SpAmA	Spanish American Authors
SpAmWW	Spanish American Women Writers
SpyFic	Spy Fiction
StaCVF	The Stanford Companion to Victorian Fiction
Str&VC	Story and Verse for Children
SupFW	Supernatural Fiction Writers
TelT	Tellers of Tales
TexWr	Texas Writers of Today
ThTwC	Thinkers of the Twentieth Century
ThrBJA	Third Book of Junior Authors
ThrtnMM	Thirteen Mistresses of Murder
Tw	The Twenties, 1917-1929
TwCA	Twentieth Century Authors
TwCPaSc	Twentieth Century Painters and Sculptors
TwCWr	Twentieth Century Writing
TwCChW	Twentieth-Century Children's Writers
TwCCr&M	Twentieth-Century Crime and Mystery Writers
TwCLC	Twentieth-Century Literary Criticism
TwCRHW	Twentieth-Century Romance and Historical Writers
TwCSFW	Twentieth-Century Science-Fiction Writers
TwCWW	Twentieth-Century Western Writers
TwCYAW	Twentieth-Century Young Adult Writers
UFOEn	The UFO Encyclopedia
WebAB	Webster's American Biographies
WebAMB	Webster's American Military Biographies
WebE&AL	Webster's New World Companion to English and American Literature
WhDW	Who Did What
WhAm	Who Was Who in America
WhAmArt	Who Was Who in American Art
WhAmP	Who Was Who in American Politics
WhCiWar	Who Was Who in the Civil War
WhFla	Who Was Who in Florida
WhJnl	Who Was Who in Journalism, 1925-1928
WhNaAH	Who Was Who in Native American History
WhNAA	Who Was Who among North American Authors, 1921-1939
WhScrn	Who Was Who on Screen
Who	Who's Who
WhoAdv	Who's Who in Advertising
WhoAm	Who's Who in America
WhoAmA	Who's Who in American Art
WhoAmJ	Who's Who in American Jewry
WhoAmL	Who's Who in American Law
WhoAmM	Who's Who in American Music: Classical
WhoAmP	Who's Who in American Politics
WhoAmW	Who's Who of American Women
WhoArab	Who's Who in the Arab World
WhoArt	Who's Who in Art
WhoAsA	Who's Who among Asian Americans
WhoAtom	Who's Who in Atoms
WhoBlA	Who's Who among Black Americans
WhoCan	Who's Who in Canada
WhoCanL	Who's Who in Canadian Literature
WhoChL	The Who's Who of Children's Literature
WhoCom	Who's Who in Comedy
WhoE	Who's Who in the East
WhoEc	Who's Who in Economics
WhoEnt	Who's Who in Entertainment
WhoEIO	Who's Who in European Institutions and Organizations
WhoFI	Who's Who in Finance and Industry
WhoFla	Who's Who in Florida, 1973/74
WhoFtbl	Who's Who in Football
WhoFrS	Who's Who in Frontier Science and Technology
WhoGen	Who's Who in Genealogy & Heraldry
WhoGov	Who's Who in Government
WhoGrA	Who's Who in Graphic Art
WhoHisp	Who's Who among Hispanic Americans
WhoHcky	Who's Who in Hockey
WhoHol	Who's Who in Hollywood, 1900-1976
WhoHr&F	Who's Who in Horror and Fantasy Fiction
WhoIns	Who's Who in Insurance
WhoJazz	Who's Who of Jazz: Storyville to Swing Street
WhoLib	Who's Who in Librarianship
WhoLibI	Who's Who in Library and Information Services
WhoLibS	Who's Who in Library Service

KEY TO SOURCE CODES

HispLC	Hispanic Literature Criticism
HispWr	Hispanic Writers
HispAmA	The Hispanic-American Almanac
HisEWW	The Historical Encyclopedia of World War II
HsB&A	The House of Beadle and Adams and Its Dime and Nickel Novels
ICPEnP	ICP (International Center of Photography) Encyclopedia of Photography
IlBBlP	An Illustrated Bio-Bibliography of Black Photographers, 1940-1988
IlDcG	An Illustrated Dictionary of Glass
IlEncMy	An Illustrated Encyclopaedia of Mysticism and the Mystery Religions
IlrAm	The Illustrator in America, 1880-1980
IlsBYP	Illustrators of Books for Young People
IlsCB	Illustrators of Children's Books
InB&W	In Black and White
InSci	Index to Scientists of the World from Ancient to Modern Times
InWom	Index to Women of the World from Ancient to Modern Times: A Supplement
IndAu	Indiana Authors and Their Books, 1816-1916
IntAu&W	The International Authors and Writers Who's Who
IntDcAA	International Dictionary of Art and Artists: Artists
IntDcT	International Dictionary of Theatre
IntDcWB	The International Dictionary of Women's Biography
IntEnSS	International Encyclopedia of the Social Sciences
IntLitE	International Literature in English
IntMed	International Medical Who's Who
IntMPA	International Motion Picture Almanac
IntWW	The International Who's Who
IntWWE	International Who's Who in Energy and Nuclear Sciences
IntWWM	International Who's Who in Music and Musicians' Directory
IntWWP	International Who's Who in Poetry
IntYB	The International Year Book and Statesmen's Who's Who
IntvTCA	Interviews and Conversations with 20th-Century Authors Writing in English
IntvWPC	Interviews with Writers of the Post-Colonial World
JeAmFiW	Jewish American Fiction Writers
JeAmHC	Jewish-American History and Culture
JrnUS	Journalists of the United States
JBA	The Junior Book of Authors
LadLa	The Lady Laureates
LatAmWr	Latin American Writers
Law&B	Law & Business Directory of Corporate Counsel
LEduc	Leaders in Education
LElec	Leaders in Electronics
LesBEnT	Les Brown's Encyclopedia of Television
LiExTwC	Literary Exile in the Twentieth Century
LiHiK	A Literary History of Kentucky
LitC	Literature Criticism from 1400 to 1800
LivgBAA	Living Black American Authors
LivgFWS	The Living Female Writers of the South
LngCEL	Longman Companion to English Literature
LngCTC	Longman Companion to Twentieth Century Literature
LuthC	Lutheran Cyclopedia
MacBEP	Macmillan Biographical Encyclopedia of Photographic Artists & Innovators
MacEA	Macmillan Encyclopedia of Architects
MagSAmL	Magill's Survey of American Literature
MagSWL	Magill's Survey of World Literature
MajAI	Major Authors and Illustrators for Children and Young Adults
MajMD	Major Modern Dramatists
MajTwCW	Major Twentieth-Century Writers
MakMC	Makers of Modern Culture
MarqDCG	Marquis Who's Who Directory of Computer Graphics
McGEWB	The McGraw-Hill Encyclopedia of World Biography
McGEWD	McGraw-Hill Encyclopedia of World Drama
McGMS	McGraw-Hill Modern Scientists and Engineers
MedHR	Medal of Honor Recipients, 1863-1978
MedPD	Media Personnel Directory
MemAm	Memorable Americans, 1750-1950
MexAmB	Mexican American Biographies
MichAu	Michigan Authors
MidE	The Middle East and North Africa
MinnWr	Minnesota Writers
ModAL	Modern American Literature
ModAWP	Modern American Women Poets
ModAWWr	Modern American Women Writers
ModArCr	Modern Arts Criticism
ModBlW	Modern Black Writers
ModBrL	Modern British Literature
ModCmwL	Modern Commonwealth Literature
ModFrL	Modern French Literature
ModGL	Modern German Literature
ModIrL	Modern Irish Literature
ModRL	Modern Romance Literatures
ModSL	Modern Slavic Literatures
ModSpP	Modern Spanish and Portuguese Literatures
ModWD	Modern World Drama
MorBMP	More Books by More People
MorJA	More Junior Authors
MorMA	More Memorable Americans, 1750-1950
MotPP	Motion Picture Performers
MouLC	Moulton's Library of Literary Criticism
MovMk	The Movie Makers
NamesHP	Names in the History of Psychology
NatCAB	The National Cyclopaedia of American Biography
NatPD	National Playwrights Directory
NegAl	The Negro Almanac
NewAmDM	The New American Dictionary of Music
NewC	The New Century Handbook of English Literature
NewCBMT	New Complete Book of the American Musical Theater
NewCon	The New Consciousness, 1941-1968
NewEScF	The New Encyclopedia of Science Fiction
NewGrDA	The New Grove Dictionary of American Music
NewOxM	The New Oxford Companion to Music
NewYTBE	The New York Times Biographical Edition
NewYTBS	The New York Times Biographical Service
NewYTET	The New York Times Encyclopedia of Television
NewbC	Newbery and Caldecott Medal Books
NewbMB	Newbery Medal Books, 1922-1955
News	Newsmakers
NinCLC	Nineteenth-Century Literature Criticism
NobelP	Nobel Prize Winners
NotAW	Notable American Women, The Modern Period
NotBlAW	Notable Black American Women
NotHsAW	Notable Hispanic American Women
NotNAT	Notable Names in the American Theatre
NotWoAT	Notable Women in the American Theatre
Novels	Novels and Novelists
ObitOF	Obituaries on File
ObitT	Obituaries from the Times
OhA&B	Ohio Authors and Their Books
OxCAmH	The Oxford Companion to American History
OxCAmL	The Oxford Companion to American Literature
OxCAmT	The Oxford Companion to American Theatre
OxCArt	The Oxford Companion to Art
OxCAusL	The Oxford Companion to Australian Literature
OxCCan	The Oxford Companion to Canadian History and Literature
OxCCanL	The Oxford Companion to Canadian Literature
OxCCanT	The Oxford Companion to Canadian Theatre

ISBN 0-8103-2899-2
90000
9 780810 328990